Criminal Law in Action

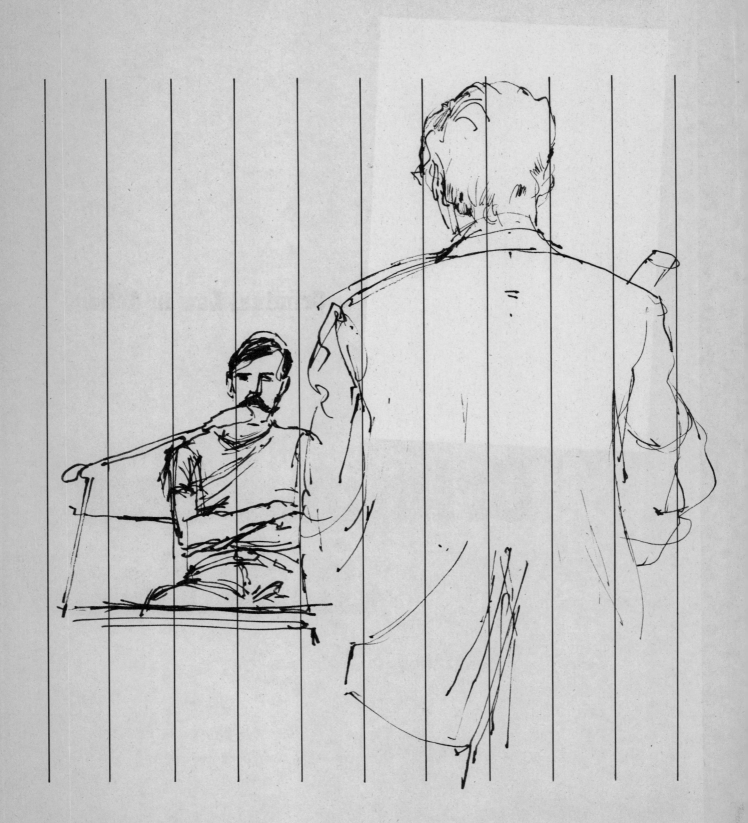

Criminal Law in Action

WILLIAM J. CHAMBLISS

HAMILTON PUBLISHING COMPANY

SANTA BARBARA, CALIFORNIA

Copyright © 1975, by John Wiley & Sons, Inc.

Published by **Hamilton Publishing Company,**
a Division of John Wiley & Sons, Inc.
All rights reserved. Published simultaneously in Canada.

Library of Congress Cataloging in Publication Data:

Chambliss, William J.   comp.

  Criminal law in action.

  1. Criminal justice, Administration of—United
States—Addresses, essays, lectures. 2. Law enforce-
ment—United States—Addresses, essays, lectures.
3. Crime and criminals—Economic aspects—United
States—Addresses, essays, lectures. I. Title.
HV8138.C484   364   74-32149

ISBN 0-471-14474-6

Printed in the United States of America

10 9 8 7 6 5 4 3 2 1

For Jeff, Kent, and Lauren

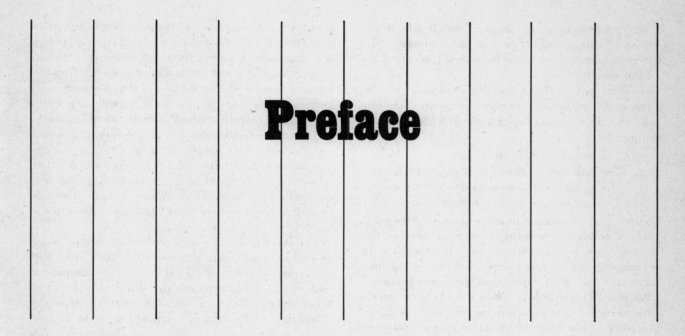

Preface

In the 1924 edition of *Criminology* Edwin Sutherland observed:

> An understanding of the nature of law is necessary in order to secure an understanding of the nature of crime. A complete explanation of the origin and enforcement of laws would be also an explanation of the violation of laws.[1]

In the competition for time and energy the study of criminal subcultures and criminal etiology has usually been given priority over the study of the relationship between crime and the criminal law. In the past decade, however, emphasis has begun to shift to the point where the sociological analysis of criminal law now has a place in the theoretical and research interests of criminologists which is consistent with Sutherland's farsighted observation.

The study of crime took a great leap forward when, about fifty years ago, social scientists realized that crime would never be explained by searching for hereditary, biological, or genetic characteristics that might differentiate criminals from noncriminals. A half-century of inquiry ensued wherein the search for social experiences replaced the search for biological or physiological traits. Today the study of crime and deviance is once more making a leap in a new direction. We have come to realize that crime is not so much a matter of individuals differing in their social experiences. Crime is rather a political phenomenon whereby some behaviors and some people are labeled "criminal," "delinquent," or "sick," while other behaviors and people are not. The study of crime thus becomes not simply a study of the social and psychological differences between "criminals" and "noncriminals." It becomes instead the systematic study of the criminal law as a living institution within which what are basically political decisions are made. The end product of these political decisions is the definition of some behaviors and some people as "criminal."

To say that crime is a political phenomenon is to open up a whole new spectrum on the question of crime. Instead of asking "why do some people commit crimes and others not" we ask "why are some acts defined as criminal while others are not." Instead of asking "why is crime more often committed in this part of a city than in that" we ask why the law enforcement agencies make more arrests "here" than "there." Rather than ask whether or not punishment

[1]Edwin H. Sutherland, *Criminology*, Philadelphia: J. B. Lippincott, 1924, p. 11.

is a natural response to deviance, we ask why different societies respond to criminal acts and what effect different responses to crime have on the criminal and on the society.

Taken together these questions circumscribe the study of the relationship between crime and the criminal law. This book is divided into four main areas of inquiry:

1. The creation of criminal laws
2. The political economy of law enforcement
3. The social organization of law enforcement
4. The impact of legal institutions

There is a vast literature in anthropology, economics, political science, psychology, sociology, and law that is addressed to these questions. In selecting the readings in this volume I have tried to take the most important and most representative examples available from all these fields. Since it is of course impossible to include even a small fraction of the available literature, it has been my intention to concentrate on empirical studies of the criminal law. But data without theory are limited and may be misleading. I have therefore taken it as my responsibility to intertwine the research papers with theoretical perspectives within which the data make sense.

In making the selection of what to incorporate in this volume, I have left out some areas as important as those that have been included. Two areas that have been omitted deserve special mention.

The focus of the book is purposefully, and at the same time unfortunately, on Anglo-American law. This focus is necessitated by the lack of comparable data from studies of the law in other cultures. Although I have included a few studies from other countries, the framework remains Ango-American out of necessity. It is to be hoped that the few studies of a comparative nature included in the volume will suggest fruitful areas for further research. Another limiting feature of this volume is that the numerous studies of the legal profession qua profession (with the accompanying questions of recruitment, training, and professional-association membership) are not represented. This decision was dictated by the desire to keep the volume relatively compact. Another reason for omitting the research on the legal profession is that the focus of this volume is more narrowly limited to the everyday events that take place in the legal process.

The impetus for this book was an attempt to revise an earlier effort published under the title *Crime and the Legal Process*. While some of the structure of that earlier book remains, the differences between this and the earlier work are much greater than are the similarities. It therefore seemed wise to re-title the book and treat it as a separate attempt. Indeed, the accumulation of research and enhancement of theoretical perspectives in the sociology of criminal law has been so stimulating in the past few years that fundamental changes have occurred in the field and in my own thinking about it.

There is still much to be done; the task of understanding any social phenomenon as complex and as central to the human condition as the law is an endless one. Here, as before, I can only hope that this work will stimulate inquiring minds to benefit from the mistakes as well as the truths contained in this volume.

W. J. C.

Contents

Preface   vii

PART 1: THE CREATION OF LEGAL NORMS

Introduction   2

1. "The Law of Vagrancy,"
   by William J. Chambliss   9
2. "Gideon's Trumpet,"
   by Anthony Lewis   26

PART 2: THE POLITICAL ECONOMY OF CRIME AND LAW ENFORCEMENT

Introduction   34

3. "Class and the Economics of Crime,"
   by David M. Gordon   35
4. "Rape: The All-American Crime,"
   by Susan Griffin   51
5. "The Political Economy of Crime:
   A Comparative Study of Nigeria and the
   United States,"
   by William J. Chambliss   62
6. "The Saints and the Roughnecks,"
   by William J. Chambliss   71

7. "From Constabulary to Police Society:
   Implications for Social Control,"
   by Evelyn L. Parks   81

PART 3: THE SOCIAL ORGANIZATION OF CRIMINAL LAW ENFORCEMENT

Introduction   96

8. "Poverty and Criminal Justice,"
   by Patricia M. Wald   98
9. "White Collar Crime:
   The Statistical Record,"
   by Edwin H. Sutherland   110
10. "Class Linkages of Legal Treatment
    of Homosexuals,"
    by Ronald A. Farrell   125
11. "Police Corruption in New York City,"
    Knapp Commission   137
12. "Vice, Corruption, Bureaucracy,
    and Power,"
    by William J. Chambliss   144
13. "The Thief and the Law:
    A Safecracker's Perspective,"
    by Harry King   159

Arrest

Introduction   166

14. "Background Characteristics of Recruit
    Police Officers,"
    by John H. McNamara   171
15. "Police Field Practices,"
    *President's Commission on Law
    Enforcement and Administration of Justice*   181
16. "The Police on Skid-Row: A Study
    of Peace Keeping,"
    by Egon Bittner   197
17. "Police Encounters with Juveniles,"
    by Irving Piliavin and Scott Briar   214
18. "The Narcotics Enforcement Pattern,"
    by Jerome H. Skolnick   222
19. "The Use of Violence by the Police,"
    *by William J. Chambliss and
    Robert B. Seidman*   237
20. "Police Brutality—Answers to Key
    Questions,"
    by Albert J. Reiss, Jr.   246

Prosecution

Introduction   258

21. "The Practice of Law as Confidence Game:
    Organizational Cooptation of a Profession,"
    by Abraham S. Blumberg   262

Trial and Sentencing

Introduction   282

22. "The Chicago Conspiracy Trial,"
    by David J. Danelski   285
23. "Vagrancy-Type Law and Its
    Administration,"
    by Caleb Foote   315
24. "The Law in a Rural Setting,"
    by Harry M. Caudill   322
25. "Sentencing and Sentences,"
    *by William J. Chambliss and
    Robert B. Seidman*   328

Imprisonment and Other Forms
of Punishment

Introduction   346

26. "Punishment and Social Structure,"
    by Georg Rusche and Otto Kirchheimer   347
27. "Race, Judicial Discretion, and the
    Death Penalty,"
    by Marvin E. Wolfgang and Marc Riedel   365

PART 4: THE IMPACT OF LEGAL
INSTITUTIONS

Introduction   380

28. "In Search of Juvenile Justice: *Gault*
    and Its Implementation,"
    *by Norman Lefstein, Vaughan Stapleton,
    and Lee Teitelbaum*   384
29. "Types of Deviance and the Effectiveness
    of Legal Sanctions,"
    by William J. Chambliss   398
30. "Murder and Capital Punishment,"
    by William C. Bailey   408
31. "Deterrence and Specific Offenses:
    Drunken Driving,"
    by Johannes Andenaes   421
32. "Sanctions and Deviance: Evidence
    and Remaining Questions,"
    by Charles R. Tittle and Charles H. Logan   426
33. "What Happens When the Police Strike,"
    by Gerald Clark   440
34. "Drug Addiction in America and England,"
    by Edwin M. Schur   450
35. "Two Studies of Legal Stigma,"
    *by Richard D. Schwartz and
    Jerome H. Skolnick*   458
36. "Mods, Rockers, and the Rest: Community
    Reactions to Juvenile Delinquency,"
    by Stanley Cohen   466

PART 5: EPILOGUE   475

Part 1

Criminal Law in Action

Part 1

The Creation of Legal Norms

PART 1 THE CREATION OF LEGAL NORMS

INTRODUCTION

In the Spring and Summer of 1973 disclosures of criminal behavior by persons in high public office struck like a bombshell at the political foundations of the United States. The "Watergate Affair," the conviction of Superior Court Judge and former State Governor Kerner on charges of accepting bribes, and a grand jury investigation of possibilities Vice President Spiro Agnew accepted bribes, brought into sharp relief a fundamental point about crime and criminal law which has long been part of the lexicon of academic criminologists: namely, that crime is not something which is limited to the violent acts of "psychopaths." Crime is a highly complex legal, political, economic, and social phenomenon which must be systematically studied from many angles if it is to be understood.

The more we have learned about crime the more we have come to realize that it is as necessary to understand how some acts and some people get defined as criminal by the legal institutions as it is to understand the subcultures and life styles of people who commit criminal acts. As a result, the focus of criminology in recent years has shifted more and more to see the sociology of criminal law as the appropriate starting point for the study of crime. A full understanding of crime must incorporate an understanding of the institutions which create, interpret, and enforce the rules which comprise the criminal law. American law has developed slowly and fitfully for at least eight hundred years. It is natural for us then to begin our inquiry by looking at the historical roots of our legal system.

ANGLO-AMERICAN LAW IN HISTORICAL PERSPECTIVE

William the Conqueror was faced with a formidable task when he took the throne of England. The kingdom he had conquered in 1066 was composed of a number of groups of people with quite divergent ways of looking at the world and equally diverse sets of values. The various social groups were not organized in such a way that they paid homage, much less taxes, to one central authority. By contemporary standards, William had conquered an anarchy whose salient characteristic was a pluralistic value system: a land divided into eight subdivisions, each with its own king. The country's only unifying characteristic was the presence of Christianity, a remnant of the Roman occupation six centuries earlier. One of William's first acts was to declare this heterogeneous conglomeration subject to his leadership and to claim all land for the crown.

He attempted to gain control over the church, which was at that time a major landholder. As a means of achieving this control William separated the lay and ecclesiastical courts of law. His moves constituted a grave threat to the economic well-being and the political power of the church. Not surprisingly, the conflict between the church and state played a major part in the history of England for several centuries, coming to a head during the reign of Henry II. The crown also asserted that it was solely responsible for peace ("the king's peace") throughout the realm. To enforce this peace, the king sent judges into the countryside. By so doing, the crown took away much of the power of the barons, and the lines of conflict between the crown, the barons, and the church were drawn.

From the time of William until the reign of Henry II a quasi-legal structure prevailed which was strongly influenced by the tribal heritage of England prior to the Norman conquest. But during the reign of Henry II, most of the fundamental features of the structure of Anglo-American law emerged.

First and foremost, Anglo-American law has inherited a reliance on force and coercion as the appropriate mechanisms for handling disputes. At an earlier time in England, the emphasis in settling disputes had been on reconciliation rather than on coercion. Thus, if a member of one kinship group had violated the rights of someone from another group, the guiding principle was to effect a reconciliation of the individuals and the groups. But the legal system emerging from the reign of William through that of Henry II emphasized the use of force by the state as the right and proper means of settling disputes.

An equally important inheritance from the earlier years of the Anglo-American legal system is the view that personal wrongs are transgressions against the *state* and that the state and *only* the state has the right to punish such acts. This principle contrasted sharply with the norms of English society prior to the time of William, when wrongs were considered a highly personal matter.

Other characteristics emerging at this time include the state's use of an ostensibly independent and unbiased government official to handle disputes between individuals and the state or between two or more persons. In modern times this is, of course, the judge.

It is also significant that the judicial function was separated from the legislative function. The legal system was so designed that those who would decide disputes would not

PART 1   THE CREATION OF LEGAL NORMS

be the same as those who made the laws. Finally, there emerged in this early period the use of a group of the accused's peers as the rightful body for determining guilt and innocence.

These innovations more than any others can be said to represent the salient structural features of the Anglo-American legal system. Much of the content and most certainly the focus of the legal norms have undergone dramatic shifts over the centuries; but the reliance on coercion through force, the use of judges, the differentiation of functions between the judiciary and the legislature, and the users of peers (juries) have remained firmly ingrained features of the legal order.

Thus, this heritage from feudal England has been more important in establishing the *structure* of the legal system than in determining the *content* of the laws. The bulk of the offenses which occupy the attention of the legal order today were unheard of in early English law, and even laws which have roots in early England, such as the Law of Theft and the Vagrancy Statutes, differ so in their content today that they are more appropriately to be seen as new laws than as continuations of old ones.

The content of the legal system has also changed through the death of many laws which at one time occupied a central place in the legal order, laws that provided penal sanctions for indebtedness being but one example of the attrition.

There have also been dramatic changes in the types of sanctions meted out for various types of offenses. In early England, punishment for even minor offenses was exceedingly severe: for example, "(I)n medieval England peasants were hanged for stealing a few eggs."*

C. Ray Jeffrey summarizes some of the more important aspects of the historical background of Anglo-American criminal law as follows:

The pattern of social change in England from 400 to 1200 was a change from tribalism to feudalism to nationalism. The *land-tie* replaced the *blood-tie* as the basis for social order.

During the tribal period there was a fusion of institutional functions in the kinship unit. This body was the political, economic, family, religious, and ecological unit. By 1200 separate institutions existed in these several areas. Political author-

ity was now in the hands of landlords. By the time of Henry II the king emerged as the supreme landlord in this feudal hierarchy. Economic organization shifted from a hunting, fishing, and pastoral economy, where the kinship group was the economic unit, to an agricultural economy, where the feudal manor was the economic unit. Each man occupied land belonging to his lord, rather than to his kin, and he was attached to this land through a personal-legal relationship known as the tenure system. Status was now based on this tenure system. Feudalism was based on a division of men into two classes: military and agricultural. Religion was now controlled by a professional hierarchy of priests and bishops who acted as both church officials and landlords. Christianity was an important aspect of the feudal system. The conjugal family did not perform the many functions performed by the tribal family. This shift from an institutional family to a companionship family is a familiar theme in sociological literature today.

A new social structure emerged in England, and as a result of these changes a new legal system came into existence. During the tribal period the legal system was in the hands of the tribal group, and justice was based on the blood-feud. As tribalism gave way to feudalism, the feud was replaced by a system of compensations. Justice passed into the hands of landlords. There was no separation of lay and ecclesiastical courts until the time of William. State law and crime came into existence during the time of Henry II as a result of this separation of State and Church, and as a result of the emergence of a central authority in England which replaced the authority of the feudal lords. Henry replaced feudal justice with state justice by means of justices in eyre, the king's peace, a system of royal courts, and a system of royal writs. Common law emerged as the law of the Crown available to all men. The myth that the common law of England is the law of the Anglo-Saxons is without historical foundation. The family was no longer involved in law and justice. The State was the offended social unit, and the State was the proper prosecutor in every case of crime. Justice was now the sole prerogative of the State. "Custom passes into law." This shift occurred historically when a political community separate from the kinship group emerged as a part of the social organization. A comparison of tribal law and state law reveals these basic differences.*

Tribal Law	State Law
Blood-tie	Territorial-tie
Collective responsibility	Individual responsibility
Family as unit of justice and order	State as unit of justice
Feud or compensation	Punishment

*Gerhard Lenski, *Power and Privilege*, New York: McGraw-Hill, 1966, p. 271; H. S. Bennett, *Life on the English Manor: A Study of Peasant Conditions, 1150-1400*, London: Cambridge University Press, 1960.

*C. Ray Jeffrey, "The Development of Crime in Early English Society," *Journal of Criminal Law, Criminology and Police Science*, vol. 47, March-April, 1957, p. 666.

PART 1   THE CREATION OF LEGAL NORMS

RECENT TRENDS

The last two hundred years have brought profound changes in the Western world, and with these changes we find equally significant alterations of the legal order. The most important of these changes are not to be found in the types of behaviors which are prohibited or in the types of punishments applied; on the contrary, the most significant changes occur in the institutionalized procedures and the institutionalized conceptions of the basic values of the legal order. For it is these perspectives which ultimately shape the legal system, although their immediate impact may be seen more readily in an alteration of the idea rather than an alteration of the fact of the legal system.

Of the changes to be mentioned here, none is more important than the twentieth century trend toward an ever increasing secularization of the legal system. The jury system, as it has developed, illustrates this general process.

Initially, the wisest composition of the jury was seen as consisting of peers chosen because they were familiar with the facts of the case. Being familiar presumably made them better able to establish the truth. Today, of course, the criteria for jury selection are almost the exact opposite: A prospective juror is not allowed to serve if he knows very much about the case prior to the trial. A similar example is the rule governing venue: If a defendant can show that the community at large is too intimately familiar with the case, then it is possible to force the trial to take place elsewhere. The tendency to conceive of deterrence as the most important, if not the only, legitimate justification for the existence of punishment is still another example of this process, for an emphasis on deterrence places increasing emphasis on the role of the law in achieving objectively defensible goals. The more traditional arguments for punishment, which suggested the need for "retribution" or the necessity of obtaining "an eye for an eye and a tooth for a tooth," have become much less persuasive in modern legal thinking than they once were. More and more the law is being structured and judged according to how well it meets certain explicit societal goals; it is no longer sufficient that the law supposedly represents a system of "natural" rights and obligations.

We have seen in very recent years what is perhaps the most important outgrowth of this trend to secularize the legal order, in that courts and legislatures have increasingly turned to empirical evidence of how the legal system works

in fact—as opposed to simply reifying the beauty of the logical structure of the law. In England, for example, criminal laws against prostitution, drug use, homosexuality, and gambling were abolished in part because there was evidence that requiring agencies to enforce these laws led more often to the corruption of the enforcers than to the reduction in the frequency of such "immoral" acts.*

The Supreme Court in the United States has recently shown an equally impressive tendency to look for empirical evidence of the "law in action" as a basis for making legal decisions. The "Miranda decision" represented a landmark case in criminal law illustrating this tendency.

The issue in the Miranda case was whether or not the police could interrogate a suspected criminal without the suspect's having first been given the right to refuse to submit to such interrogation. The Supreme Court held in this classic decision that evidence (including confessions) thus gathered was inadmissible in court and could not be used as a basis for finding a defendant guilty. It was certainly not a new principle: the Court had always held that a defendant's civil liberties had to be protected and that the police could not use undue pressure (such as physical brutality) to obtain a confession. As an illustration of the increasing sensitivity of the legal system to empirical data, however, what is significant about the Miranda decision is the fact that the Court did not rest its case simply by reaffirming the rights which are guaranteed by the logical structure (blueprint) of the legal norms; rather, the Court attempted to assess what was in fact taking place in police stations as officers enforced the laws. To accomplish this, the Court analyzed the contents of police training manuals to determine the tactics and strategies suggested in these manuals for police to use to obtain confessions. It was on the basis of the contradiction between these practices and the spirit of the legal system that the Supreme Court established new rules for ensuring that defendants not receive undue pressure from police.†

In present times administrative boards have emerged as institutionalized mechanisms replacing activities previously contained within the legal system. The juvenile court movement begun at the turn of the century has resulted in

---

*Wolfenden Report in Parliament, *Criminal Law Review,* England, 1959.
†*Miranda v. Arizona in Official Reports of the Supreme Court,* vol. 384, 1966, U. S. part 3, pp. 436-718, 982-995.

the virtual withdrawal of the traditional legal processing of juveniles after arrest. Although the juvenile court retains a judge, this is in most cases simply an anachronism with little real consequence for the functioning of the court. In point of fact, the juvenile court is manned and manipulated, for better or for worse, by professionally trained social workers whose tie to the legal order is only tangential.

A further illustration of the trend toward replacing the legal system with administrative boards is found in Nils Christie's analysis of the use of welfare boards to handle alcoholics.* Although we have seen only the beginnings of such programs in the United States, the change has been virtually complete in England and in many other European countries. It seems likely that the trend will take on increasing importance in the future and that we shall see a gradual withdrawal of strictly legal handling of more and more types of heretofore criminal behavior.†

The climate of the legal order is thus dramatically different in the twentieth century from what has ever been the case in our history. There is widespread agreement on the value of developing an increasingly rational system for meting out justice. Equally important is the fact that there is a willingness to consider the events which actually take place in the legal process, and not just the structure of the law in its abstract majesty, as evidence to be reckoned with in guiding changes in the legal structure. In recent years we have also seen the trend toward an increasing reliance on statutes combined with a gradual shift away from using the criminal law as the sole entity prescribing the handling of persons who have violated the law.

THEORIES OF LEGAL CHANGE

How can we account for the changes which take place in the criminal law and what are the dynamics through which these changes occur? Theories of the origin of criminal law parallel rather closely general theories of society. The chief division is between those theories that see the dynamic of society as best understood in terms of conflict, as contrasted with those theories that see society as best under-

stood in terms of consensus.* Generally, these two perspectives are referred to as "conflict" and "consensus" models of society. With respect to the sociology of criminal law the two models make quite different fundamental assumptions: the conflict model emphasizes the role of conflicts between social classes and interest groups as the moving force behind the creation and implementation of criminal laws; the consensus model emphasizes the shared interests of everyone in a society and the consensus (either articulated or inarticulated) over fundamental values which this shared interest creates. Until recently, consensus theories dominated the anthropological, sociological, and political science perspective on crime and criminal law. The natural-law view that the law is a straightforward reflection and translation of the "volksgeist" (the "spirit of the people") anchors the most extreme position deriving from the consensus model. The consensus perspective is well summarized by Jerome Hall when he argues that "criminal law represents a sustained effort to preserve important social values from serious harm and to do so not arbitrarily but in accordance with rational methods directed toward the discovery of just ends."†

In recent years, however, the conflict perspective has regained considerable favor among social scientists as political events (such as urban riots and political corruption) have forced a re-evaluation of traditional consensual views. In contrast to consensus theories, the conflict model sees law as being created out of the conflict between social classes and vested interest groups. The Marxian view that "in every era the ruling ideas are the ideas of the ruling class" anchors the conflict perspective. More generally, conflict theory sees the creation and enforcement of criminal law as best understood as stemming from the conflicts inherent in the unequal distribution of wealth, power, and control that characterizes capitalist economic systems.

As is always the case in the development of social thought these two general models have spawned a wide variety of more specific theories of legal change. The more

---

*Nils Christie, "Temperance Boards: A Study of Welfare Law," *Social Problems,* vol. 12, Spring, 1965, pp. 415-428.

†For an elaboration of the role of the lawyer in this process, see Willard Hurst, "The Legal Profession," *Wisconsin Law Review,* vol. 1966, Fall, pp. 969-978.

---

*For a detailed analysis of this argument, see William J. Chambliss and Robert B. Seidman, *Law, Order and Power,* Reading, Mass.: Addison-Wesley, 1971; Richard Quinney, *The Social Reality of Crime,* Boston: Little, Brown, 1970; Austin Turk, *Criminality and Legal Order,* Chicago: Rand McNally, 1969.

†Jerome Hall, *General Principles of Criminal Law,* Indianapolis: Bobbs-Merrill, 1947, p. 1.

PART 1   THE CREATION OF LEGAL NORMS

important theories derived from the conflict perspective include the following:

1. theories that emphasize the role of "moral entrepreneurs," the role of particular groups of persons who organize to achieve legal changes which they think are essential for the well-being of society;*
2. theories that emphasize the importance of bureaucratic interests in the rationalization of problems that inhere in society;†
3. theories that emphasize the conflicts that inhere between vested interest groups vying for the favors of state power through the use of legal changes;**
4. theories that emphasize the inherent conflicts between those who rule and those who are ruled and which see the criminal law as incorporating rules for enforcing the interests and ideologies of the ruling classes.‡

The consensus model has been equally prolific in spawning theories of legal change. Among the more influential theories are:

1. theories that see the law as a reflection of "perceived social needs" which all reasonable men agree must be met if society is to continue;‡‡
2. theories closely related to the above, but somewhat different in emphasis, that see the criminal law as an expression of what is in the "public interest"—that is, the interests of the vast majority of the members of a particular society;*
3. theories that see the law as a reflection of the "moral indignation" or "shared popular viewpoint" of a particularly influential or important segment of the society;†
4. theories that see the law as an expression of the most fundamental values that inhere in all societies.

In the following pages we will review the more important theories, and assess them with regard to their ability to explain what we know of the creation of criminal laws. As shall become apparent in the studies that follow, none of these positions does justice to the complexity and vitality of the social processes which inhere in the creation of criminal laws. In the end it will be clear, however, that an analysis based on conflict models is of more general utility than is the consensus framework.

STUDIES OF LAW CREATION

One of the earliest attempts to systematically study the creation of criminal laws was Jerome Hall's investigation of the emergence of the law of theft in England.** Hall writes:

> The report of any law case is a human document. Illuminated with but a bit of imagination, even the technical words written in a musty volume portray a vivid drama. The dead awaken, contestants battle hotly for the things they value; and powerful forces penetrate the courtroom, driving the actors to extend themselves to their uttermost limits. The final opinion, deliberately expressed, may conceal within its austere form a life-struggle. Most cases, to be sure, are merely cumulative in their effect, moving in well beaten paths, with some inevitable deviation but by and large within the lines laid down. Occasionally, however, comes a case of tremendous importance. It affects the gentlemen on the bench greatly; despite their efforts to preserve the appearance of conformity to precedent, it is clear that they struck out in a definitely new direction.
>
> Such a case, decided in 1473, was designated the Carrier's Case.
>
> The facts are simple enough: the defendant was hired to carry certain bales to Southampton. Instead of fulfilling his obligation, he carried the goods to another place, broke open the bales

*Howard Becker, *The Outsiders,* New York: The Free Press of Glencoe, 1963; Joseph Gusfield, *Symbolic Crusade: Status Politics and the American Temperance Movement,* Urbana: University of Illinois Press, 1963; William J. Chambliss and Robert B. Seidman, *Law, Order and Power,* Reading, Mass.: Addison-Wesley, 1971.

†William J. Chambliss, "Vice, Corruption, Bureaucracy, and Power," *Wisconsin Law Review,* vol. 1971, no. 4, pp. 1150-1173.

**Richard Quinney, *The Social Reality of Crime,* Boston: Little, Brown, 1970.

‡Richard Quinney, "Crime Control in Capitalist Society: A Critical Philosophy of Legal Order," *Issues in Criminology,* vol. 8, no. 1, Spring, 1973, pp. 75-99; Richard Quinney, *Critique of Legal Order,* Boston: Little, Brown, 1974; Georg Rusche and Otto Kirchheimer, *Punishment and Social Structure,* New York: Russell and Russell, 1939, 1967; Karl Renner, *The Institutions of Private Law,* London: Routledge and Kegan Paul, 1957; William J. Chambliss and Robert B. Seidman, *Law, Order and Power,* Reading, Mass.: Addison-Wesley, 1971.

‡‡Emile Durkheim, *The Division of Labor in Society,* Glencoe, Ill.: The Free Press, 1957, Jerome Hall, *Theft, Law and Society* (revised edition), Indianapolis: Bobbs-Merrill, 1952.

*C. Auerbach, L. K. Garrison, W. Hurst, and S. Mermin, *The Legal Process,* San Francisco: Chandler, 1961.

†Svend Ranulf, *Moral Indignation and Middle Class Psychology,* New York: Schocken, 1964.

**Jerome Hall, *Theft, Law and Society* (revised edition), Indianapolis: Bobbs-Merrill, 1952.

PART 1 THE CREATION OF LEGAL NORMS

and took the contents. He was apprehended and charged with felony.

The case was discussed at length, at least on two occasions, before and by the most illustrious judges of the time, among whom were Brian, the Chief Justice, Choke, and Nedham; attorneys Hussey and Molineux represented the Crown.

Brian, one of the soundest of English judges, contended throughout the proceedings that no felony had been committed. The defendant had possession, said Brian, "by a bailing and delivery lawfully"; and "what he himself has he cannot take with *vi et armis* nor against the peace; therefore it cannot be felony nor trespass."

Against this position, it was argued:

1. There was no bailment but, instead, "a bargain to take and carry" which did not vest possession if the carrier's intention was unlawful at the time he received the goods.
2. Granted that there was a bailment, felony was committed by subsequently taking the property *animo furandi*.
3. The bailment was terminated by taking the goods to a place other than Southampton and "breaking bulk," that is, opening the bales.
4. The defendant had possession of the containers or wrappers only but not of the contents of the bales.
5. The case should be decided not according to common law but "according to the law of nature" (this was urged by the Chancellor).

The defendant was finally held guilty of felony by a majority of the judges.*

The Carrier Case raises a central question for the sociology of criminal law: what happens when social conditions (especially economic and political conditions) change such that the established laws do not adequately protect the interests of the more powerful classes? Hall's study makes it clear on the one hand that at the time of the Carrier Case there was *no* legal prohibition against taking the goods of another person if he or she had entrusted those goods to your care. But commerce, trade, and the transportation of goods was becoming an increasingly important part of England's economy during this historical period. The judges deciding the Carrier Case had then to choose between creating a new law to protect merchants who entrusted their goods to a carrier or permitting the lack of such legal protection to undermine trade and the merchant classes' economic interests. The court decided to act in the interests of the merchants despite the lack of a law:

In the absence of any other even remotely relevant sanction in the criminal law, the only choice was—guilty of larceny or not guilty of any offense.

But it may be a matter of some wonder why the change in law did not come from the legislature rather than from a court which was compelled to disguise its decision in fictitious terms in order to save the face of the existing doctrine. . . . Here it must suffice to recall first, that Edward rarely summoned Parliament; second, that the sharp distinctions we are accustomed to draw regarding a division of powers cannot be applied accurately to the political instrumentalities of fifteenth century England; and, lastly, that the method actually used was, because of the relationship between the Crown and the Star Chamber, by far the simplest.

We are now in a position to visualize the case and the problem presented to the judges as a result of the legal, political, and economic conditions. On the one hand, the criminal law at the time is clear. On the other hand, the whole complex aggregate of political and economic conditions thrusts itself upon the court. The more powerful forces prevailed—that happened which in due course must have happened under the circumstances. The most powerful forces of the time were interrelated very intimately and at many points: the New Monarchy and the *nouveau riche*—the mercantile class; the business interests of both and the consequent need for a secure carrying trade; the wool and textile industry, the most valuable, by far, in all the realm; wool and cloth, the most important exports; these exports and the foreign trade; this trade and Southampton, chief trading city with the Latin countries for centuries; the numerous and very influential Italian merchants who bought English wool and cloth inland and shipped them from Southampton. The great forces of an emerging modern world, represented in the above phenomena, necessitated the elimination of a formula which had outgrown its usefulness. A new set of major institutions required a new rule. The law, lagging behind the needs of the times, was brought into more harmonious relationship with the other institutions by the decision rendered in the Carrier's Case.*

Hall's investigation into the law of theft is a powerful statement of the role of political and economic conditions in determining the kinds of acts that will be called criminal.

Does the case of the law of theft represent evidence in support of the conflict or the consensus theory? Clearly, it would be stretching the data to see the judiciary's acts as a reflection of consensus. Were there consensus, the

---

Ibid., p. 5.

Ibid., pp. 32-33.

judiciary in all likelihood would not have had to settle the case at all but the legislature would have done so expeditiously. The fact that legal fictions were necessary to justify the court's decision also suggests the lack of a consensus. It is more in line with the facts presented to see the law of theft as taking its form as a result of the interrelationship of "the most powerful forces of the time . . . : the New Monarchy and the *nouveau riche*—the mercantile class; the business interests of both and the consequent need for a secure carrying trade. . . ."

A similar conclusion is also suggested by the following article which is an analysis of the vagrancy laws in England and the United States. Note, however, in the following study the important role that *conflict* between the ruling classes and the peasants or workers plays in forming the definition of behavior as criminal.

1

The Law of Vagrancy

WILLIAM J. CHAMBLISS

LEGAL INNOVATION: THE EMERGENCE OF THE LAW OF VAGRANCY IN ENGLAND

There is general agreement among legal scholars that the first full-fledged vagrancy statute was passed in England in 1349.[1] As is usually the case with legislative innovations, however, this statue was preceded by laws which established a climate favorable to such change. The most significant forerunner to the 1349 vagrancy statute was in 1274 when it was provided:

> Because that abbies and houses of religion have been overcharged and sore grieved, by the resort of great men and other, so that their goods have not been sufficient for themselves, whereby they have been greatly hindered and impoverished, that they cannot maintain themselves, nor such charity as they have been accustomed to do; it is provided, that none shall come to eat or lodge in any house of religion, or any other's foundation than of his own, at the costs of the house, unless he is required by the governor of the home before his coming hither. (3 Ed. 1 c. 1)[2]

Even more to the point was the history of the vagrancy statutes from 1349 onward; a history of legislative enactment and innovation designed to pro-

Source: "A Sociological Analysis of the Law of Vagrancy," *Social Problems*, Vol. 12, Summer, 1964, pp. 46-67. By permission of the author and publisher.

vide labor for the established economic elites of the society. Of considerable importance in this analysis is to note that as the economic resources of the society change (from feudal agrarianism to commerce and trade) the content and focus of the criminal law changes.

In 1349 the first vagrancy statute was passed and the wording of this statute made its intention quite clear:

> Because that many valiant beggars, as long as they may live of begging, do refuse to labor, giving themselves to idleness and vice, and sometimes to theft and other abominations; it is ordained, that none upon pain of imprisonment shall, under the colour of pity or alms, give any thing to such which may labour, or presume to favor them towards their desires; so that thereby they may be compelled to labour for their necessary living.

It was further provided by this statute that:

> . . . every man and woman, of what condition he be, free or bond, able in body, and within the age of threescore years, not living in merchandize nor exercising any craft, nor having of his own whereon to live, nor proper land whereon to occupy himself, and not serving any other, if he in convenient service (his estate considered) be required to serve, shall be bounded to serve him which shall him require. . . . And if any refuse,

he shall on conviction by two true men, . . . be committed to gaol till he find surety to serve.

And if any workman or servant, of what estate or condition he be, retained in any man's service, do depart from the said service without reasonable cause or license, before the term agreed on, he shall have pain of imprisonment (23 Ed. 3)

This statute also stipulated that the workers should receive a standard wage. In 1351 this statute was strengthened:

And none shall go out of the town where he dwelled in winter, to serve the summer, if he may serve in the same town (25 Ed. 3 (1351)).

By 34 Ed. 3 (1360) the punishment for these acts became imprisonment for fifteen days and if they "do not justify themselves by the end of that time, to be sent to gaol till they do."

The prime mover for the creation of these laws was the Black Death which struck England about 1348. Among the many disastrous consequences the plague had upon the social structure was the fact that it decimated the labor force. It is estimated that by the time the pestilence had run its course at least fifty percent of the population of England had died from the plague. This decimation of the labor force would necessitate rather drastic innovations in any society but its impact was heightened in England where, at the time, the economy was highly dependent upon a ready supply of cheap labor.

Even before the pestilence, the availability of an adequate supply of cheap labor was becoming a problem for the feudal landowners. The crusades and various wars had made money necessary to the lords, and, as a result, the lords frequently agreed to sell the serfs their freedom in order to obtain the needed funds. The serfs, for their part, sought to escape from serfdom (by "fair means" or "foul") because the larger towns which were becoming commercial and trade centers during this period could offer the serf greater personal freedom as well as a higher standard of living:

By the middle of the 14th century the outward uniformity of the manorial system had become in practice considerably varied . . . for the peasant had begun to drift to the towns and it was unlikely that the old village life in its unpleasant aspects should not be resented. Moreover the constant wars against France and Scotland were fought mainly with mercenaries

after Henry III's time and most villages contributed to the new armies. The bolder serfs either joined the armies or fled to the towns, and even in the villages the free men who held by villein tenure were as eager to commute their services as the serfs were to escape. Only the amount of "free" labor available enabled the lord to work his demesne in many places (Bradshaw: p. 54).

Bradshaw (ibid.) says, regarding the effect of the Black Death,

. . . in 1348 the Black Death reached England and the vast mortality that ensued destroyed that reserve of labour which alone had made the manorial system even nominally possible.

The immediate result of these events was, of course, no surprise: Wages for the "free" man rose considerably, and this increased on the one hand the landowner's problems and on the other hand the plight of the unfree tenant. For although wages increased for the personally free laborers it, of course, did not necessarily add to the standard of living of the serf; if anything it worsened his position because the landowner would be hard pressed to pay for the personally free labor which he needed. Thus it would become more and more difficult to maintain the standard of living for the serf which had heretofore been supplied. The serf had no alternative but flight if he chose to better his position. Furthermore, flight usually meant both freedom and better conditions since the possibility of work in the new weaving industry was great and the chance of being caught was small (ibid., p. 57).

It was under these conditions that we find the first vagrancy statutes emerging. There is little question but that these statutes were designed for one express purpose: to force laborers (whether personally free or unfree) to accept employment at a low wage in order to insure the landowner an adequate supply of labor at a price he could afford to pay. Caleb Foote concurs with this interpretation when he notes:

The anti-migratory policy behind vagrancy legislation began as an essential complement of the wage stabilization legislation which accompanied the breakup of feudalism and the depopulation caused by the Black Death. By the Statutes of Labourers in 1349–1351, every able-bodied person without other means of support was required to work for wages fixed at the level preceding the Black Death; it was unlawful to accept more, or to refuse an offer to work, or to flee from one county to another to avoid offers of work or to seek higher wages, or to give alms to able-bodied beggars who refused to work (Foote: 1958, p. 615).

In short, as Foote says in another place, this was an "attempt to make the vagrancy statutes a substitute for serfdom" (ibid.). This same conclusion is equally apparent from the wording of the statute:

> Because great part of the people, and especially of workmen and servants, late died in pestilence; many seeing the necessity of masters, and great scarcity of servants, will not serve without excessive wages, and some rather willing to beg in idleness than by labour to get their living: it is ordained, that every man and woman, of what condition he be, free or bond, able in body and within the age of three-score years, not living in merchandise, (etc.) be required to serve . . .

The innovation in the law, then, was a direct result of the aforementioned changes which had occurred in the social setting. The law was clearly and consciously designed to serve the interests of the ruling class of feudal landlords at the expense of the serfs or working classes. The vagrancy laws were designed to alleviate a condition defined by the lawmakers as undesirable. The solution was to attempt to force a reversal, as it were, of a social process which was well underway; that is, to curtail mobility of laborers in such a way that labor would not become a commodity for which the landowners would have to compete.

A SHIFT IN FOCAL CONCERN

Following the squelching of the Peasants' Revolt in 1381, the services of the serfs to the lord "tended to become less and less exacted, although in certain forms they lingered on till the seventeenth century . . . By the sixteenth century few knew that there were any bondmen in England . . . and in 1575 Queen Elizabeth listened to the prayers of almost the last serfs in England . . . and granted them manumission" (Bradshaw: p. 61).

In view of this change we would expect corresponding changes in the vagrancy laws. Beginning with the lessening of punishment in the statute of 1530, we find these changes. Instead of remaining dormant (or becoming more so) or being negated altogether, however, the vagrancy statutes experienced a shift in focal concern. With this shift the statutes served a new and equally important function for the ruling class of England. The first statute

which indicates this change was in 1530. In this statute (22 H. 8. c. 12) it was stated:

> If any person, being whole and mighty in body, and able to labour, be taken in begging, or be vagrant and can give no reckoning how he lawfully gets his living . . . and all other idle persons going about, some of them using divers and subtle crafty and unlawful games and plays, and some of them feigning themselves to have knowledge of . . . crafty sciences . . . shall be punished as provided.

What is most significant about this statute is the shift from an earlier concern with laborers to a concern with *criminal* activities. To be sure, the stipulation of persons "being whole and mighty in body, and able to labour, be taken in begging, or be vagrant" sounds very much like the concerns of the earlier statutes. Some important differences are apparent, however, when the rest of the statute includes those who "can give no reckoning how he lawfully gets his living"; "some of them using divers subtil and unlawful games and plays." This is the first statute which specifically focuses upon these kinds of criteria for adjudging someone a vagrant.

It is significant that in this statute the severity of punishment is increased so as to be greater not only than provided by the 1530 statute but the punishment is more severe than that which had been provided by *any* of the pre-1530 statutes as well. For someone who is merely idle and gives no reckoning of how he makes his living the offender shall be:

> . . . had to the next market town, or other place where they (the constables) shall think most convenient, and there to be tied to the end of a cart naked, and to be beaten with whips throughout the same market town or other place, till his body be bloody by reason of such whipping (22 H. 8. c. 12 (1530)).

But, for those who use "divers and subtil crafty and unlawful games and plays," etc., the punishment is "whipping at two days together in manner aforesaid" (ibid.). For the second offense, such persons are:

> . . . scourged two days, and the third day to be put upon the pillory from nine of the clock till eleven before noon of the same day and to have one of his ears cut off (ibid.).

And, if he offend the third time, "to have like punishment with whipping, standing on the pillory and to have his other ear cut off."

This statute (1) makes a distinction between types of offenders and applies the more severe punishment to those who are clearly engaged in "criminal" activities, (2) mentions a specific concern with categories of "unlawful" behavior, and (3) applies a type of punishment (cutting off the ear) generally reserved for offenders who are defined as likely to be fairly serious criminals.

Only five years later we find for the first time that the punishment of death is applied to the crime of vagrancy. We also note a change in terminology in the statute:

> . . . and if any ruffians . . . after having been once apprehended . . . shall wander, loiter, or idle use themselves and play the vagabonds . . . shall be eftsoons not only whipped again, but shall have the gristle of his right ear clean cut off. And if he shall again offend, he shall be committed to gaol till the next session; and being there convicted upon indictment, he shall have judgment to suffer pains and execution of death, as a felon, as an enemy of the commonwealth (27 H. 8. c. 25 (1535)).

It is significant that the statute now makes persons who repeat the crime of vagrancy felons. During this period then, the focal concern of the vagrancy statutes becomes a concern for the control of felons and is no longer primarily concerned with the movement of laborers.

These statutory changes were a direct response to changes taking place in England's social structure during this period. We have already pointed out that feudalism was decaying rapidly. Concomitant with the breakup of feudalism was an increased emphasis upon commerce and trade. The commercial emphasis in England at the turn of the sixteenth century is of particular importance in the development of vagrancy laws. With commercialism came considerable traffic bearing valuable goods. Where there were 169 important merchants in the middle of the fourteenth century, there were 3,000 merchants engaged in foreign trade alone at the beginning of the sixteenth century, (Hall: op. cit., p. 21). England became highly dependent upon commerce for its economic surplus. Italians conducted a great deal of the commerce of England during this early period and were held in low repute by the populace. They were subject to attacks by citizens and, more important, were frequently robbed of their goods while transporting them. "The general insecurity of the

times made any transportation hazardous. The special risks to which the alien merchant was subjected gave rise to the royal practice of issuing formally executed covenants of safe conduct through the realm" (ibid., p. 23).

Such a situation not only called for the enforcement of existing laws but also called for the creation of new laws which would facilitate the control of persons preying upon merchants transporting goods. The vagrancy statutes were revived in order to fulfill just such a purpose. Persons who had committed no serious felony but who were suspected of being capable of doing so could be apprehended and incapacitated through the application of vagrancy laws once these laws were refocused so as to include "any ruffians . . . (who) shall wander, loiter, or idle use themselves and play the vagabonds . . ." (H. 8. c. 25 (1535)).

The new focal concern is continued in 1 Ed. 6. c. 3 (1547) and in fact is made more general so as to include:

> Whoever man or woman, being not lame, impotent, or so aged or diseased that he or she cannot work, not having whereon to live, shall be lurking in any house, or loitering or idle wandering by the highway side, or in streets, cities, towns, or villages, not applying themselves to some honest labour, and so continuing for three days; or running away from their work; every such person shall be taken for a vagabond. And . . . upon conviction of two witnesses . . . the same loiterer (shall) be marked with a hot iron in the breast with a letter V, and adjudged him to the person bringing him, to be his slave for two years . . .

Should the vagabond run away, upon conviction, he was to be branded by a hot iron with the letter S on the forehead and to be henceforth declared a slave forever. And in 1571 there is modification of the punishment to be inflicted, whereby the offender is to be "branded on the chest with the letter V" (for vagabond). And, if he is convicted the second time, the brand is to be made on the forehead. It is worth noting here that this method of punishment, which first appeared in 1530 and is repeated here with somewhat more force, is also an indication of a change in the type of person to whom the law is intended to apply. For it is likely that nothing so permanent as branding would be applied to someone who was wandering but looking for work, or at worst merely idle and not particularly dangerous *per se*. On the other hand, it could well be applied to someone who was likely to be engaged in other criminal activities in connection with being "vagrant."

By 1571 in the statute of 14 E. 1. c. 5 the shift in focal concern is fully developed:

> All rogues, vagabonds, and sturdy beggars shall . . . be committed to the common gaol . . . shall be grievously whipped, and burnt thro the gristle of the right ear with a hot iron of the compass of an inch about; . . . And for the second offense, he shall be adjudged a felon, unless some person will take him for two years in to his service. And for the third offense, he shall be adjudged guilty of felony without benefit of clergy.

And there is included a long list of persons who fall within the statute: "proctors, procurators, idle persons going about using subtil, crafty and unlawful games or plays; and some of them feigning themselves to have knowledge of . . . absurd sciences . . . and all fencers, bearwards, common players in interludes, and minstrels . . . all jugglers, pedlars, tinkers, petty chapmen . . . and all counterfeiters of licenses, passports and users of the same." The major significance of this statute is that it includes all the previously defined offenders and adds some more. Significantly, those added are more clearly criminal types, counterfeiters, for example. It is also significant that there is the following qualification of this statute: "Provided also, that this act shall not extend to cookers, or harvest folks, that travel for harvest work, corn or hay."

The emphasis upon the criminalistic aspect of vagrants continues in Chapter 17 of the same statute:

> Whereas divers *licentious* persons wander up and down in all parts of the realm, to countenance their *wicked behavior;* and do continually assemble themselves armed in the highways, and elsewhere in troops, *to the great terror* of her majesty's true subjects, the *impeachment of her laws,* and the disturbance of the peace and tranquility of the realm; and whereas many outrages are daily committed by these dissolute persons, and more are likely to ensue if speedy remedy be not provided. (Emphasis added.)

With minor variations (e.g., offering a reward for the capture of a vagrant) the statutes remain essentially of this nature until 1743. In 1743 there was once more an expansion of the types of persons in-cluded such that "all persons going about as patent gatherers, or gatherers of alms, under pretense of loss by fire or other casualty; or going about as collectors for prisons, gaols, or hospitals; all persons playing of betting at any unlawful games; and all persons who run away and leave their wives or children . . . all persons wandering abroad, and lodging in ale-houses, barns, out-houses, or in the open air, not giving good account of themselves" were types of offenders added to those already included.

By 1743 the vagrancy statutes had apparently been sufficiently reconstructed by the shifts of concern so as to be once more a useful instrument in the creation of social solidarity. This function has apparently continued down to the present day in England. The changes from 1743 to the present have all been in the direction of clarifying or expanding the categories covered but little has been introduced to change either the meaning or the impact of this branch of the law.

We can summarize this shift in focal concern by quoting from Halsbury. He has noted that in the vagrancy statutes:

> . . . elaborate provision is made for the relief and incidental control of destitute wayfarers. These latter, however, form but a small portion of the offenders aimed at by what are known as the Vagrancy Laws, . . . many offenders who are in no ordinary sense of the word vagrants, have been brought under the laws relating to vagrancy, and the great number of the offenses coming within the operation of these laws have little or no relation to the subject of poor relief, but are more properly directed towards the prevention of crime, the preservation of good order, and the promotion of social economy. (Halsbury: pp. 606-607)

Before leaving this section it is perhaps pertinent to make a qualifying remark. We have emphasized how the vagrancy statutes underwent a shift in focal concern as the social setting changed. The shift in focal concern is not meant to imply that the later focus of the statutes represents a completely new law. It will be recalled that even in the first vagrancy statutes there was reference to those who "do refuse labor, giving themselves to idleness and vice and sometimes to theft and other abominations." Thus the possibility of criminal activities resulting from persons who refuse to labor was recognized even in the earliest statute. The fact remains, however, that the major emphasis in this statute and in the statutes which followed the first one was always upon the "refusal to labor" or "begging." The "criminalistic" aspect of such persons was relatively unimportant. Later, as we have shown, the criminalistic potential becomes of paramount importance. The thread runs back to the earliest statute but the reason for the statutes' existence as well as the focal concern of the statutes is quite different in 1743 than it was in 1349.

VAGRANCY LAWS IN THE UNITED STATES

In general, the vagrancy laws of England, as they stood in the middle eighteenth century, were simply adopted by the states. There were some exceptions to this general trend. For example, Maryland restricted the application of vagrancy laws to "free" Negroes. In addition, for *all* states the vagrancy laws were even more explicitly concerned with the control of criminals and undesirables than had been the case in England. New York, for example, explicitly defines prostitutes as being a category of vagrants during this period. These exceptions do not, however, change the general picture significantly and it is quite appropriate to consider the United States' vagrancy laws as following from England's of the middle eighteenth century with relatively minor changes. The control of criminals and undesirables was the *raison d'etre* of the vagrancy laws in the U.S. This is as true today as it was in 1750. As Caleb Foote's analysis of the application of vagrancy statutes in the Philadelphia court shows, these laws are presently applied indiscriminately to persons considered a "nuisance." Foote suggests that "the chief significance of this branch of the criminal law lies in its quantitative impact and administrative usefulness." (Foote: op. cit., p. 613) Then it appears that in America the trend begun in England in the sixteenth, seventeenth and eighteenth centuries has been carried to its logical extreme and the laws are now used principally as a mechanism for "clearing the streets" of the derelicts who inhabit the "skid rows" and "Bowerys" of our large urban areas.

Since the 1800's there has been an abundant source of prospects to which the vagrancy laws have been applied. These have been primarily those persons deemed by the police and the courts to be either actively involved in criminal activities or at least peripherally involved. In this context, then, the statutes have changed very little. The functions served by the statutes in England of the late eighteenth century are still being served today in both England and the United States. The locale has changed somewhat and it appears that the present-day application of vagrancy statutes is focused upon the arrest and confinement of the "down and outers" who inhabit certain sections of our larger cities but the impact has remained constant. The lack of change in the vagrancy statutes, then, can be seen as a reflection of the society's perception of a continuing need to control some of its "suspicious" or "undesirable" members.

A word of caution is in order lest we leave the impression that this administrative purpose is the sole function of vagrancy laws in the U.S. today. Although it is our contention that this is generally true it is worth remembering that, during certain periods of our recent history and to some extent today, these laws have also been used to control the movement of workers. This was particularly the case during the depression years, and California is infamous for its use of vagrancy laws to restrict the admission of migrants from other states. (Edwards *vs* California. 314 U.S.: 160 (1941) The vagrancy statutes, because of their history, still contain germs within them which make such effects possible. Their main purpose, however, is clearly no longer the control of laborers but rather the control of the undesirable, the criminal and the "nuisance."

DISCUSSION

The foregoing analysis of the vagrancy laws has demonstrated that these laws were legislative innovation which reflected the socially perceived necessity of providing an abundance of cheap labor to landowners during a period when serfdom was breaking down and when the pool of available labor was depleted. With the eventual breakup of feudalism the need for such laws eventually disappeared and the increased dependence of the economy upon industry and commerce rendered the former use of the vagrancy statutes unnecessary. As a result, for a substantial period the vagrancy statutes were dormant, undergoing only minor changes and, presumably, being applied infrequently. Finally, the vagrancy laws were subjected to considerable alteration through a shift in the focal concern of the statutes. Whereas in their inception the laws focused upon the "idle" and "those refusing to labor," after the turn of the sixteenth century, emphasis came to be upon "rogues," "vagabonds," and others who were suspected of being engaged in criminal activities. During this period the focus was particularly upon "roadmen" who preyed upon citizens who transported goods from one place to another. The increased importance of commerce to England during this period made it necessary that some protection be given persons engaged in this enterprise and the vagrancy statutes provided one source for such protection by refocusing the acts to be included under these statutes.

Comparing the results of this analysis with the findings of Hall's study of theft we see a good deal of correspondence. Of major importance is the fact that both analyses demonstrate the truth of Hall's assertion that "the functioning of courts is significantly related to concomitant cultural needs, and this applies to the law of procedure as well as to substantive law." (Hall: op. cit., p. XII)

Our analysis of the vagrancy laws also indicates that when changed social conditions create a perceived need for legal changes, these alterations will be effected through a revision and refocusing of existing statutes. This process was demonstrated in Hall's analysis of theft as well as in our analysis of vagrancy. In the case of vagrancy, the laws were dormant when the focal concern of the laws was shifted so as to provide control over potential criminals. In the case of theft the laws were reinterpreted (interestingly, by the courts and not by the legislature) so as to include persons who were transporting goods for a merchant but who absconded with the contents of the packages transported.

It also seems probable that when the social conditions change and previously useful laws are no longer useful there will be long periods when these laws will remain dormant. It is less likely that they will be officially negated. During this period of dormancy it is the judiciary which has principal responsibility for *not* applying the statutes. It is possible that one finds statutes being negated only when the judiciary stubbornly applies laws which do not have substantial public support. An example of such laws in contemporary times would be the "Blue Laws." Most states still have laws prohibiting the sale of retail goods on Sunday yet these laws are rarely applied. The laws are very likely to remain but to be dormant unless a recalcitrant judge or a vocal minority of the population insists that the laws be applied. When this happens we can anticipate that the statutes will be negated. Should there arise a perceived need to curtail retail selling under some special circumstances, then it is likely that these laws will undergo a shift in focal concern much like the shift which characterized the vagrancy laws. Lacking such application the laws will simply remain dormant except for rare instances where they will be negated.

This analysis of the vagrancy statutes (and Hall's analysis of theft as well) has demonstrated the important emergence and role of ruling classes in the alteration of laws. The vagrancy laws emerged in order to provide the powerful landowners with a ready supply of cheap labor. When this no longer seemed necessary, and particularly when the landowners were neither dependent upon cheap labor nor so powerful, the laws became dormant. Finally a new ruling class emerged and the laws were then altered so as to afford some protection to them. These findings are thus in agreement with Weber's contention that "status groups" determine the content of the law. (Rheinstein: 1954) The findings are inconsistent, on the other hand, with the perception of the law as simply a reflection of "public opinion" as is sometimes noted in the literature. (Friedman: 1959)

FOOTNOTES

[1] For a more complete listing of most of the statutes used in this study see Burn, *History of the English Poor Laws.*

[2] Citations of English statutes should be read as follows: 3 Ed. 1 c. 1 refers to the third act of Edward the First.

REFERENCES

Auerback, D., Garrison, K., Hurst, W., and Mermin, S., *The Legal Process: An Introduction to Decision-Making by Judicial, Legislative, Executive, and Administrative Agencies*, San Francisco: Chandler (1961).

Bradshaw, F. *A Social History of England*, London: University of London Press (1915).

Carson, W. G. O. "The Sociology of Crime and the Emergence of Criminal Laws," paper presented at the British Sociological Association, London (April 1971).

Chambliss, William J., *Crime and The Legal Process*, New York: McGraw-Hill (1969).

Chambliss, William J., and Seidman, Robert B., *Law, Order and Power*, Reading, Massachusetts: Addison-Wesley (1971).

Durkheim, Emile, *The Division of Labor in Society*, Glencoe, Illinois: The Free Press (1949).

Duster, Troy, *The Legislation of Morality: Law, Drugs and Moral Judgement*, New York: Free Press (1970).

Foote, Caleb, "Vagrancy-type Law and its Administration," *University of Pennsylvania Law Review*, Vol. 104 (1956) pp. 603–650.

Foucault, Michael, *Madness and Civilization: A History of Insanity in the Age of Reason*, New York: Pantheon Books (1965).

Friedman, Lawrence, and Macaulay, Stewart, *Law and the Behavioral Sciences*, Indianapolis: Bobbs-Merrill (1969).

Friedman, W., *Law in a Changing Society*, Berkeley: University of California Press (1959).

Gusfield, Joseph R., *Symbolic Crusade: Status Politics and the American Temperance Movement*, Urbana: University of Illinois Press (1963).

Halsbury, Earl of, *The Laws of England*, Bell Yard, Temple Bar, Butterworth & Co. (1912).

Hall, Jerome, *Theft, Law, and Society*, Indianapolis: Bobbs-Merrill, Revised Edition (1952).

Holdsworth, Sir William, *A History of English Law*, Vol. 3, Boston: Little, Brown (1924).

Hurst, J. Willard, *Law and Conditions of Freedom*, Madison: University of Wisconsin Press (1956).

Hurst, J. Willard, *The Growth of American Law: The Law Makers*, Boston: Little, Brown (1950).

Jeffrey, C. Ray, "The Development of Crime in Early English Society," *Journal of Criminal Law, Criminology and Police Science*, Vol. 47, (March-April 1957), pp. 647–666.

Lemert, Edwin M., *Social Action and Legal Change: Revolution Within the Juvenile Court*, Chicago: Aldine (1970).

Lemert, Edwin M., "Legislating Change in the Juvenile Court," *Wisconsin Law Review* (Spring 1967), pp. 421–448.

Lindesmith, Alfred R., *The Addict and The Law*, Bloomington: Indiana University Press (1965).

Lindesmith, Alfred R., *Addiction and Opiates*, Chicago: Aldine (1968).

Quinney, Richard, *The Social Reality of Crime*, Boston: Little, Brown (1970).

Ranulf, Svend, *The Jealousy of the Gods*, Vols. 1 and 2, London: Williams and Northgate Ltd. (1933).

Ranulf, Svend, *Moral Indignation and Middle Class Psychology*, Copenhagen: Levin and Monksgard (1938).

Roby, Pamela A., "Politics and Criminal Law: Revision of the New York State Penal Law on Prostitution," *Social Problems* (Summer 1969), pp. 83–109.

Schwartz, Richard, and Skolnick, Jerome, *Society and The Legal Order*, New York: Basic Books (1971).

Sinclair, Andrew, *Era of Excess: A Social History of the Prohibition Movement*, New York: Harper and Row (1964).

Stephen, J. F., *A History of the Criminal Law of England*, Vol. 1, London: Macmillan (1883).

Walker, Nigel, *Crime and Insanity in England*, (two volumes), Edinburgh: The University Press (1968).

Williams, Glanville L., *The Proof of Guilt: A Study of English Criminal Trial*, London: Stevens (1963).

PART 1 THE CREATION OF LEGAL NORMS

The more recent history of the vagrancy statutes has continued to repeat the same basic process. During times of harvest (in states where agriculture is big business) vagrancy statutes are enforced as a means of providing cheap labor.* Conversely, during periods of recession when there is an over-abundance of cheap labor these same statutes are used to restrict the mobility of the unemployed.†

These historical data are essential if we are to comprehend the rule creation process but they cannot tell us what the process is today. Presumably the role of the ruling class in the creation of criminal laws could have changed substantially in recent years. The available evidence suggests that this has not happened. Indeed, what evidence there is suggests that *even those laws which appear to be contrary to the interests of those who control the economic resources are in fact created to help them increase their profits.*

Since the 1900's there has been a heady growth in America of criminal laws ostensibly designed to curb the excesses of private enterprise. The Sherman anti-trust laws, pure food and drug laws, restrictions on the use of "unfair competition" and the like have emerged as a whole new area of criminal law. On the surface it would appear that these laws represent strong evidence that under certain circumstances criminal laws are passed which are purposely and explicitly contrary to the interests of the most powerful economic interests of the society. Closer examination reveals, however, that even laws that are, on the surface, inimical to the interests of those who control the resources of the society are laws which in fact were promoted and shaped by those very same groups as a means of enhancing and improving their control over the means of production.

Gabriel Kolko has provided historical analysis of the emergence of laws regulating the railroad and meatpacking industries which demonstrate quite clearly that in these areas the laws were promoted and shaped by large corporations in an effort to control competition from smaller companies and to insure better markets for the large companies' products.**

In the latter part of the nineteenth century the railroad industry was in a state of chaos created by intense competition and national economic crises. In June, 1877 a general strike of railroad workers surprised and incapacitated the industry. One consequence of the strike was to establish the role that the state would have in conflicts between workers and industry:

> Out of the crisis came a working view of the role of the state in industrial society which was consistently applied during the next three decades: if for some reason the power of various key business interests was endangered, even for causes of their own making, the state was to intervene to preserve their dominant position.*

The fact that this principle emerged from the strike was doubtless no surprise to the railroad owners. They had, after all, become established and powerful largely through the cooperation of the state in the early years of their development.† The strike, however, underlined for them the value to be had from stronger cooperation with the federal bureaucracy.

There thus began a movement within the railroad industry itself to seek federal regulation of the industry. Previous efforts at pooling by competitive railroads had been largely a failure and the industry had remained intensely competitive.

Profits were low for many companies and bankruptcies not uncommon. Eventually the major railroad companies came to realize that federal regulation which would establish uniform prices at a level guaranteeing profits to the industry was an acceptable and desirable solution. It was, in effect, the use of criminal law legislation to benefit the larger, established railroads to the disadvantage of the smaller. Price and policy regulation by the Federal Government reduced competition and thus eliminated the possibility that a small company might take business away from a larger one. Although widely touted as anti-monopoly legislation, the establishment of the Interstate Commerce Commission and the statutes controlling railroad activities was essentially a move to encourage monopolies within the railroad industry.

The history of criminal law legislation geared ostensibly to regulate the unsanitary practices of the meatpacking industry shows the same underlying motivation. The large meatpacking firms were suffering financially in com-

---

*James P. Spradley, *You Owe Yourself a Drunk,* Boston: Little, Brown, 1970.
†*Edwards v. California,* 314 S: 1941, p. 160.
**Gabriel Kolko, *The Triumph of Conservatism,* New York: The Free Press of Glencoe, 1963; *Railroads and Regulations,* Princeton: Princeton University Press, 1965.

*Ibid., 1965, p. 12.
†Willard Hurst, *The Growth of American Law: The Law Makers,* Boston: Little, Brown, 1950; *Law and Conditions in France,* Madison: University of Wisconsin Press, 1956.

PART 1 THE CREATION OF LEGAL NORMS

petition with smaller firms who were able to undersell them. The entire industry engaged in incredibly unsanitary processing practices which resulted in widespread illness. The larger firms were also being hurt by the fact that the often unhealthy meat sold abroad was reducing the demand in Europe for American meat products. A solution to both problems for the large corporations was legislation creating government inspection of meat processing. This would, of course, raise the cost of producing the meat but for the large firms the increased cost would be minimal as it could be spread over a large output. For the small firms, however, the increased cost would destroy their competitive advantage. Simultaneously, meat inspection laws would improve the health qualities and thereby enable American manufacturers to compete favorably for European markets. Realizing this led the large meatpackers to lobby for federal regulations to control the industry. The government responded to these pressures by passing laws making it a crime to produce meat under unsanitary conditions. The legislation thus aided the large meatpackers in their competition with smaller firms. Upton Sinclair, who inadvertently popularized the unsanitary conditions in the meatpacking industry (he was mainly concerned with working conditions when he wrote in 1906 but it was sanitation that became the issue), accurately described both the reason for passing and the effects of the meatpacking regulations:

> The Federal inspection of meat was, historically, established at the packer's request; . . . it is maintained and paid for by the people of the United States for the benefit of the packers; . . . men wearing the blue uniforms and brass buttons of the United States service are employed for the purpose of certifying to the nations of the civilized world that all the diseased and tainted meat which happens to come into existence in the United States of America is carefully sifted out and consumed by the American people.*

During the legislative debates establishing federal inspection of meat, the large meatpackers were consulted and helped draw up the bills. Samuel H. Cowan, the lawyer for the National Livestock Association, was asked to write a bill acceptable to the packers, which he did. When President Roosevelt criticized the bill, Senator Wadsworth responded:

> I told you on Wednesday night when I submitted the bill to you, that the packers insisted before our committee on having a rigid

inspection law passed. Their life depends on it. They placed no obstacle in our way . . .*

When the bill was finally passed and the head of the Department of Agriculture announced to a gathering of the large meatpackers his department's intention to strictly and rigidly enforce the new laws he was greeted with a round of applause from the industry. For the new laws would, as George Perkins wrote to J. P. Morgan, ". . . be of very great advantage . . . as it will practically give [the meatpackers] a government certificate for their goods . . ."†

Economic interests also become involved in criminal law legislation in order to protect themselves against laws that would interfere with their profits. This process was illustrated and an important set of general principles concerning criminal definitions illuminated by the passage in the United States of The Comprehensive Drug Control Act of 1970.** This statute was designed to control the distribution and use of "dangerous drugs" and included the controversial provision that law enforcement agents could enter private dwellings without knocking in order to search and investigate for the presence of dangerous drugs. In the course of legislative hearings it became apparent that legislation designed to control the use and distribution of drugs in the United States was circumscribed by the fact that legislators would *not* endorse legislation inimical to the interests of the pharmaceutical industry even in the face of overwhelming evidence that the industry was responsible for much of the widespread use of drugs. The drug problem was carefully defined and publicized by the drug industry and legislators as a problem involving "freaky youth" and lower class slumdwellers despite substantial evidence indicating that the dangers of drug use were by no means limited to these classes of persons.

The Comprehensive Drug Abuse Control Act was a bill introduced to the Congress by President Nixon with, predictably, the strong support of two of his major law enforcement officers: Attorney General John Mitchell and

---

*Upton Sinclair, *The Jungle*, Cambridge, Mass.: Bentley Roberts, 1906.

*Gabriel Kolko, *The Triumph of Conservatism*, New York: The Free Press of Glencoe, 1963, p. 106.

†*Ibid.*

**This section is based on James M. Graham, "Profits at All Costs: Amphetamine Politics on Capitol Hill," *Society*, Jan., 1972, pp. 14-72. For a discussion of economic interest in the legislation of laws controlling pollution and safety standards in factories, see W. G. O. Carson, "The Sociology of Crime and the Emergence of Criminal Laws," paper presented at the British Sociological Association, London, April, 1971.

PART 1   THE CREATION OF LEGAL NORMS

the Director of the Bureau of Narcotics and Dangerous Drugs, John Ingersoll.

The bill, as drafted by the Nixon administration with consultation from representatives of the drug industry, was tantamount to providing heretofore unheard of powers to the law enforcement bureaucracies of the state and federal governments in the enforcement of laws controlling the distribution and possession of "drugs." Significantly, however, the drugs that received the greatest emphasis were those that were either imported or produced easily by individuals: heroin, marijuana, and LSD being the principal examples. Drugs which were produced by pharmaceutical manufacturers, even though they were generally sold illegally, were left virtually uncontrolled in the bill. This came about not by accident but through the concerted efforts of the pharmaceutical industry to see that their economic interests were protected.

The issue, so far as the pharmacists were concerned, centered on the manufacture of amphetamines, metaphetamines (referred to as "speed"), and two drugs closely related to these: Librium and Valium.

In a series of testimonies and hearings before various congressional committees and on the floor of the two houses the following facts were brought to light.

Each year in the United States the pharmaceutical industry produces between *eight and ten billion* amphetamine pills. These pills are consumed mainly by the white, middle class American—the housewife, the businessman, students, physicians, and athletes. According to testimony by representatives from the medical profession and the National Institute of Mental Health, many of the consumers of these pills have become psychologically dependent upon them. Furthermore, two of the drugs—Librium and Valium—are, according to testimony before the Congress, likely to lead to extreme depression and suicide. Dr. Stanley Cohen of the National Institute of Mental Health testified that prolonged use of these drugs was common and that it could result in malnutrition, prolonged psychotic states, heart irregularities, convulsions, hepatitis, and sustained brain damage.*

The Bureau of Narcotics and Dangerous Drugs provided the Congress with a report that pinpointed Valium and Librium as being involved in thirty-six suicides and 750 attempted suicides.

Dr. John D. Griffith of the Vanderbilt Medical School stated: "Amphetamine addiction is more widespread, more incapacitating, more dangerous and socially disrupting than narcotic addiction." He further testified that "making these drugs available for obesity and depression has proved to be quite harmful to the public."*

The Director of Student Health Services at the University of Utah testified:

> Amphetamines provide one of the major ironies of the whole field of drug abuse. We continue to insist that they are good drugs when used under medical supervision, but their greatest use turns out to be frivolous, illegal and highly destructive to the user.†

These protestations of danger to the public and inherent problems of addiction, suicide, and the like may or may not be accurate. They are, in any event, no more questionable than the evidence provided on the horrors and dangers of other drugs such as LSD, marijuana and heroin which are not part of the profit system of the pharmaceutical companies.

The failure of Congress or the state bureaucracies concerned with "crime" to include these drugs in the same category as the more widely publicized ones did not result from the presentation of any evidence contradicting the findings mentioned above. It resulted simply from a willingness or a desire to ignore evidence that would have forced the passage of a law inimical to the interests of the drug industry.

That the drug industry profits greatly from the current freedom to manufacture and distribute these drugs is also clearly documented in the hearings. Hoffman-LaRoche Laboratories, producers of Valium and Librium, earned a profit in one year of over four million dollars on these two drugs alone.

Most of the eight billion pills were sold legally through prescription provided by doctors. Many, however, were produced by these firms and diverted into the illegal market. The Bureau of Narcotics and Dangerous Drugs estimated that between seventy-five and ninety percent of the amphetamines on the illegal market had been produced legally by American drug companies. Some of these pills get into the illegal market through forged prescriptions,

*House Hearings, February, 1970, pp. 606, 607, 610.

*Ibid., pp. 616, 618.
†Ibid., pp. 636, 641.

theft, and fraud. But the drug industry is clearly a willing and cooperative victim of some of these practices. Narcotics bureau officers reported that it was possible to simply write drug companies using fake addresses and stationery and obtain massive quantities of the drugs. One agent reported obtaining twenty-five thousand pills by sending a letter to a drug company and signing his name as a medical doctor. The prescriptions on amphetamines and related drugs also invite misuse in that it is possible to write the prescription for an indefinite supply enabling the prescription holder to return to the drug store at will to have the prescription refilled.

Expert testimony was also forthcoming that the real medical needs of the society could be met by, at most, the production of only a few thousand (instead of eight or ten billion) pills a year. Dr. John Griffith of Vanderbilt University Medical School testified that "a few thousand tablets would supply the whole medical needs of the country."*

There was even considerable evidence presented that the amphetamines were of almost no medical use whatsoever, irrespective of the dangers that inhered in their widespread distribution. Congressman Claude Pepper of Florida reported that his Select Committee on Crime had, in the Fall of 1969, distributed questionnaires to medical deans and health organizations throughout the United States. Of 53 responses received by his committee only one suggested that the drug had any use whatsoever and this one suggested that its use was limited to "early stages of a diet program." A representative from the National Institute of Mental Health (Dr. Stanley Cohen) estimated that 99 percent of the prescriptions were supposedly for dietary purposes. Obesity thus becomes a legitimate excuse to get high on speed.

The testimony and reports of medical experts were not, of course, the only side presented at the congressional hearings. At every stage in the history of the bill the pharmaceutical interests were well represented. The Director of the Bureau of Narcotics and Dangerous Drugs admitted under questioning that representatives from the drug industry had been involved in the drafting of the bill for the administration.

During the congressional hearings the drug industry lobbyists testified, as did leading figures from the industry.

The testimony invariably emphasized the danger of "speed freaks" but denied that the industry had any responsibility for such things. Further the industry apologists stressed the medicinal value of amphetamines—a value largely contradicted by independent testimony. Finally, the industry spokesman insisted that present controls were adequate and that government intervention would violate the freedom of the industry necessary for it to serve the public interest.

In the end all testimony and facts which were critical of the drug industry's view were simply swept under the rug. The pharmaceutical companies employed lobbyists, the national pharmaceutical associations sent representatives, and the Congress passed the bill without controlling the manufacture and distribution of any of the drugs from which the drug industry profits. In this way Congress avoided two problems in one: on the one hand, it did not provide legislation that would have angered the drug industry; on the other hand, they did pass a law which made it possible to more readily arrest, prosecute, and convict those powerless members of society who engage in the taking of drugs, the profits of which did not go to the established industries. There is no way to interpret this legislation as a sincere attempt to do something about drug abuse; it is in consequence and by design an example of how the laws reflect the interests of those in power at the expense (both financial and psychological) of those who lack the economic and therefore political power to influence the legislative process. The Comprehensive Drug Abuse Control Act of 1970 which was strongly supported by President Nixon and Attorney General Mitchell as an important piece of ammunition in the arsenal against crime was in effect an important piece of ammunition in the arsenal of the drug industry to reduce competition from unorganized entrepreneurs.

Can we, then, conclude that *all* criminal laws emerge as a result of the actions and interest of ruling elites? Unfortunately we cannot. History rarely supplies us with such clearcut evidence favoring one or another universal principle. Innumerable instances abound where laws emerge and become institutionalized as a consequence of special interest groups which are *not* necessarily connected to or acting in behalf of the ruling classes.

One example of great significance for the operation of the criminal law today is the emergence of criminal laws prohibiting the sale, distribution, and use of narcotics including opium and its derivatives (the most important of which

---

*Ibid., p. 458.

PART 1   THE CREATION OF LEGAL NORMS

is heroin), marijuana, cocaine, acid, and the barbiturates.

In the late eighteen and early nineteen hundreds when opium first appeared on the American market it was touted by leading pharmaceutical companies as a "miracle drug" that "harmlessly" solved all sorts of problems from headaches and rheumatism to boredom. Heroin was available without prescription from druggists and mail order houses.

In 1914 the Federal Government passed the Harrison Act. This law established the first attempt by the government to in any way involve itself with the growing traffic in drugs. The Harrison Act "was passed as a revenue measure and made absolutely no direct mention of addicts or addiction."* According to Alfred Lindesmith the purpose of the Harrison Act was simply to make the matter of drug distribution a part of the public record.

The Treasury Department was given authority to oversee the collection of the revenue from the newly passed tax on drugs. In the course of the next twenty to thirty years, the government carefully selected cases to try and appeal through the criminal courts until the Harrison Act came to be interpreted by the courts as a law making it illegal to be a drug addict and illegal for anyone, including physicians, to sell or prescribe drugs to patients for the purpose of relieving symptoms caused by addiction.

Furthermore, the federal agencies responsible for enforcing the drug laws have often established agency guidelines which were inconsistent with the laws and the court. Lindesmith concludes: ". . . the present system of dealing with addicts is irrational and inconsistent and . . . was not established by legislative intention or by court decisions but rather by administrative action with the Treasury Department."

It is also clear that those branches of the Federal Government authorized to enforce drug laws have been instrumental in shaping and passing state laws making addiction a crime. So too have they been active and effective in constantly expanding the types of products defined as "dangerous drugs." Especially significant in this respect are the activities of the Federal Narcotics Bureau in the 1930's which culminated in the inclusion of marijuana as a "dangerous drug":

The Treasury Department's Bureau of Narcotics furnished most

of the enterprise that produced the marijuana tax act . . . the Federal Bureau of Narcotics cooperated actively with the National Conference of Commissioners on Uniform State Laws in developing uniform laws on narcotics, stressing among other matters the need to control marijuana use.*

An analysis of juvenile court legislation in California has also shown the power of law enforcement bureaucracies in creating law.† Lemert's analysis of the emergence and functioning of the California Youth Authority makes clear how bureaucratic needs may determine the shape of law:

. . . the pressing need for a budget to support the C.Y.A.'s Division of Institutions has meant that where the choice has had to be made between upgrading juvenile court operation through new legislation and maintaining dominant organizational interests, the latter has prevailed . . . the need to support and administer existing institutions, as well as construct new ones, soon established budgetary priority for the Division of Institutions, and came to occupy the largest share of time, energies, and attention of administrators and staff. Recruitment practices, in-training programs, and job assignments tended to preserve a custodial pattern of action within the Division of Institutions, despite the California Youth Authority's informal dedication and official allegiance to the purposes of individualized treatment.**

It is likely that these cases do little more than expose the more visible examples of bureaucratic involvement in the creation of laws. The general rule of law creation that emerges is that bureaucracies will use their resources, power, and influence to obtain passage and suppression of laws that represent the interests of the bureaucracies themselves. The "public interest" or the long-range goal of law are largely irrelevant or at least are only secondary to the interests of the bureaucracies in running and expanding trouble-free organizations.

We see, then, with these investigations of opiate and marijuana laws, the important role played by government agencies in the development of criminal laws. Although those who manage these large governmental bureaucracies may have considerable influence, and may generally represent the interest of the ruling class, they also represent their own class interests. Thus, the conflict-ruling-elite model must be modified to take into account the important

---

*Alfred R. Lindesmith, "Federal Law and Drug Addiction," *Social Problems,* vol. 7, Summer, 1959, p. 48.

*Howard Becker, *The Outsiders,* New York: The Free Press of Glencoe, 1963, p. 8.
†Edwin M. Lemert, *Social Action and Legal Change: Revolution Within the Juvenile Court,* Chicago: Aldine, 1970.
**Ibid.,* p. 52, 56.

PART 1   THE CREATION OF LEGAL NORMS

role sometimes played by government bureaucracies in the creation of criminal laws.

PUBLIC MORALITY AND MORAL ENTREPRENEURS

Part of the mythology that surrounds the law is the view that new laws are created as a result of a change in the values of "the people." This perspective, which is often espoused by social scientists as well as lawyers, sees an assumed "value-consensus" of the community as the root of all law. As we have seen from the data presented, such a view scarcely does justice to the realities of legislation. There is, nevertheless, a substantial body of data which indicates that public views on morality *do* affect legislation, especially those views of segments of the public which get representation by groups of moral entrepreneurs —that is, groups organized to influence law making and enforcement according to their view of morality.

Some of the earliest systematic work on the issue of public indignation and criminal law legislation was done by the Danish Sociologist Svend Ranulf in the two classical studies, *The Jealousy of the Gods* and *Moral Indignation and Middle Class Psychology*. Ranulf shows by careful historical analysis that in both Greece and Europe the "disinterested tendency to punish" for moral breaches emerges with the development of a lower middle class.

Ranulf's argument is basically that until a lower middle class emerges there is no pressure for the state to take the role of a disinterested third party in disputes; rather, disputes are handled between the particular people involved with some mediation by a third party (perhaps appointed by the state) but without the state itself assuming a role as enforcer of abstract moral principles. With the emergence of a lower middle class, however, Ranulf argues, there is pressure on the law to change and become the keeper of public morality. The lower middle class manages this change in law by a general and widespread expression of "moral indignation" over acts committed by persons in other (presumably less moral) social classes. Ranulf's explanation for this process is that the moral indignation of the lower middle class stems from a basic tendency of the lower middle class to envy the position of the more affluent classes.

More recently Joseph Gusfield and Troy Duster have contributed impressive evidence for the argument that public indignation is a force behind criminal law creation.* In his

analysis of the emergence of prohibition laws Gusfield has documented the incredibly important influence on criminal law that the rural middle class was able to have during the early years of the twentieth century when they became an organized social movement which was able to effectively lobby for federal legislation prohibiting the sale and consumption of alcoholic beverages. Gusfield's argument, which he presents most persuasively, is that the loss of power, status, and economic well-being experienced by the small town and rural middle classes at this time led them to express their dissatisfaction with the way society was changing by focusing on the immorality of alcohol. This focused energy was successful in electing a President sympathetic with their viewpoint, and ultimately in creating one of the most bizarre periods of criminal law practice the nation has ever known.

Further evidence of the effects of public indignation on the emergence and shape of the criminal law is also provided by an examination of the role of groups organized to protect the "public interest." In the United States much of the law governing criminal procedure has been written and rewritten by groups of moral entrepreneurs, especially the American Civil Liberties Union and the National Association for the Advancement of Colored People.* The ACLU has been particularly active in criminal law cases where their concern has been with police procedures. In a series of landmark decisions of the United State Supreme Court, which virtually re-write the laws governing police behavior, the ACLU provided funds and legal counsel. These groups, although protecting the rights of the lower classes, are themselves composed of middle class members of the community and supported by financial contributions from that same middle class.

The important point to keep in mind, however, is not so much the immediate impetus for the legislation but the fact that it grows out of conflicts between various social classes and interest groups in the society. The downwardly mobile middle class needed legislation to protect its morality and its social standing precisely because there were other classes which did not agree with or defer to its viewpoint. The NAACP, the ACLU, and the currently popular consumer protection groups *are* in many cases effective spokesmen for the lower and middle classes, and are effec-

---

Duster, *The Legislation of Morality: Law, Drugs and Moral Judgment,* New York: The Free Press of Glencoe, 1970.
*William J. Chambliss and Robert B. Seidman, *Law, Order and Power,* Reading, Mass.: Addison-Wesley, 1971.

---

*Joseph R. Gusfield, *Symbolic Crusade: Status Politics and the American Temperance Movement,* Urbana: University of Illinois Press, 1963; Troy

tive to some degree in obtaining legislation which is inimical to the immediate interests of the ruling classes. But it is a mistake to conclude that "the people" are thus the fountainhead from which laws spring. Rather it is clear that it is the conflict between social class interests and particular interest groups that determines the parameters of the criminal law. Most often, as the evidence presented indicates, the ruling class has its way in the formation and implementation of criminal laws. However the persistence and importance of the conflicts resolved through law necessarily creates occasions where well organized groups representing non-ruling class interests manage to effect important legislation.

Put another way, "public opinion" as a source of law is a misleading conceptualization precisely because it does not specify what "public" refers to. If it refers to "every right-minded citizen" then it is highly unlikely that in complex, stratified, industrialized societies there are very many things on which there is any "public" opinion since there is such widespread disagreement. Certainly the recent legislation making it possible to obtain divorces without legal counsel (a piece of legislation opposed by the powerful Bar Association), or laws legalizing abortion (opposed by some powerful religious groups), were passed as a result of concerted efforts by a very small segment of the population; and it seems likely that most people were unaware that these efforts were even being made.

A consensual moral indignation of the middle class is thus a rare event and in any event no guarantee that the law will change unless the indignation coalesces into a working organization with specific roles and financial backing.

Middle class organizations are, for the most part, unable to combat or counteract the forces of the classes who control the economic resources of the society. As we saw earlier in the history of criminal law legislation, the economic elites' interests are protected by their ability to directly influence legislation and by their mobilization of bias which flows from their position in the society. During the discussion of the Dangerous Drug Act of 1970, for example, the interests of the law enforcement bureaucracies and the drug industry were so fully represented that the moral indignation of the middle class, which was ostensibly the basis for the passage of the law, was simply an excuse used to legitimize a law which was first and foremost a reflection of the wishes of more powerful interests.

The group of moral entrepreneurs who represent the indignation of at least some segment of the middle class fare best when they engage less potent forces than the economic elites. In particular their effect on criminal law legislation is likely to be most noticeable where they engage the law enforcement bureaucracies or only small businesses.

Such was the case in a recent debate in New York over revision of the laws concerning prostitution.* The issue arose over article 230 (one of approximately 520 sections) of the 1965 New York State Penal Law. Sections 230.00, 230.05, and 230.10 of the code provide:

230.00 *Prostitution*

A person is guilty of prostitution when such person engages or agrees or offers to engage in sexual conduct with another person in return for a fee.

Prostitution is a violation. L. 1965, c. 1030, cff. Sept. 1, 1967.

230.05 *Patronizing a prostitute*

A person is guilty of patronizing a prostitute when:

1. Pursuant to a prior understanding, he pays a fee to another person as compensation for such person or a third person having engaged in sexual conduct with him; or

2. He pays or agrees to pay a fee to another person pursuant to an understanding that in return therefor such person or a third person will engage in sexual conduct with him; or

3. He solicits or requests another person to engage in sexual conduct with him in return for a fee.

Patronizing a prostitute is a violation. L. 1965, c. 1030, eff. Sept. 1, 1967.

230.10 *Prostitution and patronizing a prostitute; no defense*

In any prosecution for prostitution or patronizing a prostitute, the sex of the two parties or prospective parties to the sexual conduct engaged in, contemplated, or solicited is immaterial, and it is no defense that:

1. Such persons were of the same sex; or

2. The person who received, agreed to receive or solicited a fee was a male and the person who paid or agreed or offered to pay such fee was a female. L. 1965, c. 1030, eff. Sept. 1, 1967.

At the time this revised code was proposed, prostitution was subject to a penalty of up to three years in a reformatory or a year in jail. Further, prostitution was, until 1960, defined by court decisions as an act committable only by a female. In 1960, by court decision, homosexuality was incorporated under the umbrella of the statute.†

---

*Pamela A. Roby, "Politics and Criminal Law: Revision of the New York State Penal Law on Prostitution," *Social Problems,* Summer, 1969, pp. 83-109.
†*Ibid.,* p. 87.

PART 1   THE CREATION OF LEGAL NORMS

The new code on prostitution made two significant changes: first it included as a violation patronizing a prostitute and, second, it greatly reduced the penalty for prostitution by making the act a "violation" rather than a crime. The maximum sentence for a "violation" is fifteen days, rather than a year, in jail.

In 1961 the Governor of New York appointed a commission to recommend needed revisions of the Penal Law and the Code of Criminal Procedure. The commission staff relied heavily on the advice of Chief Justice John M. Murtagh, a judge nationally known for his concern with criminal procedures in dealing with prostitution. The commission members also relied on Great Britain's *Wolfenden Report,* the model penal codes of the American Bar Association, and procedures in other states.

After four years of work the commission held "Public Hearings" on the proposed penal code revision. "The Public" was probably unaware of the event but some special interest groups were not. Of the 520 articles only the one dealing with prostitution was revised as a result of these hearings. The major change wrought was the addition of "patronizing a prostitute" as a violation, something which was *not* included in the commission's original proposed code. The major proponent for including "patronizing" was the American Social Health Association, which argued that the only way to effectively control the spread of disease was by punishing the patron. The Association's view was buttressed by arguments from Dorris Clarke, Attorney and retired Chief Probation Officer of the N.Y. City Magistrates Court. Further support came from testimony of an independent doctor who argued that since both customer and prostitute were guilty, both should be punished.

Combating this position was Judge Murtagh and a few spokesmen for the police who argued that the police needed to have the confidence of customers in order to get testimony against prostitutes.

The opposition was, at this point, no match in number or organization and thus the patron clause was written into the law.

On the eve of the new law going into effect the police relaxed their enforcement policies. Subsequently a rumor circulated that there was an influx of prostitutes into the city. The source of the rumor is not clear but:

New York politicians, businessmen, and the police may have begun to talk about an influx of prostitutes and the need for a "cleanup" because they were dissatisfied with the law becoming "soft" on prostitutes.*

During this time police department representatives began telling newsmen of increases in prostitution.

The commission that had drafted the new law denied these allegations. In any event, in August of 1967 midtown businessmen and the New York Hotel Association along with politicians and government officials pressured the police to get rid of the prostitutes in the area of Times Square.

Approximately two weeks before the new law was to become effective the police made a series of raids around Times Square and arrested suspected prostitutes by the score! On August 20th alone 121 were arrested on Times Square. Between August and September 23, 1300 arrests were made. Most of those which *followed* the date when the new law became effective (September 1st) were for loitering or disorderly conduct.

The New York Civil Liberties Union, the Legal Aid Society, and a New York judge all made vociferous protests over the mass arrest of persons for disorderly conduct and loitering when it was obvious, even to the police, that these charges would not stand up in court. The NYCLU reported on September 22, 1967:

In a press release, the New York Civil Liberties Union protested police practices in the "Times Square cleanup campaign". The NYCLU reported, "Literally hundreds of women have been arrested and charged with disorderly conduct during the summer months, and the situation still continues." ". . . there is a conspiracy on the part of the police to deprive these women of their civil right by arresting them on insubstantial charges." ". . . women are being arrested in a dragnet and charged with disorderly conduct and loitering in order to raise the number of arrests." ". . . many innocent girls are undoubtedly being caught in the net and the entire practice is an outrageous perversion of the judicial process. Furthermore, women who refuse to submit to the unlawful practices of the police have been manhandled."

The Union reported Judge Basel saying, "I don't doubt that most of them are prostitutes, but it is a violation of the civil liberties of these girls. Even streetwalkers are entitled to their Constitutional rights. The District Attorney moved in all these cases to have the charges thrown out, but in every case the girls

---

Ibid., p. 94.

PART 1   THE CREATION OF LEGAL NORMS

were arrested after it was too late for night court, so they were kept over night with no substantial charges pending against them."*

The police roundup continued. From September 23rd to September 30th another 1100 arrests were made. These arrests brought the total from August 20th to September 30th to 2,400; this total was only 200 fewer arrests in six weeks than had been reported during the preceding six months. Significantly, only 6% of the arrests for violation of the prostitution ordinance involved the arrest of patrons despite the fact that the only legal basis for arresting prostitutes was for a policeman to observe a patron offering and a prostitute accepting a fee.

Thus began a campaign by the police department in cooperation with the Hotel Association and businessmen in the area to change those parts of the new penal code that liberalized the prostitution laws. In September, 1967 the police department prefiled amendments to be considered by the 1968 legislature. These amendments in effect would have given the police almost complete discretion in the arrest of suspected prostitutes; they would have returned prostitution to the status of a crime thus increasing the penalties and these amendments would have effectively enabled the police to avoid the application of the law to patrons without formally changing this part of the penal code.

The Mayor of New York City created a committee to look into the new law and the problem of prostitution. The committee in the end recommended that prostitution be reclassified a crime instead of its present status as a "violation"; thereby the penalty would have increased from 15 days to one year in jail. But the committee did *not* recommend adopting any of the other changes advocated by the police and the Hotel Association. When this proposal was presented before the state legislature it went to a Senate committee which voted *against* sending the bill back to the Senate: thus the law was kept as passed in 1967 at least for another year. In the end, the welfare, civil liberties, and Bar Association interests dominated over the interests of the police and the businessmen with respect to the severity of the sanctions and the criteria for making an arrest. The police and businessmen held sway over

enforcement policies but this did *not* culminate in any immediate change in the law.

The New York Bar, NYCLU, and Legal Aid Society along with some prominent public figures proved to be more potent forces in shaping the formal law than did the police and the Hotel Owners Association.

The analysis of the New York controversy over prostitution makes this point. For the most part the controversy over the new law was limited to different groups of moral entrepreneurs from the middle class: civil liberties and welfare groups on the one side, police and small businessmen on the other. The issue was largely irrelevant to the economic elites of the state or even the city, and they were as a result apathetic. To the extent that the upper classes were represented at all in the debate, the new legislation was tacitly supported, judging from the support given by the Bar Associations and Commissions in their suggested revisions. This case also illustrates how police, prosecutorial, and judicial discretion can subvert the law. The 1965 revision made patrons, who doubtless represented the entire spectrum of social classes, equally culpable. The police, however, through selective enforcement rendered this aspect of the law virtually meaningless and forced reconsideration by the law makers.

The moving force in the creation of criminal laws is conflict. Who takes the mantle and engages the courts in the resolution of the conflict is usually determined by the resources available to the interested parties. Occasionally, however, a major innovation in criminal law stems from the concerted effort of only one person. This is particularly likely at the Appellate Court level. The legislature passes the laws but the interpretation of the laws which will bind the courts in the administration of punishment and the application of the laws derives from Appellate Court decisions. It will be recalled that it was Appellate Court decisions that played a central role in the development of the drug laws in the United States.

In 1962 one man, a convicted felon in a Florida prison, persisted in his effort to gain a hearing before the United States Supreme Court. As a result of his efforts a fundamental part of the procedures for handling suspected criminals was changed. The man's name was Clarence Earl Gideon. His story and the effect of his efforts on the criminal law is described in the following article by Anthony Lewis.

Ibid., p. 55.

2

Gideon's Trumpet

ANTHONY LEWIS

In the morning mail of January 8, 1962, the Supreme Court of the United States received a large envelope from Clarence Earl Gideon, prisoner No. 003826, Florida State Prison, P. O. Box 221, Raiford, Florida. Like all correspondence addressed to the Court generally rather than to any particular justice or Court employee, it went to a room at the top of the great marble steps so familiar to Washington tourists. There a secretary opened the envelope. As the return address had indicated, it was another petition by a prisoner without funds asking the Supreme Court to get him out of jail—another, in the secretary's eyes, because pleas from prisoners were so familiar a part of her work. She walked into the next room and put the envelope on the desk of an assistant clerk of the Supreme Court, Michael Rodak, Jr.

Mr. Rodak, among other duties, concerns himself with what the Supreme Court calls its Miscellaneous Docket. This is made up mostly of cases brought by persons who are too poor to have their court papers printed or to pay the usual fee of one hundred dollars

for docketing a case in the Supreme Court—bringing it there. A federal statute permits persons to proceed in any federal court *in forma pauperis*, in the manner of a pauper, without following the usual forms or paying the regular costs. The only requirement in the statute is that the litigant "make affidavit that he is unable to pay such costs or give security therefor."

The Supreme Court's own rules show special concern for *in forma pauperis* cases. Rule 53 allows an impoverished person to file just one copy of a petition, instead of the forty ordinarily required, and states that the Court will make "due allowance" for technical errors so long as there is substantial compliance. In practice, the men in the Clerk's Office —a half dozen career employees, who effectively handle the Court's relations with the outside world— stretch even the rule of substantial compliance. Rule 53 also waives the general requirement that documents submitted to the Supreme Court be printed. It says that *in forma pauperis* applications should be typewritten "whenever possible," but in fact handwritten papers are accepted.

Gideon's were written in pencil. They were done in carefully formed printing, like a schoolboy's, on lined sheets evidently provided by the Florida prison. Printed at the top of each sheet, under the heading Correspondence Regulations, was a set of rules ("Only 2 letters each week . . . written on one side only . . . letters must be written in English . . .") and the warning: MAIL WILL NOT BE DELIVERED WHICH DOES NOT CONFORM TO THESE RULES. Gideon's punctuation and spelling were full of surprises, but there was also a good deal of practiced, if archaic, legal jargon, such as "Comes now the petitioner. . . ." It seemed likely to Rodak that Gideon had a copy of the Supreme Court Rules.

The first of the documents in the envelope was a two-page affair headed "Motion for leave to proceed in forma pauperis" and including the notarized affidavit that the statute requires. A quick check indicated to Rodak that this prisoner had substantially complied with the rules. He appeared, for example, to have met the requirement that criminal cases be brought to the Supreme Court within ninety days of the lower court decision. Gideon had applied to the Florida Supreme Court for a writ of habeas corpus—an order freeing him on the ground that he was illegally imprisoned. He enclosed a copy of that application and of a brief order of the Florida court denying it. The Florida ruling against him, which he wanted the Supreme Court of the United States to review, was dated October 30, 1961, less than ninety days before.

There was very little in what he had sent to the Court to portray Clarence Earl Gideon the man. His age, his color, his criminal record if any—not even these basic facts appeared, much less any details for a more complete portrait. Because the case came from the South, one's assumption might have been that he was a Negro. He was not.

Gideon was a fifty-one-year-old white man who had been in and out of prisons much of his life. He had served time for four previous felonies, and he bore the physical marks of a destitute life: a wrinkled, prematurely aged face, a voice and hands that trembled, a frail body, white hair. He had never been a professional criminal or a man of violence; he just could not seem to settle down to work, and so he had made his way by gambling and occasional thefts. Those who had known him, even the men who had arrested him and those who were now his jailers, considered Gideon a perfectly harmless human being, rather likeable, but one tossed aside by life. Anyone meeting him for the first time would be likely to regard him as the most wretched of men.

And yet a flame still burned in Clarence Earl Gideon. He had not given up caring about life or freedom; he had not lost his sense of injustice. Right now he had a passionate—some thought almost irrational—feeling of having been wronged by the State of Florida, and he had the determination to try to do something about it. Although the Clerk's Office could not be expected to remember him, this was in fact his second petition to the Supreme Court. The first had been returned for failure to include a pauper's affidavit, and the Clerk's Office had enclosed a copy of the rules and a sample affidavit to help him do better next time. Gideon persevered.

Assistant Clerk Rodak, knowing and caring nothing for any of this, stamped Gideon's papers and gave them a number—890 Miscellaneous, meaning that the case was the 890th entered on the Miscellaneous Docket in the October Term, 1961. (Supreme Court terms, which usually run from October into June, are formally designated by the month in which they begin.) On a green file card a secretary typed the number and the title of the case: Clarence Earl Gideon, petitioner, versus H. G. Cochran, Jr., Director, Division of Corrections, State of Florida, respondent. Then the papers were put into a large red folder and tied with a string. (Red is the color for Miscellaneous cases; regular prepaid cases, on what is called the Appellate Docket, go into blue folders.) The Gideon folder was dispatched to the file room, one floor down, by an electric dumbwaiter.

Sometimes Rodak or his colleague in the Clerk's Office, Edward Schade, looking over the confused and often unintelligible prisoners' petitions that come before them, will spot one with an impressive legal claim. Their view has nothing whatever to do with the action the Supreme Court may take, since only the nine justices act for the Court and they do not discuss the merits of cases with the employees in the Clerk's Office. Still, just in the office, it enlivens things to say once in a while: "Here's one that I'll bet will be granted."

PART 1   THE CREATION OF LEGAL NORMS

No one said that about *Gideon v. Cochran*, No. 890 Miscellaneous, October Term, 1961. In the Clerk's Office it had no ring of history to it. It was just one of nine *in forma pauperis* cases that arrived in the mail on January 8, 1962. Four others were, like Gideon's, criminal cases from the state courts —from Iowa, Washington, New York and Illinois. Two were appeals from federal convictions. One was a civil case, a claim by an unhappy and unaffluent author that someone had plagiarized his copyrighted play. The last was so confused that the Clerk's Office was unable to put it in any category at all.

Gideon's main submission was a five-page document entitled "Petition for a Writ of Certiorari Directed to the Supreme Court State of Florida." A writ of certiorari is a formal device to bring a case up to the Supreme Court from a lower court. In plain terms Gideon was asking the Supreme Court to hear his case.

What was his case? Gideon said he was serving a five-year term for "the crime of breaking and entering with the intent to commit a misdemeanor, to wit, petty larceny." He had been convicted of breaking into the Bay Harbor Poolroom in Panama City, Florida. Gideon said his conviction violated the due-process clause of the Fourteenth Amendment to the Constitution, which provides that "No state shall . . . deprive any person of life, liberty, or property, without due process of law." In what way had Gideon's trial or conviction assertedly lacked "due process of law"? For two of the petition's five pages it was impossible to tell. Then came this pregnant statement:

"When at the time of the petitioners trial he ask the lower court for the aid of counsel, the court refused this aid. Petitioner told the court that this Court made decision to the effect that all citizens tried for a felony crime should have aid of counsel. The lower court ignored this plea."

Five more times in the succeeding pages of his penciled petition Gideon spoke of the right to counsel. To try a poor man for a felony without giving him a lawyer, he said, was to deprive him of due process of law. There was only one trouble with the argument, and it was a problem Gideon did not men-

tion. Just twenty years before, in the case of *Betts v. Brady*, the Supreme Court had rejected the contention that the due-process clause of the Fourteenth Amendment provided a flat guarantee of counsel in state criminal trials.

Betts v. Brady was a decision that surprised many persons when made and that had been a subject of dispute ever since. For a majority of six to three, Justice Owen J. Roberts said the Fourteenth Amendment provided no universal assurance of a lawyer's help in a state criminal trial. A lawyer was constitutionally required only if to be tried without one amounted to "a denial of fundamental fairness." The crucial passage in the opinion read:

"Asserted denial [of due process of law] is to be tested by an appraisal of the totality of facts in a given case. That which may, in one setting, constitute a denial of fundamental fairness, shocking to the universal sense of justice, may, in other circumstances, and in the light of other considerations, fall short of such denial. In the application of such a concept there is always the danger of falling into the habit of formulating the guarantee into a set of hard and fast rules the application of which in a given case may be to ignore the qualifying factors. . . ."

Later cases had refined the rule of *Betts v. Brady*. To prove that he was denied "fundamental fairness" because he had no counsel, the poor man had to show that he was the victim of what the Court called "special circumstances." Those might be his own illiteracy, ignorance, youth, or mental illness, the complexity of the charge against him or the conduct of the prosecutor or judge at the trial.

But Gideon did not claim any "special circumstances." His petition made not the slightest attempt to come within the sophisticated rule of *Betts v. Brady*. Indeed, there was nothing to indicate he had ever heard of the case or its principle. From the day he was tried Gideon had had one idea: That under the Constitution of the United States he, a poor man, was flatly entitled to have a lawyer provided to help in his defense.

Gideon was tried on August 4, 1961, in the Circuit Court of the Fourteenth Judicial Circuit of Florida, in and for Bay County, before Judge Robert L. McCrary, Jr. The trial transcript begins as follows:

Lewis: Gideon's Trumpet

THE COURT: The next case on the docket is the case of the State of Florida, Plaintiff, versus Clarence Earl Gideon, Defendant. What says the State, are you ready to go to trial in this case?

MR. HARRIS: (William E. Harris, Assistant State Attorney): The State is ready, your Honor.

THE COURT: What says the Defendant? Are you ready to go to trial?

THE DEFENDANT: I am not ready, your Honor.

THE COURT: Did you plead not guilty to this charge by reason of insanity?

THE DEFENDANT: No sir.

THE COURT: Why aren't you ready?

THE DEFENDANT: I have no counsel.

THE COURT: Why do you not have counsel? Did you not know that your case was set for trial today?

THE DEFENDANT: Yes sir, I knew it was set for trial today.

THE COURT: Why, then, did you not secure counsel and be prepared to go to trial?

The Defendant answered the Court's question, but spoke in such low tones that it was not audible.

THE COURT: Come closer up, Mr. Gideon, I can't understand you, I don't know what you said, and the Reporter didn't understand you either.

At this point the Defendant arose from his chair where he was seated at the Counsel Table and walked up and stood directly in front of the Bench, facing his Honor, Judge McCrary.

THE COURT: Now tell us what you said again, so we can understand you, please.

THE DEFENDANT: Your Honor, I said: I request this Court to appoint counsel to represent me in this trial.

THE COURT: Mr. Gideon, I am sorry, but I cannot appoint counsel to represent you in this case. Under the laws of the State of Florida, the only time the court can appoint counsel to represent a Defendant is when that person is charged with a capital offense. I am sorry, but I will have to deny your request to appoint counsel to defend you in this case.

THE DEFENDANT: The United States Supreme Court says I am entitled to be represented by counsel.

THE COURT: Let the record show that the defendant has asked the court to appoint counsel to represent him in this trial and the court denied the request and informed the defendant that the only time the court could appoint counsel to represent a defendant was in cases where the defendant was charged with a capital offense. The defendant stated to the court that the United States Supreme Court said he was entitled to it.

Gideon was wrong, of course. The United States Supreme Court had not said he was entitled to counsel; in *Betts v. Brady* and succeeding cases it had said quite the opposite. But that did not necessarily make Gideon's petition futile, for the Supreme Court never speaks with absolute finality when it interprets the Constitution. From time to time—with due solemnity, and after much searching of conscience— the Court has overruled its own decisions. Although he did not know it, Clarence Earl Gideon was calling for one of those great occasions in legal history. He was asking the Supreme Court to change its mind.

The United States Supreme Court did in fact change its mind. It ruled in favor of Gideon and thereby established a principle which all state and federal courts have subsequently been bound to follow, namely that every citizen must be represented by counsel if he requests it. As we shall see in later chapters, the dictates of the Supreme Court do not always force lower courts, prosecuting attorneys, and police departments to actually implement the intention of the decision—there are ingenious ways devised to avoid doing what the court has decreed—but nonetheless at least the formal requirements of the law were dramatically changed through the efforts of one man.

DISCUSSION AND CONCLUSION

Between the Star Chamber in fifteenth century England where a group of judges defined what would be theft in order to protect the interests of the ruling classes, and the United States Supreme Court in mid-twentieth century where an impoverished petty criminal's petition was the basis for redefining the accused's rights in criminal procedures, lies a vast array of criminal laws that have been created, contradicted, and reformulated. Constructing a general theory that can account for such a wide range of

PART 1 THE CREATION OF LEGAL NORMS

events is no simple task. It is not surprising that such efforts often fall short of their goal.

Two general models of rule creation have dominated sociological and legal efforts to explain the emergence and alteration of criminal laws: the "consensus" and the "conflict" models. "Consensus" theories would seem to have their greatest support from criminal laws about which there is widespread agreement, such as laws prohibiting violence, theft, rape, murder, and the like. It is important to distinguish, however, between consensus as a *source* of legal innovation and consensus as a *consequence* of that innovation. Certainly in today's world there are few people who argue that murder should not be a crime. It is noteworthy, however, that in early England what is legally murder today was not an act about which the state would concern itself. Rather, such acts were viewed as a dispute between different clans to be adjudicated according to their own wishes without state interference. And as we have seen, even laws of theft were not enacted as a result of public opinion but were instead enacted to protect the interests of certain powerful classes.

All of this is not to say that laws never emerge on the heels of widespread public opinion. It is to say, however, that this is rare and in any event accounts for but a small segment of the criminal law in America today. The more useful model is clearly one that sees the emergence of criminal laws as a result of conflicts inherent in the structure of the society.

It is also quite apparent from the data that the ruling class (defined as those who control the economic resources of the society) *do* strongly influence what kinds of behavior will be defined as criminal and what will not; so, too, judging from the evidence, do bureaucratic agencies, special interest groups such as moral entrepreneurs, and even individuals with a "cause." All of these are at times able to manipulate legislation and court decisions to be in line with their own image of what the law should reflect.

There are, then, three major inputs into the law making process: (1) economic crises which threaten the interests of the ruling class, (2) bureaucratic needs as perceived by those who manage the bureaucracy, and (3) moral entrepreneurs who seek to change the law so that it comes more into line with their vision of justice.*

What seems to be most congenial with this data, then, is a conflict mode of legal change. The starting point for this model is the recognition that modern, industrialized society is composed of numerous social classes and interest groups who compete for the favors of the state. Not all of these classes and groups are equally powerful. Some have more to offer (economically, persuasively, or politically) to the lawmakers and government officials. Those with more to offer will more often have their interests represented in the criminal law than will others. Thus, when changes in social structure or economic crises impair the economic interests of the ruling class, the lawmakers are quick to respond.

A society divided into social classes where there are great differences in wealth, power, and privilege is also a society in which conflict between social classes is omnipresent. So long as class conflicts are latent, those who sit at the top of the political and economic structure can manipulate the criminal laws to suit their own purposes. But when class conflict breaks into open rebellion, as it often does in such societies,* the state must enact legislation and the courts re-interpret laws in ways that are perceived as solutions to the conflict. During these times it is to be expected that the courts and legislators will simultaneously create criminal laws which provide the state with greater control over those groups who are engaged in acts disruptive to the status quo, and laws which may appear to alleviate the conditions which can be construed as having given rise to the manifest social conflicts. Once these dual measures of oppression and appeasement have had their desired effect—that is, when the instant manifest conflict has been subdued—then the power of the ruling class will reassert itself and even the concessions which were given in the heat of the conflict may gradually be eroded. In the end the plight of the powerless may have been slightly improved, but the class structure of the society insures that the underlying conflicts and the role of the criminal law as an arm of those who rule will prevail.

In between crises, or perhaps as an adjunct to the legislative-judicial innovations taking place because of

---

*Most broadly conceived, each of these sources may be summarized under the concept of "interest groups," but such a general concept does little more than provide an umbrella under which to put these various social processes. It seems wiser to accept the fact that there are three sources of criminal law creation than to perhaps distort their relative significance by attempting to place them all under a single causal variable. See Richard Quinney, *The Social Reality of Crime,* Boston: Little, Brown, 1971.

*For a brief history of rebellions in America, see Richard E. Rubenstein, *Rebels in Eden,* Boston: Little, Brown, 1970.

PART 1   THE CREATION OF LEGAL NORMS

them, bureaucracies can mobilize and moral entrepreneurs organize to plead their case before the lawmaking bodies. Without the changes in economic structure that accompanied England's transition from feudalism to capitalism the laws of theft and vagrancy would not have taken the form they did, and without the riots, demonstrations, and rebellions of the 1960's Gideon's Trumpet would never have been blown. These innovations would have remained uninitiated while in their stead special interest groups or bureaucratic officials or economic elites would simply have held sway over the creation of laws specially geared to their interests.

Part 2

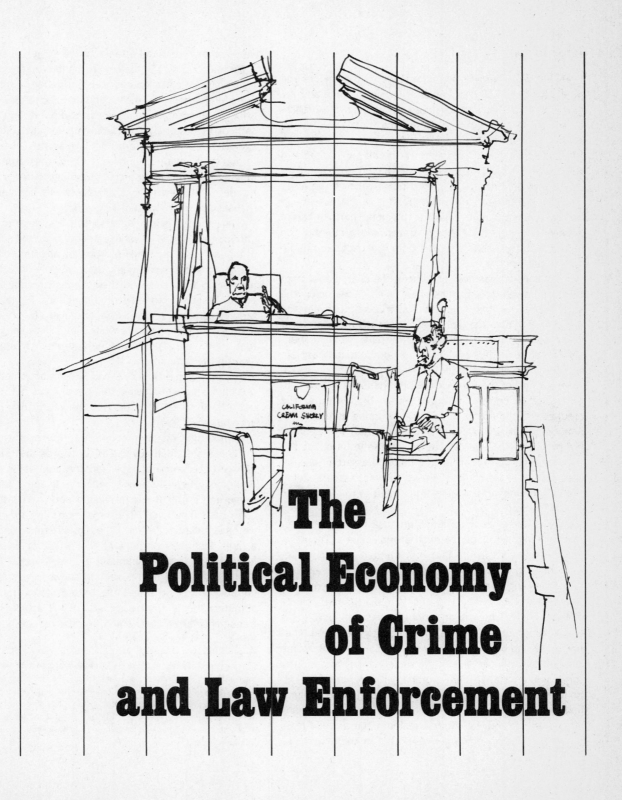

The
Political Economy
of Crime
and Law Enforcement

PART 2 THE POLITICAL ECONOMY OF CRIME AND LAW ENFORCEMENT

INTRODUCTION

In recent years social scientists, lawyers, and the general public have paid a great deal of attention to crime and the criminal law. Of particular interest has been the realization that the police and to some extent all law enforcing agencies discriminate against the poor in general and Blacks, Chicanos, and Indians in particular. This concern with discrimination in the law was forced onto the consciousness of America by ghetto riots, police brutality at conventions and peace demonstrations, and the reaction of law enforcement officials to the long hair, unkempt appearance, and casual use of drugs among many of the college and high school youths from "respectable middle class families."

Yet this new awareness of some of the characteristics of the criminal law process has often failed to see below the surface because it is blind to the relationship between the criminal law and the political and economic system of which the criminal law is an integral part. That relationship must be understood if we are to adequately explain why the law works as it does.

In this part of the book we take up the issue of how people come to commit criminal acts. In particular the emphasis in the article is on the reinforcing nature of the relationship between criminal behavior and the criminal law process. The intention of this part is to introduce the behavioral background which is then addressed in the succeeding part of the book, where we discuss in greater detail the law enforcement process from arrest to the imposition of punishment.

In a very real sense societies produce their own crime. Although in most modern industrialized societies there is a rough consensus on the fact that murder, robbery, rape, theft, and kidnapping are acts which the state must respond to by imposing legal sanctions, there is little consensus on what other acts should be considered criminal. Since offenses such as murder and robbery constitute only a very small proportion of the acts which occupy the attention of the police and courts, it is necessarily true that most crime is created by the decision of the society to pay attention to some acts and label them criminal while ignoring others. Policemen in the United States, Sweden, and Finland make more arrests for drunkenness every year than for any other crime. Rarely is anyone arrested in the United States for failing to come regularly to work, but failing to work is a very common criminal offense in the Soviet Union.

On the other side of the coin is the fact that every society also systematically ignores some criminal offenses while punishing others. In most capitalist economies, political bribery and corruption are widespread but rarely if ever the subject of systematic investigation by law enforcement agencies. Organized criminal syndicates operate with impunity in many countries, committing criminal acts ranging from providing illegal gambling to drugs and even murder while unemployed derelicts are arrested by the thousands for being drunk in public.

Even for the same offense the response of the law enforcement agencies varies depending on the social class of the law violator. While persons are arrested for shooting craps in a ghetto apartment, upper middle class businessmen are playing poker in their homes for stakes that the ghetto resident can only dream about. Fights between family members on skid row are likely to bring official action from law enforcers while similar or even more violent fights in upper class neighborhoods are handled "within the family."

The following article by David M. Gordon, an economist, presents a more detailed statement of some of these implications of these remarks for the study of crime and criminal law.

Following Gordon's economic interpretation is an insightful statement by Susan Griffin of the relationship between the crime of rape and the political economy of America. Then a study comparing selected features of crime and criminal law in Nigeria and the United States contrasts "functional" and "dialectic" (a variant of what we have called "conflict") theories of crime, and another article describes crime and the effect of criminal law enforcement in two delinquent groups.

The last article in this section shows how criminal law enforcement has changed the United States from a "constabulary" to a "police society." This article is then a transition into Part III, which looks at the social organization of law enforcement.*

---

*For some recent analyses of the issues raised in this section, see the following: Ian Taylor, Paul Maiton, and Jack Young, *The New Criminology: For a Social Theory of Deviance,* London: Routledge and Kegan Paul, 1973; Richard Quinney, *Critique of Legal Order,* Boston: Little, Brown, 1974; Austin Turk, *Criminality and Legal Order,* Chicago: Rand-McNally, 1969; William J. Chambliss and Milton Mankoff, *Whose Law, What Order?,* Santa Barbara: Hamilton, in press.

3

Class and the Economics of Crime

DAVID M. GORDON

Then in his second semester at Eastern District High School, he gave up working in school altogether. "I don't really know why, and I don't want to rationalize about it, but it may have been that I had been systematically de-educated. With all the emphasis on discipline, all the fire gets damped down. I knew I had a given role in society, and you wonder what do you need to know about Plato to fix the engine of an automobile. Anyhow, I flew apart, I began cutting classes, gambling in the bathroom, the whole bit . . . I picked pockets. I was a little crook.

(Nine months in a reformatory intervened.) When he came out, Franklin K. Lane High School never jelled, and eventually he began to hustle. "I took a bunch of nothing jobs—they lasted a month on the average, and then I'd go to the movies instead. I bounced around, I'd hustle when it was necessary—gambling, numbers, a little petty larceny. And when I was 19 I committed a burglary and that was the end of the ball game."

. . . From the story of a 30-year-old black ex-con[1]

Crime in the United States has become another domestic "crisis." Crime rates have been soaring. Central city residents hide in their homes at night,

Source: "Class and the Economics of Crime," *The Review of Radical Political Economics*, Vol. 3, No. 3, Summer, 1971, pp. 51–72. By permission of the author and publisher.

frightened by the ubiquitous muggers. Public efforts to prevent crime have mushroomed into a veritable military campaign; like our other recent war adventures, the campaign seems essentially to have failed. Compounding the sense of crisis, inmates have been rebelling in the prisons, forging what one observer recently called a "low-visibility revolution."[2]

Although sociologists and criminologists have been studying the problem of crime for years, economists have largely ignored it. Suddenly, at the end of the 1960's, they strode confidently into the breach. Applying the standard tools of neo-classical economics, they promised to guide us toward "optimal" crime prevention and control. In his pioneering essay, Gary Becker explains how easily the problem can be understood (3, p. 170): ". . . a useful theory of criminal behavior can dispense with special theories of anomic, psychological inadequacies, or inheritance of special traits and simply extend the economist's usual analysis of choice."

The orthodox analysis seems to me to offer neither a valid framework within which to understand the problem of crime nor a useful guide toward its solution. In this essay, I have tried to articulate an alternative radical economic analysis of crime in the United States. The essay applies some of the basic tools of radical theory to try to illuminate the causes of crime in this country and to explain our failures to curb its growth. The paper has three sections. The first section provides a brief descriptive summary of the nature and extent of crime in America. The second section very briefly surveys some of the conventional public perspectives motivating our efforts to control crime and outlines recent orthodox economic analyses of the problem. The third section suggests a radical economic analysis of crime, arguing that we cannot realistically expect to "solve" the problem of crime in the United States without first effecting a fundamental redistribution of power in our society.

CRIME IN AMERICA

Several useful summaries of the nature and extent of American crime are easily available.[3] Based on those sources, the following paragraphs outline the most important questions about the problem of crime which any economic analysis must try to resolve.

It seems important to emphasize, first of all, that crime is ubiquitous in the United States. Our laws are so pervasive that one must virtually retire to a hermitage in order to avoid committing a crime. According to a national survey conducted in 1965 by the President's Crime Commission (32, p. 5), 91 percent of all adult Americans "admitted that they had committed acts for which they might have received jail or prison sentences." The Crime Commission also found that in 1965 "more than two million Americans were received in prisons or juvenile training schools, or placed on probation"—well over two percent of the labor force. Criminal behavior, it appears, is clearly a norm and not an aberration.

Given that ubiquity, one should also emphasize the extraordinary selectivity of our attention to the problem of crime. We focus all our paranoia about "law'n'order" and "safe streets" on a limited number of crimes while we totally ignore many other kinds of crime, equally serious and of much greater economic importance.

The crimes on which the public *does* concentrate its fears and cannons are often lumped together as "urban" or "violent" crimes. These crimes can be usefully summarized by those for which the FBI accumulates a general statistical Index. Seven

"Index Crimes" are traced in the Bureau's periodic Crime Report: willful homicide, forcible rape, aggravated assault, robbery, larceny (of more than $50), and motor vehicle theft.

Some basic facts about these seven fearsome crimes are well-known. The measured incidence of the Index Crimes has been increasing rapidly in the United States in the past 10 to 15 years.[4] The Index Crimes occur twice as frequently in large cities as they do on average throughout the country. Within large cities, they occur most frequently in ghetto areas. The threat and tragedy of violent crime notwithstanding, almost all of these crimes are economically motivated; Clark concludes quite simply (8, p. 38) that "their main purpose is to obtain money or property." Fully seven-eighths of Index Crimes are crimes against property and only one-eighth are crimes against person. Moreover, many of the relatively few "violent" crimes against person occur inadvertently in the process of committing crimes against property.

A large part of the crime against property is committed by youth. Clark concludes from the scattered statistics (8, p. 54) that half of all property crime is committed by people under twenty-one.[5] Certainly more important in considering the evolution of public attitudes, Blacks commit disproportionate numbers of these seven Index Crimes (and are also disproportionately the victims of the same crimes). Although arrest rates bear an obviously spurious relationship to the actual incidence of crime, some of the figures seem astonishing.[6] In 1968, for instance, official statistics indicate that 61 percent of those arrested for robbery were Black and nearly half of those arrested for aggravated assault were Black, despite the fact that Blacks represented only twelve percent of the population. And the public exaggerates these figures even further; public attitudes often appear to presume that *all* of the Index Crimes are committed by Blacks and that every Black male is on the verge of committing a crime.[7]

The crimes our society chooses consistently to *ignore* seem just as obvious. Many kinds of relatively hidden crimes, most of them called, "white-collar" crimes, occur both frequently and profitably. Tax evasion, price fixing, embezzlement, swindling and consumer fraud capture billions of dollars every year. Clark provides some simple examples of the magnitudes of these kinds of crime (8, p. 38):

> Illicit gains from white-collar crime far exceed those of all other crime combined . . . One corporate price-fixing conspiracy criminally converted more money each year it continued than all of the hundreds of thousands of burglaries, larcenies, or thefts in the entire nation during those same years. Reported bank embezzlements cost ten times more than bank robberies each year.

As Clark also notes, the public and the media choose to pay almost no attention to either the existence or the causes of those kinds of crime.

The selectivity of public opinion is matched by the biases of our governmental system of law enforcement and the administration of justice. The system prosecutes and punishes some crimes and criminals heavily while leaving others alone. Some defenders of the system occasionally argue that it concentrates most heavily on those crimes of the greatest magnitude and importance, but the data do not support this view: the Index Crimes on which the system focuses account for small proportions of the total personal harm and property loss resulting from crime in the United States. For example, deaths resulting from "willful homicide" are one-fifth as frequent as deaths from motor vehicle accidents; although many experts ascribe nearly half of motor vehicle accidents to mechanical failure, the system rarely pays attention to those liable for that failure. The economic loss attributable to Index Crimes against property—robbery, burglary, and so on—are one-fifth the losses attributable to embezzlement, fraud and unreported commercial theft, and yet the system concentrates almost exclusively, on the former.

One can much more reasonably argue that the selectivity of our police, courts and prisons corresponds to the relative *class status* of those who perpetrate different kinds of crimes. We seem to have a dual system of justice in this country, as both the Crime Commission (32) and Goldfarb (13) have most clearly shown. The public system concentrates on crimes committed by the poor, while crimes by the more affluent are left to private auspices. Our prisons function, as Goldfarb notes, like a "national poorhouse," swallowing the poor, chewing them up and occasionally spitting them back at the larger society. When the more affluent get in trouble, in contrast, private psychiatric and counselling assistance supplant prosecution. Goldfarb concludes (13, p. 312; Goldfarb's emphasis): ". . . in the classes of offenses committed by rich and poor *equally*, it is rarely the rich who end up behind bars."[8]

None of the system's selectivity seems to work, finally, as we claim that we intend it to work. The public seems to think that concentration on a few crimes will at least improve the effectiveness of the system in controlling those few crimes—leading to greater prevention and deterrence and perhaps equally to greater rehabilitation. Buoyed by that hope, the various governments in the United States spent roughly $4.2 billion on police, prisons and the courts in 1965, while private individuals and corporations spent an additional $1.9 billion on prevention and insurance. And yet, despite those billions, our system of law enforcement and the administration of justice appears not only to be failing to curb the growth of crime but actually to be *exacerbating* the criminality it seeks selectively to control. The prisons themselves are veritable factories of crime; Clark notes (8, p. 212): "Jails and prisons in the United States today are more often than not manufacturers of crime. Of those who come to jail undecided, capable either of criminal conduct or of lives free of crime, most are turned to crime." More generally, very few of those who get started in crime ever actually leave it as a result of the system's deterrent or rehabilitative effects. According to Clark's statistical summaries (8, p. 55), roughly half of those released from prison eventually return, and fully 80 percent of serious crime is committed by "repeaters" —by those who have been convicted of crime before.

These very brief descriptive observations clearly suggest the questions an economic analysis must seek to answer about the problem of crime: *why* is there so much crime? Why do the public and the government concentrate so selectively on such a small part of the criminal activity in this country? And why do all our billions of dollars fail so miserably in curbing even that small part of the total problem?

CONVENTIONAL ANALYSIS

Conventional public analyses of crime divide roughly into two views—"conservative" and "liberal"—which tend to agree on basic assumptions and to diverge as they debate the specifics of crime prevention and control.

The conservative perspective on crime has an appealing simplicity.[9] Since conservatives believe that the social "order" is ultimately rational and is adequately reflected in the laws of our governments, they also believe that those who violate it can be regarded as "irrational" citizens and social misfits. The more violent the crimes, the more seriously we must regard their consequences. And since criminals (and especially violent ones) act irrationally, we can deter and prevent their actions only by responding to them with comparably irrational actions—principally by the threat or application of raw force. Toward that end, conservatives engage in two kinds of policy calculations. First, they discuss the potential deterrence of a variety of crime-prevention techniques. If only enough deterrent force could be mustered, they assume, crime could be stopped. Typically, they urge more police and more equipment to prevent crime. Second, they tend to favor preventive detention as a necessary means of protecting the social order from the threat of probable criminality; they make their argument, normally, on relatively pragmatic grounds.[10]

Liberals tend to regard the problem of criminal activity as a more complicated dilemma.[11] They agree that those who violate the "social order" can indeed be regarded as "irrational." At the same time, however, liberals regard the interactions of individuals with society as extremely complex processes, fraught with imperfections, and they are likely to argue that some individuals are much more likely than others to be *pushed* toward the irrationality of criminal behavior; we should therefore try to avoid *blaming* some criminals for their irrational acts. And since different individuals are pushed in very different ways by different social circumstances, there is a wide variety of behavior among criminals. The Crime Commission concludes (32, p. 5), "No single formula, no single theory, no single general-

ization can explain the vast range of behavior called crime."

Some of these heterogeneous crimes are more serious than others, liberals continue, because they are more violent and therefore more threatening. Liberals tend to agree with conservatives and the FBI that the FBI Crime Index adequately encompasses the potentially most violent crimes. But liberals tend to disagree with conservatives in arguing that these kinds of relatively violent crimes cannot simply be prevented by force, that they cannot ultimately be curbed until the social imperfections which underlie them are eliminated. The prevalence of "violent" crime among youth, Blacks and ghetto residents derives from the diseases of poverty and racism in American society; given those basic social imperfections, as the Crime Commission argues (35, p. 5), ". . . it is probable that crime will continue to increase . . . unless there are drastic changes in general social and economic conditions."

Can we do nothing about crime until we eliminate the sores of poverty and racism? Liberals respond ambivalently, but they often argue that we can marginally improve our prevention of crime and our treatment of criminals if we can at least marginally rationalize our system of law enforcement and administration of justice. We need more research, more analysis, more technology, more money, better administration, and more numerous and professional personnel.[12]

In the past few years, redressing an historic neglect, several orthodox economists have tried to clarify our analysis of criminal behavior and our evaluation of alternative public policies to combat it.[13] Although a few 19th-century classical economists like Jeremy Bentham had originally applied economics to the analysis of the problem of crime, as Becker (3) and Tullock (49) note, economists since then have generally ignored the problem. Recent advances in neoclassical micro-economic theory permit us, we are now told, to "extend the economist's usual analysis of choice" to an analysis of criminal behavior and its "optimal" prevention and punishment. Since each of the recent applications of orthodox economics outlines the mode of analysis rather clearly and the approach so directly reflects the more general predispositions of orthodox microeconomics, a few very brief observations about the orthodox analysis are sufficient to clarify its differences with both the "public" perspectives outlined above and the radical analysis developed below.

The central and most important thrust of the orthodox analysis is that criminal behavior, like any other economic activity, is eminently rational; in this important respect, the economists differ fundamentally with the conventional liberal and conservative public views. Becker formulates this central contention quite simply (3, p. 176):

> . . . a person commits an offense if the expected utility to him exceeds the utility he could get by using his time and other resources at other activities. Some persons become 'criminals,' therefore, not because their basic motivation differs from that of other persons, but because their benefits and costs differ.

More specifically, individuals are assumed to calculate the returns to and the risks of "legitimate" employment and "criminal" activity and base their choices between those two modes of activity on their cost/benefit calculations. Stigler adds (42, p. 530), "The details of occupational choice in illegal activity are not different from those encountered in the legitimate occupations."

Given those assumptions of rationality, orthodox economists argue that we can construct some "optimal" social policies to combat crime. They assume, first of all, that there is a social welfare function through which the costs and benefits of criminal offenses to each member of society can be translated into a common metric. Society (through its several governments) should then try to minimize the "social loss" from criminal offenses as measured by the social welfare function. In their formulation of the parameters of these calculations, they hypothesize that criminals respond quite sensitively in their own decision-making to variations in the level and probability of punishment. They also assume, as Becker puts it (3, p. 174), that "the more that is spent on policemen, court personnel, and specialized equipment, the easier it is to discover offenses and convict offenders." They then proceed to the final argu-

ment: we can choose (through our governments) some combination of punishment levels and social expenditures—with expenditures determining the probability of capture and conviction—which will minimize our social losses from crime subject to the revenue constraints in our public and private budgets.

Behind the orthodox economic analysis lie two obvious and fundamental assumptions. First, although the assumption is rarely made explicit, the analysis assumes that governments behave in democratic societies in such a way that everyone's preferences have an equal chance of influencing the final outcome, that public policy formulations can adequately reflect the costs and benefits of criminal offenses to all individuals in society.[14]

Second, orthodox economists assume some simple and identifiable relationships between the amount of money we actually spend on prevention and enforcement, the amount of prevention and enforcement we would *like to achieve*, and the amount of prevention and enforcement we can *actually achieve*. This involves the assumption, noted above, that larger expenditures monotonically increase the probability of apprehension and conviction. It also involves another, related assumption—that the level of government expenditures on prevention and punishment accurately reflects society's desired level of prevention and enforcement instead of, for example, the influence of vested interests in maximizing expenditures; if a state or locality spends more on its police, courts and prisons, *ceteris paribus*, orthodox economists assume that they do so because they seek to deter crime more effectively through the (expected) increase in the probability of arrest and punishment, and not for any other reason.

A RADICAL ANALYSIS OF CRIME

This section outlines the structure of a radical economic analysis of crime in the United States. Many points in the argument will seem quite obvious, simple elaborations of common sense. Other points will bear some important similarities to one or another of the views described in the preceding section. Taken together, however, the arguments in the following analysis seem to me to provide a more useful, coherent, and realistic interpretation of the problem than the more conventional models. In the analysis, I have tried as simply as possible to apply some general hypotheses of radical economic analysis to a discussion of the specific problem of crime in this country.[15]

The analysis has five separate parts. The first tries to explain a basic behavioral *similarity* among all the major kinds of crime in the United States. Given that fundamental similarity, the second part seeks to explain the most important dimensions of *difference* among various crimes in this country. Given a delineation of the sources of difference among crimes, the third part attempts an historical explanation of the sources of those sources of difference—analysis, as it were, of the underlying causes of some immediate causes of difference. The fourth part argues that we cannot easily reverse history, that we cannot easily alter the fundamental social structures and trends which have produced the problem of crime today. A final section provides a brief review of the central hypotheses of the argument and some comments on its implications.

Competitive capitalism and rational crime   Capitalist societies depend, as radicals often argue, on basically competitive forms of social and economic interaction and upon substantial inequalities in the allocation of social resources. Without inequalities, it would be much more difficult to induce workers to work in alienating environments. Without competition and a competitive ideology, workers might not be inclined to struggle to improve their relative income and status in society by working harder. Finally, although rights of property are protected, capitalist societies do not guarantee economic security to most of its individual members. Individuals must fend for themselves, finding the best available opportunities to provide for themselves and their families. At the same time, history bequeaths a corpus of laws and statutes to any social epoch which may or may not correspond to the social morality of that epoch. Inevitably, at any point in time, many of the "best" opportunities for economic survival open to different citizens will violate some of these historically-determined laws. Driven by the fear

of economic insecurity and by a competitive desire to gain some of the goods unequally distributed throughout the society, many individuals will eventually become "criminals." As Adam Smith himself admitted in *The Wealth of Nations* (41, p. 670), "Where there is no property . . . civil government is not so necessary."

In that respect, therefore, radicals would argue that nearly all crimes in capitalist societies represent perfectly *rational* responses to the structure of institutions upon which capitalist societies are based. Crimes of many different varieties constitute functionally similar responses to the organization of capitalist institutions, for those crimes help provide a means of survival in a society within which survival is never assured. Three different kinds of crime in the United States provide the most important examples of this functionally similar rationality among different kinds of crime: ghetto crime, organized crime, and corporate (or "white-collar") crime.[16]

It seems especially clear, first of all, that ghetto crime is committed by people responding quite reasonably to the structure of economic opportunities available to them. Only rarely, it appears, can ghetto criminals be regarded as raving, irrational, anti-social lunatics.[17] The "legitimate" jobs open to many ghetto residents, especially to young black males, typically pay low wages, offer relatively demanding assignments and carry the constant risk of layoff. In contrast, many kinds of crime "available" in the ghetto often bring higher monetary return, even higher social status, and—at least in some cases like numbers running—sometimes carry relatively low risk of arrest and punishment.[18] Given those alternative opportunities, the choice between "legitimate" and "illegitimate" activities is often quite simple. As Arthur Dunmeyer, a black hustler from Harlem, has put it (5, p. 292):

> In some cases this is the way you get your drug dealers and prostitutes and your numbers runners . . . They see that these things are the only way that they can compete in the society, to get some sort of status. They realize that there aren't any real doors open to them, and so, to commit crime was the only thing to do, they can't go back.

The fact that these activities are often "illegal"

sometimes doesn't really matter; since life out of jail often seems as bad as life inside prison, the deterrent effect of punishment is negligible. Dunmeyer expresses this point clearly as well (5, p. 293):

> It is not a matter of a guy saying, "I want to go to jail (or) I am afraid of jail." Jail is on the street just like it is on the inside. The same as, like when you are in jail, they tell you, "Look, if you do something wrong you are going to be put in the hole." You are still in jail, in the hole or out of the hole. You are in jail in the street or behind bars. It is the same thing . . .

In much the same way, organized crime represents a perfectly rational kind of economic activity.[19] Activities like gambling and prostitution are illegal for varieties of historical reasons, but there is a demand for those activities nonetheless. As Donald Cressey writes (10, p. 294), "The American confederation of criminals thrives because a large minority of citizens demands the illicit goods and services it has for sale." Clark makes the same point (8, p. 68), arguing that organized crimes are essentially "consensual crimes . . . , desired by the consuming public." The simple fact that they are both illegal and in such demand provides a simple explanation for the secrecy, relative efficiency and occasional violence of those who provide them. In nearly every sense, for example, the organization of the heroin industry bears as rational and reasonable a relationship to the nature of the product as the structures of the tobacco and alcoholic beverages industries bear to the nature of their own products.[20]

Finally, briefly to amplify the third example, corporate crime also represents a quite rational response to life in capitalist societies. Corporations exist to protect and augment the capital of their owners. If it becomes difficult to perform that function one way, corporate officials will quite inevitably try to do it another. When Westinghouse and General Electric conspired to fix prices, for instance, they were resorting to one of many possible devices for limiting the potential threat of competition to their price structures. Similarly, when Ford and General Motors proliferate new car model after new car model, each differing only slightly from its siblings, they are choosing to protect their price structures by product differentiation. In one case, the corporations were using oligopolistic power quite directly. In the other,

they rely on the power of advertising to generate demand for the differentiated products. In the context of the perpetual and highly competitive race among corporations for profits and capital accumulation, each response seems quite reasonable. In his pioneering studies of corporate crime, Sutherland made the same points about corporate crime and linked their behavior to lower-class criminality (44, p. 310):

> I have attempted to demonstrate that businessmen violate the law with great frequency. . . . If these conclusions are correct, it is very clear that the criminal behavior of businessmen cannot be explained by poverty, in the usual sense, or by bad housing or lack of recreational facilities or feeblemindedness or emotional instability. Business leaders are capable, emotionally-balanced and in no sense pathological. . . The assumption that an offender must have some such pathological distortion of the intellect or the emotions seems to me absurd, and if it is absurd regarding the crimes of businessmen, it is equally absurd regarding the crimes of persons in the lower economic class.

Class institutions and differences among crimes If most crime in the United States in one way or another reflects the same kind of rational response to the insecurity and inequality of capitalist institutions, what explains the manifold differences among different kinds of crime? Some crimes are much more violent than others, some are much more heavily prosecuted, and some are much more profitable. Why?

As a first step in explaining differences among crimes, I would apply the general perspective in a relatively straightforward manner, arguing quite simply that many of the most important differences among different kinds of crime in this country are determined by the *structure of class institutions* in our society and by the *class biases* of the State. That argument has two separate components.

First, I would argue that many of the important differences among crimes in this society derive quite directly from the different socio-economic classes to which individuals belong. Relatively affluent citizens have access to jobs in large corporations, to institutions involved in complicated paper transactions involving lots of money, and to avenues of relatively unobtrusive communication. Members of these classes who decide to break the law, as Clark puts it (8, p. 38), have "an easier, less offensive, less visible way of doing wrong." Those raised in poverty, on the other hand, do not have such easy access to money. If they are to obtain it criminally, they must impinge on those who already have it or direct its flow. As Robert Morgenthau has written (25, p. 20), those growing up in the ghetto "will probably never have the opportunity to embezzle funds from a bank or to promote a multimillion dollar stock fraud scheme. The criminal ways which we encourage (them) to choose will be those closest at hand—from vandalism to mugging to armed robbery."

Second, I would argue that the biases of our police, courts and prisons *explain* the relative violence of many crimes—that many of the differences in the degree of violence among different kinds of crime do not cause the selectivity of public concern about those crimes but *are in fact caused by* that selectivity. For a variety of historical reasons, as I noted above, we have a dual system of justice in this country; the police, courts and prisons pay careful attention to only a few crimes. It is only natural, as a result, that those who run the highest risks of arrest and conviction may have to rely on the threat or commission of violence in order to protect themselves. Many kinds of ghetto crimes generate violence, for instance, because the participants are severely prosecuted for their crimes and must try to protect themselves however they can. Other kinds of ghetto crimes are openly tolerated by the police, like the numbers racket, and those crimes rarely involve violence. It may be true, as Clark argues (8, p. 39), that "violent crime springs from a violent environment," but violent environments like the ghetto do not always produce violent crimes. Those crimes to which the police pay attention usually involve violence, while those which the police tend to ignore quite normally do not. In similar ways, organized crime has become violent historically, as Cressey especially argues (10), principally because its participants are often prosecuted. As long as that remains true, the suppliers of illegal goods require secrecy, organization and a bit of violence to protect their livelihood. Completely in contrast, corporate

crime does not require violence because it is ignored by the police; corporate criminals can safely assume they do not face the threat of jail and do not therefore have to cover their tracks with the threat of harming those who betray them. When Lockheed Aircraft accountants and executives falsified their public reports in order to disguise cost over-runs on the C-5A airplane in 1967 and 1968, for instance, they did not have to force Defense Department officials at knife-point to play along with their falsifications. As Robert Sherrill reports in his investigation of the Lockheed affair (40, p. 43), the Defense Department officials were entirely willing to cooperate. "This sympathy," Sherrill writes, "was reflected in orders from top Air Force officials to withhold information regarding Lockheed's dilemma from all reports that would be widely circulated." If only local police were equally sympathetic to the "dilemmas" of street-corner junkies, the violent patterns of drug-related crimes might be considerably transformed.[21]

In short, it seems important to view some of the most important differences among crimes—differences in their violence, their style and their impact —as fundamental outgrowths of the class structure of society and the class biases of our major institutions, including the State and its system of enforcement and administration of justice. Given that argument, it places a special burden on attempts to explain the historical sources of the duality of the public system of justice in this country, for that duality, coupled with the class biases of other institutions, plays such an important role in determining the patterns of American crime.

The sources of duality   One can explain the duality of our public system of justice quite easily, it seems to me, if one is willing to view the State through the radical perspective. The analysis involves answers to two separate questions. First, one must ask why the State *ignores* certain kinds of crimes, especially white-collar crimes and corporate crimes. Second, given that most crimes among the poor claim the poor as their victims, one must ask why the State bothers to worry so incessantly about those crimes.

The answer to the first question draws directly from the radical theory of the State. According to the radical theory, the government in a capitalist society like the United States exists primarily to preserve the stability of the system which provides, preserves and protects returns to the owners of capital. As long as crimes among the corporate class tend in general to harm members of other classes, like those in the "consuming" class, the State will not spontaneously move to prevent those crimes from taking place. On the other hand, as Paul Sweezy has especially argued (45), the State may be pressured either nominally or effectively to prosecute the wealthy if their criminal practices become so egregiously offensive that their victims may move to overthrow the system itself. In those cases, the State may punish individual members of the class in order to protect the interests of the entire class. Latent opposition to the practices of corporations may be forestalled, to pick several examples, by token public efforts to enact and enforce anti-trust, truth-in-lending, anti-pollution, industrial safety and auto safety legislation. As James Ridgeway has most clearly shown in the case of pollution (37), however, the gap between the enactment of the statutes and their effective enforcement seems quite cavernous.[22]

The answer to the second question seems slightly more complicated historically. Public responses to crime among the poor have changed periodically throughout American history, responding both to changes in the patterns of the crimes themselves and to changes in public morality. The subtlety of that historical process would be difficult to trace in this kind of discussion, but some patterns do seem clear.

Earlier in American history, as Clark has pointed out (8, pp. 55–56), we tended to ignore many crimes among the poor because those crimes rarely impinged upon the lives of the more affluent. Gambling, prostitution, dope and robbery seemed to flourish in the slums of the early 20th century, and the police rarely moved to intervene. More recently, however, some of the traditional patterns of crime have changed. Two dimensions of change seem most important. On the one hand, much of the crime has moved out of the ghettos. As Clark explains (8, p. 55), "Our concern arose when social dynamics and population movements brought crime and addiction out of the slums and inflicted it on or threatened the powerful and well-to-do." On the other hand, the styles in

which ghetto criminals have fulfilled their criminal intent may have grown more hostile since World War II, flowing through what I have elsewhere called the "promised land effect" (in 15), after the title of the book by Claude Brown (4). As Brown points out, second-generation Northern Blacks—the sons and daughters of Southern migrants born in Northern slums—have relatively little reason to hope that their lives will improve. Their parents migrated in search of better times, but some of those born in the North probably believe that their avenues for escape from poverty have disappeared. Brown puts it well (4, p. 8):

> The children of these disillusioned colored pioneers inherited the total lot of their parents—the disappointments, the anger. To add to their misery, they had little hope of deliverance. For where does one run to when he's already in the promised land?

Out of frustration, some of the crime among younger ghetto-born Blacks may be more vengeful now, more concerned with sticking it to whitey. Coupled with the spread of ghetto crime into other parts of the city, this symbolic expression of vengefulness undoubtedly heightens the fear that many affluent citizens feel about ghetto crime. Given their influence with the government, they quite naturally have moved toward increasing public attention to the prevention and punishment of crimes among the poor.

Once the patterns of public duality have been established, of course, they acquire a momentum and dynamic all their own. To begin with, vested interests develop, deriving their livelihood and status from the system. The prison system, like the defense industry, becomes a power of its own, with access to public bureaucracies, with workers to support and with power to defend. Eldridge Cleaver has made special note of this feature of our public system (9, p. 185):

> The only conclusion one can draw is that the parole system is a procedure devised primarily for the purpose of running people in and out of jail—most of them black—in order to create and maintain a lot of jobs for the white prison system. In California, which I know best—and I'm sure it's the same in other states—there are thousands and thousands of people who draw their living directly or indirectly from the prison system; all the clerks, all the guards, all the bailiffs, all the

people who sell goods to the prisons. They regard the inmates as a sort of product from which they all draw their livelihood, and the part of the crop they keep exploiting most are the black inmates.

In much the same way, the police become an interest and a power of their own.[23] They are used and manipulated by the larger society to enforce the law selectively; as Clark writes (8, p. 137), "We send police to maintain order, to arrest, to jail—and to ignore vital laws also intended to protect life and to prevent death . . ." As agents of selective social control, the police also inevitably become the focus of increasing animosity among those they are asked selectively to control. Manipulated by the larger society, hated by those at the bottom, the police tend to develop the mentality, as Westley (50) has called it, of a "garrison." They eventually seek to serve neither the interests of the larger society nor the interests of the law but the interests of the garrison. One reaches the point, finally, where police interests interject an intermediate membrane screening the priorities of the state and society on the one hand and the interests of their victims on the other. Westley concludes (50): "When enforcement of the law conflicts with the ends of the police, the law is not enforced. When it supports the ends of the police, they are fully behind it. When it bears no relation to the ends of the police, they enforce it as a matter of routine."

The implausibility of reform   One needs to ask, finally, whether these patterns can be changed and the trends reversed. Can we simultaneously eradicate the causes of crime and reform our dual system of justice? At the heart of that question lies the question posed at the beginning of this essay, for it simultaneously raises the necessity of explaining the failures of our present system to prevent the crime it seeks most systematically to control.

I would argue, quite simply, that reform is implausible unless we change the basic institutions upon which capitalism in the United States depends. We cannot legitimately expect to eradicate the initial causes of crime for two reasons. First, capitalism depends quite substantially on the preservation of the conditions of competition and inequality. Those conditions, as I argued above, will tend to lead almost inevitably to relatively pervasive criminal behavior; without those conditions, the capitalist system would scarcely work at all. Second, as many have argued, the general presence of racism in this country, though capitalists may not in fact have created it, tends to support and maintain the power of the capitalists as a class by providing cheap labor and dividing the working class. Given the substantial control of capitalists over the policies and priorities of the State, we cannot easily expect to prod the State to eliminate the fundamental causes of racism in this country. In that respect, it seems likely that the particular inequalities facing Blacks and their consequent attraction to the opportunities available in crime seem likely to continue.

Given expectations that crime will continue, it seems equally unlikely that we shall be able to reform our systems of prosecution and punishment in order to mitigate their harmful effects on criminals and to equalize their treatment of different kinds of crime. First and superficially, as I noted above, several important and powerful vested interests have acquired a stake in the current system and seem likely to resist efforts to change it. Second and more fundamentally, the cumulative effect of the patterns of crime, violence, prosecution and punishment in this country play an important role in helping legitimize and stabilize the capitalist system. Although capitalists as a class may not have created the current patterns of crime and punishment, those patterns currently serve their interests in several different ways. We should expect that the capitalists as a class will hardly be eager to push reform of the system. Given their relative reluctance to reform the system, we should expect to be able to push reform only in the event that we can substantially change the structure of power to which the State responds.

The current patterns of crime and punishment help support the capitalist system in three different ways. First, the pervasive patterns of selective enforcement seem to reinforce a prevalent ideology in this society that individuals, rather than institutions, are to blame for social problems. Individuals are criminally prosecuted for motor accidents because of negligent or drunken driving, for instance, but auto manufacturers are never criminally prosecuted for the negligent construction of unsafe cars or for their roles in increasing the likelihood of death through air pollution. Individual citizens are often prosecuted and punished for violence and for resisting arrest, equally, but those agents of institutions, like police and prison guards, or institutions themselves, like Dow Chemical, are never prosecuted for inflicting unwarranted violence on others. These patterns of selectivity reinforce our pervasive preconceptions of the invulnerability of institutions, leading us to blame ourselves for social failure; this pattern of individual blame, as Edwards and MacEwan have especially argued (11), plays an important role in legitimizing the basic institutions of this kind of capitalist society.

Second, and critically important, the patterns of crime and punishment manage "legitimately" to neutralize the potential opposition to the system of many of our most oppressed citizens. In particular, the system serves ultimately to keep thousands of men out of the job market or trapped in the secondary labor market by perpetuating a set of institutions which serves functionally to feed large numbers of Blacks (and poor whites) through the cycle of crime, imprisonment, parole, and recidivism. The system has this same ultimate effect in many different ways. It locks up many for life, first of all, guaranteeing that those potentially disaffected souls keep "out of trouble." For those whom it occasionally releases, it tends to drive them deeper into criminality, intensifying their criminal and violent behavior, filling their heads with paranoia and hatred, keeping them perpetually on the run and unable, ultimately, to organize with others to change the institutions which pursue them. Finally, it blots their records with the stigma of criminality, effectively precluding the reform of even those who vow to escape the system and go "straight" by denying them many decent employment opportunities.[24]

The importance of this neutralization should not be underestimated. If all young black men in this country do not eventually become criminals, most of them are conscious of the trap into which they might fall. George Jackson has written from prison (20), "Blackmen born in the U.S. and fortunate enough to

live past the age of eighteen are conditioned to accept the inevitability of prison. For most of us, it simply looms as the next phase in a sequence of humiliations." And once they are trapped, the cycle continues almost regardless of the will of those involved. Prison, parole and the eventual return to prison become standard points on the itinerary. Cleaver has written (9, pp. 154–155):

> I noticed that every time I went back to jail, the same guys who were in Juvenile Hall with me were also there again. They arrived there soon after I got there, or a little bit before I left. They always seemed to make the scene. In the California prison system, they carry you from Juvenile Hall to the old folks' colony, down in San Luis Obispo, and wait for you to die. Then they bury you there . . . I noticed these waves, these generations . . . graduating classes moving up from Juvenile Hall, all the way up.

And those who succeed finally in understanding the trap and in pulling themselves out of it, like Malcolm X, Claude Brown, Eldridge Cleaver and George Jackson, seem to succeed precisely because they understand how debilitating the cycle becomes, how totally dehumanizing it will remain. Another black ex-con has perfectly expressed the sudden insight which allowed him to pull out of the trap (6):

> It didn't take me any time to decide I wasn't going back to commit crimes. Because it's stupid, it's a trap, it only makes it easier for them to neutralize you. It's hard to explain, because you can't say it's a question of right and wrong, but of being free or (being) trapped.

If the system did not effect this neutralization, if so many of the poor were not trapped in the debilitating system of crime and punishment, then they might otherwise gather the strength to oppose the system which reinforces their misery. Like many other institutions in this country, the system of crime and punishment serves an important function for the capitalist class by dividing and weakening those who might potentially seek to overthrow the capitalist system. Although the capitalists have not created the system, in any direct sense, they would doubtless hate to have to do without it.[25]

The third and perhaps most important functionally supportive role of the current patterns of crime and punishment is that those patterns allow us to ignore some basic issues about the relationships in our

PART 2   THE POLITICAL ECONOMY OF CRIME AND LAW ENFORCEMENT

society between institutions and individuals. By treating criminals as animals and misfits, as enemies of the state, we are permitted to continue avoiding some basic questions about the dehumanizing effects of our social institutions. We keep our criminals out of sight, so we are never forced to recognize and deal with the psychic punishment we inflict on them. Like the schools and the welfare system, the legal system turns out, upon close inspection, to rob most of its "clients" of the last vestiges of their personal dignity. Each one of those institutions, in its own way, helps us forget about the responsibilities we might alternatively assume for providing the best possible environment within which all of us could grow and develop as individuals. Cleaver sees this "role" of the system quite clearly (9, pp. 179–182):

> Those who are now in prisons could be put through a process of real rehabilitation before their release . . . By rehabilitation I mean they would be trained for jobs that would not be an insult to their dignity, that would give them some sense of security, that would allow them to achieve some brotherly connection with their fellow man. But for this kind of rehabilitation to happen on a large scale would entail the complete reorganization of society, not to mention the prison system. It would call for the teaching of a new set of ethics, based on the principle of cooperation, as opposed to the presently dominating principle of competition. It would require the transformation of the entire moral fabric of this country . . .

By keeping its victims so thoroughly hidden and rendering them so apparently inhuman, our system of crime and punishment allows us to forget how sweeping a "transformation" of our social ideology we would require in order to begin solving the problem of crime. The more we forget, the more protected capitalists remain from a thorough re-examination of the ideological basis of the institutions upon which they depend.

Summary and implications   It seems useful briefly to summarize the analysis outlined in this section, in order both to emphasize the connections among its arguments and to clarify its differences with other "models" of crime and punishment. Most crimes in this country share a single important similarity—they represent rational responses to the competitiveness and inequality of life in capitalist societies. (In this emphasis on the rationality of crime, the anal-

ysis differs with the "conventional public analyses" of crime and resembles the orthodox economic approach.) Many crimes seem very different at the same time, but many of their differences—in character and degree of violence—can usefully be explained by the structure of class institutions in this country and the duality of the public system of the enforcement and administration of justice. (In this central deployment of the radical concepts of class and the class-biased State, the analysis differs fundamentally with both the "public" and the orthodox economic perspectives.) That duality, in turn, can fruitfully be explained by a dynamic view of the class-biased role of public institutions and the vested interests which evolve out of the state's activities. For many reasons, finally, it seems unlikely that we can change the patterns of crime and punishment, for the kinds of changes we would need would appear substantially to threaten the stability of the capitalist system. If we managed somehow to eliminate ghetto crime, for instance, the competitiveness, inequalities and racism of our institutions would tend to reproduce it. And if, by chance, the pattern of ghetto crime was not reproduced, the capitalists might simply have to invent some other way of neutralizing the potential opposition of so many black men, against which they might once again be forced to rebel with "criminal acts." It is in that sense of fundamental causality that we must somehow change the entire structure of institutions in this country in order to eliminate the causes of crime.

Could any of this be any different in any society? Is it not inevitable that criminals must be severely punished and that vast quantities of social resources must be applied to "deter" potential criminality? I don't see why. It seems entirely possible to imagine a radically different kind of society in which social institutions would serve the needs of citizens and foster their development as creative human beings, and, as a natural consequence, in which "criminals" would be treated in the ways that many families deal with those family members who betray the family trust. John Griffiths has projected a society in which legal and penal institutions would be motivated by this "Family Model," where social response to criminal behavior would be motivated by an underlying assumption, as Griffiths writes (18, p. 371), "of reconcilable—even mutually supportive—interest, a state of love."[20] Such a society would "make plain that while the criminal has transgressed, we do not therefore cut him off from us; our concern and dedication to his well-being continue. We have punished him and drawn him back in among us; we have not cast him out to fend for himself against our systematic enmity." In such a society, rather than forcing the criminal to admit his failure and reform himself, we would all admit our mutual failures and seek to reform the total community—in which effort the criminal would play an important, constructive and educative role. The distance of that vision simply indicates how deeply our present treatment of criminals is imbedded in the basic institutional structure of this country.

FOOTNOTES

[1] Quoted in B. G. Chevigny (6).

[2] See Ronald L. Goldfarb, "The Horror of Prisons," *The New York Times*, October 28, 1970, p. 47.

[3] For two very brief summaries of data, see the first two reading selections in the chapter on crime in Gordon, ed. (15). For the two most useful general summaries, see Clark (8) and the Report of the President's Commission on Law Enforcement and the Administration of Justice (32). Another useful summary is contained in Wolfgang (55). For more detail, see the appendices to the Crime Commission Report (33), (34), (35). For interesting critical comments on the Crime Commission Report, see Wilson (51).

[4] The statistical increase may be misleading, of course, because many kinds of crime are much more likely to be reported now than comparable crimes of thirty or forty years ago. See Clark (8).

[5] Violent crimes, on the other hand, are more frequently committed by adults; as Clark explains it (8, p. 55), "It takes longer to harden the young to violence."

[6] The reason that the arrest rates may be spurious is that, as the Crime Commission Report (32), Clark (8), and Goldfarb (13) have documented, blacks are much more likely than whites to be arrested whether they have committed a crime or not. Despite that immeasurable bias in the arrest statistics, it is nonetheless assumed that Blacks commit a much larger percentage of most crimes than their share of urban population.

[7] Fred P. Graham provides a useful analysis of the myths and realities of black crime in a recent article (17).

[8] It is one thing to cite this "duality" as fact, of course, and quite another thing to explain it. I shall cite it now as a phenomenon requiring explanation and try to explain it later.

[9] For the clearest exposition of the conservative view on crime, see Banfield (2).

[10] Banfield has formulated the conservative equation (2, p. 184): "If some people's freedom is not abridged by law-enforcement agencies, that of others will be abridged by law breakers. The question, therefore, is not whether abridging the freedom of those who may commit serious crimes is an evil—it is—but whether it is a lesser or a greater one than the alternative." For a description of the Nixon Administration's basically conservative position, see Harris (19). For a superb analysis of the legal aspects of the major Nixon crime legislation, see Packer (31).

[11] The clearest expressions of the liberal view on crime are contained in three reports of Presidential commissions published in the late 1960's: The Presidential Commission on Law Enforcement and the Administration of Justice (32), the National Advisory Commission on Civil Disorders (27), and the National Commission on Violence (28).

[12] See Wolfgang (55, p. 275) and the Commission on Violence Report (28, p. 40) for explicit statements of this inclination.

[13] For the most notable pieces of recent literature, see Becker (3), Stigler (42), Thurow (46), and Tullock (48, 49). Some attempts have been made to apply the orthodox analysis empirically; for one such attempt, see Landes (22).

[14] Becker admits (3, p. 209), that the analysis is hampered by "the absence of a reliable theory of political decision-making." Tullock is the only one who makes the underlying political assumption precise and explicit. He writes (48, p. II-2): "My first general assumption, then, is that the reader is not in a position to assure himself of special treatment in any legal system. That is, if I argue that the reader should favor a law against theft, one of the basic assumptions will be that he does not have a real opportunity to get a law enacted which prohibits theft by everyone else but leaves him free to steal himself." He adds that this assumption ". . . will . . . underlie all of the specific proposals" he makes in his manuscript.

[15] I am relying, essentially, on the general hypotheses outlined and evoked in Edwards and MacEwan (11), Gordon, ed. (15), and other recent radical works. For two useful discussions of the meaning of the radical concept of class, especially as Marx used the term, see Ossowski (29) and Tucker (47). For two summaries of the radical theory of the State, see Sweezy (45) and Milliband (24).

[16] This is not meant to imply, obviously, that there would be no crime in a communist society in which perfectly secure equal support was provided for all. It suggests, quite simply, that one would have to analyze crime in such a society with reference to a different set of ideas and a different set of institutions.

[17] Our knowledge of ghetto crime draws primarily from the testimony of several ex-ghetto criminals, as in Brown (4), Cleaver (9), Jackson (20), and Malcolm X (23). For other more analytic studies, see Shaw and McKay (39), and Wolfgang and Ferracuti (54). For interesting evidence on the different attitudes toward crime of poor and middle-class youth, see Goodwin (14). For a bit of empirical evidence on the critical interaction between job prospects and rates of recidivism, see Evans (12).

[18] For more on the structure of jobs available, see Chapter Two in Gordon, ed. (15). One often finds informal support for such contentions. A Manhattan prostitute once said about her crimes, "What is there to say. We've got a living to earn. There wouldn't be any prostitution if there weren't a demand for it." Quoted in the *New York Times*, May 29, 1970. A black high school graduate discussed the problem at greater length with an interviewer in a recent book (quoted in Goro [16], p. 146): "That's why a lot of brothers are out on the street now, stinging, robbing people, mugging, 'cause when they get a job, man, they be doing their best, and the white man get jealous 'cause he feel this man could do

better than he doing. 'I got to get rid of him.' So they fire him, so a man, he lose his pride . . . They give you something, and then they take it away from you . . . There's no reason for you to be stealing. That's a lie! If you're a thief, I'd advise you to be a good thief. 'Cause you working, Jim, you ain't going to succeed unless you got some kind of influence."

[19]For two of the best available analyses of organized crime, see Cressey (10) and Morris and Hawkins (26).

[20]As Cressey points out (10), for instance, it makes a great deal of sense in the heroin industry for the supplier to seek a monopoly on the source of the heroin but to permit many individual sellers of heroin at its final destination, usually without organization backing, because the risks occur primarily at the consumers' end.

[21]Many would argue, along these lines, that heroin addicts would not be prone either to violence or to crime if heroin were legal and free. The fact that it is illegal and that the police go after its consumers means that a cycle of crime and violence is established from which it becomes increasingly difficult to escape.

[22]This argument rests on an assumption, of course, that one learns more about the priorities of the state by looking at its patterns of enforcement than at the nature of its statutes. This seems quite reasonable. The statutory process is often cumbersome, whereas the patterns of enforcement can sometimes be changed quite easily. (Stigler [42] makes the same point.) Furthermore, as many radicals would argue, the State in democratic societies can often support the capitalist class most effectively by selective enforcement of the laws, rather than by selective legislation. For varieties of relatively complicated historical reasons, selective enforcement of the law seems to arouse less fear for the erosion of democratic tradition than selective legislation itself. As long as we have statutes which nominally outlaw racial inequality, for instance, inadequate enforcement of those laws seems to cause relatively little furor; before we had such laws in this country, protests against the selective statutes could ultimately be mounted.

[23]For some useful references on the police, see P. Chevigny (7), Westley (50), and Wilson (52). For a review of that literature, with some very interesting comments about the police, see Kempton (21). For one discussion of the first hints of evidence that there may not, in fact, be any kind of identifiable relationship between the number of police we have and their effectiveness, see Reeves (36).

[24]For the most devastating story I've seen about how the neutralization occurs to even the most innocent of ghetto Blacks, see Asinof (1).

[25]One should not underestimate the importance of this effect for quantitative as well as qualitative reasons. In July 1968, for instance, an estimated 140,000 blacks were serving time in penal institutions at federal, state, and local levels. If the percentage of black males in prison had been as low as the proportions of white men (controlling for age), there would have been only 25,000 blacks in jail. If those extra 115,000 black men were not in prison, they would likely be unemployed or intermittently employed. (See Evans [12]). In addition, official labor force figures radically undercount the number of blacks in the census because many black males are simply missed by the census-taker. In July 1968, almost one million black males were "missed" in that way. On the arbitrary assumption that one-fifth of those "missing males" were in one way or another evading the law, involved in hustling, or otherwise trapped in the legal system, then a total of 315,000 black men who might be unemployed were it not for the effects of the law were not counted in "measured" unemployment statistics. Total "measured" black male unemployment in July 1968 was 317,000, so that the total black unemployment problem might be nearly twice as large as we "think" it is were it not for the selective effects of our police, courts and prisons on black men.

[26]Griffiths' article attempts to offer a reply to an earlier legal article by Packer (30). In his essay, Griffiths contrasts the "Family Model of the Criminal Process" with what he calls the "Battle Model of the Criminal Process"—a model which he argues motivates both the theory and the reality of our social treatment of criminals.

REFERENCES

1. Eliot Asinof, *People vs. Blutcher* (New York: Viking, 1970).

2. Edward C. Banfield, *The Unheavenly City* (Boston: Little, Brown, 1970).

3. Gary Becker, "Crime and Punishment: An Economic Approach," *Journal of Political Economy*, March/April 1968.

4. Claude Brown, *Manchild in the Promised Land* (New York: Macmillan, 1965)

5. Claude Brown and Arthur Dunmeyer, "A Way of Life in the Ghetto," in Gordon, ed. (15).

6. Bell Gale Chevigny, "After the Death of Jail," *The Village Voice*, July 10, 1969. Partially reprinted in Gordon, ed. (15).

7. Paul Chevigny, *Police Power* (New York: Pantheon, 1969).

8. Ramsey Clark, *Crime in America* (New York: Simon and Schuster, 1970).

9. Eldridge Cleaver, *Post-Prison Writings and Speeches* (New York: A Ramparts Book by Random House, 1969).

10. Donald Cressey, *Theft of the Nation: The Structure and Operations of Organized Crime* (New York: Harper & Row, 1969).

11. Richard Edwards, Arthur MacEwan, et al., "A Radical Approach to Economics," *American Economic Review*, May 1970, Reprinted in Gordon, ed. (15).

12. Robert Evans, Jr. "The Labor Market and Parole Success," *Journal of Human Resources*, Spring 1968.

13. Ronald Goldfarb, "Prison: The National Poorhouse," *The New Republic*, November, 1969. Reprinted in Gordon, ed. (15).

14. Leonard Goodwin, "Work Orientations of the Underemployed Poor," *Journal of Human Resources,* Fall 1969.

15. David M. Gordon, ed., *Problems in Political Economy: An Urban Perspective* (Lexington, Mass.: D. C. Heath, 1971).

16. Herb Goro, *The Block* (New York: Random House, 1970).

17. Fred P. Graham, "Black Crime: The Lawless Image," *Harper's,* September, 1970.

18. John Griffiths, "Ideology in Criminal Procedure, or a Third 'Model' of the Criminal Process," *Yale Law Journal,* January, 1970.

19. Richard Harris, *Justice* (New York: Dutton, 1970).

20. George Jackson, *Soledad Brother* (New York: Bantam Books, 1970).

21. Murray Kempton, "Cops," *The New York Review of Books,* November 5, 1970.

22. William Landes, "An Economic Analysis of the Courts," *Journal of Law and Economics,* April, 1970.

23. Malcolm X, *Autobiography* (New York: Grove Press, 1964).

24. Ralph Milliband, *The State in Capitalist Society* (New York: Basic Books, 1969).

25. Robert Morgenthau, "Equal Justice and the Problem of White Collar Crime," *The Conference Board Record,* August, 1969.

26. Norval Morris and Gordon Hawkins, *The Honest Politician's Guide to Crime Control* (Chicago: University of Chicago Press, 1969).

27. National Advisory Commission on Civil Disorders, *Report* (New York: Bantam Books, 1968).

28. National Commission on the Causes and Prevention of Violence, *To Establish Justice, To Insure Domestic Tranquility* (New York: Bantam Books, 1970).

29. Stanislaw Ossowski, *Class Structure in the Social Consciousness* (New York: Free Press, 1963), trans. by Sheila Patterson.

30. Herbert Packer, "Two Models of the Criminal Process," *University of Pennsylvania Law Review,* 1964.

31. _____, "Nixon's Crime Program and What It Means," *New York Review of Books,* October 22, 1970.

32. President's Commission on Law Enforcement and Administration of Justice, *The Challenge of Crime in a Free Society* (Washington: U.S. Government Printing Office, 1967).

33. _____, *Corrections* (Washington: U.S. Government Printing Office, 1967).

34. _____, *The Courts* (Washington: U.S. Government Printing Office, 1967).

35. _____, *Crime and Its Impact—An Assessment* (Washington: U.S. Government Printing Office, 1967).

36. Richard Reeves, "Police: Maybe They Should Be Doing Something Different," *The New York Times,* January 24, 1971.

37. James Ridgeway, *The Politics of Ecology,* (New York: Dutton, 1970).

38. Arnold Rose, *The Power Structure: Political Process in America* (New York: Oxford University Press, 1968).

39. Clifford Shaw and Henry McKay, *Juvenile Delinquency and Urban Areas* (Chicago: University of Chicago Press, 1969).

40. Robert Sherrill, "The Convenience of Being Lockheed," *Scanlan's Monthly,* August 1970.

41. Adam Smith, *The Wealth of Nations* (New York: Modern Library, 1937).

42. George Stigler, "The Optimum Enforcement of Laws," *Journal of Political Economy,* May/June 1970.

43. Edmund H. Sutherland, *Principles of Criminology,* 6th ed. (Philadelphia: Lippincott, 1960).

44. _____, "The Crime of Corporations," in Gordon, ed. (15).

45. Paul Sweezy, "The State," Chapt. XIII of *The Theory of Capitalist Development* (New York: Monthly Review Press, 1968). Partially reprinted in Gordon, ed. (15).

46. Lester C. Thurow, "Equity and Efficiency in Justice," *Public Policy,* Summer, 1970.

47. Robert Tucker, *The Marxian Revolutionary Idea* (New York: W. W. Norton, 1969).

48. Gordon Tullock, *General Standards: The Logic of Law and Ethics,* Virginia Polytechnic Institute, 1968, unpublished manuscript.

49. _____, "An Economic Approach to Crime," *Social Science Quarterly*, June 1969.

50. William Westley, *Violence and Police* (Cambridge, Mass.: M.I.T. Press, 1970).

51. James Q. Wilson, "Crime in the Streets," *The Public Interest*, No. 5 (Fall 1966).

52. _____, *Varieties of Police Behavior* (New York: Basic Books, 1969).

53. Robert Paul Wolff, *The Poverty of Liberalism* (Boston: Beacon Press, 1968).

54. Marvin E. Wolfgang and Franco Ferracuti, *The Subculture of Violence* (New York: Barnes and Noble, 1967).

55. Marvin E. Wolfgang, "Urban Crime," in James Q. Wilson, ed., *The Metropolitan Enigma* (Cambridge, Mass.: Harvard University Press, 1968).

4

Rape: The All-American Crime

SUSAN GRIFFIN

I

I have never been free of the fear of rape. From a very early age I, like most women, have thought of rape as a part of my natural environment—something to be feared and prayed against like fire or lightning. I never asked why men raped; I simply thought it one of the many mysteries of human nature.

I was, however, curious enough about the violent side of humanity to read every crime magazine I was able to ferret away from my grandfather. Each issue featured at least one "sex crime," with pictures of a victim, usually in a pearl necklace, and of the ditch or the orchard where her body was found. I was never certain why the victims were always women, nor what the motives of the murderer were, but I did guess that the world was not a safe place for women. I observed that my grandmother was meticulous about locks, and quick to draw the shades before anyone removed so much as a shoe. I sensed that danger lurked outside.

Source: "Rape: The All-American Crime," *Ramparts*, Vol. 10, No. 3, September, 1971, pp. 26-35. By permission of the author.

At the age of eight, my suspicions were confirmed. My grandmother took me to the back of the house where the men wouldn't hear, and told me that strange men wanted to do harm to little girls. I learned not to walk on dark streets, not to talk to strangers, or get into strange cars, to lock doors, and to be modest. She never explained why a man would want to harm a little girl, and I never asked.

If I thought for a while that my grandmother's fears were imaginary, the illusion was brief. That year, on the way home from school, a schoolmate a few years older than I tried to rape me. Later, in an obscure aisle of the local library (while I was reading *Freddy the Pig*) I turned to discover a man exposing himself. Then, the friendly man around the corner was arrested for child molesting.

My initiation to sexuality was typical. Every woman has similar stories to tell—the first man who attacked her may have been a neighbor, a family friend, an uncle, her doctor, or perhaps her own father. And women who grow up in New York City always have tales about the subway.

But though rape and the fear of rape are a daily part of every woman's consciousness, the subject is so rarely discussed by that unofficial staff of male intellectuals (who write the books which study seem-· ingly every other form of male activity) that one begins to suspect a conspiracy of silence. And indeed, the obscurity of rape in print exists in marked contrast to the frequency of rape in reality, for *forcible rape is the most frequently committed violent crime in America today*. The Federal Bureau of Investigation classes three crimes as violent: murder, aggravated assault and forcible rape. In 1968, 31,060 rapes were *reported*. According to the FBI and independent criminologists, however, to approach accuracy this figure must be multiplied by at least a factor of ten to compensate for the fact that most rapes are not reported; when these compensatory mathematics are used, there are more rapes committed than aggravated assaults and homicides.

When I asked Berkeley, California's Police Inspector in charge of rape investigation if he knew why men rape women, he replied that he had not spoken with "these people and delved into what really makes them tick, because that really isn't my job. . . ." However, when I asked him how a woman might prevent being raped, he was not so reticent, "I wouldn't advise any female to go walking around alone at night . . . and she should lock her car at all times." The Inspector illustrated his warning with a grisly story about a man who lay in wait for women in the back seats of their cars, while they were shopping in a local supermarket. This man eventually murdered one of his rape victims. "Always lock your car," the Inspector repeated, and then added, without a hint of irony, "Of course, you don't have to be paranoid about this type of thing."

The Inspector wondered why I wanted to write about rape. Like most men he did not understand the urgency of the topic, for, after all, men are not raped. But like most women I had spent considerable time speculating on the true nature of the rapist. When I was very young, my image of the "sexual offender" was a nightmarish amalgamation of the bogey man and Captain Hook: he wore a black cape, and he cackled. As I matured, so did my image of the rapist. Born into the psychoanalytic age, I tried to "understand" the rapist. Rape, I came to believe, was only one of many unfortunate evils produced by sexual repression. Reasoning by tautology, I con-

cluded that any man who would rape a woman must be out of his mind.

Yet, though the theory that rapists are insane is a popular one, this belief has no basis in fact. According to Professor Menachem Amir's study of 646 rape cases in Philadelphia, *Patterns in Forcible Rape*, men who rape are not abnormal. Amir writes, "Studies indicate that sex offenders do not constitute a unique or psychopathological type; nor are they as a group invariably more disturbed than the control groups to which they are compared." Alan Taylor, a parole officer who has worked with rapists in the prison facilities at San Luis Obispo, California, stated the question in plainer language, "Those men were the most normal men there. They had a lot of hang-ups, but they were the same hang-ups as men walking out on the street."

Another canon in the apologetics of rape is that, if it were not for learned social controls, all men would rape. Rape is held to be natural behavior, and not to rape must be learned. But in truth rape is not universal to the human species. Moreover, studies of rape in our culture reveal that, far from being impulsive behavior, most rape is planned. Professor Amir's study reveals that in cases of group rape (the "gangbang" of masculine slang) 90 percent of the rapes were planned; in pair rapes, 83 percent of the rapes were planned; and in single rapes, 58 percent were planned. These figures should significantly discredit the image of the rapist as a man who is suddenly overcome by sexual needs society does not allow him to fulfill.

Far from the social control of rape being learned, comparisons with other cultures lead one to suspect that, in our society, it is rape itself that is learned. (The fact that rape is against the law should not be considered proof that rape is not in fact encouraged as part of our culture.)

This culture's concept of rape as an illegal, but still understandable, form of behavior is not a universal one. In her study *Sex and Temperament*, Margaret Mead describes a society that does not share our views. The Arapesh do not ". . . have any conception of the male nature that might make rape understandable to them." Indeed our interpretation of rape is a product of our conception of the nature of male sexuality. A common retort to the question, why don't women rape men, is the myth that men have greater sexual needs, that their sexuality is more urgent than women's. And it is the nature of human beings to want to live up to what is expected of them.

And this same culture which expects aggression from the male expects passivity from the female. Conveniently, the companion myth about the nature of female sexuality is that all women secretly want to be raped. Lurking beneath her modest female exterior is a subconscious desire to be ravished. The following description of a stag movie, written by Brenda Starr in Los Angeles' underground paper, *Everywoman*, typifies this male fantasy. The movie "showed a woman in her underclothes reading on her bed. She is interrupted by a rapist with a knife. He immediately wins her over with his charm and they get busy sucking and fucking." An advertisement in the *Berkeley Barb* reads, "Now as all women know from their daydreams, rape has a lot of advantages. Best of all it's so simple. No preparation necessary, no planning ahead of time, no wondering if you should or shouldn't; just whang! bang!" Thanks to Masters and Johnson even the scientific canon recognizes that for the female, "whang! bang!" can scarcely be described as pleasurable.

Still, the male psyche persists in believing that, protestations and struggles to the contrary, deep inside her mysterious feminine soul, the female victim has wished for her own fate. A young woman who was raped by the husband of a friend said that days after the incident the man returned to her home, pounded on the door and screamed to her, "Jane, Jane. You loved it. You know you loved it."

The theory that women like being raped extends itself by deduction into the proposition that most or much of rape is provoked by the victim. But this too is only myth. Though provocation, considered a mitigating factor in a court of law, may consist of only "a gesture," according to the Federal Commission on Crimes of Violence, only 4 percent of reported rapes involved any precipitative behavior by the woman.

The notion that rape is enjoyed by the victim is also convenient for the man who, though he would not commit forcible rape, enjoys the idea of its existence, as if rape confirms that enormous sexual potency which he secretly knows to be his own. It is for the pleasure of the armchair rapist that detailed accounts of violent rapes exist in the media. Indeed, many men appear to take sexual pleasure from nearly all forms of violence. Whatever the motivation, male sexuality and violence in our culture seem to be inseparable. James Bond alternately whips out his revolver and his cock, and though there is no known connection between the skills of gun-fighting and love-making, pacifism seems suspiciously effeminate.

In a recent fictional treatment of the Manson case, Frank Conroy writes of his vicarious titillation when describing the murders to his wife:

> "Every single person there was killed." She didn't move. "It sounds like there was torture," I said. As the words left my mouth I knew there was no need to say them to frighten her into believing that she needed me for protection.

The pleasure he feels as his wife's protector is inextricably mixed with pleasure in the violence itself. Conroy writes, "I was excited by the killings, as one is excited by catastrophe on a grand scale, as one is alert to pre-echoes of unknown changes, hints of unrevealed secrets, rumblings of chaos. . . ."

The attraction of the male in our culture to violence and death is a tradition Manson and his admirers are carrying on with tireless avidity (even presuming Manson's innocence, he dreams of the purification of fire and destruction). It was Malraux in his *Anti-Memoirs* who said that, for the male, facing death was *the* illuminating experience analogous to childbirth for the female. Certainly our culture does glorify war and shroud the agonies of the gunfighter in veils of mystery.

And in the spectrum of male behavior, rape, the perfect combination of sex and violence, is the penultimate act. Erotic pleasure cannot be separated from culture, and in our culture male eroticism is wedded to power. Not only should a man be taller and stronger than a female in the perfect love-match, but he must also demonstrate his superior strength in gestures of dominance which are perceived as amorous. Though the law attempts to make a clear division between rape and sexual intercourse, in fact the courts find it difficult to distinguish between a case where the decision to copulate was mutual and one where a man forced himself upon his partner.

The scenario is even further complicated by the expectation that, not only does a woman mean "yes" when she says "no," but that a really decent woman ought to begin by saying "no," and then be led down the primrose path to acquiescence. Ovid, the author of Western Civilization's most celebrated sex-manual, makes this expectation perfectly clear:

> . . . and when I beg you to say "yes," say "no." Then let me lie outside your bolted door. . . . So Love grows strong. . . .

That the basic elements of rape are involved in all heterosexual relationships may explain why men often identify with the offender in this crime. But to regard the rapist as the victim, a man driven by his inherent sexual needs to take what will not be given him, reveals a basic ignorance of sexual politics. For in our culture heterosexual love finds an erotic expression through male dominance and female submission. A man who derives pleasure from raping a woman clearly must enjoy force and dominance as much or more than the simple pleasures of the flesh. Coitus cannot be experienced in isolation. The weather, the state of the nation, the level of sugar in the blood—all will affect a man's ability to achieve an orgasm. If a man can achieve sexual pleasure after terrorizing and humiliating the object of his passion, and in fact while inflicting pain upon her, one must assume he derives pleasure directly from terrorizing, humiliating and harming a woman. According to Amir's study of forcible rape, on a statistical average the man who has been convicted of rape was found to have a normal sexual personality, tending to be different from the normal, well-adjusted male only in having a greater tendency to express violence and rage.

And if the professional rapist is to be separated from the average dominant heterosexual, it may be mainly a quantitative difference. For the existence of rape as an index to masculinity is not entirely metaphorical. Though this measure of masculinity seems to be more publicly exhibited among "bad boys" or aging bikers who practice sexual initiation through group rape, in fact, "good boys" engage in the same rites to prove their manhood. In Stockton,

a small town in California which epitomizes silent-majority America, a bachelor party was given last summer for a young man about to be married. A woman was hired to dance "topless" for the amusement of the guests. At the high point of the evening the bridegroom-to-be dragged the woman into a bedroom. No move was made by any of his companions to stop what was clearly going to be an attempted rape. Far from it. As the woman described, "I tried to keep him away—told him of my Herpes Genitalis, et cetera, but he couldn't face the guys if he didn't screw me." After the bridegroom had finished raping the woman and returned with her to the party, far from chastising him, his friends heckled the woman and covered her with wine.

It was fortunate for the dancer that the bridegroom's friends did not follow him into the bedroom for, though one might suppose that in group rape, since the victim is outnumbered, less force would be inflicted on her, in fact, Amir's studies indicate, "the most excessive degrees of violence occurred in group rape." Far from discouraging violence, the presence of other men may in fact encourage sadism, and even cause the behavior. In an unpublished study of group rape by Gilbert Geis and Duncan Chappell, the authors refer to a study by W. H. Blanchard which relates, "The leader of the male group . . . apparently precipitated and maintained the activity, despite misgivings, because of a need to fulfill the role that the other two men had assigned to him. 'I was scared when it began to happen,' he says. 'I wanted to leave but I didn't want to say it to the other guys—you know—that I was scared.'"

Thus it becomes clear that not only does our culture teach men the rudiments of rape, but society, or more specifically other men, encourage the practice of it.

II

Every man I meet wants to protect me. Can't figure out what from.

—Mae West

If a male society rewards aggressive, domineering sexual behavior, it contains within itself a sexual schizophrenia. For the masculine man is also expected to prove his mettle as a protector of women.

To the naive eye, this dichotomy implies that men fall into one of two categories: those who rape and those who protect. In fact, life does not prove so simple. In a study euphemistically entitled "Sex Aggression by College Men," it was discovered that men who believe in a double standard of morality for men and women, who in fact believe most fervently in the ultimate value of virginity, are more liable to commit "this aggressive variety of sexual exploitation."

(At this point in our narrative it should come as no surprise that Sir Thomas Malory, creator of that classic tale of chivalry, *The Knights of the Round Table*, was himself arrested and found guilty for repeated incidents of rape.)

In the system of chivalry, men protect women against men. This is not unlike the protection relationship which the mafia established with small businesses in the early part of this century. Indeed, chivalry is an age-old protection racket which depends for its existence on rape.

According to the male mythology which defines and perpetuates rape, it is an animal instinct inherent in the male. The story goes that sometime in our pre-historical past, the male, more hirsute and burly than today's counterparts, roamed about an uncivilized landscape until he found a desirable female. (Oddly enough, this female is *not* pictured as more muscular than the modern woman.) Her mate does not bother with courtship. He simply grabs her by the hair and drags her to the closest cave. Presumably, one of the major advantages of modern civilization for the female has been the civilizing of the male. We call it chivalry.

But women do not get chivalry for free. According to the logic of sexual politics, we too have to civilize our behavior. (Enter chastity. Enter virginity. Enter monogamy.) For the female, civilized behavior means chastity before marriage and faithfulness within it. Chivalrous behavior in the male is supposed to protect that chastity from involuntary defilement. The fly in the ointment of this otherwise peaceful system is the fallen woman. She does not behave. And therefore she does not deserve protection. Or, to use another argument, a major tenet of the same value system: what has once been defiled cannot again be violated. One begins to suspect that it is the behavior of the fallen woman, and not that of the male, that civilization aims to control.

The assumption that a woman who does not respect the double standard deserves whatever she gets (or at the very least "asks for it") operates in the courts today. While in some states a man's previous rape convictions are not considered admissible evidence, the sexual reputation of the rape victim is considered a crucial element of the facts upon which the court must decide innocence or guilt.

The court's respect for the double standard manifested itself particularly clearly in the case of the People v. Jerry Plotkin. Mr. Plotkin, a 36-year-old jeweler, was tried for rape last spring in a San Francisco Superior Court. According to the woman who brought the charges, Plotkin, along with three other men, forced her at gunpoint to enter a car one night in October, 1970. She was taken to Mr. Plotkin's fashionable apartment where he and the three other men first raped her and then, in the delicate language of the *S.F. Chronicle*, "subjected her to perverted sex acts." She was, she said, set free in the morning with the warning that she would be killed if she spoke to anyone about the event. She did report the incident to the police who then searched Plotkin's apartment and discovered a long list of names of women. Her name was on the list and had been crossed out.

In addition to the woman's account of her abduction and rape, the prosecution submitted four of Plotkin's address books containing the names of hundreds of women. Plotkin claimed he did not know all of the women since some of the names had been given to him by friends and he had not yet called on them. Several women, however, did testify in court that Plotkin had, to cite the *Chronicle*, "lured them up to his apartment under one pretext or another, and forced his sexual attentions on them."

Plotkin's defense rested on two premises. First, through his own testimony Plotkin established a reputation for himself as a sexual libertine who frequently picked up girls in bars and took them to his house where sexual relations often took place. He was the Playboy. He claimed that the accusation of rape, therefore, was false—this incident had simply been one of many casual sexual relationships, the victim one of many playmates. The second premise of the defense was that his accuser was also a sexual libertine. However, the picture created of the young woman (fully 13 years younger than Plotkin) was not akin to the light-hearted, gay-bachelor image projected by the defendant. On the contrary, the day after the defense cross-examined the woman, the *Chronicle* printed a story headlined, "Grueling Day for Rape Case Victim." (A leaflet passed out by women in front of the courtroom was more succinct: "Rape was committed by four men in a private apartment in October; on Thursday, it was done by a judge and a lawyer in a public courtroom.")

Through skillful questioning fraught with innuendo, Plotkin's defense attorney James Martin MacInnis portrayed the young woman as a licentious opportunist and unfit mother. MacInnis began by asking the young woman (then employed as a secretary) whether or not it was true that she was "familiar with liquor" and had worked as a "cocktail waitress." The young woman replied (the *Chronicle* wrote "admitted") that she had worked once or twice as a cocktail waitress. The attorney then asked if she had worked as a secretary in the financial district but had "left that employment after it was discovered that you had sexual intercourse on a couch in the office." The woman replied, "That is a lie. I left because I didn't like working in a one-girl office. It was too lonely." Then the defense asked if, while working as an attendant at a health club, "you were accused of having a sexual affair with a man?" Again the woman denied the story, "I was never accused of that."

Plotkin's attorney then sought to establish that his client's accuser was living with a married man. She responded that the man was separated from his wife. Finally he told the court that she had "spent the night" with another man who lived in the same building.

At this point in the testimony the woman asked Plotkin's defense attorney, "Am I on trial? . . . It is embarrassing and personal to admit these things to all these people. . . . I did not commit a crime. I am a human being." The lawyer, true to the chivalry of his class, apologized and immediately resumed questioning her, turning his attention to her chil-

dren. (She is divorced, and the children at the time of the trial were in a foster home.) "Isn't it true that your two children have a sex game in which one gets on top of another and they—" "That is a lie!" the young woman interrupted him. She ended her testimony by explaining "They are wonderful children. They are not perverted."

The jury, divided in favor of acquittal ten to two, asked the court stenographer to read the woman's testimony back to them. After this reading, the Superior Court acquitted the defendant of both the charges of rape and kidnapping.

According to the double standard a woman who has had sexual intercourse out of wedlock cannot be raped. Rape is not only a crime of aggression against the body; it is a transgression against chastity as defined by men. When a woman is forced into a sexual relationship, she has, according to the male ethos, been violated. But she is also defiled if she does not behave according to the double standard, by maintaining her chastity, or confining her sexual activities to a monogamous relationship.

One should not assume, however, that a woman can avoid the possibility of rape simply by behaving. Though myth would have it that mainly "bad girls" are raped, this theory has no basis in fact. Available statistics would lead one to believe that a safer course is promiscuity. In a study of rape done in the District of Columbia, it was found that 82 percent of the rape victims had a "good reputation." Even the Police Inspector's advice to stay off the streets is rather useless, for almost half of reported rapes occur in the home of the victim and are committed by a man she has never before seen. Like indiscriminate terrorism, rape can happen to any woman, and few women are ever without this knowledge.

But the courts and the police, both dominated by white males, continue to suspect the rape victim, *sui generis*, of provoking or asking for her own assault. According to Amir's study, the police tend to believe that a woman without a good reputation cannot be raped. The rape victim is usually submitted to countless questions about her own sexual mores and behavior by the police investigator. This preoccupation is partially justified by the legal requirements for prosecution in a rape case. The rape victim must have been penetrated, and she must have made it clear to her assailant that she did not want penetration (unless of course she is unconscious). A refusal to accompany a man to some isolated place to allow him to touch her does not in the eyes of the court, constitute rape. She must have said "no" at the crucial genital moment. And the rape victim, to qualify as such, must also have put up a physical struggle—unless she can prove that to do so would have been to endanger her life.

But the zealous interest the police frequently exhibit in the physical details of a rape case is only partially explained by the requirements of the court. A woman who was raped in Berkeley was asked to tell the story of her rape four different times "right out in the street," while her assailant was escaping. She was then required to submit to a pelvic examination to prove that penetration had taken place. Later, she was taken to the police station where she was asked the same questions again: "Were you forced?" "Did he penetrate?" "Are you sure your life was in danger and you had no other choice?" This woman had been pulled off the street by a man who held a 10-inch knife at her throat and forcibly raped her. She was raped at midnight and was not able to return to her home until five in the morning. Police contacted her twice again in the next week, once by telephone at two in the morning and once at four in the morning. In her words, "The rape was probably the least traumatic incident of the whole evening. If I'm ever raped again, . . . I wouldn't report it to the police because of all the degradation. . . . "

If white women are subjected to unnecessary and often hostile questioning after having been raped, third world women are often not believed at all. According to the white male ethos (which is not only sexist but racist), third world women are defined from birth as "impure." Thus the white male is provided with a pool of women who are fair game for sexual imperialism. Third world women frequently do not report rape and for good reason. When blues singer Billie Holliday was 10 years old, she was taken off to a local house by a neighbor and raped. Her mother brought the police to rescue her, and she was taken to the local police station crying and bleeding:

> When we got there, instead of treating me and Mom like somebody who called the cops for help, they treated me like I'd killed somebody. . . . I guess they had me figured for having enticed this old goat into the whorehouse. . . . All I know for sure is they threw me into a cell . . . a fat white matron . . . saw I was still bleeding, she felt sorry for me and gave me a couple glasses of milk. But nobody else did anything for me except give me filthy looks and snicker to themselves.
>
> After a couple of days in a cell they dragged me into a court. Mr. Dick got sentenced to five years. They sentenced me to a Catholic institution.

Clearly the white man's chivalry is aimed only to protect the chastity of "his" women.

As a final irony, that same system of sexual values from which chivalry is derived has also provided womankind with an unwritten code of behavior, called femininity, which makes a feminine woman the perfect victim of sexual aggression. If being chaste does not ward off the possibility of assault, being feminine certainly increases the chances that it will succeed. To be submissive is to defer to masculine strength; is to lack muscular development or any interest in defending oneself; is to let doors be opened, to have one's arm held when crossing the street. To be feminine is to wear shoes which make it difficult to run; skirts which inhibit one's stride; underclothes which inhibit the circulation. Is it not an intriguing observation that those very clothes which are thought to be flattering to the female and attractive to the male are those which make it impossible for a woman to defend herself against aggression?

Each girl as she grows into womanhood is taught fear. Fear is the form in which the female internalizes both chivalry and the double standard. Since, biologically speaking, women in fact have the same if not greater potential for sexual expression as do men, the woman who is taught that she must behave differently from a man must also learn to distrust her own carnality. She must deny her own feelings and learn not to act from them. She fears herself. This is the essence of passivity, and of course, a woman's passivity is not simply sexual but functions to cripple her from self-expression in every area of her life.

Passivity itself prevents a woman from ever considering her own potential for self-defense and forces her to look to men for protection. The woman is taught fear, but this time fear of the other; and yet her only relief from this fear is to seek out the other. Moreover, the passive woman is taught to regard herself as impotent, unable to act, unable even to perceive, in no way self-sufficient, and, finally, as the object and not the subject of human behavior. It is in this sense that a woman is deprived of the status of a human being. She is not free to be.

III

Since Ibsen's Nora slammed the door on her patriarchal husband, woman's attempt to be free has been more or less fashionable. In this 19th century portrait of a woman leaving her marriage, Nora tells her husband, "Our home has been nothing but a playroom. I have been your doll-wife just as at home I was papa's doll-child." And, at least on the stage, "The Doll's House" crumbled, leaving audiences with hope for the fate of the modern woman. And today, as in the past, womankind has not lacked examples of liberated women to emulate: Emma Goldman, Greta Garbo and Isadora Duncan all denounced marriage and the double standard, and believed their right to freedom included sexual independence; but still their example has not affected the lives of millions of women who continue to marry, divorce and remarry, living out their lives dependent on the status and economic power of men. Patriarchy still holds the average woman prisoner not because she lacks the courage of an Isadora Duncan, but because the material conditions of her life prevent her from being anything but an object.

In the *Elementary Structures of Kinship*, Claude Levi-Strauss gives to marriage this universal description, "It is always a system of exchange that we find at the origin of the rules of marriage." In this system of exchange, a woman is the "most precious possession." Levi-Strauss continues that the custom of including women as booty in the marketplace is still so general that "a whole volume would not be sufficient to enumerate instances of it." Levi-Strauss makes it clear that he does not exclude Western Civilization from his definition of "universal" and cites examples from modern wedding ceremonies. (The marriage ceremony is still one in which the

husband and wife become one, and "that one is the husband.")

The legal proscription against rape reflects this possessory view of women. An article in the 1952–53 *Yale Law Journal* describes the legal rationale behind laws against rape: "In our society sexual taboos, often enacted into law, buttress a system of monogamy based upon the law of 'free bargaining' of the potential spouses. Within this process the woman's power to withhold or grant sexual access is an important bargaining weapon." Presumably then, laws against rape are intended to protect the right of a woman, not for physical self-determination, but for physical "bargaining." The article goes on to explain explicitly why the preservation of the bodies of women is important to men:

The consent standard in our society does more than protect a significant item of social currency for women; it fosters, and is in turn bolstered by, a masculine pride in the exclusive possession of a sexual object. The consent of a woman to sexual intercourse awards the man a privilege of bodily access, a personal "prize" whose value is enhanced by sole ownership. An additional reason for the man's condemnation of rape may be found in the threat to his status from a decrease in the "value" of his sexual possession which would result from forcible violation.

The passage concludes by making clear whose interest the law is designed to protect. "The man responds to this undercutting of his status as *possessor* of the girl with hostility toward the rapist; no other restitution device is available. The law of rape provides an orderly outlet for his vengeance." Presumably the female victim in any case will have been sufficiently socialized so as not to consciously feel any strong need for vengeance. If she does feel this need, society does not speak to it.

The laws against rape exist to protect rights of the male as possessor of the female body, and not the right of the female over her own body. Even without this enlightening passage from the *Yale Law Review*, the laws themselves are clear: In no state can a man be accused of raping his wife. How can any man steal what already belongs to him? It is in the sense of rape as theft of another man's property that Kate Millett writes, "Traditionally rape has been viewed as an offense one male commits against another—a matter of abusing his woman." In raping another man's woman, a man may aggrandize his own manhood and concurrently reduce that of another man. Thus a man's honor is not subject directly to rape, but only indirectly, through "his" woman.

If the basic social unit is the family, in which the woman is a possession of her husband, the superstructure of society is a male hierarchy, in which men dominate other men (or patriarchal families dominate other patriarchal families). And it is no small irony that, while the very social fabric of our male-dominated culture denies women equal access to political, economic and legal power, the literature, myth and humor of our culture depicts women not only as the power behind the throne, but the real source of the oppression of men. The religious version of this fairy tale blames Eve for both carnality and eating of the tree of knowledge, at the same time making her gullible to the obvious devices of a serpent. Adam, of course, is merely the trusting victim of love. Certainly this is a biased story. But no more biased than the one television audiences receive today from the latest slick comedians. Through a media which is owned by men, censored by a State dominated by men, all the evils of this social system which make a man's life unpleasant are blamed upon "the wife." The theory is: were it not for the female who waits and plots to "trap" the male into marriage, modern man would be able to achieve Olympian freedom. She is made the scapegoat for a system which is in fact run by men.

Nowhere is this more clear than in the white racist use of the concept of white womanhood. The white male's open rape of black women, coupled with his overweening concern for the chastity and protection of his wife and daughters, represents an extreme of sexist and racist hypocrisy. While on the one hand she was held up as the standard for purity and virtue, on the other the Southern white woman was never asked if she wanted to be on a pedestal, and in fact any deviance from the male-defined standards for white womanhood was treated severely. (It is a powerful commentary on American racism that the historical role of Blacks as slaves, and thus possessions without power, has robbed black women of

legal and economic protection through marriage. Thus black women in Southern society and in the ghettoes of the North have long been easy game for white rapists.) The fear that black men would rape white women was, and is, classic paranoia. Quoting from Ann Breen's unpublished study of racism and sexism in the South *"The New South: White Man's Country,"* Frederick Douglass legitimately points out that, had the black man wished to rape white women, he had ample opportunity to do so during the civil war when white women, the wives, sisters, daughters and mothers of the rebels, were left in the care of Blacks. But yet not a single act of rape was committed during this time. The Ku Klux Klan, who tarred and feathered black men and lynched them in the honor of the purity of white womanhood, also applied tar and feathers to a Southern white woman accused of bigamy, which leads one to suspect that Southern white men were not so much outraged at the violation of the woman as a person, in the few instances where rape was actually committed by black men, but at the violation of his property rights. In the situation where a black man was found to be having sexual relations with a white woman, the white woman could exercise skin-privilege, and claim that she had been raped, in which case the black man was lynched. But if she did not claim rape, she herself was subject to lynching.

In constructing the myth of white womanhood so as to justify the lynching and oppression of black men and women, the white male has created a convenient symbol of his own power which has resulted in black hostility toward the white "bitch," accompanied by an unreasonable fear on the part of many white women of the black rapist. Moreover, it is not surprising that after being told for two centuries that he wants to rape white women, occasionally a black man does actually commit that act. But it is crucial to note that the frequency of this practice is outrageously exaggerated in the white mythos. Ninety percent of reported rape is intra- not inter-racial.

In *Soul on Ice*, Eldridge Cleaver has described the mixing of a rage against white power with the internalized sexism of a black man raping a white woman. "Somehow I arrived at the conclusion that, as a matter of principle, it was of paramount importance for me to have an antagonistic, ruthless attitude toward white women. . . . Rape was an insurrectionary act. It delighted me that I was defying and trampling upon the white man's law, upon his system of values and that I was defiling his women—and this point, I believe, was the most satisfying to me because I was very resentful over the historical fact of how the white man has used the black woman." Thus a black man uses white women to take out his rage against white men. But in fact, whenever a rape of a white woman by a black man does take place, it is again the white man who benefits. First, the act itself terrorizes the white woman and makes her more dependent on the white male for protection. Then, if the woman prosecutes her attacker, the white man is afforded legal opportunity to exercise overt racism. Of course, the knowledge of the rape helps to perpetuate two myths which are beneficial to white male rule—the bestiality of the black man and the desirability of white women. Finally, the white man surely benefits because he himself is not the object of attack—he has been allowed to stay in power.

Indeed, the existence of rape in any form is beneficial to the ruling class of white males. For rape is a kind of terrorism which severely limits the freedom of women and makes women dependent on men. Moreover, in the act of rape, the rage that one man may harbor toward another higher in the male hierarchy can be deflected toward a female scapegoat. For every man there is always someone lower on the social scale on whom he can take out his aggressions. And that is any woman alive.

This oppressive attitude towards women finds its institutionalization in the traditional family. For it is assumed that a man "wears the pants" in his family—he exercises the option of rule whenever he so chooses. Not that he makes all the decisions—clearly women make most of the important day-to-day decisions in a family. But when a conflict of interest arises, it is the man's interest which will prevail. His word, in itself, is more powerful. He lords it over his wife in the same way his boss lords it over him, so that the very process of exercising his power becomes as important an act as obtaining

whatever it is his power can get for him. This notion of power is key to the male ego in this culture, for the two acceptable measures of masculinity are a man's power over women and his power over other men. A man may boast to his friends that "I have 20 men working for me." It is also aggrandizement of his ego if he has the financial power to clothe his wife in furs and jewels. And, if a man lacks the wherewithal to acquire such power, he can always express his rage through equally masculine activities—rape and theft. Since male society defines the female as a possession, it is not surprising that the felony most often committed together with rape is theft. As the following classic tale of rape points out, the elements of theft, violence and forced sexual relations merge into an indistinguishable whole.

The woman who told this story was acquainted with the man who tried to rape her. When the man learned that she was going to be staying alone for the weekend, he began early in the day a polite campaign to get her to go out with him. When she continued to refuse his request, his chivalrous mask dropped away:

"I had locked all the doors because I was afraid, and I don't know how he got in; it was probably through the screen door. When I woke up, he was shaking my leg. His eyes were red, and I knew he had been drinking or smoking. I thought I would try to talk my way out of it. He started by saying that he wanted to sleep with me, and then he got angrier and angrier, until he started to say, 'I want pussy,' 'I want pussy.' Then, I got scared and tried to push him away. That's when he started to force himself on me. It was awful. It was the most humiliating, terrible feeling. He was forcing my legs apart and ripping my clothes off. And it was painful. I did fight him—he was slightly drunk and I was able to keep him away. I had taken judo a few years back, but I was afraid to throw a chop for fear that he'd kill me. I could see he was getting more and more violent. I was thinking wildly of some way to get out of this alive, and then I said to him, 'Do you want money. I'll give you money.' We had money but I was also thinking that if I got to the back room I could telephone the police—as if the police would have even helped. It was a stupid thing to think of because obviously he would follow me. And he did. When he saw me pick up the phone, he tried to tie the cord around my neck. I screamed at him that I did have the money in another room, that I was going to call the police because I was scared, but that I would never tell anybody what happened. It would be an absolute secret. He said, okay, and I went to get the money. But when he got it, all of a sudden he got this crazy look in his eye and he said to me, 'Now I'm going to kill you.' Then I started saying my prayers. I knew there was nothing I could do. He started to hit me—I still wasn't sure if he wanted to rape me at this point—or just to kill me. He was hurting me, but hadn't yet gotten me into a strangle-hold because he was still drunk and off balance. Somehow we pushed into the kitchen where I kept looking at this big knife. But I didn't pick it up. Somehow, no matter how much I hated him at that moment, I still couldn't imagine putting the knife in his flesh, and then I was afraid he would grab it and stick it into me. Then he was hitting me again and somehow we pushed through the back door of the kitchen and onto the porch steps. We fell down the steps and that's when he started to strangle me. He was on top of me. He just went on and on until finally I lost consciousness. I did scream, though my screams sounded like whispers to me. But what happened was that a cab driver happened by and frightened him away. The cab driver revived me—I was out only a minute at the most. And then I ran across the street and I grabbed the woman who was our neighbor and screamed at her, 'Am I alive? Am I still alive?'"

Rape is an act of aggression in which the victim is denied her self-determination. It is an act of violence which, if not actually followed by beatings or murder, nevertheless always carries with it the threat of death. And finally, rape is a form of mass terrorism, for the victims of rape are chosen indiscriminately, but the propagandists for male supremacy broadcast that it is women who cause rape by being unchaste or in the wrong place at the wrong time—in essence, by behaving as though they were free.

The threat of rape is used to deny women employment. (In California, the Berkeley Public Library, until pushed by the Federal Employment Practices Commission, refused to hire female shelvers because of perverted men in the stacks.) The fear of rape keeps women off the streets at night. Keeps women at home. Keeps women passive and modest for fear that they be thought provocative.

It is part of human dignity to be able to defend oneself, and women are learning. Some women have learned karate; some to shoot guns. And yet we will not be free until the threat of rape and the atmosphere of violence is ended, and to end that the nature of male behavior must change.

But rape is not an isolated act that can be rooted out from patriarchy without ending patriarchy itself. The same men and power structure who victimize women are engaged in the act of raping Vietnam, raping black people and the very earth we live upon. Rape is a classic act of domination where, in the words of Kate Millett, "the emotions of hatred, contempt, and the desire to break or violate personality," takes place. This breaking of the personality characterizes modern life itself. No simple reforms can eliminate rape. As the symbolic expression of the white male hierarchy, rape is the quintessential act of our civilization, one which, Valerie Solanis warns, is in danger of "humping itself to death."

5

The Political Economy of Crime:

A Comparative Study of Nigeria and the United States

WILLIAM J. CHAMBLISS

Criminology shares in common with all other social thought the fact that the research we do and the explanations we divine flow from and reflect the general theoretical perspective within which we work. In the social sciences two perspectives dominate our work. These are commonly referred to as the "functional" and "dialectic" models of society.[1] In the study of crime these two models are intimately associated with the work of Emile Durkheim and Karl Marx.

The starting point for both Marx and Durkheim is that we can understand crime (or any social phenomena for that matter) only if we can articulate and describe the *consequences* which the event has for the larger set of social relations in which the event is implicated. In this sense then both perspectives are "functional" (van den Berghe, 1964), though the dialectic argues that the equilibrium produced by functional interrelation is necessarily a temporary state of a changing historical process and *not,* as the functional perspective suggests, an "ingredient of all healthy societies" (Durkheim, 1958: 67). For

Source: Sawyer F. Sylvester, Jr., and Edward Sagarin, *Politics and Crime,* New York: Praeger, 1974, pp. 17–30. By permission of the author and publisher.

Marx a "healthy society" would be one free of class conflict and therefore free of crime.

The dialectic and functional models diverge rather sharply on the issue of what exactly is contributed by crime to "all healthy societies." For Durkheim, crime's most important function (i.e., consequence) in society was its role in establishing and preserving the moral boundaries of the community (1960: 102):

Crime brings together upright consciences and concentrates them. We have only to notice what happens, particularly in a small town, when some moral scandal has just been committed. They stop each other on the street. They visit each other. They seek to come together to talk of the event and to wax indignant in common. From all the similar impressions which are exchanged, for all the temper that gets itself expressed, there emerges a unique temper . . . which is everybody's without being anybody's in particular. That is the public temper.

For Marx the most important contribution made by crime to society (or function of crime in society) is its contribution to temporary economic stability in an economic system that is inherently unstable. (Marx, n.d.: 375–76).

. . . crime takes a part of the superfluous population off the labor market and thus reduces competition among the laborers—up to a certain point preventing wages from falling below the minimum—the struggle against crime absorbs another part of this population. Thus the criminal comes in as one of those natural 'counterweights' which bring about a correct balance and open up a whole perspective of 'useful' occupations . . . the criminal . . . produces the whole of the police and of criminal justice, constables, judges, hangmen, juries, etc.; and all these different lines of business, which form equally many categories of the social division of labor, develop different capacities of the human spirit, create new needs and new ways of satisfying them. Torture alone has given rise to the most ingenious mechanical inventions, and employed many honorable craftsmen in the production of its instruments.

In addition Marx (1964: 225–30) viewed crime as contributing to political stability by legitimizing the state's monopoly on violence and justifying political and legal control of the masses.

More specifically the two perspectives suggest the following differing interpretations of crime:

Functional Hypotheses	*Dialectic Hypotheses*
1. Acts are criminal because they offend the morality of the people.	1. An act is criminal because it is in the interests of the ruling class to so define it.
2. Persons are labeled criminal because their behavior has gone beyond the tolerance limits of the community's conscience.	2. Persons are labeled criminal because so defining them serves the interests of the ruling class.
3. The lower classes are more likely to be arrested because they commit more crimes.	3. The lower classes are labeled criminal and the bourgeoisie is not because the bourgeoisie's control of the means of production gives them control of the state and law enforcement as well.
4. Crime is a constant in societies. All societies need and produce crime.	4. Crime varies from society to society depending on the political and economic structures of the society.
5. As societies become more specialized in the division of labor, more and more laws will reflect contractual disputes and penal laws will become less and less significant.	5. As capitalist societies industrialize the division between social classes will grow and penal laws will increasingly have to be passed and enforced to maintain temporary stability by curtailing violent confrontations between social classes.
6. Socialist and capitalist societies should have the same amounts of crime where they have comparable rates of industrialization and bureaucratization.	6. Socialist and capitalist societies should have significantly different crime rates since class conflict will be less in socialist societies and therefore the amount of crime lower as well.
7. Crime makes people more aware of the interests they have in common.	7. Defining certain people as criminal permits greater control of the proletariat.
8. Crime creates a tighter hold between and leads to greater solidarity among members of the community.	8. Crime directs the hostility of the oppressed away from the oppressors and towards their own class.

Elsewhere I have investigated the extent to which the two paradigms are compatible with data on the creation of criminal laws (Chambliss, 1963). In this paper I hope to shed light on the relative utility of the two models in explaining the distribution and content of criminal behavior. To do this I will report on the results of a comparative study of crime and criminal law enforcement in Nigeria and the United States.

DATA COLLECTION

Our data comes from research in the United States—principally Seattle, Washington—and Nigeria, principally Ibadan. The research methods employed are mainly those of a participant observer. In Seattle the research spanned almost 10 years (1962–1972) and in Ibadan the research took place during 1967–68. In both cities the data was gathered through extensive interviewing of informants from all sides of the criminal law—criminals, professional thieves, racketeers, prostitutes, government officials, police officers, businessmen and members of various social class levels in the community. The sampling was what sociologists have come to call (with more than a slight bit of irony) "convenience samples." Any other sampling procedure is simply impossible in the almost impenetrable world of crime and law enforcement.

Nigeria and America share in common the fact that they inherited British common law at the time of their independence. Independence came somewhat later for Nigeria than for America, but the legal systems inherited were very similar. As a result both countries share much the same foundation in statutes and common law principles. While differences exist, they are not, for our purposes, of any great significance.

In both Nigeria and the United States it is a crime punishable by imprisonment and fine for any public official to accept a bribe, to solicit a bribe, or to give special favors to a citizen for monetary considerations. It is also against the law in both countries to run gambling establishments, to engage in or solicit for prostitutes, to sell liquor that has not been inspected and stamped by a duly appointed agency of the government, to run a taxi service without a license, and so on. And, of course, both nations share the more obvious restrictions on murder, theft, robbery, rape and the standard array of criminal offenses. In both countries there is a striking similarity in the types of laws that do *not* and those that do get enforced.[2]

CRIME AND LAW ENFORCEMENT IN NIGERIA

In both Nigeria and the United States many laws can be and are systematically violated with impunity by those who control the political or economic resources of the society. Particularly relevant are those laws that restrict such things as bribery, racketeering (especially gambling), prostitution, drug distribution and selling, usury and the whole range of criminal offenses committed by businessmen in the course of their businesses (white collar crimes).

In Nigeria the acceptance of bribes by government officials is blatantly public and virtually universal. When the vice-president of a large research organization that was just getting established in Nigeria visited the head of the Nigerian Customs he was told by the Customs Director that "at the outset it is important that we both understand that the customs office is corrupt from the top to the bottom." Incoming American professors were usually asked by members of the faculty at the university if they would be willing to exchange their American dollars on the black market at a better exchange rate than banks would offer. In at least one instance the Nigerian professor making this request was doing so for the military governor of the state within which the university was located. Should the incoming American fail to meet a colleague who would wish to make an illegal transfer of funds he would in all likelihood be approached by any number of other citizens in high places. For example, the vice-president of the leading bank near the university would often approach American professors and ask if they would like to exchange their money through him personally and thereby receive a better exchange rate than was possible if they dealt directly through the bank.

At the time of my study, tithes of this sort were paid at every level. Businessmen desiring to establish businesses found their way blocked interminably by bureaucratic red tape until the proper amount of "dash" has been given to someone with the power to effect the result desired. Citizens riding buses were asked for cigarettes and small change by army soldiers who manned check points. The soldiers, in turn, had to pay a daily or weekly tithe to superior officers in order to be kept at this preferential assignment. At the border one could bring French wine, cigarettes, and many other prohibited commodities into Nigeria, so long as prior arrangements had been made with the customs officers either in Lagos or at the check point itself. The prior arrangements include payment of a bribe.

As a result of bribes and payoffs, there flourished a large and highly profitable trade in a wide variety of vices. Prostitution was open and rampant in all of the large cities of Nigeria—it was especially well developed in those cities where commerce and industry brought large numbers of foreigners. Gambling establishments, located mainly in large European style hotels, and managed incidentally by Italian visitors, catered to the moneyed set with a variety of games of chance competitive with Monte Carlo or Las Vegas. There was a large illicit liquor trade (mostly a home-brewed gin-like drink) as well as a smaller but nevertheless profitable trade in drugs that received political and legal protection through payoffs to high-level officials.

In at least Ibadan and Lagos gangs of professional thieves operated with impunity. These gangs of thieves were well organized and included the use of beggars and young children as cover for theft activities. The links to the police were sufficient to guarantee that suspects would be treated leniently— usually allowed to go with no charges being brought. In one instance an entire community within the city of Ibadan was threatened by thieves with total destruction. The events leading up to this are revealing. The community, which I shall call Lando, had been victimized by a gang of thieves who broke into homes and stole valuable goods. The elders of Lando hired four men to guard the community. When thieves came one evening the hired guards caught and killed three of them. The next day the Oba of the community was called on by two men from another part of the city. These men expressed grave concern that some of their compatriots had been killed in Lando. The Oba informed them that if any other thieves came to Lando they would be dealt with similarly. The thieves' representatives advised the Oba that if such a thing happened the thieves would burn the community to the ground. When the Oba said he would call the police it was pointed out to him that the chief of police was the brother-in-law of one of the thieves. Ultimately an agreement was reached whereby the thieves agreed to stop stealing in Lando in return for the Oba's promise that the thieves could sell their stolen property in Lando on market day.

Ibadan is a very cosmopolitan city which lies in the Yoruba section of western Nigeria. Although dominated by the Yoruba there are nonetheless large numbers of Hausa, Ibo and other ethnic groups in the city. The Hausa who are strongly Muslim, while the Yoruba are roughly 50% Christian, occupy a ghetto within Ibadan which is almost exclusively Hausa. Despite the fact that the Hausa are an immigrant group where one might expect the crime rate to be high, there are very few Hausa arrested for crime. This is particularly impressive since there is general belief that the Hausa are responsible for some of the more efficient and effective groups of professional thieves in the area. The explanation for this apparently lies in the fact that the Hausa have a strong leadership which intervenes with payoffs and cash to government and police officials, whenever a member of their community is in any difficulty.

Payment of bribes to the police is usually possible whenever an arrest is likely. An incoming American who illegally photographed an airport was allowed to go (without even destroying his film) upon payment of $15 to the arresting officer. Six dollars was sufficient for the wife of an American professor to avoid arrest for reckless driving. A young son of a wealthy merchant was arrested on numerous occasions for being drunk, driving without a license, stealing and getting into fights. On every occasion the police returned him to the custody of his parents without charges being filed when the father paid the arresting officer (or the policemen on the desk) $30 to $45.

Such practices were not atypical but were instead the usual procedure. It was said, and research bears this out, that one with money could pay to be excused from any type or amount of crime.

TABLE 1

Arrest Rate for 1000 Population,
Ibadan, Nigeria, 1967

Immigrant Areas	Indigenous Area	Hausa Area
1.41	.61	.54

Who, then, did get arrested? In general those who lacked either the money or the political influence to fix a criminal charge. The most common arrest of youth was for "street trading"—that is, selling items on the street. The second most frequent offense was "being away from home" or "sleeping out without protection." Among adults, "suspiciousness," public indecency, intoxication and being with no visible means of support were the most common offenses. Although robbery, theft and burglary were common offenses (in a sample of 300 residents of Ibadan, 12.7% reported having been the victim of burglary) arrests for these offenses were much less frequent.

Anyone who has lived or traveled in foreign countries will not be surprised by these findings. What is usually not recognized, however, is that these same kinds of things characterize crime and criminal law enforcement in the United States (and possibly every other nation) as well.

CRIME AND LAW ENFORCEMENT IN SEATTLE

Seattle, like Ibadan, is a city of 1,000,000 people with its own police, government and set of laws inherited from Great Britain. In Seattle, as in Ibadan, one can find any type of vice that suits the palate. One must travel away from the middle and upper-class suburbs that ring the city and venture into the never-never land of skidrow derelicts, the black ghetto, or a few other pockets of rundown hotels, cafes and cabarets that are sprinkled along freeways and by the docks. Here one can find prostitution, gambling, usury, drugs, pornography, bootleg liquor, bookmaking and pinball machines. Simply in terms of profit, gambling and usury are most important.

Gambling ranges from bookmaking (at practically every street corner in the center of the city) to open poker games, bingo parlors, off-track betting, casinos, roulette and dice games (concentrated in a few locations and also floating out into the suburban country clubs and fraternal organizations) and innumerable two and five dollar stud-poker games scattered liberally throughout the city.

The most conspicuous card games take place from about 10 in the morning (it varies slightly from one "fun house" to the next) until midnight. But there are a number of other 24 hour games that run constantly. In the more public games the limit ranges from $1 to $5 for each bet; in the more select games that run 24 hours a day there is a "pot limit" or "no limit" rule. These games are reported to have betting as high as $20,000 and $30,000. I have seen a bet made and called for $1,000 in one of these games. During this game, which was the highest stakes game I witnessed in the six years of the study, the police lieutenant in charge of the vice squad was called in to supervise the game—not, need I add, to break up the game or make any arrests, only to insure against violence.

Prostitution covers the usual range of ethnic group, age, shape and size of female. It is also found in houses with madams *à la* New Orleans stereotype, on the street through pimps, or in a suburban apartment building or hotels. Prices range from $5 for a short time with a street walker to $200 for a night with a lady who has her own apartment (which she usually shares with her boyfriend who is discreetly gone during business operations).

High interest loans are easy to arrange through stores that advertise "your signature is worth $5,000." It is really worth considerably more; it may in fact be worth your life. The interest rates vary from a low of 20% for three months to as high as 100% for varying periods. Repayment is demanded not through the courts but through the help of "the Gaspipe Gang" who call on recalcitrant debtors and use physical force to bring about payment. The "interest only" repayment is the most popular alternative practiced by borrowers, and is preferred by the loan sharks as well. The longer repayment can be prolonged, the more advantageous it is to the loan agents.

Pinball machines are readily available throughout the city and most of them pay off in cash.

The gambling, prostitution, drug distribution, pornography, and usury (high interest loans) which flourish in the lower-class center of the city do so with the compliance, encouragement and cooperation of the major political and law enforcement officials in the city. There is in fact a symbiotic relationship between the law enforcement-political organizations of the city and a group of *local* (as distinct from national) men who control the distribution of vices.

The payoffs and briberies in Seattle are complex. The simpler and more straightforward are those made by each gambling establishment. A restaurant or cabaret with cardroom attached had to pay around $200 each month to the police and $200 to the "syndicate." In reality these were two branches of the same group of men, but the payoffs were made separately. Anyone who refused these payments was harassed by fire inspectors, health inspectors, licensing difficulties and even physical violence from enforcers who worked for the crime cabal in the city. Similarly, places with pinball machines, pornography, bookmaking or prostitution had to pay regularly to the "bagman" who collected a fee for the police. Payoffs to policemen were also required of tow truck operators, cabaret owners and other businesses where police cooperation was necessary. Tow truck drivers carried with them a matchbox with $3 in it, and when asked for a light by the policeman who had called them to the scene of an accident, they gave them the matchbox with the money inside. Cabaret owners paid according to how large their business was. The police could extract payoffs because the laws were so worded as to make it virtually impossible to own a profitable cabaret without violating the law. For example, it was illegal to have an entertainer closer than 25 feet to the nearest customer. A cabaret, to comply with this ordinance, would have had to have a night club the size of a large ballroom at which point the atmosphere would have been too sterile as to drive customers away, not to mention the fact that such large spaces are exceedingly expensive in the downtown section of the city. Thus, the police could, if they chose, close down a cabaret on a moment's notice. Payoffs were a necessary investment to assure that the police would not so choose.

The trade in licenses was notoriously corrupt. It was generally agreed by my informants that to get a tow truck license one had to pay a bribe of $10,000; a cardroom license was $25,000; taxicab licenses were unavailable as were licenses for distributing pinball machines or juke boxes. These licenses had all been issued to members of the syndicate that controlled the rackets, and no outsiders were permitted in.

There were innumerable instances of payoffs to politicians and government officials for real estate deals, businesses and stock transactions. In each case the participants were a combination of local businessmen, racketeers, local politicians and government officials.

Interestingly there is also a minority ghetto within Seattle where one would expect to find a high crime rate. In Seattle this is the Japanese-American section of the city. It is widely believed that the Japanese-Americans have a very low propensity to crime. This is usually attributed to the family-centered orientation of the Japanese-American community.

There is some evidence, however, that this perspective is largely a self-fulfilling prophecy (Nagasawa, 1965; Chambliss and Nagasawa, 1969). Table 2 shows a comparison between the self-reported delinquency and arrest rates of Japanese-American youth for a selected year. The data suffers, of course, from problems inherent in such comparisons but nonetheless the point cannot be gainsaid that the actual crime rate among Japanese-American youth is considerably higher than the conventional view would suggest.[3]

TABLE 2

Comparison of Arrests (for 1963) and Self-Reported Delinquency Involvement, by Racial Groups[a]

	% Arrested	% Self-reporting High Delinquency Involvement[b]
White	11	53
Black	36	52
Japanese	2	36

[a]Based on data from Nagasawa (1965); see also Chambliss and Nagasawa (1969).
[b]A self-reported delinquency scale was developed and the respondents were divided so that 50% of the sample was categorized as having high and 50% as having low delinquent involvement.

Thus we see that in both the Hausa area of Ibadan and the Japanese-American section of Seattle there is reason to suspect a reasonably high crime rate but official statistics show an exceptionally low one. When discussing Hausa crime earlier, I attributed this fact to the payoffs made by Hausa leaders to the police and other government officials. Somewhat the same sort of system prevails in Seattle as well, especially with regard to the rackets. Whereas prostitutes, pornography shops, gambling establishments, cabaret operators and tow truck operators must pay off individually to the police and the syndicate, the Japanese-American community did so *as a community*. The tithe was collected by a local businessman and was paid to the police and the syndicate in a group sum. Individual prostitutes and vice racketeers might at times have to do special favors for a policeman or political figure, but by and large the payoffs were made collectively rather than individually.

PART 2   THE POLITICAL ECONOMY OF CRIME AND LAW ENFORCEMENT

This collective payoff was in large measure a result of the same characteristic of both the Hausa and the Japanese-American communities, namely the heterogeneous social class nature of the community. Typically, wealthy or middle-class members of the lower-class white slum or the black ghetto moved out of these areas as rapidly as their incomes permitted. So too with Yoruba, Ibo or other ethnic groups in Ibadan. But many, though certainly not all, upper and middle-class Hausa in Ibadan, and Japanese-Americans in Seattle retained their residence in their respective communities. As a result the enforcement of any law became more problematic for law enforcement agencies. Arrests made of any youth or adult always carried with it the possibility that the suspect would have a politically influential parent or friend. There was also the possibility that a payoff of some sort (including political patronage) would override the policeman's efforts. Since there was also the necessity to hide from the middle and upper-class the extent to which the police closed their eyes to the rackets, it was then convenient to avoid having many police in the Hausa and Japanese-American community. The myth of these areas as "no crime" sections of the city was thus very convenient. By contrast since only those members of the middle and upper-class who were seeking the vices would come to the skidrow area or the black ghetto, then the presence of the police was not problematic and in fact helped to assure the "respectable" citizen that he could partake of his prurient interests without fear of being the victim of a robbery or of any violence.

As in Nigeria, all of this corruption, bribery and blatant violation of the law was taking place, while arrests were being made and people sent to jail or prison for other offenses. In Seattle over 70% of all arrests during the time of the study were for public drunkenness (Spradley, 1970: 120). It was literally the case that the police were arresting drunks on one side of a building while on the other side a vast array of other offenses were being committed.

DISCUSSION

What, then, are we to conclude from these admittedly brief sketches of selected aspects of crime and law enforcement in Nigeria and America? The most obvious conclusion is that these law enforcement systems are not organized to reduce crime or to enforce the public morality. They are rather organized to manage crime by cooperating with the most criminal groups and enforcing laws against those whose crimes are a minimal threat to the society. In doing so the law enforcers end up as crime producers. By promising profit and security to those criminals who engage in organized criminal activities from which the political and legal systems can profit, law enforcement practices produce crime by selecting and encouraging the perpetuation of criminal careers.

This general conclusion is clearly in line with the postulates we earlier derived from the dialectic perspective. The findings are incompatible with the relevant postulates derived from the functional perspective. Particularly relevant are postulates 1–3. The data from this comparative study clearly supports the argument that criminal acts which serve the interests of the ruling class will go unsanctioned while those that do not will be punished. It seems likely, although not necessarily proven by these data, that we can much better explain the propensity to violate the law as a consequence of economic interests than we can explain it as a consequence of socialization into particular value-sets of normative systems. The lawyers in the prosecuting attorney's office, the judges on the bench as well as the policeman on the beat all shared an anticriminal set of values and norms but they nonetheless took bribes and encouraged racketeering because it was in their economic interests to do so.

The question as to whether crime contributes to social solidarity (the functional argument) or is an economic product (the dialectic argument) is difficult to untangle because of the vagueness of the claims. "Social solidarity" would, presumably, suggest that crime increases consensus. But the prevalence of widespread graft and vice in Nigeria and America would seem to reflect and perpetuate dissensus rather than consensus. It would seem that a much more plausible characterization derives from the dialectic position that crime is an economic product in view of the intimate tie-in between businessmen, politicians, law enforcers and racketeers that has been discovered.

The present study does not bear directly on the other propositions outlined above. We can nonetheless speculate on the relative merits of the two perspectives. Erikson (1965) has published an extremely imaginative account of the causes and effects of crime on the Puritan communities of New England. His data showed quite clearly that the leaders of the community (that is, those who controlled the political and economic resources of the community) used crime as a convenient label to pin on groups who threatened their position. By this technique there was a semblance of peace immediately following each of the "crime waves." The peace, needless to say, was gained at the expense of those individuals and groups who had previously threatened the monopoly on power that the entrenched power-holders had. Erikson interprets the rseults of these encounters between various groups and social classes as leading to increased social solidarity. This may be the case; however, it is equally clear that the increased solidarity was short-lived for, by Erikson's own account there were three major crime waves produced by the leaders of the community within a relatively short period of time.

Postulates 4–6 deal with expected differences between societies. The functional argument implies that societies at comparable levels of industrialization should share comparable crime rates. Crime statistics are notoriously unreliable, so that we are really whistling in the dark on this issue. It is, however, worth noting that if we were to rank other societies according to the degree to which the resources of the society have been distributed throughout the population, we might find some interesting comparisons. America's crime rate is probably among the highest in the world and its resources the most concentrated in the hands of a few. China's resources seem to be far more equitably distributed and the crime rate correspondingly lower. Sweden and Norway are, if my impression is correct, somewhere in between the extremes of China and the United States on both variables. And one gets the impression that crime in East Germany is far less prevalent than is the case in West Germany. But lacking reliable data these are only highly impressionistic observations.

SUMMARY

Comparative data from research on crime and law enforcement in Nigeria and the United States has been used to shed light on the relative utility of postulates derived from the functional and dialectic theoretical models. The existence of widespread corruption in the political and legal systems of both countries and the prevalence of vices, coupled with the fact that most of the law enforcement energy is devoted to the arrest and processing of minor offenses committed by persons at the bottom of the social class hierarchy, suggest the superiority of the dialectic model.

FOOTNOTES

[1] I have chosen to use the term "dialectic" rather than the more familiar "conflict" model because the latter has unfortunately been used to include pluralist models which are quite incompatible with the more routine viewpoint which divides social thought along the most important dimension of criticism.

[2] Throughout the paper we rely on data from Ibadan and Seattle as a basis for discussing the patterns of both countries. This leap may disturb some and if so then you may consider the study as speaking only to the two cities with only a promise of application more generally. From a variety of research studies and my own impressions I am convinced that what is true of Ibadan and Seattle is also true throughout both countries; but whether or not this is the case should not affect the overall conclusions of this inquiry.

[3] For an excellent discussion of relative rates of delinquency by social class and corroborating evidence for the view expressed in the paper, see Travis Hirsch, *Causes of Delinquency*, Berkeley and Los Angeles: University of California Press, 1971.

REFERENCES

Chambliss, William J., "The state, the law and the definition of behavior as criminal or delinquent." In Daniel Glaser, ed., Handbook of Criminology. Chicago: Rand McNally, 1963.

Chambliss, William J., and Richard H. Nagasawa, "On the validity of official statistics." Journal of Research in Crime and Delinquency, January, 1969, 71–77.

Durkheim, Emile, The Rules of Sociological Method. Glencoe: Free Press, 1958.

Durkheim, Emile, The Division of Labor in Society. Glencoe: Free Press, 1960.

Erikson, Kai, Wayward Puritans. New York: Wiley, 1965.

Marx, Karl, Theories of Surplus Value. Vol. 1. Moscow: Foreign Language Publishing House, n.d.

PART 2   THE POLITICAL ECONOMY OF CRIME AND LAW ENFORCEMENT

Marx, Karl, The State and the Law. In T. B. Bottomore, ed., Karl Marx: Selected Writings in Sociology and Philosophy. New York: McGraw-Hill, 1964.

Nagasawa, Richard H., Delinquency and Non-Delinquency: A Study of Status Problems and Perceived Opportunity. Unpublished M.A. thesis. Seattle: University of Washington, 1965.

Spradley, James Q., You Owe Yourself a Drunk. Boston: Little, Brown, 1970.

Van den Berghe, Pierre L., "Functionalism and dialectics." American Sociological Review, 695–705, 1964.

6

The Saints and the Roughnecks

WILLIAM J. CHAMBLISS

Eight promising young men—children of good, stable, white upper-middle-class families, active in school affairs, good pre-college students—were some of the most delinquent boys at Hanibal High School. While community residents and parents knew that these boys occasionally sowed a few wild oats, they were totally unaware that sowing wild oats completely occupied the daily routine of these young men. The Saints were constantly occupied with truancy, drinking, wild driving, petty theft and vandalism. Yet not one was officially arrested for any misdeed during the two years I observed them.

This record was particularly surprising in light of my observations during the same two years of another gang of Hanibal High School students, six lower-class white boys known as the Roughnecks. The Roughnecks were constantly in trouble with police and community even though their rate of delinquency was about equal with that of the Saints. What was the cause of this disparity? the result? The following consideration of the activities, social class and community perceptions of both gangs may provide some answers.

Source: "The Saints and the Roughnecks," *Society*, Vol. 11, No. 11, November-December, 1973, pp. 24–31. By permission of the author and publisher.

THE SAINTS FROM MONDAY TO FRIDAY

The Saints' principal daily concern was with getting out of school as early as possible. The boys managed to get out of school with minimum danger that they would be accused of playing hooky through an elaborate procedure for obtaining "legitimate" release from class. The most common procedure was for one boy to obtain the release of another by fabricating a meeting of some committee, program or recognized club. Charles might raise his hand in his 9:00 chemistry class and asked to be excused—a euphemism for going to the bathroom. Charles would go to Ed's math class and inform the teacher that Ed was needed for a 9:30 rehearsal of the drama club play. The math teacher would recognize Ed and Charles as "good students" involved in numerous school activities and would permit Ed to leave at 9:30. Charles would return to his class, and Ed would go to Tom's English class to obtain his release. Tom would engineer Charles' escape. The strategy would continue until as many of the Saints as possible were freed. After a stealthy trip to the car (which had been parked in a strategic spot), the boys were off for a day of fun.

Over the two years I observed the Saints, this pattern was repeated nearly every day. There were variations on the theme, but in one form or another, the boys used this procedure for getting out of class and then off the school grounds. Rarely did all eight of the Saints manage to leave school at the same time. The average number avoiding school on the days I observed them was five.

Having escaped from the concrete corridors the boys usually went either to a pool hall on the other (lower-class) side of town or to a cafe in the suburbs. Both places were out of the way of people the boys were likely to know (family or school officials), and both provided a source of entertainment. The pool hall entertainment was the generally rough atmosphere, the occasional hustler, the sometimes drunk proprietor and, of course, the game of pool. The cafe's entertainment was provided by the owner. The boys would "accidentally" knock a glass on the floor or spill cola on the counter—not all the time, but enough to be sporting. They would also bend spoons, put salt in sugar bowls and generally tease whoever was working in the cafe. The owner had opened the cafe recently and was dependent on the boys' business which was, in fact, substantial since between the horsing around and the teasing they bought food and drinks.

THE SAINTS ON WEEKENDS

On weekends the automobile was even more critical than during the week, for on weekends the Saints went to Big Town—a large city with a population of over a million 25 miles from Hanibal. Every Friday and Saturday night most of the Saints would meet between 8:00 and 8:30 and would go into Big Town. Big Town activities included drinking heavily in taverns or nightclubs, driving drunkenly through the streets, and committing acts of vandalism and playing pranks.

By midnight on Fridays and Saturdays the Saints were usually thoroughly high, and one or two of them were often so drunk they had to be carried to the cars. Then the boys drove around town, calling obscenities to women and girls; occasionally trying (unsuccessfully so far as I could tell) to pick girls up; and driving recklessly through red lights and at high speeds with their lights out. Occasionally they played "chicken." One boy would climb out the

back window of the car and across the roof to the driver's side of the car while the car was moving at high speed (between 40 and 50 miles an hour); then the driver would move over and the boy who had just crawled across the car roof would take the driver's seat.

Searching for "fair game" for a prank was the boys' principal activity after they left the tavern. The boys would drive alongside a foot patrolman and ask directions to some street. If the policeman leaned on the car in the course of answering the question, the driver would speed away, causing him to lose his balance. The Saints were careful to play this prank only in an area where they were not going to spend much time and where they could quickly disappear around a corner to avoid having their license plate number taken.

Construction sites and road repair areas were the special province of the Saints' mischief. A soon-to-be repaired hole in the road inevitably invited the Saints to remove lanterns and wooden barricades and put them in the car, leaving the hole unprotected. The boys would find a safe vantage point and wait for an unsuspecting motorist to drive into the hole. Often, though not always, the boys would go up to the motorist and commiserate with him about the dreadful way the city protected its citizenry.

Leaving the scene of the open hole and the motorist, the boys would then go searching for an appropriate place to erect the stolen barricade. An "appropriate place" was often a spot on the highway near a curve in the road where the barricade would not be seen by an oncoming motorist. The boys would wait to watch an unsuspecting motorist attempt to stop and (usually) crash into the wooden barricade. With saintly bearing the boys might offer help and understanding.

A stolen lantern might well find its way onto the back of a police car or hang from a street lamp. Once a lantern served as a prop for a reenactment of the "midnight ride of Paul Revere" until the "play," which was taking place at 2:00 AM in the center of a main street of Big Town, was interrupted by a police car several blocks away. The boys ran, leaving the lanterns on the street, and managed to avoid being apprehended.

Abandoned houses, especially if they were located in out-of-the-way places, were fair game for destruction and spontaneous vandalism. The boys would break windows, remove furniture to the yard and tear it apart, urinate on the walls and scrawl obscenities inside.

Through all the pranks, drinking and reckless driving the boys managed miraculously to avoid being stopped by police. Only twice in two years was I aware that they had been stopped by a Big City policeman. Once was for speeding (which they did every time they drove whether they were drunk or sober), and the driver managed to convince the policeman that it was simply an error. The second time they were stopped they had just left a nightclub and were walking through an alley. Aaron stopped to urinate and the boys began making obscene remarks. A foot patrolman came into the alley, lectured the boys and sent them home. Before the boys got to the car one began talking in a loud voice again. The policeman, who had followed them down the alley, arrested this boy for disturbing the peace and took him to the police station where the other Saints gathered. After paying a $5.00 fine, and with the assurance that there would be no permanent record of the arrest, the boy was released.

The boys had a spirit of frivolity and fun about their escapades. They did not view what they were engaged in as "delinquency," though it surely was by any reasonable definition of that word. They simply viewed themselves as having a little fun and who, they would ask, was really hurt by it? The answer had to be no one, although this fact remains one of the most difficult things to explain about the gang's behavior. Unlikely though it seems, in two years of drinking, driving, carousing and vandalism no one was seriously injured as a result of the Saints' activities.

THE SAINTS IN SCHOOL

The Saints were highly successful in school. The average grade for the group was "B," with two of the boys having close to a straight "A" average. Almost all of the boys were popular and many of them held offices in the school. One of the boys was vice-president of the student body one year. Six of the boys played on athletic teams.

At the end of their senior year, the student body selected ten seniors for special recognition as the "school wheels"; four of the ten were Saints. Teachers and school officials saw no problem with any of these boys and anticipated that they would all "make something of themselves."

How the boys managed to maintain this impression is surprising in view of their actual behavior while in school. Their technique for covering truancy was so successful that teachers did not even realize that the boys were absent from school much of the time. Occasionally, of course, the system would backfire and then the boy was on his own. A boy who was caught would be most contrite, would plead guilty and ask for mercy. He inevitably got the mercy he sought.

Cheating on examinations was rampant, even to the point of orally communicating answers to exams as well as looking at one another's papers. Since none of the group studied, and since they were primarily dependent on one another for help, it is surprising that grades were so high. Teachers contributed to the deception in their admitted inclination to give these boys (and presumably others like them) the benefit of the doubt. When asked how the boys did in school, and when pressed on specific examinations, teachers might admit that they were disappointed in John's performance, but would quickly add that they "knew that he was capable of doing better," so John was given a higher grade than he had actually earned. How often this happened is impossible to know. During the time that I observed the group, I never saw any of the boys take homework home. Teachers may have been "understanding" very regularly.

One exception to the gang's generally good performance was Jerry, who had a "C" average in his junior year, experienced disaster the next year and failed to graduate. Jerry had always been a little more nonchalant than the others about the liberties he took in school. Rather than wait for someone to come get him from class, he would offer his own excuse and leave. Although he probably did not miss any more classes than most of the others in the group, he did not take the requisite pains to cover his absences. Jerry was the only Saint whom I ever heard talk back to a teacher. Although teachers often called him a "cut up" or a "smart kid," they never referred to him as a troublemaker or as a kid headed for trouble. It seems likely, then, that Jerry's failure his senior year and his mediocre performance his junior year were consequences of his not playing the game the proper way (possibly because he was disturbed by his parents' divorce). His teachers regarded him as "immature" and not quite ready to get out of high school.

THE POLICE AND THE SAINTS

The local police saw the Saints as good boys who were among the leaders of the youth in the community. Rarely, the boys might be stopped in town for speeding or for running a stop sign. When this happened the boys were always polite, contrite and pled for mercy. As in school, they received the mercy they asked for. None ever received a ticket or was taken into the precinct by the local police.

The situation in Big City, where the boys engaged in most of their delinquency, was only slightly different. The police there did not know the boys at all, although occasionally the boys were stopped by a patrolman. Once they were caught taking a lantern from a construction site. Another time they were stopped for running a stop sign, and on several occasions they were stopped for speeding. Their behavior was as before: contrite, polite and penitent. The urban police, like the local police, accepted their demeanor as sincere. More important, the urban police were convinced that these were good boys just out for a lark.

THE ROUGHNECKS

Hanibal townspeople never perceived the Saints' high level of delinquency. The Saints were good boys who just went in for an occasional prank. After all, they were well dressed, well mannered and had nice cars. The Roughnecks were a different story. Although the two gangs of boys were the same age, and both groups engaged in an equal amount of wild-oat sowing, everyone agreed that the not-so-well-dressed, not-so-well-mannered, not-so-rich boys were heading for trouble. Townspeople would say,

"You can see the gang members at the drugstore, night after night, leaning against the storefront (sometimes drunk) or slouching around inside buying cokes, reading magazines, and probably stealing old Mr. Wall blind. When they are outside and girls walk by, even respectable girls, these boys make suggestive remarks. Sometimes their remarks are downright lewd."

From the community's viewpoint, the real indication that these kids were in for trouble was that they were constantly involved with the police. Some of them had been picked up for stealing, mostly small stuff, of course, "but still it's stealing small stuff that leads to big time crimes." "Too bad," people said. "Too bad that these boys couldn't behave like the other kids in town; stay out of trouble, be polite to adults, and look to their future."

The community's impression of the degree to which this group of six boys (ranging in age from 16 to 19) engaged in delinquency was somewhat distorted. In some ways the gang was more delinquent than the community thought; in other ways they were less.

The fighting activities of the group were fairly readily and accurately perceived by almost everyone. At least once a month, the boys would get into some sort of fight, although most fights were scraps between members of the group or involved only one member of the group and some peripheral hanger-on. Only three times in the period of observation did the group fight together: once against a gang from across town, once against two blacks and once against a group of boys from another school. For the first two fights the group went out "looking for trouble"—and they found it both times. The third fight followed a football game and began spontaneously with an argument on the football field between one of the Roughnecks and a member of the opposition's football team.

Jack had a particular propensity for fighting and was involved in most of the brawls. He was a prime mover of the escalation of arguments into fights.

More serious than fighting, had the community been aware of it, was theft. Although almost everyone was aware that the boys occasionally stole things, they did not realize the extent of the activity. Petty stealing was a frequent event for the Roughnecks. Sometimes they stole as a group and coordinated their efforts; other times they stole in pairs. Rarely did they steal alone.

The thefts ranged from very small things like paperback books, comics and ballpoint pens to expensive items like watches. The nature of the thefts varied from time to time. The gang would go through a period of systematically shoplifting items from automobiles or school lockers. Types of thievery varied with the whim of the gang. Some forms of thievery were more profitable than others, but all thefts were for profit, not just thrills.

Roughnecks siphoned gasoline from cars as often as they had access to an automobile, which was not very often. Unlike the Saints, who owned their own cars, the Roughnecks would have to borrow their parents' cars, an event which occurred only eight or nine times a year. The boys claimed to have stolen cars for joy rides from time to time.

Ron committed the most serious of the group's offenses. With an unidentified associate the boy attempted to burglarize a gasoline station. Although this station had been robbed twice previously in the same month, Ron denied any involvement in either of the other thefts. When Ron and his accomplice approached the station, the owner was hiding in the bushes beside the station. He fired both barrels of a double-barreled shotgun at the boys. Ron was severely injured; the other boy ran away and was never caught. Though he remained in critical condition for several months, Ron finally recovered and served six months of the following year in reform school. Upon release from reform school, Ron was put back a grade in school, and began running around with a different gang of boys. The Roughnecks considered the new gang less delinquent than themselves, and during the following year Ron had no more trouble with the police.

The Roughnecks, then, engaged mainly in three types of delinquency: theft, drinking and fighting. Although community members perceived that this gang of kids was delinquent, they mistakenly believed that their illegal activities were primarily drinking, fighting and being a nuisance to passersby. Drinking was limited among the gang members, although it did occur, and theft was much more prevalent than anyone realized.

Drinking would doubtless have been more prevalent had the boys had ready access to liquor. Since they rarely had automobiles at their disposal, they could not travel very far, and the bars in town would not serve them. Most of the boys had little money, and this, too, inhibited their purchase of alcohol. Their major source of liquor was a local drunk who would buy them a fifth if they would give him enough extra to buy himself a pint of whiskey or a bottle of wine.

The community's perception of drinking as prevalent stemmed from the fact that it was the most obvious delinquency the boys engaged in. When one of the boys had been drinking, even a casual observer seeing him on the corner would suspect that he was high.

There was a high level of mutual distrust and dislike between the Roughnecks and the police. The boys felt very strongly that the police were unfair and corrupt. Some evidence existed that the boys were correct in their perception.

The main source of the boys' dislike for the police undoubtedly stemmed from the fact that the police would sporadically harass the group. From the standpoint of the boys, these acts of occasional enforcement of the law were whimsical and uncalled for. It made no sense to them, for example, that the police would come to the corner occasionally and threaten them with arrest for loitering when the night before the boys had been out siphoning gasoline from cars and the police had been nowhere in sight. To the boys, the police were stupid on the one hand, for not being where they should have been and catching the boys in a serious offense, and unfair on the other hand, for trumping up "loitering" charges against them.

From the viewpoint of the police, the situation was quite different. They knew, with all the confidence necessary to be a policeman, that these boys were engaged in criminal activities. They knew this partly from occasionally catching them, mostly from circumstantial evidence ("the boys were around when those tires were slashed"), and partly because the police shared the view of the community in general that this was a bad bunch of boys. The best the police could hope to do was to be sensitive to the fact that these boys were engaged in illegal acts and arrest them whenever there was some evidence that they had been involved. Whether or not the boys had in fact committed a particular act in a particular way was not especially important. The police had a broader view: their job was to stamp out these kids' crimes; the tactics were not as important as the end result.

Over the period that the group was under observation, each member was arrested at least once. Several of the boys were arrested a number of times and spent at least one night in jail. While most were never taken to court, two of the boys were sentenced to six months' incarceration in boys' schools.

THE ROUGHNECKS IN SCHOOL

The Roughnecks' behavior in school was not particularly disruptive. During school hours they did not all hang around together, but tended instead to spend most of their time with one or two other members of the gang who were their special buddies. Although every member of the gang attempted to avoid school as much as possible, they were not particularly successful and most of them attended school with surprising regularity. They considered school a burden —something to be gotten through with a minimum of conflict. If they were "bugged" by a particular teacher, it could lead to trouble. One of the boys, Al, once threatened to beat up a teacher and, according to the other boys, the teacher hid under a desk to escape him.

Teachers saw the boys the way the general community did, as heading for trouble, as being uninterested in making something of themselves. Some were also seen as being incapable of meeting the academic standards of the school. Most of the teachers expressed concern for this group of boys and were willing to pass them despite poor performance, in the belief that failing them would only aggravate the problem.

The group of boys had a grade point average just slightly above "C." No one in the group failed either grade, and no one had better than a "C" average.

They were very consistent in their achievement or, at least, the teachers were consistent in their perception of the boys' achievement.

Two of the boys were good football players. Herb was acknowledged to be the best player in the school and Jack was almost as good. Both boys were criticized for their failure to abide by training rules, for refusing to come to practice as often as they should, and for not playing their best during practice. What they lacked in sportsmanship they made up for in skill, apparently, and played every game no matter how poorly they had performed in practice or how many practice sessions they had missed.

TWO QUESTIONS

Why did the community, the school and the police react to the Saints as though they were good, upstanding, nondelinquent youths with bright futures but to the Roughnecks as though they were tough, young criminals who were headed for trouble? Why did the Roughnecks and the Saints in fact have quite different careers after high school—careers which, by and large, lived up to the expectations of the community?

The most obvious explanation for the differences in the community's and law enforcement agencies' reactions to the two gangs is that one group of boys was "more delinquent" than the other. Which group *was* more delinquent? The answer to this question will determine in part how we explain the differential responses to these groups by the members of the community and, particularly, by law enforcement and school officials.

In sheer number of illegal acts, the Saints were the more delinquent. They were truant from school for at least part of the day almost every day of the week. In addition, their drinking and vandalism occurred with surprising regularity. The Roughnecks, in contrast, engaged sporadically in delinquent episodes. While these episodes were frequent, they certainly did not occur on a daily or even a weekly basis.

The difference in frequency of offenses was probably caused by the Roughnecks' inability to obtain liquor and to manipulate legitimate excuses from school. Since the Roughnecks had less money than the Saints, and teachers carefully supervised their school activities, the Roughnecks' hearts may have been as black as the Saints', but their misdeeds were not nearly as frequent.

There are really no clear-cut criteria by which to measure qualitative differences in antisocial behavior. The most important dimension of the difference is generally referred to as the "seriousness" of the offenses.

If seriousness encompasses the relative economic costs of delinquent acts, then some assessment can be made. The Roughnecks probably stole an average of about $5.00 worth of goods a week. Some weeks the figure was considerably higher, but these times must be balanced against long periods when almost nothing was stolen.

The Saints were more continuously engaged in delinquency but their acts were not for the most part costly to property. Only their vandalism and occasional theft of gasoline would so qualify. Perhaps once or twice a month they would siphon a tankful of gas. The other costly items were street signs, construction lanterns and the like. All of these acts combined probably did not quite average $5.00 a week, partly because much of the stolen equipment was abandoned and presumably could be recovered. The difference in cost of stolen property between the two groups was trivial, but the Roughnecks probably had a slightly more expensive set of activities than did the Saints.

Another meaning of seriousness is the potential threat of physical harm to members of the community and to the boys themselves. The Roughnecks were more prone to physical violence; they not only welcomed an opportunity to fight; they went seeking it. In addition, they fought among themselves frequently. Although the fighting never included deadly weapons, it was still a menace, however minor, to the physical safety of those involved.

The Saints never fought. They avoided physical conflict both inside and outside the group. At the same time, though, the Saints frequently endangered their own and other people's lives. They did so almost every time they drove a car, especially if they had been drinking. Sober, their driving was risky; under the influence of alcohol it was horren-

dous. In addition, the Saints endangered the lives of others with their pranks. Street excavations left unmarked were a very serious hazard.

Evaluating the relative seriousness of the two gangs' activities is difficult. The community reacted as though the behavior of the Roughnecks was a problem, and they reacted as though the behavior of the Saints was not. But the members of the community were ignorant of the array of delinquent acts that characterized the Saints' behavior. Although concerned citizens were unaware of much of the Roughnecks' behavior as well, they were much better informed about the Roughnecks' involvement in delinquency than they were about the Saints'.

VISIBILITY

Differential treatment of the two gangs resulted in part because one gang was infinitely more visible than the other. This differential visibility was a direct function of the economic standing of the families. The Saints had access to automobiles and were able to remove themselves from the sight of the community. In as routine a decision as to where to go to have a milkshake after school, the Saints stayed away from the mainstream of community life. Lacking transportation, the Roughnecks could not make it to the edge of town. The center of town was the only practical place for them to meet since their homes were scattered throughout the town and any noncentral meeting place put an undue hardship on some members. Through necessity the Roughnecks congregated in a crowded area where everyone in the community passed frequently, including teachers and law enforcement officers. They could easily see the Roughnecks hanging around the drugstore.

The Roughnecks, of course, made themselves even more visible by making remarks to passersby and by occasionally getting into fights on the corner. Meanwhile, just as regularly, the Saints were either at the cafe on one edge of town or in the pool hall at the other edge of town. Without any particular realization that they were making themselves inconspicuous, the Saints were able to hide their time-wasting. Not only were they removed from the mainstream of traffic, but they were almost always inside a building.

On their escapades the Saints were also relatively invisible, since they left Hanibal and travelled to Big City. Here, too, they were mobile, roaming the city, rarely going to the same area twice.

DEMEANOR

To the notion of visibility must be added the difference in the responses of group members to outside intervention with their activities. If one of the Saints was confronted with an accusing policeman, even if he felt he was truly innocent of a wrongdoing, his demeanor was apologetic and penitent. A Roughneck's attitude was almost the polar opposite. When confronted with a threatening adult authority, even one who tried to be pleasant, the Roughneck's hostility and disdain were clearly observable. Sometimes he might attempt to put up a veneer of respect, but it was thin and was not accepted as sincere by the authority.

School was no different from the community at large. The Saints could manipulate the system by feigning compliance with the school norms. The availability of cars at school meant that once free from the immediate sight of the teacher, the boys could disappear rapidly. And this escape was well enough planned that no administrator or teacher was nearby when the boys left. A Roughneck who wished to escape for a few hours was in a bind. If it were possible to get free from class, downtown was still a mile away, and even if he arrived there, he was still very visible. Truancy for the Roughnecks meant almost certain detection, while the Saints enjoyed almost complete immunity from sanctions.

BIAS

Community members were not aware of the transgressions of the Saints. Even if the Saints had been less discreet, their favorite delinquencies would have been perceived as less serious than those of the Roughnecks.

In the eyes of the police and school officials, a boy who drinks in an alley and stands intoxicated on the street corner is committing a more serious offense than is a boy who drinks to inebriation in a nightclub or a tavern and drives around afterwards in a car.

Similarly, a boy who steals a wallet from a store will be viewed as having committed a more serious offense than a boy who steals a lantern from a construction site.

Perceptual bias also operates with respect to the demeanor of the boys in the two groups when they are confronted by adults. It is not simply that adults dislike the posture affected by boys of the Roughneck ilk; more important is the conviction that the posture adopted by the Roughnecks is an indication of their devotion and commitment to deviance as a way of life. The posture becomes a cue, just as the type of the offense is a cue, to the degree to which the known transgressions are indicators of the youths' potential for other problems.

Visibility, demeanor and bias are surface variables which explain the day-to-day operations of the police. Why do these surface variables operate as they do? Why did the police choose to disregard the Saints' delinquencies while breathing down the backs of the Roughnecks?

The answer lies in the class structure of American society and the control of legal institutions by those at the top of the class structure. Obviously, no representative of the upper class drew up the operational chart for the police which led them to look in the ghettoes and on streetcorners—which led them to see the demeanor of lower-class youth as troublesome and that of upper-middle-class youth as tolerable. Rather, the procedures simply developed from experience—experience with irate and influential upper-middle-class parents insisting that their son's vandalism was simply a prank and his drunkenness only a momentary "sowing of wild oats"—experience with cooperative or indifferent, powerless, lower-class parents who acquiesced to the laws' definition of their son's behavior.

ADULT CAREERS OF THE SAINTS AND THE ROUGHNECKS

The community's confidence in the potential of the Saints and the Roughnecks apparently was justified. If anything, the community members underestimated the degree to which these youngsters would turn out "good" or "bad."

Seven of the eight members of the Saints went on to college immediately after high school. Five of the boys graduated from college in four years. The sixth one finished college after two years in the army, and the seventh spent four years in the air force before returning to college and receiving a B.A. degree. Of these seven college graduates, three went on for advanced degrees. One finished law school and is now active in state politics, one finished medical school and is practicing near Hanibal, and one boy is now working for a Ph.D. The other four college graduates entered submanagerial, managerial or executive training positions with larger firms.

The only Saint who did not complete college was Jerry. Jerry had failed to graduate from high school with the other Saints. During his second senior year, after the other Saints had gone on to college, Jerry began to hang around with what several teachers described as a "rough crowd"—the gang that was heir apparent to the Roughnecks. At the end of his second senior year, when he did graduate from high school, Jerry took a job as a used-car salesman, got married and quickly had a child. Although he made several abortive attempts to go to college by attending night school, when I last saw him (ten years after high school) Jerry was unemployed and had been living on unemployment for almost a year. His wife worked as a waitress.

Some of the Roughnecks have lived up to community expectations. A number of them were headed for trouble. A few were not.

Jack and Herb were the athletes among the Roughnecks and their athletic prowess paid off handsomely. Both boys received unsolicited athletic scholarships to college. After Herb received his scholarship (near the end of his senior year), he apparently did an about-face. His demeanor became very similar to that of the Saints. Although he remained a member in good standing of the Roughnecks, he stopped participating in most activities and did not hang around the corner as often.

Jack did not change. If anything, he became more prone to fighting. He even made excuses for accepting the scholarship. He told the other gang members that the school had guaranteed him a "C"

average if he would come to play football—an idea that seems far-fetched, even in this day of highly competitive recruiting.

During the summer after graduation from high school, Jack attempted suicide by jumping from a tall building. The jump would certainly have killed most people trying it, but Jack survived. He entered college in the fall and played four years of football. He and Herb graduated in four years, and both are teaching and coaching in high schools. They are married and have stable families. If anything, Jack appears to have a more prestigious position in the community than does Herb, though both are well respected and secure in their positions.

Two of the boys never finished high school. Tommy left at the end of his junior year and went to another state. That summer he was arrested and placed on probation on a manslaughter charge. Three years later he was arrested for murder; he pleaded guilty to second degree murder and is serving a 30-year sentence in the state penitentiary.

Al, the other boy who did not finish high school, also left the state in his senior year. He is serving a life sentence in a state penitentiary for first degree murder.

Wes is a small-time gambler. He finished high school and "bummed around." After several years he made contact with a bookmaker who employed him as a runner. Later he acquired his own area and has been working it ever since. His position among the bookmakers is almost identical to the position he had in the gang; he is always around but no one is really aware of him. He makes no trouble and he does not get into any. Steady, reliable, capable of keeping his mouth closed, he plays the game by the rules, even though the game is an illegal one.

That leaves only Ron. Some of his former friends reported that they had heard he was "driving a truck up north," but no one could provide any concrete information.

REINFORCEMENT

The community responded to the Roughnecks as boys in trouble, and the boys agreed with that perception. Their pattern of deviancy was reinforced, and breaking away from it became increasingly un-likely. Once the boys acquired an image of themselves as deviants, they selected new friends who affirmed that self-image. As that self-conception became more firmly entrenched, they also became willing to try new and more extreme deviances. With their growing alienation came freer expression of disrespect and hostility for representatives of the legitimate society. This disrespect increased the community's negativism, perpetuating the entire process of commitment to deviance. Lack of a commitment to deviance works the same way. In either case, the process will perpetuate itself unless some event (like a scholarship to college or a sudden failure) external to the established relationship intervenes. For two of the Roughnecks (Herb and Jack), receiving college athletic scholarships created new relations and culminated in a break with the established pattern of deviance. In the case of one of the Saints (Jerry), his parents' divorce and his failing to graduate from high school changed some of his other relations. Being held back in school for a year and losing his place among the Saints had sufficient impact on Jerry to alter his self-image and virtually to assure that he would not go on to college as his peers did. Although the experiments of life can rarely be reversed, it seems likely in view of the behavior of the other boys who did not enjoy this special treatment by the school that Jerry, too, would have "become something" had he graduated as anticipated. For Herb and Jack outside intervention worked to their advantage; for Jerry it was his undoing.

Selective perception and labelling—finding, processing and punishing some kinds of criminality and not others—means that visible, poor, nonmobile, outspoken, undiplomatic "tough" kids will be noticed, whether their actions are seriously delinquent or not. Other kids, who have established a reputation for being bright (even though underachieving), disciplined and involved in respectable activities, who are mobile and monied, will be invisible when they deviate from sanctioned activities. They'll sow their wild oats—perhaps even wider and thicker than their lower-class cohorts—but they won't be noticed. When it's time to leave adolescence most will follow the expected path, settling into the ways of the middle class, remembering fondly the delinquent but unnoticed fling of their youth. The Roughnecks and others like them may turn around, too. It is more likely that their noticeable deviance will have been so reinforced by police and community that their lives will be effectively channelled into careers consistent with their adolescent background.

7

From Constabulary to Police Society:

Implications for Social Control

EVELYN L. PARKS

The history of social control in the United States is the history of transition from "constabulary" to "police society" in which the proliferation of criminal laws, enforcement officials, criminal courts and prisons was not essentially for the protection of the "general welfare" of society but was for the protection of the interests and lifestyles of but one segment of society —those holding positions of wealth, "respectability," and power.

The establishment of a police society in the United States made possible a new conception of law and order in which more effective control of the population was feasible. Central to this conception were laws governing the private behavior of citizens where no self-defined victims are involved—the vice laws. Thus, the growth of the police was necessary for the growth of both law and crime.

TRANSITION FROM A CONSTABULARY TO A POLICE SOCIETY

The first official responsible for the enforcement of law and order in the New World was the constable.

Source: "From Constabulary to Police Society," *Catalyst*, No. 5, Summer, 1970, pp. 1–22. By permission of the author and publisher.

The law as written was oppressive—outlawing swearing, lying, sabbath breaking, and night walking— and gave to the constable almost totalitarian powers to enforce the laws.[1] However, the constable did not use his power to discover and punish deviation from the established laws. Rather, he assisted complaining citizens if and when they sought his help. This reflected the conception of law during colonial times: the written law was regarded as an ideal, rather than as prescriptions actually to be enforced.

Initially, the constableship was a collective responsibility which all able-bodied men were expected to assume. It was not a specialized occupation or an income producing job, but a service to the community. The constableship was so thankless a task, however, that as early as 1653, fines were sometimes levied against anyone refusing to serve.[2]

The constable served only during the day. At night, the towns formed a citizens' watch or nightwatch. Supposedly, each adult male took his turn, but as with the constable those who could hired substitutes. In contrast to our present police the concerns of the nightwatch were more closely related to the general welfare. They included looking out for fires, reporting the time, and describing the weather.

Thus, there was no *one* specialized agency responsible for social control. Not only was the power divided between the constable and the nightwatch, but initially, both were volunteer services rotated among the citizens. This lack of specialization of enforcement of law and order extended to a comparative lack of specialization in the punishment of offenders. Although prisons were constructed as early as 1637, they were almost never kept in good enough condition to prevent jailbreaks. The financial costs of jails was considered prohibitive; corporal punishments, such as whippings, were preferred.[3] Thus, there was no specialized penal system, staffed and available.

Early police The constabulary was not able to survive the growth of urban society and the concomitant economic specialization. Charles Reith writes that voluntary observance of the laws

> can be seen to have never survived in effective form the advent of community prosperity, as this brings into being, inevitably, differences in wealth and social status, and creates, on this basis, classes and parties and factions with or without wealth and power and privileges. In the presence of these divisions, community unanimity in voluntary law observance disappears and some other means of securing law observance and the maintenance of authority and order must be found.[4]

By 1800 in the larger cities the constabulary had changed from a voluntary position to a quasi-professional one, being either appointed or elected and providing an income. Some people resisted this step, claiming that such police were threats to civil liberty, and that they performed duties each citizen should perform himself. However, in the 1840's and 1850's, the nightwatch was gradually incorporated into an increasingly professionalized police, establishing twenty-four hour responsibility and in other ways beginning to institute the type of law enforcement that we have today.[5]

In the 1850's, cities began to employ detectives. The earliest detectives represented an attempt to apply the conception of the constableship to urban society. That is, the duties of the detective were to assist in recovering stolen property, not to prevent crime. However, this application of the constableship to the emerging urban society proved ineffective.

For one thing, to recover stolen property effectively, familiarity with criminals was a necessary qualification and quite naturally ex-criminals were often hired. For another, detectives became corrupted through taking advantage of a system known as compromises. Under this system, it was legal for a thief to negotiate with the robbed owner and agree to return part of the stolen goods, if the thief could remain free. Detectives, however, would often supplement their salaries by accepting thieves' offers of a portion of the stolen goods in exchange for their immunity.[6]

Understandably, detectives were reluctant to devote their time to anything other than large-scale robbery. Murder, an amateur crime at this time, went uninvestigated. Detectives essentially served the private interests of big business at the expense of the general public.

By 1880, the detective force as such had acquired such adverse publicity that in most places they were formally abolished. Their functions and services however were incorporated into the regular police. Compromises were no longer legally acceptable.

Historical sources of the change from constabulary to police Central to the development of the professional police is the development of economic inequality. Seldon Bacon in his study of the development of the municipal police sees the increasing economic specialization and the resulting "class stratification" as the primary cause for the development of police.[7] He argues that specialists could exploit the increasing dependence of the populace on their services. Cities responded by creating specialized offices of independent inspectors who attempted to prevent exploitation or cheating of the populace. For example, the necessity in New Amsterdam to rely on specialized suppliers of firewood led as early as 1658 to the employment of firewood inspectors. Regulation of butchers, bakers, and hack drivers showed the same consequences of the inability of the citizen to rely on his own resources in a period of increasing specialization.[8]

By the time of the emergence of the professional police, the list of regulatory or inspectorial officials had grown quite long. Bacon describes the development of "the night police, the market police, street police, animal police, liquor police, the vagabond and stranger police, vehicle police, fire police, election police, Sunday police and so on."[9] Gradually, many of these special police or inspectors were removed from the professional police to other municipal agencies. "Only slowly did regulation for the public good and the maintenance of order become themselves specializations and the full-time career police develop."[10]

The other central element in the development of the professional police was rioting, which is closely related to economic inequality. Usually, riots are an attempt by the have-nots to seek a redress of grievances from those with power and wealth. The solid citizens, on the other hand, wanted to prevent riots, to stop the disturbances in the streets. An official history of the Buffalo Police states that in March of 1834 complaints of riot and disorder continued to pour in upon the Mayor. "Rowdies paraded the streets at night, unmolested, and taxpayers became alarmed regarding both life and property."[11] Roger Lane writes of Boston, that "The problem of mob violence . . . soon compelled the municipality to take a more significant step, to create a new class of permanent professional officers with new standards of performance."[12]

David Bordua and Albert Reiss write:

> The paramilitary form of early police bureaucracy was a response not only, or even primarily, to crime *per se*, but to the possibility of riotous disorder. Not crime and danger but the "criminal" and "dangerous classes" as part of the urban social structure led to the formation of uniformed and military organized police. Such organizations intervened between the propertied elites and the propertyless masses who were regarded as politically dangerous as a class.[13]

Riots became so frequent that the traditional method of controlling them by use of military forces became less and less effective. Military forces were unable to arrive at the scene of trouble before rioting had already reached uncontrollable proportions. This illustrates how the military may be able temporarily to enforce laws but are ineffective for sustained law enforcement.[14] The police, not the military, represent the continued presence of the central political authority.

Furthermore, in a riot situation, the direct use of social and economic superiors as the agents of suppression increases class violence.

> If the power structure armed itself and fought a riot or a rebellious people, this created more trouble and tension than the original problem. But, if one can have an independent police which fights the mob, then antagonism is directed toward police, not the power structure. A paid professional police seems to separate "constitutional" authority from social and economic dominance.[15]

These trends towards the establishment of a paramilitary police were given further impetus by the Civil War. It was the glory of the Army uniform that helped the public accept a uniformed police. Previously, the police themselves, as well as the public, had objected to uniforms as implying a police state with the men as agents of the king or ruler. A uniformed police was seen as contradictory to the ideals of the American Revolution, to a republic of free men.[16] But after 1860 the police began to carry guns, although at first unofficially. Within twenty years, however, most cities were furnishing guns along with badges.

The professional police and the new concept of law As the cities changed from a constabulary to a professional police, so was there a change in the conception of law. Whereas the constable had only investigated crimes in which a citizen had complained, the new professional police, were expected to *prevent* crime. A preventive conception of law requires that the police take the initiative and seek out those engaged in violating the law—those engaged in specific behaviors that are designated as illegal. Once an individual has been arrested for breaking a law, he is then identified, labelled and treated as a criminal. The whole person then becomes a criminal—not just an individual who has broken a law. Since now too, professional police were responsible for maintaining public order—seen as preventing crime—they came to respond to individuals who committed unlawful acts as criminal persons—as wholly illegitimate.

Processing people through this machinery stigmatizes people—i.e., publicly identifies the whole person in terms of only certain of his behavior patterns. At the same time, this often leads to acceptance by such persons of that identity. In this and other ways the transition to police society *created* the underworld. A professional police creates a professional underworld.[17]

The "yellow press" which had emerged by the middle of the nineteenth century, focused on crime and violence. This helped confirm the new definition and stigmatization of the criminal person. Reporters obtained their stories by attending police courts. Police court reportage became so popular that even the conservative press eventually came to adopt it. And the police became guides to the newly discovered underworld.[18]

The establishment of a professional police concerned with prevention increases the power of the state. Roger Lane writes:

> Before the 1830's the law in many matters was regarded as the expression of an ideal. The creation of a strong police raised the exciting possibility that the ideal might be realized, that morality could be enforced and the state made an instrument of social regeneration.[19]

With the idea of prevention, then, law loses its status as only an ideal and becomes a real prescription actually to be enforced.

Those involved in the Reform Movements of the 1830's were quick to demand the services of the new police. Although they had originally objected to hiring paid, daytime police, they soon began to welcome the police as part of the reform movement, seeing the police as "moral missionaries" eventually eliminating crime and vice.[20] As Howard Becker writes, "The final outcome of a moral crusade is a police force."[21]

During the first half of the 19th century, the professional police increasingly took over and expanded the duties of the constableship. This led to the police themselves becoming specialists in the maintenance of public order, which involved a transition to emphasizing the prevention of crime, and the role of law as ideal became an attempt to enforce laws as real prescriptions governing conduct. In this way the police, as an agency of the state, took over the function of social control from the members of the local community. The historical sources of the change were economic inequality and increasing riots. Thus, the police became an agency of those with wealth and power, for suppressing the attempts by the have-nots to re-distribute the wealth and power.

Thus, the professional police gave the upper classes an extremely useful and powerful mechanism for maintaining the unequal distribution of wealth and power: Law, which is proclaimed to be for the general welfare, is in fact an instrument in class warfare. This is most clearly demonstrated by looking at the history of the vice laws. Social control is at its greatest when the state has the power to govern the private behavior of citizens—when the state can declare illegal and punish acts in which all parties are willing participants.

THE VICE LAWS AS SOCIAL CONTROL: THE CASE OF ALCOHOL

The most celebrated vice problem in America is the use of alcohol. The use of alcohol dates back to early colonial times, during which nearly everybody drank: men, women, and children—it was an indispensable part of living. Drinking was usually family-centered and family-controlled, or part of community events.[22]

In early colonial times, mostly wine and beer were imbibed, with hard liquor (distilled spirits) in third place. However, hard liquor was much easier to transport as well as less subject to spoilage than wine and beer or the grains from which they were derived. As the colonies developed a market economy, this pushed the manufacturing and selling of hard liquors rather than beer and wine. The manufacturing and selling of hard liquor became an important part of the developing colonial commerce. "During the years immediately preceding the Revolution, more than 600,000 gallons were shipped abroad annually."[23]

As the manufacturing changed from wine and beer to hard liquor, so did the drinking habits of the colonists. By the end of the eighteenth century about ninety per cent of the alcohol consumed in this country was in the form of hard liquor. "By 1807, it is recorded that Boston had one distillery for every forty inhabitants—but only two breweries."[24]

Just as the drinking began to change from beer and wine to hard liquor, so also, around 1750, the context began to change from a family activity to an individual one. Men, especially young, unattached men, and other "peripheral segments" of society, began to do most of the drinking.[25] Saloons and taverns, instead of the home, became the place to drink.

These changes brought about a great increase in the amount and frequency of intoxication. Spirits are more intoxicating than either wine or beer, and the context of the saloon places no restrictions on consumption. The thirty years preceding and the fifty years following the American Revolution was an era of extremely heavy drinking.[26]

The Temperance & Prohibition Movement As the amount and frequency of drunkenness increased so did social concern about drinking. Drunkenness was often accompanied by destructive behavior. Intoxication came to be seen "as a threat to the personal well-being and property of peaceful citizens."[27] In this way, the call to moderation was an attempt to control those who were seen as a threat by the "solid" citizens. And so the Temperance Movement began in the last half of the eighteenth century.

In the 1830's the Temperance Movement altered its goal from moderation to abstinence. Why did abstinence, rather than moderation, become the symbol of respectability? Joseph R. Gusfield, who has interpreted the Temperance/Prohibition movement in terms of its symbolic meanings and status conflicts, considers the Temperance Movement and ultimately Prohibition as a quest for honor and power. Gusfield argues that coercive reform, or the change from temperance to abstinence, became necessary with the decline of the pre-civil war Federalist aristocracy and the rise to social and political importance of the "common man," that which is symbolized by Andrew Jackson's election to the presidency.[28]

> To make the new common man respond to the moral ideals of the old order, was both a way of maintaining the prestige of the old aristocracy and an attempt to control the character of the political electorate.[29]

Lyman Beecher, a leading Temperance leader, puts it more forcefully.

> When the laboring classes are contaminated, the right to suffrage becomes the engine of destruction . . . As intemperance increases, the power of taxation will come more and more into the hands of men of intemperate habits and desperate fortunes; of course, the laws will gradually become subservient to the debtor and less efficacious in protecting the rights of property.[30]

The insistence on total abstinence came just when the country's drinking habits were becoming more moderate and changing from hard liquors back again to wine and beer. In 1800, when most drinking was of hard liquor 90% of the white population was from Britain. By 1840, the immigration of ethnic groups from southern, central, and eastern Europe (where drinking habits were of wine and beer) acted as a moderating influence on the drinking habits of the nation.[31] Only total abstinence, then, would be a symbol of power and respectability—moderation was not enough to indicate superiority.

The change from moderation to abstinence was reflected in the laws of Massachusetts. In 1835, a Massachusetts statute revision made single incidences of drunkenness a punishable offense. Prior to this only the habitually drunk were usually arrested. In Boston, the number of drunk arrests jumped from the few hundred annually during the 1830's to several thousand in the 1840's and 1850's. Even before the middle of the century, Theodore Parker believed that "the 'rude tuition' of courts and constables was improving the drinking habits of the Irish immigrants."[32] In 1841, the Boston Society for the Suppression of Intoxication petitioned for a doubling of the police force.[33]

Thus, the Temperance/Prohibition Movement was an effort to control the "dangerous classes," to make them conform to middle class standards of respectability. As is so often the case, the stated goals of improving society or helping the unfortunates muted the fact that this "help" came in the form of control —the police power of the state. Not only did alcohol use come to be universally defined as a social problem, but criminal law and police enforcement was commonly seen as the solution to the problem.

The thought and research of seemingly all fields could be used to support the claims of the prohibitionists. Based on research done in the last half of the nineteenth century, scientists began to describe the negative effects alcohol has on the human body, and for the first time, claimed that even moderate drinking might cause liver, kidney, and heart diseases.[34]

PART 2   THE POLITICAL ECONOMY OF CRIME AND LAW ENFORCEMENT

In 1914, psychiatrists and neurologists meeting in Chicago adopted a resolution concluding that the availability of alcoholic beverages caused a large amount of mental, moral, and physical degeneracy and urged the medical profession "to take the lead in securing prohibitory legislation."[35]

Temperance groups were even able to utilize mortality studies done by insurance companies. A study drawing on the experience of two million policy holders between 1885 and 1908, concluded that those who drank the equivalent of only two glasses of beer each day showed a mortality rate of 18% higher than average. Furthermore, those who drank two ounces or more of alcohol each day were found to have a mortality rate of 86% higher than insured lives in general.[36]

Social workers, lawyers and judges began to claim that alcohol played an important role in crime. On the basis of a study of 13,402 convicts in twelve different states, the community leaders of one city concluded that "intemperance had been the sole cause of crime in 16 per cent of the cases, the primary cause in 31 per cent, and one of the causes in nearly 50 per cent."[37] Alcohol was also claimed to be an important factor in prostitution and venereal disease. (One physician reported that 70 per cent of all venereal infection in men under 25 was contracted while under the influence of alcohol.)[38]

In addition, Prohibitionists claimed the use of alcoholic beverages was an important factor in domestic unhappiness and broken homes. "According to a study by the U.S. Bureau of the Census, for the years 1887–1906, nearly 20% of all divorces were granted for reasons of intemperance."[39]

Even notable academicians argued that alcohol was one of the chief factors creating crime and that the state ought to abolish it.[40] A noted sociologist felt that instituting national prohibition would reduce crime and poverty, improve the position of women and children, benefit the home, purify politics, and elevate the status of the wage earner.[41]

The Volstead Act and enforcement The Prohibitionists were successful and in 1918, the Volstead Act was passed. As is well known, the attempt to enforce the Volstead Act resulted in corruption unparalleled in American history. Stories of dry agents and other gov-

ernmental personnel responsible for enforcement conniving with smugglers or accepting bribes appeared in the newspapers day after day. For example, in Philadelphia, a grand jury investigation in 1928 showed that one police "inspector had $193,533.22 in his bank account, another had $102,829.45, and a third had $40,412.75. One police captain had accumulated a nest egg of $133,845.86, and nine had bank accounts ranging from $14,607.44 to $68,905.89."[42]

By the fall of 1923 in Philadelphia, things were so bad that the mayor requested President Harding to lend the city the services of Brigadier General Smedley D. Butler of the Marine Corps, a famous soldier of World War I. General Butler arrived and began a whirlwind round of raids and arrests. At first it appeared he would succeed in enforcing the Volstead Act, but then: places were found empty when raids were attempted (they had been warned); the courts would dismiss cases brought before them. General Butler stuck it out for two years before returning to the Marine Corps declaring the job had been a waste of time: "trying to enforce the law in Philadelphia," he said, "was worse than any battle I was ever in."[43]

When the Volstead Act was passed, the justice department made no special preparation to handle extra violators. The result is that within a few months federal courts throughout the country were overwhelmed by the number of dry cases, and Emory R. Buckner, United States Attorney from New York, told a congressional committee in 1926 that

> . . . violators of the Volstead Act were being brought into the Federal Building in New York City at the rate of about fifty thousand a year, and the United States Attorney's office was five months behind in the preliminary steps of preparing cases.[44]

The volume of law-breakers was so tremendous that those who could pay the fines and/or bribe the officials, went free. A jury trial was impossible.[45]

And so goes the story of the attempt to enforce Prohibition. It is generally thought of as such a fiasco, such an aberration of American justice that those who study it feel a need for an explanation of its existence. This need for explanation, however, usually does not extend to our other vice laws, such as drug laws, which are still seen as supporting democracy and justice for all.

THE VICE LAWS AS SOCIAL CONTROL: THE CASE OF NARCOTIC DRUGS

The scientific condemnation of the dangers involved in the use of alcohol did not extend even to warnings about the dangers in the use of opium and its derivatives. Indeed, the use of such drugs was systematically encouraged in the nineteenth century. Opium constituted the main therapeutic agent of medical men for more than two thousand years—through the nineteenth century. A physician writes:

> Even in the last half of the 19th century, there was little recognition of and less attention paid to overindulgence in or abuse of opium. It was a panacea for all ills. When a person became dependent upon it so that abstinence symptoms developed if a dose or two were missed, more was taken for the aches and pains and other discomforts of abstinence, just as it was taken for similar symptoms from any other cause.[46]

In 1804 a German chemist isolated morphine. In this country, morphine began to be applied hypodermically in the 1850's. At first, it was declared that administration through the skin, as opposed to through the mouth, was *not* habit forming. Although there were soon isolated warnings that the hypodermic habit was even harder to break than the oral habit, the majority of textbooks on the practice of medicine failed to issue any warning of the dangers of the hypodermic use of morphine until 1900.[47]

In 1898 heroin was isolated. Heroin is approximately three times as powerful as morphine and morphine is more potent than opium. Opium is generally smoked while its derivatives are taken orally or with hypodermic needles.[48] At first it was also claimed that heroin was free from addiction-forming properties, possessing many of the virtues and none of the dangers of morphine and codeine. Heroin was even recommended as a treatment for those addicted to morphine and codeine. For the next few years, doctors continued to report in medical journals, on the curative and therapeutic value of heroin, either omitting any reference to addiction, or assuming any addiction to be very mild and much less bothersome than morphine addiction. It was 1910 before the medical profession began to warn of the addictive dangers of heroin.[49]

Throughout the nineteenth century, if overindulgence was necessary, many preferred addiction to narcotics than alcohol. In 1889 a doctor observed:

> The only grounds on which opium in lieu of alcohol can be claimed as reformatory are that it is less inimical to healthy life than alcohol, that it calms in place of exciting the baser passions, and hence is less productive of acts of violence and crime; in short, that as a whole the use of morphine in place of alcohol is but a choice of evils, and by far the lesser. . . .
>
> I might, had I time and space, enlarge by statistics to prove the law-abiding qualities of opium-eating peoples, but of this anyone can perceive somewhat for himself, if he carefully watches and reflects on the quiet, introspective gaze of the morphine habitue and compares it with the riotous devil-may-care leer of the drunkard.[50]

During the nineteenth century it was primarily the respectable rather than the criminal classes who used the drug. It has been suggested that part of the reason the use of opium became so popular at this time was that the respectable people "who crave the effect of a stimulant but will not risk their reputation for temperance by taking alcoholic beverages."[51]

Drugs could be purchased openly and cheaply from the drugstores. Not only could the narcotics themselves be bought, but many kinds of opiate-containing patent medicines were advertised. Anyone interested could buy paregoric, laudanum, tincture of opium, morphine, Womslow's Soothing Syrup, Godfrey's Cordial, McMumn's Elixir of Opium, or others.[52] "The more you drink," one tonic advertised, "the more you want." Mothers fed their babies 750,000 bottles of opium-laced syrup a year.[53]

Whereas white Americans previously had used opium in all other derivative forms, the smoking of opium was introduced by Chinese immigrants in California, and was outlawed in San Francisco in 1875.[54] This is the first time opium or any of its derivatives was outlawed in the United States. It appears that the legislation outlawing opium was an attempt to control the Chinese immigrants, to make them conform to the "American Way of Life," much as the drinking laws in Boston in the 1830's, and 1840's were used to control the Irish immigrants.

The Harrison Act and enforcement In 1914 Congress passed the Harrison Act. While with the Volstead

Act it is clear that total abstinence was the goal and intent of the law, it is unclear as to the actual intentions of Congress when the Harrison Act was passed. Some authors contend that the Harrison Act was intended only as a revenue measure, attempting to tax drugs. The desire was to regulate the use of drugs, not to impose abstinence. The careful wording of the Harrison Act which allows for medical doctors to treat or prescribe drugs for addict-patients is referred to as evidence. Whatever the original intentions of Congress, through a series of Supreme Court rulings, by 1922 the Harrison Act came to mean total abstinence for all.[55]

As with the Volstead Act, legislation of the Harrison Act was easier than enforcement. It is difficult to enforce laws preventing activities in which all parties are willing participants. This is especially true when the contraband object is very small in size. In this way, the existence of laws prohibiting crimes without victims increases the power of the police as it necessitates and legitimates a close surveillance of the population.

In order to enforce laws preventing activities in which there is no citizen-complaint, police must develop an information system and much of police energy is devoted to finding law-breakers.[56] "The informer system has become such an intrinsic component of police work that the abilities of a professional detective have come to be defined in terms of his capacity to utilize this system."[57] Or as Westley puts it: "a detective is as good as his stool pigeon." Westley adds further that the solutions to crimes are largely the result of bargains detectives make with underworld figures.[58]

The relation of detective to informer is illustrated by the following newspaper report on the retirement of Mr. Dean J. Gavin, Detective Sgt. of the Buffalo police, after thirty-four years of police work, seventeen of them as a member of the Narcotics Squad.

His contacts in the underworld are legion. And when he sends out a message seeking information on anything from a burglary to a narcotics delivery, the tenants in crime's jungle make certain that Dean Gavin gets the answers.

The criminals who maintain the information-gathering network for Detective Sgt. Gavin have a universal contempt for the police . . . but they respect him.[59]

Police, then, need informers to enforce the vice laws. The existence of vice laws assures the police of a sizeable group who are in need of the favors and generosity of the police, and thus are willing to serve as informers for those favors. Police can reward the cooperative informer by reduced sentences or failure to prosecute. The stiffer and more severe the penalty, the greater the amount of bargaining power or discretion in the hands of the police—the greater the penalty, the greater the power of the police.

The police-informer system rests on the ability of the police to withhold prosecution if they desire. This means the cooperation of the District Attorney and even the courts is necessary. An informer system assumes the absence of an injured party, and of a citizen complainant.

The difficulty of enforcing laws without a complainant is clearly shown in the enforcement of the narcotic laws. The addict-informer becomes the chief source of information for violation of the narcotic laws. Police attempt to arrest the big-time operator through the addict informer. "The Bureau of Narcotics is authorized to pay the 'operating expenses' of informants whose information leads to seizure of drugs in illicit traffic."[60] Narcotic agents will supply informants with drugs, money to purchase drugs, or allow him to steal for money to purchase drugs. Thus, the law permits narcotic agents to do precisely what it forbids the doctor—supply the addicted with drugs.

Some lawyers have been disturbed at the Federal Bureau's dependence on informers. In a 1960 decision, Judge David Bazelon of the U. S. Court of Appeals for the District of Columbia Circuit criticized the Narcotic bureau:

It is notorious that the narcotic informer is often himself involved in the narcotics traffic and is often paid for his information in cash, narcotics, immunity from prosecution, or lenient punishment . . . Under such stipulation it is to be expected that the informer will not infrequently reach for shadowy leads, or even seek to incriminate the innocent.[61]

In March, 1959, in New York, a district judge acquitted a defendant who had been enticed into addiction by an informer for the Bureau of Narcotics. The judge said the defendant's participation in the crime "was a creation of the productivity of law-enforcement officers."[62]

Once an individual is labeled an addict by the police, there is no restraint on their power. Police can break into a known addict's residence. If they find narcotics in his possession or marks on his arm, they can demand that he "rat" on his source or spend ninety days in jail and face the "cold turkey" treatment. Once an individual has had "narcotic" dealings with the police, he can expect further dealings. If he should object to strong arm methods or lack of "due process," the police can threaten to punish him with the full force of the laws.

It appears then, that the enforcement of laws against activities in which there is no citizen complainant does not occur along legal lines. Establishing laws which proscribe such activities and establishing a police force to discover and prosecute persons who engage in such activities maximizes the possibilities of social control, in that it necessitates and legitimates a close surveillance of the population.

SELECTIVE ENFORCEMENT OF THE VICE LAWS: THE IMMUNITY OF THE POWERFUL

It has been argued that the police and the legal system serve the interests of the powerful. This has been shown previously in that the powerful are able to get their own moral values passed as laws of the land—this is part of the definition of power. Also, however, they appear to be immune from the application or enforcement of the law. This can be substantiated by looking at the mechanics of enforcement. The police tend to divide the populace into two groups —the criminal and the non-criminal—and treat each accordingly. In police academies the recruits are told: "There are two kinds of people you arrest: those who pay the fine and those who don't."[63]

William Westley asked the policeman in his study to describe the section of the general public that likes the police. Replies included:

"The law-abiding element likes the police. Well the people that are settled down are polite to policemen, but the floater —people who move around—are entirely different. They think we are after them."[64]

Westley concludes that "the better class of people," those from better residential neighborhoods and skilled workers, are treated with politeness and friendliness, because "that is the way to make them like you." In the policeman's relation to the middle class, "The commission of a crime by an individual is not enough to classify him a criminal."[65]

He sees these people [middle class] as within the law, that is, as being within the protection of the law, and as a group he has to observe the letter of the law in his treatment of them. Their power forces him to do so. No distinction is gained from the apprehension of such a person. Essentially, they do not fall into the category of potential criminals.[66]

Whereas, for people in the slums, the patrolman feels that roughness is necessary, both to make them respect the policeman and to maintain order and conformity. Patrolmen are aware that it is slum dwellers' lack of power which enables him to use roughness and ignore "due process."

Skolnick writes that the police wish that "civil liberties people" would recognize the differences that police follow in applying search and seizure laws to respectable citizens and to criminals.[67]

The immunity of those with power and wealth to having the law apply to them is so traditional that the police in one city were able to apply the normally withheld law enforcement to political officials as a measure of collective bargaining. The report of the activities of the Police Locust Club (police union), of Rochester, New York on the front page of the local newspaper is remarkable.

The first move was to ticket cars owned by public officials for violations of the state Motor Vehicle Law.

According to the club president, Ralph Boryszewski, other steps will include:

Refusal to 'comply with requests from politicians for favors for themselves and their friends . . .'

Cracking down on after-hours spots and gambling establishments 'which have been protected through the silent consent of public officials.'

"These evils have existed as long as the police department has, and the public should know what's going on," Boryszewski said today. The slowdown is "really a speedup in enforcement of the law," he said. "The public won't be hurt, we're after the men who think they're above the law."[68]

A Vermont urologist was charged with failure to file an income tax return for the years 1962, 1963, and 1964. However, he entered a plea of nolo on the 1964 charge only. "The judge said he accepted the lesser plea solely because it might jeopardize the doctor's standing in the medical profession."[69]

Drug users who fail to fit the "dope fiend" image, that is, drug users who are from the "respectable" or upper classes, are not regarded as narcotic criminals and do not become part of the official reports. When the addict is a well-to-do professional man, such as a physician or lawyer, and is well spoken and well educated, then prosecutors, policemen, and judges alike seem to agree that "the harsh penalties of the law . . . were surely not intended for a person like this, and, by an unspoken agreement, arrangements are quietly made to exempt him from such penalties."[70] The justification usually offered for not arresting addicted doctors and nurses is that they do not resort to crime to obtain drugs and are productive members of the community. "The only reason that users in the medical profession do not commit the crimes against property which other addicts do, is, of course, that drugs are available to them from medical sources."[71]

The more laws a nation passes, the greater the possible size of the criminal population. In 1912, Roscoe Pound pointed out "of one hundred thousand persons arrested in Chicago in 1912, more than one-half were held for violation of legal precepts which did not exist twenty-five years before."[72] Ten years ago, it was established that "the number of crimes for which one may be prosecuted has at least doubled since the turn of the century."[73]

The increase has been in misdemeanors, not felonies. Sutherland and Gehlke, studying trends from 1900–1930, found little increase in laws dealing with murder or robbery. "The increase came in areas where there was no general agreement: public morals, business ethics, and standards of health and safety."[74]

The prevention of felonies, and the protection of the community from acts of violence, is usually given as the *raison d'etre* of criminal law and the justification for a police system and penal sanctions. Yet, most police activity is concerned with misdemeanors, not felonies. Seldon Bacon writes

What are the crimes which hurt society so often and so intensely that the society must react to such disorder and must react in an effective way (i.e. with organizations, equip-

ment, and specialization)? The answer of the modern criminologist to this question is felonies. The case studies however, clearly indicate that society does not react in these ways to felonies nearly as much as to misdemeanors. Indeed, the adjustment to felonious activity is a secondary if not a tertiary sphere of action. Moreover, judicial studies of the present day point to the same findings, misdemeanor cases outnumber felony cases 100 to 1. Yet the criminologists without exception have labored almost exclusively in the sphere of felonies.[75]

One writer noted that "in the three years from 1954 through 1956 arrests for drunkenness in Los Angeles constituted between 43 and 46 per cent of all arrest bookings."[76] The importance of this is not in the prevalence of drunkenness as much as it is in the easy rationale afforded the police for maintaining order and conformity, for "keeping the peace."[77] Now that marijuana smoking is apparently so widespread, laws preventing its use give police an excuse to arrest anyone they see as a threat to "order."

Becker writes, "In America, only about six out of every hundred major crimes known to police result in jail sentences."[78] In addition, only about twenty per cent of original reports find their way into criminal statistics.[79] It appears then, that the police have considerable discretion in deciding which violators to punish, or in deciding when an individual has committed a violation.

The greater the number of punitive laws, and the stiffer the penalties, the easier it is to attempt enforcement of any *one* law. Police threaten prostitutes with arrest, using the threat to get a lead on narcotic arrests; if the prostitute informs, then there is no arrest or reduced charges.[80] Liquor laws can be used to regulate or control "homosexual" bars.[81] Burglary informants as well as narcotic informants are usually addicts. Skolnick writes, "In general, burglary detectives permit informants to commit narcotic offenses, while narcotic detectives allow informants to steal."[82]

As early as 1906, Professor Ernst Freund commented upon the range of criminal legislation. "Living under free institutions we submit to public regulation and control in ways that appear inconceivable to the spirit of oriental despotism."[83]

As the laws increase in range and number, the population is criminalized, especially the population from low-economic background, minority racial groups, or non-conformists in other ways. John I. Kitsuse writes about those labeled as deviant.

> For in modern society, the socially significant differentiation of deviants from the non-deviant population is increasingly contingent upon circumstances of situation, place, social and personal biography, and the bureaucratically organized activities of agencies of control.[84]

CONCLUSION

The attempt to enforce vice laws, as laws prohibiting activities in which there is no self-defined victim, is frequently referred to as the attempt to enforce "conventional morality." The implication is that other laws, like laws proscribing murder, have something like a metaphysical transcultural base. Today, however, many conventional sociologists and criminologists have come to the conclusion that *all* activities of police and criminal courts, not just those concerned with vice laws, enforce the moral order—enforce conformity—rather than enforce the law. Bordua and Reiss write, "police above all link daily life to central authority; moral consensus is extended through the police as an instrument of legitimate coercion."[85] Alan Silver sees the extension of moral consensus and the development of the professional police as aspects of the same historical development—the "police are official representatives of the moral order."[86]

This appears to be an apparent conclusion when one realizes that "nothing is a crime which the law does not so regard and punish."[87] As Durkheim suggests, yesterday's bad taste is today's criminal law.[88] Or, as Becker writes, "Deviance is not a quality of the act the person commits, but rather a consequence of the application by others of rules and sanctions to an 'offender'."[89] F. L. Wines writes:

> Crime is not a character which attaches to an act . . .
>
> It is a complex relation which the law created between itself and the law breaker. The law creates crime. It therefore creates the criminal, because crime cannot be said to exist apart from the criminal.[90]

As Saint Paul said, "Without the law, sin is dead." Instituting prohibitive laws against any activity establishes the "language of punishment." The existence of "the autocratic criminal law . . . compels and accustoms men to control their fellows without their consent and against their wills. It conveys to them the idea that such must be and is inevitable."[91]

For purposes of social control, then, the effects of laws prohibiting murder and beer drinking are the same. The enforcement of both serves to maintain the unequal distribution of power and wealth.

It appears, therefore, that there are no substantive distinctions among the ideas of enforcing the moral order, enforcing conventional morality, enforcing conformity, enforcing the law, and maintaining the unequal distribution of power. Crimes are violations of those moral values that the nation-state enforces through punitive law. The morality enforced is always the morality of those in power and it is primarily enforced upon those without power. That a group's morality and value system is enforced is part of the definition of its having power. To put it thus, the unequal distribution of power and wealth is maintained in part by police enforcement of the morality and value system of those with power and wealth.

The vast number of our laws provides the means for selective enforcement, and selective enforcement means the immunity of the rich and powerful. The greater the number of laws, the easier it is to control those without power and wealth. The content of the laws is not crucial for purposes of social control. What is crucial is the power to establish the "language of punishment" (or conversely, "the language of legitimacy"), the power to institute both the enforcers of law—the police—and the violators of law—the criminals.

FOOTNOTES

[1]Carl Bridenbaugh, *Cities in the Wilderness: The First Century of Urban Life in America* (New York: A. A. Knopf, [1938] 1955), p. 64.
[2]*Ibid.*, p. 65.
[3]Carl Bridenbaugh, *Cities in Revolt: Urban Life in America* 1743–1776 (New York: A. A. Knopf, 1955), p.119.
[4]Charles Reith, *The Blind Eye of History: A Study of the Origins of the Present Police Era*, (London: Farber and Farber, 1952), p. 210.
[5]David Bordua and Albert Reiss, Jr., "Law Enforcement," in Paul F. Lazarsfeld and others, *The Uses of Sociology* (New York: Basic Books, Inc., 1967), p. 276.
[6]Edward Crapsey, *The Nether Side of New York* (New York: Sheldon and Co., 1872), pp. 15–16. Today, "compromises" sometimes occur in civil

rather than criminal court cases, or as "out of court" settlements, available only in white-collar criminality. See Edwin H. Sutherland, "White Collar Criminality" in *Radical Perspectives on Social Problems*, ed. by Frank Lindenfeld (New York: Macmillan Co., 1968), pp. 149–159.

[7] Seldon Bacon, *The Early Development of American Municipal Police*, (unpublished Ph.D Dissertation, Yale University, 1939), Vol. I and II.

[8] Bacon, *op. cit.*, Vol. I, cited in Bordua and Reiss, *op. cit.*, p. 277.

[9] *Ibid.*, pp. 279–80.

[10] Bordua and Reiss, *op. cit.*, p. 280.

[11] Mark S. Hubbell, *Our Police and Our City: A Study of the Official History of the Buffalo Police Department* (Buffalo: Bensler and Wesley, 1893), pp. 57–58.

[12] Roger Lane, *Policing the City—Boston 1822–1885* (Cambridge: Harvard University Press, 1967), p. 26.

[13] Bordua and Reiss, *op. cit.*, p. 282.

[14] Reith, *op. cit.*, p. 19.

[15] Alan Silver, "The Demand for Order in Civil Society: A Review of Some Themes in the History of Urban Crime, Police, and Riot," in David J. Bordua, *The Police: Six Sociological Essays* (New York: Wiley, 1967), pp. 11–12.

[16] Raymond Fosdick, *American Police Systems* (New York: The Century Co., 1921), p.70.

[17] See Lane, *op. cit.*, p. 54.

[18] *Ibid.*, p. 50.

[19] *Ibid.*, p. 222.

[20] *Ibid.*, p. 49.

[21] Howard S. Becker, *Outsiders: Studies in the Sociology of Deviance* (Glencoe: The Free Press, 1963), p. 156.

[22] Robert Straus, "Alcohol," in Robert K. Merton and Robert A. Nisbet, eds., *Contemporary Social Problems* (New York: Harcourt, Brace, and World, Inc., Second ed. 1966), p. 244.

[23] Herbert Asbury, *The Great Illusion: An Informal History of Prohibition* (Garden City, New York: Doubleday and Co., Inc.), p. 7.

[24] Straus, *op. cit.*, p. 245.

[25] Asbury, *op. cit.*, pp. 13–14, Straus, *op. cit.*, p. 246.

[26] Asbury, *op. cit.*, p. 13.

[27] Straus, *op. cit.*, p. 246.

[28] Joseph R. Gusfield, *Symbolic Crusade: Status Politics and the American Temperance Movement* (Urbana: University of Illinois Press, 1966).

[29] *Ibid.*, p. 21.

[30] Lyman Beecher, *Six Sermons on Intemperance* (New York: American Trust Society, 1843), pp. 57–58, quoted in Gusfield, *ibid.*, p. 43.

[31] Straus, *op. cit.*, p. 249.

[32] Lane, *op. cit.*, p. 49.

[33] *Ibid.*

[34] J. H. Timberlake, *Prohibition and the Progressive Movement 1900–1920* (Cambridge: Harvard University Press, 1963), p. 41.

[35] *Anti-Saloon League, Proceedings*, 1919, pp. 45–46, quoted in *Ibid.*, p. 47.

[36] Edward B. Phelps, "The Mortality from Alcohol in the United States—the Results of a Recent Investigation of the Contributory Relation with Each of the Assigned Causes of Adult Mortality," International Congress of Hygiene and Demography, *Transactions*, 1912 (6 vols., Washington, 1913), Vol. I, pp. 813–822, quoted in Timberlake, *op. cit.*, pp. 54–55.

[37] John Koren, *Economic Aspects of the Liquor Problem* (Boston, 1899) p. 30, quoted in Timberlake, *op. cit.*, p. 57.

[38] John B. Huber, "The Effects of Alcohol," *Collier's Weekly*, Vol. 57, June 3, 1916, p. 32, quoted in Timberlake, *op. cit.*, p. 58.

[39] George Elliot Howard, "Alcohol and Crime: A Study in Social Causation," *The American Journal of Sociology*, Vol. 24, July 1918, p. 79, quoted in Timberlake, *op. cit.*, p. 58.

[40] Howard, *op. cit.*, pp. 61–64, and 80, quoted in Timberlake, *op. cit.*, p. 60.

[41] Edward A. Ross, "Prohibition as a Sociologist Sees It," *Harper's Monthly Magazine*, Vol. 142, January, 1921, p. 188; this article was reprinted in Ross' *The Social Trend* (New York, 1922), pp. 137–160, and quoted in Timberlake, *op. cit.*, pp. 60–61.

[42] Asbury, *op. cit.*, p. 185.

[43] *Ibid.*, p. 186.

[44] *Ibid.*, p. 169.

[45] *Ibid.*, pp. 169–170.

[46] Nathan E. Eddy, "The History of the Development of Narcotics," *Law and Contemporary Problems*, vol. 22, Winter, 1957, p. 3.

[47] Charles E. Terry and Mildred Pellens, *The Opium Problem* (New York: Haddon Craftsmen, 1928), p. 72.

[48] Alfred R. Lindesmith, *Addiction and Opiates* (Chicago: Aldine, 1968 ed. [first published 1947]), p. 208.

[49] Terry and Pellens, *op. cit.*, pp. 78–85.

[50] J. R. Black, "Advantages for Substituting the Morphia Habit for the Incurably Alcoholic," *Cincinnati Lancet-Clinic*, vol. 22, 1889, pp. 537–541, quoted in Lindesmith, *op. cit.*, pp. 211–212.

[51] Rufus King, "Narcotic Drug Laws and Enforcement Policies," *Law and Contemporary Problems*, vol. 22, Winter, 1957, p. 113.

[52] Lindesmith, *op. cit.*, p. 210.

[53] Stanley Meisler, "Federal Narcotics Czar," *The Nation*, February 20, 1960, p. 159.

[54] Terry and Pellens, *op. cit.*, p. 73.

[55] See Lindesmith, *op. cit.*, p. 6, and King, *op. cit.*, p. 121.

[56] See Jerome Skolnick and J. Richard Woodworth, "Bureaucracy, Information and Social Control: A Study of Morals Detail," in Bordua, (ed.), *The Police: Six Sociological Essays*, *op. cit.*, pp. 99–136.

[57] Jerome H. Skolnick, *Justice Without Trial: Law Enforcement in Democratic Society* (New York: Wiley and Sons, Inc.,), p. 238.

[58] William A. Westley, *The Police: A Sociological Study of Law, Custom, and Morality* (unpublished Ph.D. Dissertation, University of Chicago, 1951), pp. 70–71.

[59] Ray Hill, "Even the Crooks He Pursues Respect Gavin," *Buffalo Evening News*, February 3, 1968, Sunday edition.

[60] Edwin M. Schur, *Crime Without Victims: Deviant Behavior and Public Policy* (Englewood-cliffs, New Jersey: Prentice-Hall, Inc., 1965), p. 135.

[61] Stanley Meisler, "Federal Narcotics Czar," *The Nation*, February 20, 1960, p. 160.

[62] *Ibid.*

[63] Wesley, *op. cit.*, p. 95.

[64] *Ibid.*, p. 161.

[65] *Ibid.*, p. 166.

[66] *Ibid.*, p. 167.

[67] Skolnick, *Justice Without Trial*, *op. cit.*, p. 147.

[68] Everson Moran, "Officials' Cars Tagged in Police 'Slowdown,'" *The Times Union*, Greater Rochester Edition, July 2, 1968, p. 1.

[69] *Rutland Daily Herald*, April 19, 1969, p. 7.

[70] Lindesmith, *The Addict and the Law*, *op. cit.*, p. 90.

[71]*Ibid.*

[72]Quoted in Frances A. Allen, "The Borderland of Criminal Law: Problems of 'Socializing' Justice." *The Social Service Review*, Vol. 32, June, 1958, p. 108.

[73]*Ibid.*

[74]Cited in Richard C. Fuller, "Morals and the Criminal Law," *Journal of Criminal Law, Criminology, and Police Science*, vol. 32, March-April, 1942, pp. 625–26.

[75]Bacon, Vol. II, *op. cit.*, p. 784.

[76]Allen, *op. cit.*, p. 111.

[77]Egon Bittner notes that "patrolmen do not really enforce the law, even when they do invoke it, but merely use it as a resource to solve certain pressing problems in keeping the peace." Egon Bittner, "The Police on Skid Row: A Study of Peace Keeping," *The American Sociological Review*, Vol. 32, Ocotber, 1967, p. 710.

[78]Becker, *op. cit.*, p. 171.

[79]Skolnick, *Justice Without Trial, op. cit.*, p. 173.

[80]*Ibid.*, p. 125.

[81]Schur, *op. cit.*, p. 81.

[82]Skolnick, *op. cit.*, p. 129.

[83]Quoted in Allen, *op. cit.*, p. 108.

[84]John I. Kitsuse, "Societal Reaction to Deviant Behavior: Problems of Theory and Method," *Social Problems*, Vol. 9, Winter, 1962, p. 256.

[85]Bordua and Reiss, *op. cit.*, p. 282.

[86]Silver, *op. cit.*, in Bordua, (ed.), *The Police: Six Sociological Essays, op. cit.*, p. 14.

[87]F. H. Wines, *Punishment and Reformation: An Historical Sketch of the Rise of the Penitentiary Systems*, (New York: Crowell and Co., 1895), p. 13.

[88]Emile Durkheim, *The Rules of Sociological Method*, 8th ed. (Glencoe: The Free Press, 1966).

[89]Becker, *op. cit.*, p. 9.

[90]Wines, *op. cit.*, p. 24.

[91]Paul Reiwald, *Society and Its Criminals*, tr. by T. E. James, (London, William Heineman, 1949), p. 302.

In the first article in this section David M. Gordon distinguished between the conservative, the liberal, and the radical perspectives of crime. These categories correspond roughly to the distinction made in Part I of the book between "consensual" and "conflict" models. Both the conservative and liberal perspectives assume a consensus: they assume that "the public" or "almost everyone" shares the same set of values which are opposed to the commission of any criminal behavior. The conflict view sees instead either a pluralistic value system within which different groups disagree in word and deed about the kinds of things that are "really criminal," or sees crime as an inevitable outgrowth of the conflicts and contradictions that inhere in the political and economic structure of the society. The latter perspective is the one argued by Gordon and the viewpoint which we concluded with in Part I after analyzing the relevant data on the emergence of criminal laws.

Thus far the evidence again seems to favor the conflict model. It is stretching the logic of the consensus argument rather badly to assume that the routinized illegal business practices of businessmen or government officials is to be understood as simply a failure of selected individuals to adhere to the consensual value system. Crime is so ubiquitous among businessmen, politicals, law enforcers, and government officials that it is "normative" in the sense that *some* criminal acts are routinely engaged in by everyone. Furthermore, a consensual model of crime and criminal law fails to direct our attention to the importance of the link between crime and the political economy. The conflict model with an emphasis upon the intimate relationship between crime and the political and economic structure of the society is much more promising in that it assumes a diversity of values both criminal and noncriminal stemming from different class interests and leading to widespread criminality across class lines though the content or form of the criminality will vary. Thus the "snatch and grab" thefts of lower class youth will not be duplicated in the middle class suburbs and the fraudulent advertising or price fixing of large corporations will not characterize the criminality of the working class.

Part 3

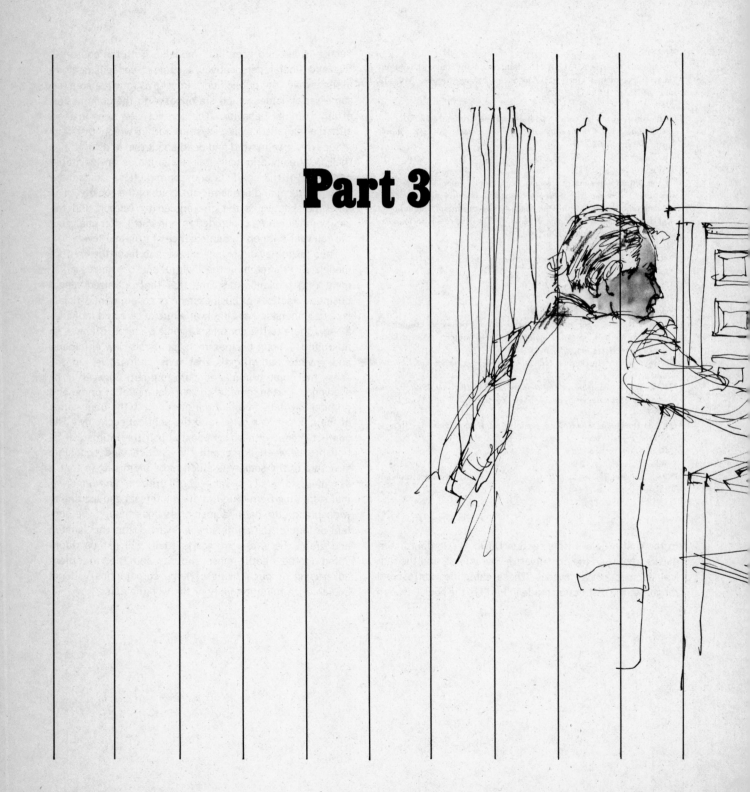

The Social Organization of Criminal Law Enforcement

PART 3   THE SOCIAL ORGANIZATION OF CRIMINAL LAW ENFORCEMENT

INTRODUCTION

One can imagine a legal system within which decisions are automatic and where the acts that are supposed to put in motion the legal machinery are clear-cut, unambiguous acts, the desirability of which is in no way open to question. But one can really only *imagine* such a system. Laws are written in language, and language is inherently ambiguous, so that no one has a copyright on *the* interpretation of what a word, much less a string of words, means. To complicate matters even further, in the Anglo-American political process these prescriptions and proscriptions which are enacted into the criminal law are usually enacted precisely because there is sufficient ambiguity so that a large number of legislators can agree to vote in favor of passage.

More complicating still is the fact that in American society the legal system must reckon with a pluralistic value system. It is simply mythological to suppose that there is *one* set of values in America upon which there is consensus. Although it may be true that there is consensus with respect to certain legal proscriptions, such as those prohibiting murder, forcible rape, and various kinds of theft, these acts are but a small segment of legal concern. On matters that occupy the bulk of legal activities and which have the greatest impact on the system, such as gambling, prostitution, homosexuality, drunkenness, and drug use, there is considerable disagreement and open debate.

Even where laws may express values with which at least one segment of the citizenry are in accord, the areas of ambiguity are likely to be great indeed. Is a youth "truant" if he slips out of study hall to have a soda? Or is he truant if he accompanies his mother to a concert when he is supposed to be in school? Has a man committed a crime when he is "under the influence of alcohol" and walking down the street, or must he be lying drunk in the gutter? Formally, these issues are left to the court to decide, but in fact each of the processing agencies must make decisions in these ambiguous areas, for it makes little sense for the police constantly to arrest persons whom the prosecutor refuses to prosecute, and it makes little sense for the prosecutor to bring charges when the judges will not try the case.

Then, too, laws are notoriously resistant to change, and this is reflected in the large numbers of laws which are "on the books" at any point in time but which clearly run counter to the prevailing mores. Most states have laws prohibiting the sale of retail merchandise on Sunday but these laws are rarely enforced. Laws exist which prohibit a man and his wife from having sexual intercourse on Sunday, and there are laws which declare it a delinquent act for a person under the age of eighteen to smoke or talk back to his parents. Any law enforcement agency attempting to enforce these rules would be likely to bring forth the wrath, not the praise, of the persons whose values it is presumably protecting.

What all these dilemmas come down to in practice is that *the administration of the criminal law is a highly selective process and involves the use of a wide range of discretion* by the agencies responsible for enforcing the law. At every step of the law enforcement process, from deciding where to send patrolmen to look for crime to determining how many years a man should be sent to prison, the organizations that are responsible for enforcing the law make decisions which have the net effect of determining what types of offenses will come to the notice of officials, what kinds of offenses and offenders will be processed, and precisely how far this processing will go. It is in the day-to-day practices and policies of the processing agencies that the law is put into effect, and *it is out of the struggle to perform their tasks in ways which maximize rewards and minimize strains for the organization and the individuals involved that the legal processing agencies shape the law.*

With a few exceptions, which are detailed below, the rewards which can be offered for nonenforcement of the law and the amount of trouble a suspected offender can create for the legal system are closely linked to the individual's social class position. Although law enforcement agencies will generally be rewarded for their conscientious and systematic processing of skid-row drunkards for "public intoxication," nothing but organizational strain and trouble is likely to emerge from efforts to process "respectable" middle class persons for the same offense. Similarly, whereas the legal system will find public support for the arrest of gamblers who handle policy numbers in the Negro ghettos, they will be rewarded only with trouble for enforcing antigambling laws against a middle class group that plays poker every Friday night.

A consequence of the unequal ability of members of different social classes to reward the legal system is that at every step of the legal process the lower class person is more likely to feel the sting of the law enforcement process.

PART 3   THE SOCIAL ORGANIZATION OF CRIMINAL LAW ENFORCEMENT

The lower class person is (1) more likely to be scrutinized and therefore to be observed in any violation of the law, (2) more likely to be arrested if discovered under suspicious circumstances, (3) more likely to spend time between arrest and trial in jail, (4) more likely to come to trial, (5) more likely to be found guilty, and (6) if found guilty more likely to receive harsh punishment than his middle or upper class counterpart. Even after sentence is passed, the built-in biases continue—among those sentenced to death for murder, lower class persons are more likely to be executed than are the others.

Patricia M. Wald analyzes the general relationship between poverty and criminal justice in a paper she wrote for the President's Crime Commission.

Edwin H. Sutherland provides us with an analysis of white collar crime and the general pattern of nonenforcement characteristic of these offenses. Following Sutherland is an article by Ronald A. Farrell which studies the effect of social class on the legal treatment of homosexuals.

8

Poverty and Criminal Justice

PATRICIA M. WALD

The great majority of those accused of crime in this country are poor. The system of criminal justice under which they are judged is rooted in certain ideals: that arrest can only be for cause; that defendants, presumed innocent until shown guilty, are entitled to pretrial freedom to aid in their own defense; that a guilty plea should be voluntary; that the allegations of wrongdoing must be submitted to the truthfinding light of the adversary system; that the sentence should be based on the gravity of the crime, yet tempered by the rehabilitative potential of the defendant; that, after rehabilitation, the offender should be accepted back into the community.

To the extent, however, that the system works less fairly for the poor man than for the affluent, the ideal is flawed.

How *does* the system work for the poor?

On almost any night in any metropolitan jurisdiction in the United States a wide range of arrests is made: petty offenses, serious misdemeanors, felonies, juvenile misconduct. These are typical:

Source: "Poverty and Criminal Justice," The President's Commission on Law Enforcement and Administration of Justice, Washington, U.S. Government Printing Office, 1967. By permission of the author and publisher. Footnotes deleted.

Defendant A is spotted by a foot patrol officer in the skid row district of town, weaving along the street. When the officer approaches him, the man begins muttering incoherently and shrugs off the officer's inquiries. When the officer seizes his arm, A breaks the hold violently, curses the officer and the police. The patrolman puts in a call for a squad car, and the man is taken to the precinct station where he is booked on a double charge of drunk and disorderly.

Defendant B, a woman, is apprehended for shoplifting a $10 dress in a downtown department store. A store detective who has been watching stops her near the door and finds the dress under her skirt. He calls a police officer who takes her to the precinct for booking on a charge of petty larceny.

Defendant C is charged with holding up a liquor store and seriously wounding the proprietor while making his getaway. His arrest follows an informer's tip and the victim's identification of his mug shot. The mug shot is a leftover from an "investigative arrest" two years before.

Defendant D, a 17-year-old Negro male, unemployed and a school dropout, is stopped by a Youth Division officer at 12:30 a.m. on a street corner while loitering with a noisy gang. There is a 10:00 p.m. curfew in effect for juveniles. The officer tells the gang to disperse and go home; D retorts that he doesn't have to and "no . . . cop can make me." The officer takes him in custody, frisks him for weapons, marches him to the precinct station, and calls his home. A man answers the phone, but is either intoxicated or unable to understand what the officer says. D is taken to the juvenile detention center for the night.

All of these defendants are poor. At every stage of the criminal process they will face the cumulative handicaps of poverty.

IN THE STATIONHOUSE

Defendant A's belt is removed to balk any attempts at suicide, and he is put in the drunk tank to sober up.

> "His cellmate lies slumped and snoring on the cell's single steel bunk, sleeping off an all-day drunk, oblivious to the shouts . . . There are at least two men in each 4 x 8 foot cell and three in some. . . . The stench of cheap alcohol, dried blood, urine and excrement covers the cell block. Except for the young man's shouts, it is quiet. Most of the prisoners are so drunk they gaze without seeing, unable to answer when spoken to. There are no lights in the cells, which form a square in the middle of the cell block. But the ring of naked light bulbs on the walls around the cell block throw light into the cells, each of which is equipped with a steel bunk. There are no mattresses. 'Mattresses wouldn't last the night,' a policeman explains. 'And with prisoners urinating all over them, they wouldn't be any good if they did last.' The only sound in the cell block is the constant flowing of water through the toilets in each cell. The toilets do not have tops, which could be torn off and broken."

Every half hour or so a policeman checks to see if the inmates are "still warm."

After sobering up, a drunk or disorderly can usually leave the lockup in four to five hours if he is able to post collateral, $10–$25. No matter how many times he has been arrested before, he will not have to appear in court if he chooses to forfeit the collateral. The drunk without money stays in jail until court the next morning. At 6 a.m., the police vans collect the residue of the precinct lockups and take them to the courthouse cell blocks to await a 10:00 arraignment.

Defendant B is booked at the precinct. Her offense is an "open and shut" case with witnesses; she is charged with petty larceny, and the files are checked to see if she has a record. Because of the frequent association among shoplifting, prostitution, and narcotics addiction, she is subjected to a compulsory physical examination. Clean, she is eligible for stationhouse bail of $500. This means cash in the full amount or a $50 premium for a bondsman. She may make one or several phone calls to a bondsman (a list hangs by the pay phone), a friend, relative, or an attorney if she knows one or can pick one out of the yellow pages. But the timing and the number of phone calls are usually a matter of police discretion, and it may be an empty right if no one answers, or if there is no telephone in the rented rooms or tenements of her friends and family. Unable to raise bail, she must await arraignment—any time from an hour to several weeks after booking.

Defendant C, suspected of robbery and aggravated assault, both felonies, is properly warned of his right to remain silent or to consult counsel before any questioning takes place. But he has no *right to an appointed lawyer before his first court appearance*, and since he cannot afford his own lawyer, his real choice is to keep quiet or sign a waiver of the right not to be questioned. For the present he prefers not to talk.

C's fingerprints and mug shot are taken, and a record check is made for any other arrests in the police files. The FBI is sent a copy of the fingerprints to check for out-of-jurisdiction offenses. He is taken to the hospital for identification by the owner-victim, then back to the liquor store so the police can replay the event and verify the victim's story as well as watch C's reaction. Street witnesses brought to the station point him out as the man they saw running from the store. C is placed in a lineup, made to strike a variety of poses and repeat the words of the holdup man. A blood smear is taken to match against some stains on the sidewalk outside the store. His room is searched for weapons, and ballistics tests are made on a gun found there.

This investigative process, steady or interrupted, may go on for many hours, even days. He is allowed to call or see his family, but their entreaties to tell all, their own woes—"what will happen to me and the kids now"—offer little solace. He may not want to involve others who can help him because they, too, would come under police scrutiny and questioning.

The interrogation (if there is any) and the investigation often precede the actual booking, so he is unsure of what charges are lodged against him. The duration of his custody is open-ended; he is not told how long it will last. If he has not been able to reach a friend or relative, no one knows for sure where he is.

In the back of his mind may linger stories he has heard about police brutality: telephone books which leave no marks, psychological bullying. Only the police are present to hear what he actually says or to observe in what condition he is when he says it. Often, in the tension of the moment and the rush of later events, he forgets what he said.

The morning following juvenile defendant D's apprehension, the arresting officer finds he has a record of prior juvenile offenses, minor thefts, truancy, gang activity. Several years ago, he was put on juvenile probation, and completed the period without further incident. The officer goes to see his parents and finds the mother, unmarried with several younger children, working a 3:00–12:00 shift in a bar. The home consists of two rooms in a dilapidated, overcrowded tenement. The mother reacts to the news by bitterly complaining of the boy, the company he keeps, the troubles he has already caused her, and the miseries yet to come. Based on the interview and D's past record, the officer decides to petition the case to juvenile court.

PRELIMINARY HEARING AND ARRAIGNMENT

Defendant A, charged with drunk and disorderly, is brought into court from the bullpen in a shuffling line of dirty, beat, unshaven counterparts, many still reeking of alcohol. Each spends an average of 90 seconds before the judge, time for the clerk to intone the charge and for the judge to ask if he desires counsel and how he pleads. Rarely does a request for counsel or a "not guilty" break the monotony of muttered "guilties." Lawyers are not often assigned in police court, and anyone who can afford his own counsel will already have been released from jail on bond—to prepare for trial at a later date or to negotiate with the city prosecutor to drop the charges.

Occasionally, an unrepresented defendant will ask for trial. If the arresting officer is present, he will be tried on the spot. There are no jury trials in drunk court. The policeman will testify that the man was "staggering," "his breath smelled of some sort of alcoholic beverage," his speech was "slurred"—"his eyes were bloodshot and glassy." The man may protest that he had only a few drinks, but there are no witnesses to support his testimony, no scientific evidence to establish his alcoholic blood level at the time of arrest, no lawyers to cross-examine the officers. If the defendant pleads not guilty and hopes he can get counsel (his own or court-assigned), he may have his trial postponed a week or two. Meanwhile, he must make bond or return to jail.

Police Court sentencing is usually done immediately after a plea. A few courts with alcoholic rehabilitation court clinics may screen for likely candidates—those not too far along on the alcoholism trail—in the detention pens. Counsel, when available, can ask for a presentence report, but delay in sentencing means jail or bail in the meantime. On a short-term offense it is seldom worth it.

Other kinds of petty offenders—disorderlies, vagrants, street ordinance violators—follow a similar pattern in court. Guilty pleas are the rule. Without counsel or witnesses it is the defendant's word against the police. Even when counsel is present, defense efforts at impeachment founder on the scanty records kept by the police in such petty offenses. The only defense may be the defendant's word—impeachable if he has a record—and hard-to-find "character witnesses" without records from his slum neighborhood.

Defendant B, the shoplifter, is arraigned in a misdemeanor court the same morning:

> "The audience section of the courtroom is usually jammed with relatives of the defendants involved, and with witnesses and complainants, as well as with defendants themselves who have been released on parole or bail. . . .
>
> "The number of reserved seats is usually inadequate for all of the attorneys and police involved in the day's cases. As a result, the attorneys usually gather close to the bench; and the police invariably also congregate inside the rail close to the door leading to the detention pen. As each case is called, the policeman will fetch from the pen the defendant whom he has arrested and bring him before the judge."

B is told of her rights, in a mass of a hundred other accused, crushed into the space between counsel table and spectators "like New Yorkers in a subway at rush hour." Marched slowly to the judge's bench "like assembly line workers in a factory, all parties operate under a climate which makes it appear that nothing may be permitted to interfere with the smooth operation of the line."

When B is before the judge, the clerk reads her a summary statement of the charges against her and recites her rights to trial and counsel, phrased in the words of the pertinent statute or court ruling. "Spoken at high speed, in a dull monotone, phrased in legal jargon, the charges and the rights are frequently unintelligible."

B can plead guilty at her first appearance or ask for a trial. She can also request an adjournment to consult or obtain counsel. The various jurisdictions differ on whether a misdemeanant who cannot afford counsel is entitled to appointed counsel. Until recently in Washington, D. C., the court appointed counsel from a "mourners' bench" and left it to the lawyer and his new client to negotiate a fee. In New York City, a Legal Aid lawyer is appointed minutes before the arraignment of an indigent defendant. In Miami, there is no representation provided for indigent misdemeanants; in Los Angeles, less than 10% of all misdemeanants have counsel at arraignment. In all events, more misdemeanants than felons lack representation. It may be harder for the defendant to qualify as an indigent misdemeanant than as an indigent felon, either because he has scraped up a small, automatically disqualifying bail bond or because the counsel fees involved are so small. Without counsel, defendant B is almost certain to plead guilty.

Even with counsel, however, pressures are strong in a high volume misdemeanor court to plead guilty and hope for, or bargain for, leniency. Assigned counsel often get no pay for representation at this level; retained counsel put into the case only the time equivalent of the $50 or $75 they can get out of it, and public defenders have only a few minutes' frantic conference with their clients outside the courtroom to decide on a plea or request for adjournment.

Trial is not an attractive prospect for an indigent misdemeanant or his lawyer. It can mean a new round of bail bonds or weeks in jail awaiting trial. Complexities of proof may be just as great as in felony trials; thorny legal issues can arise: problems of illegal search and seizure, unlawful arrests, or coerced confessions. But public funds are almost never available for investigators or expert witnesses in these courts. Preliminary hearings are usually waived because lawyers cannot take the time. Witness fees—75 cents a day in misdemeanor cases in the General Sessions Court of the District of Columbia—are noncompensatory. Constant adjournments and calendar breakdowns wear down even a persevering defendant, his underpaid lawyer, and his reluctant witnesses. Few legal reputations are made in misdemeanor courts. The trials are more informal, the judges apt to be less learned in the law than in higher courts. There is generally no court reporter unless the defendant hires his own, which he seldom can afford. In general, upsetting the routine of misdemeanor court by demanding a trial is a risky proposition: it can operate as a lever to bargain with the prosecutor for a shorter sentence or dismissal, but it can also antagonize the prosecutor and judge, resulting in a stiffer sentence on conviction.

Only defendants with money can afford to play the waiting game. Lawyers assured of reasonable fees can invest the time and energy to prepare for trial if bargaining for leniency ends in a stalemate. Their clients do not suffer from tactical maneuvers that delay the ultimate trial. The prosecutor, cannily recognizing their potential "follow through," may capitulate earlier in the game. In contrast the indigent's attempts at bargaining are confined to a few hours or days after arraignment and, declining in vigor, reflect the inescapable fact that he has the most to lose from each new delay.

After the police have completed their investigation, defendant C is brought before a judge for preliminary hearing. Charged with robbery and aggravated assault, a determination is made on whether he should be bound over to the grand jury. If the police cannot justify the charges, they could be dismissed at this juncture, but if C has already confessed, his admissions can be introduced against him; so can other incriminating post-arrest developments, including lineup identifications, fingerprints, etc. At the preliminary hearing, the defendant has the option of asserting his right to have the government present its case. Appearance of counsel here may be crucial. The defendant may not fully understand that if he waives, he loses one of his best and most effective chances to discover the identity of the government's key witnesses and the nature of the government's evidence. Adroit cross-examination at the preliminary hearing can expose and freeze inconsistencies in testimony before government witnesses have time to reflect and to consult extensively with the prosecution; valuable ground work may be laid for later impeachment at trial.

But the indigent defendant may not always be offered assigned counsel at his first appearance before a judicial officer. Without counsel, few felony suspects are adept enough to probe evidentiary weaknesses by cross-examining prosecution witnesses; few are experienced enough to weigh the pros and cons of taking the stand themselves. Since he has been in police custody from the time of his arrest, the defendant has had no opportunity to line up defense witnesses. Even if, by some extraordinary effort, he succeeded in constructing a plausible defense or in challenging the government's case, no stenographic record of the preliminary examination would be available without costly advance arrangements.

Bail in felony cases is ordinarily set for the first time at the preliminary hearing. For armed robbery and aggravated assault, it may be as high as $25,000, requiring a $2,500 premium that poor defendants cannot raise. With no defense lawyer to argue for lower bail, the prosecutor's recommendation will ordinarily stand. Even in cities where projects are operating to release worthy defendants without bail, the indigent's roots in the community usually must be solid, his record comparatively clean of past felonies. On the other hand, financial ability to make bail can be a mixed blessing. It may disqualify him from obtaining assigned counsel then, or later on arraignment.

When he is bound over to the grand jury, the detained defendant enters a legal limbo. Even if counsel were appointed for the preliminary hearing, his duties have ceased, and appointment of new counsel awaits action of the grand jury. Without a lawyer, the defendant can do nothing to affect the grand jury's deliberations or to identify key witnesses.

In jail, the defendant is thrown among convicted criminals. He marks out his days in idleness. Outside problems proliferate and contacts crumble. He is the target of constant jailhouse advice on "copping a plea" from fellow inmates. Weeks, months go by, often with no word from the courts or the lawyers on the progress of his case. If the grand jury finally declines to indict, his case may be "kicked downstairs" for reinstatement of misdemeanor charges. This process may take additional weeks while witnesses are recalled to swear to the new complaint and a new prosecutor assigned to the case. Only when the misdemeanor information is filed and a new arraignment date set is he notified that the felony charges have been dismissed.

When an indictment is handed down, the accused felon is brought from jail for arraignment, this time in the felony court where he will be tried. Counsel is now offered the indigent defendant. Bail must be reset by the judge to cover the period until trial, sometimes months away. An adjournment may be necessary to decide on a plea. Many indigents, energies sapped by prolonged periods in jail, waive counsel and plead guilty immediately. Yet a plea of not guilty is often necessary to buy time for negotiating with the prosecutor on reduction of the charges, dropping some charges in exchange for a plea to others, prosecuting multiple charges or indictments separately or concurrently. Occasionally only a token bargaining effort is required because of the pressures of the calendar on the court and prosecutors, but usually defense counsel's success is comprised of many factors: his reputation and the intensity of his commitment to the case; his capacity for engaging the prosecution with pretrial motion and writs; his resources for proceeding to a full-scale trial; his willingness to challenge illegal police or prosecutorial tactics. To bargain expertly, counsel must be able to probe the strengths and weaknesses of the prosecution's case, to realize and fulfill the potential of his own. He must acquire a sure knowledge of all the permutations and combinations of pleas and penalties that are possible under the indictment. Intangibles enter the picture; the defendant must impose full trust in his counsel's strategic judgment, be willing to accept his assessment of the prospects and alternatives.

As soon as the petition involving defendant D is filed in juvenile court, the court's intake worker decides whether to proceed with the case. If she thinks the family can control the boy and he is likely to avoid trouble again, she can dismiss the case or place him on informal probation for a few months. To make the decision, she has to assess the child himself, his home situation, his school, and police record.

In D's case, the lack of home supervision, his mother's self-admitted defeat in holding him in line, and his record of one previous probation rule out dismissal. The decision is made to charge him with violation of the curfew and disorderly conduct and to bring him before the juvenile court that afternoon. (Had the offense been more serious, he might have been waived to an adult court for a full-scale criminal trial.) In a few jurisdictions, the child and parents will be asked if they want a lawyer when a decision to petition the case is made; if they have no money, counsel will be assigned. In most jurisdictions, however, there is no procedure for assignment of counsel before hearing.

The first hearing before the juvenile judge decides whether D has committed some act which, under the statutes, gives the court jurisdiction. Juvenile court proceedings are informal, not open to the public, not usually recorded. The judge, in the presence of D's mother, will ask the boy if he wants counsel. Most juvenile court defendants lacking funds waive counsel. The judge asks if D admits the allegation of the petition; nothing is said about his right to remain silent. Most juveniles concede "involvement" readily. If the child denies the facts alleged, the case is set down for trial at a later date, and he is either sent back to the detention home or released to his own parents in the interim. D, who has been this route before, admits his offense, and the judge postpones disposition until a social study can be made by the court. In the meantime, out of school without a job

or 24-hour supervision at home, he is remanded to detention.

At the detention home, D is one of the older inmates. In the group are other 16–18-year-olds awaiting waiver decisions, trials or dispositions for auto thefts, housebreakings, burglaries, and narcotics offenses. They are questioned by the police while detained. Because of the transient, short-term population, the school program is a haphazard, undisciplined one. D has been out of school over a year and has no interest in renewing his formal education. The home provides a different kind of education: He learns details of other inmates' exploits, tricks for dealing with the police, names of friends to contact or stay clear of in training schools; he gets a first exposure to the future jailhouse crowd, is initiated into homosexual rites.

"I could do everything I wanted to do—steal, fight, curse, play, and nobody could take me and put me anywhere. I was already in the only place they could put me. I had found a way to get away with everything I wanted to do . . . I was doing things to people that I never would have done out on the street, but I didn't care. It didn't make sense to be in the Youth House if you were only going to do the things you did out on the street."

PREPARATION AND TRIAL

C prepares for trial, although plea bargaining continues up to the time of entering the courthouse. As the momentum of pretrial preparation mounts, pressures to compromise increase. Pretrial motions involving full-scale hearings are time-consuming, require extensive research and investigation, and can delay trial for months. Yet they are often the vitals of the defense strategy. The suspect should be taken to the scene of the arrest to replay his account of what happened. Other witnesses to the incident have to be located and their stories recorded. The legal precedents must be researched. New counsel must familiarize himself with any evidence adduced at an earlier preliminary hearing. All of this takes time and money while the defendant languishes in jail.

Challenging a confession before trial means obtaining a copy of the admission itself and since the *Miranda* decision a copy of any written waiver of the defendant's right to counsel. A moment-by-moment account of how and when it was obtained from the defendant must be developed by subpoenaing the police log in the case, and having the defendant examined—physically and psychologically—for signs of incapacity or compulsion, as soon as possible after he made the statements. A motion for severance means a painstaking analysis of the prejudice of a joint trial, as well as discovery motions to obtain a codefendant's admissions. Motions for a change of venue must assess the prejudice of pretrial publicity and obtain assurances that the new forum is in a jurisdiction willing to accept the burden of an indigent defendant. Efforts to exclude wiretaps or electronic bugs may demand acoustical engineers, debugging experts, blueprint specialists. Search and seizure motions in narcotics cases require that the arresting officers be interviewed on the details of the seizure, and what probable cause they had for suspecting possession or making the arrest.

And there are larger problems. Motions for tactical delay have little appeal to a client in jail. Even a successful motion to dismiss the indictment—unless it concludes the case—merely signals the start of the process all over again and interminable months more in detention.

If he proposes to plead his client not guilty by reason of insanity, an indigent's counsel encounters formidable obstacles. He can have him committed to a public hospital for observation and diagnosed by government psychiatrists, who then report back to the court on the defendant's capacity to stand trial and his mental responsibility for the alleged criminal acts. If they report him sane and responsible, counsel has the option of abandoning the defense or relying on cross-examination to discredit the examiner. If, however, the defendant can afford to hire his own psychiatrist—or better still, several (at $25 an hour)—to examine the patient, he may produce a contradiagnosis to put before the jury. The defense psychiatrist can speak confidently of the quality of the state's psychiatric report, the talents of the staff, and the acceptability of the methodology employed. With an expert stalemate, the jury will be less inhibited in making up their own minds.

Perhaps more important, the psychiatrist preparing the state's initial diagnosis does so in the sobering knowledge that it will undergo the close scrutiny of an outside professional who has had ample opportunity to observe and examine the patient. His participation in the psychiatric dialogue that precedes the formal report may make the difference between a contested and an uncontested plea.

Tracking down ordinary defense witnesses in the slums to support the defendant's alibi or to act as character witnesses often has a Runyanesque aspect to it. The defendant in jail tells his counsel he has known the witnesses for years but only by the name of "Toothpick," "Malachi Joe," or "Jet." He does not know where they live or if they have a phone. If he could get out and look himself, he is sure he could find them at the old haunts, but his descriptive faculties leave something to be desired. Since a subpoena cannot be issued for "Toothpick," of no known address, counsel sets off on a painstaking, often frustrating, search of the defendant's neighborhood. He stops children at play; he attempts door-to-door conversations with hostile and suspicious slum-dwellers; he haunts the local bars; he even asks the police on the beat for help. If he finally locates the witnesses, they must be "collared" and cajoled into coming to court; otherwise, they will probably ignore a subpoena. They must be reassured—if possible—that there will be no retaliation from police or prosecutors, that they will not themselves be held in jail as material witnesses. Fare for the trip to court must be dredged up from somewhere, lost days' pay replaced. Rarely can they tolerate more than one trip, if their testimony is postponed, they slip back into oblivion.

A defendant in jail cannot help counsel locate witnesses, persuade them to testify, nor restage his story on the actual scene. He is unavailable for spot calls to check details or last-minute conferences to plan strategy; jail may be on the edge of town and the visiting hours inconvenient for busy counsel.

But often there is no alibi, no insanity plea, no defensive pyrotechnics. The indigent must meet the government's case head-on and seek to exploit evidentiary weaknesses. Ideally, he needs to size up his opposition in advance of trial, to know who the witnesses are and what they will say; to obtain the results of scientific tests on blood, narcotics, fingerprints, handwriting, ballistic tests on weapons, exhibits taken from the scene or from the defendant himself, and reports on medical examination of the victim.

In the absence of a cadre of independent investigators, the defendant has to rely for this information on pretrial criminal discovery. But neither the names of government witnesses nor their prior statements to the police or to the grand jury, even those of a codefendant, are generally available in advance through discovery; their stories cannot be checked out for error—purposeful or inadvertent. They cannot even be contacted personally to see if they have any information helpful to the defense. Their FBI records cannot be secured.

The indigent defendant, on the other hand, must often disclose what he expects his witnesses to testify in order to obtain a free subpoena. The government has its corps of fingerprint, ballistics, and handwriting specialists; it has laboratories in which to test and analyze the evidence. The government also possesses the real evidence itself: the prints, the bullet, the blood, the signature. The results of these tests may be available through discovery, but to counter these tests effectively the defense needs its own experts to view the original evidence. This means double trips and double expert fees, once to analyze and again to testify. Funds from public sources for expert defense witnesses are always limited; often they are nonexistent.

The defendant can have his case tried to a jury or a judge. Detained defendants and those with assigned counsel are more apt to choose a judge; jury calendars are notoriously backlogged, and the penalty for demanding a jury trial may be a stiffer sentence. Adjournments are frequent, and the attrition rate for defense witnesses high. There may be subtler reasons, too, for bypassing a jury. The make-up of many juries is middle-class oriented—small businessmen, accountants, housewives. Slum residents are not so likely to be on the voter registration lists from which the juries are drawn. If they are, they are not attracted to jury duty; usually they cannot afford long absences from their jobs.

The outcome of C's trial depends on a number of factors: his counsel's ability to discredit government witnesses on cross-examination; his successful refutation of scientific evidence or tests; his ability to keep any confessions out of evidence; his success in convincing the judge that the defendant could not be the man involved or that he was somewhere else at the time.

Skillful cross-examination is most effective "when the questions are based on facts rather than on intuition . . . it often takes days or weeks to secure a witness or scientific proof which can destroy a fabricated story. If the fabricated story is not revealed until trial, it may be too late."

But indigent defense counsel must rely too often on spotting surface inconsistencies in a witness' testimony or on comparing testimony on the stand with prior statements made available in the courtroom only after the witness has testified. The statements must then be perused under the impatient eyes of judge and jury while the trial is stalled.

Defense witnesses pose strategic obstacles, even when they actually appear. They are likely to be shabbily dressed, inarticulate, unsophisticated, testy, nervous, and vulnerable to prosecution efforts at impeachment. The effect on a predominantly white collar jury can be prejudicial.

The defendant himself runs a similar risk. A detained defendant often comes to the courtroom pallid, unshaven, dishevelled, demoralized, a victim of the jailhouse blues. He comes and goes through a special door that the jury soon learns leads to the detention pen beyond. He is always closely accompanied by a police escort or marshal.

A defendant under courtroom guard raises tactical as well as psychological problems. During the trial his lawyer may need to consult with him privately in the courtroom, but his guard is always in range. There can be no productive lunch or recess conferences, no quick trips to locate last-minute rebuttal witnesses, no pretrial warm-ups or post-trial replays. Should surprise witnesses or evidence materialize, the indigent's defense counsel must face such crises alone.

In most cases, the trial will end in a guilty verdict. But even an acquitted defendant often faces debts, no job, broken family ties. Should there be a hung

jury and retrial ordered, a transcript of the trial becomes an urgent necessity: to find contradictions in
the prosecution's case, to prepare to impeach witnesses, to reevaluate trial strategy. But transcripts
for retrial are not routinely provided indigents. Nor
is the defendant now likely to be any freer to participate in the crucial work of preparing for his second
trial than he was for the first.

After the verdict, the judge can admit the defendant to bail pending sentence, or he can refuse bail
altogether. A new bail premium may be necessary
to continue his freedom. If he has been detained to
this point, it is unlikely that he will be released now.

Had defendant D chosen to deny the charges
against him in juvenile court, he would have faced
many of the same problems of locating witnesses and
refuting prosecution evidence that confront his adult
counterparts. In most juvenile courts, he would not,
however, have had the benefit of assigned counsel,
let alone investigative help. Even with counsel the
chances of acquittal would be slim. The rules of
evidence applicable in many juvenile courts do not
bar hearsay or illegally obtained evidence to establish his involvement. He may even have been forced
to testify himself. The child can be excluded from
the courtroom at the judge's discretion. There may
be no court record to appeal from; in only a few
places can he demand a jury. The standard of proof
is a preponderance of evidence, not guilt beyond a
reasonable doubt. If adjudicated a delinquent,
there could be an immediate disposition at trial;
more likely he will be sent back to the detention
center while the court's staff conducts a social study
into his background to recommend what should be
done with him.

SENTENCING AND APPEAL

Defendant A, drunk and disorderly, will be sentenced on the spot. The sentence may be suspended
if he has no lengthy record. Otherwise, he may be
fined $30 (or 30 days) or given a short sentence
(10–90 days) in the local jail or workhouse. But
even a short jail sentence can play havoc with a marginal offender's precarious existence—day-to-day
jobs and rented rooms are gone when he gets back,
his tenuous ties to the neighborhood cut.

A poor, petty offender rarely appeals his conviction. Appeal is often discretionary with the courts if
the fine does not exceed $50. There is a 3-day limit
on filing, and no mention of his appeal right is made
in court. Usually, he has no counsel. By the time
an appeal would be heard, his sentence is served; a
stay would have to be conditional on an appeal bond
of perhaps $500–1,000.

Misdemeanant B, convicted of petty larceny, will
probably not receive a presentence investigation. If
she has counsel, her lawyer can, of course, present
his own information and plea to the court, citing her
job status, her family responsibilities, her penitent
attitude—all the reasons why the court should not
disrupt a life with some semblance of normality. An
offer to make restitution to the victim for any monetary loss or to pay hospital bills can be effective at
this juncture. It may also be impossible if the
defendant is impoverished.

In certain kinds of cases, the court will realize
that a promise to seek private psychiatric treatment
on release holds out a better promise of recovery and
safety to the community than a nontherapeutic jail
sentence. However, if the defendant or her lawyer
can satisfy none of these alternatives, she may go to
prison for several months. And any appeal rights
may be illusory. Free counsel may not be available
on appeal, even in serious misdemeanors.

When felony defendant C appears for sentencing,
there will probably be a presentence report in his
file. The contents of the report, however, will usually be inaccessible to him or his counsel in accordance with a general policy of nondisclosure. The
probation officer will have been to the jail to talk to
him and to report his "attitude," "his rehabilitative
potential." He will also have been to see his family
and friends, employers, neighbors, and enemies.
The report will contain a potpourri of their narratives
and the investigator's own conclusions. Dedicated
counsel may try to supplement this report with an
investigation of his own. If possible, he will advance
rehabilitation plans for his client in an effort to
avoid prison. But often harried by other business,
assigned counsel may have to defer judgment to the
probation office. For whatever reasons—the defendant's appearance or demeanor, his lack of a job or

strong family ties after months in jail—defendants with assigned counsel and defendants detained before trial receive prison sentences more often than the rest.

After sentence, if there is a right to appeal, the indigent must be furnished counsel and a transcript or whatever record is necessary for an adequate appeal. But often there are time limits on how promptly the appeal must be filed, even if counsel has not been appointed. In such cases, the defendant will have to write the petition or file the notice of appeal himself. In such event, he or his lawyer may still have to absorb much of the cost of appeal.

Appeals can prolong the proceedings excruciatingly. Unable to raise new bail, the indigent defendant may languish months in jail—without credit toward his sentence. If he elects to begin serving sentence, he may be sent to a state penitentiary, far from counsel. And successful appeal, while sometimes bringing release, more often means only a new trial and an interminable replay of the whole process.

In the period after D is adjudicated a delinquent, a court social worker will conduct a background investigation preparatory to holding a dispositional hearing. She will talk to D in the detention home and to his supervisors to see how he is "adjusting." His mother, his school teachers, his neighbors will be contacted. His earlier probation file will be checked. If there is any possibility of emotional or mental aberration, psychological or neurological studies can be ordered. All this will go into her report, along with her conclusions: "He is a bad influence on younger boys"; he "disobeys" his mother; he is "untruthful."

In D's case, the factual recitation will be typical of that of a majority of youths before the court: No father in the home, mother works, intermittent periods on welfare, home life overcrowded, turbulent and disorganized, constant evictions, poor early school adjustment, habitual truancy, dropout at 16, suspected vandalism, early sex adventures, neighborhood a drop-site for stolen cars, a hangout for addicts, pushers, prostitutes, a battleground for gang wars. Since school, he has held a few jobs, for short periods only: car washer, kitchen help,

road gang. Mother is ambivalent toward him, alternatively possessive and rejecting. He is a loner, with no active membership in church or social organizations.

The report is complete, and D is brought under guard from the detention center to court. He may not have seen his mother since the last visiting day —if she came to see him then. He has no lawyer. The judge has been handed the social study prior to court, and the social worker is there to elaborate on the report or to answer questions. The child or his parent has no right to see the study. The social worker may have concluded that the boy must be removed from his home because his mother cannot control him, or because there are no daytime or evening supervision resources in his neighborhood to see that he stays in line.

Theoretically, the mother (or counsel if the youth were represented) could counter with job offers, possible rehabilitative programs, vocational training, or Job Corps placement to prove institutionalization was not necessary. A more affluent parent could offer a special private school, outpatient psychiatric treatment, or group counselling for the whole family. Witnesses could be offered to show the boy's redeeming features and his potential for constructive action and growth.

In D's case none of these possibilities are available. The judge listens to the social worker and to the child and his mother—often antagonistic to one another—then commits the boy to juvenile training school for an indeterminate period, not to exceed his twenty-first year.

PRISON, PROBATION, AND PAROLE

Defendant B, the shoplifter, is ultimately granted probation. She will be required to report to a probation officer downtown at the court at his convenience. She must stay in the area. She cannot change jobs, move, alter her marital status without permission, frequent places where liquor is sold, or stay out late. She cannot associate with other law offenders. She must obey all laws. If she does not have a job, she must try "diligently" to get one. Restitution may have to be made. In some counties, the costs of providing her with a legal defense must be repaid as a condition of probation.

In the slum areas where life is lived on the streets and in the bars, where a sizable percentage of local residents are past offenders, the conditions of probation may not be realistic. Probationers, like other slum-dwellers, probably have a greater chance of being "picked up" for a minor street offense because of where and how they live. Now, because of their special status (probationers' names are generally listed at their local precinct), they may attract even closer official attention in areas which police are trying to "keep clean."

Probation officers exercise their discretion as to how to handle "technical violations" in different ways. If the officer and his probationer hit it off well, the officer will hesitate to be rigid, but in many cases the wide social gap between the middle-class officer and his lower-class client inhibits such rapport. The officer can ignore minor rule infractions, recognize the day-to-day pressures of existence, help the probationer to overcome his anti-authority bias. Or he can blow the whistle on every technicality, assuring the probationer's quick return to jail.

If revocation is threatened, the probationer in many jurisdictions will get neither notice nor a hearing. Assignment of counsel to indigent probationers is an accident of jurisdiction. An unrepresented probationer can be refused access to the probation officer's reports or files; confrontation and cross-examination of unidentified accusers may be impossible. Bail may or may not be available during the proceeding. A full-scale probation hearing, like a trial on the main offense, often involves a contest of facts and requires witnesses, evidence, searching cross-examination, for which the indigent is totally without resources.

Defendant C, the indigent hold-up man, has been sentenced to prison. Left behind are a wife and children, snowballing debts. In prison, he can contribute nothing to his dependents' existence. His prison earnings, if any, are meager and are consumed primarily in commissary items—cigarettes, soap, candy. He may be drawn into the prison rackets to earn more. If the prison is distant from his neighborhood, he can expect few visitors to make the time-consuming and expensive trip.

His prison work duty often reflects the same educational and skill deficiencies that plagued him on the outside. He is apt to relate poorly to the prison's middle-class staff.

While in prison, he may try to institute collateral attacks on his conviction by writing judges and public officials his version of how he was wronged. Occasionally such a letter with surface merit will provoke a judge to grant a hearing, but the aid of counsel and supporting investigative resources, seldom available, may be indispensable to success.

At the end of one-third of his sentence, he may petition for parole, and reapply yearly if he is turned down. Parole applications take into account the nature of the man's crime, his pre-prison record, his "institutional adjustment." Even when granted, however, parole may depend on his having a job waiting for him and an approved place to live. A prisoner may wait months after parole has been granted for these conditions to materialize, or until he can be mandatorily released—when his sentence less "good time" is finished.

Back on the street, living on the dole of relatives, or working at a transient job, he starts anew. Parole conditions prevent him from leaving the area, from associating with ex-cons like himself, from carrying weapons, drinking, going to "undesirable places," changing addresses, marrying or cohabiting extra-maritally, from driving a car without permission. Because of his record, he cannot work in a bar, restaurant, hospital, and in some places not even in a barber shop. He cannot afford the compensating luxury of further training or education. Old debts have mounted while he was in prison, or he has acquired new debts since his return.

In desperation, some parolees actually ask to be returned; others revert to crime for supplemental income. The parolee can always be sent back to jail for technical violations or new offenses. He is troubled by the threat of police harassment—rightly or wrongly—which can lead to revocation. If he is charged with a new offense, he can go back to prison before, not after, the revocation hearing. He usually has no right to assigned counsel at such a hearing.

In the juvenile training school (typically in a rural setting far from the inner city where he lives and often inaccessible by public transportation), D sees his family infrequently; his companionship is concentrated in the ranks of fellow delinquents.

> "Warwick had real criminals . . . it seemed like just about everybody at Warwick not only knew how to pick locks but knew how to cross wires in cars and get them started without keys. Just about everybody knew how to pick pockets and roll reefers, and a lot of cats knew how to cut drugs. They knew how much sugar to put with heroin to make a cap or a bag. There was so much to learn . . . One of the most interesting things I learned about was faggots. Before I went to Warwick, I used to look down on faggots like they were something dirty. But while I was up there, I met some faggots who were pretty nice guys . . ."

Insufficient staff and an overcrowded institution provide little casework, no therapy, too much opportunity for abuse of the weak and nonconforming inmates. For persistent misbehavior he can in many instances be transferred administratively to an adult prison. The institution decides when he is ready for release, and even then it may be delayed if his home remains "unsuitable." When release does come, it is usually conditional, revocable for "unsatisfactory adjustment" as well as for infringement of rules or or new law violations. He can be kept on a ward status indefinitely until the agency asks the court to terminate it. If he commits a new violation, the boy goes back into detention to await new court action. When he is finally discharged, D's juvenile record, while not open to public inspection, can be used to impeach him in later court proceedings, or included in any pre-sentence report for an adult court. It follows him into the Army. A potential employer's request for a police clearance as a prerequisite to employment will expose it.

CONCLUSION

Poverty breeds crime. The poor are arrested more often, convicted more frequently, sentenced more harshly, rehabilitated less successfully than the rest of society. So long as the social conditions that produce poverty remain, no reforms in the criminal process will eliminate this imbalance. But we can ease the burdens of poverty by assuring the poor those basic procedural rights which our society ostensibly grants all citizens: the right to be represented by competent counsel early enough in the process to preserve other rights; the right to prepare an adequate defense, the right to be free until convicted, the right not to be jailed solely because of lack of money to remit a fine or make restitution, the right to parole, the right to a clean start after prison. In withholding these fundamentals from any citizen, society reveals a poverty of its own.

9

White Collar Crime: The Statistical Record

EDWIN H. SUTHERLAND

In order to secure more definite information regarding the crimes of persons of the upper socio-economic class, an attempt has been made to tabulate the decisions of courts and administrative commissions against seventy of the largest manufacturing, mining, and mercantile corporations. The seventy large corporations used in this analysis are, with two exceptions, included in each of two lists of the 200 largest non-financial corporations in the United States. One of these lists was prepared by Berle and Means in 1929, and the other by the Temporary National Economic Committee in 1938. From these lists were excluded the public utility corporations, including transportation and communications corporations, and the corporations in one other industry. This left 68 corporations common to both lists. To these were added two corporations which appeared in the list for 1938 and not in the list for 1929. The list of seventy corporations is, therefore, unselected except as to size and type of specialization, with the two exceptions mentioned, and neither of these exceptions was selected with knowledge of its rank among large corporations as to violations of laws.

The present analysis covers the life careers of

Source: *White Collar Crime* by Edwin H. Sutherland. Copyright © 1949, by Holt, Rinehart and Winston, Inc. Reprinted by permission of Holt, Rinehart and Winston, Inc.

the seventy corporations. The average life of these corporations is approximately 45 years, but decisions as to the date of origin are arbitrary in a few cases. The analysis also includes the decisions against the subsidiaries of the seventy large corporations, as listed in the standard manuals, for the period the subsidiaries have been under the control of the parent corporations.

The analysis is concerned with the following types of violations of laws: restraint of trade; misrepresentation in advertising; infringement of patents, trademarks, and copyrights; "unfair labor practices" as defined by the National Labor Relations Law and a few decisions under other labor laws; rebates; financial fraud and violation of trust; violations of war regulations; and some miscellaneous offenses. All of the cases included in the tabulation are violations of law, most of them may properly be defined as crimes, and the others are closely allied to criminal behavior.

The sources of information regarding these violations of law are the decisions of the federal, state, and, in a few cases, municipal courts, as published in *Federal Reporter* and the *American State Reports*; the published decisions of the Federal Trade Commission, the Interstate Commerce Commission, the Securities and Exchange Commission, the National

Labor Relations Board, and, for the period 1924–1927, of the Federal Food and Drug Administration. These official reports have been supplemented, as to infringement, by the reports on infringement cases listed in the *Official Gazette* of the Patent Office, and as to violations of law in general, by reports of decisions in newspapers. The *New York Times* has been used, especially because its material has been indexed since 1913. The name of each of the seventy corporations and its subsidiaries was checked against the index of each of these series of reports and of the *New York Times*.

The enumeration of decisions as reported in these sources is certainly far short of the total number of decisions rendered against these seventy corporations. First, many of the decisions of the lower courts are not published in the series of federal and state reports, and many of them are not published in accessible newspapers. Second, many suits are settled out of court and no outcome reported in the series of reports or in newspapers. The number of suits initiated against the seventy corporations, which dropped out of sight after preliminary motions and which were presumably settled out of court, is approximately 50 percent of the number included in the tabulation in this chapter. Many of these probably involved violations of law and could have been tabulated as such if more complete information had been available. Third, the Food and Drug Administration has not published its decisions by names of offenders except during the years 1924–1927. Fourth, many of the decisions are indexed under such names as "John Doe Trade Association," or "John Doe *et al*." Consequently, many of the seventy corporations which have been defendants in those suits were not discovered because their names did not appear in the indexes, and often were not even mentioned in the published reports. Finally, many of the subsidiaries

of these corporations are not listed in the financial manuals and could not be identified for the present study.

A decision against one of the seventy corporations is the unit in this tabulation. If a decision is made in one suit against three of the seventy corporations, it is counted three times, once against each of the three corporations. Also, if a criminal suit and an equity suit are initiated against one corporation for essentially the same overt behavior, and a decision is made against the corporation in each of these suits, two decisions are counted. This obviously involves some duplication. On the other hand, one decision may contain scores of counts, each of which charges a specific violation of law and may also refer to a policy which has been in operation for a decade or longer; this decision, nevertheless, is counted only once.

The term "decision" is used here to include not only the formal decisions and orders of courts, but also the decisions of administrative commissions, stipulations accepted by the court or commission, settlements ordered or approved by the court, confiscation of food as in violation of the Pure Food Law, and, in three cases, which will be explained in a later chapter, opinions of courts that the defendant had violated the law at an earlier time even though the court then dismissed the suit.

The enumeration of the decisions which have been discovered is presented in Table I. This shows that each of the seventy large corporations has one or more decisions against it, with a maximum of 50. The total number of decisions is 980, and the average per corporation is 14.0. Sixty corporations have decisions against them for restraint of trade, 53 for infringement, 44 for unfair labor practices, 43 for miscellaneous offenses, 28 for misrepresentation in advertising, and 26 for rebates.

TABLE I

Decisions by Courts and Commissions against Seventy Large Corporations, by Types of Laws Violated

Corporation*	Restraint of Trade	Misrepresentation in Ads	Infringement	Unfair Labor	Rebates	Other	Total
1	12	6	2	11	6	13	50
2	12	1	1	10	5	21	50
3	6	2	22	9	—	1	40

PART 3   THE SOCIAL ORGANIZATION OF CRIMINAL LAW ENFORCEMENT

TABLE I—(Continued)

Corporation*	Restraint of Trade	Misrepresentation in Ads	Infringement	Unfair Labor	Rebates	Other	Total
4	1	12	15	5	—	6	39
5	—	18	20	1	—	—	39
6	22	—	6	—	—	3	31
7	1	2	8	15	1	1	28
8	9	2	5	2	5	3	26
9	19	—	2	—	2	2	25
10	13	2	9	—	—	1	25
11	21	—	4	—	—	—	25
12	21	—	3	—	—	1	25
13	7	—	—	—	10	6	23
14	—	12	11	—	—	—	23
15	8	3	—	1	—	7	19
16	11	—	3	2	3	—	19
17	10	1	5	2	—	1	19
18	4	—	1	9	3	2	19
19	—	1	9	1	—	7	18
20	—	5	13	—	—	—	18
21	4	—	4	2	—	7	17
22	6	—	3	3	4	1	17
23	—	—	10	1	—	4	15
24	4	—	1	3	3	3	14
25	2	—	1	4	2	5	14
26	3	—	2	5	4	—	14
27	7	—	4	3	—	—	14
28	1	1	4	3	—	5	14
29	3	—	1	9	—	1	14
30	7	1	—	5	—	—	13
31	1	8	1	1	—	2	13
32	7	2	1	—	1	1	12
33	8	1	1	—	1	1	12
34	3	—	3	5	—	1	12
35	3	—	—	7	1	—	11
36	1	—	6	2	—	1	10
37	3	4	1	—	1	1	10
38	6	1	1	1	—	1	10
39	1	3	1	1	1	2	9
40	6	—	1	—	—	1	8
41	5	—	3	—	—	—	8
42	1	1	4	2	—	—	8
43	1	—	—	3	1	3	8
44	2	—	2	—	2	2	8
45	1	2	2	3	—	—	8
46	3	1	2	1	—	1	8
47	2	—	—	3	2	1	8
48	5	—	—	1	1	—	7
49	1	1	2	3	—	—	7

TABLE I—(Continued)

Corporation*	Restraint of Trade	Misrepresentation in Ads	Infringement	Unfair Labor	Rebates	Other	Total
50	1	—	—	4	1	1	7
51	6	—	1	—	—	—	7
52	—	—	5	2	—	—	7
53	—	—	5	—	—	2	7
54	3	—	1	1	1	—	6
55	1	—	—	2	2	1	6
56	1	—	3	—	—	2	6
57	2	—	1	1	2	—	6
58	1	—	—	3	1	—	5
59	5	—	—	—	—	—	5
60	2	—	1	2	—	—	5
61	2	—	1	—	—	2	5
62	3	—	1	—	—	1	5
63	—	—	2	2	—	—	4
64	1	1	1	—	—	—	3
65	—	2	—	—	—	1	3
66	2	1	—	—	—	—	3
67	—	—	—	2	—	—	2
68	1	—	—	—	—	1	2
69	1	—	—	—	—	—	1
70	1	—	—	—	—	—	1
Total	307	97	222	158	66	130	980

*The corporations are designated by number rather than name for reasons stated in the Preface. The numbers were assigned on the basis of total number of decisions; a corporation retains the same number in all Tables.

Table II presents an analysis of the 980 decisions by types of jurisdictions of the courts and commissions which rendered the decisions. This shows that 158 decisions were made against 41 of the seventy large corporations by criminal courts, 298 decisions against 59 of the corporations by civil courts, and 129 decisions against 43 corporations by equity courts. This gives a total of 583 decisions by courts.

The essential characteristic of crime is that it is behavior which is prohibited by the State as an injury to the State and against which the State may react, at least as a last resort, by punishment. The two abstract criteria generally regarded by legal scholars as necessary elements in a definition of crime are legal description of an act as socially harmful and legal provision of a penalty for the act.[1]

The first of these criteria—legal definition of a social harm—applies to all of the classes of acts which are included in the 980 decisions tabulated above. This can be readily determined by the words in the statutes—"crime" or "misdemeanor" in some, and "unfair," "discrimination," or "infringement" in all of the others. The persons injured may be divided into two groups: first, a relatively small number of persons engaged in the same occupation as the offenders or in related occupations, and, second, the general public either as consumers or as constituents of the social institutions which are affected by the violations of the laws. The antitrust laws are designed to protect competitors and also to protect the institution of free competition as the regulator of the economic system, and thereby to protect consumers against arbitrary prices; and to protect the institution of democracy against the dangers of great concentration of wealth in the hands of monopolies. Laws against false advertising are designed to protect

PART 3   THE SOCIAL ORGANIZATION OF CRIMINAL LAW ENFORCEMENT

TABLE II
Decisions by Courts and Commissions against Thirty-three Large Corporations
for Violations of Specified Laws, by Jurisdictions and Procedures

Corporations	Court		Commission				Total
	Criminal	Civil	Equity	Order	Confiscation	Settlement	
1	18	4	4	17	7	—	50
2	18	3	6	10	13	—	50
3	1	23	4	12	—	—	40
4	—	18	2	19	—	—	39
5	—	20	—	19	—	—	39
6	—	15	13	3	—	—	31
7	2	8	—	18	—	—	28
8	4	6	3	13	—	—	26
9	10	10	2	1	—	2	25
10	4	9	5	6	—	1	25
11	—	11	10	4	—	—	25
12	—	10	10	4	—	1	25
13	12	3	7	—	—	1	23
14	—	12	—	11	—	—	23
15	7	4	—	6	2	—	19
16	10	3	1	5	—	—	19
17	3	6	3	6	—	1	19
18	3	2	4	10	—	—	19
19	2	9	5	2	—	—	18
20	—	13	—	5	—	—	18
21	6	4	4	3	—	—	17
22	2	5	1	9	—	—	17
23	2	10	2	1	—	—	15
24	3	3	3	4	—	1	14
25	3	1	4	6	—	—	14
26	3	2	1	8	—	—	14
27	4	4	1	5	—	—	14
28	2	5	—	5	—	2	14
29	1	1	1	11	—	—	14
30	3	—	1	9	—	—	13
31	1	1	1	9	—	1	13
32	6	1	—	5	—	—	12
33	6	1	1	3	1	—	12

competitors against unfair competition and also to protect consumers against fraud. The National Labor Relations Law is designed to protect employees against coercion by employers and also to protect the general public against interferences with commerce due to strikes and lockouts. The laws against infringements are designed to protect the owners of patents, copyrights, and trademarks against deprivation of their property and against unfair competition, and also to protect the institution of patents and copyrights, which was established in order to "promote the progress of science and the useful arts." Violations of these laws are legally defined as injuries to the parties specified.

Each of these laws has a logical basis in the common law and is an adaptation of the common law to modern social organization. False advertising is related to common law fraud, and infringement to larceny. The National Labor Relations Law, as an attempt to prevent coercion, is related to the common law prohibition of restrictions on freedom in the form of assault, false imprisonment, and extortion. For at least two centuries prior to the enactment of the modern antitrust laws the common law was moving against restraint of trade, monopoly, and unfair competition.

Each of the four types of laws under consideration, with the possible exception of the laws regarding infringements, grew primarily out of considerations of the welfare of the organized society. In this respect they are analogous to the laws of the earliest societies, where crimes were largely limited to injuries such as treason, in which the organized society was the victim and particular persons suffered only as they were members of the organized society. Subsequent criminal laws have been concerned principally with person-to-person injuries, as in larceny, and the State has taken jurisdiction over the procedures principally in order to bring private vengeance under public control. The interest of the State in such behavior is secondary and derivative. In this sense, the four laws under consideration may properly be regarded as criminal laws in a more fundamental sense than the laws regarding larceny.

Each of the four laws provides a penal sanction and thus meets the second criterion in the definition of crime. Consequently, each of the adverse decisions under these four laws, except certain decisions under the infringement laws, is a decision that a crime was committed. This conclusion will be explained by analysis of the penal sanctions provided in the four laws.

The Sherman Antitrust Law stated explicitly that a violation of the law is a misdemeanor. Three methods of enforcement of this law are provided, each involving procedures regarding misdemeanors. First, it may be enforced by the usual criminal prosecution, resulting in the imposition of fine or imprisonment. Second, the attorney general of the United States and the several district attorneys are given the "duty" of "repressing and preventing" violations of the law by petitions for injunctions, and violations of the injunctions are punishable as contempt of court. This method of enforcing a criminal law was an invention and, as will be explained pres-

ently, is the key to the interpretation of the differential implementation of the criminal law as applied to white collar criminals. Third, parties who are injured by violations of the law are authorized to sue for damages, with a mandatory provision that the damages awarded be three times the injuries suffered. These damages in excess of reparation are penalties for violation of the law. They are payable to the injured party in order to induce him to take the initiative in the enforcement of the criminal law and in this respect are similar to the earlier methods of private prosecutions under the criminal law. All three of these methods of enforcement are based on decisions that a criminal law was violated and therefore that a crime was committed; the decisions of a civil court or a court of equity as to these violations are as good evidence of criminal behavior as is the decision of a criminal court. Judge Carpenter stated in regard to the injunctions under the antitrust law: "The Supreme Court in upholding them necessarily has determined that the things which were enjoined were crimes, as defined by one at least of the first three sections of the Act."[2]

The Sherman Antitrust Law has been supplemented by the Federal Trade Commission Law, the Clayton Act, and several other laws relating to restraint of trade. Some of these supplementary laws define violations as crimes and provide the conventional penalties, but most of them do not make explicit the criminality of the violations of law. A large proportion of the cases dealt with under these supplementary laws could be dealt with instead under the original Sherman Law, which is explicitly a criminal law, or under the antitrust laws of the several states, which also are in most states explicitly criminal laws. In practice, violations of these supplementary laws are customarily dealt with by the Federal Trade Commission. This Commission has two principal sanctions under its control, namely: the stipulation and the cease and desist order. The Commission may, after the violation of law has been proved, accept a stipulation from the corporation that it will not violate the law in the future. Such stipulations are customarily restricted to the minor or technical violations. If a stipulation is violated or if no stipulation is accepted, the Commission may issue a cease and desist order; this is equivalent to a court's injunction except that violation is not punishable as contempt. If the Commission's desist order is violated, the Commission may apply to the court for an injunction, the violation of which is punishable as contempt. By an amendment to the Federal Trade Commission Law in the Wheeler-Lea Act of 1938, an order of the Commission becomes "final" if not officially questioned within a specified time and thereafter its violation is punishable by a civil fine. Thus, although certain interim procedures may be used in the enforcement of these antitrust laws, fines or imprisonment for contempt are available as means of enforcement if the interim procedures fail. In this respect the interim procedures are similar to probation in ordinary criminal cases. An unlawful act is not defined as criminal by the fact that it is punished, but by the fact that it is punishable. Larceny is as truly a crime when the thief is placed on probation as when he is committed to prison. The argument may be made that punishment for contempt of court is not punishment for violation of the original law and that, therefore, the original law does not contain a penal sanction. This reasoning is specious since the original law provides the injunction with its penalty as a part of the procedure for enforcement. Consequently, all of the decisions made under the antitrust laws are decisions that the corporations committed crimes.[3]

The laws regarding false advertising, as included in the decisions under consideration, are of two types. First, false advertising in the form of false labels is defined in the Pure Food and Drug Law as a misdemeanor and is punishable by a fine. Second, false advertising generally is defined in the Federal Trade Commission Act as unfair competition. Cases of the second type are under the jurisdiction of the Federal Trade Commission, which uses the same procedures as in antitrust cases. Penal sanctions are available, therefore, under these laws and all of the decisions in false advertising cases are decisions that the corporations committed crimes.

The National Labor Relations Law of 1935 defines a violation as "unfair labor practice." The National Labor Relations Board is authorized to make official decisions as to violations of the law and, in case of

violation, to issue desist orders and also to make certain remedial orders, such as reimbursement of employees who have been dismissed or demoted because of activities in collective bargaining. If an order is violated, the Board may apply to the court for enforcement, and a violation of the order of the court is punishable as contempt. Thus, all of the decisions under this law, which is enforceable by penal sanctions, are decisions that crimes were committed.[4]

The laws regarding infringements are more complex than those previously described. Infringements of a copyright or of a patented design are defined in the federal statutes as misdemeanors, punishable by fines. Decisions against the seventy corporations have been made in seven cases under the copyright law and in no cases, so far as discovered, on charges of infringement of patented designs. Other infringements are not explicitly defined in the federal statutes on patents and trademarks as crimes, although many state laws have so defined infringements of trademarks.[5] Nevertheless, these infringements may be criminal under federal statutes in either of two respects. First, the statutes provide that damages awarded to injured owners of patents or trademarks may be greater than the injuries actually suffered; these are punitive damages and constitute one form of punishment. Although these punitive damages are not mandatory as under the Sherman Antitrust Law, they are not explicitly limited to wanton and malicious infringements. Also, the rule in federal trademark cases is that an account of profits is taken only when the infringement involves wrongful intent to defraud the original owner or deceive the public. These decisions, therefore, are equivalent to convictions in criminal trials. On these principles three of the decisions against the seventy corporations in patent cases and six in trademark cases are classified as criminal convictions. Second, agents of the Federal Trade Commission may initiate actions against infringers as unfair competition. Infringements proceeded against in this manner may be punished in the same manner as violations of the antitrust laws, namely, by stipulations, desist orders, and fines or imprisonment for violations of desist orders. Five decisions in infringement cases against the seventy corporations are classified as criminal actions in this sense. This gives a total of 21 decisions in infringement cases which may be classified as evidence of criminal behavior of the seventy corporations. Of the 222 decisions on infringements, 201 are left unaccounted for in terms of criminality.

The evidence in some of these cases and in the descriptions of general practices regarding patents and trademarks justifies an estimate that a large proportion of the 201 cases—perhaps half—involved wilful appropriation of the property of others and might have resulted in penalties under state or federal laws if the injured parties had approached the behavior from the point of view of crime. In spite of this estimate, the 201 decisions are not included as evidence of criminal behavior.

The laws in regard to financial manipulations, such as violations of trust, stock market manipulations, stock watering, and misrepresentation in the sale of securities, are generally based on the laws of fraud or violation of trust. A poor man was recently sentenced in Indiana to serve one to seven years in the state prison on conviction of false pretenses; he had listed with a finance company household goods, which he did not own, as a means of securing a loan. The same law applies to corporations but it is seldom used when corporations misrepresent their assets. The judicial decisions have tended toward higher standards of protection of stockholders and of the public, and the Securities and Exchange Commission has been organized to implement these laws. Most of the regulations imposed by this Commission during the last decade and a half were in accordance with some of the earlier decisions of courts.[6]

The penalties presented in the preceding section as definitive of crime were limited to fines, imprisonment, and punitive damages. In addition, the stipulation, the desist order, and the injunction without reference to contempt have the attributes of punishment in a limited manner. This is evident both in the fact that they result in some suffering on the part of the corporation against which they are issued, and also in the fact that they were designed by legislators and administrators to produce suffering. The suffering takes the form of public shame,

which is an important aspect of all penalties. This was illustrated in extreme form in the colonial penalty of sewing the letter "T" on the clothing of a thief. In England the Bread Act of 1836 and the Adulteration of Seeds Act of 1869 provided as a penalty the publication in the newspaper of the details regarding the crimes of adulteration of these products; the Public Health Act of 1891 authorized the court to order a person twice convicted of selling meat unfit for human consumption to fix a sign on his place of business of a size to be specified by the court, stating that he had been convicted twice of violating this law. Stipulations, desist orders, and injunctions to some extent resemble these publicity penalties of England. That the publication of the stipulation in Federal Trade Commission cases is a punishment is attested by Lowell B. Mason, a member of the Commission.[7]

That this suffering is designed is apparent from the sequence of sanctions used by the Federal Trade Commission. The stipulation involves the least publicity and is used for minor violations. The desist order is used if the stipulation is violated and also if the violation of the law is appraised by the Commission as wilful and major. The desist order involves more public shame than the stipulation. The shame resulting from the stipulation and the desist order is somewhat mitigated by the argument of the corporations that such orders are merely the acts of bureaucrats. Still more shameful to the corporation is an injunction issued by a court. The shame resulting from an injunction is sometimes mitigated and the corporation's face is saved by taking a consent decree, or making a plea of *nolo contendere*. The corporation may insist that the consent decree is not an admission that it violated the law. For example, the meat-packers took a consent decree in an antitrust case in 1921, with the explanation that they had not knowingly violated any law and were consenting to the decree without attempting to defend themselves because they wished to cooperate with the government in every possible way. This patriotic motivation appeared questionable, however, after the packers fought during the next decade and a half for a modification of the decree, so that it was approximately fifteen years before the decree was fully executed. The plea of *nolo contendere* was first used in antitrust cases in 1910, but has been used in hundreds of cases since that date. This plea at the same time saves the face of the corporation and protects the corporation against suits for damages, since the decision in a case in which the plea is *nolo contendere* may not be used as evidence in other cases.[8] The sequence of stipulation, desist order, and injunction indicates that the variations in public shame are designed; also, the arguments and tactics used by corporations to protect themselves against public shame in connection with these orders indicate that the corporations recognize them as punishments.

The conclusion in this semantic portion of the analysis is that 779 of the 980 decisions against the seventy large corporations are decisions that crimes were committed.

This conclusion may be questioned on the ground that the rules of proof and evidence used in reaching many of these decisions were not the same as the rules used in criminal courts. This involves, especially, the proof of criminal intent and the presumption of innocence. These rules of criminal intent and presumption of innocence, however, are not required in all prosecutions in criminal courts and the number of exceptions authorized by statutes is increasing. In many states a person may be committed to prison without protection of one or both of these rules on charges of statutory rape, bigamy, adultery, passing bad checks, selling mortgaged property, defrauding a hotel keeper, and other offenses.[9] Jerome Hall and others who include *mens rea* as one of the essential and universal criteria of crime justify their position by the argument that exceptions such as those mentioned above are "bad law."[10] The important consideration here is that the criteria which have been used in defining white collar crimes are not categorically different from the criteria used in defining some other crimes. The proportion of decisions rendered against corporations without the protection of the rules of criminal intent and presumption of innocence is probably greater than the proportion rendered against other criminals, but a difference in proportions does not make the violations of law by corporations categori-

cally different from the violations of law by other criminals. Moreover, the difference in proportion, as the procedures actually operate, is not great. On the one hand, many of the defendants in usual criminal cases, being in relative poverty, do not get good defense and consequently secure little benefit from these rules; on the other hand, the Commissions come close to observing these rules of proof and evidence although they are not required to do so. This is illustrated by the procedure of the Federal Trade Commission in regard to advertisements. Each year the Commission examines several hundred thousand advertisements and appraises about 50,000 of them as probably false. From the 50,000, it selects about 1,500 as patently false. For example, an advertisement of gum-wood furniture as "mahogany" would seldom be an accidental error and would generally result from a state of mind which deviated from honesty by more than the natural tendency of human beings to feel proud of their handiwork.

The preceding discussion has shown that these seventy corporations committed crimes according to 779 decisions, and also has shown that the criminality of their behavior was not made obvious by the conventional procedures of the criminal law but was blurred and concealed by special procedures. This differential implementation of the law as applied to the crimes of corporations eliminates or at least minimizes the stigma of crime. This differential implementation of the law began with the Sherman Antitrust Law of 1890. As previously described, this law is explicitly a criminal law and a violation of the law is a misdemeanor no matter what procedure is used. The customary policy would have been to rely on criminal prosecution as the method of enforcement. But a clever invention was made in the provision of an injunction to enforce a criminal law; this was an invention in that it was a direct reversal of previous case law. Also, private parties were encouraged by treble damages to enforce a criminal law by suits in civil courts. In either case, the defendant did not appear in the criminal court and the fact that he had committed a crime did not appear on the face of the proceedings.

The Sherman Antitrust Law, in this respect, became the model in practically all subsequent procedures authorized to deal with the crimes of corporations. When the Federal Trade Commission Bill and the Clayton Bill were introduced in Congress, they contained the conventional criminal procedures; these were eliminated in committee discussions, and other procedures which did not carry the external symbols of criminal process were substituted. The violations of these laws are crimes, as has been shown above, but they are treated as though they were not crimes, with the effect and probably the intention of eliminating the stigma of crime.

This policy of eliminating the stigma of crime is illustrated in the following statement by Wendell Berge, at the time assistant to the head of the antitrust division of the Department of Justice, in a plea for abandonment of the criminal prosecutions under the antitrust law and the authorization of civil procedures with civil fines as a substitute.

> While civil penalties may be as severe in their financial effects as criminal penalties, yet they do not involve the stigma that attends indictment and conviction. Most of the defendants in antitrust cases are not criminals in the usual sense. There is no inherent reason why antitrust enforcement requires branding them as such.[11]

If a civil fine were substituted for a criminal fine, a violation of the antitrust law would be as truly a crime as it is now. The thing which would be eliminated is the stigma of crime. Consequently, the stigma of crime has become a penalty in itself, which may be imposed in connection with other penalties or withheld, just as it is possible to combine imprisonment with a fine or have a fine without imprisonment. A civil fine is a financial penalty without the additional penalty of stigma, while a criminal fine is a financial penalty with the additional penalty of stigma.

When the stigma of crime is imposed as a penalty, it places the defendant within the popular stereotype of "the criminal." In primitive society "the criminal" was substantially the same as "the stranger,"[12] while in modern society the stereotype is limited largely to the lower socio-economic class. Seventy-five percent of the persons committed to state prisons are probably not, aside from their unesteemed cultural attainments, "criminals in the usual sense of

the word." It may be excellent policy to eliminate the stigma of crime from violations of law by both the upper and lower classes, but we are not here concerned with policy.

White collar crime is similar to juvenile delinquency in respect to the stigma. In both cases the procedures of the criminal law are modified so that the stigma of crime will not attach to the offenders. The stigma of crime has been less completely eliminated from juvenile delinquency than from white collar crimes because the procedures for the former are a less complete departure from conventional criminal procedures, because most juvenile delinquents come from the lower class, and because the juveniles are not organized to protect their good names. Because these juvenile delinquents have not been successfully freed from the stigma of crime, they have been generally held to be within the scope of the theories of criminal behavior and in fact provide a large part of the data for criminology. Because the external symbols have been more completely eliminated from white collar crimes, these crimes have generally not been included within the scope of criminology. These procedural symbols, however, are not the essential elements in criminality, and white collar crime belongs logically within the scope of criminology, just as does juvenile delinquency.

Those who insist that moral culpability is a necessary element in crime argue that criminality is lacking in the violations of laws which have eliminated the stigma from crime. This involves the general question of the relation of criminal law to the mores. The laws with which we are here concerned are not arbitrary, as is the regulation that one must drive on the right side of the street. The Sherman Antitrust Law, for example, represents a settled tradition in favor of free competition and free enterprise. This ideology is obvious in the resentment against communism. A violation of the antitrust law is a violation of strongly entrenched moral sentiments. The value of these laws is questioned principally by persons who believe in a more collectivistic system, and these persons are limited to two principal groups, namely, the socialists and the leaders of Big Business. When the business leaders, through corporate activities, violate the antitrust law, they are violating the moral sentiments of practically all sections of the American public except the socialists.

The other laws for the regulation of business are similarly rooted in moral sentiments. Violations of these laws, to be sure, do not call forth as much resentment as do murder and rape, but not all laws in the penal code involve equal resentments by the public. We divide crimes into felonies, which elicit more resentment, and misdemeanors, which elicit less resentment. Within each of these classes, again, the several statutes may be arranged in order of the degree of atrocity of the behavior. White collar crimes, presumably, would be in the lower part of the range in this respect but not entirely out of the range. Moreover, very few of the ordinary crimes arouse much resentment in the ordinary citizen unless the crimes are very spectacular or unless he or his immediate friends are affected. The average citizen, reading in the morning newspaper that the home of an unknown person has been burglarized by another unknown person, has no appreciable increase in blood pressure. Fear and resentment develop in the modern city principally as the result of an accumulation of crimes, as depicted in crime rates or in general descriptions. Such resentment develops under those circumstances both as to white collar crimes and other crimes. Finally, not all parts of the society react in the same manner against the violations of a particular law. It is true that one's business associates do not regard a violation of a business regulation as atrocious. It is true, also, that people in certain slum areas do not regard larceny by their neighbors as atrocious, for they will ordinarily give assistance to these neighbors who are being pursued by the agents of criminal justice.

The differential implementation of the law as it applies to large corporations may be explained by three factors, namely, the status of the businessman, the trend away from punishment, and the relatively unorganized resentment of the public against white collar crimes. Each of these will be described.

First, the methods used in the enforcement of any law are an adaptation to the characteristics of the prospective violators of that law, as appraised by the legislators and the judicial and administrative personnel. The appraisals regarding businessmen, who are the prospective violators of the law now under consideration, include a combination of fear and admiration. Those who are responsible for the system of criminal justice are afraid to antagonize businessmen; among other consequences, such antagonism may result in a reduction in contributions to the campaign funds needed to win the next election. The amendment to the Pure Food and Drug Law of 1938 explicitly excludes from the penal provisions of that law the advertising agencies and media (that is, principally, newspapers and journals) which participate in the misrepresentation. Accessories to crimes are customarily included within the scope of the criminal law, but these accessories are very powerful and influential in the determination of public opinion and they are made immune. Probably much more important than fear, however, is the cultural homogeneity of legislators, judges, and administrators with businessmen. Legislators admire and respect businessmen and cannot conceive of them as criminals; businessmen do not conform to the popular stereotype of "the criminal." The legislators are confident that these respectable gentlemen will conform to the law as the result of very mild pressure. The most powerful group in medieval society secured relative immunity from punishment by "benefit of clergy," and now our most powerful group secures relative immunity by "benefit of business," or more generally by "high social status." The statement of Daniel Drew, a pious old fraud, describes the working of the criminal law with accuracy: "Law is like a cobweb; it's made for flies and the smaller kind of insects, so to speak, but lets the big bumblebees break through. When technicalities of the law stood in my way, I have always been able to brush them aside easy as anything."

This interpretation meets with considerable opposition from persons who insist that this is an egalitarian society in which all men are equal in the eyes of the law. It is not possible to give a complete demonstration of the validity of this interpretation of class differences, but four types of evidence are presented in the following paragraphs as partial demonstration.

The Department of Justice is authorized to use both criminal prosecutions and petitions in equity to enforce the Sherman Antitrust Law. The Department has selected the method of criminal prosecution in a larger proportion of cases against trade unions than of cases against corporations, although the law was enacted primarily because of fear of the corporations. From 1890 to 1929, the Department of Justice initiated 438 actions under this law with decisions favorable to the United States. Of the actions against business firms and associations of business firms, 27 percent were criminal prosecutions, while of the actions against trade unions 71 percent were criminal prosecutions.[13] This shows that the Department of Justice has been more inclined to use a method which carries with it the stigma of crime against trade unions than against business firms.

The method of criminal prosecution in enforcement of the Sherman Antitrust Law has varied from one presidential administration to another. It was seldom used in the administrations of the presidents who are popularly appraised as friendly toward business, namely, McKinley, Harding, Coolidge, and Hoover.

Businessmen suffered their greatest loss of prestige in the depression which began in 1929. It was precisely in this period of low status of businessmen that the most strenuous efforts were made to enforce the old laws and enact new laws for the regulation of businessmen. The appropriations for this purpose were multiplied several times and persons were selected for their vigor in administration of the law, with the result that the number of decisions against the seventy corporations was quadrupled in the next decade.

The Federal Trade Commission Law states that a violation of the law by a corporation shall be deemed to be also a violation by the officers and directors of the corporation. Businessmen, however, are seldom convicted in criminal courts, and several cases have been reported, like the six percent case in the automobile industry, in which corporations were convicted while the persons who directed the corporations were acquitted. Executives of corporations are convicted in criminal courts principally when they use methods of crime similar to the methods of the lower socio-economic class.

A second factor in the explanation of the differential implementation of the law as applied to white collar criminals is the trend away from penal methods. This trend advanced more rapidly in the area of white collar crimes than that of other crimes. The trend is seen in general in the almost complete abandonment of the extreme penalties of death and physical torture; in the supplanting of conventional penal methods by non-penal methods such as probation and the case-work methods which accompany probation; and in the supplementing of penal methods by non-penal methods, as in the development of case work and educational policies in prisons. These decreases in penal methods are examined by a series of social changes: the increased power of the lower socio-economic class upon which previously most of the penalties were inflicted; the inclusion within the scope of the penal laws of a large part of the upper socio-economic class as illustrated by traffic regulations; the increased social interaction among the classes, which has resulted in increased understanding and sympathy; the failure of penal methods to make substantial reductions in crime rates; and the weakening hold on the legal profession and others of the individualistic and hedonistic psychology which had placed great emphasis on pain in the control of behavior. To some extent overlapping those just mentioned, is the fact that punishment, which was previously the chief reliance for control in the home, the school, and the church, has tended to disappear from those institutions, leaving the State without cultural support for its own penal methods.[14]

The third factor in the differential implementation of the law in the area of white collar crime is the relatively unorganized resentment of the public toward white collar crime. Three reasons for the different relation between law and mores in this area may be given. (a) The violations of law by businessmen are complex and their effects diffused. They are not simple and direct attacks by one person on another person, as is assault and battery. Many of the white collar crimes can be appreciated only by persons who are experts in the occupations in which they occur. A corporation often violates a law for a decade or longer before the administrative agencies or the public become aware of the violation. The effects of these crimes may be diffused over a long period of time and perhaps among millions of people, with no particular person suffering much at a particular time. (b) The public agencies of communication do not express the organized moral sentiments of the community as to white collar crimes, in part because the crimes are complicated and not easily presented as news, but probably in greater part because these agencies of communication are owned or controlled by businessmen and because these agencies are themselves involved in the violations of many of these laws. Public opinion in regard to picking pockets would not be well organized if most of the information regarding this crime came to the public directly from the pickpockets themselves. This failure of the public agencies may be illustrated by the almost complete lack of attention by newspapers to the evidence presented in the trial of A. B. Dick and other business machine companies that these companies maintained a sabotage school in Chicago in which their employees were trained to sabotage the machines of rival companies, and even machines of their own companies if the supplies of rival companies were being used.[15] Many newspapers did not even mention this decision, and those which did mention it placed a brief paragraph on an inner page. Analogous behavior of trade unions, with features as spectacular as in this case, would have been presented with large headlines on the front page of hundreds of newspapers. (c) These laws for the regulation of business belong to a relatively new and specialized part of the statutes. The old common law crimes, as continued in the regular penal codes, were generally limited to person-to-person attacks, which might have been committed by any person in any society.

In the more complex society of the present day, legislatures have felt compelled to regulate many special occupations and other special groups. The penal code of California, for instance, contains an index of penal provisions in the statutes outside of the penal code, which are designed to regulate barbers, plumbers, farmers, corporations, and other special groups. This index occupies 46 pages, and the complete statutes to which reference is made in the index occupy many hundreds of pages. This illustrates the great expansion of penal laws beyond the simple requirements of earlier societies. The teachers of criminal law, who generally confine their attention to the old penal code, miss the larger part of the penal law of the modern state. Similarly, the

public is not generally aware of many of these specialized provisions, and consequently the resentment of the public is not organized.

For the three reasons which have been presented, the public does not have the same organized resentment against white collar crimes as against certain of the serious felonies. The relation between the law and mores, finally, tends to be circular. The laws, to a considerable extent, are crystallizations of the mores, and each act of enforcement of the laws tends to re-enforce the mores. The laws regarding white collar crimes, which conceal the criminality of the behavior, have been less effective than other criminal laws in re-enforcing the mores.

The answers to the questions posed at the beginning of this chapter may be summarized in the following propositions: First, the white collar crimes which are discussed in this book have the general criteria of criminal behavior, namely, legal definition of social injuries and legal provision of penal sanctions. They are therefore cognate with other crimes. Second, these white collar crimes have generally not been regarded by criminologists as cognate with other crimes and as within the scope of theories of criminal behavior because the administrative and judicial procedures have been different for these violations of criminal law than for other violations of criminal law. Third, this differential implementation of the criminal law as applied to businessmen is explained by the status of the businessmen, the trend away from punitive methods, and the relatively unorganized resentment of the public toward white collar crimes.

Since this analysis is concerned with violations of laws by corporations, a brief description of the relation of the corporation to the criminal law is necessary. Three or four generations ago the courts with unanimity decided that corporations could not commit crimes. These decisions were based on one or more of the following principles. First, since the corporation is a legislative artifact and does not have a mind or soul, it cannot have criminal intent and therefore cannot commit a crime. Second, since a corporation is not authorized to do unlawful acts, the agents of a corporation are not authorized to do unlawful acts. If those agents commit unlawful acts, they do so in their personal capacity and not in their capacity as agents. They may be punished, therefore, as persons but not as agents. Third, with a few exceptions, the only penalties that can be imposed on corporations, if found guilty of crimes, are fines. These fines are injuries to stockholders rather than to the agents who are directly responsible for the violations of the laws. Therefore, as a matter of policy, the agents rather than the stockholders should be punished.

In contrast with earlier practice, corporations are now frequently convicted of crimes. Corporations have been convicted of larceny, manslaughter, keeping disorderly houses, breaking the Sabbath, destruction of property, and a variety of other crimes.[16] Such decisions involve reversal of the three principles on which the earlier decisions were based. First, the corporation is not merely a legislative artifact. Associations of persons existed prior to the law and some of these associations have been recognized as entities by legislatures. These corporations and other associations are instrumental in determining legislation. Consequently legislation is in part an artifact of corporations, just as corporations are in part an artifact of legislatures.[17] Second, the requirement that criminal intent be demonstrated has been eliminated from an increasing number of criminal laws, as has been described above. Third, the location of responsibility has been extremely difficult in many parts of modern society, and responsibility is certainly a much more complicated concept than is ordinarily believed. The old employers' liability laws, which were based on the principle of individual responsibility, broke down because responsibility for industrial accidents could not be located. Workmen's compensation laws were substituted, with their principle that the industrial establishment should bear the cost of industrial accidents. Some attention has been given to the location of responsibility for decisions in the policies of large corporations.[18] Although responsibility for actions of particular types may be located, power to modify such actions lies also at various other points. Owing largely to the complexity of this concept, the question of individual responsibility is frequently waived and penalties are imposed on corporations. This does, to be sure, affect the stockholders who may have almost no power in making decisions as to policy; the same thing is true of other penalties which have been suggested as substitutes for fines on corporations, namely, dissolution of the corporation, suspension of business for a specified time, restriction of sphere of action of the corporation, confiscation of goods, publicity, surety for good behavior, and supervision by the court.

Two questions may be raised regarding the responsibility of corporations from the point of view of the statistical tabulation of violations of law presented in an earlier chapter. The first is whether a corporation should be held responsible for the action of a special department of the corporation. The advertising department, for example, may prepare and distribute advertisements which violate the law. The customary plea of the executives of the corporation is that they were ignorant of and not responsible for the action of the special department. This plea is akin to the alibi of the ordinary criminal and need not be taken seriously. The departments of a corporation know that their recognition by the executives of the corporation depends on results and that few questions will be asked if results are achieved. In the rare case in which the executives are not only unaware of but sincerely opposed to the policy of a particular department, the corporation is customarily held responsible by the court. That is the only question of interest in the present connection. Consequently, an illegal act is reported as the act of the corporation without consideration of the location of responsibility within the corporation.

The second question is concerned with the relation between the parent corporation and the subsidiaries. This relationship varies widely from one corporation to another and even within one corporate system. When subsidiaries are prosecuted for violations of law, the parent company generally pleads ignorance of the methods which were used by the subsidiary. This, again, is customarily an alibi, although it may be true in some cases. For instance, the automobile corporations generally insist that the labor policy of each subsidiary is determined by that subsidiary and is not within the control of the parent company. However, when a labor controversy arose

PART 3   THE SOCIAL ORGANIZATION OF CRIMINAL LAW ENFORCEMENT

in a plant in Texas and a settlement was proposed by the labor leaders, the personnel department of that plant replied: "We must consult Detroit." They reported the following morning: "Detroit says 'no.'" For the present purpose, the corporation and its subsidiaries are treated as a unit, without regard to the location of responsibility within the unit.

FOOTNOTES

[1] The most thorough analysis of crime from the point of view of the legal definition is Jerome Hall, *Principles of Criminal Law* (Indianapolis, 1947). He lists seven criteria of crime: "(1) certain external consequences ('harms'), (2) which are legally forbidden (principle of legality); (3) conduct; (4) *mens rea;* (5) the fusion, 'concurrence,' of *mens rea* and conduct; (6) a 'causal' relationship between the legally forbidden harms and the voluntary misconduct; and (7) (legally prescribed) punishment" (p. 11). The position taken in the present chapter is in most respects consistent with Hall's definition; certain differences will be considered later.

[2] U. S. vs. Swift, 188 F 92 (1911).

[3] A few of the decisions on restraint of trade were made under the Packers and Stockyards Act. The penal sanctions in this Act are essentially the same as in the Federal Trade Commission Act.

[4] Violations of the federal Fair Labor Standards Act and of most of the state labor laws are defined as misdemeanors.

[5] For a list of such state laws see Walter J. Derenburg, *Trade Mark Protection and Unfair Trading* (New York, 1936), pp. 861–1012.

[6] Orville C. Snyder, "Criminal Breach of Trust and Corporate Mismanagement," *Miss. Law Jour.,* 11:123–151, 262–289, 368–389, December, 1938 and April, 1939; A. A. Berle, "Liability for Stock Market Manipulation," *Columbia Law Rev.,* 31:264–279, February, 1931; David L. Dodd, *The Judicial Valuation of Property for Stock-Issue Purposes* (New York, 1930).

[7] Lowell B. Mason, "FTC Stipulation—Friend of Advertiser," *Chicago Bar Record,* 26:310 f., May, 1945.

[8] Paul E. Hadlick, *Criminal Prosecutions under the Sherman Antitrust Act* (Washington, 1939), pp. 131–132.

[9] Livingston Hall, "Statutory Law of Crimes, 1887–1936," *Harvard Law Rev.,* 50:616–653, February, 1937.

[10] Jerome Hall, *op. cit.,* ch. X.

[11] Wendell Berge, "Remedies Available to the Government under the Sherman Act," *Law and Contemporary Problems,* 7:111, January, 1940.

[12] On the role of the stranger in punitive justice, see Ellsworth Faris, "The Origin of Punishment," *Intern. Journ. of Ethics,* 25:54–67, October, 1914; George H. Mead, "The Psychology of Punitive Justice," *Amer. Journ. Sociol.,* 23:577–602, March, 1918; F. Znaniecki, *Social Actions* (New York, 1936), pp. 345–408.

[13] Percentages compiled from cases listed in the report of the Department of Justice, *"Federal Antitrust Laws, 1938."*

[14] The trend away from penal methods suggests that the penal sanction may not be a completely adequate criterion in the definition of crime.

[15] *New York Times,* March 26, 1948, pp. 31, 37.

[16] George F. Canfield, "Corporate Responsibility for Crime," *Columbia Law Rev.,* 14:469–481, June, 1941; Frederic P. Lee, "Corporate Liability," *Columbia Law Rev.,* 28:1–28, February, 1928; Max Radin, "Endless Problem of Corporate Personality," *Columbia Law Rev.,* 32:643–667, April, 1932.

[17] For a summary of classical theories of corporate personality, see Frederick Hallis, *Corporate Personality* (London, 1930). See also, Henri Lévy-Brühl, "Collective Personality in the Law," *Annales Sociologiques,* series C, no. 3, 1938.

[18] Robert A. Gordon, *Business Leadership in the Large Corporation* (Washington, 1945).

10

Class Linkages of Legal Treatment of Homosexuals

RONALD A. FARRELL

Data on the relationship of social status to crime and legal treatment are limited and contradictory. Most studies utilizing official statistics have shown an overrepresentation of lower-class people in criminal populations (Glueck, 1934; Caldwell, 1931; Shaw and McKay, 1943; and others). Likewise a recent study of the legal treatment of consenting adult homosexuals in Los Angeles County found that only 3.7% of the felony and 10% of the misdemeanor defendants were professional men.

A number of social scientists have maintained, however, that the law enforcement processes tend to select those from the lower classes (see especially Sutherland, 1949). In the earlier literature, Warner and Lunt (1941: 373–377)[1] and Useem et al. (1942)[2] offer research support for this point of view. More recent studies lend additional support. For example, Gallo et al. (1966: 741) found that in one small upper-class community there were no arrests for homosexual sex offenses in the period of 1962–1964. Similarly,

in Allegheny County, Pennsylvania, Goldman (1964: 587–590) found that the policeman's decision regarding the disposition in a case of a juvenile arrest is influenced by his impression of the offender and by a series of pressures brought to bear on him by the community, both of which circumstances are related to the boy's family background, attitude, personality, and so on. And finally, studies utilizing the anonymous questionnaire procedure have offered empirical evidence indicating no significant relationship between delinquent behavior and socioeconomic status (Nye et al., 1958; Akers, 1964; Empey and Erickson, 1966).[3] Thus, the lower classes may be no more criminal than the middle and upper classes, but may simply be less successful in evading punishment.

Studies have also shown that there are differentials in legal treatment according to race. Negroes are more likely to be arrested, indicted, and convicted than are whites who commit the same offenses (Lemert and Rosberg, 1948) and are less likely than whites to receive probation or a suspended sentence (Axelrad, 1952). Although the more severe legal treatment of Negroes may be due in part to racial

Source: "Class Linkages of Legal Treatment of Homosexuals," by Ronald A. Farrell is reprinted from *Criminology*, Vol. 9, No. 1 (May 1971), pp. 49–67, by permission of the Publisher, Sage Publications, Inc.

prejudice, it is likely that the Negro-white differential may be a class variation, since Negroes are found for the most part in the lower social classes.

Other studies have also shown that there are differences in the kinds and forms of offenses committed by members of different classes. The ratio of lower-class persons represented in official statistics on sex offenses is somewhat lower than that for figures on most conventional crime, and, in fact, the crime rates of the lower classes may be lower than those of other classes for homosexual sex offenses (Kinsey et al., 1948: 327–393). Regarding the forms that an offense might take, Myerhoff and Myerhoff (1964) found that although the middle-class delinquent may engage in as many antisocial activities as do lower-class youngsters, factors interact to prevent these activities from coming to the attention of the authorities, or if the middle-class youngsters are apprehended, prevent them from being officially handled or recorded. They point out, for example, that homosexuals from the middle class exercise more discretion, judgment, and self-possession than those from the lower class. Leznoff and Westley (1955) found likewise. They report that there is a relationship between occupation and overt versus secret homosexuality. The overt homosexual tends to fit into an occupation of low status rank; the secret homosexual into an occupation with relatively high status rank.

The literature, then, indicates that statutory possibilities alone may not provide a realistic picture of the offender's legal status. The class position appears to be of considerable importance. The form that the offense takes, the social image that the individual presents, the attitude of the police, judges, juries, and the public toward the offender and his behavior, and possibly a combination of factors related to legal protection (obtaining bail, effectiveness of legal counsel, and the like), all of which are related to one's social class position, may influence the legal treatment.

THE PROBLEM

Regarding law enforcement practices and adult male homosexual sex offenses, there are no controlled studies either supporting or disproving the claim that the implementation of the law differs according to the class position of the offender. This is a field, therefore, wherein knowledge of the legal treatment imposed on individuals from different class levels should be especially valuable. This study, therefore, is a pilot study carried out to explore this relationship.

For purposes of this research, an adult male homosexual sex offender was defined as a male, eighteen years or older, who made homosexual overtures to, or voluntarily had sexual contact with, another male. Although it is not a crime to be a homosexual, homosexual acts among adults, as well as between adults and minors, and in private, as well as in public, are unlawful in all American jurisdictions, with the exception of Illinois. These acts usually come under the law of sodomy.[4] The jurisdiction in which this study was made distinguished between sodomy by mouth or anus (a felony which brings a sentence of a fine or imprisonment by separate and solitary confinement or both) and assault or solicitation to commit sodomy (also a felony, but bringing a sentence of a lesser fine or imprisonment for a shorter period by separate and solitary confinement or both). Those who assaulted or solicited were in some instances charged with "disorderly conduct," "public indecency," and the like. These labels imply any act involving limited physical contact or merely a "proposition." These and similar statutes are also applied to those arrested for transvestism. A number of the offenses also come under the charge of corrupting the morals of a minor or contributing to the delinquency of a minor. In this jurisdiction, the homosexual may also be subject to long-term incarceration, for treatment under a special "sex offender" law (for discussion of "sex offender" or "sex psychopath" laws, see Szasz, 1963: 213–214; 1965: 125–130; Bowman and Engle, 1956: 578.)

THE SAMPLE

The data that follow were collected from a sample of 108 offenders who received legal treatment during a five-year period in a large urban jurisdiction in the United States.[5] Several years ago, this jurisdiction established a diagnostic center, whose purpose is to provide the judges with a better understanding of guilty defendants so that sentencing will be more meaningful. The center has maintained an established policy of examining sexual offenders routinely. Consequently, all homosexual sex offenders, after their charge but prior to their trial, are seen at the center, where an exhaustive examination is done on their psychological condition and social background. If the examination reveals that the defendant was not responsible for his actions as a result of insanity, the center recommends psychiatric commitment. Otherwise, this information is summarized and forwarded to the presiding judge at the time of the trial for his use in the event that the defendant is found guilty.

The major purpose of this study is to summarize from case records, the social class backgrounds, details of offense, and legal dispositions of 108 offenders who were seen in conjunction with this center. These 108 cases represent a 100% sample of all adult males who were arrested and held for court for homosexual offenses during the five-year period. In the absence of true probability sampling, however, it can only be assumed that these cases are roughly representative of the American, male, big-city, apprehended homosexual sex offender population. Furthermore, since the reaction of legal authorities to homosexuals is likely to vary considerably among different jurisdictions, these findings on legal treatment should not be interpreted as the general situation. In fact, the presence of a diagnostic center in this jurisdiction, in itself, implies some degree of uniqueness. Nevertheless, the sample includes minor and major offenders and offenders who were, after their return to the court, given heavy or light sentences, fined, or placed on probation, and so on.

THE HYPOTHESIS AND PROCEDURE

The principal hypothesis is that the lower-status homosexual sex offenders more frequently come in contact with the law and receive more severe legal treatment. The hypothesis will be tested first by briefly examining the social status[6] of offenders. Next, legal treatment[7] in relation to social status will be considered. In analyzing the treatment of offenders, since only 108 cases are involved and since

dividing them into all the headings and subheadings employed in the general study would have left few or no cases in some of the subdivisions, only the major headings will be employed in the statistical breakdown. Legal treatment will be divided into three levels of severity:

(1) severe (incarceration including psychiatric commitment);

(2) moderate (probation with or without psychiatric treatment); and

(3) mild (a fine or less—only one defendant was fined—includes suspended sentence, not guilty, dismissed, and voluntary psychiatric treatment).

Because of a clustering of cases at the lower-status levels, social status will be divided into the following three categories:

(1) lower-lower class;

(2) upper-lower class; and

(3) middle class (includes also those few cases falling above the middle class).

The chi-square analysis will be used and relationships will be accepted as statistically significant at the .10 level. After analyzing the relationship between the legal treatment and social status of all 108 offenders, the relationship will be reexamined while holding each of a number of possible intervening variables constant. Here, Cramér's V test[8] will be used to measure the relative strength of these relationships. The variables controlled for are the offender's prior offense record, age of the youngest object, degree of consent, setting of the act, type of act, and finally, these interdependent variables (except prior offense record) will be treated as one variable and labeled "severity of offense."[9] In controlling for severity of offense, offenses will be divided (according to the degree of presence of unfavorable legal and criminological factors) into three categories: (1) severe, (2) moderate, and (3) milder.

FINDINGS

In terms of Warner's classification, homosexuals who were arrested and held for court in this jurisdiction occupy a low social status and presumably a lower status than the general population of homosexuals. The figures in Table 1 show that 75.9% of these offenders come from the two lower classes. Generally, they are characterized by a low level of education (58.4% did not complete high school), poor homes, and low incomes (of those for whom data was available, 63.3% had yearly incomes of less than $4,000)[10] which are acquired through either public or private assistance or through unskilled or semi-skilled manual work.

Since the variables that influence apprehension or omission by the police are so numerous, any explanations must be clearly labeled as plausible interpretations. First, the fact that most offenders from the higher social strata carry out their acts under low visibility would seem to be very important. Most departments are probably most interested in containing open "subcultural" homosexuality, public solicitation (especially of minors), and acts of a more aggravated nature. Typical law enforcement, therefore, strives to effect arrests through the use of plain-clothes detectives set up as decoys who may be solicited by overt homosexuals (Jacobs, 1963; Gallo et al., 1966; Schur, 1965: 80–81), through harassment of their known meeting places, such as "gay" bars (Gallo et al., 1966; Schur, 1965: 81), and through individual complaints. Homosexual activity

TABLE 1
Social Status of Offenders

Social Status	n	%
Upper-upper class	—	—
Lower-upper class	3	(2.8)
Upper-middle class	7	(6.5)
Lower-middle class	16	(14.8)
Upper-lower class	43	(39.8)
Lower-lower class	39	(36.1)
Total	108	(100)

which is carried on in a "discreet" manner is not likely to become known to the public, and if it does, it is not likely to produce strong discontent and complaints. Even when homosexual activity of this nature is known to the police, as long as it is not producing a negative societal reaction, they may view it as having less than serious social consequences and adopt what they interpret to be the public's attitude of "live and let live." Second, among those who are

suspected or known to have committed a homosexual act, those who possess additional qualities concurring with the stereotypic image of the homosexual are more likely to be labeled, rejected, and legally processed. Since lower-class homosexuals are more effeminate in mannerisms and appearance (Leznoff and Westley, 1955: 260), and since these attributes are an important part of the homosexual stereotype (Simmons, 1965), the lower-class homosexual is more likely to experience social rejection in the form of complaints to the police. Furthermore, complaints against persons possessing effeminate attributes may more frequently result in arrest and a formal charge since the judgments of the legal authorities regarding possible guilt may also be influenced by the popular stereotype. It should also be noted that even in the absence of complaints, effeminate mannerisms and appearance are obviously more likely to attract the direct attention of the police. And finally, there is at least a possibility that the higher-status homosexual can play blackmail fees (Gebhard et al., 1965: 354–355; Sherwin, 1966: 118), therefore avoiding exposure, use his power and influence with the legal authorities, or may simply be so well respected (even by the legal authorities) that he is relatively immune to legal processes.

When the social status of offenders was observed in relation to their legal treatment, the figures indicated that those from the lower classes received the more severe treatment. The relationship (shown in Table 2) indicates that 66.7% of the offenders from the lower-lower class, as compared with 25.6% from the upper-lower class, and with 7.7% from the middle class, received incarceration. Without controlling for any of the possible intervening variables, the figures in Table 2 indicate a very highly significant relationship between social status and legal treatment.

The question remains, however, as to whether offenders from the lower social strata received the more severe legal treatment because of more unfavorable legal factors related to their offense. In an attempt to partially answer this question, Table 3 shows a distribution of the sample, broken by status, on the possible determinants of more severe legal treatment. The figures show significant differences

TABLE 2

Legal Treatment and Social Status of Offenders

Legal Treatment	Social Status						Total
	Middle Class		Upper-Lower Class		Lower-Lower Class		
	n	%	n	%	n	%	
Incarceration	2	(7.7)	11	(25.6)	26	(66.7)	39
Probation	8	(30.8)	17	(39.5)	6	(15.4)	31
Fine or less	16	(61.5)	15	(34.9)	7	(17.9)	38
Total	26	(100)	43	(100)	39	(100)	108

$x^2 = 29.851$ with 4 d^f $P < .001$
$V = .372$

TABLE 3

Social Status and Determinants of More Severe Legal Treatment[a]

Determinants	Social Status						X^2	V
	Middle Class		Upper-Lower Class		Lower-Lower Class			
	n	%	n	%	n	%		
Total	26	(100)	43	(100)	39	(100)		
Prior offense record	8	(30.8)	27	(62.8)	33	(84.9)	19.340 with 2 d^f $P < .001$	.424
Object a minor	20	(76.9)	29	(67.4)	23	(59.0)	2.280 with 2 d^f NS	.145
Offender acted violently	2	(7.7)	6	(14.0)	7	(17.9)	1.372 with 2 d^f NS	.113
Object unwilling	7	(26.9)	11	(25.6)	15	(38.5)	1.812 with 2 d^f NS	.129
Act occurred in public	17	(65.4)	22	(51.2)	24	(61.5)	1.606 with 2 d^f NS	.122
Involving penetration	20	(76.9)	33	(76.7)	23	(59.0)	3.802 with 2 d^f NS	.188

[a.] Numbers and percentages total more than 100% because of multiple classifications.

among the classes only with regard to prior offense record. In these cases, the lower classes are more heavily represented. It should be noted, however, that although a disproportionately large number of the lower-class offenders have a prior criminal record, there is at least the possibility that the legal treatment initially given these offenders was influenced by their social status.

To provide for the possible interrelatedness of some of these items, offenses were scaled and divided into severe, moderate, and milder offense categories. These categories were then observed in relation to social status. The figures, represented in Table 4, show no significant differences among the classes on this combined item.

Next, each of the separate items and the combined item were held constant while the relationship between social status and legal treatment was reexamined within each of the analytically discerned categories. Table 5 shows the significance levels of the relationship after controlling for each of these items. The table shows that the relationship, although reduced in significance in some instances, was retained for all items. The chi-square value of the relationship was reduced for the first time to a ten percent probability level, however, on the

TABLE 4
Severity of Offense and Social Status of Offenders

| | Social Status | | | | | | |
| | Middle Class | | Upper-Lower Class | | Lower-Lower Class | | |
Severity Level	n	%	n	%	n	%	Total
Severe	11	(42.3)	21	(48.8)	17	(43.6)	49
Moderate	10	(38.5)	13	(30.2)	11	(28.2)	34
Milder	5	(19.2)	9	(20.9)	11	(28.2)	25
Total	26	(100)	43	(100)	39	(100)	108

$x^2 = 1.446$ with 4 d^f NS
$V = .081$

TABLE 5
Significance Levels for Relationship of Legal Treatment
and Social Status Controlling for Intervening Variables

Variable Controlled For	x^2	V
Prior offense record	10.838 with 4 d^f $P < .05$	.282
First offender	15.948 with 4 d^f $P < .01$	.446
Object a minor	19.268 with 4 d^f $P < .001$	.366
Object an adult	13.929 with 4 d^f $P < .01$	.440
Involving unwillingness or violence	19.117 with 4 d^f $P < .001$	.446
Involving consent	11.829 with 4 d^f $P < .05$	.316
Involving penetration	13.898 with 4 d^f $P < .01$	.302
Involving assault or solicitation	20.286 with 4 d^f $P < .001$	.563
Severe offense	18.200 with 4 d^f $P < .01$	.431
Moderate offense	8.374 with 4 d^f $P < .10$	.351
Milder offense	8.030 with 4 d^f $P < .10$	.401

moderate and milder offense items. Table 6 shows the relationship for all three severity categories. The figures show that, although the relationship appears to be statistically weakened in the moderate and milder offense categories, the differences are very slight and may be largely the result of a smaller number of observed cases in the latter two categories, rather than of any significant changes in the trend of legal treatment.

It may be concluded, then, that the hypothesis has been supported. The data show that a disproportionately large number of the homosexuals who are arrested and held for court are from the lower classes, and that these offenders receive more severe legal treatment than higher-status persons, even when guilty of roughly similar offenses. Since the data do not represent an exhaustive survey of all possible intervening variables, however, all explanations of the foregoing relationships must, again, be clearly labeled as plausible interpretations.

The economic factors which would appear to be operating in favor of the higher-status offender are presumably his ability to pay bail and finance effective legal counsel. Many lower-class defendants are unable to furnish bail and are, thus, more likely to be convicted and severely sentenced than are defendants charged with similar offenses who are free on bail. The jail defendant is under the handicap in that he looks guilty, and this is especially so for the defendant who is brought to court in custody, and is usually without a job to which he can return if placed on probation (Foote, 1955). A factor which could be empirically tested in this study, and may be related to the ability to finance effective legal counsel, was the time lapse between arrest and trial.

Table 7 shows the legal treatment and time lapse for offenders. The figures indicate that a delay in court proceedings was very likely to result in milder treatment. The relationship shows that only 19.4% of the offenders being tried during or after the fourth

TABLE 6
Legal Treatment and Social Status for Severity of Offense Categories

Legal Treatment	Middle Class		Upper-Lower Class		Lower-Lower Class		Total
	n	%	n	%	n	%	
Severe Offense:							
Incarceration	—	—	6	(28.6)	12	(70.6)	18
Probation	3	(27.3)	8	(38.1)	1	(5.9)	12
Fine or less	8	(72.7)	7	(33.3)	4	(23.5)	19
Total	11	(100)	21	(100)	17	(100)	49

$x^2 = 18.200$ with 4 d^f P < .01
V = .431

Moderate Offense:							
Incarceration	2	(20)	3	(23)	8	(72.7)	13
Probation	4	(40)	5	(38.5)	2	(18.2)	11
Fine or less	4	(40)	5	(38.5)	1	(9.1)	10
Total	10	(100)	13	(100)	11	(100)	34

$x^2 = 8.374$ with 4 d^f P < .10
V = .351

Milder Offense:							
Incarceration			2	(22.2)	6	(54.5)	8
Probation	1	(20)	4	(44.4)	3	(27.3)	8
Fine or less	4	(80)	3	(33.3)	2	(18.2)	9
Total	5	(100)	9	(100)	11	(100)	25

$x^2 = 8.030$ with 4 d^f P < .10
V = .401

TABLE 7
Legal Treatment of Offenders and Time Lapse between Arrest and Trial

Legal Treatment	Time Lapse Between Arrest and Trial							
	3 Months or Less		4 Months or More		Not Known		Total	
	n	%	n	%	n	%	n	%
Incarceration	25	(62.5)	13	(19.4)	1	(100)	39	(36.1)
Probation	7	(17.5)	24	(35.8)	—	—	31	(28.7)
Fine or less	8	(20.0)	30	(44.8)	—	—	38	(35.2)
Total	40	(100)	67	(100)	1	(100)	108	(100)

$x^2 = 20.330$ with 2 d^f P < .001
V = .436

month following arrest, as compared with 62.5% that were tried during the first three months, received incarceration. The figures, furthermore, show a reverse trend for those receiving probation or a fine or less. Further analysis of these data in Table 8 show that the higher-status offenders were those able to secure the delay in trial. The figures show that 84.6% of the offenders from the middle class, as compared with 72% from the upper-lower class and 35.9% from the lower-lower class were able to delay their trials beyond three months.

TABLE 8
Time Lapse between Arrest and Trial and Social Status of Offenders

| | Social Status | | | | | | |
| | Middle Class | | Upper-Lower Class | | Lower-Lower Class | | |
Time Lapse	n	%	n	%	n	%	Total
3 months or less	4	(15.4)	12	(28)	24	(61.5)	40
4 months or less	22	(84.6)	31	(72)	14	(35.9)	67
Not known	—		—		1	(2.5)	1
Total	26	(100)	43	(100)	39	(100)	108

$x^2 = 17.809$ with 2 d^f P < .001
V = .408

The foregoing data, then, show that the higher-status offender's ability to obtain delays in court proceedings may have been an important determinant of his legal treatment. These findings are not surprising, since a delay in court proceedings would enable the defense to better prepare its case. An additional element, and one that may be particularly relevant to emotionally charged crimes such as sex offenses, is that the delay may allow time for public discontent to die down. This would appear to be especially important in cases involving children, violence, or other aggravating circumstances which are likely to produce strong public resentment and pressure for a conviction and severe penalty.

Other factors which would also appear to be operating in favor of higher-status offenders are as follows: First, as has already been pointed out, higher-status homosexuals are not as effeminate in mannerisms and appearance. This factor may raise considerable doubt of guilt in the minds of prosecutors, judges, and jury members, since their judgments may be influenced by the popular homosexual stereotype. On the other hand, they may be convinced of the lower-class individual's guilt, since he is likely to possess such attributes. Second, since upper-strata socialization emphasizes training in the social graces, it is likely that these offenders will possess the ability to sell themselves more effectively when on trial. Third, since prosecutors, judges, and jury members having higher participation and influence are from the middle class (Strodtbeck, 1957), they are more likely to identify with these offenders. Putting themselves in the offender's predicament, they may be inclined toward a milder

legal treatment. Fourth, when higher-status individuals are found out, they are likely to suffer loss of status, prestige, and often jobs and incomes as well. As a result, there is sometimes a public feeling, shared possibly by judges and juries, to the effect that such persons have already paid for a substantial portion of their crime and will be deterred from future deviance by the mere fact of their appearance in court, their financial loss, and the disgrace and humiliation which they have suffered as a result of their conduct. On the other hand, judges and juries may feel presumably that lower-status offenders have no status to lose and therefore status loss cannot serve as either a punishment or a deterrent. And finally, a strong possibility exists that the courts may simply assume that the social stability (job, family, and the like) of the higher-status offenders will reduce the likelihood of future offenses and therefore give milder legal treatment. This would seem to be an especially high probability in jurisdictions with diagnostic centers, since their recommendation to the court may be influenced by such factors. In the jurisdiction from which this sample was drawn, such an influence should be operative only in the event that the defendant is found to be insane or guilty. In any event, it must be acknowledged that the offender's social status may influence the diagnostic center's evaluation and recommendation and ultimately the court's disposition of the case.

SUMMARY

This study has examined the relationship between the social status and legal treatment of adult male homosexual sex offenders. The variables controlled for were the offender's prior offense record, age of the youngest object, degree of consent, whether the act occurred in public, the type of act, and, finally, these interdependent variables (except prior offense record) were treated as one and labeled "severity of offense." The data, from case records of 108 offenders held for court, support the hypothesis in that they show a disproportionately large number of the offenders were from the lower classes and that these offenders received more severe legal treatment than higher-status persons, even when guilty of roughly similar offenses.

The fact that few of these offenders are from the middle class was accounted for by the probability that middle-class homosexuals carry out their acts under low visibility and do not possess the effeminate attributes which may attract public attention or persuade legal authorities of guilt. There also exists at least the possibility that middle-class offenders can pay blackmail, use their power to influence the police, or be so well respected that they are relatively immune to legal processes. The significant relationship which was found between the legal treatment and social status of offenders was accounted for by the presumably greater possibility of higher-status offenders being able to pay bail, finance effective legal counsel, present a favorable image when on trial, and to receive the empathy of middle-class persons judging them. Furthermore, those passing judgment may feel that middle-class offenders have paid for a substantial portion of their crime through the status loss which they are likely to have suffered, or that their social stability will reduce the likelihood of future offenses.

In conclusion, along with the variables considered here, future studies should attempt to acquire data on whether the defendant was released on bail, the quality of legal counsel, the different judges presiding over the trials, whether there was a jury trial, more detailed information on the prior offense record, the diagnostic center's recommendation to the court, and the degree to which the offender's appearance concurs with the popular homosexual stereotype. These factors presumably influence legal treatment and require further carefully controlled investigation.

FOOTNOTES

[1] Reporting on their study of a New England community, these authors point out that although a disproportionate number of arrests were of members of the two lowest classes, interviews with police indicated "that the same acts committed in the higher and lower classes resulted in fewer arrests for those who were better placed socially."

[2] This study of a small South Dakota town found that local police were expected to deal severely with lower-class delinquents on the theory that they come from bad stock and must be deterred through strict punishment, while offenders from the higher class are considered "accidental" or "queer" cases that do not reflect on their families and are consequently released after warning.

[3] These researchers found not only that respondents reported a large number of undetected violations and the number of violations differed little from one status level to another, but also that middle-class respondents committed the most serious offenses.

[4] In addition to homosexual acts, sodomy laws cover certain acts between heterosexual partners, acts with animals, fowls, or corpses, and, in one or two states, mutual masturbation or incitement to masturbation. These laws do not display the degree of specificity usually required in the statutory definitions of crime (for a discussion of the laws, see Bowman and Engle, 1956; St John-Stevas, 1961).

[5] This jurisdiction had a population size of more than one million in 1960.

[6] In classifying offenders by social status, the system of six classes was used. The scales used are modifications of those used by Warner et al. (1949: 123, 154) in the Jonesville study. The factors scaled are, respectively, occupation, education, income source, and dwelling area.

[7] The following is a generally inclusive list of treatments given offenders, which are ranked from the most severe to the very mild: (1) incarceration; (2) commitment to a state institution for the criminally insane, mentally ill, or mentally defective; (3) probation with private or outpatient psychiatric treatment; (4) probation without an order of psychiatric treatment; (5) fine; (6) suspended sentence; (7) acquitted; and (8) case ignored, not prosecuted or dismissed because of insufficient evidence or lack of sufficiency in the point of law of a pleading or state of facts alleged.

[8] This measure is defined as: $V^2 = \dfrac{x^2}{N \text{ Min } (r\text{-}1,\, c\text{-}1)} = \dfrac{\phi^2}{M\,(r\text{-}1,\, c\text{-}1)}$. V is used here since it can attain unity even in those instances when the number of rows and columns are not equal.

[9] In measuring severity of offense, the following index was used: (a) age status of youngest object: (minor; adult); (b) degree of consent: (involving violence; unwillingness [includes cases in which the object was a police officer or child under age 11]; consent); (c) setting of the act: (public; private); (d) type of act: (penetration of the mouth or anus; assault to perform a homosexual act [includes masturbation]; public solicitation).

[10] The total yearly income was not obtained for eighteen (16.7%) of the offenders studied.

REFERENCES

AKERS, R. L. (1964) "Socioeconomic status and delinquent behavior: a retest." J. of Research in Crime and Delinquency (January): 38–46.

AXELRAD, S. (1952) "Negro and white institutionalized delinquents." Amer. J. of Sociology 57 (May): 569–574.

BOWMAN, K. M. and B. ENGLE (1956) "A psychiatric evaluation of laws of homosexuality." Amer. J. of Psychiatry 112 (February): 577–583.

CALDWELL, M. G. (1931) "The economic status of the families of delinquent boys in Wisconsin." Amer. J. of Sociology 37 (September): 231–239.

EMPEY, L. T. and M. L. ERICKSON (1966) "Hidden delinquency and social status." Social Forces 4 (June): 546–554.

FOOTE, C. (1955) "The bail system and equal justice." Federal Probation 19 (September): 43–48.

GALLO, J. J. (1965–1966) "The consenting adult homosexual and the law." UCLA Law Rev. 13: 686–742.

GEBHARD, P. H., J. H. GAGNON, W. B. POMEROY, and C. V. CHRISTENSON (1965) Sex Offenders. New York: Harper & Row.

GLUECK, S. and E. T. GLUECK (1934) 1000 Juvenile Delinquents. Cambridge, Mass.: Harvard Univ. Press.

GOLDMAN, N. (1964) "The disposition of juvenile arrests by urban police," pp. 577–590 in E. W. Burgess and D. J. Bogue (eds.) Contributions to Urban Sociology. Chicago: Univ. of Chicago Press.

JACOBS, H. (1963) "Decoy enforcement of homosexual laws." Univ. of Pennsylvania Law Rev. 112 (December): 259–284.

KINSEY, A. C., W. B. POMEROY and C. E. MARTIN (1948) Sexual Behavior in the Human Male. Philadelphia: W. B. Saunders.

LEMERT, E. M. and J. ROSBERG (1948) "The administration of justice to minority groups in Los Angeles County." Univ. of California Pubns. in Culture and Society 2: 1–28.

LEZNOFF, M. and W. A. WESTLEY (1955) "The homosexual community." Social Problems 3 (July): 257–263.

MYERHOFF, H. L. and B. G. MYERHOFF (1964) "Field observation of middle class gangs." Social Forces 42 (March): 328–336.

NYE, I., J. F. SHORT, Jr., and V. J. OLSEN (1958) "Socioeconomic status and delinquent behavior." Amer. J. of Sociology 63 (January): 381–389.

SCHUR, E. M. (1965) Crimes Without Victims. Englewood Cliffs, N. J.: Prentice-Hall.

SHAW, C. and H. D. MCKAY (1943) Juvenile Delinquency and Urban Areas. Chicago: Univ. of Chicago Press.

SHERWIN, R. V. (1966) "The law and sexual relationships." J. of Social Issues 22 (April): 109–122.

SIMMONS, J. L. (1965) "Public stereotypes of deviants." Social Problems 13 (Fall): 223–232.

ST JOHN-STEVAS, N. (1961) Life, Death and the Law. London: Eyre & Spottiswoods.

STRODTBECK, F. L. (1957) "Social status in jury deliberations." Amer. Soc. Rev. 22 (December): 713–719.

SUTHERLAND, E. H. (1949) White Collar Crime. New York: Dryden Press.

SZASZ, T. S. (1965) "Legal and moral aspects of homosexuality," pp. 124–139 in J. Marmor (ed.) Sexual Inversion. New York: Basic Books.

——— (1963) Law, Liberty and Psychiatry. New York: Macmillan.

USEEM, J., P. TANGENT, and R. USEEM (1942) "Stratification in a prairie town." Amer. Soc. Rev. 7 (June): 331–342.

WARNER, W. L. and P. S. LUNT (1941) The Social Life of a Modern Community. New Haven: Yale Univ. Press.

WARNER, W. L., M. MEEKER, and K. EELLS (1949) Social Class in America. Chicago: Science Research Associated.

PART 3   THE SOCIAL ORGANIZATION OF CRIMINAL LAW ENFORCEMENT

That systematic bias in law enforcement is not intentional should be perfectly obvious. But, as we saw in the article, "The Saints and the Roughnecks," even so elementary a decision as assessing the meaning of the demeanor of an arrested youth, the police and other law enforcement personnel invariably give "the break" to people who possess middle class symbols and middle class ways of doing things. A "tough" or "cool" demeanor on the part of a youth is likely to be interpreted as meaning that the youth is a more serious and recalcitrant delinquent than is a youth who appears concerned, contrite, and penitent. Yet one could certainly argue on sociological grounds that such an assumption is not at all justified. The urban Black culture, for example, certainly encourages the expression of a cool posture for the male irrespective of his involvement in illegal behavior. The middle class culture, by contrast, encourages at least a show of respect for authority and an appearance of compliance with middle class values. These differences in demeanor, then, mean in effect that a lower class youth, especially a Black lower class youth, is considerably more likely to be processed than is a middle class youth.

Furthermore, the transgressions of lower class persons are much more *visible* than the transgressions of middle class persons. Crowded living conditions create an environment in which most behavior, even that which occurs in one's own home, is susceptible to screening by the neighbors and by law enforcement officials. Domestic disputes, drinking to excess, and other quasi-illegal acts are much more likely to be seen in the lower classes than in the middle classes. Even the delinquent acts of juveniles are most visible among lower class persons than among middle class persons. Middle class adolescents generally have access to automobiles; many of them have their own cars. And the automobile provides an avenue of escape from the scrutiny of the law enforcers: Drinking can be done in out-of-the-way places; delinquent acts can be committed in neighboring communities rather than near one's own home. The lower class adolescent, by contrast, will find such mobility difficult to manage. If he drinks, he must do so in an alley; if he gambles, he is not protected by the security of his parents' home; indeed, for the urban lower class adolescent even so private an act as sexual relations is likely to be carried out in relatively more public arenas than is the case for the middle class adolescent who has the privacy at least of his car.

Gambling is an excellent example of the difference in visibility for adults as well as for adolescents. In a large house a group of middle class men wishing to gamble can find a room where other members of the family will not be disturbed by the game. In a small apartment with a large number of people, the lower class male will have less opportunity to gamble in his own home. He is more likely to find an alleyway or the back room of a public place a more convenient place to gamble. But the middle class person is protected from scrutiny by the police in the privacy of his own home, whereas the lower class gambler is exposing himself to the sanctions of the legal system by gambling in public.

The deviance of the poor is more visible in a diversity of subtle ways. Being more frequently involved with governmental agencies, such as those that dispense welfare, vastly increases the possibility of deviance being officially discovered. In their study of a police department's morals detail, Skolnick and Woodworth found that the discovery of statutory-rape cases by the police was largely dependent on referrals from welfare agencies:

> The influence of poverty on the discovery of statutory rapes is obvious; the largest single source of reports is from the family support division (40%). At the time of the study ADC aid could be given to a mother only if her real property was worth less than $5,000 and her personal property less than $600. One social worker reported that most applicants possessed no real property; those who had originally owned such property had exhausted its value prior to applying for aid. Thus, *statutory rape is punished mainly among the poor who become visible by applying for maternity aid from welfare authorities.A* (Emphasis added)

Official statistics are generally interpreted as evidence that problems with drinking, fighting, and gambling are concentrated in lower class areas. Yet these statistics do not tell a story of differences in the frequency or seriousness of these acts; they simply reflect the fact that middle class affluence affords a shield against public scrutiny which is not enjoyed by members of the lower class. The weight of the evidence indicates that to a significant degree the legal system's processing of law violators involves the arrest and prosecution of lower class persons for doing in public what middle and upper class persons do in private.

Stinchcombe has argued that the institution of privacy is an effective barrier to legal intervention because it is a strongly held value in America.B But there is more involved in the differential application of the statutes than compli-

PART 3   THE SOCIAL ORGANIZATION OF CRIMINAL LAW ENFORCEMENT

ance with an institutional norm protecting privacy. Law enforcement agencies do not hesitate to violate this and a host of other norms when such violation is organizationally rewarding. Thus we find the police violating the privacy of slum dwellers with considerable regularity; we find law enforcement agents resorting to the illegal use of violence against politically impotent offenders; and we find a patterned and widespread use of violence by police to obtain confessions. Law enforcement agencies systematically violate strongly held norms of behavior when it is in their best interests to do so. The failure of the legal system to exploit the potential source of offenses that is offered by middle and upper class law violators does not derive from the strength of the institution of privacy; it derives instead from the very rational choice on the part of the legal system to pursue those violators that the community will reward them for pursuing and to ignore those violators who have the capability of causing trouble for the agencies.

But the ways in which the legal system and crime interact to create exceptions to this general maxim of social class discrimination are as important sociologically as is the general pattern. First, of course, a middle or upper class citizen may commit an act sufficiently heinous so that he loses his power to interfere with the smooth running of the law enforcement machinery. A well-to-do offender will, nevertheless, receive the benefit of mercy at every step of the criminal-legal process. The arresting officer will be courteous, the prosecutor will inform the offender of his legal rights, and the judge and jury will be understanding and lenient in the sentence. But if the offense is serious enough, the legal system will generally be rewarded for having brought the guilty party to trial. Indeed, the risk of not getting a guilty conviction may be greater than when a bum is involved, but the rewards are greater as well. The public, the news media, and colleagues will be much readier to praise the officers, prosecutors, and judges who find a wealthy person guilty of committing a serious offense than they will the officer who has arrested the same alcoholic who has been in and out of jail a hundred times.

From the standpoint of the administration of criminal law, a far more important exception to the general maxim that the law is enforced against lower but not middle and upper class persons is the special relationship which emerges between organized and professional criminals and the legal system. Despite the fact that organized and professional criminals operate in, and are members of, the lower class, these groups generally enjoy considerable immunity from the imposition of legal sanctions. How this works is spelled out in the following articles.

11

Police Corruption in New York City

KNAPP COMMISSION

THE EXTENT OF POLICE CORRUPTION

We found corruption to be widespread. It took various forms depending upon the activity involved, appearing at its most sophisticated among plainclothesmen assigned to enforcing gambling laws. In the five plainclothes divisions where our investigations were concentrated we found a strikingly standardized pattern of corruption. Plainclothesmen, participating in what is known in police parlance as a "pad," collected regular biweekly or monthly payments amounting to as much as $3,500 from each of the gambling establishments in the area under their jurisdiction, and divided the take in equal shares. The monthly share per man (called the "nut") ranged from $300 to $400 in midtown Manhattan to $1,500 in Harlem. When supervisors were involved they received a share and a half. A newly assigned plainclothesman was not entitled to his share for about two months, while he was checked out for reliability, but the earnings lost by the delay were made up to

Source: Report by the Commission to Investigate Allegations of Police Corruption in New York City, Whitman Knapp, Chairman, August 3, 1972. By permission of the authors and publisher.

him in the form of two months' severance pay when he left the division.

Evidence before us led us to the conclusion that the same pattern existed in the remaining divisions which we did not investigate in depth. This conclusion was confirmed by events occurring before and after the period of our investigation. Prior to the Commission's existence, exposures by former plainclothesman Frank Serpico had led to indictments or departmental charges against nineteen plainclothesmen in a Bronx division for involvement in a pad where the nut was $800. After our public hearings had been completed, an investigation conducted by the Kings County District Attorney and the Department's Internal Affairs Division—which investigation neither the Commission nor its staff had even known about—resulted in indictments and charges against thirty-seven Brooklyn plainclothesmen who had participated in a pad with a nut of $1,200. The manner of operation of the pad involved in each of these situations was in every detail identical to that described at the Commission hearings, and in each almost every plainclothesman in the division, including supervisory lieutenants, was implicated.

PART 3   THE SOCIAL ORGANIZATION OF CRIMINAL LAW ENFORCEMENT

Corruption in narcotics enforcement lacked the organization of the gambling pads, but individual payments—known as "scores"—were commonly received and could be staggering in amount. Our investigation, a concurrent probe by the State Investigation Commission, and prosecutions by federal and local authorities all revealed a pattern whereby corrupt officers customarily collected scores in substantial amounts from narcotics violators. These scores were either kept by the individual officer or shared with a partner and, perhaps, a superior officer. They ranged from minor shakedowns to payments of many thousands of dollars, the largest narcotics payoff uncovered in our investigation having been $80,000. According to information developed by the SIC and in recent federal investigations, the size of this score was by no means unique.

Corruption among detectives assigned to general investigative duties also took the form of shakedowns of individual targets of opportunity. Although these scores were not in the huge amounts found in narcotics, they not infrequently came to several thousand dollars.

Uniformed patrolmen assigned to street duties were not found to receive money on nearly so grand or organized a scale, but the large number of small payments they received present an equally serious if less dramatic problem. Uniformed patrolmen, particularly those assigned to radio patrol cars, participated in gambling pads more modest in size than those received by plainclothes units and received regular payments from construction sites, bars, grocery stores, and other business establishments. These payments were usually made on a regular basis to sector car patrolmen and on a haphazard basis to others. While individual payments to uniformed men were small, mostly under $20, they were often so numerous as to add substantially to a patrolman's income. Other less regular payments to uniformed patrolmen included those made by after-hours bars, bottle clubs, tow trucks, motorists, cab drivers, parking lots, prostitutes, and defendants wanting to fix their cases in court. Another practice found to be widespread was the payment of gratuities by policemen to other policemen to expedite normal police procedures or to gain favorable assignments.

Sergeants and lieutenants who were so inclined participated in the same kind of corruption as the men they supervised. In addition, some sergeants had their own pads from which patrolmen were excluded.

Although the Commission was unable to develop hard evidence establishing that officers above the rank of lieutenant received payoffs, considerable circumstantial evidence and some testimony so indicated. Most often when a superior officer is corrupt, he uses a patrolman as his "bagman" who collects for him and keeps a percentage of the take. Because the bagman may keep the money for himself, although he claims to be collecting for his superior, it is extremely difficult to determine with any accuracy when the superior actually is involved.

Of course, not all policemen are corrupt. If we are to exclude such petty infractions as free meals, an appreciable number do not engage in any corrupt activities. Yet, with extremely rare exceptions, even those who themselves engage in no corrupt activities are involved in corruption in the sense that they take no steps to prevent what they know or suspect to be going on about them.

It must be made clear that—in a little over a year with a staff having as few as two and never more than twelve field investigators—we did not examine every precinct in the Department. Our conclusion that corruption is widespread throughout the Department is based on the fact that information supplied to us by hundreds of sources within and without the Department was consistently borne out by specific observations made in areas we were able to investigate in detail.

THE NATURE AND SIGNIFICANCE OF POLICE CORRUPTION

Corruption, although widespread, is by no means uniform in degree. Corrupt policemen have been described as falling into two basic categories: "meat-eaters" and "grass-eaters." As the names might suggest, the meat-eaters are those policemen who, like Patrolman William Phillips who testified at our hearings, aggressively misuse their police powers for personal gain. The grass-eaters simply accept the payoffs that the happenstances of police work throw their way. Although the meat-eaters get the huge payoffs that make the headlines, they represent a small percentage of all corrupt policemen. The truth is, the vast majority of policemen on the take don't deal in huge amounts of graft.

And yet, grass-eaters are the heart of the problem. Their great numbers tend to make corruption "respectable." They also tend to encourage the code of silence that brands anyone who exposes corruption a traitor. At the time our investigation began, any policeman violating the code did so at his peril. The result was described in our interim report: "The rookie who comes into the Department is faced with the situation where it is easier for him to become corrupt than to remain honest."

More importantly, although meat-eaters can and have been individually induced to make their peace with society, the grass-eaters may be more easily reformed. We believe that, given proper leadership and support, many police who have slipped into corruption would exchange their illicit income for the satisfaction of belonging to a corruption-free Department in which they could take genuine pride.

The problem of corruption is neither new, nor confined to the police. Reports of prior investigations into police corruption, testimony taken by the Commission, and opinions of informed persons both within and without the Department make it abundantly clear that police corruption has been a problem for many years. Investigations have occurred on the average of once in twenty years since before the turn of the century, and yet conditions exposed by one investigation seem substantially unchanged when the next one makes its report. This doesn't mean that the police have a monopoly on corruption. On the contrary, in every area where police corruption exists it is paralleled by corruption in other agencies of government, in industry and labor, and in the professions.

Our own mandate was limited solely to the police. There are sound reasons for such a special concern with police corruption. The police have a unique place in our society. The policeman is expected to "uphold the law" and "keep the peace." He is charged with everything from traffic control to riot control. He is expected to protect our lives and our property. As a result, society gives him special powers and prerogatives, which include the right and obligation to bear arms, along with the authority to take away our liberty by arresting us.

Symbolically, his role is even greater. For most people, the policeman is the law. To them, the law is administered by the patrolman on the beat and the captain in the station house. Little wonder that the public becomes aroused and alarmed when the police are charged with corruption or are shown to be corrupt.

DEPARTMENTAL ATTITUDES TOWARD POLICE CORRUPTION

Although this special concern is justified, public preoccupation with police corruption as opposed to corruption in other agencies of government inevitably seems unfair to the policeman. He believes that he is unjustly blamed for the results of corruption in other parts of the criminal-justice system. This sense of unfairness intensifies the sense of isolation and hostility to which the nature of police work inevitably gives rise.

Feelings of isolation and hostility are experienced by policemen not just in New York, but everywhere. To understand these feelings one must appreciate an important characteristic of any metropolitan police department, namely an extremely intense group loyalty. When properly understood, this group loyalty can be used in the fight against corruption. If misunderstood or ignored, it can undermine anticorruption activities.

Pressures that give rise to this group loyalty include the danger to which policemen are constantly exposed and the hostility they encounter from society at large. Everyone agrees that a policeman's life is a dangerous one, and that his safety, not to mention his life, can depend on his ability to rely on a fellow officer in a moment of crisis. It is less generally realized that the policeman works in a sea of hostility. This is true, not only in high crime areas, but throughout the City. Nobody, whether a burglar or a Sunday motorist, likes to have his activities interfered with. As a result, most citizens, at one time or another, regard the police with varying degrees of hostility. The policeman feels, and naturally often returns, this hostility.

Two principal characteristics emerge from this group loyalty: suspicion and hostility directed at any outside interference with the Department, and an intense desire to be proud of the Department. This mixture of hostility and pride has created what the Commission has found to be the most serious road-block to a rational attack upon police corruption: a stubborn refusal at all levels of the Department to acknowledge that a serious problem exists.

The interaction of stubbornness, hostility, and pride has given rise to the so-called "rotten-apple" theory. According to this theory, which bordered on official Department doctrine, any policeman found to be corrupt must promptly be denounced as a rotten apple in an otherwise clean barrel. It must never be admitted that his individual corruption may be symptomatic of underlying disease.

This doctrine was bottomed on two basic premises: First, the morale of the Department requires that there be no official recognition of corruption, even though practically all members of the Department know it is in truth extensive; second, the Department's public image and effectiveness require official denial of this truth.

The rotten-apple doctrine has in many ways been a basic obstacle to meaningful reform. To begin with, it reinforced and gave respectability to the code of silence. The official view that the Department's image and morale forbade public disclosure of the extent of corruption inhibited any officer who wished to disclose corruption and justified any who preferred to remain silent. The doctrine also made difficult, if not impossible, any meaningful attempt at managerial reform. A high command unwilling to acknowledge that the problem of corruption is extensive cannot very well argue that drastic changes are necessary to deal with that problem. Thus neither the Mayor's Office nor the Police Department took adequate steps to see that such changes were made when the need for them was indicated by the charges made by Officers Frank Serpico and David Durk in 1968. This was demonstrated in the Commission's second set of public hearings in December 1971.

Finally, the doctrine made impossible the use of one of the most effective techniques for dealing with any entrenched criminal activity, namely persuading a participant to help provide evidence against his partners in crime. If a corrupt policeman is merely an isolated rotten apple, no reason can be given for not exposing him the minute he is discovered. If, on the other hand, it is acknowledged that a corrupt officer is only one part of an apparatus of corruption, common sense dictates that every effort should be made to enlist the offender's aid in providing the evidence to destroy the apparatus.

THE COMMISSION'S ACTIONS

The Commission examined and rejected the premises upon which the rotten-apple doctrine rested. We concluded that there was no justification for fearing that public acknowledgment of the extent of corruption would damage the image and effectiveness of the Department. We are convinced that instead of damaging its image a realistic attitude toward corruption could only enhance the Department's credibility. The conditions described in the Commission's public hearings came as no surprise to the large numbers of City residents who had experienced them for years. If then, the Department makes it a point to acknowledge corrupt conditions the public already knows to exist, it can hardly damage its image. On the contrary, it can only promote confidence in the Department's good-faith desire to deal with those conditions.

The Commission looked at the question of morale in much the same way. We did not—and do not—believe that the morale of the average policeman is enhanced by a commanding officer who insists on denying facts that the policeman knows to be true. We believed—and continue to believe—that such false denials can only undercut the policeman's confidence in his commander. If a policeman listens to his commander solemnly deny the existence of an obvious corrupt situation, the policeman can draw only one of two conclusions: either the commander is hopelessly naive or he is content to let the corruption continue.

Once we had rejected the premises of the rotten-apple doctrine, the Commission determined to employ one of the techniques that adherence to the doctrine had made impossible, namely to persuade formerly corrupt police officers to work with us in providing evidence of continuing corruption.

The mere decision to use the technique did not automatically produce a body of officers able and eager to assist us in this manner. Indeed, knowledgeable persons assured us that the code of silence was so strong that we would never find a corrupt officer who could be persuaded to assist in exposing corruption. We ultimately did persuade four officers, including Detective Robert L. Leuci and Patrolmen William Phillips, Edward Droge and Alfonso Jannotta to undertake undercover work. Of these, all but Detective Leuci did so under the compulsion of having been caught by Commission investigators. Patrolmen Phillips and Droge testified at public hearings held in October 1971. Patrolman Jannotta was unavailable due to illness at the time of the hearings. The information disclosed by Detective Leuci was so vital that we did not, since our time was limited, feel justified in keeping it to ourselves. Leuci and the Commission staff members who had debriefed him and worked with him on his initial undercover operations were turned over to the federal government for the long-term investigation which was required. Leuci's work as a federal undercover agent is now resulting in the series of important narcotics-related indictments being obtained by United States Attorney Whitney North Seymour, Jr.

Success in persuading these officers to assist in the investigation was a first step in demonstrating that the rotten-apple doctrine was invalid. Patrolman Phillips' three days of testimony about systematic corruption in various parts of the Department, corroborated by tape-recorded conversations with many police officers and others, was in itself enough to make the doctrine seem untenable. Patrolman Droge described how departmental pressures gradually converted an idealistic rookie into an increasingly bold finder of bribes and payoffs. Former Patrolman Waverly Logan, who volunteered to testify about corruption in which he had been involved, corroborated Droge's testimony and went on to tell about policemen in Harlem who received monthly as much as $3,000 each in narcotics graft. Patrolman Logan also introduced the Commission to two addicts who were willing to work with us in obtaining evidence to corroborate these assertions. The Commission's work with these addicts produced movies and recorded conversations of policemen selling narcotics. Some of the narcotics were paid for with merchandise the policemen believed to be stolen. Captain Daniel McGowan, a police officer of unquestioned integrity and experienced in anticorruption work, testified that the picture of corruption presented by Patrolmen Phillips, Droge, and Logan was an accurate one. In addition, there was testimony from, among others, a Harlem gambler, Commission agents describing their investigations, and witnesses in the business community revealing corrupt police dealings with the hotel and construction industries. Recorded conversations and movies documented instances of police corruption, including gambling and narcotics payoffs, fixing court cases, and shaking down a tow-truck operator. The cumulative effect of these two weeks of testimony made it not only unrealistic but absurd for anyone thereafter to adhere to the rotten-apple doctrine, either publicly or privately.

The doctrine did not die easily. Institutional pressures within the Department seemed to force the high command to continue giving lip service to the doctrine even when speaking out against corruption. Commissioner Murphy in his early statements about corruption regularly included a pointed statement indicting that the corruption in the Department was limited to a few officers. On one occasion he went so far as to imply that there were no more than about 300 corrupt police officers in the entire Department. After Patrolman Phillips had completed two of his three days of testimony at our public hearings, Commissioner Murphy found it necessary to discount his testimony of widespread corruption, referring to him as a "rogue cop."

However, one week later, after Phillips had completed his testimony and had been followed by Patrolmen Logan and Droge and others, the Department, speaking through First Deputy Commissioner William H. T. Smith, forthrightly rejected the rotten-apple doctrine by name. Smith defined it as standing for the proposition that "police departments are essentially free of corruption except for the presence of a few corrupt officers who have managed to slip into police service and also into key assignments such as gambling investigations, despite rigorously applied screening procedures designed to keep them out." He said that traditional police strategy had been to react defensively whenever a scandal arose by "promising to crack down on graft, to go after the 'rogue cops,' to get rid of 'rotten apples.'" Smith said the Department now rejected this approach "not just on principle, but because as a way of controlling corruption it had utterly failed." He acknowledged that the result of adherence to the theory had been a breakdown in public confidence: ". . . they [the public] are sick of 'bobbing for rotten apples' in the police barrel. They want an entirely new barrel that will never again become contaminated."

CHANGING DEPARTMENTAL ATTITUDES

The public hearings, in addition to helping bring about official abandonment of the rotten-apple doctrine, have had dramatic effect on the way members of the Department discuss corruption. This change was graphically described shortly after our hearings by former Assistant Chief Inspector Sidney C. Cooper in colorful language: "Not very long ago we talked about corruption with all the enthusiasm of a group of little old ladies talking about venereal disease. Now there is a little more open discussion about combatting graft as if it were a public health problem." In short, the first barrier to a realistic look at corruption has been overcome: the problem has been officially, and unofficially, acknowledged.

Some time after the public hearings were over, it was revealed that Detective Leuci had been doing undercover work for the federal government for over a year and a half, and that he had been doing it with both the knowledge and protection of the Department's high command. News also began to spread throughout the Department that other formerly corrupt policemen were doing undercover work for the Department's Internal Affairs Division and for at least one district attorney's office. These revelations had considerable impact, both direct and indirect, upon attitudes toward corruption within the Department.

To put the direct impact in proper perspective, it should be pointed out that any criminal activity, within a police department or elsewhere, cannot thrive unless all of its participants are able to main-

tain confidence in each other. Patrolman Phillips' testimony made this very clear. In testifying about his own corrupt activities, he described how he could, by making a few telephone calls within five or ten minutes, "check out" the reliability of any other officer whose assistance he might require in a corrupt enterprise. By way of illustration, he described instances where he had been similarly checked out while doing undercover work for the Commission. This ability to check out, and rely upon, an officer with whom one has had no previous contact rested on the assumption—unchallenged before the advent of our Commission—that no police officer who had once become involved in corruption could ever be persuaded to disclose the corruption of others. The actions of Detective Leuci and Patrolmen Phillips and Droge and of others as yet unnamed who are presently working undercover have undermined this assumption.

Even more important was the indirect effect produced by general knowledge that the undercover activities of these formerly corrupt policemen had been known to—and protected by—the Department's high command. Traditionally, the rank and file have shown a deep cynicism, well justified by history, concerning pronouncements of new police commissioners. They carefully examine the new commissioner's every word and action, searching for "messages": Does he mean business? Can he stand up against institutional pressures?

The initial lack of clarity in Commissioner Murphy's statements on the rotten-apple theory and his "rogue cop" reaction to the first widely publicized defiance of the code of silence were interpreted by some as suggesting a lack of commitment to total war on corruption. However, the Department's final repudiation of the doctrine, and the general knowledge that the Department was using and protecting policemen who had agreed to do undercover work, gave reassurance to the doubters.

In short, we believe that the Department's recent reactions to the Commission's activities have promoted realistic self-criticism within the Department. This spirit of self-criticism is an encouraging sign. For one thing, it is becoming less unusual for police officers to report evidence of police corruption. If this tendency continues, the day may be approaching when the rookie coming into the Department will not be pressured toward corruption, but can count on finding support for his desire to remain honest.

The present situation is quite like that existing at the close of previous investigations. A considerable momentum for reform has been generated, but not enough time has elapsed to reverse attitudes that have been solidifying for many years in the minds of both the public and the police.

After previous investigations, the momentum was allowed to evaporate.

The question now is: Will history repeat itself? Or does society finally realize that police corruption is a problem that must be dealt with and not just talked about once every twenty years?

Both immediate and long-term actions are mandatory. The reforms already initiated within the Department must be completed and expanded; there must be changes, both legislative and administrative, to curb pressures toward police corruption and to facilitate its control; and the momentum generated by the events before and during the life of this Commission must be maintained.

12

Vice, Corruption, Bureaucracy, and Power

WILLIAM J. CHAMBLISS

I. INTRODUCTION[1]

At the turn of the century Lincoln Steffens made a career and helped elect a president by exposing corruption in American cities.[2] In more recent years the task of exposure has fallen into the generally less daring hands of social scientists who, unlike their journalistic predecessors, have gathered their information from police departments, attorney generals' offices, and grand jury records.[3] Unfortunately, this difference in source of information has probably distorted the descriptions of organized crime and may well have led to premature acceptance of the Justice Department's long-espoused view regarding the existence of a national criminal organization.[4] It almost certainly has led to an over-emphasis on the *criminal* in organized crime and a corresponding de-emphasis on *corruption* as an institutionalized component of America's legal-political system.[5] Concomitantly, it has obscured perception of the degree to which the structure of America's law and politics creates and perpetuates syndicates that supply the vices in our major cities.

Source: "Vice, Corruption, Bureaucracy, and Power," *Wisconsin Law Review*, Vol. 1971, No. 4, pp. 1130–1155. By permission of the author and publisher.

Getting into the bowels of the city, rather than just the records and IBM cards of the bureaucracies, brings the role of corruption into sharp relief. Organized crime becomes not something that exists outside law and government but is instead a creation of them, or perhaps more accurately, a hidden but nonetheless integral part of the governmental structure. The people most likely to be exposed by public inquiries (whether conducted by the FBI, a grand jury, or the Internal Revenue Service) may officially be outside of government, but the cabal of which they are a part is organized around, run by, and created in the interests of economic, legal, and political elites.

Study of Rainfall West (a pseudonym), the focus of this analysis of the relationship between vice and the political and economic system, dramatically illustrates the interdependency. The cabal that manages the vices is composed of important businessmen, law enforcement officers, political leaders, and a member of a major trade union. Working for, and with, this cabal of respectable community members is a staff which coordinates the daily activities of prostitution, gambling, bookmaking, the sale and distribution of drugs, and other vices.

Representatives from each of these groups comprising the political and economic power centers of the community, meet regularly to distribute profits, discuss problems, and make the necessary organizational and policy decisions essential to the maintenance of a profitable, trouble-free business.

A. Data collection The data reported in this paper were gathered over a period of seven years, from 1962 to 1969. Most came from interviews with persons who were members of either the vice syndicate, law enforcement agencies, or both. The interviews ranged in intensity from casual conversations to extended interviewing, complete with tape recording, at frequent intervals over the full seven years of the study. In addition, I participated in many, though not all, of the vices that comprise the cornerstone upon which corruption of the law enforcement agencies is laid.

There is, of course, considerable latitude for discretion on my part as to what I believe ultimately characterizes the situation. Obviously not everyone told the same story, nor did I give equal credibility to all information acquired. The story that does emerge, however, most closely coincides with my own observations and with otherwise inexplicable facts. I am confident that the data are accurate, valid, and reliable; but this cannot be demonstrated by pointing to unbiased sampling, objective measures, and the like for, alas, in this type of research such procedures are impossible.

B. The setting: Rainfall West Rainfall West is practically indistinguishable from any other city of a million population. The conspicuous bulk of the population—the middle class—shares with its contemporaries everywhere a smug complacency and a firm belief in the intrinsic worth of the area and the city. Their particular smugness may be exaggerated due to relative freedom from the urban blight that is so often the fate of larger cities and to the fact that Rainfall West's natural surroundings attract tourists, thereby providing the citizenry with confirmation of their faith that this is, indeed, a "chosen land!"[6]

However, an invisible, although fairly large minority of the population, do not believe they live in the promised land. These are the inhabitants of the slums and ghettos that make up the center of the city. Camouflaging the discontent of the center are urban renewal programs which ring the slums with brick buildings and skyscrapers. But satisfaction is illusory; it requires only a slight effort to get past this brick and mortar and into the not-so-enthusiastic city center—a marked contrast to the wildly bubbling civic center located less than a mile away. Despite the ease of access, few of those living in the suburbs and working in the area surrounding the slums take the time to go where the action is. Those who do go for specific reasons: to bet on a football game, to find a prostitute, to see a dirty movie, or to obtain a personal loan that would be unavailable from conventional financial institutions.

II. BUREAUCRATIC CORRUPTION AND ORGANIZED CRIME: A STUDY IN SYMBIOSIS

Laws prohibiting gambling, prostitution, pornography, drug use, and high interest rates on personal loans are laws about which there is a conspicuous lack of consensus. Even persons who agree that such behavior is improper and should be controlled by law disagree on the proper legal response. Should persons found guilty of committing such acts be imprisoned, or counselled? Reflecting this dissension, large groups of people, some with considerable political power, insist on their right to enjoy the pleasures of vice without interference from the law.

In Rainfall West, those involved in providing gambling and other vices enjoy pointing out that their services are profitable because of the demand for them by members of the respectable community. Prostitutes work in apartments which are on the fringes of the lower class area of the city, rather than in the heart of the slums, precisely because they must maintain an appearance of ecological respectability so that their clients will not feel contaminated by poverty. While professional pride may stimulate exaggeration on the part of the prostitutes, their verbal reports are always to the effect that "all" of their clients are "very important people." My own observations of the comings and goings in several apartment houses where prostitutes work generally verified the girls' claims. Of some fifty persons seen going to prostitutes' rooms in apartment houses, only one was dressed in anything less casual than a business suit.

Observations of panorama—pornographic films shown in the back rooms of restaurants and game rooms—also confirmed the impression that the principal users of vice are middle and upper class clientele. During several weeks of observations, over seventy percent of the consumers of these pornographic vignettes were well dressed, single-minded visitors to the slums, who came for fifteen or twenty minutes of viewing and left as inconspicuously as possible. The remaining thirty percent were poorly dressed, older men who lived in the area.

Information on gambling and bookmaking in the permanently established or floating games is less readily available. Bookmakers report that the bulk of their "real business" comes from "doctors, lawyers and dentists" in the city:

It's the big boys—your professionals—who do the betting down here. Of course, they don't come down themselves; they either send someone or they call up. Most of them call up, 'cause I know them or they know Mr. _____ [one of the key figures in the gambling operation.]

Q. How 'bout the guys who walk off the street and bet?

A. Yeh; well, they're important. They do place bets and they sit around here and wait for the results. But that's mostly small stuff. I'd be out of business if I had to depend on them guys.

The poker and card games held throughout the city are of two types: (1) the small, daily game that caters almost exclusively to local residents of the area or working-class men who drop in for a hand or two while they are driving their delivery route or on their lunch hour; (2) and the action game which takes place twenty-four hours a day, and is located in more obscure places such as a suite in a downtown hotel. Like the prostitutes, these games are located on the edges of the lower class areas. The action games are the playground of well-dressed men who were by manner, finances, and dress clearly well-to-do businessmen.

Then, of course, there are the games, movies, and gambling nights at private clubs—country clubs, Elks, Lions, and Masons clubs—where gambling is a mainstay. Gambling nights at the different clubs vary in frequency. The largest and most exclusive country club in Rainfall West has a funtime once a month at which one can find every conceivable variety of gambling and a limited, but fairly sophisticated, selection of pornography. Although admission is presumably limited to members of the club, it is relatively easy to gain entrance simply by joining with a temporary membership, paying a two dollar fee at the door. Other clubs, such as the local fraternal organizations, have pinball machines present at all times; some also provide slot machines. Many of these clubs have ongoing poker and other gambling card games, run by people who work for the crime cabal. In all of these cases, the vices cater exclusively to middle and upper class clients.

Not all the business and professional men in Rainfall West partake of the vices. Instead, some of the leading citizens sincerely oppose the presence of vice in their city. Even larger members of the middle and working classes are adamant in their opposition to vice of all kinds. On occasion, they make their views forcefully known to the politicians and law enforcement officers, thus requiring these public officials to express their own opposition and appear to be snuffing out vice by enforcing the law.

The law enforcement system is thus placed squarely in the middle of two essentially conflicting demands. On the one hand, their job obligates them to enforce the law, albeit with discretion; at the same time, considerable disagreement rages over whether or not some acts should be subject to legal sanction. This conflict is heightened by the fact that some influential persons in the community insist that all laws be rigorously enforced while others demand that some laws not be enforced, at least not against themselves.

Faced with such a dilemma and such an ambivalent situation, the law enforcers do what any well managed bureaucracy would do under similar circumstances—they follow the line of least resistance. Using the discretion inherent in their positions, they resolve the problem by establishing procedures which minimize organizational strains and which provide the greatest promise of rewards for the organization and the individuals involved. Typically, this means that law enforcers adopt a tolerance policy towards the vices, selectively enforcing these laws only when it is to their advantage to do so. Since the persons demanding enforcement are generally middle class persons who rarely venture into the less prosperous sections of the city, the enforcers can control visibility and minimize complaints by merely regulating the ecological location of the vices. Limiting the visibility of such activity as sexual deviance, gambling, and prostitution appeases those persons who demand the enforcement of applicable laws. At the same time, since controlling visibility does not eliminate access for persons sufficiently interested to ferret out the tolerated vice areas, those demanding such services are also satisfied.

This policy is also advantageous because it renders the legal system capable of exercising considerable control over potential sources of real trouble. For example, since gambling and prostitution are profitable, competition among persons desiring to provide these services is likely. Understandably, this competition is prone to become violent. If the legal system cannot control those running these vices, competing groups may well go to war to obtain dominance over the rackets. If, however, the legal system cooperates with one group, there will be a sufficient concentration of power to avoid these uprisings. Similarly, prostitution can be kept clean if the law enforcers cooperate with the prostitutes; the law can thus minimize the chance, for instance, that a prostitute will steal money from a customer. In this and many other ways, the law enforcement system maximizes its visible effectiveness by creating and supporting a shadow government that manages the vices.

Initially this may require bringing in people from other cities to help set up the necessary organizational structure. Or it may mean recruiting and training local talent or simply co-opting, coercing, or purchasing the knowledge and skills of entrepreneurs who are at the moment engaged in vice operations. When made, this move often involves considerable strain, since some of those brought in may be uncooperative. Whatever the particulars, the ultimate result is the same: a syndicate emerges—composed of politicians, law enforcers, and citizens—capable of supplying and controlling the vices in the city. The most efficient cabal is invariably one that contains representatives of all the leading centers of power. Businessmen must be involved because of their political influence and their ability to control the mass media. This prerequisite is illustrated by the case of a fledgling magazine which published an article intimating that several leading politicians were corrupt. Immediately major advertisers canceled their advertisements in the magazine. One large chain store refused to sell that issue of the magazine in any of its stores. And when one of the leading cabal members was accused of accepting bribes, a number of the community's most prominent businessmen sponsored a large advertisement declaring their unfailing support for and confidence in the integrity of this "outstanding public servant."

The cabal must also have the cooperation of businessmen in procuring the loans which enable them individually and collectively to purchase legitimate businesses, as well as to expand the vice enterprises. A member of the banking community is therefore a considerable asset. In Rainfall West the vice president of one of the local banks (who was an investigator for a federal law enforcement agency before he entered banking) is a willing and knowledgeable participant in business relations with cabal members. He not only serves on the board of directors of a loan agency controlled by the cabal, but also advises cabal members on how to keep their earnings a secret. Further he sometimes serves as a go-between, passing investment tips from the cabal onto other businessmen in the community. In this way the cabal serves the economic interests of businessmen indirectly as well as directly.

The political influence of the cabal is more directly obtained. Huge, tax free profits make it possible for the cabal to generously support political candidates of its choice. Often the cabal assists both candidates in an election, thus assuring itself of influence regardless of who wins. While usually there is a favorite, ultra-cooperative candidate who receives the greater proportion of the contributions, everyone is likely to receive something.

III. THE BUREAUCRACY

Contrary to the prevailing myth that universal rules govern bureaucracies, the fact is that in day-to-day operations rules can—and must—be selectively applied. As a consequence, some degree of corruption is not merely a possibility, but rather is a virtual certainty which is built into the very structure of bureaucratic organizations.

The starting point for understanding this structural invitation to corruption is the observation that application of all the rules and procedures comprising the foundation of an organization inevitably admits of a high degree of discretion. Rules can only specify what should be done when the actions being considered fall clearly into unambiguously specifiable categories, about which there can be no reasonable grounds of disagreement or conflicting interpretation. But such categories are a virtual impossibility, given the inherently ambiguous nature of language. Instead, most events fall within the penumbra of the bureaucratic rules where the discretion of office-holders must hold sway.

Since discretionary decisionmaking is recognized as inevitable in effect, all bureaucratic decisions become subject to the discretionary will of the office-holder. Moreover, if one has a reason to look, vagueness and ambiguity can be found in any rule, no matter how carefully stipulated. And if ambiguity and vagueness are not sufficient to justify particularistic criteria being applied, contradictory rules or implications of rules can be readily located which have the same effect on justifying the decisions which, for whatever reason the office-holder wishes, can be used to enforce his position. Finally, since organizations characteristically develop their own set of common practices which take on the status of rules (whether written or unwritten), the entire process of applying rules becomes totally dependent on the discretion of the office-holder. The bureaucracy thus has its own set of precedents which can be invoked in cases where the articulated rules do not provide precisely the decision desired by the office-holder.

Ultimately, the office-holder has license to apply rules derived from a practically bottomless set of choices. Individual self-interest then depends on one's ability to ingratiate himself to office-holders at all levels in order to ensure that the rules most useful to him are applied. The bureaucracy therefore is not a rational institution with universal standards, but is instead, irrational and particularistic. It is a type of organization in which the organization's reason for being is displaced by a set of goals that often conflict with the organization's presumed purposes. This is precisely the consequence of the organizational response to the dilemma created by laws prohibiting the vices. Hence, the bureaucratic nature of law enforcement and political organization makes possible the corruption of the legal-political bureaucracy.

In the case of Rainfall West the goal of maintaining a smooth functioning organization takes precedence over all other institutional goals. Where conflict arises between the long-range goals of the law and the short-range goal of sustaining the organization, the former lose out, even at the expense of undermining the socially agreed-upon purposes for which the organization presumably exists.

Yet, the law-enforcement agency's tendency to follow the line of least resistance of maintaining organizational goals in the face of conflicting demands necessarily embodies a choice as to whose demands will be followed. For bureaucracies are not equally susceptible to all interests in the society. They do not fear the castigation, interference, and disruptive potential of the alcoholics on skid row or the cafe-owners in the slums. In fact, some residents of the black ghetto in Rainfall West and of other lower class areas of the city have been campaigning for years to rid their communities of the gambling casinos, whore houses, pornography stalls, and bookmaking operations. But these pleas fall on deaf ears. The letters they write and the committees they form receive no publicity and create no stir in the smoothly functioning organizations that occupy the political and legal offices of the city. On the other hand, when the president of a large corporation in the city objected to the "slanderous lies" being spread about one of the leading members of the crime cabal in Rainfall West, the magazine carrying the "lies" was removed from newstand sale, and the editors lost many of their most profitable advertisers. Similarly, when any question of the honesty or integrity of policemen, prosecuting attorneys, or judges involved in the cabal is raised publicly, it is either squelched before aired (the editor of the leading daily newspaper in Rainfall West is a long-time friend of one of the cabal's leading members) or it arouses the denial of influential members of the banking community (especially those bankers whose institutions loan money to cabal members), as well as leading politicans, law enforcement officers, and the like.

In short, bureaucracies are susceptible to differential influence, according to the economic and political power of the groups attempting to exert influence. Since every facet of politics and the mass media is subject to reprisals by cabal members and friends, exposition of the ongoing relationship between the cabal and the most powerful economic groups in the city is practically impossible.

The fact that the bureaucrats must listen to the economic elites of the city and not the have-nots is then one important element that stimulates the growth and maintenance of a crime cabal. But the links between the elites and the cabal are more than merely spiritual. The economic elite of the city does not simply play golf with the political and legal elite. There are in fact significant economic ties between the two groups.

The most obvious nexus is manifested by the campaign contributions from the economic elite to the political and legal elites. We need not dwell on this observation here; it has been well documented in innumerable other studies.[7] However, what is not well recognized is that the crime cabal is itself an important source of economic revenue for the economic elite. In at least one instance, the leading bankers and industrialists of the city were part of a multi-million dollar stock swindle engineered and manipulated by the crime cabal with the assistance of confidence-men from another state. This entire case was shrouded in such secrecy that eastern newspapers were calling people at the University of Rainfall West to find out why news about the scandal was not forthcoming from local wire services. When the scandal was finally exposed the fact that industrialists and cabal members heavily financed the operation (and correspondingly reaped the profits) was conveniently ignored in the newspapers and the courts; the evil-doers were limited to the outsiders who were in reality the front men for the entire confidence operation.

In a broader sense, key members of the economic elite in the community are also members of the cabal. While the day-to-day, week-to-week operations of the cabal are determined by the criminal-political-legal elite, the economic elite benefits mightily from the cabal. Not surprisingly, any threat to the cabal is quickly squelched by the economic elite under the name of "concerned citizens," which indeed they are.

The crime cabal is thus an inevitable outgrowth of the political economy of American cities. The ruling elites from every sphere benefit economically and socially from the presence of a smoothly running cabal. Law enforcement and government bureaucracies function best when a cabal is part of the governmental structure. And the general public is satisfied when control of the vices gives an appearance of respectability, but a reality of availability.

IV. VICE IN RAINFALL WEST

The vices available in Rainfall West are varied and tantalizing. Gambling ranges from bookmaking (at practically every street corner in the center of the city) to open poker games, bingo parlors, off-track betting, casinos, roulette and dice games (concentrated in a few locations and also floating out into the suburban country clubs and fraternal organizations), and innumerable two and five dollar stud-poker games scattered liberally throughout the city.

The most conspicuous card games take place from about ten in the morning—varying slightly from one fun house to the next—until midnight. A number of other twenty-four hour games run constantly. In the more public games, the limit ranges from one to five dollars for each bet; in the more select twenty-four hours a day games, there is a pot limit or no limit rule. These games are reported to have betting as high as twenty and thirty thousand dollars. I saw a bet made and called for a thousand dollars in one of these games. During this game, the highest stakes game I witnessed in six years of the study, the police lieutenant in charge of the vice squad was called in to supervise the game—not, need I add, to break up the game or make any arrests, but only to insure against violence.

Prostitution covers the usual range of ethnic group, age, shape, and size of female. It is found in houses with madams *a la* the New Orleans stereotype, on the street through pimps, or in suburban apartment buildings and hotels. Prices range from five dollars for a short time with a street walker to two hundred dollars for a night with a lady who has her own apartment (which she usually shares with her boyfriend who is discreetly gone during business operations).

High interest loans are easy to arrange through stores that advertise, "your signature is worth $5,000." It is really worth considerably more; it may in fact be worth your life. The interest rates vary from a low of 20 percent for three months to as high as 100 percent for varying periods. Repayment is demanded not through the courts, but through the help of "The Gaspipe Gang," who call on recalcitrant debtors and use physical force to bring about payment. "Interest only" repayment is the most popular alternative practiced by borrowers and is preferred by the loan sharks as well. The longer repayment can be prolonged, the more advantageous the loan is to the agent.

Pinball machines are readily available throughout the city, most of them paying off in cash.

The gambling, prostitution, drug distribution, pornography, and usury which flourish in the lower class center of the city do so with the compliance, encouragement, and cooperation of the major political and law enforcement officials in the city. There is in fact a symbiotic relationship between the law enforcement-political organizations of the city and a group of *local,* as distinct from national, men who control the distribution of vices.

V. CORRUPTION IN RAINFALL WEST

In the spring of 19— a businessman whom I shall call Mr. Van Meter sold his restaurant and began looking for a new investment when he noticed an advertisement in the paper which read:

> Excellent investment opportunity for someone with $30,000 cash to purchase the good will and equipment of a long established restaurant in down town area. . . .

After making the necessary inquiries, inspecting the business, and evaluating its potential, Mr. Van Meter purchased it. In addition to the restaurant, the business consisted of a card room which was legally licensed by the city, operating under a publicly acknowledged tolerance policy which allowed card games, including poker, to be played. These games were limited by the tolerance policy to a maximum $1.00 limit for each bet.

Thus, Mr. Van Meter had purchased a restaurant with a built-in criminal enterprise. It was never clear whether he was, at the time of purchasing the business, fully aware of the criminal nature of the card room. Certainly the official tolerance policy was bound to create confusion over the illegality of gambling in the licensed card rooms. The full extent to which this purchase involved Mr. Van Meter in illegal activities crystallized immediately upon purchase of the property.[8]

> [W]e had just completed taking the inventory of [the restaurant]. I was then handed the $60,000 keys of the premises by Mr. Bataglia, and he approached me and said, "Up until now, I have never discussed with you the fact that we run a bookmaking operation here, and that we did not sell this to you; however if you wish to have this operation continue here, you must place another $5,000 to us, and we will count you in. Now, if you do not buy it, we will put out this bookmaking operation, and you will go broke." "In other words," Mr. Bataglia continued, "we will use you, and you need us." I told Mr. Bataglia that I did not come to this town to bookmake or to operate any form of rackets, and I assumed that I had purchased a legitimate business. Mr. Bataglia said, "You have purchased a legitimate business; however, you must have the bookmaking operation in order to survive." I promptly kicked him out of the place.

The question of how "legitimate" the business Mr. Van Meter had purchased was is not so simple as he thought. It was, to be sure, a licensed operation; there was a license to operate the restaurant, a license to operate the card room attached to the restaurant, and a license to operate the cigar stand (where much of the bookmaking operation had taken place before Mr. Van Meter purchased the place). These licenses, although providing a "legitimate business," also had the effect of making the owner of the business constantly in violation of the law, for the laws were so constructed that no one could possibly operate a "legitimate" business "legally". Thus, anyone operating the business was vulnerable to constant harassment and even closure by the authorities if he failed to cooperate with law enforcement personnel.

The card room attached to the business was the most flagrant example of a legitimate enterprise that was necessarily run illegally. The city of Rainfall West had adopted by ordinance a tolerance policy towards gambling. This tolerance policy consisted of permitting card rooms, which were then licensed by the city, pinball machines that paid off money to winners, and panorama shows. The city ordinance allowed a maximum one dollar bet at the card table in rooms such as those in Mr. Van Meter's restaurant.

This ordinance was in clear and open violation of state law. The State Attorney General had publicly stated that the tolerance policy of the city was illegal and that the only policy for the state was that all gambling was illegal. Despite these rulings from higher state officials, the tolerance policy continued and flourished in the city although it did so illegally.

This general illegality of the card room was not, however, easily enforceable against any one person running a card room without enforcement against all persons running card rooms. There were, however, wrinkles in the tolerance policy ordinance which made it possible discriminately to close down one card room without being forced to take action against all of them. This was accomplished in part by the limit of one dollar on a bet. The card room was allowed to take a certain percentage of the pot from each game, but the number of people playing and the amount of percentage permitted did not allow one to make a profit if the table limit remained at one dollar. Furthermore, since most people gambling wanted to bet more, they would not patronize a card room that insisted on the one dollar limit. Mr. Van Meter, like all other card room operators, allowed a two to five dollar limit. The ordinance was written in such a way that, in reality, everyone would be in violation of it. It was therefore possible for the police to harass or close down whatever card rooms they chose at their own discretion.

The health and fire regulations of the city were also written in such a way that no one could comply with all the ordinances. It was impossible to serve meals and still avoid violation of the health standards required. Thus, when the health or fire department chose to enforce the rules, they could do so selectively against whatever business they chose.

The same set of circumstances governed the cabaret licenses in the city. The city ordinances required that every cabaret have a restaurant attached; the restaurant, the ordinance stated, had to comprise at least seventy five percent of the total floor space of the cabaret and restaurant combined. Since there was a much higher demand for cabarets than restaurants in the central section of the city, this meant that cabaret owners were bound by law to have restaurants attached some of which would necessarily lose money. Moreover, these restaurants had to be extremely large in order to constitute seventy five percent of the total floor space. For a one-hundred square foot cabaret, an attached three-hundred square foot restaurant was required. The cabaret owners burden was further increased by an ordinance governing the use of entertainers in the cabaret, requiring that any entertainer be at least twenty five feet from the nearest customer during her act. Plainly, the cabaret had to be absolutely gigantic to accommodate any customers after a twenty five foot buffer zone encircled the entertainer. Combined with the requirement that this now very large cabaret had to have attached to it a restaurant three times as large, the regulatory scheme simply made it impossible to run a cabaret legally.

The effect of such ordinances was to give the police and the prosecuting attorney complete discretion in choosing who should operate gambling rooms, cabarets, and restaurants. This discretion was used to force payoffs to the police and cooperation with the criminal syndicate.

Mr. Van Meter discovered the payoff system fairly early in his venture:

I found shortages that were occurring in the bar, and asked an employee to explain them, which he did, in this manner: "The money is saved to pay the 'juice' of the place." I asked him what was the "juice." He said in this city you must "pay to stay." Mr. Davis said, "You pay for the beat-man [from the police department] $250.00 per month. That takes care of the various shifts, and you must pay the upper brass, also $200.00 each month. A beat-man collects around the first of each month, and another man collects for the upper brass. You get the privilege to stay in business." That is true; however, you must remember that it is not what they will do for you, but what they will do to you, if you don't make these payoffs as are ordered. "If I refuse, what then?" I asked.

"The *least* that could happen to you is you will lose your business."

During the next three months, Mr. Van Meter made the payoffs required. He refused, however, to allow the bookmaking operation back into the building or to hire persons to run the card room and bar whom members of the organized crime syndicate and the police recommended to him for the job. He also fired one employee whom he found was taking bets while tending bar.

In August of the same year, a man whom Mr. Van Meter had known prior to buying the restaurant met him in his office:

Mr. Danielski met with me in my office and he came prepared to offer me $500 per month—in cash deductions—of my remaining balance of the contract owing against (the restaurant) if I would give him the bookmaking operation, and he would guarantee me another $800 a month more business. He warned that if he wanted to give my establishment trouble, he would go to a certain faction of the police department; if he wanted me open, he would go to another faction. "So do some thinking on the subject, and I will be in on Monday for your answer." Monday, I gave Mr. Danielski his answer. The answer was no.

In June of 19—, a man by the name of Joe Link, who I found later was a second-string gang member of Mr. Bataglia's, made application to me to operate my card room. I did give him the opportunity to operate the card room because I had known him some 20 years ago when he was attending the same high school that I was. After I had refused the offer of Mr. Danielski, Mr. Joe Link had received orders from Mr. Danielski and Mr. Bataglia to run my customers out and in any way he could, cripple my operation to bring me to terms. I terminated Mr. Link on November 6, 19—, and shortly after, after I had removed Mr. Link, Police Officer Herb C. conferred with me in my office, and Officer Herb C. said that I had better re-appoint Mr. Link in my card room; that his superiors were not happy with me. If I did not return Mr. Link to his former position, then it would be necessary to clear anyone that I wanted to replace Mr. Link with. Officer C. felt that no one else would be acceptable. He further stated I had better make a decision soon, because he would not allow the card room to run without an approved boss. I informed Officer C. that I would employ anyone I chose in my card room or in any other department. Officer C. said "Mr. Van Meter, you, I think, do not realize how powerful a force you will be fighting or how deep in City Hall this reaches. Even I am not let know all the bosses or where the money goes." I did not return Mr. Link, as I was ordered by Officer

C., and I did select my own card room bosses.

On November 7, 19—, I received a phone call stating that I soon would have a visitor who was going to shoot me between the eyes if I did not comply with the demands to return Mr. Link to his former position.

The crime cabal in Rainfall West (including police officers, politicians and members of the organized criminal syndicate), like the criminal law which underpins it, relies on the threat of coercion to maintain order. That threat, however, is not an empty one. Although Mr. Van Meter was not "shot between the eyes" as threatened, others who defied the cabal were less fortunate. Although it has never been established that any of the suspicious deaths that have taken place involving members of crime cabal were murder, the evidence, nonetheless, points rather strongly in that direction. Eric Tandlin, former county auditor for Rainfall West, is but one of thirteen similar cases which occurred from 1955–1969.

Tandlin had been county auditor for seventeen years. He kept his nose clean, did the bidding of the right politicans, and received a special gift every Christmas for his cooperation. In the course of doing business with the politicians and criminals, he also developed extensive knowledge of the operations. Suddenly, without warning or expectation on his part, Eric was not supported by his party, for re-election as auditor, losing the nomination to the brother-in-law of the chief of police. It was a shock from which Eric did not soon recover. He began drinking heavily and frequenting the gambling houses; he also began talking a great deal. One Friday evening, he made friends with a reporter who promised to put him in touch with someone from the attorney general's office. Saturday night at 6:30, just as the card rooms were being prepared for the evening, word spread through the grapevine along First Street that Eric had been done in: "Danielski took Eric for a walk down by the bay."

The Sunday morning paper carried a small front page story:

Eric Tandlin aged forty seven was found drowned in back bay yesterday at around 5:00 p.m. The Coroner's office listed the cause of death as possible suicide. Friends said Mr. Tandlin who had been county auditor for many years until his defeat in the primaries last fall had been despondent over his failure to be re-elected.

The coroner, who was the brother-in-law of the chief of police, described the probable cause of death as "suicide." The people of Miriam Street knew better. They also knew that this was a warning not to talk to reporters, sociologists, or anyone else "nosing around." In the last few years the cabal has been responsible for the deaths of several of its members. Drowning is a favorite method of eliminating troublemakers, because it is difficult to ascertain whether or not the person fell from a boat by accident, was held under water by someone else, or committed suicide.[9] L. S., who was in charge of a portion of the pinball operations, but who came into disfavor with the cabal, was found drowned at the edge of a lake near his home. J. B., an assistant police chief who had been a minor member of the cabal for years, drowned while on a fishing trip aboard one of the yachts owned by a leading member of the cabal. In both instances the coroner, who was the brother-in-law of one of the leading cabal members, diagnosed the deaths as "accidental drownings." Over the years, he has often made that diagnosis when cabal members or workers in the organization have met with misfortune.

Other deaths have been arranged in more traditional ways. At least one man, for example, was shot in an argument in a bar. The offender was tried before a judge who has consistently shown great compassion for any crimes committed by members of the cabal (although he has compensated for this leniency with cabal members by being unusually harsh in cases against blacks who appear before him), and the case was dismissed for lack of evidence.

However, murder is not the preferred method of handling uncooperative people. Far better, in the strategy of the crime cabal, is the time-honoured technique of blackmail and co-optation. The easiest and safest tactic is to purchase the individual for a reasonable amount, as was attempted with Mr. Van Meter. If this fails, then some form of blackmail or relatively minor coercion may be in order.

For instance, Sheriff McCallister was strongly supported by the cabal in his bid for office. Campaign contributions were generously provided since McCallister was running against a local lawyer who was familiar with the goings-on of the cabal and had vowed to attack its operations. McCallister won the election—cabal candidates almost never lose local elections—but underwent a dramatic change-of-heart shortly thereafter. He announced in no uncertain terms that he would not permit the operation of gambling houses in the country, although he did not intend to do anything about the operations within the city limits since that was not his jurisdiction. Nevertheless the country, he insisted, would be kept clean.

The cabal was as annoyed as it was surprised. The country operations were only a small portion of the total enterprise, but they were nonetheless important, and no one wanted to give up the territory. Further, the prospect of closing down the lay-off center operating in the country was no small matter. The center is crucial to the entire enterprise, because it is here that the results of horse races and other sports events come directly to the bookmakers. The center also enables the cabal to protect itself against potential bankruptcy. When the betting is particularly heavy in one direction, bets are laid off by wiring Las Vegas where the national betting pattern always takes care of local variations. Clearly, something had to be done about McCallister.

No man is entirely pure, and McCallister was less pure than many. He had two major weaknesses: gambling and young girls. One weekend shortly after he took office a good friend of his asked if he would like to go to Las Vegas for the weekend. He jumped at the opportunity. While the weekend went well in some respects, McCallister was unlucky at cards. When he flew back to Rainfall West Sunday night, he left $14,000 worth of I. O. U's in Las Vegas.

Monday morning one of the cabal chiefs visited McCallister in his office. The conversation went like this:

Say, Mac, I understand you was down in Vegas over the weekend.

Yeah.

Hear you lost a little bit at the tables, Mac.

Uuh-huh.

Well the boys wanted me to tell you not to worry about those pieces of paper you left. We got them back for you.

I don't. . . .

Also, Mac, we thought you might like to have a momento of your trip; so we brought you these pictures. . . .

The "momentos" were pictures of McCallister in a hotel room with several young girls. Thereafter things in the country returned to normal.

Lest one think the cabal exploitative, it should be noted that McCallister was not kept in line by the threat of exposure alone. He was, in fact, subsequently placed on the payroll in the amount of one thousand dollars a month. When his term as sheriff was over, an appointment was arranged for him to the state parole board. He was thus able to continue serving the cabal in a variety of ways for the rest of his life. Cooperation paid off much better than would have exposure.

Threats from outside the organization are more rare than are threats from within. Nevertheless, they occur and must be dealt with in the best possible way. Since no set strategy exists, each incident is handled in its own way. During Robert Kennedy's days as attorney general, the federal attorney for the state began a campaign to rid the state of the members of the cabal. People who held political office were generally immune, but some of the higher-ups in the operational section of the cabal were indicted. Ultimately five members of the cabal, including a high ranking member of the local Teamsters' Union, were sentenced to prison. The entire affair was scandalous; politicians whose lives depended on the cabal fought the nasty business with all their power. They were able to protect the major leaders of the cabal and to avert exposure of the cabal politicians. However, some blood ran, and it was a sad day for the five sentenced to prison terms. Yet the organization remained intact and, indeed, the five men who went to prison continued to receive their full share of profits from the cabal enterprises. Corruption continued unabated, and the net effect on organized crime in the state was nil.

One reason that Mr. Van Meter was not "shot between the eyes" was that, although not fully cooperative, he was nonetheless paying into the cabal four hundred and fifty dollars a month in "juice." Eventually he cut down on these payments. When this happened Mr. Van Meter became a serious prob-

lem for the cabal, and something more than mere threats was necessary:

No extortion was paid by me directly to them, but it involved a third party. Some time shortly after the first of each month, the sum of $250.00 was paid to (the above mentioned) Officer C., which he presumably divided up with other patrolmen on the beat. Two hundred dollars each month was given to (another bagman) for what the boys termed as "It was going to the upper braid." The $200.00 per month was paid each month from June 19— with payment of $200.00 being made in January 19—. After that I refused to make further payments. . . . After some wrangling back and forth, I just told them that I would not pay any more. They said, "Well, we will take $100.00 per month on a temporary basis." I paid $100.00 per month for the next twelve months. Early the next year I had planned to cut off all payments to the patrolmen. . . . About the 8th of July the explosion occurred. Police officers Merrill and Lynch conducted a scare program; jerked patrons off stools, ran others out of my establishment; Patrolman Lynch ordered my card room floorman into the rest room; and ordered my card room closed. When my floorman came out of the rest room, he left white and shaking and never to be seen in the city again.

Following this incident, Mr. Van Meter met with his attorney, the chief of police, and a former mayor. Although the meeting was cordial, he was told they could do nothing unless he could produce affidavits substantiating his claims. He did so, but quickly became enmeshed in requests and demands for more affidavits, while the prosecuting attorney's office resisted cooperating.

The refusal of cooperation from the prosecuting attorney was not surprising. What Mr. Van Meter did not realize was that the prosecuting attorney was the key political figure behind the corruption of the legal and political machinery. He was also the political boss of the county and had great influence on state politics, coming as he did from the most populous area of the state. Over the years his influence had been used to place men in key positions throughout the various government bureaucracies, including the police department, the judiciary, the city council, and relevant governmental agencies such as the tax office and the licensing bureau.

There was, however, a shift in emphasis for a short time in the cabal's dealings with Mr. Van Meter. They offered to buy his business at the price he had paid for it. But when he refused, the pace of harassment increased. Longshoremen came into his restaurant and started fights. Police stood around the card room day and night observing. City health officials would come to inspect the cooking area during mealtimes, thereby delaying the food being served to customers; the fire department made frequent visits to inspect fire precautions. On several occasions, Mr. Van Meter was cited for violating health and safety standards.

Finally, he was called to the city council to answer an adverse police report stating that he allowed drunks and brawling in his establishment. At the hearing, he was warned that he would lose all of his licenses if a drunk were ever again found in his restaurant.

During the next six months, the pressure on Mr. Van Meter continued at an ever increasing rate. Longshoremen came into the restaurant and card room and picked fights with customers, employees, and Mr. Van Meter himself. The health department chose five o'clock in the evening several days running to inspect the health facilities of the establishment. The fire inspector came at the lunch hour to inspect the fire equipment, writing up every minor defect detectable. Toward the end of Mr. Van Meter's attempt to fight the combine of the government, the police force, and the criminal syndicate, he received innumerable threats to his life. Bricks and stones were thrown through the windows of his building. Ultimately, he sold his business back to the man from whom he had purchased it at a loss of thirty thousand dollars and left the city.

The affair caused considerable consternation among the legal-political-criminal cabal which controlled and profited from the rackets in Rainfall West. In the "good old days" the problem would have been quickly solved, one informant remarked, "by a bullet through the fat slob's head." But ready resort to murder as a solution to problems was clearly frowned upon by the powers that operated organized crime in Rainfall West. Although the syndicate had been responsible for many murders over the past ten years, these murders were limited to troublesome persons *within* the syndicate. As nearly as

could be determined, no outsider had been murdered for a number of years.

Overall the gambling, bookmaking, pinball, and usury operations grossed at least twenty five million dollars a year in the city alone. It was literally the case that drunks were arrested on the street for public intoxication while gamblers made thousands of dollars and policemen accepted bribes five feet away.

Payoffs, bribes, and associated corruption were not limited solely to illegal activities. To obtain a license for tow-truck operations one had to pay ten thousand dollars to the licensing bureau; a license for a taxi franchise cost fifteen thousand dollars. In addition, taxi drivers who sold bootleg liquor (standard brand liquors sold after hours or on Sunday) or who would steer customers to prostitutes or gambling places, paid the beat policeman and the sergeant of the vice squad. Tow-truck operators also paid the policeman who called the company when an accident occurred.

As one informant commented:

> When I would go out on a call for a policeman I would always carry matchbooks with three dollars tucked behind the covers. I would hand this to the cops when I came to the scene of the accident.
>
> Q. Did every policeman accept these bribes?
>
> A. No. Once in a while you would run into a cop who would say he wasn't interested. But that was rare. Almost all of them would take it.

Most of the cabarets, topless bars, and taverns were owned either directly or indirectly by members of the organized crime syndicate. Thus, the syndicate not only controlled the gambling enterprises, but also "legitimate" businesses associated with night life as well. In addition, several of the hotels and restaurants were also owned by the syndicate. Ownership of these establishments was disguised in several ways, such as placing them formally in the name of a corporation with a board of directors who were really front-men for the syndicate or placing them in the names of relatives of syndicate members. It should further be underlined that the official ownership by the syndicate must be interpreted to mean by all of the members who were in the political and legal bureaucracies and simultaneously members of the syndicate, as well as those who were solely involved in the day-to-day operations of the vice syndicate.

The governing board of the syndicate consisted of seven men, four of whom held high positions in the government and three of whom were responsible for the operation of the various enterprises. The profits were split among these seven men. We are *not* then talking about a syndicate that paid off officials, but about a syndicate that is part and parcel of the government, although not subject to election.

VI. CONCLUSION

There is abundant data indicating that what is true in Rainfall West is true in virtually every city in the United States and has been true since at least the early 1900's. Writing at the turn of the century, Lincoln Steffens observed that "the spirit of graft and of lawlessness is the American spirit." He went on to describe the results of his inquiries:

> in the very first study—St. Louis—the startling truth lay bare that corruption was not merely political; it was financial, commercial, social; the ramifications of boodle were so complex, various and far-reaching, that our mind could hardly grasp them. . . . St. Louis exemplified boodle; Minneapolis Police graft; Pittsburgh a political and Industrial machine; Philadelphia general civil corruption. . . .[10]

In 1931, after completing an inquiry into the police, the National Commission on Law Observance and Enforcement concluded:

> Nearly all of the large cities suffer from an alliance between politicians and criminals. For example, Los Angeles was controlled by a few gamblers for a number of years. San Francisco suffered similarly some years ago and at one period in its history was so completely dominated by the gamblers that three prominent gamblers who were in control of the politics of the city and who quarrelled about the appointment of the police chief settled their quarrel by shaking dice to determine who would name the chief for the first two years, who for the second two years, and who for the third.
>
> Recently the gamblers were driven out of Detroit by the commissioner. These gamblers were strong enough politically to oust this commissioner from office despite the fact that he was recognized by police chiefs as one of the strongest and ablest police executives in America. For a number of years Kansas City, Mo., was controlled by a vice ring and no interference with their enterprises was tolerated. Chicago, *despite its unenviable reputation*, is but one of numerous cities

where the police have frequently been betrayed by their elected officials.[11]

Frank Tannenbaum once noted:

> It is clear that the evidence at hand—that a considerable measure of the crime in the community is made possible and perhaps inevitable by the peculiar connection that exists between the political organizations of our large cities and the criminal activities of various gangs that are permitted and even encouraged to operate.[12]

Similarly, the Kefauver Commission summarized the results of its extensive investigation into organized crime in 1951:

> (1) There is a nationwide crime syndicate known as the Mafia, whose tentacles are found in many large cities. It has international ramifications which appear most clearly in connection with the narcotics traffic.
>
> (2) Its leaders are usually found in control of the most lucrative rackets in their cities.
>
> (3) There are indications of centralized direction and control of these rackets, but leadership appears to be in a group rather than in a single individual.[13]

And in 1969, Donald R. Cressey, using data gathered from the attorney general of the United States and local Crime Commission, capsulized the state of organized crime in the U. S.:

> In the United States, criminals have managed to put together an organization which is at once a nationwide illicit cartel and a nationwide confederation. This organization is dedicated to amassing millions of dollars by means of extortion, and from usury, the illicit sale of lottery tickets, chances on the outcome of horse races and athletic events, narcotics and untaxed liquor.[14]

The frequency of major scandals linking organized criminals with leading political and legal figures suggests the same general conclusion. Detroit, Chicago, Denver, Reading, Pennsylvania, Columbus and Cleveland, Ohio, Miami, New York, Boston, and a horde of other cities have been scandalized and cleansed innumerable times.[15] Yet organized crime persists and, in fact, thrives. Despite periodic forays, exposures, and reform movements prompted by journalists, sociologists, and politicians, organized crime has become an institution in the United States and in many other parts of the world as well.[16]

Once established, the effect of a syndicate on the entire legal and political system is profound. Maintenance of order in such an organization requires the use of extra-legal procedures since, obviously, the law cannot always be relied on to serve the interests of the crime cabal. The law can harass uncooperative people; it can even be used to send persons to prison on real or faked charges. But to make discipline and obedience certain, it is often necessary to enforce the rules of the syndicate in extra-legal ways. To avoid detection of these procedures, the police, prosecuting attorney's office, and judiciary must be organized in ways that make them incapable of discovering events that the cabal does not want disclosed. In actual practice, policemen, prosecutors, and judges who are *not* members of the cabal must not be in a position to investigate those things that the syndicate does not want investigated. The military chain of command of the police is, of course, well-suited to such a purpose. So, in fact, is the availability of such subtle but nonetheless important sanctions as relegating uncooperative policemen to undesirable positions in the department. Conversely, cooperative policemen are rewarded with promotions, prestigious positions on the force, and of course a piece of the action.

Another consequence is widespread acceptance of petty graft. The matchbox fee for accident officers is but one illustration. Free meals and cigarettes, bottles of whiskey at Christmas, and the like are practically universal in the police department. Television sets, cases of expensive whiskey, and on occasion new automobiles or inside information on investments are commonplace in the prosecuting attorney's office.

Significantly, the symbiotic relationship between organized crime and the legal system not only negates the law enforcement function of the law vis-à-vis these types of crimes but actually increases crime in a number of ways. Perhaps most important, gradual commitment to maintaining the secrecy of the relationship in turn necessitates the commission of crimes other than those involved in the vices per se. At times, it becomes necessary to intimidate through physical punishment and even to murder recalcitrant members of the syndicate. Calculating the extent of such activities is risky business. From 1955 to 1969 in Rainfall West, a conservative estimate of the number of persons killed by the syndi-

cate is fifteen. However, estimates range as high as "hundreds." Although such information is impossible to verify in a manner that creates confidence, it is virtually certain that some murders have been perpetrated by the syndicate in order to protect the secrecy of their operations. It is also certain that the local law enforcement officials, politicians and businessmen involved with the syndicate have cooperated in these murders.

The location of the vices in the ghettos and slums of the city may well contribute to a host of other types of criminality as well. The disdain which ghetto residents have for the law and law enforcers is likely derived from more than simply their own experiences with injustice and police harassment. Their day-to-day observations that criminal syndicates operate openly and freely in their areas with complete immunity from punishment, while persons standing on a corner or playing cards in an apartment are subject to arrest, can not help but affect their perception of the legal system. We do not know that such observations undermine respect for and willingness to comply with the law, but that conclusion would not seem unreasonable.

It is no accident that whenever the presence of vice and organizations that provide the vices is exposed to public view by politicians, exposure is always couched in terms of organized crime. The question of corruption is conveniently left in the shadows. Similarly, it is no accident that organized crime is inevitably seen as consisting of an organization of criminals with names like Valachi, Genovesse and Joe Bonana. Yet the data from the study of Rainfall West, as well as that of earlier studies of vice, makes it abundantly clear that this analysis is fundamentally misleading.

I have argued, and I think the data demonstrate quite convincingly, that the people who run the organizations which supply the vices in American cities are members of the business, political, and law enforcement communities—not simply members of a criminal society. Furthermore, it is also clear from this study that corruption of political-legal organization is a critical part of the life-blood of the crime cabal. The study of organized crime is thus a misnomer; the study should consider corruption, bureaucracy, and power. By relying on governmental agencies for their information on vice and the rackets, social scientists and lawyers have inadvertently contributed to the miscasting of the issue in terms that are descriptively biased and theoretically sterile. Further, they have been diverted from sociologically interesting and important issues raised by the persistence of crime cabals. As a consequence, the real significance of the existence of syndicates has been overlooked; for instead of seeing these social entities as intimately tied to, and in symbiosis with, the legal and political bureaucracies of the state, they have emphasized the criminality of only a portion of those involved. Such a view contributes little to our knowledge of crime and even less to attempts at crime control.

FOOTNOTES

[1] I am grateful to W. G. O. Carson, Terence Morris, Paul Rock, Charles Michener, Patrick Douglas, Donald Cressey, and Robert Seidman for helpful comments on earlier versions of this paper.

[2] L. STEFFENS, THE SHAME OF THE CITIES (1904). *See* THE AUTOBIOGRAPHY OF LINCOLN STEFFENS (1931).

[3] D. CRESSEY, THEFT OF THE NATION (1969); Gardiner, *Wincanton: The Politics of Corruption*, Appendix B of THE PRESIDENT'S COMMISSION ON LAW ENFORCEMENT AND ADMINISTRATION OF JUSTICE, TASK FORCE REPORT: ORGANIZED CRIME (1967); in W. CHAMBLISS, CRIME AND THE LEGAL PROCESS 103 (1969).

[4] The view of organized crime as controlled by a national syndicate appears in D. CRESSEY, *supra* note 2. For a criticism of this view see H. MORRIS & G. HAWKINS, THE HONEST POLITICIANS GUIDE TO CRIME CONTROL (1970).

[5] Most recent examples of this are D. CRESSEY, *supra* note 2; H. MORRIS & G. HAWKINS, *supra* note 3; King, *Wild Shots in the War on Crime*, 20 J. PUB. LAW 85 (1971); Lynch & Phillips, *Organized Crime-Violence and Corruption*, 20 J. PUB. LAW 59 (1971); McKeon, *The Incursion By Organized Crime Into Legitimate Business*, 20 J. PUB.

LAW 117 (1971); Schelling, *What is the Business of Organized Crime?*, 20 J. PUB. LAW 71 (1971); Thrower, *Symposium: Organized Crime, Introduction*, 20 J. PUB. LAW 33 (1971); Tyler, *Sociodynamics of Organized Crime*, 20 J. PUB. LAW 41 (1971). For a discussion of the importance of studying corruption see W. CHAMBLISS, *supra* note 2, at 89; W. CHAMBLISS & R. SEIDMAN, LAW, ORDER AND POWER (1971); McKitvick, *The Study of Corruption*, 72 POL. SCI. Q. 502 (1957).

[6] Thinking of one's own residence as a "chosen land" need not of course be connected with any objectively verifiable evidence. A small Indian farm town where the standard of living is scarcely ever above the poverty level has painted signs on sidewalks which read "Isn't God good to Indians?" Any outside observer knowing something of the hardships and disadvantages that derive from living in this town might well answer an unequivocal "no." Most members of this community nevertheless answer affirmatively.

[7] *See generally* G. DORNHOFF, WHO RULES AMERICA? (1969); OVERA, PRESIDENTIAL CAMPAIGN FUNDS (1946); J. SHANNON, MONEY AND POLITICS (1959); OVERA, MONEY IN ELECTIONS (1932); Bernstein, *Private Wealth and Public Office: The High Cost of Campaigning* 22 THE NATION 77 (1966).

[8] All quotations are from taped interviews. The names of persons and places are fictitious.

[9] According to one informant: "Murder is the easiest crime of all to get away with. There are 101 ways to commit murder that are guaranteed to let you get away with it." He might have added that this was especially true when the coroner, the prosecuting attorney and key policy officials were cooperating with the murderers.

[10] *See* L. STEFFENS, THE SHAME OF THE CITIES 151 (1904).

[11] Garrett & Monroe, *Police Conditions in the United States*, 14 NAT'L COMM'N ON LAW OBSERVANCE AND ENFORCEMENT REPORT ON POLICE 45 (1931).

[12] F. TANNENBAUM, CRIME AND THE COMMUNITY 128 (1938).

[13] PRESIDENT'S COMMISSION ON LAW ENFORCEMENT AND ADMINISTRATION OF JUSTICE, THE CHALLENGE OF CRIME IN A FREE SOCIETY 7 (1967).

[14] D. CRESSEY, *supra* note 3. For a discussion of similar phenomena in Great Britain see N. LUCAS, BRITAIN'S GANGLAND (1969). *See also* D. BELL, END OF IDEOLOGY (1960).

[15] Wilson, *The Police and their Problems: A Theory*, 12 PUB. POLICY 189 (1963).

[16] *See* McMullen, *A Theory of Corruption*, 9 SOC. REV. 181 (1961).

13

The Thief and the Law:

A Safecracker's Perspective

HARRY KING

"... the only people that really profit from theft is the fix, the judge and the district attorney."

Frankly, after sitting down and analyzing it I come to the conclusion that the only people that really profit from theft is the fix, the judge, and the district attorney. They're the guys who make the money, not the guy who stole it. The guy who stole it is always getting pinched, and they're shaking him down for what he's got. I've had 'em flat pinch me on the street and shake me right down, take me in the car and shake me down and take every penny I had on me. Tell me to get out of the car. I've had that happen, and I didn't say nothing; I had no recourse.

In the old days we used to take and make a deal with the police. We knew we were going to make a deal, or the dicks knew we were going to, and they would have a lot of unsolved crimes. So, to make it easier for everybody we'd just what we called "clean the slate" for them. They'd say, "I got fifteen capers here we haven't been able to solve, will you clean them up for us?" That's all. We'd just sign a confession, I mean it wasn't really a confession. We didn't even know where these capers were. But they

Source: *Box Man: A Professional Thief's Journey*, as told to and edited by Bill Chambliss, New York: Harper and Row, 1972. By permission of the author and publisher.

never used them against us or anything. It was just to clean the slate for the police department. Our attorney had probably come down and talked to us and asked us if we would do it because he wanted a favor from a policeman, or something like that. You scratch my back, I'll scratch yours. So we would go ahead and do it, knowing that they wouldn't do nothin'.

There was more principles between the thieves and the police department in those days. Now they tell me that a policeman will say yes and turn right around and do no.

When I was rooting we were very close to some policemen. In Portland we used to have to pay off 20 percent to the chief of dicks and a lot of times the guy we beat would holler for five times as much as we got and we would have to give the Chief 20 percent of what they hollered for although he knew it was wrong. You see the criminals haven't got all the rackets; the worst ones are the upright members of society.

Every town has a criminal attorney who is the fix. The jailer would tell you who the fix in town was, or the bull that pinched you because he'd get a commission from the attorney, you know, for it. Everybody wants to tell you. Especially a box man, he's usually got money so they all wanna get cut in on the action. Then they got ten percent of what the attorney gets as his fee, so you have no trouble findin' out.

The attorney will come to see you and talk to you. He asks you where you're from and usually trys to check and see if you're gonna run or not. After he talks to you a little bit why you usually know somebody that he knows, another box man around the country or something, and he'll get you out on bail, get the bail cut down, and get you out on it or take you right out that night on bail. Then you go down and see him the next day and ask him what the score is and he'll tell you it'll cost you so much to get this cut down to a petty larceny beef and that's all there is to it. It's just that simple if the town's not hot.

If the town's hot, and somebody's gotta go to the joint, if you're an outsider you're probably the one to go. But if he can beat it he flat tells you how much it'll be. He has to give the district attorney so much, and possibly the judge, not necessarily the district attorney, might be an assistant in the office that he deals with. Sometimes you can square the beef in the city court and get it dropped. And the dick, if they've got the handout why they get a piece of the action too. Everybody's got their hand out, haven't they?

You won't take off when you're out on bond because that bondsman, you see, it's like the last time, my bond was $100,000 and you didn't customarily put a thief on a $100,000 bond, but my word's good so the bondsman signed for it. You can't just take off when a guy's a right guy you just can't take and dump him by runnin' off; that would be foolish to do, because the next time you needed a bond, you wouldn't get the bond, because they're just like safemen, I mean, word gets around. Well, now I can go to New York City and tell them to call Portland and the bondsman there will tell you I'm all right. So even in New York they'll sign a bond and they'll let me out on the cuff because they know I'll go right out and go to work and get it.

Sometimes you're forced into a trial, but not usually. Only about one quarter the time. You wouldn't plead not guilty because a box man, if you're caught, you're right on the caper. They don't pick you up after. The [criminal] lawyer usually couldn't plead before a jury—I got a lawyer in Portland: I listened to him plead a case in the jury room one day and he almost hung this guy. And I told him afterwards, "If I ever have to go to a jury, don't you ever plead for me."

But if he's a fix, that's his field, you see, that's all he understands is connections. I've never found a fix that's a good trial lawyer. A fix has got it all fixed before you go to court and then the district attorney will get up and recommend this way or that way if it goes that far and you'll be granted probation, parole, or whatever they're gonna grant or ask for dismissal if you got enough money, which is a little raw so they don't very often do that. But it's all cut and dried. You know what you're gonna get before you go down to court. I've been to court hundreds of times but I've only been to prison five times.

They can't dismiss the case as a rule. It's pretty raw to do that. They suspend the sentence. They just forget about it. If you're on parole, you don't necessarily stay there, it's not a good idea to stay where you were sentenced. The safe squad is usually pretty unhappy about you getting a parole and all they want to do is lock you up. Like Edgar Hoover, he says, "Commit the crime, lock him up, that's the easiest way to take care of him." And they'll roust you and give you a bad time if you've got a suspended sentence or parole, so you usually try and transfer someplace else. Of course, they don't want you there, either, as soon as they find out who you are.

Sometimes you can't get the fix. You run into places, if it is real hot. I've gone into towns and looked the town over and you don't know anybody, you don't contact anybody, and some towns never publish the crime news, outside of murder or something like that, but stickups, box jobs, they don't publish them. So you go in and you don't know whether this town is red hot and you go out and root and you get snatched. You get down there, they're looking for somebody like you and nothing in the world will save you, I don't care what kind of a connection you got. People want a clean town, so they grab the first guy that they can hang on, make a big issue out of it and send him to the joint. Everybody settles down, and "see what a pure town we got." The thieves that was really making the money, they just go on about their business.

The last time I was rootin' I used a policeman for a point man and we built such a fire in Portland, on ourselves that when they did catch us they threw everything but the book at us. You know, and the fix was absolutely useless. I hired a fix but only to cut it down. To throw some of those beefs off me. I will show ya. My bondsman down there put up a $25,000 bond for me. I was being held in the county jail. They'd caught us cold-turkey, right out on this job by accident. A paper boy got a squint at us and my partner just as we walked across in the doorway and he called the bulls and they came out and we were completely surrounded, you know, when we came out of the joint. Half of the money disappeared, in transit, but they just left us alone, you know, and let us go ahead and finish it and then come out.

Well, my lawyer came down to see me right away and he said, "I'll have Joe bail you out." Well, then, Joe was on his way up to the jail to do it when this dick that I knew came up to see me. And he told me, "They got fifty beefs down there they're going to put on you." And I said, "Man, they can't prove them beefs, none of 'em, some of them are mine and some ain't, but they can't prove them." And he said, "No, but Oregon as you know, indicts guys and lets the judge decide whether they're guilty or not." So he said, "All they've got to do is throw them down in front of the grand jury and the grand jury'll indict you." I said, "Oh, I don't think they'll do that." And Joe comes up and put his $25,000 down and before I could get out and be released, they had me on another beef at $100,000. So I bowed my neck and sent for Joe and told him, "Well, I want out." My word was good enough for him for that and he said, "All right, I'll go get the bonds and get you out." And he went down to get 'em and while he was gone, they come up and stood right there with papers for another indictment. Waiting for me to get out.

So sometimes, you got to be thrown to the lions. The district attorney will resort to that, the district attorney has to have so many convictions a year. If you created a big furor in the town. My picture was in the papers for three weeks after we got pinched. And we were Number One news. That's when they can't fix it. All you can do then is try to get all the beefs throwed off except one and go to the pen for that one. That's how come you do actually go in spite of the fix. They all are in business and they have to show some results.

And with the publicity I had, well, in fact when I beat five years off the sentence and got out on probation, there was an awful storm. Why I can't even go to Portland now. You know, without them causing trouble over it. If I was still stealing I'd tear that town apart because I know I can beat 'em for a long time, I know that. But if I was going to do that, I would go from here to down there and have guys case off those joints for me and go from here down to Portland and knock 'em off and come back here and laugh at 'em. And let 'em blow their cork. But, you can't fix some of those, you just can't. And I don't mean by that that you can't fix a murder beef because you can. You know, but sometimes the heat's on too much and you just got to go ahead and go, that's all.

There's a lot of guys that do time who get real good connections and a normal beef they can fix. Two or three box men that I know in Portland, went down the same way but they were small-time box men. When they finally really got nailed, was when they knocked off a canteen—that has all this candy business—they got quite a large sum off that. And the canteen had a lot of strength, you know, they raised so much hell about it day after day. Where the average Hoosier—he believes the police department. He goes down there and says, "Well, I was robbed last night." And he goes home and says they'll catch the thief next week. The bulls know who it was so they go out and shake the guy down and get some dough off him or pinch him and the lawyer gets some dough, and that's all there is to it. There is no publicity. But if it's a big beef, then everybody gets interested in it because they don't like that heat on. I've seen beefs where all the thieves get mad over it because they all got to leave town over it. And they'd all be mad at the guys that done it.

I went to prison five times and each time it was the same thing, approximately. You know, too much heat. See, when I work, I work real hard. I just believe in it. I mean, it's silly to make $1,000 and go out and spend it, you're broke again. That's perpetual motion. So I don't believe that way. I say, "Well, if we're going to work, we get in a mood for everything and it is let's just keep on plowing, you know, just keep going right on down the line till we got a chunk of money, then lay off."

If you get picked up in a small town, you can deal with the D.A. personally, you know, he gets so few chances to take any dough, that when a thief comes into town, you know, why, he comes out in person and talks with him. He cuts out the attorney and everything else. I've had that happen several times, when I'd get pinched, like that. But little towns are so hard to work in because you can't case the joint off, you know. The Hoosiers know one another real well. And the bull on the beat knows everybody in town—knows where he's supposed to be and what time he's supposed to be home and what he's doing in that neck of the woods and everything else. When he sees a stranger, a couple times in a evening, why right away he begins to think. And some of those little town-clowns are pretty sharp, they've been there for a long time, they get pretty sharp. They wouldn't compete with one in the city, but they're very clever in their own districts.

To give you an illustration of the fix. Recently Danny was released from Montana on parole. He came to Seattle. A short time later he was arrested for possession of narcotics. He had a real sharp lawyer who could do business with the D.A. He went up and got the D.A. straightened around. After getting the case squared around they went to court. The judge was told that in as much as Danny was going to be violated and taken back to the joint they thought they should save time and money and drop the charge. The judge did this. Then the attorney for Danny flew over to Montana. He told the parole board that Danny was being held and tried for possession of narcotics in Seattle and that he thought they should continue Danny's parole. The parole board went along with the idea, not knowing that Danny had the charges dropped here. So consequently Danny remains on parole to this day, no charges against him or anything.

The fix does business with the district attorney and very seldom does he talk to the judge directly. Then when they go to court the judge usually goes along with the district attorney. Quite often the money that's given to the D.A. is split with the judge.

I automatically come in contact with corruption everywhere. But there is a great many people, judges, attorneys, policemen who are honest, extremely so, and I come in contact with the other kind; it is essential that I do. Any attorney I have is automatically a fix. Which 90 percent of the criminal attorneys are, nothing but fixes. They can't take a case before a jury and win. And the policemen that I know are the policemen that will take money. The judges I know, district attorneys I know are all corrupt but I don't say they are all that way. I will say a hell of a good percent of them are. But the point is you can get a fix anywhere; Salt Lake City, Los Angeles, Las Vegas, any of them. Just find a connection that's all.

To fix the average beef costs around four to five thousand dollars. It would be less for petty larceny; they're not much trouble unless they have been in the bulls' hair a lot. And if they have, they want to put him away. They won't listen, you know—nobody can fix it.

In a lot of places if two men are arrested they will come up and tell you that one is going to the joint and one is going to spring. And one of the guys is going and they have to decide who it will be. Is that justice? No, that's what is got me so mixed up. That blindfold should be really permanently tied on there.

There is no such thing as justice in criminal courts. If you've got the money you get the fix. If you haven't got the money, you don't get it. It's just that plain and that simple. A woman set fire to her home in Portland and her father's extremely wealthy. Murder is not a bailable offense. While this woman was in jail they passed a law allowing murder to be bailed out. She was immediately bailed out and was turned loose by the jury. She deliberately set fire to her home and burned up two or three of her children. She admitted it. It was a premeditated crime, incidentally. But she was turned loose. How can you expect these guys and kids to believe that there is justice? You can't convince these kids of that when they go up there in these detention homes five or six times. Those things have to be changed.

I'll tell you a little story that I have just seen. I'm down talking to a parole officer one day pertaining to a stabbing. He said he had to take care of it right away. He was supposed to make a pre-sentence of this guy. He sits there and reads what little information has been given to him. He determines what recommendation he is going to make to the judge. He was supposed to have personally investigated this man. I don't condemn him because he is so crowded. But the point is that he sat right there and recommended that the man be placed on probation from what he had. That's not right. That's not the answer to it.

When I was younger and the bulls would take you in you knew right then that you were gonna get a dumping [a beating]. But that didn't do no good either. But right here in this police department they still give you a thumping. I know a friend of mine was killed for shooting at a policeman. They beat him so badly that when they sent him to Walla Walla he died. It was from that beating.

But as a whole there is police violence in Seattle only in a minor way, Portland in a minor way, San Francisco in a major way, L.A. in a major way only they take you to the outlying jails to accomplish it now where there is no danger of the newspapers getting a hold of it. But they will use the brutal methods. I've been through both sides of it; where they treat you with kid gloves and where they are brutal.

When I was a kid in the penitentiary they were very brutal. They threw you in a black hole and they left you there. If you made any noise three or four of them would come in and beat you up. It was very simple. There was just as much crime then as there is today.

The FBI doesn't break heads anymore at all. It's an illusion that they didn't at one time. They were just as vicious as anybody was. We go through an era, you know. Edgar Hoover is a very dedicated man. He has only one thing in this world that he wants to accomplish and that's to solve the crime and put the person in jail. That's all. He doesn't believe in paroles or anything. At one time, when he first started out, he got a hold of the whip and as the boss he was a pretty vicious man. You probably don't recall, but they shot their own man one time, they were so anxious. Edgar Hoover shot at his own

man one time trying to make a name for himself. They have got out of that. They have got to the point where they have become so successful that they don't need to use those methods anymore.

The only way you can beat the law is by moving all the time. The law is easy to beat as long as you keep moving all the time. But you have to continually move. We've proved that stealing can be very profitable by moving around all the time. I'm a great one for testing out systems and we went from right here in Seattle to Miami one time and stole ourselves silly. We made a terrific amount of money but we never was pinched once because we kept right on moving. And the FBI will tell you that as long as you keep moving, it's awfully hard for them to get you. You'll notice that they never catch any of these most wanted men till they sit down someplace. As long as those guys keep moving, they can't catch them. There's nothing for you to take a hold of, you know, to get the guy. See, you got to commit crimes and keep moving and they won't get you, unless it's just an accident. But the minute you sit down they'll get you because it's the bull's job to know all the thieves in that town. That's what makes them smart dicks.

They call these guys "camera-eye dicks." Well, that's guys that look at mug-shots all the time; men wanted here and there all around the country and they look at them mug-shots and they walk out on the street and start lookin' around. That's why I never go down to skid road or nothing when I'm stealing. I never go but to the best places. 'Cause the bulls never go there. And I can go in town and stay there as long as I want—within reason—and then I'll never be bothered. Never.

I don't dress like a thief, or pimp or anything. After I grew up and began to look around, found out that I could spot these thieves, you know, a block away the way they dressed and stuff in the old days, I quit dressing like them. I didn't think that it was so smart, anymore. I was raised in what they called the "hoodlums" in San Francisco out of 16th and Mission. It was just a collection of kids—tough kids—out there. I was the only one that wasn't tough I guess, in the whole district. But they all dressed the same. And they thought it was smart. That's when I learned not to. The bulls would come down and roust us and we didn't know how they could spot us. 'Cause we all wore the same caps and shirts. That's when I changed my style of dressing.

In the East, they stay right in one area most of the time. They stay right in New York City, it's so big. You know, they stay there. You give them a year's operation and every bull in New York will know about them, if it's in their field. But then they have the syndicate to fix it if they get busted. Out here they move around from Seattle to Portland, San Francisco to Los Angeles, Salt Lake–Phoenix, like that and it's hard for them bulls to keep up. Today they've got this teletype and stuff where they trade information and the minute they see any inkling of a guy leaving one town and going to another, they teletype it. They put that information together.

The FBI has the money to build it up and they have developed the best techniques that there are and they draw the greatest men in that field to solve a crime. They really don't have to worry anymore. Each one of their agents now is a general agent who can be turned loose on any type of crime. I wouldn't say the FBI are particularly better people. An illustration is that one of their agents in the East tried to sell some evidence that they had to some criminals. And one held up a bank in California, an ex-agent. So they are not better, but they are better with techniques. They are getting things more their way like in the fingerprint system. They are getting more laws passed that are to their benefit. This makes it easier for them to overcome laws.

If you were to read all the laws that have been sneaked in by Hoover and passed, you wouldn't believe it. You actually haven't any rights. You have violated the federal laws so many times it's pathetic. Everyone has. But in your case he doesn't want you. He wants me, the criminal. But it helps him to catch me. You would be surprised at the people who commit crimes today, businessmen who are really con men, and there is nothing they can do. Not a thing can they do to prosecute them. I'm very much against that type of crime.

The FBI has got beyond a brutal stage. They are cold-blooded, when they pull out that pistol they are going to kill you. They don't shoot at your legs or arms to cripple you. They shoot to kill. They carry that 357 magnum and no man carries a gun

that big unless he intends to kill someone. That's a brutality in a sense, I guess. I don't really know if it is necessary to carry a gun. I would say off hand that it is like carrying a shotgun; but a shotgun is inconvenient and that's the only reason they don't carry one of them.

The FBI has sent policemen to schools. They have made the FBI school available. I think the school is in Washington, D. C. They have what they call a coordinator. The FBI has a man here who just hangs around the police station. All he does is coordinate between the FBI and the police.

The police department has all the reason in the world to be afraid of the FBI. They [the police] are shaking down guys all the time; prostitutes, criminals, bootleggers. So they are very much afraid of the FBI. The FBI is aware of that. It shows they overlook that. Because the policemen is there. He is there to stay. They don't dare start prosecuting the whole police department or they will get no cooperation. And no police department can get along without the stool-pigeon. The city police has more access to stool-pigeons than the FBI does. So the FBI, being smarter, they cooperate with the city police.

No police department, FBI or otherwise can get along without the stool-pigeon. I would say that 50 percent of their crimes are solved by stool-pigeons. Without them they can't get along. The FBI does not trust the city police in any manner, shape or form. I know two or three agents here real well. I've known them for years. One of them, in fact, was assigned to me at one time and tailed me around. I got tired of it and stepped in a doorway and he lost me for a minute. When he went by I told him that I was going to get a cup of coffee and why didn't we go together. That shook him up. He reminds me of it every once in awhile. Now we are pretty good friends. I also remind him once in awhile that there is a phrase in the Bible that says, "Thou Shalt Not Kill." Usually it perturbs him a great deal when I tell him that. He has no answer to it. I just do it for meanness for I know that he has to carry a gun. But that's defeat in my mind. I never carried a gun because I knew that someday I would have to kill somebody. That's what you carry a gun for. So I never carried one. Because I don't believe it's man's prerogative to take a life.

Arrest

PART 3   THE SOCIAL ORGANIZATION OF CRIMINAL LAW ENFORCEMENT

INTRODUCTION

Police decisions and practices doubtless have a greater effect on the shape of the legal system than those of any other law enforcement agency. Each year in the United States approximately six million persons are arrested. Most of these arrests are for relatively minor offenses. In 1970, for example, police departments reporting to the Federal Bureau of Investigation reported 6,257,000 arrests, of which only 920,000 (15%) were for offenses which are categorized by the FBI as "Type I" or "major" offenses. Even this figure distorts somewhat the seriousness of most of the offenses for which arrests are made. It is clear, however, that well over 80% of the arrests made by police are for minor, albeit not necessarily inconsequential, offenses. This in part accounts for the fact that, of the over four million arrests made each year, fewer than one hundred thousand persons (2 or 3%) are sent to prison. Most of the persons arrested never appear in court, many are released after booking, some are held in jail for only a short time, and still others appear in court but spend only a short time in a city or county jail.

The President's Crime Commission conducted a national survey to locate the number of persons in the population who had been victims of crime and to see what subsequently happened to their cases.* The findings illustrate the sifting process of the legal system in macrocosm (see Table 1). Of the 2077 cases of victimization reported in

TABLE 1

Total cases	2007
Police notified	1024
Police came	787
Police called incident a crime	593
Arrest made	120
Trial	50
"Proper" conviction*	27

*As characterized by the victim.

Source: P. H. Ennis, "Criminal victimization in the United States: a report of a national survey." A report of a research study submitted to the President's Commission on Law Enforcement and Administration of Justice, Field Surveys II, U. S. Government Printing Office, 1967, p. 49.

*President's Commission on Law Enforcement and Administration of Justice, The Challenge of Crime in a Free Society, Washington: U.S. Government Printing Office, 1967.

the survey, only 120, or just 5% culminated in trials. The major single cause of legal inaction was a failure on the part of the victims to report the crimes to the police: 51% of the victims reported not having told the police about the incident. The reduction of the over 1000 cases that remained to 120 ending in trials is largely accomplished by the discretionary powers of the various legal processing agencies.

A more detailed accounting, which will further illuminate the role of official discretion in criminal-law procedures, shows a still more dramatic reduction in the number of persons who make their way through the legal process and move from arrest to conviction. A recent survey of law-enforcement activities in Washington, D.C. provides data that are fairly representative* (see Table 2). In Washington, D.C. in 1965 there were 25,648 felonies known to the police, and there were 6266 arrests. We do not know, unfortunately, what percentage of the felonies known were accounted for by these 6266 arrests (since one arrest might account for fifteen felonies), nor do we know how many persons might have been arrested but turned loose by police at the time of initial contact or after screening at police headquarters. We do know, however, that of these 6266 arrests over 50% were released from felony charges. After screening by the prosecutor's office there remained an estimated 2379 adults charged with felonies by the prosecutor. The remaining cases were either dismissed or had charges reduced to misdemeanor offenses. Later in the process, after grand jury hearings, 1526 persons were indicted and convictions were obtained in 981 cases. Of these convictions, 273 were appealed and no final disposition was available at the time of the report. However, in the appeals court of the District of Columbia, the number of appeals granted averages around 20% of the cases appealed, so it is a fair estimate that around forty-five of the appeals were granted. Thus, during the course of legal process approximately 85% of the persons arrested for felonies avoided a felony conviction or, conversely, of the persons arrested for felonies only 15% were ultimately convicted.

The majority of those arrested are released from criminal prosecution; the remainder are charged with lesser (misdemeanor) offenses. Even the figure of 15% is an underestimate of the impact of the legal process on the distribution

*Report of the President's Commission on Crime in the District of Columbia, Washington: U.S. Government Printing Office, 1967.

PART 3   THE SOCIAL ORGANIZATION OF CRIMINAL LAW ENFORCEMENT

of persons arrested, since it does not include those persons who are released by the police and never come to the attention of the prosecutor.

With nothing save these raw statistics to judge the legal process by, the picture that emerges is nonetheless quite revealing. First it is clear that the bulk of the criminal law enforcement effort is directed towards minor infractions of the law—drunkenness, vagrancy, disorderly conduct, and the like. Second, even within the small proportion of the serious offenses (which at most accounts for only twenty percent of the total arrests) the vast majority of these offenses never culminate in a criminal conviction. To understand the process we must know in some detail precisely what takes place in the organizations responsible for "enforcing the law."

Even apparently insignificant and obvious decisions made at the policing level may have profound consequences in determining specifically who is processed through the legal system, and, more generally, what the law in action really means.

The relatively minor and apparently straightforward decision of how to distribute available police manpower has important consequences. Obviously, even in police state societies there are not enough police to permit the constant surveillance of every citizen or even of every square mile of territory. Where then, should the police be distributed so that they will be likely to detect crime? The answer is as simple as the question: where the most crime occurs. But the answer to the question of where the most crime occurs may not be as simple as it looks. Generally,

TABLE 2
Disposition of Adults Arrested for Felonies in Washington, D.C., during 1965.

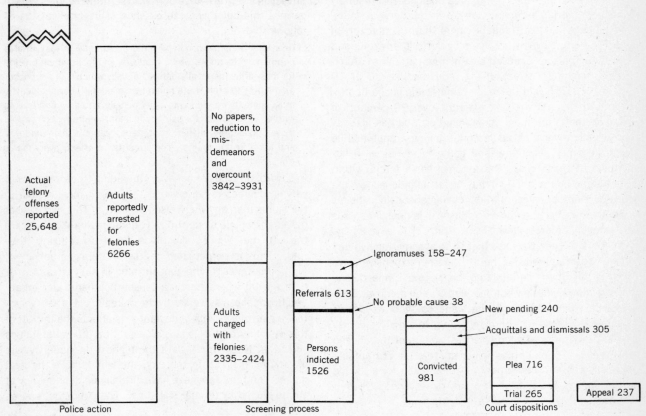

From President's Commission on Crime and Law Enforcement in Washington, D.C., U.S. Government Printing Office, 1967.

the evidence for where the most crimes occur consists in past records. If the central district of a city has had the highest crime rates in years past, then that is where the police must focus their attention today. But behind this simple logic is a potentially dangerous cycle: it is possible that the only reason the central section, or any other section, has shown a higher crime rate in the past is because police were there to look for it. Thus it is quite possible that the police, by this apparently simple decision with an obvious direction implied, may well contribute to the maintenance of a self-fulfilling prophecy which finds crime prevalent where we look for it, not because of the inherent criminality of the areas surveyed, but merely because crime is sufficiently widespread so that any area that was inundated by policemen would show a correspondingly high crime rate.

Weight is added to this interpretation when it is realized that a "high crime rate" for an area does not mean simply that there are large numbers of rapes, murders, assaults, and robberies. Most, probably more than 80 percent, of the crime effort by law enforcers consists in arresting and processing persons accused of very minor offenses: drunkenness, vagrancy, streetwalking, and the like. Over 10 percent (101,763) of the major crimes were accounted for by auto theft. Yet the vast majority (over 90 percent) of the auto thefts are more accurately described as joyrides and usually involve an adolescent's taking an automobile for a short period of time and going for a ride with it.* In most of these cases the automobile is found within twenty-four hours where it has been abandoned by the thieves. Another category which characteristically includes a number of offenses whose seriousness is questionable is the category of larceny over $50. Thirty or forty years ago it might have been the case that to steal something valued at over $50 required the theft of a rather expensive commodity, but this is certainly no longer true. Indeed, one hubcap from most new automobiles is valued at over $50. To place such offenses in the same category as crimes against the person and burglary is to give a distorted view of the seriousness of such offenses. Much of the alleged increase in serious crimes in recent years is attributable to an increase in the number of autos taken for a joyride rather than to an increase in other, more serious types of offenses.

Furthermore, even among the major crimes, the bulk of these (roughly 80 percent) are crimes against property, a fact which contrasts rather sharply with the widespread belief that most police activities center on crimes against the person, such as assault, murder, and rape.

These facts suggest, then, that the arrest rate in any area is largely a function of the police making arrests for relatively minor offenses. Although the data are not available for an accurate assessment, casual observation would suggest that the frequency of drunkenness, gambling, and numerous other offenses is probably as great in the middle-class respectable neighborhoods as it is in the lower-class slums. The middle-class transgressions, however, are "invisible," not just because the police do not as thoroughly survey the areas in search of transgressions but also because middle-class wrongdoings (as defined by law) typically take place in private. As was pointed out earlier, privacy is a very effective barrier to scrutiny. James Wilson defines this point and the essence of its implications as follows:

> In a slum neighborhood, personal and family privacy is at a premium. The doors, walls, windows, and locks which provide for most of us the legally-defined privacy which it is the policeman's duty to protect are much less meaningful to people who must share their rooms with other persons and their apartments with other families. Particularly in warm weather, such people move outside, sit on their front steps, lean out their windows, and loiter in the streets. The street is, in effect, every man's front room.*

In a word, all types of behavior, including transgressions of varying degrees of seriousness, are much more visible in the slums than anywhere else in the city. This fact is what moves the police to scrutinize with considerably more care the activities which take place. And scrutinizing, they find. Thus is perpetuated the self-fulfilling prophecy of high crime rates' being concentrated in slum areas.

In one city where there is a densely populated area inhabited by Japanese as well as by the more typical urban Negro, the degree of visibility of deviant acts affects the impact of this visibility on the legal process. The official statistics show that Negro youth have the highest delinquency rate of any racial group in the city; the whites have the next highest; and the Japanese have virtually no delinquency at all, as judged by official statistics. The police believe, as

---

*Jerome Hall, *Theft, Law and Society,* Indianapolis: Bobbs-Merrill, 1935, ch. 6.

*James Q. Wilson, "The Police and Their Problems: A Theory," *Public Policy,* vol. 12, 1963, p. 195.

PART 3   THE SOCIAL ORGANIZATION OF CRIMINAL LAW ENFORCEMENT

do most of the people in the community who are in any way connected with youth and youth problems, that the Japanese youth are of a different cut than most groups; families are more solidary; the adults form a more homogeneous and tight-knit community; and as a consequence, youthful involvement in delinquency is exceedingly rare. Believing this, the police devote little time to surveying the Japanese community. Patrolmen are assigned in large numbers to the Negro ghetto and to the skid-row area, but few are assigned to survey the area encompassing the Japanese community. Furthermore, the Japanese socioeconomic level is considerably higher than that of the Negroes; consequently, the residences are more likely to be "private" in the way that conventional middle-class residences are private, thus affording an added barrier to the visibility of transgressions.

Richard Nagasawa, utilizing a self-reported delinquency index, obtained responses on involvement in delinquency from a sample of Japanese, Negro, and white youth attending high school in the area with the highest delinquency rates of the city.* His findings (see Table 1) suggest that while the Japanese youth do have a somewhat lower rate of involvement in delinquency than white or Negro youths,

TABLE 3
Comparison of Arrests (for 1963) and Self-Reported Delinquency Involvement by Racial Groups

	Percent of Each Group Arrested during 1963	*Percent of Each Group Classified as High Delinquency Involvement on the Basis of Self-Reported Delinquency**
White	11	53
Negro	36	52
Japanese	2	36

*A self-reported delinquency scale was developed, and the respondents were divided so that 50 percent of the sample was categorized as having high and 50 percent as having low delinquent involvement.

*Richard H. Nagasawa, "Delinquency and Non-delinquency: A Study of Status Problems and Perceived Opportunity," unpublished Master's thesis, University of Washington, Seattle, Washington, 1965. See Travis Hirsch, *Causes of Delinquency,* Berkeley and Los Angeles: University of California Press, 1969, for an excellent discussion of self-report and official delinquency studies.

they are scarcely "delinquency-free," as is generally assumed. The really striking contrast which emerges between the official rates (as measured by police statistics) and the self-reported rates of the three groups can be explained by differences in the visibility of the acts but certainly not by differences in the propensity of the youths in the various groups to commit transgressions, as judged by their self-reported involvement.

The general point to be made here is that police decisions have a good deal of a "self-fulfilling" quality. Precisely how many more offenses would be observed in areas of more sparse and more affluent populations it is impossible to guess. But we should look rather carefully at the assumption that previous crime rates are an adequate index of the propensity of one group to commit more crimes as compared with some other group. Statistics and legal action concerning even apparently obvious offenses such as murder and rape are likely to be very biased against lower-class areas for much the same reason that statistics on minor offenses are. Murder is one of the more difficult crimes to hide, yet it is proportionately more difficult for someone in a lower-class area to hide than it is for someone in a middle-class area. In addition, the police are understandably more reluctant to bring charges of murder against a respectable member of the community than they are against someone who is viewed as being suspect.

Data on rape may well be similarly biased. Doubtless many more rapes occur than are reported because of the unwillingness of victims to have it publicly known that the rape took place. If the rape occurs in an automobile or in the privacy of a home, then the likelihood of the event's becoming public is totally dependent on the victim's taking action. If, on the other hand, the rape occurs in an alley or in an apartment where shouts are easily heard by neighbors, then the fact of the rape is far more likely to become public. Indeed, rather than acting as a source of shame, a rape under these circumstances may make the offended person feel compelled to file a complaint in order to demonstrate publicly that she was not a willing partner. Where the event occurs out of public view there is considerably less incentive for making an official report.

The police also contribute to the high incidence of crime in certain areas by adopting policies which encourage the concentration of tolerated but criminal activities in certain ecological areas of the city. Thus, as was pointed out earlier, the fact that the police tolerate gambling, prostitution, homosexual bars, and the distribution of pornography only in the poorer, more run-down sections of the city ensures that these sections will have a higher incidence of crime (at least with respect to the above-mentioned crimes). It also increases the likelihood that assaults, drinking, and the like will occur since in American culture these are frequently concomitants of enjoying the vices.

Once the policeman goes out on the beat (or into a patrol car) the process continues. Even if one is committed to arresting all violators of the law (which virtually no policeman can do) considerable discretion is called for. How does a policeman decide, for example, that something is amiss and should be looked into? Where policemen are assigned the same beat for some period of time, one of the most often-used techniques for making such a decision is to search for "unusual" events. To the uninitiated, things which appear to be unusual events may not be so at all. A policeman may, for example, ignore the fact that a woman comes running from her house screaming that

someone is going to kill her. If this has happened every Friday night at approximately the same time for a year, then the policeman may well have decided that it is not significant. Or, if the same shopkeeper is always engaged in an apparently violent argument with the same customer every week, the policeman may well continue on his appointed rounds without so much as even a second look into the store. In fact, what may stand out in his routine as an unusual event is the absence of a shouting argument or the absence of a drunk from a street corner. This weighing of events is a highly selective procedure and is yet another in a series of sociologically significant events which shape the legal process.

The articles that follow pursue the topic of police practices by providing a wide range of studies from the recruitment and training of police officers to the field practices routinely engaged in by the police on the beat. We also take up the controversial question of the use of violence by the police and the consequences of this for the law enforcement process at the level of arrest.

14

Background Characteristics of Recruit Police Officers

JOHN H. McNAMARA

Many of the attitudes and past experiences of newly appointed recruit police officers are relevant to a discussion of the functions of recruit training for the uncertainties of police work. Immediately after a patrolman was first appointed to the department he, along with a number of other recruits, began his formal training. Prior to his appointment he had been subjected to a number of examinations and investigations. He must have passed a written civil service examination which was considered by the personnel department to serve not only as an intelligence test, but also as a test of knowledge concerning police work.[1]

Following the civil service written test, the candidate is required to pass qualifying medical and physical tests. Finally, the candidate had to be approved by the unit conducting his "character investigation." The character investigation was an attempt to assess the degree to which a candidate would be likely to withstand the ethical and psychological risks involved in police work. The investigation was somewhat

Source: "Uncertainties in Police Work: Recruits' Backgrounds and Training," David J. Bordua (ed.), *The Police*, New York: John Wiley, 1967, pp. 191–207. Copyright © 1967 John Wiley & Sons, Inc. Reprinted by permission of John Wiley & Sons, Inc.

comprehensive in that the investigation of each candidate required approximately twenty-five man-hours of the investigators. They attempted to construct a pattern of each candidate's character from such data as his occupational history, financial status, conduct in school or in the military, sexual habits, and criminal or delinquent experiences of the candidate, his friends, and his relatives. Interviews conducted by an investigator with a candidate were considered valuable because the investigator could personally assess the degree to which the candidate was cooperative and truthful. These interviews often approximated a stress interview in which the reaction of the candidate to the authority of the investigator (usually a police sergeant) was recorded. Thus, a candidate was given a foretaste of the semimilitary model governing interaction between superordinate and subordinate even before he was appointed to the force.

The recommendation of the investigator that the candidate be approved or disapproved or that a "hearing board" pass on the suitability of the candidate was governed by the phrase, "All doubts about a candidate should be resolved in favor of the department." In effect this meant that any candidate about whom there was doubt should not be approved. In each of two groups of patrolmen in the study, only two-thirds of the candidates were approved by the character investigation unit. Of a combined total of 272 patrolmen in the two groups, 27% were referred to the hearing board and the remaining 7% were disapproved of but later hired as a result of a hearing board's recommendation or as a result of civil service limitations on the police commissioner's discretion regarding appointments. Although the candidate's first encounter with the department may seem somewhat harsh, the selection procedures in departments which employ the polygraph or lie detector routinely are equally, if not more, harsh.

As a result of recruiting, the selection program, and the self-selection of candidates, newly appointed patrolmen tended to be primarily from the lower-middle-class segments of the population. If we use the measure of their fathers' eleven major occupations for three combined groups of 574 recruit patrolmen relative to the distribution of the labor force for the New York "S.M.S.A." as reported in the 1960 U.S. census, it is clear that the recruits are not drawn from families in the "higher skill" segments of the population (Table 1).

The recruits themselves, as a group, had held at least one full-time job treated by the census classification as being a "higher skill" occupation than their fathers. Table 2 presents the percentages of the "highest skill" full-time occupations prior to entrance into the police force. Generational and age differences between the recruits and their fathers as well as the shifting nature of work are relevant to a comparison of the percentages of recruits and their fathers classified as having clerical or sale occupations. The mean age of the recruits at the time they listed their occupations was 24.3 years of age. Two-thirds of the group were between the ages of 21 and 24 inclusive. The increasing need for personnel in the "tertiary" areas of work also accounts in part for the generational differences.

TABLE 1

Occupational Levels of Police Recruits' Fathers

Occupational Level	Percent of of Recruits' Fathers	Percent, Work Force, New York S.M.S.A.
Professional, technical, managers, officials, proprietors	10.8	22.2
Clerical, sales	9.4	27.2
Craftsmen, foremen	19.3	11.3
Operatives	16.6	17.3
Service, household workers	28.1*	11.8
Laborers	5.7	3.4
Not reported	10.1	6.7

*One-third of the recruits' fathers in this category were recorded as having the occupation of police officer or an occupation involving police-type duties, for example, private detective or watchman.

TABLE 2

Prior Full-Time "Highest Skill" Occupation of Recruits

Occupational Level	Percentage of Recruits
Professional managers, etc.	7
Clerical, sales	44
Skilled, foremen, craftsmen	22
Operatives, kindred	12
Service, household	8
Unskilled, laborer	3
Not reported	4

The recruits further tend not to be from the more educated segments of the population. In order to be appointed to the force, a recruit was required to have a high school degree. Of one combined group of 574 recruits, however, 21% had not earned a diploma but had "equivalency degrees," given upon passing an examination. In this same group, less than 2% had earned their Bachelor of Arts degree and 28% had had some college at the time they were tested.

Given the socioeconomic level of the recruits, we hypothesized that they would be somewhat more authoritarian than the general population and thus would score somewhat higher on the F-scale, but not as high as many sociologists posit.[2] One group of 166 recruits was tested prior to their entrance into the police academy, and another group of 294 recruits was tested in their third month of training in the academy. Both groups had a mean of 4.15 and a standard deviation of .65 on the F-scale. Adorno et al.[3] report mean scores of 4.19 and 4.06

respectively for 61 "working-class men" and 343 "maritime school men." The authors also report a mean of 3.84 and a standard deviation of 1.10 for a group of 1518 subjects of varying background characteristics.

For sociologists who propose that recruits are attracted to police work by the power residing in the role these mean scores may be surprisingly low. The main attraction of the work for recruits, however, seemed more to be found in the civil service security coupled with the relatively high economic benefits associated with the job. In support of this it was found that a large proportion of each incoming group of recruits had taken entrance examinations for both the police department and the fire department. The latter had similar job security conditions and economic benefits but fewer openings and more stringent physical requirements. A number of police recruits, moreover, expressed their preference for the fire department primarily because of their dislike of dealing with the public in police work. Further, although a number of men who resigned from the police department to join the fire department, the police department gained almost no personnel who resigned from the fire department.

Additionally, the recruits' responses to a "punitiveness" scale constructed by Nettler from responses of a sample of 939 community leaders in a metropolitan area seem relatively nonpunitive.[4] (See Table 3.) The scale scores of 157 recruits in their first week of training at the police academy were markedly lower than those of the community leaders. (The scale requires the respondent to indicate which societal response—treatment or punishment—is appro-

TABLE 3

Percentage Distributions of Scale Types:
Punitiveness Scale (in Per Cent)

Scale Types	Community Leaders*	Police Recruits
IV (punitive)	17	2
III	20	12
II	10	17
I	40	39
0 (nonpunitive)	13	31

*See Nettler, *loc. cit.*

priate for different types of juvenile deviants.) This comparison may be inappropriate, since there is a large age difference as well as a regional difference between the two samples, and recruits might identify more closely with juvenile deviants. Since the questionnaires were not anonymous, the recruits' responses may have been subjected to a "social desirability" influence and hence lower than they might have been. Recruits are probably somewhat sensitive to any imputations of tendencies toward "police brutality." It would seem that recruits were less interested in "disinterested punishment"[5] than in avoiding some harm to themselves or to certain other people.

RELEVANCE OF RECRUITS' BACKGROUNDS FOR LEGAL UNCERTAINTIES

From the above discussion we see that the recruits are likely to be drawn from different segments of the population than those from which legislators and jurists are drawn. Thus, there exists a potential set of tensions between police and law-makers' definitions of crime and ranking of seriousness of different crimes. For example, the courts tend to treat violations of vice laws as minor offenses, but police departments traditionally expend a great deal of time and manpower in the search for marijuana users, prostitutes, homosexuals, etc. In this connection, the author heard the chief magistrate of New York City, at a meeting of a police officers' association, request that fewer arrests of narcotics addicts be made in view of the lack of both court and treatment facilities.

Although the recruits score on the F-scale within the limits expected on the basis of their socioeconomic origins, their group mean score still exceeds the overall mean of a "purposive" sample (intended to test a cross-section) presented in the original study by Adorno *et al*.[6] Therefore it could be predicted that the recruits would be less likely than the general public to appreciate the subtleties and qualifying conditions that are associated with both substantive and procedural criminal law. Moreover, the academy relied mainly on classroom presentation and study in order to transmit some understanding of the laws police enforce. We also hypothesized that this reliance on the classroom for teaching law to the recruits would be problematic in view of the limited formal academic backgrounds of the recruits.

Similarly, given the socioeconomic backgrounds of the recruits, one could predict that their view of the effects of a less punitive court orientation would be quite different from that of court personnel. We examined the responses to an item asked of 294 recruits in their third month of training to indicate whether they agree with a number of reasons offered to explain ". . . why some citizens assault police." A statistically significant difference existed between recruits dichotomized into two groups on the basis of their fathers' occupations. Recruits with fathers in the higher skill classification were less likely to feel that the leniency of courts and laws accounts for assaults on the police (Table 4).

TABLE 4
Responses to "Courts and the Laws Are too Lenient" as One Reason Why Citizens Assault Police (Recruits Differentiated by Fathers' Occupations)

Fathers' Occupation	Actually Is a Reason	Do Not Know, Uncertain	Not Actually a Reason
Higher skill*	74	15	41
Lower skill	97	33	34
$p < .05$ (Chi-square$=6.58$; $df=2$)			

*Higher-skill occupations are professional, managerial, technical, clerical, sales, skilled, craftsmen, and foremen. Lower-skill occupations are all others.

This difference in attitudes regarding the determinants of assaultive behavior implies not only a difference in attitudes toward the courts and laws but also a difference in their attempts later to reduce the frequency of intensity of these assaults. It might be hypothesized that recruits who see the responsibility for these assaults as that of the courts and laws do not see it as that of the police department or the individual officer. The recruits, however, still dichotomized by their fathers' occupational skill level, do not respond differently to three other possible reasons why citizens assault police: "Some arrests are unlawful," "Some people are handled poorly," and "Police aren't firm enough." The differentiated responses to the item concerning the leniency of

courts and law seem to reflect a belief concerning the existence of this leniency as much as a belief in the effects of leniency.

RELEVANCE OF RECRUITS' BACKGROUNDS FOR UNCERTAINTIES REGARDING POLICE PRESTIGE

When recruits were asked to indicate the prestige that the general public might assign to police work relative to other career possibilities they had entertained or to other jobs they had prior to coming into the police department, they were likely to consider police work as more socially *prestigious* (Table 5). Further, as recruits moved from considering remote (career possibilities) to more proximate (prior) jobs, they tended to indicate that police work increased its level of relative prestige in the eyes of the general public. Thus, although 34% considered past career possibilities more prestigious than police work, only 14% considered jobs they had actually had to be more prestigious than police work. The recruits clearly considered their new employment in the department as a step for themselves at the time they joined the force.

Even though approximately two-thirds of the recruits considered police work to be equally or more prestigious than other career possibilities they had seriously considered, the recruits were not so convinced that police work as a career fared so well in the relative prestige assigned to it by the general public. In general and similar to more experienced patrolmen, police recruits do not see the position of patrolman as possessing much prestige. For example, only 12% of one sample of 171 recruits agreed or strongly agreed with the statement "The respect that citizens have for a patrolman and his position has been steadily increasing over the years," whereas 72% disagreed or strongly disagreed with the statement. Thus, although the recruits consider police work to be more prestigious for themselves, they do not consider the position as one which is increasing its share of respect. There may be some difficulty in treating "respect" as synonymous with "prestige." The notion of respect accorded police often was equated with fear of police. Whether this latter component predominated in the responses to the item cannot be determined from the data. Perhaps

TABLE 5

Percentages of Recruits' Estimates of Relative Prestige Assigned by the "General Public" to Recruits' Past Job or Career Possibilities and to Past Jobs

| | Prestige of Other Jobs Relative to Police Work | | | | | |
Careers or Jobs	Much Higher (1–1.9)*	Somewhat Higher (2–2.9)	About the Same (3–3.9)	Somewhat Lower (4–4.9)	Much Lower (5)	N
Past career possibilities of greatest interest	8	26	40	22	5	257**
Jobs recruits had "good chance of getting" when they joined police department	7	18	37	28	10	166
Prior full-time, "nontemporary" jobs of recruits	4	10	26	46	13	268

*Mean ranks were computed for each respondent, with a value of 1 assigned to "much higher," 2 to "somewhat higher," etc.

**Only recruits ranking the jobs in each of the above categories were considered in computing the percentages. The total number of respondents was 279. (Two groups were combined.)

the distinction made by recruits is one between a descriptive statement (prestige) and a normative statement (respect). That is, although the job involves an increase in the personal mana of the recruits, they believe there is not presently enough mana imputed to the role of the patrolman.[7]

It might be predicted that this feeling of insufficient respect for the role of the patrolman might become more salient for the recruits after they leave the academy and begin their work in the field units. But in a follow-up of the group of 171 recruits it was found that the percentage disagreeing or strongly disagreeing with the statement "Respect . . . for a patrolman and his position has been steadily increasing over the years" changed only 1% after they had been working in the field for one year. Nevertheless, the underlying attitude that patrolmen are not bettering their degree of respect may come to have a different meaning for an individual patrolman who, as one consequence of this attitude, feels he cannot rely on a high degree of public respect in carrying out his duties.

RELEVANCE OF RECRUITS' BACKGROUNDS FOR UNCERTAINTIES REGARDING EFFECTIVE INTERPERSONAL TACTICS

As indicated above, the recruits tend to be relatively homogeneous with respect to socioeconomic background, educational level, and scores on the F-scale. (The standard deviation was lower than that of any of

the groups reported by Adorno et al.).[8] They are also homogeneous in religion (in one combined group of 567 recruits, 80% were Catholic, 15% Protestant, and 4% Jewish), ethnicity (in a combined group of 565 recruits, 5% were Negro and 95% white, and it is the author's impression that less than 1% of the recruits were of Puerto Rican background), and age (two-thirds of the group of 574 were between the ages of 21 and 24 inclusive).

The homogeneity of police recruits, while perhaps desirable in some regards, particularly for ease of administrative practice, implies an immediate problem in terms of their ability to do veridical role-taking with the many different types of citizens that make up the heterogeneous urban population of New York. Given the recruits' homogeneity, the department was not able to select each man carefully for his optimal first assignment. Instead, the primary consideration in assigning men to precinct duty was the ease of commuting from their residence precinct to their assigned precinct. (Police officers could not be assigned to precincts in which they lived primarily because they would find it difficult to make impartial judgments in their interactions with the public.)

Equally important from the standpoint of the recruits' role-taking skills, is that the recruits are homogeneous in specific dimensions. For example, their somewhat high average score on the F-scale implies some difficulty in veridical role-taking.[9] Similarly, the fact that only 5% of the recruits were

Negroes and less than 1% were of Puerto Rican background implies immediately some role-taking problems because of a lack of common experience or shared perspective in dealing with Negroes and Puerto Ricans who together comprise 22% of the population of New York City. This is, of course, particularly problematic, since members of these groups are predominantly in the lowest socioeconomic strata, and these strata are over-represented in interactions with police, whether in regard to crimes or to the personal "service functions" served by police officers.

The socioeconomic level of recruits similarly implies certain difficulties regarding veridical role-taking. Schatzman and Strauss found a significant difference between middle-class and lower-class patterns of role-taking in which lower-class interviewees were characterized by a "relative insensitivity to disparities in perspective" between themselves and the interviewers as well as by a "notable assumption of correspondence in imagery."[10] In general, the lower-class subjects were far less able to perceive others as being members of different classes with different types of roles; that is, they were less able to impose a more impersonal or abstract frame of reference on others divorced from the others' unique identities. As Newcomb *et al.* point out, accurate perception of others requires that the perceiver have available to him some general principles or concepts with which to account for his observations of others.[11] Although the recruits do not come from the lowest socioeconomic segments, they do come from the segments in which the high skill occupations are underrepresented. Thus, their ability to do "interpersonal testing" was perhaps less marked than if the department had been able to recruit from the economically more favored segments of the population.

Of course, the characteristics of the citizen with whom a police officer is interacting must be taken into consideration in any discussion of the determinants of his effective interpersonal testing. For the most part, the most problematic or potentially problematic situations were those involving members of the lower socioeconomic strata and police officers in interaction. And even though middle-class persons may be generally more successful in role-taking, it is also a commonplace finding that similarity of background between two persons increases the accuracy of any role-taking between the two. Hence, the increase in role-taking skills that would follow upon the selection of a larger proportion of recruits from among the middle socioeconomic strata might be offset by the decrease in similarity of backgrounds between the more problematic citizens from the lower strata and such police officers.

At least one other consideration is relevant to this discussion of socioeconomic background and role-taking skills. Increased empathy between two persons may also be associated with increased sympathy between the two. As Turner has pointed out, role-taking may or may not involve taking the "standpoint of the other," that is, accepting the other's point of view as one's own.[12] The inappropriateness of a police officer's accepting the point of view of a prisoner who is resisting arrest while threatening the officer with a knife seems clear enough. If similarity of background were the primary basis for veridical role-taking, then it would be more likely that a role-taker would also take over the standpoint of the other for his own than if some other basis were primary, for example, low scores on the F-scale, whatever the identity of the relevant variable being measured by the F-scale.

Some of the characteristics of the recruits are also relevant to their ability to bring about effective *clarifications of their expectations* for citizens with whom they are interacting. Schatzman and Strauss have identified communication differences between lower- and middle-class subjects as involving the middle-class practice of using many ". . . devices to supply context and clarify meaning" and of being especially sensitive to communication problems with persons who fail to share their individual viewpoints or frames of reference.[13] It is relevant to note that the "decoders" in this study were middle-class interviewers. Even if all police were from the middle classes or above, their communication "devices" and sensitivity to communication problems would perhaps be more appropriate for other members of the middle classes than for members of the lower classes. Nevertheless, the skills involved in specifying expectations would be of great value to a police officer in view of the high degree of stress and consequent "narrowing of perception" which many of his interactants are experiencing at the time he is with them.

Recruits also tend not to have had much experience as supervisors prior to their coming into the department. In one group of 295 recruits the percentage having had any supervisory experience was 30.1. In the same group of 295 only 17% had had more than six months' experience as supervisors. This is not an unexpected finding in view of the usual age structure of the recruit groups. In another group of 279 recruits, 181 had been in the military for a mean period of 3.3 years. Of the 181 with service experience, 57% had had three or more years in the service and 54% had held the rank of E-4 or above. Of course, some of these latter ranks were specialist rather than line ranks; the recruits had approximately the same distribution of ranks relative to their length of service as do service personnel in general.

In view of the relatively little supervisory experience that recruits have had, it should be expected that they would have had little experience in clarifying expectations to persons in a subordinate or lower status position. This experience would undoubtedly aid them in being able to find and present desirable alternative modes of compliance with their expectations to citizens with whom they must interact. The extent to which past supervisory experience would aid in this regard, however, is also a function of a number of other conditions such as the specific nature of the task, the degree to which the lower-status person subscribes to the norms underlying the expectations of the higher status person, the specificity of the role relationship between the two, and so on. Thus, supervisory experience alone is not a sufficient condition for the recruit's ability to clarify expectations.

There seems to be little in the recruits' backgrounds that would point to their being unusually adept at *exploiting or utilizing the values of citizens* in attempting to gain their compliance. Since the recruits are homogeneous with respect to a number of social and psychological factors, it could be hypothesized that they might support one anothers' values

to the point where it becomes difficult for them to see many citizens' values as anything but wrong or at least not legitimate. Such an orientation makes it unlikely that a police officer would do much veridical role-taking or have much awareness of the existence of different citizens' values.

Furthermore, the problem for police officers in suspending their own values in order to consider a citizen's values different from their own would be more a problem for recruits with high F-scale scores and for those from the lower socioeconomic segments. We can hypothesize that recruits with these characteristics have a relatively ethnocentric orientation, and therefore they would be more likely to rely on the use or threat of force to gain compliance.

Similarly, the recruits' backgrounds do not particularly indicate an ability to effect a *presentation of self* as decisive or as impersonally concerned with a citizen and his problems. The recruits' relatively young ages and their lack of supervisory experience imply little opportunity to develop the skill of dissembling their uncertainties regarding an appropriate line of action.

In addition, since they are not recruited from the middle classes in which tension-binding and the cultivation of "manners" are more likely to predominate, the recruits would be relatively less able to effect an impersonal presentation of self. "Acting out" of problems is to some extent valued behavior in lower-middle and lower classes, especially when their members are confronted with status challenges of the sort that police officers constantly face. The notion of "disinterested punishment" is characteristically a middle-class orientation, and members of lower socioeconomic strata are far more likely to inject themselves more directly into the punishment of deviants.

RELEVANCE OF RECRUITS' BACKGROUNDS FOR ORGANIZATIONAL UNCERTAINTIES

Since a large proportion of the recruits have had some experience in the military services, the use of negative sanctions and the appearance of close supervision that together constitute the *semimilitary model* would not be unfamiliar to many of them. In addition, the majority of recruits have not been employed before in jobs where they were loosely supervised or where the use of negative sanctions was likely to be considered highly inappropriate by their supervisors. Therefore, the newly appointed recruits should not experience much of a "culture shock" with regard to the police department's expressed policy of supervision. The specific actual practices of supervisors may later concern them, but in general the recruits seem to feel that close and strict supervision is common and is appropriate for patrolmen.

The responses of one group of 171 recruits in their first week of training support the above assertion. Their responses to items A and B in Table 6—approximately two-thirds either agree or strongly agree with the items—indicate that the recruits expect supervision to be close and strict. Their responses to items C and D further indicate they do not consider such supervision as negatively affecting the performance of patrolmen.

Not only are the recruits prepared for the general orientation of close and strict supervision, but they also regard this type of supervision favorably. After recruits complete their training and have been assigned to the field for some time, they maintain approximately the same point of view regarding the existence of close and strict supervision. A combined group, which includes the group just discussed, was tested at a point when 137 had had one year and 83 patrolmen had had two years of work in the field. The percentage of the combined experienced group in agreement with item A (Table 6) was again 67%. These in agreement with item B changed only six points from 63% to 57%.

There was, however, a different degree of change with regard to the evaluation of this sort of supervision. Those patrolmen in agreement with item C as recruits constituted only 9% of the group, but after some field experience those of the combined group in agreement increased to 25% of the group. Similarly, 19% of the patrolmen as recruits were in agreement with item B, but 32% of the combined group were in agreement after their field experience. Although it is difficult to tell whether this reflected specific experiences of the patrolmen or a more general change in their evaluation of the dominant supervisory style in the department, there is little doubt that the patrolmen shifted toward a more negative evaluation of that style. In the discussion of the organizational sources of uncertainty, we explored the implications of such an evaluation and hypothesized the primary difficulty to be that patrolmen need to feel some sense of autonomy in order to make appropriate decisions in stressful situations.

The more negative evaluation of supervision made by officers after their field experience seemed to be related, to some extent, to an increased perception of the sanctions used by supervisors as being of a punitive nature. The responses to the following item are relevant: "Patrolmen are frequently found guilty of violating departmental rules and procedures and are consequently penalized severely." Twenty percent of the group of 171 were in agreement with this statement at the outset of their recruit training; after some field experience, 33% of the combined group were in agreement. Further, within the group of experienced patrolmen, those with two years' as

TABLE 6
Recruits' Perception of Semimilitary Aspects of Department (in Per Cent)

Item	No Answer	Strongly Agree	Agree	Uncertain	Disagree	Strongly Disagree
A	1	11	56	17	15	0
B	1	19	44	14	20	2
C	1	3	6	39	46	5
D	2	2	17	31	38	10

Item A: "Generally, police supervisors manage to observe patrolmen at work very closely."
Item B: "The department expects supervisors to deal with their patrolmen in a very strict manner."
Item C: "One of the major problems with law enforcement is that each patrolman is not given enough latitude by his supervisors to handle the police problem in his area of responsibility."
Item D: "Patrolmen often fail to take necessary police action due to a feeling that supervisors will disapprove of their actions."

contrasted with those with one year's experience tended more to be in agreement with the statement. Thirty-eight percent of the group with two years' experience agreed with the statement.

Recruits at the outset of their careers in the department seemed to be well aware that any violation of the rules and regulations of the department could be the basis for disciplinary action against patrolmen. Of the group of 171 recruits 91% agreed and only 4% disagreed with this paraphrased passage from the preface to the *Rules and Procedures*. It is interesting to note that although there was little change in the distribution of responses to this statement after the training and field experience, there was some increase in the amount of disagreement—from 4% to 5% at the end of training to 8% after one year of field experience. A comparable group of patrolmen with two years' experience had 13% of its responses in disagreement with the statement. It appears that experience tends somewhat to meliorate the rather strict or literal interpretation of this part of the preface to the *Rules and Procedures* but only slightly, since 83% of the patrolmen with one year's field experience still were in agreement with the item.

The degree of awareness of the "rat rule," as so designated, is quite different. In a group of 107 recruits tested at the beginning and at the end of their training, both times only five correctly identified the meaning of "rat rule" presented along with other words and phrases associated with police work. Since the recruits were scheduled to be familiarized with the "rat rule" during their fourteenth hour of instruction at the academy, we must assume that the instructors at the academy probably did not refer to the rule by the above designation. Although the group was not asked again to define the phrase when they were tested after two years in the field, we may be sure that the phrase was familiar then to more than five of the group.

The same group of 107 recruits was questioned about their *career aspirations* during their first week of training. The modal choice for the assignment the recruits "would most like to have after ten years on the job" was the detective division. Thirty-eight percent indicated this assignment as their most desired career pattern. In another group of 296 recruits tested during their third month of training, 58% chose the detective division as their most desired assignment after ten years.

The recruits not only considered an assignment to the detective division to be the ideal assignment but they also *expected* to be given this assignment after their first ten years on the force. Thirty-two percent (the modal response) of the group of 107 recruits so indicated in response to an item asking "What assignment do you think you will have ten years from now?" (Forty-one percent failed to indicate any assignment in response to this item.)

It was hypothesized that the recruits' socio-economic backgrounds might account for their interest in and expectations about an assignment to the detective division. But there was no significant difference between recruits whose fathers' occupations were characterized as in the top three skill levels of the census classification and other recruits with regard to both their expected and desired assignments in the tenth year on the force. The choice of the detective career pattern is more akin to the modal choice of airline pilot made by high school male students in that the work of a detective is strongly glamorized in the mass media. It is also considered to be a high status appointment by officers. Further, assignment to the detective division for many obviates the long hours of study that seem necessary for patrolmen to pass the civil service examinations for promotion to sergeant and above.

Eventually the goal of becoming a detective apparently changed for many of the recruits. In a group of officers tested after they completed either one or two years' experience in the field, the percentage *still* desiring appointment to the detective division "after ten years on the job" shifted to 28%. The percentage that still *expected* to be detectives "after ten years on the job" shifted even more markedly to only 16%. (As recruits, those *expecting* to be detectives in ten years constituted anywhere from 32% to 55% in different samples.)

This shift away from the detective career pattern was accompanied by an increased acceptance of the civil service promotional pattern as well as an increased acceptance of both the desirability and likelihood of being assigned to the patrol force after ten years. Those *desiring* an assignment to the patrol force after ten years shifted from 6% of the group of 107 new recruits to 20% in the group of experienced patrolmen. Those *expecting* to be assigned at the end of ten years to patrol duties also shifted— from 12% among the recruits to 33% among the experienced officers. It would seem then that the career aspirations of police were tempered by a more realistic appraisal of the available opportunities.

In this section dealing with background characteristics of the recruits we have attempted to show how the recruits are prepared to cope with the uncertainties of police work as well as with the requirements of the police academy. We noted that the recruits are better prepared to cope with uncertainties stemming from organizational sources and from the perceived low prestige attached to the role of police officer by the general public. On the other hand, their background characteristics and attitudes at the outset of their careers in police work do not prepare the recruits as well for the uncertainties regarding the use of effective interpersonal skills and the uncertainties stemming from considerations of the legality of police actions.

One major task for the recruit training school of the police academy would then seem clear: a systematic attempt to give the recruit the appropriate knowledge and attitudes that would reduce the uncertainties regarding the legality of his actions as well as a systematic attempt to move the recruits toward an acquisition of interpersonal skills.

FOOTNOTES

[1] See L. R. Eilbert, J. H. McNamara and V. L. Hanson, *Research on Selection and Training for Police Recruits: First Annual Report*, American Institute for Research, Pittsburgh, Pa., 1961, p. 4, for a brief discussion of the relationship between scores on one civil service examination and scores on the Otis intelligence test. The product-moment correlation between the two sets of scores was .54.

[2] The F-scale is an instrument for measuring the authoritarian personality syndrome.

[3] T. W. Adorno *et al.*, *The Authoritarian Personality*, New York, Harper and Brothers (1950), esp. pp. 255–8.

[4] G. Nettler, "Cruelty, Dignity and Determinism," *American Sociological Review*, Vol. 24, No. 3 (1959), esp. p. 380.

[5] See Nettler, *op. cit.*, p. 377, in which he cites Ranulf's thesis that disinterested punishment is characteristically a middle-class phenomenon.

[6] T. W. Adorno *et al.*, *op. cit.*, p. 258.

[7] See E. Goffman, "The Nature of Deference and Demeanor," *American Anthropologist*, Vol. 58 (1956), pp. 473–502, for an application of the concept of mana to interaction in urban society.

[8] T. W. Adorno *et al.*, *op. cit.*, p. 258.

[9] See T. M. Newcomb, R. H. Turner and P. E. Converse, *Social Psychology* (New York, Holt, Rinehart and Winston, 1965), pp. 172–9, for a discussion of the negative relationships found between scores on the F-scale and veridical role-taking.

[10] L. Schatzman and A. Strauss, "Social Class and Modes of Communication," *American Journal of Sociology*, Vol. 60 (1955), pp. 329–38.

[11] T. M. Newcomb *et al.*, *op. cit.*, p. 177.

[12] R. H. Turner, "Role-Taking, Role Standpoint, and Reference-Group Behavior," *American Journal of Sociology*, Vol. 61 (1956), pp. 316–28. Reprinted in *Approaches, Contexts and Problems of Social Psychology*, E. E. Sampson, (ed.) (Englewood Cliffs, N. J., Prentice-Hall, 1964, pp. 219–31.)

[13] L. Schatzman and A. Strauss, *op. cit.*

15

Police Field Practices

PRESIDENT'S COMMISSION ON LAW ENFORCEMENT
AND ADMINISTRATION OF JUSTICE

A community's attitude toward the police is influenced most by the action of individual officers on the street. While community relations units, neighborhood advisory committees, and fair procedures for processing citizen complaints are essential for reducing existing friction between the police and the community, these programs will have little enduring effect if persons are not treated justly in their contacts with police officers. This is particularly true of persons in slums or minority group neighborhoods who, because of more frequent contact with the police, are more aware of police practices.

Although many allegations of police misconduct or discriminatory treatment are unwarranted, Commission surveys reveal that police practices exist which cannot be justified. For example, the Commission found that abusive treatment of minority groups and the poor continues to occur. Many established police policies—such as the use of arrests for investigative purposes—alienate the community and have no legal basis. Departments

Source: "Police Field Practices," President's Commission on Law Enforcement and Administration of Justice, *Task Force Report: The Police*, Washington: U.S. Government Printing Office, 1967. Footnotes deleted.

may utilize procedures, such as the use of dogs to control crowds, without balancing the potential harm to police-community relations. And some valuable law enforcement techniques, like field interrogation, are frequently abused to the detriment of community relations. Too few departments give necessary guidance to assist their personnel in resolving potentially explosive social and criminal problems.

It is not possible for the police to enforce the law and preserve the peace without incurring some hostility and resentment. This is inherent in the very nature of police work. The major criticisms of the police, however, result from the particular methods used in accomplishing these functions. The purpose of this section is to examine police practices which appear to antagonize certain portions of the community, to determine the propriety of such practices, to show the need for all departments to establish reasoned policies governing police practices, and to analyze the sometimes competing considerations which must be weighed before establishing such policies.

This section does not constitute an effort to determine whether particular police practices are unconstitutional. Plainly, some practices described in this section, such as physical abuse, are illegal; others raise constitutional questions; and still others may be constitutional but unwise. Here the sole focus is on police practices which do or may affect community relations regardless of constitutional issues.

POLICE CONTACTS WITH CITIZENS ON THE STREET

It is extremely difficult for a policeman to maintain his composure in all street situations even though this is expected and demanded of him in nearly all police departments. For example, the Law Enforcement Code of Ethics, which has been adopted by nearly all departments and police associations, requires the following:

> I will * * * maintain courageous calm in the face of danger, scorn, or ridicule; develop self-restraint; and be constantly mindful of the welfare of others.
>
> I will never act officiously or permit personal feelings, prejudices, animosities or friendships to influence my decisions * * *. I will enforce the law courteously and appropriately without fear or favor, malice or ill will, never employing unnecessary force or violence * * *

But the capability of a policeman, and particularly one who works in a high-crime rate or slum neighborhood, to act in a restrained manner is constantly tested. There are countless pressures which increase the difficulty of performing police work calmly and with restraint. Typically, an officer is expected to maintain order on the street, to keep "a clean beat," to disperse mobs, to remove "undesirables," whether or not legal tools for accomplishing these results are available. A policeman's authority is daily challenged by unruly juveniles anxious to detect any weakness or fear. In dangerous neighborhoods, he may be mocked, threatened, or even spat upon. Police work requires that policemen continually see the tragedy of victimized citizens and the sordid lives of the reprehensible and unfortunate elements of the community. And, a policeman must always live with the prospect that he may be subject to attack without warning.

Even if an officer is of the highest quality, his work and the people with whom he must deal may cause him to become disillusioned or angry. If he is not of the highest quality or if he has not been properly trained, if he is prejudiced or hotheaded, he may succumb to his anger or resentment and physically or verbally abuse someone who offends him.

The problems of police-citizen contacts are multiplied and exacerbated when the citizens involved are youths. Youths commit a large and increasing proportion of crimes. They are out and around, noticeable to the patrolling officer. They travel in groups, which may make them appear more suspicious and at least potentially harder to control. They spend time in such local gathering places as pool halls, recreation centers, record shops, and street corners, and they often acquire information useful to the police. The antipathy toward the police that they might have at any age by virtue of race, neighborhood, or experience is heightened by youth's natural dislike for authority.

It is hardly surprising that youths and policemen are not always on the best of terms. Various factors influence their reactions to and relations with each other. Informal street contacts are rarely recorded, and little factual information is available about their real extent and nature. Several recent studies and field research projects, however, have begun to explore the causes of friction between police and juveniles.

In one study, a series of interviews was conducted with San Francisco gang boys—white, Mexican, and Negro—over a 2-year period. While the survey was limited to gang members, it has broader significance both because its observations and analyses deal with activities of the boys independent of their gangs and because gangs and their members probably have greater contact than other youths with the police.

As the San Francisco observers point out, besides needing to obtain information from youths and to apprehend them when they have violated the law, the police also feel an obligation to receive respectful behavior from them, both to symbolize their law-abiding attitude and to attest their acceptance of the particular police officer's authority. The youths in question, however, feel an equal need to establish and maintain their autonomy—a need that, in the case of many lower class gang boys, has been a way of life since they were children and successfully asserted their independence of overworked, ineffectual, or absent parents. One of the most tangible ways in which gang boys assert autonomy is their claim to control of a street corner, city block, or other geographical area as the inviolable site of their activities. But the gang's private hangout is also the policeman's beat and:

> Although the boys attempt either subtly or violently to convince outsiders that their behavior at the hangout is a strictly private affair, the police tend to insist with equal conviction that all behavior on public property is their legitimate concern.

According to one sociologist, the Chicago police illustrate the conflict by saying, when displeased by a gang's hangout behavior, "Give me that corner!"

The struggle for street corner control may be the backdrop for encounters between police and juveniles, but it is the more pointed, circumscribed encounters—stops, searches, trips to the stationhouse—that shape their views of each other. As the San Francisco sociologists point out, when policemen are suspicious of youths in a strange neighborhood, or their furtive actions, or their gathering together in groups, they are often supported in their suspicions by common sense and experience, as well as by want of alternative means to solve crimes and preserve public order. But feeling themselves both demeaned and challenged, the youths may react with more or less open defiance and hostility, slouching or smirking or answering the officers in an offhand or uncooperative manner, thereby challenging the policeman, in turn, to "put-up-or-shut-up." In that situation the officers, fearful of losing face and sacrificing authority on future occasions, may feel virtually forced either to arrest the juveniles for a vague or minor offense (suspicion of robbery, loitering, disturbing the peace, violating curfew regulations) or to make it appear that they are being let go out of the goodness of the officer's heart. The San Francisco study concludes that "this is why criminal records of many gang boys are often heavily laced with such charges as 'suspicion of robbery' and 'suspicion of rape.'" Similarly, a study of disorderly conduct arrests of both adults and juveniles in the District of Columbia found that in almost a quarter of them the arrest had been made only for loud and boisterous talking or obscene remarks to the police.

The San Francisco gang study, in taped interviews of youths, found that the appearances of authority thereby gained is more than offset by the resentment and disrespect created:

> One day we were standing on the corner about three blocks from school and this juvenile officer comes up. He say, "Hey you boys! Come here!" So everybody else walked over there. But this one stud made like he didn't hear him. So the cop say, "Hey punk! Come here!" So the stud sorta look up like he hear him and start walking over. But he walking over real slow. So the cop walk over there and grab him by the collar and throw him down and put the handcuffs on him, saying, "When I call you next time come see what I want!" So everybody was standing by the car, and he say, "All right you black * * * ! Get your * * * home!" Just like that. And he handcuffed the stud and took him to juvenile hall for nothing. Just for standing there looking at him.

Demeanor appears to affect police disposition after arrest as well as arrest in the first instance. Juvenile officers and patrolmen interviewed in the San Francisco study estimated that demeanor is the major factor in 50 to 60 percent of juvenile dispositions. Another study of juvenile offenders reports police officials in agreement that "defiance on the part of a boy will lead to juvenile court quicker than anything else." The more general significance of demeanor is illustrated by a study of a western police department, in which it was found that charges against speeders, prostitutes, and other offenders depended in large part on the suspect's demeanor.

Not all policemen equate unusual attire or surroundings with actual or potential lawlessness, and not all interpret defiance as need or justification for custody. This distinction is not lost on youths:

> Those two studs out in Lakeview wouldn't always be on our back for playing neither. We'd be standing on the corner pulling some kinda phoney (!) * * *, and they'd pull up to find out if we was up to something. But they talked to us nice. They wouldn't let us get away with nothing, and, I mean, them cats would bust you if they had to. But they talked to us nice.

Such officers—as the gang boy himself points out—are not necessarily softer, more lenient, or less effective. But by avoiding ethnic slurs, by recognizing and making allowance for the exuberance and the naturally combative and nonconforming attitudes of adolescents, these policemen allow adolescents to escape the uncomfortable spotlight of constant suspicion. Such a spotlight is not only frequently undeserved but it may encourage the youths to act as their audience, the police officers, appear to expect.

Verbal abuse and discourtesy Commission studies reveal that there are abuses in some cities which range from simple discourtesy to clearly unwarranted excessive use of force against persons of all ages. In focusing on such abuses, it is important to bear in mind that in the large majority of instances officers were observed to handle themselves with courage and often with restraint. Therefore, it is important that the following material not be read as a general description of the conduct of all police officers, but rather as a description of certain conduct which cannot be tolerated regardless how frequent or infrequent it may be.

No matter is more important to police-community relations than the manner in which police officers talk to people on the street. The Michigan State survey found that while allegations of excessive physical force receive the most attention, verbal abuse and discourtesy were probably greater irritants to community relations. If officers are abusive, insulting, or condescending, the most insignificant contact can become an occasion which arouses hostility against the police. On the other hand, if police officers are polite, forthright, respectful, and, where appropriate, friendly, a field interrogation, a traffic ticket, or even an arrest can actually increase the respect of the citizen, as well as others who see the incident, for the police.

Commission surveys revealed that a number of officers treat citizens in a demeaning manner. In one Commission study, observations were made in several cities of several hundred routine contacts between police and citizens, usually in a home or on the street. Most of the persons interviewed were witnesses, bystanders, and victims, rather than suspects. The study showed 9 percent of the persons received a polite request from the officers; 5 percent received an impersonal summons which was neither polite nor nasty; 66 percent were interrogated without introduction; and 15 percent of the interrogations began with a brusque or nasty command like "Come 'ere, punk" or "Get your * * * over here, pork chop."

Discriminatory statements, in particular, produce both anger and strong counterprejudice among mi-

nority groups. The use of racial epithets, such as "nigger," "coon," "boy," and "Pancho" appears to be widespread, even though their use is condemned by responsible police administrators. The President's Commission on Crime in the District of Columbia found that "offensive terms such as 'boy' or 'nigger' are too often used by officers of the Department" and that "in most cases, the language is chosen deliberately to demean the citizen and demonstrate the superiority of the officer." And a study of police handling of juveniles in two police departments stated that, while the observer never heard derogatory remarks made to Negroes by officers on the professionalized force, he heard dozens of insults and derogatory remarks by officers in the less professionalized department. It is precisely this type of language which solidifies the conflict between minority groups and the police.

Many police departments have regulations which require that citizens be treated with courtesy and respect and train their officers accordingly. One of the most far-reaching is that of the San Diego Police Department:

> We should treat all juveniles as we would want our own children treated, even the "hard core young hoodlum," for our job is to help juveniles toward good citizenship and build respect for the police and not to create "cop-haters" and criminals. *Always be fair, impartial, honest, and constructive.* [Emphasis in original.]

A similar rule might properly be applied to adults as well.

But the general instructions of most departments are neither sufficiently forceful nor specific as to the manner in which police officers should conduct themselves with regard to citizens. General police statements concerning the need for courtesy are not enough. All departments, for example, should formulate clear policies which prohibit the use of racial epithets. A similar recommendation was made by the President's Commission on Crime in the District of Columbia:

> The chief of police should issue a directive concerning verbal abuse of citizens by police officers, which identifies and prohibits the use of trigger words such as "boy" or "nigger." The Metropolitan Police Department should make it clear that violation of its order will be cause for disciplinary

procedures. Current department statements on the subject, which urge that "undue familiarity with the use of such terms as 'bud,' 'Junior,' 'Mac,' be avoided, are neither sufficiently forceful nor directly related to the problems of the community.

Shortly after that report, the chief of police issued a more specific directive than had previously existed.

Other police departments also prohibit certain forms of address. For example, the Chicago Police Department has the following policy:

> At all times Departmental personnel will:
> 1. Never show any bias or prejudice against race, religion, or any other group or individual.
> 2. Act, speak, and conduct themselves in such a manner as to treat all persons with complete courtesy and with that respect due to every person as a human being.
> 3. Never "talk down" to any group or individual or engage in the use of derogatory terms such as "nigger," "boy," "wop," "kike," "chink," "shine," "burrhead," "dago," "polack," "bohunk," and the like * * *

Some departments, such as Baltimore, require that their officers address persons as Mr. _____, Mrs. _____, Sir, or Madam. Such forms of address should be used as a matter of common courtesy.

Of course, it is often difficult for officers to be respectful when dealing with citizens who are abusive or disrespectful. But, as was expressed by the President's Commission on Crime in the District of Columbia after it deplored the use of abusive language both by police and citizens: "Officers must be held to a higher standard of conduct in performing their official duties." This view was also expressed by O. W. Wilson, the superintendent of police in Chicago:

> The officer * * * must remember that there is no law against making a policeman angry and that he cannot charge a man with offending him. Until the citizen acts overtly in violation of the law, he should take no action against him, least of all lower himself to the level of the citizen by berating and demeaning him in a loud and angry voice. The officer who withstands angry verbal assaults builds his own character and raises the standard of the department.

Consequently, if citizens show disrespect for an officer, such conduct, alone, while reprehensible, does not justify making an arrest or taking other action.

Finally, police officers should be encouraged to talk to citizens about nonpolice matters while on duty, as they are in New York, rather than prohibited from conducting such conversations with citizens. The BSSR survey of three Washington, D. C., precincts shows that hostility in Negro males declines as informal contacts with the police increase. These contacts allow the police to establish friendships rather than having solely the role of making arrests and interrogations.

Physical misconduct   Unjustified use of force, like verbal abuse, cannot be tolerated in law enforcement. Many persons, and particularly those from minority groups, believe that police officers sometimes or even frequently engage in excessive or unnecessary physical force. The Commission was not able to determine the extent of physical abuse by policemen in this country since recent studies have generally not been systematic. Earlier studies, however, found that police brutality was a significant problem. For example, the National Commission on Law Observance and Enforcement (the Wickersham Commission), which reported to President Hoover in 1931, found considerable evidence of police brutality. The President's Commission on Civil Rights, appointed by President Truman, made a similar finding in 1947. And in 1961, the U. S. Civil Rights Commission concluded that "police brutality is still a serious problem throughout the United States."

The Commission believes that physical abuse is not as serious a problem as it was in the past. The few statistics which do exist suggest small numbers of cases involving excessive use of force. Although the relatively small number of reported complaints cannot be considered an accurate measure of the total problem, most persons, including civil rights leaders, believe that verbal abuse and harassment, not excessive use of force, is the major police-community relations problem today. It is clear, however, that excessive force remains a serious problem in parts of the South. There are too many well-documented instances of brutality against Negroes and civil rights workers in the recent past to doubt that it still occurs today. For example, during the Mississippi march in the summer of 1966, State, county and local law enforcement officers on several occasions struck demonstrators. On numerous other occasions, law enforcement officers have watched white citizens attack civil rights demonstrators or have otherwise failed to prevent or halt private violence.

Moreover, one study undertaken by the Commission also determined that excessive use of force still remains as a significant problem outside the South as well. During this study, Commission observers systematically accompanied police officers on regular patrol in a number of major cities—primarily in high crime and slum precincts—for periods ranging from 5 to 8 weeks. During the survey, observers witnessed, during 850 8-hour patrols, 5,339 police-citizen encounters—encounters which included police contacts with suspects, witnesses, victims, and bystanders. While watching these encounters, Commission observers reported that there were 20 instances where officers used force where none was clearly required or where its use was plainly excessive. Of the incidents observed, most did not appear to be based upon racial prejudice. More than half of those subjected to excessive force were white. Almost all of the victims appeared to be poor. They included drunks, sexual deviates, or juveniles who were regarded by the police as hoodlums, and most appeared to contest verbally the police officer's authority. Three of the 20 examples of the incidents observed are as follows:

White officers responded to a man with a gun * * * and heard three shots fired. Then the white man with the gun got a drop on the officer—somehow they got the gun away and handcuffed him (gun was a 12 gauge 1905 musket). When they got him to the station garage, they kicked him all over, but the principal one was the officer who had been in danger when the man had the drop on him. He beat him as the others held him up. I got to the scene and the lockup man whistled for them to stop but they didn't. The Lieutenant arrived with everyone else and said there's going to be a beef on this one so cover it up and go find the empty shells. Someone call an ambulance (he needed it badly). Then the Lieutenant took complete control. They got the shells, got a complainant who said the three shots were an attempt to kill the officer, and he would sign a complaint, say he called an ambulance, etc. They wrote a cover for the incident. The officer who beat the man most was shaken by then but the others gave him support, telling him how brave he was and how wise he had been

not to kill the guy at the scene, etc. They then set about to put all the stories in order and I was carefully notified of it in detail so I would have it straight. I had enough rapport with these officers that they talked about it even after. The man was in pretty bad shape when he got to the hospital.

*   *   *   *   *

The officers were flagged down by a white man and woman. "The man who flagged us down said a Negro was inside the (public transportation station) causing trouble. The woman said he had sworn at her as did the man. One said: 'What's a nigger doing here; he should be down on * * *' The two white officers went in and grabbed him. They shoved him into a phone booth. Both officers beat him with fists and a flashlight and also hit him in the groin, then they dragged him out and kept him on his knees. He said he had just been released from a mental hospital that day. He begged them not to hit him again and let him go back to the hospital. One officer said: 'Don't you like us Nigger; we're here to help you! You're a crazy nigger.' They took him to the car and he kept begging them not to hurt him. Then they put him on the wrong bus—he wanted to go to the hospital and they sent him the wrong way. The last thing the Negro man said was: 'You police just like to shoot and beat people.' Officer No. 1 said: 'Get moving nigger or I'll shoot you.' The offender was crying and bleeding as he was put on the bus. Officer No. 2 said: 'He won't be back.'"

*   *   *   *   *

The dispatch was drunks in a cemetery. "We found the drunks sleeping in the cemetery. They were white men between 25 and 45 years of age. Officer No. 1 (white) ripped the shirt off one drunk in searching him. He also hit him in the groin with his nightstick. Officer No. 2 ripped back of pants of another drunk. The officers laughed as they forced them to climb over the fence and they laughed because the buttocks of the one was completely exposed. One officer said: 'I ought to run you * * * in.' As they left over the fence, another said: 'Those * * * * * won't be back—a bunch of * * * winos.'"

While this limited study gave the Commission no basis for stating the extent to which police officers use force, it did confirm that such conduct still exists in the cities where observations were made.

One other study conducted in a large city revealed that when juveniles show disrespect to officers, many of the officers prefer to settle the challenge to their authority by physical means. This study indicated that certain officers would justify their use of force by deliberately provoking the juvenile until he could be considered to be resisting arrest. This technique is described in the statements of one police officer and one juvenile taken during interviews in this city:

> For example, when you stop a fellow for a routine questioning, say a wise guy, and he starts talking back to you and telling you that you are no good and that sort of thing. You know you can take a man in on a disorderly conduct charge, but you can practically never make it stick. So what you do in a case like this is to egg the guy on until he makes a remark where you can justifiably slap him, and then if he fights back, you can call it resisting arrest.

> *   *   *   *   *

> Another reason why they beat up on you is because they always have the advantage over you. The cop might say, "You done this." And you might say, "I didn't!" And he'll say, "Don't talk back to me or I'll go upside your head!" You know, and then they say they had a right to hit you or arrest you because you were talking back to an officer or resisting arrest, and you were merely trying to explain or tell him that you hadn't done what he said you'd done. One of those kinds of things. Well, that means you in the wrong when you get downtown anyway. You're always in the wrong."

A survey of policemen in one midwestern city in 1951 also indicated that many officers had misconceptions about when they are justified in using force. Officers were asked to respond to this question: "When do you think a policeman is justified in roughing a man up?" They gave the following responses:

Reason	*Percentage*
Disrespect for police	37
To obtain information	19
For the hardened criminal	7
When you know the man is guilty	3
For sex criminals	3
When impossible to avoid	23
To make an arrest	8

The interviews provided considerable detail concerning the officers' rationale. They believed that the use of force to obtain evidence which would justify an arrest in a felony case was acceptable—"to rough him up a little, up to a point * * * You feel that the end justifies the means." Force was seen to be permissible with sex criminals when the officer knew that a person was guilty, did not have enough evidence, and considered it necessary to ensure that the criminal was punished. The officers said that

force was justified in cases involving disrespect such as:

> I was on the beat, and I was taking [a man] down to the station. There were people following us. He kept saying that I wasn't in the army. Well, he kept going on like that, and I finally had to bust him one. I had to do it. The people would have thought I was afraid otherwise.

The officers believed that the only way to treat certain groups of people, including Negroes and the poor, is to treat them roughly. On the other hand, this study did conclude that illegal force was not used as frequently and with as little provocation as the officers' statements would suggest.

To prevent physical abuse by police officers requires that all police departments take great care in selecting personnel, formulate strong policies on permissible conduct, dismiss officers who engage in physical misconduct, regularly review personnel practices, comprehensively investigate all complaints made against individual officers, and strongly discipline those officers who misbehave. . . . Policies should be formulated to bar not only unnecessary force but describe, to the extent possible, the amount of force which is permissible for making arrests and carying out other police activities. Such policies can best be enforced if all officers who use physical force for any reason are required to report in writing the circumstances under which the force was used.

Discrimination The University of California study found that members of minority groups in Philadelphia and San Diego generally believed that discrimination is practiced against both middle class and poor persons from minority groups. Polls of minority groups show similar results. It is extremely difficult to establish the extent to which such allegations are accurate since discrimination is likely to be only one of several factors which affect an officer's decision in any particular situation. Negroes, other minority groups, and the poor are arrested and probably stopped in disproportion to their numbers. However, these groups frequently live in high-crime areas. Consequently, normal, completely fair police work would doubtless produce the arrest or stopping of larger numbers of these groups.

Two studies of referrals to juvenile courts in several cities found that the police referred significantly more

Negro than white juveniles for the same types of offenses, particularly for minor offenses. Another study of police handling of juveniles in two large cities found that the eastern, nonprofessional police force referred three times as many Negro juveniles to court as whites. On the other hand, the western, more professional police force tended to treat similar types of offenders alike. And, the Commission's study, based on observation of routine police work in several northern cities, found that the police did not discriminate between whites and Negroes of the same economic class; instead, police conduct seemed to depend on economic status and on whether the person was a drunk, a homosexual, or otherwise an outcast.

As was described earlier, a high percentage of Negroes believe that the police provide inadequate protection in minority communities. Lack of protection can take the form of police being slow to respond to calls, having inadequate personnel, or tending to ignore offenses by one minority person against another in contrast to those by members of minority groups against whites or whites against whites. While the lack of attention paid to investigating violations against others of the same race is probably decreasing, it still exists in many localities. For example, the American Bar Foundation study undertaken in mid-1950's found that it exists especially in large cities and particularly as to serious offenses such as aggravated assault.

Police officers should not base decisions to arrest, stop, use force, or the like, in whole or in part, on race, poverty, or civil rights activity. All decisions must be based on objective evidence which creates suspicion, proof of guilt, or threat of danger to the officer or public, as the law requires.

Field interrogation In many communities, field interrogations are a major source of friction between the police and minority groups. Many minority group leaders strongly contend that field interrogations are predominantly conducted in slum communities, that they are used indiscriminately, and that they are conducted in an abusive and unfriendly manner.

The police consider field interrogations to be an important method of preventing and investigating crime, since they rarely encounter a crime in progress. Normally, by the time a police officer has arrived at a crime scene, the perpetrator has fled, people have gathered, and confusion has ensued. Further, the police believe that they can prevent much crime if they are permitted to stop and question persons whose behavior strongly suggests that a criminal act is being contemplated:

A law enforcement officer in the performance of his duties will be confronted with innumerable situations in which it seems necessary to make some inquiry of a person whose name he does not know, and whom, if further action is not taken, he is most unlikely ever to find again. An inquiry may appear appropriate because such a person is behaving in a suspicious or unusual manner which suggests a possible involvement in crime. Thus, he may be a person running with a heavy package at 2:00 a.m. in a business neighborhood. Or he may correspond to a description of the perpetrator of a recent crime, but because he is traveling in an automobile it is impossible to be sure. Or he may be walking down a street at night, looking into the windows of parked cars.

The person to whom the officer would like to direct an inquiry may clearly not be involved in criminality. He may be a person who was near the scene of a crime, and thus a potential source of information. Or it may be impossible to tell in advance whether the person to be stopped is a suspect or a source of information.

The limits of police authority to stop persons briefly for purposes of criminal investigation are unclear in most jurisdictions. In some States, there is specific statutory authority for officers to stop suspicious persons. For example, a recently enacted statute in New York gives an officer authority to stop for questioning a person whom "he reasonably suspects is committing, has committed, or is about to commit" a felony or other specified crimes and authorizes the officer to use whatever force is necessary to effectuate such stops.

In most States, however, there is no specific statute which defines this authority. As a result, police departments are given little guidance as to when a person may be stopped, whether or how long he may be detained, whether force may be used to detain him, what degree of force may be used, whether a person may be searched, whether he may be compelled to answer certain questions, and under what circumstances he must be advised of his legal rights.

A few police departments have policies governing the conduct of field interrogations. Training materials of the Oakland, Calif. Police Dept., for example, carefully describe the types of persons who should be stopped; the San Diego, Calif. Police Dept. specifically forbids officers to restrain persons being questioned against their will; and the Tampa, Fla. Police Dept. defines conditions under which a person may be searched.

The Commission believes that there is a definite need to authorize the police to stop suspects and possible witnesses of major crimes, to detain them for brief questioning if they will not voluntarily cooperate, and to search such suspects for dangerous weapons when such a precaution is necessary. This need was also recognized by the reporters for the American Law Institute Model Pre-Arraignment Code Project:

> If, as some have argued, the only power to restrain a person, even briefly, is by arresting him on reasonable grounds to believe him guilty of a crime, the police will be foreclosed from responding to confused, emergency situations in the way that seems most natural and rational. For in such circumstances, where a crime may have been committed and a suspect or important witness is about to disappear, it seems irrational to deprive the officer of the opportunity to "freeze" the situation for a short time, so that he may make inquiry and arrive at a considered judgment about further action to be taken. To deny the police such a power would be too high a price in effective policing and in the police's respect for the good sense of the rules that govern them, in order to avoid brief inconveniences that most innocent persons would be prepared to undergo.

Misuse of field interrogations, however, is causing serious friction with minority groups in many localities. This is becoming particularly true as more police departments adopt "aggressive patrol" in which officers are encouraged routinely to stop and question persons on the street who are unknown to them, who are suspicious, or whose purpose for being abroad is not readily evident. The Michigan State survey found that both minority group leaders and persons sympathetic to minority groups throughout the country were almost unanimous in labelling field interrogation as a principal problem in police-community relations:

> * * * race has an undue influence on who is stopped.

> * * * practice is o.k., but the way it was carried out was unfriendly, abusive, etc. Not against method, but how it is used.

> Personally, I found it offensive and was affronted on occasions of its use in New York.

> Spanish-Americans are picked up sooner.

> Many Negroes stopped in other neighborhoods and questioned. Happens more to Negroes than to others.

The Commission has found that field interrogations, used sometimes in conjunction with aggressive, preventive patrol, are often conducted on a broad-scale basis by many police departments. First, field interrogations are often conducted with little or no basis for suspicion. In San Diego, written reports were made of over 200,000 stops in 1965 and there were probably about as many stops which were not recorded. The effect on attitudes which can result is revealed by the following comment of a lower income Negro:

> When they stop everybody, they say, well, they haven't seen you around, you know, they want to get to know your name, and all this. I can see them stopping you one time, but the same police stopping you every other day, and asking you the same old question.

A study of juvenile offenses in a western city with high police standards found that Negroes were stopped more frequently than other juveniles "often even in the absence of evidence that an offense had been committed."

Second, field interrogations are sometimes used in a way which discriminates against minority groups, the poor, and the juvenile. For example, the Michigan State survey found, on the basis of riding with patrol units in two cities, that members of minority groups were often stopped, particularly if found in groups, in the company of white people, or at night in white neighborhoods, and that this caused serious problems. Similarly, in a midwestern city, using aggressive patrol and field interrogations seems to cause, as in San Diego, the major problem in police-community relations. In contrast, in Philadelphia the field interrogation is used less and is not a major item of criticism by minority groups or others.

Finally, field interrogations are frequently conducted in a discourteous or otherwise offensive manner which is particularly irritating to the citizen. For example, even in San Diego, where officers are instructed specifically and at length to give the citizen an explanation and to act courteously, the University of California study found that an explanation is frequently not given. In some cities, searches are made in a high proportion of instances not for the purpose of protecting the officer but to obtain drugs or other incriminating evidence. In New York, for example, where searches are permitted only when the officer reasonably believes he is in bodily danger, searches were made in 81.6 percent of stops reported. However, a Commission survey of police practices in several large cities, found that one out of every five persons frisked was carrying a dangerous weapon—10 percent were carrying guns and another 10 percent knives.

While the same problems exist as to field interrogations of juveniles as with adults, there are also additional difficulties. As was described earlier, juveniles are subjected to particularly close scrutiny by police officers. The study in San Francisco, for example, found that juveniles are frequently stopped when they travel outside their own neighborhoods:

> If we go someplace, they tell us to go on home. Because every time we go somewhere we mostly go in big groups and they don't want us. One time we was talking in Steiner Street. So a cop drove up and he say, "Hey! Hanky and panky! Come here!" And he say, "You all out of bounds, get back on the other side of Steiner Street."

> *   *   *   *   *

> If boys from Hunter's Point or Fillmore [Negro neighborhoods in San Francisco] go in all white districts, the police will stop you and ask you where you from. If you say Fillmore or Hunter's Point, they'll take you down to the station and run checks on you. Any burglaries, any purse snatchings, anything.

The same study also found that the police are suspicious and make field interrogations of certain individuals because of clothing, hair, and walking mannerisms:

> Why do they pick us up? They don't pick everybody up. They just pick up the ones with the hats on and trench coats and conks [a Negro hair style]. If you got long hair and hats on, something like this one, you gonna get picked up.

> Especially a conk. And the way you dress. Sometimes, like if you've got on black pants, better not have on no black pants or bends [a kind of trouser] or levis. They think you going to rob somebody. And don't have a head scarf on your head. They'll bust you for having a head scarf.

> *   *   *   *   *

> The way you walk sometimes. * * * Don't try to be cool. You know. They'll bust you for that. * * * Last night a cop picked me up for that. He told me I had a bad walk. He say, "You think you're bad."

White youths who wear the clothes and have the look of possible delinquents are likewise stopped sometimes without evidence of criminality.

The study concluded that the juveniles understood being sought and interrogated for their illegal activity:

> If you done something and you be lying and yelling when the boys from juvy come around and they catch you lying, well, what you gonna do? You gonna complain 'cause you was caught? Hell man, you can't do that. You did something and you was caught and that's the way it goes.

But they were indignant about field interrogation for offenses they did not commit—when "we were just minding our own business when the cops came along." And they particularly resented being singled out because of their clothes or hair: "Hell man, them cops is supposed to be out catching criminals! They ain't paid to be lookin' after my *hair!*" The juveniles consider this harassment by the police as a policy of confinement by a "foreign army of occupation."

In order to balance the need for field interrogations and the harmful effect on police-community relations which may result from their indiscriminate use, State legislatures should define the extent of police authority to stop and question persons, and police departments should adopt detailed policies governing this authority whether or not legislation exists. Such legislation and policies should have the following principles:

● Field interrogations should be conducted only when an officer has reason to believe that a person is about to commit or has committed a crime, or that a crime has been committed and he has knowledge of material value to the investigation.

- Field interrogations should not be used at all for minor crimes like vagrancy and loitering.
- Adequate reason should be based on the actions of the person, his presence near the scene of a crime, and similar factors raising substantial suspicion, and not on race, poverty, or youth.
- The stop should be limited in time. The sole purposes should be: (a) to obtain the citizen's identification; (b) to verify it by readily available information; (c) to request cooperation in the investigation of a crime; and (d) to verify by readily available information any account of his presence or any other information given by the person.
- The citizen should be addressed politely and should receive a suitable explanation of the reason for the stop.
- An officer should be allowed to conduct a search of the person only if he has reason to believe that his safety or the safety of others so requires.
- Officers should be required to file a report each time a stop is made in order to record the circumstances and persons involved. Even greater care should be taken with these records, than with arrest records so that the police do not use them to establish the delinquency or bad character of the person stopped. Moreover, the records should not be available to persons outside of public law enforcement agencies.

One of the most difficult questions in connection with a stop and attendant search is whether the results or fruits of a search other than weapons, should be used by police. While there are serious objections to barring evidence of crime discovered in a lawful search, the admissibility of evidence such as betting slips or narcotics found during a stop may encourage the misuse of the search power.

EXERCISE OF THE ARREST POWER

Arrests for investigation Although there is no legal basis for arresting persons simply as a means of detaining them while an investigation of their possible involvement in crime is conducted, this has been a common practice in a number of departments.

The American Bar Foundation study of police practices in three midwestern States found that in cities with substantial crime problems, arrests are often made on suspicion—such as refusing to answer questions or giving an equivocal answer during a field interrogation. In 1960, the Washington, D. C. Police Department made 4,684 arrests for investigation, but only 257 (5.5 percent) of the arrested persons were ever charged with the commission of a specific offense. Of those arrested, 1,349 were held for 8 hours or more. This practice was abolished in 1963 as a result of a study in 1962 condemning it.

In Detroit, from 1947 to 1956, 219,053 arrests of a total of 658,808 nontraffic arrests were listed by the police department as arrests for investigations. In 1956, of 73,827 arrests, only 40,641 persons were formally charged with commission of an offense; 33,186, or 45 percent, were arrested for investigation. Of the latter, only 6,490 were subsequently charged with a crime and the others were released without charge. The suspect would be detained for an average of at least 3 days before release or before being brought before a magistrate. Authority for the practice was provided in the police manual. The 1964 police department statistics still showed that 8,140 arrests out of 63,125 nontraffic arrests were classified merely as "detention."

Sixteen of fifty-five departments responding to a Commission survey in 1966 admitted the use of investigative arrests. In Baltimore, for example, 3,719 (6.6 percent) of the 56,160 nontraffic arrests during 1964 were recorded as arrests for investigation. Of those arrested on this basis, 98 percent were dismissed without going before a magistrate.

Occasionally, police departments engage in dragnet arrests on suspicion after serious crimes have been committed. In Detroit, in December 1960 and January 1961, after a series of rapes and murders of women, persons were stopped on the street, searched, and in about 1,000 cases arrested. In 1964, after two brothers killed one policeman and seriously wounded another, Baltimore police officers searched more than 300 homes, most belonging to Negroes, looking for the gunman. The searches were often made in the middle of the night and were based almost entirely on anonymous tips. The U. S. Court of Appeals for the Fourth Circuit stated:

PART 3   THE SOCIAL ORGANIZATION OF CRIMINAL LAW ENFORCEMENT

Lack of respect for the police is conceded to be one of the factors generating violent outbursts in Negro communities. The invasions so graphically depicted in this case "could" happen in prosperous suburban neighborhoods, but the innocent victims know only that wholesale raids do not happen elsewhere and did happen to them. Understandably they feel that such illegal treatment is reserved for those elements who the police believe cannot or will not challenge them.

As reported in the Uniform Crime Reports prepared by the Federal Bureau of Investigation, 76,346 arrests for suspicion were listed for the year 1965, in jurisdictions with approximately 70 percent of the Nation's population. These statistics almost certainly understate the number of investigative arrests in the country. In jurisdictions where the practice is not permitted, such arrests are frequently made by using the drunkenness, vagrancy, and other petty offense laws. Similarly, the American Bar Foundation found that in the three States it studied, a common practice was to arrest a suspicious person and then book him for an offense which occurs frequently in the area or for an offense for which he resembled generally the person wanted. A captain in a Kansas sheriff's department said that it was no problem to arrest a person without a specific offense in mind since "it is no difficult matter to find some sort of a 'want' on the State teletype that will fit the man's description." An instructor in a training session said that "[It] is a poor policeman who cannot find a description to fit the suspect, as you officers have at least 30 days of daily bulletins in your notebooks."

One nationally recognized governmental consulting firm, which has done considerable consulting with police agencies, recently reported that the widespread use of investigative arrests demonstrates inadequate policy, supervision, and investigative personnel:

> The practice of allowing or perhaps even condoning such arrests reflects an unawareness of the impropriety and, in fact, the illegality of most such arrests. It has developed as a result of failure to formulate policy and adequate procedures on the part of the chief and the command staff.
>
> Aside from the legal and constitutional implications of arrests for "suspicion" or "for investigation," the frequency of occurrence of such arrests tends to reflect upon the competency and attitude of the investigator, and quality of inves-

tigations surrounding the cases for which these arrests are made * * *.

> Thus, it may be seen that departments and individual investigators who tend to rely heavily upon indiscriminate and casual arrests of known criminals, suspects, and others will generally perform rather inadequate and unprofessional investigations.

Arrests for investigation or on suspicion, whatever label is attached, should be abolished by all departments that now utilize them. This practice has long been a source of justified community hostility. They not only seriously inconvenience the citizen or even result in his incarceration, but they result in an arrest record which may greatly affect his present or future employment.

Arrests for harassment The police in some cities use their arrest power to harass persons whom they do not intend to prosecute because of insufficient evidence or because of the practice of the courts in giving light sentences. The harassment arrest is primarily used as a mechanism for annoying persons who are allegedly involved in vice practices such as prostitution, gambling, or illegal liquor sales. The American Bar Foundation study found in Detroit, during 1956–57, for example, over 1,000 arrests were made for gambling and liquor violations during a 6-month period in one precinct. Ultimately, however, only 60 cases were presented for prosecution. These arrests were made because, as an assistant prosecutor commented: "the prosecutor's office and the police department are forced to find other means of punishing, harassing, and generally making life uneasy for the gamblers."

The same study found that as many as 40 or 50 prostitutes a night were arrested and released the next day because they were found on the street in an area where prostitution was practiced and they had a prior record of arrests for prostitution. Negro women with white men were almost always charged. A police official asserted that the arrests were part of "a harassment program. The police department has no other means of dealing with prostitution."

Similarly, in Cleveland, of 1,202 women arrested and taken to a particular precinct in a Negro area of Cleveland for investigation in connection with prostitution, 1,075 were Negro. Only 96 were charged. The 224 white men arrested were all released on the stated ground that they were needed to testify against the women. The uniform release of these men has been a cause of great resentment in the Negro community.

While the police are under considerable pressure to contain vice within a community and to keep undesirable persons off the street, the current practice of using the arrest power in situations in which there is no intent to submit the case for prosecution is deplorable. Police departments, therefore, should establish policies which specifically prevent illegal harassment arrests, and which direct that arrests be made only if probable cause exists that a crime has been committed.

Arrests for minor crimes Arrests for minor crimes, such as vagrancy, disorderly conduct, use of obscene language, loitering, failure to move on, blocking the street or sidewalk, drunkenness, drinking in public, and curfew violations, constitute almost one-half of all arrests made each year in the United States. There is evidence that such arrests create great antagonism against police officers in slum communities. For example, many complaints filed with the review board in Philadelphia involve such ordinances and not a single complaint has involved an incident during commission of a felony. The reason for hostility resulting from minor crimes is probably that while most offenders know when they have committed major crimes and expect that they will be arrested for them, the issue as to most alleged minor crimes is not as clear and the offender does not usually believe, whether or not he has acted illegally, that he has done anything sufficiently wrong to justify arrest. The comments of two men in Harlem suggest the antagonism that can result:

> A bunch of us could be playing some music, or dancing, which we have as an outlet for ourselves. We can't dance in the house, we don't have clubs or things like that, so we're out on the sidewalk, right on the sidewalk; we might feel like doing dancing, or one might want to play something on his horn. Right away here comes a cop. "You're disturbing the peace!" No one has said anything, you understand; no one has made a complaint. Everyone is enjoying themselves.

> But here comes one cop, and he'll want to chase everyone. And gets mad. I mean, he gets mad! We aren't mad. He comes into the neighborhood, aggravated and mad.

>   *   *   *   *   *

> Last night, for instance, the officer stopped some fellas on 125th Street * * *. [T]he officer said, "All right, everybody get off the street or inside!" Now, it's very hot. We don't have air-conditioned apartments in most of these houses up here, so where are we going if we get off the streets? We can't go back in the house because we almost suffocate. So we sit down on the curb, or stand on the sidewalk, or on the steps, things like that, till the wee hours of the morning, expecially in the summer when it's too hot to go up. Now where were we going? But he came out with his nightstick and wants to beat people on the head, and wanted to—he arrested one fellow. The other fellow said, "Well, I'll move, but you don't have to talk to me like a dog."

Minor crime statutes are frequently misused. They are employed as a means of clearing undesirables or unsightly persons from the street or driving them out of town, aiding the police in detaining a suspected person during an investigation of a more serious crime, and regulating street activity in slum neighborhoods. Often, under pressure from the community, the police will "declare a war on bums, prostitutes, homosexuals, and narcotic traffickers" by making wholesale arrests for vagrancy, disorderly conduct, drunkenness, or loitering. Justice William O. Douglas found that in Tucson, between 1958 and 1960, the poor were discouraged to come to the city for employment by the policy of picking "up any vags spotted within the city limits." In 1966, a District of Columbia judge found that "the typical accused under [the vagrancy] law is a miserable derelict whose principal offense is poverty and affinity for cheap wine, or an individual, male or female, suspected of engaging in prostitution or homosexuality." The court concluded that the "basic design" of the vagrancy law is "preventive conviction imposed upon those who because of their background and behavior are more likely than the general public to commit crimes and * * * the statute contemplates such convictions even though no overt criminal act has been committed or can be proved." Recent studies of the use of public drunkenness statutes in two cities found that they were often employed to arrest skid row types who were not drunk but were aesthetically displeasing. Until 1965, one department was arresting women under an ordinance which made it a crime for a "woman of notorious character" to walk or ride up "the streets of this city."

This practice is even more harmful to a person than an unwarranted field interrogation, since the suspect is not merely stopped, but he is arrested and confined, at least until he can make bail. While such arrests may serve some investigative value to the police, there is grave question as to their propriety.

The American Bar Foundation, in its study of 1956–57, found that the "Police assume that these [vagrancy] statutes are intended primarily as aids to investigation." For example, if the police desire to undertake an in-custody investigation of a person, and investigative arrests are not used, they often arrest a person for violating a vagrancy-type statute. In one observation made during the American Bar Foundation study, a man was seen near a pawn shop with a jacket on his arm. When questioned, he said that he was unemployed because he had just come to the city to find work and that he had no identification because his wallet had been stolen; he also gave other evasive answers. The officers arrested him for vagrancy because they suspected him of burglary but lacked evidence. Similarly, a man suspected of homicide was arrested for vagrancy so that a prolonged investigation could be made while he served his sentence. Other statutes were found to be used for the same purpose. A man suspected of carrying narcotics, whom the officers did not have evidence to arrest, was arrested for a minor traffic violation which would ordinarily result in a warning and his car was searched.

Arrests for failure to move on, loitering, blocking the sidewalk, or public drinking are predominantly made in slum neighborhoods. One reason is that more officers are stationed in these neighborhoods because of the greater amount of serious crime. As a result, residents sometimes charge "over policing" at the same time they seek more protection from crimes such as robbery and burglary. Minor crime statutes, however, are also more used in poor areas because it is harder to keep order there. As a precinct captain in Washington, D. C. stated:

> We do tend to enforce the drunk laws more rigidly on 14th Street than in, say, Crestwood, a better part of the precinct. If we overlooked things on 14th Street, we would have a more serious problem.

The source of these difficulties in enforcement of minor crime statutes reaches beyond the police. The community often demands that the police rid the city of undesirable persons, harass persons engaged in vice activities, and keep the unsightly off the streets, even though the police do not have legal means of doing so. Thus, until the public recognizes the dilemma facing the police in regulating such behavior, the police will continue to be placed in an untenable position.

As recommended in chapter 5 of the General Report, the content and use of minor crime statutes should be carefully reexamined in all communities. Obviously, certain minor crime statutes are necessary in order to regulate reasonable conduct on the street. If persons are disorderly and disturb others, if they block the streets and sidewalk, if they use obscene language in public, police action is warranted. Many existing statutes, however, which base criminality on suspicious conduct, a prior record, or poverty, are of questionable legal validity and usually of considerable harm to community relations.

At least some minor crime statutes should be eliminated. In chapter 9 of the General Report, the Commission recommended the abolition of criminal drunkenness statutes. Besides its other virtues, this would reduce the tension which frequently results, particularly in minority communities, from the arrest of drunks. The neighborhood reaction would doubtless be different if citizens knew, as the Commission recommends, that drunks were merely taken to a sobering up facility and then released or treated.

Most statutes which are used to regulate street conduct are so broad that almost unlimited discretion is given to the police officer to arrest persons on the street or, as with a failure-to-move-on statute, to regulate conduct by the threat of arrest. Such statutes should be amended to cover only conduct which reasonably disturbs the public or is an immediate threat to the peace. Even if this is done, however, there would still be a need for police departments to formulate guidelines concerning their permissible use.

The guidelines should clearly bar discriminatory enforcement of minor crime statutes either against individuals or in particular neighborhoods. The District of Columbia Crime Commission Report noted that "until recently, there were no criteria issued by the police to assist the officer in exercising * * * discretion wisely."

Arrest quotas It is often alleged that police officers and perhaps even precincts have arrest quotas. As a result, it is contended, officers who have not made a sufficient number of arrests begin to make frivolous or marginally warranted arrests relating to minor crimes and that supervising officers order patrolmen to clear the streets of drunks and the like. The police, on the other hand, generally deny that such quotas exist.

The difficulty in determining whether arrest quotas exist is that they need not be absolute requirements. The effect is virtually the same if precincts and individual officers are expected to make an approximate number of arrests as evidence that they are carrying out their responsibilities in a diligent and effective manner. Such expectations can be as effective as a regulation.

The Commission has little evidence that police forces use quotas for evaluating officers. Two Commission surveys did find, however, that, in both a midwestern and a western city, one means by which superior officers evaluated officers was by the number of field interrogations each had made. In one of those cities a ranking officer stated:

> Our first line supervisors [Sergeants] have a responsibility to keep statistics on each officer's production—not an average, but his production—to find out whether a particular officer's performance is consistent with what his [s]quad's average might be. As a result, if a particular man is low, we expect an explanation.

Police work is far too complicated and delicate a job to judge an officer's work or qualifications for promotion on the number of arrests he has made. Furthermore, arrest quotas, if they exist as either explicit requirements or implied expectations, can lead to improper activity by policemen. Patrolling officers have the complex and difficult responsibility of exercising their discretion based on the circumstances of the particular case. No part of this calcu-

lation should consist of the number of arrests the officer has made in comparison to a preestablished quota or expectation set by the department.

USE OF FIREARMS TO APPREHEND OR ARREST SUSPECTS

Police use of firearms to apprehend suspects often strains community relations or even results in serious disturbances. For example, the San Francisco riot of 1966 started after a juvenile was shot and killed while fleeing from a stolen car. Severe tensions were aroused in Los Angeles during May 1966, after an officer's firearm accidentally discharged and killed a man who had refused to stop his automobile until it was forced to the curb. In St. Louis, disturbances began in September 1966 after police officers shot and killed a person who had his hands handcuffed behind him in a police car located in the courtyard of police headquarters. The police assert that the suspect threatened officers in the car with a tear gas pistol he had in his belt behind him which the officers had failed to find in a search earlier.

When studied objectively and unemotionally, particular uses of firearms by police officers are often unwarranted. For example, an American Bar Foundation study revealed one instance where a foot patrolman signaled a speeding driver to stop. When the driver did not, the officer fired five times at the speeding car.

A study by an American Civil Liberties Union affiliate in a medium-sized city found that officers fired guns more than 300 times in a 2-year period and over one-third were during automobile chases involving juveniles. An average of 240 persons per year were fatally injured by police between 1950 and 1960. The Michigan State study concluded that police officers often use guns indiscriminately and that this was due, in large part, to overemphasis of danger in police work. While the murder of a single police officer is a tragedy, as of 1955, the rate of total police fatalities while on duty (including accidents) was 33 fatalities per 100,000 officers which was less than the rate of deaths on duty in mining (94), agriculture (55), construction (76), and transportation (44).

It is surprising and alarming that few police departments provide their officers with careful instruction on the circumstances under which the use of a firearm is permissible. For example, a 1961 survey of Michigan police forces found that 27 out of 49 had no firearms policies. A survey in 1964, of 45 of the 51 American cities of over 250,000 population, found that 3 had no written firearms policy, and, while others had comprehensive policy statements, many were quite limited. For example, one simply prohibited warning shots, one instructed its officers to "exercise the greatest possible caution," and 10 urged officers to use "good judgment." While it is true that many departments have oral firearms policies, these policies have normally developed through customary practices that rarely are the product of careful analysis and are usually not well understood by patrolmen.

16

The Police on Skid-Row:

A Study of Peace Keeping

EGON BITTNER

The prototype of modern police organization, the Metropolitan Police of London, was created to replace an antiquated and corrupt system of law enforcement. The early planners were motivated by the mixture of hardheaded business rationality and humane sentiment that characterized liberal British thought of the first half of the nineteenth century.[1] Partly to meet the objections of a parliamentary committee, which was opposed to the establishment of the police in England, and partly because it was in line with their own thinking, the planners sought to produce an instrument that could not readily be used in the play of internal power politics but which would, instead, advance and protect conditions favorable to industry and commerce and to urban civil life in general. These intentions were not very specific and had to be reconciled with the existing structures of governing, administering justice, and

keeping the peace. Consequently, the locus and mandate of the police in the modern polity were ill-defined at the outset. On the one hand, the new institution was to be a part of the executive branch of government, organized, funded, and staffed in accordance with standards that were typical for the entire system of the executive. On the other hand, the duties that were given to the police organization brought it under direct control of the judiciary in its day-to-day operation.

The dual patronage of the police by the executive and the judiciary is characteristic for all democratically governed countries. Moreover, it is generally the case, or at least it is deemed desirable, that judges *rather than* executive officials have control over police use and procedure.[2] This preference is based on two considerations. First, in the tenets of the democratic creed, the possibility of direct control of the police by a government in power is repugnant.[3] Even when the specter of the police state in its more ominous forms is not a concern, close ties between those who govern and those who police are viewed as a sign of political corruption.[4] Hence, mayors, governors, and cabinet officers—although the nominal superiors of the police—tend to maintain,

Source: "The Police on Skid-Row: A Study of Peace Keeping," *American Sociological Review*, Vol. 32, October, 1967, pp. 699–715. By permission of the author and publisher. This research was supported in part by Grant 64-1-35 from the California Department of Mental Hygiene. The author gratefully acknowledges the help received from Fred Davis, Sheldon Messinger, Leonard Schatzman, and Anselm Strauss in the preparation of this paper.

or to pretend, a hands-off policy. Second, it is commonly understood that the main function of the police is the control of crime. Since the concept of crime belongs wholly to the law, and its treatment is exhaustively based on considerations of legality, police procedure automatically stands under the same system of review that controls the administration of justice in general.

By nature, judicial control encompasses only those aspects of police activity that are directly related to full-dress legal prosecution of offenders. The judiciary has neither the authority nor the means to direct, supervise, and review those activities of the police that do not result in prosecution. Yet such other activities are unavoidable, frequent, and largely within the realm of public expectations. It might be assumed that in this domain of practice the police are under executive control. This is not the case, however, except in a marginal sense.[5] Not only are police departments generally free to determine what need be done and how, but aside from informal pressures they are given scant direction in these matters. Thus, there appear to exist two relatively independent domains of police activity. In one, their methods are constrained by the prospect of the future disposition of a case in the courts; in the other, they operate under some other consideration and largely with no structured and continuous outside constraint. Following the terminology suggested by Michael Banton, they may be said to function in the first instance as "law officers" and in the second instance as "peace officers."[6] It must be emphasized that the designation "peace officer" is a residual term, with only some vaguely presumptive content. The role, as Banton speaks of it, is supposed to encompass all occupational routines not directly related to making arrests, without, however, specifying what determines the limits of competence and availability of the police in such actions.

Efforts to characterize a large domain of activities of an important public agency have so far yielded only negative definitions. We know that they do not involve arrests; we also know that they do not stand under judicial control, and that they are not, in any important sense, determined by specific executive or legislative mandates. In police textbooks and manuals, these activities receive only casual attention, and the role of the "peace officer" is typically stated in terms suggesting that his work is governed mainly by the individual officer's personal wisdom, integrity, and altruism.[7] Police departments generally keep no records of procedures that do not involve making arrests. Policemen, when asked, insist that they merely use common sense when acting as "peace officers," though they tend to emphasize the elements of experience and practice in discharging the role adequately. All this ambiguity is the more remarkable for the fact that peace keeping tasks, i.e., procedures not involving the formal legal remedy of arrest, were explicitly built into the program of the modern police from the outset.[8] The early executives of the London police saw with great clarity that their organization had a dual function. While it was to be an arm of the administration of justice, in respect of which it developed certain techniques for bringing offenders to trial, it was also expected to function apart from, and at times in lieu of, the employment of full-dress legal procedure. Despite its early origin, despite a great deal of public knowledge about it, despite the fact that it is routinely done by policemen, no one can say with any clarity what it means to do a good job of keeping the peace. To be sure, there is vague consensus that when policemen direct, aid, inform, pacify, warn, discipline, roust, and do whatever else they do without making arrests, they do this with some reference to the circumstances of the occasion and, thus, somehow contribute to the maintenance of the peace and order. Peace keeping appears to be a solution to an unknown problem arrived at by unknown means.

The following is an attempt to clarify conceptually the mandate and the practice of keeping the peace. The effort will be directed not to the formulation of a comprehensive solution of the problem but to a detailed consideration of some aspects of it. Only in order to place the particular into the overall domain to which it belongs will the structural determinants of keeping the peace in general be discussed. By structural determinants are meant the typical situations that policemen perceive as *demand conditions* for action without arrest. This will be followed by a description of peace keeping in skid-row districts, with the object of identifying those aspects of it that constitute a *practical skill*.

Since the major object of this paper is to elucidate peace keeping practice as a skilled performance, it is necessary to make clear how the use of the term is intended.

Practical skill will be used to refer to those methods of doing certain things, and to the information that underlies the use of the methods, that *practitioners themselves* view as proper and efficient. Skill is, therefore, a stable orientation to work tasks that is relatively independent of the personal feelings and judgments of those who employ it. Whether the exercise of this skilled performance is desirable or not, and whether it is based on correct information or not, are specifically outside the scope of interest of this presentation. The following is deliberately confined to a description of what police patrolmen consider to be the reality of their work circumstances, what they do, and what they feel they must do to do a good job. That the practice is thought to be determined by normative standards of skill minimizes but does not eliminate the factors of personal interest or inclination. Moreover, the distribution of skill varies among practitioners in the very standards they set for themselves. For example, we will show that patrolmen view a measure of rough informality as good practice vis-a-vis skid-row inhabitants. By this standard, patrolmen who are "not rough enough," or who are "too tough," or whose roughness is determined by personal feelings rather than by situational exigencies, are judged to be poor craftsmen.

The description and analysis are based on twelve months of field work with the police departments of two large cities west of the Mississippi. Eleven weeks of this time were spent in skid-row and skid-row-like districts. The observations were augmented by approximately one hundred interviews with police officers of all ranks. The formulations that will be proposed were discussed in these interviews. They were recognized by the respondents as elements of standard practice. The respondents' recognition was often accompanied by remarks indicating that they had never thought about things in this way and that they were not aware how standardized police work was.

STRUCTURAL DEMAND CONDITIONS OF PEACE KEEPING

There exist at least five types of relatively distinct circumstances that produce police activities that do not involve invoking the law and that are only in a trivial sense determined by those considerations of legality but merely that there is no legal directive that informs the acting policeman whether what he does must be done or how it is to be done. In these circumstances, policemen act as all-purpose and terminal remedial agents, and the confronted problem is solved in the field. If these practices stand under any kind of review at all, and typically they do not, it is only through internal police department control.

1. Although the executive branch of government generally refrains from exercising a controlling influence over the direction of police interest, it manages to extract certain performances from it. Two important examples of this are the supervision of certain licensed services and premises and the regulation of traffic.[9] With respect to the first, the police tend to concentrate on what might be called the moral aspects of establishments rather than on questions relating to the technical adequacy of the service. This orientation is based on the assumption that certain types of businesses lend themselves to exploitation for undesirable and illegal purposes. Since this tendency cannot be fully controlled, it is only natural that the police will be inclined to favor licensees who are at least cooperative. This, however, transforms the task from the mere scrutiny of credentials and the passing of judgments, to the creation and maintenance of a network of connections that conveys influence, pressure, and information. The duty to inspect is the background of this network, but the resulting contacts acquire tenders, shopkeepers, and hotel clerks become, for patrolmen, a resource that must be continuously serviced by visits and exchanges of favors. While it is apparent that this condition lends itself to corrupt exploitation by individual officers, even the most flawlessly honest policeman must participate in this network of exchanges if he is to function adequately. Thus, engaging in such exchanges

becomes an occupational task that demands attention and time.

Regulation of traffic is considerably less complex. More than anything else, traffic control symbolizes the autonomous authority of policemen. Their commands generally are met with unquestioned compliance. Even when they issue citations, which seemingly refer the case to the courts, it is common practice for the accused to view the allegation as a finding against him and to pay the fine. Police officials emphasize that it is more important to be circumspect than legalistic in traffic control. Officers are often reminded that a large segment of the public has no other contacts with the police, and that the field lends itself to public relations work by the line personnel.[10]

2. Policemen often do not arrest persons who have committed minor offenses in circumstances in which the arrest is technically possible. This practice has recently received considerable attention in legal and sociological literature. The studies were motivated by the realization that "police decisions not to invoke the criminal process determine the outer limits of law enforcement."[11] From these researches, it was learned that the police tend to impose more stringent criteria of law enforcement on certain segments of the community than on others.[12] It was also learned that, from the perspective of the administration of justice, the decisions not to make arrests often are based on compelling reasons.[13] It is less well appreciated that policemen often not only refrain from invoking the law formally but also employ alternative sanctions. For example, it is standard practice that violators are warned not to repeat the offense. This often leads to patrolmen's "keeping an eye" on certain persons. Less frequent, though not unusual, is the practice of direct disciplining of offenders, especially when they are juveniles, which occasionally involves inducing them to repair the damage occasioned by their misconduct.[14]

The power to arrest and the freedom not to arrest can be used in cases that do not involve patent offenses. An officer can say to a person whose behavior he wishes to control, "I'll let you go this time!" without indicating to him that he could not have been arrested in any case. Nor is this always deliberate misrepresentation, for in many cases the law is sufficiently ambiguous to allow alternative interpretations. In short, not to make an arrest is rarely, if ever, merely a decision not to act; it is most often a decision to act alternatively. In the case of minor offenses, to make an arrest often is merely one of several possible proper actions.

3. There exists a public demand for police intervention in matters that contain no criminal and often no legal aspects.[15] For example, it is commonly assumed that officers will be available to arbitrate quarrels, to pacify the unruly, and to help in keeping order. They are supposed also to aid people in trouble, and there is scarcely a human predicament imaginable for which police aid has not been solicited and obtained at one time or another. Most authors writing about the police consider such activities only marginally related to the police mandate. This view fails to reckon with the fact that the availability of these performances is taken for granted and the police assign a substantial amount of their resources to such work. Although this work cannot be subsumed under the concept of legal action, it does involve the exercise of a form of authority that most people associate with the police. In fact, no matter how trivial the occasion, the device of "calling the cops" transforms any problem. It implies that a situation is, or is getting, out of hand. Police responses to public demands are always oriented to this implication, and the risk of proliferation of troubles makes every call a potentially serious matter.[16]

4. Certain mass phenomena of either a regular or a spontaneous nature require direct monitoring. Most important is the controlling of crowds in incipient stages of disorder. The specter of mob violence frequently calls for measures that involve coercion, including the use of physical force. Legal theory allows, of course, that public officials are empowered to use coercion in situations of imminent danger.[17] Unfortunately, the doctrine is not sufficiently specific to be of much help as a rule of practice. It is based on the assumption of

the adventitiousness of danger, and thus does not lend itself readily to elaborations that could direct the routines of early detection and prevention of untoward developments. It is interesting that the objective of preventing riots by informal means posed one of the central organizational problems for the police in England during the era of the Chartists.[18]

5. The police have certain special duties with respect to persons who are viewed as less than fully accountable for their actions. Examples of those eligible for special consideration are those who are under age[19] and those who are mentally ill.[20] Although it is virtually never acknowledged explicitly, those receiving special treatment include people who do not lead "normal" lives and who occupy a pariah status in society. This group includes residents of ethnic ghettos, certain types of bohemians and vagabonds, and persons of known criminal background. The special treatment of children and of sick persons is permissively sanctioned by the law, but the special treatment of others is, in principle, opposed by the leading theme of legality and the tenets of the democratic faith.[21] The important point is not that such persons are arrested more often than others, which is quite true, but that they are perceived by the police as producing a special problem that necessitates continuous attention and the use of special procedures.

The five types of demand conditions do not exclude the possibility of invoking the criminal process. Indeed, arrests do occur quite frequently in all these circumstances. But the concerns generated in these areas cause activities that usually do not terminate in an arrest. When arrests are made, there exist, at least in the ideal, certain criteria by reference to which the arrest can be judged as having been made more or less properly, and there are some persons who, in the natural course of events, actually judge the performance.[22] But for actions not resulting in arrest there are no such criteria and no such judges. How, then, can one speak of such actions as necessary and proper? Since there does not exist any official answer to this query, and since policemen act in the role of "peace officers" pretty much without external direction or constraint, the question comes down to asking how the policeman himself knows whether he has any business with a person he does not arrest, and if so, what that business might be. Furthermore, if there exists a domain of concerns and activities that is largely independent of the law enforcement mandate, it is reasonable to assume that it will exercise some degree of influence on how and to what ends the law is invoked in cases of arrests.

Skid-row presents one excellent opportunity to study these problems. The area contains a heavy concentration of persons who do not live "normal" lives in terms of prevailing standards of middle-class morality. Since the police respond to this situation by intensive patrolling, the structure of peace keeping should be readily observable. Needless to say, the findings and conclusions will not be necessarily generalizable to other types of demand conditions.

THE PROBLEM OF KEEPING THE PEACE IN SKID-ROW

Skid-row has always occupied a special place among the various forms of urban life. While other areas are perceived as being different in many ways, skid-row is seen as completely different. Though it is located in the heart of civilization, it is viewed as containing aspects of the primordial jungle, calling for missionary activities and offering opportunities for exotic adventure. While each inhabitant individually can be seen as tragically linked to the vicissitudes of "normal" life, allowing others to say "here but for the Grace of God go I," those who live there are believed to have repudiated the entire role-casting scheme of the majority and to live apart from normalcy. Accordingly, the traditional attitude of civic-mindedness toward skid-row has been dominated by the desire to contain it and to salvage souls from its clutches.[23] The specific task of containment has been left to the police. That this task pressed upon the police some rather special duties has never come under explicit consideration, either from the government that expects control or from the police departments that implement it. Instead, the prevailing method of carrying out the task is to assign patrolmen to the area on a fairly permanent basis and to allow them to work out their own ways of running things. External influence is confined largely to the supply of support and facilities, on the one hand, and to occasional expressions of criticism about the overall conditions, on the other. Within the limits of available resources and general expectations, patrolmen are supposed to know what to do and are free to do it.[24]

Patrolmen who are more or less permanently assigned to skid-row districts tend to develop a conception of the nature of their "domain" that is surprisingly uniform. Individual officers differ in many aspects of practice, emphasize different concerns, and maintain different contacts, but they are in fundamental agreement about the structure of skid-row life. This relatively uniform conception includes an implicit formulation of the problem of keeping the peace in skid-row.

In the view of the experienced patrolman, life on skid-row is fundamentally different from life in other parts of society. To be sure, they say, around its geographic limits the area tends to blend into the surrounding environment, and its population always encompasses some persons who are only transitionally associated with it. Basically, however, skid-row is perceived as the natural habitat of people who lack the capacities and commitments to live "normal" lives on a sustained basis. The presence of these people defines the nature of social reality in the area. In general, and especially in casual encounters, the presumption of incompetence and of the disinclination to be "normal" is the leading theme for the interpretation of all actions and relations. Not only do people approach one another in this manner, but presumably they also expect to be approached in this way, and they conduct themselves accordingly.

In practice, the restriction of interactional possibilities that is based on the patrolman's stereotyped conception of skid-row residents is always subject to revision and modification toward particular individuals. Thus, it is entirely possible, and not unusual, for patrolmen to view certain skid-row inhabitants in terms that involve non-skid-row aspects of normality. Instances of such approaches and relationships invariably involve personal acquaintance and the knowledge of a good deal of individually qualifying

information. Such instances are seen, despite their relative frequency, as exceptions to the rule. The awareness of the possibility of breakdown, frustration, and betrayal is ever-present, basic wariness is never wholly dissipated, and undaunted trust can never be fully reconciled with presence on skid-row.

What patrolmen view as normal on skid-row—and what they also think is taken for granted as "life as usual" by the inhabitants—is not easily summarized. It seems to focus on the idea that the dominant consideration governing all enterprise and association is directed to the occasion of the moment. Nothing is thought of as having a background that might have led up to the present in terms of some compelling moral or practical necessity. There are some exceptions to this rule, of course: the police themselves, and those who run certain establishments, are perceived as engaged in important and necessary activities. But in order to carry them out they, too, must be geared to the overall atmosphere of fortuitousness. In this atmosphere, the range of control that persons have over one another is exceedingly narrow. Good faith, even where it is valued, is seen merely as a personal matter. Its violations are the victim's own hard luck, rather than demonstrable violations of property. There is only a private sense of irony at having been victimized. The overall air is not so much one of active distrust as it is one of irrelevance of trust; as patrolmen often emphasize, the situation does not necessarily cause all relations to be predatory, but the possibility of exploitation is not checked by the expectation that it will not happen.

Just as the past is seen by the policeman as having only the most attenuated relevance to the present, so the future implications of present situations are said to be generally devoid of prospective coherence. No venture, especially no joint venture, can be said to have a strongly predictable future in line with its initial objectives. It is a matter of adventitious circumstance whether or not matters go as anticipated. That which is not within the grasp of momentary control is outside of practical social reality.

Though patrolmen see the temporal framework of the occasion of the moment mainly as a lack of trustworthiness, they also recognize that it involves more than merely the personal motives of individuals. In addition to the fact that everybody *feels* that things matter only at the moment, irresponsibility takes an *objectified* form on skid-row. The places the residents occupy, the social relations they entertain, and the activities that engage them are not meaningfully connected over time. Thus, for example, address, occupation, marital status, etc., matter much less on skid-row than in any other part of society. The fact that present whereabouts, activities, and affiliations imply neither continuity nor direction means that life on skid-row lacks a socially structured background of accountability. Of course, everybody's life contains some sequential incongruities, but in the life of a skid-row inhabitant every moment is an accident. That a man has no "address" in the future that could be in some way inferred from where he is and what he does makes him a person of *radically reduced visibility*. If he disappears from sight and one wishes to locate him, it is virtually impossible to systematize the search. All one can know with relative certainty is that he will be somewhere on some skid-row and the only thing one can do is to trace the factual contiguities of his whereabouts.

It is commonly known that the police are expert in finding people and that they have developed an exquisite technology involving special facilities and procedures of sleuthing. It is less well appreciated that all this technology builds upon those socially structured features of everyday life that render persons findable in the first place.

Under ordinary conditions, the query as to where a person is can be addressed, from the outset, to a restricted realm of possibilities that can be further narrowed by looking into certain places and asking certain persons. The map of whereabouts that normally competent persons use whenever they wish to locate someone is constituted by the basic facts of membership in society. Insofar as membership consists of status incumbencies, each of which has an adumbrated future that substantially reduces unpredictability, it is itself a guarantee of the order within which it is quite difficult to get lost. Membership is thus visible not only now but also as its own projection into the future. It is in terms of this prospective availability that the skid-row inhabitant is a

person of reduced visibility. His membership is viewed as extraordinary because its extension into the future is *not* reduced to a restricted realm of possibilities. Neither his subjective dispositions, nor his circumstances, indicate that he is oriented to any particular long-range interests. But, as he may claim every contingent opportunity, his claims are always seen as based on slight merit or right, at least to the extent that interfering with them does not constitute a substantial denial of his freedom.

This, then, constitutes the problem of keeping the peace on skid-row. Considerations of monetary expediency are seen as having unqualified priority as maxims of conduct; consequently, the controlling influences of the pursuit of sustained interests are presumed to be absent.

THE PRACTICES OF KEEPING THE PEACE IN SKID-ROW

From the perspective of society as a whole, skid-row inhabitants appear troublesome in a variety of ways. The uncommitted life attributed to them is perceived as inherently offensive; its very existence arouses indignation and contempt. More important, however, is the feeling that persons who have repudiated the entire role-status casting system of society, persons whose lives forever collapse into a succession of random moments, are seen as constituting a practical risk. As they have nothing to forsake, nothing is thought safe from them.[25]

The skid-row patrolman's concept of his mandate includes an awareness of this presumed risk. He is constantly attuned to the possibility of violence, and he is convinced that things to which the inhabitants have free access are as good as lost. But his concern is directed toward the continuous condition of peril *in the area* rather than *for society in general*. While he is obviously conscious of the presence of many persons who have committed crimes outside of skid-row and will arrest them when they come to his attention, this is a peripheral part of his routine activities. In general, the skid-row patrolman and his superiors take for granted that his main business is to keep the peace and enforce the laws *on skid-row*, and that he is involved only incidentally in protecting society at large. Thus, his task is formulated basically as the protection of putative predators from one another. The maintenance of peace and safety is difficult because everyday life on skid-row is viewed as an open field for reciprocal exploitation. As the lives of the inhabitants lack the prospective coherence associated with status incumbency, the realization of self-interest does not produce order. Hence, mechanisms that control risk must work primarily from without.

External containment, to be effective, must be oriented to the realities of existence. Thus, the skid-row patrolman employs an approach that he views as appropriate to the *ad hoc* nature of skid-row life. The following are the three most prominent elements of this approach. First, the seasoned patrolman seeks to acquire a richly particularized knowledge of people and places in the area. Second, he gives the consideration of strict culpability a subordinate status among grounds for remedial sanction. Third, his use and choice of coercive interventions is determined mainly by exigencies of situations and with little regard for possible long range effects on individual persons.

The particularization of knowledge The patrolman's orientation to people on skid-row is structured basically by the presupposition that if he does not know a man personally there is very little that he can assume about him. This rule determines his interaction with people who live on skid-row. Since the area also contains other types of persons, however, its applicability is not universal. To some such persons it does not apply at all, and it has a somewhat mitigated significance with certain others. For example, some persons encountered on skid-row can be recognized immediately as outsiders. Among them are workers who are employed in commercial and industrial enterprises that abut the area, persons who come for the purpose of adventurous "slumming," and some patrons of second-hand stores and pawn shops. Even with very little experience, it is relatively easy to identify these people by appearance, demeanor, and the time and place of their presence. The patrolman maintains an impersonal attitude toward them, and they are, under ordinary circumstances, not the objects of his attention.[26]

Clearly set off from these outsiders are the residents and the entire corps of personnel that services skid-row. It would be fair to say that one of the main routine activities of patrolmen is the establishment and maintenance of familiar relationships with individual members of these groups. Officers emphasize their interest in this, and they maintain that their grasp of and control over skid-row is precisely commensurate with the extent to which they "know the people." By this they do not mean having a quasi-theoretical understanding of human nature but rather the common practice of individualized and reciprocal recognition. As this group encompasses both those who render services on skid-row and those who are serviced, individualized interest is not always based on the desire to overcome uncertainty. Instead, relations with service personnel become absorbed into the network of particularized attention. Ties between patrolmen, on the other hand, and businessmen, managers, and workers, on the other hand, are often defined in terms of shared or similar interests. It bears mentioning that many persons live *and* work on skid-row. Thus, the distinction between those who service and those who are serviced is not a clearcut dichotomy but a spectrum of affiliations.

As a general rule, the skid-row patrolman possesses an immensely detailed factual knowledge of his beat. He knows, and knows a great deal about, a large number of residents. He is likely to know every person who manages or works in the local bars, hotels, shops, stores, and missions. Moreover, he probably knows every public and private place inside and out. Finally, he ordinarily remembers countless events of the past which he can recount by citing names, dates and places with remarkable precision. Though there are always some threads missing in the fabric of information, it is continuously woven and mended even as it is being used. New facts, however, are added to the texture, not in terms of structured categories but in terms of adjoining known realities. In other words, the content and organization of the patrolman's knowledge is primarily ideographic and only vestigially, if at all, nomothetic.

Individual patrolmen vary in the extent to which they make themselves available or actively pursue personal acquaintances. But even the most aloof are continuously greeted and engaged in conversations that indicate a background of individualistic associations. While this scarcely has the appearance of work, because of its casual character, patrolmen do not view it as an optional activity. In the course of making their rounds, patrolmen seem to have access to every place, and their entry causes no surprise or consternation. Instead, the entry tends to lead to informal exchanges of small talk. At times the rounds include entering hotels and gaining access to rooms or dormitories, often for no other purpose than asking the occupants how things are going. In all this, patrolmen address innumerable persons by name and are in turn addressed by name. The conversational style that characterizes these exchanges is casual to an extent that by non-skid-row standards might suggest intimacy. Not only does the officer himself avoid all terms of deference and respect but he does not seem to expect or demand them. For example, a patrolman said to a man radiating an alcoholic glow on the street, "You've got enough of a heat on now; I'll give you ten minutes to get your ass off the street!" Without stopping, the man answered, "Oh, why don't you go and piss in your own pot!" The officer's only response was, "All right, in ten minutes you're either in bed or on your way to the can."

This kind of expressive freedom is an intricately limited privilege. Persons of acquaintance are entitled to it and appear to exercise it mainly in routinized encounters. But strangers, too, can use it with impunity. The safe way of gaining the privilege is to respond to the patrolman in ways that do not challenge his right to ask questions and issue commands. Once the concession is made that the officer is entitled to inquire into a man's background, business, and intentions, and that he is entitled to obedience, there opens a field of colloquial license. A patrolman seems to grant expressive freedom in recognition of a person's acceptance of his access to areas of life ordinarily defined as private and subject to coercive control only under special circumstances. While patrolmen accept and seemingly even cultivate the rough *quid pro quo* of informality, and while they do not expect sincerity, candor, or obedience in their dealings with the inhabitants, they do not allow the rejection of their approach.

The explicit refusal to answer questions of a personal nature and the demand to know why the questions are asked significantly enhances a person's chances of being arrested on some minor charge. While most patrolmen tend to be personally indignant about this kind of response and use the arrest to compose their own hurt feelings, this is merely a case of affect being in line with the method. There are other officers who proceed in the same manner without taking offense, or even with feelings of regret. Such patrolmen often maintain that their colleagues' affective involvement is a corruption of an essentially valid technique. The technique is oriented to the goal of maintaining operational control. The patrolman's conception of this goal places him hierarchically above whomever he approaches, and makes him the sole judge of the propriety of the occasion. As he alone is oriented to this goal, and as he seeks to attain it by means of individualized access to persons, those who frustrate him are seen as motivated at best by the desire to "give him a hard time" and at worst by some darkly devious purpose.

Officers are quite aware that the directness of their approach and the demands they make are difficult to reconcile with the doctrines of civil liberties, but they maintain that they are in accord with the general freedom of access that persons living on skid-row normally grant one another. That is, they believe that the imposition of personalized and far-reaching control is in tune with standard expectancies. In terms of these expectancies, people are not so much denied the right to privacy as they are seen as not having any privacy. Thus, officers seek to install themselves in the center of people's lives and let the consciousness of their presence play the part of conscience.

When talking about the practical necessity of an aggressively personal approach, officers do not refer merely to the need for maintaining control over lives that are open in the direction of the untoward. They also see it as the basis for the supply of certain valued services to inhabitants of skid-row. The coerced or conceded access to persons often imposes on the patrolman tasks that are, in the main, in line with these persons' expressed or implied interest. In asserting this connection, patrolmen note that they frequently help people to obtain meals, lodging, employment, that they direct them to welfare and health services, and that they aid them in various other ways. Though patrolmen tend to describe such services mainly as the product of their own altruism, they also say that their colleagues who avoid them are simply doing a poor job of patrolling. The acceptance of the need to help people is based on the realization that the hungry, the sick, and the troubled are a potential source of problems. Moreover, that patrolmen will help people is part of the background expectancies of life on skid-row. Hotel clerks normally call policemen when someone gets so sick as to need attention; merchants expect to be taxed, in a manner of speaking, to meet the pressing needs of certain persons; and the inhabitants do not hesitate to accept, solicit, and demand every kind of aid. The domain of the patrolman's service activity is virtually limitless, and it is no exaggeration to say that the solution of every conceivable problem has at one time or another been attempted by a police officer. In one observed instance, a patrolman unceremoniously entered the room of a man he had never seen before. The man, who gave no indication that he regarded the officer's entry and questions as anything but part of life as usual, related a story of having had his dentures stolen by his wife. In the course of the subsequent rounds, the patrolman sought to locate the woman and the dentures. This did not become the evening's project but was attended to while doing other things. In the densely matted activities of the patrolman, the questioning became one more strand, not so much to be pursued to its solution as a theme that organized the memory of one more man known individually. In all this, the officer followed the precept formulated by a somewhat more articulate patrolman: "If I want to be in control of my work and keep the street relatively peaceful, I have to know the people. To know them I must gain their trust, which means that I have to be involved in their lives. But I can't be soft like a social worker because unlike him I cannot call the cops when things go wrong. I am the cops!"[27]

The restricted relevance of culpability It is well known that policemen exercise discretionary freedom in invoking the law. It is also conceded that, in some

measure, the practice is unavoidable. This being so, the outstanding problem is whether or not the decisions are in line with the intent of the law. On skid-row, patrolmen often make decisions based on reasons that the law probably does not recognize as valid. The problem can best be introduced by citing an example.

A man in a relatively mild state of intoxication (by skid-row standards) approached a patrolman to tell him that he had a room in a hotel, to which the officer responded by urging him to go to bed instead of getting drunk. As the man walked off, the officer related the following thoughts: Here is a completely lost soul. Though he probably is no more than thirty-five years old, he looks to be in his fifties. He never works and he hardly ever has a place to stay. He has been on the street for several years and is known as "Dakota." During the past few days, "Dakota" has been seen in the company of "Big Jim." The latter is an invalid living on some sort of pension with which he pays for a room in the hotel to which "Dakota" referred and for four weekly meal tickets in one of the restaurants on the street. Whatever is left he spends on wine and beer. Occasionally, "Big Jim" goes on drinking sprees in the company of someone like "Dakota." Leaving aside the consideration that there is probably a homosexual background in the association, and that it is not right that "Big Jim" should have to support the drinking habit of someone else, there is the more important risk that if "Dakota" moves in with "Big Jim" he will very likely walk off with whatever the latter keeps in his room. "Big Jim" would never dream of reporting the theft; he would just beat the hell out of "Dakota" after he sobered up. When asked what could be done to prevent the theft and the subsequent recriminations, the patrolman proposed that in this particular case he would throw "Big Jim" into jail if he found him tonight and then tell the hotel clerk to throw "Dakota" out of the room. When asked why he did not arrest "Dakota," who was, after all, drunk enough to warrant an arrest, the officer explained that this would not solve anything. While "Dakota" was in jail "Big Jim" would continue drinking and would either strike up another liaison or embrace his old buddy after he had been released. The only thing to do was to get "Big Jim" to sober up, and the only sure way of doing this was to arrest him.

As it turned out, "Big Jim" was not located that evening. But had he been located and arrested on a drunk charge, the fact that he was intoxicated would not have been the real reason for proceeding against him, but merely the pretext. The point of the example is not that it illustrates the tendency of skid-row patrolmen to arrest persons who would not be arrested under conditions of full respect for their legal rights. To be sure, this too happens. In the majority of minor arrest cases, however, the criteria the law specifies are met. But it is the rare exception that the law is invoked merely because the specifications of the law are met. That is, compliance with the law is merely the outward appearance of an intervention that is actually based on altogether different considerations. Thus, it could be said that patrolmen do not really enforce the law, even when they do invoke it, but merely use it as a resource to solve certain pressing practical problems in keeping the peace. This observation goes beyond the conclusion that many of the lesser norms of the criminal law are treated as defeasible in police work. It is patently not the case that skid-row patrolmen apply the legal norms while recognizing many exceptions to their applicability. Instead, the observation leads to the conclusion that in keeping the peace on skid-row, patrolmen encounter certain matters they attend to by means of coercive action, e.g., arrests. In doing this, they invoke legal norms that are available, and with some regard for substantive appropriateness. Hence, the problem patrolmen confront is not which drunks, beggars, or disturbers of the peace should be arrested and which can be let go as exceptions to the rule. Rather, the problem is whether, when someone "needs" to be arrested, he should be charged with drunkenness, begging, or disturbing the peace. Speculating further, one is almost compelled to infer that virtually any set of norms could be used in this manner, provided that they sanction relatively common forms of behavior.

The reduced relevance of culpability in peace keeping practice on skid-row is not readily visible. As mentioned, most arrested persons were actually found in the act, or in the state, alleged in the arrest record. It becomes partly visible when one views the treatment of persons who are not arrested even though all the legal grounds for an arrest are present. Whenever such persons are encountered and can be induced to leave, or taken to some shelter, or remanded to someone's care, then patrolmen feel, or at least maintain, that an arrest would serve no useful purpose. That is, whenever there exist means for controlling the troublesome aspects of some person's presence in some way alternative to an arrest, such means are preferentially employed, provided, of course, that the case in hand involves only a minor offense.[28]

The attenuation of the relevance of culpability is most visible when the presence of legal grounds for an arrest could be questioned, i.e., in cases that sometimes are euphemistically called "preventive arrests." In one observed instance, a man who attempted to trade a pocket knife came to the attention of a patrolman. The initial encounter was attended by a good deal of levity and the man willingly responded to the officer's inquiries about his identity and business. The man laughingly acknowledged that he needed some money to get drunk. In the course of the exchange it came to light that he had just arrived in town, traveling in his automobile. When confronted with the demand to lead the officer to the car, the man's expression became serious and he pointedly stated that he would not comply because this was none of the officer's business. After a bit more prodding, which the patrolman initially kept in the light mood, the man was arrested on a charge involving begging. In subsequent conversation the patrolman acknowledged that the charge was only speciously appropriate and mainly a pretext. Having committed himself to demanding information he could not accept defeat. When this incident was discussed with another patrolman, the second officer found fault not with the fact that the arrest was made on a pretext but with the first officer's own contribution to the creation of conditions that made it unavoidable. "You see," he continued, "there is always the risk that the man is testing you and you must let him know what is what. The best among us can usually keep the upper hand in such situations without making arrests. But when it comes down to the wire, then you can't let them get away with it."

Finally, it must be mentioned that the reduction of the significance of culpability is built into the normal order of skid-row life, as patrolmen see it. Officers almost unfailingly say, pointing to some particular person, "I know that he knows that I know that some of the things he 'owns' are stolen, and that nothing can be done about it." In saying this, they often claim to have knowledge of such a degree of certainty as would normally be sufficient for virtually any kind of action except legal proceedings. Against this background, patrolmen adopt the view that the law is not merely imperfect and difficult to implement, but that on skid-row, at least, the association between delict and sanction is distinctly occasional. Thus, to implement the law naïvely, i.e., to arrest someone *merely* because he committed some minor offense, is perceived as containing elements of injustice.

Moreover, patrolmen often deal with situations in which questions of culpability are profoundly ambiguous. For example, an officer was called to help in settling a violent dispute in a hotel room. The object of the quarrel was a supposedly stolen pair of trousers. As the story unfolded in the conflicting versions of the participants, it was not possible to decide who was the complainant and who was alleged to be the thief, nor did it come to light who occupied the room in which the fracas took place, or whether the trousers were taken from the room or to the room. Though the officer did ask some questions, it seemed, and was confirmed in later conversation, that he was there not to solve the puzzle of the missing trousers but to keep the situation from getting out of hand. In the end, the exhausted participants dispersed, and this was the conclusion of the case. The patrolman maintained that no one could unravel mysteries of this sort because "these people take things from each other so often that no one could tell what 'belongs' to whom." In fact, he suggested, the terms owning, stealing, and swindling, in their strict sense, do not really belong on skid-row, and all efforts to distribute guilt and innocence according to some rational formula of justice are doomed to failure.

It could be said that the term "curb-stone justice" that is sometimes applied to the procedures of patrolmen in skid-rows contains a double irony. Not only is the procedure not legally authorized, which is the intended irony in the expression, but it does not even pretend to distribute deserts. The best among the patrolmen, according to their own standards, use the law to keep skid-row inhabitants from sinking deeper into the misery they already experience. The worst, in terms of these same standards, exploit the practice for personal aggrandizement or gain. Leaving motives aside, however, it is easy to see that if culpability is not the salient consideration leading to an arrest in cases where it is patently obvious, then the practical patrolman may not view it as being wholly out of line to make arrests lacking in formal legal justification. Conversely, he will come to view minor offense arrests made solely because legal standards are met as poor craftsmanship.

The background of ad hoc decision making When skid-row patrolmen are pressed to explain their reasons for minor offense arrests, they most often mention that it is done for the protection of the arrested person. This, they maintain, is the case in virtually all drunk arrests, in the majority of arrests involving begging and other nuisance offenses, and in many cases involving acts of violence. When they are asked to explain further such arrests as the one cited earlier involving the man attempting to sell the pocket knife, who was certainly not arrested for his own protection, they cite the consideration that belligerent persons constitute a much greater menace on skid-row than any place else in the city. The reasons for this are twofold. First, many of the inhabitants are old, feeble, and not too smart, all of which makes them relatively defenseless. Second, many of the inhabitants are involved in illegal activities and are known as persons of bad character, which does not make them credible victims or witnesses. Potential predators realize that the resources society has mobilized to minimize the risk of criminal victimization do not protect the predator himself. Thus, reciprocal exploitation constitutes a preferred risk. The high vulnerability of everybody on skid-row is public knowledge and causes every seemingly aggressive act to be seen as a potentially grave risk.

When, in response to all this, patrolmen are confronted with the observation that many minor offense arrests they make do not seem to involve a careful evaluation of facts before acting, they give the following explanations: First, the two reasons of protection and prevention represent a global background, and in individual cases it may sometimes not be possible to produce adequate justification on these grounds. Nor is it thought to be a problem of great moment to estimate precisely whether someone is more likely to come to grief or to cause grief when the objective is to prevent the proliferation of troubles. Second, patrolmen maintain that some of the seemingly spur-of-the-moment decisions are actually made against a background of knowledge of facts that are not readily apparent in the situations. Since experience not only contains this information but also causes it to come to mind, patrolmen claim to have developed a special sensitivity for qualities of appearances that allow an intuitive grasp of probable tendencies. In this context, little things are said to have high informational value and lead to conclusions without the intervention of explicitly reasoned chains of inferences. Third, patrolmen readily admit that they do not adhere to high standards of adequacy of justification. They do not seek to defend the adequacy of their method against some abstract criteria of merit. Instead, when questioned, they assess their methods against the background of a whole system of *ad hoc* decision making, a system that encompasses the courts, correction facilities, the welfare establishment, and medical services. In fact, policemen generally maintain that their own procedures not only measure up to the workings of this system but exceed them in the attitude of carefulness.

In addition to these recognized reasons, there are two additional background factors that play a significant part in decisions to employ coercion. One has to do with the relevance of situational factors, and the other with the evaluation of coercion as relatively insignificant in the lives of the inhabitants.

There is no doubt that the nature of the circumstances often has decisive influence on what will be done. For example, the same patrolman who arrested the man trying to sell his pocket knife was observed dealing with a young couple. Though the officer was clearly angered by what he perceived as insolence and threatened the man with arrest, he merely ordered him and his companion to leave the street. He saw them walking away in a deliberately slow manner and when he noticed them a while later, still standing only a short distance away from the place of encounter, he did not respond to their presence. The difference between the two cases was that in the first there was a crowd of amused bystanders, while the latter case was not witnessed by anyone. In another instance, the patrolman was directed to a hotel and found a father and son fighting about money. The father occupied a room in the hotel and the son occasionally shared his quarters. There were two other men present, and they made it clear that their sympathies were with the older man. The son was whisked off to jail without much study of the relative merits of the conflicting claims. In yet another case, a middle-aged woman was forcefully evacuated from a bar even after the bartender explained that her loud behavior was merely a response to goading by some foul-mouthed youth.

In all such circumstances, coercive control is exercised as a means of coming to grips with situational exigencies. Force is used against particular persons but is incidental to the task. An ideal of "economy of intervention" dictates in these and similar cases that the person whose presence is most likely to perpetuate the troublesome development be removed. Moreover, the decision as to who is to be removed is arrived at very quickly. Officers feel considerable pressure to act unhesitatingly, and many give accounts of situations that got out of hand because of desires to handle cases with careful consideration. However, even when there is no apparent risk of rapid proliferation of trouble, the tactic of removing one or two persons is used to control an undesirable situation. Thus, when a patrolman ran into a group of four men sharing a bottle of wine in an alley, he emptied the remaining contents of the bottle into the gutter, arrested one man—who was no more and no less drunk than the others—and let the others disperse in various directions.

The exigential nature of control is also evident in the handling of isolated drunks. Men are arrested because of where they happen to be encountered. In this, it matters not only whether a man is found in a conspicuous place or not, but also how far away he is from his domicile. The further away he is, the less likely it is that he will make it to his room, and the more likely the arrest. Sometimes drunk arrests are made mainly because the police van is available. In one case a patrolman summoned the van to pick up an arrested man. As the van was pulling away from the curb the officer stopped the driver because he sighted another drunk stumbling across the street. The second man protested saying that he "wasn't even half drunk yet." The patrolman's response was "OK, I'll owe you half a drunk." In sum, the basic routine of keeping the peace on skid-row involves a process of matching the resources of control with situational exigencies. The overall objective is to reduce the total amount of risk in the area. In this, practicality plays a considerably more important role than legal norms. Precisely because patrolmen see legal reasons for coercive action much more widely distributed on skid-row than could ever be matched by interventions, they intervene not in the interest of law enforcement but in the interest of producing relative tranquility and order on the street.

Taking the perspective of the victim of coercive measures, one could ask why he, in particular, has to bear the cost of keeping the aggregate of troubles down while others, who are equally or perhaps even more implicated, go scot-free. Patrolmen maintain that the *ad hoc* selection of persons for attention must be viewed in the light of the following consideration: Arresting a person on skid-row on some minor charge may save him and others a lot of trouble, but it does not work any real hardships on the arrested person. It is difficult to overestimate the skid-row patrolman's feeling of certainty that his coercive and disciplinary actions toward the inhabitants have but the most passing significance in their lives. Sending a man to jail on some charge that will hold him for a couple of days is seen as a matter of such slight importance to the affected person that it could hardly give rise to scruples. Thus, every indication that a coercive measure should be taken is accompanied by the realization "I might as well, for all it matters to him." Certain realities of life on skid-row furnish

the context for this belief in the attenuated relevance of coercion in the lives of the inhabitants. Foremost among them is that the use of police authority is seen as totally unremarkable by everybody on skid-row. Persons who live or work there are continuously exposed to it and take its existence for granted. Shopkeepers, hotel clerks, and bartenders call patrolmen to rid themselves of unwanted and troublesome patrons. Residents expect patrolmen to arbitrate their quarrels authoritatively. Men who receive orders, whether they obey them or not, treat them as part of life as usual. Moreover, patrolmen find that disciplinary and coercive actions apparently do not affect their friendly relations with the persons against whom these actions are taken. Those who greet and chat with them are the very same men who have been disciplined, arrested, and ordered around in the past, and who expect to be thus treated again in the future. From all this, officers gather that though the people on skid-row seek to evade police authority, they do not really object to it. Indeed, it happens quite frequently that officers encounter men who welcome being arrested and even actively ask for it. Finally, officers point out that sending someone to jail from skid-row does not upset his relatives or his family life, does not cause him to miss work or lose a job, does not lead to his being reproached by friends and associates, does not lead to failure to meet commitments or protect investments, and does not conflict with any but the most passing intentions of the arrested person. Seasoned patrolmen are not oblivious to the irony of the fact that measures intended as mechanisms for distributing deserts can be used freely because these measures are relatively impotent in their effects.

SUMMARY AND CONCLUSIONS

It was the purpose of this paper to render an account of a domain of police practice that does not seem subject to any system of external control. Following the terminology suggested by Michael Banton, this practice was called keeping the peace. The procedures employed in keeping the peace are not determined by legal mandates but are, instead, responses to certain demand conditions. From among several demand conditions, we concentrated on the one produced by the concentration of certain types of persons in districts known as skid-row. Patrolmen maintain that the lives of the inhabitants of the area are lacking in prospective coherence. The consequent reduction in the temporal horizon of predictability constitutes the main problem of keeping the peace on skid-row.

Peace keeping procedure on skid-row consists of three elements. Patrolmen seek to acquire a rich body of concrete knowledge about people by cultivating personal acquaintance with as many residents as possible. They tend to proceed against persons mainly on the basis of perceived risk, rather than on the basis of culpability. And they are more interested in reducing the aggregate total of troubles in the area than in evaluating individual cases according to merit.

There may seem to be a discrepancy between the skid-row patrolman's objective of preventing disorder and his efforts to maintain personal acquaintance with as many persons as possible. But these efforts are principally a tactical device. By knowing someone individually the patrolman reduces ambiguity, extends trust and favors, but does not grant immunity. The informality of interaction on skid-row always contains some indications of the hierarchical superiority of the patrolman and the reality of his potential power lurks in the background of every encounter.

Though our interest was focused initially on those police procedures that did not involve invoking the law, we found that the two cannot be separated. The reason for the connection is not given in the circumstance that the roles of the "law officer" and the "peace officer" are enacted by the same person and thus are contiguous. According to our observations, patrolmen do not act alternatively as one or the other, with certain actions being determined by the intended objective of keeping the peace and others being determined by the duty to enforce the law. Instead, we have found that *peace keeping occasionally acquires the external aspects of law enforcement*. This makes it specious to inquire whether or not police discretion in invoking the law conforms with the intention of some specific legal formula. The real reason behind an arrest is virtually always the actual state of particular social situations, or of the skid-row area in general.

We have concentrated on those procedures and considerations that skid-row patrolmen regard as necessary, proper, and efficient relative to the circumstances in which they are employed. In this way, we attempted to disclose the conception of the mandate to which the police feel summoned. It was entirely outside the scope of the presentation to review the merits of this conception and of the methods used to meet it. Only insofar as patrolmen themselves recognized instances and patterns of malpractice did we take note of them. Most of the criticism voiced by officers had to do with the use of undue harshness and with the indiscriminate use of arrest powers when these were based on personal feelings rather than the requirements of the situation. According to prevailing opinion, patrolmen guilty of such abuses make life unnecessarily difficult for themselves and for their co-workers. Despite disapproval of harshness, officers tend to be defensive about it. For example, one sergeant who was outspokenly critical of brutality, said that though in general brutal men create more problems than they solve, "they do a good job in some situations for which the better men have no stomach." Moreover, supervisory personnel exhibit a strong reluctance to direct their subordinates in the particulars of their work performance. According to our observations, control is exercised mainly through consultation with superiors, and directives take the form of requests rather than orders. In the background of all this is the belief that patrol work on skid-row requires a great deal of discretionary freedom. In the words of the same sergeant quoted above, "a good man has things worked out in his own ways on his beat and he doesn't need anybody to tell him what to do."

The virtual absence of disciplinary control and the demand for discretionary freedom are related to the idea that patrol work involves "playing by ear." For if it is true that peace keeping cannot be systematically generalized, then, of course, it cannot be organizationally constrained. What the seasoned patrolman means, however, in saying that he "plays by ear" is that he is making his decisions while being attuned to the realities of complex situations about which he has immensely detailed knowledge. This studied aspect of peace keeping generally is not made explicit, nor is the tyro or the outsider made aware of it. Quite to the contrary, the ability to discharge the duties associated with keeping the peace is viewed as a reflection of an innate talent of "getting along with people." Thus, the same demands are made of barely initiated officers as are made of experienced practitioners. Correspondingly, beginners tend to think that they can do as well as their more knowledgeable peers. As this leads to inevitable frustrations, they find themselves in a situation that is conducive to the development of a particular sense of "touchiness." Personal dispositions of individual officers are, of course, of great relevance. But the license of discretionary freedom and the expectation of success under conditions of autonomy, without any indication that the work of the successful craftsman is based on an acquired preparedness for the task, is ready-made for failure and malpractice. Moreover, it leads to slipshod practices of patrol that also infect the standards of the careful craftsman.

The uniformed patrol, and especially the foot patrol, has a low preferential value in the division of labor of police work. This is, in part, at least, due to the belief that "anyone could do it." In fact, this belief is thoroughly mistaken. At present, however, the recognition that the practice requires preparation, and the process of obtaining the preparation itself, is left entirely to the practitioner.

FOOTNOTES

[1] The bill for a Metropolitan Police was actually enacted under the sponsorship of Robert Peel, the Home Secretary in the Tory Government of the Duke of Wellington. There is, however, no doubt that it was one of the several reform tendencies that Peel assimilated into Tory politics in his long career. Cf. J. L. Lyman, "The Metropolitan Police Act of 1829," *Journal of Criminal Law, Criminology and Police Science,* 55 (1964), 141–154.

[2] Jerome Hall, "Police and Law in a Democratic Society," *Indiana Law Journal,* 28 (1953), 133–177. Though other authors are less emphatic on this point, judicial control is generally taken for granted. The point has been made, however, that in modern times judicial control over the police has been asserted mainly because of the default of any other general controlling authority, cf. E. L. Barrett, Jr., "Police Practice and the Law," *California Law Review,* 50 (1962), 11–55.

[3] A. C. German, F. D. Day and R. R. J. Gallati, *Introduction to Law Enforcement,* Springfield, Ill.: C. C. Thomas, 1966; "One concept, in particular, should be kept in mind. A dictatorship can never exist unless the police system of the country is under the absolute control of the dictator. There is no other way to uphold a dictatorship except by terror, and the instrument of this total terror is the secret police, whatever its name. In every country where freedom has been lost, law enforcement has been a dominant instrument in destroying it" (p. 80).

[4] The point is frequently made; cf. Raymond B. Fosdick, *American Police Systems,* New York: Century Company, 1920; Bruce Smith, *Police Systems in the United States,* 2nd rev. ed., New York: Harper, 1960.

[5] The executive margin of control is set mainly in terms of budgetary determinations and the mapping of some formal aspects of the organization of departments.

[6] Michael Banton, *The Policeman in the Community,* New York: Basic Books, 1964, pp. 6–7 and 127 ff.

[7] R. Bruce Holmgren, *Primary Police Functions,* New York: William C. Copp, 1962.

[8] Cf. Lyman, *op. cit.,* p. 153; F. C. Mather, *Public Order in the Age of the Chartists,* Manchester: Manchester University Press, 1959, chapter IV. See also Robert H. Bremer, "Police, Penal and Parole Policies in Cleveland and Toledo," *American Journal of Economics and Sociology,* 14 (1955), 387–398, for similar recognition in the United States at about the turn of this century.

[9] Smith, *op. cit.,* pp. 15 ff.

[10] Orlando W. Wilson, "Police Authority in a Free Society," *Journal of Criminal Law, Criminology and Police Science,* 54 (1964), 175–177.

[11] Joseph Goldstein, "Police Discretion Not to Invoke the Criminal Process," *Yale Law Journal,* 69 (1960), 543.

[12] Jerome Skolnick, *Justice without Trial,* New York: Wiley, 1966.

[13] Wayne LaFave, "The Police and Nonenforcement of the Law," *Wisconsin Law Review* (1962), 104–137 and 179–239.

[14] Nathan Goldman, *The Differential Selection of Juvenile Offenders for Court Appearance,* National Research and Information Center, National Council on Crime and Delinquency, 1963, pp. 114 ff.

[15] Elaine Cumming, Ian Cumming and Laura Edell, "Policeman as Philosopher, Guide and Friend," *Social Problems,* 12, (1965), 276–286.

[16] There is little doubt that many requests for service are turned down by the police, especially when they are made over the telephone or by mail, cf. LaFave, *op. cit.,* p. 212, n. 124. The uniformed patrolman, however, finds it virtually impossible to leave the scene without becoming involved in some way or another.

[17] Hans Kelsen, *General Theory of Law and State,* New York: Russell & Russell, 1961, pp. 278–279; H. L. A. Hart, *The Concept of Law,* Oxford: Clarendon Press, 1961, pp. 20–21.

[18] Mather, *op. cit.;* see also, Jenifer Hart, "Reform of the Borough Police, 1835–1856," *English History Review,* 70 (1955), 411–427.

[19] Francis A. Allen, *The Borderland of Criminal Justice,* Chicago: University of Chicago Press, 1964.

[20] Egon Bittner, "Police Discretion in Emergency Apprehension of Mentally Ill Persons," *Social Problems,* 14 (1967), 278–292.

[21] It bears mentioning, however, that differential treatment is not unique with the police, but is also in many ways representative for the administration of justice in general; cf. J. E. Carlin, Jan Howard and S. L. Messinger, "Civil Justice and the Poor," *Law and Society,* 1 (1966), 9–89; Jacobus tenBroek (ed.) *The Law of the Poor,* San Francisco: Chandler Publishing Co., 1966.

[22]This is, however, true only in the ideal. It is well known that a substantial number of persons who are arrested are subsequently released without ever being charged and tried, cf. Barrett, *op. cit*.

[23]The literature on skid-row is voluminous. The classic in the field is Nels Anderson, *The Hobo*, Chicago: University of Chicago Press, 1923. Samuel E. Wallace, *Skid-Row as a Way of Life*, Totowa, New Jersey: The Bedminster Press, 1965, is a more recent descriptive account and contains a useful bibliography. Donald A. Bogue, *Skid-Row in American Cities*, Chicago: Community and Family Center, University of Chicago, 1963, contains an exhaustive quantitative survey of Chicago skid-row.

[24]One of the two cities described in this paper also employed the procedure of the "round-up" of drunks. In this, the police van toured the skid-row area twice daily, during the mid-afternoon and early evening hours, and the officers who manned it picked up drunks they sighted. A similar procedure is used in New York's Bowery and the officers who do it are called "condition men." Cf. *Bowery Project*, Bureau of Applied Social Research, Columbia University, Summary Report of a Study Undertaken under Contract Approved by the Board of Estimates, 1963, mimeo., p. 11.

[25]An illuminating parallel to the perception of skid-row can be found in the more traditional concept of vagabondage. Cf. Alexandre Vexliard, *Introduction à la Sociologie du Vagabondage*, Paris: Libraire Marcel Rivière, 1956, and "La Disparition du Vagabondage comme Fleau Social Universel," *Revue de L'Institut de Sociologie* (1963), 53–79. The classic account of English conditions up to the 19th century is C. J. Ribton-Turner, *A History of Vagrants and Vagrancy and Beggars and Begging*, London: Chapman and Hall, 1887.

[26]Several patrolmen complained about the influx of "tourists" into skid-row. Since such "tourists" are perceived as seeking illicit adventure, they receive little sympathy from patrolmen when they complain about being victimized.

[27]The same officer commented further, "If a man looks for something, I might help him. But I don't stay with him till he finds what he is looking for. If I did, I would never get to do anything else. In the last analysis, I really never solve any problems. The best I can hope for is to keep things from getting worse."

[28]When evidence is present to indicate that a serious crime has been committed, considerations of culpability acquire a position of priority. Two such arrests were observed, both involving checkpassers. The first offender was caught *in flagrante delicto*. In the second instance, the suspect attracted the attention of the patrolman because of his sickly appearance. In the ensuing conversation the man made some remarks that led the officer to place a call with the Warrant Division of his department. According to the information that was obtained by checking records, the man was a wanted checkpasser and was immediately arrested.

17

Police Encounters with Juveniles

IRVING PILIAVIN and SCOTT BRIAR

As the first of a series of decisions made in the channeling of youthful offenders through the agencies concerned with juvenile justice and corrections, the disposition decisions made by police officers have potentially profound consequences for apprehended juveniles.[1] Thus arrest, the most severe of the dispositions available to police, may not only lead to confinement of the suspected offender but also bring him loss of social status, restriction of educational and employment opportunities, and future harassment by law-enforcement personnel.[2] According to some criminologists, the stigmatization resulting from police apprehension, arrest, and detention actually reinforces deviant behavior.[3] Other authorities have suggested, in fact, that this stigmatization serves as the catalytic agent initiating delinquent careers.[4] Despite their presumed significance, however, little empirical analysis has been reported regarding the factors influencing, or consequences resulting from, police actions with juvenile offenders. Furthermore, while some studies of police encounters with adult offenders have been reported, the extent

Source: "Police Encounters with Juveniles," *American Journal of Sociology*, Vol. 70, September, 1964, pp. 206–214. Copyright © 1964 by the University of Chicago Press. By permission of the author and publisher.

to which the findings of these investigations pertain to law-enforcement practices with youthful offenders is not known.[5]

The above considerations have led the writers to undertake a longitudinal study of the conditions influencing, and consequences flowing from, police actions with juveniles. In the present paper findings will be presented indicating the influence of certain factors on police actions. Research data consist primarily of notes and records based on nine months' observation of all juvenile officers in one police department.[6] The officers were observed in the course of their regular tours of duty.[7] While these data do not lend themselves to quantitative assessments of reliability and validity, the candor shown by the officers in their interviews with the investigators and their use of officially frowned-upon practices while under observation provide some assurance that the materials presented below accurately reflect the typical operations and attitudes of the law-enforcement personnel studied.

The setting for the research, a metropolitan police department serving an industrial city with approximately 450,000 inhabitants, was noted within the community it served and among law enforcement officials elsewhere for the honesty and superior quality of its personnel. Incidents involving criminal activity or brutality by members of the department had been extremely rare during the ten years preceding this study; personnel standards were comparatively high; and an extensive training program was provided to both new and experienced personnel. Juvenile Bureau members, the primary subjects of this investigation, differed somewhat from other members of the department in that they were responsible for delinquency prevention as well as law enforcement, that is, juvenile officers were expected to be knowledgeable about conditions leading to crime and delinquency and to be able to work with community agencies serving known or potential juvenile offenders. Accordingly, in the assignment of personnel to the Juvenile Bureau, consideration was given not only to an officer's devotion to and reliability in law enforcement but also to his commitment to delinquency prevention. Assignment to the Bureau was of advantage to policemen seeking promotions. Consequently, many officers requested transfer to this unit, and its personnel comprised a highly select group of officers.

In the field, juvenile officers operated essentially as patrol officers. They cruised assigned beats and, although concerned primarily with juvenile offenders, frequently had occasion to apprehend and arrest adults. Confrontations between the officers and juveniles occurred in one of the following three ways, in order of increasing frequency: (1) encounters resulting from officers' spotting officially "wanted" youths; (2) encounters taking place at or near the scene of offenses reported to police headquarters; and (3) encounters occurring as the result of officers' directly observing youths either committing offenses or in "suspicious circumstances." However, the probability that a confrontation would take place between officer and juvenile, or that a particular disposition of an identified offender would be made, was only in part determined by the knowledge that an offense had occurred or that a particular juvenile had committed an offense. The bases for and utilization of non-offense related criteria by police in accosting and disposing of juveniles are the focuses of the following discussion.

SANCTIONS FOR DISCRETION

In each encounter with juveniles, with the minor exception of officially "wanted" youths,[8] a central task confronting the officer was to decide what official action to take against the boys involved. In making these disposition decisions, officers could select any one of five discrete alternatives:

1. Outright release
2. Release and submission of a "field interrogation report" briefly describing the circumstances initiating the police-juvenile confrontation
3. "Official reprimand" and release to parents or guardian
4. Citation to juvenile court
5. Arrest and confinement in juvenile hall

Dispositions 3, 4, and 5 differed from the others in two basic respects. First, with rare exceptions, when an officer chose to reprimand, cite, or arrest a boy, he took the youth to the police station. Second, the reprimanded, cited, or arrested boy acquired an official police "record," that is, his name was officially recorded in Bureau files as a juvenile violator.

Analysis of the distribution of police disposition decisions about juveniles revealed that in virtually every category of offense the full range of official disposition alternatives available to officers was employed. This wide range of discretion resulted primarily from two conditions. First, it reflected the reluctance of officers to expose certain youths to the stigmatization presumed to be associated with official police action. Few juvenile officers believed that correctional agencies serving the community could effectively help delinquents. For some officers this attitude reflected a lack of confidence in rehabilitation techniques; for others, a belief that high case loads and lack of professional training among correctional workers vitiated their efforts at treatment. All officers were agreed, however, that juvenile justice and correctional processes were essentially concerned with apprehension and punishment rather than treatment. Furthermore, all officers believed that some aspects of these processes (e.g., judicial definition of youths as delinquents and removal of delinquents from the community), as well as some of the possible consequences of these processes (e.g., intimate institutional contact with "hard-core" delinquents, as well as parental, school, and conventional peer disapproval or rejection), could reinforce what previously might have been only a tentative proclivity toward delinquent values and behavior. Consequently, when officers found reason to doubt that a youth being confronted was highly committed toward deviance, they were inclined to treat him with leniency.

Second, and more important, the practice of discretion was sanctioned by police-department policy. Training manuals and departmental bulletins stressed that the disposition of each juvenile offender was not to be based solely on the type of infraction he committed. Thus while it was departmental policy to "arrest and confine all juveniles who have committed a felony or misdemeanor involving theft, sex offense, battery, possession of dangerous weapons, prowling, peeping, intoxication, incorrigibility, and disturbance of the peace," it was acknowledged that "such considerations as age, attitude and prior criminal record might indicate that a different disposition would be more appropriate."[9] The official justification for discretion in processing juvenile offenders, based on the preventive aims of the Juvenile Bureau, was that each juvenile violator should be dealt with solely on the basis of what was best for him.[10] Unofficially, administrative legitimation of discretion was further justified on the grounds that strict enforcement practices would overcrowd court calendars and detention facilities, as well as dramatically increase juvenile crime rates—consequences to be avoided because they would expose the police department to community criticism.[11]

In practice, the official policy justifying use of discretion served as a demand that discretion be exercised. As such, it posed three problems for juvenile officers. First, it represented a departure from the traditional police practice with which the juvenile officers themselves were identified, in the sense that they were expected to justify their juvenile disposition decisions not simply by evidence proving a youth had committed a crime—grounds on which police were officially expected to base their dispositions of non-juvenile offenders[12]—but in the *character* of the youth. Second, in disposing of juvenile offenders, officers were expected, in effect, to make judicial rather than ministerial decisions.[13] Third, the shift from the offense to the offender as the basis for determining the appropriate disposition substantially increased the uncertainty and ambiguity for officers in the situation of apprehension because no explicit rules existed for determining which disposition different types of youths should receive. Despite these problems, officers were constrained to base disposition decisions on the character of the apprehended youth, not only because they wanted to be fair, but because persistent failure to do so could result in judicial criticism, departmental censure, and, they believed, loss of authority with juveniles.[14]

DISPOSITION CRITERIA

Assessing the character of apprehended offenders posed relatively few difficulties for officers in the case of youths who had committed serious crimes such as robbery, homicide, aggravated assault, grand theft, auto theft, rape, and arson. Officials generally regarded these juveniles as confirmed delinquents simply by virtue of their involvement in offenses of this magnitude.[15] However, the infraction committed did not always suffice to determine the appropriate disposition for some serious offenders;[16] and, in the case of minor offenders, who comprised over 90 percent of the youths against whom police took action, the violation per se generally played an insignificant role in the choice of disposition. While a number of minor offenders were seen as serious delinquents deserving arrest, many others were perceived either as "good" boys whose offenses were atypical of their customary behavior, as pawns of undesirable associates or, in any case, as boys for whom arrest was regarded as an unwarranted and possibly harmful punishment. Thus, for nearly all minor violators and for some serious delinquents, the assessment of character—the distinction between serious delinquents, "good" boys, misguided youths, and so on—and the dispositions which followed from these assessments were based on the youths' personal characteristics and not their offenses.

Despite this dependence of disposition decisions on the personal characteristics of these youths, however, police officers actually had access only to very limited information about boys at the time they had to decide what to do with them. In the field, officers typically had no data concerning the past offense records, school performance, family situation, or personal adjustment of apprehended youths.[17] Furthermore, files at police headquarters provided data only about each boy's prior offense record. Thus both the decision made in the field—whether or not to bring the boy in—and the decision made at the station—which disposition to invoke—were based largely on cues which emerged from the interaction between the officer and the youth, cues from which the officer inferred the youth's character. These cues included the youth's group affiliations, age, race, grooming, dress, and demeanor. Older juveniles, members of known delinquent gangs, Negroes, youths with well-oiled hair, black jackets, and soiled denims or jeans (the presumed uniform of "tough" boys), and boys who in their interactions with officers did not manifest what were considered to be appropriate signs of respect tended to receive the more severe dispositions. Other than prior record, the most important of the above cues was a youth's *demeanor*. In the opinion of juvenile patrolmen themselves the demeanor of apprehended juveniles was a major determinant of their decisions for 50–60 percent of the juvenile cases they processed.[18] A less subjective indication of the association between a youth's demeanor and police disposition is provided by Table 1, which presents the police dispositions for sixty-six youths whose encounters with police were observed in the course of this study.[19] For purposes of this analysis, each youth's demeanor in the encounter was classified as either cooperative or uncooperative.[20] The results clearly reveal a marked association between youth demeanor and the severity of police dispositions.

The cues used by police to assess demeanor were fairly simple. Juveniles who were contrite about their infractions, respectful to officers, and fearful of the sanctions that might be employed against them tended to be viewed by patrolmen as basically law-abiding or at least "salvageable." For these youths it was usually assumed that informal or formal reprimand would suffice to guarantee their future con-

formity. In contrast, youthful offenders who were fractious, obdurate, or who appeared nonchalant in their encounters with patrolmen were likely to be viewed as "would-be tough guys" or "punks" who fully deserved the most severe sanction: arrest. The following excerpts from observation notes illustrate the importance attached to demeanor by police in making disposition decisions.

1. The interrogation of "A" (an 18-year-old upper-lower-class white male accused of statutory rape) was assigned to a police sergeant with long experience on the force. As I sat in his office while we waited for the youth to arrive for questioning, the sergeant expressed his uncertainty as to what he should do with this young man. On the one hand, he could not ignore the fact that an offense had been committed; he had been informed, in fact, that the youth was prepared to confess to the offense. Nor could he overlook the continued pressure from the girl's father (an important political figure) for the police to take severe action against the youth. On the other hand, the sergeant had formed a low opinion of the girl's moral character, and he considered it unfair to charge "A" with statutory rape when the girl was a willing partner to the offense and might even have been the instigator of it. However, his sense of injustice concerning "A" was tempered by his image of the youth as a "punk," based, he explained, on information he had received that the youth belonged to a certain gang, the members of which were well known to, and disliked by, the police.

TABLE 1

Severity of Police Disposition by Youth's Demeanor

	Youth's Demeanor		
Severity of Police Disposition	Co-operative	Unco-operative	Total
Arrest (most severe)	2	14	16
Citation or official reprimand	4	5	9
Informal reprimand	15	1	16
Admonish and release (least severe)	24	1	25
TOTAL	45	21	66

Nevertheless, as we prepared to leave his office to interview "A," the sergeant was still in doubt as to what he should do with him.

As we walked down the corridor to the interrogation room, the sergeant was stopped by a reporter from the local newspaper. In an excited tone of voice, the reporter explained that his editor was pressing him to get further information about the case. The newspaper had printed some of the facts about the girl's disappearance, and as a consequence the girl's father was threatening suit against the paper for defamation of the girl's character. It would strengthen the newspaper's position, the reporter explained, if the police had information indicating that the girl's associates, particularly the youth the sergeant was about to interrogate, were persons of disreputable character. This stimulus seemed to resolve the sergeant's uncertainty. He told the reporter, "unofficially," that the youth was known to be an undesirable person, citing as evidence his membership in the delinquent gang. Furthermore, the sergeant added that he had evidence that this youth had been intimate with the girl over a period of many months. When the reporter asked if the police were planning to do anything to the youth, the sergeant answered that he intended to charge the youth with statutory rape.

In the interrogation, however, three points quickly emerged which profoundly affected the sergeant's judgment of the youth. First, the youth was polite and cooperative; he consistently addressed the officer as "sir," answered all questions quietly, and signed a statement implicating himself in numerous counts of statutory rape. Second, the youth's intentions toward the girl appeared to have been honorable; for example, he said that he wanted to marry her eventually. Third, the youth was not in fact a member of the gang in question. The sergeant's attitude became increasingly sympathetic, and after we left the interrogation room he announced his intention to "get 'A' off the hook," meaning that he wanted to have the charges against "A" reduced or, if possible, dropped.

2. Officers "X" and "Y" brought into the police station a seventeen-year-old white boy who, along with two older companions, had been found in a home having sex relations with a fifteen-year-old girl. The boy responded to police officers' queries slowly and with obvious disregard. It was apparent that his lack of deference toward the officers and his failure to evidence concern about his situation were irritating his questioners. Finally, one of the officers turned to me and, obviously angry, commented that in his view the boy was simply a "stud" interested only in sex, eating, and sleeping. The policemen conjectured that the boy "probably already had knocked up half a dozen girls." The boy ignored these remarks, except for an occasional impassive stare at the patrolmen. Turning to the boy, the officer remarked, "What the hell am I going to do with you?" And again the boy simply returned the officer's gaze. The latter then said, "Well, I guess we'll just have to put you away for a while." An arrest report was then made out and the boy was taken to Juvenile Hall.

Although anger and disgust frequently characterized officers' attitudes toward recalcitrant and impassive juvenile offenders, their manner while processing these youths was typically routine, restrained, and without rancor. While the officers' restraint may have been due in part to their desire to avoid accusation and censure, it also seemed to reflect their inurement to a frequent experience. By and large, only their occasional "needling" or insulting of a boy gave any hint of the underlying resentment and dislike they felt toward many of these youths.[21]

PREJUDICE IN APPREHENSION AND DISPOSITION DECISIONS

Compared to other youths, Negroes and boys whose appearance matched the delinquent stereotype were more frequently stopped and interrogated by patrolmen—often even in the absence of evidence that an offense had been committed[22]—and usually were given more severe dispositions for the same violations. Our data suggest, however, that these selective apprehension and disposition practices resulted not only from the intrusion of long-held prejudices of individual police officers but also from certain job-related experiences of law-enforcement personnel.

First, the tendency for police to give more severe dispositions to Negroes and to youths whose appearance corresponded to that which police associated with delinquents partly reflected the fact, observed in this study, that these youths also were much more likely than were other types of boys to exhibit the sort of recalcitrant demeanor which police construed as a sign of the confirmed delinquent. Further, officers assumed, partly on the basis of departmental statistics, that Negroes and juveniles who "look tough" (e.g., who wear chinos, leather jackets, boots, etc.) commit crimes more frequently than do other types of youths.[23] In this sense, the police justified their selective treatment of these youths along epidemiological lines: that is, they were concentrating their attention on those youths whom they believed were most likely to commit delinquent acts. In the words of one highly placed official in the department:

> If you know that the bulk of your delinquent problem comes from kids who, say, are from 12 to 14 years of age, when you're out on patrol you are much more likely to be sensitive to the activities of juveniles in this age bracket than older or younger groups. This would be good law enforcement practice. The logic in our case is the same except that our delinquency problem is largely found in the Negro community and it is these youths toward whom we are sensitized.

As regards prejudice per se, eighteen of twenty-seven officers interviewed openly admitted a dislike for Negroes. However, they attributed their dislike to experiences they had, as policemen, with youths from this minority group. The officers reported that Negro boys were much more likely than non-Negroes to "give us a hard time," be uncooperative, and show no remorse for their transgressions. Recurrent exposure to such attitudes among Negro youth, the officers claimed, generated their antipathy toward Negroes. The following excerpt is typical of the views expressed by these officers:

> They (Negroes) have no regard for the law or for the police. They just don't seem to give a damn. Few of them are interested in school or getting ahead. The girls start having illegitimate kids before they are 16 years old and the boys are always "out for kicks." Furthermore, many of these kids try to run you down. They say the damnedest things to you and they seem to have absolutely no respect for you as an adult. I admit I am prejudiced now, but frankly I don't think I was when I began police work.

IMPLICATIONS

It is apparent from the findings presented above that the police officers studied in this research were permitted and even encouraged to exercise immense latitude in disposing of the juveniles they encountered. That is, it was within the officer's discretionary authority, except in extreme limiting cases, to decide which juveniles were to come to the attention of the courts and correctional agencies and thereby be identified officially as delinquents. In exercising this discretion policemen were strongly guided by the demeanor of those who were apprehended, a practice which ultimately led, as seen above, to certain youths' (particularly Negroes[24] and boys dressed in the style of "toughs") being treated more severely than other juveniles for comparable offenses.

But the relevance of demeanor was not limited only to police disposition practices. Thus, for example, in conjunction with police crime statistics the criterion of demeanor led police to concentrate their surveillance activities in areas frequented or inhabited by Negroes. Furthermore, these youths were accosted more often than others by officers on patrol simply because their skin color identified them as potential troublemakers. These discriminatory practices—and it is important to note that they are discriminatory, even if based on accurate statistical information—may well have self-fulfilling consequences. Thus it is not unlikely that frequent encounters with police, particularly those involving youths innocent of wrongdoing, will increase the hostility of these juveniles toward law enforcement personnel. It is also not unlikely that the frequency of such encounters will in time reduce their significance in the eyes of apprehended juveniles, thereby leading these youths to regard them as "routine." Such responses to police encounters, however, are those which law enforcement personnel perceive as indicators of the serious delinquent. They thus serve to vindicate and reinforce officers' prejudices, leading to closer surveillance of Negro districts, more frequent encounters with Negro youths, and so on in a vicious circle. Moreover, the consequences of this chain of events are reflected in police statistics showing a disproportionately high percentage of Negroes among juvenile offenders, thereby providing

PART 3   THE SOCIAL ORGANIZATION OF CRIMINAL LAW ENFORCEMENT

"objective" justification for concentrating police attention on Negro youths.

To a substantial extent, as we have implied earlier, the discretion practiced by juvenile officers is simply an extension of the juvenile-court philosophy, which holds that in making legal decisions regarding juveniles, more weight should be given to the juvenile's character and life-situation than to his actual offending behavior. The juvenile officer's disposition decisions—and the information he used as a basis for them—are more akin to the discriminations made by probation officers and other correctional workers than they are to decisions of police officers dealing with non-juvenile offenders. The problem is that such clinical-type decisions are not restrained by mechanisms comparable to the principles of due process and the rules of procedure governing police decisions regarding adult offenders. Consequently, prejudicial practices by police officers can escape notice more easily in their dealings with juveniles than with adults.

The observations made in this study serve to underscore the fact that the official delinquent, as distinguished from the juvenile who simply commits a delinquent act, is the product of a social judgment, in this case a judgment made by the police. He is a delinquent because someone in authority has defined him as one, often on the basis of the public face he has presented to officials rather than of the kind of offense he has committed.

FOOTNOTES

[1] This study was supported by Grant MH-06328-02, National Institute of Mental Health, United States Public Health Service.

[2] Richard D. Schwartz and Jerome H. Skolnick, "Two Studies of Legal Stigma," *Social Problems*, X (April, 1962), 133–42; Sol Rubin, *Crime and Juvenile Delinquency* (New York: Oceana Publications, 1958); B. F. McSally, "Finding Jobs for Released Offenders," *Federal Probation*, XXIV (June, 1960), 12–17; Harold D. Lasswell and Richard C. Donnelly, "The Continuing Debate over Responsibility: An Introduction to Isolating the Condemnation Sanction," *Yale Law Journal*, LXVIII (April, 1959), 869–99.

[3] Richard A. Cloward and Lloyd E. Ohlin, *Delinquency and Opportunity* (Glencoe, Ill.: Free Press, 1960), pp. 124–30.

[4] Frank Tannenbaum, *Crime and the Community* (New York: Columbia University Press, 1936), pp. 17–20; Howard S. Becker, *Outsiders: Studies in the Sociology of Deviance* (New York: Free Press of Glencoe, 1963), chaps. i and ii.

[5] For a detailed accounting of police discretionary practices, see Joseph Goldstein, "Police Discretion Not to Invoke the Criminal Process: Low-visibility Decisions in the Administration of Justice," *Yale Law Journal*, LXIX (1960), 543–94; Wayne R. LaFave, "The Police and Non-enforcement of the Law—Part I," *Wisconsin Law Review*, January, 1962, pp. 104–37; S. H. Kadish, "Legal Norms and Discretion in the Police and Sentencing Processes," *Harvard Law Review*, LXXV (March, 1962), 904–31.

[6] Approximately thirty officers were assigned to the Juvenile Bureau in the department studied. While we had an opportunity to observe all officers in the Bureau during the study, our observations were concentrated on those who had been working in the Bureau for one or two years at least. Although two of the officers in the Juvenile Bureau were Negro, we observed these officers on only a few occasions.

[7] Although observations were not confined to specific days or work shifts, more observations were made during evenings and weekends because police activity was greatest during these periods.

[8] "Wanted" juveniles usually were placed under arrest or in protective custody, a practice which in effect relieved officers of the responsibility for deciding what to do with these youths.

[9] Quoted from a training manual issued by the police department studied in this research.

[10] Presumably this also implied that police action with juveniles was to be determined partly by the offenders' need for correctional services.

[11] This was reported by beat officers as well as supervisory and administrative personnel of the juvenile bureau.

[12] In actual practice, of course, disposition decisions regarding adult offenders also were influenced by many factors extraneous to the offense per se.

[13] For example, in dealing with adult violators, officers had no disposition alternative comparable to the reprimand-and-release category, a disposition which contained elements of punishment but did not involve mediation by the court.

[14] The concern of officers over possible loss of authority stemmed from their belief that court failure to support arrests by appropriate action would cause policemen to "lose face" in the eyes of juveniles.

[15] It is also likely that the possibility of negative publicity resulting from the failure to arrest such violators—particularly if they became involved in further serious crime—brought about strong administrative pressure for their arrest.

[16] For example, in the year preceding this research, over 30 percent of the juveniles involved in burglaries and 12 percent of the juveniles committing auto theft received dispositions other than arrest.

[17] On occasion, officers apprehended youths whom they personally knew to be prior offenders. This did not occur frequently, however, for several reasons. First, approximately 75 percent of apprehended youths had no prior official records; second, officers periodically exchanged patrol areas, thus limiting their exposure to, and knowledge about, these areas; and third, patrolmen seldom spent more than three or four years in the juvenile division.

[18] While reliable subgroup estimates were impossible to obtain through observation because of the relatively small number of incidents observed, the importance of demeanor in disposition decisions appeared to be much less significant with known prior offenders.

[19]Systematic data were collected on police encounters with seventy-six juveniles. In ten of these encounters the police concluded that their suspicions were groundless, and consequently the juveniles involved were exonerated; these ten cases were eliminated from this analysis of demeanor. (The total number of encounters observed was considerably more than seventy-six, but systematic data-collection procedures were not instituted until several months after observations began.)

[20]The data used for the classification of demeanor were the written records of observations made by the authors. The classifications were made by an independent judge not associated with this study. In classifying a youth's demeanor as cooperative or uncooperative, particular attention was paid to: (1) the youth's responses to police officers' questions and requests; (2) the respect and deference—or lack of these qualities—shown by the youth toward police officers; and (3) police officers' assessments of the youth's demeanor.

[21]Officers' animosity toward recalcitrant or aloof offenders appeared to stem from two sources: moral indignation that these juveniles were self-righteous and indifferent about their transgressions, and resentment that these youths failed to accord police the respect they believed they deserved. Since the patrolmen perceived themselves as honestly and impartially performing a vital community function, warranting respect and deference from the community at large, they attributed the lack of respect shown them by these juveniles to the latter's immorality.

[22]The clearest evidence for this assertion is provided by the over-representation of Negroes among "innocent" juveniles accosted by the police. As noted, of the seventy-six juveniles on whom systematic data were collected, ten were exonerated and released without suspicion. Seven, or two-thirds of these ten "innocent" juveniles were Negro, in contrast to the allegedly "guilty" youths, less than one-third of whom were Negro. The following incident illustrates the operation of this bias: One officer, observing a youth walking along the street, commented that the youth "looks suspicious" and promptly stopped and questioned him. Asked later to explain what aroused his suspicion, the officer explained, "He was a Negro wearing dark glasses at midnight."

[23]While police statistics did not permit an analysis of crime rates by appearance, they strongly supported officers' contentions concerning the delinquency rate among Negroes. Of all male juveniles processed by the police department in 1961, for example, 40.2 percent were Negro and 33.9 percent were white. These two groups comprised at that time, respectively, about 22.7 percent and 73.6 percent of the population in the community studied.

[24]An uncooperative demeanor was presented by more than one-third of the Negro youths but by only one-sixth of the white youths encountered by the police in the course of our observations.

18

The Narcotics Enforcement Pattern

JEROME H. SKOLNICK

ROUTINE ACTIVITY AND THE PETTY INFORMANT

In a municipal police department, vice control officers, like all plainclothesmen, spend a portion of their working hours on surveillance, simply riding in unmarked cars on street patrol. But vice control men spend much less time in this fashion than patrol division detectives, since they frequently are able to "create" crimes through the leads of informants, while patrol division detectives must await the report of a felony before they can take action. Thus, the patrol detective—who rides alone, while vice control men team up in pairs—may find boredom a major enemy. Entire evenings may pass when patrolling detectives do nothing other than drive a car slowly around a city for eight hours. After a while, the detective may feel gratitude for the felon who provides him with activity.

Much of the generative activity in enforcing narcotics crimes takes place within the police station. This is not because narcotics police are lazy but because the nature of narcotics crime requires that

invocation of activity be based upon receipt of messages.[1] Thus, all detectives, but especially narcotics detectives, do a lot of work on the telephone. Many of the informants (some of whom are transients) do not have telephones of their own, and others prefer not to be called at home by a policeman. As a result, the narcotics policeman is continually being called to the telephone.

Not all informing, however, takes place over the telephone. Petty informants seem to enjoy wandering into the separate quarters of the vice control squad, and narcotics officers must be available to greet and chat with them. Indeed, due to their constant need for information, narcotics officers encourage informants to "drop in." To this end, the Westville vice control squad is not only quartered separately from the rest of the police department but it even has a special entrance through which informants can pass unobserved by other policemen.

During the evening being described, Sergeant Harris was visited by a long-time addict and regular informant for the vice control squad, who was a mercenary, paid for his information. Members of the vice control squad suspected him of "dealing a little methedrine" himself and had another addict-informant keeping an eye on him. Actually, each addict-informant accused the other of dealing methedrine, but the vice control squad had been unable to convict either.

The informant, especially one who seems odd or eccentric, is in an advantageous position, since he can gain a fairly accurate idea of the physical location of members of the narcotics detail by the simple expedient of telephoning them. Narcotics officers, however, are alert to deceptive techniques used by informants and take care to counteract these whenever possible. From the officers' point of view, the least serious is the petty informant dealer who, for instance, drops around to the police station to impress the officers that he is "working" in their interest. There are evidently two reasons for the policeman's indulgent response to the maneuvers of an informant of this type. First, although the policeman sees through his artifices, such an informant may sometimes produce useful information and is consequently tolerated. Indeed, the policeman may feel genuinely sorry for such a man. In my experience, most policemen can empathize somewhat with the petty addict-informant. I have several times heard various vice squad detectives express the notion that such-and-such an informant "could have been somebody if he hadn't gotten hooked on that stuff. It's terrible what it does to you." In addition, the petty informant is typically not a symbolic assailant but is perceived as something of a pitiful figure, rather like a punch-drunk prizefighter.

Perhaps the more important reason, however, is instrumental. An informant would at most risk using "only" a so-called dangerous drug when visiting the narcotics detail, since such use constitutes a misdemeanor rather than a felony. Consequently, in the narcotics officer's scale of values, the user simply does not constitute a "good pinch." In practice, therefore, although such an informant does not have a "license" to operate, neither do the narcotics police strive to bring about his apprehension. Of course, if he were to be caught selling drugs illegally, he would surely be arrested (even if only to be released again in return for information).

Police take most seriously deceptive techniques whereby informants attempt to use their working relations with law enforcement officers for positive personal gain. This situation poses the gravest dilemma for detectives by suspending them between the ideals of morality and the demands of efficiency. For example, when informant A says that B is in possession of an illegal object, there is often reason to suspect A's motives. Within the system, the morally acceptable motive is to extricate oneself from a difficult situation. It is not that such motivation is positively countenanced either by the police or by the informants themselves. But if the situation of the informant is perceived as an equilibrium with a set of minuses on one side and pluses on the other, it is seen as understandable for a man in a minus situation to bring himself back to normal. Thus, when the petty informant gives information in exchange for money to purchase drugs, or to avoid a penal sanction, his motives are acceptable, and the police feel no hesitancy in engaging his services.

However, the police do not consider it morally acceptable for a man to inform to gain positive benefits. Policemen may not personally like the idea, but they sometimes find themselves in a position of having to use information given by people who are vengeful, or worse yet, who will gain some unlawful benefit from the arrest of another, such as freedom to take over another seller's clientele if he is sent to jail or the opportunity to strip clean of resalable articles the premises of a man who has been arrested. What troubles police most is the "set-up," the "planting," for instance, of a good supply of narcotics in addict A's house by B to take A "out of the scene." Suspicious of being deceived, police usually check carefully an informant's story if the context makes it appear the informant is somehow being positively rewarded. Policemen have few, if any, moral reservations about setting a trap for a suspected felon on their own initiative. What hurts both pride and morality is to permit a false trap to be set by one "criminal" for another.

SETTING UP A "GOOD PINCH"

In what follows, the events of the "good pinch" evening are described. They are also interpreted in light of how organizational commitments of the police influence their capacity to observe the rule of law.

Shortly after the petty informant left, a telephone call came in from another addict-informant, Charlie, who was scheduled for preliminary hearing on a charge of possession for sale with one prior conviction. Charlie reported that a couple of addicts had stolen a large supply of drugs from a warehouse or drugstore, and had "split up the loot" in his "pad." He could not provide the address of the thieves, although he had visited one of them and thought he might be able to find his way there again. (According to the police, "hypes" find it difficult to remember addresses. Thus, an uninformed narcotics officer might believe an addict to be lying when he claimed to be unable to remember a friend's address.)

Charlie also reported a rumor that one of the thieves, Dave, had been robbed by another addict, Bill. Charlie didn't know where Bill lived either, but he knew a close friend of Bill's who was living in Cedarville. Charlie reasoned that if Bill had any "stuff," it would be likely that Bill's friend, Archie, would also have gotten some.

On the strength of Charlie's tip, Sergeant Harris decided it would be worthwhile to try to locate Archie, since he was well known to the police as an addict. Archie's address was on file, and some checking revealed Archie to be living in the Bismarck Hotel in Cedarville. Before we left, the Sergeant called the Cedarville vice control squad (consisting of two men), explaining that this was his way of maintaining good relations with adjacent police departments. In addition, the Sergeant notified the State of California narcotics agents, who are invited by the Westville police department to make use of the office space and equipment of the Westville vice control.

The Westville Police Department, especially the vice control squad, is proud of its relations with other law enforcement agencies. This working relationship is important for the efficient enforcement of the narcotics laws, since state agents and the local police provide each other with complementary services. The Westville vice control squad has three resources that state agents lack: they possess greater knowledge of local conditions, have the services of a well-developed network of local informants, and are allowed to arrest for "marks" alone—tiny red bruises that indicate recent use of narcotics. (Using narcotics or "being under the influence" is itself a misdemeanor under Section 11721 of the penal code).[2] State agents typically do not arrest for "marks," since their chief interest is to uncover large sources of illegal narcotics. The arrest for "marks," however, is an added value in the vice control officer's resources in bargaining for information and thus enables the Westville vice control squad to initiate cases more effectively than can state police. Finally, the Westville squad can call for the services of the local patrol police when "extra bodies" are required.

The state agents are better equipped than the local vice control squad to follow through on cases, especially those involving large quantities of narcotics. Since they have statewide jurisdiction, state police can take a plane from, for instance, San Francisco to Los Angeles to investigate a lead on a supplier in the other city. Furthermore, large amounts of money are sometimes required to make incriminating purchases of opiates or heroin, especially in transactions coming over the border from Mexico. Westville police have neither the funds nor the jurisdiction to handle this type of law enforcement operation. Therefore, local and state police complement each other, the local police by initiating small arrests and the state police by having the resources to track down the bigger "pinches." As will be shown, narcotics arrests are seen as a series of increasingly larger steps up a ladder, at the top of which is the narcotics officer's prize: the "source."

CREATING AN INFORMANT

We left Westville in two cars—four state agents in a flashy-looking hard top convertible, and the Sergeant, and another state agent and I in the 1963 blue Plymouth sedan well known to addicts in the area. As we drove up to the hotel in Cedarville, we spotted the two local vice control men, looking like two professional football players on their way to a Friday night movie. One of the state agents recognized a car that seemed to be Archie's, which of course suggested that Archie was either in his room or nearby. Three state agents stayed outside while two of the state agents, the Cedarville vice control man, Sergeant Harris and I entered the hotel.

Inside the hotel, the chief state agent approached the desk clerk and asked whether Archie was in the hotel. The clerk said he thought he was, but that he might well be in another (Dominick's) room. Three policemen and I went to Dominick's room on the third floor, and two went to Archie's second-floor room with a key they obtained from the clerk. Approaching Dominick's room on tiptoe, we heard several men's voices. One policeman suggested that somebody ought to go downstairs and tell the other policemen that Dominick's room was occupied. I volunteered, because I wanted to see what the other policemen were doing in the meantime.

When I arrived they were searching Archie's room. (I relayed the message to the policemen downstairs.) The room served as a painting studio for Archie, and most of the space was crammed with paints, bottles, and canvasses at different stages of completion in an apparently haphazard disarray. The officers, who by my observation were skilled at searching without changing the appearance of the room, had been looking mainly through drawers. They rearranged the little they had upset and the three of us went upstairs.

Legally, the police are not permitted to enter a room and make a search without a warrant, except "incident" to an arrest of some person in the room. Thus, they cannot search an empty room without a warrant, even if they see marijuana on the table through a window. In California, unless a search has some reasonable relationship to an arrest, it becomes an unlawful exploratory search.[3] The practice of making an unlawful exploratory search of the room of a suspected criminal is, so far as I could tell on several occasions, accepted by both the Westville police and the state police. As one policeman commented:

"Of course, it's not exactly legal to take a peek beforehand. It's not one of the things you usually talk about as a police technique. But if you find something, you back off and figure out how you can do it legal. And if you don't find anything, you don't have to waste a lot of time."

The policeman does not feel legally constrained in conducting an exploratory examination of suspicious premises. Even less does he feel *morally* at fault in conducting a prior search of a known addict's room for narcotics.

The process by which the policeman justifies his unlawful exploratory search is similar to that by which many criminals justify theirs. Thus, the policeman distinguishes between *legality* and *morality*, just as the criminal does, and as we all do to a certain extent. The prostitute, for example, justifies her activity by asserting that she engages in an enterprise her "trick" desires. The confidence man rationalizes his deceptions with the belief that "there is a bit of larceny in the soul of every man" and that his motives are no different from his victims'. The civil-rights "sit-in" justifies his "trespass" on grounds of a higher morality. Similarly, the policeman countenances *his* unlawful exploration by pointing to the difficulties of his job and asserting that his activity has no adverse effect upon the person whose property is unlawfully searched, *provided* that person is not a criminal. Thus, the policeman typically alleges that unless he conducts unlawful searches, for example, dangerous addicts might escape capture; furthermore, he maintains that innocent persons have no cause for complaint.

When the group reassembled, it was decided to break into Dominick's room, but without kicking the door in. The following strategy was used: one of the Cedarville vice control men knocked on Dominick's door, and said, "Phone," imitating the Spanish accent of the desk clerk. From inside the door, Dominick said, "What?" and the officer repeated, "Phone." Dominick opened the door slightly, and as he did, several policemen pushed inside.

At this point, it was important for the narcotics officers to keep talking in a friendly, calm tone. "Well, hello, Archie," Sergeant Harris said, "just relax and everybody stay where they are and everything is going to be okay." Archie and Dominick began to protest that they hadn't done anything wrong, and it wasn't nice of the police to "just come busting into" the room this way.

The denial of guilt in this case was important for the police because it implied that the suspect would not mind having his arms examined. Had the suspect refused to answer, and ordered the police out in absence of a warrant, the police would again have been on shaky legal ground. So far, their suspicion of Archie was based on a reliable informant's word that Archie probably had some "stuff," since he was a friend of an addict who, the informant had heard, was "dealing." This vague, hearsay information was also insufficient legally to establish probable cause for a frisk and an examination of his body.[4] What the policeman required was a tactic to circumvent the legal restrictions.

By denying his guilt, the suspect gives the policeman an opening wedge. He can say, as Sergeant Harris did, "Okay, Archie, you know it's my job to check you out," simultaneously grabbing Archie's arm and pulling up the shirtsleeve. Before Archie had an opportunity to emit the words suggested by the look of protest on his face, the Sergeant had his fingers on a pair of tiny red "marks" in the crook of the elbow. By finding the marks in the way he had, the Sergeant had introduced new elements into the legal situation. First, he could reasonably claim that Archie had "volunteered" to show his arms and that no physical coercion was used. More important, from the Sergeant's point of view, by finding marks, he had established reasonable cause for arresting Archie as a man "under the influence" of narcotics. In addition, the legality of the arrest further established a basis for a thorough search, after the exploratory "peek," although it is arguable whether the means of entry would be upheld by an appellate court.

We might ask why the suspect did not assert his legal rights and demand a search warrant as soon as the door was opened. There were several reasons. First, he was physically coerced (albeit by indirection, since no actual violence was used). Five physically well-constituted, armed men (plus one middle-sized unarmed professor) broke in unexpectedly and stood around with no-nonsense looks on their faces. At that moment, it would have taken an act of heroism to order them out.

Second, these men did represent authority. To a certain extent, the suspect must interpret the policeman's behavior as being proper, for the policeman represents the state. His very being conveys an impression of legitimacy to this type of addict, an occupant of a cheap hotel room, a user of narcotics, a struggling painter. In addition to being surprised and upset, the suspect may not be entirely aware of his legal rights, and the police in this situation did not advise him of his rights.

Furthermore, Archie was, after all, a known addict and had previous experiences with the police. Consequently, there was on his part an anticipation of future encounters. If he acted like a "wise-guy" this time (by ordering the police to leave), he could have "the book thrown at him" the next. One narcotics detective reported that no known addict had ever refused him permission to make an examination for "marks," even though there was no legal justification for a search. I have seen a detective pull to the curb and ask a man how things are going, adding, "You wouldn't happen to be dirty, would you?" The detective may look, or just wish the man well and leave.

Finally, there is for the suspect in a room, as for the man stopped by the police on the street, the genuine possibility of innocence combined with the mildness of the request. The police are, after all, making a seemingly innocuous request, permission to glance at the crook of an elbow. Objectively, its fulfillment demands no more exertion than the common courtesy of giving a match or the correct time to a stranger. In a nonlegal context, it might almost be insulting to refuse. In the situation, however, we might think the insulted party would be the suspect; it is far more degrading to be suspected of being an addict than to be asked for a match. But for the already convicted user, most of the stigma has already been manifested. Having once been proved culpable, the suspect can hardly claim to be shocked by the suspicion of use. All of these factors combine to impede assertion of legal rights. Furthermore, if the addict is innocent, the police leave, with the suspect disturbed but not substantially harmed.

The failure to consider such facts by appellate courts and civil liberties lawyers puzzles and annoys the policeman. He claims that he would never do this sort of thing to a respectable citizen, and that the law should somehow recognize the difference in its search-and-seizure rules between respectable citizens and known criminals. Since the search-and-seizure rules are based on concepts of probability, a degree of irrationality in ignoring probabilities associated with an individual's past *status* as an addict cannot be denied. The policeman is far less interested in questions of constitutionality than in the reasonableness of a *working* system.

The criminal law, however, largely because it is so heavily influenced by constitutional requirements, is not necessarily administratively rational. Indeed the principle of legality often stands in opposition to the principle of administrative rationality. Like the policeman, the addict typically does not perceive interactions against a background of higher legal requirements. He operates according to the normative assumptions of everyday life, emphasizing the factual. He knows he is an addict, that he will sometimes be in possession of narcotics and, fearing that he will be discovered, he is not going to unduly antagonize the police. Of all types of "criminality," addiction is undoubtedly the most difficult, because the addict must anticipate continual and relatively uncontrolled participation in the forbidden activity, and, therefore, repeated contact with police.

Moreover, the experienced addict knows much about how police operate and what they are after. He knows they are not interested in a "vag" addict who possesses only a supply of drugs sufficient for immediate personal use. On the other side, the policeman is confident that his behavior is not going to be the subject of an appellate court decision. If no incriminating evidence has been found, it is hardly likely the addict will sue in tort, or even lodge a complaint with the police department, partly because of the practical ineffectiveness of such remedies, but mainly because the addict has an expectation of continuing relations with the police.

The policeman's encounter with the addict is a game with a twist. Each playing is influenced by the anticipation of future games. As a result, it is difficult to describe, in any single instance, the values held by the competing parties, since these are modified by each party's subjective assessment of what his opponent's strength will be in future encounters. Thus, the addict would not sue in tort, nor would he complain to the police department about a narcotics officer's behavior, because this would be taken as an affront by the policeman. Such aggressive behavior on the part of the addict toward the policeman would doubtless lead to another sort of game situation in the future where the addict would be defined as an enemy. Outcomes of games played between superordinates and subordinates are going to vary greatly depending on the conception the authority has of his antagonist. Typically, when no incriminating evidence is discovered, the addict is happy to forget the affair. By the same token, when incriminating evidence is discovered, the policeman expects the addict to "cop out" (confess) sometime during the adjudicative process. In the present case, the copping out occurred early, exactly as anticipated.

> The sergeant, the supervising state agent, and the suspect went back upstairs to the suspect's room for interrogation. The purpose was to convince Archie to purchase narcotics from Bill under surveillance. When we reached his room, the state agent opened the conversation by saying, "Look, Archie, you know the score. Tell us how much stuff you've got—and you know you'd better tell us the truth, because we're going to search anyway." Archie showed the agent a "fit" (eyedropper and hypodermic needle) and some pills in the bathroom. The agent found other pills that Archie claimed were vitamins. Additional questions revealed that Archie had been purchasing his drugs from Bill. Archie also said that Bill had quite a lot and that he understood Bill had gotten his supply by "burning" (stealing from) a third person whom Archie didn't know.

> Since Archie's story was consistent with the one the police had gotten from the original informant, Charlie, they offered Archie a deal. In return for his "cooperation" (calling Bill and making a "connection" with him that night), they would overlook his "marks" (thus saving him a probable period of ninety days in the county jail). Archie hesitated and tried to argue his way out, but it was perfectly evident that he understood the futility of his argument, especially since he had informed for them in the past. Within a span of ten minutes, Archie agreed to "cooperate." He said, however, that he owed Bill fourteen dollars and couldn't "make a buy from him" unless he could say he would pay him the "bread." The police offered to provide the money, and Archie called Bill, who, according to Archie, had agreed to a sale.

TRIAL BY POLICE

At this point, any lingering doubt the police might have had as to Bill's guilt was erased. They had been only slightly uncertain after the original informant, Charlie, had called and told them that he had personally seen Dave and another addict divide up the spoils of a theft of narcotics and dangerous drugs and that Dave had in turn been robbed by Bill. Now that Archie had "testified" to the effect that Bill was dealing narcotics, any remaining residue of "reasonable doubt" was obliterated.

The use of legal terminology emphasizes the similarity between the reasoning processes of the policeman and those employed by the formal evidentiary standards governing determinations of guilt or innocence. An eyewitness had established that a crime had been committed, and knew the identity of one of the culprits. In addition, he had given hearsay testimony (not admissible in a courtroom) that one of the original culprits had been robbed by a third party, Bill. Although no eyewitness observed this robbery, another witness testified to its effects:

Archie not only gave hearsay testimony that Bill "had plenty of stuff," but in addition said that he, Archie, had personally purchased narcotics from Bill. The evidence in this "case" was circumstantial, but strong (depending on the weight conferred on the testimony of the chief witnesses). Moreover, the testimony was given against a background of police experience with the typical behavior patterns of addicts. The stories told by the informants not only fit together, thereby reinforcing the validity of each, but conformed generally to the policeman's conception of usual addict behavior. Therefore, so far as the police were concerned, reliable witnesses had provided circumstantial evidence and eyewitness testimony sufficient to convict Bill.

The standards used by the police to assess Bill's guilt were not unlike those employed by the trial court. (Of course, only one side of the case was stated, since Bill had been given no opportunity to testify or bring witnesses on his own behalf; but for the police this omission was irrelevant.) The evidentiary standards employed by the police in this case are obvious and are those to which reasonable men seem naturally to gravitate. For instance, African tribal judges, as described by Gluckman, employed reasoning similar to that the policeman uses to assess the addict's guilt and to that English and American jurists would likely employ if placed in the social situation of the policeman. Gluckman says:

> Judges work not only with standards of reasonable behaviour for upright incumbents of particular social positions, but also with standards of behaviour which are reasonably interpreted as those of particular kinds of wrongdoers. There are social stereotypes of how thieves, adulterers, and other malefactors act. If the witnessed actions of a defendant assemble into one of these stereotypes, he is found guilty, though the judges prefer direct evidence to convict.[5]

In effect, the behavior reported about Bill fit the stereotype of the guilty addict-seller, although guilt had by no means been judicially established. Consequently, for the police, the job now was not to convince themselves of the suspect's guilt, but to demonstrate it in a fashion that would satisfy two closely related requirements: the maintenance of the informer system, and the standard of evidence sufficient to convict in court.

It is instructive to consider the probable legal outcome if at this time the police had decided to arrest Bill on the strength of the evidence presented. In court, Charlie's testimony about Bill's activities would be objected to and upheld as irrelevant, immaterial, and hearsay. Charlie did not see Bill rob Dave of narcotics but had merely heard of this through the addict grapevine. Although Archie's testimony would be admissible, he would be the sole prosecution witness, and any competent defense attorney could destroy Archie's credibility by bringing out that he was a narcotics addict who had been offered a deal in return for testimony. Thus, the case would turn on the testimony of a single vulnerable prosecution witness. By practical courtroom standards, the State at this point had no case against Bill, although by police standards Bill was guilty beyond a reasonable doubt.

Therefore, the police needed Archie's agreement to purchase narcotics from Bill to satisfy judicial criteria for conviction. The primary reason for requiring Archie to "make a buy," however, was not to establish probable cause, but to determine the location of the narcotics and establish that the suspect possessed narcotics, either on his person or "constructively" in his home, or his car or even on the person of a female companion.[6] Because Bill was a user-dealer and therefore likely to have his supply close at hand, his apprehension would be relatively easy. By contrast, if he had been a nonuser-dealer, it would have been much more difficult for the police to capture him successfully, since nonuser-dealers do not generally care whether the narcotics are close at hand. Indeed, from his familiarity with the law about possession, the nonaddict-dealer is likely to have a "stash" or a "stash pad" somewhere removed from his own residence, perhaps at the home of a girl friend, or even in any of the numerous places in the public domain that can serve as "stashes,"[7] such as trees, directional signs, the undersides of benches and so forth.

There is an important law enforcement distinction to be drawn between popularly reported *transport stashes*—false heels, false bottomed suitcases, diaphragms—and *storage stashes*. Although it is difficult to deceive police in a search of one's self and immediate effects, it is equally difficult for the police to prove a legal connection between an individual and a stash of narcotics stuffed behind the stairway carpeting of an open apartment house. Thus a "buy" is often required to ascertain the location of the narcotics. In the present case, for example, Bill might have had a "stash" half a block away, in a neighbor's backyard. Archie's job was to trigger Bill into getting his supply, not so much for the police to see where it was, as where it was not.

> The police conducted an extended interrogation of Archie about how much "stuff" Bill had, how long he had it, how much he had on hand, and where he kept it. Archie said he thought Bill had gotten the "stuff" about two weeks earlier and had been "shooting and dealing" during this period, but that he wasn't sure exactly how much Bill had on hand, and he certainly didn't know where Bill kept it. Consequently, the police drove to Bill's place in Westville, after Archie had called Bill and told him he had the "bread" he owed him. The police watched Archie enter. He came out more quickly than expected and drove to an appointed spot for a rendezvous. There Archie explained that Bill said he wasn't dressed and didn't want to sell anything tonight, but that he'd give him something in the morning.

The question the police had to resolve was whether they should break into Bill's that night, or wait until morning for Archie to make a buy. After some discussion, it was decided for two reasons to break in immediately. First, it was felt that the longer the wait before breaking in on the suspect, the less likely he would be caught with a sizable amount (large enough to warrant a charge of possession for sale rather than mere possession) or, worst of all, from the policeman's view, they would merely be able to charge him with being "under the influence." When an addict has a large supply over a period of time, he is likely to have built up his habit with the free access. This, coupled with the knowledge that Bill had already sold a portion of his original holdings, made the police reluctant to wait longer.

Second, Bill was on parole, and was required to take the Nalline test weekly. In 1957 the California legislature authorized the court to require the Nalline test as a condition of probation, if the court has reason to believe that the probationer is a narcotics user.[8] The easily administered test involves reading the size of the subject's pupil, followed by an injec-

tion of the drug. According to the developer, prior use of an opiate will cause the diameter of the pupil to enlarge, the size of the increase being related to the amount used. Occasional use results in practically no change in pupillary diameter, while absence of narcotics is revealed by reduction of the diameter of the pupil.[9]

If the addict is taking the Nalline test, he will therefore usually be a probationer or a parolee. Even though the test is technically "voluntary" in that the addict signs an "Authorization and Waiver" form, addicts do not generally like it, and submit only as an alternative to jail or state prison. For example, a petty user (a so-called "vag" addict)[10] may receive a sentence of ninety days in the county jail with judgment suspended for as long as three years, provided he takes and passes the Nalline test during this time. He is thus liable for the entire period of suspended judgment to examination for use of narcotics[11] by his probation or parole officer, who often delegates his authority to the police.

Relations between probation officers and police are apt to be difficult, especially when the probationer is a narcotics addict. In this situation, it is mainly the probation officer who is placed in an ambiguous position between therapist and policeman.[12] The policeman's goal is, by contrast, much more clearly defined. His immediate task is to make narcotics arrests using every resource at his command. One of his prime resources is the addict. To the extent, however, that policemen make use of addict-probationers, probation officers fear that the addict will be reintroduced into the world of criminality from which he has so recently emerged, interfering with his potential rehabilitation.

The relations between probation officers and police vary from jurisdiction to jurisdiction. In some, they may be hostile. Westville vice control officers were proud of their cordial relations with the probation department and with parole officers. In general, the police have led the probation officers to believe that whenever a probationer-addict is used as an informant, the probation officer will routinely be informed. Indeed, the police department has one man assigned to the Nalline testing program, who also acts as liaison to the probation department.

Meetings between the two departments are held weekly and telephone conversations may occur many times each day. Actually, the police do not routinely disclose the names of their informants to the probation officers but do supply them with information about their probationers' behavior, especially when the behavior seems to be illegal. In return for this information, probation officers (and parole officers) will cooperate with police by giving information, and more importantly by authorizing police to make an arrest as a violation of probation or parole when the police require such authorization.

The police were already apprised of Bill's failure to present himself for the Nalline test the preceding week, and as a result suspected he had been using narcotics. The Sergeant was on friendly terms with Bill's parole officer, and counted on him for support in an arrest of Bill for parole violation. That is, although the parole officer had not specifically requested that Bill be arrested, the Sergeant depended upon the parole officer's willingness to affirm he had so requested should the issue arise. As in many systems of so-called rational procedure, the actual practice depends on independently created strategies for avoiding the sanctions of regulation, rather than on formal delegation of authority.

The problem for the police then became how to break into Bill's apartment. Especially in vice control, police frequently must kick doors in sharply and quickly, without giving advance notice of their intentions to the suspect. The purpose of such violent entries is evident: to counteract the speed with which the suspect must destroy or hide incriminating evidence. Thus, a floating crap game can take on the appearance of a discussion group in seconds. Similarly, narcotics are easily flushed down a toilet, and most addicts will stash their supply near one. Even the word "supply," however, is misleading because it connotes a substantial amount of matter, when actually large quantities of narcotics are measured in ounces. As a result, the policeman must be able to control the suspect's behavior before a brush of his hand destroys his cache.

In this case, the police questioned Archie on the layout of Bill's apartment. Archie thought it would be difficult for the police to find incriminating evidence on Bill. He explained

the house had a front and rear door, with a heavy chain and bolt on the front door, and creaky stairs in the rear. It would be, the police figured, a "tough pad to crack." Finally, Sergeant Harris constructed what turned out to be an effective plan. He called for a "beat car" with flashing red light and uniformed patrolmen to pull up in the street in front of the house, and instructed the patrolmen to make a lot of noise. They were to pound on the front door, demand admission, and if not admitted immediately, kick the door in. In the meantime, he detailed three men up the back stairs while the beat car was driving up front, correctly anticipating that Bill's attention would be riveted on the front of the house when he saw the flashing red light and the beat car outside. This gave the three plainclothesmen sufficient time to station themselves outside the rear door, without being heard going upstairs.

As assumed, Bill panicked when he saw the patrolmen heading for the front door and ran across the length of the apartment to the kitchen in the rear. The top half of the rear door was made of glass and the plainclothesmen stationed outside could see Bill run in and attempt to hide a package of white powder under the refrigerator. Whether they kicked the door in before, after, or simultaneously with Bill's attempt to dispose of the heroin, I cannot say, since I was at the front door behind the uniformed policemen. The fact is, however, that Bill was caught in the act.

The case described above was a "good pinch." It resulted in a charge and conviction of possession for sale upon the defendant's plea of guilty. Because of his youth, the seller was given a relatively light six-month term in the county jail, and his wife was given thirty days. Some time later, I interviewed the wife in the county jail, quite by accident, in connection with part of the study concerning defendants' perceptions of the criminal process. It was clear she did not recall this "Dr. Skolnick" who was interviewing her as one of the "policemen" involved in her arrest. (I was visible throughout the arrest proceedings and the subsequent interrogation, but this new context offered a new identity.) She was pleased with the way her case had gone and felt that both she and her husband had "gotten off" lightly. They each felt, she reported, that they had committed a serious crime, the police had treated them well, the judge had been understanding and the defense attorney, a public defender, competent. Whatever resentment she held was toward the unknown "fink" who had "ratted" on them to the police. The police, however, were perceived as men doing their jobs, an impression they convey well.

THE BIG CASE

Cases like the one now discussed occur so rarely that no special term, other than "big case" or "big one," develops to describe them. This case yielded the largest amount of narcotics confiscated in three years by the Westville department. Since there was much secrecy, it was fortunate that the apprehension took place after rapport had been established with the Westville vice control squad. A member of this squad informed me of developments and invited me (via an unexpected telephone call to my home one evening) to observe the proceedings when "the caper was scheduled to go down."

A major difference between the ordinary "good pinch" and the big narcotics case is whether the ultimate source has been tapped. In the typical "good pinch," narcotics officers make every effort to apprehend a larger dealer. Since Bill had stolen his narcotics from a drugstore, he was himself the ultimate source, and the police could make no further arrests. Most of the time, narcotics officers are not able to arrest important men in the dealership hierarchy, nor are they able to confiscate more than a small proportion of the annual narcotics traffic. In the State of California, a man offering to sell a pound of heroin was regarded by narcotics agents at the federal, state and local levels whom I interviewed as being about "as big as they come." Such a man, of course, purchases his narcotics from another dealer who usually is foreign and therefore may be outside the jurisdiction of federal agents. Since the flow of narcotics is part of an international traffic, even federal agents are usually unable to reach high into ultimate sources of supply.[13]

The analysis of this "big case" illustrates two principles: first, how its enforcement pattern affords the police more leeway in complying with legal rules; and second, how such cases aid the police to acquire the commodities they need to carry out the enforcement of middle-sized cases. In any case, the Westville narcotics detail apprehended a nonuser-dealer whose activities they had been following for almost two years. The nonuser-dealer, the straight businessman in narcotics, is more difficult to apprehend than the man who sells and also takes narcotics. When the "heat is on," or when he perceives it to be "on," the nonuser-dealer can keep away from his source of supply more easily than the addict-dealer. As long as the narcotics are hidden in a neutral stash, the dealer need not be concerned about police apprehension. All involved—the police, the addict, the dealer—are well aware of the implications attached to possession, and perhaps more importantly, to nonpossession of narcotics. Thus, the police always fear that when they set up a "buy," the seller will not show up with the "stuff" on his person.[14]

The apprehension of the nonuser-dealer involved the use of several petty informants, plus diligent and patient police work. The police finally took a room where they were able to keep him under constant surveillance and caught him selling several "balloons" of heroin. When apprehended, nonuser-dealers do not usually agree to serve as informants, since they are themselves exceptionally "good pinches," and are more "reliable businessmen" than addicts. In this case, however, partly because of the persuasive abilities of the police, but largely because there was bigger game in the offing, it was possible, through the cooperation of the district attorney's office, to offer a substantial reduction in charges.

Cooperation here meant more and was more dangerous than the cooperation demanded of Archie. Archie merely had to "make a buy." In this case, however, the strategy was to have a state agent make a series of purchases. Where nonuser-dealers are involved, speed of apprehension is not as important as is patience. Unlike the user-dealer, the nonuser is unlikely to consume his supply. The aim is not to catch him quickly but to bring him to the point where he purchases quantities as large as the abundance of his source will permit him to offer. To bring him to this point, he must come to trust his purchaser. Accordingly, the strategy of the narcotics police required the local dealer to make several purchases and to introduce another "buyer" provided by the state police.

The advantage of this strategy is that it allows the purchaser to risk exposure through public testimony.

The informant who performs the introduction is still under suspicion, but he can always claim that the state agent was introduced to him by a third party, just as he introduced the agent to the source. In the Pirandello-like setting of a narcotics investigation, it is difficult for an accused party to sort out the actual identities and loyalties of those with whom he has been involved. If the accused chooses to go to trial, however, the true identity of the man who testifies that he purchased narcotics from the accused is revealed. Where the State's witness is a narcotics officer, law enforcement need not be concerned about disclosing identity and, furthermore, can rely on him to testify persuasively. (Police, in my experience, make excellent witnesses.) The only drawback for the police arises from a concern for police resources; each time a policeman participates in such a maneuver he too is partly "burned" and loses some of his value as an undercover agent. Given budgetary limitations, the police can afford to use narcotics agents only in the bigger cases. It is also true that the speed of apprehension typically required in smaller cases normally does not permit police to be used as *agents provocateurs*. Thus, in the "good pinch" described above, a police agent could not have been substituted for Archie since by the time necessary introductions and purchases could have been made, the *corpus delicti* would have been consumed.

In that "good pinch" only one purchase was made. Here there were four, each large. The state agent was introduced to the sellers, the Gomez brothers, by the informant who represented the agent as a friend "dealing" in the northwestern United States, and able to dispose of large amounts of heroin. The agent was first introduced to the dealer's younger brother, Arthur, who was a partner, but evidently did not personally have the "connections." The agent was especially skillful in using his knowledge of narcotics and his demeanor to impress the younger Gomez that he was an "old-time Mexican dealer" rather than a flashy newcomer. The younger Gomez agreed to let the agent have three ounces of heroin in exchange for cash, and also two ounces on "consignment."

About two weeks later, after payment had been made on the consignment purchase, several recorded telephone calls were made over a four-day period to the older brother Charles. He continued to promise delivery of heroin to the agent, but on each day "backed off," claiming to be unable to locate his "connection." The agent also made a recorded telephone call to the dealer's girl friend during which she told him that Charles was trying to contact the "connection." A week later the agent recorded two telephone calls to Charles arranging for the delivery of heroin to Westville. It was agreed that Charles and Arthur would fly to the local airport, to be met by the agent. On the appointed day, the agent purchased five ounces of heroin[15] from the brothers for close to twenty-one hundred dollars. There was no recording of the actual transaction, but several state agents and members of the Westville narcotics detail observed it from a distance.

At this point, the police saw their next move as luring the defendants to a place where a transaction could be "bugged" by a concealed microphone. Accordingly, the state agent telephoned Charles Gomez and told him he was fearful of the "heat" at the airport, and had arranged for the next deal to take place in a Westville motel room. Two days later, the dealer and his girl friend appeared at the motel, where the agent purchased approximately ten ounces of heroin for twenty-eight hundred dollars. Several other narcotics police were observing near the motel and a hidden camera took a photograph of the dealer entering the motel room. The purchase went off smoothly, however, and any suspicions Gomez might have held were evidently allayed.

A week later the agent called the brothers and made arrangements to purchase as much as twenty-two ounces of narcotics later in the week, in the same Westville motel room. This was to be the setting for the "big pinch," the exchange of five thousand dollars for at least a pound of heroin, with, presumably, the remainder on consignment. The younger Gomez agreed to come and the events leading to arrest were initiated. It was decided that the agent would give the money to the younger Gomez, who was scheduled to arrive with the heroin at eight in the evening. Following the transfer, the younger Gomez was expected to call his older brother and tell him that everything "had come off okay" and that he would arrive home in the morning. After this phone call, the police planned for the agent to call the elder Gomez and to indicate that there was a "panic"[16] on, and that if the brother could come up that night with another dozen or so ounces of heroin, the agent could pay for it.

Anticipation of a "big case" arouses much anxiety in the police. With each successful purchase, the stakes become higher. There already was enough evidence to arrest and, in all likelihood, to convict the Gomez brothers. But the aim of the police was, at this point, to implicate the brothers as fully and as clearly as possible. Indeed, at a certain point the big case becomes almost an aesthetic matter, and style, defined by the personal satisfactions of the narcotics policeman, counts for almost as much as results. Unfortunately, from the policeman's viewpoint, the expectation of a "big case" not only arouses personal anxiety, but also requires unusual cooperation among law enforcement organizations. This increases the number of men involved, the personal tensions of each, and thus the possibility that the charade will be revealed to the offender.

In the present case these factors resulted in several mishaps that destroyed the aesthetic of this night's work, but which also, against the background of prior incriminating encounters with the offenders, made little legal difference. First, the younger Gomez failed to arrive on schedule. When he did arrive somewhat unexpectedly, the state agent was in conversation with three Westville police officers. Gomez, the state agent later reported, had asked him what was going on, and the agent replied that he was asking directions from these strangers about where to meet the helicopter. (One of the police commented, "This guy Gomez must really be stupid. Any one of our nickel-and-dime dealers here in Westville would have smelled the heat a mile away.") At the time, however, the state agent did not know whether the dealer had caught on to the trap. He could not be certain at how to interpret the dealer's lateness. It might have been, as Gomez explained, that he had difficulty getting the heroin from his connection. But the agent also was concerned that Gomez had become suspicious, arrived early, had hidden the heroin, then returned to the airport. Without the heroin, the evening's plan would be a failure. Nor could the agent be sure that Gomez was not armed; a report that he might be had been received from police in another part of the state.

Under these circumstances, it is not surprising that the usually cool state agent missed the highway turnoff to the motel and arrived twenty minutes late. In the meantime, the police at the motel were becoming increasingly fidgety. Two policemen (and the writer) were stationed in the room next to where the "buy" was to take place, to record the conversation and to be available for assistance should the dealer be armed. Five policemen were in the motel manager's office with equipment for recording the expected telephone conversation with Charles Gomez, and another policeman (along with a newspaperman) was stationed across the courtyard as an additional check on Gomez's movements.

Gomez and the state agent arrived in the room at about 10:30 P.M. In the adjoining room the recording equipment had failed, which not only meant the loss of a recorded conversation of the narcotics purchase, but also heightened concern for the agent's safety and caused partial inability to keep track of Gomez. Presumably, if he left the room, the agent across the courtyard would see him and notify the police in the manager's office via the walkie-talkies with which each of the three police locations were equipped. About fifteen minutes after Gomez arrived, we in the adjoining room were informed by walkie-talkie that Gomez had telephoned his brother to say that everything was okay. We were also told that the detectives in the office had evidently recorded this conversation, but that they were going to listen to the record to make sure. So far everything was proceeding as planned. Fifteen minutes later we were told that Gomez was in custody in the manager's office.

This is what had happened. Gomez decided after his telephone call to go to the lobby to buy a soft drink. When he left, the walkie-talkie in the surveillance room did not respond. The agent became so flustered he forgot to use the telephone to warn the other officers of Gomez's impending arrival. Gomez entered the lobby from a side entrance, because it was a shorter distance from the room, and literally walked into a bevy of policemen listening intently to the recording of Arthur Gomez speaking to Charles. Whether the policemen or the dealer was more surprised, I cannot say. At that point, however, it was incumbent that the police arrest Arthur.

Shortly after Arthur was taken into custody, he was brought out into the courtyard and photographed by the newsmen. The problem for the police at this point was to convince Arthur Gomez to call his brother Charles and to persuade him to come to Westville with additional narcotics. Arthur finally complied about two hours later when, in my opinion, he believed his brother would know that something had gone wrong. In any event, Charles did not arrive the next morning, but was arrested at his home by the state and local police of his area. Both men finally pleaded guilty to two counts of possession for sale and were sentenced to three years in San Quentin prison. The sentence of the younger Gomez was suspended (partly on the recommendation of the police for his "cooperation" in making the telephone call), but he was required to serve the first year of his suspended sentence in the county jail.

The following day a story appeared in the local Westville newspaper with an eight-column headline and front-page pictures reporting that a one-and-one-half-million dollar "dope ring" had been "smashed." The size of the dope ring was reported in the newspaper headline according to the ultimate possible price of the narcotics on the illicit retail market. Actually, the "pound" of narcotics confiscated contained only 6 percent pure heroin. Such a quantity does go a long way on the retail market, but not nearly as far as the newspaper story suggested.

Such stories serve several functions for the narcotics police. This sort of report gives the policeman public recognition as a reward for his services. In this case, however, the police did not personally feel that they deserved as much recognition as they received. Although the case had yielded an acceptable outcome, it did not "come off" with the smoothness which they regard as the fundamental satisfaction of narcotics work. This is not to say that the police were dissatisfied; rather events

had spoiled an unusual opportunity for a masterful arrest and transformed it into a less than craftsman-like occasion.

Another purpose served by exaggerated newspaper treatment of narcotics cases is to indicate to the public that "dope rings" are in common operation, but that the police are able to "smash" them. To a certain extent, however, the "dope ring" referred to in the newspaper article was itself "created" by the narcotics police. This is not to say that Charles Gomez was not a criminal purveyor of narcotics; but when law enforcement agencies themselves become major purchasers of narcotics, they make someone like Gomez a much more important-appearing dealer than he would have been had not close to twelve thousand dollars worth of narcotics been purchased from him by the state. In this sense, then, in the "big case," narcotics police inevitably are part of the "dope rings" they themselves help to create.

Finally, newspaper stories of this kind serve the more important function of giving the narcotics police support in their campign for increasingly severe penalties against those trafficking in narcotics. These penalties, as we indicated, provide the police with greater commodities to maintain the information system enabling "good pinches."

SUMMARY AND CONCLUSION

This chapter has described the work of the narcotics officer at three levels: his routine activities, especially with petty informants; the "good pinch"; and "the big case." These levels were shown to be interrelated, since narcotics enforcement typically involves the apprehension of a hierarchy of offenders. Therefore, for that reason, because the ordinary addict is a criminal, actually and symbolically, and also in conformity to a belief that the way to destroy the narcotics traffic is to rid the community of customers, the police pursue the petty user.[17]

In those instances where a petty user has enough narcotics in his possession to lay the basis for a felony charge, his arrest is considered a "good pinch." The apprehension of a petty user affords a degree of satisfaction to the police, but not nearly so much as participation in a "big case," especially when a nonuser-dealer is caught. The latter is considered part of the organized narcotics traffic; bringing about his conviction is therefore regarded as especially meritorious.

Beyond these reasons for the policeman's preference of the "big case" arrest over the "good pinch" is another important consideration. The "big case" provides the policeman with the conditions under which conventional and constitutional standards of legality may best be met. Thus, a typical difference in conditions underlying the two types of arrests is the amount of time the police have: little in the "good pinch," much in the "big case." Greater time permits the police to obtain warrants, allows the offender to make several observed infractions of the law, and enables the police to make more adquate records of infractions.

The main reason the police are able to keep more adequate records in the "big case" revolves around the most important condition distinguishing these two types of arrests. In the "good pinch," the informant is typically an addict, while in the "big case," the informant is typically a narcotics officer. This difference is also related to the amount of time available; since the police must move quickly in the "good pinch," they usually have insufficient time to establish a new identity for the policeman, whereas the addict comes equipped with his own.

Not only is the policeman a better record keeper than the addict-informant but he is also a more persuasive witness during the trial. Even if the informant were able to give convincing testimony, he would be asked to take the stand only in rare instances, since the policeman is usually obliged to protect the informer's criminal status. It is therefore ironic that the cases in which the policeman least prefers to participate arise as test cases to restrict the limits of his behavior. In the narcotics area, a "big case" is rarely the subject of an appellate judicial decision for the simple reason that the "big case" provides the policeman with the conditions under which constitutional standards of legality may best be met.[18] From the policeman's point of view, meeting these standards is preferable to not meeting them, but he is not so concerned about the standards in the abstract. The meeting of constitutional requirements is primarily a way to demonstrate

his ability to do his job well; that is the principal concern of the detective.

FOOTNOTES

[1] If the idea that policemen are slow to arrive at the scene of a crime is true, the cause is typically overwork rather than laziness. Policemen seem inclined toward physical activity, provided it occurs in an authoritative context. They do not care to be sent on errands and above all dislike paper work. They seem to enjoy most of all, the processes of investigation: talking, telephoning, going "out on the street." These activities are of course the ones where their authority is most evident and exercised.

[2] Until 1962, one could be arrested in Westville for *being* an addict. However, that was declared unconstitutional in *Robinson v. California*, 370 U. S. 660 (1962).

[3] See Rex Collings, Jr., "Toward Workable Rules of Search and Seizure —an Amicus Curiae Brief," *California Law Review*, 50 (1962), 443 [citing *People v. Molarius*, 146 Cal. App. 2d 129, 303 P. 2d 350 (1956)].

[4] See Frank J. Remington, "The Law Relating to 'On the Street' Detention, Questioning, and Frisking," *Journal of Criminal Law, Criminology and Police Science*, 51 (December, 1960), pp. 386–394.

[5] Max Gluckman, *The Judicial Process Among the Barotse of Northern Rhodesia* (Glencoe, New York: The Free Press, 1955), p. 359.

[6] A person is in possession of a narcotic when it is under his dominion and control, and, to his knowledge, either is carried on his person or in his presence, the possession thereof is immediate, accessible, and exclusive to him, provided, however, that two or more persons may have joint possession and the possession may be individual, through an agent or joint with another. *People v. Bigelow*, 104 Cal. App. 2d 380, 388. Cited by Fricke, *California Criminal Law*, 8th ed., 1961, p. 395.

[7] For a discussion of stashes in an institutional setting, see Erving Goffman, *Asylums* (Garden City, New York: Anchor Books, 1961), pp. 248 ff.

[8] The use of Nalline (a Merck & Co., Inc., trademark for the narcotic, N-allynormorphine) for the diagnosis of addiction was first explored by Dr. Harris Isbell and his associates at the United States Public Health Service Hospital in Lexington, Kentucky, and was further developed by Dr. James Terry, Medical Officer of the Sheriff's staff of the Alameda County, California, Rehabilitation Center. It is now used as a means of controlling addiction in several California counties.

[9] For additional information on the technical, administrative, medical, and legal aspects of the Nalline test, see the following: Harris Isbell, "Nalline—A Specific Narcotic Antagonist: Clinical and Pharmacologic Observations," *The Merck Report*, 62 (April, 1953), 23–26; J. G. Terry, "Nalline: An Aid to Detecting Narcotics Users," *California Medicine*, 85 (November, 1956), 299–301; A. Wikler, H. F. Fraser, and Harris Isbell, "N-allynormorphine: Effects of Single Doses and Precipitation of Acute Abstinence Syndromes during Addiction to Morphine, Methadone, or Heroin in Man (Post Addicts)," *Journal of Pharmacology and Experimental Therapy*, 109 (September, 1953), 8–20; Stewart Weinberg, "Nalline as an Aid in the Detection and Control of Users of Narcotics," *California Law Review*, 48 (1960), 282–294; Thorvald T. Brown, Chapter IX, "The Nalline Test," in *The Enigma of Drug Addiction* (Springfield, Illinois: Charles C Thomas, 1961), pp. 287–334; and Ernest B. Smith, *Nalline Examinations of Narcotic Addicts: Analysis of*

Deterrent Effects, unpublished M.A. thesis, Department of Criminology, University of California, Berkeley, 1960.

[10]The term stems from the days when police used to arrest users under the vagrancy laws. Presently, Sec. 11721 of the Penal Code serves the same purpose.

[11]It has happened, but rarely, that a vag addict chooses ninety days in jail over three years of Nalline.

[12]Lloyd E. Ohlin, Herman Piven, and Donnell M. Pappenfort, "Major Dilemmas of the Social Worker in Probation and Parole," *National Probation and Parole Association Journal,* 2 (July, 1956), 211–225.

[13]Official Treasury Department figures indicate that in 1961, 40.26 kilograms of heroin and 20.25 kilograms of other narcotics drugs were seized or purchased by federal authorities; in 1962, 87.80 kilograms of heroin and 21.55 kilograms of other narcotics were seized or purchased by federal agents. The Treasury Department Bureau of Narcotics makes no official estimate of the amount of heroin used annually in the United States, but agents interviewed agreed that the amount confiscated is a small percentage of the amount used. (The figures cited above are given in the Bureau of Narcotics report *Traffic in Opium and Other Dangerous Drugs,* Washington, D. C.: Government Printing Office, 1963, p. 66.)

[14]A shrewd nonuser-dealer had the Westville narcotics police completely stymied at the time of this writing. His mode of operation was based on a skillful combination of use of assistants and of negotiation to take advantage of protections afforded the defendant in the criminal process. He personally handled neither cash nor heroin, and never associated himself with a direct exchange of one for the other. He would have the buyer give his assistant the money for the heroin and would telephone the buyer the next day giving the location of the stash. Furthermore, he had developed a reputation for trustworthiness among his customers; so much so that the head of the Westville narcotics detail ruefully acknowledged, "He gives good quantity and good quality. The only way we'll ever get him is through a conspiracy charge."

[15]An ounce of heroin is not necessarily an ounce of pure heroin. Usually what is purchased has already been "cut." Most of the heroin sold by the Gomez brothers was about 6 percent pure.

[16]When an area runs dry of narcotics, addicts in that area, because of their pressing need, will be enormously anxious to the point of panic, and hence the term.

[17]See generally the panel on "Law Enforcement and Controls" and especially the statement by John C. Cross in *Proceedings of the White House Conference on Narcotic and Drug Abuse* (Washington, D. C.: Government Printing Office, 1962), pp. 23–65.

[18]One recent important case—which was indeed a "good pinch"—was the case of *People v. Ker,* 374 U.S. 23 (1963). Although this decision in some respects limits the policemen's actions, it also recognizes the special circumstances under which narcotics police perform their duties.

19

The Use of Violence by the Police

WILLIAM J. CHAMBLISS
and ROBERT B. SEIDMAN

The American policeman regards himself as the embodiment of society's legitimate power of violence. When in uniform, he carries a billyclub, he wears an ammunition belt and a holster with a gun in it, his handcuffs dangle from the belt, he frequently sports a crash helmet, and he carries mace and other incapacitating chemicals. The tools of his trade are instruments of violence.

Society equips the police with the capacity for violence not for the individual benefit of the policeman, but for its own benefit. The result, however, has a dual thrust. Sometimes violence must be used to accomplish society's immediate purposes, e.g. to subdue a violent robber in order to arrest him and make him amenable to the criminal proceedings. Sometimes, however, it must be used by the policeman in his own defense. It is the nature of a policeman's day-to-day work, that he may occasionally come in contact with the most violent elements in society. Police work is probably the only peacetime occupation in which sudden death by knifing or gun-

Source: *Law, Order and Power*, Reading, Mass.: Addison-Wesley, 1971, pp. 274–286. By permission of the author and publisher.

shot constitutes a significant occupational hazard. The society therefore equips the policeman with instruments of violence for his own protection, because it is in society's interest that he be able to protect himself; and the police are generally regarded as having a job which is infinitely more dangerous than any other occupation. This conception is in part due to the stereotyped image of police work as consisting in the arrest and pursuit of persons who commit crimes of violence and destruction such as rape, arson, murder, armed robbery, and the like. In point of fact, the policeman is only rarely called upon to arrest or pursue persons engaged in crimes where violence is even remotely possible. The bulk of his day-to-day activities consists in "peace-keeping"—settling domestic quarrels, watching people come and go on streets where crimes rarely occur, arresting a drunk, or rescuing a cat from an ice floe in the local river. Eighty percent of the arrests made by the police every year are for very minor offenses; over fifty percent of the arrests are for drunkenness alone. Few policemen are threatened with severe bodily harm in any year, and even fewer are actually killed. Table 1 shows a comparison

PART 3   THE SOCIAL ORGANIZATION OF CRIMINAL LAW ENFORCEMENT

TABLE 1
Comparison of the Number of Policemen Killed in the Line of Duty with the Number of Persons Killed by the Police[1]

Year		Persons Killed by Police			Police Killed in Line of Duty
	Total	*White*	*Black*	*Other*	
1956	226	123	101	2	46
1957	228	119	106	3	45
1958	229	111	116	2	49
1959	227	110	115	2	49
1960	245	125	119	1	48
1961	237	134	100	3	71
1962	187	89	93	2	78
1963	246	111	129	2	88
1964	278	134	141	3	88
1965	271	154	114	3	83
Average per year	237	109	103	2	64

between the number of policemen killed every year and the number of persons killed by policemen every year. There are, on the average, four times as many people killed by policemen as there are policemen killed in the line of duty. Further, given that many of the seventy-odd policemen killed each year die in automobile accidents and other noncriminal events, it is clear that the number of police killed each year by "criminals" is much smaller than the impression given to the public in law-enforcement propaganda. Indeed, firemen, who are generally regarded as having a relatively safe occupation, are more likely to be killed in the line of duty than are policemen.

These facts notwithstanding, the policeman's job is regarded as a highly dangerous one. That some policemen are killed is sufficiently impressive to underscore the dangerous nature of the job, although the public image and the image of the police themselves exaggerate the real danger considerably.

Police in other countries are even less likely to meet with violence than are the police in the United States. In England it is an extremely rare event when a police officer is killed in the line of duty. Police work in England is generally regarded as an exceedingly safe occupation. Certainly streetcar conductors and bus drivers are in much greater danger of being maimed or killed in the line of duty than are British police officers. The same holds true in most Scandinavian and European countries.

The norms which define the permissible use of violence by a policeman are appropriate to the purposes for which he is given the instruments of violence. He is permitted to use force either to effectuate the official purposes of taking certain categories of criminals into custody or preventing certain sorts of crimes, or to defend himself. The law provides, however, that he use only the minimum amount of force necessary to effectuate these purposes.

The laws which specify the norms for the policeman's role, therefore, do not give him any general license to apply force. Instead, they give him a limited privilege. It is a defense to any charge of police hitting or wounding or killing that the police officer was acting within the scope of his duties or in self-defense. The Wisconsin Criminal Code, for example, provides in part:

939.45. *Privilege.* The fact that the actor's conduct is privileged, although otherwise criminal, is a defense to a prosecution for any crime based on that conduct. The defense of privilege can be claimed under any of the following circumstances: . . .

2   When the actor's conduct is in defense of persons or property under any of the circumstances described in s. 939.48 (relating to self-defense and the defense of others) or 939.49 (relating to the defense of property). While reasonable force can be used to prevent or terminate an unlawful interference with property, "it is not reasonable to intentionally use force intended or likely to

cause death or great bodily harm for the sole purpose of defense of one's property," or

3　When the actor's conduct is in good faith and is an apparently authorized and reasonable fulfillment of any duties of a public office; or

4　When the actor's conduct is a reasonable accomplishment of a lawful arrest . . .

The critical question concerning the content of these norms, of course, is the word "reasonable." This is a concept frequently used in law. It has a dual aspect. In the first place, all of us use the question of "reasonableness" as a test of truth. If John claims that he agreed to sell to Mark a ten-year-old Ford sedan in poor condition for an agreed price of $3000, and Mark agrees that he promised to buy the car, but claims that the agreed price was $250, and there is evidence that the market price of such a used car was $250, most of us would tend to believe Mark rather than John. Here we are using the concept of what is "reasonable" in a factual sense, for that report of conduct is more likely to be true, which matches our knowledge of the everyday conduct of most of us.

More frequently, however, the word "reasonable" is used in law to mask a normative concept. It is used by courts and legislatures to cover a variety of cases too wide for precise definition. A legislature cannot be expected to lay out with precision for all possible cases the amount of force which one is entitled to use in effecting an arrest. Instead, in the Wisconsin statute, the legislature says only that the use of force is not criminal when part of a "reasonable accomplishment" of a lawful arrest, leaving for courts and juries to give the word "reasonable" specific contents in specific situations.

Appellate courts have given some content to the term through their decisions. In general, the word "reasonable" has come to mean "necessary." Was the force used no more than was necessary to accomplish the purpose for which the privilege to use force was given? The Wisconsin statute with respect to self-defense codifies the rule which has been evolved in most common-law jurisdictions:

939.48. *Self-Defense and Defense of Others.* (1) A person is privileged to threaten or intentionally use force against another for the purpose of preventing or terminating what he reasonably believes to be an unlawful interference with his person by such other person. The actor may intentionally use only such force or threat thereof as he reasonably believes is necessary to prevent or terminate the interference. He may not intentionally use force which is intended or likely to cause death or great bodily harm unless he reasonably believes that such force is necessary to prevent imminent death or great bodily harm to himself.

The same rule applies in matters of arrest: The police officer is entitled to use only so much force as is necessary to accomplish the arrest.

That the police in general have not internalized the norms defining the permissible use of violence seems quite clear from numerous studies. In a survey[2] of policemen in a midwestern city in 1951, officers were asked to respond to this question: "When do you think a policeman is justified in roughing a man up?" They responded as follows:

Reason	Percentage
Disrespect for police	37
To obtain information	19
For the hardened criminal	7
When you know the man is guilty	3
For sex criminals	3
When impossible to avoid	23
To make an arrest	8

The officers believed that "the only way to treat certain groups of people including Negroes and the poor, is to treat them roughly."[3]

A more recent study conducted for the President's Commission on Crime and Law Enforcement documented through observations the frequency and severity of violence by police as they carried out the routines of their jobs. Researchers recorded their observations in the cities of Boston, Chicago, and Washington, D.C., which were gathered by sitting in patrol cars and monitoring booking and lockup procedures in high-crime precincts for seven weeks, seven days a week. They divided the use of physical force by the police into two categories:[4] First, force was considered undue, unreasonable or unwarranted "only in those cases in which a policeman struck the citizen with his hands, fist, feet or body, or where he used a weapon of some kind— such as a nightstick or a pistol." Secondly, a physical assault on a citizen was judged to be "improper" or , "unnecessary" only when force was used in one or more of the following ways:

1 If a policeman physically assaulted a citizen and then failed to make an arrest; proper use involves an arrest.

2 If the citizen being arrested did not, by word or deed, resist the policeman; force should be used if it is necessary to make an arrest.

3 If the policeman, even though there was resistance to the arrest, could easily have restrained the citizen in other ways.

4 If a large number of policemen were present and could have assisted in subduing the citizen in the station, in lockup, and in the interrogation room.

5 If an offender was handcuffed and made no attempt to flee or offer violent resistance.

6 If the citizen resisted arrest, but the use of force continued even after the citizen was subdued.

This survey of police methods disclosed thirty-seven cases during the period of investigation in which force was used improperly. Forty-four citizens were assaulted by the police during this period. In thirteen of these cases the use of force occurred in the station house when at least four other policemen were present. In about half of these cases the person assaulted by the police was bruised but not seriously hurt; in three cases the person assaulted required hospitalization. The following case was reported, not as necessarily representative, but at least as an indication of the way in which undue force is sometimes used by the police:

The watch began rather routinely as the policemen cruised the district. Their first radio dispatch came at about 5:30 p.m. They were told to investigate two drunks in a cemetery. On arriving they found two white men "sleeping one off." Without questioning the men, the older policeman began to search one of them, ripping his shirt and hitting him in the groin with a nightstick. The younger policeman, as he searched the second, ripped away the seat of his trousers, exposing his buttocks. The policemen then prodded the men toward the cemetery fence and forced them to climb it, laughing at the plight of the drunk with the exposed buttocks. As the drunks went over the fence, one policeman shouted, "I ought to run you fuckers in." The other remarked to the observer, "Those assholes won't be back; a bunch of shitty winos."[5]

Not long after they returned to their car, the policemen stopped a woman who had made a left turn improperly. She was treated very politely, and the younger policeman, who wrote the ticket, later commented to the observer "Nice lady." At 7:30 they were dispatched to check a suspicious auto. After a quick check, the car was marked abandoned.

Shortly after a 30-minute break for a 7:30 "lunch" the two policemen received a dispatch to take a burglary report. Arriving at a slum walkup, the police entered a room where an obviously drunk white man in his late 40's insisted that someone had entered and stolen his food and liquor. He kept insisting that it had been taken and that he had been forced to borrow money to buy beer. The younger policeman, who took the report, kept harassing the man, alternating between mocking and badgering him with rhetorical questions. "You say your name is Half-A-Wit (for Hathaway)? Do you sleep with niggers? How did you vote on the bond issue? Are you sure that's all that's missing? Are you a virgin yet?" The man responded to all of this with the seeming vagueness and joviality of the intoxicated, expressing gratitude for the policemen's help as they left. The older policeman remarked to the observer as they left, "Ain't drunks funny?"

For the next little happened, but as the two were moving across the precinct shortly after 10 p.m., a white man and a woman in their 50's flagged them down. Since they were obviously "substantial" middle-class citizens of the district, the policemen listened to their complaints that a Negro man was causing trouble inside the public-transport station from which they had just emerged. The woman said that he had sworn at her. The older policeman remarked, "What's a nigger doing up here? He should be down on Franklin Road."

With that, they ran into the station and grabbed the Negro man who was inside. Without questioning him, they shoved him into a phone booth and began beating him with their fists and a flashlight. They also hit him in the groin. Then they dragged him out and kept him on his knees. He pleaded that he had just been released from a mental hospital that day and, begging not to be hit again, asked them to let him return to the hospital. One policeman said: "Don't you like us, nigger? I like to beat niggers and rip out their eyes." They took him outside to their patrol car. Then they decided to put him on a bus, telling him that he was returning to the hospital; they deliberately put him on a bus going in the opposite direction. Just before the Negro boarded the bus, he said, "You police just like to shoot and beat people." The first policeman replied, "Get moving, nigger, or I'll shoot you." The man was crying and bleeding as he was put on the bus. Leaving the scene, the younger policeman commented, "He won't be back."[6]

For the rest of the evening, the two policemen kept looking for drunks and harassing any they found. They concluded the evening by being dispatched to an address where, they were told, a man was being held for the police. No one answered their knock. They left.

Another case is also illustrative:

White officers responded to a man with a gun . . . and heard three shots fired. Then the white man with the gun got a drop on the officer—somehow they got the gun away and handcuffed him (gun was a 12 gauge 1905 musket). When they got him to the station garage, they kicked him all over, but the principal one was the officer who had been in danger when the man had the drop on him. He beat him as the others held him up. I got to the scene and the lockup man whistled for them to stop but they didn't. The Lieutenant arrived with everyone else and said there's going to be a beef on this one so cover it up and go find the empty shells. Someone call an ambulance (he needed it badly). Then the Lieutenant took complete control. They got the shells, got a complainant who said the three shots were an attempt to kill the officer, and he would sign a complaint, said he called an ambulance, etc. They wrote a cover for the incident. The officer who beat the man most was shaken by then but the others gave him support, telling him how brave he was and how wise he had been not to kill the guy at the scene, etc. They then set about to put all the stories in order and I was carefully notified of it in detail so I would have it straight. I had enough rapport with these officers that they talked about it even after. The man was in pretty bad shape when he got to the hospital.[7]

The researcher also observed assaults on suspects in lockups and station houses.

It is important to keep in mind that in many of these cases the police were well aware that they were being observed. One can only understand their willingness to behave in such a manner despite the presence of observers by realizing that from the perspective of the police their actions were completely justified. Indeed, it is standard police rhetoric to refer to anyone who objects to such practices as "bleeding hearts"—an expression reminiscent of President Johnson's comment about "nervous nellies" who opposed the escalation of the Vietnam War. The police respond to criticisms of their tactics with rhetorical questions about the desire of some "softheaded fools" who want them to treat everyone with "TLC" (tender loving care).

It is undoubtedly the case, however, that in the presence of observers the police are more reticent in the use of undue force than they would be otherwise. If violence is a common pattern of police behavior even in the presence of observers, then such violence is bound to occur when the police are not under observation, if only because we all have the tendency to rely on established patterns of actions, and also because of the aroused emotions of the moment. But in all likelihood the observed frequency of violence represents a sizable reduction over what routinely takes place. Thus it seems safe to assume that however much violence was discovered in this study, it was an underestimate of the actual amount of violence taking place.

Although the estimate of the overall frequency of undue police violence is undoubtedly conservative, nonetheless, the frequency is quite high. Using as a base the 643 white suspects encountered by the police during the period of study, the researchers report a rate of police abuse of 41.9 per 1000 suspects. This rate is much higher, incidentally, than the rates of crimes of violence among the population, and almost one thousand times as high as the murder rate in the United States. For black defendants, the abuse rate is lower but still of some consequence. Of 751 black suspects 17 experienced undue use of force—a rate of 22.6 per 1000.

There is no ready explanation for the unusual finding that blacks experience less violence at the hands of the police than whites of the same social class. Indeed, the data reported earlier on the number of persons killed by police indicated that blacks were much more likely to be killed than whites, considering their proportion in the population. The two findings, then, are in conflict. It would be premature to conclude from these observations that the blacks are less likely to be the recipient of police violence than whites are, and much other impressionistic evidence suggests just the reverse of this is the case. It seems likely that this discrepancy has something to do with the characteristics of this particular study rather than reflecting a general tendency in the police departments. Certainly if the cities studied were in the south, it would have been most surprising if the same results were obtained. Until more data becomes available, we should hold this question in abeyance.

The important finding for the analysis at hand is that the poor are much more likely to be on the receiving end of illegal police violence than other groups in the society. Black or white, the likelihood of being a victim of police brutality is highly correlated with being poor. It is the poor man in the slums, be he a white wino or a black teenager, who faces the prospect of being brutalized by the police. In the words of the report, "the lower class bears the brunt of victimization by the police."

As was the case in the responses to the questionnaire mentioned earlier in this chapter, a frequent reason for the use of unwarranted force and violence by the police was the attempt to "instill respect" in the citizens for the police. One policeman commented to the observer: "On the street you can't beat them. But when you get them to the station, you can instill some respect in them." The research team found that open defiance of police authority was present in 39% of the cases where the police used undue force. It is important to realize, however, that:

> Open defiance of police authority . . . is what the policeman defines as *his* authority, not necessarily "official" authority. Indeed in 40% of the cases that the police considered open defiance, the policeman never executed an arrest.[8]

There are indications that the tendency of police to be overly quick in reacting with violence has increased dramatically since the onset of urban riots in the black ghettos, the increased frequency of peace demonstrations, and the emergence of militant and quasimilitary groups of Blacks advocating self-protection for the black community. The police response to these changes in the American scene has generally been repressive and intimidating. The consequence has been that police are more likely to use undue force when arresting or questioning Blacks than they have been previously, though the tendency has always been strong. When the police attempt to exert total control over the situation, it often means that they would resort to violence at the slightest provocation or perhaps when no provocation is forthcoming save the appearance of "the man." The following case is illustrative:

> A black man was stopped for making an illegal left turn. He was a large man with a beard and semi-hippie attire. The police officer approached the car and pushed the man up against the side; when the black man objected to the treatment the officer and his partner beat the man to the ground. A further beating was administered at the station house.[9]

The police in this particular city reported that they were "very wary" of black men with beards and Afro-style clothing. It was the feeling of the police that all such men were potentially dangerous to the policeman's safety and that therefore the latter had to keep the upper hand at all times, even to the point of using violence *before* any was used toward him.

In several cities the police and prosecuting attorneys' offices have gone on open campaigns to harass and intimidate members of the Black Panthers. In Oakland, California, off-duty policemen once entered the offices of the Black Panther Party and shot holes in a picture of Huey Newton which was hanging on the wall. In New York City, off-duty policemen once attacked and beat up Blacks in a courtroom. In Seattle, the police, at the direction of a prosecuting attorney, have indiscriminately arrested and unnecessarily used force against members of the Black Panther Party.

The use of force in cases of crowd and riot control is another problem entirely. In the case of brutality or excessive violence by an individual officer, it is traditionally argued by police apologists that the problem is not systemic but individual to the officers involved. In many cases involving crowd control, however, the excessive use of violence by the police involved seems to be on such a wide scale that it is hard to believe that the incident was not officially encouraged or condoned. For example, a national news magazine described how the police ejected students conducting a sit-in at Columbia University in 1968: At one building,

> police threw dozens of students from inside the building to rows of policemen and plainclothesmen outside, where some were punched, kicked and hit with clubs and handcuffs. One blond girl was thrown to the brick sidewalk and beaten unconscious . . . In some areas (of the campus) the police behaved with restraint; in others they were vicious.[10]

Similar stories could be quoted of police action at a substantial number of civil rights demonstrations, student demonstrations, and riots. Since in every case there are well-documented stories and even motion pictures showing policemen beating citizens even after they had fallen to the ground, there can be little doubt that the police in such a case had gone beyond the legitimate use of force provided for by the statutes.

The best-investigated instance of police violence during demonstrations is provided by the "Walker Report," which is an analysis of the riot that occurred during the Democratic National Convention in Chicago in 1968. During the convention large numbers of demonstrators gathered in the city to protest against the war in Vietnam, the method of selecting presidential candidates, and the "establishment." The response of the police, according to the report prepared for the National Commission on the Causes and Prevention of Violence, was to employ large-scale force and violence. The report termed the disturbance in Chicago a "police riot."

The control of the police power completely broke down. Demonstrators, reporters, passersby, and onlookers were indiscriminately attacked, beaten, and assaulted by policemen:

> police action was not confined . . . to necessary force even in clearing the park: A young man and his girl friend were both grabbed by officers. He screamed "We're going, we're going," but they threw him into the pond. The officers grabbed the girl, knocked her to the ground, dragged her along the embankment and hit her with their batons on her head, arms, back and legs. The boy tried to scramble up the embankment to her, but police shoved him back in the water at least twice. He finally got to her and tried to pull her in the water, away from the police. He was clubbed on the head five or six times. An officer shouted, "Let's get the fucking bastards," but the boy pulled her in the water and the police left.

Like the incident described above, much of the violence witnessed in Old Town that night seems malicious or mindless:

> There were pedestrians. People who were not part of the demonstration were coming out of a tavern to see what the demonstration was . . . and the officers indiscriminately started beating everybody on the street who was not a policeman.

Another scene:

> There was a group of about six police officers that moved in and started beating two youths. When one of the officers pulled back his nightstick to swing, one of the youths grabbed it from behind and started beating on the officer. At this point about ten officers left everybody else and ran after this youth, who turned down Wells and ran to the left.
>
> But the officers went to the right, picked up another youth, assuming he was the one they were chasing, and took him into an empty lot and beat him. And when they got him to the ground, they just kicked him ten times—the wrong youth, the innocent youth who had been standing there.

A federal legal official relates an experience of Tuesday evening:

> "I then walked one block north where I met a group of 12–15 policemen. I showed them my identification and they permitted me to walk with them. The police walked one block west. Numerous people were watching us from their windows and balconies. The police yelled profanities at them, taunting them to come down where the police would beat them up. The police stopped a number of people on the street demanding identification. They verbally abused each pedestrian and pushed one or two without hurting them. We walked back to Clark Street and began to walk north where the police stopped a number of people who appeared to be protesters, and ordered them out of the area in a very abusive way. One protester who was walking in the opposite direction was kneed in the groin by a policeman who was walking towards him. The boy fell to the ground and swore at the policeman who picked him up and threw him to the ground. We continued to walk toward the command post. A derelict who appeared to be very intoxicated, walked up to the policeman and mumbled something that was incoherent. The policeman pulled from his belt a tin container and sprayed its contents into the eyes of the derelict, who stumbled around and fell on his face.
>
> "It was on these nights that the police violence against media representatives reached its peak. Much of it was plainly deliberate. A newsman was pulled aside on Monday by a detective acquaintance of his who said: 'The word is being passed to get newsmen.' Individual newsmen were warned, 'You take my picture tonight and I'm going to get you.' Cries of 'get the camera' preceded individual attacks on photographers."

A newspaper photographer describes Old Town on Monday at about 9:00 P.M.:

> "When the people arrived at the intersection of Wells and Division, they were not standing in the streets. Suddenly a column of policemen ran out from the alley. They were reinforcements. They were under control but there seemed to be no direction. One man was yelling, 'Get them up on the sidewalks, turn them around.' Very suddenly the police charged the people on the sidewalks and began beating their heads. A line of cameramen was 'trapped' along with the crowd along the sidewalks, and the police went down the line chopping away at the cameras."

A network cameraman reports that on the same night:

> "I just saw this guy coming at me with his nightstick and I had the camera up. The tip of his stick hit me right in the mouth, then I put my tongue up there and I noticed that my tooth was gone. I turned around then to try to leave and then

this cop came up behind me with his stick and he jabbed me in the back.

"All of a sudden these cops jumped out of the police cars and started just beating the hell out of people. And before anything else happened to me, I saw a man holding a Bell & Howell camera with big wide letters on it, saying 'CBS.' He apparently had been hit by a cop. And cops were standing around and there was blood streaming down his face. Another policeman was running after me and saying, 'Get the fuck out of here.' And I heard another guy scream, 'Get their fucking cameras.' And the next thing I know I was being hit on the head, and I think on the back, and I was forced down on the ground at the corner of Division and Wells."[11]

After the "police riot" in Chicago, 101 demonstrators were hospitalized for injuries sustained in attacks by policemen. An additional 425 persons were treated at seven medical facilities set up by the Medical Committee for Human Rights. Over 200 more persons were treated by the Committee's mobile medical teams, and the committee estimated that over 400 persons were given first aid for tear gas or mace.[12]

Reports of police actions in cities that have experienced riots in the black ghettos are similar. The number of civilians killed is difficult to estimate because of the police effort to suppress such statistics, but reliable estimates for the riot in Newark, New Jersey, alone range from thirty-five to well over fifty. Of these civilians killed, according to one of the participants, only a very small handful were shot while breaking the law; almost all the rest were shot while they were in the area but not engaged in any illegal activity.[13]

The typical response of police departments to public criticism of such behavior by large groups of officers is to close ranks in defense. The standard excuse is that the police met with "resistance." For example, after the Columbia incident referred to above, the New York Commissioner of Police is reported to have said that "his men encountered 'a good deal of resistance' when they entered the buildings (to eject the demonstrators)."[14] Sometimes the fact that demonstrators used vile and abusive language at the police or spat at them is given as the excuse: "After all, the police are human." However, a policeman's privilege of using violence, as the Wisconsin statute states, extends to self-defense

only in cases of "unreasonable interference with his person." The use of abusive language is not an interference with the person. Similarly, during the Democratic Convention in Chicago in 1968, the police were shown on television screens across the country swinging night sticks and beating numerous demonstrators. In this case, the police and the mayor of the city defended the police action by arguing that they had had advance knowledge of the potential violence of some of the demonstrators, including the fact that some of the demonstrators were armed with lethal weapons. The police and public officials in this instance justified the excessive use of violence by the police on the grounds that the police were potentially endangered.

The use of violence *in excess* of the amount necessary to accomplish the purposes for which the right to use violence is granted is the limiting case of crime-control, where the police are in fact themselves punishing the suspect for the claimed misconduct, basing the punishment entirely on their own perceptions of guilt and, frequently, their own conception of what constitutes criminal behavior, and where all the procedural protections of accusation, hearing, and sentencing are abandoned.

It must be stressed that the tendency for the police to use violence is not a necessary outcome of police organization in complex societies. In England large peace demonstrations have apparently met with cooperative and patient police reaction. Indeed, policemen have even been attacked by demonstrators and refused to respond with violence. In a recent British demonstration where thousands of people were marching, where the police had been forewarned that some of the marchers were planning to destroy public buildings and physically attack the police, where rumors had reached the police that "outside agitators" were coming to stir the crowd to riot, the police responded with great restraint and a general unwillingness to use violence even in the face of violence being used against them. Reports have it that by the end of the day, the demonstrators who remained into the night eventually joined hands with the policemen and concluded the day's march with song—with the policemen joining in.

Although systematic data are not available, what

evidence there is suggests that the police in the United States are among the most violent in the world. However, even in the United States there are wide variations in the propensity of different law enforcement agencies to resort to violence in the treatment of suspects. What little evidence there is suggests that federal prisoners are less likely to be the victims of violence than state prisoners. Arnold Trebach interviewed inmates in penitentiaries in New Jersey, Pennsylvania, and in a federal prison and found 54% of the New Jersey prisoners claiming that the police had either used or threatened to use violence, 41% of the Philadelphia prisoners making the same claim (and this was mainly the threat of violence), and 22% of the federal prisoners making this claim. Furthermore, 70% of the federal prisoners responded that they had been "treated well" by the federal police.[15]

The reasons for the police violence also vary. In the study cited above, 70% of the New Jersey prisoners who had been subjected to violence maintained that this was done to coerce confessions, whereas there were very few such claims either in Philadelphia or among federal prisoners. Indeed, among the New Jersey prisoners 22% claimed that they had signed confessions as a consequence of police violence, but none of the Philadelphia prisoners and only 5% of the federal prisoners made similar claims.

Is police brutality a recent phenomenon? If not, why has it suddenly been pressed into public concern?

There can be little doubt that police brutality is as American as apple pie and has almost as long a history. It has been hidden for generations, along with the Other America, by the walls that separate the middle class and the urban poor. In recent years, the growing loss of legitimacy of the American government has led to widespread civil rights demonstrations, anti-war demonstrations, and campus protests. Police brutality could no longer be hidden. Urban riots have frequently been diagnosed as having been triggered by police violence, and urban riots cannot be concealed. The same militancy which has brought about civil rights demonstrations has induced Blacks to challenge police brutality on a variety of levels. The long-continued pressure of moral enterpreneurs, such as the American Civil Liberties Union, has succeeded in casting some light on the dark shadows of police station back rooms.

FOOTNOTES

[1] U. S. Office of Vital Statistics Official Reports, 1951–1965.
[2] William A. Westley, "Violence and the Police," *Am. J. Soc.*, 59, 1951, pp. 34–38.
[3] *Ibid.*, p. 40.
[4] All unacknowledged quotations and conclusions in the following discussion are from Albert J. Reiss, Jr., "The Use of Physical Force in Police Work," report prepared for the President's Commission on Law Enforcement and Administration of Justice, University of Michigan, Ann Arbor, 1966, pp. 16 ff.
[5] Also quoted in the Commission's *Task Force Report: The Police*, p. 182.
[6] *Ibid.*
[7] *Ibid.*
[8] Reiss, *op. cit.*, pp. 16 ff.
[9] William J. Chambliss, field notes.
[10] *Newsweek*, May 13, 1968, p. 60.
[11] *The Walker Report: Violence in Chicago*, "Rights in Conflict," Bantam, New York, 1968, pp. 5–8.
[12] *Ibid.*, pp. 353–354.
[13] Thomas Hayden, *Rebellion in Newark*, Random House, New York, 1967.
[14] *Time*, May 17, 1968, p. 59.
[15] Arnold S. Trebach, *The Rationing of Justice*, Rutgers University Press, New Brunswick, N. J., 1964, pp. 40–41.

20

Police Brutality— Answers to Key Questions

ALBERT J. REISS, JR.

"For three years, there has been through the courts and the streets a dreary procession of citizens with broken heads and bruised bodies against few of whom was violence needed to effect an arrest. Many of them had done nothing to deserve an arrest. In a majority of such cases, no complaint was made. If the victim complains, his charge is generally dismissed. The police are practically above the law."

This statement was published in 1903, and its author was the Hon. Frank Moss, a former police commissioner of New York City. Clearly, today's charges of police brutality and mistreatment of citizens have a precedent in American history—but never before has the issue of police brutality assumed the public urgency it has today. In Newark, in Detroit, in Watts, in Harlem, and, in fact, in practically every city that has had a civil disturbance, "deep hostility between police and ghetto" was, reports the Kerner Commission, "a primary cause of the riots."

Whether or not the police accept the words "police brutality," the public now wants some plain answers

to some plain questions. How widespread is police mistreatment of citizens? Is it on the increase? Why do policemen mistreat citizens? Do the police mistreat Negroes more than whites?

To find some answers, 36 people working for the Center of Research on Social Organization observed police-citizen encounters in the cities of Boston, Chicago, and Washington, D. C. For seven days a week, for seven weeks during the summer of 1966, these observers, with police permission, sat in patrol cars and monitored booking and lockup procedures in high-crime precincts.

Obtaining information about police mistreatment of citizens is no simple matter. National and state civil-rights commissions receive hundreds of complaints charging mistreatment—but proving these allegations is difficult. The few local civilian-review boards, such as the one in Philadelphia, have not produced any significant volume of complaints leading to the dismissal or disciplining of policemen for alleged brutality. Generally, police chiefs are silent on the matter, or answer charges of brutality with vague statements that they will investigate any complaints brought to their attention. Rank-and-file policemen are usually more outspoken: They often

Source: Reprinted by permission of Transaction, Inc., from *Society*, Vol. 5, No. 8, July/August 1968. Copyright © 1968 by Transaction, Inc.

insinuate that charges of brutality are part of a conspiracy against them, and against law and order.

THE MEANING OF BRUTALITY

What citizens mean by police brutality covers the full range of police practices. These practices, contrary to the impression of many civil-rights activists, are not newly devised to deal with Negroes in our urban ghettos. They are ways in which the police have traditionally behaved in dealing with certain citizens, particularly those in the lower classes. The most common of these practices are:

- the use of profane and abusive language,
- commands to move on or get home,
- stopping and questioning people on the street or searching them and their cars,
- threats to use force if not obeyed,
- prodding with a nightstick or approaching with a pistol, and
- the actual use of physical force or violence itself.

Citizens and the police do not always agree on what constitutes proper police practice. What is "proper," or what is "brutal," it need hardly be pointed out, is more a matter of judgment about what someone did than a description of what police do. What is important is not the practice itself but what it means to the citizen. What citizens object to and call "police brutality" is really the judgment that they have not been treated with the full rights and dignity owing citizens in a democratic society. Any practice that degrades their status, that restricts their freedom, that annoys or harasses them, or that uses physical force is frequently seen as unnecessary and unwarranted. More often than not, they are probably right.

Many police practices serve only to degrade the citizen's sense of himself and his status. This is particularly true with regard to the way the police use language. Most citizens who have contact with the police object less to their use of four-letter words than to *how* the policeman talks to them. Particularly objectionable is the habit policemen have of "talking down" to citizens, of calling them names that deprecate them in their own eyes and those of others. More than one Negro citizen has complained:

"They talk down to me as if I had no name—like 'boy' or 'man' or whatever, or they call me 'Jack' or by my first name. They don't show me no respect."

Members of minority groups and those seen as nonconformists, for whatever reason, are the most likely targets of status degradation. Someone who has been drinking may be told he is a "bum" or a "shitty wino." A woman walking alone may be called a "whore." And a man who doesn't happen to meet a policeman's standard of how one should look or dress may be met with the remark, "What's the matter, you a queer?" A white migrant from the South may be called a "hillbilly" or "shitkicker"; a Puerto Rican, a "porkchop"; a young boy, a "punk kid." When the policeman does not use words of status degradation, his manner may be degrading. Citizens want to be treated as people, not as "nonpersons" who are talked about as if they were not present.

That many Negroes believe that the police have degraded their status is clear from surveys in Watts, Newark, and Detroit. One out of every five Negroes in our center's post-riot survey in Detroit reports that the police have "talked down to him." More than one in ten says a policeman has "called me a bad name."

To be treated as "suspicious" is not only degrading, but is also a form of harassment and a restriction on the right to move freely. The harassing tactics of the police—dispersing social street-gatherings, the indiscriminate stopping of Negroes on foot or in cars, and commands to move on or go home—are particularly common in ghetto areas.

Young people are the most likely targets of harassing orders to disperse or move on. Particularly in summer, ghetto youths are likely to spend lots of time in public places. Given the inadequacy of their housing and the absence of community facilities, the street corner is often their social center. As the police cruise the busy streets of the ghetto, they frequently shout at groups of teenagers to "get going" or "get home." Our observations of police practices show that *white as well as Negro youths* are often harassed in this way.

Frequently the policeman may leave the car and threaten or force youths to move on. For example, one summer evening as the scout car cruised a busy street of a white slum, the patrolmen observed three white boys and a girl on a corner. When told to move on, they mumbled and grumbled in undertones, angering the police by their failure to comply. As they slowly moved off, the officers pushed them along the street. Suddenly one of the white patrolmen took a lighted cigarette from a 15-year-old boy and stuck it in his face, pushing him forward as he did so. When the youngsters did move on, one policeman remarked to the observer that the girl was "nothing but a whore." Such tactics can only intensify resentment toward the police.

Police harassment is not confined to youth. One in every four adult Negroes in Detroit claims he has been stopped and questioned by the police without good reason. The same proportion claim they have been stopped in their cars. One in five says he has been searched unnecessarily; and one in six says that his car was searched for no good reason. The members of an interracial couple, particularly a Negro man accompanying a white woman, are perhaps the most vulnerable to harassment.

What citizens regard as police brutality many policemen consider necessary for law enforcement. While degrading epithets and abusive language may no longer be considered proper by either police commanders or citizens, they often disagree about other practices related to law enforcement. For example, although many citizens see "stop and question" or "stop and frisk" procedures as harassment, police commanders usually regard them merely as "aggressive prevention" to curb crime.

PHYSICAL FORCE—OR SELF-DEFENSE?

The nub of the police-brutality issue seems to lie in police use of physical force. By law, the police have the right to use such force if necessary to make an arrest, to keep the peace, or to maintain public order. But just how much force is necessary or proper?

This was the crucial problem we attempted to answer by placing observers in the patrol cars and in the precincts. Our 36 observers, divided equally between Chicago, Boston, and Washington, were responsible for reporting the details of all situations

where police used physical force against a citizen. To ensure the observation of a large number of encounters, two high-crime police precincts were monitored in Boston and Chicago; four in Washington. At least one precinct was composed of primarily Negro residents, another primarily of whites. Where possible, we also tried to select precincts with considerable variation in social-class composition. Given the criterion of a high crime rate, however, people of low socioeconomic status predominated in most of the areas surveyed.

The law fails to provide simple rules about what—and how much—force that policemen can properly use. The American Bar Foundation's study *Arrest*, by Wayne La Fave, put the matter rather well, stating that the courts of all states would undoubtedly agree that in making an arrest a policeman should use only that amount of force he reasonably believes necessary. But La Fave also pointed out that there is no agreement on the question of when it is better to let the suspect escape than to employ "deadly" force.

Even in those states where the use of deadly force is limited by law, the kinds of physical force a policeman may use are not clearly defined. No kind of force is categorically denied a policeman, since he is always permitted to use deadly force in self-defense.

This right to protect himself often leads the policeman to argue self-defense whenever he uses force. We found that many policemen, whether or not the facts justify it, regularly follow their use of force with the charge that the citizen was assaulting a policeman or resisting arrest. Our observers also found that some policemen even carry pistols and knives that they have confiscated while searching citizens; they carry them so they may be placed at a scene should it be necessary to establish a case of self-defense.

Of course, not all cases of force involve the use of *unnecessary* force. Each instance of force reported by our observers was examined and judged to be either necessary or unnecessary. Cases involving simple restraint—holding a man by the arm—were deliberately excluded from consideration, even though a policeman's right to do so can, in many instances, be challenged. In judging when police force is "unwarranted," "unreasonable," or "undue," we rather deliberately selected only those cases in which a policeman struck the citizen with his hands, fist, feet, or body, or where he used a weapon of some kind—such as a nightstick or a pistol. In these cases, had the policeman been found to have used physical force improperly, he could have been arrested on complaint and, like any other citizen, charged with a simple or aggravated assault. A physical assault on a citizen was judged to be "improper" or "unnecessary" only if force was used in one or more of the following ways:

- If a policeman physically assaulted a citizen and then failed to make an arrest; proper use involves an arrest.
- If the citizen being arrested did not, by word or deed, resist the policeman; force should be used only if it is necessary to make the arrest.
- If the policeman, even though there was resistance to the arrest, could easily have restrained the citizen in other ways.
- If a large number of policemen were present and could have assisted in subduing the citizen in the station, in lockup, and in the interrogation rooms.
- If an offender was handcuffed and made no attempt to flee or offer violent resistance.
- If the citizen resisted arrest, but the use of force continued even after the citizen was subdued.

In the seven-week period, we found 37 cases in which force was used improperly. In all, 44 citizens had been assaulted. In 15 of these cases, no one was arrested. Of these, 8 had offered no verbal or physical resistance whatsoever, while 7 had.

An arrest was made in 22 of the cases. In 13, force was exercised in the station house when at least four other policemen were present. In two cases, there was no verbal or physical resistance to the arrest, but force was still applied. In two other cases, the police applied force to a handcuffed offender in a field setting. And in five situations, the offender did resist arrest, but the policeman continued to use force even after he had been subdued.

Just how serious was the improper use of force in these 44 cases? Naturally there were differences in degree of injury. In about one-half of the cases, the citizens appeared little more than physically bruised; in three cases, the amount of force was so great that the citizen had to be hospitalized. Despite the fact that cases can easily be selected for their dramatic rather than their representative quality, I want to present a few to give a sense of what the observers saw and reported as undue use of force.

OBSERVING ON PATROL

In the following two cases, the citizens offered no physical or verbal resistance, and the two white policemen made no arrest. It is the only instance in which the observers saw the same two policemen using force improperly more than once.

The police precinct in which these incidents occurred is typical of those found in some of our larger cities, where the patrolmen move routinely from gold coast to slum. There are little islands of the rich and poor, of old Americans and new, of recent migrants and old settlers. One moves from high-rise areas of middle- and upper-income whites through an area of the really old Americans—Indians—to an enclave of the recently arrived. The recently arrived are primarily those the policemen call "hillbillies" (migrants from Kentucky and Tennessee) and "porkchops" (Puerto Ricans). There are ethnic islands of Germans and Swedes. Although there is a small area where Negroes live, it is principally a precinct of whites. The police in the district are, with one exception, white.

On a Friday in the middle of July, the observer arrived for the 4 to 12 midnight watch. The beat car that had been randomly chosen carried two white patrolmen—one with 14 years of experience in the precinct, the other with three.

The watch began rather routinely as the policemen cruised the district. Their first radio dispatch came at about 5:30 P.M. They were told to investigate two drunks in a cemetery. On arriving they found two white men "sleeping it off." Without questioning the men, the older policeman began to search one of them, ripping his shirt and hitting him in the groin with a nightstick. The younger policeman, as he searched the second, ripped away the seat of his trousers, exposing his buttocks. The policemen then prodded the men toward the cemetery fence and forced them to climb it, laughing at the plight of the drunk with the exposed buttocks. As the drunks went over the fence, one policeman shouted, "I ought to run you fuckers in!" The other remarked to the observer, "Those assholes won't be back; a bunch of shitty winos."

Not long after they returned to their car, the policemen stopped a woman who had made a left turn improperly. She was treated very politely, and the younger policeman, who wrote the ticket, later commented to the observer, "Nice lady." At 7:30 they were dispatched to check a suspicious auto. After a quick check, the car was marked abandoned.

Shortly after a 30-minute break for a 7:30 "lunch," the two policemen received a dispatch to take a burglary report. Arriving at a slum walkup, the police entered a room where an obviously drunk white man in his late 40s insisted that someone had entered and stolen his food and liquor. He kept insisting that it had been taken and that he had been forced to borrow money to buy beer. The younger policeman, who took the report, kept harassing the man, alternating between mocking and badgering him with rhetorical questions. "You say your name is Half-A-Wit [for Hathaway]? Do you sleep with niggers? How did you vote on the bond issue? Are you sure that's all that's missing? Are you a virgin yet?" The man responded to all of this with the seeming vagueness and joviality of the intoxicated, expressing gratitude for the policemen's help as they left. The older policeman remarked to the observer as they left, "Ain't drunks funny?"

For the next hour little happened, but as the two were moving across the precinct shortly after 10 P.M., a white man and a woman in their 50s flagged them down. Since they were obviously "substantial" middle-class citizens of the district, the policemen listened to their complaints that a Negro man was causing trouble inside the public-transport station from which they had just emerged. The woman said that he had sworn at her. The older policeman remarked, "What's a nigger doing up here? He should be down on Franklin Road!"

With that, they ran into the station and grabbed the Negro man who was inside. Without questioning

him, they shoved him into a phone booth and began beating him with their fists and a flashlight. They also hit him in the groin. Then they dragged him out and kept him on his knees. He pleaded that he had just been released from a mental hospital that day and, begging not to be hit again, asked them to let him return to the hospital. One policeman said: "Don't you like us, nigger? I like to beat niggers and rip out their eyes." They took him outside to their patrol car. Then they decided to put him on a bus, telling him that he was returning to the hospital; they deliberately put him on a bus going in the opposite direction. Just before the Negro boarded the bus, he said, "You police just like to shoot and beat people." The first policeman replied, "Get moving, nigger, or I'll shoot you." The man was crying and bleeding as he was put on the bus. Leaving the scene, the younger policeman commented, "He won't be back."

For the rest of the evening, the two policemen kept looking for drunks and harassing any they found. They concluded the evening by being dispatched to an address where, they were told, a man was being held for the police. No one answered their knock. They left.

The station house has long been suspected of harboring questionable police practices. Interrogation-room procedures have been attacked, particularly because of the methods the police have used to get confessions. The drama of the confession in the interrogation room has been complete with bright lights and physical torture. Whether or not such practices have ever existed on the scale suggested by popular accounts, confessions in recent years, even by accounts of offenders, have rarely been accompanied by such high drama. But recently the interrogation room has come under fire again for its failure to protect the constitutional rights of the suspect to remain silent and to have legal counsel.

BACKSTAGE AT THE STATION

The police station, however, is more than just a series of cubicles called interrogation rooms. There are other rooms and usually a lockup as well. Many of these are also hidden from public view. It is not surprising, then, that one-third of all the observations of the undue use of force occurred within the station.

In any station there normally are several policemen present who should be able to deal with almost any situation requiring force that arises. In many of the situations that were observed, as many as seven and eight policemen were present, most of whom simply stood by and watched force being used. The custom among policemen, it appeared, is that you intervene only if a fellow policeman needs help, or if you have been personally offended or affronted by those involved.

Force is used unnecessarily at many different points and places in the station. The citizen who is not cooperative during the booking process may be pushed or shoved, have his handcuffs twisted with a nightstick, have his foot stomped, or be pulled by the hair. All of these practices were reported by policemen as ways of obtaining "cooperation." But it was clear that the booking could have been completed without any of this harassment.

The lockup was the scene of some of the most severe applications of force. Two of the three cases requiring hospitalization came about when an offender was "worked over" in the lockup. To be sure, the arrested are not always cooperative when they get in the lockup, and force may be necessary to place them in a cell. But the amount of force observed hardly seemed necessary.

One evening an observer was present in the lockup when two white policemen came in with a white man. The suspect had been handcuffed and brought to the station because he had proved obstreperous after being arrested for a traffic violation. Apparently he had been drinking. While waiting in the lockup, the man began to urinate on the floor. In response, the policemen began to beat the man. They jumped him, knocked him down, and beat his head against the concrete floor. He required emergency treatment at a nearby hospital.

At times a policeman may be involved in a kind of escalation of force. Using force appropriately for an arrest in the field seemingly sets the stage for its later use, improperly, in the station. The following case illustrates how such a situation may develop:

Within a large city's high-crime rate precinct,

occupied mostly by Negroes, the police responded to an "officer in trouble" call. It is difficult to imagine a call that brings a more immediate response, so a large number of police cars immediately converged at an intersection of a busy public street where a bus had been stopped. Near the bus, a white policeman was holding two young Negroes at gun point. The policeman reported that he had responded to a summons from the white bus-driver complaining that the boys had refused to pay their fares and had used obscene language. The policeman also reported that the boys swore at him, and one swung at him while the other drew a screwdriver and started toward him. At that point, he said, he drew his pistol.

The policeman placed one of the offenders in handcuffs and began to transport both of them to the station. While driving to the station, the driver of one car noted that the other policeman, transporting the other boy, was struggling with him. The first policeman stopped and entered the other patrol car. The observer reported that he kept hitting the boy who was handcuffed until the boy appeared completely subdued. The boy kept saying, "You don't have any right to beat me. I don't care if you kill me."

After the policemen got the offenders to the station, although the boys no longer resisted them, the police began to beat them while they were handcuffed in an interrogation room. One of the boys hollered: "You can't beat me like this! I'm only a kid, and my hands are tied." Later one of the policemen commented to the observer: "On the street you can't beat them. But when you get to the station, you can instill some respect in them."

Cases where the offender resists an arrest provide perhaps the most difficulty in judging the legitimacy of the force applied. An encounter that began as a dispatch to a disturbance at a private residence was one case about which there could be honest difference in judgment. On arrival, the policemen—one white, the other Negro—met a white woman who claimed that her husband, who was in the back yard and drunk, had beaten her. She asked the policemen to "take him in." The observer reported that the police found the man in the house. When they attempted to take him, he resisted by placing his hands between the doorjamb. Both policemen then grabbed him. The Negro policeman said, "We're going to have trouble, so let's finish it right here." He grabbed the offender and knocked him down. Both policemen then wrestled with the man, handcuffed him, and took him to the station. As they did so, one of the policemen remarked, "These sons of bitches want to fight, so you have to break them quick."

A MINIMAL PICTURE?

The reader, as well as most police administrators, may be skeptical about reports that policemen used force in the presence of observers. Indeed, one police administrator, indignant over reports of undue use of force in his department, seemed more concerned that the policemen had permitted themselves to be observed behaving improperly than he was about their improper behavior. When demanding to know the names of the policemen who had used force improperly so he could discharge them—a demand we could not meet, since we were bound to protect our sources of information—he remarked, "Any officer who is stupid enough to behave that way in the presence of outsiders deserves to be fired."

There were and are a number of reasons why our observers were able to see policemen behaving improperly. We entered each department with the full cooperation of the top administrators. So far as the men in the line were concerned, our chief interest was in how citizens behave toward police, a main object of our study. Many policemen, given their strong feelings against citizens, fail to see that their own behavior is equally open to observation. Furthermore, our observers are trained to fit into a role of trust—one that is genuine, since most observers are actually sympathetic to the plight of the policeman, if not to his behavior.

Finally, and this is a fact all too easily forgotten, people cannot change their behavior in the presence of others as easily as many think. This is particularly true when people become deeply involved in certain situations. The policeman not only comes to "trust" the observer in the law-enforcement situation —regarding him as a source of additional help if necessary—but, when he becomes involved in a dispute with a citizen, he easily forgets that an observer is present. Partly because he does not know what else to do, in such situations the policeman behaves "normally." But should one cling to the notion that most policemen modify their behavior in the presence of outsiders, one is left with the uncomfortable conclusion that our cases represent a minimal picture of actual misbehavior.

Superficially it might seem that the use of an excessive amount of force against citizens is low. In only 37 of 3826 encounters observed did the police use undue force. Of the 4604 white citizens in these encounters, 27 experienced an excessive amount of force—a rate of 5.9 for every 1000 citizens involved. The comparable rate for 5960 Negroes, of whom 17 experienced an excessive amount of force, is 2.8. Thus, whether one considers these rates high or low, the fact is that the *rate of excessive force for all white citizens in encounters with the police is twice that for Negro citizens*.

A rate depends, however, upon selecting a population that is logically the target of force. What we have just given is a rate for *all* citizens involved in encounters with the police. But many of these citizens are not logical targets of force. Many, for example, simply call the police to complain about crimes against themselves or their property. And others are merely witnesses to crimes.

The more logical target population consists of citizens whom the police allege to be offenders—a population of suspects. In our study, there were 643 white suspects, 27 of whom experienced undue use of force. This yields an abuse rate of 41.9 per 1000 white suspects. The comparable rate for 751 Negro suspects, of whom 17 experienced undue use of force, is 22.6 per 1000. If one accepts these rates as reasonably reliable estimates of the undue force against suspects, then there should be little doubt that in major metropolitan areas the sort of behavior commonly called "police brutality" is far from rare.

Popular impression casts police brutality as a racial matter—white police mistreating Negro citizens. The fact is that white suspects are more liable to being treated improperly by the police than Negro suspects are. This, however, should not be confused with the chances a citizen takes of being mistreated.

In two of the cities we studied, Negroes are a minority. The chances, then, that any Negro has of being treated improperly are, perhaps, more nearly comparable to that for whites. If the rates are comparable, then one might say that the application of force unnecessarily by the police operates without respect to the race of an offender.

Many people believe that the race of the policeman must affect his use of force, particularly since many white policemen express prejudice against Negroes. Our own work shows that in the police precincts made up largely of Negro citizens, over three-fourths of the policemen express prejudice against Negroes. Only 1 percent express sympathetic attitudes. But as sociologists and social psychologists have often shown, prejudice and attitudes do not necessarily carry over into discriminatory actions.

Our findings show that there is little difference between the rate of force used by white and by Negro policemen. Of the 54 policemen observed using too much force, 45 were white and 9 were Negro. For every 100 white policemen, 8.7 will use force; for every 100 Negro policemen, 9.8 will. What this really means, though, is that about one in every 10 policemen in high-crime rate areas of cities sometimes uses force unnecessarily.

Yet, one may ask, doesn't prejudice enter into the use of force? Didn't some of the policemen who were observed utter prejudiced statements toward Negroes and other minority-group members? Of course they did. But the question of whether it was their prejudice or some other factor that motivated them to mistreat Negroes is not so easily answered.

Still, even though our figures show that a white suspect is more liable to encounter violence, one may ask whether white policemen victimize Negroes more than whites. We found, for the most part, that they do not. Policemen, both Negro and white, are most likely to exercise force against members of their *own* race:

- 67 percent of the citizens victimized by white policemen were white.
- 71 percent of the citizens victimized by Negro policemen were Negro.

To interpret these statistics correctly, however, one should take into account the differences in opportunity policemen have to use force against members of their own and other races. Negro policemen, in the three cities we studied, were far *less* likely to police white citizens than white policemen were to police Negroes. Negro policemen usually policed other Negroes, while white policemen policed both whites and Negroes about equally. In total numbers, then, more white policemen than Negro policemen used force against Negroes. But this is explained by the fact that whites make up 85 percent of the police force, and more than 50 percent of all policemen policing Negroes.

Though no precise estimates are possible, the facts just given suggest that white policemen, even though they are prejudiced toward Negroes, do not discriminate against Negroes in the excessive use of force. The use of force by the police is more readily explained by police culture than it is by the policeman's race. Indeed, in the few cases where we observed a Negro policeman using unnecessary force against white citizens, there was no evidence that he did so because of his race.

The disparity between our findings and the public's sense that Negroes are the main victims of police brutality can easily be resolved if one asks how the public becomes aware of the police misusing force.

THE VICTIMS AND THE TURF

Fifty years ago, the immigrants to our cities—Eastern and Southern Europeans such as the Poles and the Italians—complained about police brutality. Today the new immigrants to our cities—mostly Negroes from the rural South—raise their voices through the civil rights movement, through black-nationalist and other race-conscious organizations. There is no comparable voice for white citizens since, except for the Puerto Ricans, they now lack the nationality organizations that were once formed to promote and protect the interests of their immigrant forebears.

Although policemen do not seem to select their victims according to race, two facts stand out. All victims were offenders, and all were from the lower class. Concentrating as we did on high-crime rate areas of cities, we do not have a representative sample of residents in any city. Nonetheless, we observed a sizable minority of middle- and upper-status citizens, some of whom were offenders. But since no middle- or upper-class offender, white or Negro, was the victim of an excessive amount of force, it appears that the lower class bears the brunt of victimization by the police.

The most likely victim of excessive force is a lower-class man of either race. No white woman and only two Negro women were victimized. The difference between the risk assumed by white and by Negro women can be accounted for by the fact that far more Negro women are processed as suspects or offenders.

Whether or not a policeman uses force unnecessarily depends upon the social setting in which the encounter takes place. Of the 37 instances of excessive force, 37 percent took place in police-controlled settings, such as the patrol car or the precinct station. Public places, usually streets, accounted for 41 percent, and 16 percent took place in a private residence. The remaining 6 percent occurred in commercial settings. This is not, of course, a random sample of settings where the police encounter suspects.

What is most obvious, and most disturbing, is that the police are very likely to use force in settings that they control. Although only 18 percent of all situations involving suspects ever ended up at the station house, 32 percent of all situations where an excessive amount of force was used took place in the police station.

No one who accepts the fact that the police sometimes use an excessive amount of force should be surprised by our finding that they often select their own turf. What should be apparent to the nation's police administrators, however, is that these settings are under their command and control. Controlling the police in the field, where the patrolman is away from direct supervision, is understandably difficult. But the station house is the police administrator's domain. The fact that one in three instances of excessive force took place in settings that can be directly controlled should cause concern among police officials.

The presence of citizens who might serve as witnesses against a policeman should deter him from undue use of force. Indeed, procedures for the review of police conduct are based on the presumption that one can get this kind of testimony. Otherwise, one is left simply with a citizen complaint and contrary testimony by the policeman—a situation in which it is very difficult to prove the citizen's allegation.

In most situations involving the use of excessive force, there were witnesses. In our 37 cases, there were bystanders present three-fourths of the time. But in only one situation did the group present sympathize with the citizen and threaten to report the policeman. A complaint was filed on that incident —the only one of the 37 observed instances of undue force in which a formal complaint was filed.

All in all, the situations where excessive force was used were devoid of bystanders who did not have a stake in being "against" the offender. Generally, they were fellow policemen, or fellow offenders whose truthfulness could be easily challenged. When a policeman uses undue force, then, he usually does not risk a complaint against himself or testimony from witnesses who favor the complainant against the policeman. This, as much as anything, probably accounts for the low rate of formal complaints against policemen who use force unnecessarily.

A striking fact is that in more than one-half of all instances of undue coercion, at least one other policeman was present who did not participate in the use of force. This shows that, for the most part, the police do not restrain their fellow policemen. On the contrary, there were times when their very presence encouraged the use of force. One man brought into the lockup for threatening a policeman with a pistol was so severely beaten by this policeman that he required hospitalization. During the beating, some fellow policemen propped the man up, while others shouted encouragement. Though the official police code does not legitimate this practice, police culture does.

VICTIMS—DEFIANT OR DEVIANT

Now, are there characteristics of the offender or his behavior that precipitate the use of excessive force by the police? Superficially, yes. Almost one-half of the cases involved open defiance of police authority (39 percent) or resisting arrest (9 percent). Open defiance of police authority, however, is what the policeman defines as *his* authority, not necessarily "official" authority. Indeed in 40 percent of the cases that the police considered open defiance, the policeman never executed an arrest—a somewhat surprising fact for those who assume that policemen generally "cover" improper use of force with a "bona fide" arrest and a charge of resisting arrest.

But it is still of interest to know what a policeman *sees* as defiance. Often he seems threatened by a simple refusal to acquiesce to his own authority. A policeman beat a handcuffed offender because, when told to sit, the offender did not sit down. One Negro woman was soundly slapped for her refusal to approach the police car and identify herself.

Important as a threat to his authority may appear to the policeman, there were many more of these instances in which the policeman did *not* respond with the use of force. The important issue seems to be whether the policeman manages to assert his authority despite the threat to it. I suspect that policemen are more likely to respond with excessive force when they define the situation as one in which there remains a question as to who is "in charge."

Similarly, some evidence indicates that harassment of deviants plays a role in the undue use of force. Incidents involving drunks made up 27 percent of all incidents of improper use of force; an additional 5 percent involved homosexuals or narcotics users. Since deviants generally remain silent victims to avoid public exposure of their deviance, they are particularly susceptible to the use of excessive force.

It is clear, though, that the police encounter many situations involving deviants where no force is used. Generally they respond to them routinely. What is surprising, then, is that the police do not mistreat deviants more than they do. The explanation may lie in the kind of relationships the police have with deviants. Many are valuable to the police because they serve as informers. To mistreat them severely would be to cut off a major source of police intelligence. At the same time, deviants are easily controlled by harassment.

Clearly, we have seen that police mistreatment of citizens exists. Is it, however, on the increase?

Citizen complaints against the police are common, and allegations that the police use force improperly are frequent. There is evidence that physical brutality exists today. But there is also evidence, from the history of our cities, that the police have long engaged in the use of unnecessary physical force. No one can say with confidence whether there is more or less of it today than there was at the turn of the century.

What we lack is evidence that would permit us to calculate comparative rates of police misuse of force for different periods of American history. Only recently have we begun to count and report the volume of complaints against the police. And the research reported in this article represents the only attempt to estimate the amount of police mistreatment by actual observation of what the police do to citizens.

LACK OF INFORMATION

Police chiefs are notoriously reluctant to disclose information that would allow us to assess the nature and volume of complaints against the police. Only a few departments have begun to report something about citizen complaints. And these give us very little information.

Consider, for example, the 1966 Annual Report released by the New Orleans Police Department. It tells us that there were 208 cases of "alleged police misconduct on which action was taken." It fails to tell us whether there were any allegations that are *not* included among these cases. Are these all the allegations that came to the attention of the department? Or are they only those the department chose to review as "police disciplinary matters"? Of the 208 cases the department considered "disciplinary matters," the report tells us that no disciplinary action was taken in 106 cases. There were 11 cases that resulted in 14 dismissals; 56 cases that resulted in 72 suspensions, fines, or loss of days; and 35 cases involving 52 written or verbal "reprimands" or "cautionings."

The failure of the report to tell us the charge against the policeman is a significant omission. We cannot tell how many of these allegations involved improper use of force, how many involved verbal abuse or harassment, how many involved police felonies or misdemeanors, and so on. In such reports, the defensive posture of the nation's police departments is all too apparent. Although the 1966 report of the New Orleans Police Department tells us much about what the police allege were the felonies and misdemeanors by citizens of New Orleans, it tells us nothing about what citizens allege was misconduct by the police!

Many responsible people believe that the use of physical brutality by the police is on the wane. They point to the fact that, at least outside the South, there are more reports of other forms of police mistreatment of citizens than reports of undue physical coercion. They also suggest that third-degree interrogations and curbstone justice with the nightstick are less common. It does not seem unreasonable, then, to assume that police practices that degrade a citizen's status or that harass him and restrict his freedom are more common than police misuse of force. But that may have always been so.

Whether or not the policeman's "sense of justice" and his use of unnecessary force have changed remains an open question. Forms may change while practices go on. To move misuse from the street to the station house, or from the interrogation room to the lockup, changes the place but not the practice itself.

Our ignorance of just what goes on between police and citizens poses one of the central issues in policing today: How can we make the police accountable to the citizenry in a democratic society and yet not hamstring them in their legitimate pursuit of law and order? There are no simple answers.

Police departments are organizations that process people. All people-processing organizations face certain common problems. But the police administrator faces a problem in controlling practice with clients that is not found in most other organizations. The problem is that police contact with citizens occurs in the community, where direct supervision is not possible. Assuming our unwillingness to spend resources for almost one-to-one supervision, the problem for the police commander is to make policemen behave properly when they are not under direct supervision. He also faces the problem of making them behave properly in the station house as well.

Historically, we have found but one way—apart from supervision—that deals with this problem. That solution is professionalization of workers. Perhaps only through the professionalization of the police can we hope to solve the problem of police malpractice.

But lest anyone optimistically assume that professionalization will eliminate police malpractice altogether, we should keep in mind that problems of malpractice also occur regularly in both law and medicine.

Prosecution

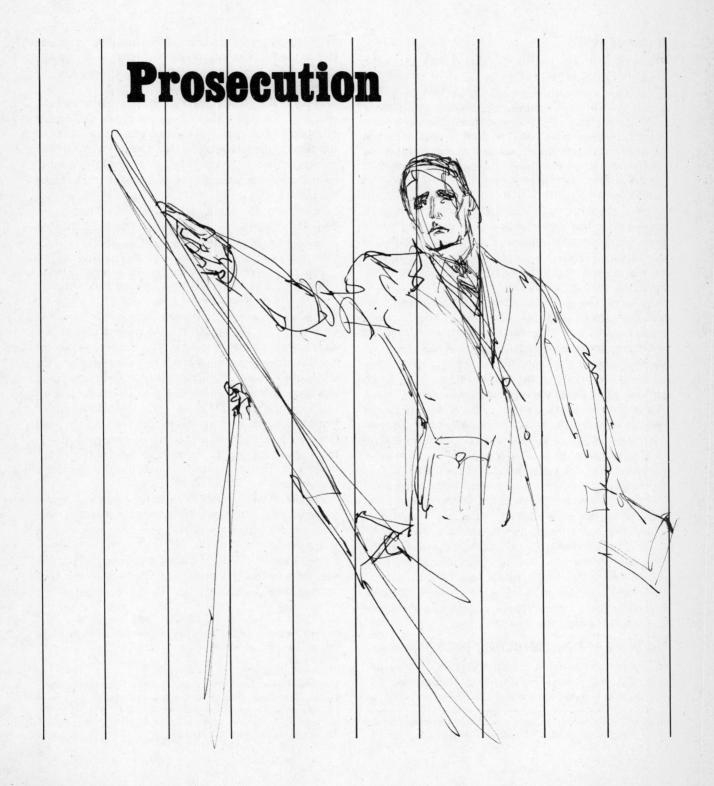

PART 3   THE SOCIAL ORGANIZATION OF CRIMINAL LAW ENFORCEMENT

INTRODUCTION

The typical situation surrounding criminal prosecution is characterized by Wayne LaFave as

> one in which the police make an arrest without a warrant and then bring the suspect to the prosecutor with a request that he approve the issuance of a warrant. The decision to arrest is clearly made by the police. The decision as to whether to charge the suspect and the selection of the charge are the responsibility of the prosecutor. The prosecutor's charging decision is manifested by his approval or refusal of the issuance of the warrant.*

For an offense to move from arrest to consideration by a court it must pass through intermediary processing by the prosecutor's office. At this stage of the legal process it is determined in which of essentially three possible ways the case is to move from arrest to court proceedings: indictment, information, or complaint.

In general, all three possibilities hinge on prosecutorial willingness to proceed. An indictment is a finding by a grand jury that there is probable cause to believe that the accused committed the crime charged. Since there is no defense before a grand jury, the grand jury considers only the evidence presented by the prosecutor. It is a rare grand jury that defies the prosecutor. An information is a charge of criminal offense filed by the prosecutor on the basis of his own determination of probable cause. A complaint by a citizen charging a man of criminal offense in most states cannot be heard in court, but must be made to the prosecutor. The prosecutor stands astride the criminal process, controlling the gates that lead to the trial court.

The articulated norms for police conduct require the police to enforce every violation of the law. Judges, too, formally are not in the position to dismiss a charge, or, if the accused is proven guilty, to find the accused not guilty, although they are given vast powers of discretion in the choice of sentence. Of the three principal actors in a criminal prosecution, the prosecutor alone is formally to decide whether or not to enforce the law, and the degree of crime with which to charge the offender.

THE SCOPE OF THE PROSECUTOR'S DISCRETION

In England, the power of prosecuting criminal cases was originally, and remains in theory today, largely lodged in the hands of private persons, who are not compelled by law to initiate such prosecutions.* When initiated, the action still resembles a private lawsuit between private parties rather than a prosecution initiated and carried on by the sovereign power.

In the United States, the office of the public prosecutor was grafted on the traditional system of private criminal litigation.† The public prosecutor thus assimilated the functions of the private prosecutor, and just as the private prosecutor had discretion whether or not to prosecute, so the public prosecutor was endowed with the same discretion.

In actuality, the prosecutor's discretion is almost unlimited. As the court said in Brack v. Wells,** a Maryland case,

> As a general rule, whether the State's Attorney does or does not institute a particular prosecution is a matter which rests in his discretion. Unless the discretion is grossly abused or such duty is compelled by statute or there is a clear showing that such duty exists, mandamus will not lie.

That is, a court will not issue a writ compelling the prosecutor to prosecute. It is true that if the power to prosecute is used in a discriminatory manner, its use may be enjoined,‡ but that is nearly the only grounds for interference with the prosecutor's discretion. Occasionally, a court has removed a prosecutor from office for failing to prosecute manifest and flagrant violations of crime within the court's jurisdiction.‡‡ However, such occasions have been rare. In practice, the prosecutor's decision to initiate a prosecution, and the degree of crime to be charged, lie entirely in his discretion. That discretion is, for all practical purposes, unreviewable.

His discretion is almost as broad if he wants to decline to prosecute a charge already laid. In some states, there are no limits placed upon the prosecutor's discretion to stop a prosecution in *media res*. In most states, however, a small element of judicial control is inserted into the process by permitting the prosecutor to initiate prosecution, but requiring judicial approval for a withdrawal of the

---

*Wayne R. LaFave, *Arrest: The Decision to Take a Suspect into Custody,* Boston: Little, Brown, 1965, p. 53. Reprinted by permission.

---

*Howard Pendleton, *Criminal Justice in England: A Study in Law Administration,* New York: Macmillan, 1931, p. 3.

†*Ibid.,* p. 5.

**184 Md. 86, 40 A 2d 319 (1944).

‡Wayne R. LaFave, *Arrest: The Decision to Take a Suspect into Custody,* Boston: Little, Brown, 1965, p. 8. Reprinted by permission.

‡‡*State ex rel. McKittrick v. Graves,* 346 Mo. 990, 144 S.W. 2d 91 (1940); see also *State v. Winnem,* 12 N.J. 152, 96 A 2d 63 (1953); *Wilbur v. Howard,* 70 F. Supp. 930 (E. D. Ky 1947).

PART 3 THE SOCIAL ORGANIZATION OF CRIMINAL LAW ENFORCEMENT

charges.* In fact, however, as in the case of the decision to prosecute, "the prosecutor's discretion in the use of *nol pros* (*nolle prosequi,* or decision not to prosecute) is an enormous power in the hands of one public official. Its use is generally not subject to publicity and public scrutiny . . ."†

The scope of the prosecutor's discretion to prosecute or not to do so can be easily justified. Even assuming the desirability of full enforcement of the law, somebody must make preliminary decisions concerning the probability of success of a prosecution—to decide whether the evidence is sufficient for conviction or whether the facts as claimed fall within or without a rule of law. Moreover, there are numerous cases in which considerations individual to a defendant suggest that invocation of the awful machinery of the criminal law is unnecessary or undesirable:

> There are many legitimate reasons for a prosecutor's failure to prosecute: where the alleged criminal act may be the result of some quarrel between neighbours and all parties are equally at fault; where the alleged criminal act may be the result of some minor domestic dispute; where an overzealous creditor may be attempting to pervert the criminal process for the purpose of collecting a civil debt; where the expense of extradition might not justify the spending of public funds to bring back a person accused of a petty crime; where a person may have committed a technical violation of the law, and a warning may be sufficient to prevent further infractions; where the evidence is so slim that it would be unfair to subject a person to the ordeal and notoriety of a prosecution—these are some of the considerations that a prosecutor must weigh before proceeding in any particular case.**

In fact, as might be predicted, the decision to prosecute at all tends to be a function of the sorts of pressure to which the prosecutor is subject. That white collar crime is treated with exceptional leniency by prosecutors has been often documented. They are crimes that frequently do not carry deep social stigmas, and hence the prosecutor rarely feels much animus toward the criminals. His values not being involved, it is easy for him to agree not to prosecute, and to leave to civil action or to the noncriminal action of a regulatory agency, the sanctioning of the individuals involved. Ferdinand Lundberg writes:

In the case of white-collar crimes of corporations, if any individual is punished (usually none is) it is only one or very few. The authorities do not dig pertinaciously with a view to ferreting out every last person who had anything to do with the case. But . . . it is different with crimes of the lower classes. In kidnapping, for example, the FBI, in addition to seizing the kidnappers, flushes to the surface anyone who (1) rented them quarters to conceal the kidnapped person or to hide in; (2) acted as unwitting agents for them in conveying messages or collecting ransom; (3) transported them; (4) in any way innocently gave aid and assistance; or (5) was a witness to any of these separate acts. The government men do such a splendid job that almost everyone except the obstetricians who brought the various parties into the world are brought to bar, where the aroused judge "breaks the book over their heads" in the course of sentencing.*

The following report of a sociologist recalling an experience when he worked as a cub newspaper reporter in a wealthy Eastern suburb illustrates the more blatant ways in which the legal system cooperates with influential members of the elite to cover up their involvements in crime.†

In 1957, I worked as a cub reporter for a Long Island 'family' newspaper, part of a large chain of papers and T.V. stations across the country. I was 20, idealistic about journalism, proud to be the weekend police reporter for all of Nassau and Suffolk counties. Old hands on the police beat for other competing papers made it a practice to call three central police information centers every few hours, then put $3.50 on their expense vouchers from the 35 stations they were suppose to have called. Dutifully, I kept on calling all 35 stations every two hours, randomly varying the order in which I went down the list each time.

This Sunday morning, just out of bed, I called the 'Clam Cove' station, second on the list. Journalistically absurd, since nothing ever happened on the 'North Shore Gold Coast,' the precinct contained nothing but vast multi-million dollar estates, and the station consisted of two men in a little booth and one squad car. I dialed, but the phone never rang at the other end. The officer had apparently just picked it up himself, and in confusion, assumed he had gotten the number he intended to dial. He was talking to me, yelling, in fact, about a murder at the "X" family estate, and telling me to get the chief of detectives out of bed, get a doctor, and get the hell over there. He thought he was talking to the county detective bureau. I finally broke in to

---

*See Note, "Prosecutor's Discretion," *University of Pennsylvania Law Review,* vol. 103, 1955, p. 1057.
†*Ibid.,* p. 1071.
**Douglas B. Wright, "Duties of a Prosecutor," *Connecticut Bar Journal,* vol. 33, 1959, p. 293. Reprinted by permission.

*Ferdinand Lundberg, *The Rich and the Super-Rich: A Study in the Power of Money Today,* New York: Lyle Stuart, 1968, p. 135. Reprinted by permission.
†Howard Boughie, "Cub Reporter," written for this volume.

introduce myself as a reporter, and after a long silence, he said simply, "Get the fuck off this phone!" and hung up.

I drove at 95 m.p.h. all the way to the "X" estate, but it still took me 20 minutes from the time of the phone call. When I got there, I wondered what was taking the detective so long. Their headquarters was only five minutes away. In the post-dawn mist, a white pillared mansion sat primly on a three-acre carpet of manicured grass. Next to it I saw the squad car from 'Clam Cove,' and then the officer, talking to a man in bare feet and pyjamas on the lawn.

He turned out to be a night watchman for a warehouse full of movie equipment stored on the estate grounds. I walked toward them and heard him say to the cop, wearily, as if he were repeating himself for the ninth time, while the cop wrote it on a note-pad, 'I heard a loud noise like a shot—it woke me up—then there was about ten, maybe fifteen seconds, then there was another shot. Then this screaming and crying and when I got to the door. . . .'

At this point I was moving quietly to my right, toward the open door of the mansion. I got to within fifteen feet of the door and I could hear a woman sobbing, and then her anguished voice, 'I killed him, O God, I killed him.' I looked inside. There was a tiled corridor, lit mainly by a yellow glow from an open bed-room door on the left. On the floor was a woman in a sequined white evening gown lying on something in a pool of blood. Then I could see that she was lying on the naked body of a man, the top half of which, from the shoulders up, was completely red and somehow distorted in shape. There was a big double-barrelled rifle on the floor just inside the bedroom doorway on the right of the corridor.

Sirens behind me jerked me around. Six sheriff's department station wagons roared into the entrance drive in the line. By my watch, it had taken them 28 minutes to get there. Detectives and sheriff's officers ran from their cars into the house, brush-ing right by me. They really looked like they knew just what to do. One cop picked up the woman and carried her into the bedroom on the right, her evening gown dripping with blood. A detective went in with a screwdriver, and soon two cops came out with the door from the left-hand bedroom. It had little holes in it at about shoulder level, and some blood spatters. The detectives with the screwdriver then knelt next to the body of the man, and pried up a piece of floor tile. It had holes in it, too.

Two more cars arrived, somebody yelled, 'Get the doctor in here,' and a man with a medical bag went inside the bedroom on the right. In the other car, I recognized a friend of mine, a freelance news photographer. He saw me, I pulled him aside, and said, 'The woman's in there with a doctor, let's get a shot. . . .' We ran around to the right side of the house, and the blinds of the bedroom window were open. Inside, the woman lay on top of the bed, wearing a clean white nightgown.

Over the end of the bed hung the bloody evening gown. The doctor was giving her an injection. My photographer friend took a picture, but no sooner had his flash gone off, than two over-coated detectives ran in our direction. I tried to tell them who I was, but they just pushed both of us back across the lawn, told us to get back to our cars. Then one detective grabbed my friend's camera and pulled out the film shot. We retreated and waited in my car for other reporters to arrive.

When they did, I told them everything I'd seen and heard. I was too upset to withhold my information for a 'scoop.' I wanted to know what it all added up to. Old George of the Mirror and Ben of the News were usually cynical and funny about the goriest of situations. I'd never seen them as serious as they were now. George finally said, 'You're going to be either the richest, or the deadest, or the wisest fuckin' cub reporter in the country before this is over.' Then he and Ben began to put it all together for me. Purely hypothetical, they said, and they argued over the likelihood of particular details, but both of them were willing to bet me every cent they had that the story would turn out this way:

They explained that the "X" family was one of the richest on the North Shore. The favourite son was the dead man, and the woman his wife, a racehorse and safari addict. The time lapse between the report to detective headquarters and their arrival on the scene was filled with telephone calls to the old man, and a deal, maybe in millions, had been worked out to protect the family name. The evidence was now being confiscated, the murderess put under sedation, and grounds for a story of acci-dental shooting were being constructed.

'You'll never hear the watchman's story in court,' said George. 'And the floor tile and door full of bullets won't show up either,' said Ben. 'The bloody evening gown never existed. Her story will be she undressed and went to sleep, then shot an intruder while she was groggy.'

'That bitch shot him in the nude as he came toward her bed-room, cool and calm, after she'd waited up all night, she stood right over him and let him have it again, to make sure.'

I didn't believe a word of it. I told my city editor everything I'd seen and heard, and related Ben and George's fantasy. He laughed, but with a slight hesitation. He told me to keep my information for 'color' on the story as it developed through con-ventional news sources. The police reported that a man had been shot in the right shoulder and forehead with an elephant gun. Mrs. "X" had been in a state of complete shock and couldn't be questioned. She was in the hospital under seda-tion. There would be an inquest in five days. The "X"'s had been at a party at the Astors the night before, going home early to retire for the night. No further information was available.

All I could turn up during those five days were the facts that Mrs. "X" was a crack shot, had hunted tigers at night, and that she and her husband had been squabbling for a month, even had a public spat at the Astors that night, and went home in a mutual fury.

At the inquest, Mrs. "X" reported she had gone to sleep, and in the early morning, had heard noises 'like a burglar was in the house.' She woke up, and in the dark hallway saw a strange figure. She grabbed her loaded rifle, which she always kept by her bedroom door because of burglar scares, and both barrels went off before she knew what was happening. As her eyes grew accustomed to the darkness, she saw that she had shot her own husband: At this point she broke down before the judge. The inquest decision was accidental shooting. Case dismissed.

George and Ben had been almost perfectly accurate in their predictions. I had seen the police change Mrs. "X"'s bloodied evening gown, obviously the one she had worn to the Astors, into a clean white nightgown. Why? To substantiate the story that she went to bed and was awakened by sounds, had shot someone in a groggy half sleep. In fact, she probably never went to sleep at all, but sat up arguing or brooding all night until the fatal outcome. I had heard the watchman tell the cop about two shots spaced several seconds apart. Why hadn't he been called to the inquest? And why didn't the bullet-riddled door and floor tile show up as evidence? The only logical conclusion from those two pieces of information would be that Mrs. "X" shot her husband the first time from across the hall, straight on through his shoulder and into the door behind him. Then, several seconds later, she stood above him, and seeing that he still lived, emptied the second barrel through his skull and into the floor.

What was all the fancy police work about the lamp and lamp-table? As they were originally placed, a bright light shone into the hallway from the husband's bedroom, clearly illuminating anyone standing there. Without such a light, the claim could be made that Mrs. "X" fired blindly into the half-dark.

No such substantiation appeared necessary at the inquest. Probably, the altered evidence needed only to be presented to the District Attorney and the Judge. Mrs. "X" was later reported to have inherited a high fortune, including $10,000 a month for support of her two children. She quickly took off for a European grand tour. The chief of the county detectives was seen driving a new Lincoln Continental a few months after the case had ended.

Right after the inquest, I ran to my city editor. What about the sequined evening gown? What about the watchman's testimony about the shots? What about the bullets in the floor tile? What about the light from his bedroom? By now I was screaming at him. He locked his door which was already closed.

'Suppose George and Ben were right,' he said. 'You're the only non-policeman who can testify to those pieces of evidence, right? You're also our weekend police reporter, right? You work with the detectives and cops by day and sometimes by night, right? They all carry guns, right? And you're still alive, right? So obviously you didn't see any of these things, right?'

I couldn't answer. He just led me to the door, and after I was outside, I heard him lock it again.

The systematic exclusion of certain classes of offenders from prosecution and the concomitant selection of others is one of the chief findings of studies of the criminal law.* We have seen earlier how white collar crimes, rapes, middle class delinquency, professional theft, and, in the preceding report, members of the upper class are protected from criminal prosecution. The dynamics of this process are investigated in the article that follows. Abraham Blumberg shows how the organization of the practice of law leads to the cooptation of lawyers and a loss of adequate legal representation for their clients.

---

*See Richard Quinney, *The American Criminal Justice System*, Boston: Little, Brown, 1974.

21

The Practice of Law as Confidence Game:

Organizational Cooptation of a Profession

ABRAHAM S. BLUMBERG

A recurring theme in the growing dialogue between sociology and law has been the great need for a joint effort of the two disciplines to illuminate urgent social and legal issues. Having uttered fervent public pronouncements in this vein, however, the respective practitioners often go their separate ways. Academic spokesmen for the legal profession are somewhat critical of sociologists of law because of what they perceive as the sociologist's preoccupation with the application of theory and methodology to the examination of legal phenomena, without regard to the solution of legal problems. Further, it is felt that "contemporary writing in the sociology of law . . . betrays the existence of painfully unsophisticated notions about the day-to-day operations of courts, legislatures and law offices."[1] Regardless of the merit of such criticism, scant attention—apart from explorations of the legal profession itself—has been given to the sociological examination of legal institutions, or their supporting ideological assumptions. Thus, for example, very little sociological effort is

expended to ascertain the validity and viability of important court decisions, which may rest on wholly erroneous assumptions about the contextual realities of social structure. A particular decision may rest upon a legally impeccable rationale; at the same time it may be rendered nugatory or self-defeating by contingencies imposed by aspects of social reality of which the lawmakers are themselves unaware.

Within this context, I wish to question the impact of three recent landmark decisions of the United States Supreme Court; each hailed as destined to effect profound changes in the future of criminal law administration and enforcement in America. The first of these, *Gideon v. Wainwright*, 372 U. S. 335 (1963) required states and localities henceforth to furnish counsel in the case of indigent persons charged with a felony.[2] The Gideon ruling left several major issues unsettled, among them the vital question: What is the precise point in time at which a suspect is entitled to counsel?[3] The answer came relatively quickly in *Escobedo v. Illinois*, 378 U. S. 478 (1964), which has aroused a storm of controversy. Danny Escobedo confessed to the murder of his brother-in-law after the police had refused to permit retained counsel to see him, although his

Source: "The Practice of Law as Confidence Game: Organizational Cooptation of a Profession," *Law and Society Review*, Vol. 1, June, 1967, pp. 15–39. By permission of the author and publisher.

lawyer was present in the station house and asked to confer with his client. In a 5–4 decision, the court asserted that counsel must be permitted when the process of police investigative effort shifts from merely investigatory to that of accusatory: "when its focus is on the accused and its purpose is to elicit a confession—our adversary system begins to operate, and, under the circumstances here, the accused must be permitted to consult with his lawyer."

As a consequence, Escobedo's confession was rendered inadmissible. The decision triggered a national debate among police, district attorneys, judges, lawyers, and other law enforcement officials, which continues unabated, as to the value and propriety of confessions in criminal cases.[4] On June 13, 1966, the Supreme Court in a 5–4 decision underscored the principle enunciated in *Escobedo* in the case of *Miranda v. Arizona*.[5] Police interrogation of any suspect in custody, without his consent, unless a defense attorney is present, is prohibited by the self-incrimination provision of the Fifth Amendment. Regardless of the relative merit of the various shades of opinion about the role of counsel in criminal cases, the issues generated thereby will be in part resolved as additional cases move toward decision in the Supreme Court in the near future. They are of peripheral interest and not of immediate concern in this paper. However, the *Gideon*, *Escobedo*, and *Miranda* cases pose interesting general questions. In all three decisions, the Supreme Court reiterates the traditional legal conception of a defense lawyer based on the ideological perception of a criminal case as an *adversary, combative* proceeding, in which counsel for the defense assiduously musters all the admittedly limited resources at his command to *defend* the accused.[6] The fundamental question remains to be answered: Does the Supreme Court's conception of the role of counsel in a criminal case square with social reality?

The task of this paper is to furnish some preliminary evidence toward the illumination of that question. Little empirical understanding of the function of defense counsel exists; only some ideologically oriented generalizations and commitments. This paper is based upon observations made by the writer during many years of legal practice in the criminal courts of a large metropolitan area. No claim is made as to its methodological rigor, although it does reflect a conscious and sustained effort for participant observation.

COURT STRUCTURE DEFINES ROLE OF DEFENSE LAWYER

The overwhelming majority of convictions in criminal cases (usually over 90 percent) are not the product of combative, trial-by-jury process at all, but instead merely involve the sentencing of the individual after a negotiated, bargained-for plea of guilty has been entered.[7] Although more recently the overzealous role of police and prosecutors in producing pretrial confessions and admissions has achieved a good deal of notoriety, scant attention has been paid to the organizational structure and personnel of the criminal court itself. Indeed, the extremely high conviction rate produced without the features of an adversary trial in our courts would tend to suggest that the "trial" becomes a perfunctory reiteration and validation of the pretrial interrogation and investigation.[8]

The institutional setting of the court defines a role for the defense counsel in a criminal case radically different from the one traditionally depicted.[9] Sociologists and others have focused their attention on the deprivations and social disabilities of such variables as race, ethnicity, and social class as being the source of an accused person's defeat in a criminal court. Largely overlooked is the variable of the court organization itself, which possesses a thrust, purpose, and direction of its own. It is grounded in pragmatic values, bureaucratic priorities, and administrative instruments. These exalt maximum production and the particularistic career designs of organizational incumbents, whose occupational and career commitments tend to generate a set of priorities. These priorities exert a higher claim than the stated ideological goals of "due process of law," and are often inconsistent with them.

Organizational goals and discipline impose a set of demands and conditions of practice on the respective professions in the criminal court, to which they respond by abandoning their ideological and professional commitments to the accused client, in the service of these higher claims of the court organization. All court personnel, including the accused's own lawyer, tend to be coopted to become agent-mediators[10] who help the accused redefine his situation and restructure his perceptions concomitant with a plea of guilty.

Of all the occupational roles in the court the only private individual who is officially recognized as having a special status and concomitant obligations is the lawyer. His legal status is that of "an officer of the court" and he is held to a standard of ethical performance and duty to his client as well as to the court. This obligation is thought to be far higher than that expected of ordinary individuals occupying the various occupational statuses in the court community. However, lawyers, whether privately retained or of the legal-aid, public defender variety, have close and continuing relations with the prosecuting office and the court itself through discreet relations with the judges via their law secretaries or "confidential" assistants. Indeed, lines of communication, influence and contact with those offices, as well as with the Office of the Clerk of the court, Probation Division, and with the press, are essential to present and prospective requirements of criminal law practice. Similarly, the subtle involvement of the press and other mass media in the court's organizational network is not readily discernible to the casual observer. Accused persons come and go in the court system schema, but the structure and its occupational incumbents remain to carry on their respective career, occupational and organizational enterprises. The individual stridencies, tensions, and conflicts a given accused person's case may present to all the participants are overcome, because the formal and informal relations of all the groups in the court setting require it. The probability of continued future relations and interaction must be preserved at all costs.

This is particularly true of the "lawyer regulars" *i.e.*, those defense lawyers, who by virtue of their continuous appearances in behalf of defendants, tend to represent the bulk of a criminal court's non-indigent case workload, and those lawyers who are not "regulars," who appear almost casually in behalf of an occasional client. Some of the "lawyer regu-

lars" are highly visible as one moves about the major urban centers of the nation, their offices line the back streets of the courthouses, at times sharing space with bondsmen. Their political "visibility" in terms of local club house ties, reaching into the judge's chambers and prosecutor's office, are also deemed essential to successful practitioners. Previous research has indicated that the "lawyer regulars" make no effort to conceal their dependence upon police, bondsmen, jail personnel. Nor do they conceal the necessity for maintaining intimate relations with all levels of personnel in the court setting as a means of obtaining, maintaining, and building their practice. These informal relations are the *sine qua non* not only of retaining a practice, but also in the negotiation of pleas and sentences.[11]

The client, then, is a secondary figure in the court system as in certain other bureaucratic settings.[12] He becomes a means to other ends of the organization's incumbents. He may present doubts, contingencies, and pressures which challenge existing informal arrangements or disrupt them; but these tend to be resolved in favor of the continuance of the organization and its relations as before. There is a greater community of interests among all the principal organizational structures and their incumbents than exists elsewhere in other settings. The accused's lawyer has far greater professional, economic, intellectual and other ties to the various elements of the court system than he does to his own client. In short, the court is a closed community.

This is more than just the case of the usual "secrets" of bureaucracy which are fanatically defended from an outside view. Even all elements of the press are zealously determined to report on that which will not offend the board of judges, the prosecutor, probation, legal-aid, or other officials, in return for privileges and courtesies granted in the past and to be granted in the future. Rather than any view of the matter in terms of some variation of a "conspiracy" hypothesis, the simple explanation is one of an on-going system handling delicate tensions, managing the trauma produced by law enforcement and administration, and requiring almost pathological distrust of "outsiders" bordering on group paranoia.

The hostile attitude toward "outsiders" is in large measure engendered by a defensiveness itself produced by the inherent deficiencies of assembly line justice, so characteristic of our major criminal courts. Intolerably large caseloads of defendants which must be disposed of in an organizational context of limited resources and personnel, potentially subject the participants in the court community to harsh scrutiny from appellate courts, and other public and private sources of condemnation. As a consequence, an almost irreconcilable conflict is posed in terms of intense pressures to process large numbers of cases on the one hand, and the stringent ideological and legal requirements of "due process of law," on the other hand. A rather tenuous resolution of the dilemma has emerged in the shape of a large variety of bureaucratically ordained and controlled "work crimes," short cuts, deviations, and outright rule violations adopted as court practice in order to meet production norms. Fearfully anticipating criticism on ethical as well as legal grounds, all the significant participants in the court's social structure are bound into an organized system of complicity. This consists of a work arrangement in which the patterned, covert, informal breaches, and evasions of "due process" are institutionalized, but are, nevertheless, denied to exist.

These institutionalized evasions will be found to occur to some degree, in all criminal courts. Their nature, scope and complexity are largely determined by the size of the court, and the character of the community in which it is located, e.g., whether it is a large, urban institution, or a relatively small rural county court. In addition, idiosyncratic, local conditions may contribute to a unique flavor in the character and quality of the criminal law's administration in a particular community. However, in most instances a variety of stratagems are employed—some subtle, some crude, in effectively disposing of what are often too large caseloads. A wide variety of coercive devices are employed against an accused-client, couched in a depersonalized, instrumental, bureaucratic version of due process of law, and which are in reality a perfunctory obeisance to the ideology of due process. These include some very explicit pressures which are exerted in some measure by all court personnel, including judges, to plead guilty and avoid trial. In many instances the sanction of a potentially harsh sentence is utilized as the visible alternative to pleading guilty, in the case of recalcitrants. Probation and psychiatric reports are "tailored" to organizational needs, or are at least responsive to the court organization's requirements for the refurbishment of a defendant's social biography, consonant with his new status. A resourceful judge can, through his subtle domination of the proceedings, impose his will on the final outcome of a trial. Stenographers and clerks, in their function as record keepers, are on occasion pressed into service in support of a judicial need to "rewrite" the record of a courtroom event. Bail practices are usually employed for purposes other than simply assuring a defendant's presence on the date of a hearing in connection with his case. Too often, the discretionary power as to bail is part of the arsenal of weapons available to collapse the resistance of an accused person. The foregoing is a most cursory examination of some of the more prominent "short cuts" available to any court organization. There are numerous other procedural strategies constituting due process deviations, which tend to become the work style artifacts of a court's personnel. Thus, only court "regulars" who are "bound in" are really accepted; others are treated routinely and in almost a coldly correct manner.

The defense attorneys, therefore, whether of the legal-aid, public defender variety, or privately retained, although operating in terms of pressures specific to their respective role and organizational obligations, ultimately are concerned with strategies which tend to lead to a plea. It is the rational, impersonal elements involving economies of time, labor, expense and a superior commitment of the defense counsel to these rationalistic values of maximum production[13] of court organization that prevail, in his relationship with a client. The lawyer "regulars" are frequently former staff members of the prosecutor's office and utilize the prestige, know-how and contacts of their former affiliation as part of their stock in trade. Close and continuing relations between the lawyer "regular" and his former colleagues in the prosecutor's office generally overshadow the relationship between the regular and his client. The continuing colleagueship of supposedly adversary counsel rests on real professional and organizational needs of a *quid pro quo*, which goes beyond the limits of an accommodation or *modus vivendi* one might ordinarily expect under the circumstances of an otherwise seemingly adversary relationship. Indeed, the adversary features which are manifest are for the most part muted and exist even in their attenuated form largely for external consumption. The principals, lawyer and assistant district attorney, rely upon one another's cooperation for their continued professional existence, and so the bargaining between them tends usually to be "reasonable" rather than fierce.

FEE COLLECTION AND FIXING

The real key to understanding the role of defense counsel in a criminal case is to be found in the area of the fixing of the fee to be charged and its collection. The problem of fixing and collecting the fee tends to influence to a significant degree the criminal court process itself, and not just the relationship of the lawyer and his client. In essence, a lawyer-client "confidence game" is played. A true confidence game is unlike the case of the emperor's new clothes wherein that monarch's nakedness was a result of inordinate gullibility and credulity. In a genuine confidence game, the perpetrator manipulates the basic dishonesty of his partner, the victim or mark, toward his own (the confidence operator's) ends. Thus, "the victim of a con scheme must have some larceny in his heart."[14]

Legal service lends itself particularly well to confidence games. Usually, a plumber will be able to demonstrate empirically that he has performed a service by clearing up the stuffed drain, repairing the leaky faucet or pipe—and therefore merits his fee. He has rendered, when summoned, a visible, tangible boon for his client in return for the requested fee. A physician, who has not performed some visible surgery or otherwise engaged in some readily discernible procedure in connection with a patient, may be deemed by the patient to have "done nothing" for him. As a consequence, medical practitioners may simply prescribe or administer by injection a place-

bo to overcome a patient's potential reluctance or dissatisfaction in paying a requested fee, "for nothing."

In the practice of law there is a special problem in this regard, no matter what the level of the practitioner or his place in the hierarchy of prestige. Much legal work is intangible either because it is simply a few words of advice, some preventive action, a telephone call, negotiation of some kind, a form filled out and filed, a hurried conference with another attorney or an official of a government agency, a letter or opinion written, or a countless variety of seemingly innocuous, and even prosaic procedures and actions. These are the basic activities, apart from any possible court appearance, of almost all lawyers, at all levels of practice. Much of the activity is not in the nature of the exercise of the traditional, precise professional skills of the attorney such as library research and oral argument in connection with appellate briefs, court motions, trial work, drafting of opinions, memoranda, contracts, and other complex documents and agreements. Instead, much legal activity, whether it is at the lowest or highest "white shoe" law firm levels, is of the brokerage, agent, sales representative, lobbyist type of activity, in which the lawyer acts for someone else in pursuing the latter's interests and designs. The service is intangible.[15]

The large scale law firm may not speak as openly of their "contacts," their "fixing" abilities, as does the lower level lawyer. They trade instead upon a facade of thick carpeting, walnut panelling, genteel low pressure, and superficialities of traditional legal professionalism. There are occasions when even the large firm is on the defensive in connection with the fees they charge because the services rendered or results obtained do not appear to merit the fee asked.[16] Therefore, there is a recurrent problem in the legal profession in fixing the amount of fee, and in justifying the basis for the requested fee.

Although the fee at times amounts to what the traffic and the conscience of the lawyer will bear, one further observation must be made with regard to the size of the fee and its collection. The defendant in a criminal case and the material gain he may have acquired during the course of his illicit activities are soon parted. Not infrequently the ill-gotten fruits of the various modes of larceny are sequestered by a defense lawyer in payment of his fee. Inexorably, the amount of the fee is a function of the dollar value of the crime committed, and is frequently set with meticulous precision at a sum which bears an uncanny relationship to that of the net proceeds of the particular offense involved. On occasion, defendants have been known to commit additional offenses while at liberty on bail, in order to secure the requisite funds with which to meet their obligations for payment of legal fees. Defense lawyers condition even the most obtuse clients to recognize that there is a firm interconnection between fee payment and the zealous exercise of professional expertise, secret knowledge, and organizational "connections" in their behalf. Lawyers, therefore, seek to keep their clients in a proper state of tension, and to arouse in them the precise edge of anxiety which is calculated to encourage prompt fee payment. Consequently, the client attitude in the relationship between defense counsel and an accused is in many instances a precarious admixture of hostility, mistrust, dependence, and sycophancy. By keeping his client's anxieties aroused to the proper pitch, and establishing a seemingly causal relationship between a requested fee and the accused's ultimate extrication from his onerous difficulties, the lawyer will have established the necessary preliminary groundwork to assure a minimum of haggling over the fee and its eventual payment.

In varying degrees, as a consequence, all law practice involves a manipulation of the client and a stage management of the lawyer-client relationship so that at least an *appearance* of help and service will be forthcoming. This is accomplished in a variety of ways, often exercised in combination with each other. At the outset, the lawyer-professional employs with suitable variation a measure of sales-puff which may range from an air of unbounding self-confidence, adequacy, and dominion over events, to that of complete arrogance. This will be supplemented by the affectation of a studied, faultless mode of personal attire. In the larger firms, the furnishings and office trappings will serve as the backdrop to help in impression management and client intimidation. In all firms, solo or large scale, an

access to secret knowledge, and to the seats of power and influence is inferred, or presumed to a varying degree as the basic vendible commodity of the practitioners.

The lack of visible end product offers a special complication in the course of the professional life of the criminal court lawyer with respect to his fee and in his relations with his client. The plain fact is that an accused in a criminal case always "loses" even when he has been exonerated by an acquittal, discharge, or dismissal of his case. The hostility of an accused which follows as a consequence of his arrest, incarceration, possible loss of job, expense and other traumas connected with his case is directed, by means of displacement, toward his lawyer. It is in this sense that it may be said that a criminal lawyer never really "wins" a case. The really satisfied client is rare, since in the very nature of the situation even an accused's vindication leaves him with some degree of dissatisfaction and hostility. It is this state of affairs that makes for a lawyer-client relationship in the criminal court which tends to be a somewhat exaggerated version of the usual lawyer-client confidence game.

At the outset, because there are great risks of nonpayment of the fee, due to the impecuniousness of his clients, and the fact that a man who is sentenced to jail may be a singularly unappreciative client, the criminal lawyer collects his fee *in advance*. Often, because the lawyer and the accused both have questionable designs of their own upon each other, the confidence game can be played. The criminal lawyer must serve three major functions, or stated another way, he must solve three problems. First, he must arrange for his fee; second, he must prepare and then, if necessary, "cool out" his client in case of defeat[17] (a highly likely contingency); third, he must satisfy the court organization that he has performed adequately in the process of negotiating the plea, so as to preclude the possibility of any sort of embarrassing incident which may serve to invite "outside" scrutiny.

In assuring the attainment of one of his primary objectives, his fee, the criminal lawyer will very often enter into negotiations with the accused's kin, including collateral relatives. In many instances, the accused himself is unable to pay any sort of fee or anything more than a token fee. It then becomes important to involve as many of the accused's kin as possible in the situation. This is especially so if the attorney hopes to collect a significant part of a proposed substantial fee. It is not uncommon for several relatives to contribute toward the fee. The larger the group, the greater the possibility that the lawyer will collect a sizable fee by getting contributions from each.

A fee for a felony case which ultimately results in a plea, rather than a trial, may ordinarily range anywhere from $500 to $1,500. Should the case go to trial, the fee will be proportionately larger, depending upon the length of the trial. But the larger the fee the lawyer wishes to exact, the more impressive his performance must be, in terms of his stage managed image as a personage of great influence and power in the court organization. Court personnel are keenly aware of the extent to which a lawyer's stock in trade involves the precarious stage management of an image which goes beyond the usual professional flamboyance, and for this reason alone the lawyer is "bound in" to the authority system of the court's organizational discipline. Therefore, to some extent, court personnel will aid the lawyer in the creation and maintenance of that impression. There is a tacit commitment to the lawyer by the court organization, apart from formal etiquette, to aid him in this. Such augmentation of the lawyer's stage-managed image as this affords, is the partial basis for the *quid pro quo* which exists between the lawyer and the court organization. It tends to serve as the continuing basis for the higher loyalty of the lawyer to the organization; his relationship with his client, in contrast, is transient, ephemeral and often superficial.

DEFENSE LAWYER AS DOUBLE AGENT

The lawyer has often been accused of stirring up unnecessary litigation, especially in the field of negligence. He is said to acquire a vested interest in a cause of action or claim which was initially his client's. The strong incentive of possible fee motivates the lawyer to promote litigation which would otherwise never have developed. However, the criminal lawyer develops a vested interest of an entirely different nature in his client's case: to limit its scope and duration rather than do battle. Only in this way can a case be "profitable." Thus, he enlists the aid of relatives not only to assure payment of his fee, but he will also rely on these persons to help him in his agent-mediator role of convincing the accused to plead guilty, and ultimately to help in "cooling out" the accused if necessary.

It is at this point that an accused-defendant may experience his first sense of "betrayal." While he had perhaps perceived the police and prosecutor to be adversaries, or possibly even the judge, the accused is wholly unprepared for his counsel's role performance as an agent-mediator. In the same vein, it is even less likely to occur to an accused that members of his own family or other kin may become agents, albeit at the behest and urging of other agents or mediators, acting on the principle that they are in reality helping an accused negotiate the best possible plea arrangement under the circumstances. Usually, it will be the lawyer who will activate next of kin in this role, his ostensible motive being to arrange for his fee. But soon latent and unstated motives will assert themselves, with entreaties by counsel to the accused's next of kin, to appeal to the accused to "help himself" by pleading. *Gemeinschaft* sentiments are to this extent exploited by a defense lawyer (or even at times by a district attorney) to achieve specific secular ends, that is, of concluding a particular matter with all possible dispatch.

The fee is often collected in stages, each installment usually payable prior to a necessary court appearance required during the course of an accused's career journey. At each stage, in his interviews and communications with the accused, or in addition, with members of his family, if they are helping with the fee payment, the lawyer employs an air of professional confidence and "inside-dopesterism" in order to assuage anxieties on all sides. He makes the necessary bland assurances, and in effect manipulates his client, who is usually willing to do and say the things, true or not, which will help his attorney extricate him. Since the dimensions of what he is essentially selling, organizational influence and expertise, are not technically and precisely measurable, the lawyer can make extravagant claims of influence and secret knowledge with impunity. Thus, lawyers frequently claim to have inside knowledge in connection with information in the hands of the D.A., police, probation officials or to have access to these functionaries. Factually, they often do, and need only to exaggerate the nature of their relationships with them to obtain the desired effective impression upon the client. But, as in the genuine confidence game, the victim who has participated is loath to do anything which will upset the lesser plea which his lawyer has "conned" him into accepting.[18]

In effect, in his role as double agent, the criminal lawyer performs an extremely vital and delicate mission for the court organization and the accused. Both principals are anxious to terminate the litigation with a minimum of expense and damage to each other. There is no other personage or role incumbent in the total court structure more strategically located, who by training and in terms of his own requirements, is more ideally suited to do so than the lawyer. In recognition of this, judges will cooperate with attorneys in many important ways. For example, they will adjourn the case of an accused in jail awaiting plea or sentence if the attorney requests such action. While explicitly this may be done for some innocuous and seemingly valid reason, the tacit purpose is that pressure is being applied by the attorney for the collection of his fee, which he knows will probably not be forthcoming if the case is concluded. Judges are aware of this tactic on the part of lawyers, who, by requesting an adjournment, keep an accused incarcerated awhile longer as a not too subtle method of dunning a client for payment. However, the judges will go along with this, on the ground that important ends are being served. Often, the only end served is to protect a lawyer's fee.

The judge will help an accused's lawyer in still another way. He will lend the official aura of his office and courtroom so that a lawyer can stage-manage an impression of an "all out" performance for the accused in justification of his fee. The judge and other court personnel will serve as a backdrop for a scene charged with dramatic fire, in which the accused's lawyer makes a stirring appeal in his behalf. With a show of restrained passion, the lawyer will intone the virtues of the accused and recite the social

deprivations which have reduced him to his present state. The speech varies somewhat, depending on whether the accused has been convicted after trial or has pleaded guilty. In the main, however, the incongruity, superficiality, and ritualistic character of the total performance is underscored by a visibly impassive, almost bored reaction on the part of the judge and other members of the court retinue.

Afterward, there is a hearty exchange of pleasantries between the lawyer and district attorney, wholly out of context in terms of the supposed adversary nature of the preceding events. The fiery passion in defense of his client is gone, and the lawyers for both sides resume their offstage relations, chatting amiably and perhaps including the judge in their restrained banter. No other aspect of their visible conduct so effectively serves to put even a casual observer on notice, that these individuals have claims upon each other. These seemingly innocuous actions are indicative of continuing organizational and informal relations, which, in their intricacy and depth, range far beyond any priorities or claims a particular defendant may have.[19]

Criminal law practice is a unique form of private law practice since it really only appears to be private practice.[20] Actually it is bureaucratic practice, because of the legal practitioner's enmeshment in the authority, discipline, and perspectives of the court organization. Private practice, supposedly, in a professional sense, involves the maintenance of an organized, disciplined body of knowledge and learning; the individual practitioners are imbued with a spirit of autonomy and service, the earning of a livelihood being incidental. In the sense that the lawyer in the criminal court serves as a double agent, serving higher organizational rather than professional ends, he may be deemed to be engaged in bureaucratic rather than private practice. To some extent the lawyer-client "confidence game," in addition to its other functions, serves to conceal this fact.

THE CLIENT'S PERCEPTION

The "cop-out" ceremony, in which the court process culminates, is not only invaluable for redefining the accused's perspectives of himself, but also in reiterating publicly in a formally structured ritual the accused person's guilt for the benefit of significant "others" who are observing. The accused not only is made to assert publicly his guilt of a specific crime, but also a complete recital of its details. He is further made to indicate that he is entering his plea of guilt freely, willingly, and voluntarily, and that he is not doing so because of any promises or in consideration of any commitments that may have been made to him by anyone. This last is intended as a blanket statement to shield the participants from any possible charges of "coercion" or undue influence that may have been exerted in violation of due process requirements. Its function is to preclude any later review by an appellate court on these grounds, and also to obviate any second thoughts an accused may develop in connection with his plea.

However, for the accused, the conception of self as a guilty person is in large measure a temporary role adaptation. His career socialization as an accused, if it is successful, eventuates in his acceptance and redefinition of himself as a guilty person.[21] However, the transformation is ephemeral, in that he will, in private, quickly reassert his innocence. Of importance is that he accept his defeat, publicly proclaim it, and find some measure of pacification in it.[22] Almost immediately after his plea, a defendant will generally be interviewed by a representative of the probation division in connection with a presentence report which is to be prepared. The very first question to be asked of him by the probation officer is: "Are you guilty of the crime to which you pleaded?" This is by way of double affirmation of the defendant's guilt. Should the defendant now begin to make bold assertions of his innocence, despite his plea of guilty, he will be asked to withdraw his plea and stand trial on the original charges. Such a threatened possibility is, in most instances, sufficient to cause an accused to let the plea stand and to request the probation officer to overlook his exclamations of innocence. The table that follows is a breakdown of the categorized responses of a random sample of male defendants in Metropolitan Court[23] during 1962, 1963, and 1964 in connection with their statements during presentence probation interviews following their plea of guilty.

It would be well to observe at the outset, that of the 724 defendants who pleaded guilty before trial,

TABLE 1

Defendant Responses as to Guilt or Innocence after Pleading Guilty

N = 724 Years — 1962, 1963, 1964

Nature of Response		N of Defendants
INNOCENT (Manipulated)	"The lawyer or judge, police or D. A. 'conned me'"	86
INNOCENT (Pragmatic)	"Wanted to get it over with" "You can't beat the system" "They have you over a barrel when you have a record"	147
INNOCENT (Advice of counsel)	"Followed my lawyer's advice"	92
INNOCENT (Defiant)	"Framed"— Betrayed by "Complainant," "Police," "Squealers," "Lawyer," "Friends," "Wife," "Girlfriend"	33
INNOCENT (Adverse social data)	Blames probation officer or psychiatrist for "Bad Report," in cases where there was pre-pleading investigation	15
GUILTY	"But I should have gotten a better deal" Blames Lawyer, D.A., Police, Judge	74
GUILTY	Won't say anything further	21
FATALISTIC (Doesn't press his "Innocence," won't admit "Guilt")	"I did it for convenience" "My lawyer told me it was only thing I could do" "I did it because it was the best way out"	248
NO RESPONSE		8
TOTAL		724

only 43 (5.94 percent) of the total group had confessed prior to their indictment. Thus, the ultimate judicial process was predicated upon evidence independent of any confession of the accused.[24]

As the data indicate, only a relatively small number (95) out of the total number of defendants actually will even admit their guilt, following the "cop-out" ceremony. However, even though they have affirmed their guilt, many of these defendants felt that they should have been able to negotiate a more favorable plea. The largest aggregate of defendants (373) were those who reasserted their "innocence" following their public profession of guilt during the "cop-out" ceremony. These defendants employed differential degrees of fervor, solemnity and credibility, ranging from really mild, wavering assertions of innocence which were embroidered with a variety of stock explanations and rationalizations, to those of an adamant, "framed" nature. Thus, the "Innocent" group, for the most part, were largely concerned with underscoring for their probation interviewer their essential "goodness" and "worthiness," despite their formal plea of guilty. Assertion of his innocence at the post-plea stage, resurrects a more respectable and acceptable self concept for the accused defendant who has pleaded guilty. A recital of the structural exigencies which precipitated his plea of guilt, serves to embellish a newly proffered claim of innocence, which many defendants mistakenly feel will stand them in good stead at the time of sentence, or ultimately with probation or parole authorities.

Relatively few (33) maintained their innocence in terms of having been "framed" by some person or agent-mediator, although a larger number (86) indicated that they had been manipulated or "conned" by an agent-mediator to plead guilty, but as indicated, their assertions of innocence were relatively mild.

A rather substantial group (147) preferred to stress the pragmatic aspects of their plea of guilty. They would only perfunctorily assert their innocence and would in general refer to some adverse aspect of their situation which they believed tended to negatively affect their bargaining leverage, including in some instances a prior criminal record.

One group of defendants (92), while maintaining their innocence, simply employed some variation of a theme of following "the advice of counsel" as a covering response, to explain their guilty plea in the light of their new affirmation of innocence.

The largest single group of defendants (248) were basically fatalistic. They often verbalized weak suggestions of their innocence in rather halting terms, wholly without conviction. By the same token, they would not admit guilt readily and were generally evasive as to guilt or innocence, preferring to stress

aspects of their stoic submission in their decision to plead. This sizable group of defendants appeared to perceive the total court process as being caught up in a monstrous organizational apparatus, in which the defendant role expectancies were not clearly defined. Reluctant to offend anyone in authority, fearful that clear-cut statements on their part as to their guilt or innocence would be negatively construed, they adopted a stance of passivity, resignation and acceptance. Interestingly, they would in most instances invoke their lawyer as being the one who crystallized the available alternatives for them, and who was therefore the critical element in their decision-making process.

In order to determine which agent-mediator was most influential in altering the accused's perspectives as to his decision to plead or go to trial (regardless of the proposed basis of the plea), the same sample of defendants were asked to indicate the person who first suggested to them that they plead guilty. They were also asked to indicate which of the persons or officials who made such suggestion, was most influential in affecting their final decision to plead.

The following table indicates the breakdown of the responses to the two questions:

TABLE 2
Role of Agent-mediators in Defendant's Guilty Plea

Person or Official	First Suggested Plea of Guilty	Influenced the Accused Most in His Final Decision to Plead
JUDGE	4	26
DISTRICT ATTORNEY	67	116
DEFENSE COUNSEL	407	411
PROBATION OFFICER	14	3
PSYCHIATRIST	8	1
WIFE	34	120
FRIENDS AND KIN	21	14
POLICE	14	4
FELLOW INMATES	119	14
OTHERS	28	5
NO RESPONSE	8	10
TOTAL	724	724

It is popularly assumed that the police, through forced confessions, and the district attorney, employing still other pressures, are most instrumental in the inducement of an accused to plead guilty.[25] As Table 2 indicates, it is actually the defendant's own counsel who is most effective in this role. Further, this phenomenon tends to reinforce the extremely rational nature of criminal law administration, for an organization could not rely upon the sort of idiosyncratic measures employed by the police to induce confessions and maintain its efficiency, high production and overall rational-legal character. The defense counsel becomes the ideal agent-mediator since, as "officer of the court" and confidant of the accused and his kin, he lives astride both worlds and can serve the ends of the two as well as his own.[26]

While an accused's wife, for example, may be influential in making him more amenable to a plea, her agent-mediator role has, nevertheless, usually been sparked and initiated by defense counsel. Further, although a number of first suggestions of a plea came from an accused's fellow jail inmates, he tended to rely largely on his counsel as an ultimate source of influence in his final decision. The defense counsel, being a crucial figure in the total organizational scheme in constituting a new set of perspectives for the accused, the same sample of defendants were asked to indicate at which stage of their contact with counsel was the suggestion of a plea made. There are three basic kinds of defense counsel available in Metropolitan Court: Legal-aid, privately retained counsel, and counsel assigned by the court (but may eventually be privately retained by the accused).

The overwhelming majority of accused persons, regardless of type of counsel, related a specific incident which indicated an urging or suggestion, either during the course of the first or second contact, that they plead guilty to a lesser charge if this could be arranged. Of all the agent-mediators, it is the lawyer who is most effective in manipulating an accused's perspectives, notwithstanding pressures that may have been previously applied by police, district attorney, judge or any of the agent-mediators that may have been activated by them. Legal-aid and assigned counsel would apparently be more likely to suggest a possible plea at the point of initial interview as response to pressures of time. In the case of the assigned counsel, the strong possibility that there is no fee involved, may be an added impetus to such a suggestion at the first contact.

In addition, there is some further evidence in Table 3 of the perfunctory, ministerial character of the system in Metropolitan Court and similar criminal courts. There is little real effort to individualize, and the lawyer's role as agent-mediator may be seen as unique in that he is in effect a double agent. Although, as "officer of the court" he mediates between the court organization and the defendant, his roles with respect to each are rent by conflicts of interest. Too often these must be resolved in favor of the organization which provides him with the means for his professional existence. Consequently, in order to reduce the strains and conflicts imposed in what is ultimately an overdemanding role obligation for him, the lawyer engages in the lawyer-client "confidence game" so as to structure more favorably an otherwise onerous role system.[27]

TABLE 3
Stage at Which Counsel Suggested Accused to Plead
N = 724

| | Counsel Type | | | | | | | |
| | Privately Retained | | Legal-aid | | Assigned | | Total | |
Contact	N	%	N	%	N	%	N	%
FIRST	66	35	237	49	28	60	331	46
SECOND	83	44	142	29	8	17	233	32
THIRD	29	15	63	13	4	9	96	13
FOURTH OR MORE	12	6	31	7	5	11	48	7
NO RESPONSE	0	0	14	3	2	4	16	2
TOTAL	190	100	487	101*	47	101*	724	100

*Rounded percentage.

CONCLUSION

Recent decisions of the Supreme Court, in the area of criminal law administration and defendant's rights, fail to take into account three crucial aspects of social structure which may tend to render the more libertarian rules as nugatory. The decisions overlook (1) the nature of courts as formal organization; (2) the relationship that the lawyer-regular *actually* has with the court organization; and (3) the character of the lawyer-client relationship in the criminal court (the routine relationships, not those unusual ones that are described in "heroic" terms in novels, movies, and TV).

Courts, like many other modern large-scale organizations, possess a monstrous appetite for the cooptation of entire professional groups as well as individuals.[28] Almost all those who come within the ambit of organizational authority, find that their definitions, perceptions and values have been refurbished, largely in terms favorable to the particular organization and its goals. As a result, recent Supreme Court decisions may have a long range effect which is radically different from that intended or anticipated. The more libertarian rules will tend to produce the rather ironic end result of augmenting the *existing* organizational arrangements, enriching court organizations with more personnel and elaborate structure, which in turn will maximize organizational goals of "efficiency" and production. Thus, many defendants will find that courts will possess an even more sophisticated apparatus for processing them toward a guilty plea!

FOOTNOTES

[1] H. W. Jones, *A View From the Bridge*, Law and Society: Supplement to Summer, 1965 Issue of Social Problems 42 (1965). See G. Geis, *Sociology, Criminology, and Criminal Law*, 7 Social Problems 40–47 (1959); N. S. Timasheff, *Growth and Scope of Sociology of Law*, in *Modern Sociological Theory in Continuity and Change* 424–49 (H. Becker & A. Boskoff, eds. 1957), for further evaluation of the strained relations between sociology and law.

[2] This decision represented the climax of a line of cases which had begun to chip away at the notion that the Sixth Amendment of the Constitution (right to assistance of counsel) applied only to the federal government, and could not be held to run against the states through the Fourteenth Amendment. An exhaustive historical analysis of the Fourteenth Amendment and the Bill of Rights will be found in C. Fairman, *Does the Fourteenth Amendment Incorporate the Bill of Rights? The Original Understanding*, 2 Stan. L. Rev. 5–139 (1949). Since the Gideon deci-

sion, there is already evidence that its effect will ultimately extend to indigent persons charged with misdemeanors—and perhaps ultimately even traffic cases and other minor offenses. For a popular account of this important development in connection with the right to assistance of counsel, see A. Lewis, *Gideon's Trumpet* (1964). For a scholarly historical analysis of the right to counsel see W. M. Beaney, *The Right to Counsel in American Courts* (1955). For a more recent comprehensive review and discussion of the right to counsel and its development, see Note, *Counsel at Interrogation*, 73 Yale L.J. 1000–57 (1964).

With the passage of the Criminal Justice Act of 1964, indigent accused persons in the federal courts will be defended by federally paid legal counsel. For a general discussion of the nature and extent of public and private legal aid in the United States prior to the Gideon case, see E. A. Brownell, *Legal Aid in the United States* (1961); also R. B. von Mehren, et al., *Equal Justice for the Accused* (1959).

[3] In the case of federal defendants the issue is clear. In *Mallory v. United States*, 354 U.S. 449 (1957), the Supreme Court unequivocally indicated that a person under federal arrest must be taken "without any unnecessary delay" before a U.S. commissioner where he will receive information as to his rights to remain silent and to assistance of counsel which will be furnished, in the event he is indigent, under the Criminal Justice Act of 1964. For a most interesting and richly documented work in connection with the general area of the Bill of Rights, see C. R. Sowle, *Police Power and Individual Freedom* (1962).

[4] See N. Y. Times, Nov. 20, 1965, p. 1, for Justice Nathan R. Sobel's statement to the effect that based on his study of 1,000 indictments in Brooklyn, N. Y., from February–April, 1965, fewer than 10% involved confessions. Sobel's detailed analysis will be found in six articles which appeared in the New York Law Journal, beginning November 15, 1965, through November 21, 1965, titled *The Exclusionary Rules in the Law of Confessions: A Legal Perspective—A Practical Perspective*. Most law enforcement officials believe that the majority of convictions in criminal cases are based upon confessions obtained by police. For example, the District Attorney of New York County (a jurisdiction which has the largest volume of cases in the United States), Frank S. Hogan, reports that confessions are crucial and indicates "if a suspect is entitled to have a lawyer during preliminary questioning . . . any lawyer worth his fee will tell him to keep his mouth shut," N. Y. Times, Dec. 2, 1965, p. 1. Concise discussions of the issue are to be found in D. Robinson, Jr., *Massiah, Escobedo and Rationales for the Exclusion of Confessions*, 56 J. Crim. L. C. & P.S. 412–31 (1965); D. C. Dowling, *Escobedo and Beyond: The Need for a Fourteenth Amendment Code of Criminal Procedure*, 56 J. Crim. L. C. & P.S. 143–57 (1965).

[5] *Miranda v. Arizona*, 384 U. S. 436 (1966).

[6] Even under optimal circumstances a criminal case is a very much one-sided affair, the parties to the "contest" being decidedly unequal in strength and resources. See A. S. Goldstein, *The State and the Accused: Balance of Advantage in Criminal Procedure*, 69 Yale L.J. 1149–99 (1960).

[7] F. J. Davis et al., *Society and the Law: New Meanings for an Old Profession* 301 (1962); L. Orfield, *Criminal Procedure from Arrest to Appeal* 297 (1947).

D. J. Newman, *Pleading Guilty for Considerations: A Study of Bargain Justice*, 46 J. Crim. L. C. & P.S. 780–90 (1954). Newman's data covered only one year, 1954, in a midwestern community, however, it is in general confirmed by my own data drawn from a far more populous area, and from what is one of the major criminal courts in the country, for a period of fifteen years from 1950 to 1964 inclusive. The English experience tends also to confirm American data, see N. Walker, *Crime and Punishment in Britain: An Analysis of the Penal System* (1965). See also D. J. Newman, *Conviction: The Determination of Guilt or Innocence Without Trial* (1966), for a comprehensive legalistic study of the guilty plea sponsored by the American Bar Foundation. The criminal court as a social system, an analysis of "bargaining" and its functions in the criminal court's organizational structure, are examined in my forthcoming book, *The Criminal Court: A Sociological Perspective*, to be published by Quadrangle Books, Chicago.

[8]G. Feifer, *Justice in Moscow* (1965). The Soviet trial has been termed "an appeal from the pretrial investigation" and Feifer notes that the Soviet "trial" is simply a recapitulation of the data collected by the pretrial investigator. The notions of a trial being a "tabula rasa" and presumptions of innocence are wholly alien to Soviet notions of justice. ". . . the closer the investigation resembles the finished script, the better. . . ." *Id.* at 86.

[9]For a concise statement of the constitutional and economic aspects of the right to legal assistance, see M. G. Paulsen, *Equal Justice for the Poor Man* (1964); for a brief traditional description of the legal profession see P. A. Freund, *The Legal Profession*, Daedalus 689–700 (1963).

[10]I use the concept in the general sense that Erving Goffman employed it in his *Asylums: Essays on the Social Situation of Mental Patients and Other Inmates* (1961).

[11]A. L. Wood, *Informal Relations in the Practice of Criminal Law*, 62 Am. J. Soc. 48–55 (1956); J. E. Carlin, *Lawyers on Their Own* 105–109 (1962); R. Goldfarb, *Ransom—A Critique of the American Bail System* 114–15 (1965). Relatively recent data as to recruitment to the legal profession, and variables involved in the type of practice engaged in, will be found in J. Ladinsky, *Careers of Lawyers, Law Practice, and Legal Institutions*, 28 Am. Soc. Rev. 47–54 (1963). See also S. Warkov & J. Zelan, *Lawyers in the Making* (1965).

[12]There is a real question to be raised as to whether in certain organizational settings, a complete reversal of the bureaucratic-ideal has not occurred. That is, it would seem, in some instances the organization appears to exist to serve the needs of its various occupational incumbents, rather than its clients. A. Etzioni, *Modern Organizations* 94–104 (1964).

[13]Three relatively recent items reported in the New York Times, tend to underscore this point as it has manifested itself in one of the major criminal courts. In one instance the Bronx County Bar Association condemned "mass assembly-line justice," which "was rushing defendants into pleas of guilty and into convictions, in violation of their legal rights." N. Y. Times, March 10, 1965, p. 51. Another item, appearing somewhat later that year reports a judge criticizing his own court system (the New York Criminal Court), that "pressure to set statistical records in disposing of cases had hurt the administration of justice." N. Y. Times, Nov. 4, 1965, p. 49. A third, and most unusual recent public discussion in the press was a statement by a leading New York appellate judge decrying "instant justice" which is employed to reduce court calendar congestion "converting our courthouses into counting houses . . . , as in most big cities where the volume of business tends to overpower court facilities." N. Y. Times, Feb. 5, 1966, p. 58.

[14]R. L. Gasser, *The Confidence Game*, 27 Fed. Prob. 47 (1963).

[15]C. W. Mills, *White Collar* 121–29 (1951); J. E. Carlin, *supra*, note 11.

[16]E. O. Smigel, *The Wall Street Lawyer* (New York: The Free Press of Glencoe, 1964), p. 309.

[17]Talcott Parsons indicates that the social role and function of the lawyer can be therapeutic, helping his client psychologically in giving him necessary emotional support at critical times. The lawyer is also said to be acting as an agent of social control in the counseling of his client and in the influencing of his course of conduct. See T. Parsons, *Essays in Sociological Theory*, 382 et. seq. (1954); E. Goffman, *On Cooling the Mark Out: Some Aspects of Adaptation to Failure, in Human Behavior and Social Processes* 482–505 (A. Rose ed., 1962). Goffman's "cooling out" analysis is especially relevant in the lawyer-accused client relationship.

[18]The question has never been raised as to whether "bargain justice," "copping a plea," or justice by negotiation is a constitutional process. Although it has become the most central aspect of the process of criminal law administration, it has received virtually no close scrutiny by the appellate courts. As a consequence, it is relatively free of legal control and supervision. But, apart from any questions of the legality of bargaining, in terms of the pressures and devices that are employed which tend to violate due process of law, there remain ethical and practical questions. The system of bargain-counter justice is like the proverbial iceberg, much of its danger is concealed in secret negotiations and its least alarming feature, the final plea, being the one presented to public view. See A. S. Trebach, *The Rationing of Justice* 74–94 (1964); Note, *Guilty Plea Bargaining: Compromises by Prosecutors to Secure Guilty Pleas*, 112 U. Pa. L. Rev. 865–95 (1964).

[19]For a conventional summary statement of some of the inevitable conflicting loyalties encountered in the practice of law, see E. E. Cheatham, *Cases and Materials on the Legal Profession* 70–79 (2d ed., 1955).

[20]Some lawyers at either end of the continuum of law practice appear to have grave doubts as to whether it is indeed a profession at all. J. E. Carlin, *op. cit.*, *supra*, note 11, at 192; E. O. Smigel, *supra*, note 16, at 304–305. Increasingly, it is perceived as a business with widespread evasion of the Canons of Ethics, duplicity and chicanery being practiced in an effort to get and keep business. The poet, Carl Sandburg, epitomized this notion in the following vignette: "Have you a criminal lawyer in this burg?" "We think so but we haven't been able to prove it on him." C. Sandburg, *The People, Yes* 154 (1936).

Thus, while there is a considerable amount of dishonesty present in law practice involving fee splitting, thefts from clients, influence peddling, fixing, questionable use of favors and gifts to obtain business or influence others, this sort of activity is most often attributed to the "solo," private practice lawyer. See A. L. Wood, *Professional Ethics Among Criminal Lawyers*, Social Problems 70–83 (1959). However, to some degree, large scale "downtown" elite firms also engage in these dubious activities. The difference is that the latter firms enjoy a good deal of immunity from these harsh charges because of their institutional and organizational advantages, in terms of near monopoly over more desirable types of practice, as well as exerting great influence in the political, economic and professional realms of power.

[21]This does not mean that most of those who plead guilty are innocent of any crime. Indeed, in many instances those who have been able to negotiate a lesser plea, have done so willingly and even eagerly. The system of justice-by-negotiation, without trial, probably tends to better serve the interests and requirements of guilty persons, who are thereby presented with formal alternatives of "half a loaf," in terms of, at worst, possibilities

of a lesser plea and a concomitant shorter sentence as compensation for their acquiescence and participation. Having observed the prescriptive etiquette in compliance with the defendant role expectancies in this setting, he is rewarded. An innocent person, on the other hand, is confronted with the same set of role prescriptions, structures and legal alternatives, and in any event, for him this mode of justice is often an ineluctable bind.

[22]"Any communicative network between persons whereby the public identity of an actor is transformed into something looked on as lower in the local scheme of social types will be called a 'status degradation ceremony.'" H. Garfinkel, *Conditions of Successful Degradation Ceremonies,* 61 Am. J. Soc. 420–24 (1956). But contrary to the conception of the "cop out" as a "status degradation ceremony," is the fact that it is in reality a charade, during the course of which an accused must project an appropriate and acceptable amount of guilt, penitence and remorse. Having adequately feigned the role of the "guilty person," his healers will engage in the fantasy that he is contrite, and thereby merits a lesser plea. It is one of the essential functions of the criminal lawyer that he coach and direct his accused-client in that role performance. Thus, what is actually involved is not a "degradation" process at all, but is instead, a highly structured system of exchange cloaked in the rituals of legalism and public professions of guilt and repentance.

[23]The name is of course fictitious. However, the actual court which served as the universe from which the data were drawn, is one of the largest criminal courts in the United States, dealing with felonies only. Female defendants in the years 1950 through 1964 constituted from 7–10% of the totals for each year.

[24]My own data in this connection would appear to support Sobel's conclusion (see note 4 *supra*), and appears to be at variance with the prevalent view, which stresses the importance of confessions in law enforcement and prosecution. All the persons in my sample were originally charged with felonies ranging from homicide to forgery; in most instances the original felony charges were reduced to misdemeanors by way of a negotiated lesser plea. The vast range of crime categories which are available, facilitates the patterned court process of plea reduction to a lesser offense, which is also usually a socially less opprobrious crime. For an illustration of this feature of the bargaining process in a court utilizing a public defender office, see D. Sudnow, *Normal Crimes: Sociological Features of the Penal Code in a Public Defender Office,* 12 Social Problems 255–76 (1964).

[25]Failures, shortcomings and oppressive features of our system of criminal justice have been attributed to a variety of sources including "lawless" police, overzealous district attorneys, "hanging" juries, corruption and political connivance, incompetent judges, inadequacy or lack of counsel, and poverty or other social disabilities of the defendant. See A. Barth, *Law Enforcement versus the Law* (1963), for a journalist's account embodying this point of view; J. H. Skolnick, *Justice without Trial: Law Enforcement in Democratic Society* (1966), for a sociologist's study of the role of the police in criminal law administration. For a somewhat more detailed, albeit legalistic and somewhat technical discussion of American police procedures, see W. R. LaFave, *Arrest: The Decision to Take a Suspect into Custody* (1965).

[26]Aspects of the lawyer's ambivalences with regard to the expectancies of the various groups who have claims upon him, are discussed in H. J. O'Gorman, *The Ambivalence of Lawyers,* paper presented at the Eastern

Sociological Association meetings, April 10, 1965.

[27]W. J. Goode, *A Theory of Role Strain,* 25 Am. Soc. Rev. 483–96 (1960); J. D. Snoek, *Role Strain in Diversified Role Sets,* 71 Am. J. Soc. 363–72 (1966).

[28]Some of the resources which have become an integral part of our courts, *e.g.,* psychiatry, social work and probation, were originally intended as part of an ameliorative, therapeutic effort to individualize offenders. However, there is some evidence that a quite different result obtains, than the one originally intended. The ameliorative instruments have been coopted by the court in order to more "efficiently" deal with a court's caseload, often to the legal disadvantage of an accused person. See F. A. Allen, *The Borderland of Criminal Justice* (1964); T. S. Szasz, *Law, Liberty and Psychiatry* (1963) and also Szasz's most recent, *Psychiatric Justice* (1965); L. Diana, *The Rights of Juvenile Delinquents: An Appraisal of Juvenile Court Procedures,* 47 J. Crim. L. C. & P.S. 561–69 (1957).

THE USE OF GUILTY PLEAS IN THE LEGAL PROCESS

A basic tenet of Anglo-American criminal proceedings is that the accused is presumed innocent until he is proved guilty in an adversary proceeding.* The adversary proceeding is supposed to be the sovereign remedy for earlier ills. It is in the courtroom, at the trial itself, that the majestic rights enshrined in the Constitution are upheld; it is there that evidence illegitimately obtained will be suppressed; it is there that the prosecution will be required to keep the high standards to which it is held; and it is there that the presence of counsel and judge will prevent oppression or overreaching by police or prosecutor, however weak, humble, or lowly the accused may be.

In fact, these things do happen in many cases that actually reach adversary, public hearings. But in the United States, it is an abnormal criminal proceeding that ends in public hearings. At least ninety percent of all criminal prosecutions result in guilty pleas, most of them after negotiations between the accused (or his lawyer) and the prosecuting attorney. To understand the nature of criminal prosecution, therefore, it is essential to understand the process by which guilty pleas are reached in so high a proportion of the cases, and to see the consequences.

There are heavy institutional pressures on the prosecutor to obtain guilty pleas. His own office is, at least in urban centers, invariably overworked. Trials are arduous. They require that witnesses be interviewed and their statements

---

*William J. Chambliss and Robert B. Seidman, *Law, Order and Power,* Reading, Mass.: Addison-Wesley, 1971.

taken, the law researched, motions drawn and filed, and perhaps an appeal briefed and argued. To the overworked prosecutor, a short hearing on plea and sentence is a welcome respite.

The police reward the prosecutor when he succeeds in obtaining a guilty plea by praise and good will. Courtroom time for many police is not paid; even when it is paid, it frequently comes in the policeman's off hours. Trials call for putting in extra time by the police, not only in court but in the preparation of testimony as well. If there was police misconduct in the gathering of evidence, a trial risks its exposure.

Judges, too, place enormous pressure on prosecutors to process the criminal docket expeditiously. In every state, there is a chronic shortage of trial judges. Dockets, both civil and criminal, get longer every year as society becomes more complex and more sophisticated, and as the number of automobile accidents continues to mount. Criminal actions take precedence over civil actions. In every civil action, however, there is a hungry lawyer with channels for placing heavy pressure on trial courts through professional associations and personal contact. Moreover, courts are always under heavy political and public pressure simply to reduce costs. Perhaps the single most frequent reason given for imposing a relatively light sentence on a guilty plea is that the accused should be rewarded for saving the state the expenses of a trial. Pressures to save money, and to expedite the criminal docket so that lawyers can get their much more lucrative civil cases tried, combine. The higher judiciary (which in most states are responsible for judicial administration) constantly place enormous pressure on lower courts to speed up the docket.

The trial judge feels very sharply the pressure of the higher judiciary to expedite the docket. This pressure comes in the form of constant judicial pressure to settle civil lawsuits without trial. In criminal cases, there is constant pressure on both the prosecutors and the defense counsel to negotiate guilty pleas. So strong is this interest of the trial judge to expedite the cases that not infrequently either the defense counsel or the prosecutor will find a way to include the judge directly in the plea-bargaining session, knowing that almost invariably the judge will put pressure on whichever party seems most willing to go to trial.

Finally, there are political incentives working on the prosecutor to obtain guilty pleas. A conviction is a conviction. In the election years, the only measure of a prosecutor's efficiency that the public seems to understand is the gross number of convictions he has obtained. Whether the convictions are for very minor offenses or for major felonies, whether they are obtained by way of guilty pleas or trials, whether they are of the highest or lowest possible charge— no matter; the essential figure is the gross number of convictions. The more trials there are, the lower will be the number of convictions.

There are, therefore, heavy institutional and bureaucratic pressures on the prosecutor to obtain guilty pleas and avert a trial. How widespread bargaining with defendants for guilty pleas has become is indicated in a *University of Pennsylvania Law Review* survey which disclosed that eighty-six percent of the prosecutors responding to their questionnaire had answered "yes" to the question: "Is it the practice of your office to make arrangements with criminal defendants (or their counsel) when appropriate, in order to obtain a plea of guilty?" The same survey revealed that these guilty pleas were obtained through bargaining with the accused. Three types of bargains most often used were promise of sentence reduction made by the prosecutor, acceptance of pleas to lesser offenses which were included in the charge, and dismissal of some counts or of other indictments. The most prevalent practice was the use of less serious charges by the prosecutors.

For the most part, then, the day-to-day activities of a prosecuting attorney in processing criminal cases is to use his office to obtain guilty pleas. The evidence indicates that in a sizable proportion of the cases processed plea-bargaining is completed between the prosecutor and the defendant without a lawyer or public defender intervening on the part of the defendant. Newman found, for example, that fifty percent of the defendants who pleaded guilty did so without the advice of or consultation with counsel.*

Judges, too, recognize that without a high proportion of guilty pleas, the whole court administration of criminal law would break down. Newman quotes a judge:† "The truth is, that a criminal court can operate only by inducing the great mass of actually guilty defendants to plead guilty, paying in leniency the price for the pleas."** In fact, however, as we have seen, the excessive case loads of the courts are

---

*Donald J. Newman, "Pleading Guilty for Considerations: A Study of Bargain Justice," *Journal of Criminal Law, Criminology and Police Science*, vol. 46, 1956, p. 780–782.
†Justice Henry T. Lummus.
**Donald J. Newman, *Conviction: The Determination of Guilt or Innocence Without Trial*, Boston: Little, Brown, 1966, p. 76.

themselves a function of decisions within the legal system.

If there is so much pressure to expedite the docket, why do law-enforcement agencies expend so much of their resources in the repeated arrest of drunkards, only to release them after a short confinement in jail and return them to their old habits?* There is, it would seem, no particular public pressure on the police or the courts to persist in this mockery of the legal system. The explanation for its continuance seems to be in the bureaucratic structure of the legal system. The arrest of "drunken," "disorderly," and "suspicious" persons provides a source of continuing evidence for the necessity to increase the size of the law-enforcement agencies. It also serves as a constant reminder to "the public" indirectly and the resource allocators directly of the "crime problem" and of the law-enforcement agencies' efforts to "do something" about it. The fact that, by their own admission, what they are doing is not really solving the problem—it is in all likelihood aggravating it—seems to be of little consequence. In the absence of any other solution—and no acceptable alternative has been found—the resource allocators must choose between supporting the present policies, with all their shortcomings, or doing nothing. Doing nothing may well be politically disastrous. The decision to "take the line of least resistance" is inevitable. The politicians support the law-enforcement agencies' requests for bigger and presumably better bureaucracies to cope with the problem, by arresting more drunks.

THE CONSEQUENCES OF THE GUILTY PLEA SYSTEM

As a result of these pressures on the prosecutors and the courts, the negotiated plea becomes, not the exception, but the rule. Negotiations between prosecutors and defense counsel become institutionalized. In Detroit, for example, there is one assistant prosecutor whose only job is to screen cases just prior to arraignment with the express purpose of singling out those cases in which guilty pleas are to be obtained for reduced charges.† In a typical trial court in Connecticut, the prosecutor has regular office hours in which to confer with defense counsel for plea-bargaining.

All the legal roles involved change radically as plea-negotiation becomes institutionalized. The police, knowing that a negotiation will take place and in order to enhance the prosecution's bargaining position, will tack on numerous charges where one charge might have sufficed as the cause of an arrest. For example, a man arrested for disorderly conduct will be charged with public intoxication, disorderly conduct, resisting arrest, and assaulting a police officer. While there may be some evidence that the additional charges can be sustained, the primary purpose of adding them to the information is to increase the pressure on the defendant to plead guilty to a "lesser" charge—namely, one of the alleged crimes, rather than standing trial for all four.

It is, of course, the pervasive vagueness of the substantive criminal law that makes such flexibility possible. As we saw, that vagueness is an important source of prosecutorial discretion. This discretion is supposed to be used, on the due-process model, to humanize the application of the rules so as to achieve "substantial justice." In fact, however, the charges as originally brought are not shaped by these considerations, but by the expectation of bargaining before trial.

The judge's role becomes warped as well. Despite the strictures of the due-process rules, the judges are completely aware that the pleas which are solemnly asserted by defendants to be free and voluntary, made without coercion or promise of benefit, are almost invariably the result of a bargain struck in the hallways. In fact, sometimes one sees a judge solemnly approving a defendant's statement that his plea was not induced by threat or promise, when the plea bargain was actually struck in the judge's chambers!

That plea-bargaining warps the judicial process from its ostensible functions is evident in those cases in which the judges approve a change in plea to a charge which the accused could not possibly have committed. For example, one of the authors of this book represented a defendant on a speeding charge in Connecticut many years ago. A conviction of speeding then resulted in an automatic loss of license for thirty days, which the defendant was loath to incur. There was considerable doubt that the prosecution could prove the speeding charge. The prosecutor offered to reduce the charge to the very minor offense of crossing a white line, usually subject to a $5 fine. The charge was appropriately reduced, and the plea solemnly recorded, although on the street in question there was no white line.

Appellate courts have condoned the practices of plea-bargaining even to the point of refusing to overturn decisions where there was no logical connection between the defendant's acts, and the crime to which he pleaded guilty.

---

*Wayne R. LaFave, *Arrest: The Decision to Take a Suspect into Custody*, Boston: Little, Brown, 1965, pp. 439–440.

†Donald J. Newman, *Conviction: The Determination of Guilt or Innocence Without Trial*, Boston: Little Brown, 1966, p. 80.

PART 3   THE SOCIAL ORGANIZATION OF CRIMINAL LAW ENFORCEMENT

A defendant in a New York court who had been charged with manslaughter was permitted to plead guilty to "attempted manslaughter in the second degree."* (An attempt at a crime is usually subject to more lenient punishment than the crime itself.) The New York penal code defines manslaughter as a homicide committed "without a design to effect death"; i.e., it is an accident. In his appeal the defendant insisted that one could not be guilty of "attempted manslaughter." One could not "attempt" an accident. The appellate court was well aware that the reduction in charge from "manslaughter" to "attempted manslaughter" which had been made in a lower court was a result of bargaining for a guilty plea between the defendant and the prosecutor. The court upheld the plea, despite the patently illogical nature of the reduced charge:

> The question on this appeal is whether this definition which includes an "intent to commit a crime" renders the plea taken by the defendant inoperative, illogical or repugnant and, therefore, invalid. We hold that it does not when a defendant knowingly accepts a plea to attempted manslaughter as was done in this case in satisfaction of an indictment charging a crime carrying a heavier penalty. In such a case, there is no violation of defendant's right to due process. The defendant declined to risk his chances with a jury. He induced the proceeding of which he now complains. He made no objection or complaint when asked in the presence of his counsel whether he had any legal cause to show why judgment should not be pronounced against him, and judgment was therefore pronounced. As a result, the range of sentence which the court could impose was cut in half—a substantial benefit to the defendant . . . While there may be question whether a plea of attempted manslaughter is technically and logically consistent, such a plea should be sustained on the ground that it was sought by the defendant and freely taken as part of a bargain which was struck for the defendant's benefit.†

Of all the roles involved in the criminal process, it is defense counsel's which is most deeply affected by the plea-bargaining system. The guilty plea represents the final submission of the accused to the crime-control model. In the very process of striking it, the defense counsel is ensnared in that model. He is transformed from an adversary upholding the values of due process to a cooperator in crime control. This transformation can be seen by examining the roles of the public defenders and the "courthouse regulars" who handle the bulk of criminal matters.

A few states have established public defender's offices. Ordinarily, a public defender is to assist only indigent defendants. The theory on which the role is built is that due process requires an adversary system, the operations of which become a sham when a defendant is without the benefit of counsel. The formal role of the public defender thus places him in perpetual and uncompromising opposition to the public prosecutor.

In fact, it does not work that way, however. Gresham Sykes has shown that even in a maximum-security penitentiary, in which guards and inmates are nominally in completely antagonistic positions, in fact the "society of captives" functions by way of successive bargains struck between guards and prisoners.* The bargaining process itself demands that the guards adopt, to a degree, the values of the convicts. In the same way, the bargaining process that is the daily business of the public defender and prosecutor ensnares the defender in the prosecutorial and police culture, the culture upholding the crime-control model of legal system. David Sudnow writes from his study of a public defender's office in California:

> In the course of routinely encountering persons charged with "petty theft," "burglary," "assault with a deadly weapon," "rape," "possession of marijuana," etc., the Public Defender gains knowledge of the typical manner in which offenses of given classes are committed, the social characteristics of the persons who regularly commit them, the features of the settings in which they occur, the types of victims often involved, and the like. He learns to speak knowledgeably of "burglars," "petty thieves," "drunks," "rapists," "narcos," etc., and to attribute to them personal biographies, modes of usual criminal activity, criminal histories, psychological characteristics, and social backgrounds.†

As the public defender learns the faces of crime, the personal characteristics and typical behavior patterns of criminals, he comes to adopt the perspective of the prosecutor's office. He adopts this perspective in part because the public defender is dependent on the prosecutor for defining the situation for him. More significantly, the public defender's office must, in fact, accept the view of the defendant adopted by the prosecutor's office if it is to operate

---

*Cited in Donald R. Cressey, "Negotiated Justice," *Criminologica*, February, 1968.
†*Ibid.*

*Gresham M. Sykes, *The Society of Captives: A Study of a Maximum Security Prison*, Princeton: Princeton University Press, 1958, pp. 56–57.
†David D. Sudnow, "Normal Crimes: Sociological Features of the Penal Code in a Public Defender's Office," *Social Problems*, vol. 12, 1965, pp. 255–276. Reprinted by permission of The Society for the Study of Social Problems.

with maximum efficiency as an organization. There will be essentially no rewards (save perhaps the vague and intangible one of serving the clients) for the public defender who too vigorously opposes the view of the prosecuting attorney. Indeed, such a stance would so effectively interrupt the "normal processes" of the organizations concerned that it would simply not be tolerated. A public defender who cooperates with the prosecuting attorney's office in securing guilty pleas from defendants will find that everything, including his superior's assessment of the quality of his work, runs in his favor.

The defense attorney, even when he is a private attorney with no formal organizational ties to the court (such as those of the public defender or court appointed lawyer, for example) is nonetheless dependent on the organization of the court and the prosecutor's office if he is to be in any way effective. Frequently the defense attorney is maximally rewarded when his case is quickly disposed of. If there is only a limited source of pay for the defense, then the attorney will not receive adequate compensation for his efforts unless he manages to obtain a plea of guilty from his client and a "deal" with the prosecutor. Indeed, the pressure to obtain a plea of guilty from the defendant or to arrange a deal rather than go to trial is omnipresent, even when the defendant has moderate financial resources. The expense of an extended trial is sufficiently great so that only the most affluent defendants can really adequately compensate a lawyer who tries his case rather than obtaining from him a plea of guilty.

In addition to this very lowly economic factor is the fact that most private attorneys who handle criminal cases become court "regulars." They appear repeatedly before the same judges, and work with the same prosecuting attorneys and the same court staff on a large number of cases. As a consequence, the attorney must operate in each case in ways that increase the likelihood of cooperation from the court and the prosecuting personnel on future cases. The court can confer many favors: low bail, easy sentences, generous continuances to permit the client to find the lawyer's fee. Judges are well aware of the importance of these favors to the private attorneys. Not infrequently, after striking a plea-bargain in the judge's presence and with his approval, a judge will say, in effect, "Well, let's go out and put on the show. We must allow the defense counsel to show his client that he is earning his fee." A lawyer who can acquire the reputation that he has "the

hex" on a particular judge will attract more clients than one against whom it is believed the judge constantly exercises his discretion adversely.

Prosecutors, too, can give favors to defense counsel. A reputation of having close and favorable relationships with a prosecutor more than any other single factor can build the practice, and hence the income and prestige, of a criminal lawyer. To reach such a position, the lawyer cannot cause difficulties for the prosecutor. Most important of all, he must be "reasonable" in his plea-bargaining—that is to say, he must keep his demands within the accepted range which prosecutors exercise their discretion.

Because of the prospective continuing relationship between the prosecutor and the "courthouse regular," the personal interests of the attorney intrude into the plea-bargaining process. A continuing relationship requires good-natured compromise. What the attorney has to compromise, however, is not his personal interests but those of his client. Frequently in a plea-bargaining session in which the same defense counsel represents several clients in different and unrelated cases, at some point one or the other party will try to bargain one case against another: "You give me that one, and I'll give you this other one." The process of bargaining itself corrupts the defense counsel and lures him into the system.

The criminal defense of a client is especially amenable to this type of corruptive influence largely because once the sentence has been imposed, there are rarely any objective criteria by which the defense attorney's performance can be judged. If a man accused of grand larceny is sentenced to only three years in prison, the sentence may represent something of a victory for the defense. Indeed, if the defense attorney can convince the defendant and his relatives that things would have been much worse if they did not enter into a bargain with the prosecutor, then such a turn of events will be viewed as a successful defense. The issue of guilt or innocence takes second place to the fact that it is almost always possible for the defense attorney, trading on his claimed professional expertise, to convince the defendant that things could have been much worse. Since the maximum punishment is rarely imposed, in fact things could generally have been worse. The plea-bargain is well adapted to clothing in an appearance of client-protection, a transaction that in fact protects the interests of the defense counsel, and through him the organizational interests of the prosecutor and trial court.

CONCLUSION

The decision to prosecute and whom to prosecute for alleged offenses, whether made by the prosecuting attorney's office or, in the case of juveniles, by the police, is one which takes its distinctive character from the bureaucratic features of this phase of law enforcement. The prosecutor will engage in bargaining with defendants whenever possible in order to make certain that he is able to achieve a high proportion of convictions without jeopardizing the efficient operations of the office of prosecuting problematic cases (e.g., politically powerful persons). When the decision to prosecute rests in the hands of the police, their decisions will reflect essentially the same perspective.

As a consequence, given the social organization of most complex societies, it is the economically and politically powerless who are most likely to be prosecuted for alleged crimes. How favorable a "bargain" one can strike with the prosecutor in the pretrial confrontations is a direct function of how politically and economically powerful the defendant is. In terms of day-to-day prosecutorial activities, what this comes down to is that the lower class, indigent, and minority group member is most likely to be prosecuted for his offenses, while the more well-to-do members of the society retain considerable immunity. The crime-control model of the legal system in fact described how the prosecutors exercise their discretion. The character of law enforcement is thus shaped more by the organizational features of the legal system than by the rules and procedures which comprise the "written" though not the "real" law.

Trial and Sentencing

INTRODUCTION

It is in a trial that all the excitement and tension that epitomize the popular conception of the criminal process are found: the crusading district attorney brings to public justice the wicked and the corrupt, the powerful and the evil alike; the bold defense attorney, aided by the resourceful (if not always completely legal) private eye, confounds villainy, tears off the veil of suspicious circumstances, and justice invariably emerges triumphant.

In fact, the trial of an issue of fact to a jury is statistically a tiny wart on the end of the criminal process. At least ninety percent of all accused persons plead guilty. Of the remainder, only a small fraction elect a jury trial.

It is intriguing that despite the tiny number of persons who actually are tried by a jury, every person who is convicted must in one way or another affirmatively waive his right to a jury trial; and, having waived his right to a jury trial, he must, as we have already seen, equally formally waive his right to any trial at all.

THE TRIAL OF AN ISSUE OF FACT

As was noted earlier, the indictment or information charges the accused of certain specific acts at a certain time and place. By pleading not guilty, the defendant serves notice that he wants the prosecution to persuade the trier—the judge or jury—of the truth of those allegations about matters of fact.

Facts are never true or false; they either exist or do not exist. Our knowledge about facts can never be true or false; it can only be more or less probable. The prosecution's burden, therefore, is to persuade the jury that the truth of the propositions alleged is sufficiently probable that it should, for the purposes of the litigation, assert that they are true.

The entire process of proof in a trial is thus aimed at establishing probabilities. The rules of evidence which control the procedures of proof, if they are properly fashioned, ought to contribute to the correct determination of the probabilities.

The first, and most important rule in a trial, therefore, must be one which limits the admissible evidence to what is relevant to the material issues in question. That is, the defendant is charged with a particular crime, and the proofs must be addressed to showing whether he committed or did not commit this, and not any other, crime, and not whether he was, in general, a good or a bad man.

Two other policies tend to limit the overriding criterion of relevance: to prevent decisions based on prejudice and to reduce confusion of issues and the length of trial. There are many bits of evidence which have little probative value, but will go far to sway a jury's passions. For example, that a defendant has committed other crimes of the same sort suggests that he is *the kind of man* likely to commit such a crime, and hence that it is more probable that *he* committed *this* crime rather than an ordinary citizen. The fact that an accused had an earlier criminal conviction almost ensures his conviction before most juries, regardless of the probabilities as suggested by the rest of the testimony. To admit testimony on a man's past character or past misdeeds not directly associated with the crime charged means in practice that the accused person is being tried not for his conduct on the occasion in question, but for his general bad character.

In general, therefore, testimony which has a high rhetorical or emotive content, but relatively low probative value, is excluded, in the interest of ensuring that the decision will be based on evidence that is directly relevant, and not on emotional bias. Thus, testimony of an accused person's bad character, of his past convictions, or of specific acts of impropriety, is not ordinarily admissible.

In addition, considerations of administrative efficiency of the trial create a set of constraints of their own. There are two principal dangers in this connection: The issues may become too complex and hence divert the attention of the jury from the material facts to be proved; and the trial may become overly long.

Problems arise chiefly with respect to the credibility of witnesses. The trier of fact usually cannot be shown a motion picture of the incident. Rather, he is almost always in the position of trying to discover whether an incident which is now history in fact took place as alleged in the charge. The information relevant to that inquiry can be acquired only through the testimony of witnesses who claim to have knowledge about the facts to be proved, or through pieces of "real evidence"—objects (documents such as letters, deeds, etc., are the most important kind) which can be brought physically into the courtroom for the examination of the trier.

Every time a witness testifies, however, the probability that what he reports to the tribunal is true depends on his credibility, which is a function of five factors: his opportunity to observe the event he is reporting; his capacity to observe; his capacity to remember; his capacity to report it to the tribunal; and his veracity. If any of these factors is called into question, his whole testimony becomes suspect, and hence the probability of the propositions about matters of fact which he reports is reduced.

Since the credibility of the witness is a central factor in determining the probability which the jury will attach to his testimony, it is always at issue. The veracity component of credibility is largely a matter of character. There is, therefore, a great temptation for the opponent to introduce every adverse incident in the witness' past in order to blacken his character in the eyes of the jury, and thus to reduce the probability to be attached to his testimony.

The danger of converting the trial of the accused into a trial of the character of the witnesses, therefore, lurks behind every trial. A host of rules have been devised to reduce this possibility (and with it, the concomitant danger of prolonging the trial unduly). The most important of these rules is embodied in the right to cross-examine witnesses.

Cross-examination—the questioning of a witness by the opponent—has been described as "the greatest legal engine ever invented for the discovery of truth . . . If we omit political considerations of broader range, then cross-examination, not trial by jury, is the great and permanent contribution of the Anglo-American system of law to improved methods of trail procedure."* In the Anglo-American system, cross-examination is the principal means of testing credibility. The idea is that by questioning the witness and shrewdly confronting him with other, conflicting evidence, the opposing counsel could force the witness to demonstrate his credibility in court in a way that cannot otherwise be accomplished.

This critical dependence on cross-examination in court procedure has many consequences. Of these, perhaps the limitation on the introduction of hearsay testimony is the most important. Hearsay testimony is testimony in which a witness in court (who is subject to cross-examination and thus to credibility test) reports what some person outside the courtroom (the extrajudicial declarant) told him about a particular matter, in order to persuade the jury of the fact as reported by the extrajudicial declarant. The value of such a report made to the jury thus is a function of the credibility of two persons: the witness and the extrajudicial

declarant. Since extrajudicial declarants are not available for cross-examination, hearsay testimony is ordinarily inadmissible. A large number of exceptions exist, mainly in cases in which it is thought that the extrajudicial declarant would be unlikely to make the report in question unless it were true, such as a statement which is against his own economic interest. In such a case, circumstantial guarantees of the credibility of the extrajudicial declarant are deemed surrogate for cross-examination.

Cross-examination has been crowned with a halo in the ideology of Anglo-American legal culture. Empirical data suggest that it may be a misplaced canonization. Opposing counsel use it as a device to discredit testimony which they know is accurate. Witnesses are confused by cross-examination; and some data suggest that, with some witnesses, the attack on their credibility makes them more stubborn and more sure of what at first was only tentatively stated. In one experimentally staged kidnapping scene, for example, cross-examination on the lapse of time resulted in errors in testimony being doubled or trebled.*

Cross-examination has also been regarded as the primary means of avoiding confusion of issues and undue prolongation of trials. With few exceptions, evidence of specific acts by a witness tending to discredit him is admissible only when it can be questioned in cross-examination. Further evidence concerning his credibility introduced solely to contradict the response elicited in cross-examination is ordinarily not permitted. Thus cross-examination has become practically the only way in which a witness' credibility can be attacked.

In a criminal trial, the prosecution, obedient to the command of the presumption of innocence, must first display its evidence, usually through witnesses. Each witness is subject to cross-examination as soon as he has completed his direct testimony. After the prosecution has furnished all its evidence, ordinarily the defense counsel will move for a judgment of dismissal, i.e., a judgment of not guilty on the ground that the prosecution has failed to prove each of the material elements as charged, even assuming the truth of the prosecution testimony. When this motion is denied, the defense will then go forward with its own testimony, each of its witnesses in turn being subject to cross-examination by the prosecution.

---

*John H. Wigmore, "A Treatise on the Anglo-American System of Evidence," Trial at Common Law, vol. 5, Boston: Little, Brown, 1940 (3rd ed.), p. 1367.

*Cited in Glanville L. Williams, The Proof of Guilt: A Study of the English Criminal Trial, London: Stevens, 1963, p. 5.

Judge Jerome Frank, a leading critic of the adversary system, has identified a variety of weaknesses in the theoretical perfection of the adversary model. His principal criticism is that, far from ensuring that all the facts are developed for the trier's consideration, the system tends to ensure that some facts will not be developed. He identifies seven reasons for this: (1) The whole atmosphere of the courtroom bewilders witnesses. (2) Lawyers, before trial, coach the witnesses who will appear for their clients. In Austrian practice, by contrast, it is the height of unethical practice for a lawyer even to talk to a potential witness before the trial. (3) Dishonest lawyers use this practice to encourage perjury. (4) Cross-examination is a device to discredit honest witnesses. (5) Lawyers refuse to concede facts which they know are true, but which they believe the opposing party cannot prove. Indeed, the Bar Association's Committee on Ethics has held that it is proper professional conduct for a lawyer in the trial of a case not to disclose to the court such facts (although he may have a professional responsibility to try to persuade his client to disclose them, and if the latter does not, to withdraw from the case). (6) Lawyers rely on surprise as a tactic. (7) Financial weakness may prevent proper investigation of the facts by one or both parties.*

---

*Jerome Frank, *Courts on Trial,* Princeton: Princeton University Press, 1949, pp. 81–85, 94–96.

The implications of the adversary system for the conduct of judge and jury is that they play relatively passive roles. The role of the judge has been transformed in the course of time. In the Middle Ages, he was indeed an umpire in a decision making process that was frequently enough literally trial by combat. In the Tudor period and the years that followed, judges took an active role in questioning witnesses and in prosecution, although the form of the adversary proceedings was nominally maintained. The advent of the modern era, with its emphasis on free private action, saw the return of the judge to his passive role of administering the rules of conflict rather than engaging in the conflict itself.

The jurors' role has likewise undergone a radical change over the centuries. From being the major source of information about the defendant's guilt they have become more and more the "impartial triers" of the facts, who listen to the proofs adduced by the two warring parties.

But all the rules of evidence, procedural safeguards, and guarantees of impartiality cannot get around the fact that the trial is in the end a human experience. As such it is subject to the whims and prejudices of the participants as well as the all-important social forces that push men to behave in ways that are incompatible with the "blueprint" of the trial as laid down in law. Nowhere has this been clearer than in the well-known trial of political activists which took place in the court of Judge Hoffman in Chicago.

22

The Chicago Conspiracy Trial

DAVID J. DANELSKI

The roots of the Chicago conspiracy trial are deep in the 1960s—in the hopes and failures of the civil rights movement, in the frustration and despair of the peace movement, in the fear of ghetto riots, in the rise of black militance, and in the flowering of a youth counterculture. As the 1960s drew to a close, dissent escalated, became more militant, and tended to converge. The political and cultural watershed of the decade was 1967; Chicago lay just beyond the divide.

THE MOVEMENTS CONVERGE

On New Year's Day of 1967 two young black men in Oakland, California—Bobby Seale and Huey P. Newton—painted a sign that said BLACK PANTHER PARTY FOR SELF DEFENSE and placed it in the window of an office they had rented.[1] The Black Panther Party, with Seale as chairman and Newton as minister of defense, held its first meeting a week later.

On 15 April Martin Luther King, Jr., Dr. Benjamin Spock, and Harry Belafonte led a march of 100,000

Source: From *Political Trials*, edited by Theodore L. Becker, copyright © 1971 by The Bobbs-Merrill Company, Inc. Reprinted by permission of the author and publisher.

persons through Manhattan's streets to the United Nations Plaza, where King and Stokely Carmichael, among others, denounced the Vietnam war. Some of the young marchers carried daffodils and shouted "Flower power!" There were also shouts of "Hell no, we won't go!" and "Hey, hey, L. B. J., how many kids did you kill today?" The demonstration, which was peaceful, had been organized by David T. Dellinger,[2] a radical Christian pacifist and disciple of the late A. J. Muste. Soon thereafter Dellinger organized the National Mobilization Committee to End the War in Vietnam.

On 19 April Congressman Bill Cramer, a Republican from Florida, rose in the House of Representatives to denounce Stokely Carmichael. It was time, he said, to put out of business men like Carmichael, who traveled from state to state with the intention of inciting riots. He reminded his colleagues of his bill that would make such activities a crime. What Carmichael is doing, he said, "is un-American and he should be put in jail."[3] In June there were racial disturbances in Tampa, Cincinnati, and Atlanta. H. Rap Brown, who had succeeded Carmichael as chairman of the Student Nonviolent Coordinating

Committee, had been in those cities just before or during the disturbances.

On 12 July the Newark riots began. Five days later, twenty-three persons—twenty-one Blacks and two whites—were dead. On 19 July, without administration support, the House of Representatives passed Cramer's anti-riot bill by a vote of 347 to 70.

In August a group of hippies led by Abbie Hoffman,[4] a self-styled cultural revolutionary, threw money away at the New York Stock Exchange. It was "a gesture of love," said Hoffman, but most of the stockbrokers and clerks on the floor of the exchange jeered, pointed, and shook their fists at the hippies.

In early October it was announced that the Democratic Party would hold its next convention in Chicago; discussions began immediately in the National Mobilization Committee for massive demonstrations in Chicago to protest the Vietnam war.

On 21 October Dellinger, with the assistance of Jerry Rubin,[5] a political hippie from Berkeley, coordinated a mass march on the Pentagon. The government hesitated to issue a permit for the march, but at the last minute one was negotiated. At the Pentagon the demonstrators physically confronted military police and federal marshals; some 600 persons were arrested. It was "a mixture of Gandhi and guerilla," said Dellinger later, and it was planned that way.[6]

Early in the morning of 28 October Huey Newton was involved in a shoot-out with two Oakland policemen. When it was over, one policeman was dead; the other officer and Newton were seriously wounded, and Newton was charged with first-degree murder.

Sometime in December, Abbie Hoffman, Jerry Rubin, and Paul Krassner met at Hoffman's Lower East Side apartment, where they discussed going to Chicago the following summer to have a Festival of Life (in contrast with the "Festival of Death"—the Democratic National Convention), and, in the course of their discussion, the Yippies were born. Hoffman tells it this way: "There we were, all stoned, rolling on the floor . . . yippie! . . . Somebody says oink and that's it, pig, it's a natural, man, we gotta win . . . Let's try success, I mean, when we went to the Pentagon we were going to get it to rise 300 feet in the air . . . so we said how about doing one that will win. And so YIPPIE was born, the Youth International Party."[7]

GETTING IT TOGETHER

In the early months of 1968 the National Mobilization Committee held many meetings about possible activities in Chicago but could reach no decision.[8] It had, however, opened a Chicago office headed by Rennie Davis,[9] a former SDS community organizer who had gone to North Vietnam the year before and joined the National Mobilization Committee upon his return. The Yippies were more decisive; they were coming to Chicago and had already contacted a number of folk singers and leaders of rock groups who tentatively agreed to participate in the Festival of Life. The Yippies were also acquiring notoriety in their attempts to freak out the system. They staged a raid on the State University of New York's Stony Brook campus soon after a police narcotics raid at the school, and held a midnight party at Grand Central Station attended by 5,000 persons. The latter affair resulted in a confrontation with New York police, fifty arrests, and many injuries.

Meanwhile, a civil rights housing bill was progressing slowly through the Senate. When the bill was debated in early March, Senator Strom Thurmond offered his "Rap Brown" amendment, which was in effect Cramer's "Stokely Carmichael" bill, and the Senate passed it by an overwhelming 84–13 vote.

In late March the National Mobilization Committee held a conference at Lake Villa, Illinois, to discuss the coordination of various protest organizations—especially the black liberation and peace groups—and the proposed Chicago protest that summer. Dellinger chaired the meeting and Hoffman and Rubin were present. Tom Hayden,[10] an SDS founder and New Left theoretician, collaborated with Rennie Davis on a position paper presented at the conference. The paper outlined a plan for a funeral march to the Chicago Amphitheatre while President Johnson was being renominated at the Democratic convention. Retired generals, admirals, and Vietnam veterans might lead the march followed by people from various constituencies. Spring and summer would be devoted to local organizing, wrote Davis and Hayden, and "the summer would be capped by three days of sustained, organized protests at the Democratic National Convention, clogging the streets of Chicago with people demanding peace, justice, and self-determination for all people." The paper clearly stated: "The campaign should not plan violence and disruption against the Democratic National Convention. It should be nonviolent and legal."[11]

After the Lake Villa conference a number of things happened in rapid succession on the national scene: President Johnson suspended the bombing of North Vietnam and declared he would not seek renomination; Eugene McCarthy and his "Children's Crusade" scored primary election upsets in New Hampshire and later in Oregon; Martin Luther King, Jr., was assassinated; in response to riots in the ghetto areas of Chicago, Mayor Richard J. Daley made his shoot-to-kill-rioters-and-maim-looters statement; the Civil Rights Act of 1968 (with Senator Thurmond's Rap Brown amendment in it) was approved by the House and became law; Robert Kennedy was assassinated on the night of his California primary victory; and Hubert H. Humphrey declared his candidacy for the presidency. During April and May few political activists seemed interested in a demonstration in Chicago. Rough handling of demonstrators during a peace march in Chicago on 27 April reinforced negative notions about demonstrations in August. But Kennedy's assassination and Humphrey's candidacy revived interest on the part of those who had earlier considered various ways to focus mass protest on Chicago during the week of the Democratic convention.

Yippie spokesmen and Mobilization leaders sought permits from the city for their festival, marches, and demonstrations. A permit was especially important for the Yippies, because without it the big rock bands would not participate in the festival. The Yippies also wanted permission for their followers to sleep in Lincoln Park. There was an ordinance against this, but there were precedents for exceptions. The Mobilization's chief demand was a line of march that would bring demonstrators within eyesight of the Amphitheatre. Hoffman and Davis negotiated with Deputy Mayor David E. Stahl. Hoffman told Stahl that the Festival of Life would be such a good thing for Chicago that the city should pay $100,000 to have it put on. For $200,000, Hoffman added, the Yippies would drop the whole thing and leave town. Having heard of the Yippie's Grand Central party and having seen some of the pre-festival literature referring to nudity, open lovemaking, and drugs for all in Lincoln Park, Chicago officials saw the Yippies and the festival as nothing but trouble, and found it impossible to permit a march to the Amphitheatre. So they delayed a decision. The Yippies and the Mobilization leaders thought that permits would be granted but, as in the march on the Pentagon, at the last minute.

On 18 August hippies and other protesters began arriving in Chicago, and still there were no permits. On the next day the Yippies and the National Mobilization filed suits in the United States District Court to require the city to grant permits. The National Mobilization case was heard by Judge William J. Lynch, a former law partner of Mayor Daley. Judge Lynch decided against the National Mobilization and the Yippies withdrew their suit. Thus matters stood on the eve of the Democratic National Convention.

CONFRONTATION

A week before the convention Davis and Hayden began recruiting and training marshals for Mobilization demonstrations. Marshals were told that their function was to protect the demonstrators, keep them nonviolent, maintain order, and prevent clashes with the police. Emphasis was placed on what to do in event of disorder. If the police charged, marshals were instructed to stall them so that demonstrators could escape. Marshals were required to accept the nonviolent tenets of the Mobilization; at least two marshals resigned during the training sessions on the ground that they could not accept such principles.

News media people, police officers, and undercover agents came to Lincoln Park to observe the training of marshals. Demonstrators practiced the *wasshoi* (Japanese snake dancing), a maneuver supposed to be effective for getting through police lines, but they were so inept at it that the maneuver was never used during convention week. There were also self-defense sessions in which karate and judo were demonstrated.

On Friday 23 August Jerry Rubin went to a pig farm, purchased a 400-pound porker, dubbed him Pigasus, and declared him a presidential candidate. While Rubin and a group of Yippies sang "God Bless America," Pigasus was released in Chicago's Civic Plaza. Rubin and some of the Yippies were arrested and Pigasus was taken into custody.

On Saturday 24 August Rubin, Hoffman, Krassner, Ed Sanders, and Allen Ginsberg met and discussed their position concerning remaining in Lincoln Park after 11 P.M. After the meeting Rubin and Hoffman stated jointly that if the police demanded it, the people should leave the park rather than be arrested or beaten. "We, not they," said the statement, "will decide when the battle begins. . . . We are not going into their jails and we aren't going to shed our blood. We're too important for that."[12] At 11 P.M. the police cleared the area. When a crowd gathered outside the park, the police tried to disperse it. Police cars were stoned and eleven persons were arrested for disorderly conduct.

On Sunday 25 August there was a peaceful march from Lincoln Park to Chicago's Loop. The marchers passed the Palmer House Hotel shouting "Free Huey!" When police gave the marchers instructions, they complied, but the police did not harass or intimidate them. That afternoon a newsman overheard Abbie Hoffman say in Lincoln Park: "If the pigs come into the park tonight we are not going to stay. But we don't want to get trapped or forced into any mass arrest situation. Everybody knows what the police are planning."[13]

Later in the afternoon a disagreement occurred between police and Yippies concerning the use of a flatbed truck in the entertainment area. Hoffman worked out a compromise with the police, but it was not communicated to the crowd, and during the confusion which followed the police used their clubs on the demonstrators. Prior to the incident a number of police officers removed their badges and nameplates.

A few hours later another confrontation took place. During this incident Hoffman, negotiating with a police commander, said the demonstrators would test their right to remain in the park after 11 P.M.; the commander said they would be arrested. "Groovy," answered Hoffman. When the police tried to clear the park many demonstrators refused to follow the instructions of the marshals and shouted obscenities at them. "Daley gives orders," one demonstrator said. "Don't give us orders, you fascist!" Hundreds of demonstrators surged from the park into the streets. A march began, but the police stopped it. Some windows were broken. More than a thousand demonstrators returned to the park. Tear gas was used, and demonstrators, newsmen, and bystanders in the area

adjacent to the park—Old Town—were chased and clubbed by the police.

On Monday 26 August the police arrested Tom Hayden and Wolfe Lowenthal in Lincoln Park, charging them with resisting arrest and letting the air out of the tires of a police car. Rennie Davis immediately led a march to the police station to protest the arrests. About 400 marchers went to the Conrad Hilton Hotel, chanting: "What do we want?" "Revolution!" "When do we want it?" "Now!" Joined by other demonstrators, the marchers paraded around the statue of General Logan in Grant Park. Some of them climbed the statue, and the police broke the arm of a demonstrator as they pulled him off.

By 8:30 that evening Hayden and Lowenthal had been released on $1,000 bonds. At that time in Lincoln Park, Abbie Hoffman told a group, "We are not here to fight anybody. If we are told to leave, then leave."[14] From 9 P.M. on, Old Town was chaotic. Crowds of up to 2,000 streamed along the streets; some persons threw bottles and other objects, some walked on the roofs of cars. At 10:45 a group of clergymen entered the park to act as a buffer between police and demonstrators. A barricade made of park benches and trash baskets was set up, and demonstrators taunted the police from behind it. When the demonstrators began to throw rocks and bottles, the police charged the barricade shouting "Kill, kill, kill!" Again demonstrators, newsmen and bystanders were clubbed by the police as the park and the Old Town area were cleared.

On Tuesday 27 August several peaceful marches and demonstrations took place. In the afternoon Jerry Rubin told a crowd in Lincoln Park that they should picket the Chicago Transit Authority bus garages in support of striking black bus drivers. In the evening, at approximately 7 P.M., Bobby Seale spoke to a crowd of some 1,500 persons in the park. According to a witness who took notes on his speech, he called for a revolution in the United States. "We will go forward," he said,

as human beings to remove pigs and hogs that are terrorizing people here and throughout the world. . . . If a pig comes and starts swinging a club, then put it over his head and lay him to the ground. It's the same thing for other groups in a similar situation when pigs will attack. If you're getting down to the nitty-gritty, you'll have some functional organization like ours to take care of pigs in a desired manner. [Seale urged Blacks to] get your shotguns, get your .357 magnums and get your .45's and everything else you can get. . . . Large groups are wrong. Get into small groups of three, four and five. Be armed and spread out so we can "stuckle" these pigs. . . . If the pigs treat us unjustly tonight, we'll have to barbecue some of that pork.[15]

Rubin also spoke, saying whites should take the same risks as the Blacks. "If they try to keep us out of the park," he said, "then we'll go to the streets."[16] A little after midnight the police began clearing the park, this time using tear gas dispensed from a truck. The crowd in the streets was smaller than the previous night, but there was more violence. Police cars and CTA buses were stoned, bottles flew at the police, and the police, now relying on tear gas to disperse the crowd, chased demonstrators and often clubbed them. Some officers brandished shotguns and revolvers, and that in itself usually dispersed small crowds. Order was not restored until about 3 A.M. There were more than 100 arrests; seven police officers had been injured and nine vehicles damaged.

That same evening an "unbirthday party" for President Johnson was celebrated at the Coliseum, an auditorium about a half mile from Grant Park. About 3,000 persons listened to rock groups and speeches. Dellinger announced there would probably be an attempt to march to the Amphitheatre the next day. Just before midnight a crowd of about 2,000 marched from the Coliseum to the Hilton. Earlier, another group had gone there from Lincoln Park. When the Coliseum group arrived, marshals, drawn from the ranks of the demonstrators, were kneeling with their arms locked facing the police, who lined the street for an entire block. At 1:35 A.M., the demonstrators were told by the deputy superintendent of police that they could remain in the park if they stayed across the street and were peaceful. At 2:10 A.M., the National Guard relieved the police. At about 4:30 A.M. Hayden spoke to the demonstrators, saying that he had "gone underground, to get the pig off my back."

Wednesday 28 August was the most violent day of the convention week. Abbie Hoffman was arrested while eating breakfast with his wife; he was charged with having an obscene word written on his forehead.

Early in the afternoon Bobby Seale made a speech in Grant Park to approximately 700 persons. He demanded that Huey Newton be freed and was quoted as saying "Burn the city . . . tear it down."[17]

At an afternoon rally, presided over by Dellinger, marshals were recruited and trained for an unsanctioned march to the Amphitheatre. During one of the speeches a young man shinnied up the flagpole near the bandshell; there were shouts from the crowd: "Tear down the flag!" Dellinger took the microphone and asked instead that the flag be lowered to halfmast in honor "of the wounded, loyal demonstrators."[18] The young man was arrested; the crowd roared "Pigs! Pigs!" and began throwing things at the police officers. Suddenly a half-dozen young men went up the flagpole, lowered the flag, and ran up a red cloth or a woman's slip. Immediately several policemen pushed through the crowd to arrest the youth who had raised the red "flag." The crowd shouted obscenities at the police, who were freely swinging their nightsticks. When Rennie Davis started toward the flagpole in an effort to quiet the demonstrators, the police yelled: "Get Davis!" As the police left the flagpole, they were pelted with stones, bottles, and other objects. Dellinger asked the people to sit down, saying, "There's much more of the program to come. Be calm! Don't be violent!"[19] The marshals, arms locked, stood between demonstrators and police. "At first," a St. Louis newspaperman said,

> the police stepped forward in unison, jabbing in an upward motion with their nightsticks. . . . Suddenly they stopped the unison and began flailing with their clubs in all directions . . . People scattered . . . some went down, screaming and cursing and moaning. I saw a number of women . . . literally run over. In the wink of an eye, the police appeared to have lost all control.[20]

Some demonstrators hurled pieces of concrete at the police, shouting "Death to the pigs!" and "Fascist bastards!" The melee lasted about twenty minutes. For some time Allen Ginsberg had been chanting *Om;* gradually the crowd joined in, and the rally resumed. Dick Gregory made a biting speech, calling Mayor Daley a "fat, red-faced hoodlum." "The cops aren't responsible," he said, "the real blame goes to Daley and the crooks downtown."[21]

PART 3 THE SOCIAL ORGANIZATION OF CRIMINAL LAW ENFORCEMENT

At approximately 4:30 P.M. Dellinger told the crowd that he would attempt to lead a nonviolent march to the Amphitheatre. "If you are looking for trouble," he said, "don't come with us. We don't want violence." Dellinger was interrupted; after holding a brief conference at the speakers' stand, he said: "I am told by some that there is a group which intends to break out of the park and that will be violent. Anyone who wishes to go with that group may, but the group I'm leading will be nonviolent."

"Tom Neuman got up," an eyewitness said, "and indicated that he felt his place in society had been taken away and that he was ready to go to the streets to get it back. He was obviously trying to arouse the crowd."[22] Some demonstrators followed him into the streets, but a crowd estimated at between 5,000 and 6,000 persons lined up for the Amphitheatre march. Negotiations dragged on for more than an hour while the crowd waited. Permission for the march was denied, and at approximately 6 P.M. one of the march leaders informed the crowd that there would be no march and asked everyone to disperse and regroup in front of the Hilton Hotel. Frantically, people tried to leave the park, which was surrounded by the police and National Guard. The guardsmen used tear gas and marshals lost control of the situation. Some four to five thousand persons had converged at the Hilton Hotel. Dodging rocks and bottles the police went through the demonstrators, clubbing them and shouting "Kill, kill, kill!" The crowd chanted: "The whole world is watching. The whole world is watching."

On Thursday 29 August Dellinger, Davis, Hayden, and Rubin asked a crowd of 2,000 in Grant Park to remain there and to march to the Amphitheatre later in the day. Hayden said, "We should be happy we came here, fought and survived. If we can survive here, we can survive in any city in the country." He went on to say: "When they injure us, we will be warriors. When they gas us, they will gas the rooms in their own hotels. And when they smash blood from our heads there will be blood from a lot of other heads."[23] Abbie Hoffman led a group of demonstrators from the park, but was stopped by National Guardsmen. Later, Dick Gregory spoke to a group at the Logan statue and introduced Deputy Superintendent of Police Rocheford, who said the police

would stop any march to the Amphitheatre, but that those who stayed in the park would not be arrested. Gregory then invited demonstrators to march to his southside home, which would take them to areas prohibited by the police. A march got underway but was blocked by National Guardsmen; a number of demonstrators were arrested. When bottles were thrown, guardsmen responded with gas. This was the last major incident of the convention week. The next day there were a few speeches in Grant Park, and then the last of the protesters returned home.

THE CHICAGO EIGHT

During the next few weeks Attorney General Ramsey Clark came under considerable political pressure to prosecute the Chicago demonstrators. A study by his staff indicated, however, that it was the Chicago police who had rioted and that there were no grounds for a federal indictment of the demonstrators. Clark instructed Thomas A. Foran,[24] the United States Attorney in Chicago, to initiate an investigation of police behavior during the convention week with a view toward prosecution.

But Chicago would not let Washington determine the matter. On 9 September Chief Judge William J. Campbell,[25] of the Federal District Court in Chicago, an old friend of Mayor Daley, took the rather unusual step of convening a federal grand jury to investigate the demonstrations. He charged the jury specifically to investigate allegations of an interstate conspiracy to incite a riot and police violations of the civil rights of demonstrators. Judge Campbell made it clear to Foran that he did not want the Justice Department involved in the grand jury proceedings. What evidence was to be presented, he said, and who should be prosecuted, would be determined solely by the grand jury, not the Justice Department. He followed the grand jury's work closely, reading the transcript of its proceedings each day and frequently summoning "the jurors before him to deliver instructions on what they should consider and in what light they should consider it."[26]

Judge Campbell was taken aback when the *Walker Report* was made public on 1 December. The report was based on an extensive study of the Chicago disorders at the request of the National Commission on the Causes and Prevention of Violence. In its summary section the report stated:

> During the week of the Democratic National Convention, the Chicago police were targets of mounting provocation by both word and act. . . . The nature of the response was unrestrained and indiscriminate police violence on many occasions, particularly at night. That violence was made all the more shocking by the fact that it was often inflicted upon persons who had broken no law, disobeyed no order, made no threat. . . , Newsmen and photographers were singled out for assault, and their equipment deliberately damaged. Fundamental police training was ignored; and officers, when on the scene, were often unable to control their men. . . . To read dispassionately the hundreds of statements describing at firsthand the events . . . is to become convinced of the presence of what can only be called a police riot.[27]

Judge Campbell questioned both the objectivity of the report and the timing of its release.

When the *Walker Report* was published, Richard M. Nixon was president-elect, and Ramsey Clark was preparing to leave the Justice Department. When asked whether he had changed his mind about not bringing charges against the Chicago demonstrators, he said: "No, and if the new administration does prosecute them, that will be a clear signal that a crackdown is on the way."[28] In the new administration as Clark's successor was John Mitchell, Nixon's campaign manager. One of the main themes of the presidential campaign was law and order; some observers expected the new administration to prosecute the Chicago demonstrators, not to help Mayor Daley save face by providing scapegoats, but as a show of support for the police throughout the country.

A couple of months after Mitchell took office he had two visitors from Chicago—Thomas A. Foran and one of his assistants, Richard G. Schultz.[29] After they went over the testimony heard by the Chicago grand jury, Mitchell asked a number of questions and then agreed that certain demonstration leaders and policemen should be prosecuted. On 20 March eight demonstration leaders and eight policemen were indicted.

"Politics, pure and simple," said Clark when he heard of the indictments. "The eight-to-eight balance makes that clear. Also, the same lawyers in the Department who reported to me that proceedings against the demonstrators could not be justified must have reported the same thing to Mitchell. But with the same information he reached a different conclusion."[30] Mitchell, however, according to an assistant United States Attorney, had more information than Clark—specifically, the expected testimony of certain Chicago undercover policemen.

The eight demonstration defendants—instantly tagged the Chicago Eight—were (in order named in the indictment) David Dellinger, Rennie Davis, Tom Hayden, Abbie Hoffman, Jerry Rubin, Lee Weiner, John Froines, and Bobby Seale. All were charged with conspiracy to cross state lines with intent to cause a riot, to interfere with law enforcement officers and firemen in the performance of their duties, and to teach and demonstrate the use of incendiary devices.[31] Twelve alleged co-conspirators were also named but not indicted. Weiner and Froines were charged with teaching and demonstrating the use of incendiary devices,[32] and the remaining defendants were charged with violating the Rap Brown law: crossing state lines with intent to cause a riot.[33] Except for Weiner and Froines, the defendants were well known.

Weiner[34] was a research assistant and Ph.D. candidate in sociology at Northwestern University; Froines,[35] an assistant professor of chemistry at the University of Oregon, had returned from England and stopped off in Chicago to spend the summer with his wife's parents. Both had been marshals in the demonstrations. One writer called them "small shots"; they had seemed so unimportant that the *Walker Report* had not even mentioned them.[36] One hypothesis for their inclusion in the indictment—which would be asserted later by their lawyers—was that the indictment was a crackdown on dissent, and Weiner and Froines represented dissent in the academic community. Another hypothesis was that their inclusion gave some substance to the government's case, for without the count involving incendiary devices, the indictment charged little more than thinking, speaking, and associating—activities generally regarded as protected by the First Amendment. Still another hypothesis was that they were included in order to provide some basis for negotiation during jury deliberations.

The defendants' names were not listed in alphabetical order. Perhaps Dellinger's name was first because, at fifty-two, he was the eldest (the others ranging in age from twenty-eight to thirty-two), and hence, in the government's view, the architect of the alleged conspiracy. It was not because the evidence against him was strongest; in many ways it was the weakest. The order of the defendants' names was perhaps not as significant as the essential mixture of political styles they represented, a mixture consistent with the explanation that the indictment was a crackdown on various kinds of dissent: Dellinger, radical pacifism; Davis and Hayden, the New Left; Hoffman and Rubin, political hippies; Weiner and Froines, academic dissent; and Seale, black militance. Seale's inclusion in the conspiracy charge made no sense to him or the other defendants; he had not met any of the defendants, except Rubin, before the trial. Moreover, during the convention week, he had been a last-minute speaking replacement for Eldridge Cleaver.

In the random assignment of cases in the United States District Court in Chicago, Judge Campbell drew *United States of America v. Dellinger et al.*, but he disqualified himself on the ground that he had worked intimately on the case with the grand jury. The case was returned for reassignment, and on 1 April it was assigned, again presumably in a random manner, to Julius Jennings Hoffman,[37] a seventy-three-year-old, conscientious, pro-government judge who had been appointed by President Eisenhower. "Hoffman," said a Chicago lawyer, "regards himself as the embodiment of everything Federal. So in criminal cases . . . he tends to see the defense and their attorneys as the enemy."[38]

NO SPEECHES, NO EMBELLISHMENTS

On 9 April the defendants were arraigned. When defense counsel—Charles R. Garry, William Kunstler, Michael J. Kennedy, Gerald B. Lefcourt, Leonard I. Weinglass, and Dennis J. Roberts—were introduced as lawyers from California, New York, and New Jersey, Judge Hoffman asked, "These men are taking bread out of the mouths of our Chicago Bar here?"[39]

The first defendant—Dellinger—was then asked to plead. "Obviously not guilty," said Dellinger, expressing the moral outrage he would later show from time to time during the trial. "The guilty parties have not been indicted." Refusing the plea, Judge Hoffman asked Dellinger again how he pleaded. Dellinger responded: "I said obviously not guilty." Again the plea was refused. "Once more," said the judge, "how do you plead?" And Dellinger answered: "I thought I made myself clear. I said not guilty." The plea was refused a third time and the judge asked Dellinger's lawyer to advise him how to plead.

KENNEDY: He has pleaded.
JUDGE HOFFMAN: He has not pleaded.
KENNEDY: He has pleaded not guilty.
JUDGE HOFFMAN: He has not pleaded, sir. All he has to say is not guilty or guilty. I don't care which. No speeches. No embellishments. How do you plead, sir?
DELLINGER: Not guilty.[40]

When Jerry Rubin was asked to plead, William Kunstler[41] began, "Just for the record—" but was interrupted by the following exchange:

JUDGE HOFFMAN: Everything we do is for the record, Mr. Kunstler.
KUNSTLER: Of course, Your Honor.
JUDGE HOFFMAN: That is why the government pays a high salary for an official reporter. I am not frightened when you say "for the record."
KUNSTLER: Yes, Your Honor—
JUDGE HOFFMAN: You see this lady. She is a very competent reporter. Anything you say and I say, or anybody says, is for the record. You have my assurance.
KUNSTLER: Your Honor, I was not trying to put the Court in terror, as you know.
JUDGE HOFFMAN: Perhaps even way out in New York you have found that I don't frighten very easily.
KUNSTLER: Maybe that works both ways.

At that point Garry intervened:

GARRY: But I do, Your Honor.
JUDGE HOFFMAN: What did you say?
GARRY: I get frightened.
JUDGE HOFFMAN: Well, we will try to put you at ease.
GARRY: Thank you, Your Honor.[42]

Rubin then raised a clenched fist and pleaded not guilty.

JUDGE HOFFMAN: Let the record show that the defendant Rubin pleaded guilty raising a clenched fist.

KUNSTLER: I have to object to that, Your Honor. He pleaded not guilty.

JUDGE HOFFMAN: Oh, he pleaded not guilty.

KUNSTLER: A Freudian slip.

JUDGE HOFFMAN: I thought with that clenched fist, he was going to change the order of things. Not guilty?

KUNSTLER: Not guilty.

JUDGE HOFFMAN: Your plea is not guilty?

RUBIN: Not guilty with a clenched fist.

JUDGE HOFFMAN: You see, I got frightened of that, Mr. Kunstler. I don't know whether that fist was directed at me or not.

KUNSTLER: No, Your Honor, it is a symbol of defiance against certain things which the defendants believe are wrong.

JUDGE HOFFMAN: Not against me. He doesn't think I am wrong yet, does he?

KUNSTLER: I won't even answer that question.[43]

The other lawyers who spoke in court that day fared not much better than Kunstler. After the arraignment, Kennedy argued a motion to grant the defense six months in which to prepare pretrial motions. In view of the complexity of the case, the large number of defendants and counsel, and the fact that the government had already worked on the case for six months, he thought the defense request was reasonable. Judge Hoffman asked Foran for his views. Foran suggested the defense be given thirty days to prepare pretrial motions and the government twenty in which to answer. Judge Hoffman ruled accordingly and set the trial for 24 September, which flabbergasted Kennedy. "Your Honor, most respectfully," he said, "has hamstrung us. . . . There is no opportunity for us to defend our clients when we have but thirty days to draw together this incredible mass of information, and slightly over three months to prepare for trial." "I never hear arguments after I rule, sir," answered Judge Hoffman. "You will learn that when you come to try this case, if you come to try it."[44]

Garry tried to get a clarification of the ruling, but Hoffman did not understand him. When he tried to explain, the judge would not listen. He said to Gary "You have tried [to explain], and you have failed. The order stands."[45] In regard to other motions, including permission for the defendants to travel, Judge Hoffman insisted that defense lawyers work out the matter by stipulation with the government.

At first Kunstler refused; later, however, seeing they could get nowhere with Judge Hoffman, the defense lawyers worked out stipulations with the government.

GARRY DROPS OUT

Defendants and lawyers alike were sorely disillusioned by Judge Hoffman. "From the very first moment of our arraignment we realized," Hayden said bitterly, after the trial, "that our fates were to be decided by a madman, Judge Julius J. Hoffman."[46] In May Kunstler filed an application asking the judge to disqualify himself. He said it was his distinct impression from the tenor of the judge's remarks, his attitude toward the defendants, and his rulings that he had a personal bias either against the defendants or for the government. This was the first of several such motions the defense made, all of which were denied. One of them irked Judge Hoffman so much that he impounded it for further action, presumably as evidence of contumacious conduct.

In July Judge Hoffman heard arguments on pretrial motions, all of which he subsequently denied. One of the most important was a motion to suppress evidence obtained by electronic surveillance. Michael Tigar, an expert on the subject, joined the defense to argue the motion. His command of the law and style of argument, a blend of grace and deference, impressed the judge. Arguing the same motion, Leonard Weinglass flatly criticized the government for wiretapping, saying that the attorney general admitted that by engaging in wiretapping the government committed criminal acts against its citizens. "Did he say that?" asked the judge sharply. "Did he use that language?" Weinglass read the attorney general's affidavit that stated federal agents had monitored telephone conversations of the defendants in order to gather intelligence for reasons of internal security.

JUDGE HOFFMAN: You were slightly in error when you said the affiant . . . said that the government "committed criminal acts." That is not the language of the affidavit, is it?

WEINGLASS: That was the justification for the wiretap and I put this question to the Court—

JUDGE HOFFMAN: I just don't like a lawyer to stand before me and say a document contains certain language when it does not.

WEINGLASS: The fact of the matter is—

JUDGE HOFFMAN: I won't argue that with you because it doesn't, and you know it doesn't. You said it did and it doesn't.[47]

Judge Hoffman carried a negative impression of Weinglass throughout the trial. He referred to him out of court as "this wild man Weinglass," and during the trial he addressed him variously as Feinglass, Weinrob, Weinstein, Feinstein, Weinrus, Weinberg, Weinramer, and once even Mr. What's Your Name. At the end of the trial, when Weinglass was sentenced for contempt of court, he mentioned Judge Hoffman's slighting him and said: "I was hopeful when I came here that after 20 weeks the Court would know my name and I didn't receive that which I thought was the minimum."[48]

Fifteen days before the trial was scheduled to begin, Garry, ill with an infected gallbladder, requested a six weeks' continuance so that he might have his gallbladder removed. His participation in the trial, he said, was of the utmost importance to the defendants because he was their chief counsel and because he was the only lawyer who had Bobby Seale's confidence. "I make this statement," he concluded, "in as serious a request as I have ever asked of a court."[49] The government strongly opposed Garry's motion. When Judge Hoffman noted that a number of lawyers had filed appearances for the defendants and that the designation of chief counsel was not recognized in the United States Code, Garry tried to explain that many of the lawyers had appeared only to prepare and argue pretrial motions or to fulfill the requirements of local counsel under the court's rules. But that made no difference to Judge Hoffman. He denied Garry's motion and issued an order requiring Bobby Seale to be brought from California, where he was in custody, for trial on 24 September. "And," Garry interjected, "he will be without counsel at that time, your Honor."[50]

On 24 September only Kunstler and Weinglass, in addition to the two local attorneys, were in court. Kennedy, Roberts, and Tigar had wired Foran stating their desire to withdraw from the case; and Lefcourt, Kunstler explained, had to take his place in the New York Black Panther trial. Kunstler told the court that he and Weinglass would each represent four defendants and had filed appearances for them that day; but, he added, the defendants took the position that they were not fully represented because Garry was not present. Foran had no objection to Kunstler and Weinglass representing all the defendants. He did object, however, to the failure of Kennedy, Lefcourt, Roberts, and Tigar to appear for the trial. In his opinion their withdrawal was "incredibly irresponsible and unprofessional."[51] But he said that the government would not ask that they be ordered to appear immediately if the defendants would represent to the court that they were satisfied with counsel then in court; he further requested "that they waive any claim that their Sixth Amendment rights are abridged." "A disgraceful suggestion," Kunstler replied.[52] Judge Hoffman responded by issuing bench warrants for the arrest of the four lawyers. Two days later they were held in contempt of court, but there was such a protest among lawyers throughout the country that the judge was persuaded to vacate the contempt findings and permit the lawyers to withdraw.

FREE THE JURY

For selection of the jury, the defendants were moved to a larger courtroom where three hundred prospective jurors were waiting. The defendants felt uneasy as they studied the predominantly white, middle-aged, middle-class citizens who were supposed to be their peers. They looked, wrote Hayden, "like a Republican State Convention. It was the Silent Majority making a rare public appearance. . . . There was hardly a Black or a young person in the room."[53] The defense challenged the use of voting lists in selecting the venire on the ground that it systematically excluded racial minorities, the young, the mobile, and those alienated from traditional electoral politics. The challenge was overruled and the judge read the indictment to the jurors.

Judge Hoffman had ruled earlier that there would be no *voir dire* examination of prospective jurors, but that the defense and the government could submit questions which he would consider. He accepted a few of the government's questions but virtually none of the defendants'. Among those excluded were: "Do you believe that young men who refuse to participate in the armed forces because of their opposition to the war are cowards, slackers, or unpatriotic?"

"Do you have any hostile feelings toward persons whose life styles differ from your own?" "Would you let your son or daughter marry a Yippie?" The one defense question accepted in substance was whether the prospective jurors had any close relatives and friends who were law enforcement officers or employees of the city, state, or federal governments.

Judge Hoffman began by asking each prospective juror whether he could be impartial in the case. The first nineteen veniremen answered, without exception, that they could not. They were excused; the judge asked the remaining veniremen to rise if they felt they could not be impartial. Thirty-eight men and women rose, and they were also excused. Individual examination of prospective jurors was surprisingly brief. The examination of Mrs. Mildred Burns was typical:

Q. What is your family situation?
A. I have a husband and one married son.
Q. Your husband's business or occupation?
A. He is a planning engineer at Argonne Laboratories.
Q. That is an agency of the government, isn't it?
A. No, it is run by the University of Chicago.
Q. University of Chicago. Is that where Mr. Fermi started?
A. Yes.
Q. How long has he been at Argonne?
A. Twenty-one years.
Q. Are you occupied with anything?
A. Part time, on and off.
Q. What did you say?
A. Part time. A friend of mine has a bakery and I help her once in a while.
Q. Selling?
A. Yes, cashier.[54]

The defense accepted Mrs. Burns as a juror, perhaps because of the mention of the University of Chicago and Mr. Fermi. As it turned out, she was one of the "hardliners" for conviction of all defendants on all counts. More, of course, was involved than what the prospective jurors said. "You scan the face and clothing," wrote Hayden, "try to catch a vibration or two, listen to the tone of voice as he answers the simple questions."[55] As the defendants participated in selection of the jury their behavior must have puzzled, if not appalled, many of the jurors. "What a scene it must have been," recalled Hayden. "Eight madmen in bright clothes passing notes, climbing over the table, whispering, laughing, arguing over

the appearance of the jurors. We were judging them, putting them down, shaking our heads, looking sharply at them, yet we were the ones on trial."[56]

The defense had seventeen and the government had six peremptory challenges for twelve jurors, and each side had two peremptory challenges for four alternate jurors. The government was willing to go to trial with the first twelve jurors in the box and tendered them to the defense. Kunstler attempted to challenge for cause jurors whose friends or relatives were police officers. Since those jurors said they could be impartial, Judge Hoffman denied the challenge. Kunstler then challenged them peremptorily. More veniremen were called and the government challengd two of them peremptorily—one a recent chemistry graduate from the University of Illinois, the other an elderly black electrician who had recently lost his job with the Pullman Company after thirty-one years of employment.

After the first few hours of jury selection, the defense felt optimistic; it had used only eight challenges, and it had accepted at least two or three jurors it believed it could count on. One was Mrs. Jean Fritz, a DesPlaines housewife, who had been seen carrying a book by James Baldwin. Another was Kristi King, a customer's representative from Crystal Lake. At twenty-three, she was the only young person on the jury, but just as important as her age was the fact that she had a sister who had worked for VISTA. And there were two black women: Mrs. Mary Butler, a widow and retired cook whose son was a food service worker at the Playboy Club, and Mrs. Evelyn Hill, a nurse's aide with dyed red hair whose husband worked as a shipping clerk. It was difficult to tell about the others. Two were men: Edward F. Kratzke, an equipment cleaner for the Chicago Transit Authority whose wife worked as a janitress in a tuberculosis sanitarium, and John M. Nelson, a self-employed house painter with a skid row address. The remaining half dozen were middle-aged white women. Three of them—Shirley Seaholm, Ruth Peterson, and Lorraine Bernacki—had children attending college, and one, Miriam Hill, had a son serving in the navy. The remaining jurors were Frieda H. Robbins, who worked as a cashier for a public utility company, and Mildred Burns, whose husband worked at Argonne Laboratories.

At this point the defendants asked for a recess for purposes of mutual consultation. They suspected the government was deliberately saving its four remaining peremptory challenges until the defendants had used all of theirs, at which time it would challenge jurors like Kristi King and Mrs. Butler. The jury, as described, had been tendered by the government. Should the defendants, with nine peremptory challenges left, accept it? That was the question they discussed and voted upon in a conference room eight feet square. "That little room," said John Froines, "was the most tension-packed place I've been in in my life."[57] The defendants believed that they could achieve no more than a hung jury in the trial, and they felt that at least some jurors were sympathetic to them; so they voted unanimously to accept the jury.

When they returned to the courtroom four alternate jurors were still to be chosen. They were regarded as important, because the trial would be a long one, and some of the alternates were likely to be regular jurors by the time the verdict was reached. Kunstler noticed that among those called as prospective alternates were a young woman, Kay S. Richards, and a black woman, Mrs. Wafer Fisher; he used the two defense challenges in a way that secured both. Thus the jury was selected, and in record time for such a case—less than a day.

During the first witness's testimony something happened which affected the composition of the jury and perhaps the outcome of the case. The families of two of the jurors—Kristi King and Ruth Peterson—had received notes saying "You are being watched. The Black Panthers."[58] The notes were reported to the FBI, and Judge Hoffman met with counsel in chambers to decide what should be done about the matter. Neither judge nor government counsel wanted the existence or contents of the notes made public, because the other jurors might learn of them. Kunstler informed Seale of the notes and told him that Foran and Schultz did not want the notes publicized. "Don't want publicity about it?" Seale retorted. "We're not going to send any stupid notes like that, man. Somebody's railroading us."[59] Seale wrote a statement for the press that was given to Hayden. Later at a press conference, Hayden told reporters of the notes and said: "What we are facing here is a frame-up on trumped-up charges." He then read from Seale's statement: "There is a plot by the FBI and other lackey pig agents to tamper with the jury and then try to blame it on the Black Panther Party."[60] When the judge heard of the press conference, he immediately ordered the jury sequestered.

Judge Hoffman questioned jurors King and Peterson about the notes. Miss King was given the note and asked if she had seen it. She said she had not. He asked if any member of her family had brought it to her attention, and she again said no. He then said: "All right. Read it, Miss King. Read it, please." After she read it aloud he asked whether, having read the note, she could continue to be fair and impartial in this case. She stared at Bobby Seale and, on the verge of tears, said, "No, sir."[61] Kunstler objected to the revealing of the contents of the note to Miss King, but it was too late. She was excused as a juror, and Kay Richards, a twenty-three-year-old computer operator, took her place. Mrs. Peterson said she had seen the note but it did not affect her impartiality. She also said she had mentioned the note to her roommate, Mrs. Burns. The latter said the note would not affect her impartiality, and both women remained as jurors. The jury was complete and underwent no further changes.

Far more was involved in this incident than the replacement of a juror. For the next four-and-a-half months the jury was to be sequestered—shut up with each other and federal marshals in hotel rooms, away from their families and loved ones. Perhaps such measures were inevitable, but they were a blow to the defense, because jurors often blame the defendants for their plight. Indeed, the jurors envied the defendants' freedom—all but Seale were out on bail during most of the trial—and at least one of them appreciated the sentiment of a sign Lee Weiner held up one day outside the courtroom as the jury boarded the bus for its hotel. It said: "Free the jury."[62]

A FREE, INDEPENDENT BLACK MAN

During the selection of the jury, Bobby Seale sat somewhat apart from the seven other defendants. He was waiting for word from Garry, who he still hoped would come to Chicago to defend him. Meanwhile Kunstler had filed two appearances for Seale—one on 22 September simply for the purpose of seeing Seale, who had just been brought cross-country in shackles and was being held incommunicado; the other a general appearance filed two days later when Kunstler and Weinglass divided the defendants among them. Seale maintains he had not agreed to be defended by Kunstler at that or any other time.[63] On the afternoon the jury was selected—25 September— Warden Moore of the Cook County Jail put in a phone call to Garry's office for Seale, and Barney Dreyfus, Garry's law partner, told him that Garry was going to the hospital the next day and could not come to Chicago to defend the Panther leader. Seale told Dreyfus that he would ask Judge Hoffman to postpone his part of the case until he could have Garry, because he could not function without him. "Let Garry know what I am doing," he said, "and then maybe after he gets out of the hospital he can go on."[64]

That night Seale, thinking about how Malcolm X and Huey Newton wanted to be lawyers and how Huey had once defended himself in California, drafted his first legal motion.[65] On a legal yellow pad, he wrote:

> I submit to Judge Julius Hoffman that the trial be postponed until a later date when I, Bobby G. Seale, can have the "legal council of my choice who is effective," Attorney Charles R. Garry and if my constitutional rights are not respected by this court then other lawyers on record here representing me, except Charles R. Garry, do not speak for me, represent me, as of this date 9-26-69. I fire them now until Charles R. Garry can be made chief counsel in this trial. . . .

When Seale signed the motion, he added, "Chairman, Black Panther Party."[66]

On the morning of the twenty-sixth, before the court session began, Seale told Kunstler he was firing all the lawyers and gave him his motion to read. "Man," said one of the defendants, "that's going to make it look like all of the defendants are splitting." No, Seale assured them. His situation was simply different than theirs; he needed Garry "and everybody knows it."[67] When the court convened, Seale walked up to the attorney's lectern and began reading his motion. Near the end of his statement, he read:

> If I am consistently denied this right of legal defense counsel of my choice who is effective by the Judge of this Court,

then I can only see the Judge as a blatant racist of the United States Court.

JUDGE HOFFMAN: Just a minute. Just a minute.

SEALE: With gross prejudicial error toward all defendants and myself.

JUDGE HOFFMAN: Just a minute. What did you say? Read that, Miss Reporter.

SEALE: I said if my constitutional rights are denied as my constitutional rights have been denied in the past in the course of this trial, et cetera, then the tenor is the act of racism and me a black man, there seems to be a form of prejudice against me even to the other defendants on the part of the Judge.[68]

Judge Hoffman was stung. He said he was a friend of the Negro people and referred more than once to his 1968 South Holland decision, the first, he pointed out, requiring school desegregation in the North. Seale's motion was denied, but that did not end the matter, for Seale fully intended to defend himself. That same day, after the government and defense attorneys made their opening statements, Seale rose to reply to some statements Schultz had made about him. "Just a minute, sir," the judge said. "Who is your lawyer?" "Charles R. Garry," Seale answered.[69] The judge then said that Kunstler might make another opening statement in behalf of Seale. Refusing, Kunstler said: "Your Honor, I cannot compromise Mr. Seale's position." Later, Kunstler made it clear that he was not directing Seale in any way. "He is," said the lawyer, "a free, independent black man who does his own direction."

JUDGE HOFFMAN: Black or white, sir—and what an extraordinary statement, "an independent black man." He is a defendant in this case. He will be calling you a racist before you are through, Mr. Kunstler.

KUNSTLER: Your Honor, I think to call him a free, independent black man will not incite his anger.[70]

Although there were references in the newspapers to Seale's disruptions, the record shows that he seldom spoke unless statements were made about him or the Black Panthers, and when he spoke, he reiterated that he had fired Kunstler and wanted to exercise his right to defend himself. If a witness testified against him, he would wait until the lawyers finished their examinations, then rise to cross-examine when he thought it was his turn. Judge Hoffman refused to let him speak, much less defend himself, and the intensity of the exchanges between the two men escalated. When Seale rose to speak, the judge often excused the jury. Seale claims that Hoffman would say deliberately in an overly loud voice: "Take the jury out! Take the jury out! I don't want to hear this man. Mr. Marshal, set that man down!" so that the reporter could not record Seale's words. "But," Seale said, "I got hip to him. I saw the tactics he was using, so every time he started raising his voice I'd raise my voice up too."[71] As time went on, Seale also used more invective, calling Judge Hoffman a fascist and a pig as well as a racist.

Eventually Schultz and Foran also felt the sharp edge of Seale's invective. On 22 October Schultz marked a photograph for identification that showed a boy wearing a sweatshirt with a clenched black fist on it, which Schultz referred to as the "black power symbol."

> SEALE: It's not a black power sign. It's a power to the people sign, and he is deliberately distorting that and that's a racist technique.
> SCHULTZ: If the Court please, this man has repeatedly called me a racist—
> SEALE: Yes, you are. You are, Dick Schultz.
> SCHULTZ: And called Mr. Foran a racist—[72]

Some observers of the trial, acknowledging that Seale was disrespectful to Judge Hoffman, said he acted with enormous dignity in asserting what he honestly believed to be his constitutional rights. All during the trial he was imprisoned (due to his scheduled appearance at another trial in New Haven on a charge of murder) and a good part of the time he was ill. The other defendants could hold press conferences and speak to groups throughout the country, but Seale's only forum was the courtroom. It is not clear whether he deliberately used the courtroom as a means of speaking to the people outside. But in asserting the right to defend himself, he spoke of many things that bothered him. Two examples:

> You denied me the right to defend myself. You think black people don't have a mind. Well, we got big minds, good minds, and we know how to come forth with constitutional rights, the so-called constitutional rights. I am not going to be quiet. I am talking in behalf of my constitutional rights, man, in behalf of myself. . . .[73]

> You have George Washington and Benjamin Franklin sitting

in a picture behind you, and they were slave owners. That's what they were. They owned slaves. You are acting in the same manner, denying me my constitutional rights . . .[74]

By 29 October Judge Hoffman was at wit's end. He could no longer tolerate Seale's calling him a racist, a fascist, and a pig and thus ordered him bound and gagged—measures that only exacerbated an already impossible situation. When Seale tried to rise and, through his gag, object, black marshals were ordered to quiet him, and their manner was not gentle. Even the cold words of the official record give a vivid picture:

> KUNSTLER: Your Honor, are we going to stop this medieval torture that is going on in this courtroom? I think this is a disgrace.
> RUBIN: This guy is putting his elbow in Bobby's mouth and it wasn't necessary at all.
> KUNSTLER: This is no longer a court of order, Your Honor; this is a medieval torture chamber. It is a disgrace. They are assaulting the other defendants also.
> RUBIN: Don't hit me in my balls, mother fucker.
> SEALE: This mother fucker [referring to the gag] is tight and it is stopping my blood.
> KUNSTLER: Your Honor, this is an unholy disgrace to the law that is going on in this room and I as an American lawyer feel a disgrace.
> FORAN: Created by Mr. Kunstler.
> KUNSTLER: Created by nothing other than what you have done to this man.
> ABBIE HOFFMAN: You come down here and watch it, Judge.
> FORAN: May the record show the outbursts are the defendant Rubin.
> SEALE: You fascist dogs, you rotten, low life son-of-a-bitch. I am glad I said it about Washington used to have slaves, the first President—
> DELLINGER: Somebody go to protect him.[75]

The defendants were sensitive men who had been in the civil rights movement from its earliest days. Being activists and protesters, they felt they should do something to express their moral outrage, and they did. On at least one occasion, Dellinger threw his body between the marshals and Seale in an effort to protect him, and once when the jury entered the courtroom, Davis ran up to it and said that the marshals had tortured Seale. On 28 October, Seale refused to rise when Judge Hoffman entered and left the courtroom, and the defendants did the same. But Seale wanted this form of protest to be his own, and after a couple of days told the white defendants, through his gag, to rise. Near the end of October, Judge Hoffman told them that if they did not cease supporting Seale, he would revoke their bail. Kunstler answered that the defendants would not let a threatened loss of their liberty stand in the way of Seale asserting his constitutional rights. Nothing further was said of the matter, and the defendants' bail continued.

Seale has a profound effect on the jurors, most of whom were frightened of him. Kay Richards said she was so afraid that she could not have convicted him. Mrs. Peterson, who received one of the threatening notes, was also "terribly afraid, no matter what she told the judge." Mrs. Fisher, a black alternate juror, told Miss Richards that after the trial was over she was afraid that Seale would pay her a visit. Mrs. Butler sympathized with Seale and tried to understand his behavior. "She didn't know why he made those outbursts but she didn't feel that he should shut up. She felt he had a reason for doing it."[76]

Binding and gagging Seale was no solution; with Judge Hoffman's consent, Hayden and Weinglass went to San Francisco on 31 October to consult Garry and to determine whether he could still defend Seale. Garry said he was still too weak after his operation, and that it was too late for him to enter the case. Nonetheless, Judge Hoffman decided there would be no more bonds or gag for Seale. There had been no deal.

Seale sat quietly as government witnesses took the stand until a deputy sheriff from San Mateo testified about Seal obtaining an airline ticket to come to Chicago in August of 1968. Seale then said he would like to approach the lectern. "You may not cross-examine, sir," the judge replied. But Seale rapidly asked the witness a series of questions punctuated by Judge Hoffman's repeated plea: "Mr. Seale, I ask you to sit down." Seal continued: "Why did you follow me . . . at the airport?" "Have you ever killed a Black Panther Party member?" "Have you ever been on any raids in the Black Panther Party's offices or Black Panther Party members' homes?"[77]

Again, Judge Hoffman went over the old arguments about whether Kunstler was Seale's lawyer and whether Seale had a constitutional right to defend himself. The judge then recessed the court, and when

he returned, found Seale guilty of sixteen instances of contempt. Before sentencing him, he said that Seale might speak. "For myself?" asked the defendant. "This," said Hoffman crisply, "is a special occasion." Seale repeated what he had said throughout the trial: he wanted either to have Garry defend him or to be allowed to defend himself; and he insisted that his requests were not contemptuous. "If a black man stands up and speaks," he explained, "if a black man asks for his rights, if a black man demands his rights . . . what do you do? You're talking about punishing. If a black man gets up and speaks in behalf of the world—" Judge Hoffman interrupted to note that if Seale was addressing him, he would have to stand. Seale retorted that earlier he was prevented from standing, and now he was required to do so. He gave up; he would go to a higher court. Judge Hoffman abruptly sentenced him to four years in prison for contempt of court and declared a mistrial in the case. "You can't call it a mistrial," said Seale. "I'm put in jail for four years for nothing? I want my coat." The audience cried "Free Bobby! Free Bobby!"[78]

THE INFORMANTS TESTIFY

When Seale was taken from the courtroom the government was in the middle of its case. David Stahl and a lawyer for the City of Chicago had testified about permit negotiations with Hoffman, Davis, and Dellinger. They told the jury that city officials had taken seriously the Yippies' plans for body painting, nude-ins at the beaches, and public fornication. Stahl also said he had taken seriously Hoffman's statement that the Yippies could call off the Festival of Life for $100,000.[79] According to Stahl, during the negotiations Hoffman had said he was prepared to tear up Chicago and the convention and even die in Lincoln Park; Davis had observed that the city's failure to grant permits was an invitation to violence; and Dellinger, who made it clear that he was not interested in violence or in disrupting the convention, had said that he believed in civil disobedience—a remark the government presumably thought incriminating.

The heart of the government's case was the testimony of three undercover policemen—Robert Pierson, William Frapolly, and Irwin Bock—and a journalism student, Dwayne Oklepek, who had been paid by a Chicago newspaper columnist to infiltrate the Mobilization. Pierson, posing as a member of a motor-cycle gang, had acted as Jerry Rubin's bodyguard, and had played his part with enthusiasm, calling his fellow officers pigs, throwing rocks at them, even being clubbed by them. Frapolly had posed as a student radical. He had joined SDS at Northeastern Illinois College and played his undercover role so well that he was expelled from the school. Bock, a navy veteran, had joined Veterans for Peace and worked himself up in the Chicago peace movement, claiming all along that he was a United Airlines employee. He did not shed his cover until after he had been interviewed by Weinglass as a possible defense witness.

Pierson testified mostly about Hoffman's and Rubin's aggressive rhetoric. "Last night's confrontation was a pretty good one," the undercover agent said to Hoffman on Monday 26 August. "Last night," Hoffman is supposed to have answered, "they pushed us out of the park, but tonight we are going to hold the park." Then Pierson said Hoffman used a "foul word": "We're going to 'F' . . . up the pigs and the convention." Schultz told Pierson to say the "foul word." He said it.

SCHULTZ: Then what did he say, please?
PIERSON: He said that "If they push us out of the park tonight, we're going to break windows," and again he used a foul word.
SCHULTZ: The same word?
PIERSON: Yes.[80]

When Hayden and Lowenthal were arrested later that day, Pierson claimed to have heard Rubin say: "We're going to get even with the 'F' . . . 'n pigs . . . We're going to hold the park, if we're pushed out, we're to 'F' . . . up the Old Town area."[81] The next day, Pierson said, Rubin showed him a newspaper picture of a policeman with a nightstick in his hand. "Look at that fat pig," Rubin said. "We should isolate one or two of the pigs and kill them." Pierson said he had agreed.[82] That night Rubin and Pierson ran through the streets together, and, according to Pierson, each of them threw a small bottle at a police car. And on Wednesday, during the flagpole incident, as demonstrators jumped up and down on a police car, Pierson said he heard Rubin yelling: "Kill the pigs! Kill the cops!"[83]

Bock, Frapolly, and Oklepek testified that on 9 August they had attended a marshals' meeting at which the Mobilization's plans for the convention protests were discussed. Their versions differed somewhat but were generally consistent. According to their narratives, all of the defendants, with the exception of Seale and Rubin, were present at the marshals' meeting. The major topic of discussion was a planned march to the Amphitheatre on 28 August. Davis explained the plan for the march, and Hayden said that he, Davis, and Hoffman had worked on plans for diversionary tactics during the march. Those tactics, Davis said, involved breaking windows, pulling fire alarms, and setting small fires. After further discussion of the march, Dellinger said he agreed with the plans and would report them to the Mobilization Steering Committee.

The undercover agents said that a discussion of Lincoln Park produced a plan to "lure" McCarthy kids and other young people into the park with sex and music and keep them after the 11 P.M. curfew; if the police used violent measures and some of the young people were injured, sympathy would be generated for the Mobilization. Hoffman said he wanted Mobilization marshals to help defend the park on 25 August. Davis said he would have them and referred to "the perimeter of defense of Lincoln Park." He expected the police to drive the demonstrators out of the park sometime after midnight; at that time, they should regroup and march south to the Loop to "tie it up and bust it up." When someone asked what would happen if the police would not let the demonstrators leave the park, Davis replied: "That's easy. We just riot." Davis also talked about a mill-in in the Loop on 26 and 27 August that would involve blocking pedestrian and motor traffic, smashing windows, running through stores, and generally shutting things down. On the last day of the convention Davis proposed a demonstration that would send the protesters home in a proper frame of mind, "if," he was quoted as saying, "there was anyone left."[84]

Of the three witnesses, Bock was the most impressive—and his testimony the most damaging. After describing the 9 August meeting, he told the court of a meeting on 21 August, when Davis again discussed the Amphitheatre march. Davis allegedly said the Mobilization had four alternatives: One, have the march as announced. Two, have a rally in Grant Park. Three, have the rally and a confrontation. And four, have the rally and take over some buildings in the Loop. These alternatives were discussed by some of the marshals later that evening at Froines's apartment. Weiner favored the fourth alternative: there should be some speeches at Grant Park inciting the crowd and then the Conrad Hilton —at least a floor of it—should be seized. The other marshals, including Froines, agreed. On 26 August Davis told a group which included Weiner, Froines, and Rubin that "the people are now ready for a little bit more. . . . We should have a wall-to-wall sit-in in front of the Conrad Hilton. . . . When the police come to break these people up, they would break into small bands and go directly into the Loop causing disturbances . . . break windows, pull fire alarm boxes, stone police cars, break street lights." Rubin added that "they could start fires in the Loop."

At a meeting on 28 August, Dellinger was said to have reported that the city would not grant a permit to march to the Amphitheatre. "If the city doesn't give in to our demands," Hayden responded, "there would be war in the streets and there should be." On 29 August Weiner told Bock, Froines, Lowenthal, and a student named Craig Shimabukuro (an unindicted co-conspirator) that they had needed Molotov cocktails the night before. "They're easy to make," Weiner said. "All it takes is gasoline, sand, rags, and bottles." Next they discussed the possibility of firebombing the Grant Park Garage. No such bombing occurred, but the next day at a Mobilization picnic near Morton Grove, Weiner, who believed that Shimabukuro had been arrested, said that if the police had waited five minutes longer they would have caught him with all the necessary materials for making Molotov cocktails.[85]

Frapolly also testified about the abortive plan to firebomb the Grant Park Garage. At the picnic, according to Frapolly's account, Froines said he had purchased butyric acid (a harmless, foul-smelling chemical) and given it to some girls who had used it the night before. Expanding on the subject, Froines talked about the need for chemists in the movement —then the protesters "could have the formulas for making tear gas, Molotov cocktails, MACE and other devices."[86]

Scores of additional government witnesses testified about statements made by the defendants. On the evening of 27 August Abbie Hoffman was allegedly overheard telling demonstrators that they were going to storm the Hilton Hotel and that they should bring rocks, bottles, and bricks. On 29 August he supposedly approached a black undercover agent and asked if he would help capture Deputy Superintendent Rocheford, who at the time was negotiating with Dick Gregory in Grant Park. Paid informers testified that Hayden made speeches in March and July in which he talked about disrupting the convention. A paid informer also testified that Dellinger told students at San Diego State College in July: "Burn your draft cards. Resist the draft. Violate the laws. Go to jail. Disrupt the United States Government in any way you can to stop this insane war." After being loudly applauded, Dellinger said "I am going to Chicago to the Democratic National Convention where there may be problems. I'll see you in Chicago."[86]

Tape recordings of speeches given at the Grant Park rally on Wednesday 28 August and films of marches were presented to the jury. The defendants could not understand why the films were offered until they saw that a number of Viet Cong flags were shown in them. Later, in his argument to the jury, Schultz would say: "And the crowd charged up the hill with their flags, red, black and Viet Cong flags. You saw films of this incident."[88]

The defendants maintained that most of the testimony concerning their conversations was fabricated or greatly distorted. Cross-examination, however, did not show that government witnesses were lying, and only occasionally exposed distortions.[89] This might be attributed to the fact that cross-examination was neither Kunstler's nor Weinglass's forte. Originally Garry was to handle this part of the defense; his absence from the trial was in this respect a great loss to the defendants. Furthermore, Judge Hoffman interpreted the rules of evidence rigorously against the defendants and generously for the government. Weinglass's repeated complaints about this double standard served only to increase Judge Hoffman's hostility toward him. And seldom did the judge explain his rulings, even when requested to do so by counsel. This gave defendants and spectators the impression that he was being arbitrary; Dellinger, for example, referred to him as the chief prosecutor in the case. At the end of the trial Judge Hoffman told Schultz: "I shall not restrict you to do something that the other side insists be done all the time. We will handle each objection as it is made."[90]

The defendants, believing they were being treated unfairly and frustrated by the failure of cross-examination to bring out what they thought was the truth, sometimes charged in open court that witnesses were lying. When Frapolly was on the stand, for example, Dellinger asked if Foran believed the witness's testimony. Then he said to Judge Hoffman: "I asked Mr. Foran if he could possibly believe one word of that. I don't believe the witness believes it. I don't think Mr. Foran believes it."[91]

Another defense response to government testimony was laughter. At one point Bock mistakenly referred to Weiner instead of Froines, and Schultz asked him a question so that he might correct himself. The defendants and their lawyers burst into laughter. Schultz appealed to Judge Hoffman, who warned the defendants that they were in a United States District Court, "not a vaudeville theatre." "But your Honor," replied Kunstler, "we are human beings, too, and when remarks are made from the witness stand which evoke laughter, I don't think it can be helped. You can't make automatons out of us or robots; we are human beings and we laugh occasionally, and if it comes irrepressibly, I don't see how that really becomes a court matter." Schultz accused Kunstler of laughing to influence the jury by creating the impression that Bock's testimony was absurd, and Kunstler answered: "I agree with Mr. Schultz. I happen to think it is absurd, and sometimes when the absurdity becomes too much, I laugh."[92]

POLITICAL THEATRE

The laughter and outbursts in court, the defendants maintained, were almost always spontaneous. There were, however, three deliberate incidents. The first occurred on 15 October when the defendants, in observance of the nationwide War Moratorium, wore black armbands and draped Viet Cong and American flags over the defense tables. When Judge Hoffman entered the courtroom, Dellinger addressed him: "Mr. Hoffman, we are observing the moratorium."

JUDGE HOFFMAN: I am Judge Hoffman, sir.

DELLINGER: I believe in equality, sir, so I prefer to call people Mr. or by their first name.

JUDGE HOFFMAN: Sit down. The clerk is about to call my cases.

DELLINGER: I wanted to explain to you we are reading the names of the war dead.

MARSHAL: Sit down.

DELLINGER: We were just reading the names of the dead from both sides.[93]

The marshals removed the flags; when the jury was brought in, Dellinger rose and asked for a moment of silence.

The second incident occurred a week later when the defendants asked if they might present a birthday cake to Bobby Seale. The cake was taken by marshals at the courtroom dooe and Davis announced loudly: "They have arrested your cake, Bobby. They arrested it."[94] The third incident took place during the final days of the trial. Angered by the revocation of Dellinger's bail, Hoffman and Rubin appeared in court the next day attired in judicial robes. While the judge watched, they threw the robes on the floor and wiped their feet on them. These acts were not mere theatre; each had an intended message, but it was not necessarily the message the jury received.

One of the reasons more such incidents did not occur was that the defendants did not need the court as a forum. During the trial they held press conferences, appeared on television, and spoke on college campuses throughout the nation. Kunstler and Weinglass did the same—to the consternation of Judge Hoffman, Foran, and Schultz. When the government suggested that such appearances were improper, Kunstler and Weinglass maintained they were simply exercising their First Amendment rights.

WOODSTOCK NATION FOR THE DEFENSE

In his opening statement at the beginning of the trial Kunstler had said: "We hope to prove before you that the evidence submitted by the defendants will show that this prosecution which you are hearing is the result of two motives on the part of the government—"

SCHULTZ: Objection as to any motive of the prosecution, if the Court please.

KUNSTLER: Your Honor, it is a proper defense to show motive.

JUDGE HOFFMAN: I sustain the objection. You may speak to the guilt or innocence of your clients, not to the motive of the Government.

KUNSTLER: Your Honor, I always thought that—

SCHULTZ: Objection to any colloquies, and arguments, your Honor.

JUDGE HOFFMAN: I sustain the objection, regardless of what you have always thought, Mr. Kunstler.[95]

Apparently the motives Kunstler intended to mention were the government's attempt to stifle dissent in the nation and to make the defendants scapegoats for Chicago's police riot during the convention.

The defense was never able to present its case concerning the government's motives. It tried when it called as witnesses former Attorney General Ramsey Clark, two of his aides—Wesley Pomeroy and Roger Wilkins—and Mayor Richard J. Daley. Pomeroy and Wilkins testified that they had consulted Daley and Foran in an effort to encourage permit negotiations between the city and the Mobilization; but government objections prevented them from saying more than that. Clark was not even allowed to take the stand. Daley testified, but Judge Hoffman refused to declare him a hostile witness, which prevented Kunstler from cross-examining him. Direct examination was fruitless. When Daley was asked about his relationship with Foran, the mayor said that Foran was one of the finest attorneys in the country. A question about the relationship between Daley and Judge Campbell was ruled objectionable, as were some eighty-two other questions. Kunstler renewed his motion to declare Daley a hostile witness but the judge denied it a second time.

Since Kunstler and Weinglass had made their opening statements, the defendants had discussed at length the kind of defense case they wanted. Hoffman and Rubin argued for imaginative theatre while Hayden advocated a fairly straight legal defense; the result was a compromise. The defense set out to do principally two things: One, show the jury (and, beyond the jury, the country) the kind of people the defendants were—their life styles, their heroes, their political views, their hopes for the future. Two, prove that they had come to Chicago to protest peacefully and that the police and their superiors were responsible for the violence during the week of the convention. The defense sought to make its case by calling three types of witnesses: rebuttal witnesses, political witnesses, and theatre witnesses.

The vast majority of defense witnesses spoke in rebuttal. Some testified that the defendants who had planned the Mobilization protests and the Festival of Life—Dellinger, Davis, Hayden, Hoffman, and Rubin—had said before the convention that they wanted no violence. The testimony of others constituted a replay—with emphasis on police violence—of the events in Lincoln Park and Grant Park during the week of the convention. Still others took the stand to rebut specific remarks made by government witnesses.

Among the political witnesses were the Reverend Jesse Jackson, Arthur Waskow, Mark Lane, Julian Bond, and Bobby Seale. By describing conversations with the defendants and reporting remarks made in their presence, they presented the defendants' political views—views with which they sympathized. Expert witnesses were also called to testify about the original meaning of the First Amendment, racism in the Democratic Party, and repression of the youth counterculture, but the jury was not allowed to hear their testimony.

Among the theatre witnesses were Arlo Guthrie, Judy Collins, Pete Seeger, and Jacques Levy. Guthrie told the story of "Alice's Restaurant," Judy Collins recited the words of "Where Have All the Flowers Gone," and Pete Seeger began reciting but finished almost singing "Wasn't That a Time." The defendants wanted the songs sung in order to give the jury some notion of their feelings and hence their intentions, but Judge Hoffman would not allow any singing. When Levy testified, the judge reminded him: "You are not in a theatre now, sir." And Foran stressed the fact that the nudity in Levy's *Oh, Calcutta!* had caused the musical to be shut down in Los Angeles.

Allen Ginsberg was, to the defendants, an ideal witness. He testified as to Abbie Hoffman's peaceful intentions and spoke for the counterculture the defendants saw themselves representing:

He [Hoffman] said that politics had become theatre and magic; that it was the manipulation of imagery through the mass media that was confusing and hypnotizing the people in the United States and making them accept a war which they did not really believe in; that people were involved in a life style which was intolerable to the younger folk, which involved brutality and police violence as well as larger violence in Vietnam, and that ourselves might be able to get together in Chicago and invite teachers to present different ideas of what is wrong with the planet; what we can do to solve the pollution crisis, what we can do to solve the Vietnam war, to present different ideas for making the society more sacred and less commercial, less materialistic, what we could do to uplevel or improve the whole tone of the trap that we felt ourselves in as the population grew and as politics became more violent and chaotic.[96]

One reporter called Foran's cross-examination of Ginsberg a form of fag baiting. Foran wanted to know how "intimate" Ginsberg's relationship was with Rubin and Hoffman, and asked about the religious significance of some of Ginsberg's sexual poems which he was asked to read to the jury. The defense decided that if the government wanted poetry, the jury should hear something relevant. Weinglass asked Ginsberg to recite the poem "Howl." "I saw the best minds of my generation destroyed by madness," the poet began as the courtroom fell silent. As he cried "Moloch! Moloch! Nightmare of Moloch!" even Judge Hoffman seemed affected. And when he finished—"They saw it all! the wild eyes! the holy yells! They bade farewell! They jumped off the roof! to solitude! waving! carrying flowers! Down to the river! into the street!"—the defendants were in tears. Foran declined to cross-examine again. He stared at Ginsberg and muttered: "Damn fag."[98]

Some of the defense witnesses actually may have helped the government's case before the jury. The cross-examination of Linda Morse is perhaps the best example. Armed with an interview she had given *Playboy*, Schultz began by showing her a photograph of a machine gun and asking her if she knew its caliber. Even Judge Hoffman was a little shaken by the question and reminded Schultz that the proceedings were not *voir dire*. Schultz, confident, assured the judge and pushed on:

SCHULTZ: You practice shooting an M-1 yourself, don't you?

MORSE: Yes, I do.

SCHULTZ: You also practice karate, don't you?

MORSE: Yes, I do.

SCHULTZ: What else do you practice?

MORSE: Just those two things.

SCHULTZ: That is for the revolution, isn't it?

MORSE: After Chicago I changed from being a pacifist to the realization that we had to defend ourselves. A non-violent revolution was impossible. I desperately wish it was possible.[99]

Schultz explored her political views and got her to admit that when the revolution came, people would gain control of American cities the way the National Liberation Front did in Vietnam. Schultz refused to accept certain answers on the ground that they were not responsive.

KUNSTLER: Your Honor, they are intensely political questions and she is trying to give a political answer to a political question.

JUDGE HOFFMAN: This is not a political case as far as I am concerned.

KUNSTLER: Well, Your Honor, as far as some of the rest of us us are concerned, it is quite a political case.

JUDGE HOFFMAN: It is a criminal case. There is an indictment here. I have the indictment right up here. I can't go into politics here in this court.

KUNSTLER: Your Honor, Jesus was accused criminally, too, and we understand really that was not truly a criminal case in the sense that it is just an ordinary—

JUDGE HOFFMAN: I didn't live at that time. I don't know. Some people think I go back that far, but I really didn't.

KUNSTLER: Well, I was assuming Your Honor had read of the incident.[100]

The defendants decided among themselves that Abbie Hoffman and Rennie Davis would testify. Rubin very much wanted to testify and the rest of the defendants, with one exception, were willing to do so. The possibility that Dellinger might take the stand was discussed, but the defense case took so much time that the defendants decided to go to the jury with only the testimony of Hoffman and Davis.

"My name is Abbie," Hoffman told the jury. I am an orphan of America. . . . I live in Woodstock Nation. . . . It is a nation of alienated young people. We carry it around with us as a state of mind in the way the Sioux Indians carried the Sioux nation around with them. It is a nation dedicated to cooperation versus competition, to the idea that people should have better means of exchange than property or money, that there should be some other basis of human interaction." He said he had not come to Chicago intending to encourage or incite anyone to commit an act of violence. When asked if he had entered into an agreement with the other defendants to encourage violence during the convention week, he answered: "An agreement? We couldn't agree on lunch."[101]

Schultz cross-examined Hoffman on the Yippies' plans for nude-ins and public fornication at Lincoln

Park. He dwelt especially on the latter until Kunstler called him a dirty old man. Schultz asked Hoffman about the plan for Yippies to assist in diversionary tactics. Hoffman answered: "Yippies would assist in diversionary tactics. . . . Never. No. That kind of an agreement with the Mobilization? We had a closer agreement with the Mayor than with the Mobilization."[102] When asked if he wanted to make it appear that the convention was being held under military conditions, Hoffman answered: "You can do that with a Yo-Yo in this country. That's quite easy. You can see just from this courtroom. Look at all the troops around. Right?"[103]

Twice Hoffman took the Fifth Amendment but changed his mind both times and answered the questions. The first time he said: "This might be incriminating. . . . Why don't I take the Fifth Amendment? I always wanted to."[104] The second time he took it in protest to a ruling by Judge Hoffman. When he answered the question he said: "All my years on the witness stand, I never heard anything like that ruling."[105] Schultz then questioned him about his statement in Grant Park about trying to capture Deputy Superintendent Rocheford. In his book, *Revolution for the Hell of It,* Hoffman had mentioned the incident, but maintained, on redirect examination, that he never intended to kidnap Rocheford. Hoffman often distinguished between what he had said and what he had written in the book.

> ABBIE HOFFMAN: Did you ask me if I had the thoughts or if I wrote I had the thoughts? There is a difference.
> SCHULTZ: It is a convenient difference, isn't it, Mr. Hoffman.
> ABBIE HOFFMAN: I don't know what you mean by that, Mr. Schultz. I have never been on trial for my thoughts before.[106]

Davis took the stand to describe the events leading up to the Mobilization's decision to hold a protest demonstration in Chicago. When he testified about the Lake Villa conference, Weinglass offered in evidence the position paper Davis and Hayden had written. The government objected on the ground, among others, that it was self-serving, and Judge Hoffman sustained the objection. "Your Honor has read the document?" asked Weinglass. "I have looked it over," the judge said. "You never read it," Davis interjected. "I was watching you. You read two

pages."[107] That exchange earned Davis a two-month sentence for contempt. Davis was able, however, to testify that the paper stated that any demonstration in Chicago "mush be legal and nonviolent." The permit negotiations were covered in detail: Davis maintained that he sincerely sought the permits because he and the Mobilization wanted a legal, nonviolent demonstration.

Davis testified about his discussions with demonstration marshals, giving a different version than that supplied by Oklepek, Frapolly, and Bock. He said that on 2 August, Bock had suggested that a balloon filled with helium be sent over the Amphitheatre. When Davis asked what it would carry, Bock answered "Anything." He told of the marches he led on Sunday and Monday and the events he observed during the rest of convention week. He also told of two beatings he received at the hands of the police.

Foran cross-examined Davis for two-and-a-half days, and admitted later that it was one of the most difficult cross-examinations in his career. Davis refused to be held to yes-or-no answers and sought to explain his responses. Foran was not always in control, which exasperated him. When he asked if Davis had heard Bock's testimony, Davis shot back: "I heard him testify falsely, yes, sir."[108] But eventually Foran got what he wanted:

> FORAN: And what you want to urge young people to do is to revolt, isn't that right?
> DAVIS: Yes, revolt. That is probably right.
> FORAN: And you stated, have you not, "that there can be no question by the time that I am through that I have every intention of urging that you revolt, that you join the movement, that you become part of a growing force for insurrection in the United States"? You have said that, haven't you?
> DAVIS: I was standing right next to Fred Hampton when I said that, and later he was murdered.[109]

On Friday 30 January Kunstler said the defense had no more witnesses and would rest its case on Monday. Over the weekend he learned that Ralph Abernathy, who had been co-chairman of the Mobilization and in Chicago during the Democratic convention, had returned to the country and was willing to testify. But Judge Hoffman would not permit him to do so, and told Kunstler to rest the defense case as he said he would. Kunstler refused:

You can't tell me that Ralph Abernathy cannot take the stand today because of the technicality of whether I made a representation. That representation was made in perfect good faith with your Honor. I did not know that Reverend Abernathy was back in the country. We have been trying to get him for a week and a half. . . . I have sat here for four and a half months and watched the objections denied and sustained by your Honor, and I know that this is not a fair trial. I know it in my heart. If I have to lose my license to practice law, and if I have to go to jail, I can't think of a better cause to go to jail for and to lose my license for—

VOICE: Right on!

KUNSTLER:—than to tell your Honor that you are doing a disservice to the law . . . everything I have learned throughout my life has come to naught, that there is no meaning in this court, and there is no law in the court—

VOICES: Right on!

KUNSTLER:—and these men are going to jail by virtue of a legal lynching—

VOICES: Right on!

KUNSTLER:—and Your Honor is wholly responsible for that, and if . . . this is what your pride is going to be built on, I can only say to Your Honor, "Good luck to you."

JUDGE HOFFMAN: Every one of those applauders—

VOICES: Right on! Right on!

JUDGE HOFFMAN: Out with those applauders.[110]

Kunstler refused to rest the defense's case without Abernathy's testimony; so Judge Hoffman stated for the record that the defense had rested.

WHO WAS LYING?

In the government's rebuttal case, Deputy Police Chief Riordan gave testimony that suggested that Dellinger had committed violent acts after his attempted march to the Amphitheatre on 28 August was prohibited. "Oh, bull shit," Dellinger burst out. "That is an absolute lie. Let's argue about what I stand for and what you stand for, but let's not make up things like that."

JUDGE HOFFMAN: I have never heard in more than a half century of the bar a man using profanity in this court or in a courtroom.

ABBIE HOFFMAN: I've never been in an obscene court, either.

JUDGE HOFFMAN: I never have as a spectator or as a judge. I never did.

KUNSTLER: You never sat here as a defendant and heard liars on the stand, Your Honor.

SCHULTZ: Now, Your Honor, I move that that statement—

How dare Mr. Kunstler—

KUNSTLER: I say it openly and fully, Your Honor.

SCHULTZ: Your Honor, we had to sit with our lips tight, listening to those defendants, to those two defendants, Mr. Hayden and Mr. Hoffman, perjure themselves.

JUDGE HOFFMAN: Don't, please.

SCHULTZ: I mean Davis and Hoffman.

KUNSTLER: A little Freudian slip, Your Honor.[111]

For that outburst, Dellinger's bail was revoked. Angered by the action, the defendants had long discussions concerning what they should do about it. Hayden argued for keeping cool. Hoffman and Rubin disagreed, and the next day they appeared in court dressed in judicial robes.

Bock, recalled, testified that he had never made a statement to Davis about a balloon carrying anything. In fact, he said, he had not even seen Davis on 2 August, the day the conversation was supposed to have occurred. Weinglass did his best during cross-examination to shake Bock's testimony. He asked if Bock had seen Davis on 27 July, but Schultz objected on the ground that the question went beyond the scope of direct examination. When the judge sustained the objection, Weinglass complained that the rules of evidence were being read restrictively against the defense. The most Weinglass was able to elicit from Bock was a statement that while he was in the navy he had heard of the balloon technique for rescuing downed flyers. In answer to a question by Kunstler, Bock said that he had not read about Davis's testimony in the newspapers. Later Kunstler asked him whether he knew that Davis had testified.

BOCK: I knew that he had testified, yes, sir.

KUNSTLER: How did you find it out?

BOCK: I read it in the paper.[112]

With that answer, Kunstler sat down.

THE LIGHTS IN CAMELOT

The government's position throughout the trial had been that the case was criminal, not political. Yet in the government's opening argument to the jury, Schultz made it sound as though the defendants were being tried because they were revolutionaries:

The point is that they came here wanting a riot, wanting people to be injured—not because they liked people being hurt, people, whether they be policemen or demonstrators, but by creating a situation of violence, where it would appear that the demonstrators were being oppressed, police would be magnetized, would be polarized, would join in with the demonstrators, and a national liberation front would be started. People would start taking to the streets to overthrow, to revolt, as Davis now uses the word—he is calling for a revolution and insurrection; this was to be the beginning.[113]

In his concluding remarks to the jury Weinglass sought to put the case in historical and political perspective. "Throughout history," he said, "it has always been easy to go along. They did it at the Salem Witch Trials. They went along in Jerusalem—"

SCHULTZ: Oh, objection, if the court please. That doesn't belong in this courtroom. That is not legitimate argument and I object to that. I object to that. I object to that.

JUDGE HOFFMAN: I see no relationship—

SCHULTZ: That is grossly improper.

JUDGE HOFFMAN: I see no relationship to the Salem Witch Trials to this courtroom. I don't think it is comparable. I sustain the objection.[114]

Kunstler sought to explain to the jury that the right to dissent in the United States—and not merely the defendants—was on trial. "These seven men," he said, "are important to us as human beings, as clients, but they are not really sitting in the dock here. We are all in the dock because what happens to them happens to all of us. What happens to them is the ultimate answer to all of us."

FORAN: Your Honor, I object to that. That is improper.

JUDGE HOFFMAN: Oh, I would question the validity of that statement. Do you object to the statement?

FORAN: Yes, Your Honor. I object to the statement.

JUDGE HOFFMAN: I sustain the objection.[115]

Later Kunstler returned to the dissent theme: "The defendants are well known. They are leaders in many areas of what we call the spectrum of dissent in the United States. That is one of the reasons they are indicted, because they are such people."

FORAN: Your Honor, I object to that. That is improper.

JUDGE HOFFMAN: The reason for their indictment is set forth in the indictment. That indictment has been read to the jurors, and it does not contain any such statement as you have just made, Mr. Kunstler. Therefore, I sustain the objection.

KUNSTLER: Your Honor, the real reason—

JUDGE HOFFMAN: I direct the jury to disregard it.

Kunstler concluded. "I think if this case does nothing else, perhaps it will bring into focus that

again we are in that moment of history when a courtroom becomes the proving ground of whether we do live free and whether we do die free."[116]

Foran made the government's closing argument. He said the defendants were highly sophisticated, educated, "evil men" whose intentions were obvious. "Davis," he said, "told you from the witness stand after two-and-a-half days of the toughest cross-examination I ever was involved in, because he was so smart and so clever and so alert, but at last he told you. 'Revolution. Insurrection.' "[117]

Later Foran returned to the theme of evil and its relation to the corruption of American youth by the defendants:

Evil is exciting and evil is interesting, and plenty of kids have a fascination for it. It is knowledge of kids like that that these sophisticated, educated psychology majors know about. They know about kids, and they know how to draw the kids together and maneuver them, and use them to accomplish their purposes. Kids in the sixties, you know, are disillusioned. There is no question about that. They feel that John Kennedy went, Bobby Kennedy went, Martin Luther King went—they were all killed—and the kids do feel the lights have gone out in Camelot, the banners are furled, and the parade is over, and this kind of thing. These guys take advantage of them. They take advantage of it personally, intentionally, evilly, and to corrupt those kids, and they use them, and they use them for their purposes . . .[118]

In conclusion, Foran said:

The lights in that Camelot kids believe in needn't go out. The banners can snap in the spring breeze. The parade will never be over if people will remember, and I go back to this quote, what Thomas Jefferson said, "Obedience to the law is the major part of patriotism." . . . You people are obligated by your oath to fulfill your obligation without fear, favor, or sympathy. Do your duty.[119]

PEOPLE WILL NO LONGER BE QUIET

While the jury was doing its duty, Judge Hoffman adjudged the defendants and their lawyers guilty of 159 contempt citations and sentenced them to jail terms ranging from two months and eight days (Weiner) to four years and thirteen days (Kunstler). There was a pattern to the dates of the citations. From the time the first witness testified on 26 September until 15 October, no defendant was cited for contumacious behavior.[120] Almost half of the defendants' contemptuous acts occurred during two brief periods —28, 29, and 30 October and 4 and 5 February— during which Bobby Seale was bound and gagged and Dellinger's bail was revoked.[121] The pattern of the lawyers' citations was somewhat different. Two-thirds of the acts for which they were punished occurred for the most part during the last thirty days of the trial. In November Kunstler had a contempt-free record. That month Weinglass had only one citation, and in December, his record was free of contempt.

Before they were sentenced the defendants and their lawyers were allowed to address the court. Dellinger referred to racism and the Vietnam war in trying to explain some of his behavior. Judge Hoffman stopped him, saying he should not "talk politics." "You have tried," answered Dellinger, "to keep what you call politics, which means the truth, out of this courtroom, just as the prosecution has." The judge asked Dellinger to say no more, but he would not stop: "You want us to be like good Germans supporting the evils of our decade and . . . when we refuse . . . you want us to be like good Jews, going quietly and politely to concentration camps. . . . People will no longer be quiet. . . . I am an old man and I am just speaking feebly, and not too well, but I reflect the spirit that will echo throughout the world."

One of Dellinger's daughters applauded, and a marshal forcibly removed her from the courtroom. "Leave my daughter alone!" Dellinger cried. "Leave my daughter alone!" "Tyrants! Tyrants!" shouted a spectator.

"Heil Hitler! Heil Hitler! Heil Hitler!" Rubin yelled at the judge. And Kunstler, weeping as he hunched over the attorney's lectern, said: "What are you doing to us? My life has come to nothing. I am not anything any more. You destroyed me and everybody else. Put me in jail now, for God's sake, and get me out of this place. Come to mine now. Come to mine now, Judge, please. Please. I beg you." Judge Hoffman, his jaws working, stared straight ahead and said nothing.[122]

Davis explained that the reason for his behavior in October was Judge Hoffman's treatment of Seale. "You know what he called me," said the judge.

DAVIS: He called you a racist, a fascist, and a pig.
JUDGE HOFFMAN: Several times.

DAVIS: Many times, and not enough.
JUDGE HOFFMAN: I will ask you to sit down.[123]

Because Hayden's statement was courteous and restrained, a genuine dialogue took place between him and the judge—the first in the trial. Judge Hoffman said it pained him to be called a racist and have obscenities shouted at him; he felt he did not deserve such treatment. Both men agreed that the trial did not work the way American trials are supposed to work. "I think the difficulty," said Hayden, "is trying to try people for . . . ideological crimes. That is what brings politics and consciousness into the courtroom."[124]

Abbie Hoffman said he had no respect for the court because he did not regard it as legitimate. Rubin said that Judge Hoffman had "done more harm to this country than any other single person alive today."[125] Weiner said that Judge Hoffman saw the Chicago Seven as defendants, but "we see ourselves as revolutionaries. You see us on trial in a criminal trial. We see ourselves under the gun of a political trial being used as a weapon in the hands of the government in an ongoing political war against dissent and youth in this country."[126] Judge Hoffman almost overlooked sentencing Froines, who said: "It's part of being a media unknown that even the Judge finally forgets you're here."[127]

The lawyers were last to speak. Weinglass humbly asked Judge Hoffman for compassion, explaining that this was his first trial before a federal court. With some difficulty he referred to the judge's slighting him and calling him Mr. Feinglass, but he confessed that in the heat of courtroom battle perhaps he too had argued somewhat zealously. Compassion was not forthcoming. "I am accustomed to having lawyers obey the rules," said the judge, "and that you consistently failed to do . . . As you may know—perhaps you don't—this is [your] first case in the federal court you just told me—the United States of America in this case is the plaintiff. 'The accuser'—Justice Cardozo says, 'the accuser has some rights.'"[128]

"I am going to make a rather unorthodox statement," the judge said to Kunstler. "If [crime] is on the increase, . . . it is due in large part to the fact that waiting in the wings are lawyers who are willing . . . to go beyond professional responsibility, professional rights, and professional duty in their defense of a defendant." The judge was leading up to a matter that had bothered him throughout the trial—Bobby Seale. "You represent yourself," he told Kunstler, "to be a leader at the Bar, . . . and you have never, never, made an attempt to say something like this to him, 'Bobby, hush. Cool it. Sit down now.' You let him go on. . . . You made no effort, no effort, to have him keep from calling a Judge of the United States District Court a pig, a fascist pig, a racist pig. . . . You let him continue speaking and repeating. If that is being a great lawyer, I do not share your view." To which Kunstler answered: "I am glad your Honor spoke because I suddenly feel nothing but compassion for you. Everything else has dropped away."[129]

THE JURY DEALS

Meanwhile the jury deliberated. Eight jurors were for conviction on all counts; four were for complete acquittal. Two of the four were Jean Fritz, the woman who had been seen carrying the Baldwin book, and Mary Butler, the retired cook. The other two were Shirley Seaholm and Frieda Robbins. Some of the jurors favoring conviction expressed strong views. One said that "the young people who demonstrated during the convention should have been shot down by the police." Another thought "the defendants should be convicted because of their appearance, their language, and their life style." A woman juror, asked if she could understand the defendants' position, replied: "Do you want your kids to grow up that way?" John Nelson, the unemployed housepainter, thought the defendants were dangerous men who were plotting to take over the country. Mrs. Miriam Hill said she resented all war protesters because her son was in the navy.[130]

Feelings ran high between the jury's two factions. Sequestration had taken its toll; one of the jurors was willing to vote either way in order to go home as soon as possible. At one point the vote was nine to three for conviction on all counts. Then the young computer operator, Kay Richards, suggested a compromise: a verdict of not guilty on the conspiracy charge and complete acquittal of Weiner and Froines. Three of the jurors who had stood firm for complete acquittal

for three days could not at first accept the compromise. They said the anti-riot law was unconstitutional. But that was not, Miss Richards explained, for them to determine; they had only to decide if the defendants had violated the law. That was the turning point; on the fourth day of deliberation, all the jurors had agreed to the compromise.

After the verdict was announced and the jury discharged, some of the jurors expressed their views on the case and the defendants. Edward Kratzke, the jury foreman, said: "I was a streetcar conductor. I've seen guys, real bums with no soul, just a body— but when they went in front of a judge, they had their hats off. These defendants wouldn't even stand up when the judge walked in. When there's no respect, we might as well give up the United States."[131] During a television interview Mrs. Ruth Peterson said the defendants "needed a good bath and to have their hair cut. . . . They had no respect for nobody, not even the marshals. When they told them to get their feet off their chairs, they just put them right back up again. I don't think that's nice."[132]

ALICE IN 1984?

Each defendant received the same sentence: five years in prison and a $5,000 fine. Court costs were also assessed against them. Before sentences were passed, each of the defendants was allowed to make a statement, his last in the trial.

David Dellinger spoke calmly. He told the judge that he felt more compassion than hostility toward him. However misguided and intolerant he thought Judge Hoffman was, Dellinger had to admit the old man had a spunky quality one had to admire. "All the way through the trial," he said to the judge, "I kept comparing you to King George III of England, . . . perhaps because you are trying to forestall a second American revolution which is in the cards."[133]

Rennie Davis was hostile. He said that from the beginning the trial was controlled by the FBI and undercover agents, and that they had lied day after day on the witness stand. "Since I did not get a jury of my peers," he said, "I look to the jury that is in the streets. My jury will be in the streets tomorrow all across this country and the verdict from my jury will keep coming in over the next five years."[134]

Tom Hayden said:

Our intention in coming to Chicago was not to incite a riot. . . . [It] was to see to it that certain things, that is, the right of every human being, the right to assemble, the right to protest, can be carried out even where the Government chooses to suspend those rights. It was because we chose to exercise those rights in Chicago . . . that we are here today. . . . We would hardly be notorious characters if they had left us alone in the streets of Chicago last year. . . . It would have been testimony to our failure as organizers. But instead we became the architects, the master minds, and the geniuses of a conspiracy to overthrow the government. We were invented. We were chosen by the government to serve as scapegoats for all that they wanted to prevent happening in the 1970's.[135]

Abbie Hoffman said he felt like Alice in Wonderland. "I am still waiting for the permits for Lincoln Park. I still think Lyndon Johnson is President. I don't understand what is going on in America, America with a 'k,' not a 'c.' . . . We are being tried as criminals. America doesn't have political trials. . . . This is a criminal trial. So it can't be a political trial. It was Alice in Wonderland coming in: now I feel like Alice in 1984 because I have lived through the winter in injustice in this trial."[136]

Jerry Rubin gave Judge Hoffman a copy of his book *Do It!* with this inscription: "Dear Julius, the demonstrations in Chicago in 1968 were the first steps in the revolution. What happened in the courtroom is the second step. Julius, you radicalized more young people than we ever could. You're the country's top Yippie." Rubin's final words were: "This is the happiest moment of my life." To which other defendants responded: "Right on!"[137]

Judge Hoffman had the last word. He said that the record in the trial and the defendants' remarks in the court that day showed they were "clearly dangerous persons" who should not be at large. "Therefore, the commitments here will be without bail."[138]

THE JURY IN THE STREETS

Rennie Davis had said his jury would be in the streets, and it was. Tens of thousands of young people protested the conviction of the Chicago defendants. They held rallies and marched in Boston, New Haven, New York, Washington, Chicago, Madison, Seattle, and Berkeley. More than 100 were arrested and some were injured. At Drew University, student response

to a speech by Senator Strom Thurmond supporting Judge Hoffman was something Abbie Hoffman might have dreamed up: they pelted Thurmond with marshmallows. The Court of Appeals for the Seventh Circuit gave the defendants their freedom pending appeal, and they and their lawyers traveled around the country speaking at colleges and universities to finance their appeal. After Kunstler spoke at the University of California at Santa Barbara, the students began a protest demonstration that culminated in the burning of a branch of the Bank of America.

Tom Hayden and several writers began books on the trial. The Toronto Workshop Company produced *Chicago 70*, a skillful blend of Chicago trial transcript and *Alice in Wonderland*. The trial had been tape recorded, and one enterprising soul bought the tapes with a view of selling recordings. A publishing house plans to print the entire transcript of the trial, some 22,000 pages. Film producers are considering making a movie of the proceedings. The trial was over, but its myth was just beginning.

THE IDEAL OF A FAIR TRIAL

Just prior to being sentenced for contempt, Bobby Seale said his case would be taken "to a higher court, possibly to the highest court in America."[139] Tom Hayden, in the same situation later, also mentioned the Supreme Court, but in a pessimistic way. He feared the trial indicated a change of direction in the courts. In support of his view he pointed to Judge G. Harrold Carswell's nomination to the Senate as a candidate for the Supreme Court, and said he doubted that a man like Carswell—who fought against "outside agitators," who was against what the defendants considered social justice, and who upheld the status quo—could overturn the rulings in the Chicago trial. "Therefore," he concluded, "for a lot of people who feel the way I do, we are in the movie *Z*. I mean there is not going to be a higher court."[140]

A few days after the trial ended the Supreme Court of the United States heard arguments in *Illinois v. Allen*,[141] a case in which a defendant charged with armed robbery acted in such a disruptive manner during his trial that the judge removed him from the court and tried him in absentia. The Court, in an opinion by Justice Black, held that the circumstances of the judge's action did not violate the defendant's constitutional rights of confrontation. In such cases, Justice Black said, "there are at least three constitutionally permissible ways for a judge to handle an obstreperous defendant like Allen: (1) bind and gag him, thereby keeping him present; (2) cite him for contempt; (3) take him out of the courtroom until he promises to conduct himself properly."[142] In deciding the Allen case the justices no doubt gave some thought to Judge Hoffman's binding and gagging of Bobby Seale. Justice Douglas, who wrote a separate opinion, almost certainly had the Chicago case in mind. "Would we," he asked, apparently referring to Seale, "tolerate removal of a defendant from the courtroom during a trial because he was insisting on his constitutional rights, albeit vociferously, no matter how obnoxious his philosophy might have been to the bench that tried him? Would we uphold contempt in that situation?"[143] And for the first time in a judicial opinion Justice Douglas officially recognized political trials and identified five of them in the nation's past: those of Spies, Debs, Mooney, Sacco and Vanzetti, and Dennis.[144]

The Court's real problems, according to Douglas, do not arise in trials like Allen's, which was "the classical criminal case without any political or subversive overtones." They arise in two other types of trials. The first are political trials that involve either political indictments or political judges. The second "are trials used by minorities to destroy the existing constitutional system and bring on repressive measures." Involved in a trial of the second variety, the defendant proceeds at his peril, for "the Constitution was not designed as an instrument for a form of rough-and-tumble contest. The social compact has room for tolerance, patience, and restraint, but not sabotage and violence." In a political trial, Justice Douglas suggested, it is the government that runs the greater risk. "Problems of political indictments and of political judges," he wrote, "raise profound questions going to the heart of the social compact. For that compact is two-sided: majorities undertake to press their grievances within limits of the Constitution and in accord with its procedures; minorities agree to abide by constitutional procedures in resisting those claims." Then he asked a crucial question

that the Court would one day face: "Does the answer to that problem involve defining the procedure for conducting political trials or does it involve the designing of constitutional methods for putting an end to them?" He suggested that the record in the Allen case was "singularly inadequate to answer those questions," and that it would "be time enough to resolve those weighty problems when a political trial reaches this Court for review." The record of the Chicago trial, if it reaches the Supreme Court, will give the justices an opportunity to consider the problems raised by Justice Douglas; clearly it was not a "classical criminal case without any political or subversive overtones."[145]

The Chicago case might never reach the Supreme Court. If it does, it is not inconceivable that it will be decided against the defendants. After all, the Court decided against Debs, Mooney, and Dennis and refused to hear the appeal of Sacco and Vanzetti. If the defendants lose on appeal, their trial may have an even greater social and political impact than if they win, since they claimed from the beginning that the trial was political and hence unfair. "The cultural value of the ideal of a fair trial," Thurman Arnold wrote,

is advanced as much by its failure as it is by its success. Any violation of the symbol of a ceremonial trial rouses persons who would be left unmoved by an ordinary nonceremonial injustice. . . . Harmless anarchists may be shot by the police. . . . Liberals will be sorry and forget. But let them be treated unfairly by a court . . . and, before dissatisfaction has died away, the prejudice or phobia which created the unfair atmosphere of the trial will receive a public analysis and examination which otherwise it would not get.[146]

The Chicago conspiracy trial is already a cause célèbre. Ultimately the people, not the courts, will decide whether justice was done.[147]

FOOTNOTES

[1]Bobby Seale, Seize the Time (New York: Random House, 1970), pp. 77–78. Seale was born in Dallas, Texas on 22 October 1936 and grew up in Berkeley. Released from the air force with a bad conduct discharge, he had difficulty finding employment and went to Merritt Junior College in West Oakland with hopes of becoming an engineer. There he met Huey Newton in the early 1960s and largely through his influence acquired political consciousness.

[2]Dellinger was born in Wakefield, Massachusetts and graduated from Yale magna cum laude in 1936. During the Spanish Civil War he drove

an ambulance for the Friends; during World War II he refused to register for the draft and served two prison terms, although as a student at Union Theological Seminary he could have claimed exemption.

[3]U. S., *Congressional Record*, 90th Cong., 1st Sess., 1967, CXIII. pt. 8, 10083–84.

[4]Hoffman was born in Worcester, Massachusetts on 30 November 1936. He received a B. A. from Brandeis in 1959 and spent a year at Berkeley doing graduate work in psychology. After brief employment as a psychologist at a Massachusetts state hospital, he worked with SNCC in Mississippi and then came to New York's Lower East Side.

[5]Rubin was a reporter for the *Cincinnati Post and Times-Star*, attended Oberlin College, graduated from the University of Cincinnati, began graduate work at Berkeley, got involved in the Free Speech Movement, dropped out of school and "out of the White Race and the Amerikan nation." *Do It!* (New York: Simon and Schuster, 1970), p. 13.

[6]Daniel Walker, *Rights in Conflict: A Report Submitted to the National Commission on the Causes and Prevention of Violence* (New York: Bantam Books, 1968), p. 22, hereinafter referred to as the *Walker Report*.

[7]Ibid., p. 43.

[8]Because the government and defense versions of what happened in Chicago during the week of the Democratic National Convention read like tales told by characters in *Akutagawa's Rashomon*, I have, in an effort to be objective, summarized the events of that week as described in the *Walker Report*, noting especially all references to the defendants. The *Walker Report* is the most comprehensive and objective study of the Chicago disorders. It is based on 3,437 statements of eyewitnesses and participants, 180 hours of motion picture film, 12,000 still photographs, and the official records of the FBI, the Chicago Police Department, and the National Guard. Daniel Walker, who supervised the study, is a prominent attorney and president of the Chicago Crime Commission, a highly regarded private organization. The study group consisted of 90 full-time and 121 part-time investigators, many of whom were lawyers or were trained by the FBI. Although the *Walker Report*'s conclusions have not been universally accepted, the facts contained in the report are generally acknowledged as accurate. For other views on the Chicago disorders, see John Schultz, *No One Was Killed* (Chicago: Big Table Publishing Co., 1969), and Jeffery St. John, *Countdown to Chaos* (Los Angeles: Nash Publishing Corp., 1969). Schultz generally sides with the demonstrators. St. John presents a view from the right and reprints in an appendix, a large portion of *The Strategy of the Confrontation: Chicago and the Democratic National Convention*, which was put out by the City of Chicago a week after the convention.

[9]Davis was born in Lansing, Michigan on 23 May 1940. At the time his father was an economics professor at Michigan State University. Davis graduated from Oberlin College and received a master's degree in labor and industrial relations from the University of Illinois.

[10]Hayden is the same age as Davis. He was born in Michigan and graduated from the University of Michigan, where he was editor of the *Michigan Daily*. He worked with SNCC in Mississippi in the early 1960s.

[11]Quoted in the *Walker Report*, p. 27.

[12]Ibid., pp. 136–37.

[13]Ibid., p. 142.

[14]Ibid., p. 167.

[15]Ibid., p. 187.

[16]Ibid.

[17]Ibid., p. 216.

[18]Ibid., p. 222.

[19]Ibid., p. 226.

[20]Ibid., p. 228.

[21]Ibid., p. 230.

[22]Ibid., pp. 230–31. Although the *Walker Report* does not mention it, Rubin and Hayden also spoke at the rally.

[23]Ibid., p. 337.

[24]Foran was born in 1924. He received a bachelor of philosophy degree from Loyola in Chicago and a law degree from the University of Detroit. He was a close political associate of Mayor Daley and in Chicago was regarded as a liberal Democrat and an able United States Attorney.

[25]Judge Campbell was born in Chicago on 19 March 1903. A protégé of Bishop B. J. Sheil, he served as his personal attorney and as counsel and director of the Catholic Youth Organization, one of the bishop's major interests. Bishop Sheil was a political liberal and a friend of Franklin Delano Roosevelt, and Campbell apparently benefited from the friendship. In 1935 he became Illinois administrator of the National Youth Administration, in 1938 United States Attorney, and in 1940, at the age of 37, a United States District Judge.

[26]Richard Harris, *Justice* (New York: E. P. Dutton, 1970), p. 70.

[27]*Walker Report*, pp. 1–5.

[28]Harris, *Justice*, P. 70.

[29]Schultz was born in 1938, attended the University of Illinois, received his law degree from DePaul University, and did postgraduate work at New York University Law School. Though he had been a member of the bar less than five years, he had acquired considerable skill as a trial lawyer and originally was to try the Chicago conspiracy case by himself. He had worked with the grand jury, written the indictment, and mastered the details of the case so well that Tom Hayden would later say that he "was an overcharged computer, a structure freak [he wore gray flannel suits and gray ties] who knew the exact details of 'criminal' meetings we had long since forgotten." "The Trial," *Ramparts* IX (July 1970), p. 26.

[30]Harris, *Justice*, p. 181.

[31]In violation of 18 U. S. C. §§ 231 (1) and (2), and 2101.

[32]In violation of 18 U. S. C. § 231 (1).

[33]In violation of 18 U. S. C. § 2101, which provides: "Whoever travels in interstate or foreign commerce, including, but not limited to, the mail, telegraph, telephone, radio, or television with intent (A) to incite a riot; or (B) to organize, promote, encourage, participate in, or carry on a riot; or (C) to commit any act of violence in furtherance of a riot; or (D) to aid or abet any person in inciting or participating in or carrying on a riot or committing any act of violence in furtherance of a riot; and who either during the course of any such travel or use or thereafter performs or attempts to perform any other overt act for any purpose specified . . . shall be fined not more than $10,000 or imprisoned not more than five years, or both."

[34]Weiner was a native of Chicago who had received a B. A. from the University of Illinois and a master's degree in social work from Loyola University.

[35]Froines was born in Oakland, California, on 13 June 1939. After graduating from Berkeley in 1962, he spent a summer working in a black voter registration project in Louisiana and then went to Yale, where he received a Ph.D. in chemistry. While at Yale he joined SDS and worked in a black community project in New Haven. His SDS affiliation led

to friendships with Davis and Hayden.

[36]Nicholas Von Hoffman, "The Chicago Conspiracy Circus," *Playboy* XVII (June 1970), p. 94.

[37]Judge Hoffman was born in Chicago on 7 July 1895. He received his legal education at Northwestern University, graduating in 1915. He practiced law until 1936 when he became secretary and counsel of the Brunswick-Balke-Collender Company, a corporation belonging to his wife's family. In 1944 he returned to law practice, contributed large sums of money to the Republican Party, and in 1947 became a judge in the Superior Court of Cook County. Six years later he was appointed to the federal bench.

[38]*New York Times*, 9 October 1969, p. 30.

[39]Trial Transcript of the Record in the Case of *United States of America v. David T. Dellinger et al.*, p. A71, hereinafter referred to as Trial Transcript.

[40]Ibid., pp. A77–A78.

[41]Kunstler was born in New York City on 7 July 1919. He graduated *magna cum laude* from Yale in 1941. He wrote poetry as a young man and privately published a book of verse entitled *Our Pleasant Vices*. He graduated from Columbia Law School in 1948, underwent executive training with Macy's, and then practiced law and worked as a writer to earn a living, writing mostly books on important trials. In 1961 he defended the Freedom Riders in Jackson, Mississippi, and thereafter represented Martin Luther King, Jr., Ralph Abernathy, H. Rap Brown, and other civil rights leaders. See his book *Deep in My Heart* (New York: William Morrow, 1966).

[42]Trial Transcript, pp. A82–A83.

[43]Ibid., pp. A83–A84.

[44]Ibid., pp. A94–A95.

[45]Ibid., p. A100.

[46]Hayden, "The Trial," p. 25.

[47]Trial Transcript, pp. A296–97.

[48]Ibid., p. 21808. Weinglass was born in 1933. He received a B. A. from George Washington University and a law degree from Yale. Admitted to the New Jersey bar in 1959, he opened an office in Newark where he represented mostly the poor and the indigent and where he met Tom Hayden.

[49]Ibid., p. A343.

[50]Ibid., p. A368.

[51]Ibid., p. A389.

[52]Ibid., pp. A391–92.

[53]Hayden, "The Trial," p. 35.

[54]Trial Transcript, pp. A597–98.

[55]Hayden, "The Trial," p. 36.

[56]Ibid., p. 37.

[57]Quoted in John Schultz, "The Struggle for the Laugh in the Courtroom," *Evergreen Review* XIV (June 1970), p. 73.

[58]Trial Transcript. pp. 458–59.

[59]Seale, *Seize the Time*, pp. 329–30.

[60]*Chicago Tribune*, 1 October 1969, p. 1.

[61]Trial Transcript, pp. 457–59.

[62]Kay S. Richards, "Chicago 7 Verdict: Step by Step," *Boston Globe*, 23 February 1970, p. 5.

[63]Seale, *Seize the Time*, pp. 323–25; Trial Transcript, p. 5363.

[64]Seale, *Seize the Time*, pp. 323–25.

[65]Bobby Seale, "A Personal Statement" in *The "Trial" of Bobby Seale* (New York: Priam Books, 1970), p. 121.

[66]Motion of Defendant Bobby G. Seale, 26 September 1969, File 69 CR 180, United States District Court, Chicago, Illinois.

[67]Seale, *Seize the Time*, p. 325.

[68]Trial Transcript, p. 5416.

[69]Ibid., p. 76.

[70]Ibid., pp. 78, 699.

[71]Seale, *Seize the Time*, p. 329.

[72]Trial Transcript, pp. 3599–3600.

[73]Ibid., p. 4344.

[74]Ibid., p. 4720. Seale's statements are remarkably similar to certain passages of Eldridge Cleaver's *Soul on Ice* (New York: Delta, 1968). See, for examples, pp. 162–63.

[75]Trial Transcript, pp. 4815–16.

[76]Richards, "Chicago 7 Verdict," *Boston Globe*, 24 February 1970, p. 24.

[77]Trial Transcript, p. 5404.

[78]Ibid., pp. 5475–84.

[79]Hoffman said the figure he mentioned for calling off the festival was $200,000.

[80]Trial Transcript, pp. 1359–60.

[81]Ibid., pp. 1371–72.

[82]Ibid., p. 1403.

[83]Ibid., p. 1459.

[84]Ibid., pp. 2496–99, 4265–67, 6212–16.

[85]Ibid., pp. 6286, 6468, 6476, 6484.

[86]Ibid., p. 4381.

[87]Ibid., pp. 2913–16.

[88]Ibid., p. 20552.

[89]In cross-examining Frapolly, Weinglass was able to get him to admit that in the same conversation in which Molotov cocktails were discussed, Froines had said that he did not know how to make them.

[90]Trial Transcript, p. 20441.

[91]Ibid., p. 4372.

[92]Ibid., pp. 6288–89.

[93]Ibid., p. 2425A.

[94]Ibid., p. 3640.

[95]Ibid., pp. 34–35.

[96]Ibid., pp. 10661–62.

[97]From "Howl," in *Howl and Other Poems*, by Allen Ginsberg. Copyright © 1956, 1959 by Allen Ginsberg. Reprinted by permission of City Lights Books.

[98]Hayden, "The Trial," p. 23.

[99]Trial Transcript, pp. 11352–53.

[100]Ibid., pp. 11359–60.

[101]Ibid., pp. 12397–400, 13003, 13005.

[102]Ibid., p. 13233.

[103]Ibid., p. 13108.

[104]Ibid., pp. 13314–15.

[105]Ibid., p. 13340.

[106]Ibid., p. 13328.

[107]Ibid., pp. 17443–44.

[108]Ibid., p. 18055.

[109]Ibid., p. 18243.

[110]Ibid., pp. 19109–13.

[111]Ibid., pp. 19669–70.

[112]Ibid., p. 20018.

[113]Ibid., pp. 20448–49.

[114]Ibid., pp. 21087–88.

[115]Ibid., p. 21091.

[116]Ibid., pp. 21110, 21222.

[117]Ibid., p. 21251.

[118]Ibid., p. 21319.

[119]Ibid., pp. 21338–39.

[120]Hoffman and Hayden were each cited for contempt prior to the first witness taking the stand, but both incidents were trivial. Hoffman blew a kiss to the jury, and Hayden greeted the jury in a friendly fashion with a power-to-the-people salute.

[121]This was initially pointed out by Harry Kalven, Jr., in his introduction to *Contempt* (Chicago: Swallow Press, Inc., 1970), p. xviii.

[122]Trial Transcript, pp. 21508–10; *Chicago Sun-Times*, 15 February 1970, p. 1.

[123]Trial Transcript, p. 21541.

[124]Ibid., p. 21587.

[125]Ibid., p. 21649.

[126]Ibid., p. 21661D.

[127]Ibid., p. 21673.

[128]Ibid., pp. 21803–05.

[129]Ibid., pp. 21746, 21749–50.

[130]Richards, "Chicago 7 Verdict," *Boston Globe*, 22 February 1970, p. 28.

[131]Hayden, "The Trial," p. 37.

[132]J. Anthony Lucas, "The Second Confrontation in Chicago," *New York Times Magazine*, 27 March 1970, p. 34.

[133]*Trial Transcript*, p. 21959.

[134]Ibid., P. 21965.

[135]Ibid., pp. 21967–68, 21972.

[136]Ibid., pp. 21992–93, 21996, 22001.

[137]Ibid., pp. 22015, 22018.

[138]Ibid., p. 22021.

[139]Ibid., p. 5480.

[140]Ibid., pp. 21583–84.

[141]397 U. S. 337 (1970).

[142]Ibid., 343–44.

[143]Ibid., 355.

[144]*Spies et al.* v. *People (The Anarchists' Case)*, 122 Ill. 1, 12 N. E. 865 (1887); *In re Debs*, 158 U. S. 564 (1887); *Mooney v. Holohan*, 294 U. S. 103 (1935); *Commonwealth* v. *Sacco et al.*, 255 Mass 369, 151 N. E. 839 (1926), 259 Mass 128, 156 N. E. 57 (1927); *Dennis et al.* v. *United States*, 341 U. S. 494 (1951).

[145]397 U. S. at 356.

[146]*The Symbols of Government* (New Haven: Yale University Press, 1935), p. 142.

[147]In addition to the sources cited, this chapter is based on interviews with and observations of some of the lawyers and defendants. I discussed the case with both Weinglass and Schultz and interviewed Froines. On May Day 1970 the Chicago Seven came to New Haven; at that time I had an opportunity to observe and listen to all of them. I also spoke briefly with Davis. Earlier I heard Kunstler give a lecture at Yale on the case. Also useful were filmed interviews of Seale and his wife.

Most cases heard in court, as suggested before, are heard before a judge only. Furthermore, most of these cases are not for serious offenses but are trials of persons charged with drunkenness, vagrancy, disorderly conduct and the like. In the next article by Caleb Foote we are provided a detailed accounting of how "vagrancy-type laws" are administered. Immediately following the Foote article is an analysis of court proceedings in rural America where the issues take on a different flavor, but the more general processes remain the same.

23

Vagrancy-Type Law and Its Administration

CALEB FOOTE

I. INTRODUCTION

This study combines analysis of the history, theory and purposes of vagrancy-type laws with a report of their administration by the police, magistrates and correctional authorities in Philadelphia. Such a dual approach is essential. Minor offenses are seldom reviewed by higher courts, and the actual limits of vagrancy are set not in the statute but by practices of police and magistrates. Conversely, an intelligent appraisal of these practices requires some historical orientation. The vagrancy laws "might be unintelligible if we did not regard them as a supplement to the old Poor Laws . . .";[1] they continue to reflect their inception in the fourteenth century when they were "a kind of substitute for the system of villainage and serfdom."[2]

The material on the administration of vagrancy-type laws was obtained by a field study of Philadelphia practices. The basic technique employed was the intermittent observation of hundreds of trials in

Source: "Vagrancy-Type Law and Its Administration," *University of Pennsylvania Law Review*, Vol. 104, 1956, pp. 603–650. By permission of the author and publisher. The historical discussion has for the most part been deleted. Footnotes have been renumbered.

the magistrates' courts during a period beginning in 1951, supplemented by interviews with a small sample of convicted vagrants at the House of Correction and the compilation of statistical information from police and House of Correction records. This method was time-consuming and in many ways unsatisfactory, but there was no alternative, for no stenographic notes of testimony are made at the trials, and the records maintained by the magistrates were useless for the purpose of this study.

It is impossible, short of a more intensive examination, to determine whether the hundreds of vagrancy, drunkenness and disorderly conduct trials which were observed were exceptional or whether they represent a fair sample of Philadelphia practices. It is believed, however, that the sample is representative. A number of different magistrates conducted the hearings, and while there were differences among them, their general attitude towards and conduct of vagrancy-type cases was remarkably similar. The fact that the observation extended from June, 1951, through March, 1954, and that the more serious abuses in magisterial practice so pervaded all of the observed hearings throughout this period make it reasonable to infer that they are typical of Philadelphia practices.

While the administrative material is drawn solely from Philadelphia, the significance of the study has broader application. No comparable study has been made elsewhere, but it is probable that many Philadelphia practices are widespread.

At a time when there is dispute as to the extent to which latitude should be accorded police and administrative action by easing the procedural and constitutional restrictions imposed by our criminal law,[3] the practices described in this study offer a revealing illustration of what happens when those restrictions are removed. Procedural due process does not penetrate to the world inhabited by the "bums" of Philadelphia, and this description of what occurs in that world is certainly relevant to the problem of how far our criminal law administration should relax constitutional and procedural controls to permit greater administrative police discretion.

II.   A VAGRANT'S DAY IN COURT

Because the issues raised by vagrancy-type law can only be understood in the context of the law's everyday administration, examples of typical proceedings in the Philadelphia magistrates' courts are a useful introduction to the problem. The enforcement efforts of the police and magistrates were conducted on a year-round basis, but from time to time during the period of this study the tempo of enforcement was stepped up with a well-publicized "drive" against vagrants. One of the more recent examples was a "cleanup" to make the newly completed Independence Mall "out of bounds for undesirables,"[4] the theory apparently being that the publicity would induce vagrants already in the city to depart and would deter "undesirables" who had planned to come to Philadelphia from entering the city. A description of one of these "cleanups" reveals many of the complex factors and motives that underlie vagrancy administration.

On January 31, 1954, the Philadelphia press reported that police had "opened a drive against vagrants and habitual drunkards in the central city area." By February 2, the drive was at its height, and that morning 56 cases were awaiting disposition when the magistrate opened the daily divisional police court for the district which included the "skid

row" and the central city area. These cases were the last items on the morning's docket, and the magistrate did not reach them until 11:04 a.m. In one of the cases there was a private prosecutor, and the hearing of evidence consumed five minutes. As court adjourned at 11:24, this left 15 minutes in which to hear the remaining 55 cases. During that time the magistrate discharged 40 defendants and found 15 guilty and sentenced them to three months terms in the House of Correction.

Four of these committed defendants were tried, found guilty and sentenced in the elapsed time of seventeen seconds from the time that the first man's name was called by the magistrate through the pronouncing of sentence upon the fourth defendant. In each of these cases the magistrate merely read off the name of the defendant, took one look at him and said, "Three months in the House of Correction." As the third man was being led out he objected, stating, "But I'm working . . . ," to which the magistrate replied, "Aw, go on."

The magistrate then called the name of one defendant several times and got no answer. Finally he said, "Where are you, Martin?" The defendant raised his hand and answered, "Right here." "You aren't going to be 'right here' for long," the magistrate said. "Three months in Correction." Another defendant was called. The magistrate stated: "I'm going to send you up for a medical examination— three months in the House of Correction."

A number of defendants were discharged with orders to get out of Philadelphia or to get out of the particular section of Philadelphia where they were arrested. "What are you doing in Philadelphia?" the magistrate asked one of these. "Just passing through." "You get back to Norristown. We've got enough bums here without you." Another defendant whose defense was that he was passing through town added, "I was in the bus station when they arrested me." "Let me see your bus ticket," the magistrate said. "The only thing that's going to save you this morning is if you have that bus ticket. Otherwise you're going to Correction for sure." After considerable fumbling the defendant produced a Philadelphia to New York ticket. "You better get on that bus quick," said the magistrate, "because if you're picked up between here and the bus station, you're a dead duck."

In discharging defendants with out-of-the-central-city addresses, the magistrate made comments such as the following:

"You stay out in West Philadelphia."

"Stay up in the fifteenth ward: I'll take care of you up there."

"What are you doing in this part of town? You stay where you belong; we've got enough bums down here without you."

Near the end of the line the magistrate called a name, and after taking a quick look said, "You're too clean to be here. You're discharged."

The next morning, the *Philadelphia Inquirer* ran an editorial under the title, "Get Bums off the Street and into Prison Cells,"[5] which noted with satisfaction that three-month sentences were being imposed and that "Chief Magistrate Clothier has threatened them with jail sentences of two years." The editorial felt that "If they have nothing worse to expect from the police than a warm cell to sleep it off for the night, the vagrants will hardly be discouraged. But two years in prison is something else again; only the most hardened bum will take a chance on that." The editorial had no suggestions on how one who was already a "bum" could avoid taking the chance.

The hearings that morning moved even more rapidly; between 50 and 60 defendants were handled between 10:39 and 10:54. Five defendants were committed under the same procedure already noted, the magistrate merely calling their names, taking one look, and then pronouncing sentence. To another he said, "You look like one, three months."

"Three months for you, Tom Harris," he said to a defendant. "I'm working," the defendant replied. "Yes, I know," the magistrate responded, "working on the Bible. Take him away, oh, and take Mr. Gurdy here back with you for another three months."

Three other defendants alleged the defense of working. Two were ignored, but the third kept insisting that he had a job with a packing company. The magistrate asked him under whom he worked, what the first name of his boss was, and finally discharged him.

"Well, what do you want to tell me?" the magistrate said to another defendant. The reply was that he was on his way to Harrisburg. "You keep going to Harrisburg, then, and don't you stop, because if you do, you're a dead duck." Other defendants from Camden and Conshohocken were told to "go back where you belong."

The court room at the 12th and Pine St. police station was jammed at these hearings. Spectators were packed in solidly behind the railing, and the defendants, all of whom were herded out at once, occupied every bit of space between the rail and the bench. The noise and confusion were continuous. . . .

This 1954 winter drive lasted for almost a month. Usually the duration was shorter, and as soon as the newspaper publicity ceased, the atmosphere at the hearings relaxed. With no drive in progress, there were fewer spectators, a higher proportion of discharges, and the magistrates sometimes took longer to hear the cases.

Hearings observed earlier at another court before other magistrates are illustrative of the unpublicized enforcement which went on between drives. At the time the court was observed, it was handling up to 1600 summary cases a month, and of necessity it worked rapidly. One of the magistrates did not even bother to hear the routine drunkenness cases; only aggravated offenders whom the police wished to have committed were brought before him, and the other defendants were automatically discharged without a hearing. The usual practice, however, was for the magistrate to tell an officer, "bring on the boarders," and for the police to herd all the vagrancy-type defendants into the courtroom at one time, a process that was frequently accompanied by general hilarity. The magistrate greeted his favorites with a broad grin; the police joked with the defendants as they shoved them along; and the loafers on the spectator's side of the railing joked about the stench. The officer who sat with the magistrate took the night list of arrests and called the defendants one by one. Some were still so drunk that they could scarcely make it across the room alone, and stood stolidly, with glazed eyes. The emaciated, gaunt, tattered appearance of some indicated both poverty and chronic alcoholism. Many of the defendants were discharged with a brief explanation:

"George, I feel sorry for you; go home and quit drinking."

"I haven't seen you for three weeks—discharged."

"You work, don't you? I know you. I know every one of you. I'm around here seven days a week, 365 days a year. Now go on and get back to work."

But there were some of the same summary convictions noted above, where as soon as a defendant's name was called, and while he was still making his way forward, the magistrate pronounced: "Three months in the House of Correction," and the police hustled the convicted man back to his cell. Presumably in these cases, listed as "drunk" on the arrest roster but as habitual drunkenness on the commitment sheet, the test of habitualness being applied was that described by several magistrates as: "When you get sick of seeing their faces, you send them to Correction."

Most of the Philadelphians were discharged, but one defendant who gave a Philadelphia address was next asked, "Do you have any proof that you live there?" "No, judge, I don't have anything with me." "Three months in the House of Correction." As another Philadelphian, summarily given the same sentence, was led away, the magistrate remarked to one of the officers, "He doesn't belong in this district. He ought to stay where he belongs."

Different magistrates followed different policies regarding out-of-town transients. Some followed the practice of discharging out-of-town defendants with a warning to leave Philadelphia immediately. Another magistrate's invariable opening gambit was the question, "Where do you live?" If the answer was anything other than a Philadelphia address, usually a three months sentence was immediately imposed. . . .

In Philadelphia many vagrant-type defendants are banished merely because their poverty—often but not always combined with alcoholism—makes them aesthetically undesirable on the city's streets and parks, a practice which carries out the Poor Law policy that pauperism alone is sufficient reason to compel people to "stay where they belong." There is, however, a second important factor involved in the policy of exclusion, banishment and control of vagrant-type defendants. It has been thought that the circumstances under which vagrant-type defendants are frequently apprehended are sufficiently suspicious to raise a reasonable inference that crim-

inal conduct other than vagrancy or drunkenness is involved. It is important to note that two quite different kinds of suspicion are involved. The alleged vagrant may be suspected of *past criminality*, the arrest for vagrancy offering the opportunity to investigate whether the suspect is wanted in another jurisdiction or has committed other crimes.[6] On the other hand, the suspicion may be of *future criminality*, the inference being that purposeful poverty is likely to lead to other crimes unless the state steps in.

The commonest judicial explanation of vagrancy's place in a penal code is based on the second of these assumptions. The traditional view expressed in cases and texts is that the vagrant mode of life denounced by the statutes is of itself a crime breeder and the vagrant "the chrysalis of every species of criminal."[7] This view appears very early in vagrancy's legislative history,[8] and courts have continued to echo the preamble of a pre-Elizabethan statute that "idleness and vagabondry is the mother and root of all thefts, robberies, and all evil acts, and other mischiefs. . . ."[9] Vagrancy statutes are viewed as "police regulations to prevent crime,"[10] to check the spread of "a parasitic disease"[11] which is not only evil in itself but "productive of innumerable vices and crimes of great magnitude."[12] Thus, the arrests are supposed to "check evil in its beginning"[13] and "prevent crime by disrupting and scattering the breeding spot."[14]

This theory that purposeful poverty will lead to other criminality has a certain basis in common sense, for if a man is idle with no means of support, "there is a great temptation to steal in order to relieve his hunger."[15] But that statement suggests the rationale's limitations, for if the necessity of self-support is what turns the vagrant to crime, that criminality may be of a very petty nature.[16] The most common example is undoubtedly begging which, although usually proscribed by statute or ordinance,[17] still retains strong public tolerance carried over from religious teaching on giving and the tradition of holy men living upon alms.[18] The sanction against begging has not repressed the practice[19] and is not vigorously enforced, with the result that there are sufficient funds to be coaxed out of the public to meet the demands of those who seek merely a meal, a bed or another drink. A man with such limited objectives is not forced into very serious criminality to obtain gratification.

Nor does it necessarily follow that one who is idle and apparently without means of support will turn to criminality. When completely down and out, he may be able to go on relief or to obtain help from friends or relatives. Many casual workers obtain jobs between periods of unemployment—which last as long as any funds remain—after which they may ship out to sea, go back to migratory agricultural labor or seasonal industrial work or even get a job right in the skid row. A man willing to undergo the very low standard of living of the stereotype vagrant may, like Thoreau in *Walden*, work at odd jobs only to the extent necessary to provide for his limited needs. Men whose stories would place them in each of these categories were interviewed at the House of Correction, and they find occasional recognition in the reported cases.[20]

No adequate studies have been found to correlate the incidence of other criminality among vagrants and thus test the validity of this breeding-ground theory. Probably no such study could be made, for police practices have little relationship to this judicially-created rationale. Even if it could be determined that persons arrested for vagrancy also had a high incidence of other criminality, little light would be thrown on the breeding ground theory, for the police make many arrests for vagrancy without regard to whether or not the arrested person falls into the status of a vagrant.

Such material as is available, however, lends weight to the belief that there is little correlation between pauperism and serious criminality. A study of the prior convictions of a sample of inmates admitted to the Philadelphia House of Correction reveals fairly high recidivism confined to other vagrancy and habitual drunkenness convictions but a low rate of recidivism for other more serious crimes.[21] Even writers who support the "breeding ground" rationale also state that it does not breed dangerous criminality.[22] The British Vagrancy Committee's exhaustive study in 1906 reported that "the witnesses who have given evidence before us agree that the vagrant class as a whole is not much addicted to the worse forms of crime, but minor offenses are very common," citing petty larcenies from the back doors of houses as an example.[23] Kinberg's study of vagrants in Sweden found a large group of tramps, hobos, vagabonds and intermittent vagrants characterized by an absence of criminality in the usual sense, and he cites other European studies showing many subjects punished innumerable times for vagrancy but with no manifestations of other forms of criminality.[24] This Philadelphia study appears to support these conclusions, for there was no indication by police and magistrates that they regarded the vagrants as dangerous potential criminals. Many, indeed, when in the grip of acute alcoholism, were more an object of pathos than anything else.

In any event this analysis is rendered somewhat academic because the police take a much more pragmatic view of suspicion as a policy behind vagrancy law. The arrests, both in Philadelphia and in other jurisdictions as revealed in reported cases, give little indication that the police are consciously suppressing a mode of life because it may lead to future criminality. Where suspicion of any sort is involved, it is suspicion of past criminality. In Philadelphia, magistrates would sometimes commit with some such explanation as "I'm going to have you investigated; there have been a lot of robberies around here." On a number of occasions one magistrate delivered a "You people may think I'm cruel" speech to the spectators at his hearings, one version of which would continue: "It may seem cruel to send all these people up like this, but you'd be surprised how many are wanted in other jurisdictions. Last month alone 50 of these men were wanted." (The month referred to was June, 1951; according to information supplied the writer at the House of Correction, only one of the commitments for that month was wanted in another jurisdiction.) This is a crude, free-swinging method of trying to solve past crimes, not an attack on a breeding place of potential criminals. . . .

One cannot escape the conclusion that the administration of vagrancy-type laws serves as an escape hatch to avoid the rigidity imposed by real or imagined defects in criminal law and procedure. To the extent that such rigidity presents a real problem and that the need for a safety valve is not merely the product of inefficiency on the part of police or prosecutors, such a problem should not be dealt with by indirection. If it is necessary to ease the prosecution's burden of proof or to legalize arrests for mere suspicion, then the grave policy and constitutional problems posed by such suggestions should be faced. If present restrictions on the laws of attempts or arrest place too onerous a burden upon the police because of the nature of modern crime, then such propositions should be discussed and resolved on their merits, as, for example, the proposals in the Uniform Arrest Act.[25]

The economic purposes which once gave vagrancy a function no longer exist, and the philosophy and practices of welfare agencies have so changed relief methods that a criminal sanction to enforce an Elizabethan poor law concept is outdated. To try to utilize a feudal statute as a weapon against modern crime and as a means of liberalizing the restrictions of criminal law and procedure is both inefficient and an invitation to the kind of abuses which this study has shown to be widespread.

It was to avoid just such abuses that the restrictions of our criminal procedure were developed. If the administrative flexibility gained by the circumvention of that procedure in vagrancy-type cases has resulted in a return of those abuses, perhaps that more than anything else demonstrates the wisdom of our traditional procedural protections.

FOOTNOTES

[1] Kenny, *Outlines of the Criminal Law*, 381 (15th ed. 1936).

[2] 3 Stephen, *History of the Criminal Law of England*, 204 (1883).

[3] See, *e.g.*, the differences of opinion within the Supreme Court on two recently decided cases: *Stein v. New York*, 346 U.S. 156 (1953); *Irvine v. California*, 347 U.S. 128 (1954).

[4] *Philadelphia Inquirer*, Aug. 9, 1955, p. 1, col. 1.

[5] *Id.*, Feb. 3, 1954, p. 30, cols. 1 & 2.

[6] For a recent example of this, see the following news item: "Tony Labandeira, 35, was released from the Dawes County jail Monday morning after serving a 10-day sentence for vagrancy during which he was questioned about the rape-slaying of Donna Sue Davis in Sioux City, Ia." *Lincoln* (Nebr.) *Star*, July 2, 1955, p. 16, col. 1.

[7] Tiedeman, *Limitations of Police Powers*, 117 (1886).

[8] The earliest reference was to vagabonds as "idle, and suspected persons." 11 Hen. 7, c. 2 (1494).

[9] 1 Edw. 6, c. 3 (1547).

[10] *In the Matter of Forbes*, 11 Abb. Pr. 52, 55 (N.Y. Sup. Ct. 1860); see *Commonwealth v. Roth*, 136 Pa. Super. 301, 304, 7 A.2d 145, 146 (1939). "The . . . idea that 'where there is smoke there must be fire' is the reason why vagrancy has been a crime for centuries." Note, 80 U. Pa. L. Rev. 565, 568 (1932).

[11] *State v. Harlow*, 174 Wash. 227, 233, 24 P.2d 601, 603 (1933).

[12] *County of Northampton v. West*, 28 Pa. 173, 175 (1857).

[13] *Levine v. State*, 110 N.J.L. 467, 470, 166 Atl. 300, 302 (Hudson County C.P. 1933).

[14] *People v. Pieri*, 269 N.Y. 315, 323, 199 N.E. 495, 498 (1936).

[15] *Daniel v. State*, 110 Ga. 915, 916, 36 S.E. 293 (1900).

[16] See notes 68–71 *infra*.

[17] *E.g.*, Colo. Stat. Ann. c. 48, § 281 (1935); Vt. Rev. Stat. § 8444 (1947). In Philadelphia several magistrates informed me that begging is punished as straight vagrancy, although no such cases were observed. Compare the tramp statute, Pa. Stat. Ann. tit. 18, § 4617 (Purdon 1945), which covers begging but which is a misdemeanor.

[18] "[T]here grew up in the course of time the theory of the religious merit of almsgiving. Charity became a means of securing forgiveness of sin to the giver, a means of grace. Almsgiving, no longer the means primarily of helping a fellow-man in need, became fundamentally a method of washing away one's sins.

"With the rise of monasticism in Christendom the religious basis of begging in the cleansing grace of charity was completed in the theory that those were of superior sanctity who forsook all their worldly possessions and depended entirely upon the charity of God's people. Thus, the religious basis of beggary had its roots deep in man's desire to free himself from sin by giving to a beggar, and on the other hand got its justification from the desire to attain salvation by becoming a beggar. From both points of view religion sanctified begging." Gillin, *Vagrancy and Begging*, 35 Am. J. Soc. 425, 426 (1929).

[19] "Excepting prohibition, there is probably no problem in which attempts at control appear to have been a more blatant and universal failure than they have in the case of begging." Gilmore, *The Beggar*, 213 (1940).

[20] *Leonard v. State*, 5 Ga. App. 494, 63 S.E. 530 (1909) (defendant who usually loafed not a vagrant when earning enough to live in meager style); *Lewis v. State*, 3 Ga. App. 322, 59 S.E. 933 (1907); *Senegal v. State*, 112 Tex. Crim. 408, 16 S.W.2d 1070 (1929) (idling around pool halls by the longshoremen with only occasional employment held not vagrancy).

[21] See Hiller & Rector, *Intake and Release Procedures in the House of Correction, Philadelphia, Pa.* (Nat'l Probation & Parole Ass'n 1953) (mimeo). For the recidivism of all 164 inmates studied, see *id.* table I at 94; of 134 males, see *id.* table K at 96–97. Of the cases studied, 61 were defendants serving vagrancy or habitual drunkenness sentences, of whom 24 appeared to be first commitments, 29 had prior commitments for vagrancy or habitual drunkenness, and only 8 had other criminal records, of which several appeared to be for minor criminality only.

[22] For an example of this confusion compare the following excerpts from Dawson, *The Vagrancy Problem* (1910):

"Dislike of regular labor makes them tramps, tramping making them criminals—the two conditions are inseparably connected as cause and effect, for their kinship lies in the very constitution and instincts of human nature. . . ." *Id.* at 37.

"It is not—in the main, at any rate—a dangerous criminal class with which we have to do, but for the most part the weak and aimless characters whose great need is the moral tonic of discipline and compulsion." *Id.* at 72.

[23] Departmental Committee on Vagrancy, Report 25 (London 1906). For an optimistic recent British report on the rehabilitative possibilities of tramps and vagrants, see editorial comment, 112 Just. P. 727 (1948).

[24] Kinsberg, *On So-called Vagrancy: A Medico-sociological Study*, 24 J. Crim. L., C. & P.S. 409, 552 (1933).

[25] Warner, *The Uniform Arrest Act*, 28 Va. L. Rev. 315, 343–47 (1942).

24

The Law in a Rural Setting

HARRY M. CAUDILL

In her checkered history Kentucky has had four written Constitutions. Beginning with the first in 1792 they were extremely democratic documents, vesting in the voters the power to elect almost every man who governs them or has charge of public affairs. The present Constitution, written in 1890, attempted to preserve undiluted the rough frontier equality whose character had been stamped on the state's people a century before. First of all the Constitutional Convention undertook to reserve all real power at the local level. A host of county and city elective officers was established. In a six-year interval the people in a typical plateau county choose the following officials: the state senator, state representative, circuit judge, Circuit Court clerk, Commonwealth attorney, County Court clerk, county judge, county attorney, tax commissioner, sheriff, coroner, eight justices of the peace, eight constables and five members of the Board of Education. In addition the people in each municipality elect a mayor, a police judge, five or six members of the Common Council, and, in some towns, a city attorney and marshal.

Source: From *Night Comes to the Cumberlands*, by Harry M. Caudill, by permission of Little, Brown and Co. in association with The Atlantic Monthly Press. Copyright © 1962, 1963 by Harry M. Caudill.

At the state level they elect a governor, lieutenant-governor, secretary of state, auditor of public accounts, treasurer, commissioner of agriculture, attorney-general and seven judges of the Court of Appeals. Most ridiculous of all they elect a clerk of the Court of Appeals. This official keeps a record of the proceedings of the state's highest court and has to earn his modest salary by electioneering among three million people in forty thousand square miles of territory.

But the state officials are a façade. The real power of government is at the base. Except for the judicial officers all this great host of local servants are paid by fees. The amount of their compensation is dependent upon their ability to collect charges from the general public. The state officials lack power to remove any of these "fee grabbers" other than the sheriffs, and there is no practical means by which malfeasance at the local level can be punished. To all intents and purposes the governor is little more than a presiding county judge. His ability to lead depends upon his capacity to persuade, because once a governor has fallen into the disfavor of the courthouse cliques his days are numbered. Dealing with a faceless multitude of county-centered and often illiterate voters, the county officials can propagandize endlessly to the detriment of a state administration, assuring its political doom regardless of the worthiness of the governor's aims. The courthouses are one hundred and twenty anchors which perpetually hold developments to the political center of the stream at a virtual standstill. At the bottom of this courthouse conservatism is a relentless determination to prevent any change that might replace fees with salaries or dilute the powers of local offices.

And what is the role of the public servant who holds office in such a setting? What kind of people knock at his door and what standards of public service do they demand of him? By what creed do they expect him to serve the holy principles of Liberty and Justice? In this most democratic of all states, how does Democracy fare?

The office of the county judge is the nerve center of the courthouse. In addition to being a judicial official charged with the trial of misdemeanors and minor civil actions, His Honor is the chief executive officer of the county. He presides over the fiscal court, directs the spending of county funds and is generally the chief "contact man" with Frankfort in political matters pertaining to the county.

His office consists of two dingy rooms. The long unpainted walls are peeling and paint hangs in scales from the ceiling. The rays of the sun struggle with small success to pierce the dirty, rain-streaked windowpanes. In the corner of the outer room a tobacco-stained cardboard box serves as a waste can.

The outer room contains the desk of his secretary and a half-dozen chairs are lined up along the walls. No matter how harassed she may be by the constant procession of callers, his secretary never fails to smile ingratiatingly—because even the smallest frown may offend a voter. From 8:30 in the morning when the office opens until 4:30 when the doors are locked, there is seldom a moment when a group of people are not waiting to "see the judge."

A day spent with the county judge in such an office in a plateau county is a revealing experience. It tells a story of the breakdown of Democracy and of the growing dependence and futility of the population. If Democracy is to eventually prevail over totalitarian ideologies the individual citizen must be able to shoulder a multitude of responsibilities and to discharge them out of a sense of duty. To do this he must possess the ability to meet social and economic problems and the willingness to grasp them. Until a generation ago the mountaineer was accustomed to "turn out" for road workings and other undertakings for community betterment. He was not paid and he did not expect to be. His willingness to work on roads and other essential projects was a holdover from the frontier where no government or government largesse existed. However, as government expanded and its benefits multiplied the old sturdiness began to dissolve. Though many frontier modes and outlooks survive and are sharply impressive, the traumas of fifty years have left a lasting imprint on the character of the mountaineer. His forefathers lived by the frontier maxim "root hog or die." They would be astounded if they could return in the spirit to behold their descendants thronging the office of the county judge to implore his assistance in a multitude of situations which, in an earlier time, would have been met by the citizens without its once occurring to them that help from any quarter was either responsible or desirable.

A moment after the judge unlocked the door to his office an elderly woman darted in behind him. The judge greeted her with an affable smile and after a moment of small talk about her family and community, he inquired her business. She drew a paper from her purse and displayed it to him. On it was scrawled in longhand: *"We the undersigned persons have contributed to help _____ who is sick and has to stay at home."* Below this caption four or five courthouse officeholders and county-seat merchants had written their names. Each of them had noted his contribution of $1.00 to the sufferer. The old lady explained that her son had a family and had been sick for a long time. "The doctors," she said, "can't find out what's the matter with him, and, as fer me, I'm almost certain it's cancer. You know, judge, how we've always voted fer you every time you ever run for anything and will again just as shore as you run. If you can help him out now when he's having such bad luck, we shore will appreciate it."

The judge sighed ruefully, because such pleas are routine, but he added his name to the list and handed the woman a dollar bill.

A moment later the secretary arrived and callers began to fill the chairs in the waiting room. Some said they had just dropped by to shake hands with the judge and had no business in particular, but three very determined gentlemen were ushered into his office. Dressed in mud-spattered overalls, they lived on a creek some eleven miles from the county seat. The state had built a rural highway into the community in 1949 and later hard-surfaced it. But long neglect had allowed the road to deteriorate badly. The spokesman for the group, a tall, raw-boned mountaineer, told their story:

"Judge, you know what kind of a shape our road is in and that it's prac'ly impossible to travel it. The ditch lines are all stopped up and there are holes all over it big enough to set a washtub in. One feller broke an axle right in the middle of the road last week. Now you know our precinct has always been one of the best in the county and you never come up there electioneering in your life that you didn't get a big vote, but if you can't do something for us now we'll sure as hell remember it if you ever run for anything else again. We ain't got no governor or he wouldn't let the roads get in the shape they're in now. We've just got to have the ditch lines cleared out and the holes filled up."

The judge attempted to mollify his angry visitors, for this was not their first visit to his office on the same business. He pointed out very courteously, however, that funds were short and that a new coat of surfacing was out of the question. He promised to send a scraper to clean out the drainage ditches, and pledged an application of gravel for the worst places in the road. He warned them, however, "The roads all over this county are going to pieces, and we simply don't have the money to keep them up. We are doing everything in our power to maintain the roads, but we just don't have the money to do a decent job."

Somewhat mollified, the men departed—but not before dropping another threat of retribution at the polls if some effective relief did not ensue.

As they left, the county attorney rapped on the door and then entered the judge's private office. The Grand Jury had adjourned the day before and, as their predecessors had done for a good many years, the jurors had blasted the county officials for allowing the

courthouse and jail to fall into filthy ruin. In a report to the circuit judge they declared that they had inspected the jail and found that structure wholly "unfit for human occupancy." The walls were cracked and broken, the roof leaked and the cells were inadequately heated. The commodes were without seats and the coal-black mattresses were without sheets. The entire facility reeked of excrement, urine and sweat. They recommended that the jail be closed and not reopened until completely renovated. They found the courthouse in almost equally foul condition, and said so in scathing terms.

The judge and the county attorney went over the report together line by line and agreed with the sentiments expressed in it. The county attorney remarked that it was a good report. "They would have been a lot more helpful, though," he said, "if they had told us where to get the money to do something about it." The judge reminded him that in several mountain counties the question of a bond issue for the construction of a new jail and courthouse had been referred to the people and sternly rejected at the polls. The county attorney opined, "If the same issue was placed on the ballot in this county you wouldn't get three votes for it out of that grand jury panel."

While he and the judge talked, proof of the jury's criticism was manifested by a vile stench which crept into the office from the public toilet in the basement of the courthouse.

When the county attorney was gone one of the county's justices of the peace brought his son-in-law to meet the judge. The justice pointed out that the fiscal court would soon have to add another man to the county road crew, and that his son-in-law desperately needed the job. The judge and justice were political allies, and His Honor agreed that the jobless son-in-law was ideally suited for the position. When this happy accord had been reached his secretary informed the judge that a deputy sheriff had arrested a speeder and that the culprit was awaiting trial. Whereupon the judge walked into the unswept little courtroom near his office and sat down behind the judicial desk.

A middle-aged man and his wife were sitting on the front bench in the section of the courtroom reserved for spectators. Nearby sat a man in overalls and an open-collared, blue workshirt. He wore a baseball player's cap and an enormous star-shaped badge was pinned to the bib of his overalls. Strapped to his side was a German Luger pistol, a memento of some distant battlefield. The judge cleared his throat and asked the officer the nature of the charge against the defendant. The deputy stood up and came forward.

"Judge," he said, "this man was driving in a very reckless way. I got behind 'im and follered 'im about four mile, and I seen his car cross the yaller line at least three times. I want a warrant chargin' 'im with reckless driving."

His Honor turned to the offender and asked what he had to say. He was from New Jersey and on his way to visit his son in Virginia. He and his wife had decided to turn aside and see the Kentucky mountains, about whose beauty they had heard so much. They had driven neither recklessly nor rapidly, and if their automobile had crossed the center line at any time it had been done inadvertently and on a relatively straight stretch of road where no other vehicles were in view.

It was obvious that the judge was impressed by the "violator's" sincerity and that he believed what he had said. He paused for a long moment and reflected upon the situation and, to one versed in mountain politics, his silent cogitations left a plainly discernible track. He weighed the fact that on the one hand he was dealing with a deputy who voted in the county and whose kinsmen and friends were equipped with razor-sharp votes. He knew that if the motorist paid no fine the deputy would be offended. The officer made his living from the fees collected in cases such as this one. If the New Jersey motorist paid a fine he must also pay the costs, six dollars of which would go into the pocket of the deputy. The guardian of the public peace would take unkindly to a dismissal of the case after he had gone to the trouble to capture the man and bring him three miles to the county seat. Weighed on the other end of the scale was a stranger who would never be here again and who, even if he paid a small fine, perhaps unjustly, would not suffer irreparably. These considerations produced the inevitable conclusion. His Honor decreed the minimum fine allowed under the statute. The total came to eighteen dollars and fifty cents. When justice had thus been meted

out the judge did not return to his office but took advantage of the opportunity to escape for lunch. When he returned at 1:00 p.m. the callers had increased in number and their problems had grown even more vexatious.

A fifty-year-old man, his wife and her father had come to tell the judge that the Welfare worker had denied his claim for public assistance. He wanted the judge to talk to her and, if necessary, to go to Frankfort and see if the claim couldn't be straightened out. He said:

"Judge, I just can't work. I can't do nary a thing. I'm sick and I've got a doctor's certificate to prove it. I worked in the mines for twenty-five years before they shut down but you know I got into bad air and ever since then when I git hot or a little bit tired I get so nervous I can't hardly stand it. I don't have a thing in the world to live on and they've turned down my claim, and I know that if you will get onto the people at Frankfort you can get it straightened out. There's a sight of people in this county that ain't as bad off as I am and they didn't have any trouble gettin' it and I'm sure not a-goin' to give up on it without seeing into it a little further."

At this juncture the man's father-in-law, a gentleman of approximately seventy-five, chimed in. He had lived with his daughter and son-in-law for three years and never had known anybody who was a harder worker. He had seen the man work an hour or two in his vegetable garden and get so nervous that he would spill his coffee when he came into the house to rest. He assured the judge that he would be the first to say so if he thought his son-in-law was "putting on."

The judge heard this tale of woe with deep respect and assured his visitors that they had his sympathy and that he would make every effort to help them. He hedged by pointing out that public assistance is administered by a state agency over which he had no control. The Welfare Department had a lot of stubborn people on its staff, some of whom, unfortunately, were quite unreasonable. He remembered that the sick man had always been his friend and stood by him in bygone years. He summed up his gratitude with the assertion, "You've scratched my back in the past and I'll try to scratch yours now. You know, turn about is fair play."

Highly gratified, the nervous man, his wife and his father-in-law left, after again reminding the judge that they sure would appreciate his help.

The next caller had been drawing State Aid but his check had been discontinued because his children had not been attending school regularly. He explained that his young-'uns had been sick. "Not sick enough to have a doctor, but feelin' bad and I just couldn't make 'em go to school a-feelin' bad. As soon as they got to feelin' better they went right back to school, and I don't know what we'll do if we don't git some help fer 'em again."

He promised that if the judge could prevail upon the Welfare worker to restore his check he would make an affidavit to send his children to school on each day when they were well enough to go.

About 3:30 in the afternoon the county truant officer (known officially by the horrendous title of Director of Pupil Personnel) made his appearance. A warrant had been sworn out charging a father with failing to send his children to school and the trial was set for that hour. The defendant was already present in the little courtroom. A few moments later the county attorney appeared to prosecute the case for the state. The truant officer explained that the defendant was the father of six children, all of whom were of elementary school age. They had not been to school in the preceding month despite his pleas that the father keep them in regular attendance. The county attorney asked the Court to impose a fine or jail sentence. The judge asked the defendant why he had not been sending his children to school. The man stalked forward and gazed around him with the uncertainty of a trapped animal. He had dressed in tattered overalls to which many patches had been affixed. He was approximately forty-five years old and it was obvious from his huge hands and stooped shoulders that he had spent many years under the low roof of a coal mine. He pleaded his defense with the eloquence of an able trial lawyer. With powerful conviction he said:

"I agree with everything that's been said. My children have not been going to school and nobody wants them to go any more than I do. I've been out of work now for four years. I've been all over this coal-field and over into Virginia and West Virginia looking for work. I've made trip after trip to Indianny, Ohio, and Michigan and I couldn't find a day's work anywhere. I drawed out my unemployment compensation over three years ago and the only income I've had since has been just a day's work now and then doing farm work for somebody. I sold my old car, my shotgun, my radio and even my watch to get money to feed my family. And now I don't have a thing in the world left that anybody would want. I'm dead-broke and about ready to give up. I live over a mile from the schoolhouse and I simply don't have any money to buy my children shoes or clothes to wear. I own a little old four-room shanty of a house and twenty acres of wore-out hillside land. Last spring the coal company that owns the coal augered it and teetotally destroyed the land. I couldn't sell the whole place for five hundred dollars if my life depended on it. Me and my oldest boy have one pair of shoes between us, and that's all. When he wears 'em I don't have any and when I wear 'em he don't have any. If it wasn't for these rations the gover'ment gives us, I guess the whole family would of been starved to death long afore now. If you want to fine me I ain't got a penny to pay it with and I'll have to lay it out in jail. If you think puttin' me in jail will help my young-'uns any, then go ahead and do it and I'll be glad of it. If the county attorney or the truant officer will find me a job where I can work out something for my kids to wear I'll be much abliged to 'em as long as I live."

At the conclusion of his declaration the judge looked uneasily around, eying the county attorney and the truant officer in the hope that some help would come from that quarter. Both gentlemen remained silent. At length the judge plied the defendant with questions. The man had a third-grade education. He had worked in the mines for a total of twenty years and had spent three years as an infantry soldier in the war against Japan. He had been fortunate, however, and had received no wounds. Consequently, he drew no pension or compensation from the Veteran's Administration. The factories to which he had applied for employment had insisted on men with more education than he possessed. They also wanted younger men. Finally the county attorney demanded to know whether he had any skill except mining coal. The answer was an emphatic "No." Then he blurted out:

"Judge, I'm not the only man in this fix on the creek where I live. They's at least a dozen other men who ain't sent their children to school for the same reason mine ain't a-goin'. They can't send 'em cause they can't get hold of any money to send 'em with. Now the county attorney and the truant officer are trying to make an example out of me. They think that if I go to jail for a week or two the rest of 'em will somehow find the money to get their kids into the schoolhouse."

He looked intently at the truant officer and demanded, "Ain't that so?" to which the truant officer hesitantly assented.

The judge mulled the problem over for a moment or two and then "filed away" the warrant. He explained that it was not being dismissed, but was being continued upon the docket indefinitely. "If the case is ever set for trial again I will write you a letter well in advance of the trial date and tell you when to be here," he said. "In the meantime go home and do the best you possibly can to make enough money to educate your children. If they don't go to school they'll never be able to make a living and when they get grown they'll be in just as bad a fix as you are in now."

The defendant thanked the judge, picked up his battered miner's cap and walked to the door. There he paused and looked back at the judge, attorney and truant officer for a long moment, as though framing a question. Then he thought better of it and closed the door behind him. His Honor had had enough for one day, and decided to go home. While he was locking the door I glanced at the headlines on the newspaper the morning mail had brought to his desk:

FEDERAL AID TO EDUCATION BILL DIES IN HOUSE COMMITTEE

BILLIONS APPROVED FOR FOREIGN AID

JOBLESS MINER KILLS SELF IN HARLAN

25

Sentencing and Sentences

WILLIAM J. CHAMBLISS
and ROBERT B. SEIDMAN

Once the plea or verdict of guilty has been recorded, the whole thrust of the procedures of criminal trial changes. Instead of following a set of norms conforming to the ideal of due process, the sentencing is controlled by norms which are frankly incompatible with the ideal. The central fact in the actual procedures, which is carefully protected by the normative structure itself, is the unbelievably wide, almost totally uncontrolled discretion of the trial judge. To understand the sentencing process, we shall consider it as a system, with its inputs, conversion processes, and outputs.

SENTENCING: INPUTS

A wide variety of inputs enter the sentencing process: information concerning the offense, information concerning the offender, pressures from public and the police and prosecuting authorities, the personality, training, and value-set of the sentencing judge, the ability and status of the defense counsel, and the personal relationships between the counsel and the court.

Source: *Law, Order and Power*, Reading, Mass.: Addison-Wesley, 1971, pp. 447–472. By permission of the authors and publisher.

The information concerning the offense is derived from a variety of sources. If there has been a trial, of course the trial judge is well aware of the facts of the particular case. In most cases, however, where there is a plea of guilty, the judge's information must come from other sources. There are always the bare facts set forth in the information to which the accused has pleaded guilty. Especially in the case of minor offenses, this is more often than not the only information which the judge will have about the matter. For example, every morning in some police or magistrate's courts one can see a long queue of landlords charged with suffering garbage cans to stand without a cover, each dutifully paying a few dollars—a standard fine set for the charge—to a clerk who has no knowledge of the circumstances of the offense other than the fact of the charge. In traffic offenses, too, a similar procedure frequently obtains. In fact, this procedure is so regularized in traffic cases that in many communities it is possible to plead guilty by mail to certain minor offenses and enclose a standard fine set forth in the policeman's ticket, which is also designed as an envelope to be used for mailing purpose.

Such routine assessment of fines occurs when two conditions are present: there is a great number of such cases so that the court cannot consider each one individually because of the constraints of time and manpower; and the offense does not touch seriously the value-set of the judge.

In more serious cases, on a plea of guilty, the prosecutor will briefly detail the facts out of which the case arose. Such a statement, which may be slanted, sometimes presents the defense counsel with Hobson's choice. If he permits the statement of the prosecutor to stand without challenge, the court may sentence on the basis of information more damaging to the accused than the defense counsel believes the facts to warrant. On the other hand, the legitimacy of the guilty plea depends on the claim that the accused acknowledges that he is in fact guilty. That acknowledgement and the repentance which it implies is the theoretical justification for the leniency which the defendant hopes to earn by his plea. To challenge the facts as set forth by the prosecutor thus places in jeopardy the entire plea, frequently carefully negotiated and delicately balanced. Accordingly, far more often than not the defense dares not challenge the prosecution's statement of the facts, so that it is only a prosecution's view of the offense that the judge ever hears. This view is of course basically the policeman's suspicions put forward as facts, since the prosecutor derives his information in almost all cases from examining the police file on the case.

In practice, however, the prosecutor only rarely presents Hobson's choice to counsel. The prosecutor, perhaps more than any other official in the criminal process, has an enormous stake in the plea-bargaining system. It is in his interest to ensure that adequate inducements are held out to defendants to plead guilty. Some of these inducements are within his power to provide. The act of sentencing, however, even after the reduction of charge, is nominally at least in the hands of the judge. It is to be expected, therefore, that prosecutors will cooperate in presenting the facts of the offense and the character of the accused in as favorable light as possible after the plea of guilty has been recorded. The *Yale Law Journal*, from 140 replies to a questionnaire sent to all federal district judges in 1956, reported that a number of judges gave as a reason for the lighter sentences delivered after guilty pleas, that frequently brutal

aspects of the crime emerge during a trial (thus leading to more severe sentences) that are not brought to light by a prosecutor's statement of the facts.[1]

Finally, the judge may learn the details of the offense from a presentence report. This report has much more significance, however, as a source of information about the offender, which is the second of the significant inputs into the sentencing process that we consider here.

As we saw in our discussion of the principles of sentencing, among the elements to be taken into account is the amenability of the accused to rehabilitative treatment. It follows that if the sentence is to fit not merely the crime but also the criminal, the judge must have some information about the accused person.

In the case of many minor crimes, practically the only information the judge can have about the accused is his superficial appearance in court. More than half the cases dealt with in the courts, even excluding traffic offenses, are relatively minor: drunkenness, disorderly conduct, vagrancy. Typically, sentences for such offenders are meted out quickly if not necessarily justly. Caleb Foote reports that the Municipal Court in Philadelphia disposed of 55 cases in 15 minutes.[2] The offenders in such cases almost invariably are persons who are regarded by the judge as having a degraded status—"winos," beggars, prostitutes, in short the "dregs of the society"— and hence so summary a method of dealing with their fates does not usually seriously disturb the middle-class conscience of the judge. Moreover, the bureaucratic pressures for efficiency, speed, and routine are again at work in subverting the individualized sentencing that is the ideal.

In more serious cases, the burden of describing the accused to the courts tends to fall on the defense counsel or the presentence investigation and report. In most jurisdictions, whether or not there is a presentence report, the defense counsel will plead for his client prior to the sentencing, at least when the offenses are serious. Frequently he will introduce letters or affidavits from "respectable" members of the community attesting to the good reputation and work habits of the accused, especially if he is a first offender. Witnesses may even be called—a minister, a teacher, or a doctor—to testify to the defendant's previous good character. The purpose of the defense counsel is to persuade the judge that the accused is basically a person of fine character, who committed the theft or assault in question through a temporary, regrettable, but most unlikely aberration.

The prosecutor's role in presenting information about the character of the accused is generally far more limited. Invariably, he will supply the most weighty bit of information relating to the accused —his previous criminal record—contained in the police files. Beyond that, however, he will only rarely oppose the defense counsel's description of the accused, and that is when he is pressed by the police or adverse publicity to obtain a heavy sentence.

Perhaps the most important source of information about the criminal is the presentence report, now increasingly common in most states. This is a report prepared by a social worker, usually attached to the Probation Department. A typical suggested form requires the case worker to supply information under the following headings: (1) offenses, (2) prior record, (3) family history, (4) home and neighborhood, (5) education, (6) religion, (7) interests and activities, (8) health (physical and mental), (9) employment, (10) resources, (11) summary, (12) plan, and (13) agencies interested.[3] Since the argument and evidence put forward by the defense counsel is obviously and admittedly biased in favor of the accused, it is inevitable that the judge will give great weight to the presentence report, prepared as it is by a professional worker presumably without a personal interest in the case. For example, for the years between 1959 and 1965, the Superior Courts of California followed the probation officer's recommendation of probation between 95.6% to 97.3% of the time. In ten judicial circuits of the United States in 1964, the trial courts followed those recommendations in 94.1% of the cases. The California courts between 1959 and 1965 failed to follow the probation officer's recommendation against probation between 12.8% and 21.6% of the time; and in the ten federal judicial circuits in 1964, the recommendations were not followed in an average of 19.7% of the cases.[4]

Public pressures constitute a significant input into the sentencing system, but one which is difficult to evaluate. That local newspapers have undertaken a campaign against a particular category of crime, or have given special publicity to a particular crime in question, plainly has some effect upon the judge's attitude toward the sentence. The Advisory Council of Judges to the National Probation and Parole Association has formally stated that:

> the judge must use public opinion constructively as an aid in sentencing, but not be dominated by it; he must respect it, but not be enslaved by it; he must lead the community toward higher standards of justice and treatment, but not be so far ahead of it that it will lose sight of him.[5]

What this Delphic statement may mean in practice, of course, is anybody's guess, but it does demonstrate that judges do take public opinion into account.

The difficulty, of course, is in determining what is "public opinion." For example, following a serious outbreak of violence in the Chicago ghetto, Mayor Daley issued a statement urging the police to shoot looters. It is only to be expected that judges, in looting cases, would respond to such a statement by imposing relatively heavier sentences in Chicago than in New York, where Mayor Lindsay stated that he did not believe it proper to shoot a teen-ager for stealing a six-pack of beer. In either case, the judge is apt to assume that the mayor's statement *is* public opinion. That there may be substantial elements of the public that disagree with either statement may be disregarded.

In fact, the "public opinion" which a judge will follow is likely to be the public opinion of those whose respect and admiration he regards as important. An English lawyer (later Lord Chancellor of England) put it nicely in a different context:

> The majority of us need the approval of their fellow citizens. Consciously or unconsciously, we spend a good deal of time looking over our shoulder to those whose esteem we value. The Conservative looks to Conservatives, the Socialist to Socialists, the lawyer to lawyers, the husband to his wife . . .[6]

Judges look to the approbation of those in their own reference group—other judges and lawyers first of all, and the upper classes generally. So the "public" opinion to which judges are most apt to defer is in fact middle-class opinion, largely as stated in the public press.

As we have suggested, in cases of pleas of guilty prosecutors rarely seek to put pressure on the court to deliver a particularly heavy sentence, for it is in their interest on such pleas to cooperate with the defense counsel to keep sentences low. They will regularly recommend relatively heavy sentences under two circumstances: at a trial and when the police insist on it. In general, the police measure their success in terms of the clearance rate, which is related to arrest and conviction, not to the severity of the sentence. As a result, they are not usually very much interested in the sentence.[7]

The police do interest themselves in the sentence in three situations. In the first place, when they have bargained for a lower sentence with an accused in exchange for a guilty plea or a confession to other unrelated crimes to help the clearance rate, they will try to persuade the prosecutor, and through him the judge, to act leniently.[8] Secondly, the police will try to obtain a heavier sentence where the arrest has been made by a highly specialized unit dealing with a specific problem, and the offender is an habitual offender who has caused the unit a great deal of trouble.[9] Finally, the police will press for a heavy sentence when the accused has been "fresh," or resisted arrest, or otherwise demonstrated a low opinion of the force.

Most prosecutors take the same position. They must cooperate with the police, for without the latter's cooperation the prosecutor's job is impossible. Many prosecutors will not agree to a reduced charge or promise to recommend a specific sentence to the trial judge without substantial agreement by the police. It is not infrequent for the prosecutor to ask the police if the accused had been properly respectful. In cases in which there are allegations of police misconduct— a false arrest or unnecessary violence—it is quite common for the prosecutor to insist on the defendant's executing a release of the arresting officer personally from liability as a condition for *nolle prosequi* or even for an agreement to permit the accused to plead guilty to a lesser charge.

The personality and value-sets of the trial judge form a most important group of inputs into the sentencing process. In most states the personality of the trial judge has been shaped by the fact that he is likely to have spent a good part of his prejudgeship training as a prosecuting attorney. He is therefore conditioned to a pro-police viewpoint and most likely will adopt the crime-control attitude.

The final significant input into the system is the ability and status of the defense counsel, and the personal relationship between the counsel and the judge. The most important aspect of this input is the character of the defense counsel as a member of the "courthouse regulars" or as a little-known outsider. Judges are interested in clearing their dockets; they, too, must meet the demands of bureaucratic efficiency. They are well aware that the lawyer's livelihood depends on the appearance that he is better able to persuade judges to impose lower sentences than others. Moreover, lawyers and judges are members of the same profession; more likely than not, they are both involved in political activities and, especially in smaller communities, may be connected by a hundred professional ties of cases handled together, and favors given and taken.

SENTENCING: CONVERSION PROCESS

All these inputs go into the sentencing process. Out of these various bits of information (or perhaps misinformation), pressures, and interpersonal relationships, the judge must fashion a specific sentence. What are the norms which determine the appropriate elements which the judge ought to take into account and which determine the nature of the decision-making process?

As we saw earlier, in fact there are *no* standards or norms which instruct the judge which elements are to be taken into account in sentencing, and what weight they are to be given. He is presented only with a statute which typically provides very broad limits within which he must set the sentence. In New York, for example, robbery in the first degree is punishable by imprisonment of not "less than ten years" nor "more than thirty years."[10] Rape in the first degree is "punishable by imprisonment for not more than twenty years."[11] Burglary in the first degree is punishable by imprisonment from ten to thirty years, burglary in the second degree "for a term not exceeding fifteen years."[12]

So long as a trial judge stays within such limits in his sentences, and in the absence of a specific statute permitting appeal of sentence (which exists in only a very few jurisdictions), an appellate court will not reduce the sentence merely because it is, in the opinion of the appellate court, excessive.[13] Even where a judge uses multiple successive sentences to increase the statutory maximum, an appellate court will not intervene, however much they may deplore the practice.[14] Nor will they intervene when the trial judge uses evidence of a crime not charged to increase the sentence. For example, in *Peterson v. United States*,[15] the defendant was convicted of the theft of a forty-cent postage stamp. The trial judge imposed the maximum penalty under the statute, stating that "the offense for which the defendant was formally found guilty" was "rather trifling." He continued, however, to say that he believed that Peterson was also guilty of subordination of perjury—a crime not charged—"which was the main reason for the severe sentence imposed." The appellate court refused to intervene in the sentence. In *U.S. v. Sacher*,[16] the federal Court of Appeals went so far as to hold that a trial court's "reason for the length of sentence would not affect its validity and should be ignored on appeal."

The origin of this sweeping and almost unchecked power of the trial judge seemingly lies embedded in the history of punishments in the common law. During the great formative period of the common law, death was the only penalty for crimes of any seriousness and for many that were not serious at all. In 1819, Sir Thomas Fowell Buxton put the number of capital offenses at 223 in England. Leon Radzinowicz maintains that, since many of the statutes in fact covered a variety of crimes, the number ought to be three or four times as much.[17] They made a crazy patchwork without rhyme, plan, or reason, as successive Parliaments mindlessly added felonies without end, each punishable by death without benefit of clergy. Arson of a dwelling house was a capital offense. So was burning a cock of hay or a threat to commit arson. But burning down a field of standing ripened wheat was not even a crime. Serious crimes and frivolous ones intermingled without distinction. If murder was a capital offense, so was the heinous conduct involved in maliciously cutting the hop-binds on the poles holding the hops on any plantation of hops.[18] On the other hand, through some weird oversight it was not even a misdemeanor to steal from a furnished house let as a whole.[19]

This intolerably broad definition of capital offenses came to be cut down by the concurrence of three fac-

tors: the frequent commutation of the death sentence by the Crown, the arbitrary understating of the value of stolen property by juries (so that there are cases reported in which juries solemnly held that the value of a £100 note was but 39 shillings, thus preventing the crime from being capital, since capital punishment began at theft of property of a value of 40 shillings); and a series of restrictive interpretations by the judges. It is from the first of these, the exercise of the royal prerogative, that the judges derived their power to assess sentence.

The royal prerogative was always entirely discretionary; it remains so to this day. In practice, punishment by death came to be inflicted on smaller and smaller numbers of those convicted by the courts, the royal prerogative being increasingly used to commute the sentences to transportation. (Indeed, many Americans today are the direct descendants of those thus freed and transported.[20]) The custom arose that judges would send a memorial to the Crown recommending transportation, which came to be followed as a matter of course by the King.[21] In 1768 the judges were in effect given the power to order any person convicted of capital offenses without benefit of clergy to be transported for any term they thought proper, or for fourteen years if no term was specially mentioned.[22] The extent of punishment for clergyable offenses, at the beginning of the eighteenth century usually nothing or at the most imprisonment for a year without hard labor,[23] was slowly increased until in the reign of George IV it included imprisonment not exceeding a year or, in some cases, a whipping, and in cases of petty larceny (and some cases of grand larceny), seven years' transportation.[24]

The power given to the judges to commute death sentences was exercised with increasing frequency. In 1805, in England and Wales, 4605 accused persons were admitted for trial; no bills were found in 730 cases; 1092 were acquitted; of the remaining 2783, 350 were sentenced to death, of whom 68 were executed, 595 were transported, 1680 were imprisoned, and 180 were sentenced to a whipping or a fine.[25]

A great wave of reform of English criminal law, led by Sir John Romilly and Jeremy Bentham, in the course of years worked a seachange over the harshness and virtual anarchy of the earlier English criminal law.[26] The result was that by 1883 (when Stephen wrote), capital punishment no longer existed in England save for a very small number of crimes: treason, murder, etc. The reform did not achieve significant rationalization of the structure of punishments, however. For example, in 1883 it was impossible to sentence a man to more than two years of hard labor or to transportation for less than five years; there was simply no sentence available which would remove anyone from society for a period of between two to five years.[27]

The tradition, however, that any punishment short of death was a matter of grace appeared to have been firmly established. The reformers regarded this extraordinary scope of discretion for the judge as part of the evil of a discretionary criminal law which they sought to change. The cardinal aim of the middle-class reformers was a world of law rather than one run at the discretion of either judges or the aristocracy in general. Romilly urged that judges should not have unlimited discretion as to punishment.[28] Bentham tried to lay down rules for punishment based on his utilitarian calculus of pleasure and pain.[29] This movement received impetus from the continent, where the revolutionary dogma of *nulla poena sine lege* had been developed precisely to eliminate the autocratic system of "arbitrary punishment" imposed by the judges.

The drive to formalize the sentencing structure and the opposing tradition that punishment was a matter of judicial discretion resolved themselves in the practice, eventually established in both England and the United States, that the legislature lays down the maximum (and sometimes minimum) punishment for the crime and within the given ranges the judges have discretion to assess the penalty. This development had a powerful ally in the modern penological principle that punishment should be adjusted to the criminal and not to the crime. The doctrine of giving the judges discretion is thus justified today, not on the ground that it is an outgrowth of the royal prerogative, which was its origin, but on ground of the new principles of penology.

The result is the sharp line drawn between the proof of a criminal act, which is subject to all the requirements of due process, and the factual basis of sentencing.

> Tribunals passing upon the guilt of a defendant always have been hedged in by strict evidentiary procedural limitations. But both before and since the American colonies became a nation, courts in this country and in England practiced a policy under which a sentencing judge could exercise a wide discretion in the sources and types of evidence used to assist him in determining the kind and extent of punishment to be imposed within limits fixed by law . . .[30]

As we saw,[31] however, the dominant principle is that sentences serve multiple purposes. Retribution, general deterrence, special deterrence, incapacitation, and rehabilitation are all permissible objectives of correctional treatment. The issue to which the discretion of the sentencing judge must be directed in the first place is how much weight to give to each objective in the case at hand. Where this issue is concerned, neither case law nor statutes provide a guide. As a result, judges can work with their own notions of penological theory without even nominal control by an authoritative principle. Since most judges come to the bench without training in penology either in law school or in their subsequent practice— usually a civil practice—they tend to respond, not to penological theory, but to the popular pressures on them.

The absence of appellate review of sentences has meant that no body of norms for sentencing has been developed.[32] In a rare American opinion discussing the question of sentencing, the court said:

> What then should be the punishment inflicted upon the defendant in this particular case? What considerations should weigh in the matter? It must be assumed that the discretion given by the (statute in question) is to be exercised by the jury or the court, as the case may be, on some rational basis, and not in an arbitrary, capricious or whimsical manner. The law, however, furnishes no precedents upon which any theory of determination of the question is to be sought.[33]

It may be doubted, however, that even if appellate courts had the power of review, as they have in a few states and in England, they would develop a coherent body of norms for sentencing. Livingston Hall concludes that

> with a few exceptions, the machinery of appellate review of sentences has not been employed by the courts which possess

it as a means of establishing any general sentencing policy. The case method of the common law has been rarely applied to sentencing; the courts do not often admit that any two sentences must bear a rational relation to each other, or are specific illustrations of general principles which may be deduced from them.[34]

The English Court of Criminal Appeal has had for a long time the power to alter sentences where it is evident that the judge acted on some wrong principle or overlooked some material factor, or that the sentence is manifestly excessive in view of the circumstances of the case.[35] The most that the Court has done, however, is to articulate a string of maxims of sentencing that, like the rubrics of statutory construction, constitute a handy grab bag from which "principles" can be chosen to justify any given sentence.

A few examples from cases in England and British Africa (where judges follow the English rules) will suffice. The leading case is *Rex v. Ball*.[36] In this case, the court made the following often quoted statement:

> In deciding the appropriate sentence a court should always be guided by certain considerations. The first and foremost is the public interest. The criminal law is publicly enforced not only with the object of punishing crime, but also in the hope of preventing it. A proper sentence passed in public can serve the public interest in two ways. It may deter others who might be tempted to try crime as seeming to offer easy money on the supposition that if the offender is caught and brought to justice, the punishment will be negligible. Such a sentence may also deter the particular criminal from committing a crime again, or induce him to turn from a criminal to an honest life . . . Our law does not, therefore, fix the sentence for a particular crime, but fixes a maximum sentence and leaves it to the court to decide what is, within that maximum, the appropriate sentence for each criminal in the particular circumstances of each case. Not only with regard to each crime, but in regard to each criminal, the court has the right and duty to decide whether to be lenient or severe.[37]

The difficulty is that when "punishing the crime" (a retributive concept), general deterrence, and special deterrence are both regarded as proper considerations to be weighed, and when there is no standard of appropriate weight to be attached to each, the courts inevitably make decisions which are in principle incompatible.

In *Rex v. Petero Mukasa*,[38] the East African Court of Appeals reduced the sentences for manslaughter pronounced on some peasants who had killed some herdsmen believing that they were thieves, on the ground that there was an indigenous Uganda custom permitting people to kill thieves caught in the act (special deterrence). Two years earlier, the same court in *Rex v. Atma Singh s/o Chanda Singh*[39] had refused to reduce the sentence of a Sikh who had not killed an adulterous wife, but had cut off her nose and ears in accordance with a claimed Sikh custom of thus dealing with unfaithful wives. The court said that the existence of so barbarous a custom demanded not a lighter sentence, but a heavier sentence (general deterrence).

In *Rex v. Ball*,[40] as we saw, the court said squarely that "the first and foremost" interest to be served is the public interest. In *Rex v. Reeves*,[41] the Court of Criminal Appeal in England reduced a sentence so that, because a codefendant had received a much lighter sentence, the accused would not suffer "a strong sense of grievance," which was hardly the primary "public interest."

In *Rex v. Schoenfield*,[42] the English court reduced a 30-year disqualification for a first offender for driving while drunk to five years, "which was a more normal period for this type of offense" (retribution). In *Rex v. Walton*,[43] the same court reduced a 3-year disqualification for a first offender for driving while drunk to 12 months.

In *Rex v. Kyle*,[44] the court said that it was proper to place an accused, otherwise a fit subject for punishment, on probation where great interest in helping him was shown by a residential community (special deterrence). In *Rex v. Mild and Reynolds*,[43] heavy sentences were upheld in a hire purchase fraud, because "hire purchase frauds are rife at present" (general deterrence).

In *Dowling v. Inspector-General of Police*,[46] the accused was convicted of sodomy. The Nigerian court said that a sentence of six months "cannot be considered excessive" when the maximum sentence for the offense was fourteen years imprisonment. Sodomy, whatever its incidence in England, is rare in Nigeria. In *Queen v. Princewell*[47] another Nigerian court sentenced the accused to one month's imprisonment for bigamy where the statute provided a maximum of seven years, remarking that the fact that polygamy was common in Nigeria distinguished the situation from one in England. The court did not mention the maximum statutory sentence as a guide to the seriousness of the offense.

The list could be increased to enormous length. Given precedents of this sort, even where, as in England and Africa, an appellate court has sought to create a body of norms for sentencing, a trial judge can always unearth a shibboleth sanctified by precedent to justify whatever sentence he wishes to impose. If he believes that a severe sentence is required, he can point to the prevalence of crime in the neighborhood, or the "intrinsic gravity" of the offense, or the past bad record of the accused, or "the normal period for this type of offense." If he wishes to justify a lenient sentence, he can invoke a possible "strong sense of grievance" by the accused, or his personal characteristics, or the relation between his sentence and the maximum sentence proposed by the statute. In sum, appellate review has failed to produce a coherent set of principles for the guidance of judicial sentencing. That it has not done so even in those jurisdictions where appeal of sentence is possible reflects not the incapacity or perverseness of judges, but the inherent ambiguity in our approach to crime and punishment.

In the absence of any norms prescribing what factors are legally significant in sentencing and what weight they are to be given, it is to be expected that the sentencing process has come to resemble not a trial of an issue of fact, but an administrative process.[48]

The essence of due process lies in the concept of an adversary proceeding. The principal consequence of the adversary proceeding is that every assertion made by one side which is subject to challenge will be examined critically before the judge. As a result, the judge will have had called to his attention all the relevant factual information and theoretical material which either side can adduce, so that there is at least a built-in assurance that his decision will not be made in ignorance. The sentencing process, however, is nowhere regarded as an adversary process. A few states do have old statutes which seek to assimilate the sentencing process to trial proceedings. For example, an old Utah statute provides that:

> When discretion is conferred upon the court as to the extent of punishment, the court, at the time of pronouncing judgment, may take into consideration any circumstances, either in aggravation or mitigation of the punishment, which may be presented to it by either party.[49]

> The circumstances must be presented by the testimony of witnesses examined in open court, except that when a witness is so ill or infirm as to be unable to attend, his deposition may be taken by a magistrate of the county, out of court, upon such notice to the adverse party as the court may direct. No affidavit or testimony or representation of any kind, verbal or written, shall be offered to or received by the court or judge thereof in aggravation or mitigation of the punishment, except as provided by this section.[50]

In most states, however, either judges are expressly authorized to receive evidence of any sort on sentencing, or no prescription at all is made concerning the matter. Even in the states which do require evidence, statutes authorizing presentence investigations and reports are treated in practice as creating an exception to the rule.

The Supreme Court, which has so assiduously constructed a due-process framework for other areas of the criminal law, has nevertheless not extended the constitutional vision of the criminal process into the posttrial proceedings as it has the pretrial proceedings. It did make an abortive excursion into the area, however. In *Townsend v. Burke*,[51] in 1948, the Court was presented with an appellant who had been sentenced to ten to twenty years imprisonment after the following enlightening dialogue:

By the Court (addressing Townsend):

Q. Townsend, how old are you?

A. Twenty-nine.

Q. You have been here before, haven't you?

A. Yes, sir.

Q. *1933, larceny of an automobile.* 1934, larceny of produce. 1930, larceny of a bicycle. 1931, entering to steal and larceny. *1938, entering to steal and larceny in Doylestown.* Were you tried up there? No, no, arrested in Doylestown. That was up on Germantown Avenue, wasn't it? You robbed a paint store. [Italics as in Supreme Court Report.]

A. No. That was my brother.

Q. You were tried for it, weren't you?

A. Yes, but I was not guilty.

Q. And 1945, this. 1936, entering to steal and larceny, 1350 Ridge Avenue. Is that your brother too?

A. No.

Q. *1937, receiving stolen goods, a saxophone.* What did you want with a saxophone? Didn't hope to play in the prison band, did you?

The Court: Ten to twenty in the Penitentiary.[52]

The three italicized charges had in fact all resulted in verdicts or judgments of not guilty. The Supreme Court held that to take these into account, whether by design or carelessness, was "inconsistent with due process of law, and such a conviction cannot stand."

A year later, in 1949, however, the Court decided *Williams v. New York.*[53] In that case, a jury found the accused guilty of first-degree murder, recommending life imprisonment. The trial judge, under a New York statute permitting him to ignore the jury's recommendation, nevertheless sentenced Williams to death. In giving his reasons for imposing the death sentence the judge discussed in open court the evidence upon which the jury had convicted. He added that this evidence had been considered in the light of additional information obtained through the court's "Probation Department, and through other sources." After the accused protested his innocence once again, the trial judge stated that the presentence report had disclosed many material facts concerning the accused's background which could not properly have been brought before the jury in its consideration of the question of guilt. He referred to some thirty burglaries which the accused was said to have committed (although he had been convicted of none of these, and had according to the presentence report, confessed to only some of them). The judge also referred to certain activities of the accused as shown by the probation report, which indicated that the appellant possessed a "morbid sexuality," and classified him as a "menace to society." The accuracy of these statements made by the judge was not challenged by the defense counsel. The Supreme Court of the United States held that the proceeding did not violate the due-process clause because the problems of sentencing were such as to make inappropriate to it the adversary procedures used in a trial.

This is a surprising result in the light of *Townsend*. If a judge chooses not to disclose the contents of a presentence report, there is no knowing whether or not he relied on precisely the sort of information that *Townsend* held it wrong to use as grounds for sentence. (The Court did nod its head in Townsend's direction by a sibylline footnote, that "What we have said is not to be accepted as a holding that the sentencing procedure is immune from scrutiny under the due-process clause," citing *Townsend*.)

The reason for the decision was the manifest conflict between modern notions of sentencing and the concept of due process:

Modern changes in the treatment of offenders make it more necessary now than a century ago for the observance of the distinctions in the evidentiary procedure in the trial and sentencing process. For indeterminate sentences and probation have resulted in an increase in the discretionary powers exercised by fixing punishments.

Under the practice of individualizing punishments, investigational techniques have been given an important role. Probation workers making reports of their investigations have not been trained to prosecute but to aid offenders. Their reports have been given a high value by conscientious judges who want to sentence persons on the best available information rather than on guesswork and inadequate information. To deprive sentencing judges of this kind of information would undermine modern penological policies that have been cautiously adopted throughout the nation after careful consideration and experimentation. We must recognize that most of the information now relied upon by the judges to guide them in the intelligent imposition of sentences would not be available if information were restricted to that given in open court by witnesses subject to cross-examination . . .[34]

The central reason why the adversary system is thought to provide a legal-rational legitimization for the decision-making process is that a rational decisional process requires that the judge be aware of all the potential alternatives for decision, their possible consequences, and the relevant theories and values, before making a decision. The *Townsend* case demonstrated the real danger that a judge, through error or design, might take into account matters that ought not to be taken into account. The judges cannot deny that the minimum requirements of a rational decision in sentencing are that the defendant be at least apprised of the factual matters on which the judge proposes to base his sentence, and that the defendant be permitted to argue against the judge's understanding of these facts. Why have the judges decided that in this one activity of sentencing the procedures which have proved in other contexts to be so attractive to them are not to be used?

The fact that the present sentencing procedure developed in a historical context based on prerogative is not a sufficient explanation. Time and time again we have seen judges impose on the criminal process new norms more closely approximating the due-process ideal. Juries have lost their power to decide the law. The accused was first permitted to have counsel and now must be supplied with one. The rules of evidence have been sharpened to exclude the irrelevant. The courts could readily have decreed a change in the traditional norms controlling sentencing.

Nor is the breadth of the investigation demanded by the newer notions of penology a sufficient explanation. In administrative proceedings requiring a far broader investigation the Constitution has been held to require a hearing, despite the difficulty of proof. In setting the rates for an electric generating company, for example, all three parties involved—the company requesting the increase, the Commission staff, and interested members of the public—customarily introduce testimony on such abstruse and complex subjects as the probable increase in the demand for power over the next decade or more, which involves predictions of population increase, the rate of family formation, the migrations into and away from the area, the probable increase in the use of electrical appliances (such as air-conditioning), the projected increase of industry in the area, the sectoral composition of the industrial expansion expected and hence its relative demand for power, the projected movement of prices in fuel, labor, and equipment, and a myriad of other factors. By contrast, the matters at issue in criminal sentencing are relatively simple.

Part of the reason may lie in the fixed pattern of evidence in a judicial proceeding. In *Williams*, the Court rested its decision in part on this ground:

> In addition to the historical basis for different evidentiary rules governing trial and sentencing procedures there are sound practical reasons for the distinction. In a trial before verdict the issue is whether a defendant is guilty of having engaged in certain criminal conduct of which he has been specifically accused. Rules of evidence have been fashioned for criminal trials which narrowly confine the trial contest to evidence that is strictly relevant to the particular offense charged. These rules rest in part on a necessity to prevent a time consuming and confusing trial of collateral issues. They were also designed to prevent tribunals concerned solely with the issue of guilt of a particular offense from being influenced to convict for that offense by evidence that the defendant had habitually engaged in other misconduct. A sentencing judge, however, is not confined to the narrow issue of guilt. His task within fixed statutory or constitutional limits is to determine the type and extent of punishment after the issue of guilt has been determined. Highly relevant—if not essential—to his selection of an appropriate sentence is the possession of the fullest information possible concerning the defendant's life and characteristics. And modern concepts individualizing punishment have made it all the more necessary that a sentencing judge not be denied an opportunity to obtain pertinent information by a requirement of rigid adherence to restrictive rules of evidence properly applicable to the trial.[55]

But this reason is hardly convincing, although this set of mind no doubt contributed to the decision in the *Williams* case itself. After all, judges have been adept at fashioning rules of evidence different from those applicable at a trial to suit the demands of administrative proceedings of all sorts, without holding that the inadequacy of the rules of evidence appropriate to a trial disqualified the hearings or required a complete abandonment of due-process standards.

One of the reasons given by the Supreme Court in *Williams* was, as might have been predicted, the now familiar bureaucratic reason of judiciary efficiency. "[T]he modern probation report draws on information concerning every aspect of a defendant's life. The type and extent of this information makes totally impractical if not impossible open court testimony with cross-examination. Such a procedure could endlessly delay criminal administration in a retrial of collateral issues."[56]

Yet even this simple reason hardly explains the sharp contradiction between the due-process standard operative elsewhere in the criminal trial (as in *Townsend*), even in sentencing, and in the actual decision in *Williams*. Whatever the reason may be, however, the consequences of the decision are plain: it leaves the judge wholly in command of the overwhelming majority of criminal cases which end in pleas of guilty, and the majority of the few cases which do go to trial and end in convictions. In all these cases, the discretion of the trial judge is essentially unfettered by norms of decision-making, exposure to public examination, or appellate review. Probably no place in the entire universe of state actions (save, perhaps, in the determinations of local Selective Service Boards) are administrative officers endowed with such wide discretion in the invocation of such awesome powers.

The contradictions that exist in endowing sentencing judges with so much power are very sharp. Due process is still the ideal to which lip service is paid. Some minimal due-process requirements are now usually held sacred. If the defendant has a counsel, he must ordinarily be present on sentencing.[57] Sentences imposed in the absence of the defendant are void.[58] The accused must be heard if he affirmatively requests a hearing, but there is no necessity that he be heard unless he makes the request.[59] Rule 32(a) of the Federal Rules of Criminal Procedure provides that the judge should ask the accused if he has anything to say before imposing the sentence, but it has been held that failure to comply with this rule by a judge does not void the sentence unless the accused has affirmatively requested to be heard and has been refused.[60]

The contradiction is well expressed in *U.S.* ex rel. *Collins v. Claudy*.[61] In that case, the court was presented with the question whether due process required a hearing on the issue of prior convictions in order for the trial judge to impose a sentence, under a recidivist statute, in excess of the maximum ordinarily permissible for the crime charged. In holding that it was, the court said:

Such post-conviction consideration of the question of recidivism serves two important purposes. It is as essential to the establishment of the legal basis of the enhanced sentence as proof of premeditation is in many states for capital punishment for murder. . . . At the same time it also enables the court to employ informed judgment in the exercise of its far-reaching discretion whether to impose additional punishment, and how much, on account of such prior conviction and attendant circumstances as the inquiry may reveal. Essential fairness dictates that the disposition of any issue thus determinative of the legal power of the tribunal and thereafter influential upon its discretion to punish a defendant must be after some notice to the accused that the issue is before the court followed by some opportunity to be heard.[62]

A hearing at which the accused is not notified of the evidence against him contained in the presentence report is, of course, hardly a hearing at which the accused can adequately present his case. Nevertheless, the suggestion that rational decision-making requires some sort of a hearing before decision suggests that the continuing requirement to legitimize every phase of the judicial process will at some point in the future resolve the existing contradiction between ideal and practice in favor of the due-process ideal.

At present, however, there are no such curbs on the sentencing judge. What are the consequences of permitting basically middle-class judges, socialized into a profession which in most of its functions serves a middle-class clientele, working within a bureaucratic framework where efficiency and smooth functioning are seen as critically important and where informed cooperation with other bureaucrats (e.g., prosecutors and police officers) are essential to efficient functioning, to have unfettered discretion in the sentencing of criminals who are mainly from the poor and minority groups?

SENTENCING: OUTPUT

The literature on sentencing is replete with examples of discriminatory, prejudiced, and highly idiosyncratic practices. Judges may develop an attitude of indifference and unconcern for the opinions of others, express highly personal and idiosyncratic values and force these values on persons who come before them.[63]

More than half the cases dealt with in the courts are of minor offenses: drunkenness, disorderly conduct, and vagrancy. The typical procedure for handling such cases is to summarily dispense with the normal legal procedures and to simply mete out sentences as quickly and efficiently as possible. Caleb Foote reports the following observations from the municipal court in Philadelphia:

that morning 56 cases were awaiting when the magistrate opened the daily divisional police court for the district which included the "skid row" and the central city area. These cases were the last items on the morning's docket, and the magistrate did not reach them until 11:04 a.m. In one of the cases there was a private prosecutor, and the hearing of evidence consumed five minutes. As court adjourned at 11:24, this left 15 minutes in which to hear the remaining 55 cases. During that time the magistrate discharged 40 defendants and found 15 guilty and sentenced them to three months terms in the House of Correction.

Four of these committed defendants were tried, found guilty and sentenced in the elapsed time of seventeen seconds from the time that the first man's name was called by the magistrate through the pronouncing of sentence upon the fourth defendant. In each of these cases the magistrate merely read off the name of the defendant, took one look at him and said, "Three months in the House of Correction." As the third man was being led out he objected, stating, "But I'm working . . . ," to which the magistrate replied, "Aw, go on."

The magistrate then called the name of one defendant several times and got no answer. Finally he said, "Where are you, Martin?" The defendant raised his hand and answered, "Right here." "You aren't going to be 'right here' for long," the magistrate said. "Three months in Correction." Another defendant was called. The magistrate stated: "I'm going to send you up for a medical examination—three months in the House of Correction."

A number of defendants were discharged with orders to get out of Philadelphia or to get out of the particular section of Philadelphia where they were arrested. "What are you doing in Philadelphia?" the magistrate asked one of these. "Just passing through." "You get back to Norristown. We've got enough bums here without you." Another defendant whose defense was that he was passing through town added, "I was in the bus station when they arrested me." "Let me see your bus ticket," the magistrate said. "The only thing that's going to save you this morning is if you have that bus ticket. Otherwise you're going to Correction for sure." After considerable fumbling the defendant produced a Philadelphia to New York ticket. "You better get on that bus quick," said the magistrate, "because if you're picked up between here and the bus station, you're a dead duck."

In discharging defendants with out-of-the-central-city addresses, the magistrate made comments such as the following:

"You stay out in West Philadelphia."

"Stay up in the fifteenth ward; I'll take care of you up there."

"What are you doing in this part of town? You stay where

you belong; we've got enough bums down here without you."

Near the end of the line the magistrate called a name, and after taking a quick look said, "You're too clean to be here. You're discharged."[64]

Among judges presiding over the Chicago Women's Court during a three-year period, Mary Owen Cameron found wide variation in different judges' propensity to use different kinds of sanctions for persons brought before the court for shoplifting.[65] The proportion of cases found "not guilty" ranged from five percent for one judge to twenty percent of the cases tried by another. One judge gave no "token sentences," while another judge meted out token sentences in fifty-five percent of the cases he handled over this period. The proportions of probation sentences ranged from a low of three percent of the jail sentences in the case of one judge to thirty-one percent of the jail sentences in the case of another judge.

Edward Green's study of sentencing practices in Philadelphia courts revealed similar differences.[66] Green categorized cases by the seriousness of the crime and compared the sentences received. He concludes: "at each level of gravity there are statistically significant differences among the judges in the severity of the sentences imposed."

Inquiries into judicial decision-making have also consistently demonstrated the operation of racial and social-class biases in the decisions of judges. Cameron's findings from the sentencing of women for shoplifting illustrate this. Judges found sixteen percent of the white women brought before them on charges of shoplifting to be "not guilty," but only four percent of the black women were found innocent. In addition, twenty-two percent of the black women as compared to four percent of the white women were sent to jail. Finally, of the twenty-one white women sentenced to jail, only two (ten percent) were to be jailed for thirty days or more; of the seventy-six black women sentenced to jail, twenty (twenty-six percent) were to be jailed for thirty days or more.

Green's Philadelphia study showed similar tendencies of judges to impose sanctions more often and more severely on Blacks than on whites. Green notes, however, that in his sample this differential treatment is obviated when prior criminal record is taken into account. Green interprets this to mean that the differential severity with which Blacks are treated in the courts does not stem from racial discrimination, but rather, it stems from the fact that Blacks are more likely to have a past criminal record. We have already seen in previous sections that at the time of arrest and arraignment, the organization of law-enforcement is such that a black man is much more likely to have a "record" than a white person is. In view of this fact, Green's discovery that past criminal records account for the higher rate and severity of black convictions may indicate no more than persistently biased processing. Nevertheless, if Green's findings are generally applicable, they suggest that at least the sentencing practices of judges are nondiscriminatory. It seems more likely, however, that Philadelphia is unique since these findings contradict the results of other investigations. We cannot answer this question with a great deal of confidence, however, since the other inquiries into sentencing practices were not controlled for seriousness of offenses. We can certainly conclude that Blacks receive harsher treatment before the courts than do whites, but we must await further research before we can adequately assess the influence of race as contrasted with other variables such as prior arrest records.

The greater severity of treatment accorded the Blacks continues after the sentencing has taken place. Between 1930 and 1964, 3849 persons were executed in the United States (see Table 1). Of these, forty-five percent (1743) were white and fifty-four percent (2064) were Black. Blacks constitute less than thirteen percent of the population; yet they contribute over fifty percent of the persons executed. Blacks are more often arrested for all kinds of capitally punishable offense than are whites, and this may account for the higher frequency of executions. For example, in 1965 there were 6509 arrests for murder and nonnegligent manslaughter in the United States, and fifty-seven percent (3704) of those arrested for murder were Blacks. To what extent these arrests are a function of discrimination against the Blacks is only a guess at this point. It is pertinent to note, however, that there are many more whites than Blacks arrested for "manslaughter due to negligence." (In 1965 there were 1833 whites arrested for this offense

and 541 Blacks.) The practice of prosecutors to bargain for guilty pleas suggests that this differential in the proportion of arrests for manslaughter by negligence may in part reflect the propensity of prosecutors to file lesser charges against whites more often than against Blacks.

That such an interpretation is plausible receives indirect support from a study by Wolfgang, Kelly, and Nolde, who report that among persons awaiting execution on "death row" in Pennsylvania, twenty percent of the whites, as compared with twelve percent of the Blacks, had their death sentences commuted. The difference is even greater for felony-murders than for nonfelony-murders.[67]

It is the black felony-murderers more than any other type of offender who suffer the death penalty. This finding is especially striking when we note that nearly three times more white than black felony-murderers have their sentences commuted.

Regional differences are rather striking. A higher proportion of Blacks are convicted and executed in the South than any other section of the country, and they are convicted there for a greater variety of crimes. Between 1930 and 1964, North Carolina executed 263 persons: 207 for murder, 47 for rape, and 9 for "other offenses."[68] Of the 263 persons executed, 199 were Blacks and 59 were whites. Thus seventy-six percent of the persons executed in North Carolina during that period were Blacks. Execution for rape is an almost exclusively Southern phenomenon. Between 1930 and 1964, there were 455 executions for rape in the United States, and all but twelve of these occurred in the South; ten of the exceptions took place in Missouri, and two in Nevada. Of the 455 persons executed for rape, 405 were Blacks, 48 were whites, and 2 were of "other races."

GUILTY PLEAS AND THE COURT

The discussion of the use of guilty pleas in Section 21.2 was focused on the role of the prosecutor. It is obvious from that discussion that the prosecutor's use of the guilty plea could not work without the complicity of the judges on the bench. If the prosecutor's recommendation for leniency was only occasionally adhered to by the judge, then the ability of the prosecutor to keep his bargain would be undermined. Or

TABLE 1

Prisoners Executed under Civil Authority, by Offense and Race (1930–1964)

Type of Offense and Race	1930 to 1939	1940 to 1949	1950 to 1959	1958	1959	1960	1961	1962	1963	1964	All Years
Total	1667	1284	717	49	49	56	42	47	21	15	3849
White	827	490	336	20	16	21	20	28	13	8	1743
Black	816	781	376	28	33	35	22	19	8	7	2064
Other	24	13	5	1	—	—	—	—	—	—	42
Murder	1515	1064	601	41	41	44	33	41	18	9	3325
White*	804	458	316	20	15	18	18	26	12	5	1657
Black*	687	595	280	20	26	26	15	15	6	4	1628
Other	24	11	5	1	—	—	—	—	—	—	40
Rape	125	200	102	7	8	8	8	4	2	6	455
White	10	19	13	—	1	—	1	2	—	3	48
Black	115	179	89	7	7	8	7	2	2	3	405
Other	—	2	—	—	—	—	—	—	—	—	2
All other offenses**	27	20	14	1	—	4	1	2	1	—	69
White†	13	13	7	—	—	3	1	—	1	—	38
Black	14	7	7	1	—	1	—	2	—	—	31

*White includes 18 females, Black, 12 females.

**24 armed robberies, 20 kidnappings, 11 burglaries, 8 espionage (6 in 1942 and 2 in 1953), and 6 aggravated assaults.

†Includes two females, both executed in 1953, one for kidnapping and one for espionage.

if the prosecutor's recommendation that the court impose a minimum sentence on the defendant were given only very cursory consideration by the court, the bargain would fall apart. In actual practice the judge and his decisions are highly influenced by the prosecutors; and thus the ability of the prosecutor to "deliver his promises" is assured. The fact that prosecutors have so much influence on the judges partly reflects the formal organization of the court. The judge is highly dependent on the information provided by the prosecutor and his staff. More important, however, is the fact that the judge will find his end of the legal system functions most effectively and efficiently if he does not interfere with the policies and programs of the prosecutor. Occasionally the close relationship between the prosecutor and the judge involves the joint sharing of graft and pay-offs. More typically the cooperative relationship evolves out of the shared interests of the judge and the prosecution in seeing that cases are dealt with expeditiously and with a minimum of strain for the court. This view was succinctly put by Justice Henry T. Lummus when he observed:

a criminal court can operate only by inducing the great mass of actually guilty defendants to plead guilty, paying in leniency the price for the pleas.[69]

Donald Newman has estimated that ninety percent of all criminal convictions are the result of a guilty plea.[70] For the most part these guilty pleas are obtained by promises of less severe sanctioning than what the defendant can anticipate if he pleads not guilty. More often than not, judges take into account the guilty plea and apply less severe sanctions. The *Yale Law Journal* sent questionnaires to 240 federal judges and received responses from 140 of them. Sixty-six percent of the respondents reported that the defendant's plea was "a relevant factor in local sentencing procedure,"[71] and the majority of the judges rewarded the defendant pleading guilty with a less severe sentence than his counterpart who had a trial.

There are any number of reasons why courts and prosecutors look with favor on guilty pleas. In one way or another, all of the reasons come down to the fact that these agencies can operate more efficiently and with less strain if the bulk of the offenders processed plead guilty. It is probable, as the quote from

Justice Lummus implies, that the courts would come to a standstill if all defendants insisted on court trials, for at present the available manpower is insufficient to withstand the onslaught of a ninety percent increase in trials. Furthermore, even if the personnel were available, trials are expensive, time-consuming, and the outcomes are rarely predictable. A guilty plea by the defendant assures that the case will be handled expeditiously. Little is gained even by the defendant by insisting on a trial when the likelihood is to incur a more severe penalty.

These practices and policies may be organizationally effective, but they create still another area of discrimination against the poor and the Blacks. Since the guilty plea is obtained by a bargain between the defendant and the court, the benefit to the defendant will depend on the strength of his bargaining position. The strength of his bargaining position, in turn, is a function of his ability to hire private counsel and of his knowledge of his legal rights and of law generally. Most middle and upper class persons arrested for crime may be as ignorant about the law as most lower class persons, but they can pay for good legal counsel to inform them of their bargaining power. The professional thief is quite sophisticated about the legal system and can also afford legal counsel. It remains for the poor to receive the brunt of the disadvantageous possibilities of "bargain justice." Since the black persons who are processed in the courts tend to be poor, they will be the ones most likely to receive the short end of the "bargain."

The judge's role in Anglo-American law in sentencing allows for at least as great discretion as do the roles of the prosecutor and the police. In some respects, the judge's role is less encumbered by organizational restrictions than is the case with other agencies in the legal system. The fact remains, however, that in actual practice the judges' decisions are likely to be just as much determined by extralegal factors as the decisions of other law enforcement agencies. The demands for efficient and orderly performance of the court take priority and create a propensity on the part of the courts to dispose of cases in ways that ensure the continued smooth functioning of the system. The consequence of such a policy is to systematically select certain categories of offenders (specifically the poor and the Black) for the most severe treatment. Thus, with all their presumed autonomy and independence from public control, judicial decisions, like decisions at every other level of the law enforcement system, nevertheless remain a function of the organizational requirements of the legal system to a much greater extent than they are a function of the blueprint that supposedly guides those decisions.

SUMMARY

The effects of bureaucratization are rarely taken into account when laws are made or when law enforcement agencies are established. Neither are these effects given any consideration when the law is designed to have certain consequences, as when criminal sentences are supposed to serve the broader purposes of society. Yet, in fact, the tendency and necessity to bureaucratize is far and away the single most important variable in determining the actual day to day functioning of the legal system and its effect is clearly shown in the sentencing of offenders. Thus the large number of persons brought before municipal courts for minor transgressions of the law leads to an almost completely automatic sentence for certain types of offenders. Furthermore, even for more serious offenses the pressure to make the decision expeditiously (which is in large part a carry-over from the heavy burden created by the large number of minor offenders handled) leads to the judges relying heavily on the advice of "specialists"—in this case probation and parole officers who make presentencing reports on offenders before the court for sentencing.

Under these circumstances, institutionalized patterns of discrimination against the poor are inevitable. They would no doubt be no less inevitable were the decisions solely in the hands of the judge (as it is ostensibly in the blueprint of the law); but were they solely in the hands of the judge the decisions would at least be more easily identifiable as reflecting the biases of a class. As things now stand, what with the trappings of "experts" and "objective personnel" who are presumably "interested only in the well-being of the offender and society" it is more difficult to discern the operation of bias and institutionalized discrimination against the poor because it is hidden behind a facade of bureaucracy. The judge can point to his "professional staff" as justification for his decisions and the "professional staff" can point to their position as an "expert" for protection against criticism.

It is only when the sum total of the sentencing is added up that the real picture begins to emerge.

FOOTNOTES

[1]Comment, "The influence of the defendant's plea on judicial determination of sentence," *Yale Law J.*, 66, 1956, p. 204 and 218.

[2]Caleb Foote, "Vagrancy-type law and its administration," *U. Pa. Law Rev.*, 104, 1956, p. 605.

[3]See Administrative Office of the United States Courts, *The Presentence Investigation Report*, Pub. No. 101 (1943); quoted in a footnote to *Williams v. New York*, 337 U. S. 241, 69 Sup. Ct. 1079, 93 L. Ed., 1337 (1949).

[4]Robert M. Carter and Leslie T. Wilkins, "Some factors in sentencing policy," *J. Criminal Law, Criminology, and Police Science*, 58, 1967, p. 503.

[5]Advisory Council of Judges of the National Probation and Parole Association, *Guides for Sentencing*, Carnegie Press, New York, 1957, p. 46.

[6]Sir Gerald Gardiner, "The purposes of criminal punishment," *Mod. Law Rev.*, 21, 1958, p. 117 at 123.

[7]Lloyd E. Ohlin and Frank J. Remington, "Sentencing structure: its effect upon systems for the administration of criminal justice," *Law and Contemporary Problems*, 23, 1958, p. 495.

[8]Jerome H. Skolnick, *Justice Without Trial*, Wiley, New York, 1966, p. 175.

[9]Ohlin and Remington, *loc. cit.*

[10]New York Penal Law, Section 2125.

[11]New York Penal Law, Section 2010.

[12]New York Penal Law, Section 407.

[13]Livingston Hall, "Reduction of criminal sentences on appeal," *Columbia Law Rev.*, 37, 1937, p. 521.

[14]*U. S. v. Steinberg*, 62 F. 2d 77 (2nd Cir., 1932), at 78.

[15]246 Fed. 118 (4th Cir., 1917).

[16]182 F. 2d 416 (2nd Cir., 1950).

[17]Leon Radzinowicz, *A History of English Criminal Law and Its Administration from 1750*, Vol. 1, Stevens, London, 1948, p. 5.

[18]*Ibid.*, p. 10.

[19]*Rex v. Palmer*, 2, Leach 692 (1795).

[20]See Sir James F. Stephen, *A History of the Criminal Law of England*, Vol. 1, Macmillan, London, 1883, p. 471.

[21]Radzinowicz, *op. cit.*, Vol. 1, pp. 110–111.

[22]8 Geo 3 c. 16.

[23]Stephen, *op. cit.*, Vol. 1, p. 468.

[24]*Ibid.*, pp. 471–472.

[25]Radzinowicz, *op. cit.*, Vol. 1, p. 160.

[26]See generally Stephen, *op. cit.*, Vol. 1, pp. 471–480.

[27]*Ibid.*, p. 483.

[28]Sir John Romilly, "Debates in the year 1810 upon Sir John Romilly's Bills for abolishing the punishment of death for stealing to the amount of forty shillings in a dwelling-house, for stealing to the amount of five shillings privately in a shop, and for stealing on navigable waters," cited in Radzinowicz, *op. cit.*, Vol. 1. p. 329.

[29]*Ibid.*, pp. 370–371.

[30]*Williams v. New York*, 337 U. S. 241, 69 S. Ct. 1079, 93 L. Ed. 1337 (1949).

[31]*Supra*, p. 449.

[32]Note, "Due process and legislative standards in sentencing," *U. Pa. Law Rev.*, 101, 1952, pp. 257–258.

[33]*Commonwealth v. Ritter*, 13 D. and C. 285 (Court of Oyer and Terminer, Philadelphia, 1930).

[34]Livingstone Hall, "Reduction of criminal sentences on appeal," *Columbia Law Rev.*, 37, 1937, pp. 521, 575. Reprinted by permission.

[35]*Rex v. Shershewsky*, [1912] Times Law Reports 364.

[36]35 Criminal Appeal Reports (England, 1951), 164; [*Rex v. Ball* (No. 2)].

[37]35 Cr. App. Rep. 164 at 165.

[38]11 E. A. C. A. 114 (Uganda, 1944).

[39]9 E. A. C. A. 69 (Kenya, 1942).

[40]35 Cr. App. Rep. (1951), 164 at 165, 166.

[41]*The Times*, October 3, 1964.

[42]*The Times*, November, 6, 1962.

[43][1963] *Criminal Law Rev.*, 62.

[44][1964] *Criminal Law Rev.*, 68.

[45][1963] *Criminal Law Rev.*, 63.

[46][1961] All N. L. R. (Nigerian Law Reports) 782 (High Court, Lagos), 12.

[47][1963] N. R. N. L. R. (Northern Region Nigerian Law Reports) 54 (High Co Jos, Northern Nigeria), 12.

[48]Kenneth C. Davis, *Discretionary Justice: A Preliminary Inquiry*, Louisiana State University Press, Baton Rouge, 1969, pp. 133–141.

[49]*Utah Code Ann.*, Section 77–35–12 (1953).

[50]*Ibid.*, Section 77–35–13 (1953).

[51]334 U. S. 736, 68 S. Ct. 1252, 92 L. Ed. 1690 (1948).

[52]334 U. S. at 739.

[53]337 U. S. 241, 69 S. Ct. 1079, 93 L. Ed. 1337 (1949).

[54]337 U. S. at 249.

[55]337 U. S. at 246.

[56]337 U. S. at 250.

[57]*Mempa v. Rhay*, 389 U. S. 129 (1967).

[58]*Prive v. Zerbst*, 268 F. 72 (N. D. Ga., 1920); *Wilson v. Johnston*, 47 F. Supp. 275 (D. Cal., 1942); *Anderson v. Denver*, 265 F. 3 (8th Cir., 1920).

[59]*Shockley v. U. S.*, 166 F. 2d 704 (9th Cir., 1948) cert. den. 334 U. S. 850, 92 L. Ed. 1173, 68 S. Ct. 1502.

[60]*Calvaresi v. U. S.*, 216 F. 2d 891 (10th Cir., 1954), reversed on other grounds, 348 U. S. 961, 99 L. Ed. 749, 75 S. Ct. 522, 523.

[61]204 F. 2d 624 (3rd Cir., 1953).

[62]204 F. 2d at 628.

[63]Edward Green, *Judicial Attitudes in Sentencing*, Macmillan, London, 1961, p. 6.

[64]Caleb Foote, "Vagrancy-type law and its administration," *U. of Pa. Law Rev.*, 104, 1 1956, pp. 605–606. Reprinted by permission of the University of Pennsylvania Law Review.

[65]Mary Owen Cameron, *The Booster and the Snitch: Department Store Shoplifting*, Free Press of Glencoe, New York, 1964, pp. 143–144.

[66]Green, *op. cit.*, pp. 67–69.

[67]Marvin E. Wolfgang, Arlene Kelly, and Hans C. Nolde, "Comparison of the executed and the commuted among admissions to death row," in Norman B. Johnson, Leonard D. Savitz, and Marvin E. Wolfgang (eds.), *The Sociology of Punishment and Correction*, Wiley, New York, 1962, pp. 63–69.

[68]These statistics are taken from Frank E. Hartung, "Trends in the use of capital punishment," *Annals of the American Academy of Political and Social Science*, November 1952, and from *The National Prisoner Statistics Bulletin*, Bureau of Prisons, Washington, D. C.

[69]Cited in Donald J. Newman, *Conviction: The Determination of Guilt or Innocence Without Trial*, Little, Brown, Boston, 1966, p. 62.

[70]*Ibid.*, p. 3.

[71]Comment, *supra* (n.1), pp. 206–207.

Imprisonment and Other Forms of Punishment

PART 3   THE SOCIAL ORGANIZATION OF CRIMINAL LAW ENFORCEMENT

INTRODUCTION

If America's police and courts are in crisis, the prison system is in a state of shock. A group of social scientists recently said at a meeting of the American Academy for the Advancement of Science:

> Many, if not all, seriously concerned criminologists now firmly believe that the total institution was an historical aberration and must be eliminated with all due haste.

The view that the prison was an "historical aberration" is dealt with in the first article in this section. Although on humanitarian and perhaps even social grounds the prison may have been more harmful than beneficial, the point made by Rusche and Kirchheimer in the following article is that imprisonment grew up as a solution to economic problems inherent in Western society as it moved from feudalism to capitalism. Punishment generally and imprisonment in particular were responses to social relations created by the political and economic relations of the time. Perhaps today what we are seeing is that the economic relations which made imprisonment viable are beginning to change. The social scientists arguing for the abolition of prisons may well represent the forerunners of changed economic and political conditions which will see the emergence of profound changes in the system of punishment in post-industrial societies. Nonetheless, it must be recognized that the form of punishment a society utilizes reflects the social relations and especially the social conflicts engendered by the society's political economy. This point is well documented by the careful historical analysis of punishment presented by Rusche and Kirchheimer in the first article. The article that follows brings us to today by analyzing the effects of race on the imposition of the death penalty. The logic of the analysis by Rusche and Kirchheimer would imply that the death penalty and other forms of punishment would be more often and more severely imposed against Blacks and other minorities than against whites, and in fact that is exactly what the results of the Wolfgang and Riedel article show.

26

Punishment and Social Structure

GEORG RUSCHE
and OTTO KIRCHHEIMER

SOCIAL CONDITIONS AND PENAL ADMINISTRATION

In the history of penal administration several epochs can be distinguished during which entirely different systems of punishment were prevalent. Penance and fines were preferred methods of punishment in the early Middle Ages. They were gradually replaced during the later Middle Ages by a harsh system of corporal and capital punishment which, in its turn, gave way to imprisonment about the seventeenth century.

Penance and fines in the later middle ages The different penal systems and their variations are closely related to the phases of economic development. In the early Middle Ages there was not much room for a system of state punishment. The law of feud and penance was essentially a law regulating relations between equals in status and wealth. It assumed the existence of sufficient land to meet the requirements of a continually increasing population without lowering their standard of living. Although the population of West-

ern and Central Europe increased rapidly after 1200, the social conditions of the lower classes remained relatively favorable, particularly on the land. The colonization of Eastern European territories by the Germans, with its constant demand for man power, enabled the agricultural population of other provinces to escape the pressure to which the landlords sometimes subjected them. The possibility of migrating to the new towns provided a similar opportunity of escape through the attainment of personal freedom. These developments induced the landlords to treat their serfs with more care. The relations between the warrior-landlords and their serfs were of a traditional character, tantamount to a precisely determined legal relationship. These conditions tended to prevent social tension and to provide that cohesion which was characteristic of the period. Criminal law played an unimportant role as a means of preserving the social hierarchy. Tradition, a well-balanced system of social dependence, and the religious acknowledgment of the established order of things were sufficient and efficient safeguards. The main emphasis of criminal law lay on the maintenance of public order between equals in status and wealth. If, in the heat of the moment or in a state of intoxication, someone

Source: *Punishment and Social Structure* (translated by Finkelstein and Kirchheimer), copyright 1939, 1967 by Columbia University Press; reprinted by Russell & Russell (New York), 1968.

committed an offense against decency, accepted morality, or religion, or severely injured or killed his neighbor—violation of property rights did not count much in this society of landowners—a solemn gathering of free men would be held to pronounce judgment and make the culprit pay *Wergeld* or do penance so that the vengeance of the injured parties should not develop into blood feud and anarchy. An English proverb says: "Buy off the spear or bear it." The chief deterrent to crime was fear of the private vengeance of the injured party. Crime was looked upon as an act of war. In the absence of a strong central power the public peace was endangered by the smallest quarrel between neighbors, as these quarrels automatically involved relatives and servants. The preservation of peace was, therefore, the primary preoccupation of criminal law. As a result of its method of private arbitration, it performed this task almost entirely by the imposition of fines.

Class distinctions were manifested by differences in the extent of penance. Penance was carefully graded according to the social status of the evildoer and of the wronged party. Although this class differentiation affected only the degree of penance at first, it was at the same time one of the principal factors in the evolution of systems of corporal punishment. The inability of lower class evildoers to pay fines in money led to the substitution of corporal punishment in their case. The penal system thus came to be more and more restricted to a minority of the population. This development can be traced in every European country. A Sion statute of 1338 provided a fine of twenty livres in assault cases; if the offender could not pay he was to receive corporal punishment by being thrown into prison and fed on bread and water until the citizens interceded or the bishop pardoned him. This statute not only illustrates the automatic character of the transformation of penance into corporal punishment, but it also shows that imprisonment was regarded as a form of corporal punishment at this time.

Criminal law and the rise of capitalism The intense class conflicts in Flanders, upper Italy, Tuscany, and upper Germany which marked the transition to capitalist forms in the fourteenth and fifteenth centuries led to the creation of a harsh criminal law directed against the lower classes. The constant increase in crime among the ranks of the poverty-stricken proletariat, especially in the big towns, made it necessary for the ruling classes to search for new methods which would make the administration of criminal law more effective. The system of punishment, with its dual regime of corporal punishment and fines, remained unchanged, however, except that different applications were made according to the class of the condemned person. Variations in the treatment of different categories of offenses and offenders became more pronounced. The private settlement of disputes involving dishonest acts, such as theft, was no longer permitted. Even the right of asylum did not apply to such cases. This did not mean that every form of offense against property was regarded as a dishonest act. Dishonesty was considered not from the angle of the property stolen or damaged but rather from the angle of the person stealing or damaging: he would be dealt with much more harshly if he happened to be homeless or of low social status. As Radbruch remarks, social and moral considerations were intermingled. Since the majority of criminals were members of the lower classes, the word "villain," originally applied to a member of a particular social class, came to indicate a judgment of moral inferiority. This distinction clearly appears in Gandinus when he writes that the *poena extraordinaria* must be determined by the judge with reference to the nature of the offense and the offender (*secundum qualitatem delicti et personae*).

Those who had enough money to pay were able to buy exemption from punishment, [while] offenders who were without means (and they made up the great majority in these hard times) were powerless to save themselves from the harsh treatment to which they were liable. By far the greater number of crimes were now crimes against property, committed by those who had no property, so that a fine would hardly have met the case. The exchequer could get nothing out of them, as Schmidt remarks. He suggests a further reason for this important change of policy, namely, that "it had become a matter of paramount importance to suppress the bands of vagabonds, beggars, and robbers who were becoming a plague on the land. In one place after another the sluice gates would open and release·a new and poisonous flood into the muddy sea of crime." The poorer the masses became, the harsher the punishments in order to deter them from crime. Physical punishment now began to increase considerably all over the country, until finally it became not merely supplementary but the regular form of punishment. Execution, mutilation, and flogging were not introduced at one stroke by any sudden revolutionary change, but gradually became the rule with changing conditions. As time went on, punishment became harsher, not milder. There was a theory that the punishment should be milder in case of doubt, but such humanizing tendencies did not meet with approval in practice. On the contrary, open war was waged between legislation and science in the matter of punishment.

Legislation was openly directed against the lower classes. Even when criminal procedure as such was the same for all estates and classes, special procedures soon arose which affected only the lower classes. Thus, Schmidt says that there was one respect in which the old arbitrary justice could not be abolished, in the persecution of habitual lower class offenders. The simplification of procedure in cases where the prisoner had been taken in *flagrante delicto* permitted the isolation of a class of outlaws for whom the provisions of the law, such as consideration of the gravity of the crime, could not fully apply. Execution, banishment, mutilation, branding, and flogging more or less exterminated the whole range of professional rogues from murderers and robbers to vagrants and gypsies. With the increase in the number of professional lower class criminals in the later Middle Ages, this arbitrary justice, according to Schmidt, became more and more common and led to a profound change in the whole administration of criminal law.

Until the fifteenth century, the death penalty and serious mutilation were used only in extreme cases to supplement the complicated and carefully differentiated system of fines, but now they became the most common measures. Judges resorted to them whenever they were convinced that the offender was a danger to society. The extraordinary increase in the number of death sentences in the course of the sixteenth century is well known. The data for England, which must be approximately correct, give us an idea of the situation prevailing throughout Europe. We are told that 72,000 major and minor thieves were hanged during the reign of Henry VIII, and that under Elizabeth vagabonds were strung up in rows, as many as three and four hundred at a time. And the population of England was then only about three million. The Nürnberg executioner, Franz Schmidt, executed 361 people during his forty-four years in office (1573–1617) and inflicted corporal punishment on only 345. Both the absolute figures in proportion to the total population and the ratio of capital to corporal punishments offer a very significant indication of the prevailing severity of punishment. Outwardly the death penalty remained the same, but it gained a new significance in principle. It was no longer the extreme penalty for serious offenses, but a means of putting allegedly dangerous individuals out of the way. In this kind of procedure, little attention was paid to the guilt or innocence of a suspect, as can be seen from the statement made by the Reichskammergericht to the Lindauer Reichstag in 1496 that innocent people were put to death without any just cause.

Exile, a most common form of punishment at this period, frequently meant a far worse fate for lower class victims than one might think. The exile escaped death in his own town, but, as often as not, the gallows awaited him in the town where he sought refuge. Exile for the rich, however, was not a very severe punishment. It meant travel for study, the establishment of business branches abroad, and even diplomatic service for the home town or native country, with the prospect of an early and glorious return.

The whole system of punishment in the later Middle Ages makes it quite clear that there was no shortage of labor, at least in the towns. As the price paid for labor decreased, the value set on human life became smaller and smaller. The hard struggle for existence molded the penal system in such a way as to make it one of the means of preventing too great an increase of population. Von Hentig quite correctly applies the idea of selection to the penal system in this connection and he shows that the system acted as a kind of artificial earthquake or famine in destroying those whom the upper classes considered unfit for society.

MERCANTILISM AND THE RISE OF IMPRISONMENT

The labor market and the state   Methods of punishment began to undergo a gradual but profound change toward the end of the sixteenth century. The possibility of exploiting the labor of prisoners now received increasing attention. Galley slavery, deportation, and penal servitude at hard labor were introduced, the first two only for a time, the third as the hesitant precursor of an institution which has lasted into the present. Sometimes they appeared together with the traditional system of fines and capital and corporal punishment; at other times they tended to displace the latter. These changes were not the result of humanitarian considerations, but of certain economic developments which revealed the potential value of a mass of human material completely at the disposal of the administration.

The rise of larger and wealthier town populations created an increased demand for certain consumer's goods. The steadiness of the demand and the growth of the financial system led to a constant extension of markets; the possibility that the entrepreneur would not be able to dispose of his products became almost negligible. Merchants from the countries which had been least affected by the new treasure were able to sell at a great profit to those which had been more strongly affected. Countries which had established trade relations with the Levant and Asia were able to export the treasure on extraordinarily profitable terms. The conquest of colonies not only led to greater importation of precious metals, with all its economic consequences, but also to an extension of markets for mass-consumption goods.

The population, after the middle of the sixteenth century, failed to keep pace with this increase in the possibility of employment. In England and in France population growth was checked by the wars of religion and other internal disturbances, and it remained very small. The most extreme case was that of Germany. As a result of the Thirty Years' War, population declined in the middle of the seventeenth century at a rate comparable only to certain local drops during the Black Death. An estimated fall from eighteen million to seven million, given by some authors, may be exaggerated, but the more conservative estimates are

impressive enough. Inama-Sternegg estimates 17.64 million in 1475, 20.95 in 1600–1620 and 13.29 in the middle of the seventeenth century. A slow increase did not set in again until the second half of the seventeenth century, and in many cases a century or more was needed to make up the loss. In the period before the Thirty Years' War real wages fell while population increased, but from 1620 to 1670 real wages rose. As Elsas has recently formulated the relationship, real wages throughout the sixteenth and seventeenth centuries followed a course contrary to the movement of prices and population: in other words, real wages corresponded to the supply of labor. . . .

This lack of constancy in the labor supply and the low productivity of labor meant a tremendous change in the position of the owning classes. At the very time when the extension of markets and the increasing requirements of technical equipment called for more invested capital, labor became a relatively scarce commodity. Capitalists of the mercantilist period could obtain labor on the open market only by paying high wages and granting favorable working conditions. When one considers the diametrically opposed conditions of the previous century, one realizes what the change must have meant to the propertied classes. The beginning of the disappearance of the labor reserve was a severe blow to those who owned the means of production. Workers had the power to insist on radical improvements in their working conditions. Accumulation of capital was necessary for the expansion of trade and manufacture, and it was being severely hampered by the new wage and labor conditions. The capitalist was obliged to turn to the state for working capital and for the restriction of wages.

The ruling classes left no means unexplored in order to overcome the condition of the labor market. A series of rigorous measures restricting the liberty of the individual was introduced. . . .

Military strategy and methods of recruiting and of maintaining military discipline were determined by the scarcity of man power. In his evaluation of Frederick II's policy, Meinecke says that the barbaric elements of his military system and, above all, the recruitment of this scum of humanity were in such close accord with his carefully thought-out demographic, financial, and economic system that everything would have fallen to pieces if he had removed a single stone from its foundation. If one needed an army at the beginning of the Thirty Years' War, unemployed mercenaries would pour in from everywhere. As industry advanced, the living standard of the workers improved and they had the possibility of a life easier and quieter than the life of the soldier. It thus became more and more difficult for governments to outbid employers, who were offering rising wages, and to recruit soldiers for their service.

Press gangs had already made their appearance by the time of the Thirty Years' War. Officers were instructed to seize passersby and force them to sign for military service. Or local authorities were required to provide the regiments with a certain number of recruits. Peasants were afraid to bring their produce to the towns, and large numbers of young people fled over the borders. Matters became still worse under Frederick William I. Local authorities in every province complained that people were being driven out of the country and that the whole economy was threatened. Recruits eventually became so expensive and rare that the Prussian king issued the famous *Kantonreglement* of 1773 in order to stop captains from quarreling with each other over recruits. The value of soldiers is also shown by the extraordinarily high prices paid to the German princes by England when she was waging her colonial wars. England fought her colonial wars almost entirely with foreigners, on the ground that her own able-bodied population could be more profitably occupied with the works and arts of peace.

The shortage of men eventually became so serious that the army had to be reinforced with criminals. In the great wars which England waged with France and Spain during the latter half of the eighteenth century it was difficult to find enough soldiers and sailors by any process of enlistment, impressment, or importation. Judges and gaolers were consulted about the fitness of convicts for military service, and the qualification was physical, not moral. The army came to be considered a kind of penal organization suited only for ne'er-do-wells, spendthrifts, black sheep, and ex-convicts. Countries even went so far as to take criminals over from other governments which did not know what to do with them. Ave-Lallemant writes that the record of almost every criminal of the eighteenth century contained instances of recruiting and subsequent desertion. This was a very practical means of avoiding prosecution until time and circumstances became more favorable. . . .

The observance of factory regulations became an urgent problem as a result of the scarcity of labor, especially of skilled labor. Strict rules were introduced to control the activity of the worker from morning prayers to the end of the day. Attempts were even made to regulate his private life, with a view to protecting him from influences likely to affect his productivity or discipline. The productivity of labor was low, and the difficulty was heightened by the large number of holidays during the year. Frequent laws were passed in order to regulate working hours, which were being reduced by the growing power of the wage earners. We hear of a twelve-hour day in Holland in the seventeenth century, a short working day when compared with the normal day of twelve to sixteen hours in seventeenth and eighteenth century France. The capstone of governmental regulation of the labor market was the prohibition of working-class organizations. Workers were severely punished for laying down their tools for higher wages or any other cause. Freedom of combination was against the whole spirit of the law, which held that labor questions were to be decided by the ruling authorities alone. . . .

From the end of the sixteenth century, the increasing scarcity of labor forced a change in the treatment of the poor, a change which is reflected in the attitudes toward beggary expressed in contemporary writing. In a pamphlet of 1641, which bears the significant title, *STANLEY'S REMEDY: Or, the Way how to Reform: Wandring Beggers, Theeves, Highway Robbers, and Pick-pockets: Or, an Abstract of his Discoverie; wherein is shewed, that Sodome's Sin of Idleness is the Poverty and Misery of this Kingdome: By some Well-wishers to the Honour of God, and the Publike Good, both of Rich and Poore,* a robber who was pardoned by Queen Elizabeth after having received a sentence of death calculated the loss sustained by the commonwealth as a result of the idleness of 80,000 beggars who could be put to useful work. The characteristic complaints of the later Middle Ages about the offenses against property and other serious crimes committed by despairing creatures who had no means of subsistence give way to complaints about the laziness of beggars and the resulting loss to the country.

The people who tramped and begged their way through the country and streamed into the towns during the mercantilist period in search of favorable living conditions were not always unable to defend themselves against social oppression, except in times of unusual distress. If the conditions offered by employers seemed too harsh, they threw themselves upon private charity in preference to regular employment. At this time, the beggars' income, like government unemployment benefits today, was the limit below which wages could not sink. Workers often became beggars when they wanted a holiday for a longer or shorter period of time, or when they sought a breathing spell in which to find more congenial or more profitable employment.

Everywhere there were bitter complaints about the shortage of labor caused by mendicancy. The repressive poor laws took this problem into consideration. In contrast to the policy at the beginning of the sixteenth century, with its chief aim the elimination of beggary, the new program was more directly economic in purpose. It sought to prevent the poor from withholding their labor power, as they used to do by begging in preference to working for low wages. A Brussels decree of 1599 established penalties for able-bodied beggars, domestic servants who left their masters, and workmen who left their employment in order to become beggars. A French decree of 1724 justified the punishment of able-bodied beggars on the ground that they really deprived the poor of bread, since they withheld their labor power from town and village. The definitions of rogue, vagabond, and sturdy beggar in an English statute of 1597 are further evidence of the change in attitude, for these terms included all laborers who refused to work at prevailing wages.

We are therefore led to the conclusion that the adoption, at the end of the seventeenth century, of a more humane method for the repression of vagrancy,

the institution of the house of correction, was also the outcome of a change in general economic conditions. The new legislative policy on begging was a direct expression of the new economic policy. With the help of its legislative and administrative machinery, the state used the labor contingent, which it found at its disposal, for the prosecution of its new aims.

The rise of the house of correction   The earliest institution created for the specific purpose of ridding the towns of vagabonds and beggars was probably the Bridewell in London (1555). The act of 1576, which we have already mentioned, provided for the establishment of similar institutions in every county. England thus led the way in time, but the development reached its peak in Holland for a number of reasons. At the end of the sixteenth century, Holland had the most highly developed capitalist system in Europe, but it did not have the reserve of labor power which existed in England after the enclosure movement. We have already referred to the high wages and favorable labor conditions prevailing in Holland, with its unusually short working day. Innovations destined to reduce the cost of production were naturally welcome. Every effort was made to draw upon all the available labor reserves, not only to absorb them into economic activity but, further, to "resocialize" them in such a way that in the future they would enter the labor market freely. . . .

It is equally certain that the houses of correction were very valuable for the national economy as a whole. Their low wages and their training of unskilled workers were important contributing factors in the rise of capitalist production. Contemporary writers and economic historians were agreed on this point. In Döpler's description, for example, great stress is laid on the enrichment of the national economy which accompanied the work of rehabilitation. The moral and material advantages of "modern" imprisonment, he says, arise because the inmates are turned aside from their wickedness to piety, from vice to virtue, from the road to destruction to the straight path of salvation, from the sloth that makes men stupid and sleepy to work that is useful for themselves and for society. When they are reformed, they will know how to earn their bread, and it is advantageous to the state that the idlers and rogues who will not work or improve their situation of their own accord should not be a burden on the industrious workers, but should be compelled to work against their will, by flogging and other means. Finally, Döpler points out, their labor in the production of useful goods will repay the initial investment. Modern students of economic history also have emphasized the economic role of the house of correction. Kulischer writes that, like orphanages, they were to be trade schools and nurseries of industry, spreading all kinds of useful things throughout the country. He argues from this that the industries begun in the houses of forced labor were regarded as contributions to the industry of the county. . . .

CHANGES IN THE FORM OF PUNISHMENT

. . . We have seen how certain economic changes helped to bring about an increase in the value placed upon human life and led the state to make practical use of the man power at its disposal. The idea of utilizing the potential labor of the criminal was not new. From time to time thoughtful men had come to the same conclusion as the inhabitants of More's Utopia, that it is unwise to execute offenders because their labor is more profitable than their death. But this idea could not be put into practice unless the dominant tendencies of the age were favorable to it. Until then, people who believed in it were considered cranks, and public practice followed those who advocated cruelty. Earlier thinkers were resurrected and hailed as misunderstood "forerunners" only after the conditions had changed.

The galley Galley slavery persisted even after the end of the economic system based upon slavery, because the strenuous and hazardous nature of the work made it difficult to recruit free men. The need for rowers became particularly urgent toward the end of the fifteenth century with the onset of the period of naval wars among the Mediterranean powers, Christian and Mohammedan. These wars gave added impetus to the old practice of drafting oarsmen from among prisoners. The number needed for a single ship was very large, three hundred and fifty for one of the big galleys, called a *galéasse,* and one hundred and eighty for a smaller boat. Decrees of Charles V and Philip II

of Spain introduced this form of punishment for major offenders as well as for beggars and vagabonds. An edict of Margaret of Parma organized vagabond hunts in the Netherlands at the instigation of Philip II who was unable to procure large enough crews for his galleys. The practice was widespread in France from the sixteenth century on. In 1771, when Joussé wrote his *Traité de la justice criminelle en France,* galley servitude was the punishment for forgers, thieves sentenced for the second time, and beggars for the third, among others. . . .

The early history of the transportation of criminals Another way of utilizing the labor power of convicts was to ship them to colonies and distant military settlements. Spain and Portugal were doing this as early as the fifteenth century, but then abandoned the practice because man power was urgently needed for the galleys. England became the first country to introduce systematic transportation of criminals, a method of punishment made necessary by her colonial expansion. The purpose of the following brief discussion is to show how this innovation in penology is analogous to galley servitude in that the need for labor power was the driving force in both cases.

Overseas colonies had huge tracts of land available for cultivation and there was a great demand for the colonial products in Europe. Each colonist, says Adam Smith,

> is eager . . . to collect laborers from all quarters, and to reward them with the most liberal wages. But those liberal wages, joined to the plenty and cheapness of land, soon make these laborers leave him, in order to become landlords themselves, and to reward, with equal liberality other laborers, who soon leave them for the same reason that they left their first master.

There was thus a constant shortage of labor in the colonies and the search for workers became a pressing problem. Settlers attempted to enslave the natives but the latter too often fled in groups to the vast open spaces of the colonies. The native population was quickly decimated by war, compulsory labor of unusual severity, and disease. The only alternative was to import workers, and that meant forced labor, in the main. The demand was so great that a new crime came into being—kidnaping. In the middle of the seventeenth century there were numerous

instances of organized bands of kidnapers in the sea-
port towns seizing children, generally of the poorer
classes, and selling them into slavery in the colonies.

In England, however, transportation was held to be
contrary to the interests of the mother country, where
workers were needed so badly. Colonization, Furniss
relates, was condemned because it reduced the number of working hands and robbed the country of their
contribution to the wealth of the nation. It was export
of the prime material of the country's wealth without
a sufficient return. As one contemporary phrased it,

> they have drained us of multitudes of our people who might
> have been serviceable at home, and advanced improvements in
> husbandry and manufactures; that this kingdom is worse peo-
> pled, by so much as they are increased; and that inhabitants
> being the wealth of a nation, by how much they are lessened,
> by so much we are poorer than when we first began to settle
> those colonies.

The simplest way to supply the needs of the colonies
without prejudice to the interests of the mother country was to send out convicts who would normally be
executed. Referring to the example of Spain, Governor Dole of Virginia wrote to the King in 1611, asking
that prisoners under sentence of death be sent to the
colony for three years. This, he thought, would be a
good way to populate the new country. Prizes were
even offered in order to encourage the importation of
convicts. . . .

With the introduction of Negro slavery in the last
decades of the seventeenth century the conditions
of the white colonial servants began to deteriorate.
From 1635 on, importers of Negroes also were given a
bonus, and the spread of the plantation system greatly
increased the demand for slave labor. There were
only 2,000 slaves in Virginia in 1671, whereas white
servants numbered about 6,000. By 1708, however,
there were 12,000 slaves, and about fifty years later
120,156. Just before the American Revolution there
were 192 ships engaged in the slave trade, and they
had a gross yearly freightage of 47,000. Such a huge
supply of workers considerably alleviated the "labor
famine" in the colonies, and the transportation of
convicts ceased to be a paying proposition, for Negro slaves tended to bring a higher price than criminals whose labor was available for only a limited
period of time.

Once transportation ceased to pay, the colonists
realized that it was a shameful business unworthy of
them. They took steps against the "humiliating obligation of receiving every year an importation of the
refuse of the British population." Furthermore, most
of the colonists consisted of people who had crossed
the ocean because they were dissatisfied with conditions at home. They based their freedom and independence on their own work, and were therefore bitter
opponents of the large plantation owners who relied
on forced labor. Their discontent was opposed by the
financial interests of the English court, however. A
great many people in England who were interested in
the new colonies considered it advantageous to increase the labor supply and to drive wages down by
transporting criminals. The colonists fought back by
means of statutes which levied a duty on the import
of poor and disabled persons as well as on persons
convicted of heinous crimes. The Declaration of
Independence and the Revolutionary War ended the
problem of making it impossible to send any more
criminals to America.

Francis Bacon once made the following pessimistic
prophecy:

> It is a shameful and unblessed thing to take the scum of people,
> and wicked condemned men, to be the people with whom you
> plant; and not only so, but it spoileth the plantation; for they
> will ever live like rogues, and not fall to work, but be lazy,
> and do mischief, and spend victuals, and be quickly weary,
> and then certify over to their country to the discredit of the
> plantation.

After quoting this passage, Holtzendorff, a nineteenth-
century German authority on criminal policy, comments that experience proved the very opposite. We
may add that the reform of convicts achieved under
the favorable social conditions in the North American
colonies proves conclusively that the categories good
and bad, honest and criminal, are strictly relative.

SOCIAL AND PENAL CONSEQUENCES OF THE INDUSTRIAL REVOLUTION

The movement for the reform of criminal law gained
real momentum during the second half of the eighteenth century. The first edition of Beccaria was
published in 1763, the *Allgemeine preussische Land-
recht* in 1794. But the basis for the new system

of punishment, the need for man power, was disappearing during the same period. We have already indicated that the reform found fertile ground only because its humanitarian principles coincided with the economic necessities of the time. Now, when attempts were being made to give practical expression to these new ideas, part of the base from which they arose had already ceased to exist. That situation was reflected in the conditions of prison life, as we can see from the descriptions in the fourth edition of Howard's *State of the Prisons in England and Wales*. Visiting the Osnabrück prison, he completely disregarded the warden's information—we are vividly reminded of similar cases today—after he saw the misery expressed in the faces of the prisoners. In Ghent, his inquiries led him to the same conclusions. We have similar evidence from Thuringia in the second half of the eighteenth century, where there were not enough instructors nor adequate markets for the commodities produced in the prisons. Lack of space made it necessary to herd people together. The report of the Weimar *Zuchthaus*, for example, said that conditions were "thoroughly bad." . . .

The house of correction grew out of a social situation in which the conditions of the labor market were favorable to the lower classes. But this situation changed. The demand for workers was satisfied and a surplus eventually developed. The population of England increased by one million in the first half of the eighteenth century, and by three million in the second half. It was 5.1 million in 1720, 6 in 1750, and 9.18 in 1801. Between 1781 and 1800 the rate of increase was 9 to 11 percent, and between 1801 and 1820, 14 to 18 percent. The population of France was 19 million in 1707, 24 in 1770, and 26 in 1789. What the ruling classes had been seeking for over a century was now an accomplished fact—relative overpopulation. Factory owners need no longer hunt for men. On the contrary, workers had to search out places of employment. The rapidly growing population could not support itself on the land, especially after certain changes had taken place in agricultural production, resulting in enclosures and large estates. From the beginning of the eighteenth century agricultural workers began to stream into the towns, a movement which reached its climax in the first decades of the nineteenth century.

The introduction of machinery at such a time was bound to have catastrophic effects. It began in the textile industry. Home spinning, which used to occupy entire districts, had been unable to satisfy the demand of the textile mills for yarn. The introduction of the spinning machine now increased the output per worker to such a degree that it became possible to develop the textile industry to meet the needs of all possible markets without relying on handspun yarn. The consequence was that spinning ceased to be one of those subsidiary home industries by means of which the poorer English people had managed to supplement their insufficient returns from the land. All the spinning was now done in factories, and men frequently found it impossible to compete with women and children. The same process of industrialization gradually spread from the cotton mills to all other enterprises. More and more people were thrown out of work, steadily increasing industrial unemployment. . . .

The increase in crime and its effect on the theory and practice of punishment The increasing sharpness of the struggle for existence brought the living standard of the working class to an incredibly low level. In England, the height of pauperism was reached between 1780 and 1830. Throughout the first half of the nineteenth century, behind the picture of growing starvation, immorality, and drunkenness we find the threat of revolution. The newly created proletariat was ready at any moment for rebellion and violence. The slogan "Bread or Blood" spread through the English factory districts in 1810, and in 1831 the silk weavers of Lyons inscribed on their banner the motto, "Vivre en travaillant ou mourir en combattant."

More and more of the impoverished masses were driven to crime. Offenses against property began to increase considerably at the end of the eighteenth century, and matters became still worse during the first decades of the nineteenth. The London statistics for the period 1821–27 give a vivid picture of the decisive part played by larceny in the general increase of convictions (Table 1, next page).

TABLE 1
Larceny in London, 1821–27

Year	Total Convictions	Convictions for Larceny
1821	8,788	6,629
1822	8,209	6,424
1823	8,204	6,452
1824	9,152	7,550
1825	9,964	8,011
1826	11,095	8,962
1827	12,564	9,803

Source: C. Lucas, *Du système pénitentiaire en Europe et aux États-Unis* (Paris, 1825), 1, p. 53.

The yearly average of convictions by Assizes and Quarter Sessions in England rose as is shown in Table 2.

TABLE 2
Convictions by Assizes and Quarter Sessions, 1805–33

Years	Convictions
1805– 6	2,649
1807– 9	2,843
1810–12	3,411
1813–15	4,443
1816–18	7,937
1819–21	9,205
1822–24	8,613
1825–27	11,212
1828–30	12,596
1831–33	14,408

Source: E. Ducpetiaux, *Statistique comparle de la criminalité. . . .* (Bruxelles, 1835), p. 41.

During this period, then, the number of convictions increased by 540%. Engels commented: "Want leaves the workingman the choice between starving slowly, killing himself speedily, or taking what he needs where he finds it—in plain English, stealing. And there is no cause for surprise that most of them prefer stealing to starvation and suicide." This general development was not limited to England by any means, as the French criminal statistics of Table 3 show.

We thus see what tremendous proportions crime reached during the great industrial crisis. Such far-reaching crises were unknown during the mercantil-

ist period in spite of all the disturbances due to war or natural causes. In describing the close connection between the crime rate and economic conditions, Pike says that the English Criminal Tables from 1810 on indicate that hard times, increased competition, or diminished demand for labor were followed by an increase in convictions for larceny and graver offenses, whereas better times were accompanied by a decrease. The year 1815, when the troops returned home and began to compete with other laborers, saw a marked increase of convictions, and so did 1825, the year of the great commercial depression. In 1835, on the other hand, a sharp drop in the price of corn, continuing the price fall of the three previous years, was accompanied by a considerable decrease in the number of prison commitments.

The ruling classes were tempted to return to the premercantilist methods of treating criminals. A demand for harsher methods became widespread, and the liberal use of imprisonment to replace the traditional forms of punishment was severely criticized. People declared that the penal system had become a humbug, and that punishment should once again become something that the wrongdoer felt to the very marrow of his bones, something that tortured and destroyed him, as the penal laws of Charles V expressed it. The ax, the whip, and starvation ought to be reintroduced in order to root out the criminals. Wagnitz stated that, although he would not advocate the gallows and the wheel as other writers had done, he would insist on permanent confinement for those miserable people who showed by repeated offenses that they were too weak to withstand the temptation of crime and were therefore incurably diseased in

TABLE 3
Larceny in France, 1825–42

Year	Total Convictions	Convictions for Larceny
1825	35,214	7,132
1828	41,120	9,400
1832	45,431	13,463
1836	54,976	14,601
1842	72,490	20,022

Source: Compiled from the annual *Compte général de l'administration de la justice criminelle.*

spirit. In 1802 the Helvetian Department of the Interior sent out a questionnaire concerning the results of the criminal code drawn up on the lines of the French code of 1795. In reply, a Zürich judge, Meyer, bitterly attacked the humanitarian effeminacy of the age and made ironic remarks about the dream of a possible elevation of mankind. He recommended the reestablishment of a qualified death penalty and corporal punishment. That his opinion was fairly representative can be seen from the fact that some cantons returned to the *Peinliche Halsgerichtsordnung* of Charles V when they regained their sovereign legislative power.

The same complaints appear in France. Debry, formerly a member of the Convention and later an administrative official under Napoleon, said that there could be no doubt that the high frequency of thefts and robberies, especially in the rural areas, was due to the weakness of the legislation on which court practice was founded. Punishments were not heavy enough. Special police and court martials were established, and the campaigns of "pacification" led to a virtual slaughter of poor outlaws, especially in the southern departments. The same tendencies were manifested in legislation. The *ad hoc* laws which had already intensified the repression in the time of the Consulate, especially the law reintroducing branding for recidivists and forgers, reached their climax in the code of 1810. This codification deviated still further from the liberal system of punishment of the revolutionary legislation. In introducing the bill before the *Tribunal*, Treilhard expressed the new official attitude toward crime when he judged the revolutionary legislation in the following language: "This famous assembly, which has distinguished itself by so many useful ideas, which has done away with so many abuses, and which has without doubt shown the best intentions, has not always guarded itself against the enthusiasm of human kindness." Garraud characterized the new system correctly when he remarked that it was particularly noteworthy for the excess of its severity, that its only interest was to strike the guilty, and that the idea of correction had no place in it. The death penalty remained unchallenged and life imprisonment was frequently applied. Excessive punishment, barbaric

mutilations, and unjust penalties like confiscation of property and loss of civil rights were its chief characteristics.

The situation had become reversed in Germany, too. Conservative students of criminal theory stated with satisfaction that the principle of retributive justice was beginning to have a salutary effect on the penal system. They returned to the view that one can get at a thief only through his skin, and whipping became a favored form of punishment once more, for it was cheap and avoided overcrowding the prisons. The most important step in this direction is represented by Anselm Feuerbach's Bavarian Criminal Code of 1813. In legal technique it was a distinctly progressive step, as compared with the eighteenth-century codifications, but in its system of punishment it followed the harsh tendencies of the period. The death penalty, life imprisonment in chains, and the house of correction were the basis of the system. . . .

New aims and methods of prison administration Imprisonment became the chief punishment throughout the western world at the very moment when the economic foundation of the house of correction was destroyed by industrial changes. English developments are particularly interesting in this connection, as they show that imprisonment was much the most frequent form of punishment even when transportation was at its height.

In 1837–39, the ratio of transportation to imprisonment was 23.5 to 100, and in 1844–46 only 15 to 100.

Imprisonment took various forms and gradations according to the gravity of the crime and the social position of the convict. It has already been indicated that class differentiations in the system of punishment were not abolished in the first half of the nineteenth century. The upper classes were not yet convinced the advantages of sacrificing to the ideology of justice and equality those of its members whose position could no longer be maintained, as in the case of Hatry and, more recently, Whitney. The official commentary on the Bavarian Criminal Code of 1813 actually attempted to justify the introduction of *Festungshaft* for the upper classes on the ground that

PART 3   THE SOCIAL ORGANIZATION OF CRIMINAL LAW ENFORCEMENT

TABLE 4
Distribution of Punishments in England, 1806–33

| Punishment | Number of Sentences | | | |
	1806–12	1813–19	1820–26	1827–33
Capital punishment	2,800	6,584	7,659	9,457
Transportation for life	76	564	1,000	2,979
21–35 years	—	—	—	13
14 years	291	1,012	1,196	4,287
10, 9, 4 years	—	3	3	3
7 years	3,660	7,823	10,828	16,221
Imprisonment with or without other punishments				
3 to 5 years	—	99	79	46
1 to 2 years	13,413	1,693	2,343	1,673
6 months to 1 year	—	5,644	8,088	9,050
Less than 6 months	—	21,787	31,988	47,620
Whipping and fines	1,027	1,487	1,832	2,225
Total	21,267	46,651	65,016	93,574

Source: Ducpetiaux, *op. cit.*, p. 51

it was not a violator of liberal ideas. It argued that the principle of equality is not abandoned when minor punishments are adapted to personal conditions as long as modifications of severe punishments are not permitted to turn into the privilege of immunity. The argument that the upper classes are more sensitive to punishment and that there is greater likelihood of suffering on the part of their families, already rejected by Beccaria, was again drawn upon to save the traditional privileges of the aristocracy. The privilege of separate confinement for the upper classes was retained in all the German countries, and especially in Prussia. Only in the second half of the century did the pressure of the Rhineland lawyers and parliamentarians, representatives of a more highly developed section of capitalist society, change *Festungshaft* from a privilege of the upper strata to a particular form of punishment for specific crimes. . . .

The 1825 report on the prison of the canton Waad, one of the most valuable documents of the whole prison literature of the period, insisted first of all that mere deprivation of liberty is no effective punishment for the lower classes. The conclusion was reached that the necessary condition for the prisoner's reentry into society is unconditional submission to authority, a conclusion which has remained unshaken by reform programs and tendencies up to the present. If the

prisoners resign themselves to a quiet, regular, and industrious life, punishment will become more tolerable for them. Once this routine becomes a habit, the first step toward improvement has been taken. As far as possible there must be a guaranty that the improvement will continue after the prisoner has been released. Obedience is demanded not so much for the smooth functioning of the prison but for the sake of the convict himself, who shall learn to submit willingly to the fate of the lower classes. That is a difficult task. Obedience to the law is simple and self-evident for the upper classes, but it is almost hopeless to lift the ragged and starved prison inmates to such a level. The chances of success were not considered very good, but the report indicated a practical method. To induce the convicts to economize, they were credited with the value of as much bread as they were able to refrain from consuming immediately. The saving was about 50 quintals a year, which went to the profit of the criminals without any added expense to the administration. The convicts learn to economize even in times of want and misery, in preparation for worse times yet to come.

All agreed that nothing beyond the barest minimum should be supplied to the prisoners. In discussing the reproduction costs of labor power as the determining factor in wages, Marx remarked that political economy deals with the worker only in his capacity as worker. . . .

We have seen that the houses of correction used to spur the inmates to greater industry by paying them according to their work or by giving them a share of the profits. They were punished only if they failed to perform their task, whether from lack of skill or from laziness. Now that it no longer paid to employ prisoners, however, they were frequently left with nothing to do. This raised the whole problem of the purpose of imprisonment, and brought its repressive, deterrent side to the fore. The way was open for the realization of the programs of reformers like Pearson and Mittelstädt, who sought to make the prisons rational and efficient means of deterring the lower classes from crime, means which would not allow the convict to perish, but which would impress him once and for all by fear and terror. England, with its large industrial reserve army, led the way. Work was introduced as a form of punishment, not as a source of profit, and moral arguments were brought forward as a justification. One experienced administrator explained in 1821 that work which was to produce profit would interfere with discipline and moral improvement, because, for purposes of manufacture, the taskmaster would seek to assemble prisoners who would otherwise not be permitted to associate with each other.

Prison labor became a method of torture, and the authorities were expert enough in inventing new forms; occupations of a purely punitive character were made as fatiguing as possible and were dragged out for unbearable lengths of time. Prisoners carried huge stones from one place to another and then back again, they worked pumps from which the water flowed back to its source, or trod mills which did no useful work. A simple form of treadwheel, easily applicable to all prisons, was devised by William Cubitt about 1818 for use in the Suffolk County Gaol at Bury, and it was from this example that the practice spread. The cheapness and simplicity of the "stepping-mill" or "everlasting staircase," as it was called, the severe physical exertion required, and the hatred engendered by "wheel-stepping" commended the new device to Quarter Sessions, and models were set up in every reformed prison, grinding corn or grinding nothing, raising water, supply-

ing power for hemp-beating, cork-cutting, or other machines. Not only was the treadwheel regarded as a success because it afforded a cheap and easy method of forcing prisoners to work, but also because it deterred persons who might use the gaol as a place of ultimate refuge.

The prisoners tried desperately to avoid such punishments. A strong outside opposition also developed on the ground that the treadwheel was so exhausting as to destroy the prisoner's health and that it often amounted to actual torture. Furthermore, it was argued, such punishment counteracted every effort to reform the prisoner's character. But official English opinion continued to favor strictly punitive labor, and it spread from prison to prison despite the attacks of the humanitarians. It was even to be found in the colonial penitentiaries of Hobart Town and Sidney.

These developments also attracted attention outside of England. A German writer insisted on the infliction of penalties having a humiliating effect; if corporal punishment is abolished, he argued, there must be a substitute like the treadmill, which would soon come to be regarded as humiliating. Mittelstädt welcomed the changes because they indicated a realization that the principles of justice demanded that imprisonment should be something more than mere deprivation of liberty and hence should entail a certain amount of positive pain and hardship. German penal practice adhered to this conception until the middle of the nineteenth century. Judges did not trouble to distinguish between different degrees of imprisonment or to fix the term according to definite principles. Legislators and judges were indifferent to prison conditions. They were content to assume that hunger, flogging, and hard labor would do their work, and that there could be no one so poor and miserable but that fear and shame would ultimately force him to do everything in his power to stay outside the prison walls. The possibility that imprisonment could lose its intimidating effects lay beyond the realm of rational thought.

MODERN PRISON REFORM AND ITS LIMITS
Rising living standards of the lower classes and the effects on criminal policy The condition of the lower classes

in Europe improved considerably in the second half, and especially in the last quarter, of the nineteenth century. Europe now entered that period of prosperity which lasted until 1914, interrupted only by minor crises. The participation of the masses in the consumption of goods formerly inaccessible to them was the consequence partly of their increased income and partly of mass production. Clapham notes that the rise in English wages in the eighties was not limited to the average wage earner in the towns, but benefited women and farm laborers as well. Sée makes the same observation for France, where wages increased slowly until 1860 and much more rapidly thereafter. In France, apart from the factors operative in Germany and England, that is, better organization of the working classes, technological progress, and mass production of consumption goods, another factor played a leading role in the improvement of lower-class conditions, namely, the lower birth rate and the consequent decrease in labor supply and increase in wages during the period of industrial expansion. In Germany, industrialization came later than in other western countries but living conditions improved nevertheless. Better transportation facilities automatically created an adjustment between standards of living in various parts of the same country. Unlike the situation in the seventeenth century, it was scarcely possible to find economic prosperity in one section and starvation in a neighboring region. Furthermore, governments began to alleviate poverty during periods of crisis. One important symptom of the improved standard of living is the decline of emigration at the very time when colonial expansion and the development of the American continent took place.

The influence of these economic developments on criminality soon became noticeable. Pike, the historian of English criminal law, remarked that prosperity and steady employment in the factories, aided perhaps by other factors, gradually softened that spirit of violence which formerly revealed itself upon the slightest provocation. The criminal statistics of the period give the same impression. The number of offenses and convictions decreased everywhere, or at least remained stationary, as the following figures show. (It should be noted that they are not entirely comparable.)

TABLE 5

Decrease in Number of Convictions, Late Nineteenth and Early Twentieth Centuries

A. Germany: Convictions of Persons above the Age of Discretion, for Petty Larceny (per 100,000 Population)*

Period	Number
1882–84	241
1885–89	206
1890–94	212
1895–99	187
1900–04	184
1905–09	181
1910–13	173

B. England: Persons Tried before Assizes, Quarter Sessions, and Summary Courts for Offenses against Property without Violence (per 100,000 Population)**

Period	Number
1876–80	200
1881–85	205
1886–90	180
1891–95	171
1896–99	146
1900–04	153
1905–09	158
1910–14	150

*Source: R. Rabl, *Strafzumessungspraxis und Kriminalitätsbewegung* (Leipzig, 1936), p. 13.
**Source: Calculated from the annual *Criminal Statistics, England and Wales*.

The value of human labor power was again seen in a different light. It is true that population increased considerably in the nineteenth century and that the period of labor scarcity had disappeared forever; but the immense expansion of industrial production in the era of imperialism provided for a maximum absorption of labor power. The senseless imprisonment of individuals became undesirable and out of step with the times. Worms, a French economist, condemned both the damaging effect of laws against usury and the unreasonable methods of dealing with crime, in one and the same sentence, written in 1870. He stated that life and liberty came to be regarded as more valuable with the change to modern industrial production, and he drew the conclusion that to shorten the days of a citizen without urgent necessity or to prolong his senseless imprisonment without incontrovertible reason at a time when everyone is regarded, morally at least, as a responsible producer would constitute a loss of forces for society. Far from being useful, it is detrimental. It has often been pointed out that the notion that it is undesirable to waste the social capital invested in members of society was one of the motivating forces in early social insurance programs. It also underlay the policy of crime prevention which the writers of the Enlightenment had earlier recommended as the best way to stop infringements upon property rights. . . .

The end of the nineteenth century marks the close of the period of antagonism between the last remnants of feudalism and the administrative bureaucracy on the one hand and the middle class on the other. As the latter strengthened their hold over the machinery of government and administration, it became less and less necessary to continue the process of formalizing criminal law as a guarantee of their social and economic position. The significance of an independent judiciary changed, too. The liberal attitude which we often find among judges in the first half of the nineteenth century gave way to strict conservatism after the reconciliation of the bourgeoisie with the bureaucratic and agrarian interests, and the ideology of independence gradually became a camouflage for the struggle against the lower classes. The orientation of criminal law was affected by these changes. "The improved relations between citizens and law," as Richard Schmidt calls this unification of the interests of the upper class, undermined the political function of the system of legal guarantees which had arisen toward the end of the eighteenth century. It was no longer necessary to protect the bourgeoisie against the arbitrariness of the administration, now that the two were largely identical. The once political question of protecting the individual in criminal procedure had become a problem of mere legal technique.

This change in the political basis coincides with the development of a sociological approach to criminal law. Statistical inquiries into the relationship between crime rates and economic fluctuations revealed the degree to which crime is a purely social phenomenon. Furthermore, the problem of penal methods was no longer viewed as a problem of maintaining a just proportion between crime and punishment; it was examined from the viewpoint of the criminal's future, the expectation of rehabilitation, and the precautions

which it was worth taking. Carried to its extreme, this approach would mean that in normal cases crime is evidence of the necessity of transferring the delinquent to a well-organized charitable institution. The ideal judge would be one who is fully conscious of society's guilt, acquits the poor defendant who pleads guilty of larceny, and gives him money for a new start. The main representatives of sociological criminology did not go this far, however. They were content to place the main burden upon social policy and to advocate a thoroughgoing rationalization of criminal justice under the exclusive domination of theological viewpoints. Criminals who do not need correction and supervision should be kept out of prisons by an extensive use of probations and fines (administrative objections are met by pointing to the economic advantages to be derived from this procedure). The short-term sentence was condemned. "There is nothing more immoral and more absurd," wrote Liszt, "than the short-term sentences of imprisonment for apprentices in crime." Criminals capable of reform should be morally reeducated with the utmost diligence. The idea of the guilt of society merges with the idea of giving the greatest possible number of productive forces back to society. The reformation of convicts is thus regarded as a good investment, and not merely as a charitable whim. A convict should be banished from society for an indefinite period only when there is no prospect for rehabilitation. This idea of criminality as a social phenomenon which can be adjusted by appropriate measures received a characteristic formulation from Prins:

> If crime broke out on chance occasions like a will-o'-the-wisp fluttering over the swamp at night, justice would only be able to strike back by chance. That is not the case. Crime tends to concentrate in a definite circle which expands or contracts under the influence of misery or prosperity. We do not grope in the dark and we can try to react with a greater chance of success.

It is interesting to note that the reformers themselves endeavored to retain all the guarantees of procedure which had been built up since the end of the eighteenth century, as well as the exact definition of legal facts which had been developed through legislation and jurisprudence. The criminal reformers of our time have welcomed the proposal to separate the determination of guilt from the imposition of the sentence; the first is to be entrusted to a qualified judge, the second to a "social physician." Such a separation of functions is the logical outcome of the attempt to safeguard the interests of both the individual and society. In spite of this attachment of the social-liberal reform school to the traditional guarantees of procedure, however, there is a definite connection between their theory and the decline of formalism in criminal law. If crime is primarily an index for more intimate knowledge of the delinquent's personality, the question of the crime which the delinquent has committed, or, if already convicted, whether he committed any crime at all in a given case, is forced into the background together with the question of those general political tendencies which sought to weaken the formalism of criminal law.

Richard Schmidt is quite right in attacking Radbruch's notion that liberalism regards punishment solely from the standpoint of society's security, and that merely repressive punishment belongs to conservatism. Schmidt points out that the strict suppression of professional criminals of proletarian origin, the most absolutistic side of a penal system which centers about society's security, would be heartily welcomed in many militarists, agrarian, capitalist, and rural middle-class circles. More recent developments have fully confirmed his view. It is significant that the least liberal portions of the reform program, such as preventive detention and all other forms of rendering prisoners harmless, have been realized much more completely than other aspects like prison reform.

Results and limits of prison reform   Before we discuss the most recent trends, we must examine the development of punishment by imprisonment in the period of relative prosperity, the period when the reform school was at its height. . . . The new policy sponsored by the reformers was to keep as many delinquents as possible out of jail by a more extensive use of fines, which we will treat later, by a probation policy, and, above all, by seeking to ameliorate the social conditions responsible for crime.

The following table shows the shifts of the prison population in France between 1884 and 1932, and in England between 1880 and 1931.

TABLE 6
Decline in Prison Population, Late Nineteenth Century and Twentieth Century

A. France: Prison Population, 1884–1932*

| | Maisons Centrales | | Maisons D'Arrêt (as of Dec. 31) | |
Year	Men	Women	Men	Women
1884	12,689	1,943	21,257	3,974
1887	11,547	1,635	21,394	3,573
1890	10,540	1,640	20,940	3,440
1891	10,054	1,439	20,336	3,338
1894	9,839	1,294	19,389	3,652
1897	8,434	1,008	15,636	2,790
1900	6,802	801	14,769	2,466
1902	5,906	673	13,941	2,152
1905	5,401	539	13,502	1,902
1909	5,540	507	13,304	1,885
1910	5,612	534	14,518	2,224
1913	6,413	726	14,123	2,219
1920	7,443	863	17,997	3,383
1921	6,247	1,086	13,920	2,911
1922	6,090	935	11,037	2,338
1925	5,529	885	12,278	2,095
1927	5,405	542	14,293	2,316
1929	4,992	573	12,537	2,038
1930	5,085	590	12,575	1,885
1931	4,662	546	11,695	1,756
1932	4,315	469	12,579	1,591

B. England: Persons Sent into Penal Servitude or Imprisoned**

Year	Number
1880	32,999
1890	24,628
1900	22,432
1905	28,257
1910	26,096
1911	23,758
1912	23,994
1913	21,463
1914	18,195
1915	11,802
1916	11,027
1917	11,930
1918	11,303
1919	12,732
1920	15,518
1921	15,756
1922	15,520
1923	14,788
1924	14,132
1925	13,580

TABLE 6 (Continued)

1926	14,537
1927	14,446
1928	13,726
1929	13,526
1930	14,294
1931	13,838

*Source: Compiled from the annual Statistique pénitentiaire.
**Source: Fox, Modern English Prison, pp. 218–19.

The tendency to substitute other forms of punishment for imprisonment was accompanied by a decrease in the length and severity of prison sentences. That is clearly shown by the following table giving the distribution of sentences in Germany from 1882 to 1934. (Note the upswing in prison sentences beginning with the crisis in 1930.)

The general tendency toward leniency is quite obvious. The house of correction is replaced by the medium prison term and the latter by short-term imprisonment or fines. The trend would be even more evident if probation statistics were presented. Rabl's studies have shown that this leniency was applied equally to all types of delinquency. . . .

It was in this social atmosphere that the literature of modern prison reform arose. Its insistence on treating crime as a psychological-medical problem, that is to say, on the social necessity of healing the prisoner if possible or of isolating him if no cure could be achieved, spread to every section of the population. Thus, Hugo Haase, in explaining the demands of the German Social Democratic Party in the field of criminal law at its 1906 convention, took the position that the common practice of acquitting members of better families in cases of larceny by the introduction of medical evidence certifying kleptomania should be extended much more widely. The *Reichsrechtliche Grundsätze über den Vollzug von Freiheitsstrafer*, an agreement between the various German states on June 7, 1923, regarding the treatment of delinquents, was perhaps the most notable example of the progressive spirit in criminal practice.

The criminologists of the modern reform school have retained the older notion that the standard of living within the prison must be below the minimum

TABLE 7
Distribution of German Sentences in Percents

Year	Death Sentence	Zuchthaus	Total Prison Sentences	Over One Year	Three Months to One Year	Less Than Three Months	Arrests	Fines
1882	.03	4.3	72.0	1.6	9.6	60.8	.46	22.2
1886	.02	3.4	68.5	2.7	11.1	54.7	.36	26.5
1893	.01	2.7	61.6	3.0	11.0	47.6	.23	33.6
1900	.01	2.1	55.6	2.9	10.7	42.0	.11	39.7
1907	.01	1.4	47.8	2.3	8.9	36.6	.08	47.5
1913	.01	1.4	44.0	2.7	9.2	32.1	.05	52.0
1918	.01	1.7	60.1	3.4	11.7	45.0	.02	32.0
1921	.02	1.4	56.9	4.3	14.3	38.3	.02	39.3
1926	.02	1.2	32.5	2.3	10.5	19.7	.42	63.2
1928	.01	0.87	28.6	1.8	8.8	18.0	.49	69.2
1930	.01	0.78	31.8	1.9	9.5	20.3	.52	66.2
1931	.008	0.81	35.9	2.1	10.7	23.1	.45	62.1
1932	.009	1.12	41.5	2.5	12.9	26.0	.46	56.3
1933	.016	1.97	44.5	3.9	15.0	25.5	.51	52.6
1934	.025	3.22	41.7	4.6	14.6	22.4	.47	54.7

Source: Compiled from the *Kriminalstatistik für das deutsche Reich* and the *Statistisches Jahrbuch für das deutsche Reich*.

standard outside. Enrico Ferri, representative of a poor country whose lower classes scarcely participated in the general improvement in European economic conditions, expressed strong opposition at the end of the nineteenth century to "this upheaval of every principle of social justice which would have prisons more convenient and more comfortable than dwellings of poor and honest folk who may, so long as they remain honest, die there of acute or chronic starvation since society assures them food and lodging only when they commit culpable acts." The problem became less acute at the turn of the century, because the progress of material culture and the general amelioration of lower class life allowed for a certain improvement in prison conditions without destroying the line of demarcation from life outside. To this extent economic developments fitted in with the aims of the reformers, but we must not lose sight of the fact that their insistence on retaining the line of demarcation set narrow limits to the possibilities of reform and surrendered it to the mercy of every crisis in the market. Even in periods of prosperity large sections of the population lack the forces necessary in the struggle for survival, especially in the larger cities. . . .

The existing social system with its need for rationalization not only restricts the extension of a repressive penal policy but also sets narrow limits to the reform program. The penal system of any given society is not an isolated phenomenon subject only to its own special laws. It is an integral part of the whole social system, and shares its aspirations and its defects. The crime rate can really be influenced only if society is in a position to offer its members a certain measure of security and to guarantee a reasonable standard of living. The shift from a repressive penal policy to a progressive program can then be raised out of the sphere of humanitarianism to constructive social activity. So long as the social consciousness is not in a position to comprehend and act upon the necessary connection between a progressive penal program and progress in general, any project for penal reform can have but doubtful success, and failures will be attributed to the inherent wickedness of human nature rather than to the social system. The inevitable consequence is a return to the pessimistic doctrine that man's evil nature can be tamed only by depressing the prison standard below that of the lowest free classes. The futility of severe punishment and cruel treatment may be proven a thousand times, but so long as society is unable to solve its social problems, repression, the easy way out, will always be accepted. It provides the illusion of security by covering the symptoms of social disease with a system of legal and moral value judgments. There is a paradox in the fact that the progress of human knowledge has made the problem of penal treatment more comprehensible and more soluble than ever, while the question of a fundamental revision in the policy of punishment seems to be further away today than ever before because of its functional dependence on the given social order.

27

Race, Judicial Discretion, and the Death Penalty

MARVIN E. WOLFGANG
and MARC RIEDEL

In *Furman v. Georgia,* the Supreme Court, by a five-to-four decision, ruled that "the imposition and carrying out of the death penalty in these cases constitutes cruel and unusual punishment in violation of the Eighth and Fourteenth Amendments."[1] The three petitioners referred to in the decision are Black; one had been convicted of a felony murder, while the other two had been convicted of rape. In each case the decision to impose the death penalty had been determined by a jury.[2]

SOME MAJOR ISSUES IN THE FURMAN CASE

Civil rights and civil liberties organizations view the *Furman* decision "as the watershed in its long struggle against capital punishment," but many of the consequences of the decision are unclear.[3] Although each of the five concurring justices filed separate opinions, and none joined in the opinion of any other, there was agreement that the death penalty constitutes cruel and unusual punishment because it is imposed infrequently and under no clear standards. In addition, the opinions of Justices William O.

Source: "Race, Judicial Discretion, and the Death Penalty," *Annals of the American Academy of Political and Social Science*. Vol. 407, May, 1973. Copyright © 1973 by the American Academy of Political and Social Science.

Douglas and Thurgood Marshall suggest that the death penalty may have been imposed in a discriminatory manner. Inseparable from these latter considerations, however, was the central issue of whether the death penalty for felony murder and rape, when imposed by a jury having discretion to mete out death or imprisonment, is constitutionally permissible.[4]

The Court concluded that the death penalty constitutes cruel and unusual punishment partly because it is infrequently and arbitrarily applied. However, that very infrequency could support both concurring and dissenting opinions and therefore really supports neither. Moreover, although the death penalty may be infrequently imposed, it is not imposed arbitrarily. Focusing on previously unpublished studies of rape and the death penalty, this paper will conclude that racial variables are systematically and consistently related to the imposition of the death penalty.

According to Justice Douglas, the Court's view of the sentencing discretion of juries was stated in *McGautha v. California:* "In light of history, experience and the present limitations of human knowledge, we find it quite impossible to say that committing to the untrammeled discretion of the jury the power to pronounce life or death in capital cases is offensive to anything in the Constitution."[5] The Court could find no constitutional dimensions in the argument that juries that have the discretion to send a person to death should be given standards by which this discretion can be exercised.

Although the Court did not conclude that standards should be given to juries in the exercise of their sentencing discretion, Justice Douglas did indicate that such jury discretion serves the function of preventing punishments for laws that are "totally repugnant to the feelings of the community. . . ."[6] Chief Justice Warren E. Burger also emphasized that the exercise of jury discretion expresses the conscience of the community. Drawing upon the *Witherspoon v. Illinois* decision, the Chief Justice concluded that juries are given sentencing discretion in death penalty cases because their selections maintain a link between community values and the penal system, "a link without which the determination of punishment could hardly reflect 'the evolving standards of decency that mark the progress of a maturing society.'"[7]

If the Court had previously held that the exercise of jury discretion in death penalty cases was not unconstitutional, how could it rule in *Furman v. Georgia* that imposition of the death penalty by a jury exercising their sentencing discretion is in violation of the Eighth and Fourteenth Amendments? It would appear that the dissenting opinion of Justice Lewis F. Powell is correct: "Having so recently reaffirmed our historic dedication to entrusting the sentencing function to the jury's 'untrammeled discretion' . . . , it is difficult to see how the Court can now hold the entire process constitutionally defective under the Eighth Amendment."[8] However, the basis for inferring cruel and unusual punishments in the imposition of the death penalty hinged on the interpretation and relationship between the Eighth and Fourteenth Amendments. Both *McGautha* and *Witherspoon* were rulings focusing on due process and equal protection clauses in the Fourteenth Amendment. Justice Douglas maintained that there is "increasing recognition of the fact that the basic theme of equal protection is implicit in 'cruel and unusual' punishment."[9] Where a penalty is imposed with extreme rarity or is arbitrarily or discriminatorily

administered, it should be considered imposed "unusually."

Justice William J. Brennan pointed out that the "Cruel and Unusual Punishments Clause is fully applicable to the States through the Due Process Clause of the Fourteenth Amendment."[10] Justice Brennan concluded that because of the *McGautha* decision, procedures have not been "constructed to guard against the totally capricious selection of criminals for the punishment of death."[11] This conclusion is based on the infrequency and apparent lack of selectivity of executions.

Among the other concurring opinions, Justice Potter Stewart simply concluded that "the Eighth and Fourteenth Amendments cannot tolerate the infliction of a sentence of death under legal systems that permit this unique penalty to be so wantonly and so freakishly imposed."[12] Justice Byron R. White recognized the right of juries to exercise their discretion in imposing the death penalty, but pointed out that it is exercised with such infrequency that "the threat of execution is too attenuated to be of substantial service to criminal justice."[13] Justice Marshall claimed that the death penalty was cruel and unusual because it was excessive and unnecessary. Giving juries "untrammeled discretion" to impose a sentence of death was "an open invitation to discrimination."[14]

The concurring opinions concluded that the exercise of jury discretion in imposing the death penalty was cruel and unusual punishment because of its infrequency, its arbitrariness, or the opportunities it afforded for discrimination. The dissenting opinions, on the other hand, pointed out that these were due process arguments outside the purview of the "cruel and unusual punishment" provision of the Eighth Amendment. In addition, three of the four dissenting justices held that the Court's decision infringed on legislative prerogatives.

From the available literature, as well as what is given in the opinions of the justices, there seems little doubt that the death penalty is infrequently or rarely imposed.[15] It is unclear, however, what infrequency of imposition per se can demonstrate. Where juries are given discretion to mete out the death penalty or imprisonment, infrequency of imposition may mean only that the jury feels there are very few cases that warrant the extreme penalty; cases receiving the death penalty, it could be claimed, may involve circumstances that raise no issue of cruel and unusual punishment.

In part, this is the position taken in the dissenting opinion of Chief Justice Burger.[16] On the other hand, infrequency of imposition may mean that cases are selected randomly[17] or on constitutionally impermissible grounds such as race,[18] a point of view suggested by the concurring opinions. Thus, infrequency of imposition appears to be supportive both of the interpretation that the exercise of jury discretion constitutes cruel and unusual punishment and the interpretation that it does not.

Two of the majority opinions characterize the jury's discretionary behavior in imposing the death penalty as "random," "capricious," "wanton," and "freakish."[19] We noted previously that the *McGautha* decision established that juries could act with "untrammeled discretion"; but the lack of standards to guide the jury in imposing the sentence of death raised no constitutional issue. If a jury exercises that discretion, it may do so in a way that is unconstitutional, but historically the behavior is not random, capricious, wanton, or freakish. As will be seen when the empirical evidence is reviewed, there are very distinct patterns of behavior which show that racial variables *are* influential in the imposition of the death penalty.

Both Justices Douglas and Marshall recognized the existence of discrimination in the imposition of the death penalty. Justice Douglas stated that

> the discretion of judges and juries in imposing the death penalty enables the penalty to be selectively applied, feeding prejudices against the accused if he is poor and despised, and lacking political clout, or if he is a member of a suspect or unpopular minority, and saving those who by social position may be in a more protected position. . . . Thus, these discretionary statutes are unconstitutional in their operation. They are pregnant with discrimination and discrimination is an ingredient not compatible with the idea of equal protection of the laws that is implicit in the ban on "cruel and unusual" punishment.[20]

If the discretionary statutes are "pregnant with discrimination," then Chief Justice Burger correctly pointed out that

legislative bodies may seek to bring their laws into compliance with the Court's ruling by providing standards for juries and judges to follow in determining the sentence in capital cases or by more narrowly defining the crimes for which the penalty is to be imposed. If such standards can be devised or the crimes more meticulously defined, the results cannot be detrimental.[21]

As a possible clue to such standards for jury use, Chief Justice Burger referred to motive or lack of motive of the perpetrator, degree of injury or suffering of the victim or victims, and the degree of brutality in the commission of the crime as prominent factors in the decision of the existing jury system.

With regard to the issue of discrimination, Justice Powell suggested that an argument

> not presented by any of the petitioners today, premised on the Equal Protection Clause, might well be made. If a Negro defendant, for instance, could demonstrate that members of his race were being singled out for more severe punishment than others charged with the same offense, a constitutional violation might be established.[22]

Putting the dissenting views of Chief Justice Burger and Justice Powell together suggests an interesting approach to the research literature. Even if the suggestions of the Chief Justice were to be followed, if statutory provisions were very specific, and if standards were constructed to guide juries, racial discrimination might still be demonstrated as an overriding consideration in sentencing. In other words, racial discrimination could be demonstrated if it were shown that variables like "amount of injury to victim" and committing a "contemporaneous offense" had no significant relation to death penalty sentencing when the race of the defendant was taken into account and while significantly higher proportions of one racial group compared to others were sentenced to death.

In the following sections the material which is presented in summary form is addressed to this very issue.

IS DIFFERENTIAL SENTENCING RACIAL DISCRIMINATION?

Of the 3,859 persons executed for all crimes since 1930, 54.6 percent have been Black or members of other racial minority groups. Of the 455 executed for rape alone, 89.5 percent have been nonwhite.[23] As census data clearly reveal, Blacks in American society have consistently represented approximately 10 percent of the United States population.

These statistics alone, of course, do not reveal elements of judicial bias in the administration of criminal law. It is also well recognized that Blacks in American society, with variations in time and place, have a criminal homicide rate that is between four and ten times greater than that of whites. Age, sex, and regional variations within the country are regularly taken into account when studies of homicide are made. There can be little argument about the fact that official police arrest and court adjudication records show a higher proportion of Blacks than of whites arrested and convicted for criminal homicide. We are not here questioning the process of the differential arrest of Blacks compared to whites nor the issue of varying degrees of evidentiary material for indictment of Blacks compared with whites. What is at issue is whether, among persons who have been convicted of capital crimes, a statistically significantly higher proportion of Blacks than of whites, all other things being relatively equal, are differentially sentenced to death. One of the important phrases in this statement is "relatively equal," for we need to know much more than is currently available about the circumstances of the crime, the previous record of the defendant, and the relationship between the victim and the offender before assertions of racial discrimination and bias can be made with utmost validity.

Many of the studies that have examined racial disparities in sentencing have attempted to control for one or more nonracial variables which might explain the differential imposition of the death penalty. The studies have been fragmentary and localized in particular states, but the findings have been in a consistent direction: Blacks are disproportionately sentenced to death.[24]

As an example of research done to determine the effects of race while taking into account the effects of nonracial variables, Wolfgang, Kelly, and Nolde analyzed the records of 439 persons sentenced to death in Pennsylvania between 1914 and 1958 for first degree murder.[25] Of 147 Blacks, only 11 percent had their sentences of death commuted to life

imprisonment; whereas of 263 whites, 20 percent had their sentences commuted. The statistical association between being executed and being Black was statistically significant ($x^2 = 4.33$; $p < 0.05$). As was asserted,

> something more than chance has operated over the years to produce this racial difference . . . because the Negro/high-execution association is statistically present, some suspicion of racial discrimination can hardly be avoided. If such a relationship had not appeared, this kind of suspicion could have been allayed; the existence of the relationship, although not "proving" differential bias by the Pardon Boards over the years since 1914, strongly suggests that such bias has existed.

In this study there was no significant difference between race and the commission of felony murder. That is, the proportion of Blacks and whites who had committed felony murder was not statistically different, yet 94 percent of black felony murderers were executed compared to 83 percent of white felony murderers. This latter was also a statistically significant difference, indicating that among offenders who had been sentenced to death and who had committed felony murder, Blacks were executed more and commuted less than whites. Finally, it was noted in general that offenders with court-appointed counsel were more likely to be executed and offenders with private counsel more likely to be commuted to life imprisonment, but even among the court-appointed counsel, a statistically significantly higher proportion of Blacks were executed than whites ($x^2 = 4.04$; $p < 0.05$). The authors concluded:

> . . . any empirical verification of previously assumed differences among persons who received society's ultimate sanction should be of value in understanding the operation of our legal principles. That race is one of these significant differences constitutes a social and political violation of the principle of equal justice. . . .[26]

In one of the early significant studies on race and capital punishment, Guy B. Johnson pointed out that the race of both the victim and the offender may be an important variable in understanding the penalties applied to homicides.[27] Using 220 homicide cases from Richmond, Virginia, from 1930 to 1939, and 330 homicides from five counties in North Carolina from 1930 to 1940, Johnson hypothesized that cases of black offenders whose victims were white would be viewed as the most serious homicides, followed by white offenders/white victims, black offenders/black victims, and white offenders/black victims.

Johnson found that of the 141 black/black cases, there were only 8 sentences of life imprisonment and no death sentences. Of the 22 cases of black offenders and white victims, 7 defendants received life imprisonment and 6 received the death penalty. Although the quality and quantity of data precluded further analysis, Johnson did conclude that "Negro versus Negro offenses are treated with undue leniency, while the Negro versus white offenses are treated with undue severity."[28]

The effects of the race of the offender, as well as racial combinations of offender and victim, on the imposition of the death penalty become more clear when studies on rape offenses are examined. Among persons sentenced to death for rape in North Carolina from 1909 to 1954, Elmer Johnson found that 56 percent of Blacks compared to 43 percent of whites were executed.[29] A Florida study of sentences for rape between 1940 and 1964 noted that only six cases, or 5 percent, of white males who raped white females received the death penalty. But of the eighty-four black males who raped white women, forty-five, or 54 percent, received the death penalty, while none of the eight white offenders who raped black females received the death penalty.[30]

Data from the Federal Bureau of Prisons suggest that racial differentials are most clear among death sentences for rape. As we noted, 405 of the 455 persons executed for rape since 1930 were black; only 2 were from other racial minorities. All of the executions for rape were in southern or border states or the District of Columbia.[31] In Louisiana, Mississippi, Oklahoma, Virginia, West Virginia, and the District of Columbia not a single white man was executed for rape over the forty-two-year period from 1930 to 1972. Together, these jurisdictions executed 66 Blacks. Arkansas, Delaware, Florida, Kentucky, and Missouri each executed 1 white man for rape since 1930, but together they have executed 71 Blacks.

Findings of racial discrimination in previous studies, as well as suspicions of racial discrimination raised by the data from the Bureau of Prisons, have been reinforced recently by more conclusive findings based on refined and detailed analyses of rape convictions in several states where rape has been a statutory capital crime. Differential sentencing has required further examination to determine whether racial discrimination exists.

RACIAL DISCRIMINATION IN THE IMPOSITION OF THE DEATH PENALTY FOR RAPE IN THE SOUTH, 1945–1965

During the summer of 1965, research was initiated to examine in detail the relationship between race and sentencing for rape in eleven southern and border states in which rape was a capital offense. The study was sponsored by the NAACP Legal Defense Fund and conducted by the Center for Studies in Criminology and Criminal Law at the University of Pennsylvania by Professors Anthony Amsterdam and Marvin E. Wolfgang.

At each step in the development and implementation of the research design, from selection of the sample to analysis of the data, the emphasis was on the use of research criteria that would increase the reliability and objectivity of the data while minimizing sources of bias and subjectivity. Interfacing with scientific demands was the selection of dimensions of inquiry that would increase understanding of racial discrimination, if it existed, in a judicial system and that would also be of possible use in subsequent litigation.

The research findings were presented as evidence in six states to support petitioners' claims of racial discrimination in the administration of the death penalty. They were part of the brief in the *Maxwell* case argued before the United States Supreme Court[32] and part of the testimony offered before a subcommittee of the House of Representatives considering bills to suspend the death penalty for two years or to abolish it.[33]

Although eighteen American jurisdictions allowed the imposition of the death penalty for rape, substantial numbers of persons have been executed for this crime during the past thirty years in only twelve: Alabama, Arkansas, Florida, Georgia, Louisiana, Maryland, Mississippi, North Carolina, South Carolina, Tennessee, Texas, and Virginia. It was decided that the study could be profitably confined to these twelve states.

In order to form an empirical basis for conclusions about the effect of racial factors on capital sentencing for rape, it was necessary to gather data about a substantial number of rape cases in each state. Moreover, a sufficiently long period of time covered by the research was necessary in order to satisfy the notion of "custom," or of an institutionalized, systematic judicial norm of sentencing behavior; hence the twenty-year period used in this study.

To meet the demands of proper statistical analysis, cases could have been obtained by seeking every rape conviction in each state for a decade, or by selecting counties by standard statistical sampling techniques over a twenty-year period. This latter process was used. For each of the twelve states, a sample of counties was chosen to represent the urban-rural and black-white demographic distributions of each state. The counties chosen comprised more than 50 percent of the total population of the twelve states.[34] For the counties included in each state sample, every case of conviction for rape from January 1, 1945 to the summer of 1965 was recorded. Maryland was initially included in the survey, but time limitations precluded full data collection in that state. Therefore, data were gathered for a twenty-year period for over 3,000 rape convictions in 230 counties in eleven states.[35]

The states included in the study were not only those that most often executed persons for rape; they also displayed an apparent racial disparity, for black offenders were more frequently executed than were white offenders. In seeking to explore the meaning of this apparent racial disparity in capital sentencing, only rape *convictions* were considered. It might be asserted that Blacks more frequently than whites commit rape, are more frequently arrested, or are more frequently charged with that offense. Whether these or any combination of these assertions were true was not questioned in this study. Instead, the focus was on the reliable and objectively ascertainable fact that defendants had been convicted for the crime of rape. Using this point of departure meant that the effect of racial factors on the criminal process prior to conviction could not be explored. There would be no way of knowing—if Blacks were disproportionately sentenced to death for rape—whether the pattern could be accounted for by a disproportionate frequency in the commission of rapes by Blacks or by a disproportionate frequency in the conviction of Blacks for rape. However, *among convicted defendants*, it was possible to determine whether black defendants were disproportionately frequently sentenced to death and, if so, whether the disproportion could be explained by nonracial variables.

In order to explore the effect of racial as well as nonracial variables on the imposition of the death penalty, it was necessary to determine which variables could be obtained from the county records of rape convictions. In addition to collecting information on the race of the defendant and the victim and on the type of sentence, information was gathered about many nonracial variables that could be construed as mitigating or aggravating circumstances. If standards were sought for sentencing in capital cases, some of the nonracial variables listed below might be seriously considered. These were the variables included in the study reported here.

1. Offender characteristics
   a. age
   b. marital status
   c. prior criminal record
   d. previous imprisonment
   e. employment status
2. Victim characteristics
   a. age
   b. marital status
   c. dependent children
   d. prior criminal record
   e. reputation for chastity
3. Nature of relations between victim and offender
   a. offender known to victim
   b. prior sexual relations
4. Circumstances of offense
   a. contemporaneous offense
   b. type of entry—authorized or unauthorized
   c. location of offense—indoor or outdoor
   d. display of weapon
   e. carrying of weapon
   f. amount of injury to victim

g. threatened victim
h. degree of force employed
i. victim made pregnant by offense
j. one or multiple offenders
k. date of offense

5. Circumstances of the trial
   a. plea
   b. defense of insanity
   c. appointed or retained counsel
   d. length of time on trial
   e. defense of consent
   f. whether defendant testified

An elaborate twenty-eight-page research schedule was constructed to obtain reliable and uniform data from records of widely varying quality in geographically dispersed locations. To reduce the amount of subjective or judgmental variation recorded by field investigators, each variable was described in a manner that focused the investigators' attention on objective facts or quantities that could be recorded on a check list.

There is little difficulty in establishing accurate schedule categories when the information to be obtained, like race or plea, is unambiguous. More difficulty occurs in obtaining reliable and objective data for items like "injury sustained by victim, companion victim, or other persons." To make reliable comparisons from case to case, a checklist of categories of predescribed injuries was developed, using brief phrases that focused the recorders' attention on specific, significant, objective details and the consequences of injuries. For example, categories for the latter item included recording whether the victim suffered "minor injury requiring no medical treatment," suffered "physical injuries requiring medical treatment, but not requiring hospitalization," or suffered "physical injuries requiring hospitalization."[36]

Thirty law students were recruited from different parts of the country to serve as field investigators. Before going into the field, the students were given a two-day orientation by the two principal investigators. The instruction process outlined in detail the research design and the legal components of the task. Emphasis was placed on the importance of providing reliable data which depended upon uniformity in the observation and recording of data. It was particularly emphasized that the investigators should not let their personal assumptions about the probable results of the study influence the manner in which they recorded the data. The field investigators were instructed to call central personnel for advice if instances arose in which they had trouble classifying their observations while in the field. After completion in the field, the schedules were forwarded to the Center for Studies in Criminology and Criminal Law for coding and statistical analysis.

The method of analysis used to determine whether the death penalty is given disproportionately frequently to Blacks employed the null hypothesis and the chi-square (X^2) statistical test, for which $p < 0.05$ was chosen as the level of significance. One major null hypothesis stated that among all defendants convicted of rape there is no significant association between the race of the defendant and the type of sentence imposed. The second major null hypothesis stated that among all defendants convicted of rape there are no significant differences between the proportions of black defendants with white victims and all other classes of rape defendants sentenced to death. Both of these hypotheses were rejected in each state analyzed.

The data were compiled and analyzed in seven states—Alabama, Arkansas, Florida, Georgia, Louisiana, South Carolina, and Tennessee—for purposes of submitting testimony in litigation conducted by the Legal Defense Fund. Each state was separately reviewed with its own set of tables and conclusions. The findings were uniformly similar for each state and the conclusions the same. In future analyses planned by the Center for Studies in Criminology and Criminal Law, all states for which data are available will be comprehensively reviewed. In the present article, only a brief summary with an illustration of the procedure can be presented. In the tables that follow, the total number of cases varies by the particular factor analyzed because of differences in the availability of information over the twenty-year period in each of the states.

Among 1,265 cases in which the race of the defendant and the sentence are known, nearly seven times as many Blacks were sentenced to death as were whites. Among the 823 Blacks convicted of rape, 110, or 13 percent, were sentenced to death; among the 442 whites convicted of rape, only 9, or 2 percent, were sentenced to death. The statistical probability that such a disproportionate number of Blacks could be sentenced to death by chance alone is less than one out of a thousand. More particularly, a statistically significantly higher proportion of black defendants whose victims were white were sentenced to death. From a total of 1,238 convicted rape defendants, 317 were black defendants with white victims, and 921 were all other racial combinations of defendant and victim—including black/white, white/white, and white/black. Of the 317 black defendants whose victims were white, 113, or approximately 36 percent, were sentenced to death. Of the 921 defendants involved in all other racial combinations of defendant and victim, only 19, or 2 percent, were sentenced to death. In short, black defendants whose victims were white were sentenced to death approximately eighteen times more frequently than defendants in any other racial combination of defendant and victim. Again, the probability of such a distribution, or such a relationship between the sentence of death and black defendants with white victims is, by chance alone, less than one out of a thousand.

But the obvious fact that there is differential sentencing by race, as shown in Tables 1 and 2, does not alone permit a conclusion of racial discrimination in sentencing. We may hypothesize, for example, that, as a group, black rape defendants more often than white defendants commit another offense along with the commission of the rape offense. It could generally be asserted that the commission of a contemporaneous offense, like burglary or robbery, is an aggravating circumstance and could account for the disproportionate frequency with which black defendants receive the death penalty.

Because of these considerations, all the nonracial variables previously listed were introduced in a further examination of the associations between race and the imposition of the death penalty.

First, each nonracial variable was examined relative to type of sentence. If no significant relationship existed between the nonracial variable and type of sentence, further analysis of that variable was not undertaken for it could at that point be concluded that no significant difference in type of sentence occurred because of that variable. Table 3, however, illustrates that there is a significant association between offenses committed contemporaneously with the rape offense and type of sentence.

If there was a significant association between the nonracial variable and sentence, the nonracial variable was then cross-tabulated with the race of the defendant. If the resulting chi-square was not significant, no further analysis was performed. There could be, however, a significant association between the nonracial variable and race, as is shown in Table 4. This table indicates that among 572 black defendants, 150, or 26 percent, had committed contemporaneous offenses, while among white defendants 45, or 15 percent, had committed contemporaneous offenses.

Table 5 would seem to add one more piece of evidence that the nonracial variable of contemporaneous offenses is a contributory factor producing a more frequent imposition of the death penalty for Blacks, particularly those with white victims. Data from this table indicate a significant association between the presence or absence of contemporaneous offenses and racial combinations of defendant and victim. Among the 146 black defendants with white victims, 40 percent had committed contemporaneous offenses, whereas only 14 percent of the 561 cases making up all other racial combinations involved contemporaneous offenses.

TABLE 1
Race of Defendants by Type of Sentence

	Death		Other		Total	
	Number	*Percent*	*Number*	*Percent*	*Number*	*Percent*
Black	110	13	713	87	823	100
White	9	2	433	98	442	100
Total	119		1146		1265	

Note: States included are Florida, Georgia, Louisiana, South Carolina, Tennessee. $X^2 = 41.9924$; $p < 0.001$.

TABLE 2
Racial Combinations of Defendant and Victim by Type of Sentence

| | Death | | Other | | Total | |
	Number	Percent	Number	Percent	Number	Percent
Black defendant and white victim	113	36	204	64	317	100
All other racial combinations of defendant and victim	19	2	902	98	921	100
Total	132		1106		1238	

Note: States included are Arkansas, Florida, Georgia, Louisiana, South Carolina, Tennessee. $X^2 = 275.7192; p < 0.001$.

TABLE 3
Contemporaneous Offense by Type of Sentence

| | Death | | Other | | Total | |
	Number	Percent	Number	Percent	Number	Percent
Contemporaneous offense	53	28	133	72	186	100
No contemporaneous offense	92	10	840	90	932	100
Total	145		973		1118	

Note: States included are Arkansas, Florida, Georgia, Louisiana, South Carolina, Tennessee. $X^2 = 39.4915; p$ 0.001.

TABLE 4
Contemporaneous Offense by Race of Defendant

| | Black | | White | | Total |
	Number	Percent	Number	Percent	Number
Contemporaneous offense	150	26	45	15	195
No contemporaneous offense	422	74	264	85	686
Total	572	100	309	100	881

Note: States included are Arkansas, Florida, Georgia, Louisiana, Tennessee. $X^2 = 15.1583; p < 0.001$.

TABLE 5
Contemporaneous Offense by Racial Combinations of Defendant and Victim

| | Black Defendant and White Victim | | All Other Racial Combinations of Defendant/Victim | | Total |
	Number	Percent	Number	Percent	Number
Contemporaneous offense	58	40	81	14	139
No contemporaneous offense	88	60	480	86	568
Total	146	100	561	100	707

Note: States included are Florida, Georgia, Tennessee. $X^2 = 45.3139; p \leq 0.001$.

Although it might appear that the presence or absence of contemporaneous offenses is a contributory factor, more refined procedure shows that it does not play a significant part in explaining the association between black defendants and the imposition of the death penalty. To perform this further analysis, the nonracial variable of contemporaneous offenses was split into two subgroups. The first subgroup included all cases in which the defendant had committed a contemporaneous offense—Table 6. Within this subgroup, chi-square analysis shows a significant association between racial combinations of defendant and victim and imposition of the death penalty. More specifically, among the fifty-eight

TABLE 6

Racial Combinations of Defendant/Victim by Type of Sentence Among All Cases
in Which Defendant Committed a Contemporaneous Offense

	Death		Other		Total	
	Number	*Percent*	*Number*	*Percent*	*Number*	*Percent*
Black defendant and white victim	22	39	36	61	58	100
All other racial combinations of defendant/victim	2	3	79	97	81	100
Total	24		115		139	

Note: States included are Florida, Georgia, Tennessee. $X^2 = 27.3231$; $p < 0.001$.

black defendants with white victims, 39 percent received the death penalty, but among all other racial combinations of defendant and victim, only 3 percent of the eighty-one defendants received the death penalty.

For the other subgroup in which no contemporaneous offenses were committed, there is also a significant association between racial combinations of defendant and victim and the imposition of the death penalty. Table 7 indicates that among the 88 black defendants with white victims, 39 percent received the death penalty, whereas among 480 cases of other racial combinations, only 2 percent received the death penalty.

It is important to repeat the final descriptive assertion derived from these data: It is not the presence of the nonracial factor of a contemporaneous offense that affects the decision to impose the death penalty more frequently on Blacks. Rather, it is the racial factor of the relationship between the defendant and victim that results in the use of the death penalty. Whether or not a contemporaneous offense has been committed, if the defendant is black and the victim is

white, the defendant is about eighteen times more likely to receive the death penalty than when the defendant is in any other racial combination of defendant and victim.

Over two dozen possibly aggravating nonracial variables that might have accounted for the higher proportion of Blacks than whites sentenced to death upon conviction of rape have been analyzed. Not one of these nonracial factors has withstood the tests of statistical significance. That is, in none of the seven states carefully analyzed can it be said that any of the nonracial factors account for the statistically significant and disproportionate number of Blacks sentenced to death for rape. This is a striking conclusion. It cannot be said that Blacks are more frequently sentenced to death because they have a longer prior criminal record than whites, because they used more force on the victim, because they committed a robbery or burglary, because they entered premises without authorization, because they used a weapon or threatened the victim with a weapon, because they had an accomplice in the commission of the rape, because they impregnated the victim, because they more fre-

TABLE 7

Racial Combinations of Defendant/Victim by Type of Sentence Among All Cases
in Which Defendant Committed No Contemporaneous Offense

	Death		Other		Total	
	Number	*Percent*	*Number*	*Percent*	*Number*	*Percent*
Black defendant and white victim	34	39	54	61	88	100
All other racial combinations of defendant/victim	9	2	471	98	480	100
Total	43		525		568	

Note: States included are Florida, Georgia, Tennessee. $X^2 = 138.4186$; $p < 0.001$.

quently attacked persons under age sixteen, and so forth. All the nonracial factors in each of the states analyzed "wash out," that is, they have no bearing on the imposition of the death penalty in disproportionate numbers upon Blacks. The only variable of statistical significance that remains is race.

CONCLUSION

In *Furman v. Georgia*, the United States Supreme Court declared the death penalty unconstitutional because it is a "cruel and unusual" punishment. That the history of this penalty has been marked by elements of racial discrimination was alluded to by at least two justices, but the Court has not directly ruled out the death penalty on this basis, which could be grounded in the Fourteenth Amendment and the "due process" dictum.

That Blacks have been disproportionately sentenced to death and executed in the United States has long been noted. But general social differentials in sentencing may not alone denote racial discrimination, or failure of Blacks to be given all due process in the administration of criminal justice. An elaborate research scheme, reported here, which collected data on capital rape convictions over a twenty-year period from 1945 to 1965 has now provided material on many nonracial variables to determine whether they, rather than race, could account for the disproportionately and significantly high frequency of Blacks sentenced to death compared to whites.

Based upon a refined statistical analysis of rape convictions in states where rape has been a capital crime, this study shows that there has been a patterned, systematic, and customary imposition of the death penalty. Far from being "freakish" or capricious, sentences of death have been imposed on Blacks, compared to whites, in a way that exceeds any statistical notion of chance or fortuity. Moreover, the systems of criminal justice in the jurisdictions studied have inflicted the death penalty on Blacks in such disproportions without statutory or other legally acceptable bases. Thus, with the benefit of a carefully designed and objectively analyzed study of these conditions, it can be concluded that the significant racial differentials found in the impo-

sition of the death penalty are indeed produced by racial discrimination.

The study has shown that racial discrimination has long existed and exists with currency above the conviction stage of the judicial process. That there may be more systematic features of racial differentials, from which discrimination may be inferred, remains for future and further research to determine. Discretion at earlier stages in the administration of justice could also carry elements of racial discrimination: arrest, hearing, plea bargaining, decisions to prosecute or drop charges, and many others, when death is a permissible penalty. Neither mandatory sanctions nor the reduction of racial discrimination at the sentencing stage would eliminate the untoward systematic effects of racial discrimination elsewhere in the processing of defendants. By declaring the death penalty unconstitutional, and reaffirming this declaration if necessary, the Supreme Court at least and at last removes the consequence of finality which differential justice has produced.

FOOTNOTES

[1] 408 U. S. at 239–240.
[2] The convictions and sentences were affirmed, *Furman v. State*, 225 Ga. 253, 167 S.E. 2d 628 (1969); *Jackson v. State*, 225 Ga. 790, 171 S.E. 2d 501 (1969); *Branch v. State*, 447 S.W. 2d 932 (Tex. Ct. Crim. App. 1969).
[3] Hugo Adam Bedau, *The Case against the Death Penalty* (New York: American Civil Liberties Union, 1973).
[4] Bedau, *Case against the Death Penalty*.
[5] 408 U. S. at 247.
[6] 408 U. S. at 245.
[7] 408 U. S. at 388.
[8] 408 U. S. at 449.
[9] 408 U. S. at 249.
[10] 408 U. S. at 257.
[11] 408 U. S. at 295.
[12] 408 U. S. at 310.
[13] 408 U. S. at 313.
[14] 408 U. S. at 365.
[15] 408 U. S. at 291–292.
[16] 408 U. S. at 389.
[17] 408 U. S. at 295, 310.
[18] 408 U. S. at 256–257, 365.
[19] 408 U. S. at 295, 310.
[20] 408 U. S. at 256, 257.
[21] 408 U. S. at 400–401.
[22] 408 U. S. at 449.

[23]Testimony of Marvin E. Wolfgang at hearings before the Subcommittee of the Committee on the Judiciary, March 16, 1972.

[24]Hugo Adam Bedau, "Capital Punishment in Oregon 1903–1964," *Oregon Law Review* 45 (1965), p. 1, and "Death Sentences in New Jersey 1907–1960," *Rutgers Law Review* 19 (1965), p. 1; William J. Bowers, *Discrimination in Capital Punishment: Characteristics of the Condemned* (unpublished transcript from The Russel B. Stearns Research Center, Northeastern University, 1972); Robert M. Carter and A. LaMont Smith, "The Death Penalty in California: A Statistical and Composite Portrait," *Crime and Delinquency* 15 (1969), p. 62; George E. Danielson, *Facts and Figures Concerning Executions in California 1938–1962*, prepared with the assistance of the Assembly Legislative Reference Service, Sacramento, 1963; Harold Garfinkel, "Research Note on Inter- and Intra-Racial Homicides," *Social Forces* 27 (1949), p. 369; Frank E. Hartung, "Trends in the Use of Capital Punishment," THE ANNALS 284 (1952), p. 8; Rupert C. Koeninger, "Capital Punishment in Texas 1924–1968," *Crime and Delinquency* 15 (1969), p. 132; Charles S. Mangum, *The Legal Status of the Negro* (Chapel Hill: University of North Carolina Press, 1940); Maryland Legislative Council, Committee on Capital Punishment, *Report*, 1962; Donald H. Partington, "The Incidence of the Death Penalty for Rape in Virginia," *Washington and Lee Law Review* 22 (1965), p. 43; James A. McCafferty, "The Death Sentence," in H. A. Bedau, ed., *The Death Penalty in America*, rev. ed. (New York: Doubleday, 1967); Ohio Legislative Service Commission, Staff Research Report no. 46, *Capital Punishment*, 1962; Pennsylvania Joint Legislative Committee on Capital Punishment, *Report*, 1961; Thorsten Sellin, "A Note on Capital Executions in the United States," *British Journal of Delinquency* 1 (1960), p. 6; "A Study of the California Penalty Jury in First-Degree Murder Trials," *Stanford Law Review* 21 (1969), p. 1297; Texas Department of Corrections, Division of Research, *A Synopsis of Offenders Receiving the Death Sentence in Texas*, Research Report no. 8, 1972; United Nations Economic and Social Council, Commission on Human Rights, *Capital Punishment in the Republic of South Africa*, unpublished working paper, 1964; Franklin H. Williams, "The Death Penalty and the Negro," *The Crisis* 67 (1960), p. 501; Edwin D. Wolf, "Abstracts of Analysis of Jury Sentencing in Capital Cases," *Rutgers Law Review* 19 (1964), p. 56.

[25]Marvin E. Wolfgang, Arlene Kelly, and Hans C. Nolde, "Comparisons of the Executed and the Commuted among Admissions to Death Row," *Journal of Criminal Law, Criminology and Police Science* 53 (September 1962), p. 301. The variables included in the study were type of murder, offender's age, race, occupation, marital status, whether native- or foreign-born, type of counsel, and reasons for commutations.

[26]*Ibid.*, p. 311.

[27]Guy B. Johnson, "The Negro and Crime," THE ANNALS 217 (September 1941), pp. 93–104.

[28]*Ibid.*, p. 98.

[29]Elmer H. Johnson, "Selective Factors in Capital Punishment," *Social Forces* 36 (December 1957), p. 165.

[30]*Rape: Selective Electrocution Based on Race* (Miami: Florida Civil Liberties Union, 1964).

[31]Bureau of Prisons, National Prisoner Statistics, *Capital Punishment 1930–1968*, Bulletin no. 45, August 1969.

[32]*Maxwell v. Bishop*, 398 U. S. 262 (1970).

[33]Wolfgang, Testimony, p. 165.

[34]The sampling plan for each state in the study was developed with the assistance of John Monroe.

[35]Deposition of written interrogatories to Marvin E. Wolfgang re *Willie Awkwright v. Asa D. Kelly, Jr. and Lamont Smith*, Case No. 5283 in the Superior Court of Tattnall County, Georgia.

[36]These particular categories were developed in an earlier study where a system of standardized description and evaluation of the degrees of injury was constructed. See Thorsten Sellin and Marvin E. Wolfgang, *The Measurement of Delinquency* (New York: Wiley, 1964).

Part 4

The Impact
of Legal Institutions

PART 4   THE IMPACT OF LEGAL INSTITUTIONS

INTRODUCTION

In the last analysis a legal system must be judged according to the impact it has. If that impact is largely deleterious to people's lives, then maintaining the system can scarcely be justified. If, on the other hand, the law contributes in some important ways to improving the lot of most of the people then there is justification for keeping it.

In this section we take up several issues related to the impact of legal institutions. First we look at the effect that laws have on the operational activities of law enforcement agencies. We touched on this subject earlier (in Part 3) when we discussed the effect of legal rules on police use of violence. Now we turn to a more systematic appraisal of specific laws. More precisely, we want to look at the impact which a series of United States Supreme Court decisions has had on the law enforcement practices of police and courts.

During the 1950's and 1960's the United States Supreme Court virtually rewrote the acceptable legal procedures for the arrest, prosecution, and trial of accused felons. We have seen earlier how the Gideon decision changed the rules under which indigent defendants could waive their right to being represented by a lawyer. During the same period the Court also passed the Miranda and Gault decisions which had equally far-reaching implications for the handling of accused persons.

MIRANDA

The issue in *Miranda* was the extent to which the police may interrogate in the station house without counsel, without advising the accused of his right to counsel or his right to keep silent. In *Escobedo v. Illinois,** in 1964, the Supreme Court had held that a statement elicited through police interrogation was inadmissible in the trial of the accused solely on the ground that the statement was elicited before indictment, but after the investigation had focused on the accused, and after the police had refused to honor his request to consult his lawyer during the course of the interrogation. In *Miranda,* the police had interrogated the accused for two hours in private without advising him of his constitutional rights; that fact alone was held to be sufficient to make the statement inadmissible.

The basis of the decision was not philosophical, but empirical. The Court quoted from police manuals of instruction, in lieu of specific observations of what actually goes on in police interrogation rooms. These manuals made it clear that the basis for successful pretrial interrogation is the overpowering of the will of the accused by the interrogator. The Court concluded that

> Even without employing brutality, the "third degree" or the specific stratagems described (in the police instruction manuals), the very fact of custodial interrogation exacts a heavy toll on the individual's liberty and trades on the weakness of individuals . . .*

The protection was woven from the dual strands of the privilege against self-incrimination and of the right to counsel. The privilege prohibited the extraction of confessions, and the right to counsel ensured that the privilege would be observed. Indeed, as Justice Jackson once observed many years before,

> Under our systems (a lawyer) deems that his sole duty is to protect his client—guilty or innocent—and that in such a capacity he owes no duty whatever to help society solve its crime problems. Under this conception of criminal procedure, any lawyer worth his salt will tell the subject in no uncertain terms to make no statement to the police under any circumstances.†

The Court then laid down a set of norms for police conduct. The test now became not whether the confession or statement of the accused was "voluntary," but whether the police had acted in a certain precisely defined way:

> To summarize, we hold that when an individual is taken into custody or otherwise deprived of his freedom by the authorities and is subjected to questioning, the privilege against self-incrimination is jeopardized. Procedural safeguards must be employed to protect the privilege, and unless other fully effective means are adopted to notify the person of his right to silence and to assure that the exercise of the right will be scrupulously honored, the following measures are required. He must be warned prior to any questioning that he has the right to remain silent, that anything he says can be used against him in a court of law, that he has the right to the presence of an attorney, and that if he cannot afford an attorney one will be appointed for him prior to any questioning if he so desires. Opportunity to exercise these rights must be afforded to him throughout the interrogation. After such warnings have been given, and such opportunity afforded him, the individual may knowingly and intelligently waive these rights and agree to answer questions or make a statement. But unless and until such warnings and waiver are demonstrated by the prosecution at trial, no evidence obtained as a result of interrogation can be used against him.**

---

*378 U. S. 478, 84 S. Ct. 1758, 12 L Ed. 2d 977 (1964).

*384 U. S. at 448–454.

†R. Jackson, concurring in *Watts v. Indiana,* 338 U. S. 49, 57.69 S. Ct. 1937, 93 L. Ed. 1801 (1947).

**384 U. S. at 478–479.

PART 4   THE IMPACT OF LEGAL INSTITUTIONS

The movement begun long ago finally came to fruition. The guarantees of due process moved forward from the mansion to the gatehouse of the law. But, as we have seen so often, this has had little significant effect on actual police practice.

THE CONSEQUENCE OF *MIRANDA*

The most complete investigation of station house interrogations yet published appears to be that conducted by members of the *Yale Law Review* staff in New Haven, Connecticut, during the summer of 1966.* An analogous investigation was conducted by the Institute of Criminal Law and Procedure in Washington, D. C.†

The principal conclusion both in New Haven and in Washington is that *Miranda* seems to have changed the practice of the police very little. In New Haven, the police appeared to be seriously interested in interrogating 61% of the suspects.** In Washington, the number of suspects interrogated by the police fell from 55% to 48% between the period just before the *Miranda* decision and the period just after it. The New Haven Police Department regulations require that the detective attempt an interrogation of every suspect arrested.

As we just saw, the *Miranda* opinion used information concerning coercive techniques of interrogation contained in police instruction manuals as surrogate for empirical data about what actually went on during such interrogations. The New Haven police did not use any of the tactics described in these manuals on 44 out of 127 suspects, but on 38 of the suspects they used three or more of these tactics. Threats as well as feigned sympathy for the suspect were used. The Yale students making the observations reported that from other evidence they had it appeared that the level of police coercive treatment had been especially subdued while, and because, they were present. Both before and after the period of observation, "the detectives frequently displayed a more hostile air . . . The police told suspects more often that they would be 'worse off' if they did not talk, played down the seriousness of the crime, swore at the suspects, and made promises of leniency."*

In neither New Haven nor Washington, apparently, did the police in even the majority of cases give the accused the *full* warnings spelled out in the *Miranda* decision. In Washington, 29% of the suspects said that they had not been given any warning, and 62% said that they had not been given the full warning. In New Haven, only 25 out of 118 suspects were given the full *Miranda* warning.

Even when given, however, the warning was hardly effective. Most of the detectives, even when they gave the warning, "incorporated into their tactical repertoires some sort of hedging on the warnings . . ." Some changed the warning slightly: "Whatever you say may be used *for* or against you in a court of law." Often, the detectives advised the suspect with some inconsistent qualifying remark, such as "You don't have to say a word, but you ought to get everything cleared up," or "You don't have to say anything, of course, *but* can you explain how . . ."†

In some of the New Haven cases the police went even further:

Even when the detective advised the suspect of his rights without these undercutting devices, he commonly de-fused the advice by implying that the suspect had better not exercise his rights, or by delivering this statement in a formalized, bureaucratic tone to indicate that his remarks were simply a routine, meaningless legalism. Often they would bring the flow of conversation to a halt and preface their remarks with "Now I am going to warn you of your rights." After they had finished the advice they would solemnly intone, "Now you have been warned of your rights," then immediately shift into a conversational tone to ask, "Now, would you like to tell me what happened?"

In the few cases where a suspect showed an interest in finding a lawyer and did not already know one, the police usually managed to head him off simply by not helping him locate one. Sometimes they refused to advise the suspect whether he should have a lawyer with him during questioning; more often they merely offered him a telephone book without further comment, and that was enough to deter him from calling a lawyer.**

In New Haven, the only constant factor affecting the detectives' giving or withholding of the full warning was the seriousness of the crime. The more serious the crime, the greater was the probability that the full *Miranda* warning

---

*Michael Wald, Richard Ayres, David W. Hess, Mark Schantz, and Charles H. Whitehead, Jr., "Interrogations in New Haven: The Impact of Miranda," *Yale Law Journal,* vol. 76, 1967, p. 1519. Reprinted by permission of The Yale Law Journal Co., and Fred B. Rothman & Co.

†Richard J. Medalie, Leonard Zeitz, and Paul Alexander, "Custodial Police Interrogation in our Nation's Capital: The Attempt to Implement Miranda," *University of Michigan Law Review,* vol. 66, 1968, p. 1347.

**Michael Wald, Richard Ayres, David W. Hess, Mark Schantz, and Charles H. Whitehead, Jr., "Interrogations in New Haven: The Impact of Miranda," *Yale Law Journal,* vol. 76, 1967, p. 1539. Reprinted by permission of The Yale Law Journal Co., and Fred B. Rothman & Co.

Ibid., p. 1531.
†*Ibid.*, p. 1552.
**Ibid.*, p. 1552.

would be given:* Moreover, the suspect was even more likely to get the warning in those cases of serious crime where the police had already enough evidence for trial, but not enough for conviction, i.e. in precisely those cases where, as we shall see, the exclusionary rule might make the difference between conviction and acquittal.

Both in Washington and in New Haven the warnings, even when given, apparently had little effect on the suspects' behavior. Many simply do not understand the serious implications of the decision to call a lawyer. In Washington, only one out of fourteen suspects asked for a lawyer. Over four out of ten gave statements to the police. In New Haven, the observers concluded that in only 6% of the cases did the *Miranda* warning affect the result.

The New Haven observers attributed the ineffectiveness of the warning to a variety of reasons. The accused persons frequently did not seem to be able to grasp the significance of making a statement, even when the warning was given, either because the warning was given in such a way as to minimize its effectiveness or because "since most suspects had little education—many could not even read— and appeared both ill-at-ease and dazed at the process," the warning had little impact. A very high proportion of those arrested by the police were in fact guilty of the crimes charged. When presented by the evidence in the possession of the police, the accused tended to try to exculpate themselves—and sank deeper into the morass.† A number of them gave statements which they believed exculpated them—for example, that in an assault case, the victim began the affray—when in fact the statements were incriminating.

In short, the *Miranda* rules, despite the great amount of controversy they have caused, seemingly have not significantly changed the conduct of either the police or the accused persons. However, it must be noted that the New Haven data were gathered in the first few months after the *Miranda* decision had been handed down. It is possible, though doubtful, that it takes a long time for rules of this sort to be internalized by the police and hence to affect police activity.

An example of slow change can perhaps be seen in the development of the confessions rule. In 1931, the Wickersham Commission reported that police used the third de-

gree with remarkable frequency.* That police brutality continues to be a factor was documented by a footnote to the *Miranda* decision itself:

see *People v. Wakat,* 415 111.610, 114 N.E. 2d 706 (1953); *Wakat v. Harlib,* 253 F. 2d 59 (C.A. 7th Cir. 1958) (Defendant suffering from broken bones, multiple bruises and injuries sufficiently serious to require eight months' medical treatment after being manhandled by five policemen); *Kier v. State,* 213 Md. 556, 132 A. 2d 494 (1957) (police doctor told accused, who was strapped to a chair completely naked, that he proposed to take hair and skin scrapings from anything that looked like blood or sperm from various parts of his body); *Bruner v. People,* 113 Colo. 114, 156 P. 2d 111 (1945) (defendant held in custody over two months, deprived of food for 15 hours, forced to submit to lie detector test when he wanted to go to the toilet); *People v. Matlock,* 51 Cal. 2d 682, 336 P. 2d 505 (defendant questioned incessantly over an evening's time, made to lie on cold board and to answer questions whenever it appeared he was getting sleepy.)†

Despite the continuation of such practices today, the level of their incidence seems to have declined. In New Haven, the observers learned from interviews both with detectives and with suspects that

there seemingly has been a substantial change in police attitudes and practices from 1960 to 1966. Both groups believe the interrogation process has become considerably less hostile; detectives are unwilling to use tactics approved seven years ago. For example, we found several instances where detectives stopped an interrogation when the letter of *Miranda* did not require them to do so. This change is probably attributable both to court decisions on the criminal law and to change in administration within the department.**

The President's Commission on Law Enforcement and the Administration of Justice came to the same conclusion:

In 1931, the Wickersham Commission reported that the extraction of confessions through physical brutality was a widespread, almost universal, police practice. During the next several years the Supreme Court issued a number of rulings that excluded

---

*Ibid., p. 1552.
†Ibid., p. 1572.

*National Commission on Law Observance and Enforcement: Report on Lawlessness in Law Enforcement, vol. 4, 1931; see Bates Booth, "Confessions and Methods Employed in Procuring Them," *University of Southern California Law Review,* vol. 4, 1930, p. 83. Paul G. Kauper, "Judicial Examination of the Accused—A Remedy for the Third Degree," *University of Michigan Law Review,* vol. 30, 1932, p. 1224.
†*Miranda v. Arizona,* 384 U. S. at 446 n7.
**Michael Wald, Richard Ayres, David M. Hess, Mark Schantz, and Charles H. Whitehead, Jr., "Interrogations in New Haven: The Impact of Miranda," *Yale Law Journal,* vol. 76, 1967, p. 1574. Reprinted by permission of The Yale Law Journal Co., and Fred B. Rothman & Co.

PART 4 THE IMPACT OF LEGAL INSTITUTIONS

such confessions as admissible evidence in court. There can be no doubt that these rulings had much to do with the fact that today the third degree is almost nonexistent.*

How the rulings of the Supreme Court in the confession cases contributed to the lowering of the level of violence during in-custody interrogation, of course, is difficult or impossible to assess. They might have contributed to it through an educative process involving the police officers generally. They might have contributed to it by offering support to a general community sentiment against brutality, and thus providing by way of community disapproval a sanction for officers who violated the norm. They might have contributed to it by creating a community climate of opinion in which the officers, as members of the community, participated.

Nevertheless, the precise *Miranda* warnings and the sort of conduct which the rulings prescribed do not seem significantly to have solved the problems with which the Court was primarily concerned. Suspects are still interrogated

---

*President's Commission on Law Enforcement and Administration of Justice, *The Challenge of Crime in a Free Society,* Washington: U. S. Government Printing Office, 1967, p. 93.

under conditions of severe psychological coercion and, sometimes, physical coercion. The prescribed warnings either are not given at all, or given incompletely, or are incomprehensible as given. Suspects are still subjected to precisely the sort of grilling which the Supreme Court has held to be over the line between questioning and coercion as drawn by the privilege against self-incrimination.

A similar pattern of discrepancy is to be found with respect to the relationship between court decisions and the juvenile court practices in handling juveniles charged with delinquency. For years juveniles had not been extended the same constitutional rights as adults even in principle. (As we have seen in practice the benefits deriving from the constitutional guarantees have largely fallen on the prosperous members of the community, both criminal and noncriminal.) But the juvenile was not even potentially protected by these guarantees. In a recent decision,* the Supreme Court extended the right to counsel, freedom from self-incrimination, right to notification of charges, and right to confrontation and countercharges to juveniles as well as adults. The impact of this decision is examined in the study that follows.

---

*In re Gault, 387 U. S. 1 87 S. Ct. 1428, 18 L. Ed. 2d 527 (1967).

28

In Search of Juvenile Justice:

Gault and Its Implementation

NORMAN LEFSTEIN
and VAUGHAN STAPLETON
and LEE TEITELBAUM

On May 15, 1967 the United States Supreme Court rendered, in *In re Gault*,[1] its first decision in the area of juvenile delinquency procedure. Commentators have repeatedly construed the rulings in *Gault* as requiring juvenile courts to adopt new and more liberal practices. The privilege against self-incrimination, and the rights to notice of charges, counsel, confrontation, and cross-examination were heretofore primarily regarded as the cornerstones of an adversary system of justice. The extension of these rights to juvenile courts would have seemed to require an overnight transformation of the court procedures.[2]

This article examines the response of three urban juvenile courts—referred to as Metro, Gotham and Zenith[3]—to the *Gault* decision. The data presented here—drawn from numerous observations of court hearings—provide some indication of the extent of the changes in juvenile proceedings. Particular attention is paid to what the Supreme Court seems to have required in *Gault*, to what juvenile courts should now be expected to do under that decision,

Source: "In Search of Juvenile Justice: *Gault* and Its Implementation," *Law and Society Review*, Vol. 3, 1969, pp. 491–562. By permission of the authors and publisher. Footnotes have been renumbered.

and to what was actually done in the observed courts. This study also provides insight into the problems encountered in the implementation of *Gault*, as well as a commentary on the structure of the juvenile hearing process.

RIGHT TO COUNSEL

In general In discussing the right to counsel, the Supreme Court in *Gault* commented:

> A proceeding where the issue is whether the child will be found to be "delinquent" and subjected to the loss of his liberty for years is comparable in seriousness to a felony prosecution. The juvenile needs the assistance of counsel to cope with problems of law, to make skilled inquiry into the facts, to insist upon regularity of the proceedings, and to ascertain whether he has a defense and to prepare and submit it. *The child "requires the guiding hand of counsel at every step in the proceedings against him."*[4]

The court then directed its attention toward ensuring that this right, established in principle, would be meaningful in operation. Rejecting the view of some courts that even if a youth does have the right to counsel there is no requirement that he be so informed,[5] the majority opinion expressly required that the juvenile and his parent be told of the child's right, and further that they be instructed that if they could not afford an attorney, one would be appointed for them.[6] The opinion also imported to the juvenile courts the concept of waiver; henceforth, counsel could be withheld from the parties only if they validly waived their rights to a lawyer.

In the delinquency cases reported in this study, compliance with the right to counsel was determined from the initial court hearings where juveniles and their parents appeared without counsel. However, two of the courts sent to the accused's parents, in advance of the first hearing, a notice which included reference to the right to counsel. In Metro, a form entitled *Notice: Legal Rights and Privileges* was delivered by a probation officer to the minor's parents, and the parents were asked to sign a return indicating their receipt of the notice. The part of the form relevant to the right to counsel reads as follows:

> You and/or your child have the right to be represented by a lawyer who will advise you as to the law and present your case in Court. If you wish to have a lawyer but are financially unable to employ one, we suggest that you contact the Legal Aid Defender's Office [giving address and phone number] or consult the yellow pages of the telephone book under "attorneys" for a listing of the Legal Aid Society Office nearest your home.

The Gotham juvenile court at the time of this study sent a summons by regular mail to the respondent and his parents containing the following information: "PARENTS, GUARDIAN or CUSTODIAN, of the juvenile and juvenile_____, have the right to retain and be represented by counsel at every stage of the proceedings."

Neither notice complies satisfactorily with the right to counsel requirement imposed by *Gault*.[7] The first carefully avoids mentioning the court's duty to appoint a lawyer for the minor, if for financial reasons one cannot be retained; the latter simply makes no mention at all of that duty. But even if the notices were complete, it is doubtful that the court's responsibility to inform the parents and juvenile of the right to counsel would be reduced. In federal criminal cases, the judge bears the responsibility of ascertaining that the defendant in fact knows of, and adequately understands, this right.

> When a defendant appears before the court without counsel, we think, as a minimum, the court, in order to discharge its duty, must advise the defendant of the seriousness of the charge, that the Constitution of the United States guarantees him the right to have the assistance of counsel for his defense, and that if he is unable to employ counsel, it is the duty of the court to appoint, and the court will appoint, counsel for him. Ordinarily, only by such an inquiry can the court be sure that the defendant understands his constitutional right . . .[8]

While it may be argued that the states are not bound to exercise all the precautions of federal criminal practice,[9] it would seem clear that the accused juvenile must be offered the right to counsel before it can be said that he has knowingly and intelligently waived it,[10] and that every presumption against such waiver must be indulged.[11] Similarly, it would seem that juvenile courts must insure that the minor and parents knew of their right to counsel, and that they understood its significance.[12] Indeed, particular care is necessary in cases involving minors in order to be assured that the youth knows he is entitled to a lawyer; in criminal prosecutions involving juveniles, it has frequently been held that the trial judge must so inform the defendant, or a subsequent waiver is invalid.[13] Since minors in delinquency proceedings are almost always younger than those prosecuted criminally, the need for a careful appraisal of rights is, if anything, more pronounced. Further support for this proposition may be found where, as in most delinquency cases, the respondent and his parents are indigent. Reliance upon written notification presupposes that the recipient can read and understand the notice, that he does so if he can, and that, if it is the parent who is given notice, the parent conveys the information in an intelligible manner to the child. These assumptions, when applied to the population typically appearing before juvenile courts, are most dubious.[14]

Degree of compliance "Full advice" has been used to describe those cases where the respondent and his parents were fully informed of the child's right to retained or appointed counsel. The following colloquy from a case in Zenith illustrates full advice:

> The judge, "You understand this is a serious charge, don't you?" "Yes." [This is response by father.] Now speaking to both the father and the boy, he continued, "I want you to know that you have the right to a private attorney, I'll appoint a public defender for you."

This case may be taken as an exemplar: the advice of rights is directed to both the parent and the youth, and it is made clear that the judge will appoint an attorney if the respondent is indigent. Although every warning should be as straightforward and complete as this one, instances where compliance was not so satisfactory have been treated as "full" for purposes of this article. For example, it is certainly not sufficient to tell only the parent that he has a right to counsel; the right to be informed runs equally to the child. Thus, if the judge specifically addresses only the parent in rendering advice of counsel, the requirements of *Gault* have not fully been met. On the other hand, if full advice was given and no person singled out, full compliance was assumed, even though only the parent responded and even though it was unclear that the child comprehended in any real sense that the right was *his*.

The judge also must clearly state that the respondent and his parent not only have the right to retained counsel, but that if they cannot afford an attorney, one will be appointed for them. If the court does not state that counsel will be appointed but merely says that a legal aid lawyer is available, the effect may not be the same. If appointment is made, the attorney is generally under an obligation to appear and either provide representation or satisfy the court that he cannot.[15] If the latter occurs, the court will be bound to appoint a substitute for him, and the defendant is assured of representation. Further, some legal aid offices require a registration fee, and in the absence of outright appointment the respondent or his parents may be required to absorb that expense or forego the legal services. Nevertheless, consistent with our practice of analyzing the data conservatively, a statement by the judge that a legal aid attorney was available has been treated as satisfying *Gault*'s requirements.[16]

On the basis of the above categorization, Zenith was found to have the highest degree of compliance with *Gault*'s mandate. Of the 18 youths in the sample of cases analyzed, 10 (or 56%) were fully advised of the right to counsel. In Metro, the extent of compliance was substantially less. Only 2 youths of a sample of 71 (3%) were fully advised of the right to representation. Gotham was the least diligent in complying with *Gault*'s requirements. In not 1 case among 59 were the parents and minor adequately advised of their right to counsel. One of two things happened: Either no mention at all was made of the right to counsel or there was "partial advice" of the right, meaning that necessary elements of the warning were omitted. A case from Metro in which the judge asked: "Mrs. C_____, did you know that you have a right to have a lawyer?" illustrates what we have termed "partial advice." The warning, phrased in the form of a question, was directed solely and explicitly to the parent, and the judge failed to state that the boy and his parent were entitled to appointed counsel if they were indigent.[17] A breakdown of the degree of compliance with the right to counsel for all three cities is shown in Table 1.

Thus, a greater attempt at compliance was made in Zenith and Metro than in Gotham. Only one case was found in Zenith where a hearing was held without any mention of the right to counsel, and in Metro, at least some form of advice was given, albeit incompletely, in more than two-thirds of the cases. Gotham, in contrast, emerged as the most resistant to the newly imposed constitutional requirements.[18]

The failure of the courts in Metro and Gotham to comply with the right to counsel requirement cannot

TABLE 1
Compliance with the Right to Counsel Requirement

Type of Compliance	Gotham		Metro		Zenith	
	N	%	N	%	N	%
Full Advice	(0)	0	(2)	3	(10)	56
Partial Advice	(9)	15	(46)	65	(7)	38
No Advice	(50)	85	(23)	32	(1)	6
Total Number of Youths	(59)		(71)		(18)	

N = number of youths.

be dismissed as a technical matter. In one-third of the sample cases in Metro, and in 85% of the Gotham cases, the error cannot be ascribed to faulty terminology nor even to imperfect comprehension of the rules set out in *Gault;* neither the parent nor the child was informed in any fashion by the courts of the right to retained or appointed counsel.[19] Even in those instances where partial but inadequate advice was rendered, the omission cannot be considered insignificant. Failure to inform the child of the right, or to state that a "free lawyer" is available as a matter of right, is a most critical omission.[20]

Prejudicial advice Heretofore, we have been concerned with the relevant legal content of the communication regarding the right to counsel. Successful communication of a message from one person to another depends on many factors other than content of the message itself. Verbal and nonverbal cues may transform a statement's meaning into something altogether different from the actual words used. In considering the extent of meaningful as well as literal compliance with *Gault*, the manner of communication is highly relevant.

Advice of the right to counsel may be rendered in such a way as to encourage the exercise of that right. When the judge says (as he did in a Zenith case), "Larry, I'd like to advise you that you are entitled to a lawyer and I'll be happy to appoint a free lawyer for you if you have no money," it may be supposed that any trepidation on the part of the youth or his parent concerning exercise of the right does not derive from the court.

The advice may be essentially neutral in quality. Consider this Zenith case:

> The judge continued that the law obliges him to tell them that they have a privilege of engaging an attorney. If they wish to get an attorney, the proceedings would be continued for them to do so. If they didn't have sufficient funds, he would appoint one.

Conversely, the advice may be given in such a manner as to discourage exercise of the right to counsel. Perhaps the most common is "a question so framed, or uttered with such emphasis, or accompanied by such non-verbal conduct of the questioner as to suggest the desired answer."[21] The following excerpt from a Zenith case is illustrative:

> After the judge informed the boys and their mothers of the charges against them, he continued very rapidly, "At this time, I'd like to inform you that you have a right to have an attorney. If you cannot afford an attorney, I'll appoint an attorney for you. Or, on the other hand, if you'd like, we can have the case heard today."
>
> The woman said something and the judge said, "I can't hear you."
>
> Then the woman said that she would like to have it heard today.
>
> The judge said, "Let the record show that Mrs. G_____, the mother of A_____, waives the right to an attorney."

It is arguable here that the judge is merely performing his duty to inform the respondent of all possible courses of action open to her. Nevertheless, the effect of a rapid delivery plus the judge's invitation that "we can have the case heard today," suggesting that proceeding without a lawyer will expedite matters and that the case can competently be placed in his hands, tends to preclude a positive consideration of the right to counsel.

By failing to respond to the misapprehensions and questions of parties, judges may effectively discourage the use of counsel. Consider the following case from Metro:

> The judge begins by saying, "Mrs. C_____, did you know that you have a right to have a lawyer?"
>
> She replied that she "didn't know." She paused, then she said, "Well, Mr. _____ [the probation officer] said that it was up to me, and I said that I didn't have any money."
>
> The judge said, "Well, one thing you have here is all kinds of lawyers." He said that they could get some at the Legal Aid Society.
>
> The mother replied, "Well, I have one, but he's so expensive."
>
> And the judge left it at this, and they went ahead and heard the case.

In this case the judge's failure to inform the respondent that the court could appoint an attorney if she could not afford one, taken with his failure to respond to her oblique reference of an inability to pay, militated against exercise of that right.

In Metro the judges consistently assumed that the written notice of right to counsel delivered before the hearing fully satisfied *Gault*. Communication between judge and respondent during the court hearing reflected an assumption by the judge that the parents and child had read the notice, understood their rights, and were waiving these rights by appearing at the hearing without an attorney. The following is a simple illustration of this:

> Addressing himself to the mother the judge states, "I take it that you came without a lawyer because you think you didn't need it."
>
> Mrs. H_____ replies, "Right."

The effect of this formulation is to discourage further and positive consideration of the right to an attorney, and the statement's directive quality is strengthened by the judge's status vis-à-vis those appearing before him.

Still another case from Metro embodies a different type of prejudice. The judge not only failed to inform the respondents that a free attorney could be appointed, but was obviously unwilling to continue the case for such an appointment.

> The judge begins by saying, "We sent a notice out to you which stated that you can get a lawyer, and furthermore that if you can't afford one that we would get you one."
>
> The father stands up and says in broken phrases, "Well we— I can't afford . . ."
>
> The judge breaks him off and says, "That's no objection, we're able to get you one, but you've decided not to have one. Right?"
>
> The father replies, "Yes."

A case from Gotham presents a classic example of a judge leading the respondent to the position desired by the court. Before the case began a bailiff entered the court and told the judge that Mr. X, a legal aid attorney, had been assigned to the case, but no one from the legal aid office had appeared. A private attorney, Mr. G_____, learned that the court might hear the case without counsel, and asked the bailiff to request an adjournment until such time as the legal aid attorney could be present. The following material is from our field notes:

> The judge, "I will not adjourn it."
>
> The bailiff, "Your honor, G_____ is not the attorney."
>
> The judge, "He needn't come in. We have proof of the matter?"
>
> The police officer, "Yes."
>
> The father and the boy entered the courtroom. The bailiff told them to be seated.
>
> The judge said, "Tell me about this charge."

> The police officer said that the youth before him was _____. He was 17 years of age. There were two complaints against the boy, one was illegal possession of marijuana, the other was illegal use of marijuana.
>
> The judge said, "What are the two charges?"
>
> The police officer answered, "Possession and unlawful use."
>
> The judge turned to the boy and his father, "Are you the boy's father?"
>
> The father said, "Yes. Can I say something. We were supposed to have an attorney here, but he's not here."
>
> The judge said, "Did you get notice of the hearing today?"
>
> The father said he didn't, but I don't think he understood the word notice, and so the boy explained it to him. And then he said he did.
>
> The judge, "When did you get notice?"
>
> The father said, "Some time ago. Our attorney was supposed to be here, but he didn't show up."
>
> The judge then read off the new notice which says that they're entitled to have an attorney, Mr. X, etc.
>
> The man said yes he knew about that, and he said, "I talked with Mr. X Monday, but there's been a mix-up." He went on to explain that there was supposed to have been someone here today. It sounded as if he had not discussed in detail the content of the case, but he had actually contacted him on Monday.
>
> The judge said, "The important thing is whether the boy had possession of narcotics or not."
>
> The father said that the boy stated that he did not have it, and he got scared when he was brought into the police station and then said it.
>
> The judge said, "I'm going to hear testimony. If Mr. X's office wants to take the blame, O.K. Swear them in. . . ." [Testimony concerning the charges was then heard by the judge.] After hearing some of the evidence during which time the boy denied that he had smoked marijuana, the judge turned to the father and said, "Now sir, I'm prepared today to place this boy on probation and let him go home. If you want to come back here next week and have this detective. . . ." He continued on to say that if he wanted to come back here and say the same thing over while the father had an attorney he may do so. The judge then said that he didn't know what he would do next week, however. [After some more conversation, the judge said], "We can go through the mechanics of the court and have cross-examination and all the rest, but this court's interest is what is best for the boy . . . I think what I'm trying to do is save everybody's time."
>
> The father then said that probation would be all right. The judge stated that he could sign the waiver. The father said that he wondered if the boy went on probation could he leave

town. He said he had been planning on going to see his grandfather.

The probation officer present spoke up and said that this would present no problems. The judge agreed, and he stated that otherwise, we'll make a federal case out of this. And if we bring the boy back with an attorney, well, after an hour, I'll still have to make the decision and it's probably not going to be so different from what I make here. Then he went on to explain that he wanted the father to understand that the boy should sign a waiver which would save him from a criminal record and from going into an adult court since this was a criminal offense. The boy went over to the table and signed it, apparently without question, and then the father was asked to come over to the table.

The foregoing case illustrates fully the coercive power of suggestion. Obviously the judge thought the case sustainable on the evidence presented by the detective and did not wish to be bothered by an attorney. The field notes also indicate that the judge had knowledge of a social record on the juvenile, which revealed that the youth had previously been before the court on a narcotics charge, but had not been adjudicated delinquent.[22]

Bureaucratic pressures may sometimes provide the impetus for biased communication. To avoid delay, a judge may fail to fully advise the child and his parents of their right to an attorney:

> The probation officer stated, "Mrs. G_____ mentioned the fact that she might want to have a lawyer."
>
> The judge, "Well, we can't have them coming down here at the last minute." The judge then commented about how hard it is to get them down here.
>
> The mother said something. The judge said, "Have you changed your mind?" The mother replied, "Yes."

Finally, the content of a message may be compro-

mised by the manner in which it is delivered. When rights are communicated to respondents in a rapid fashion, allowing no time for an answer, the communication must be deemed prejudicial. In the following example (a case in Metro) the rapidity with which the information was given plus the obvious desire to hear the case without delay undoubtedly discouraged exercise of the rights mentioned:

> Referee, "You have the right to be represented by an attorney and the right to cross-examine witnesses, and you do not have to say anything, either an admission or denial, if you don't want to. All right, officer, what is the situation?"

"Prejudicial advice" of the right to counsel was found almost uniformly where less than "full advice" of the right was rendered. Only three cases were observed where full advice was given in a manner deemed to be prejudicial, two in Zenith and one in Metro. A complete breakdown reflecting "prejudicial advice" together with "full," "partial," and "no advice," reveals the patterns in Table 2.

PRIVILEGE AGAINST SELF-INCRIMINATION

In general The privilege against self-incrimination was largely unrecognized in delinquency proceedings before the Supreme Court's decision in *Gault*.[23] Even those courts and authorities that held that the privilege was in some way appropriate in juvenile court hearings felt it unnecessary or even inadvisable to inform the minor of this right.[24] In *Gault*, the Supreme Court rejected the argument that the youth and his parent should not be advised of the right to silence,[25] and held that: "The constitutional privilege against self-incrimination is applicable in the case of juveniles as it is with respect to adults."[26]

TABLE 2
Compliance with the Right to Counsel Requirement*

Type of Compliance	Gotham		Metro		Zenith	
	N	%	N	%	N	%
Full advice	(0)	0	(1)	1	(8)	44
Full advice—also prejudicial	(0)	0	(1)	1	(2)	11
Partial advice	(7)	12	(15)	21	(6)	33
Partial advice—also prejudicial	(2)	3	(31)	44	(1)	6
No advice	(50)	85	(23)	32	(1)	6
Total number of youths	(59)		(71)		(18)	

*Percents may not add to 100 due to rounding.

In criminal prosecutions, the defendant is exempt from answering all questions, since each may be incriminating.[27] While in principle the prosecution could call the defendant to the stand to determine whether he chose to exercise his right of refusing to answer any questions, no court has approved this practice.[28] Even the calling of a codefendant in a criminal case, without his having made a valid waiver, is a violation of the defendant's privilege.[29] Furthermore, the prosecutor is barred from commenting upon the accused's failure to testify, and no inference may properly be drawn from such failure.[30]

Now that *Gault* has extended the privilege against self-incrimination to delinquency proceedings, it seems clear that an uncounseled juvenile must be informed that he need not say anything before a single question is asked and, if he does testify, a valid waiver of the privilege must have been made. In *Johnson v. Zerbst*,[31] the Supreme Court established that every reasonable presumption against waiver of basic constitutional rights must be indulged. Relying upon the *Johnson* case, a federal court of appeals has held that: "Waiver of the privilege [against self-incrimination] must be informed and intelligent. There can be no waiver if the defendants do not know their rights. The rule must be the same, we think, when the record is silent or inconclusive concerning knowledge."[32] In *Miranda v. Arizona*,[33] invoking the *Johnson* decision and *Carnley v. Cochran*,[34] the Supreme Court held that waiver of the privilege against self-incrimination during in-custody interrogation, in the absence of an attorney, cannot be presumed from a silent record.

State courts have come to much the same conclusion. In *People v. Chlebowy*,[35] an unrepresented defendant was asked by the court if he wished to take the stand at the conclusion of the prosecution's case. He said that he did, and was thereupon sworn and examined by the judge. The reviewing court reversed, holding that the trial judge was required to inform the accused that he did not have to testify, that no inference could be drawn from his failure to testify, and that what he said could be used against him:

> When a defendant goes to trial upon a charge of a criminal nature without the benefit of counsel, it is the duty of the court to be alert to protect the defendant's rights. Good practice requires that any suggestion by the court that the defendant take the stand be coupled with advice as to his privilege against self-incrimination. The defendant may not be called to the stand in a criminal case unless he waives his privilege. He cannot be charged with a waiver of the privilege unless it appears that he was aware of its existence and its surrounding safeguards and voluntarily and intelligently elected to refrain from asserting it.[36]

Surely these rules applied to protect adults are even more appropriate when a juvenile is involved.

In this study, advice of the privilege against self-incrimination was considered relevant in all cases in our final sample, except those continued for a lawyer or witness, or dismissed without a hearing. It may appear that this approach fails to take into account the effect of a respondent's guilty plea which, in criminal prosecutions, is usually said to waive the privilege against self-incrimination.[37] When an uncounseled defendant in a criminal case enters a guilty plea, attack upon an ensuing conviction normally is directed to the validity of the plea itself, or to the competency of the waiver of counsel pursuant to which the plea was accepted. The issue of self-incrimination does not arise, since the guilty plea is not considered testimonial in nature and, once entered, it is deemed to waive the privilege. However, in many juvenile courts, certainly in Gotham and Metro, we are persuaded that the relevancy of the privilege against self-incrimination should not be related to whether the respondent admits the offense. The informality in these courts all too often leads to a blurring of procedural lines. It is often unclear whether the juvenile admits or denies the offense, and occasionally he is never even asked. Sometimes when a youth is asked to state his position, the judge has already heard the evidence against him. In criminal cases, by contrast, the plea-taking process occurs at a separate arraignment hearing; if a defendant subsequently wishes to plead guilty and withdraw a not guilty plea entered at arraignment, the record provides a clear statement of what has happened.

Although the procedure in Zenith provided that a definite plea be taken before the adjudication hearing, no such hearing existed in either Metro or Gotham. Thus no plea was taken in the usual sense in these two cities, but during the proceedings the youth

Lefstein, Stapleton, Teitelbaum: Juvenile Justice

usually was asked whether he committed the alleged act, or if he had anything to say. While sometimes there was an "admission" by the respondent, it was not a guilty plea, but a self-incriminatory statement in the testimonial sense. Therefore these admissions have been seen to pose self-incrimination issues. Similarly, in *Gault*, the alleged admissions by the respondent to the juvenile court judge were viewed as self-incriminatory statements.[38] *In re Butterfield*,[39] a recent decision of a California appellate court, provides a further illustration. After the respondent and her mother were advised of and purportedly waived the right to counsel, the charges were read. At this point, there was the following dialogue:

MR. PALMA [Deputy Probation Officer]: Now, Rachelle, did you understand the petition that was read?

THE MINOR: Yes.

MR. PALMA: Are these allegations true?

THE MINOR: Yes.

MR. PALMA: Will you explain to the Court what happened at the time?

THE MINOR: I just got suspended from school, and my aunt came and picked me up and she said that she thought she was going to put me back in Juvenile Hall and I just—she left the house and I got in the cabinet and took some medication.

MR. PALMA: What was your reason for taking the medication, Rachelle?

THE MINOR: I didn't want to go back to Juvenile Hall.

MR. PALMA: Request the petition be sustained.

THE COURT: All right . . .[40]

The reviewing court, in reversing the adjudication, analyzed the case as follows:

No evidence other than the minor's admission was received. The adjudication was one of "delinquency" because it found her guilty of disobedience to a court order and committed her to confinement in a correctional institution. It was used "against" her in the sense that it formed the entire evidentiary

basis for the judgment. *The statement was self-incriminating. She had no prior warning and there is no evidence that she had any awareness of her right to refrain from self-incrimination. Evidentiary use of her self-incriminating statement without that awareness infected the hearing with a violation of due process.*[41]

Degree of compliance Full advice of the privilege against self-incrimination requires that the minor be informed that he need not answer any questions before any questions are in fact put to him. We did not assume in our analysis that the judge was bound to advise the respondent that no inference would be drawn from his failure to speak, although this is arguably required by *Gault*. The Supreme Court stated the issue as: "whether . . . an admission by the juvenile may be used against him in the absence of clear and unequivocal evidence that the admission was *made with knowledge that he* was not obliged to speak and *would not be penalized for remaining silent*."[42] The import of the Court's language seems to be that unless a youth has been so informed, any statement he may make is improperly obtained.[43] Had this criterion been used there would not have been any case in the three cities where the privilege was fully implemented.

In Zenith, the relevant sample for purposes of the privilege against self-incrimination contained only six cases, due to the large number continued for an attorney. In two of these the youths were fully advised of the privilege. The remaining four juveniles were not advised at all, and all entered admissions. Since Zenith employs a formal plea-taking procedure, it can forcefully be argued that the requirements of the privilege did not apply in these cases.

In Metro, of a relevant sample of 62 cases, 18 respondents (29%) were advised of the right to remain silent. In 44 cases (71%), the privilege was never mentioned. In Gotham, the sample contained 53

TABLE 3

Compliance with the Privilege against Self-Incrimination Requirement

Type of Compliance	Gotham		Metro		Zenith	
	N	%	N	%	N	%
Full advice	(0)	0	(18)	29	(2)	33
No advice[44]	(53)	100	(44)	71	(4)	67
Total number of youths	(53)		(62)		(6)	

relevant cases, and in not one of these was mention made of the privilege against self-incrimination. As explained previously, in neither Metro nor Gotham was an admission by the juvenile considered a waiver of the privilege.

Prejudicial advice   We found that advice of the privilege invariably was communicated in a prejudicial manner in Metro. Frequently the warning was transmitted very quickly, and the proceeding continued without further reference to the privilege. Both the speed with which the information was communicated and the abrupt change of subject, without waiting for an answer, clearly tended to discourage exercise of the privilege. In one hearing a judge informed eight boys involved in a single offense of their privilege not to testify in the following way:

> Initially, the judge made comments to the effect that all boys were involved in the arson, although some may have taken part in different ways. After these statements, the judge stated, "Now, none of you have to answer anything. You don't have to say anything. I'll start with A_____." The judge asks A_____ if he was involved saying, "A_____?" And A_____ says, "Yes."

The judge then received admissions or denials from all eight boys without first ascertaining whether any of the youths actually wanted to invoke the privilege. Subsequently all of the boys testified. The privilege against self-incrimination was particularly relevant in this case because there was no presentation of evidence, with the exception of extrajudicial confessions made to police officers by five of the boys. Three of the boys during the hearing repudiated their confessions and denied involvement, but all were adjudicated delinquent.

Advice of the privilege also was classified as prejudicial when the judge, after giving the warning, immediately invited the respondent to forego his right of silence. Consider these examples from Metro:

> The judge first asked the boy if it was true that he stole the merchandise in question from the company. After receiving a response from the boy which is unclear [Although the statement of the child was unclear, the judge treated the case as a denial.], the judge stated, after a detective from the department store was sworn in, "B_____, you don't have to tell us anything unless you want to, but you can tell us if you want to."

*   *   *

> The judge says, "All right, B_____, you don't have to say a word here, but you may do so if you wish. Swear them in. You can talk or be quiet."

The court's conduct here cannot be considered neutral. By swearing the respondent, the uniform rule in criminal cases that a defendant has a right not to be called or sworn as part of his privilege is breached.[45] In addition, an explicit invitation to testify may make it difficult for some juveniles to decline. During a coroner's inquest in a South Dakota case,[46] the state's attorney observed that the 18-year-old defendant was present, but stated that he would not call him to testify. The coroner then said: "Did you hear what the state's attorney said, Mr. Halvorsen? He's not going to call on you to testify. You have the right if you so wish on your own behalf to come up and be sworn and testify."[47] The Supreme Court of South Dakota held that the information given was insufficient, and further that: "After . . . it was announced that he would not be called, but had a right to come forward and testify in his own behalf, he was not free to exercise an uncoerced volition."[48] The status of the juvenile court judge, as perceived by those appearing before him, may be expected to strengthen the impact of the invitation to testify, thereby weakening or entirely negating any previous statement of the right.

While there were no youths in Gotham who were fully or even prejudicially advised of their right to remain silent, there was one case that demonstrated a unique and imaginative response to the privilege against self-incrimination requirement:

> The judge began, "Are you the boy's mother?"
>
> "Yes."
>
> "Have you talked with the boy about this?"
>
> "Yes."
>
> "Does he admit it?"
>
> "Yes."

By asking the boy's mother if the child had admitted his involvement, the judge circumvented the self-incrimination issue. Subsequently, the youth testified, denied his guilt, but was adjudicated delinquent.

Table 4 reveals patterns of compliance for the following three categories: full advice on the privilege, full advice—also prejudicial, and no advice.

TABLE 4
Compliance with the Privilege against Self-Incrimination Requirement

Type of Compliance	Gotham		Metro		Zenith
	N	%	N	%	N
Full advice	(0)	0	(1)	2	(2)
Full advice—also prejudicial	(0)	0	(17)	27	(0)
No advice	(53)	100	(44)	71	(4)
Total number of youths	(53)		(62)		(6)

In Metro, consideration of literal compliance with the requirement, (i.e., whether the privilege was mentioned to the respondent) revealed that in 17 cases (27%) the privilege was accorded.[49] However, when an analysis is made of the manner and meaningfulness of the communication, the instances of full nonprejudicial compliance with the privilege are reduced to 1 case (2%).

RIGHT TO CONFRONTATION

In general In *Gault*, the only evidence against the respondent, except for an invalid admission, was a probation officer's secondhand account of the respondent's conversation with the complaining witness. The complainant, a woman, allegedly told the probation officer that Gerald Gault had spoken obscene words to her over the telephone, but she failed to testify in court, and the trial judge explicitly stated that her presence was unnecessary.[50] Noting its recent extension of the sixth amendment confrontation clause to state criminal prosecutions,[51] the Supreme Court held: "Absent a valid confession adequate to support the determination of the Juvenile Court, confrontation and sworn testimony by witnesses available for cross examination were essential for a finding of 'delinquency.' . . ."[52]

The Court's holding may be interpreted as differentiating between evidence that the juvenile court may receive, and evidence upon which a constitutionally sufficient delinquency adjudication must be founded.[53] In any event, it is clear that a delinquency finding must, in light of *Gault*, satisfy normal standards of confrontation.

The principal objective of the right to confrontation is to secure an opportunity for the accused to cross-examine the witnesses against him.[54] To that extent, constitutional significance is accorded to the eviden-

tiary rule against hearsay.[55] In criminal cases, failure of confrontation typically occurs where statements of a third party are related by a witness. The impropriety lies in receiving evidence not subject to cross-examination.

The informality of juvenile courts presents a situation rarely found in criminal prosecutions. In delinquency cases a necessary witness frequently does not appear, and no evidence is introduced in lieu of the anticipated testimony. In an auto theft case, for instance, the owner of the stolen car may not be present to testify that the vehicle is his and that it was taken without his authority. Instead, a police liaison officer or some other court official will read the charge at the beginning of the hearing, and the charge will include allegations of ownership and theft. While no testimony has been given, these allegations are nevertheless before the court, and their truth is frequently accepted. In criminal cases, the failure to produce a key witness would be treated as a failure to prove essential elements of the crime, and result in dismissal. During this analysis, when we encountered similar failures in proof which were ignored by the juvenile courts, the confrontation was classified as inadequate.

The same standards of relevancy used to identify the privilege against self-incrimination cases were applied to determine cases in the right to confrontation category. Although a guilty plea excuses confrontation in criminal cases by making it unnecessary for the state to prove its case, for reasons noted in the discussion of the privilege against self-incrimination in Gotham and Metro, a juvenile's admission or denial was not considered decisive.

Degree of compliance Satisfactory implementation of the right to confrontation normally requires that every essential witness testify whenever there is not a guilty plea. Because formal pleas were never rendered in Metro and Gotham, it could be argued that all necessary witnesses should have testified in every hearing. However, we rejected this argument, principally because we wanted to know whether all necessary witnesses were *present*, not whether in fact they *testified*. The objective was to determine to what degree the action of the juvenile court judge in *Gault*, when he stated that the complainant did not have to be present, was unusual, or whether it would occur even after the Supreme Court's decision. Moreover, it was not difficult to report accurately who was present during a hearing, but our observers sometimes did experience difficulty in reporting everyone who spoke and the complete substance of what they said. If, during an informal hearing with multiple parties, suddenly everyone spoke at once, the observer might have missed one or more "witness's testimony." With these concerns in mind, the following categories were formulated: "full confrontation"—all essential witnesses present in the courtroom regardless of whether they testified; "partial confrontation"—one or more of several essential witnesses present regardless of whether any testified; and "no confrontation"—no essential witnesses present. The table below shows the data analyzed according to these categories.

In Zenith, of the seven cases deemed relevant for purposes of the right to confrontation, full opportunity for cross-examination of witnesses was found in three cases, and no confrontation in four. But in the four cases lacking confrontation, admissions to the offense were entered by the respondent, and, as noted previously, the plea-taking procedure is sufficiently formalized in Zenith to make it comparable with criminal cases. Indeed, the pattern in Zenith is normally what one expects in a formal prosecutorial system—full confrontation afforded when there is

a denial and no confrontation if an admission is entered.

In Gotham the right to confrontation was more frequently afforded the respondent than were the other requirements of *Gault*. In 20 of 53 cases (38%), there was full confrontation; but in 16 cases (30%), only some of the necessary witnesses were present and available for cross-examination, and none were present in 17 cases (32%). In Metro, by contrast, the majority of cases, 42 (68%), fell into the "partial confrontation" category. Complete failure of confrontation was relatively rare, occurring in only 6 cases (10%), and full confrontation was found in 14 cases (22%).

FOOTNOTES

[1] 387 U. S. 1 (1967).

[2] Prior to Gault, courts had divided sharply on the existence and operation of these rights at the adjudicative hearing. While it was held that the juvenile could not be denied the assistance of counsel already retained, *see In re* Poulin, 100 N.H. 458, 129 A.2d 672 (1957), the rights announced in Gideon v. Wainwright, 372 U. S. 335 (1963) were not generally made available in juvenile courts. Some state statutes provided that whether counsel should be appointed was a matter for the court's discretion. *E.g.*, Ala. Code Ann. tit. 13, §359 (1959); Cal. Welf. & Inst. Code §§633, 634, 679, 700 (1961) (mandatory where felony charge involved); Colo. Rev. Stat. §22-8-6 (1964); Ark. Stat. Ann. 45-227 (1964); Mich. Comp. Laws Ann. §712A.17 (Supp. 1968); Nev. Rev. Stat. §62.085 (1961); N.D. Century Code §27-16-25 (1960); W. Va. Code §49.04 [13] (1961); Wis. Stat. Ann. §48-25-6 (1957). Others mentioned only a right to retained counsel. *E.g.*, Me. Rev. Stat. Ann. tit. 15, §2609 (1964); Miss. Code Ann. §7185.08 (1942); Mo. Stat. Ann. §211.211 (1959); Ohio Rev. Code Ann. §2151.35 (1964); R. I. Gen. Laws §§14-1-30, 14-1-58 (1961). A few states required appointment of counsel for the indigent, at least upon request. Idaho Code §16-1631 (Supp. 1968); Ill. Rev. Stat. ch. 37, §701-20 (1967); Iowa Code Ann. ch. 232, §232.28 (Supp. 1965); Kan. Gen. Stat. §38.821 (1963) (guardian ad litem); Minn. Stat. Ann. §260.155(2) (Supp. 1967); Ore. Rev. Stat. §419.498 (Supp. 1967). In the jurisdictions where the right to counsel in delinquency proceedings was not treated by statute, predictably, the

TABLE 5

Compliance with the Right to Confrontation Requirement

Type of Compliance	Gotham		Metro		Zenith
	N	%	N	%	N
Full Confrontation	(20)	38	(14)	22	(3)
Partial Confrontation	(16)	30	(42)	68	(0)
No Confrontation	(17)	32	(6)	10	(4)
Total number of youths	(53)		(62)		(7)

Lefstein, Stapleton, Teitelbaum: Juvenile Justice

decisions were split. *Compare* Application of Gault, 99 Ariz. 181, 407 P.2d 760 (1965); People v. Fifield, 136 Cal. App. 2d 741, 289 P.2d 303 (1955) *with In re* Poff, 135 F. Supp. 224 (D.D.C. 1955); Shioutakon v. District of Columbia, 246 F.2d 666 D.D.C. 1956).

The privilege against self-incrimination was by and large unrecognized in delinquency cases prior to Gault. *See* P. Driscoll, *The Privilege Against Self-Incrimination in Juvenile Proceedings*, 15 JUV. CT. JUDGES J. 17 (1964); N. Lefstein, In re Gault, *Juvenile Courts and Lawyers*, 53 A.B.A.J. 811 (1967); PRESIDENT'S COMMISSION ON LAW ENFORCEMENT AND ADMINISTRATION OF CRIMINAL JUSTICE, TASK FORCE REPORT: JUVENILE DELINQUENCY AND YOUTH CRIME 37 (1967). Some courts indicated that the privilege did not apply to juvenile courts since they were civil rather than criminal in nature. *In re* Santillanes, 47 N.M. 140, 138 P.2d 503 (1943); *In re* Holmes, 379 Pa. 599, 109 A.2d 523 (1954), *cert denied*, 348 U. S. 973; *In re* Lewis, 51 Wn. 2d 193, 316 P.2d 907 (1957). The Arizona Supreme Court in Application of Gault, *supra*, without expressly holding that the privilege applied in Arizona delinquency hearings, took the position adopted by the UNITED STATES CHILDREN'S BUREAU in its STANDARDS FOR JUVENILE AND FAMILY COURTS (1966) that while the right to silence may exist in some sense, the child and his parents need not be informed of it.

Juvenile courts had frequently taken the position that strict application of ordinary rules of criminal procedure would substantially interfere with the relationship between child and the court. Thus admission of hearsay evidence was held not to invalidate an adjudication of delinquency in *In re* Holmes, *supra*, State *ex rel.* Christiansen v. Christiansen, 119 Utah 361, 227 P.2d 760 (1951), and *In re* Bentley, 246 Wis. 69, 16 N.W. 2d 390 (1944). On much the same theory, the rule preventing the use of unsworn testimony in ascertaining essential facts was not extended to delinquency proceedings in some courts. State *ex rel.* Christiansen v. Christiansen, *supra;* State v. Scholl, 167 Wis. 504, 167 N.W. 830 (1918). Other jurisdictions, however, concluded that the use of hearsay and unsworn testimony was improper. *In re* Sippy, 97 A. 2d 455 (D.C. Mun. Ct. App. 1953); *In re* Mantell, 157 Neb. 900, 62 N.W. 2d 308 (1954).

[3]The decision to use fictional names for the three project cities was encouraged by the project's Advisory Board.

[4]387 U. S. 1, 36 (emphasis added).

[5]*See* Note, *Juvenile Delinquents: The Police, State Courts, and Individualized Justice*, 79 HARV. L. REV. 775, 797 (1966).

[6]387 U. S. 1, 41.

[7]Nor did the notices in these two cities or in Zenith satisfy Gault's requirement that the parent and the child be served written, timely, and specific notice of the charges. 387 U. S. at 32-33. In Metro, a written notice was served with a copy of the petition attached, but it was not directed to the child as the Supreme Court in Gault required. Although in Gotham both parent and child were afforded written and timely notice, the charge frequently was indicated only by the initials of the offense. For example, the offense of "deportment endangering health and general welfare" appeared in notices as "Juvenile Delinquency: DEHGW." Moreover, even when the offense could be deciphered, a specific factual description of the conduct was still missing. *See In Re* Wylie, 231 A.2d 81 (D.C. Ct. App. 1967); N. Dorsen & D. Rezneck, *In Re Gault and the Future of Juvenile Law*, 1 FAM. L.Q. 1, 14 (Dec. 1967). In Zenith, written notice of the charge was not sent to the youth or his parents. Instead, the parties were informed verbally of the date and time of their first scheduled court hearing, and when a parent appeared a bailiff thrust into his hand a printed form to sign, which purported to waive service of process. The substance of the form was rarely—if ever—explained, and the consequences of waiver never discussed. The child typically was not asked to sign the waiver form. Only after the parent had signed was a copy of the petition containing the charge given to the parent or child. Clearly this procedure did not constitute timely fulfillment of Gault's notice of charges requirement. Nor did the purported waiver of service by the parent appear to have been "knowing and intelligent." *See* Carnley v. Cochran, 369 U. S. 506 (1962); Johnson v. Zerbst, 304 U. S. 458 (1938). The procedure also failed to circumvent a statutory requirement that summons and a copy of the petition be served on the parties at least three days before the first court hearing.

[8]Cherrie v. United States, 179 F.2d 94, 96 (10th Cir. 1949). *See* W. Thompson, *The Judge's Responsibility on a Plea of Guilty*, 62 W. VA. L. REV. 213, 216 (1960).

[9]*See* Comment, *Waiver of the Right to Counsel in State Court Cases: The Effect of* Gideon v. Wainright, 31 U. CHI. L. REV. 591, 594-95 (1964).

[10]*See* Carnley v. Cochran, 369 U. S. 506 (1962).

[11]*Id.*; Johnson v. Zerbst, 304 U. S. 458 (1938).

[12]*See* Von Moltke v. Gillies, 332 U. S. 708, 723-24 (1948) (plurality opinion by Black, J.); Cherrie v. United States, *supra* note 8; Snell v. United States, 174 F.2d 580 (10th Cir. 1949); People v. Hardin, 207 Cal. App. 2d 336, 24 Cal. Rptr. 563 (Dist. Ct. App. 1962).

[13]*See* Uverges v. Pennsylvania, 335 U. S. 437 (1948) (17 years old); People v. Devanish, 285 App. Div. 826, 136 N.Y.S.2d 759 (1955) (16 years old); *In re* Gooding, 338 P.2d 114 (Okla. Crim. 1959) (18 years old). *Accord* United States *ex rel.* Brown v. Fay, 242 F. Supp. 273 (S.D.N.Y. 1965) (16 years old); People v. Byroads, 24 App. Div.2d 732, 263 N.Y.S.2d 401 (1965) (17 years old) (mem.); United States *ex rel.* Slebodnik v. Pennsylvania, 343 F.2d 605 (3rd Cir. 1965) (applying Pennsylvania law to a 17-year-old).

[14]Certainly there is much evidence to indicate that receipt and endorsement of a paper does not necessarily imply knowledge of the contents of the matter signed. The failure of poor persons to know and understand their commercial contracts has been carefully researched, *see* D. CAPLOVITZ, THE POOR PAY MORE 188-89 (1967), and the lack of education frequently found among the urban poor is unquestionable. *See* PRESIDENT'S COMMISSION ON LAW ENFORCEMENT AND ADMINISTRATION OF JUSTICE, THE CHALLENGE OF CRIME IN A FREE SOCIETY 69-70 (1967).

It is also now quite clear that juvenile courts are, in practice, courts for the poor.

> The upper and middle classes show surprising agility in keeping their delinquent children out of the court. In some cases we can be sure that a petition has not been filed against an offending middle-class youngster because restitution has been supplied to the victim of the child's misconduct. In other cases, the upper and middle-class youths have been shielded against juvenile court adjudications by their parents' ability to provide privately arranged corrective treatment. After an adjudication, a person of means can often arrange for the use of private facilities not available to the poor.

Paulsen, *Juvenile Courts, Family Courts, and the Poor Man, in* THE LAW OF THE POOR 310, 372 (J. tenBroek, ed. 1966).

PART 4   THE IMPACT OF LEGAL INSTITUTIONS

[15]See Powell v. Alabama, 287 U. S. 45, 73 (1932): "Attorneys are officers of the court, and are bound to render services when required by such appointment."

[16]This manner of informing of the right to appointed counsel was very common in Metro, and was incorporated into the written notice of rights sent to the parents of those appearing before the juvenile court. See text at note 7, *supra*. Because of the classification adopted, it is unnecessary to consider whether appointment to "Legal Aid," though entered on the record and formally made, is satisfactory where, as in Zenith, appointment is not made to an individual practitioner and the Legal Aid Office is not established as an office licensed to practice law and would, apparently, not technically be bound by an appointment.

[17]See United States *ex rel.* Brown v. Fay, 242 F. Supp. 243 (D.C.N.Y. 1965); People v. Byroads, 24 App. Div.2d 732, 263 N.Y.S.2d 401 (1965).

[18]It may be argued that Gotham's juvenile court was merely awaiting the anticipated changes in the rules of court. If this is a plausible argument, however, it does not abrogate the authority of the Supreme Court's decision in Gault. Indeed, if anything, it indicated the power of juvenile court tradition in resisting change.

[19]As noted previously, the written notice of counsel supplied in these two cities was also deficient.

[20]See Cherrie v. United States, 179 F.2d 94 (10th Cir. 1949); Thompson, *supra* note 8.

[21]E. D. MORGAN, BASIC PROBLEMS OF EVIDENCE (Joint Committee on Continuing Legal Education of the American Law Institute and the American Bar Association 1963), quoted in E. Webb, The Interview, or The Only Wheel in Town, 23 (unpublished ms. Northwestern University, undated).

[22]Although foreknowledge of a juvenile's prior history may well constitute prejudicial error, traditional juvenile court philosophy and practice has tended to support procedures whereby the judge becomes familiar with the youth's background before an adjudication hearing. See generally, E. Krasnow, *Social Investigation Reports in the Juvenile Courts: Their Uses and Abuses*, 12 CRIME & DELIN. 151 (1966); Teitelbaum, *The Use of Social Reports in Juvenile Court Adjudications*, 7 J. FAM. L. 425 (1967).

[23]See In re Santillanes, 47 N.M. 140, 138 P.2d 503 (1943); Driscoll, *supra* note 2; PRESIDENT'S COMMISSION ON LAW ENFORCEMENT AND ADMINISTRATION OF JUSTICE, *supra* note 2.

[24]See Application of Gault, 99 Ariz. 181, 407 P.2d 760 (1965); UNITED STATES CHILDREN'S BUREAU, STANDARDS FOR JUVENILE AND FAMILY COURTS 72 (1966).

[25]387 U. S. 1, 51-52.

[26]Id. at 55.

[27]8 J. WIGMORE, EVIDENCE §2260, at 369 (McNaughten Rev. 1961).

[28]Id. at §2268, p. 406, and cases cited at n. 6. THE UNIFORM RULES OF EVIDENCE, rule 23 (1), provides a typical statement of the principle: "Every person has in a criminal action in which he is an accused a privilege not to be called as a witness and not to testify."

[29]See United States v. Housing Foundation of America, 176 F.2d 665

(3d Cir. 1959).

[30]Griffin v. California, 380 U. S. 609 (1965).

[31]304 U. S. 458 (1938).

[32]Wood v. United States, 128 F.2d 265, 277 (D.C. Cir. 1942).

[33]384 U. S. 436, 475 (1966).

[34]369 U. S. 506 (1962).

[35]78 N.Y.S.2d 596 (Sup. Ct. 1948).

[36]Id. at 600. See People v. Glaser, 238 Cal. App.2d 819, 48 Cal. Rptr. 427 (1965), *cert. denied*, 385 U. S. 880, *reh. denied*, 385 U. S. 965; State v. De Cola, 33 N.J. 335, 164 A.2d 729 (1960) (grand jury investigation); People v. Morett, 69 N.Y.S.2d 540 (App. Div. 1947); State v. Halvorsen, 110 N.W.2d 132 (S.D. 1961) (coroner's inquest).

[37]United States v. Gernie, 252 F.2d 664 (2d Cir. 1958), *cert. denied*, 356 U. S. 968, *reh. denied*, 357 U. S. 944; Knox v. State, 234 Md. 203, 198 A.2d 285 (1964); Commonwealth *ex-rel.* Blackman v. Banmiller, 405 Pa. 560, 176 A.2d 682 (1962); State v. Nelson, 65 Wash. 2d 189, 396 P.2d 540 (1964). See United States v. Cioffi, 242 F.2d 473 (2d Cier. 1957), *cert. denied*, 353 U. S. 975; People v. Sierra, 117 Cal. App. 2d 649, 256 P. 2d 577 (1953). *But see* Wood v. United States, 128 F.2d 265 (D.C. Cir. 1942).

[38]387 U. S. at 42-57, *passim*.

[39]61 Cal. Rptr. 874 (1967).

[40]Id. at 877, n. 5.

[41]Id. at 877 (emphasis added).

[42]387 U. S. 1, 44 (emphasis added).

[43]Cf. People v. Chlebowy, *supra* note 31.

[44]A "partial advice" category, used in Tables 1 and 2, *supra*, to describe compliance with the right to counsel, is inappropriate in analyzing the privilege against self-incrimination. Since the only requirement for compliance with the privilege is that the juvenile be informed of his right to silence, advice must be either full or not at all.

[45]8 WIGMORE, EVIDENCE §2268, at 406, and cases cited at n. 6.

[46]State v. Halvorsen, 110 N.W.2d 132 (S.D. 1961).

[47]Id. at 134.

[48]Id. at 136-37.

[49]See Table 3 *supra*.

[50]387 U. S. at 43.

[51]Pointer v. Texas, 380 U. S. 400 (1965); Douglas v. Alabama, 380 U. S. 415 (1965).

[52]387 U. S. at 56.

[53]See Dorsen & Rezneck, *supra* note 7, at 20; Teitelbaum, *supra* note 22, at 431. *Cf.* CAL. WELF. & INST'NS. CODE §701 (1966), which permits the juvenile court to admit any evidence that is relevant and material, but requires that a finding of delinquency be supported by a preponderance of the evidence admissible in criminal cases.

[54]5 WIGMORE, EVIDENCE §1395 (3d ed. 1940).

[55]See Pointer v. Texas, 380 U. S. 400 (1965); Dorsen & Rezneck, *supra* note 7, at 20; Note, *Confrontation and the Hearsay Rule*, 75 YALE L.J. 1434 (1966); Comment, *Federal Confrontation: A Not Very Clear Say on Hearsay*, 13 U.C.L.A. L. REV. 366, 372 (1966).

PART 4 THE IMPACT OF LEGAL INSTITUTIONS

Studies such as the preceding, of the impact of law in the role performance of police, prosecutors, and judges, strongly suggest that merely changing legal rules will *not* dramatically change the performance of whole institutional (political-economic) and organizational (especially bureaucratic) forces which inherently dictate violation of the rules.

THE DETERRENT INFLUENCE OF PUNISHMENT

The court decisions that dictate appropriate procedures for law enforcement agencies do *not* include within them any direct sanctions against policemen, prosecutors or judges who violate the law. Indirectly, lower law decisions may be overturned if a defendant appeals, but this is almost the *only* sanction operative. The situation is of course very different for the average citizen who violates criminal laws.

Criminal laws are criminal precisely because they are prescriptions which carry penalties (fines, imprisonment, or both) for those who are found guilty of violating them. A question of main concern to the sociology of criminal law is the extent to which the imposition of punishment deters people from committing crime.

The second article in this section, "Types of Deviance and the Effectiveness of Legal Sanctions," attempts to construct a theoretical paradigm for understanding the deterrent influence of the threat or the imposition of penal sanctions. Following this, William C. Bailey analyzes the effect of capital punishment on murder, and subsequent articles take up the issue of deterrence in its various facets, including what happens when police strike, how different drug programs effect recidivism, and finally whether labeling people as criminal leads to further criminality.

29

Types of Deviance and the Effectiveness of Legal Sanctions

WILLIAM J. CHAMBLISS

In the last analysis a legal system must be judged according to the impact it has on the social order. If that impact is largely deleterious to the lives of men, then maintaining the legal system can scarcely be justified. If, on the other hand, the law contributes in some important ways to the goals of society and its members, then there is justification for keeping it. And, of course, if the legal system is useful in certain ways but deleterious in others, then this condition cries out for changes to increase its effectiveness while maintaining those aspects found to have desirable consequences.

Not all of the presumed consequences of the law are equally amenable to empirical verification. For example, the idea that if a person commits a criminal act the state must punish him because this is the only way to restore the balance of nature to its proper order is not amenable to systematic investigation. Such a position rests, ultimately, on the purely philosophical assumption that retribution for wrongdoings is intrinsically valuable.

Source: "Types of Deviance and the Effectiveness of Legal Sanctions," *Wisconsin Law Review*, Summer, 1967, pp. 703–719. By permission of the author and publisher. The author is indebted to Robert Seidman for valuable assistance in the preparation of this article.

Such vague and ill-defined assertions about the consequences of the law have in recent years been relegated to a much less important place than the more directly demonstrable question of whether or not the presence of laws and the imposition of punishment acts as a deterrent to crime.[1] As Schwartz and Skolnick point out:

> Legal thinking has moved increasingly toward a sociologically meaningful view of the legal system. Sanctions, in particular, have come to be regarded in functional terms. In criminal law, for instance, sanctions are said to be designed to prevent recidivism by rehabilitating, restraining or executing the offender. They are also said to be intended to deter others from the performance of similar acts and, sometimes, to provide a channel for the expression of retaliatory motives.[2]

The social sciences have been concerned principally with the question of deterrence, for it is here that the impact of the legal system is most amenable to empirical and systematic evaluation.[3]

I. THE DETERRENT INFLUENCE OF CAPITAL PUNISHMENT

The question of the deterrent influence of capital punishment has occupied the forefront in criminological research into deterrence for years. The preponderance of the evidence indicates that capital punishment does not act as a deterrent to murder. This general conclusion is based on a number of observations and researches that have demonstrated:

1. That murder rates have remained constant despite trends away from the use of capital punishment;

2. that within the United States where one state has abolished capital punishment and another has not, the murder rate is no higher in the abolition state than in the retention state; and

3. that apparently the possible consequences of the act of murder are not considered by the murderer at the time of the offense.

Some of the evidence substantiating these three conclusions is presented below.[4]

There has been a very clear tendency throughout the Western World to eliminate capital punishment. In the United States this trend away from capital punishment has taken several forms. To begin with, there has been a rapid decline in the number of states where capital punishment is mandatory if an accused is found guilty; in 1924 the death penalty was mandatory in eight states, but by 1964 it was not mandatory in any. There has also been a tendency to impose the death sentence less and less frequently. Eighty percent of those persons sentenced to death in 1933–1934 were ultimately executed; the figure was 81 percent in 1940–1945. But from 1960 to 1964 only 34 percent of the persons sentenced to death have been executed.

There has also been a steady increase in the number of states that have abolished capital punishment for various crimes. In 1920 only six states had abolished capital punishment; by 1957 the number of such states had risen to eight; and by 1965, 13 states had formally abolished capital punishment. Perhaps even more significant is the rapid decline in the number of persons actually executed. In 1951 there were 105 executions in the United States. The number of executions has steadily and precipitously declined since that time, with 15 executions in 1964, 7 in 1965, and only 1 in 1966.

Thus we see in the United States a steady and rapid alteration in the propensity to administer capital punishment. From the standpoint of deterrence, the significance of this trend is that during this same period

we find *no significant change* in the murder rate (see Table 1). It would seem that if the presence of capital punishment either in principle or in fact, were a deterrent to murder, then the murder rate should have gone up as both the potential and the actual use of capital punishment declined.

TABLE 1
Comparison of Prisoners Executed under Civil Authority and Murder Rate, 1951–1966.

Year	Number of Persons Executed	Murder Rate (per 100,000 population)
1951	105	4.8
1952	83	5.0
1953	62	4.8
1954	81	4.8
1955	76	4.8
1956	65	4.9
1957	65	4.9
1958	49	4.7
1959	49	4.8
1960	56	5.1
1961	42	4.7
1962	47	4.5
1963	21	4.5
1964	15	4.8
1965	7	5.1
1966	1	5.6

A similar conclusion emerges when the murder rates of states that have retained the death penalty are compared with the murder rates of states that have abolished it.[5] This general conclusion also holds true when one compares contiguous states—states that presumably are relatively homogeneous culturally, but where one state has retained the death penalty and the other has not (see Table 2).

The states that have *abolished* the death penalty do not show a substantially higher murder rate when compared with states that have retained it. In four of the five pairs of states included in the table, the abolition state has a lower murder rate. In one pair the abolition state has a higher rate. The differences are slight in every instance, and the only safe conclusion possible from this data is that there is no greater propensity to murder when capital punishment is not a possibility than when it is. The point is not that abolishing capital punishment decreases the murder

TABLE 2[6]
Annual Average Murder Rates in Selected Contiguous States

	Murder Rate 1959–1964
Rhode Island[a]	1.1
Connecticut[b]	1.5
Wisconsin[a]	1.3
Illinois[b]	5.1
Minnesota[a]	1.1
Iowa[b]	1.2
Wisconsin[a]	1.3
Iowa[b]	1.2
Michigan[a]	3.4
Indiana[b]	3.5

[a] abolition states
[b] death penalty states

rate; rather, since the murder rate does not increase, one must conclude that capital punishment is not an effective deterrent.

The same conclusion is also suggested by a study of the murder rate in Philadelphia immediately preceding and following particularly well-publicized executions. If executing someone for a capital crime is a deterrent, one would expect its influence to be at a peak when an execution was imminent or had just occurred. But Savitz found no difference in the murder rate immediately prior to and following such executions.[7]

Some of these studies rest on the analysis of data that have serious limitations, and none of the data are as perfect as one would like. However, given the preponderance of evidence, it seems safe to conclude that capital punishment does not act as an effective deterrent to murder. This conclusion about capital punishment does not apply to punishment generally since, as is well recognized, murder and other capital offenses are usually shrouded with a great deal of emotional involvement on the part of the offender. Thus, one might well expect punishment to be less effective precisely because such offenses are less dictated by "rational" considerations of gain or loss. Therefore, one must look at what the evidence indicates about different types of offenses.[8]

II. DRUG ADDICTION AND THE LAW[9]

There is a saying among drug addicts that "once the monkey's on your back, you never shake him off." The empirical research on drug addiction strongly

supports this contention. In a study of 800 addicts who were followed after treatment, it was found that 81.6 percent of them had relapsed within the first year, 93.9 percent within three years and 96.7 percent within five years.[10] The federally run hospitals at Lexington and Fort Worth report similar recidivism rates among persons treated at these hospitals. The President's Commission on Law Enforcement and Administration of Justice has also concluded that there is a high relapse rate.[11]

Even among persons who are presumably the most likely to be rehabilitated through treatment, the recidivism rate is exceedingly high. Synanon, an organization for the treatment of drug addicts in Los Angeles, accepts only those addicts who volunteer for treatment. In addition to volunteering, the addicts must agree to undergo rather severe "hazing" policies in order to demonstrate the sincerity of their desire to abstain from drug use. Given these conditions, it is reasonable to presume that Synanon treats only those persons whose desire to "kick the habit" is very strong. But even with these persons, the proportion who fail to complete the treatment program is in excess of 70 percent of all those who initially apply.[12]

For the question of the deterrent influence of punishment, the significance of these statistics comes from the realization that concomitant with this propensity to recidivate has been the constantly increasing effort of the federal government to punish drug users severely. The Bureau of Narcotics has increased its efforts at control, and the formal sanctions have drastically increased in severity. Under certain federal statutes, an offender can be sentenced to prison for six years with no possibility of parole, thus making drug use one of the most severely punished crimes in the United States.

This evidence, then, suggests that drug addiction, like murder, is relatively unaffected by the threat or the imposition of punishment. But one may still raise the question of whether it is justifiable to generalize these findings to all types of offenses. Indeed, at least in one respect, drug addiction and murder share in common something that is lacking in many other types of offenses. Both of these acts are "expressive" —the act is committed because it is pleasurable in and of itself and not because it is a route to some other goal.

III. THE VIOLATION OF PARKING REGULATIONS

If murder and drug addiction anchor one extreme in a typology of criminal acts, parking law violations anchor the other. Probably no one violates parking laws simply because it is pleasurable to do so—rather, people violate these laws primarily because to do so is *instrumental* to the attainment of some other goal. Does the imposition of punishment have the same effect on parking law violators as it had on drug addicts and murderers?

A study of the violation of parking regulations by university faculty found that the propensity to violate these rules is directly related to the likelihood that offenders will be published.[13] In this study, a sample of faculty members was interviewed, with records being checked to establish the validity of the interview data. Information was gathered on the sample's tendency to violate the regulations during a two and one-half year period when the sanctions that could be imposed were slight and when the regulations were only sporadically enforced. Significantly, during this period over one-third of the sample reported complying with the regulations despite the mild and rarely enforced sanctions. The other members of the sample, however, reported varying degrees of rule violation, ranging from one recalcitrant who parked illegally daily (even on the lawn beside his office) and who "saved the tickets to play solitaire with," to persons who violated occasionally in order to deliver a package on campus.

There was a dramatic shift in the tendency to violate the regulations when official policies changed. In January 1956 the campus police force was greatly increased in size, thus enabling adequate coverage of all parking areas. Fines were increased from the previously established figure of 1 dollar for every offense to 1 dollar for the first offense, 3 dollars for the second offense, and 5 dollars for the third and subsequent offenses during any 12 month period. Most importantly, during this second period of more severe sanctions, illegal parking could (and did) result in the violator's car being towed away at his own expense. These changes were sufficient to alter considerably the faculty's compliant behavior. Where there had been 13 frequent violators during the light sanctioning period, there were only 2 after the change. Even

these 2 violators had changed their patterns of violation considerably. One reported violating frequently, but only for a few minutes while he delivered something to a building, thus minimizing his chances of being ticketed. The other reported violating only by illegally parking in a place where he had never received a ticket, and he further commented that had he received a ticket he would have stopped parking there. Thus, in effect, all 13 frequent violators showed a reduction in the propensity to violate the laws after sanctions were imposed.

IV. WHITE-COLLAR CRIMES

Although the data are less systematic than one might wish, studies on the impact of enforcement on the business connected crimes show results similar to the impact of sanctions on parking violators. Where penal sanctions are imposed there is a decline in the propensity to violate the law. Clinard summarized the findings from his study of black market violations during World War II as follows:

> [During the first stage of enforcement] . . . the public and business had been developing an attitude that the OPA did not mean business, that violations would be followed with only minor actions, usually simply a warning letter, and that the penalties described in the regulations were virtually meaningless. New types of violations were rapidly being devised and spreading from business concern to business concern and from consumer to consumer. . . .
>
> As the economy was rapidly getting out of hand with this slow hit-and miss method of price control, the government on April 28, 1942, froze the prices on nearly all uncontrolled commodities. . . . This regulation provided: "Persons violating any provision of this Regulation are subject to the criminal penalties, civil enforcement actions, and suits for treble damages provided by the Emergency Price Control Act of 1942. . . ."
>
> . . . [T]he penalty of imprisonment, even for a short period of time, was the punishment most feared by businessmen, according to their own statements; yet it was seldom invoked as a deterrent for others. A survey of wholesale food dealers' opinions, for example, revealed that they considered imprisonment a far more effective penalty than any other government action, including fines. In fact, some 65 percent of them made such a statement. They made remarks such as the following about jail sentences: "Jail is the only way; nobody wants to go to jail." "Everybody gets panicky at the thought of a jail sentence." "A jail sentence is dishonorable; it jeopardizes the reputation." . . . These expressions are in marked contrast

to the attitudes of the same men toward the imposition of fines and other monetary penalties: "They don't hurt anybody." . . . "People are making enough money nowadays to pay a fine easily."[14]

Clinard also reports that in districts where the OPA regulations were enforced, compliance with the rules was much more prevalent than where enforcement was lax. In one midwestern city two automobile dealers were heavily fined and one was sent to prison. Clinard reports that numerous dealers commented that they were unwilling to take the risk of being sent to prison, and the regulations were complied with. By contrast, a company that had handled over 300,000 pounds of meat in 5 months and had charged prices of 7 to 11 cents a pound in excess of the allowed ceiling was found guilty of violating the regulations. The convicted defendants were fined only 250 dollars each and given a 30-day suspended sentence. The OPA district enforcement attorney stated that attempts to enforce the regulations were simply "laughed at" after this case.

The expressed reaction of persons sentenced to jail for violation of the Sherman Antitrust law suggests a similar impact. When sentenced, George Burens, a General Electric Company vice-president who was fined 4,000 dollars and given 30 days in jail, said, "There goes my whole life. Who's going to want to hire a jailbird?"[15]

V. THE SNITCH AND BOOSTER

Cameron's study of shoplifting throws still more light on the impact of punishment as a deterrent. Cameron points out that there are two types of shoplifters: the "Snitch" and the "Booster." The Booster is a professional thief whose principal form of theft is shoplifting. The Snitch (or pilferer), in contrast, is generally a respectable citizen (usually a middle-class housewife) who shoplifts in order to obtain goods she could not otherwise afford.[16] Cameron was able to check on the recidivism of persons apprehended by careful examination of department store files. Once a person is apprehended by a store detective, a card is filed with her picture; every store in the city has access to this file. Thus it is quite likely that any previous arrest will be known. Cameron found that persons who were professional thieves invariably had prior arrest records in the stores' files but that the Snitches

almost never did. For the Snitches, one arrest was almost always sufficient to insure that she would never be arrested again. It is possible, but quite unlikely, that the Snitch simply became more careful after having been arrested once. It is more likely that she was in fact deterred from further shoplifting by the experience.

> Among pilferers who are apprehended and interrogated by the store police but set free without formal charge, there is very little or no recidivism. . . .
>
> [O]nce arrested, interrogated, and in their own perspective, perhaps humiliated, pilferers apparently stop pilfering. The rate of recidivism is amazingly low. The reward of shoplifting, whatever it is, is not worth the cost to reputation and self-esteem. . . .
>
> One woman was observed who, thoroughly shaken as the realization of her predicament began to appear to her, interrupted her protestations of innocence from time to time, overwhelmed at the thought of how some particular person in her "in-group" would react to her arrest. Her conversation with the interrogator ran somewhat as follows: "I didn't intend to take the dress. I just wanted to see it in the daylight. [She had stuffed it into a shopping bag and carried it out of the store.] Oh, what will my husband do? I did intend to pay for it. It's all a mistake. Oh, my God, what will my mother say! I'll be glad to pay for it. See, I've got the money with me. Oh, my children! They can't find out I've been arrested! I'd never be able to face them again!" . . .
>
> The contrast in behavior between the pilferer and the recognized and self-admitted thief is striking. The experienced thief either already knows what to do or knows precisely where and how to find out. His emotional reactions may involve anger directed at himself or at features in the situation around him, but he is not at a loss for reactions. He follows the prescribed modes of behavior, and knows, either because of prior experience or through the vicarious experiences of acquaintances, what arrest involves by way of obligations and rights. He has some familiarity with bonding practice and either already has or knows how to find a lawyer who will act for him.[17]

These findings suggest that the amateur shoplifter, or the Snitch, will be deterred from further criminality by the imposition of punishment while the professional thief will be little affected by it.

The Cameron findings on professional thieves are also corroborated by other investigations. Lemert's study of the systematic check forger suggests that receiving an occasional jail sentence is merely part of the life of being a professional thief; it is accepted as one of the "hazards of the business," just as other occupational groups accept certain undesirable characteristics of their work as inevitable hazards.[18] That arrest and jail sentence do not interrupt the ongoing interpersonal relations of professional thieves is undoubtedly an important element in rendering the punishment relatively ineffective.

But this fatalistic acceptance of imprisonment as an inevitability should not be interpreted to mean that the professional thief is wholly unresponsive to the threat of punishment. On the contrary, a much greater proportion of a thief's energy is devoted to avoiding capture and imprisonment than is devoted to stealing. Although serving an occasional sentence apparently does not deter the professional thief from crime, it must be remembered that, for a reasonably competent and skillful thief, prison sentences occur relatively infrequently.[19]

VI. A TYPOLOGY OF CRIME AND DETERRENCE

The preceding summary of research findings on the deterrent influence of punishment on various types of crimes suggests some interesting contrasts. First is the contrast between acts that are "expressive" and acts that are "instrumental." Murder as an expressive act is quite resistant to punishment as a deterrent, as is drug addiction; instrumental acts, such as violating parking regulations and shoplifting by middle-class housewives, are more likely to be influenced by the threat or imposition of punishment.

The other major distinction suggested by the research is between persons who are highly committed to crime as a way of life and persons whose commitment is low. Cameron talks about this distinction in contrasting the Booster and the Snitch. She argues that this distinction is essentially a difference in the group support for their transgressions perceived by these different categories of offenders. More generally, one could say that persons with a high commitment perceive group support, conceive of themselves as criminal, and pattern their way of life around their involvement in criminality. Persons with low commitment would, of course, exhibit the reverse of these characteristics.

By combining these two dimensions of criminality and offender, it is possible to construct a typology of criminal acts with clear implications for the likelihood that a combination of offender and offense will respond to punishment by reducing their involvement in crime. The hypothesis is that where a high commitment to crime as a way of life is combined with involvement in an act that is expressive, one finds the greatest resistance to deterrence through threat of punishment. At the other extreme are acts where commitment to crime is low and where the act is instrumental (such as the Snitch, the white-collar criminal, or the parking law violator). Here we would expect both general and specific deterrence to be maximally effective (see Table 3).

TABLE 3
Types of Deviance

| | | Type of Act | |
		Instrumental	Expressive
Degree of Commitment to Crime as a Way of Life	High	Professional thief Booster Some check forgers Some murderers	Most drug addicts Some murderers Some sex offenders
	Low	Snitch Parking law violator White-collar criminal Some murderers	Most murderers Some drug addicts Most sex offenders

While we can assert with some confidence that the remaining two types—high commitment-instrumental and low commitment-expressive—will fall between the two polar types, it is somewhat more difficult to know which of these types will be more responsive to punishment. It seems likely, however, that the impulsive nature of expressive acts, even when commitment to crime is low, will make such acts less amenable to punishment than instrumental acts, even though commitment is high.

We have, then, the following hierarchy of types that can be ranked according to whether or not they are likely to be deterred by punishment or the threat of it:

Most likely to be deterred: low commitment-
  instrumental
high commitment-
  instrumental

Least likely to be deterred: low commitment-
expressive
high commitment-
expressive

In considering this typology, it must be stressed that the sociological types represented by it do not correspond perfectly with legal types. If they did, there would be no reason for developing the typology. For example, the legal category "murder" contributes cases to at least three of the four sociological types. Probably in over 90 percent of the cases,[20] murder is an expressive act where the commitment to crime as a way of life is low. Typically, murder occurs in an argument between two people. But there are other types of murder that would fit into the instrumental category of offenses; gangland murders, which constitute only a very small portion of the total number of murders, would, of course, be such a type. Murdering someone to collect insurance and sundry other profit-making schemes would represent instrumental types of offenses where commitment is probably low.

The above argument can now be used to throw more light on the earlier discussion of the deterrent influence of capital punishment. For if this theory is correct, then low commitment-instrumental murders should be deterred by the threat of punishment. That capital punishment does not deter now becomes dependent on the fact that most murders are expressive types of offenses.[21]

If this typology has the kind of general utility in predicting the deterrent influence of punishment that research findings suggest it should have, then a truly rational system of justice is one that will maximize its effectiveness by imposing criminal sanctions where these act as an effective deterrent, and at the same time develop alternatives to punishment where it is found to be ineffective. The implication of the foregoing analysis would be that the legal system will have little effect in reducing the frequency of such things as excessive drinking, drug use, most murders, most sex offenses, and aggravated assault. For these behaviors, alternative mechanisms of social control must be instituted.

Ironically, most of the criminal-legal effort is devoted to processing and sanctioning those persons *least* likely to be deterred by legal sanctions. Most arrests and most convictions are for relatively minor offenses, most of which are unlikely to be deterred by imposing sanctions. In 1965, for example, police reported 4,955,047 arrests to the FBI. Only 834,296 of them were for offenses that the FBI categorizes as "Type I," or "major," crimes.[22] There is even reason to question whether this statistic is an overestimate of the proportion that are major crimes since 101,763 of these arrests were for auto theft, which in over 90 percent of the cases consists of an adolescent's borrowing an automobile for a short period of time and going for a "joy ride." In any event, well over 80 percent of the arrests made by the police are for relatively minor offenses. Although some of these offenses might be responsive to sanctions, most will not. Drunkenness accounts for a larger share of arrests made than any other single offense—in 1965, 1,535,040 arrests were for drunkenness, and this represents almost one-third of the total arrests made. Furthermore, when drunkenness-related[23] offenses are added together, they constitute *almost 50 percent* of all criminal arrests.[24] Finally, when arrests for other offenses unlikely to be deterred are considered, such as drug law violations (most of which are arrests of drug addicts),[25] aggravated assault, vandalism, and sex offenses, then the proportion of the arrests for offenses not likely to be deterred by imposing sanctions approaches 60 percent.

That arresting persons for drunkenness is not likely to be an effective deterrent is implied by the typology. Indeed, since the bulk of such arrests are of the chronic skid row inebriate, such persons fall into the category of offenders least likely to be deterred: those with high commitment to a criminal way of life (in this case the criminal way of life consists of persistent drunkenness) and those whose acts are expressive. Studies of such offenders bear out this expectation. In their study of chronic police court inebriates, Pittman and Gordon found that the majority of these offenders were persons who had been through the "revolving door" of the police station and jail innumerable times.

The results of our investigation negate completely the assumption that incarceration acts as a deterrent to the chronic public inebriate. . . . Of the 1,357 men committed to the Monroe County Penitentiary in 1954 on charges of public intoxication or allied offenses, only 5 were newcomers to prison life. About one-third of these men—455 to be exact—were there for their second to tenth round. Nearly 6 out of 10 (80 men) had been committed from 10 to 25 times to a penal institution, and 96 men had served 25 or more jail terms. Our study group, a random sample of their kind, includes men who have been arrested 81, 90 and 110 times for public intoxication. There is no question about it: jailing has not deterred them from further public drunkenness.[26]

Pittman and Gordon's claims are a little stronger than their data warrant. While it is true that the persons studied in the county jail show a failure of penal sanctions to deter, it may well be that many more persons who are no longer in jail but who have been arrested previously were subsequently deterred. Thus, this evidence can only be taken as suggestive, but it seems unlikely that the findings would be much different even if sampling procedures had been more reliable.

These findings contrast nicely with the common observation that systematic arrests for driving while intoxicated act as a deterrent. Many casual observers have claimed that the Scandinavian practice of arresting and severely sanctioning persons who drive while under the influence of alcohol, has the effect of greatly reducing the frequency of such events and (perhaps more importantly) of reducing the frequency with which accidents occur as a consequence of driving under the influence.[27] Since this offense would fall logically into the category of an instrumental act (the drinking may be expressive, but driving while drunk would clearly be instrumental by the definition given earlier[28]), then such a finding is precisely what would be expected by the theory.

By contrast, persons likely to be deterred by imposing sanctions are, in general, the most likely to escape them. As Sutherland's analysis of white-collar crime has shown, violators of the Sherman Antitrust law are relatively free from criminal prosecution, though the imposition of punishment would be maximally effective with this type of offense.[29] Professional thieves likewise enjoy a surprising immunity from sanctions.[30]

The incompatibility of current legal practices with the data and theoretical perspective presented here is summed up in the way the legal system typically responds to violation of antidrug laws. Relatively miniscule amounts of the legal system's energies and potentials are devoted to the development of techniques and procedures that would increase the efficiency with which persons responsible for importing, wholesaling, and distributing drugs for illegal resale are prosecuted. By contrast, great ingenuity is shown in the enforcement of antidrug laws against persons buying drugs for their own consumption. Included in these techniques are ingenious, albeit quasi-legal, methods of searching dwellings without a warrant and then, if anything is found, obtaining a warrant to make a second, "legal" search; entrapping prospective buyers; and using as informers drug addicts who are paid for informing by being given drugs for their own consumption.[31] The likelihood that drug addicts will be deterred by sanctions, regardless of how severe or likely sanctioning may be, is exceedingly small. The wholesalers, importers, and distributors, by contrast, are generally ignored; but sanctions, if imposed, would be far more likely to be effective. As Lindesmith has pointed out, the present policy of arresting addicts and ignoring the profiteers makes about as much sense as believing that the wholesale arrest of drunks along the bowery would have curtailed the violation of prohibition laws.[32]

VII. CONCLUSION

Before spelling out the implications of the foregoing analysis, it is essential that two general disclaimers be underlined. First, it must be reiterated that this article has assumed that deterrence is the only legitimate purpose for imposing criminal sanctions. As the Schwartz and Skolnick quotation[33] indicates, this view is increasingly shared by lawyers and social scientists.[34]

But there are some who would disagree with this position and who would claim other, equally important purposes for imposing criminal sanctions. A person may be arrested to protect him from possible harm; drunks, for example, may be put in jail to keep them from freezing to death or from having their money stolen. Or, laws may be kept "on the books" because what they express contributes something valuable to the moral climate of the society, irrespective of whether or not they are enforced. A detailed analysis of the almost infinite number of purposes claimed for the criminal law is beyond the scope of this article. No matter what such an analysis might indicate as the various legitimate purposes of the law, the fact remains that, at the very least, deterrence is a major, if not the only, purpose. Therefore, it is justifiable to consider the implications of the foregoing analysis assuming deterrence to be the sole purpose of the criminal law.

A second qualification is the tentative nature of the theory suggested here. At this point, it is of greater concern that one ask the right question than that one come up with the right answer.

On the assumption, then, that the theory presented here will be confirmed by further research, what are the policy implications? One implication is quite clear. Current practices of the legal system in focusing on persons whose acts are principally expressive in character is accomplishing very little vis-à-vis deterrence. Furthermore, the failure to develop techniques for imposing sanctions on instrumental type offenders omits a potentially important function for the legal order.

More specifically, what does the theory imply for lawmakers? Is it possible to write laws so that they will take into account such things as the instrumental or expressive character of criminal acts? Can laws be written to take into account the person's degree of commitment to crime as a way of life? Although the task is not a simple one, the law has proven its capacity for taking into account far greater subtleties than these. Indeed, in many instances similar distinctions are made in the law. Laws imposing different penal sanctions for the "habitual offender" come close to selecting persons who are "committed to crime as a way of life." Unfortunately, such laws also pull into their net persons who are habitually expressive offenders. Indeed, one suspects that such laws are more often used to permanently incarcerate sexual offenders (who are likely to be expressive types of offenders) than to permanently incarcerate professional thieves.

Similarly, laws differentiate persons who have intent and those who do not. The notion of intent is not sufficient to differentiate expressive and instrumental acts, but the possibility of doing so through a similar legal category is certainly not farfetched.

It is conceivable that the law might prescribe, for offenders who committed an act as a means to achieving some other goal, a punishment different than the punishment prescribed for persons who committed an act because the act was satisfying in and of itself. Presumably, courts and penal institutions attempt to do this for some offenders: Arsonists, for example, are likely to receive quite different treatment if they burned a building for the pure pleasure of it than if they burned the building because it was insured for more than it was worth.

These current practices suggest that the precedent and even the mechanisms exist for making such distinctions within the legal order. The problem, then, is not that the law is unable to take such things into account; rather, the problem is that the empirical data to tell us what distinctions should be made have not been available. Then, too, there is the more basic problem of confidence in the data that is available. We are better off making social policies based on less-than-perfect data than making social policies based on no data at all. Currently, the law is based on virtually no data at all; could we really go very far wrong if we changed our policies on the basis of only tentative conclusions? It seems unlikely that things would be any worse, and there is always the chance that they would be considerably better.

FOOTNOTES

[1]*See* the discussions in Andenaes, *The General Preventive Effects of Punishment*, 114 U. PA. L REV. 949 (1966); Andenaes, *General Prevention—Illusions of Reality?*, 43 J. CRIM. L.C. & P.S. 176 (1952).

[2]Schwartz & Skolnick, *Two Studies of Legal Stigma*, 10 SOC. PROBLEMS 133 (1962).

[3]Legal writers typically distinguish between general deterrence (the deterrence of potential law violators) and specific deterrence (the deterrence of a violator from committing further transgressions). While this disctinction may be useful in the abstract, it is difficult to maintain in empirical research and may in fact obscure more than it clarifies. Therefore, this article will adopt the more inclusive conception of deterrence without differentiating general and specific consequences.

[4]For an excellent compilation of data and relevant discussions on capital punishment, *see* CAPITAL PUNISHMENT (T. Sellin ed. 1967).

[5]*See* Schuessler, *The Deterrent Influence of the Death Penalty*, 284 ANNALS 54 (1952).

[6]This table is a revision and updating of the table to be found in *id*. at 58.

[7]Savitz, *A Study of Capital Punishment*, 49 J. CRIM. L.C. & P.S. 338 (1958).

[8]The importance of looking at types of offenses is noted in the Andenaes articles cited in note 1 *supra*.

[9]The following discussion is limited to the use of opiates and its derivatives, principally heroin and morphine; whether other so-called durgs would show the same characteristics is as yet unknown.

[10]A. LINDESMITH, OPIATE ADDICTION 49 (1957).

[11]PRESIDENT'S COMM'N ON LAW ENFORCEMENT AND ADMINISTRATION OF JUSTICE, THE CHALLENGE OF CRIME IN A FREE SOCIETY 225-26 (1967). *See also* E. SCHUR, DRUG ADDICTION IN AMERICA AND ENGLAND 61-63 (1962).

[12]Volkman & Cressey, *Differential Association and the Rehabilitation of Drug Addicts*, 69 AM. J. SOCIOLOGY 129 (1963).

[13]Chambliss, *The Deterrent Influence of Punishment*, 12 CRIME & DELINQUENCY 70 (1966).

[14]M. CLINARD, THE BLACK MARKET 59-60, 243-45 (1952).

[15]Apparently someone wanted to hire jailbirds: Of the seven men who received jail sentences, all but one were employed at the same or higher levels with either their own companies or similar ones a year later.

[16]To the layman, all shoplifters are frequently viewed as being "kleptomaniacs." Cameron reports that few, if any, shoplifters are impulsive thieves. *See* M. CAMERON, THE BOOSTER AND THE SNITCH (1966).

[17]*Id.*, at 151, 163-65.

[18]Lemert, *The Behavior of the Systematic Check Forger*, 6 SOC. PROBLEMS 141 (1958).

[19]*See* E. SUTHERLAND, THE PROFESSIONAL THIEF (1937) and note 30 *infra*.

[20]M. WOLFGANG, PATTERNS IN CRIMINAL HOMICIDE 191 (1958).

[21]The policy question raised by this argument is a sticky one. Assuming that institutional-type murders are deterred by capital punishment (a conclusion that is consistent with the preceding argument), then should we continue to impose capital punishment generally for murder in order to achieve that deterrent effect? The answer to this query must of course take into account the costs of such a policy. The cost of deterring instrumental murderers with capital punishment is to execute persons who would not be deterred by the threat of punishment because their acts are expressive; and in the case of murder, this represents the vast bulk of the offenders. The argument becomes even more complicated when one takes into account that in all likelihood an instrumental murderer faces a lesser possiblity of having sanctions imposed and this fact inevitably flows from the different types of offenses. One can only raise those issues here and hope that others will help pursue the answers.

[22]FBI, UNIFORM CRIME REPORTS—1965, at 108.

[23]Violation of liquor laws, driving while under the influence of alcohol, disorderly conduct, and vagrancy.

[24]Total arrests in 1965 were 4,955,047; arrests for drunkenness-related offenses totaled 2,467,089. FBI, *supra* note 22, at 108-10.

[25]*See* A. LINDESMITH, THE ADDICT AND THE LAW (1966).

[26]D. PITTMAN & C. GORDON, REVOLVING DOOR 139-40 (1958).

[27]Andenaes, *The General Preventive Effects of Punishment*, 114 U. PA. L. REV. 949, 968-70 (1966).

[28]*See* p. 708 *supra*.

[29]E. SUTHERLAND, WHITE COLLAR CRIME 42 (1949).

[30]A professional safecracker of the author's acquaintance estimated that he had been arrested for safecracking (burglary) 300 times in a career spanning some 45 years but that he had received only three prison sentences from these 300 arrests. His immunity from prosecution stemmed principally from his ability to "fix" any criminal charges brought against him.

[31]For evidence of these practices, *see* J. SKOLNICK, JUSTICE WITHOUT TRIAL 112-63 (1966); A. LINDESMITH, *supra* note 25. Some of these practices have also been described by officials of the Federal Bureau of Narcotics. *See* H. ANSLINGER & W. TOMPKINS, THE TRAFFIC IN NARCOTICS (1953); Illicit Narcotics Traffic, *Hearings Before the Subcomm. on Improvements In the Federal Criminal Code of the Senate Comm. on the Judiciary*, 84th Cong., 1st Sess., pt. 5 (1956) ("The Causes, Treatment, and Rehabilitation of Drug Addicts").

[32]A similar thing is true for many, perhaps most, other types of offenses. The expressive murderer is probably more likely to be maximally punished than is the instrumental murderer; the skid row drunkard is probably more likely to be punished than the drunken driver; the juvenile who commits vandalistic acts is more vulnerable than the one who shoplifts.

[33]*See* text accompanying note 2 *supra*.

[34]For an example of a jurist who takes this position, *see* Commonwealth v. Ritter, 13 Pa. D. & C. 285 (Ct. of O. & T., Philadelphia County 1930).

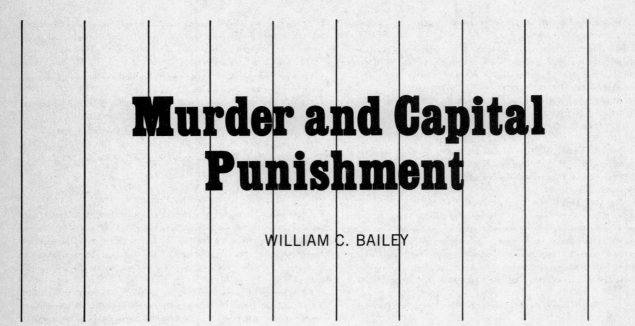

Murder and Capital Punishment

WILLIAM C. BAILEY

Research on the relationship between homicide and capital punishment in the past decade has been virtually nonexistent (Bedau, 1971).[1] Apparently the early investigations by Bye (1919), Sutherland (1925), Kirkpatrick (1925), and Vold (1932) and later examinations by Sellin (1967, 1955), Schuessler (1952), and Savitz (1958) have convinced most students of homicide that the ineffectiveness of the death penalty as a deterrent to murder has been clearly demonstrated (Gibbs, 1968). In short, for most authorities the question of the death penalty is a dead issue, for the preponderance of evidence indicates that capital punishment *does not* act as an effective deterrent to murder (Chambliss, 1967, 1969; Morris and Zimring, 1969; Reckless, 1969; Daleschall, 1969; Quinney, 1970; Bloch and Geis, 1970; Taft and England, 1968; Clark, 1971; Johnson, 1964; Knudten, 1970; Sellin, 1967, 1959, 1955; Schuessler, 1952; The President's Commission on Law Enforcement and Administration of Justice, 1967).[2]

Not everyone remains convinced, however, of this conclusion. In a recent examination of the capital

Source: This article was prepared for this volume.

punishment question, Bedau (1970) argues that most criminologists skeptical of capital punishment have not come to this conclusion by a critical examination of the evidence, but rather because of their adherence to a theory of violent crimes that excludes the influence of the threat of punishment.[3] Furthermore, careful examination of the literature reveals much of the evidence usually cited as questioning the death penalty as a deterrent to murder to be less than conclusive. With few exceptions, deterrence investigations of capital punishment suffer from a number of serious theoretical and methodological shortcomings that must not be overlooked (Bedau, 1970; Gibbs, 1968; Erickson and Gibbs, 1962; Sutherland and Cressey, 1970). Before examining these, however, and the scope of the present investigation, it would first be of value to briefly review the available evidence.

PREVIOUS RESEARCH

The conclusion that capital punishment has no deterrent effect on murder stems primarily from three types of investigations: (1) comparative analyses of homicide rates for states which differ in the legal provision for the death penalty, (2) longitudinal investigations of states' homicide rates before and after the abolition and/or restoration of the death penalty, and (3) longitudinal analyses of homicide rates just before and just after publicity of executions.[4]

By far the most common approach to testing the deterrent effect of the death penalty has been to compare homicide rates of abolitionist and retentionist states (Sutherland and Cressey, 1970). As illustrated in Table I, these investigations have gener-

ally shown rates of homicide in the latter states to be two to three times higher than in the former; a finding quite contrary to what deterrence theory would predict (Sutherland, 1925; Sutherland and Cressey, 1970; Schuessler, 1952). Such comparisons have usually been ruled invalid, however, for the groupings of the two types of states are not uniform with respect to other possibly important etiological factors—population composition, social structure and cultural patterns (Sutherland, 1925; Schuessler, 1952).[5]

To meet this objection, Sutherland (1925), Schuessler (1952), and Sellin (1967) compared homicide rates of abolitionist states with neighboring capital punishment states. Table II reports annual average homicide rates for selected years for four groupings of contiguous abolition and retentionist states.

As reflected in Table II, these investigations have consistently led researchers to one of two conclusions: one, abolitionist states have slightly lower homicide rates than their death penalty neighbors (Sutherland, 1925; Sutherland and Cressey, 1970), or two, it is impossible to differentiate capital punishment from abolitionist states by solely examining offense rates (Schuessler, 1952; Sellin, 1967; Chambliss, 1969; Bloch and Geis, 1970).[6]

TABLE I

Homicide Rates for Death Penalty and Adolition States for Selected Years[a]

Year	Abolition States	Death Penalty States
1928	4.2	8.8
1933	3.7	10.5
1938	2.2	7.6
1943	2.1	5.5
1949	2.2	6.0
1953	2.2	5.9
1958	2.1	5.3
1963	2.6	4.9
1968	3.9	6.7
1971	4.9	8.1

[a]Rates are computed per 100,000 population

TABLE II

Annual Average Homicide Rates for Thirteen States Selected According to Contiguity[a]

State	1931–35	1936–40	1941–46	1959–64	1967–71
Rhode Island[b]	1.8	1.5	1.0	1.0	2.8
Connecticut	2.4	2.0	1.9	1.4	2.9
Michigan[b]	5.0	3.6	3.4	3.8	8.3
Indiana	6.2	4.3	3.2	3.6	4.7
Wisconsin[b]	2.4	1.7	1.5	1.3	2.2
Illinois	9.6	5.7	4.4	4.9	8.6
Minnesota[b]	3.1	1.7	1.6	1.1	2.0
Iowa[c]	2.6	1.7	1.3	1.1	1.7
Kansas[d]	6.2	3.6	3.0	2.5	4.2
Colorado	7.5	5.5	3.7	4.8	5.5
Missouri	11.1	6.6	5.3	9.2	9.2
Nebraska	3.7	1.7	1.8	2.2	2.6
Oklahoma	11.0	7.2	5.6	5.9	6.3

[a]Rates are computed per 100,000 population
[b]Abolition state
[c]Abolition state since 1965
[d]Abolition between 1931 and 1935

PART 4   THE IMPACT OF LEGAL INSTITUTIONS

Furthermore, examinations of the relationship between the risk of execution (number of executions for murder per 1,000 homicides) in retentionist states and homicide rates have shown no discernible correlation between these two factors (Knudten, 1970; Gibbons, 1968; Bedau, 1967; Taft and England, 1968; Sellin, 1967, 1955; Johnson, 1964; Schuessler, 1952). For example, the homicide rates for the four states leading in the use of capital punishment during 1960 were: New York 2.9, California 3.9, Texas 8.7, and Arkansas 8.6. Rates for contiguous death penalty states making less use of the death penalty were: Pennsylvania 2.8, Oregon 2.2, Oklahoma 7.5, and Missouri 4.6, respectively (Taft and England, 1968). As Sellin (1955, 23) reports, "It is impossible to draw any inference . . . that there is a relationship between a large number of executions, small numbers of executions, continuous executions, no executions, and what happens to the homicide rate." He goes on to say, "the conclusion is inevitable that the presence of the death penalty—in law or practice—does not influence homicide death rates" (1967, 138).

Comparative examinations of homicide rates before and after abolition, and in some cases the restoration of the death penalty, provide a second important source of evidence on the question of capital punishment. These investigations reveal that states that have abolished the death penalty have generally experienced no unusual increase in homicide rate, nor has the reintroduction of the death penalty (eleven states have abolished the death penalty but later restored it) been followed by a significant decrease in the level of homicides (Clark, 1971; Sutherland and Cressey, 1970; Bedau, 1967; Taft and England, 1968; Mattick, 1966; Sellin, 1959; Schuessler, 1952). Abolition has sometimes been followed by an increase in the homicide rate and sometimes not, and so is the case with the reintroduction of the death penalty. The important point is that changes in offense rates for these states almost exactly parallel those of neighboring states where no changes in the laws regulating the death penalty occurred (Sutherland and Cressey, 1970). In sum, explanation of homicide rates in abolitionist and retentionist states must be sought elsewhere than the presence or absence of capital punishment (Clark, 1971; Sutherland and Cressey, 1970; Taft and England, 1968; Sellin, 1967; Sutherland, 1934).

Longitudinal analyses of abolition for many European countries have also led investigators to a similar conclusion. For example, as noted in Table III, abolition of the death penalty in Sweden (1921) and the Netherlands (1870) was not followed by a significant increase in the homicide rate as deterrence theory would predict.

TABLE III

Annual Average Homicide Rates for Sweden (1861–1942) and the Netherlands (1850–1927) for Selected Years[a]

Sweden[b]		*Netherlands*[c]	
	Homicide		*Homicide*
Period	*Rate*	*Period*	*Rate*
1861–1877	1.12	1850–1859	.96
1878–1898	.90	1860–1869	1.46
1899–1904	.96	1870–1880[d]	.83
1905–1913	.86	1881–1890	1.17
1914–1916	.72	1891–1900	1.41
1920–1932[d]	.52	1901–1910	1.25
1933–1938	.46	1911–1920	1.32
1939–1942	.47	1921–1927	.60

[a] Source: Schuessler, 1952.

[b] Rates are computed per 100,000 population.

[c] Rates are computed per 1,000,000 population.

[d] Sweden abolished the death penalty in 1921, with abolition in 1870 for the Netherlands.

To the contrary, the homicide rate continued to drop in Sweden after abolition with only a slight but not permanent increase in rate for the Netherlands after abolition. Further as Calvert (1931) reports from an extensive survey of the international literature, in no single instance for all the countries of the world is there evidence of a permanent increase in homicide after abolition. In fact, for many nations the homicide rate has fallen after abolition.

A third source of evidence commonly cited as questioning the effectiveness of the death penalty has come from investigations of the effect that publicity has on homicide rates. Deterrence theory suggests that publicity surrounding mass executions would have the effect of deterring would-be killers. Dann's (1935) early analysis of homicide rates in Philadelphia sixty days before and sixty days after the execution of five killers, however, revealed no significant difference in rates before and after this highly publicized event. In a more recent investigation in Philadelphia, Savitz (1958) examined the rate of capital crimes eight weeks before and eight weeks after the well-publicized sentencing of four men to death. Examination of homicide rates in both the areas where the offenses occurred and where the offenders lived revealed no significant difference in rates before and after sentencing. Each of these investigations as well as a similar study in Chicago (Mattick, 1966) indicates "that homicides fluctuate independently of news coverage, executions and commutations of sentences in capital cases" (Sutherland and Cressey, 1970, 333). In sum, historical and comparative analyses like those cited above for both this country and abroad as well as case study and clinical observations (Thomas, 1957; Cuthbert, 1970; Gillin, 1946; Menninger, 1968; Palmer, 1960; Lawes, 1932) have brought most criminologists to what Sellin (1959) has termed the "inevitable conclusion," that the death penalty has no discernible effect as a deterrent to murder.[7] As indicated above, however, not all students of homicide would appear ready to accept this conclusion. Careful examination of the above investigations reveals that each suffers from a number of serious theoretical and methodological limitations. We might now briefly examine some of these.

Deterrence theory suggests that if punishment is to act as an effective deterrent to crime it must be: (1) severe enough to outweigh the potential pleasures crime might bring, (2) administered with certainty,[8] (3) administered promptly,[9] (4) administered publicly,[10] and (5) applied with the proper judicial attitude[11] (Beccaria, 1809; Bentham, 1843; Ross, 1901; Barnes and Teeters, 1951; Bloch and Geis, 1962; Johnson, 1964; Caldwell, 1965; Gibbs, 1968; Taft and England, 1968; Sutherland and Cressey, 1970). Each of these principles of punishment is seen by deterrence advocates as essential for maximum protection. For the most part, however, only one aspect of capital punishment—its severity—has been examined as a deterrent to murder. Little attention has been paid to the certainty of the death penalty, with examinations of the remaining three aspects of punishment being completely absent from the literature.

In sum, the question of the death penalty as a deterrent to murder has only been examined in the most narrow theoretical sense. Deterrence theory has simply never really been tried and given a "fair chance." (Puttkammer, 1953). As Jeffery (1965, 299) states, "The lesson to be learned from capital punishment is not that punishment does not deter, but that the improper and sloppy use of punishment does not deter . . ."

Of methodological concern, each of the above studies rests upon a number of unproven empirical assumptions, some of which appear highly questionable (Bedau, 1970).[12] These primarily concern the adequacy of using available aggregate homicide statistics, issued by the Federal Bureau of Investigation and the Public Health Service, as an index of murder in examining the deterrent effect of the death penalty.[13]

In the United States, generally only one type of homicide—murder in the first degree—is punishable by death, with murder in the second degree and voluntary manslaughter usually being punished by imprisonment (Sellin, 1959). Typically, however, investigations of the death penalty have operationally defined premeditated murder as homicide, a much more inclusive offense category. This practice has been necessitated by the fact that no alternative statistics are currently available on a nationwide basis that break down homicide by type and degree.[14] "In a word, there is no exact information anywhere as to the volume of capital crimes in the United States" (Bedau, 1967, 56). As a result, investigators have been forced to make a large and possibly erroneous assumption whether they use police or mortality statistics, that the proportion of first degree murders to total homicides remains constant so that statistics on the latter provide a reasonably good indicator of capital offenses.

Most investigators have accepted this essentially untestable assumption out of necessity (Sellin, 1959; Schuessler, 1952; Sutherland, 1925). Some, however, have attempted to justify this practice on empirical grounds. Schuessler (1952) for example, argues that the high degree of correspondence between police, prisoner and mortality statistics on homicide —not murder—clearly suggests the plausibility of the above assumption. A careful examination of his reasoning, however, reveals his argument to be quite unconvincing (Bailey, 1973).[15]

What the situation "boils down" to is that no one has succeeded in accurately counting the number of capital offenses hidden in the available homicide statistics in order to test this assumption (Sellin, 1967).[16] Nor have there been any serious attempts to seek alternative data on capital homicides. As it stands, we are forced to take it on the authority of experienced criminologists (Sutherland, 1925; Schuessler, 1952; Sellin, 1967, 1959) that available homicide statistics permit an adequate test of the death penalty as a deterrent (Bedau, 1967). This is clearly a regrettable situation for so much of the debate over the death penalty seems to turn on the validity of this assumption. Even more regrettable is the fact that investigators have not attempted to look beyond the limitations of the available statistics to seek data better suited to address the capital punishment question.[17] In short, the attitude that "the available data may not be good but they're the best we've got," has produced nothing of significance on the question of the death penalty in the last decade. Clearly additional research is needed in this important area. The research reported here is an attempt to go beyond some of the limitations of past investigations by examining the death penalty question with alternative homicide data.

THE PRESENT INVESTIGATION

The research reported here is a further examination of the relationship between homicide and capital punishment. Our approach is similar to that of Schuessler (1952) and Sellin (1959, 1967) with one important exception; the murder data examined here permit a direct rather than indirect assessment of the relationship between capital homicides and the death penalty.

As noted above, the Federal Bureaus of Investigation and Prisons and the Public Health Service *do not* report statistics on first degree murder, the only type of homicide generally punishable by death. Rather, figures are only available from these sources for the "catch-all" offense categories of murder and non-negligent manslaughter or homicide. The use of

these data has seriously limited past investigations of capital punishment (Sellin, 1967).

To avoid this problem and obtain theoretically appropriate data on first degree murder, a survey was conducted of all State Bureaus of Corrections throughout the United States. Letters were sent to each agency requesting information on the number of convicted first degree murderers referred to penal institutions in 1967 and 1968. For states with no central corrections authority, individual inquiries were sent to each penal institution in the state requesting the needed information.

Admissions data were only requested for the years 1967 and 1968 for two reasons. First, initial inquiries to corrections authorities revealed the referral statistics for prior years (before 1967) were in many cases not available. Second, this investigation was initially launched late in 1970, and referral statistics in many cases had not yet been compiled for 1969. Consequently, reasonably complete data could only be obtained for the two years surveyed.

For states with central correction bureaus, responses to our inquiry were usually immediate. In some cases, however, the needed statistics had not been compiled and a survey of records was required. In a few such cases, over a year elapsed before the data were provided, and in eight cases we were refused the needed statistics because they were either nowhere available, or would be too costly to compile. In total, complete figures were received from 41 states.[18] States unable to supply the needed data include: Mississippi, Arkansas, Georgia, South Carolina, Missouri, Pennsylvania, Arizona and Alaska.[19]

FIRST DEGREE MURDER

In our request, agencies were asked to report the number of persons convicted and referred to penal institutions for first degree murder. Due to variation in homicide statutes across the country, a definition of murder in the first degree was provided with our inquiry to assure comparability of the data.[20] Only for the state of Florida was it found impossible to "break down" homicide referrals by degree. Consequently, this state was dropped from the analysis.[21] In the remaining cases whenever there was initially any doubt as to the type of homicide reported, the question was quickly resolved by examining the state's homicide statutes.

SECOND DEGREE MURDER

With our request for first degree murder statistics, prison officials were also asked to report admissions for murder in the second degree. Second degree murder, although usually not thought of as of theoretical importance in studies of the death penalty, is considered here for two important reasons. First, it is fairly well recognized that many offenders initially charged with first degree murder are later recharged with Murder II in exchange for "copping a plea." In other words, many actual first degree murders end up in court and prison statistics as second degree murders (Gibbons, 1968).[22] We can only speculate how common this practice is in the absence of hard data, but this factor would certainly seem worthy of consideration in this investigation.

Second, despite the fact that first degree murder is the only capital homicide in most states, deterrence theory suggests that the death penalty may have a deterrent effect for other forms of homicide as well. The fact that society so condemns the taking of another's life that it demands the life of the offender ". . . helps to engender attitudes of dislike, contempt, disgust, and even horror for these acts, and thus contributes to the development of personal forces hostile to crime" (Caldwell, 1965, 425–426). In fact, the subtle, unconscious effect of criminal law and punishment, as opposed to the cool, conscious calculation of punishment, was believed by Beccaria (1809) and Bentham (1843) to be the major mechanism of deterrence.

LIMITATIONS OF THE DATA

It should be kept clearly in mind that the figures reported here refer solely to persons convicted of first and second degree murder and referred to state penal institutions. The data may not be interpreted as reflecting: (1) the total number of first and second degree murders committed in a state, (2) the number of persons accused of murder in the first and second degree, nor (3) the number of persons tried for Murder I and II. Further, these data may not be interpreted as completely accurately reflecting the total number of persons convicted of Murder I and II. Undoubtedly, a few persons convicted of murder were referred to mental rather than correctional institutions. The number here is probably quite small, however. Wolfgang (1958), for example, reports that only 17 of 621 homicide offenders (2.7%) were declared insane by the courts.[23] In sum, our data do reflect, although probably with slight error, the number of convictions for murder in the first and second degree for the states and years surveyed.

COMPARISON OF DEATH PENALTY AND ABOLITION STATES

Data in Table IV report mean offense rates of first and second degree murder, total murder and homicide for the states and years surveyed. Comparison of figures for abolition and capital punishment states reveals that for both years rates for each offense are

TABLE IV

Mean Offense Rates for First and Second Degree Murder, Total Murders and Homicide for Death Penalty and Abolition States, 1967 and 1968[a]

Offense	Abolition States		Capital Punishment States		All States[b]	
	1967	1968	1967	1968	1967	1968
First Degree Murder	.18	.21	.47	.58	.31	.50
Second Degree Murder	.30	.43	.92	1.03	.73	.89
Total Murders	.48	.64	1.38	1.59	1.15	1.38
Homicide[c]	2.72	3.09	5.90	6.04	4.85	5.48

[a]Offense rates are computed per 100,000 population

[b]Mean rates are only computed for the states surveyed in this investigation

[c]Source: Federal Bureau of Investigation, *Uniform Crime Reports*, 1968 (Washington, D. C.: 60–65)

substantially higher for death penalty states. For 1967, rates for all four offenses are at least twice as large as those for states without the death penalty. Similarly, mean offense rates for 1968 for death penalty states also substantially exceed those for abolition states ranging from a high of 1.9 times larger for second degree murder to a low of 1.6 times higher for homicide.

Comparison of rates for death penalty and abolition states with the mean rates for all states surveyed also reflects the disparity between the two types of states.[24] For both years, average rates for all four offenses are below the nation's average for abolition states, while rates for capital punishment states exceed the national average for each offense. A state-by-state comparison of rates in each type of state with the average for the country further reveals that for both years combined: (1) 88% of the abolition states have first degree murder rates below the nation's average, while only 52% of the retentionist states are below the mean, (2) for second degree murder, 91% of the abolition states have rates below the mean while again only 52% of the death penalty states are below the national average, (3) all (100%) of the states that have abolished the death penalty have rates of total murder below the country's average, whereas only 48% of the capital punishment states are below the average, and (4) for the offense of homicide, 83% of the abolition states have rates below the nation's average while again only 48% of the death penalty states fall in this category.

In sum, comparison of offense rates both between death penalty and abolition states as well as comparison of rates for each with the nation's average, reveals rates of Murder I, Murder II, total murder and homicide to be substantially higher in capital punishment jurisdictions. These findings are consistent with those reported by Schuessler (1952) and Sellin (1967, 1955) for the offense of homicide, but quite contrary to what deterrence theory would predict. Some, however, as Schuessler (1952) points out, have objected to comparing average offense rates for death penalty and abolition states for such comparisons ignore other possibly important etiological factors. To meet this objection, comparison of "matched" capital punishment and abolition states would seem warranted.

COMPARISON OF CONTIGUOUS CAPITAL PUNISHMENT AND ABOLITION STATES

To meet the above objection the usual practice has been to compare the homicide rates of neighboring death penalty and abolition states. Table V reports rates of first and second degree murder, total murder and homicide for eight groupings of contiguous capital punishment and abolition states for 1967 and 1968.[25]

Inspection of these data reveals a very similar picture to that reported above where mean offense rates for the two types of states were examined. Inspection of the first grouping of states (Maine, Vermont, New Hampshire) for first degree murder for 1967 reveals that the rate for Maine, an abolitionist state, exceeds that for New Hampshire, a death penalty state, whereas the opposite holds when the rates for Vermont, also an abolitionist state, and New Hampshire are compared. When such comparisons are repeated within all groupings of contiguous states for 1967, 67% of the comparisons show death penalty states to have higher Murder I rates than their abolitionist neighbors, while the opposite holds for only 20% of the comparisons. In 13% of the comparisons rates for both types of states are the same.

For 1968, comparison of first degree murder rates for the two types of states reveals a very similar picture to the former year. For this year, 64% of the comparisons within neighboring groups of states show rates to be higher in capital punishment jurisdictions, while rates are only higher in 29% of the cases for abolitionist states. Seven percent of the comparisons show rates of Murder I to be the same for both types of states.

Further inspection of Table V indicates a very similar pattern for the remaining three offenses. Comparison of abolition and death penalty states for these offenses, as well as Murder I, are summarized in Table VI.

Comparison of figures reported in Table VI between contiguous death penalty and abolition jurisdictions for Murder II, total murder and homicide for both years reveals that for at least 60% or more of the states compared, rates are higher in the former jurisdictions. In contrast, rates in abolition states only exceed those in neighboring death penalty states in no more than 40% of the cases compared.

TABLE V
Rates of First and Second Degree Murder, Total Murder and Homicide for Death Penalty and Abolition States, 1967 and 1968[a]

State	First Degree Murder		Second Degree Murder		Total Murder		Homicide[b]	
	1967	1968	1967	1968	1967	1968	1967	1968
Maine[c]	.50	.40	.30	.50	.80	.90	.4	3.0
Vermont[c]	.00	.50	.75	.00	.75	.50	3.1	2.6
New Hampshire	.14	.14	.00	.43	.14	.57	2.0	1.4
Rhode Island[c]	.00	.00	.11	.67	.11	.67	2.2	2.4
Connecticut	.28	.23	1.21	1.10	1.49	1.33	2.4	2.5
Massachusetts	.09	.28	.20	.54	.29	.82	2.8	3.5
Michigan[c]	.34	.44	.76	.78	1.11	1.22	6.2	7.3
Indiana	.16	.29	.32	.35	.48	.64	3.7	4.7
Ohio	.43	.55	.66	.71	1.09	1.26	5.2	5.3
Minnesota[c]	.08	.05	.14	.19	.22	.24	1.6	2.2
Wisconsin[c]	.26	.29	.21	.60	.47	.89	1.9	2.2
Iowa[c]	.07	.04	.21	.21	.28	.25	1.5	1.7
Illinois	.63	.96	1.17	1.46	1.80	2.42	7.3	8.1
North Dakota[c]	.00	.00	.00	.00	.00	.00	0.2	1.1
South Dakota	.00	.29	2.00	1.29	2.00	1.58	3.7	3.8
Montana	.00	.00	.14	.43	.14	.43	2.4	3.3
Washington	.09	.06	.44	.36	.53	.42	3.1	3.6
Oregon[c]	.30	.15	.45	.50	.75	.65	3.1	3.2
Idaho	.57	1.00	.43	1.14	1.00	2.14	4.3	2.3
West Virginia[c]	.33	.33	.61	.67	.94	1.00	4.6	5.5
Virginia	1.02	.72	1.31	1.37	2.33	2.09	7.3	8.3
New York[c]	.14	[d]	.11	[d]	.25	[d]	5.4	6.5
New Jersey	.24	.27	.74	.66	.96	.93	3.9	5.1

[a]Offense rates are computed per 100,000 population
[b]Source: Federal Bureau of Investigation, Uniform Crime Reports, 1968 (Washington, D.C.: 60–65).
[c]Abolition states
[d]Murder I and II statistics were not available for New York for 1968

TABLE VI
Summary of Comparison of Offense Rates for First and Second Degree Murder, Total Murder and Homicide for Contiguous Abolition and Death Penalty States[a]

Offense	Year	Higher Rates for Death Penalty States		Higher Rates for Abolition States		Rates Tied for Both Types of States	
		No.	%	No.	%	No.	%
First Degree Murder	1967	10	67	3	20	2	13
	1968	9	64	4	29	1	7
Second Degree Murder	1967	9	60	6	40	0	0
	1968	9	64	5	36	0	0
Total Murder	1967	10	67	5	33	0	0
	1968	11	79	3	21	0	0
Homicide	1967	10	67	4	27	1	7
	1968	9	60	6	40	0	0

[a]Figures in the number (No.) columns refer to the total number of cases where comparison of contiguous death penalty and abolition states show rates to be (a) higher in the former, (b) higher in the latter, or (c) the same for both types of jurisdictions.

In sum, figures for Murder I, Murder II, total murder and homicide for contiguous capital punishment and abolition states reveal rates for all four offenses to be generally higher in death penalty jurisdictions. These findings are consistent with earlier examinations of homicide, but quite contrary to what deterrence theory would lead us to expect (Schuessler, 1952; Sellin, 1967).

OFFENSE RATES AND THE CERTAINTY OF PUNISHMENT

Proponents of punishment argue that if legal sanctions are to act as effective deterrents, they must be "real." That is, if the probability of punishment is slight or non-existent, it will not deter no matter how severe. This point would seem of particular importance in examining past investigations of the death penalty. As Gibbs (1968, 518) points out, much of the evidence on the inefficiency of the death penalty is based upon normative legal differences among political units, "(e.g., whether or not there is a statutory provision for the death penalty)" not the actual use of capital punishment. No one would argue that the death penalty could be an effective deterrent if it is never used. Accordingly, the important question would appear to be, "how are differences in the use of the death penalty in retentionist states related to offense rates in these jurisdictions?" The relationship between offense rates and risk of execution has been previously examined but only for the offense of homicide (Schuessler, 1952; Sellin, 1967). To provide a more refined examination of this question, average execution rates (operationally defined as the total number of executions during the last five years per 1000 homicides for these years) are correlated with rates of first and second degree murder, total murder and homicide for 1967 and 1968.[26] Results of this analysis are reported in Table VII.

Deterrence theory would suggest the higher the execution rate the lower the rate of capital homicides in death penalty states. Inspection of figures in row one of Table VII reveals only a slight inverse relationship between execution rates and rates of first degree murder. Although both of the coefficients are in the predicted direction, neither is statistically sig-

nificant at the .05 level nor does either permit as much as 4% explained variation in Murder I rates.

TABLE VII

Correlation[a] of Rates of First and Second Degree Murder, Total Murder and Homicide with Execution Rates for 27 Death Penalty States, 1967 and 1968

Offense	*1967*	*1968*
First Degree Murder	−.137	−.194
Second Degree Murder	−.167	−.351
Total Murder	−.180	−.302[b]
Homicide	−.166	−.039

[a]Coefficients are Pearson product moment correlations
[b]P < .05

Further inspection of Table VII reveals a very similar pattern for the remaining three offenses. As with Murder I, each of the coefficients is in the expected negative direction, but only the correlation for second degree murder for 1968 reaches statistical significance at the .05 level. Even here, however, only approximately 12% of variation in offense rate can be accounted for by executions.

In sum, for both years surveyed, the association between execution rates and rates of first and second degree murder, total murder and homicide are in the predicted direction. For neither year, however, nor for a single offense are the negative correlations as substantial as deterrence theory would suggest.

SUMMARY AND CONCLUSION

Despite the length and intensity of the debate over capital punishment, the role of the death penalty as a deterrent to murder remains a question not yet resolved. Comparative analyses of homicide rates for abolition and death penalty states as well as longitudinal examinations of homicide rates before and after abolition have brought most "careful" investigators to what Sellin (1959) has termed the inevitable conclusion: that the death penalty has no discernible effect as a deterrent to murder.[27] Careful examination of death penalty investigations, however, reveals both theoretical and methodological shortcomings that must not be ignored. On the former level, primarily only one aspect of the death penalty—its severity—has been examined, with one equally important, if not more important, aspects of punishment usually being ignored. Methodologically, a major difficulty with most investigations centers around the use of homicide—not first degree murder—statistics in examining the presumed deterrent effect of capital punishment. This practice rests upon the very questionable assumption that homicide statistics reported by the Federal Bureau of Investigation and the Public Health Service provide a "reasonably" good index of murder in the first degree, the offense of concern in examining the death penalty.

To provide a more refined and theoretically sound examination of the relationship between the death penalty and capital homicide, a survey was conducted of state bureaus of prisons throughout the country requesting admission statistics for first and second degree murder for 1967 and 1968. Examination of these data, along with homicide statistics issued by the Federal Bureau of Investigation for death penalty and abolition states revealed that: (1) average rates for all three offenses are consistently higher for death penalty than abolitionist jurisdictions, (2) rates for all three offenses are also consistently higher for retentionist states than their abolitionist neighbors, and (3) execution rates in death penalty states are only slightly inversely related to rates for all three offenses.

In sum, the evidence reported here falls within the negative pattern of findings of death penalty investigations which span some five decades (Bye, 1919; Sutherland, 1925). Our findings should not be viewed however, as simply "one more" investigation questioning the death penalty. As noted above, by our examining the question of capital punishment with figures for *capital homicide* a major objection to past investigations would appear to have been met. Nor, however, should our findings be interpreted as proving the ineffectiveness of the death penalty. There remain a number of theoretical and methodological questions about capital punishment yet to be examined, the importance of which would seem reflected by the continued efforts of such scholars as Messinger, Skolnick, Wolfgang, Zeisel and Bedau (1972) and others to probe deeper into the question

of the death penalty.[28] Hopefully criminologists will accept the challenge of moving beyond the traditional, but sterile, types of death penalty research that has characterized the last decade and probe deeper into the question of capital punishment.[29]

FOOTNOTES

[1]Despite the United States Supreme Court's recent ruling on the constitutionality of the death penalty, the question of capital punishment as a deterrent to crime remains an issue of both theoretical and practical importance. First, despite the length and intensity of the capital punishment debate both here and abroad, the role of the death penalty as a deterrent remains a question not yet resolved. (Gibbs, 1968; Van den Haag, 1969; Bedau, 1970) Second, in their recent ruling the Supreme Court *did not* categorically reject the death penalty as cruel and unusual punishment under the 8th Amendment. Rather, the high court only ruled capital punishment to be unconstitutional under certain conditions. Further, as evidenced by recent developments in the states of California and Florida, the high court *did not* forbid states to continue to legislate certain offenses as capital. Third, the Supreme Court's partial rejection of the death penalty was a 5 to 4 decision. There is no assurance that the balance of the court might not change in the near future, nor that the court might reconsider the death penalty question with the opposite result. One only needs to look at the case of thirteen states in this country that abolished the death penalty only to later restore it. Lastly, despite the reduced use of the death penalty in this country and abroad over the past few decades, its provision remains throughout much of the world, and clearly provides an issue worthy of further exploration (Gibbs, 1968; Van den Haag, 1969; Bedau, 1970).

[2]The sentiment of most sociologists on the question of capital punishment is probably well reflected in this often cited statement by Barnes and Teeters (1959, 314):

> Not a single assumption underlying the theory of capital punishment can be squared with the facts about human nature and social conduct that have been established through the progress of scientific and sociological thought in the last century and a half. In fact, the whole concept of capital punishment is scientifically and historically on a par with astrological medicine, the belief in witchcraft, or the rejection of biological evolution.

[3]In addition, McClellan (1961) points out that much of the evidence gathered on the deterrence question is questionable for it would appear to have been collected for the sole purpose of disproving the deterrent value claimed for punishment.

[4]In addition, Sellin's (1955, 1967) examinations of police safety and prison homicides, respectively, and the death penalty, are also often cited in discussions of capital punishment as a deterrent to homicide.

[5]Schuessler (1952) points out that this criticism indirectly affirms that the relative occurrence of murder is the result of a combination of social circumstances of which punishment is only one.

[6]Even this matching procedure has been objected to by some. Van den Haag (1969), for example, argues that past attempts to match similar

abolitionist and capital punishment states, have been unsuccessful for the two types of states are often "not similar enough." He fails to mention, however, in what way they are not similar enough.

[7] As Bedau (1970) points out, a review of Sellin's writings on the death penalty, which span from 1953–67, reveal a certain vacillation in the conclusions he draws. At times, he categorically denies the death penalty as a deterrent to homicide, and at other times he denies it as a superior deterrent to life imprisonment as a deterrent to homicide; two quite different conclusions.

[8] Both Beccaria (1809) and Bentham (1843) argued that the threat of punishment must be certain if it is to be real. If the probability of being detected and apprehended are slight or nonexistent, the threat of punishment will not be effective no matter how severe.

[9] In Beccaria's (1809, 76–76) words:

An immediate punishment is more useful; because the smaller the interval of time between the punishment and the crime, the stronger and more lasting will be the association of the two ideas of 'crime' and 'punishment,' so that they may be considered, one as the cause and the other as the unavoidable and necessary effect . . .

[10] Ross (1901), for example, argues that punishment should not only be administered publicly, but ceremoniously for it thus becomes a more powerful means of intimidating both the accused and onlookers.

[11] To act as an effective deterrent punishment must be rid of its personal element. As Ross (1901) argues; punishment must appear as a blow from God or Justice, not from the victor.

[12] Bedau (1970, 545) lists four such common assumptions. These are: (1) "homicides as measured by vital statistics are in a generally constant ratio to criminal homicides," (2) "the years for which the evidence has been gathered are representative and not atypical," (3) "however much fluctuations in the homicide rate owe to other factors, there is a non-negligible proportion which is a function of the severity of the penalty," and (4) "the deterrent effect of a penalty is not significantly weakened by its infrequent imposition."

[13] The homicide offense category used by the F.B.I. is "Murder and non-negligent manslaughter." It is defined as, "all willful felonious homicides as distinguished from deaths caused by negligence" (1970, 61). The Public Health Service defines homicide as "a death resulting from an injury purposely inflicted by another person." Intent to kill is not required to classify a death as a homicide. For instance, a death from an injury received during a fight is classified as a homicide even though there may have been no intent to kill. Other examples are the abandonment of newly born infants, or the accidental shooting of a bystander during an armed robbery (1967, 9).

The Federal Bureau of Prisons also provides statistics on homicide referrals to state and federal institutions which have been used as an index of murder. Their homicide category includes all types of murder and both negligent and non-negligent manslaughter (1970, 2).

As clearly reflected in the above definitions, these homicide offense categories depart substantially from most state's definitions of first degree murder; the offense of theoretical concern with the death penalty.

[14] Since the designation of guilt of murder in the first degree is a matter for the courts to decide, judicial statistics on court dispositions would provide a much more adequate indicator of capital homicides than existing sources. Unfortunately, the Federal Bureau of the Census discontinued gathering court statistics in 1945, under the title of *Judicial Criminal Statistics*.

[15] For an examination and empirical assessment of Schuessler's argument, see Bailey (1973).

[16] Students of homicide have long recognized and complained about the absence of adequate statistics on capital homicides (Wolfgang, 1958; Vold, 1932). To date, however, little to no progress has been made in filling this void (Bedau, 1967).

[17] This lack of concern for improved data by which to examine the death penalty question may well reflect the negative bias toward the death penalty that Bedau (1970) and McClellan (1961) attribute to many homicide investigators.

[18] For the states of Virginia, New Jersey, Oregon, Minnesota, and Connecticut, statistics were only available for the fiscal years 1967 and 1968. Further, statistics were only available for 1967 for the state of New Jersey. These cases were included in the analysis.

[19] With few exceptions, our investigation was received with interest and cooperation by state correctional authorities.

[20] Murder in the first degree typically includes the elements of premeditation and malice aforethought, while Murder in the second degree lacks the element of premeditation. "Premeditation designates intent to violate the law formulated prior to the activity," while "malice aforethought refers to the simple presence of intent to kill at the time of the act" (Gibbons, 1968, 346). To be convicted of Murder I, both premeditation and malice aforethought must be proven, where Murder II only requires proof of the latter.

[21] This is an unfortunate loss for Florida reported a total of 191 combined Murder I and II convictions for 1967 and 256 combined convictions for 1968.

[22] It should also be noted, however, that it is a fairly common practice in many prosecutor's offices to initially charge nearly all homicide suspects with Murder I, and "bargain down" thereafter. Whether these two practices "balance out" one another in the statistics can only be guessed at.

[23] Guttmacher (1960) estimates that at most only 2–4% of homicide offenders are found legally insane.

[24] For 1967, mean rates for first and second degree murder, total murder and homicide are .31, .73, 1.15, and 4.85, respectively. For 1968, corresponding rates are .50, .89, 1.38, and 5.48.

[25] Maine, Vermont, Rhode Island, Michigan, Minnesota, Wisconsin, Iowa, North Dakota, Oregon, West Virginia, Hawaii, and New York are normally considered abolition states. The death penalty may be prescribed, however, in Vermont, Rhode Island, North Dakota, and New York for certain offenses (see: Finkel, 1967; Bedau, 1967).

[26] Figures on homicide are used in the denominator of the execution index for figures for Murder I—the more appropriate offense—are not available for these years. A five year time interval in computing average execution rates was selected to provide greater stability in rate and to allow sufficient time for the presumed deterrent effect of executions to be realized.

[27] As Bedau (1970) points out, most investigations have not addressed themselves to the question of the death penalty as a deterrent, but rather to the question of whether the death penalty is a superior deterrent to "life" imprisonment. The latter, of course, is the issue of concern in this investigation.

[28] In a recent NAACP Conference on the death penalty, attended by Messinger, Skolnick, Wolfgang, Zeisel, Bedau and others, alarm was expressed over the "paucity of reliable social science evidence" on this important issue and the need for continued empirical research to address

◦

the still unanswered questions regarding the death penalty. (Bedau, 1973, 9, 12).

[29]This research is "sterile" in the sense that the same basic research designs, subject to the same theoretical and methodological shortcomings, have characterized most works since Sutherland's (1932), Schuessler's (1952) and Sellin's (1955, 1959) early investigations.

REFERENCES

BAILEY, WILLIAM C. (1973) "First and Second Degree Murder: Some Empirical Evidence," Cleveland, Ohio (mimeographed).

BARNES, HARRY E. and NEGLEY K. TEETERS (1959) *New Horizons in Criminology*. Englewood Cliffs, New Jersey: Prentice-Hall.

BECCARIA, CESARE (1809) *Essays on Crimes and Punishment*, 1st American Edition. New York: Gould Publishers.

BEDAU, HUGO A. (1967) *The Death Penalty in America*. Revised Edition. Garden City, New Jersey: Doubleday and Company, Inc.

———— (1971) "The Death Penalty in America," *Federal Probation*, 35, No. 2; 32–43.

———— (1973a) *The Case Against the Death Penalty*. New York: American Civil Liberties Union.

———— (1973b) "The Future of Capital Punishment: A Problem for Law and the Social Sciences." Project Statement Submitted to Russell Sage Foundation. Medford, Massachusetts (mimeographed).

BENTHAM, JEREMY (1843) *Principles of Penal Law*. Edinburgh.

BLOCH, HERBERT A., and GILBERT GEIS (1962) *Man, Crime and Society*. New York: Random House.

BYE, RAYMOND T. (1919) *Capital Punishment in the United States:* Committee on Philanthropic Labor of Philadelphia Yearly Meeting of Friends.

CALDWELL, ROBERT G. (1965) *Criminology*. New York: Ronald Press.

CALVERT, ERIC ROY (1931) *The Death Penalty Inquiry*. London: Gallancz Publishers.

CHAMBLISS, WILLIAM J. (1966) "The Deterrent Influence of Punishment," *Psychological Monographs*, Vol. 57.

———— (1967) "Types of Deviance and the Effectiveness of Legal Sanctions," *Wisconsin Law Review*, August, 1967.

———— (1969) *Crime and the Legal Process*, New York: McGraw-Hill.

CLARK, RAMSEY (1971) *Crime in America*. New York: John Simon & Schuster.

CUTHBERT, T. MARTIN (1970) "A Portfolio of Murders," *British Journal of Psychiatry*, 116: 1–10.

DANN, ROBERT H. (1935) The Deterrent Effect of Capital Punishment, *Friends Social Service Series*, Bulletin No. 29, Third Month.

DOLESCHAL, EUGENE (1969) "The Deterrent Effect of Legal Punishment," *Information Review on Crime and Delinquency*, 1, 1–17.

ERICKSON, MAYNARD L. and JACK P. GIBBS (1972) "The Deterrence Question: Some Alternative Methods of Analysis," Tucson, Arizona (mimeographed).

FEDERAL BUREAU OF THE CENSUS (1945) Judicial Criminal Statistics. Washington, D.C.

FEDERAL BUREAU OF INVESTIGATION (1968) *Crime in the United States: Uniform Crime Reports–1967*. Washington, D.C.

———— (1970) *Crime in the United States: Uniform Crime Reports–1970*. Washington, D.C.

FEDERAL BUREAU OF PRISONS (1970) *National Prisoner Statistics: State Prisoners: Admissions & Releases, 1970*. Washington, D.C.

FINKEL, ROBERT H. (1967) "A Survey of Capital Offenses," in William J. Chambliss (ed.), *Crime and the Legal Process*. New York: McGraw-Hill Book Co.

GIBBONS, DON C. (1968) *Society, Crime and Criminal Careers*. Englewood Cliffs, New Jersey: Prentice-Hall.

GIBBS, JACK P. (1968) "Crime, Punishment and Deterrence," *Southwestern Social Science Quarterly*, 48 (March): 515–530.

GILLIN, JOHN L. (1946) *The Wisconsin Prisoner*. Madison: University of Wisconsin Press.

GUTTMACHER, MANFRED (1960) *Mind of the Murderer*. New York: Farrar, Strauss and Cudahy.

JEFFERY, C. R. (1965) "Criminal Behavior and Learning Theory," *Journal of Criminal Law, Criminology and Police Science*, 56 (September): 294–300.

JOHNSON, ELMER HUBERT (1964) *Crime, Correction and Society*. Homewood, Ill.: The Dorsey Press.

KIRKPATRICK, CLIFFORD (1925) *Capital Punishment*. Philadelphia: Committee on Philanthropic

Labor of Philadelphia Yearly Meeting of Friends.

KNUDTEN, RICHARD D. (1970) *Crime in a Complex Society*. Homewood, Ill.: The Dorsey Press.

LAWES, LOUIS E. (1932) *Twenty Thousand Years in Sing Sing*. New York: Long and Smith.

MATTICK, HANS W. (1966) *The Unexplained Death: An Analysis of Capital Punishment*, 2nd ed. Chicago: John Howard Association.

McCLELLAN, GRANT S. (ed.) (1961) *Capital Punishment*. New York: H. W. Wilson Co.

MENNINGER, KARL (1968) *The Crime of Punishment*. New York: The Viking Press.

MESSINGER, SHELDON, JEROME SKOLNICK, MARVIL WOLFGANG, HANS ZEISEL, AND HUGO BEDAU (1972) NAACP Legal Defense And Educational Fund, Inc., Conference. New York. October.

MORRIS, NORVAL AND FRANK ZIMRING (1969) "Deterrence and Corrections," *Annals*, 381: 137–146.

PALMER, STUART (1960) *A Study of Murder*. New York: Thomas Y. Crowell Co.

PRESIDENT'S COMMISSION ON LAW ENFORCEMENT AND ADMINISTRATION OF JUSTICE (1967) *The Challenge of Crime in a Free Society*. Washington, D.C.

PUBLIC HEALTH SERVICE (1967) *Homicide in the United States: 1950–1964*. Washington, D.C.

PUTTKAMMER, ERNST W. (1953) *Administration of Criminal Law*. Chicago: University of Chicago Press.

QUINNEY, RICHARD A. (1970) *The Social Reality of Crime*. Boston: Little, Brown.

RECKLESS, WALTER C. (1969) "The Use of the Death Penalty," *Crime and Delinquency*, 15, No. 1: 43–56.

ROSS, E. A. (1901) *Social Control*. Cleveland: Case Western Reserve University Press.

SAVITZ, LEONARD D. (1958) "A Study of Capital Pun-

ishment," *Journal of Criminal Law and Criminology*, 49 (November–December): 338–341.

SCHUESSLER, KARL A. (1952) "The Deterrent Influence of the Death Penalty," *Annals of American Academy of Political and Social Science*, 284: 54–63.

SELLIN, THORSTEN (ed.) (1955) Quoted from Royal Commission on Capital Punishment (1949–1953). Report Great Britain Parliament. (Papers by Command md. 8932.) September. London: H. M. Stationary Office: 17–24.

——— (1959) *The Death Penalty*. Philadelphia: American Law Institute.

——— (1967) *Capital Punishment*. New York: Harper & Row, Publishers.

SUTHERLAND, EDWIN H. (1925) "Murder and the Death Penalty," *Journal of the American Institute of Criminal Law and Criminology*, 51: 522–529.

——— (1934) *Principles of Criminology*. Chicago: J. B. Lippincott Co.

SUTHERLAND, EDWIN H. AND DONALD R. CRESSEY (1970) *Principles of Criminology*. 7th Edition. Philadelphia: J. B. Lippincott Co.

TAFT, DONALD R. AND RALPH W. ENGLAND (1968) *Criminology*. 4th Edition. New York: Macmillan.

THOMAS, TREVOR (1964) *This Life We Take*, 3rd Edition. Washington, D.C.: Friends Committee on Legislation.

VAN DEN HAAG, ERNEST (1969) "On Deterrence and the Death Penalty," *Journal of Criminal Law, Criminology and Police Science*, 60, No. 2: 141–147.

VOLD, GEORGE B. (1932) "Can the Death Penalty Prevent Crime?" *The Prison Journal*, October: 3–8.

WOLFGANG, MARVIN E. (1958) *Patterns in Criminal Homicide*. New York: John Wiley and Sons, Inc.

31

Deterrence and Specific Offenses: Drunken Driving

JOHANNES ANDENAES

For many years the Scandinavian states have had strict legislation against drunken driving, coupled with strict enforcement policies. In Norway, for example, the law prohibits driving when the blood alcohol level exceeds .05 percent. Any person suspected of drunken driving must submit to a blood test. Upon conviction, the driver's license is automatically revoked for one year and, in addition, the consistent policy of the courts has been to impose a prison sentence. This strict policy seems to have had a considerable effect on driver attitudes with regard to driving under the influence of alcohol, and drunken driving now causes a very small percentage of highway accidents.[1] However, this legislation has been in force since a time when there were far fewer automobiles and accidents than today. It is therefore impossible to demonstrate statistically the impact of the legislation.

The situation is different in Great Britain, which recently adopted a new highway safety act.[2] The new legislation retained existing provisions which led to conviction only in cases involving a high degree of intoxication but added a new offense: driving

Source: "Deterrence and Specific Offenses," *University of Chicago Law Review*, Vol. 38, 1971, pp. 537–580. By permission of the author and publisher.

with an undue proportion of alcohol in the blood. The prescribed limit is eighty milligrams of alcohol in one hundred milliliters of blood (.08 percent). If the police have reasonable cause to believe that a driver has been drinking or has committed a moving traffic offense, they may ask the driver to take a breath test. The police may always request a breath test if the driver has been involved in an accident.[3] If the test indicates that the driver's blood alcohol content is probably above the legal limit, he may be arrested and taken to the police station. There the driver is requested either to submit to a blood test or, if he refuses, to furnish two urine samples for analysis. Failure to cooperate with these requests renders the driver liable to the same penalties that attach to driving with the proscribed blood alcohol content. Upon conviction for the new offense, the driver's license is automatically revoked for one year, except in extraordinary circumstances, and the driver is also subject to a fine of up to £ 100, four months imprisonment, or both.

An intensive publicity campaign, beginning two weeks prior to the effective date of the Act (October 9, 1967) and continuing for four months, accompanied passage of the new law. The campaign, estimated to have cost nearly £ 350,000, was particularly intense in the beginning and during the December holiday season. News coverage and comments in the press, radio and television provided additional publicity for the new law. As a result, there was great public awareness of the new law, and unusual interest in highway safety in general.

Highway accident statistics were carefully compiled to gauge the effect of the new legislation. This is one of the few instances in which an effort has been made to learn the precise effects of a new policy. According to official figures, highway accidents decreased substantially after the Act took effect.[4] The table below is compiled from those figures.

In the first nine months of 1967 there was no consistent trend in the incidence of highway accidents; there was an increase over the previous year during some months and a decrease in others. Overall, there was a two percent decrease in casualties as compared with 1966. Total traffic was estimated to have increased from 1966 by five percent in October, two percent in November, and to have decreased one percent in December. Neither the figures for 1966 nor those for the first nine months of 1967 reflect any remarkable change in comparison with previous years. In the 1950's and 1960's there had been a slow but steady upward trend in highway casualties. The annual number of fatalities had increased from about 5,000 in the early 1950's to approximately 8,000 during the period from 1964 to 1966.

After the passage of the Highway Safety Act of 1967, there was a larger decrease in serious accidents than in minor accidents. This result is in harmony with the findings of previous highway accident research showing that accidents involving drivers with blood alcohol levels over .08 percent tend to be more serious than the average accident.[5] Different drinking and driving habits during the holidays may explain the great reduction during the Christmas season. While changes in weather conditions may influence the figures for each month, the consistency of the figures is remarkable.

A striking pattern emerges if the accidents are correlated to the periods of the day in which they occurred. During working hours (8 a.m. to 6 p.m.) the decrease is slight: two percent of fatal and serious accidents in October and November; seven percent in December. Between 8 p.m. and 4 a.m. the figures were thirty-six percent in October, thirty-eight percent in November and forty-one percent in December. For the early morning hours considered alone they were even higher. The inevitable conclusion is that, in this socially important area, new legislation has had a considerable impact on people's behavior, at least temporarily.[6]

A study of about half of the fatal accidents in Great Britain in December, 1964, and January, 1965, showed that thirty percent of the fatally injured drivers had more than .05 percent blood alcohol content. Twenty-three percent of the fatally injured drivers had more than .08 percent blood alcohol content and twelve percent had more than .15 percent. Seventy-five percent of the drivers killed between 10 p.m. and 2 a.m. had at least .05 percent blood alcohol content compared with ten percent of the drivers killed between 6 a.m. and noon.[7] These figures do not mean, of course, that drinking was the cause of the accident in all cases, but the implications are obvious.

Several alternative hypotheses which might be thought to explain the decrease in highway accidents in Great Britain deserve discussion. It may be argued that increased awareness of the dangers of drunken driving rather than the threat of punishment led to the reduction in the number of accidents. This theory credits the publicity campaign rather than the law itself for causing the decrease. This argument, however, does not appear to be supported by the facts. There had been long-standing public discussion of the problem of drunken driving, and the publicity

Percentage Decrease in Highway Casualties in Great Britain, October to December, 1967, Compared with Same Period in 1966

	Oct.*	Nov.	Dec.	Oct.-Dec.	Christmas
Fatalities	17	20	33	23	36
Seriously injured	15	15	22	17	30
Slightly injured	11	13	20	15	

*Figures for October represent the period after the Act took effect.

campaign began two weeks before the new law took effect. Yet, in the first eight days of October, 1967, there was a reduction in highway casualties (compared with the same period in 1966) of only two percent—the same reduction obtained in the first nine months of 1967. In that portion of October after the Act took effect, the reduction was twelve percent. The decrease in fatalities was one percent in the eight days of October before the Act took effect and seventeen percent for the remainder of the month. Moreover, surveys conducted among drivers in September, 1967, and January, 1968, showed that drivers' toleration of drinking and driving and their opinion of the amount they could drink without affecting their driving remained substantially unchanged.[8] It seems clear that the dramatic reduction in highway accidents is directly attributable to the new legislation. The report of the surveys concluded that the publicity campaign had been valuable only in the sense that it made drivers aware of the new law.

Even if this conclusion is accepted, it does not necessarily follow that the explanation for the decrease in highway accidents is the effect of the new law on alcohol consumption before driving. An alternative hypothesis is that drivers, expecting increased police surveillance during the period immediately following the effective date of the new Act, exercised greater caution in driving quite apart from the Act's effect on alcohol consumption. It may well be that some part of the reduction of accidents is due to this factor. However, the distribution of the decrease in accidents according to time of day indicates that the most important factor was change in drinking and driving habits.

An important question is whether the effects of the new law are permanent. Other cases exist where an initial reduction in the commission of the proscribed offense, resulting from a new law accompanied by intensive publicity, has been followed by an eventual return to the previous level.[9] There is some indication of a similar development in Great Britain. In the last three months of the first year in which the Act was in effect, fatalities were nine percent less than in the previous year, seriously injured seven percent and slightly injured seven percent.[10] While these decreases are less impressive than those for the months

immediately following the effective date of the Act, the development is somewhat ambiguous. As stated above, December is probably the month in which the most social drinking occurs. In December, 1967, the decrease from the 1966 level was thirty-three percent and in December, 1968, the decrease was thirty-two percent. The figures for seriously injured were twenty-two and nineteen percent and for slightly injured, twenty and eighteen percent. Thus, the reduction in the level of casualties for this month was practically the same as in the first year of the law's operation. It is possible that other safety measures introduced by the Ministry of Transport during the year influenced these figures. Nevertheless, the Ministry's conclusion "that a fair proportion of the reductions are being maintained, although it is clearly too early to assess the long term effects,"[11] seems well founded. Postmortem examinations of fatally injured drivers revealed that the percentage of such drivers with blood alcohol content of over .08 percent fell from a previous average of twenty-eight percent to fifteen percent in the first year after the effective date of the Act.[12]

For the first twelve months after the effective date of the Act the total reduction in casualties compared to the previous year was ten percent. This represents 1,152 fewer fatalities, 11,177 fewer seriously injured and 28,130 fewer slightly injured. Opinion polls indicate that a majority of the population favors the new Act. But when fifteen percent of drivers who are fatally injured in highway accidents have blood alcohol content of over .08 percent and eleven percent have over .15 percent, a serious drunken driving problem still exists. It would be interesting to have comparable information from the Scandinavian countries, where drunken driving legislation is older and stricter.

A decrease in the deterrent effectiveness of the new law with the passage of time can be interpreted in three ways:

(1) The publicity in connection with the Act created an exaggerated fear of detection for drunken driving. Later, drivers began to make a more realistic assessment of the risk of detection, and consequently the deterrent effect was weakened. The law had been "oversold." In addition, many loopholes in

the law gradually became public knowledge, thus reducing the deterrent effect.

(2) The motivating force of a risk is dependent not only on the intellectual knowledge of the risk, but also on the degree of awareness. If, for example, one witnesses a traffic accident, his awareness of the risks of driving is greatly increased. In the same way, it can be assumed that the risk created by a new law is fresh in the minds of drivers, especially if enactment is accompanied by intense publicity. This high degree of risk awareness is gradually weakened, even when no reassessment of the risk is made. It is impossible to maintain the same level of publicity after the initial period of the Act's operation, and even if this were attempted, public sensitivity would probably be reduced when the publicity lost its news interest. Thus, a certain decrease in the "shock effect" of new legislation must be expected as a normal development.

(3) To the extent that the immediate reduction of highway casualties is due not to a changed pattern of alcohol consumption, but to the general driver expectation of more intense traffic control, the effect of the new law will necessarily be temporary.

These considerations could have been evaluated more effectively had surveys of drivers been made periodically. This would have been an important supplement to the accident statistics and would have revealed more about the psychological effects which led to the decreases. The survey research that has been done failed to cover such questions as how drivers assess the risk of detection.

The foregoing discussion has been concerned primarily with the awareness of the risk of punishment. However, I do not intend to imply that the effects of the new legislation are a result only of fear. Although survey research does not indicate a change in attitudes toward drinking and driving per se,[13] the desire to obey the law may well have played a considerable role in the change in behavior. Therefore, it cannot be assumed that similar legislation, even when enforced in the same manner as in Great Britain, will have the same effects in a country whose citizens view obedience to the law differently. My personal view, however, is that the major factor in the

success of the British legislation is mere deterrence. Creation of similar awareness of risk in a different society would have similar results if the drinking patterns and the social characteristics of the drivers were approximately the same.

Statistical evidence of the general preventive effects of punishment is scarce. What broader conclusions can be drawn from the British experience? Why do the British statistics yield the unequivocal results which are usually so difficult to obtain? Two points should be mentioned.

First, driving under the influence of alcohol differs from traditional crimes in that conduct not previously criminal has been made criminal, and it is therefore possible to measure the total impact of the new law. Crimes such as murder, robbery, rape and burglary remain substantially the same from one generation to the next. Changes relevant to the deterrent effect of the law usually concern the level of penalties or the level of enforcement. With such crimes, instead of measuring the total impact of the criminal provisions, there is the more difficult task of measuring the marginal effect of a change in the penalty or the degree of enforcement.

Second, in this case statistics of highway accidents provide an independent measure of the effects of the law. It is thus possible to avoid many of the difficulties of measuring the extent of violations. When the scope of a penal law is extended or contracted, it is theoretically possible to measure the total impact of the extension or contraction of the law. But "before" and "after" tests in these situations are especially difficult because criminal statistics do not provide a "before" measure for conduct that is now criminal or an "after" measure for conduct that has ceased to be a crime.

It should be noted that the number of highway accidents resulting from drinking may not be presumed to vary directly with the number of violations of the drunken driving laws. The effect of the law often may be that the driver reduces his consumption in order to decrease the risk of detection, even though his blood alcohol content remains higher than the maximum legal limit. Because the risk of an accident increases as the amount of alcohol increases, such reductions in consumption may be very important in relation to the goals of the law. If the legal limit is low, a high proportion of fringe violators may be of minor importance for highway safety. Since the aim of the law is to promote highway safety, the influence of the law on the number of accidents is a better measure of its efficacy than would be "before" and "after" statistics on the number of drivers whose blood alcohol content exceeds the limit.

Since the change in accident statistics shows the total impact of the new legislation, it is a poor basis for forecasting the effects of changes in the level of penalties or in the stringency of enforcement. Norwegians generally accept the proposition that non-suspension of prison sentences imposed on drunken driving has been very important in promoting the deterrent effect of the law. In Great Britain, the sentence usually consists of a fine and temporary loss of the driver's license. This contrast gives reason for questioning the importance of prison sentences. Perhaps fines and license revocation can achieve almost the same results as prison sentences; but further discussion on this point would require a much more thorough study.

For several reasons, a stronger deterrent effect may be expected from drunken driving laws than from laws against many other types of offenses. Driving under the influence of alcohol is not restricted to a criminal sub-culture, and it is not subject to severe moral condemnation. Nor is it behavior triggered by strong emotions. The decision whether or not to drink is usually made deliberately, as a rational choice; and the motivation to commit the offense is not strong. The law interferes only slightly with personal liberty. It asks the citizen neither to stop drinking nor to stop driving. It merely prohibits combining the two activities. Thus, the drunken driving situation is one in which common sense tells us that the risk of punishment can be expected to have more effect than in the case of many other offenses. This point should not, however, be overstated. There is no standard of the normal or average crime to which drunken driving is an exception. Every offense must be considered separately. Indeed, the motivational situation in many socially important types of offenses may be more similar to drunken driving than, for example, to murder or rape.

As enforcement of a law becomes more effective and penalties for its violation become stricter, the class of lawbreakers becomes more abnormal. It is no doubt correct that drunken driving was common throughout the population before the passage of strict criminal sanctions. Distribution of the violators is not so widespread after the passage of the new legislation. The composition of the class of drunken drivers will be altered. Instead of a fairly random sample of drivers, the drunken drivers will be primarily the problem drinkers and those with previous records for drunken driving—people less amenable to being deterred. This fact must be taken into account in forecasting the effect of any increase in the level of enforcement or punishment of an offense which is already strictly enforced and punished. He who invests in increased severity, has to expect diminishing returns.

32

Sanctions and Deviance:

Evidence and Remaining Questions

CHARLES R. TITTLE
and CHARLES H. LOGAN

The last few years have witnessed a resurgence of interest among social scientists in the possible effects of negative sanctions in producing conformity to norms. During the first half of this century deterrence ideas were often the object of debate and research. Debate, however, was usually conducted on an ideological level, and the extant research generally suggested that punishment was of minor importance as a behavioral influence (Ball, 1955; Tappan, 1960: 243–255). As a result, many social scientists came to regard the question as either theoretically uninteresting or as empirically non-problematic.

For instance, most major theories of deviance developed in this century have given little attention to the role of sanctions. Instead they have emphasized special motivations stemming from socialization into unusual normative contexts, failure of conventional socialization, psychodynamic problems, or pressures generated by social contexts (Cohen, 1966). In addition, general theories of social order or social organization have seldom attributed major significance to sanctions as a means of generating conformity.

Source: "Sanctions and Deviance: Evidence and Remaining Questions," *Law and Society Review*, Spring, 1973, pp. 371–382. By permission of the authors and publisher.

Confidence that the deterrence issue has been empirically resolved is evident in much criminological writing. For instance, one criminological classic unabashedly asserts that punishment "does not deter . . . [nor] does it act as a deterrent upon others . . ." (Tannenbaum, 1938: 478), while a well-known contemporary criminology text concludes that one of the limitations of legal punishment is that "it does not prevent crime in others or prevent relapse into crime" (Reckless, 1967: 508).

Such conclusions are typically based on two kinds of evidence. The most widely cited concerns the relationship between capital punishment and homicide (Sutherland and Cressey, 1966; 335–353). This literature includes studies comparing homicide rates of similar social units differing in legal provision for capital punishment (Schuessler, 1952; Sellin, 1967), studies comparing homicide rates of the same social units at times when capital punishment was operative and at times when it was not (Schuessler, 1952; Walker, 1965: 238–241; Mattick, 1963), studies of homicide frequency immediately following 1935), and illustrative case or historical materials (Horton and Leslie, 1965: 165–169; Barnes and Teeters, 1959: 315–317). This work has been interpreted as remarkably consistent in discounting a deterrent effect for capital punishment (Morris and Hawkins, 1969; Walker, 1965).

While death penalty research focused on the effect of punishment (or legal provision for punishment) in deterring potential offenders generally, a second body of literature treated the question of whether punishment other than death or permanent incarceration deters future deviance among those who personally experience the punishment (*i.e.*, does punishment reduce recidivism?). A study of corporal punishment found it ineffective in deterring further offense (Caldwell, 1944), and a study of both serious and minor offenders (Morris, 1951) found no correlation between cumulative duration of separate, very short sentences ("days in") and cumulative length of time between discharges and reconvictions ("days out"). Furthermore, recidivism rates for released convicts were generally reported to be quite high (Glueck and Glueck, 1943: 121; Vold, 1954; Westover, 1958). Laboratory experiments with animals also provided some indirect evidence for the pessimistic view of sanctions. Although the effectiveness of punishment in conditioning animals has been controversial, the prevailing interpretation, up until recently, seems to have been that negative reinforcement is at best inefficient as a behavioral conditioner (Skinner, 1953; Bandura, 1962).[1]

Some evidence in past research did suggest that the probability of sanction was an important variable for some types of deviance and in some circumstances. For instance, illustrative historical material showed that in some cases policy immobilization was followed by increased crime, that increased police surveillance was followed by decreases in illegal behavior, and that employment of technical innovations in police techniques preceded dramatic declines in various types of deviance (Toby, 1964; Andenaes, 1952; Hall, 1952). Nevertheless the bulk of the research seemed to indicate to most scholars that the idea of deterrence was not empirically valid.

CONTEMPORARY PERSPECTIVES

Recent shifts in attention from the deviant act itself to social reactions to deviance (Gibbs, 1966), however, have led sociologists to reconsider negative

sanctions as independent variables. The result has been a critical reassessment of death penalty and recidivism research and the stimulation of broader research interests concerned with the relationship between sanctions and behavior.

Critics of capital punishment research have pointed up a number of deficiencies (Tappan, 1960: 253–255; Walker, 1965: 241; Zimring, 1971; Logan, 1971a), the most important of which is the failure of the research to consider the probability (or the perceived probability) of imposition of the death penalty rather than simply the legal provision for its imposition. It has been pointed out that the mere presence or absence of a possible death penalty may be irrelevant as a deterrent to murder, but that the deterrent effect of a death penalty imposed with a fairly high degree of certainty is still unknown. Only Schuessler's study of capital punishment attempted to take this variable into account (Schuessler, 1952). He devised a crude index of the certainty of execution for the various states of the U. S. Despite the fact that he was dealing with conditions that tend to reduce an association (low probability cases and an attenuated distribution), he nevertheless found a negative (−.29), although non-significant, correlation between certainty and the homicide rate.

Second, historical examples or anecdotal material cited as evidence against the deterrent theory have been shown to be predicated on faulty logic (Walker, 1965: 238; Zimring, 1971). The fact that crime still occurs despite the presence of capital punishment is insufficient basis for inference without additional data concerning the number of non-criminals who may have been deterred by consideration of the possible penalty. In like manner, confessions of convicted murderers indicating that they did not take the penalty into account cannot permit inferences about the number of potential murderers who may have taken it into account.

Third, it has been observed that even if the validity of the capital punishment studies were impeccable, they would still permit only the conclusion that capital punishment adds nothing additional in deterrent power above that which may be generated by all other punishments to which potential offenders are subject. A really meaningful test of the deterrent effect of capital punishment would require that it be compared with the alternative of no punishment at all. If the threat of death does not deter murder to any greater extent than simply the threat of imprisonment, this cannot be interpreted to mean that all types of sanctions are ineffective for all types of deviant acts. This is especially true since homicide is generally considered to be a special kind of deviance (Chambliss, 1967). Thus, even though the death penalty literature provides a reasonable rationale for abolishing capital punishment in modern society, it does not afford an adequate basis for drawing conclusions about the deterrent effect of sanctions in general.

Similarly, the recidivism literature has been found deficient in addressing the issue of whether negative sanctions generate conformity. First, and most important, recidivism studies are relevant only to the question of whether punishment affects the future behavior of those punished. It is theoretically defensible to postulate that punishment might generate more deviance for those punished, but at the same time still be a powerful deterrent for those not punished (Tittle, 1969; Thorsell and Klemke, 1972). Indeed, the same mechanisms that possibly generate secondary deviance (stigmatization and labeling) may deter the non-stigmatized (Lemert, 1967). In any case, recidivism is of only slight significance compared to the question of general deterrence. Even 100 percent success in specific deterrence (*i.e.*, complete elimination of recidivism) would have little impact on crime rates, since only a tiny proportion of offenders are ever in a position to become recidivists in the first place (Gould and Namenwirth, 1971: 256–257).

Second, even with regard to the question of specific deterrence (future behavior of the punished), the recidivism literature is far from compelling. One problem in the use of such data is that recidivism may stem from ancillary conditions involved in incarceration that negate the deterrent effect of punishment. For example, increased fear of sanction—the deterrent objective of imprisonment—may be eroded by socialization into a deviant subculture or by association with deviant role models while incarcerated (Clemmer, 1940; Wheeler, 1961). Similarly, lack

of recidivism may result from rehabilitative efforts undertaken while the individual was in prison rather than from deterrence based on fear of punishment. Recidivism rates, therefore, probably indicate more about the conditions under which punishment is administered than about the punishment *per se*.

Furthermore, the most valid test of the specific deterrent effect of legal sanctions would be one that compared recidivism rates of those punished with the recidivism of offenders who escaped any contact with the law. There are really no data of this type (see Uniform Crime Reports, 1967: 37 for the closest approximation—re-arrest is highest for those whose cases were previously dismissed or who were acquitted), but it is hard to imagine that offenders who escape arrest or detection would be less likely to repeat an offense than those who are processed through the legal system (Packer, 1968: 46). Comparison of probationers with incarcerees does suggest that recidivism is greatest among the incarcerees (Levin, 1971), but there is probably a selective factor involved (Wilkins, 1969), and probation is itself a form of legal sanction. Consequently, one might be justified in concluding from such comparisons that incarceration adds nothing in deterrent power above what is achieved with the lesser penalty, but he would not be justified in concluding that incarceration or punishment in general is not a deterrent.

But even apart from these considerations, the recidivism data provide a weak platform to support an anti-deterrent argument. Logical and interpretative difficulties are paramount (Walker, 1965: 242–260; Wilkins, 1969), and in addition, the data are less contrary to the deterrence argument than is usually assumed. While there are many variations and complexities, the available follow-up data suggest that only about 35 percent of the released inmates return to prison (Glaser, 1964: 13–35). Moreover, a recent study conducted by the FBI suggests that legal sanctions may be more of a specific deterrent than even the FBI is willing to admit. All arrestees released in 1963 were traced six years by means of FBI arrests reports. Although 65 percent were re-arrested on some charge within six years, only 23 percent (40 percent of those re-arrested during the first four years) had been reconvicted by the end of the fourth year (Uniform Crime Reports, 1967: 41), and extrapolation suggests that the overall reconviction rate is far below 35 percent.[2]

Third, the pessimistic conclusions drawn from laboratory work have been tempered by contemporary work that points up the limitations of conditioning principles, particularly when applied to people, and demonstrates that under some circumstances aversive control is both effective and efficient (Bandura, 1969: 293–353). In addition, recent work shows that vicarious reinforcement (social learning), including negative reinforcement, may play an important part in human behavior determination (Bandura, 1969: 118–216; Bandura and Walters, 1963).

RECENT RESEARCH

In addition to reassessment of capital punishment and recidivism research, contemporary perspectives have led to a series of studies which suggest that sanctions may be more important than previously thought.

Direct investigative evidence Some of the most significant data comes from laboratory work on vicarious reinforcement (Bandura, 1969: 118–216; Bandura and Walters, 1963). Fascinating experiments have demonstrated that behavior in many circumstances can be influenced by fear of punishment or anticipation of reward generated by observing others being punished or rewarded for various kinds of behavior. If such effects are generalizable to larger contexts, it may indicate that general deterrence of deviance (or generation of conformity), to the extent that it occurs, is possible because citizens vicariously identify with those who are punished for having been caught in deviance. And, of course, the same process might account for the failure of general deterrence since much crime goes unpunished and is often rewarding.

Additional evidence stems from a series of sociological and social psychological investigations addressed to one or another aspect of this problem. One was a study of parking violations on a Midwestern university campus (Chambliss, 1966). Chambliss reported findings to indicate that an increase in severity and certainty of penalties led to a significant reduction in violations by many faculty members, especially by those who had previously been frequent violators. But he also found that for a significant proportion of the sample the change in sanctions was irrelevant, since some never violated the rules anyway and others only violated infrequently.

A second investigation was conducted by Schwartz and Orleans (1967; see also Schwartz, 1969). With the cooperation of the Internal Revenue Service they were able to relate degree of tax compliance to "sanction threat" and "conscience appeal." Subjects were randomly assigned to treatment and control groups. Prior to submission of tax returns, one group was subjected to an interview containing questions that suggested the possibility of sanction for dishonesty in reporting income. Another group was asked questions designed to remind them of their moral obligations, while a third group was interviewed but asked no "conscience appeal" or "sanction threat" questions. A fourth group was not interviewed. The results showed that both "sanction threats" and "conscience appeals" could induce greater conformity (both treatment groups had significantly higher reported income than the control groups), but "conscience appeal" was found to be more effective. The degree of effectiveness of each of the inducements, however, was found to vary by social characteristics of the respondents, particularly socioeconomic status. It was further discovered that "sanction threats" apparently generated, among a minority of subjects (35 percent), attempts to make up through greater deduction what they had "lost" in more honest reporting of income. Thus, despite the fact that the independent variables were not really "threats" or "conscience appeals," and there was no measurement of the perceived reality or perceived probability of imposition of the "sanction," the study strongly suggests that reminding individuals of the possibility of negative sanctions does help secure conformity. But it seems that bringing to mind possible sanctions may not be as effective in achieving compliance with norms as bringing to mind other things.

Sinha (1967) conducted an experiment in which a difficult task was attempted by pairs of individuals, one of whom was a stooge. Successful completion of the task merited a financial reward. According to the rules, the subject was not to help in actual performance of the task but was only to give instructions. Material aid in response to requests for help, therefore, represented cheating. In one condition the subjects were threatened with punishment for violation, but not in the other. The results showed significantly fewer individuals cheating in the sanction threat condition. The data revealed, however, that among those who broke the rules, the number of violations in the sanction threat condition did not differ significantly from the non-threat condition. Hence, the results suggest that sanctions may be successful deterrents only for potential offenders. Once norms are violated, the sanction threat loses its potency for inhibiting further violations.

These studies were followed by two similar investigations undertaken simultaneously but independently. In one, Gibbs (1968) calculated, from FBI and prisoner statistics, indexes of severity and certainty of imprisonment for homicide. Analysis of the relationship between these indexes and the homicide rate by states of the U. S. revealed a substantial negative association. The findings therefore suggested a deterrent effect for imprisonment that increases with greater probability of lengthy incarceration.

Tittle's research (1969) employed official statistics to construct indexes of certainty and severity of imprisonment for each of seven major offense categories and for a total category of felonies. These indexes were based on a logic similar to that used by Gibbs but were somewhat different in actual content. The results of the analysis of the relationship between these indexes and crime rates for states of the U. S. led to a conclusion that high probability of imprisonment was associated with lower crime rates. The efficacy of severity of punishment, however, appeared to be limited to the offense of homicide. Further analysis suggested a complex interaction between certainty and severity of punishment in their influence on various offense rates. In general it appeared that certainty of imprisonment was associated with lower crime rates independently of severity while severity was associated with lower crime rates only for particular levels of certainty.

The Gibbs and Tittle articles almost immediately stimulated scholarly response. Gray and Martin

(1969) re-analyzed Gibbs' data and Bailey, Martin, and Gray (1971) and Logan (1971a and 1972) reanalyzed Tittle's data using more rigorous and demanding techniques. In all instances the original findings were confirmed except that Logan's results suggested that severity of punishment was more important than originally thought. Chiricos and Waldo (1970), however, employed indexes modeled after Tittle's and examined the relationships between the certainty and severity of imprisonment and crime rates for various periods of time, and attempted to relate percentage changes in the indexes from one time period to another. They noted a great deal of inconsistency in the results and concluded that the evidence could not be accepted as support for deterrence theory. Furthermore, they challenged the validity of the research by Tittle and Gibbs on the grounds that the procedures used produced spurious results. They argued that the simulation technique used by Tittle to estimate the degree of possible spurious association produced by the fact that the ratios representing the independent and the dependent variables contained a figure common to the numerator of one and the denominator of the other was not correct.

Logan (1971a and 1971b) responded to the Chiricos and Waldo attack by pointing out: (1) that their findings concerning certainty of imprisonment and crime rates are actually quite consistent and impressive (they concede this point but argue that it is an artifact); (2) that relating percentage changes between two indexes is misleading and unreliable, especially since slight and erratic changes can show up as strong and widely varying percentages where the base on which the percentage is calculated is low; (3) that arbitrary selection of widely separated points in time for computation of the measures of change in indexes is illegitimate; and (4) that by studying only specific offenses and small time periods without the inclusion of a "total offense" category they maximized the likelihood of an unstable finding. Bailey, Gray, and Martin (1971) in another critique showed that much of the data used by Chiricos and Waldo were incomparable and incomplete. Furthermore, both responses to the Chiricos and Waldo paper demonstrated that the methodological attack on the work of Gibbs and Tittle was without merit. Thus the conclusions in support of deterrence theory appear to be well-grounded, and some basis for interpreting the Chiricos and Waldo finding concerning certainty of punishment as supportive of the deterrence hypothesis has been established.

Three other investigations using official statistics have provided additional supportive data. In one, Logan (1971a) examined original arrest data provided by the FBI. Using higher order statistical techniques, he found a general negative relationship between crime rate and probability of arrest for all offenses except homicide. In a second, Phillips (1972) standardized a measure of crime rate to take account of varied etiological factors and employed a probability model for analysis. His work showed that a major portion of the variance in homicide rate is attributable to certainty and severity of punishment.

A third study analyzed the relationship between arrest clearance rates and crime for all the counties and municipalities in Florida (Tittle and Rowe, 1973a). The results clearly support a deterrent argument, although the effect was found to be contingent upon the probability of arrest reaching a certain minimal level (about 30 percent).

A different type of research has been reported by Salem and Bowers. They related the severity of sanctioning policy in academic contexts to the incidence of self-reported rule-breaking by samples of students. In one analysis (1970), they found a negative relationship between severity of sanctioning policy and incidence of most types of offense, although the magnitude of the relationship varied considerably from offense to offense. They argued that the apparent deterrent effect was probably not direct, but rather resulted from the general normative climate that prevailed. But in a later, more careful analysis (Bowers and Salem, 1972) they concluded that the sanctioning policy had no effect at all, but was rather a dependent variable representing response to deviant behavior. If their later analysis using only one type of deviance is representative of all the deviances considered in the study, then the Salem and Bowers data represent a contradiction to deterrence theory in regard to severity of sanction. But had the investigators been able to take into account the certainty or perceived certainty of the imposition

of the penalties rather than simply the formal policy, the results might have been different.

Jensen's study (1969) of the relationship between beliefs about the probability of apprehension/punishment and delinquency (both self-reported and official) among adolescents provides further confirmation of the idea that sanctions affect behavior. Although his measure of "probability belief" was very crude, being the expressed agreement with a statement concerning high probability of apprehension/punishment for delinquent offenses generally, the data still reveal a negative relationship between perceived certainty and delinquency. The magnitudes of those associations are not compelling, but they are especially interesting because they deal with deterrence at the primary level of cognition. The findings point toward the possibility that deterrence may be more a matter of belief than of reality. Actual characteristics of sanctions such as severity, certainty, or even simple possibility may be important only to the extent that they generate particular kinds of beliefs about the consequences of deviance. Jensen's work suggests considerable misperception of the actual probability of apprehension/punishment (shared misunderstanding). It is possible that the effectiveness of sanctions hinges on the perceived certainty of their imposition, a factor which may vary from individual to individual and from social group to social group.

Some data on this point are provided by Waldo and Chiricos (1972). They surveyed a random sample of students at a southern university concerning perceptions and knowledge of sanction characteristics and two types of criminal behavior—marijuana use and theft. They found that perceived certainty of apprehension and penalty were strongly related in an inverse direction with both forms of self-reported illegal behavior, although they were more strongly related to marijuana use than to theft. The authors interpreted their findings to indicate that perceived certainty of formal sanctions does serve as a deterrent, but that such deterrence is more likely to be operative with respect to crimes that lack wide moral support. Where a norm is morally buttressed, deterrence on an official level may be secondary to deterrence by informal sanctions or to control by internalized inhibitions. The authors were unable to find support for deterrence ideas concerning perceived severity of sanctions, although a more straightforward measure and more sophisticated analysis might have led to greater confidence in the finding.

Finally, the effect on classroom cheating of a sanction threat and a moral appeal were tested experimentally (Tittle and Rowe, 1973b). The experiment demonstrated that this type deviance could be substantially deterred by a threat of detection and punishment. The study also revealed a differential effect for females and for those who had greater need to cheat. The evidence was interpreted as strongly supportive of deterrence theory, at least in a situation where a norm lacks moral support, behavior is instrumental, and there is little commitment on the part of the offenders to the deviance.

Indirect investigative evidence Other research has addressed the deterrence question more indirectly. One such study used questionnaire responses of college students (Rettig and Rawson, 1963). The students were asked to judge the probability that a hypothetical person would engage in different kinds of unethical behavior under varied conditions. The conditions represented variations in the utility of the act, the probability of apprehension and the severity of punishment, the intent of the act, and the type of victim. The findings indicated that severity of punishment was the most important source of variation, of the six considered, in predictions of probable actions of the hypothetical characters.

Rettig and Pasamanick (1964) conducted a similar study in which the same questionnaire was administered to students who had one year previously participated in an experiment where they were required to perform an essentially impossible task for pay. Any reported success represented unethical conduct. They found that previously identified cheaters were far less sensitive to punishment as a determinant of behaviors by the hypothetical individuals. Based on the assumption that the subjects were reflecting their own sensitivities in judging the behavior of the hypothetical persons, they concluded that "the reinforcement value of a censure is the most significant determinant which

predicts unethical behavior" (Rettig and Pasamanick, 1964: 112).

Rettig (1964) extended this general approach by comparing the "ethical risk sensitivity" of reformatory inmates and a matched sample of college students. Prisoners' predictions as to whether a hypothetical bank teller would embezzle funds were affected more by the teller's perception of severity of censure than by consideration of gain, expectancy of discovery, or intention to steal versus intention to borrow. Students did not differ from prisoners in the primacy of severity of censure as a determinant, but the students' predictions were affected more than the prisoners' by considerations of gain and likelihoods of detection.

Sinha (1968) refined the original Rawson and Rettig study by changing somewhat the scale and hypothetical situations and by including other ethically dubious behaviors. He found that decisions apparently involved varying sets of considerations for various types of ethical situations and decisions. Although expectancy of censure was found to have the highest mean importance, it was concluded that expectancy of censure and reinforcement value are interrelated so that the reinforcement value of a censure is contingent upon its expectancy.

Another study compared a sample of incarcerated delinquents with a sample of non-delinquents in terms of accuracy of knowledge about probability of arrest and conviction for various crimes, likelihood that they might commit various criminal acts, and for those who thought they might commit the deviant acts, perceptions of the probability that they would be arrested and convicted (Claster, 1967). Although the findings revealed no significant differences between delinquents and non-delinquents in knowledge of the probability of arrest and conviction, they did show that delinquents who thought they might commit various hypothetical crimes perceived the probability of personal arrest and conviction to be lower than did the non-delinquents who thought they might commit the hypothetical crimes.

Piliavin and his associates focused on the question of whether the potential "personal cost" of informal sanctions differentiated delinquents from non-delinquents (Piliavin, Hardyck, and Vadum, 1968) and whether this variable allowed prediction of cheating behavior in a laboratory situation (Piliavin, Vadum, and Hardyck, 1969). They measured the personal costs of informal sanctions with questionnaire responses concerning the importance of evaluation by significant others such as parents and teachers. In a survey they found a negative relationship between score on the "costs" scale and delinquency, and in a laboratory experiment they found that "low cost" boys cheated more than "high cost" boys.

Horai and Tedeschi (1969) were interested in the extent to which one person can induce obedience to commands by the use of sanctions. They had college students play an interpersonal game (Prisoners' Dilemma) in which one party was able to employ sanctions in an effort to induce the other player to act contrary to his self-interest. They varied the probability that the sanction would be imposed (credibility) and the magnitude of the sanction (severity). Both credibility and severity were found to be related to degree of compliance. Faley and Tedeschi (1971) repeated the experiment with ROTC cadets, varying the status of the threatener as well as the severity and credibility of the threats. The results showed greater compliance to threats issued by high status persons than by low status persons, and they confirmed that credibility and severity were significant influences on degree of compliance. Gahagan, *et al*. (1970) repeated the experiment, varying the pattern of punishment as well as the credibility. They found no effect for patterning, but did confirm the importance of credibility. Thus these experiments suggest that compliance to commands is influenced by sanction threats.

These studies are all suggestive that negative sanctions have an important bearing on behavior. But the data are too oblique and the studies too dependent upon dubious assumptions to permit confident interpretation of the results in terms of the deterrence hypothesis. Rettig and Rawson did not ask the subjects to assess how they themselves would behave in the hypothetical situations; they were simply asked to predict behavior of the hypothetical person. Thus

they were probably measuring what variables the subjects thought are generally operative in behavior determination but not necessarily the ones which are. Claster neglected to examine directly the relationship between self-assessed likelihood of deviant behavior and perceptions of the probability of arrest and conviction. He reports only differences in perceived probability of sanctions between delinquents and non-delinquents who admitted the likelihood of hypothetical deviant behavior. The Piliavin studies did not measure the subjects' perceptions of the probability that significant others would find out their transgressions, the likelihood that "costs" would ensue from discovery, nor even the probability of getting caught. They simply assumed that all these probabilities were high or at least high enough to produce an effect. And finally, the studies involving interpersonal control did not provide real rewards for winning. Moreover, obedience to commands by an individual may be quite different than conformity to social norms or laws.

Case material Additional evidence consists of recently compiled illustrative or historical case material. Important variations have been observed in some types of crimes when police were immobilized (Clark, 1969; Andenaes, 1966), and some evidence of decrease in crime following the employment of technical innovations in police techniques or of greater surveillance have been recorded (Zimring, 1971: 68–73; Walker, 1965: 241–242; Conklin, 1972: 143; Cramton, 1969). Probably the best data of this type have been reported by Ross, Campbell, and Glass (1970). They studied the effect of the British breathalyser law of 1967, using time series data. The legislation provided for suspected drinkers or traffic offenders to be tested on the spot with breath machines and, if ultimately convicted in court, to receive a mandatory penalty. If fewer traffic casualties can be taken as an indicator of fewer cases of drinking while driving, then the data demonstrate considerable effect. Since the law was designed to increase the probabilty of detection and penalty for the offense, the results constitute impressive support for a deterrent hypothesis.

Case material concerning severity of penalties, however, has not supported a deterrent effect for sanctions (Tornudd, 1968), and some which presumably does reveal such an effect is questionable (see Campbell and Ross, 1968; Glass, 1968). The most unequivocal example is a study by Schwartz (1968). His analysis of rape in Philadelphia before and after increased penalties provided no basis for concluding that increased severity of sanctions significantly affected the amount of rape. Thus, the case material compiled in recent years is generally consistent with other research in suggesting that sanctions may have some deterrent effect when the certainty of imposition is reasonably high, but that severity of sanctions in the absence of certainty has little bearing on deviance.

EMPIRICAL ISSUES

Almost all research since 1960 supports the view that negative sanctions are significant variables in the explanation of conformity and deviance. Therefore social scientists would appear to be on firm ground in at least treating the issue of deterrence as an open question. Enough suggestive evidence has been compiled to warrant systematic research efforts and to mandate serious theoretical consideration of the role of sanctions in human behavior and social organization. It is clear, however, that the evidence is not conclusive. At this point we can safely say only that sanctions apparently have some deterrent effect under some circumstances. It is now necessary to undertake careful research in an attempt to specify the conditions under which sanctions are likely to be important influences on behavior. Consideration of past research suggests many gaps in our knowledge. A variety of questions must be investigated before effective theory building can be undertaken and before social science can claim to speak with much confidence about the role of sanctions in human affairs.

First, the influence of type of norm on degree of deterrence that is likely to result from the application of sanctions must be established. Sociological literature suggests that some types of norms are likely to be obeyed irrespective of sanctions, while others are likely to be disobeyed frequently despite provisions for sanctions. Yet there is little empirical data on the question. Norms vary in the degree of their generality, their importance, their legitimacy, and their legal status. It is necessary to establish: (1) whether sanctions are more likely to be successful in producing conformity to rules that are widely shared or to those that are specific to a given situation, (2) the relative effectiveness of sanctions in deterring violations of rules generally felt to be very important and in deterring those of less importance, (3) the extent to which "legitimate" as opposed to "arbitrary" rules are subject to enforcement by sanctions, (4) whether deterrence is more likely with legal norms than for other norms, and (5) whether rules that have moral support are more enforceable by sanctions than are those that lack such moral support.

Second, it must be determined how characteristics of given types of behavior affect the degree of likely deterrence of deviance. Variations along this dimension include the perceived intrinsic or utilitarian rewards of different types of behavior as well as the rationality (subject to reasoned calculation as opposed to emotionality or impulsiveness) of different kinds of behavior. Furthermore, deterrence may be more or less effective depending upon the motivations which lead to given acts of deviance. Thus one could imagine that acts of rebellion, acts designed to create martyrdom, or acts for the purpose of reinforcing deviant identities would be less deterrable than acts that have private utility for the actor. By the same token, deviance that stems from a sense of injustice may be less deterrable than deviance that stems from attempts to exploit others. Another possibly important distinction in this regard concerns the position of the act in a series of potential deviant acts. Thus a first offense may be more sensitive to sanctions than are repeated offenses. Some experimental evidence suggests that once a sanction threat has failed to deter, its potency as a deterrent to further rule-breaking is eroded. This distinction is akin to the frequently noted difference between general and specific deterrence. General deterrence is said to occur when potential offenders are deterred by fear of sanction while specific deterrence refers to inhibition of repeated acts of deviance by those who have been sanctioned.

Third, the way in which deterrence of deviance varies by characteristics of potential rule-breakers has to be specified. Such things as social class, age, sex, race, social visibility, personal alienation from the political and social system, and moral commitments to the norms may be major determinants of whether a deterrent effect is probable in a given situation (Zimring and Hawkins, 1968).

Fourth, the way in which variations in sanction characteristics themselves influence the likely degree of conformity must be clarified. Characteristics of sanctions which might be important in this regard are: (1) the probability of imposition of the sanction, (2) the severity of the sanction, (3) whether the sanction is imposed on an informal or formal level, (4) the status of the sanctioner, and (5) the celerity with which the sanction is applied (Clark and Gibbs, 1965). Not only must the importance of each of these dimensions be specified, but also their interrelationship in influencing conformity in various contexts must be clarified. It may be that some sanction characteristics can become operative only when a certain level has been reached with respect to another characteristic. Thus it could be that formal sanctions can be effective only if reinforced by informal sanctions or if the certainty of imposition is high. In like manner, severity of sanction may be important only when minimal levels of certainty exist.

But more important than the actual character of sanctions may be beliefs or perceptions about the characteristics of sanctions. It is entirely possible that ignorance of sanction characteristics constitutes the major deterrent mechanism (if such a mechanism is operative), at least with respect to legal norms. After all, the probability of sanction is in reality very slight (Logan, 1971a) and the severity of punishment frequently turns out to be relatively light (National Prisoner Statistics, N. D.). Yet the general anxiety that stems from uncertainty may influence the behavior of some in a very powerful way. If primary deterrence (individual fear of sanctions) does influence behavior, then cognitions could well be linked to variations in rates of deviance, independent of the actual situation. For example, it seems likely that the lesser propensity of middle class people to engage in ordinary crime may stem partly from a gross over-estimate of the likelihood of apprehension for them personally and a conception of punishment as more severe than it really is. They typically have little personal contact with legal processes and therefore have no realistic basis for judgment. Lower class persons, on the other hand, usually have enough contact with the legal system to know that the likelihood of apprehension and punishment is slight and to know that typical punishments are not unbearable. But even if objective knowledge about sanctions were uniform throughout society, people from different groups would still have differing perceptions of the personal costs to them that would be entailed by different sanctions. Hence, perceptions of sanctions is a crucial variable for further analysis.

While it seems reasonable to postulate that perceptions of sanction characteristics are related to amounts and kinds of deviance, it is also important to note that the relationship might not be straightforward or linear. For some, a given amount of perceived risk may add an incentive for deviance (Werthman, 1969). But this incentive may diminish beyond a certain point—the risk may become so great that it is no longer a gamble. For such persons the relationship between perceived sanction characteristics and deviance probability would be U-shaped. For others the relationship may be linear or log linear. These are only speculative possibilities; the point is that the relationship between actual or perceived characteristics of sanctions and probability of deviance for individuals or for social collectivities is unknown.

Furthermore, the relation between sanctions and deviance is probably circular, at least for legal sanctions. Identifying the causal effects of sanctions on deviance and accurately describing their strengths and forms under different conditions will necessitate separation of the reciprocal effects that increased amounts of deviance may have on sanction-reactions.

Fifth, the interrelationship of the above described variables in the generation of conformity must be clarified. It is possible that the problem is far more complex than has been assumed. Some evidence already indicates that characteristics of sanctions may interact in important ways. But when one adds to that complexity the possible interrelationship of characteristics of norms, of potential offenders, and of the behavior, it may well turn out that the occurrence of deterrence is highly specific.

Finally, the relative importance of sanction threats compared to other variables that are thought to be important in determining conformity or deviance needs to be explored in the varied situations described above. Social scientists attribute significance to variables such as moral commitments, belief as to the amount of deviance that is occurring, imputed legitimacy of the normative system, peer pressures or acceptance, relative deprivation, self-conception, and symbolically learned motivations (see Cohen, 1966). But we do not know how important each is, relative to the others, nor how important sanctions are relative to these variables. Understanding of conformity/deviance, or the role of sanctions, will not be adequate until we can make statements about how much of each factor is generally or specifically operative in the production of conformity.

It should be obvious that addressing these issues empirically will require much work, ingenuity, and attention by social scientists. The job requires a wide range of data gathered in a myriad of circumstances, using a variety of research methods. Productive outcomes will necessitate sharper definitions and conceptual formulations than have typically been employed in the past. Moreover, in an area so prone to ideological disputation, considerable effort may be required simply to keep alive a spirit of objective inquiry. Progress, therefore, will not be easily accomplished. But if our objective is to understand social order, we must accept the challenge and continue to seek empirical answers to many long-neglected questions concerning negative sanctions and behavior.

FOOTNOTES

[1] Despite recent comprehensive reviews of the punishment literature which conclude that punishment can be highly effective in eliminating behavioral responses (Azrin and Holz, 1966; Bandura, 1969: 293–353), some continue to interpret punishment studies as indicating little effectiveness and are even willing to generalize from laboratory punishment of animals to social sanctioning of humans (Appel and Peterson, 1965; Jeffery, 1965).

[2] UCR neglects to report convictions in subsequent years, but one can extrapolate. In so doing, however, it is necessary to consider the possibility that the number reconvicted may have risen as people arrested during the first four years came to trial after that date and additional arrests were made. Given that lag time in the judicial process is rarely more than two years, and that most of those re-arrested during the six years were taken into custody during the first two years (66 percent), it is reasonable to assume that the vast majority of re-arrestees had been tried by the end of the fourth year. If we assume, moreover, that the 40 percent reconviction of arrestees applies only to those arrested during the first two years of the follow-up and we project this conviction rate to cover all those arrested from the third through the sixth years, we arrive at a total reconviction rate of 26 percent for the original sample of releasees. Furthermore, during the fifth and sixth years an increment of only two percent per year in additional arrests were added. Hence the reconviction rate of offenders released in 1963 would appear to be well below 35 percent even if one projects the follow-up far beyond the original six years.

REFERENCES

ANDENAES, JOHS (1966) "The General Preventive Effects of Punishment," 114 University of Pennsylvania Law Review 949–83.

———— (1952) "General Prevention—Illusion or Reality?" 43 Journal of Criminal Law, Criminology, and Police Science 176–98.

APPEL, JAMES B. AND NEIL J. PETERSON (1965) "What's Wrong with Punishment?" 56 Journal of Criminal Law, Criminology, and Police Science 450–53.

AZRIN, N. H. AND W. C. HOLZ (1966) "Punishment," in WERNER K. HONIG (ed.), Operant Behavior: Areas of Research and Application. New York: Appleton-Century-Crofts.

BAILEY, WILLIAM C., LOUIS N. GRAY AND DAVID J. MARTIN (1971) "On Punishment and Crime (Chiricos and Waldo, 1970): Some Methodological Commentary," 19 Social Problems 284–89.

———— AND DAVID J. MARTIN AND LOUIS N. GRAY (1971) "Crime and Deterrence: A Correlation Analysis," unpublished paper: mimeograph.

BALL, JOHN C. (1955) "The Deterrence Concept in Criminology and Law," 46 Journal of Criminal Law, Criminology, and Police Science 347–54.

BANDURA, ALBERT (1962) "Punishment Revisited," 26 Journal of Consulting Psychology 298–301.

———— (1969) Principles of Behavior Modification. New York: Holt, Rinehart and Winston.

———— AND RICHARD H. WALTERS (1963) Social Learning and Personality Development. New York: Holt, Rinehart and Winston.

BARNES, HARRY E. AND NEGLEY K. TEETERS (1959) New Horizons in Criminology. Englewood Cliffs, New Jersey: Prentice-Hall.

BOWERS, WILLIAM J., AND RICHARD G. SALEM (1972) "Severity of Formal Sanctions as a Repressive Response to Deviant Behavior," 6 Law and Society Review 427–41.

CALDWELL, ROBERT G. (1944) "The Deterrent Influence of Corporal Punishment upon Prisoners Who Have Been Whipped," 2 American Sociological Review 171–77.

CAMPBELL, DONALD T. AND H. LAURENCE ROSS (1968) "The Connecticut Crackdown on Speeding: Time Series Data in Quasi-Experimental Analysis," 3 Law and Society Review 33–35.

CHAMBLISS, WILLIAM J. (1966) "The Deterrent Influence of Punishment," 12 Crime and Delinquency 70–75.

———— (1967) "Types of Deviance and the Effectiveness of Legal Sanctions," Wisconsin Law Review 703–19.

CHIRICOS, THEODORE G. AND GORDON P. WALDO (1970) "Punishment and Crime: An Examination of Some Empirical Evidence," 18 Social Problems 200–17.

CLARK, ALEXANDER L. AND JACK P. GIBBS (1965) "Social Control: A Reformulation," 12 Social Problems 398–415.

CLARK, GERALD (1969) "Black Tuesday in Montreal: What Happens When the Police Strike," November 16 New York Times Magazine 45ff.

CLASTER, DANIEL S. (1967) "Comparisons of Risk Perception between Delinquents and Non-Delinquents," 58 Journal of Criminal Law, Criminology, and Police Science 80–86.

CLEMMER, DONALD (1940) The Prison Community. Boston: Christopher Publishing Company.

COHEN, ALBERT K. (1966) Deviance and Control. Englewood Cliffs, New Jersey: Prentice-Hall.

CONKLIN, JOHN E. (1972) Robbery and the Criminal Justice System. Philadelphia: J. B. Lippincott.

CRAMTON, ROGER C. (1969) "Driver Behavior and Legal Sanctions: A Study of Deterrence," 67 Michigan Law Review 421–54.

DANN, ROBERT H. (1935) "The Deterrent Effect of Capital Punishment," Friends Social Science Bulletin, No. 29: Philadelphia, Pa. As described in Mattick, 1963.

FALEY, THOMAS AND JAMES T. TEDESCHI (1971) "Status and Reactions to Threats," 17 Journal of Personality and Social Psychology 192–99.

GAHAGAN, JAMES, J. T. TEDESCHI, THOMAS FALEY, AND SVENN LINDSKOLD (1970) "Patterns of Punishment and Reactions to Threats," 80 Journal of Social Psychology 115–16.

GIBBS, JACK P. (1966) "Conceptions of Deviant Behavior: The Old and the New," 9 Pacific Sociological Review 9–14.

———— (1968) "Crime, Punishment and Deterrence," 48 Southwestern Social Science Quarterly 515–530.

GLASER, DANIEL (1964) The Effectiveness of a Prison and Parole System. Indianapolis: Bobbs-Merrill.

GLASS, GENE V. (1968) "Analysis of Data on the Connecticut Speeding Crackdown as a Times-Series Quasi-Experiment," 3 Law and Society Review 55–76.

GLUECK, ELEANOR AND SHELDON GLUECK (1943) Criminal Careers in Retrospect. New York: The Commonwealth Fund.

GOULD, LEROY AND ZVI NAMENWIRTH (1971) "Contrary Objectives: Crime Control and Rehabilitation of Criminals," in JACK DOUGLAS (ed.), Crime and Justice in American Society. Indianapolis: Bobbs-Merrill.

GRAY, LOUIS N. AND DAVID J. MARTIN (1969) "Punishment and Deterrence: Another Analysis of Gibbs' Data," 50 Social Science Quarterly 389–95.

HALL, JEROME (1952) Theft, Law, and Society. (2nd Edition.) Indianapolis: Bobbs-Merrill.

HORAI, J. AND J. T. TEDESCHI (1969) "Effects of Credibility and Magnitude of Punishment on Compliance to Threats," 12 Journal of Personality and Social Psychology 164–69.

HORTON, PAUL B. AND GERALD R. LESLIE (1965) The Sociology of Social Problems. New York: Appleton-Century-Crofts.

JEFFERY, C. R. (1965) "Criminal Behavior and Learning Theory," 56 Journal of Criminal Law, Criminology and Police Science 294–300.

JENSEN, GARY F. (1969) "'Crime Doesn't Pay': Correlates of a Shared Misunderstanding," 17 Social Problems 189–201.

LEMMERT, EDWIN (1967) "The Concept of Secondary Deviation," in Human Deviance, Social Problems, and Social Control. Englewood Cliffs, New Jersey: Prentice-Hall.

LEVIN, MARTIN A. (1971) "Policy Evaluation and Recidivism," 6 Law and Society Review 17–46.

LOGAN, CHARLES H. (1971a) Legal Sanctions and Deterrence from Crime. Unpublished Ph.D. dissertation, Indiana University.

——— (1971b) "On Punishment and Crime (Chiricos and Waldo, 1970): Some Methodological Commentary," 19 Social Problems 280–84.

——— (1972) "General Deterrent Effects of Imprisonment," 51 Social Forces 64–73.

MATTICK, HANS (1963) The Unexamined Death. Chicago: John Howard Association.

MORRIS, NORVAL (1951) The Habitual Offender. Cambridge: Harvard University Press.

——— AND GORDON HAWKINS (1969) "From Murder and from Violence, Good Lord, Deliver Us," 10 Midway 63–95.

NATIONAL PRISONER STATISTICS (N.D.) Prisoners Released from State and Federal Institutions, 1960. Washington, D.C.: Bureau of Prisons, U.S. Justice Department.

PACKER, HERBERT L. (1968) The Limits of the Criminal Sanction. Stanford: Stanford University Press.

PHILLIPS, LLAD (1972) "Crime Control: The Case for Deterrence," unpublished paper presented at the American Enterprise Institute Conference on the Economics of Crime and Punishment. Washington, D.C. July 17–18.

PILIAVIN, IRVING M., JANE ÁLLYN HARDYCK AND ARLENE C. VADUM (1968) "Constraining Effects of Personal Costs on the Transgressions of Juve-

niles," 10 Journal of Personality and Social Psychology 227–31.

——— A. C. VADUM AND J. A. HARDYCK (1969) "Delinquency, Personal Costs, and Parental Treatment: A Test of a Cost-Reward Model," 60 Journal of Criminal Law, Criminology, and Police Science 165–72.

RECKLESS, WALTER C. (1967) The Crime Problem. (4th Edition.) New York: Appleton-Century-Crofts.

RETTIG, SALOMON (1964) "Ethical Risk Sensitivity in Male Prisoners," 4 British Journal of Criminology 582–90.

——— AND BENJAMIN PASAMANICK (1964) "Differential Judgment of Ethical Risk by Cheaters and Non-Cheaters," 69 Journal of Abnormal and Social Psychology 109–13.

——— AND HARVE E. RAWSON (1963) "The Risk Hypothesis in Predictive Judgments of Unethical Behavior," 66 Journal of Abnormal and Social Psychology 243–48.

ROSS, H. LAURENCE, DONALD T. CAMPBELL AND GENE V. GLASS (1970) "Determining the Social Effects of a Legal Reform: The British 'Breath-alyser' Crackdown of 1967," 13 American Behavioral Scientist 493–509.

SALEM, RICHARD G. AND WILLIAM J. BOWERS (1970) "Severity of Formal Sanctions as a Deterrent to Deviant Behavior," 5 Law and Society Review 21–40.

SAVITZ, LEONARD (1958) "A Study in Capital Punishment," 49 Journal of Criminal Law, Criminology, and Police Science 328–41.

SCHUESSLER, KARL F. (1952) "The Deterrent Influence of the Death Penalty," 284 The Annals 54–62.

SCHWARTZ, BARRY (1968) "The Effect in Philadelphia of Pennsylvania's Increased Penalties for Rape and Attempted Rape," 59 Journal of Criminal Law, Criminology, and Police Science 509–15.

SCHWARTZ, RICHARD D. (1969) "Sanctions and Compliance," paper read at the annual meeting of the American Sociological Association, San Francisco.

_____ AND SONYA ORLEANS (1967) "On Legal Sanctions," 34 The University of Chicago Law Review 274–300.

SELLIN, THORSTEN (1967) "Homicides in Retentionist and Abolitionist States," in Capital Punishment. New York: Harper and Row.

SINHA, JAI B. P. (1967) "Ethical Risk and Censure-Avoiding Behavior," 71 Journal of Social Psychology 267–75.

_____ (1968) "A Note on Ethical Risk Hypothesis," 76 Journal of Social Psychology 117–22.

SKINNER, B. F. (1953) Science and Human Behavior. New York: Macmillan.

SUTHERLAND, EDWIN H. AND DONALD R. CRESSEY (1966) Principles of Criminology. Philadelphia: J. B. Lippincott.

TANNENBAUM, FRANK (1938) Crime and the Community. Boston: Ginn and Company.

TAPPAN, PAUL W. (1960) Crime, Justice, and Correction. Boston: Ginn and Company.

THORSELL, BERNARD A. AND LLOYD W. KLEMKE (1972) "The Labeling Process: Reinforcement and Deterrent?" 6 Law and Society Review 393–403.

TITTLE, CHARLES R. (1969) "Crime Rates and Legal Sanctions," 16 Social Problems 409–23.

_____ AND ALAN R. ROWE (1973a) "Certainty of Arrest and Crime Rates: A Further Test of the Deterrence Hypothesis," Social Force (forthcoming).

_____ AND ALAN R. ROWE (1973b) "Moral Appeal, Sanction Threat, and Deviance: an Experimental Test," Social Problems (forthcoming).

TOBY, JACKSON (1964) "Is Punishment Necessary?" 55 Journal of Criminal Law, Criminology, and Police Science 332–337.

TORNUDD, PATRIK (1968) "The Preventive Effect of Fines for Drunkenness," in Scandinavian Studies in Criminology, Vol. 2. Oslo: Universitetsforlaget.

UNIFORM CRIME REPORTS (1967) U.S. Department of Justice. Washington, D.C.: Government Printing Office.

VOLD, GEORGE B. (1954) "Does the Prison Reform?" 293 The Annals 42–50.

WALDO, GORDON P. AND THEODORE G. CHIRICOS (1972) "Perceived Penal Sanction and Self-Reported Criminality: A Neglected Approach to Deterrence Research," 19 Social Problems 522–40.

WALKER, NIGEL (1965) Crime and Punishment in Britain. Edinburgh: University of Edinburgh Press.

WERTHMAN, CARL (1969) "Delinquency and Moral Character," in DONALD R. CRESSEY AND DAVID A. WARD (eds.), Delinquency, Crime, and Social Process. New York: Harper and Row.

WESTOVER, HARRY C. (1958) "Is Prison Rehabilitation Successful?" 22 Federal Probation 3–6.

WHEELER, STANTON (1961) "Socialization in Correctional Communities," 26 American Sociological Review 697–712.

WILKINS, LESLIE T. (1969) Evaluation of Penal Measures. New York: Random House.

ZIMRING, FRANK E. (1971) Perspectives on Deterrence. Public Health Service Publication No. 2056, NIMH Center for Studies of Crime and Delinquency, U.S. Government Printing Office.

_____ AND GORDON HAWKINS (1968) "Deterrence and Marginal Groups," Journal of Research in Crime and Delinquency 100–114.

33

What Happens When the Police Strike

GERALD CLARK

On the day Montreal became a city without police-men, Gilles Madore unsuspectingly left his home as usual at 9:30 A.M. to drive to work. Madore, a 32-year-old bank inspector, had been filling in for the past few months as manager of the City & District Savings Bank branch at the corner of St. Denis Street and St. Joseph Boulevard, almost entirely a French-speaking residential area with only a splash of English and Italian. It was a perfect October day —clear and crisp—and during the 15-minute drive Madore noted that the trees were at their peak of gold and crimson. He was listening to the car radio, but since it was an FM all-music station, he caught no bulletins. Madore, in fact, did not know the police had walked off the job until he arrived at the bank and a nervous teller greeted him with the news that the city was wipe open to criminals. "Don't worry," Madore said reassuringly. "We're a small branch. Holdup men won't come here." Besides, this was a Tuesday, by experience the quietest day in the week for bank robberies.

Source: "What Happens When the Police Strike," *New York Times Magazine*, November 16, 1969, pp. 79–97. © 1969 by The New York Times Company. Reprinted by permission.

Madore was not alone in his ignorance of the strike. Most Montrealers were only now beginning to hear of it, for there had been no forewarning, no build-up. The morning newscasts had carried, as a routine item, the report that police were to meet in the Paul Sauvé Arena at 9 A.M. to hear the results of an arbitration board's findings on wages and other issues that had remained unsettled for almost a year. But no one had anticipated a walkout; it was illegal for policemen and firefighters to strike.

At about the time Madore was learning of the de-velopment, another tall—and rather rugged—Mon-trealer, René St. Martin, was also receiving a sketchy fill-in. St. Martin, 25, was a patrolman, first class, assigned to cruisers. He had worked the 4 P.M.-to-midnight shift and, after a few hours' sleep, had now arrived at court as a witness in a stolen-car case. But, St. Martin discovered, no cases were being heard; few police witnesses had shown up. Shop stewards of the union, the Montreal Policemen's Brotherhood, had made the rounds of 25 station houses around 7:30 A.M.—and calls had gone out over police radio bands—to get men to leave their posts at once, to assemble in the arena even before the planned session. Men arriving for the 8 A.M.

Clark: What Happens When the Police Strike

shift also were told that the arbitration board's decisions were so distasteful that everyone had better head for the meeting. Even members of the Sûreté, the detective branch, turned in their sidearms and took off.

To St. Martin it was a surprise—and shock—to realize that a full strike was under way. He got into his car and drove the 10 miles to the arena in the northeast end of the city. By now scores of blue-and-white police cruisers were double- and triple-parked, along with scores of motorcycles. St. Martin arrived at about 11 A.M. and, as it developed, stayed there until midnight. With him were almost all of the other 3,780 men of the Montreal police force.

Thus, on Oct. 7, the largest city in Canada, and one of the most civilized cities in the world, found what it was like to be without police protection during a day and night. Before the ordeal was over, a psychologist would shoot and kill a burglar; another man—a provincial police corporal—would be slain, and 49 persons would be wounded or injured in rioting. Nine bank holdups, almost a tenth of the total for the whole of last year, would be committed, along with 17 other robberies at gunpoint. Ordinarily disciplined, peaceful citizens would go wild, smashing 1,000 plate glass windows in the heart of the city and looting shop displays. The losses and damage would exceed $1-million.

But the gray statistics alone would not be very meaningful. It was on the social and psychological levels that the story held its horror. For the real message was about the "thin blue line"—the phrase used by Sgt. Guy Marcil, president of the Policemen's Brotherhood—that separates civilization from chaos and anarchy.

Essentially, it was not the rise in professional crime—12 times the normal—that counted. It was the way political grievances, and private and group frustrations, shot to the surface when no one was around to enforce the law. These included: an attack by taxi drivers on a company holding an exclusive franchise to provide limousine service at Montreal's International Airport; an attack by French-Canadian separatists on symbols of the "English Establishment"; an attack on the Mayor's property by social

agitators who contend that not enough is being done for the poor; an attack on the United States Consulate by anti-Americans; and then, simply, an attack on a code of ethics and behavior by conventional men and women who chose to join a mob.

At the outset, a few of Montreal's English-speaking people, who number about one-fifth of the population, thought the Quebec revolution had commenced. But for the most people the day itself was reasonably calm. Apart from traffic tie-ups, the public experienced few inconveniences. At first there was a fear that accident victims might suffer, since police handle the cruising ambulances. Early on, a radio dispatcher tried to get an ambulance to respond to a call. The driver, instead, asked the dispatcher for directions to the Paul Sauvé Arena. Minutes later the radio went dead as dispatchers themselves left for the North End. But by then hospitals and private ambulance services had begun to take over.

It was not even accurate to say that the city was entirely without police. At headquarters, 47 officers —all of them ineligible for membership in the union— remained on duty, relaying distress calls to the Quebec Provincial Police (Q.P.P.) who started to send their own cruisers into city districts. By 10 A.M. 200 members of the Q.P.P. were mustered, and 40 brown-and-yellow alien cruisers were on the streets. It was not quite the same as the city force's 686 cars, motorcycles and other vehicles, but it was comforting nonetheless. Then a news bulletin at 10:30 A.M. alarmed the public: firemen, disgruntled over an arbitration board decision affecting them only a day earlier, were walking out of 45 stations and joining police at the arena. Yet even here there soon came an encouraging note. The city would not be completely vulnerable; the firefighters had decided to leave behind emergency teams of nine men in each of Montreal's 10 districts, enough to operate a pump and ladder truck.

Soon, however, it was apparent that the provincial police—most of them drawn from the local administrative office or brought in from outlying areas and unacquainted with city streets—could not keep pace with the kind of alarms municipal police handle as routine. Gilles Madore, at his branch, heard rumors that the banks would be ordered to close and the army summoned. As the morning progressed, he began to feel some apprehension. Customers paused to relay reports of holdups elsewhere. While Madore still believed his branch was safe (after all, it kept none of the large sums that downtown branches must keep for business firms), the first holdup of the day, at 11:15 A.M., had been at a Bank of Montreal branch in Pointe St. Charles, a slum district. Three men had entered the bank, two of them wearing Halloween masks and carrying pistols, the other wearing a brown paper bag with eye holes and carrying a shotgun. The nine employes kept their hands in the air while one of the bandits fired two shots at the lock of a teller's cash drawer. The haul was not large—a little more than $3,000—and the men were out of there in two minutes. It took the Q.P.P. 10 minutes to arrive. This was to form the pattern of the day. Time was on the side of the lawless.

The regular professional bank robbery in Montreal runs frequently to smoothly choreographed trios, with one man—usually armed with an impressive weapon like a submachine gun or shotgun—covering the staff while the other two leap over the counter to grab the money. The entire operation is supposed to be over within 30 seconds, at the most 45 seconds, because experienced hands know that an alert teller or manager will press a silent alarm connected to a protection service which in turn is linked with police headquarters. It takes 30 seconds from the moment the alarm is pressed until the message reaches the police; usually the nearest cruiser is not more than a minute or a minute and a half away. So, two minutes is the most any bandits can figure on; to give themselves a reasonable margin they rarely spend more than a quarter of that time.

René St. Martin, after 10 months on radio cars, was familiar with the technique of bank robbers. But his mind was elsewhere. He was listening to the speeches of union leaders, and he was in a quandary. While he supported the case made by the union, he believed essential services should not be allowed to strike. St. Martin likes being a policeman, and he does not feel—or at least did not until this moment—that the Montreal public is particularly hostile to the department or ungrateful to it. Fringe groups may shout "pigs" or "fuzz," but generally one does not hear such derogatory terms about Montreal policemen. On the contrary, there is an admiration for the way they have developed over the past few years into a remarkably good force: young, clean-cut recruits, efficient, honest, with the most rigorous training in the country and, until the walkout, a high level of discipline.

Certainly there was little public awareness of discontent in the ranks. During Expo 67 the Brotherhood went along with a city request for labor peace and accepted an unfavorable contract. Since then, however, the union had felt itself ignored, cut off by an administration that would not acknowledge the argument that Montreal patrolmen were entitled to at least the same income as police in Toronto, Canada's second largest city. St. Martin did not need reminders of how difficult his job was, though speaker after speaker pointed to the hazards in Montreal. It has the usual student troubles; last February rioters at Sir George Williams University barricaded themselves in a computer center and destroyed it. In addition, police must contend with a distinctive political situation: secessionists who are determined to break the Province of Quebec away from the rest of Canada often engage in terrorism. More than 100 bomb incidents have been recorded in the past two years, while street demonstrations, increasing in ferocity, have tested the 110-man riot squad. A senior observer from the Toronto Police Department who had studied several American riot squads in action said publicly that he had seen none to compare with Montreal's for deftness and effectiveness.

The plain fact was that Montreal police—who are expected to be bilingual on top of everything else—sustained in the line of duty three times the number of injuries of Toronto police and were paid considerably less. St. Martin, with five years' experience, received $7,300 a year, while his counterpart in Toronto received $9,112. The Brotherhood had demanded $9,200. Now—after 11 months of costly negotiation, conciliation and arbitration—it was told it would get $8,480. "Public garbage!" cried President Marcil. The smoky, noisy arena fell silent when the policemen's veteran chaplain, the Rev. Bertrand-Marie Boulay, a 50-year-old Dominican, exhorted them to keep to their fight: "You must stand shoulder to shoulder with your president and your negotiators, and your chaplain will be there, near the head of the line."

Now the men were just going to stay there—not "on strike" but in a "study session"—until they got what they were after. Carloads of sandwiches were brought in. Men pushed their folding chairs into squares and played a popular police card game called "pitch." Reminiscing about it later, St. Martin said he was hoping the decision to settle or not to settle would be taken from him. He was sure that in a matter of a few hours the provincial government would enact legislation compelling the strikers to go back to work, or that prominent industrialists would say, "*C'est assez ça,*" and persuade municipal authorities to offer improvements.

But there was no sign of either. Instead, there was simply a vague promise from the chairman of the city's executive committee, Lucien Saulnier, that the administration would reassess the findings of the arbitration board. Saulnier arrived at the Paul Sauvé Arena at midday, spoke for a few noncommittal minutes and left while some strikers jeered and others cheered. St. Martin thought it took a man "*qui a du guts*" to enter the arena.

Saulnier, though an elected councilor, in effect is city manager. While he is the cool and adroit administrator, Jean Drapeau, the Mayor since 1960, is the colorful and imaginative impresario who has transformed Montreal—always attractive but rather backward—into a lively and urbane and advanced metropolis. When financial experts said Montreal could not afford a subway, Drapeau not only built one; he made the Métro a showplace, with each of its score of stations of different artistic motif. Town planners from around the world came to admire and study the rejuvenated center of the city with its skyscrapers and underground plazas consisting of hundreds of shops and dozens of fine restaurants and theaters.

Montrealers, who possessed San Franciscans' sense of superiority and pride in their city, would deny Drapeau nothing. It was Drapeau who sold a skeptical Canada on staging, on man-made islands in the St. Lawrence River, what turned out to be the highly successful Expo 67. And later, when he threatened to resign if the one-season Expo was not continued as the annual Man and His World, townspeople rallied in such strength that the Federal and provincial governments agreed to a scheme underwriting part of any deficit. This year, Drapeau, at 53, hardly slowed down. His showmanship was unerring when he helped promote a National League franchise for a town with no obvious proclivity to baseball. Drapeau saw his Expos, of bush-league caliber, establish a first-season record by drawing 1.2 million fans.

But all of this effort took money and a distorted sense of priorities. The city fell notoriously behind in a slum clearance, low-cost housing, social service and better pay for civic employes. There was growing resentment that the Mayor was too busy with frills to pay attention to routine affairs. Strikers at the Paul Sauvé Arena held aloft placards sayings, "*Drapeau au poteau*" ("Drapeau to the gallows"). Drapeau, in fact, was at this moment of crisis on his way home from St. Louis, Mo., where he had gone to participate in a Canadian trade show. Only a month earlier he had attended another opening—of his own restaurant, Le Vaisseau d'Or, Ship of Gold.

Even though many people wondered what a Mayor was doing moonlighting, this was no ordinary restaurant. In characteristic Drapeau style, he defined it as a concert hall where one could, incidentally, dine. A 16-member orchestra played Bach, Vivaldi, and Mozart while patrons ate a seven-course meal in the recreated opulence of a Montreal mansion's living room of the eighteen-nineties. A dinner for two, with drinks and wine, cost about $40. The figure was not entirely lost on social agitators who pointed out that the maximum allowance for a family of four on welfare was $40 a week. In an area with almost 7.5 percent unemployment, the city had 27,000 welfare cases representing 70,000 men, women, and children. But more graphically, a Montreal Labor Council study indicated that 38 percent of the total population lived in poverty or near the poverty line.

Three weeks after the opening of Le Vaisseau d'Or, a bundle of dynamite, estimated at 15 sticks, exploded outside Drapeau's two-story home in the East End of Montreal. No one was injured, but the house was demolished. Investigation failed to show whether the terrorists were political foes, social fanatics, labor extremists, Maoists or separatists who resented Drapeau's efforts to make Montreal an international capital rather than a unilingual French-Canadian haven.

One could almost be sure, in view of the absence of police from the streets, that Le Vaisseau d'Or would now be a target. But at the moment a more prosaic crime was in the making. Shortly before 1 P.M. a man about 23 years of age walked into a branch of the Canadian Imperial Bank of Commerce on Mount Royal Avenue East, stood in line at a teller's position and shoved across the counter a note: "Silence. Ceci est un holdup." The teller was an English-speaking woman who could not read French. But she could understand "holdup." Moreover, she saw what looked like the handle of a gun sticking from the man's pocket. He collected close to $1,000, in the process striking a blow for bilingualism.

By now some of the outlying bank branches were closing down in self-defense. Downtown branches, which had brought in private security guards, were untouched, but holdups were taking place with greater frequency in the residential districts. At 1:45 P.M. Gilles Madore received a phone call from the head office telling him to allow in only known customers. His branch is modern and, with the exception of garish brown tile covering the side of the counter, quite attractive; the glass front gives it an appearance of spaciousness. Madore double-locked the glass door himself. Five minutes later, as he was preparing to go to lunch, he saw from the big window of his office three hooded men—one carrying a shotgun—running toward the bank.

Madore instinctively pressed the silent alarm. The men banged on the door and then, frustrated, retreated to an adjacent lane. They were obviously professionals. The hoods they wore—knitted ski masks, covering the entire head, face and neck, with slits for the eyes and mouth—are favored by old hands. Seconds later, they were back. This time the man with the shotgun smashed the butt against the door. The glass fell away, and the men stepped inside. By now half of the staff of 12 had fled to the tiny kitchen. The other six waited, Madore beside

the entrance to the manager's office. The man with the shotgun told him, "Bouges pas, toi—je vais te descendre" (Don't move—or I'll bring you down"). As Madore remembers it, "I didn't move."

The other men, clutching revolvers, advanced to the other side of the counter. There was little conversation, but when a teller hesitated in handing over the key to his cash drawer, one of the bandits slapped his face. The yield from all the cash drawers came to $2,000. Under normal circumstances, the bandits should have made their escape by now. But the shotgun man, the lookout man, did not even bother to glance into the street to see if anyone had spotted them. Nor did he trouble to count aloud to 30—a common practice to warn that time is up. Instead, he instructed the cashier to open the cash box, kept for tellers, in the big vault. The men scooped up $4,000 in U. S. banknotes, $7,000 in Canadian funds and $15,000 in travelers' checks, making a grand total of $28,000—the biggest haul of the day. On the way out, the man with the shotgun paused at the water fountain and took a long drink. The duration of the operation was between four and five minutes. Provincial police arrived at 2:10 P.M., 20 minutes after Madore had sounded the alarm.

The delays were not always due to the heavy pressures on the provincial police or their unfamiliarity with Montreal's streets. Some of the strikers, after monitoring the Q.P.P. radio, ambushed and seized seven provincial cruisers responding to calls. The number was selected deliberately, for the Q.P.P. drew on seven radio bands and the strikers were able to muddle all of them with the cruisers' transmitters. For a while this strategy forced the provincial police, whom the strikers regarded as strike-breakers, to keep only two-thirds of their cars on the road. The rest remained at headquarters to take orders directly.

Most of the men at the arena were unaware of the ugliness outside, and when René St. Martin managed to reach a phone, he found his wife Andrée in a mood of dejection. Their 22-month-old son, Stéphane, was asleep, but their 3-year-old daughter Josée, was looking at television scenes of the arena and saying, "My daddy is there." It was not easy to get along on take-home pay of $105.42 a week, and

Andrée knew the men were entitled to a better deal. But, as she later recalled it, "I am a mother, and I thought of the agony of some other woman whose child might be lying bleeding on the street, or who might be lost. . . ."

The afternoon was surprisingly tranquil. Holdups, though plentiful, were of a routine nature. At 3:05 P.M. two men with submachine guns entered the jewelry store of Roland Handfield on Jean Talon Street East and announced: "This is a holdup. Lay down on the floor." Handfield and his two clerks obeyed without hesitation. The men proceeded to fill a bag with rings, bracelets, and other items valued at from $3,000 to $4,000—and then one of them said, "Three minutes. Let's go." A car, the motor running, was waiting at the corner.

At another small jewelry store, Bijouteric Borduas, a 23-year-old clerk, Pauline Deschambault, thought it was so dull and orderly in the streets and in the shops that surely the police must be back at work. Then she heard the bell tinkle as the front door opened, and she saw two young men walk in, unmasked but holding revolvers. She screamed and ran to the back of the store. The lone male clerk was told to flop behind the counter. A few minutes later, the men departed with about $6,700 in rings and watches.

The Perrette Dairy Ltd., with its chain of 40 shops in the city, reported five holdups, compared with the usual average of one a month. At 6:50 P.M., at the branch at 6030 Sherbrooke Street West, a customer selected a package of cheese and, instead of paying for it, pulled a pistol from his pocket. The solitary clerk emptied the till of $107, forgetting the manager's injunction to keep ginger ale bottles within reach and heave them at any thief. Before the day ended, there had been a total of 26 armed robberies in all districts.

By early evening the provincial police had 500 men in action; another 300 were en route to Montreal from posts as far as Sept-Iles, 510 miles away. Lucien Saulnier made a radio and television appeal for people to "be calm and vigilant," stay home and protect their property. One woman said she had not worried about the situation until she heard this dramatic message. Another woman, young and pretty, was afraid to walk to the bus stop after a dental appointment; she thought she might be attacked or raped (there were no reported rape cases). She set about to make herself look old and uninteresting by dropping her glasses to the tip of her nose; she also covered a fresh coiffure with a pocket rain bonnet and tried to add inches to her miniskirt by pulling it low on her hips. It was only much later, when she had recovered from her moments of terror, that she was able to say wryly: "Have you any idea what it's like trying to walk in an extended miniskirt?"

Most people appeared relaxed, even if some behaved irrationally. Metropolitan Montreal numbers 2.5 million inhabitants, but only half live in the city proper, where the strike was taking place. The others live in separate municipalities—some of them, like Westmount and Outremont, enclaves surrounded by the City of Montreal—with their own police and fire services. None of these was on strike. However, a Westmount resident, arriving home at 7 P.M. from work, found his way barred by the door chain, a device never before used by his wife. "What's the idea?" he asked her. She replied that Saulnier had told people to be on guard. Another man returned from work to find that every light in his home in Outremont had been switched on; his wife was certain this would ward off intruders.

As it happened, the population, at the start, did heed Saulnier. It kept away from the downtown areas. A visitor driving along Ste. Catherine, the biggest shopping and entertainment street, would have thought it a Sunday rather than Tuesday evening. Theaters, cinemas and restaurants functioned. It was just that the traffic was light and shushed. But not everywhere. Around City Hall, in the old quarter of Montreal, several taxis started hooting their horns before forming a procession and driving west to Barré and Mountain Streets. At that point, approximately 7:30 P.M., began the buildup for a night of havoc.

Other cabs headed downtown to join the cavalcade, and by the time it reached its objective, the garage of Murray Hill Limousine Service Ltd., it numbered 75 vehicles—carrying not only cabbies but political extremists. An alliance had been formed between the Mouvement de Libération du

Taxi, which could claim a membership of no more than 100 of Montreal's 10,000 cab drivers, and the Front de Libération Populaire, a small group of Maoists and student radicals who charged that a "fascist Drapeau-Saulnier administration had sold out taxi drivers' interests to the capitalists." In fact, it was a Federal concession that had given Murray Hill the sole right to pick up passengers at Montreal's airport, in return for guaranteed service. But the grievance was an old one among drivers of city taxi associations.

For separatists and terrorists, with no riot squad to restrain them, this was obviously a night to make political gain in the wider goal of removing Quebec from "English domination." Murray Hill, as an example, was owned by an English-speaking Montrealer, Charles Hershorn, whose home had been bombed a year ago.

At 8:03 P.M. a Q.P.P. radio dispatcher sent four cars to Murray Hill. They fumbled through unfamiliar back streets flanked on the north by railway yards and on the south by the waterfront. At 8:08 P.M. another four cars were told to get there in a hurry. By now demonstrators were chanting, *"Québec aux Québécois,"* and throwing rocks and Molotov cocktails. The targets of the fire bombs were four Murray Hill buses and four cars in the parking lot, and quickly they were aflame. Demonstrators pushed one of the burning buses down an incline to crash into the barred garage doors. The tactics were terrifying to the Murray Hill employes inside; they were sitting above underground storage tanks containing 18,000 gallons of gasoline. Firemen, forced back by the rioters, were compelled to set up hoses at a distance. Then a guard on the roof of the two-story building opened fire on the crowd with a 12-gauge shotgun. "How big is the crowd?" a Q.P.P. dispatcher asked over the radio. "Over 200," replied a cruiser, "and impossible to control." A city police striker, using a hijacked car transmitter, cut in— and a Q.P.P. man cursed him.

By now a second guard was shooting from the garage roof, and there was return fire from a tenement roof across the road. It was the first time that street war of this type had ever struck Montreal, and when

it was ended, a provincial plainclothesman, Cpl. Robert Dumas, 35, was its chief victim. Dumas, a member of the Q.P.P. antisubversive squad, had been one of the first police on the site. He entered the Murray Hill garage to phone for reinforcements; then, racing out to try to halt rioters tossing Molotov cocktails, he was fatally wounded by a shotgun blast. Another 19 persons—some cabbies, some youths— were taken to hospitals with buckshot wounds. Thirty more suffered injuries at Murray Hill and in the subsequent bouts that took place as the crowd began moving, around 10:30 P.M., up the hill.

The next destination was the Queen Elizabeth Hotel, chosen because Murray Hill had a concession there; thus it deserved to have its storefront windows smashed. From here it was a short and logical step to the Sheraton–Mount Royal Hotel, for the same reason. But on the way, the demonstrators paused at the Windsor Hotel, where Mayor Drapeau's restaurant was located in the basement level. Drapes were ripped down, glassware smashed and small fires set. By now Drapeau, having landed from St. Louis an hour and a half earlier, was in City Hall receiving reports of the growing violence.

The streets in Drapeau's beloved heart of the city—the complex around Place Ville Marie and the Ste. Catherine Street area—were beginning to fill with more than the original couple of hundred separatist and agitators who had started out with an organized line of attack. Arriving from all directions, looters and vandals were hitting out indiscriminately. A provincial police officer radioed headquarters: "Send help to the corner of Peel and Ste. Catherine. People are breaking windows at the Bank of Nova Scotia." Minutes later: "We need more help. We are 25 against 500."

For two uninterrupted, chaotic hours the plunderers went to work, barely touched by the undermanned and bewildered Q.P.P. At one point young people surrounded a parked cruiser, rocking it and blocking the doors so the occupants could not escape. All along central Ste. Catherine Street, for a stretch of 21 blocks, the shattering of $300,000 worth of plate glass windows was hardly heard above the roar of the mob and the incessant ringing of unanswered alarm bells. In the distance sirens sounded. Their screech receded, however, as a new touch was added. Provincial police were receiving more and more calls about other riots in widely scattered parts of the city, only to find them fictitious. Later, Q.P.P. Director Maurice St. Pierre was to suggest the calls came from strikers.

In all, something like 156 shops had windows smashed and display contents hauled away—stereo units, radios, fur coats, dresses, an assortment of goods. The major department stores—Eaton's, Simpson's, Morgan's—were hit, along with lesser ones. Pink Poodle, a medium-priced women's specialty shop, caught it from two directions. While the ordinary looters were content to strip Pink Poodle's window mannequins of $3,000 worth of garments, professional burglars entered the premises through a back door and made off with 150 fur and cloth coats valued at $20,000.

There were riffraff out that night and maybe some poor people; but also there were so-called respectable, middle-class people. A well-dressed man, with a fur coat over each arm, scampered down Ste. Catherine Street shouting, "One for my wife, one for my girl friend." There were some orderly people, too. A middle-aged man, seeing a young man reaching for a fur coat, tried to talk him out of it— whereupon he was set upon by two other looters for interfering. At Seltzer Drugs, where the window offered transistor sets, hair dryers and other fairly expensive items, a woman reached for a yellow box of Kleenex, ripped away the wrapping and stuffed the tissue into her handbag. She laughed aloud, for no one in particular to hear, as though to proclaim that suddenly she had a license to break the rules.

Or maybe she simply needed to blow her nose, and in the spirit of gaiety took the Kleenex. For in a sense there was also a carnival atmosphere, a pre-Christmas festivity about the street. There was nothing furtive in the stealing. Many of the people who now descended on Ste. Catherine Street, drawn by radio and television accounts, were content to stand by as spectators; but some, when they saw windows smashed, helped themselves to what was inside. Often they seemed to wait for just the right window

to be smashed. But with no bothersome police around—at one stage a busload of Q.P.P., arriving from out of town, drove along Ste. Catherine Street without any pause in the looting—a sense of fear was absent.

At the Paul Sauvé Arena, René St. Martin heard the Brotherhood president, Guy Marcil, announce that the Quebec Legislature had ordered the strikers back to work by one minute past midnight, or they would face severe fines and loss of accreditation as a trade union. Some men hissed. "We must obey," said Marcil. St. Martin was glad that the decision was, at last, made for him. But he felt it was not the Government's threat alone that got the men back on the beat. "It was," he said, "the way the rioters and looters were tearing our city to ribbons."

At 12:57 A.M. Montreal city police calls returned to the air. The 17-hour trial was over, and people cheered the first familiar blue-and-white cruisers that arrived at the corner of Peel and Ste. Catherine Streets. The police grinned back and began the business of chasing off the remaining looters and, along with the Q.P.P., making 104 arrests.

Many angles were left for later examination. Political extremists, after leaving the Sheraton–Mount Royal Hotel, shattered windows at nearby McGill University. But this was predictable, since separatists consider McGill a bastion of the English Establishment. Equally foreseeable was the small routine march on McGregor Avenue, where demonstrators threw stones through the windows of the United States Consulate while they left untouched in the same block consulates of Israel, West Germany, Switzerland and Italy. Nor was there any special significance to the other crimes—except, as might be expected, that there were more than usual.

For instance, 456 burglaries were reported for 17 hours, compared with the normal 350 for a whole week. The pattern and timetable suggested that professionals, rather than amateurs, were at work. From 9 A.M. to 11 A.M., before criminals could be assured a police strike was indeed underway, no major incidents were logged. Then the signals began to come in from banks. After the banks closed, four jewelry stores in succession were held up. When jewelers shut down, at 6 P.M., the drug stores and food stores raised the alarm. The police, in making their analysis, did not believe that a single, massive gang was involved. Rather, several compact groups were thought to be operating, independently but with a common and logical program of attack based on known schedules of business establishments.

It was the behavior of ordinary people at night that caused the most perplexity and anxiety. No special denominator tied together the shops they looted; some were owned by Catholics, some by Protestants, some by Jews; some represented "English" interests, others "French" interests. Men and women of every kind and variety flocked to the Ste. Catherine Street area because it was here that the action, set off initially by organized extremists, was taking place. And then they abandoned inhibitions.

A German-trained psychologist, Dr. Paul Fircks, received a visitor in his home and explained the phenomenon. He did so by citing from a volume that is now a classic, "The Crowd: a Study of the Popular Mind," written in 1897 by a French psychologist, Gustave Le Bon. The crowd—the mob—is amoral, and if the law relaxes, the people in the crowd act out their impulses. Morals and ethics are externalized by the presence of the police; if the police are not there, the mob does as it pleases. It is the believer in individuality who stands back, who refuses to join the mob, who rejects looting, who behaves in a civilized fashion. "But the majority of people," adds Fircks, "join mobs when given an opportunity. Germany has shown this. Hitler was a genius who created out of supposed individuals a crowd, a mob."

Fircks, who is 67 and Russian-born, lived in Germany from 1934 to 1947. His own story is directly related to what happened in Montreal on what has come to be known as "Black Tuesday." A widower, Fircks lives alone with his cat, Baroness, in a large home in a high-income residential district where burglaries are frequent. Shortly before midnight he prepared to retire; but having heard the late news, and of the troubles downtown, he decided to take extra precautions.

Fircks, who practices psychotherapy, including hypnosis, remembered that in his office in the base-

ment was a .32-caliber revolver that he had recently taken from a patient. He fetched it, went upstairs to his bedroom, bolted the door and slipped into bed—the revolver on the table next to him. When he awoke, it was to the sound of someone jimmying the bedroom door. Fircks fired three times, and when he descended found at the foot of the stairs the body of a man who, it turned out, was a 39-year-old habitual burglar.

What was Fircks's reaction? "I went through two world wars and the Nazis. No burglar is going to frighten me. Besides, I teach my patients to be aggressive. If you have an aggresive attitude, you cannot be afraid."

But shooting and killing even a burglar? "I looked at the man lying here, and I cursed him. I thought: How does he dare? Who does he think he is to threaten me, to come into my home this way?"

The day after the strike a Montreal editor received a phone call from an American newspaper friend in Washington. "What was the final toll up there?" asked the Washingtonian. When the answer was, "Two men killed, one a policeman, the other a burglar," the reaction was quick and astonished: "My God, if that happened here in Washington, if the police went on strike, the private hate lists would come out so fast we'd have a blood bath."

It was only in retrospect that Montrealers sensed how close a grim experience had come to gross tragedy. During the rioting and looting many people, sitting in suburban homes and watching television, thought it must be happening to a city in a foreign country. The awakening the next morning was acute when they traveled to downtown offices and saw the debris and damage. But the awful part was the realization that terrorists had selected relatively few targets, and that by and large the mob that later emerged was a good-natured one rather than vicious. No explosive bombs were thrown, no one cried out in a crusade of personal vendetta or racial or religious war. But if there is a next time with more targets and objectives, the thin blue line might indeed prove thin.

Each person had his own particular message to remember. For Dr. Fircks it was short and clear:

"Never allow a policeman to strike, because then the mob comes together."

For Jean-Paul Gilbert, Montreal police director, there was no need for the harsh reminder that "a municipal force is a must in our society." A comparatively small number of men, familiar with local geography and conditions, can maintain peace in a city. Despite the good intentions and resources of the Q.P.P., who ultimately pressed 100 cruisers into service, Montreal was virtually without protection. Even the effectiveness of the army—a token force of the Royal 22d Regiment arrived as the strike was ending and mounted guard at City Hall—is questionable, according to Gilbert, unless soldiers are trained in crowd control. Thus he is a firm advocate of intensive coordination, in training and deployment, among forces on the national, state or provincial and municipal levels. The concept arouses misgivings among civil libertarians who fear growing police powers.

What did Black Tuesday teach Constable St. Martin? "That some people are like animals. You can expect teenagers to be undisciplined and wild, but it was shocking to see adults behave this way."

To his wife, Andrée, the police were wrong in striking or, worse still, were guilty of bad public relations, of spoiling an image: "They could have demonstrated how bitter they were if perhaps 1,000 at a time had assembled in the arena while the rest continued to protect the city."

Gilles Madore, the bank inspector, thinking not only of the illegality of the strike but of the way strikers ambushed cars of the Q.P.P.—in effect, committing such crimes as kidnapping and stealing—says: "If I had a priest who sinned and then asked me not to sin, I would hardly have faith in him. It is the same for the police. They have no right to go against the law and then expect others to obey it."

But Madore also believes that Montreal police are hard-working and efficient, and deserve to be paid more. There was little public opposition, in fact, when Lucien Saulnier announced 16 days after policemen were back on the job that a contract agreement had been reached. The city would boost a first-class constable's salary to $8,750—$270 above the arbitration board's award and, taking into account fringe benefits, effective parity with Toronto. If there was any overall public indictment, it was against the Drapeau-Saulnier administration for failing to anticipate the mood of policemen.

The lesson for many people, apart from discovery of their vulnerability, was that society cannot legislate against strikes among civil servants unless it is prepared to guarantee that they will have no cause to feel aggrieved. Here was a body of men with a strong sense of discipline and responsibility, yet it felt impelled to lash out. The huge inflow of letters to the press contained the expected words of condemnation—the strike was illegitimate, misguided, shocking. Yet, curiously, the letters also showed a remarkable sense of fairness, of soul-searching, as though each man and woman was peering into his or her own background and values to find reasons for the walkout.

"Our police forces," wrote one woman, "are underpaid and underarmed. Yet society demands that they do their duty. I say society has a duty to them first. That entails our trust, our respect, our support and maintenance to match their dangerous task of protecting society."

34

Drug Addiction in America and England

EDWIN M. SCHUR

There are in the United States about 60,000 opiate addicts, the Federal Bureau of Narcotics estimates, and some medical experts believe that 1,000,000 is closer to the actual number of those addicted to morphine, heroin, and related drugs. Neither figure, however startling, indicates in itself the far-reaching ramifications of the addiction problem. For a complicated web of corruption, degradation, vicious police practice, and secondary crime has developed around the use of narcotics in America. At its center stands the punitive anti-addict policy embodied in our narcotic laws.

The country's first major legislative effort to control narcotics, the Harrison Act, was to set the direction for all future legislation in this field. The law, passed by Congress in 1914 and still in effect, was essentially a tax measure designed to regulate the handling of narcotics by distributors and dispensers. While saying nothing about addicts as such, it was very broadly interpreted to mean that a doctor's "good faith" prescription of narcotics to an addict

was itself improper; and since this law's enactment, few medical practitioners have cared to take the risk of trying to help a narcotics patient with his problems. In recent years, considerably more stringent anti-narcotics legislation has been enacted—much of it, paradoxically, tending to perpetuate the very condition meant to be cured. The Boggs Act provided minimum mandatory sentences for all narcotics offenses—it followed the 1951 Kefauver Committee's investigations publicizing the narcotics problem. Four years later, a Senate subcommittee's investigation, under the chairmanship of then Senator Price Daniel, led to the federal Narcotics Control Act of 1956, which both raises previous minimum sentences for violations and permits the death penalty to be imposed on adults found guilty of selling heroin to persons under eighteen. This law—like most of the country's drug statutes—fails to provide the proper distinction between the addict and the peddler who is a non-addict: the *mere fact* of possession, purchase, sale, or transfer of narcotics is made punishable. So, too, a vast array of state laws prohibits the unauthorized possession and transfer of narcotics; finally, in several states, addiction is in itself a crime.

Source: "Drug Addiction in America and England," *Commentary*, Vol. 30, September, 1960, pp. 241–248. Copyright © 1960 by the American Jewish Committee.

The legal position of the American addict was neatly summed up by Dr. Herbert Berger in testimony before the Daniel committee: "It is illegal to prescribe narcotics for an addict, it is illegal to fill a prescription for an addict, it is illegal for an addict to possess narcotics, or in some states, even a syringe or other material which he might use for the taking of narcotics." Addicts, he continued, have been almost completely isolated from the medical profession, "the one group of individuals who might have brought to them some relief from their present deplorable state."

It is this very isolation which has pushed the addict straight into the black market. The addict's inability to get to the doctor obviously furnishes the economic incentive that supports the thriving underworld traffic in drugs. "It is precisely our law enforcement efforts," one authority has remarked, "and nothing else, that keeps the price of drugs, nearly worthless in themselves, so high as to attract an endless procession of criminal entrepreneurs to keep the traffic flowing." This crucial supply-and-demand factor was granted even by Commissioner of Narcotics Harry J. Anslinger—though seemingly he never tires of applauding the laws he administers; he wrote (along with W. F. Tompkins) that "the diversion of supplies from the regular medical channels causes a sharp rise in prices in the domestic illegal market, and the consequent large profits from a constant temptation and incentive to smugglers who are still able to obtain the drug abroad at comparatively modest prices." According to one estimate—a conservative one—a supply of heroin purchased abroad for $1,500 would be likely to wholesale in New York for around $6,000; split up for retailing throughout the country, it might eventually bring $200,000.

The high price of illegal drugs almost invariably forces the addict into crime. Although some law enforcement authorities take a different view of addict crime, social scientists generally agree that its main cause lies in the addict's need for money to buy drugs in the illicit market. Addicts have comparatively high arrest rates for nonviolent property crimes (and for prostitution), and comparatively low rates for violent offenses against the person (rape, assault, homicide). In a recent report on juvenile drug use in New York, Professors Isidor Chein and Eva Rosenfeld stated:

> The average addicted youngster spends about forty dollars a week on drugs, often as much as seventy dollars. He is too young and unskilled to be able to support his habit by his earnings. The connection between drug use and delinquency for "profit" has been established beyond any doubt. Apart from the users' own free admission of having committed crimes like burglary, there is independent evidence that in those areas of the city where drug rates went up, the proportion of juvenile delinquencies likely to result in cash incomes also went up, while the proportion of delinquencies which are primarily behavior disturbances (rape, assault, auto theft, disorderly conduct) went down. Available knowledge about the behavior of drug users in juvenile gangs also indicates that they show preferences for income-producing delinquencies, as against participation in gang warfare, vandalism, and general hell-raising.

But our narcotics laws do worse than just foster this black market situation: if only indirectly, they promote the spread of addiction. The drug peddler who profits by supplying narcotics obviously stands to gain if he can enlarge his market. This means creating new addicts. Likewise addicts themselves turn to the selling of drugs in the effort to finance their own habit. It is not hard to understand why the illicit narcotics traffic has assumed the proportions of big business. A Daniel committee report, issued in 1956, stated that this traffic "now costs over $500 million per year, to say nothing of the human lives shortened or destroyed."

The underworld traffic in drugs is, plainly, too enormous for existing law enforcement agencies to handle. The Federal Bureau of Narcotics, with headquarters in Washington and district offices in key areas throughout the country, has a staff of only some four hundred employees; there is, in addition, a considerably wider interlocking anti-narcotics police network, comprising the Bureau and at least segments of the regular police organizations in most states. (Attempts to seize contraband drugs at the point of entry into the country have largely failed, and the failure has been reviewed in two ways. Critics of current policy insist that if people want drugs badly enough to pay high prices for them, a way always will be found to make the drugs available. Enforcement officers, on the other hand, stress the prohibitive man-power requirements of effective smuggling control. All would perhaps agree with Commissioner Anslinger's oft quoted statement that the combined forces of the army, the navy, the Narcotics Bureau, and the Federal Bureau of Investigation could not stop the smuggling of narcotics.)

Narcotics agents have been forced to rely heavily on addict informers. But—as a police expert has pointed out—"whenever addicts are used as informers, the peddlers either cut off their supply, thus forcing them out of the community, or arrange to have them murdered." Although anti-narcotics drives have employed police decoys, and searches and seizures which raised serious questions of constitutionality, even these extreme methods have failed to achieve any impressive results. Recent reports of the Federal Bureau of Investigation cite some 7,000 or more annual arrests for violations of state narcotics laws alone, yet there is little reason to believe that these represent more than a fraction of all the violations that occurred.[1]

Whatever impact the enforcement effort does have is felt most strongly not by the big-time narcotics profiteer, but by the addict himself. Four grades of sellers in the American drug traffic were listed by a New York Academy of Medicine report in 1955: the importer, who is rarely an addict; the professional wholesaler, also rarely an addict; the peddler, who may be an addict; and the pusher, an addict who sells to get funds for his own drug supply. Despite those occasional—and well-publicized—exposés of "dope rings" and "drug syndicates," enforcement efforts in this country have had little effect at the "executive level" of the drug traffic. Any limited success has been mainly at the expense of the addicts, the pushers, perhaps the peddlers. Professor Alfred Lindesmith recently described the "long, shabby, pitiful parade of indigent drug users and petty offenders, mostly Negroes," seen in the Chicago Narcotics Court and other municipal courts throughout the country. As he points out, "The notion that punishing these victims will deter the lords of the dope traffic is as naïve as supposing that the bootlegging enterprises of the late Al Capone could have been destroyed by arresting drunks on West Madison Street or Times Square."

This perfervid anti-addict activity has been coupled with a modest effort to develop a medical treatment program for addicts. The U. S. Public Health Service hospitals for addicts at Lexington, Kentucky, and Fort Worth, Texas, accept both voluntary patients and those committed to the hospitals on conviction of violating federal narcotics laws. A comprehensive treatment routine includes gradual withdrawal from drugs, vocational and recreational activities, and some kind of psychotherapy. This program, too, has had only a limited success. It is recognized by most experts that relapse in addiction cases is the rule rather than the exception. Dr. Hubert Berger, already cited, has stated that the relapse rate probably approaches 90 percent ("and most addicts seem to think it exceeds that figure"). As he points out, "We in medicine do not accept with equanimity any treatment that fails to achieve cure in even 5 percent of the cases of any specified disease. Yet the United States government is committed to a plan of action which fails more than 90 percent of the time."

Nor can expansion of treatment facilities be expected to solve the addiction problem. All such efforts suffer from the general tenor of American narcotics policy—a policy based upon compulsion. The addict cannot be "cured" against his will—a fact too often overlooked; and once treated, there is no way of insuring that he will remain abstinent. Commissioner Anslinger is, of course, a staunch advocate of the compulsory confinement (for treatment) of addicts; and perhaps he unwittingly reflects the attitude implicit in such an approach when he writes: "The great majority of addicts are parasitic. This parasitic drug addict is a tremendous burden on the community. He represents a continuing problem to the police through his depredations against society." In this statement of the Commissioner's, suggesting that the addict is more a public enemy than a troubled person, we see embodied the official approach to addiction in the United States. Condemned by the "public," hounded by the police, exploited by the black marketeer, and ravaged by the physiological and psychological pressures of his own condition, the addict has no choice, finally, but to act as though he really were a "public enemy."

In sharp contrast is the situation of addicts in Great Britain. At one time it was possible to obtain opiates in Britain (as it was in the United States) without prescription at the neighborhood chemist's, and unrecognized addiction was widespread. Yet today estimates of the number of addicts in the United Kingdom run from between 300 to 1200. British addicts commit little serious crime, and there are no signs that the juvenile population is succumbing to addiction. Neither is there a large-scale black market in narcotics; the government reports with confidence that, "The addict who is also a 'pusher' is seldom encountered in the United Kingdom." Most British addicts are nativeborn whites, over thirty years of age, and about one-quarter of them are in the medical and allied professions.

Underlying this altogether different, and far happier, narcotics situation in Great Britain is, I believe, the sane approach that the British have to the general question of addiction. To the British, addicts are persons in need of medical attention, and doctors may (if certain broad conditions are satisfied) legally supply the wanted narcotics—under the National Health Service at nominal cost. The Dangerous Drugs Act (Britain's major narcotics law, first passed in 1920) places stringent controls on the import, manufacture, sale, and possession of narcotic drugs. Careful records are required of all drug transactions, subject to periodic inspection, and the Home Office warns doctors that "the continued supply of dangerous drugs to a patient solely for the gratification of addiction" is not considered legitimate. However, the ruling principle (as established by a Ministry of Health committee in 1926) is that narcotics may properly be administered to addicts after prolonged attempt at cure if "the drug cannot be safely discontinued entirely, on account of the severity of the withdrawal symptoms produced" or if the patient, "while capable of leading a useful and relatively normal life when a certain minimum dose is regularly administered, becomes incapable of this when the drug is entirely discontinued." There is no formal registration of addicts, but doctors are requested to inform the Home Office of any addicts coming under their care. While addicts may undergo treatment at some public hospitals and private nursing homes, there is no compulsory treatment in Great Britain, nor do any state institutions specialize in the treatment of addicts.

This entire approach has worked remarkably well. Not only has the estimated number of addicts remained low, it has actually decreased—from 700 in 1935 to 359 in 1957. All the evidence indicates that there are very few addicts other than those receiving their supplies through legal channels. No sizable underworld drug traffic exists. The addict furnishes no economic incentive for contraband peddling, and needn't become a thief or prostitute to pay for drugs. Apparently, the few addicts who are convicted of crimes usually have committed minor violations in order to get a little more of the drug than the doctor provided. Generally speaking, addiction and underworld life are not closely connected—one reason, perhaps, why few young people in Britain (even among the delinquents) have taken up the use of opiate drugs.

Certainly the British practice is not perfect—an addict occasionally forges a prescription for extra drugs or manages to get drugs from two doctors at once, and some doctors illegally divert drugs to their own use; but these abuses are not widespread. It would seem that by refusing to treat the addict as a criminal, Britain has kept him from becoming one. In short, the British addict is not a social menace.

What is more, not only does the British approach to addiction work—where the American does not—but the former appears to make much greater sense in light of our up-to-date medical and sociological knowledge. Misinformation about the nature of opiate addiction is widespread in the United States.[2] Many Americans continue to accept what Professor Alfred Lindesmith has labeled the " 'dope fiend' mythology." Addicts are pictured as violent and ruthless degenerates—a picture quite at odds with the known effects of opiates, which are, in fact, depressants. Opiate drugs relieve pain, decrease anxiety, relax the muscles, and induce drowsiness and euphoria; and anyone who has observed long-time addicts taking their shots knows that ordinarily the addict displays relief rather than excitement when he injects the drug. Thus, opiates, since they slow down the system rather than stimulate it, ordinarily do not propel the addict into violent crime. The claim that they promote sex orgies is equally fallacious—opiates in fact inhibit the sexual functions, often to the point of producing impotence in the male. The general deleterious effects of the drug upon the addict himself have also been greatly exaggerated. On the whole, the addict, unless deprived of his drug, probably suffers less organic harm than does the chronic alcoholic.

Yet there is little doubt that characteristic behavioral problems do arise from the regular taking of narcotics. Almost always, the addict experiences difficulties in sexual adjustment. Several American studies reveal, for example, a high rate of marital instability among known addicts. Although comparable information is not available regarding British addicts, the data that have been collected suggest that addiction interferes with normal sexual functioning even where the addict is free from persecution. American research also indicates that addiction makes satisfactory occupational adjustment very difficult. As Charles Winick has pointed out, "So akin to sleep is the effect of an opiate that the addict refers to it as being 'on the nod,' 'stoned,' 'out of this world,' 'half awake and half asleep.' His ability to earn a living is also likely to be impaired because he has to spend so much time procuring his drugs that he may literally have no time to work." Almost every study of addicts has found, however, that there are some persons who can and do work effectively while taking opiates. Many doctor-addicts appear able to carry on their work satisfactorily, as have any number of creative artists who were addicted. Furthermore, the addict's ability to function in a job situation is not determined solely by the effects of the drug on him—in Britain the addict is not compelled to spend all his time seeking out drugs, nor is he under the great financial pressure of his American counterpart. But by and large, it seems indisputable that many, perhaps even most, opiate addicts find it difficult to hold down a full-time job with any consistent regularity.

Other aspects of addict behavior are far less predictable, being determined almost entirely by social rather than physiological factors. Thus, the assertions that addicts are basically "criminal types"

is unsound. If addicts are basically criminal or if the drugs themselves cause criminal behavior, why do we find in Britain a low rate of addict crime? All available evidence indicates that it is not addiction itself, but the punitive approach to addiction, which produces antisocial behavior in addicts.

An increasing emphasis, in recent years, on the question of causation has served to advance our total understanding of addiction and of the addict. Much of the professional literature on the causes of addiction asserts that drug-taking is a form of (or a result of) mental illness. Psychoanalysts, for instance, stress such factors as oral fixation and unconscious homosexuality, and many psychiatrists attribute addiction to unsatisfactory family relations, feelings of inadequacy, and similar personality matters. In essence, the psychological approach holds that particular individuals are predisposed to addiction; that addiction is primarily a symptom of some underlying psychic disturbance. But this kind of explanation is not entirely satisfactory. As Lindesmith has pointed out, the belief in a predisposition to addiction ignores the fact that probably all "normal" persons who have imagined themselves immune and who have taken opiates steadily for any length of time, have become addicted. Furthermore, even the psychologists have recognized that some addicts are not otherwise abnormal; this category of "normal addicts" would seem to contradict the idea of psychological predisposition. Then too, psychologists have studied the personalities of addicts only after they became addicted and there is no way of distinguishing between resultant and causative traits. Starting with the assumption that a person must be abnormal to become an addict, it is all too easy to find the addict's personality problems. Lindesmith believes that disapproval of addiction invariably colors the diagnosis:

Addicts are said to become addicted because they have feelings of frustration, lack of self-confidence, and need the drug to bolster themselves up. Lack of self-confidence is taken as a criterion of psychopathy or of weakness. But another person becomes addicted, it is said, because of "curiosity" and a "willingness to try anything once" and this too is called abnormal. Thus, self-confidence and the lack of self-confidence are both signs of abnormality. The addict is evidently judged in advance. He is damned if he is self-confident and he is damned if he is not.

The belief that addiction reflects some psychological disturbance also ignores sociocultural variations in the distribution of addiction. How does one explain the fact that in some societies the regular use of narcotics is socially acceptable? Or that in Britain and America there is a disproportionately large number of addicts in the medical profession? Clearly psychological predisposition is not a complete explanation.

Sociologists and social psychologists have related addiction to slum dwelling, family background, minority-group status, and subcultural influence. But these approaches, too, fail as universal theories. Lindesmith, in his book *Opiate Addiction,* has perhaps developed the only really comprehensive theory acceptable to sociologists. He was intrigued by the fact that some of the persons receiving prolonged administration of narcotics (e.g., for relief of pain) do not become addicts—even though experiencing the drug's physiological effects, they develop no independent craving for the drug which persists when tolerance and withdrawal distress are no longer experienced. On the basis of intensive interviews with sixty addicts (together with a careful reading of addiction literature), Lindesmith concluded that ultimately addiction must be attributed to the learning process: "The knowledge of ignorance of the meaning of withdrawal distress and the use of opiates thereafter determines whether or not the individual will become addicted." The addicts Lindesmith interviewed had all understood the withdrawal symptoms and then used the drugs to avoid them; furthermore, he could find no case in which this process did not result in addiction. This approach does not, it is true, provide a basis for selecting out from the general population those individuals destined to become addicts, but this was not Lindesmith's aim. What his theory does, is describe the general process by which people (whoever they may be) become drug addicts. The doctor's peculiar susceptibility to addiction, in the light of this explanation, becomes understandable. Knowing that narcotics relieve pain and anxiety, and having easy access to them (and often believing he can take opiates without becoming addicted), the

doctor, not surprisingly, may succumb. Once addicted, he realizes he must continue taking the drug. Lindesmith's approach may not be a particularly dramatic one, but it does explain, at least in part, *all* cases of addiction.

Clearly, none of these findings supports the American treatment of the addict: as a public enemy. Whether the addict is in fact sick or not, criminal he is not. Why then is it that Americans continue to treat addicts as they do? The persistence of our blatantly ineffective drug laws suggest that they are crucially bound up with other social values and institutions.

It has already been noted here that the narcotics traffic has developed into a form of big business, and as Robert Merton states, "in strictly economic terms, there is no relevant difference between the provision of licit and illicit goods and services." Specifically, then, the drug peddler serves positive economic functions by providing goods for which there is a very real demand. (Such illicit entrepreneurship seems particularly well adapted to the American ethos. Rum-running during Prohibition was, of course, the classic case; another good example is the continuing provision of illegal abortion facilities.) Max Lerner has argued that the narcotics pusher "represents the principle of creating a market, inherent in the market economy." This particular market is vitally dependent upon current drug policies; if addicts were supplied legally with low-cost drugs, the market would collapse.

In some respects, law enforcement authorities may also have a sort of vested interest in maintaining the status quo. Rufus King has argued that the Narcotics Division of the Treasury Department (the early enforcement arm of the narcotics laws, known since 1930 as the Federal Narcotics Bureau), "succeeded in creating a very large criminal class for itself to police (i.e., the whole doctor-patient-addict-peddler community), instead of the very small one that Congress had intended (the smuggler and the peddler)." How else can one explain the continuing support of policies which run counter to common sense and the vast bulk of available evidence—policies which cannot help but perpetuate the drug traffic? Why else would Commissioner Anslinger keep on asserting, as he did in a recent article, that the essence of the addiction problem is "hoodlumism," and that, "In a sense it may be true that every hoodlum is a psychiatric problem but in a practical sense one must treat the bank robber, the gambler, and the thief as criminals"?

The American treatment of addicts may also be attributed to the addict's serving as a convenient scapegoat—one more enemy in the perpetual battle against crime and immorality of which Americans seem so fond. In his perceptive essay, "Crime as an American Way of Life," Daniel Bell stressed that, "In no other country have there been such spectacular attempts to curb human appetites and brand them as illicit, and nowhere else such glaring failures. From the start America was at one and the same time a frontier community where 'everything goes,' and the fair country of the Blue Laws. . . . In America the enforcement of public morals has been a continuing feature of our history." Even well-informed persons who have discarded the stereotyped image of the addict as a violent criminal may continue to condemn him, instead, for his passivity, since opiates, because of their slowing-down effects, produce the "un-American" reaction of avoiding encounters with the environment. In the United States, where a gospel of work (of the sort Max Weber described in *The Protestant Ethic and the Spirit of Capitalism*) may be said to prevail, even part-time idleness is not easily tolerated. Indeed, opiate addiction produces the kind of behavior which, in many respects, is directly opposite to that most highly prized in our society. Erich Fromm has referred to the "marketing orientation": "Success depends largely on how well a person sells himself on the market, how well he gets his personality across, how nice a 'package' he is; whether he is 'cheerful,' 'sound,' 'aggressive,' 'reliable,' 'ambitious.' . . ." The addict is hardly likely to conform to this model.

An additional support for the official position regarding addicts has been the medical profession's failure to insist on its responsibility for their treatment. Only recently have there been indications of a change in this attitude. In 1955, a committee of the New York Academy of Medicine, holding that "the most effective way to eradicate drug addiction is to take the profit out of the illicit drug traffic," proposed a national network of federally controlled clinics at which addicts could receive low-cost drugs. In 1958, a joint committee of the American Medical Association and the American Bar Association called for the establishment of an experimental clinic to see what would happen if a group of addicts received drugs free under medical supervision. This proposal followed a report by the American Medical Association's Council on Mental Health urging that "narcotic addiction should be viewed, much more than it has been in the past, as an illness and that there should be a progressive movement in the direction of treating addiction medically rather than punitively." The Council approved the idea of eventually "endorsing regulations somewhat similar to those currently in force in England." The Narcotics Bureau and other law enforcement agencies have vehemently opposed all such proposals, arguing that there really is nothing new or special about the British approach. It is pointed out (with supporting British quotations) that Britain permits no "indiscriminate" prescribing of narcotics; that prescribing for "the mere gratification of addiction" is not allowed; and that narcotic drugs are subject to "strict control." These statements are true enough, but when used, as here, to suggest that the British practice is no different from our own, they are totally misleading. As already mentioned, in Britain it is the doctor who decides when a person should receive narcotics. Doctors are not imprisoned for treating addicts (as some have been in the United States). The few prosecutions for over-prescribing have in fact been unsuccessful—the court upholding the doctor's professional judgment in such matters.

Critics sometimes indiscriminately link the British approach and all reform proposals with a "clinic system" which, they point out, was once unsuccessfully attempted in the United States. It is not certain, however, that these clinics—which operated between 1912 and 1925 in over forty American cities and dispensed low-cost drugs to addicts—were a complete failure. Some accounts would indicate that certain clinics were quite successful, and that the government (with the support of organized medicine) shut them all down largely on the evidence of the least efficient one, that in New York. The 1957

American Medical Association report on addiction states that, "Reasons for closing the clinics are obscure." The AMA's stand in the 1920's undoubtedly was based in part on medical considerations (some doctors still believe that to supply the addict with drugs is to abandon the attempt to "cure"), but at the same time it constituted an easy way out; the treatment of drug addiction is a bothersome and often unrewarding process. If the recent change in medical opinion is followed by pressure for actual changes in policy, there may be substantial hope for a new approach to addiction in the United States.

Just as there are many factors which have inhibited addiction reform, so there is no simple explanation for the great hold narcotic drugs seem to have upon Americans. The apolitical hipster may think to develop a new type of radicalism by deliberately courting psychopathy—drugs, violence, and mystical sexuality are his answer to the bomb, the cult of commodities, and the miseries of the mass society. The intellectual who comes to despair of the value of reason alone may seek through drugs to "transcend the self," to achieve new insights and experience new kinds of intense feeling. The minority-group or disturbed adolescent may attempt to create around the use of drugs a way of life which appears to offer him the prestige and self-esteem he is deprived of by the larger society. The general combination of tension and tedium which plagues many Americans today may lead to narcotics use, just as it may lead to reliance on alcohol, aspirin, or tranquilizers. Whatever the case, short of eradicating all the social conditions breeding addiction we must concentrate on formulating a sane policy toward the addicts.

Although legislative committees and other official bodies constantly demand "narcotics reform," they almost always take for granted the general desirability of our current policies. It is quite clear that American policies have not worked, primarily because of the vicious supply-and-demand cycle they set in motion. What is needed is an absolute reversal of our current attitudes and laws. The addict will get his drugs, no matter how hard the law enforcers try to stop him, and the only sensible course of action is to try to substitute medical supervision for police persecution. But, one may ask, would something like the British approach work in the United States? There is no way of knowing until we actually put such a policy to the test. It has been argued that supplying addicts will not reduce criminality; the addict, critics of the British system say, will not be content with the amount he gets legally. While it is true that with increasing tolerance to his drug the addict usually wants more and more of it, the British experience indicates that some addicts can, under favorable circumstances, get along reasonably well on legally prescribed limited doses. Certainly we have everything to gain and nothing to lose by instituting at least an experimental clinic through which to test the British approach.

Some would yet argue that we must condemn addiction, if for no other reason than that it is a "vice." Yet on what grounds can we call drug addiction a vice? Is it as morally reprehensible as the criminality and degradation to which we in this country have driven the addict? Similarly, is it really true (as officials sometimes contend) that the American public would never countenance a non-punitive approach to addiction? Public condemnation of the addict is as much a product of our current policy as it is a cause of that policy. The British people (though equally decent and "right thinking") appear quite capable of accepting intelligent efforts to deal with addiction. Americans may very well be able to do the same, once they are aware of the basic facts about addiction and addiction policies.

FOOTNOTES

[1] Like many social problems in America, addiction is concentrated in the big cities—and particularly in the most crowded and underprivileged areas of those cities. Thus, Negroes have a disproportionately high rate of narcotics arrests (in terms of their proportion to the general population), and police officials claim that they make up a large segment of the total addict population. Although the extent of juvenile addiction has sometimes been exaggerated, a considerable number of juveniles and young adults do use drugs.

[2] While marijuana is often linked indiscriminately with the opiates, opiate addiction and the habitual use of marijuana have entirely different effects. The opiate addict experiences a severe withdrawal illness if deprived of his drug; he physiologically requires it to avoid the painful syndrome. The marijuana user, on the other hand, ordinarily suffers no extreme reaction to deprivation, and has no such physiological attachment. For this reason, the use of marijuana does not pose really urgent social problems of the sort raised by opiate addiction, even though an intelligent policy regarding opiate addiction probably would reduce the use of marijuana.

35

Two Studies of Legal Stigma

RICHARD D. SCHWARTZ
and JEROME H. SKOLNICK

Legal thinking has moved increasingly toward a sociologically meaningful view of the legal system. Sanctions, in particular, have come to be regarded in functional terms.[1] In criminal law, for instance, sanctions are said to be designed to prevent recidivism by rehabilitating, restraining, or executing the offender. They are also said to be intended to deter others from the performance of similar acts and, sometimes, to provide a channel for the expression of retaliatory motives. In such civil actions as tort or contract, monetary awards may be intended as retributive and deterrent, as in the use of punitive damages, or may be regarded as *quid pro quo* to compensate the plaintiff for his wrongful loss.

While these goals comprise an integral part of the rationale of law, little is known about the extent to which they are fulfilled in practice. Lawmen do not as a rule make such studies, because their traditions and techniques are not designed for a systematic examination of the operation of the legal system in action, especially outside the courtroom. Thus, when extra-legal consequences—e.g., the social stigma of a prison sentence—are taken into account

Source: "Two Studies of Legal Stigma," *Social Problems*, Vol. 10, Fall, 1962, pp. 133–142. By permission of the authors and publisher.

at all, it is through the discretionary actions of police, prosecutor, judge, and jury. Systematic information on a variety of unanticipated outcomes, those which benefit the accused as well as those which hurt him, might help to inform these decision makers and perhaps lead to changes in substantive law as well. The present paper is an attempt to study the consequences of stigma associated with legal accusation.

From a sociological viewpoint, there are several types of indirect consequences of legal sanctions which can be distinguished. These include differential deterrence, effects on the sanctionee's associates, and variations in the degree of deprivation which sanction imposes on the recipient himself.

First, the imposition of sanction, while intended as a matter of overt policy to deter the public at large, probably will vary in its effectiveness as a deterrent, depending upon the extent to which potential offenders perceive themselves as similar to the sanctionee. Such "differential deterrence" would occur if white-collar anti-trust violators were restrained by the conviction of General Electric executives, but not by invocation of the Sherman Act against union leaders.

The imposition of a sanction may even provide an unintended incentive to violate the law. A study of factors affecting compliance with federal income tax laws provides some evidence of this effect.[2] Some respondents reported that they began to cheat on their tax returns only *after* convictions for tax evasion had been obtained against others in their jurisdiction. They explained this surprising behavior by noting that the prosecutions had always been conducted against blatant violators and not against the kind of moderate offenders which they then became. These respondents were, therefore, unintentionally educated to the possibility of supposedly "safe" violations.

Second, deprivations or benefits may accrue to non-sanctioned individuals by virtue of the web of affiliations that join them to the defendant. The wife and family of a convicted man may, for instance, suffer from his arrest as much as the man himself. On the other hand, they may be relieved by his absence if the family relationship has been an unhappy one. Similarly, whole groups of persons may be affected by sanctions to an individual, as when discriminatory practices increase because of a highly publicized crime attributed to a member of a given minority group.

Finally, the social position of the defendant himself will serve to aggravate or alleviate the effects of any given sanction. Although all three indirect consequences may be interrelated, it is the third with which this paper will be primarily concerned.

FINDINGS

The subjects studied to examine the effects of legal accusation on occupational positions represented two extremes: lower-class unskilled workers charged with assault, and medical doctors accused of malpractice. The first project lent itself to a field experiment, while the second required a survey design. Because of differences in method and substance, the studies cannot be used as formal controls for each other. Taken together, however, they do suggest that the indirect effects of sanctions can be powerful, that they can produce unintended harm or unexpected benefit and that the results are related to officially unemphasized aspects of the social context in which the sanctions are administered. Accordingly, the two studies will be discussed together, as bearing on one another. Strictly speaking, however, each can, and properly should, stand alone as a separate examination of the unanticipated consequences of legal sanctions.

Study I. The effects of a criminal court record on the employment opportunities of unskilled workers In the field experiment, four employment folders were prepared, the same in all respects except for the criminal court record of the applicant. In all of the folders he was described as a thirty-two-year-old single male of unspecified race, with a high school training in mechanical trades, and a record of successive short-term jobs as a kitchen helper, maintenance worker, and handyman. These characteristics are roughly typical of applicants for unskilled hotel jobs in the Catskill resort area of New York State where employment opportunities were tested.[3]

The four folders differed only in the applicant's reported record of criminal court involvement. The first folder indicated that the applicant had been convicted and sentenced for assault; the second, that he had been tried for assault and acquitted; the third, also tried for assault and acquitted, but with a letter from the judge certifying the finding of not guilty and reaffirming the legal presumption of innocence. The fourth folder made no mention of any criminal record.

A sample of one hundred employers was utilized. Each employer was assigned to one of four "treatment" groups.[4] To each employer only one folder was shown; this folder was one of the four kinds mentioned above, the selection of the folder being determined by the treatment group to which the potential employer was assigned. The employer was asked whether he could "use" the man described in the folder. To preserve the reality of the situation and make it a true field experiment, employers were never given any indication that they were participating in an experiment. So far as they knew, a legitimate offer to work was being made in each showing of the folder by the "employment agent."

The experiment was designed to determine what employers would do in fact if confronted with an employment applicant with a criminal record. The questionnaire approach used in earlier studies[5] seemed ill-adapted to the problem, since respondents confronted with hypothetical situations might be particularly prone to answer in what they considered a socially acceptable manner. The second alternative —studying job opportunities of individuals who had been involved with the law—would have made it very difficult to find comparable groups of applicants and potential employers. For these reasons, the field experiment reported here was utilized.

Some deception was involved in the study. The "employment agent"—the same individual in all hundred cases—was in fact a law student who was working in the Catskills during the summer of 1959 as an insurance adjuster. In representing himself as being both an adjuster and an employment agent, he was assuming a combination of roles which is not uncommon there. The adjuster role gave him an opportunity to introduce a single application for employment casually and naturally. To the extent that the experiment worked, however, it was inevitable that some employers should be led to believe that they had immediate prospects of filling a job opening. In those instances where an offer to hire was made, the "agent" called a few hours later to say that the applicant had taken another job. The field experimenter attempted in such instances to locate a satisfactory replacement by contacting an employment agency in the area. Because this procedure was used and since the jobs involved were of relatively minor consequence, we believe that the deception caused little economic harm.

As mentioned, each treatment group of twenty-five employers was approached with one type of folder. Responses were dichotomized: those who expressed a willingness to consider the applicant in any way were termed positive; those who made no response or who explicitly refused to consider the candidate were termed negative. Our results consist of comparisons between positive and negative responses, thus defined, for the treatment groups.

Of the twenty-five employers shown the "no record" folder, nine gave positive responses. Subject to reservations arising from chance variations in sampling we take this as indicative of the "ceiling" of jobs available for this kind of applicant under the given field conditions. Positive responses by these employers may be compared with those in the other treatment groups to obtain an indication of job opportunities lost because of the various legal records.

Of the twenty-five employers approached with the "convict" folder, only one expressed interest in the

applicant. This is a rather graphic indication of the effect which a criminal record may have on job opportunities. Care must be exercised, of course, in generalizing the conclusions to other settings. In this context, however, the criminal record made a major difference.

From a theoretical point of view, the finding leads toward the conclusion that conviction constitutes a powerful form of "status degradation"[6] which continues to operate after the time when, according to the generalized theory of justice underlying punishment in our society, the individual's "debt" has been paid. A record of conviction produces a durable if not permanent loss of status. For purposes of effective social control, this state of affairs may heighten the deterrent effect of conviction—though that remains to be established. Any such contribution to social control, however, must be balanced against the barriers imposed upon rehabilitation of the convict. If the ex-prisoner finds difficulty in securing menial kinds of legitimate work, further crime may become an increasingly attractive alternative.[7]

Another important finding of this study concerns the small number of positive responses elicited by the "accused but acquitted" applicant. Of the twenty-five employers approached with this folder, three offered jobs. Thus, the individual accused but acquitted of assault has almost as much trouble finding even an unskilled job as the one who was not only accused of the same offense, but also convicted.

From a theoretical point of view, this result indicates that permanent lowering of status is not limited to those explicitly singled out by being convicted of a crime. As an ideal outcome of American Justice, criminal procedure is supposed to distinguish between the "guilty" and those who have been acquitted. Legally controlled consequences which follow the judgment are consistent with this purpose. Thus, the "guilty" are subject to fine and imprisonment, while those who are acquitted are immune from these sanctions. But deprivations may be imposed on the acquitted, both before and after victory in court. Before trial, legal rules either permit or require arrest and detention. The suspect may be faced with the expense of an attorney and a bail bond if he is to mitigate these limitations on his privacy and freedom. In addition, some pre-trial deprivations are imposed without formal legal permission. These may include coercive questioning, use of violence, and stigmatization. And, as this study indicates, some deprivations not under the direct control of the legal process may develop or persist after an official decision of acquittal has been made.

Thus two legal principles conflict in practice. On the one hand, "a man is innocent until proven guilty." On the other, the accused is systematically treated as guilty under the administration of criminal law until a functionary or official body—police, magistrate, prosecuting attorney, or trial judge or jury—decides that he is entitled to be free. Even then, the results of treating him as guilty persist and may lead to serious consequences.

The conflict could be eased by measures aimed at reducing the deprivations imposed on the accused, before and after acquittal. Some legal attention has been focused on pre-trial deprivations. The provision of bail and counsel, the availability of habeas corpus, limitations on the admissibility of coerced confessions, and civil actions for false arrest are examples of measures aimed at protecting the rights of the accused before trial. Although these are often limited in effectiveness, especially for individuals of lower socioeconomic status, they at least represent some concern with implementing the presumption of innocence at the pre-trial stage.

By contrast, the courts have done little toward alleviating the post-acquittal consequences of legal accusation. One effort along these lines has been employed in the federal courts, however. Where an individual has been accused and exonerated of a crime, he may petition the federal courts for a "Certificate of Innocence" certifying this fact.[8] Posses-

sion of such a document might be expected to alleviate post-acquittal deprivations.

Some indication of the effectiveness of such a measure is found in the responses of the final treatment group. Their folder, it will be recalled, contained information on the accusation and acquittal of the applicant, but also included a letter from a judge addressed "To whom it may concern" certifying the applicant's acquittal and reminding the reader of the presumption of innocence. Such a letter might have had a boomerang effect, by reemphasizing the legal involvement of the applicant. It was important, therefore, to determine empirically whether such a communication would improve or harm the chances of employment. Our findings indicate that it increased employment opportunities, since the letter folder elicited six positive responses. Even though this fell short of the nine responses to the "no record" folder, it doubled the number for the "accused but acquitted" and created a significantly greater number of job offers than those elicited by the convicted record. This suggests that the procedure merits consideration as a means of offsetting the occupational loss resulting from accusation. It should be noted, however, that repeated use of this device might reduce its effectiveness.

The results of the experiment are summarized in Table 1. The differences in outcome found there indicate that various types of legal records are systematically related to job opportunities. It seems fair to infer also that the trend of job losses corresponds with the apparent punitive intent of the authorities. Where the man is convicted, that intent is presumably greatest. It is less where he is accused but acquitted and still less where the court makes an effort to emphasize the absence of a finding of guilt.

TABLE 1
Effect of Four Types of Legal Folder on Job Opportunities (in Percent)

	No Record (N = 25)	Acquitted with Letter (N = 25)	Acquitted without Letter (N = 25)	Convicted (N = 25)	Total (N = 100)
Positive response	36	24	12	4	19
Negative response	64	76	88	96	81
Total	100	100	100	100	100

Nevertheless, where the difference in punitive intent is ideally greatest, between conviction and acquittal, the difference in occupational harm is very slight. A similar blurring of this distinction shows up in a different way in the next study.

Study II. The effects on defendants of suits for medical malpractice As indicated earlier, the second study differed from the first in a number of ways: method of research, social class of accused, relationship between the accused and his "employer," social support available to accused, type of offense and its possible relevance to occupational adequacy. Because the two studies differ in so many ways, the reader is again cautioned to avoid thinking of them as providing a rigorous comparative examination. They are presented together only to demonstrate that legal accusation can produce unanticipated deprivations, as in the case of Study I, or unanticipated benefits, as in the research now to be presented. In the discussion to follow, some of the possible reasons for the different outcomes will be suggested.

The extra-legal effects of a malpractice suit were studied by obtaining the records of Connecticut's leading carrier of malpractice insurance. According to these records, a total of 69 doctors in the state had been sued in 64 suits during the post World War II period covered by the study, September, 1945, to September, 1959.[9] Some suits were instituted against more than one doctor, and four physicians had been sued twice. Of the total of 69 physicians, 58 were questioned. Interviews were conducted with the approval of the Connecticut Medical Association by Robert Wyckoff, whose extraordinary qualifications for the work included possession of both the M.D. and LL.B. degrees. Dr. Wyckoff was able to secure detailed responses to his inquiries from all doctors contacted.

Twenty of the respondents were questioned by personal interview, 28 by telephone, and the remainder by mail. Forty-three of those reached practiced principally in cities, eleven in suburbs, and four in rural areas. Seventeen were engaged in general practice and forty-one were specialists. The sample proved comparable to the doctors in the state as a whole in age, experience, and professional qualifications.[10] The range was from the lowest professional stratum to chiefs of staff and services in the state's most highly regarded hospitals.

Of the 57 malpractice cases reported, doctors clearly won 38; nineteen of these were dropped by the plaintiff and an equal number were won in court by the defendant doctor. Of the remaining nineteen suits, eleven were settled out of court for a nominal amount, four for approximately the amount the plaintiff claimed and four resulted in judgment for the plaintiff in court.

The malpractice survey did not reveal widespread occupational harm to the physicians involved. Of the 58 respondents, 52 reported no negative effects of the suit on their practice, and five of the remaining six, all specialists, reported that their practice *improved* after the suit. The heaviest loser in court (a radiologist), reported the largest gain. He commented, "I guess all the doctors in town felt sorry for me because new patients started coming in from doctors who had not sent me patients previously." Only one doctor reported adverse consequences to his practice. A winner in court, this man suffered physical and emotional stress symptoms which hampered his later effectiveness in surgical work. The temporary drop in his practice appears to have been produced by neurotic symptoms and is therefore only indirectly traceable to the malpractice suit. Seventeen other doctors reported varying degrees of personal dissatisfaction and anxiety during and after the suit, but none of them reported impairment of practice. No significant relationship was found between outcome of the suit and expressed dissatisfaction.

A protective institutional environment helps to explain these results. No cases were found in which a doctor's hospital privileges were reduced following the suit. Neither was any physician unable later to obtain malpractice insurance, although a handful found it necessary to pay higher rates. The State Licensing Commission, which is headed by a doctor, did not intervene in any instance. Local medical societies generally investigated charges through their ethics and grievances committees, but where they took any action, it was almost always to recommend or assist in legal defense against the suit.

DISCUSSION

Accusation has different outcomes for unskilled workers and doctors in the two studies. How may these be explained? First, they might be nothing more than artifacts of research method. In the field experiment, it was possible to see behavior directly, i.e., to determine how employers act when confronted with what appears to them to be a realistic opportunity to hire. Responses are therefore not distorted by the memory of the respondent. By contrast, the memory of the doctors might have been consciously or unconsciously shaped by the wish to create the impression that the public had not taken seriously the accusation leveled against them. The motive for such a distortion might be either to protect the respondent's self-esteem or to preserve an image of public acceptance in the eyes of the interviewer, the profession, and the public. Efforts of the interviewer to assure his subjects of anonymity—intended to offset these effects—may have succeeded or may, on the contrary, have accentuated an awareness of the danger. A related type of distortion might have stemmed from a desire by doctors to affect public attitudes toward malpractice. Two conflicting motives might have been expected to enter here. The doctor might have tended to exaggerate the harm caused by an accusation, especially if followed by acquittal, in order to turn public opinion toward legal policies which would limit malpractice liability. On the other hand, he might tend to underplay extra-legal harm caused by a legally insufficient accusation in order to discourage potential plaintiffs from instituting suits aimed at securing remunerative settlements and/or revenge for grievances. Whether these diverse motives operated to distort doctors' reports and, if so, which of them produced the greater degree of distortion is a matter for speculation. It is only suggested here that the interview method is more subject to certain types of distortion than the direct behavioral observations of the field experiment.

Even if such distortion did not occur, the results may be attributable to differences in research design. In the field experiment, a direct comparison is made between the occupational position of an accused and an identical individual not accused at a single point in time. In the medical study, effects were inferred through retrospective judgment, although checks on actual income would have no doubt confirmed these judgments. Granted that income had increased, many other explanations are available to account for

it. An improvement in practice after a malpractice suit may have resulted from factors extraneous to the suit. The passage of time in the community and increased experience may have led to a larger practice and may even have masked negative effects of the suit. There may have been a general increase in practice for the kinds of doctors involved in these suits, even greater for doctors not sued than for doctors in the sample. Whether interviews with a control sample could have yielded sufficiently precise data to rule out these possibilities is problematic. Unfortunately, the resources available for the study did not enable such data to be obtained.

A third difference in the two designs may affect the results. In the field experiment, full information concerning the legal record is provided to all of the relevant decision makers, i.e., the employers. In the medical study, by contrast, the results depend on decisions of actual patients to consult a given doctor. It may be assumed that such decisions are often based on imperfect information, some patients knowing little or nothing about the malpractice suit. To ascertain how much information employers usually have concerning the legal record of the employee and then supply that amount would have been a desirable refinement, but a difficult one. The alternative approach would involve turning the medical study into an experiment in which full information concerning malpractice (e.g., liable, accused but acquitted, no record of accusation) was supplied to potential patients. This would have permitted a comparison of the effects of legal accusation in two instances where information concerning the accusation is constant. To carry out such an experiment in a field situation would require an unlikely degree of cooperation, for instance by a medical clinic which might ask patients to choose their doctor on the basis of information given them. It is difficult to conceive of an experiment along these lines which would be both realistic enough to be valid and harmless enough to be ethical.

If we assume, however, that these methodological problems do not invalidate the basic finding, how may it be explained? Why would unskilled workers accused but acquitted of assault have great difficulty getting jobs, while doctors accused of malpractice—whether acquitted or not—are left unharmed or more sought after than before?

First, the charge of criminal assault carries with it the legal allegation and the popular connotation of intent to harm. Malpractice, on the other hand, implies negligence or failure to exercise reasonable care. Even though actual physical harm may be greater in malpractice, the element of intent suggests that the man accused of assault would be more likely to repeat his attempt and to find the mark. However, it is dubious that this fine distinction could be drawn by the lay public.

Perhaps more important, all doctors and particularly specialists may be immune from the effects of a malpractice suit because their services are in short supply.[11] By contrast, the unskilled worker is one of many and therefore likely to be passed over in favor of someone with a "cleaner" record.

Moreover, high occupational status, such as is demonstrably enjoyed by doctors,[12] probably tends to insulate the doctor from imputations of incompetence. In general, professionals are assumed to possess uniformly high ability, to be oriented toward community service, and to enforce adequate standards within their own organization.[13] Doctors in particular receive deference, just because they are doctors, not only from the population as a whole but even from fellow professionals.[14]

Finally, individual doctors appear to be protected from the effects of accusation by the sympathetic and powerful support they receive from fellow members of the occupation, a factor absent in the case of unskilled, unorganized laborers.[15] The medical society provides advice on handling malpractice actions, for instance, and referrals by other doctors sometimes increase as a consequence of the sympathy felt for the malpractice suit victim. Such assistance is further evidence that the professional operates as "a community within a community,"[16] shielding its members from controls exercised by formal authorities in the larger society.

In order to isolate these factors, additional studies are needed. It would be interesting to know, for instance, whether high occupational status would protect a doctor acquitted of a charge of assault. Information on this question is sparse. Actual instances of assaults by doctors are probably very rare. When and if they do occur, it seems unlikely that they would lead to publicity and prosecution, since police and prosecutor discretion might usually be employed to quash charges before they are publicized. In the rare instances in which they come to public attention, such accusations appear to produce a marked effect because of the assumption that the pressing of charges, despite the status of the defendant, indicates probable guilt. Nevertheless, instances may be found in which even the accusation of first degree murder followed by acquittal appears to have left the doctor professionally unscathed.[17] Similarly, as a test of the group protection hypothesis, one might investigate the effect of an acquittal for assault on working men who are union members. The analogy would be particularly instructive where the union plays an important part in employment decisions, for instance in industries which make use of a union hiring hall.

In the absence of studies which isolate the effect of such factors, our findings cannot readily be generalized. It is tempting to suggest after an initial look at the results that social class differences provide the explanation. But subsequent analysis and research might well reveal significant intra-class variations, depending on the distribution of other operative factors. A lower class person with a scarce specialty and a protective occupational group who is acquitted of a lightly regarded offense might benefit from the accusation. Nevertheless, class in general seems to correlate with the relevant factors to such an extent that in reality the law regularly works to the disadvantage of the already more disadvantaged classes.

CONCLUSION

Legal accusation imposes a variety of consequences, depending on the nature of the accusation and the characteristics of the accused. Deprivations occur, even though not officially intended, in the case of unskilled workers who have been acquitted of assault charges. On the other hand, malpractice actions— even when resulting in a judgment against the doctor —are not usually followed by negative consequences and sometimes have a favorable effect on the professional position of the defendant. These differences in outcome suggest two conclusions: one, the need for more explicit clarification of legal goals; two, the importance of examining the attitudes and social structure of the community outside the courtroom if the legal process is to hit intended targets, while avoiding innocent bystanders. Greater precision in communicating goals and in appraising consequences of present practices should help to make the legal process an increasingly equitable and effective instrument of social control.

FOOTNOTES

[1] Legal sanctions are defined as changes in life conditions imposed through court action.

[2] Richard D. Schwartz, "The Effectiveness of Legal Controls: Factors in the Reporting of Minor Items of Income on Federal Income Tax Returns." Paper presented at the annual meeting of the American Sociological Association, Chicago, 1959.

[3] The generality of these results remains to be determined. The effects of criminal involvement in the Catskill area are probably diminished, however, by the temporary nature of employment, the generally poor qualifications of the work force, and the excess of demand over supply of unskilled labor there. Accordingly, the employment differences among the four treatment groups found in this study are likely, if anything, to be *smaller* than would be expected in industries and areas where workers are more carefully selected.

[4] Employers were not approached in pre-selected random order, due to a misunderstanding of instructions on the part of the law student who carried out the experiment during a three and one-half week period. Because of this flaw in the experimental procedure, the results should be treated with appropriate caution. Thus, chi-squared analysis may not properly be utilized. (For those used in this measure, $P < .05$ for Table 24–1.)

[5] Sol Rubin, *Crime and Juvenile Delinquency*, New York: Oceana, 1958, pp. 151–56.

[6] Harold Garfinkel, "Conditions of Successful Degradation Ceremonies," *American Journal of Sociology*, 61 (March, 1956), pp. 420–24.

[7] Severe negative effects of conviction on employment opportunities have been noted by Sol Rubin, *Crime and Juvenile Delinquency*, New York: Oceana, 1958. A further source of employment difficulty is inherent in licensing statutes and security regulations which sometimes preclude convicts from being employed in their pre-conviction occupation or even in the trades which they may have acquired during imprisonment. These effects may, however, be counteracted by bonding arrangements, prison associations, and publicity programs aimed at increasing confidence in and sympathy for ex-convicts. See also, B. F. McSally, "Finding Jobs for Released Offenders," *Federal Probation*, 24 (June, 1960), pp. 12–17; Harold D. Lasswell and Richard C. Donnelly, "The Continuing Debate over Responsibility: An Introduction to Isolating the Condemnation Sanction," *Yale Law Journal*, 68 (April, 1959), pp. 869–99; Johannes Andenaes, "General Prevention—Illusion or Reality?" *J. Criminal Law*, 43 (July–August, 1952), pp. 176–98.

[8] 28 United States Code, Secs. 1495, 2513.

[9] A spot check of one county revealed that the Company's records covered every malpractice suit tried in the courts of that county during this period.

[10] No relationship was found between any of these characteristics and the legal or extra-legal consequences of the lawsuit.

[11] See Eliot Freidson, "Client Control and Medical Practice," *American Journal of Sociology*, 65 (January, 1960), pp. 374–82. Freidson's point is that practitioners are more subject to client control than specialists are. Our findings emphasize the importance of professional as compared to client control, and professional protection against a particular form of client control, extending through both branches of the medical profession. However, what holds for malpractice situations may not be true of routine medical practice.

[12] National Opinion Research Center, "Jobs and Occupations: A Popular Evaluation," *Opinion News*, 9 (Sept., 1947), pp. 3–13. More recent studies in several countries tend to confirm the high status of the physician. See Alex Inkeles, "Industrial Man: The Relation of Status to Experience, Perception and Value," *American Journal of Sociology*, 66 (July, 1960), pp. 1–31.

[13] Talcott Parsons, *The Social System*, Glencoe: The Free Press, 1951, pp. 454–73; and Everett C. Hughes, *Men and Their Work*, Glencoe: The Free Press, 1958.

[14] Alvin Zander, Arthur R. Cohen, and Ezra Stotland, *Role Relations in the Mental Health Professions*, Ann Arbor: Institute for Social Research, 1957.

[15] Unions sometimes act to protect the seniority rights of members who, discharged from their jobs upon arrest, seek re-employment following their acquittal.

[16] See William J. Goode, "Community within a Community: The Professions," *American Sociological Review*, 22 (April, 1957), pp. 194–200.

36

Mods, Rockers and the Rest:

Community Reactions to Juvenile Delinquency

STANLEY COHEN

This paper deals with one part of a research project being carried out within a certain theoretical framework in criminology and the broader field of the sociology of deviance. To understand why certain aspects of the subject matter—the Mods and Rockers phenomenon—are being considered rather than others, it is necessary to provide a brief statement of this framework.

THEORETICAL FRAMEWORK

The main purpose of the research project is to investigate social reaction to deviant behaviour. The rationale behind this approach was first set out in a strangely neglected textbook by Lemert[1] and systematized more recently by Becker.[2] This approach views deviance as a transactional process, the result of interaction between the person who commits an act and those who respond to it. Social reaction to deviance, the crucial variable in this approach, is largely ignored in conventional research in criminology and social deviance. In the field of juvenile delinquency, for example, the bulk of research is directed towards

Source: "Mods, Rockers and the Rest," *The Howard Journal* (12), London, 1967, pp. 121–130. By permission of the author and publisher.

the taxonomic tabulation of the delinquents' traits (or attitudes, or values) in an attempt to see how delinquents differ from non-delinquents.[3] On this basis causal theories are constructed. But the deviant act is not, or not only, deviant *per se*, it has to be defined and treated as such by the community. Social problems are what people think they are—there is an objective and verifiable situation, but also a subjective awareness of it and a definition by certain people that the situation is inimical to their interests and that something should be done about it.[4] The damage to art treasures by floods is a 'problem' to those whose commercial and aesthetic values are tied up with the preservation of art treasures. If this group of people didn't exist, there would be no problem. In the same way, the delinquent is a problem, but a problem *for someone*.

So when Becker writes that society creates deviance, he does not mean this in the conventional sense of there being social factors in the individual's situation which prompt his action, but that '. . . social groups create deviance by making the rules whose infractions constitute deviance, and by applying these rules to particular persons and labelling them as outsiders.' From this point of view, deviance is not a quality of the act the person commits, but rather a consequence of the application by others of rules and sanctions to an 'offender.'[5] The audience, not the actor, is the crucial variable.

One effect of community reaction is to confirm the deviant in his self-identity. When the community reacts negatively to a person's deviation from valued norms he tends to define his situation largely in terms of the reaction. He takes a new self-concept, identifies himself in a new light and even begins to act like the stereotype of him. James Baldwin has vividly described the position of many Negroes in these terms: he notes how his father '. . . was defeated long before he died because . . . he really believed what white people said about him' and warned his nephew: 'You can only be destroyed by believing that you really are what the white world calls a nigger.'[6]

This reaction sequence sets into operation what Wilkins calls a 'deviation-amplifying system'[7] and the present research is aimed at observing the workings of this sort of system. The sequence would run something like this:

1. Initial deviation from valued norms, leading to:
2. Punitive reaction by the community (which may lead to the segregation of groups and marking them as deviant):
3. Development of a deviant self-identity and behaviour appropriate to this identity:
4. Further punitive reaction, etc.

Although it is not within the scope of this [paper] to develop the theme, it should be pointed out that this sort of analysis is not just a manipulation of theoretical models. As Wilkins himself has made very clear, the implications for social policy, in the fields of both treatment and prevention, are considerable. Schur has recently used this type of model to examine the impact of public policy on abortion, homosexuality, and drug addiction.[8] He shows, for example, how policy based often upon vital misconceptions about the nature of deviant behaviour, may be expressed in legal prescriptions. This 'criminalization' of deviance then forces the individual into reinforcing a criminal self-image that creates problems for himself and society at large. The classic example, of course, is the creation of the addict sub-culture as partly at least a consequence of the public stereotype (the 'dope fiend') and repressive legislation. In the context of compulsory hospitalization, treatment may just reinforce the self-image.

THE PRESENT STUDY

Deviance is not a 'thing' which can be observed and studied. The term is a conceptual category and all we have are types of behaviour that have been classified as deviant. For research purposes we have to choose one of these types and juvenile delinquency is simply one such type that can be studied. Again though, juvenile delinquency is not a concrete enough category for this type of study—the term is a legal definition and not a behavioural syndrome. So, for reasons including its topical importance as a subject in its own right, the unit of study for this section of the project was narrowed down to what is classifiable (for want of a less emotive word) as 'hooliganism.' The Mods and Rockers phenomenon of the last three years, particularly in the form it took of disturbances and so-called riots at English seaside resorts over bank holiday weekends, provides an archetypal example of this behaviour.

Because we are using the transactional framework to explore certain aspects of the community reaction, the study is necessarily self-limiting. It does not attempt to provide a comprehensive account of the whole phenomenon e.g. in historical terms or in terms of subcultural theory.

METHOD

In an exploratory study of this nature there are few guidelines on which method to use for collecting data. In the event almost all possible methods were tried. These included:—content analysis of all press cuttings covering the period Easter 1964–August 1966 (national as well as relevant local press); 65 interviews carried out with a quota sample of spectators on the Brighton sea-front during Whitsun 1965; various other interviews with local figures, e.g. newspaper editors, local government officials, hotel proprietors, M.P.'s etc.; and personal observation of crowd behaviour, police action and court hearings. (The final research report will also use data from 140 intensive interviews carried out in a London

Borough on the more general topic of attitudes to delinquency.)

THE INITIAL DEVIATION

Clacton is an East Coast resort not particularly well known for the range of amusements it provides for its younger visitors. Easter 1963 was worse than usual —it was cold and wet, in fact the coldest Easter Sunday for eighty years. The shopkeepers and the stall-owners were irritated by the lack of business and the young people milling around had their own irritation fanned by rumours of cafe owners and barmen refusing to serve some of them. A few groups started roughing around and for the first time the Mods and Rockers factions, a division at that time only vaguely in the air, started separating out. Those on bikes and scooters roared up and down, windows were broken, some beach huts were wrecked, one boy fired a starting pistol in the air. The vast number of young people crowding the streets, the noise, everyone's general irritation and the often panicky actions of an unprepared and undermanned police force, made the two days seem rather frightening.

One of the most significant features about Clacton is that there appear to have been present a number of what the police would call 'troublemakers'—mainly Rockers from the East End or small East Anglian villages. Contrasted with the fringe supporters, these are the same hard core who in race riots and other crowd situations are predisposed to take the initiative and to respond violently to what is perceived as police provocation. All the 24 boys charged in the Clacton court claimed that they had been the unlucky ones, that they had been picked out at random. Yet 23 out of the 24 had previous convictions—the police's chances of picking out 23 previous offenders at random out of a crowd of say a thousand, is one in a couple of million.

As we shall show, many aspects of the Mods and Rockers have parallels in the class of phenomena known as mass delusion. These studies[9] show that the first stage is invariably a real event—the delusion or hysteria is created because the initial event is reported in such a way as to set in motion a cumulative sequence which serves to fulfill the expectations created by the earlier events. In terms of our model this is an amplifying process.

THE PROCESS OF AMPLIFICATION

One of the most important elements in the reaction to deviance is the growth of a generalized set of beliefs to explain the behaviour. Once the first stage of reporting is past, the community feels the need to make sense of what has occurred—this is especially the case when the event is perceived as a dislocation of the smooth running of things: the killing of a policeman, a political assassination, a natural disaster. People look for explanations, self-styled experts proclaim favourite theories, stereotypes are confirmed or new ones are created, words acquire a symbolic meaning—'Aberfan,' 'Dallas,' 'Braybrook Street,' 'Clacton.'

In the case of deviancy, these generalised beliefs invariably involve spurious attribution; all sorts of traits are attributed to the deviant and, on the basis of little or no evidence, a whole set of misconceptions arise. Let us give a few examples of some of these elements.

'Violence and Damage'—it was widely believed that the Mods and Rockers caused widespread damage and were involved in violent assaults on each other or 'innocent holidaymakers.' In fact the amount of damage done was not excessive—in the three-year period there were less than ten cases of malicious damage—in Hastings, August 1964, for example, one of the 'big' events, there were four charges of malicious damage out of 64 arrests.

During Whitsun 1964, although there were 54 arrests in Bournemouth the damage was £ 100, in Brighton with 76 arrests the damage was £ 400, in Margate with 64 arrests the damage was £ 250. Compare these figures to the *real* cost to the resorts which was in extra police charges: the four successive bank holidays between Easter 1965 and Easter 1966 cost the Brighton Council an extra £ 13,000. The amount of serious violence similarly was negligible—only one tenth of the original Clacton offenders were charged with offenses involving violence. In Margate, Whitsun 1964, supposedly the most violent weekend, where according to the *Daily Express* (19/5/64) 'The 1964 boys smeared the traditional postcard scene with blood and violence,' there were two not very serious stabbings and one man dropped onto a flower bed. The typical offense was using threatening behaviour or obstructing the police.

Leaving aside the obvious inconvenience caused to adults by crowds of youths milling about on the pavements and beach, few innocent holidaymakers were the victims of violence—the targets were members of a rival group or, more often, the police.

'Loss of trade'—it was widely believed that the troubles scared potential visitors away and the resorts suffered financially. The evidence for this is at best dubious. Papers quoted figures from Brighton for Whitsun 1964 showing that the number of deckchairs hired had dropped by 8,000 on the previous year's weekend. This drop was attributed to the effects of the Mods and Rockers. Analyses of other figures, however, show that the total number of visitors was probably more—the reason why fewer deckchairs were hired was that Whit Monday was one of the coldest for decades—the temperature had dropped overnight by 14° F. and the beaches were virtually deserted. Interviews and observation suggest that if anything, the Mods and Rockers attracted some visitors and by the end of 1965 certainly, the happenings were part of the Brighton scene—the pier, whelks and the Mods and Rockers could all be taken in on a day trip.

'Affluent Youth'—attitudes and opinions are often shaped and bolstered up by legends and myths. One of the most recurrent of the Mods and Rockers myths was the one about the boy who told the Margate magistrates that he would pay his £75 fine with a cheque. This myth was frequently used to justify the image of the Mods and Rockers are classless, affluent, and scooter or motor-bike owners. The story was in itself true enough—what few papers bothered to publish and what they all knew, was that the boy's offer was a pathetic gesture of bravado. He later admitted that not only did he not have the £75 cheque but did not even have a bank account and had never signed a cheque in his life. The affluence image has very little factual basis. The Clacton offenders had on them an average of 15/- for the whole bank holiday weekend. The best off was a window cleaner earning £15 a week, but more typical were a market assistant earning £7 10s. and a 17-year-old clerk earning £5 14s. The average take-home pay in a sample of offenders from Margate, Whitsun 1964, was £11 per week. The classless image is also none too accurate—the typical Rocker was an unskilled manual worker, the

typical Mod a semi-skilled manual worker.[10] In all cases, the majority of young people present hitched or came down by train or coach. The scooter and motor-bike riders were a minority, albeit a noisy and ubiquitous minority.

A detailed analysis of a number of other such images, shows that a large component of the deviation is, in Lemert's term, 'putative': 'The putative deviation is that portion of the societal definition of the deviant which has no foundation in his objective behaviour.'[11] Why is this sort of belief system important?

In the first place the stereotypes implied in the putative deviation serve to sensitize the community to any sign of incipient deviance. A previously ambiguous situation which may have been 'written off' as a Saturday night brawl now becomes re-interpreted as a 'Mods and Rockers clash.' In the weeks following the first two or three major happenings, a number of such incidents were reported from widely scattered localities. Minor scuffles and fights and increased police vigilance were reported by the Press under such headings as 'Mods and Rockers Strike Again.' There were also numerous false alarms—after Whitsun 1964 for example, the police in Stamford Hill after answering a false alarm stated that 'people are a bit jumpy after the trouble on the coast.' This type of sensitization which turns non-events into events, is exactly the same process noted by students of mass delusion. In a state of hypersuggestibility following the reporting of a 'Mad Bomber' or a 'Phantom Anaesthetist' or a 'Sex Fiend On The Loose' ambiguous events are re-interpreted to fit into the belief. This is made easier when there is a composite stereotype available with readily identifiable symbols such as clothes. To the residents of Brighton, any boy between fourteen and twenty wearing a fur-collared anorak was a Mod. At the end of one Bank Holiday the police stood at the station putting back on the trains all 'suspicious looking' arrivals who could not prove that they were local residents.

Another way in which beliefs are important in amplifying deviance is that they serve to legitimate the action of society's agents of control. *If* you are dealing with a group that is vicious, destructive, causing your community a financial loss, and symbolically repudiating your cherished values, then you are justified to respond punitively. *If*, moreover, this is an affluent horde of scooter-riders, then 'fines won't touch them' and you have to propose confiscation of their scooters, forced labour camps, corporal punishment, turning the fire hoses on them. By the logic of their own definitions, the agents of control have to escalate the measures they take and propose to take to deal with the problem. So by Easter 1965 the magistrates in Brighton were employing the highly dubious practice of remanding young people in custody as a form of extra-legal punishment. Bail was refused not on the merits of the individual case but as a matter of principle—the ostensible reason given by the magistrates for remand as being to enable the police to make enquiries, was not in fact the reason given in court when bail was opposed. The police opposed bail on the grounds that if the boys were allowed to go free justice would not be done and that the public would not be protected. On the flimsiest evidence a boy, who by the police's own account had done nothing more than refuse to 'move along,' would be certified as an 'unruly person,' refused bail and remanded in custody in an adult prison—in some cases for up to three weeks. A test case of this sort when taken before a Judge in Chambers resulted in the immediate release of a 16-year-old boy from prison on bail. Although precise data is difficult to obtain, at least 20 cases have been traced of successful appeals on the grounds of wrongful arrests or disproportionately high sentences. There is no doubt that in certain cases, admittedly under conditions of extreme physical and psychological strain and under direct provocation, arrests were made quite arbitrarily and with unnecessary violence. In one instance, arrested youths were observed being pushed through a gauntlet of police punches before literally being thrown into the van.

Informal agents of social control also took up extreme positions. On the initiative of a group of senior aldermen and councillors, the Brighton Council overwhelmingly passed a resolution calling for the setting up of compulsory labour camps for Mods and Rockers. A group of Great Yarmouth businessmen and hotel-keepers set up a Safeguard Committee which seriously debated a scheme of setting up road blocks outside the town to prevent any invasion.

We have discussed three types of processes identifiable in the reaction: the growth of generalised beliefs, which contain a putative element, the sensitization to deviance and the escalation of methods of social control. To evaluate the effects of the reaction on the self-image we would need a more complicated type of research design than has been used here—a longitudinal study of the impact of community reaction on young people's self concepts. At present we can only use the overt behaviour as the dependent variable and assume that this behaviour is consonant with the actors' self-image.

In the first place, as we have seen, the behaviour was often 'created' because of community sensitization. The atmosphere of expectancy present at the seaside resorts resulted in incidents being created out of nothing.

> Two boys stopped to watch a very drunk old tramp dancing about on the beach. They started throwing pennies at his feet. Within 45 seconds there were at least a hundred people gathered round and in 60 seconds the police were there. I turned my back on the crowd to watch the spectators gathering on the promenade above and by the time I turned back, two policemen were leading a boy away from the crowd.
> —(*Notes*, Brighton, Easter 1965).

Incidents such as these were created by sensitivity on the part of both audience and actors. There was a sense among the young people that they had to play to the gallery; the literal gallery of the adults lining the railing as at a bullfight, and the photographers running around from one event to the other; and the metaphorical gallery of the consumers of the mass media who had read in their morning papers 'Seaside Resorts Prepare for the Hooligans' Invasion.' The control agents, especially the police, created deviance not only in the sense of provoking the more labile members of the crowd into losing their tempers, but in Becker's sense of making the rules whose infraction constituted deviance. So, for example, certain areas were designated in advance as 'trouble spots.' If a number of youths were congregating in one of these trouble spots even for legitimate reasons (such as sheltering from the rain) they could be moved along, because policy was to keep these spots free. If one refused to move along he could be arrested and charged with wilful obstruction. (Under Sec. 51(3) Police Act 1964.)

Another significant effect of the reaction was, in Tannenbaum's phrase, the 'dramatisation of evil.'

The adult reaction was not only negative—it could hardly have been otherwise—but it was hostile in the melodramatic sense. There was the famous speech by a Margate magistrate about his town being '. . . polluted by hordes of hooligans . . . these long-haired mentally unstable petty little hoodlums, these sawdust Caesars who can only find courage like rats hunting in packs'; there were the newspaper headlines about 'vermin'; there was the show of force on the spot —police dogs, horses, walkie talkies, water board vans converted into squad cars; there were scenes like the police ceremoniously marching a group of youths through a street lined with spectators.

One way in which this hostility was reacted to was by returning it in kind. In the first series of events, the crowd, with the exception of the hard core referred to earlier, maintained fairly good humoured relations with the police. Attacks were disrespectful gestures such as knocking of helmets rather than malicious. In the 1966 incidents, the atmosphere was more tense. The lines had hardened:

> A policeman walked quite peacefully between two rows of boys near the aquarium. Some of them started whistling the Z-car theme and one shouted out 'Sprachen the Deutsch Constable?'
> —(*Notes*, Brighton, Easter 1966).

Another way in which the conflict was hardened was between the two groups themselves. Although the Mods and Rockers represent two very different consumer styles—the Mods the more glossy fashion-conscious teenager, the Rockers the tougher, reactionary tradition—the antagonism between the two groups is not very deep, they have much more in common, particularly their working class membership. There was initially nothing like the gang rivalry supposed to characterise the American type of conflict gang caricatured in West Side Story, in fact there was nothing like a gang. Commercial and media exploitation of the Mod-Rocker difference, and misguided attempts to explain the whole situation of unrest in terms of this difference, hardened the barriers. The groups were merely loose collectivities or crowds within which there was occasionally some more structured grouping based on territorial loyalty, e.g. 'The Walthamstow Boys,' 'The Lot From Eltham.' Constant repetition of the gang image made these collectivities see themselves as gangs and behave in a gang

fashion. Yablonsky has noted the same process in his study of delinquent gangs as near groups.[12]

THE ROLE OF THE MASS MEDIA

Without being able to consider here all the mechanisms through which the reaction was amplified, it is necessary to comment on the most important of these, the mass media. One must remember that in mass society one's view of deviance is usually second hand. In the hypothetical village community one might have been able to react to the village idiot in terms of first-hand impressions. In mass society images arrive already processed—policymakers can and do make decisions about say delinquents or drug addicts on the basis of the most crude and misleading images. In the case of the Mods and Rockers the media were responsible to a large extent for the putative deviance. An analysis, for example, of the House of Commons debate on 'Juvenile Delinquency and Hooliganism' (27th April 1964) shows the extent to which the images and stereotypes provided by the media were the basis for theories and policy proposals.

It is not just that the newspapers exaggerated the amount of behaviour—this is more or less inevitable. Estimates in any crowd situation such as a political rally or sporting event are notoriously inaccurate. What was more important was the manner of presentation—the sensational headlines, the interviews with dramatic characters and subtle techniques well known to war correspondents, such as reporting the same incident twice. Another effective technique was the misleading juxtaposition of headlines—on at least three occasions headlines such as 'Mod Found Dead in Sea,' 'Boy Falls to Death from Cliff' were used as sub-headings in Mods and Rockers reports. In every case the deaths had no connection at all with the disturbances and were pure accidents.

The chief roles of the media seem to have been in transmitting the stereotypes and creating an expectancy before each event that something was going to happen. This last role was particularly taken by the local press which highlighted reports about local traders arming themselves with tear gas, citizens forming vigilante patrols, etc.

DIFFERENTIAL REACTION

It is, of course, a fallacy to think of the mass media influencing a purely passive audience. Communication is responded to selectively, and the sort of questions we would like to answer are:—to what extent were the stereotypes and images absorbed by the community? How did the reaction crystallize into attitudes and opinions (e.g. about causes and solutions)? How were these attitudes affected by variables such as social class, education, political membership? Why did the reaction take the form it did?

The final research report will attempt to answer these questions. A preliminary analysis of the data from the Brighton sample only, suggests that the following type of generalisations might emerge:—

1. The reaction of the general public is less intense and less stereotypical than the reaction reflected in the mass media.

2. Local residents in the areas affected are more punitive than out of town visitors and the public in general.

3. Little difference between the Labour and Conservative groups were found. Except at the extreme of authoritarianism, political preference does not correlate with attitudes to delinquency.

4. The two most frequent single causes given for the Mods and Rockers events are 'boredom' and 'too much money.'

5. A dimension such as 'punitiveness' is too gross to measure attitudes to deviant behaviour. Certain groups, particularly working class and upper class, can at the same time be 'tolerant' of the behaviour and also devise the most punitive solutions for dealing with the behaviour when it is perceived as 'going too far.' The middle class less often makes this distinction.

CONCLUSION

It must be emphasised again that as this is an analysis of the ways in which social reaction impinges upon the genesis and amplification of deviance, little has been said about the behaviour itself. This does not mean that one is trying to deny an objective reality or even less trying to present the Mods and Rockers as innocent victims of conspiracy and discrimination. Social forces work in far more subtle ways. Although people *were* inconvenienced or hurt, and there were fights and vandalism, there is at the very least enough

evidence to suggest that the development of this behaviour was not independent of the reaction it provoked. Can one go further and say that the transactional theory is proved?

Clearly the present study is not a complete validation. For one thing, the crucial variable of the deviant self identity has not been measured and it might be a defect of the theory that this type of variable is peculiarly difficult to operationalise. There are problems in the model immediately apparent—for example why does the Wilkins-type of amplification sequence ever stop? Theoretically something like the Teddy Boy movement should have carried on growing. We know that this did not happen and there are already signs that the Mods and Rockers are going the same way. There are obviously factors 'outside' the model to account for these changes. Another problem is why not everybody exposed to the same definitions develops the appropriate self-image.

Until such questions are answered, we can only conclude that transactional theory provides a potentially useful framework for studying deviance. In the case of the Mods and Rockers at least, it gives an additional dimension to any other causal explanation.

FOOTNOTES

[1] Lemert, E. M., *Social Pathology*, London: McGraw-Hill, 1951.

[2] Becker, H. S., *Outsiders, Studies in the Sociology of Deviance*, New York: Free Press, 1963.

[3] Deutcher, I., 'Some Relevant Directions for Research in Juvenile Delinquency,' in Rose, A. R. (Ed.) *Human Behaviour and Social Processes*, London: Routledge and Kegan Paul, 1962, pp. 468–481.

[4] Fuller, R. C., and Meyers, R. R., 'Some Aspects of a Theory of Social Problems,' *Amer. Sociol. Rev. 6*, February, 1941, pp. 24–32.

[5] Becker, op. cit., p. 9.

[6] Baldwin, J., *The Fire Next Time*, Penguin, 1964, p. 13.

[7] Wilkins, L., *Social Deviance*, London, Tavistock, 1964. See also the preceding paper in this book.

[8] Schur, E. M., *Crimes Without Victims, Deviant Behaviour and Public Policy*, New Jersey: Prentice Hall, 1965.

[9] Johnson, D. M., 'The Phantom Anaesthetist of Mattoon,' *Journal of Abnormal and Social Psychology*, 40, 1945, pp. 175–186 etc.

[10] Barker, P. and Little, A., 'The Margate Offenders: A Survey,' *New Society*, Vol. 4, No. 96, 30th July 1964, pp. 6–10.

[11] Lemert, op. cit., p. 56.

[12] Yablonsky, L., *The Violent Gang*, New York: Collier Macmillan, 1962.

Part 5

Epilogue

PART 5   EPILOGUE

Between the idea
And the reality
Between the motion
And the act
Falls the Shadow
   —T. S. Eliot
      "The Hollow Men"

It may be true, as Mark Twain once warned, that it is dangerous to depart too quickly from our myths. But the contrary argument also has something in it: that if we are to ever deal effectively with our reality we must understand it better than the myths usually enable us to do. It is the latter belief that has guided the preparation of this book.

Few people would find fault with the ideology that underpins the legal systems of Western societies. One might well argue against the laws that protect the sanctity of private property, that provide special advantage in contracts to the more powerful party, that define as criminal acts committed by the lower class but as noncriminal more deleterious acts committed by those who control the resources of the society. But the fundamental notions of a system of law that applies equally to everyone (men and women), that provides everyone with a chance for a fair and impartial hearing before officials appointed for their skill and independence from outside influence, and a system that contains within it carefully devised procedural rules to guarantee the individual citizen freedom from unjust accusations or sanctions is on the surface easily defended. Most people would probably also acknowledge that a legal system that effectively controls the actions of some few people who refuse to live by standards accepted by "all healthy consciences" in the community is a desirable institution.

Such a view of the legal system is of course widespread. The mass media, textbooks, journalists, politicians, and ordinary citizens frequently espouse the value and the absolute necessity for having the legal system that prevails. So too do many social scientists who by their theories and their research look narrowly at the inner workings of the legal process and ignore the larger questions of how that system is a reflection of the political and economic institutions of which it is a part.

The studies and perspectives contained in this book are testimony to the fact that the idealized conception of Western law that is so all-pervasive is a myth. At the root of the myth is the belief that the outcome of the criminal law process is mainly a function of the rules and procedures that govern the system. The fact is that the reality of the criminal law in action is determined by political and economic forces that create social relations attended to by the police departments, prosecuting attorney's offices, courts, prisons, and every other bureaucratic agency charged with the responsibility of "upholding the law."

Rather than being an impartial, value-neutral arm of "the people" expressing their collective sentiments, the criminal law in action is a reflection of the struggles that inhere in a class society dominated by divisions between social classes. In this struggle the agencies that enforce and interpret the laws are inevitably reflecting the interests and values of those who control the economic and political pinnacles of power and resources in the society. That this is not a new condition of life is attested to by the fact that the same thing has been true throughout the history of Western society. That it must inevitably remain true is a question not yet answered. We can be certain, however, that without pursuing the quest for a system that comes closer to our ideals we will lack the knowledge to do anything about it.

For too many years a structural-functional perspective on the criminal law process dominated the thinking of American social science. The basic assumptions of that perspective were that the criminal law was a set of rules stipulated by legislatures and courts which reflected the most fundamental beliefs of the people in the society. The structural-functional view also saw the criminal law as fulfilling certain fundamental needs of the society. The most basic problem with this view was a failure to specify exactly who "the people" were whose interests, views and needs were being satisfied by the legal system. The studies in this volume have demonstrated that the functions served by the criminal law in action are clearly linked to the interests and privileges of the upper classes but are scarcely serving "the people" in general.

Sociology in general and criminology in particular are in the throes of what Thomas E. Kuhn has called a "paradigm revolution." That is, sociology and criminology are moving rapidly away from the previously accepted structural-functional analysis and are seeking more adequate understanding through the development of an alternative—in this case the conflict—paradigm.

The emergent paradigm in criminology and the sociology of criminal law is one which emphasizes social conflict as the moving force behind the criminal law in action. The social relations which are part of the class, labor, and productive systems of capitalist societies are seen as more

PART 5 EPILOGUE

important in determining the content and functioning of the criminal law process than are the values, norms, and beliefs of "the society."

This shift in paradigms means much more than merely a shift in the theories we use. It means more than merely explaining the same facts with new causal models. It provides us with a whole new set of concepts, categories, and perspectives with which to view the events that comprise the criminal law in action. It also provides us with a new set of moral imperatives and implications for social action. If, for example, we view the criminal law and its shortcomings as basically adequate with a few minor problematic areas that need adjustment, then we are inclined to study the parts and tinker with the problems. If, however, we view the criminal law process as a reflection of fundamental characteristics of the political economy of the society, then it is only by changing that political economy that we can hope to fundamentally change the real effect of the criminal law.

Theories should be judged not only according to how well they order the empirical data with which we are concerned; they should be judged as well in terms of whether they provide a critical perspective for understanding and changing the social reality. The perspective in this book and the researches we have collected manage both these responsibilities in ways that are promising. Fulfillment remains for the future.

5 New and Enhanced Material in Each Chapter

Added and revised material reflects major changes and discoveries in the field. This edition includes over 2,000 new reference citations. A list of new material can be found in the Preface for Instructors.

6 Beautiful Graphics and Photographs

Visually stunning, the graphics and photos effectively illustrate major points and enhance student interest and understanding.

"The tables, charts, photos, and . . . specific pedagogical tools enhance the experience rather than being a distraction."

Joseph Kishton, *University of North Carolina–Wilmington*

7 Outstanding Pedagogical Features

Outstanding pedagogical features support students' mastery of the material.

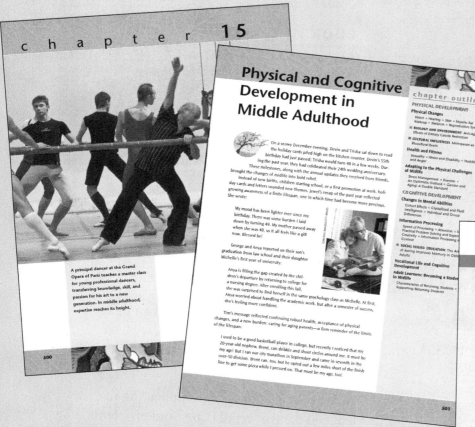

CHAPTER INTRODUCTIONS

Chapter openers begin with an outline and an engaging real-life story.

END-OF-CHAPTER SUMMARIES

Chapter summaries are organized by learning objectives, encouraging active study. They also include bolded key terms, which help students acquire and master the vocabulary of the field.

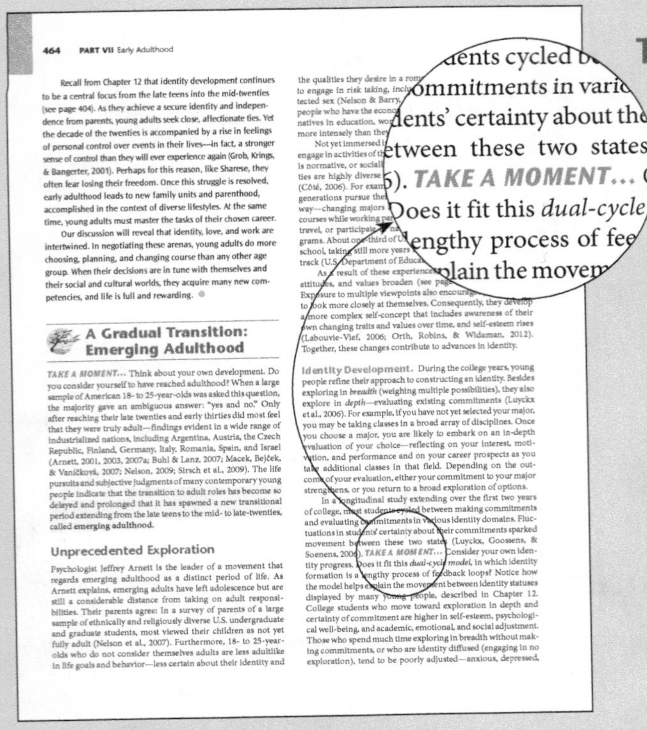

TAKE A MOMENT

Built into the text narrative, this feature engages students by asking them to "take a moment" to think about an important point, integrate information on human development, or engage in an exercise or an application to clarify a challenging concept.

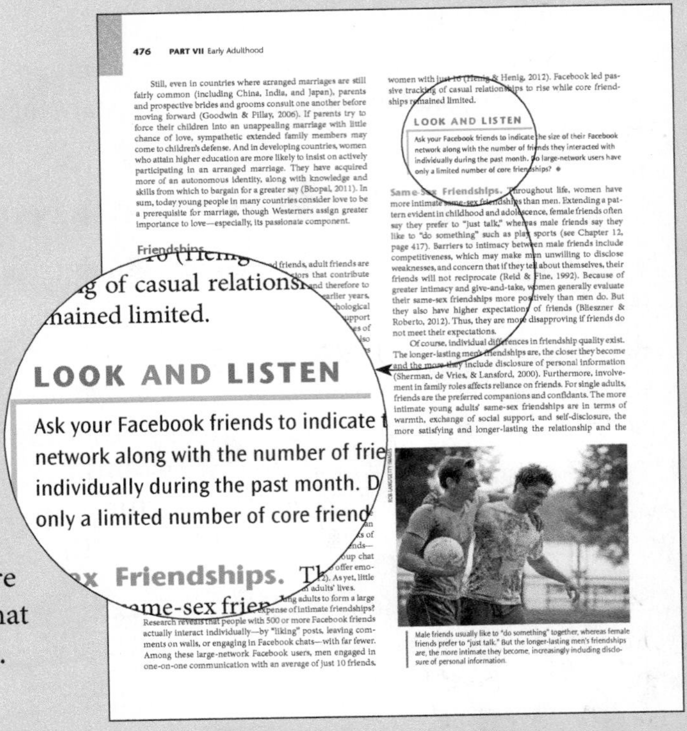

LOOK AND LISTEN

This *New* active-learning feature asks students to observe what real individuals say and do; speak with or observe parents, teachers, or other professionals; and inquire into community programs and practices that influence children, adolescents, and adults.

ASK YOURSELF QUESTIONS

REVIEW questions help students recall and comprehend information they have just read.

CONNECT questions help students build an image of the whole person by integrating what they have learned across age periods and domains of development.

APPLY questions encourage the application of knowledge to controversial issues and problems faced by children, adolescents, adults, and professionals who work with them.

REFLECT questions help make the study of human development personally meaningful by asking students to reflect on their own development and life experiences. Each question is answered on the text's MyDevelopmentLab website.

Recall from Chapter 12 that identity development continues to be a central focus from the late teens into the mid-twenties (see page 404). As they achieve a secure identity and independence from parents, young adults seek close, affectionate ties. Yet the decade of the twenties is accompanied by a rise in feelings of personal control over events in their lives—in fact, a stronger sense of control than they will ever experience again (Grob, Krings, & Bangerter, 2001). Perhaps for this reason, like Sharese, they often fear losing their freedom. Once this struggle is resolved, early adulthood leads to new family units and parenthood, accomplished in the context of diverse lifestyles. At the same time, young adults must master the tasks of their chosen career.

Our discussion will reveal that identity, love, and work are intertwined. In negotiating these arenas, young adults do more choosing, planning, and changing course than any other age group. When their decisions are in tune with themselves and their social and cultural worlds, they acquire many new competencies, and life is full and rewarding. ●

A Gradual Transition: Emerging Adulthood

TAKE A MOMENT... Think about your own development. Do you consider yourself to have reached adulthood? When a large sample of American 18- to 25-year-olds was asked this question, the majority gave an ambiguous answer: "yes and no." Only after reaching their late twenties and early thirties did most feel that they were truly adult—findings evident in a wide range of industrialized nations, including Argentina, Austria, the Czech Republic, Finland, Germany, Italy, Romania, Spain, and Israel (Arnett, 2001, 2003, 2007a; Buhl & Lanz, 2007; Macek, Bejček, & Vaníčková, 2007; Nelson, 2009; Sirsch et al., 2009). The life pursuits and subjective judgments of many contemporary young people indicate that the transition to adult roles has become so delayed and prolonged that it has spawned a new transitional period extending from the late teens to the mid- to late-twenties, called emerging adulthood.

Unprecedented Exploration

Psychologist Jeffrey Arnett is the leader of a movement that regards emerging adulthood as a distinct period of life. As Arnett explains, emerging adults have left adolescence but are still a considerable distance from taking on adult responsibilities. Their parents agree: In a survey of parents of a large sample of ethnically and religiously diverse U.S. undergraduate and graduate students, most viewed their children as not yet fully adult (Nelson et al., 2007). Furthermore, 18- to 25-year-olds who do not consider themselves adults are less adultlike in life goals and behavior—less certain about their identity and

the qualities they desire in a rom... to engage in risk taking (Nelson & Barry, ... tected sex (Nelson & Barry, ... people who have the econo... natives in education, wo... more intensely than the...

Not yet immersed in ... engage in activities of d... is normative, or social... ties are highly diverse ... (Côté, 2006). For exam... generations pursue their ... way—changing majors ... courses while working pa... travel, or participating ... About one-third of U.S. ... school, taking still more years ... track (U.S. Department of Educa...

As a result of these experience... attitudes, and values broaden (see pag... Exposure to multiple viewpoints also encourage... to look more closely at themselves. Consequently, they develop a more complex self-concept that includes awareness of their own changing traits and values over time, and self-esteem rises (Labouvie-Vief, 2006; Orth, Robins, & Widaman, 2012). Together, these changes contribute to advances in identity.

Identity Development. During the college years, young people refine their approach to constructing an identity. Besides exploring in *breadth* (weighing multiple possibilities), they also explore in *depth*—evaluating existing commitments (Luyckx et al., 2006). For example, if you have not yet selected your major, you may be taking classes in a broad array of disciplines. Once you choose a major, you are likely to embark on an in-depth evaluation of your choice—reflecting on your interest, motivation, and performance on your career prospects as you take additional classes in that field. Depending on the outcome of your evaluation, either your commitment to your major strengthens, or you return to a broad exploration of options.

In a longitudinal study extending over the first two years of college, most students cycled between making commitments and evaluating commitments in various identity domains. Fluctuations in students' certainty about their commitments sparked movement between these two states (Luyckx, Goossens, & Soenens, 2006). *TAKE A MOMENT...* Consider your own identity progress. Does it fit this *dual-cycle* model, in which identity formation is a lengthy process of feedback loops? Notice how the model helps explain the movement between identity statuses displayed by many young people, described in Chapter 12. College students who move toward exploration in depth and certainty of commitment are higher in self-esteem, psychological well-being, and academic, emotional, and social adjustment. Those who spend much time exploring in breadth without making commitments, or who are identity foreclosed (engaging in no exploration), tend to be poorly adjusted—anxious, depressed,

Still, even in countries where arranged marriages are still fairly common (including China, India, and Japan), parents and prospective brides and grooms consult one another before moving forward (Goodwin & Pillay, 2006). If parents try to force their children into an unappealing marriage with little chance of love, sympathetic extended family members may come to children's defense. And in developing countries, women who attain higher education are more likely to insist on actively participating in an arranged marriage. They have acquired more of an autonomous identity, along with knowledge and skills from which to bargain for a greater say (Bhopal, 2011). In sum, today young people in many countries consider love to be a prerequisite for marriage, though Westerners assign greater importance to love—especially its passionate component.

Friendships

...g of casual relationsh... ...mained limited.

LOOK AND LISTEN

Ask your Facebook friends to indicate ... network along with the number of frie... individually during the past month. D... only a limited number of core friend...

...x Friendships. Th... ...ame-sex frien... Research reveals that people with 500 or more Facebook friends actually interact individually—by "liking" posts, leaving comments on walls, or engaging in Facebook chats—with far fewer. Among these large-network Facebook users, men engaged in one-on-one communication with an average of just 10 friends.

women with just 10 (Hening & Henig, 2012). Facebook led passive tracking of casual relationships to rise while core friendships remained limited.

LOOK AND LISTEN

Ask your Facebook friends to indicate the size of their Facebook network along with the number of friends that they interacted with individually during the past month. Do large-network users have only a limited number of core friendships? ●

Same-Sex Friendships. Throughout life, women have more intimate same-sex friendships than men. Extending a pattern evident in childhood and adolescence, female friends often say they prefer to "just talk," whereas male friends say they like to "do something" such as play sports (see Chapter 12, page 417). Barriers to intimacy between male friends include competitiveness, which may make men unwilling to disclose weaknesses, and concern that if they talk about themselves, their friends will not reciprocate (Reid & Fine, 1992). Because of greater intimacy and give-and-take, women generally evaluate their same-sex friendships more positively than men do. But they also have higher expectations of friends (Blieszner & Roberto, 2012). Thus, they are more disapproving if friends do not meet their expectations.

Of course, individual differences in friendship quality exist. The longer-lasting men's friendships are, the closer they become and the more they include disclosure of personal information (Sherman, de Vries, & Lansford, 2000). Furthermore, involvement in family roles affects reliance on friends. For single adults, friends are the preferred companions and confidants. The more intimate young adults' same-sex friendships are in terms of warmth, exchange of social support, and self-disclosure, the more satisfying and longer-lasting the relationship and the

Male friends usually like to "do something" together, whereas female friends prefer to "just talk." But the longer-lasting men's friendships are, the more intimate they become, increasingly including disclosure of personal information.

perspective point out that people frequently rise above self-interest to defend others' rights. For example, moral leaders in business—rather than resorting to Stage 2 reasoning—endorse trust, integrity, good faith, and just laws and codes of conduct (Damon, 2004; Gibbs, 2006). Also, adolescents and adults are well aware of the greater adequacy of higher-stage moral reasoning, which some people act on despite highly corrupt environments. Most individuals who engage in sudden altruistic action may have previously considered relevant moral issues so thoroughly that their moral judgment activates automatically, triggering an immediate response (Gibbs et al., 2009a; Pizaro & Bloom, 2003). In these instances, people who appear to be engaging in after-the-fact moral justification are actually behaving with great forethought.

In sum, the cognitive-developmental approach to morality has done much to clarify our profound moral potential. And despite opposition, Kohlberg's central assumption—that with age, humans everywhere construct a deeper understanding of fairness and justice that guides moral action—remains powerfully influential.

Gender Typing

As Sabrina entered adolescence, she began to worry about walking, talking, eating, dressing, laughing, and competing in ways consistent with a feminine gender role. According to one hypothesis, the arrival of adolescence is typically accompanied by **gender intensification**—increased gender stereotyping of attitudes and behavior, and movement toward a more traditional gender identity. Research on gender intensification, however, is mixed, with some studies finding evidence for it and others reporting few instances (Basow & Rubin, 1999; Galambos, Almeida, & Petersen, 1990; Huston & Alvarez, 1990; Priess, Lindberg, & Hyde, 2009). When gender intensification is evident, it seems to be stronger for adolescent girls. Although girls continue to be less gender-typed than boys, some may feel less free to experiment with "other-gender" activities and behaviors than they did in middle childhood.

In young people who do exhibit gender intensification, biological, social, and cognitive factors likely are involved. As puberty magnifies sex differences in appearance, teenagers may spend more time thinking about themselves in gender-linked ways. Pubertal changes might also prompt gender-typed pressures from others. Parents with traditional gender-role beliefs may encourage "gender-appropriate" activities and behavior more than they did earlier (Crouter et al., 2007; Shanahan et al., 2007). And when adolescents start to date, they may become more gender-typed as a way of increasing their attractiveness (Maccoby, 1998). Finally, cognitive changes—might make young people more concerned with what others think—might heighten teenagers' more responsive to gender-role expectations.

Gender intensification declines by late adolescence, but not all affected young people move beyond it to the same degree. Teenagers who are encouraged to explore non-gender-typed options and to question the value of gender stereotypes for

themselves and society are more likely to build an androgynous gender identity (see Chapter 8, page 276). Overall, androgynous adolescents, especially girls, tend to be psychologically healthier—more self-confident, more willing to speak their own mind, better-liked by peers, and identity-achieved (Bronstein, 2006; Dusek, 1987; Harter, 2006).

For some young people, early adolescence is a time of gender intensification. Pubertal changes in appearance, traditional gender-role expectations of parents, and increased concern with what others think can prompt a move toward a more traditional gender identity.

REVIEW How does an understanding of ideal reciprocity contribute to moral development? Why are Kohlberg's Stages 3 and 4 morally mature?

CONNECT How might the exploration of values and goals associated with healthy identity development contribute to a decline in adolescent gender intensification?

APPLY Tam grew up in a small village culture, Lydia in a large industrial city. At age 15, Tam reasons at Kohlberg's Stage 3, Lydia at Stage 4. What factors might account for the difference?

REFLECT Do you favor a cognitive-developmental or a pragmatic approach to morality, or both? Explain, drawing on research evidence and personal experiences.

The Family

Franca and Antonio remember their son Louis's freshman year of high school as a difficult time. Because of a demanding project at work, Franca was away from home many evenings and weekends. In her absence, Antonio took over, but a series of business declined and he had to cut costs at his hardware store, he, too, had less time for the family. That year, Louis and two friends

FEATURE BOXES

See page v for a complete listing of feature boxes.

Biology and Environment boxes highlight the growing attention to the complex, bidirectional relationship between biology and environment. Examples include *A Case of Epigenesis: Smoking During Pregnancy Alters Gene Expression; Children with Attention-Deficit Hyperactivity Disorder; Anti-Aging Effects of Dietary Calorie Restriction;* and *Religious Involvement and Quality of Life in the Final Year.*

Cultural Influences boxes deepen the attention to culture threaded throughout the text and accentuate both cross-cultural and multicultural variations in development—for example, *Immigrant Youths: Adapting to a New Land; Impact of Ethnic and Political Violence on Children; Is Emerging Adulthood Really a Distinct Period of Development?;* and *The New Old Age.*

Social Issues boxes discuss the impact of social conditions on children, adolescents, and adults and emphasize the need for sensitive social policies to ensure their well-being:

New! **Social Issues: Education** boxes focus on home, school, and community influences on learning. Examples include *Baby Learning from TV and Video: The Video Deficit Effect; Media Multitasking Disrupts Attention and Learning; Magnet Schools: Equal Access to High-Quality Education;* and *The Art of Acting Improves Memory in Older Adults.*

New! **Social Issues: Health** boxes address values and practices relevant to physical and mental health. Examples include *Family Chaos Undermines Children's Well-Being; The Nurse–Family Partnership: Reducing Maternal Stress and Enhancing Child Development Through Social Support; A Cross-National Perspective on Health Care and Other Policies for Parents and Newborn Babies;* and *Interventions for Caregivers of Older Adults with Dementia.*

APPLYING WHAT WE KNOW TABLES

This feature summarizes research-based applications, speaking directly to students as parents or future parents and to those pursuing different careers or areas of study, such as teaching, health care, counseling, or social work.

See page v for a complete listing of Applying What We Know tables.

MILESTONES TABLES

These beautifully illustrated tables summarize major developments within each topical area, providing a convenient overview of the chronology of development.

IN-TEXT HIGHLIGHTED KEY TERMS WITH DEFINITIONS

Mastery of terms is promoted through in-text highlighting of key-term and concept definitions.

END-OF-CHAPTER TERM LIST, AND END-OF-BOOK GLOSSARY

Key terms also appear in an end-of-chapter page-referenced term list and an end-of-book page-referenced glossary.

8 *Unsurpassed Technology— MyDevelopmentLab*

Authored by Laura Berk, MyDevelopmentLab for *Development Through the Lifespan* engages students through personalized learning and helps instructors with course preparation, content delivery, and assessment. It helps students better prepare for class, quizzes, and exams. It provides educators with a dynamic set of tools for tracking individual and class performance.

- A **Personalized Study Plan** organizes students' study needs into three levels: Remember, Understand, and Apply.

- The **Gradebook** helps students track progress and get immediate feedback. Automatically graded assessments flow into the Gradebook, which can be viewed in MyDevelopmentLab or exported.

- The **eText** allows students to highlight relevant passages and add notes. Access the eText through a laptop, iPad, or tablet—or download the free app to use on tablets.

- **Extensive video footage** includes *New* video segments such as Preterm Birth, Autism, First-Grade Science Education, Civic Engagement in Adolescence, Changing Parent–Adolescent Relationships, Adult Obesity, and Surrogacy.

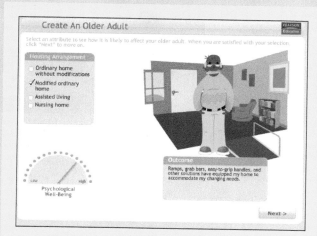

- **Multimedia simulations** include *New* Language Development, Create an Older Adult, and Working Memory.

- **Careers in Human Development** explains how studying lifespan development is essential for a wide range of career paths. This tool features over 25 career overviews, which contain interviews with actual practitioners, educational requirements, typical day-to-day activities, and links to websites for additional information.

- **Biographies** of major figures in the field. Examples include Erik Erikson, Jean Piaget, Lev Vygotsky, and Lawrence Kohlberg.

- *New* **MyVirtualLife** includes two simulations. In the first, students observe the effects of their parenting decisions on a child's development. In the second, they simulate their own progress through adulthood, making personal choices and reflecting on their lives.

MyDevelopmentLab can be used by itself or linked to any learning management system. To learn more about how the new MyDevelopmentLab combines learning applications with powerful assessment, visit **www.mydevelopmentlab.com**.

9 Valuable Teaching Resources

MyDevelopmentLab for *Development Through the Lifespan*. Authored by Laura Berk, MyDevelopmentLab includes a variety of assessments that enable continuous evaluation of students' learning. Extensive video footage, multimedia simulations, "Careers in Human Development," and interactive activities—all unique to *Development Through the Lifespan*—are also included. See previous page.

Instructor's Resource Manual (IRM). Each chapter includes a Chapter-at-a-Glance grid, Brief Chapter Summary, Learning Objectives, detailed Lecture Outlines, Learning Activities, "Ask Yourself" questions with answers, Suggested Student Readings, and Media Materials list.

Test Bank. The test bank contains more than 2,000 multiple-choice and essay questions, all of which are page-referenced to the chapter content and also classified by type.

Pearson MyTest. This secure online environment allows instructors to easily create exams, study guide questions, and quizzes from any computer with an Internet connection.

PowerPoint Presentation. The PowerPoint presentation provides outlines and illustrations of key topics for each chapter of the text.

***Explorations in Lifespan Development* DVD and Guide.** This *New* DVD is over four hours in length and contains over 60 four- to ten-minute narrated segments, designed for effective classroom use, that illustrate the many theories, concepts, and milestones of human development. *New* additions include Preterm Birth, Autism, First-Grade Science Education, Civic Engagement in Adolescence, Changing Parent–Adolescent Relationships, Adult Obesity, and Surrogacy.

10 Pearson Choices

These alternatives to the traditional printed textbook are available for *Development Through the Lifespan.*

MyDevelopmentLab with eTextbook offers a full digital version of the print book and is readable on iOS and Android tablets. Students can get access to MyDevelopmentLab with the print book or save even more by purchasing online access at **www.mydevelopmentlab.com.**

Books à la Carte is a convenient, three-hole-punched, loose-leaf version of the traditional text at a discounted price—allowing students to carry only what they need to class. The Books à la Carte edition is also available with MyDevelopmentLab access.

CourseSmart eTextbook offers the same content as the printed text in a convenient online format—with highlighting, online search, and printing capabilities. Learn more at **www.coursesmart.com.**

Laura E. Berk

Development Through the Lifespan

Fourth Custom Edition for Mt. San Antonio College

Taken from:
Development Through the Lifespan, Sixth Edition
by Laura E. Berk

Pearson Learning Solutions, 501 Boylston Street, Suite 900, Boston, MA 02116
A Pearson Education Company
www.pearsoned.com

Printed in the United States of America

8 9 10 11 12 V0UD 19 18 17 16 15

000200010271850969

ML

PEARSON   ISBN 10: 1-269-60354-X
ISBN 13: 978-1-269-60354-6

About the Author

Laura E. Berk is a distinguished professor of psychology at Illinois State University, where she has taught human development to both undergraduate and graduate students for more than three decades. She received her bachelor's degree in psychology from the University of California, Berkeley, and her master's and doctoral degrees in child development and educational psychology from the University of Chicago. She has been a visiting scholar at Cornell University, UCLA, Stanford University, and the University of South Australia.

Berk has published widely on the effects of school environments on children's development, the development of private speech, and the role of make-believe play in development. Her research has been funded by the U.S. Office of Education and the National Institute of Child Health and Human Development. It has appeared in many prominent journals, including *Child Development, Developmental Psychology, Merrill-Palmer Quarterly, Journal of Abnormal Child Psychology, Development and Psychopathology*, and *Early Childhood Research Quarterly*. Her empirical studies have attracted the attention of the general public, leading to contributions to *Psychology Today* and *Scientific American*. She has also been featured on National Public Radio's *Morning Edition* and in *Parents Magazine, Wondertime*, and *Reader's Digest*.

Berk has served as a research editor of *Young Children* and as a consulting editor for *Early Childhood Research Quarterly*. Currently, she is associate editor of the *Journal of Cognitive Education and Psychology*. She is a frequent contributor to edited volumes on early childhood development, having recently authored chapters on the importance of parenting, on make-believe play, and on the kindergarten child. She has also written the article on social development for *The Child: An Encyclopedic Companion;* the article on Vygotsky for the *Encyclopedia of Cognitive Science;* and the chapter on storytelling as a teaching strategy for *Voices of Experience: Memorable Talks from the National Institute on the Teaching of Psychology* (Association for Psychological Science). She is coauthor of the forthcoming chapter on make-believe play and self-regulation in the *Sage Handbook of Play in Early Childhood*.

Berk's books include *Private Speech: From Social Interaction to Self-Regulation; Scaffolding Children's Learning: Vygotsky and Early Childhood Education; Landscapes of Development: An Anthology of Readings;* and *A Mandate for Playful Learning in Preschool: Presenting the Evidence*. In addition to *Development Through the Lifespan*, she is author of the best-selling texts *Child Development* and *Infants, Children, and Adolescents*, published by Pearson. Her book for parents and teachers is *Awakening Children's Minds: How Parents and Teachers Can Make a Difference*.

Berk is active in work for children's causes. In addition to service in her home community, she is a member of the national board of directors and chair of the Chicago advisory board of Jumpstart, a nonprofit organization that provides intensive literacy intervention to thousands of low-income preschoolers across the United States, using college and university students as interveners. Berk is a fellow of the American Psychological Association, Division 7: Developmental Psychology.

Brief Contents

PART I: Theory and Research in Human Development

1 History, Theory, and Research Strategies 2

PART II: Foundations of Development

2 Genetic and Environmental Foundations 44

3 Prenatal Development, Birth, and the Newborn Baby 78

PART III: Infancy and Toddlerhood: The First Two Years

4 Physical Development in Infancy and Toddlerhood 118

5 Cognitive Development in Infancy and Toddlerhood 150

6 Emotional and Social Development in Infancy and Toddlerhood 182

PART IV: Early Childhood: Two to Six Years

7 Physical and Cognitive Development in Early Childhood 214

8 Emotional and Social Development in Early Childhood 254

PART V: Middle Childhood: Six to Eleven Years

9 Physical and Cognitive Development in Middle Childhood 288

10 Emotional and Social Development in Middle Childhood 328

PART VI: Adolescence: The Transition to Adulthood

11 Physical and Cognitive Development in Adolescence 360

12 Emotional and Social Development in Adolescence 400

PART VII: Early Adulthood

13 Physical and Cognitive Development in Early Adulthood 430

14 Emotional and Social Development in Early Adulthood 462

PART VIII: Middle Adulthood

15 Physical and Cognitive Development in Middle Adulthood 500

16 Emotional and Social Development in Middle Adulthood 530

PART IX: Late Adulthood

17 Physical and Cognitive Development in Late Adulthood 562

18 Emotional and Social Development in Late Adulthood 602

PART X: The End of Life

19 Death, Dying, and Bereavement 638

Observation Guide I

Features at a Glance

SOCIAL ISSUES: HEALTH

Family Chaos Undermines Children's Well-Being   26
The Pros and Cons of Reproductive Technologies   54
The Nurse–Family Partnership: Reducing Maternal Stress and Enhancing
    Child Development Through Social Support   94
A Cross-National Perspective on Health Care and Other Policies for Parents
    and Newborn Babies   104
Does Child Care in Infancy Threaten Attachment Security and Later
    Adjustment?   202
Emotional Intelligence   313
Children's Eyewitness Testimony   355
Lesbian, Gay, and Bisexual Youths: Coming Out to Oneself and
    Others   376
The Obesity Epidemic: How Americans Became the Heaviest People in the
    World   440
Childhood Attachment Patterns and Adult Romantic Relationships   474
Partner Abuse   482
Generative Adults Tell Their Life Stories   534
Grandparents Rearing Grandchildren: The Skipped-Generation
    Family   548
Interventions for Caregivers of Older Adults with Dementia   586
Elder Suicide   612
Voluntary Active Euthanasia: Lessons from Australia and the
    Netherlands   657

SOCIAL ISSUES: EDUCATION

Baby Learning from TV and Video: The Video Deficit Effect   159
Children's Questions: Catalyst for Cognitive Development   232
Young Children Learn About Gender Through Mother–Child
    Conversations   275
School Recess—A Time to Play, a Time to Learn   298
Magnet Schools: Equal Access to High-Quality Education   321
Media Multitasking Disrupts Attention and Learning   394
Development of Civic Engagement   413
Masculinity at Work: Men Who Choose Nontraditional Careers   458
The Art of Acting Improves Memory in Older Adults   523

BIOLOGY AND ENVIRONMENT

Resilience   10
A Case of Epigenesis: Smoking During Pregnancy Alters Gene
    Expression   74
The Mysterious Tragedy of Sudden Infant Death Syndrome   110
Brain Plasticity: Insights from Research on Brain-Damaged Children and
    Adults   126
"Tuning In" to Familiar Speech, Faces, and Music: A Sensitive Period for
    Culture-Specific Learning   141
Infantile Amnesia   164
Parental Depression and Child Development   186
Development of Shyness and Sociability   192
"Mindblindness" and Autism   241
Children with Attention-Deficit Hyperactivity Disorder   304
Bullies and Their Victims   342
Sex Differences in Spatial Abilities   390
Two Routes to Adolescent Delinquency   424
Telomere Length: A Marker of the Impact of Life Circumstances on
    Biological Aging   433
Anti-Aging Effects of Dietary Calorie Restriction   505
What Factors Promote Psychological Well-Being in Midlife?   540
What Can We Learn About Aging from Centenarians?   566
Religious Involvement and Quality of Life in the Final Year   609
Music as Palliative Care for Dying Patients   653

CULTURAL INFLUENCES

The Baby Boomers Reshape the Life Course   12
Immigrant Youths: Adapting to a New Land   32
The African-American Extended Family   66
Cultural Variation in Infant Sleeping Arrangements   129
Social Origins of Make-Believe Play   168
The Powerful Role of Paternal Warmth in Development   204
Children in Village and Tribal Cultures Observe and Participate in Adult
    Work   236
Cultural Variations in Personal Storytelling: Implications for Early
    Self-Concept   257
Ethnic Differences in the Consequences of Physical Punishment   267
Impact of Ethnic and Political Violence on Children   353
Identity Development Among Ethnic Minority Adolescents   406
Is Emerging Adulthood Really a Distinct Period of Development?   467
Menopause as a Biocultural Event   508
Cultural Variations in Sense of Usefulness in Late Life   576
The New Old Age   607
Cultural Variations in Mourning Behavior   664

APPLYING WHAT WE KNOW

Steps Prospective Parents Can Take Before Conception to Increase the
    Chances of a Healthy Baby   57
Do's and Don'ts for a Healthy Pregnancy   96
Soothing a Crying Baby   111
Reasons to Breastfeed   131
Features of a High-Quality Home Life: The HOME Infant–Toddler
    Subscales   171
Signs of Developmentally Appropriate Infant and Toddler Child Care   172
Supporting Early Language Learning   179
Encouraging Affectionate Ties Between Infants and Their Preschool
    Siblings   205
Helping Toddlers Develop Compliance and Self-Control   209
Features of a High-Quality Home Life for Preschoolers: The HOME Early
    Childhood Subscales   244
Signs of Developmentally Appropriate Early Childhood Programs   247
Helping Children Manage Common Fears of Early Childhood   259
Positive Parenting   268
Regulating TV and Computer Use   272
Providing Developmentally Appropriate Organized Sports in Middle
    Childhood   297
Signs of High-Quality Education in Elementary School   319
Fostering a Mastery-Oriented Approach to Learning   335
Helping Children Adjust to Their Parents' Divorce   349
Handling Consequences of Teenagers' New Cognitive Capacities   386
Supporting High Achievement in Adolescence   393
Supporting Healthy Identity Development   405
Preventing Sexual Coercion   449
Resources That Foster Resilience in Emerging Adulthood   468
Keeping Love Alive in a Romantic Partnership   475
Strategies That Help Dual-Earner Couples Combine Work and Family
    Roles   495
Reducing Cancer Incidence and Deaths   511
Reducing the Risk of Heart Attack   512
Managing Stress   515
Facilitating Adult Reentry to College   527
Ways Middle-Aged Parents Can Promote Positive Ties with Their Adult
    Children   546
Relieving the Stress of Caring for an Aging Parent   551
Ingredients of Effective Retirement Planning   557
Increasing the Effectiveness of Educational Experiences for Older
    Adults   598
Fostering Adaptation to Widowhood in Late Adulthood   624
Discussing Concerns About Death with Children and Adolescents   644
Communicating with Dying People   650
Suggestions for Resolving Grief After a Loved One Dies   663

Contents

A Personal Note to Students   *xv*
Preface for Instructors   *xvi*

PART I
Theory and Research in Human Development

chapter 1
History, Theory, and Research Strategies   2

A Scientific, Applied, and Interdisciplinary Field   5

Basic Issues   5
Continuous or Discontinuous Development?   6
One Course of Development or Many?   6
Relative Influence of Nature and Nurture?   7

The Lifespan Perspective: A Balanced Point of View   7
Development Is Lifelong   8
Development Is Multidimensional and Multidirectional   9
Development Is Plastic   9
■ BIOLOGY AND ENVIRONMENT *Resilience*   10
Development Is Influenced by Multiple, Interacting Forces   10
■ CULTURAL INFLUENCES *The Baby Boomers Reshape the Life Course*   12

Scientific Beginnings   14
Darwin: Forefather of Scientific Child Study   14
The Normative Period   14
The Mental Testing Movement   15

Mid-Twentieth-Century Theories   15
The Psychoanalytic Perspective   15
Behaviorism and Social Learning Theory   17
Piaget's Cognitive-Developmental Theory   18

Recent Theoretical Perspectives   20
Information Processing   20
Developmental Cognitive Neuroscience   21
Ethology and Evolutionary Developmental Psychology   22
Vygotsky's Sociocultural Theory   23
Ecological Systems Theory   24
■ SOCIAL ISSUES: HEALTH *Family Chaos Undermines Children's Well-Being*   26

Comparing and Evaluating Theories   27

Studying Development   27
Common Research Methods   28
■ CULTURAL INFLUENCES *Immigrant Youths: Adapting to a New Land*   32
General Research Designs   34
Designs for Studying Development   35

Ethics in Lifespan Research   39
Summary   41
Important Terms and Concepts   43

PART II
Foundations of Development

chapter 2
Genetic and Environmental Foundations   44

Genetic Foundations   46
The Genetic Code   46
The Sex Cells   46
Boy or Girl?   47
Multiple Offspring   47
Patterns of Genetic Inheritance   48
Chromosomal Abnormalities   52

Reproductive Choices   53
Genetic Counseling   53
■ SOCIAL ISSUES: HEALTH *The Pros and Cons of Reproductive Technologies*   54
Prenatal Diagnosis and Fetal Medicine   56
Adoption   57

Environmental Contexts for Development   59
The Family   59
Socioeconomic Status and Family Functioning   61
Poverty   61
Affluence   62
Beyond the Family: Neighborhoods, Towns, and Cities   63
The Cultural Context   65
■ CULTURAL INFLUENCES *The African-American Extended Family*   66

Understanding the Relationship Between Heredity and Environment   69
The Question, "How Much?"   70
The Question, "How?"   71
■ BIOLOGY AND ENVIRONMENT *A Case of Epigenesis: Smoking During Pregnancy Alters Gene Expression*   74

Summary   75
Important Terms and Concepts   77

chapter 3
Prenatal Development, Birth, and the Newborn Baby   78

Prenatal Development   80
Conception   80
Period of the Zygote   80

Period of the Embryo 82
Period of the Fetus 83

Prenatal Environmental Influences 85
Teratogens 85
Other Maternal Factors 92

■ SOCIAL ISSUES: HEALTH *The Nurse–Family Partnership:
Reducing Maternal Stress and Enhancing Child Development
Through Social Support 94*

The Importance of Prenatal Health Care 95

Childbirth 96
The Stages of Childbirth 96
The Baby's Adaptation to Labor and Delivery 97
The Newborn Baby's Appearance 97
Assessing the Newborn's Physical Condition: The Apgar Scale 98

Approaches to Childbirth 98
Natural, or Prepared, Childbirth 99
Home Delivery 99

Medical Interventions 100
Fetal Monitoring 100
Labor and Delivery Medication 100
Cesarean Delivery 101

Preterm and Low-Birth-Weight Infants 101
Preterm versus Small-for-Date Infants 102
Consequences for Caregiving 102
Interventions for Preterm Infants 102

■ SOCIAL ISSUES: HEALTH *A Cross-National Perspective on Health
Care and Other Policies for Parents and Newborn Babies 104*

Birth Complications, Parenting, and Resilience 105

The Newborn Baby's Capacities 106
Reflexes 106
States 108

■ BIOLOGY AND ENVIRONMENT *The Mysterious Tragedy of Sudden
Infant Death Syndrome 110*

Sensory Capacities 112
Neonatal Behavioral Assessment 114

Adjusting to the New Family Unit 115

Summary 115

Important Terms and Concepts 117

PART III

Infancy and Toddlerhood: The First Two Years

chapter 4

Physical Development in Infancy and Toddlerhood 118

Body Growth 120
Changes in Body Size and Muscle–Fat Makeup 120
Individual and Group Differences 121
Changes in Body Proportions 121

Brain Development 121
Development of Neurons 121
Neurobiological Methods 122
Development of the Cerebral Cortex 124
Sensitive Periods in Brain Development 125

■ BIOLOGY AND ENVIRONMENT *Brain Plasticity: Insights from
Research on Brain-Damaged Children and Adults 126*

Changing States of Arousal 128

■ CULTURAL INFLUENCES *Cultural Variation in Infant Sleeping
Arrangements 129*

Influences on Early Physical Growth 130
Heredity 130
Nutrition 130
Malnutrition 132

Learning Capacities 133
Classical Conditioning 133
Operant Conditioning 134
Habituation 134
Imitation 135

Motor Development 136
The Sequence of Motor Development 137
Motor Skills as Dynamic Systems 137
Fine-Motor Development: Reaching and Grasping 139

Perceptual Development 140
Hearing 140

■ BIOLOGY AND ENVIRONMENT *"Tuning In" to Familiar Speech,
Faces, and Music: A Sensitive Period for Culture-Specific Learning 141*

Vision 142
Intermodal Perception 145
Understanding Perceptual Development 146

Summary 148

Important Terms and Concepts 149

chapter 5

Cognitive Development in Infancy and Toddlerhood 150

Piaget's Cognitive-Developmental Theory 152
Piaget's Ideas About Cognitive Change 152
The Sensorimotor Stage 153
Follow-Up Research on Infant Cognitive Development 155
Evaluation of the Sensorimotor Stage 158

■ SOCIAL ISSUES: EDUCATION *Baby Learning from TV and Video:
The Video Deficit Effect 159*

Information Processing 161
A General Model of Information Processing 161
Attention 163
Memory 163

■ BIOLOGY AND ENVIRONMENT *Infantile Amnesia 164*

Categorization 164
Evaluation of Information-Processing Findings 166

The Social Context of Early Cognitive Development 167

■ CULTURAL INFLUENCES *Social Origins of Make-Believe Play 168*

Individual Differences in Early Mental Development   *169*
Infant and Toddler Intelligence Tests   *169*
Early Environment and Mental Development   *170*
Early Intervention for At-Risk Infants and Toddlers   *173*

Language Development   *174*
Theories of Language Development   *174*
Getting Ready to Talk   *175*
First Words   *176*
The Two-Word Utterance Phase   *177*
Individual and Cultural Differences   *177*
Supporting Early Language Development   *178*

Summary   *180*

Important Terms and Concepts   *181*

 c h a p t e r   6
Emotional and Social Development in Infancy and Toddlerhood   182

Erikson's Theory of Infant and Toddler Personality   *184*
Basic Trust versus Mistrust   *184*
Autonomy versus Shame and Doubt   *184*

Emotional Development   *185*
Development of Basic Emotions   *185*

■ **BIOLOGY AND ENVIRONMENT** *Parental Depression and Child Development*   *186*

Understanding and Responding to the Emotions of Others   *188*
Emergence of Self-Conscious Emotions   *188*
Beginnings of Emotional Self-Regulation   *189*

Temperament and Development   *190*
The Structure of Temperament   *190*
Measuring Temperament   *191*
Stability of Temperament   *191*

■ **BIOLOGY AND ENVIRONMENT** *Development of Shyness and Sociability*   *192*

Genetic and Environmental Influences   *193*
Temperament and Child Rearing: The Goodness-of-Fit Model   *194*

Development of Attachment   *195*
Bowlby's Ethological Theory   *196*
Measuring the Security of Attachment   *197*
Stability of Attachment   *198*
Cultural Variations   *198*
Factors That Affect Attachment Security   *199*
Multiple Attachments   *201*

■ **SOCIAL ISSUES: HEALTH** *Does Child Care in Infancy Threaten Attachment Security and Later Adjustment?*   *202*

■ **CULTURAL INFLUENCES** *The Powerful Role of Paternal Warmth in Development*   *204*

Attachment and Later Development   *206*

Self-Development   *206*
Self-Awareness   *206*
Categorizing the Self   *208*
Self-Control   *208*

Summary   *210*
Important Terms and Concepts   *211*
 **MILESTONES**   *Development in Infancy and Toddlerhood*   **212**

PART IV

Early Childhood: Two to Six Years

 c h a p t e r   7
Physical and Cognitive Development in Early Childhood   214

PHYSICAL DEVELOPMENT   *216*

A Changing Body and Brain   *216*
Skeletal Growth   *217*
Brain Development   *217*

Influences on Physical Growth and Health   *219*
Heredity and Hormones   *219*
Nutrition   *219*
Infectious Disease   *220*
Childhood Injuries   *221*

Motor Development   *223*
Gross-Motor Development   *223*
Fine-Motor Development   *224*
Individual Differences in Motor Skills   *225*

COGNITIVE DEVELOPMENT   *226*

Piaget's Theory: The Preoperational Stage   *226*
Advances in Mental Representation   *226*
Make-Believe Play   *226*
Symbol–Real-World Relations   *227*
Limitations of Preoperational Thought   *228*
Follow-Up Research on Preoperational Thought   *230*
Evaluation of the Preoperational Stage   *231*

■ **SOCIAL ISSUES: EDUCATION** *Children's Questions: Catalyst for Cognitive Development*   *232*

Piaget and Education   *233*

Vygotsky's Sociocultural Theory   *233*
Private Speech   *233*
Social Origins of Early Childhood Cognition   *234*
Vygotsky and Education   *235*
Evaluation of Vygotsky's Theory   *235*

■ **CULTURAL INFLUENCES** *Children in Village and Tribal Cultures Observe and Participate in Adult Work*   *236*

Information Processing   *236*
Attention   *236*
Memory   *237*
The Young Child's Theory of Mind   *238*
Early Childhood Literacy   *240*

■ BIOLOGY AND ENVIRONMENT *"Mindblindness" and Autism* 241

Early Childhood Mathematical Reasoning 242

Individual Differences in Mental Development 243
Home Environment and Mental Development 244
Preschool, Kindergarten, and Child Care 244
Educational Media 246

Language Development 248
Vocabulary 248
Grammar 249
Conversation 250
Supporting Language Development in Early Childhood 250

Summary 251

Important Terms and Concepts 253

c h a p t e r   8

Emotional and Social Development in Early Childhood   254

Erikson's Theory: Initiative versus Guilt 256

Self-Understanding 256
Foundations of Self-Concept 256

■ CULTURAL INFLUENCES *Cultural Variations in Personal Storytelling: Implications for Early Self-Concept* 257

Emergence of Self-Esteem 257

Emotional Development 258
Understanding Emotion 258
Emotional Self-Regulation 259
Self-Conscious Emotions 259
Empathy and Sympathy 260

Peer Relations 261
Advances in Peer Sociability 261
First Friendships 262
Peer Relations and School Readiness 263
Parental Influences on Early Peer Relations 263

Foundations of Morality 264
The Psychoanalytic Perspective 264
Social Learning Theory 265

■ CULTURAL INFLUENCES *Ethnic Differences in the Consequences of Physical Punishment* 267

The Cognitive-Developmental Perspective 268
The Other Side of Morality: Development of Aggression 269

Gender Typing 273
Gender-Stereotyped Beliefs and Behavior 273
Biological Influences on Gender Typing 273
Environmental Influences on Gender Typing 274

■ SOCIAL ISSUES: EDUCATION *Young Children Learn About Gender Through Mother–Child Conversations* 275

Gender Identity 276
Reducing Gender Stereotyping in Young Children 278

Child Rearing and Emotional and Social Development 278
Styles of Child Rearing 278
What Makes Authoritative Child Rearing Effective? 280
Cultural Variations 280
Child Maltreatment 281

Summary 284

Important Terms and Concepts 285

MILESTONES   *Development in Early Childhood* 286

P A R T   V

**Middle Childhood:
Six to Eleven Years**

c h a p t e r   9

Physical and Cognitive Development in Middle Childhood   288

PHYSICAL DEVELOPMENT 290

Body Growth 290

Common Health Problems 290
Nutrition 291
Overweight and Obesity 291
Vision and Hearing 293
Illnesses 293
Unintentional Injuries 294

Motor Development and Play 294
Gross-Motor Development 294
Fine-Motor Development 295
Sex Differences 296
Games with Rules 296
Shadows of Our Evolutionary Past 297

■ SOCIAL ISSUES: EDUCATION *School Recess—A Time to Play, a Time to Learn* 298

Physical Education 298

COGNITIVE DEVELOPMENT 299

Piaget's Theory: The Concrete Operational Stage 299
Concrete Operational Thought 299
Limitations of Concrete Operational Thought 301
Follow-Up Research on Concrete Operational Thought 301
Evaluation of the Concrete Operational Stage 302

Information Processing 302
Working-Memory Capacity 302
Executive Function 303
Attention 303

■ BIOLOGY AND ENVIRONMENT *Children with Attention-Deficit Hyperactivity Disorder* 304

Memory Strategies 304
Knowledge and Memory 305

Culture, Schooling, and Memory Strategies   *306*
The School-Age Child's Theory of Mind   *306*
Cognitive Self-Regulation   *307*
Applications of Information Processing to Academic
   Learning   *307*

Individual Differences in Mental Development   *309*
Defining and Measuring Intelligence   *309*
Recent Efforts to Define Intelligence   *310*
Explaining Individual and Group Differences in IQ   *312*

■ SOCIAL ISSUES: HEALTH   *Emotional Intelligence*   *313*

Language Development   *316*
Vocabulary   *316*
Grammar   *316*
Pragmatics   *316*
Learning Two Languages   *317*

Learning in School   *318*
Class Size   *318*
Educational Philosophies   *319*
Teacher–Student Interaction   *320*

■ SOCIAL ISSUES: EDUCATION   *Magnet Schools: Equal Access to
High-Quality Education*   *321*

Grouping Practices   *321*
Teaching Children with Special Needs   *322*
How Well Educated Are U.S. Children?   *323*

Summary   *325*

Important Terms and Concepts   *327*

chapter 10

**Emotional and Social Development
in Middle Childhood   328**

Erikson's Theory: Industry versus Inferiority   *330*

Self-Understanding   *330*
Self-Concept   *330*
Self-Esteem   *331*
Influences on Self-Esteem   *331*

Emotional Development   *335*
Self-Conscious Emotions   *335*
Emotional Understanding   *335*
Emotional Self-Regulation   *336*

Moral Development   *336*
Moral and Social-Conventional Understanding   *336*
Understanding Individual Rights   *337*
Understanding Diversity and Inequality   *337*

Peer Relations   *339*
Peer Groups   *339*
Friendships   *340*
Peer Acceptance   *341*

■ BIOLOGY AND ENVIRONMENT   *Bullies and Their Victims*   *342*

Gender Typing   *343*
Gender-Stereotyped Beliefs   *343*
Gender Identity and Behavior   *344*

Family Influences   *345*
Parent–Child Relationships   *345*
Siblings   *345*
Only Children   *346*
Divorce   *346*
Blended Families   *349*
Maternal Employment and Dual-Earner Families   *350*

Some Common Problems of Development   *352*
Fears and Anxieties   *352*
Child Sexual Abuse   *352*

■ CULTURAL INFLUENCES   *Impact of Ethnic and Political Violence on
Children*   *353*

Fostering Resilience in Middle Childhood   *354*

■ SOCIAL ISSUES: HEALTH   *Children's Eyewitness Testimony*   *355*

Summary   *356*

Important Terms and Concepts   *357*

MILESTONES   ***Development in Middle
Childhood*   *358***

PART VI

Adolescence:
The Transition to Adulthood

chapter 11

**Physical and Cognitive
Development in Adolescence   360**

PHYSICAL DEVELOPMENT   *362*

Conceptions of Adolescence   *362*
The Biological Perspective   *362*
The Social Perspective   *362*
A Balanced Point of View   *362*

Puberty: The Physical Transition to Adulthood   *363*
Hormonal Changes   *363*
Body Growth   *363*
Motor Development and Physical Activity   *364*
Sexual Maturation   *365*
Individual Differences in Pubertal Growth   *366*
Brain Development   *367*
Changing States of Arousal   *368*

The Psychological Impact of Pubertal Events   *368*
Reactions to Pubertal Changes   *368*
Pubertal Change, Emotion, and Social Behavior   *369*
Pubertal Timing   *370*

Health Issues   *371*
Nutritional Needs   *371*
Eating Disorders   *372*
Sexuality   *373*

■ SOCIAL ISSUES: HEALTH   *Lesbian, Gay, and Bisexual Youths:
Coming Out to Oneself and Others*   *376*

Sexually Transmitted Diseases *376*
Adolescent Pregnancy and Parenthood *378*
Substance Use and Abuse *380*

COGNITIVE DEVELOPMENT 382

Piaget's Theory: The Formal Operational Stage *382*
Hypothetico-Deductive Reasoning *382*
Propositional Thought *383*
Follow-Up Research on Formal Operational Thought *383*

An Information-Processing View of Adolescent Cognitive Development 384
Scientific Reasoning: Coordinating Theory with Evidence *385*
How Scientific Reasoning Develops *385*

Consequences of Adolescent Cognitive Changes *386*
Self-Consciousness and Self-Focusing *386*
Idealism and Criticism *387*
Decision Making *387*

Sex Differences in Mental Abilities *388*
Verbal Abilities *388*
Mathematical Abilities *388*

■ **BIOLOGY AND ENVIRONMENT** *Sex Differences in Spatial Abilities* *390*

Learning in School *391*
School Transitions *391*
Academic Achievement *392*

■ **SOCIAL ISSUES: EDUCATION** *Media Multitasking Disrupts Attention and Learning* *394*

Dropping Out *396*

Summary *397*

Important Terms and Concepts *399*

chapter 12
Emotional and Social Development in Adolescence 400

Erikson's Theory: Identity versus Role Confusion *402*

Self-Understanding *402*
Changes in Self-Concept *402*
Changes in Self-Esteem *402*
Paths to Identity *403*
Identity Status and Psychological Well-Being *404*
Factors Affecting Identity Development *404*

Moral Development *405*

■ **CULTURAL INFLUENCES** *Identity Development Among Ethnic Minority Adolescents* *406*

Kohlberg's Theory of Moral Development *407*
Are There Sex Differences in Moral Reasoning? *409*
Coordinating Moral, Social-Conventional, and Personal Concerns *409*
Influences on Moral Reasoning *410*
Moral Reasoning and Behavior *411*
Religious Involvement and Moral Development *412*
Further Challenges to Kohlberg's Theory *412*

■ **SOCIAL ISSUES: EDUCATION** *Development of Civic Engagement* *413*

Gender Typing *414*

The Family *414*
Parent–Child Relationships *415*
Family Circumstances *416*
Siblings *416*

Peer Relations *417*
Friendships *417*
Cliques and Crowds *419*
Dating *420*

Problems of Development *421*
Depression *421*
Suicide *422*
Delinquency *423*

■ **BIOLOGY AND ENVIRONMENT** *Two Routes to Adolescent Delinquency* *424*

Summary *426*

Important Terms and Concepts *427*

MILESTONES *Development in Adolescence* *428*

PART VII
Early Adulthood

chapter 13
Physical and Cognitive Development in Early Adulthood 430

PHYSICAL DEVELOPMENT 432

Biological Aging Is Under Way in Early Adulthood *432*
Aging at the Level of DNA and Body Cells *432*

■ **BIOLOGY AND ENVIRONMENT** *Telomere Length: A Marker of the Impact of Life Circumstances on Biological Aging* *433*

Aging at the Level of Tissues and Organs *434*

Physical Changes *434*
Cardiovascular and Respiratory Systems *434*
Motor Performance *436*
Immune System *437*
Reproductive Capacity *437*

Health and Fitness *438*
Nutrition *439*

■ **SOCIAL ISSUES: HEALTH** *The Obesity Epidemic: How Americans Became the Heaviest People in the World* *440*

Exercise *443*
Substance Abuse *444*
Sexuality *445*
Psychological Stress *449*

COGNITIVE DEVELOPMENT *450*

Changes in the Structure of Thought *450*
Perry's Theory: Epistemic Cognition *451*
Labouvie-Vief's Theory: Pragmatic Thought and
Cognitive-Affective Complexity *452*

Expertise and Creativity *453*

The College Experience *454*
Psychological Impact of Attending College *454*
Dropping Out *455*

Vocational Choice *455*
Selecting a Vocation *455*
Factors Influencing Vocational Choice *456*

■ **SOCIAL ISSUES: EDUCATION** *Masculinity at Work: Men Who
Choose Nontraditional Careers* *458*

Vocational Preparation of Non-College-Bound Young Adults *459*

Summary *460*

Important Terms and Concepts *461*

chapter 14
Emotional and Social Development in Early Adulthood 462

A Gradual Transition: Emerging Adulthood *464*
Unprecedented Exploration *464*
Cultural Change, Cultural Variation, and Emerging
Adulthood *466*

■ **CULTURAL INFLUENCES** *Is Emerging Adulthood Really a Distinct
Period of Development?* *467*

Risk and Resilience in Emerging Adulthood *467*

Erikson's Theory: Intimacy versus Isolation *469*

**Other Theories of Adult Psychosocial
Development** *470*
Levinson's Seasons of Life *470*
Vaillant's Adaptation to Life *470*
The Social Clock *471*

Close Relationships *472*
Romantic Love *472*

■ **SOCIAL ISSUES: HEALTH** *Childhood Attachment Patterns and
Adult Romantic Relationships* *474*

Friendships *476*
Loneliness *477*

The Family Life Cycle *478*
Leaving Home *478*
Joining of Families in Marriage *479*

■ **SOCIAL ISSUES: HEALTH** *Partner Abuse* *482*

Parenthood *483*

The Diversity of Adult Lifestyles *486*
Singlehood *486*
Cohabitation *487*
Childlessness *488*
Divorce and Remarriage *489*
Varied Styles of Parenthood *490*

Career Development *492*
Establishing a Career *492*
Women and Ethnic Minorities *493*
Combining Work and Family *494*

Summary *496*

Important Terms and Concepts *497*

MILESTONES *Development in Early
Adulthood* *498*

PART VIII
Middle Adulthood

chapter 15
Physical and Cognitive Development in Middle Adulthood 500

PHYSICAL DEVELOPMENT *502*

Physical Changes *502*
Vision *502*
Hearing *503*
Skin *503*
Muscle–Fat Makeup *504*
Skeleton *504*
Reproductive System *504*

■ **BIOLOGY AND ENVIRONMENT** *Anti-Aging Effects of Dietary
Calorie Restriction* *505*

■ **CULTURAL INFLUENCES** *Menopause as a Biocultural Event* *508*

Health and Fitness *508*
Sexuality *509*
Illness and Disability *509*
Hostility and Anger *513*

Adapting to the Physical Challenges of Midlife *514*
Stress Management *514*
Exercise *515*
An Optimistic Outlook *516*
Gender and Aging: A Double Standard *516*

COGNITIVE DEVELOPMENT *517*

Changes in Mental Abilities *517*
Cohort Effects *517*
Crystallized and Fluid Intelligence *518*
Individual and Group Differences *519*

Information Processing *520*
Speed of Processing *520*
Attention *521*
Memory *522*

■ **SOCIAL ISSUES: EDUCATION** *The Art of Acting Improves
Memory in Older Adults* *523*

Practical Problem Solving and Expertise *524*

Creativity *524*
Information Processing in Context *525*

Vocational Life and Cognitive Development *525*

Adult Learners: Becoming a Student in Midlife *526*
Characteristics of Returning Students *526*
Supporting Returning Students *526*

Summary *528*

Important Terms and Concepts *529*

c h a p t e r 16

Emotional and Social Development in Middle Adulthood **530**

Erikson's Theory: Generativity versus Stagnation *532*
■ SOCIAL ISSUES: HEALTH *Generative Adults Tell Their Life Stories* *534*

Other Theories of Psychosocial Development in Midlife *535*
Levinson's Seasons of Life *535*
Vaillant's Adaptation to Life *536*
Is There a Midlife Crisis? *536*
Stage or Life Events Approach *537*

Stability and Change in Self-Concept and Personality *538*
Possible Selves *538*
Self-Acceptance, Autonomy, and Environmental Mastery *538*
Coping with Daily Stressors *539*
■ BIOLOGY AND ENVIRONMENT *What Factors Promote Psychological Well-Being in Midlife?* *540*
Gender Identity *540*
Individual Differences in Personality Traits *542*

Relationships at Midlife *543*
Marriage and Divorce *543*
Changing Parent–Child Relationships *544*
Grandparenthood *545*
Middle-Aged Children and Their Aging Parents *547*
■ SOCIAL ISSUES: HEALTH *Grandparents Rearing Grandchildren: The Skipped-Generation Family* *548*
Siblings *552*
Friendships *552*

Vocational Life *553*
Job Satisfaction *553*
Career Development *554*
Career Change at Midlife *555*
Unemployment *556*
Planning for Retirement *556*

Summary *558*

Important Terms and Concepts *559*

MILESTONES *Development in Middle Adulthood* *560*

PART IX

Late Adulthood

c h a p t e r 17

Physical and Cognitive Development in Late Adulthood **562**

PHYSICAL DEVELOPMENT *564*

Life Expectancy *564*
Variations in Life Expectancy *564*
Life Expectancy in Late Adulthood *565*
Maximum Lifespan *566*
■ BIOLOGY AND ENVIRONMENT *What Can We Learn About Aging from Centenarians?* *566*

Physical Changes *567*
Nervous System *568*
Sensory Systems *568*
Cardiovascular and Respiratory Systems *570*
Immune System *571*
Sleep *571*
Physical Appearance and Mobility *571*
Adapting to Physical Changes of Late Adulthood *572*

Health, Fitness, and Disability *575*
■ CULTURAL INFLUENCES *Cultural Variations in Sense of Usefulness in Late Life* *576*
Nutrition and Exercise *577*
Sexuality *578*
Physical Disabilities *579*
Mental Disabilities *582*
■ SOCIAL ISSUES: HEALTH *Interventions for Caregivers of Older Adults with Dementia* *586*
Health Care *588*

COGNITIVE DEVELOPMENT *589*

Memory *591*
Deliberate versus Automatic Memory *591*
Associative Memory *591*
Remote Memory *592*
Prospective Memory *593*

Language Processing *593*

Problem Solving *594*

Wisdom *595*

Factors Related to Cognitive Maintenance Change *596*

Cognitive Interventions *597*

Lifelong Learning *597*
Types of Programs *597*
Benefits of Continuing Education *599*

Summary *599*

Important Terms and Concepts *601*

chapter 18
Emotional and Social Development in Late Adulthood 602

Erikson's Theory: Ego Integrity versus Despair   *604*

Other Theories of Psychosocial Development in Late Adulthood   *604*
Peck's Tasks of Ego Integrity and Joan Erikson's Gerotranscendence   *604*
Labouvie-Vief's Emotional Expertise   *605*
Reminiscence   *606*

Stability and Change in Self-Concept and Personality   *606*
Secure and Multifaceted Self-Concept   *606*
■ CULTURAL INFLUENCES   *The New Old Age*   *607*

Agreeableness, Acceptance of Change, and Openness to Experience   *608*
Spirituality and Religiosity   *608*

■ BIOLOGY AND ENVIRONMENT   *Religious Involvement and Quality of Life in the Final Year*   *609*

Contextual Influences on Psychological Well-Being   *610*
Control versus Dependency   *610*
Physical Health   *611*
Negative Life Changes   *611*
Social Support   *611*

■ SOCIAL ISSUES: HEALTH   *Elder Suicide*   *612*

A Changing Social World   *614*
Social Theories of Aging   *614*
Social Contexts of Aging: Communities, Neighborhoods, and Housing   *616*

Relationships in Late Adulthood   *620*
Marriage   *620*
Gay and Lesbian Partnerships   *621*
Divorce, Remarriage, and Cohabitation   *621*
Widowhood   *622*
Never-Married, Childless Older Adults   *623*
Siblings   *624*
Friendships   *624*
Relationships with Adult Children   *625*
Relationships with Adult Grandchildren and Great-Grandchildren   *626*
Elder Maltreatment   *627*

Retirement   *629*
The Decision to Retire   *629*
Adjustment to Retirement   *630*
Leisure and Volunteer Activities   *631*

Optimal Aging   *632*

Summary   *633*

Important Terms and Concepts   *635*

MILESTONES   *Development in Late Adulthood*   *636*

chapter 19
Death, Dying, and Bereavement 638

How We Die   *640*
Physical Changes   *640*
Defining Death   *640*
Death with Dignity   *641*

Understanding of and Attitudes Toward Death   *642*
Childhood   *642*
Adolescence   *643*
Adulthood   *644*
Death Anxiety   *645*

Thinking and Emotions of Dying People   *646*
Do Stages of Dying Exist?   *646*
Contextual Influences on Adaptations to Dying   *647*

A Place to Die   *650*
Home   *651*
Hospital   *651*
Nursing Home   *652*
The Hospice Approach   *652*

■ BIOLOGY AND ENVIRONMENT   *Music as Palliative Care for Dying Patients*   *653*

The Right to Die   *654*
Passive Euthanasia   *654*
Voluntary Active Euthanasia   *656*

■ SOCIAL ISSUES: HEALTH   *Voluntary Active Euthanasia: Lessons from Australia and the Netherlands*   *657*

Assisted Suicide   *658*

Bereavement: Coping with the Death of a Loved One   *659*
Grief Process   *659*
Personal and Situational Variations   *660*
Bereavement Interventions   *663*

■ CULTURAL INFLUENCES   *Cultural Variations in Mourning Behavior*   *664*

Death Education   *665*

Summary   *666*

Important Terms and Concepts   *667*

Glossary   *G-1*

References   *R-1*

Name Index   *NI-1*

Subject Index   *SI-1*

Observation Guide   *I*

A Personal Note to Students

My more than 30 years of teaching human development have brought me in contact with thousands of students like you—students with diverse college majors, future goals, interests, and needs. Some are affiliated with my own field, psychology, but many come from other related fields—education, sociology, anthropology, family studies, social service, nursing, and biology, to name just a few. Each semester, my students' aspirations have proved to be as varied as their fields of study. Many look toward careers in applied work—counseling, caregiving, nursing, social work, school psychology, and program administration. Some plan to teach, and a few want to do research. Most hope someday to become parents, whereas others are already parents who come with a desire to better understand and rear their children. And almost all arrive with a deep curiosity about how they themselves developed from tiny infants into the complex human beings they are today.

My goal in preparing this sixth edition of *Development Through the Lifespan* is to provide a textbook that meets the instructional goals of your course as well as your personal interests and needs. To achieve these objectives, I have grounded this book in a carefully selected body of classic and current theory and research. In addition, the text highlights the lifespan perspective on development and the interacting contributions of biology and environment to the developing person. It also illustrates commonalities and differences among ethnic groups and cultures and discusses the broader social contexts in which we develop. I have provided a unique pedagogical program that will assist you in mastering information, integrating various aspects of development, critically examining controversial issues, applying what you have learned, and relating the information to your own life.

I hope that learning about human development will be as rewarding for you as I have found it over the years. I would like to know what you think about both the field of human development and this book. I welcome your comments; please feel free to send them to me at Department of Psychology, Box 4620, Illinois State University, Normal, IL 61790.

Laura E. Berk

Preface for Instructors

My decision to write *Development Through the Lifespan* was inspired by a wealth of professional and personal experiences. First and foremost were the interests and concerns of hundreds of students of human development with whom I have worked in over three decades of college teaching. Each semester, their insights and questions have revealed how an understanding of any single period of development is enriched by an appreciation of the entire lifespan. Second, as I moved through adult development myself, I began to think more intensely about factors that have shaped and reshaped my own life course—family, friends, mentors, co-workers, community, and larger society. My career well-established, my marriage having stood the test of time, and my children launched into their adult lives, I felt that a deeper grasp of these multiple, interacting influences would help me better appreciate where I had been and where I would be going in the years ahead. I was also convinced that such knowledge could contribute to my becoming a better teacher, scholar, family member, and citizen. And because teaching has been so central and gratifying to my work life, I wanted to bring to others a personally meaningful understanding of lifespan development.

The years since *Development Through the Lifespan* first appeared have been a period of considerable expansion and change in theory and research. This sixth edition represents these rapidly transforming aspects of the field, with a wealth of new content and teaching tools:

■ *Diverse pathways of change are highlighted.* Investigators have reached broad consensus that variations in biological makeup and everyday tasks lead to wide individual differences in paths of change and resulting competencies. This edition pays more attention to variability in development and to recent theories—including ecological, sociocultural, and dynamic systems—that attempt to explain it. Multicultural and cross-cultural findings, including international comparisons, are enhanced throughout the text. Biology and Environment and Cultural Influences boxes also accentuate the theme of diversity in development.

■ *The lifespan perspective is emphasized.* As in previous editions, the lifespan perspective—development as lifelong, multidimensional, multidirectional, plastic, and embedded in multiple contexts—continues to serve as a unifying approach to understanding human change and is woven thoroughly into the text.

■ *The complex bidirectional relationship between biology and environment is given greater attention.* Accumulating evidence on development of the brain, motor skills, cognitive and language competencies, temperament and personality, emotional and social understanding, and developmental problems underscores the way biological factors emerge in, are modified by, and share power with experience. Interconnections between biology and environment are integral to the lifespan perspective and are revisited throughout the text narrative and in the Biology and Environment boxes with new and updated topics.

■ *Inclusion of interdisciplinary research is expanded.* The move toward viewing thoughts, feelings, and behavior as an integrated whole, affected by a wide array of influences in biology, social context, and culture, has motivated developmental researchers to strengthen their ties with other fields of psychology and with other disciplines. Topics and findings included in this edition increasingly reflect the contributions of educational psychology, social psychology, health psychology, clinical psychology, neurobiology, pediatrics, geriatrics, sociology, anthropology, social service, and other fields.

■ *The links among theory, research, and applications are strengthened.* As researchers intensify their efforts to generate findings relevant to real-life situations, I have placed even greater weight on social policy issues and sound theory- and research-based applications. Further applications are provided in the Applying What We Know tables, which give students concrete ways of building bridges between their learning and the real world.

■ *The role of active student learning is made more explicit.* TAKE A MOMENT..., a feature built into the chapter narrative, asks students to think deeply and critically or to engage in an exercise or application as they read. Ask Yourself questions at the end of each major section have been thoroughly revised and expanded to promote four approaches to engaging actively with the subject matter—*Review, Connect, Apply,* and *Reflect.* This feature assists students in thinking about what they have learned from multiple vantage points. A new **LOOK AND LISTEN** feature asks students to observe what real children, adolescents, and adults say and do; speak with them or with professionals invested in their well-being; and inquire into community programs and practices that influence lifespan development. In addition, highlighting of key terms within the text narrative reinforces student learning in context.

Text Philosophy

The basic approach of this book has been shaped by my own professional and personal history as a teacher, researcher, and parent. It consists of seven philosophical ingredients that I regard as essential for students to emerge from a course with a thorough understanding of lifespan development. Each theme is woven into every chapter:

1. **An understanding of the diverse array of theories in the field and the strengths and shortcomings of each.** The first chapter begins by emphasizing that only knowledge of multiple theories can do justice to the richness of human

development. As I take up each age period and domain of development, I present a variety of theoretical perspectives, indicate how each highlights previously overlooked aspects of development, and discuss research that evaluates it. Consideration of contrasting theories also serves as the context for an evenhanded analysis of many controversial issues.

2. **A grasp of the lifespan perspective as an integrative approach to development.** I introduce the lifespan perspective as an organizing framework in the first chapter and refer to and illustrate its assumptions throughout the text, in an effort to help students construct an overall vision of development from conception to death.

3. **Knowledge of both the sequence of human development and the processes that underlie it.** Students are provided with a discussion of the organized sequence of development along with processes of change. An understanding of process—how complex combinations of biological and environmental events produce development—has been the focus of most recent research. Accordingly, the text reflects this emphasis. But new information about the timetable of change has also emerged. In many ways, the very young and the old have proved to be far more competent than they were believed to be in the past. In addition, many milestones of adult development, such as finishing formal education, entering a career, getting married, having children, and retiring, have become less predictable. Current evidence on the sequence and timing of development, along with its implications for process, is presented for all periods of the lifespan.

4. **An appreciation of the impact of context and culture on human development.** A wealth of research indicates that people live in rich physical and social contexts that affect all domains of development. Throughout the book, students travel to distant parts of the world as I review a growing body of cross-cultural evidence. The text narrative also discusses many findings on socioeconomically and ethnically diverse people within the United States. Furthermore, the impact of historical time period and cohort membership receives continuous attention. In this vein, gender issues— the distinctive but continually evolving experiences, roles, and life paths of males and females—are granted substantial emphasis. Besides highlighting the effects of immediate settings, such as family, neighborhood, and school, I make a concerted effort to underscore the influence of larger social structures—societal values, laws, and government policies and programs—on lifelong well-being.

5. **An understanding of the joint contributions of biology and environment to development.** The field recognizes more powerfully than ever before the joint roles of hereditary/constitutional and environmental factors—that these contributions to development combine in complex ways and cannot be separated in a simple manner. Numerous examples of how biological dispositions can be maintained as well as transformed by social contexts are presented throughout the book.

6. **A sense of the interdependency of all domains of development—physical, cognitive, emotional, and social.** Every chapter emphasizes an integrated approach to human development. I show how physical, cognitive, emotional, and social development are interwoven. Within the text narrative, and in a special series of Ask Yourself questions at the end of major sections, students are referred to other sections of the book to deepen their grasp of relationships among various aspects of change.

7. **An appreciation of the interrelatedness of theory, research, and applications.** Throughout this book, I emphasize that theories of human development and the research stimulated by them provide the foundation for sound, effective practices with children, adolescents, and adults. The link among theory, research, and applications is reinforced by an organizational format in which theory and research are presented first, followed by practical implications. In addition, a current focus in the field—harnessing knowledge of human development to shape social policies that support human needs throughout the lifespan—is reflected in every chapter. The text addresses the current condition of children, adolescents, and adults in the United States and elsewhere in the world and shows how theory and research have combined with public interest to spark successful interventions. Many important applied topics are considered, such as family planning, infant mortality, maternal employment and child care, teenage pregnancy and parenthood, domestic violence, exercise and adult health, religiosity and well-being, lifelong learning, grandparents rearing grandchildren, caring for aging adults with dementia, adjustment to retirement, optimal aging, and palliative care for the dying.

Text Organization

I have chosen a chronological organization for *Development Through the Lifespan*. The book begins with an introductory chapter that describes the scientific history of the field, influential theories, and research strategies. It is followed by two chapters on the foundations of development. Chapter 2 combines an overview of genetic and environmental contexts into a single integrated discussion of these multifaceted influences on development. Chapter 3 is devoted to prenatal development, birth, and the newborn baby. With this foundation, students are ready to look closely at seven major age periods: infancy and toddlerhood (Chapters 4, 5, and 6), early childhood (Chapters 7 and 8), middle childhood (Chapters 9 and 10), adolescence (Chapters 11 and 12), early adulthood (Chapters 13 and 14), middle adulthood (Chapters 15 and 16), and late adulthood (Chapters 17 and 18). Topical chapters within each chronological division cover physical development, cognitive development, and emotional and social development. The book concludes with a chapter on death, dying, and bereavement (Chapter 19).

The chronological approach assists students in thoroughly understanding each age period. It also eases the task of integrating the various domains of development because each is discussed in close proximity. At the same time, a chronologically organized book requires that theories covering several age periods be presented piecemeal. This creates a challenge for students, who must link the various parts together. To assist with this task, I frequently remind students of important earlier achievements before discussing new developments, referring back to related sections with page references. Also, chapters or sections devoted to the same topic (for example, cognitive development) are similarly organized, making it easier for students to draw connections across age periods and construct an overall view of developmental change.

New Coverage in the Sixth Edition

Lifespan development is a fascinating and ever-changing field of study, with constantly emerging new discoveries and refinements in existing knowledge. The sixth edition represents this burgeoning contemporary literature, with over 2,000 new citations. Cutting-edge topics throughout the text underscore the book's major themes. Here is a sampling:

CHAPTER 1: Updated Biology and Environment box on resilience • Updated section on developmental cognitive neuroscience • Increased coverage of evolutionary developmental psychology, with special attention to the adaptiveness of human longevity • Expanded illustrations at all levels of Bronfenbrenner's ecological model • New Social Issues: Health box on how family chaos undermines children's well-being • Updated Cultural Influences box on immigrant youths • Clarified explanation of sequential designs

CHAPTER 2: Updated Social Issues: Health box on the pros and cons of reproductive technologies • Updated section on development of adopted children • Enhanced attention to the impact of poverty on development • Expanded introduction to family influences on development, including the importance of coparenting • Updated research on neighborhood influences on children's physical and mental health • Current statistics on the condition of children, families, and the aged in the United States compared with other Western nations • Introduction to the concept of gene–environment interaction, with illustrative research findings • Expanded section on epigenesis, including new examples of environmental influences on gene expression • New Biology and Environment box highlighting a case of epigenesis—prenatal smoking modifies gene expression

CHAPTER 3: Enhanced attention to fetal brain development, sensory capacities, and behavior • Expanded and updated consideration of a wide range of teratogens • New evidence on the long-term consequences of emotional stress during pregnancy • New findings on older maternal age and prenatal and birth complications • Updated evidence on the contributions of doula support to the birth process and to newborn adjustment • New research on parenting and development of preterm and low-birth-weight infants • Expanded and updated Social Issues: Health box on health care and other policies for parents and newborn babies, including cross-national infant mortality rates and the importance of generous parental leave • New Social Issues: Health box on the Nurse–Family Partnership—reducing maternal stress and enhancing child development through social support • Updated findings on the roles of impaired brain functioning, maternal smoking, and maternal drug abuse in sudden infant death syndrome (SIDS) • New evidence on the role of sleep in infant learning • New research on the impact of "proximal care"—extensive holding of young babies—in reducing infant crying • Updated research on touch sensitivity in newborns, including techniques for reducing infant stress to painful medical procedures

CHAPTER 4: Updated introduction to major methods of assessing brain functioning, including the EEG geodesic sensor net (GSN) and near-infrared spectroscopy (NIRS) • Updated discussion of advances in brain development, with special attention to the prefrontal cortex • New research on children adopted from Romanian orphanages, including neurobiological evidence bearing on the question of whether infancy is a sensitive period of development • Updated Cultural Influences box on cultural variation in infant sleeping arrangements • Updated section on breastfeeding • New dynamic systems research on development of walking and reaching • Updated evidence on how caregiving practices and physical surroundings contribute to development of infant motor skills • Enhanced attention to cultural influences—including infant sleep and motor development • New evidence on the perceptual narrowing effect in speech, music, and species-related face perception, and in gender- and race-related face perception • Expanded and updated section on intermodal perception, including its contributions to all aspects of psychological development

CHAPTER 5: Revised and updated section on infant and toddler imitation, revealing toddlers' ability to infer others' intentions • New section on symbolic understanding, including toddlers' developing grasp of words and pictures as symbolic tools • New Social Issues: Education box on baby learning from TV and video, including discussion of the video deficit effect • Revised section introducing information-processing concepts, including working memory, automatic processes, speed of processing, and executive function • New evidence on similarity of infant and toddler recall memory to memory processing in older children and adults • Revised and updated section on infant and toddler categorization skills • New research on babies' joint attention and preverbal gestures, revealing their developing capacity to participate in cooperative processes necessary for effective communication • Updated findings on toddlers' earliest spoken words, including cultural variations • New findings on adult–child conversation and early vocabulary development, with special attention to SES differences

CHAPTER 6: New research on consequences of effortful control—the self-regulatory dimension of temperament—for cognitive, emotional, and social development • Special attention to the role of child genotype in parenting effects on temperament • Updated evidence on contextual factors that contribute to changes in attachment pattern over time • Revised and updated section on consequences of early availability of a consistent caregiver for attachment security, emotion processing, and adjustment, highlighting studies of children adopted from Eastern European orphanages • New evidence on contributions of fathers' play to attachment security and emotional and social adjustment • Updated findings on employed fathers' increased involvement in caregiving • Revised and updated Social Issues: Health box on child care, attachment, and later development • New evidence on toddlers' scale errors, with implications for body self-awareness • Updated research on the impact of sensitive caregiving on early self-development

CHAPTER 7: Increased attention to brain development in early childhood, with special attention to the prefrontal cortex and executive function • Updated statistics and research on the health status of U.S. young children, including tooth decay, childhood immunizations, and overall health status • New research on development of handedness, including cultural variations • Expanded attention to the impact of adult mealtime practices on children's eating behavior • New evidence on preschoolers' magical beliefs • Revised and updated section on preschoolers' understanding of symbol–real-world relations • New research on cultural variations in effective scaffolding • New Social Issues: Education box on children's questions as a catalyst for cognitive development • Updated discussion of gains in executive function in early childhood, including attention, inhibition, and planning • Recent findings on toddlers' early, implicit false-belief understanding and its relationship to preschoolers explicit grasp of false belief • New evidence on cognitive attainments and social experiences that contribute to mastery of false belief • Enhanced discussion of SES differences in emergent literacy and math knowledge • Updated discussion of the effects of television and computers on academic learning • New research on preschoolers' strategies for word learning, including cultural variations

CHAPTER 8: Updated consideration of emotional self-regulation in early childhood, including the influence of temperament and parenting • Enhanced Cultural Influences box on ethnic differences in the consequences of physical punishment • New section on the role of positive peer relations in school readiness • New longitudinal evidence on the relationship of early corporal punishment to later behavior problems • Enhanced attention to aggressive children's distorted view of the social world • Updated discussion of parent training programs to reduce child conduct problems, with special attention to Incredible Years • New Social Issues: Education box on young children's learning about gender through mother–child conversations • New section on cultural variations in communication within gender-segregated peer groups • New findings on the harmful impact of parental psychological control on children's adjustment • Updated consideration of consequences of child maltreatment, including new evidence on central nervous system damage

CHAPTER 9: Revised and updated section on overweight and obesity, including current U.S. prevalence rates, international comparisons, and coverage of contributing factors and consequences • Updated statistics on physical activity and fitness among U.S. school-age children • New sections on working-memory capacity and executive function in middle childhood, with implications for academic learning • Revised and updated Biology and Environment box on children with attention-deficit hyperactivity disorder • New research on development of planning in middle childhood • Updated evidence on the school-age child's theory of mind • Updated Social Issues: Education box on emotional intelligence • Discussion of secular trends in IQ, including implications for understanding ethnic variations in IQ • Attention to the impact of the U.S. No Child Left Behind Act on quality of U.S. education • Updated research on academic achievement of U.S. children with limited English proficiency • Expanded consideration of the impact of biased teacher judgments on ethnic minority children's academic achievement • New research on educational consequences of widespread SES and ethnic segregation in American schools • New Social Issues: Education box on magnet schools as a means of attaining equal access to high-quality education • Revised and updated section on U.S. academic achievement in international perspective, including comparisons with high-performing nations

CHAPTER 10: Enhanced attention to cultural variations in self-concept, with special attention to Asian versus U.S. comparisons • Updated research on parenting practices and children's achievement-related attributions, including the influence of cultural values on likelihood of developing learned helplessness • Expanded and updated section on children's understanding of diversity and inequality, development of racial and ethnic prejudice, and strategies for reducing prejudice • New findings on peer acceptance, including implications of peer-acceptance categories for bullying and victimization • Updated Biology and Environment box on bullies and their victims • New evidence on sex differences in development of gender identity in middle childhood • Expanded attention to the role of effective coparenting in children's adjustment to parental divorce and remarriage • New research on the implications of self-care and after-school programs for school-age children's adjustment • Revised and updated Cultural Influences box on impact of ethnic and political violence on children • Updated findings on the consequences of child sexual abuse

CHAPTER 11: New section on adolescent brain development, focusing on the imbalance between the cognitive control network and the emotional/social network, with implications for teenage reward-seeking, emotional reactivity, and risk-taking • Updated evidence on teenage pregnancy and parenthood prevention and intervention strategies • New findings on key elements of effective sex education programs • Expanded and updated research on adolescent decision making • Updated consideration of factors contributing to sex differences in spatial and mathematical abilities, including cultural valuing of gender equality • New research on the impact of school transitions on adolescent adjustment • Enhanced consideration of teacher and peer supports for academic achievement • Updated discussion of factors contributing to dropping out of school • New Social Issues: Education box on the impact of "media multitasking" on learning

CHAPTER 12: New research on personal and social factors contributing to identity development in adolescence • Updated Social Issues: Health box on adolescent suicide • Updated evidence on adolescents' capacity to integrate moral, social-conventional, and personal concerns • Enhanced consideration of factors that promote moral identity, along with its relationship to moral behavior • Updated Social Issues: Education box on development of civic engagement • New evidence on gender intensification in adolescence • Updated section on parenting and adolescent autonomy, including research on immigrant families • Expanded and updated section on Internet friendships, with special attention to teenagers' use of social networking sites • New evidence on associations among parent, friend, and dating-partner relationships • New findings on long-term outcomes of multisystemic therapy for violent juvenile offenders

CHAPTER 13: Updated Biology and Environment box on telomere length as a marker of the impact of life circumstances on biological aging • New controversial evidence on the role of free radicals in aging • New research on SES variations in adult health • Updated statistics on the continued worldwide rise in adult overweight and obesity, including a revised Social Issues: Health box on environmental factors contributing to the U.S. obesity epidemic • New findings on negative stereotyping and discrimination experienced by overweight adults • Enhanced discussion of treatment of adult obesity • New evidence on the Internet as a contemporary way to initiate dating relationships • Updated research on psychological stress and unfavorable health outcomes • Enhanced discussion of the psychological impact of attending college, including bene-

fits of opportunities to interact with racially and ethnically diverse peers • New findings on the role of gender stereotypes in women's likelihood of choosing STEM careers • Updated Social Issues: Education box on men who choose nontraditional careers

CHAPTER 14: Revised and updated section on emerging adulthood, including new findings on emerging adults' religiosity, spirituality, and commitment to community service • Enhanced discussion of the controversy over whether emerging adulthood really is a distinct period of development • Special attention to parenting of emerging adults, including "helicopter parenting" • Updated consideration of increasingly flexible age-graded expectations for early adulthood life events • Updated consideration of factors that contribute to enduring romantic relationships • New findings on social networking sites as contexts for early adulthood friendship • Expanded discussion of the rise in average age of leaving the parental home • Increased attention to parent–young-adult child relationships • New findings on sharing of household tasks in dual-earner marriages, including cross-national evidence • Updated research on relationship qualities and communication skills contributing to marital satisfaction • Attention to the role of American individualism in the high U.S. divorce and remarriage rates • Updated consideration of the dramatic increase in never-married single parents, including SES and ethnic variations • New findings on career development in early adulthood, with special attention to obstacles to success faced by women and ethnic minorities • Enhanced discussion of combining work and family

CHAPTER 15: Updated Biology and Environment box on anti-aging effects of dietary calorie restriction • Updated evidence on the risks of hormone therapy to reduce physical discomforts of menopause • New survey findings on sexual activity of U.S. middle-aged adults • Updated sections on risk of cancer and heart disease in midlife • New research on gains in effective coping in middle adulthood • Updated evidence on the neurobiological basis of declines in processing speed with age • New findings on midlife changes in attention and memory • New Social Issues: Education box on how lessons in the art of acting improve memory in older adults

CHAPTER 16: Enhanced consideration of the contribution of parenting to generativity in midlife • New research on cultural variations in the link between midlife physical changes and psychological well-being • Updated Social Issues: Health box on grandparents rearing grandchildren in skipped-generation families • Updated evidence on relationships between middle-aged adults and their aging parents, including ethnic variations • New findings on midlife intergenerational assistance to both children and aging parents • Enhanced discussion of care of aging parents in poor health, with emphasis on gender disparities, ethnic variations, and emotional, physical, and financial consequences • New research on middle-aged adults' use of social networking sites • Updated discussion of the glass ceiling in career advancement faced by women and ethnic minorities • New evidence on career change at midlife, with special attention to blue-collar workers • Discussion of the impact of the late-2000s recession on delayed retirement

CHAPTER 17: Updated statistics on life expectancy in late adulthood, including gender and SES variations • Updated international comparisons in healthy life expectancy • New research on brain development, including neurological changes that enable older adults to compensate for declines in central nervous system functioning • Updated findings on risk and protective factors associated with various aspects of physical aging • New evidence on cultural variations in older adults' sense of personal control, with implications for coping with physical impairments • Updated section on assistive technologies • Expanded and updated discussion of stereotypes of aging, including stereotype threat, with implications for physical and cognitive performance • Updated consideration of SES and ethnic variations in health in late adulthood • Expanded consideration of progress in compression of morbidity • Updated survey findings on sexual activity in late adulthood • New findings on neurological changes associated with Alzheimer's disease, including efforts to understand how abnormal amyloid and tau damage neurons • New evidence on genetic and environmental risks for Alzheimer's, and on protective factors, with special emphasis on diet, education, and physical activity • Updated Social Issues: Health box on interventions for caregivers of older adults with dementia, with increased attention to respite and caregiving skills • Enhanced attention to use of selective optimization with compensation in adapting to cognitive changes • Expanded discussion of episodic memory and prospective memory in late adulthood • Updated research on everyday problem solving in late adulthood • Enhanced consideration of the impact of cognitive

training on older adults' mental functioning, including broadening programs to target self-efficacy • New evidence on the rapid rise in use of computers and the Internet among older people

CHAPTER 18: Updated research on reminiscence in late adulthood • New findings on personality development in late adulthood, with special attention to openness to experience • Enhanced consideration of the benefits of spirituality and religiosity in late life, including a new Biology and Environment box on religious involvement and quality of life in the final year • Consideration of sustaining an effective person–environment fit in older adults' social contexts, including caregiving and housing arrangements • Updated discussion of socioemotional selectivity theory and related research • New research on divorce, remarriage, and cohabitation in late adulthood, including aging baby boomers' use of online dating services • Updated findings on late-life friendships • New evidence on retirement as a dynamic process with multiple transitions and wide individual variation

CHAPTER 19: Updated research on diverse factors influencing people's adaptation to dying • Updated discussion of dying at home, in hospitals, and in nursing homes • New findings on hospice, including reducing patient suffering, improving family functioning, and increasing ability to sustain patient care at home • Updated statistics on public attitudes toward passive euthanasia, voluntary active euthanasia, and assisted suicide • Updated statistics on Oregon residents dying by legalized assisted suicide • New research on the role of expressions of happiness and humor in bereavement adjustment • New evidence on bereavement interventions, with special attention to support groups based on the dual-process model of coping with loss

Acknowledgments

The dedicated contributions of many individuals helped make this book a reality and contributed to refinements and improvements in this sixth edition. An impressive cast of reviewers provided many helpful suggestions, constructive criticisms, and enthusiasm for the organization and content of the text. I am grateful to each one of them.

Reviewers for the Sixth Edition

Cheryl Anagnopoulos, Black Hills State University
Carolyn M. Barry, Loyola University
Lori Bica, University of Wisconsin, Eau Claire
Linda Curry, Texas Christian University
Manfred Diehl, Colorado State University
Mary Anne Erickson, Ithaca College
Karen Fingerman, University of Texas, Austin
Linda Halgunseth, Pennsylvania State University
Melinda Heinz, Iowa State University
Joseph Kishton, University of North Carolina, Wilmington
Dale Lund, California State University, San Bernardino
Debra McGinnis, Oakland University
Celinda Reese-Melancon, Oklahoma State University
Mathew Shake, Western Kentucky University
Kim Shifren, Towson University
Gregory Smith, Kent State University
Stephanie Stein, Central Washington University
JoNell Strough, West Virginia University
Bruce Thompson, University of Southern Maine
Laura Thompson, New Mexico State University

Reviewers for Previous Editions

Gerald Adams, University of Guelph
Jackie Adamson, South Dakota School of Mines and Technology
Paul C. Amrhein, University of New Mexico
Cheryl Anagnopoulos, Black Hills State University
Doreen Arcus, University of Massachusetts, Lowell
René L. Babcock, Central Michigan University
Sherry Beaumont, University of Northern British Columbia
W. Keith Berg, University of Florida
James A. Bird, Weber State University
Toni Bisconti, University of Akron
Joyce Bishop, Golden West College
Kimberly Blair, University of Pittsburgh
Tracie L. Blumentritt, University of Wisconsin—La Crosse
Ed Brady, Belleville Area College
Michele Y. Breault, Truman State University
Dilek Buchholz, Weber State University
Lanthan Camblin, University of Cincinnati
Judith W. Cameron, Ohio State University
Joan B. Cannon, University of Massachusetts, Lowell
Michael Caruso, University of Toledo
Susan L. Churchill, University of Nebraska—Lincoln
Gary Creasey, Illinois State University

Rhoda Cummings, University of Nevada—Reno
Rita M. Curl, Minot State University
Carol Lynn Davis, University of Maine
Lou de la Cruz, Sheridan Institute
Byron Egeland, University of Minnesota
Beth Fauth, Utah State University
Karen Fingerman, Purdue University
Maria P. Fracasso, Towson University
Elizabeth E. Garner, University of North Florida
Laurie Gottlieb, McGill University
Dan Grangaard, Austin Community College
Clifford Gray, Pueblo Community College
Marlene Groomes, Miami Dade College
Laura Gruntmeir, Redlands Community College
Laura Hanish, Arizona State University
Traci Haynes, Columbus State Community College
Vernon Haynes, Youngstown State University
Bert Hayslip, University of North Texas
Bob Heller, Athabasca University
Karl Hennig, St. Francis Xavier University
Paula Hillman, University of Wisconsin—Whitewater
Deb Hollister, Valencia Community College
Hui-Chin Hsu, University of Georgia
Lera Joyce Johnson, Centenary College of Louisiana
Janet Kalinowski, Ithaca College
Kevin Keating, Broward Community College
Wendy Kliewer, Virginia Commonwealth University
Marita Kloseck, University of Western Ontario
Karen Kopera-Frye, University of Nevada, Reno
Valerie Kuhlmeier, Queens University
Deanna Kuhn, Teachers College, Columbia University
Rebecca A. López, California State University—Long Beach
Dale Lund, California State University, San Bernardino
Pamela Manners, Troy State University
Ashley Maynard, University of Hawaii
Robert B. McLaren, California State University, Fullerton
Kate McLean, University of Toronto at Mississauga
Randy Mergler, California State University
Karla K. Miley, Black Hawk College
Carol Miller, Anne Arundel Community College
Teri Miller, Milwaukee Area Technical College
David Mitchell, Kennesaw State University
Steve Mitchell, Somerset Community College
Gary T. Montgomery, University of Texas, Pan American
Feleccia Moore-Davis, Houston Community College
Ulrich Mueller, University of Victoria
Karen Nelson, Austin College
Bob Newby, Tarleton State University
Jill Norvilitis, Buffalo State College
Patricia O'Brien, University of Illinois at Chicago
Nancy Ogden, Mount Royal College
Peter Oliver, University of Hartford
Verna C. Pangman, University of Manitoba
Robert Pasnak, George Mason University
Ellen Pastorino, Gainesville College

Julie Patrick, West Virginia University
Marion Perlmutter, University of Michigan
Warren H. Phillips, Iowa State University
Leslee K. Polina, Southeast Missouri State University
Dana Plude, University of Maryland
Dolores Pushkar, Concordia University
Leon Rappaport, Kansas State University
Pamela Roberts, California State University, Long Beach
Stephanie J. Rowley, University of North Carolina
Elmer Ruhnke, Manatee Community College
Randall Russac, University of North Florida
Marie Saracino, Stephen F. Austin State University
Edythe H. Schwartz, California State University—Sacramento
Bonnie Seegmiller, City University of New York, Hunter College
Richard Selby, Southeast Missouri State University
Aurora Sherman, Oregon State University
Carey Sherman, University of Michigan
David Shwalb, Southeastern Louisiana University
Paul S. Silverman, University of Montana
Judi Smetana, University of Rochester
Glenda Smith, North Harris College
Jacqui Smith, University of Michigan
Jeanne Spaulding, Houston Community College
Thomas Spencer, San Francisco State University
Bruce Stam, Chemeketa Community College
JoNell Strough, West Virginia University
Vince Sullivan, Pensacola Junior College
Bruce Thompson, University of Southern Maine
Laura Thompson, New Mexico State University
Mojisola Tiamiyu, University of Toledo
Ruth Tincoff, Harvard University
Joe Tinnin, Richland College
Catya von Károlyi, University of Wisconsin—Eau Claire
L. Monique Ward, University of Michigan
Rob Weisskirch, California State University, Fullerton
Nancy White, Youngstown State University
Ursula M. White, El Paso Community College
Carol L. Wilkinson, Whatcom Community College
Lois J. Willoughby, Miami-Dade Community College
Paul Wink, Wellesley College
Deborah R. Winters, New Mexico State University

I cannot begin to express what a great pleasure it has been, once again, to work with Tom Pauken, Managing Editor, who oversaw the preparation of the third and fifth editions of *Development Through the Lifespan* and who returned to edit this sixth edition. His careful review of manuscript, keen organizational skills, responsive day-to-day communication, insightful suggestions, astute problem solving, interest in the subject matter, and thoughtfulness greatly enhanced the quality of the text and eased the immense challenges that arose during its preparation. Judy Ashkenaz, Development Editor, carefully reviewed and commented on each chapter, helping to ensure that every thought and concept would be clearly expressed and well-developed. She also assisted with preparation of photo specifications, drafting of photo captions and chapter summaries, and, as needs arose, graciously took on extra tasks, including updating of diverse aspects of the Instructor's Resource Manual. Rachel Trapp, editorial assistant, has been extraordinary. In addition to spending countless hours searching, gathering, and organizing scholarly literature, she assisted with an array of editorial and production tasks. In a pinch, she diligently took over the responsibility of preparing and editing many of the assessments in MyDevelopmentLab (MDL).

The supplements package benefited from the talents and dedication of several other individuals. Leah Shriro revised the IRM brief summaries and lecture outlines. Kimberly Michaud prepared a superb Test Bank and many of the MDL assessments. Judy Ashkenaz designed and wrote a highly attractive Power-Point presentation. Maria Henneberry and Phil Vandiver of Contemporary Visuals in Bloomington, IL, prepared an artistic and inspiring set of new video segments addressing diverse topics in lifespan development.

Donna Simons, Senior Production Project Manager, coordinated the complex production tasks that resulted in an exquisitely beautiful sixth edition. I am grateful for her keen aesthetic sense, attention to detail, flexibility, efficiency, and thoughtfulness. I thank Sarah Evertson for photo research that contributed to the exceptional photographs that illustrate the text narrative. Margaret Pinette provided outstanding copyediting and careful compilation of the references list, and Julie Hotchkiss offered meticulous proofreading.

Wendy Albert, Executive Marketing Manager, prepared the beautiful print ads and informative e-mails to the field about *Development Through the Lifespan*, Sixth Edition. She has also ensured that accurate and clear information reached Pearson Education's sales force and that the needs of prospective and current adopters were met.

A final word of gratitude goes to my family, whose love, patience, and understanding have enabled me to be wife, mother, teacher, researcher, and text author at the same time. My sons, David and Peter, grew up with my texts, passing from childhood to adolescence and then to adulthood as successive editions were written. David has a special connection with the books' subject matter as an elementary school teacher. Peter is now an experienced attorney, and his vivacious and talented wife Melissa joins a new generation of university faculty dedicated to creative teaching and research. All three continue to enrich my understanding through reflections on events and progress in their own lives. Last, but certainly not least, I thank my husband, Ken, for joining me on a wonderfully fulfilling lifespan journey. Over the past two decades, he willingly made room in our lives for the immensely demanding endeavor of authoring six editions of *Development Through the Lifespan*. His reflections, support, and astute counsel made all the difference during the project's final months.

Laura E. Berk

Legend for Photos Accompanying Sofie's Story

Sofie's story is told in Chapters 1 and 19, from her birth to her death. The photos that appear at the beginning of Chapter 1 follow her through her lifespan and include family members of two succeeding generations.

Page 2

1. Sofie, age 18, high school graduation in 1926.
2. Sofie as a baby, with her mother in 1908.
3. Sofie, age 6, with her brother, age 8, in 1914.
4. Sofie's German passport.
5. Sofie, age 60, and daughter Laura on Laura's wedding day in 1968.
6. Sofie and Phil in 1968, less than two years before Sofie died.
7. Sofie's grandsons, David and Peter, ages 5 and 2, children of Laura and Ken.
8. Laura, Ken, and sons Peter and David, ages 10 and 13, on the occasion of David's Bar Mitzvah in 1985.
9. Peter and Melissa on their wedding day in 2007.
10. Laura, Ken, sons David and Peter, and Peter's wife Melissa, with acclaimed pianist Awadagin Pratt, at the naming of a Pratt Foundation piano scholarship in Sofie's memory.

Page 3

Sofie, age 61, and her first grandchild, Ellen, October 1969, less than three months before Sofie died.

Page 4

Sofie and Phil in their mid-thirties, during World War II, when they became engaged.

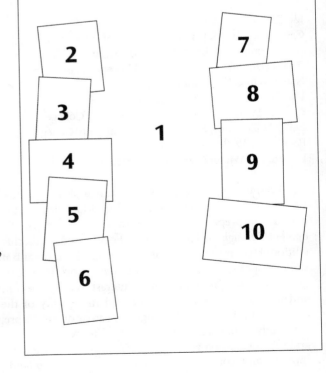

Development Through the Lifespan

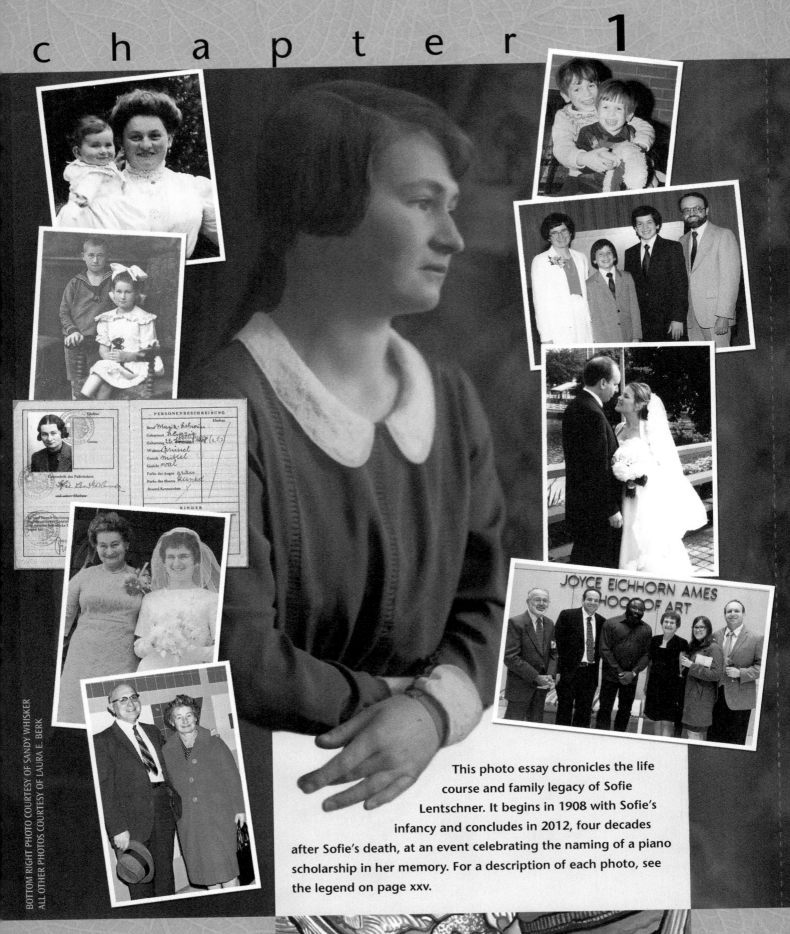

This photo essay chronicles the life course and family legacy of Sofie Lentschner. It begins in 1908 with Sofie's infancy and concludes in 2012, four decades after Sofie's death, at an event celebrating the naming of a piano scholarship in her memory. For a description of each photo, see the legend on page xxv.

History, Theory, and Research Strategies

Sofie Lentschner was born in 1908, the second child of Jewish parents who made their home in Leipzig, Germany, a city of thriving commerce and cultural vitality. Her father was a successful businessman and community leader, her mother a socialite well-known for her charm, beauty, and hospitality. As a baby, Sofie displayed the determination and persistence that would be sustained throughout her life. She sat for long periods inspecting small objects with her eyes and hands. The single event that consistently broke her gaze was the sound of the piano in the parlor. As soon as Sofie could crawl, she steadfastly pulled herself up to finger its keys and marveled at the tinkling sounds.

By the time Sofie entered elementary school, she was an introspective child, often ill at ease at the festive parties that girls of her family's social standing were expected to attend. She immersed herself in schoolwork, especially in mastering foreign languages—a regular part of German elementary and secondary education. Twice a week, she took piano lessons from the finest teacher in Leipzig. By the time Sofie graduated from high school, she spoke English and French fluently and had become an accomplished pianist. Whereas most German girls of her time married by age 20, Sofie postponed serious courtship in favor of entering the university. Her parents began to wonder whether their intense, studious daughter would ever settle into family life.

Sofie wanted marriage as well as education, but her plans were thwarted by the political turbulence of her times. When Hitler rose to power in the early 1930s, Sofie's father, fearing for the safety of his wife and children, moved the family to Belgium. Conditions for Jews in Europe quickly worsened. The Nazis plundered Sofie's family home and confiscated her father's business. By the end of the 1930s, Sofie had lost contact with all but a handful of her aunts, uncles, cousins, and childhood friends, many of whom (she later learned) were herded into cattle cars and transported to Nazi death camps at Auschwitz and Chelmno, Poland. In 1939, as anti-Jewish laws and atrocities intensified, Sofie's family fled to the United States.

COURTESY OF LAURA E. BERK

As Sofie turned 30, her parents, convinced that she would never marry and would need a career for financial security, agreed to support her return to school. Sofie earned two master's degrees, one in music and the other in librarianship. Then, on a blind date, she met Philip, a U.S. army officer. Philip's calm, gentle nature complemented Sofie's intensity and worldliness. Within six months they married. During the next four

chapter outline

A Scientific, Applied, and Interdisciplinary Field

Basic Issues

Continuous or Discontinuous Development? • One Course of Development or Many? • Relative Influence of Nature and Nurture?

The Lifespan Perspective: A Balanced Point of View

Development Is Lifelong • Development Is Multidimensional and Multidirectional • Development Is Plastic • Development Is Influenced by Multiple, Interacting Forces

■ **BIOLOGY AND ENVIRONMENT** Resilience

■ **CULTURAL INFLUENCES** The Baby Boomers Reshape the Life Course

Scientific Beginnings

Darwin: Forefather of Scientific Child Study • The Normative Period • The Mental Testing Movement

Mid-Twentieth-Century Theories

The Psychoanalytic Perspective • Behaviorism and Social Learning Theory • Piaget's Cognitive-Developmental Theory

Recent Theoretical Perspectives

Information Processing • Developmental Cognitive Neuroscience • Ethology and Evolutionary Developmental Psychology • Vygotsky's Sociocultural Theory • Ecological Systems Theory

■ **SOCIAL ISSUES: HEALTH** Family Chaos Undermines Children's Well-Being

Comparing and Evaluating Theories

Studying Development

Common Research Methods • General Research Designs • Designs for Studying Development

■ **CULTURAL INFLUENCES** Immigrant Youths: Adapting to a New Land

Ethics in Lifespan Research

years, two daughters and a son were born. Soon Sofie's father became ill, his health shattered by the strain of uprooting his family and losing his home and business. After months of being bedridden, he died of heart failure.

When World War II ended, Philip left the army and opened a small men's clothing store. Sofie divided her time between

caring for the children and helping Philip in the store. Now in her forties, she was a devoted mother, but few women her age were still rearing young children. As Philip struggled with the business, he spent longer hours at work, and Sofie often felt lonely. She rarely touched the piano, which brought back painful memories of youthful life plans shattered by war.

Sofie's sense of isolation and lack of fulfillment frequently left her short-tempered. Late at night, she and Philip could be heard arguing.

As Sofie's children grew older, she returned to school again, this time to earn a teaching credential. Finally, at age 50, she launched a career. For the next decade, she taught German and French to high school students and English to newly arrived immigrants. Besides easing her family's financial difficulties, she felt a gratifying sense of accomplishment and creativity. These years were among the most energetic and satisfying of Sofie's life. She had an unending enthusiasm for teaching—for transmitting her facility with language, her first-hand knowledge of the consequences of hatred and oppression, and her practical understanding of how to adapt to life in a new land. She watched her children, whose young lives were free of the trauma of war, adopt many of her values and commitments and begin their marital and vocational lives at the expected time.

Sofie approached age 60 with an optimistic outlook. Released from the financial burden of paying for their children's college education, she and Philip looked forward to greater leisure. Their affection and respect for each other deepened.

Once again, Sofie began to play the piano. But this period of contentment was short-lived.

One morning, Sofie awoke and felt a hard lump under her arm. Several days later, her doctor diagnosed cancer. Sofie's spirited disposition and capacity to adapt to radical life changes helped her meet the illness head on. She defined it as an enemy to be fought and overcome. As a result, she lived five more years. Despite the exhaustion of chemotherapy, Sofie maintained a full schedule of teaching duties and continued to visit and run errands for her elderly mother. But as she weakened physically, she no longer had the stamina to meet her classes. Bedridden for the last few weeks, she slipped quietly into death with Philip at her side. The funeral chapel overflowed with hundreds of Sofie's students. She had granted each a memorable image of a woman of courage and caring.

One of Sofie's three children, Laura, is the author of this book. Married a year before Sofie died, Laura and her husband, Ken, often think of Sofie's message, spoken privately to them on the eve of their wedding day: "I learned from my own life and marriage that you must build a life together but also a life apart. You must grant each other the time, space, and support to forge your own identities, your own ways of expressing yourselves and giving to others. The most important ingredient of your relationship must be respect."

Laura and Ken settled in a small midwestern city, near Illinois State University, where they have served on the faculty for many years—Laura in the Department of Psychology, Ken in the Department of Mathematics. They have two sons, David and Peter, to whom Laura has related many stories about Sofie's life and who carry her legacy forward. David shares his grandmother's penchant for teaching; he is a second-grade teacher. Peter, a lawyer, shares his grandmother's love of music, and his wife Melissa—much like Sofie—is both a talented linguist and a musician. When Peter asked Melissa to marry him, he placed a family heirloom on her finger—an engagement ring that had belonged to Sofie's aunt, who perished in a Nazi death camp. In the box that held the ring, Melissa found a written copy of the story of Sofie and her family.

Sofie also had a lifelong impact on many of her students. A professor of human development wrote to Laura:

I have been meaning to contact you for a while. I teach a class in lifespan development. When I opened the textbook and saw the pictures of your mother, I was very surprised. I took high school German classes from her. I remember her as a very tough teacher who both held her students accountable and cared about each and every one of us. That she was an incredible teacher did not really sink in until I went to Germany during my [college] years and was able to both understand German and speak it.

Sofie's story raises a wealth of fascinating issues about human life histories:

- What determines the features that Sofie shares with others and those that make her unique—in physical characteristics, mental capacities, interests, and behaviors?
- What led Sofie to retain the same persistent, determined disposition throughout her life but to change in other essential ways?
- How do historical and cultural conditions—for Sofie, the persecution that destroyed her childhood home, caused the death of family members and friends, and led her family to flee to the United States—affect well-being throughout life?
- How does the timing of events—for example, Sofie's early exposure to foreign languages and her delayed entry into marriage, parenthood, and career—affect development?
- What factors—both personal and environmental—led Sofie to die sooner than expected?

These are central questions addressed by **developmental science,** a field of study devoted to understanding constancy and change throughout the lifespan (Lerner, 2006; Lerner et al., 2011). Great diversity characterizes the interests and concerns of investigators who study development. But all share a single goal: to identify those factors that influence consistencies and transformations in people from conception to death. ●

A Scientific, Applied, and Interdisciplinary Field

The questions just listed are not merely of scientific interest. Each has *applied,* or practical, importance as well. In fact, scientific curiosity is just one factor that led the study of development to become the exciting field it is today. Research about development has also been stimulated by social pressures to improve people's lives. For example, the beginning of public education in the early twentieth century led to a demand for knowledge about what and how to teach children of different ages. The interest of the medical profession in improving people's

health required an understanding of physical development, nutrition, and disease. The social service profession's desire to treat emotional problems and to help people adjust to major life events, such as divorce, job loss, war, natural disasters, or the death of loved ones, required information about personality and social development. And parents have continually sought expert advice about child-rearing practices and experiences that would promote their children's well-being.

Our large storehouse of information about development is *interdisciplinary.* It has grown through the combined efforts of people from many fields of study. Because of the need for solutions to everyday problems at all ages, researchers from psychology, sociology, anthropology, biology, and neuroscience have joined forces in research with professionals from education, family studies, medicine, public health, and social service, to name just a few. Together, they have created the field as it exists today—a body of knowledge that is not just scientifically important but also relevant and useful.

 ## Basic Issues

Developmental science is a relatively recent endeavor. Studies of children did not begin until the late nineteenth and early twentieth centuries. Investigations into adult development, aging, and change over the life course emerged only in the 1960s and 1970s (Elder & Shanahan, 2006). But speculations about how people grow and change have existed for centuries. As they combined with research, they inspired the construction of *theories* of development. A **theory** is an orderly, integrated set of statements that describes, explains, and predicts behavior. For example, a good theory of infant–caregiver attachment would (1) *describe* the behaviors of babies of 6 to 8 months of age as they seek the affection and comfort of a familiar adult, (2) *explain* how and why infants develop this strong desire to bond with a caregiver, and (3) *predict* the consequences of this emotional bond for future relationships.

Theories are vital tools for two reasons. First, they provide organizing frameworks for our observations of people. In other words, they *guide and give meaning* to what we see. Second, theories that are verified by research provide a sound basis for practical action. Once a theory helps us *understand* development, we are in a much better position to know *how to improve* the welfare and treatment of children and adults.

As we will see, theories are influenced by the cultural values and belief systems of their times. But theories differ in one important way from mere opinion or belief: A theory's continued existence depends on *scientific verification*. Every theory must be tested using a fair set of research procedures agreed on by the scientific community, and the findings must endure, or be replicated over time.

Within the field of developmental science, many theories exist, offering very different ideas about what people are like and how they change. The study of development provides no ultimate truth because investigators do not always agree on the meaning of what they see. Also, humans are complex beings; they change physically, mentally, emotionally, and socially. No single theory has explained all these aspects. But the existence of many theories helps advance knowledge as researchers continually try to support, contradict, and integrate these different points of view.

This chapter introduces you to major theories of human development and research strategies used to test them. In later chapters, we will return to each theory in greater detail and will also introduce other important but less grand theories. Although there are many theories, we can easily organize them by looking at the stand they take on three basic issues: (1) Is the course of development continuous or discontinuous? (2) Does one course of development characterize all people, or are there many possible courses? (3) What are the roles of genetic and environmental factors—nature and nurture—in development? Let's look closely at each of these issues.

Continuous or Discontinuous Development?

How can we best describe the differences in capacities among infants, children, adolescents, and adults? As Figure 1.1 illustrates, major theories recognize two possibilities.

One view holds that infants and preschoolers respond to the world in much the same way as adults do. The difference between the immature and mature being is simply one of *amount or complexity*. For example, when Sofie was a baby, her perception of a piano melody, memory for past events, and ability to categorize objects may have been much like our own. Perhaps her only limitation was that she could not perform

these skills with as much information and precision as we can. If this is so, then changes in her thinking must be **continuous**—a process of gradually augmenting the same types of skills that were there to begin with.

According to a second view, infants and children have *unique ways of thinking, feeling, and behaving*, ones quite different from adults. If so, then development is **discontinuous**—a process in which new ways of understanding and responding to the world emerge at specific times. From this perspective, Sofie could not yet perceive, remember, and categorize experiences as a mature person can. Rather, she moved through a series of developmental steps, each of which has unique features, until she reached the highest level of functioning.

Theories that accept the discontinuous perspective regard development as taking place in **stages**—*qualitative* changes in thinking, feeling, and behaving that characterize specific periods of development. In stage theories, development is like climbing a staircase, with each step corresponding to a more mature, reorganized way of functioning. The stage concept also assumes that people undergo periods of rapid transformation as they step up from one stage to the next. In other words, change is fairly sudden rather than gradual and ongoing.

Does development actually occur in a neat, orderly sequence of stages? This ambitious assumption has faced significant challenges. Later in this chapter, we will review some influential stage theories.

One Course of Development or Many?

Stage theorists assume that people everywhere follow the same sequence of development. Yet the field of human development is becoming increasingly aware that children and adults live in

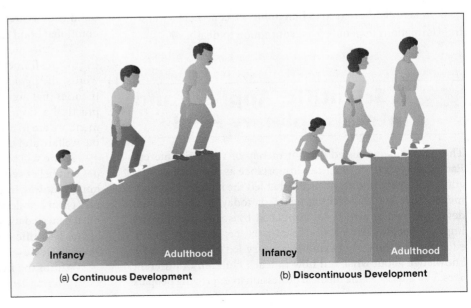

FIGURE 1.1 **Is development continuous or discontinuous?** (a) Some theorists believe that development is a smooth, continuous process. Individuals gradually add more of the same types of skills. (b) Other theorists think that development takes place in discontinuous stages. People change rapidly as they step up to a new level and then change very little for a while. With each new step, the person interprets and responds to the world in a reorganized, qualitatively different way. As we will see later, still other theorists believe that development is characterized by both continuous and discontinuous change.

(a) **Continuous Development**   Infancy   Adulthood

(b) **Discontinuous Development**   Infancy   Adulthood

distinct **contexts**—unique combinations of personal and environmental circumstances that can result in different paths of change. For example, a shy individual who fears social encounters develops in very different contexts from those of an outgoing agemate who readily seeks out other people (Kagan, 2003, 2008a). Children and adults in non-Western village societies have experiences in their families and communities that differ sharply from those of people in large Western cities. These different circumstances foster different intellectual capacities, social skills, and feelings about the self and others (Shweder et al., 2006).

As you will see, contemporary theorists regard the contexts that shape development as many-layered and complex. On the personal side, they include heredity and biological makeup. On the environmental side, they include both immediate settings—home, school, and neighborhood—and circumstances more remote from people's everyday lives: community resources, societal values, and historical time period. Finally, researchers today are more conscious than ever before of cultural diversity in development.

Relative Influence of Nature and Nurture?

In addition to describing the course of human development, each theory takes a stand on a major question about its underlying causes: Are genetic or environmental factors more important? This is the age-old **nature–nurture controversy.** By *nature,* we mean the hereditary information we receive from our parents at the moment of conception. By *nurture,* we mean the complex forces of the physical and social world that influence our biological makeup and psychological experiences before and after birth.

Although all theories grant roles to both nature and nurture, they vary in emphasis. Consider the following questions: Is the developing person's ability to think in more complex ways largely the result of a built-in timetable of growth, or is it primarily influenced by stimulation from parents and teachers? Do children acquire language rapidly because they are genetically predisposed to do so or because parents teach them from an early age? And what accounts for the vast individual differences among people—in height, weight, physical coordination, intelligence, personality, and social skills? Is nature or nurture more responsible?

A theory's position on the roles of nature and nurture affects how it explains individual differences. Theorists who emphasize *stability*—that individuals who are high or low in a characteristic (such as verbal ability, anxiety, or sociability) will remain so at later ages—typically stress the importance of *heredity.* If they regard environment as important, they usually point to *early experiences* as establishing a lifelong

pattern of behavior. Powerful negative events in the first few years, they argue, cannot be fully overcome by later, more positive ones (Bowlby, 1980; Sroufe et al., 2010). Other theorists, taking a more optimistic view, see development as having substantial **plasticity** throughout life—as open to change in response to influential experiences (Baltes, Lindenberger, & Staudinger, 2006; Overton, 2010).

Throughout this book, you will see that investigators disagree, often sharply, on the question of *stability versus plasticity.* Their answers often vary across *domains,* or aspects, of development. Think back to Sofie's story, and you will see that her linguistic ability and persistent approach to challenges were stable over the lifespan. In contrast, her psychological well-being and life satisfaction fluctuated considerably.

The Lifespan Perspective: A Balanced Point of View

So far, we have discussed basic issues of human development in terms of extremes—solutions favoring one side or the other. But as we trace the unfolding of the field, you will see that the positions of many theorists have softened. Today, some theorists believe that both continuous and discontinuous changes occur. Many acknowledge that development has both universal features and features unique to each individual and his or her contexts. And a growing number regard heredity and environment as inseparably interwoven, each affecting the potential of the other to modify the child's traits and capacities (Gottlieb, 2007; Overton, 2010; Rutter, 2007).

These balanced visions owe much to the expansion of research from a nearly exclusive focus on the first two decades

Since the 1960s, researchers have moved from focusing only on child development to investigating development over the entire life course. This woman and her companions on a river rafting trip illustrate the health, vitality, and life satisfaction of many contemporary older adults.

of life to include development during adulthood. In the first half of the twentieth century, it was widely assumed that development stopped at adolescence. Infancy and childhood were viewed as periods of rapid transformation, adulthood as a plateau, and aging as a period of decline. The changing character of the North American population awakened researchers to the idea that gains in functioning are lifelong.

Because of improvements in nutrition, sanitation, and medical knowledge, *average life expectancy* (the number of years an individual born in a particular year can expect to live) gained more in the twentieth century than in the preceding 5,000 years. In 1900, life expectancy was just under age 50; today, it is 78.5 years in the United States and even higher in most other industrialized nations, including neighboring Canada. Life expectancy continues to increase; in the United States, it is predicted to reach 84 years in 2050. Consequently, there are more older adults—a worldwide trend that is especially striking in developed countries. People age 65 and older accounted for about 4 percent of the U.S. population in 1900, 7 percent in 1950, and 13 percent in 2010 (U.S. Census Bureau, 2012b).

Older adults are not only more numerous but also healthier and more active. Challenging the earlier stereotype of the withering person, they have contributed to a profound shift in our view of human change and the factors that underlie it. Increasingly, researchers are envisioning *development as a dynamic system*—a perpetually ongoing process, extending from conception to death, that is molded by a complex network of biological, psychological, and social influences (Lerner et al., 2011). A leading dynamic systems approach is the **lifespan perspective.** Four assumptions make up this broader view: that development is (1) lifelong, (2) multidimensional and multidirectional, (3) highly plastic, and (4) affected by multiple, interacting forces (Baltes, Lindenberger, & Staudinger, 2006; Smith & Baltes, 1999; Staudinger & Lindenberger, 2003).

Development Is Lifelong

According to the lifespan perspective, no single age period is supreme in its impact on the life course. Rather, events occurring during each major period, summarized in Table 1.1, can have equally powerful effects on future change. Within each period, change occurs in three broad domains: *physical, cognitive,* and *emotional/social,* which we separate for convenience of discussion (see Figure 1.2 for a description of each). Yet, as you already know from reading the first part of this chapter, these domains are not really distinct; they overlap and interact.

Every age period has its own agenda, its unique demands and opportunities that yield some similarities in development across many individuals. Nevertheless, throughout life, the challenges people face and the adjustments they make are highly diverse in timing and pattern, as the remaining assumptions make clear.

TABLE 1.1 **Major Periods of Human Development**

PERIOD	APPROXIMATE AGE RANGE	BRIEF DESCRIPTION
Prenatal	Conception to birth	The one-celled organism transforms into a human baby with remarkable capacities to adjust to life outside the womb.
Infancy and toddlerhood	Birth–2 years	Dramatic changes in the body and brain support the emergence of a wide array of motor, perceptual, and intellectual capacities and first intimate ties to others.
Early childhood	2–6 years	During the "play years," motor skills are refined, thought and language expand at an astounding pace, a sense of morality is evident, and children establish ties with peers.
Middle childhood	6–11 years	The school years are marked by improved athletic abilities; more logical thought processes; mastery of basic literacy skills; advances in self-understanding, morality, and friendship; and the beginnings of peer-group membership.
Adolescence	11–18 years	Puberty leads to an adult-sized body and sexual maturity. Thought becomes abstract and idealistic and school achievement more serious. Adolescents begin to establish autonomy from the family and to define personal values and goals.
Early adulthood	18–40 years	Most young people leave home, complete their education, and begin full-time work. Major concerns are developing a career, forming an intimate partnership, and marrying, rearing children, or establishing other lifestyles.
Middle adulthood	40–65 years	Many people are at the height of their careers and attain leadership positions. They must also help their children begin independent lives and their parents adapt to aging. They become more aware of their own mortality.
Late adulthood	65 years–death	People adjust to retirement, to decreased physical strength and health, and often to the death of a spouse. They reflect on the meaning of their lives.

Physical Development
Changes in body size, proportions, appearance, functioning of body systems, perceptual and motor capacities, and physical health

Cognitive Development
Changes in intellectual abilities, including attention, memory, academic and everyday knowledge, problem solving, imagination, creativity, and language

Emotional and Social Development
Changes in emotional communication, self-understanding, knowledge about other people, interpersonal skills, friendships, intimate relationships, and moral reasoning and behavior

FIGURE 1.2 Major domains of development. The three domains are not really distinct. Rather, they overlap and interact.

Development Is Multidimensional and Multidirectional

Think back to Sofie's life and how she continually faced new demands and opportunities. From a lifespan perspective, the challenges and adjustments of development are *multidimensional*— affected by an intricate blend of biological, psychological, and social forces.

Lifespan development is also *multidirectional,* in at least two ways. First, development is not limited to improved performance. Rather, at every period, it is a joint expression of growth and decline. When Sofie directed her energies toward mastering languages and music as a school-age child, she gave up refining other skills to their full potential. Later, when she chose to become a teacher, she let go of other career options. Although gains are especially evident early in life, and losses during the final years, people of all ages can improve current skills and develop new ones, including skills that compensate for reduced functioning (Lang, Rohr, & Williger, 2010; Scheibe, Freund, & Baltes, 2007). Most older adults, for example, devise compensatory techniques for dealing with their increasing memory failures. They may rely more on external aids, such as calendars and lists, or generate new internal strategies, such as visualizing exactly where they will be and what they will be doing when they must keep an appointment or take medication (de Frias & Dixon, 2005).

Second, besides being multidirectional over time, change is multidirectional within each domain of development. Although some qualities of Sofie's cognitive functioning (such as memory) probably declined in her mature years, her knowledge of both English and French undoubtedly grew throughout her life. And she also developed new forms of thinking. For example, Sofie's wealth of experience and ability to cope with diverse problems led her to become expert in practical matters—a quality of reasoning called *wisdom.* Recall Sofie's wise advice to Laura and Ken on the eve of their wedding day. We will consider the development of wisdom in Chapter 17. Notice in these examples how the lifespan perspective includes both continuous and discontinuous change.

Development Is Plastic

Lifespan researchers emphasize that development is plastic at all ages. Consider Sofie's social reserve in childhood and her decision to study rather than marry as a young adult. As new opportunities arose, Sofie moved easily into marriage and childbearing in her thirties. And although parenthood and financial difficulties posed challenges to Sofie's and Philip's happiness, their relationship gradually became richer and more fulfilling. In Chapter 17, we will see that intellectual performance also remains flexible with advancing age. Older adults respond to

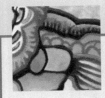

Biology and Environment

Resilience

This boy's close, affectionate relationship with his father promotes resilience. A strong bond with at least one parent who combines warmth with appropriate expectations for maturity can shield children from the damaging effects of stressful life conditions.

John and his best friend, Gary, grew up in a rundown, crime-ridden, inner-city neighborhood. By age 10, each had experienced years of family conflict followed by parental divorce. Reared from then on in mother-headed households, John and Gary rarely saw their fathers. Both dropped out of high school and were in and out of trouble with the police.

Then their paths diverged. By age 30, John had fathered two children with women he never married, had spent time in prison, was unemployed, and drank alcohol heavily. In contrast, Gary had returned to finish high school, had studied auto mechanics at a community college, and had become manager of a gas station and repair shop. Married with two children, he had saved his earnings and bought a home. He was happy, healthy, and well-adapted to life.

A wealth of evidence shows that environmental risks—poverty, negative family interactions and parental divorce, job loss, mental illness, and drug abuse—predispose children to future problems (Masten & Gewirtz, 2006; Sameroff, 2006; Wadsworth & Santiago, 2008). Why did

Gary "beat the odds" and come through unscathed?

Research on **resilience**—the ability to adapt effectively in the face of threats to development—is receiving increased attention as investigators look for ways to protect young people from the damaging effects of stressful life conditions (Masten & Powell, 2003). This interest has been inspired by long-term studies on the relationship of life stressors in childhood to competence and adjustment in adolescence and adulthood (Werner, 2013). In each study, some individuals were shielded from negative outcomes, whereas others had lasting problems. Four broad factors offered protection from the damaging effects of stressful life events.

Personal Characteristics

A child's genetically influenced characteristics can reduce exposure to risk or lead to experiences that compensate for early stressful events. High intelligence and socially valued talents (in music or athletics, for example) increase the chances that a child will have rewarding experiences in school and in the community that offset the impact of a stressful home life. Temperament is particularly

powerful. Children who have easygoing, sociable dispositions and who can readily inhibit negative emotions and impulses tend to have an optimistic outlook on life and a special capacity to adapt to change—

---

special training with substantial (but not unlimited) gains in a wide variety of mental abilities (Stine-Morrow & Basak, 2011).

Evidence on plasticity reveals that aging is not an eventual "shipwreck," as has often been assumed. Instead, the metaphor of a "butterfly"—of metamorphosis and continued potential—provides a far more accurate picture of lifespan change. Still, development gradually becomes less plastic, as both capacity and opportunity for change are reduced. And plasticity varies greatly across individuals. Some children and adults experience more diverse life circumstances. Also, as the Biology and Environment box above indicates, some adapt more easily than others to changing conditions.

Development Is Influenced by Multiple, Interacting Forces

According to the lifespan perspective, pathways of change are highly diverse because *development is influenced by multiple*

forces: biological, historical, social, and cultural. Although these wide-ranging influences can be organized into three categories, they work together, combining in unique ways to fashion each life course.

Age-Graded Influences. Events that are strongly related to age and therefore fairly predictable in when they occur and how long they last are called **age-graded influences.** For example, most individuals walk shortly after their first birthday, acquire their native language during the preschool years, reach puberty around age 12 to 14, and (for women) experience menopause in their late forties or early fifties. These milestones are influenced by biology, but social customs—such as starting school around age 6, getting a driver's license at age 16, and entering college around age 18—can create age-graded influences as well. Age-graded influences are especially prevalent in childhood and adolescence, when biological changes are rapid and cultures impose many age-related experiences to ensure

qualities that elicit positive responses from others. In contrast, emotionally reactive and irritable children often tax the patience of people around them (Vanderbilt-Adriance & Shaw, 2008; Wang & Deater-Deckard, 2013). For example, both John and Gary moved several times during their childhoods. Each time, John became anxious and angry. Gary looked forward to making new friends and exploring a new neighborhood.

A Warm Parental Relationship

A close relationship with at least one parent who provides warmth, appropriately high expectations, monitoring of the child's activities, and an organized home environment fosters resilience (Masten & Shaffer, 2006; Taylor, 2010). But this factor (as well as the next one) is not independent of children's personal characteristics. Children who are relaxed, socially responsive, and able to deal with change are easier to rear and more likely to enjoy positive relationships with parents and other people. At the same time, some children develop more attractive dispositions as a result of parental warmth and attention (Gulotta, 2008).

Social Support Outside the Immediate Family

The most consistent asset of resilient children is a strong bond with a competent, caring adult. For children who do not have a close bond with either parent, a grand-parent, aunt, uncle, or teacher who forms a special relationship with the child can promote resilience (Masten & Reed, 2002). Gary received support in adolescence from his grandfather, who listened to Gary's concerns and helped him solve problems. In addition, Gary's grandfather had a stable marriage and work life and handled stressors skillfully. Consequently, he served as a model of effective coping.

Associations with rule-abiding peers who value school achievement are also linked to resilience (Tiet, Huizinga, & Byrnes, 2010). But children who have positive relationships with adults are far more likely to establish these supportive peer ties.

Community Resources and Opportunities

Community supports—good schools, convenient and affordable health care and social services, libraries, and recreation centers—foster both parents' and children's well-being. In addition, opportunities to participate in community life help older children and adolescents overcome adversity. Extracurricular activities at school, religious youth groups, scouting, and other organizations teach important social skills, such as cooperation, leadership, and contributing to others' welfare. As participants acquire these competencies, they gain in self-reliance, self-esteem, and community commitment (Benson et al., 2006). As a college student, Gary volunteered for Habitat for Humanity, joining a team building affordable housing in low-income neighborhoods. Community involvement offered Gary opportunities to form meaningful relationships, which further strengthened his resilience.

Research on resilience highlights the complex connections between heredity and environment. Armed with positive characteristics, which stem from native endowment, favorable rearing experiences, or both, children and adolescents can act to reduce stressful situations.

But when many risks pile up, they are increasingly difficult to overcome (Obradović et al., 2009). To inoculate children against the negative effects of risk, interventions must not only reduce risks but also enhance children's protective relationships at home, in school, and in the community. This means attending to both the person and the environment—strengthening the individual's capacities while also reducing hazardous experiences.

For these 18-year-olds, moving into their college dorm is a major life transition, offering new freedoms and responsibilities. Entering college is an age-graded influence, occurring at about the same age for most young people.

YOON S. BYUN/THE BOSTON GLOBE/GETTY IMAGES

that young people acquire the skills they need to participate in their society.

History-Graded Influences. Development is also profoundly affected by forces unique to a particular historical era. Examples include epidemics, wars, and periods of economic prosperity or depression; technological advances, such as the introduction of television, computers, and the Internet; and changes in cultural values, such as attitudes toward women and ethnic minorities. These **history-graded influences** explain why people born around the same time—called a *cohort*—tend to be alike in ways that set them apart from people born at other times.

Consider the *baby boomers*, a term used to describe people born between 1946 and 1964, the post–World War II period during which birth rates soared in most Western nations. This population increase was especially sharp in the United States: By 1960, the prewar birth rate had nearly doubled, yielding the

Cultural Influences

The Baby Boomers Reshape the Life Course

From 1946 to 1964, 92 percent of all American women of childbearing age gave birth, averaging almost four children each—a new baby every 8 seconds (Croker, 2007). This splurge of births, which extended for nearly two decades, yielded a unique generation often credited with changing the world. Today, the baby boomers comprise more than 80 million adults—nearly 30 percent of the U.S. population (U.S. Census Bureau, 2012). Most are middle aged, with the oldest having recently entered late adulthood.

Several interrelated factors sparked the post–World War II baby boom. Many people who had postponed marriage and parenthood throughout the Great Depression of the 1930s started families in the 1940s, once the economy had improved. With the end of World War II, returning GIs also began to have children. As these two cohorts focused on childbearing, they gave birth to babies who otherwise would have been spaced out over 10 to 15 years. And as economic prosperity accelerated in the 1950s, making larger families affordable, more people

married at younger ages and had several children closely spaced, which led the baby boom to persist into the 1960s (Stewart & Malley, 2004). Finally, after a war, the desire to make babies generally strengthens. Besides replacing massive loss of life, new births signify hope that "human life will continue" (Croker, 2007, p. 9).

Compared with the previous generation, many more young baby boomers were economically privileged. They were also the recipients of deep emotional investment from their parents, who—having undergone the deprivations of depression and war—often ranked children as the most enduring benefit of their adult lives. These factors may have engendered optimism, confidence, even a sense of entitlement (Elder, Nguyen, & Caspi, 1985). At the same time, their huge numbers—evident in overflowing school classrooms—may have sparked an intense struggle for individual recognition. By the time the boomers reached early adulthood, this set of traits led critics to label them a narcissistic, indulged, "me" generation.

Rock star Bono, born in 1960, is a "trailing edge" baby boomer who, like many in his cohort, has a strong sense of social responsibility. Here he holds a child at a health clinic in Lesotho. Bono is a leader in the fight against AIDS and poverty in Africa.

From the mid-1960s to the early 1970s, the "leading-edge" baby boomers (born in the late 1940s and early 1950s) entered colleges and universities in record numbers, becoming better educated than any previous generation. This cohort—self-focused, socially aware, and in search of distinction—broke away from their parents'

largest gain in the nation's history. The sheer size of the baby-boom generation made it a powerful social force from the time its members became young adults; today, the baby boomers are redefining our view of middle and late adulthood (see the Cultural Influences box above).

LOOK AND LISTEN

Identify a history-graded influence in your life, and speculate about its impact on people your age. Then ask someone a generation older than you to identify a history-graded influence in his or her life and to reflect on its impact. ●

Nonnormative Influences. Age-graded and history-graded influences are *normative*—meaning typical, or average—because each affects large numbers of people in a similar way. **Nonnormative influences** are events that are irregular: They happen to just one person or a few people and do not follow a

predictable timetable. Consequently, they enhance the multi-directionality of development. Nonnormative influences that had a major impact on the direction of Sofie's life included piano lessons in childhood with an inspiring teacher; delayed marriage, parenthood, and career entry; and a battle with cancer. Because they occur haphazardly, nonnormative events are difficult for researchers to capture and study. Yet, as each of us can attest from our own experiences, they can affect us in powerful ways.

Nonnormative influences have become more powerful and age-graded influences less so in contemporary adult development. Compared with Sofie's era, much greater diversity exists today in the ages at which people finish their education, enter careers, get married, have children, and retire. Indeed, Sofie's "off-time" accomplishments would have been less unusual had she been born two generations later! Age remains a powerful organizer of everyday experiences, and age-related expectations have certainly not disappeared. But age markers have blurred, and they vary across ethnic groups and cultures. The increasing

family- and marriage-centered lifestyles. Starting in the mid-sixties, marriage rates declined, age of first marriage rose, and divorce rates increased. And the baby boomers responded to the turbulence of those times—the assassination of President Kennedy in 1963, the Vietnam War, and growing racial tensions—by mobilizing around the antiwar, civil rights, and women's movements, yielding a generation of student activists.

By the time the "trailing-edge" boomers (born in the late 1950s and early 1960s) came of age, these movements had left an enduring mark. Even as they turned toward family life and career development, the boomers continued to search for personal meaning, self-expression, and social responsibility. By midlife, the generation had produced an unusually large number of socially concerned writers, teachers, filmmakers, and labor and community organizers, as well as innovative musicians and artists (Cole & Stewart, 1996; Dickstein, 1992). And a multitude of ordinary citizens worked to advance social causes.

In addition, as baby-boom women entered the labor market and struggled for career advancement and equal pay, their self-confidence grew, and they paved the way for the next generation: On average, younger women attained this same level of self-confidence at a much earlier age (Stewart & Ostrove, 1998; Twenge, 1997, 2001). And as baby-boom activists pressed for gender and racial equality, they influenced national policy. The 1960s saw laws passed that banned discrimination in employment practices, in racial access to public accommodations, and in sale or rental of housing. By the 1970s, progress in civil rights served as the springboard for the gay and lesbian rights movement.

Today, the baby boomers are the largest generation ever to have entered middle age, and they are healthier, better educated, and financially better off than any previous midlife cohort (Whitbourne & Willis, 2006). Their sense of self-empowerment and innovativeness is bringing new vitality to this period of the lifespan, including efforts to increase the personal meaningfulness of their careers and to deepen their lifelong engagement with social causes. Yet another concern of baby-boom midlifers is an intense desire to control the physical changes of aging (Hooyman & Kiyak, 2011). Far more than their predecessors, they resist growing old, as indicated by their interest in a wide array of anti-aging products and

procedures—from cosmetics to Botox to plastic surgery—that are now a multi-billion-dollar U.S. industry.

Nevertheless, it is important to note that the baby boomers—though advantaged as a generation—are diverse in health status and sense of control over their lives. Those higher in education and income considerably better off. And because retirement savings were heavily hit by the economic recession of 2007 to 2009, many are working longer than they otherwise had planned.

What lies ahead as this gigantic population bulge moves into late adulthood? Most analysts focus on societal burdens, such as rising social security and health-care costs. At the same time, as the boomers continue to build on the foundation laid in middle age, they could become "our only increasing natural resource" (Freedman, 1999). After retirement, they will have more time to care about others—and more relevant experience and years left to do so—than any previous generation. Policies and programs aimed at recruiting older adults into volunteer and service roles may be one of the most effective ways to "channel good will into good deeds," combat social ills, and enhance development during all periods of life.

role of nonnormative events in the life course adds to the fluid nature of lifespan development.

Notice that instead of a single line of development, the lifespan perspective emphasizes many potential pathways and outcomes—an image more like tree branches extending in diverse directions, which may undergo both continuous and stagewise transformations (see Figure 1.3). Now let's turn to scientific foundations of the field as a prelude to major theories that address various aspects of change.

FIGURE 1.3 The lifespan view of development. Rather than envisioning a single line of stagewise or continuous change (see Figure 1.1 on page 6), lifespan theorists conceive of development as more like tree branches extending in diverse directions. Many potential pathways are possible, depending on the contexts that influence the individual's life course. Each branch in this treelike image represents a possible skill within one of the major domains of development. The crossing of the branches signifies that the domains—physical, cognitive, emotional, and social—are interrelated.

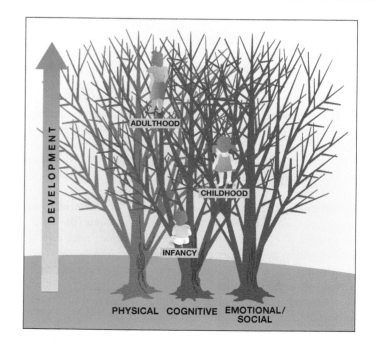

ASK YOURSELF

REVIEW Distinguish age-graded, history-graded, and nonnormative influences on lifespan development. Cite an example of each in Sofie's story.

CONNECT What stand does the lifespan perspective take on the issue of *one course of development or many?* How about the relative influence of *nature and nurture?* Explain.

APPLY Anna, a high school counselor, has devised a program that integrates classroom learning with vocational training to help adolescents at risk for school dropout stay in school and transition smoothly to work life. What is Anna's position on *stability versus plasticity* in development? Explain.

REFLECT Describe an aspect of your development that differs from a parent's or a grandparent's when he or she was your age. Using influences highlighted by the lifespan perspective, explain this difference in development.

Scientific Beginnings

Scientific study of human development dates back to the late nineteenth and early twentieth centuries. Early observations of human change were soon followed by improved methods and theories. Each advance contributed to the firm foundation on which the field rests today.

Darwin: Forefather of Scientific Child Study

British naturalist Charles Darwin (1809–1882) observed the infinite variation among plant and animal species. He also saw that within a species, no two individuals are exactly alike. From these observations, he constructed his famous *theory of evolution.*

The theory emphasized two related principles: *natural selection* and *survival of the fittest.* Darwin explained that certain species survive in particular environments because they have characteristics that fit with, or are adapted to, their surroundings. Other species die off because they are less well-suited to their environments. Individuals within a species who best meet the environment's survival requirements live long enough to reproduce and pass their more beneficial characteristics to future generations. Darwin's (1859/1936) emphasis on the adaptive value of physical characteristics and behavior found its way into important developmental theories.

During his explorations, Darwin discovered that early prenatal growth is strikingly similar in many species. Other scientists concluded from Darwin's observations that the development of the human child follows the same general plan as the evolution of the human species. Although this belief eventually proved inaccurate, efforts to chart parallels between child growth and human evolution prompted researchers to make careful observations of all aspects of children's behavior. Out of these first attempts to document an idea about development, scientific child study was born.

The Normative Period

G. Stanley Hall (1844–1924), one of the most influential American psychologists of the early twentieth century, is generally regarded as the founder of the child study movement (Cairns & Cairns, 2006). He also foreshadowed lifespan research by writing one of the few books of his time on aging. Inspired by Darwin's work, Hall and his well-known student Arnold Gesell (1880–1961) devised theories based on evolutionary ideas. They regarded development as a *maturational process*—a genetically determined series of events that unfold automatically, much like a flower (Gesell, 1933; Hall, 1904).

Hall and Gesell are remembered less for their one-sided theories than for their intensive efforts to describe all aspects of

Darwin's theory of evolution emphasizes the adaptive value of physical characteristics and behavior. Affection and care in families promote survival and psychological well-being throughout the lifespan. Here, a son helps his father adjust to using a walker.

development. This launched the **normative approach,** in which measures of behavior are taken on large numbers of individuals, and age-related averages are computed to represent typical development. Using this procedure, Hall constructed elaborate questionnaires asking children of different ages almost everything they could tell about themselves—interests, fears, imaginary playmates, dreams, friendships, everyday knowledge, and more. Similarly, through careful observations and parent interviews, Gesell collected detailed normative information on the motor achievements, social behaviors, and personality characteristics of infants and children.

Gesell was also among the first to make knowledge about child development meaningful to parents by informing them of what to expect at each age. If the timetable of development is the product of millions of years of evolution, as Gesell believed, then children are naturally knowledgeable about their needs. His child-rearing advice recommended sensitivity to children's cues (Thelen & Adolph, 1992). Along with Benjamin Spock's *Baby and Child Care,* Gesell's books became a central part of a rapidly expanding child development literature for parents.

The Mental Testing Movement

While Hall and Gesell were developing their theories and methods in the United States, French psychologist Alfred Binet (1857–1911) was also taking a normative approach to child development, but for a different reason. In the early 1900s, Binet and his colleague Theodore Simon were asked by Paris school officials to find a way to identify children with learning problems who needed to be placed in special classes. To address these practical educational concerns, Binet and Simon constructed the first successful intelligence test.

In 1916, at Stanford University, Binet's test was adapted for use with English-speaking children. Since then, the English version has been known as the *Stanford-Binet Intelligence Scale.* Besides providing a score that could successfully predict school achievement, the Binet test sparked tremendous interest in individual differences in development. Comparisons of the scores of people who vary in gender, ethnicity, birth order, family background, and other characteristics became a major focus of research. And intelligence tests moved quickly to the forefront of the nature–nurture controversy.

 # Mid-Twentieth-Century Theories

In the mid-twentieth century, the study of human development expanded into a legitimate discipline. As it attracted increasing interest, a variety of theories emerged, each of which continues to have followers today. In these theories, the European concern with the individual's inner thoughts and feelings contrasts sharply with the North American academic focus on scientific precision and concrete, observable behavior.

The Psychoanalytic Perspective

In the 1930s and 1940s, as more people sought help from professionals to deal with emotional difficulties, a new question had to be addressed: How and why do people become the way they are? To treat psychological problems, psychiatrists and social workers turned to an emerging approach to personality development that emphasized each individual's unique life history.

According to the **psychoanalytic perspective,** people move through a series of stages in which they confront conflicts between biological drives and social expectations. How these conflicts are resolved determines the person's ability to learn, to get along with others, and to cope with anxiety. Among the many individuals who contributed to the psychoanalytic perspective, two were especially influential: Sigmund Freud, founder of the psychoanalytic movement, and Erik Erikson.

Freud's Theory. Freud (1856–1939), a Viennese physician, sought a cure for emotionally troubled adults by having them talk freely about painful events of their childhoods. Working with these recollections, he examined the unconscious motivations of his patients and constructed his **psychosexual theory,** which emphasizes that how parents manage their child's sexual and aggressive drives in the first few years is crucial for healthy personality development.

In Freud's theory, three parts of the personality—id, ego, and superego—become integrated during five stages, summarized in Table 1.2 on page 16. The *id,* the largest portion of the mind, is the source of basic biological needs and desires. The *ego,* the conscious, rational part of personality, emerges in early infancy to redirect the id's impulses so they are discharged in acceptable ways.

Between 3 and 6 years of age, the *superego,* or conscience, develops as parents insist that children conform to the values of society. Now the ego faces the increasingly complex task of reconciling the demands of the id, the external world, and conscience (Freud, 1923/1974). For example, when the id impulse to grab an attractive toy from a playmate confronts the superego's warning that such behavior is wrong, the ego must mediate between these two forces, deciding which will win the inner struggle or, alternatively, work out a compromise, such as asking for a turn with the toy. According to Freud, the relations established among the id, ego, and superego during the preschool years determine the individual's basic personality.

Freud (1938/1973) believed that during childhood, sexual impulses shift their focus from the oral to the anal to the genital regions of the body. In each stage, parents walk a fine line between permitting too much or too little gratification of their child's basic needs. If parents strike an appropriate balance, then children grow into well-adjusted adults with the capacity for mature sexual behavior and investment in family life.

Freud's theory was the first to stress the influence of the early parent–child relationship on development. But his perspective was eventually criticized. First, it overemphasized the influence of sexual feelings in development. Second, because it

TABLE 1.2 Freud's Psychosexual Stages and Erikson's Psychosocial Stages Compared

APPROXIMATE AGE	FREUD'S PSYCHOSEXUAL STAGE	ERIKSON'S PSYCHOSOCIAL STAGE
Birth–1 year	*Oral:* The new ego directs the baby's sucking activities toward breast or bottle. If oral needs are not met, the individual may develop such habits as thumb sucking, fingernail biting, overeating, or smoking.	*Basic trust versus mistrust:* From warm, responsive care, infants gain a sense of trust, or confidence, that the world is good. Mistrust occurs if infants are neglected or handled harshly.
1–3 years	*Anal:* Toddlers and preschoolers enjoy holding and releasing urine and feces. If parents toilet train before children are ready or make too few demands, conflicts about anal control may appear in the form of extreme orderliness or disorder.	*Autonomy versus shame and doubt:* Using new mental and motor skills, children want to decide for themselves. Parents can foster autonomy by permitting reasonable free choice and not forcing or shaming the child.
3–6 years	*Phallic:* As preschoolers take pleasure in genital stimulation, Freud's Oedipus conflict for boys and Electra conflict for girls arise: Children feel a sexual desire for the other-sex parent. To avoid punishment, they give up this desire and adopt the same-sex parent's characteristics and values. As a result, the superego is formed, and children feel guilty when they violate its standards.	*Initiative versus guilt:* Through make-believe play, children gain insight into the person they can become. Initiative—a sense of ambition and responsibility— develops when parents support their child's sense of purpose. But if parents demand too much self-control, children experience excessive guilt.
6–11 years	*Latency:* Sexual instincts die down, and the superego strengthens as the child acquires new social values from adults and same-sex peers.	*Industry versus inferiority:* At school, children learn to work and cooperate with others. Inferiority develops when negative experiences at home, at school, or with peers lead to feelings of incompetence.
Adolescence	*Genital:* With puberty, sexual impulses reappear. Successful development during earlier stages leads to marriage, mature sexuality, and child rearing.	*Identity versus role confusion:* By exploring values and vocational goals, the young person forms a personal identity. The negative outcome is confusion about future adult roles.
Early adulthood		*Intimacy versus isolation:* Young adults establish intimate relationships. Because of earlier disappointments, some individuals cannot form close bonds and remain isolated.
Middle adulthood		*Generativity versus stagnation:* Generativity means giving to the next generation through child rearing, caring for others, or productive work. The person who fails in these ways feels an absence of meaningful accomplishment.
Old age		*Integrity versus despair:* Integrity results from feeling that life was worth living as it happened. Older people who are dissatisfied with their lives fear death.

© OLIVE PIERCE/BLACK STAR

Erik Erikson

was based on the problems of sexually repressed, well-to-do adults in nineteenth-century Viennese society, it did not apply in other cultures. Finally, Freud had not studied children directly.

Erikson's Theory. Several of Freud's followers took what was useful from his theory and improved on his vision. The most important of these neo-Freudians is Erik Erikson (1902–1994), who expanded the picture of development at each stage. In his **psychosocial theory,** Erikson emphasized that in addition to mediating between id impulses and superego demands, the ego makes a positive contribution to development, acquiring attitudes and skills that make the individual an active, contribut-

ing member of society. A basic psychosocial conflict, which is resolved along a continuum from positive to negative, determines healthy or maladaptive outcomes at each stage. As Table 1.2 shows, Erikson's first five stages parallel Freud's stages, but Erikson added three adult stages.

Unlike Freud, Erikson pointed out that normal development must be understood in relation to each culture's life situation. For example, in the 1940s, he observed that Yurok Indians of the northwest coast of the United States deprived babies of breastfeeding for the first 10 days after birth and instead fed them a thin soup. At age 6 months, infants were abruptly weaned—if necessary, by having the mother leave for a few days.

A child of the Kazakh people of Mongolia observes closely as her grandfather demonstrates how to train an eagle to hunt small animals, essential for the heavily meat-based Kazakh diet. As Erikson recognized, this parenting practice is best understood in relation to the competencies valued and needed in Kazakh culture.

From our cultural vantage point, these practices seem cruel. But Erikson explained that because the Yurok depended on salmon, which fill the river just once a year, the development of considerable self-restraint was essential for survival. In this way, he showed that child rearing is responsive to the competencies valued and needed by an individual's society.

Contributions and Limitations of the Psychoanalytic Perspective.

A special strength of the psychoanalytic perspective is its emphasis on the individual's unique life history as worthy of study and understanding. Consistent with this view, psychoanalytic theorists accept the *clinical,* or *case study, method,* which synthesizes information from a variety of sources into a detailed picture of the personality of a single person. (We will discuss this method further at the end of this chapter.) Psychoanalytic theory has also inspired a wealth of research on many aspects of emotional and social development, including infant–caregiver attachment, aggression, sibling relationships, child-rearing practices, morality, gender roles, and adolescent identity.

Despite its extensive contributions, the psychoanalytic perspective is no longer in the mainstream of human development research. Psychoanalytic theorists may have become isolated from the rest of the field because they were so strongly committed to in-depth study of individuals that they failed to consider other methods. In addition, many psychoanalytic ideas, such as psychosexual stages and ego functioning, are so vague that they are difficult or impossible to test empirically (Crain, 2005; Thomas, 2005).

Nevertheless, Erikson's broad outline of lifespan change captures the essence of psychosocial attainments during each major period of the life course. We will return to it, along with other perspectives inspired by Erikson's theory, in later chapters.

Behaviorism and Social Learning Theory

As the psychoanalytic perspective gained in prominence, the study of development was also influenced by a very different perspective. According to **behaviorism,** directly observable events—stimuli and responses—are the appropriate focus of study. North American behaviorism began in the early twentieth century with the work of John Watson (1878–1958), who, rejecting the psychoanalytic concern with the unseen workings of the mind, set out to create an objective science of psychology.

Traditional Behaviorism. Watson was inspired by Russian physiologist Ivan Pavlov's studies of animal learning. Pavlov knew that dogs release saliva as an innate reflex when they are given food. But he noticed that his dogs were salivating before they tasted any food—when they saw the trainer who usually fed them. The dogs, Pavlov reasoned, must have learned to associate a neutral stimulus (the trainer) with another stimulus (food) that produces a reflexive response (salivation). Because of this association, the neutral stimulus alone could bring about a response resembling the reflex. Eager to test this idea, Pavlov successfully taught dogs to salivate at the sound of a bell by pairing it with the presentation of food. He had discovered *classical conditioning.*

Watson wanted to find out if classical conditioning could be applied to children's behavior. In a historic experiment, he taught Albert, an 11-month-old infant, to fear a neutral stimulus—a soft white rat—by presenting it several times with a sharp, loud sound, which naturally scared the baby. Little Albert, who at first had reached out eagerly to touch the furry rat, began to cry and turn his head away at the sight of it (Watson & Raynor, 1920). In fact, Albert's fear was so intense that researchers eventually challenged the ethics of studies like this one. Watson concluded that environment is the supreme force in development and that adults can mold children's behavior by carefully controlling stimulus–response associations. He viewed development as a continuous process—a gradual increase with age in the number and strength of these associations.

Another form of behaviorism was B. F. Skinner's (1904–1990) *operant conditioning theory.* According to Skinner, the frequency of a behavior can be increased by following it with a wide variety of *reinforcers,* such as food, praise, or a friendly smile. It can also be decreased through *punishment,* such as disapproval or withdrawal of privileges. As a result of Skinner's work, operant conditioning became a broadly applied learning principle. We will consider these conditioning techniques further in Chapter 4.

Social Learning Theory. Psychologists wondered whether behaviorism might offer a more direct and effective explanation of the development of social behavior than the less precise concepts of psychoanalytic theory. This sparked approaches that built on the principles of conditioning, offering expanded views of how children and adults acquire new responses.

Several kinds of **social learning theory** emerged. The most influential, devised by Albert Bandura (1925–), emphasizes *modeling,* also known as *imitation* or *observational learning,* as a powerful source of development. The baby who claps her hands after her mother does so, the child who angrily hits a playmate in the same way that he has been punished at home, and the teenager who wears the same clothes and hairstyle as her friends at school are all displaying observational learning. In his early work, Bandura found that diverse factors affect children's motivation to imitate: their own history of reinforcement or punishment for the behavior, the promise of future reinforcement or punishment, and even vicarious reinforcement or punishment (observing the model being reinforced or punished).

Bandura's work continues to influence much research on social development. But today, his theory stresses the importance of *cognition,* or thinking. In fact, the most recent revision of Bandura's (1992, 2001) theory places such strong emphasis on how we think about ourselves and other people that he calls it a *social-cognitive* rather than a social learning approach.

In Bandura's revised view, children gradually become more selective in what they imitate. From watching others engage in self-praise and self-blame and through feedback about the worth of their own actions, children develop *personal standards* for behavior and *a sense of self-efficacy*—the belief that their own abilities and characteristics will help them succeed. These cognitions guide responses in particular situations (Bandura, 1999, 2001). For example, imagine a parent who often remarks, "I'm glad I kept working on that task, even though it was hard," who explains the value of persistence, and who encourages it by saying, "I know you can do a good job on that homework!" Soon the child starts to view herself as hardworking and high-achieving and selects people with these characteristics as models. In this way, as individuals acquire attitudes, values, and convictions about themselves, they control their own learning and behavior.

Contributions and Limitations of Behaviorism and Social Learning Theory. Behaviorism and social learning theory have been helpful in treating a wide range of adjustment problems. **Behavior modification** consists of procedures that combine conditioning and modeling to eliminate undesirable behaviors and increase desirable responses. It has been used to relieve a wide range of difficulties in children and adults, ranging from poor time management and unwanted habits to serious problems, such as language delays, persistent aggression, and extreme fears (Martin & Pear, 2011).

Nevertheless, many theorists believe that behaviorism and social learning theory offer too narrow a view of important environmental influences, which extend beyond immediate reinforcement, punishment, and modeled behaviors to people's rich physical and social worlds. Behaviorism and social learning theory have also been criticized for underestimating people's contributions to their own development. Bandura, with his emphasis on cognition, is unique among theorists whose work grew out of the behaviorist tradition in granting children and adults an active role in their own learning.

Piaget's Cognitive-Developmental Theory

If one individual has influenced research on child development more than any other, it is Swiss cognitive theorist Jean Piaget (1896–1980). North American investigators had been aware of Piaget's work since 1930. But they did not grant it much attention until the 1960s, mainly because Piaget's ideas were at odds with behaviorism, which dominated North American psychology in the mid-twentieth century (Cairns & Cairns, 2006). Piaget did not believe that children's learning depends on reinforcers, such as rewards from adults. According to his **cognitive-developmental theory,** children actively construct knowledge as they manipulate and explore their world.

Piaget's Stages. Piaget's view of development was greatly influenced by his early training in biology. Central to his theory is the biological concept of *adaptation* (Piaget, 1971). Just as structures of the body are adapted to fit with the environment, so structures of the mind develop to better fit with, or represent,

Social learning theory recognizes that children acquire many skills through modeling. By observing and imitating her mother, this Vietnamese preschooler learns to use chopsticks.

TABLE 1.3

Piaget's Stages of Cognitive Development

STAGE	PERIOD OF DEVELOPMENT	DESCRIPTION	
Sensorimotor	Birth–2 years	Infants "think" by acting on the world with their eyes, ears, hands, and mouth. As a result, they invent ways of solving sensorimotor problems, such as pulling a lever to hear the sound of a music box, finding hidden toys, and putting objects into and taking them out of containers.	
Preoperational	2–7 years	Preschool children use symbols to represent their earlier sensori-motor discoveries. Development of language and make-believe play takes place. However, thinking lacks the logic of the two remaining stages.	
Concrete operational	7–11 years	Children's reasoning becomes logical. School-age children understand that a certain amount of lemonade or play dough remains the same even after its appearance changes. They also organize objects into hierarchies of classes and subclasses. However, children think in a logical, organized fashion only when dealing with concrete information they can perceive directly.	
Formal operational	11 years on	The capacity for abstract, systematic thinking enables adolescents, when faced with a problem, to start with a hypothesis, deduce testable inferences, and isolate and combine variables to see which inferences are confirmed. Adolescents can also evaluate the logic of verbal statements without referring to real-world circumstances.	

Jean Piaget

the external world. In infancy and early childhood, Piaget claimed, children's understanding is different from adults'. For example, he believed that young babies do not realize that an object hidden from view—a favorite toy or even the mother—continues to exist. He also concluded that preschoolers' thinking is full of faulty logic. For example, children younger than age 7 commonly say that the amount of a liquid changes when it is poured into a different-shaped container. According to Piaget, children eventually revise these incorrect ideas in their ongoing efforts to achieve an *equilibrium,* or balance, between internal structures and information they encounter in their everyday worlds.

In Piaget's theory, as the brain develops and children's experiences expand, they move through four broad stages, each characterized by qualitatively distinct ways of thinking. Table 1.3 provides a brief description of Piaget's stages. Cognitive development begins in the *sensorimotor stage* with the baby's use of the senses and movements to explore the world. These action patterns evolve into the symbolic but illogical thinking of the preschooler in the *preoperational stage.* Then cognition is transformed into the more organized, logical reasoning of the school-age child in the *concrete operational stage.* Finally, in the *formal operational stage,* thought becomes the abstract, systematic reasoning system of the adolescent and adult.

Piaget devised special methods for investigating how children think. Early in his career, he carefully observed his three infant children and presented them with everyday problems, such as an attractive object that could be grasped, mouthed,

In Piaget's concrete operational stage, school-age children think in an organized, logical fashion about concrete objects. This 7-year-old understands that the quantity of pie dough remains the same after he changes its shape from a ball to a flattened circle.

kicked, or searched for. From their responses, Piaget derived his ideas about cognitive changes during the first two years. To study childhood and adolescent thought, Piaget adapted the clinical method of psychoanalysis, conducting open-ended *clinical interviews* in which a child's initial response to a task served as the basis for Piaget's next question. We will look more closely at this technique when we discuss research methods later in this chapter.

Contributions and Limitations of Piaget's Theory. Piaget convinced the field that children are active learners whose minds consist of rich structures of knowledge. Besides investigating children's understanding of the physical world, Piaget explored their reasoning about the social world. His stages have sparked a wealth of research on children's conceptions of themselves, other people, and human relationships. In practical terms, Piaget's theory encouraged the development of educational philosophies and programs that emphasize discovery learning and direct contact with the environment.

Despite Piaget's overwhelming contributions, his theory has been challenged. Research indicates that Piaget underestimated the competencies of infants and preschoolers. When young children are given tasks scaled down in difficulty and relevant to their everyday experiences, their understanding appears closer to that of the older child and adult than Piaget assumed. Also, adolescents generally reach their full intellectual potential only in areas of endeavor in which they have had extensive education and experience (Kuhn, 2008). These findings have led many researchers to conclude that cognitive maturity depends heavily on the complexity of knowledge sampled and the individual's familiarity with the task.

Furthermore, many studies show that children's performance on Piagetian problems can be improved with training—findings that call into question Piaget's assumption that discovery learning rather than adult teaching is the best way to foster development (Klahr & Nigam, 2004; Siegler & Svetina, 2006). Critics also point out that Piaget's stagewise account pays insufficient attention to social and cultural influences on development. Finally, some lifespan theorists disagree with Piaget's conclusion that no major cognitive changes occur after adolescence. Several have proposed important transformations in adulthood (Labouvie-Vief, 2006; Moshman, 2011; Perry, 1970/1998).

Today, the field of developmental science is divided over its loyalty to Piaget's ideas (Desrochers, 2008). Those who continue to find merit in Piaget's stages often accept a modified view—one in which changes in thinking take place more gradually than Piaget believed (Case, 1998; Demetriou et al., 2002; Fischer & Bidell, 2006; Halford & Andrews, 2006). Among those who disagree with Piaget's stage sequence, some have embraced an approach that emphasizes continuous gains in children's cognition: information processing. And still others have been drawn to theories that focus on the role of children's social and cultural contexts. We take up these approaches in the next section.

ASK YOURSELF

REVIEW What aspect of behaviorism made it attractive to critics of the psychoanalytic perspective? How did Piaget's theory respond to a major limitation of behaviorism?

CONNECT Although social learning theory focuses on social development and Piaget's theory on cognitive development, each has enhanced our understanding of other domains. Mention an additional domain addressed by each theory.

APPLY A 4-year-old becomes frightened of the dark and refuses to go to sleep at night. How would a psychoanalyst and a behaviorist differ in their views of how this problem developed?

REFLECT Describe a personal experience in which you received feedback from another person that strengthened your sense of self-efficacy—belief that your abilities and characteristics will help you succeed.

Recent Theoretical Perspectives

New ways of understanding the developing person are constantly emerging—questioning, building on, and enhancing the discoveries of earlier theories. Today, a burst of fresh approaches and research emphases is broadening our understanding of lifespan development.

Information Processing

In the 1970s and 1980s, researchers turned to the field of cognitive psychology for ways to understand the development of thinking. The design of digital computers that use mathematically specified steps to solve problems suggested to psychologists that the human mind might also be viewed as a symbol-manipulating system through which information flows—a perspective called **information processing** (Klahr & MacWhinney, 1998; Munakata, 2006). From the time information is presented to the senses at *input* until it emerges as a behavioral response at *output*, information is actively coded, transformed, and organized.

Information-processing researchers often design flowcharts to map the precise steps individuals use to solve problems and complete tasks, much like the plans devised by programmers to get computers to perform a series of "mental operations." They seek to clarify how both task characteristics and cognitive limitations—for example, memory capacity or available knowledge—influence performance (Birney & Sternberg, 2011). To see the usefulness of this approach, let's look at an example.

In a study of problem solving, a researcher provided a pile of blocks varying in size, shape, and weight and asked school-age

FIGURE 1.4 **Information-processing flowchart showing the steps that a 5-year-old used to solve a bridge-building problem.** Her task was to use blocks varying in size, shape, and weight, some of which were planklike, to construct a bridge across a "river" (painted on a floor mat) too wide for any single block to span. The child discovered how to counterweight and balance the bridge. The arrows reveal that, even after building a successful counterweight, she returned to earlier, unsuccessful strategies, which seemed to help her understand why the counterweight approach worked. (Adapted from Thornton, 1999.)

children to build a bridge across a "river" (painted on a floor mat) that was too wide for any single block to span (Thornton, 1999). Figure 1.4 shows one solution: Two planklike blocks span the water, each held in place by the counterweight of heavy blocks on the bridge's towers. Whereas older children easily built successful bridges, only one 5-year-old did. Careful tracking of her efforts revealed that she repeatedly tried unsuccessful strategies, such as pushing two planks together and pressing down on their ends to hold them in place. But eventually, her experimentation triggered the idea of using the blocks as counterweights. Her mistaken procedures helped her understand why the counterweight approach worked.

Many information-processing models exist. Some, like the one just considered, track children's mastery of one or a few tasks. Others describe the human cognitive system as a whole (Gopnik & Tenenbaum, 2007; Johnson & Mareschal, 2001; Westermann et al., 2006). These general models are used as guides for asking questions about broad changes in thinking: Does a child's ability to solve problems become more organized and "planful" with age? Why is information processing slower among older than younger adults? Are declines in memory during old age evident on all types of tasks or only some?

Like Piaget's theory, the information-processing approach regards people as actively making sense of their own thinking (Halford, 2005; Munakata, 2006). But unlike Piaget's theory, it does not divide development into stages. Rather, most information-processing researchers regard the thought processes studied—perception, attention, memory, planning strategies, categorization of information, and comprehension of written and spoken prose—as similar at all ages but present to a lesser or greater extent. Their view of development is one of continuous change.

A great strength of the information-processing approach is its commitment to rigorous research methods. Because it has

provided precise accounts of how children and adults tackle many cognitive tasks, its findings have important implications for education (Blumenfeld, Marx, & Harris, 2006; Siegler, 2009). But information processing has fallen short in some respects. It has been better at analyzing thinking into its components than at putting them back together into a comprehensive theory. And it has little to say about aspects of cognition that are not linear and logical, such as imagination and creativity.

Developmental Cognitive Neuroscience

Over the past three decades, as information-processing research has expanded, a new area of investigation arose, called **developmental cognitive neuroscience**. It brings together researchers from psychology, biology, neuroscience, and medicine to study the relationship between changes in the brain and the developing person's cognitive processing and behavior patterns.

Improved methods for analyzing brain activity while children and adults perform various tasks have greatly enhanced knowledge of relationships between brain functioning, cognitive capacities, and behavior (Pennington, Snyder, & Roberts, 2007; Westermann et al., 2007). Armed with these brain-imaging techniques (which we will consider in Chapter 4), neuroscientists are tackling questions like these: How does genetic makeup combine with specific experiences at various ages to influence the growth and organization of the young child's brain? What transformations in the brain make it harder for adolescents and adults than for children to acquire a second language? What neurological changes are related to declines in speed of thinking, memory, and other aspects of cognitive processing in old age?

During the first five years, the brain is highly plastic—especially open to growth as a result of experience. But it retains considerable plasticity throughout life. Neuroscientists are making rapid progress in identifying the types of experiences that support or undermine brain development at various ages. They are also clarifying the brain bases of many learning and behavior disorders, and they are contributing to effective interventions by examining the impact of various intervention techniques on both brain functioning and behavior (Durston & Conrad, 2007; Luciana, 2007; Schlaggar & McCandliss, 2007). Although much remains to be discovered, developmental cognitive neuroscience is already transforming our understanding of development and yielding major practical applications throughout the lifespan.

An advantage of having many theories is that they encourage researchers to attend to previously neglected dimensions of people's lives. The final three perspectives we will discuss focus on *contexts* for development. The first of these views emphasizes that the development of many capacities is influenced by our long evolutionary history.

Ethology and Evolutionary Developmental Psychology

Ethology is concerned with the adaptive, or survival, value of behavior and its evolutionary history. Its roots can be traced to the work of Darwin. Two European zoologists, Konrad Lorenz and Niko Tinbergen, laid its modern foundations. Watching diverse animal species in their natural habitats, Lorenz and Tinbergen observed behavior patterns that promote survival. The best known of these is *imprinting*, the early following behavior of certain baby birds, such as geese, that ensures that the young will stay close to the mother and be fed and protected from danger. Imprinting takes place during an early, restricted period of development (Lorenz, 1952). If the mother goose is absent during this time but an object resembling her in important features is present, young goslings may imprint on it instead.

Observations of imprinting led to a major concept in human development: the *critical period*. It refers to a limited time span during which the individual is biologically prepared to acquire certain adaptive behaviors but needs the support of an appropriately stimulating environment. Many researchers have investigated whether complex cognitive and social behaviors must be learned during certain time periods. For example, if children are deprived of adequate food or physical and social stimulation during their early years, will their intelligence be impaired? If language learning is impeded in childhood due to limited parent–child communication, is the capacity to acquire language later reduced?

In later chapters, we will see that the term *sensitive period* applies better to human development than the strict notion of a critical period (Bornstein, 1989). A **sensitive period** is a time that is optimal for certain capacities to emerge and in which the individual is especially responsive to environmental influences. However, its boundaries are less well-defined than those of a critical period. Development can occur later, but it is harder to induce.

Inspired by observations of imprinting, British psychoanalyst John Bowlby (1969) applied ethological theory to the understanding of the human infant–caregiver relationship. He argued that infant smiling, babbling, grasping, and crying are built-in social signals that encourage the caregiver to approach, care for, and interact with the baby. By keeping the parent near, these behaviors help ensure that the infant will be fed, protected from danger, and provided with stimulation and affection necessary for healthy growth. The development of attachment in humans is a lengthy process that leads the baby to form a deep affectionate tie with the caregiver (Thompson, 2006). Bowlby believed that this bond has lifelong consequences for human relationships. In later chapters, we will consider research that evaluates this assumption.

Observations by ethologists have shown that many aspects of social behavior, including emotional expressions, aggression, cooperation, and social play, resemble those of our primate relatives. Recently, researchers have extended this effort in a new area of research called **evolutionary developmental psychology**. It seeks to understand the adaptive value of specieswide cognitive, emotional, and social competencies as those competencies change with age Geary, 2006b; King & Bjorklund, 2010). Evolutionary developmental psychologists ask questions like these: What role does the newborn's visual preference for facelike stimuli play in survival? Does it support older infants' capacity to distinguish familiar caregivers from unfamiliar people? Why do children play in gender-segregated groups? What do they learn from such play that might lead to adult gender-typed behaviors, such as male dominance and female investment in caregiving?

MARTIN HARVEY/GETTY IMAGES/PETER ARNOLD

Ethology focuses on the adaptive, or survival, value of behavior and on similarities between human behavior and that of other species, especially our primate relatives. Observing this chimpanzee mother cuddling her infant helps us understand the human caregiver–infant relationship.

Human longevity may have adaptive value. It enables younger family members to draw on older adults' knowledge and sage advice when tackling life's challenges.

As these examples suggest, evolutionary psychologists are not just concerned with the genetic and biological roots of development. They recognize that humans' large brain and extended childhood resulted from the need to master an increasingly complex environment, so they are also interested in learning (Bjorklund, Causey, & Periss, 2009). And they realize that today's lifestyles differ so radically from those of our evolutionary ancestors that certain evolved behaviors—such as life-threatening risk taking in adolescents and male-to-male violence—are no longer adaptive (Blasi & Bjorklund, 2003).

Recently, evolutionary psychologists have begun to address the adaptiveness of human longevity—why adults live as much as one-fourth to one-third of their years after their children are grown (Greve & Bjorklund, 2009). The most common explanation involves the support that grandparents (especially grandmothers) offer in rearing young grandchildren, which is associated with higher birth and child-survival rates. Another view emphasizes the adaptive value of older adults' vast knowledge, experience, and sage advice—a rich resource for younger members of the family or social group as they tackle life's many challenges.

In sum, evolutionary developmental psychology aims to understand the *person–environment system* throughout the lifespan. The next contextual perspective we will discuss, Vygotsky's sociocultural theory, serves as an excellent complement to the evolutionary viewpoint because it highlights social and cultural contexts for development.

Vygotsky's Sociocultural Theory

The field of human development has recently seen a dramatic increase in studies addressing the cultural context of people's lives. Investigations that make comparisons across cultures, and between ethnic groups within cultures, provide insight into whether developmental pathways apply to all people or are limited to particular environmental conditions (Goodnow, 2010).

Today, much research is examining the relationship of *culturally specific beliefs and practices* to development. The contributions of Russian psychologist Lev Vygotsky (1896–1934) have played a major role in this trend. Vygotsky's (1934/1987) perspective, called **sociocultural theory,** focuses on how *culture*—the values, beliefs, customs, and skills of a social group—is transmitted to the next generation. According to Vygotsky, *social interaction*—in particular, cooperative dialogues with more knowledgeable members of society—is necessary for children to acquire the ways of thinking and behaving that make up a community's culture. Vygotsky believed that as adults and more expert peers help children master culturally meaningful activities, the communication between them becomes part of children's thinking. As children internalize the features of these dialogues, they can use the language within them to guide their own thought and actions and to acquire new skills (Berk & Harris, 2003; Winsler, Fernyhough, & Montero, 2009). The young child instructing herself while working a puzzle or setting a table for dinner has begun to produce the same kind of guiding comments that an adult previously used to help her master important tasks.

Vygotsky's theory has been especially influential in the study of cognitive development. Vygotsky agreed with Piaget that children are active, constructive beings. But whereas Piaget emphasized children's independent efforts to make sense of their world, Vygotsky viewed cognitive development as a *socially mediated process,* in which children depend on assistance from adults and more-expert peers as they tackle new challenges.

A Cambodian girl learns traditional dance forms from her grandmother. She acquires a culturally valued skill by interacting with an older, more experienced member of her culture.

In Vygotsky's theory, children undergo certain stagewise changes. For example, when they acquire language, they gain in ability to participate in dialogues with others, and mastery of culturally valued competencies surges forward. When children enter school, they spend much time discussing language, literacy, and other academic concepts—experiences that encourage them to reflect on their own thinking (Bodrova & Leong, 2007; Kozulin, 2003). As a result, they advance dramatically in reasoning and problem solving.

At the same time, Vygotsky stressed that dialogues with experts lead to continuous changes in cognition that vary greatly from culture to culture. Consistent with this view, a major finding of cross-cultural research is that cultures select tasks for their members, and social interaction surrounding those tasks leads to competencies essential for success in a particular culture. For example, in industrialized nations, teachers help people learn to read, drive a car, or use a computer. Among the Zinacanteco Indians of southern Mexico, adult experts guide young girls as they master complicated weaving techniques (Greenfield, 2004; Greenfield, Maynard, & Childs, 2000). In Brazil and other developing nations, child candy sellers with little or no schooling develop sophisticated mathematical abilities as the result of buying candy from wholesalers, pricing it in collaboration with adults and experienced peers, and bargaining with customers on city streets (Saxe, 1988).

Research stimulated by Vygotsky's theory reveals that people in every culture develop unique strengths. But Vygotsky's emphasis on culture and social experience led him to neglect the biological side of development. Although he recognized the importance of heredity and brain growth, he said little about

their role in cognitive change. Furthermore, Vygotsky's focus on social transmission of knowledge meant that, compared with other theorists, he placed less emphasis on children's capacity to shape their own development. Followers of Vygotsky grant the individual and society more balanced, mutually influential roles (Nelson, 2007a; Rogoff, 2003).

Ecological Systems Theory

Urie Bronfenbrenner (1917–2005) is responsible for an approach that has moved to the forefront of the field because it offers the most differentiated and complete account of contextual influences on development. **Ecological systems theory** views the person as developing within a complex *system* of relationships affected by multiple levels of the surrounding environment. Because the child's biologically influenced dispositions join with environmental forces to mold development, Bronfenbrenner characterized his perspective as a *bioecological model* (Bronfenbrenner, 2005; Bronfenbrenner & Morris, 2006).

Bronfenbrenner envisioned the environment as a series of nested structures, including but also extending beyond the home, school, neighborhood, and workplace settings in which people spend their everyday lives (see Figure 1.5). Each layer of the environment joins with the others to powerfully affect development.

The Microsystem. The innermost level of the environment, the **microsystem**, consists of activities and interaction patterns in the person's immediate surroundings. Bronfenbrenner emphasized that to understand development at this level, we

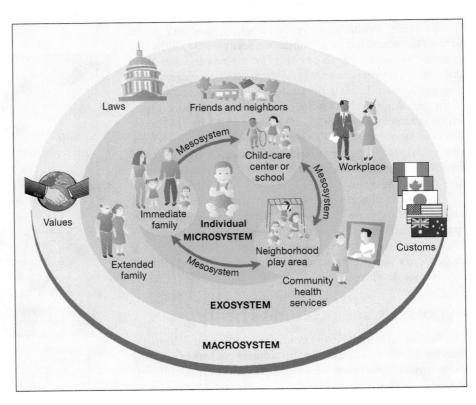

FIGURE 1.5 Structure of the environment in ecological systems theory. The *microsystem* concerns relations between the developing person and the immediate environment; the *mesosystem*, connections among immediate settings; the *exosystem*, social settings that affect but do not contain the developing person; and the *macrosystem*, the values, laws, customs, and resources of the culture that affect activities and interactions at all inner layers. The *chronosystem* (not pictured) is not a specific context. Instead, it refers to the dynamic, ever-changing nature of the person's environment.

© ELLEN B. SENISI PHOTOGRAPHY

A father says good-bye to his daughter at the start of the school day. The child's experiences at school (microsystem) and the father's experiences at work (exosystem) affect the father–daughter relationship.

must keep in mind that all relationships are *bidirectional*. For example, adults affect children's behavior, but children's biologically and socially influenced characteristics—their physical attributes, personalities, and capacities—also affect adults' behavior. A friendly, attentive child is likely to evoke positive, patient reactions from parents, whereas an irritable or distractible child is more likely to receive impatience, restriction, and punishment. When these reciprocal interactions occur often over time, they have an enduring impact on development (Crockenberg & Leerkes, 2003).

Third parties—other individuals in the microsystem—also affect the quality of any two-person relationship. If they are supportive, interaction is enhanced. For example, when parents encourage each other in their child-rearing roles, each engages in more effective parenting. In contrast, marital conflict is associated with inconsistent discipline and hostile reactions toward children. In response, children often react with fear and anxiety or with anger and aggression, and the well-being of both parent and child suffers (Caldera & Lindsey, 2006; Low & Stocker, 2012).

The Mesosystem. The second level of Bronfenbrenner's model, the **mesosystem,** encompasses connections between microsystems. For example, a child's academic progress depends not just on activities that take place in classrooms but also on parent involvement in school life and on the extent to which academic learning is carried over into the home (Jeynes, 2012). Among adults, how well a person functions as spouse and parent at home is affected by relationships in the workplace, and vice versa (Gottfried, Gottfried, & Bathurst, 2002).

The Exosystem. The **exosystem** consists of social settings that do not contain the developing person but nevertheless affect experiences in immediate settings. These can be formal organizations, such as the board of directors in the individual's workplace, religious institution, or community health and welfare services. Flexible work schedules, paid maternity and paternity leave, and sick leave for parents whose children are ill are examples of ways that work settings can help parents rear children and, indirectly, enhance the development of both adult and child. Exosystem supports can also be informal. Children are affected by their parents' social networks—friends and extended-family members who provide advice, companionship, and even financial assistance. Research confirms the negative impact of a breakdown in exosystem activities. Families who are socially isolated, with few personal or community-based ties, show increased rates of conflict and child abuse (Coulton et al., 2007). Refer to the Social Issues: Health box on page 26 for an additional illustration of the power of the exosystem to affect family functioning and children's development.

The Macrosystem. The outermost level of Bronfenbrenner's model, the **macrosystem,** consists of cultural values, laws, customs, and resources. The priority that the macrosystem gives to the needs of children and adults affects the support they receive at inner levels of the environment. For example, in countries that require generous workplace benefits for employed parents and set high standards for the quality of child care, children are more likely to have favorable experiences in their immediate settings. And when the government provides a generous pension plan for retirees, it supports the well-being of older people.

LOOK AND LISTEN

Ask a parent to explain his or her most worrisome child-rearing challenge. Cite one source of support at each level of Bronfenbrenner's model that could ease parental stress and promote child development. ●

A Dynamic, Ever-Changing System. According to Bronfenbrenner, the environment is not a static force that affects people in a uniform way. Instead, it is ever-changing. Whenever individuals add or let go of roles or settings in their lives, the breadth of their microsystems changes. These shifts in contexts—or *ecological transitions,* as Bronfenbrenner called them—are often important turning points in development. Starting school, entering the workforce, marrying, becoming a parent, getting divorced, moving, and retiring are examples.

Bronfenbrenner called the temporal dimension of his model the **chronosystem** (the prefix *chrono* means "time"). Life changes can be imposed externally or, alternatively, can arise from within the person, since individuals select, modify, and create many of their own settings and experiences. How they do so depends on their age; their physical, intellectual, and personality characteristics; and their environmental opportunities. Therefore, in ecological systems theory, development is neither

Social Issues: Health

Family Chaos Undermines Children's Well-Being

Virtually all of us can recall days during our childhoods when family routines—regular mealtime, bedtime, homework time, and parent–child reading and playtimes—were disrupted, perhaps because of a change in a parent's job, a family illness, or a busy season of after-school sports. In some families, however, absence of daily structure is nearly constant, yielding a chaotic home life that interferes with healthy development (Fiese & Winter, 2010). An organized family life provides a supportive context for warm, involved parent–child interaction, which is essential to children's well-being.

Family chaos is linked to economic disadvantage—especially, single mothers with limited incomes struggling to juggle the challenges of transportation, shift jobs, unstable child-care arrangements, and other daily hassles. But chaos is not limited to such families.

Surveys reveal that among U.S. families as a whole, mothers' time with children has remained fairly stable over the past three decades, and fathers' time has increased (Galinsky, Aumann, & Bond, 2009). But the way many parents spend that time has changed. Across income levels and ethnic groups, both mothers and fathers report more multitasking while caring for children—for example, using mealtimes not just to eat but also to check homework, read to children, and plan family outings and celebrations (Bianchi & Raley, 2005; Serpell et al., 2002). Consequently, disruption in one family routine can disrupt others.

Possibly because of this compression of family routines, today's parents and children consistently say they have too little time together (Opinion Research Corporation, 2009). For example, only slightly more than half of U.S. families report eating together three to five times per week (CASA, 2006). Frequency of family meals is

associated with wide-ranging positive outcomes—in childhood, enhanced language development and academic achievement, fewer behavior problems, and time spent sleeping; and in adolescence, reduced sexual risk taking, alcohol and drug use, and mental health problems. Shared mealtimes also increase the likelihood of a healthy diet and protect against obesity and adolescent eating disorders (Adam, Snell, & Pendry, 2007; Fiese & Schwartz, 2008). As these findings suggest, regular mealtimes are a general indicator of an organized family life and positive parent involvement.

But family chaos can prevail even when families do engage in joint activities. Unpredictable, disorganized family meals involving harsh or lax parental discipline and hostile, disrespectful communication are associated with children's adjustment difficulties (Fiese, Foley, & Spagnola, 2006). As family time becomes pressured and overwhelming, its orderly structure diminishes, and warm parent–child engagement disintegrates.

Diverse circumstances can trigger a pileup of limited parental emotional resources, breeding family chaos. In addition to *microsystem* and *mesosytem* influences (parents with mental health problems, parental separation and divorce, single parents with few or no supportive relationships), the *exosystem* is powerful: When family time is at the mercy of external forces—parents commuting several hours a day to and from work, child-care

arrangements often failing, parents experiencing excessive workplace pressures or job loss—family routines are threatened.

Family chaos contributes to children's behavior problems, above and beyond its negative impact on parenting effectiveness (Coldwell, Pike, & Dunn, 2008; Fiese & Winter, 2010). Chaotic surroundings induce in children a sense of being hassled and feelings of powerlessness, which engender anxiety and low self-esteem.

Exosystem and macrosystem supports—including work settings with favorable family policies and high-quality child care that is affordable and reliable—can help prevent escalating demands on families that give way to chaos (Repetti & Wang, 2010). In one community, a child-care center initiated a take-home dinner program. Busy parents could special-order a healthy, reasonably priced family meal, ready to go at day's end to aid in making the family dinner a routine that enhances children's development.

© MICHAEL NEWMAN/PHOTOEDIT

A chaotic home life interferes with warm, relaxed parent–child interaction and contributes to behavior problems. Exosystem influences, such as excessive workplace pressures, can trigger disorganized family routines.

controlled by environmental circumstances nor driven solely by inner dispositions. Rather, people are both products and producers of their environments: The person and the environment form a network of interdependent effects. Our discussion of resilience on pages 10–11 illustrates this idea. We will see many more examples in later chapters.

ASK YOURSELF

REVIEW Explain how each recent theoretical perspective regards children and adults as active contributors to their own development.

CONNECT Is ecological systems theory compatible with assumptions of the lifespan perspective—development as lifelong, multidirectional, highly plastic, and influenced by multiple, interacting forces? Explain.

APPLY Mario wants to find out precisely how children of different ages recall stories. Anna is interested in how adult–child communication in different cultures influences children's storytelling. Which theoretical perspective has Mario probably chosen? How about Anna? Explain.

REFLECT To illustrate the chronosystem in ecological systems theory, select an important event from your childhood, such as a move to a new neighborhood, a class with an inspiring teacher, or parental divorce. How did the event affect you? How might its impact have differed had you been five years younger? How about five years older?

Comparing and Evaluating Theories

In the preceding sections, we reviewed major theoretical perspectives in human development research. They differ in many respects. First, they focus on different domains of development. Some, such as the psychoanalytic perspective and ethology, emphasize emotional and social development. Others, such as Piaget's cognitive-developmental theory, information processing, and Vygotsky's sociocultural theory, stress changes in thinking. The remaining approaches—behaviorism, social learning theory, evolutionary developmental psychology, ecological systems theory, and the lifespan perspective—discuss many aspects of human functioning. Second, every theory contains a point of view about development. *TAKE A MOMENT...* As we conclude our review of theoretical perspectives, identify the stand each theory takes on the controversial issues presented at the beginning of this chapter. Then check your analysis against Table 1.4 on page 28.

Finally, we have seen that every theory has strengths and limitations. Perhaps you are attracted to some theories but have doubts about others. As you read more about development in later chapters, you may find it useful to keep a notebook in which you test your theoretical likes and dislikes against the evidence. Don't be surprised if you revise your ideas many times, just as theorists have done since scientific study of development began.

Studying Development

In every science, research is usually based on a *hypothesis*—a prediction about behavior drawn from a theory. Theories and hypotheses, however, merely initiate the many activities that result in sound evidence on human development. Conducting research according to scientifically accepted procedures involves many steps and choices. Investigators must decide which participants, and how many, to include. Then they must figure out what the participants will be asked to do and when, where, and how many times each will be seen. Finally, they must examine and draw conclusions from their data.

In the following sections, we look at research strategies commonly used to study human development. We begin with common *research methods*—the specific activities of participants, such as taking tests, answering questionnaires, responding to interviews, or being observed. Then we turn to *research designs*—overall plans for research studies that permit the best possible test of the investigator's hypothesis. Finally, we discuss ethical issues involved in doing research with human participants.

Why learn about research strategies? Why not leave these matters to research specialists and concentrate, instead, on what is known about the developing person and how this knowledge can be applied? There are two reasons. First, each of us must be a wise and critical consumer of knowledge. Knowing the strengths and limitations of various research strategies is important in separating dependable information from misleading results. Second, individuals who work directly with children or adults may be in a unique position to build bridges between research and practice by conducting studies, either on their own or in partnership with experienced investigators. Community agencies such as schools, mental health facilities, and parks and recreation programs are increasingly collaborating with researchers in designing, implementing, and evaluating interventions aimed at enhancing development (Guerra, Graham, & Tolan, 2011). To broaden these efforts, a basic understanding of the research process is essential.

LOOK AND LISTEN

Ask a teacher, counselor, social worker, or nurse to describe a question about development he or she would like researchers to address. After reading the rest of this chapter, recommend research strategies best suited to answering that question, citing their strengths and limitations. ●

TABLE 1.4

Stances of Major Theories on Basic Issues in Human Development

THEORY	CONTINUOUS OR DISCONTINUOUS DEVELOPMENT?	ONE COURSE OF DEVELOPMENT OR MANY?	RELATIVE INFLUENCE OF NATURE AND NURTURE?
Psychoanalytic perspective	*Discontinuous:* Psychosexual and psychosocial development takes place in stages.	*One course:* Stages are assumed to be universal.	*Both nature and nurture:* Innate impulses are channeled and controlled through child-rearing experiences. *Early experiences* set the course of later development.
Behaviorism and social learning theory	*Continuous:* Development involves an increase in learned behaviors.	*Many possible courses:* Behaviors reinforced and modeled may vary from person to person.	*Emphasis on nurture:* Development is the result of conditioning and modeling. *Both early and later experiences* are important.
Piaget's cognitive-developmental theory	*Discontinuous:* Cognitive development takes place in stages.	*One course:* Stages are assumed to be universal.	*Both nature and nurture:* Development occurs as the brain grows and children exercise their innate drive to discover reality in a generally stimulating environment. *Both early and later experiences* are important.
Information processing	*Continuous:* Children and adults change gradually in perception, attention, memory, and problem-solving skills.	*One course:* Changes studied characterize most or all children and adults.	*Both nature and nurture:* Children and adults are active, sense-making beings who modify their thinking as the brain grows and they confront new environmental demands. *Both early and later experiences* are important.
Ethology and evolutionary developmental psychology	*Both continuous and discontinuous:* Children and adults gradually develop a wider range of adaptive behaviors. Sensitive periods occur in which qualitatively distinct capacities emerge fairly suddenly.	*One course:* Adaptive behaviors and sensitive periods apply to all members of a species.	*Both nature and nurture:* Evolution and heredity influence behavior, and learning lends greater flexibility and adaptiveness to it. In sensitive periods, *early experiences* set the course of later development.
Vygotsky's sociocultural theory	*Both continuous and discontinuous:* Language development and schooling lead to stagewise changes. Dialogues with more expert members of society also lead to continuous changes that vary from culture to culture.	*Many possible courses:* Socially mediated changes in thought and behavior vary from culture to culture.	*Both nature and nurture:* Heredity, brain growth, and dialogues with more expert members of society jointly contribute to development. *Both early and later experiences* are important.
Ecological systems theory	*Not specified.*	*Many possible courses:* Biologically influenced dispositions join with environmental forces at multiple levels to mold development in unique ways.	*Both nature and nurture:* The individual's characteristics and the reactions of others affect each other in a bidirectional fashion. *Both early and later experiences* are important.
Lifespan perspective	**Both continuous and discontinuous: Continuous gains and declines and discontinuous, stagewise emergence of new skills occur.**	**Many possible courses: Development is influenced by multiple, interacting biological, psychological, and social forces, many of which vary from person to person, leading to diverse pathways of change.**	**Both nature and nurture: Development is multidimensional, affected by an intricate blend of hereditary and environmental factors. Emphasizes plasticity at all ages. *Both early and later experiences* are important.**

Common Research Methods

How does a researcher choose a basic approach to gathering information? Common methods include systematic observation, self-reports (such as questionnaires and interviews), clinical or case studies of a single individual, and ethnographies of the life circumstances of a specific group of people. Table 1.5 summarizes the strengths and limitations of each of these methods.

Systematic Observation. Observations of the behavior of children and adults can be made in different ways. One approach is to go into the field, or natural environment, and record the behavior of interest—a method called **naturalistic observation.**

A study of preschoolers' responses to their peers' distress provides a good example (Farver & Branstetter, 1994). Observing 3- and 4-year-olds in child-care centers, the researchers recorded each instance of crying and the reactions of nearby

TABLE 1.5 Strengths and Limitations of Common Research Methods

METHOD	DESCRIPTION	STRENGTHS	LIMITATIONS
SYSTEMATIC OBSERVATION			
Naturalistic observation	Observation of behavior in natural contexts	Reflects participants' everyday lives.	Cannot control conditions under which participants are observed.
Structured observation	Observation of behavior in a laboratory, where conditions are the same for all participants	Grants each participant an equal opportunity to display the behavior of interest.	May not yield observations typical of participants' behavior in everyday life.
SELF-REPORTS			
Clinical interview	Flexible interviewing procedure in which the investigator obtains a complete account of the participant's thoughts	Comes as close as possible to the way participants think in everyday life. Great breadth and depth of information can be obtained in a short time.	May not result in accurate reporting of information. Flexible procedure makes comparing individuals' responses difficult.
Structured interview, questionnaires, and tests	Self-report instruments in which each participant is asked the same questions in the same way	Permits comparisons of participants' responses and efficient data collection. Researchers can specify answer alternatives that participants might not think of in an open-ended interview.	Does not yield the same depth of information as a clinical interview. Responses are still subject to inaccurate reporting.
CLINICAL, OR CASE STUDY, METHOD			
	A full picture of one individual's psychological functioning, obtained by combining interviews, observations, and test scores	Provides rich, descriptive insights into factors that affect development.	May be biased by researchers' theoretical preferences. Findings cannot be applied to individuals other than the participant.
ETHNOGRAPHY			
	Participant observation of a culture or distinct social group. By making extensive field notes, the researcher tries to capture the culture's unique values and social processes	Provides a more complete description than can be derived from a single observational visit, interview, or questionnaire.	May be biased by researchers' values and theoretical preferences. Findings cannot be applied to individuals and settings other than the ones studied.

children—whether they ignored, watched, commented on the child's unhappiness, scolded or teased, or shared, helped, or expressed sympathy. Caregiver behaviors—explaining why a child was crying, mediating conflict, or offering comfort—were noted to see if adult sensitivity was related to children's caring responses. A strong relationship emerged. The great strength of naturalistic observation is that investigators can see directly the everyday behaviors they hope to explain.

Naturalistic observation also has a major limitation: Not all individuals have the same opportunity to display a particular behavior in everyday life. In the study just described, some children might have witnessed a child crying more often than others or been exposed to more cues for positive social responses from caregivers. For these reasons, they might have displayed more compassion.

Researchers commonly deal with this difficulty by making **structured observations,** in which the investigator sets up a laboratory situation that evokes the behavior of interest so that every participant has equal opportunity to display the response. In one such study, 2-year-olds' emotional reactions to harm that

they thought they had caused were observed by asking each of them to take care of a rag doll that had been modified so its leg would fall off when the child picked it up. To make the child feel at fault, once the leg detached, an adult "talked for" the doll by saying, "Ow!" Researchers recorded children's facial expressions of sadness and concern for the injured doll, efforts to help the doll, and body tension—responses that indicated remorse and a desire to make amends for the mishap. In addition, mothers were asked to engage in brief conversations about emotions with their children (Garner, 2003). Toddlers whose mothers more often explained the causes and consequences of emotion were more likely to express concern for the injured doll.

The procedures used to collect systematic observations vary, depending on the research problem posed. Sometimes investigators choose to analyze the entire stream of behavior—everything said and done over a certain time period. In one study, researchers wanted to find out whether maternal sensitivity in infancy and early childhood contributes to readiness for formal schooling at age 6 (Hirsh-Pasek & Burchinal, 2006). Between ages 6 months and 4½ years, the investigators periodically

© ELLEN B. SENISI PHOTOGRAPHY

In naturalistic observation, the researcher goes into the field and records the behavior of interest. Here, a researcher observes children at preschool. She may be focusing on their playmate choices, cooperation, helpfulness, or conflicts.

videotaped mother–child 15-minute play sessions. Then they rated each session for many behaviors—maternal positive emotion, support, stimulating play, and respect for the child's autonomy. These ingredients of sensitivity did predict better language and academic progress when the children reached kindergarten.

Researchers have devised ingenious ways of observing difficult-to-capture behaviors. For example, to record instances of bullying, a group of investigators set up video cameras overlooking a classroom and a playground and had fourth to sixth graders wear small, remote microphones and pocket-sized transmitters (Craig, Pepler, & Atlas, 2000). Results revealed that bullying occurred often—at rates of 2.4 episodes per hour in the classroom and 4.5 episodes per hour on the playground. Yet only 15 to 18 percent of the time did teachers take steps to stop the harassment.

Systematic observation provides invaluable information on how children and adults actually behave, but it tells us little about the reasoning behind their responses. For that information, researchers must turn to self-report techniques.

Self-Reports. Self-reports ask research participants to provide information on their perceptions, thoughts, abilities, feelings, attitudes, beliefs, and past experiences. They range from relatively unstructured interviews to highly structured interviews, questionnaires, and tests.

In a **clinical interview,** researchers use a flexible, conversational style to probe for the participant's point of view. In the following example, Piaget questioned a 5-year-old child about his understanding of dreams:

> *Where does the dream come from?*—I think you sleep so well that you dream.—*Does it come from us or from outside?*—From outside.—*When you are in bed and you dream, where is the*

dream?—In my bed, under the blanket. I don't really know. If it was in my stomach, the bones would be in the way and I shouldn't see it.—*Is the dream there when you sleep?*—Yes, it is in the bed beside me. (Piaget, 1926/1930, pp. 97–98)

Although a researcher conducting clinical interviews with more than one participant would typically ask the same first question to establish a common task, individualized prompts are used to provide a fuller picture of each person's reasoning.

The clinical interview has two major strengths. First, it permits people to display their thoughts in terms that are as close as possible to the way they think in everyday life. Second, the clinical interview can provide a large amount of information in a fairly brief period. For example, in an hour-long session, we can obtain a wide range of information on child rearing from a parent or on life circumstances from an older adult—much more than we could capture by observing for the same amount of time.

A major limitation of the clinical interview has to do with the accuracy with which people report their thoughts, feelings, and experiences. Some participants, wishing to please the interviewer, may make up answers that do not represent their actual thinking. When asked about past events, some may have trouble recalling exactly what happened. And because the clinical interview depends on verbal ability and expressiveness, it may underestimate the capacities of individuals who have difficulty putting their thoughts into words.

The clinical interview has also been criticized because of its flexibility. When questions are phrased differently for each participant, responses may reflect the manner of interviewing rather than real differences in the way people think about a topic. **Structured interviews** (including tests and questionnaires), in which each participant is asked the same set of questions in the same way, eliminate this problem. These instruments are also much more efficient. Answers are briefer, and researchers can obtain written responses from an entire group simultaneously. Furthermore, by listing answer alternatives, researchers can specify the activities and behaviors of interest—ones that participants might not think of in an open-ended clinical interview. For example, when parents were asked what they considered "the most important thing for children to prepare them for life," 62 percent checked "to think for themselves" when this choice appeared on a list. Yet only 5 percent thought of this during a clinical interview (Schwarz, 1999).

Nevertheless, structured interviews do not yield the same depth of information as a clinical interview. And they can still be affected by the problem of inaccurate reporting. Currently, more researchers are combining the two approaches to see if they yield consistent findings (Yoshikawa et al., 2008). And blending the two methods is likely to offer a clearer picture than either method can alone.

The Clinical, or Case Study, Method. An outgrowth of psychoanalytic theory, the **clinical,** or **case study, method** brings together a wide range of information on one person,

Using the clinical, or case study, method, this researcher interacts with a 3-year-old during a home visit. Interviews and observations will contribute to an in-depth picture of this child's psychological functioning.

including interviews, observations, and test scores. The aim is to obtain as complete a picture as possible of that individual's psychological functioning and the experiences that led up to it.

The clinical method is well-suited to studying the development of certain types of individuals who are few in number but vary widely in characteristics. For example, the method has been used to find out what contributes to the accomplishments of *prodigies*—extremely gifted children who attain adult competence in a field before age 10 (Moran & Gardner, 2006). Consider Adam, a boy who read, wrote, and composed musical pieces before he was out of diapers. By age 4, Adam was deeply involved in mastering human symbol systems—French, German, Russian, Sanskrit, Greek, the computer programming language BASIC, ancient hieroglyphs, music, and mathematics. Adam's parents provided a home rich in stimulation and reared him with affection, firmness, and humor. They searched for schools in which he could both develop his abilities and form rewarding social relationships. He graduated from college at age 18 and continued to pursue musical composition (Goldsmith, 2000). Would Adam have realized his abilities without the chance combination of his special gift and nurturing, committed parents? Probably not, researchers concluded (Feldman, 2004).

The clinical method yields richly detailed case narratives that offer valuable insights into the many factors influencing development. Nevertheless, like all other methods, it has drawbacks. Because information often is collected unsystematically and subjectively, researchers' theoretical preferences may bias their observations and interpretations. In addition, investigators cannot assume that their conclusions apply, or generalize, to anyone other than the person studied (Stanovich, 2013). Even

when patterns emerge across several cases, it is wise to confirm these with other research strategies.

Methods for Studying Culture. To study the impact of culture, researchers adjust the methods just considered or tap procedures specially devised for cross-cultural and multicultural research (Triandis, 2007). Which approach investigators choose depends on their research goals.

Sometimes researchers are interested in characteristics that are believed to be universal but that vary in degree from one society to the next: Are parents warmer or more directive in some cultures than others? How strong are gender stereotypes in different nations? In each instance, several cultural groups will be compared, and all participants must be questioned or observed in the same way. Therefore, researchers draw on the observational and self-report procedures we have already considered, adapting them through translation so they can be understood in each cultural context. For example, to study cultural variation in parenting practices, the same questionnaire, asking for ratings on such items as "I often hug and kiss my child" or "I scold my child when his/her behavior does not meet my

This Western researcher spent months living among the Efe people of the Republic of Congo in an effort to understand their way of life. Here he observes young children sharing food.

Cultural Influences

Immigrant Youths: Adapting to a New Land

Over the past several decades, a rising tide of immigrants has come to North America, fleeing war and persecution in their homelands or seeking better life chances. Today, nearly one-fourth of U.S. children and adolescents have foreign-born parents, making them the fastest growing sector of the U.S. youth population. About 20 percent of these young people are foreign-born themselves, mostly from Latin America, the Caribbean, and Asia (Hernandez, Denton, & Macartney, 2008; Suárez-Orozco, Todorova, & Qin, 2006).

How well are immigrant youths adapting to their new country? To find out, researchers use multiple research methods—academic testing, questionnaires assessing psychological adjustment, and in-depth ethnographies.

Academic Achievement and Adjustment

Although educators and laypeople often assume that the transition to a new country has a negative impact on psychological well-being, evidence reveals that children of immigrant parents adapt well. Students who are first-generation (foreign-born) and second-generation (American-born, with immigrant parents) often achieve in school as well as or better than students of native-born parents (Fuligni, 2004; Hao & Woo, 2012; Hernandez, Denton, & Macartney, 2008). Findings on psychological adjustment are similar. Compared with their agemates, adolescents from immigrant families are less likely to commit delinquent and violent acts, to use drugs and alcohol, or to have early sex. They are also less likely to be obese or to have missed school because of illness. And they tend to report just as high, and at times higher, self-esteem as young people with native-born parents (Fuligni, 1998; Saucier et al., 2002; Supple & Small, 2006).

These outcomes are strongest for Chinese, Filipino, Japanese, Korean, and East Indian youths, less dramatic for other ethnicities (Fuligni, 2004; Louie, 2001; Portes & Rumbaut, 2005). Variation in adjustment is greater among Mexican, Central American, and Southeast Asian (Hmong, Cambodian, Laotian, Thai, and Vietnamese) young people, who show elevated rates of school failure and dropout, delinquency, teenage parenthood, and drug use. Disparities in parental economic resources, education, English-language proficiency, and support of children contribute

These Hmong boys perform in an ethnic festival in St. Paul, Minnesota, where many Hmong immigrants have settled. Cultural values that foster allegiance to family and community promote high achievement and protect many immigrant youths from involvement in risky behaviors.

expectations," is given to all participants (Wu et al., 2002). Still, investigators must be mindful of cultural differences in familiarity with being observed and with responding to self-report instruments, which may bias their findings (Van de Vijver, Hofer, & Chasiotis, 2010).

At other times, researchers want to uncover the *cultural meanings* of children's and adults' behaviors by becoming as familiar as possible with their way of life. To achieve this goal, investigators rely on a method borrowed from the field of anthropology—**ethnography.** Like the clinical method, ethnographic research is a descriptive, qualitative technique. But instead of aiming to understand a single individual, it is directed toward understanding a culture or a distinct social group through *participant observation.* Typically, the researcher spends months, and sometimes years, in the cultural community, participating in its daily life. Extensive field notes are gathered, consisting of a mix of observations, self-reports from members of the culture, and careful interpretations by the investigator (Miller, Hengst, & Wang, 2003; Shweder et al., 2006). Later, these notes are put together into a description of the community that tries to capture its unique values and social processes.

The ethnographic method assumes that entering into close contact with a social group will allow researchers to understand the beliefs and behaviors of its members in a way that is not possible with an observational visit, interview, or questionnaire. Some ethnographies take in many aspects of experience, as one team of researchers did in describing what it is like to grow up in a small American town. Others focus on one or a few settings and issues—for example, barriers to effective parent–school communication in a Mexican-American community or African-Caribbean adults' reactions to a diagnosis

to these trends (García Coll & Marks, 2009; Pong & Landale, 2012).

Still, many first- and second-generation youths whose parents face considerable financial hardship and who speak little English are successful (Hao & Woo, 2012; Hernandez, Denton, & Macartney, 2008). Factors other than income are responsible—notably, family values and strong ethnic-community ties.

Family and Community Influences

Ethnographies reveal that immigrant parents view education as the surest way to improve life chances (García Coll & Marks, 2009; Goldenberg et al., 2001). Aware of the challenges their children face, they typically emphasize trying hard. They remind their children that, because educational opportunities were not available in their native countries, they themselves are often limited to menial jobs. And while preserving their culture's values, these parents also make certain adaptations—for example, supporting education for daughters even though their culture of origin endorses it only for sons.

Adolescents from these families internalize their parents' valuing of education, endorsing it more strongly than agemates with native-born parents (Fuligni, 2004;

Su & Costigan, 2008). Because minority ethnicities usually stress allegiance to family and community over individual goals, first- and second-generation young people feel a strong sense of obligation to their parents. They view school success as both their own and their parents' success and as a way of repaying their parents for the hardships they have endured (Bacallao & Smokowski, 2007; Fuligni, Yip, & Tseng, 2002). Both family relationships and school achievement protect these youths from delinquency, early pregnancy and drug use, and other risky behaviors (see the Biology and Environment box on resilience on pages 10–11).

Immigrant parents of successful youths typically develop close ties to an ethnic community, which exerts additional control through a high consensus on values and constant monitoring of young people's activities. The following comments capture the power of these family and community forces:

Elizabeth, age 16, from Vietnam, straight-A student, like her two older sisters: "My parents know pretty much all the kids in the neighborhood. . . . Everybody here knows everybody else. It's hard to get away with much." (Zhou & Bankston, 1998, pp. 93, 130)

Juan, teenager from Mexico: A really big part of the Hispanic population [is] being close to family, and the family being a priority all the time. I hate people who say, "Why do you want to go to a party where your family's at? Don't you want to get away from them?" You know, I don't really get tired of them. I've always been really close to them. That connection to my parents, that trust that you can talk to them, that makes me Mexican. (Bacallao & Smokowski, 2007, p. 62)

The experiences of well-adjusted immigrant youths are not problem-free. Chinese adolescents who had arrived in the United States within the previous year described their adjustment as very difficult because they were not proficient in English and, as a result, found many everyday tasks challenging and felt socially isolated (Yeh et al., 2008). Young immigrants also encounter racial and ethnic prejudices and experience tensions between family values and the new culture—challenges we will take up in Chapter 12. In the long term, however, family and community cohesion, supervision, and high expectations promote favorable outcomes.

of high blood pressure, signaling elevated risk for heart disease (Higginbottom, 2006; Peshkin, 1997; Valdés, 1998). Notice how such ethnographic evidence is vital in designing effective educational and health interventions. Increasingly, researchers are supplementing traditional self-report and observational methods with ethnography when they suspect that unique meanings underlie cultural differences, as the Cultural Influences box above reveals.

Ethnographers strive to minimize their own influence on the culture they are studying by becoming part of it. Nevertheless, as with clinical studies, investigators' cultural values and theoretical commitments sometimes lead them to observe selectively or misinterpret what they see. In addition, the findings of ethnographic studies cannot be assumed to generalize beyond the people and settings in which the research was conducted.

ASK YOURSELF

REVIEW Why might a researcher choose structured observation over naturalistic observation? How about the reverse?

CONNECT What strengths and limitations do the clinical, or case study, method and ethnography have in common?

APPLY A researcher wants to study the thoughts and feelings of parents on active duty in the military and those of their school-age and adolescent children. Which method should she use? Why?

REFLECT Reread the description of nonnormative influences on page 12, and cite an example from your own life. Which method would be best suited to studying the impact of such a nonnormative event on development?

General Research Designs

In deciding on a research design, investigators choose a way of setting up a study that permits them to test their hypotheses with the greatest certainty possible. Two main types of designs are used in all research on human behavior: *correlational* and *experimental*.

Correlational Design. In a **correlational design,** researchers gather information on individuals, generally in natural life circumstances, without altering their experiences. Then they look at relationships between participants' characteristics and their behavior or development. Suppose we want to answer such questions as, Do parents' styles of interacting with their children have any bearing on children's intelligence? Does the arrival of a baby influence a couple's marital satisfaction? Does the death of a spouse in old age affect the surviving partner's physical health and psychological well-being? In these and many other instances, the conditions of interest are difficult or impossible to arrange and control and must be studied as they currently exist.

Correlational studies have one major limitation: We cannot infer cause and effect. For example, if we were to find that parental interaction is related to children's intelligence, we would not know whether parents' behavior actually *causes* intellectual differences among children. In fact, the opposite is possible: The behaviors of highly intelligent children may be so attractive that they cause parents to interact more favorably. Or a third variable that we did not even consider, such as the amount of noise and distraction in the home, may cause changes in both parental interaction and children's intelligence.

In correlational studies and in other types of research designs, investigators often examine relationships by using a

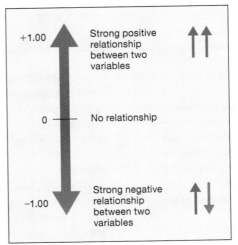

FIGURE 1.6 **The meaning of correlation coefficients.** The magnitude of the number indicates the *strength* of the relationship. The sign of the number (+ or –) indicates the *direction* of the relationship.

correlation coefficient—a number that describes how two measures, or variables, are associated with each other. We will encounter the correlation coefficient in discussing research findings throughout this book, so let's look at what it is and how it is interpreted. A correlation coefficient can range in value from +1.00 to –1.00. The *magnitude,* or *size, of the number* shows the *strength of the relationship.* A zero correlation indicates no relationship; the closer the value is to +1.00 or –1.00, the stronger the relationship (see Figure 1.6). For instance, a correlation of –.78 is high, –.52 is moderate, and –.18 is low. Note, however, that correlations of +.52 and –.52 are equally strong. The *sign of the number* (+ or –) refers to the *direction of the relationship.* A positive sign (+) means that as one variable *increases,* the other also *increases.* A negative sign (–) indicates that as one variable *increases,* the other *decreases.*

Let's look at some examples of how a correlation coefficient works. One researcher reported a +.55 correlation between a measure of maternal language stimulation and the size of children's vocabularies at 2 years of age (Hoff, 2003). This is a moderate correlation, which indicates that mothers who spoke more to their toddlers had children who were more advanced in language development. In two other studies, maternal sensitivity was modestly associated with children's cooperativeness in consistent ways. First, maternal warmth and encouragement during play correlated positively with 2-year-olds' willingness to comply with their mother's directive to clean up toys, at +.34 (Feldman & Klein, 2003). Second, the extent to which mothers spoke harshly, interrupted, and controlled their 4-year-olds' play correlated negatively with children's compliance, at –.31 for boys and –.42 for girls (Smith et al., 2004).

All these investigations found correlations between parenting and young children's behavior. *TAKE A MOMENT...* Are you tempted to conclude that the maternal behaviors influenced children's responses? Although the researchers in these studies suspected this was so, they could not be sure of cause and effect.

Will the death of her husband affect this elderly widow's physical health and psychological well-being? A correlational design can be used to answer this question, but it does not permit researchers to determine the precise cause of their findings.

© TONY FREEMAN/PHOTOEDIT

Can you think of other possible explanations? Finding a relationship in a correlational study does suggest that tracking down its cause—using a more powerful experimental strategy, if possible—would be worthwhile.

Experimental Design. An **experimental design** permits inferences about cause and effect because researchers use an evenhanded procedure to assign people to two or more treatment conditions. In an experiment, the events and behaviors of interest are divided into two types: independent and dependent variables. The **independent variable** is the one the investigator expects to cause changes in another variable. The **dependent variable** is the one the investigator expects to be influenced by the independent variable. Cause-and-effect relationships can be detected because the researcher directly *controls* or *manipulates* changes in the independent variable by exposing participants to the treatment conditions. Then the researcher compares their performance on measures of the dependent variable.

In one *laboratory experiment,* investigators explored the impact of adults' angry interactions on children's adjustment (El-Sheikh, Cummings, & Reiter, 1996). They hypothesized that the way angry encounters end (independent variable) affects children's emotional reactions (dependent variable). Four- and 5-year-olds were brought to a laboratory one at a time, accompanied by their mothers. One group was exposed to an *unresolved-anger treatment,* in which two adult actors entered the room and argued but did not work out their disagreements. The other group witnessed a *resolved-anger treatment,* in which the adults ended their disputes by apologizing and compromising. When witnessing a follow-up adult conflict, children in the resolved-anger treatment showed less distress, as measured by fewer anxious facial expressions, less freezing in place, and less seeking of closeness to their mothers. The experiment revealed that anger resolution can reduce the stressful impact of adult conflict on children.

In experimental studies, investigators must take special precautions to control for participants' characteristics that could reduce the accuracy of their findings. For example, in the study just described, if a greater number of children from homes high in parental conflict ended up in the unresolved-anger treatment, we could not tell what produced the results—the independent variable or the children's backgrounds. To protect against this problem, researchers engage in **random assignment** of participants to treatment conditions. By using an unbiased procedure, such as drawing numbers out of a hat or flipping a coin, investigators increase the chances that participants' characteristics will be equally distributed across treatment groups.

Modified Experimental Designs: Field and Natural Experiments. Most experiments are conducted in laboratories, where researchers can achieve the maximum possible control over treatment conditions. But, as we have already indicated, findings obtained in laboratories may not always apply to everyday situations. In *field experiments,* investigators capitalize on opportunities to assign participants randomly to treatment conditions in natural settings. In the experiment just described, we can conclude that the emotional climate established by adults affects children's behavior in the laboratory. But does it also do so in daily life?

Another study helps answer this question. Ethnically diverse, poverty-stricken families with a 2-year-old child were scheduled for a home visit, during which researchers assessed family functioning and child problem behaviors by asking parents to respond to questionnaires and videotaping parent–child interaction. Then the families were randomly assigned to either a brief intervention condition, called the Family Check-Up, or a no-intervention control group. The intervention consisted of three home-based sessions in which a consultant gave parents feedback about their child-rearing practices and their child's adjustment, explored parents' willingness to improve, and identified community services appropriate to each family's needs (Dishion et al., 2008). Findings showed that families assigned to the Family Check-Up (but not controls) gained in positive parenting, which predicted a reduction in child problem behaviors—sometimes still evident a year later, when participating children were reassessed at age 3. Highly problematic children benefited most from this brief, early intervention.

Often researchers cannot randomly assign participants and manipulate conditions in the real world. Sometimes they can compromise by conducting *natural, or quasi-, experiments,* comparing treatments that already exist, such as different family environments, schools, workplaces, or retirement villages. These studies differ from correlational research only in that groups of participants are carefully chosen to ensure that their characteristics are as much alike as possible. In this way, investigators do their best to rule out alternative explanations for their treatment effects. But, despite these efforts, natural experiments cannot achieve the precision and rigor of true experimental research.

To help you compare correlational and experimental designs, Table 1.6 on page 36 summarizes their strengths and limitations. It also includes an overview of designs for studying development, to which we turn next.

Designs for Studying Development

Scientists interested in human development require information about the way research participants change over time. To answer questions about development, they must extend correlational and experimental approaches to include measurements at different ages. Longitudinal and cross-sectional designs are special *developmental* research strategies. In each, age comparisons form the basis of the research plan.

The Longitudinal Design. In a **longitudinal design,** participants are studied repeatedly, and changes are noted as they get older. The time spanned may be relatively short (a few months to several years) or very long (a decade or even a lifetime). The longitudinal approach has two major strengths. First, because it tracks the performance of each person over time,

TABLE 1.6
Strengths and Limitations of Research Designs

DESIGN	DESCRIPTION	STRENGTHS	LIMITATIONS
GENERAL			
Correlational	The investigator obtains information on participants without altering their experiences.	Permits study of relationships between variables.	Does not permit inferences about cause-and-effect relationships.
Experimental	Through random assignment of participants to treatment conditions, the investigator manipulates an independent variable and examines its effect on a dependent variable. Can be conducted in the laboratory or the natural environment.	Permits inferences about cause-and-effect relationships.	When conducted in the laboratory, findings may not generalize to the real world. In *field experiments,* control over the treatment is usually weaker than in the laboratory. In *natural,* or *quasi-, experiments,* lack of random assignment substantially reduces the precision of research.
DEVELOPMENTAL			
Longitudinal	The investigator studies the same group of participants repeatedly at different ages.	Permits study of common patterns and individual differences in development and relationships between early and later events and behaviors.	Age-related changes may be distorted because of participant dropout, practice effects, and cohort effects.
Cross-sectional	The investigator studies groups of participants differing in age at the same point in time.	More efficient than the longitudinal design. Not plagued by such problems as participant dropout and practice effects.	Does not permit study of individual developmental trends. Age differences may be distorted because of cohort effects.
Sequential	The investigator conducts several similar cross-sectional or longitudinal studies (called sequences). These might study participants over the same ages but in different years, or they might study participants over different ages but during the same years.	When the design includes longitudinal sequences, permits both longitudinal and cross-sectional comparisons. Also reveals cohort effects. Permits tracking of age-related changes more efficiently than the longitudinal design.	May have the same problems as longitudinal and cross-sectional strategies, but the design itself helps identify difficulties.

researchers can identify common patterns as well as individual differences in development. Second, longitudinal studies permit investigators to examine relationships between early and later events and behaviors. Let's illustrate these ideas.

A group of researchers wondered whether children who display extreme personality styles—either angry and explosive or shy and withdrawn—retain the same dispositions when they become adults. In addition, the researchers wanted to know what kinds of experiences promote stability or change in personality and what consequences explosiveness and shyness have for long-term adjustment. To answer these questions, the researchers delved into the archives of the Guidance Study, a well-known longitudinal investigation initiated in 1928 at the University of California, Berkeley, and continued for several decades (Caspi, Elder, & Bem, 1987, 1988).

Results revealed that the two personality styles were moderately stable. Between ages 8 and 30, a good number of individuals remained the same, whereas others changed substantially. When stability did occur, it appeared to be due to a "snowballing effect," in which children evoked responses from adults and peers that acted to maintain their dispositions. Explosive

youngsters were likely to be treated with anger, whereas shy children were apt to be ignored. As a result, the two types of children came to view their social worlds differently. Explosive children regarded others as hostile; shy children regarded them as unfriendly (Caspi & Roberts, 2001). Together, these factors led explosive children to sustain or increase their unruliness and shy children to continue to withdraw.

Persistence of extreme personality styles affected many areas of adult adjustment. For men, the results of early explosiveness were most apparent in their work lives, in the form of conflicts with supervisors, frequent job changes, and unemployment. Since few women in this sample of an earlier generation worked after marriage, their family lives were most affected. Explosive girls grew up to be hotheaded wives and mothers who were especially prone to divorce. Sex differences in the long-term consequences of shyness were even greater. Men who had been withdrawn in childhood were delayed in marrying, becoming fathers, and developing stable careers. However, perhaps because a withdrawn, unassertive style was socially acceptable for females in the mid-twentieth century, women who had shy personalities showed no special adjustment problems.

Problems in Conducting Longitudinal Research.

Despite their strengths, longitudinal investigations pose a number of problems. For example, participants may move away or drop out of the research for other reasons. This biases the sample so that it no longer represents the population to whom researchers would like to generalize their findings. Also, from repeated study, people may become more aware of their own thoughts, feelings, and actions and revise them in ways that have little to do with age-related change. In addition, they may become "test-wise." Their performance may improve as a result of *practice effects*—better test-taking skills and increased familiarity with the test—not because of factors commonly associated with development.

The most widely discussed threat to longitudinal findings is **cohort effects** (see page 11): Individuals born in the same time period are influenced by a particular set of historical and cultural conditions. Results based on one cohort may not apply to people developing at other times. For example, unlike the findings on female shyness described in the preceding section, which were gathered in the 1950s, today's shy adolescent girls and young women tend to be poorly adjusted—a difference that may be due to changes in gender roles in Western societies. Shy young people, whether male or female, feel more anxious, depressed, and lonely and may do less well in educational and career attainment than their agemates (Caspi et al., 2003; Karevold et al., 2012; Mounts et al., 2006). Similarly, a longitudinal study of lifespan development would probably result in quite different findings if it were carried out in the first decade of the twenty-first century, around the time of World War II, or during the Great Depression of the 1930s.

Cohort effects don't just operate broadly on an entire generation. They also occur when specific experiences influence some groups of individuals but not others in the same generation. For example, children who witnessed the terrorist attacks of September 11, 2001 (either because they were near Ground Zero or because they saw injury and death on TV), or who lost a parent in the disaster, were far more likely than other children to display persistent emotional problems, including intense fear, anxiety, and depression (Mullett-Hume et al., 2008; Pfeffer et al., 2007; Rosen & Cohen, 2010). A study of one New York City sample suggested that as many as one-fourth of the city's children were affected (Hoven et al., 2005).

The Cross-Sectional Design.

The length of time it takes for many behaviors to change, even in limited longitudinal studies, has led researchers to turn toward a more convenient strategy for studying development. In the **cross-sectional design,** groups of people differing in age are studied at the same point in time. The cross-sectional design is an efficient strategy for describing age-related trends. And because participants are measured only once, researchers need not be concerned about such difficulties as participant dropout or practice effects.

A study in which students in grades 3, 6, 9, and 12 filled out a questionnaire about their sibling relationships provides a good illustration (Buhrmester & Furman, 1990). Findings revealed that

Cohort effects are particular historical and cultural conditions that affect individuals born in the same time period. Young people who witnessed Barack Obama and his family celebrating his election victory in 2008 and again in 2012 came away with a new sense of what is possible for members of America's ethnic minorities.

sibling interaction was characterized by greater equality and less power assertion with age. Also, feelings of sibling companionship declined in adolescence. The researchers thought that several factors contributed to these age differences. As later-born children become more competent and independent, they no longer need, and are probably less willing to accept, direction from older siblings. And as adolescents move from psychological dependence on the family to greater involvement with peers, they may have less time and emotional need to invest in siblings. As you will see in Chapter 12, subsequent research has confirmed these intriguing ideas about the development of sibling relationships.

Problems in Conducting Cross-Sectional Research.

Despite its convenience, cross-sectional research does not provide evidence about development at the level at which it actually occurs: the individual. For example, in the cross-sectional study of sibling relationships just discussed, comparisons are limited to age-group averages. We cannot tell if important individual differences exist. Indeed, longitudinal findings reveal that adolescents vary considerably in the changing quality of their sibling relationships. Although many become more distant, others become more supportive and intimate, still others more rivalrous and antagonistic (Branje et al., 2004; Kim et al., 2006; Whiteman & Loken, 2006).

Cross-sectional studies—especially those that cover a wide age span—have another problem. Like longitudinal research, they can be threatened by cohort effects. For example, comparisons of 10-year-old cohorts, 20-year-old cohorts, and 30-year-old cohorts—groups born and reared in different years—may not really represent age-related changes. Instead, they may reflect unique experiences associated with the historical period in which the age groups were growing up.

Improving Developmental Designs. Researchers have devised ways of building on the strengths and minimizing the weaknesses of longitudinal and cross-sectional approaches. Several modified developmental designs have resulted.

Sequential Designs. To overcome some of the limitations of traditional developmental designs, investigators sometimes use **sequential designs,** in which they conduct several similar cross-sectional or longitudinal studies (called *sequences*). The sequences might study participants over the same ages but in different years, or they might study participants over different ages but during the same years. Figure 1.7 illustrates the first of these options. As it also reveals, some sequential designs combine longitudinal and cross-sectional strategies, an approach that has two advantages:

- We can find out whether cohort effects are operating by comparing participants of the same age who were born in different years. In the example in Figure 1.7, we can compare the three longitudinal samples at ages 20, 30, and 40. If they do not differ, we can rule out cohort effects.

- We can make longitudinal and cross-sectional comparisons. If outcomes are similar in both, then we can be especially confident about our findings.

In a study that used the design in Figure 1.7, researchers wanted to find out whether adult personality development progresses as Erikson's psychosocial theory predicts (Whitbourne et al., 1992). Questionnaires measuring Erikson's stages were given to three cohorts of 20-year-olds, each born a decade apart. The cohorts were reassessed at ten-year intervals. Consistent with Erikson's theory, longitudinal and cross-sectional gains in identity and intimacy occurred between ages 20 and 30—a trend unaffected by historical time period. But a powerful cohort effect emerged for consolidation of the sense of industry: At age 20, Cohort 1 scored substantially below Cohorts 2 and 3. Look at Figure 1.7 again and notice that members of Cohort 1 reached age 20 in the mid-1960s. As college students, they were part of an era of political protest that reflected disenchantment with the work ethic. Once out of college, they caught up with the other cohorts in industry, perhaps as a result of experiencing the pressures of the work world. Followed up in 2001 at age 54, Cohort 1 showed a decline in focus on identity issues and a gain in ego integrity over middle adulthood—trends expected to continue through late adulthood (Sneed, Whitbourne, & Culang, 2006). Future tracking of Cohorts 2 and 3 will reveal whether they, too, follow this Erikson-predicted psychosocial path.

By uncovering cohort effects, sequential designs help explain diversity in development. Yet to date only a small number of sequential studies have been conducted.

Combining Experimental and Developmental Designs. Perhaps you noticed that all the examples of longitudinal and cross-sectional research we have considered permit only correlational, not causal, inferences. Yet causal information is desirable, both for testing theories and for finding ways to enhance development. Sometimes researchers can explore the causal link between experiences and development by experimentally manipulating the experiences. If, as a result, development improves, then we have strong evidence for a causal association. Today, research that combines an experimental strategy with either a longitudinal or a cross-sectional approach is becoming increasingly common.

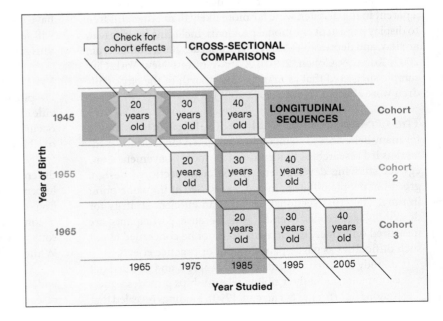

FIGURE 1.7 Example of a sequential design. Three cohorts, born in 1945 (blue), 1955 (pink), and 1965 (green), are followed longitudinally from 20 to 40 years of age. The design permits the researcher to check for cohort effects by comparing people of the same age who were born in different years. In a study that used this design, the 20-year-olds in Cohort 1 differed substantially from the 20-year-olds in Cohorts 2 and 3, indicating powerful history-graded influences. This design also permits longitudinal and cross-sectional comparisons. Similar findings lend additional confidence in the results.

ASK YOURSELF

REVIEW Explain how cohort effects can affect the findings of both longitudinal and cross-sectional studies. How do sequential designs reveal cohort effects?

CONNECT Review the study of the Family Check-Up, described on page 35. Explain how it combines an experimental with a developmental design. What are the independent and dependent variables? Is its developmental approach longitudinal or cross-sectional?

APPLY A researcher compares older adults with chronic heart disease to those with no major health problems and finds that the first group scores lower on mental tests. Can the researcher conclude that heart disease causes a decline in intellectual functioning in late adulthood? Explain.

REFLECT Suppose a researcher asks you to enroll your baby in a 10-year longitudinal study. What factors would lead you to agree and stay involved? Do your answers shed light on why longitudinal studies often have biased samples?

 ## Ethics in Lifespan Research

Research into human behavior creates ethical issues because, unfortunately, the quest for scientific knowledge can sometimes exploit people. For this reason, special guidelines for research have been developed by the federal government, by funding agencies, and by research-oriented associations, such as the American Psychological Association (2002) and the Society for Research in Child Development (2007). Table 1.7 presents a summary of basic research rights drawn from these guidelines. *TAKE A MOMENT...* After examining them, read about the following research situations, each of which poses a serious ethical dilemma. What precautions do you think should be taken in each instance?

● In a study of moral development, an investigator wants to assess children's ability to resist temptation by videotaping their behavior without their knowledge. She promises 7-year-olds a prize for solving difficult puzzles but tells them not to look at a classmate's correct solutions, which are deliberately placed at the back of the room. Informing children ahead of time that cheating is being studied or that their behavior is being monitored will destroy the purpose of the study.

● A researcher wants to study the impact of mild daily exercise on the physical and mental health of elderly patients in nursing homes. He consults each resident's doctor to make sure that the exercise routine will not be harmful. But when he seeks the residents' consent, he finds that many do not comprehend the purpose of the research. And some appear to agree simply to relieve feelings of isolation and loneliness.

As these examples indicate, when children or the aged take part in research, the ethical concerns are especially complex. Immaturity makes it difficult or impossible for children to evaluate for themselves what participation in research will mean. And because mental impairment rises with very advanced age, some older adults cannot make voluntary and informed choices (Dubois et al., 2011; Society for Research in Child Development, 2007). And the life circumstances of others make them unusually vulnerable to pressure for participation.

TABLE 1.7

Rights of Research Participants

RESEARCH RIGHT	DESCRIPTION
Protection from harm	Participants have the right to be protected from physical or psychological harm in research. If in doubt about the harmful effects of research, investigators should seek the opinion of others. When harm seems possible, investigators should find other means for obtaining the desired information or abandon the research.
Informed consent	All participants, including children and the elderly, have the right to have explained to them, in language appropriate to their level of understanding, all aspects of the research that may affect their willingness to participate. When children are participants, informed consent of parents as well as of others who act on the child's behalf (such as school officials) should be obtained, preferably in writing. Older adults who are cognitively impaired should be asked to appoint a surrogate decision maker. If they cannot do so, then someone should be named by an institutional review board (IRB) after careful consultation with relatives and professionals who know the person well. All participants have the right to discontinue participation in the research at any time.
Privacy	Participants have the right to concealment of their identity on all information collected in the course of research. They also have this right with respect to written reports and any informal discussions about the research.
Knowledge of results	Participants have the right to be informed of the results of research in language that is appropriate to their level of understanding.
Beneficial treatments	If experimental treatments believed to be beneficial are under investigation, participants in control groups have the right to alternative beneficial treatments if they are available.

Sources: American Psychological Association, 2002; Society for Research in Child Development, 2007.

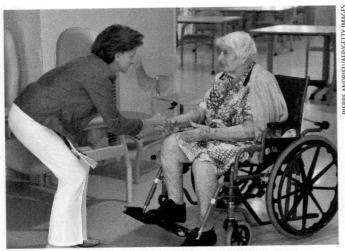

PIERRE ANDRIEU/AFP/GETTY IMAGES

Older adults should not be arbitrarily excluded from research. Most require only typical informed-consent procedures, and their participation brings both personal and scientific benefits. But for some elders, including those who reside in settings for the chronically ill, informed consent may necessitate the assistance of a surrogate decision maker.

Virtually every organization that has devised ethical principles for research has concluded that conflicts arising in research situations often do not have simple right-or-wrong answers. The ultimate responsibility for the ethical integrity of research lies with the investigator. But researchers are advised—and often required—to seek advice from others. Committees for this purpose exist in colleges, universities, and other institutions. These *institutional review boards (IRBs)* weigh the costs of the research to participants in terms of inconvenience and possible psychological or physical injury against the study's value for advancing knowledge and improving conditions of life. If there are any risks to participants' safety and welfare that the research does not justify, then preference is always given to the participants' interests.

The ethical principle of *informed consent* requires special interpretation when participants cannot fully appreciate the research goals and activities. Parental consent is meant to protect the safety of children, whose ability to decide is not yet mature. But as soon as children are old enough to appreciate the purpose of the research, and certainly by age 7, their own informed consent should be obtained in addition to parental consent. Around this age, changes in children's thinking permit them to better understand basic scientific principles and the needs of others. Researchers should respect and enhance these new capacities by giving school-age children a full explanation of research activities in language they can understand (Fisher, 1993). Extra care must be taken when telling children that the information they provide will be kept confidential and that they can end their participation at any time. Even adolescents may not understand, and sometimes do not believe, these promises (Bruzzese & Fisher, 2003; Ondrusek et al., 1998).

Most older adults require no more than the usual informed-consent procedures. Yet many investigators set upper age limits in studies relevant to the elderly, thereby excluding the oldest

adults (Bayer & Tadd, 2000). Older adults should not be stereotyped as incompetent to decide about their own participation or to engage in research activities. Nevertheless, extra measures must be taken to protect those who are cognitively impaired or who reside in settings for the chronically ill. As noted, some individuals may agree to participate simply to engage in rewarding social interaction. Yet participation should not be automatically withheld, since it can result in personal as well as scientific benefits. In these instances, potential participants should be asked to appoint a surrogate decision maker. If they cannot do so, then someone should be named by an IRB, after careful consultation with relatives and professionals who know the person well. As an added precaution, if the elderly person is incapable of consenting and the risks of the research are more than minimal, then the study should not be done unless it is likely to benefit the participant directly (Dubois et al., 2011).

Finally, all ethical guidelines advise that special precautions be taken in the use of deception and concealment, as occurs when researchers observe people from behind one-way mirrors, give them false feedback about their performance, or do not tell them the truth about the real purpose of the research. When these kinds of procedures are used, *debriefing,* in which the investigator provides a full account and justification of the activities, occurs after the research session is over. But young children often lack the cognitive skills to understand the reasons for deceptive procedures, and despite explanations, even older children may leave the research situation with their belief in the honesty of adults undermined. Ethical standards permit deception if investigators satisfy IRBs that a study's potential benefits to society are great enough to justify infringing on participants' right to informed consent and risking other harm (Fisher, 2005). Nevertheless, because deception may have serious emotional consequences for some youngsters, many experts in research ethics believe that investigators should use it with children only if the risk of harm is minimal.

ASK YOURSELF

REVIEW What special steps must investigators take in conducting studies of children and the aged to ensure protection from harm and informed consent?

CONNECT In the field experiment on the Family Check-Up (see page 35), why is it ethically important for the researchers to offer the intervention, or a beneficial alternative, to the no-intervention control group after completion of the study?

APPLY As a researcher gathered observations of the activities of several elderly adults with cognitive impairments in a nursing home, one resident said, "Stop watching me!" How should the researcher respond, and why?

REFLECT What ethical safeguards do you regard as vital in conducting research that requires deception of children?

SUMMARY

A Scientific, Applied, and Interdisciplinary Field
(p. 5)

What is developmental science, and what factors stimulated expansion of the field?

● **Developmental science** is an interdisciplinary field devoted to understanding human constancy and change throughout the lifespan. Research on human development has been stimulated by both scientific curiosity and social pressures to improve people's lives.

Basic Issues (p. 5)

Identify three basic issues on which theories of human development take a stand.

● Each **theory** of human development takes a stand on three basic issues: (1) Is development a **continuous** process, or does it proceed in a series of **discontinuous stages?** (2) Does one general course of development characterize all individuals, or do many possible courses exist, depending on the distinct **contexts** in which children and adults live? (3) Is development determined primarily by genetic or environmental factors (the **nature–nurture controversy**), and are individual differences stable or characterized by substantial **plasticity?**

The Lifespan Perspective: A Balanced Point of View
(p. 7)

Describe the lifespan perspective on development.

● The **lifespan perspective** is a balanced view that envisions development as a dynamic system. It is based on assumptions that development is lifelong, multidimensional (affected by biological, psychological, and social forces), multidirectional (a joint expression of growth and decline), and plastic (open to change through new experiences).

● According to the lifespan perspective, the life course is influenced by multiple, interacting forces, which can be organized into three categories: (1) **age-graded influences,** which are predictable in timing and duration; (2) **history-graded influences,** unique to a particular historical era; and (3) **nonnormative influences,** unique to one or a few individuals.

Scientific Beginnings (p. 14)

Describe the major early influences on the scientific study of development.

● Darwin's theory of evolution influenced important developmental theories and inspired scientific child study. In the early twentieth century, Hall and Gesell introduced the **normative approach,** which produced a large body of descriptive facts about development.

● Binet and Simon constructed the first successful intelligence test, which sparked interest in individual differences in development and led to a heated controversy over nature versus nurture.

Mid-Twentieth-Century Theories (p. 15)

What theories influenced human development research in the mid-twentieth century?

● In the 1930s and 1940s, psychiatrists and social workers turned to the **psychoanalytic perspective** for help in treating people's emotional problems. In Freud's **psychosexual theory,** the individual moves through five stages, during which three portions of the personality—id, ego, and superego—become integrated. Erikson's **psychosocial theory** expands Freud's theory by emphasizing the development of culturally relevant attitudes and skills and the lifespan nature of development.

● As the psychoanalytic perspective gained in prominence, **behaviorism** and **social learning theory** emerged, emphasizing the study of directly observable events—stimuli and responses—and the principles of conditioning and modeling. These approaches led to the use of **behavior modification** to eliminate undesirable behaviors and increase desirable responses.

● In contrast to behaviorism, Piaget's **cognitive-developmental theory** emphasizes children's active role in constructing knowledge as they manipulate and explore their world. According to Piaget, children move through four stages, from the baby's sensorimotor action patterns to the adolescent's capacity for abstract, systematic thinking. Piaget's work has stimulated a wealth of research on children's thinking and encouraged educational programs that emphasize discovery learning.

Recent Theoretical Perspectives (p. 20)

Describe recent theoretical perspectives on human development.

● **Information processing** views the mind as a complex symbol-manipulating system, much like a computer. Because this approach provides precise accounts of how children and adults tackle cognitive tasks, its findings have important implications for education.

● Researchers in **developmental cognitive neuroscience** study the relationship between changes in the brain and the development of cognitive processing and behavior patterns. They have made progress in identifying the types of experiences to which the brain is sensitive at various ages and in clarifying the brain bases of many learning and behavior disorders.

- Three contemporary perspectives emphasize contexts of development. **Ethology** stresses the adaptive value of behavior and inspired the **sensitive period** concept. In **evolutionary developmental psychology,** which extends this emphasis, researchers seek to understand the person–environment system throughout the lifespan.

- Vygotsky's **sociocultural theory,** which focuses on how culture is transmitted from one generation to the next through social interaction, views cognitive development as a socially mediated process. Through cooperative dialogues with more expert members of society, children come to use language to guide their own thought and actions and acquire culturally relevant knowledge and skills.

- **Ecological systems theory** views the individual as developing within a complex system of relationships affected by multiple, nested layers of the surrounding environment— **microsystem, mesosystem, exosystem,** and **macrosystem.** The **chronosystem** represents the dynamic, ever-changing nature of individuals and their experiences.

Comparing and Evaluating Theories (p. 27)

Identify the stand taken by each major theory on the three basic issues of human development.

- Theories vary in their focus on different domains of development, in their view of how development occurs, and in their strengths and weaknesses. (For a full summary, see Table 1.4 on page 28.)

Studying Development (p. 27)

Describe methods commonly used in research on human development.

- **Naturalistic observations,** gathered in everyday environments, permit researchers to see directly the everyday behaviors they hope to explain. In contrast, **structured observations,** which take place in laboratories, give every participant an equal opportunity to display the behaviors of interest.

- Self-report methods can be flexible and open-ended like the **clinical interview,** which permits participants to express their thoughts in ways similar to their thinking in everyday life. Alternatively, **structured interviews** (including tests and questionnaires) are more efficient, permitting researchers to ask about activities and behaviors that participants may not think of in an open-ended interview. Investigators use the **clinical,** or **case study, method** to gain an in-depth understanding of a single individual.

- Researchers have adapted observational and self-report methods to permit direct comparisons of cultures. To uncover the cultural meanings of behavior, they rely on **ethnography,** engaging in participant observation.

Distinguish between correlational and experimental research designs, noting the strengths and limitations of each.

- The **correlational design** examines relationships between variables without altering people's experiences. The **correlation coefficient** is often used to measure the association between variables. Correlational studies do not permit inferences about cause and effect, but they can identify relationships that are worth exploring with a more powerful experimental strategy.

- An **experimental design** permits cause-and-effect inferences. Researchers manipulate an **independent variable** by exposing participants to two or more treatment conditions. Then they determine what effect this variable has on a **dependent variable. Random assignment** to treatment conditions reduces the chances that participant characteristics will affect the accuracy of experimental findings.

- Field and natural, or quasi-, experiments compare treatments in natural environments. However, these approaches are less rigorous than laboratory experiments.

Describe designs for studying development, noting the strengths and limitations of each.

- In the **longitudinal design,** participants are studied repeatedly over time, permitting researchers to identify common patterns and individual differences in development and to examine relationships between early and later events and behaviors. Longitudinal research poses several problems, including biased sampling, practice effects, and **cohort effects**— difficulty generalizing to people developing at other historical times.

- The **cross-sectional design,** in which groups of people differing in age are studied at the same point in time, is an efficient way to study age-related trends, but it is limited to comparisons of age-group averages. Cross-sectional studies, especially those that cover a wide age span, are also vulnerable to cohort effects.

- By comparing participants of the same age who were born in different years, investigators use **sequential designs** to discover whether cohort effects are operating. When sequential designs combine longitudinal and cross-sectional strategies, researchers can see if outcomes are similar, adding confidence to their findings.

- When researchers combine experimental and developmental designs, they can examine causal influences on development.

Ethics in Lifespan Research (p. 39)

What special ethical concerns arise in research on human development?

- Because the quest for scientific knowledge has the potential to exploit people, the ethical principle of informed consent requires special safeguards for children and for elderly people who are cognitively impaired or who live in settings for the care of the chronically ill. The use of deception in research with children is especially risky because it may undermine their basic faith in the honesty of adults.

Important Terms and Concepts

age-graded influences (p. 10)
behavior modification (p. 18)
behaviorism (p. 17)
chronosystem (p. 25)
clinical interview (p. 30)
clinical, or case study, method (p. 30)
cognitive-developmental theory (p. 18)
cohort effects (p. 37)
contexts (p. 7)
continuous development (p. 6)
correlational design (p. 34)
correlation coefficient (p. 34)
cross-sectional design (p. 37)
dependent variable (p. 35)
developmental cognitive neuroscience (p. 21)
developmental science (p. 5)
discontinuous development (p. 6)

ecological systems theory (p. 24)
ethnography (p. 32)
ethology (p. 22)
evolutionary developmental psychology (p. 22)
exosystem (p. 25)
experimental design (p. 35)
history-graded influences (p. 11)
independent variable (p. 35)
information processing (p. 20)
lifespan perspective (p. 8)
longitudinal design (p. 35)
macrosystem (p. 25)
mesosystem (p. 25)
microsystem (p. 24)
naturalistic observation (p. 28)
nature–nurture controversy (p. 7)
nonnormative influences (p. 12)

normative approach (p. 15)
plasticity (p. 7)
psychoanalytic perspective (p. 15)
psychosexual theory (p. 15)
psychosocial theory (p. 16)
random assignment (p. 35)
resilience (p. 10)
sensitive period (p. 22)
sequential designs (p. 38)
social learning theory (p. 18)
sociocultural theory (p. 23)
stage (p. 6)
structured interview (p. 30)
structured observation (p. 29)
theory (p. 5)

© ELLEN B. SENISI PHOTOGRAPHY

Heredity and environment combine in intricate ways, making members of this large extended family both alike and different in physical characteristics and behavior.

Genetic and Environmental Foundations

chapter outline

Genetic Foundations

The Genetic Code • The Sex Cells • Boy or Girl? • Multiple Offspring • Patterns of Genetic Inheritance • Chromosomal Abnormalities

Reproductive Choices

Genetic Counseling • Prenatal Diagnosis and Fetal Medicine • Adoption

■ **SOCIAL ISSUES: HEALTH** The Pros and Cons of Reproductive Technologies

Environmental Contexts for Development

The Family • Socioeconomic Status and Family Functioning • Poverty • Affluence • Beyond the Family: Neighborhoods, Towns, and Cities • The Cultural Context

■ **CULTURAL INFLUENCES** The African-American Extended Family

Understanding the Relationship Between Heredity and Environment

The Question, "How Much?" • The Question, "How?"

■ **BIOLOGY AND ENVIRONMENT** A Case of Epigenesis: Smoking During Pregnancy Alters Gene Expression

"It's a girl!" announces the doctor, holding up the squalling newborn baby as her parents gaze with amazement at their miraculous creation. "A girl! We've named her Sarah!" exclaims the proud father to eager relatives waiting for news of their new family member.

As we join these parents in thinking about how this wondrous being came into existence and imagining her future, we are struck by many questions. How could this baby, equipped with everything necessary for life outside the womb, have developed from the union of two tiny cells? What ensures that Sarah will, in due time, roll over, walk, talk, make friends, learn, imagine, and create—just like other typical children born before her? Why is she a girl and not a boy, dark-haired rather than blond, calm and cuddly instead of wiry and energetic? What difference will it make that Sarah is given a name and place in one family, community, nation, and culture rather than another?

To answer these questions, this chapter takes a close look at the foundations of development: heredity and environment. Because nature has prepared us for survival, all humans have features in common. Yet each of us is also unique. *TAKE A MOMENT...* Think about several of your friends, and jot down the most obvious physical and behavioral similarities between them and their parents. Did you find that

© LAURA DWIGHT PHOTOGRAPHY

one person shows combined features of both parents, another resembles just one parent, whereas a third is not like either parent? These directly observable characteristics are called **phenotypes.** They depend in part on the individual's **genotype**—the complex blend of genetic information that determines our species and influences all our unique characteristics. Yet phenotypes are also affected by each person's lifelong history of experiences.

We begin our discussion with a review of basic genetic principles that help explain similarities and differences among us in appearance and behavior. Then we turn to aspects of the environment that play powerful roles throughout the lifespan. Finally, we consider the question of how nature and nurture *work together* to shape the course of development. ●

Genetic Foundations

Each of us is made up of trillions of units called *cells*. Within every cell (except red blood cells) is a control center, or *nucleus,* containing rodlike structures called **chromosomes,** which store and transmit genetic information. Human chromosomes come in 23 matching pairs (an exception is the XY pair in males, which we will discuss shortly). Each member of a pair corresponds to the other in size, shape, and genetic functions, with one chromosome inherited from the mother and one from the father (see Figure 2.1).

The Genetic Code

Chromosomes are made up of a chemical substance called **deoxyribonucleic acid, or DNA.** As Figure 2.2 shows, DNA is a long, double-stranded molecule that looks like a twisted ladder. Each rung of the ladder consists of a specific pair of chemical substances called *bases,* joined together between the two sides. It is this sequence of base pairs that provides genetic instructions. A **gene** is a segment of DNA along the length of the chromosome. Genes can be of different lengths—perhaps 100 to several thousand ladder rungs long. An estimated 20,000 to 25,000 genes lie along the human chromosomes (Human Genome Program, 2008).

We share some of our genetic makeup with even the simplest organisms, such as bacteria and molds, and most of it with other mammals, especially primates. Between 98 and 99 percent of chimpanzee and human DNA is identical. This means that only a small portion of our heredity is responsible for the traits that make us human, from our upright gait to our extraordinary language and cognitive capacities. And the genetic variation from one human to the next is even less! Individuals around the world are about 99.1 percent genetically identical (Gibbons et al., 2004). But it takes a change in only a single base pair to influence human traits. And such tiny changes can combine in unique ways across multiple genes, thereby amplifying variability within the human species.

A unique feature of DNA is that it can duplicate itself through a process called **mitosis.** This special ability permits the one-celled fertilized ovum to develop into a complex human being composed of a great many cells. Refer again to Figure 2.2, and you will see that during mitosis, the chromosomes copy themselves. As a result, each new body cell contains the same number of chromosomes and genetic information.

Genes accomplish their task by sending instructions for making a rich assortment of proteins to the *cytoplasm,* the area surrounding the cell nucleus. Proteins, which trigger chemical reactions throughout the body, are the biological foundation on which our characteristics are built. How do humans, with far fewer genes than scientists once thought (only twice as many as the worm or fly), manage to develop into such complex beings? The answer lies in the proteins our genes make, which break up and reassemble in staggering variety—about 10 to 20 million altogether. Simpler species have far fewer proteins. Furthermore, the communication system between the cell nucleus and cytoplasm, which fine-tunes gene activity, is more intricate in humans than in simpler organisms. Within the cell, wide-ranging environmental factors modify gene expression (Lashley, 2007). So even at this microscopic level, biological events are the result of *both* genetic and nongenetic forces.

The Sex Cells

New individuals are created when two special cells called **gametes,** or sex cells—the sperm and ovum—combine. A gamete contains only 23 chromosomes, half as many as a regular body cell. Gametes are formed through a cell division process called **meiosis,** which halves the number of chromosomes normally present in body cells. When sperm and ovum unite at conception, the resulting cell, called a **zygote,** will again have 46 chromosomes.

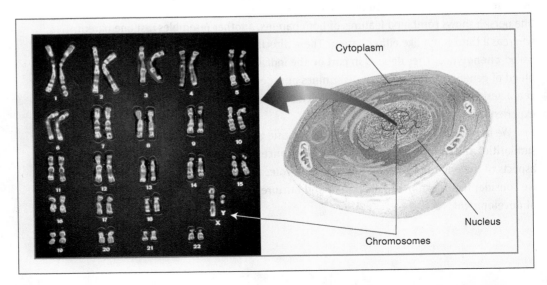

FIGURE 2.1 A karyotype, or photograph, of human chromosomes. The 46 chromosomes shown on the left were isolated from a human cell, stained, greatly magnified, and arranged in pairs according to decreasing size of the upper "arm" of each chromosome. The twenty-third pair, XY, reveals that the cell donor is a male. In a female, this pair would be XX. (© CNRI/ Science Photo Library/Photo Researchers, Inc.)

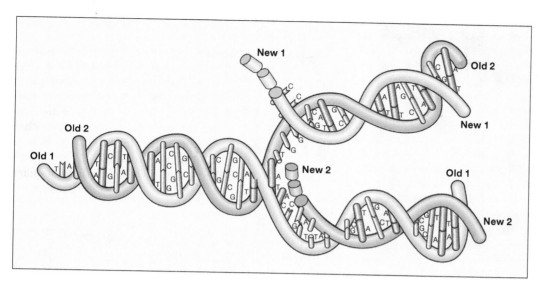

FIGURE 2.2 DNA's ladder-like structure. This figure shows that the pairings of bases across the rungs of the ladder are very specific: Adenine (A) always appears with thymine (T), and cytosine (C) always appears with guanine (G). Here, the DNA ladder duplicates by splitting down the middle of its ladder rungs. Each free base picks up a new complementary partner from the area surrounding the cell nucleus.

In meiosis, the chromosomes pair up and exchange segments, so that genes from one are replaced by genes from another. Then chance determines which member of each pair will gather with others and end up in the same gamete. These events make the likelihood extremely low—about 1 in 700 trillion—that nontwin siblings will be genetically identical (Gould & Keeton, 1996). The genetic variability produced by meiosis is adaptive: It increases the chances that at least some members of a species will cope with ever-changing environments and will survive.

In the male, four sperm are produced when meiosis is complete. Also, the cells from which sperm arise are produced continuously throughout life. For this reason, a healthy man can father a child at any age after sexual maturity. In the female, meiosis results in just one ovum. In addition, the female is born with a bank of ova already present in her ovaries, though recent findings suggest that new ova may arise from ovarian stem cells later on (White et al., 2012). Nevertheless, females can bear children for only three to four decades. Still, there are plenty of female sex cells. About 1 to 2 million are present at birth, 40,000 remain at adolescence, and approximately 350 to 450 will mature during a woman's childbearing years (Moore & Persaud, 2008).

Boy or Girl?

Return to Figure 2.1 and note that 22 of the 23 pairs of chromosomes are matching pairs, called **autosomes** (meaning *not* sex chromosomes). The twenty-third pair consists of **sex chromosomes.** In females, this pair is called XX; in males, it is called XY. The X is a relatively large chromosome, whereas the Y is short and carries little genetic material. When gametes form in males, the X and Y chromosomes separate into different sperm cells. The gametes that form in females all carry an X chromosome. Therefore, the sex of the new organism is determined by whether an X-bearing or a Y-bearing sperm fertilizes the ovum.

Multiple Offspring

Ruth and Peter, a couple I know well, tried for several years to have a child, without success. When Ruth reached age 33, her doctor prescribed a fertility drug, and twins—Jeannie and Jason—were born. Jeannie and Jason are **fraternal,** or **dizygotic, twins,** the most common type of multiple offspring, resulting from the release and fertilization of two ova. Genetically, they are no more alike than ordinary siblings. Table 2.1 summarizes genetic and environmental factors that

TABLE 2.1 Maternal Factors Linked to Fraternal Twinning

FACTOR	DESCRIPTION
Ethnicity	Occurs in 4 per 1,000 births among Asians, 8 per 1,000 births among whites, 12 to 16 per 1,000 births among blacks[a]
Family history of twinning	Occurs more often among women whose mothers and sisters gave birth to fraternal twins
Age	Rises with maternal age, peaking between 35 and 39 years, and then rapidly falls
Nutrition	Occurs less often among women with poor diets; occurs more often among women who are tall and overweight or of normal weight as opposed to slight body build
Number of births	Is more likely with each additional birth
Fertility drugs and in vitro fertilization	Is more likely with fertility hormones and in vitro fertilization (see page 54), which also increase the chances of bearing triplets, quadruplets, or quintuplets

[a]Worldwide rates, not including multiple births resulting from use of fertility drugs.
Sources: Hall, 2003; Hoekstra et al., 2008; Lashley, 2007.

These identical, or monozygotic, twins were created when a duplicating zygote separated into two clusters of cells, which developed into two individuals with the same genetic makeup.

increase the chances of giving birth to fraternal twins. Older maternal age, fertility drugs, and in vitro fertilization (to be discussed shortly) are major causes of the dramatic rise in fraternal twinning and other multiple births in industrialized nations over the past several decades (Machin, 2005; Russell et al., 2003). Currently, fraternal twins account for 1 in about every 60 births in the United States (U.S. Department of Health and Human Services, 2010a).

Twins can be created in another way. Sometimes a zygote that has started to duplicate separates into two clusters of cells that develop into two individuals. These are called **identical**, or **monozygotic, twins** because they have the same genetic makeup. The frequency of identical twins is the same around the world—about 1 in every 330 births (Hall, 2003). Animal research has uncovered a variety of environmental influences that prompt this type of twinning, including temperature changes, variation in oxygen levels, and late fertilization of the ovum. In a minority of cases, the identical twinning runs in families, suggesting a genetic influence (Lashley, 2007).

During their early years, children of single births often are healthier and develop more rapidly than twins. Jeannie and Jason, like most twins, were born early—three weeks before Ruth's due date. And, like other premature infants—as you will see in Chapter 3—they required special care after birth. When the twins came home from the hospital, Ruth and Peter had to divide time between them. Perhaps because neither baby received as much attention as the average single infant, Jeannie and Jason walked and talked several months later than most other children their age, though both caught up by middle childhood (Lytton & Gallagher, 2002). Parental energies are further strained after the birth of triplets, whose early development is slower than that of twins (Feldman, Eidelman, & Rotenberg, 2004).

Patterns of Genetic Inheritance

Jeannie has her parents' dark, straight hair; Jason is curly-haired and blond. Patterns of genetic inheritance—the way genes from each parent interact—explain these outcomes. Recall that, except for the XY pair in males, all chromosomes come in matching pairs. Two forms of each gene occur at the same place on the chromosomes, one inherited from the mother and one from the father. Each form of a gene is called an **allele**. If the alleles from both parents are alike, the child is **homozygous** and will display the inherited trait. If the alleles differ, then the child is **heterozygous**, and relationships between the alleles determine the phenotype.

Dominant–Recessive Inheritance. In many heterozygous pairings, **dominant–recessive inheritance** occurs: Only one allele affects the child's characteristics. It is called *dominant*; the second allele, which has no effect, is called *recessive*. Hair color is an example. The allele for dark hair is dominant (we can represent it with a capital *D*), whereas the one for blond hair is recessive (symbolized by a lowercase *b*). A child who inherits a homozygous pair of dominant alleles *(DD)* and a child who inherits a heterozygous pair *(Db)* will both be dark-haired, even though their genotypes differ. Blond hair (like Jason's) can result only from having two recessive alleles *(bb)*. Still, heterozygous individuals with just one recessive allele *(Db)* can pass that trait to their children. Therefore, they are called **carriers** of the trait.

Some human characteristics that follow the rules of dominant–recessive inheritance are listed in Tables 2.2 and 2.3.

TABLE 2.2 **Examples of Dominant and Recessive Characteristics**

DOMINANT	RECESSIVE
Dark hair	Blond hair
Normal hair	Pattern baldness
Curly hair	Straight hair
Nonred hair	Red hair
Facial dimples	No dimples
Normal hearing	Some forms of deafness
Normal vision	Nearsightedness
Farsightedness	Normal vision
Normal vision	Congenital eye cataracts
Normally pigmented skin	Albinism
Double-jointedness	Normal joints
Type A blood	Type O blood
Type B blood	Type O blood
Rh-positive blood	Rh-negative blood

Note: Many normal characteristics that were previously thought to be due to dominant–recessive inheritance, such as eye color, are now regarded as due to multiple genes. For the characteristics listed here, there still seems to be general agreement that the simple dominant–recessive relationship holds.

Source: McKusick, 2011.

TABLE 2.3

Examples of Dominant and Recessive Diseases

DISEASE	DESCRIPTION	MODE OF INHERITANCE	INCIDENCE	TREATMENT
AUTOSOMAL DISEASES				
Cooley's anemia	Pale appearance, retarded physical growth, and lethargic behavior begin in infancy.	Recessive	1 in 500 births to parents of Mediterranean descent	Frequent blood transfusion; death from complications usually occurs by adolescence.
Cystic fibrosis	Lungs, liver, and pancreas secrete large amounts of thick mucus, leading to breathing and digestive difficulties.	Recessive	1 in 2,000 to 2,500 Caucasian births; 1 in 16,000 births to North Americans of African descent	Bronchial drainage, prompt treatment of respiratory infection, dietary management. Advances in medical care allow survival with good life quality into adulthood.
Phenylketonuria (PKU)	Inability to metabolize the amino acid phenylalanine, contained in many proteins, causes severe central nervous system damage in the first year of life.	Recessive	1 in 8,000 births	Placing the child on a special diet results in average intelligence and normal lifespan. Subtle deficits in memory, planning, decision making, and problem solving are often present.
Sickle cell anemia	Abnormal sickling of red blood cells causes oxygen deprivation, pain, swelling, and tissue damage. Anemia and susceptibility to infections, especially pneumonia, occur.	Recessive	1 in 500 births to North Americans of African descent	Blood transfusions, painkillers, prompt treatment of infection. No known cure; 50 percent die by age 55.
Tay-Sachs disease	Central nervous system degeneration, with onset at about 6 months, leads to poor muscle tone, blindness, deafness, and convulsions.	Recessive	1 in 3,600 births to Jews of European descent and to French Canadians	None. Death occurs by 3 to 4 years of age.
Huntington disease	Central nervous system degeneration leads to muscular coordination difficulties, mental deterioration, and personality changes. Symptoms usually do not appear until age 35 or later.	Dominant	1 in 18,000 to 25,000 births to North Americans	None. Death occurs 10 to 20 years after symptom onset.
Marfan syndrome	Tall, slender build; thin, elongated arms and legs; and heart defects and eye abnormalities, especially of the lens. Excessive lengthening of the body results in a variety of skeletal defects.	Dominant	1 in 5,000 to 10,000 births	Correction of heart and eye defects is sometimes possible. Death from heart failure in young adulthood is common.
X-LINKED DISEASES				
Duchenne muscular dystrophy	Degenerative muscle disease. Abnormal gait, loss of ability to walk between 7 and 13 years of age.	Recessive	1 in 3,000 to 5,000 male births	None. Death from respiratory infection or weakening of the heart muscle usually occurs in adolescence.
Hemophilia	Blood fails to clot normally; can lead to severe internal bleeding and tissue damage.	Recessive	1 in 4,000 to 7,000 male births	Blood transfusions. Safety precautions to prevent injury.
Diabetes insipidus	Insufficient production of the hormone vasopressin results in excessive thirst and urination. Dehydration can cause central nervous system damage.	Recessive	1 in 2,500 male births	Hormone replacement.

Note: For recessive disorders listed, carrier status can be detected in prospective parents through a blood test or genetic analyses. For all disorders listed, prenatal diagnosis is available (see page 56).
Sources: Kliegman et al., 2008; Lashley, 2007; McKusick, 2011.

As you can see, many disabilities and diseases are the product of recessive alleles. One of the most frequently occurring recessive disorders is *phenylketonuria,* or *PKU,* which affects the way the body breaks down proteins contained in many foods. Infants born with two recessive alleles lack an enzyme that converts one of the basic amino acids that make up proteins (phenylalanine) into a byproduct essential for body functioning (tyrosine). Without this enzyme, phenylalanine quickly builds to toxic levels that damage the central nervous system. By 1 year, infants with PKU are permanently mentally retarded.

Despite its potentially damaging effects, PKU provides an excellent illustration of the fact that inheriting unfavorable genes does not always lead to an untreatable condition. All U.S. states require that each newborn be given a blood test for PKU. If the disease is found, doctors place the baby on a diet low in phenylalanine. Children who receive this treatment nevertheless show mild deficits in certain cognitive skills, such as memory, planning, decision making, and problem solving, because even small amounts of phenylalanine interfere with brain functioning (DeRoche & Welsh, 2008). But as long as dietary treatment begins early and continues, children with PKU usually attain an average level of intelligence and have a normal lifespan.

In dominant–recessive inheritance, if we know the genetic makeup of the parents, we can predict the percentage of children in a family who are likely to display or carry a trait. Figure 2.3 illustrates this for PKU. For a child to inherit the condition, each parent must have a recessive allele.

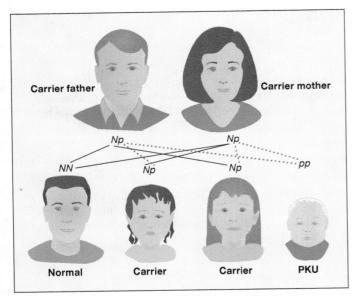

FIGURE 2.3 Dominant–recessive mode of inheritance, as illustrated by PKU. When both parents are heterozygous carriers of the recessive gene *(p),* we can predict that 25 percent of their offspring are likely to be normal *(NN),* 50 percent are likely to be carriers *(Np),* and 25 percent are likely to inherit the disorder *(pp).* Notice that the PKU-affected child, in contrast to his siblings, has light hair. The recessive gene for PKU affects more than one trait. It also leads to fair coloring.

Only rarely are serious diseases due to dominant alleles. Think about why this is so. Children who inherit the dominant allele always develop the disorder. They seldom live long enough to reproduce, so the harmful dominant allele is eliminated from the family's heredity in a single generation. Some dominant disorders, however, do persist. One is *Huntington disease,* a condition in which the central nervous system degenerates. Why has this disorder endured? Its symptoms usually do not appear until age 35 or later, after the person has passed the dominant gene to his or her children.

Incomplete Dominance. In some heterozygous circumstances, the dominant–recessive relationship does not hold completely. Instead, we see **incomplete dominance,** a pattern of inheritance in which both alleles are expressed in the phenotype, resulting in a combined trait, or one that is intermediate between the two.

The *sickle cell trait,* a heterozygous condition present in many black Africans, provides an example. *Sickle cell anemia* (see Table 2.3) occurs in full form when a child inherits two recessive genes. They cause the usually round red blood cells to become sickle (crescent-moon) shaped, especially under low-oxygen conditions. The sickled cells clog the blood vessels and block the flow of blood, causing intense pain, swelling, and tissue damage. Despite medical advances that today allow 85 percent of affected children to survive to adulthood, North Americans with sickle cell anemia have an average life expectancy of only 55 years (Driscoll, 2007). Heterozygous individuals are protected from the disease under most circumstances. However, when they experience oxygen deprivation—for example, at high altitudes or after intense physical exercise—the single recessive allele asserts itself, and a temporary, mild form of the illness occurs.

The sickle cell allele is common among black Africans for a special reason. Carriers of it are more resistant to malaria than are individuals with two alleles for normal red blood cells. In Africa, where malaria is common, these carriers survived and reproduced more frequently than others, leading the gene to be maintained in the black population. But in regions of the world where the risk of malaria is low, the frequency of the gene is declining. For example, only 8 percent of African Americans are carriers, compared with 20 percent of black Africans (National Center for Biotechnology Information, 2007).

X-Linked Inheritance. Males and females have an equal chance of inheriting recessive disorders carried on the autosomes, such as PKU and sickle cell anemia. But when a harmful allele is carried on the X chromosome, **X-linked inheritance** applies. Males are more likely to be affected because their sex chromosomes do not match. In females, any recessive allele on one X chromosome has a good chance of being suppressed by a dominant allele on the other X. But the Y chromosome is only about one-third as long and therefore lacks many corresponding genes to override those on the X. A well-known example is *hemophilia,* a disorder in which the blood fails to clot normally.

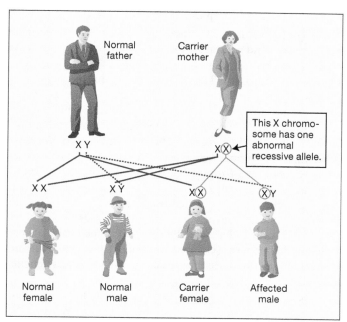

FIGURE 2.4 X-linked inheritance. In the example shown here, the allele on the father's X chromosome is normal. The mother has one normal and one abnormal recessive allele on her X chromosomes. By looking at the possible combinations of the parents' alleles, we can predict that 50 percent of these parents' male children are likely to have the disorder and 50 percent of their female children are likely to be carriers of it.

Figure 2.4 shows its greater likelihood of inheritance by male children whose mothers carry the abnormal allele.

Besides X-linked disorders, many sex differences reveal the male to be at a disadvantage. Rates of miscarriage, infant and childhood deaths, birth defects, learning disabilities, behavior disorders, and mental retardation all are higher for boys (Butler & Meaney, 2005). It is possible that these sex differences can be traced to the genetic code. The female, with two X chromosomes, benefits from a greater variety of genes. Nature, however, seems to have adjusted for the male's disadvantage. Worldwide, about 106 boys are born for every 100 girls, and judging from miscarriage and abortion statistics, an even greater number of males are conceived (United Nations, 2011).

Nevertheless, in recent decades the proportion of male births has declined in many industrialized countries, including the United States, Canada, and European nations (Jongbloet et al., 2001). Some researchers attribute the trend to a rise in stressful living conditions, which heighten spontaneous abortions, especially of male fetuses (Catalano et al., 2010). In support of this hypothesis, a California study spanning the decade of the 1990s revealed that the percentage of male fetal deaths increased in months in which unemployment (a major stressor) also rose above its typical level (Catalano et al., 2009).

Genomic Imprinting. More than 1,000 human characteristics follow the rules of dominant–recessive and incomplete-dominance inheritance (McKusick, 2011). In these cases,

whichever parent contributes a gene to the new individual, the gene responds in the same way. Geneticists, however, have identified some exceptions. In **genomic imprinting,** alleles are *imprinted,* or chemically *marked,* so that one pair member (either the mother's or the father's) is activated, regardless of its makeup (Hirasawa & Feil, 2010). The imprint is often temporary; it may be erased in the next generation, and it may not occur in all individuals.

Imprinting helps us understand certain puzzling genetic patterns. For example, children are more likely to develop diabetes if their father, rather than their mother, suffers from it. And people with asthma or hay fever tend to have mothers, not fathers, with the illness. Imprinting is involved in several childhood cancers and in *Prader-Willi syndrome,* a disorder with symptoms of mental retardation and severe obesity (Butler, 2009). It may also explain why Huntington disease, when inherited from the father, tends to emerge at an earlier age and to progress more rapidly (Gropman & Adams, 2007).

Genomic imprinting can also operate on the sex chromosomes, as *fragile X syndrome*—the most common inherited cause of mental retardation—reveals. In this disorder, which affects about 1 in 4,000 males and 1 in 6,000 females, an abnormal repetition of a sequence of DNA bases occurs on the X chromosome, damaging a particular gene. About 25 to 30 percent of individuals with fragile X syndrome also have symptoms of *autism,* a serious disorder usually diagnosed in early childhood that involves impaired social interaction, delayed or absent language and communication, and repetitive motor behavior (Schwarte, 2008). The defective gene at the fragile site is expressed only when it is passed from mother to child (Hagerman et al., 2009). Because the disorder is X-linked, males are more severely affected.

Mutation. Although less than 3 percent of pregnancies result in the birth of a baby with a hereditary abnormality, these children account for about 20 percent of infant deaths and contribute substantially to lifelong impaired physical and mental functioning (U.S. Department of Health and Human Services, 2010a). How are harmful genes created in the first place? The answer is **mutation,** a sudden but permanent change in a segment of DNA. A mutation may affect only one or two genes, or it may involve many genes, as in the chromosomal disorders we will discuss shortly. Some mutations occur spontaneously, simply by chance. Others are caused by hazardous environmental agents.

Although nonionizing forms of radiation—electromagnetic waves and microwaves—have no demonstrated impact on DNA, ionizing (high-energy) radiation is an established cause of mutation. Women who receive repeated doses before conception are more likely to miscarry or to give birth to children with hereditary defects. The incidence of genetic abnormalities, such as physical malformations and childhood cancer, is also higher in children whose fathers are exposed to radiation in their occupation. However, infrequent and mild exposure to radiation does not cause genetic damage (Jacquet, 2004). Rather, high doses over a long period impair DNA.

The examples just given illustrate *germline mutation,* which takes place in the cells that give rise to gametes. When the affected individual mates, the defective DNA is passed on to the next generation. In a second type, called *somatic mutation,* normal body cells mutate, an event that can occur at any time of life. The DNA defect appears in every cell derived from the affected body cell, eventually becoming widespread enough to cause disease (such as cancer) or disability.

It is easy to see how disorders that run in families can result from germline mutation. But somatic mutation may be involved in these disorders as well. Some people harbor a genetic susceptibility that causes certain body cells to mutate easily in the presence of triggering events (Weiss, 2005). This helps explain why some individuals develop serious illnesses as a result of smoking, exposure to pollutants, or psychological stress, while others do not.

Somatic mutation shows that each of us does not have a single, permanent genotype. Rather, the genetic makeup of each cell can change over time. Somatic mutation increases with age, raising the possibility that it contributes to the age-related rise in disease and to the aging process itself (Salvioli et al., 2008).

Finally, although virtually all mutations that have been studied are harmful, some spontaneous ones (such as the sickle cell allele in malaria-ridden regions of the world) are necessary and desirable. By increasing genetic variation, they help individuals adapt to unexpected environmental challenges. Scientists, however, seldom go looking for mutations that underlie favorable traits, such as an exceptional talent or sturdy immune system. They are far more concerned with identifying and eliminating unfavorable genes that threaten health and survival.

Polygenic Inheritance. So far, we have discussed patterns of inheritance in which people either display a particular trait or do not. These cut-and-dried individual differences are much easier to trace to their genetic origins than are characteristics that vary on a continuum among people, such as height, weight, intelligence, and personality. These traits are due to **polygenic inheritance,** in which many genes influence the characteristic in question. Polygenic inheritance is complex, and much about it is still unknown. In the final section of this chapter, we will discuss how researchers infer the influence of heredity on human attributes when they do not know the precise patterns of inheritance.

Chromosomal Abnormalities

Besides harmful recessive alleles, abnormalities of the chromosomes are a major cause of serious developmental problems. Most chromosomal defects result from mistakes occurring during meiosis, when the ovum and sperm are formed. A chromosome pair does not separate properly, or part of a chromosome breaks off. Because these errors involve far more DNA than problems due to single genes, they usually produce many physical and mental symptoms.

Down Syndrome. The most common chromosomal disorder, occurring in 1 out of every 770 live births, is *Down syndrome.* In 95 percent of cases, it results from a failure of the twenty-first pair of chromosomes to separate during meiosis, so the new individual receives three of these chromosomes rather than the normal two. For this reason, Down syndrome is sometimes called *trisomy 21.* In other, less frequent forms, an extra broken piece of a twenty-first chromosome is attached to another chromosome (called *translocation* pattern). Or an error occurs during the early stages of mitosis, causing some but not all body cells to have the defective chromosomal makeup (called *mosaic* pattern) (U.S. Department of Health and Human Services, 2012a). Because the mosaic type involves less genetic material, symptoms may be less extreme.

The consequences of Down syndrome include mental retardation, memory and speech problems, limited vocabulary, and slow motor development. Affected individuals also have distinct physical features—a short, stocky build, a flattened face, a protruding tongue, almond-shaped eyes, and (in 50 percent of cases) an unusual crease running across the palm of the hand. In addition, infants with Down syndrome are often born with eye cataracts, hearing loss, and heart and intestinal defects (U.S. Department of Health and Human Services, 2012a). Because of medical advances, fewer individuals with Down syndrome die early than was the case in the past. Many survive into their fifties and a few into their sixties to eighties. However, more than half of affected individuals who live past age 40 show symptoms of *Alzheimer's disease,* the most common form of dementia (Wiseman et al., 2009). Genes on chromosome 21 are linked to this disorder.

© ROBIN NELSON/PHOTOEDIT

Despite impaired development, this toddler with Down syndrome benefits from growing up in a stimulating, caring environment. As his physical therapist engages him in water play, he benefits intellectually, physically, and emotionally.

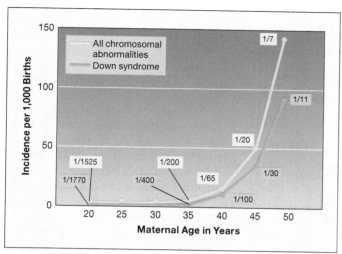

FIGURE 2.5 Risk of Down syndrome and all chromosomal abnormalities by maternal age. Risk rises sharply after age 35. (From R. L. Schonberg & C. J. Tifft, 2007, "Birth Defects and Prenatal Diagnosis," from *Children with Disabilities*, 6/e, M. L. Batshaw, L. Pellegrino, & N. J. Roizen, editors, p. 85. Baltimore: Paul H. Brookes Publishing Co, Inc. Adapted by permission.)

Infants with Down syndrome smile less readily, show poor eye-to-eye contact, have weak muscle tone, and explore objects less persistently (Slonims & McConachie, 2006). But when parents encourage them to engage with their surroundings, Down syndrome children develop more favorably. They also benefit from infant and preschool intervention programs, although emotional, social, and motor skills improve more than intellectual performance (Carr, 2002). Clearly, environmental factors affect how well children with Down syndrome fare.

As Figure 2.5 shows, the risk of bearing a Down syndrome baby rises dramatically with maternal age. But exactly why older mothers are more likely to release ova with meiotic errors is not yet known (Martin, 2008). In about 5 to 10 percent of cases, the extra genetic material originates with the father. Some studies suggest a role for advanced paternal age, while others show no age effects (De Souza, Alberman, & Morris, 2009; Dzurova & Pikhart, 2005; Sherman et al., 2005).

Abnormalities of the Sex Chromosomes. Disorders of the autosomes other than Down syndrome usually disrupt development so severely that miscarriage occurs. When such babies are born, they rarely survive beyond early childhood. In contrast, sex chromosome disorders often are not recognized until adolescence when, in some deviations, puberty is delayed. The most common problems involve the presence of an extra chromosome (either X or Y) or the absence of one X in females.

Research has discredited a variety of myths about individuals with sex chromosome disorders. For example, males with *XYY syndrome* are not necessarily more aggressive and antisocial than XY males. And most children with sex chromosome disorders do not suffer from mental retardation. Rather, their intellectual problems are usually very specific. Verbal difficulties—for

example, with reading and vocabulary—are common among girls with *triple X syndrome* and boys with *Klinefelter syndrome,* both of whom inherit an extra X chromosome. In contrast, girls with *Turner syndrome,* who are missing an X, have trouble with spatial relationships—for example, drawing pictures, telling right from left, following travel directions, and noticing changes in facial expressions (Kesler, 2007; Lawrence et al., 2003; J. L. Simpson et al., 2003). Brain-imaging evidence confirms that adding to or subtracting from the usual number of X chromosomes alters the development of certain brain structures, yielding particular intellectual deficits (Cutter et al., 2006; Itti et al., 2006).

ASK YOURSELF

REVIEW Cite evidence indicating that both heredity and environment contribute to the development of individuals with PKU and Down syndrome.

REVIEW Using your knowledge of X-linked inheritance, explain why males are more vulnerable than females to miscarriage, infant death, genetic disorders, and other problems.

CONNECT Referring to ecological systems theory (Chapter 1, pages 24–27), explain why parents of children with genetic disorders often experience increased stress. What factors, within and beyond the family, can help these parents support their children's development?

APPLY Gilbert's genetic makeup is homozygous for dark hair. Jan's is homozygous for blond hair. What proportion of their children are likely to be dark-haired? Explain.

 Reproductive Choices

Two years after they married, Ted and Marianne gave birth to their first child. Kendra appeared to be a healthy infant, but by 4 months her growth had slowed, and she was diagnosed with Tay-Sachs disease (see Table 2.3 on page 49). When Kendra died at 2 years of age, Ted and Marianne were devastated. Although they did not want to bring another infant into the world who would endure such suffering, they badly wanted to have a child.

In the past, many couples with genetic disorders in their families chose not to bear a child at all rather than risk the birth of an abnormal baby. Today, genetic counseling and prenatal diagnosis help people make informed decisions about conceiving, carrying a pregnancy to term, or adopting a child.

Genetic Counseling

Genetic counseling is a communication process designed to help couples assess their chances of giving birth to a baby with a hereditary disorder and choose the best course of action in view of risks and family goals (Resta et al., 2006). Individuals

Social Issues: Health

The Pros and Cons of Reproductive Technologies

Some couples decide not to risk pregnancy because of a history of genetic disease. Many others—in fact, one-sixth of all couples who try to conceive—discover that they are infertile. And some never-married adults and gay and lesbian partners want to bear children. Today, increasing numbers of individuals are turning to alternative methods of conception—technologies that, although they fulfill the wish for parenthood, have become the subject of heated debate.

Donor Insemination and In Vitro Fertilization

For several decades, *donor insemination*—injection of sperm from an anonymous man into a woman—has been used to overcome male reproductive difficulties. In recent years, it has also permitted women without a male partner to become pregnant. Donor insemination is 70 to 80 percent successful, resulting in about 40,000 deliveries and 52,000 newborn babies in the United States each year (Wright et al., 2008).

In vitro fertilization is another reproductive technology that has become increasingly common. Since the first "test tube" baby was born in England in 1978, 1 percent of all children in developed countries—about 60,000 babies in the United States—have been conceived through this technique annually (Centers for Disease Control and Prevention, 2011e). With in vitro fertilization, a woman is given hormones that stimulate the ripening of several ova. These are removed surgically and placed in a dish of nutrients, to which sperm are added. Once an ovum is fertilized and begins to

duplicate into several cells, it is injected into the mother's uterus.

By mixing and matching gametes, pregnancies can be brought about when either or both partners have a reproductive problem. Usually, in vitro fertilization is used to treat women whose fallopian tubes are permanently damaged. But a recently developed technique permits a single sperm to be injected directly into an ovum, thereby overcoming most male fertility problems. And a "sex sorter" method helps ensure that couples who carry X-linked diseases (which usually affect males) have a daughter. Fertilized ova and sperm can even be frozen and stored in embryo banks for use at some future time, thereby guaranteeing healthy zygotes should age or illness lead to fertility problems.

The overall success rate of in vitro fertilization is about 35 percent. However, success declines steadily with age, from 40 percent in women younger than age 35 to 8 percent in women age 43 and older (Pauli et al., 2009).

Children conceived through these methods may be genetically unrelated to one or both of their parents. In addition, most parents who have used in vitro fertilization do not tell their children about their origins. Does lack of genetic ties or secrecy surrounding these techniques interfere with parent–child relationships? Perhaps because of a strong desire for parenthood, caregiving is actually somewhat warmer for young children conceived through donor insemination or in vitro fertilization. Also, in vitro infants are as securely attached to their parents, and in vitro children and adolescents as well-adjusted, as their counterparts who were naturally conceived

(Golombok et al., 2004; Punamaki, 2006; Wagenaar et al., 2011).

Although reproductive technologies have many benefits, serious questions have arisen about their use. In many countries, including the United States, doctors are not required to keep records of donor characteristics, though information about the child's genetic background might be crucial in the case of serious disease (Adamson, 2005). Another concern is that the in vitro "sex sorter" method will lead to parental sex selection, thereby eroding the moral value that boys and girls are equally precious.

Furthermore, about 50 percent of in vitro procedures result in multiple births. Most are twins, but 9 percent are triplets and higher-order multiples. Consequently, among in vitro babies, the rate of low birth weight is nearly three times as high as in the general population (Wright et al., 2008). Risk of major birth defects also doubles because of many factors, including drugs used to induce ripening of ova and delays in fertilizing the ova outside the womb (Machin, 2005; Neri, Takeuchi, & Palermo, 2008). In sum, in vitro fertilization poses greater risks than natural conception to infant survival and healthy development.

Surrogate Motherhood

An even more controversial form of medically assisted conception is *surrogate motherhood*. In this procedure, in vitro fertilization may be used to impregnate a woman (called a surrogate) with a couple's fertilized ovum. Alternatively, sperm from a man whose partner is infertile may be used to inseminate the surrogate, who agrees to turn the baby over to the natural father. The child is then adopted by his partner. In both cases, the surrogate is paid a fee for her childbearing services.

likely to seek counseling are those who have had difficulties bearing children—for example, repeated miscarriages—or who know that genetic problems exist in their families. In addition, women who delay childbearing past age 35 are often candidates for genetic counseling. After this time, the overall rate of chromosomal abnormalities rises sharply (refer again to Figure 2.5). But because younger mothers give birth in far greater numbers

than older mothers, they bear the majority of babies with genetic defects. Therefore, some experts argue that maternal needs, not age, should determine referral for genetic counseling (Berkowitz, Roberts, & Minkoff, 2006).

If a family history of mental retardation, psychological disorders, physical defects, or inherited diseases exists, the genetic counselor interviews the couple and prepares a *pedigree*,

Although most of these arrangements proceed smoothly, those that end up in court highlight serious risks for all concerned. In one case, both parties rejected the infant with severe disabilities who resulted from the pregnancy. In several others, the surrogate mother wanted to keep the baby, or the couple changed their mind during the pregnancy. These children came into the world in the midst of conflict that threatened to last for years.

Because surrogacy usually involves the wealthy as contractors for infants and the less economically advantaged as surrogates, it may promote exploitation of financially needy women. In addition, most surrogates already have children of their own, and knowledge that their mother would give away a baby may cause these children to worry about the security of their own family circumstances.

Fertility drugs and in vitro fertilization often result in multiple births. These quadruplets are healthy, but babies born with the aid of reproductive technologies are at high risk for low birth weight and major birth defects.

New Reproductive Frontiers

Reproductive technologies are evolving faster than societies can weigh the ethics of these procedures. Doctors have used donor ova from younger women in combination with in vitro fertilization to help postmenopausal women become pregnant. Most recipients are in their forties, but several women in their fifties and sixties, and a few at age 70, have given birth. These cases raise questions about bringing children into the world whose parents may not live to see them reach adulthood. Based on U.S. life expectancy data, 1 in 3 mothers and 1 in 2 fathers having a baby at age 55 will die before their child enters college (U.S. Census Bureau, 2012).

Currently, experts are debating other reproductive options. At donor banks, customers can select ova or sperm on the basis of physical characteristics and even IQ. And scientists are devising ways to alter the DNA of human ova, sperm, and embryos to protect against hereditary disorders—techniques that could be used to engineer other desired characteristics. Many worry that these practices are dangerous steps toward selective breeding through "designer babies"—controlling offspring characteristics by manipulating genetic makeup.

Although new reproductive technologies permit many barren couples to rear healthy newborn babies, laws are needed to regulate such practices. In Australia, New Zealand, Sweden, and Switzerland, individuals conceived with donated gametes have a right to information about their genetic origins (Frith, 2001). Pressure from those working in the field of assisted reproduction may soon lead to a similar policy in the United States. Australia, Canada, and the Netherlands prohibit any genetic alteration of human gametes, with other nations following suit (Isasi, Nguyen, & Knoppers, 2006). But some scientists argue that this total ban is too restrictive because it interferes with serving therapeutic needs.

In the case of surrogate motherhood, the ethical problems are so complex that 11 U.S. states and the District of Columbia have sharply restricted the practice (Human Rights Campaign, 2008). Australia, Canada, and many European nations have banned it, arguing that the status of a baby should not be a matter of commercial arrangement. Denmark, France, and Italy have prohibited in vitro fertilization for women past menopause. At present, little is known about the psychological consequences of being a product of these procedures. Research on how such children grow up, including later-appearing medical conditions and knowledge and feelings about their origins, is important for weighing the pros and cons of these techniques.

a picture of the family tree in which affected relatives are identified. The pedigree is used to estimate the likelihood that parents will have an abnormal child, using the genetic principles discussed earlier in this chapter. For many disorders, molecular genetic analyses (in which DNA is examined) can reveal whether the parent is a carrier of the harmful gene. Carrier detection is possible for all the recessive diseases listed in Table 2.3 on page 49, as well as others, and for fragile X syndrome.

When all the relevant information is in, the genetic counselor helps people consider appropriate options. These include taking a chance and conceiving, choosing from among a variety of reproductive technologies (see the Social Issues: Health box above), or adopting a child.

Prenatal Diagnosis and Fetal Medicine

If couples who might bear an abnormal child decide to conceive, several **prenatal diagnostic methods**—medical procedures that permit detection of developmental problems before birth—are available (see Table 2.4). Women of advanced maternal age are prime candidates for *amniocentesis* or *chorionic villus sampling.* Except for *maternal blood analysis,* however, prenatal diagnosis should not be used routinely because of injury risks to the developing organism.

Prenatal diagnosis has led to advances in fetal medicine. For example, by inserting a needle into the uterus, doctors can administer drugs to the fetus. Surgery has been performed to repair such problems as heart, lung, and diaphragm malformations, urinary tract obstructions, and neural defects. Fetuses with blood disorders have been given blood transfusions. And those with immune deficiencies have received bone marrow transplants that succeeded in creating a normally functioning immune system (Deprest et al., 2010).

These techniques frequently result in complications, the most common being premature labor and miscarriage (Schonberg & Tifft, 2007). Yet parents may be willing to try almost any option, even one with only a slim chance of success. Currently, the medical profession is struggling with how to help parents make informed decisions about fetal surgery.

Advances in *genetic engineering* also offer hope for correcting hereditary defects. As part of the Human Genome Project—an ambitious international research program aimed at deciphering the chemical makeup of human genetic material (genome)— researchers have mapped the sequence of all human DNA base pairs. Using that information, they are "annotating" the genome—identifying all its genes and their functions, including their protein products and what these products do. A major goal is to understand the estimated 4,000 human disorders, those due to single genes and those resulting from a complex interplay of multiple genes and environmental factors.

TABLE 2.4 Prenatal Diagnostic Methods

METHOD	DESCRIPTION
Amniocentesis	The most widely used technique. A hollow needle is inserted through the abdominal wall to obtain a sample of fluid in the uterus. Cells are examined for genetic defects. Can be performed by the 14th week after conception; 1 to 2 more weeks are required for test results. Small risk of miscarriage.
Chorionic villus sampling	A procedure that can be used if results are desired or needed very early in pregnancy. A thin tube is inserted into the uterus through the vagina, or a hollow needle is inserted through the abdominal wall. A small plug of tissue is removed from the end of one or more chorionic villi, the hairlike projections on the chorion, the membrane surrounding the developing organism. Cells are examined for genetic defects. Can be performed at 9 weeks after conception; results are available within 24 hours. Entails a slightly greater risk of miscarriage than amniocentesis. Also associated with a small risk of limb deformities, which increases the earlier the procedure is performed.
Fetoscopy	A small tube with a light source at one end is inserted into the uterus to inspect the fetus for defects of the limbs and face. Also allows a sample of fetal blood to be obtained, permitting diagnosis of such disorders as hemophilia and sickle cell anemia, as well as neural defects (see below). Usually performed between 15 and 18 weeks after conception but can be done as early as 5 weeks. Entails some risk of miscarriage.
Ultrasound	High-frequency sound waves are beamed at the uterus; their reflection is translated into a picture on a video screen that reveals the size, shape, and placement of the fetus. By itself, permits assessment of fetal age, detection of multiple pregnancies, and identification of gross physical defects. Also used to guide amniocentesis, chorionic villus sampling, and fetoscopy. Sometimes combined with magnetic resonance imaging (see page 123 in Chapter 4) to detect physical abnormalities with greater accuracy. When used five or more times, may increase the chances of low birth weight.
Maternal blood analysis	By the second month of pregnancy, some of the developing organism's cells enter the maternal bloodstream. An elevated level of alpha-fetoprotein may indicate kidney disease, abnormal closure of the esophagus, or neural tube defects, such as anencephaly (absence of most of the brain) and spina bifida (bulging of the spinal cord from the spinal column). Isolated cells can be examined for genetic defects.
Ultrafast magnetic resonance imaging (MRI)	Sometimes used as a supplement to ultrasound, where brain or other abnormalities are detected and MRI can provide greater diagnostic accuracy. The ultrafast technique overcomes image blurring due to fetal movements. No evidence of adverse effects.
Preimplantation genetic diagnosis	After in vitro fertilization and duplication of the zygote into a cluster of about 8 to 10 cells, 1 or 2 cells are removed and examined for hereditary defects. Only if that sample is free of detectable genetic disorders is the fertilized ovum implanted in the woman's uterus.

Sources: Hahn & Chitty, 2008; Jokhi & Whitby, 2011; Kumar & O'Brien, 2004; Moore & Persaud, 2008; Sermon, Van Steirteghem, & Liebaers, 2004.

Applying What We Know

Steps Prospective Parents Can Take Before Conception to Increase the Chances of a Healthy Baby

Recommendation	Explanation
Arrange for a physical exam.	A physical exam before conception permits detection of diseases and other medical problems that might reduce fertility, be difficult to treat during pregnancy, or affect the developing organism.
Consider your genetic makeup.	Find out if anyone in your family has had a child with a genetic disease or disability. If so, seek genetic counseling before conception.
Reduce or eliminate toxins under your control.	Because the developing organism is highly sensitive to damaging environmental agents during the early weeks of pregnancy (see Chapter 3), couples trying to conceive should avoid drugs, alcohol, cigarette smoke, radiation, pollution, chemical substances in the home and workplace, and infectious diseases. Furthermore, they should stay away from ionizing radiation and some industrial chemicals that are known to cause mutations.
Ensure proper nutrition.	A doctor-recommended vitamin–mineral supplement, begun before conception, helps prevent many prenatal problems. It should include folic acid, which reduces the chances of neural tube defects, prematurity, and low birth weight (see Chapter 3, page 92).
Consult your doctor after 12 months of unsuccessful efforts at conception.	Long periods of infertility may be due to undiagnosed spontaneous abortions, which can be caused by genetic defects in either partner. If a physical exam reveals a healthy reproductive system, seek genetic counseling.

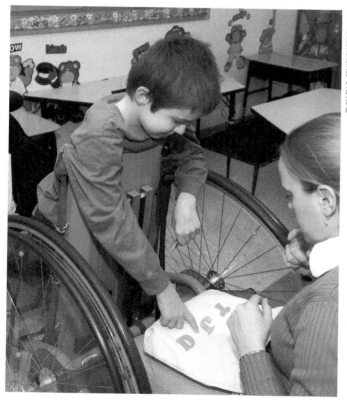

This 10-year-old has Duchenne muscular dystrophy, a hereditary degenerative muscle disease that is likely to lead to early death. In the future, such children may benefit from gene-based treatments for hereditary disorders.

Already, thousands of genes have been identified, including those involved in hundreds of diseases, such as cystic fibrosis; Duchenne muscular dystrophy; Huntington disease; Marfan syndrome; heart, digestive, blood, eye, and nervous system abnormalities; and many forms of cancer (National Institutes of Health, 2012). As a result, new treatments are being explored, such as *gene therapy*—correcting genetic abnormalities by delivering DNA carrying a functional gene to the cells. In recent experiments, gene therapy relieved symptoms in hemophilia patients and in patients with severe immune system dysfunction. A few, however, experienced serious side effects (Gillet et al., 2009). In another approach, called *proteomics,* scientists modify gene-specified proteins involved in biological aging and disease (Van Eyk & Dunn, 2008).

Genetic treatments seem some distance in the future for most single-gene defects, however, and even farther off for diseases involving multiple genes that combine in complex ways with each other and the environment. Applying What We Know above summarizes steps that prospective parents can take before conception to protect the genetic health of their child.

Adoption

Adults who are infertile, who are likely to pass along a genetic disorder, or who are older and single but want a family are turning to adoption in increasing numbers. Those who have children by birth, too, sometimes choose to expand their families through adoption. Adoption agencies try to ensure a good fit

Memuna, adopted at age 6, and her American parents and siblings visit Memuna's extended family in Sierra Leone. Several years earlier, civil-war militia attacks took the lives of Memuna's birth parents. Her adoptive parents are helping her forge an identity that blends her Sierra Leone and U.S backgrounds.

COURTESY OF THE MCSHANE FAMILY

by seeking parents of the same ethnic and religious background as the child and, where possible, trying to choose parents who are the same age as typical biological parents. Because the availability of healthy babies has declined (fewer young unwed mothers give up their babies than in the past), more people in North America and Western Europe are adopting from other countries or accepting children who are past infancy or who have known developmental problems (Schweiger & O'Brien, 2005).

Adopted children and adolescents—whether or not they are born in their adoptive parents' country—tend to have more learning and emotional difficulties than other children, a difference that increases with the child's age at time of adoption (van den Dries et al., 2009; van IJzendoorn, Juffer, & Poelhuis, 2005; Verhulst, 2008). Various explanations exist for adoptees' more problematic childhoods. The biological mother may have been unable to care for the child because of problems believed to be partly genetic, such as alcoholism or severe depression, and may have passed this tendency to her offspring. Or perhaps she experienced stress, poor diet, or inadequate medical care during pregnancy—factors that can affect the child (as we will see in Chapter 3). Furthermore, children adopted after infancy often have a preadoptive history of conflict-ridden family relationships, lack of parental affection, neglect and abuse, or deprived institutional rearing. Finally, adoptive parents and children, who are genetically unrelated, are less alike in intelligence and personality than are biological relatives—differences that may threaten family harmony.

Despite these risks, most adopted children fare well, and those with preexisting problems usually make rapid progress (Arcus & Chambers, 2008; Bimmel et al., 2003). In a study of internationally adopted children in the Netherlands, sensitive maternal care and secure attachment in infancy predicted cognitive and social competence at age 7 (Stams, Juffer, & van IJzendoorn, 2002). And children with troubled family histories who are adopted at older ages generally improve in feelings of trust and affection for their adoptive parents, as they come to feel loved and supported (Veríssimo & Salvaterra, 2006). As we will see in Chapter 4, however, later-adopted children—especially those with multiple early-life adversities—are more likely than their agemates to have persistent cognitive, emotional, and social problems.

By adolescence, adoptees' lives are often complicated by unresolved curiosity about their roots. Some have difficulty accepting the possibility that they may never know their birth parents. Others worry about what they would do if their birth parents suddenly reappeared. Adopted teenagers also face a more challenging process of defining themselves as they try to integrate aspects of their birth family and their adoptive family into their emerging identity. Nevertheless, the decision to search for birth parents is usually postponed until early adulthood, when marriage and childbirth may trigger it.

Despite concerns about their origins, most adoptees appear well-adjusted as adults. When parents have been warm, open, and supportive in their communication about adoption, their children typically forge a positive sense of self (Brodzinsky, 2011). And as long as their parents took steps to help them learn about their heritage in childhood, young people adopted into a different ethnic group or culture generally develop identities that are healthy blends of their birth and rearing backgrounds (Nickman et al., 2005; Thomas & Tessler, 2007).

As we conclude our discussion of reproductive choices, perhaps you are wondering how things turned out for Ted and Marianne. Through genetic counseling, Marianne discovered a history of Tay-Sachs disease on her mother's side of the family. Ted had a distant cousin who died of the disorder. The genetic counselor explained that the chances of giving birth to another affected baby were 1 in 4. Ted and Marianne took the risk. Their son Douglas is now 12 years old. Although Douglas is a carrier of the recessive allele, he is a normal, healthy boy. In a few years, Ted and Marianne will tell Douglas about his genetic history and explain the importance of seeking genetic counseling and testing before he has children of his own.

ASK YOURSELF

REVIEW Why is genetic counseling called a *communication process?* Who should seek it?

CONNECT How does research on adoption reveal resilience? Which factor related to resilience (see Chapter 1, pages 10–11) is central in positive outcomes for adoptees?

APPLY Imagine that you must counsel a couple considering in vitro fertilization using donor ova to overcome infertility. What medical and ethical risks would you raise?

REFLECT Suppose you are a carrier of fragile X syndrome and want to have children. Would you choose pregnancy, adoption, or surrogacy? If you became pregnant, would you opt for prenatal diagnosis? Explain your decisions.

 # Environmental Contexts for Development

Just as complex as genetic inheritance is the surrounding environment—a many-layered set of influences that combine to help or hinder physical and psychological well-being. *TAKE A MOMENT...* Think back to your childhood, and jot down a brief description of events and people that you believe significantly influenced your development. Next, do the same for your adult life. Do the items on your list resemble those of my students, who mostly mention experiences that involve their families? This emphasis is not surprising, since the family is the first and longest-lasting context for development. Other influences that make most students' top ten are friends, neighbors, school, workplace, and community and religious organizations.

Return to Bronfenbrenner's ecological systems theory, discussed in Chapter 1. It emphasizes that environments extending beyond the *microsystem*—the immediate settings just mentioned—powerfully affect development. Indeed, my students rarely mention one important context. Its impact is so pervasive that we seldom stop to think about it in our daily lives. This is the *macrosystem*, or broad social climate of society—its values and programs that support and protect human development. All people need help with the demands of each period of the lifespan—through affordable housing and health care, safe neighborhoods, good schools, well-equipped recreational facilities, and high-quality child care and other services that permit them to meet both work and family responsibilities. And some people, because of poverty or individual tragedies, need considerably more help than others.

In the following sections, we take up these contexts for development. Because they affect every age and aspect of change, we will return to them in later chapters. For now, our discussion emphasizes that environments, as well as heredity, can enhance or create risks for development.

The Family

In power and breadth of influence, no other microsystem context equals the family. The family creates unique bonds among people. Attachments to parents and siblings are usually lifelong and serve as models for relationships in the wider world. Within the family, children learn the language, skills, and social and moral values of their culture. And people of all ages turn to family members for information, assistance, and pleasurable interaction. Warm, gratifying family ties predict physical and psychological health throughout development. In contrast, isolation or alienation from the family is often associated with developmental problems (Deković & Buist, 2005; Parke & Buriel, 2006).

Contemporary researchers view the family as a network of interdependent relationships (Bornstein & Sawyer, 2006; Bronfenbrenner & Morris, 2006). Recall from ecological systems theory that *bidirectional influences* exist in which the behaviors of each family member affect those of others. Indeed, the very term *system* implies that the responses of family members are related. These system influences operate both directly and indirectly.

Direct Influences. The next time you have a chance to observe family members interacting, watch carefully. You are likely to see that kind, patient communication evokes cooperative, harmonious responses, whereas harshness and impatience engender angry, resistive behavior. Each of these reactions, in turn, forges a new link in the interactive chain. In the first instance, a positive message tends to follow; in the second, a negative or avoidant one is likely.

LOOK AND LISTEN

Observe several parent–young child pairs in a context where parents are likely to place limits on children's behavior. How does quality of parent communication seem to influence the child's response? How does the child's response affect the parent's subsequent interaction? ●

These observations fit with a wealth of research on the family system. Studies of families of diverse ethnicities show that when parents are firm but warm, children tend to comply

© LAURA DWIGHT PHOTOGRAPHY

Family relationships are bidirectional, in that each member's behaviors affect those of others. This father's affectionate involvement evokes attentiveness and cooperation from his son, which promote further parental warmth and caring.

with their requests. And when children cooperate, their parents are likely to be warm and gentle in the future. In contrast, children whose parents discipline harshly and impatiently are likely to refuse and rebel. And because children's misbehavior is stressful, parents may increase their use of punishment, leading to more unruliness by the child (Stormshak et al., 2000; Whiteside-Mansell et al., 2003). This principle also applies to other two-person family relationships—siblings, marital partners, parent and adult child. In each case, the behavior of one family member helps sustain a form of interaction in the other that either promotes or undermines psychological well-being.

Indirect Influences. The impact of family relationships on development becomes even more complicated when we consider that interaction between any two members is affected by others present in the setting. Recall from Chapter 1 that Bronfenbrenner calls these indirect influences the effect of *third parties.*

Third parties can serve as supports for or barriers to development. For example, when a marital relationship is warm and considerate, mothers and fathers are more likely to engage in effective **coparenting,** mutually supporting each other's parenting behaviors. Such parents are warmer, praise and stimulate their children more, and nag and scold them less. Effective coparenting, in turn, fosters a positive marital relationship (Morrill et al., 2010). In contrast, parents whose marriage is tense and hostile often interfere with one another's child-rearing efforts, are less responsive to children's needs, and are more likely to criticize, express anger, and punish (Caldera & Lindsey, 2006; McHale et al., 2002b).

Children who are chronically exposed to angry, unresolved parental conflict have serious emotional problems resulting from disrupted emotional security (Cummings & Merrilees, 2010; Schacht, Cummings, & Davies, 2009). These include both *internalizing difficulties* (especially among girls), such as feeling worried and fearful and trying to repair their parents' relationship; and *externalizing difficulties* (especially among boys), including anger and aggression (Cummings, Goeke-Morey, & Papp, 2004). These child problems can further disrupt parents' marital relationship.

Yet even when third parties strain family ties, other members may help restore effective interaction. Grandparents, for example, can promote children's development both directly, by responding warmly to the child, and indirectly, by providing parents with child-rearing advice, models of child-rearing skill, and even financial assistance. Of course, as with any indirect influence, grandparents can sometimes be harmful. When relations between grandparents and parents are quarrelsome, parent–child communication may suffer.

Adapting to Change. Think back to the *chronosystem* in Bronfenbrenner's theory (see page 25 in Chapter 1). The interplay of forces within the family is dynamic and ever-changing. Important events, such as the birth of a baby, a change of jobs, or the addition to the household of an elderly parent in declining health, create challenges that modify existing relationships. The way such events affect family interaction depends on the support other family members provide and on the developmental status of each participant. For example, the arrival of a new baby prompts very different reactions in a toddler than in a school-age child. And caring for an ill elderly parent is more stressful for a middle-aged adult still rearing children than for an adult of the same age who has no child-rearing responsibilities.

Historical time period also contributes to a dynamic family system. In recent decades, a declining birth rate, a high divorce rate, expansion of women's roles, and postponement of parenthood have led to a smaller family size. This, combined with a longer lifespan, means that more generations are alive, with fewer members in the youngest ones, leading to a "top-heavy" family structure. Young people today are more likely to have older relatives than at any time in history—a circumstance that can be enriching as well as a source of tension. In sum, as this complex intergenerational system moves through time, relationships are constantly revised as members adjust to their own and others' development as well as to external pressures.

Nevertheless, some general patterns in family functioning do exist. In the United States and other industrialized nations, one important source of these consistencies is socioeconomic status.

Socioeconomic Status and Family Functioning

People in industrialized nations are stratified on the basis of what they do at work and how much they earn for doing it—factors that determine their social position and economic well-being. Researchers assess a family's standing on this continuum through an index called **socioeconomic status (SES)**, which combines three related, but not completely overlapping, variables: (1) years of education and (2) the prestige of one's job and the skill it requires, both of which measure social status; and (3) income, which measures economic status. As SES rises and falls, people face changing circumstances that profoundly affect family functioning.

SES is linked to timing of marriage and parenthood and to family size. People who work in skilled and semiskilled manual occupations (for example, construction workers, truck drivers, and custodians) tend to marry and have children earlier as well as give birth to more children than people in professional and technical occupations. The two groups also differ in values and expectations. For example, when asked about personal qualities they desire for their children, lower-SES parents tend to emphasize external characteristics, such as obedience, politeness, neatness, and cleanliness. In contrast, higher-SES parents emphasize psychological traits, such as curiosity, happiness, self-direction, and cognitive and social maturity (Duncan & Magnuson, 2003; Hoff, Laursen, & Tardif, 2002; Tudge et al., 2000).

These differences are reflected in family interaction. Parents higher in SES talk to, read to, and otherwise stimulate their infants and preschoolers more. With older children and adolescents, they use more warmth, explanations, and verbal praise; set higher academic and other developmental goals; and allow their children to make more decisions. Commands ("You do that because I told you to"), criticism, and physical punishment all occur more often in low-SES households (Bush & Peterson, 2008; Mandara et al., 2009).

Education contributes substantially to these variations in child rearing. Higher-SES parents' interest in providing verbal stimulation and nurturing inner traits is supported by years of schooling, during which they learned to think about abstract, subjective ideas and, thus, to invest in their children's cognitive and social development (Mistry et al., 2008; Vernon-Feagins et al., 2008). At the same time, greater economic security enables parents to devote more time, energy, and material resources to fostering their children's psychological characteristics (Cheadle & Amato, 2011; Votruba-Drzal, 2003). In contrast, high levels of stress sparked by economic insecurity contribute to low-SES parents' reduced provision of stimulating interaction and activities as well as greater use of coercive discipline (Chin & Phillips, 2004; Conger & Donnellan, 2007). Because of limited education and low social status, many lower-SES parents feel a sense of powerlessness in their relationships beyond the home. At work, for example, they must obey rules of others in positions of authority. When they get home, their parent–child interaction seems to duplicate these experiences—but now they are in authority. Higher-SES parents, in contrast, typically have more control over their own lives. At work, they are used to making independent decisions and convincing others of their point of view. At home, they are more likely to teach these skills to their children (Greenberger, O'Neil, & Nagel, 1994).

Poverty

When families slip into poverty, development is seriously threatened. Consider Zinnia Mae, who grew up in a close-knit black community located in a small southeastern American city (Heath, 1990). As unemployment struck the community and citizens moved away, 16-year-old Zinnia Mae caught a ride to Atlanta. Two years later, she was the mother of a daughter and twin boys, and she had moved into high-rise public housing.

Zinnia Mae worried constantly about scraping together enough money to put food on the table, finding babysitters so she could go to the laundry or grocery, freeing herself from rising debt, and finding the twins' father, who had stopped sending money. The children had only one set meal—breakfast; otherwise, they ate whenever they were hungry or bored. Their play space was limited to the living room sofa and a mattress on the floor. Toys consisted of scraps of a blanket, spoons and food cartons, a small rubber ball, a few plastic cars, and a roller skate abandoned in the building. At a researcher's request, Zinnia Mae agreed to tape record her interactions with her children. Cut off from family and community ties and overwhelmed by financial strain and feelings of helplessness, she found herself unable to join in activities with her children. In 500 hours of tape, she started a conversation with them only 18 times.

Although poverty rates in the United States declined slightly in the 1990s, in recent years they have risen. Today, about 15 percent—46 million Americans—are affected. Those hit hardest are parents under age 25 with young children and older adults who live alone. Poverty is also magnified among ethnic minorities and women. For example, more than 21 percent of U.S. children are poor, a rate that climbs to 32 percent for Hispanic children, 34 percent for Native-American children, and 38 percent for African-American children. For single mothers with preschool children and elderly women on their own, the poverty rate is close to 50 percent (DeNavas-Walt, Proctor, & Smith, 2011; U.S. Census Bureau, 2012).

At a homeless shelter, a mother helps her 7-year-old with a home-work assignment. But many homeless children suffer from developmental delays and emotional stress that interfere with school achievement.

Joblessness, a high divorce rate, a lower remarriage rate among women than men, widowhood, and (as we will see later) inadequate government programs to meet family needs are responsible for these disheartening statistics. The poverty rate is higher among children than any other age group. And of all Western nations, the United States has the highest percentage of extremely poor children. Nearly 10 percent of U.S. children live in deep poverty (at less than half the poverty threshold, the income level judged necessary for a minimum living standard). In contrast, in Denmark, Finland, Norway, and Sweden, child poverty rates have remained at 5 percent or less for two decades, and deep child poverty is rare (UNICEF, 2007, 2010b). The earlier poverty begins, the deeper it is, and the longer it lasts, the more devastating are its effects. Children of poverty are more likely than other children to suffer from lifelong poor physical health, persistent deficits in cognitive development and academic achievement, high school dropout, mental illness, and antisocial behavior (Aber, Jones, & Raver, 2007; Morgan et al., 2009; Ryan, Fauth, & Brooks-Gunn, 2006).

The constant stressors that accompany poverty gradually weaken the family system. Poor families have many daily hassles—bills to pay, the car breaking down, loss of welfare and unemployment payments, something stolen from the house, to name just a few. When daily crises arise, family members become depressed, irritable, and distracted; and hostile interactions increase (Conger & Donnellan, 2007; Kohen et al., 2008).

Negative outcomes are especially severe in single-parent families and families who must live in poor housing and dangerous neighborhoods—conditions that make everyday existence even more difficult, while reducing social supports that help people cope with economic hardship (Hart, Atkins, & Matsuba, 2008; Leventhal & Brooks-Gunn, 2003).

Besides poverty, another problem—one that has become more common in the past 30 years—has reduced the life chances of many children and adults. Approximately 3.5 million people in the United States experience homelessness in a given year. The majority are adults on their own, many of whom suffer from serious mental illness. But about 38 percent of the homeless are children (National Coalition for the Homeless, 2009). The rise in homelessness is mostly due to two factors: a decline in the availability of government-supported, low-cost housing and the release of large numbers of mentally ill people from institutions, without an increase in community treatment programs to help them adjust to ordinary life and get better.

Most homeless families consist of women with children under age 5. Besides health problems (which affect the majority of homeless people), many homeless children suffer from developmental delays and chronic emotional stress due to harsh, insecure daily lives (Pardeck, 2005). An estimated 25 to 30 percent who are old enough do not go to school. Those who do enroll achieve less well than other poverty-stricken children because of poor attendance and health and emotional difficulties (Obradović et al., 2009; Shinn et al., 2008).

Affluence

Despite their advanced education and great material wealth, affluent parents—those in prestigious and high-paying occupations—too often fail to engage in family interaction and parenting that promote favorable development. In several studies, researchers tracked the adjustment of youths growing up in high-SES suburbs (Luthar & Latendresse, 2005a). By seventh grade, many showed serious problems that worsened in high school. Their school grades were poor, and they were more likely than low-SES youths to engage in alcohol and drug use and to report high levels of anxiety and depression (Luthar & Becker, 2002; Luthar & Goldstein, 2008). Furthermore, among affluent (but not low-SES) teenagers, substance use was correlated with anxiety and depression, suggesting that wealthy youths took drugs to self-medicate—a practice that predicts persistent abuse (Luthar & Sexton, 2004).

Why are so many affluent youths troubled? Compared to their better-adjusted counterparts, poorly adjusted affluent young people report less emotional closeness and supervision from their parents, who lead professionally and socially demanding lives. As a group, wealthy parents are nearly as physically and emotionally unavailable to their youngsters as parents coping

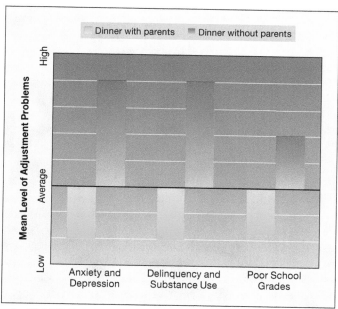

FIGURE 2.6 **Relationship of regularly eating dinner with parents to affluent youths' adjustment problems.** Compared with sixth graders who often ate dinner with their parents, those who rarely did so were far more likely to display anxiety and depression, delinquency and substance use, and poor school grades, even after many other aspects of parenting were controlled. In this study, frequent family mealtimes also protected low-SES youths from delinquency and substance use and from classroom learning problems. (Adapted from Luthar & Latendresse, 2005b.)

with serious financial strain. At the same time, these parents often make excessive demands for achievement (Luthar & Becker, 2002). Adolescents whose parents value their accomplishments more than their character are more likely to have academic and emotional problems.

For both affluent and low-SES youths, a simple routine—eating dinner with parents—is associated with a reduction in adjustment difficulties, even after many other aspects of parenting are controlled (see Figure 2.6) (Luthar & Latendresse, 2005b). Interventions that make wealthy parents aware of the high costs of a competitive lifestyle and minimal family time are badly needed.

Beyond the Family: Neighborhoods, Towns, and Cities

As the concepts of *mesosystem* and *exosystem* in ecological systems theory make clear, connections between family and community are vital for psychological well-being. From our discussion of poverty, perhaps you can see why: In poverty-stricken urban areas, community life is usually disrupted. Families move often, parks and playgrounds are in disarray, and community centers providing organized leisure time activities do not exist. In such neighborhoods, family violence, child abuse and neglect, child and youth internalizing and externalizing difficulties, adult criminal behavior, and depression and declines in cognitive

functioning in older adults are especially high (Aneshensel et al., 2007; Chen, Howard, & Brooks-Gunn, 2011; Dunn, Schaefer-McDaniel, & Ramsay, 2010; Lang et al., 2008). In contrast, strong family ties to the surrounding social context—as indicated by frequent contact with friends and relatives and regular church, synagogue, or mosque attendance—reduce stress and enhance adjustment.

Neighborhoods. Let's look closely at the functions of communities in the lives of children and adults by beginning with the neighborhood. *TAKE A MOMENT...* What were your childhood experiences like in the yards, streets, and parks surrounding your home? How did you spend your time, whom did you get to know, and how important were these moments to you?

Neighborhoods offer resources and social ties that play an important part in children's development. In several studies, low-SES families were randomly assigned vouchers to move out of public housing into neighborhoods varying widely in affluence. Compared with their peers who remained in poverty-stricken areas, children and youths who moved into low-poverty neighborhoods showed substantially better physical and mental health and school achievement (Goering, 2003; Leventhal & Brooks-Gunn, 2003).

Neighborhood resources have a greater impact on economically disadvantaged than well-to-do young people. Higher-SES families are less dependent on their immediate surroundings for social support, education, and leisure pursuits. They can afford to transport their children to lessons and entertainment and, if necessary, to better-quality schools in distant parts of the community. In low-income neighborhoods, in-school and after-school programs that substitute for lack of other resources by providing art, music, sports, scouting, and other enrichment activities are associated with improved academic performance and a reduction in emotional and behavior problems in middle childhood (Peters, Petrunka, & Arnold, 2003; Vandell, Reisner, & Pierce, 2007). Neighborhood organizations and informal social activities contribute to favorable development in adolescence, including increased self-confidence, school achievement, and educational aspirations (Barnes et al., 2007; Gonzales et al., 1996).

Yet in dangerous, disorganized neighborhoods, high-quality activities for children and adolescents are scarce. Even when they are available, crime and social disorder limit young people's access, and parents overwhelmed by financial and other stressors are less likely to encourage their children to participate (Dearing et al., 2009; Dynarski et al., 2004). Thus, the neediest children and youths are especially likely to miss out on these development-enhancing activities.

LOOK AND LISTEN

Ask several parents to list their school-age children's regular lessons and other enrichment activities. Then inquire about home and neighborhood factors that either encourage or impede their children's participation. ●

The Better Beginnings, Better Futures Project of Ontario, Canada, is a government-sponsored set of pilot programs aimed at preventing the dire consequences of neighborhood poverty. The most successful of these efforts, using a local elementary school as its base, provided children with in-class, before- and after-school, and summer enrichment activities. Workers also visited each child's parents regularly, informed them about community resources, and encouraged their involvement in the child's school and neighborhood life. And a communitywide component focused on improving the quality of the neighborhood as a place to live, by offering leadership training and adult education programs and organizing safety initiatives and special events and celebrations (Peters, 2005; Peters, Petrunka, & Arnold, 2003). Evaluations as children reached grades 3, 6, and 9 revealed wide-ranging benefits compared with children and families living in other poverty neighborhoods without this set of programs (Peters et al., 2010). Among these were parents' sense of improved marital satisfaction, family functioning, effective child rearing, and community involvement, and gains in children's academic achievement and social adjustment, including positive relationships with peers and adults and a reduction in emotional and behavior problems.

This 5-year-old enjoys working with volunteers at a community garden sponsored by the Boys & Girls Clubs of America. Neighborhood resources are especially important for the development of economically disadvantaged children and youths.

As these outcomes suggest, neighborhoods also affect adults' well-being. An employed parent who can rely on a caring neighbor or community program for child-rearing assistance and who lives in a safe area gains access to valuable information and services, effective child-rearing role models, and peace of mind essential for productive work. In low-SES areas with high resident stability and social cohesion, where neighbors collaborate in keeping the environment clean and watching out for vandalism and other crimes, adults report less stress, which in turn predicts substantially better physical health (Boardman, 2004; Feldman & Steptoe, 2004).

During late adulthood, neighborhoods become increasingly important because people spend more time in their homes. Despite the availability of planned housing for older adults, about 90 percent remain in regular housing, usually in the same neighborhood where they lived during their working lives (U.S. Census Bureau, 2012b). Proximity to relatives and friends is a significant factor in the decision to move or stay put late in life. In the absence of nearby family members, older adults mention neighbors and nearby friends as resources they rely on most for physical and social support (Hooyman & Kiyak, 2011).

Towns and Cities. Neighborhoods are embedded in towns and cities, which also mold children's and adults' daily lives. In rural areas and small towns, children and youths are more likely to be given important work tasks—caring for livestock, operating the snowplow, or playing in the town band. They usually perform these tasks alongside adults, who instill in them a strong sense of responsibility and teach them practical and social skills needed to sustain their community. Compared with large urban areas, small towns also offer stronger connections between settings that influence children's lives. For example, because most citizens know each other and schools serve as centers of community life, contact between teachers and parents occurs often—an important factor in promoting children's academic achievement (Hill & Taylor, 2004).

Adults in small towns participate in more civic groups, such as school board or volunteer fire brigade. And they are more likely to occupy positions of leadership because a greater proportion of residents are needed to meet community needs (Elder & Conger, 2000). In late adulthood, people residing in small towns and suburbs have neighbors who are more willing to provide assistance. As a result, they form a greater number of warm relationships with nonrelatives.

Of course, small-town residents cannot visit museums, go to professional baseball games, or attend orchestra concerts on a regular basis. The variety of settings is not as great as in a large city. In small towns, however, active involvement in the community is likely to be greater throughout the lifespan. Also, public places in small towns are relatively safe and secure. Responsible adults are present in almost all settings to keep an eye on children and youths. And older adults feel safer—a strong contributor to how satisfied they are with their place of residence (Shields et al., 2002). These conditions are hard to match in today's urban environments.

The Cultural Context

Our discussion in Chapter 1 emphasized that human development can be fully understood only when viewed in its larger cultural context. In the following sections, we expand on this theme by taking up the role of the *macrosystem* in development. First, we discuss ways that cultural values and practices affect environmental contexts for development. Second, we consider how healthy development depends on laws and government programs that shield people from harm and foster their well-being.

Cultural Values and Practices. Cultures shape family interaction and community settings beyond the home—in short, all aspects of daily life. Many of us remain blind to aspects of our own cultural heritage until we see them in relation to the practices of others.

TAKE A MOMENT… Consider the question, Who should be responsible for rearing young children? How would you answer it? Here are some typical responses from my students: "If parents decide to have a baby, then they should be ready to care for it." "Most people are not happy about others intruding into family life." These statements reflect a widely held opinion in the United States—that the care and rearing of children, and paying for that care, are the duty of parents, and only parents. This view has a long history—one in which independence, self-reliance, and the privacy of family life emerged as central American values (Halfon & McLearn, 2002). It is one reason, among others, that the public has been slow to endorse government-supported benefits for all families, such as high-quality child care and paid employment leave for meeting family needs. And it has also contributed to the large number of U.S. families who remain poor, even though family members are gainfully employed (Gruendel & Aber, 2007; UNICEF, 2007, 2010).

Although the culture as a whole may value independence and privacy, not all citizens share the same values. Some belong to **subcultures**—groups of people with beliefs and customs that differ from those of the larger culture. Many ethnic minority groups in the United States have cooperative family structures, which help protect their members from the harmful effects of poverty. As the Cultural Influences box on page 66 indicates, the African-American tradition of **extended-family households,** in which three or more generations live together, is a vital feature of black family life that has enabled its members to survive, despite a long history of prejudice and economic deprivation. Within the extended family, grandparents play meaningful

roles in guiding younger generations; adults who face employment, marital, or child-rearing difficulties receive assistance and emotional support; and caregiving is enhanced for children and the elderly. Active, involved extended families also characterize other minorities, such as Asian, Native-American, and Hispanic subcultures (Becker et al., 2003; Harwood et al., 2002).

Our discussion so far reflects a broad dimension on which cultures and subcultures differ: the extent to which *collectivism* versus *individualism* is emphasized. In **collectivist societies,** people define themselves as part of a group and stress group goals over individual goals. In **individualistic societies,** people think of themselves as separate entities and are largely concerned with their own personal needs (Triandis, 1995, 2005). As these definitions suggest, the two cultural patterns are associated with two distinct views of the self. Collectivist societies value an *interdependent self,* which stresses social harmony, obligations and responsibility to others, and collaborative endeavors. In contrast, individualistic societies value an *independent self,* which emphasizes personal exploration, discovery, achievement, and individual choice in relationships. Both interdependence and independence, in varying mixtures, are part of the makeup of every person (McAdams & Cox, 2010; Tamis-LeMonda et al., 2008). But societies vary greatly in the extent to which they emphasize each alternative and—as later chapters will reveal—instill it in their young.

Although individualism tends to increase as cultures become more complex, cross-national differences remain. The United States is strongly individualistic, whereas most Western European countries lean toward collectivism. As we will see next, collectivist versus individualistic values have a powerful impact on a nation's approach to protecting the well-being of its children, families, and aging citizens.

Public Policies and Lifespan Development. When widespread social problems arise, such as poverty, homelessness, hunger, and disease, nations attempt to solve them through **public policies**—laws and government programs designed to improve current conditions. For example, when poverty increases and families become homeless, a country might decide to build more low-cost housing, provide economic aid to homeowners having difficulty making mortgage payments, raise the minimum wage, and increase welfare benefits. When reports indicate that many children are not achieving well in school, federal and state governments might grant more tax money to school districts, strengthen teacher preparation, and make sure that help reaches children who need it most. And when senior citizens have difficulty making ends meet because of inflation, a nation might increase its social security benefits.

Nevertheless, U.S. public policies safeguarding children and youths have lagged behind policies for older adults. And compared with other industrialized nations, both sets of policies have been especially slow to emerge in the United States.

Cultural Influences

The African-American Extended Family

The African-American extended family can be traced to the African heritage of most black Americans. In many African societies, newly married couples do not start their own households. Instead, they live with a large extended family, which assists its members with all aspects of daily life. This tradition of maintaining a broad network of kin ties traveled to North America during the period of slavery. Since then, it has served as a protective shield against the destructive impact of poverty and racial prejudice on African-American family life. Today, more black than white adults have relatives other than their own children living in the same household. African-American parents also live closer to kin, often establish family-like relationships with friends and neighbors, see more relatives during the week, and perceive them as more important figures in their lives (Boyd-Franklin, 2006; McAdoo & Younge, 2009).

By providing emotional support and sharing essential resources, the African-American extended family helps reduce the stress of poverty and single parenthood. Extended-family members often help with child rearing, and adolescent mothers living in extended families are more likely to complete high school and get a job and less likely to be on welfare than mothers living on their own—factors that in turn benefit children's well-being (Gordon, Chase-Lansdale, & Brooks-Gunn, 2004; Trent & Harlan, 1994).

For single mothers who were very young at the time of their child's birth, extended-family living continues to be associated with more positive mother–child interaction during the preschool years. Otherwise, establishing an independent household with the help of nearby relatives is related to improved child rearing. Perhaps this arrangement permits the more mature teenage mother who has developed effective parenting skills to implement them (Chase-Lansdale, Brooks-Gunn, & Zamsky, 1994). In families rearing adolescents, kinship support increases the likelihood of effective parenting, which is related to adolescents' self-reliance, emotional well-being, and reduced antisocial behavior (Simons et al., 2006; Taylor, 2010).

Finally, the extended family plays an important role in transmitting African-American culture. Compared with nuclear-family households (which include only parents and their children), extended-family arrangements place more emphasis on cooperation and on moral and religious

© JEFF GREENBERG/THE IMAGE WORKS

Three generations celebrate together at a neighborhood festival. Strong bonds with extended family members have helped protect many African-American children against the destructive impact of poverty and racial prejudice.

values. And older black adults, such as grandparents and great-grandparents, regard educating children about their African heritage as especially important (Mosely-Howard & Evans, 2000; Taylor, 2000). Family reunions—sometimes held in grandparents' and great-grandparents' hometowns in the South—are especially common among African Americans, giving young people a strong sense of their roots (Boyd-Franklin, 2006). These influences strengthen family bonds, protect children's development, and increase the chances that the extended-family lifestyle will carry over to the next generation.

Policies for Children, Youths, and Families. We have already seen that although many U.S. children fare well, a large number grow up in environments that threaten their development. As Table 2.5 reveals, the United States does not rank well on any key measure of children's health and well-being.

The problems of children and youths extend beyond the indicators in the table. Despite improved health-care provisions signed into law in 2010, the United States remains the only industrialized nation in the world without a universal, publicly funded health-care system. Approximately 10 percent

TABLE 2.5 **How Does the United States Compare to Other Nations on Indicators of Children's Health and Well-Being?**

INDICATOR	U.S. RANK[a]	SOME COUNTRIES THE UNITED STATES TRAILS
Childhood poverty (among 24 industrialized nations considered)	24th	Canada, Czech Republic, Germany, United Kingdom, Norway, Sweden, Poland, Spain[b]
Infant deaths in the first year of life (worldwide)	28th	Canada, Hong Kong, Ireland, Singapore, Spain
Teenage birth rate (among 28 industrialized nations considered)	28th	Australia, Canada, Czech Republic, Denmark, Hungary, Iceland, Poland, Slovakia
Public expenditure on education as a percentage of gross domestic product[c] (among 22 industrialized nations considered)	12th	Belgium, France, Iceland, New Zealand, Portugal, Spain, Sweden
Public expenditure on early childhood education and child care as a percentage of gross domestic product[c] (among 14 industrialized nations considered)	9th	Austria, Germany, Italy, Netherlands, France, Sweden
Public expenditure on health as a percentage of total health expenditure, public plus private (among 27 industrialized nations considered)	26th	Austria, Australia, Canada, France, Hungary, Iceland, Switzerland, New Zealand

[a]1 = highest, or best, rank.

[b]U.S. childhood poverty and, especially, deep poverty rates greatly exceed poverty in these nations. For example, the poverty rate is 12 percent in the United Kingdoms, 9.5 percent in Canada, 6 percent in the Czech Republic, 4 percent in Norway, and 2.5 percent in Sweden. Deep poverty affects just 2.5 percent of children in Canada, and a fraction of 1 percent in the other countries just listed.

[c]Gross domestic product is the value of all goods and services produced by a nation during a specified time period. It provides an overall measure of a nation's wealth.

Sources: Canada Campaign 2000, 2009; OECD, 2010a, 2010b; U.S. Census Bureau, 2012; U.S. Department of Education, 2012.

of U.S. children—most in low-income families—have no health insurance (Kenney et al., 2010). Furthermore, the United States has been slow to move toward national standards and funding for child care. Affordable care is in short supply, and much of it is substandard in quality (Lamb & Ahnert, 2006; Muenchow & Marsland, 2007). In families affected by divorce, weak enforcement of child support payments heightens poverty in mother-headed households. When non-college-bound young people finish high school, many lack the vocational preparation they need to contribute fully to society. And 8 percent of 16- to 24-year-olds who dropped out of high school have not returned to earn a diploma (U.S. Department of Education, 2012b).

Why have attempts to help children and youths been difficult to realize in the United States? A complex set of political and economic forces is involved. Cultural values of self-reliance and privacy have made government hesitant to become involved in family matters. Furthermore, good social programs are expensive, and they must compete for a fair share of a country's economic resources. Children can easily remain unrecognized in this process because they cannot vote or speak out to protect their own interests, as adult citizens do (Ripple & Zigler, 2003). Instead, they must rely on the goodwill of others to become an important government priority.

Policies for Older Adults. Until well into the twentieth century, the United States had few policies in place to protect its aging population. For example, Social Security benefits, which address the income needs of retired citizens who contributed

to society through prior employment, were not awarded until the late 1930s. Yet most Western nations had social security systems in place a decade or more earlier (Karger & Stoesz, 2010). In the 1960s, U.S. federal spending on programs for older adults expanded rapidly. Medicare, a national health insurance program for older people that pays partial health-care costs, was initiated. But it mainly covers acute care services and requires participants to pay part of those costs, too. This leaves about half of elderly health spending to be covered by supplemental private insurance, government health insurance for the poor, or out-of-pocket payments (U.S. Department of Health and Human Services, 2011g).

Social Security and Medicare consume 96 percent of the U.S. federal budget for the elderly; only 4 percent is devoted to other programs. Consequently, U.S. programs for the aged have been criticized for neglecting social services (Hooyman & Kiyak, 2011). To meet this need, a national network for planning, coordinating, and delivering assistance to the aged has been established. Approximately 630 Area Agencies on Aging operate at regional and local levels, assessing community needs and offering communal and home-delivered meals, self-care education, elder abuse prevention, and a wide range of other social services. But limited funding means that the Area Agencies help far too few people in need.

As noted earlier, many senior citizens—especially women, ethnic minorities, and those living alone—remain in dire economic straits. Those who had interrupted employment histories, held jobs without benefits, or suffered lifelong poverty are

Many U.S. ethnic-minority older adults are poverty-stricken. This Native American, who lives in a remote Alaskan village, depends on an itinerant nurse for routine medical care.

not eligible for Social Security. Although all Americans age 65 and older are guaranteed a minimum income, the guaranteed amount is below the poverty line—the amount judged necessary for bare subsistence by the federal government. Furthermore, Social Security benefits are rarely adequate as a sole source of retirement income; they must be supplemented through other pensions and family savings. But a substantial percentage of U.S. aging citizens do not have access to these resources. Therefore, they are more likely than other age groups to be among the "near poor" (U.S. Department of Health and Human Services, 2010f).

Nevertheless, the U.S. aging population is financially much better off now than in the past. Today, older adults are a large, powerful, well-organized constituency, far more likely than children or low-income families to attract the support of politicians. As a result, the number of aging poor has declined from 1 out of 3 people in 1960 to 1 out of 10 in the early twenty-first century (U.S. Census Bureau, 2012). And senior citizens are healthier and more independent than ever before. Still, as Figure 2.7 shows, aging adults in the United States are less well off than those in many other Western nations, which provide more generous, government-funded income supplements to older adults.

Looking Toward the Future. Despite the worrisome state of many children, families, and aging citizens, efforts are being made to improve their condition. Throughout this book, we will discuss many successful programs that could be expanded. Also, growing awareness of the gap between what we know and what we do to better people's lives has led experts

in developmental science to join with concerned citizens as advocates for more effective policies. As a result, several influential interest groups devoted to the well-being of children or older adults have emerged.

In the United States, the Children's Defense Fund (CDF)—a private, nonprofit organization founded by Marian Wright Edelman in 1973—engages in public education, legal action, drafting of legislation, congressional testimony, and community organizing. It also publishes many reports on U.S. children's condition, government-sponsored programs that serve children and families, and research-based proposals for improving those programs. To learn more about the Children's Defense Fund, visit its website at *www.childrensdefense.org*. Another energetic advocacy organization is the National Center for Children in Poverty, dedicated to advancing the economic security, health, and welfare of U.S. children in low-income families by informing policy makers of relevant research. To explore its activities, visit *www.nccp.org*.

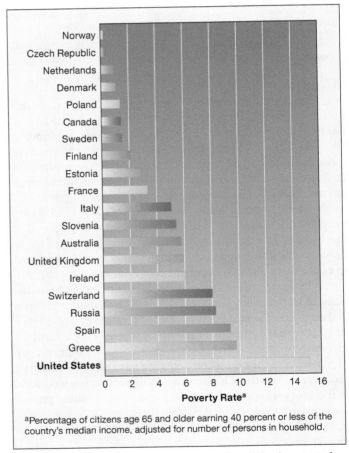

^aPercentage of citizens age 65 and older earning 40 percent or less of the country's median income, adjusted for number of persons in household.

FIGURE 2.7 **Percentage of older adults living in poverty in 20 industrialized nations.** Among the countries listed, the United States has the highest rate of older adults living in poverty. Public expenditures on social security and other income guarantees for senior citizens are far greater in the highly ranked nations than in the United States. (Adapted from Luxembourg Income Study, 2011.)

About half of Americans over age 50, both retired and employed, are members of AARP (originally known as the American Association of Retired Persons). Founded by Ethel Percy Andrus in 1958, AARP has a large and energetic lobbying staff that works for increased government benefits of all kinds for the aged. Every two years, it releases *The Policy Book,* an in-depth compilation of AARP policy positions that form the basis for advocacy activities in diverse areas, including income, health care, social services, housing, and personal and legal rights. Among AARP's programs is an effort to mobilize elderly voters, an initiative that keeps lawmakers highly sensitive to policy proposals affecting older Americans. A description of AARP and its activities can be found at *www.aarp.org.*

Besides strong advocacy, public policies that enhance development depend on policy-relevant research that documents needs and evaluates programs to spark improvements. Today, more researchers are collaborating with community and government agencies to enhance the social relevance of their investigations. They are also doing a better job of disseminating their findings in easily understandable, compelling ways, through reports to government officials, websites aimed at increasing public understanding, and collaborations with the media to ensure accurate and effective reporting in newspaper stories, magazine articles, and radio and television documentaries (Shonkoff & Bales, 2011). In these ways, researchers are helping to create the sense of immediacy about the condition of children, families, and the aged that is necessary to spur a society into action.

At this California resource center, low-income families learn about healthy eating and also receive food. Policy-relevant research helps make the case for programs like this one by documenting pressing needs of children and families.

© DAVID BACON/THE IMAGE WORKS

Understanding the Relationship Between Heredity and Environment

So far in this chapter, we have discussed a wide variety of genetic and environmental influences, each of which has the power to alter the course of development. Yet people who are born into the same family (and who therefore share both genes and environments) are often quite different in characteristics. We also know that some individuals are affected more than others by their homes, neighborhoods, and communities. How do scientists explain the impact of heredity and environment when they seem to work in so many different ways?

Behavioral genetics is a field devoted to uncovering the contributions of nature and nurture to this diversity in human traits and abilities. All contemporary researchers agree that both heredity and environment are involved in every aspect of development. But for polygenic traits (those due to many genes), such as intelligence and personality, scientists are a long way from knowing the precise hereditary influences involved. Although they are making progress in identifying variations in DNA sequences associated with complex traits, so far these genetic markers explain only a small amount of variation in human behavior, and a minority of cases of most psychological disorders (Plomin & Davis, 2009). For the most part, scientists are still limited to investigating the impact of genes on complex characteristics indirectly.

Some believe that it is useful and possible to answer the question of *how much each factor contributes* to differences among people. A growing consensus, however, regards that question as unanswerable. These investigators believe that heredity and environment are inseparable (Gottlieb, Wahlsten, & Lickliter, 2006; Lerner & Overton, 2008). The important question, they maintain, is *how nature and nurture work together.* Let's consider each position in turn.

The Question, "How Much?"

To infer the role of heredity in complex human characteristics, researchers use special methods, the most common being the *heritability estimate.* Let's look closely at the information this procedure yields, along with its limitations.

Heritability. **Heritability estimates** measure the extent to which individual differences in complex traits in a specific population are due to genetic factors. We will take a brief look at heritability findings on intelligence and personality here and will return to them in later chapters, when we consider these topics in greater detail. Heritability estimates are obtained from **kinship studies,** which compare the characteristics of family members. The most common type of kinship study compares identical twins, who share all their genes, with fraternal twins, who, on average, share only half. If people who are genetically more alike are also more similar in intelligence and personality, then the researcher assumes that heredity plays an important role.

Kinship studies of intelligence provide some of the most controversial findings in the field of developmental science. Some experts claim a strong genetic influence, whereas others believe that heredity is barely involved. Currently, most kinship findings support a moderate role for heredity. When many twin studies are examined, correlations between the scores of identical twins are consistently higher than those of fraternal twins. In a summary of more than 10,000 twin pairs, the correlation for intelligence was .86 for identical twins and .60 for fraternal twins (Plomin & Spinath, 2004).

Researchers use a complex statistical procedure to compare these correlations, arriving at a heritability estimate ranging from 0 to 1.00. The value for intelligence is about .50 for child and adolescent twin samples in Western industrialized nations. This suggests that differences in genetic makeup explain half the variation in intelligence. However, heritability increases through middle adulthood, with some estimates as high as .80 (Baird & Bergeman, 2011; Haworth et al., 2010). As we will see later, one explanation is that, compared to children, adults exert greater personal control over their intellectual experiences—for example, how much time they spend reading or solving challenging problems. Adopted children's mental test scores are more strongly related to their biological parents' scores than to those of their adoptive parents, offering further support for the role of heredity (Petrill & Deater-Deckard, 2004).

Heritability research also reveals that genetic factors are important in personality. For frequently studied traits, such as sociability, anxiety, agreeableness, and activity level, heritability estimates obtained on child, adolescent, and young adult twins are moderate, in the .40s and .50s (Caspi & Shiner, 2006; Rothbart & Bates, 2006; Wright et al., 2008). Unlike intelligence, however, heritability of personality does not increase over the lifespan (Heiman et al., 2003; Loehlin et al., 2005).

Twin studies of schizophrenia—a psychological disorder involving delusions and hallucinations, difficulty distinguishing fantasy from reality, and irrational and inappropriate behaviors—consistently yield high heritabilities, around .80. The role of heredity in antisocial behavior and major depression, though still apparent, is less strong, with heritabilities in the .30s and .40s (Faraone, 2008). Again, adoption studies support these results. Biological relatives of schizophrenic and depressed adoptees are more likely than adoptive relatives to share the same disorder (Plomin et al., 2001; Ridenour, 2000; Tienari et al., 2003).

Limitations of Heritability. The accuracy of heritability estimates depends on the extent to which the twin pairs studied reflect genetic and environmental variation in the population. Within a population in which all people have very similar home, school, and community experiences, individual differences in intelligence and personality would be largely genetic, and heritability estimates would be close to 1.00. Conversely, the more environments vary, the more likely they are to account for individual differences, yielding lower heritability estimates. In twin studies, most of the twin pairs are reared together under highly similar conditions. Even when separated twins are available for study, social service agencies have often placed them in advantaged homes that are alike in many ways (Rutter et al.,

Adriana and Tamara, identical twins separated at birth by adoption, were unaware of each other's existence. When they met at age 20, they discovered many similarities—academic achievement, love of dancing, and even taste in clothing. Clearly, heredity contributes to psychological characteristics. Nevertheless, generalizing from twin evidence to the population is controversial.

2001). Because the environments of most twin pairs are less diverse than those of the general population, heritability estimates are likely to exaggerate the role of heredity.

Heritability estimates are controversial measures because they can easily be misapplied. For example, high heritabilities have been used to suggest that ethnic differences in intelligence, such as the poorer performance of black children compared to white children, have a genetic basis (Jensen, 1969, 1998, 2001; Rushton & Jensen, 2005, 2006). Yet this line of reasoning is widely regarded as incorrect. Heritabilities computed on mostly white twin samples do not tell us what causes test score differences between ethnic groups. We have already seen that large economic and cultural differences are involved. In Chapter 9, we will discuss research indicating that when black children are adopted into economically advantaged homes at an early age, their scores are well above average and substantially higher than those of children growing up in impoverished families.

Perhaps the most serious criticism of heritability estimates has to do with their limited usefulness. Though interesting, these statistics give us no precise information on how intelligence and personality develop or how children might respond to environments designed to help them develop as far as possible (Baltes, Lindenberger, & Staudinger, 2006). Indeed, the heritability of children's intelligence increases as parental education and income increase—that is, as children grow up in conditions that allow them to make the most of their genetic endowment. In impoverished environments, children are prevented from realizing their potential. Consequently, enhancing experiences through interventions—such as increasing parent education and income and providing high-quality preschool or child care—has a greater impact on development (Bronfenbrenner & Morris, 2006; Turkheimer et al., 2003).

In sum, although heritability estimates confirm that heredity contributes to a broad array of complex traits, they tell us nothing about how environment can modify genetic influences. Still, scientists often rely on positive heritabilities before initiating more costly molecular analyses in search of specific genes that contribute to personality traits and disorders.

The Question, "How?"

Today, most researchers view development as the result of a dynamic interplay between heredity and environment. How do nature and nurture work together? Several concepts shed light on this question.

Gene–Environment Interaction. The first of these ideas is **gene–environment interaction**, which means that because of their genetic makeup, individuals differ in their responsiveness to qualities of the environment (Rutter, 2011). In other words, people have unique, genetically influenced reactions to particular experiences. Let's explore this idea in Figure 2.8. Gene–environment interaction can apply to any characteristic; here it is illustrated for intelligence. Notice that

when environments vary from extremely unstimulating to highly enriched, Ben's intelligence increases steadily, Linda's rises sharply and then falls off, and Ron's begins to increase only after the environment becomes modestly stimulating.

Gene–environment interaction highlights two important points. First, it shows that because each of us has a unique genetic makeup, we respond differently to the same environment. Notice in Figure 2.8 how a poor environment results in similarly low scores for all three individuals. But when the environment provides a moderate level of stimulation, Linda is by far the best-performing child. And in a highly enriched environment, Ben does best, followed by Ron, both of whom now outperform Linda. Second, sometimes different gene–environment combinations can make two people look the same! For example, if Linda is reared in a minimally stimulating environment, her score will be about 100—average for people in general. Ben and Ron can also obtain this score, but to do so, they must grow up in a fairly enriched home (Gottlieb, Wahlsten, & Lickliter, 2006).

Recently, researchers have made strides in identifying gene–environment interactions in personality development. In Chapter 6 we will see that young children with a gene that increases their risk of an emotionally reactive temperament respond especially strongly to variations in parenting quality (Pluess & Belsky, 2011). When parenting is favorable, they gain control over their emotions and adjust as well or better than other children. But when parenting is unfavorable, they become increasingly irritable, difficult, and poorly adjusted, more so than children not at genetic risk.

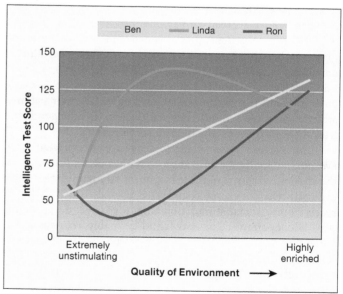

FIGURE 2.8 Gene–environment interaction, illustrated for intelligence by three children who differ in responsiveness to quality of the environment. As environments vary from extremely unstimulating to highly enriched, Ben's intelligence test score increases steadily, Linda's rises sharply and then falls off, and Ron's begins to increase only after the environment becomes modestly stimulating.

Canalization. Another way of understanding how heredity and environment combine comes from the concept of **canalization**—the tendency of heredity to restrict the development of some characteristics to just one or a few outcomes. A behavior that is strongly canalized develops similarly in a wide range of environments; only strong environmental forces can change it (Waddington, 1957). For example, infant perceptual and motor development seems to be strongly canalized because all normal human babies eventually roll over, reach for objects, sit up, crawl, and walk. It takes extreme conditions to modify these behaviors or cause them not to appear. In contrast, intelligence and personality are less strongly canalized; they vary much more with changes in the environment.

When we look at behaviors constrained by heredity, we can see that canalization is highly adaptive. Through it, nature ensures that children will develop certain species-typical skills under many rearing conditions, thereby promoting survival.

Gene–Environment Correlation.

A major problem in trying to separate heredity and environment is that they are often correlated (Rutter, 2011; Scarr & McCartney, 1983). According to the concept of **gene–environment correlation,** our genes influence the environments to which we are exposed. The way this happens changes with age.

Passive and Evocative Correlation. At younger ages, two types of gene–environment correlation are common. The first is called *passive* correlation because the child has no control over it. Early on, parents provide environments influenced by their own heredity. For example, parents who are good athletes emphasize outdoor activities and enroll their children in swimming and gymnastics. Besides being exposed to an "athletic environment," the children may have inherited their parents' athletic ability. As a result, they are likely to become good athletes for both genetic and environmental reasons.

The second type of gene–environment correlation is *evocative*. Children evoke responses that are influenced by the child's heredity, and these responses strengthen the child's original style. For example, an active, friendly baby is likely to receive more social stimulation than a passive, quiet infant. And a cooperative, attentive child probably receives more patient and sensitive interactions from parents than an inattentive, distractible child. In support of this idea, the less genetically alike siblings are, the more their parents treat them differently, in both warmth and negativity. Thus, parents' treatment of identical twins is highly similar, whereas their treatment of fraternal twins and nontwin biological siblings is only moderately so. And little resemblance exists in parents' warm and negative interactions with unrelated stepsiblings (see Figure 2.9) (Reiss, 2003).

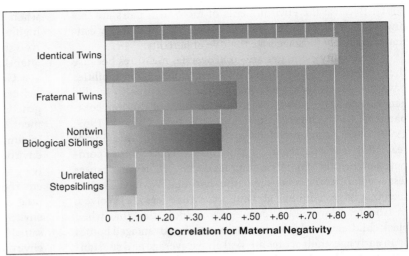

FIGURE 2.9 Similarity in mothers' interactions for pairs of siblings differing in genetic relatedness. The correlations shown are for maternal negativity. The pattern illustrates evocative gene–environment correlation. Identical twins evoke similar maternal treatment because of their identical heredity. As genetic resemblance between siblings declines, the strength of the correlation drops. Mothers vary their interactions as they respond to each child's unique genetic makeup. (Adapted from Reiss, 2003.)

Active Correlation. At older ages, *active* gene–environment correlation becomes common. As children extend their experiences beyond the immediate family and are given the freedom to make more choices, they actively seek environments that fit with their genetic tendencies. The well-coordinated, muscular child spends more time at after-school sports, the musically talented child joins the school orchestra and practices his violin, and the intellectually curious child is a familiar patron at her local library.

This tendency to actively choose environments that complement our heredity is called **niche-picking** (Scarr & McCartney, 1983). Infants and young children cannot do much niche-picking because adults select environments for them. In contrast, older children, adolescents, and adults are increasingly in charge of their environments.

Niche-picking explains why pairs of identical twins reared apart during childhood and later reunited may find, to their surprise, that they have similar hobbies, food preferences, and vocations—a trend that is especially marked when twins' environmental opportunities are similar (Plomin, 1994). Niche-picking also helps us understand why identical twins become somewhat more alike, and fraternal twins and adopted siblings less alike, in intelligence with age (Bouchard, 2004; Loehlin, Horn, & Willerman, 1997). And niche-picking sheds light on why adult identical twins, compared to fraternal twins and other adults, select more similar spouses and best friends—in height, weight, personality, political attitudes, and other characteristics (Rushton & Bons, 2005).

The influence of heredity and environment is not constant but changes over time. With age, genetic factors may become more important in influencing the environments we experience and choose for ourselves.

This mother shares her love of the piano with her daughter, who also may have inherited her mother's musical talent. When heredity and environment are correlated, the influence of one cannot be separated from the influence of the other.

Environmental Influences on Gene Expression.

Notice how, in the concepts just considered, heredity is granted priority. In gene–environment interaction, it affects responsiveness to particular environments. In canalization, it restricts the development of certain behaviors. Similarly, gene–environment correlation is viewed as driven by genetics, in that children's genetic makeup causes them to receive, evoke, or seek experiences that actualize their hereditary tendencies (Plomin, 2009; Rutter, 2011).

A growing number of researchers take issue with the supremacy of heredity, arguing that it does not dictate children's experiences or development in a rigid way. In one study, boys with a genetic tendency toward antisocial behavior (based on the presence of a gene on the X chromosome known to predispose both animals and humans to aggression) were no more aggressive than boys without this gene, *unless* they also had a history of severe child abuse (Caspi et al., 2002). Boys with and without the gene did not differ in their experience of abuse, indicating that the "aggressive genotype" did not increase exposure to abuse. And in a large Finnish adoption study, children whose biological mothers had schizophrenia but who were being reared by healthy adoptive parents showed little mental

illness—no more than a control group with healthy biological and adoptive parents. In contrast, schizophrenia and other psychological impairments piled up in adoptees whose biological and adoptive parents were both disturbed (Tienari et al., 2003; Tienari, Wahlberg, & Wynne, 2006).

Furthermore, parents and other caring adults can *uncouple* unfavorable gene–environment correlations by providing children with positive experiences that modify the expression of heredity, yielding favorable outcomes. For example, in a study that tracked the development of 5-year-old identical twins, pair members tended to resemble each other in level of aggression. And the more aggression they displayed, the more maternal anger and criticism they received (a gene–environment correlation). Nevertheless, some mothers treated their twins differently. When followed up at age 7, twins who had been targets of more maternal negativity engaged in even more antisocial behavior. In contrast, their better-treated, genetically identical counterparts showed a reduction in disruptive acts (Caspi et al., 2004). Good parenting protected them from a spiraling, antisocial course of development.

Accumulating evidence reveals that the relationship between heredity and environment is not a one-way street, from genes to environment to behavior. Rather, like other system influences considered in this and the previous chapter, it is *bidirectional:* Genes affect people's behavior and experiences, but their experiences and behavior also affect gene expression (Diamond, 2009; Gottlieb, 2003; Rutter, 2007). Researchers call this view of the relationship between heredity and environment the *epigenetic framework* (Gottlieb, 1998, 2007). It is depicted in Figure 2.10. **Epigenesis** means development resulting from ongoing, bidirectional exchanges between heredity and all levels of the environment. To illustrate, providing a baby with a

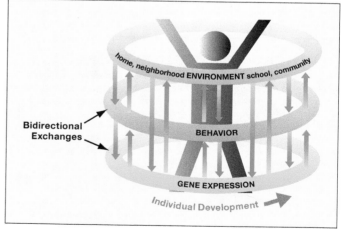

FIGURE 2.10 The epigenetic framework. Development takes place through ongoing, bidirectional exchanges between heredity and all levels of the environment. Genes affect behavior and experiences. Experiences and behavior also affect gene expression. (Adapted from Gottlieb, 2007.)

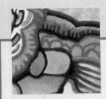

Biology and Environment

A Case of Epigenesis: Smoking During Pregnancy Alters Gene Expression

A wealth of experimental research with animals confirms that environment can modify the genome in ways that have no impact on a gene's sequence of base pairs but nevertheless affect the operation of that gene (Zhang & Meaney, 2010). This epigenetic interplay, in which a gene's impact on the individual's phenotype depends on the gene's context, is now being vigorously investigated in humans.

Maternal smoking during pregnancy is among the risk factors for *attention-deficit hyperactivity disorder (ADHD)*—one of the most common disorders of childhood, which we will take up in greater detail in Chapter 9. ADHD symptoms—inattention, impulsivity, and overactivity—typically result in serious academic and social problems. Some studies report that individuals who are homozygous for a chromosome-5 gene (DD) containing a special repeat of base pairs are at increased risk for ADHD, though other research has not confirmed any role for this gene (Fisher et al., 2002; Gill et al., 1997; Waldman et al., 1998).

Animal evidence suggests that one reason for this inconsistency may be that environmental influences associated with ADHD—such as prenatal exposure to toxins—modify the gene's activity. To test this possibility, researchers recruited several hundred mothers and their 6-month-old babies, obtaining infant blood samples for molecular genetic analysis and asking mothers whether they smoked regularly during pregnancy (Kahn et al., 2003). At a 5-year follow-up, parents responded to a widely used behavior rating scale that assesses children for ADHD symptoms.

Findings revealed that by itself, the DD genotype was unrelated to impulsivity, overactivity, or oppositional behavior. But children whose mothers had smoked during pregnancy scored higher in these behaviors than children of nonsmoking mothers. Furthermore, as Figure 2.11 shows, 5-year-olds with both prenatal nicotine exposure and the DD genotype obtained substantially higher impulsivity, overactivity, and oppositional scores than all other groups—outcomes that persisted even after a variety of other factors (quality of the home environment and maternal ethnicity, marital status, and post-birth smoking) had been controlled.

Another investigation following participants into adolescence yielded similar findings, suggesting that the epigenetic effect persists (Becker et al.,

Because his mother smoked during pregnancy, this baby may be at risk for attention-deficit hyperactivity disorder (ADHD). Prenatal nicotine exposure seems to alter expression of a chromosome-5 gene in ways that greatly heighten impulsivity, overactivity, and oppositional behavior.

2008). What processes might account for it? In animal research, tobacco smoke stimulates the DD genotype to release chemicals in the brain that that promote impulsivity and overactivity (Ernst, Moolchan, & Robinson, 2001). These behaviors, in turn, often evoke harsh, punitive parenting, which triggers defiance in children.

The DD genotype is widespread, present in more than 50 percent of people. Thus, the majority of children prenatally exposed to nicotine are at high risk for learning and behavior problems (refer to page 88 in Chapter 3). Growing evidence indicates that other genes, in epigenetic interplay with as yet unknown environmental factors, also contribute to ADHD symptoms (Hudziak & Rettew, 2009).

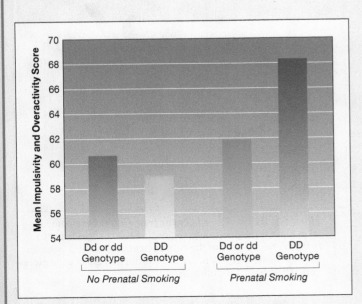

FIGURE 2.11 Combined influence of maternal prenatal smoking and genotype on impulsivity and overactivity at age 5. In the absence of prenatal smoking, 5-year-olds who were homozygous for a chromosome-5 gene (DD) showed no elevation in impulsivity and overactivity (orange bar) compared with children of other genotypes (Dd or dd) (red bar). Among children of all genotypes, prenatal smoking was associated with an increase in these behaviors (green and purple bars). And the combination of prenatal smoking and DD genotype greatly magnified impulsivity and overactivity (purple bar). Children's oppositional behavior followed a similar epigenetic pattern. (Adapted from Kahn et al., 2003.)

healthy diet increases brain growth, leading to new connections between nerve cells, which transform gene expression. This opens the door to new gene–environment exchanges—for example, advanced exploration of objects and interaction with caregivers, which further enhance brain growth and gene expression. These ongoing, bidirectional influences foster cognitive and social development. In contrast, harmful environments can negatively affect gene expression (see the Biology and Environment box on page 74 for an example) (Blair & Raver, 2012). And at times, the impact is so profound that later experiences can do little to change characteristics (such as intelligence and personality) that originally were flexible.

A major reason that researchers are interested in the nature–nurture issue is that they want to improve environments so that people can develop as far as possible. The concept of epigenesis reminds us that development is best understood as a series of complex exchanges between nature and nurture. Although people cannot be changed in any way we might desire, environments can modify genetic influences. The success of any attempt to improve development depends on the characteristics we want to change, the genetic makeup of the individual, and the type and timing of our intervention.

ASK YOURSELF

REVIEW What is epigenesis, and how does it differ from gene–environment interaction and gene–environment correlation? Provide an example of epigenesis.

CONNECT Explain how each of the following concepts supports the conclusion that genetic influences on human characteristics are not constant but change over time: somatic mutation (page 52), niche-picking (page 72), and epigenesis (page 73).

APPLY Bianca's parents are accomplished musicians. At age 4, Bianca began taking piano lessons. By age 10, she was accompanying the school choir. At age 14, she asked to attend a special music high school. Explain how gene–environment correlation promoted Bianca's talent.

REFLECT What aspects of your own development—for example, interests, hobbies, college major, or vocational choice—are probably due to niche-picking? Explain.

SUMMARY

Genetic Foundations (p. 46)

What are genes, and how are they transmitted from one generation to the next?

- Each individual's **phenotype,** or directly observable characteristics, is a product of both **genotype** and environment. **Chromosomes,** rodlike structures within the cell nucleus, contain our hereditary endowment. Along their length are **genes,** segments of **deoxyribonucleic acid (DNA)** that send instructions for making a rich assortment of proteins to the cell's cytoplasm.

- **Gametes,** or sex cells, result from a cell division process called **meiosis,** in which each individual receives a unique set of genes from each parent. Once sperm and ovum unite, the resulting **zygote** starts to develop into a complex human being through cell duplication, or **mitosis.**

- If the fertilizing sperm carries an X chromosome, the child will be a girl; if it contains a Y chromosome, a boy. **Fraternal,** or **dizygotic, twins** result when two ova are released from the mother's ovaries and each is fertilized. **Identical,** or **monozygotic, twins** develop when a zygote divides in two during the early stages of cell duplication.

© F4FOTO/ALAMY

Describe various patterns of genetic inheritance.

- **Homozygous** individuals have two identical **alleles,** or forms of a gene. If the alleles differ, the individual is **heterozygous,** and relationships between the alleles determine the phenotype. In **dominant–recessive inheritance,** only individuals with two recessive alleles display the recessive trait. Heterozygous individuals display only the dominant trait and are **carriers** of the recessive trait. In **incomplete dominance,** both alleles are expressed in the phenotype.

- In **X-linked inheritance,** a harmful allele is carried on the X chromosome and, therefore, is more likely to affect males. In **genomic imprinting,** one parent's allele is activated, regardless of its makeup.

- Harmful genes arise from **mutation,** which can occur spontaneously or be caused by hazardous environmental agents. Germline mutation affects the cells that give rise to gametes; somatic mutation can occur in body cells at any time of life.

- Human traits that vary on a continuum, such as intelligence and personality, result from **polygenic inheritance**—the effects of many genes.

Describe major chromosomal abnormalities, and explain how they occur.

- Most chromosomal abnormalities result from errors during meiosis. The most common, Down syndrome, results in physical defects and mental retardation. **Sex chromosome** disorders, such as XYY, triple X, Klinefelter, and Turner syndromes, are milder than defects of the **autosomes,** usually causing specific intellectual problems but not mental retardation.

Reproductive Choices

(p. 53)

What procedures can assist prospective parents in having healthy children?

- **Genetic counseling** helps couples at risk for giving birth to children with genetic abnormalities decide whether or not to conceive. **Prenatal diagnostic methods** permit early detection of developmental problems.

- Reproductive technologies such as donor insemination, in vitro fertilization, surrogate motherhood, and postmenopausal-assisted childbirth enable individuals to become parents who otherwise would not, but they raise serious legal and ethical concerns.

- Many parents who are infertile or at high risk of transmitting a genetic disorder decide to adopt. Although adopted children have more learning and emotional problems than children in general, most fare well in the long run. Warm, sensitive parenting predicts favorable development.

COURTESY OF THE MCSHANE FAMILY

Environmental Contexts for Development (p. 59)

Describe family functioning from the perspective of ecological systems theory, along with aspects of the environment that support family well-being and development.

- The first and foremost context for development is the family, a dynamic system characterized by bidirectional influences, in which each member's behaviors affect those of others. Both direct and indirect influences operate within the family system, which must continually adjust to new events and changes in its members.

AP IMAGES/JENNI GIRTMAN

- **Socioeconomic status (SES)** profoundly affects family functioning. Higher-SES families tend to be smaller, to emphasize psychological traits, and to engage in warm, verbally stimulating interaction with children. Lower-SES families often stress external characteristics and use more commands, criticism, and physical punishment. Many affluent parents are physically and emotionally unavailable, thereby impairing their children's adjustment. Poverty and homelessness can seriously undermine development.

- Connections between family and community are vital for psychological well-being. Stable, socially cohesive neighborhoods in which residents have access to social support and enrichment activities promote favorable development in both children and adults. Compared with urban environments, small towns foster greater community involvement, warm ties among nonrelatives, and a sense of safety among the elderly.

RICHARD W. RODRIGUEZ/AP IMAGES FOR BOYS & GIRLS CLUBS OF AMERICA

- The values and practices of cultures and **subcultures** affect all aspects of daily life. **Extended-family households,** which are common among many ethnic minority groups, help protect family members from the negative effects of poverty and other stressful life conditions.

- **Collectivist societies,** which emphasize group needs and goals, and **individualistic societies,** which emphasize individual well-being, take different approaches to devising **public policies** to address social problems. Largely because of its strongly individualistic values, U.S. policies safeguarding children and families, as well as those safeguarding older adults, lag behind those of other Western nations.

© DAVID BACON/THE IMAGE WORKS

Understanding the Relationship Between Heredity and Environment

(p. 69)

Explain the various ways heredity and environment may combine to influence complex traits.

- **Behavioral genetics** is a field that examines the contributions of nature and nurture to diversity in human traits and abilities. Researchers use **kinship studies** to compute **heritability estimates,** which measure the extent to which genetic factors influence complex traits such as intelligence and personality. However, the accuracy and usefulness of heritability estimates have been challenged.

- According to the concepts of **gene–environment interaction** and **canalization,** heredity influences each individual's unique response to varying environments. **Gene–environment correlation** and **niche-picking** describe how genes affect the environments to which individuals are exposed. **Epigenesis** reminds us that development is best understood as a series of complex exchanges between heredity and all levels of the environment.

Important Terms and Concepts

allele (p. 48)
autosomes (p. 47)
behavioral genetics (p. 69)
canalization (p. 72)
carrier (p. 48)
chromosomes (p. 46)
collectivist societies (p. 65)
coparenting (p. 60)
deoxyribonucleic acid (DNA) (p. 46)
dominant–recessive inheritance (p. 48)
epigenesis (p. 73)
extended-family household (p. 65)
fraternal, or dizygotic, twins (p. 47)
gametes (p. 46)

gene (p. 46)
gene–environment correlation (p. 72)
gene–environment interaction (p. 71)
genetic counseling (p. 53)
genomic imprinting (p. 51)
genotype (p. 45)
heritability estimate (p. 70)
heterozygous (p. 48)
homozygous (p. 48)
identical, or monozygotic, twins (p. 48)
incomplete dominance (p. 50)
individualistic societies (p. 65)
kinship studies (p. 70)
meiosis (p. 46)

mitosis (p. 46)
mutation (p. 51)
niche-picking (p. 72)
phenotype (p. 45)
polygenic inheritance (p. 52)
prenatal diagnostic methods (p. 56)
public policies (p. 65)
sex chromosomes (p. 47)
socioeconomic status (SES) (p. 61)
subculture (p. 65)
X-linked inheritance (p. 50)
zygote (p. 46)

ELIZABETH FLORES/MCT/NEWSCOM

An expectant mother reacts with amazement on hearing the robust heartbeat of her nearly full-term fetus. High-quality prenatal care and preparation for the events of childbirth enable her to approach labor and delivery with confidence and excitement.

Prenatal Development, Birth, and the Newborn Baby

chapter outline

Prenatal Development

Conception • Period of the Zygote • Period of the Embryo • Period of the Fetus

Prenatal Environmental Influences

Teratogens • Other Maternal Factors • The Importance of Prenatal Health Care

■ **SOCIAL ISSUES: HEALTH** The Nurse–Family Partnership: Reducing Maternal Stress and Enhancing Child Development Through Social Support

Childbirth

The Stages of Childbirth • The Baby's Adaptation to Labor and Delivery • The Newborn Baby's Appearance • Assessing the Newborn's Physical Condition: The Apgar Scale

Approaches to Childbirth

Natural, or Prepared, Childbirth • Home Delivery

Medical Interventions

Fetal Monitoring • Labor and Delivery Medication • Cesarean Delivery

Preterm and Low-Birth-Weight Infants

Preterm versus Small-for-Date Infants • Consequences for Caregiving • Interventions for Preterm Infants

■ **SOCIAL ISSUES: HEALTH** A Cross-National Perspective on Health Care and Other Policies for Parents and Newborn Babies

Birth Complications, Parenting, and Resilience

The Newborn Baby's Capacities

Reflexes • States • Sensory Capacities • Neonatal Behavioral Assessment

■ **BIOLOGY AND ENVIRONMENT** The Mysterious Tragedy of Sudden Infant Death Syndrome

Adjusting to the New Family Unit

When I met Yolanda and Jay one fall in my child development class, Yolanda was just two months pregnant. Approaching age 30, married for several years, and their careers well under way, they had decided to have a baby. To prepare for parenthood, they enrolled in my evening section, arriving once a week after work full of questions: "How does the baby grow before birth?" "When is each organ formed?" "Has its heart begun to beat?" "Can it hear, feel, or sense our presence?"

Most of all, Yolanda and Jay wanted to do everything possible to make sure their baby would be born healthy. Yolanda started to wonder about her diet and whether she should keep up her daily aerobic workout. And she asked me whether an aspirin for a headache, a glass of wine at dinner, or a few cups of coffee during work and study hours might be harmful.

In this chapter, we answer Yolanda and Jay's questions, along with a great many more that scientists have asked about the events before birth. First, we trace prenatal development, paying special attention to environmental supports for healthy growth, as well as damaging influences that threaten the child's health and survival. Next, we turn to the events of childbirth. Today, women in industrialized nations have many choices about where and how they give birth, and hospitals go to great lengths to make the arrival of a new baby a rewarding, family-centered event.

Yolanda and Jay's son Joshua reaped the benefits of his parents' careful attention to his needs during pregnancy. He was strong, alert, and healthy at birth. Nevertheless, the birth process does not always go smoothly. We will consider the pros and cons of medical interventions, such as pain-relieving drugs and surgical deliveries, designed to ease a difficult birth and protect the health of mother and baby. Our discussion also addresses the development of infants born underweight or too early. We conclude with a close look at the remarkable capacities of newborns. ●

ARIEL SKELLEY/GETTY IMAGES/BLEND IMAGES

Prenatal Development

The sperm and ovum that unite to form the new individual are uniquely suited for the task of reproduction. The ovum is a tiny sphere, measuring ¹⁄₁₇₅ inch in diameter—barely visible to the naked eye as a dot the size of the period at the end of this sentence. But in its microscopic world, it is a giant—the largest cell in the human body. The ovum's size makes it a perfect target for the much smaller sperm, which measure only ¹⁄₅₀₀ inch.

Conception

About once every 28 days, in the middle of a woman's menstrual cycle, an ovum bursts from one of her *ovaries,* two walnut-sized organs located deep inside her abdomen, and is drawn into one of two *fallopian tubes*—long, thin structures that lead to the hollow, soft-lined uterus (see Figure 3.1). While the ovum is traveling, the spot on the ovary from which it was released, now called the *corpus luteum,* secretes hormones that prepare the lining of the uterus to receive a fertilized ovum. If pregnancy does not occur, the corpus luteum shrinks, and the lining of the uterus is discarded two weeks later with menstruation.

The male produces sperm in vast numbers—an average of 300 million a day—in the *testes,* two glands located in the *scrotum,* sacs that lie just behind the penis. In the final process of maturation, each sperm develops a tail that permits it to swim long distances, upstream in the female reproductive tract, through the *cervix* (opening of the uterus) and into the fallopian tube, where fertilization usually takes place. The journey is difficult, and many sperm die. Only 300 to 500 reach the ovum, if one happens to be present. Sperm live for up to 6 days and can lie in wait for the ovum, which survives for only 1 day after being released into the fallopian tube. However, most conceptions result from intercourse occurring during a three-day period—on the day of ovulation or during the 2 days preceding it (Wilcox, Weinberg, & Baird, 1995).

With conception, the story of prenatal development begins to unfold. The vast changes that take place during the 38 weeks of pregnancy are usually divided into three phases: (1) the period of the zygote, (2) the period of the embryo, and (3) the period of the fetus. As we look at what happens in each, you may find it useful to refer to Table 3.1, which summarizes milestones of prenatal development.

Period of the Zygote

The period of the zygote lasts about two weeks, from fertilization until the tiny mass of cells drifts down and out of the fallopian tube and attaches itself to the wall of the uterus. The zygote's first cell duplication is long and drawn out; it is not complete until about 30 hours after conception. Gradually, new cells are added at a faster rate. By the fourth day, 60 to 70 cells exist that form a hollow, fluid-filled ball

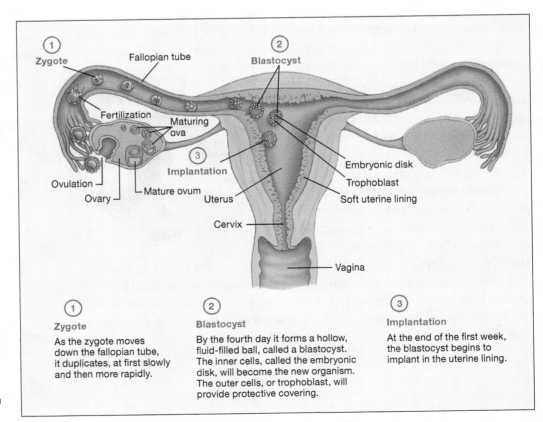

FIGURE 3.1 Female reproductive organs, showing fertilization, early cell duplication, and implantation. (From *Before We Are Born,* 6th ed., by K. L. Moore & T. V. N. Persaud, p. 87. Copyright © 2003, reprinted with permission from Elsevier, Inc.)

① Zygote
As the zygote moves down the fallopian tube, it duplicates, at first slowly and then more rapidly.

② Blastocyst
By the fourth day it forms a hollow, fluid-filled ball, called a blastocyst. The inner cells, called the embryonic disk, will become the new organism. The outer cells, or trophoblast, will provide protective covering.

③ Implantation
At the end of the first week, the blastocyst begins to implant in the uterine lining.

TABLE 3.1
Milestones of Prenatal Development

TRIMESTER	PERIOD	WEEKS	LENGTH AND WEIGHT	MAJOR EVENTS
First	Zygote	1		The one-celled zygote multiplies and forms a blastocyst.
		2		The blastocyst burrows into the uterine lining. Structures that feed and protect the developing organism begin to form—*amnion, chorion, yolk sac, placenta,* and *umbilical cord.*
	Embryo	3–4	¼ inch (6 mm)	A primitive brain and spinal cord appear. Heart, muscles, ribs, backbone, and digestive tract begin to develop.
		5–8	1 inch (2.5 cm); ½ ounce (4 g)	Many external body structures (face, arms, legs, toes, fingers) and internal organs form. The sense of touch begins to develop, and the embryo can move.
	Fetus	9–12	3 inches (7.6 cm); less than 1 ounce (28 g)	Rapid increase in size begins. Nervous system, organs, and muscles become organized and connected, and new behavioral capacities (kicking, thumb sucking, mouth opening, and rehearsal of breathing) appear. External genitals are well-formed, and the fetus's sex is evident.
Second		13–24	12 inches (30 cm); 1.8 pounds (820 g)	The fetus continues to enlarge rapidly. In the middle of this period, fetal movements can be felt by the mother. Vernix and lanugo keep the fetus's skin from chapping in the amniotic fluid. Most of the brain's neurons are in place by 24 weeks. Eyes are sensitive to light, and the fetus reacts to sound.
Third		25–38	20 inches (50 cm); 7.5 pounds (3,400 g)	The fetus has a good chance of survival if born during this time. Size increases. Lungs mature. Rapid brain development causes sensory and behavioral capacities to expand. In the middle of this period, a layer of fat is added under the skin. Antibodies are transmitted from mother to fetus to protect against disease. Most fetuses rotate into an upside-down position in preparation for birth.

Source: Moore, Persaud, & Torchia, 2013.
Photos (from top to bottom): © Claude Cortier/Photo Researchers, Inc.; © G. Moscoso/Photo Researchers, Inc.; © John Watney/Photo Researchers, Inc.; © James Stevenson/Photo Researchers, Inc.; © Lennart Nilsson, *A Child Is Born*/Scanpix.

called a *blastocyst* (refer again to Figure 3.1). The cells on the inside, called the *embryonic disk,* will become the new organism; the outer ring of cells, termed the *trophoblast,* will become the structures that provide protective covering and nourishment.

Implantation. Between the seventh and ninth days, **implantation** occurs: The blastocyst burrows deep into the uterine lining. Surrounded by the woman's nourishing blood, it starts to grow in earnest. At first, the trophoblast (protective outer layer) multiplies fastest. It forms a membrane, called the **amnion,** that encloses the developing organism in *amniotic fluid,* which helps keep the temperature of the prenatal world constant and provides a cushion against any jolts caused by the woman's movement. A *yolk sac* emerges that produces blood cells until the liver, spleen, and bone marrow are mature enough to take over this function (Moore, Persaud, & Torchia, 2013).

The events of these first two weeks are delicate and uncertain. As many as 30 percent of zygotes do not survive this period. In some, the sperm and ovum do not join properly. In others, cell duplication never begins. By preventing implantation in these cases, nature eliminates most prenatal abnormalities (Sadler, 2010).

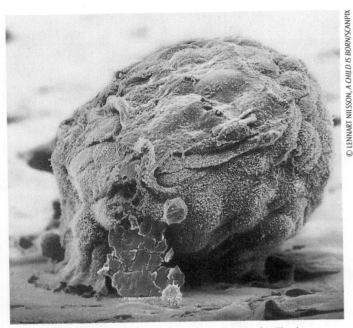

© LENNART NILSSON, *A CHILD IS BORN*/SCANPIX

Period of the zygote: seventh to ninth day. The fertilized ovum duplicates rapidly, forming a hollow ball of cells, or blastocyst, by the fourth day after fertilization. Here the blastocyst, magnified thousands of times, burrows into the uterine lining between the seventh and ninth day.

The Placenta and Umbilical Cord. By the end of the second week, cells of the trophoblast form another protective membrane—the **chorion**, which surrounds the amnion. From the chorion, tiny hairlike *villi*, or blood vessels, emerge.[1] As these villi burrow into the uterine wall, the *placenta* starts to develop. By bringing the embryo's and mother's blood close together, the **placenta** permits food and oxygen to reach the organism and waste products to be carried away. A membrane forms that allows these substances to be exchanged but prevents the mother's and embryo's blood from mixing directly.

The placenta is connected to the developing organism by the **umbilical cord**, which first appears as a tiny stalk and, during the course of pregnancy, grows to a length of 1 to 3 feet. The umbilical cord contains one large vein that delivers blood loaded with nutrients and two arteries that remove waste products. The force of blood flowing through the cord keeps it firm, so it seldom tangles while the embryo, like a space-walking astronaut, floats freely in its fluid-filled chamber (Moore, Persaud, & Torchia, 2013).

By the end of the period of the zygote, the developing organism has found food and shelter. These dramatic beginnings take place before most mothers know they are pregnant.

---

[1]Recall from Table 2.4 on page 56 that *chorionic villus sampling* is the prenatal diagnostic method that can be performed earliest, at nine weeks after conception.

Period of the Embryo

The period of the **embryo** lasts from implantation through the eighth week of pregnancy. During these brief six weeks, the most rapid prenatal changes take place as the groundwork is laid for all body structures and internal organs.

Last Half of the First Month. In the first week of this period, the embryonic disk forms three layers of cells: (1) the *ectoderm*, which will become the nervous system and skin; (2) the *mesoderm*, from which will develop the muscles, skeleton, circulatory system, and other internal organs; and (3) the *endoderm*, which will become the digestive system, lungs, urinary tract, and glands. These three layers give rise to all parts of the body.

At first, the nervous system develops fastest. The ectoderm folds over to form the **neural tube**, or primitive spinal cord. At 3½ weeks, the top swells to form the brain. While the nervous system is developing, the heart begins to pump blood, and the muscles, backbone, ribs, and digestive tract appear. At the end of the first month, the curled embryo—only ¼ inch long—consists of millions of organized groups of cells with specific functions.

The Second Month. In the second month, growth continues rapidly. The eyes, ears, nose, jaw, and neck form. Tiny buds become arms, legs, fingers, and toes. Internal organs are more distinct: The intestines grow, the heart develops separate chambers, and the liver and spleen take over production of blood cells so that the yolk sac is no longer needed. Changing body proportions cause the embryo's posture to become more upright.

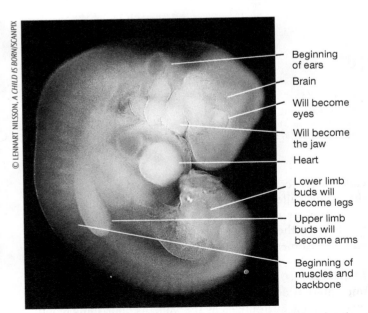

© LENNART NILSSON, *A CHILD IS BORN*/SCANPIX

- Beginning of ears
- Brain
- Will become eyes
- Will become the jaw
- Heart
- Lower limb buds will become legs
- Upper limb buds will become arms
- Beginning of muscles and backbone

Period of the embryo: fourth week. This 4-week-old embryo is only ¼-inch long, but many body structures have begun to form. The primitive tail will disappear by the end of the embryonic period.

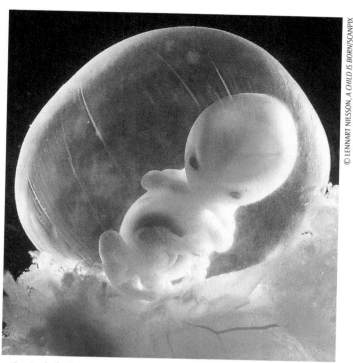

Period of the embryo: seventh week. The embryo's posture is more upright. Body structures—eyes, nose, arms, legs, and internal organs—are more distinct. An embryo this age responds to touch. It can also move, although at less than one inch long and one ounce in weight, it is till too tiny to be felt by the mother.

At 7 weeks, production of *neurons* (nerve cells that store and transmit information) begins deep inside the neural tube at the astounding pace of more than 250,000 per minute (Nelson, 2011). Once formed, neurons begin traveling along tiny threads to their permanent locations, where they will form the major parts of the brain.

At the end of this period, the embryo—about 1 inch long and ¹/₇ ounce in weight—can already sense its world. It responds to touch, particularly in the mouth area and on the soles of the feet. And it can move, although its tiny flutters are still too light to be felt by the mother (Moore, Persaud, & Torchia, 2013).

Period of the Fetus

The period of the **fetus,** from the ninth week to the end of pregnancy, is the longest prenatal period. During this "growth and finishing" phase, the organism increases rapidly in size.

The Third Month. In the third month, the organs, muscles, and nervous system start to become organized and connected. When the brain signals, the fetus kicks, bends its arms, forms a fist, curls its toes, turns its head, opens its mouth, and even sucks its thumb, stretches, and yawns. Body position changes occur as often as 25 times per hour (Einspieler, Marschik, & Prechtl, 2008). The tiny lungs begin to expand and contract in

an early rehearsal of breathing movements. By the twelfth week, the external genitals are well-formed, and the sex of the fetus can be detected with ultrasound (Sadler, 2010). Other finishing touches appear, such as fingernails, toenails, tooth buds, and eyelids. The heartbeat can now be heard through a stethoscope.

Prenatal development is sometimes divided into **trimesters,** or three equal time periods. At the end of the third month, the *first trimester* is complete.

The Second Trimester. By the middle of the second trimester, between 17 and 20 weeks, the new being has grown large enough that the mother can feel its movements. A white, cheeselike substance called **vernix** protects its skin from chapping during the long months spent bathing in the amniotic fluid. White, downy hair called **lanugo** also appears over the entire body, helping the vernix stick to the skin.

At the end of the second trimester, many organs are well-developed. And most of the brain's billions of neurons are in place; few will be produced after this time. However, *glial cells,* which support and feed the neurons, continue to increase rapidly throughout the remaining months of pregnancy, as well as after birth. Consequently, brain weight increases tenfold from the twentieth week until birth (Roelfsema et al., 2004). At the same time, neurons begin forming *synapses,* or connections, at a rapid pace.

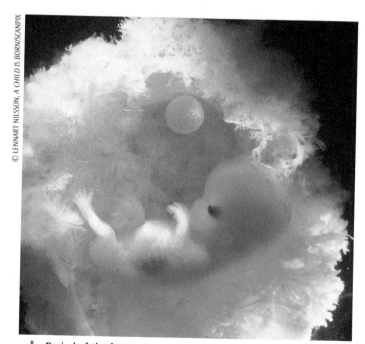

Period of the fetus: eleventh week. The fetus grows rapidly. At 11 weeks, the brain and muscles are better connected. The fetus can kick, bend its arms, and open and close its hands and mouth, and suck its thumb. Notice the yolk sac, which shrinks as the internal organs take over its function of producing blood cells.

Brain growth means new behavioral capacities. The 20-week-old fetus can be stimulated as well as irritated by sounds. And if a doctor looks inside the uterus using fetoscopy (see Table 2.4 on page 56), fetuses try to shield their eyes from the light with their hands, indicating that sight has begun to emerge (Moore, Persaud, & Torchia, 2013). Still, a fetus born at this time cannot survive. Its lungs are immature, and the brain cannot yet control breathing and body temperature.

The Third Trimester. During the final trimester, a fetus born early has a chance for survival. The point at which the baby can first survive, called the **age of viability,** occurs sometime between 22 and 26 weeks (Moore, Persaud, & Torchia, 2013). A baby born between the seventh and eighth months, however, usually needs oxygen assistance to breathe. Although the brain's respiratory center is now mature, tiny air sacs in the lungs are not yet ready to inflate and exchange carbon dioxide for oxygen.

The brain continues to make great strides. The *cerebral cortex,* the seat of human intelligence, enlarges. As neural connectivity and organization improve, the fetus spends more time awake. At 20 weeks, fetal heart rate reveals no periods of alertness. But by 28 weeks, fetuses are awake about 11 percent of the time, a figure that rises to 16 percent just before birth (DiPietro et al., 1996). Between 30 and 34 weeks, fetuses show rhythmic alternations between sleep and wakefulness that gradually increase in organization (Rivkees, 2003). Around this time, synchrony between fetal heart rate and motor activity peaks: A rise in heart rate is usually followed within 5 seconds by a burst of motor activity (DiPietro et al., 2006). These are clear signs that coordinated neural networks are beginning to form in the brain.

By the end of pregnancy, the fetus also takes on the beginnings of a personality. Fetal activity is linked to infant temperament. In one study, more active fetuses during the third trimester became 1-year-olds who could better handle frustration and 2-year-olds who were less fearful, in that they more readily interacted with toys and with an unfamiliar adult in a laboratory (DiPietro et al., 2002). Perhaps fetal activity is an indicator of healthy neurological development, which fosters adaptability in childhood. The relationships just described, however, are only modest. As we will see in Chapter 6, sensitive caregiving can modify the temperaments of children who have difficulty adapting to new experiences.

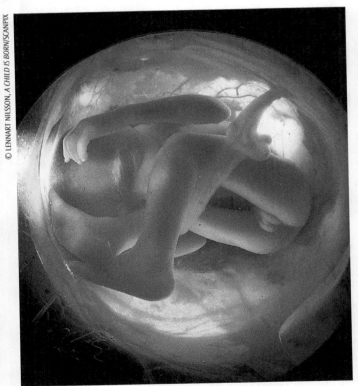

Period of the fetus: twenty-second week. This fetus is almost one foot long and weighs slightly more than one pound. Its movements can be felt easily by the mother and by other family members who place a hand on her abdomen. If born now, the fetus has a slim chance of surviving.

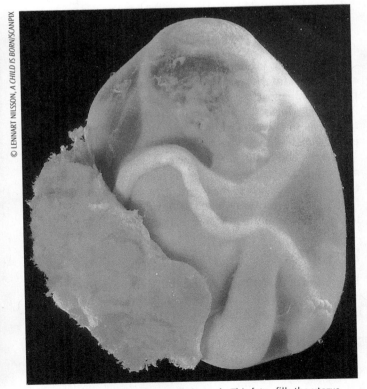

Period of the fetus: thirty-sixth week. This fetus fills the uterus. To nourish it, the umbilical cord and placenta have grown large. Notice the vernix (a cheeselike substance) on the skin, which protects it from chapping. The fetus has accumulated fat to aid temperature regulation after birth. In two more weeks, it will be full-term.

The third trimester brings greater responsiveness to stimulation. Between 23 and 30 weeks, connections form between the cerebral cortex and brain regions involved in pain sensitivity. By this time, painkillers should be used in any surgical procedures (Lee et al., 2005). Around 28 weeks, fetuses blink their eyes in reaction to nearby sounds (Kisilevsky & Low, 1998; Saffran, Werker, & Werner, 2006). And at 30 weeks, fetuses presented with a repeated auditory stimulus against the mother's abdomen initially react with a rise in heart rate and body movements. But over the next 5 to 6 minutes, responsiveness gradually declines, indicating *habituation* (adaptation) to the sound. If the stimulus is reintroduced after a 10-minute delay, heart rate falls off far more quickly (Dirix et al., 2009). This suggests that fetuses can remember for at least a brief period.

Within the next six weeks, fetuses distinguish the tone and rhythm of different voices and sounds. They show systematic heart rate changes to a male versus a female speaker, to the mother's voice versus a stranger's, to a stranger speaking their native language (English) versus a foreign language (Mandarin Chinese), and to a simple familiar melody (descending tones) versus an unfamiliar melody (ascending tones) (Granier-Deferre et al., 2003; Huotilainen et al., 2005; Kisilevsky et al., 2003, 2009; Lecanuet et al., 1993). And in one clever study, mothers read aloud Dr. Seuss's lively book *The Cat in the Hat* for the last six weeks of pregnancy. After birth, their infants learned to turn on recordings of the mother's voice by sucking on nipples. They sucked hardest to hear *The Cat in the Hat*—the sound they had come to know while still in the womb (DeCasper & Spence, 1988).

In the final three months, the fetus gains more than 5 pounds and grows 7 inches. In the eighth month, a layer of fat is added to assist with temperature regulation. The fetus also receives antibodies from the mother's blood that protect against illnesses, since the newborn's own immune system will not work well until several months after birth. In the last weeks, most fetuses assume an upside-down position, partly because of the shape of the uterus and also because the head is heavier than the feet. Growth slows, and birth is about to take place.

ASK YOURSELF

REVIEW Why is the period of the embryo regarded as the most dramatic prenatal period? Why is the period of the fetus called the "growth and finishing" phase?

CONNECT How is brain development related to fetal capacities and behavior?

APPLY Amy, two months pregnant, wonders how the embryo is being fed and what parts of the body have formed. "I don't look pregnant yet, so does that mean not much development has taken place?" she asks. How would you respond to Amy?

Prenatal Environmental Influences

Although the prenatal environment is far more constant than the world outside the womb, many factors can affect the embryo and fetus. Yolanda and Jay learned that parents—and society as a whole—can do a great deal to create a safe environment for development before birth.

Teratogens

The term **teratogen** refers to any environmental agent that causes damage during the prenatal period. Scientists chose this label (from the Greek word *teras*, meaning "malformation" or "monstrosity") because they first learned about harmful prenatal influences from cases in which babies had been profoundly damaged. But the harm done by teratogens is not always simple and straightforward. It depends on the following factors:

- *Dose.* As we discuss particular teratogens, you will see that larger doses over longer time periods usually have more negative effects.

- *Heredity.* The genetic makeup of the mother and the developing organism plays an important role. Some individuals are better able than others to withstand harmful environments.

- *Other negative influences.* The presence of several negative factors at once, such as additional teratogens, poor nutrition, and lack of medical care, can worsen the impact of a harmful agent.

- *Age.* The effects of teratogens vary with the age of the organism at time of exposure. To understand this last idea, think of the *sensitive period* concept introduced in Chapter 1. A sensitive period is a limited time span in which a part of the body or a behavior is biologically prepared to develop rapidly. During that time, it is especially sensitive to its surroundings. If the environment is harmful, then damage occurs, and recovery is difficult and sometimes impossible.

Figure 3.2 on page 86 summarizes prenatal sensitive periods. In the *period of the zygote*, before implantation, teratogens rarely have any impact. If they do, the tiny mass of cells is usually so damaged that it dies. The *embryonic period* is the time when serious defects are most likely to occur because the foundations for all body parts are being laid down. During the *fetal period*, teratogenic damage is usually minor. However, organs such as the brain, ears, eyes, teeth, and genitals can still be strongly affected.

The effects of teratogens go beyond immediate physical damage. Some health effects are delayed and may not show up for decades. Furthermore, psychological consequences may occur indirectly, as a result of physical damage. For example, a defect resulting from drugs the mother took during pregnancy can affect others' reactions to the child as well as the child's

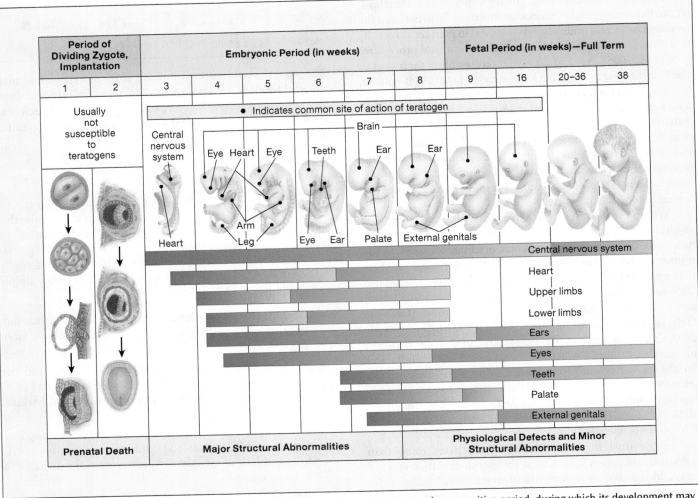

Period of Dividing Zygote, Implantation		Embryonic Period (in weeks)						Fetal Period (in weeks)—Full Term			
1	2	3	4	5	6	7	8	9	16	20–36	38

FIGURE 3.2 Sensitive periods in prenatal development. Each organ or structure has a sensitive period, during which its development may be disturbed. Blue horizontal bars indicate highly sensitive periods. Green horizontal bars indicate periods that are somewhat less sensitive to teratogens, although damage can occur. (Adapted from *Before We Are Born*, 7th ed., by K. L. Moore and T. V. N. Persaud, p. 313. Copyright © 2008, reprinted with permission from Elsevier, Inc.)

ability to explore the environment. Over time, parent–child interaction, peer relations, and cognitive, emotional, and social development may suffer. Furthermore, prenatally exposed children may be less resilient in the face of environmental risks, such as single parenthood, parental emotional disturbance, or maladaptive parenting (Yumoto, Jacobson, & Jacobson, 2008). As a result, their long-term adjustment may be compromised.

Notice how an important idea about development discussed in earlier chapters is at work here: *bidirectional influences* between child and environment. Now let's look at what scientists have discovered about a variety of teratogens.

Prescription and Nonprescription Drugs. In the early 1960s, the world learned a tragic lesson about drugs and prenatal development. At that time, a sedative called *thalidomide* was widely available in Canada, Europe, and South America. When taken by mothers 4 to 6 weeks after conception, thalidomide produced gross deformities of the embryo's arms

and legs and, less frequently, damage to the ears, heart, kidneys, and genitals. About 7,000 infants worldwide were affected (Moore, Persaud, & Torchia, 2013). As children exposed to thalidomide grew older, many scored below average in intelligence. Perhaps the drug damaged the central nervous system directly. Or the child-rearing conditions of these severely deformed youngsters may have impaired their intellectual development.

Another medication, a synthetic hormone called *diethylstilbestrol (DES)*, was widely prescribed between 1945 and 1970 to prevent miscarriages. As daughters of these mothers reached adolescence and young adulthood, they showed unusually high rates of cancer of the vagina, malformations of the uterus, and infertility. When they tried to have children, their pregnancies more often resulted in prematurity, low birth weight, and miscarriage than those of non-DES-exposed women. Young men showed an increased risk of genital abnormalities and cancer of the testes (Goodman, Schorge, & Greene, 2011; Hammes & Laitman, 2003).

Currently, the most widely used potent teratogen is a vitamin A derivative called *Accutane* (known by the generic name *isotretinoin*), prescribed to treat severe acne and taken by hundreds of thousands of women of childbearing age in industrialized nations. Exposure during the first trimester results in eye, ear, skull, brain, heart, and immune system abnormalities (Honein, Paulozzi, & Erickson, 2001). Accutane's packaging warns users to avoid pregnancy by using two methods of birth control, but many women do not heed this advice (Garcia-Bournissen et al., 2008).

Indeed, any drug with a molecule small enough to penetrate the placental barrier can enter the embryonic or fetal bloodstream. Yet many pregnant women continue to take over-the-counter medications without consulting their doctors. Aspirin is one of the most common. Several studies suggest that regular aspirin use is linked to low birth weight, infant death around the time of birth, poorer motor development, and lower intelligence scores in early childhood, although other research fails to confirm these findings (Barr et al., 1990; Kozer et al., 2003; Streissguth et al., 1987). Coffee, tea, cola, and cocoa contain another frequently consumed drug, caffeine. High doses increase the risk of low birth weight (Brent, Christian, & Diener, 2011). And persistent intake of antidepressant medication is linked to an elevated incidence of premature delivery and birth complications, including respiratory distress, and to high blood pressure in infancy (Lund, Pedersen, & Henriksen, 2009; Roca et al., 2011; Udechuku et al., 2010).

Because children's lives are involved, we must take findings like these seriously. At the same time, we cannot be sure that these frequently used drugs actually cause the problems just mentioned. Often mothers take more than one drug. If the embryo or fetus is injured, it is hard to tell which drug might be responsible or whether other factors correlated with drug taking are at fault. Until we have more information, the safest course of action is the one Yolanda took: Avoid these drugs entirely. Unfortunately, many women do not know that they are pregnant during the early weeks of the embryonic period, when exposure to medications (and other teratogens) can be of greatest threat.

Illegal Drugs. The use of highly addictive mood-altering drugs, such as cocaine and heroin, has become more widespread, especially in poverty-stricken inner-city areas, where these drugs provide a temporary escape from a daily life of hopelessness. Nearly 4 percent of U.S. pregnant women take these substances (Substance Abuse and Mental Health Services Administration, 2011).

Babies born to users of cocaine, heroin, or methadone (a less addictive drug used to wean people away from heroin) are at risk for a wide variety of problems, including prematurity, low birth weight, physical defects, breathing difficulties, and death around the time of birth (Bandstra et al., 2010; Howell, Coles, & Kable, 2008; Schuetze & Eiden, 2006). In addition, these infants are born drug-addicted. They are often feverish and irritable and have trouble sleeping, and their cries are abnormally shrill and piercing—a common symptom among stressed newborns (Bauer et al., 2005). When mothers with many problems of their own must care for these babies, who are difficult to calm down, cuddle, and feed, behavior problems are likely to persist.

Throughout the first year, heroin- and methadone-exposed infants are less attentive to the environment than nonexposed babies, and their motor development is slow. After infancy, some children get better, while others remain jittery and inattentive. The kind of parenting they receive may explain why problems persist for some but not for others (Hans & Jeremy, 2001).

Evidence on cocaine suggests that some prenatally exposed babies develop lasting difficulties. Cocaine constricts the blood vessels, causing oxygen delivered to the developing organism to fall for 15 minutes following a high dose. It also can alter the production and functioning of neurons and the chemical balance in the fetus's brain. These effects may contribute to an array of cocaine-associated physical defects, including eye, bone, genital, urinary tract, kidney, and heart deformities; brain hemorrhages and seizures; and severe growth retardation (Covington et al., 2002; Feng, 2005; Salisbury et al., 2009). Several studies report perceptual, motor, attention, memory, language, and impulse-control problems that persist into the preschool and school years (Bandstra et al., 2011; Dennis et al., 2006; Lester & Lagasse, 2010; Linares et al., 2006).

Other investigations, however, reveal no major negative effects of prenatal cocaine exposure (Behnke et al., 2006; Frank et al., 2005; Hurt et al., 2009). These contradictory findings indicate how difficult it is to isolate the precise damage caused by illegal drugs. Cocaine users vary greatly in the amount, potency, and purity of the cocaine they ingest. Also, they often take several drugs, display other high-risk behaviors, suffer from poverty and other stresses, and engage in insensitive caregiving—factors that worsen outcomes for children (Jones,

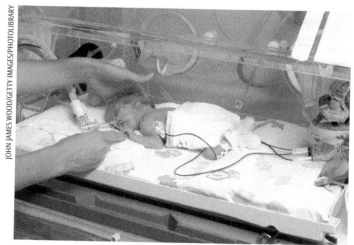

This infant, born many weeks before his due date, breathes with the aid of a respirator. Prematurity and low birth weight can result from a variety of environmental influences during pregnancy, including maternal drug and tobacco use.

2006). But researchers have yet to determine exactly what accounts for findings of cocaine-related damage in some studies but not in others.

Another illegal drug, marijuana, is used more widely than heroin and cocaine. Researchers have linked prenatal marijuana exposure to smaller head size (a measure of brain growth); attention, memory, and academic achievement difficulties; impulsivity and overactivity; and depression as well as anger and aggression in childhood and adolescence (Goldschmidt et al., 2004; Gray et al., 2005; Huizink & Mulder, 2006; Jutras-Aswad et al., 2009). As with cocaine, however, lasting consequences are not well-established. Overall, the effects of illegal drugs are far less consistent than the impact of two legal substances to which we now turn: tobacco and alcohol.

Tobacco. Although smoking has declined in Western nations, an estimated 14 percent of U.S. women smoke during their pregnancies (Tong et al., 2009). The best-known effect of smoking during the prenatal period is low birth weight. But the likelihood of other serious consequences, such as miscarriage, prematurity, cleft lip and palate, blood vessel abnormalities, impaired heart rate and breathing during sleep, infant death, and asthma and cancer later in childhood, also increases (Geerts et al., 2012; Howell, Coles, & Kable, 2008; Jaakkola & Gissler, 2004; Mossey et al., 2009). The more cigarettes a mother smokes, the greater the chances that her baby will be affected. And if a pregnant woman stops smoking at any time, even during the third trimester, she reduces the likelihood that her infant will be born underweight and suffer from future problems (Klesges et al., 2001).

Even when a baby of a smoking mother appears to be born in good physical condition, slight behavioral abnormalities may threaten the child's development. Newborns of smoking mothers are less attentive to sounds, display more muscle tension, are more excitable when touched and visually stimulated, and more often have colic (persistent crying). These findings suggest subtle negative effects on brain development (Law et al., 2003; Sondergaard et al., 2002). Consistent with this view, prenatally exposed children and adolescents tend to have shorter attention spans, difficulties with impulsivity and overactivity, poorer memories, lower mental test scores, and higher levels of disruptive, aggressive behavior (Espy et al., 2011; Fryer, Crocker, & Mattson, 2008; Lindblad & Hjern, 2010).

Exactly how can smoking harm the fetus? Nicotine, the addictive substance in tobacco, constricts blood vessels, lessens blood flow to the uterus, and causes the placenta to grow abnormally. This reduces the transfer of nutrients, so the fetus gains weight poorly. Also, nicotine raises the concentration of carbon monoxide in the bloodstreams of both mother and fetus. Carbon monoxide displaces oxygen from red blood cells, damaging the central nervous system and slowing body growth in the fetuses of laboratory animals (Friedman, 1996). Similar effects may occur in humans.

From one-third to one-half of nonsmoking pregnant women are "passive smokers" because their husbands, relatives, or co-workers use cigarettes. Passive smoking is also related to low birth weight, infant death, childhood respiratory illnesses, and possible long-term attention, learning, and behavior problems (Best, 2009; Pattenden et al., 2006). Clearly, expectant mothers should avoid smoke-filled environments.

Alcohol. In his moving book *The Broken Cord*, Michael Dorris (1989), a Dartmouth College anthropology professor, described what it was like to rear his adopted son Abel (called Adam in the book), whose biological mother drank heavily throughout pregnancy and died of alcohol poisoning shortly after his birth. A Sioux Indian, Abel was born with **fetal alcohol spectrum disorder (FASD)**, a term that encompasses a range of physical, mental, and behavioral outcomes caused by prenatal alcohol exposure. Children with FASD are given one of three diagnoses, which vary in severity:

1. **Fetal alcohol syndrome (FAS),** distinguished by (a) slow physical growth, (b) a pattern of three facial abnormalities (short eyelid openings; a thin upper lip; a smooth or flattened philtrum, or indentation running from the bottom of the nose to the center of the upper lip), and (c) brain injury,

Left photo: This 5-year-old's mother drank heavily during pregnancy. Her widely spaced eyes, thin upper lip, and flattened philtrum are typical of fetal alcohol syndrome (FAS). *Right photo:* This 12-year-old has the small head and facial abnormalities of FAS. She also shows the mental impairments and slow growth that accompany the disorder.

evident in a small head and impairment in at least three areas of functioning—for example, memory, language and communication, attention span and activity level (overactivity), planning and reasoning, motor coordination, or social skills. Other defects—of the eyes, ears, nose, throat, heart, genitals, urinary tract, or immune system—may also be present. Abel was diagnosed as having FAS. As is typical for this disorder, his mother drank heavily throughout pregnancy.

2. **Partial fetal alcohol syndrome (p-FAS),** characterized by (a) two of the three facial abnormalities just mentioned and (b) brain injury, again evident in at least three areas of impaired functioning. Mothers of children with p-FAS generally drank alcohol in smaller quantities, and children's defects vary with the timing and length of alcohol exposure. Furthermore, recent evidence suggests that paternal alcohol use around the time of conception can alter gene expression (see page 73 in Chapter 2), thereby contributing to symptoms (Ouko et al., 2009).

3. **Alcohol-related neurodevelopmental disorder (ARND),** in which at least three areas of mental functioning are impaired, despite typical physical growth and absence of facial abnormalities. Again, prenatal alcohol exposure, though confirmed, is less pervasive than in FAS (Chudley et al., 2005; Loock et al., 2005).

Even when provided with enriched diets, FAS babies fail to catch up in physical size during infancy and childhood. Mental impairment associated with all three FASD diagnoses is also permanent: In his teens and twenties, Abel Dorris had trouble concentrating and keeping a routine job, and he suffered from poor judgment. For example, he would buy something and not wait for change or would wander off in the middle of a task. He died at age 23, after being hit by a car.

The more alcohol a woman consumes during pregnancy, the poorer the child's motor coordination, speed of information processing, reasoning, and intelligence and achievement test scores during the preschool and school years (Burden, Jacobson, & Jacobson, 2005; Korkman, Kettunen, & Autti-Raemoe, 2003; Mattson, Calarco, & Lang, 2006). In adolescence and early adulthood, FASD is associated with persisting attention and motor-coordination deficits, poor school performance, trouble with the law, inappropriate social and sexual behaviors, alcohol and drug abuse, and lasting mental health problems, including depression and high emotional reactivity to stress (Barr et al., 2006; Fryer, Crocker, & Mattson, 2008; Hellemans et al., 2010; Howell et al., 2006; Streissguth et al., 2004).

How does alcohol produce its devastating effects? First, it interferes with production and migration of neurons in the primitive neural tube. Brain-imaging research reveals reduced brain size, damage to many brain structures, and abnormalities in brain functioning, including the electrical and chemical activity involved in transferring messages from one part of the brain to another (Coles et al., 2011; Haycock, 2009). Second, the body uses large quantities of oxygen to metabolize alcohol. A pregnant woman's heavy drinking draws away oxygen that the developing organism needs for cell growth.

About 25 percent of U.S. mothers report drinking at some time during their pregnancies. As with heroin and cocaine, alcohol abuse is higher in poverty-stricken women. On some Native-American reservations, the incidence of FAS is as high as 10 to 20 percent (Szlemko, Wood, & Thurman, 2006; Tong et al., 2009). Unfortunately, when affected girls later become pregnant, the poor judgment caused by the syndrome often prevents them from understanding why they themselves should avoid alcohol. Thus, the tragic cycle is likely to be repeated in the next generation.

How much alcohol is safe during pregnancy? Even mild drinking, less than one drink per day, is associated with reduced head size and body growth among children followed into adolescence (Jacobson et al., 2004; Martinez-Frias et al., 2004). Recall that other factors—both genetic and environmental—can make some fetuses more vulnerable to teratogens. Therefore, no amount of alcohol is safe. Couples planning a pregnancy and expectant mothers should avoid alcohol entirely.

Radiation. Defects due to ionizing radiation were tragically apparent in children born to pregnant women who survived the bombing of Hiroshima and Nagasaki during World War II. Similar abnormalities surfaced in the nine months following the 1986 Chernobyl, Ukraine, nuclear power plant accident. After each disaster, the incidence of miscarriage and babies born with underdeveloped brains, physical deformities, and slow physical growth rose dramatically (Double et al., 2011; Schull, 2003). Evacuation of residents in areas near the Japanese

© CAROLINE PENN/CORBIS

This child's deformities are linked to radiation exposure early in pregnancy, caused by the Chernobyl nuclear power plant disaster in 1986. She is also at risk for low intelligence and language and emotional disorders.

nuclear facility damaged by the March 2011 earthquake and tsunami was intended to prevent these devastating outcomes.

Even when a radiation-exposed baby seems normal, problems may appear later. For example, even low-level radiation, resulting from industrial leakage or medical X-rays, can increase the risk of childhood cancer (Fattibene et al., 1999). In middle childhood, prenatally exposed Chernobyl children had abnormal brain-wave activity, lower intelligence test scores, and rates of language and emotional disorders two to three times greater than those of nonexposed Russian children. Furthermore, the more tension parents reported, due to forced evacuation from their homes and worries about living in irradiated areas, the poorer their children's emotional functioning (Loganovskaja & Loganovsky, 1999; Loganovsky et al., 2008). Stressful rearing conditions seemed to combine with the damaging effects of prenatal radiation to impair children's development.

Environmental Pollution. In industrialized nations, an astounding number of potentially dangerous chemicals are released into the environment. More than 75,000 are in common use in the United States, and many new pollutants are introduced each year. When 10 newborns were randomly selected from U.S. hospitals for analysis of umbilical cord blood, researchers uncovered a startling array of industrial contaminants—287 in all (Houlihan et al., 2005). They concluded that many babies are "born polluted" by chemicals that not only impair prenatal development but increase the chances of health problems and life-threatening diseases later on.

Certain pollutants cause severe prenatal damage. In the 1950s, an industrial plant released waste containing high levels of *mercury* into a bay providing seafood and water for the town of Minamata, Japan. Many children born at the time displayed physical deformities, mental retardation, abnormal speech, difficulty in chewing and swallowing, and uncoordinated movements. High levels of prenatal mercury exposure disrupt production and migration of neurons, causing widespread brain damage (Clarkson, Magos, & Myers, 2003; Hubbs-Tait et al., 2005). Prenatal mercury exposure from maternal seafood diets predicts deficits in speed of cognitive processing and motor, attention, and verbal test performance during the school years (Boucher et al., 2010; Debes et al., 2006). Pregnant women are wise to avoid eating long-lived predatory fish, such as swordfish, albacore tuna, and shark, which are heavily contaminated with mercury.

For many years, *polychlorinated biphenyls (PCBs)* were used to insulate electrical equipment until research showed that, like mercury, they entered waterways and the food supply. In Taiwan, prenatal exposure to high levels of PCBs in rice oil resulted in low birth weight, discolored skin, deformities of the gums and nails, brain-wave abnormalities, and delayed cognitive development (Chen & Hsu, 1994; Chen et al., 1994). Steady, low-level PCB exposure is also harmful. Women who frequently ate PCB-contaminated fish, compared with those who ate little or no fish, had infants with lower birth weights, smaller heads, persisting attention and memory difficulties, and

lower intelligence test scores in childhood (Boucher, Muckle, & Bastien, 2009; Jacobson & Jacobson, 2003; Stewart et al., 2008).

Another teratogen, *lead,* is present in paint flaking off the walls of old buildings and in certain materials used in industrial occupations. High levels of prenatal lead exposure are related to prematurity, low birth weight, brain damage, and a wide variety of physical defects. Even at low levels, affected infants and children show slightly poorer mental and motor development (Bellinger, 2005; Jedrychowski et al., 2009).

Finally, prenatal exposure to dioxins—toxic compounds resulting from incineration—is linked to brain, immune system, and thyroid damage in babies and to an increased incidence of breast and uterine cancers in women, perhaps through altering hormone levels (ten Tusscher & Koppe, 2004). Even tiny amounts of dioxin in the paternal bloodstream cause a dramatic change in sex ratio of offspring: Affected men father nearly twice as many girls as boys (Ishihara et al., 2007). Dioxin seems to impair the fertility of Y-bearing sperm prior to conception.

Infectious Disease. About 5 percent of women in industrialized nations catch an infectious disease while pregnant. Although most of these illnesses, such as the common cold, seem to have no impact, a few—as Table 3.2 illustrates—can cause extensive damage.

Viruses. In the mid-1960s, a worldwide epidemic of *rubella* (three-day, or German, measles) led to the birth of more than 20,000 American babies with serious defects and to 13,000 fetal and newborn deaths. Consistent with the sensitive-period concept, the greatest damage occurs when rubella strikes during the embryonic period. More than 50 percent of infants whose mothers become ill during that time show deafness; eye deformities, including cataracts; heart, genital, urinary, intestinal, bone, and dental defects; and mental retardation. Infection during the fetal period is less harmful, but low birth weight, hearing loss, and bone defects may still occur. The organ damage inflicted by prenatal rubella often leads to lifelong health problems, including severe mental illness, diabetes, cardiovascular disease, and thyroid and immune-system dysfunction in adulthood (Brown, 2006; Duszak, 2009).

Routine vaccination in infancy and childhood has made new rubella outbreaks unlikely in industrialized nations. But an estimated 100,000 cases of prenatal infection continue to occur worldwide, primarily in developing countries in Africa and Asia with weak or absent immunization programs (Bale, 2009).

The *human immunodeficiency virus (HIV),* which can lead to *acquired immune deficiency syndrome (AIDS),* a disease that destroys the immune system, has infected increasing numbers of women over the past three decades. In developing countries, where 95 percent of new infections occur, more than half affect women. In South Africa, for example, nearly 30 percent of all pregnant women are HIV-positive (South African Department of Health, 2009). Untreated HIV-infected expectant mothers pass the deadly virus to the developing organism 20 to 30 percent of the time.

TABLE 3.2

Effects of Some Infectious Diseases During Pregnancy

DISEASE	MISCARRIAGE	PHYSICAL MALFORMATIONS	MENTAL RETARDATION	LOW BIRTH WEIGHT AND PREMATURITY
VIRAL				
Acquired immune deficiency syndrome (AIDS)	✗	?	✔	?
Chickenpox	✗	✔	✔	✔
Cytomegalovirus	✔	✔	✔	✔
Herpes simplex 2 (genital herpes)	✔	✔	✔	✔
Mumps	✔	?	✗	✗
Rubella (German measles)	✔	✔	✔	✔
BACTERIAL				
Chlamydia	✔	?	✗	✔
Syphilis	✔	✔	✔	?
Tuberculosis	✔	?	✔	✔
PARASITIC				
Malaria	✔	✗	✗	✔
Toxoplasmosis	✔	✔	✔	✔

✔ = established finding, ✗ = no present evidence, ? = possible effect that is not clearly established.
Sources: Jones, Lopez, & Wilson, 2003; Kliegman et al., 2008; Mardh, 2002; O'Rahilly & Müller, 2001.

AIDS progresses rapidly in infants. By 6 months, weight loss, diarrhea, and repeated respiratory illnesses are common. The virus also causes brain damage, as indicated by seizures, gradual loss in brain weight, and delayed mental and motor development. Nearly half of prenatal AIDS babies die by 1 year of age and 90 percent by age 3 (Devi et al., 2009). Antiretroviral drug therapy reduces prenatal AIDS transmission by as much as 95 percent, with no harmful consequences of drug treatment for children. These medications have led to a dramatic decline in prenatally acquired AIDS in Western nations. Although distribution is increasing, antiretroviral drugs are still not widely available in impoverished regions of the world (UNICEF, 2010a).

As Table 3.2 reveals, the developing organism is especially sensitive to the family of herpes viruses, for which no vaccine or treatment exists. Among these, *cytomegalovirus* (the most frequent prenatal infection, transmitted through respiratory or sexual contact) and *herpes simplex 2* (which is sexually transmitted) are especially dangerous. In both, the virus invades the mother's genital tract, infecting babies either during pregnancy or at birth.

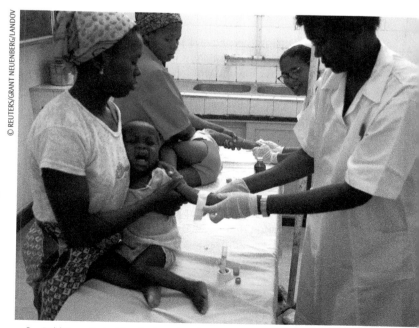

Babies are tested for the HIV virus in a clinic in Mozambique, Africa. Prenatal treatment with antiretroviral drugs reduces transmission of AIDS from mother to child by as much as 95 percent.

Bacterial and Parasitic Diseases. Table 3.2 also includes several bacterial and parasitic diseases. Among the most common is *toxoplasmosis,* caused by a parasite found in many animals. Pregnant women may become infected from eating raw or undercooked meat or from contact with the feces of infected cats. About 40 percent of women who have the disease transmit it to the developing organism. If it strikes during the first trimester, it is likely to cause eye and brain damage. Later infection is linked to mild visual and cognitive impairments (Jones, Lopez, & Wilson, 2003). Expectant mothers can avoid toxoplasmosis by making sure that the meat they eat is well-cooked, having pet cats checked for the disease, and turning over the care of litter boxes to other family members.

Other Maternal Factors

Besides avoiding teratogens, expectant parents can support the development of the embryo and fetus in other ways. In healthy, physically fit women, regular moderate exercise, such as walking, swimming, biking, or an aerobic workout, is related to increased birth weight (Olson et al., 2009). However, frequent, vigorous exercise, especially late in pregnancy, results in lower birth weight than in healthy, nonexercising controls (Clapp et al., 2002; Leet & Flick, 2003). Most women, however, do not engage in sufficient moderate exercise during pregnancy to promote their own and their baby's health (Poudevigne & O'Connor, 2006). An expectant mother who remains fit experiences fewer physical discomforts in the final weeks.

In the following sections, we examine other maternal factors—nutrition, emotional stress, blood type, age, and previous births.

Nutrition. During the prenatal period, when children are growing more rapidly than at any other time, they depend totally on the mother for nutrients. A healthy diet that results in a weight gain of 25 to 30 pounds (10 to 13.5 kilograms) helps ensure the health of mother and baby.

Prenatal malnutrition can cause serious damage to the central nervous system. The poorer the mother's diet, the greater the loss in brain weight, especially if malnutrition occurred during the last trimester. During that time, the brain is increasing rapidly in size, and a maternal diet high in all the basic nutrients is necessary for it to reach its full potential. An inadequate diet during pregnancy can also distort the structure of the liver, kidney, pancreas, and other organs, resulting in lifelong health problems, including cardiovascular disease and diabetes in adulthood (Barker, 2008; Whincup et al., 2008).

Because poor nutrition suppresses development of the immune system, prenatally malnourished babies frequently catch respiratory illnesses (Chandra, 1991). In addition, they are often irritable and unresponsive to stimulation. In poverty-stricken families, these effects quickly combine with a stressful home life. With age, low intelligence and serious learning problems become more apparent (Pollitt, 1996).

Many studies show that providing pregnant women with adequate food has a substantial impact on the health of their newborn babies. Yet the growth demands of the prenatal period require more than just increased quantity of food. Vitamin–mineral enrichment is also crucial. For example, taking a folic acid supplement around the time of conception greatly reduces by more than 70 percent abnormalities of the neural tube, such as *anencephaly* and *spina bifida* (see Table 2.4 on page 56). Folic acid supplementation early in pregnancy also reduces the risk of other physical defects, including cleft lip and palate, urinary tract abnormalities, and limb deformities. Furthermore, adequate folic acid intake during the last 10 weeks of pregnancy cuts in half the risk of premature delivery and low birth weight (Goh & Koren, 2008; MCR Vitamin Study Research Group, 1991; Scholl, Hediger, & Belsky, 1996).

Because of these findings, U.S. government guidelines recommend that all women of childbearing age consume 0.4 milligrams of folic acid per day. For women who have previously had a pregnancy affected by neural tube defect, the recommended amount is 4 to 5 milligrams (dosage must be carefully monitored, as excessive intake can be harmful) (American Academy of Pediatrics, 2006). About half of U.S. pregnancies are unplanned, so government regulations mandate that bread, flour, rice, pasta, and other grain products be fortified with folic acid.

When poor nutrition persists throughout pregnancy, infants usually require more than dietary improvement. Successful interventions must also break the cycle of apathetic mother–baby interactions. Some do so by teaching parents how to interact effectively with their infants, while others focus on stimulating infants to promote active engagement with their physical and social surroundings (Grantham-McGregor et al., 1994; Grantham-McGregor, Schofield, & Powell, 1987).

Although prenatal malnutrition is highest in poverty-stricken regions of the world, it is not limited to developing countries. The U.S. Special Supplemental Food Program for Women, Infants, and Children (WIC), which provides food packages to low-income pregnant women, reaches about 90 percent of those who qualify because of their extremely low incomes (U.S. Department of Agriculture, 2011b). But many U.S. women who need nutrition intervention are not eligible for WIC.

Emotional Stress. When women experience severe emotional stress during pregnancy, their babies are at risk for a wide variety of difficulties. Intense anxiety—especially during the first two trimesters—is associated with higher rates of miscarriage, prematurity, low birth weight, infant respiratory and digestive illnesses, colic (persistent infant crying), sleep disturbances, and irritability during the child's first three years (Field, 2011; Lazinski, Shea, & Steiner, 2008; van der Wal, van Eijsden, & Bonsel, 2007).

How can maternal stress affect the fetus? *TAKE A MOMENT...* To understand this process, list the changes you sensed in your own body the last time you were under stress.

When we experience fear and anxiety, stress hormones released into our bloodstream—such as *epinephrine* (adrenaline) and *cortisol*, known as the "flight or fight" hormones—cause us to be "poised for action." Large amounts of blood are sent to parts of the body involved in the defensive response—the brain, the heart, and the muscles in the arms, legs, and trunk. Blood flow to other organs, including the uterus, is reduced. As a result, the fetus is deprived of a full supply of oxygen and nutrients.

Maternal stress hormones also cross the placenta, causing a dramatic rise in fetal stress hormones (evident in the amniotic fluid) and, therefore, in fetal heart rate, blood pressure, blood glucose, and activity level (Kinsella & Monk, 2009; Weinstock, 2008). Excessive fetal stress may permanently alter fetal neurological functioning, thereby heightening stress reactivity in later life. In several studies, infants and children of mothers who experienced severe prenatal anxiety displayed cortisol levels that were either abnormally high or abnormally low, both of which signal reduced physiological capacity to manage stress. Consistent with these findings, such children are more upset than their agemates when faced with novel or challenging experiences—effects that persist into adolescence and early adulthood (Entringer et al., 2009; Van den Bergh et al., 2008).

Furthermore, maternal emotional stress during pregnancy predicts childhood weakened immune system functioning and increased susceptibility to infectious disease (Nielsen et al., 2011). It is also associated with diverse negative behavioral outcomes, including anxiety, short attention span, anger, aggression, overactivity, and lower mental test scores, above and beyond the impact of other risks, such as maternal prenatal maternal smoking, low birth weight, postnatal maternal anxiety, and low SES (de Weerth & Buitelaar, 2005; Gutteling et al., 2006; Lazinski, Shea, & Steiner, 2008; Loomans et al., 2011).

But stress-related prenatal complications are greatly reduced when mothers have partners, other family members, and friends who offer social support (Glover, Bergman, & O'Connor, 2008). The relationship of social support to positive pregnancy outcomes and subsequent child development is particularly strong for low-income women, who often lead highly stressful lives (see the Social Issues: Health box on page 94).

Rh Factor Incompatibility. When inherited blood types of mother and fetus differ, serious problems sometimes result. The most common cause of these difficulties is **Rh factor incompatibility.** When the mother is Rh-negative (lacks the Rh blood protein) and the father is Rh-positive (has the protein), the baby may inherit the father's Rh-positive blood type. If even a little of a fetus's Rh-positive blood crosses the placenta into the Rh-negative mother's bloodstream, she begins to form antibodies to the foreign Rh protein. If these enter the fetus's system, they destroy red blood cells, reducing the oxygen supply to organs and tissues. Mental retardation, miscarriage, heart damage, and infant death can occur.

It takes time for the mother to produce Rh antibodies, so firstborn children are rarely affected. The danger increases with each additional pregnancy. Fortunately, Rh incompatibility can

be prevented in most cases. After the birth of each Rh-positive baby, Rh-negative mothers are routinely given a vaccine to prevent the buildup of antibodies.

Maternal Age. In Chapter 2, we noted that women who delay childbearing until their thirties or forties face increased risk of infertility, miscarriage, and babies born with chromosomal defects. Are other pregnancy complications more common for older mothers? Research indicates that healthy women in their thirties have about the same rates as those in their twenties (Bianco et al., 1996; Dildy et al., 1996; Prysak, Lorenz, & Kisly, 1995). Thereafter, as Figure 3.3 reveals, complication rates increase, with a sharp rise among women age 50 to 55—an age at which because of menopause (end of menstruation) and aging reproductive organs, few women can conceive naturally (Salihu et al., 2003; Usta & Nassar, 2008).

In the case of teenage mothers, does physical immaturity cause prenatal complications? As we will see in Chapter 11, nature tries to ensure that once a girl can conceive, she is physically ready to carry and give birth to a baby. Infants born to teenagers have a higher rate of problems, but not directly because of maternal age. Most pregnant teenagers come from low-income backgrounds, where stress, poor nutrition, and health problems are common. Also, many are afraid to seek medical care or, in the United States, do not have access to care because they lack health insurance (U.S. Department of Health and Human Services, 2011a).

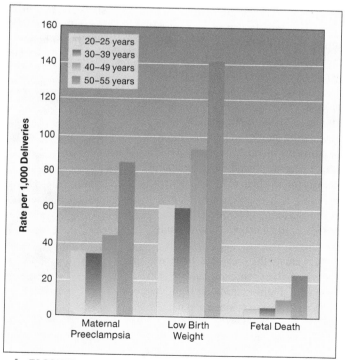

FIGURE 3.3 **Relationship of maternal age to prenatal and birth complications.** Complications increase after age 40, with a sharp rise between 50 and 55 years. See page 95 for a description of preeclampsia. (Adapted from Salihu et al., 2003.)

Social Issues: Health

The Nurse–Family Partnership: Reducing Maternal Stress and Enhancing Child Development Through Social Support

At age 17, Denise—an unemployed high-school dropout living with her disapproving parents—gave birth to Tara. Having no one to turn to for help during pregnancy and beyond, Denise felt overwhelmed and anxious much of the time. Tara was premature and cried uncontrollably, slept erratically, and suffered from frequent minor illnesses throughout her first year. When she reached school age, she had trouble keeping up academically, and her teachers described her as distractible, unable to sit still, angry, and uncooperative.

The Nurse–Family Partnership, currently implemented in hundreds of counties across 42 U.S. states, is a voluntary home visiting program for first-time, low-income expectant mothers like Denise. Its goals are to reduce pregnancy and birth complications, promote competent early caregiving, and improve family conditions, thereby protecting children from lasting adjustment difficulties. A registered nurse visits the home weekly during the first month after enrollment, twice a month during the remainder of pregnancy and through the middle of the child's second year, and then monthly until age 2. In these sessions, the nurse provides the mother with intensive social support—a sympathetic ear; assistance in accessing health and other community services and the help of family members (especially fathers and grandmothers); and encouragement to finish high school, find work, and engage in future family planning.

To evaluate the program's effectiveness, researchers randomly assigned large samples of mothers at risk for high prenatal stress (due to teenage pregnancy, poverty, and other negative life conditions) to nurse-visiting or comparison conditions (just prenatal care, or prenatal care plus infant referral for developmental problems). Families were followed through their child's school-age years and, in one experiment, into adolescence (Kitzman et al., 2010; Olds et al., 2004, 2007; Rubin et al., 2011).

As kindergartners, Nurse–Family Partnership children obtained higher language and intelligence test scores. And at both ages 6 and 9, the children of home-visited mothers in the poorest mental health during pregnancy exceeded comparison children in academic achievement and displayed fewer behavior problems. Furthermore, from their baby's birth on, home-visited mothers were on a more favorable life course: They had fewer subsequent births, longer intervals between their first and second births, more frequent contact with the child's father, more stable intimate partnerships, less welfare dependence, and a greater sense of control over their lives—key factors in reducing subsequent prenatal stress and in protecting children's development. Perhaps for these reasons, 12-year-old children of home-visited mothers continued to be advantaged in academic achievement and reported less alcohol use and drug-taking than comparison-group agemates.

Other findings revealed that professional nurses, compared with trained paraprofessionals, were far more effective in preventing outcomes associated with prenatal stress, including high infant fearfulness to novel stimuli and delayed mental development (Olds et al., 2002). Nurses were probably more proficient in individualizing program guidelines to fit the strengths and challenges faced by each family. They also might have had unique legitimacy as experts in the eyes of stressed mothers, more easily convincing them to take steps to reduce pregnancy complications that can trigger persisting developmental problems—such as those Tara displayed.

The Nurse–Family Partnership is highly cost-effective (Dawley, Loch, & Bindrich, 2007). For $1 spent, it saves more than $5 in public spending on pregnancy complications, preterm births, and child and youth learning and behavior problems.

COURTESY OF NURSE–FAMILY PARTNERSHIP

The Nurse–Family Partnership provides this first-time mother with regular home visits from a registered nurse. In follow-up research, children of home-visited mothers developed more favorably—cognitively, emotionally, and socially—than comparison children.

The Importance of Prenatal Health Care

Yolanda had her first prenatal appointment three weeks after missing her menstrual period. After that, she visited the doctor's office once a month until she was seven months pregnant, then twice during the eighth month. As birth grew near, Yolanda's appointments increased to once a week. The doctor kept track of her general health, her weight gain, the capacity of her uterus and cervix to support the fetus, and the fetus's growth.

Yolanda's pregnancy, like most others, was free of complications. But unexpected difficulties can arise, especially if mothers have health problems. For example, the 5 percent of pregnant women who have diabetes need careful monitoring. Extra glucose in the diabetic mother's bloodstream causes the fetus to grow larger than average, making pregnancy and birth problems more common. Maternal high blood glucose also compromises prenatal brain development: It is linked to poorer memory and learning in infancy and early childhood (deRegnier et al., 2007). Another complication, experienced by 5 to 10 percent of pregnant women, is *preeclampsia* (sometimes called *toxemia*), in which blood pressure increases sharply and the face, hands, and feet swell in the last half of pregnancy. If untreated, preeclampsia can cause convulsions in the mother and fetal death. Usually, hospitalization, bed rest, and drugs can lower blood pressure to a safe level (Vidaeff, Carroll, & Ramin, 2005). If not, the baby must be delivered at once.

Unfortunately, 6 percent of pregnant women in the United States wait until after the first trimester to seek prenatal care or receive none at all. Inadequate care is far more common among adolescent and low-income, ethnic-minority mothers. Their infants are three times as likely to be born underweight and five times as likely to die as are babies of mothers who receive early medical attention (Child Trends, 2012). Although the poorest of these mothers are eligible for government-sponsored health services, many low-income women do not qualify. As we will see when we take up birth complications, in nations where affordable medical care is universally available, such as Australia, Canada, Japan, and European countries, late-care pregnancies and maternal and infant health problems are greatly reduced.

LOOK AND LISTEN

List prenatal environmental factors that can compromise later academic performance and social adjustment. Ask several adults who hope someday to be parents to explain what they know about each factor. How great is their need for prenatal education? ●

Besides financial hardship, some mothers have other reasons for not seeking early prenatal care. These include *situational barriers* (difficulty finding a doctor, getting an appointment, and arranging transportation) and *personal barriers* (psychological

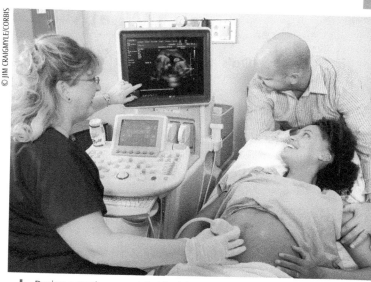

During a routine prenatal visit, this couple views an ultrasound image of their twins. All pregnant women need regular prenatal care to protect their health and that of their babies.

stress, the demands of taking care of other young children, family crises, and ambivalence about the pregnancy). Many also engage in high-risk behaviors, such as smoking and drug abuse, which they do not want to reveal to health professionals (Daniels, Noe, & Mayberry, 2006; Maupin et al., 2004). These women, who receive little or no prenatal care, are among those who need it most!

Clearly, public education about the importance of early and sustained prenatal care for all pregnant women is badly needed. Refer to Applying What We Know on page 96, which lists "do's and don'ts" for a healthy pregnancy, based on our discussion of the prenatal environment.

ASK YOURSELF

REVIEW Why is it difficult to determine the prenatal effects of many environmental agents, such as drugs and pollution?

CONNECT How do teratogens illustrate the notion of epigenesis, presented in Chapter 2, that environments can affect gene expression (see page 73 to review)?

APPLY Nora, pregnant for the first time, believes that a few cigarettes and a glass of wine a day won't be harmful. Provide Nora with research-based reasons for not smoking or drinking.

REFLECT If you had to choose five environmental influences to publicize in a campaign aimed at promoting healthy prenatal development, which ones would you choose, and why?

Applying What We Know

Do's and Don'ts for a Healthy Pregnancy

Do	Don't
Do make sure that you have been vaccinated against infectious diseases that are dangerous to the embryo and fetus, such as rubella, before you get pregnant. Most vaccinations are not safe during pregnancy.	Don't take any drugs without consulting your doctor.
Do see a doctor as soon as you suspect that you are pregnant, and continue to get regular medical checkups throughout pregnancy.	Don't smoke. If you have already smoked during part of your pregnancy, cut down or, better yet, quit. If other members of your family smoke, ask them to quit or to smoke outside.
Do eat a well-balanced diet and take vitamin–mineral supplements, as prescribed by your doctor, both prior to and during pregnancy. Gain 25 to 30 pounds gradually.	Don't drink alcohol from the time you decide to get pregnant.
Do obtain literature from your doctor, library, or bookstore about prenatal development. Ask your doctor about anything that concerns you.	Don't engage in activities that might expose your embryo or fetus to environmental hazards, such as radiation or chemical pollutants. If you work in an occupation that involves these agents, ask for a safer assignment or a leave of absence.
Do keep physically fit through moderate exercise. If possible, join a special exercise class for expectant mothers.	Don't engage in activities that might expose your embryo or fetus to harmful infectious diseases, such as toxoplasmosis.
Do avoid emotional stress. If you are a single expectant mother, find a relative or friend on whom you can rely for emotional support.	Don't choose pregnancy as a time to go on a diet.
Do get plenty of rest. An overtired mother is at risk for pregnancy complications.	Don't gain too much weight during pregnancy. A very large weight gain is associated with complications.
Do enroll in a prenatal and childbirth education class with your partner or other companion. When parents know what to expect, the nine months before birth can be one of the most joyful times of life.	

Childbirth

Although Yolanda and Jay completed my course three months before their baby was born, both agreed to return the following spring to share their experiences with my next class. Two-week-old Joshua came along as well. Yolanda and Jay's story revealed that the birth of a baby is one of the most dramatic and emotional events in human experience. Jay was present throughout Yolanda's labor and delivery. Yolanda explained:

> By morning, we knew I was in labor. It was Thursday, so we went in for my usual weekly appointment. The doctor said, yes, the baby was on the way, but it would be a while. He told us to go home and relax and come to the hospital in three or four hours. We checked in at 3 in the afternoon; Joshua arrived at 2 o'clock the next morning. When, finally, I was ready to deliver, it went quickly; a half hour or so and some good hard pushes, and there he was! His face was red and puffy, and his head was misshapen, but I thought, "Our son! I can't believe he's really here."

Jay was also elated by Joshua's birth. "I wanted to support Yolanda and to experience as much as I could. It was awesome, indescribable," he said, holding Joshua over his shoulder and patting and kissing him gently. In the following sections, we explore the experience of childbirth, from both the parents' and the baby's point of view.

The Stages of Childbirth

It is not surprising that childbirth is often referred to as labor. It is the hardest physical work a woman may ever do. A complex series of hormonal changes between mother and fetus initiates the process, which naturally divides into three stages (see Figure 3.4):

1. *Dilation and effacement of the cervix.* This is the longest stage of labor, lasting an average of 12 to 14 hours with a first birth and 4 to 6 hours with later births. Contractions of the uterus gradually become more frequent and powerful, causing the cervix, or uterine opening, to widen and thin to nothing, forming a clear channel from the uterus into the birth canal, or vagina.
2. *Delivery of the baby.* This stage is much shorter, lasting about 50 minutes for a first birth and 20 minutes in later births. Strong contractions of the uterus continue, but the mother also feels a natural urge to squeeze and push with her abdominal muscles. As she does so with each contraction, she forces the baby down and out.
3. *Delivery of the placenta.* Labor comes to an end with a few final contractions and pushes. These cause the placenta to separate from the wall of the uterus and be delivered in about 5 to 10 minutes.

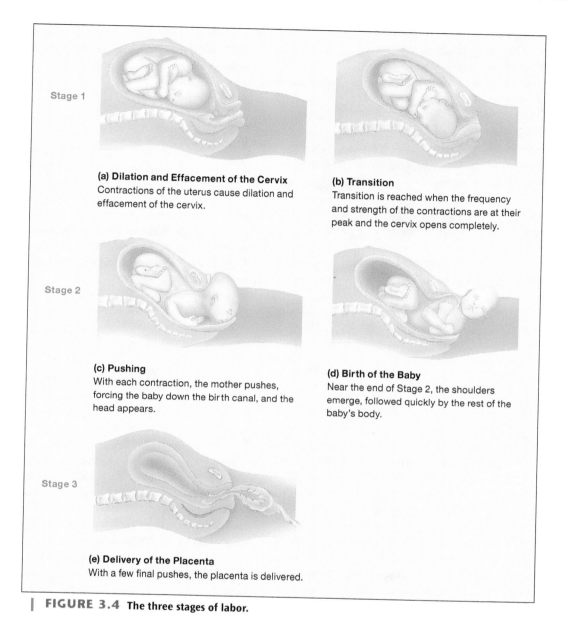

(a) Dilation and Effacement of the Cervix
Contractions of the uterus cause dilation and effacement of the cervix.

(b) Transition
Transition is reached when the frequency and strength of the contractions are at their peak and the cervix opens completely.

(c) Pushing
With each contraction, the mother pushes, forcing the baby down the birth canal, and the head appears.

(d) Birth of the Baby
Near the end of Stage 2, the shoulders emerge, followed quickly by the rest of the baby's body.

(e) Delivery of the Placenta
With a few final pushes, the placenta is delivered.

| FIGURE 3.4 The three stages of labor.

The Baby's Adaptation to Labor and Delivery

At first glance, labor and delivery seem like a dangerous ordeal for the baby. The strong contractions exposed Joshua's head to a great deal of pressure, and they squeezed the placenta and the umbilical cord repeatedly. Each time, Joshua's supply of oxygen was temporarily reduced.

Fortunately, healthy babies are well-equipped to withstand these traumas. The force of the contractions causes the infant to produce high levels of stress hormones. Unlike during pregnancy, when excessive stress endangers the fetus, during childbirth high levels of infant cortisol and other stress hormones are adaptive. They help the baby withstand oxygen deprivation by

sending a rich supply of blood to the brain and heart (Gluckman, Sizonenko, & Bassett, 1999). In addition, stress hormones prepare the baby to breathe by causing the lungs to absorb any remaining fluid and by expanding the bronchial tubes (passages leading to the lungs). Finally, stress hormones arouse the infant into alertness. Joshua was born wide awake, ready to interact with the surrounding world.

The Newborn Baby's Appearance

Parents are often surprised at the odd-looking newborn—a far cry from the storybook image they may have had in their minds. The average newborn is 20 inches long and 7½ pounds in weight; boys tend to be slightly longer and heavier than girls.

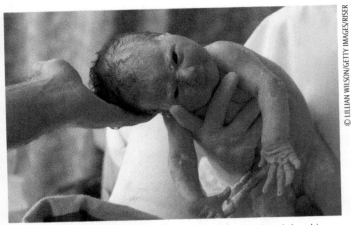

To accommodate the well-developed brain, a newborn's head is large in relation to the trunk and legs. This newborn's body readily turns pink as she takes her first few breaths.

The head is large in comparison to the trunk and legs, which are short and bowed. This combination of a large head (with its well-developed brain) and a small body means that human infants learn quickly in the first few months of life. But, unlike most other mammals, they cannot get around on their own until much later.

Even though newborn babies may not match parents' idealized image, some features do make them attractive (Luo, Li, & Lee, 2011). Their round faces, chubby cheeks, large foreheads, and big eyes make adults feel like picking them up and cuddling them.

Assessing the Newborn's Physical Condition: The Apgar Scale

Infants who have difficulty making the transition to life outside the uterus require special help at once. To assess the newborn's

physical condition quickly, doctors and nurses use the **Apgar Scale.** As Table 3.3 shows, a rating of 0, 1, or 2 on each of five characteristics is made at 1 minute and again at 5 minutes after birth. A combined Apgar score of 7 or better indicates that the infant is in good physical condition. If the score is between 4 and 6, the baby needs assistance in establishing breathing and other vital signs. If the score is 3 or below, the infant is in serious danger and requires emergency medical attention. Two Apgar ratings are given because some babies have trouble adjusting at first but do quite well after a few minutes (Apgar, 1953).

Approaches to Childbirth

Childbirth practices, like other aspects of family life, are molded by the society of which mother and baby are a part. In many village and tribal cultures, expectant mothers are well-acquainted with the childbirth process. For example, the Jarara of South America and the Pukapukans of the Pacific Islands treat birth as a vital part of daily life. The Jarara mother gives birth in full view of the entire community, including small children. The Pukapukan girl is so familiar with the events of labor and delivery that she frequently can be seen playing at it. Using a coconut to represent the baby, she stuffs it inside her dress, imitates the mother's pushing, and lets the nut fall at the proper moment. In most nonindustrialized cultures, women are assisted—though often not by medical personnel—during labor and delivery. Among the Mayans of the Yucatán, the mother leans against the body of a woman called the "head helper," who supports her weight and breathes with her during each contraction (Jordan, 1993; Mead & Newton, 1967).

In Western nations, childbirth has changed dramatically over the centuries. Before the late 1800s, birth usually took place at home and was a family-centered event. The industrial revolution brought greater crowding to cities, along with new health

TABLE 3.3 **The Apgar Scale**

SIGN[a]	RATING		
	0	1	2
Heart rate	No heartbeat	Under 100 beats per minute	100 to 140 beats per minute
Respiratory effort	No breathing for 60 seconds	Irregular, shallow breathing	Strong breathing and crying
Reflex irritability (sneezing, coughing, and grimacing)	No response	Weak reflexive response	Strong reflexive response
Muscle tone	Completely limp	Weak movements of arms and legs	Strong movements of arms and legs
Color[b]	Blue body, arms, and legs	Body pink with blue arms and legs	Body, arms, and legs completely pink

[a]To remember these signs, you may find it helpful to use a technique in which the original labels are reordered and renamed as follows: color = **A**ppearance; heart rate = **P**ulse; reflex irritability = **G**rimace; muscle tone = **A**ctivity; and respiratory effort = **R**espiration. Together, the first letters of the new labels spell **Apgar.**
[b]The skin tone of nonwhite babies makes it difficult to apply the "pink" color criterion. However, newborns of all races can be rated for pinkish glow resulting from the flow of oxygen through body tissues.
Source: Apgar, 1953.

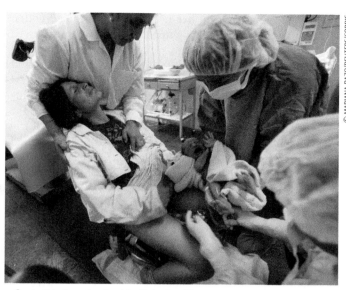

In this Peruvian health clinic, families are encouraged to incorporate practices of their village culture into the birth experience. Here, a familiar attendant soothes a new mother as her baby is delivered.

problems. As a result, childbirth moved from home to hospital, where the health of mothers and babies could be protected. Once doctors assumed responsibility for childbirth, women's knowledge of it declined, and relatives and friends no longer participated (Borst, 1995).

By the 1950s and 1960s, women had begun to question the medical procedures that had come to be used routinely during labor and delivery. Many felt that routine use of strong drugs and delivery instruments had robbed them of a precious experience and was often neither necessary nor safe for the baby. Gradually, a natural childbirth movement arose in Europe and spread to North America. Its purpose was to make hospital birth as comfortable and rewarding for mothers as possible. Today, most hospitals offer birth centers that are family-centered and homelike. *Freestanding birth centers,* which permit greater maternal control over labor and delivery, including choice of delivery positions, presence of family members and friends, and early contact between parents and baby, also exist. And a small number of North American women reject institutional birth entirely and choose to have their babies at home.

Natural, or Prepared, Childbirth

Yolanda and Jay chose **natural,** or **prepared, childbirth**—a group of techniques aimed at reducing pain and medical intervention and making childbirth a rewarding experience. Most natural childbirth programs draw on methods developed by Grantly Dick-Read (1959) in England and Fernand Lamaze (1958) in France. These physicians recognized that cultural attitudes had taught women to fear the birth experience. An anxious, frightened woman in labor tenses muscles, turning the mild pain that sometimes accompanies strong contractions into intense pain.

In a typical natural childbirth program, the expectant mother and a companion (a partner, relative, or friend) participate in three activities:

- *Classes.* Yolanda and Jay attended a series of classes in which they learned about the anatomy and physiology of labor and delivery. Knowledge about the birth process reduces a mother's fear.

- *Relaxation and breathing techniques.* During each class, Yolanda was taught relaxation and breathing exercises aimed at counteracting the pain of uterine contractions.

- *Labor coach.* Jay learned how to help Yolanda during childbirth by reminding her to relax and breathe, massaging her back, supporting her body, and offering encouragement and affection.

Social support is important to the success of natural childbirth techniques. In Guatemalan and American hospitals that routinely isolated patients during childbirth, some mothers were randomly assigned a *doula*—a Greek word referring to a trained lay attendant—who stayed with them throughout labor and delivery, talking to them, holding their hands, and rubbing their backs to promote relaxation. These mothers had fewer birth complications, and their labors were several hours shorter than those of women who did not have supportive companionship. Guatemalan mothers who received doula support also interacted more positively with their babies after delivery, talking, smiling, and gently stroking (Kennell et al., 1991; Sosa et al., 1980).

Other studies indicate that mothers who are supported during labor and delivery—either by a lay birth attendant or by a relative or friend with doula training—less often have cesarean (surgical) deliveries or need medication to control pain. Also, their babies' Apgar scores are higher, and they are more likely to be breastfeeding at a two-month follow-up (Campbell et al., 2006, 2007; Hodnett et al., 2003; McGrath & Kennell, 2008). Social support also makes Western hospital-birth customs more acceptable to women from parts of the world where assistance from family and community members is the norm (Dundek, 2006).

LOOK AND LISTEN

Talk to several mothers about social supports available to them during labor and delivery. From the mothers' perspectives, how did those supports (or lack of support) affect the birth experience? ●

Home Delivery

Home birth has always been popular in certain industrialized nations, such as England, the Netherlands, and Sweden. The number of American women choosing to have their babies at home rose during the 1970s and 1980s but remains small, at less than 1 percent (U.S. Department of Health and Human Services, 2011a). Although some home births are attended by

After a home birth, the midwife and a lay attendant provide support to the new mother. For healthy women attended by a well-trained doctor or midwife, home birth is as safe as hospital birth.

doctors, many more are handled by *certified nurse–midwives,* who have degrees in nursing and additional training in child-birth management.

Is it just as safe to give birth at home as in a hospital? For healthy women who are assisted by a well-trained doctor or midwife, it seems so because complications rarely occur (Fullerton, Navarro, & Young, 2007; Wax, Pinette, & Cartin, 2010). However, if attendants are not carefully trained and prepared to handle emergencies, the rate of infant death is high (Mehlmadrona & Madrona, 1997). When mothers are at risk for any kind of complication, the appropriate place for labor and delivery is the hospital, where life-saving treatment is available.

Medical Interventions

Four-year-old Melinda walks with a halting, lumbering gait and has difficulty keeping her balance. She has *cerebral palsy,* a general term for a variety of impairments in muscle coordination caused by brain damage before, during, or just after birth. For about 10 percent of these children, including Melinda, brain damage was caused by **anoxia,** or inadequate oxygen supply, during labor and delivery (Bracci, Perrone, & Buonocore, 2006). Melinda was also in **breech position,** turned so that the buttocks or feet would be delivered first, and the umbilical

cord was wrapped around her neck. Her mother had gotten pregnant accidentally, was frightened and alone, and arrived at the hospital at the last minute. Had she come to the hospital earlier, doctors could have monitored Melinda's condition and delivered her surgically as soon as squeezing of the umbilical cord led to distress, thereby reducing the damage or preventing it entirely.

In cases like Melinda's, medical interventions are clearly justified. But in others, they can interfere with delivery and even pose new risks. In the following sections, we examine some commonly used medical procedures during childbirth.

Fetal Monitoring

Fetal monitors are electronic instruments that track the baby's heart rate during labor. An abnormal heartbeat may indicate that the baby is in distress due to anoxia and needs to be delivered immediately. Continuous fetal monitoring, which is required in most U.S. hospitals, is used in over 80 percent of American births (Natale & Dodman, 2003). The most popular type of monitor is strapped across the mother's abdomen throughout labor. A second, more accurate method involves threading a recording device through the cervix and placing it directly under the baby's scalp.

Fetal monitoring is a safe medical procedure that has saved the lives of many babies in high-risk situations. But in healthy pregnancies, it does not reduce the already low rates of infant brain damage and death (Haws et al., 2009). Furthermore, most infants have some heartbeat irregularities during labor, so critics worry that fetal monitors identify many babies as in danger who, in fact, are not. Monitoring is linked to an increase in the number of cesarean (surgical) deliveries, which we will discuss shortly (Thacker & Stroup, 2003). In addition, some women complain that the devices are uncomfortable, prevent them from moving easily, and interfere with the normal course of labor.

Still, fetal monitors will probably continue to be used routinely in the United States, even though they are not necessary in most cases. Doctors fear that they will be sued for malpractice if an infant dies or is born with problems and they cannot show that they did everything possible to protect the baby.

Labor and Delivery Medication

Some form of medication is used in more than 80 percent of U.S. births (Althaus & Wax, 2005). *Analgesics,* drugs used to relieve pain, may be given in mild doses during labor to help a mother relax. *Anesthetics* are a stronger type of painkiller that blocks sensation. Currently, the most common approach to controlling pain during labor is *epidural analgesia,* in which a regional pain-relieving drug is delivered continuously through a catheter into a small space in the lower spine. Unlike older spinal block procedures, which numb the entire lower half of the body, epidural analgesia limits pain reduction to the pelvic region. Because the mother retains the capacity to feel the pressure of the contractions and to move her trunk and legs, she is able to push during the second stage of labor.

Although pain-relieving drugs help women cope with childbirth and enable doctors to perform essential medical interventions, they also can cause problems. Epidural analgesia, for example, weakens uterine contractions. As a result, labor is prolonged, and the chances of cesarean (surgical) delivery increase (Nguyen et al., 2010). And because drugs rapidly cross the placenta, exposed newborns tend to have lower Apgar scores, to be sleepy and withdrawn, to suck poorly during feedings, and to be irritable when awake (Caton et al., 2002; Eltzschig, Lieberman, & Camann, 2003; Emory, Schlackman, & Fiano, 1996). Although no confirmed long-term consequences for development exist, the negative impact of these drugs on the newborn's adjustment supports the current trend to limit their use.

Cesarean Delivery

A **cesarean delivery** is a surgical birth; the doctor makes an incision in the mother's abdomen and lifts the baby out of the uterus. Forty years ago, cesarean delivery was rare. Since then, cesarean rates have climbed internationally, reaching 16 percent in Finland, 23 percent in New Zealand, 26 percent in Canada, 30 percent in Australia, and 32 percent in the United States (OECD, 2011b).

Cesareans have always been warranted by medical emergencies, such as Rh incompatibility, premature separation of the placenta from the uterus, or serious maternal illness or infection (for example, the herpes simplex 2 virus, which can infect the baby during a vaginal delivery). Cesareans are also justified in breech births, in which the baby risks head injury or anoxia (as in Melinda's case). But the infant's exact position makes a difference: Certain breech babies fare just as well with a normal delivery as with a cesarean (Giuliani et al., 2002). Sometimes the doctor can gently turn the baby into a head-down position during the early part of labor.

Until recently, many women who have had a cesarean have been offered the option of a vaginal birth in subsequent pregnancies. But new evidence indicates that compared with repeated cesareans, a natural labor after a cesarean is associated with slightly increased rates of rupture of the uterus and infant death (Cahill & Macones, 2007). As a result, the rule, "Once a cesarean, always a cesarean," has made a comeback.

Repeated cesareans, however, do not explain the worldwide rise in cesarean deliveries. Instead, medical control over childbirth is largely responsible. Because many needless cesareans are performed, pregnant women should ask questions about the procedure before choosing a doctor. Although the operation itself is safe, mother and baby require more time for recovery. Anesthetic may have crossed the placenta, making cesarean newborns sleepy and unresponsive and at increased risk for breathing difficulties (McDonagh, Osterweil, & Guise, 2005).

ASK YOURSELF

REVIEW Describe the features and benefits of natural childbirth. What aspect contributes greatly to favorable outcomes, and why?

CONNECT How might use of epidural analgesia negatively affect the parent–newborn relationship? Explain how your answer illustrates bidirectional influences between parent and child, emphasized in ecological systems theory.

APPLY On seeing her newborn baby for the first time, Caroline exclaimed, "Why is she so out of proportion?" What observations prompted Caroline to ask this question? Explain why her baby's appearance is adaptive.

REFLECT If you were an expectant parent, would you choose home birth? Why or why not?

Preterm and Low-Birth-Weight Infants

Babies born three weeks or more before the end of a full 38-week pregnancy or who weigh less than 5½ pounds (2,500 grams) have for many years been referred to as "premature." A wealth of research indicates that premature babies are at risk for many problems. Birth weight is the best available predictor of infant survival and healthy development. Many newborns who weigh less than 3½ pounds (1,500 grams) experience difficulties that are not overcome, an effect that becomes stronger as length of pregnancy and birth weight decrease (see Figure 3.5 on page 102) (Baron & Rey-Casserly, 2010; Bolisetty et al., 2006; Dombrowski, Noonan, & Martin, 2007). Brain abnormalities, frequent illness, inattention, overactivity, sensory impairments, poor motor coordination, language delays, low intelligence test scores, deficits in school learning, and emotional and behavior problems are some of the difficulties that persist through childhood and adolescence and into adulthood (Aarnoudse-Moens, Weiglas-Kuperus, & van Goudoever, 2009; Clark et al., 2008; Delobel-Ayoub et al., 2009; Nosarti et al., 2011).

About 1 in 13 American infants is born underweight. Although the problem can strike unexpectedly, it occurs especially often among poverty-stricken women (U.S. Department of Health and Human Services, 2011a). These mothers, as noted earlier, are more likely to be undernourished and to be exposed to other harmful environmental influences. In addition, they often do not receive adequate prenatal care.

Recall from Chapter 2 that prematurity is also common in multiple births. About 60 percent of twins and more than 90 percent of triplets are born early and low birth weight (U.S. Department of Health and Human Services, 2011a). Because space inside the uterus is restricted, multiples gain less weight than singletons in the second half of pregnancy.

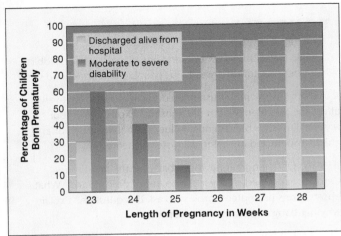

FIGURE 3.5 Rates of infant survival and child disabilities by length of pregnancy. In a follow-up of more than 2,300 babies born between 23 and 28 weeks gestation, the percentage who survived decreased and the percentage who displayed moderate to severe disabilities (assessed during the preschool years) increased with reduced length of pregnancy. Severe disabilities included cerebral palsy (unlikely to ever walk), severely delayed mental development, deafness, and blindness. Moderate disabilities included cerebral palsy (able to walk with assistance), moderately delayed mental development, and hearing impairments partially correctable with a hearing aid. (Adapted from Bolisetty et al., 2006.)

Preterm versus Small-for-Date Infants

Although low-birth-weight infants face many obstacles to healthy development, most go on to lead normal lives; about half of those born at 23 to 24 weeks gestation and weighing only a couple of pounds at birth have no disability (refer again to Figure 3.5). To better understand why some babies do better than others, researchers divide them into two groups. **Preterm infants** are those born several weeks or more before their due date. Although they are small, their weight may still be appropriate, based on time spent in the uterus. **Small-for-date infants** are below their expected weight considering length of the pregnancy. Some small-for-date infants are actually full-term. Others are preterm infants who are especially underweight.

Of the two types of babies, small-for-date infants usually have more serious problems. During the first year, they are more likely to die, catch infections, and show evidence of brain damage. By middle childhood, they are smaller in stature, have lower intelligence test scores, are less attentive, achieve more poorly in school, and are socially immature (Hediger et al., 2002; O'Keefe et al., 2003; Sullivan et al., 2008). Small-for-date infants probably experienced inadequate nutrition before birth. Perhaps their mothers did not eat properly, the placenta did not function normally, or the babies themselves had defects that prevented them from growing as they should. Consequently, small-for-date infants are especially likely to suffer from prenatal neurological impairments that permanently weaken their capacity to manage stress (Wust et al., 2005).

Even among preterm newborns whose weight is appropriate for length of pregnancy, just seven more days—from

34 to 35 weeks—greatly reduces rates of illness, costly medical procedures, and lengthy hospital stays (Gladstone & Katz, 2004). And despite being relatively low-risk for disabilities, a substantial number of 34-week preterms are below average in physical growth and mildly to moderately delayed in cognitive development in early and middle childhood (Morse et al., 2009; Pietz et al., 2004; Stephens & Vohr, 2009). And in an investigation of over 120,000 New York City births, babies born even 1 or 2 weeks early showed slightly lower reading and math scores at a third-grade follow-up than children who experienced a full-length prenatal period (Noble et al., 2012). These outcomes persisted even after controlling for other factors linked to achievement, such as birth weight and SES. Yet doctors often induce births several weeks preterm, under the misconception that these babies are developmentally "mature."

Consequences for Caregiving

Imagine a scrawny, thin-skinned infant whose body is only a little larger than the size of your hand. You try to play with the baby by stroking and talking softly, but he is sleepy and unresponsive. When you feed him, he sucks poorly. During the short, unpredictable periods in which he is awake, he is usually irritable.

The appearance and behavior of preterm babies can lead parents to be less sensitive in caring for them. Compared with full-term infants, preterm babies—especially those who are very ill at birth—are less often held close, touched, and talked to gently. At times, mothers of these infants resort to interfering pokes and verbal commands in an effort to obtain a higher level of response from the baby (Barratt, Roach, & Leavitt, 1996; Feldman, 2007). This may explain why preterm babies as a group are at risk for child abuse.

Research reveals that distressed, emotionally reactive preterm infants are especially susceptible to the effects of parenting quality: Among a sample of preterm 9-month-olds, the combination of infant negativity and angry or intrusive parenting yielded the highest rates of behavior problems at 2 years of age. But with warm, sensitive parenting, distressed preterm babies' rates of behavior problems were the lowest (Poehlmann et al., 2011). When they are born to isolated, poverty-stricken mothers who cannot provide good nutrition, health care, and parenting, the likelihood of unfavorable outcomes increases. In contrast, parents with stable life circumstances and social supports usually can overcome the stresses of caring for a preterm infant (Ment et al., 2003). In these cases, even sick preterm babies have a good chance of catching up in development by middle childhood.

These findings suggest that how well preterm infants develop has a great deal to do with the parent–child relationship. Consequently, interventions directed at supporting both sides of this tie are more likely to help these infants recover.

Interventions for Preterm Infants

A preterm baby is cared for in a special Plexiglas-enclosed bed called an *isolette*. Temperature is carefully controlled because these babies cannot yet regulate their own body temperature effectively. To help protect the baby from infection, air is filtered before it enters the isolette. When a preterm infant is fed through a stomach tube, breathes with the aid of a respirator, and receives medication through an intravenous needle, the isolette can be very isolating indeed! Physical needs that otherwise would lead to close contact and other human stimulation are met mechanically.

Special Infant Stimulation. In proper doses, certain kinds of stimulation can help preterm infants develop. In some intensive care nurseries, preterm babies can be seen rocking in suspended hammocks or lying on waterbeds designed to replace the gentle motion they would have received while still in the mother's uterus. Other forms of stimulation have also been used—an attractive mobile or a tape recording of a heartbeat, soft music, or the mother's voice. These experiences promote faster weight gain, more predictable sleep patterns, and greater alertness (Arnon et al., 2006; Marshall-Baker, Lickliter, & Cooper, 1998).

Touch is an especially important form of stimulation. In baby animals, touching the skin releases certain brain chemicals that support physical growth—effects believed to occur in humans as well. When preterm infants were massaged several times each day in the hospital, they gained weight faster and, at the end of the first year, were advanced in mental and motor development over preterm babies not given this stimulation (Field, 2001; Field, Hernandez-Reif, & Freedman, 2004).

In developing countries where hospitalization is not always possible, skin-to-skin "kangaroo care" is the most readily available intervention for promoting the survival and recovery of preterm babies. It involves placing the infant in a vertical position between the mother's breasts or next to the father's chest (under the parent's clothing) so the parent's body functions as a human incubator. Kangaroo care offers fathers a unique opportunity to increase their involvement in caring for the preterm newborn. Because of its many physical and psychological benefits, the technique is often used in Western nations as a supplement to hospital intensive care.

Kangaroo skin-to-skin contact fosters improved oxygenation of the baby's body, temperature regulation, sleep, breastfeeding, alertness, and infant survival (Conde-Agudelo, Belizan, & Diaz-Rossello, 2011; Lawn et al., 2010). In addition, the kangaroo position provides the baby with gentle stimulation of all sensory modalities: hearing (through the parent's voice), smell (through proximity to the parent's body), touch (through skin-to-skin contact), and visual (through the upright position). Mothers and fathers practicing kangaroo care feel more confident about caring for their fragile babies and interact more sensitively and affectionately with them (Dodd, 2005; Feldman, 2007).

Together, these factors may explain why preterm babies given many hours of kangaroo care in their early weeks, compared to those given little or no such care, score higher on measures of mental and motor development during the first year (Charpak, Ruiz-Peláez, & Figueroa, 2005; Feldman, 2007). Because of its diverse benefits, more than 80 percent of U.S. hospitals now offer kangaroo care to preterm newborns (Field et al., 2006).

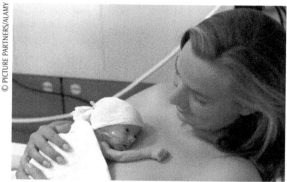

Top photo: A father in El Salvador uses skin-to-skin "kangaroo care" with his infant as part of a hospital program that teaches parents techniques for promoting survival and development in preterm and underweight babies. *Bottom photo:* Here, a U.S. mother uses kangaroo care with her fragile newborn.

Training Parents in Infant Caregiving Skills. Interventions that support parents of preterm infants generally teach them about the infant's characteristics and promote caregiving skills. For parents with adequate economic and personal resources to care for a preterm infant, just a few sessions of coaching in recognizing and responding to the baby's needs are linked to enhanced parent–infant interaction, reduced infant crying and improved sleep, more rapid language development in the second year, and steady gains in mental test scores that equal those of full-term children by middle childhood (Achenbach et al., 1990; Newnham, Milgrom, & Skouteris, 2009).

When preterm infants live in stressed, low-income households, long-term, intensive intervention is required to reduce developmental problems. In the Infant Health and Development

Social Issues: Health

A Cross-National Perspective on Health Care and Other Policies for Parents and Newborn Babies

These fathers in Stockholm take advantage of Sweden's parental leave program, the most generous in the world, which provides them with two weeks of birth leave followed by 16 months of paid leave at 80 percent of prior earnings.

nfant mortality—the number of deaths in the first year of life per 1,000 live births—is an index used around the world to assess the overall health of a nation's children. Although the United States has the most up-to-date health-care technology in the world, it has made less progress in reducing infant deaths than many other countries. Over the past three decades, it has slipped in the international rankings, from seventh in the 1950s to twenty-eighth in 2012. Members of America's poor ethnic minorities are at greatest risk. African-American and Native-American babies are nearly twice as likely as white infants to die in the first year of life (U.S. Census Bureau, 2012a, 2012b).

Neonatal mortality, the rate of death within the first month of life, accounts for 67 percent of the infant death rate in the United States. Two factors are largely responsible for neonatal mortality. The first is serious physical defects, most of which cannot be prevented. The percentage of babies born with physical defects is about the same in all ethnic and income groups. The second leading cause of neonatal mortality is low birth weight, which is largely preventable. African-American and Native-American babies are twice as likely as white infants to be born early and underweight (U.S. Census Bureau, 2012b).

Widespread poverty and weak health-care programs for mothers and young children are largely responsible for these trends.

Each country in Figure 3.6 that outranks the United States in infant survival provides all its citizens with government-sponsored health-care benefits. And each takes extra steps to make sure that pregnant mothers and babies have access to good nutrition, high-quality medical care, and social and economic supports that promote effective parenting.

For example, all Western European nations guarantee women a certain number of prenatal visits at very low or no cost. After a baby is born, a health professional routinely visits the home to provide counseling about infant care and to arrange continuing medical services. Home assistance is especially extensive in the Netherlands. For a token fee, each mother is granted a specially trained maternity helper, who assists with infant care, shopping, housekeeping, meal preparation, and the care of other children during the days after delivery (Zwart, 2007).

Paid, job-protected employment leave is another vital societal intervention for new parents. Canadian mothers are eligible for 15 weeks' maternity leave at 55 percent of prior earnings (up to a maximum of

$485 per week), and Canadian mothers or fathers can take an additional 35 weeks of parental leave at the same rate. Paid leave is widely available in other industrialized nations as well. Sweden has the most generous parental leave program in the world. Mothers can begin maternity leave 60 days prior to expected delivery, extending it to six weeks after birth; fathers are granted two weeks of birth leave. In addition, either parent can take full leave for 16 months at 80 percent of prior earnings, followed by an additional three months at a modest flat rate. Each parent is also entitled to another 18 months of unpaid leave. Furthermore, many countries supplement basic paid

---

Project, preterm babies born into poverty received a comprehensive intervention that combined medical follow-up, weekly parent training sessions, and cognitively stimulating child care from 1 to 3 years of age. More than four times as many intervention children as controls (39 versus 9 percent) were within normal range at age 3 in intelligence, psychological adjustment, and physical growth (Bradley et al., 1994). In addition, mothers in the intervention group were more affectionate and more often encouraged play and cognitive mastery in their children—one reason their 3-year-olds may have been developing so favorably (McCarton, 1998).

At ages 5 and 8, children who had attended the child-care program regularly—for more than 350 days over the three-year period—continued to show better intellectual functioning. The more they attended, the higher they scored, with greater gains among those whose birth weights were higher—between 4½ and 5½ pounds (2,001 to 2,500 grams). In contrast, children who attended only sporadically gained little or even lost ground (Hill, Brooks-Gunn, & Waldfogel, 2003). These findings confirm that babies who are both preterm and economically disadvantaged require *intensive* intervention. And special strategies, such

leave. In Germany, for example, after a fully paid three-month leave, a parent may take one more year at a flat rate and three additional years at no pay (OECD, 2006; Waldfogel, 2001).

Yet in the United States, the federal government mandates *only 12 weeks of unpaid leave* for employees in businesses with at least 50 workers. Most women, however, work in smaller businesses, and many of those who work in large enough companies cannot afford to take unpaid leave (Hewlett, 2003). Similarly, though paternal leave predicts fathers' increased involvement in infant care at the end of the first year, many fathers take little or none at all (Nepomnyaschy & Waldfogel, 2007; OECD, 2006). In 2002, California became the first state to guarantee a mother or father paid leave—up to six weeks at half salary, regardless of the size of the company. Since then, Hawaii, New Jersey, New York, Rhode Island, and the territory of Puerto Rico have passed similar legislation.

Nevertheless, six weeks of childbirth leave (the norm in the United States) is not enough. When a family is stressed by a baby's arrival, leaves of six weeks or less are linked to increased maternal anxiety, depression, marital dissatisfaction, sense of role overload (conflict between work and family responsibilities), and negative interactions with the baby. A longer leave (12 weeks or more) predicts favorable

maternal mental health, supportive marital interaction, and sensitive caregiving (Feldman, Sussman, & Zigler, 2004; Hyde et al., 2001). Single women and their babies are most hurt by the absence of a generous national paid-leave policy. These mothers, who are usually the sole source of support for their families, can least afford to take time from their jobs.

In countries with low infant mortality rates, expectant parents need not wonder how or where they will get health care and other resources to support their baby's development. The powerful impact of universal, high-quality health care, generous parental leave, and other social services on maternal and infant well-being provides strong justification for these policies.

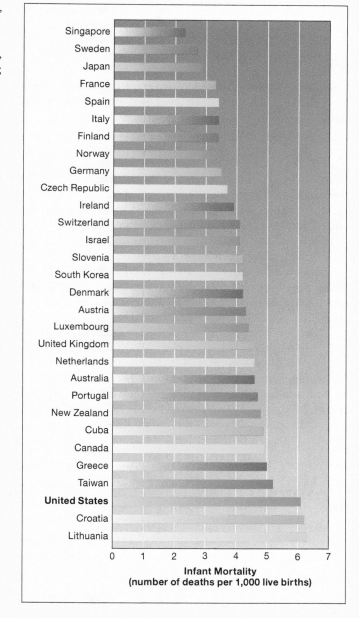

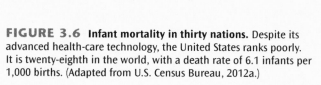

FIGURE 3.6 Infant mortality in thirty nations. Despite its advanced health-care technology, the United States ranks poorly. It is twenty-eighth in the world, with a death rate of 6.1 infants per 1,000 births. (Adapted from U.S. Census Bureau, 2012a.)

as extra adult–child interaction, may be necessary to achieve lasting changes in children with the lowest birth weights.

Nevertheless, even the best caregiving environments cannot "fix" the enormous biological risks associated with extremely low birth weight. A better course of action would be to prevent this serious threat to infant survival and development. The high rate of underweight babies in the United States—one of the worst in the industrialized world—could be greatly reduced by improving the health and social conditions described in the Social Issues: Health box above.

Birth Complications, Parenting, and Resilience

In the preceding sections, we considered a variety of birth complications. Now let's try to put the evidence together. Can any general principles help us understand how infants who survive a traumatic birth are likely to develop? A landmark study carried out in Hawaii provides some answers.

In 1955, Emmy Werner and Ruth Smith began to follow nearly 700 infants on the island of Kauai who had experienced mild, moderate, or severe birth complications. Each was matched, on the basis of SES and ethnicity, with a healthy newborn (Werner & Smith, 1982). Findings showed that the likelihood of long-term difficulties increased if birth trauma was severe. But among mildly to moderately stressed children, those growing up in stable families did almost as well on measures of intelligence and psychological adjustment as those with no birth problems. Children exposed to poverty, family disorganization, and mentally ill parents often developed serious learning difficulties, behavior problems, and emotional disturbance.

The Kauai study tells us that as long as birth injuries are not overwhelming, a supportive home environment can restore children's growth. But the most intriguing cases in this study were the handful of exceptions. A few children with both fairly serious birth complications and troubled family environments grew into competent adults who fared as well as controls in career attainment and psychological adjustment. Werner and Smith found that these children relied on factors outside the family and within themselves to overcome stress. Some had attractive personalities that drew positive responses from relatives, neighbors, and peers. In other instances, a grandparent, aunt, uncle, or babysitter provided the needed emotional support (Werner, 1989, 2001; Werner & Smith, 1992).

Do these outcomes remind you of the characteristics of resilient children, discussed in Chapter 1? The Kauai study and other similar investigations reveal that the impact of early biological risks often wanes as children's personal characteristics and social experiences contribute increasingly to their functioning (Laucht, Esser, & Schmidt, 1997; Resnick et al., 1999). In sum, when the overall balance of life events tips toward the favorable side, children with serious birth problems can develop successfully.

The Newborn Baby's Capacities

Newborn infants have a remarkable set of capacities that are crucial for survival and for evoking attention and care from parents. In relating to the physical and social world, babies are active from the very start.

Reflexes

A **reflex** is an inborn, automatic response to a particular form of stimulation. Reflexes are the newborn baby's most obvious organized patterns of behavior. As Jay placed Joshua on a table in my classroom, we saw several. When Jay bumped the side of the table, Joshua reacted by flinging his arms wide and bringing them back toward his body. As Yolanda stroked Joshua's cheek, he turned his head in her direction. *TAKE A MOMENT...* Look at Table 3.4 and see if you can name the newborn reflexes that Joshua displayed.

Some reflexes have survival value. The rooting reflex helps a breastfed baby find the mother's nipple. Babies display it only when hungry and touched by another person, not when they touch themselves (Rochat & Hespos, 1997). At birth, babies adjust their sucking pressure to how easily milk flows from the nipple (Craig & Lee, 1999). And if sucking were not automatic, our species would be unlikely to survive for a single generation!

A few reflexes form the basis for complex motor skills that will develop later. The stepping reflex looks like a primitive walking response. Unlike other reflexes, it appears in a wide range of situations—with the newborn's body in a sideways or upside-down position, with feet touching walls or ceilings, and even with legs dangling in the air (Adolph & Berger, 2006).

ASK YOURSELF

REVIEW Sensitive care can help preterm infants recover, but they are less likely than full-term newborns to receive such care. Explain why.

CONNECT List factors discussed in this chapter that increase the chances that an infant will be born underweight. How many of these factors could be prevented by better health care for expectant mothers?

APPLY Cecilia and Adena each gave birth to a 3-pound baby seven weeks preterm. Cecilia is single and on welfare. Adena and her partner are happily married and earn a good income. Plan an intervention appropriate for helping each baby develop.

REFLECT Many people object to the use of extraordinary medical measures to save extremely low-birth-weight babies because of their high risk for serious developmental problems. Do you agree or disagree? Explain.

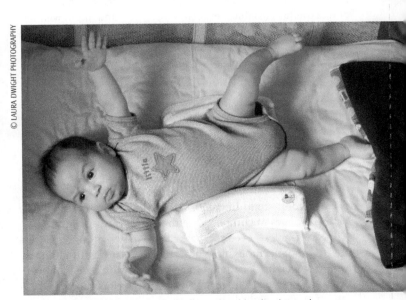

© LAURA DWIGHT PHOTOGRAPHY

In the Moro reflex, loss of support or a sudden loud sound causes the baby to extend the legs and throw the arms outward in an "embracing" motion.

TABLE 3.4

Some Newborn Reflexes

REFLEX	STIMULATION	RESPONSE	AGE OF DISAPPEARANCE	FUNCTION
Eye blink	Shine bright light at eyes or clap hand near head.	Infant quickly closes eyelids.	Permanent	Protects infant from strong stimulation
Rooting	Stroke cheek near corner of mouth.	Head turns toward source of stimulation.	3 weeks (becomes voluntary turning at this time)	Helps infant find the nipple
Sucking	Place finger in infant's mouth.	Infant sucks finger rhythmically.	Replaced by voluntary sucking after 4 months	Permits feeding
Moro	Hold infant horizontally on back and let head drop slightly, or produce a sudden loud sound against surface supporting infant.	Infant makes an "embracing" motion by arching back, extending legs, throwing arms outward, and then bringing arms in toward the body.	6 months	In human evolutionary past, may have helped infant cling to mother
Palmar grasp	Place finger in infant's hand and press against palm.	Infant spontaneously grasps finger.	3–4 months	Prepares infant for voluntary grasping
Tonic neck	Turn head to one side while infant is lying awake on back.	Infant lies in a "fencing position." One arm is extended in front of eyes on side to which head is turned, other arm is flexed.	4 months	May prepare infant for voluntary reaching
Stepping	Hold infant under arms and permit bare feet to touch a flat surface.	Infant lifts one foot after another in stepping response.	2 months in infants who gain weight quickly; sustained in lighter infants	Prepares infant for voluntary walking
Babinski	Stroke sole of foot from toe toward heel.	Toes fan out and curl as foot twists in.	8–12 months	Unknown

Sources: Knobloch & Pasamanick, 1974; Prechtl & Beintema, 1965; Thelen, Fisher, & Ridley-Johnson, 1984.

One reason that babies frequently engage in the alternating leg movements of stepping is their ease compared with other movement patterns; repetitive movement of just one leg or of both legs at once requires more effort.

In infants who gain weight quickly in the weeks after birth, the stepping reflex drops out because thigh and calf muscles are not strong enough to lift the baby's chubby legs. But if the lower part of the infant's body is dipped in water, the reflex reappears because the buoyancy of the water lightens the load on the baby's muscles (Thelen, Fisher, & Ridley-Johnson, 1984). When stepping is exercised regularly, babies make more reflexive stepping movements and are likely to walk several weeks earlier than if stepping is not practiced (Zelazo et al., 1993). However, there is no special need for infants to practice the stepping reflex because all normal babies walk in due time.

Several reflexes help parents and infants establish gratifying interaction. A baby who searches for and successfully finds the nipple, sucks easily during feedings, and grasps when the hand is touched encourages parents to respond lovingly and feel competent as caregivers. Reflexes can also help caregivers comfort the baby because they permit infants to control distress and amount of stimulation. For example, on short trips with Joshua to the grocery store, Yolanda brought along a pacifier. If he became fussy, sucking helped quiet him until she could feed, change, or hold him.

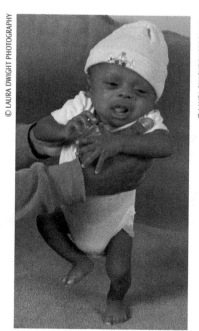

When held upright under the arms, newborns show a reflexive stepping response, which forms the basis for later walking.

The palmar grasp reflex is so strong during the first week after birth that many infants can use it to support their entire weight.

Refer to Table 3.4 again, and you will see that most newborn reflexes disappear during the first six months. Researchers believe that this is due to a gradual increase in voluntary control over behavior as the cerebral cortex develops. Pediatricians test reflexes carefully because reflexes can reveal the health of the baby's nervous system. Weak or absent reflexes, overly rigid or exaggerated reflexes, and reflexes that persist beyond the point in development when they should normally disappear can signal brain damage (Schott & Rossor, 2003; Zafeiriou, 2000).

States

Throughout the day and night, newborn infants move in and out of five **states of arousal,** or degrees of sleep and wakefulness, described in Table 3.5. During the first month, these states alternate frequently. The most fleeting is quiet alertness, which usually moves quickly toward fussing and crying. Much to the relief of their fatigued parents, newborns spend the greatest amount of time asleep—about 16 to 18 hours a day. Because the fetus tends to synchronize periods of rest and activity with those of the mother, newborns sleep more at night than during the day (Heraghty et al., 2008). Nevertheless, young babies' sleep–wake cycles are affected more by fullness–hunger than by darkness–light (Davis, Parker, & Montgomery, 2004).

However, striking individual differences in daily rhythms exist that affect parents' attitudes toward and interactions with the baby. A few newborns sleep for long periods, increasing the energy their well-rested parents have for sensitive, responsive care. Other babies cry a great deal, and their parents must exert great effort to soothe them. If these parents do not succeed, they may feel less competent and less positive toward their infant.

Furthermore, from birth on, arousal patterns have implications for cognitive development. Babies who spend more time alert probably receive more social stimulation and opportunities to explore and, therefore, may have a slight advantage in mental development (Sadeh et al., 2007; Smart & Hiscock, 2007). And as with adults, sleep enhances babies' learning and memory. In one study, eye-blink responses and brain-wave recordings revealed that sleeping newborns readily learned that a tone would be followed by a puff of air to the eye (Fifer et al., 2010). Because young infants spend so much time sleeping, the capacity to learn about external stimuli during sleep may be essential for adaptation to their surroundings.

Of the states listed in Table 3.5, the two extremes—sleep and crying—have been of greatest interest to researchers. Each tells us something about normal and abnormal early development.

Sleep. Observing Joshua as he slept, Yolanda and Jay wondered why his eyelids and body twitched and his rate of breathing varied. Sleep is made up of at least two states. During irregular, or **rapid-eye-movement (REM), sleep,** brain-wave activity is remarkably similar to that of the waking state. The eyes dart beneath the lids; heart rate, blood pressure, and breathing are uneven; and slight body movements occur. In contrast, during regular, or **non-rapid-eye-movement (NREM), sleep,** the body is almost motionless, and heart rate, breathing, and brain-wave activity are slow and even.

Like children and adults, newborns alternate between REM and NREM sleep. However, they spend far more time in the REM state than they ever will again. REM sleep accounts for 50 percent of a newborn baby's sleep time. By 3 to 5 years, it has declined to an adultlike level of 20 percent (Louis et al., 1997).

Why do young infants spend so much time in REM sleep? In older children and adults, the REM state is associated with dreaming. Babies probably do not dream, at least not in the same way we do. But researchers believe that the stimulation of REM sleep is vital for growth of the central nervous system. Young infants seem to have a special need for this stimulation because they spend little time in an alert state, when they can

TABLE 3.5 **Infant States of Arousal**

STATE	DESCRIPTION	DAILY DURATION IN NEWBORN
Regular, or NREM, sleep	The infant is at full rest and shows little or no body activity. The eyelids are closed, no eye movements occur, the face is relaxed, and breathing is slow and regular.	8–9 hours
Irregular, or REM, sleep	Gentle limb movements, occasional stirring, and facial grimacing occur. Although the eyelids are closed, occasional rapid eye movements can be seen beneath them. Breathing is irregular.	8–9 hours
Drowsiness	The infant is either falling asleep or waking up. Body is less active than in irregular sleep but more active than in regular sleep. The eyes open and close; when open, they have a glazed look. Breathing is even but somewhat faster than in regular sleep.	Varies
Quiet alertness	The infant's body is relatively inactive, with eyes open and attentive. Breathing is even.	2–3 hours
Waking activity and crying	The infant shows frequent bursts of uncoordinated body activity. Breathing is very irregular. Face may be relaxed or tense and wrinkled. Crying may occur.	1–4 hours

Source: Wolff, 1966.

get input from the environment. In support of this idea, the percentage of REM sleep is especially great in the fetus and in preterm babies, who are even less able than full-term newborns to take advantage of external stimulation (de Weerd & van den Bossche, 2003; Peirano, Algarin, & Uauy, 2003).

Because newborns' normal sleep behavior is organized and patterned, observations of sleep states can help identify central nervous system abnormalities. In infants who are brain-damaged or who have experienced birth trauma, disturbed REM–NREM sleep cycles are often present. Babies with poor sleep organization are likely to be behaviorally disorganized and, therefore, to have difficulty learning and evoking caregiver interactions that enhance their development. In the preschool years, they show delayed motor, cognitive, and language development (de Weerd & van den Bossche, 2003; Feldman, 2006; Holditch-Davis, Belyea, & Edwards, 2005). And the brain-functioning problems that underlie newborn sleep irregularities may culminate in sudden infant death syndrome, a major cause of infant mortality (see the Biology and Environment box on page 110).

Crying. Crying is the first way that babies communicate, letting parents know they need food, comfort, or stimulation. During the weeks after birth, all infants have some fussy periods when they are difficult to console. But most of the time, the nature of the cry, combined with the experiences leading up to it, helps guide parents toward its cause. The baby's cry is a complex stimulus that varies in intensity, from a whimper to a message of all-out distress (Gustafson, Wood, & Green, 2000; Wood, 2009). As early as the first few weeks, infants can be identified by the unique vocal "signature" of their cries, which helps parents locate their baby from a distance (Gustafson, Green, & Cleland, 1994).

Young infants usually cry because of physical needs. Hunger is the most common cause, but babies may also cry in response to temperature change when undressed, a sudden noise, or a painful stimulus. Newborns (as well as older babies) often cry at the sound of another crying baby (Dondi, Simion, & Caltran, 1999; Geangu et al., 2010). Some researchers believe that this response reflects an inborn capacity to react to the suffering of others. Furthermore, crying typically increases during the early weeks, peaks at about 6 weeks, and then declines (Barr, 2001). Because this trend appears in many cultures with vastly different infant care practices, researchers believe that normal readjustments of the central nervous system underlie it. *TAKE A MOMENT...* The next time you hear an infant cry, notice your own reaction. The sound stimulates strong feelings of arousal and discomfort in men and women, parents and nonparents alike (Murray, 1985). This powerful response is probably innately programmed in humans to make sure that babies receive the care and protection they need to survive.

Soothing Crying Infants. Although parents do not always interpret their baby's cry correctly, their accuracy improves with experience. At the same time, they vary widely in responsiveness.

To soothe his crying infant, this father rocks her gently while talking softly.

Parents who are high in empathy (ability to take the perspective of others in distress) and who hold "child-centered" attitudes toward infant care (for example, believe that babies cannot be spoiled by being picked up) are more likely to respond quickly and sensitively to a crying baby (Leerkes, 2010; Zeifman, 2003).

Fortunately, there are many ways to soothe a crying baby when feeding and diaper changing do not work (see Applying What We Know on page 111). The technique that Western parents usually try first, lifting the baby to the shoulder and rocking or walking, is highly effective. Another common soothing method is swaddling—wrapping the baby snugly in a blanket. The Quechua, who live in the cold, high-altitude desert regions of Peru, dress young babies in layers of clothing and blankets that cover the head and body, a practice that reduces crying and promotes sleep (Tronick, Thomas, & Daltabuit, 1994). It also allows the baby to conserve energy for early growth in the harsh Peruvian highlands.

LOOK AND LISTEN

In a public setting, watch several parents soothe their crying babies. What techniques did the parents use, and how successful were they? ●

Biology and Environment

The Mysterious Tragedy of Sudden Infant Death Syndrome

illie awoke with a start one morning and looked at the clock. It was 7:30, and Sasha had missed both her night waking and her early morning feeding. Wondering if she was all right, Millie and her husband Stuart tiptoed into the room. Sasha lay still, curled up under her blanket. She had died silently during her sleep.

Sasha was a victim of **sudden infant death syndrome (SIDS),** the unexpected death, usually during the night, of an infant under 1 year of age that remains unexplained after thorough investigation. In industrialized nations, SIDS is the leading cause of infant mortality between 1 and 12 months, accounting for about 20 percent of these deaths in the United States (Mathews & MacDorman, 2008).

SIDS victims usually show physical problems from the beginning. Early medical records of SIDS babies reveal higher rates of prematurity and low birth weight, poor Apgar scores, and limp muscle tone. Abnormal heart rate and respiration and disturbances in sleep–wake activity and in REM–NREM cycles while asleep are also involved (Cornwell & Feigenbaum, 2006; Kato et al., 2003). At the time of death, many SIDS babies have a mild respiratory infection (Blood-Siegfried, 2009). This seems to increase the chances of respiratory failure in an already vulnerable baby.

Mounting evidence suggests that impaired brain functioning is a major contributor to SIDS. Between 2 and 4 months, when SIDS is most likely to occur, reflexes decline and are replaced by voluntary, learned responses. Neurological weaknesses may prevent SIDS babies from acquiring behaviors that replace defensive reflexes (Lipsitt, 2003). As a result, when breathing difficulties occur during sleep, infants do not wake up, shift their position, or cry out for help. Instead, they simply give in to oxygen

deprivation and death. In support of this interpretation, autopsies reveal that the brains of SIDS babies contain unusually low levels of serotonin (a brain chemical that assists with arousal when survival is threatened) as well as other abnormalities in centers that control breathing and arousal (Duncan et al., 2010).

Several environmental factors are linked to SIDS. Maternal cigarette smoking, both during and after pregnancy, as well as smoking by other caregivers, doubles risk of the disorder. Babies exposed to cigarette smoke arouse less easily from sleep and have more respiratory infections (Richardson, Walker, & Horne, 2009; Shah, Sullivan, & Carter, 2006). Prenatal abuse of drugs that depress central nervous system functioning (alcohol, opiates, and barbiturates) increases the risk of SIDS as much as fifteenfold (Hunt & Hauck, 2006). Babies of drug-abusing mothers are especially likely to display SIDS-related brain abnormalities (Kinney, 2009).

SIDS babies are also more likely to sleep on their stomachs than on their backs and often are wrapped very warmly in clothing and blankets. Infants who sleep on their stomachs less often wake when their breathing is disturbed (Richardson, Walker, & Horne, 2008). In other cases, healthy babies sleeping face down on soft bedding may die from continually breathing their own exhaled breath.

Quitting smoking and drug taking, changing an infant's sleeping position, and removing a few bedclothes can reduce the incidence of SIDS. For example, if women refrained from smoking while pregnant, an estimated 30 percent of SIDS cases would be prevented. Public education campaigns that encourage parents to put their infants down on their backs have cut the incidence of SIDS in half in many Western nations (Moon, Horne, & Hauck, 2007). Another

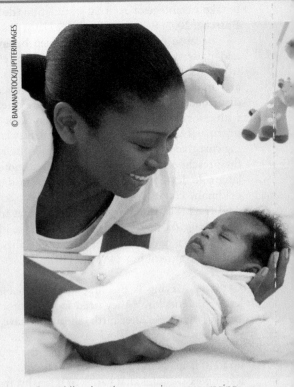

Public education campaigns encouraging parents to put their infants down on their backs to sleep have helped reduce the incidence of SIDS by more than half in many Western nations.

protective measure is pacifier use: Sleeping babies who suck arouse more easily in response to breathing and heart-rate irregularities (Li et al., 2006). Nevertheless, compared with white infants, SIDS rates are two to six times as high in poverty-stricken minority groups, where parental stress, substance abuse, reduced access to health care, and lack of knowledge about safe sleep practices are widespread (Colson et al., 2009; Pickett, Luo, & Lauderdale, 2005).

When SIDS does occur, surviving family members require a great deal of help to overcome a sudden and unexpected death. As Millie commented six months after Sasha's death, "It's the worst crisis we've ever been through. What's helped us most are the comforting words of others who've experienced the same tragedy."

Applying **What We Know**

Soothing a Crying Baby

Method	Explanation
Talk softly or play rhythmic sounds.	Continuous, monotonous, rhythmic sounds (such as a clock ticking, a fan whirring, or peaceful music) are more effective than intermittent sounds.
Offer a pacifier.	Sucking helps babies control their own level of arousal.
Massage the baby's body.	Stroking the baby's torso and limbs with continuous, gentle motions relaxes the baby's muscles.
Swaddle the baby.	Restricting movement and increasing warmth often soothe a young infant.
Lift the baby to the shoulder and rock or walk.	This combination of physical contact, upright posture, and motion is an effective soothing technique, causing young infants to become quietly alert.
Take the baby for a short car ride or a walk in a baby carriage; swing the baby in a cradle.	Gentle, rhythmic motion of any kind helps lull the baby to sleep.
Combine several of the methods just listed.	Stimulating several of the baby's senses at once is often more effective than stimulating only one.
If these methods do not work, let the baby cry for a short period.	Occasionally, a baby responds well to just being put down and, after a few minutes, will fall asleep.

Sources: Campos, 1989; Evanoo, 2007; Lester, 1985; Reisman, 1987.

In many tribal and village societies and non-Western developed nations (such as Japan), babies are in physical contact with their caregivers almost continuously. Infants in these cultures show shorter bouts of crying than their American counterparts (Barr, 2001). When Western parents choose to practice "proximal care" by holding their babies extensively, amount of crying

Like the Quechua of Peru, the Mongol people of Central Asia heavily swaddle their babies, a practice that reduces crying and promotes sleep while also protecting infants from the region's harsh winters.

in the early months is reduced by about one-third (St James-Roberts et al., 2006).

But not all research indicates that rapid parental responsiveness reduces infant crying (van IJzendoorn & Hubbard, 2000). Parents must make reasoned choices about what to do on the basis of culturally accepted practices, the suspected reason for the cry, and the context in which it occurs—for example, in the privacy of their own home or while having dinner at a restaurant. Fortunately, with age, crying declines. Virtually all researchers agree that parents can lessen older babies' need to cry by encouraging more mature ways of expressing their desires, such as gestures and vocalizations.

Abnormal Crying. Like reflexes and sleep patterns, the infant's cry offers a clue to central nervous system distress. The cries of brain-damaged babies and those who have experienced prenatal and birth complications are often shrill, piercing, and shorter in duration than those of healthy infants (Boukydis & Lester, 1998; Green, Irwin, & Gustafson, 2000). Even newborns with a fairly common problem—*colic,* or persistent crying—tend to have high-pitched, harsh-sounding cries (Zeskind & Barr, 1997). Although the cause of colic is unknown, certain newborns, who react especially strongly to unpleasant stimuli, are susceptible. Because their crying is intense, they find it harder to calm down than other babies (Barr et al., 2005; St James-Roberts et al., 2003). Colic generally subsides between 3 and 6 months.

Most parents try to respond to a crying baby with extra care and attention, but sometimes the cry is so unpleasant and the infant so difficult to soothe that parents become frustrated, resentful, and angry. Preterm and ill babies are more likely to be abused by highly stressed parents, who sometimes mention a high-pitched, grating cry as one factor that caused them to lose control and harm the baby (St James-Roberts, 2007). We will discuss a host of additional influences on child abuse in Chapter 8.

Sensory Capacities

On his visit to my class, Joshua looked wide-eyed at my bright pink blouse and turned to the sound of his mother's voice. During feedings, he lets Yolanda know through his sucking rhythm that he prefers the taste of breast milk to plain water. Clearly, Joshua has some well-developed sensory capacities. In the following sections, we explore the newborn's responsiveness to touch, taste, smell, sound, and visual stimulation.

Touch. In our discussion of preterm infants, we saw that touch helps stimulate early physical growth. As we will see in Chapter 6, it is vital for emotional development as well. Therefore, it is not surprising that sensitivity to touch is well-developed at birth. The reflexes listed in Table 3.4 on page 107 reveal that the newborn baby responds to touch, especially around the mouth, on the palms, and on the soles of the feet (Humphrey, 1978). Newborns even use touch to investigate their world. When small objects are placed in their palms, they can distinguish shape (prism versus cylinder) and texture (smooth versus rough), as indicated by their tendency to hold on longer to objects with an unfamiliar shape or texture (Sann & Streri, 2007, 2008).

At birth, infants are highly sensitive to pain. If male newborns are circumcised, anesthetic is sometimes not used because of the risk of giving drugs to a very young infant. Babies often respond with a high-pitched, stressful cry and a dramatic rise in heart rate, blood pressure, palm sweating, pupil dilation, and muscle tension (Lehr et al., 2007; Warnock & Sandrin, 2004). Brain-imaging research suggests that because of central nervous system immaturity, preterm babies, particularly males, feel the pain of a medical injection especially intensely (Bartocci et al., 2006).

Recent research establishing the safety of certain local anesthetics for newborns promises to ease the pain of these procedures. Offering a nipple that delivers a sugar solution is also helpful; it quickly reduces crying and discomfort in young babies, preterm and full-term alike. Breast milk may be especially effective: Even the smell of the milk of the baby's mother reduces infant distress to a routine blood-test heelstick more effectively than the odor of another mother's milk or of formula (Nishitani et al., 2009). And combining sweet liquid with gentle holding by the parent lessens pain even more. Research on infant mammals indicates that physical touch releases *endorphins*—painkilling chemicals in the brain (Axelin, Salanterä, & Lehtonen, 2006; Gormally et al., 2001).

Allowing a baby to endure severe pain overwhelms the nervous system with stress hormones, which can disrupt the child's developing capacity to handle common, everyday stressors. The result is heightened pain sensitivity, sleep disturbances, feeding problems, and difficulty calming down when upset (Mitchell & Boss, 2002).

Taste and Smell. Facial expressions reveal that newborns can distinguish several basic tastes. Like adults, they relax their facial muscles in response to sweetness, purse their lips when the taste is sour, and show a distinct archlike mouth opening when it is bitter (Steiner, 1979; Steiner et al., 2001). These reactions are important for survival: The food that best supports the infant's early growth is the sweet-tasting milk of the mother's breast. Not until 4 months do babies prefer a salty taste to plain water, a change that may prepare them to accept solid foods (Mennella & Beauchamp, 1998).

Nevertheless, newborns can readily learn to like a taste that at first evoked either a neutral or a negative response. For example, babies allergic to cow's-milk formula who are given a soy- or other vegetable-based substitute (typically very strong and bitter-tasting) soon prefer it to regular formula (Harris, 1997). A taste previously disliked can come to be preferred when it is paired with relief of hunger.

As with taste, certain odor preferences are present at birth. For example, the smell of bananas or chocolate causes a relaxed, pleasant facial expression, whereas the odor of rotten eggs makes the infant frown (Steiner, 1979). During pregnancy, the amniotic fluid is rich in tastes and smells that vary with the mother's diet—early experiences that influence newborns' preferences. In a study carried out in the Alsatian region of France, where anise is frequently used to flavor foods, researchers tested newborns for their reaction to the anise odor (Schaal, Marlier, & Soussignan, 2000). The mothers of some babies had regularly consumed anise during the last two weeks of pregnancy; the other mothers had never consumed it. When presented with the anise odor on the day of birth, the babies of non-anise-consuming mothers were far more likely to turn away with a negative facial expression (see Figure 3.7). These different reactions were still apparent four days later, even though all mothers had refrained from consuming anise during this time.

In many mammals, the sense of smell plays an important role in feeding and in protecting the young from predators by helping mothers and babies identify each other. Although smell is less well-developed in humans, traces of its survival value remain.

Immediately after birth, babies placed face down between their mother's breasts spontaneously latch on to a nipple and begin sucking within an hour. If one breast is washed to remove its natural scent, most newborns grasp the unwashed breast, indicating that they are guided by smell (Varendi & Porter, 2001). At 4 days of age, breastfed babies prefer the smell of their own mother's breast to that of an unfamiliar lactating mother (Cernoch & Porter, 1985). And both breast- and bottle-fed 3- to 4-day-olds orient more to the smell of unfamiliar human milk than to formula milk, indicating that (even without postnatal

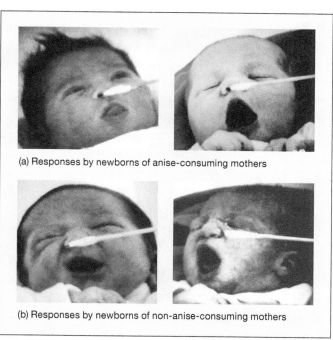

(a) Responses by newborns of anise-consuming mothers

(b) Responses by newborns of non-anise-consuming mothers

FIGURE 3.7 Examples of facial expressions of newborns exposed to the odor of anise whose mothers' diets differed in anise-flavored foods during late pregnancy. (a) Babies of anise-consuming mothers spent more time turning toward the odor and sucking, licking, and chewing. (b) Babies of non-anise-consuming mothers more often turned away with a negative facial expression. (From B. Schaal, L. Marlier, & R. Soussignan, 2000, "Human Foetuses Learn Odours from Their Pregnant Mother's Diet," *Chemical Senses, 25,* p. 731. © 2000 Oxford University Press. Reprinted by permission of Oxford University Press and Dr. Benoist Schaal.)

exposure) the odor of human milk is more attractive to newborns (Marlier & Schaal, 2005). Newborns' dual attraction to the odor of their mother and to that of breast milk helps them locate an appropriate food source and, in the process, begin to distinguish their caregiver from other people.

Hearing. Newborn infants can hear a wide variety of sounds, and their sensitivity improves greatly over the first few months (Saffran, Werker, & Werner, 2006; Tharpe & Ashmead, 2001). At birth, infants prefer complex sounds, such as noises and voices, to pure tones. And babies only a few days old can tell the difference between a variety of sound patterns: a series of tones arranged in ascending versus descending order; tone sequences with a rhythmic downbeat (as in music) versus those without; utterances with two versus three syllables; the stress patterns of words ("*ma*-ma" versus "ma-*ma*"); happy-sounding speech as opposed to speech with negative or neutral emotional qualities; and even two languages spoken by the same bilingual speaker, as long as those languages differ in their rhythmic features—for example, French versus Russian (Mastropieri & Turkewitz, 1999; Ramus, 2002; Sansavini, Bertoncini, & Giovanelli, 1997; Trehub, 2001; Winkler et al., 2009).

Young infants listen longer to human speech than structurally similar nonspeech sounds (Vouloumanos & Werker,

2004). And they can detect the sounds of any human language. Newborns make fine-grained distinctions among many speech sounds. For example, when given a nipple that turns on a recording of the "*ba*" sound, babies suck vigorously and then slow down as the novelty wears off. When the sound switches to "*ga*," sucking picks up, indicating that infants detect this subtle difference. Using this method, researchers have found only a few speech sounds that newborns cannot discriminate. Their ability to perceive sounds not found in their own language is more precise than an adult's (Aldridge, Stillman, & Bower, 2001; Jusczyk & Luce, 2002). These capacities reveal that the baby is marvelously prepared for the awesome task of acquiring language.

TAKE A MOMENT... Listen carefully to yourself the next time you talk to a young baby. You will probably speak in ways that highlight important parts of the speech stream—use a slow, high-pitched, expressive voice with a rising tone at the ends of phrases and sentences and a pause before continuing. Adults probably communicate this way because they notice that infants are more attentive when they do so. Indeed, newborns prefer speech with these characteristics (Saffran, Werker, & Werner, 2006). In addition, they will suck more on a nipple to hear a recording of their mother's voice than that of an unfamiliar woman and to hear their native language as opposed to a foreign language (Moon, Cooper, & Fifer, 1993; Spence & DeCasper, 1987). These preferences may have developed from hearing the muffled sounds of the mother's voice before birth.

Vision. Vision is the least-developed of the newborn baby's senses. Visual structures in both the eye and the brain are not yet fully formed. For example, cells in the *retina*, the membrane lining the inside of the eye that captures light and transforms it into messages that are sent to the brain, are not as mature or densely packed as they will be in several months. The optic nerve that relays these messages, and the visual centers in the brain that receive them, will not be adultlike for several years. And the muscles of the *lens*, which permit us to adjust our visual focus to varying distances, are weak (Kellman & Arterberry, 2006).

As a result, newborns cannot focus their eyes well, and **visual acuity,** or fineness of discrimination, is limited. At birth, infants perceive objects at a distance of 20 feet about as clearly as adults do at 600 feet (Slater et al., 2010). In addition, unlike adults (who see nearby objects most clearly), newborn babies see unclearly across a wide range of distances (Banks, 1980; Hainline, 1998). As a result, images such as the parent's face, even from close up, look quite blurred.

Although they cannot yet see well, newborns actively explore their environment by scanning it for interesting sights and tracking moving objects. However, their eye movements are slow and inaccurate (von Hofsten & Rosander, 1998). Joshua's captivation with my pink blouse reveals that he is attracted to bright objects. But although newborns prefer to look at colored rather than gray stimuli, they are not yet good at discriminating colors. It will take about four months for color vision to become adultlike (Kellman & Arterberry, 2006).

Neonatal Behavioral Assessment

A variety of instruments permit doctors, nurses, and researchers to assess the behavior of newborn babies. The most widely used, T. Berry Brazelton's **Neonatal Behavioral Assessment Scale (NBAS),** evaluates the newborn's reflexes, muscle tone, state changes, responsiveness to physical and social stimuli, and other reactions (Brazelton & Nugent, 1995). An instrument consisting of similar items, the Neonatal Intensive Care Unit Network Neurobehavioral Scale (NNNS), is specially designed for use with newborns at risk for developmental problems because of low birth weight, preterm delivery, prenatal substance exposure, or other conditions (Lester & Tronick, 2004). Scores are used to recommend appropriate interventions and to guide parents in meeting their baby's unique needs.

The NBAS has been given to many infants around the world. As a result, researchers have learned about individual and cultural differences in newborn behavior and how child-rearing practices can maintain or change a baby's reactions. For example, NBAS scores of Asian and Native-American babies reveal that they are less irritable than Caucasian infants. Mothers in these cultures often encourage their babies' calm dispositions through holding and nursing at the first signs of discomfort (Muret-Wagstaff & Moore, 1989; Small, 1998). The Kipsigis of rural Kenya, who highly value infant motor maturity, massage babies regularly and begin exercising the stepping reflex shortly after birth. These customs contribute to Kipsigis babies' strong but flexible muscle tone at 5 days of age (Super & Harkness, 2009). In Zambia, Africa, close mother–infant contact throughout the day quickly changes the poor NBAS scores of undernourished newborns. When reassessed at 1 week of age, a once unresponsive newborn appears alert and contented (Brazelton, Koslowski, & Tronick, 1976).

TAKE A MOMENT... Using these examples, can you explain why a single neonatal assessment score is not a good predictor of later development? Because newborn behavior and parenting combine to influence development, *changes in scores* over the first week or two of life (rather than a single score) provide the best estimate of the baby's ability to recover from the stress of birth. NBAS "recovery curves" predict intelligence and absence of emotional and behavior problems with moderate success well into the preschool years (Brazelton, Nugent, & Lester, 1987; Ohgi et al., 2003a, 2003b).

In some hospitals, health professionals use the NBAS or the NNNS to help parents get to know their newborns through discussion or demonstration of the capacities these instruments assess. Parents who participate in these programs, compared with no-intervention controls, interact more confidently and effectively with their babies (Browne & Talmi, 2005; Bruschweiler-Stern, 2004). Although lasting effects on development have not been demonstrated, NBAS-based interventions are useful in helping the parent–infant relationship get off to a good start.

© JEFFREY L. ROTMAN/CORBIS

Similar to women in the Zambian culture, this mother of the El Molo people of northern Kenya carries her baby all day, providing close physical contact, a rich variety of stimulation, and ready feeding.

ASK YOURSELF

REVIEW What functions does REM sleep serve in young infants? Can sleep tell us anything about the health of the newborn's central nervous system? Explain.

CONNECT How do the diverse capacities of newborn babies contribute to their first social relationships? Provide as many examples as you can.

APPLY After a difficult delivery, Jackie observes her 2-day-old daughter Kelly being given the NBAS. Kelly scores poorly on many items. Seeing this, Jackie wonders if Kelly will develop normally. How would you respond to Jackie's concern?

REFLECT Are newborns more competent than you thought they were before you read this chapter? Which of their capacities most surprised you?

Adjusting to the New Family Unit

Because effective parental care is crucial for infant survival and optimal development, nature helps prepare expectant mothers and fathers for their new role. Toward the end of pregnancy, mothers begin producing the hormone oxytocin, which stimulates uterine contractions; causes the breasts to "let down" milk; induces a calm, relaxed mood; and promotes responsiveness to the baby (Russell, Douglas, & Ingram, 2001). And fathers show hormonal changes around the time of birth that are compatible with those of mothers—specifically, slight increases in *prolactin* (a hormone that stimulates milk production in females) and *estrogens* (sex hormones produced in larger quantities in females) and a drop in *androgens* (sex hormones produced in larger quantities in males) (Numan & Insel, 2003; Wynne-Edwards, 2001). These changes, which are induced by fathers' contact with the mother and baby, predict positive emotional reactions to infants and paternal caregiving (Feldman et al., 2010; Leuner, Glasper, & Gould, 2010).

Although birth-related hormones can facilitate caregiving, their release and effects may depend on experiences, such as a positive couple relationship. Furthermore, humans can parent effectively without experiencing birth-related hormonal changes, as successful adoption reveals. And as we have seen, a great many factors—from family functioning to social policies—are involved in good infant care.

Indeed, the early weeks after the baby's arrival are full of profound challenges. The mother needs to recuperate from childbirth. If she is breastfeeding, energies must be devoted to

working out this intimate relationship. The father must become a part of this new threesome while supporting the mother in her recovery. At times, he may feel ambivalent about the baby, who constantly demands and gets the mother's attention. And as we will see in Chapter 6, siblings—especially those who are young and firstborn—understandably feel displaced. They sometimes react with jealousy and anger.

While all this is going on, the tiny infant is assertive about his urgent physical needs, demanding to be fed, changed, and comforted at odd times of the day and night. The family schedule becomes irregular and uncertain. Yolanda spoke candidly about the changes she and Jay experienced:

> When we brought Joshua home, he seemed so small and helpless, and we worried about whether we would be able to take proper care of him. It took us 20 minutes to change the first diaper! I rarely feel rested because I'm up two to four times every night, and I spend a good part of my waking hours trying to anticipate Joshua's rhythms and needs. If Jay weren't so willing to help by holding and walking Joshua, I think I'd find it much harder.

How long does this time of adjustment to parenthood last? In Chapter 14, we will see that when marital relationships are positive, social support is available, and families have sufficient income, the stress caused by the birth of a baby remains manageable. Nevertheless, as one pair of counselors who have worked with many new parents pointed out, "As long as children are dependent on their parents, those parents find themselves preoccupied with thoughts of their children. This does not keep them from enjoying other aspects of their lives, but it does mean that they never return to being quite the same people they were before they became parents" (Colman & Colman, 1991, p. 198).

SUMMARY

Prenatal Development
(p. 80)

List the three periods of prenatal development, and describe the major milestones of each.

- The period of the zygote lasts about two weeks, from fertilization until **implantation** of the blastocyst in the uterine lining. During this time, structures that will support prenatal growth begin to form, including the **placenta** and the **umbilical cord.**

- During the period of the **embryo,** weeks 2 through 8, the groundwork is laid for all body structures. The **neural tube** forms and the nervous system starts to develop. Other organs follow rapidly. By the end of this period, the embryo responds to touch and can move.

- The period of the **fetus,** lasting until the end of pregnancy, involves dramatic increase in body size and completion of physical structures. At the end of the second **trimester,** most of the brain's neurons are in place.

- The fetus reaches the **age of viability** at the beginning of the third trimester, between 22 and 26 weeks. The brain continues to develop rapidly, and new sensory and behavioral capacities emerge. Gradually the lungs mature, the fetus fills the uterus, and birth is near.

Prenatal Environmental Influences (p. 85)

Cite factors that influence the impact of teratogens, noting agents that are known teratogens.

- The impact of **teratogens** varies with the amount and length of exposure, genetic makeup of mother and fetus, presence or absence of other harmful agents, and age of the organism at time of exposure. The developing organism is especially vulnerable during the embryonic period.

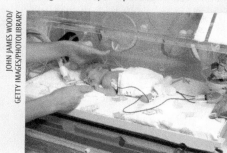

JOHN JAMES WOOD/
GETTY IMAGES/PHOTOLIBRARY

- The most widely used potent teratogen is Accutane, a drug used to treat severe acne. The prenatal impact of other commonly used medications, such as aspirin and caffeine, is hard to separate from other factors correlated with drug taking.

- Babies born to users of cocaine, heroin, or methadone are at risk for a wide variety of problems, including prematurity, low birth weight, physical defects, breathing difficulties, and death around the time of birth.

- Infants whose parents use tobacco are often born underweight, may have physical defects, and are at risk for long-term attention, learning, and behavior problems. Maternal alcohol consumption can lead to **fetal alcohol spectrum disorder (FASD)**. **Fetal alcohol syndrome (FAS)** involves slow physical growth, facial abnormalities, and mental impairments. Milder forms—**partial fetal alcohol syndrome (p-FAS)** and **alcohol-related neurodevelopmental disorder (ARND)**—affect children whose mothers consumed smaller quantities of alcohol.

© SHUTTERSTOCK

- Prenatal exposure to high levels of ionizing radiation, mercury, PCBs, lead, and dioxins leads to physical malformations and severe brain damage. Low-level exposure has been linked to cognitive deficits and emotional and behavioral disorders.

- Among infectious diseases, rubella causes a wide range of abnormalities. Babies with prenatally transmitted HIV rapidly develop AIDS, leading to brain damage and early death. Cytomegalovirus, herpes simplex 2, and toxoplasmosis can also be devastating to the embryo and fetus.

Describe the impact of additional maternal factors on prenatal development.

- Prenatal malnutrition can lead to low birth weight, organ damage, and suppression of immune system development. Vitamin–mineral enrichment, including folic acid, can prevent prenatal and birth complications.

- Severe emotional stress is linked to many pregnancy complications and may permanently alter fetal neurological functioning, thereby magnifying future stress reactivity. Its negative impact can be reduced by providing the mother with social support. **Rh factor incompatibility**—an Rh-negative mother carrying an Rh-positive fetus—can lead to oxygen deprivation, brain and heart damage, and infant death.

- Other than the risk of chromosomal abnormalities in older women, maternal age through the thirties is not a major cause of prenatal problems. Poor health and environmental risks associated with poverty are the strongest predictors of pregnancy complications.

Why is early and regular health care vital during the prenatal period?

- Unexpected difficulties, such as preeclampsia, can arise, especially in mothers with preexisting health problems. Prenatal health care is especially critical for women unlikely to seek it, including those who are young and poor.

Childbirth (p. 96)

Describe the three stages of childbirth, the baby's adaptation to labor and delivery, and the newborn baby's appearance.

- In the first stage of childbirth, contractions widen and thin the cervix. In the second stage, the mother feels an urge to push the baby through the birth canal. In the final stage, the placenta is delivered. During labor, infants produce high levels of stress hormones, which help them withstand oxygen deprivation, clear the lungs for breathing, and arouse them into alertness at birth.

- Newborn babies have large heads, small bodies, and facial features that make adults feel like cuddling them. The **Apgar Scale** assesses the baby's physical condition at birth.

Approaches to Childbirth (p. 98)

Describe natural childbirth and home delivery, noting benefits and concerns associated with each.

- In **natural,** or **prepared, childbirth,** the expectant mother and a companion attend classes about labor and delivery, master relaxation and breathing techniques to counteract pain, and prepare for coaching during childbirth. Social support from a partner, relative, or doula reduces the length of labor and the incidence of birth complications.

- Home birth is safe for healthy mothers who are assisted by a well-trained doctor or midwife, but mothers at risk for complications are safer giving birth in a hospital.

Medical Interventions (p. 100)

List common medical interventions during childbirth, circumstances that justify their use, and any dangers associated with each.

- **Fetal monitors** help save the lives of many babies at risk for **anoxia** because of pregnancy and birth complications. When used routinely, however, they may identify infants as in danger who, in fact, are not.

- Use of analgesics and anesthetics to control pain, though necessary in complicated deliveries, can prolong labor and may have negative affects on the newborn's adjustment.

- **Cesarean deliveries** are warranted by medical emergency or serious maternal illness and for many babies who are in **breech position.** However, many unnecessary cesareans are performed.

Preterm and Low-Birth-Weight Infants (p. 101)

Describe risks associated with preterm birth and low birth weight, along with effective interventions.

- Low birth weight, most common in infants born to poverty-stricken women, is a major cause of neonatal and **infant mortality** and many developmental problems. Compared with **preterm infants,** whose weight is appropriate for time spent in the uterus, **small-for-date infants** usually have longer-lasting difficulties.

© ERNESTO BONILLA/XINHUA PRESS/CORBIS

- Some interventions provide special stimulation in the intensive care nursery. Others teach parents how to care for and interact with their babies. Preterm infants in stressed, low-income households need long-term, intensive intervention.

Birth Complications, Parenting, and Resilience (p. 105)

What factors predict positive outcomes in infants who survive a traumatic birth?

- When infants experience birth trauma, a supportive home environment can help restore their growth. Even infants with fairly serious birth complications can recover with the help of favorable experiences with parents, relatives, neighbors, and peers.

The Newborn Baby's Capacities (p. 106)

Describe the newborn baby's reflexes and states of arousal, including sleep characteristics and ways to soothe a crying baby.

- **Reflexes** are the newborn baby's most obvious organized patterns of behavior. Some have survival value, others provide the foundation for voluntary motor skills, and still others help parents and infants establish gratifying interaction.

© LAURA DWIGHT PHOTOGRAPHY

- Newborns move in and out of five **states of arousal** but spend most of their time asleep. Sleep includes at least two states, **rapid-eye-movement (REM) sleep** and **non-rapid-eye-movement (NREM) sleep.** Newborns spend about 50 percent of sleep time in REM sleep, which provides them with stimulation essential for central nervous system development.

- A crying baby stimulates strong feelings of discomfort in nearby adults. The intensity of the cry and the experiences that led up to it help parents identify what is wrong. Once feeding and diaper changing have been tried, a highly effective soothing technique is lifting the baby to the shoulder and rocking and walking.

Describe the newborn baby's sensory capacities.

- The senses of touch, taste, smell, and sound are well-developed at birth. Newborns use touch to investigate their world, are sensitive to pain, prefer sweet tastes and smells, and orient toward the odor of their own mother's lactating breast.

- Newborns can distinguish a variety of sound patterns and prefer complex sounds. They are especially responsive to human speech, can detect the sounds of any human language, and prefer their mother's voice.

- Vision is the least developed of the newborn's senses. At birth, focusing ability and **visual acuity** are limited. In exploring the visual field, newborn babies are attracted to bright objects but have difficulty discriminating colors.

Why is neonatal behavioral assessment useful?

- The most widely used instrument for assessing the behavior of the newborn infant, Brazelton's **Neonatal Behavioral Assessment Scale (NBAS),** has helped researchers understand individual and cultural differences in newborn behavior. Sometimes it is used to teach parents about their newborn's capacities.

© JEFFREY L. ROTMAN/CORBIS

Adjusting to the New Family Unit (p. 115)

Describe typical changes in the family after the birth of a new baby.

- The new baby's arrival is exciting but stressful, as the mother recuperates from childbirth and the family schedule becomes irregular and uncertain. When parents have a positive relationship as well as social support and adequate income, adjustment problems are usually temporary.

Important Terms and Concepts

age of viability (p. 84)
alcohol-related neurodevelopmental disorder (ARND) (p. 89)
amnion (p. 81)
anoxia (p. 100)
Apgar Scale (p. 98)
breech position (p. 100)
cesarean delivery (p. 101)
chorion (p. 82)
embryo (p. 82)
fetal alcohol spectrum disorder (FASD) (p. 88)
fetal alcohol syndrome (FAS) (p. 88)

fetal monitors (p. 100)
fetus (p. 83)
implantation (p. 81)
infant mortality (p. 104)
lanugo (p. 83)
natural, or prepared, childbirth (p. 99)
Neonatal Behavioral Assessment Scale (NBAS) (p. 114)
neural tube (p. 82)
non-rapid-eye-movement (NREM) sleep (p. 108)
placenta (p. 82)

preterm infants (p. 102)
rapid-eye-movement (REM) sleep (p. 108)
reflex (p. 106)
Rh factor incompatibility (p. 93)
small-for-date infants (p. 102)
states of arousal (p. 108)
sudden infant death syndrome (SIDS) (p. 110)
teratogen (p. 85)
trimesters (p. 83)
umbilical cord (p. 82)
vernix (p. 83)
visual acuity (p. 113)

© ELLEN B. SENISI PHOTOGRAPHY

Infants acquire new motor skills by building on previously acquired capacities. Eager to explore her world, this baby practices the art of crawling. Once she can fully move on her own, she will make dramatic strides in understanding her surroundings.

Physical Development in Infancy and Toddlerhood

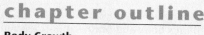

chapter outline

Body Growth

Changes in Body Size and Muscle–Fat Makeup • Individual and Group Differences • Changes in Body Proportions

Brain Development

Development of Neurons • Neurobiological Methods • Development of the Cerebral Cortex • Sensitive Periods in Brain Development • Changing States of Arousal

■ **BIOLOGY AND ENVIRONMENT** Brain Plasticity: Insights from Research on Brain-Damaged Children and Adults

■ **CULTURAL INFLUENCES** Cultural Variation in Infant Sleeping Arrangements

Influences on Early Physical Growth

Heredity • Nutrition • Malnutrition

Learning Capacities

Classical Conditioning • Operant Conditioning • Habituation • Imitation

Motor Development

The Sequence of Motor Development • Motor Skills as Dynamic Systems • Fine-Motor Development: Reaching and Grasping

Perceptual Development

Hearing • Vision • Intermodal Perception • Understanding Perceptual Development

■ **BIOLOGY AND ENVIRONMENT** "Tuning In" to Familiar Speech, Faces, and Music: A Sensitive Period for Culture-Specific Learning

On a brilliant June morning, 16-month-old Caitlin emerged from her front door, ready for the short drive to the child-care home where she spent her weekdays while her mother, Carolyn, and her father, David, worked. Clutching a teddy bear in one hand and her mother's arm with the other, Caitlin descended the steps. "One! Two! Threeee!" Carolyn counted as she helped Caitlin down. "How much she's changed," Carolyn thought to herself, looking at the child who, not long ago, had been a newborn. With her first steps, Caitlin had passed from *infancy* to *toddlerhood*—a period spanning the second year of life. At first, Caitlin did, indeed, "toddle" with an awkward gait, tipping over frequently. But her face reflected the thrill of conquering a new skill.

As they walked toward the car, Carolyn and Caitlin spotted 3-year-old Eli and his father, Kevin, in the neighboring yard. Eli dashed toward them, waving a bright yellow envelope. Carolyn bent down to open the envelope and took out a card. It read, "Announcing the arrival of Grace Ann. Born: Cambodia. Age: 16 months." Carolyn turned to Kevin and Eli. "That's wonderful news! When can we see her?"

"Let's wait a few days," Kevin suggested. "Monica's taken Grace to the doctor this morning. She's underweight and malnourished." Kevin described Monica's first night with Grace in a hotel room in Phnom Penh. Grace lay on the bed, withdrawn and fearful. Eventually she fell asleep, gripping crackers in both hands.

HOANG DINH NAM/AFP/GETTY IMAGES

Carolyn felt Caitlin's impatient tug at her sleeve. Off they drove to child care, where Vanessa had just dropped off her 18-month-old son, Timmy. Within moments, Caitlin and Timmy were in the sandbox, shoveling sand into plastic cups and buckets with the help of their caregiver, Ginette.

A few weeks later, Grace joined Caitlin and Timmy at Ginette's child-care home. Although still tiny and unable to crawl or walk, she had grown taller and heavier, and her sad, vacant gaze had given way to an alert expression, a ready smile, and an enthusiastic desire to imitate and explore. When Caitlin headed for the sandbox, Grace stretched out her arms, asking Ginette to carry her there, too. Soon Grace was pulling herself up at every opportunity. Finally, at age 18 months, she walked!

This chapter traces physical growth during the first two years—one of the most remarkable and busiest times of development. We will see how rapid changes in the infant's body and brain support learning, motor skills, and perceptual capacities. Caitlin, Grace, and Timmy will join us along the way to illustrate individual differences and environmental influences on physical development. ●

Body Growth

TAKE A MOMENT... The next time you're walking in your neighborhood park or at the mall, note the contrast between infants' and toddlers' physical capabilities. One reason for the vast changes in what children can do over the first two years is that their bodies change enormously—faster than at any other time after birth.

Changes in Body Size and Muscle–Fat Makeup

By the end of the first year, a typical infant's height is about 32 inches—more than 50 percent greater than at birth. By 2 years, it is 75 percent greater (36 inches). Similarly, by 5 months of age, birth weight has doubled, to about 15 pounds. At 1 year it has tripled, to 22 pounds, and at 2 years it has quadrupled, to about 30 pounds.

Figure 4.1 illustrates this dramatic increase in body size. But rather than making steady gains, infants and toddlers grow in little spurts. In one study, children who were followed over the first 21 months of life went for periods of 7 to 63 days with no growth, then added as much as half an inch in a 24-hour period! Almost always, parents described their babies as irritable and

Chris at 7 weeks

Chris at 7 months

Chris at 11 months

Chris at 22 months

Mai at 11 months

Mai at birth

Mai at 8 months

Mai at 22 months

FIGURE 4.1 Body growth during the first two years. These photos depict the dramatic changes in body size and proportions during infancy and toddlerhood in two individuals—a boy, Chris, and a girl, Mai. In the first year, the head is quite large in proportion to the rest of the body, and height and weight gain are especially rapid. During the second year, the lower portion of the body catches up. Notice, also, how both children added "baby fat" in the early months of life and then slimmed down, a trend that continues into middle childhood.

very hungry on the day before the spurt (Lampl, 1993; Lampl, Veldhuis, & Johnson, 1992).

One of the most obvious changes in infants' appearance is their transformation into round, plump babies by the middle of the first year. This early rise in "baby fat," which peaks at about 9 months, helps the small infant maintain a constant body temperature. In the second year, most toddlers slim down, a trend that continues into middle childhood (Fomon & Nelson, 2002). In contrast, muscle tissue increases very slowly during infancy and will not reach a peak until adolescence. Babies are not very muscular; their strength and physical coordination are limited.

Individual and Group Differences

In infancy, girls are slightly shorter and lighter than boys, with a higher ratio of fat to muscle. These small sex differences persist throughout early and middle childhood and are greatly magnified at adolescence. Ethnic differences in body size are apparent as well. Grace was below the *growth norms* (height and weight averages for children her age). Early malnutrition contributed, but even after substantial catch-up, Grace—as is typical for Asian children—remained below North American norms. In contrast, Timmy is slightly above average, as African-American children tend to be (Bogin, 2001).

Children of the same age also differ in *rate* of physical growth; some make faster progress toward a mature body size than others. But current body size is not enough to tell us how quickly a child's physical growth is moving along. Although Timmy is larger and heavier than Caitlin and Grace, he is not physically more mature. In a moment, you will see why.

The best estimate of a child's physical maturity is *skeletal age,* a measure of bone development. It is determined by X-raying the long bones of the body to see the extent to which soft, pliable cartilage has hardened into bone, a gradual process that is completed in adolescence. When skeletal ages are examined, African-American children tend to be slightly ahead of Caucasian children at all ages, and girls are considerably ahead of boys. At birth, the sexes differ by about 4 to 6 weeks, a gap that widens over infancy and childhood (Tanner, Healy, & Cameron, 2001). This greater physical maturity may contribute to girls' greater resistance to harmful environmental influences. As noted in Chapter 2, girls experience fewer developmental problems than boys and have lower infant and childhood mortality rates.

Changes in Body Proportions

As the child's overall size increases, different parts of the body grow at different rates. Two growth patterns describe these changes. The first is the **cephalocaudal trend**—from the Latin for "head to tail." During the prenatal period, the head develops more rapidly than the lower part of the body. At birth, the head takes up one-fourth of total body length, the legs only one-third. Notice how, in Figure 4.1, the lower portion of the body catches up. By age 2, the head accounts for only one-fifth and the legs for nearly one-half of total body length.

In the second pattern, the **proximodistal trend,** growth proceeds, literally, from "near to far"—from the center of the body outward. In the prenatal period, the head, chest, and trunk grow first, then the arms and legs, and finally the hands and feet. During infancy and childhood, the arms and legs continue to grow somewhat ahead of the hands and feet.

Brain Development

At birth, the brain is nearer to its adult size than any other physical structure, and it continues to develop at an astounding pace throughout infancy and toddlerhood. We can best understand brain growth by looking at it from two vantage points: (1) the microscopic level of individual brain cells and (2) the larger level of the cerebral cortex, the most complex brain structure and the one responsible for the highly developed intelligence of our species.

Development of Neurons

The human brain has 100 to 200 billion **neurons,** or nerve cells that store and transmit information, many of which have thousands of direct connections with other neurons. Unlike other body cells, neurons are not tightly packed together. Between them are tiny gaps, or **synapses,** where fibers from different neurons come close together but do not touch (see Figure 4.2). Neurons send messages to one another by releasing chemicals called **neurotransmitters,** which cross the synapse.

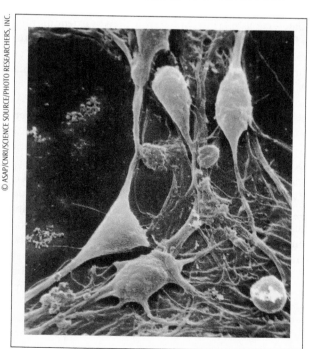

FIGURE 4.2 Neurons and their connective fibers. This photograph of several neurons, taken with the aid of a powerful microscope, shows the elaborate synaptic connections that form with neighboring cells.

© ASAP/CNRI/SCIENCE SOURCE/PHOTO RESEARCHERS, INC.

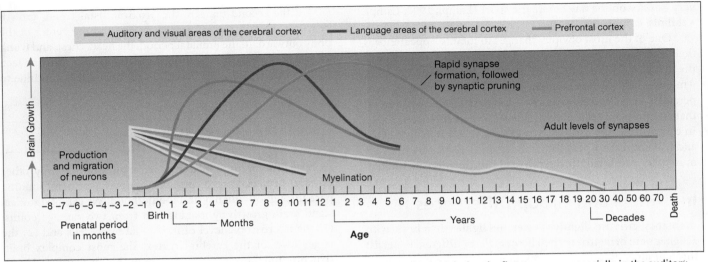

FIGURE 4.3 **Major milestones of brain development.** Formation of synapses is rapid during the first two years, especially in the auditory, visual, and language areas of the cerebral cortex. The prefrontal cortex undergoes more extended synaptic growth. In each area, overproduction of synapses is followed by synaptic pruning. The prefrontal cortex is among the last regions to attain adult levels of synaptic connections—in mid- to late adolescence. Myelination occurs at a dramatic pace during the first two years, more slowly through childhood, followed by an acceleration at adolescence and then a reduced pace in early adulthood. The multiple yellow lines indicate that the timing of myelination varies among different brain areas. For example, neural fibers myelinate over a longer period in the language areas, and especially in the prefrontal cortex, than in the visual and auditory areas. (Adapted from Thompson & Nelson, 2001.)

The basic story of brain growth concerns how neurons develop and form this elaborate communication system. Figure 4.3 summarizes major milestones of brain development. In the prenatal period, neurons are produced in the embryo's primitive neural tube. From there, they migrate to form the major parts of the brain (see Chapter 3, page 82). Once neurons are in place, they differentiate, establishing their unique functions by extending their fibers to form synaptic connections with neighboring cells. During the first two years, neural fibers and synapses increase at an astounding pace (Huttenlocher, 2002; Moore, Persaud, & Torchia, 2013). A surprising aspect of brain growth is **programmed cell death,** which makes space for these connective structures: As synapses form, many surrounding neurons die—20 to 80 percent, depending on the brain region (de Haan & Johnson, 2003; Stiles, 2008). Fortunately, during the prenatal period, the neural tube produces far more neurons than the brain will ever need.

As neurons form connections, *stimulation* becomes vital to their survival. Neurons that are stimulated by input from the surrounding environment continue to establish synapses, forming increasingly elaborate systems of communication that support more complex abilities. At first, stimulation results in a massive overabundance of synapses, many of which serve identical functions, thereby ensuring that the child will acquire the motor, cognitive, and social skills that our species needs to survive. Neurons that are seldom stimulated soon lose their synapses, in a process called **synaptic pruning** that returns neurons not needed at the moment to an uncommitted state so they can support future development. In all, about 40 percent of synapses are pruned during childhood and adolescence to reach the adult level (Webb, Monk, & Nelson, 2001). For this process to advance, appropriate stimulation of the child's brain is vital during periods in which the formation of synapses is at its peak (Bryk & Fisher, 2012).

If few new neurons are produced after the prenatal period, what causes the dramatic increase in brain size during the first two years? About half the brain's volume is made up of **glial cells,** which are responsible for **myelination,** the coating of neural fibers with an insulating fatty sheath (called *myelin*) that improves the efficiency of message transfer. Glial cells multiply rapidly from the fourth month of pregnancy through the second year of life—a process that continues at a slower pace through middle childhood and accelerates again in adolescence. Gains in neural fibers and myelination are responsible for the extraordinary gain in overall size of the brain—from nearly 30 percent of its adult weight at birth to 70 percent by age 2 (Johnson, 2011; Knickmeyer et al., 2008).

Brain development can be compared to molding a "living sculpture." First, neurons and synapses are overproduced. Then, cell death and synaptic pruning sculpt away excess building material to form the mature brain—a process jointly influenced by genetically programmed events and the child's experiences. The resulting "sculpture" is a set of interconnected regions, each with specific functions—much like countries on a globe that communicate with one another (Johnston et al., 2001). This "geography" of the brain permits researchers to study its developing organization and the activity of its regions using neurobiological methods.

Neurobiological Methods

Table 4.1 describes major measures of brain functioning. The first two methods detect changes in *electrical activity* in the cerebral cortex. In an *electroencephalogram (EEG),* researchers examine *brain-wave patterns* for stability and organization—signs of mature functioning of the cortex. And as the person

TABLE 4.1
Methods for Measuring Brain Functioning

METHOD	DESCRIPTION
Electroencephalogram (EEG)	Electrodes embedded in a head cap record electrical brain-wave activity in the brain's outer layers—the cerebral cortex. Today, researchers use an advanced tool called a geodesic sensor net (GSN) to hold interconnected electrodes (up to 128 for infants and 256 for children and adults) in place through a cap that adjusts to each person's head shape, yielding improved brain-wave detection.
Event-related potentials (ERPs)	Using the EEG, the frequency and amplitude of brain waves in response to particular stimuli (such as a picture, music, or speech) are recorded in multiple areas of the cerebral cortex. Enables identification of general regions of stimulus-induced activity.
Functional magnetic resonance imaging (fMRI)	While the person lies inside a tunnel-shaped apparatus that creates a magnetic field, a scanner magnetically detects increased blood flow and oxygen metabolism in areas of the brain as the individual processes particular stimuli. The scanner typically records images every 1 to 4 seconds; these are combined into a computerized moving picture of activity anywhere in the brain (not just its outer layers). Not appropriate for children younger than age 5 to 6, who cannot remain still during testing.
Positron emission tomography (PET)	After injection or inhalation of a radioactive substance, the person lies on an apparatus with a scanner that emits fine streams of X-rays, which detect increased blood flow and oxygen metabolism in areas of the brain as the person processes particular stimuli. As with fMRI, the result is a computerized image of "online" activity anywhere in the brain. Not appropriate for children younger than age 5 to 6.
Near-infrared spectroscopy (NIRS)	Using thin, flexible optical fibers attached to the scalp through a head cap, infrared (invisible) light is beamed at the brain; its absorption by areas of the cerebral cortex varies with changes in blood flow and oxygen metabolism as the individual processes particular stimuli. The result is a computerized moving picture of active areas in the cerebral cortex. Unlike fMRI and PET, NIRS is appropriate for infants and young children, who can move within limited range.

processes a particular stimulus, *event-related potentials (ERPs)* detect the general location of brain-wave activity—a technique often used to study preverbal infants' responsiveness to various stimuli, the impact of experience on specialization of specific brain regions, and atypical brain functioning in individuals with learning and emotional problems (DeBoer, Scott, & Nelson, 2007; deRegnier, 2005).

Neuroimaging techniques, which yield detailed, three-dimensional computerized pictures of the entire brain and its active areas, provide the most precise information about which brain regions are specialized for certain capacities and about abnormalities in brain functioning. The most promising of these methods is *functional magnetic resonance imaging (fMRI).* Unlike *positron emission tomography (PET),* fMRI does not depend on X-ray photography, which requires injection of a radioactive substance. Rather, when an individual is exposed to a stimulus, fMRI detects changes in blood flow and oxygen metabolism throughout the brain magnetically, yielding a colorful, moving picture of parts of the brain used to perform a given activity (see Figure 4.4a, b, and c).

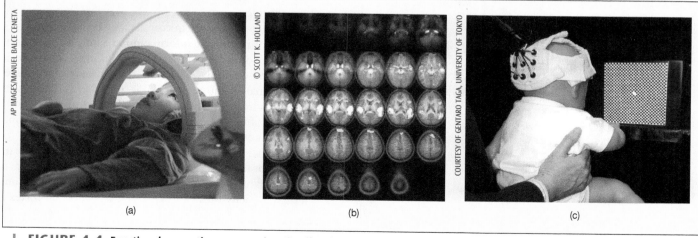

FIGURE 4.4 Functional magnetic resonance imaging (fMRI) and near-infrared spectroscopy (NIRS). (a) This 6-year-old is part of a study that uses fMRI to find out how his brain processes light and motion. (b) The fMRI image shows which areas of the child's brain are active while he views changing visual stimuli. (c) Here, NIRS is used to investigate a 2-month-old's response to a visual stimulus. During testing, the baby can move freely within a limited range. (Photo (c) from G. Taga, K. Asakawa, A. Maki, Y. Konishi, & H. Koisumi, 2003, "Brain Imaging in Awake Infants by Near-Infrared Optical Topography," *Proceedings of the National Academy of Sciences, 100,* p. 10723. Reprinted by permission.)

Because PET and fMRI require that the participant lie as motionless as possible for an extended time, they are not suitable for infants and young children (Nelson, Thomas, & de Haan, 2006). A neuroimaging technique that works well in infancy and early childhood is *near-infrared spectroscopy (NIRS),* in which infrared (invisible) light is beamed at regions of the cerebral cortex to measure blood flow and oxygen metabolism while the child attends to a stimulus (refer again to Table 4.1). Because the apparatus consists only of thin, flexible optical fibers attached to the scalp using a head cap, a baby can sit on the parent's lap and move during testing—as Figure 4.4c illustrates (Hespos et al., 2010). But unlike PET and fMRI, which map activity changes throughout the brain, NIRS examines only the functioning of the cerebral cortex.

Development of the Cerebral Cortex

The **cerebral cortex** surrounds the rest of the brain, resembling half of a shelled walnut. It is the largest brain structure, accounting for 85 percent of the brain's weight and containing the greatest number of neurons and synapses. Because the cerebral cortex is the last part of the brain to stop growing, it is sensitive to environmental influences for a much longer period than any other part of the brain.

Regions of the Cerebral Cortex. Figure 4.5 shows specific functions of regions of the cerebral cortex, such as receiving information from the senses, instructing the body to move, and thinking. The order in which cortical regions develop corresponds to the order in which various capacities emerge in the infant and growing child. For example, a burst of activity

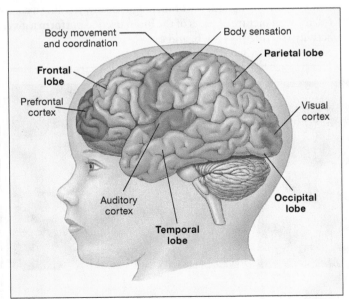

FIGURE 4.5 The left side of the human brain, showing the cerebral cortex. The cortex is divided into different lobes, each containing a variety of regions with specific functions. Some major regions are labeled here.

occurs in the auditory and visual cortexes and in areas responsible for body movement over the first year—a period of dramatic gains in auditory and visual perception and mastery of motor skills (Johnson, 2011). Language areas are especially active from late infancy through the preschool years, when language development flourishes (Pujol et al., 2006; Thompson, 2000).

The cortical regions with the most extended period of development are the *frontal lobes.* The **prefrontal cortex,** lying in front of areas controlling body movement, is responsible for thought—in particular, consciousness, inhibition of impulses, integration of information, and use of memory, reasoning, planning, and problem-solving strategies. From age 2 months on, the prefrontal cortex functions more effectively. But it undergoes especially rapid myelination and formation and pruning of synapses during the preschool and school years, followed by another period of accelerated growth in adolescence, when it reaches an adult level of synaptic connections (Nelson, 2002; Nelson, Thomas, & de Haan, 2006; Sowell et al., 2002).

Lateralization and Plasticity of the Cortex. The cerebral cortex has two *hemispheres,* or sides, that differ in their functions. Some tasks are done mostly by the left hemisphere, others by the right. For example, each hemisphere receives sensory information from the side of the body opposite to it and controls only that side.[*] For most of us, the left hemisphere is largely responsible for verbal abilities (such as spoken and written language) and positive emotion (such as joy). The right hemisphere handles spatial abilities (judging distances, reading maps, and recognizing geometric shapes) and negative emotion (such as distress) (Banish & Heller, 1998; Nelson & Bosquet, 2000). In left-handed people, this pattern may be reversed or, more commonly, the cerebral cortex may be less clearly specialized than in right-handers.

Why does this specialization of the two hemispheres, called **lateralization,** occur? Studies using fMRI reveal that the left hemisphere is better at processing information in a sequential, analytic (piece-by-piece) way, a good approach for dealing with communicative information—both verbal (language) and emotional (a joyful smile). In contrast, the right hemisphere is specialized for processing information in a holistic, integrative manner, ideal for making sense of spatial information and regulating negative emotion. A lateralized brain may have evolved because it enabled humans to cope more successfully with changing environmental demands (Falk, 2005). It permits a wider array of functions to be carried out effectively than if both sides processed information exactly the same way.

Researchers study the timing of brain lateralization to learn more about **brain plasticity.** A highly plastic cerebral cortex, in which many areas are not yet committed to specific functions, has a high capacity for learning. And if a part of the cortex is

---

[*]The eyes are an exception. Messages from the right half of each retina go to the right hemisphere; messages from the left half of each retina go to the left hemisphere. Thus, visual information from *both* eyes is received by *both* hemispheres.

damaged, other parts can take over tasks it would have handled. But once the hemispheres lateralize, damage to a specific region means that the abilities it controls cannot be recovered to the same extent or as easily as earlier.

At birth, the hemispheres have already begun to specialize. Most newborns show greater activation (detected with either ERP or NIRS) in the left hemisphere while listening to speech sounds or displaying a positive state of arousal. In contrast, the right hemisphere reacts more strongly to nonspeech sounds and to stimuli (such as a sour-tasting fluid) that evoke negative emotion (Davidson, 1994; Fox & Davidson, 1986; Hespos et al., 2010).

Nevertheless, research on brain-damaged children and adults offers dramatic evidence for substantial plasticity in the young brain, summarized in the Biology and Environment box on page 126. Furthermore, early experience greatly influences the organization of the cerebral cortex. For example, deaf adults who, as infants and children, learned sign language (a spatial skill) depend more than hearing individuals on the right hemisphere for language processing (Neville & Bavelier, 2002). And toddlers who are advanced in language development show greater left-hemispheric specialization for language than their more slowly developing agemates (Luna et al., 2001; Mills et al., 2005). Apparently, the very process of acquiring language and other skills promotes lateralization.

In sum, the brain is more plastic during the first few years than it will ever be again. An overabundance of synaptic connections supports brain plasticity, ensuring that young children will acquire certain capacities even if some areas are damaged. And although the cortex is programmed from the start for hemispheric specialization, experience greatly influences the rate and success of its advancing organization.

Sensitive Periods in Brain Development

Both animal and human studies reveal that early, extreme sensory deprivation results in permanent brain damage and loss of functions—findings that verify the existence of sensitive periods in brain development. For example, early, varied visual experiences must occur for the brain's visual centers to develop normally. If a 1-month-old kitten is deprived of light for just three or four days, these areas of the brain degenerate. If the kitten is kept in the dark during the fourth week of life and beyond, the damage is severe and permanent (Crair, Gillespie, & Stryker, 1998). And the general quality of the early environment affects overall brain growth. When animals reared from birth in physically and socially stimulating surroundings are compared with those reared under depleted conditions, the brains of the stimulated animals are larger and heavier and show much denser synaptic connections (Sale, Berardi, & Maffei, 2009).

Human Evidence: Victims of Deprived Early Environments. For ethical reasons, we cannot deliberately deprive some infants of normal rearing experiences and observe the impact on their brains and competencies. Instead, we must turn to natural experiments, in which children were victims of deprived early environments that were later rectified. Such studies have revealed some parallels with the animal evidence just described.

For example, when babies are born with cataracts (clouded lenses, preventing clear visual images) in both eyes, those who have corrective surgery within four to six months show rapid improvement in vision, except for subtle aspects of face perception, which require early visual input to the right hemisphere to develop (Le Grand et al., 2003; Maurer, Mondloch, & Lewis, 2007). The longer cataract surgery is postponed beyond infancy, the less complete the recovery in visual skills. And if surgery is delayed until adulthood, vision is severely and permanently impaired (Lewis & Maurer, 2005).

Studies of infants placed in orphanages who were later exposed to ordinary family rearing confirm the importance of a generally stimulating physical and social environment for psychological development. In one investigation, researchers followed the progress of a large sample of children transferred between birth and 3½ years from extremely deprived Romanian orphanages to adoptive families in Great Britain (Beckett et al., 2006; O'Connor et al., 2000; Rutter et al., 1998, 2004, 2010). On arrival, most were impaired in all domains of development. Cognitive catch-up was impressive for children adopted before 6 months, who attained average mental test scores in childhood and adolescence, performing as well as a comparison group of early-adopted British-born children.

But Romanian children who had been institutionalized for more than the first six months showed serious intellectual

These children in an orphanage in Romania receive little adult contact or stimulation. The longer they remain in this barren environment, the more likely they are to display profound impairments in all domains of development.

Biology and Environment

Brain Plasticity: Insights from Research on Brain-Damaged Children and Adults

In the first few years of life, the brain is highly plastic. It can reorganize areas committed to specific functions in ways that the mature brain cannot. Consistently, adults who suffered brain injuries in infancy and early childhood show fewer cognitive impairments than adults with later-occurring injuries (Holland, 2004; Huttenlocher, 2002). Nevertheless, the young brain is not totally plastic. When it is injured, its functioning is compromised. The extent of plasticity depends on several factors, including age at time of injury, site of damage, and skill area. Furthermore, plasticity is not restricted to childhood. Some reorganization after injury also occurs in the mature brain.

Brain Plasticity in Infancy and Early Childhood

In a large study of children with injuries to the cerebral cortex that occurred before birth or in the first six months of life, language and spatial skills were assessed repeatedly into adolescence (Akshoomoff et al., 2002; Stiles, 2001a; Stiles et al., 2005, 2008). All the children had experienced early brain seizures or hemorrhages. Brain-imaging techniques (fMRI and PET) revealed the precise site of damage.

Regardless of whether injury occurred in the left or right cerebral hemisphere, the children showed delays in language development that persisted until about 3½ years of age. That damage to either hemisphere affected early language competence indicates that at first, language functioning is broadly distributed in the brain. But by age 5, the children caught up in vocabulary and grammatical skills. Undamaged areas—in either the left or the right hemisphere—had taken over these language functions.

Compared with language, spatial skills were more impaired after early brain injury. When preschool through adolescent-age youngsters were asked to copy designs, those with early right-hemispheric damage had trouble with holistic processing—accurately representing the overall shape. In contrast, children with left-hemispheric damage captured the basic shape but omitted fine-grained

details. Nevertheless, the children improved in drawing skills with age—gains that do not occur in brain-injured adults (Akshoomoff et al., 2002; Stiles et al., 2003, 2008).

Clearly, recovery after early brain injury is greater for language than for spatial skills. Why is this so? Researchers speculate that spatial processing is the older of the two capacities in our evolutionary history and, therefore, more lateralized at birth (Stiles, 2001b; Stiles et al., 2002, 2008). But early brain injury has far less impact than later injury on *both* language and spatial skills. In sum, the young brain is remarkably plastic.

The Price of High Plasticity in the Young Brain

Despite impressive recovery of language and (to a lesser extent) spatial skills, children with early brain injuries show deficits in a wide range of complex mental abilities during the school years. For example, their reading and math progress is slow. And in telling stories, they produce simpler narratives than age-mates without early brain injuries (although many catch up in narrative skills by early adolescence) (Reilly, Bates, & Marchman, 1998; Reilly et al., 2004). Furthermore, the more brain tissue destroyed in infancy or early childhood, the poorer children score on intelligence tests (Anderson et al., 2006).

High brain plasticity, researchers explain, comes at a price. When healthy brain regions take over the functions of damaged areas, a "crowding effect" occurs: Multiple tasks must be done by a smaller-than-usual volume of brain tissue (Stiles, 2012). Consequently, the brain processes information less quickly and accurately than it would if it were intact. Complex mental abilities of all kinds suffer into middle childhood, and often longer, because performing them well requires considerable space in the cerebral cortex.

Brain Plasticity in Adulthood

Brain plasticity is not restricted to early childhood. Though far more limited, reorganization in the brain can occur later, even in adulthood. For example, adult stroke

© JIM WEST/THE IMAGE WORKS

This preschooler, who experienced brain damage in infancy, has been spared massive impairments because of early, high brain plasticity. A teacher guides his hand in drawing shapes to strengthen spatial skills, which are more impaired than language.

victims often display considerable recovery, especially in response to stimulation of language and motor skills. Brain-imaging techniques reveal that structures adjacent to the permanently damaged area or in the opposite cerebral hemisphere reorganize to support the impaired ability (Kalra & Ratan, 2007; Murphy & Corbett, 2009).

In infancy and childhood, the goal of brain growth is to form neural connections that ensure mastery of essential skills. Animal research reveals that plasticity is greatest while the brain is forming many new synapses; it declines during synaptic pruning (Murphy & Corbett, 2009). At older ages, specialized brain structures are in place, but after injury they can still reorganize to some degree. The adult brain can produce a small number of new neurons. And when an individual practices relevant tasks, the brain strengthens existing synapses and generates new ones (Nelson, Thomas, & de Haan, 2006).

Plasticity seems to be a basic property of the nervous system. Researchers hope to discover how experience and brain plasticity work together throughout life, so they can help people of all ages—with and without brain injuries—develop at their best.

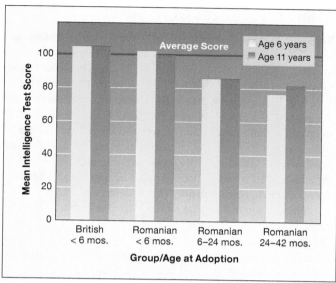

FIGURE 4.6 Relationship of age at adoption to mental test scores at ages 6 and 11 among British and Romanian adoptees. Children transferred from Romanian orphanages to British adoptive homes in the first six months of life attained average scores and fared as well as British early-adopted children, suggesting that they had fully recovered from extreme early deprivation. Romanian children adopted after 6 months of age performed well below average. And although those adopted after age 2 improved between ages 6 and 11, they continued to show serious intellectual deficits. (Adapted from Beckett et al., 2006.)

deficits (see Figure 4.6). Although they improved in test scores during middle childhood and adolescence, they remained substantially below average. And most displayed at least three serious mental health problems, such as inattention, overactivity, unruly behavior, and autistic-like symptoms (social disinterest, stereotyped behavior) (Kreppner et al., 2007, 2010).

Neurobiological findings indicate that early, prolonged institutionalization leads to a generalized decrease in activity in the cerebral cortex, especially the prefrontal cortex, which governs complex cognition and impulse control. Neural fibers connecting the prefrontal cortex with other brain structures involved in control of emotion are also reduced (Eluvathingal et al., 2006; Nelson, 2007b). And activation of the left cerebral hemisphere, governing positive emotion, is diminished relative to right cerebral activation, governing negative emotion (McLaughlin et al., 2011).

Additional evidence confirms that the chronic stress of early, deprived orphanage rearing disrupts the brain's capacity to manage stress, with long-term physical and psychological consequences. In another investigation, researchers followed the development of children who had spent their first eight months or more in Romanian institutions and were then adopted into Canadian homes (Gunnar et al., 2001; Gunnar & Cheatham, 2003). Compared with agemates adopted shortly after birth, these children showed extreme stress reactivity, as indicated by high concentrations of the stress hormone *cortisol* in their saliva—a physiological response linked to persistent illness,

retarded physical growth, and learning and behavior problems, including deficits in attention and control of anger and other impulses. The longer the children spent in orphanage care, the higher their cortisol levels—even 6½ years after adoption. In other investigations, orphanage children displayed abnormally low cortisol—a blunted physiological stress response that may be the central nervous system's adaptation to earlier, frequent cortisol elevations (Loman & Gunnar, 2010).

Appropriate Stimulation. Unlike the orphanage children just described, Grace, whom Monica and Kevin had adopted in Cambodia at 16 months of age, showed favorable progress. Two years earlier, they had adopted Grace's older brother, Eli. When Eli was 2 years old, Monica and Kevin sent a letter and a photo of Eli to his biological mother, describing a bright, happy child. The next day, the Cambodian mother tearfully asked an adoption agency to send her baby daughter to join Eli and his American family. Although Grace's early environment was very depleted, her biological mother's loving care—holding gently, speaking softly, playfully stimulating, and breastfeeding—may have prevented irreversible damage to her brain.

In the Bucharest Early Intervention Project, about 200 institutionalized Romanian babies were randomized into conditions of either care as usual or transfer to high-quality foster families between ages 5 and 30 months. Specially trained social workers provided foster parents with counseling and support. Follow-ups between 2½ and 4 years revealed that the foster-care group exceeded the institutional-care group in intelligence test scores, language skills, emotional responsiveness, and EEG and ERP assessments of brain activity (Nelson et al., 2007; Smyke et al., 2009). On all measures, the earlier the foster placement, the better the outcome. But consistent with an early sensitive period, the foster-care group remained behind never-institutionalized agemates living with Bucharest families.

In addition to impoverished environments, ones that overwhelm children with expectations beyond their current capacities interfere with the brain's potential. In recent years, expensive early learning centers have sprung up, in which infants are trained with letter and number flash cards and slightly older toddlers are given a full curriculum of reading, math, science, art, gym, and more. There is no evidence that these programs yield smarter "superbabies" (Hirsh-Pasek & Golinkoff, 2003). To the contrary, trying to prime infants with stimulation for which they are not ready can cause them to withdraw, thereby threatening their interest in learning and creating conditions much like stimulus deprivation!

How, then, can we characterize appropriate stimulation during the early years? To answer this question, researchers distinguish between two types of brain development. The first, **experience-expectant brain growth,** refers to the young brain's rapidly developing organization, which depends on ordinary experiences—opportunities to explore the environment, interact with people, and hear language and other sounds. As a result of millions of years of evolution, the brains of all infants, toddlers, and young children *expect* to encounter these experiences

Experience-expectant brain growth occurs naturally, through ordinary, stimulating experiences. This toddler exploring a mossy log enjoys the type of activity that best promotes brain development in the early years.

and, if they do, grow normally. The second type of brain development, **experience-dependent brain growth,** occurs throughout our lives. It consists of additional growth and refinement of established brain structures as a result of specific learning experiences that vary widely across individuals and cultures (Greenough & Black, 1992). Reading and writing, playing computer games, weaving an intricate rug, and practicing the violin are examples. The brain of a violinist differs in certain ways from the brain of a poet because each has exercised different brain regions for a long time.

Experience-expectant brain growth occurs early and naturally, as caregivers offer babies and preschoolers age-appropriate play materials and engage them in enjoyable daily routines—a shared meal, a game of peekaboo, a bath before bed, a picture book to talk about, or a song to sing. The resulting growth provides the foundation for later-occurring, experience-dependent development (Huttenlocher, 2002; Shonkoff & Phillips, 2001). No evidence exists for a sensitive period in the first five or six years for mastering skills that depend on extensive training, such as reading, musical performance, or gymnastics. To the contrary, rushing early learning harms the brain by overwhelming its neural circuits, thereby reducing the brain's sensitivity to the everyday experiences it needs for a healthy start in life.

Changing States of Arousal

Rapid brain growth means that the organization of sleep and wakefulness changes substantially between birth and 2 years, and fussiness and crying also decline. The newborn baby takes round-the-clock naps that total about 16 to 18 hours (Davis, Parker & Montgomery, 2004). Total sleep time declines slowly; the average 2-year-old still needs 12 to 13 hours. But periods of sleep and wakefulness become fewer and longer, and the sleep–wake pattern increasingly conforms to a night–day schedule. Most 6- to 9-month-olds take two daytime naps; by about 18 months, children generally need only one nap. Finally, between ages 3 and 5, napping subsides (Iglowstein et al., 2003).

These changing arousal patterns are due to brain development, but they are also affected by cultural beliefs and practices and individual parents' needs (Super & Harkness, 2002). Dutch parents, for example, view sleep regularity as far more important than the U.S. parents do. And whereas U.S. parents regard a predictable sleep schedule as emerging naturally from within the child, Dutch parents believe that a schedule must be imposed, or the baby's development might suffer (Super et al., 1996; Super & Harkness, 2010). At age 6 months, Dutch babies are put to bed earlier and sleep, on average, 2 hours more per day than their U.S. agemates.

Motivated by demanding work schedules and other needs, many Western parents try to get their babies to sleep through the night as early as 3 to 4 months by offering an evening feeding—a practice that may be at odds with young infants' neurological capacities. Not until the middle of the first year is the secretion of *melatonin,* a hormone within the brain that promotes drowsiness, much greater at night than during the day (Sadeh, 1997).

Furthermore, as the Cultural Influences box on the following page reveals, isolating infants to promote sleep is rare elsewhere in the world. When babies sleep with their parents, their average sleep period remains constant at three hours from 1 to 8 months of age. Only at the end of the first year, as REM sleep (the state that usually prompts waking) declines, do infants move in the direction of an adultlike sleep–waking schedule (Ficca et al., 1999).

Even after infants sleep through the night, they continue to wake occasionally. In studies carried out in Australia, Israel, and the United States, night wakings increased around 6 months and again between 1½ and 2 years and then declined (Armstrong, Quinn, & Dadds, 1994; Scher, Epstein, & Tirosh, 2004; Scher et al., 1995). As Chapter 6 will reveal, around the middle of the first year, infants are forming a clear-cut attachment to their familiar caregiver and begin protesting when he or she leaves. And the challenges of toddlerhood—the ability to range farther from the caregiver and increased awareness of the self as separate from others—often prompt anxiety, evident in disturbed sleep and clinginess. When parents offer comfort, these behaviors subside.

LOOK AND LISTEN

Interview a parent of a baby about sleep challenges. What strategies has the parent tried to ease these difficulties? Are the techniques likely to be effective, in view of evidence on infant sleep development? ●

Cultural Influences

Cultural Variation in Infant Sleeping Arrangements

Western child-rearing advice from experts strongly encourages nighttime separation of baby from parent. For example, the most recent edition of Benjamin Spock's *Baby and Child Care* recommends that babies sleep in their own room by 3 months of age, explaining, "By 6 months, a child who regularly sleeps in her parents' room may feel uneasy sleeping anywhere else" (Spock & Needlman, 2012, p. 62). And the American Academy of Pediatrics (2012) has issued a controversial warning that parent–infant bedsharing may increase the risk of sudden infant death syndrome (SIDS).

Yet parent–infant "cosleeping" is the norm for approximately 90 percent of the world's population, in cultures as diverse as the Japanese, the rural Guatemalan Maya, the Inuit of northwestern Canada, and the !Kung of Botswana. Japanese and Korean children usually lie next to their mothers in infancy and early childhood, and many continue to sleep with a parent or other family member until adolescence (Takahashi, 1990; Yang & Hahn, 2002). Among the Maya, mother–infant bedsharing is interrupted only by the birth of a new baby, when the older child is moved next to the father or to another bed in the same room (Morelli et al., 1992). Bedsharing is also common in U.S. ethnic minority families (McKenna & Volpe, 2007). African-American children, for example, frequently fall asleep with their parents and remain with them for part or all of the night (Buswell & Spatz, 2007).

Cultural values—specifically, collectivism versus individualism (see Chapter 2)—strongly influence infant sleeping arrangements. In one study, researchers interviewed Guatemalan Mayan mothers and American middle-SES mothers about their sleeping practices. Mayan mothers stressed the importance of promoting an *interdependent self,* explaining that cosleeping builds a close parent–child bond, which is necessary for children to learn the ways of people around them. In contrast, American mothers emphasized an *independent self,* mentioning their desire to instill early autonomy, prevent bad habits, and protect their own privacy (Morelli et al., 1992).

Over the past two decades, cosleeping has increased in Western nations. An estimated 13 percent of U.S. infants routinely bedshare, and an additional 30 to 35 percent sometimes do (Buswell & Spatz, 2007; Willinger et al., 2003). Proponents of the practice say that it helps infants sleep, makes breastfeeding more convenient, and provides valuable bonding time (McKenna & Volpe, 2007).

During the night, cosleeping babies breastfeed three times longer than infants who sleep alone. Because infants arouse to nurse more often when sleeping next to their mothers, some researchers believe that cosleeping may actually help safeguard babies at risk for SIDS (see page 110 in Chapter 3). Consistent with this view, SIDS is rare in Asian cultures where cosleeping is widespread, including Cambodia, China, Japan, Korea, Thailand, and Vietnam (McKenna, 2002; McKenna & McDade, 2005). And contrary to popular belief, cosleeping does not reduce mothers' total sleep time, although they experience more brief awakenings, which permit them to check on their baby (Mao et al., 2004).

Infant sleeping practices affect other aspects of family life. For example, Mayan babies doze off in the midst of ongoing family activities and are carried to bed by their mothers. In contrast, for many American parents, bedtime often involves a lengthy, elaborate ritual. Perhaps bedtime struggles, so common in Western homes but rare elsewhere in the world, are related to the stress young children feel when they must fall asleep without assistance (Latz, Wolf, & Lozoff, 1999).

Critics warn that bedsharing will promote emotional problems, especially excessive dependency. Yet a study following children from the end of pregnancy through age 18 showed that young people who had bedshared in the early years were no different from others in any aspect of adjustment (Okami, Weisner, & Olmstead, 2002). Another

This Vietnamese mother and child sleep together—a practice common in their culture and around the globe. Hard wooden sleeping surfaces protect cosleeping children from entrapment in soft bedding.

ERIC LAFFORGUE/GAMMA-RAPHO VIA GETTY IMAGES

concern is that infants might become trapped under the parent's body or in soft bedding and suffocate. Parents who are obese or who use alcohol, tobacco, or illegal drugs do pose a serious risk to their sleeping babies, as does the use of quilts and comforters or an overly soft mattress (American Academy of Pediatrics, 2012; Willinger et al., 2003).

But with appropriate precautions, parents and infants can cosleep safely (McKenna & Volpe, 2007). In cultures where cosleeping is widespread, parents and infants usually sleep with light covering on hard surfaces, such as firm mattresses, floor mats, and wooden planks, or infants sleep in a cradle or hammock next to the parents' bed (McKenna, 2001, 2002). And when sharing the same bed, infants typically lie on their back or side facing the mother—positions that promote frequent, easy communication between parent and baby and arousal if breathing is threatened.

Finally, breastfeeding mothers usually assume a distinctive sleeping posture: They face the infant, with knees drawn up under the baby's feet and arm above the baby's head. Besides facilitating feeding, the position prevents the infant from sliding down under covers or up under pillows (Ball, 2006). Because this posture is also seen in female great apes while sharing sleeping nests with their infants, researchers believe it may have evolved to enhance infant safety.

ASK YOURSELF

REVIEW How do overproduction of synapses and synaptic pruning support infants' and children's ability to learn?

CONNECT Explain how inappropriate stimulation—either too little or too much—can impair cognitive and emotional development in the early years.

APPLY Which infant enrichment program would you choose: one that emphasizes gentle talking and touching and social games, or one that includes reading and number drills and classical music lessons? Explain.

REFLECT What is your attitude toward parent–infant cosleeping? Is it influenced by your cultural background? Explain.

Influences on Early Physical Growth

Physical growth, like other aspects of development, results from a complex interplay between genetic and environmental factors. Heredity, nutrition, and emotional well-being all affect early physical growth.

Heredity

Because identical twins are much more alike in body size than fraternal twins, we know that heredity is important in physical growth (Estourgie-van Burk et al., 2006; Touwslager et al., 2011). When diet and health are adequate, height and rate of physical growth are largely influenced by heredity. In fact, as long as negative environmental influences such as poor nutrition and illness are not severe, children and adolescents typically show *catch-up growth*—a return to a genetically influenced growth path once conditions improve. Still, the brain, the heart, the digestive system, and many other internal organs may be permanently compromised (Hales & Ozanne, 2003). (Recall the consequences of inadequate prenatal nutrition for long-term health, discussed on page 92 in Chapter 3.)

Genetic makeup also affects body weight: The weights of adopted children correlate more strongly with those of their biological than of their adoptive parents (Kinnunen, Pietilainen, & Rissanen, 2006). At the same time, environment—in particular, nutrition—plays an especially important role.

Nutrition

Nutrition is especially crucial for development in the first two years because the baby's brain and body are growing so rapidly. Pound for pound, an infant's energy needs are twice those of an adult. Twenty-five percent of babies' total caloric intake is devoted to growth, and infants need extra calories to keep rapidly developing organs functioning properly (Meyer, 2009).

Breastfeeding versus Bottle-Feeding. Babies need not only enough food but also the right kind of food. In early infancy, breastfeeding is ideally suited to their needs, and bottled formulas try to imitate it. Applying What We Know on the following page summarizes major nutritional and health advantages of breastfeeding.

Because of these benefits, breastfed babies in poverty-stricken regions are much less likely to be malnourished and 6 to 14 times more likely to survive the first year of life. The World Health Organization recommends breastfeeding until age 2 years, with solid foods added at 6 months. These practices, if widely followed, would save the lives of more than a million infants annually (World Health Organization, 2012b). Even breastfeeding for just a few weeks offers some protection against respiratory and intestinal infections, which are devastating to young children in developing countries. Also, because a nursing mother is less likely to get pregnant, breastfeeding helps increase spacing between siblings, a major factor in reducing infant and childhood deaths in nations with widespread poverty. (Note, however, that breastfeeding is not a reliable method of birth control.)

Yet many mothers in the developing world do not know about these benefits. In Africa, the Middle East, and Latin America, most babies get some breastfeeding, but fewer than 40 percent are exclusively breastfed for the first six months, and one-third are fully weaned from the breast before 1 year (UNICEF, 2009). In place of breast milk, mothers give their babies commercial formula or low-grade nutrients, such as rice water or highly diluted cow or goat milk. Contamination of these foods as a result of poor sanitation is common and often leads to illness and infant death. The United Nations has encouraged all hospitals and maternity units in developing countries to promote breastfeeding as long as mothers do not have viral or bacterial infections (such as HIV or tuberculosis) that can be

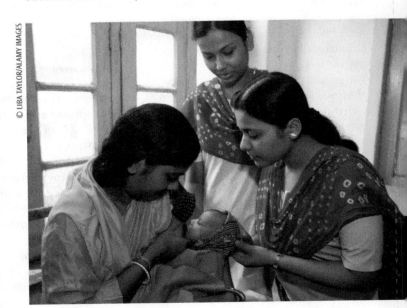

Midwives in India support a mother as she learns to breastfeed her infant. Breastfeeding is especially important in developing countries, where it helps protect babies against life-threatening infections and early death.

Applying What We Know

Reasons to Breastfeed

Nutritional and Health Advantages	Explanation
Provides the correct balance of fat and protein	Compared with the milk of other mammals, human milk is higher in fat and lower in protein. This balance, as well as the unique proteins and fats contained in human milk, is ideal for a rapidly myelinating nervous system.
Ensures nutritional completeness	A mother who breastfeeds need not add other foods to her infant's diet until the baby is 6 months old. The milks of all mammals are low in iron, but the iron contained in breast milk is much more easily absorbed by the baby's system. Consequently, bottle-fed infants need iron-fortified formula.
Helps ensure healthy physical growth	One-year-old breastfed babies are leaner (have a higher percentage of muscle to fat), a growth pattern that persists through the preschool years and that may help prevent later overweight and obesity.
Protects against many diseases	Breastfeeding transfers antibodies and other infection-fighting agents from mother to child and enhances functioning of the immune system. Compared with bottle-fed infants, breastfed babies have far fewer allergic reactions and respiratory and intestinal illnesses. Breast milk also has anti-inflammatory effects, which reduce the severity of illness symptoms. Breastfeeding in the first four months is linked to lower blood cholesterol levels in adulthood and, thereby, may help prevent cardiovascular disease.
Protects against faulty jaw development and tooth decay	Sucking the mother's nipple instead of an artificial nipple helps avoid malocclusion, a condition in which the upper and lower jaws do not meet properly. It also protects against tooth decay due to sweet liquid remaining in the mouths of infants who fall asleep while sucking on a bottle.
Ensures digestibility	Because breastfed babies have a different kind of bacteria growing in their intestines than do bottle-fed infants, they rarely suffer from constipation or other gastrointestinal problems.
Smooths the transition to solid foods	Breastfed infants accept new solid foods more easily than bottle-fed infants, perhaps because of their greater experience with a variety of flavors, which pass from the maternal diet into the mother's milk.

Sources: American Academy of Pediatrics, 2005; Buescher, 2001; Michels et al., 2007; Owen et al., 2008; Rosetta & Baldi, 2008; Weyermann, Rothenbacher, & Brenner, 2006.

transmitted to the baby. Today, most developing countries have banned the practice of giving free or subsidized formula to new mothers.

Partly as a result of the natural childbirth movement, breastfeeding has become more common in industrialized nations, especially among well-educated women. Today, 74 percent of American mothers breastfeed, but more than half stop by 6 months (Centers for Disease Control and Prevention, 2011a). Not surprisingly, mothers who return to work sooner wean their babies from the breast earlier (Kimbro, 2006). But mothers who cannot be with their infants all the time can still combine breast- and bottle-feeding. The U.S. Department of Health and Human Services (2010a) advises exclusive breastfeeding for the first 6 months and inclusion of breast milk in the baby's diet until at least 1 year.

Women who do not breastfeed sometimes worry that they are depriving their baby of an experience essential for healthy psychological development. Yet breastfed and bottle-fed infants in industrialized nations do not differ in quality of the mother–infant relationship or in later emotional adjustment (Fergusson & Woodward, 1999; Jansen, de Weerth, & Riksen-Walraven, 2008). Some studies report a slight advantage in intelligence test performance for children and adolescents who were breastfed, after controlling for many factors. Most, however, find no cognitive benefits (Der, Batty, & Deary, 2006).

Are Chubby Babies at Risk for Later Overweight and Obesity? From early infancy, Timmy was an enthusiastic eater who nursed vigorously and gained weight quickly. By 5 months, he began reaching for food on his mother's plate. Vanessa wondered: Was she overfeeding Timmy and increasing his chances of becoming overweight?

Most chubby babies thin out during toddlerhood and early childhood, as weight gain slows and they become more active. Infants and toddlers can eat nutritious foods freely without risk of becoming overweight. But recent evidence does indicate a strengthening relationship between rapid weight gain in infancy and later obesity (Botton et al., 2008; Chomtho et al., 2008). The trend may be due to the rise in overweight and obesity among adults, who promote unhealthy eating habits in their young children. Interviews with 1,500 U.S. parents of 4- to 24-month-olds revealed that many routinely served older infants and toddlers french fries, pizza, candy, sugary fruit drinks, and soda. On average, infants consumed 20 percent and toddlers 30 percent more calories than they needed. At the same time, as many as one-fourth ate no fruits and one-third no vegetables (Siega-Riz et al., 2010).

How can concerned parents prevent their infants from becoming overweight children and adults? One way is to breastfeed for the first six months, which is associated with slower early weight gain (Gunnarsdottir et al., 2010). Another is to avoid giving them foods loaded with sugar, salt, and saturated fats. Once toddlers learn to walk, climb, and run, parents can also provide plenty of opportunities for energetic play. Finally, because research shows a correlation between excessive television viewing and overweight in older children, parents should limit the time very young children spend in front of the TV.

Malnutrition

Osita is an Ethiopian 2-year-old whose mother has never had to worry about his gaining too much weight. When she weaned him at 1 year, there was little for him to eat besides starchy rice-flour cakes. Soon his belly enlarged, his feet swelled, his hair fell out, and a rash appeared on his skin. His bright-eyed curiosity vanished, and he became irritable and listless.

In developing countries and war-torn areas where food resources are limited, malnutrition is widespread. Recent evidence indicates that about 27 percent of the world's children suffer from malnutrition before age 5 (World Health Organization, 2010). The 10 percent who are severely affected suffer from two dietary diseases.

Marasmus is a wasted condition of the body caused by a diet low in all essential nutrients. It usually appears in the first year of life when a baby's mother is too malnourished to produce enough breast milk and bottle-feeding is also inadequate. Her starving baby becomes painfully thin and is in danger of dying.

Osita has **kwashiorkor,** caused by an unbalanced diet very low in protein. The disease usually strikes after weaning, between 1 and 3 years of age. It is common in regions where children get just enough calories from starchy foods but little protein. The child's body responds by breaking down its own protein reserves, which causes the swelling and other symptoms that Osita experienced.

Children who survive these extreme forms of malnutrition grow to be smaller in all body dimensions and suffer from lasting damage to the brain, heart, liver, or other organs (Müller & Krawinkel, 2005). When their diets do improve, they tend to gain excessive weight (Uauy et al., 2008). A malnourished body protects itself by establishing a low basal metabolism rate, which may endure after nutrition improves. Also, malnutrition may disrupt appetite control centers in the brain, causing the child to overeat when food becomes plentiful.

Learning and behavior are also seriously affected. In one long-term study of marasmic children, an improved diet led to some catch-up growth in height, but not in head size (Stoch et al., 1982). The malnutrition probably interfered with growth of neural fibers and myelination, causing a permanent loss in brain weight. And animal evidence reveals that a deficient diet alters the production of neurotransmitters in the brain—an effect that can disrupt all aspects of development (Haller, 2005). These children score low on intelligence tests, show poor fine-motor coordination, and have difficulty paying attention (Galler et al., 1990; Liu et al., 2003). They also display a more intense stress response to fear-arousing situations, perhaps caused by the constant, gnawing pain of hunger (Fernald & Grantham-McGregor, 1998).

Inadequate nutrition is not confined to developing countries. Because government-supported supplementary food programs do not reach all families in need, an estimated 21 percent of U.S. children suffer from *food insecurity*—uncertain access to enough food for a healthy, active life. Food insecurity is especially high among single-parent families (35 percent) and low-income ethnic minority families—for example, Hispanics and African Americans (25 and 27 percent, respectively) (U.S. Department of Agriculture, 2011a). Although few of these children have marasmus or kwashiorkor, their physical growth and ability to learn are still affected.

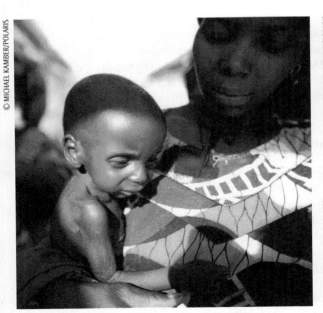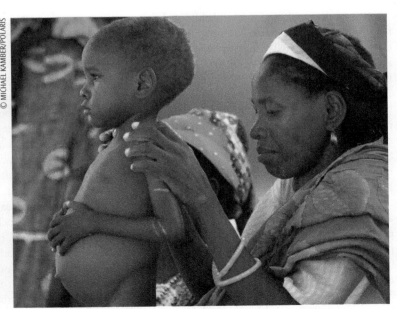

Left photo: This baby of Niger, Africa, has marasmus, a wasted condition caused by a diet low in all essential nutrients. *Right photo:* The swollen abdomen of this toddler, also of Niger, is a symptom of kwashiorkor, which results from a diet very low in protein. If these children survive, they are likely to be growth stunted and to suffer from lasting organ damage and serious cognitive and emotional impairments.

ASK YOURSELF

REVIEW Explain why breastfeeding can have lifelong consequences for the development of babies born in poverty-stricken regions of the world.

CONNECT How are bidirectional influences between parent and child involved in the impact of malnutrition on psychological development?

APPLY Eight-month-old Shaun is well below average in height and painfully thin. What serious growth disorder does he likely have, and what type of intervention, in addition to dietary enrichment, will help restore his development? (Hint: See page 92 in Chapter 3.)

REFLECT Imagine that you are the parent of a newborn baby. Describe feeding practices you would use, and ones you would avoid, to prevent overweight and obesity.

Learning Capacities

Learning refers to changes in behavior as the result of experience. Babies come into the world with built-in learning capacities that permit them to profit from experience immediately. Infants are capable of two basic forms of learning, which were introduced in Chapter 1: classical and operant conditioning. They also learn through their natural preference for novel stimulation. Finally, shortly after birth, babies learn by observing others; they can imitate the facial expressions and gestures of adults.

Classical Conditioning

Newborn reflexes, discussed in Chapter 3, make **classical conditioning** possible in the young infant. In this form of learning, a neutral stimulus is paired with a stimulus that leads to a reflexive response. Once the baby's nervous system makes the connection between the two stimuli, the neutral stimulus produces the behavior by itself. Classical conditioning helps infants recognize which events usually occur together in the everyday world, so they can anticipate what is about to happen next. As a result, the environment becomes more orderly and predictable. Let's take a closer look at the steps of classical conditioning.

As Carolyn settled down in the rocking chair to nurse Caitlin, she often stroked Caitlin's forehead. Soon Carolyn noticed that each time she did this, Caitlin made sucking movements. Caitlin had been classically conditioned. Figure 4.7 shows how it happened:

1. Before learning takes place, an **unconditioned stimulus** (UCS) must consistently produce a reflexive, or **unconditioned, response** (UCR). In Caitlin's case, sweet breast milk (UCS) resulted in sucking (UCR).

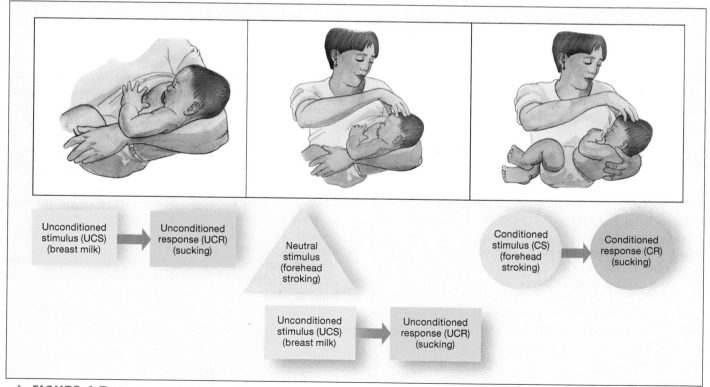

FIGURE 4.7 The steps of classical conditioning. This example shows how a mother classically conditioned her baby to make sucking movements by stroking the baby's forehead at the beginning of feedings.

2. To produce learning, a *neutral stimulus* that does not lead to the reflex is presented just before, or at about the same time as, the UCS. Carolyn stroked Caitlin's forehead as each nursing period began. The stroking (neutral stimulus) was paired with the taste of milk (UCS).

3. If learning has occurred, the neutral stimulus by itself produces a response similar to the reflexive response. The neutral stimulus is then called a **conditioned stimulus (CS)**, and the response it elicits is called a **conditioned response (CR)**. We know that Caitlin has been classically conditioned because stroking her forehead outside the feeding situation (CS) results in sucking (CR).

If the CS is presented alone enough times, without being paired with the UCS, the CR will no longer occur, an outcome called *extinction*. In other words, if Carolyn repeatedly strokes Caitlin's forehead without feeding her, Caitlin will gradually stop sucking in response to stroking.

Young infants can be classically conditioned most easily when the association between two stimuli has survival value. In the example just described, learning which stimuli regularly accompany feeding improves the infant's ability to get food and survive (Blass, Ganchrow, & Steiner, 1984).

In contrast, some responses, such as fear, are very difficult to classically condition in young babies. Until infants have the motor skills to escape unpleasant events, they have no biological need to form these associations. After age 6 months, however, fear is easy to condition. In Chapter 6, we will discuss the development of fear and other emotional reactions.

Operant Conditioning

In classical conditioning, babies build expectations about stimulus events in the environment, but their behavior does not influence the stimuli that occur. In **operant conditioning**, infants act, or *operate*, on the environment, and stimuli that follow their behavior change the probability that the behavior will occur again. A stimulus that increases the occurrence of a response is called a **reinforcer**. For example, sweet liquid *reinforces* the sucking response in newborns. Removing a desirable stimulus or presenting an unpleasant one to decrease the occurrence of a response is called **punishment**. A sour-tasting fluid *punishes* newborns' sucking response, causing them to purse their lips and stop sucking entirely.

Many stimuli besides food can serve as reinforcers of infant behavior. For example, newborns will suck faster on a nipple when their rate of sucking produces interesting sights and sounds, including visual designs, music, or human voices (Floccia, Christophe, & Bertoncini, 1997). As these findings suggest, operant conditioning is a powerful tool for finding out what stimuli babies can perceive and which ones they prefer.

As infants get older, operant conditioning includes a wider range of responses and stimuli. For example, researchers have hung mobiles over the cribs of 2- to 6-month-olds. When the baby's foot is attached to the mobile with a long cord, the infant can, by kicking, make the mobile turn. Under these conditions, it takes only a few minutes for infants to start kicking vigorously (Rovee-Collier, 1999; Rovee-Collier & Barr, 2001). As you will see in Chapter 5, operant conditioning with mobiles is frequently used to study infants' memory and their ability to group similar stimuli into categories. Once babies learn the kicking response, researchers see how long and under what conditions they retain it when exposed again to the original mobile or to mobiles with varying features.

Operant conditioning also plays a vital role in the formation of social relationships. As the baby gazes into the adult's eyes, the adult looks and smiles back, and then the infant looks and smiles again. As the behavior of each partner reinforces the other, both continue their pleasurable interaction. In Chapter 6, we will see that this contingent responsiveness contributes to the development of infant–caregiver attachment.

Habituation

At birth, the human brain is set up to be attracted to novelty. Infants tend to respond more strongly to a new element that has entered their environment, an inclination that ensures that they will continually add to their knowledge base. **Habituation** refers to a gradual reduction in the strength of a response due to repetitive stimulation. Looking, heart rate, and respiration rate may all decline, indicating a loss of interest. Once this has occurred, a new stimulus—a change in the environment—causes responsiveness to return to a high level, an increase called **recovery**. For example, when you walk through a familiar space, you notice things that are new and different—a recently hung picture on the wall or a piece of furniture that has been moved. Habituation and recovery make learning more efficient by focusing our attention on those aspects of the environment we know least about.

Researchers investigating infants' understanding of the world rely on habituation and recovery more than any other learning capacity. For example, a baby who first *habituates* to a visual pattern (a photo of a baby) and then *recovers* to a new one (a photo of a bald man) appears to remember the first stimulus and perceive the second one as new and different from it. This method of studying infant perception and cognition, illustrated in Figure 4.8, can be used with newborns, including preterm infants (Kavšek & Bornstein, 2010). It has even been used to study the fetus's sensitivity to external stimuli—for example, by measuring changes in fetal heart rate when various repeated sounds are presented (see page 85 in Chapter 3).

Recovery to a new stimulus, or novelty preference, assesses infants' *recent memory*. **TAKE A MOMENT...** Think about what happens when you return to a place you have not seen for a long time. Instead of attending to novelty, you are likely to focus on aspects that are familiar: "I recognize that—I've been here before!" Like adults, infants shift from a novelty preference to a familiarity preference as more time intervenes between habituation and test phases in research. That is, babies recover to the familiar stimulus rather than to a novel stimulus (see Figure 4.8)

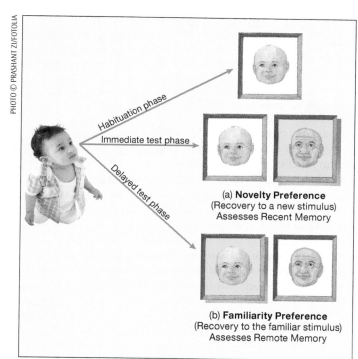

Habituation phase

Immediate test phase

Delayed test phase

(a) Novelty Preference
(Recovery to a new stimulus)
Assesses Recent Memory

(b) Familiarity Preference
(Recovery to the familiar stimulus)
Assesses Remote Memory

FIGURE 4.8 **Using habituation to study infant perception and cognition.** In the habituation phase, infants view a photo of a baby until their looking declines. In the test phase, infants are again shown the baby photo, but this time it appears alongside a photo of a bald-headed man. (a) When the test phase occurs soon after the habituation phase (within minutes, hours, or days, depending on the age of the infants), participants who remember the baby face and distinguish it from the man's face show a *novelty preference;* they recover to (spend more time looking at) the new stimulus. (b) When the test phase is delayed for weeks or months, infants who continue to remember the baby face shift to a *familiarity preference;* they recover to the familiar baby face rather than to the novel man's face.

(Bahrick, Hernandez-Reif, & Pickens, 1997; Courage & Howe, 1998; Flom & Bahrick, 2010; Richmond, Colombo, & Hayne, 2007). By focusing on that shift, researchers can also use habituation to assess *remote memory,* or memory for stimuli to which infants were exposed weeks or months earlier.

As Chapter 5 will reveal, habituation research has greatly enriched our understanding of how long babies remember a wide range of stimuli. And by varying stimulus features, researchers can use habituation and recovery to study babies' ability to categorize stimuli as well.

Imitation

Babies come into the world with a primitive ability to learn through **imitation**—by copying the behavior of another person. For example, Figure 4.9 shows a human newborn imitating two adult facial expressions (Meltzoff & Moore, 1977). The newborn's capacity to imitate extends to certain gestures, such as head and index-finger movements, and has been demonstrated in many ethnic groups and cultures (Meltzoff & Kuhl,

1994; Nagy et al., 2005). As the figure illustrates, even newborn primates, including chimpanzees (our closest evolutionary relatives), imitate some behaviors (Ferrari et al., 2006; Myowa-Yamakoshi et al., 2004).

Although newborns' capacity to imitate is widely accepted, a few studies have failed to reproduce the human findings (see, for example, Anisfeld et al., 2001). And because newborn mouth and tongue movements occur with increased frequency to almost any arousing change in stimulation (such as lively music or flashing lights), some researchers argue that certain newborn "imitative" responses are actually mouthing—a common early

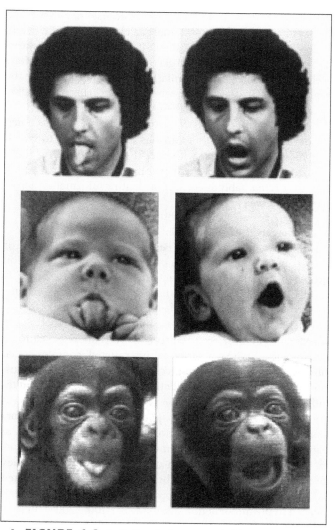

FIGURE 4.9 **Imitation by human and chimpanzee newborns.** The human infants in the middle row imitating (left) tongue protrusion and (right) mouth opening are 2 to 3 weeks old. The chimpanzee imitating both facial expressions is 2 weeks old. (From A. N. Meltzoff & M. K. Moore, 1977, "Imitation of Facial and Manual Gestures by Human Neonates," *Science, 198,* p. 75. Copyright © 1977 by AAAS. Reprinted with permission of the AAAS and A. N. Meltzoff. And from M. Myowa-Yamakoshi et al., 2004, "Imitation in Neonatal Chimpanzees [Pan Troglodytes]." *Developmental Science, 7,* p. 440. Copyright 2004 by Blackwell Publishing. Reproduced with permission of John Wiley & Sons Ltd.)

exploratory response to interesting stimuli (Jones, 2009). Furthermore, imitation is harder to induce in babies 2 to 3 months old than just after birth. Therefore, skeptics believe that the newborn imitative capacity is little more than an automatic response that declines with age, much like a reflex (Heyes, 2005).

Others claim that newborns—both primates and humans—imitate a variety of facial expressions and head movements with effort and determination, even after short delays—when the adult is no longer demonstrating the behavior (Meltzoff & Moore, 1999; Paukner, Ferrari, & Suomi, 2011). Furthermore, these investigators argue that imitation—unlike reflexes—does not decline. Human babies several months old often do not imitate an adult's behavior right away because they first try to play familiar social games—mutual gazing, cooing, smiling, and waving their arms. But when an adult models a gesture repeatedly, older human infants soon get down to business and imitate (Meltzoff & Moore, 1994). Similarly, imitation declines in baby chimps around 9 weeks of age, when mother–baby mutual gazing and other face-to-face exchanges increase.

According to Andrew Meltzoff, newborns imitate much as older children and adults do—by actively trying to match body movements they *see* with ones they *feel* themselves make (Meltzoff, 2007). Later we will encounter evidence that young infants are remarkably adept at coordinating information across sensory systems.

Indeed, scientists have identified specialized cells in motor areas of the cerebral cortex in primates—called **mirror neurons**—that underlie these capacities (Ferrari & Coudé, 2011). Mirror neurons fire identically when a primate hears or sees an action and when it carries out that action on its own (Rizzolatti & Craighero, 2004). Human adults have especially elaborate systems of mirror neurons, which enable us to observe another's behavior (such as smiling or throwing a ball) while simulating the behavior in our own brain. Mirror neurons are believed to be the biological basis of a variety of interrelated, complex social abilities, including imitation, empathic sharing of emotions, and understanding others' intentions (Iacoboni, 2009; Schulte-Ruther et al., 2007).

Brain-imaging findings support a functioning mirror-neuron system as early as 6 months of age. Using NIRS, researchers found that the same motor areas of the cerebral cortex were activated in 6-month-olds and in adults when they observed a model engage in a behavior that could be imitated (tapping a box to make a toy pop out) as when they themselves engaged in the motor action (Shimada & Hiraki, 2006). In contrast, when infants and adults observed an object that appeared to move on its own, without human intervention (a ball hanging from the ceiling on a string, swinging like a pendulum), motor areas were not activated.

Still, Meltzoff's view of newborn imitation as a flexible, voluntary capacity remains controversial. Mirror neurons, though possibly functional at birth, undergo an extended period of development (Bertenthal & Longo, 2007; Lepage & Théoret, 2007). Similarly, as we will see in Chapter 5, the capacity to imitate expands greatly over the first two years. But however limited it is at birth, imitation is a powerful means of learning. Using imitation, infants explore their social world, not only learning from other people but getting to know them by matching their behavioral states. As babies notice similarities between their own actions and those of others, they experience other people as "like me" and, thus, learn about themselves (Meltzoff, 2007). In this way, infant imitation may serve as the foundation for understanding others' thoughts and feelings, which we take up in Chapter 6. Finally, caregivers take great pleasure in a baby who imitates their facial gestures and actions, which helps get the infant's relationship with parents off to a good start.

ASK YOURSELF

REVIEW Provide an example of classical conditioning, of operant conditioning, and of habituation/recovery in young infants. Why is each type of learning useful?

CONNECT Which learning capacities contribute to an infant's first social relationships? Explain, providing examples.

APPLY Nine-month-old Byron has a toy with large, colored push buttons on it. Each time he pushes a button, he hears a nursery tune. Which learning capacity is the manufacturer of this toy taking advantage of? What can Byron's play with the toy reveal about his perception of sound patterns?

 ## Motor Development

Carolyn, Monica, and Vanessa each kept a baby book, filled with proud notations about when their children first held up their heads, reached for objects, sat by themselves, and walked alone. Parents are understandably excited about these new motor skills, which allow babies to master their bodies and the environment in new ways. For example, sitting upright gives infants a new perspective on the world. Reaching permits babies to find out about objects by acting on them. And when infants can move on their own, their opportunities for exploration multiply.

Babies' motor achievements have a powerful effect on their social relationships. When Caitlin crawled at 7½ months, Carolyn and David began to restrict her movements by saying no and expressing mild impatience. When she walked three days after her first birthday, the first "testing of wills" occurred (Biringen et al., 1995). Despite her mother's warnings, she sometimes pulled items from shelves that were off limits. "I said, 'Don't do that!'" Carolyn would say firmly, taking Caitlin's hand and redirecting her attention.

At the same time, newly walking babies more actively attend to and initiate social interaction (Clearfield, Osborn, & Mullen, 2008; Karasik et al., 2011). Caitlin frequently toddled over to her parents to express a greeting, give a hug, or show them objects of interest. Carolyn and David, in turn, increased their expressions of affection and playful activities. And when Caitlin encountered risky situations, such as a sloping walkway or a dangerous object, Carolyn and David intervened, combining emotional warnings with rich verbal and gestural information that helped Caitlin notice critical features of her surroundings, regulate her motor actions, and acquire language (Campos et al., 2000; Karasik et al., 2008). Caitlin's delight as she worked on new motor skills triggered pleasurable reactions in others, which encouraged her efforts further. Motor, social, cognitive, and language competencies developed together and supported one another.

The Sequence of Motor Development

Gross-motor development refers to control over actions that help infants get around in the environment, such as crawling, standing, and walking. *Fine-motor development* has to do with smaller movements, such as reaching and grasping. Table 4.2 shows the average age at which U.S. infants and toddlers achieve a variety of gross- and fine-motor skills. It also presents the age ranges during which most babies accomplish each skill, indicating large individual differences in *rate* of motor progress. Also, a baby

who is a late reacher will not necessarily be a late crawler or walker. We would be concerned about a child's development only if many motor skills were seriously delayed.

Historically, researchers assumed that motor skills were separate, innate abilities that emerged in a fixed sequence governed by a built-in maturational timetable. This view has long been discredited. Rather, motor skills are interrelated. Each is a product of earlier motor attainments and a contributor to new ones. And children acquire motor skills in highly individual ways. For example, before her adoption, Grace spent most of her days lying in a hammock. Because she was rarely placed on her tummy and on firm surfaces that enabled her to move on her own, she did not try to crawl. As a result, she pulled to a stand and walked before she crawled! Babies display such skills as rolling, sitting, crawling, and walking in diverse orders rather than in the sequence implied by motor norms (Adolph, Karasik, & Tamis-LeMonda, 2010).

Motor Skills as Dynamic Systems

According to **dynamic systems theory of motor development,** mastery of motor skills involves acquiring increasingly complex

TABLE 4.2
Gross- and Fine-Motor Development in the First Two Years

MOTOR SKILL	AVERAGE AGE ACHIEVED	AGE RANGE IN WHICH 90 PERCENT OF INFANTS ACHIEVE THE SKILL
When held upright, holds head erect and steady	6 weeks	3 weeks–4 months
When prone, lifts self by arms	2 months	3 weeks–4 months
Rolls from side to back	2 months	3 weeks–5 months
Grasps cube	3 months, 3 weeks	2–7 months
Rolls from back to side	4½ months	2–7 months
Sits alone	7 months	5–9 months
Crawls	7 months	5–11 months
Pulls to stand	8 months	5–12 months
Plays pat-a-cake	9 months, 3 weeks	7–15 months
Stands alone	11 months	9–16 months
Walks alone	11 months, 3 weeks	9–17 months
Builds tower of two cubes	11 months, 3 weeks	10–19 months
Scribbles vigorously	14 months	10–21 months
Walks up stairs with help	16 months	12–23 months
Jumps in place	23 months, 2 weeks	17–30 months
Walks on tiptoe	25 months	16–30 months

Note: These milestones represent overall age trends. Individual differences exist in the precise age at which each milestone is attained.
Sources: Bayley, 1969, 1993, 2005.
Photos: (top) © Laura Dwight Photography; (middle) © Laura Dwight Photography; (bottom) © Elizabeth Crews/The Image Works

systems of action. When motor skills work as a system, separate abilities blend together, each cooperating with others to produce more effective ways of exploring and controlling the environment. For example, control of the head and upper chest combine into sitting with support. Kicking, rocking on all fours, and reaching combine to become crawling. Then crawling, standing, and stepping are united into walking (Adolph & Berger, 2006; Thelen & Smith, 1998).

Each new skill is a joint product of four factors: (1) central nervous system development, (2) the body's movement capacities, (3) the goals the child has in mind, and (4) environmental supports for the skill. Change in any element makes the system less stable, and the child starts to explore and select new, more effective motor patterns.

The broader physical environment also profoundly influences motor skills. Infants with stairs in their home learn to crawl up stairs at an earlier age and also more readily master a back-descent strategy—the safest but also the most challenging position because the baby must turn around at the top, give up visual guidance of her goal, and crawl backward (Berger, Theuring, & Adolph, 2007). And if children were reared on the moon, with its reduced gravity, they would prefer jumping to walking or running!

LOOK AND LISTEN

Spend an hour observing a newly crawling or walking baby. Note the goals that motivate the baby to move, along with the baby's effort and motor experimentation. Describe parenting behaviors and features of the environment that promote mastery of the skill. ●

When a skill is first acquired, infants must refine it. For example, in trying to crawl, Caitlin often collapsed on her tummy and moved backward. Soon she figured out how to propel herself forward by alternately pulling with her arms and pushing with her feet, "belly-crawling" in various ways for several weeks (Vereijken & Adolph, 1999). As babies attempt a new skill, related, previously mastered skills often become less secure. As the novice walker experiments with balancing the body vertically over two small moving feet, balance during sitting may become temporarily less stable (Chen et al., 2007). In learning to walk, toddlers practice six or more hours a day, traveling the length of 29 football fields! Gradually their small, unsteady steps change to a longer stride, their feet move closer together, their toes point to the front, and their legs become symmetrically coordinated (Adolph, Vereijken, & Shrout, 2003). As movements are repeated thousands of times, they promote new synaptic connections in the brain that govern motor patterns.

Dynamic systems theory shows us why motor development cannot be genetically determined. Because it is motivated by exploration and the desire to master new tasks, heredity can map it out only at a general level. Rather than being *hardwired* into the nervous system, behaviors are *softly assembled,* allowing for different paths to the same motor skill (Adolph, 2008; Thelen & Smith, 2006).

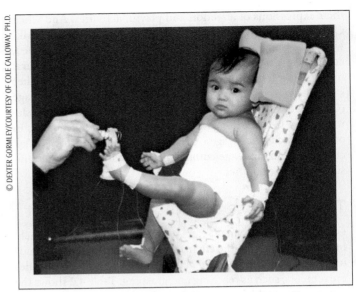

FIGURE 4.10 Reaching "feet first." When sounding toys were held in front of babies' hands and feet, they reached with their feet as early as 8 weeks of age, a month or more before they reached with their hands. This 2½-month-old skillfully explores an object with her foot.

Dynamic Motor Systems in Action. To find out how babies acquire motor capacities, some studies have tracked their first attempts at a skill until it became smooth and effortless. In one investigation, researchers held sounding toys alternately in front of infants' hands and feet, from the time they showed interest until they engaged in well-coordinated reaching and grasping (Galloway & Thelen, 2004). As Figure 4.10 shows, the infants violated the normative sequence of arm and hand control preceding leg and foot control, shown in Table 4.2. They first reached for the toys with their feet—as early as 8 weeks of age, at least a month before reaching with their hands!

Why did babies reach "feet first"? Because the hip joint constrains the legs to move less freely than the shoulder constrains the arms, infants could more easily control their leg movements. When they first tried reaching with their hands, their arms actually moved *away* from the object! Consequently, foot reaching required far less practice than hand reaching. As these findings confirm, rather than following a strict, predetermined pattern, the order in which motor skills develop depends on the anatomy of the body part being used, the surrounding environment, and the baby's efforts.

Cultural Variations in Motor Development. Cross-cultural research further illustrates how early movement opportunities and a stimulating environment contribute to motor development. Over half a century ago, Wayne Dennis (1960) observed infants in Iranian orphanages who were deprived of the tantalizing surroundings that induce infants to acquire motor skills. These babies spent their days lying on their backs in cribs, without toys to play with. As a result, most did not move on their own until after 2 years of age. When they finally did move, the constant experience of lying on their backs led them to scoot in a sitting position rather than crawl on their hands and knees. Because babies who scoot come up against furniture with their feet, not their hands, they are far less likely to pull themselves to a standing position in preparation for walking. Indeed, by 3 to 4 years of age, only 15 percent of the Iranian orphans were walking alone.

Cultural variations in infant-rearing practices affect motor development. *TAKE A MOMENT...* Take a quick survey of several parents you know: Should sitting, crawling, and walking be deliberately encouraged? Answers vary widely from culture to culture. Japanese mothers, for example, believe such efforts are unnecessary (Seymour, 1999). Among the Zinacanteco Indians of southern Mexico and the Gusii of Kenya, rapid motor progress is actively discouraged. Babies who walk before they know enough to keep away from cooking fires and weaving looms are viewed as dangerous to themselves and disruptive to others (Greenfield, 1992).

In contrast, among the Kipsigis of Kenya and the West Indians of Jamaica, babies hold their heads up, sit alone, and walk considerably earlier than North American infants. In both societies, parents emphasize early motor maturity, practicing formal exercises to stimulate particular skills (Adolph, Karasik, & Tamis-LeMonda, 2010). In the first few months, babies are seated in holes dug in the ground, with rolled blankets to keep them upright. Walking is promoted by frequently standing babies in adults' laps, bouncing them on their feet, and exercising the stepping reflex (Hopkins & Westra, 1988; Super, 1981). As parents in these cultures support babies in upright postures and rarely put them down on the floor, their infants usually skip crawling—a motor skill regarded as crucial in Western nations!

Finally, because it decreases exposure to "tummy time," the current Western practice of having babies sleep on their backs to protect them from SIDS (see page 110 in Chapter 3) delays gross motor milestones of rolling, sitting, and crawling

This West Indian mother of Jamaica "walks" her baby up her body in a deliberate effort to promote early mastery of walking.

(Majnemer & Barr, 2005; Scrutton, 2005). Regularly exposing infants to the tummy-lying position during waking hours prevents these delays.

Fine-Motor Development: Reaching and Grasping

Of all motor skills, reaching may play the greatest role in infant cognitive development. By grasping things, turning them over, and seeing what happens when they are released, infants learn a great deal about the sights, sounds, and feel of objects.

Reaching and grasping, like many other motor skills, start out as gross, diffuse activity and move toward mastery of fine movements. Figure 4.11 illustrates some milestones of reaching

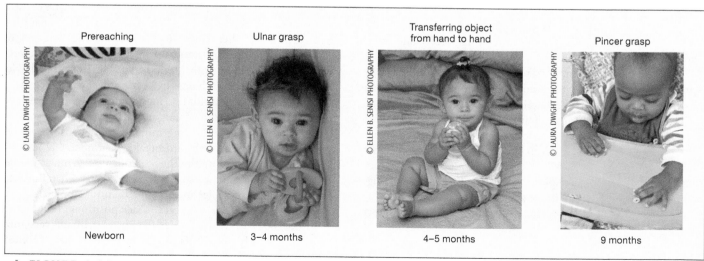

Prereaching   Ulnar grasp   Transferring object from hand to hand   Pincer grasp

Newborn   3–4 months   4–5 months   9 months

FIGURE 4.11 Some milestones of reaching and grasping. The average age at which each skill is attained is given. (Ages from Bayley, 1969; Rochat, 1989.)

over the first nine months. Newborns make poorly coordinated swipes or swings, called *prereaching*, toward an object in front of them, but because of poor arm and hand control they rarely contact the object. Like newborn reflexes, prereaching drops out around 7 weeks of age. Yet these early behaviors suggest that babies are biologically prepared to coordinate hand with eye in the act of exploring (Rosander & von Hofsten, 2002; von Hofsten, 2004).

At about 3 to 4 months, as infants develop the necessary eye, head, and shoulder control, reaching reappears as purposeful, forward arm movements in the presence of a nearby toy and gradually improves in accuracy (Bhat, Heathcock, & Galloway, 2005; Spencer et al., 2000). By 5 to 6 months, infants reach for an object in a room that has been darkened during the reach by switching off the lights—a skill that improves over the next few months (Clifton et al., 1994; McCarty & Ashmead, 1999). Early on, vision is freed from the basic act of reaching so it can focus on more complex adjustments. By 7 months, the arms become more independent; infants reach for an object by extending one arm rather than both (Fagard & Pezé, 1997). During the next few months, infants become more efficient at reaching for moving objects—ones that spin, change direction, and move sideways, closer, or farther away (Fagard, Spelke, & von Hofsten, 2009; Wentworth, Benson, & Haith, 2000).

Once infants can reach, they modify their grasp. The newborn's grasp reflex is replaced by the *ulnar grasp*, a clumsy motion in which the fingers close against the palm. Still, even 4-month-olds adjust their grasp to the size and shape of an object—a capacity that improves over the first year as infants orient the hand more precisely and do so in advance of contacting the object (Barrett, Traupman, & Needham, 2008; Witherington, 2005). Around 4 to 5 months, when infants begin to sit up, both hands become coordinated in exploring objects. Babies of this age can hold an object in one hand while the other scans it with the fingertips, and they frequently transfer objects from hand to hand (Rochat & Goubet, 1995). By the end of the first year, infants use the thumb and index finger opposably in a well-coordinated *pincer grasp*. Then the ability to manipulate objects greatly expands. The 1-year-old can pick up raisins and blades of grass, turn knobs, and open and close small boxes.

Between 8 and 11 months, reaching and grasping are well-practiced, so attention is released from the motor skill to events that occur before and after attaining the object. For example, 10-month-olds easily adjust their reach to anticipate their next action. They reach for a ball faster when they intend to throw it than when they intend to drop it carefully through a narrow tube (Claxton, Keen, & McCarty, 2003). Around this time, too, infants begin to solve simple problems that involve reaching, such as searching for and finding a hidden toy.

Finally, the capacity to reach for and manipulate an object increases infants' attention to the way an adult reaches for and plays with that same object (Hauf, Aschersleben, & Prinz, 2007). As babies watch what others do, they broaden their understanding of others' behaviors and of the range of actions that can be performed on various objects.

ASK YOURSELF

REVIEW Cite evidence that motor development is a joint product of biological, psychological, and environmental factors.

CONNECT Provide several examples of how motor development influences infants' attainment of cognitive and social competencies.

APPLY List everyday experiences that support mastery of reaching, grasping, sitting, and crawling. Why should caregivers place young infants in a variety of waking-time body positions?

REFLECT Do you favor early, systematic training of infants in motor skills such as crawling, walking, and stair climbing? Why or why not?

Perceptual Development

In Chapter 3, you learned that the senses of touch, taste, smell, and hearing—but not vision—are remarkably well-developed at birth. Now let's turn to a related question: How does perception change over the first year? Our discussion will address hearing and vision, the focus of almost all research. Recall that in Chapter 3, we used the word *sensation* to talk about these capacities. It suggests a fairly passive process—what the baby's receptors detect when exposed to stimulation. Now we use the word *perception*, which is active: When we perceive, we organize and interpret what we see.

As we review the perceptual achievements of infancy, you may find it hard to tell where perception leaves off and thinking begins. The research we are about to discuss provides an excellent bridge to the topic of Chapter 5—cognitive development during the first two years.

Hearing

On Timmy's first birthday, Vanessa bought several CDs of nursery songs, and she turned one on each afternoon at naptime. Soon Timmy let her know his favorite tune. If she put on "Twinkle, Twinkle," he stood up in his crib and whimpered until she replaced it with "Jack and Jill." Timmy's behavior illustrates the greatest change in hearing over the first year of life: Babies organize sounds into increasingly elaborate patterns.

Between 4 and 7 months, infants display a sense of musical phrasing: They prefer Mozart minuets with pauses between phrases to those with awkward breaks (Krumhansl & Jusczyk, 1990). Around 6 to 7 months, they can distinguish musical tunes on the basis of variations in rhythmic patterns, including beat structure (duple or triple) and accent structure (emphasis on the first note of every beat unit or at other positions) (Hannon & Johnson, 2004). And by the end of the first year, infants recognize the same melody when it is played in different keys (Trehub, 2001). As we will see shortly, 6- to 12-month-olds make comparable discriminations in human speech: They readily detect sound regularities that will facilitate later language learning.

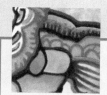

Biology and Environment

"Tuning In" to Familiar Speech, Faces, and Music: A Sensitive Period for Culture-Specific Learning

To share experiences with members of their family and community, babies must become skilled at making perceptual discriminations that are meaningful in their culture. As we have seen, at first babies are sensitive to virtually all speech sounds, but around 6 months, they narrow their focus, limiting the distinctions they make to the language they hear and will soon learn.

The ability to perceive faces shows a similar **perceptual narrowing effect**—perceptual sensitivity that becomes increasingly attuned with age to information most often encountered. After habituating to one member of each pair of faces in Figure 4.12, 6-month-olds were shown the familiar and novel faces side-by-side. For both pairs, they recovered to (looked longer at) the novel face, indicating that they could discriminate individual faces of both humans and monkeys equally well (Pascalis, de Haan, & Nelson, 2002). But at 9 months, infants no longer showed a novelty preference when viewing the monkey pair. Like adults, they could distinguish only the human faces. Similar findings emerge with sheep faces: 4- to 6-months-olds easily distinguish them, but 9- to 11-month olds no longer do (Simpson et al., 2011).

The perceptual narrowing effect appears again in musical rhythm perception. Western adults are accustomed to the even-beat pattern of Western music—repetition of the same rhythmic structure in every measure of a tune—and easily notice rhythmic changes that disrupt this familiar beat. But present them with music that does not follow this typical Western rhythmic form—Baltic folk tunes, for example—and they fail to pick up on rhythmic-pattern deviations. Six-month-olds, however, can detect such disruptions in both Western and non-Western melodies. But by 12 months, after added exposure to Western music, babies are no longer aware of deviations in foreign musical rhythms, although their sensitivity to Western rhythmic structure remains unchanged (Hannon & Trehub, 2005b).

Several weeks of regular interaction with a foreign-language speaker and of daily opportunities to listen to non-Western music fully restore 12-month-olds' sensitivity to wide-ranging speech sounds and music rhythms (Hannon & Trehub, 2005a; Kuhl, Tsao, & Liu, 2003). Similarly, 6-month-olds given three months of training in discriminating individual monkey faces, in which each image is labeled with a distinct name ("Carlos," "Iona") instead of the generic label "monkey," retain their ability to discriminate monkey faces at 9 months (Scott & Monesson, 2009). Adults given similar extensive experiences, by contrast, show little improvement in perceptual sensitivity.

Taken together, these findings suggest a heightened capacity—or sensitive period—in the second half of the first year, when babies are biologically prepared to "zero in"

FIGURE 4.12 Discrimination of human and monkey faces. Which of these pairs is easiest for you to tell apart? After habituating to one of the photos in each pair, infants were shown the familiar and the novel face side-by-side. For both pairs, 6-month-olds recovered to (looked longer at) the novel face, indicating that they could discriminate human and monkey faces equally well. By 12 months, babies lost their ability to distinguish the monkey faces. Like adults, they showed a novelty preference only to human stimuli. (From O. Pascalis et al., 2002, "Is Face Processing Species-Specific During the First Year of Life?" *Science, 296,* p. 1322. Copyright © 2002 by AAAS. Reprinted by permission from AAAS.)

on socially meaningful perceptual distinctions. Notice how, between 6 and 12 months, learning is especially rapid across several domains (speech, faces, and music) and is easily modified by experience. This suggests a broad neurological change—perhaps a special time of experience-expectant brain growth (see page 127) in which babies analyze everyday stimulation of all kinds similarly, in ways that prepare them to participate in their cultural community.

Speech Perception. Recall from Chapter 3 that newborns can distinguish nearly all sounds in human languages and that they prefer listening to human speech over nonspeech sounds, and to their native tongue rather than a foreign language. As infants listen to people talking, they learn to focus on meaningful sound variations. ERP brain-wave recordings reveal that around 5 months, babies become sensitive to syllable stress patterns in their own language (Weber et al., 2004). Between 6 and 8 months, they start to "screen out" sounds not used in their native tongue (Anderson, Morgan, & White, 2003; Polka & Werker, 1994). As the Biology and Environment box above explains, this increased responsiveness to native-language sounds is part of a general "tuning" process in the second half of the first year—a possible sensitive period in which infants acquire a range of perceptual skills for picking up socially important information.

Soon after, infants focus on larger speech segments that are critical to figuring out meaning. They recognize familiar words in spoken passages and listen longer to speech with clear clause and phrase boundaries (Johnson & Seidl, 2008; Jusczyk & Hohne, 1997; Soderstrom et al., 2003). Around 7 to 9 months, infants extend this sensitivity to speech structure to individual words: They begin to divide the speech stream into wordlike units (Jusczyk, 2002; Saffran, Werker, & Werner, 2006).

Analyzing the Speech Stream. How do infants make such rapid progress in perceiving the structure of language? Research shows that they have an impressive **statistical learning capacity**. By analyzing the speech stream for patterns—repeatedly occurring sequences of sounds—they acquire a stock of speech structures for which they will later learn meanings, long before they start to talk around age 12 months.

For example, when presented with controlled sequences of nonsense syllables, babies listen for statistical regularities: They locate words by distinguishing syllables that often occur together (indicating they belong to the same word) from syllables that seldom occur together (indicating a word boundary). Consider the English word sequence *pretty#baby*. After listening to the speech stream for just one minute (about 60 words), 8-month-olds discriminate a word-internal syllable pair *(pretty)* from a word-external syllable pair *(ty#ba)*. They prefer to listen to new speech that preserves the word-internal pattern (Saffran, Aslin, & Newport, 1996; Saffran & Thiessen, 2003).

Once infants locate words, they focus on the words and, around 7 to 8 months, identify regular syllable-stress patterns—for example, in English and Dutch, that the onset of a strong syllable *(hap*-py, *rab*-bit) often signals a new word (Swingley, 2005; Thiessen & Saffran, 2007). By 10 months, babies can detect words that start with weak syllables, such as "sur*prise,*" by listening for sound regularities before and after the words (Jusczyk, 2001; Kooijman, Hagoort, & Cutler, 2009).

Clearly, babies have a powerful ability to extract patterns from complex, continuous speech. Some researchers believe that infants are innately equipped with a general statistical learning capacity for detecting structure in the environment, which they also apply to nonspeech auditory information and to visual stimulation. Consistent with this idea, ERP recordings suggest that newborns perceive patterns in both sequences of speech syllables and sequences of tones (Kudo et al., 2011; Teinonen et al., 2009). And 2-month-olds detect regularities in sequences of visual stimuli (Kirkham, Slemmer, & Johnson, 2002).

Vision

For exploring the environment, humans depend on vision more than any other sense. Although at first a baby's visual world is fragmented, it undergoes extraordinary changes during the first 7 to 8 months of life.

Visual development is supported by rapid maturation of the eye and visual centers in the cerebral cortex. Recall from Chapter 3 that the newborn baby focuses and perceives color poorly. Around 2 months, infants can focus on objects about as well as adults can, and their color vision is adultlike by 4 months (Kellman & Arterberry, 2006). *Visual acuity* (fineness of discrimination) improves steadily, reaching 20/80 by 6 months and an adult level of about 20/20 by 4 years (Slater et al., 2010). Scanning the environment and tracking moving objects improve over the first half-year as infants better control their eye movements and build an organized perceptual world (Johnson, Slemmer, & Amso, 2004; von Hofsten & Rosander, 1998).

As babies explore their visual field, they figure out the characteristics of objects and how they are arranged in space. To understand how they do so, let's examine the development of two aspects of vision: depth and pattern perception.

Depth Perception. *Depth perception* is the ability to judge the distance of objects from one another and from ourselves. It is important for understanding the layout of the environment and for guiding motor activity.

Figure 4.13 shows the *visual cliff*, designed by Eleanor Gibson and Richard Walk (1960) and used in the earliest studies of depth perception. It consists of a Plexiglas-covered table with a platform at the center, a "shallow" side with a checkerboard pattern just under the glass, and a "deep" side with a checkerboard several feet below the glass. The researchers found that crawling babies readily crossed the shallow side, but most reacted with fear to the deep side. They concluded that around the time infants crawl, most distinguish deep from shallow surfaces and avoid drop-offs.

The visual cliff shows that crawling and avoidance of drop-offs are linked, but not how they are related or when depth perception first appears. Subsequent research has looked at babies' ability to detect specific depth cues, using methods that do not require that they crawl.

Motion is the first depth cue to which infants are sensitive. Babies 3 to 4 weeks old blink their eyes defensively when an object moves toward their face as if it is going to hit (Nánez & Yonas, 1994). *Binocular depth cues* arise because our two eyes have slightly different views of the visual field. The brain blends these two images, resulting in perception of depth. Research in which two overlapping images are projected before the baby, who wears special goggles to ensure that each eye receives only one image, reveals that sensitivity to binocular cues emerges between 2 and 3 months and improves rapidly over the first year (Birch, 1993; Brown & Miracle, 2003). Finally, beginning at 3 to 4 months and strengthening between 5 and 7 months, babies display sensitivity to *pictorial depth cues*—the ones artists often use to make a painting look three-dimensional. Examples include receding lines that create the illusion of perspective, changes in texture (nearby textures are more detailed than faraway ones), overlapping objects (an object partially hidden by another object is perceived to be more distant), and shadows cast on surfaces (indicating a separation in space between

FIGURE 4.13 The visual cliff. Plexiglas covers the deep and shallow sides. By refusing to cross the deep side and showing a preference for the shallow side, this infant demonstrates the ability to perceive depth.

the object and the surface) (Kavšek, Yonas, & Granrud, 2012; Shuwairi, Albert, & Johnson, 2007).

Why does perception of depth cues emerge in the order just described? Researchers speculate that motor development is involved. For example, control of the head during the early weeks of life may help babies notice motion and binocular cues. Around the middle of the first year, the ability to turn, poke, and feel the surface of objects promotes sensitivity to pictorial cues as infants pick up information about size, texture, and three-dimensional shape (Bushnell & Boudreau, 1993; Soska, Adolph, & Johnson, 2010). And as we will see next, one aspect of motor progress—independent movement—plays a vital role in refinement of depth perception.

Independent Movement and Depth Perception.

At 6 months, Timmy started crawling. "He's fearless!" exclaimed Vanessa. "If I put him down in the middle of my bed, he crawls right over the edge. The same thing happens by the stairs." Will Timmy become wary of the side of the bed and the staircase as

he becomes a more experienced crawler? Research suggests that he will. Infants with more crawling experience (regardless of when they started to crawl) are far more likely to refuse to cross the deep side of the visual cliff (Campos et al., 2000).

From extensive everyday experience, babies gradually figure out how to use depth cues to detect the danger of falling. But because the loss of body control that leads to falling differs greatly for each body position, babies must undergo this learning separately for each posture. In one study, 9-month-olds who were experienced sitters but novice crawlers were placed on the edge of a shallow drop-off that could be widened (Adolph, 2002, 2008). While in the familiar sitting position, infants avoided leaning out for an attractive toy at distances likely to result in falling. But in the unfamiliar crawling posture, they headed over the edge, even when the distance was extremely wide! And newly walking babies, while avoiding sharp drop-offs, career down slopes and over uneven surfaces without making the necessary postural adjustments, even when their mothers discourage them from proceeding! Thus, they fall frequently (Adolph et al., 2008; Joh & Adolph, 2006). As infants discover how to avoid falling in different postures and situations, their understanding of depth expands.

Crawling experience promotes other aspects of three-dimensional understanding. For example, seasoned crawlers are better than their inexperienced agemates at remembering object locations and finding hidden objects (Bai & Bertenthal, 1992; Campos et al., 2000). Why does crawling make such a difference?

Infants must learn to use depth cues to avoid falling in each new position—sitting, crawling, walking—and in various situations. As this 10-month-old takes her first steps, she uses vision to make postural adjustments, and her understanding of depth expands.

TAKE A MOMENT... Compare your own experience of the environment when you are driven from one place to another with what you experience when you walk or drive yourself. When you move on your own, you are much more aware of landmarks and routes of travel, and you take more careful note of what things look like from different points of view. The same is true for infants. In fact, crawling promotes a new level of brain organization, as indicated by more organized EEG brain-wave activity in the cerebral cortex (Bell & Fox, 1996). Perhaps crawling strengthens certain neural connections, especially those involved in vision and understanding of space.

Pattern Perception. Even newborns prefer to look at patterned rather than plain stimuli (Fantz, 1961). As they get older, infants prefer more complex patterns. For example, 3-week-old infants look longest at black-and-white checkerboards with a few large squares, whereas 8- and 14-week-olds prefer those with many squares (Brennan, Ames, & Moore, 1966).

A general principle, called **contrast sensitivity**, explains early pattern preferences (Banks & Ginsburg, 1985). *Contrast* refers to the difference in the amount of light between adjacent regions in a pattern. If babies are *sensitive to* (can detect) the contrast in two or more patterns, they prefer the one with more

contrast. To understand this idea, look at the checkerboards in the top row of Figure 4.14. To us, the one with many small squares has more contrasting elements. Now look at the bottom row, which shows how these checkerboards appear to infants in the first few weeks of life. Because of their poor vision, very young babies cannot resolve the small features in more complex patterns, so they prefer to look at the large, bold checkerboard. Around 2 months, when detection of fine-grained detail has improved, infants become sensitive to the contrast in complex patterns and spend more time looking at them (Gwiazda & Birch, 2001). Contrast sensitivity continues to increase during infancy and childhood.

In the early weeks of life, infants respond to the separate parts of a pattern. They stare at single, high-contrast features and have difficulty shifting their gaze away toward other interesting stimuli (Hunnius & Geuze, 2004a, 2004b). At 2 to 3 months, when scanning ability and contrast sensitivity improve, infants thoroughly explore a pattern's features, pausing briefly to look at each part (Bronson, 1994).

Once babies take in all aspects of a pattern, they integrate the parts into a unified whole. Around 4 months, babies are so good at detecting pattern organization that they perceive subjective boundaries that are not really present. For example, they perceive a square in the center of Figure 4.15a, just as you do (Ghim, 1990). Older infants carry this sensitivity to subjective form further, applying it to complex, moving stimuli. For example, 9-month-olds look much longer at an organized series of blinking lights that resembles a human being walking than at an upside-down or scrambled version (Bertenthal, 1993). At 12 months, infants detect familiar objects represented by incomplete drawings, even when as much as two-thirds of the drawing is missing (see Figure 4.15b) (Rose, Jankowski, & Senior, 1997). As these findings reveal, infants' increasing knowledge of objects and actions supports pattern perception.

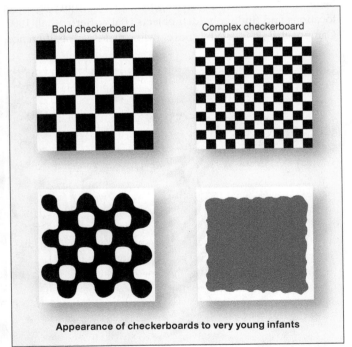

Bold checkerboard   Complex checkerboard

Appearance of checkerboards to very young infants

FIGURE 4.14 The way two checkerboards differing in complexity look to infants in the first few weeks of life. Because of their poor vision, very young infants cannot resolve the fine detail in the *complex checkerboard*. It appears blurred, like a gray field. The large, *bold checkerboard* appears to have more contrast, so babies prefer to look at it. (Adapted from M. S. Banks & P. Salapatek, 1983, "Infant Visual Perception," in M. M. Haith & J. J. Campos [Eds.], *Handbook of Child Psychology: Vol. 2. Infancy and Developmental Psychobiology* [4th ed.], p. 504. Copyright © 1983 by John Wiley & Sons, Inc. Reproduced with permission of John Wiley & Sons, Inc.)

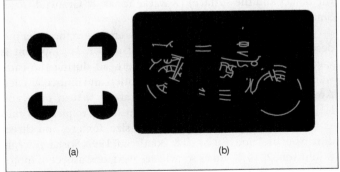

(a)   (b)

FIGURE 4.15 Subjective boundaries in visual patterns. (a) Do you perceive a square in the middle of the figure? By 4 months of age, infants do, too. (b) What does the image, missing two-thirds of its outline, look like to you? By 12 months, infants detect a motorcycle. After habituating to the incomplete motorcycle image, they were shown an intact motorcycle figure paired with a novel form. Twelve-month-olds recovered to (looked longer at) the novel figure, indicating that they recognized the motorcycle pattern on the basis of very little visual information. (Adapted from Ghim, 1990; Rose, Jankowski, & Senior, 1997.)

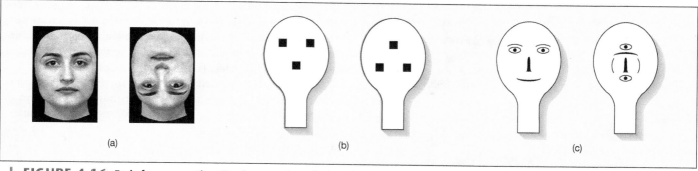

FIGURE 4.16 **Early face perception.** Newborns prefer to look at the photo of a face (a) and the simple pattern resembling a face (b) over the upside-down versions. (c) When the complex drawing of a face on the left and the equally complex, scrambled version on the right are moved across newborns' visual field, they follow the face longer. But if the two stimuli are stationary, infants show no preference for the face until around 2 months of age. (From Cassia, Turati, & Simion, 2004; Johnson, 1999; Mondloch et al., 1999.)

Face Perception. Infants' tendency to search for structure in a patterned stimulus also applies to face perception. Newborns prefer to look at photos and simplified drawings of faces with features arranged naturally (upright) rather than unnaturally (upside-down or sideways) (see Figure 4.16a) (Cassia, Turati, & Simion, 2004; Mondloch et al., 1999). They also track a facelike pattern moving across their visual field farther than they track other stimuli (Johnson, 1999). And although they rely more on high-contrast, outer features (hairline and chin) than inner features to distinguish real faces, newborns prefer photos of faces with eyes open and a direct gaze (Farroni et al., 2002; Turati et al., 2006). Yet another amazing capacity is their tendency to look longer at both human and animal faces judged by adults as attractive—a preference that may be the origin of the widespread social bias favoring physically attractive people (Quinn et al., 2008; Slater et al., 2010).

Some researchers claim that these behaviors reflect a built-in capacity to orient toward members of one's own species, just as many newborn animals do (Johnson, 2001; Slater et al., 2011). Others assert that newborns prefer any stimulus in which the most salient elements are arranged horizontally in the upper part of a pattern—like the "eyes" in Figure 4.16b (Turati, 2004). Possibly, however, a bias favoring the facial pattern promotes such preferences. Still other researchers argue that newborns are exposed to faces more often than to other stimuli—early experiences that could quickly "wire" the brain to detect faces and prefer attractive ones (Nelson, 2001).

Although newborns respond to facelike structures, they cannot discriminate a complex facial pattern from other, equally complex patterns (see Figure 4.16c). But from repeated exposures to their mother's face, they quickly learn to prefer her face to that of an unfamiliar woman, although they mostly attend to its broad outlines. Around 2 months, when they can combine pattern elements into an organized whole, babies prefer a complex drawing of the human face to other equally complex stimulus arrangements (Dannemiller & Stephens, 1988). And they clearly prefer their mother's detailed facial features to those of another woman (Bartrip, Morton, & de Schonen, 2001).

Around 3 months, infants make fine distinctions among the features of different faces—for example, between photographs of two strangers, even when the faces are moderately similar (Farroni et al., 2007). At 5 months—and strengthening over the second half-year—infants perceive emotional expressions as meaningful wholes. They treat positive faces (happy and surprised) as different from negative ones (sad and fearful) (Bornstein & Arterberry, 2003; Ludemann, 1991).

Experience influences face processing, leading babies to form group biases at a tender age. As early as 3 months, infants prefer and more easily discriminate among female faces than among male faces (Quinn et al., 2002; Ramsey-Rennels & Langlois, 2006). The greater time infants spend with female adults explains this effect, since babies with a male primary caregiver prefer male faces. Furthermore, 3- to 6-month-olds exposed mostly to members of their own race prefer to look at the faces of members of that race and more easily detect differences among those faces (Bar-Haim et al., 2006; Kelly et al., 2007, 2009). This own-race face preference is absent in babies who have frequent contact with members of other races, and it can be reversed through exposure to racial diversity (Sangrigoli et al., 2005). *TAKE A MOMENT...* Notice how early experience promotes *perceptual narrowing* with respect to gender and racial information in faces, as occurs for species information, discussed in the Biology and Environment box on page 141.

Clearly, extensive face-to-face interaction with caregivers contributes to infants' refinement of face perception. And as babies recognize and respond to the expressive behavior of others, face perception supports their earliest social relationships.

Up to this point, we have considered the infant's sensory systems one by one. Now let's examine their coordination.

Intermodal Perception

Our world provides rich, continuous *intermodal stimulation*—simultaneous input from more than one modality, or sensory system. In **intermodal perception,** we make sense of these running streams of light, sound, tactile, odor, and taste information, perceiving them as integrated wholes. We know, for example,

© GERI ENGBERG/THE IMAGE WORKS

This baby exploring the surface of a guitar readily picks up amodal information, such as common rate, rhythm, duration, and temporal synchrony, in the visual appearance and sounds of its moving strings.

that an object's shape is the same whether we see it or touch it, that lip movements are closely coordinated with the sound of a voice, and that dropping a rigid object on a hard surface will cause a sharp, banging sound.

Recall that newborns turn in the general direction of a sound and reach for objects in a primitive way. These behaviors suggest that infants expect sight, sound, and touch to go together. Research reveals that babies perceive input from different sensory systems in a unified way by detecting *amodal sensory properties*—information that overlaps two or more sensory systems, such as rate, rhythm, duration, intensity, temporal synchrony (for vision and hearing), and texture and shape (for vision and touch). Consider the sight and sound of a bouncing ball or the face and voice of a speaking person. In each event, visual and auditory information occur simultaneously and with the same rate, rhythm, duration, and intensity.

Even newborns are impressive perceivers of amodal properties. After touching an object (such as a cylinder) placed in their palms, they recognize it visually, distinguishing it from a different-shaped object (Sann & Streri, 2007). And they require just one exposure to learn the association between the sight and sound of a toy, such as a rhythmically jangling rattle (Morrongiello, Fenwick, & Chance, 1998).

Within the first half-year, infants master a remarkable range of intermodal relationships. Three- to 4-month-olds can match faces with voices on the basis of lip–voice synchrony, emotional expression, and even age and gender of the speaker (Bahrick, Netto, & Hernandez-Reif, 1998). Between 4 and 6 months, infants can perceive and remember the unique face–voice pairings of unfamiliar adults (Bahrick, Hernandez-Reif, & Flom, 2005).

How does intermodal perception develop so quickly? Young infants seem biologically primed to focus on amodal information. Their detection of amodal relations—for example,

the common tempo and rhythm in sights and sounds—precedes and seems to provide the basis for detecting more specific intermodal matches, such as the relation between a particular person's face and the sound of her voice or between an object and its verbal label (Bahrick, Hernandez-Reif, & Flom, 2005).

Intermodal sensitivity is crucial for perceptual development. In the first few months, when much stimulation is unfamiliar and confusing, it enables babies to notice meaningful correlations between sensory inputs and rapidly make sense of their surroundings (Bahrick, Lickliter, & Flom, 2004).

In addition to easing perception of the physical world, intermodal perception facilitates social and language processing. For example, as 3- to 4-month-olds gaze at an adult's face, they initially require both vocal and visual input to distinguish positive from negative emotional expressions (Walker-Andrews, 1997). Only later do infants discriminate positive from negative emotion in each sensory modality—first in voices (around 4 to 5 months), later (from 5 months on) in faces (Bahrick, Hernandez-Reif, & Flom, 2005). Furthermore, in speaking to infants, parents often provide temporal synchrony between words, object motions, and touch—for example, saying "doll" while moving a doll and having it touch the infant. This greatly increases the chances that babies will remember the association between the word and the object (Gogate & Bahrick, 1998, 2001).

LOOK AND LISTEN

While watching a parent and infant playing, list instances of parental intermodal stimulation and communication. What is the baby likely learning about people, objects, or language from each intermodal experience? ●

In sum, intermodal perception fosters all aspects of psychological development. When caregivers provide many concurrent sights, sounds, and touches, babies process more information and learn faster (Bahrick, 2010). Intermodal perception is yet another fundamental capacity that assists infants in their active efforts to build an orderly, predictable world.

Understanding Perceptual Development

Now that we have reviewed the development of infant perceptual capacities, how can we put together this diverse array of amazing achievements? Widely accepted answers come from the work of Eleanor and James Gibson. According to the Gibsons' **differentiation theory**, infants actively search for *invariant features* of the environment—those that remain stable—in a constantly changing perceptual world. In pattern perception, for example, young babies search for features that stand out and orient toward faces. Soon they thoroughly explore a stimulus, noticing *stable relationships* among its features. As a result, they detect patterns, such as complex designs and individual faces. Similarly, infants analyze the speech stream for regularities, detecting words, word-order sequences, and—within words—

FIGURE 4.17 Acting on the environment plays a major role in perceptual differentiation. Crawling and walking change the way babies perceive a sloping surface. The newly crawling infant on the left plunges headlong down the slope. He has not yet learned that it affords the possibility of falling. The toddler on the right, who has been walking for more than a month, approaches the slope cautiously. Experience in trying to remain upright but frequently tumbling over has made him more aware of the consequences of his movements. He perceives the incline differently than he did at a younger age.

DR. KAREN E. ADOLPH, INFANT ACTION LAB, NEW YORK UNIVERSITY

syllable-stress patterns. The development of intermodal perception also reflects this principle. Babies seek out invariant relationships—first, amodal properties, such as common rate and rhythm, in a voice and face, and later, more detailed associations, such as unique voice–face matches.

The Gibsons described their theory as *differentiation* (where *differentiate* means "analyze" or "break down") because over time, the baby detects finer and finer invariant features among stimuli. In addition to pattern perception and intermodal perception, differentiation applies to depth perception. Recall how sensitivity to motion precedes detection of fine-grained pictorial features. So one way of understanding perceptual development is to think of it as a built-in tendency to seek order and consistency—a capacity that becomes increasingly fine-tuned with age (Gibson, 1970; Gibson, 1979).

Infants constantly look for ways in which the environment *affords possibilities for action* (Gibson, 2000, 2003). By exploring their surroundings, they figure out which things can be grasped, squeezed, bounced, or stroked and whether a surface is safe to cross or presents the possibility of falling (Adolph & Eppler, 1998, 1999). And from handling objects, babies become more aware of a variety of observable object properties (Perone et al., 2008). As a result, they differentiate the world in new ways and act more competently.

To illustrate, recall how infants' changing capabilities for independent movement affect their perception. When babies crawl, and again when they walk, they gradually realize that a sloping surface *affords the possibility of falling* (see Figure 4.17). With added weeks of practicing each skill, they hesitate to crawl or walk down a risky incline. Experience in trying to keep their balance on various surfaces makes crawlers and walkers more aware of the consequences of their movements. Crawlers come to detect when surface slant places so much body weight on their arms that they will fall forward, and walkers come to sense when an incline shifts body weight so their legs and feet can no longer hold them upright. Learning is gradual and effortful because newly crawling and walking babies cross many types

of surfaces in their homes each day (Adolph, 2008; Adolph & Joh, 2009). As they experiment with balance and postural adjustments to accommodate each, they perceive surfaces in new ways that guide their movements. As a result, they act more competently.

As we conclude our discussion of infant perception, it is only fair to note that some researchers believe that babies do more than make sense of experience by searching for invariant features and action possibilities: They also *impose meaning on* what they perceive, constructing categories of objects and events in the surrounding environment. We have seen the glimmerings of this *cognitive* point of view in this chapter. For example, older babies *interpret* a familiar face as a source of pleasure and affection and a pattern of blinking lights as a moving human being. This cognitive perspective also has merit in understanding the achievements of infancy. In fact, many researchers combine these two positions, regarding infant development as proceeding from a perceptual to a cognitive emphasis over the first year of life.

ASK YOURSELF

REVIEW Using examples, explain why intermodal perception is vital for infants' developing understanding of their physical and social worlds.

CONNECT According to differentiation theory, perceptual development reflects infants' active search for invariant features. Provide examples from research on hearing, pattern perception, and intermodal perception.

APPLY After several weeks of crawling, Ben learned to avoid going headfirst down a steep incline. Now he has started to walk. Can his parents trust him not to try walking down a steep surface? Explain.

SUMMARY

Body Growth (p. 120)

Describe major changes in body growth over the first two years.

- Height and weight gains are greater during the first two years than at any other time after birth. Body fat is laid down quickly during the first nine months, whereas muscle development is slow and gradual. Body proportions change as growth follows the **cephalocaudal and proximodistal trends.**

Brain Development (p. 121)

Describe brain development during infancy and toddlerhood, including appropriate stimulation to support the brain's potential.

- Early in development, the brain grows faster than any other organ of the body. Once **neurons** are in place, they rapidly form **synapses.** To communicate, neurons release chemicals called **neurotransmitters,** which cross synapses. **Programmed cell death** makes space for neural fibers and synapses. Neurons that are seldom stimulated lose their synapses in a process called **synaptic pruning. Glial cells,** responsible for **myelination,** multiply rapidly through the second year, contributing to large gains in brain weight.

- The **cerebral cortex** is the largest, most complex brain structure and the last to stop growing. Its frontal lobes, which contain the **prefrontal cortex,** have the most extended period of development. Gradually, the hemispheres of the cerebral cortex specialize, a process called **lateralization.** But in the first few years of life, there is high **brain plasticity,** with many areas not yet committed to specific functions.

- Both heredity and early experience contribute to brain organization. Stimulation of the brain is essential during sensitive periods, when the brain is developing most rapidly. Prolonged early deprivation can impair functioning of the cerebral cortex, especially the prefrontal cortex, and interfere with the brain's capacity to manage stress, with long-term physical and psychological consequences.

- Appropriate early stimulation promotes **experience-expectant brain growth,** which depends on ordinary experiences. No evidence exists for a sensitive period in the first few years for **experience-dependent brain growth,** which relies on specific learning experiences. In fact, environments that overwhelm children with inappropriately advanced expectations can undermine the brain's potential.

© ALAMY

How does the organization of sleep and wakefulness change over the first two years?

- Infants' changing arousal patterns are primarily affected by brain growth, but the social environment also plays a role. Periods of sleep and wakefulness become fewer but longer, increasingly conforming to a night–day schedule. Parents in Western nations try to get their babies to sleep through the night much earlier than parents throughout most of the world, who are more likely to sleep with their babies.

Influences on Early Physical Growth (p. 130)

Cite evidence that heredity and nutrition both contribute to early physical growth.

- Twin and adoption studies reveal that heredity contributes to body size and rate of physical growth.

- Breast milk is ideally suited to infants' growth needs. Breastfeeding protects against disease and prevents malnutrition and infant death in poverty-stricken areas of the world.

- Most infants and toddlers can eat nutritious foods freely without risk of becoming overweight. However, because of unhealthy parental feeding practices, the relationship between rapid weight gain in infancy and later obesity is strengthening.

- **Marasmus** and **kwashiorkor,** two dietary diseases caused by malnutrition, affect many children in developing countries. If prolonged, they can permanently stunt body growth and brain development.

Learning Capacities (p. 133)

Describe infant learning capacities, the conditions under which they occur, and the unique value of each.

- **Classical conditioning** is based on the infant's ability to associate events that usually occur together in the everyday world. Infants can be classically conditioned most easily when the pairing of an **unconditioned stimulus (UCS)** and a **conditioned stimulus (CS)** has survival value.

- In **operant conditioning,** infants act on the environment, and their behavior is followed by either **reinforcers,** which increase the occurrence of a preceding behavior, or **punishment,** which either removes a desirable stimulus or presents an unpleasant one to decrease the occurrence of a response. In young infants, interesting sights and sounds and pleasurable caregiver interaction serve as effective reinforcers.

- **Habituation** and **recovery** reveal that at birth, babies are attracted to novelty. Novelty preference (recovery to a novel stimulus) assesses recent memory, whereas familiarity preference (recovery to the familiar stimulus) assesses remote memory.

- Newborns have a primitive ability to imitate adults' facial expressions and gestures. **Imitation** is a powerful means of learning, which contributes to the parent–infant bond. Specialized cells called **mirror neurons** underlie infants' capacity to imitate, but whether imitation is a voluntary capacity in newborns remains controversial.

Motor Development (p. 136)

Describe dynamic systems theory of motor development, along with factors that influence motor progress in the first two years.

- According to **dynamic systems theory of motor development,** children acquire new motor skills by combining existing skills into increasingly complex systems of action. Each new skill is a joint product of central nervous system development, the body's movement possibilities, the child's goals, and environmental supports for the skill.

- Movement opportunities and a stimulating environment contribute to motor development, as shown by observations of infants learning to crawl and walk in varying contexts. Cultural values and child-rearing customs also contribute to the emergence and refinement of motor skills.

- During the first year, infants perfect reaching and grasping. Reaching gradually becomes more accurate and flexible, and the clumsy ulnar grasp is transformed into a refined pincer grasp.

Perceptual Development (p. 140)

What changes in hearing, depth and pattern perception, and intermodal perception take place during infancy?

- Infants organize sounds into increasingly complex patterns and, as part of the **perceptual narrowing effect,** begin to "screen out" sounds not used in their native tongue by the middle of the first year. An impressive **statistical learning capacity** enables babies to detect regular sound patterns, for which they will later learn meanings.

- Rapid maturation of the eye and visual centers in the brain supports the development of focusing, color discrimination, and visual acuity during the first half-year. The ability to scan the environment and track moving objects also improves.

- Research on depth perception reveals that responsiveness to motion cues develops first, followed by sensitivity to binocular and then to pictorial cues. Experience in crawling enhances depth perception and other aspects of three-dimensional understanding, but babies must learn to avoid drop-offs for each body position.

- **Contrast sensitivity** explains infants' early pattern preferences. At first, babies stare at single, high-contrast features. At 2 to 3 months, they thoroughly explore a pattern's features and start to detect pattern organization. Over time, they discriminate increasingly complex, meaningful patterns.

- Newborns prefer to look at and track simple, facelike stimuli, but researchers disagree on whether they have a built-in tendency to orient toward human faces. Around 2 months, they recognize and prefer their mother's facial features, and at 3 months, they distinguish the features of different faces. Starting at 5 months, they perceive emotional expressions as meaningful wholes.

- From the start, infants are capable of **intermodal perception**—combining information across sensory modalities. Detection of amodal relations (such as common tempo or rhythm) may provide the basis for detecting other intermodal matches.

Explain differentiation theory of perceptual development.

- According to **differentiation theory,** perceptual development is a matter of detecting invariant features in a constantly changing perceptual world. Acting on the world plays a major role in perceptual differentiation. From a more cognitive perspective, infants also impose meaning on what they perceive. Many researchers combine these two ideas.

Important Terms and Concepts

brain plasticity (p. 124)
cephalocaudal trend (p. 121)
cerebral cortex (p. 124)
classical conditioning (p. 133)
conditioned response (CR) (p. 134)
conditioned stimulus (CS) (p. 134)
contrast sensitivity (p. 144)
differentiation theory (p. 146)
dynamic systems theory of motor development (p. 137)
experience-dependent brain growth (p. 128)
experience-expectant brain growth (p. 127)

glial cells (p. 122)
habituation (p. 134)
imitation (p. 135)
intermodal perception (p. 145)
kwashiorkor (p. 132)
lateralization (p. 124)
marasmus (p. 132)
mirror neurons (p. 136)
myelination (p. 122)
neurons (p. 121)
neurotransmitters (p. 121)
operant conditioning (p. 134)

perceptual narrowing effect (p. 141)
prefrontal cortex (p. 124)
programmed cell death (p. 122)
proximodistal trend (p. 121)
punishment (p. 134)
recovery (p. 134)
reinforcer (p. 134)
statistical learning capacity (p. 142)
synapses (p. 121)
synaptic pruning (p. 122)
unconditioned response (UCR) (p. 133)
unconditioned stimulus (UCS) (p. 133)

A father encourages his child's curiosity and delight in discovery. With the sensitive support of caring adults, infants' and toddlers' cognition and language develop rapidly.

Cognitive Development in Infancy and Toddlerhood

When Caitlin, Grace, and Timmy gathered at Ginette's child-care home, the playroom was alive with activity. The three spirited explorers, each nearly 18 months old, were bent on discovery. Grace dropped shapes through holes in a plastic box that Ginette held and adjusted so the harder ones would fall smoothly into place. Once a few shapes were inside, Grace grabbed the box and shook it, squealing with delight as the lid fell open and the shapes scattered around her. The clatter attracted Timmy, who picked up a shape, carried it to the railing at the top of the basement steps, and dropped it overboard, then followed with a teddy bear, a ball, his shoe, and a spoon. Meanwhile, Caitlin pulled open a drawer, unloaded a set of wooden bowls, stacked them in a pile, knocked it over, and then banged two bowls together.

As the toddlers experimented, I could see the beginnings of spoken language—a whole new way of influencing the world. "All gone baw!" Caitlin exclaimed as Timmy tossed the bright red ball down the basement steps. "Bye-bye," Grace chimed in, waving as the ball disappeared from sight. Later that day, Grace revealed the beginnings of make-believe. "Night-night," she said, putting her head down and closing her eyes, ever so pleased that she could decide for herself when and where to go to bed.

© ELLEN B. SENSI PHOTOGRAPHY

Over the first two years, the small, reflexive newborn baby becomes a self-assertive, purposeful being who solves simple problems and starts to master the most amazing human ability: language. Parents wonder, how does all this happen so quickly? This question has also captivated researchers, yielding a wealth of findings along with vigorous debate over how to explain the astonishing pace of infant and toddler cognition.

In this chapter, we take up three perspectives on early cognitive development: Piaget's *cognitive-developmental theory, information processing,* and Vygotsky's *sociocultural theory.* We also consider the usefulness of tests that measure infants' and toddlers' intellectual progress. Finally, we look at the beginnings of language. We will see how toddlers' first words build on early cognitive achievements and how, very soon, new words and expressions greatly increase the speed and flexibility of their thinking. Throughout development, cognition and language mutually support each other. ●

chapter outline

Piaget's Cognitive-Developmental Theory

Piaget's Ideas About Cognitive Change ● The Sensorimotor Stage ● Follow-Up Research on Infant Cognitive Development ● Evaluation of the Sensorimotor Stage

■ **SOCIAL ISSUES: EDUCATION** Baby Learning from TV and Video: The Video Deficit Effect

Information Processing

A General Model of Information Processing ● Attention ● Memory ● Categorization ● Evaluation of Information-Processing Findings

■ **BIOLOGY AND ENVIRONMENT** Infantile Amnesia

The Social Context of Early Cognitive Development

■ **CULTURAL INFLUENCES** Social Origins of Make-Believe Play

Individual Differences in Early Mental Development

Infant and Toddler Intelligence Tests ● Early Environment and Mental Development ● Early Intervention for At-Risk Infants and Toddlers

Language Development

Theories of Language Development ● Getting Ready to Talk ● First Words ● The Two-Word Utterance Phase ● Individual and Cultural Differences ● Supporting Early Language Development

Piaget's Cognitive-Developmental Theory

Swiss theorist Jean Piaget inspired a vision of children as busy, motivated explorers whose thinking develops as they act directly on the environment. Influenced by his background in biology, Piaget believed that the child's mind forms and modifies psychological structures so they achieve a better fit with external reality. Recall from Chapter 1 that in Piaget's theory, children move through four stages between infancy and adolescence. During these stages, all aspects of cognition develop in an integrated fashion, changing in a similar way at about the same time.

Piaget's first stage, the **sensorimotor stage,** spans the first two years of life. Piaget believed that infants and toddlers "think" with their eyes, ears, hands, and other sensorimotor equipment. They cannot yet carry out many activities inside their heads. But by the end of toddlerhood, children can solve practical, everyday problems and represent their experiences in speech, gesture, and play. To appreciate Piaget's view of how these vast changes take place, let's consider some important concepts.

Piaget's Ideas About Cognitive Change

According to Piaget, specific psychological structures—organized ways of making sense of experience called **schemes**—change with age. At first, schemes are sensorimotor action patterns. For example, at 6 months, Timmy dropped objects in a fairly rigid way, simply letting go of a rattle or teething ring and watching with interest. By 18 months, his "dropping scheme" had become deliberate and creative. In tossing objects down the basement stairs, he threw some in the air, bounced others off walls, released some gently and others forcefully. Soon, instead of just acting on objects, he will show evidence of thinking before he acts. For Piaget, this change marks the transition from sensorimotor to preoperational thought.

In Piaget's theory, two processes, *adaptation* and *organization,* account for changes in schemes.

Adaptation. *TAKE A MOMENT...* The next time you have a chance, notice how infants and toddlers tirelessly repeat actions that lead to interesting effects. **Adaptation** involves building schemes through direct interaction with the environment. It consists of two complementary activities, *assimilation* and *accommodation.* During **assimilation,** we use our current schemes to interpret the external world. For example, when Timmy dropped objects, he was assimilating them to his sensorimotor "dropping scheme." In **accommodation,** we create new schemes or adjust old ones after noticing that our current ways of thinking do not capture the environment completely. When Timmy dropped objects in different ways, he modified his dropping scheme to take account of the varied properties of objects.

According to Piaget, the balance between assimilation and accommodation varies over time. When children are not changing

© LAURA DWIGHT PHOTOGRAPHY

In Piaget's theory, first schemes are sensorimotor action patterns. As this 11-month-old repeatedly experiments with her dropping scheme, her dropping behavior becomes more deliberate and varied.

much, they assimilate more than they accommodate—a steady, comfortable state that Piaget called cognitive *equilibrium.* During rapid cognitive change, however, children are in a state of *disequilibrium,* or cognitive discomfort. Realizing that new information does not match their current schemes, they shift from assimilation toward accommodation. After modifying their schemes, they move back toward assimilation, exercising their newly changed structures until they are ready to be modified again.

Each time this back-and-forth movement between equilibrium and disequilibrium occurs, more effective schemes are produced. Because the times of greatest accommodation are the earliest ones, the sensorimotor stage is Piaget's most complex period of development.

Organization. Schemes also change through **organization,** a process that takes place internally, apart from direct contact with the environment. Once children form new schemes, they rearrange them, linking them with other schemes to create a strongly interconnected cognitive system. For example, eventually Timmy will relate "dropping" to "throwing" and to his developing understanding of "nearness" and "farness." According to Piaget, schemes truly reach equilibrium when they become part of a broad network of structures that can be jointly applied to the surrounding world (Piaget, 1936/1952).

In the following sections, we will first describe infant development as Piaget saw it, noting research that supports his observations. Then we will consider evidence demonstrating that, in some ways, babies' cognitive competence is more advanced than Piaget believed.

The Sensorimotor Stage

The difference between the newborn baby and the 2-year-old child is so vast that Piaget divided the sensorimotor stage into six substages, summarized in Table 5.1. Piaget based this sequence on his own three children—a very small sample. He observed his son and two daughters carefully and also presented them with everyday problems (such as hidden objects) that helped reveal their understanding of the world.

According to Piaget, at birth infants know so little that they cannot explore purposefully. The **circular reaction** provides a special means of adapting their first schemes. It involves stumbling onto a new experience caused by the baby's own motor activity. The reaction is "circular" because, as the infant tries to repeat the event again and again, a sensorimotor response that first occurred by chance strengthens into a new scheme. Consider Caitlin, who at age 2 months accidentally made a smacking noise after a feeding. Finding the sound intriguing, she tried to repeat it until she became quite expert at smacking her lips.

The circular reaction initially centers on the infant's own body but later turns outward, toward manipulation of objects. In the second year, it becomes experimental and creative, aimed at producing novel outcomes. Infants' difficulty inhibiting new and interesting behaviors may underlie the circular reaction. This immaturity in inhibition seems to be adaptive, helping to ensure that new skills will not be interrupted before they strengthen (Carey & Markman, 1999). Piaget considered revisions in the circular reaction so important that, as Table 5.1 shows, he named the sensorimotor substages after them.

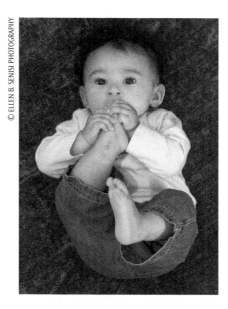

This 3-month-old tries to repeat a newly discovered action—sucking her toes—in a primary circular reaction that helps her gain voluntary control over her behavior.

Repeating Chance Behaviors. Piaget saw newborn reflexes as the building blocks of sensorimotor intelligence. In Substage 1, babies suck, grasp, and look in much the same way, no matter what experiences they encounter. In one amusing example, Carolyn described how 2-week-old Caitlin lay on the bed next to her sleeping father. Suddenly, he awoke with a start. Caitlin had latched on and begun to suck on his back!

Around 1 month, as babies enter Substage 2, they start to gain voluntary control over their actions through the *primary circular reaction,* by repeating chance behaviors largely motivated by basic needs. This leads to some simple motor habits, such as sucking their fist or thumb. Babies in this substage also begin to vary their behavior in response to environmental demands. For example, they open their mouths differently for a nipple than for a spoon. And they start to anticipate events. When hungry, 3-month-old Timmy would stop crying as soon as Vanessa entered the room—a signal that feeding time was near.

TABLE 5.1
Summary of Piaget's Sensorimotor Stage

SENSORIMOTOR SUBSTAGE	TYPICAL ADAPTIVE BEHAVIORS
1. Reflexive schemes (birth–1 month)	Newborn reflexes (see Chapter 3, page 107)
2. Primary circular reactions (1–4 months)	Simple motor habits centered around the infant's own body; limited anticipation of events
3. Secondary circular reactions (4–8 months)	Actions aimed at repeating interesting effects in the surrounding world; imitation of familiar behaviors
4. Coordination of secondary circular reactions (8–12 months)	Intentional, or goal-directed, behavior; ability to find a hidden object in the first location in which it is hidden (object permanence); improved anticipation of events; imitation of behaviors slightly different from those the infant usually performs
5. Tertiary circular reactions (12–18 months)	Exploration of the properties of objects by acting on them in novel ways; imitation of novel behaviors; ability to search in several locations for a hidden object (accurate A–B search)
6. Mental representation (18 months–2 years)	Internal depictions of objects and events, as indicated by sudden solutions to problems; ability to find an object that has been moved while out of sight (invisible displacement); deferred imitation; and make-believe play

During Substage 3, from 4 to 8 months, infants sit up and reach for and manipulate objects. These motor achievements strengthen the *secondary circular reaction,* through which babies try to repeat interesting events in the surrounding environment that are caused by their own actions. For example, 4-month-old Caitlin accidentally knocked a toy hung in front of her, producing a fascinating swinging motion. Over the next three days, Caitlin tried to repeat this effect, gradually forming a new "hitting" scheme. Improved control over their own behavior permits infants to imitate others' behavior more effectively. However, they usually cannot adapt flexibly and quickly enough to imitate novel behaviors. Therefore, although they enjoy watching an adult demonstrate a game of pat-a-cake, they are not yet able to participate.

Intentional Behavior. In Substage 4, 8- to 12-month-olds combine schemes into new, more complex action sequences. As a result, actions that lead to new schemes no longer have a hit-or-miss quality—*accidentally* bringing the thumb to the mouth or *happening* to hit the toy. Instead, 8- to 12-month-olds can engage in **intentional,** or **goal-directed, behavior,** coordinating schemes deliberately to solve simple problems. Consider Piaget's famous object-hiding task, in which he shows the baby an attractive toy and then hides it behind his hand or under a cover. Infants of this substage can find the object by coordinating two schemes—"pushing" aside the obstacle and "grasping" the toy. Piaget regarded these *means–end action sequences* as the foundation for all problem solving.

Retrieving hidden objects reveals that infants have begun to master **object permanence,** the understanding that objects continue to exist when out of sight. But this awareness is not yet complete. Babies still make the *A-not-B search error:* If they reach several times for an object at a first hiding place (A), then see it moved to a second (B), they still search for it in the first

hiding place (A). Consequently, Piaget concluded, they do not have a clear image of the object as persisting when hidden from view.

Infants in Substage 4, who can better anticipate events, sometimes use their capacity for intentional behavior to try to change those events. At 10 months, Timmy crawled after Vanessa when she put on her coat, whimpering to keep her from leaving. Also, babies can now imitate behaviors slightly different from those they usually perform. After watching someone else, they try to stir with a spoon, push a toy car, or drop raisins into a cup (Piaget, 1945/1951).

In Substage 5, from 12 to 18 months, the *tertiary circular reaction,* in which toddlers repeat behaviors with variation, emerges. Recall how Timmy dropped objects over the basement steps, trying first this action, then that, then another. This deliberately exploratory approach makes 12- to 18-month-olds better problem solvers. For example, Grace figured out how to fit a shape through a hole in a container by turning and twisting it until it fell through and how to use a stick to get toys that were out of reach. According to Piaget, this capacity to experiment leads to a more advanced understanding of object permanence. Toddlers look for a hidden toy in several locations, displaying an accurate A–B search. Their more flexible action patterns also permit them to imitate many more behaviors—stacking blocks, scribbling on paper, and making funny faces.

Mental Representation. Substage 6 brings the ability to create **mental representations**—internal depictions of information that the mind can manipulate. Our most powerful mental representations are of two kinds: (1) *images,* or mental pictures of objects, people, and spaces; and (2) *concepts,* or categories in which similar objects or events are grouped together. We use a mental image to retrace our steps when we've misplaced something or to imitate another's behavior long after observing it. By thinking in concepts and labeling them (for example, "ball" for all rounded, movable objects used in play), we become more efficient thinkers, organizing our diverse experiences into meaningful, manageable, and memorable units.

Piaget noted that 18- to 24-month-olds arrive at solutions suddenly rather than through trial-and-error behavior. In doing so, they seem to experiment with actions inside their heads— evidence that they can mentally represent their experiences. For example, at 19 months, Grace—after bumping her new push toy against a wall—paused for a moment as if to "think," then immediately turned the toy in a new direction.

Representation also enables older toddlers to solve advanced object permanence problems involving *invisible displacement—* finding a toy moved while out of sight, such as into a small box while under a cover. It permits **deferred imitation**—the ability to remember and copy the behavior of models who are not present. And it makes possible **make-believe play,** in which children act out everyday and imaginary activities. As the sensorimotor stage draws to a close, mental symbols have become major instruments of thinking.

© LAURA DWIGHT PHOTOGRAPHY

To find the toy hidden under the cloth, a 10-month-old engages in intentional, goal-directed behavior—the basis for all problem solving.

Follow-Up Research on Infant Cognitive Development

Many studies suggest that infants display a wide array of understandings earlier than Piaget believed. Recall the operant conditioning research reviewed in Chapter 4, in which newborns sucked vigorously on a nipple to gain access to interesting sights and sounds. This behavior, which closely resembles Piaget's secondary circular reaction, shows that infants explore and control the external world long before 4 to 8 months. In fact, they do so as soon as they are born.

To discover what infants know about hidden objects and other aspects of physical reality, researchers often use the **violation-of-expectation method.** They may *habituate* babies to a physical event (expose them to the event until their looking declines) to familiarize them with a situation in which their knowledge will be tested. Or they may simply show babies an *expected event* (one that follows physical laws) and an *unexpected event* (a variation of the first event that violates physical laws). Heightened attention to the unexpected event suggests that the infant is "surprised" by a deviation from physical reality and, therefore, is aware of that aspect of the physical world.

The violation-of-expectation method is controversial. Some researchers believe that it indicates limited awareness of physical events—not the full-blown, conscious understanding that was Piaget's focus in requiring infants to act on their surroundings, as in searching for hidden objects (Campos et al., 2008; Munakata, 2001). Others maintain that the method reveals only babies' perceptual preference for novelty, not their knowledge of the physical world (Bremner, 2010; Cohen, 2010; Kagan, 2008). Let's examine this debate in light of recent evidence.

Object Permanence. In a series of studies using the violation-of-expectation method, Renée Baillargeon and her collaborators claimed to have found evidence for object permanence in the first few months of life. Figure 5.1 illustrates one of these studies (Aguiar & Baillargeon, 2002; Baillargeon & DeVos, 1991). After habituating to a short and a tall carrot moving behind a screen, infants were given two test events: (1) an *expected event,* in which the short carrot moved behind a screen, could not be seen in its window, and reappeared on the other side; and (2) an *unexpected event,* in which the tall carrot moved behind a screen, could not be seen in its window (although it was taller than the window's lower edge), and reappeared. Infants as young as 2½ to 3½ months looked longer at the unexpected event, suggesting that they had some awareness that an object moved behind a screen would continue to exist.

Additional violation-of-expectation studies yielded similar results, suggesting that infants look longer at a wide variety of unexpected events involving hidden objects (Newcombe, Sluzenski, & Huttenlocher, 2005; Wang, Baillargeon, & Paterson, 2005). Still, several researchers using similar procedures failed to confirm Baillargeon's findings (Cohen & Marks, 2002; Schöner & Thelen, 2006; Sirois & Jackson, 2012). And, as previously

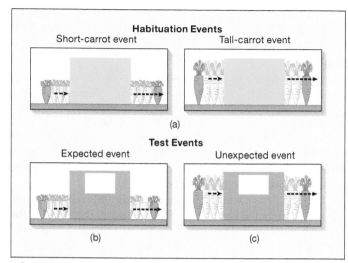

FIGURE 5.1 Testing young infants for understanding of object permanence using the violation-of-expectation method. (a) First, infants were habituated to two events: a short carrot and a tall carrot moving behind a yellow screen, on alternate trials. Next, the researchers presented two test events. The color of the screen was changed to help infants notice its window. (b) In the *expected event,* the carrot shorter than the window's lower edge moved behind the blue screen and reappeared on the other side. (c) In the *unexpected event,* the carrot taller than the window's lower edge moved behind the screen and did not appear in the window, but then emerged intact on the other side. Infants as young as 2½ to 3½ months looked longer at the *unexpected event,* suggesting that they had some understanding of object permanence. (Adapted from R. Baillargeon & J. DeVos, 1991, "Object Permanence in Young Infants: Further Evidence," *Child Development, 62,* p. 1230. © 1991, John Wiley and Sons. Reproduced with permission of John Wiley & Sons Ltd.)

noted, critics question what babies' looking preferences tell us about what they actually understand.

But another type of looking behavior suggests that young infants are aware that objects persist when out of view. Four- and 5-month-olds will track a ball's path of movement as it disappears and reappears from behind a barrier, even gazing ahead to where they expect it to emerge (Bertenthal, Longo, & Kenny, 2007; Rosander & von Hofsten, 2004). With age, babies are more likely to fixate on the predicted place of the ball's reappearance and wait for it—evidence of an increasingly secure grasp of object permanence.

In related research, 6-month-olds' ERP brain-wave activity was recorded as the babies watched two events on a computer screen. In one event, a black square moved until it covered an object, then moved away to reveal the object (object permanence). In the other, as a black square began to move across an object, the object disintegrated (object disappearance) (Kaufman, Csibra, & Johnson, 2005). Only while watching the first event did the infants show a particular brain-wave pattern in the right temporal lobe—the same pattern adults exhibit when told to sustain a mental image of an object.

If young infants do have some notion of object permanence, how do we explain Piaget's finding that even babies capable of reaching do not try to search for hidden objects before 8 months of age? Consistent with Piaget's theory, searching for hidden objects is a true cognitive advance because infants solve some object-hiding tasks before others: Ten-month-olds search for an object placed on a table and covered by a cloth before they search for an object that a hand deposits under a cloth (Moore & Meltzoff, 1999). In the second, more difficult task, infants seem to expect the object to reappear in the hand from which it initially disappeared. When the hand emerges without the object, they conclude that there is no other place the object could be. Not until 14 months can most babies infer that the hand deposited the object under the cloth.

Once 8- to 12-month-olds search for hidden objects, they make the A-not-B search error. Some research suggests that they search at A (where they found the object previously) instead of B (its most recent location) because they have trouble inhibiting a previously rewarded response (Diamond, Cruttenden, & Neiderman, 1994). Another possibility is that after finding the object several times at A, they do not attend closely when it is hidden at B (Ruffman & Langman, 2002).

A more comprehensive explanation is that a complex, dynamic system of factors—having built a habit of reaching toward A, continuing to look at A, having the hiding place at B appear similar to the one at A, and maintaining a constant body posture—increases the chances that the baby will make the A-not-B search error. Disrupting any one of these factors increases 10-month-olds' accurate searching at B (Thelen et al., 2001). In addition, older infants are still perfecting reaching and grasping (see Chapter 3) (Berger, 2010). If these motor skills are challenging, babies have little attention left to focus on inhibiting their habitual reach toward A.

LOOK AND LISTEN

Using an attractive toy and cloth, try several object-hiding tasks with 8- to 14-month-olds. Is their searching behavior consistent with research findings? ●

In sum, mastery of object permanence is a gradual achievement. Babies' understanding becomes increasingly complex with age: They must distinguish the object from the barrier concealing it, keep track of the object's whereabouts, and use this knowledge to obtain the object (Cohen & Cashon, 2006; Moore & Meltzoff, 2008). Success at object search tasks coincides with rapid development of the frontal lobes of the cerebral cortex (Bell, 1998). Also crucial are a wide variety of experiences perceiving, acting on, and remembering objects.

Mental Representation. In Piaget's theory, before about 18 months of age, infants are unable to mentally represent experience. Yet 8- to 10-month-olds' ability to recall the location of hidden objects after delays of more than a minute, and 14-month-olds' recall after delays of a day or more, indicate that babies construct mental representations of objects and their whereabouts (McDonough, 1999; Moore & Meltzoff, 2004). And in studies of deferred imitation and problem solving, representational thought is evident even earlier.

Deferred and Inferred Imitation. Piaget studied imitation by noting when his three children demonstrated it in their everyday behavior. Under these conditions, a great deal must be known about the infant's daily life to be sure that deferred imitation—which requires infants to represent a model's past behavior—has occurred.

Laboratory research suggests that deferred imitation is present at 6 weeks of age! Infants who watched an unfamiliar adult's facial expression imitated it when exposed to the same adult the next day (Meltzoff & Moore, 1994). As motor capacities improve, infants copy actions with objects. In one study, an adult showed 6- and 9-month-olds a novel series of actions with a puppet: taking its glove off, shaking the glove to ring a bell inside, and replacing the glove. When tested a day later, infants who had seen the novel actions were far more likely to imitate them (see Figure 5.2). And when researchers paired a second, motionless puppet with the first puppet a day before the demonstration, 6-month-olds generalized the novel actions to this new, very different-looking puppet (Barr, Marrott, & Rovee-Collier, 2003).

Between 12 and 18 months, toddlers use deferred imitation skillfully to enrich their range of sensorimotor schemes. They retain modeled behaviors for at least several months, copy the actions of peers as well as adults, and imitate across a change in context—for example, enact at home a behavior seen at child care (Klein & Meltzoff, 1999; Meltzoff & Williamson, 2010). The ability to recall modeled behaviors in the order they occurred—evident as early as 6 months—also strengthens over the second year (Bauer, 2006; Rovee-Collier & Cuevas, 2009). And when toddlers imitate in correct sequence, they remember more behaviors (Knopf, Kraus, & Kressley-Mba, 2006).

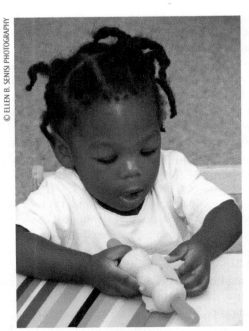

© ELLEN B. SENISI PHOTOGRAPHY

Through deferred imitation, toddlers greatly expand their sensorimotor schemes. While imitating, this 2-year-old encounters a problem faced by all cookie bakers at one time or another.

(a)　　　　　(b)

COURTESY OF CAROLYN ROVEE-COLLIER

FIGURE 5.2 Testing infants for deferred imitation. After researchers performed a novel series of actions with a puppet, this 6-month-old imitated the actions a day later—at left, removing the glove; at right, shaking the glove to ring a bell inside. With age, gains in recall are evident in deferred imitation of others' behaviors over longer delays.

Toddlers even imitate rationally, by *inferring* others' intentions! Fourteen-month-olds are more likely to imitate purposeful than accidental behaviors (Carpenter, Akhtar, & Tomasello, 1998). And they adapt their imitative acts to a model's goals. If 12-month-olds see an adult perform an unusual action for fun (make a toy dog enter a miniature house by jumping through the chimney, even though its door is wide open), they copy the behavior. But if the adult engages in the odd behavior because she *must* (she makes the dog go through the chimney only after first trying to use the door and finding it locked), 12-month-olds typically imitate the more efficient action (putting the dog through the door) (Schwier et al., 2006).

Between 14 and 18 months, toddlers become increasingly adept at imitating actions an adult *tries* to produce, even if these are not fully realized (Bellagamba, Camaioni, & Colonnesi, 2006; Olineck & Poulin-Dubois, 2007, 2009). On one occasion, Ginette attempted to pour some raisins into a bag but missed, spilling them onto the counter. A moment later, Grace began dropping the raisins into the bag, indicating that she had inferred Ginette's goal.

Problem Solving. As Piaget indicated, around 7 to 8 months, infants develop intentional means–end action sequences, which they use to solve simple problems, such as pulling on a cloth to obtain a toy resting on its far end (Willatts, 1999). Soon after, infants' representational skills permit more effective problem solving than Piaget's theory suggests.

By 10 to 12 months, infants can *solve problems by analogy*—apply a solution strategy from one problem to other relevant problems. In one study, babies were given three similar problems, each requiring them to overcome a barrier, grasp a string, and pull it to get an attractive toy. The problems differed in many aspects of their superficial features—texture and color of the string, barrier, and floor mat and type of toy (horse, doll, or car). For the first problem, the parent demonstrated the solution and encouraged the infant to imitate. Babies obtained the toy more readily with each additional problem (Chen, Sanchez, & Campbell, 1997). Similarly, 12-month-olds who were repeatedly presented

with a spoon in the same orientation (handle to one side) readily adapted their motor actions when the spoon was presented with the handle to the other side, successfully transporting food to their mouths most of the time (McCarty & Keen, 2005).

These findings reveal that at the end of the first year, infants form flexible mental representations of how to use tools to get objects. They have some ability to move beyond trial-and-error experimentation, represent a solution mentally, and use it in new contexts.

Symbolic Understanding. One of the most momentous early attainments is the realization that words can be used to cue mental images of things not physically present—a symbolic capacity called **displaced reference** that emerges around the first birthday. It greatly expands toddlers' capacity to learn about the world through communicating with others. Observations of 12-month-olds reveal that they respond to the label of an absent toy by looking at and gesturing toward the spot where it usually rests (Saylor, 2004). As memory and vocabulary improve, skill at displaced reference expands.

But at first, toddlers have difficulty using language to acquire new information about an absent object—an ability that is essential to learn from symbols. In one study, an adult taught 19- and 22-month-olds a name for a stuffed animal—"Lucy" for a frog. Then, with the frog out of sight, the toddler was told that some water had spilled, so "Lucy's all wet!" Finally, the adult showed the toddler three stuffed animals—a wet frog, a dry frog, and a pig—and said, "Get Lucy!" (Ganea et al., 2007). Although all the children remembered that Lucy was a frog, only the 22-month-olds identified the wet frog as Lucy. This capacity to use language as a flexible symbolic tool—to modify and enrich existing mental representations—improves gradually into the preschool years.

Awareness of the symbolic function of pictures also emerges in the second year. Even newborns perceive a relation between a picture and its referent, as indicated by their preference for looking at a photo of their mother's face (see page 145 in Chapter 4). At the same time, infants do not treat pictures as symbols.

Rather, they touch, rub, and pat a color photo of an object, or pick it up and manipulate it. These behaviors, which reveal confusion about the picture's true nature, decline after 9 months, becoming rare around 18 months (DeLoache et al., 1988; DeLoache & Ganea, 2009).

As long as pictures strongly resemble real objects, by the middle of the second year toddlers treat them symbolically. After hearing a novel label ("blicket") applied to a color photo of an unfamiliar object, most 15- to 24-month-olds—when presented with both the real object and its picture and asked to indicate the "blicket"—gave a symbolic response. They selected either the real object or both the object and its picture, not the picture alone (Ganea et al., 2009). Around this time, toddlers increasingly use pictures as vehicles for communicating with others and acquiring new knowledge (Ganea, Pickard, & DeLoache, 2008). They point to, name, and talk about pictures, and they can apply something learned from a book with realistic-looking pictures to real objects, and vice versa.

But even after coming to appreciate the symbolic nature of pictures, young children have difficulty grasping the distinction between some pictures (such as line drawings) and their referents, as we will see in Chapter 8. How do infants and toddlers interpret another ever-present, pictorial medium—video? Turn to the Social Issues: Education box on the following page to find out.

Evaluation of the Sensorimotor Stage

Table 5.2 summarizes the remarkable cognitive attainments we have just considered. *TAKE A MOMENT...* Compare this table with Piaget's description of the sensorimotor substages in Table 5.1 on page 153. You will see that infants anticipate events, actively search for hidden objects, master the A–B object search, flexibly vary their sensorimotor schemes, engage in make-believe play, and treat pictures and video images symbolically

within Piaget's time frame. Yet other capacities—including secondary circular reactions, understanding of object properties, first signs of object permanence, deferred imitation, problem solving by analogy, and displaced reference of words—emerge earlier than Piaget expected. These findings show that the cognitive attainments of infancy do not develop together in the neat, stepwise fashion that Piaget assumed.

Recent research raises questions about Piaget's view of how infant development takes place. Consistent with Piaget's ideas, sensorimotor action helps infants construct some forms of knowledge. For example, in Chapter 4, we saw that crawling enhances depth perception and ability to find hidden objects, and handling objects fosters awareness of object properties. Yet we have also seen that infants comprehend a great deal before they are capable of the motor behaviors that Piaget assumed led to those understandings. How can we account for babies' amazing cognitive accomplishments?

Alternative Explanations. Unlike Piaget, who thought young babies constructed all mental representations out of sensorimotor activity, most researchers now believe that infants have some built-in cognitive equipment for making sense of experience. But intense disagreement exists over the extent of this initial understanding. As we have seen, much evidence on young infants' cognition rests on the violation-of-expectation method. Researchers who lack confidence in this method argue that babies' cognitive starting point is limited (Campos et al., 2008; Cohen, 2010; Cohen & Cashon, 2006; Kagan, 2008). For example, some believe that newborns begin life with a set of biases for attending to certain information and with general-purpose learning procedures—such as powerful techniques for analyzing complex perceptual information. Together, these capacities enable infants to construct a wide variety of schemes (Bahrick, 2010; Huttenlocher, 2002; Quinn, 2008; Rakison, 2010).

TABLE 5.2 Some Cognitive Attainments of Infancy and Toddlerhood

AGE	COGNITIVE ATTAINMENTS
Birth–1 month	Secondary circular reactions using limited motor skills, such as sucking a nipple to gain access to interesting sights and sounds
1–4 months	Awareness of object permanence, object solidity, and gravity, as suggested by violation-of-expectation findings; deferred imitation of an adult's facial expression over a short delay (one day)
4–8 months	Improved knowledge of object properties and basic numerical knowledge, as suggested by violation-of-expectation findings; deferred imitation of an adult's novel actions on objects over a short delay (one to three days)
8–12 months	Ability to search for a hidden object when covered by a cloth; ability to solve simple problems by analogy to a previous problem
12–18 months	Ability to search in several locations for a hidden object, when a hand deposits it under a cloth, and when it is moved from one location to another (accurate A–B search); deferred imitation of an adult's novel actions on objects after long delays (at least several months) and across a change in situation (from child care to home); rational imitation, inferring the model's intentions; displaced reference of words
18 months–2 years	Ability to find an object moved while out of sight (invisible displacement); deferred imitation of actions an adult tries to produce, even if these are not fully realized; deferred imitation of everyday behaviors in make-believe play; beginning awareness of pictures and video as symbols of reality

TAKE A MOMENT... Which of the capacities listed in the table indicate that mental representation emerges earlier than Piaget believed?

Social Issues: Education

Baby Learning from TV and Video: The Video Deficit Effect

Children first become TV and video viewers in early infancy, as they are exposed to programs watched by parents and older siblings or to shows aimed at viewers not yet out of diapers, such as the Baby Einstein products. About 40 percent of U.S. 3-month-olds watch regularly, a figure that rises to 90 percent at age 2, a period during which average viewing time increases from just under an hour to 1½ hours a day (Zimmerman, Christakis, & Meltzoff, 2007). Although parents assume that babies learn from TV and videos, research indicates that they cannot take full advantage of them.

Initially, infants respond to videos of people as if viewing people directly—smiling, moving their arms and legs, and (by 6 months) imitating actions of a televised adult. But they confuse the images with the real thing (Barr, Muentener, & Garcia, 2007; Marian, Neisser, & Rochat, 1996). When shown videos of attractive toys, 9-month-olds manually explored the screen, as they do with pictures. By 19 months, touching and grabbing had declined in favor of pointing at the images (Pierroutsakos & Troseth, 2003). Nevertheless, toddlers continue to have difficulty applying what they see on video to real situations.

In a series of studies, some 2-year-olds watched through a window while a live adult hid an object in an adjoining room, while others watched the same event on a video screen. Children in the direct viewing condition retrieved the toy easily; those in the video condition had difficulty (Troseth, 2003; Troseth & DeLoache, 1998).

This **video deficit effect**—poorer performance after a video than a live demonstration—has also been found for 2-year-olds' deferred imitation, word learning, and means–end problem solving (Deocampo, 2003; Hayne, Herbert, & Simcock, 2003; Krcmar, Grela, & Linn, 2007).

One explanation is that 2-year-olds typically do not view a video character as offering socially relevant information. After an adult on video announced where she hid a toy, few 2-year-olds searched (Schmidt, Crawley-Davis, & Anderson, 2007). In contrast, when the adult uttered the same words while standing in front of the child, 2-year-olds promptly retrieved the object.

Toddlers seem to discount information on video as relevant to their everyday experiences because people do not look at and converse with them directly or establish a shared focus on objects, as their caregivers do. In one study, researchers gave some 2-year-olds an interactive video experience (using a two-way, closed-circuit video system). An adult on video interacted with the child for five minutes—calling the child by name, talking about the child's siblings and pets, waiting for the child to respond, and playing interactive games (Troseth, Saylor, & Archer, 2006). Compared with 2-year-olds who viewed the same adult in a noninteractive video, those in the interactive condition

This baby thinks the child she sees on the TV screen is real. Not until she is about 2½ will she understand how onscreen images relate to real people and objects.

were far more likely to use a verbal cue from a person on video to retrieve a toy.

Around age 2½, the video deficit effect declines. Before this age, the American Academy of Pediatrics (2001) recommends against mass media exposure. In support of this advice, amount of TV viewing is negatively related to 8- to 18-month-olds' language progress (Tanimura et al., 2004; Zimmerman, Christakis, & Meltzoff, 2007). And 1- to 3-year-old heavy viewers tend to have attention, memory, and reading difficulties in the early school years (Christakis et al., 2004; Zimmerman & Christakis, 2005).

When toddlers do watch TV and video, it is likely to work best as a teaching tool when it is rich in social cues—close-ups of characters who look directly at the camera, address questions to viewers, and pause to invite their response. Repetition of video programs also helps children over age 2 make sense of video content.

Others, convinced by violation-of-expectation findings, believe that infants start out with impressive understandings. According to this **core knowledge perspective,** babies are born with a set of innate knowledge systems, or *core domains of thought.* Each of these prewired understandings permits a ready grasp of new, related information and therefore supports early, rapid development (Carey & Markman, 1999; Leslie, 2004; Spelke, 2004; Spelke & Kinzler, 2007). Core knowledge theorists argue that infants could not make sense of the complex

stimulation around them without having been genetically "set up" in the course of evolution to comprehend its crucial aspects.

Researchers have conducted many studies of infants' *physical knowledge,* including object permanence, object solidity (that one object cannot move through another), and gravity (that an object will fall without support). Violation-of-expectation findings suggest that in the first few months, infants have some awareness of all these basic object properties and quickly build on this knowledge (Baillargeon, 2004; Hespos & Baillargeon,

2008; Luo & Baillargeon, 2005; Spelke, 2000). Core knowledge theorists also assume that an inherited foundation of *linguistic knowledge* enables swift language acquisition in early childhood—a possibility we will consider later in this chapter. Furthermore, these theorists argue, infants' early orientation toward people initiates rapid development of *psychological knowledge*—in particular, understanding of mental states, such as intentions, emotions, desires, and beliefs, which we will address further in Chapter 6.

Research even suggests that infants have basic *numerical knowledge*. In the best-known study, 5-month-olds saw a screen raised to hide a single toy animal and then watched a hand place a second toy behind the screen. Finally the screen was removed to reveal either one or two toys. If infants kept track of the two objects (requiring them to add one object to another), then they should look longer at the unexpected, one-toy display—which is what they did (see Figure 5.3) (Wynn, Bloom, & Chiang, 2002). These findings and those of similar investigations suggest that babies can discriminate quantities up to three and use that knowledge to perform simple arithmetic—both addition and subtraction (in which two objects are covered and one object is removed) (Kobayashi et al., 2004; Kobayashi, Hiraki, & Hasegawa, 2005; Wynn, Bloom, & Chiang, 2002).

Additional evidence suggests that 6-month-olds can distinguish among large sets of items, as long as the difference between those sets is very great—at least a factor of two. For example, they can tell the difference between 8 and 16 dots but not between

Did this toddler learn to build a block tower by repeatedly acting on objects, as Piaget assumed? Or did he begin life with innate knowledge that helps him understand objects and their relationships quickly, with little hands-on exploration?

6 and 12 (Lipton & Spelke, 2004; Xu, Spelke, & Goddard, 2005). As a result, some researchers believe that infants can represent approximate large-number values, in addition to the small-number discriminations evident in Figure 5.3.

But like other violation-of-expectation results, babies' numerical capacities are controversial. In experiments similar to those just described, looking preferences were inconsistent

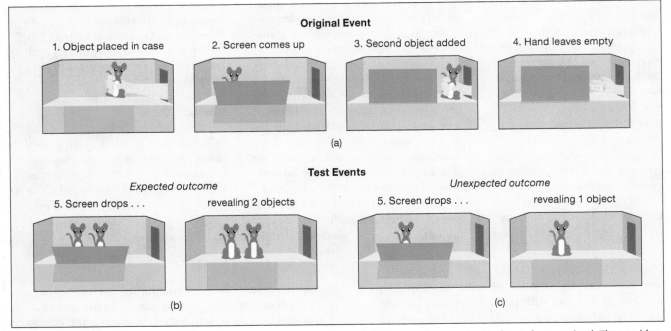

FIGURE 5.3 **Testing infants for basic number concepts.** (a) First, infants saw a screen raised in front of a toy animal. Then an identical toy was added behind the screen. Next, the researchers presented two outcomes. (b) In the *expected outcome*, the screen dropped to reveal two toy animals. (c) In the *unexpected outcome*, the screen dropped to reveal one toy animal. Five-month-olds shown the unexpected outcome looked longer than did 5-month-olds shown the expected outcome. The researchers concluded that infants can discriminate the quantities "one" and "two" and use that knowledge to perform simple addition: 1 + 1 = 2. A variation of this procedure suggested that 5-month-olds could also do simple subtraction: 2 – 1 = 1. (From K. Wynn, 1992, "Addition and Subtraction by Human Infants." *Nature,* 358, p. 749. © 1992 by Nature Publishing Group. Adapted with permission of Macmillan Publishers, Ltd.)

(Langer, Gillette, & Arriaga, 2003; Wakeley, Rivera, & Langer, 2000). These researchers point out that claims for infants' knowledge of number concepts are surprising, in view of other research indicating that before 14 to 16 months, toddlers have difficulty making less-than and greater-than comparisons between small sets. And not until the preschool years do children answer correctly when asked to add and subtract small sets.

The core knowledge perspective, while emphasizing native endowment, acknowledges that experience is essential for children to extend this initial knowledge. But so far, it has said little about which experiences are most important in each core domain of thought and how those experiences advance children's thinking. Despite ongoing challenges from critics, core knowledge research has sharpened the field's focus on specifying the starting point of human cognition and carefully tracking the changes that build on it.

Piaget's Legacy. Follow-up research on Piaget's sensorimotor stage yields broad agreement on two issues. First, many cognitive changes of infancy are gradual and continuous rather than abrupt and stagelike, as Piaget thought (Bjorklund, 2012; Courage & Howe, 2002). Second, rather than developing together, various aspects of infant cognition change unevenly because of the challenges posed by different types of tasks and infants' varying experience with them. These ideas serve as the basis for another major approach to cognitive development—*information processing*.

Before we turn to this alternative point of view, let's recognize Piaget's enormous contributions. Piaget's work inspired a wealth of research on infant cognition, including studies that challenged his theory. Today, researchers are far from consensus on how to modify or replace his account of infant cognitive development, and some believe that his general approach continues to make sense and fits most of the evidence (Cohen, 2010). Piaget's observations also have been of great practical value. Teachers and caregivers continue to look to the sensorimotor stage for guidelines on how to create developmentally appropriate environments for infants and toddlers.

ASK YOURSELF

REVIEW Using the text discussion on pages 155–158, construct your own summary table of infant and toddler cognitive development. Which entries in your table are consistent with Piaget's sensorimotor stage? Which ones develop earlier than Piaget anticipated?

APPLY Several times, after her father hid a teething biscuit under a red cup, 12-month-old Mimi retrieved it easily. Then Mimi's father hid the biscuit under a nearby yellow cup. Why did Mimi persist in searching for it under the red cup?

REFLECT What advice would you give the typical U.S. parent about permitting an infant or toddler to watch as much as 1 to 1½ hours of TV or video per day? Explain.

Information Processing

Information-processing researchers agree with Piaget that children are active, inquiring beings. But instead of providing a single, unified theory of cognitive development, they focus on many aspects of thinking, from attention, memory, and categorization skills to complex problem solving.

Recall from Chapter 1 that the information-processing approach frequently relies on computer-like flowcharts to describe the human cognitive system. Information-processing theorists are not satisfied with general concepts, such as assimilation and accommodation, to describe how children think. Instead, they want to know exactly what individuals of different ages do when faced with a task or problem (Birney & Sternberg, 2011; Miller, 2009). The computer model of human thinking is attractive because it is explicit and precise.

A General Model of Information Processing

Most information-processing researchers assume that we hold information in three parts of the mental system for processing: the *sensory register,* the *short-term memory store,* and the *long-term memory store* (see Figure 5.4 on page 162). As information flows through each, we can use *mental strategies* to operate on and transform it, increasing the chances that we will retain information, use it efficiently, and think flexibly, adapting the information to changing circumstances. To understand this more clearly, let's look at each component of the mental system.

First, information enters the **sensory register,** where sights and sounds are represented directly and stored briefly. *TAKE A MOMENT...* Look around you, and then close your eyes. An image of what you saw persists for a few seconds, but then it decays, or disappears, unless you use mental strategies to preserve it. For example, by *attending to* some information more carefully than to other information, you increase the chances that it will transfer to the next step of the information-processing system.

In the second part of the mind, the **short-term memory store,** we retain attended-to information briefly so we can actively "work" on it to reach our goals. One way of looking at the short-term store is in terms of its *basic capacity,* often referred to as *short-term memory:* how many pieces of information can be held at once for a few seconds. But most researchers endorse a contemporary view of the short-term store, which offers a more meaningful indicator of its capacity, called **working memory**— the number of items that can be briefly held in mind while also engaging in some effort to monitor or manipulate those items. Working memory can be thought of as a "mental workspace" that we use to accomplish many activities in daily life. From childhood on, researchers assess changes in working-memory capacity by presenting individuals with lists of items (such as numerical digits or short sentences), asking them to "work" on the items (for example, repeat the digits backward or remember the final word of each sentence in correct order), and seeing how well they do.

FIGURE 5.4 Model of the human information-processing system. Information flows through three parts of the mental system: the *sensory register*, the *short-term memory store*, and the *long-term memory store*. In each, mental strategies can be used to manipulate information, increasing the efficiency and flexibility of thinking and the chances that information will be retained. The *central executive* is the conscious, reflective part of the mental system. It coordinates incoming information with information already in the system, decides what to attend to, and oversees the use of strategies.

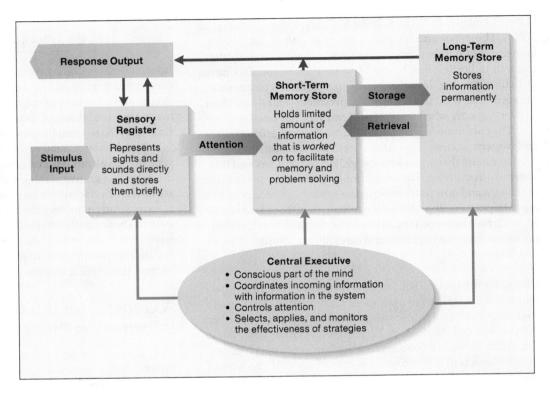

The sensory register can take in a wide panorama of information. Short-term and working memory are far more restricted, though their capacity increases steadily from early childhood to early adulthood—on a verbatim digit-span task tapping short-term memory, from about 2 to 7 items; and on working-memory tasks, from about 2 to 5 items (Cowan & Alloway, 2009). Still, individual differences are evident at all ages. By engaging in a variety of basic cognitive procedures, such as focusing attention on relevant items and repeating (rehearsing) them rapidly, we increase the chances that information will be retained and accessible to ongoing thinking.

To manage the cognitive system's activities, the **central executive** directs the flow of information, implementing the basic procedures just mentioned and also engaging in more sophisticated activities that enable complex, flexible thinking. For example, the central executive coordinates incoming information with information already in the system, and it selects, applies, and monitors strategies that facilitate memory storage, comprehension, reasoning, and problem solving (Pressley & Hilden, 2006). The central executive is the conscious, reflective part of our mental system. It ensures that we think purposefully, to attain our goals.

The more effectively the central executive joins with working memory to process information, the better learned cognitive activities will be and the more *automatically* we can apply them. Consider the richness of your thinking while you automatically drive a car. **Automatic processes** are so well-learned that they require no space in working memory and, therefore, permit us to focus on other information while performing them. Furthermore, the more effectively we process information in working memory,

the more likely it will transfer to the third, and largest, storage area—**long-term memory**, our permanent knowledge base, which is unlimited. In fact, we store so much in long-term memory that *retrieval*—getting information back from the system—can be problematic. To aid retrieval, we apply strategies, just as we do in working memory. Information in long-term memory is *categorized* by its contents, much like a library shelving system that enables us to retrieve items by following the same network of associations used to store them in the first place.

Information-processing research indicates that several aspects of the cognitive system improve during childhood and adolescence: (1) the *basic capacity* of its stores, especially working memory; (2) the *speed* with which information is worked on; and (3) the *functioning of the central executive*. Together, these changes make possible more complex forms of thinking with age (Case, 1998; Kail, 2003).

Gains in working-memory capacity are due in part to brain development, but greater processing speed also contributes. Fast, fluent thinking frees working-memory resources to support storage and manipulation of additional information. Furthermore, researchers have become increasingly interested in studying the development of **executive function**—the diverse cognitive operations and strategies that enable us to achieve our goals in cognitively challenging situations (Welsh, Friedman, & Spieker, 2008). These include controlling attention, suppressing impulses, coordinating information in working memory, and flexibly directing and monitoring thought and behavior. As we will see, gains in working memory capacity and aspects of executive function are under way in the first two years; dramatic strides will follow in childhood and adolescence.

Attention

Recall from Chapter 4 that around 2 to 3 months of age, infants shift from focusing on single, high-contrast features to exploring objects and patterns more thoroughly. Besides attending to more aspects of the environment, infants gradually become more efficient at managing their attention, taking in information more quickly. Habituation research reveals that preterm and newborn babies require a long time—about 3 to 4 minutes—to habituate and recover to novel visual stimuli. But by 4 or 5 months, they need as little as 5 to 10 seconds to take in a complex visual stimulus and recognize it as different from a previous one (Rose, Feldman, & Jankowski, 2001; Slater et al., 1996).

One reason that very young babies' habituation times are so much longer is their difficulty disengaging attention from a stimulus (Colombo, 2002). When Carolyn held up a colorful rattle, 2-month-old Caitlin stared intently until, unable to break her gaze, she burst into tears. The ability to shift attention from one stimulus to another improves by 4 months—a change believed to be due to development of structures in the cerebral cortex controlling eye movements (Blaga & Colombo, 2006; Posner & Rothbart, 2007).

Over the first year, infants attend to novel and eye-catching events. In the second year, as toddlers become increasingly capable of intentional behavior (refer back to Piaget's Substage 4), attraction to novelty declines (but does not disappear) and *sustained attention* improves, especially when children play with toys. A toddler who engages even in simple goal-directed behavior, such as stacking blocks or putting them in a container, must sustain attention to reach the goal (Ruff & Capozzoli, 2003). As plans and activities gradually become more complex, the duration of attention increases.

Memory

Operant conditioning and habituation provide windows into early memory. Both methods show that retention of visual events increases dramatically over infancy and toddlerhood.

Using operant conditioning, researchers study infant memory by teaching 2- to 6-month-olds to move a mobile by kicking a foot tied to it with a long cord. Two-month-olds remember how to activate the mobile for 1 to 2 days after training, and 3-month-olds for one week. By 6 months, memory increases to two weeks (Rovee-Collier, 1999; Rovee-Collier & Bhatt, 1993). Around the middle of the first year, babies can manipulate switches or buttons to control stimulation. When 6- to 18-month-olds pressed a lever to make a toy train move around a track, duration of memory continued to increase with age; 13 weeks after training, 18-month-olds still remembered how to press the lever (see Figure 5.5) (Hartshorn et al., 1998).

Even after 2- to 6-month-olds forget an operant response, they need only a brief prompt—an adult who shakes the mobile—to reinstate the memory (Hildreth & Rovee-Collier, 2002). And when 6-month-olds are given a chance to reactivate the response themselves for just a couple of minutes, their memory not only returns but extends dramatically, to about

17 weeks (Hildreth, Sweeney, & Rovee-Collier, 2003). Perhaps permitting the baby to generate the previously learned behavior strengthens memory because it reexposes the child to more aspects of the original learning situation.

Habituation studies show that infants learn and retain a wide variety of information just by watching objects and events, without being physically active. Sometimes, they do so for much longer time spans than in operant conditioning studies. Babies are especially attentive to the movements of objects and people. In one investigation, 5½-month-olds remembered a woman's captivating action (such as blowing bubbles or brushing hair) seven weeks later, as indicated by a *familiarity preference* (see page 135 in Chapter 4) (Bahrick, Gogate, & Ruiz, 2002). The babies were so attentive to the woman's action that they did not remember her face, even when tested 1 minute later for a *novelty preference*.

In Chapter 4, we saw that 3- to 5-month-olds are excellent at discriminating faces. But their memory for the faces of unfamiliar people and for other visual patterns is short-lived—at 3 months, only about 24 hours, and at the end of the first year, several days to a few weeks (Fagan, 1973; Pascalis, de Haan, & Nelson, 1998). By contrast, 3-month-olds' memory for the unusual movements of objects (such as a metal nut swinging on the end of a string) persists for at least three months (Bahrick, Hernandez-Reif, & Pickens, 1997).

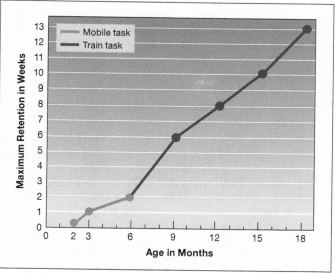

FIGURE 5.5 Increase in retention in two operant conditioning tasks from 2 to 18 months. Two- to 6-month-olds were trained to make a kicking response that turned a mobile. Six- to 18-month-olds were trained to press a lever that made a toy train move around a track. Six-month-olds learned both responses and retained them for an identical length of time, indicating that the tasks are comparable. Consequently, researchers could plot a single line tracking gains in retention of operant responses from 2 to 18 months of age. The line shows that memory improves dramatically. (From C. Rovee-Collier & R. Barr, 2001, "Infant Learning and Memory," in G. Bremner & A. Fogel, [Eds.], *Blackwell Handbook of Infant Development*, Oxford, U.K.: Blackwell, p. 150. © 2001, 2004 by Blackwell Publishing Ltd. Reproduced with permission of John Wiley & Sons Ltd.)

Biology and Environment

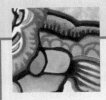

Infantile Amnesia

If infants and toddlers recall many aspects of their everyday lives, how do we explain **infantile amnesia**—that most of us cannot retrieve events that happened to us before age 3? The reason cannot be merely the passage of time because we can recall many personally meaningful one-time events from both the recent and the distant past: the day a sibling was born or a move to a new house—recollections known as **autobiographical memory.**

Several accounts of infantile amnesia exist. One theory credits brain development, suggesting that vital changes in the prefrontal cortex pave the way for an *explicit* memory system—one in which children remember deliberately rather than *implicitly,* without conscious awareness (Nelson, 1995). But mounting evidence indicates that even young infants engage in conscious recall (Bauer, 2006; Rovee-Collier & Cuevas, 2009). Their memory processing is not fundamentally different from that of children and adults.

Another conjecture is that older children and adults often use verbal means for storing information, whereas infants' and toddlers' memory processing is largely nonverbal—an incompatibility that may prevent long-term retention of early experiences. To test this idea, researchers sent two adults to the homes of 2- to 4-year-olds with an unusual toy that the children were likely to remember: The Magic Shrinking Machine, shown in Figure 5.6. One adult showed the child how, after inserting an object in an opening on top of the machine and turning a crank that activated flashing lights and musical sounds, the child could retrieve a smaller, identical object (discretely dropped down a chute by the second adult) from behind a door on the front of the machine.

A day later, the researchers tested the children to see how well they recalled the event. Their nonverbal memory—based on acting out the "shrinking" event and recognizing the "shrunken" objects in photos—was excellent. But even when they had the vocabulary, children younger than age 3 had trouble describing features of the "shrinking" experience. Verbal recall increased sharply between ages 3 and 4—the period during which children "scramble over the

amnesia barrier" (Simcock & Hayne, 2003, p. 813). In a second study, preschoolers could not translate their nonverbal memory for the game into language 6 months to 1 year later, when their language had improved dramatically. Their verbal reports were "frozen in time," reflecting their limited language skill at the age they played the game (Simcock & Hayne, 2002).

These findings help us reconcile infants' and toddlers' remarkable memory skills with infantile amnesia. During the first few years, children rely heavily on nonverbal memory techniques, such as visual images and motor actions. As language develops, preschoolers can use it to refer to preverbal memories. But their ability to do so is fragile, requiring strong contextual cues, such as direct exposure to the physical setting of the to-be-recalled experience (Morris & Baker-Ward, 2007). Only after age 3 do children often represent events verbally and participate in elaborate conversations with adults about them. As children encode autobiographical events in verbal form, they use language-based cues to retrieve them, increasing the accessibility of these memories at later ages (Peterson, Warren, & Short, 2011).

By 10 months, infants remember both novel actions and features of objects involved in those actions equally well (Horst, Oakes, & Madole, 2005). Thus, over the second half-year, sensitivity to object appearance increases. This change is fostered by infants' increasing ability to manipulate objects, which helps them learn about objects' observable properties.

So far, we have discussed only **recognition**—noticing when a stimulus is identical or similar to one previously experienced. It is the simplest form of memory: All babies have to do is indicate (by kicking, pressing a lever, or looking) that a new stimulus is identical or similar to a previous one. **Recall** is more challenging because it involves remembering something not present. But by the second half of the first year, infants are capable of recall, as indicated by their ability to find hidden objects and engage in deferred imitation. Recall, too, improves steadily with age. For example, 1-year-olds can retain short sequences of adult-modeled behaviors for up to 3 months, and 1½-year-olds can do so for as long as 12 months (Rovee-Collier & Cuevas, 2009).

Long-term recall depends on connections among multiple regions of the cerebral cortex, especially with the prefrontal cortex. During infancy and toddlerhood, these neural circuits develop rapidly (Nelson, Thomas, & de Haan, 2006). Yet a puzzling finding is that older children and adults no longer recall their earliest experiences! See the Biology and Environment box above for a discussion of *infantile amnesia.*

Categorization

Even young infants can *categorize,* grouping similar objects and events into a single representation. Categorization reduces the enormous amount of new information infants encounter every day, helping them learn and remember (Rakison, 2010).

Creative variations of operant conditioning research with mobiles have been used to investigate infant categorization. One such study, of 3-month-olds, is described and illustrated in

Other findings indicate that the advent of a clear self-image contributes to the end of infantile amnesia (Howe, Courage, & Rooksby, 2009). Toddlers who were advanced in development of a sense of self demonstrated better verbal memories a year later while conversing about past

events with their mothers (Harley & Reese, 1999).

Very likely, both neurobiological change and social experience contribute to the decline of infantile amnesia. Brain development and adult–child interaction may jointly foster self-awareness, language, and

improved memory, which enable children to talk with adults about significant past experiences (Bauer, 2007). As a result, preschoolers begin to construct a long-lasting autobiographical narrative of their lives and enter into the history of their family and community.

  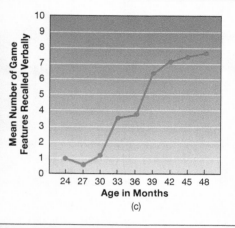

(a)   (b)   (c)

FIGURE 5.6 **The Magic Shrinking Machine, used to test young children's verbal and nonverbal memory of an unusual event.** After being shown how the machine worked, the child participated in selecting objects from a polka-dot bag, dropping them into the top of the machine (a), and turning a crank, which produced a "shrunken" object (b). When tested the next day, 2- to 4-year-olds' nonverbal memory for the event was excellent. But below 36 months, verbal recall was poor, based on the number of features recalled about the game during an open-ended interview (c). Recall improved between 36 and 48 months, the period during which infantile amnesia subsides. (From G. Simcock & H. Hayne, 2003, "Age-Related Changes in Verbal and Nonverbal Memory During Early Childhood," *Developmental Psychology, 39,* pp. 807, 809. Copyright © 2003 by the American Psychological Association. Reprinted with permission of the American Psychological Association. *Photos:* Ross Coombes/Courtesy of Harlene Hayne.)

Figure 5.7 on page 166. Similar investigations reveal that in the first few months, babies categorize stimuli on the basis of shape, size, and other physical properties (Wasserman & Rovee-Collier, 2001). By 6 months of age, they can categorize on the basis of two correlated features—for example, the shape and color of an alphabet letter (Bhatt et al., 2004). This ability to categorize using clusters of features prepares babies for acquiring many complex everyday categories.

Habituation has also been used to study infant categorization. Researchers show babies a series of pictures belonging to one category and then see whether they recover to (look longer at) a picture that is not a member of the category. Findings reveal that in the second half of the first year, as long as they have sufficient familiarity with category members, infants group objects into an impressive array of categories—food items, furniture, birds, land animals, air animals, sea animals, plants, vehicles, kitchen utensils, and spatial location ("above" and "below," "on" and "in") (Bornstein, Arterberry, & Mash, 2010; Casasola,

Cohen, & Chiarello, 2003; Oakes, Coppage, & Dingel, 1997). Besides organizing the physical world, infants of this age categorize their emotional and social worlds. They sort people and their voices by gender and age, have begun to distinguish emotional expressions, separate people's natural actions (walking) from other motions, and expect people (but not inanimate objects) to move spontaneously (Spelke, Phillips, & Woodward, 1995; see also Chapter 4, pages 144–145).

Babies' earliest categories are based on similar overall appearance or prominent object part: legs for animals, wheels for vehicles. By the second half of the first year, more categories appear to be based on subtle sets of features (Cohen, 2003; Mandler, 2004; Quinn, 2008). Older infants can even make categorical distinctions when the perceptual contrast between two categories is minimal (birds versus airplanes).

As they gain experience in comparing to-be-categorized items in varied ways and as their store of verbal labels expands, toddlers start to categorize flexibly: When 14-month-olds are

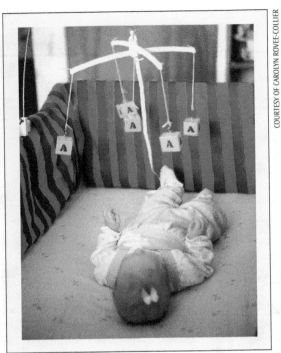

COURTESY OF CAROLYN ROVEE-COLLIER

FIGURE 5.7 Investigating infant categorization using operant conditioning. Three-month-olds were taught to kick to move a mobile that was made of small blocks, all with the letter *A* on them. After a delay, kicking returned to a high level only if the babies were shown a mobile whose elements were labeled with the same form (the letter *A*). If the form was changed (from *A*s to *2*s), infants no longer kicked vigorously. While making the mobile move, the babies had grouped together its features. They associated the kicking response with the category *A* and, at later testing, distinguished it from the category *2*. (Bhatt, Rovee-Collier, & Weiner, 1994; Hayne, Rovee-Collier, & Perris, 1987.)

given four balls and four blocks, some made of soft rubber and some of rigid plastic, their sequence of object touching reveals that after classifying by shape, they can switch to classifying by material (soft versus hard) if an adult calls their attention to the new basis for grouping (Ellis & Oakes, 2006).

In addition to touching and sorting, toddlers' categorization skills are evident in their play behaviors. After watching an adult give a toy dog a drink from a cup, most 14-month-olds shown a rabbit and a motorcycle offered the drink only to the rabbit (Mandler & McDonough, 1998). They clearly understood that certain actions are appropriate for some categories of items (animals) and not others (vehicles).

By the end of the second year, toddlers' grasp of the animate–inanimate distinction expands. Nonlinear motions are typical of animates (a person or a dog jumping), linear motions of inanimates (a car or a table pushed along a surface). At 18 months, toddlers more often imitate a nonlinear motion with a toy that has animate-like parts (legs), even if it represents an inanimate (a bed). At 22 months, displaying a fuller understanding, they imitate a nonlinear motion only with toys in the animate category (a cat but not a bed) (Rakison, 2005, 2006). They seem to realize that whereas animates are self-propelled and therefore

have varied paths of movement, inanimates move only when acted on, in highly restricted ways.

Researchers disagree on how toddlers gradually shift from categorizing on the basis of prominent perceptual features (things with flapping wings and feathers belong to one category; things with rigid wings and a smooth surface to another) to categorizing on a conceptual basis, grouping objects by their common function or behavior (birds versus airplanes, dogs versus cats) (Oakes et al., 2009; Rakison & Lupyan, 2008). But all acknowledge that exploration of objects and expanding knowledge of the world contribute. In addition, adult labeling of a set of objects with a consistently applied word ("Look at the car!" "Do you see the car?") calls babies' attention to commonalities among objects, fostering categorization as early as 3 to 4 months of age (Ferry, Hespos, & Waxman, 2010). Toddlers' vocabulary growth, in turn, fosters categorization (Cohen & Brunt, 2009; Waxman, 2003).

Variations among languages lead to cultural differences in development of categories. Korean toddlers, who learn a language in which object names are often omitted from sentences, develop object-sorting skills later than their English-speaking counterparts (Gopnik & Choi, 1990). At the same time, Korean contains a common word, *kkita,* with no English equivalent, referring to a tight fit between objects in contact (a ring on a finger, a cap on a pen), and Korean toddlers are advanced in forming the spatial category "tight fit" (Choi et al., 1999).

Evaluation of Information-Processing Findings

The information-processing perspective underscores the continuity of human thinking from infancy into adult life. In attending to the environment, remembering everyday events, and categorizing objects, Caitlin, Grace, and Timmy think in ways that are remarkably similar to our own, though their mental processing is far from proficient. Findings on memory and categorization join with other research in challenging Piaget's view of early cognitive development. Infants' capacity to recall events and to categorize stimuli attests, once again, to their ability to mentally represent their experiences.

Information-processing research has contributed greatly to our view of infants and toddlers as sophisticated cognitive beings. But its central strength—analyzing cognition into its components, such as perception, attention, memory, and categorization—is also its greatest drawback: Information processing has had difficulty putting these components back together into a broad, comprehensive theory.

One approach to overcoming this weakness has been to combine Piaget's theory with the information-processing approach, an effort we will explore in Chapter 9. A more recent trend has been the application of a *dynamic systems view* (see Chapter 4, pages 137–138) to early cognition. In this approach, researchers analyze each cognitive attainment to see how it results from a complex system of prior accomplishments and the child's current goals (Spencer & Perone, 2008; Thelen & Smith, 2006).

Once these ideas are fully tested, they may move the field closer to a more powerful view of how the minds of infants and children develop.

The Social Context of Early Cognitive Development

Recall the description at the beginning of this chapter of Grace dropping shapes into a container. Notice that she learns about the toy with Ginette's help. With adult support, Grace will gradually become better at matching shapes to openings and dropping them into the container. Then she will be able to perform this and similar activities on her own.

Vygotsky's sociocultural theory emphasizes that children live in rich social and cultural contexts that affect the way their cognitive world is structured (Bodrova & Leong, 2007; Rogoff, 2003). Vygotsky believed that complex mental activities have their origins in social interaction. Through joint activities with more mature members of their society, children master activities and think in ways that have meaning in their culture.

A special Vygotskian concept explains how this happens. The **zone of proximal** (or potential) **development** refers to a range of tasks too difficult for the child to do alone but possible with the help of more skilled partners. To understand this idea, think about how a sensitive adult (such as Ginette) introduces a child to a new activity. The adult picks a task that the child can master but that is challenging enough that the child cannot do it by herself. As the adult guides and supports, the child joins in the interaction and picks up mental strategies. As her competence increases, the adult steps back, permitting the child to take more responsibility for the task. This form of teaching—known as *scaffolding*—promotes learning at all ages, and we will consider it further in Chapter 7.

Vygotsky's ideas have been applied mostly to older children, who are more skilled in language and social communication. Recently, however, his theory has been extended to infancy and toddlerhood. Recall that babies are equipped with capacities that ensure that caregivers will interact with them. Then adults adjust the environment and their communication in ways that promote learning adapted to their cultural circumstances.

A study by Barbara Rogoff and her collaborators (1984) illustrates this process. Placing a jack-in-the-box nearby, the researchers watched how several adults played with Rogoff's son and daughter over the first two years. In the early months, the adults tried to focus the baby's attention by working the toy and, as the bunny popped out, saying something like "My, what happened?" By the end of the first year, when the baby's cognitive and motor skills had improved, interaction centered on how to use the toy. The adults guided the baby's hand in turning the crank and putting the bunny back in the box. During the second year, adults helped from a distance, using gestures and verbal prompts, such as making a turning motion with the hand near the crank. Research indicates that this fine-tuned support is related to advanced play, language, and problem solving in toddlerhood and early childhood (Bornstein et al., 1992; Charman et al., 2001; Tamis-LeMonda & Bornstein, 1989).

As early as the first year, cultural variations in social experiences affect mental strategies. In the jack-in-the-box example, adults and children focused their attention on a single activity. This strategy, common in Western middle-SES homes, is well-suited to lessons in which children master skills apart from the everyday situations in which they will later use those skills. In contrast, Guatemalan Mayan adults and babies often attend to several events at once. For example, one 12-month-old skillfully put objects in a jar while watching a passing truck and blowing into a toy whistle (Chavajay & Rogoff, 1999). Processing several competing events simultaneously may be vital in cultures where children largely learn through keen observation of others' ongoing activities. Children of Guatemalan Mayan, Mexican, and Native-American parents without extensive education continue to display this style of attention well into middle childhood (Chavajay & Rogoff, 2002; Correa-Chavez, Rogoff, & Mejía-Arauz, 2005; Philips, 1983).

Earlier we saw how infants and toddlers create new schemes by acting on the physical world (Piaget) and how certain skills become better developed as children represent their experiences more efficiently and meaningfully (information processing). Vygotsky adds a third dimension to our understanding by emphasizing that many aspects of cognitive development are socially mediated. The Cultural Influences box on page 168 presents additional evidence for this idea, and we will see even more in the next section.

Using simple words and gestures, this mother brings a challenging task—rotating the plane's propeller—within her toddler's zone of proximal development. By adjusting her communication to suit the child's needs, she transfers mental strategies to him and promotes learning.

Cultural Influences

Social Origins of Make-Believe Play

© CAROLINE PENN/PANOS PICTURES

A Kenyan child guides his younger brother in pretend play. In cultures where sibling caregiving is common, make-believe play is more frequent and complex with older siblings than with mothers.

One of the activities my husband, Ken, used to do with our two sons when they were young was to bake pineapple upside-down cake, a favorite treat. One Sunday afternoon when a cake was in the making, 21-month-old Peter stood on a chair at the kitchen sink, busily pouring water from one cup to another.

"He's in the way, Dad!" complained 4-year-old David, trying to pull Peter away from the sink.

"Maybe if we let him help, he'll give us room," Ken suggested. As David stirred the batter, Ken poured some into a small bowl for Peter, moved his chair to the side of the sink, and handed him a spoon.

"Here's how you do it, Petey," instructed David, with a superior air. Peter watched as David stirred, then tried to copy his motion. When it was time to pour the batter, Ken helped Peter hold and tip the small bowl.

"Time to bake it," said Ken.

"Bake it, bake it," repeated Peter, watching Ken slip the pan into the oven.

Several hours later, we observed one of Peter's earliest instances of make-believe play. He got his pail from the sandbox and, after filling it with a handful of sand, carried it into the kitchen and put it down on the floor in front of the oven. "Bake it, bake it," Peter called to Ken. Together, father and son placed the pretend cake in the oven.

Piaget and his followers concluded that toddlers discover make-believe independently, once they are capable of representational schemes. Vygotsky challenged this view, pointing out that society provides children with opportunities to represent culturally meaningful activities in play. Make-believe, like other complex mental activities, is first learned under the guidance of experts (Berk, Mann, & Ogan, 2006). In the example just described, Peter extended his capacity to represent daily events when Ken drew him into the baking task and helped him act it out in play.

Current evidence supports the idea that early make-believe is the combined result of children's readiness to engage in it and social experiences that promote it. In one observational study of U.S. middle-SES toddlers, 75 to 80 percent of make-believe involved mother–child interaction (Haight & Miller, 1993). At 12 months, almost all play episodes were initiated by mothers, but by the end of the second year, half of pretend episodes were initiated by each.

During make-believe, mothers offer toddlers a rich array of cues that they are pretending—looking and smiling at the child more, making more exaggerated movements, and using more "we" talk (acknowledging that pretending is a joint endeavor) than they do during the same real-life event (Lillard, 2007). These maternal cues encourage toddlers to join in and probably facilitate their ability to distinguish pretend from real acts, which strengthens over the second and third years (Lillard & Witherington, 2004; Ma & Lillard, 2006).

Also, when adults participate, toddlers' make-believe is more elaborate (Keren et al., 2005). They are more likely to combine pretend acts into complex sequences, as Peter did when he put sand in the bucket (making the batter), carried it into the kitchen, and, with Ken's help, put it in the oven (baking the cake). The more parents pretend with their toddlers, the more time their children devote to make-believe.

In some cultures, such as those of Indonesia and Mexico, where extended-family households and sibling caregiving are common, make-believe is more frequent and complex with older siblings than with mothers. As early as age 3 to 4, children provide rich, challenging stimulation to their younger brothers and sisters, take these teaching responsibilities seriously, and, with age, become better at them (Zukow-Goldring, 2002). In a study of Zinacanteco Indian children of southern Mexico, by

age 8, sibling teachers were highly skilled at showing 2-year-olds how to play at everyday tasks, such as washing and cooking (Maynard, 2002). They often guided toddlers verbally and physically through the task and provided feedback.

In Western middle-SES families, older siblings less often teach deliberately but still serve as influential models of playful behavior. In a study of New Zealand families of Western European descent, when both a parent and an older sibling were available, toddlers more often imitated the actions of the sibling, especially when siblings engaged in make-believe (Barr & Hayne, 2003).

As we will see in Chapter 7, make-believe play is a major means through which children extend their cognitive skills and learn about important activities in their culture. Vygotsky's theory, and the findings that support it, tell us that providing a stimulating physical environment is not enough to promote early cognitive development. In addition, toddlers must be invited and encouraged by more skilled members of their culture to participate in the social world around them. Parents and teachers can enhance early make-believe by playing often with toddlers, guiding and elaborating on their make-believe themes.

ASK YOURSELF

REVIEW What impact does toddlers' more advanced play with toys have on the development of attention?

CONNECT List techniques parents can use to *scaffold* the development of categorization in infancy and toddlerhood, and explain why each is effective.

APPLY When Timmy was 18 months old, his mother stood behind him, helping him throw a large ball into a box. As his skill improved, she stepped back, letting him try on his own. Using Vygotsky's ideas, explain how Timmy's mother is supporting his cognitive development.

REFLECT Describe your earliest autobiographical memory. How old were you when the event occurred? Do your responses fit with research on infantile amnesia?

Individual Differences in Early Mental Development

Because of Grace's deprived early environment, Kevin and Monica had a psychologist give her one of many tests available for assessing mental development in infants and toddlers. Worried about Timmy's progress, Vanessa also arranged for him to be tested. At age 22 months, he had only a handful of words in his vocabulary, played in a less mature way than Caitlin and Grace, and seemed restless and overactive.

The cognitive theories we have just discussed try to explain the *process* of development—how children's thinking changes. Mental tests, in contrast, focus on cognitive *products*. Their goal is to measure behaviors that reflect development and to arrive at scores that *predict* future performance, such as later intelligence, school achievement, and adult vocational success. This concern with prediction arose nearly a century ago, when French psychologist Alfred Binet designed the first successful intelligence test, which predicted school achievement (see Chapter 1). It inspired the design of many new tests, including ones that measure intelligence at very early ages.

Infant and Toddler Intelligence Tests

Accurately measuring infants' intelligence is a challenge because babies cannot answer questions or follow directions. All we can do is present them with stimuli, coax them to respond, and observe their behavior. As a result, most infant tests emphasize perceptual and motor responses. But new tests are being developed that also tap early language, cognition, and social behavior, especially with older infants and toddlers.

One commonly used test, the *Bayley Scales of Infant and Toddler Development,* is suitable for children between 1 month

and 3½ years. The most recent edition, the Bayley-III, has three main subtests: (1) the Cognitive Scale, which includes such items as attention to familiar and unfamiliar objects, looking for a fallen object, and pretend play; (2) the Language Scale, which assesses understanding and expression of language—for example, recognition of objects and people, following simple directions, and naming objects and pictures; and (3) the Motor Scale, which includes gross and fine motor skills, such as grasping, sitting, stacking blocks, and climbing stairs (Bayley, 2005).

Two additional Bayley-III scales depend on parental report: (4) the Social-Emotional Scale, which asks caregivers about such behaviors as ease of calming, social responsiveness, and imitation in play; and (5) the Adaptive Behavior Scale, which asks about adaptation to the demands of daily life, including communication, self-control, following rules, and getting along with others.

Computing Intelligence Test Scores. Intelligence tests for infants, children, and adults are scored in much the same way—by computing an **intelligence quotient (IQ),** which indicates the extent to which the raw score (number of items passed) deviates from the typical performance of same-age individuals. To make this comparison possible, test designers engage in **standardization**—giving the test to a large, representative sample and using the results as the *standard* for interpreting scores. The standardization sample for the Bayley-III included 1,700 infants, toddlers, and young preschoolers, reflecting the U.S. population in SES and ethnic diversity.

Within the standardization sample, performances at each age level form a **normal distribution,** in which most scores cluster around the mean, or average, with progressively fewer falling toward the extremes (see Figure 5.8 on page 170). This *bell-shaped distribution* results whenever researchers measure individual differences in large samples. When intelligence tests are standardized, the mean IQ is set at 100. An individual's IQ is higher or lower than 100 by an amount that reflects how much

A trained examiner administers a test based on the Bayley Scales of Infant Development to a 1-year-old sitting in her mother's lap. Compared with earlier editions, the Bayley-III Cognitive and Language Scales better predict preschool mental test performance.

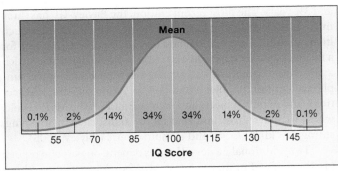

FIGURE 5.8 Normal distribution of intelligence test scores. To determine the percentage of same-age individuals in the population a person with a certain IQ outperformed, add the figures to the left of that IQ score. For example, an 8-year-old child with an IQ of 115 scored better than 84 percent of the population of 8-year-olds.

his or her test performance deviates from the standardization-sample mean.

The IQ offers a way of finding out whether an individual is ahead, behind, or on time (average) in mental development compared with others of the same age. For example, if Timmy's score is 100, then he did better than 50 percent of his agemates. A child with an IQ of 85 did better than only 16 percent, whereas a child with an IQ of 130 outperformed 98 percent. The IQs of 96 percent of individuals fall between 70 and 130; only a few achieve higher or lower scores.

Predicting Later Performance from Infant Tests. Despite careful construction, most infant tests—including previous editions of the Bayley—predict later intelligence poorly. Infants and toddlers easily become distracted, fatigued, or bored during testing, so their scores often do not reflect their true abilities. And infant perceptual and motor items differ from the tasks given to older children, which increasingly emphasize verbal, conceptual, and problem-solving skills. In contrast, the Bayley-III Cognitive and Language Scales, which better dovetail with childhood tests, are good predictors of preschool mental test performance (Albers & Grieve, 2007). But because most infant test scores do not tap the same dimensions of intelligence assessed in older children, they are conservatively labeled **developmental quotients (DQs)** rather than IQs.

Infant tests are somewhat better at making long-term predictions for extremely low-scoring babies. Today, they are largely used for *screening*—helping to identify for further observation and intervention babies who are likely to have developmental problems.

As an alternative to infant tests, some researchers have turned to information-processing measures, such as habituation, to assess early mental progress. Their findings show that speed of habituation and recovery to novel visual stimuli are among the best available infant predictors of IQ from early childhood through early adulthood (Fagan, Holland, & Wheeler, 2007; Kavsek, 2004; McCall & Carriger, 1993). Habituation and recovery seem to be an especially effective early index of intelligence because they assess memory as well as quickness and

flexibility of thinking, which underlie intelligent behavior at all ages (Colombo, 2002; Colombo et al., 2004). The consistency of these findings has prompted designers of the Bayley-III to include items that tap such cognitive skills as habituation, object permanence, and categorization.

Early Environment and Mental Development

In Chapter 2, we indicated that intelligence is a complex blend of hereditary and environmental influences. Many studies have examined the relationship of environmental factors to infant and toddler mental test scores. As we consider this evidence, you will encounter findings that highlight the role of heredity as well.

Home Environment. The **Home Observation for Measurement of the Environment (HOME)** is a checklist for gathering information about the quality of children's home lives through observation and parental interview (Caldwell & Bradley, 1994). Applying What We Know on the following page lists factors measured by HOME during the first three years. Each is positively related to toddlers' mental test performance. Regardless of SES and ethnicity, an organized, stimulating physical setting and parental affection, involvement, and encouragement of new skills repeatedly predict better language and IQ scores in toddlerhood and early childhood (Fuligni, Han, & Brooks-Gunn, 2004; Linver, Martin, & Brooks-Gunn, 2004; Tamis-LeMonda et al., 2004; Tong et al., 2007). The extent to which parents talk to infants and toddlers is particularly important. It contributes strongly to early language progress, which, in turn, predicts intelligence and academic achievement in elementary school (Hart & Risley, 1995).

Yet we must interpret these correlational findings cautiously. In all the studies, children were reared by their biological parents, with whom they share not just a common environment but also a common heredity. Parents who are genetically more intelligent may provide better experiences while also giving birth to genetically brighter children, who evoke more stimulation from

A mother plays actively and affectionately with her baby. Parental warmth, attention, and verbal communication predict better language and IQ scores in toddlerhood and early childhood.

Applying What We Know

Features of a High-Quality Home Life: The HOME Infant–Toddler Subscales

Home Subscale	Sample Item
Emotional and verbal responsiveness of the parent	Parent caresses or kisses child at least once during observer's visit.
	Parent spontaneously speaks to child twice or more (excluding scolding) during observer's visit.
Parental acceptance of the child	Parent does not interfere with child's actions or restrict child's movements more than three times during observer's visit.
Organization of the physical environment	Child's play environment appears safe and free of hazards.
Provision of appropriate play materials	Parent provides toys or interesting activities for child during observer's visit.
Parental involvement with the child	Parent tends to keep child within visual range and to look at child often during observer's visit.
Opportunities for variety in daily stimulation	Child eats at least one meal per day with mother and/or father, according to parental report.
	Child frequently has a chance to get out of house (for example, accompanies parent on trips to grocery store).

Sources: Bradley, 1994; Bradley et al., 2001.

their parents. Research supports this hypothesis, which refers to *gene–environment correlation* (see Chapter 2, page 72) (Saudino & Plomin, 1997). But heredity does not account for the entire association between home environment and mental test scores. Family living conditions—both HOME scores and affluence of the surrounding neighborhood—continue to predict children's IQ beyond the contribution of parental IQ and education (Chase-Lansdale et al., 1997; Klebanov et al., 1998).

How can the research summarized so far help us understand Vanessa's concern about Timmy's development? Ben, the psychologist who tested Timmy, found that he scored only slightly below average. Ben talked with Vanessa about her child-rearing practices and watched her play with Timmy. A single parent who worked long hours, Vanessa had little energy for Timmy at the end of the day. Ben also noticed that Vanessa, anxious about Timmy's progress, tended to pressure him, dampening his active behavior and bombarding him with directions: "That's enough ball play. Stack these blocks."

Ben explained that when parents are intrusive in these ways, infants and toddlers are likely to be distractible, play immaturely, and do poorly on mental tests (Bono & Stifter, 2003; Stilson & Harding, 1997). He coached Vanessa in how to interact sensitively with Timmy, while also assuring her that Timmy's current performance need not forecast his future development. Warm, responsive parenting that builds on toddlers' current capacities is a much better indicator than an early mental test score of how children will do later.

Infant and Toddler Child Care.

Today, more than 60 percent of U.S. mothers with a child under age 2 are employed (U.S. Census Bureau, 2012b). Child care for infants and toddlers has become common, and its quality—though not as influential as parenting—affects mental development. Research consistently

shows that infants and young children exposed to poor-quality child care—whether they come from middle-class or from low-SES homes—score lower on measures of cognitive and social skills (Belsky et al., 2007b; Hausfather et al., 1997; NICHD Early Child Care Research Network, 2000b, 2001, 2003b, 2006). In contrast, good child care can reduce the negative impact of a stressed, poverty-stricken home life, and it sustains the benefits of growing up in an economically advantaged family (Lamb & Ahnert, 2006; McCartney et al., 2007; NICHD Early Child Care Research Network, 2003b).

In contrast to most European countries and to Australia and New Zealand, where child care is nationally regulated and funded to ensure its quality, reports on U.S. child care raise serious concerns. Standards are set by the individual states and vary widely. In studies of quality, only 20 to 25 percent of U.S. child-care centers and family child-care settings (in which a caregiver cares for children in her home) provided infants and toddlers with sufficiently positive, stimulating experiences to promote healthy psychological development. Most settings offered substandard care (NICHD Early Childhood Research Network, 2000a, 2004).

LOOK AND LISTEN

Ask several employed parents of infants or toddlers to describe what they sought in a child-care setting, along with challenges they faced in finding child care. Are the parents knowledgeable about the ingredients of high-quality care? ●

Unfortunately, many U.S. children from low-income families experience inadequate child care (Brooks-Gunn, 2004). But U.S. settings providing the very worst care tend to serve middle-SES families. These parents are especially likely to place their

Applying What We Know

Signs of Developmentally Appropriate Infant and Toddler Child Care

Program Characteristics	Signs of Quality
Physical setting	Indoor environment is clean, in good repair, well-lighted, and well-ventilated. Fenced outdoor play space is available. Setting does not appear overcrowded when children are present.
Toys and equipment	Play materials are appropriate for infants and toddlers and are stored on low shelves within easy reach. Cribs, highchairs, infant seats, and child-sized tables and chairs are available. Outdoor equipment includes small riding toys, swings, slide, and sandbox.
Caregiver–child ratio	In child-care centers, caregiver–child ratio is no greater than 1 to 3 for infants and 1 to 6 for toddlers. Group size (number of children in one room) is no greater than 6 infants with 2 caregivers and 12 toddlers with 2 caregivers. In family child care, caregiver is responsible for no more than 6 children; within this group, no more than 2 are infants and toddlers. Staffing is consistent, so infants and toddlers can form relationships with particular caregivers.
Daily activities	Daily schedule includes times for active play, quiet play, naps, snacks, and meals. It is flexible rather than rigid, to meet the needs of individual children. Atmosphere is warm and supportive, and children are never left unsupervised.
Interactions among adults and children	Caregivers respond promptly to infants' and toddlers' distress; hold, talk to, sing to, and read to them; and interact with them in a manner that respects the individual child's interests and tolerance for stimulation.
Caregiver qualifications	Caregiver has some training in child development, first aid, and safety.
Relationships with parents	Parents are welcome anytime. Caregivers talk frequently with parents about children's behavior and development.
Licensing and accreditation	Child-care setting, whether a center or a home, is licensed by the state. In the United States, voluntary accreditation by the National Association for the Education of Young Children *(www.naeyc.org/academy),* or the National Association for Family Child Care *(www.nafcc.org)* is evidence of an especially high-quality program.

Sources: Copple & Bredekamp, 2009.

children in for-profit centers, where quality tends to be lowest. Low-SES children more often attend publicly subsidized, non-profit centers, which have smaller group sizes and better teacher–child ratios (Lamb & Ahnert, 2006). Still, child-care quality for low-SES children varies widely. And probably because of greater access to adult stimulation, infants and toddlers in high-quality family child care score higher than those in center care in cognitive and language development (NICHD Early Child Care Research Network, 2000b).

See Applying What We Know above for signs of high-quality care for infants and toddlers, based on standards for **developmentally appropriate practice.** These standards, devised by the U.S. National Association for the Education of Young Children, specify program characteristics that serve young children's developmental and individual needs, based on both current research and consensus among experts. Caitlin, Grace, and Timmy are fortunate to be in family child care that meets these standards.

Child care in the United States is affected by a macrosystem of individualistic values and weak government regulation and funding. Furthermore, many parents think that their children's child-care experiences are better than they really are. Unable to identify good care, they do not demand it (Helburn, 1995). In recent years, recognizing that child care is in a state of crisis, the U.S. federal government and some states have allocated

additional funds to subsidize its cost, primarily for low-income families. Though far from meeting the need, this increase in resources has had a positive impact on child-care quality and accessibility (Children's Defense Fund, 2009).

High-quality child care, with a generous caregiver–child ratio, well-trained caregivers, and developmentally appropriate activities, can be especially beneficial to children from low-SES homes.

Good child care is a cost-effective means of protecting children's well-being. And much like the programs we are about to consider, it can serve as effective early intervention for children whose development is at risk.

Early Intervention for At-Risk Infants and Toddlers

Children living in poverty are likely to show gradual declines in intelligence test scores and to achieve poorly when they reach school age (Bradley et al., 2001; Gutman, Sameroff, & Cole, 2003). These problems are largely due to stressful home environments that undermine children's ability to learn and increase the likelihood that they will remain poor as adults (McLoyd, Aikens, & Burton, 2006). A variety of intervention programs have been developed to break this tragic cycle of poverty. Although most begin during the preschool years (we will discuss these in Chapter 7), a few start during infancy and continue through early childhood.

In center-based interventions, children attend an organized child-care or preschool program where they receive educational, nutritional, and health services, and their parents receive child-rearing and other social service supports. In home-based interventions, a skilled adult visits the home and works with parents, teaching them how to stimulate a very young child's development. In most programs of either type, participating children score higher than untreated controls on mental tests by age 2. The earlier intervention begins, the longer it lasts, and the greater its scope and intensity, the better participants' cognitive and academic performance is throughout childhood and adolescence (Brooks-Gunn, 2004; Ramey, Ramey, & Lanzi, 2006; Sweet & Appelbaum, 2004).

The Carolina Abecedarian Project illustrates these favorable outcomes. In the 1970s, more than 100 infants from poverty-stricken families, ranging in age from 3 weeks to 3 months, were randomly assigned to either a treatment group or a control group. Treatment infants were enrolled in full-time, year-round child care through the preschool years. There they received stimulation aimed at promoting motor, cognitive, language, and social skills and, after age 3, literacy and math concepts. Special emphasis was placed on rich, responsive adult–child verbal communication. All children received nutrition and health services; the primary difference between treatment and controls was the intensive child-care experience.

As Figure 5.9 shows, by 12 months of age, the IQs of the two groups diverged. Treatment children sustained their advantage until last tested—at age 21. In addition, throughout their school years, treatment youths achieved considerably higher scores in reading and math. These gains translated into more years of schooling completed, higher rates of college enrollment and employment in skilled jobs, and lower rates of drug use and adolescent parenthood (Campbell et al., 2001, 2002; Campbell & Ramey, 2010).

Recognition of the power of intervening as early as possible led the U.S. Congress to provide limited funding for services

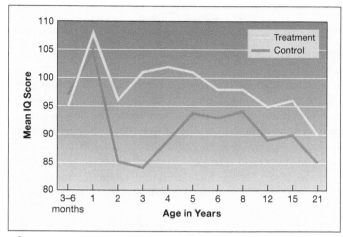

FIGURE 5.9 IQ scores of treatment and control children from infancy to 21 years in the Carolina Abecedarian Project. At 1 year, treatment children outperformed controls, an advantage consistently maintained through age 21. The IQ scores of both groups declined gradually during childhood and adolescence—a trend probably due to the damaging impact of poverty on mental development. (Adapted from Campbell et al., 2001.)

directed at infants and toddlers who already have serious developmental problems or who are at risk for problems because of poverty. Early Head Start, begun in 1995, currently has 1,000 sites serving about 100,000 low-income children and their families (Early Head Start National Resource Center, 2011). A recent evaluation, conducted when children reached age 3, showed that intervention led to warmer, more stimulating parenting, a reduction in harsh discipline, gains in cognitive and language development, and lessening of child aggression (Love et al., 2005; Love, Chazan-Cohen, & Raikes, 2007; Raikes et al., 2010). The strongest effects occurred at sites mixing center- and home-based services. Though not yet plentiful enough to meet the need, such programs are a promising beginning.

ASK YOURSELF

REVIEW What probably accounts for the finding that speed of habituation and recovery to novel visual stimuli predicts later IQ better than most infant mental test scores?

CONNECT Using what you learned about brain development in Chapter 4, explain why it is best to initiate intervention for poverty-stricken children in the first two years rather than later.

APPLY Fifteen-month-old Joey's developmental quotient (DQ) is 115. His mother wants to know exactly what this means and what she should do to support his mental development. How would you respond?

REFLECT Suppose you were seeking a child-care setting for your baby. What would you want it to be like, and why?

Language Development

Improvements in perception and cognition during infancy pave the way for an extraordinary human achievement—language. In Chapter 4, we saw that by the second half of the first year, infants make dramatic progress in distinguishing the basic sounds of their language and in segmenting the flow of speech into word and phrase units. They also start to comprehend some word meanings and, around 12 months of age, say their first word. Sometime between 1½ and 2 years, toddlers combine two words (Gleason, 2009). By age 6, children understand the meaning of about 10,000 words, speak in elaborate sentences, and are skilled conversationalists.

To appreciate this awesome task, think about the many abilities involved in your own flexible use of language. When you speak, you must select words that match the underlying concepts you want to convey. To be understood, you must pronounce words correctly. Then you must combine them into phrases and sentences using a complex set of grammatical rules. Finally, you must follow the rules of everyday conversation—take turns, make comments relevant to what your partner just said, and use an appropriate tone of voice. How do infants and toddlers make such remarkable progress in launching these skills?

Theories of Language Development

In the 1950s, researchers did not take seriously the idea that very young children might be able to figure out important properties of language. Children's regular and rapid attainment of language milestones suggested a process largely governed by maturation, inspiring the nativist perspective on language development. In recent years, new evidence has spawned the interactionist perspective, which emphasizes the joint roles of children's inner capacities and communicative experiences.

The Nativist Perspective. According to linguist Noam Chomsky's (1957) *nativist* theory, language is a unique human accomplishment, etched into the structure of the brain. Focusing on grammar, Chomsky reasoned that the rules of sentence organization are too complex to be directly taught to or discovered by even a cognitively sophisticated young child. Rather, he proposed that all children have a **language acquisition device (LAD)**, an innate system that contains a *universal grammar*, or set of rules common to all languages. It enables children, no matter which language they hear, to understand and speak in a rule-oriented fashion as soon as they pick up enough words.

Are children biologically primed to acquire language? Recall from Chapter 4 that newborn babies are remarkably sensitive to speech sounds. And children everywhere reach major language milestones in a similar sequence. Also, the ability to master a grammatically complex language system seems unique to humans, as efforts to teach language to nonhuman primates—using either specially devised artificial symbol systems or sign language—have met with limited success. Even after extensive training, chimpanzees (who are closest to humans in terms of evolution) master only a basic vocabulary and short word combinations, and they produce these far less consistently than human preschoolers (Tomasello, Call, & Hare, 2003).

Furthermore, evidence that childhood is a *sensitive period* for language acquisition is consistent with Chomsky's idea of a biologically based language program. Researchers have examined the language competence of deaf adults who acquired their first language—American Sign Language (ASL), a gestural system used by the deaf—at different ages. The later learners, whose parents chose to educate them through speech and lip-reading, did not acquire spoken language because of their profound deafness. Consistent with the sensitive-period notion, those who learned ASL in adolescence or adulthood never became as proficient as those who learned in childhood (Mayberry, 2010; Newport, 1991; Singleton & Newport, 2004).

But challenges to Chomsky's theory suggest that it, too, provides only a partial account of language development. First, researchers have had great difficulty specifying Chomsky's universal grammar. Chomsky's critics doubt that one set of rules can account for the extraordinary variation in grammatical forms among the world's 5,000 to 8,000 languages (Christiansen & Chater, 2008; Evans & Levinson, 2009; Tomasello, 2005). Second, children do not acquire language as quickly as nativist theory suggests. They refine and generalize many grammatical forms gradually, engaging in much piecemeal learning and making errors along the way. As we will see in Chapter 9, complete mastery of some grammatical forms, such as the passive voice, is not achieved until well into middle childhood (Tager-Flusberg & Zukowski, 2009; Tomasello, 2006). This suggests that more experimentation and learning are involved than Chomsky assumed.

Finally, recall from Chapter 4 that for most people, language is housed largely in the left hemisphere of the cerebral cortex, consistent with Chomsky's notion of a brain prepared to process language. But our discussion also revealed that language areas in the cortex *develop* as children acquire language. Although the left hemisphere is biased for language processing, if it is injured in the early years, other regions take over (see page 126 in Chapter 4). So localization of language in the left hemisphere is not necessary for effective language use. Furthermore, brain-imaging research shows that many regions of the cerebral cortex participate in language activities to differing degrees, depending on the language skill and the individual's mastery of that skill (Shafer & Garrido-Nag, 2007).

The Interactionist Perspective. Recent ideas about language development emphasize *interactions* between inner capacities and environmental influences. One type of interactionist theory applies the information-processing perspective to language development. A second type emphasizes social interaction.

Some information-processing theorists assume that children make sense of their complex language environments by applying powerful cognitive capacities of a general kind (Bates, 2004; Elman, 2001; Munakata, 2006; Saffran, 2009). These theorists note that brain regions housing language also govern similar perceptual and cognitive abilities, such as the capacity

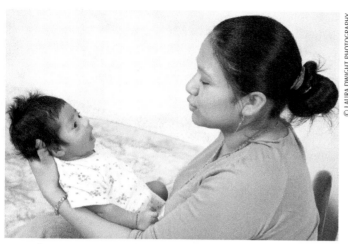

Infants communicate from the very beginning of life, as this interchange between a mother and her 1-month-old illustrates. How will this child become a fluent speaker of her native language within just a few years? Theorists disagree sharply on answers to this question.

to analyze musical and visual patterns (Saygin et al., 2004; Saygin, Leech, & Dick, 2010).

Other theorists blend this information-processing view with Chomsky's nativist perspective. They agree that infants are amazing analyzers of speech and other information. But, they argue, these capacities probably are not sufficient to account for mastery of higher-level aspects of language, such as intricate grammatical structures (Aslin & Newport, 2009). They also point out that grammatical competence may depend more on specific brain structures than the other components of language. When 2- to 2½-year-olds and adults listened to short sentences—some grammatically correct, others with phrase-structure violations—both groups showed similarly distinct ERP brain-wave patterns

for each sentence type in the left frontal and temporal lobes of the cerebral cortex (Oberecker & Friederici, 2006; Oberecker, Friedrich, & Friederici, 2005). This suggests that 2-year-olds process sentence structures using the same neural system as adults do. Furthermore, in studies of older children and adults with left-hemispheric brain damage, grammar is more impaired than other language functions (Stromswold, 2000).

Still other interactionists emphasize that children's social skills and language experiences are centrally involved in language development. In this *social-interactionist* view, an active child, well-endowed for making sense of language, strives to communicate. In doing so, she cues her caregivers to provide appropriate language experiences, which help her relate the content and structure of language to its social meanings (Bohannon & Bonvillian, 2009; Chapman, 2006).

Among social interactionists, disagreement continues over whether or not children are equipped with specialized language abilities (Lidz, 2007; Shatz, 2007; Tomasello, 2003, 2006). Nevertheless, as we chart the course of language development, we will encounter much support for their central premise—that children's social competencies and language experiences greatly affect their language progress. In reality, native endowment, cognitive-processing strategies, and social experience probably operate in different balances with respect to each aspect of language. Table 5.3 provides an overview of early language milestones that we will examine in the next few sections.

Getting Ready to Talk

Before babies say their first word, they make impressive progress toward understanding and speaking their native tongue. They listen attentively to human speech, and they make speechlike sounds. As adults, we can hardly help but respond.

TABLE 5.3

Milestones of Language Development During the First Two Years

APPROXIMATE AGE	MILESTONE
2 months	Infants coo, making pleasant vowel sounds.
4 months on	Infants observe with interest as the caregiver plays turn-taking games, such as pat-a-cake and peekaboo.
6 months on	Infants babble, adding consonants to their cooing sounds and repeating syllables. By 7 months, babbling starts to include many sounds of spoken languages.
	Infants begin to comprehend a few commonly heard words.
8–12 months	Infants become more accurate at establishing joint attention with the caregiver, who often verbally labels what the baby is looking at.
	Infants actively participate in turn-taking games, trading roles with the caregiver.
	Infants use preverbal gestures, such as showing and pointing, to influence others' goals and behavior and to convey information.
12 months	Babbling includes sound and intonation patterns of the child's language community.
	Speed and accuracy of word comprehension increase rapidly.
	Toddlers say their first recognizable word.
18–24 months	Spoken vocabulary expands from about 50 to 200 to 250 words.
	Toddlers combine two words.

Cooing and Babbling.

Around 2 months, babies begin to make vowel-like noises, called **cooing** because of their pleasant "oo" quality. Gradually, consonants are added, and around 6 months, **babbling** appears, in which infants repeat consonant–vowel combinations in long strings, such as "bababababa" or "nananananana."

Babies everywhere (even those who are deaf) start babbling at about the same age and produce a similar range of early sounds. But for babbling to develop further, infants must be able to hear human speech. In hearing-impaired babies, these speech-like sounds are greatly delayed. And a deaf infant not exposed to sign language will stop babbling entirely (Oller, 2000).

As infants listen to spoken language, babbling expands to include a broader range of sounds. Around 7 months, it starts to include many sounds common in spoken languages. As caregivers respond to infant babbles, babies modify their babbling to include sound patterns like those in the adult's speech (Goldstein & Schwade, 2008). By 8 to 10 months, babbling reflects the sound and intonation patterns of children's language community, some of which are transferred to their first words (Boysson-Bardies & Vihman, 1991).

Deaf infants exposed to sign language from birth babble with their hands much as hearing infants do through speech (Petitto & Marentette, 1991). Furthermore, hearing babies of deaf, signing parents produce babblelike hand motions with the rhythmic patterns of natural sign languages (Petitto et al., 2001, 2004). This sensitivity to language rhythm—evident in both spoken and signed babbling—supports both discovery and production of meaningful language units.

Becoming a Communicator.

At birth, infants are prepared for some aspects of conversational behavior. For example, newborns initiate interaction through eye contact and terminate it by looking away. By 3 to 4 months, infants start to gaze in the same general direction adults are looking—a skill that becomes more accurate at 10 to 11 months, as babies realize that others' focus offers information about their communicative intentions (to talk about an object) or other goals (to obtain an object) (Brooks & Meltzoff, 2005; Senju, Csibra, & Johnson, 2008). This **joint attention,** in which the child attends to the same object or event as the caregiver, who often labels it, contributes greatly to early language development. Infants and toddlers who frequently experience it sustain attention longer, comprehend more language, produce meaningful gestures and words earlier, and show faster vocabulary development (Brooks & Meltzoff, 2008; Carpenter, Nagell, & Tomasello, 1998; Flom & Pick, 2003; Silvén, 2001).

Between 4 and 6 months, interactions between caregivers and babies begin to include *give-and-take*, as in pat-a-cake and peekaboo games. At first, the parent starts the game and the baby is an amused observer. But even 4-month-olds are sensitive to the structure and timing of these interactions, smiling more to an organized than to a disorganized peekaboo exchange (Rochat, Querido, & Striano, 1999). By 12 months, babies participate

This baby uses a preverbal gesture to draw his caregiver's attention to a picture. The caregiver's verbal response promotes the baby's transition to spoken language.

actively, trading roles with the caregiver. In this way, they practice the turn-taking pattern of conversation, a vital context for acquiring language and communication skills. Infants' play maturity and vocalizations during games predict advanced language progress in the second year (Rome-Flanders & Cronk, 1995).

At the end of the first year, babies use *preverbal gestures* to direct adults' attention, to influence their behavior, and to convey helpful information (Tomasello, Carpenter, & Liszkowski, 2007). For example, Caitlin held up a toy to show it, pointed to the cupboard when she wanted a cookie, and pointed at her mother's car keys lying on the floor. Carolyn responded to these gestures and also labeled them ("That's your bear!" "You want a cookie!" "Oh, there are my keys!"). In this way, toddlers learn that using language leads to desired results. Soon toddlers integrate words with gestures, using the gesture to expand their verbal message, as in pointing to a toy while saying "give" (Capirci et al., 2005). Gradually, gestures recede, and words become dominant. But the earlier toddlers form word–gesture combinations, the faster their vocabulary growth, the sooner they produce two-word utterances at the end of the second year, and the more complex their sentences at age 3½ (Özçaliskan & Goldin-Meadow, 2005; Rowe & Goldin-Meadow, 2009).

First Words

In the second half of the first year, infants begin to understand word meanings. When 6-month-olds listened to the word "Mommy" or "Daddy" while looking at side-by-side videos of their parents, they looked longer at the video of the named parent (Tincoff & Jusczyk, 1999). First spoken words, around 1 year, build on the sensorimotor foundations Piaget described and on categories children have formed. In a study tracking the first 10 words used by several hundred U.S. and Chinese (both Mandarin- and Cantonese-speaking) babies, important people ("Mama," "Dada"), common objects ("ball," "bread"), and sound effects ("woof-woof," "vroom") were mentioned most often. Action words ("hit," "grab," "hug") and social routines ("hi," "bye"), though also appearing in all three groups, were more often produced by Chinese than U.S. babies, and the Chinese babies also named more important people—differences we will consider shortly (Tardif et al., 2008). In their first 50 words, toddlers rarely name things that just *sit there*, like "table" or "vase."

When young children first learn words, they sometimes apply them too narrowly, an error called **underextension**. At 16 months, Caitlin used "bear" only to refer to the worn and tattered bear she carried nearly constantly. As vocabulary expands, a more common error is **overextension**—applying a word to a wider collection of objects and events than is appropriate. For example, Grace used "car" for buses, trains, trucks, and fire engines. Toddlers' overextensions reflect their sensitivity to categories (MacWhinney, 2005). They apply a new word to a group of similar experiences: "car" to wheeled objects, "open" to opening a door, peeling fruit, and untying shoelaces. This suggests that children often overextend deliberately because they have difficulty recalling or have not acquired a suitable word. And when a word is hard to pronounce, toddlers are likely to substitute a related one they can say (Bloom, 2000). As vocabulary and pronunciation improve, overextensions disappear.

Overextensions illustrate another important feature of language development: the distinction between language *production* (the words children use) and language *comprehension* (the words they understand). At all ages, comprehension develops ahead of production. A 2-year-old who refers to trucks, trains, and bikes as "car" may look at or point to these objects correctly when given their names (Naigles & Gelman, 1995). Still, the two capacities are related. The speed and accuracy of toddlers' comprehension of spoken language increase dramatically over the second year. And toddlers who are faster and more accurate in comprehension tend to show more rapid growth in words understood and produced as they approach age 2 (Fernald, Perfors, & Marchman, 2006). Quick comprehension frees space in working memory for picking up new words and for the more demanding task of using them to communicate.

The Two-Word Utterance Phase

Young toddlers add to their spoken vocabularies at a rate of one to three words per week. Gradually, the number of words learned accelerates. Because gains in word production between 18 and 24 months are so impressive (one or two words per day), many researchers concluded that toddlers undergo a *spurt in vocabulary*—a transition from a slower to a faster learning phase. But recent evidence indicates that most children show a steady increase in rate of word learning that continues through the preschool years (Ganger & Brent, 2004).

How do toddlers build their vocabularies so quickly? In the second year, they improve in ability to categorize experience, recall words, and grasp others' social cues to meaning, such as eye gaze, pointing, and handling objects (Dapretto & Bjork, 2000; Golinkoff & Hirsh-Pasek, 2006; Liszkowski, Carpenter, & Tomasello, 2007). In Chapter 7, we will consider young children's specific strategies for word learning.

Once toddlers produce 200 to 250 words, they start to combine two words: "Mommy shoe," "go car," "more cookie." These two-word utterances are called **telegraphic speech** because, like a telegram, they focus on high-content words, omitting smaller, less important ones. Children the world over use them to express an impressive variety of meanings.

Two-word speech consists largely of simple formulas ("more + X," "eat + X"), with different words inserted in the "X" position. Toddlers rarely make gross grammatical errors, such as saying "chair my" instead of "my chair." But their word-order regularities are usually copies of adult word pairings, as when the parent says, "How about *more sandwich?*" or "Let's see if you can *eat the berries*" (Tomasello, 2003; Tomasello & Brandt, 2009). These findings indicate that young children first acquire "concrete pieces of language" from frequent word pairings they hear. Only gradually do they generalize from those pieces to construct word-order and other grammatical rules (Tomasello, 2006). As we will see in Chapter 7, children master grammar steadily over the preschool years.

Individual and Cultural Differences

Although children typically produce their first word around their first birthday, the range is large, from 8 to 18 months—variation due to a complex blend of genetic and environmental influences. Earlier we saw that Timmy's spoken language was delayed, in part because of Vanessa's tense, directive communication with him. But Timmy is also a boy, and many studies show that girls are slightly ahead of boys in early vocabulary growth (Fenson et al., 1994; Van Hulle, Goldsmith, & Lemery, 2004). The most common explanation is girls' faster rate of physical maturation, believed to promote earlier development of the left cerebral hemisphere.

Temperament matters, too. Shy toddlers often wait until they understand a great deal before trying to speak. Once they do speak, their vocabularies increase rapidly, although they remain slightly behind their agemates (Spere et al., 2004). Temperamentally negative toddlers also acquire language more slowly because their high emotional reactivity diverts them from processing linguistic information (Salley & Dixon, 2007).

The quantity of caregiver–child conversation and richness of adults' vocabularies also play a strong role (Zimmerman et al., 2009). Commonly used words for objects appear early in toddlers' speech, and the more often their caregivers use a particular noun, the sooner young children produce it (Goodman, Dale, & Li, 2008). Mothers talk more to toddler-age girls than to boys, and parents converse less often with shy than with sociable children (Leaper, Anderson, & Sanders, 1998; Patterson & Fisher, 2002).

Low-SES children, who receive less verbal stimulation in their homes than higher-SES children, usually have smaller vocabularies (Hoff, 2006). Limited parent–child book reading is a major factor. On average, a middle-SES child is read to for 1,000 hours between 1 and 5 years, a low-SES child for only 25 hours (Neuman, 2003). As a result, low-SES kindergartners have vocabularies only one-fourth as large as those of their higher SES agemates (Lee & Burkam, 2002). And low-income children are also behind in early literacy knowledge and later reading achievement, as we will see in Chapter 7.

Furthermore, 2-year-olds' spoken vocabularies vary substantially across languages—about 180 to 200 words for children acquiring Swedish, 250 to 300 words for children acquiring English, and 500 words for children acquiring Mandarin Chinese (Bleses et al., 2008; Tardif et al., 2009). In Swedish, a complicated system of speech sounds makes syllable and word boundaries challenging to discriminate and pronounce. In contrast, Mandarin Chinese has many short words with easy-to-pronounce initial consonants. Within Mandarin words, each syllable is given one of four distinct tones, aiding discrimination.

Young children have distinct styles of early language learning. Caitlin and Grace, like most toddlers, used a **referential style**; their vocabularies consisted mainly of words that refer to objects. A smaller number of toddlers use an **expressive style**; compared with referential children, they produce many more social formulas and pronouns ("thank you," "done," "I want it"). These styles reflect early ideas about the functions of language. Grace, for example, thought words were for naming things. In contrast, expressive-style children believe words are for talking about people's feelings and needs (Bates et al., 1994). The vocabularies of referential-style toddlers grow faster because all languages contain many more object labels than social phrases.

What accounts for a toddler's language style? Rapidly developing referential-style children often have an especially active interest in exploring objects. They also eagerly imitate their parents' frequent naming of objects (Masur & Rodemaker, 1999). Expressive-style children tend to be highly sociable, and their parents more often use verbal routines ("How are you?" "It's no trouble") that support social relationships (Goldfield, 1987).

The two language styles are also linked to culture. Nouns are particularly common in the vocabularies of English-speaking toddlers, but Chinese, Japanese, and Korean toddlers have more words for social routines. Mothers' speech in each culture reflects this difference (Choi & Gopnik, 1995; Fernald & Morikawa, 1993; Tardif, Gelman, & Xu, 1999). American mothers frequently label objects when interacting with their babies. Asian mothers, perhaps because of a cultural emphasis on the importance of group membership, teach social routines as soon as their children begin to speak.

At what point should parents be concerned if their child talks very little or not at all? If a toddler's language is greatly delayed when compared with the norms in Table 5.3 (page 175),

then parents should consult the child's doctor or a speech and language therapist. Late babbling may be a sign of slow language development that can be prevented with early intervention (Fasolo, Marjorano, & D'Odorico, 2008). Some toddlers who do not follow simple directions or who, after age 2, have difficulty putting their thoughts into words may suffer from a hearing impairment or a language disorder that requires immediate treatment.

Supporting Early Language Development

Consistent with the interactionist view, a rich social environment builds on young children's natural readiness to acquire language. For a summary of how caregivers can consciously support early language development, see Applying What We Know on the following page. Caregivers also do so unconsciously—through a special style of speech.

Adults in many cultures speak to babies in **infant-directed speech (IDS)**, a form of communication made up of short sentences with high-pitched, exaggerated expression, clear pronunciation, distinct pauses between speech segments, and repetition of new words in a variety of contexts ("See the *ball*," "The *ball* bounced!") (Fernald et al., 1989; O'Neill et al., 2005). Deaf parents use a similar style of communication when signing to their deaf babies (Masataka, 1996).

By using infant-directed speech, this father speaks in ways that are sensitive to his daughter's language needs and encourages her to join in. Dialogues about picture books are especially powerful sources of early language learning.

Applying **What We Know**

Supporting Early Language Learning

Strategy	Consequence
Respond to coos and babbles with speech sounds and words.	Encourages experimentation with sounds that can later be blended into first words. Provides experience with turn-taking pattern of human conversation.
Establish joint attention, and comment on what child sees.	Predicts earlier onset of language and faster vocabulary development.
Play social games, such as pat-a-cake and peekaboo.	Provides experience with the turn-taking pattern of human conversation.
Engage toddlers in joint make-believe play.	Promotes all aspects of conversational dialogue.
Engage toddlers in frequent conversations.	Predicts faster early language development and academic success during the school years.
Read to toddlers often, engaging them in dialogues about picture books.	Provides exposure to many aspects of language, including vocabulary, grammar, communication skills, and information about written symbols and story structures.

IDS builds on several communicative strategies we have already considered: joint attention, turn-taking, and caregivers' sensitivity to toddlers' preverbal gestures. In this example, Carolyn uses IDS with 18-month-old Caitlin:

Caitlin: "Go car."

Carolyn: "Yes, time to go in the car. Where's your jacket?"

Caitlin: *[Looks around, walks to the closet.]* "Dacket!" *[Points to her jacket.]*

Carolyn: "There's that jacket! *[She helps Caitlin into the jacket.]* On it goes! Let's zip up. *[Zips up the jacket.]* Now, say bye-bye to Grace and Timmy."

Caitlin: "Bye-bye, G-ace. Bye-bye, Te-te.

Carolyn: "Where's your bear?"

Caitlin: *[Looks around.]*

Carolyn: *[Pointing.]* "See? By the sofa." *[Caitlin gets the bear.]*

From birth on, infants prefer IDS over other adult talk, and by 5 months they are more emotionally responsive to it (Aslin, Jusczyk, & Pisoni, 1998). Parents constantly fine-tune the length and content of their utterances to fit their children's needs—adjustments that foster word learning and enable toddlers to join in (Cameron-Faulkner, Lieven, & Tomasello, 2003; Rowe, 2008). As we saw earlier, parent–toddler conversation—especially, reading and talking about picture books—strongly predicts language development and reading success during the school years.

LOOK AND LISTEN

While observing a parent and toddler playing, describe how the parent adapts his or her language to the child's needs. Did the parent use IDS? ●

Do social experiences that promote language development remind you of those that strengthen cognitive development in general? IDS and parent–child conversation create a *zone of proximal development* in which children's language expands. In contrast, impatience with and rejection of children's efforts to talk lead them to stop trying and result in immature language skills (Baumwell, Tamis-LeMonda, & Bornstein, 1997; Cabrera, Shannon, & Tamis-LeMonda, 2007). In the next chapter, we will see that sensitivity to children's needs and capacities supports their emotional and social development as well.

ASK YOURSELF

REVIEW Why is the social interactionist perspective attractive to many investigators of language development? Cite evidence that supports it.

CONNECT Cognition and language are interrelated. List examples of how cognition fosters language development. Next, list examples of how language fosters cognitive development.

APPLY Fran frequently corrects her 17-month-old son Jeremy's attempts to talk and—fearing that he won't use words—refuses to respond to his gestures. How might Fran be contributing to Jeremy's slow language progress?

REFLECT Find an opportunity to speak to an infant or toddler. Did you use IDS? What features of your speech are likely to promote early language development, and why?

SUMMARY

Piaget's Cognitive-Developmental Theory (p. 152)

According to Piaget, how do schemes change over the course of development?

- By acting on the environment, children move through four stages in which psychological structures, or **schemes,** achieve a better fit with external reality.

- Schemes change in two ways: through **adaptation,** which is made up of two complementary activities—**assimilation** and **accommodation**—and through **organization,** the internal rearrangement of schemes into a strongly interconnected cognitive system.

Describe the major cognitive achievements of the sensorimotor stage.

- In the **sensorimotor stage,** the **circular reaction** provides a means of adapting first schemes, and the newborn's reflexes gradually transform into the flexible action patterns of the older infant. Eight- to 12-month-olds develop **intentional,** or **goal-directed, behavior** and begin to understand **object permanence.**

- Between 18 and 24 months, **mental representation** is evident in sudden solutions to sensorimotor problems, mastery of object permanence problems involving invisible displacement, **deferred imitation,** and **make-believe play.**

What does follow-up research reveal about the accuracy of Piaget's sensorimotor stage?

- Many studies suggest that infants display certain understandings earlier than Piaget believed. Some awareness of object permanence, as revealed by the **violation-of-expectation method** and object-tracking research, may be evident in the first few months.

- Around the first birthday, babies attain **displaced reference,** the realization that words may stand for things not physically present. By the middle of the second year, toddlers treat realistic-looking pictures symbolically; around 2½ years, they grasp the symbolic meaning of video.

- Today, researchers believe that newborns have more built-in equipment for making sense of their world than Piaget assumed, although they disagree on how much initial understanding infants have. According to the **core knowledge perspective,** infants are born with core domains of thought that support early, rapid cognitive development. Research suggests that infants have basic physical, linguistic, psychological, and numerical knowledge.

© EDITH HELD/CORBIS

- Broad agreement exists that many cognitive changes of infancy are continuous rather than stagelike and that various aspects of cognition develop unevenly rather than in an integrated fashion.

Information Processing (p. 161)

Describe the information-processing view of cognitive development.

- Most information-processing researchers assume that we hold information in three parts of the mental system for processing: the **sensory register,** the **short-term memory store,** and **long-term memory.** The **central executive** joins with **working memory**—our "mental workspace"—to process information effectively, increasing the chances that it will transfer to our permanent knowledge base. Well-learned **automatic processes** require no space in working memory, permitting us to focus on other information while performing them.

- Gains in **executive function**—including attention, impulse control, and coordinating information in working memory—are under way in the first two years. Dramatic advances will follow in childhood and adolescence.

What changes in attention, memory, and categorization take place during the first two years?

- With age, infants attend to more aspects of the environment and take information in more quickly. In the second year, attention to novelty declines and sustained attention improves.

- Young infants are capable of **recognition** memory. By the second half of the first year, they also engage in **recall.** Both improve steadily with age.

- Infants group stimuli into increasingly complex categories, and toddlers' categorization gradually shifts from a perceptual to a conceptual basis. In the second half of the first year, infants have begun to grasp the animate–inanimate distinction, an understanding that expands during toddlerhood.

Describe contributions and limitations of the information-processing approach to our understanding of early cognitive development.

- Information-processing findings challenge Piaget's view of infants as purely sensorimotor beings who cannot mentally represent experiences. But information processing has not yet provided a broad, comprehensive theory of children's thinking.

The Social Context of Early Cognitive Development (p. 167)

How does Vygotsky's concept of the zone of proximal development expand our understanding of early cognitive development?

- Vygotsky believed that infants master tasks within the **zone of proximal development**—ones just ahead of their current capacities—through the support and guidance of more skilled partners. As early as the first year, cultural variations in social experiences affect mental strategies.

Individual Differences in Early Mental Development (p. 169)

Describe the mental testing approach and the extent to which infant tests predict later performance.

- The mental testing approach measures intellectual development in an effort to predict future performance. Scores are arrived at by computing an **intelligence quotient (IQ),** which compares an individual's test performance with that of a **standardization** sample of same-age individuals, whose scores form a **normal distribution.**

- Infant tests consisting largely of perceptual and motor responses predict later intelligence poorly. As a result, scores on infant tests are called **developmental quotients (DQs),** rather than IQs. Speed of habituation and recovery to visual stimuli are better predictors of future performance.

Discuss environmental influences on early mental development, including home, child care, and early intervention for at-risk infants and toddlers.

- Research with the **Home Observation for Measurement of the Environment (HOME)** shows that an organized, stimulating home environment and parental encouragement, involvement, and affection repeatedly predict early mental test scores. Although the HOME–IQ relationship is partly due to heredity, family living conditions also affect mental development.

- Infant and toddler child care is increasingly common, and its quality has a major impact on mental development. Standards for **developmentally appropriate practice** specify program characteristics that meet young children's developmental needs.

- Intensive intervention beginning in infancy and extending through early childhood can prevent the gradual declines in intelligence and the poor academic performance of many poverty-stricken children.

Language Development
(p. 174)

Describe theories of language development, and indicate how much emphasis each places on innate abilities and environmental influences.

- Chomsky's *nativist* theory regards children as naturally endowed with a **language acquisition device (LAD).** Consistent with this perspective, mastery of a complex language system is unique to humans, and childhood is a sensitive period for language acquisition.

- Recent theories view language development as resulting from interactions between inner capacities and environmental influences. Some interactionists apply the information-processing perspective to language development. Others emphasize the importance of children's social skills and language experiences.

Describe major language milestones in the first two years, individual differences, and ways adults can support early language development.

- Infants begin **cooing** at 2 months and **babbling** at about 6 months. Around 10 to 11 months, their skill at establishing **joint attention** improves, and soon they use preverbal gestures. Adults can encourage language progress by responding to infants' coos and babbles, playing turn-taking games, establishing joint attention and labeling what babies see, and responding verbally to infants' preverbal gestures.

- Around 12 months, toddlers say their first word. Young children often make errors of **underextension** and **overextension.** Once vocabulary reaches 200 to 250 words, two-word utterances called **telegraphic speech** appear. At all ages, language comprehension is ahead of production.

- Girls show faster language progress than boys, and reserved, cautious toddlers may wait before trying to speak. Most toddlers use a **referential style** of language learning; their early words consist largely of names for objects. Some use an **expressive style,** in which social formulas and pronouns are common and vocabulary grows more slowly.

- Adults in many cultures speak to young children in **infant-directed speech (IDS),** a simplified form of language that is well suited to their learning needs. Parent–toddler conversation is a good predictor of early language development and reading success during the school years.

Important Terms and Concepts

accommodation (p. 152)
adaptation (p. 152)
assimilation (p. 152)
autobiographical memory (p. 164)
automatic processes (p. 162)
babbling (p. 176)
central executive (p. 162)
circular reaction (p. 153)
cooing (p. 176)
core knowledge perspective (p. 159)
deferred imitation (p. 154)
developmentally appropriate practice (p. 172)
developmental quotient (DQ) (p. 170)
displaced reference (p. 157)
executive function (p. 162)

expressive style of language learning (p. 178)
Home Observation for Measurement of the Environment (HOME) (p. 170)
infant-directed speech (IDS) (p. 178)
infantile amnesia (p. 164)
intelligence quotient (IQ) (p. 169)
intentional, or goal-directed, behavior (p. 154)
joint attention (p. 176)
language acquisition device (LAD) (p. 174)
long-term memory (p. 162)
make-believe play (p. 154)
mental representation (p. 154)
normal distribution (p. 169)
object permanence (p. 154)
organization (p. 152)

overextension (p. 177)
recall (p. 164)
recognition (p. 164)
referential style of language learning (p. 178)
scheme (p. 152)
sensorimotor stage (p. 152)
sensory register (p. 161)
short-term memory store (p. 161)
standardization (p. 169)
telegraphic speech (p. 177)
underextension (p. 177)
video deficit effect (p. 159)
violation-of-expectation method (p. 155)
working memory (p. 161)
zone of proximal development (p. 167)

This father takes time to build a strong, affectionate bond with his infant daughter. His warmth and sensitivity engender a sense of security in the baby—a vital foundation for all aspects of early development.

Emotional and Social Development in Infancy and Toddlerhood

As Caitlin reached 8 months of age, her parents noticed that she had become more fearful. One evening, when Carolyn and David left her with a babysitter, she wailed as they headed for the door—an experience she had accepted easily a few weeks earlier. Caitlin and Timmy's caregiver Ginette also observed an increasing wariness of strangers. When she turned to go to another room, both babies dropped their play to crawl after her. At the mail carrier's knock at the door, they clung to Ginette's legs, reaching out to be picked up.

At the same time, each baby seemed more willful. Removing an object from the hand produced little response at 5 months. But at 8 months, when Timmy's mother, Vanessa, took away a table knife he had managed to reach, Timmy burst into angry screams and could not be consoled or distracted.

All Monica and Kevin knew about Grace's first year was that she had been deeply loved by her destitute, homeless mother. Separation from her, followed by a long journey to an unfamiliar home, had left Grace in shock. At first she was extremely sad, turning away when Monica or Kevin picked her up. But as Grace's new parents held her close, spoke gently, and satisfied her craving for food, Grace returned their affection. Two weeks after her arrival, her despondency gave way to a sunny, easygoing disposition. She burst into a wide grin, reached out at the sight of Monica and Kevin, and laughed at her brother Eli's funny faces. As her second birthday approached, she pointed to herself, exclaiming "Gwace!" and laid claim to treasured possessions. "Gwace's chicken!" she would announce at mealtimes, sucking the marrow from the drumstick, a practice she had brought with her from Cambodia.

© CLAIRE STOUT/ALAMY

Taken together, the children's reactions reflect two related aspects of personality development during the first two years: close ties to others and a sense of self. We begin with Erikson's psychosocial theory, which provides an overview of personality development during infancy and toddlerhood. Then, as we chart the course of emotional development, we will discover why fear and anger became more apparent in Caitlin's and Timmy's range of emotions by the end of the first year. Our attention then turns to individual

chapter outline

Erikson's Theory of Infant and Toddler Personality

Basic Trust versus Mistrust • Autonomy versus Shame and Doubt

Emotional Development

Development of Basic Emotions • Understanding and Responding to the Emotions of Others • Emergence of Self-Conscious Emotions • Beginnings of Emotional Self-Regulation

■ **BIOLOGY AND ENVIRONMENT** Parental Depression and Child Development

Temperament and Development

The Structure of Temperament • Measuring Temperament • Stability of Temperament • Genetic and Environmental Influences • Temperament and Child Rearing: The Goodness-of-Fit Model

■ **BIOLOGY AND ENVIRONMENT** Development of Shyness and Sociability

Development of Attachment

Bowlby's Ethological Theory • Measuring the Security of Attachment • Stability of Attachment • Cultural Variations • Factors That Affect Attachment Security • Multiple Attachments • Attachment and Later Development

■ **SOCIAL ISSUES: HEALTH** Does Child Care in Infancy Threaten Attachment Security and Later Adjustment?

■ **CULTURAL INFLUENCES** The Powerful Role of Paternal Warmth in Development

Self-Development

Self-Awareness • Categorizing the Self • Self-Control

differences in temperament. We will examine genetic and environmental contributions to these differences and their consequences for future development.

Next, we take up attachment to the caregiver, the child's first affectionate tie. We will see how the feelings of security that grow out of this important bond support the child's sense of independence and expanding social relationships.

Finally, we focus on early self-development. By the end of toddlerhood, Grace recognized herself in mirrors and photographs, labeled herself as a girl, and showed the beginnings of self-control. "Don't touch!" she instructed herself one day as she resisted the desire to pull a lamp cord out of its socket. Cognitive advances combine with social experiences to produce these changes during the second year. ●

Erikson's Theory of Infant and Toddler Personality

Our discussion of major theories in Chapter 1 revealed that the psychoanalytic perspective is no longer in the mainstream of human development research. But one of its lasting contributions is its ability to capture the essence of personality during each period of development. Recall that Sigmund Freud believed that psychological health and maladjustment could be traced to the quality of the child's relationships with parents during the early years. Although Freud's preoccupation with the channeling of biological drives and his neglect of important experiences beyond infancy and early childhood came to be heavily criticized, the basic outlines of his theory were accepted and elaborated in several subsequent theories. The most influential is Erik Erikson's *psychosocial theory,* also introduced in Chapter 1.

Basic Trust versus Mistrust

Erikson accepted Freud's emphasis on the importance of the parent–infant relationship during feeding, but he expanded and enriched Freud's view. A healthy outcome during infancy, Erikson believed, does not depend on the *amount* of food or oral stimulation offered but rather on the *quality* of caregiving: relieving discomfort promptly and sensitively, holding the infant gently, waiting patiently until the baby has had enough milk, and weaning when the infant shows less interest in breast or bottle.

Erikson recognized that no parent can be perfectly in tune with the baby's needs. Many factors affect parental responsiveness—personal happiness, current life conditions (for example, additional young children in the family), and culturally valued child-rearing practices. But when the *balance of care* is sympathetic and loving, the psychological conflict of the first year— **basic trust versus mistrust**—is resolved on the positive side. The trusting infant expects the world to be good and gratifying, so he feels confident about venturing out and exploring it. The

mistrustful baby cannot count on the kindness and compassion of others, so she protects herself by withdrawing from people and things around her.

Autonomy versus Shame and Doubt

With the transition to toddlerhood, Freud viewed the parents' manner of toilet training as decisive for psychological health. In Erikson' view, toilet training is only one of many influential experiences. The familiar refrains of newly walking, talking toddlers—"No!" "Do it myself!"—reveal that they have entered a period of budding selfhood. They want to decide for themselves, not just in toileting but also in other situations. The conflict of toddlerhood, **autonomy versus shame and doubt,** is resolved favorably when parents provide young children with suitable guidance and reasonable choices. A self-confident, secure 2-year-old has parents who do not criticize or attack him when he fails at new skills—using the toilet, eating with a spoon, or putting away toys. And they meet his assertions of independence with tolerance and understanding—for example, by giving him an extra five minutes to finish his play before leaving for the grocery store. In contrast, when parents are over- or undercontrolling, the outcome is a child who feels forced and shamed and who doubts his ability to control his impulses and act competently on his own.

In sum, basic trust and autonomy grow out of warm, sensitive parenting and reasonable expectations for impulse control starting in the second year. If children emerge from the first few years without sufficient trust in caregivers and without a healthy sense of individuality, the seeds are sown for adjustment problems. Adults who have difficulty establishing intimate ties, who are overly dependent on a loved one, or who continually doubt their own ability to meet new challenges may not have fully mastered the tasks of trust and autonomy during infancy and toddlerhood.

On a visit to a science museum, a 2-year-old insists on exploring a flight simulator. As the mother supports her toddler's desire to "do it myself," she fosters a healthy sense of autonomy.

Emotional Development

TAKE A MOMENT... Observe several infants and toddlers, noting the emotions each displays, the cues you rely on to interpret the baby's emotional state, and how caregivers respond. Researchers have conducted many such observations to find out how babies convey their emotions and interpret those of others. They have discovered that emotions play powerful roles in organizing the attainments that Erikson regarded as so important: social relationships, exploration of the environment, and discovery of the self (Halle, 2003; Saarni et al., 2006).

Think back to the *dynamic systems perspective* introduced in Chapters 1 and 4. As you read about early emotional development in the sections that follow, notice how emotions are an integral part of young children's dynamic systems of action. Emotions energize development. At the same time, they are an aspect of the system that develops, becoming more varied and complex as children reorganize their behavior to attain new goals (Campos, Frankel, & Camras, 2004; Thompson, Winer, & Goodvin, 2011).

Because infants cannot describe their feelings, determining exactly which emotions they are experiencing is a challenge. Cross-cultural evidence reveals that people around the world associate photographs of different facial expressions with emotions in the same way (Ekman, 2003; Ekman & Friesen, 1972). These findings inspired researchers to analyze infants' facial patterns to determine the range of emotions they display at different ages. But to express a particular emotion, infants, children, and adults actually use diverse responses—not just facial expressions but also vocalizations and body movements—which vary with their developing capacities, goals, and contexts. Therefore, to infer babies' emotions as accurately as possible, researchers are best off attending to multiple interacting behavioral cues and seeing how they vary across situations believed to elicit different emotions (Lewis, 2000, 2008).

Development of Basic Emotions

Basic emotions—happiness, interest, surprise, fear, anger, sadness, and disgust—are universal in humans and other primates and have a long evolutionary history of promoting survival. Do infants come into the world with the ability to express basic emotions? Although signs of some emotions are present, babies' earliest emotional life consists of little more than two global arousal states: attraction to pleasant stimulation and withdrawal from unpleasant stimulation (Camras et al., 2003; Fox, 1991). Only gradually do emotions become clear, well-organized signals.

According to one view, sensitive, contingent caregiver communication, in which parents selectively mirror aspects of the baby's diffuse emotional behavior, helps infants construct emotional expressions that more closely resemble those of adults (Gergely & Watson, 1999). With age, face, voice, and posture start to form organized patterns that vary meaningfully with environmental events. For example, Caitlin typically responded to her parents' playful interaction with a joyful face, pleasant

babbling, and a relaxed posture, as if to say, "This is fun!" In contrast, an unresponsive parent often evokes a sad face, fussy sounds, and a drooping body (sending the message, "I'm despondent") or an angry face, crying, and "pick-me-up" gestures (as if to say, "Change this unpleasant event!") (Weinberg & Tronick, 1994; Yale et al., 1999). Gradually, emotional expressions become well-organized and specific—and therefore provide more precise information about the baby's internal state.

Four basic emotions—happiness, anger, sadness, and fear—have received the most research attention. Let's see how they develop.

Happiness. Happiness—expressed first in blissful smiles and later through exuberant laughter—contributes to many aspects of development. When infants achieve new skills, they smile and laugh, displaying delight in motor and cognitive mastery. As the smile encourages caregivers to be affectionate and stimulating, the baby smiles even more (Aksan & Kochanska, 2004). Happiness binds parent and baby into a warm, supportive relationship that fosters the infant's developing competencies.

During the early weeks, newborn babies smile when full, during REM sleep, and in response to gentle touches and sounds, such as stroking of the skin, rocking, and the mother's soft, high-pitched voice. By the end of the first month, infants smile at dynamic, eye-catching sights, such as a bright object jumping suddenly across their field of vision. Between 6 and 10 weeks, the parent's communication evokes a broad grin called the **social smile** (Lavelli & Fogel, 2005; Sroufe & Waters, 1976). These changes parallel the development of infant perceptual capacities—in particular, sensitivity to visual patterns, including the human face (see Chapter 4). And social smiling becomes better-organized and stable as babies learn to use it to evoke and sustain pleasurable face-to-face interaction.

Laughter, which appears around 3 to 4 months, reflects faster processing of information than smiling. But, as with smiling, the first laughs occur in response to very active stimuli, such as the parent saying playfully, "I'm gonna get you!" and kissing the baby's tummy. As infants understand more about their world, they laugh at events with subtler elements of surprise, such as a silent game of peekaboo (Sroufe & Wunsch, 1972).

Around the middle of the first year, infants smile and laugh more when interacting with familiar people, a preference that strengthens the parent–child bond. Between 8 and 10 months, infants more often interrupt their play with an interesting toy to relay their delight to an attentive adult (Venezia et al., 2004). And like adults, 10- to 12-month-olds have several smiles, which vary with context—a broad, "cheek-raised" smile in response to a parent's greeting; a reserved, muted smile for a friendly stranger; and a "mouth-open" smile during stimulating play (Bolzani et al., 2002; Messinger & Fogel, 2007). By the end of the first year, the smile has become a deliberate social signal.

Anger and Sadness. Newborn babies respond with generalized distress to a variety of unpleasant experiences, including hunger, painful medical procedures, changes in body temperature, and too much or too little stimulation. From 4 to 6 months

Biology and Environment

Parental Depression and Child Development

About 8 to 10 percent of women experience chronic depression— mild to severe feelings of sadness, distress, and withdrawal that continue for months or years. Often, the beginnings of this emotional state cannot be pinpointed. In other instances, depression emerges or strengthens after childbirth but fails to subside as the new mother adjusts to hormonal changes in her body and gains confidence in caring for her baby. This is called *postpartum depression*.

Although it is less recognized and studied, fathers, too, experience chronic depression. About 3 to 5 percent of fathers report symptoms after the birth of a child (Madsen & Juhl, 2007; Thombs, Roseman, & Arthurs, 2010). Parental depression can interfere with effective parenting and seriously impair children's development. Genetic makeup increases the risk of depressive illness, but social and cultural factors are also involved.

Maternal Depression

During Julia's pregnancy, her husband, Kyle, showed so little interest in the baby that Julia worried that having a child might be a mistake. Then, shortly after Lucy was born, Julia's mood plunged. She felt anxious and weepy, overwhelmed by Lucy's needs, and angry at loss of control over her own schedule. When Julia approached Kyle about her own fatigue and his unwillingness to help with the baby, he snapped that she was over-reacting. Julia's childless friends stopped by just once to see Lucy but did not call again.

Julia's depressed mood quickly affected her baby. In the weeks after birth, infants of depressed mothers sleep poorly, are less attentive to their surroundings, and have elevated levels of the stress hormone cortisol (Field, 1998). The more extreme the depression and the greater the number of stressors in a mother's life (such as marital discord, little or no social support, and poverty), the more the parent–child relationship suffers (Simpson et al., 2003). Julia rarely smiled at,

comforted, or talked to Lucy, who responded to her mother's sad, vacant gaze by turning away, crying, and often looking sad or angry herself (Feldman et al., 2009; Field, 2011). Julia, in turn, felt guilty and inadequate, and her depression deepened. By age 6 months, Lucy showed symptoms common in babies of depressed mothers—delays in motor and mental development, an irritable mood, and attachment difficulties (Cornish et al., 2005; McMahon et al., 2006).

When maternal depression persists, the parent–child relationship worsens. Depressed mothers view their infants more negatively than independent observers do (Forman et al., 2007). And they use inconsistent discipline—sometimes lax, at other times too forceful. As we will see in later chapters, children who experience these maladaptive parenting practices often have serious adjustment problems. Some withdraw into a depressed mood themselves; others become impulsive and aggressive. In one study, infants born to mothers who were depressed during pregnancy were four times as likely as babies of nondepressed mothers to have engaged in violent antisocial behavior (such as fighting, bullying, assault with a weapon,

---

into the second year, angry expressions increase in frequency and intensity (Braungart-Rieker, Hill-Soderlund, & Karrass, 2010). Older infants also react with anger in a wider range of situations—when an interesting object or event is removed, an expected pleasant event does not occur, their arms are restrained, the caregiver leaves for a brief time, or they are put down for a nap (Camras et al., 1992; Stenberg & Campos, 1990; Sullivan & Lewis, 2003).

Why do angry reactions increase with age? As infants become capable of intentional behavior (see Chapter 5), they want to control their own actions and the effects they produce. They are also more persistent about obtaining desired objects (Mascolo & Fischer, 2007). Furthermore, older infants are better at identifying who caused them pain or removed a toy. The rise in anger is also adaptive. New motor capacities enable an angry infant to defend herself or overcome an obstacle (Izard & Ackerman, 2000). Finally, anger motivates caregivers to relieve the baby's distress and, in the case of separation, may discourage them from leaving again soon.

Although expressions of sadness also occur in response to pain, removal of an object, and brief separations, they are less frequent than anger (Alessandri, Sullivan, & Lewis, 1990).

But when caregiver–infant communication is seriously disrupted, infant sadness is common—a condition that impairs all aspects of development (see the Biology and Environment box above).

Fear. Like anger, fear rises from the second half of the first year into the second year (Braungart-Rieker, Hill-Soderland, & Karrass, 2010). Older infants hesitate before playing with a new toy, and newly crawling infants soon back away from heights (see Chapter 4). But the most frequent expression of fear is to unfamiliar adults, a response called **stranger anxiety**. Many infants and toddlers are quite wary of strangers, although the reaction does not always occur. It depends on several factors: temperament (some babies are generally more fearful), past experiences with strangers, and the current situation. When an unfamiliar adult picks up the infant in a new setting, stranger anxiety is likely. But if the adult sits still while the baby moves around and a parent is nearby, infants often show positive and curious behavior (Horner, 1980). The stranger's style of interaction—expressing warmth, holding out an attractive toy, playing a familiar game, and approaching slowly rather than abruptly— reduces the baby's fear.

and extreme bodily harm) by age 16, after other stressors in the mother's life that could contribute to youth antisocial conduct had been controlled (Hay et al., 2010).

Paternal Depression

Paternal depression is also linked to dissatisfaction with marriage and family life after childbirth and to other life stressors, including job loss and divorce (Bielawska-Batorowicz & Kossakowska-Petrycka, 2006). In a study of a large representative sample of British parents and babies, researchers assessed depressive symptoms of fathers shortly after birth and again the following year. Then they tracked the children's development into the preschool years. Persistent paternal depression was, like maternal depression, a strong predictor of child behavior problems—especially overactivity, defiance, and aggression in boys (Ramchandani et al., 2008).

Paternal depression is linked to frequent father–child conflict as children grow older (Kane & Garber, 2004). Over time, children subjected to parental negativity develop a pessimistic world view—one in which they lack self-confidence and perceive their parents and other people as threatening. Children who

constantly feel endangered are especially likely to become overly aroused in stressful situations, easily losing control in the face of cognitive and social challenges (Sturge-Apple et al., 2008). Although children of depressed parents may inherit a tendency toward emotional and behavior problems, quality of parenting is a major factor in their adjustment.

Interventions

Early treatment is vital to prevent parental depression from interfering with the parent–child relationship. Julia's doctor referred her to a therapist, who helped Julia and Kyle with their marital problems. At times, antidepressant medication is prescribed.

In addition to alleviating parental depression, therapy that encourages depressed mothers to revise their negative views of their babies and to engage in emotionally positive, responsive caregiving is vital for reducing young children's attachment and other developmental problems (Forman et al., 2007). When a depressed parent does not respond easily to treatment, a warm relationship with the other parent or another caregiver can safeguard children's development (Mezulis, Hyde, & Clark, 2004).

This father appears completely disengaged from his wife and toddler. If his depression continues, disruptions in the parent–child relationship will likely lead to serious child behavior problems.

Cross-cultural research reveals that infant-rearing practices can modify stranger anxiety. Among the Efe hunters and gatherers of the Republic of Congo, where the maternal death rate is high, infant survival is safeguarded by a collective caregiving system in which, starting at birth, Efe babies are passed from one adult to another. Consequently, Efe infants show little stranger anxiety (Tronick, Morelli, & Ivey, 1992). In contrast, among infants in Israeli kibbutzim (cooperative agricultural settlements), who live in isolated communities vulnerable to terrorist attacks, wariness of strangers is widespread. By the end of the first year, when infants look to others for cues about how to respond emotionally, kibbutz babies display greater stranger anxiety than their city-reared counterparts (Saarni et al., 2006).

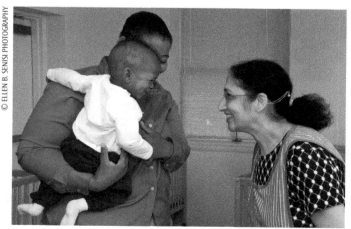

Stranger anxiety appears in many infants after 6 months of age. But this baby, safe in his mother's arms, also expresses curiosity, reaching out warily toward an unfamiliar adult who eases his fear by smiling and approaching slowly.

LOOK AND LISTEN

While observing an 8- to 18-month-old with his or her parent, gently approach the baby, offering a toy. Does the baby respond with stranger anxiety? To better understand the baby's behavior, ask the parent to describe his or her temperament and past experiences with strangers. ●

The rise in fear after age 6 months keeps newly mobile babies' enthusiasm for exploration in check. Once wariness develops, babies use the familiar caregiver as a **secure base,** or point from which to explore, venturing into the environment and then returning for emotional support. As part of this adaptive system, encounters with strangers lead to two conflicting tendencies: approach (indicated by interest and friendliness) and avoidance (indicated by fear). The infant's behavior is a balance between the two.

Eventually, as cognitive development enables toddlers to discriminate more effectively between threatening and non-threatening people and situations, stranger anxiety and other fears of the first two years decline. Fear also wanes as toddlers acquire more strategies for coping with it, as you will see when we discuss emotional self-regulation.

Understanding and Responding to the Emotions of Others

Infants' emotional expressions are closely tied to their ability to interpret the emotional cues of others. We have seen that in the first few months, babies match the feeling tone of the caregiver in face-to-face communication. Some researchers claim that infants respond in kind to others' emotions through a built-in, automatic process of *emotional contagion* (Stern, 1985). Others, however, believe that infants acquire these emotional contingencies through operant conditioning—for example, learning that a smile generally triggers pleasurable feedback and that distress prompts a comforting response (Saarni et al., 2006).

Around 3 to 4 months, infants can match the emotion in a voice with the appropriate face of a speaking person, and they become sensitive to the structure and timing of face-to-face interactions. When they gaze, smile, or vocalize, they now expect their social partner to respond in kind, and they reply with positive vocal and emotional reactions (Markova & Legerstee, 2006; Rochat, Striano, & Blatt, 2002). Within these exchanges, babies become increasingly aware of the range of emotional expressions (Montague & Walker-Andrews, 2001). Recall from Chapter 4 (see page 136) that out of this early imitative communication, infants start to view others as "like me"—an awareness believed to lay the foundation for understanding others' thoughts and feelings (Meltzoff, 2007).

From 5 months on, infants perceive facial expressions as organized patterns (see Chapter 4). Responding to emotional expressions as organized wholes suggests that these signals are becoming meaningful to babies. As skill at establishing joint attention improves, infants realize that an emotional expression not only has meaning but is also a meaningful reaction to a specific object or event (Moses et al., 2001; Tomasello, 1999).

Once these understandings are in place, beginning at 8 to 10 months, infants engage in social referencing—actively seeking emotional information from a trusted person in an uncertain situation (Mumme et al., 2007). Many studies show that the caregiver's emotional expression (happy, angry, or fearful) influences whether a 1-year-old will be wary of strangers, play with an unfamiliar toy, or cross the deep side of the visual cliff (see page 143) (de Rosnay et al., 2006; Stenberg, 2003; Striano & Rochat, 2000). The caregiver's voice—either alone or combined with a facial expression—is more effective than a facial expression alone (Kim, Walden, & Knieps, 2010; Vaish & Striano, 2004). The voice conveys both emotional and verbal information, and the baby need not turn toward the adult but, instead, can focus on evaluating the novel event.

Parents can take advantage of social referencing to teach their baby how to react to many everyday events. And around the middle of the second year, as toddlers begin to appreciate that others' emotional reactions may differ from their own, social referencing allows them to compare their own and others' assessments of events. In one study, an adult showed 14- and 18-month-olds broccoli and crackers and acted delighted with one food but disgusted with the other. When asked to share the food, 18-month-olds gave the adult whichever food she appeared to like, regardless of their own preferences (Repacholi & Gopnik, 1997).

In sum, in social referencing, toddlers move beyond simply reacting to others' emotional messages. They use those signals to evaluate the safety and security of their surroundings, to guide their own actions, and to gather information about others' intentions and preferences. These experiences, along with cognitive and language development, probably help toddlers refine the meanings of emotions—for example, happiness versus surprise, anger versus fear—during the second year (Gendler, Witherington, & Edwards, 2008; Saarni et al., 2006).

Emergence of Self-Conscious Emotions

Besides basic emotions, humans are capable of a second, higher-order set of feelings, including guilt, shame, embarrassment, envy, and pride. These are called self-conscious emotions because each involves injury to or enhancement of our sense of self. We feel guilt when we have harmed someone and want to correct the wrongdoing. When we are ashamed or embarrassed, we have negative feelings about our behavior, and we want to retreat so others will no longer notice our failings. In contrast, pride reflects delight in the self's achievements, and we are inclined to tell others what we have accomplished and to take on further challenges (Saarni et al., 2006).

Self-conscious emotions appear in the middle of the second year, as 18- to 24-month-olds become firmly aware of the self as a separate, unique individual. Toddlers show shame and embarrassment by lowering their eyes, hanging their heads, and hiding their faces with their hands. They show guiltlike reactions, too, like the 22-month-old who returned a toy she had grabbed and patted her upset playmate. Pride also emerges around this time, and envy by age 3 (Barrett, 2005; Garner, 2003; Lewis et al., 1989).

Besides self-awareness, self-conscious emotions require an additional ingredient: adult instruction in *when* to feel proud, ashamed, or guilty. Parents begin this tutoring early when they say, "Look how far you can throw that ball!" or "You should feel ashamed for grabbing that toy!" Self-conscious emotions play important roles in children's achievement-related and moral behaviors. The situations in which adults encourage these feelings vary from culture to culture. In Western individualistic nations, most children are taught to feel pride in personal

A mother praises her 2-year-old's success at tower-building. To experience self-conscious emotions, such as pride, young children need self-awareness as well as adult instruction.

achievement—throwing a ball the farthest, winning a game, and (later on) getting good grades. In collectivist cultures such as China and Japan, calling attention to individual success evokes embarrassment and self-effacement. And violating cultural standards by failing to show concern for others—a parent, a teacher, or an employer—sparks intense shame (Akimoto & Sanbonmatsu, 1999; Lewis, 1992).

Beginnings of Emotional Self-Regulation

Besides expressing a wider range of emotions, infants and toddlers begin to manage their emotional experiences. **Emotional self-regulation** refers to the strategies we use to adjust our emotional state to a comfortable level of intensity so we can accomplish our goals (Eisenberg & Spinrad, 2004; Thompson & Goodvin, 2007). When you remind yourself that an anxiety-provoking event will be over soon, suppress your anger at a friend's behavior, or decide not to see a scary horror film, you are engaging in emotional self-regulation.

Emotional self-regulation requires voluntary, effortful management of emotions. This capacity for *effortful control* improves gradually, as a result of development of the prefrontal cortex and the assistance of caregivers, who help children manage intense emotion and teach them strategies for doing so (Fox & Calkins, 2003; Rothbart, Posner, & Kieras, 2006). Individual differences in control of emotion are evident in infancy and, by early childhood, play such a vital role in children's adjustment that—as we will see later—effortful control is considered a major dimension of temperament. A good start in regulating emotion during the first two years contributes greatly to autonomy and mastery of cognitive and social skills (Eisenberg et al., 2004; Lawson & Ruff, 2004).

In the early months, infants have only a limited capacity to regulate their emotional states. When their feelings get too intense, they are easily overwhelmed. They depend on the soothing interventions of caregivers—being lifted to the shoulder, rocked, gently stroked, and talked to softly—for distraction and reorienting of attention.

More effective functioning of the prefrontal cortex increases the baby's tolerance for stimulation. Between 2 and 4 months, caregivers build on this capacity by initiating face-to-face play and attention to objects. In these interactions, parents arouse pleasure in the baby while adjusting the pace of their behavior so the infant does not become overwhelmed and distressed. As a result, the baby's tolerance for stimulation increases further (Kopp & Neufeld, 2003).

By 4 to 6 months, the ability to shift attention helps infants control emotion. Babies who more readily turn away from unpleasant events or engage in self-soothing are less prone to distress (Crockenberg & Leerkes, 2003). At the end of the first year, crawling and walking enable infants to regulate emotion more effectively by approaching or retreating from various situations.

Infants whose parents "read" and respond contingently and sympathetically to their emotional cues tend to be less fussy and fearful, to express more pleasurable emotion, to be more interested in exploration, and to be easier to soothe (Braungart-Rieker, Hill-Soderlund, & Karrass, 2010; Crockenberg & Leerkes, 2004; Volling et al., 2002). In contrast, parents who respond impatiently or angrily or who wait to intervene until the infant has become extremely agitated reinforce the baby's rapid rise to intense distress. When caregivers fail to regulate stressful experiences for babies, brain structures that buffer stress may not develop properly, resulting in an anxious, reactive child who has a reduced capacity for managing emotional problems (Blair & Raver, 2012; Feldman, 2007).

Caregivers also provide lessons in socially approved ways of expressing feelings. As early as the first few months, parents encourage infants to suppress negative emotion by imitating their expressions of interest, happiness, and surprise more often than their expressions of anger and sadness. Boys get more of this training than girls, in part because boys have a harder time regulating negative emotion (Else-Quest et al., 2006; Malatesta et al., 1986). As a result, the well-known sex difference—females as emotionally expressive and males as emotionally controlled—is promoted at a tender age. Collectivist cultures place particular emphasis on socially appropriate emotional behavior. Compared with Americans, Japanese and Chinese adults discourage the expression of strong emotion in babies (Fogel, 1993; Kuchner, 1989). By the end of the first year, Chinese and Japanese infants smile and cry less than American infants (Camras et al., 1998; Gartstein et al., 2010).

Toward the end of the second year, a vocabulary for talking about feelings—"happy," "surprised," "scary," "yucky," "mad"—develops rapidly, but toddlers are not yet good at using language to manage their emotions. Temper tantrums tend to occur when an adult rejects their demands, particularly when toddlers are fatigued or hungry (Mascolo & Fischer, 2007). Toddlers whose parents are emotionally sympathetic but set limits (by not giving in to tantrums), who distract the child by offering acceptable alternatives, and who later suggest better ways to handle adult refusals display more effective anger-regulation strategies and social skills during the preschool years (Lecuyer & Houck, 2006).

Patient, sensitive parents also encourage toddlers to describe their internal states. Then, when 2-year-olds feel distressed, they can guide caregivers in helping them (Cole, Armstrong, & Pemberton, 2010). For example, while listening to a story about monsters, Grace whimpered, "Mommy, scary." Monica put the book down and gave Grace a comforting hug.

ASK YOURSELF

REVIEW Why do many infants show stranger anxiety in the second half of the first year? What factors can increase or decrease wariness of strangers?

CONNECT Why do children of depressed parents have difficulty regulating emotion (see pages 186–187)? What implications do their weak self-regulatory skills have for their response to cognitive and social challenges?

APPLY At age 14 months, Reggie built a block tower and gleefully knocked it down. But at age 2, he called to his mother and pointed proudly to his tall block tower. What explains this change in Reggie's emotional behavior?

REFLECT Describe several recent instances illustrating how you typically manage negative emotion. How might your early experiences, gender, and cultural background have influenced your style of emotional self-regulation?

Temperament and Development

From early infancy, Caitlin's sociability was unmistakable. She smiled and laughed while interacting with adults and, in her second year, readily approached other children. Meanwhile, Monica marveled at Grace's calm, relaxed disposition. At 19 months, she sat contented in a highchair through a two-hour family celebration at a restaurant. In contrast, Timmy was active and distractible. Vanessa found herself chasing him as he dropped one toy, moved on to the next, and climbed on chairs and tables.

When we describe one person as cheerful and "upbeat," another as active and energetic, and still others as calm, cautious, persistent, or prone to angry outbursts, we are referring to **temperament**—early-appearing, stable individual differences in reactivity and self-regulation. *Reactivity* refers to quickness and intensity of emotional arousal, attention, and motor activity. *Self-regulation*, as we have seen, refers to strategies that modify that reactivity (Rothbart & Bates, 2006). The psychological traits that make up temperament are believed to form the cornerstone of the adult personality.

In 1956, Alexander Thomas and Stella Chess initiated the New York Longitudinal Study, a groundbreaking investigation of the development of temperament that followed 141 children from early infancy well into adulthood. Results showed that temperament can increase a child's chances of experiencing psychological problems or, alternatively, protect a child from the negative effects of a highly stressful home life. At the same time, Thomas and Chess (1977) discovered that parenting practices can modify children's temperaments considerably.

These findings stimulated a growing body of research on temperament, including its stability, biological roots, and interaction with child-rearing experiences. Let's begin to explore these issues by looking at the structure, or makeup, of temperament and how it is measured.

The Structure of Temperament

Thomas and Chess's model of temperament inspired all others that followed. When detailed descriptions of infants' and children's behavior obtained from parent interviews were rated on nine dimensions of temperament, certain characteristics clustered together, yielding three types of children:

- The **easy child** (40 percent of the sample) quickly establishes regular routines in infancy, is generally cheerful, and adapts easily to new experiences.

- The **difficult child** (10 percent of the sample) is irregular in daily routines, is slow to accept new experiences, and tends to react negatively and intensely.

- The **slow-to-warm-up child** (15 percent of the sample) is inactive, shows mild, low-key reactions to environmental stimuli, is negative in mood, and adjusts slowly to new experiences.

Note that 35 percent of the children did not fit any of these categories. Instead, they showed unique blends of temperamental characteristics.

The difficult pattern has sparked the most interest because it places children at high risk for adjustment problems—both anxious withdrawal and aggressive behavior in early and middle childhood (Bates, Wachs, & Emde, 1994; Ramos et al., 2005; Thomas, Chess, & Birch, 1968). Compared with difficult children, slow-to-warm-up children present fewer problems in the early years. However, they tend to show excessive fearfulness and slow, constricted behavior in the late preschool and school years, when they are expected to respond actively and quickly in classrooms and peer groups (Chess & Thomas, 1984; Schmitz et al., 1999).

Today, the most influential model of temperament is Mary Rothbart's, described in Table 6.1. It combines related traits proposed by Thomas and Chess and other researchers, yielding a concise list of just six dimensions. For example, "distractibility" and "attention span and persistence" are considered opposite ends of the same dimension, which is labeled "attention span/persistence." A unique feature of Rothbart's model is inclusion of both "fearful distress" and "irritable distress," which distinguish between reactivity triggered by fear and reactivity due to frustration. And the model deletes overly broad dimensions, such as

TABLE 6.1 **Rothbart's Model of Temperament**

DIMENSION	DESCRIPTION
REACTIVITY	
Activity level	Level of gross-motor activity
Attention span/persistence	Duration of orienting or interest
Fearful distress	Wariness and distress in response to intense or novel stimuli, including time to adjust to new situations
Irritable distress	Extent of fussing, crying, and distress when desires are frustrated
Positive affect	Frequency of expression of happiness and pleasure
SELF-REGULATION	
Effortful control	Capacity to voluntarily suppress a dominant, reactive response in order to plan and execute a more adaptive response

regularity of body functions and intensity of reaction (Rothbart, Ahadi, & Evans, 2000; Rothbart & Mauro, 1990). A child who is regular in sleeping is not necessarily regular in eating or bowel habits. And a child who smiles and laughs intensely is not necessarily intense in fear, irritability, or motor activity.

Rothbart's dimensions represent the three underlying components included in the definition of temperament: (1) *emotion* ("fearful distress," "irritable distress," "positive affect," and "soothability"), (2) *attention* ("attention span/persistence"), and (3) *action* ("activity level"). According to Rothbart, individuals differ not only in their reactivity on each dimension but also in the self-regulatory dimension of temperament, **effortful control**—the capacity to voluntarily suppress a dominant response in order to plan and execute a more adaptive response (Rothbart, 2003; Rothbart & Bates, 2006). Variations in effortful control are evident in how effectively a child can focus and shift attention, inhibit impulses, and manage negative emotion.

Beginning in early childhood, effortful control predicts favorable development and adjustment in cultures as diverse as China and the United States (Zhou, Lengua, & Wang, 2009). Positive outcomes include persistence, task mastery, academic achievement, cooperation, moral maturity (such as concern about wrongdoing and willingness to apologize), and positive social behaviors of sharing and helpfulness (Eisenberg, 2010; Harris et al., 2007; Kochanska & Aksan, 2006; Posner & Rothbart, 2007; Valiente et al., 2010). Effortful control is also associated with children's resistance to stress (David & Murphy, 2007). Perhaps children high in effortful control are better able to shift attention away from disturbing events and their own anxiety to more positive features of their social environments.

TAKE A MOMENT... Turn back to page 162 in Chapter 5 to review the concept of executive function, and note its resemblance to effortful control. These converging concepts, which are associated with similar positive outcomes, reveal that the same mental activities lead to effective regulation in both the cognitive and emotional/social domains.

Measuring Temperament

Temperament is often assessed through interviews or questionnaires given to parents. Behavior ratings by pediatricians, teachers, and others familiar with the child and laboratory observations by researchers have also been used. Parental reports are convenient and take advantage of parents' depth of knowledge about their child across many situations (Gartstein & Rothbart, 2003). Although information from parents has been criticized as biased, parental reports are moderately related to researchers' observations of children's behavior (Majdandžić & van den Boom, 2007; Mangelsdorf, Schoppe, & Buur, 2000). And parent perceptions are useful for understanding how parents view and respond to their child.

Observations by researchers in the home or laboratory avoid the subjectivity of parental reports but can lead to other inaccuracies. In homes, observers find it hard to capture rare but important events, such as infants' response to frustration. And in the unfamiliar lab setting, fearful children who calmly avoid certain experiences at home may become too upset to complete the session (Wachs & Bates, 2001). Still, researchers can better control children's experiences in the lab. And they can conveniently combine observations of behavior with physiological measures to gain insight into the biological bases of temperament.

Most neurobiological research has focused on children who fall at opposite extremes of the positive-affect and fearful-distress dimensions of temperament: **inhibited, or shy, children,** who react negatively to and withdraw from novel stimuli, and **uninhibited, or sociable, children,** who display positive emotion to and approach novel stimuli. As the Biology and Environment box on page 192 reveals, biologically based reactivity—evident in heart rate, hormone levels, and measures of brain activity—differentiates children with inhibited and uninhibited temperaments.

Stability of Temperament

Young children who score low or high on attention span, irritability, sociability, shyness, or effortful control tend to respond similarly when assessed again several months to a few years later and, occasionally, even into the adult years (Caspi et al., 2003; Kochanska & Knaack, 2003; Majdandžić & van den Boom, 2007; Rothbart, Ahadi, & Evans, 2000; van den Akker et al., 2010). However, the overall stability of temperament is low in infancy and toddlerhood and only moderate from the preschool years on (Putnam, Samson, & Rothbart, 2000).

Why isn't temperament more stable? A major reason is that temperament itself develops with age. To illustrate, let's look at irritability and activity level. Recall from Chapter 3 that most babies fuss and cry in the early months. As infants better regulate their attention and emotions, many who initially seemed irritable become calm and content. In the case of activity level, the meaning of the behavior changes. At first, an active, wriggling

Biology and Environment

Development of Shyness and Sociability

Two 4-month-old babies, Larry and Mitch, visited the laboratory of Jerome Kagan, who observed their reactions to various unfamiliar experiences. When exposed to new sights and sounds, such as a moving mobile decorated with colorful toys, Larry tensed his muscles, moved his arms and legs with agitation, and began to cry. In contrast, Mitch remained relaxed and quiet, smiling and cooing.

As toddlers, Larry and Mitch returned to the laboratory, where they experienced several procedures designed to induce uncertainty. Electrodes were placed on their bodies and blood pressure cuffs on their arms to measure heart rate; toy robots, animals, and puppets moved before their eyes; and unfamiliar people behaved in unexpected ways or wore novel costumes. While Larry whimpered and quickly withdrew, Mitch watched with interest, laughed, and approached the toys and strangers.

On a third visit, at age 4½, Larry barely talked or smiled during an interview with an unfamiliar adult. In contrast, Mitch asked questions and communicated his pleasure at each new activity. In a playroom with two unfamiliar peers, Larry pulled back and watched, while Mitch quickly made friends.

In longitudinal research on several hundred children, Kagan found that about 20 percent of 4-month-old babies were, like Larry, easily upset by novelty; 40 percent, like Mitch, were comfortable, even delighted, with new experiences. About 20 to 30 percent of these groups retained their temperamental styles as they grew older (Kagan, 2003; Kagan & Saudino, 2001; Kagan et al., 2007). But most children's dispositions became less extreme over time. Biological makeup and child-rearing experiences jointly influenced stability and change in temperament.

Neurobiological Correlates of Shyness and Sociability

Individual differences in arousal of the *amygdala,* an inner brain structure devoted to processing emotional information, contribute to these contrasting temperaments. In shy,

inhibited children, novel stimuli easily excite the amygdala and its connections to the prefrontal cortex and the sympathetic nervous system, which prepares the body to act in the face of threat. In sociable, uninhibited children, the same level of stimulation evokes minimal neural excitation (Kagan & Fox, 2006). While viewing photos of unfamiliar faces, adults who had been classified as inhibited in the second year of life showed greater fMRI activity in the amygdala than adults who had been uninhibited as toddlers (Schwartz et al., 2003). And additional neurobiological responses known to be mediated by the amygdala distinguish these two emotional styles:

- *Heart rate.* From the first few weeks of life, the heart rates of shy children are consistently higher than those of sociable children, and they speed up further in response to unfamiliar events (Schmidt et al., 2007; Snidman et al., 1995).

- *Cortisol.* Saliva concentrations of the stress hormone cortisol tend to be higher, and to rise more in response to a stressful event, in shy than in sociable children (Schmidt et al., 1997, 1999; Zimmermann & Stansbury, 2004).

- *Pupil dilation, blood pressure, and skin surface temperature.* Compared with sociable children, shy children show greater pupil dilation, rise in blood pressure, and cooling of the fingertips when faced with novelty (Kagan et al., 1999, 2007).

Furthermore, shy infants and preschoolers show greater EEG activity in the right than in the left frontal lobe of the cerebral cortex, which is associated with negative emotional reactivity; sociable children show the opposite pattern (Fox et al., 2008; Kagan et al., 2007). Neural activity in the amygdala, which is transmitted to the frontal lobes, probably contributes to these differences.

Child-Rearing Practices

According to Kagan, extremely shy or sociable children inherit a physiology that biases them toward a particular temperamental style. Yet heritability research indicates that

A strong physiological response to uncertain situations prompts this toddler to cling to her father. With patient but insistent encouragement, her parents can help her overcome the urge to retreat.

genes contribute only modestly to shyness and sociability (Kagan & Fox, 2006).

Child-rearing practices affect the chances that an emotionally reactive baby will become a fearful child. Warm, supportive parenting reduces shy infants' and preschoolers' intense physiological reaction to novelty, whereas cold, intrusive parenting heightens anxiety (Coplan, Arbeau, & Armer, 2008; Hane et al., 2008). And if parents overprotect infants and young children who dislike novelty, they make it harder for their child to overcome an urge to retreat. Parents who make appropriate demands for their child to approach new experiences help shy youngsters develop strategies for regulating fear (Rubin & Burgess, 2002).

When inhibition persists, it leads to excessive cautiousness, low self-esteem, and loneliness. In adolescence, persistent shyness increases the risk of severe anxiety, especially social phobia—intense fear of being humiliated in social situations (Kagan & Fox, 2006). For inhibited children to acquire effective social skills, parenting must be tailored to their temperaments—a theme we will encounter again in this and later chapters.

infant tends to be highly aroused and uncomfortable, whereas an inactive baby is often alert and attentive. Once infants move on their own, the reverse is so! An active crawler is usually alert and interested in exploration, whereas an inactive baby may be fearful and withdrawn.

These discrepancies help us understand why long-term prediction from early temperament is best achieved after age 3, when styles of responding are better established (Roberts & DelVecchio, 2000). In line with this idea, between age 2½ and 3, children improve substantially and also perform more consistently across a wide range of tasks requiring effortful control, such as waiting for a reward, lowering their voice to a whisper, succeeding at games like "Simon Says," and selectively attending to one stimulus while ignoring competing stimuli (Kochanska, Murray, & Harlan, 2000; Li-Grining, 2007). Researchers believe that around this time, areas in the prefrontal cortex involved in suppressing impulses develop rapidly (Gerardi-Caulton, 2000; Rothbart & Bates, 2006).

Nevertheless, the ease with which children manage their reactivity in early childhood depends on the type and strength of the reactive emotion involved. Preschoolers who were highly fearful as toddlers score slightly better than their agemates in effortful control. In contrast, angry, irritable toddlers tend to be less effective at effortful control at later ages (Bridgett et al., 2009; Kochanska & Knaack, 2003).

In sum, many factors affect the extent to which a child's temperament remains stable, including development of the biological systems on which temperament is based, the child's capacity for effortful control, and the success of her efforts, which depend on the quality and intensity of her emotional reactivity. When we consider the evidence as a whole, the low to moderate stability of temperament makes sense. It also confirms that experience can modify biologically based temperamental traits considerably, although children rarely change from one extreme to another—that is, shy toddlers practically never become highly sociable, and irritable toddlers seldom become easy-going. With these ideas in mind, let's turn to genetic and environmental contributions to temperament and personality.

Genetic and Environmental Influences

The word *temperament* implies a genetic foundation for individual differences in personality. Research indicates that identical twins are more similar than fraternal twins across a wide range of temperamental and personality traits (Bouchard, 2004; Bouchard & Loehlin, 2001; Caspi & Shiner, 2006; Goldsmith, Pollak, & Davidson, 2008). In Chapter 2, we noted that heritability estimates suggest a moderate role for heredity in temperament and personality: About half of individual differences have been attributed to differences in genetic makeup.

Nevertheless, genetic influences vary with the temperamental trait and with the age of individuals studied. For example, heritability estimates are higher for expressions of negative emotion than for positive emotion. And the role of heredity is considerably less in infancy than in childhood and later years, when temperament becomes more stable (Wachs & Bates, 2001).

Although genetic influences are clear, environment is also powerful. For example, persistent nutritional and emotional deprivation profoundly alters temperament, resulting in maladaptive emotional reactivity. Recall from Chapter 4 that even after dietary improvement, children exposed to severe malnutrition in infancy remain more distractible and fearful than their agemates. And infants reared in deprived orphanages are easily overwhelmed by stressful events. Their poor regulation of emotion results in inattention and weak impulse control, including frequent expressions of anger (see page 127).

Other evidence confirms that heredity and environment often jointly contribute to temperament, since a child's approach to the world affects the experiences to which she is exposed—an instance of gene–environment correlation (see page 72 in Chapter 2). To see how this works, let's look at ethnic and gender differences.

Ethnic and Gender Differences. Compared with American Caucasian infants, Chinese and Japanese babies tend to be less active, irritable, vocal, more easily soothed when upset, and better at quieting themselves (Kagan et al., 1994; Lewis, Ramsay, & Kawakami, 1993). Chinese and Japanese babies are also more fearful and inhibited, remaining closer to their mothers in an unfamiliar playroom and displaying more anxiety when interacting with a stranger (Chen, Wang, & DeSouza, 2006).

These variations may have genetic roots, but they are supported by cultural beliefs and practices. Japanese mothers usually say that babies come into the world as independent beings who must learn to rely on their mothers through close physical contact. American mothers typically believe just the opposite—that they must wean babies away from dependency toward autonomy. And while Asian cultures tend to view calmness as an ideal emotional state, Americans highly value the arousal and excitement generated by new places and activities (Kagan, 2010). Consistent with these beliefs, Asian mothers interact gently, soothingly, and gesturally with their babies, whereas Caucasian mothers use a more active, stimulating, verbal approach (Rothbaum et al., 2000a). Also, recall from our discussion of emotional self-regulation that Chinese and Japanese adults discourage babies from expressing strong emotion, which contributes further to their infants' tranquility.

Similarly, gender differences in temperament are evident as early as the first year, suggesting a genetic foundation. Boys are more active and daring, more irritable when frustrated, and slightly more impulsive—factors that contribute to their higher injury rates throughout childhood and adolescence. And girls' large advantage in effortful control undoubtedly contributes to their greater compliance, better school performance, and lower incidence of behavior problems (Eisenberg et al., 2004; Else-Quest et al., 2006). At the same time, parents more often encourage their young sons to be physically active and their daughters to seek help and physical closeness—through the toys they provide (trucks and footballs for boys, dolls and tea sets for girls) and through more positive reactions when the child exhibits temperamental traits consistent with gender stereotypes (Bryan & Dix, 2009; Ruble, Martin, & Berenbaum, 2006).

Children's Unique Experiences. In families with several children, an additional influence on temperament is at work. *TAKE A MOMENT...* Ask several parents to describe each of their children's personalities. You will see that they often look for differences between siblings: "She's a lot more active," "He's more sociable," "She's far more persistent." As a result, parents often regard siblings as more distinct than other observers do. In a large study of 1- to 3-year-old twin pairs, parents rated identical twins as resembling each other less in temperament than researchers' ratings indicated. And whereas researchers rated fraternal twins as moderately similar, parents viewed them as somewhat opposite in temperamental style (Saudino, 2003).

Parents' tendency to emphasize each child's unique qualities affects their child-rearing practices. In an investigation of identical-twin toddlers, mothers' differential treatment predicted differences in psychological adjustment. The twin who received more warmth and less harshness was more positive in mood and social behavior (Deater-Deckard et al., 2001). Each child, in turn, evokes responses from caregivers that are consistent with parental beliefs and the child's developing temperament.

Besides different experiences within the family, siblings have distinct experiences with teachers, peers, and others in their community that affect personality development. And in middle childhood and adolescence, they often seek ways to differ from one another. For all these reasons, both identical and fraternal twins tend to become increasingly dissimilar in personality with age (Loehlin & Martin, 2001; McCartney, Harris, & Bernieri, 1990). In sum, temperament and personality can be understood only in terms of complex interdependencies between genetic and environmental factors.

Temperament and Child Rearing: The Goodness-of-Fit Model

If a child's disposition interferes with learning or getting along with others, adults must gently but consistently counteract the child's maladaptive style. Thomas and Chess (1977) proposed a **goodness-of-fit model** to describe how temperament and environment together can produce favorable outcomes. Goodness of fit involves creating child-rearing environments that recognize each child's temperament while encouraging more adaptive functioning.

Difficult children (who withdraw from new experiences and react negatively and intensely) frequently experience parenting that fits poorly with their dispositions, putting them at high risk for later adjustment problems. By the second year, their parents tend to resort to angry, punitive discipline, which undermines the development of effortful control. As the child reacts with defiance and disobedience, parents become increasingly stressed (Bridgett et al., 2009; Paulussen-Hoogeboom et al., 2007). As a result, they continue their coercive tactics and also discipline inconsistently, at times rewarding the child's noncompliance by giving in to it. These practices sustain and even increase the child's irritable, conflict-ridden style (van Aken et al., 2007; Pesonen et al., 2008).

© CORBIS

A parent's firm but affectionate approach to discipline can help temperamentally difficult children gain in effortful control, managing negative emotion.

In contrast, when parents are positive and sensitive, which helps babies regulate emotion, difficultness declines by age 2 or 3 (Feldman, Greenbaum, & Yirmiya, 1999). In toddlerhood and childhood, parental sensitivity, support, clear expectations, and limits foster effortful control, also reducing the likelihood that difficultness will persist (Cipriano & Stifter, 2010; Raikes et al., 2007).

Recent evidence indicates that temperamentally difficult children function much worse than other children when exposed to inept parenting, yet benefit most from good parenting (Pluess & Belsky, 2011). Using molecular genetic analyses, researchers are investigating gene–environment interactions (see page 71 in Chapter 2) that explain this finding. In one study, 2-year-olds with a chromosome 17 gene that interferes with functioning of the neurotransmitter serotonin (involved in regulating negative mood) became increasingly irritable as their mothers' anxiety about parenting increased (Ivorra et al., 2010). Maternal anxiety had little impact on toddlers without this genetic marker. In another investigation, preschoolers with this gene benefited, especially, from positive parenting. With affection and support, their capacity for effortful control equaled that of agemates with a low-risk genotype (Kochanska, Philibert, & Barry, 2009).

Cultural values also affect the fit between parenting and child temperament, as research in China illustrates. In the past, collectivist values, which discourage self-assertion, led Chinese adults to evaluate shy children positively (Chen, Rubin, & Li, 1995; Chen et al., 1998). But rapid expansion of a market economy in China, which requires assertiveness and sociability for success, may be responsible for a change in Chinese parents' and teachers' attitudes toward childhood shyness (Chen, Wang, & DeSouza, 2006; Yu, 2002). In a study of Shanghai fourth graders, the association between shyness and adjustment changed over time. Whereas shyness was positively correlated with teacher-rated competence, peer acceptance, leadership, and academic achievement in 1990, these relationships weakened in 1998 and reversed in 2002, when they mirrored findings of Western research (see Figure 6.1) (Chen et al., 2005). But in rural areas of China, positive valuing of shyness persists, and shy children in rural communities continue to enjoy high social status and are well-adjusted (Chen, Wang, & Cao, 2011). Cultural context makes a difference in whether shy children fare well or poorly.

An effective match between rearing conditions and child temperament is best accomplished early, before unfavorable temperament–environment relationships produce maladjustment. Both difficult and shy children benefit from warm, accepting parenting that makes firm but reasonable demands for mastering new experiences. The goodness-of-fit model reminds us that children have unique dispositions that adults must accept. Parents can neither take full credit for their children's virtues nor be blamed for all their faults. But parents can turn an environment that exaggerates a child's problems into one that builds on the child's strengths.

As we will see next, goodness of fit is also at the heart of infant–caregiver attachment. This first intimate relationship grows out of interaction between parent and baby, to which the emotional styles of both partners contribute.

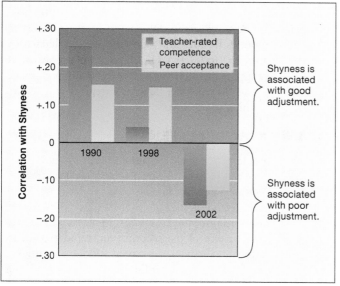

FIGURE 6.1 Changes over time in correlations between shyness and adjustment among Chinese fourth graders. In 1990, shy Chinese children appeared well-adjusted. But as China's market economy expanded and valuing of self-assertion and sociability increased, the direction of the correlations shifted. In 2002, shyness was negatively associated with adjustment. These findings are for teacher-rated competence and peer acceptance. Those for leadership (holding offices in student organizations) and academic achievement changed similarly. (Adapted from Chen et al., 2005.)

ASK YOURSELF

REVIEW How do genetic and environmental factors work together to influence temperament? Cite several examples from research.

CONNECT Explain how findings on ethnic and gender differences in temperament illustrate gene–environment correlation, discussed on page 72 in Chapter 2.

APPLY Mandy and Jeff are parents of 2-year-old inhibited Sam and 3-year-old difficult Maria. Explain the importance of effortful control to Mandy and Jeff, and suggest ways they can strengthen it in each of their children.

REFLECT How would you describe your temperament as a young child? Do you think your temperament has remained stable, or has it changed? What factors might be involved?

 Development of Attachment

Attachment is the strong affectionate tie we have with special people in our lives that leads us to feel pleasure when we interact with them and to be comforted by their nearness in times of stress. By the second half of the first year, infants have become attached to familiar people who have responded to their needs.

TAKE A MOMENT... Watch how babies of this age single out their parents for special attention. When the parent enters the room, the baby breaks into a broad, friendly smile. When she picks him up, he pats her face, explores her hair, and snuggles against her. When he feels anxious or afraid, he crawls into her lap and clings closely.

Freud first suggested that the infant's emotional tie to the mother is the foundation for all later relationships. Contemporary research indicates that—although the parent–infant bond is vitally important—later development is influenced not just by early attachment experiences but also by the continuing quality of the parent–child relationship.

Attachment has also been the subject of intense theoretical debate. Recall that the *psychoanalytic perspective* regards feeding as the central context in which caregivers and babies build this close emotional bond. *Behaviorism,* too, emphasizes the importance of feeding, but for different reasons. According to a well-known behaviorist explanation, infants learn to prefer the mother's soft caresses, warm smiles, and tender words because these events are paired with tension relief as she satisfies the baby's hunger.

Although feeding is an important context for building a close relationship, attachment does not depend on hunger satisfaction. In the 1950s, a famous experiment showed that rhesus monkeys reared with terry-cloth and wire-mesh "surrogate

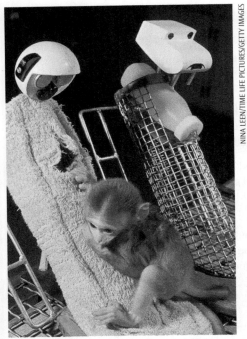

NINA LEEN/TIME LIFE PICTURES/GETTY IMAGES

Baby monkeys reared with "surrogate mothers" preferred to cling to a soft terry-cloth "mother" over a wire-mesh "mother" holding a bottle—evidence that parent–infant attachment is based on more than satisfaction of hunger.

mothers" clung to the soft terry-cloth substitute, even though the wire-mesh "mother" held the bottle and infants had to climb onto it to be fed (Harlow & Zimmerman, 1959). Human infants, too, become attached to family members who seldom feed them, including fathers, siblings, and grandparents. And toddlers in Western cultures who sleep alone and experience frequent daytime separations from their parents sometimes develop strong emotional ties to cuddly objects, such as blankets and teddy bears, that play no role in infant feeding!

Bowlby's Ethological Theory

Today, **ethological theory of attachment,** which recognizes the infant's emotional tie to the caregiver as an evolved response that promotes survival, is the most widely accepted view. John Bowlby (1969), who first applied this idea to the infant–caregiver bond, retained the psychoanalytic idea that quality of attachment to the caregiver has profound implications for the child's feelings of security and capacity to form trusting relationships.

At the same time, Bowlby was inspired by Konrad Lorenz's studies of imprinting (see Chapter 1). Bowlby believed that the human infant, like the young of other animal species, is endowed with a set of built-in behaviors that help keep the parent nearby to protect the infant from danger and to provide support for exploring and mastering the environment (Waters & Cummings, 2000). Contact with the parent also ensures that the baby will be fed, but Bowlby pointed out that feeding is not the basis for attachment. Rather, attachment can best be understood in an evolutionary context in which survival of the species—through ensuring both safety and competence—is of utmost importance.

According to Bowlby, the infant's relationship with the parent begins as a set of innate signals that call the adult to the baby's side. Over time, a true affectionate bond forms, supported by new cognitive and emotional capacities as well as by a history of warm, sensitive care. Attachment develops in four phases:

1. *Preattachment phase* (birth to 6 weeks). Built-in signals—grasping, smiling, crying, and gazing into the adult's eyes—help bring newborn babies into close contact with other humans, who comfort them. Babies of this age recognize their own mother's smell, voice, and face (see Chapters 3 and 4). But they are not yet attached to her, since they do not mind being left with an unfamiliar adult.

2. *"Attachment-in-the-making" phase* (6 weeks to 6–8 months). During this phase, infants respond differently to a familiar caregiver than to a stranger. For example, at 4 months, Timmy smiled, laughed, and babbled more freely when interacting with his mother and quieted more quickly when she picked him up. As infants learn that their own actions affect the behavior of those around them, they begin to develop a *sense of trust*—the expectation that the caregiver will respond when signaled—but they still do not protest when separated from her.

3. *"Clear-cut" attachment phase* (6–8 months to 18 months–2 years). Now attachment to the familiar caregiver is evident. Babies display **separation anxiety,** becoming upset when their trusted caregiver leaves. Like stranger anxiety (see page 186), separation anxiety does not always occur; it depends on infant temperament and the current situation. But in many cultures, separation anxiety increases between 6 and 15 months. Besides protesting the parent's departure, older infants and toddlers try hard to maintain her presence. They approach, follow, and climb on her in preference to others. And they use the familiar caregiver as a secure base from which to explore.

LOOK AND LISTEN

Watch an 8- to 18-month-old at play for 20 to 30 minutes. Describe the baby's use of the parent or other familiar caregiver as a secure base from which to explore. ●

4. *Formation of a reciprocal relationship* (18 months to 2 years and on). By the end of the second year, rapid growth in representation and language permits toddlers to understand some of the factors that influence the parent's coming and going and to predict her return. As a result, separation protest declines. Now children negotiate with the caregiver, using requests and persuasion to alter her goals. For example, at age 2, Caitlin asked Carolyn and David to read a story before leaving her with a babysitter. The extra time with her parents, along with a better understanding of where they were going ("to have dinner with Uncle Charlie") and when they would be back ("right after you go to sleep"), helped Caitlin withstand her parents' absence.

Because this 2-year-old has the language and representational skills to predict his mother's return, separation anxiety declines. He accepts his mother's departure.

According to Bowlby (1980), out of their experiences during these four phases, children construct an enduring affectionate tie to the caregiver that they can use as a secure base in the parents' absence. This image serves as an **internal working model,** or set of expectations about the availability of attachment figures and their likelihood of providing support during times of stress. The internal working model becomes a vital part of personality, serving as a guide for all future close relationships (Bretherton & Munholland, 2008).

Consistent with these ideas, as early as the second year, toddlers form attachment-related expectations about parental comfort and support. In one study, securely attached 12- to 16-month-olds looked longer at a video of an unresponsive caregiver (inconsistent with their expectations) than a video of a responsive caregiver. Insecurely attached toddlers, in contrast, did not distinguish between the two (Johnson, Dweck, & Chen, 2007; Johnson et al., 2010). With age, children continually revise and expand their internal working model as their cognitive, emotional, and social capacities increase and as they interact with parents and form other bonds with adults, siblings, and friends.

Measuring the Security of Attachment

Although all family-reared babies become attached to a familiar caregiver by the second year, the quality of this relationship varies. Some infants appear relaxed and secure in the presence of the caregiver; they know they can count on her for protection and support. Others seem anxious and uncertain.

A widely used laboratory procedure for assessing the quality of attachment between 1 and 2 years of age is the **Strange Situation.** In designing it, Mary Ainsworth and her colleagues (1978) reasoned that securely attached infants and toddlers should use the parent as a secure base from which to explore an unfamiliar playroom. In addition, when the parent leaves, an unfamiliar adult should be less comforting than the parent. The Strange Situation takes the baby through eight short episodes

in which brief separations from and reunions with the parent occur (see Table 6.2).

Observing infants' responses to these episodes, researchers identified a secure attachment pattern and three patterns of insecurity; a few babies cannot be classified (Ainsworth et al., 1978; Barnett & Vondra, 1999; Main & Solomon, 1990; Thompson, 2006). Although separation anxiety varies among the groups, the baby's reunion responses define attachment quality. *TAKE A MOMENT...* From the description at the beginning of this chapter, which pattern do you think Grace displayed after adjusting to her adoptive family?

- **Secure attachment.** These infants use the parent as a secure base. When separated, they may or may not cry, but if they do, it is because the parent is absent and they prefer her to the stranger. When the parent returns, they actively seek contact, and their crying is reduced immediately. About 60 percent of North American infants in middle-SES families show this pattern. (In low-SES families, a smaller proportion of babies show the secure pattern, with higher proportions falling into the insecure patterns.)

- **Avoidant attachment.** These infants seem unresponsive to the parent when she is present. When she leaves, they usually are not distressed, and they react to the stranger in much the same way as to the parent. During reunion, they

TABLE 6.2

Episodes in the Strange Situation

EPISODE	EVENTS	ATTACHMENT BEHAVIOR OBSERVED
1	Researcher introduces parent and baby to playroom and then leaves.	
2	Parent is seated while baby plays with toys.	Parent as a secure base
3	Stranger enters, is seated, and talks to parent.	Reaction to unfamiliar adult
4	Parent leaves room. Stranger responds to baby and offers comfort if baby is upset.	Separation anxiety
5	Parent returns, greets baby, and offers comfort if necessary. Stranger leaves room.	Reaction to reunion
6	Parent leaves room.	Separation anxiety
7	Stranger enters room and offers comfort.	Ability to be soothed by stranger
8	Parent returns, greets baby, offers comfort if necessary, and tries to reinterest baby in toys.	Reaction to reunion

Note: Episode 1 lasts about 30 seconds; each of the remaining episodes lasts about 3 minutes. Separation episodes are cut short if the baby becomes very upset. Reunion episodes are extended if the baby needs more time to calm down and return to play.
Source: Ainsworth et al., 1978.

avoid or are slow to greet the parent, and when picked up, they often fail to cling. About 15 percent of North American infants in middle-SES families show this pattern.

- **Resistant attachment.** Before separation, these infants seek closeness to the parent and often fail to explore. When the parent leaves, they are usually distressed, and on her return they combine clinginess with angry, resistive behavior, sometimes hitting and pushing. Many continue to cry after being picked up and cannot be comforted easily. About 10 percent of North American infants in middle-SES families show this pattern.

- **Disorganized/disoriented attachment.** This pattern reflects the greatest insecurity. At reunion, these infants show confused, contradictory behaviors—for example, looking away while the parent is holding them or approaching the parent with flat, depressed emotion. Most display a dazed facial expression, and a few cry out unexpectedly after having calmed down or display odd, frozen postures. About 15 percent of North American infants in middle-SES families show this pattern.

An alternative method, the **Attachment Q-Sort,** suitable for children between 1 and 4 years, depends on home observation (Waters et al., 1995). Either the parent or a highly trained observer sorts 90 behaviors ("Child greets mother with a big smile when she enters the room," "If mother moves very far, child follows along") into nine categories ranging from "highly descriptive" to "not at all descriptive" of the child. Then a score, ranging from high to low in security, is computed.

Because the Q-Sort taps a wider array of attachment-related behaviors than the Strange Situation, it may better reflect the parent–infant relationship in everyday life. However, the Q-Sort method is time-consuming, requiring a nonparent informant to spend several hours observing the child before sorting the descriptors, and it does not differentiate between types of insecurity. The Q-Sort responses of expert observers correspond well with babies' secure-base behavior in the Strange Situation, but parents' Q-Sorts do not (van IJzendoorn et al., 2004). Parents of insecure children, especially, may have difficulty accurately reporting their child's attachment behaviors.

Stability of Attachment

Research on the stability of attachment patterns between 1 and 2 years of age yields a wide range of findings (Thompson, 2000, 2006). A close look at which babies stay the same and which ones change yields a more consistent picture. Quality of attachment is usually secure and stable for middle-SES babies experiencing favorable life conditions. And infants who move from insecurity to security typically have well-adjusted mothers with positive family and friendship ties. Perhaps many became parents before they were psychologically ready but, with social support, grew into the role.

In contrast, in low-SES families with many daily stresses and little social support, attachment generally moves away from

security or changes from one insecure pattern to another (Belsky et al., 1996; Fish, 2004; Levendosky et al., 2011; Vondra et al., 2001). In one long-term follow-up of a poverty-stricken sample, many securely attached infants ended up insecure when reassessed in early adulthood. Child maltreatment, maternal depression, and poor family functioning in adolescence distinguished these young people from the few who stayed securely attached (Weinfield, Sroufe, & Egeland, 2000; Weinfield, Whaley, & Egeland, 2004).

These findings indicate that securely attached babies more often maintain their attachment status than insecure babies. The exception is disorganized/disoriented attachment, an insecure pattern that is either highly stable or that consistently predicts insecurity of another type in adolescence and early adulthood (Aikens, Howes, & Hamilton, 2009; Hesse & Main, 2000; Sroufe et al., 2005; Weinfield, Whaley, & Egeland, 2004). As you will soon see, many disorganized/disoriented infants and children experience extremely negative caregiving, which may disrupt emotional self-regulation so severely that confused, ambivalent feelings toward parents often persist.

Cultural Variations

Cross-cultural evidence indicates that attachment patterns may have to be interpreted differently in certain cultures. For example, as Figure 6.2 reveals, German infants show considerably more avoidant attachment than American babies do.

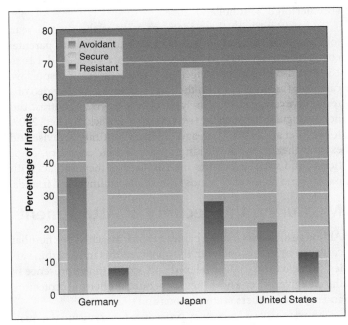

FIGURE 6.2 A cross-cultural comparison of infants' reactions in the Strange Situation. A high percentage of German babies seem avoidantly attached, whereas a substantial number of Japanese infants appear resistantly attached. Note that these responses may not reflect true insecurity. Instead, they are probably due to cultural differences in child-rearing practices. (Adapted from van IJzendoorn & Kroonenberg, 1988; van IJzendoorn & Sagi-Schwartz, 2008.)

Dogon mothers of Mali, West Africa, stay close to their babies and respond promptly and gently to infant hunger and distress. With their mothers consistently available, none of the Dogon babies show avoidant attachment.

But German parents value independence and encourage their infants to be nonclingy (Grossmann et al., 1985). In contrast, a study of infants of the Dogon people of Mali, Africa, revealed that none showed avoidant attachment to their mothers (True, Pisani, & Oumar, 2001). Even when grandmothers are primary caregivers (as they are with firstborn sons), Dogon mothers remain available, holding their babies close and nursing promptly in response to hunger and distress.

Japanese infants, as well, rarely show avoidant attachment (refer again to Figure 6.2). Rather, many are resistantly attached, but this reaction may not represent true insecurity. Japanese mothers rarely leave their babies in others' care, so the Strange Situation probably induces greater stress in them than in infants who experience frequent maternal separations (Takahashi, 1990). Also, Japanese parents view the attention seeking that is part of resistant attachment as a normal indicator of infants' efforts to satisfy dependency and security needs (Rothbaum et al., 2007). Despite such cultural variations, the secure pattern is still the most common attachment quality in all societies studied (van IJzendoorn & Sagi-Schwartz, 2008).

Factors That Affect Attachment Security

What factors might influence attachment security? Researchers have looked closely at four important influences: (1) early availability of a consistent caregiver, (2) quality of caregiving,

(3) the baby's characteristics, and (4) family context, including parents' internal working models.

Early Availability of a Consistent Caregiver. What happens when a baby does not have the opportunity to establish a close tie to a caregiver? To find out, researchers followed the development of infants in a British institution with a good caregiver–child ratio and a rich selection of books and toys. However, staff turnover was so rapid that the average child had 50 caregivers by age 4½! Many of these children became "late adoptees" who were placed in homes after age 4. Most developed deep ties with their adoptive parents, indicating that a first attachment can develop as late as 4 to 6 years of age (Hodges & Tizard, 1989; Tizard & Rees, 1975). But these children were more likely to display attachment difficulties, including an excessive desire for adult attention, "overfriendliness" to unfamiliar adults and peers, failure to check back with the parent in anxiety-arousing situations, and few friendships.

Children who spent their first year or more in deprived Eastern European orphanages—though also able to bond with their adoptive parents—show elevated rates of attachment insecurity (van den Dries et al., 2009; Smyke et al., 2010). And they, too, are at high risk for emotional and social difficulties. Whereas many are indiscriminately friendly, others are sad, anxious, and withdrawn. These symptoms typically persist and are associated with wide-ranging mental health problems in middle childhood and adolescence, including cognitive impairments, inattention and hyperactivity, depression, and either social avoidance or aggressive behavior (Kreppner et al., 2007, 2010; Rutter et al., 2007, 2010; Zeanah, 2000).

Furthermore, as early as 7 months, institutionalized children show reduced ERP brain waves in response to facial expressions of emotion and have trouble discriminating such expressions—outcomes that suggest disrupted formation of neural structures involved in "reading" emotions (Parker et al., 2005). Consistent with these findings, in adopted children with longer institutional stays, the volume of the *amygdala* (see page 192) is atypically large (Tottenham et al., 2011). The larger the amygdala, the worse adopted children perform on tasks assessing understanding of emotion and the poorer their emotional self-regulation. Overall, the evidence indicates that fully normal emotional development depends on establishing a close tie with a caregiver early in life.

Quality of Caregiving. Dozens of studies report that **sensitive caregiving**—responding promptly, consistently, and appropriately to infants and holding them tenderly and carefully—is moderately related to attachment security in diverse cultures and SES groups (Belsky & Fearon, 2008; De Wolff & van IJzendoorn, 1997; van IJzendoorn et al., 2004). In contrast, insecurely attached infants tend to have mothers who engage in less physical contact, handle them awkwardly or "routinely," and are sometimes resentful and rejecting, particularly in response to infant distress (Ainsworth et al., 1978; Isabella, 1993; McElwain & Booth-LaForce, 2006; Pederson & Moran, 1996).

This mother and baby engage in a sensitively tuned form of communication called interactional synchrony, in which they match emotional states, especially positive ones. Among Western infants, this style of communication predicts secure attachment.

VICKY KASALA PRODUCTIONS/GETTY/DIGITAL VISION

Also, in studies of Western babies, a special form of communication called **interactional synchrony** separates the experiences of secure from insecure babies. It is best described as a sensitively tuned "emotional dance," in which the caregiver responds to infant signals in a well-timed, rhythmic, appropriate fashion. In addition, both partners match emotional states, especially the positive ones (Bigelow et al., 2010; Isabella & Belsky, 1991; Nievar & Becker, 2008). Earlier we saw that sensitive face-to-face play, in which interactional synchrony occurs, also helps infants regulate emotion.

Cultures, however, vary in their view of sensitivity toward infants. Among the Gusii people of Kenya, for example, mothers rarely cuddle, hug, or interact playfully with their babies, although they are very responsive to their infants' needs. Yet most Gusii infants appear securely attached (LeVine et al., 1994). This suggests that security depends on attentive caregiving, not necessarily on moment-by-moment contingent interaction. Puerto Rican mothers, who highly value obedience and socially appropriate behavior, often physically direct and limit their babies' actions—a caregiving style linked to attachment security in Puerto Rican culture (Carlson & Harwood, 2003). Yet in many Western cultures, such physical control and restriction of exploration predict insecurity (Belsky & Fearon, 2008; Whipple, Bernier, & Mageau, 2011).

Compared with securely attached infants, avoidant babies tend to receive overstimulating, intrusive care. Their mothers might, for example, talk energetically to them while they are looking away or falling asleep. By avoiding the mother, these infants appear to be escaping from overwhelming interaction. Resistant infants often experience inconsistent care. Their mothers are unresponsive to infant signals. Yet when the baby begins to explore, these mothers interfere, shifting the infant's attention back to themselves. As a result, the baby is overly dependent as well as angry at the mother's lack of involvement (Cassidy & Berlin, 1994; Isabella & Belsky, 1991).

Highly inadequate caregiving is a powerful predictor of disruptions in attachment. Child abuse and neglect (topics we will consider in Chapter 8) are associated with all three forms of attachment insecurity. Among maltreated infants, disorganized/disoriented attachment is especially high (van IJzendoorn, Schuengel, & Bakermans-Kranenburg, 1999). Persistently depressed mothers, mothers with very low marital satisfaction, and parents suffering from a traumatic event, such as serious illness or loss of a loved one, also tend to promote the uncertain behaviors of this pattern (Campbell et al., 2004; Madigan et al., 2006; Moss et al., 2005). And some mothers of disorganized/disoriented infants engage in frightening, contradictory, and unpleasant behaviors, such as looking scared, teasing the baby, holding the baby stiffly at a distance, roughly pulling the baby by the arm, or seeking reassurance from the upset child (Abrams, Rifkin, & Hesse, 2006; Lyons-Ruth, Bronfman, & Parsons, 1999; Moran et al., 2008).

Infant Characteristics. Because attachment is the result of a *relationship* that builds between two partners, infant characteristics should affect how easily it is established. In Chapter 3 we saw that prematurity, birth complications, and newborn illness make caregiving more taxing. In families under stress, these difficulties are linked to attachment insecurity (Poehlmann & Fiese, 2001). But at-risk newborns whose parents have the time and patience to care for them fare quite well in attachment security (Brisch et al., 2005; Cox, Hopkins, & Hans, 2000).

Babies whose temperament is emotionally reactive and difficult are more likely to develop later insecure attachments (van IJzendoorn et al., 2004; Vaughn, Bost, & van IJzendoorn, 2008). Again, however, caregiving is involved. In a study extending from birth to age 2, difficult infants more often had highly anxious mothers—a combination that, by the second year, often resulted in a "disharmonious relationship" characterized by both maternal insensitivity and attachment insecurity (Symons, 2001).

Other research focusing on disorganized/disoriented attachment has uncovered gene–environment interactions (Gervai, 2009). In one investigation, mothers' experience of unresolved loss of a loved one or other trauma was associated with attachment disorganization only in infants with a chromosome-11 gene linked to deficient self-regulation (van IJzendoorn & Bakermans-Kranenburg, 2006). Babies with this genetic marker, who face special challenges in managing intense emotion, were more negatively affected by maternal adjustment problems.

If children's temperaments determined attachment security, we would expect attachment, like temperament, to be at least moderately heritable. Yet the heritability of attachment is virtually nil (Roisman & Fraley, 2008). In fact, about two-thirds of siblings establish similar attachment patterns with their parent, although the siblings often differ in temperament (Cole, 2006; Dozier et al., 2001). This suggests that most parents try to adjust their caregiving to each child's individual needs.

Why don't infant characteristics show strong relationships with attachment quality? Their influence probably depends on goodness of fit. From this perspective, *many* child attributes can lead to secure attachment as long as caregivers sensitively adjust their behavior to fit the baby's needs (Seifer & Schiller, 1995). Interventions that teach parents to interact with difficult-to-care-for infants are highly successful in enhancing both sensitive care and attachment security (Velderman et al., 2006). But when parents' capacity is strained—by their own personalities or by stressful living conditions—then infants with illnesses, disabilities, and difficult temperaments are at risk for attachment problems.

Family Circumstances.

Shortly after Timmy's birth, his parents divorced and his father moved to a distant city. Anxious and distracted, Vanessa placed 1-month-old Timmy in Ginette's child-care home and began working 50-hour weeks to make ends meet. On days Vanessa stayed late at the office, a babysitter picked Timmy up, gave him dinner, and put him to bed. Once or twice a week, Vanessa went to get Timmy from child care. As he neared his first birthday, Vanessa noticed that unlike the other children, who reached out, crawled, or ran to their parents, Timmy ignored her.

Timmy's behavior reflects a repeated finding: Job loss, a failing marriage, and financial difficulties can undermine attachment by interfering with parental sensitivity. These stressors can also affect babies' sense of security directly, by altering the emotional climate of the family (for example, exposing them to angry adult interactions) or by disrupting familiar daily routines (Finger et al., 2009; Raikes & Thompson, 2005). (See the Social Issues: Health box on pages 202–203 to find out how child care affects early emotional development.) Social support fosters attachment security by reducing parental stress and improving the quality of parent–child communication (Belsky & Fearon, 2002b; Moss et al., 2005). Ginette's sensitivity was helpful, as was the parenting advice Vanessa received from Ben, a psychologist. As Timmy turned 2, his relationship with his mother seemed warmer.

Parents' Internal Working Models.

Parents bring to the family context their own history of attachment experiences, from which they construct internal working models that they apply to the bonds they establish with their children. Monica, who recalled her mother as tense and preoccupied, expressed regret that they had not had a closer relationship. Is her image of parenthood likely to affect Grace's attachment security?

To assess parents' internal working models, researchers ask them to evaluate childhood memories of attachment experiences (Main & Goldwyn, 1998). Parents who discuss their childhoods with objectivity and balance, regardless of whether their experiences were positive or negative, tend to have securely attached children. In contrast, parents who dismiss the importance of early relationships or describe them in angry, confused ways usually have insecurely attached children and are less warm, sensitive, and encouraging of learning and mastery (Behrens, Hesse, & Main, 2007; Coyl, Newland, & Freeman, 2010; Steele, Steele, & Fonagy, 1996; van IJzendoorn, 1995).

But we must not assume any direct transfer of parents' childhood experiences to quality of attachment with their own children. Internal working models are *reconstructed memories* affected by many factors, including relationship experiences over the life course, personality, and current life satisfaction. Longitudinal research reveals that negative life events can weaken the link between an individual's own attachment security in infancy and a secure internal working model in adulthood. And insecurely attached babies who become adults with insecure internal working models often have lives that, based on self-reports in adulthood, are filled with family crises (Waters et al., 2000; Weinfield, Sroufe, & Egeland, 2000).

In sum, our early rearing experiences do not destine us to become either sensitive or insensitive parents. Rather, the way we *view* our childhoods—our ability to come to terms with negative events, to integrate new information into our working models, and to look back on our own parents in an understanding, forgiving way—is far more influential in how we rear our children than the actual history of care we received (Bretherton & Munholland, 2008).

Multiple Attachments

Babies develop attachments to a variety of familiar people—not just mothers but also fathers, grandparents, siblings, and professional caregivers. Although Bowlby (1969) believed that infants are predisposed to direct their attachment behaviors to a single special person, especially when they are distressed, his theory allowed for these multiple attachments.

Fathers.

When anxious or unhappy, most babies prefer to be comforted by their mother. But this preference typically declines over the second year. And when babies are not distressed, they approach, vocalize to, and smile equally often at both parents (Bornstein, 2006; Parke, 2002).

Fathers' sensitive caregiving and interactional synchrony with infants, like mothers', predict attachment security (Lundy, 2003; van IJzendoorn et al., 2004). But as infancy progresses, mothers and fathers in many cultures, including Australia, Canada, Germany, India, Israel, Italy, Japan, and the United States, tend to interact differently with their babies. Mothers devote more time to physical care and expressing affection, fathers to playful interaction (Freeman & Newland, 2010; Roopnarine et al., 1990).

Mothers and fathers also play differently. Mothers more often provide toys, talk to infants, and gently play conventional

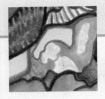

Social Issues: Health

Does Child Care in Infancy Threaten Attachment Security and Later Adjustment?

Are infants who experience daily separation from their employed parents and early placement in child care at risk for attachment insecurity and development problems? Some researchers think so, but others disagree. Let's look closely at the evidence.

Attachment Quality

Some studies suggest that babies placed in full-time child care before 12 months of age are more likely to display insecure attachment in the Strange Situation (Belsky, 2001, 2005). But the best current evidence—from the National Institute of Child Health and Development (NICHD) Study of Early Child Care, the largest longitudinal investigation to date, including more than 1,300 infants and their families—confirms that nonparental care by itself does not affect attachment quality (NICHD Early Child Care Research Network, 1997, 2001). Rather, the relationship between child care and emotional well-being depends on both family and child-care experiences.

Family Circumstances

We have seen that family conditions affect children's attachment security and later adjustment. Findings of the NICHD Study confirmed that parenting quality, assessed using a combination of maternal sensitivity and HOME scores (see page 171 in Chapter 5), exerted a more powerful impact on children's adjustment than did exposure to child care (NICHD Early Childhood Research Network, 1998; Watamura et al., 2011).

For employed parents, balancing work and caregiving can be stressful. Mothers who are fatigued and anxious because they feel overloaded by work and family pressures may respond less sensitively to their babies, thereby risking the infant's security. And as paternal involvement in caregiving has risen (see page 203), many more U.S. fathers in dual-earner families also report work–family life conflict (Galinsky, Aumann, & Bond, 2009).

Quality and Extent of Child Care

Nevertheless, poor-quality child care may contribute to a higher rate of insecure attachment. In the NICHD Study, when babies were exposed to combined home and child-care risk factors—insensitive caregiving at home along with insensitive caregiving in child care, long hours in child care, or more than one child-care arrangement—the rate of attachment insecurity increased. Overall, mother–child interaction was more favorable when children attended higher-quality child care and also spent fewer hours in child care (NICHD Early Child Care Research Network, 1997, 1999).

Furthermore, when these children reached age 3, a history of higher-quality child care predicted better social skills (NICHD Early Child Care Research Network, 2002b). However, at age 4½ to 5, children averaging more than 30 child-care hours per week displayed more behavior problems, especially defiance, disobedience, and aggression. For those who had been in child-care centers as opposed to family child-care homes, this outcome persisted through elementary school (Belsky et al., 2007; NICHD Early Child Care Research Network, 2003a, 2006).

But these findings do not necessarily mean that child care causes behavior problems. Rather, heavy exposure to substandard care, which is widespread in the United States, may promote these difficulties, especially when combined with family risk factors. A closer look at the NICHD participants during the preschool years revealed that those in both poor-quality home and child-care environments fared worst in social skills and problem behaviors, whereas those in both high-quality home and child-child care environments fared best. In between

---

games like pat-a-cake and peekaboo. In contrast, fathers—especially with their infant sons—tend to engage in highly stimulating physical play with bursts of excitement that increase as play progresses (Feldman, 2003). As long as fathers are also sensitive, this stimulating, startling play style helps babies regulate emotion in intensely arousing situations, including novel physical environments and play with peers (Cabrera et al., 2007; Hazen et al., 2010; Paquette, 2004). In a German study, fathers' sensitive, challenging play with preschoolers predicted favorable emotional and social adjustment from kindergarten to early adulthood (Grossmann et al., 2008).

Play is a vital context in which fathers build secure attachments (Newland, Coyl, & Freeman, 2008). It may be especially influential in cultures such as Japan, where long work hours prevent most fathers from sharing in infant caregiving (Hewlett, 2004). In many Western nations, however, a strict division of parental roles—mother as caregiver, father as playmate—has changed over the past several decades in response to women's workforce participation and to cultural valuing of gender equality.

LOOK AND LISTEN

Observe parents at play with infants at home or a family gathering. Describe both similarities and differences in mothers' and fathers' behaviors. Are your observations consistent with research findings? ●

A recent U.S. national survey of several thousand employed workers indicated that U.S. fathers under age 29 devote about 85 percent as much time to children as mothers do—on average, just over 4 hours per workday, nearly double the hours young

were preschoolers in high-quality child care but poor-quality homes (Watamura et al., 2011). These children benefited from the *protective influence* of high-quality child care.

Evidence from other industrialized nations confirms that full-time child care need not harm children's development. In Australia, for example, infants who spend full days in government-funded, high-quality child-care centers have a higher rate of secure attachment than infants informally cared for by relatives, friends, or babysitters. And amount of time spent in child care is unrelated to Australian children's behavior problems (Love et al., 2003).

Still, some children may be particularly stressed by long child-care hours. Many infants, toddlers, and preschoolers attending child-care centers for full days show a mild increase in saliva concentrations of cortisol across the day—a pattern that does not occur on days they spend at home. In one study, children rated as highly fearful by their caregivers experienced an especially sharp increase in cortisol levels (Watamura et al., 2003). Inhibited children may find the constant company of large numbers of peers particularly stressful.

Conclusions

Taken together, research suggests that some infants may be at risk for attachment insecurity and later adjustment problems due to inadequate child care, long hours in such care, and the joint pressures their parents experience from full-time employment and parenthood. But it is inappropriate to use these findings to justify a reduction in child-care services. When family incomes are limited or mothers who want to work are forced to stay at home, children's emotional security is not promoted.

Instead, it makes sense to increase the availability of high-quality child care and to relieve work–family-life conflict by providing parents with paid employment leave (see page 105 in Chapter 3) and opportunities for part-time work. In the NICHD study, part-time (as opposed to full-time) employment during the baby's first year was associated with greater maternal sensitivity and a higher-quality home environment, which yielded more favorable development in early childhood (Brooks-Gunn, Han, & Waldfogel, 2010).

Finally, for child care to foster attachment security, the professional caregiver's relationship with the baby is vital. When caregiver–child ratios are generous, group sizes are small, and caregivers are educated

High-quality child care, with generous caregiver–child ratios, small group sizes, and knowledgeable caregivers, can be part of a system that promotes all aspects of development, including attachment security.

about child development and child rearing, caregivers' interactions are more positive and children develop more favorably (McCartney et al., 2007; NICHD Early Child Care Research Network, 2000b, 2002a, 2006). Child care with these characteristics can become part of an ecological system that relieves parental and child stress, thereby promoting healthy attachment and development.

---

fathers reported three decades ago. Although fathers age 29 to 42 spend somewhat less time with children, their involvement has also increased substantially (see Figure 6.3). Today, nearly one-third of U.S. employed women say that their spouse or partner shares equally in or takes most responsibility for child-care tasks (Galinsky, Aumann, & Bond, 2009). Paternal availability to children is fairly similar across SES and ethnic groups, with one exception: Hispanic fathers spend more time engaged,

FIGURE 6.3 **Average amount of time per workday U.S. employed mothers and fathers reported spending with their children (age 12 and younger) in 1977 and 2008.** In national surveys of several thousand employed parents, mothers' time with children remained fairly stable from 1977 to 2008; fathers' time increased substantially. (Adapted from Galinsky, Aumann, & Bond, 2009.)

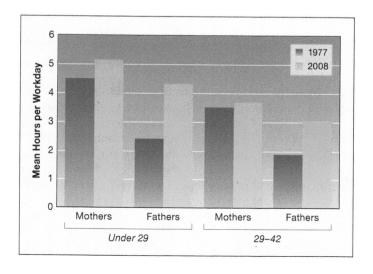

Cultural Influences

The Powerful Role of Paternal Warmth in Development

In studies of many societies and ethnic groups around the world, researchers coded paternal expressions of love and nurturance—evident in such behaviors as cuddling, hugging, comforting, playing, verbally expressing love, and praising the child's behavior. Fathers' affectionate involvement predicted later cognitive, emotional, and social competence as strongly as did mothers' warmth—and occasionally more strongly (Rohner & Veneziano, 2001; Veneziano, 2003). And in Western cultures, paternal warmth and secure attachment protected children against a wide range of difficulties, including childhood emotional and behavior problems and adolescent substance abuse and delinquency (Grant et al., 2000; Michiels et al., 2010; Nelson & Coyne, 2009; Tacon & Caldera, 2001).

Fathers who devote little time to physical caregiving express warmth through play. In a German study, fathers' play sensitivity—accepting toddlers' play initiatives, adapting play behaviors to toddlers' capacities, and responding appropriately to toddlers' expressions of emotion—predicted children's secure internal working models of attachment during middle childhood and adolescence (Grossmann et al., 2002). Through play, fathers seemed to transfer to young

children a sense of confidence about parental support, which may strengthen their capacity to master many later challenges.

What factors promote paternal warmth? Cross-cultural research reveals a consistent association between the amount of time fathers spend near infants and toddlers and their expressions of caring and affection (Rohner & Veneziano, 2001). Consider the Aka hunters and gatherers of Central Africa, where fathers spend more time in physical proximity to their babies than in any other known society. Aka fathers are within arm's reach of infants more than half the day, and they pick up, cuddle, and play with their babies at least five times as often as fathers in other hunting-and-gathering societies. Why are Aka fathers so involved? The bond between Aka husband and wife is unusually cooperative and intimate. Throughout the day, couples share hunting, food preparation, and social and leisure activities. The more time Aka parents are together, the greater the father's loving interaction with his baby (Hewlett, 1992).

In Western cultures as well, happily married fathers whose partners cooperate with them in parenting spend more time with and interact more effectively with infants. In contrast, marital dissatisfaction

In diverse cultures, fathers' warmth predicts long-term favorable cognitive, emotional, and social development.

is associated with insensitive paternal care (Brown et al., 2010; Lundy, 2002; Sevigny & Loutzenhiser, 2010). Clearly, fathers' warm relationships with their partners and their babies are closely linked. Evidence for the power of paternal affection, reported in virtually every culture and ethnic group studied, is reason to encourage and support fathers in nurturing care of young children.

---

probably because of the particularly high value that Hispanic cultures place on family involvement (Cabrera & García Coll, 2004; Parke et al., 2004).

Mothers in dual-earner families tend to engage in more playful stimulation of their babies than mothers who are at home full-time (Cox et al., 1992). But fathers who are primary caregivers retain their arousing play style (Lamb & Oppenheim, 1989). These highly involved fathers typically are less gender-stereotyped in their beliefs; have sympathetic, friendly personalities; often had fathers who were more involved in rearing them; and regard parenthood as an especially enriching experience (Cabrera et al., 2000; Levy-Shiff & Israelashvili, 1988).

Fathers' involvement with babies unfolds within a complex system of family attitudes and relationships. A warm

marital bond promotes both parents' sensitivity and involvement and children's attachment security, but it is particularly important for fathers (Brown et al., 2010; Lamb & Lewis, 2004). See the Cultural Influences box above for cross-cultural evidence documenting this conclusion—and also highlighting the powerful role of paternal warmth in children's development.

Siblings. Despite declines in family size, 80 percent of North American and European children grow up with at least one sibling (Dunn, 2004). The arrival of a new baby is a difficult experience for most preschoolers, who often become demanding, clingy, and deliberately naughty for a time. Attachment security also declines, especially for children over age 2 (old

Applying What We Know

Encouraging Affectionate Ties Between Infants and Their Preschool Siblings

Suggestion	Description
Spend extra time with the older child.	To minimize the older child's feelings of being deprived of affection and attention, set aside time to spend with her. Fathers can be especially helpful, planning special outings with the preschooler and taking over care of the baby so the mother can be with the older child.
Handle sibling misbehavior with patience.	Respond patiently to the older sibling's misbehavior and demands for attention, recognizing that these reactions are temporary. Give the preschooler opportunities to feel proud of being more grown-up than the baby. For example, encourage the older child to assist with feeding, bathing, dressing, and offering toys, and show appreciation for these efforts.
Discuss the baby's wants and needs.	By helping the older sibling understand the baby's point of view, parents can promote friendly, considerate behavior. Say, for example, "He's so little that he just can't wait to be fed," or "He's trying to reach his rattle, and he can't."
Express positive emotion toward your partner and engage in effective coparenting.	When parents mutually support each other's parenting behavior, their good communication helps the older sibling cope adaptively with jealousy and conflict.

enough to feel threatened and displaced) and for those with mothers under stress (Baydar, Greek, & Brooks-Gunn, 1997; Teti et al., 1996).

Yet resentment is only one feature of a rich emotional relationship that soon develops between siblings. Older children also show affection and concern—kissing and patting the baby and calling out, "Mom, he needs you," when the infant cries. By the end of the first year, babies usually spend much time with older siblings and are comforted by the presence of a preschool-age brother or sister during short parental absences. Throughout childhood, children continue to treat older siblings as attachment figures, turning to them for comfort in stressful situations when parents are unavailable (Seibert & Kerns, 2009).

Nevertheless, individual differences in sibling relationships emerge soon after the new baby's arrival. Certain temperamental traits—high emotional reactivity or activity level—increase the chances of sibling conflict (Brody, Stoneman, & McCoy, 1994; Dunn, 1994). And maternal warmth toward both children is related to positive sibling interaction and to preschoolers' support of a distressed younger sibling (Volling, 2001; Volling & Belsky, 1992). In contrast, maternal harshness and lack of involvement are linked to antagonistic sibling relationships (Howe, Aquan-Assee, & Bukowski, 2001).

Finally, a good marriage and effective coparenting are linked to preschool siblings' capacity to cope adaptively with jealousy and conflict (Volling, McElwain, & Miller, 2002). Perhaps good communication between parents serves as a model of effective problem solving. It may also foster a generally happy family environment, giving children less reason to feel jealous.

Refer to Applying What We Know above for ways to promote positive sibling relationships between babies and

preschoolers. Siblings offer a rich social context in which young children learn and practice a wide range of skills, including affectionate caring, conflict resolution, and control of hostile and envious feelings.

© LAURA DWIGHT PHOTOGRAPHY

The arrival of a baby brother or sister is a difficult experience for most preschoolers. Maternal warmth toward both children assures the older sibling of continuing parental love and is related to positive sibling interaction.

Attachment and Later Development

According to psychoanalytic and ethological theories, the inner feelings of affection and security that result from a healthy attachment relationship support all aspects of psychological development. Consistent with this view, an extended longitudinal study found that preschoolers who had been securely attached as babies were rated by their teachers as higher in self-esteem, social skills, and empathy than were their insecurely attached counterparts, who displayed more behavior problems. When studied again at age 11 in summer camp, children who had been secure infants continued to be more socially competent, as judged by camp counselors. And as these well-functioning school-age children became adolescents and young adults, they continued to benefit from more supportive social networks, formed more stable and gratifying romantic relationships, and attained higher levels of education (Elicker, Englund, & Sroufe, 1992; Sroufe, 2002; Sroufe et al., 2005).

For some researchers, these findings indicate that secure attachment in infancy causes improved cognitive, emotional, and social competence in later years. Yet contrary evidence exists. In other longitudinal studies, secure infants generally fared better than insecure infants, but not always (Fearon et al., 2010; McCartney et al., 2004; Schneider, Atkinson, & Tardif, 2001; Stams, Juffer, & van IJzendoorn, 2002).

What accounts for this inconsistency? Mounting evidence indicates that *continuity of caregiving* determines whether attachment security is linked to later development (Lamb et al., 1985; Thompson, 2006). Children whose parents respond sensitively not just in infancy but also in later years are likely to develop favorably. In contrast, children of parents who react insensitively or who, over a long period, are exposed to a negative family climate tend to establish lasting patterns of avoidant, resistant, or disorganized behavior and are at greater risk for developmental difficulties.

A close look at the relationship between parenting and children's adjustment supports this interpretation. Disorganized/disoriented attachment, a pattern associated with serious parental psychological problems and highly maladaptive caregiving, is strongly linked to both internalizing and externalizing difficulties in childhood (Lyons-Ruth, Easterbrooks, & Cibelli, 1997; Moss et al., 2006). And when a large sample of children were tracked from ages 1 to 3 years, those experiencing secure attachment followed by sensitive parenting scored highest in cognitive, emotional, and social outcomes. Those experiencing insecure attachment followed by parental insensitivity scored lowest, while those with mixed histories of attachment and maternal sensitivity scored in between (Belsky & Fearon, 2002a).

Although a secure attachment in infancy does not guarantee good parenting, it does launch the parent–child relationship on a positive path. An early warm, positive parent–child tie, sustained over time, predicts a more confident and complex self-concept, more advanced emotional understanding, more effective social skills, a stronger sense of moral responsibility, and higher motivation to achieve in school (Thompson, 2006, 2008).

But the effects of early attachment security are *conditional*—dependent on the quality of the baby's future relationships. Finally, as we will see again in future chapters, attachment is just one of the complex influences on children's psychological development.

ASK YOURSELF

REVIEW What factors explain stability in attachment pattern for some children and change for others? Are these factors also involved in the link between attachment in infancy and later development? Explain.

CONNECT List the diverse factors that affect the parent–infant child bond, and discuss how research confirms the role of each level of ecological systems theory in attachment security.

APPLY What attachment pattern did Timmy display when Vanessa arrived home from work, and what factors probably contributed to it?

REFLECT How would you characterize your internal working model? What factors, in addition to your relationship with your parents, might have influenced it?

Self-Development

Infancy is a rich formative period for the development of both physical and social understanding. In Chapter 5, you learned that infants develop an appreciation of the permanence of objects. In this chapter, we have seen that over the first year, infants recognize and respond appropriately to others' emotions and distinguish familiar from unfamiliar people. That both objects and people achieve an independent, stable existence for the infant implies that knowledge of the self as a separate, permanent entity is also emerging.

Self-Awareness

When Carolyn held Caitlin in front of a mirror, as early as the first few months Caitlin smiled and returned friendly behaviors to her image. At what age did she realize that the charming baby gazing and smiling back was herself?

Beginnings of Self-Awareness. At birth, infants sense that they are distinct from their surroundings. For example, newborns display a stronger rooting reflex in response to external stimulation (an adult's finger touching their cheek) than to self-stimulation (their own hand contacting their cheek) (Rochat & Hespos, 1997). Newborns' remarkable capacity for *intermodal perception* (see page 145 in Chapter 4) supports the beginnings of self-awareness (Rochat, 2003). As they feel their own touch, feel and watch their limbs move, and feel and hear themselves cry, babies experience intermodal matches that differentiate their own body from surrounding bodies and objects.

Over the first few months, infants distinguish their own visual image from other stimuli, but their self-awareness is limited—expressed only in perception and action. When shown two side-by-side video images of their kicking legs, one from their own perspective (camera behind the baby) and one from an observer's perspective (camera in front of the baby), 3-month-olds looked longer at the observer's view (Rochat, 1998). By 4 months, infants look and smile more at video images of others than at video images of themselves, indicating that they treat another person (as opposed to the self) as a social partner (Rochat & Striano, 2002).

Self-Recognition. During the second year, toddlers become consciously aware of the self's physical features. In several studies, 9- to 28-month-olds were placed in front of a mirror. Then, under the pretext of wiping the baby's face, each mother rubbed red dye on her child's nose or forehead. Younger babies typically touched the mirror as if the red mark had nothing to do with themselves. But those older than 20 months touched or rubbed their noses or foreheads, indicating awareness of their unique appearance (Bard et al., 2006; Lewis & Brooks-Gunn, 1979).

Around age 2, **self-recognition**—identification of the self as a physically unique being—is well under way. Children point to themselves in photos and refer to themselves by name or with a personal pronoun ("I" or "me") (Lewis & Ramsay, 2004). Soon children identify themselves in images with less detail and fidelity than mirrors. Around age 2½, most reach for a sticker surreptitiously placed on top of their heads when shown themselves in a live video, and around age 3 most recognize their own shadow (Cameron & Gallup, 1988; Suddendorf, Simcock, & Nielsen, 2007).

Nevertheless, toddlers make **scale errors,** attempting to do things that their body size makes impossible. For example, they will try to put on dolls' clothes, sit in a doll-sized chair, or walk through a doorway too narrow for them to pass through (Brownell, Zerwas, & Ramani, 2007; DeLoache, Uttal, & Rosengren, 2004). Possibly, toddlers lack an accurate understanding of their own body dimensions. Alternatively, they may simply be exploring the consequences of squeezing into restricted spaces, as they are far less likely to try when the risk of harming themselves is high (the too-narrow doorway is next to a ledge where they could fall) (Franchak & Adolph, 2012). Scale errors decline around age 2, but many 2½-year-olds still make them.

What experiences contribute to gains in self-awareness? During the first year, as infants act on the environment, they probably notice effects that help them sort out self, other people, and objects (Nadel, Prepin, & Okanda, 2005; Rochat, 2001). For example, batting a mobile and seeing it swing in a pattern different from the infant's own actions informs the baby about the relation between self and physical world. Smiling and vocalizing at a caregiver who smiles and vocalizes back helps clarify the relation between self and social world. The contrast between

This 20-month-old's response to her mirror image indicates that she recognizes her unique physical features and is aware of herself as a separate being, distinct from other people and objects.

these experiences helps infants sense that they are separate from external reality.

Cultural variations exist in early self-development. Urban German and Greek toddlers attain mirror self-recognition earlier than toddlers of the Nso people of Cameroon, a collectivist farming society that highly values social harmony and responsibility to others (Keller et al., 2004, 2005). Compared to their German and Greek counterparts, Nso mothers engage in less face-to-face communication and object stimulation and more body contact and physical stimulation of their babies. German and Greek practices reflect a *distal parenting style* common in cultures that emphasize independence; the Nso practice a *proximal parenting style* typical in cultures that promote interdependence. In line with these differences, Nso proximal parenting is associated with later attainment of self-recognition but earlier emergence of toddlers' compliance with adult requests (see Figure 6.4 on page 208).

Self-Awareness and Early Emotional and Social Development. Self-awareness quickly becomes a central part of children's emotional and social lives. Recall that self-conscious emotions depend on a strengthening sense of self. Self-awareness also leads to first efforts to appreciate others' perspectives. Older toddlers who have experienced sensitive

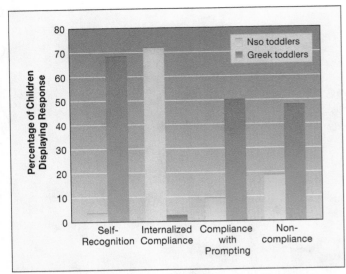

FIGURE 6.4 Self-recognition and compliance among Nso and Greek toddlers. At 10 and 20 months, toddlers were tested for mirror self-recognition and for compliance (they were told not to open a transparent container with an attractive food). Among Greek toddlers, whose culture values independence, many more had attained self-recognition. But Nso toddlers, reared in an interdependent culture, were greatly advanced in compliance (following directions without prompting), whereas Greek toddlers either needed reminders or did not comply. (Adapted from Keller et al., 2004.)

caregiving draw on their advancing cognitive, language, and social skills to express first signs of **empathy**—the ability to understand another's emotional state and *feel with* that person, or respond emotionally in a similar way. For example, they communicate concern when others are distressed and may offer what they themselves find comforting—a hug, a reassuring comment, or a favorite doll or blanket (Hoffman, 2000; Moreno, Klute, & Robinson, 2008).

At the same time, toddlers demonstrate clearer awareness of how to upset others. One 18-month-old heard her mother talking to another adult about an older sibling: "Anny is really frightened of spiders" (Dunn, 1989, p. 107). The innocent-looking toddler ran to the bedroom, returned with the toy spider, and pushed it in front of Anny's face!

Categorizing the Self

By the end of the second year, language becomes a powerful tool in self-development. Between 18 and 30 months, children develop a **categorical self** as they classify themselves and others on the basis of age ("baby," "boy," or "man"), sex ("boy" or "girl"), physical characteristics ("big," "strong"), and even goodness versus badness ("I a good girl." "Tommy mean!") and competencies ("Did it!" "I can't") (Stipek, Gralinski, & Kopp, 1990).

Toddlers use their limited understanding of these social categories to organize their own behavior. As early as 17 months, they select and play in a more involved way with toys that are stereotyped for their own gender—dolls and tea sets for girls, trucks and cars for boys. Their ability to label their own gender predicts a sharp rise in these play preferences over the next few months (Zosuls et al., 2009). Then parents encourage gender-typed behavior by responding more positively when toddlers display it (Ruble, Martin, & Berenbaum, 2006). As we will see in Chapter 8, gender typing increases dramatically in early childhood.

Self-Control

Self-awareness also contributes to effortful control, evident in toddlers' strengthening capacity to inhibit impulses, manage negative emotion, and behave in socially acceptable ways. Indeed, a firmer sense of self may underlie the increasing stability and organization of effortful control in the third year (see page 193). To behave in a self-controlled fashion, children must think of themselves as separate, autonomous beings who can direct their own actions. And they must have the representational and memory capacities to recall a caregiver's directive ("Caitlin, don't touch that light socket!") and apply it to their own behavior.

As these capacities emerge between 12 and 18 months, toddlers first become capable of **compliance**. They show clear awareness of caregivers' wishes and expectations and can obey simple requests and commands. And as every parent knows, they can also decide to do just the opposite! But for most, assertiveness and opposition occur alongside compliance with an eager, willing spirit, which suggests that the child is beginning to adopt the adult's directives as his own (Dix et al., 2007; Kochanska, Murray, & Harlan, 2000). Compliance quickly leads to toddlers' first consciencelike verbalizations—for example, correcting the self by saying "No!" before touching a delicate object or jumping on the sofa.

This toddler demonstrates compliance and the beginnings of self-control as she helps her father wash dishes. She eagerly joins in the task, suggesting that she is adopting the adult's directives as her own.

Applying **What We Know**

Helping Toddlers Develop Compliance and Self-Control

Suggestion	Rationale
Respond to the toddler with sensitivity and encouragement.	Toddlers whose parents are sensitive and supportive actively resist at times, but they are also more compliant and self-controlled.
Provide advance notice when the toddler must stop an enjoyable activity.	Toddlers find it more difficult to stop a pleasant activity that is already under way than to wait before engaging in a desired action.
Offer many prompts and reminders.	Toddlers' ability to remember and comply with rules is limited; they need continuous adult oversight and patient assistance.
Respond to self-controlled behavior with verbal and physical approval.	Praise and hugs reinforce appropriate behavior, increasing the likelihood that it will occur again.
Encourage selective and sustained attention (see Chapter 5, page 163).	Development of attention is related to self-control. Children who can shift attention from a captivating stimulus and focus on a less attractive alternative are better at controlling their impulses.
Support language development (see Chapter 5, page 179).	In the second year, children begin to use language to remind themselves of adult expectations and to delay gratification.
Gradually increase rules in a manner consistent with the toddler's developing capacities.	As cognition and language improve, toddlers can follow more rules related to safety, respect for people and property, family routines, manners, and simple chores.

Researchers often study self-control by giving children tasks that, like the situations just mentioned, require **delay of gratification**—waiting for an appropriate time and place to engage in a tempting act. Between ages 1½ and 3, children show an increasing capacity to wait before eating a treat, opening a present, or playing with a toy (Vaughn, Kopp, & Krakow, 1984). Children who are advanced in development of attention and language tend to be better at delaying gratification (Else-Quest et al., 2006). These findings help explain why girls are typically more self-controlled than boys.

Like effortful control in general, young children's capacity to delay gratification is influenced by both biologically based temperament and quality of caregiving (Kochanska & Aksan, 2006; Kochanska & Knaack, 2003). Inhibited children find it easier to wait than angry, irritable children do. But toddlers who experience parental warmth and simple (as opposed to lengthy, detailed) statements that patiently redirect their behavior are more likely to be cooperative and resist temptation (Blandon & Volling, 2008; Hakman & Sullivan, 2009). Such parenting—which encourages and models patient, nonimpulsive behavior—is particularly important for temperamentally reactive children. In one study, anger-prone 7-month-olds with gentle, responsive mothers became eagerly compliant 15-month-olds (Kochanska, Aksan, & Carlson, 2005). Angry infants with insensitive mothers, by contrast, developed into strikingly uncooperative toddlers.

As self-control improves, parents gradually increase the range of rules they expect toddlers to follow, from safety and respect for property and people to family routines, manners, and simple chores (Gralinski & Kopp, 1993). Still, toddlers' control

over their own actions depends on constant parental oversight and reminders. Several prompts ("Remember, we're going to go in just a minute") and gentle insistence were usually necessary to get Caitlin to stop playing so that she and her parents could go on an errand. Applying What We Know above summarizes ways to help toddlers develop compliance and self-control.

As the second year of life drew to a close, Carolyn, Monica, and Vanessa were delighted at their children's readiness to learn the rules of social life. As we will see in Chapter 8, advances in cognition and language, along with parental warmth and reasonable demands for maturity, lead preschoolers to make tremendous strides in this area.

ASK YOURSELF

REVIEW What competencies are necessary for the emergence of compliance and self-control?

CONNECT What type of early parenting fosters the development of emotional self-regulation, secure attachment, and self-control? Why, in each instance, is it effective?

APPLY Len, a caregiver of 1- and 2-year-olds, wonders whether toddlers recognize themselves. List signs of self-recognition in the second year that Len can observe.

REFLECT Do you think that "the terrible twos," a commonly used expression to characterize toddler behavior, is an apt description? Explain.

SUMMARY

Erikson's Theory of Infant and Toddler Personality (p. 184)

According to Erikson's psychosocial theory, how do infants and toddlers resolve the psychological conflicts of the first two years?

- Warm, responsive caregiving leads infants to resolve the psychological conflict of **basic trust versus mistrust** on the positive side. During toddlerhood, **autonomy versus shame and doubt** is resolved favorably when parents provide appropriate guidance and reasonable choices. If children emerge from the first few years without sufficient trust and autonomy, the seeds are sown for adjustment problems.

Emotional Development (p. 185)

Describe the development of basic emotions over the first year.

- During the first half-year, **basic emotions** gradually become clear, well-organized signals. The **social smile** appears between 6 and 10 weeks, laughter around 3 to 4 months. Happiness strengthens the parent–child bond and both reflects and supports physical and cognitive mastery.

- Anger and fear, especially in the form of **stranger anxiety**, increase in the second half of the first year as infants' cognitive and motor capacities improve. Newly mobile babies use the familiar caregiver as a **secure base** from which to explore.

Summarize changes during the first two years in understanding others' emotions, expression of self-conscious emotions, and emotional self-regulation.

- The ability to understand others' emotional expressions improves over the first year. At 8 to 10 months, infants engage in **social referencing,** actively seeking emotional

information from caregivers in uncertain situations. By the middle of the second year, toddlers appreciate that others' emotional reactions may differ from their own.

- During toddlerhood, self-awareness and adult instruction provide the foundation for **self-conscious emotions,** such as guilt, shame, embarrassment, envy, and pride. **Emotional self-regulation** emerges as the prefrontal cortex functions more effectively and as caregivers build on the infants' increasing tolerance for stimulation. When caregivers are emotionally sympathetic but set limits, children develop more effective anger-regulation strategies in the preschool years.

Temperament and Development (p. 190)

What is temperament, and how is it measured?

- **Temperament** refers to early-appearing, stable individual differences in reactivity and self-regulation. The New York Longitudinal Study identified three patterns: the **easy child,** the **difficult child,** and the **slow-to-warm-up child.** Mary Rothbart's model of temperament includes **effortful control,** the ability to regulate one's reactivity.

- Temperament is assessed through parental reports, behavior ratings by others familiar with the child, and laboratory observations. Most neurobiological research has focused on distinguishing **inhibited,** or **shy, children** from **uninhibited,** or **sociable, children.**

What roles do heredity and environment play in the stability of temperament?

- Temperament shows only low to moderate stability. Gene–environment correlation influences the experiences to which children are exposed, and experience modifies temperamental traits. Ethnic and gender differences may have a genetic foundation but are supported by cultural beliefs and practices.

- According to the **goodness-of-fit model,** parenting practices that fit well with the child's temperament help children achieve more adaptive functioning. Temperamentally difficult children are especially responsive to both positive and negative parenting.

Development of Attachment (p. 195)

Describe the development of attachment during the first two years.

- **Ethological theory,** the most widely accepted perspective on **attachment,** recognizes the infant's emotional tie to the caregiver as an evolved response that promotes survival. In early infancy, a set of built-in behaviors encourages the parent to remain close to the baby.

- Around 6 to 8 months, **separation anxiety** and use of the caregiver as a secure base indicate that a true attachment bond has formed. As representation and language develop, separation protest declines. From early caregiving experiences, children construct an **internal working model** that guides future close relationships.

How do researchers measure attachment security, what factors affect it, and what are its implications for later development?

- Using the **Strange Situation,** a laboratory technique for assessing the quality of attachment between 1 and 2 years, researchers have identified four attachment patterns: **secure, avoidant, resistant,** and **disorganized/ disoriented.** The **Attachment Q-Sort,** a home observation method suitable for 1- to 4-year-olds, yields a score ranging from high to low in security.

- Securely attached babies more often maintain their attachment pattern than insecure babies, although the disorganized/disoriented pattern is highly stable. Cultural conditions must be considered in interpreting attachment patterns.

- Attachment quality is influenced by early availability of a consistent caregiver, quality of caregiving, the fit between the baby's temperament and parenting practices, and family circumstances. **Sensitive caregiving** is moderately related to attachment security. In Western cultures, **interactional synchrony** characterizes the experiences of securely attached babies.

- Continuity of caregiving is the crucial factor determining whether attachment security is linked to later development. If caregiving improves, children can recover from an insecure attachment history.

Describe infants' capacity for multiple attachments.

- Infants develop strong affectionate ties to fathers, who tend to engage in more exciting, physical play with babies than mothers do. Early in the first year, infants begin to build rich emotional relationships with siblings that mix affection and caring with rivalry and resentment. Individual differences in the quality of sibling relationships are influenced by temperament and parenting.

Self-Development (p. 206)

Describe the development of self-awareness in infancy and toddlerhood, along with the emotional and social capacities it supports.

- At birth, infants sense that they are physically distinct from their surroundings, an awareness that is promoted by their capacity for intermodal perception. Around age 2, **self-recognition**—identification of the self as a physically unique being—is well under way. However, toddlers make **scale errors,** attempting to do things that their body size makes impossible.

- Self-awareness is associated with the beginnings of **empathy,** the ability to feel with another person. As language strengthens and toddlers compare themselves to others, they develop a **categorical self** based on age, sex, physical characteristics, goodness versus badness, and competencies.

- Self-awareness provides the foundation for the emergence of **compliance** between 12 and 18 months and gains in **delay of gratification** between 1½ and 3 years. Children who are advanced in development of attention and language and who have warm, encouraging parents tend to be more self-controlled.

Important Terms and Concepts

attachment (p. 195)
Attachment Q-Sort (p. 198)
autonomy versus shame and doubt (p. 184)
avoidant attachment (p. 197)
basic emotions (p. 185)
basic trust versus mistrust (p. 184)
categorical self (p. 208)
compliance (p. 208)
delay of gratification (p. 209)
difficult child (p. 190)
disorganized/disoriented attachment (p. 198)
easy child (p. 190)

effortful control (p. 191)
emotional self-regulation (p. 189)
empathy (p. 208)
ethological theory of attachment (p. 196)
goodness-of-fit model (p. 194)
inhibited, or shy, child (p. 191)
interactional synchrony (p. 200)
internal working model (p. 197)
resistant attachment (p. 198)
scale errors (p. 207)
secure attachment (p. 197)
secure base (p. 187)

self-conscious emotions (p. 188)
self-recognition (p. 207)
sensitive caregiving (p. 199)
separation anxiety (p. 196)
slow-to-warm-up child (p. 190)
social referencing (p. 188)
social smile (p. 185)
stranger anxiety (p. 186)
Strange Situation (p. 197)
temperament (p. 190)
uninhibited, or sociable, child (p. 191)

milestones

Development in Infancy and Toddlerhood

Birth–6 months

PHYSICAL

- Height and weight increase rapidly. (120)
- Newborn reflexes decline. (107–108)
- Distinguishes basic tastes and odors; shows preference for sweet-tasting foods. (112)
- Responses can be classically and operantly conditioned. (133–134)
- Habituates to unchanging stimuli; recovers to novel stimuli. (134–135)
- Sleep is increasingly organized into a night–day schedule. (128)
- Holds head up, rolls over, and grasps objects. (137, 139)
- Perceives auditory and visual stimuli as organized patterns. (140, 142, 144)
- Shows sensitivity to motion, then binocular, and finally pictorial depth cues. (142)
- Recognizes and prefers human facial pattern; recognizes features of mother's face. (145)
- Masters a wide range of intermodal (visual, auditory, and tactile) relationships. (146)

COGNITIVE

- Engages in immediate and deferred imitation of adults' facial expressions. (135–136, 156)
- Repeats chance behaviors that lead to pleasurable and interesting results. (153–154)

- Has some awareness of many physical properties (including object permanence) and basic numerical knowledge. (155, 160)
- Recognition memory for visual events improves. (163)
- Attention becomes more efficient and flexible. (163)
- Forms categories based on objects' similar physical properties. (165–166)

LANGUAGE

- Coos and, by end of this period, babbles. (176)
- Begins to establish joint attention with caregiver, who labels objects and events. (176)

EMOTIONAL/SOCIAL

- Social smile and laughter emerge. (185)
- Matches feeling tone of caregiver in face-to-face communication; later, expects matched responses. (188)

- Emotional expressions become well-organized and meaningfully related to environmental events. (185)

- Regulates emotion by shifting attention and self-soothing. (189)
- Awareness of self as physically distinct from surroundings increases. (206–207)

7–12 months

PHYSICAL

- Approaches adultlike sleep–wake schedule. (128)
- Sits alone, crawls, and walks. (137)

- Reaching and grasping improve in flexibility and accuracy; shows refined pincer grasp. (140)
- Intermodal perception continues to improve. (146)

COGNITIVE

- Engages in intentional, or goal-directed, behavior. (154)
- Finds object hidden in an initial location. (154)
- Recall memory improves, as indicated by gains in deferred imitation of adults' actions with objects. (156–157, 164)
- Solves simple problems by analogy to a previous problem. (157)
- Categorizes objects on the basis of subtle sets of features, even when the perceptual contrast between categories is minimal. (165)

Note: Numbers in parentheses indicate the page or pages on which each milestone is discussed.

LANGUAGE

- Babbling expands to include many sounds of spoken languages and patterns of the child's language community. (176)
- Joint attention with caregiver becomes more accurate. (176)
- Takes turns in games, such as pat-a-cake and peekaboo. (176)
- Comprehends some word meanings. (176)
- Uses preverbal gestures (showing, pointing) to influence others' behavior. (176)

- Around end of this period, understands displaced reference of words and says first words. (157, 176)

EMOTIONAL/SOCIAL

- Smiling and laughter increase in frequency and expressiveness. (185–186)
- Anger and fear increase in frequency and intensity. (185–186)
- Stranger anxiety and separation anxiety appear. (186, 196)
- Uses caregiver as a secure base for exploration. (187–188)
- Shows "clear-cut" attachment to familiar caregivers. (196)
- Increasingly detects the meaning of others' emotional expressions and engages in social referencing. (188)
- Regulates emotion by approaching and retreating from stimulation. (189)

13–18 months

PHYSICAL

- Height and weight gain are rapid, but not as great as in first year. (120)
- Walking is better coordinated. (138)
- Manipulates small objects with improved coordination. (140)

COGNITIVE

- Explores the properties of objects by acting on them in novel ways. (154)
- Searches in several locations for a hidden object. (154)
- Engages in deferred imitation of adults' actions with objects over longer delays and across a change in context—for example, from child care to home. (156)
- Sustained attention improves. (163)
- Recall memory improves further. (164)
- Sorts objects into categories. (166)
- Realizes that pictures can symbolize real objects. (158)

LANGUAGE

- Steadily adds to vocabulary. (175, 177)
- By end of this period, produces 50 words. (175)

EMOTIONAL/SOCIAL

- Joins in play with familiar adults and siblings. (201–202, 205)

- Realizes that others' emotional reactions may differ from one's own. (188)
- Complies with simple directives. (208)

19–24 months

PHYSICAL

- Jumps, walks on tiptoe, and runs. (137)
- Manipulates small objects with good coordination. (140)

COGNITIVE

- Solves simple problems suddenly, through representation. (154)
- Finds a hidden object that has been moved while out of sight. (154)
- Engages in make-believe play, using simple actions experienced in everyday life. (154, 168)

- Engages in deferred imitation of actions an adult tries to produce, even if not fully realized. (157)
- Categorizes objects conceptually, on the basis of common function or behavior. (166)

LANGUAGE

- Produces 200 to 250 words. (175)
- Combines two words. (177)

EMOTIONAL/SOCIAL

- Self-conscious emotions (shame, embarrassment, guilt, envy, and pride) emerge. (188–189)
- Acquires a vocabulary for talking about feelings. (189)
- Begins to use language to assist with emotional self-regulation. (189–190)
- Begins to tolerate caregiver's absences more easily; separation anxiety declines. (197)
- Recognizes image of self and, by end of this period, uses own name or personal pronoun to refer to self. (207)
- Less often makes scale errors. (207)
- Shows signs of empathy. (207–208)
- Categorizes self and others on the basis of age, sex, physical characteristics, and goodness and badness. (208)
- Shows gender-stereotyped toy preferences. (208)
- Self-control, as indicated by delay of gratification, emerges.

© LAURA DWIGHT PHOTOGRAPHY

Rich opportunities for playful
exploration and peer collaboration
contribute vitally to preschoolers'
rapidly advancing cognitive and
language skills.

Physical and Cognitive Development in Early Childhood

For more than a decade, my fourth-floor office window overlooked the preschool and kindergarten play yard of our university laboratory school. On mild fall and spring mornings, the doors of the classrooms swung open, and sand table, easels, and large blocks spilled out into a small courtyard. Alongside the building was a grassy area with jungle gyms, swings, a playhouse, and a flower garden planted by the children. Beyond it lay a circular path lined with tricycles and wagons. Each day, the setting was alive with activity.

The years from 2 to 6 are often called "the play years," since play blossoms during this time and supports every aspect of development. Our discussion opens with the physical attainments of early childhood—growth in body size and improvements in motor coordination. We look at genetic and environmental factors that support these changes and at their intimate connection with other domains of development.

© ELLEN B. SENISI PHOTOGRAPHY

Then we explore early childhood cognition, beginning with Piaget's preoperational stage. Recent research, along with Vygotsky's sociocultural theory and information processing, extends our understanding of preschoolers' cognitive competencies. Next, we address factors that contribute to early childhood mental development—the home environment, the quality of preschool and child care, and the many hours young children spend watching television and using computers. We conclude with the dramatic expansion of language in early childhood. ●

chapter outline

PHYSICAL DEVELOPMENT

A Changing Body and Brain

Skeletal Growth • Brain Development

Influences on Physical Growth and Health

Heredity and Hormones • Nutrition • Infectious Disease • Childhood Injuries

Motor Development

Gross-Motor Development • Fine-Motor Development • Individual Differences in Motor Skills

COGNITIVE DEVELOPMENT

Piaget's Theory: The Preoperational Stage

Advances in Mental Representation • Make-Believe Play • Symbol–Real-World Relations • Limitations of Preoperational Thought • Follow-Up Research on Preoperational Thought • Evaluation of the Preoperational Stage • Piaget and Education

■ **SOCIAL ISSUES: EDUCATION** Children's Questions: Catalyst for Cognitive Development

Vygotsky's Sociocultural Theory

Private Speech • Social Origins of Early Childhood Cognition • Vygotsky and Education • Evaluation of Vygotsky's Theory

■ **CULTURAL INFLUENCES** Children in Village and Tribal Cultures Observe and Participate in Adult Work

Information Processing

Attention • Memory • The Young Child's Theory of Mind • Early Childhood Literacy • Early Childhood Mathematical Reasoning

■ **BIOLOGY AND ENVIRONMENT** "Mindblindness" and Autism

Individual Differences in Mental Development

Home Environment and Mental Development • Preschool, Kindergarten, and Child Care • Educational Media

Language Development

Vocabulary • Grammar • Conversation • Supporting Language Development in Early Childhood

PHYSICAL DEVELOPMENT

A Changing Body and Brain

In early childhood, body growth tapers off from the rapid rate of the first two years. On average, children add 2 to 3 inches in height and about 5 pounds in weight each year. Boys continue to be slightly larger than girls. As "baby fat" drops off further, children gradually become thinner, although girls retain somewhat more body fat than boys, who are slightly more muscular. As Figure 7.1 shows, by age 5 the top-heavy, bowlegged, potbellied toddler has become a more streamlined, flat-tummied, longer-legged child with body proportions similar to those of adults. Consequently, posture and balance improve—changes that support gains in motor coordination.

Individual differences in body size are even more apparent during early childhood than in infancy and toddlerhood. Speeding around the bike path in the play yard, 5-year-old Darryl—at 48 inches tall and 55 pounds—towered over his kindergarten classmates. (The average North American 5-year-old boy is 43 inches tall and weighs 42 pounds.) Priti, an Asian-Indian child, was unusually small because of genetic factors linked to her cultural ancestry. Hal, a Caucasian child from a poverty-stricken home, was well below average for reasons we will discuss shortly.

PHOTOS OF CHRIS © BOB DAEMMRICH PHOTOGRAPHY. PHOTOS OF MARIEL © JIM WEST PHOTOGRAPHY

Chris at 3 years

Chris at 3½ years

Chris at 4½ years

Chris at 5 years

Mariel at 2½ years

Mariel at 4 years

Mariel at 4½ years

Mariel at 5 years

FIGURE 7.1 Body growth during early childhood. During the preschool years, children grow more slowly than in infancy and toddlerhood. Chris and Mariel's bodies became more streamlined, flat-tummied, and longer-legged. Boys continue to be slightly taller, heavier, and more muscular than girls. But generally, the two sexes are similar in body proportions and physical capacities.

Skeletal Growth

The skeletal changes of infancy continue throughout early childhood. Between ages 2 and 6, approximately 45 new *epiphyses,* or growth centers in which cartilage hardens into bone, emerge in various parts of the skeleton. X-rays of these growth centers enable doctors to estimate children's *skeletal age,* or progress toward physical maturity (see page 121 in Chapter 4)—information helpful in diagnosing growth disorders.

By the end of the preschool years, children start to lose their primary, or "baby," teeth. Genetic factors heavily influence the age at which they do so. For example, girls, who are ahead of boys in physical development, lose teeth earlier. Environmental influences also matter: Prolonged malnutrition delays the appearance of permanent teeth, whereas overweight and obesity accelerate it (Hilgers et al., 2006).

Diseased baby teeth can affect the health of permanent teeth, so preventing decay in primary teeth is essential—by brushing consistently, avoiding sugary foods, drinking fluoridated water, and getting topical fluoride treatments and sealants (plastic coatings that protect tooth surfaces). Another factor is exposure to tobacco smoke, which suppresses children's immune system, including the ability to fight bacteria responsible for tooth decay. Young children in homes with regular smokers are at increased risk for decayed teeth (Hanioka et al., 2011).

Unfortunately, an estimated 28 percent of U.S. preschoolers have tooth decay, a figure that rises to 50 percent in middle childhood and 60 percent by age 18. Causes include poor diet and inadequate health care—factors that are more likely to affect low-SES children. About 30 percent of U.S. children living in poverty have untreated dental caries (National Institutes of Health, 2011).

Brain Development

Between ages 2 and 6, the brain increases from 70 percent of its adult weight to 90 percent. At the same time, preschoolers improve in a wide variety of skills—physical coordination, perception, attention, memory, language, logical thinking, and imagination.

By age 4, many parts of the cerebral cortex have overproduced synapses. In some regions, such as the prefrontal cortex, the number of synapses is nearly double the adult value. Together, synaptic growth and myelination of neural fibers result in a high energy need. In fact, fMRI evidence reveals that energy metabolism in the cerebral cortex reaches a peak around this age (Huttenlocher, 2002; Nelson, Thomas, & de Haan, 2006). *Synaptic pruning* follows: Neurons that are seldom stimulated lose their connective fibers, and the number of synapses gradually declines. By age 8 to 10, energy consumption of most cortical regions diminishes to near-adult levels (Nelson, 2002). And cognitive capacities increasingly localize in distinct neural systems, reflecting a developmental shift toward a more fine-tuned, efficient neural organization (Tsujimoto, 2008).

EEG, NIRS, and fMRI measures of neural activity indicate especially rapid growth from early to middle childhood

© LAURA DWIGHT PHOTOGRAPHY

A 5-year-old illustrates gains in executive function, supported by rapid growth of the prefrontal cortex, as she engages in an activity that challenges her capacity to attend, remember, and plan.

in areas of the prefrontal cortex devoted to various aspects of executive function. These include inhibition of impulses, attention, memory, and planning and organizing behavior—capacities that advance markedly over the preschool years (Bunge & Wright, 2007; Durston & Casey, 2006). Furthermore, for most children, the left cerebral hemisphere is especially active between 3 and 6 years and then levels off. In contrast, activity in the right hemisphere increases steadily throughout early and middle childhood (Thatcher, Walker, & Giudice, 1987; Thompson et al., 2000). These findings fit nicely with what we know about several aspects of cognitive development. Language skills (typically housed in the left hemisphere) increase at an astonishing pace in early childhood, and they support children's improved executive function. In contrast, spatial skills (usually located in the right hemisphere), such as giving directions, drawing pictures, and recognizing geometric shapes, develop gradually over childhood and adolescence.

Differences in rate of development between the two hemispheres suggest that they are continuing to *lateralize* (specialize in cognitive functions). Let's take a closer look at brain lateralization in early childhood by focusing on handedness.

Handedness. Research on handedness, along with other evidence covered in Chapter 4, supports the joint contribution of nature and nurture to brain lateralization. By age 6 months, infants typically display a smoother, more efficient movement when reaching with their right than their left arm. This difference, believed to be biologically based, may contribute to the right-handed bias of most children by the end of the first year (Hinojosa, Sheu, & Michael, 2003; Rönnqvist & Domellöf, 2006). Gradually, handedness extends to additional skills.

Handedness reflects the greater capacity of one side of the brain—the individual's **dominant cerebral hemisphere**—to carry out skilled motor action. Other important abilities are generally located on the dominant side as well. For right-handed people—in Western nations, 90 percent of the population—language is housed in the left hemisphere with hand control. For the left-handed 10 percent, language is occasionally located in the right hemisphere or, more often, shared between the hemispheres (Szaflarski et al., 2012). This indicates that the brains of left-handers tend to be less strongly lateralized than those of right-handers.

Left-handed parents show only a weak tendency to have left-handed children (Vuoksimaa et al., 2009). One genetic theory proposes that most children inherit a gene that *biases* them for right-handedness and a left-dominant cerebral hemisphere. But that bias is not strong enough to overcome experiences that might sway children toward a left-hand preference (Annett, 2002). Even prenatal events may profoundly affect handedness. Both identical and fraternal twins are more likely than ordinary siblings to differ in hand preference, probably because twins usually lie in opposite orientations in the uterus (Derom et al., 1996). The orientation of most singleton fetuses—facing toward the left—is believed to promote greater control over movements on the body's right side (Previc, 1991).

Handedness also involves practice. It is strongest for complex skills requiring extensive training, such as eating with utensils, writing, and engaging in athletic activities. And wide cultural differences exist. For example, in tribal and village cultures, the rate of left-handedness is relatively high. But in a study of one such society in New Guinea, individuals who had attended school in childhood were far more likely to be extremely right-handed—findings that highlight the role of experience (Geuze et al., 2012).

Although rates of left-handedness are elevated among people with mental retardation and mental illness, atypical brain lateralization is probably not responsible for these individuals' problems. Rather, early damage to the left hemisphere may have caused their disabilities while also leading to a shift in handedness. In support of this idea, left-handedness is associated with prenatal and birth difficulties that can result in brain damage, including maternal stress, prolonged labor, prematurity, Rh incompatibility, and breech delivery (Kurganskaya, 2011; Rodriguez & Waldenström, 2008).

Most left-handers, however, have no developmental problems. In fact, left- and mixed-handed youngsters are slightly advantaged in speed and flexibility of thinking, and they are more likely than their right-handed agemates to develop outstanding verbal and mathematical talents (Flannery & Liederman, 1995; Gunstad et al., 2007). More even distribution of cognitive functions across both brain hemispheres may be responsible.

Other Advances in Brain Development. Besides the cerebral cortex, several other areas of the brain make strides during early childhood (see Figure 7.2). All of these changes involve establishing links between parts of the brain, increasing the coordinated functioning of the central nervous system.

At the rear and base of the brain is the **cerebellum,** a structure that aids in balance and control of body movement. Fibers linking the cerebellum to the cerebral cortex grow and myelinate from birth through the preschool years, contributing to dramatic gains in motor coordination: By the end of the preschool years, children can play hopscotch, throw and catch a

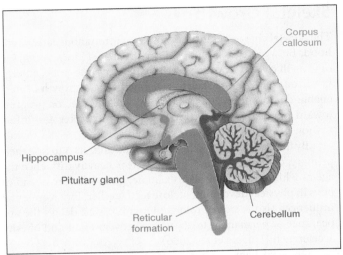

FIGURE 7.2 Cross-section of the human brain, showing the location of the cerebellum, the reticular formation, the hippocampus, and the corpus callosum. These structures undergo considerable development during early childhood. Also shown is the pituitary gland, which secretes hormones that control body growth (see page 219).

ball with well-coordinated movements, and print letters of the alphabet. Connections between the cerebellum and cerebral cortex also support thinking (Diamond, 2000): Children with damage to the cerebellum usually display both motor and cognitive deficits, including problems with memory, planning, and language (Noterdaeme et al., 2002; Riva & Giorgi, 2000).

The **reticular formation,** a structure in the brain stem that maintains alertness and consciousness, generates synapses and myelinates throughout childhood and into adolescence. Neurons in the reticular formation send out fibers to other brain regions. Many go to the prefrontal cortex, contributing to improvements in sustained, controlled attention.

An inner-brain structure called the **hippocampus,** which plays a vital role in memory and in images of space that help us find our way, undergoes rapid synapse formation and myelination in the second half of the first year, when recall memory and independent movement emerge. Over the preschool and elementary school years, the hippocampus and surrounding areas of the cerebral cortex continue to develop swiftly, establishing connections with one another and with the prefrontal cortex (Nelson, Thomas, & de Haan, 2006). These changes support the dramatic gains in memory and spatial understanding of early and middle childhood.

The **corpus callosum** is a large bundle of fibers connecting the two cerebral hemispheres. Production of synapses and myelination of the corpus callosum peak between 3 and 6 years, then continue more slowly through adolescence (Thompson et al., 2000). The corpus callosum supports smooth coordination of movements on both sides of the body and integration of many aspects of thinking, including perception, attention, memory, language, and problem solving. The more complex the task, the more essential is communication between the hemispheres.

Growth and myelination of fibers linking the cerebellum to the cerebral cortex contribute to improved motor coordination and thinking, enabling this child to master a game that requires him to play hopscotch while also throwing a ball.

ASK YOURSELF

REVIEW What aspects of brain development underlie the tremendous gains in language, thinking, and motor control of early childhood?

CONNECT What stand on the nature–nurture issue do findings on development of handedness support? Explain, using research findings.

APPLY Dental checkups reveal a high incidence of untreated tooth decay in a U.S. preschool program serving low-income children. Using findings presented in this and previous chapters, list possible contributing factors.

REFLECT How early, and to what extent, did you experience tooth decay in childhood? What factors might have been responsible?

 ## Influences on Physical Growth and Health

As we consider factors affecting growth and health in early childhood, you will encounter some familiar themes. Heredity remains important, but environmental factors—good nutrition, relative freedom from disease, and physical safety—are also essential.

Heredity and Hormones

The impact of heredity on physical growth is evident throughout childhood. Children's physical size and rate of growth are related to those of their parents (Bogin, 2001). Genes influence growth by controlling the body's production of hormones. The **pituitary gland,** located at the base of the brain, plays a critical role by releasing two hormones that induce growth.

The first, **growth hormone (GH),** is necessary for development of all body tissues except the central nervous system and the genitals. Children who lack GH reach an average mature height of only 4 to 4½ feet. When treated early with injections of GH, such children show catch-up growth and then grow at a normal rate, becoming much taller than they would have without treatment (Bright, Mendoza, & Rosenfeld, 2009).

A second pituitary hormone, **thyroid-stimulating hormone (TSH),** prompts the thyroid gland in the neck to release *thyroxine,* which is necessary for brain development and for GH to have its full impact on body size. Infants born with a deficiency of thyroxine must receive it at once, or they will be mentally retarded. Once the most rapid period of brain development is complete, thyroxine deficiency no longer affects the central nervous system but still causes children to grow more slowly than average. With prompt treatment, however, such children catch up in body growth and eventually reach normal size (Salerno et al., 2001).

Nutrition

With the transition to early childhood, many children become unpredictable, picky eaters. One father I know wistfully recalled how his son, as a toddler, eagerly sampled Chinese food: "Now, at age 3, the only thing he'll try is the ice cream!"

Preschoolers' appetites decline because their growth has slowed. Their wariness of new foods is also adaptive. If they stick to familiar foods, they are less likely to swallow dangerous substances when adults are not around to protect them (Birch & Fisher, 1995). Parents need not worry about variations in amount eaten from meal to meal. Preschoolers compensate for eating little at one meal by eating more at a later one (Hursti, 1999).

Though they eat less, preschoolers require a high-quality diet, including the same foods adults need, but in smaller amounts. Fats, oils, and salt should be kept to a minimum because of their link to high blood pressure and heart disease in adulthood. Foods high in sugar should be eaten only in small amounts to prevent tooth decay and protect against overweight and obesity—a topic we will take up in Chapter 9.

Children tend to imitate the food choices of people they admire, both adults and peers. For example, in Mexico, where children often see family members enjoying peppery foods, preschoolers enthusiastically eat chili peppers, whereas most U.S. children reject them (Birch, Zimmerman, & Hind, 1980). Repeated, unpressured exposure to a new food also increases acceptance (Fuller et al., 2005). For example, serving broccoli or tofu increases children's liking for these healthy foods. In contrast, offering sweet fruit or soft drinks promotes "milk avoidance" (Black et al., 2002).

As this child's grandmother shows him how to eat with chopsticks, he also acquires a taste for foods commonly served in his culture.

Although children's healthy eating depends on a wholesome food environment, too much parental control limits children's opportunities to develop self-control. When parents offer bribes ("Finish your vegetables, and you can have an extra cookie") children tend to like the healthy food less and the treat more (Birch, Fisher, & Davison, 2003).

LOOK AND LISTEN

Arrange to join a family with at least one preschooler for a meal, and closely observe parental mealtime practices. Are they likely to promote healthy eating habits? Explain. ●

Finally, as indicated in earlier chapters, many children in the United States and in developing countries lack access to sufficient high-quality food to support healthy development. Five-year-old Hal rode a bus from a poor neighborhood to our laboratory preschool. His mother's welfare check barely covered her rent, let alone food. Hal's diet was deficient in protein and in essential vitamins and minerals—iron (to prevent anemia and support central nervous system processes), calcium (to support development of bones and teeth), vitamin A (to help maintain eyes, skin, and a variety of internal organs), and vitamin C (to facilitate iron absorption and wound healing). These are the most common deficiencies of the preschool years (Ganji, Hampl, & Betts, 2003).

Hal was small for his age, pale, inattentive, and unruly at preschool. By the school years, low-SES U.S. children are, on average, ½ to 1 inch shorter than their economically advantaged counterparts (Cecil et al., 2005; Yip, Scanlon, & Trowbridge, 1993). And throughout childhood and adolescence, a nutritionally deficient diet is associated with attention and memory difficulties, lower intelligence and achievement test scores, and behavior problems—especially hyperactivity and aggression—

even after family factors that might account for these relationships are controlled (Liu et al., 2004; Lukowski et al., 2010; Slack & Yoo, 2005).

Infectious Disease

One day, I noticed that Hal had been absent from the play yard for several weeks, so I asked Leslie, his preschool teacher, what was wrong. "Hal's been hospitalized with the measles," she explained. "He's had difficulty recovering—lost weight when there wasn't much to lose in the first place." In well-nourished children, ordinary childhood illnesses have no effect on physical growth. But when children are undernourished, disease interacts with malnutrition in a vicious spiral, with potentially severe consequences.

Infectious Disease and Malnutrition. Hal's reaction to the measles is commonplace in developing nations, where a large proportion of the population lives in poverty and many children do not receive routine immunizations. Illnesses such as measles and chicken pox, which typically do not appear until after age 3 in industrialized nations, occur much earlier. Poor diet depresses the body's immune system, making children far more susceptible to disease. Of the 7.5 million annual deaths of children under age 5 worldwide, 98 percent are in developing countries and 65 percent are due to infectious diseases (World Health Organization, 2012a).

Disease, in turn, is a major contributor to malnutrition, hindering both physical growth and cognitive development. Illness reduces appetite and limits the body's ability to absorb foods, especially in children with intestinal infections. In developing countries, widespread diarrhea, resulting from unsafe water and contaminated foods, leads to growth stunting and nearly 1 million childhood deaths each year (World Health Organization, 2012a). Studies carried out in the slums and shantytowns of Brazil and Peru reveal that the more persistent diarrhea is in early childhood, the shorter children are in height and the lower they score on mental tests during the school years (Checkley et al., 2003; Niehaus et al., 2002).

Most developmental impairments and deaths due to diarrhea can be prevented with nearly cost-free *oral rehydration therapy (ORT),* in which sick children are given a solution of glucose, salt, and water that quickly replaces fluids the body loses. Since 1990, public health workers have taught nearly half the families in the developing world how to administer ORT. Also, supplements of zinc (essential for immune system functioning), which cost only 30 cents for a month's supply, substantially reduce the incidence of severe diarrhea (Aggarwal, Sentz, & Miller, 2007).

Immunization. In industrialized nations, childhood diseases have declined dramatically during the past half-century, largely as a result of widespread immunization of infants and young children. Hal got the measles because, unlike his classmates from more economically advantaged homes, he did not receive a full program of immunizations.

About 30 percent of U.S. preschoolers lack essential immunizations. The rate rises to 32 percent for poverty-stricken children, many of whom do not receive full protection until age 5 or 6, when it is required for school entry (U.S. Department of Health and Human Services, 2010e). In contrast, fewer than 10 percent of preschoolers lack immunizations in Denmark and Norway, and fewer than 7 percent in Canada, the Netherlands, Sweden, and the United Kingdom (World Health Organization, 2010).

Why does the United States lag behind these countries in immunization? As noted in earlier chapters, many U.S. children do not have access to the health care they need. In 1994, all medically uninsured children in the United States were guaranteed free immunizations, a program that has led to gains in immunization rates.

Inability to pay for vaccines is only one cause of inadequate immunization. Parents with stressful daily lives or without health benefits of their own often fail to schedule vaccination appointments, and those without a primary care physician do not want to endure long waits in crowded U.S. public health clinics (Falagas & Zarkadoulia, 2008). Some parents have been influenced by media reports suggesting a link between a mercury-based preservative used for decades in vaccines and a rise in the number of children diagnosed with autism. But large-scale studies show no association with autism and no consistent effects on cognitive performance (Richler et al., 2006; Stehr-Green et al., 2003; Thompson et al., 2007). Still, as a precautionary measure, mercury-free versions of childhood vaccines are now available.

In areas where many parents have refused to immunize their children, outbreaks of whooping cough and rubella have occurred, with life-threatening consequences (Kennedy & Gust, 2008; Tuyen & Bisgard, 2003). Public education programs directed at increasing parental knowledge about the importance and safety of timely immunizations are badly needed.

Childhood Injuries

More than any other child in the preschool classroom, 3-year-old Tommy had trouble sitting still and paying attention. Instead, he darted from one place and activity to another. One day, he narrowly escaped serious injury when he put his mother's car into gear while she was outside scraping ice from its windows. The vehicle rolled through a guardrail and over the side of a 10-foot concrete underpass, where it hung until rescue workers arrived. Police charged Tommy's mother with failure to use a restraint seat for a child younger than age 8.

Unintentional injuries are the leading cause of childhood mortality in industrialized nations. As Figure 7.3 reveals, the United States ranks poorly in these largely preventable events. About 20 percent of U.S. childhood deaths and 50 percent of adolescent deaths result from injuries (Centers for Disease Control and Prevention, 2012b). And among injured children and youths who survive, thousands suffer pain, brain damage, and permanent physical disabilities.

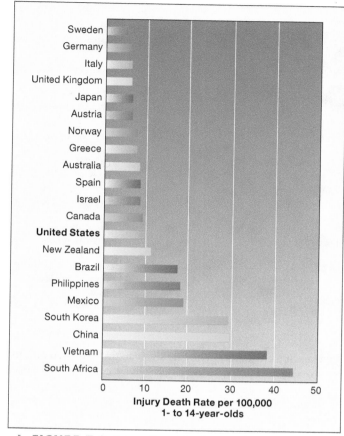

FIGURE 7.3 International death rates due to unintentional injury among 1- to 14-year-olds. Compared with other industrialized nations, the United States has a high injury rate, largely because of widespread childhood poverty and shortages of high-quality child care. Injury death rates are many times higher in developing nations, where poverty, rapid population growth, overcrowding in cities, and inadequate safety measures endanger children's lives. (Adapted from World Health Organization, 2008.)

Auto and traffic accidents, drownings, and burns are the most common injuries during early and middle childhood (Safe Kids USA, 2011b). Motor vehicle collisions are by far the most frequent source of injury across all ages, ranking as the leading cause of death among children more than 1 year old.

Factors Related to Childhood Injuries. The common view of childhood injuries as "accidental" suggests they are due to chance and cannot be prevented (Sleet & Mercy, 2003). In fact, these injuries occur within a complex *ecological system* of individual, family, community, and societal influences—and we can do something about them.

Because of their higher activity level and greater impulsivity and risk taking, boys are 1.5 times more likely to be injured than girls (Safe Kids USA, 2008). Children with certain temperamental and personality characteristics—inattentiveness, overactivity, irritability, defiance, and aggression—are also at greater risk (Ordonana, Caspi, & Moffitt, 2008; Schwebel & Gaines, 2007). As we saw in Chapter 6, these children present

Childhood injury rates are especially high in developing countries with weak public safety measures. These Cambodian children play unsupervised in a poverty-stricken, rundown neighborhood near a former dump site.

child-rearing challenges. They are likely to protest when placed in auto seat restraints, to refuse to take a companion's hand when crossing the street, and to disobey even after repeated instruction and discipline.

Poverty, single parenthood, and low parental education are also strongly associated with injury (Dudani, Macpherson, & Tamim, 2010; Schwebel & Brezausek, 2007). Parents who must cope with many daily stresses often have little energy to monitor the safety of their children. And their rundown homes and neighborhoods pose further risks (Dal Santo et al., 2004).

Broad societal conditions also affect childhood injury. In developing countries, the rate of death from injury before age 15 is five times as high as in developed nations and soon may exceed disease as the leading cause of childhood mortality (World Health Organization, 2008). Rapid population growth, overcrowding in cities, and heavy road traffic combined with weak safety measures are major causes. Safety devices, such as car safety seats and bicycle helmets, are neither readily available nor affordable.

Childhood injury rates are high in the United States because of extensive poverty, shortages of high-quality child care (to supervise children in their parents' absence), and a high rate of births to teenagers, who are not ready for parenthood. But U.S. children from advantaged families are also at considerably greater risk for injury than children in Western Europe (World Health Organization, 2008). This indicates that besides reducing poverty and teenage pregnancy and upgrading the status of child care, additional steps are needed to ensure children's safety.

Preventing Childhood Injuries. Childhood injuries have many causes, so a variety of approaches are needed to reduce them. Laws prevent many injuries by requiring car

safety seats, child-resistant caps on medicine bottles, flameproof clothing, and fencing around backyard swimming pools (the site of 50 percent of early childhood drownings) (Brenner & Committee on Injury, Violence, and Poison Protection, 2003). Communities can help by modifying their physical environments. Playgrounds, a common site of injury, can be covered with protective surfaces (Safe Kids USA, 2008). Free, easily installed window guards can be given to families in high-rise apartment buildings to prevent falls. And media campaigns can inform parents and children about safety issues.

But even though they know better, many parents and children behave in ways that compromise safety. About 27 percent of U.S. parents (like Tommy's mother) fail to place their preschoolers in car safety seats. And 84 percent of infant seats and 40 percent of child booster seats are improperly used (Safe Kids USA, 2011a). American parents, especially, seem willing to ignore familiar safety practices, perhaps because of the high value they place on individual rights and personal freedom (Damashek & Peterson, 2002).

Furthermore, many parents begin relying on children's knowledge of safety rules, rather than controlling access to hazards, as early as 2 or 3 years of age—a premature transition associated with a rise in home injuries (Morrongiello, Ondejko, & Littlejohn, 2004). But even older preschoolers spontaneously recall only about half the safety rules their parents teach them. And even with well-learned rules, they need supervision to ensure they comply (Morrongiello, Midgett, & Shields, 2001).

Parent interventions that highlight risk factors and that model and reinforce safety practices are effective in reducing home hazards and childhood injuries (Kendrick et al., 2008). But attention must also be paid to family conditions that can prevent childhood injury: relieving crowding in the home, providing social supports to ease parental stress, and teaching parents to use effective discipline—a topic we take up in Chapter 8.

ASK YOURSELF

REVIEW To effectively prevent childhood injury, why are diverse approaches essential? Cite examples at several levels of the *ecological system.*

CONNECT Using research on malnutrition, show how physical growth and health in early childhood result from a continuous, complex interplay between heredity and environment.

APPLY One day, Leslie prepared a new snack to serve at preschool: celery stuffed with ricotta cheese. The first time she served it, few children touched it. How can Leslie encourage her students to accept the snack? What tactics should she avoid?

REFLECT Ask a parent or other family member whether, as a preschooler, you were a picky eater, suffered from many infectious diseases, or sustained any serious injuries. In each instance, what factors might have been responsible?

Motor Development

TAKE A MOMENT... Observe several 2- to 6-year-olds at play in a neighborhood park, preschool, or child-care center. You will see that an explosion of new motor skills occurs in early childhood, each of which builds on the simpler movement patterns of toddlerhood.

During the preschool years, children continue to integrate previously acquired skills into more complex, *dynamic systems*. Then they revise each new skill as their bodies grow larger and stronger, their central nervous systems develop, their environments present new challenges, and they set new goals.

Gross-Motor Development

As children's bodies become more streamlined and less top-heavy, their center of gravity shifts downward, toward the trunk. As a result, balance improves greatly, paving the way for new motor skills involving large muscles of the body. By age 2, preschoolers' gaits become smooth and rhythmic—secure enough that soon they leave the ground, at first by running and later by jumping, hopping, galloping, and skipping.

As children become steadier on their feet, their arms and torsos are freed to experiment with new skills—throwing and catching balls, steering tricycles, and swinging on horizontal bars and rings. Then upper- and lower-body skills combine into more refined actions. Five- and 6-year-olds simultaneously steer and pedal a tricycle and flexibly move their whole body when

© ELLEN B. SENISI PHOTOGRAPHY

As balance improves, preschoolers can combine upper- and lower-body skills into more refined actions, such as walking on stilts.

throwing, catching, hopping, and jumping. By the end of the preschool years, all skills are performed with greater speed and endurance. Table 7.1 provides a closer look at gross-motor development in early childhood.

TABLE 7.1

Changes in Gross- and Fine-Motor Skills During Early Childhood

AGE	GROSS-MOTOR SKILLS	FINE-MOTOR SKILLS
2–3 years	Walks more rhythmically; hurried walk changes to run Jumps, hops, throws, and catches with rigid upper body Pushes riding toy with feet; little steering	Puts on and removes simple items of clothing Zips and unzips large zippers Uses spoon effectively
3–4 years	Walks up stairs, alternating feet, and down stairs, leading with one foot Jumps and hops, flexing upper body Throws and catches with slight involvement of upper body; still catches by trapping ball against chest Pedals and steers tricycle	Fastens and unfastens large buttons Serves self food without assistance Uses scissors Copies vertical line and circle Draws first picture of person, using tadpole image
4–5 years	Walks down stairs, alternating feet Runs more smoothly Gallops and skips with one foot Throws ball with increased body rotation and transfer of weight on feet; catches ball with hands Rides tricycle rapidly, steers smoothly	Uses fork effectively Cuts with scissors following line Copies triangle, cross, and some letters
5–6 years	Increases running speed Gallops more smoothly; engages in true skipping Displays mature, whole-body throwing and catching pattern; increases throwing speed Rides bicycle with training wheels	Uses knife to cut soft food Ties shoes Draws person with six parts Copies some numbers and simple words

Sources: Cratty, 1986; Haywood & Getchell, 2009; Malina & Bouchard, 1991.

Fine-Motor Development

Fine-motor skills, too, take a giant leap forward in the preschool years. As control of the hands and fingers improves, young children put puzzles together, build with small blocks, cut and paste, and string beads. To parents, fine-motor progress is most apparent in two areas: (1) children's care of their own bodies, and (2) the drawings and paintings that fill the walls at home, child care, and preschool.

Self-Help Skills. As Table 7.1 shows, young children gradually become self-sufficient at dressing and feeding. But parents must be patient about these abilities: When tired and in a hurry, young children often revert to eating with their fingers. And the 3-year-old who dresses himself may end up with his shirt on inside out, his pants on backward, and his left snow boot on his right foot! Perhaps the most complex self-help skill of early childhood is shoe tying, mastered around age 6. Success requires a longer attention span, memory for an intricate series of hand movements, and the dexterity to perform them. Shoe tying illustrates the close connection between motor and cognitive development, as do two other skills: drawing and writing.

Drawing. When given crayon and paper, even toddlers scribble in imitation of others. Gradually, marks on the page take on meaning. A variety of cognitive factors combine with fine-motor control to influence changes in children's artful representations (Golomb, 2004). These include the realization that pictures can serve as symbols, improved planning and spatial understanding, and the emphasis that the child's culture places on artistic expression.

Typically, drawing progresses through the following sequence:

1. *Scribbles.* At first, children's gestures rather than the resulting scribbles contain the intended representation. For example, one 18-month-old made her crayon hop and, as it produced a series of dots, explained, "Rabbit goes hop-hop" (Winner, 1986).

2. *First representational forms.* Around age 3, children's scribbles start to become pictures. Often children make a gesture with the crayon, notice that they have drawn a recognizable shape, and then label it (Winner, 1986). Few 3-year-olds spontaneously draw so others can tell what their picture represents. But when adults draw with children and point out the resemblances between drawings and objects, preschoolers' pictures become more comprehensible and detailed (Braswell & Callanan, 2003).

   A major milestone in drawing occurs when children use lines to represent the boundaries of objects, enabling 3- and 4-year-olds to draw their first picture of a person. Fine-motor and cognitive limitations lead the preschooler to reduce the figure to the simplest form that still looks human: the universal "tadpole" image, a circular shape with lines attached, shown on the left in Figure 7.4.

3. *More realistic drawings.* Five- and 6-year-olds create more complex drawings, like the one on the right in Figure 7.4, containing more conventional human and animal figures, with the head and body differentiated. Older preschoolers' drawings still contain perceptual distortions because they have just begun to represent depth (Cox & Littlejohn, 1995). This free depiction of reality makes their artwork look fanciful and inventive.

LOOK AND LISTEN

Visit a preschool or child-care center where artwork by 3- to 5-year-olds is plentiful. Note age differences in the complexity of children's drawings. ●

FIGURE 7.4 Examples of young children's drawings. The universal tadpolelike shape that children use to draw their first picture of a person is shown on the left. The tadpole soon becomes an anchor for greater details that sprout from the basic shape. By the end of the preschool years, children produce more complex, differentiated pictures like the one on the right, drawn by a 6-year-old child. (*Left:* Reprinted by permission from *Artful Scribbles* by Howard Gardner. Available from Basic Books, an imprint of The Perseus Books Group. Copyright © 1982. *Right:* From E. Winner, "Where Pelicans Kiss Seals," *Psychology Today, 20*[8], August 1986, p. 35. Reprinted by permission from the collection of Ellen Winner.)

The complex drawings of these kindergartners in Suzhou, China, benefit from adult expectations that young children learn to draw well and from the rich artistic traditions of Chinese culture.

Cultural Variations in Development of Drawing. In cultures with rich artistic traditions, children create elaborate drawings that reflect the conventions of their culture. Adults encourage young children by offering suggestions, modeling ways to draw, and asking them to label their pictures. Peers, as well, discuss one another's drawings and copy from one another's work (Braswell, 2006). All of these practices enhance young children's drawing progress.

But in cultures with little interest in art, even older children and adolescents produce simple forms. In the Jimi Valley, a remote region of Papua New Guinea with no indigenous pictorial art, many children do not go to school and therefore have little opportunity to develop drawing skills. When a Western researcher asked nonschooled Jimi 10- to 15-year-olds to draw a human figure for the first time, most produced nonrepresentational scribbles and shapes or simple "stick" images resembling preschoolers' tadpolelike shapes (Martlew & Connolly, 1996). These forms seem to be a universal beginning in drawing. Once children realize that lines must evoke human features, they find solutions to figure drawing that follow the general sequence described earlier.

Early Printing. When preschoolers first try to write, they scribble, making no distinction between writing and drawing. Around age 4, writing shows some distinctive features of print, such as separate forms arranged in a line on the page. But children often include picturelike devices—for example, a circular shape for "sun" (Ehri & Roberts, 2006). Only gradually, between ages 4 and 6, as they learn to name alphabet letters and link them with language sounds, do children realize that writing stands for language.

Preschoolers' first attempts to print often involve their name, generally using a single letter. "How do you make a *D?*" my older son, David, asked at age 3½. When I printed a large uppercase *D*, he tried to copy. "*D* for David," he proclaimed, quite satisfied with his backward, imperfect creation. By age 5, David printed his name clearly enough for others to read but, like many children, continued to reverse some letters until well into second grade. Until children start to read, they do not find it useful to distinguish between mirror-image forms, such as *b* and *d* and *p* and *q* (Bornstein & Arterberry, 1999).

Individual Differences in Motor Skills

Wide individual differences exist in the ages at which children reach motor milestones. A tall, muscular child tends to move more quickly and to acquire certain skills earlier than a short, stocky youngster. And as in other domains, parents and teachers probably provide more encouragement to children with biologically based motor-skill advantages.

Sex differences in motor skills are evident in early childhood. Boys are ahead of girls in skills that emphasize force and power. By age 5, they can broad-jump slightly farther, run slightly faster, and throw a ball about 5 feet farther. Girls have an edge in fine-motor skills and in certain gross-motor skills that depend on balance and agility, such as hopping and skipping (Fischman, Moore, & Steele, 1992; Haywood & Getchell, 2009). Boys' greater muscle mass and, in the case of throwing, slightly longer forearms contribute to their skill advantages. And girls' greater overall physical maturity may be partly responsible for their better balance and precision of movement.

From an early age, boys and girls are usually encouraged into different physical activities. For example, fathers are more likely to play catch with their sons than with their daughters. Sex differences in motor skills increase with age, but they remain small throughout childhood (Greendorfer, Lewko, & Rosengren, 1996). This suggests that social pressures for boys, more than girls, to be active and physically skilled exaggerate small, genetically based sex differences.

Children master the motor skills of early childhood during everyday play. Aside from throwing (where direct instruction is helpful), preschoolers exposed to gymnastics, tumbling, and other formal lessons do not make faster progress. When children have access to play spaces appropriate for running, climbing, jumping, and throwing and are encouraged to use them, they respond eagerly to these challenges. Similarly, fine-motor skills can be supported through daily routines, such as pouring juice and dressing, and through play that involves puzzles, construction sets, drawing, painting, sculpting, cutting, and pasting.

Finally, the social climate created by adults can enhance or dampen preschoolers' motor development. When parents and

HANG XINGWEI/XINHUA /LANDOV

teachers criticize a child's performance, push specific motor skills, or promote a competitive attitude, they risk undermining children's self-confidence and, in turn, their motor progress (Berk, 2006). Adult involvement in young children's motor activities should focus on fun rather than on winning or perfecting the "correct" technique.

ASK YOURSELF

REVIEW Describe typical changes in children's drawings during early childhood, along with factors that contribute to those changes.

CONNECT How are experiences that best support preschoolers' motor development consistent with experience-expectant brain growth of the early years? (Return to page 128 in Chapter 4 to review.)

APPLY Mabel and Chad want to do everything they can to support their 3-year-old daughter's motor development. What advice would you give them?

COGNITIVE DEVELOPMENT

One rainy morning, as I observed in our laboratory preschool, Leslie, the children's teacher, joined me at the back of the room. "Preschoolers' minds are such a blend of logic, fantasy, and faulty reasoning," Leslie reflected. "Every day, I'm startled by the maturity and originality of what they say and do. Yet at other times, their thinking seems limited and inflexible."

Leslie's comments sum up the puzzling contradictions of early childhood cognition. Hearing a loud thunderclap outside, 3-year-old Sammy exclaimed, "A magic man turned on the thunder!" Even after Leslie explained that thunder is caused by lightning, not by a person turning it on, Sammy persisted: "Then a magic lady did it."

In other respects, Sammy's thinking was surprisingly advanced. At snack time, he accurately counted, "One, two, three, four!" and then got four cartons of milk, one for each child at his table. But when his snack group included more than four children, Sammy's counting broke down. And after Priti dumped out her raisins, scattering them in front of her on the table, Sammy asked, "How come you got lots, and I only got this little bit?" He didn't realize that he had just as many raisins; his were simply all bunched up in a tiny red box.

To understand Sammy's reasoning, we turn first to Piaget's and Vygotsky's theories and evidence highlighting the strengths and limitations of each. Then we consider additional research on young children's cognition inspired by the information-processing perspective, address factors that contribute to individual differences in mental development, and look at the dramatic expansion of language in early childhood.

Piaget's Theory: The Preoperational Stage

As children move from the sensorimotor to the **preoperational stage,** which spans the years 2 to 7, the most obvious change is an extraordinary increase in representational, or symbolic, activity. Infants and toddlers' mental representations are impressive, but in early childhood, representational capacities blossom.

Advances in Mental Representation

Piaget acknowledged that language is our most flexible means of mental representation. By detaching thought from action, language permits far more efficient thinking than was possible earlier. When we think in words, we overcome the limits of our momentary experiences. We can deal with past, present, and future at once and combine concepts in unique ways, as when we imagine a hungry caterpillar eating bananas or monsters flying through the forest at night.

But Piaget did not regard language as the primary ingredient in childhood cognitive change. Instead, he believed that sensorimotor activity leads to internal images of experience, which children then label with words (Piaget, 1936/1952). In support of Piaget's view, children's first words have a strong sensorimotor basis (see Chapter 5). In addition, infants and toddlers acquire an impressive range of categories long before they use words to label them (see page 127). But as we will see, Piaget underestimated the power of language to spur children's cognition.

Make-Believe Play

Make-believe play is another excellent example of the development of representation in early childhood. Piaget believed that through pretending, young children practice and strengthen newly acquired representational schemes. Drawing on his ideas, several investigators have traced the development of make-believe during the preschool years.

Development of Make-Believe. One day, Sammy's 20-month-old brother, Dwayne, visited the classroom. Dwayne wandered around, picked up a toy telephone receiver, said, "Hi, Mommy," and then dropped it. Next, he found a cup, pretended to drink, and then toddled off again. Meanwhile, Sammy joined Vance and Priti in the block area for a space shuttle launch.

"That can be our control tower," Sammy suggested, pointing to a corner by a bookshelf. "Countdown!" he announced, speaking into his "walkie-talkie"—a small wooden block. "Five, six, two, four, one, blastoff!" Priti made a doll push a pretend button, and the rocket was off!

Comparing Dwayne's pretend play with Sammy's, we see three important changes that reflect the preschool child's growing symbolic mastery:

- *Play detaches from the real-life conditions associated with it.* In early pretending, toddlers use only realistic objects—a

Make-believe play increases in sophistication during the preschool years. Children pretend with less realistic toys and increasingly coordinate make-believe roles, such as bus driver and passengers.

toy telephone to talk into or a cup to drink from. Their earliest pretend acts usually imitate adults' actions and are not yet flexible. Children younger than age 2, for example, will pretend to drink from a cup but refuse to pretend a cup is a hat (Rakoczy, Tomasello, & Striano, 2005). They have trouble using an object (cup) that already has an obvious use as a symbol of another object (hat).

After age 2, children pretend with less realistic toys (a block for a telephone receiver). Gradually, they can imagine objects and events without any support from the real world, as Sammy's imaginary control tower illustrates (O'Reilly, 1995; Striano, Tomasello, & Rochat, 2001). And by age 3, they flexibly understand that an object (a yellow stick) may take on one fictional identity in one pretend game (a toothbrush) and another fictional identity (a carrot) in a different pretend game (Wyman, Rakoczy, & Tomasello, 2009).

• *Play becomes less self-centered.* At first, make-believe is directed toward the self—for example, Dwayne pretends to feed only himself. Soon, children direct pretend actions toward other objects, as when a child feeds a doll. Early in the third year, they become detached participants, making a doll feed itself or pushing a button to launch a rocket (McCune, 1993). Increasingly, preschoolers realize that agents and recipients of pretend actions can be independent of themselves.

• *Play includes more complex combinations of schemes.* Dwayne can pretend to drink from a cup, but he does not yet combine pouring and drinking. Later, children combine schemes with those of peers in **sociodramatic play**, the make-believe with others that is under way by the end of the second year and increases rapidly in complexity during early childhood (Kavanaugh, 2006). Already, Sammy and his classmates can create and coordinate several roles in an elaborate plot. By the end of early childhood, children have a sophisticated understanding of role relationships and story lines (Göncü, 1993).

LOOK AND LISTEN

Observe the make-believe play of several 2- to 4-year-olds. Describe pretend acts that exemplify important developmental changes. ●

In sociodramatic play, children display awareness that make-believe is a representational activity—an understanding that strengthens over early childhood (Lillard, 2003; Rakoczy, Tomasello, & Striano, 2004; Sobel, 2006). *TAKE A MOMENT...* Listen closely to a group of preschoolers as they assign roles and negotiate make-believe plans: "You *pretend to be* the astronaut, I'll *act like* I'm operating the control tower!" In communicating about pretend, children think about their own and others' fanciful representations—evidence that they have begun to reason about people's mental activities.

Benefits of Make-Believe. Today, Piaget's view of make-believe as mere practice of representational schemes is regarded as too limited. Play not only reflects but also contributes to children's cognitive and social skills. Compared with social non-pretend activities (such as drawing or putting puzzles together), during sociodramatic play preschoolers' interactions last longer, show more involvement, draw more children into the activity, and are more cooperative (Creasey, Jarvis, & Berk, 1998).

It is not surprising, then, that preschoolers who spend more time at sociodramatic play are seen as more socially competent by their teachers (Connolly & Doyle, 1984). And many studies reveal that make-believe strengthens a wide variety of mental abilities, including sustained attention, memory, logical reasoning, language and literacy, imagination, creativity, and the ability to reflect on one's own thinking, regulate one's own emotions and behavior, and take another's perspective (Bergen & Mauer, 2000; Berk, Mann, & Ogan, 2006; Elias & Berk, 2002; Hirsh-Pasek et al., 2009; Lindsey & Colwell, 2003; Ogan & Berk, 2009; Ruff & Capozzoli, 2003). We will return to the topic of early childhood play in this and the next chapter.

Symbol–Real-World Relations

To make believe and draw—and to understand other forms of representation, such as photographs, models, and maps—preschoolers must realize that each symbol corresponds to something specific in everyday life. In Chapter 5, we saw that by the middle of the second year, children grasp the symbolic function of realistic-looking photos, and around age 2½, of TV and video. When do children comprehend other challenging symbols—for example, three-dimensional models of real-world spaces?

In one study, 2½- and 3-year-olds watched an adult hide a small toy (Little Snoopy) in a scale model of a room and then were asked to retrieve it. Next, they had to find a larger toy (Big Snoopy) hidden in the room that the model represented. Not until age 3 could most children use the model as a guide to finding Big Snoopy in the real room (DeLoache, 1987). The 2½-year-olds did not realize that the model could be both *a toy room* and *a symbol of another room.* They had trouble with **dual representation**—viewing a symbolic object as both an object

Preschoolers who experience a variety of symbols come to understand dual representation—for example, that this dollhouse is an object in its own right but can also stand for another, a full-sized house where people live.

in its own right and a symbol. In support of this interpretation, when researchers made the model room less prominent as an object, by placing it behind a window and preventing children from touching it, more 2½-year-olds succeeded at the search task (DeLoache, 2000, 2002). Recall, also, that in make-believe play, 1½- to 2-year-olds cannot use an object that has an obvious use (cup) to stand for another object (hat). Likewise, 2-year-olds do not yet grasp that a line drawing—an object in its own right—also represents real-world objects.

Similarly, when presented with objects disguised in various ways and asked what each "looks like" and what each "is really and truly," preschoolers have difficulty. For example, when asked whether a stone painted to look like an egg "is really and truly" an egg, children younger than age 6 often responded "yes" (Flavell, Green, & Flavell, 1987). But simplify these appearance–reality tasks by permitting children to solve them nonverbally, by selecting from an array of objects the one that "really" has a particular identity, and most 3-year-olds perform well (Deák, Ray, & Brenneman, 2003). They realize that an object can be one thing (a stone) while symbolizing another (an egg).

How do children grasp the dual representation of symbolic objects? When adults point out similarities between models and real-world spaces, 2½-year-olds perform better on the find-Snoopy task (Peralta de Mendoza & Salsa, 2003). Also, insight into one type of symbol–real-world relation helps preschoolers master others. For example, children regard realistic-looking pictures as symbols early because a picture's primary purpose is to stand for something; it is not an interesting object in its own right (Preissler & Carey, 2004; Simcock & DeLoache, 2006). And 3-year-olds who can use a model of a room to locate Big Snoopy readily transfer their understanding to a simple map (Marzolf & DeLoache, 1994). In sum, experiences with diverse symbols—photos, picture books, make-believe, and maps—help preschoolers appreciate that one object can stand for another.

Limitations of Preoperational Thought

Aside from gains in representation, Piaget described preschoolers in terms of what they *cannot* understand (Beilin, 1992). As the term *preoperational* suggests, he compared them to older, more competent children who have reached the concrete operational stage. According to Piaget, young children are not capable of *operations*—mental actions that obey logical rules. Rather, their thinking is rigid, limited to one aspect of a situation at a time, and strongly influenced by the way things appear at the moment.

Egocentrism. For Piaget, the most fundamental deficiency of preoperational thinking is **egocentrism**—failure to distinguish others' symbolic viewpoints from one's own. He believed that when children first mentally represent the world, they tend to focus on their own viewpoint and simply assume that others perceive, think, and feel the same way they do.

Piaget's most convincing demonstration of egocentrism involves his *three-mountains problem,* described in Figure 7.5. He also regarded egocentrism as responsible for preoperational children's *animistic thinking*—the belief that inanimate objects have lifelike qualities, such as thoughts, wishes, feelings, and intentions (Piaget, 1926/1930). Recall Sammy's firm insistence that someone must have turned on the thunder. According to Piaget, because young children egocentrically assign human purposes to physical events, magical thinking is common during the preschool years.

Piaget argued that preschoolers' egocentric bias prevents them from *accommodating,* or reflecting on and revising their faulty reasoning in response to their physical and social worlds. To understand this shortcoming, let's consider some additional tasks that Piaget gave to children.

FIGURE 7.5 Piaget's three-mountains problem. Each mountain is distinguished by its color and by its summit. One has a red cross, another a small house, and the third a snow-capped peak. Children at the preoperational stage respond egocentrically. They cannot select a picture that shows the mountains from the doll's perspective. Instead, they simply choose the photo that reflects their own vantage point.

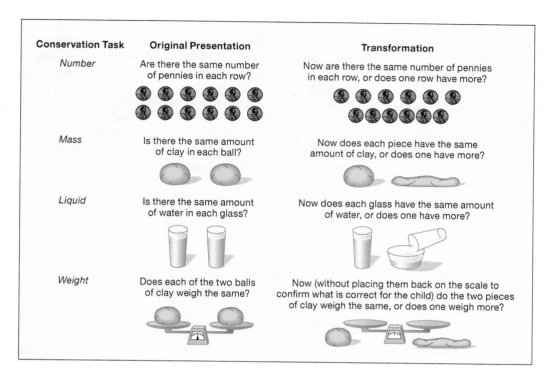

FIGURE 7.6 **Some Piagetian conservation tasks.** Children at the preoperational stage cannot yet conserve. These tasks are mastered gradually over the concrete operational stage. Children in Western nations typically acquire conservation of number, mass, and liquid sometime between 6 and 7 years and of weight between 8 and 10 years.

Inability to Conserve. Piaget's famous conservation tasks reveal a variety of deficiencies of preoperational thinking. **Conservation** refers to the idea that certain physical characteristics of objects remain the same, even when their outward appearance changes. At snack time, Priti and Sammy had identical boxes of raisins, but when Priti spread her raisins out on the table, Sammy was convinced that she had more.

In another conservation task involving liquid, the child is shown two identical tall glasses of water and asked if they contain equal amounts. Once the child agrees, the water in one glass is poured into a short, wide container, changing its appearance but not its amount. Then the child is asked whether the amount of water has changed. Preoperational children think the quantity has changed. They explain, "There is less now because the water is way down here" (that is, its level is so low) or, "There is more now because it is all spread out." Figure 7.6 illustrates other conservation tasks that you can try with children.

The inability to conserve highlights several related aspects of preoperational children's thinking. First, their understanding is *centered,* or characterized by **centration.** They focus on one aspect of a situation, neglecting other important features. In conservation of liquid, the child *centers* on the height of the water, failing to realize that changes in width compensate for changes in height. Second, children are easily distracted by the *perceptual appearance* of objects. Third, children treat the initial and final states of the water as unrelated events, ignoring the *dynamic transformation* (pouring of water) between them.

The most important illogical feature of preoperational thought is its **irreversibility,** an inability to mentally go through a series of steps in a problem and then reverse direction, returning to the starting point. *Reversibility* is part of every logical operation. After Priti spills her raisins, Sammy cannot reverse

by thinking, "I know that Priti doesn't have more raisins than I do. If we put them back in that little box, her raisins and my raisins would look just the same."

Lack of Hierarchical Classification. Preoperational children have difficulty with **hierarchical classification**—the organization of objects into classes and subclasses on the basis of similarities and differences. Piaget's famous *class inclusion problem,* illustrated in Figure 7.7, demonstrates this limitation. Preoperational children center on the overriding feature, red. They do not think reversibly by moving from the whole class (flowers) to the parts (red and blue) and back again.

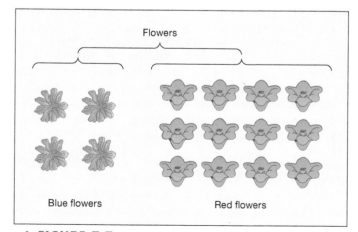

FIGURE 7.7 **A Piagetian class inclusion problem.** Children are shown 16 flowers, 4 of which are blue and 12 of which are red. Asked, "Are there more red flowers or flowers?" the preoperational child responds, "More red flowers," failing to realize that both red and blue flowers are included in the category "flowers."

Follow-Up Research on Preoperational Thought

Over the past three decades, researchers have challenged Piaget's view of preschoolers as cognitively deficient. Because many Piagetian problems contain unfamiliar elements or too many pieces of information for young children to handle at once, preschoolers' responses do not reflect their true abilities. Piaget also missed many naturally occurring instances of effective reasoning by preschoolers.

Egocentric, Animistic, and Magical Thinking.

Do young children really believe that a person standing elsewhere in a room sees exactly what they see? When researchers use simplified tasks with familiar objects, 3-year-olds show clear awareness of others' vantage points, such as recognizing how something looks to another person who is looking at it through a color filter (Moll & Meltzoff, 2011). Even 2-year-olds realize that what they see sometimes differs from what another person sees. When asked to help an adult looking for a lost object, 24-month-olds—but not 18-month-olds—handed her a toy resting behind a bucket that was within the child's line of sight but not visible to the adult (Moll & Tomasello, 2006).

Nonegocentric responses also appear in young children's conversations. For example, preschoolers adapt their speech to fit the needs of their listeners. Four-year-olds use shorter, simpler expressions when talking to 2-year-olds than to agemates or adults (Gelman & Shatz, 1978). And in describing objects, children do not use such words as "big" and "little" in a rigid, egocentric fashion. Instead, they *adjust* their descriptions to allow for context. By age 3, children judge a 2-inch shoe as small when seen by itself (because it is much smaller than most shoes) but as big for a tiny 5-inch-tall doll (Ebeling & Gelman, 1994).

In Chapter 5, we saw that toddlers have already begun to infer others' intentions (see page 157). And in his later writings, Piaget (1945/1951) did describe preschoolers' egocentrism as a *tendency* rather than an inability. As we revisit the topic of perspective taking, we will see that it develops gradually throughout childhood and adolescence.

Piaget also overestimated preschoolers' animistic beliefs. Even young infants have begun to distinguish animate from inanimate, as indicated by their developing categorical distinctions between living and nonliving things (see page 166). By age 2½, children give psychological explanations ("he likes to" or "she wants to") for people and occasionally for animals, but rarely for objects (Hickling & Wellman, 2001). In addition, preschoolers rarely attribute biological properties (like eating and growing) to robots, indicating that they are well aware that even a self-moving robot with lifelike features is not alive. They often say that robots have perceptual and psychological capacities—for example, seeing, thinking, and remembering (Jipson & Gelman, 2007; Subrahmanyam, Gelman, & Lafosse, 2002). But these responses result from incomplete knowledge about certain objects, and they decline with age.

Similarly, preschoolers think that magic accounts for events they otherwise cannot explain, as in Sammy's magical explanation of thunder (Rosengren & Hickling, 2000). Consequently, most 3- and 4-year-olds believe in the supernatural powers of fairies, goblins, and other enchanted creatures. Furthermore, older 3-year-olds and 4-year-olds think that violations of physical laws (walking through a wall) and mental laws (turning on the TV just by thinking about it) require magic more than violations of social conventions (taking a bath with shoes on) (Browne & Woolley, 2004). These responses indicate that preschoolers' notions of magic are flexible and appropriate.

Between ages 4 and 8, as children gain familiarity with physical events and principles, their magical beliefs decline. They figure out who is really behind Santa Claus and the Tooth Fairy, and they realize that the antics of magicians are due to trickery (Subbotsky, 2004). And increasingly, children say that characters and events in fantastical stories aren't real (Woolley & Cox, 2007). Still, because children entertain the possibility that something imaginary might materialize, they may react with anxiety to scary stories, TV shows, and nightmares.

Logical Thought.

Many studies show that when preschoolers are given tasks that are simplified and relevant to their everyday lives, they do not display the illogical characteristics that Piaget saw in the preoperational stage. For example, when a conservation-of-number task is scaled down to include only three items instead of six or seven, 3-year-olds perform well (Gelman, 1972). And when asked carefully worded questions about what happens to a substance (such as sugar) after it is dissolved in water, most 3- to 5-year-olds know that the substance is conserved—that it continues to exist, can be tasted, and makes the liquid heavier, even though it is invisible in the water (Au, Sidle, & Rollins, 1993; Rosen & Rozin, 1993).

Preschoolers' ability to reason about transformations is evident on other problems. They can engage in impressive *reasoning by analogy* about physical changes. Presented with the picture-matching problem "Play dough is to cut-up play dough as apple is to . . . ?," even 3-year-olds choose the correct answer (a cut-up apple) from a set of alternatives, several of which (a bitten apple, a cut-up loaf of bread) share physical features with the right choice (Goswami, 1996). These findings indicate that in familiar contexts, preschoolers can overcome appearances and think logically about cause and effect.

Finally, even without detailed biological or mechanical knowledge, preschoolers understand that the insides of animals are responsible for certain cause–effect sequences (such as willing oneself to move) that are impossible for nonliving things, such as machines (Gelman, 2003; Keil & Lockhart, 1999). Preschoolers seem to use illogical reasoning only when grappling with unfamiliar topics, too much information, or contradictory facts that they cannot reconcile.

Categorization.

Despite their difficulty with Piagetian class inclusion tasks, preschoolers organize their everyday knowledge into nested categories at an early age. By the beginning of early childhood, children's categories include objects that go together because of their common function, behavior, or natural kind (animate versus inanimate), despite varying widely in perceptual features.

These 4-year-olds understand that a category ("dinosaurs") can be based on underlying characteristics ("cold-blooded"), not just on perceptual features such as upright posture and scaly skin.

easily move back and forth between basic-level categories and *general categories,* such as "furniture." And they break down basic-level categories into *subcategories,* such as "rocking chairs" and "desk chairs."

Preschoolers' rapidly expanding vocabularies and general knowledge support their impressive skill at categorizing. As they learn more about their world, they devise ideas about underlying characteristics that category members share—for example, that a combination of physical features, internal organs, and behaviors determines an animal's identity (Gelman & Koenig, 2003). Also, adults label and explain categories to children, and picture-book reading is a rich context for doing so (Gelman & Kalish, 2006). In conversing about books, parents provide information ("Penguins live at the South Pole, swim, catch fish, and have thick layers of fat and feathers that help them stay warm") that guides children's inferences about the structure of categories. Furthermore, as the Social Issues: Education box on page 232 indicates, young children ask many questions about their world and usually get informative answers, which are well-suited to advancing their conceptual understanding.

In sum, although preschoolers' category systems are less complex than those of older children and adults, they already have the capacity to classify hierarchically and on the basis of nonobvious properties. And they use logical, causal reasoning to identify the interrelated features that form the basis of a category and to classify new members.

Indeed, 2- to 5-year-olds readily draw appropriate inferences about nonobservable characteristics shared by category members (Gopnik & Nazzi, 2003). For example, after being told that a bird has warm blood and that a stegosaurus (dinosaur) has cold blood, preschoolers infer that a pterodactyl (labeled a dinosaur) has cold blood, even though it closely resembles a bird.

During the second and third years, and perhaps earlier, children's categories differentiate. They form many *basic-level categories*—ones that are at an intermediate level of generality, such as "chairs," "tables," and "beds." By the third year, children

Evaluation of the Preoperational Stage

Table 7.2 provides an overview of the cognitive attainments of early childhood. *TAKE A MOMENT...* Compare them with Piaget's description of the preoperational child on pages 228–229.

TABLE 7.2

Some Cognitive Attainments of Early Childhood

APPROXIMATE AGE	COGNITIVE ATTAINMENTS
2–4 years	Shows a dramatic increase in representational activity, as reflected in language, make-believe play, drawing, understanding of symbol–real-world relations, and categorization
	Takes the perspective of others in simplified, familiar situations and in everyday, face-to-face communication
	Distinguishes animate beings from inanimate objects; denies that magic can alter everyday experiences
	Grasps conservation, notices transformations, reverses thinking, and understands many cause-and-effect relationships in familiar contexts
	Categorizes objects on the basis of common function, behavior, and natural kind, not just perceptual features. Uses logical, causal reasoning to identify interrelated features that form the basis of a category
	Sorts familiar objects into hierarchically organized categories
4–7 years	Becomes increasingly aware that make-believe (and other thought processes) are representational activities
	Replaces beliefs in magical creatures and events with plausible explanations

Social Issues: Education

Children's Questions: Catalyst for Cognitive Development

"Dad, what's that?" asked 4-year-old Emily as her father chopped vegetables for dinner.

"It's an onion," her father said.

"Is an onion a fruit?" Emily asked.

"It's a vegetable," her father replied. "A root vegetable because it grows underground."

Emily wrinkled her nose. "Why does it smell yucky?"

"I don't know," her father admitted. "But after dinner we can look it up online and find out."

When young children converse with adults, they ask, on average, more than one question per minute! Do inquisitive children like Emily really want answers to their many questions? Or are they—as their parents sometimes conclude—merely clamoring for attention?

An analysis of diaries that parents diverse in SES and ethnicity kept of their children's questions and of audio recordings of parent–child interactions revealed that at every age between 1 and 5 years, 70 to 90 percent of children's questions were information-seeking ("What's that [pointing to a crawfish]?") as opposed to non-information-seeking ("Can I have a cookie?") (Chouinard, 2007). And from age 2 on, children increasingly built on their fact-oriented questions

with follow-up questions that asked for causes and explanations ("What do crawfish eat?" "Why does it have claws?"). By age 3½, these sets of "building questions" made up about half of children's questions, confirming that preschoolers ask questions purposefully, to obtain clarifying information about things that puzzle them.

Unlike information obtained in other ways, answers to children's questions provide them with the precise knowledge they need at the precise moment they need it. And the content of children's questions is related to their cognitive development. At a time when vocabulary is advancing rapidly, about 60 percent of 1½- to 2-year-olds' questions ask for names of objects. With age, preschoolers increasingly ask about function ("What's it do?"), activity ("What's he doing?"), state ("Is she hungry?"), and theory of mind ("How does the pilot *know* where to fly?").

The usefulness of children's questions depends on adults' answers. Most of the time, parents respond informatively. If they do not, preschoolers are amazingly persistent: They ask again until they get the information they want. Parents adjust the complexity of their answers to fit their

CULTURA/MOOF/GETTY IMAGES

Preschoolers' questions are often purposeful efforts to understand things that puzzle them. Because adults' answers provide the precise knowledge children need at the precise moment they need it, question-asking is a powerful source of cognitive development.

children's maturity (Callanan & Oakes, 1992). To a question like "Why does the light come on?" 3-year-olds typically get simpler, "prior cause" explanations ("I turned on the switch"). Slightly older children frequently get "mechanism" explanations ("The switch allows electricity to reach the light bulb").

Clearly, asking questions is a major means through which children strive to attain adultlike understandings. Children's questions offer parents and teachers a fascinating window into their factual and conceptual knowledge, along with a wealth of opportunities to help them learn.

The evidence as a whole indicates that Piaget was partly wrong and partly right about young children's cognitive capacities. When given simplified tasks based on familiar experiences, preschoolers show the beginnings of logical thinking, which suggests that they attain logical operations gradually.

Evidence that preschoolers can be trained to perform well on Piagetian problems also supports the idea that operational thought is not absent at one point in time and present at another (Ping & Goldin-Meadow, 2008; Siegler & Svetina, 2006). Over time, children rely on increasingly effective mental (as opposed to perceptual) approaches to solving problems. For example, children who cannot use counting to compare two sets of items do not conserve number (Rouselle, Palmers, & Noël, 2004; Sophian, 1995). Once preschoolers can count, they apply this

skill to conservation-of-number tasks involving just a few items. As counting improves, they extend the strategy to problems with more items. By age 6, they understand that number remains the same after a transformation as long as nothing is added or taken away (Halford & Andrews, 2006). Consequently, they no longer need to count to verify their answer.

The gradual development of logical operations poses yet another challenge to Piaget's assumption of abrupt change toward logical reasoning around age 6 or 7. Does a preoperational stage really exist? Some no longer think so. Recall from Chapter 5 that according to the information-processing perspective, children work out their understanding of each type of task separately, and their thought processes are basically the same at all ages—just present to a greater or lesser extent.

Other experts think the stage concept is still valid, with modifications. For example, some *neo-Piagetian theorists* combine Piaget's stage approach with the information-processing emphasis on task-specific change (Case, 1998; Halford & Andrews, 2006). They believe that Piaget's strict stage definition must be transformed into a less tightly knit concept, one in which a related set of competencies develops over an extended period, depending on brain development and specific experiences. These investigators point to evidence that as long as the complexity of tasks and children's exposure to them are carefully controlled, children approach those tasks in similar, stage-consistent ways (Andrews & Halford, 2002; Case & Okamoto, 1996). For example, in drawing pictures, preschoolers depict objects separately, ignoring their spatial arrangement. In understanding stories, they grasp a single story line but have trouble with a main plot plus one or more subplots.

This flexible stage notion recognizes the unique qualities of early childhood thinking. At the same time, it provides a better account of why, as Leslie put it, "Preschoolers' minds are such a blend of logic, fantasy, and faulty reasoning."

Piaget and Education

Three educational principles derived from Piaget's theory continue to have a major impact on both teacher training and classroom practices, especially during early childhood:

- *Discovery learning.* In a Piagetian classroom, children are encouraged to discover for themselves through spontaneous interaction with the environment. Instead of presenting ready-made knowledge verbally, teachers provide a rich variety of activities designed to promote exploration, including art, puzzles, table games, dress-up clothing, building blocks, books, measuring tools, and musical instruments.

- *Sensitivity to children's readiness to learn.* In a Piagetian classroom, teachers introduce activities that build on children's current thinking, challenging their incorrect ways of viewing the world. But they do not try to hasten development by imposing new skills before children indicate interest or readiness.

- *Acceptance of individual differences.* Piaget's theory assumes that all children go through the same sequence of development, but at different rates. Therefore, teachers must plan activities for individual children and small groups, not just for the whole class. In addition, teachers evaluate educational progress in relation to the child's previous development, rather than on the basis of normative standards, or average performance of same-age peers.

Like his stages, educational applications of Piaget's theory have met with criticism. Perhaps the greatest challenge has to do with his insistence that young children learn mainly through acting on the environment (Brainerd, 2003). In the next section, we will see that young children also rely on language-based routes to knowledge.

ASK YOURSELF

REVIEW Select two of the following features of preoperational thought: egocentrism, a focus on perceptual appearances, difficulty reasoning about transformations, and lack of hierarchical classification. Present evidence indicating that preschoolers are more capable thinkers than Piaget assumed.

CONNECT Make-believe play promotes both cognitive and social development (see page 227). Explain why this is so.

APPLY Three-year-old Will understands that his tricycle isn't alive and can't feel or move on its own. But at the beach, while watching the sun dip below the horizon, Will exclaimed, "The sun is tired. It's going to sleep!" What explains this apparent contradiction in Will's reasoning?

REFLECT On the basis of what you have read, do you accept Piaget's claim for a preoperational stage of cognitive development? Explain.

Vygotsky's Sociocultural Theory

Piaget's deemphasis on language as a source of cognitive development brought on yet another challenge, this time from Vygotsky's sociocultural theory, which stresses the social context of cognitive development. During early childhood, rapid growth of language broadens preschoolers' participation in social dialogues with more knowledgeable individuals, who encourage them to master culturally important tasks. Soon children start to communicate with themselves in much the same way they converse with others. This greatly enhances their thinking and ability to control their own behavior. Let's see how this happens.

Private Speech

TAKE A MOMENT... Watch preschoolers as they play and explore the environment, and you will see that they frequently talk out loud to themselves. For example, as Sammy worked a puzzle, he said, "Where's the red piece? Now, a blue one. No, it doesn't fit. Try it here."

Piaget (1923/1926) called these utterances *egocentric speech,* reflecting his belief that young children have difficulty taking the perspectives of others. Their talk, he said, is often "talk for self" in which they express thoughts in whatever form they happen to occur, regardless of whether a listener can understand. Piaget believed that cognitive development and certain social experiences eventually bring an end to egocentric speech. Specifically, through disagreements with peers, children see that others hold viewpoints different from their own. As a result, egocentric speech declines.

A preschooler explores the possibilities of a handful of soap bubbles with the aid of private speech. Research supports Vygotsky's theory that children use private speech to guide their thinking and behavior.

Vygotsky (1934/1987) disagreed with Piaget's conclusions. Because language helps children think about their mental activities and behavior and select courses of action, Vygotsky saw it as the foundation for all higher cognitive processes, including controlled attention, deliberate memorization and recall, categorization, planning, problem solving, and self-reflection. In Vygotsky's view, children speak to themselves for self-guidance. As they get older and find tasks easier, their self-directed speech is internalized as silent, *inner speech*—the internal verbal dialogues we carry on while thinking and acting in everyday situations.

Over the past three decades, almost all studies have supported Vygotsky's perspective (Berk & Harris, 2003; Winsler, 2009). As a result, children's self-directed speech is now called **private speech** instead of egocentric speech. Research shows that children use more of it when tasks are appropriately challenging (neither too easy nor too hard), after they make errors, or when they are confused about how to proceed. With age, as Vygotsky predicted, private speech goes underground, changing into whispers and silent lip movements. Furthermore, children who freely use private speech during a challenging activity are more attentive and involved and show better task performance than their less talkative agemates (Al-Namlah, Fernyhough, & Meins, 2006; Lidstone, Meins, & Fernyhough, 2010; Winsler, Naglieri, & Manfra, 2006).

Social Origins of Early Childhood Cognition

Where does private speech come from? Recall from Chapter 5 that Vygotsky believed that children's learning takes place within the *zone of proximal development*—a range of tasks too difficult for the child to do alone but possible with the help of adults and more skilled peers. Consider the joint activity of Sammy and his mother as she helps him put together a difficult puzzle:

Sammy: I can't get this one in. *[Tries to insert a piece in the wrong place.]*

Mother: Which piece might go down here? *[Points to the bottom of the puzzle.]*

Sammy: His shoes. *[Looks for a piece resembling the clown's shoes but tries the wrong one.]*

Mother: Well, what piece looks like this shape? *[Points again to the bottom of the puzzle.]*

Sammy: The brown one. *[Tries it, and it fits; then attempts another piece and looks at his mother.]*

Mother: Try turning it just a little. *[Gestures to show him.]*

Sammy: There! *[Puts in several more pieces while his mother watches.]*

Sammy's mother keeps the puzzle within his zone of proximal development, at a manageable level of difficulty. To do so, she engages in **scaffolding**—adjusting the support offered during a teaching session to fit the child's current level of performance. When the child has little notion of how to proceed, the adult uses direct instruction, breaking the task into manageable units, suggesting strategies, and offering rationales for using them. As the child's competence increases, effective scaffolders gradually and sensitively withdraw support, turning over responsibility to the child. Then children take the language of these dialogues, make it part of their private speech, and use this speech to organize their independent efforts.

What evidence supports Vygotsky's ideas on the social origins of cognitive development? In several studies, children whose parents were effective scaffolders used more private speech, were more successful when attempting difficult tasks on their own, and were advanced in overall cognitive development (Berk & Spuhl, 1995; Conner & Cross, 2003; Mulvaney et al., 2006). Adult cognitive support—teaching in small steps and offering strategies—predicts gains in children's thinking. And among Caucasian-American parent–child pairs, adult emotional support—offering encouragement and allowing the child to take over the task—predicts children's effort (Neitzel & Stright, 2003).

Nevertheless, effective scaffolding varies among cultures, as an investigation of Hmong families who had emigrated from Southeast Asia to the United States illustrates. Unlike Caucasian-American parents, who emphasize independence by encouraging their children to think of ways to approach a task, Hmong parents—who highly value interdependence and child obedience—frequently tell their children what to do (for example, "Put this piece here, then this piece on top of it") (Stright, Herr, & Neitzel, 2009). Among Caucasian-American children, such directive scaffolding is associated with kindergartners' lack of self-control and behavior problems. Among Hmong children, however, it predicts greater rule following, organization, and task completion.

Finally, although children benefit from working on tasks with same-age peers, their planning and problem solving improve more when their partner is either an "expert" peer (especially capable at the task) or an adult. And peer disagreement (emphasized by Piaget) is less important in fostering cognitive development than the extent to which children resolve differences of opinion and cooperate (Kobayashi, 1994; Tudge, 1992).

Vygotsky and Education

Both Piagetian and Vygotskian classrooms accept individual differences and provide opportunities for children's active participation. But a Vygotskian classroom goes beyond independent discovery to promote *assisted discovery*. Teachers guide children's learning, tailoring their interventions to each child's zone of proximal development. Assisted discovery is aided by *peer collaboration,* as children of varying abilities work in groups, teaching and helping one another.

Vygotsky (1933/1978) saw make-believe play as the ideal social context for fostering cognitive development in early childhood. As children create imaginary situations, they learn to follow internal ideas and social rules rather than their immediate impulses. For example, a child pretending to go to sleep follows the rules of bedtime behavior. A child imagining himself as a father and a doll as a child conforms to the rules of parental behavior. According to Vygotsky, make-believe play is a unique, broadly influential zone of proximal development in which children try out a wide variety of challenging activities and acquire many new competencies.

Turn back to page 227 to review findings that make-believe play enhances a diverse array of cognitive and social skills. Pretending is also rich in private speech—a finding that supports its role in helping children bring action under the control of thought (Krafft & Berk, 1998). And preschoolers who spend more time engaged in sociodramatic play are better at taking personal responsibility for following classroom rules and at regulating emotion (Berk, Mann, & Ogan, 2006; Lemche et al., 2003). These findings support the role of make-believe in children's increasing self-control.

Evaluation of Vygotsky's Theory

In granting social experience a fundamental role in cognitive development, Vygotsky's theory underscores the vital role of teaching and helps us understand the wide cultural variation in children's cognitive skills. Nevertheless, it has not gone unchallenged. Verbal communication may not be the only means through which children's thinking develops—or even, in some cultures, the most important means. When Western parents scaffold their young children's mastery of challenging tasks, their verbal communication resembles the teaching that takes place in school, where their children will spend years preparing for adult life. In cultures that place less emphasis on schooling and literacy, parents often expect children to take greater responsibility for acquiring new skills through keen observation and participation in community activities (Paradise & Rogoff, 2009; Rogoff, 2003). (See the Cultural Influences box on page 236).

To account for children's diverse ways of learning through involvement with others, Barbara Rogoff (1998, 2003) suggests the term **guided participation,** a broader concept than scaffolding. It refers to shared endeavors between more expert and less expert participants, without specifying the precise features of communication. Consequently, it allows for variations across situations and cultures.

Finally, Vygotsky's theory says little about how basic motor, perceptual, attention, memory, and problem-solving skills, discussed in Chapters 4 and 5, contribute to socially transmitted higher cognitive processes. For example, his theory does not address how these elementary capacities spark changes in children's social experiences, from which more advanced cognition springs (Miller, 2009; Moll, 1994). Piaget paid far more attention than Vygotsky to the development of basic cognitive processes. It is intriguing to speculate about the broader theory that might exist today if Piaget and Vygotsky—the two twentieth-century giants of cognitive development—had had a chance to meet and weave together their extraordinary accomplishments.

© ELLEN B. SENISI PHOTOGRAPHY

In this Vygotsky-inspired classroom, 4- and 5-year-olds benefit from peer collaboration. As they jointly make music, their conductor ensures that each player stays on beat.

ASK YOURSELF

REVIEW Describe features of social interaction that support children's cognitive development. How does such interaction create a zone of proximal development?

CONNECT Explain how Piaget's and Vygotsky's theories complement each other. How would classroom practices inspired by these theories be similar? How would they be different?

APPLY Tanisha sees her 5-year-old son, Toby, talking aloud to himself as he plays. She wonders whether she should discourage this behavior. Use Vygotsky's theory to explain why Toby talks to himself. How would you advise Tanisha?

REFLECT When do you use private speech? Does it serve a self-guiding function for you, as it does for children? Explain.

Cultural Influences

Children in Village and Tribal Cultures Observe and Participate in Adult Work

In Western societies, the role of equipping children with the skills they need to become competent workers is assigned to school. In early childhood, middle-SES parents' interactions with children emphasize child-focused activities designed to prepare children to succeed in school—especially adult–child conversations and play that enhance language, literacy, and other academic knowledge. In village and tribal cultures, children receive little or no schooling, spend their days in contact with adult work, and start to assume mature responsibilities in early childhood (Rogoff et al., 2003). Consequently, parents have little need to rely on conversation and play to teach children.

A study comparing 2- and 3-year-olds' daily lives in four cultures—two U.S. middle-SES suburbs, the Efe hunters and gatherers of the Republic of Congo, and a Mayan agricultural town in Guatemala—documented these differences (Morelli, Rogoff, & Angelillo, 2003). In the U.S. communities, young children had little access to adult work and spent much time conversing and playing with adults. In contrast, the Efe and Mayan children rarely engaged in these child-focused activities. They spent their days close to—and frequently observing—adult work, which often took place in or near the Efe campsite or the Mayan family home.

An ethnography of a remote Mayan village in Yucatán, Mexico, shows that when young children are legitimate onlookers and participants in a daily life structured around adult work, their competencies differ from those of Western preschoolers (Gaskins, 1999; Gaskins, Haight, & Lancy, 2007). Yucatec Mayan adults are subsistence farmers. Men tend cornfields, aided by sons age 8 and older. Women prepare meals, wash clothes, and care for the livestock and garden, assisted by daughters and by sons too young to work in the fields. Children join in these activities from the second year on. When not participating, they are expected to be self-sufficient. Young children make many nonwork decisions for themselves—how much to sleep and eat, what to wear, and even when to start school. As a result, Yucatec Mayan preschoolers are highly competent at self-care. In contrast, their make-believe play is limited; when it occurs, they usually imitate adult work. Otherwise, they watch others—for hours each day.

Yucatec Mayan parents rarely converse or play with preschoolers or scaffold their learning. Rather, when children imitate adult tasks, parents conclude that they are ready for more responsibility. Then they assign chores, selecting tasks the child can

A Mayan 3-year-old imitates her mother in balancing a basket of laundry on her head. Children in Guatemalan Mayan culture observe and participate in the work of their community from an early age.

do with little help so that adult work is not disturbed. If a child cannot do a task, the adult takes over and the child observes, reengaging when able to contribute.

Expected to be autonomous and helpful, Yucatec Mayan children seldom ask others for something interesting to do. From an early age, they can sit quietly for long periods—through a lengthy religious service or a three-hour truck ride to town. And when an adult directs them to do a chore, they respond eagerly to the type of command that Western children frequently avoid or resent. By age 5, Yucatec Mayan children spontaneously take responsibility for tasks beyond those assigned.

Information Processing

Return to the model of information processing discussed on page 161 in Chapter 5. Recall that information processing focuses on cognitive operations and mental strategies that children use to transform stimuli flowing into their mental systems. As we have already seen, early childhood is a period of dramatic strides in mental representation. And the various components of *executive function* that enable children to succeed in cognitively challenging situations—including attention, impulse control, coordinating information in memory, and planning—show impressive gains (Welsh, Friedman, & Spieker, 2008). Preschoolers also become more aware of their own

mental life and begin to acquire academically relevant knowledge important for school success.

Attention

As parents and teachers know, preschoolers—compared with school-age children—spend shorter times involved in tasks and are easily distracted. But recall from Chapter 5 that sustained attention improves in toddlerhood, a trend that continues during early childhood.

Inhibition. A major reason is a steady gain in children's ability to inhibit impulses and keep their mind on a competing goal. Consider a task in which the child must tap once when the adult

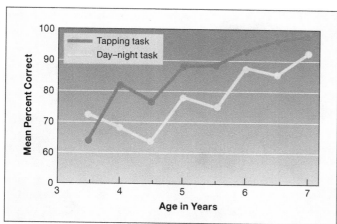

FIGURE 7.8 **Gains between ages 3 and 7 in performance on tasks requiring children to inhibit an impulse and focus on a competing goal.** In the tapping task, children had to tap once when the adult tapped twice and tap twice when the adult tapped once. In the day–night task, children had to say "night" to a picture of the sun and "day" to a picture of the moon with stars. (From A. Diamond, 2004, "Normal Development of Prefrontal Cortex from Birth to Young Adulthood: Cognitive Functions, Anatomy, and Biochemistry," as appeared in D. T. Stuss & R. T. Knight, [Eds.], *Principles of Frontal Lobe Function,* New York: Oxford University Press, p. 474. Reprinted by permission of Adele Diamond.)

taps twice and tap twice when the adult taps once or must say "night" to a picture of the sun and "day" to a picture of the moon with stars. As Figure 7.8 shows, 3- and 4-year-olds make many errors. But by age 6 to 7, children find such tasks easy (Johnson, Im-Bolter, & Pascual-Leone, 2003; Kirkham, Cruess, & Diamond, 2003). They can resist the "pull" of their attention toward a dominant stimulus—a skill that, as early as age 3 to 5, predicts social maturity as well as reading and math achievement from kindergarten through high school (Blair & Razza, 2007; Duncan et al., 2007; Rhoades, Greenberg, & Domitrovich, 2009).

Gains in inhibition are linked to development of the cerebral cortex, especially the prefrontal cortex (see page 217). But relevant experiences are also crucial. In *Tools of the Mind*—a preschool curriculum inspired by Vygotsky's theory—scaffolding of attention skills is woven into virtually all classroom activities. For example, teachers provide external aids to support attention (a child might hold a drawing of an ear as a reminder to listen during story time); lead games requiring frequent inhibition and memory for instructions; and encourage make-believe play, which helps children follow rules and use thought to guide behavior (Bodrova & Leong, 2007). When preschoolers from low-income families were randomly assigned to either Tools of the Mind or comparison classrooms, Tools children performed substantially better on end-of-year tasks assessing inhibition and other attentional capacities (Diamond et al., 2007).

Planning. By the end of early childhood, children become better at *planning*—thinking out a sequence of acts ahead of time and allocating attention accordingly to reach a goal. As long as tasks are not too complex, 5-year-olds can generate and follow a plan, such as deciding in which of two locations to store

a camera so an agemate, who wants to take a photo of a kangaroo, can retrieve the camera before arriving at the kangaroo's cage (McColgan & McCormack, 2008). Although younger children have trouble reasoning about a sequence of future events they have never before experienced, 4-year-olds can reason effectively about a short sequence of past events. For example, on a path with several landmarks they just traveled, they can identify the likely location of lost object (Friedman & Scholnick, 1997; Kaller et al., 2008).

Children learn much from cultural tools that support planning—directions for playing games, patterns for construction, recipes for cooking—especially when they collaborate with more expert planners. When 4- to 7-year-olds were observed jointly constructing a toy with their mothers, the mothers provided basic information about the usefulness of plans and how to implement specific steps: "Do you want to look at the picture and see what goes where? What piece do you need first?" After working with their mothers, younger children more often referred to the plan when building on their own (Gauvain, 2004; Gauvain, de la Ossa, & Hurtado-Ortiz, 2001). When parents encourage planning in everyday activities, from loading the dishwasher to packing for a vacation, they help children plan more effectively.

Memory

Unlike infants and toddlers, preschoolers have the language skills to describe what they remember, and they can follow directions on memory tasks. As a result, memory becomes easier to study in early childhood.

Recognition and Recall. *TAKE A MOMENT...* Show a young child a set of 10 pictures or toys. Then mix them up with some unfamiliar items, and ask the child to point to the ones in the original set. You will find that preschoolers' *recognition* memory—ability to tell whether a stimulus is the same as or similar to one they have seen before—is remarkably good. In fact, 4- and 5-year-olds perform nearly perfectly.

Now keep the items out of view, and ask the child to name the ones she saw. This more challenging task requires *recall*—that the child generate a mental image of an absent stimulus. Young children's recall is much poorer than their recognition. At age 2, they can recall no more than one or two of the items, at age 4 only about three or four (Perlmutter, 1984).

Improvement in recall in early childhood is strongly associated with language development, which greatly enhances long-lasting representations of past experiences (Melby-Lervag & Hulme, 2010; Ornstein, Haden, & Elischberger, 2006). But even preschoolers with good language skills recall poorly because they are not skilled at using **memory strategies**—deliberate mental activities that improve our chances of remembering. Preschoolers do not yet *rehearse,* or repeat items over and over to remember. Nor do they *organize,* grouping together items that are alike (all the animals together, all the vehicles together) so they can easily retrieve them by thinking of their similar characteristics—even when they are trained to do so (Gathercole, Adams, & Hitch, 1994).

Why do young children seldom use memory strategies? One reason is that strategies tax their limited working memories (see page 161 in Chapter 5). Preschoolers have difficulty holding on to pieces of information and applying a strategy at the same time.

Memory for Everyday Experiences. Think about the difference between your recall of listlike information and your memory for everyday experiences—what researchers call **episodic memory.** In remembering lists, you recall isolated bits, reproducing them exactly as you originally learned them. In remembering everyday experiences, you recall complex, meaningful information. Between 3 and 6 years, children improve sharply in memory for relations among stimuli—for example, in a set of photos, remembering not only the animals they saw but their contexts, such as a bear emerging from a tunnel or a zebra tied to a tree (Lloyd, Doydum, & Newcombe, 2009). The capacity to bind together stimuli supports an increasingly rich episodic memory in early childhood.

Memory for Familiar Events. Like adults, preschoolers remember familiar, repeated events—what you do when you go to preschool or have dinner—in terms of **scripts,** general descriptions of what occurs and when it occurs in a particular situation. Young children's scripts begin as a structure of main acts. For example, when asked to tell what happens at a restaurant, a 3-year-old might say, "You go in, get the food, eat, and then pay." Although first scripts contain only a few acts, they are almost always recalled in correct sequence (Bauer, 2002, 2006). With age, scripts become more elaborate, as in this 5-year-old's account of going to a restaurant: "You go in. You can sit in a booth or at a table. Then you tell the waitress what you want. You eat. If you want dessert, you can have some. Then you pay and go home" (Hudson, Fivush, & Kuebli, 1992).

Scripts help children (and adults) organize and interpret everyday experiences. Once formed, they can be used to predict what will happen in the future. Children rely on scripts in make-believe play and when listening to and telling stories. Scripts also support children's earliest efforts at planning as they represent sequences of actions that lead to desired goals (Hudson & Mayhew, 2009).

Memory for One-Time Events. In Chapter 5, we considered a second type of everyday memory—*autobiographical memory,* or representations of personally meaningful, one-time events. As preschoolers' cognitive and conversational skills improve, their descriptions of special events become better organized in time, more detailed, and related to the larger context of their lives (Fivush, 2001).

Adults use two styles to elicit children's autobiographical narratives. In the *elaborative style,* they follow the child's lead, ask varied questions, add information to the child's statements, and volunteer their own recollections and evaluations of events. For example, after a trip to the zoo, the parent might say, "What was the first thing we did? Why weren't the parrots in their cages? I thought the lion was scary. What did you think?" In contrast, adults who use the *repetitive style* provide little information and

As this toddler talks with his mother about past experiences, she responds in an elaborative style, asking varied questions and contributing her own recollections. Through such conversations, she enriches his autobiographical memory.

keep repeating the same questions regardless of the child's interest: "Do you remember the zoo? What did we do at the zoo?" Preschoolers who experience the elaborative style recall more information about past events, and they also produce more organized and detailed personal stories when followed up one to two years later (Cleveland & Reese, 2005; Farrant & Reese, 2000).

As children talk with adults about the past, they not only improve their autobiographical memory but also create a shared history that strengthens close relationships and self-understanding. Parents and preschoolers with secure attachment bonds engage in more elaborate reminiscing (Bost et al., 2006; Fivush & Reese, 2002). And 5- and 6-year-olds of elaborative-style parents describe themselves in clearer, more consistent ways (Bird & Reese, 2006).

Girls produce more organized and detailed narratives than boys. Compared with Asian children, Western children produce narratives with more talk about their own thoughts, emotions, and preferences. These differences fit with variations in parent–child conversations. Parents reminisce in greater detail and talk more about the emotional significance of events with daughters (Fivush, 2009). And collectivist cultural valuing of interdependence leads many Asian parents to discourage children from talking about themselves. Chinese parents, for example, engage in less detailed and evaluative past-event dialogues with their preschoolers (Fivush & Wang, 2005; Wang, 2006a).

Consistent with these early experiences, women report an earlier age of first memory and more vivid early memories than men. And Western children and adults' autobiographical memories include earlier, more detailed events that focus more on their own roles than do the memories of Asians, who tend to highlight the roles of others (Wang, 2006b, 2008).

The Young Child's Theory of Mind

As representation of the world, memory, and problem solving improve, children start to reflect on their own thought processes. They begin to construct a *theory of mind,* or coherent set of ideas about mental activities. This understanding is also called **metacognition,** or "thinking about thought" (the prefix *meta-* means "beyond" or "higher"). As adults, we have a complex appreciation of our inner mental worlds, which we use to interpret our own and others' behavior and to improve our performance on various tasks. How early are children aware of their mental lives, and how complete and accurate is their knowledge?

Awareness of Mental Life. At the end of the first year, babies view people as intentional beings who can share and influence one another's mental states, a milestone that opens the door to new forms of communication—joint attention, social referencing, preverbal gestures, and spoken language. These early milestones serve as the foundation for later mental understandings. In longitudinal research, 10-month-olds' ability to discern others' intentions predicted theory-of-mind competence at age 4 (Wellman et al., 2008). As they approach age 2, children display a clearer grasp of others' emotions and desires, evident in their realization that people often differ from one another and from themselves in likes, dislikes, wants, needs, and wishes ("Mommy like broccoli. Daddy like carrots. I no like carrots.").

As 2-year-olds' vocabularies expand, their first verbs include such words as *want, think, remember,* and *pretend* (Wellman, 2002). By age 3, children realize that thinking takes place inside their heads and that a person can think about something without seeing, touching, or talking about it (Flavell, Green, & Flavell, 1995). But 2- to 3-year-olds' verbal responses indicate that they think that people always behave in ways consistent with their *desires* and do not understand that less obvious, more interpretive mental states, such as *beliefs,* also affect behavior.

Between ages 3 and 4, children increasingly refer to their own and others' thoughts and beliefs (Wellman, 2011). And from age 4 on, they say that both *beliefs* and *desires* determine behavior. Dramatic evidence for this advance comes from games that test whether preschoolers realize that *false beliefs*—ones that do not represent reality accurately—can guide people's actions.

TAKE A MOMENT... For example, show a child two small closed boxes—a familiar Band-Aid box and a plain, unmarked box (see Figure 7.9). Then say, "Pick the box you think has the Band-Aids in it." Children usually pick the marked container. Next, open the boxes and show the child that, contrary to her own belief, the marked one is empty and the unmarked one contains the Band-Aids. Finally, introduce the child to a hand puppet and explain, "Here's Pam. She has a cut, see? Where do you think she'll look for Band-Aids? Why would she look in there? Before you looked inside, did you think that the plain box contained Band-Aids? Why?" (Bartsch & Wellman, 1995). Only a handful of 3-year-olds can explain Pam's—and their own—false beliefs, but many 4-year-olds can.

Nevertheless, growing evidence indicates that toddlers may have an *implicit* grasp of false belief—revealed by their nonverbal behaviors. For example, most 18-month-olds—after witnessing an object moved from one box to another while an adult was not looking—helped the adult, when he tried to open the original box, locate the object in the new box (Buttelmann,

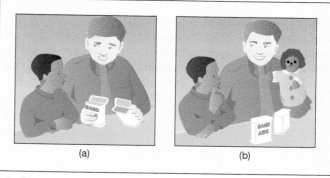

FIGURE 7.9 Example of a false-belief task. (a) An adult shows a child the contents of a Band-Aid box and of an unmarked box. The Band-Aids are in the unmarked container. (b) The adult introduces the child to a hand puppet named Pam and asks the child to predict where Pam would look for the Band-Aids and to explain Pam's behavior. The task reveals whether children understand that without having seen that the Band-Aids are in the unmarked container, Pam will hold a false belief.

Carpenter, & Tomasello, 2009). And 15- to 18-month-olds' looking behaviors—in violation-of-expectation studies and in investigations of their anticipatory glances toward the location they expect an adult to reach for an object—yield similar findings (Baillargeon, Scott, & He, 2010; Senju et al., 2011).

Performance on these implicit false-belief tasks predicts later *explicit* understanding, evident in the verbal explanations of older preschoolers (San Juan & Astington, 2012; Thoermer et al., 2012). Still, investigators disagree sharply on the depth of toddlers' insights. Some argue that they have fully formed representations, others that their awareness is limited.

Among children of diverse cultural and SES backgrounds, explicit false-belief understanding strengthens after age 3½, becoming more secure between ages 4 and 6 (Amsterlaw & Wellman, 2006; Callaghan et al., 2005; Flynn, 2006). During that time, it becomes a powerful tool for understanding oneself and others and a good predictor of social skills (Harwood & Farrar, 2006; Hughes, Ensor, & Marks, 2010). It is also associated with early reading ability, probably because it helps children comprehend story narratives (Astington & Pelletier, 2005).

Factors Contributing to Preschoolers' Theory of Mind. How do children develop a theory of mind at such a young age? Language, executive function, make-believe play, and social experiences all contribute.

Many studies indicate that language ability strongly predicts preschoolers' false-belief understanding (Milligan, Astington, & Dack, 2007). Children who spontaneously use, or who are trained to use, mental-state words in conversation are especially likely to pass false-belief tasks (Hale & Tager-Flusberg, 2003; San Juan & Astington, 2012). Among the Quechua people of the Peruvian highlands, whose language lacks mental-state terms, children have difficulty with false-belief tasks for years after children in industrialized nations have mastered them (Vinden, 1996). In contrast, Chinese languages have verb markers that can label the word *believe* as decidedly false. When adults use those markers in false-belief tasks, Chinese preschoolers perform better (Tardif, Wellman, & Cheung, 2004).

Several aspects of preschoolers' executive function—the ability to inhibit inappropriate responses, to reason about events inconsistent with immediate reality (for example, how to have avoided walking indoors with muddy shoes), and to plan—predict mastery of false belief (Drayton et al., 2011; Hughes & Ensor, 2007; Müller et al., 2012). Gains in inhibition are strongly related to mastery of false belief, perhaps because false-belief tasks require suppression of an irrelevant response—the tendency to assume that others share their own knowledge and beliefs (Birch & Bloom, 2003; Carlson, Moses, & Claxton, 2004).

Social experience also promotes understanding of the mind. In longitudinal research, mothers of securely attached babies were more likely to comment appropriately on their infants' mental states: "Do you *remember* Grandma?" "You really *like* that swing!" These mothers continued to describe their children, when they reached preschool age, in terms of mental characteristics: "She's got a mind of her own!" This maternal "mind-mindedness" was positively associated with later performance on false-belief and other theory-of-mind tasks (Meins et al., 1998, 2003; Ruffman et al., 2006). Secure attachment is also related to more elaborative parent–child narratives, including discussions of mental states—conversations that expose preschoolers to concepts and language that help them think about their own and others' mental lives (Ontai & Thompson, 2008; Taumoepeau & Ruffman, 2006).

Also, preschoolers with siblings who are children (but not infants)—especially older siblings or two or more siblings—tend to be more aware of false belief because they are exposed to more family talk about others' perspectives (Jenkins et al., 2003; McAlister & Peterson, 2006, 2007). Similarly, preschool friends who often engage in mental-state talk—as children do during make-believe play—are ahead in false-belief understanding (de Rosnay & Hughes, 2006). Style of adult–child interaction contributes, too. Discourse involving well-connected exchanges in which each speaker's remark is related to the other's previous remark predicts preschoolers' theory-of-mind progress (Ontai & Thompson, 2010). In line with Vygotsky's theory, these exchanges offer children extra opportunities to talk about inner states, receive feedback, and become increasingly aware of their own and others' mental activities.

Core knowledge theorists (see Chapter 5, page 159) believe that to profit from the social experiences just described, children must be biologically prepared to develop a theory of mind. They claim that children with *autism*, for whom mastery of false belief is either greatly delayed or absent, are deficient in the brain mechanism that enables humans to detect mental states. See the Biology and Environment box on the following page to find out more about the biological basis of reasoning about the mind.

Limitations of Preschoolers' Understanding of Mental Life. Though surprisingly advanced, preschoolers' awareness of mental activities is far from complete. For example, 3- and 4-year-olds are unaware that people continue to think while they wait, look at pictures, listen to stories, or read books—when there are no obvious cues that they are thinking (Flavell, Green, & Flavell, 1993, 1995, 2000). And children younger than age 5 pay little attention to the *process* of thinking. When asked about subtle distinctions between mental states, such as *know* and *forget*, they express confusion (Lyon & Flavell, 1994). And they believe that all events must be directly observed to be known. They do not understand that *mental inferences* can be a source of knowledge (Miller, Hardin, & Montgomery, 2003).

These findings suggest that preschoolers view the mind as a passive container of information. As they move into middle childhood, they will increasingly see it as an active, constructive agent—a change we will consider further in Chapter 9.

Early Childhood Literacy

One week, Leslie's students created a make-believe grocery store. They brought empty food boxes from home, placed them on shelves in the classroom, labeled items with prices, and made paper money for use at the cash register. A sign at the entrance announced the daily specials: "APLS BNS 5¢" ("apples bananas 5¢").

As such play reveals, preschoolers understand a great deal about written language long before they learn to read or write in conventional ways. This is not surprising: Children in industrialized nations live in a world filled with written symbols. Each day, they observe and participate in activities involving storybooks, calendars, lists, and signs. Children's active efforts to construct literacy knowledge through informal experiences are called **emergent literacy**.

Young preschoolers search for units of written language as they "read" memorized versions of stories and recognize familiar signs, such as "PIZZA." But they do not yet understand the symbolic function of the elements of print (Bialystok & Martin, 2003). Many preschoolers think that a single letter stands for a whole word or that each letter in a person's signature represents

Preschoolers acquire literacy knowledge informally through participating in everyday activities involving written symbols. Here a young chef "jots down" a phone order for a take-out meal.

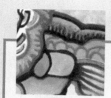

Biology and Environment

"Mindblindness" and Autism

Michael stood at the water table in Leslie's classroom, repeatedly filling a plastic cup and dumping out its contents—dip–splash, dip–splash—until Leslie came over and redirected his actions. Without looking at Leslie's face, Michael moved to a new repetitive pursuit: pouring water from one cup into another and back again. As other children entered the play space and conversed, Michael hardly noticed.

Michael has *autism* (a term that means "absorbed in the self"), the most severe behavior disorder of childhood. Like other children with autism, by age 3 he displayed deficits in three core areas of functioning. First, he had only limited ability to engage in nonverbal behaviors required for successful social interaction, such as eye gaze, facial expressions, gestures, imitation, and give-and-take. Second, his language was delayed and stereotyped. He used words to echo what others said and to get things he wanted, not to exchange ideas. Third, he engaged in much less make-believe play than other children (Frith, 2003; Walenski, Tager-Flusberg, & Ullman, 2006). And Michael showed another typical feature of autism: His interests were narrow and overly intense. For example, one day he sat for more than an hour spinning a toy Ferris wheel.

Researchers agree that autism stems from abnormal brain functioning, usually due to genetic or prenatal environmental causes. Beginning in the first year, children with the disorder have larger-than-average brains, perhaps due to massive overgrowth of synapses and lack of synaptic pruning, which accompanies normal development of cognitive, language, and communication skills (Courchesne, Carper, & Akshoomoff, 2003).

Furthermore, the amygdala, devoted to emotion processing (see page 192 in Chapter 6), grows especially large in childhood, followed by a greater than average reduction in size in adolescence and adulthood. This deviant growth pattern is believed to contribute to the deficits in emotional responsiveness and social interaction involved in the disorder

(Schumann et al., 2009; Schumann & Amaral, 2010). fMRI studies reveal that autism is also associated with reduced activity in areas of the cerebral cortex involved in processing emotional and social responsiveness and with weaker connections between the amygdala and the temporal lobes (important for processing facial expressions) (Monk et al., 2010; Théoret et al., 2005).

Mounting evidence reveals that children with autism have a deficient theory of mind. Long after they reach the intellectual level of an average 4-year-old, they have great difficulty with false belief. Most find it hard to attribute mental states to themselves or others (Steele, Joseph, & Tager-Flusberg, 2003). They rarely use mental-state words, such as *believe, think, know, feel,* and *pretend*.

As early as the second year, children with autism show deficits in capacities believed to contribute to an understanding of mental life. Compared with other children, they have difficulty distinguishing facial expressions and less often establish joint attention, engage in social referencing, or imitate an adult's novel behaviors (Chawarska & Shic, 2009; Mundy & Stella, 2000; Vivanti et al., 2008). Furthermore, they are relatively insensitive to eye gaze as a cue to what a speaker is talking about. Instead, they often assume that another person's language refers to what they themselves are looking at—a possible reason for their frequent nonsensical expressions (Baron-Cohen, Baldwin, & Crowson, 1997).

Do these findings indicate that autism is due to impairment in an innate, core brain function, which leaves the child "mindblind" and therefore unable to engage in human sociability? Some researchers think so (Baron-Cohen & Belmonte, 2005; Scholl & Leslie, 2000). But others point out that individuals with mental retardation but not autism also do poorly on tasks assessing mental understanding (Yirmiya et al., 1998). This suggests that some kind of general intellectual impairment may be involved.

This child, who has autism, is barely aware of his teacher and classmates. His "mindblindness" might be due to a basic deficit in social awareness, a general impairment in executive function, or a deficit in holistic processing.

One conjecture is that children with autism are impaired in executive function. This leaves them deficient in skills involved in flexible, goal-oriented thinking, including shifting attention to relevant aspects of a situation, inhibiting irrelevant responses, applying strategies to hold information in working memory, and generating plans (Joseph & Tager-Flusberg, 2004; Robinson et al., 2009).

Another possibility is that children with autism display a peculiar style of information processing, preferring to process the parts of stimuli over patterns and coherent wholes (Happé & Frith, 2006). Deficits in thinking flexibly and in holistic processing of stimuli would each interfere with understanding the social world because social interaction requires quick integration of information from various sources and evaluation of alternative possibilities.

It is not clear which of these hypotheses is correct. Some research suggests that impairments in social awareness, flexible thinking, processing coherent wholes, and verbal ability contribute independently to autism (Morgan, Maybery, & Durkin, 2003; Pellicano et al., 2006). Perhaps several biologically based deficits underlie the tragic social isolation of children like Michael.

a separate name. Children revise these ideas as their cognitive capacities improve, as they encounter writing in many contexts, and as adults help them with written communication. Gradually, they notice more features of written language and depict writing that varies in function, as in the "story" and "grocery list" in Figure 7.10.

Eventually, children figure out that letters are parts of words and are linked to sounds in systematic ways, as seen in the invented spellings typical between ages 5 and 7. At first, children rely on sounds in the names of letters, as in "ADE LAFWTS KRMD NTU A LAVATR" ("eighty elephants crammed into a[n] elevator"). Soon they grasp sound–letter correspondences and learn that some letters have more than one common sound and that context affects their use (McGee & Richgels, 2012).

Literacy development builds on a broad foundation of spoken language and knowledge about the world (Dickinson, Golinkoff, & Hirsh-Pasek, 2010). Over time, children's language and literacy progress facilitate each other. **Phonological awareness**—the ability to reflect on and manipulate the sound structure of spoken language, as indicated by sensitivity to changes in sounds within words, to rhyming, and to incorrect pronunciation—is a strong predictor of emergent literacy knowledge (Paris & Paris, 2006). When combined with sound–letter knowledge, it enables children to isolate speech segments and link them with their written symbols. Vocabulary and grammatical skills are also influential.

The more informal literacy-related experiences young children have, the better their language and emergent literacy development and their later reading skills (Dickinson & McCabe, 2001; Speece et al., 2004). Pointing out letter–sound correspondences and playing language–sound games enhance children's awareness of the sound structure of language and how it is represented in print (Ehri & Roberts, 2006). *Interactive reading,* in which adults discuss storybook content with preschoolers, promotes many aspects of language and literacy development. And

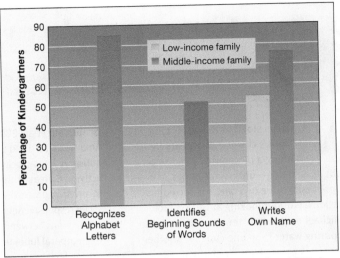

FIGURE 7.11 **Some kindergarten reading readiness skills by family income.** The gap in emergent literacy development between entering-kindergarten students from low-income and middle-income families is large. (Adapted from Lee & Burkham, 2002.)

adult-supported writing activities that focus on narrative, such as preparing a letter or a story, also have wide-ranging benefits. Each of these literacy experiences is linked to improved reading achievement in middle childhood (Hood, Conlon, & Andrews, 2008; Senechal & LeFevre, 2002; Storch & Whitehurst, 2001).

Compared to their economically advantaged agemates, preschoolers from low-income families have far fewer home and preschool language and literacy learning opportunities—a gap that translates into large differences in skills vital for reading readiness at kindergarten entry (see Figure 7.11) and into widening disparities in reading achievement during the school years (Hoff, 2013; Turnbull et al., 2009). When teachers of low-income preschoolers were given a tuition-free college course on effective early childhood literacy instruction, they readily offered many more literacy activities in their classrooms (Dickinson & Sprague, 2001). And providing parents with children's books, along with guidance in how to stimulate literacy learning in preschoolers, greatly enhances literacy activities in the home (High et al., 2000; Huebner & Payne, 2010).

Early Childhood Mathematical Reasoning

Mathematical reasoning, like literacy, builds on informally acquired knowledge. Between 14 and 16 months, toddlers display a beginning grasp of **ordinality,** or order relationships between quantities—for example, that 3 is more than 2, and 2 is more than 1. And 2-year-olds often indicate without counting that a set of items has "lots," "many," or "little" in relation to others (Ginsburg, Lee, & Boyd, 2008). By the time children turn 3, most can count rows of about five objects, although they do not yet know exactly what the words mean. For example, when asked for *one,* they give one item, but when asked for *two, three, four,* or *five,* they usually give a larger, but incorrect, amount. Nevertheless, 2½- to 3½-year-olds understand that a number

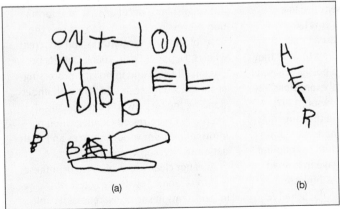

FIGURE 7.10 **A story (a) and a grocery list (b) written by a 4-year-old child.** This child's writing has many features of real print. It also reveals an awareness of different kinds of written expression. (From McGee, Lea M.; Richgels, Donald J., *Literacy's Beginnings: Supporting Young Readers and Writers,* 4th Ed., © 2004, p. 76. Reprinted and electronically reproduced by permission of Pearson Education, Inc. Upper Saddle River, New Jersey.)

word refers to a unique quantity—that when a number label changes (for example, from *five* to *six*), the number of items should also change (Sarnecka & Gelman, 2004).

By age 3½ to 4, most children have mastered the meaning of numbers up to 10, count correctly, and grasp the vital principle of **cardinality**—that the last number in a counting sequence indicates the quantity of items in a set (Geary, 2006a). Mastery of cardinality increases the efficiency of children's counting.

Around age 4, children use counting to solve arithmetic problems. At first, their strategies are tied to the order of numbers as presented; to add 2 + 4, they count on from 2 (Bryant & Nunes, 2002). But soon they experiment with other strategies and eventually arrive at the most efficient, accurate approach—in this example, beginning with the higher digit. Around this time, children realize that subtraction cancels out addition. Knowing, for example, that 4 + 3 = 7, they can infer without counting that 7 − 3 = 4 (Rasmussen, Ho, & Bisanz, 2003). Grasping basic arithmetic rules facilitates rapid computation, and with enough practice, children recall answers automatically.

When adults provide many occasions for counting, comparing quantities, and talking about number concepts, children acquire these understandings sooner (Ginsburg, Lee, & Boyd, 2008). Math proficiency at kindergarten entry predicts math achievement years later, in elementary and secondary school (Duncan et al., 2007; Romano et al., 2010).

As with emergent literacy, children from low-SES families begin kindergarten with considerably less math knowledge than their economically advantaged agemates—a gap due to differences in environmental supports. In an early childhood math curriculum called *Building Blocks,* materials that promote math concepts and skills enable teachers to weave math into many preschool daily activities, from building blocks to art and stories (Clements & Sarama, 2008). Compared with agemates randomly assigned to other preschool programs, low-SES preschoolers experiencing Building Blocks showed substantially greater year-end gains in math concepts and skills, including counting, sequencing, and arithmetic computation.

This board game helps preschoolers acquire basic math knowledge by affording many opportunities to count, compare quantities, and talk about number concepts.

ASK YOURSELF

REVIEW Describe a typical 4-year-old's understanding of mental activities, noting both strengths and limitations.

CONNECT Cite evidence on the development of preschoolers' memory, theory of mind, and literacy and mathematical understanding that is consistent with Vygotsky's sociocultural theory.

APPLY Lena wonders why her son's preschool teacher provides extensive playtime in learning centers instead of formal lessons in literacy and math skills. Explain to Lena why adult-supported play is the best way for preschoolers to develop academically.

REFLECT Describe informal experiences important for literacy and math development that you experienced while growing up. How do you think those experiences contributed to your academic progress in school?

Individual Differences in Mental Development

Five-year-old Hal sat in a testing room while Sarah gave him an intelligence test. Some of Sarah's questions were *verbal.* For example, she showed him a picture of a shovel and said, "Tell me what this is"—an item measuring vocabulary. She tested his memory by asking him to repeat sentences and lists of numbers back to her. To assess Hal's spatial reasoning, Sarah used *nonverbal* tasks: Hal copied designs with special blocks, figured out the pattern in a series of shapes, and indicated what a piece of paper folded and cut would look like when unfolded (Roid, 2003; Wechsler, 2002).

Sarah knew that Hal came from an economically disadvantaged family. When low-SES and certain ethnic minority preschoolers are bombarded with questions by an unfamiliar adult, they sometimes react with anxiety. Also, such children may not define the testing situation in achievement terms but, instead, may settle for lower performance than their abilities allow. Sarah spent time playing with Hal before she began testing and encouraged him while testing was in progress. Under these conditions, low-SES preschoolers improve in performance (Bracken, 2000).

The questions Sarah asked Hal tap knowledge and skills that not all children have equal opportunity to learn. In Chapter 9, we will take up the hotly debated issue of *cultural bias* in mental testing. For now, keep in mind that intelligence tests do not sample all human abilities, and performance is affected by cultural and situational factors (Sternberg, 2005). Nevertheless, test scores remain important: By age 6 to 7, they are good predictors of later IQ and academic achievement, which are related to vocational success in industrialized societies. Let's see how the environments in which preschoolers spend their days—home, preschool, and child care—affect mental test performance.

Applying What We Know

Features of a High-Quality Home Life for Preschoolers: The HOME Early Childhood Subscales

Subscale	Sample Item
Cognitive stimulation through toys, games, and reading material	Home includes toys that teach colors, sizes, and shapes.
Language stimulation	Parent converses with child at least twice during observer's visit.
Organization of the physical environment	All visible rooms are reasonably clean and minimally cluttered.
Emotional support: parental pride, affection, and warmth	Parent spontaneously praises child's qualities or behavior twice during observer's visit. Parent caresses, kisses, or hugs child at least once during observer's visit.
Stimulation of academic behavior	Child is encouraged to learn colors.
Parental modeling and encouragement of social maturity	Parent introduces interviewer to child.
Opportunities for variety in daily stimulation	Family member takes child on one outing (picnic, shopping) at least every other week.
Avoidance of physical punishment	Parent neither slaps nor spanks child during observer's visit.

Sources: Bradley, 1994; Bradley et al., 2001.

Home Environment and Mental Development

A special version of the *Home Observation for Measurement of the Environment (HOME),* covered in Chapter 5, assesses aspects of 3- to 6-year-olds' home lives that support mental development (see Applying What We Know above). Preschoolers who develop well intellectually have homes rich in educational toys and books. Their parents are warm and affectionate, stimulate language and academic knowledge, and arrange interesting outings. They also make reasonable demands for socially mature behavior—for example, that the child perform simple chores and behave courteously toward others. And these parents resolve conflicts with reason instead of physical force and punishment (Bradley & Caldwell, 1982; Espy, Molfese, & DiLalla, 2001; Roberts, Burchinal, & Durham, 1999).

As we saw in Chapter 2, these characteristics are less often seen in low-SES families. When parents manage, despite low education and income, to obtain high HOME scores, their preschoolers do substantially better on tests of intelligence and measures of language and emergent literacy skills (Berger, Paxson, & Waldfogel, 2009; Foster et al., 2005; Mistry et al., 2008). And in a study of low-SES African-American 3- and 4-year-olds, HOME cognitive stimulation and emotional support subscales predicted reading achievement four years later (Zaslow et al., 2006). These findings highlight the vital role of home environmental quality in children's mental development.

Preschool, Kindergarten, and Child Care

Children between ages 2 and 6 spend even more time away from their homes and parents than infants and toddlers do. Largely because of the rise in maternal employment, over the past several decades the number of young children enrolled in preschool or child care has steadily increased to more than 60 percent in the United States (U.S. Census Bureau, 2012b).

A *preschool* is a program with planned educational experiences aimed at enhancing the development of 2- to 5-year-olds. In contrast, *child care* refers to a variety of arrangements for supervising children. With age, children tend to shift from home-based to center-based programs. Many children, however, experience several types of arrangements at once (Federal Interagency Forum on Child and Family Statistics, 2011).

The line between preschool and child care is fuzzy. In response to the needs of employed parents, many U.S. preschools, as well as most public school kindergartens, have increased their hours from half to full days (U.S. Department of Education, 2012b). At the same time, good child care should provide the same high-quality educational experiences that an effective preschool does.

Types of Preschool and Kindergarten. Preschool and kindergarten programs range along a continuum from child-centered to teacher-directed. In **child-centered programs,** teachers provide a variety of activities from which children select, and much learning takes place through play. In contrast, in **academic programs,** teachers structure children's learning, teaching letters, numbers, colors, shapes, and other academic skills through formal lessons, often using repetition and drill.

Despite evidence that formal academic training in early childhood undermines motivation and emotional well-being, preschool and kindergarten teachers have felt increased pressure to take this approach. Young children who spend much time passively sitting and completing worksheets display more stress behaviors (such as wiggling and rocking), have less confidence in their abilities, prefer less challenging tasks, and are less advanced in motor, academic, language, and social skills at the end of the school year (Marcon, 1999a; Stipek et al., 1995). Follow-ups reveal lasting effects through elementary school in poorer study habits and achievement (Burts et al., 1992; Hart et al., 1998, 2003). These outcomes are strongest for low-SES children.

A special type of child-centered approach is *Montessori education,* devised a century ago by Italian physician Maria Montessori, who originally applied her method to poverty-stricken children. Features of Montessori schooling include materials specially designed to promote exploration and discovery, child-chosen activities, and equal emphasis on academic and social development (Lillard, 2007). In an evaluation of public preschools serving mostly urban minority children in Milwaukee, researchers compared students randomly assigned to either Montessori or other classrooms (Lillard & Else-Quest, 2006). Five-year-olds who had completed two years of Montessori education outperformed controls in literacy and math skills, false-belief understanding, concern with fairness in solving conflicts with peers, and cooperative play with classmates.

Early Intervention for At-Risk Preschoolers.
In the 1960s, as part of the "War on Poverty" in the United States, many intervention programs for economically disadvantaged preschoolers were initiated in an effort to address learning problems before formal schooling begins. The most extensive of these federal programs, **Project Head Start,** began in 1965. A typical Head Start center provides children with a year or two of preschool, along with nutritional and health services. Parent involvement is central to the Head Start philosophy. Parents serve on policy councils, contribute to program planning, work directly with children in classrooms, attend special programs on parenting and child development, and receive services directed at their own emotional, social, and vocational needs. Currently, Head Start serves about 904,000 children and their families across the nation (Head Start Bureau, 2010).

More than two decades of research have established the long-term benefits of preschool intervention. The most extensive of these studies combined data from seven interventions implemented by universities or research foundations. Results showed that poverty-stricken children who attended programs scored higher in IQ and achievement than controls during the first two to three years of elementary school. After that, differences declined (Lazar & Darlington, 1982). But on real-life measures of school adjustment, children and adolescents who had received intervention remained ahead. They were less likely to be placed in special education or retained in grade, and a greater number graduated from high school.

A separate report on one program—the High/Scope Perry Preschool Project—revealed benefits lasting well into adulthood. Two years' exposure to cognitively enriching preschool was associated with increased employment and reduced pregnancy and delinquency rates in adolescence. At age 27, those who had attended preschool were more likely than no-preschool controls to have graduated from high school and college, have higher earnings, be married, and own their own home—and

Project Head Start provides children from poverty-stricken families with preschool education and nutritional and health services. High-quality early educational intervention has benefits lasting into adulthood.

less likely to have been involved with the criminal justice system (see Figure 7.12). In the most recent follow-up, at age 40, the intervention group sustained its advantage on all measures of life success, including education, income, family life, and law-abiding behavior (Schweinhart, 2010; Schweinhart et al., 2005).

Do effects on school adjustment of these well-designed and well-delivered programs generalize to Head Start and other community-based preschool interventions? Findings are similar, though not as strong. Head Start preschoolers, who are more economically disadvantaged than children in other programs,

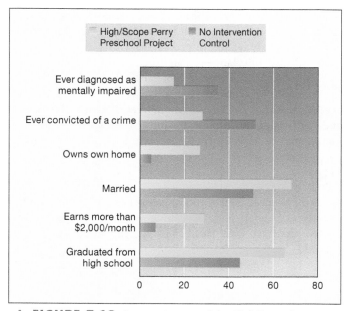

FIGURE 7.12 Some outcomes of the High/Scope Perry Preschool Project on follow-up at age 27. Although two years of a cognitively enriching preschool program did not eradicate the effects of growing up in poverty, children who received intervention were advantaged over no-intervention controls on all measures of life success when they reached adulthood. (Adapted from Schweinhart, 2010; Schweinhart et al., 2005.)

have more severe learning and behavior problems. And quality of services often does not equal that of model university-based programs (Barnett, 2011). But interventions of high quality are associated with diverse, long-lasting favorable outcomes, including higher rates of high school graduation and college enrollment and lower rates of adolescent drug use and delinquency (Garces, Thomas, & Currie, 2002; Love et al., 2006; Mashburn, 2008).

A consistent finding is that gains in IQ and achievement test scores from attending Head Start and other interventions quickly dissolve. In the Head Start Impact Study, a nationally representative sample of 5,000 Head Start 3- and 4-year-olds was randomly assigned to one year of Head Start or to a control group that could attend other types of preschool programs (U.S. Department of Health and Human Services, 2010d). By year's end, Head Start 3-year-olds exceeded controls in vocabulary, emergent literacy, and math skills; 4-year-olds in vocabulary, emergent literacy, and color identification. But except for language skills, academic advantages were no longer evident by end of first grade.

What explains these disappointing results? Head Start children typically enter inferior public schools in poverty-stricken neighborhoods, which undermine the benefits of preschool education (Brooks-Gunn, 2003; Ramey, Ramey, & Lanzi, 2006). An exception is the Chicago Child–Parent Centers—a program emphasizing literacy intervention and parent involvement that began at age 3 and continued through third grade—in which gains in academic achievement were still evident in junior high school (Reynolds & Temple, 1998).

Still, the improved school adjustment that results from attending a one- or two-year Head Start program is impressive. Program effects on parents may contribute: The more involved parents are in Head Start, the better their child-rearing practices and the more stimulating their home learning environments—factors positively related to preschoolers' task persistence and year-end academic, language, and social skills (Marcon, 1999b; McLoyd, Aikens, & Burton, 2006; Parker et al., 1999).

Head Start is highly cost-effective when compared with the cost of providing special education, treating criminal behavior, and supporting unemployed adults. Economists estimate a lifetime return to society of $300,000 to $500,000 on an investment of about $17,000 per preschool child—a potential total savings of many billions of dollars if every poverty-stricken preschooler in the United States were enrolled (Heckman et al., 2010). Because of limited funding, however, only 60 percent of poverty-stricken 3- and 4-year-olds attend some type of preschool program, with Head Start serving just half of these children (Magnuson & Shager, 2010).

Child Care. We have seen that high-quality early intervention can enhance the development of economically disadvantaged children. As noted in Chapter 5, however, much U.S. child care lacks quality. Preschoolers exposed to substandard child care, especially for long hours, score lower in cognitive and social skills and higher in behavior problems (Belsky, 2006; Lamb & Ahnert, 2006; NICHD Early Child Care Research Network, 2003b, 2006). Externalizing difficulties are especially likely to endure through middle childhood and into adolescence after extensive exposure to mediocre case (Belsky et al., 2007b; Vandell et al., 2010).

In contrast, good child care enhances cognitive, language, and social development, especially for low-SES children—effects that persist into elementary school and, for academic achievement, adolescence (Belsky et al., 2007b; Burchinal, Vandergrift, & Pianta, 2010; NICHD Early Child Care Research Network, 2006; Vandell et al., 2010). And in a study that followed very-low-income children over the preschool years, center-based care was more strongly associated with cognitive gains than were other child-care arrangements, probably because centers are more likely to provide a systematic educational program (Loeb et al., 2004).

Applying What We Know on the following page summarizes characteristics of high-quality early childhood programs, based on standards for developmentally appropriate practice devised by the U.S. National Association for the Education of Young Children. These standards offer a set of worthy goals as the United States strives to upgrade child-care and educational services for young children.

Educational Media

Besides home and preschool, young children spend much time in another learning environment: electronic media, including both television and computers. In the industrialized world, nearly all homes have at least one television set, and most have two or more. And more than 90 percent of U.S. children live in homes with one or more computers, 80 percent of which have an Internet connection, usually a high-speed link (Rideout, Foehr, & Roberts, 2010; U.S. Census Bureau, 2012b).

Educational Television. Sammy's favorite TV program, *Sesame Street,* uses lively visual and sound effects to stress basic literacy and number concepts and puppet and human characters to teach general knowledge, emotional and social understanding, and social skills. Today, *Sesame Street* is broadcast in more than 140 countries, making it the most widely viewed children's program in the world (Sesame Workshop, 2009).

Time devoted to watching children's educational programs is associated with gains in early literacy and math skills and academic progress in elementary school (Ennemoser & Schneider, 2007; Linebarger et al., 2004; Wright et al., 2001). Consistent with these findings, one study reported a link between preschool viewing of *Sesame Street* and other similar educational programs and getting higher grades, reading more books, and placing more value on achievement in high school (Anderson et al., 2001).

Sesame Street has modified its previous rapid-paced format in favor of more leisurely episodes with a clear story line. Children's programs with slow-paced action and easy-to-follow narratives, such as *Arthur & Friends, The Magic School Bus,* and *Wishbone,* lead to more elaborate make-believe play in early childhood and to greater recall of program content and gains in vocabulary and reading skills in the early school grades than programs that simply provide information (Linebarger &

Applying What We Know

Signs of Developmentally Appropriate Early Childhood Programs

Program Characteristics	Signs of Quality
Physical setting	Indoor environment is clean, in good repair, and well-ventilated. Classroom space is divided into richly equipped activity areas, including make-believe play, blocks, science, math, games and puzzles, books, art, and music. Fenced outdoor play space is equipped with swings, climbing equipment, tricycles, and sandbox.
Group size	In preschools and child-care centers, group size is no greater than 18 to 20 children with two teachers.
Caregiver–child ratio	In preschools and child-care centers, teacher is responsible for no more than 8 to 10 children. In child-care homes, caregiver is responsible for no more than 6 children.
Daily activities	Children select many of their own activities and learn through experiences relevant to their own lives, mainly in small groups or individually. Teachers facilitate children's involvement, accept individual differences, and adjust expectations to children's developing capacities.
Interactions between adults and children	Teachers move among groups and individuals, asking questions, offering suggestions, and adding more complex ideas. Teachers use positive guidance techniques, such as modeling and encouraging expected behavior and redirecting children to more acceptable activities.
Teacher qualifications	Teachers have college-level specialized preparation in early childhood development, early childhood education, or a related field.
Relationships with parents	Parents are encouraged to observe and participate. Teachers talk frequently with parents about children's behavior and development.
Licensing and accreditation	Child-care setting, whether a center or a home, is licensed by the state. Voluntary accreditation by the National Association for the Education of Young Children *(www.naeyc.org/academy)* or the National Association for Family Child Care *(www.nafcc.org)* is evidence of an especially high-quality program.

Source: Copple & Bredekamp, 2009.

Piotrowski, 2010; Singer & Singer, 2005). Narratively structured educational TV eases processing demands, freeing up space in working memory for applying program content to real-life situations.

Despite the spread of computers, television remains the dominant form of youth media. The average U.S. 2- to 6-year-old watches TV programs and videos from 1½ to 2⅔ hours a day. In middle childhood, viewing time increases to an average of 3½ hours a day, before declining slightly in adolescence (Rideout, Foehr, & Roberts, 2010; Rideout & Hamel, 2006).

Low-SES, African-American, and Hispanic children are more frequent viewers, perhaps because few alternative forms of entertainment are available in their neighborhoods or affordable for their parents. Also, parents with limited education are more likely to engage in practices that heighten TV viewing, including leaving the TV on all day and eating family meals in front of it (Rideout, Foehr, & Roberts, 2010). About one-third of U.S. preschoolers and 70 percent of school-age children and adolescents have a TV set in their bedroom; these children spend from 40 to 90 more minutes per day watching than age-mates without one (Rideout & Hamel, 2006).

Does extensive TV viewing take children away from worthwhile activities? Persistent background TV distracts infants and preschoolers from their play, diminishing time spent in focused attention and involvement with a set of toys (Courage & Howe, 2010). The more preschool and school-age children watch

prime-time shows and cartoons, the less time they spend reading and interacting with others and the poorer their academic skills (Ennemoser & Schneider, 2007; Huston et al., 1999; Wright et al., 2001). Whereas educational programs can be beneficial, watching entertainment TV—especially heavy viewing—detracts from children's school success and social experiences.

Learning with Computers. More than one-fourth of 4- to 6-year-olds use a computer regularly, with preschoolers of higher-SES parents having greater computer access (Calvert et al., 2005). And because computers can have rich educational benefits, many early childhood classrooms include computer learning centers. Kindergartners who use computers to draw or write produce more elaborate pictures and text, make fewer writing errors, and edit their work much as older children do. And combining everyday and computer experiences with math manipulatives is especially effective in promoting math concepts and skills (Clements & Sarama, 2003).

Simplified computer languages that children can use to make designs or build structures introduce them to programming skills. As long as adults support children's efforts, computer programming promotes improved problem solving and metacognition because children must plan and reflect on their thinking to get their programs to work. Furthermore, while programming, children are especially likely to help one another and to persist in the face of challenge (Nastasi & Clements, 1994; Resnick & Silverman, 2005).

As with television, children spend much time using computers for entertainment purposes, especially game playing. Both media are rife with gender stereotypes and violence. We will consider their impact on emotional and social development in the next chapter.

ASK YOURSELF

REVIEW What findings indicate that child-centered rather than academic preschools and kindergartens are better suited to fostering academic development?

CONNECT Compare outcomes resulting from preschool intervention programs with those from interventions beginning in infancy (see page 173 in Chapter 5). Which are more likely to lead to lasting cognitive gains? Explain.

APPLY Your senator has heard that IQ gains resulting from Head Start do not last, so he plans to vote against additional funding. Write a letter explaining why he should support Head Start.

REFLECT How much and what kinds of TV viewing and computer use did you engage in as a child? How do you think your home media environment influenced your development?

 # Language Development

Language is intimately related to virtually all cognitive changes discussed in this chapter. Between ages 2 and 6, children make momentous advances in language. Their remarkable achievements, as well as their mistakes along the way, reveal their active, rule-oriented approach to language learning.

Vocabulary

At age 2, Sammy had a spoken vocabulary of about 250 words. Buy age 6 he will have acquired around 10,000 words (Bloom, 1998). To accomplish this feat, Sammy acquired about five new words each day. How do children build their vocabularies so quickly? Research shows that they can connect new words with their underlying concepts after only a brief encounter, a process called **fast-mapping**. Preschoolers can even fast-map two or more new words encountered in the same situation (Wilkinson, Ross, & Diamond, 2003).

Types of Words. Children in many Western and non-Western language communities fast-map labels for objects especially rapidly because these refer to concepts that are easy to perceive. When adults point to, label, and talk about an object, they help the child figure out the word's meaning (Gershoff-Stowe & Hahn, 2007). Soon children add verbs *(go, run, broke)*, which require more complex understandings of relationships between objects and actions. Children learning Chinese, Japanese, and Korean—languages in which nouns are often omitted from adult sentences, while verbs are stressed—

acquire verbs more readily than their English-speaking agemates (Kim, McGregor, & Thompson, 2000; Tardif, 2006). Gradually, preschoolers add modifiers *(red, round, sad)*. Among those that are related in meaning, first they make general distinctions *(big–small),* then more specific ones *(tall–short, high–low, wide–narrow)* (Stevenson & Pollitt, 1987).

To fill in for words they have not yet learned, children as young as age 3 coin new words using ones they already know—for example, "plant-man," for a gardener, "crayoner" for a child using crayons. Preschoolers also extend language meanings through metaphor—like the 3-year-old who described a stomachache as a "fire engine in my tummy" (Winner, 1988). Young preschoolers' metaphors involve concrete sensory comparisons: "Clouds are pillows," "Leaves are dancers." Once vocabulary and general knowledge expand, children also appreciate nonsensory comparisons: "Friends are like magnets," "Time flies by" (Keil, 1986; Özçaliskan, 2005). As a result, young children sometimes communicate in amazingly vivid and memorable ways.

Strategies for Word Learning. Preschoolers figure out the meanings of new words by contrasting them with words they already know. How do they discover which concept each word picks out? One speculation is that early in vocabulary growth, children adopt a *mutual exclusivity bias*—the assumption that words refer to entirely separate (nonoverlapping) categories (Markman, 1992). Consistent with this idea, when 2-year-olds hear the labels for two distinct novel objects (for example, *clip* and *horn*), they assign each word correctly, to the whole object and not just a part of it (Waxman & Senghas, 1992).

Indeed, children's first several hundred nouns refer mostly to objects well-organized by shape. And learning of nouns based on the perceptual property of shape heightens young children's attention to the distinctive shapes of other objects (Smith et al., 2002; Yoshida & Smith, 2003). This *shape bias* helps preschoolers master additional names of objects, and vocabulary accelerates.

Once the name of a whole object is familiar, on hearing a new name for the object, 2- and 3-year-olds set aside the mutual exclusivity bias. For example, if the object (bottle) has a distinctively shaped part (spout), children readily apply the new label to it (Hansen & Markman, 2009). Still, mutual exclusivity and object shape cannot account for preschoolers' remarkably flexible responses when objects have more than one name. Children often call on other components of language in these instances.

According to one proposal, preschoolers figure out many word meanings by observing how words are used in the structure of sentences (Gleitman et al., 2005; Naigles & Swenson, 2007). Consider an adult who says, "This is a *citron* one," while showing the child a yellow car. Two- and 3-year-olds conclude that a new word used as an adjective for a familiar object (car) refers to a property of that object (Hall & Graham, 1999; Imai & Haryu, 2004). As preschoolers hear the word in various sentence structures ("That lemon is bright *citron*"), they refine its meaning.

Young children also take advantage of rich social information that adults frequently provide, while drawing on their own expanding ability to infer others' intentions, desires, and perspectives (Akhtar & Tomasello, 2000). In one study, an adult

© ELLEN B. SENISI PHOTOGRAPHY

Young children rely on any useful information available to add to their vocabularies. As he makes a bird feeder, this preschooler attends to a variety of perceptual, social, and linguistic cues to grasp the meanings of unfamiliar words, such as *pine cone, spread, dip, bird seed,* and *munching sparrow.*

performed an action on an object and then used a new label while looking back and forth between the child and the object, as if inviting the child to play. Two-year-olds concluded that the label referred to the action, not the object (Tomasello & Akhtar, 1995). By age 3, children can even use a speaker's recently expressed desire ("I really want to play with the *riff*") to figure out the label belonging to one of two novel objects (Saylor & Troseth, 2006).

Adults also inform children directly about which of two or more words to use—by saying, for example, "You can call it a sea creature, but it's better to say *dolphin*." Preschoolers' vocabularies grow more quickly when they have parents who provide such clarifying information (Callanan & Sabbagh, 2004).

Explaining Vocabulary Development. Children acquire vocabulary so efficiently and accurately that some theorists believe that they are innately biased to induce word meanings using certain principles, such as mutual exclusivity (Lidz, Gleitman, & Gleitman, 2004; Woodward & Markman, 1998). But critics point out that a small set of built-in, fixed principles cannot account for the flexible manner in which children master vocabulary (Deák, 2000). And many word-learning strategies cannot be innate because children acquiring different languages use different approaches to mastering the same meanings.

An alternative view is that vocabulary growth is governed by the same cognitive strategies that children apply to non-linguistic information. According to one account, children draw on a *coalition* of cues—perceptual, social, and linguistic—which shift in importance with age (Golinkoff & Hirsh-Pasek, 2006, 2008). Infants rely solely on perceptual features. Toddlers and young preschoolers, while still sensitive to perceptual features (such as object shape), increasingly attend to social cues—the speaker's direction of gaze, gestures, and expressions of desire and intention (Hollich, Hirsh-Pasek, & Golinkoff, 2000; Pruden et al., 2006). And as language develops further, linguistic cues—

sentence structure and intonation (stress, pitch, and loudness)—play larger roles.

Preschoolers are most successful at figuring out new word meanings when several kinds of information are available (Saylor, Baldwin, & Sabbagh, 2005). Researchers have just begun to study the multiple cues that children use for different kinds of words and how their combined strategies change with development.

Grammar

Between ages 2 and 3, English-speaking children use simple sentences that follow a subject–verb–object word order. Children learning other languages adopt the word orders of the adult speech to which they are exposed.

Basic Rules. Studies of children acquiring diverse languages reveal that their first use of grammatical rules is piecemeal—limited to just a few verbs. As children listen for familiar verbs in adults' speech, they expand their own utterances containing those verbs, relying on adult speech as their model (Gathercole, Sebastián, & Soto, 1999; Lieven, Pine, & Baldwin, 1997). Sammy, for example, added the preposition *with* to the verb *open* ("You open with scissors") but not to the word *hit* ("He hit me stick").

To test preschoolers' ability to generate novel sentences that conform to basic English grammar, researchers had them use a new verb in the subject–verb–object form after hearing it in a different construction, such as passive: "Ernie is getting *gorped* by the dog." The percentage of children who, when asked what the dog was doing, could respond, "He's *gorping* Ernie," rose steadily with age. But not until age 3½ to 4 could the majority of children apply the subject–verb–object structure broadly, to newly acquired verbs (Chan et al., 2010; Tomasello, 2003, 2006).

Once children form three-word sentences, they make small additions and changes to words that enable them to express meanings flexibly and efficiently. For example, they add *-s* for plural (*cats*), use prepositions (*in* and *on*), and form various tenses of the verb *to be* (*is, are, were, has been, will*). English-speaking children master these grammatical markers in a regular sequence, starting with those that involve the simplest meanings and structures (Brown, 1973; de Villiers & de Villiers, 1973).

When preschoolers acquire these markers, they sometimes overextend the rules to words that are exceptions—a type of error called **overregularization.** "My toy car *breaked*" and "We each have two *foots*" are expressions that appear between ages 2 and 3 (Maratsos, 2000; Marcus, 1995).

Complex Structures. Gradually, preschoolers master more complex grammatical structures, although they do make mistakes. In first creating questions, 2- to 3-year-olds use many formulas: "Where's *X*?" "Can I *X*?" (Dabrowska, 2000; Tomasello, 1992, 2003). Question asking remains variable for the next couple of years. An analysis of one child's questions revealed that he inverted the subject and verb when asking certain questions but not others ("What she will do?" "Why he can go?") The correct expressions were the ones he heard most often in his mother's speech (Rowland & Pine, 2000). And sometimes children produce errors in subject–verb agreement ("Where does the dogs play?") and in subject case ("Where can me sit?") (Rowland, 2007).

Similarly, children have trouble with some passive sentences. When told, "The car was pushed by the truck," young preschoolers often make a toy car push a truck. By age 5, they understand such expressions, but full mastery of the passive form is not complete until the end of middle childhood (Lempert, 1990; Tomasello, 2006).

Nevertheless, preschoolers' grasp of grammar is remarkable. By age 4 to 5, they form embedded sentences ("I think *he will come*"), tag questions ("Dad's going to be home soon, *isn't he?*"), and indirect objects ("He showed *his friend* the present"). As the preschool years draw to a close, children use most of the grammatical constructions of their language competently (Tager-Flusberg & Zukowski, 2009).

Explaining Grammatical Development. Evidence that grammatical development is an extended process has raised questions about Chomsky's nativist theory (to review, see page 174 in Chapter 5). Some experts believe that grammar is a product of general cognitive development—children's tendency to search for consistencies and patterns of all sorts. These *information-processing theorists* believe that children notice which words appear in the same positions in sentences and are similarly combined with other words (Chang, Dell, & Bock, 2006; Tomasello, 2003, 2011). Over time, they group words into grammatical categories and use them appropriately in sentences.

Still other theorists, while also focusing on how children process language, agree with the essence of Chomsky's theory. One idea proposes that the grammatical categories into which children group word meanings are innate—present at the outset (Pinker, 1999). Critics, however, point out that children's early word combinations do not show a grasp of grammar. Still another theory holds that children do not start with innate knowledge but, rather, have a *special language-making capacity*—a set of procedures for analyzing the language they hear, which supports the discovery of grammatical regularities (Slobin, 1985, 1997). Controversy persists over whether a universal language-processing device exists or whether children who hear different languages devise unique strategies (Lidz, 2007; Marchman & Thal, 2005).

Conversation

Besides acquiring vocabulary and grammar, children must learn to engage in effective and appropriate communication. This practical, social side of language is called **pragmatics**, and preschoolers make considerable headway in mastering it.

As early as age 2, children are skilled conversationalists. In face-to-face interaction, they take turns and respond appropriately to their partners' remarks (Pan & Snow, 1999). With age, the number of turns over which children can sustain interaction and their ability to maintain a topic over time increase. By age 4, children adjust their speech to fit the age, sex, and social status of their listeners. For example, in acting out roles with hand puppets, they use more commands when playing socially dominant and male roles (teacher, doctor, father) but speak more politely and use more indirect requests when playing less dominant and female roles (student, patient, mother) (Anderson, 2000).

Preschoolers' conversational skills occasionally do break down—for example, when talking on the phone. Here is an excerpt from one 4-year-old's phone conversation with his grandfather:

Grandfather:	How old will you be?
John:	Dis many. *[Holding up four fingers.]*
Grandfather:	Huh?
John:	Dis many. *[Again holding up four fingers.]* (Warren & Tate, 1992, pp. 259–260)

Young children's conversations appear less mature in highly demanding situations in which they cannot see their listeners' reactions or rely on typical conversational aids, such as gestures and objects to talk about. But when asked to tell a listener how to solve a simple puzzle, 3- to 6-year-olds give more specific directions over the phone than in person, indicating that they realize the need for more verbal description on the phone (Cameron & Lee, 1997). Between ages 4 and 8, both conversing and giving directions over the phone improve greatly. Telephone talk provides yet another example of how preschoolers' competencies depend on the demands of the situation.

Supporting Language Development in Early Childhood

How can adults foster preschoolers' language development? As in toddlerhood, conversational give-and-take with adults, either at home or in preschool, is consistently related to language progress (Hart & Risley, 1995; NICHD Early Child Care Research Network, 2000b).

Sensitive, caring adults use additional techniques that promote early language skills. When children use words incorrectly or communicate unclearly, they give helpful, explicit feedback, such as, "I can't tell which ball you want. Do you mean the large red one?" But they do not overcorrect, especially when children make grammatical mistakes. Criticism discourages children from freely using language in ways that lead to new skills.

© WAVE ROYALTY FREE/ALAMY

Responding to his 3-year-old child, this father expands her brief sentences and recasts them into accurate form—techniques that inform children about correct grammar.

Instead, adults often provide indirect feedback about grammar by using two strategies, often in combination: **recasts**—restructuring inaccurate speech into correct form, and **expansions**—elaborating on children's speech, increasing its complexity (Bohannon & Stanowicz, 1988; Chouinard & Clark, 2003). For example, if a child says, "I gotted new red shoes," the parent might respond, "Yes, you got a pair of new red shoes." After such corrective input, 2- to 4-year-olds often shift to correct forms—improvements still evident several months later (Saxton, Backley, & Gallaway, 2005). However, the impact of such feedback has been challenged. The techniques are not used in all cultures and, in a few investigations, did not affect children's grammar (Strapp & Federico, 2000; Valian, 1999). Rather than eliminating errors, perhaps expansions and recasts model grammatical alternatives and encourage children to experiment with them.

LOOK AND LISTEN

In a 30- to 60-minute observation of a 2- to 4-year-old and his or her parent, note grammatical errors the child makes and adult feedback. How often does the parent reformulate child errors or ask clarifying questions? How does the child respond? ●

Do the findings just described remind you once again of Vygotsky's theory? In language, as in other aspects of intellectual growth, parents and teachers gently prompt children to take the next step forward. Children strive to master language because they want to connect with other people. Adults, in turn, respond to children's desire to become competent speakers by listening attentively, elaborating on what children say, modeling correct usage, and stimulating children to talk further. In the next chapter, we will see that this combination of warmth and encouragement of mature behavior is at the heart of early childhood emotional and social development as well.

ASK YOURSELF

REVIEW Provide a list of recommendations for supporting language development in early childhood, noting research that supports each.

CONNECT Explain how children's strategies for word learning support the interactionist perspective on language development, described on pages 174–175 in Chapter 5.

APPLY Sammy's mother explained to him that the family would take a vacation in Miami. The next morning, Sammy announced, "I gotted my bags packed. When are we going to Your-ami?" What explains Sammy's errors?

SUMMARY

PHYSICAL DEVELOPMENT

A Changing Body and Brain (p. 216)

Describe body growth and brain development during early childhood.

- Children grow more slowly in early childhood than they did in the first two years, and they become longer and leaner. New growth centers emerge in the skeleton, and by the end of early childhood, children start to lose their primary teeth.

- Areas of the prefrontal cortex devoted to various aspects of executive function develop rapidly. The left cerebral hemisphere is especially active, supporting preschoolers' expanding language skills and improved executive function.

- Hand preference, reflecting an individual's **dominant cerebral hemisphere,** strengthens during early childhood. Research on handedness supports the joint contribution of nature and nurture to brain lateralization.

- In early childhood, fibers linking the **cerebellum** to the cerebral cortex grow and myelinate, enhancing motor coordination and thinking. The **reticular formation,** responsible for alertness and consciousness; the **hippocampus,** which plays a vital role in memory and spatial orientation; and the **corpus callosum,** connecting the two cerebral hemispheres, also develop rapidly.

Influences on Physical Growth and Health (p. 219)

Describe the effects of heredity, nutrition, and infectious disease on physical growth in early childhood.

- Heredity controls production and release of two hormones from the **pituitary gland: growth hormone (GH),** which is necessary for development of almost all body tissues, and **thyroid-stimulating hormone (TSH),** which affects brain development and body size.

- As growth rate slows, preschoolers' appetites decline, and many become picky eaters. Repeated, unpressured exposure to new foods promotes healthy, varied eating.

GETTY IMAGES/RED CHOPSTICKS

- Dietary deficiencies, especially in protein, vitamins, and minerals, can affect growth and are associated with attention and memory difficulties, academic and behavior problems, and greater susceptibility to infectious diseases. Disease also contributes to malnutrition, especially when intestinal infections cause persistent diarrhea.

- Immunization rates are lower in the United States than in other industrialized nations because many children lack access to health care. Parental stress and misconceptions about vaccine safety also contribute.

What factors increase the risk of unintentional injuries, and how can childhood injuries be prevented?

- Unintentional injuries are the leading cause of childhood mortality in industrialized nations. Victims are more likely to be boys; to be temperamentally inattentive, overactive, irritable, defiant, and aggressive; and to be growing up in stressed, poverty-stricken families.
- Effective injury prevention includes passing laws that promote child safety; creating safer home, travel, and play environments; improving public education; changing parent and child behaviors; and providing social supports to ease parental stress.

Motor Development (p. 223)

Cite major milestones of gross- and fine-motor development in early childhood, and describe individual differences.

- As the child's center of gravity shifts toward the trunk, balance improves, paving the way for new gross-motor achievements. Preschoolers run, jump, hop, gallop and eventually skip, throw, and catch, and generally become better coordinated.
- Improved control of the hands and fingers leads to dramatic gains in fine-motor skills. Preschoolers gradually become self-sufficient at dressing and feeding.
- By age 3, children's scribbles become pictures. With age, their drawings increase in complexity and realism, influenced by their culture's artistic traditions. Preschoolers also try to print alphabet letters and, later, words.

- Body build and opportunity for physical play affect motor development. Sex differences that favor boys in force and power and girls in balance and fine movements are partly genetic, but environmental pressures exaggerate them. Children master the motor skills of early childhood through informal play experiences.

COGNITIVE DEVELOPMENT

Piaget's Theory: The Preoperational Stage (p. 226)

Describe cognitive advances and limitations during the preoperational stage.

- Rapid advances in mental representation mark the beginning of Piaget's **preoperational stage.** Make-believe, which supports many aspects of development, becomes increasingly complex, evolving into **sociodramatic play** with peers. Gradually, children become capable of **dual representation**—viewing a symbolic object as both an object in its own right and a symbol.
- Preoperational children's **egocentrism**—their inability to imagine others' perspectives—contributes to **centration,** a focus on perceptual appearances, and **irreversibility.** As a result, preschoolers fail **conservation** and **hierarchical classification** tasks.

What does follow-up research reveal about the accuracy of Piaget's preoperational stage?

- When young children are given simplified tasks relevant to their everyday lives, their performance appears more mature than Piaget assumed. Preschoolers recognize others' perspectives, distinguish animate from inanimate objects, reason by analogy about physical transformations, understand cause-and-effect relationships, and organize knowledge into hierarchical categories.
- Evidence that operational thinking develops gradually over the preschool years challenges Piaget's stage concept. Some theorists propose a more flexible view of stages.

What educational principles can be derived from Piaget's theory?

- A Piagetian classroom promotes discovery learning, sensitivity to children's readiness to learn, and acceptance of individual differences.

Vygotsky's Sociocultural Theory (p. 233)

Explain Vygotsky's perspective on the social origins and significance of children's private speech.

- Unlike Piaget, Vygotsky regarded language as the foundation for all higher cognitive processes. According to Vygotsky, **private speech,** or language used for self-guidance, emerges out of social communication as adults and more skilled peers help children master appropriately challenging tasks. Private speech is eventually internalized as silent, inner speech.

- **Scaffolding**—adjusting teaching support to fit children's current needs and suggesting strategies—promotes gains in children's thinking.

Describe applications of Vygotsky's theory to education, and evaluate his major ideas.

- A Vygotskian classroom emphasizes assisted discovery—verbal guidance from teachers and peer collaboration. Make-believe play is a vital zone of proximal development that promotes many competencies.
- **Guided participation,** a broader concept than scaffolding, recognizes cultural and situational variations in shared endeavors between more expert and less expert participants.

Information Processing (p. 236)

How do attention and memory change during early childhood?

- Preschoolers' attention gradually becomes more sustained, and planning improves. But compared with older children, they spend less time involved in tasks and are less systematic in planning.
- Preschoolers' recognition memory is remarkably good, but their recall for listlike information is poor because they use **memory strategies** less effectively than older children.
- **Episodic memory**—memory for everyday experiences—improves greatly in early childhood. Like adults, preschoolers remember recurring events as **scripts,** which become increasingly elaborate with age. When adults use an elaborative style of conversing with children about the past, children's autobiographical memory becomes more organized and detailed.

Describe the young child's theory of mind.

- Preschoolers begin to construct a theory of mind, evidence of their capacity for **metacognition.** Language, executive function, and social experiences all contribute. Toddlers' nonverbal behaviors suggest an implicit awareness that people can hold false beliefs; around age 4, children's understanding becomes explicit.

● Preschoolers regard the mind as a passive container of information rather than as an active, constructive agent.

Summarize children's literacy and mathematical knowledge during early childhood.

● Children's active efforts to figure out how written symbols convey meaning are known as **emergent literacy.** Preschoolers revise these ideas as their cognitive capacities improve, as they encounter writing in many contexts, and as adults help them with written communication. **Phonological awareness** is a strong predictor of emergent literacy knowledge.

● Toddlers display a beginning grasp of **ordinality.** By age 4, preschoolers understand **cardinality** and use counting to solve arithmetic problems, eventually arriving at the most efficient, accurate approach. Adults promote children's mathematical knowledge by providing many occasions for counting, comparing quantities, and talking about number concepts.

Individual Differences in Mental Development (p. 243)

Discuss the impact of home, educational programs, child care, and media on preschoolers' mental development.

● By age 6 to 7, intelligence test scores are good predictors of later IQ and academic achievement. Children growing up in warm, stimulating homes with parents who make reasonable demands for mature behavior develop well intellectually.

● Preschool and kindergarten programs include both **child-centered programs,** in which much learning takes place through play, and **academic programs,** in which teachers train children in academic skills, often using repetition and drill. Emphasizing formal academic instruction undermines young children's motivation and negatively influences later achievement.

● **Project Head Start** is the most extensive U.S. federally funded preschool program for low-income children. High-quality preschool intervention results in immediate IQ and achievement gains and long-term improvements in school adjustment. Parent involvement in Head Start is positively related to more stimulating home environments, with benefits for children's academic, language, and social skills. Good child care enhances cognitive, language, and social development, especially for low-SES children.

● Children pick up many cognitive skills from educational television programs. Programs with slow-paced action and easy-to-follow story lines foster more elaborate make-believe play and gains in vocabulary and reading skills. But heavy exposure to entertainment TV is associated with poorer academic skills.

● Computers can have rich educational benefits when young children use them to draw or write, combine computer experiences with math manipulatives, or learn programming skills.

Language Development (p. 248)

Trace the development of vocabulary, grammar, and conversational skills in early childhood.

● Supported by **fast-mapping,** preschoolers' vocabularies increase dramatically. Initially, they rely heavily on the perceptual cue of object shape to expand their vocabulary. With age, they increasingly draw on social and linguistic cues.

● Between ages 2 and 3, children adopt the basic word order of their language. As preschoolers gradually master grammatical rules, they sometimes overextend them in a type of error called **overregularization.** By the end of early childhood, children have acquired complex grammatical forms.

● **Pragmatics** is the practical, social side of language. Two-year-olds are already skilled conversationalists in face-to-face interaction. By age 4, children adapt their speech to their listener's age, sex, and social status.

Cite factors that support language learning in early childhood.

● Conversational give-and-take with more skilled speakers fosters language progress. Adults provide explicit feedback on the clarity of children's language and indirect feedback about grammar through **recasts** and **expansions.**

Important Terms and Concepts

academic programs (p. 244)
cardinality (p. 243)
centration (p. 229)
cerebellum (p. 218)
child-centered programs (p. 244)
conservation (p. 229)
corpus callosum (p. 218)
dominant cerebral hemisphere (p. 217)
dual representation (p. 227)
egocentrism (p. 228)
emergent literacy (p. 240)
episodic memory (p. 238)

expansions (p. 251)
fast-mapping (p. 248)
growth hormone (GH) (p. 219)
guided participation (p. 235)
hierarchical classification (p. 229)
hippocampus (p. 218)
irreversibility (p. 229)
memory strategies (p. 237)
metacognition (p. 239)
ordinality (p. 242)
overregularization (p. 249)
phonological awareness (p. 242)

pituitary gland (p. 219)
pragmatics (p. 250)
preoperational stage (p. 226)
private speech (p. 234)
Project Head Start (p. 245)
recasts (p. 251)
reticular formation (p. 218)
scaffolding (p. 234)
scripts (p. 238)
sociodramatic play (p. 227)
thyroid-stimulating hormone (TSH) (p. 219)

© ELLEN B. SENISI PHOTOGRAPHY

During the preschool years, children make great strides in understanding the thoughts and feelings of others, and they build on these skills as they form first friendships—special relationships marked by attachment and common interests.

Emotional and Social Development in Early Childhood

chapter outline

Erikson's Theory: Initiative versus Guilt

Self-Understanding

Foundations of Self-Concept • Emergence of Self-Esteem

■ **CULTURAL INFLUENCES** Cultural Variations in Personal Storytelling: Implications for Early Self-Concept

Emotional Development

Understanding Emotion • Emotional Self-Regulation • Self-Conscious Emotions • Empathy and Sympathy

Peer Relations

Advances in Peer Sociability • First Friendships • Peer Relations and School Readiness • Parental Influences on Early Peer Relations

Foundations of Morality

The Psychoanalytic Perspective • Social Learning Theory • The Cognitive-Developmental Perspective • The Other Side of Morality: Development of Aggression

■ **CULTURAL INFLUENCES** Ethnic Differences in the Consequences of Physical Punishment

Gender Typing

Gender-Stereotyped Beliefs and Behaviors • Biological Influences on Gender Typing • Environmental Influences on Gender Typing • Gender Identity • Reducing Gender Stereotyping in Young Children

■ **SOCIAL ISSUES: EDUCATION** Young Children Learn About Gender Through Mother–Child Conversations

Child Rearing and Emotional and Social Development

Styles of Child Rearing • What Makes Authoritative Child Rearing Effective? • Cultural Variations • Child Maltreatment

As the children in Leslie's classroom moved through the preschool years, their personalities took on clearer definition. By age 3, they voiced firm likes and dislikes as well as new ideas about themselves. "Stop bothering me," Sammy said to Mark, who had reached for Sammy's beanbag as Sammy aimed it toward the mouth of a large clown face. "See, I'm great at this game," Sammy announced with confidence, an attitude that kept him trying, even though he missed most of the throws.

The children's conversations also revealed early notions about morality. Often they combined adults' statements about right and wrong with forceful attempts to defend their own desires. "You're 'posed to share," stated Mark, grabbing the beanbag out of Sammy's hand.

"I was here first! Gimme it back," demanded Sammy, pushing Mark. The two boys struggled until Leslie intervened, provided an extra set of beanbags, and showed them how they could both play.

© LAURA DWIGHT PHOTOGRAPHY

As the interaction between Sammy and Mark reveals, preschoolers quickly become complex social beings. Young children argue, grab, and push, but cooperative exchanges are far more frequent. Between ages 2 and 6, first friendships form, in which children converse, act out complementary roles, and learn that their own desires for companionship and toys are best met when they consider others' needs and interests.

The children's developing understanding of their social world was especially apparent in their growing attention to the dividing line between male and female. While Priti and Karen cared for a sick baby doll in the housekeeping area, Sammy, Vance, and Mark transformed the block corner into a busy intersection. "Green light, go!" shouted police officer Sammy as Vance and Mark pushed large wooden cars and trucks across the floor. Already, the children preferred peers of their own gender, and their play themes mirrored their culture's gender stereotypes.

This chapter is devoted to the many facets of early childhood emotional and social development. We begin with Erik Erikson's theory, which provides an overview of personality change in the preschool years. Then we consider children's concepts of themselves, their insights into their social and moral worlds, their gender typing, and their increasing ability to manage their emotional and social behaviors. Finally, we ask, What is effective child rearing? And we discuss the complex conditions that support good parenting or lead it to break down. ●

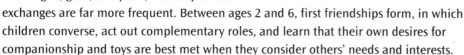

Erikson's Theory: Initiative versus Guilt

Erikson (1950) described early childhood as a period of "vigorous unfolding." Once children have a sense of autonomy, they become less contrary than they were as toddlers. Their energies are freed for tackling the psychological conflict of the preschool years: **initiative versus guilt.** As the word *initiative* suggests, young children have a new sense of purposefulness. They are eager to tackle new tasks, join in activities with peers, and discover what they can do with the help of adults. They also make strides in conscience development.

Erikson regarded play as a means through which young children learn about themselves and their social world. Play permits preschoolers to try new skills with little risk of criticism and failure. It also creates a small social organization of children who must cooperate to achieve common goals. Around the world, children act out family scenes and highly visible occupations—police officer, doctor, and nurse in Western societies, rabbit hunter and potter among the Hopi Indians, hut builder and spear maker among the Baka of West Africa (Göncü, Patt, & Kouba, 2004).

Recall that Erikson's theory builds on Freud's psychosexual stages (see Chapter 1, page 16). In Freud's Oedipus and Electra conflicts, to avoid punishment and maintain parents' affection, children form a *superego,* or conscience, by *identifying* with the same-sex parent. As a result, they adopt the moral and gender-role standards of their society. For Erikson, the negative

A Guatemalan 3-year-old pretends to shell corn. By acting out family scenes and highly visible occupations, young children around the world develop a sense of initiative, gaining insight into what they can do and become in their culture.

outcome of early childhood is an overly strict superego that causes children to feel too much guilt because they have been threatened, criticized, and punished excessively by adults. When this happens, preschoolers' exuberant play and bold efforts to master new tasks break down.

Although Freud's ideas are no longer accepted as satisfactory explanations of conscience development, Erikson's image of initiative captures the diverse changes in young children's emotional and social lives. Early childhood is, indeed, a time when children develop a confident self-image, more effective control over their emotions, new social skills, the foundations of morality, and a clear sense of themselves as boy or girl.

Self-Understanding

The development of language enables young children to talk about their own subjective experience of being. In Chapter 7, we noted that young children acquire a vocabulary for talking about their inner mental lives and gain in understanding of mental states. As self-awareness strengthens, preschoolers focus more intently on qualities that make the self unique. They begin to develop a **self-concept,** the set of attributes, abilities, attitudes, and values that an individual believes defines who he or she is.

Foundations of Self-Concept

Ask a 3- to 5-year-old to tell you about himself, and you are likely to hear something like this: "I'm Tommy. See, I got this new red T-shirt. I'm 4 years old. I can wash my hair all by myself. I have a new Tinkertoy set, and I made this big, big tower." Preschoolers' self-concepts consist largely of observable characteristics, such as their name, physical appearance, possessions, and everyday behaviors (Harter, 2006; Watson, 1990).

By age 3½, children also describe themselves in terms of typical emotions and attitudes—"I'm happy when I play with my friends"; "I don't like scary TV programs"; "I usually do what Mommy says"—suggesting a beginning understanding of their unique psychological characteristics (Eder & Mangelsdorf, 1997). And by age 5, children's degree of agreement with such statements coincides with maternal reports of their personality traits, indicating that older preschoolers have a sense of their own timidity, agreeableness, and positive or negative affect (Brown et al., 2008). But preschoolers do not yet say, "I'm helpful" or "I'm shy." Direct references to personality traits must wait for greater cognitive maturity.

A warm, sensitive parent–child relationship seems to foster a more positive, coherent early self-concept. In one study, 4-year-olds with a secure attachment to their mothers were more likely than their insecurely attached agemates to describe themselves in favorable terms at age 5—with statements that reflect agreeableness and positive affect (Goodvin et al., 2008). Also recall from Chapter 7 that securely attached preschoolers participate in more elaborative parent–child conversations about personally experienced events, which help them understand themselves (see page 240).

Cultural Influences

Cultural Variations in Personal Storytelling: Implications for Early Self-Concept

Preschoolers of many cultural backgrounds participate in personal storytelling with their parents. Striking cultural differences exist in parents' selection and interpretation of events in these narratives, affecting the way children view themselves.

In one study, researchers spent thousands of hours studying the storytelling practices of six middle-SES Irish-American families in Chicago and six middle-SES Chinese families in Taiwan. From extensive videotapes of adults' conversations with the children from age 2½ to 4, the investigators identified personal stories and coded them for content (Miller, Fung, & Mintz, 1996; Miller et al., 1997, 2012).

Parents in both cultures discussed pleasurable holidays and family excursions in similar ways and with similar frequency. But five times more often than the Irish-American parents, the Chinese parents told long stories about their preschooler's previous misdeeds—using impolite language, writing on the wall, or playing in an overly rowdy way. These narratives, often sparked by a current misdeed, were used as opportunities to educate: Parents conveyed stories with warmth and

caring, stressed the impact of misbehavior on others ("You made Mama lose face"), and often ended with direct teaching of proper behavior and a moral lesson ("Saying dirty words is not good"). By contrast, in the few instances in which Irish-American stories referred to transgressions, parents downplayed their seriousness, attributing them to the child's spunk and assertiveness.

Early narratives about the child launch preschoolers' self-concepts on culturally distinct paths (Miller, Fung, & Koven, 2007). Influenced by Confucian traditions of strict discipline and social obligations, Chinese parents integrated these values into their stories, affirming the importance of not disgracing the family and explicitly conveying expectations for improvement in the story's conclusion. Although Irish-American parents disciplined their children, they rarely dwelt on misdeeds in storytelling. Rather, they cast the child's shortcomings in a positive light, perhaps to promote self-esteem.

Whereas most Americans believe that favorable self-esteem is crucial for healthy development, Chinese adults generally see it as unimportant or even negative—as impeding the child's willingness to listen

RONNIE KAUFMAN/LARRY HIRSHOWITZ/ GETTY IMAGES/BLEND IMAGES

A Chinese mother speaks gently to her child about proper behavior. Chinese parents often tell preschoolers stories that point out the negative impact on others of the child's misdeeds. The Chinese child's self-concept, in turn, emphasizes social obligations.

and be corrected (Miller et al., 2002). Consistent with this view, the Chinese parents did little to cultivate their child's individuality. Instead, they used storytelling to guide the child toward responsible behavior. Hence, the Chinese child's self-image emphasizes obligations to others, whereas the American child's is more autonomous.

As early as age 2, parents use narratives of past events to impart rules, standards for behavior, and evaluative information about the child: "You added the milk when we made the mashed potatoes. That's a very important job!" (Nelson, 2003). As the Cultural Influences box above reveals, these self-evaluative narratives are a major means through which caregivers imbue the young child's self-concept with cultural values.

As they talk about personally significant events and as their cognitive skills advance, preschoolers gradually come to view themselves as persisting over time. Around age 4, children first become certain that a video image of themselves replayed a few minutes after it was filmed is still "me" (Povinelli, 2001). Similarly, when researchers asked 3- to 5-year-olds to imagine a future event (walking next to a waterfall) and to envision a future personal state by choosing from three items (a raincoat, money, a blanket) the one they would need to bring with them, performance—along with future-state justifications ("I'm gonna get wet")—increased sharply from age 3 to 4 (Atance & Meltzoff, 2005).

Emergence of Self-Esteem

Another aspect of self-concept emerges in early childhood: **self-esteem,** the judgments we make about our own worth and the feelings associated with those judgments. *TAKE A MOMENT...* Make a list of your own self-judgments. Notice that, besides a global appraisal of your worth as a person, you have a variety of separate self-evaluations concerning how well you perform at different activities. These evaluations are among the most important aspects of self-development because they affect our emotional experiences, future behavior, and long-term psychological adjustment.

By age 4, preschoolers have several self-judgments—for example, about learning things in school, making friends, getting along with parents, and treating others kindly (Marsh, Ellis, & Craven, 2002). But because they have difficulty distinguishing between their desired and their actual competence, they usually rate their own ability as extremely high and underestimate task

After creating a "camera" and "flash," this pre-schooler pretends to take pictures. Her high self-esteem contributes greatly to her initiative in mastering many new skills.

difficulty, as when Sammy asserted, despite his many misses, that he was great at beanbag throwing (Harter, 2003, 2006).

High self-esteem contributes greatly to preschoolers' initiative during a period in which they must master many new skills. By age 3, children whose parents patiently encourage while offering information about how to succeed are enthusiastic and highly motivated. In contrast, children whose parents criticize their worth and performance give up easily when faced with a challenge and express shame and despondency after failing (Kelley, Brownell, & Campbell, 2000). Adults can avoid promoting these self-defeating reactions by adjusting their expectations to children's capacities, scaffolding children's attempts at difficult tasks (see Chapter 7, page 234), and pointing out effort and improvement in children's behavior.

Emotional Development

Gains in representation, language, and self-concept support emotional development in early childhood. Between ages 2 and 6, children make strides in emotional abilities that, collectively, researchers refer to as *emotional competence* (Halberstadt, Denham, & Dunsmore, 2001; Saarni et al., 2006). First, preschoolers gain in emotional understanding, becoming better able to talk about feelings and to respond appropriately to others' emotional signals. Second, they become better at emotional self-regulation—in particular, at coping with intense negative emotion. Finally, preschoolers more often experience *self-conscious emotions* and *empathy*, which contribute to their developing sense of morality.

Parenting strongly influences preschoolers' emotional competence. Emotional competence, in turn, is vital for successful peer relationships and overall mental health.

Understanding Emotion

Early in the preschool years, children refer to causes, consequences, and behavioral signs of emotion, and over time their understanding becomes more accurate and complex (Stein & Levine, 1999). By age 4 to 5, children correctly judge the causes of many basic emotions ("He's happy because he's swinging very high"; "He's sad because he misses his mother"). Preschoolers' explanations tend to emphasize external factors over internal states, a balance that changes with age (Levine, 1995). After age 4, children appreciate that both desires and beliefs motivate behavior (Chapter 7). Then their grasp of how internal factors can trigger emotion expands.

Preschoolers can also predict what a playmate expressing a certain emotion might do next. Four-year-olds know that an angry child might hit someone and that a happy child is more likely to share (Russell, 1990). And they realize that thinking and feeling are interconnected—that a person reminded of a previous sad experience is likely to feel sad (Lagattuta, Wellman, & Flavell, 1997). Furthermore, they come up with effective ways to relieve others' negative feelings, such as hugging to reduce sadness (Fabes et al., 1988).

At the same time, preschoolers have difficulty interpreting situations that offer conflicting cues about how a person is feeling. When asked what might be happening in a picture of a happy-faced child with a broken bicycle, 4- and 5-year-olds tended to rely only on the emotional expression: "He's happy because he likes to ride his bike." Older children more often reconciled the two cues: "He's happy because his father promised to help fix his broken bike" (Gnepp, 1983; Hoffner & Badzinski, 1989). As in their approach to Piagetian tasks, preschoolers focus on the most obvious aspect of an emotional situation to the neglect of other relevant information.

The more parents label emotions, explain them, and express warmth and enthusiasm when conversing with preschoolers, the more "emotion words" children use and the better developed their emotional understanding (Fivush & Haden, 2005; Laible & Song, 2006). In one study, mothers who explained feelings and who negotiated and compromised during conflicts with their 2½-year-olds had children who, at age 3, were advanced in emotional understanding and used similar strategies to resolve disagreements (Laible & Thompson, 2002). Furthermore, 3- to 5-year-olds who are securely attached to their mothers better understand emotion. Attachment security is related to warmer and more elaborative parent–child narratives, including discussions of feelings that highlight the emotional significance of events (Laible, 2004; Laible & Song, 2006; Raikes & Thompson, 2006).

As preschoolers learn about emotion from interacting with adults, they engage in more emotion talk with siblings and friends, especially during make-believe play (Hughes & Dunn, 1998). Make-believe, in turn, contributes to emotional understanding, especially when children play with siblings (Youngblade & Dunn, 1995). The intense nature of the sibling relationship, combined with frequent acting out of feelings, makes pretending an excellent context for learning about emotions.

Applying What We Know

Helping Children Manage Common Fears of Early Childhood

Fear	Suggestion
Monsters, ghosts, and darkness	Reduce exposure to frightening stories in books and on TV until the child is better able to sort out appearance from reality. Make a thorough "search" of the child's room for monsters, showing him that none are there. Leave a night-light burning, sit by the child's bed until he falls asleep, and tuck in a favorite toy for protection.
Preschool or child care	If the child resists going to preschool but seems content once there, the fear is probably separation. Provide a sense of warmth and caring while gently encouraging independence. If the child fears being at preschool, find out what is frightening—the teacher, the children, or a crowded, noisy environment. Provide extra support by accompanying the child and gradually lessening the amount of time you are present.
Animals	Do not force the child to approach a dog, cat, or other animal that arouses fear. Let the child move at her own pace. Demonstrate how to hold and pet the animal, showing the child that when treated gently, the animal is friendly. If the child is larger than the animal, emphasize this: "You're so big. That kitty is probably afraid of you!"
Intense fears	If a child's fear is intense, persists for a long time, interferes with daily activities, and cannot be reduced in any of the ways just suggested, it has reached the level of a *phobia*. Sometimes phobias are linked to family problems, and counseling is needed to reduce them. At other times, phobias diminish without treatment as the child's capacity for emotional self-regulation improves.

As early as 3 to 5 years of age, knowledge about emotions is related to children's friendly, considerate behavior, willingness to make amends after harming another, and constructive responses to disputes with agemates (Dunn, Brown, & Maguire, 1995; Garner & Estep, 2001; Hughes & Ensor, 2010). Also, the more preschoolers refer to feelings when interacting with playmates, the better liked they are by their peers (Fabes et al., 2001). Children seem to recognize that acknowledging others' emotions and explaining their own enhance the quality of relationships.

Emotional Self-Regulation

Language also contributes to preschoolers' improved *emotional self-regulation* (Cole, Armstrong, & Pemberton, 2010). By age 3 to 4, children verbalize a variety of strategies for adjusting their emotional arousal to a more comfortable level. For example, they know they can blunt emotions by restricting sensory input (covering their eyes or ears to block out an unpleasant sight or sound), talking to themselves ("Mommy said she'll be back soon"), or changing their goals (deciding that they don't want to play anyway after being excluded from a game) (Thompson & Goodvin, 2007). As children use these strategies, emotional outbursts decline. *Effortful control*—in particular, inhibiting impulses and shifting attention—also continues to be vital in managing emotion during early childhood. Three-year-olds who can distract themselves when frustrated tend to become cooperative school-age children with few problem behaviors (Gilliom et al., 2002).

Warm, patient parents who use verbal guidance, including suggesting and explaining strategies and prompting children to generate their own, strengthen children's capacity to handle stress (Colman et al., 2006; Morris et al., 2011). In contrast, when parents rarely express positive emotion, dismiss children's feelings as unimportant, and have difficulty controlling their own anger, children have continuing problems in managing emotion (Hill et al., 2006; Katz & Windecker-Nelson, 2004; Thompson & Meyer, 2007).

As with infants and toddlers, preschoolers who experience negative emotion intensely find it harder to shift attention away from disturbing events and inhibit their feelings. They are more likely to be anxious and fearful, respond with irritation to others' distress, react angrily or aggressively when frustrated, and get along poorly with teachers and peers (Chang et al., 2003; Eisenberg et al., 2005; Raikes et al., 2007). Because these emotionally reactive children become increasingly difficult to rear, they are often targets of ineffective parenting, which compounds their poor self-regulation.

Adult–child conversations that prepare children for difficult experiences also foster emotional self-regulation (Thompson & Goodman, 2010). Parents who discuss what to expect and ways to handle anxiety offer strategies that children can apply. Nevertheless, preschoolers' vivid imaginations and incomplete grasp of the distinction between appearance and reality make fears common in early childhood. See Applying What We Know above for ways adults can help young children manage fears.

Self-Conscious Emotions

One morning in Leslie's classroom, a group of children crowded around for a bread-baking activity. Leslie asked them to wait patiently while she got a baking pan. But Sammy reached over to feel the dough, and the bowl tumbled off the table. When Leslie returned, Sammy looked at her, then covered his eyes with his hands and said, "I did something bad." He felt ashamed and guilty.

As their self-concepts develop, preschoolers become increasingly sensitive to praise and blame or to the possibility of such feedback. They more often experience *self-conscious emotions*—feelings that involve injury to or enhancement of their sense of self (see Chapter 6). By age 3, self-conscious emotions are clearly linked to self-evaluation (Lewis, 1995; Thompson, Meyer, & McGinley, 2006). But because preschoolers are still developing standards of excellence and conduct, they depend on the messages of parents, teachers, and others who matter to them to know *when* to feel proud, ashamed, or guilty, often viewing adult expectations as obligatory rules ("Dad said you're 'posed to take turns") (Thompson, Meyer, & McGinley, 2006).

When parents repeatedly comment on the worth of the child and her performance ("That's a bad job! I thought you were a good girl!"), children experience self-conscious emotions intensely—more shame after failure, more pride after success. In contrast, parents who focus on how to improve performance ("You did it this way; now try doing it that way") induce moderate, more adaptive levels of shame and pride and greater persistence on difficult tasks (Kelley, Brownell, & Campbell, 2000; Lewis, 1998).

Among Western children, intense shame is associated with feelings of personal inadequacy ("I'm stupid"; "I'm a terrible person") and with maladjustment—withdrawal and depression as well as intense anger and aggression toward those who participated in the shame-evoking situation (Lindsay-Hartz, de Rivera, & Mascolo, 1995; Mills, 2005). In contrast, guilt—when it occurs in appropriate circumstances and is neither excessive nor accompanied by shame—is related to good adjustment. Guilt helps children resist harmful impulses, and it motivates a misbehaving child to repair the damage and behave more considerately (Mascolo & Fischer, 2007; Tangney, Stuewig, & Mashek, 2007). But overwhelming guilt—involving such high emotional distress that the child cannot make amends—is linked to depressive symptoms as early as age 3 (Luby et al., 2009).

Finally, the consequences of shame for children's adjustment may vary across cultures. As illustrated in the Cultural Influences box on page 267 and on page 189 in Chapter 6, people in Asian collectivist societies, who define themselves in relation to their social group, view shame as an adaptive reminder of an interdependent self and of the importance of others' judgments (Bedford, 2004).

Empathy and Sympathy

Another emotional capacity that becomes more common in early childhood is *empathy,* which serves as an important motivator of **prosocial,** or **altruistic, behavior**—actions that benefit another person without any expected reward for the self (Spinrad & Eisenberg, 2009). Compared with toddlers, preschoolers rely more on words to communicate empathic feelings, a change that indicates a more reflective level of empathy. When a 4-year-old received a Christmas gift that she hadn't included on her list for Santa, she assumed it belonged to another little girl and pleaded with her parents, "We've got to give it back—

As children's language skills and capacity to take the perspective of others improve, empathy also increases, motivating prosocial, or altruistic, behavior.

Santa's made a big mistake. I think the girl's crying 'cause she didn't get her present!"

Yet in some children, empathizing—*feeling with* an upset adult or peer and responding emotionally in a similar way—does not yield acts of kindness and helpfulness but, instead, escalates into personal distress. In trying to reduce these feelings, the child focuses on his own anxiety rather than the person in need. As a result, empathy does not lead to **sympathy**—feelings of concern or sorrow for another's plight.

Temperament plays a role in whether empathy occurs and whether it prompts sympathetic, prosocial behavior or self-focused personal distress. Children who are sociable, assertive, and good at regulating emotion are more likely to empathize with others' distress, display sympathetic concern, and engage in prosocial behavior, helping, sharing, and comforting others in distress (Bengtsson, 2005; Eisenberg et al., 1998; Valiente et al., 2004). In contrast, when poor emotion regulators are faced with someone in need, they react with facial and physiological indicators of distress—frowning, lip biting, a rise in heart rate, and a sharp increase in EEG brain-wave activity in the right cerebral hemisphere (which houses negative emotion)—indications that they are overwhelmed by their feelings (Jones, Field, & Davalos, 2000; Pickens, Field, & Nawrocki, 2001).

As with other aspects of emotional development, parenting affects empathy and sympathy. When parents are warm, encourage emotional expressiveness, and show sensitive, empathic concern for their preschoolers' feelings, children are likely to react in a concerned way to the distress of others—relationships that persist into adolescence and early adulthood (Koestner, Franz, & Weinberger, 1990; Michalik et al., 2007; Strayer & Roberts, 2004). Besides modeling sympathy, parents can help shy children manage excessive anxiety and aggressive children regulate intense anger. They can also teach children the importance of kindness and can intervene when they display inappropriate emotion—strategies that predict high levels of sympathetic responding (Eisenberg, 2003).

In contrast, punitive parenting disrupts empathy at an early age (Valiente et al., 2004). In one study, physically abused preschoolers at a child-care center rarely expressed concern at a peer's unhappiness but, rather, reacted with fear, anger, and physical attacks (Klimes-Dougan & Kistner, 1990). The children's behavior resembled their parents' insensitive responses to others' suffering.

Peer Relations

As children become increasingly self-aware and better at communicating and understanding others' thoughts and feelings, their skill at interacting with peers improves rapidly. Peers provide young children with learning experiences they can get in no other way. Because peers interact on an equal footing, children must keep a conversation going, cooperate, and set goals in play. With peers, children form friendships—special relationships marked by attachment and common interests. Let's look at how peer interaction changes over the preschool years.

Advances in Peer Sociability

Mildred Parten (1932), one of the first to study peer sociability among 2- to 5-year-olds, noticed a dramatic rise with age in joint, interactive play. She concluded that social development proceeds in a three-step sequence. It begins with **nonsocial activity**—unoccupied, onlooker behavior and solitary play. Then it shifts to **parallel play,** in which a child plays near other children with similar materials but does not try to influence their behavior. At the highest level are two forms of true social interaction. In **associative play,** children engage in separate activities but exchange toys and comment on one another's behavior. Finally, in **cooperative play,** a more advanced type of interaction, children orient toward a common goal, such as acting out a make-believe theme.

Follow-Up Research on Peer Sociability. Longitudinal evidence indicates that these play forms emerge in the order suggested by Parten but that later-appearing ones do not replace earlier ones in a developmental sequence (Rubin, Bukowski, & Parker, 2006). Rather, all types coexist in early childhood.

TAKE A MOMENT... Watch children move from one type of play to another in a play group or preschool classroom, and you will see that they often transition from onlooker to parallel to cooperative play and back again (Robinson et al., 2003). Preschoolers seem to use parallel play as a way station—a respite from the demands of complex social interaction and a crossroad to new activities. And although nonsocial activity declines with age, it is still the most frequent form among 3- to 4-year-olds and accounts for a third of kindergartners' free-play time. Also, both solitary and parallel play remain fairly stable from 3 to 6 years, accounting for as much of the child's play as cooperative interaction (Rubin, Fein, & Vandenberg, 1983).

We now understand that the *type,* not the amount, of solitary and parallel play changes in early childhood. In studies of preschoolers' play in Taiwan and the United States, researchers rated the *cognitive maturity* of nonsocial, parallel, and cooperative play, using the categories shown in Table 8.1 on page 262. Within each play type, older children displayed more cognitively mature behavior than younger children (Pan, 1994; Rubin, Watson, & Jambor, 1978).

Often parents wonder whether a preschooler who spends much time playing alone is developing normally. But only *certain types* of nonsocial activity—aimless wandering, hovering near peers, and functional play involving repetitive motor action—are cause for concern. Children who watch peers without playing are usually temperamentally inhibited—high in social fearfulness (Coplan et al., 2004; Rubin, Bukowski, & Parker, 2006). And preschoolers who engage in solitary, repetitive behavior (banging blocks, making a doll jump up and down) tend to be immature, impulsive children who find it difficult to regulate anger and aggression (Coplan et al., 2001). In the classroom, both reticent and impulsive children tend to experience peer ostracism (Coplan & Arbeau, 2008).

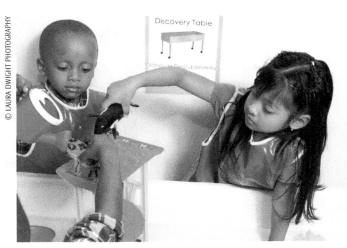

These 4-year-olds (left) engage in parallel play. Cooperative play (right) develops later than parallel play, but preschool children continue to move back and forth between the two types of sociability, using parallel play as a respite from the complex demands of cooperation.

TABLE 8.1

Developmental Sequence of Cognitive Play Categories

PLAY CATEGORY	DESCRIPTION	EXAMPLES
Functional play	Simple, repetitive motor movements with or without objects, especially common during the first two years	Running around a room, rolling a car back and forth, kneading clay with no intent to make something
Constructive play	Creating or constructing something, especially common between 3 and 6 years	Making a house out of toy blocks, drawing a picture, putting together a puzzle
Make-believe play	Acting out everyday and imaginary roles, especially common between 2 and 6 years	Playing house, school, or police officer; acting out storybook or television characters

Source: Rubin, Fein, & Vandenberg, 1983.

But most preschoolers with low rates of peer interaction simply like to play alone, and their solitary activities are positive and constructive. Children who prefer solitary play with art materials, puzzles, and building toys are typically well-adjusted youngsters who, when they do play with peers, show socially skilled behavior (Coplan & Armer, 2007). Still, a few preschoolers who engage in such age-appropriate solitary play—again, more often boys—are rebuffed by peers. Perhaps because quiet play is inconsistent with the "masculine" gender role, boys who engage in it are at risk for negative reactions from both parents and peers and, eventually, for adjustment problems (Coplan et al., 2001, 2004).

Cultural Variations. Peer sociability in collectivist societies, which stress group harmony, takes different forms than in individualistic cultures (Chen & French, 2008). For example, children in India generally play in large groups, which require high levels of cooperation. Much of their behavior is imitative, occurs in unison, and involves close physical contact. In a game called Bhatto Bhatto, children act out a script about a trip to the market, touching one another's elbows and hands as they pretend to cut and share a tasty vegetable (Roopnarine et al., 1994).

Agta village children in the Philippines play a tug-of-war game. Large-group, highly cooperative play is typical of peer sociability in collectivist societies.

As another example, Chinese preschoolers—unlike American preschoolers, who tend to reject reticent classmates—are typically willing to include a quiet, reserved child in play (Chen et al., 2006). In Chapter 6, we saw that until recently collectivist values, which discourage self-assertion, led to positive evaluations of shyness in China (see pages 194–195). Apparently, this benevolent attitude persists in the play behaviors of Chinese young children.

Cultural beliefs about the importance of play also affect early peer associations. Caregivers who view play as mere entertainment are less likely to provide props or to encourage pretend than those who value its cognitive and social benefits (Farver & Wimbarti, 1995). Preschoolers of Korean-American parents, who emphasize task persistence as vital for learning, spend less time than Caucasian-American children in joint make-believe and more time unoccupied and in parallel play (Farver, Kim, & Lee, 1995).

Recall the description of children's daily lives in a Mayan village culture on page 236 in Chapter 7. Mayan parents do not promote children's play—yet Mayan children are socially competent (Gaskins, 2000). Perhaps Western-style sociodramatic play, with its elaborate materials and wide-ranging themes, is particularly important for social development in societies where the worlds of children and adults are distinct. It may be less crucial in village cultures where children participate in adult activities from an early age.

First Friendships

As preschoolers interact, first friendships form that serve as important contexts for emotional and social development. To adults, friendship is a mutual relationship involving companionship, sharing, understanding of thoughts and feelings, and caring for and comforting each other in times of need. In addition, mature friendships endure over time and survive occasional conflicts.

Preschoolers understand something about the uniqueness of friendship. They say that a friend is someone "who likes you," with whom you spend a lot of time playing, and with whom you share toys. But friendship does not yet have a long-term, enduring quality based on mutual trust (Damon, 1988a; Hartup, 2006). "Mark's my best friend," Sammy would declare on days when the boys got along well. But when a dispute arose, he would reverse himself: "Mark, you're not my friend!"

Nevertheless, interactions between young friends are unique. Preschoolers give far more reinforcement—greetings, praise, and compliance—to children they identify as friends, and they also receive more from them. Friends are more cooperative and emotionally expressive—talking, laughing, and looking at each other more often than nonfriends do (Hartup, 2006; Vaughn et al., 2001). Furthermore, children who begin kindergarten with friends in their class or readily make new friends adjust to school more favorably (Ladd, Birch, & Buhs, 1999; Ladd & Price, 1987). Perhaps the company of friends serves as a secure base from which to develop new relationships, enhancing children's feelings of comfort in the new classroom.

Peer Relations and School Readiness

The ease with which kindergartners make new friends and are accepted by their classmates predicts cooperative participation in classroom activities and self-directed completion of learning tasks—behaviors linked to gains in achievement (Ladd, Birch, & Buhs, 1999; Ladd, Buhs, & Seid, 2000). The capacity to form friendships enables kindergartners to integrate themselves into classroom environments in ways that foster both academic and social competence. In a longitudinal follow-up of a large sample of 4-year-olds, children of average intelligence but with above-average social skills fared better in academic achievement in first grade than children of equal mental ability who were socially below average (Konold & Pianta, 2005).

Because social maturity in early childhood contributes to later academic performance, a growing number of experts propose that kindergarten readiness be assessed in terms of not just academic skills but also social skills (Ladd, Herald, & Kochel, 2006; Thompson & Raikes, 2007). Preschool programs, too, should attend to these vital social prerequisites. Warm, responsive teacher–child interaction is vital, especially for shy, impulsive, and emotionally negative children, who are at risk for social difficulties. In studies involving several thousand 4-year-olds in public preschools in six states, teacher sensitivity and emotional support were strong predictors of children's social competence, both during preschool and after kindergarten entry (Curby et al., 2009; Mashburn et al., 2008).

Parental Influences on Early Peer Relations

Children first acquire skills for interacting with peers within the family. Parents influence children's peer sociability both *directly*, through attempts to influence children's peer relations, and *indirectly*, through their child-rearing practices and play behaviors (Ladd & Pettit, 2002; Rubin et al., 2005).

Direct Parental Influences. Preschoolers whose parents frequently arrange informal peer play activities tend to have larger peer networks and to be more socially skilled (Ladd, LeSieur, & Profilet, 1993). In providing play opportunities, parents show children how to initiate peer contacts. And parents' skillful suggestions for managing conflict, discouraging teasing,

Parents' play with children, especially same-sex children, contributes to social competence. By playing with his father as he would with a peer, this child acquires social skills that facilitate peer interaction.

and entering a play group are associated with preschoolers' social competence and peer acceptance (Mize & Pettit, 2010; Parke et al., 2004b).

Indirect Parental Influences. Many parenting behaviors not directly aimed at promoting peer sociability nevertheless influence it. For example, secure attachments to parents are linked to more responsive, harmonious peer interaction, larger peer networks, and warmer, more supportive friendships during the preschool and school years (Laible, 2007; Lucas-Thompson & Clarke-Stewart, 2007; Wood, Emmerson, & Cowan, 2004). The sensitive, emotionally expressive communication that contributes to attachment security may be responsible.

Parent–child play seems particularly effective for promoting peer interaction skills. During play, parents interact with their child on a "level playing field," much as peers do. And perhaps because parents play more with children of their own sex, mothers' play is more strongly linked to daughters' competence, fathers' play to sons' competence (Lindsey & Mize, 2000; Pettit et al., 1998).

As we have seen, some preschoolers already have great difficulty with peer relations. In Leslie's classroom, Robbie was one of them. Wherever he happened to be, comments like "Robbie ruined our block tower" and "Robbie hit me for no reason" could be heard. As we take up moral development in the next section, you will learn more about how parenting contributed to Robbie's peer problems.

Foundations of Morality

Children's conversations and behavior provide many examples of their developing moral sense. By age 2, they use words to evaluate behavior as "good" or "bad" and react with distress to aggressive or potentially harmful behaviors (Kochanska, Casey, & Fukumoto, 1995). And we have seen that children of this age share toys, help others, and cooperate in games—early indicators of considerate, responsible prosocial attitudes.

Adults everywhere take note of this budding capacity to distinguish right from wrong. Some cultures have special terms for it. The Utku Indians of Hudson Bay say the child develops *ihuma* (reason). The Fijians believe that *vakayalo* (sense) appears. In response, parents hold children more responsible for their behavior (Dunn, 2005). By the end of early childhood, children can state many moral rules: "Don't take someone's things without asking!" "Tell the truth!" In addition, they argue over matters of justice: "You sat there last time, so it's my turn." "It's not fair. He got more!"

All theories of moral development recognize that conscience begins to take shape in early childhood. And most agree that at first, the child's morality is *externally controlled* by adults. Gradually, it becomes regulated by *inner standards*. Truly moral individuals do not do the right thing just to conform to others' expectations. Rather, they have developed compassionate concerns and principles of good conduct, which they follow in many situations.

Each major theory emphasizes a different aspect of morality. Psychoanalytic theory stresses the *emotional side* of conscience development—in particular, identification and guilt as motivators of good conduct. Social learning theory focuses on how *moral behavior* is learned through reinforcement and modeling. Finally, the cognitive-developmental perspective emphasizes *thinking*—children's ability to reason about justice and fairness.

The Psychoanalytic Perspective

Recall that according to Freud, young children form a *superego*, or conscience, by *identifying* with the same-sex parent, whose moral standards they adopt. Children obey the superego to avoid *guilt*, a painful emotion that arises each time they are tempted to misbehave. Moral development, Freud believed, is largely complete by 5 to 6 years of age.

Today, most researchers disagree with Freud's view of conscience development. In his theory (see page 256), fear of punishment and loss of parental love motivate conscience formation and moral behavior. Yet children whose parents frequently use threats, commands, or physical force tend to violate standards often and feel little guilt, whereas parental warmth and responsiveness predict greater guilt following transgressions (Kochanska et al., 2002, 2005, 2008). And if a parent withdraws love after misbehavior—for example, refuses to speak to or states a dislike for the child—children often respond with high levels of self-blame, thinking "I'm no good," or "Nobody loves me." Eventually, to protect themselves from overwhelming guilt, these children may deny the emotion and, as a result, also develop a weak conscience (Kochanska, 1991; Zahn-Waxler et al., 1990).

Inductive Discipline. In contrast, conscience formation is promoted by a type of discipline called **induction,** in which an adult helps the child notice feelings by pointing out the effects of the child's misbehavior on others. For example, a parent might say, "She's crying because you won't give back her doll" (Hoffman, 2000). When generally warm parents provide explanations that match the child's capacity to understand, while firmly insisting that the child listen and comply, induction is effective as early as age 2. Preschoolers whose parents use it are more likely to refrain from wrongdoing, confess and repair damage after misdeeds, and display prosocial behavior (Kerr et al., 2004; Volling, Mahoney, & Rauer, 2009; Zahn-Waxler, Radke-Yarrow, & King, 1979).

A teacher uses inductive discipline to explain to a child the impact of her transgression on others, pointing out classmates' feelings. Induction encourages empathy, sympathy, and commitment to moral standards.

The success of induction may lie in its power to motivate children's active commitment to moral standards. Induction gives children information about how to behave that they can use in future situations. By emphasizing the impact of the child's actions on others, it encourages empathy and sympathy (Krevans & Gibbs, 1996). And giving children reasons for changing their behavior encourages them to adopt moral standards because they make sense.

In contrast, discipline that relies too heavily on threats of punishment or withdrawal of love makes children so anxious and frightened that they cannot think clearly enough to figure out what they should do. As a result, these practices do not get children to internalize moral rules (Eisenberg, Fabes, & Spinrad, 2006).

The Child's Contribution. Although good discipline is crucial, children's characteristics also affect the success of parenting techniques. Twin studies suggest a modest genetic contribution to empathy (Knafo et al., 2009). More empathic children require less power assertion and are more responsive to induction.

Temperament is also influential. Mild, patient tactics—requests, suggestions, and explanations—are sufficient to prompt guilt reactions in anxious, fearful preschoolers (Kochanska et al., 2002). But with fearless, impulsive children, gentle discipline has little impact. Power assertion also works poorly. It undermines the child's capacity for effortful control, which strongly predicts good conduct, empathy, sympathy, and prosocial behavior (Kochanska & Aksan, 2006; Kochanska & Knaack, 2003). Parents of impulsive children can foster conscience development by ensuring a secure attachment relationship and combining firm correction with induction (Kochanska, Aksan, & Joy, 2007). When children are so low in anxiety that parental disapproval causes them little discomfort, a close parent–child bond motivates them to listen to parents as a means of preserving an affectionate, supportive relationship.

The Role of Guilt. Although little support exists for Freudian ideas about conscience development, Freud was correct that guilt is an important motivator of moral action. Inducing *empathy-based guilt* (expressions of personal responsibility and regret, such as "I'm sorry I hurt him") by explaining that the child is harming someone and has disappointed the parent is a means of influencing children without using coercion. Empathy-based guilt reactions are associated with stopping harmful actions, repairing damage caused by misdeeds, and engaging in future prosocial behavior (Baumeister, 1998; Eisenberg, Eggum, & Edwards, 2010). At the same time, parents must help children deal with guilt feelings constructively—by guiding them to make up for immoral behavior rather than minimizing or excusing it.

But contrary to what Freud believed, guilt is not the only force that compels us to act morally. Nor is moral development complete by the end of early childhood. Rather, it is a gradual process, extending into adulthood.

Social Learning Theory

According to social learning theory, morality does not have a unique course of development. Rather, moral behavior is acquired just like any other set of responses: through reinforcement and modeling.

Importance of Modeling. *Operant conditioning*—reinforcement for good behavior with approval, affection, and other rewards—is not enough for children to acquire moral responses. For a behavior to be reinforced, it must first occur spontaneously. Yet many prosocial acts, such as sharing, helping, or comforting an unhappy playmate, occur so rarely at first that reinforcement cannot explain their rapid development in early childhood. Rather, social learning theorists believe that children learn to behave morally largely through *modeling*—observing and imitating people who demonstrate appropriate behavior (Bandura, 1977; Grusec, 1988). Once children acquire a moral response, reinforcement in the form of praise increases its frequency (Mills & Grusec, 1989).

Many studies show that having helpful or generous models increases young children's prosocial responses. And certain characteristics of models affect children's willingness to imitate:

- *Warmth and responsiveness.* Preschoolers are more likely to copy the prosocial actions of a warm, responsive adult than those of a cold, distant adult (Yarrow, Scott, & Waxler, 1973). Warmth seems to make children more attentive and receptive to the model and is itself an example of a prosocial response.

- *Competence and power.* Children admire and therefore tend to imitate competent, powerful models—especially older peers and adults (Bandura, 1977).

- *Consistency between assertions and behavior.* When models say one thing and do another—for example, announce that "it's important to help others" but rarely engage in helpful acts—children generally choose the most lenient standard of behavior that adults demonstrate (Mischel & Liebert, 1966).

Models are most influential in the early years. In one study, toddlers' eager, willing imitation of their mothers' behavior predicted moral conduct (not cheating in a game) and guilt following transgressions at age 3 (Forman, Aksan, & Kochanska, 2004). At the end of early childhood, children who have had consistent exposure to caring adults have internalized prosocial rules and follow them whether or not a model is present (Mussen & Eisenberg-Berg, 1977).

Effects of Punishment. Many parents know that yelling at, slapping, and spanking children for misbehavior are ineffective disciplinary tactics. A sharp reprimand or physical force to restrain or move a child is justified when immediate obedience is necessary—for example, when a 3-year-old is about to run into the street. In fact, parents are most likely to use forceful methods under these conditions. But to foster long-term goals, such as acting kindly toward others, they tend to rely on warmth and reasoning (Kuczynski, 1984). And in response to very serious transgressions, such as lying and stealing, they often combine power assertion with reasoning (Grusec, 2006; Grusec & Goodnow, 1994).

Frequent punishment, however, promotes only immediate compliance, not lasting changes in behavior. For example, Robbie's parents often punished by hitting, criticizing, and shouting at him. But as soon as they were out of sight, Robbie usually engaged in the unacceptable behavior again. The more harsh threats, angry physical control, and physical punishment children experience, the more likely they are to develop serious, lasting mental health problems. These include weak internalization of moral rules; depression, aggression, antisocial behavior, and poor academic performance in childhood and adolescence; and depression, alcohol abuse, criminality, and partner and child abuse in adulthood (Afifi et al., 2006; Bender et al., 2007; Gershoff, 2002a; Kochanska, Aksan, & Nichols, 2003; Lynch et al., 2006).

Repeated harsh punishment has wide-ranging, undesirable side effects:

- Parents often spank in response to children's aggression (Holden, Coleman, & Schmidt, 1995). Yet the punishment itself models aggression!

- Harshly treated children develop a chronic sense of being personally threatened, which prompts a focus on their own distress rather than a sympathetic orientation to others' needs.

- Children who are frequently punished learn to avoid the punishing adult, who, as a result, has little opportunity to teach desirable behaviors.

- By stopping children's misbehavior temporarily, harsh punishment gives adults immediate relief. For this reason, a punitive adult is likely to punish with greater frequency over time, a course of action that can spiral into serious abuse.

- Children, adolescents, and adults whose parents used *corporal punishment*—the use of physical force to inflict pain but not injury—are more accepting of such discipline (Deater-Deckard et al., 2003; Vitrup & Holden, 2010). In this way, use of physical punishment may transfer to the next generation.

Although corporal punishment spans the SES spectrum, its frequency and harshness are elevated among less educated, economically disadvantaged parents (Lansford et al., 2004, 2009). And consistently, parents with conflict-ridden marriages and with mental health problems (who are emotionally reactive, depressed, or aggressive) are more likely to be punitive and also to have hard-to-manage children, whose disobedience evokes more parental harshness (Berlin et al., 2009; Erath et al., 2006; Taylor et al., 2010). These parent–child similarities suggest that heredity contributes to the link between punitive discipline and children's adjustment difficulties.

But heredity is not a complete explanation. Return to page 73 in Chapter 2 to review findings indicating that good parenting can shield children who are genetically at risk for aggression

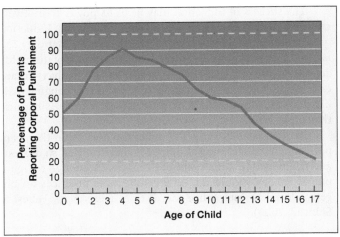

FIGURE 8.1 Prevalence of corporal punishment by children's age. Estimates are based on the percentage of parents in a nationally representative U.S. sample of nearly 1,000 reporting one or more instances of spanking, slapping, pinching, shaking, or hitting with a hard object in the past year. Physical punishment increases sharply during early childhood and then declines, but it is high at all ages. (From M. A. Straus & J. H. Stewart, 1999, "Corporal Punishment by American Parents: National Data on Prevalence, Chronicity, Severity, and Duration, in Relation to Child and Family Characteristics," *Clinical Child and Family Psychology Review, 2,* p. 59. Adapted with kind permission from Springer Science+Business Media and Murray A. Straus.)

and antisocial activity from developing those behaviors. Furthermore, longitudinal studies reveal that parental harshness and corporal punishment predict child and adolescent emotional and behavior problems, even after child, parenting, and family characteristics that might otherwise account for the relationship were controlled (Berlin et al., 2009; Lansford et al., 2009, 2011; Taylor et al., 2010).

In view of these findings, the widespread use of corporal punishment by American parents is cause for concern. Surveys of nationally representative samples of U.S. families reveal that although corporal punishment increases from infancy to age 5 and then declines, it is high at all ages (see Figure 8.1) (Gershoff et al., 2012; Straus & Stewart, 1999). Repeated use of physical punishment is more common with toddlers and preschoolers. And more than one-fourth of physically punishing parents report having used a hard object, such as a brush or a belt (Gershoff, 2002b).

A prevailing American belief is that corporal punishment, if implemented by caring parents, is harmless, perhaps even beneficial. But as the Cultural Influences box on the following page reveals, this assumption is valid only under conditions of limited use in certain social contexts.

Alternatives to Harsh Punishment. Alternatives to criticism, slaps, and spankings can reduce the side effects of punishment. A technique called **time out** involves removing children from the immediate setting—for example, by sending them to their rooms—until they are ready to act appropriately. When a child is out of control, a few minutes in time out can be

Cultural Influences

Ethnic Differences in the Consequences of Physical Punishment

In an African-American community, six elders, who had volunteered to serve as mentors for parents facing child-rearing challenges, met to discuss parenting issues at a social service agency. Their attitudes toward discipline were strikingly different from those of the white social workers who had brought them together. Each elder argued that successful child rearing required appropriate physical tactics. At the same time, they voiced strong disapproval of screaming or cursing at children, calling such out-of-control parental behavior "abusive." Ruth, the oldest and most respected member of the group, characterized good parenting as a complex combination of warmth, teaching, talking nicely, and disciplining physically. She related how an older neighbor advised her to handle her own children when she was a young parent:

> She said to me says, don't scream . . . you talk to them real nice and sweet and when they do something ugly . . . she say you get a nice little switch and you won't have any trouble with them and from that day that's the way I raised 'em. (Mosby et al., 1999, pp. 511–512)

In several studies, corporal punishment predicted externalizing problems similarly among white, black, Hispanic, and Asian children (Gershoff et al., 2012; Pardini, Fite, & Burke, 2008). But other investigations point to ethnic variations.

In one, researchers followed several hundred families for 12 years, collecting information from mothers on disciplinary strategies in early and middle childhood and from both mothers and their children on youth problem behaviors in adolescence (Lansford et al., 2004). Even after many child and family characteristics were controlled, the findings were striking: In Caucasian-American families, physical punishment was positively associated with adolescent aggression and antisocial behavior. In African-American families, by contrast, the more mothers had disciplined physically in childhood, the less their teenagers displayed angry, acting-out behavior and got in trouble at school and with the police.

According to the researchers, African-American and Caucasian-American parents tend to mete out physical punishment differently. In black families, such discipline is typically culturally approved and often mild, delivered in a context of parental warmth, and aimed at helping children become responsible adults. White parents, in contrast, consider physical punishment to be wrong, so when they resort to it, they are usually highly agitated and rejecting of the child (Dodge, McLoyd, & Lansford, 2006). As a result, many black children may view spanking as a practice carried out with their best interests in mind, whereas white children may regard it as an "act of personal aggression" (Gunnoe & Mariner, 1997, p. 768).

In support of this view, when several thousand ethnically diverse children were followed from the preschool through the early school years, spanking was associated

In African-American families, discipline often includes mild physical punishment. Because the practice is culturally approved and delivered in a context of parental warmth, children may view it as an effort to encourage maturity, not as an act of aggression.

with a rise in behavior problems if parents were cold and rejecting, but not if they were warm and supportive (McLoyd & Smith, 2002). And in another study, spanking predicted depressive symptoms only among African-American children whose mothers disapproved of the practice and, as a result, tended to use it when they were highly angry and frustrated (McLoyd et al., 2007).

These findings are not an endorsement of physical punishment. Other forms of discipline, including time out, withdrawal of privileges, and the positive strategies listed on page 268, are far more effective. But it is noteworthy that the meaning and impact of physical discipline vary sharply with its intensity level, context of warmth and support, and cultural approval.

---

enough to change behavior while also giving angry parents time to cool off (Morawska & Sanders, 2011). Another approach is *withdrawal of privileges,* such as watching a favorite TV program. Like time out, removing privileges allows parents to avoid using harsh techniques that can easily intensify into violence.

When parents do decide to use punishment, they can increase its effectiveness in three ways:

- *Consistency.* Permitting children to act inappropriately on some occasions but scolding them on others confuses them, and the unacceptable act persists (Acker & O'Leary, 1996).

- *A warm parent–child relationship.* Children of involved, caring parents find the interruption in parental affection that accompanies punishment especially unpleasant. They want to regain parental warmth and approval as quickly as possible.

- *Explanations.* Providing reasons for mild punishment helps children relate the misdeed to expectations for future behavior. This approach leads to a far greater reduction in misbehavior than using punishment alone (Larzelere et al., 1996).

Applying What We Know

Positive Parenting

Strategy	Explanation
Use transgressions as opportunities to teach.	When a child engages in harmful or unsafe behavior, intervene firmly, and then use induction, which motivates children to make amends and behave prosocially.
Reduce opportunities for misbehavior.	On a long car trip, bring back-seat activities that relieve children's restlessness. At the supermarket, converse with children and let them help with shopping. As a result, children learn to occupy themselves constructively when options are limited.
Provide reasons for rules.	When children appreciate that rules are rational, not arbitrary, they are more likely to strive to follow the rules.
Arrange for children to participate in family routines and duties.	By joining with adults in preparing a meal, washing dishes, or raking leaves, children develop a sense of responsible participation in family and community life and acquire many practical skills.
When children are obstinate, try compromising and problem solving.	When a child refuses to obey, express understanding of the child's feelings ("I know it's not fun to clean up"), suggest a compromise ("You put those away, I'll take care of these"), and help the child think of ways to avoid the problem in the future. Responding firmly but kindly and respectfully increases the likelihood of willing cooperation.
Encourage mature behavior.	Express confidence in children's capacity to learn and appreciation for effort and cooperation: "You gave that your best!" "Thanks for helping!" Adult encouragement fosters pride and satisfaction in succeeding, thereby inspiring children to improve further.

Sources: Berk, 2001; Grusec, 2006.

Positive Relationships, Positive Parenting. The most effective forms of discipline encourage good conduct—by building a mutually respectful bond with the child, letting the child know ahead of time how to act, and praising mature behavior. When sensitivity, cooperation, and shared positive emotion are evident in joint activities between parents and preschoolers, children show firmer conscience development—expressing empathy after transgressions, playing fairly in games, and considering others' welfare (Kochanska et al., 2005, 2008). Parent–child closeness leads children to heed parental demands because the child feels a sense of commitment to the relationship.

See Applying What We Know above for ways to parent positively. Parents who use these strategies focus on long-term social and life skills—cooperation, problem solving, and consideration for others. As a result, they greatly reduce the need for punishment.

The Cognitive-Developmental Perspective

The psychoanalytic and behaviorist approaches to morality focus on how children acquire ready-made standards of good conduct from adults. In contrast, the cognitive-developmental perspective regards children as *active thinkers* about social rules. As early as the preschool years, children make moral judgments, deciding what is right or wrong on the basis of concepts they construct about justice and fairness (Gibbs, 2010a; Turiel, 2006).

Young children have some well-developed ideas about morality. As long as researchers emphasize people's intentions, 3-year-olds say that a person with bad intentions—someone who deliberately frightens, embarrasses, or otherwise hurts another—is more deserving of punishment than a well-intentioned person

© MAURITIUS IMAGES GMBH/ALAMY

With parental encouragement, these sisters follow their route on a map during a long car trip. This positive parenting strategy keeps them constructively involved and reduces the likelihood of misbehavior.

(Helwig, Zelazo, & Wilson, 2001; Jones & Thompson, 2001). Around age 4, children know that a person who expresses an insincere intention—saying, "I'll come over and help you rake leaves," while not intending to do so—is lying (Maas, 2008). And 4-year-olds approve of telling the truth and disapprove of lying, even when a lie remains undetected (Bussey, 1992).

Furthermore, preschoolers distinguish **moral imperatives,** which protect people's rights and welfare, from two other types of rules and expectations: **social conventions,** customs determined solely by consensus, such as table manners and politeness rituals (saying "hello," "please," "thank you"); and **matters of personal choice,** such as friends, hairstyle, and leisure activities, which do not violate rights and are up to the individual (Killen, Margie, & Sinno, 2006; Nucci, 1996; Smetana, 2006). Interviews with 3- and 4-year-olds reveal that they judge moral violations (stealing an apple) as more wrong than violations of social conventions (eating ice cream with your fingers). And preschoolers' concern with personal choice, conveyed through statements like "I'm gonna wear *this* shirt," serves as the springboard for moral concepts of individual rights, which will expand greatly in middle childhood and adolescence (Nucci, 2005).

Within the moral domain, however, preschool and young school-age children tend to reason *rigidly,* making judgments based on salient features and consequences while neglecting other important information. For example, they are more likely than older children to claim that stealing and lying are always wrong, even when a person has a morally sound reason for doing so (Lourenco, 2003). Their explanations for why hitting others is wrong, even in the absence of rules against hitting, are simplistic and centered on physical harm: "When you get hit, it hurts, and you start to cry" (Nucci, 2008). And their focus on outcomes means that they fail to realize that a promise is still a promise, even if it is unfulfilled (Maas, 2008; Maas & Abbeduto, 2001).

Still, preschoolers' ability to distinguish moral imperatives from social conventions is impressive. How do they do so? According to cognitive-developmental theorists, they *actively make sense* of their experiences (Turiel, 2006). They observe that after a moral offense, peers respond with strong negative emotion, describe their own injury or loss, tell another child to stop, or retaliate. And an adult who intervenes is likely to call attention to the victim's rights and feelings. In contrast, violations of social convention elicit less intense peer reactions. And in these situations, adults usually demand obedience without explanation or point to the importance of keeping order.

Cognition and language support preschoolers' moral understanding, but social experiences are vital. Disputes with siblings and peers over rights, possessions, and property allow preschoolers to negotiate, compromise, and work out their first ideas about justice and fairness. Children also learn from warm, sensitive parental communication and from observing the way adults handle rule violations to protect the welfare of others (Turiel & Killen, 2010). Children who are advanced in moral thinking tend to have parents who adapt their communications about fighting, honesty, and ownership to what their children can understand, tell stories with moral implications, encourage prosocial behavior, and gently stimulate the child to think further, without being hostile or critical (Janssens & Deković, 1997; Walker & Taylor, 1991a).

Preschoolers who verbally and physically assault others, often with little or no provocation, are already delayed in moral reasoning (Helwig & Turiel, 2004; Sanderson & Siegal, 1988). Without special help, such children show long-term disruptions in moral development, deficits in self-control, and ultimately an antisocial lifestyle.

The Other Side of Morality: Development of Aggression

Beginning in late infancy, all children display aggression at times. As interactions with siblings and peers increase, so do aggressive outbursts. By the second year, aggressive acts with two distinct purposes emerge. Initially, the most common is **proactive** (or *instrumental*) **aggression,** in which children act to fulfill a need or desire—obtain an object, privilege, space, or social reward, such as adult or peer attention—and unemotionally attack a person to achieve their goal. The other type, **reactive** (or *hostile*) **aggression,** is an angry, defensive response to provocation or a blocked goal and is meant to hurt another person (Dodge, Coie, & Lynam, 2006; Little et al., 2003).

Proactive and reactive aggression come in three forms, which are the focus of most research:

- **Physical aggression** harms others through physical injury—pushing, hitting, kicking, or punching others or destroying another's property.
- **Verbal aggression** harms others through threats of physical aggression, name-calling, or hostile teasing.
- **Relational aggression** damages another's peer relationships through social exclusion, malicious gossip, or friendship manipulation.

Although verbal aggression is always direct, physical and relational aggression can be either *direct* or *indirect.* For example, hitting injures a person directly, whereas destroying property inflicts physical harm indirectly. Similarly, saying, "Do what I say, or I won't be your friend," conveys relational aggression directly, while spreading rumors, refusing to talk to a peer, or manipulating friendships by saying behind someone's back, "Don't play with her; she's a nerd," do so indirectly.

In early childhood, verbal aggression gradually replaces physical aggression (Alink et al., 2006; Tremblay et al., 1999). And proactive aggression declines as preschoolers' improved capacity to delay gratification enables them to avoid grabbing others' possessions. But reactive aggression in verbal and relational forms tends to rise over early and middle childhood (Côté et al., 2007; Tremblay, 2000). Older children are better able to recognize malicious intentions and, as a result, more often respond in hostile ways.

By age 17 months, boys are more physically aggressive than girls—a difference found throughout childhood in many cultures

These preschoolers display proactive aggression, pushing and grabbing as they argue over a game. As children learn to compromise and share, and as their capacity to delay gratification improves, proactive aggression declines.

(Baillargeon et al., 2007; Card et al., 2008). The sex difference is due in part to biology—in particular, to male sex hormones (androgens) and temperamental traits (activity level, irritability, impulsivity) on which boys exceed girls. Gender-role conformity is also important. As soon as preschoolers are aware of gender stereotypes—that males and females are expected to behave differently—physical aggression drops off more sharply for girls than for boys (Fagot & Leinbach, 1989).

Although girls have a reputation for being both more verbally and relationally aggressive than boys, the sex difference is small (Crick et al., 2004, 2006; Crick, Ostrov, & Werner, 2006). Beginning in the preschool years, girls concentrate most of their aggressive acts in the relational category. Boys inflict harm in more variable ways and, therefore, display overall rates of aggression that are much higher than girls'.

At the same time, girls more often use indirect relational tactics that—in disrupting intimate bonds especially important to girls—can be particularly mean. Whereas physical attacks are usually brief, acts of indirect relational aggression may extend for hours, weeks, or even months (Nelson, Robinson, & Hart, 2005; Underwood, 2003). In one instance, a 6-year-old girl formed a "pretty-girls club" and—for nearly an entire school year—convinced its members to exclude several classmates by saying they were "ugly and smelly."

An occasional aggressive exchange between preschoolers is normal. But children who are emotionally negative, impulsive, and disobedient are prone to early, high rates of physical or relational aggression (or both) that often persist, placing them at risk for internalizing and externalizing difficulties, social skills deficits, and antisocial activity in middle childhood and adolescence (Campbell et al., 2006; Côté et al., 2007; Vaillancourt et al., 2003). These negative outcomes, however, depend on child-rearing conditions.

The Family as Training Ground for Aggressive Behavior. "I can't control him, he's impossible," Robbie's mother, Nadine, complained to Leslie one day. When Leslie asked if Robbie might be troubled by something happening at home, she discovered that his parents fought constantly and resorted to harsh, inconsistent discipline. The same child-rearing practices that undermine moral internalization—love withdrawal, power assertion, critical remarks, physical punishment, and inconsistent discipline—are linked to aggression from early childhood through adolescence in diverse cultures, with most of these practices predicting both physical and relational forms (Bradford et al., 2003; Casas et al., 2006; Côté et al., 2007; Gershoff et al., 2010; Kuppens et al., 2009; Nelson et al., 2006a).

In families like Robbie's, anger and punitiveness quickly create a conflict-ridden family atmosphere and an "out-of-control" child. The pattern begins with forceful discipline, which occurs more often with stressful life experiences, a parent with an unstable personality, or a difficult child (Dodge, Coie, & Lynam, 2006). Typically, the parent threatens, criticizes, and punishes, and the child angrily resists until the parent "gives in." As these cycles become more frequent, they generate anxiety and irritability among other family members, who soon join in the hostile interactions. Compared with siblings in typical families, preschool siblings who have critical, punitive parents are more aggressive toward one another. Destructive sibling conflict, in turn, quickly spreads to peer relationships, contributing to poor impulse control and antisocial behavior by the early school years (Garcia et al., 2000; Ostrov, Crick, & Stauffacher, 2006).

Boys are more likely than girls to be targets of harsh, inconsistent discipline because they are more active and impulsive and therefore harder to control. When children who are extreme in these characteristics are exposed to emotionally negative, inept parenting, their capacity for emotional self-regulation, empathic responding, and guilt after transgressions is disrupted (Eisenberg, Eggum, & Edwards, 2010). Consequently, they lash out when disappointed, frustrated, or faced with a sad or fearful victim.

Children subjected to these family processes acquire a distorted view of the social world, often seeing hostile intent where it does not exist and, as a result, making many unprovoked attacks (Lochman & Dodge, 1998; Orbio de Castro et al., 2002). And some, who conclude that aggression "works" to access rewards and control others, callously use it to advance their own goals and are unconcerned about causing suffering in others—an aggressive style associated with later more severe conduct problems, violent behavior, and delinquency (Marsee & Frick, 2010).

Highly aggressive children tend to be rejected by peers, to fail in school, and (by adolescence) to seek out deviant peer groups that lead them toward violent delinquency and adult criminality. We will consider this life-course path of antisocial activity in Chapter 12.

Violent Media and Aggression. In the United States, 57 percent of TV programs between 6 A.M. and 11 P.M. contain violent scenes, often portraying repeated aggressive acts that go unpunished. Victims of TV violence are rarely shown experiencing serious harm, and few programs condemn violence or depict other ways of solving problems (Center for Communication and Social Policy, 1998). Verbally and relationally aggressive acts are particularly frequent in reality TV shows (Coyne, Robinson, & Nelson, 2010). And violent content is 9 percent above average in children's programming, with cartoons being the most violent.

LOOK AND LISTEN

Watch a half-hour of Saturday morning cartoons and a prime-time movie on TV, and tally the number of violent acts, including those that go unpunished. How often did violence occur in each type of program? What do young viewers learn about the consequences of violence? ●

Reviewers of thousands of studies have concluded that TV violence increases the likelihood of hostile thoughts and emotions and of verbally, physically, and relationally aggressive behavior (Comstock & Scharrer, 2006; Ostrov, Gentile, & Crick, 2006). And a growing number of studies confirm that playing violent video games has similar effects (Anderson et al., 2008; Hofferth, 2010). Although young people of all ages are susceptible, preschool and young school-age children are especially likely to imitate TV violence because they believe that much TV fiction is real and accept what they see uncritically.

Violent programming not only creates short-term difficulties in parent and peer relations but also has lasting negative consequences. In several longitudinal studies, time spent watching TV in childhood and adolescence predicted aggressive behavior in adulthood, after other factors linked to TV viewing (such as prior child and parent aggression, IQ, parent education, family income, and neighborhood crime) were controlled (see

Watching TV violence increases the likelihood of hostile thoughts and emotions and aggressive behavior. Playing violent video games has similar effects.

SHANNON FAGAN/GETTY IMAGES/PHOTOGRAPHER'S CHOICE

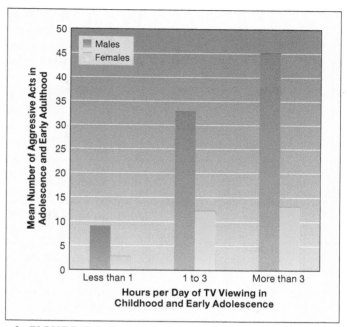

FIGURE 8.2 Relationship of television viewing in childhood and early adolescence to aggressive acts in adolescence and early adulthood. Interviews with more than 700 parents and youths revealed that the more TV watched in childhood and early adolescence, the greater the annual number of aggressive acts committed by the young person, as reported in follow-up interviews at ages 16 and 22. (Adapted from Johnson et al., 2002.)

Figure 8.2) (Graber et al., 2006; Huesmann, 1986; Huesmann et al., 2003; Johnson et al., 2002). Aggressive children and adolescents have a greater appetite for violent TV and computer games. And boys devote more time to violent media than girls, in part because of male-oriented themes of conquest and adventure. But even in nonaggressive children, violent TV sparks hostile thoughts and behavior; its impact is simply less intense (Bushman & Huesmann, 2001).

The ease with which television and video games can manipulate children's attitudes and behavior has led to strong public pressure to improve media content. In the United States, the First Amendment right to free speech has hampered efforts to regulate TV broadcasting. Instead, all programs must be rated for violent and sexual content, and all new TV sets are required to contain the V-chip, which allows parents to block undesired material. In general, parents bear most responsibility for regulating their children's exposure to media violence and other inappropriate content. As with the V-chip for TV, parents can control children's Internet access by using filters or programs that monitor website visits. Yet surveys of U.S. parents indicate that 20 to 30 percent of preschoolers and about half of school-age children experience no limits on TV or computer use at home. Some children begin visiting websites without parental supervision as early as age 4 (Rideout, Foehr, & Roberts, 2010; Rideout & Hamel, 2006; Varnhagen, 2007). Applying What We Know on page 272 lists strategies parents can use to protect their children from undesirable TV and computer fare.

Applying What We Know

Regulating TV and Computer Use

Strategy	Description
Limit TV viewing and computer use.	Parents should provide clear rules limiting children's TV and computer use and stick to them. The TV or computer should not be used as a babysitter for young children. Placing a TV or a computer in a child's bedroom substantially increases use and makes the child's activity hard to monitor.
Avoid using TV or computer time as a reward.	When TV or computer access is used as a reward or withheld as a punishment, children become increasingly attracted to it.
When possible, watch TV with children.	By raising questions about realism in TV depictions, expressing disapproval of on-screen behavior, and encouraging discussion, adults help children understand and evaluate TV content.
Link TV content to everyday learning experiences.	Parents can extend TV learning in ways that encourage children to engage actively with their surroundings. For example, a program on animals might spark a trip to the zoo, a visit to the library for a book about animals, or new ways of observing and caring for the family pet.
Model good TV and computer practices.	Parents' media behavior—avoiding excessive TV and computer use and limiting exposure to harmful content—influences their children's media behavior.

Helping Children and Parents Control Aggression.
Treatment for aggressive children is best begun early, before their antisocial behavior becomes well-practiced and difficult to change. Breaking the cycle of hostilities between family members and promoting effective ways of relating to others are crucial.

Leslie suggested that Robbie's parents enroll in a parent training program aimed at improving the parenting of children with conduct problems. In one approach, called *Incredible Years*, parents complete 18 weekly group sessions facilitated by two professionals, who teach positive parenting techniques for promoting preschool and school-age children's academic, emotional, and social skills and for managing disruptive behaviors (Webster-Stratton & Reid, 2010b). A complementary six-day training program for teachers, aimed at improving classroom management strategies and strengthening children's social skills, is also available. And a 22-week program intervenes directly with children, teaching appropriate classroom behavior, self-control, and social skills.

Evaluations in which families with aggressive children were randomly assigned to either Incredible Years or control groups reveal that the program is highly effective at improving parenting and reducing child behavior problems. Combining parent training with teacher and/or child intervention strengthens child outcomes (Webster-Stratton & Herman, 2010). And effects of parent training endure. In one long-term follow-up, 75 percent of young children with serious conduct problems whose parents participated in Incredible Years were well-adjusted as teenagers (Webster-Stratton & Reid, 2010a; Webster-Stratton, Rinaldi, & Reid, 2011).

Other interventions focus on modifying aggressive children's distorted social perspectives, by encouraging them to attend to nonhostile social cues, seek additional information

before acting, and take the perspective of others, which promotes empathy and sympathetic concern for others. Another approach is to teach effective conflict-resolution skills. At preschool, Robbie participated in a social problem-solving intervention. Over several months, he met with Leslie and a small group of classmates to act out common conflicts using puppets, discuss alternatives for settling disputes, and practice successful strategies. Children who receive such training show gains in social competence still present several months later (Bierman & Powers, 2009; Shure & Aberson, 2005).

Finally, Robbie's parents sought counseling for their marital problems. When parents receive help in coping with stressors in their own lives, interventions aimed at reducing children's aggression are even more effective (Kazdin & Whitley, 2003).

ASK YOURSELF

REVIEW What experiences help children differentiate moral imperatives, social conventions, and matters of personal choice?

CONNECT What must parents do to foster conscience development in fearless, impulsive children? How does this illustrate the concept of goodness of fit (see page 194 in Chapter 6)?

APPLY Alice and Wayne want their two children to become morally mature, caring individuals. List some parenting practices they should use and some they should avoid.

REFLECT Which types of punishment for a misbehaving preschooler do you endorse, and which types do you reject? Why?

Gender Typing

Gender typing refers to any association of objects, activities, roles, or traits with one sex or the other in ways that conform to cultural stereotypes (Liben & Bigler, 2002). In Leslie's classroom, girls spent more time in the housekeeping, art, and reading corners, while boys gathered more often in spaces devoted to blocks, woodworking, and active play. Already, the children had acquired many gender-linked beliefs and preferences and tended to play with peers of their own sex.

The same theories that provide accounts of morality have been used to explain children's gender typing: *social learning theory*, with its emphasis on modeling and reinforcement, and *cognitive-developmental theory*, with its focus on children as active thinkers about their social world. As we will see, neither is adequate by itself. *Gender schema theory*, a third perspective that combines elements of both, has gained favor. In the following sections, we consider the early development of gender typing.

Gender-Stereotyped Beliefs and Behavior

Even before children can label their own sex consistently, they have begun to acquire common associations with gender—men as rough and sharp, women as soft and round. In one study, 18-month-olds linked such items as fir trees and hammers with males, although they had not yet learned comparable feminine associations (Eichstedt et al., 2002). Recall from Chapter 6 that around age 2, children use such words as *boy, girl, lady,* and *man* appropriately. As soon as gender categories are established, children sort out what they mean in terms of activities and behavior.

Preschoolers associate toys, articles of clothing, tools, household items, games, occupations, colors (blue and pink), and behaviors (physical and relational aggression) with one sex or the other (Banse et al., 2010; Giles & Heyman, 2005; Poulin-Dubois et al., 2002). And their actions reflect their beliefs, not only in play preferences but in personality traits as well. As we have seen, boys tend to be more active, impulsive, assertive, and physically aggressive. Girls tend to be more fearful, dependent, emotionally sensitive, compliant, advanced in effortful control, and skilled at understanding self-conscious emotions and at inflicting indirect relational aggression (Bosacki & Moore, 2004; Else-Quest et al., 2006; Underwood, 2003).

During early childhood, gender-stereotyped beliefs strengthen—so much so that many children apply them as blanket rules rather than as flexible guidelines. When children were asked whether gender stereotypes could be violated, half or more of 3- and 4-year-olds answered "no" to clothing, hairstyle, and play with certain toys (Barbie dolls and G.I. Joes) (Blakemore, 2003). Furthermore, most 3- to 6-year-olds are firm about not wanting to be friends with a child who violates a gender stereotype (a boy who wears nail polish, a girl who plays with trucks) or to attend a school where such violations are allowed (Ruble et al., 2007).

Early in the preschool years, gender typing is well under way. Girls tend to play with girls and are drawn to toys and activities that emphasize nurturance and cooperation.

The rigidity of preschoolers' gender stereotypes helps us understand some commonly observed everyday behaviors. When Leslie showed her class a picture of a Scottish bagpiper wearing a kilt, the children insisted, "Men don't wear skirts!" During free play, they often exclaimed that girls can't be police officers and boys don't take care of babies. These one-sided judgments are a joint product of gender stereotyping in the environment and young children's cognitive limitations (Trautner et al., 2005). Most preschoolers do not yet realize that characteristics *associated with* being male or female—activities, toys, occupations, hairstyle, and clothing—do not *determine* a person's sex.

Biological Influences on Gender Typing

The sex differences just described appear in many cultures around the world (Munroe & Romney, 2006; Whiting & Edwards, 1988). Certain ones—male activity level and physical aggression, female emotional sensitivity, and preference for same-sex playmates—are widespread among mammalian species (de Waal, 1993, 2001). According to an evolutionary perspective, the adult life of our male ancestors was largely oriented toward competing for mates, that of our female ancestors toward rearing children. Therefore, males became genetically primed for dominance and females for intimacy, responsiveness, and cooperativeness. Evolutionary theorists claim that family and cultural forces can influence the intensity of biologically based sex differences. But experience cannot eradicate aspects of gender typing that served adaptive functions in human history (Konner, 2010; Maccoby, 2002).

Experiments with animals reveal that prenatally administered androgens increase active play and aggression and suppress maternal caregiving in both male and female mammals

(Sato et al., 2004). Eleanor Maccoby (1998) argues that sex hormones also affect human play styles, leading to rough, noisy movements among boys and calm, gentle actions among girls. Then, as children interact with peers, they choose partners whose interests and behaviors are compatible with their own. Preschool girls increasingly seek out other girls and like to play in pairs because they share a preference for quieter activities involving cooperative roles. Boys come to prefer larger-group play with other boys, who share a desire to run, climb, play-fight, compete, and build up and knock down (Fabes, Martin, & Hanish, 2003). At age 4, children spend three times as much time with same-sex as with other-sex playmates. By age 6, this ratio has climbed to 11 to 1 (Martin & Fabes, 2001).

Even stronger support for the role of biology in human gender typing comes from research on girls exposed prenatally to high levels of androgens, due either to normal variation in hormone levels or to a genetic defect. In both instances, these girls showed more "masculine" behavior—a preference for trucks and blocks over dolls, for active over quiet play, and for boys as playmates—even when parents encouraged them to engage in gender-typical play (Cohen-Bendahan, van de Beek, & Berenbaum, 2005; Pasterski et al., 2005).

Research on boys with low early androgen exposure, either because production by the testes is reduced or because body cells are androgen-insensitive, also yields consistent findings (Jürgensen et al., 2007). The greater the degree of impairment, the more these boys display "feminine" behaviors, including toy choices and preference for girl playmates.

Environmental Influences on Gender Typing

A wealth of evidence reveals that environmental forces—at home, at school, and in the community—build on genetic influences to promote vigorous gender typing in early childhood.

Parents. Beginning at birth, parents have different expectations of sons than of daughters. Many parents prefer that their children play with "gender-appropriate" toys. And they tend to describe achievement, competition, and control of emotion as important for sons and warmth, "ladylike" behavior, and closely supervised activities as important for daughters (Brody, 1999; Turner & Gervai, 1995).

Actual parenting practices reflect these beliefs. Parents give their sons toys that stress action and competition (guns, cars, tools, footballs) and their daughters toys that emphasize nurturance, cooperation, and physical attractiveness (dolls, tea sets, jewelry) (Leaper, 1994; Leaper & Friedman, 2007). Parents also actively reinforce independence in boys and closeness and dependency in girls. For example, parents react more positively when a son plays with cars and trucks, demands attention, runs and climbs, or tries to take toys from others. When interacting with daughters, they more often direct play activities, provide help, encourage participation in household tasks, make supportive statements (approval, praise, and agreement), and refer to emotions (Clearfield & Nelson, 2006; Fagot & Hagan, 1991;

Of the two sexes, boys are more gender-typed. Fathers, especially, promote "masculine" behavior in their preschool sons through activities that stress action and competition.

Kuebli, Butler, & Fivush, 1995). Gender-typed play contexts amplify these communication differences. For example, when playing housekeeping, mothers engage in high rates of supportive emotion talk with girls (Leaper, 2000).

As these findings suggest, language is a powerful indirect means for teaching children about gender stereotypes. Earlier we saw that most young children hold rigid beliefs about gender. Although their strict views are due in part to cognitive limitations, they also draw on relevant social experiences to construct these beliefs. Even parents who believe strongly in gender equality unconsciously use language that highlights gender distinctions and informs children about traditional gender roles (see the Social Issues: Education box on the following page).

LOOK AND LISTEN

Observe a parent discussing a picture book with a 3- to 6-year-old. How many times did the parent make generic statements about gender? How about the child? Did the parent accept or correct the child's generic utterances? ●

Of the two sexes, boys are more gender-typed. Fathers, especially, are more insistent that boys conform to gender roles. They place more pressure to achieve on sons than on daughters and are less tolerant of "cross-gender" behavior in sons—more concerned when a boy acts like a "sissy" than when a girl acts like a "tomboy" (Sandnabba & Ahlberg, 1999; Wood, Desmarais, & Gugula, 2002). Parents who hold nonstereotyped values and consciously avoid behaving in these ways have children who are less gender-typed (Brody, 1997; Tenenbaum & Leaper, 2002).

Teachers. Teachers often act in ways that extend gender-role learning. Several times, Leslie caught herself emphasizing gender distinctions when she called out, "Will the girls line up on one side and the boys on the other?" or pleaded, "Boys, I wish you'd quiet down like the girls!"

Social Issues: Education

Young Children Learn About Gender Through Mother–Child Conversations

© ELLEN B. SENISI PHOTOGRAPHY

In an investigation of the power of language to shape preschoolers' beliefs about gender, mothers were asked to converse with their 2- to 6-year-olds about picture books containing images both consistent and inconsistent with gender stereotypes (Gelman, Taylor, & Nguyen, 2004). Each picture was accompanied by the question, "Who can X?" where X was the activity on the page.

A detailed analysis of picture-book conversations revealed that mothers' directly expressed gender attitudes were neutral, largely because they mostly posed questions to their children, such as, "Who's driving that boat?" "Who can be a sailor? Boys and girls?" But by age 4, children often voiced stereotypes ("No, only boys can do that!"), and nearly one-third of the time, mothers affirmed them ("OK, only boys"). In other instances mothers either moved on or repeated the question. But rarely—just 2 percent of the time—did they explicitly counter a child's stereotype, and usually only when the book itself included stereotype-inconsistent pictures.

Although the mothers were not asked to discuss gender, they called attention to it even when they did not need to do so. In English, many nouns referring to people convey age-related information *(kid, baby, 2-year-old, preschooler, teenager, grownup, senior),* whereas only a few encode gender *(male, female, sister, brother, aunt, uncle).* Yet when referring to persons, mothers called attention to gender more than half the time, even though the people shown in the books varied as much in age as in gender. Referring often to gender encourages young children to sort the social world into gender categories.

Furthermore, both mothers and children frequently expressed *generic utterances*—ones that were broad in scope, referring to many, or nearly all, males and females: "Boys can be sailors." "Most girls don't like trucks." Even generics that were gender-neutral ("Lots of girls in this book") or that denied a stereotype ("Boys can be ballet dancers") prompted children to view individuals of the same gender as alike and to ignore exceptions.

Mothers' and children's use of generics increased with age (see Figure 8.3). At age 2, mothers introduced these generalizations nearly three times as often as children. But by age 6 children were producing generics more often than mothers. Generics were especially common in speech to and from boys, likely contributing to boys' stronger gender typing.

Even though these mothers over-

While reading, this mother may unconsciously teach her child to see the world in gender-linked terms—by referring to gender unnecessarily or by making generic statements ("Most girls prefer X"; "Boys usually don't like X").

whelmingly believed in gender equality, in conversing with their children, they provided a wealth of implicit cues that foster gender-stereotyping. Adults can combat children's gender stereotyped beliefs by refraining from labeling gender unnecessarily (substituting *friend* for *boy* or *girl*), using references to individuals ("That person wants to be firefighter") or qualifiers ("Some boys and some girls want to be firefighters"), countering children's stereotypical claims, and discussing gender biases in language with children and asking them to avoid using gender labels and generics.

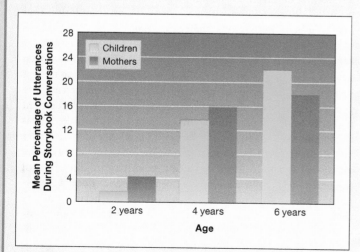

FIGURE 8.3 Mothers' and children's use of generic reference to gender during storybook conversations. Mothers' and children's use of generics increased dramatically with age. At age 2, mothers produced more generics than children. By age 6, children produced more generics than mothers. (From S. A. Gelman, M. G. Taylor, & S. P. Nguyen, "Mother–Child Conversations About Gender," *Monographs of the Society for Research in Child Development*, 69[1, Serial No. 275], p. 46. © 2004 The Society for Research in Child Development, Inc. Reproduced with permission of John Wiley & Sons Ltd)

Like parents, preschool teachers give girls more encouragement to participate in adult-structured activities. Girls frequently cluster around the teacher, following directions, whereas boys are attracted to play areas where teachers are minimally involved (Campbell, Shirley, & Candy, 2004; Powlishta, Serbin, & Moller, 1993). As a result, boys and girls practice different social behaviors. Compliance and bids for help occur more often in adult-structured contexts; assertiveness, leadership, and creative use of materials in unstructured pursuits.

Furthermore, as early as kindergarten, teachers give more overall attention (both positive and negative) to boys than to girls—a difference evident in diverse countries, including China, England, and the United States. They tend to praise boys more for their academic knowledge, perhaps as a means of motivating them because boys' school performance is behind that of girls. Teachers also use more disapproval and controlling discipline with boys (Chen & Rao, 2011; Davies, 2008; Swinson & Harrop, 2009). They seem to expect boys to misbehave more often—a belief based partly on boys' actual behavior and partly on gender stereotypes.

Peers. The more preschoolers play with same-sex partners, the more their behavior becomes gender-typed—in toy choices, activity level, aggression, and adult involvement (Martin & Fabes, 2001). By age 3, same-sex peers positively reinforce one another for gender-typed play by praising, imitating, or joining in. In contrast, when preschoolers engage in "cross-gender" activities—for example, when boys play with dolls or girls with cars and trucks—peers criticize them. Boys are especially intolerant of cross-gender play in other boys (Thorne, 1993). A boy who frequently crosses gender lines is likely to be ostracized by other boys, even when he does engage in "masculine" activities!

Children also develop different styles of social influence in gender-segregated peer groups. To get their way in large-group play, boys often rely on commands, threats, and physical force. Girls' preference for playing in pairs leads to greater concern with a partner's needs, evident in girls' use of polite requests, persuasion, and acceptance. Girls soon find that these tactics succeed with other girls but not with boys, who ignore their courteous overtures (Leaper, 1994; Leaper, Tenenbaum, & Shaffer, 1999). Boys' unresponsiveness gives girls another reason to stop interacting with them.

Over time, children come to believe in the "correctness" of gender-segregated play, which further strengthens gender segregation and gender-stereotyped activities (Martin et al., 1999). As boys and girls separate, *in-group favoritism*—more positive evaluations of members of one's own gender—becomes another factor that sustains the separate social worlds of boys and girls, resulting in "two distinct subcultures" of knowledge, beliefs, interests, and behaviors (Maccoby, 2002).

Although gender segregation is pervasive, cultural variations exist in the extent of gender-typed communication within such groups. African-American and Hispanic girls from low-SES families tend to be more assertive and independent when interacting with one another and with boys than are Caucasian-

American girls (Goodwin, 1998). Similarly, in a comparison of Chinese and U.S. preschoolers' play, Chinese girls used more direct commands and criticism when interacting with same- and other-sex peers (Kyratzis & Guo, 2001). In cultures where interdependence is highly valued, perhaps children do not feel a need to work as hard at maintaining same-sex peer relations through traditional interaction.

The Broader Social Environment. Finally, although children's everyday environments have changed to some degree, they continue to present many examples of gender-typed behavior—in occupations, leisure activities, media portrayals, and achievements of men and women. As we will see next, children soon come to view not just their social surroundings but also themselves through a "gender-biased lens"—a perspective that can seriously restrict their interests and learning opportunities.

Gender Identity

As adults, each of us has a **gender identity**—an image of oneself as relatively masculine or feminine in characteristics. By middle childhood, researchers can measure gender identity by asking children to rate themselves on personality traits. A child or adult with a "masculine" identity scores high on traditionally masculine items (such as *ambitious, competitive,* and *self-sufficient*) and low on traditionally feminine items (such as *affectionate, cheerful,* and *soft-spoken*). Someone with a "feminine" identity does the reverse. And a substantial minority (especially females) have a gender identity called **androgyny,** scoring high on both masculine and feminine personality characteristics.

Gender identity is a good predictor of psychological adjustment. "Masculine" and androgynous children and adults have higher self-esteem than "feminine" individuals (Boldizar, 1991; DiDonato & Berenbaum, 2011; Harter, 2006). In line with their flexible self-definitions, androgynous individuals are more adaptable—able to show masculine independence or feminine sensitivity, depending on the situation (Huyck, 1996; Taylor & Hall, 1982). The existence of an androgynous identity demonstrates that children can acquire a mixture of positive qualities traditionally associated with each gender—an orientation that may best help them realize their potential.

Emergence of Gender Identity. How do children develop a gender identity? According to *social learning theory,* behavior comes before self-perceptions. Preschoolers first acquire gender-typed responses through modeling and reinforcement and only later organize these behaviors into gender-linked ideas about themselves. In contrast, *cognitive-developmental theory* maintains that self-perceptions come before behavior. Over the preschool years, children acquire a cognitive appreciation of the permanence of their sex. They develop **gender constancy**—a full understanding of the biologically based permanence of their gender, including the realization that sex remains the same even if clothing, hairstyle, and play activities change. Then children use this knowledge to guide their behavior.

Children younger than age 6 who watch an adult dress a doll in "other-gender" clothing typically insist that the doll's sex has also changed (Chauhan, Shastri, & Mohite, 2005; Fagot, 1985). Attainment of gender constancy is strongly related to ability to pass verbal appearance–reality tasks (see page 228 in Chapter 7) (Trautner, Gervai, & Nemeth, 2003). Indeed, gender constancy tasks can be considered a type of appearance–reality problem, in that children must distinguish what a person looks like from who he or she really is.

In many cultures, young children do not have access to basic biological knowledge about gender because they rarely see members of the other sex naked. But giving preschoolers information about genital differences does not result in gender constancy. Those who have such knowledge usually say changing a doll's clothing will not change its sex, but when asked to justify their responses, they do not refer to sex as an innate, unchanging quality of people (Szkrybalo & Ruble, 1999). This suggests that cognitive immaturity, not social experience, is responsible for preschoolers' difficulty grasping the permanence of sex.

Is cognitive-developmental theory correct that gender constancy is responsible for children's gender-typed behavior? Evidence for this assumption is weak. "Gender-appropriate" behavior appears so early in the preschool years that its initial appearance must result from modeling and reinforcement, as social learning theory suggests. Although outcomes are not entirely consistent, some evidence suggests that gender constancy actually contributes to the emergence of more flexible gender-role attitudes during the school years (Ruble et al., 2007). But overall, the impact of gender constancy on gender typing is not great. As research in the following section reveals, gender-role adoption is more powerfully affected by children's beliefs about how close the connection must be between their own gender and their behavior.

Gender Schema Theory. **Gender schema theory** is an information-processing approach that combines social learning and cognitive-developmental features. It explains how environmental pressures and children's cognitions work together to shape gender-role development (Martin & Halverson, 1987; Martin, Ruble, & Szkrybalo, 2002). At an early age, children pick up gender-typed preferences and behaviors from others. At the same time, they organize their experiences into *gender schemas,* or masculine and feminine categories, that they use to interpret their world. As soon as preschoolers can label their own gender, they select gender schemas consistent with it ("Only boys can be doctors" or "Cooking is a girl's job") and apply those categories to themselves. Their self-perceptions then become gender-typed and serve as additional schemas that children use to process information and guide their own behavior.

We have seen that individual differences exist in the extent to which children endorse gender-typed views. Figure 8.4 shows different cognitive pathways for children who often apply gender schemas to their experiences and those who rarely do (Liben & Bigler, 2002). Consider Billy, who encounters a doll. If Billy is a *gender-schematic child,* his *gender-salience filter* immediately makes gender highly relevant. Drawing on his prior learning, he asks himself, "Should boys play with dolls?" If he answers "yes" and the toy interests him, he will explore it and learn more about it. If he answers "no," he will avoid the "gender-inappropriate" toy. But if Billy is a *gender-aschematic child*—one

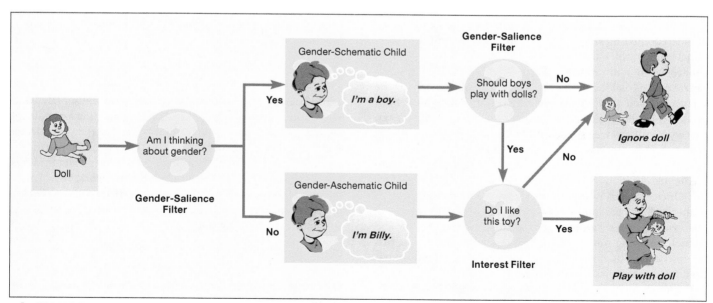

FIGURE 8.4 Cognitive pathways for gender-schematic and gender-aschematic children. In *gender-schematic children,* the gender-salience filter immediately makes gender highly relevant: Billy sees a doll and thinks, "I'm a boy. Should boys play with dolls?" Drawing on his experiences, he answers "yes" or "no." If he answers "yes" and the doll interests him, he plays with the doll. If he answers "no," he avoids the "gender-inappropriate" toy. *Gender-aschematic children* rarely view the world in gender-linked terms: Billy simply asks, "Do I like this toy?" and responds on the basis of his interests. (Reprinted by permission of Rebecca Bigler.)

who seldom views the world in gender-linked terms—he simply asks himself, "Do I like this toy?" and responds on the basis of his interests.

Gender-schematic thinking is so powerful that when children see others behaving in "gender-inconsistent" ways, they often cannot remember the information or distort it to make it "gender-consistent." For example, when shown a picture of a male nurse, they may remember him as a doctor (Martin & Ruble, 2004). And because gender-schematic preschoolers typically conclude, "What I like, children of my own sex will also like," they often use their own preferences to add to their gender biases (Liben & Bigler, 2002). For example, a girl who dislikes oysters may conclude that only boys like oysters even though she has never actually been given information promoting such a stereotype. At least partly for this reason, young children's gender schemas contain both culturally standard and nonstandard ideas (Tennenbaum et al., 2010). Not until well into the school years do children's gender schemas fully resemble those of adults.

Reducing Gender Stereotyping in Young Children

How can we help young children avoid rigid gender schemas that restrict their behavior and learning opportunities? No easy recipe exists. Biology clearly affects children's gender typing, channeling boys toward active, competitive play and girls toward quieter, more intimate interaction. But most aspects of gender typing are not built into human nature (Ruble, Martin, & Berenbaum, 2006).

Because young children's cognitive limitations lead them to assume that cultural practices determine gender, parents and teachers are wise to try to delay preschoolers' exposure to gender-stereotyped messages. Adults can begin by limiting traditional gender roles in their own behavior and by providing children with nontraditional alternatives. For example, parents can take turns making dinner, bathing children, and driving the family car, and they can give their sons and daughters both trucks and dolls and both pink and blue clothing. Teachers can ensure that all children spend time in both adult-structured and unstructured activities. Adults can also avoid using language that conveys gender stereotypes and can shield children from media presentations that do so.

Once children notice the vast array of gender stereotypes in their society, parents and teachers can point out exceptions. For example, they can arrange for children to see men and women pursuing nontraditional careers and can explain that interests and skills, not sex, should determine a person's occupation. Research shows that such reasoning is highly effective in reducing children's tendency to view the world in a gender-biased fashion. By middle childhood, children who hold flexible beliefs about what boys and girls can do are more likely to notice instances of gender discrimination (Brown & Bigler, 2004). And as we will see next, a rational approach to child rearing promotes healthy, adaptable functioning in many other areas as well.

Child Rearing and Emotional and Social Development

In this and previous chapters, we have seen how parents can foster children's competence—by building a parent–child relationship based on affection and cooperation, by serving as models and reinforcers of mature behavior, by using reasoning and inductive discipline, and by guiding and encouraging children's mastery of new skills. Now let's put these practices together into an overall view of effective parenting.

Styles of Child Rearing

Child-rearing styles are combinations of parenting behaviors that occur over a wide range of situations, creating an enduring child-rearing climate. In a landmark series of studies, Diana Baumrind (1971) gathered information on child rearing by watching parents interact with their preschoolers. Her findings, and those of others who have extended her work, reveal three features that consistently differentiate an effective style from less effective ones: (1) acceptance and involvement, (2) control, and (3) autonomy granting (Gray & Steinberg, 1999; Hart, Newell, & Olsen, 2003). Table 8.2 shows how child-rearing styles differ in these features.

Authoritative Child Rearing. The **authoritative child-rearing style**—the most successful approach—involves high acceptance and involvement, adaptive control techniques, and appropriate autonomy granting. Authoritative parents are warm, attentive, and sensitive to their child's needs. They establish an enjoyable, emotionally fulfilling parent–child relationship that

TABLE 8.2 **Features of Child-Rearing Styles**

CHILD-REARING STYLE	ACCEPTANCE AND INVOLVEMENT	CONTROL	AUTONOMY GRANTING
Authoritative	Is warm, responsive, attentive, patient, and sensitive to the child's needs	Makes reasonable demands for maturity and consistently enforces and explains them	Permits the child to make decisions in accord with readiness Encourages the child to express thoughts, feelings, and desires When parent and child disagree, engages in joint decision making when possible
Authoritarian	Is cold and rejecting and frequently degrades the child	Makes many demands coercively, using force and punishment Often uses psychological control, withdrawing love and intruding on the child's individuality	Makes decisions for the child Rarely listens to the child's point of view
Permissive	Is warm but overindulgent or inattentive	Makes few or no demands for maturity	Permits the child to make many decisions before the child is ready
Uninvolved	Is emotionally detached and withdrawn	Makes few or no demands for maturity	Is indifferent to the child's decision making and point of view

draws the child into close connection. At the same time, authoritative parents exercise firm, reasonable control. They insist on appropriate maturity, give reasons for their expectations, and use disciplinary encounters as "teaching moments" to promote the child's self-regulation. Finally, authoritative parents engage in gradual, appropriate autonomy granting, allowing the child to make decisions in areas where he is ready to do so (Kuczynski & Lollis, 2002; Russell, Mize, & Bissaker, 2004).

Throughout childhood and adolescence, authoritative parenting is linked to many aspects of competence—an upbeat mood, self-control, task persistence, cooperativeness, high self-esteem, social and moral maturity, and favorable school performance (Amato & Fowler, 2002; Aunola, Stattin, & Nurmi, 2000; Gonzalez & Wolters, 2006; Mackey, Arnold, & Pratt, 2001; Milevsky et al., 2007; Steinberg, Darling, & Fletcher, 1995).

Authoritarian Child Rearing. The **authoritarian child-rearing style** is low in acceptance and involvement, high in coercive control, and low in autonomy granting. Authoritarian parents appear cold and rejecting. To exert control, they yell, command, criticize, and threaten. "Do it because I said so!" is their attitude. They make decisions for their child and expect the child to accept their word unquestioningly. If the child resists, authoritarian parents resort to force and punishment.

Children of authoritarian parents are more likely to be anxious, unhappy, and low in self-esteem and self-reliance. When frustrated, they tend to react with hostility and, like their parents, resort to force when they do not get their way. Boys, especially, show high rates of anger and defiance. Although girls also engage in acting-out behavior, they are more likely to be dependent, lacking interest in exploration, and overwhelmed by challenging tasks (Hart, Newell, & Olsen, 2003; Kakihara et al., 2010; Thompson, Hollis, & Richards, 2003). Children and adolescents exposed to the authoritarian style typically do poorly

in school, but because of their parents' concern with control, they tend to achieve better and to commit fewer antisocial acts than peers with undemanding parents—that is, whose parents use one of the styles we will consider next (Steinberg, Blatt-Eisengart, & Cauffman, 2006).

In addition to unwarranted direct control, authoritarian parents engage in a more subtle type called **psychological control**—behaviors that intrude on and manipulate children's verbal expression, individuality, and attachments to parents. In an attempt to decide virtually everything for the child, these parents frequently interrupt or put down the child's ideas, decisions, and choice of friends. When they are dissatisfied, they withdraw love, making their affection or attention contingent on the child's compliance. They also hold excessively high expectations that do not fit the child's developing capacities. Children subjected to psychological control exhibit adjustment problems involving both anxious, withdrawn behavior and defiance and aggression—especially the relational form, which (like parental psychological control) damages relationships through manipulation and exclusion (Barber et al., 2005; Kuppens et al., 2009; Nelson et al., 2006; Silk et al., 2003).

Permissive Child Rearing. The **permissive child-rearing style** is warm and accepting but uninvolved. Permissive parents are either overindulgent or inattentive and, thus, engage in little control. Instead of gradually granting autonomy, they allow children to make many of their own decisions at an age when they are not yet capable of doing so. Their children can eat meals and go to bed whenever they wish and can watch as much television as they want. They do not have to learn good manners or do any household chores. Although some permissive parents truly believe in this approach, many others simply lack confidence in their ability to influence their child's behavior (Oyserman et al., 2005).

Children of permissive parents tend to be impulsive, disobedient, and rebellious. Compared with children whose parents exert more control, they are also overly demanding and dependent on adults, and they show less persistence on tasks, poorer school achievement, and more antisocial behavior. The link between permissive parenting and dependent, nonachieving, rebellious behavior is especially strong for boys (Barber & Olsen, 1997; Baumrind, 1971; Steinberg, Blatt-Eisengart, & Cauffman, 2006).

Uninvolved Child Rearing. The **uninvolved child-rearing style** combines low acceptance and involvement with little control and general indifference to issues of autonomy. Often these parents are emotionally detached and depressed and so overwhelmed by life stress that they have little time and energy for children. At its extreme, uninvolved parenting is a form of child maltreatment called *neglect*. Especially when it begins early, it disrupts virtually all aspects of development (see Chapter 6, page 200). Even with less extreme parental disengagement, children and adolescents display many problems—poor emotional self-regulation, school achievement difficulties, depression, anger, and antisocial behavior (Aunola, Stattin, & Nurmi, 2000; Kurdek & Fine, 1994; Schroeder et al., 2010).

What Makes Authoritative Child Rearing Effective?

Like all correlational findings, the relationship between the authoritative style and children's competence is open to interpretation. Perhaps parents of well-adjusted children are authoritative because their youngsters have especially cooperative dispositions. But although temperamentally fearless, impulsive children and emotionally negative, difficult children are more likely to evoke coercive, inconsistent discipline, extra warmth and firm control succeed in modifying these children's maladaptive styles (Cipriano & Stifter, 2010; Kochanska, Philibert, & Barry, 2009; Pettit et al., 2007).

Longitudinal research indicates that authoritative child rearing promotes maturity and adjustment in children of diverse temperaments (Hart, Newell, & Olsen, 2003; Rubin, Burgess, & Coplan, 2002). And a variant of authoritativeness in which parents exert strong control over the child's behavior—becoming directive but not coercive—yields just as favorable long-term outcomes as a more democratic approach (Baumrind, Larzelere, & Owens, 2010). Indeed, as the findings on temperament and parenting just mentioned illustrate, some children, because of their dispositions, require "heavier doses" of certain authoritative features.

In sum, authoritative child rearing seems to create a positive emotional context for parental influence in the following ways:

- Warm, involved parents who are secure in the standards they hold for their children provide models of caring concern as well as confident, self-controlled behavior.

- Children are far more likely to comply with and internalize control that appears fair and reasonable, not arbitrary.

- By making demands and engaging in autonomy granting that match children's ability to take responsibility for their own behavior, authoritative parents convey a sense of competence to their children, which fosters favorable self-esteem and cognitive and social maturity.

- Supportive aspects of the authoritative style, including parental acceptance, involvement, and rational control, are a powerful source of *resilience*, protecting children from the negative effects of family stress and poverty (Beyers et al., 2003).

LOOK AND LISTEN

Ask several parents to explain their style of child rearing, inquiring about acceptance and involvement, control, and autonomy granting. Look, especially, for variations in authoritativeness—more or less control over the child's behavior—along with parents' rationales. ●

Cultural Variations

Although authoritative parenting is broadly advantageous, parents of different ethnicities often have distinct child-rearing beliefs and practices that reflect cultural values. Let's take some examples.

Compared with Western parents, Chinese parents describe their parenting as more controlling. They are more directive in

© JANINE WIEDEL PHOTOLIBRARY/ALAMY

In Caribbean families of African origins, respect for parental authority is paired with high parental warmth—a combination that promotes competence and family loyalty.

teaching and scheduling their children's time, as a way of fostering self-control and high achievement. Chinese parents may appear less warm than Western parents because they withhold praise, which they believe results in self-satisfied, poorly motivated children (Chao, 1994; Chen et al., 2001). Chinese parents report expressing affection and using induction and other reasoning-oriented discipline as much as American parents do, but they more often shame a misbehaving child (see page 257), withdraw love, and use physical punishment (Cheah et al., 2009; Shwalb et al., 2004; Wu et al., 2002). When these practices become excessive, resulting in an authoritarian style high in psychological or coercive control, Chinese children display the same negative outcomes as Western children: poor academic achievement, anxiety, depression, and aggressive behavior (Chan, 2010; Nelson et al., 2006; Pong, Johnston, & Chen, 2010).

In Hispanic families, Asian Pacific Island families, and Caribbean families of African and East Indian origins, firm insistence on respect for parental authority is paired with high parental warmth—a combination suited to promoting cognitive and social competence and family loyalty (Halgunseth, Ispa, & Rudy, 2006; Roopnarine & Evans, 2007). Hispanic fathers often spend much time with their children and are warm and sensitive (Cabrera & Bradley, 2012). In Caribbean families that have immigrated to the United States, fathers' authoritativeness—but not mothers'—predicted preschoolers' literacy and math skills, probably because Caribbean fathers take a larger role in guiding their children's academic progress (Roopnarine et al., 2006).

Although wide variation exists, low-SES African-American parents tend to expect immediate obedience, regarding strictness as fostering self-control and a watchful attitude in risky surroundings. Consistent with these beliefs, African-American parents who use more controlling strategies tend to have more cognitively and socially competent children (Brody & Flor, 1998). Recall, also, that a history of physical punishment is associated with a reduction in antisocial behavior among African-American youths but with an increase among Caucasian Americans (see page 267). Most African-American parents who use strict, "no-nonsense" discipline use physical punishment sparingly and combine it with warmth and reasoning.

These cultural variations remind us that child-rearing styles must be viewed in their larger context. As we have seen, many factors contribute to good parenting: personal characteristics of child and parent, SES, access to extended family and community supports, cultural values and practices, and public policies.

As we turn to the topic of child maltreatment, our discussion will underscore, once again, that effective child rearing is sustained not just by the desire of mothers and fathers to be good parents. Almost all want to be. Unfortunately, when vital supports for parenting break down, children—as well as parents—can suffer terribly.

Child Maltreatment

Child maltreatment is as old as human history, but only recently has the problem been widely acknowledged and research aimed

at understanding it. Perhaps public concern has increased because child maltreatment is especially common in large industrialized nations. In the most recently reported year, about 700,000 U.S. children (9 out of every 1,000) were identified as victims (U.S. Department of Health and Human Services, 2011b). Most cases go unreported, so the true figures are much higher.

Child maltreatment takes the following forms:

- *Physical abuse:* Assaults, such as kicking, biting, shaking, punching, or stabbing, that inflict physical injury
- *Sexual abuse:* Fondling, intercourse, exhibitionism, commercial exploitation through prostitution or production of pornography, and other forms of exploitation
- *Neglect:* Failure to meet a child's basic needs for food, clothing, medical attention, education, or supervision
- *Emotional abuse:* Acts that could cause serious mental or behavioral disorders, including social isolation, repeated unreasonable demands, ridicule, humiliation, intimidation, or terrorizing

Parents commit more than 80 percent of abusive incidents. Other relatives account for about 7 percent. The remainder are perpetrated by parents' unmarried partners, school officials, camp counselors, and other adults. Mothers engage in neglect more often than fathers, whereas fathers engage in sexual abuse more often than mothers. Maternal and paternal rates of physical and emotional abuse are fairly similar. Infants and young preschoolers are at greatest risk for neglect; preschool and school-age children for physical, emotional, and sexual abuse (Trocomé & Wolfe, 2002; U.S. Department of Health and Human Services, 2011b). Because most sexual abuse victims are identified in middle childhood, we will pay special attention to this form of maltreatment in Chapter 10.

Each year, fourth to sixth graders across Los Angeles County enter a poster contest to celebrate National Child Abuse Prevention Month. This 2012 winner expresses a heartfelt appeal: "Don't Let Our Children Live in Fear." (Gillian Lih Bautista, 6th Grade, St. Genevieve Elementary, Panorama City, CA. Courtesy ICAN Associates, Los Angeles County Inter-Agency Council on Child Abuse and Neglect, ican4kids.org.)

Origins of Child Maltreatment. Early findings suggested that child maltreatment was rooted in adult psychological disturbance (Kempe et al., 1962). But although child maltreatment is more common among disturbed parents, no single "abusive personality type" exists. Parents who were abused as children do not necessarily become abusers (Buchanan, 1996; Simons et al., 1991). And sometimes even "normal" parents harm their children!

For help in understanding child maltreatment, researchers turned to *ecological systems theory* (see Chapters 1 and 2). They discovered that many interacting variables—at the family, community, and cultural levels—contribute. The more risks present, the greater the likelihood of abuse or neglect (see Table 8.3).

The Family. Within the family, children whose characteristics make them more challenging to rear are more likely to become targets of abuse. These include premature or very sick babies and children who are temperamentally difficult, are inattentive and overactive, or have other developmental problems. Child factors, however, only slightly increase the risk (Jaudes & Mackey-Bilaver, 2008; Sidebotham et al., 2003). Whether such children are maltreated largely depends on parents' characteristics.

Maltreating parents are less skillful than other parents in handling discipline confrontations. They also suffer from biased thinking about their child. For example, they often attribute their baby's crying or their child's misdeeds to a stubborn or bad disposition, evaluate child transgressions as worse than they are, and feel powerless in parenting—perspectives that lead them to move quickly toward physical force (Bugental & Happaney, 2004; Crouch et al., 2008).

Once abuse begins, it quickly becomes part of a self-sustaining relationship. The small irritations to which abusive parents react—a fussy baby, a preschooler who will not mind immediately—soon become bigger ones. Then the harshness increases. By the preschool years, abusive and neglectful parents

seldom interact with their children. When they do, the communication is almost always negative (Wolfe, 2005).

Most parents have enough self-control not to respond with abuse to their child's misbehavior or developmental problems. Other factors combine with these conditions to prompt an extreme response. Abusive parents react to stressful situations with high emotional arousal. And low income, low education (less than a high school diploma), unemployment, alcohol and drug use, marital conflict, overcrowded living conditions, frequent moves, and extreme household disorganization are common in abusive homes (Wekerle et al., 2007; Wulczyn, 2009). These conditions increase the chances that parents will be too overwhelmed to meet basic child-rearing responsibilities or will vent their frustrations by lashing out at their children.

The Community. The majority of abusive and neglectful parents are isolated from both formal and informal social supports. Because of their life histories, many have learned to mistrust and avoid others and are poorly skilled at establishing and maintaining positive relationships. Also, maltreating parents are more likely to live in unstable, rundown neighborhoods that provide few links between family and community, such as preschool programs, recreation centers, and religious institutions (Coulton et al., 2007; Guterman et al., 2009). They lack "lifelines" to others and have no one to turn to for help during stressful times.

The Larger Culture. Cultural values, laws, and customs profoundly affect the chances that child maltreatment will occur when parents feel overburdened. Societies that view violence as an appropriate way to solve problems set the stage for child abuse.

Although the United States has laws to protect children from maltreatment, widespread support exists for use of physical force with children (refer back to page 266). Many countries—including Austria, Croatia, Cyprus, Denmark, Finland,

TABLE 8.3	Factors Related to Child Maltreatment
FACTOR	**DESCRIPTION**
Parent characteristics	Psychological disturbance; alcohol and drug abuse; history of abuse as a child; belief in harsh physical discipline; desire to satisfy unmet emotional needs through the child; unreasonable expectations for child behavior; young age (most under 30); low educational level
Child characteristics	Premature or very sick baby; difficult temperament; inattentiveness and overactivity; other developmental problems
Family characteristics	Low income; poverty; homelessness; marital instability; social isolation; physical abuse of mother by husband or boyfriend; frequent moves; large families with closely spaced children; overcrowded living conditions; disorganized household; lack of steady employment; other signs of high life stress
Community	Characterized by violence and social isolation; few parks, child-care centers, preschool programs, recreation centers, or religious institutions to serve as family supports
Culture	Approval of physical force and violence as ways to solve problems

Sources: U.S. Department of Health and Human Services, 2011b; Wekerle & Wolfe, 2003; Whipple, 2006.

Germany, Israel, Italy, Latvia, Norway, Sweden, and Uruguay—have outlawed corporal punishment, a measure that dampens both physical discipline and abuse (Zolotor & Puzia, 2010). Furthermore, all industrialized nations except the United States and France now prohibit corporal punishment in schools. The U.S. Supreme Court has twice upheld the right of school officials to use corporal punishment. Fortunately, 31 U.S. states and the District of Columbia have passed laws that ban it.

Consequences of Child Maltreatment. The family circumstances of maltreated children impair the development of emotional self-regulation, empathy and sympathy, self-concept, social skills, and academic motivation. Over time, these youngsters show serious adjustment problems—cognitive deficits (including impaired working memory and executive function), severe depression, aggressive behavior, peer difficulties, substance abuse, and violent crime—that persist into adulthood (Gould et al., 2010; Kaplow & Widom, 2007; Sanchez & Pollak, 2009).

How do these damaging consequences occur? Think back to our earlier discussion of hostile cycles of parent–child interaction. For abused children, these are especially severe. Also, a family characteristic strongly associated with child abuse is partner abuse (Graham-Bermann & Howell, 2011). Clearly, the home lives of abused children overflow with experiences that evoke profound distress and with opportunities to learn to use aggression to solve problems.

Furthermore, demeaning parental messages, in which children are ridiculed, humiliated, rejected, or terrorized, result in low self-esteem, high anxiety, self-blame, and efforts to escape from extreme psychological pain—at times severe enough to lead to attempted suicide in adolescence. At school, maltreated children present serious discipline problems (Wolfe, 2005). Their noncompliance, poor motivation, and cognitive immaturity interfere with academic achievement, further undermining their chances for life success.

Finally, repeated abuse is associated with central nervous system damage, including abnormal EEG brain-wave activity; fMRI-detected reduced size and impaired functioning of the cerebral cortex, corpus callosum, and cerebellum; and atypical production of the stress hormone cortisol—initially too high but, after months of abuse, often too low. Over time, the massive trauma of persistent abuse seems to blunt children's normal physiological response to stress (Cicchetti, 2007; Hart & Rubia, 2012). These effects increase the chances that cognitive and emotional problems will endure.

Preventing Child Maltreatment. Because child maltreatment is embedded in families, communities, and society as a whole, efforts to prevent it must be directed at each of these levels. Many approaches have been suggested, from teaching high-risk parents effective child-rearing strategies to developing broad social programs aimed at improving community services and economic conditions.

We have seen that providing social supports to families is effective in easing parental stress. This approach sharply reduces child maltreatment. Parents Anonymous, a U.S. organization with affiliate programs around the world, helps child-abusing parents learn constructive parenting practices, largely through social supports. Its local chapters offer self-help group meetings, daily phone calls, and regular home visits to relieve social isolation and teach child-rearing skills.

Early intervention aimed at strengthening both child and parent competencies can reduce child maltreatment. Healthy Families America, a program that began in Hawaii and has spread to 440 sites across the United States and Canada, identifies at-risk families during pregnancy or at birth. Each receives three years of home visitation, in which a trained worker helps parents manage crises, encourages effective child rearing, and puts parents in touch with community services (Healthy Families America, 2011). In an evaluation of its effectiveness, Healthy Families home visitation alone reduced only neglect, not abuse (Duggan et al., 2004). But adding a *cognitive component* dramatically increased its impact. When home visitors helped parents change negative appraisals of their children—by countering inaccurate interpretations (for example, that the baby is behaving with malicious intent) and by working on solving child-rearing problems—physical punishment and abuse dropped sharply after one year of intervention (Bugental et al., 2002).

Even with intensive treatment, some adults persist in their abusive acts. An estimated 1,500 U.S. children, most of them infants and preschoolers, die from maltreatment each year (U.S. Department of Health and Human Services, 2011b). When parents are unlikely to change their behavior, the drastic step of separating parent from child and legally terminating parental rights is the only justifiable course of action.

Child maltreatment is a sad note on which to end our discussion of a period of childhood that is so full of excitement, awakening, and discovery. But there is reason to be optimistic. Great strides have been made over the past several decades in understanding and preventing child maltreatment.

ASK YOURSELF

REVIEW Is the concept of authoritative parenting useful for understanding effective parenting across cultures? Explain.

CONNECT Which child-rearing style is most likely to be associated with inductive discipline, and why?

APPLY Chandra heard a news report about 10 severely neglected children, living in squalor in an inner-city tenement. She wondered, "Why would parents so mistreat their children?" How would you answer Chandra?

REFLECT How would you classify your parents' child-rearing styles? What factors might have influenced their approach to parenting?

SUMMARY

Erikson's Theory: Initiative versus Guilt (p. 256)

What personality changes take place during Erikson's stage of initiative versus guilt?

- Preschoolers develop a new sense of purposefulness as they grapple with Erikson's psychological conflict of **initiative versus guilt.** A healthy sense of initiative depends on exploring the social world through play, cooperating with peers to achieve common goals, and forming a conscience through identification with the same-sex parent.

Self-Understanding (p. 256)

Describe preschoolers' self-concepts and the development of self-esteem.

- As preschoolers think more intently about themselves, they construct a **self-concept** consisting largely of observable characteristics and typical emotions and attitudes. A warm, sensitive parent–child relationship seems to foster a more positive, coherent early self-concept.

- During early childhood, high **self-esteem** contributes to a mastery-oriented approach to the environment. But even a little adult disapproval can undermine a young child's self-esteem and enthusiasm for learning.

Emotional Development (p. 258)

Identify changes in understanding and expressing emotion during early childhood, citing factors that influence those changes.

- Preschoolers' impressive understanding of the causes, consequences, and behavioral signs of basic emotions is supported by cognitive and language development, secure attachment, and conversations about feelings. By age 3

to 4, children are aware of various strategies for emotional self-regulation. Temperament and parental communication about coping strategies influence preschoolers' capacity to handle stress and negative emotion.

- As their self-concepts develop, preschoolers more often experience self-conscious emotions. They depend on feedback from parents and other adults to know when to feel each of these emotions.

- Empathy also becomes more common. Temperament and parenting influence the extent to which empathy leads to **sympathy** and results in **prosocial,** or **altruistic, behavior.**

Peer Relations (p. 261)

Describe peer sociability and friendship in early childhood, citing cultural and parental influences on early peer relations.

- During early childhood, peer interaction increases as children move from **nonsocial activity** to **parallel play,** then to **associative** and **cooperative play.** Nevertheless, both solitary and parallel play remain common.

- Sociodramatic play seems especially important in societies where child and adult worlds are distinct. In collectivist cultures, play generally occurs in large groups and is highly cooperative.

- Preschoolers understand something about the uniqueness of friendship, but their friendships do not yet have an enduring quality. Children's social maturity contributes to later academic performance. Parents affect peer sociability both directly, through attempts to influence their child's peer relations, and indirectly, through their child-rearing practices.

Foundations of Morality (p. 264)

What are the central features of psychoanalytic, social learning, and cognitive-developmental approaches to moral development?

- Psychoanalytic theory emphasizes the emotional side of moral development, especially identification and guilt as motivators of good conduct. Contrary to Freud's theory, conscience formation is promoted not by fear of punishment and loss of parental love but by **induction,** in which an adult points out the effects of the child's misbehavior on others.

- Social learning theory focuses on how moral behavior is learned through reinforcement and modeling. Effective adult models of prosocial responses are warm and powerful, and they practice what they preach.

- Alternatives to harsh punishment such as **time out** and withdrawal of privileges can help parents avoid undesirable side effects of punishment. Parents can increase the effectiveness of punishment by being consistent, maintaining a warm parent–child relationship, and offering explanations.

- The cognitive-developmental perspective views children as active thinkers about social rules. By age 4, children consider intentions in making moral judgments and distinguish truthfulness from lying. Preschoolers also distinguish **moral imperatives** from **social conventions** and **matters of personal choice.** However, they tend to reason rigidly about morality, focusing on outcomes and on physical harm.

Describe the development of aggression in early childhood, including family and media influences and effective approaches to reducing aggressive behavior.

- During early childhood, **proactive aggression** declines while **reactive aggression** increases. Proactive and reactive aggression come in three forms: **physical aggression** (more common in boys), **verbal aggression,** and **relational aggression.**

- Ineffective discipline and a conflict-ridden family atmosphere promote children's aggression, as does media violence. Effective approaches to reducing aggressive behavior include training parents in effective child-rearing practices, teaching children conflict-resolution skills, helping parents cope with stressors in their own lives, and shielding children from violent media.

Gender Typing (p. 273)

Discuss genetic and environmental influences on preschoolers' gender-stereotyped beliefs and behavior.

- **Gender typing** is well under way in the pre-school years. Preschoolers acquire a wide range of gender-stereotyped beliefs, often applying them rigidly.

- Prenatal sex hormones contribute to boys' higher activity level and rougher play and to children's preference for same-sex playmates. But parents, teachers, peers, and the broader social environment also encourage many gender-typed responses.

Describe and evaluate theories that explain the emergence of gender identity.

- Although most people have a traditional **gender identity,** some are **androgynous,** combining both masculine and feminine characteristics. Masculine and androgynous identities are linked to better psychological adjustment.

- According to social learning theory, pre-schoolers first acquire gender-typed responses through modeling and reinforcement and then organize these behaviors into gender-linked ideas about themselves. Cognitive-developmental theory maintains that children must master **gender constancy** before they develop gender-typed behavior, though evidence for this assumption is weak.

- **Gender schema theory** combines features of social learning and cognitive-developmental perspectives. As children acquire gender-typed preferences and behaviors, they form masculine and feminine categories, or gender schemas, that they apply to themselves and their world.

Child Rearing and Emotional and Social Development (p. 278)

Describe the impact of child-rearing styles on children's development, and note cultural variations in child rearing.

- Three features distinguish major **child-rearing styles:** (1) acceptance and involvement, (2) control, and (3) autonomy granting. In contrast to the **authoritarian, permissive,** and **uninvolved** styles, the **authoritative style** promotes cognitive, emotional, and social competence. Warmth, explanations, and reasonable demands for mature behavior account for the effectiveness of this style. **Psychological control,** associated with authoritarian parenting, contributes to adjustment problems.

- Certain ethnic groups, including Chinese, Hispanic, Asian Pacific Island, and African-American, combine parental warmth with high levels of control. But when control becomes harsh and excessive, it impairs academic and social competence.

Discuss the multiple origins of child maltreatment, its consequences for development, and effective prevention.

- Maltreating parents use ineffective discipline, hold a negatively biased view of their child, and feel powerless in parenting. Unmanageable parental stress and social isolation greatly increase the likelihood of abuse and neglect. Societal approval of physical force as a means of solving problems promotes child abuse.

- Maltreated children are impaired in emotional self-regulation, empathy and sympathy, self-concept, social skills, and academic motivation. The trauma of repeated abuse is associated with central nervous system damage and serious, lasting adjustment problems. Successful prevention requires efforts at the family, community, and societal levels.

Important Terms and Concepts

androgyny (p. 276)
associative play (p. 261)
authoritarian child-rearing style (p. 279)
authoritative child-rearing style (p. 278)
child-rearing styles (p. 278)
cooperative play (p. 261)
gender constancy (p. 276)
gender identity (p. 276)
gender schema theory (p. 277)
gender typing (p. 273)

induction (p. 264)
initiative versus guilt (p. 256)
matters of personal choice (p. 269)
moral imperatives (p. 269)
nonsocial activity (p. 261)
parallel play (p. 261)
permissive child-rearing style (p. 279)
physical aggression (p. 269)
proactive aggression (p. 269)
prosocial, or altruistic, behavior (p. 260)

psychological control (p. 279)
reactive aggression (p. 269)
relational aggression (p. 269)
self-concept (p. 256)
self-esteem (p. 257)
social conventions (p. 269)
sympathy (p. 260)
time out (p. 266)
uninvolved child-rearing style (p. 280)
verbal aggression (p. 269)

milestones

Development in Early Childhood

2 years

PHYSICAL

- Throughout early childhood, height and weight increase more slowly than in toddlerhood. (216)
- Balance improves; walks more rhythmically; hurried walk changes to run. (223)
- Jumps, hops, throws, and catches with rigid upper body. (223)
- Puts on and removes simple items of clothing. (223)
- Uses spoon effectively. (223)
- First drawings are gestural scribbles. (224)

COGNITIVE

- Make-believe becomes less dependent on realistic objects, less self-centered, and more complex; sociodramatic play increases. (226–227)
- Understands the symbolic function of photos and realistic-looking pictures. (228)

- Takes the perspective of others in simplified, familiar situations and in face-to-face communication. (230)
- Recognition memory is well-developed. (237)
- Shows awareness of the distinction between inner mental and outer physical events. (239)
- Begins to count. (242)

LANGUAGE

- Vocabulary increases rapidly. (248)
- Uses a coalition of cues—perceptual and, increasingly, social and linguistic—to figure out word meanings. (249)
- Speaks in simple sentences that follow basic word order of native language, gradually adding grammatical markers. (249)
- Displays effective conversational skills. (250)

EMOTIONAL/SOCIAL

- Understands causes, consequences, and behavioral signs of basic emotions. (258)
- Begins to develop self-concept and self-esteem. (256–258)
- Shows early signs of developing moral sense—verbal evaluations of own and others' actions and distress at harmful behaviors. (264)
- May display proactive (instrumental) aggression. (269)
- Gender-stereotyped beliefs and behavior increase. (273)

PHYSICAL

- Running, jumping, hopping, throwing, and catching become better coordinated. (223)
- Pedals and steers tricycle. (223)

- Galloping and one-foot skipping appear. (223)
- Fastens and unfastens large buttons. (223)
- Uses scissors. (223)
- Uses fork effectively. (223)
- Draws first picture of a person, using tadpole image. (224)

COGNITIVE

- Understands the symbolic function of drawings and of models of real-world spaces. (224, 227–228)
- Distinguishes appearance from reality. (228)
- Grasps conservation, reasons about transformations, reverses thinking, and understands cause–effect sequences in familiar contexts. (230)
- Sorts familiar objects into hierarchically organized categories. (231)
- Uses private speech to guide behavior during challenging tasks. (234)
- Improves in sustained attention. (236–237)
- Uses scripts to recall familiar events. (238)
- Understands that both beliefs and desires determine behavior. (239)
- Knows the meaning of numbers up to 10, counts correctly, and grasps cardinality. (243)

Note: Numbers in parentheses indicate the page or pages on which each milestone is discussed.

LANGUAGE

- Aware of some meaningful features of written language. (242)
- Coins new words based on known words; extends language meanings through metaphor. (248)
- Masters increasingly complex grammatical structures, occasionally overextending grammatical rules to exceptions. (249–250)
- Adjusts speech to fit the age, sex, and social status of listeners. (250)

EMOTIONAL/SOCIAL

- Describes self in terms of observable characteristics and typical emotions and attitudes. (256)
- Has several self-esteems, such as learning things in school, making friends, getting along with parents, and treating others kindly. (257)
- Emotional self-regulation improves. (259)
- Experiences self-conscious emotions more often. (260)
- Relies more on language to express empathy. (260)

- Engages in associative and cooperative play with peers, in addition to parallel play. (261)
- Forms first friendships, based on pleasurable play and sharing of toys. (262)
- Distinguishes truthfulness from lying. (269)
- Distinguishes moral imperatives from social conventions and matters of personal choice. (269)
- Proactive aggression declines, while reactive aggression (verbal and relational) increases. (269)
- Preference for same-sex playmates strengthens. (274)

5–6 years

PHYSICAL

- Starts to lose primary teeth. (217)
- Increases running speed, gallops more smoothly, and engages in true skipping. (223)
- Displays mature, flexible throwing and catching patterns. (223)
- Uses knife to cut soft foods. (223)
- Ties shoes. (223, 224)

- Draws more complex pictures. (224)
- Copies some numbers and simple words; prints name. (223, 225)

COGNITIVE

- Magical beliefs decline. (230)
- Improves in ability to distinguish appearance from reality. (228)

- Improves in sustained attention and planning. (237)
- Recognition, recall, scripted memory, and autobiographical memory improve. (237–238)

- Understanding of false belief strengthens. (239)

LANGUAGE

- Understands that letters and sounds are linked in systematic ways. (242)
- Uses invented spellings. (242)
- By age 6, vocabulary reaches about 10,000 words. (248)
- Uses most grammatical constructions competently. (250)

EMOTIONAL/SOCIAL

- Improves in emotional understanding (ability to interpret, predict, and influence others' emotional reactions). (258)

- Has acquired many morally relevant rules and behaviors. (265)
- Gender-stereotyped beliefs and behavior and preference for same-sex playmates continue to strengthen. (274)
- Understands gender constancy. (276–277)

© ELLEN B. SENISI PHOTOGRAPHY

During a science lesson, sixth graders use a map to chart catastrophic weather events around the world. An improved capacity to remember, reason, and reflect on one's own thinking makes middle childhood a time of dramatic advances in academic learning and problem solving.

Physical and Cognitive Development in Middle Childhood

"I'm on my way, Mom!" hollered 10-year-old Joey as he stuffed the last bite of toast into his mouth, slung his book bag over his shoulder, dashed out the door, jumped on his bike, and headed down the street for school. Joey's 8-year-old sister Lizzie followed, pedaling furiously until she caught up with Joey. Rena, the children's mother and one of my colleagues at the university, watched from the front porch as her son and daughter disappeared in the distance.

"They're branching out," Rena told me over lunch that day as she described the children's expanding activities and relationships. Homework, household chores, soccer teams, music lessons, scouting, friends at school and in the neighborhood, and Joey's new paper route were all part of the children's routine. "It seems the basics are all there. I don't have to monitor Joey and Lizzie constantly anymore. Being a parent is still challenging, but it's more a matter of refinements—helping them become independent, competent, and productive individuals."

Joey and Lizzie have entered middle childhood—the years from 6 to 11. Around the world, children of this age are assigned new responsibilities. For children in industrialized nations, middle childhood is often called the "school years" because its onset is marked by the start of formal schooling. In village and tribal cultures, the school may be a field or a jungle. But universally in this period, children are guided by mature members of society toward real-world tasks that increasingly resemble those they will perform as adults.

© ELLEN B. SENISI PHOTOGRAPHY

This chapter focuses on physical and cognitive development in middle childhood. By age 6, the brain has reached 90 percent of its adult weight, and the body continues to grow slowly. In this way, nature gives school-age children the mental powers to master challenging tasks as well as added time to acquire the knowledge and skills essential for life in a complex social world.

We begin by reviewing typical growth trends, gains in motor skills, and special health concerns. Then we return to Piaget's theory and the information-processing approach for an overview of cognitive changes. Next, we examine genetic and environmental contributions to IQ scores, which often enter into educational decisions. Our discussion continues with the further blossoming of language. Finally, we turn to the importance of schools in children's learning and development. ●

chapter outline

PHYSICAL DEVELOPMENT

Body Growth

Common Health Problems

Nutrition • Overweight and Obesity • Vision and Hearing • Illnesses • Unintentional Injuries

Motor Development and Play

Gross-Motor Development • Fine-Motor Development • Sex Differences • Games with Rules • Shadows of Our Evolutionary Past • Physical Education

■ **SOCIAL ISSUES: EDUCATION** School Recess—A Time to Play, a Time to Learn

COGNITIVE DEVELOPMENT

Piaget's Theory: The Concrete Operational Stage

Concrete Operational Thought • Limitations of Concrete Operational Thought • Follow-Up Research on Concrete Operational Thought • Evaluation of the Concrete Operational Stage

Information Processing

Working-Memory Capacity • Executive Function • Attention • Memory Strategies • Knowledge and Memory • Culture, Schooling, and Memory Strategies • The School-Age Child's Theory of Mind • Cognitive Self-Regulation • Applications of Information Processing to Academic Learning

■ **BIOLOGY AND ENVIRONMENT** Children with Attention-Deficit Hyperactivity Disorder

Individual Differences in Mental Development

Defining and Measuring Intelligence • Recent Efforts to Define Intelligence • Explaining Individual and Group Differences in IQ

■ **SOCIAL ISSUES: HEALTH** Emotional Intelligence

Language Development

Vocabulary • Grammar • Pragmatics • Learning Two Languages

Learning in School

Class Size • Educational Philosophies • Teacher–Student Interaction • Grouping Practices • Teaching Children with Special Needs • How Well-Educated Are American Children?

■ **SOCIAL ISSUES: EDUCATION** Magnet Schools: Equal Access to High-Quality Education

PHYSICAL DEVELOPMENT

 ## Body Growth

Physical growth during the school years continues at the slow, regular pace of early childhood. At age 6, the average North American child weighs about 45 pounds and is 3½ feet tall. Over the next few years, children add about 2 to 3 inches in height and 5 pounds in weight each year (see Figure 9.1). Between ages 6 and 8, girls are slightly shorter and lighter than boys. By age 9, this trend reverses as girls approach the dramatic adolescent growth spurt, which occurs two years earlier in girls than in boys.

Because the lower portion of the body is growing fastest, Joey and Lizzie appeared longer-legged than they had in early childhood. They grew out of their jeans more quickly than their jackets and frequently needed larger shoes. As in early childhood, girls have slightly more body fat and boys more muscle. After age 8, girls begin accumulating fat at a faster rate, and they will add even more during adolescence (Siervogel et al., 2000).

During middle childhood, the bones of the body lengthen and broaden. But ligaments are not yet firmly attached to bones, and this, combined with increasing muscle strength, gives chil-dren the unusual flexibility needed to perform cartwheels and handstands. As their bodies become stronger, many children experience a greater desire for physical exercise. Nighttime "growing pains"—stiffness and aches in the legs—are common as muscles adapt to an enlarging skeleton (Evans, 2008).

Between ages 6 and 12, all 20 primary teeth are lost and replaced by permanent ones, with girls losing their teeth slightly earlier than boys. For a while, the permanent teeth seem much too large. Gradually, growth of facial bones, especially the jaw and chin, causes the child's face to lengthen and mouth to widen, accommodating the newly erupting teeth.

Common Health Problems

Children from economically advantaged homes, like Joey and Lizzie, are at their healthiest in middle childhood, full of energy and play. The cumulative effects of good nutrition, combined with rapid development of the body's immune system, offer greater protection against disease. At the same time, growth in lung size permits more air to be exchanged with each breath, so children are better able to exercise vigorously without tiring.

Andy at 8 years

Andy at 6 years

Amy at 8 years

Amy at 6 years

Andy at 9 years

Andy at 10½ years

Amy at 9 years

Amy at 10½ years

FIGURE 9.1 Body growth during middle childhood. School-age children continue the slow, regular pattern of growth they showed in early childhood. But around age 9, girls begin to grow at a faster rate than boys. At age 10½, Amy was taller, heavier, and more mature-looking than Andy.

Not surprisingly, poverty continues to be a powerful predictor of ill health during the school years. Because economically disadvantaged U.S. families often lack health insurance (see Chapter 7), many children do not have regular access to a doctor. A substantial number also lack such basic necessities as a comfortable home and regular meals.

Nutrition

School-age children need a well-balanced, plentiful diet to provide energy for successful learning in school and increased physical activity. With their increasing focus on friendships and new activities, many children spend little time at the table, and the percentage who eat dinner with their families drops sharply between ages 9 and 14. Family dinnertimes have waned in general over the past two decades. Yet eating an evening meal with parents leads to a diet higher in fruits, vegetables, grains, and milk products and lower in soft drinks and fast foods (Burgess-Champoux et al., 2009; Fiese & Schwartz, 2008).

School-age children say that they "feel better" and "focus better" after eating healthy foods and that they feel sluggish, "like a blob," after eating junk foods (O'Dea, 2003). Consistent with these informal reports, even mild nutritional deficits can affect cognitive functioning. Among school-age children from middle- to high-SES families, insufficient dietary iron and folate predicted slightly lower mental test performance (Arija et al., 2006).

As we saw in earlier chapters, many poverty-stricken children in developing countries and in the United States suffer from serious and prolonged malnutrition. Unfortunately, malnutrition that persists from infancy or early childhood into the school years usually leads to permanent physical and mental damage (Grantham-McGregor, Walker, & Chang, 2000; Liu et al., 2003). Government-sponsored supplementary food programs from the early years through adolescence can prevent these effects.

Overweight and Obesity

Mona, a very heavy child in Lizzie's class, often watched from the sidelines during recess. When she did join in games, she was slow and clumsy, the target of unkind comments: "Move it, Tubs!" Most afternoons, she walked home from school alone while the other children gathered in groups, talking, laughing, and chasing. At home, Mona sought comfort in high-calorie snacks.

Mona suffers from **obesity,** a greater-than-20-percent increase over healthy weight, based on *body mass index (BMI)*—a ratio of weight to height associated with body fat. (A BMI above the 85th percentile for a child's age and sex is considered *overweight,* a BMI above the 95th percentile *obese.*) During the past several decades, a rise in overweight and obesity has occurred in many Western nations, with large increases in Canada, Germany, Israel, Greece, Ireland, New Zealand, the United Kingdom, and especially the United States. Today, 32 percent of U.S. children and adolescents are overweight, more than half of them extremely so: 17 percent are obese—trends that are worsening (Ogden et al., 2010; World Health Organization, 2012c, 2013a).

Obesity rates are also increasing rapidly in developing countries, as urbanization shifts the population toward sedentary lifestyles and diets high in meats and energy-dense refined foods (World Health Organization, 2012c, 2013a). In China, for example, where obesity was nearly nonexistent a generation ago, today 20 percent of children are overweight and 7 percent obese—a nearly fivefold increase over the past 25 years, with boys affected more than girls (Ding, 2008). In addition to lifestyle changes, a prevailing belief in Chinese culture that excess body fat signifies prosperity and health—carried over from a half-century ago, when famine caused millions of deaths—has contributed to this alarming upsurge. High valuing of sons may induce Chinese parents to offer boys especially generous portions of energy-dense foods that are now widely available.

Overweight rises with age, from 21 percent among U.S. preschoolers to 35 percent among school-age children and adolescents. An estimated 70 percent of affected teenagers become overweight adults (U.S. Department of Health and Human Services, 2011f). Besides serious emotional and social difficulties, obese children are at risk for lifelong health problems. Symptoms that begin to appear in the early school years—high blood pressure, high cholesterol levels, respiratory abnormalities, and insulin resistance—are powerful predictors of heart disease, circulatory difficulties, type 2 diabetes, gallbladder disease, sleep and digestive disorders, many forms of cancer, and early death (Krishnamoorthy, Hart, & Jelalian, 2006; World Cancer Research Fund, 2007). Furthermore, obesity has caused a dramatic rise in cases of diabetes in children, sometimes leading to early, severe complications, including stroke, kidney failure, and circulatory problems that heighten the risk of eventual blindness and leg amputation (Hannon, Rao, & Arslanian, 2005).

Causes of Obesity. Not all children are equally at risk for excessive weight gain. Overweight children tend to have overweight parents, and identical twins are more likely to share the disorder than fraternal twins. But heredity accounts for only a *tendency* to gain weight (Kral & Faith, 2009). The importance of environment is apparent in the consistent relationship of low SES to overweight and obesity in industrialized nations, especially among ethnic minorities—in the United States, African-American, Hispanic, and Native-American children and adults (Anand et al., 2001; Ogden et al., 2010). Factors responsible include lack of knowledge about healthy diet; a tendency to buy high-fat, low-cost foods; and family stress, which can prompt overeating. Recall, also, that children who were undernourished in their early years are at risk for later excessive weight gain (see page 132 in Chapter 4).

Parental feeding practices also contribute to childhood obesity. Some parents anxiously overfeed, interpreting almost all their child's discomforts as a desire for food. Others pressure their children to eat, a practice common among immigrant parents and grandparents who, as children themselves, survived periods of food deprivation. Still other parents are overly controlling, restricting when, what, and how much their child eats and constantly worrying about weight gain (Moens, Braet,

& Soetens, 2007). In each case, parents fail to help children learn to regulate their own food intake. Also, parents of overweight children often use high-fat, sugary foods to reinforce other behaviors, leading children to attach great value to treats (Sherry et al., 2004).

Because of these experiences, obese children soon develop maladaptive eating habits. They are more responsive than normal-weight individuals to external stimuli associated with food—taste, sight, smell, time of day, and food-related words—and less responsive to internal hunger cues (Jansen et al., 2003; Temple et al., 2007). They also eat faster, a behavior that appears as early as 18 months of age (Drabman et al., 1979).

Another factor consistently associated with weight gain is insufficient sleep (Nielsen, Danielsen, & Sørensen, 2011). Reduced sleep may increase time available for eating, leave children too fatigued for physical activity, or disrupt the brain's regulation of hunger and metabolism.

Overweight children are less physically active than their normal-weight peers. Inactivity is both cause and consequence of excessive weight gain. Research reveals that the rise in childhood obesity is due in part to the many hours U.S. children spend watching television. In a study that tracked children's TV viewing from ages 4 to 11, the more TV children watched, the more body fat they added: Children who devoted more than 3 hours per day to TV accumulated 40 percent more fat than those devoting less than 1¾ hours (see Figure 9.2) (Proctor et al., 2003). Watching TV reduces time spent in physical exercise, and TV ads encourage children to eat fattening, unhealthy snacks. Children permitted to have a TV in their bedroom—a practice linked to especially high TV viewing—are at even further risk for overweight (Adachi-Mejia et al., 2007).

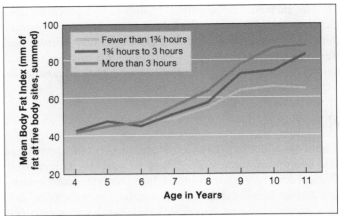

FIGURE 9.2 Relationship of television viewing to gains in body fat from ages 4 to 11. Researchers followed more than 100 children longitudinally, collecting information on hours per day of television viewing and on body fat, measured in millimeters of skinfold thickness at five body sites (upper arms, shoulders, abdomen, trunk, and thighs). The more TV children watched, the greater the gain in body fat. At ages 10 to 11, the difference between children watching fewer than 1¾ hours and those watching more than 3 hours had become large. (Adapted from M. H. Proctor et al., 2003, "Television Viewing and Change in Body Fat from Preschool to Early Adolescence: The Framingham Children's Study," *International Journal of Obesity, 27,* p. 831. Reprinted by permission from Macmillan Publishers Ltd.)

Finally, the broader food environment affects the incidence of obesity. Over the past three decades, the number of families who frequently eat meals outside the home has risen dramatically. Eating in restaurants or at relatives', neighbors', or friends' homes, as opposed to at home, substantially increases children's overall food consumption, including high-calorie drinks, fast foods, and snacks, and their risk of weight gain (Ayala et al., 2008; Poti & Popkin, 2011).

Consequences of Obesity. Unfortunately, physical attractiveness is a powerful predictor of social acceptance. In Western societies, both children and adults rate obese youngsters as less likable than other children, stereotyping them as lazy, sloppy, ugly, stupid, self-doubting, and deceitful (Kilpatrick & Sanders, 1978; Penny & Haddock, 2007; Tiggemann & Anesbury, 2000). In school, obese children and adolescents are often socially isolated. They report more emotional, social, and school difficulties, including peer teasing and consequent low self-esteem, depression, and (among obese teenagers) suicidal thoughts and suicide attempts. Persistent obesity from childhood into adolescence predicts serious disorders, including defiance, aggression, and severe depression (Puhl & Latner, 2007; Young-Hyman et al., 2006). As we will see in Chapter 13, these psychological consequences combine with continuing discrimination to result in reduced life chances in close relationships and employment.

Treating Obesity. In Mona's case, the school nurse suggested that Mona and her obese mother enter a weight-loss pro-

Parental unhealthy feeding practices—frequent take-out meals consisting of foods high in calories and fat—and a physically inactive lifestyle play major roles in these siblings' excessive weight gain.

© OCEAN/CORBIS

gram together. But Mona's mother, unhappily married for many years, had her own reasons for overeating and rejected this idea. In one study, only one-fourth of overweight parents judged their overweight children to have a weight problem (Jeffrey, 2004). Consistent with these findings, most obese children do not get any treatment.

The most effective interventions are family-based and focus on changing behaviors (Oude et al., 2009). In one program, both parent and child revised eating patterns, exercised daily, and reinforced each other with praise and points for progress, which they exchanged for special activities and times together. The more weight parents lost, the more their children lost (Wrotniak et al., 2004). Follow-ups after five and ten years showed that children maintained their weight loss more effectively than adults—a finding that underscores the importance of early intervention (Epstein, Roemmich, & Raynor, 2001). Treatment programs that focus on both diet and lifestyle can yield substantial, long-lasting weight reduction among children and adolescents (Eliakim et al., 2004; Nemet et al., 2005). But these interventions work best when parents' and children's weight problems are not severe.

Children consume one-third of their daily caloric intake at school. Therefore, schools can also help reduce obesity by serving healthier meals, ensuring regular physical activity, and offering weight reduction programs. Because obesity is expected to rise further without broad prevention strategies, many U.S. states and cities have passed obesity-reduction legislation (Levi et al., 2009). Among measures taken are weight-related school screenings for all children, improved school nutrition standards, additional school recess time and physical education, school-based obesity awareness and weight-reduction programs, and menu nutrition labeling (including calorie counts) in chain and fast-food restaurants.

LOOK AND LISTEN

Contact your state government to find out about its childhood obesity prevention legislation. Can its policies be improved? ●

Vision and Hearing

The most common vision problem in middle childhood is *myopia,* or nearsightedness. By the end of the school years, it affects nearly 25 percent of children—a rate that rises to 60 percent by early adulthood. Heredity plays a role: Identical twins are more likely than fraternal twins to share the condition (Pacella et al., 1999). And worldwide, it occurs far more frequently in Asian than in Caucasian populations (Feldkámper & Schaeffel, 2003). Early biological trauma also can induce myopia. School-age children with low birth weights show an especially high rate, believed to result from immaturity of visual structures, slower eye growth, and a greater incidence of eye disease (O'Connor et al., 2002).

When parents warn their children not to read in dim light or sit too close to the TV or computer screen, their concern

("You'll ruin your eyes!") is well-founded. In diverse cultures, the more time children spend reading, writing, using the computer, and doing other close work, the more likely they are to be myopic (Pan, Ramamurthy, & Saw, 2012; Rahi, Cumberland, & Peckham, 2011). Consequently, myopia is one of the few health conditions to increase with SES. Fortunately, it can be overcome easily with corrective lenses.

During middle childhood, the Eustachian tube (canal that runs from the inner ear to the throat) becomes longer, narrower, and more slanted, preventing fluid and bacteria from traveling so easily from the mouth to the ear. As a result, middle-ear infections, common in infancy and early childhood, become less frequent. Still, about 3 to 4 percent of the school-age population, and as many as 20 percent of low-SES children, develop permanent hearing loss as a result of repeated untreated infections (Ryding et al., 2002). With regular screening for both vision and hearing, defects can be corrected before they lead to serious learning difficulties.

Illnesses

Children experience a somewhat higher rate of illness during the first two years of elementary school than later because of exposure to sick children and an immune system that is still developing. About 15 to 20 percent of U.S. children have chronic diseases and conditions (including physical disabilities) (Van Cleave, Gortmaker, & Perrin, 2010). By far the most common—accounting for about one-third of childhood chronic illness and the most frequent cause of school absence and childhood hospitalization—is *asthma,* in which the bronchial tubes (passages that connect the throat and lungs) are highly sensitive (Bonilla et al., 2005). In response to a variety of stimuli, such as cold weather, infection, exercise, allergies, and emotional stress, they fill with mucus and contract, leading to coughing, wheezing, and serious breathing difficulties.

From 1980 to 1997, the prevalence of asthma among U.S. children more than doubled and then stabilized at 9 percent (Akinbami et al., 2009). Although heredity contributes to asthma, researchers believe that environmental factors are necessary to spark the illness. Boys, African-American children, and children who were born underweight, whose parents smoke, or who live in poverty are at greatest risk (Federico & Liu, 2003; Pearlman et al., 2006). The higher rate and greater severity of asthma among African-American and poverty-stricken children may be the result of pollution in inner-city areas (which triggers allergic reactions), stressful home lives, and lack of access to good health care. Childhood obesity is also related to asthma in middle childhood, perhaps due to high levels of blood-circulating inflammatory substances associated with body fat (Story, 2007).

About 2 percent of U.S. children have more severe chronic illnesses, such as sickle cell anemia, cystic fibrosis, diabetes, arthritis, cancer, and AIDS. Painful medical treatments, physical discomfort, and changes in appearance often disrupt the sick child's daily life, making it difficult to concentrate in school and separating the child from peers. As the illness worsens, family stress increases (LeBlanc, Goldsmith, & Patel, 2003). For these reasons, chronically ill children are at risk for academic, emotional, and social difficulties.

A strong link exists between good family functioning and child well-being for chronically ill children, just as it does for physically healthy children (Drotar et al., 2006). Interventions that foster positive family relationships help parent and child cope with the disease and improve children's adjustment. These include health education, counseling, parent and peer support groups, and disease-specific summer camps, which teach children self-help skills and give parents time off from the demands of caring for an ill youngster.

Unintentional Injuries

As we conclude our discussion of threats to school-age children's health, let's return to the topic of unintentional injuries (discussed in detail in Chapter 7). As Figure 9.3 shows, injury fatalities increase from middle childhood into adolescence, with rates for boys rising considerably above those for girls.

Motor vehicle accidents, involving children as passengers or pedestrians, continue to be the leading cause of injury, followed by bicycle accidents (Bailar-Heath & Valley-Gray, 2010). Pedestrian injuries most often result from midblock dart-outs, bicycle accidents from disobeying traffic signals and rules. When many stimuli impinge on them at once, young school-age children often fail to think before they act. They need frequent reminders, supervision, and prohibitions against venturing into busy traffic on their own.

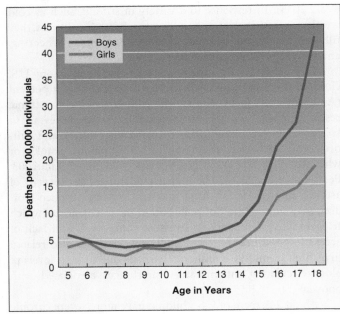

FIGURE 9.3 U.S. rates of injury mortality from middle childhood to adolescence. Injury fatalities increase with age, and the gap between boys and girls expands. Motor vehicle (passenger and pedestrian) accidents are the leading cause, with bicycle injuries next in line. (From National Center for Injury Prevention and Control, 2012.)

Effective school-based prevention programs use extensive modeling and rehearsal of safety practices, give children feedback about their performance along with praise and tangible rewards for acquiring safety skills, and provide occasional booster sessions (Zins et al., 1994). Parents, who often overestimate their child's safety knowledge and physical abilities, must be educated about children's age-related safety capacities (Schwebel & Bounds, 2003). One vital safety measure is insisting that children wear protective helmets while bicycling, in-line skating, skateboarding, or using scooters. This simple precaution leads to a 25 percent reduction in risk of head injury, a leading cause of permanent disability and death in school-age children (Macpherson & Spinks, 2007; Wesson et al., 2008).

Highly active, impulsive, risk-taking children, many of whom are boys, remain especially susceptible to injury in middle childhood. Although they have just as much safety knowledge as their peers, they are far less likely to implement it. Parents tend to be particularly lax in intervening in the dangerous behaviors of such children, especially under conditions of persistent marital conflict or other forms of mental distress (Schwebel et al., 2011, 2012). The greatest challenge for prevention programs is reaching these children and reducing their exposure to hazardous situations.

Motor Development and Play

TAKE A MOMENT... Visit a park on a pleasant weekend afternoon, and watch several preschool and school-age children at play. You will see that gains in body size and muscle strength support improved motor coordination in middle childhood. And greater cognitive and social maturity enables older children to use their new motor skills in more complex ways. A major change in children's play takes place at this time.

Gross-Motor Development

During the school years, running, jumping, hopping, and ball skills become more refined. Third to sixth graders burst into sprints as they race across the playground, jump quickly over rotating ropes, engage in intricate hopscotch patterns, kick and dribble soccer balls, bat at balls pitched by their classmates, and balance adeptly as they walk heel-to-toe across narrow ledges. These diverse skills reflect gains in four basic motor capacities:

- *Flexibility.* Compared with preschoolers, school-age children are physically more pliable and elastic, a difference that can be seen as they swing bats, kick balls, jump over hurdles, and execute tumbling routines.

- *Balance.* Improved balance supports many athletic skills, including running, hopping, skipping, throwing, kicking, and the rapid changes of direction required in many team sports.

Improved physical flexibility, balance, agility, and force, along with more efficient information processing, are evident in these 8-year-olds' soccer skills.

- *Agility.* Quicker and more accurate movements are evident in the fancy footwork of dance and cheerleading and in the forward, backward, and sideways motions used to dodge opponents in tag and soccer.

- *Force.* Older youngsters can throw and kick a ball harder and propel themselves farther off the ground when running and jumping than they could at earlier ages (Haywood & Getchell, 2009).

Along with body growth, more efficient information processing plays a vital role in improved motor performance. During middle childhood, the capacity to react only to relevant information increases. And steady gains in reaction time occur, with 11-year-olds responding twice as quickly as 5-year-olds (Kail, 2003; Largo et al., 2001). Because 6- and 7-year-olds are seldom successful at batting a thrown ball, T-ball is more appropriate for them than baseball. Similarly, handball, four-square, and kickball should precede instruction in tennis, basketball, and football.

Fine-Motor Development

Fine-motor development also improves over the school years. On rainy afternoons, Joey and Lizzie experimented with yo-yos, built model airplanes, and wove potholders on small looms. Like many children, they took up musical instruments, which demand considerable fine-motor control.

Gains in fine-motor skill are especially evident in children's writing and drawing. By age 6, most children can print the alphabet, their first and last names, and the numbers from 1 to 10 with reasonable clarity. Their writing is large, however, because they make strokes with the entire arm rather than just the wrist and fingers. Children usually master uppercase letters first because their horizontal and vertical motions are easier to control than the small curves of the lowercase alphabet. Legibility

of writing gradually increases as children produce more accurate letters with uniform height and spacing. These improvements prepare children for mastering cursive writing by third grade.

Children's drawings show dramatic gains in middle childhood. By the end of the preschool years, children can accurately copy many two-dimensional shapes, and they integrate these into their drawings. Some depth cues have also begun to appear, such as making distant objects smaller than near ones (Braine et al., 1993). Around 9 to 10 years, the third dimension is clearly evident through overlapping objects, diagonal placement, and converging lines. Furthermore, as Figure 9.4 below shows, school-age children not only depict objects in considerable detail but also relate them to one another as part of an organized whole (Case, 1998; Case & Okamoto, 1996).

FIGURE 9.4 **Increase in organization, detail, and depth cues in school-age children's drawings.** *TAKE A MOMENT...* Compare both drawings to the one by a 6-year-old on page 224 in Chapter 7. In the drawing by an 8-year-old on the top, notice how all parts are depicted in relation to one another and with greater detail. Integration of depth cues increases dramatically over the school years, as shown in the drawing on the bottom, by an 11-year-old. Here, the third dimension is indicated by overlapping objects and diagonal lines, as well as by making distant objects appear smaller than near ones.

Sex Differences

Sex differences in motor skills extend into middle childhood and, in some instances, become more pronounced. Girls have an edge in fine-motor skills of handwriting and drawing and in gross-motor capacities that depend on balance and agility, such as hopping and skipping. But boys outperform girls on all other gross-motor skills, especially throwing and kicking (Cratty, 1986; Haywood & Getchell, 2009).

School-age boys' genetic advantage in muscle mass is not large enough to account for their gross-motor superiority. Rather, the social environment plays a larger role. Research confirms that parents hold higher expectations for boys' athletic performance, and children readily absorb these messages. From first through twelfth grades, girls are less positive than boys about the value of sports and their own sports ability—differences explained in part by parental beliefs (Fredricks & Eccles, 2002). The more strongly girls believe that females are incompetent at sports (such as hockey or soccer), the lower they judge their own ability and the poorer they actually perform (Belcher et al., 2003; Chalabaev, Sarrazin & Fontayne, 2009).

Educating parents about the minimal differences between school-age boys' and girls' physical capacities and sensitizing them to unfair biases against promotion of girls' athletic ability may help increase girls' self-confidence and participation in athletics. And greater emphasis on skill training for girls, along with increased attention to their athletic achievements, is also likely to help. As a positive sign, compared with a generation ago, many more girls now participate in individual and team sports such as gymnastics and soccer (National Council of Youth Sports, 2008; Sabo & Veliz, 2011). Middle childhood is a crucial time to encourage girls' sports participation because during this period, children start to discover what they are good at and make some definite skill commitments.

Games with Rules

The physical activities of school-age children reflect an important advance in quality of play: Games with rules become common. Children around the world engage in an enormous variety of informally organized games, including variants on popular sports such as soccer, baseball, and basketball. In addition to the best-known childhood games, such as tag, jacks, and hopscotch, children have invented hundreds of other games, including red rover, statues, leapfrog, kick the can, and prisoner's base (Kirchner, 2000).

Gains in perspective taking—in particular, the ability to understand the roles of several players in a game—permit this transition to rule-oriented games. These play experiences, in turn, contribute greatly to emotional and social development. Child-invented games usually rely on simple physical skills and a sizable element of luck. As a result, they rarely become contests of individual ability. Instead, they permit children to try out different styles of cooperating, competing, winning, and losing with little personal risk. Also, in their efforts to organize a game, children discover why rules are necessary and

With their coach's encouragement, these young softball players are likely to view themselves as good at sports and to continue playing. In contrast, coaches who criticize and overemphasize competition promote early athletic dropout.

which ones work well. As we will see in Chapter 10, these experiences help children form more mature concepts of fairness and justice.

School-age children today spend less time engaged in informal outdoor play—a change that reflects parental concerns about neighborhood safety as well as competition for children's time from TV, video games, and the Internet. Another factor is the rise in adult-organized sports, such as Little League baseball and soccer and hockey leagues, which fill many hours that children used to devote to spontaneous play. About half of U.S. children—60 percent of boys and 37 percent of girls—participate in organized sports at some time between ages 5 and 18 (National Council of Youth Sports, 2008).

For most children, joining community athletic teams is associated with increased self-esteem and social skills (Daniels & Leaper, 2006; Fletcher, Nickerson, & Wright, 2003). Among shy children, sports participation seems to foster self-confidence and a decline in social anxiety, perhaps because it provides a sense of group belonging and a basis for communicating with peers (Findlay & Coplan, 2008). And children who view themselves as good at sports are more likely to continue playing on teams in adolescence, which predicts greater participation in sports and other physical fitness activities in early adulthood (Kjønniksen, Anderssen, & Wold, 2009; Marsh et al., 2007).

In some cases, though, the arguments of critics—that youth sports overemphasize competition and substitute adult control for children's natural experimentation with rules and strategies—are valid. Coaches and parents who criticize rather than encourage can prompt intense anxiety in some children, setting the stage for emotional difficulties and early athletic dropout, not elite performance (Tofler, Knapp, & Drell, 1998; Wall &

Applying What We Know

Providing Developmentally Appropriate Organized Sports in Middle Childhood

Suggestion	Description
Build on children's interests.	Permit children to select from among appropriate activities the ones that suit them best. Do not push children into sports they do not enjoy.
Teach age-appropriate skills.	For children younger than age 9, emphasize basic skills, such as kicking, throwing, and batting, and simplified games that grant all participants adequate playing time.
Emphasize enjoyment.	Permit children to progress at their own pace and to play for the fun of it, whether or not they become expert athletes.
Limit the frequency and length of practices.	Adjust practice time to children's attention spans and need for unstructured time with peers, with family, and for homework. Two practices a week, each no longer than 30 minutes for younger school-age children and 60 minutes for older school-age children, are sufficient.
Focus on personal and team improvement.	Emphasize effort, skill gains, and teamwork rather than winning. Avoid criticism for errors and defeat, which promotes anxiety and avoidance of athletics.
Discourage unhealthy competition.	Avoid all-star games and championship ceremonies that recognize individuals. Instead, acknowledge all participants.
Permit children to contribute to rules and strategies.	Involve children in decisions aimed at ensuring fair play and teamwork. To strengthen desirable responses, reinforce compliance rather than punishing noncompliance.

Côté, 2007). See Applying What We Know above for ways to ensure that athletic leagues provide children with positive learning experiences.

LOOK AND LISTEN

Observe a youth athletic league game, such as soccer, baseball, or hockey. Do coaches and parents encourage children's effort and skill gains, or are they overly focused on winning? Cite examples of adult and child behaviors. ●

Shadows of Our Evolutionary Past

TAKE A MOMENT... While watching children in your neighborhood park, notice how they sometimes wrestle, roll, hit, and run after one another, alternating roles while smiling and laughing. This friendly chasing and play-fighting is called **rough-and-tumble play.** It emerges in the preschool years and peaks in middle childhood, and children in many cultures engage in it with peers whom they like especially well (Pellegrini, 2004).

Children's rough-and-tumble play resembles the social behavior of many other young mammals. It seems to originate in parents' physical play with babies, especially fathers' with sons (see page 202 in Chapter 6). And it is more common among boys, probably because prenatal exposure to androgens (male sex hormones) predisposes boys toward active play (see Chapter 8).

In our evolutionary past, rough-and-tumble play may have been important for developing fighting skill (Power, 2000). It also helps children form a **dominance hierarchy**—a stable ordering of group members that predicts who will win when conflict arises. Observations of arguments, threats, and physical

attacks between children reveal a consistent lineup of winners and losers that becomes increasingly stable in middle childhood, especially among boys. Once school-age children establish a dominance hierarchy, hostility is rare (Pellegrini & Smith,

In our evolutionary past, rough-and-tumble play—which can be distinguished from aggression by its friendly quality—may have been important for developing fighting skill and establishing dominance hierarchies.

Social Issues: Education

School Recess—A Time to Play, a Time to Learn

When 7-year-old Whitney's family moved to a new city, she left a school with three daily recess periods for one with just a single 15-minute break per day, which her second-grade teacher cancelled if any child misbehaved. Whitney, who had previously enjoyed school, complained daily of headaches and an upset stomach. Her mother, Jill, thought, "My child is stressing out because she can't move all day!" After Jill and other parents successfully appealed to the school board to add a second recess period, Whitney's symptoms vanished (Rauber, 2006).

In recent years, recess—with its rich opportunities for child-organized play and peer interaction—has diminished or disappeared in many U.S. elementary schools (Ginsburg, 2007; Pellegrini & Holmes, 2006). Under the assumption that extra time for academics will translate into achievement gains, 7 percent of U.S. schools no longer provide recess to students as young as second grade. And over half of schools that do have recess now schedule it just once a day (U.S. Department of Education, 2012b).

Yet rather than subtracting from classroom learning, recess periods boost it! Research dating back more than 100 years confirms that distributing cognitively demanding tasks over a longer time by introducing regular breaks enhances attention and performance at all ages. Such breaks are particularly important for children. In a series of studies, elementary school students were more attentive in the classroom after recess than before it—an effect that was greater for second than fourth graders (Pellegrini, Huberty, & Jones, 1995). Teacher ratings of classroom disruptive behavior also decline for children who have more than 15 minutes of recess a day (Barros, Silver, & Stein, 2009).

In other research, kindergartners' and first graders' engagement in peer conversation and games during recess positively predicted academic achievement, even

Recess offers rich opportunities for child-organized play and games that provide practice in social skills while also promoting physical and academic competence.

after other factors that might explain the relationship (such as previous achievement) were controlled (Pellegrini, 1992; Pellegrini et al., 2002). Recall from Chapter 8 that children's social maturity contributes substantially to academic competence. Recess is one of the few remaining contexts devoted to child-organized games that provide practice in vital social skills—cooperation, leadership, followership, and inhibition of aggression—under adult supervision rather than adult direction. As children transfer these skills to the classroom, they may participate in discussions, collaborate, follow rules, and enjoy academic pursuits more—factors that enhance motivation and achievement.

1998; Roseth et al., 2007). Children seem to use play-fighting as a safe context to assess the strength of a peer before challenging that peer's dominance.

As children reach puberty, individual differences in strength become apparent, and rough-and-tumble play declines. When it does occur, its meaning changes: Adolescent boys' rough-and-tumble is linked to aggression (Pellegrini, 2003). Unlike children, teenage rough-and-tumble players "cheat," hurting their opponent. In explanation, boys often say that they are retaliating, apparently to reestablish dominance. Thus, a play behavior that limits aggression in childhood becomes a context for hostility in adolescence.

Physical Education

Physical activity supports many aspects of children's development—health, sense of self-worth, and the cognitive and social skills necessary for getting along with others. Yet to devote more time to academic instruction, U.S. elementary schools have cut

back on recess, despite its contribution to all domains of development (see the Social Issues: Education box above). Similarly, although almost most U.S. states require some physical education, only six require it in every grade, and only one mandates at least 30 minutes per school day in elementary school and 45 minutes in middle and high school. Not surprisingly, physical inactivity among school-age children is pervasive: Fewer than one-third of 6- to 17-year-olds engage in at least moderate-intensity activity for 60 minutes per day and vigorous activity (involving breathing hard and sweating) for 20 minutes, recommended for good health (National Association for Sport and Physical Education, 2010).

Many experts believe that schools should not only offer more physical education classes but also change the content of these programs. Training in competitive sports, often a high priority, is unlikely to reach the least physically fit youngsters, who avoid activities demanding a high level of skill. Instead, programs should emphasize enjoyable, informal games and individual exercise—pursuits most likely to endure.

Physically fit children tend to become active adults who reap many benefits (Kjønniksen, Torsheim, & Wold, 2008; Tammelin et al., 2003). These include greater physical strength, resistance to many illnesses (from colds and flu to cancer, diabetes, and heart disease), enhanced psychological well-being, and a longer life.

COGNITIVE DEVELOPMENT

"Finally!" 6-year-old Lizzie exclaimed the day she entered first grade. "Now I get to go to real school, just like Joey!" Lizzie walked into her classroom confidently, pencils, crayons, and writing pad in hand, ready for a more disciplined approach to learning. In a single morning, she and her classmates wrote in journals, met in reading groups, worked on addition and subtraction, and sorted leaves gathered for a science project. As Lizzie and Joey moved through the elementary school grades, they tackled increasingly complex tasks and became more accomplished at reading, writing, math skills, and general knowledge of the world.

To understand the cognitive attainments of middle childhood, we turn to research inspired by Piaget's theory and the information-processing perspective. And we look at expanding definitions of intelligence that help us appreciate individual differences. Our discussion continues with language, which blossoms further in these years. Finally, we consider the role of schools in children's development.

Piaget's Theory: The Concrete Operational Stage

When Lizzie visited my child development class as a 4-year-old, Piaget's conservation problems confused her (see Chapter 7, page 229). For example, when water was poured from a tall,

narrow container into a short, wide one, she insisted that the amount of water had changed. But when Lizzie returned at age 8, she found these tasks easy. "Of course it's the same!" she exclaimed. "The water's shorter, but it's also wider. Pour it back," she instructed the college student who was interviewing her. "You'll see, it's the same amount!"

Concrete Operational Thought

Lizzie has entered Piaget's **concrete operational stage,** which extends from about 7 to 11 years. Compared with early childhood, thought is far more logical, flexible, and organized.

Conservation. The ability to pass *conservation tasks* provides clear evidence of *operations*—mental actions that obey logical rules. Notice how Lizzie is capable of *decentration*, focusing on several aspects of a problem and relating them, rather than centering on just one. She also demonstrates **reversibility,** the capacity to think through a series of steps and then mentally reverse direction, returning to the starting point. Recall from Chapter 7 that reversibility is part of every logical operation. It is solidly achieved in middle childhood.

Classification. Between ages 7 and 10, children pass Piaget's *class inclusion problem* (see page 229). This indicates that they are more aware of classification hierarchies and can focus on relations between a general category and two specific categories at the same time—that is, on three relations at once (Hodges & French, 1988; Ni, 1998). Collections—stamps, coins, baseball cards, rocks, bottle caps—become common in middle childhood. At age 10, Joey spent hours sorting and resorting his baseball cards, grouping them first by league and team, then by playing position and batting average. He could separate the players into a variety of classes and subclasses and easily rearrange them.

An improved ability to categorize underlies children's interest in collecting objects during middle childhood. This 9-year-old sorts and organizes her extensive shell collection.

Seriation. The ability to order items along a quantitative dimension, such as length or weight, is called **seriation.** To test for it, Piaget asked children to arrange sticks of different lengths from shortest to longest. Older preschoolers can put the sticks in a row, but they do so haphazardly, making many errors. In contrast, 6- to 7-year-olds create the series efficiently, moving in an orderly sequence from the smallest stick, to the next largest, and so on.

The concrete operational child can also seriate mentally, an ability called **transitive inference.** In a well-known transitive inference problem, Piaget showed children pairings of sticks of different colors. From observing that Stick *A* is longer than Stick *B* and Stick *B* is longer than Stick *C*, children must infer that *A* is longer than *C*. Like Piaget's class inclusion task, transitive inference requires children to integrate three relations at once—in this instance, *A–B*, *B–C*, and *A–C*. When researchers take steps to ensure that children remember the premises (*A–B* and *B–C*), 7-year-olds can grasp transitive inference (Andrews & Halford, 1998; Wright, 2006).

Spatial Reasoning. Piaget found that school-age children's understanding of space is more accurate than that of preschoolers. Let's consider children's **cognitive maps**—mental representations of familiar large-scale spaces, such as their neighborhood or school. Drawing a map of a large-scale space requires considerable perspective-taking skill. Because the entire space cannot be seen at once, children must infer its overall layout by relating its separate parts.

Preschoolers and young school-age children include *landmarks* on the maps they draw, but their arrangement is not always accurate. They do better when asked to place stickers showing the location of desks and people on a map of their classroom. But if the map is rotated to a position other than the orientation of the classroom, they have difficulty (Liben & Downs, 1993).

Around age 8 to 10, children's maps become better organized, showing landmarks along an *organized route of travel*. At the same time, children are able to give clear, well-organized instructions for getting from one place to another by using a "mental walk" strategy—imagining another person's movements along a route (Gauvain & Rogoff, 1989). By the end of middle childhood, children combine landmarks and routes into an *overall view of a large-scale space*. And they readily draw and read maps of extended outdoor environments, even when the orientation of the map and the space it represents do not match (Liben, 2009). Ten- to 12-year-olds also grasp the notion of *scale*—the proportional relation between a space and its representation on a map (Liben, 2006).

LOOK AND LISTEN

Ask a 6- to 8-year-old and a 9- to 12-year-old to draw a neighborhood map showing important landmarks, such as the school, a friend's house, or a shopping area. In what ways do the children's maps differ? ●

Cultural frameworks influence children's map making. In many non-Western communities, people rarely use maps for way-finding but rely on information from neighbors, street vendors, and shopkeepers. Also, compared to their Western agemates, non-Western children less often ride in cars and more often walk, which results in intimate neighborhood knowledge. When older school-age children in small cities in India and in the United States drew maps of their neighborhoods, the Indian children represented a rich array of landmarks and aspects of social life, such as people and vehicles, in a small area surrounding their home. The U.S. children, in contrast, drew a more formal, extended space, highlighting main streets and key directions (north–south, east–west) but including few landmarks (see Figure 9.5) (Parameswaran, 2003). Although the U.S. children's maps scored higher in cognitive maturity, this difference reflected cultural interpretations of the task. When asked to create a map to "help people find their way," the Indian children drew spaces as far-reaching and organized as the U.S. children's.

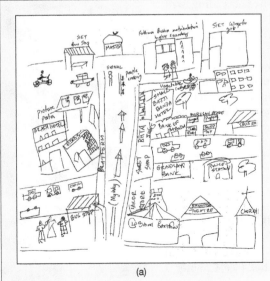 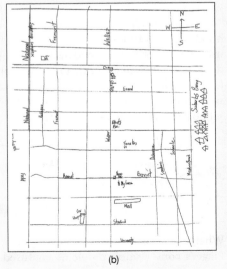

FIGURE 9.5 **Maps drawn by older school-age children from India and the United States.** (a) The Indian child depicted many landmarks and features of social life in a small area near her home. (b) The U.S. child drew a more extended space and highlighted main streets and key directions but included few landmarks and people. (Reprinted from *Journal of Environmental Psychology*, Vol. 23, No. 4, G. Parameswaran, 2003, "Experimenter Instructions as a Mediator in the Effects of Culture on Mapping One's Neighborhood," pp. 415–416. Copyright 2003, with permission from Elsevier.)

(a)   (b)

Limitations of Concrete Operational Thought

As the name of this stage suggests, concrete operational thinking suffers from one important limitation: Children think in an organized, logical fashion only when dealing with concrete information they can perceive directly. Their mental operations work poorly with abstract ideas—ones not apparent in the real world. Consider children's solutions to transitive inference problems. When shown pairs of sticks of unequal length, Lizzie easily engaged in transitive inference. But she had difficulty with a hypothetical version of this task: "Susan is taller than Sally, and Sally is taller than Mary. Who is the tallest?" Not until age 11 or 12 can children solve this problem.

That logical thought is at first tied to immediate situations helps account for a special feature of concrete operational reasoning: Children master concrete operational tasks step by step. For example, they usually grasp conservation of number first, followed by conservation of length, liquid, and mass, and then weight. This *continuum of acquisition* (or gradual mastery) of logical concepts is another indication of the limitations of concrete operational thinking (Fischer & Bidell, 1991). Rather than coming up with general logical principles that they apply to all relevant situations, school-age children seem to work out the logic of each problem separately.

Follow-Up Research on Concrete Operational Thought

According to Piaget, brain development combined with experience in a rich and varied external world should lead children everywhere to reach the concrete operational stage at about the same time. Yet recent evidence indicates that specific cultural and school practices have much to do with mastery of Piagetian tasks (Rogoff, 2003). And information-processing research helps explain the gradual mastery of logical concepts in middle childhood.

The Impact of Culture and Schooling. In tribal and village societies, conservation is often delayed. Among the Hausa of Nigeria, who live in small agricultural settlements and rarely send their children to school, even basic conservation tasks—number, length, and liquid—are not understood until age 11 or later (Fahrmeier, 1978). This suggests that participating in relevant everyday activities helps children master conservation and other Piagetian problems. Joey and Lizzie, for example, think of fairness in terms of equal distribution—a value emphasized in their culture. They frequently divide materials, such as crayons or treats, equally among their friends. Because they often see the same quantity arranged in different ways, they grasp conservation early.

The very experience of going to school seems to promote mastery of Piagetian tasks. When children of the same age are tested, those who have been in school longer do better on transitive inference problems (Artman & Cahan, 1993). Opportunities

This Zinacanteco Indian girl of southern Mexico learns the centuries-old practice of backstrap weaving. Although Zinacanteco children might do poorly on Piaget's tasks, they are adept at the complex mental transformations involved in converting warp strung on a loom into woven cloth.

to seriate objects, to learn about order relations, and to remember the parts of complex problems are probably responsible. Yet certain informal nonschool experiences can also foster operational thought. Around age 7 to 8, Zinacanteco Indian girls of southern Mexico, who learn to weave elaborately designed fabrics as an alternative to schooling, engage in mental transformations to figure out how a warp strung on a loom will turn out as woven cloth—reasoning expected at the concrete operational stage. American children of the same age, who do much better than Zinacanteco children on Piagetian tasks, have great difficulty with these weaving problems (Maynard & Greenfield, 2003).

On the basis of such findings, some investigators have concluded that the forms of logic required by Piagetian tasks do not emerge spontaneously but, rather, are heavily influenced by training, context, and cultural conditions. Does this view remind you of Vygotsky's sociocultural theory, discussed in earlier chapters?

An Information-Processing View of Concrete Operational Thought. The gradual mastery of logical concepts in middle childhood raises a familiar question about Piaget's theory: Is an abrupt stagewise transition to logical thought the best way to describe cognitive development in middle childhood?

Some *neo-Piagetian theorists* argue that the development of operational thinking can best be understood in terms of gains in information-processing speed rather than a sudden shift to a new stage (Halford & Andrews, 2006). For example, Robbie Case (1996, 1998) proposed that, with practice, cognitive schemes demand less attention and become more automatic. This frees up space in *working memory* so children can focus on combining old schemes and generating new ones. For instance, the child who sees water poured from one container to another recognizes that the height of the liquid changes. As this understanding becomes routine, the child notices that the width of the water changes as well. Soon children coordinate these observations, and they grasp conservation of liquid. Then, as this logical idea becomes well-practiced, the child transfers it to more demanding situations, such as weight.

Once the schemes of a Piagetian stage are sufficiently automatic, enough working memory is available to integrate them into an improved representation. As a result, children acquire *central conceptual structures*—networks of concepts and relations that permit them to think more effectively about a wide range of situations (Case, 1996, 1998). The central conceptual structures that emerge from integrating concrete operational schemes are broadly applicable principles that result in increasingly complex, systematic reasoning, which we will discuss in Chapter 11 in the context of formal operational thought.

Case and his colleagues—along with other information-processing researchers—have examined children's performance on a wide variety of tasks: solving arithmetic word problems, understanding stories, drawing pictures, and interpreting social situations. In each task, preschoolers typically focus on only one dimension. In understanding stories, for example, they grasp only a single story line. By the early school years, they combine two story lines into a single plot. Around 9 to 11 years, children integrate multiple dimensions (Case, 1998; Halford & Andrews, 2006). They tell coherent stories with a main plot and several subplots.

Case's theory helps explain why many understandings appear in specific situations at different times rather than being mastered all at once. First, different forms of the same logical insight, such as the various conservation tasks, vary in their processing demands, with those acquired later requiring more space in working memory. Second, children's experiences vary widely. A child who often listens to and tells stories but rarely draws pictures displays more advanced central conceptual structures in storytelling. Compared with Piaget's, Case's theory better accounts for unevenness in cognitive development.

Evaluation of the Concrete Operational Stage

Piaget was correct that school-age children approach many problems in more organized, rational ways than preschoolers. But disagreement continues over whether this difference occurs because of *continuous* improvement in logical skills or *discontinuous* restructuring of children's thinking (as Piaget's stage idea assumes). Many researchers think that both types of change may be involved (Case, 1998; Demetriou et al., 2002; Fischer & Bidell, 2006; Halford & Andrews, 2006).

During the school years, children apply logical schemes to many more tasks. In the process, their thought seems to change qualitatively—toward a more comprehensive grasp of the underlying principles of logical thought. Piaget himself recognized this possibility in evidence for gradual mastery of conservation and other tasks. So perhaps some blend of Piagetian and information-processing ideas holds the greatest promise for explaining cognitive development in middle childhood.

Information Processing

In contrast to Piaget's focus on overall cognitive change, the information-processing perspective examines separate aspects of thinking. Working-memory capacity, as noted in our discussion of Case's theory, continues to increase in middle childhood. And school-age children make great strides in executive function, yielding significant advances in attention, planning, memory, and self-regulation. Each contributes vitally to academic learning.

Working-Memory Capacity

Improved performance on working-memory tasks (see page 161 in Chapter 5) is supported by brain development. And working memory—as we have seen in our discussion of Case's theory—benefits from enhanced speed of thinking. Time needed to process information on a wide variety of cognitive tasks declines rapidly between ages 6 and 12, likely due to myelination and synaptic pruning in the cerebral cortex (Kail, 1993, 1997). A faster thinker can hold on to and operate on more information in working memory (Luna et al., 2004; Nettelbeck & Burns, 2010). Still, individual differences in working-memory capacity exist, and they are of particular concern because they predict intelligence test scores and academic achievement in diverse subjects (Colom et al., 2007; Gathercole et al., 2005).

Indeed, children with persistent learning difficulties in reading and math are often deficient in working-memory capacity (Alloway, 2009; Gathercole et al., 2006). Reduced working memory creates a bottleneck for learning. Observations of elementary school children with limited working memories revealed that they often failed at school assignments that made heavy memory demands (Gathercole, Lamont, & Alloway, 2006). They could not follow complex instructions, lost their place in tasks with multiple steps, and frequently gave up before finishing their work. The children struggled because they could not hold in mind sufficient information to complete assignments.

Compared to their economically advantaged agemates, children from poverty-stricken families are more likely to score low on working-memory tasks—a strong contributor to their generally poorer academic achievement (Farah et al., 2006; Noble, McCandliss, & Farah, 2007). In one study, years of childhood spent in poverty predicted reduced working-memory capacity in early adulthood (Evans & Schamberg, 2009). Childhood neurobiological measures of stress—elevated blood pressure and stress hormone levels, including cortisol—largely explained this poverty–working-memory association. Chronic stress, as we saw in Chapter 4, can impair brain structure and function, especially in the prefrontal cortex and its connections with the hippocampus, which govern working-memory capacity.

Interventions are needed that reduce memory loads so children with limited working memories can learn. Effective approaches include communicating in short sentences with familiar vocabulary, repeating task instructions, breaking complex tasks into manageable parts, and encouraging children to use external memory aids (such as lists of useful spellings when writing or number lines when doing math) (Gathercole & Alloway, 2008). Do these techniques remind you of *scaffolding,* a style of teaching introduced in Chapter 7 known to promote cognitive development?

Executive Function

Our discussion in Chapter 7 revealed that early childhood is a vital time for laying the foundations of executive function. During the school years, a time of continued development of the prefrontal cortex, executive function undergoes its most energetic period of development (Welsh, 2002). Children handle increasingly difficult tasks that require the integration of working memory, inhibition, planning, flexible use of strategies, and self-monitoring and self-correction of behavior (Luciana, 2003; Welsh, Pennington, & Groisser, 1991).

Heritability evidence suggests substantial genetic influence on various aspects of executive function, including combining information in working memory, controlling attention, and inhibiting inappropriate responses (Hansell et al., 2001; Polderman et al., 2009; Young et al., 2009). And molecular genetic analyses are identifying specific genes related to severely deficient functioning of executive components, such as attention and inhibition, which (as we will soon see) contributes to learning and behavior disorders, such as attention-deficit hyperactivity disorder (ADHD).

But in both typically and atypically developing children, heredity combines with environmental contexts to influence executive function. In Chapter 3, we reviewed evidence indicating that prenatal teratogens can impair impulse control, attention, planning, and other executive processes. And as with working memory, poverty and stressful living conditions can undermine executive function, with powerfully negative consequences for academic achievement and social adjustment (Blair

Middle childhood is a period of dramatic gains in executive function. This complex map-making project requires fourth graders to coordinate relevant information in working memory, inhibit inappropriate responses, flexibly implement strategies, and monitor their progress, redirecting unsuccessful efforts.

& Raver, 2012). As we turn now to the development of an array of executive processes, our discussion will confirm that supportive home and school experiences are essential for their optimal development.

Attention

In middle childhood, attention becomes more selective, adaptable, and planful. First, children become better at deliberately attending to just those aspects of a situation that are relevant to their goals. Researchers study this increasing selectivity of attention by introducing irrelevant stimuli into a task and seeing how well children attend to its central elements. Selective attention improves sharply between ages 6 and 10, with gains continuing throughout adolescence (Gomez-Perez & Ostrosky-Solis, 2006; Tabibi & Pfeffer, 2007; Vakil et al., 2009).

Second, older children are better at flexibly adapting their attention to task requirements. When asked to sort cards with pictures that vary in both color and shape, children age 5 and older readily switch their basis of sorting from color to shape when asked to do so. Younger children typically persist in sorting in just one way (Brooks et al., 2003; Zelazo, Carlson, & Kesek, 2008). And when studying for a spelling test, 10-year-old Joey was much more likely than Lizzie to devote most attention to the words he knew least well (Masur, McIntyre, & Flavell, 1973).

Finally, planning, which requires children to coordinate attention skills with other cognitive processes, improves greatly in middle childhood (Gauvain, 2004; Scholnick, 1995). On tasks with many parts, school-age children make decisions about what to do first and what to do next in an orderly fashion. Having many opportunities to practice planning helps them imagine future possibilities, postpone action in favor of evaluating alternatives, organize task materials (such as items on a

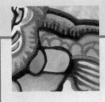

Biology and Environment

Children with Attention-Deficit Hyperactivity Disorder

While the other fifth graders worked quietly at their desks, Calvin squirmed, dropped his pencil, looked out the window, and fiddled with his shoelaces. "Hey Joey," he yelled across the room, "wanna play ball after school?" But the other children weren't eager to play with Calvin, who was physically awkward and failed to follow the rules of the game. He had trouble taking turns at bat and, in the outfield, looked elsewhere when the ball came his way. Calvin's desk was a chaotic mess. He often lost pencils, books, and other school materials, and he had difficulty remembering assignments and due dates.

Symptoms of ADHD

Calvin is one of 3 to 7 percent of U.S. school-age children with **attention-deficit hyperactivity disorder (ADHD),** which involves inattention, impulsivity, and excessive motor activity resulting in academic and social problems (American Psychiatric Association, 2000). Boys are diagnosed about four times as often as girls. However, many girls with ADHD seem to be overlooked, either because their symptoms are less flagrant or because of a gender bias: A difficult, disruptive boy is more likely to be referred for treatment (Biederman et al., 2005).

Children with ADHD cannot stay focused on a task that requires mental effort for more than a few minutes. They often act impulsively, ignoring social rules and lashing out with hostility when frustrated. Many, though not all, are *hyperactive,* exhausting parents and teachers and irritating other children with their excessive motor activity. For a child to be diagnosed with ADHD, these symptoms must have appeared before age 7 as a persistent problem.

Because of their difficulty concentrating, children with ADHD score 7 to 15 points lower than other children on intelligence tests (Barkley, 2002). Researchers agree that executive function deficiencies underlie ADHD symptoms. According to one view, children with ADHD are impaired in capacity to inhibit action in favor of thought—a basic difficulty resulting in wide-ranging inadequacies in executive processing and, therefore, in impulsive, disorganized behavior (Barkley, 2003a). Another hypothesis is that ADHD is the direct result of a cluster of executive processing problems that interfere with ability to guide one's own actions (Brown, 2006). Research confirms that children with ADHD do poorly on tasks requiring sustained attention; find it hard to ignore irrelevant information; have difficulty with memory, planning, reasoning, and problem solving in academic and social situations; and often fail to manage frustration and intense emotion (Barkley, 2003b, 2006).

Origins of ADHD

ADHD runs in families and is highly heritable: Identical twins share it more often than fraternal twins (Freitag et al., 2010; Rasmussen et al., 2004). Children with ADHD show abnormal brain functioning, including reduced electrical and blood-flow activity and structural abnormalities in the

---

grocery list), and remember the steps of their plan so they can attend to each one in sequence. Parents can foster planning by encouraging it in everyday activities, from loading the dishwasher to preparing for a vacation. In one study, discussions involving planning with school-age children predicted planning in adolescence (Gauvain & Huard, 1999). The demands of school tasks—and teachers' explanations of how to plan—also contribute to gains in planning.

The attentional strategies just considered are crucial for success in school. Unfortunately, some children have grave difficulties paying attention. See the Biology and Environment box above for a discussion of the serious learning and behavior problems of children with attention-deficit hyperactivity disorder.

Memory Strategies

As attention improves, so do *memory strategies,* deliberate mental activities we use to store and retain information. When Lizzie had a list of things to learn—for example, the state capitals of the United States—she immediately used **rehearsal**—repeating the information to herself. This memory strategy first appears in the early grade school years. Soon after, a second strategy becomes common: **organization**—grouping related items together (for example, all state capitals in the same part of the country) (Schneider, 2002).

Perfecting memory strategies requires time and effort. Eight-year-old Lizzie rehearsed in a piecemeal fashion. After being given the word *cat* in a list of items, she said, "Cat, cat, cat." But 10-year-old Joey used a more effective approach: He combined previous words with each new item, saying, "Desk, man, yard, cat, cat." This more active rehearsal approach, in which neighboring words create contexts for one another that trigger recall, yields much better memory (Lehman & Hasselhorn, 2007, 2010). Furthermore, whereas Lizzy organized by everyday association (hat–head, carrot–rabbit), Joey grouped items *taxonomically,* based on common properties (clothing, food, animals) and, thus, into fewer categories—an efficient procedure yielding dramatic memory gains (Bjorklund et al., 1994). And Joey used organization in a wide range of memory tasks, whereas Lizzie used it only when categorical relations among items were obvious.

prefrontal cortex and in other areas involved in attention, inhibition of behavior, and other aspects of motor control (Mackie et al., 2007; Sowell et al., 2003). Also, the brains of children with ADHD grow more slowly and are about 3 percent smaller in overall volume, with a thinner cerebral cortex, than those of unaffected agemates (Narr et al., 2009; Shaw et al., 2007). Several genes that disrupt functioning of neurotransmitters involved in inhibition and cognitive processing have been implicated in the disorder (Bobb et al., 2006; Faraone & Mick, 2010).

At the same time, ADHD is associated with environmental factors. Prenatal teratogens—such as tobacco, alcohol, and environmental pollutants—are linked to inattention and hyperactivity. And they can combine with certain genotypes to greatly increase risk of the disorder (see page 74 in Chapter 2). Furthermore, children with ADHD are more likely to come from homes in which marriages are unhappy and family stress is high (Bernier & Siegel, 1994). But a stressful home life rarely causes ADHD. Rather, these children's behaviors can contribute to family problems, which intensify the child's preexisting difficulties.

Treating ADHD

Calvin's doctor eventually prescribed stimulant medication, the most common treatment for ADHD. As long as dosage is carefully regulated, these drugs reduce activity level and improve attention, academic performance, and peer relations for about 70 percent of children who take them (Greenhill, Halperin, & Abikoff, 1999). Stimulant medication seems to increase activity in the prefrontal cortex, thereby improving the child's capacity to sustain attention and to inhibit off-task behavior.

Nevertheless, drug treatment cannot teach children to compensate for inattention and impulsivity. The most effective treatment approach combines medication with interventions that model and reinforce appropriate academic and social behavior (Smith, Barkley, & Shapiro, 2006).

Family intervention is also important. Inattentive, overactive children strain the patience of parents, who are likely to react punitively and inconsistently—a child-

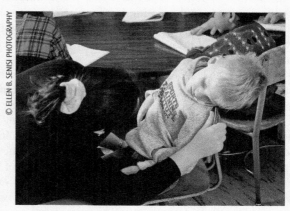

This child frequently engages in disruptive behavior at school. Children with ADHD have great difficulty staying on task and often act impulsively, ignoring social rules.

rearing style that strengthens defiant, aggressive behavior. In fact, in 50 to 75 percent of cases, these two sets of behavior problems occur together (Goldstein, 2011).

ADHD is usually a lifelong disorder. Adults with ADHD continue to need help in structuring their environments, regulating negative emotion, selecting appropriate careers, and understanding their condition as a biological deficit rather than a character flaw.

Furthermore, Joey often combined several strategies—for example, organizing items, then stating the category names, and finally rehearsing. The more strategies children apply simultaneously and consistently, the better they remember (Hock, Park, & Bjorklund, 1998; Schwenck, Bjorklund, & Schneider, 2007). Younger school-age children often try out various memory strategies but use them less systematically and successfully than older children. Still, their tendency to experiment allows them to discover which strategies work best and how to combine them effectively. Indeed, children experiment with strategies when faced with many cognitive challenges—an approach that enables them to gradually "home in" on the most effective techniques (Siegler, 1996, 2007).

By the end of middle childhood, children start to use **elaboration**—creating a relationship, or shared meaning, between two or more pieces of information that do not belong to the same category. For example, to learn the words *fish* and *pipe,* you might generate the verbal statement or mental image, "The fish is smoking a pipe." This highly effective memory technique, which requires considerable effort and space in working memory, becomes increasingly common in adolescence and early adulthood (Schneider & Pressley, 1997).

Because organization and elaboration combine items into *meaningful chunks,* they permit children to hold onto much more information and, as a result, further expand working memory. In addition, when children link a new item to information they already know, they can *retrieve* the new item easily by thinking of other items associated with it. As we will see, this also contributes to improved memory during the school years.

Knowledge and Memory

During middle childhood, the long-term knowledge base grows larger and becomes organized into increasingly elaborate, hierarchically structured networks. This rapid growth of knowledge helps children use strategies and remember (Schneider, 2002). In other words, knowing more about a topic makes new information more meaningful and familiar so it is easier to store and retrieve.

In a test of this idea, researchers classified fourth graders as either experts or novices in knowledge of soccer and then gave both groups lists of soccer and nonsoccer items to learn. Experts remembered far more items on the soccer list (but not on the nonsoccer list) than novices. And during recall, experts' listing of items was better organized, as indicated by clustering of items into categories (Schneider & Bjorklund, 1992). This superior organization at retrieval suggests that highly knowledgeable children organize information in their area of expertise with little or no effort. Consequently, experts can devote more working-memory resources to using recalled information for reasoning and problem solving.

But knowledge is not the only important factor in children's strategic memory processing. Children who are expert in an area are usually highly motivated. As a result, they not only acquire knowledge more quickly but also *actively use what they know* to add more. In contrast, academically unsuccessful children fail to ask how previously stored information can clarify new material. This, in turn, interferes with the development of a broad knowledge base (Schneider & Bjorklund, 1998). So extensive knowledge and use of memory strategies support one another.

Culture, Schooling, and Memory Strategies

Children and adults usually use memory strategies when they need to remember information for its own sake. On many other occasions, memory occurs as a natural byproduct of participation in daily activities (Rogoff, 2003).

A repeated finding is that people in non-Western cultures who lack formal schooling rarely use or benefit from instruction in memory strategies because they see no practical reason to use these techniques (Rogoff & Chavajay, 1995). Tasks that require children to recall isolated bits of information, which are common in school, strongly motivate use of memory strategies. In fact, Western children get so much practice with this type of learning that they do not refine techniques that rely on cues available in everyday life, such as spatial location and arrangement

An 8-year-old of the Dorze people of Ethiopia winds cotton onto a bobbin for his father, a skilled weaver. Despite his keen memory for the complex steps involved in preparing the bobbin, this child might have difficulty recalling the isolated bits of information that school tasks often require.

of objects. For example, Guatemalan Mayan 9-year-olds do slightly better than their U.S. agemates when told to remember the placement of 40 familiar objects in a play scene. U.S. children often rehearse object names when it would be more effective to keep track of spatial relations (Rogoff & Wadell, 1982). The development of memory strategies, then, is not just a product of a more competent information-processing system. It also depends on task demands and cultural circumstances.

The School-Age Child's Theory of Mind

During middle childhood, children's *theory of mind*, or set of ideas about mental activities, becomes more elaborate and refined. Recall from Chapter 7 that this awareness of thought is often called *metacognition*. School-age children's improved ability to reflect on their own mental life is another reason that their thinking advances.

Unlike preschoolers, who view the mind as a passive container of information, older children regard it as an active, constructive agent that selects and transforms information (Kuhn, 2000). Consequently, they have a much better understanding of cognitive processes and the impact of psychological factors on performance. For example, with age, school-age children become increasingly aware of effective memory strategies and why they work (Alexander et al., 2003). They also grasp relationships between mental activities—for example, that remembering is crucial for understanding and that understanding strengthens memory (Schwanenflugel, Henderson, & Fabricius, 1998).

Furthermore, school-age children's understanding of sources of knowledge expands. They realize that people can extend their knowledge not just by directly observing events and talking to others but also by making *mental inferences* (Miller, Hardin, & Montgomery, 2003). This grasp of inference enables knowledge of *false belief* to expand. In several studies, researchers told children complex stories involving one character's belief about a second character's belief. Then the children answered questions about what the first character thought the second character would do (see Figure 9.6). By age 6 to 7, children were aware that people form beliefs about other people's beliefs and that these second-order beliefs can be wrong! Appreciation of *second-order false belief* enables children to pinpoint the reasons that another person arrived at a certain belief (Astington, Pelletier, & Homer, 2002; Miller, 2009; Naito & Seki, 2009). This assists them greatly in understanding others' perspectives.

Indeed, shortly thereafter, around age 7 to 8, children grasp that two people are likely to interpret the same event—such as an ambiguous fragment removed from a larger drawing they have never seen—differently, no matter what beliefs or other biases they bring to the situation (Lalonde & Chandler, 2002). They realize that the same reality can be construed in many ways.

Besides more complex thinking and language, experiences that foster awareness of mental activities contribute to school-age children's more reflective, process-oriented view of the mind. In a study of rural children of Cameroon, Africa, those who attended school performed much better on theory-of-mind tasks (Vinden, 2002). In school, teachers often call attention to the

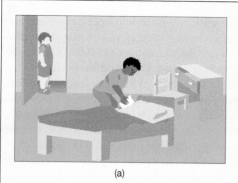

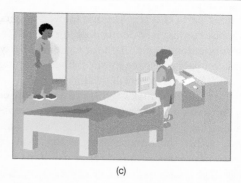

(a)

Jason has a letter from a friend. Lisa wants to read the letter, but Jason doesn't want her to. Jason puts the letter under his pillow.

(b)

Jason leaves the room to help his mother.

(c)

While Jason is gone, Lisa takes the letter and reads it. Jason returns and watches Lisa, but Lisa doesn't see Jason. Then Lisa puts the letter in Jason's desk.

FIGURE 9.6 A second-order false-belief task. After relating the story in the sequence of pictures, the researcher asks a second-order false-belief question: "Where does Lisa think Jason will look for the letter? Why?" Around age 7, children answer correctly—that Lisa thinks Jason will look under his pillow because Lisa doesn't know that Jason saw her put the letter in the desk. (Adapted from Astington, Pelletier, & Homer, 2002.)

workings of the mind by asking children to remember mental steps, share points of view with peers, and evaluate their own and others' reasoning.

Cognitive Self-Regulation

Although metacognition expands, school-age children often have difficulty putting what they know about thinking into action. They are not yet good at **cognitive self-regulation,** the process of continuously monitoring progress toward a goal, checking outcomes, and redirecting unsuccessful efforts. For example, Lizzie is aware that she should group items when memorizing, reread a complicated paragraph to make sure she understands it, and relate new information to what she already knows. But she does not always engage in these activities.

To study cognitive self-regulation, researchers sometimes look at the impact of children's awareness of memory strategies on how well they remember. By second grade, the more children know about memory strategies, the more they recall—a relationship that strengthens over middle childhood (Pierce & Lange, 2000). And when children apply a strategy consistently, their knowledge of strategies strengthens, resulting in a bidirectional association between metacognition and strategy use that enhances self-regulation (Schlagmüller & Schneider, 2002).

Why does cognitive self-regulation develop gradually? Monitoring and controlling task outcomes is cognitively demanding, requiring constant evaluation of effort and progress. Throughout elementary and secondary school, self-regulation predicts academic success (Valiente et al., 2008; Zimmerman & Cleary, 2009). Students who do well in school know whether their learning is going well. If they encounter obstacles, they take steps to address them—for example, organize the learning environment, review confusing material, or seek support from more expert adults or peers. This active, purposeful approach contrasts sharply with the passive orientation of students who achieve poorly.

Parents and teachers play vital roles in promoting children's self-regulation (Larkin, 2010). In one study, researchers observed parents helping their children with problem solving during the summer before third grade. Parents who patiently pointed out important features of the task and suggested strategies had children who, in the classroom, more often discussed ways to approach problems and monitored their own performance (Stright et al., 2002). Explaining the effectiveness of strategies is particularly helpful because it provides a rationale for future action.

Children who acquire effective self-regulatory skills develop a sense of *academic self-efficacy*—confidence in their own ability, which supports future self-regulation (Zimmerman & Moylan, 2009). Unfortunately, some children receive messages from parents and teachers that seriously undermine their academic self-esteem and self-regulatory skills. We will consider these *learned-helpless* children, along with ways to help them, in Chapter 10.

Applications of Information Processing to Academic Learning

Fundamental discoveries about the development of information processing have been applied to children's learning of reading and mathematics. Researchers are identifying the cognitive ingredients of skilled performance, tracing their development, and pinpointing differences in cognitive skills between good and poor learners. They hope, as a result, to design teaching methods that will improve children's learning.

Reading. Reading makes use of many skills at once, taxing all aspects of our information-processing system. Joey and Lizzie must perceive single letters and letter combinations, translate them into speech sounds, recognize the visual appearance of many common words, hold chunks of text in working memory while interpreting their meaning, and combine the meanings of various parts of a text passage into an understandable whole. Because reading is so demanding, most or all of these skills must be done automatically. If one or more are poorly developed, they will compete for space in our limited working memories, and reading performance will decline.

As children make the transition from emergent literacy to conventional reading, *phonological awareness* (see page 242 in Chapter 7) continues to predict reading (and spelling) progress. Other information-processing skills also contribute. Gains in processing speed foster children's rapid conversion of visual symbols into sounds (McBride-Chang & Kail, 2002). Visual scanning and discrimination play important roles and improve with reading experience (Rayner, Pollatsek, & Starr, 2003). Performing all these skills efficiently releases working memory for higher-level activities involved in comprehending the text's meaning.

Until recently, researchers were involved in an intense debate over how to teach beginning reading. Those who took a **whole-language approach** argued that from the beginning, children should be exposed to text in its complete form—stories, poems, letters, posters, and lists—so that they can appreciate the communicative function of written language. According to this view, as long as reading is kept whole and meaningful, children will be motivated to discover the specific skills they need. Other experts advocated a **phonics approach**, believing that children should first be coached on *phonics*—the basic rules for translating written symbols into sounds. Only after mastering these skills should they get complex reading material.

Many studies show that children learn best with a mixture of both approaches. In kindergarten and first and second grades, teaching that includes phonics boosts reading scores, especially for children who lag behind in reading progress (Stahl & Miller, 2006; Xue & Meisels, 2004). And when teachers combine real reading and writing with teaching of phonics and engage in other excellent teaching practices—encouraging children to tackle reading challenges and integrating reading into all school subjects—first graders show far greater literacy progress (Pressley et al., 2002).

Why might combining phonics with whole language work best? Learning relationships between letters and sounds enables children to *decode,* or decipher, words they have never seen before. Children who enter school low in phonological awareness make far better reading progress when given training in phonics (Casalis & Cole, 2009). Yet too much emphasis on basic skills may cause children to lose sight of the goal of reading: understanding. Children who read aloud fluently without registering meaning know little about effective metacognitive reading strategies—for example, that they must read more carefully if they will be tested than if they are reading for pleasure, or that explaining a passage in their own words is a good way to assess comprehension. Providing instruction aimed at increasing knowledge and use of reading strategies enhances reading performance from third grade on (McKeown & Beck, 2009; Paris & Paris, 2006).

Mathematics. Mathematics teaching in elementary school builds on and greatly enriches children's informal knowledge of number concepts and counting. Written notation systems and formal computational procedures enhance children's ability to represent numbers and compute. Over the early elementary school years, children acquire basic math facts through a combination of frequent practice, experimentation with diverse computational procedures (through which they discover faster, more accurate techniques), reasoning about number concepts, and teaching that conveys effective strategies. Eventually children retrieve answers automatically and apply this knowledge to more complex problems.

Arguments about how to teach mathematics resemble those in reading, pitting drill in computing against "number sense," or understanding. Again, a blend of both approaches is most beneficial (Fuson, 2009). In learning basic math, poorly performing students use cumbersome techniques or try to retrieve answers from memory too soon. They have not sufficiently experimented with strategies to see which are most effective and to reorganize their observations in logical, efficient ways—for example, noticing that multiplication problems involving 2 (2×8) are equivalent to addition doubles ($8 + 8$). On tasks that assess their understanding of math concepts, their performance is weak (Canobi, 2004; Canobi, Reeve, & Pattison, 2003). This suggests that encouraging students to apply strategies and making sure they understand why certain strategies work well are essential for solid mastery of basic math.

A similar picture emerges for more complex skills, such as carrying in addition, borrowing in subtraction, and operating with decimals and fractions. Children taught by rote cannot apply the procedure to new problems. Instead, they persistently make mistakes, following a "math rule" that they recall incor-

By using manipulative materials to understand number and place value, these first graders gain conceptual knowledge that helps them become more effective math problem solvers.

rectly because they do not understand it (Carpenter et al., 1999). Consider the following subtraction errors:

$$
\begin{array}{r}
427 \\
-\,138 \\
\hline
311
\end{array}
\qquad
\begin{array}{r}
7{,}002 \\
-\,5{,}445 \\
\hline
1{,}447
\end{array}
$$

In the first problem, the child subtracts a smaller from a larger digit, regardless of which is on top. In the second, the child skips columns with zeros in a borrowing operation, and the bottom digit is written as the answer.

Children who are given rich opportunities to experiment with problem solving, to grasp the reasons behind strategies, and to evaluate solution techniques seldom make such errors. In one study, second graders taught in these ways not only mastered correct procedures but even invented their own successful strategies, some of which were superior to standard, school-taught methods (Fuson & Burghard, 2003).

In Asian countries, students receive a variety of supports for acquiring mathematical knowledge and often excel at both math reasoning and computation. Use of the metric system helps Asian children grasp place value. The consistent structure of number words in Asian languages (*ten-two* for 12, *ten-three* for 13) also makes this idea clear (Miura & Okamoto, 2003). And because Asian number words are shorter and more quickly pronounced, more digits can be held in working memory at once, increasing the speed of thinking. Furthermore, Chinese parents provide their preschoolers with extensive practice in counting and adding—experiences that contribute to the superiority of Chinese over U.S. children's math knowledge even before school entry (Siegler & Mu, 2008; Zhou et al., 2006). Finally, as we will see later in this chapter, compared with lessons in the United States, those in Asian classrooms devote more time to exploring math concepts and strategies and less to drill and repetition.

ASK YOURSELF

REVIEW Cite evidence that school-age children view the mind as an active, constructive agent.

CONNECT Explain why gains in working-memory capacity and executive-function skills are vital for mastery of reading and math in middle childhood.

APPLY Lizzie knows that if you have difficulty learning part of a task, you should devote extra attention to that part. But she plays each of her piano pieces from beginning to end instead of practicing the hard parts. What explains Lizzie's failure to engage in cognitive self-regulation?

REFLECT In your own elementary school math education, how much emphasis was placed on computational drill and how much on understanding of concepts? How do you think that balance affected your interest and performance in math?

 Individual Differences in Mental Development

Around age 6, IQ becomes more stable than it was at earlier ages, and it correlates moderately well with academic achievement, typically around .50 to .60. And children with higher IQs are more likely when they grow up to attain higher levels of education and enter more prestigious occupations (Brody, 1997; Deary et al., 2007). Because IQ predicts school performance and educational attainment, it often enters into educational decisions. Do intelligence tests accurately assess the school-age child's ability to profit from academic instruction? Let's look closely at this controversial issue.

Defining and Measuring Intelligence

Virtually all intelligence tests provide an overall score (the IQ), which represents *general intelligence*, or reasoning ability, along with an array of separate scores measuring specific mental abilities. But intelligence is a collection of many capacities, not all of which are included on currently available tests (Carroll, 2005; Sternberg, 2005). Test designers use a complicated statistical technique called *factor analysis* to identify the various abilities that intelligence tests measure. It identifies which sets of test items cluster together, meaning that test-takers who do well on one item in a cluster tend to do well on the others. Distinct clusters are called *factors,* each of which represents an ability. See Figure 9.7 on page 310 for items typically included in intelligence tests for children.

The intelligence tests given from time to time in classrooms are *group-administered tests.* They permit large numbers of students to be tested at once and are useful for instructional planning and for identifying children who require more extensive evaluation with *individually administered tests.* Unlike group tests, which teachers can give with minimal training, individually administered tests demand considerable training and experience to give well. The examiner not only considers the child's answers but also observes the child's behavior, noting such reactions as attention to and interest in the tasks and wariness of the adult. These observations provide insight into whether the test results accurately reflect the child's abilities. Two individual tests—the Stanford-Binet and the Wechsler—are often used to identify highly intelligent children and to diagnose children with learning problems.

The contemporary descendant of Alfred Binet's first successful intelligence test is the *Stanford-Binet Intelligence Scales,* Fifth Edition, for individuals from age 2 to adulthood. In addition to general intelligence, it assesses five intellectual factors: general knowledge, quantitative reasoning, visual–spatial processing, working memory, and basic information processing (such as speed of analyzing information). Each factor includes both a verbal mode and a nonverbal mode of testing, yielding 10 subtests in all (Roid, 2003). The nonverbal subtests, which do not require spoken language, are especially useful when

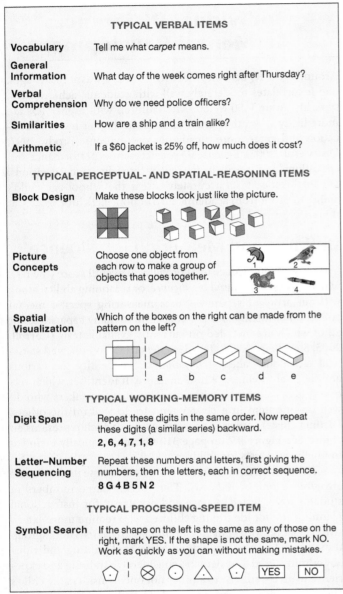

TYPICAL VERBAL ITEMS

Vocabulary — Tell me what *carpet* means.

General Information — What day of the week comes right after Thursday?

Verbal Comprehension — Why do we need police officers?

Similarities — How are a ship and a train alike?

Arithmetic — If a $60 jacket is 25% off, how much does it cost?

TYPICAL PERCEPTUAL- AND SPATIAL-REASONING ITEMS

Block Design — Make these blocks look just like the picture.

Picture Concepts — Choose one object from each row to make a group of objects that goes together.

Spatial Visualization — Which of the boxes on the right can be made from the pattern on the left?

TYPICAL WORKING-MEMORY ITEMS

Digit Span — Repeat these digits in the same order. Now repeat these digits (a similar series) backward.
2, 6, 4, 7, 1, 8

Letter–Number Sequencing — Repeat these numbers and letters, first giving the numbers, then the letters, each in correct sequence.
8 G 4 B 5 N 2

TYPICAL PROCESSING-SPEED ITEM

Symbol Search — If the shape on the left is the same as any of those on the right, mark YES. If the shape is not the same, mark NO. Work as quickly as you can without making mistakes.

FIGURE 9.7 Test items like those on commonly used intelligence tests for children. The verbal items emphasize culturally loaded, fact-oriented information. The perceptual- and spatial-reasoning, working-memory, and processing-speed items emphasize aspects of information processing and are assumed to assess more biologically based skills.

assessing individuals with limited English, hearing impairments, or communication disorders. The knowledge and quantitative reasoning factors emphasize culturally loaded, fact-oriented information, such as vocabulary and arithmetic problems. In contrast, the visual–spatial processing, working-memory, and basic information-processing factors are assumed to be less culturally biased (see the spatial visualization item in Figure 9.7).

The *Wechsler Intelligence Scale for Children (WISC-IV)* is the fourth edition of a widely used test for 6- through 16-year-olds (Wechsler, 2003). It measures general intelligence and four broad factors: verbal reasoning, perceptual (or visual–spatial) reasoning, working memory, and processing speed. Each factor is made up of two or three subtests, yielding 10 separate scores in all. The WISC-IV was designed to downplay culturally dependent knowledge, which is emphasized on only one factor (verbal reasoning). According to the test designers, the result is the most "culture-fair" intelligence test available (Williams, Weis, & Rolfhus, 2003). The WISC was also the first test to be standardized on children representing the total population of the United States, including ethnic minorities.

Recent Efforts to Define Intelligence

As we have seen, mental tests now tap important aspects of information processing. In line with this trend, some researchers combine the mental testing approach to defining intelligence with the information-processing approach. They believe that once we identify the processing skills that separate individuals who test well from those who test poorly, we will know more about how to intervene to improve performance. These investigators conduct *componential analyses* of children's test scores. This means that they look for relationships between aspects (or components) of information processing and children's intelligence test scores.

Processing speed, assessed in terms of reaction time on diverse cognitive tasks, is moderately related to IQ (Deary, 2001; Li et al., 2004). Individuals whose nervous systems function more efficiently, permitting them to take in information and manipulate it quickly, appear to have an edge in intellectual skills.

But flexible attention, memory, and reasoning strategies are as important as efficient thinking in predicting IQ, and they explain some of the association between response speed and good test performance (Lohman, 2000; Miller & Vernon, 1992). Children who apply strategies effectively acquire more knowledge and can retrieve it rapidly—advantages that carry over to mental test performance. Similarly, available space in working memory depends in part on effective inhibition (the ability to keep one's mind from straying to irrelevant thoughts). Inhibition and sustained and selective attention are among a wide array of attentional skills that are good predictors of IQ (Schweizer, Moosbrugger, & Goldhammer, 2006).

The componential approach has one major shortcoming: It regards intelligence as entirely due to causes within the child. Throughout this book, we have seen how cultural and situational factors affect children's thinking. Robert Sternberg has expanded componential approach into a comprehensive theory that regards intelligence as a product of inner and outer forces.

Sternberg's Triarchic Theory. As Figure 9.8 shows, Sternberg's (2001, 2005, 2008) **triarchic theory of successful intelligence** identifies three broad, interacting intelligences: (1) *analytical intelligence,* or information-processing skills; (2) *creative intelligence,* the capacity to solve novel problems; and (3) *practical intelligence,* application of intellectual skills in everyday situations. Intelligent behavior involves balancing all

FIGURE 9.8 Sternberg's triarchic theory of successful intelligence. People who behave intelligently balance three interrelated intelligences—analytical, creative, and practical—to achieve success in life, defined by their personal goals and the requirements of their cultural communities.

three to succeed in life according to one's personal goals and the requirements of one's cultural community.

Analytical Intelligence. *Analytical intelligence* consists of the information-processing components that underlie all intelligent acts: applying strategies, acquiring task-relevant and metacognitive knowledge, and engaging in self-regulation. But on mental tests, processing skills are used in only a few of their potential ways, resulting in far too narrow a view of intelligent behavior.

Creative Intelligence. In any context, success depends not only on processing familiar information but also on generating useful solutions to new problems. People who are *creative* think more skillfully than others when faced with novelty. Given a new task, they apply their information-processing skills in exceptionally effective ways, rapidly making these skills automatic so that working memory is freed for more complex aspects of the situation. Consequently, they quickly move to high-level performance. Although all of us are capable of some creativity, only a few individuals excel at generating novel solutions.

Practical Intelligence. Finally, intelligence is a *practical*, goal-oriented activity aimed at *adapting to, shaping*, or *selecting environments*. Intelligent people skillfully *adapt* their thinking to fit with both their desires and the demands of their everyday worlds. When they cannot adapt to a situation, they try to *shape*,

or change, it to meet their needs. If they cannot shape it, they *select* new contexts that better match their skills, values, or goals. Practical intelligence reminds us that intelligent behavior is never culture-free. Children with certain life histories do well at the behaviors required for success on intelligence tests and adapt easily to the testing conditions. Others, with different backgrounds, may misinterpret or reject the testing context. Yet such children often display sophisticated abilities in daily life—for example, telling stories, engaging in complex artistic activities, or interacting skillfully with other people.

The triarchic theory highlights the complexity of intelligent behavior and the limitations of current intelligence tests in assessing that complexity. For example, out-of-school, practical forms of intelligence are vital for life success and help explain why cultures vary widely in the behaviors they regard as intelligent (Sternberg et al., 2000). When researchers asked ethnically diverse parents to describe an intelligent first grader, Caucasian Americans mentioned cognitive traits. In contrast, ethnic minorities (Cambodian, Filipino, Vietnamese, and Mexican immigrants) identified noncognitive capacities—motivation, self-management, and social skills (Okagaki & Sternberg, 1993). According to Sternberg, mental tests can easily underestimate, and even overlook, the intellectual strengths of some children, especially ethnic minorities.

Gardner's Theory of Multiple Intelligences. In yet another view of how information-processing skills underlie intelligent behavior, Howard Gardner's (1983, 1993, 2000) **theory of multiple intelligences** defines intelligence in terms of distinct sets of processing operations that permit individuals to engage in a wide range of culturally valued activities. Dismissing the idea of general intelligence, Gardner proposes at least eight independent intelligences (see Table 9.1 on page 312).

According to Gardner, people are capable of at least eight distinct intelligences. Through a project aimed at improving sea turtle nesting habitats, these children expand and enrich their naturalist intelligence.

TABLE 9.1 **Gardner's Multiple Intelligences**

INTELLIGENCE	PROCESSING OPERATIONS	END-STATE PERFORMANCE POSSIBILITIES
Linguistic	Sensitivity to the sounds, rhythms, and meaning of words and the functions of language	Poet, journalist
Logico-mathematical	Sensitivity to, and capacity to detect, logical or numerical patterns; ability to handle long chains of logical reasoning	Mathematician
Musical	Ability to produce and appreciate pitch, rhythm (or melody), and aesthetic quality of the forms of musical expressiveness	Instrumentalist, composer
Spatial	Ability to perceive the visual–spatial world accurately, to perform transformations on those perceptions, and to re-create aspects of visual experience in the absence of relevant stimuli	Sculptor, navigator
Bodily-kinesthetic	Ability to use the body skillfully for expressive as well as goal-directed purposes; ability to handle objects skillfully	Dancer, athlete
Naturalist	Ability to recognize and classify all varieties of animals, minerals, and plants	Biologist
Interpersonal	Ability to detect and respond appropriately to the moods, temperaments, motivations, and intentions of others	Therapist, salesperson
Intrapersonal	Ability to discriminate complex inner feelings and to use them to guide one's own behavior; knowledge of one's own strengths, weaknesses, desires, and intelligences	Person with detailed, accurate self-knowledge

Sources: Gardner, 1993, 1998, 2000.

Gardner believes that each intelligence has a unique biological basis, a distinct course of development, and different expert, or "end-state," performances. At the same time, he emphasizes that a lengthy process of education is required to transform any raw potential into a mature social role (Connell, Sheridan, & Gardner, 2003). Cultural values and learning opportunities affect the extent to which a child's intellectual strengths are realized and the ways they are expressed.

Gardner's list of abilities has yet to be firmly grounded in research. Neurological evidence for the independence of his abilities is weak. Some exceptionally gifted individuals have abilities that are broad rather than limited to a particular domain (Piirto, 2007). And research with mental tests suggests that several of Gardner's intelligences (linguistic, logico-mathematical, and spatial) have common features. Nevertheless, Gardner calls attention to several intelligences not tapped by IQ scores. For example, his interpersonal and intrapersonal intelligences include a set of capacities for dealing with people and understanding oneself. As the Social Issues: Health box on the following page indicates, researchers are attempting to define, measure, and foster these vital abilities.

Explaining Individual and Group Differences in IQ

When we compare individuals in terms of academic achievement, years of education, and occupational status, it quickly becomes clear that certain sectors of the population are advantaged over others. In trying to explain these differences, researchers have compared the IQ scores of ethnic and SES groups. American black children and adolescents score, on average, 10 to 12 IQ points below American white children. Although the difference has been shrinking over the past several decades, a substantial gap remains (Edwards & Oakland, 2006; Flynn, 2007; Nisbett, 2009). Hispanic children fall midway between black and white children, and Asian Americans score slightly higher than their white counterparts—about 3 points (Ceci, Rosenblum, & Kumpf, 1998).

The gap between middle- and low-SES children—about 9 points—accounts for some of the ethnic differences in IQ, but not all. Matching black and white children on parental education and income reduces the black–white IQ gap by a third to a half (Brooks-Gunn et al., 2003). Of course, IQ varies greatly *within* each ethnic and SES group. Still, these group differences are large enough and of serious enough consequence that they cannot be ignored.

In the 1970s, the IQ nature–nurture controversy escalated after psychologist Arthur Jensen (1969) published a controversial monograph entitled, "How Much Can We Boost IQ and Scholastic Achievement?" Jensen claimed—and still maintains—that heredity is largely responsible for individual, ethnic, and SES variations in intelligence (Jensen, 1998, 2001; Rushton & Jensen, 2006, 2010). His work sparked an outpouring of research and responses, including ethical challenges reflecting deep concern that his conclusions would fuel social prejudices. Richard Herrnstein and Charles Murray rekindled the controversy with *The Bell Curve* (1994). Like Jensen, they argued that heredity contributes substantially to individual and SES differences in IQ, and they implied that heredity plays a sizable role in the black–white IQ gap. Let's look closely at some important evidence.

Nature versus Nurture. In Chapter 2, we introduced the *heritability estimate.* The most powerful evidence on the

Social Issues: Health

Emotional Intelligence

During recess, Emily handed a birthday party invitation to every fifth-grade girl except Claire, who looked on sadly as her classmates chattered about the party. But one of Emily's friends, Jessica, looked troubled. Pulling Emily aside, she exclaimed, "Why'd you do that? You hurt Claire's feelings—you embarrassed her! If you bring invitations to school, you've got to give everybody one!" After school, Jessica comforted Claire, saying, "If you aren't invited, I'm not going, either!"

Jessica's IQ is only slightly above average, but she excels at *emotional intelligence*—a term that has captured public attention because of popular books suggesting that it is an overlooked set of skills that can greatly improve life success (Goleman, 1995, 1998). According to one influential definition, **emotional intelligence** refers to a set of emotional abilities that enable individuals to process and adapt to emotional information (Salovey & Pizarro, 2003). To measure it, researchers have devised items tapping emotional skills that enable people to manage their own emotions and interact competently with others. One test requires individuals to identify and rate the strength of emotions expressed in photographs of faces (emotional perception), to reason about emotions in social situations (emotion understanding), to identify which emotions promote certain thoughts and activities (emotional facilitation), and to evaluate the effectiveness of strategies for controlling negative emotions (emotion regulation). Factor analyses of the scores of hundreds of test-takers identified several emotional capacities as well as a higher-order general factor (Mayer, Salovey, & Caruso, 2003).

Emotional intelligence is no more than modestly related to IQ. And among school-age children, adolescents, and adults, it is positively associated with self-esteem, empathy, prosocial behavior, cooperation, leadership skills, and life satisfaction and negatively related to drug and alcohol use, dependency, depression, and aggressive behavior (Brackett, Mayer, & Warner, 2004; Mavroveli et al., 2009; Petrides et al., 2006). In adulthood, emotional intelligence predicts many aspects of workplace success, including managerial effectiveness, productive co-worker relationships, and job performance (Mayer, Salovey, & Caruso, 2008).

Only a few assessments of emotional intelligence are available for children. These require careful training of teachers in observing and recording children's emotional skills during everyday activities, gathering information from parents, and taking ethnic backgrounds into account (Denham,

The 9-year-old on the right displays high emotional intelligence, accurately identifying his friend's emotion as anger and calmly talking over their disagreement.

2005). As more and better measures are devised, they may help identify children with weak social and emotional competencies who would profit from intervention (Stewart-Brown & Edmunds, 2007).

The concept of emotional intelligence has increased teachers' awareness that providing experiences that meet students' social and emotional needs can improve their adjustment. Lessons that teach emotional understanding, respect and caring for others, strategies for regulating emotion, and resistance to unfavorable peer pressure—using active learning techniques that provide skill practice both in and out of the classroom—are becoming more common (Bowkett & Percival 2011).

---

heritability of IQ involves twin comparisons. The IQ scores of identical twins (who share all their genes) are more similar than those of fraternal twins (who are genetically no more alike than ordinary siblings). On the basis of this and other kinship evidence, researchers estimate that about half the differences in IQ among children can be traced to their genetic makeup.

Recall, however, that heritabilities risk overestimating genetic influences and underestimating environmental influences (Grigorenko, 2000; Plomin, 2003). And heritability estimates do not reveal the complex processes through which genes and experiences influence intelligence as children develop.

Adoption studies offer a wider range of information. When young children are adopted into caring, stimulating homes, their IQs rise substantially compared with the IQs of nonadopted

children who remain in economically deprived families (van IJzendoorn, Juffer, & Poelhuis, 2005). But adopted children benefit to varying degrees. In one investigation, children of two extreme groups of biological mothers—those with IQs below 95 and those with IQs above 120—were adopted at birth by parents who were well above average in income and education. During the school years, the children of the low-IQ biological mothers scored above average in IQ. But they did not do as well as children of high-IQ biological mothers placed in similar adoptive families (Loehlin, Horn, & Willerman, 1997). Adoption research confirms that heredity and environment contribute jointly to IQ.

Adoption research also sheds light on the black–white IQ gap. In two studies, African-American children adopted into economically well-off white homes during the first year of life scored high on intelligence tests, attaining mean IQs of 110 and 117 by middle childhood (Moore, 1986; Scarr & Weinberg, 1983). The IQ gains of black children "reared in the culture of the tests and schools" are consistent with a wealth of evidence that poverty severely depresses the intelligence of ethnic minority children (Nisbett, 2009).

Furthermore, dramatic *secular trend* in mental test performance—a generational rise in average IQ in both industrialized nations and the developing world—supports the role of environmental factors. The greatest gains have occurred on tests of spatial reasoning—tasks often assumed to be "culture fair" and, therefore, more genetically based (Flynn, 2007). The existence of a large, environmentally induced secular trend that exceeds the black–white IQ gap presents another major challenge to the assumption that ethnic variations in IQ are mostly genetic.

Cultural Influences. A controversial question raised about ethnic differences in IQ has to do with whether they result from *test bias*. If a test samples knowledge and skills that not all groups of children have had equal opportunity to learn, or if the testing situation impairs the performance of some groups but not others, then the resulting score is a biased, or unfair, measure.

Some experts claim that because IQ predicts academic achievement equally well for majority and minority children, intelligence tests are fair to both groups. The tests, they say, represent success in the common culture (Edwards & Oakland, 2006; Jensen, 2002). Others believe that lack of exposure to certain communication styles and knowledge, along with negative stereotypes about the test-taker's ethnic group, can undermine children's performance (Ceci & Williams, 1997; Sternberg, 2005). Let's look at the evidence.

Communication Styles. Ethnic minority families often foster unique language skills that do not match the expectations of most classrooms and testing situations. An observational study carried out in low-SES African-American homes in a southeastern U.S. city revealed that the black parents rarely asked their children knowledge-training questions ("What color is it?" "What's this story about?"), which are typical of middle-SES white parents and of tests and classrooms. Instead, the black parents asked analogy questions ("What's that like?") or story-starter questions ("Did you hear Sally this morning?") that called for elaborate responses about everyday events and had no "right" answer. These experiences led the black children to develop complex verbal skills at home. But their language emphasized storytelling and emotional and social concerns rather than factual knowledge. When the black children started school, many were unfamiliar with and confused by the "objective" questions they encountered on tests and in classrooms.

Furthermore, many ethnic minority parents without extensive schooling prefer a *collaborative style of communication* when completing tasks with children. They work together in a coordinated, fluid way, each focused on the same aspect of the problem. This pattern of adult–child engagement has been observed in Native-American, Canadian Inuit, Hispanic, and Guatemalan Mayan cultures (Chavajay & Rogoff, 2002; Crago, Annahatak, & Ningiuruvik, 1993; Paradise & Rogoff, 2009). With increasing education, parents establish a *hierarchical style of communication,* like that of classrooms and tests. The parent directs each child to carry out an aspect of the task, and children work independently. This sharp discontinuity between home and school practices may contribute to low-SES minority children's lower IQs and school performance.

Knowledge. Many researchers argue that IQ scores are affected by specific information acquired as part of majority-culture upbringing. Consistent with this view, low-SES African-American children often miss vocabulary words on mental tests that have alternative meanings in their cultural community—for example, interpreting the word *frame* as "physique" and *wrapping* as "rapping," referring to the style of music (Champion, 2003a).

Even nonverbal test items, such as spatial reasoning, depend on learning opportunities. For example, using small blocks to duplicate designs and playing video games requiring mental rotation of visual images increase success on spatial tasks (Dirks, 1982; Maynard, Subrahmanyam, & Greenfield, 2005). Low-income minority children, who often grow up in more "people-oriented" than "object-oriented" homes, may lack toys and games that promote certain intellectual skills.

Furthermore, the sheer amount of time a child spends in school predicts IQ. When children of the same age enrolled in different grades are compared, those who have been in school longer score higher on intelligence tests (Ceci, 1991, 1999). Taken together, these findings indicate that children's exposure to the knowledge and ways of thinking valued in classrooms has a sizable impact on their intelligence test performance.

Stereotypes. Imagine trying to succeed at an activity when the prevailing attitude is that members of your group are incompetent. **Stereotype threat**—the fear of being judged on the basis of a negative stereotype—can trigger anxiety that interferes

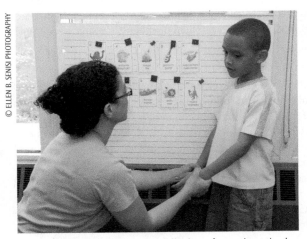

School-age children, especially those from stigmatized groups, become increasingly conscious of ethnic stereotypes. Fear of being judged on the basis of a negative stereotype may be behind this child's reluctance to try a new task in school.

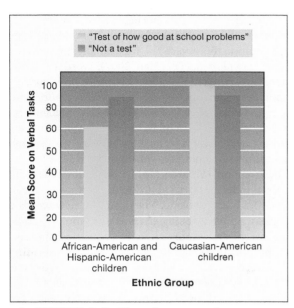

FIGURE 9.9 Effect of stereotype threat on test performance. Among African-American and Hispanic-American children who were aware of ethnic stereotypes, being told that verbal tasks were a "test of how good children are at school problems" led to far worse performance than being told the tasks were "not a test." These statements had little impact on the performance of Caucasian-American children. (Adapted from McKown & Weinstein, 2003.)

with performance. Mounting evidence confirms that stereotype threat undermines test taking in children and adults (McKown & Strambler, 2009; Steele, 1997). For example, researchers gave African-American, Hispanic, and Caucasian 6- to 10-year-olds verbal tasks. Some children were told that the tasks were "not a test." Others were told they were "a test of how good children are at school problems"—a statement designed to induce stereotype threat in the ethnic minority children (McKown & Weinstein, 2003). Among children who were aware of ethnic stereotypes (such as "black people aren't smart"), African Americans and Hispanics performed far worse in the "test" condition than in the "not a test" condition. Caucasian children, in contrast, performed similarly in both conditions (see Figure 9.9).

Over middle childhood, children become increasingly conscious of ethnic stereotypes, and those from stigmatized groups are especially mindful of them. By early adolescence, many low-SES minority students start to devalue doing well in school, saying it is not important to them (Cooper & Huh, 2008). Self-protective disengagement, sparked by stereotype threat, may be responsible. This weakening of motivation can have serious, long-term consequences. Research shows that self-discipline—effort and delay of gratification—predicts school performance at least as well as, and sometimes better than, IQ does (Duckworth & Seligman, 2005).

Reducing Cultural Bias in Testing. Although not all experts agree, many acknowledge that IQ scores can underestimate the intelligence of children from ethnic minority groups. A special concern exists about incorrectly labeling minority

children as slow learners and assigning them to remedial classes, which are far less stimulating than regular school experiences. To avoid this danger, test scores need to be combined with assessments of children's adaptive behavior—their ability to cope with the demands of their everyday environments. The child who does poorly on an intelligence test yet plays a complex game on the playground or figures out how to rewire a broken TV is unlikely to be mentally deficient.

In addition, culturally relevant testing procedures enhance minority children's test performance. In an approach called **dynamic assessment,** an innovation consistent with Vygotsky's zone of proximal development, an adult introduces purposeful teaching into the testing situation to find out what the child can attain with social support. Research shows that children's receptivity to teaching and their capacity to transfer what they have learned to novel problems contribute substantially to gains in test performance (Haywood & Lidz, 2007; Sternberg & Grigorenko, 2002). In one study, Ethiopian 6- and 7-year-olds who had recently immigrated to Israel scored well below their Israeli-born agemates on spatial reasoning tasks. The Ethiopian children had little experience with this type of thinking. After several dynamic assessment sessions in which the adult suggested effective strategies, the Ethiopian children's scores rose sharply, nearly equaling those of the Israeli-born children (Tzuriel & Kaufman, 1999). They also transferred their learning to new test items.

In view of its many problems, should intelligence testing in schools be suspended? Most experts reject this solution. Without testing, important educational decisions would be based only on subjective impressions, perhaps increasing discriminatory placement of minority children. Intelligence tests are useful when interpreted carefully by psychologists and educators who are sensitive to cultural influences on test performance. And despite their limitations, IQ scores continue to be fairly accurate measures of school learning potential for the majority of Western children.

This teacher uses dynamic assessment, tailoring instruction to students' individual needs—an approach that reveals what each child can learn with social support.

ASK YOURSELF

REVIEW Using Sternberg's triarchic theory and Gardner's theory of multiple intelligences, explain the limitations of current intelligence tests in assessing the diversity of human intelligence.

CONNECT Explain how dynamic assessment is consistent with Vygotsky's zone of proximal development and with scaffolding. (See Chapter 7, page 234.)

APPLY Josefina, a Hispanic fourth grader, does well on homework assignments. But when her teacher announces, "It's time for a test to see how much you've learned," Josefina usually does poorly. How might stereotype threat explain this inconsistency?

REFLECT Do you think that intelligence tests are culturally biased? What observations and evidence influenced your conclusions?

Language Development

Vocabulary, grammar, and pragmatics continue to develop in middle childhood, though less obviously than at earlier ages. In addition, children's attitude toward language undergoes a fundamental shift: They develop language awareness.

Schooling contributes greatly to these language competencies. Reflecting on language is extremely common during reading instruction. And fluent reading is a major new source of language learning (Ravid & Tolchinsky, 2002). As we will see, an improved ability to reflect on language grows out of literacy and supports many complex language skills.

Vocabulary

During the elementary school years, vocabulary increases fourfold, eventually exceeding comprehension of 40,000 words. On average, children learn about 20 new words each day, a rate of growth greater than in early childhood. In addition to the word-learning strategies discussed in Chapter 7, school-age children add to their vocabularies by analyzing the structure of complex words. From *happy* and *decide*, they quickly derive the meanings of *happiness* and *decision* (Larsen & Nippold, 2007). They also figure out many more word meanings from context (Nagy & Scott, 2000).

As at earlier ages, children benefit from conversation with more expert speakers, especially when their partners use and explain complex words (Weizman & Snow, 2001). But because written language contains a far more diverse and complex vocabulary than spoken language, reading contributes enormously to vocabulary growth. Children who engage in as little as 21 minutes of independent reading per day are exposed to nearly 2 million words per year (Cunningham & Stanovich, 1998).

As their knowledge expands and becomes better organized, older school-age children think about and use words more precisely: In addition to the verb *fall*, for example, they also use *topple, tumble,* and *plummet* (Berman, 2007). Word definitions also illustrate this change. Five- and 6-year-olds offer concrete descriptions referring to functions or appearance—*knife:* "when you're cutting carrots"; *bicycle:* "it's got wheels, a chain, and handlebars." By the end of elementary school, synonyms and explanations of categorical relationships appear—for example, *knife:* "something you could cut with. A saw is like a knife. It could also be a weapon" (Wehren, De Lisi, & Arnold, 1981). This advance reflects older children's ability to deal with word meanings on an entirely verbal plane. They can add new words to their vocabulary simply by being given a definition.

School-age children's more reflective, analytical approach to language permits them to appreciate the multiple meanings of words—to recognize, for example, that many words, such as *cool* or *neat*, have psychological as well as physical meanings: "What a cool shirt!" or "That movie was really neat!" This grasp of double meanings permits 8- to 10-year-olds to comprehend subtle metaphors, such as "sharp as a tack" and "spilling the beans" (Nippold, Taylor, & Baker, 1996; Wellman & Hickling, 1994). It also leads to a change in children's humor. Riddles and puns that alternate between different meanings of a key word are common: "Hey, did you take a bath?" "Why, is one missing?"

LOOK AND LISTEN

Record examples of 8- to 10-year-olds' humor, or examine storybooks for humor aimed at second through fourth graders. Does it require a grasp of the multiple meanings of words? ●

Grammar

During the school years, mastery of complex grammatical constructions improves. For example, English-speaking children use the passive voice more frequently, and they more often extend it from an abbreviated form ("It broke") into full statements ("The glass was broken by Mary") (Israel, Johnson, & Brooks, 2000; Tomasello, 2006). Although the passive form is challenging, language input makes a difference. When adults speak a language that emphasizes full passives, such as Inuktitut (spoken by the Inuit people of Arctic Canada), children produce them earlier (Allen & Crago, 1996).

Another grammatical achievement of middle childhood is advanced understanding of infinitive phrases—the difference between "John is eager to please" and "John is easy to please" (Berman, 2007; Chomsky, 1969). Like gains in vocabulary, appreciation of these subtle grammatical distinctions is supported by an improved ability to analyze and reflect on language.

Pragmatics

Improvements in *pragmatics*, the communicative side of language, also occur. Conversational strategies become more refined.

For example, school-age children are better at phrasing things to get their way. When an adult refuses to hand over a desired object, 9-year-olds, but not 5-year-olds, state their second requests more politely (Axia & Baroni, 1985).

Furthermore, as a result of improved memory, ability to take the perspective of listeners, and conversations with adults about past experiences, children's narratives increase in organization, detail, and expressiveness. A typical 4- or 5-year-old's narrative states what happened: "We went to the lake. We fished and waited. Paul caught a huge catfish." Six- and 7-year-olds add orienting information (time, place, participants) and connectives ("next," "then," "so," "finally") that lend coherence to the story. Gradually, narratives lengthen into a *classic form* in which events not only build to a high point but resolve: "After Paul reeled in the catfish, Dad cleaned and cooked it. Then we ate it all up!" And evaluative comments rise dramatically, becoming common by age 8 to 9: "The catfish tasted great. Paul was so proud!" (Melzi & Ely, 2009; Ukrainetz et al., 2005).

Because children pick up the narrative styles of significant adults in their lives, their narrative forms vary widely across cultures. For example, instead of the *topic-focused style* of most Caucasian-American school-age children, who describe an experience from beginning to end, African-American children often use a *topic-associating style* in which they blend several similar anecdotes. One 9-year-old related having a tooth pulled, then described seeing her sister's tooth pulled, next told how she had removed one of her baby teeth, and concluded, "I'm a pullin-teeth expert . . . call me, and I'll be over" (McCabe, 1997, p. 164). As a result, African-American children's narratives are usually longer and more complex than those of white children (Champion, 2003b).

The ability to generate clear oral narratives enhances reading comprehension and prepares children for producing longer, more explicit written narratives. In families who regularly eat meals together, children are advanced in language and literacy development (Snow & Beals, 2006). Mealtimes offer many opportunities to relate personal stories.

© TAMPA BAY TIMES/MELISSA LYTTLE/THE IMAGE WORKS

In families who regularly eat meals together, children are advanced in language and literacy development. Mealtimes offer many opportunities to relate complex, extended personal stories.

Learning Two Languages

Joey and Lizzie speak only one language—English, their native tongue. Yet throughout the world, many children grow up *bilingual,* learning two languages and sometimes more than two. An estimated 20 percent of U.S. children—10 million in all—speak a language other than English at home (U.S. Census Bureau, 2012b).

Bilingual Development. Children can become bilingual in two ways: (1) by acquiring both languages at the same time in early childhood or (2) by learning a second language after mastering the first. Children of bilingual parents who teach them both languages in infancy and early childhood separate the language systems early on and attain early language milestones according to a typical timetable (Conboy & Thal, 2006; Genesee & Nicoladis, 2007; Weikum et al., 2007). When school-age children acquire a second language after they already speak a first language, they generally take five to seven years to attain speaking and writing skills on a par with those of native-speaking agemates (Paradis, 2007).

As with first-language development, a *sensitive period* for second-language development exists. Mastery must begin sometime in childhood for most second-language learners to attain full proficiency (Hakuta, Bialystok, & Wiley, 2003). But a precise age cutoff for a decline in second-language learning has not been established. Rather, a continuous age-related decrease from childhood to adulthood occurs.

A large body of research shows that bilingualism has positive consequences for development. Children who are fluent in two languages outperform others on tests of selective attention, inhibition of irrelevant information, analytical reasoning, concept formation, and cognitive flexibility (Bialystok et al., 2009; Carlson & Meltzoff, 2008). They are also advanced in certain aspects of language awareness, such as detection of errors in grammar and meaning. And children readily transfer their phonological awareness skills in one language to the other, especially if the two languages share phonological features, as Spanish and English do (Siegal, Iozzi, & Surian, 2009; Snow & Kang, 2006). These capacities, as noted earlier, enhance reading achievement.

Bilingual Education. The advantages of bilingualism provide strong justification for bilingual education programs in schools. In Canada, about 7 percent of elementary school students are enrolled in *language immersion programs,* in which English-speaking children are taught entirely in French for several years. This strategy succeeds in developing children who are proficient in both languages and who, by grade 6, achieve as well in reading, writing, and math as their counterparts in the regular English program (Harley & Jean, 1999; Holobow, Genesee, & Lambert, 1991; Turnbull, Hart, & Lapkin, 2003).

In the United States, fierce disagreement exists over the question of how best to educate ethnic minority children with limited English proficiency. Some believe that time spent communicating in the child's native tongue detracts from English-language achievement, which is crucial for success in school and at work. Other educators, committed to developing minority children's native language while fostering mastery of English, note that providing instruction in the native tongue lets minority children know that their heritage is respected. It also prevents inadequate proficiency in both languages. Minority children who gradually lose the first language as a result of being taught the second end up limited in both languages for a time (Ovando & Collier, 1998). This circumstance leads to serious academic difficulties and is believed to contribute to high rates of school failure and dropout among low-SES Hispanic young people, who make up nearly 50 percent of the U.S. language-minority population.

At present, public opinion and educational practice favor English-only instruction. Many U.S. states have passed laws declaring English to be their official language, creating conditions in which schools have no obligation to teach minority students in languages other than English. Yet in classrooms where both languages are integrated into the curriculum, minority children are more involved in learning and acquire the second language more easily—gains that predict better academic achievement (Guglielmi, 2008). In contrast, when teachers speak only in a language children can barely understand, minority children display frustration, boredom, and escalating academic difficulties (Kieffer, 2008). This downward spiral in achievement is greatest in high-poverty schools, where resources to support the needs of language-minority children are scarce.

Supporters of U.S. English-only education often point to the success of Canadian language immersion programs, in which classroom lessons are conducted in the second language. But Canadian parents enroll their children in immersion classrooms voluntarily, and both French and English are majority languages that are equally valued in Canada. For U.S. non-English-speaking minority children, whose native languages are not valued by the larger society, a different strategy seems necessary: one that promotes children's native-language skills while they learn English.

The child on the left, a native Spanish speaker, benefits from an English–Spanish bilingual classroom, which sustains her native language while she masters English. And her native-English-speaking classmate has the opportunity to begin learning Spanish!

ASK YOURSELF

REVIEW Cite examples of how language awareness fosters language progress.

CONNECT How can bilingual education promote ethnic minority children's cognitive and academic development?

APPLY Ten-year-old Shana arrived home from soccer practice and remarked, "I'm wiped out!" Megan, her 5-year-old sister, looked puzzled. "What did'ya wipe out, Shana?" Megan asked. Explain Shana's and Megan's different understandings of this expression.

REFLECT Did you acquire a second language at home or study one in school? If so, when did you begin, and how proficient are you? What changes would you make in your second-language learning, and why?

Learning in School

Evidence cited throughout this chapter indicates that schools are vital forces in children's cognitive development. How do schools exert such a powerful influence? Research looking at schools as complex social systems—class size, educational philosophies, teacher–student relationships, and larger cultural context—provides important insights. As you read about these topics, refer to Applying What We Know on the following page, which summarizes characteristics of high-quality education in elementary school.

Class Size

As each school year began, Rena telephoned the principal's office to ask, "How large will Joey's and Lizzie's classes be?" Her concern is well-founded. In a large field experiment, more than 6,000 Tennessee kindergartners were randomly assigned to three class types: "small" (13 to 17 students), "regular" (22 to 25 students) with only a teacher, and regular with a teacher plus a full-time teacher's aide. These arrangements continued into third grade. Compared with students in regular-size classes, small-class students—especially ethnic minority children—scored higher in reading and math achievement each year (Mosteller, 1995). These gains persist from fourth through ninth grades, after children return to regular-size classes (Finn, Gerber, & Boyd-Zaharias, 2005; Nye, Hedges, & Konstantopoulos, 2001). And small-class size predicts academic progress even after diverse measures of teacher quality have been controlled (Brühwiler & Blatchford, 2011).

Why is small class size beneficial? With fewer children, teachers spend less time disciplining and more time teaching and giving individual attention. Also, children who learn in smaller groups show better concentration, higher-quality class participation, and more favorable attitudes toward school (Blatchford et al., 2003, 2007; Blatchford, Bassett, & Brown, 2005).

Applying What We Know

Signs of High-Quality Education in Elementary School

Classroom Characteristics	Signs of Quality
Class size	Optimum class size is no larger than 18 children.
Physical setting	Space is divided into richly equipped activity centers—for reading, writing, playing math or language games, exploring science, working on construction projects, using computers, and engaging in other academic pursuits. Spaces are used flexibly for individual and small-group activities and whole-class gatherings.
Curriculum	The curriculum helps children both achieve academic standards and make sense of their learning. Subjects are integrated so that children apply knowledge in one area to others. The curriculum is implemented through activities responsive to children's interests, ideas, and everyday lives, including their cultural backgrounds.
Daily activities	Teachers provide challenging activities that include opportunities for small-group and independent work. Groupings vary in size and makeup of children, depending on the activity and on children's learning needs. Teachers encourage cooperative learning and guide children in attaining it.
Interactions between teachers and children	Teachers foster each child's progress and use intellectually engaging strategies, including posing problems, asking thought-provoking questions, discussing ideas, and adding complexity to tasks. They also demonstrate, explain, coach, and assist in other ways, depending on each child's learning needs.
Evaluations of progress	Teachers regularly evaluate children's progress through written observations and work samples, which they use to enhance and individualize teaching. They help children reflect on their work and decide how to improve it. They also seek information and perspectives from parents on how well children are learning and include parents' views in evaluations.
Relationship with parents	Teachers forge partnerships with parents. They hold periodic conferences and encourage parents to visit the classroom anytime, to observe and volunteer.

Source: Copple & Bredekamp, 2009.

Educational Philosophies

Teachers' educational philosophies play a major role in children's learning. Two philosophical approaches have received most research attention. They differ in what children are taught, the way they are believed to learn, and how their progress is evaluated.

Traditional versus Constructivist Classrooms. In a **traditional classroom,** the teacher is the sole authority for knowledge, rules, and decision making. Students are relatively passive—listening, responding when called on, and completing teacher-assigned tasks. Their progress is evaluated by how well they keep pace with a uniform set of standards for their grade.

A **constructivist classroom,** in contrast, encourages students to *construct* their own knowledge. Although constructivist approaches vary, many are grounded in Piaget's theory, which views children as active agents who reflect on and coordinate their own thoughts rather than absorbing those of others. A glance inside a constructivist classroom reveals richly equipped learning centers, small groups and individuals solving self-chosen problems, and a teacher who guides and supports in response to children's needs. Students are evaluated by considering their progress in relation to their own prior development.

In the United States, the pendulum has swung back and forth between these two views. In the 1960s and early 1970s,

constructivist classrooms gained in popularity. Then, as concern arose over the academic progress of children and youths, a "back-to-basics" movement arose, and classrooms returned to traditional instruction. This style, still prevalent today, has become increasingly pronounced as a result of the U.S. No Child Left Behind Act, signed into law in 2001 (Darling-Hammond, 2010; Ravitch, 2010). Because it places heavy pressure on teachers and school administrators to improve achievement test scores, it has narrowed the curricular focus in many schools to preparing students to take such tests.

Although older elementary school children in traditional classrooms have a slight edge in achievement test scores, constructivist settings are associated with many other benefits—gains in critical thinking, greater social and moral maturity, and more positive attitudes toward school (DeVries, 2001; Rathunde & Csikszentmihalyi, 2005; Walberg, 1986). And as noted in Chapter 7, when teacher-directed instruction is emphasized in preschool and kindergarten, it actually undermines academic motivation and achievement, especially in low-SES children.

New Philosophical Directions. New approaches to education, grounded in Vygotsky's sociocultural theory, capitalize on the rich social context of the classroom to spur children's learning. In these **social-constructivist classrooms,** children participate in a wide range of challenging activities with teachers and peers, with whom they jointly construct understandings. As children acquire knowledge and strategies through working together, they become competent, contributing members of their classroom community and advance in cognitive and social development (Bodrova & Leong, 2007; Palincsar, 2003). Vygotsky's emphasis on the social origins of higher cognitive processes has inspired the following educational themes:

- *Teachers and children as partners in learning.* A classroom rich in both teacher–child and child–child collaboration transfers culturally valued ways of thinking to children.

- *Experiences with many types of symbolic communication in meaningful activities.* As children master reading, writing, and mathematics, they become aware of their culture's communication systems, reflect on their own thinking, and bring it under voluntary control. *TAKE A MOMENT...* Can you identify research presented earlier in this chapter that supports this theme?

- *Teaching adapted to each child's zone of proximal development.* Assistance that both responds to current understandings and encourages children to take the next step helps ensure that each child makes the best progress possible.

According to Vygotsky, besides teachers, more expert peers can spur children's learning, as long as they adjust the help they provide to fit the less mature child's zone of proximal development. Consistent with this idea, mounting evidence confirms that peer collaboration promotes development only under certain conditions. A crucial factor is **cooperative learning,** in which small groups of classmates work toward common goals—by resolving differences of opinion, sharing responsibilities, and providing one another with sufficient explanations to correct misunderstandings. And when more expert students cooperate with less expert students, both benefit in achievement and self-esteem (Ginsburg-Block, Rohrbeck, & Fantuzzo, 2006; Renninger, 1998).

These children attending a rural school in Laos cooperate easily while completing a writing assignment. Their Western cultural-majority agemates, in contrast, typically require extensive guidance to succeed at cooperative learning.

LOOK AND LISTEN

Ask an elementary school teacher to sum up his or her educational philosophy. Is it closest to a traditional, constructivist, or social-constructivist view? Has the teacher encountered any obstacles to implementing that philosophy? Explain. ●

Because Western cultural-majority children regard competition and independent work as natural, they typically require extensive guidance to succeed at cooperative learning. In several studies, groups of students trained in collaborative processes displayed more cooperative behavior, gave clearer explanations, enjoyed learning more, and made greater academic progress in diverse school subjects than did untrained groups (Gillies, 2000, 2003; Terwel et al., 2001; Webb et al., 2008). Teaching through cooperative learning broadens Vygotsky's concept of the zone of proximal development, from a child in collaboration with a more expert partner (adult or peer) to multiple partners with diverse expertises, stimulating and encouraging one another.

Teacher–Student Interaction

Elementary school students describe good teachers as caring, helpful, and stimulating—behaviors associated with gains in motivation, achievement, and positive peer relations (Hughes & Kwok, 2006, 2007; Hughes, Zhang, & Hill, 2006; O'Connor & McCartney, 2007). But too many U.S. teachers emphasize repetitive drill over higher-level thinking, such as grappling with ideas and applying knowledge to new situations (Sacks, 2005).

Of course, teachers do not interact in the same way with all children. Well-behaved, high-achieving students typically get more encouragement and praise, whereas unruly students have more conflicts with teachers and receive more criticism from them (Henricsson & Rydell, 2004). Caring teacher–student relationships have an especially strong impact on the achievement and social behavior of low-SES minority students (Baker, 2006; Crosno, Kirkpatrick, & Elder, 2004). But overall, higher-SES students—who tend to be higher-achieving and to have fewer discipline problems—have more supportive relationships with teachers (Jerome, Hamre, & Pianta, 2009; Pianta, Hamre, & Stuhlman, 2003).

Unfortunately, once teachers' attitudes toward students are established, they can become more extreme than is warranted by students' behavior. Of special concern are **educational self-fulfilling prophecies:** Children may adopt teachers' positive or negative views and start to live up to them. This effect is especially strong when teachers emphasize competition and publicly compare children, regularly favoring the best students (Kuklinski & Weinstein, 2001; Weinstein, 2002).

Teacher expectations have a greater impact on low-achieving than high-achieving students (Madon, Jussim, & Eccles, 1997). When a teacher is critical, high achievers can fall back on their history of success. Low-achieving students' sensitivity to self-fulfilling prophecies can be beneficial when teachers believe in them. But biased teacher judgments are usually slanted in a negative direction. In one study, African-American and Hispanic elementary school students taught by high-bias teachers (who

Social Issues: Education

Magnet Schools: Equal Access to High-Quality Education

Each school-day morning, Emma leaves her affluent suburban neighborhood, riding a school bus to a magnet school in an impoverished, mostly Hispanic inner-city community. In her sixth-grade class, she settles into a science project with her friend, Maricela, who lives in the local neighborhood. The girls use a thermometer, ice water, and a stopwatch to determine which of several materials is the best insulator, recording and graphing their data. Throughout the school, which specializes in innovative math and science teaching, students diverse in SES and ethnicity learn side-by-side.

Despite the 1954 U.S. Supreme Court *Brown v. Board of Education* decision ordering schools to desegregate, school integration has receded since the late 1980s, as federal courts canceled their integration orders and returned this authority to states and cities. Today, the racial divide in American education is deepening (Frankenburg & Orfield, 2007). African-American children are just as likely to attend a school that serves a mostly black population as they were in the 1960s; Hispanic children are even more segregated. And when minority students attend ethnically mixed schools, they typically do so with other minorities.

U.S. schools in low-income neighborhoods are vastly disadvantaged in funding and therefore in educational opportunities, largely because public education is primarily supported by local property taxes. Federal and state grants-in-aid are not sufficient to close this funding gap between rich and poor districts (Darling-Hammond, 2010). Consequently, dilapidated school buildings, inexperienced teachers, and poor-quality educational resources are widespread in inner-city neighborhoods (Kozol, 2005). The negative impact on student achievement is severe.

Third graders at a fine-arts magnet school jointly create a painting. The ethnically diverse learning environments of many magnet schools enhance academic achievement, especially among low-SES minority students.

Magnet schools offer a solution. In addition to the usual curriculum, they emphasize a specific area of interest—such as performing arts, math and science, or technology. Families outside the school neighborhood are attracted to magnet schools (hence the name) by their rich academic offerings. Often magnets are located in low-income minority areas, where they serve the neighborhood student population. Other students, who apply and are admitted by lottery, are bussed in—many from well-to-do city and suburban neighborhoods. In another model, all students—including those in the surrounding neighborhood—must apply. In either case, magnet schools are voluntarily desegregated.

Research confirms that less segregated education enhances minority student achievement (Linn & Welner, 2007). Is this so for magnet schools? A Connecticut study comparing seventh to tenth graders enrolled in magnet schools with those whose lottery numbers were not drawn and who therefore attended other city schools confirmed that magnet students showed greater gains in reading and math achievement over a two-year period (Bifulco, Cobb, & Bell, 2009). These outcomes were strongest for low-SES, ethnic minority students.

By high school, the higher-achieving peer environments of ethnically diverse schools encourage more students to pursue higher education (Franklin, 2012). In sum, magnet schools are a promising approach to overcoming the negative forces of SES and ethnic isolation in American schools.

---

expected them to do poorly) showed substantially lower end-of-year achievement than their counterparts taught by low-bias teachers (McKown & Weinstein, 2008). Recall our discussion of *stereotype threat*. A child in the position of confirming a negative stereotype may respond with anxiety and reduced motivation, amplifying a negative self-fulfilling prophecy.

Grouping Practices

In many schools, students are assigned to *homogeneous* groups or classes in which children of similar ability levels are taught together. Homogeneous grouping can be a potent source of self-fulfilling prophecies. Low-group students—who as early as first grade are more likely to be low-SES, minority, and male—get more drill on basic facts and skills, engage in less discussion, and progress at a slower pace. Gradually, they decline in self-esteem and motivation and fall further behind in achievement (Lleras & Rangel, 2009; Worthy, Hungerford-Kresser, & Hampton, 2009). Unfortunately, widespread SES and ethnic segregation in U.S. schools consigns large numbers of low-SES minority students to a form of schoolwide homogeneous grouping. Refer to the Social Issues: Education box above to find out how magnet schools foster heterogeneous learning contexts, thereby reducing achievement differences between SES and ethnic minority groups.

Another way schools can increase the *heterogeneity* of student groups is to combine two or three adjacent grades.(In *multigrade classrooms,* academic achievement, self-esteem, and attitudes toward school are usually more favorable than in the single-grade arrangement(Lloyd, 1999; Ong, Allison, & Haladyna, 2000). Perhaps multigrade grouping decreases competition and promotes *cooperative learning,* which also fosters these positive outcomes (see page 320).

Teaching Children with Special Needs

We have seen that effective teachers flexibly adjust their teaching strategies to accommodate students with a wide range of characteristics. These adjustments are especially challenging at the very low and high ends of the ability distribution. How do schools serve children with special learning needs?

Children with Learning Difficulties. U.S. legislation mandates that schools place children who require special supports for learning in the "least restrictive" (as close to normal as possible) environments that meet their educational needs. In **inclusive classrooms,** students with learning difficulties learn alongside typical students in the regular educational setting for all or part of the school day—a practice designed to prepare them for participation in society and to combat prejudices against individuals with disabilities (Kugelmass & Ainscow, 2004). Largely as the result of parental pressures, an increasing number of students experience *full inclusion*—full-time placement in regular classrooms.

Some students in inclusive classrooms have *mild mental retardation:* Their IQs fall between 55 and 70, and they also show problems in adaptive behavior, or skills of everyday living (American Psychiatric Association, 2000). But the largest number—5 to 10 percent of school-age children—have **learning disabilities,** great difficulty with one or more aspects of learning, usually reading. As a result, their achievement is considerably behind what would be expected on the basis of their IQ. Sometimes deficits express themselves in other ways—for example, as severe inattention, which depresses both IQ and achievement (recall our discussion of ADHD on pages 304–305). The problems of students with learning disabilities cannot be traced to any obvious physical or emotional difficulty or to environmental disadvantage. Instead, deficits in brain functioning are involved (Waber, 2010). In many instances, the cause is unknown.

Although some students benefit academically from inclusion, many do not. Achievement gains depend on both the severity of the disability and the support services available (Downing, 2010). Furthermore, children with disabilities are often rejected by regular-classroom peers. Students with mental retardation are overwhelmed by the social skills of their classmates; they cannot interact adeptly in a conversation or game. And the processing deficits of some students with learning disabilities lead to problems in social awareness and responsiveness (Kelly & Norwich, 2004; Lohrmann & Bambara, 2006).

Does this mean that students with special needs cannot be served in regular classrooms? Not necessarily. Often these

In this inclusive first-grade classroom, a teacher encourages special-needs students' active participation. They are likely to do well if they receive support from a special education teacher and if their regular classroom teacher minimizes comparisons and promotes positive peer relations.

children do best when they receive instruction in a resource room for part of the day and in the regular classroom for the remainder (Weiner & Tardif, 2004). In the resource room, a special education teacher works with students on an individual and small-group basis. Then, depending on their progress, children join regular classmates for different subjects and amounts of time.

Special steps must to be taken to promote peer relations in inclusive classrooms. Cooperative learning and peer-tutoring experiences in which teachers guide children with learning difficulties and their classmates in working together lead to friendly interaction, improved peer acceptance, and achievement gains (Fuchs et al., 2002a, 2002b). Teachers can also prepare their class for the arrival of a student with special needs. Under these conditions, inclusion may foster emotional sensitivity and prosocial behavior among regular classmates.

Gifted Children. In Joey and Lizzie's school, some children are **gifted,** displaying exceptional intellectual strengths. One or two students in every grade have IQ scores above 130, the standard definition of giftedness based on intelligence test performance. High-IQ children, as we have seen, have keen memories and an exceptional capacity to solve challenging academic problems. Yet recognition that intelligence tests do not sample the entire range of human mental skills has led to an expanded conception of giftedness.

Creativity and Talent. Creativity is the ability to produce work that is original yet appropriate—something others have not thought of that is useful in some way (Kaufman & Sternberg, 2007; Sternberg, 2003). A child with high potential for creativity can be designated as gifted. Tests of creative capacity tap **divergent thinking**—the generation of multiple and unusual possibilities when faced with a task or problem. Divergent thinking contrasts with **convergent thinking,** which involves arriving at a single correct answer and is emphasized on intelligence tests (Guilford, 1985).

FIGURE 9.10 **Responses of an 8-year-old who scored high on a figural measure of divergent thinking.** This child was asked to make as many pictures as she could from the circles on the page. The titles she gave her drawings, from left to right, are as follows: "Dracula," "one-eyed monster," "pumpkin," "Hula-Hoop," "poster," "wheelchair," "earth," "stop-light," "planet," "movie camera," "sad face," "picture," "beach ball," "the letter *O*," "car," "glasses." Tests of divergent thinking tap only one of the complex cognitive contributions to creativity. (Reprinted by permission of Laura E. Berk.)

Because highly creative children (like high-IQ children) are often better at some tasks than others, a variety of tests of divergent thinking are available (Runco, 1992; Torrance, 1988). A verbal measure might ask children to name uses for common objects (such as a newspaper). A figural measure might ask them to create drawings based on a circular motif (see Figure 9.10). A "real-world problem" measure requires students to suggest solutions to everyday problems. Responses can be scored for the number of ideas generated and their originality.

Yet critics point out that these measures are poor predictors of creative accomplishment in everyday life because they tap only one of the complex cognitive contributions to creativity (Plucker & Makel, 2010). Also involved are defining new and important problems, evaluating divergent ideas, choosing the most promising, and calling on relevant knowledge to understand and solve problems (Sternberg, 2003; Lubart, Georgsdottir, & Besançon, 2009).

Consider these ingredients, and you will see why people usually demonstrate creativity in only one or a few related areas. Partly for this reason, definitions of giftedness have been extended to include **talent**—outstanding performance in a specific field. Case studies reveal that excellence in creative writing, mathematics, science, music, visual arts, athletics, or leadership has roots in specialized interests and skills that first appear in childhood (Moran & Gardner, 2006). Highly talented children are biologically prepared to master their domain of interest, and they display a passion for doing so.

But talent must be nurtured. Studies of the backgrounds of talented children and highly accomplished adults often reveal

warm, sensitive parents who provide a stimulating home life, are devoted to developing their child's abilities, and provide models of hard work. These parents are reasonably demanding but not driving or overambitious (Winner, 2000, 2003). They arrange for caring teachers while the child is young and for more rigorous master teachers as the talent develops.

Many gifted children and adolescents are socially isolated, partly because their highly driven, nonconforming, and independent styles leave them out of step with peers and partly because they enjoy solitude, which is necessary to develop their talents. Still, gifted children desire gratifying peer relationships, and some—more often girls than boys—try to become better-liked by hiding their abilities. Compared with their typical agemates, gifted youths, especially girls, report more emotional and social difficulties, including low self-esteem and depression (Reis, 2004; Winner, 2000).

Finally, whereas many talented youths become experts in their fields, few become highly creative. Rapidly mastering an existing field requires different skills than innovating in that field (Moran & Gardner, 2006). The world, however, needs both experts and creators.

Educating the Gifted. Debate about the effectiveness of school programs for the gifted typically focuses on factors irrelevant to giftedness—whether to provide enrichment in regular classrooms, pull children out for special instruction (the most common practice), or advance brighter students to a higher grade. Overall, gifted children fare well academically and socially within each of these models, as long as the special activities provided do not reinforce academic convergent thinking to the detriment of problem solving, critical thinking, and creativity (Guignard & Lubart, 2007).

Gardner's theory of multiple intelligences has inspired several model programs that provide enrichment to all students in diverse disciplines. Meaningful activities, each tapping a specific intelligence or set of intelligences, serve as contexts for assessing strengths and weaknesses and, on that basis, teaching new knowledge and original thinking (Gardner, 2000; Hoerr, 2004). For example, linguistic intelligence might be fostered through storytelling or playwriting; spatial intelligence through drawing, sculpting, or taking apart and reassembling objects; and kinesthetic intelligence through dance or pantomime.

Evidence is still needed on how well these programs nurture children's talents and creativity. But they have already succeeded in one way—by highlighting the strengths of some students who previously had been considered unexceptional or even at risk for school failure (Kornhaber, 2004). Consequently, they may be especially useful in identifying talented low-SES, ethnic minority children, who are underrepresented in school programs for the gifted (McBee, 2006).

How Well-Educated Are U.S. Children?

Our discussion of schooling has largely focused on how teachers can support the education of children. Yet many factors—both within and outside schools—affect children's learning. Societal values, school resources, quality of teaching, and parental encouragement all play important roles. These multiple influences are especially apparent than when schooling is examined in cross-cultural perspective.

In international studies of reading, mathematics, and science achievement, young people in China, Korea, and Japan are consistently top performers. Among Western nations, Australia, Canada, Finland, the Netherlands, and Switzerland are also in the top tier. But U.S. students typically perform at or below the international averages (see Figure 9.11) (Programme for International Student Assessment, 2009).

Why do U.S. students fall behind in academic accomplishment? According to international comparisons, instruction in the United States is less challenging, more focused on absorbing facts, and less focused on high-level reasoning and critical

Finnish students explain the results of a static electricity experiment. Their country's education system—designed to cultivate initiative, problem solving, and creativity in all students—has nearly eliminated SES variations in achievement.

thinking than in other countries. According to a growing number of experts, the U.S. No Child Left Behind Act has contributed to these trends because it mandates severe sanctions for schools whose students do not meet targeted goals on achievement tests—initially, student transfers to higher-performing schools; and ultimately, staff firing, closure, state takeover, or other restructuring (Darling-Hammond, 2010; Noguera, 2010; Ravitch, 2010). Furthermore, compared with top-achieving countries, the United States is far less equitable in the quality of education it provides to its low-income and ethnic minority students. And U.S. teachers vary much more in training, salaries, and teaching conditions.

Finland is a case in point. Its nationally mandated curricula, teaching practices, and assessments are aimed at cultivating initiative, problem solving, and creativity—vital abilities needed for success in the twenty-first century. Finnish teachers are highly trained: They must complete several years of graduate-level education at government expense (Sahlberg, 2010). And Finnish education is grounded in equal opportunity for all—a policy that has nearly eliminated SES variations in achievement.

In-depth research on learning environments in Asian nations, such as Japan, Korea, and Taiwan, also highlights social forces that foster strong student learning. Among these is cultural valuing of effort. Whereas American parents and teachers tend to regard native ability as the key to academic success, Japanese, Korean, and Taiwanese parents and teachers believe that all children can succeed academically with enough effort. Asian parents devote many more hours to helping their children with homework (Stevenson, Lee, & Mu, 2000). And Asian children, influenced by collectivist values, typically view striving to achieve as a moral obligation—part of their responsibility to family and community (Hau & Ho, 2010).

As in Finland, all students in Japan, Korea, and Taiwan receive the same nationally mandated, high-quality curriculum that encourages high-level thinking, delivered by teachers who are well-prepared, highly respected in their society, and far

	Country	Average Math Achievement Score
High-Performing Nations	China (Shanghai)	600
	Singapore	562
	China (Hong Kong)	555
	Korea	546
	Taiwan	543
	Finland	541
	Switzerland	534
	Japan	529
	Canada	527
	Netherlands	526
	China (Macao)	525
	New Zealand	519
	Belgium	515
	Australia	514
	Germany	513
Intermediate-Performing Nations	Iceland	507
	Denmark	503
	Norway	498
	France	497
International Average = 496	Austria	496
	Poland	495
	Sweden	494
	Czech Republic	493
	United Kingdom	492
	Hungary	490
	Luxembourg	489
	United States	**487**
	Ireland	487
	Portugal	487
	Italy	483
	Spain	483
Low-Performing Nations	Russian Federation	468
	Greece	466
	Turkey	445
	Bulgaria	428

FIGURE 9.11 Average mathematics scores of 15-year-olds by country. The Programme for International Student Assessment measured achievement in many nations around the world. In its most recent comparison of countries' performance, the United States performed below the international average in math; in reading and science, its performance was about average. (Adapted from Programme for International Student Assessment, 2009.)

better paid than U.S. teachers (Kang & Hong, 2008; U.S. Department of Education, 2012a).

The Finnish and Asian examples underscore the need for American families, schools, and the larger society to work together to upgrade education. Recommended strategies, verified by research, include:

- providing intellectually challenging, relevant instruction with real-world applications
- strengthening teacher education
- supporting parents in creating stimulating home learning environments and monitoring their children's academic progress
- investing in high-quality preschool education, so every child arrives at school ready to learn
- vigorously pursuing school improvements that reduce the large inequities in quality of education between SES and ethnic groups (Economic Policy Institute, 2010).

SUMMARY

PHYSICAL DEVELOPMENT

Body Growth (p. 290)

Describe major trends in body growth during middle childhood.

- During middle childhood, physical growth continues at a slow, regular pace. Bones lengthen and broaden, and permanent teeth replace the primary teeth. By age 9, girls overtake boys in physical size.

Common Health Problems (p. 290)

Describe the causes and consequences of serious nutritional problems in middle childhood, giving special attention to obesity.

- Many poverty-stricken children in developing countries and in the United States continue to suffer from serious and prolonged malnutrition, which can permanently impair physical and mental development.

- Overweight and **obesity** have increased dramatically in both industrialized and developing nations, especially in the United States. Although heredity contributes to obesity, parental feeding practices, maladaptive eating habits, reduced sleep, lack of exercise, and diets high in meats and energy-dense refined foods are more powerful influences.

- Obese children are rated as less likable by peers and adults and have serious adjustment problems. The most effective interventions are family-based and focus on changing parents' and children's eating patterns and lifestyles. Schools can help by serving healthier meals and ensuring regular physical activity.

What vision and hearing problems are common in middle childhood?

- The most common vision problem, myopia, is influenced by heredity, early biological trauma, and time spent doing close work. It is one of the few health conditions that increases with SES.

- Although ear infections decline during the school years, many low-SES children experience some hearing loss because of repeated untreated middle-ear infections.

What factors contribute to illness during the school years, and how can these health problems be reduced?

- Children experience more illnesses during the first two years of elementary school than later because of exposure to sick children and an immature immune system.

- The most common cause of school absence and childhood hospitalization is asthma. Although heredity contributes to asthma, environmental factors—pollution, stressful home lives, lack of access to good health care, and the rise in childhood obesity—have led to an increase in the disease, especially among African-American and poverty-stricken children.

- Children with severe chronic illnesses are at risk for academic, emotional, and social difficulties, but positive family relationships improve adjustment.

Describe changes in the occurrence of unintentional injuries in middle childhood, and cite effective interventions.

- Unintentional injuries increase from middle childhood into adolescence, especially for boys. Auto and bicycle accidents account for most of the rise. Effective school-based prevention programs use modeling, rehearsal, and rewards for acquiring safety skills.

© OCEAN/CORBIS

Motor Development and Play (p. 294)

Cite major changes in motor development and play during middle childhood.

- Gains in flexibility, balance, agility, and force, along with more efficient information processing, contribute to school-age children's improved gross-motor performance.

- Fine-motor development also improves. Children's writing becomes more legible, and their drawings increase in organization, detail, and depth cues.

- Although girls outperform boys in fine-motor skills, boys outperform girls in all gross-motor skills except those requiring balance and agility. Parents' higher expectations for boys' athletic performance play a large role.

- Games with rules become common during the school years, contributing to emotional and social development. Children, especially boys, also engage in **rough-and-tumble play,** friendly play-fighting that helps establish a **dominance hierarchy** among group members.

- Most U.S. school-age children are not active enough for good health, in part because of cutbacks in recess and physical education.

COGNITIVE DEVELOPMENT

Piaget's Theory: The Concrete Operational Stage (p. 299)

What are the major characteristics of concrete operational thought?

- In the **concrete operational stage,** children's thought becomes more logical, flexible, and organized. Mastery of conservation demonstrates decentration and **reversibility** in thinking.

- School-age children are also better at hierarchical classification and **seriation,** including **transitive inference.** Their spatial reasoning improves, evident in their ability to create **cognitive maps** representing familiar large-scale spaces.

- Concrete operational thought is limited in that children do not come up with general logical principles. They master concrete operational tasks step by step.

Discuss follow-up research on concrete operational thought.

- Specific cultural practices, especially those associated with schooling, promote children's mastery of Piagetian tasks.

- Some researchers attribute the gradual development of operational thought to gains in information-processing speed. Case's neo-Piagetian theory proposes that with practice, cognitive schemes become more automatic, freeing up space in working memory for combining old schemes and generating new ones. Eventually, children consolidate schemes into central conceptual structures, which enable them to coordinate and integrate multiple dimensions.

Information Processing (p. 302)

Describe gains in working-memory capacity and executive function, along with the development of attention and memory in middle childhood.

- Brain development contributes to increases in processing speed and expansion of working memory, which predicts intelligence test scores and academic achievement. As the prefrontal cortex continues to develop, children make great strides in executive function.

- Attention becomes more selective, adaptable, and planful, and memory strategies also improve. **Rehearsal** appears first, followed by **organization** and then **elaboration.** With age, children combine memory strategies.

- Development of the long-term knowledge base makes new information easier to store and retrieve. Children's motivation to use what they know also contributes to memory development. Memory strategies are promoted by learning activities in school.

Describe the school-age child's theory of mind and capacity to engage in self-regulation.

- School-age children regard the mind as an active, constructive agent, yielding a better understanding of cognitive processes, including effective memory strategies, mental inference, and second-order false belief. **Cognitive self-regulation** develops gradually, improving with adult instruction in strategy use.

Discuss current controversies in teaching reading and mathematics to elementary school children.

- Skilled reading draws on all aspects of the information-processing system. A combination of **whole language** and **phonics** is most effective for teaching beginning reading. Teaching that blends practice in basic skills with conceptual understanding also is best in mathematics.

Individual Differences in Mental Development (p. 309)

Describe major approaches to defining and measuring intelligence.

- Most intelligence tests yield an overall score as well as scores for separate intellectual factors. During the school years, IQ becomes more stable and correlates moderately with academic achievement.

- Componential analyses identify information-processing skills that contribute to mental test performance. Processing speed and flexible attention, memory, and reasoning strategies are positively related to IQ.

- Sternberg's **triarchic theory of successful intelligence** identifies three broad, interacting intelligences: analytical intelligence (information-processing skills), creative intelligence (capacity to solve novel problems), and practical intelligence (application of intellectual skills in everyday situations).

- Gardner's **theory of multiple intelligences** identifies at least eight distinct mental abilities. It has stimulated efforts to define, measure, and foster **emotional intelligence.**

Describe evidence indicating that both heredity and environment contribute to intelligence.

- Heritability estimates and adoption research indicate that intelligence is a product of both heredity and environment. Adoption studies indicate that environmental factors underlie the black–white IQ gap.

- IQ scores are affected by culturally influenced communication styles and knowledge. **Stereotype threat** triggers anxiety that interferes with test performance. **Dynamic assessment** helps many minority children perform more competently on mental tests.

Language Development
(p. 316)

Describe changes in school-age children's vocabulary, grammar, and pragmatics, and cite the advantages of bilingualism for development.

- Language awareness contributes to school-age children's language progress. They have a more precise and flexible understanding of word meanings and use more complex grammatical constructions and conversational strategies. Their narratives increase in organization, detail, and expressiveness.

- Mastery of a second language must begin in childhood for full proficiency to occur. Bilingualism has positive consequences for cognitive development and aspects of language awareness. In Canada, language immersion programs succeed in developing children who are proficient in both English and French. In the United States, bilingual education that combines instruction in the native tongue and in English supports ethnic minority children's academic learning.

Learning in School (p. 318)

Describe the impact of class size and educational philosophies on children's motivation and academic achievement.

- Smaller classes in the early elementary grades promote lasting gains in academic achievement. Older elementary school students in **traditional classrooms** have a slight edge in achievement test scores over those in **constructivist classrooms,** who gain in critical thinking, social and moral maturity, and positive attitudes toward school.

- Students in **social-constructivist classrooms** benefit from working collaboratively in meaningful activities and from teaching adapted to each child's zone of proximal development. **Cooperative learning** promotes achievement and self-esteem.

Discuss the role of teacher–student interaction and grouping practices in academic achievement.

- Caring, helpful, and stimulating teaching fosters children's motivation, achievement, and peer relations. **Educational self-fulfilling prophecies** have a greater impact on low than high achievers and are especially likely to occur in classrooms that emphasize competition and public evaluation. Heterogeneous grouping in multigrade classrooms promotes favorable self-esteem and school attitudes and higher achievement.

Under what conditions is placement of children with learning difficulties in regular classrooms successful?

- The success of **inclusive classrooms** for students with mild mental retardation and **learning disabilities** depends on meeting individual learning needs and promoting positive peer relations.

Describe the characteristics of gifted children and current efforts to meet their educational needs.

- **Giftedness** includes high IQ, **creativity,** and **talent.** Tests of creativity that tap **divergent** rather than **convergent thinking** focus on only one of the ingredients of creativity. Highly talented children generally have parents and teachers who nurture their exceptional abilities. Gifted children benefit from educational programs that build on their special strengths.

How well-educated are U.S. children compared with children in other industrialized nations?

- In international studies, young people in Asian nations are consistently top performers, whereas U.S. students typically perform at or below international averages. Compared with top-achieving countries, education in the United States is more focused on absorbing facts, less focused on high-level reasoning and critical thinking, and less equitable across SES groups.

Important Terms and Concepts

attention-deficit hyperactivity disorder (ADHD) (p. 304)
cognitive maps (p. 300)
cognitive self-regulation (p. 307)
concrete operational stage (p. 299)
constructivist classroom (p. 319)
convergent thinking (p. 322)
cooperative learning (p. 320)
creativity (p. 322)
divergent thinking (p. 322)
dominance hierarchy (p. 297)

dynamic assessment (p. 315)
educational self-fulfilling prophecies (p. 320)
elaboration (p. 305)
emotional intelligence (p. 313)
gifted (p. 322)
inclusive classrooms (p. 322)
learning disabilities (p. 322)
obesity (p. 291)
organization (p. 304)
phonics approach (p. 308)
rehearsal (p. 304)

reversibility (p. 299)
rough-and-tumble play (p. 297)
seriation (p. 300)
social-constructivist classroom (p. 319)
stereotype threat (p. 314)
talent (p. 323)
theory of multiple intelligences (p. 311)
traditional classroom (p. 319)
transitive inference (p. 300)
triarchic theory of successful intelligence (p. 310)
whole-language approach (p. 308)

© ELLEN B. SENISI PHOTOGRAPHY

Social understanding expands greatly in middle childhood. Like others their age around the world, these third graders choose friends based on personal qualities, and they count on those friends for understanding and emotional support.

Emotional and Social Development in Middle Childhood

chapter outline

Erikson's Theory: Industry versus Inferiority

Self-Understanding

Self-Concept • Self-Esteem • Influences on Self-Esteem

Emotional Development

Self-Conscious Emotions • Emotional Understanding • Emotional Self-Regulation

Moral Development

Moral and Social-Conventional Understanding • Understanding Individual Rights • Understanding Diversity and Inequality

Peer Relations

Peer Groups • Friendships • Peer Acceptance

■ **BIOLOGY AND ENVIRONMENT** Bullies and Their Victims

Gender Typing

Gender-Stereotyped Beliefs • Gender Identity and Behavior

Family Influences

Parent–Child Relationships • Siblings • Only Children • Divorce • Blended Families • Maternal Employment and Dual-Earner Families

Some Common Problems of Development

Fears and Anxieties • Child Sexual Abuse • Fostering Resilience in Middle Childhood

■ **CULTURAL INFLUENCES** Impact of Ethnic and Political Violence on Children

■ **SOCIAL ISSUES: HEALTH** Children's Eyewitness Testimony

Late one afternoon, Rena heard her son Joey burst through the front door, run upstairs, and phone his best friend Terry. "Terry, gotta talk to you," Joey pleaded breathlessly. "Everything was going great until I got that word—*porcupine*," Joey went on, referring to the fifth-grade spelling bee at school that day. "Just my luck! *P-o-r-k,* that's how I spelled it! I can't believe it. Maybe I'm not so good at social studies," Joey confided, "but I *know* I'm better at spelling than that stuck-up Belinda Brown. I knocked myself out studying those spelling lists. Then *she* got all the easy words. If I *had* to lose, why couldn't it be to a nice person?"

Joey's conversation reflects new emotional and social capacities. By entering the spelling bee, he shows *industriousness,* the energetic pursuit of meaningful achievement in his culture—a major change of middle childhood. Joey's social understanding has also expanded: He can size up strengths, weaknesses, and personality characteristics. Furthermore, friendship means something different to Joey than it did earlier—he counts on his best friend, Terry, for understanding and emotional support.

For an overview of the personality changes of middle childhood, we return to Erikson's theory. Then we look at children's views of themselves and of others, their moral understanding, and their peer relationships. Each increases in complexity as children reason more effectively and spend more time in school and with agemates.

Despite changing parent–child relationships, the family remains powerfully influential in middle childhood. Today, family lifestyles are more diverse than ever before. Through Joey and his younger sister Lizzie's experiences with parental divorce, we will see that family functioning is far more important than family structure in ensuring children's well-being. Finally, we look at some common emotional problems of middle childhood. ●

ELISA CICINELLI/GETTY IMAGES/BRAND X PICTURES

Erikson's Theory: Industry versus Inferiority

According to Erikson (1950), children whose previous experiences have been positive enter middle childhood prepared to redirect their energies from the make-believe of early childhood into realistic accomplishment. Erikson believed that the combination of adult expectations and children's drive toward mastery sets the stage for the psychological conflict of middle childhood, **industry versus inferiority,** which is resolved positively when children develop a sense of competence at useful skills and tasks. In cultures everywhere, adults respond to children's improved physical and cognitive capacities by making new demands, and children are ready to benefit from those challenges.

In industrialized nations, the beginning of formal schooling marks the transition to middle childhood. With it comes literacy training, which prepares children for a vast array of specialized careers. In school, children discover their own and others' unique capacities, learn the value of division of labor, and develop a sense of moral commitment and responsibility. The danger at this stage is *inferiority,* reflected in the pessimism of children who lack confidence in their ability to do things well. This sense of inadequacy can develop when family life has not prepared children for school life or when teachers and peers destroy children's self-confidence with negative responses.

Erikson's sense of industry combines several developments of middle childhood: a positive but realistic self-concept, pride in accomplishment, moral responsibility, and cooperative participation with agemates. How do these aspects of self and social relationships change over the school years?

The industriousness of middle childhood involves responding to new expectations for realistic accomplishment. In the informal, encouraging atmosphere of this classroom in India, children come to view themselves as responsible, capable, and cooperative.

Self-Understanding

In middle childhood, children begin to describe themselves in terms of psychological traits, compare their own characteristics with those of their peers, and speculate about the causes of their strengths and weaknesses. These transformations in self-understanding have a major impact on self-esteem.

Self-Concept

During the school years, children refine their self-concept, organizing their observations of behaviors and internal states into general dispositions. A major change takes place between ages 8 and 11, as the following self-description by an 11-year-old illustrates:

> My name is A. I'm a human being. I'm a girl. I'm a truthful person. I'm not pretty. I do so-so in my studies. I'm a very good cellist. I'm a very good pianist. I'm a little bit tall for my age. I like several boys. I like several girls. I'm old-fashioned. I play tennis. I am a very good swimmer. I try to be helpful. I'm always ready to be friends with anybody. Mostly I'm good, but I lose my temper. I'm not well-liked by some girls and boys. I don't know if I'm liked by boys or not. (Montemayor & Eisen, 1977, pp. 317–318)

Instead of specific behaviors, this child emphasizes competencies: "I'm a very good cellist" (Damon & Hart, 1988). She also describes her personality, mentioning both positive and negative traits: "truthful" but short-tempered. Older school-age children are far less likely than younger children to describe themselves in extreme, all-or-none ways.

These evaluative self-descriptions result from school-age children's frequent **social comparisons**—judgments of their appearance, abilities, and behavior in relation to those of others. For example, Joey observed that he was "better at spelling" than his peers but "not so good at social studies." Whereas 4- to 6-year-olds can compare their own performance to that of one peer, older children can compare multiple individuals, including themselves (Butler, 1998; Harter, 2006).

What factors account for these revisions in self-concept? Cognitive development affects the changing *structure* of the self. School-age children, as we saw in Chapter 9, can better coordinate several aspects of a situation in reasoning about their physical world. Similarly, in the social realm, they combine typical experiences and behaviors into stable psychological dispositions, blend positive and negative characteristics, and compare their own characteristics with those of many peers (Harter, 2003, 2006).

The changing *content* of self-concept is a product of both cognitive capacities and feedback from others. Sociologist George Herbert Mead (1934) proposed that a well-organized psychological self emerges when children adopt a view of the self that resembles others' attitudes toward the child. Mead's ideas indicate that *perspective-taking skills*—in particular, an improved ability to infer what other people are thinking—are crucial for developing a self-concept based on personality traits. School-age children become better at "reading" others' messages and internalizing their expectations. As they do so, they form an *ideal self* that they use to evaluate their real self. A large discrepancy between the two, as we will see shortly, can undermine self-esteem.

In middle childhood, children look to more people beyond the family for information about themselves as they enter a wider range of settings in school and community. And self-descriptions now include frequent reference to social groups: "I'm a Boy Scout, a paper boy, and a Prairie City soccer player," said Joey. As children move into adolescence, although parents and other adults remain influential, self-concept is increasingly vested in feedback from close friends (Oosterwegel & Oppenheimer, 1993).

LOOK AND LISTEN

Ask several 8- to 11-year-old children to tell you about themselves. Do their self-descriptions include personality traits (both positive and negative), social comparisons, and references to social groups? ●

But recall that the content of self-concept varies from culture to culture. In earlier chapters, we noted that Asian parents stress harmonious interdependence, whereas Western parents stress independence and self-assertion. When asked to recall personally significant past experiences (their last birthday, a time their parent scolded them), U.S. school-age children gave longer accounts including more personal preferences, interests, skills, and opinions. Chinese children, in contrast, more often referred to social interactions and to others. Similarly, in their self-descriptions, U.S. children listed more personal attributes ("I'm smart," "I like hockey"), Chinese children more attributes involving group membership and relationships ("I'm in second grade," "My friends are crazy about me") (Wang, 2006b; Wang, Shao, & Li, 2010).

Finally, although school-age children from diverse cultures view themselves as more knowledgeable about their own inner attributes than significant adults, Japanese children credit their parents and teachers with considerably more knowledge than Western children do (Mitchell et al., 2010, p. 249). Perhaps because of their more interdependent self, Japanese children assume that their inner states are more transparent to others.

Self-Esteem

Recall that most preschoolers have extremely high self-esteem. But as children enter school and receive much more feedback about how well they perform compared with their peers, self-esteem differentiates and also adjusts to a more realistic level.

A Hierarchically Structured Self-Esteem. Researchers have asked children to indicate the extent to which statements such as "I am good at reading" or "I'm usually the one chosen for games" are true of themselves. By age 6 to 7, children in diverse Western cultures have formed at least four broad self-evaluations: academic competence, social competence, physical/athletic competence, and physical appearance. Within these are more refined categories that become increasingly distinct

with age (Marsh, 1990; Marsh & Ayotte, 2003; Van den Bergh & De Rycke, 2003). Furthermore, the capacity to view the self in terms of stable dispositions permits school-age children to combine their separate self-evaluations into a general psychological image of themselves—an overall sense of self-esteem (Harter, 2003, 2006). As a result, self-esteem takes on the hierarchical structure shown in Figure 10.1 on page 332.

Children attach greater importance to certain self-evaluations than to others. Although individual differences exist, during childhood and adolescence, perceived physical appearance correlates more strongly with overall self-worth than any other self-esteem factor (Klomsten, Skaalvik, & Espnes, 2004; Shapka & Keating, 2005). Emphasis on appearance—in the media, by parents and peers, and in society—has major implications for young people's overall satisfaction with themselves.

Changes in Level of Self-Esteem. Self-esteem declines during the first few years of elementary school as children evaluate themselves in various areas (Marsh, Craven, & Debus, 1998; Wigfield et al., 1997). Typically, the drop is not great enough to be harmful. Most (but not all) children appraise their characteristics and competencies realistically while maintaining an attitude of self-respect. Then, from fourth grade on, self-esteem rises for the majority of young people, who feel especially good about their peer relationships and athletic capabilities (Impett et al., 2008; Twenge & Campbell, 2001).

Influences on Self-Esteem

From middle childhood on, individual differences in self-esteem become increasingly stable (Trzesniewski, Donnellan, & Robins, 2003). And positive relationships among self-esteem, valuing of various activities, and success at those activities emerge and strengthen. Academic self-esteem predicts how important, useful, and enjoyable children judge school subjects to be, willingness to try hard, achievement, and eventual career choice (Denissen, Zarrett, & Eccles, 2007; Valentine, DuBois, & Cooper, 2004; Whitesell et al., 2009). Children with high social self-esteem are consistently better-liked by classmates (Jacobs et al., 2002). And as we saw in Chapter 9, sense of athletic competence is positively associated with investment in and performance at sports.

A profile of low self-esteem in all areas is linked to anxiety, depression, and increasing antisocial behavior (DuBois et al., 1999; Kim & Cicchetti, 2006; Robins et al., 2001). What social influences might lead self-esteem to be high for some children and low for others?

Culture. Cultural forces profoundly affect self-esteem. An especially strong emphasis on social comparison in school may explain why Chinese and Japanese children, despite their higher academic achievement, score lower than U.S. children in self-esteem—a difference that widens with age (Harter, 2006; Hawkins, 1994; Twenge & Crocker, 2002). In Asian classrooms, competition is tough and achievement pressure is high. At the same time, because their culture values social harmony, Asian children tend to be reserved about judging themselves positively but generous in their praise of others (Falbo et al., 1997).

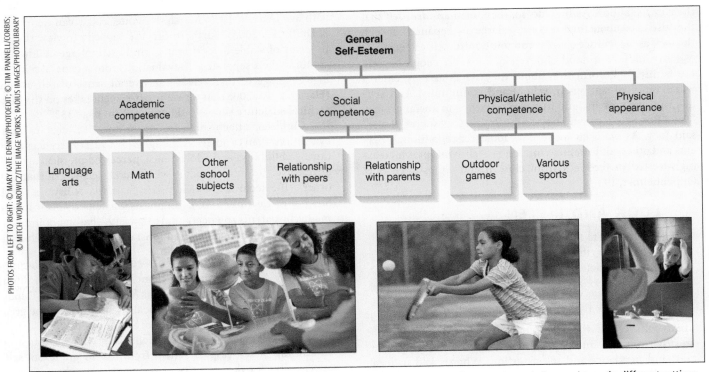

FIGURE 10.1 **Hierarchical structure of self-esteem in the mid-elementary school years.** From their experiences in different settings, children form at least four separate self-esteems: academic competence, social competence, physical/athletic competence, and physical appearance. These differentiate into additional self-evaluations and combine to form a general sense of self-esteem.

Gender-stereotyped expectations also affect self-esteem. In one study, the more 5- to 8-year-old girls talked with friends about the way people look, watched TV shows focusing on physical appearance, and perceived their friends as valuing thinness, the greater their dissatisfaction with their physical self and the lower their overall self-esteem a year later (Dohnt & Tiggemann, 2006). In academic self-judgments, girls score higher in language arts self-esteem, whereas boys have higher math, science, and physical/athletic self-esteem—even when children of equal skill levels are compared (Fredricks & Eccles, 2002; Jacobs et al., 2002; Kurtz-Costes et al., 2008). At the same time, girls exceed boys in self-esteem dimensions of close friendship and social acceptance. And despite a widely held assumption that boys' overall self-worth is much higher than girls', the difference is slight (Marsh & Ayotte, 2003; Young & Mroczek, 2003). Girls may think less well of themselves because they internalize this negative cultural message.

Compared with their Caucasian agemates, African-American children tend to have slightly higher self-esteem, possibly because of warm extended families and a stronger sense of ethnic pride (Gray-Little & Hafdahl, 2000). Finally, children and adolescents who attend schools or live in neighborhoods where their SES and ethnic groups are well-represented feel a stronger sense of belonging and have fewer self-esteem problems (Gray-Little & Carels, 1997).

An 11-year-old performs a traditional African dance at a community Kwanzaa celebration. A stronger sense of ethnic pride may be partly responsible for African-American children's higher self-esteem relative to their Caucasian agemates.

Child-Rearing Practices. Children whose parents use an *authoritative* child-rearing style (see Chapter 8) feel especially good about themselves (Lindsey et al., 2008; Wilkinson, 2004). Warm, positive parenting lets children know that they are accepted as competent and worthwhile. And firm but appropriate expectations, backed up with explanations, help them evaluate their own behavior against reasonable standards.

Controlling parents—those who too often help or make decisions for their child—communicate a sense of inadequacy to children. Having parents who are repeatedly disapproving and insulting is also linked to low self-esteem (Kernis, 2002; Pomerantz & Eaton, 2000). Children subjected to such parenting need constant reassurance, and many rely heavily on peers to affirm their self-worth—a risk factor for adjustment difficulties, including aggression and antisocial behavior (Donnellan et al., 2005). In contrast, indulgent parenting is correlated with unrealistically high self-esteem. These children tend to lash out at challenges to their overblown self-images and, thus, are also likely to be hostile and aggressive (Hughes, Cavell, & Grossman, 1997; Thomaes et al., 2008).

American cultural values have increasingly emphasized a focus on the self that may lead parents to indulge children and boost their self-esteem too much. The self-esteem of U.S. youths rose sharply from the 1970s to the 1990s—a period in which much popular parenting literature advised promoting children's self-esteem (Twenge & Campbell, 2001). Yet compared with previous generations, American youths are achieving less well and displaying more antisocial behavior and other adjustment problems (Berk, 2005). Research confirms that children do not benefit from compliments ("You're terrific") that have no basis in real accomplishment (Damon, 1995). Rather, the best way to foster a positive, secure self-image is to encourage children to strive for worthwhile goals. Over time, a bidirectional relationship emerges: Achievement fosters self-esteem, which contributes to further effort and gains in performance (Gest, Domitrovich, & Welsh, 2005; Marsh et al., 2005).

What can adults do to promote, and to avoid undermining, this mutually supportive relationship between motivation and self-esteem? Some answers come from research on the precise content of adults' messages to children in achievement situations.

Achievement-Related Attributions. *Attributions* are our common, everyday explanations for the causes of behavior—our answers to the question, "Why did I or another person do that?" Notice how Joey, in talking about the spelling bee at the beginning of this chapter, attributes his disappointing performance to *luck* (Belinda got all the easy words) and his usual success to *ability* (he *knows* he's a better speller than Belinda). Joey also appreciates that *effort* matters: "I knocked myself out studying those spelling lists."

Cognitive development permits school-age children to separate all these variables in explaining performance (Dweck, 2002). Those who are high in academic self-esteem and motivation make **mastery-oriented attributions,** crediting their successes to ability—a characteristic they can improve through trying hard and can count on when facing new challenges. And they attribute failure to factors that can be changed or controlled, such as insufficient effort or a very difficult task (Heyman & Dweck, 1998). Whether these children succeed or fail, they take an industrious, persistent approach to learning.

In contrast, children who develop **learned helplessness** attribute their failures, not their successes, to ability. When they succeed, they conclude that external factors, such as luck, are responsible. Unlike their mastery-oriented counterparts, they believe that ability is fixed and cannot be improved by trying hard (Cain & Dweck, 1995). When a task is difficult, these

A 7-year-old in a woodworking class seeks additional information on how to assemble a jewelry box. Using this mastery-oriented, effortful approach to overcoming obstacles, his performance will improve over time.

children experience an anxious loss of control—in Erikson's terms, a pervasive sense of inferiority. They give up without really trying.

Children's attributions affect their goals. Mastery-oriented children seek information on how best to increase their ability through effort. Hence, their performance improves over time (Blackwell, Trzesniewski, & Dweck, 2007). In contrast, learned-helpless children focus on obtaining positive and avoiding negative evaluations of their fragile sense of ability. Over time, their ability no longer predicts how well they do (Pomerantz & Saxon, 2001). Because they fail to connect effort with success, learned-helpless children do not develop the metacognitive and self-regulatory skills necessary for high achievement (see Chapter 9). Lack of effective learning strategies, reduced persistence, and a sense of loss of control sustain one another in a vicious cycle (Chan & Moore, 2006).

Influences on Achievement-Related Attributions. What accounts for the different attributions of mastery-oriented and learned-helpless children? Adult communication plays a key role (Pomerantz & Dong, 2006.) Children with a learned-helpless style often have parents who believe that their child is not very capable and must work harder than others to succeed. When the child fails, the parent might say, "You can't do that, can you? It's OK if you quit." When the child succeeds, the parent might offer feedback that evaluates the child's traits ("You're so smart"). Such trait statements—even when positive—encourage children to adopt a fixed view of ability, which leads them to question their competence in the face of challenges (Mueller & Dweck, 1998).

Teachers' messages also affect children's attributions. Teachers who attribute children's failures to insufficient effort, who are caring and helpful, and who emphasize learning over getting good grades tend to have mastery-oriented students (Anderman et al., 2001; Natale et al., 2009). In contrast, students with unsupportive teachers often regard their performance as externally controlled (by teachers or by luck), withdraw from learning activities, and decline in achievement—outcomes that lead children to doubt their ability (Skinner, Zimmer-Gembeck, & Connell, 1998).

For some children, performance is especially likely to be undermined by adult feedback. Despite their higher achievement, girls more often than boys blame poor performance on lack of ability. When girls do not do well, they tend to receive messages from teachers and parents that their ability is at fault, and negative stereotypes (for example, that girls are weak at math) undermine their interest and effort (Bleeker & Jacobs, 2004; Cole et al., 1999). And as Chapter 9 revealed, low-SES ethnic minority students often receive less favorable feedback from teachers, especially when assigned to homogeneous groups of poorly achieving students—conditions that result in a drop in academic self-esteem and achievement (Harris & Graham, 2007).

LOOK AND LISTEN

Observe a school-age child working on a challenging homework assignment under the guidance of a parent or other adult. What features of the adult's communication likely foster mastery-oriented attributions? How about learned helplessness? Explain. ●

Finally, cultural values affect the likelihood that children will develop learned helplessness. Asian parents and teachers are more likely than their American counterparts to view effort as key to success and as a moral responsibility—messages they transmit to children (Mok, Kennedy, & Moore, 2011; Pomerantz, Ng, & Wang, 2008). Asians also attend more to failure than to success because failure indicates where corrective action is needed. Americans, in contrast, focus more on success because it enhances self-esteem. Observations of U.S. and Chinese mothers' responses to their fourth and fifth graders' puzzle solutions revealed that the U.S. mothers offered more praise after success, whereas the Chinese mothers more often pointed out the child's inadequate performance. And Chinese mothers made more task-relevant statements aimed at ensuring that children exerted sufficient effort ("You concentrated on it": "You got only 6 out of 12") (see Figure 10.2) (Ng, Pomerantz, & Lam, 2007). When children continued with the task after mothers left the room, the Chinese children showed greater gains in performance.

Fostering a Mastery-Oriented Approach. Attribution research suggests that well-intended messages from adults sometimes undermine children's competence. An intervention called *attribution retraining* encourages learned-helpless children to believe that they can overcome failure by exerting more effort. Children are given tasks difficult enough that they will experience some failure, followed by repeated feedback that helps them revise their attributions: "You can do it if you try harder." After they succeed, children receive additional feedback—"You're really good at this" or "You really tried hard on that one"—so that they attribute their success to both ability and effort, not chance. Another approach is to encourage low-effort students to focus less on grades and more on mastering a task

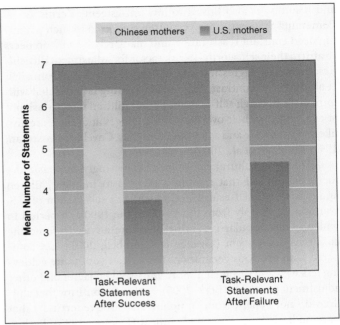

FIGURE 10.2 Chinese and U.S. mothers' task-relevant statements in response to their fourth-grade child's success or failure on puzzle tasks. Observations revealed that regardless of whether their child had just succeeded or failed, Chinese mothers were more likely than U.S. mothers to make task-relevant statements aimed at ensuring that the child exerted high effort. (Adapted from Ng, Pomerantz, & Lam, 2007.)

for individual improvement (Hilt, 2004; Yeh, 2010). Instruction in effective strategies and self-regulation is also vital, to compensate for development lost in this area and to ensure that renewed effort pays off (Wigfield et al., 2006).

Attribution retraining is best begun early, before children's views of themselves become hard to change. An even better approach is to prevent learned helplessness, using the strategies summarized in Applying What We Know on the following page.

ASK YOURSELF

REVIEW How does level of self-esteem change in middle childhood, and what accounts for these changes?

CONNECT What cognitive changes, described in Chapter 9, support the transition to a self-concept emphasizing competencies, personality traits, and social comparisons?

APPLY Should parents promote children's self-esteem by telling them they're "smart" or "wonderful"? Are children harmed if they do not feel good about everything they do? Why or why not?

REFLECT Recall your own attributions for academic successes and failures when you were in elementary school. What are those attributions like now? What messages from others may have contributed to your attributions?

Applying What We Know

Fostering a Mastery-Oriented Approach to Learning

Strategy	Description
Provision of tasks	Select tasks that are meaningful, responsive to a diversity of student interests, and appropriately matched to current competence so that the child is challenged but not overwhelmed.
Parent and teacher encouragement	Communicate warmth, confidence in the child's abilities, the value of achievement, and the importance of effort in success. Model high effort in overcoming failure. (For teachers) Communicate often with parents, suggesting ways to foster children's effort and progress. (For parents) Monitor schoolwork; provide scaffolded assistance that promotes knowledge of effective strategies and self-regulation.
Performance evaluations	Make evaluations private; avoid publicizing success or failure through wall posters, stars, privileges for "smart" children, or prizes for "best" performance. Emphasize individual progress and self-improvement.
School environment	Offer small classes, which permit teachers to provide individualized support for mastery. Provide for cooperative learning and peer tutoring, in which children assist one another; avoid ability grouping, which makes evaluations of children's progress public. Accommodate individual and cultural differences in learning styles. Create an atmosphere that sends a clear message that all students can learn.

Sources: Hilt, 2004; Wigfield et al., 2006.

Emotional Development

Greater self-awareness and social sensitivity support gains in emotional competence in middle childhood. Changes take place in experience of self-conscious emotions, emotional understanding, and emotional self-regulation.

Self-Conscious Emotions

In middle childhood, the self-conscious emotions of pride and guilt become clearly governed by personal responsibility. Children experience pride in a new accomplishment and guilt over a transgression, even when no adult is present (Harter & Whitesell, 1989). Also, children no longer report guilt for any mishap, as they did earlier, but only for intentional wrongdoing, such as ignoring responsibilities, cheating, or lying (Ferguson, Stegge, & Damhuis, 1991).

Pride motivates children to take on further challenges, whereas guilt prompts them to make amends and to strive for self-improvement. But in Chapter 8 we noted that excessive guilt is linked to depressive symptoms. And harsh, insensitive reprimands from adults ("Everyone else can do it! Why can't you?") can lead to intense shame, which is particularly destructive, yielding both internalizing and externalizing problems (see page 260).

Emotional Understanding

School-age children's understanding of mental activity means that, unlike preschoolers, they are likely to explain emotion by referring to internal states, such as happy or sad thoughts, rather than to external events (Flavell, Flavell, & Green, 2001). Also, between ages 6 and 12, children become more aware of circumstances likely to spark mixed emotions, each of which may be positive or negative and may differ in intensity (Larsen, To, & Fireman, 2007; Pons et al., 2003). For example, recalling the birthday present he received from his grandmother, Joey reflected, "I was very happy that I got something but a little sad that I didn't get just what I wanted."

Appreciating mixed emotions helps children realize that people's expressions may not reflect their true feelings (Misailidi, 2006; Saarni, 1999). It also fosters awareness of self-conscious emotions. For example, between ages 6 and 7, children improve sharply in ability to distinguish pride from happiness and surprise (Tracy, Robins, & Lagattuta, 2005). And 8- and 9-year-olds understand that pride combines two sources of happiness—joy in accomplishment and joy that a significant person recognized that accomplishment (Harter, 1999). Furthermore, children of this age can reconcile contradictory facial and situational cues in figuring out another's feelings (see page 258 in Chapter 8).

As with self-understanding, gains in emotional understanding are supported by cognitive development and social experiences, especially adults' sensitivity to children's feelings and willingness to discuss emotions. Together, these factors lead to a rise in empathy as well. As children move closer to adolescence, advances in perspective taking permit an empathic response not just to people's immediate distress but also to their general life condition (Hoffman, 2000). As Joey and Lizzie imagined how people who are chronically ill or hungry feel and

Detroit-area schoolchildren prepare meal packages for families in need. Gains in emotional understanding and perspective taking enable children to expand their empathic responding to include people's general life condition.

evoked those emotions in themselves, they gave part of their allowance to charity and joined in fundraising projects through school, community center, and scouting.

Emotional Self-Regulation

Rapid gains in emotional self-regulation occur in middle childhood. As children engage in social comparison and care more about peer approval, they must learn to manage negative emotion that threatens their self-esteem.

By age 10, most children shift adaptively between two general strategies for managing emotion. In **problem-centered coping,** they appraise the situation as changeable, identify the difficulty, and decide what to do about it. If problem solving does not work, they engage in **emotion-centered coping,** which is internal, private, and aimed at controlling distress when little can be done about an outcome (Kliewer, Fearnow, & Miller, 1996; Lazarus & Lazarus, 1994). For example, when faced with an anxiety-provoking test or an angry friend, older school-age children view problem solving and seeking social support as the best strategies. But when outcomes are beyond their control—for example, after receiving a bad grade—they opt for distraction or try to redefine the situation: "Things could be worse. There'll be another test." School-age children's improved ability to appraise situations and reflect on thoughts and feelings means that, compared with preschoolers, they more often use these internal strategies to manage emotion (Brenner & Salovey, 1997).

Furthermore, through interacting with parents, teachers, and peers, school-age children become more knowledgeable about socially approved ways to display negative emotion. They increasingly prefer verbal strategies ("Please stop pushing and wait your turn") to crying, sulking, or aggression (Shipman et al., 2003). Young school-age children justify these more mature displays of emotion by mentioning avoidance of punishment or adult approval but, by third grade, they begin to emphasize concern for others' feelings. Children with this awareness are rated as especially helpful, cooperative, and socially responsive

by teachers and as better-liked by peers (Garner, 1996; McDowell & Parke, 2000).

When emotional self-regulation has developed well, school-age children acquire a sense of *emotional self-efficacy*—a feeling of being in control of their emotional experience (Saarni, 2000; Thompson & Goodman, 2010). This fosters a favorable self-image and an optimistic outlook, which further help children face emotional challenges. As at younger ages, school-age children whose parents respond sensitively and helpfully when the child is distressed are emotionally well-regulated—generally upbeat in mood and also empathic and prosocial. In contrast, poorly regulated children often experience hostile, dismissive parental reactions to distress (Davidov & Grusec, 2006; Zeman, Shipman, & Suveg, 2002). These children are overwhelmed by negative emotion, a response that interferes with empathy and prosocial behavior.

Moral Development

Recall from Chapter 8 that preschoolers pick up many morally relevant behaviors through modeling and reinforcement. By middle childhood, they have had time to internalize rules for good conduct: "It's good to help others in trouble" or "It's wrong to take something that doesn't belong to you." This change leads children to become considerably more independent and trustworthy.

In Chapter 8, we also saw that children do not just copy their morality from others. As the cognitive-developmental approach emphasizes, they actively think about right and wrong. An expanding social world, the capacity to consider more information when reasoning, and perspective taking lead moral understanding to advance greatly in middle childhood.

Moral and Social-Conventional Understanding

During the school years, children construct a flexible appreciation of moral rules. By age 7 to 8, they no longer say truth telling is always good and lying is always bad but also consider prosocial and antisocial intentions. They evaluate certain types of truthfulness very negatively—for example, blunt statements, particularly when made in public contexts where they are especially likely to have negative social consequences (telling a classmate that you don't like her drawing) (Bussey, 1999; Ma et al., 2011). And although both Chinese and Canadian schoolchildren consider lying about antisocial acts "very naughty," Chinese children—influenced by collectivist values—more often rate lying favorably when the intention is modesty, as when a student who has thoughtfully picked up litter from the playground says, "I didn't do it" (Lee et al., 1997, 2001). Similarly, Chinese children are more likely to favor lying to support the group at the expense of the individual (saying you're sick so, as a poor singer, you won't harm your class's chances of winning a singing competition). In contrast, Canadian children more often favor lying to support the individual at the expense of the group (claiming that a friend who is a poor speller is actually a

This 10-year-old understands the moral implications of observing social conventions, such as expressing respect for his country's flag. He also grasps that flag burning might be justifiable as a form of freedom of expression in another context—a country that treats its citizens unfairly.

good speller because he wants to participate in a spelling competition) (Fu et al., 2007).

As children's ideas about justice take into account an increasing number of variables, they clarify and link moral imperatives and social conventions. School-age children, for example, distinguish social conventions with a clear *purpose* (not running in school hallways to prevent injuries) from ones with no obvious justification (crossing a "forbidden" line on the playground). They regard violations of purposeful social conventions as closer to moral transgressions (Buchanan-Barrow & Barrett, 1998). With age, they also realize that people's *intentions* and the *contexts* of their actions affect the moral implications of violating a social convention. In one study, 8- to 10-year-olds stated that because of a flag's symbolic value, burning it to express disapproval of a country or to start a cooking fire is worse than burning it accidentally. But they recognized that flag burning is a form of freedom of expression, and most agreed that it would be acceptable in a country that treated its citizens unfairly (Helwig & Prencipe, 1999).

Children in Western and non-Western cultures reason similarly about moral and social-conventional concerns (Neff & Helwig, 2002; Nucci, 2002, 2005, 2008). When a directive is fair and caring, such as telling children to stop fighting or to share candy, school-age children view it as right, regardless of who states it—a principal, a teacher, or a child with no authority. In contrast, even in Korean culture, which places a high value on deference to authority, 7- to 11-year-olds evaluate negatively a teacher's or principal's order to engage in immoral acts, such as stealing or refusing to share—a response that strengthens with age (Kim, 1998; Kim & Turiel, 1996). In sum, children everywhere seem to realize that higher principles, independent of rule and authority, must prevail when people's personal rights and welfare are at stake.

Understanding Individual Rights

When children challenge adult authority, they typically do so within the personal domain. As their grasp of moral imperatives

and social conventions strengthens, so does their conviction that certain choices, such as hairstyle, friends, and leisure activities, are up to the individual. A Colombian child illustrated this passionate defense of personal control when asked if a teacher had the right to tell a student where to sit during circle time. In the absence of a moral reason from the teacher, the child declared, "She should be able to sit wherever she wants" (Ardila-Rey & Killen, 2001, p. 249).

Notions of personal choice, in turn, enhance children's moral understanding. As early as age 6, children view freedom of speech and religion as individual rights, even if laws exist that deny those rights (Helwig, 2006). And they regard laws that discriminate against individuals—for example, denying certain people access to medical care or education—as wrong and worthy of violating (Helwig & Jasiobedzka, 2001). In justifying their responses, children appeal to personal privileges and, by the end of middle childhood, to the importance of individual rights for maintaining a fair society.

At the same time, older school-age children place limits on individual choice, depending on circumstances. While they believe that nonacademic matters (such as where to go on field trips) are best decided democratically, they regard the academic curriculum as the province of teachers, based on teachers' superior ability to make such choices (Helwig & Kim, 1999). And fourth graders faced with conflicting moral and personal concerns—such as whether or not to befriend a classmate of a different race or gender—typically decide in favor of kindness and fairness (Killen et al., 2002). Partly for this reason, as we will see next, prejudice usually declines during middle childhood.

Understanding Diversity and Inequality

By the early school years, children associate power and privilege with white people and poverty and inferior status with people of color. They do not necessarily acquire these views directly from parents or friends, whose attitudes are often different from their own (Aboud & Doyle, 1996). Rather, children seem to pick up prevailing societal attitudes from implicit messages in the media and elsewhere in their environments. Powerful sources include social contexts that present a world sorted into groups, such as racial and ethnic segregation in schools and communities.

In-Group and Out-Group Biases: Development of Prejudice. Studies in diverse Western nations confirm that by age 5 to 6, white children generally evaluate their own racial group favorably and other racial groups less favorably or negatively. *In-group favoritism* emerges first; children simply prefer their own group, generalizing from self to similar others (Bennett et al., 2004; Nesdale et al., 2004). And the ease with which a trivial group label supplied by an adult can induce in-group favoritism is striking. In one study, Caucasian-American 5-year-olds were told that they were members of a group based on T-shirt color. Although no information was provided about group status and the children never met any group members, they still displayed vigorous in-group favoritism

(Dunham, Baron, & Carey, 2011). When shown photos of unfamiliar agemates wearing either an in-group or an out-group shirt, the children claimed to like members of their own group better, gave them more resources, and engaged in positively biased recall of group members' behavior.

Out-group prejudice requires a more challenging social comparison between in-group and out-group. But it does not take long for white children to acquire negative attitudes toward ethnic minority out-groups when such attitudes are encouraged by circumstances in their environments. When white Canadian 4- to 7-year-olds living in a white community and attending nearly all-white schools sorted positive and negative adjectives into boxes labeled as belonging to a white child and a black child, out-group prejudice emerged at age 5. Unfortunately, many minority children show a reverse pattern: *out-group favoritism,* in which they assign positive characteristics to the privileged white majority and negative characteristics to their own group (Averhart & Bigler, 1997; Corenblum, 2003).

But recall that with age, children pay more attention to inner traits. The capacity to classify the social world in multiple ways enables school-age children to understand that people who look different need not think, feel, or act differently (Aboud, 2008). Consequently, voicing of negative attitudes toward minorities declines. After age 7 to 8, both majority and minority children express in-group favoritism, and white children's prejudice against out-group members often weakens (Nesdale et al., 2005; Ruble et al., 2004).

Yet even in children aware of the injustice of discrimination, prejudice can operate unintentionally and without awareness—as it does in many white adults (Dunham, Baron, & Banaji, 2006). Consider a study in which German and Dutch 9- to 15-year-olds were presented with pictures of Turkish and Moroccan immigrants, the largest ethnic minority groups in the two countries. Each was followed by a target picture with either emotionally positive or negative content, which the participants were asked to categorize quickly as either positive or negative by pressing a key (Degner & Wentura, 2010). With age, the participants responded more rapidly when negative rather than positive target pictures followed the immigrant images. Negative affect toward the ethnic minorities "spilled over" to the target pictures—evidence for automatic prejudice.

Findings like these raise the question of whether the decline in overt racial bias during middle childhood is a true decrease or whether it reflects older children's growing awareness of widely held standards that deem prejudice to be inappropriate—or both. Around age 10, white children start to avoid talking about race to appear unbiased, just as many adults do (Apfelbaum et al., 2008). At least to some degree, then, older school-age children's desire to present themselves in a socially acceptable light may contribute to reduced expressions of out-group prejudice.

Nevertheless, the extent to which children hold racial and ethnic biases varies, depending on the following personal and situational factors:

- *A fixed view of personality traits.* Children who believe that people's personality traits are fixed rather than change-

able often judge others as either "good" or "bad." Ignoring motives and circumstances, they readily form prejudices on the basis of limited information. For example, they might infer that "a new child at school who tells a lie to get other kids to like her" is simply a bad kid (Levy & Dweck, 1999).

- *Overly high self-esteem.* Children (and adults) with very high self-esteem are more likely to hold racial and ethnic prejudices (Baumeister et al., 2003; Bigler, Brown, & Markell, 2001). These individuals seem to belittle disadvantaged people or groups to justify their own extremely favorable, yet insecure, self-evaluations. Furthermore, children who say their own ethnicity makes them feel especially "good"—and thus perhaps socially superior—are more likely to display in-group favoritism and out-group prejudice (Pfeifer et al., 2007).

- *A social world in which people are sorted into groups.* The more adults highlight group distinctions and the less interracial contact children experience in their families, schools, and communities, the more likely white children will express in-group favoritism and out-group prejudice (Killen et al., 2010).

Reducing Prejudice. Research confirms that an effective way to reduce prejudice is through intergroup contact, in which racially and ethnically different children have equal status, work toward common goals, and become personally acquainted, and in which parents and teachers expect them to engage in such interaction. Children assigned to cooperative learning groups with peers of diverse backgrounds show low levels of prejudice in their expressions of likability and in their behavior. For example, they form more cross-race friendships (Pettigrew & Tropp, 2006). Sharing thoughts and feelings with close, cross-race friends, in turn, reduces even subtle, unintentional prejudices (Turner, Hewstone, & Voci, 2007). But these positive effects seem not to generalize to out-group members who are not part of these learning teams.

THE STAR-LEDGER/STEVE HOCKSTEIN/THE IMAGE WORKS

Third graders perform a traditional Chinese dance at their culturally diverse school. Long-term contact and collaboration with members of other ethnic groups reduces prejudice.

Long-term contact and collaboration among neighborhood, school, and community groups may be the best way to reduce prejudice (Rutland, Killen, & Abrams, 2010). Classrooms that expose children to ethnic diversity, teach them to value those differences, directly address the damage caused by prejudice, and encourage perspective taking and empathy both prevent children from forming negative biases and reduce already acquired biases (Dweck, 2009).

Finally, inducing children to view others' traits as changeable, by discussing with them the many possible influences on those traits, is helpful. The more children believe that people can change their personalities, the more they report liking and perceiving themselves as similar to members of disadvantaged out-groups. Furthermore, children who believe in the changeability of human attributes spend more time volunteering to help the needy (Karafantis & Levy, 2004). Volunteering may, in turn, promote a changeable view of others by helping children take the perspective of the underprivileged and appreciate the social conditions that lead to disadvantage.

ASK YOURSELF

REVIEW How does emotional self-regulation improve in middle childhood? What implications do these changes have for children's self-esteem?

CONNECT Cite examples of how older children's capacity to take more information into account enhances their emotional and moral understanding.

APPLY Ten-year-old Marla says her classmate Bernadette will never get good grades because she's lazy. Jane believes that Bernadette tries but can't concentrate because her parents are divorcing. Why is Marla more likely than Jane to develop prejudices?

REFLECT Did you attend an integrated elementary school? Why is school integration vital for reducing racial and ethnic prejudice?

Peer Relations

In middle childhood, the society of peers becomes an increasingly important context for development. Peer contact, as we have seen, contributes to perspective taking and understanding of self and others. These developments, in turn, enhance peer interaction. Compared with preschoolers, school-age children resolve conflicts more effectively, using persuasion and compromise (Mayeux & Cillessen, 2003). Sharing, helping, and other prosocial acts also increase. In line with these changes, aggression declines. But the drop is greatest for physical attacks (Côté et al., 2007). As we will see, verbal and relational aggression continue as children form peer groups.

Peer Groups

TAKE A MOMENT... Watch children in the schoolyard or neighborhood, and notice how often they gather in groups of three to a dozen or more. In what ways are members of the same group noticeably alike?

By the end of middle childhood, children display a strong desire for group belonging. They form **peer groups,** collectives that generate unique values and standards for behavior and a social structure of leaders and followers. Peer groups organize on the basis of proximity (being in the same classroom) and similarity in sex, ethnicity, academic achievement, popularity, and aggression (Rubin, Bukowski, & Parker, 2006).

The practices of these informal groups lead to a "peer culture" that typically involves a specialized vocabulary, dress code, and place to "hang out." As children develop these exclusive associations, the codes of dress and behavior that grow out of them become more broadly influential. Schoolmates who deviate—by "kissing up" to teachers, wearing the wrong kind of shirt or shoes, or tattling on classmates—are often rebuffed, becoming targets of critical glances and comments. These customs bind peers together, creating a sense of group identity. Within the group, children acquire many social skills—cooperation, leadership, followership, and loyalty to collective goals.

Most school-age children believe a group is wrong to exclude a peer (Killen, Crystal, & Watanabe, 2002). Nevertheless, children do exclude, often using relationally aggressive tactics. Peer groups—at the instigation of their leaders, who can be skillfully aggressive—frequently oust no longer "respected" children. Some of these castouts, whose own previous behavior toward outsiders reduces their chances of being included elsewhere, turn to other low-status peers with poor social skills (Farmer et al., 2010; Werner & Crick, 2004). Socially anxious

DAVID ROTH/GETTY IMAGES/TAXI

These boys have probably established a peer-group structure of leaders and followers as they gather for joint activities. Their relaxed body language and similar way of dressing suggest a strong sense of group belonging.

children, when ousted, often become increasingly peer-avoidant and thus more isolated (Buhs, Ladd, & Herald-Brown, 2010). In either case, opportunities to acquire socially competent behavior diminish. As excluded children's class participation declines, their academic achievement suffers.

School-age children's desire for group membership can also be satisfied through formal group ties such as scouting, 4-H, and religious youth groups. Adult involvement holds in check the negative behaviors associated with children's informal peer groups. And through working on joint projects and helping in their communities, children gain in social and moral maturity (Vandell & Shumow, 1999).

Friendships

Whereas peer groups provide children with insight into larger social structures, friendships contribute to the development of trust and sensitivity. During the school years, friendship becomes more complex and psychologically based. Consider the following 8-year-old's ideas:

> *Why is Shelly your best friend?* Because she helps me when I'm sad, and she shares. . . . *What makes Shelly so special?* I've known her longer, I sit next to her and got to know her better. . . . *How come you like Shelly better than anyone else?* She's done the most for me. She never disagrees, she never eats in front of me, she never walks away when I'm crying, and she helps me with my homework. . . . *How do you get someone to like you?* . . . If you're nice to [your friends], they'll be nice to you. (Damon, 1988b, pp. 80–81)

As these responses show, friendship has become a mutually agreed-on relationship in which children like each other's personal qualities and respond to one another's needs and desires. And once a friendship forms, *trust* becomes its defining feature. School-age children state that a good friendship is based on acts of kindness that signify that each person can be counted on to support the other (Hartup & Abecassis, 2004). Consequently, older children regard violations of trust, such as not helping when others need help, breaking promises, and gossiping behind the other's back, as serious breaches of friendship.

LOOK AND LISTEN

Ask an 8- to 11-year-old to tell you what he or she looks for in a best friend. Is *trust* centrally important? Does the child mention personality traits, just as school-age children do in describing themselves? ●

Because of these features, school-age children's friendships are more selective. Whereas preschoolers say they have lots of friends, by age 8 or 9, children name only a handful of good friends. Girls, who demand greater closeness than boys, are more exclusive in their friendships (Markovits, Benenson, & Dolensky, 2001).

In addition, children tend to select friends similar to themselves in age, sex, ethnicity, and SES. Friends also resemble one another in personality (sociability, inattention/hyperactivity, aggression, depression), popularity, academic achievement,

School-age children tend to select friends who are similar to themselves in personality and academic achievement. And friendships are fairly stable: These fourth graders are likely to remain friends for at least a full school year.

prosocial behavior, and judgments (including biased perceptions) of other people (Hartup, 2006; Mariano & Harton, 2005). But friendship opportunities offered by children's environments also affect their choices. As noted earlier, in integrated classrooms with mixed-race collaborative learning groups, students form more cross-race friendships.

Over middle childhood, high-quality friendships remain fairly stable, with about 50 to 70 percent enduring over a school year, and some for several years (Berndt, 2004). But context is influential, with friendships spanning several situations—such as school, religious institution, and children of parents' friends— more likely to persist (Troutman & Fletcher, 2010). At the same time, stability increases with age as friendships become psychologically based and, therefore, higher in sharing thoughts and feelings, social support, and prosocial behavior.

School-age friends not only behave more prosocially but also disagree with each other more than nonfriends. At the same time, they use negotiation to resolve conflicts more often than nonfriends do. Friends seem to realize that close relationships can survive disagreements if friends are secure in their liking for each other (Hartup, 2006). Clearly, friendship serves as an important context in which children learn to tolerate criticism and resolve disputes.

Yet the impact of friendships on children's development depends on the nature of those friends. Children who bring kindness and compassion to their friendships strengthen each other's prosocial tendencies and form more lasting ties. When aggressive children make friends, the relationship is often riddled with hostile interaction and is at risk for breakup, especially when just one member of the pair is aggressive (Ellis & Zarbatany, 2007). Aggressive girls' friendships are high in exchange of private feelings but full of jealousy, conflict, and betrayal. Aggressive boys' friendships involve frequent expressions of anger, coercive statements, physical attacks, and enticements to rule-breaking behavior (Bagwell & Coie, 2004; Crick & Nelson, 2002; Werner & Crick, 2004). These findings indicate that the social problems of aggressive children operate within their closest peer ties.

Peer Acceptance

Peer acceptance refers to likability—the extent to which a child is viewed by a group of agemates, such as classmates, as a worthy social partner. Unlike friendship, likability is not a mutual relationship but a one-sided perspective, involving the group's view of an individual. Nevertheless, certain social skills that contribute to friendship also enhance peer acceptance. Better-accepted children tend to have more friends and more positive relationships with them (Lansford et al., 2006).

To assess peer acceptance, researchers usually use self-reports that measure *social preferences*—for example, asking children to identify classmates whom they "like very much" or "like very little" (Hymel et al., 2004). Another approach assesses *social prominence*—children's judgments of the peers most of their classmates admire. Only moderate correspondence exists between the classmates children identify as prominent (looked up to by many others) and those they say they personally prefer (Prinstein & Cillessen, 2003).

Children's self-reports yield four general categories of peer acceptance:

- **Popular children,** who get many positive votes (are well-liked)
- **Rejected children,** who get many negative votes (are disliked)
- **Controversial children,** who get a large number of positive and negative votes (are both liked and disliked)
- **Neglected children,** who are seldom mentioned, either positively or negatively

About two-thirds of students in a typical elementary school classroom fit one of these categories (Coie, Dodge, & Coppotelli, 1982). The remaining one-third, who do not receive extreme scores, are *average* in peer acceptance.

Peer acceptance is a powerful predictor of psychological adjustment. Rejected children, especially, are anxious, unhappy, disruptive, and low in self-esteem. Both teachers and parents rate them as having a wide range of emotional and social problems. Peer rejection in middle childhood is also strongly associated with poor school performance, absenteeism, dropping out, substance use, depression, antisocial behavior, and delinquency in adolescence and with criminality in early adulthood (Ladd, 2005; Laird et al., 2001; Rubin, Bukowski, & Parker, 2006).

However, earlier influences—children's characteristics combined with parenting practices—may largely explain the link between peer acceptance and adjustment. School-age children with peer-relationship problems are more likely to have weak emotion regulation skills and to have experienced family stress due to low income, insensitive child rearing, and coercive discipline (Cowan & Cowan, 2004; Trentacosta & Shaw, 2009). Nevertheless, peer rejection adds to the risk of maladjustment, beyond rejected children's maladaptive behavioral styles (Sturaro et al., 2011).

Determinants of Peer Acceptance. Why is one child liked while another is rejected? A wealth of research reveals that social behavior plays a powerful role.

Popular Children. Two subtypes of popular children exist. The majority are **popular-prosocial children,** who combine academic and social competence, performing well in school and communicating with peers in sensitive, friendly, and cooperative ways (Cillessen & Bellmore, 2004). A smaller number are admired for their socially adept yet belligerent behavior. These **popular-antisocial children** include "tough" boys—athletically skilled but poor students who cause trouble and defy adult authority—and relationally aggressive boys and girls who enhance their own status by ignoring, excluding, and spreading rumors about other children (Rodkin et al., 2000; Rose, Swenson, & Waller, 2004; Vaillancourt & Hymel, 2006).

Although peer admiration gives popular-antisocial children some protection against lasting adjustment difficulties, their antisocial acts require intervention (Prinstein & La Greca, 2004; Rodkin et al., 2006). With age, peers like these high-status, aggressive youths less and less, eventually condemning their nasty tactics and rejecting them.

Rejected Children. Rejected children display a wide range of negative social behaviors. The largest subtype, **rejected-aggressive children,** show high rates of conflict, physical and relational aggression, and hyperactive, inattentive, and impulsive behavior. They are usually deficient in perspective taking, misinterpreting the innocent behaviors of peers as hostile and to blaming others for their social difficulties (Crick, Casas, & Nelson, 2002; Dodge, Coie, & Lynam, 2006; Hoza et al., 2005). Compared with popular-aggressive children, they are more extremely antagonistic. In contrast, **rejected-withdrawn children** are passive and socially awkward. These timid children are overwhelmed by social anxiety, hold negative expectations for treatment by peers, and worry about being scorned and attacked (Hart et al., 2000; Rubin, Bowker, & Gazelle, 2010; Troop-Gordon & Asher, 2005).

Rejected children are excluded by peers as early as kindergarten. Soon their classroom participation declines, their feelings of loneliness rise, their academic achievement falters, and they want to avoid school (Buhs, Ladd, & Herald-Brown, 2010; Gooren et al., 2011). Most have few friends, and some have none—a circumstance that predicts severe adjustment difficulties (Ladd et al., 2011; Pedersen et al., 2007).

Both types of rejected children are at risk for peer harassment. But as the Biology and Environment box on page 342 reveals, rejected-aggressive children also act as bullies, and rejected-withdrawn children are especially likely to be victimized.

LOOK AND LISTEN

Contact a nearby elementary school or a school district to find out what practices are in place to prevent bullying. Inquire about a written antibullying policy, and request a copy. ●

Controversial and Neglected Children. Consistent with the mixed peer opinion they engender, controversial children display a blend of positive and negative social behaviors. They are hostile and disruptive, but they also engage in positive, prosocial acts. Even though some peers dislike them, they have

Biology and Environment

Bullies and Their Victims

Follow the activities of aggressive children over a school day, and you will see that they reserve their hostilities for certain peers. A particularly destructive form of interaction is **peer victimization,** in which certain children become targets of verbal and physical attacks or other forms of abuse. What sustains these repeated assault–retreat cycles between pairs of children?

About 20 percent of children are bullies, while 25 percent are repeatedly victimized. Most bullies are boys who use both physically, verbally, and relationally aggressive tactics, but a considerable number of girls bombard vulnerable classmates with verbal and relational hostility (Cook et al., 2010). As bullies move into adolescence, gender harassment increases—powerful youths (more often boys) delivering insults of a sexual nature against weaker agemates, and heterosexual youths targeting sexual minority peers (Pepler et al., 2006). Furthermore, many youths amplify their attacks through electronic means. About 20 to 40 percent of youths have experienced "cyberbullying" through text messages, e-mail, chat rooms, or other electronic tools (Tokunaga, 2010). They often do not report it to parents or adults at school.

Many bullies are disliked because of their cruelty. But a substantial number are socially prominent youngsters, who are broadly admired for their physical attractiveness, leadership, or athletic abilities (Vaillancourt et al., 2010c). To preserve their high social status, bullies often target already peer-rejected children, whom classmates are unlikely to defend (Veenstra et al., 2010). This helps explain why peers rarely intervene to help victims, and why 20 to 30 percent of onlookers actually encourage bullies, even joining in (Salmivalli & Voeten, 2004).

Chronic victims tend to be passive when active behavior is expected. On the playground, they hang around chatting or wander on their own. When bullied, they give in, cry, and assume defensive postures (Boulton, 1999). Biologically based traits—an inhibited temperament and a frail physical appearance—contribute to victimization. But victims also have histories of resistant attachment, overly controlling child rearing, and maternal overprotection—parenting that prompts anxiety, low self-esteem, and dependency, resulting in a fearful demeanor that marks these children as vulnerable (Snyder et al., 2003). Victims' adjustment problems include depression, loneliness, poor school performance, unruly behavior, and school avoidance (Paul & Cillessen, 2003). And like persistent child abuse, victimization is linked to impaired production of cortisol, suggesting a disrupted physiological response to stress (Vaillancourt et al., 2010b).

Aggression and victimization are not polar opposites. One-third to one-half of victims are also aggressive. Occasionally, they retaliate against powerful bullies, who respond by abusing them again—a cycle that sustains their victim status (Kochenderfer-Ladd, 2003). Among rejected children, these bully/victims are the most despised. They often have histories of extremely maladaptive parenting, including child abuse. This combination of highly negative home and peer experiences places them at severe risk for maladjustment (Kowalski, Limber, & Agatston, 2008).

Interventions that change victimized children's negative opinions of themselves and that teach them to respond in nonreinforcing ways to their attackers are helpful. Another way to assist victimized children is to help them form and maintain a gratifying friendship. When children have a close friend to whom they can turn for

Some bullies are high-status youngsters, but many are disliked, or become so, because of their cruelty. And chronic victims are often easy targets—physically weak, passive, and inhibited.

help, bullying episodes usually end quickly. Anxious, withdrawn children with a close friend have fewer adjustment problems than those with no friends (Fox & Boulton, 2006; Laursen et al., 2007).

Although modifying victimized children's behavior can help, this does not mean they are to blame. The best way to reduce bullying is to change youth environments (including school, sports programs, recreation centers, and neighborhoods), promoting prosocial attitudes and behaviors. Effective approaches include developing school and community codes against bullying; teaching child bystanders to intervene; strengthening adult supervision of high-bullying areas in schools, such as hallways and schoolyard; enlisting parents' assistance in changing bullies' behaviors; and (if necessary) moving socially prominent bullies to another class or school (Kiriakidis & Kavoura, 2010; Vaillancourt et al., 2010a).

© ELLEN B. SENISI PHOTOGRAPHY

qualities that protect them from social exclusion. They have as many friends as popular children and are happy with their peer relationships (de Bruyn & Cillessen, 2006; Newcomb, Bukowski, & Pattee, 1993). But like their popular-antisocial and rejected-aggressive counterparts, they often bully others and engage in calculated relational aggression to sustain their dominance (DeRosier & Thomas, 2003; Putallaz et al., 2007).

Perhaps the most surprising finding is that neglected children, once thought to be in need of treatment, are usually well-adjusted. Although they engage in low rates of interaction, most are just as socially skilled as average children. They do not report feeling lonely or unhappy, and when they want to, they can break away from their usual pattern of playing alone, cooperating well with peers and forming positive, stable friendships (Ladd & Burgess, 1999; Ladd et al., 2011). Neglected, socially competent children remind us that an outgoing, gregarious personality style is not the only path to emotional well-being.

Helping Rejected Children. A variety of interventions exist to improve the peer relations and psychological adjustment of rejected children. Most involve coaching, modeling, and reinforcing positive social skills, such as how to initiate interaction with a peer, cooperate in play, and respond to another child with friendly emotion and approval. Several of these programs have produced lasting gains in social competence and peer acceptance (Asher & Rose, 1997; DeRosier, 2007). Combining social-skills training with other treatments increases their effectiveness. Rejected children are often poor students, whose low academic self-esteem magnifies negative reactions to teachers and classmates. Intensive academic tutoring improves both school achievement and social acceptance (O'Neill et al., 1997).

Still another approach focuses on training in perspective taking and in solving social problems. But many rejected-aggressive children are unaware of their poor social skills and do not take responsibility for their social failures (Mrug, Hoza, & Gerdes, 2001). Rejected-withdrawn children, in contrast, are likely to develop a *learned-helpless* approach to peer difficulties—concluding, after repeated rebuffs, that they will never be liked (Wichmann, Coplan, & Daniels, 2004). Both types of children need help attributing their peer difficulties to internal, changeable causes.

As rejected children gain in social skills, teachers must encourage peers to alter their negative opinions. Accepted children often selectively recall their negative acts while overlooking their positive ones (Mikami, Lerner, & Lun, 2010; Peets et al., 2007). Consequently, even in the face of contrary evidence, rejected children's negative reputations tend to persist. Teachers' praise and expressions of liking can modify peer judgments.

Finally, because rejected children's socially incompetent behaviors often originate in a poor fit between the child's temperament and parenting practices, interventions focusing on the child alone may not be sufficient (Bierman & Powers, 2009). Without interventions directed at improving the quality of parent–child interaction, rejected children may soon return to their old behavior patterns.

 # Gender Typing

Children's understanding of gender roles broadens in middle childhood, and their gender identities (views of themselves as relatively masculine or feminine) change as well. We will see that development differs for boys and girls, and it can vary considerably across cultures.

Gender-Stereotyped Beliefs

Research in many countries reveals that stereotyping of personality traits increases steadily in middle childhood, becoming adultlike around age 11 (Best, 2001; Heyman & Legare, 2004). For example, children regard "tough," "aggressive," "rational," and "dominant" as masculine and "gentle," "sympathetic," and "dependent" as feminine (Serbin, Powlishta, & Gulko, 1993).

Children derive these distinctions from observing sex differences in behavior as well as from adult treatment. When helping a child with a task, for example, parents (especially fathers) behave in a more mastery-oriented fashion with sons, setting higher standards, explaining concepts, and pointing out important features of tasks—particularly during gender-typed pursuits, such as science activities (Tenenbaum & Leaper, 2003; Tenenbaum et al., 2005). Furthermore, parents less often encourage girls to make their own decisions. And both parents and teachers more often praise boys for knowledge and accomplishment, girls for obedience (Good & Brophy, 2003; Leaper, Anderson, & Sanders, 1998; Pomerantz & Ruble, 1998).

Also in line with adult stereotypes, school-age children quickly figure out which academic subjects and skill areas are "masculine" and which are "feminine." They often regard reading, spelling, art, and music as more for girls and mathematics, athletics, and mechanical skills as more for boys (Cvencek, Meltzoff, & Greenwald, 2011; Eccles, Jacobs, & Harold, 1990). These attitudes influence children's preferences for and sense of competence at certain subjects. As we saw earlier (page 332), boys tend to feel more competent at math, science, and athletics, whereas girls feel more competent at language arts—gender differences still evident after controlling for actual performance.

An encouraging sign is that some gender-stereotyped beliefs about achievement may be changing. In several recent investigations carried out in Canada, France, and the United States, a majority of elementary and secondary students disagreed with the idea that math is a "masculine" subject (Martinot & Désert, 2007; Plante, Théoret, & Favreau, 2009; Rowley et al. 2007). And when Canadian students were given the option of rating math as a "feminine" subject (not offered in previous studies), an impressive number expressed the view that it is predominantly feminine. The overwhelming majority of these young people, however, continued to view language arts traditionally—as largely "feminine." And they still perceived girls to do better in language arts than in math.

Although school-age children are aware of many stereotypes, they also develop a more open-minded view of what males and females *can do* (Trautner et al., 2005). As with racial stereotypes (see page 338), the ability to classify flexibly contributes to this change. School-age children realize that a person's sex is not a certain predictor of his or her personality traits, activities, and behavior. Similarly, by the end of middle childhood, most children regard gender typing as socially rather than biologically influenced (Taylor, Rholdes, & Gelman, 2009).

Nevertheless, acknowledging that people *can* cross gender lines does not mean that children always *approve* of doing so. In one longitudinal study, between ages 7 and 13, children of both genders became more open-minded about girls being offered the same opportunities as boys. This increasing flexibility, however, was less pronounced among boys (Crouter et al., 2007). Furthermore, many school-age children take a harsh view of certain violations—boys playing with dolls and wearing girls' clothing, girls acting noisily and roughly. They are especially intolerant when boys engage in these "cross-gender" acts, which children regard as nearly as bad as moral transgressions (Blakemore, 2003; Levy, Taylor, & Gelman, 1995).

An 8-year-old launches the rocket she made in her school's Young Astronaut Club. Whereas school-age boys usually stick to "masculine" pursuits, girls experiment with a wider range of options.

Gender Identity and Behavior

From third to sixth grade, boys tend to strengthen their identification with "masculine" personality traits, whereas girls' identification with "feminine" traits declines. While still leaning toward the "feminine" side, girls are more *androgynous* than boys—more likely to describe themselves as having some "other-gender" characteristics (Serbin, Powlishta, & Gulko, 1993). And whereas boys usually stick to "masculine" pursuits, many girls experiment with a wider range of options—from cooking and sewing to sports and science fairs—and more often consider traditionally male future work roles, such as firefighter or astronomer (Liben & Bigler, 2002).

These changes are due to a mixture of cognitive and social forces. School-age children of both sexes are aware that society attaches greater prestige to "masculine" characteristics. For example, they rate "masculine" occupations as having higher status than "feminine" occupations (Liben, Bigler, & Krogh, 2001). And they more often regard a novel job (such as *clipster*, "a person who tests batteries") as higher in status and as appropriate "for both men and woman" when it is portrayed with a male worker than with a female worker (Liben, Bigler, & Krogh, 2001; Weisgram, Bigler, & Liben, 2010). Messages from adults and peers are also influential. In Chapter 8, we saw that parents (especially fathers) are far less tolerant when sons, as opposed to daughters, cross gender lines. Similarly, a tomboyish girl can make her way into boys' activities without losing the approval of her female peers, but a boy who engages in "feminine" pursuits is likely to be ridiculed and rejected.

As school-age children make social comparisons and characterize themselves in terms of stable dispositions, their gender identity expands to include the following self-evaluations, which greatly affect their adjustment:

- *Gender typicality*—the degree to which the child feels similar to others of the same gender. Although children need not be highly gender-typed to view themselves as gender-typical, their psychological well-being depends, to some degree, on feeling that they "fit in" with their same-sex peers (Egan & Perry, 2001).

- *Gender contentedness*—the degree to which the child feels comfortable with his or her gender assignment, which also promotes happiness.

- *Felt pressure to conform to gender roles*—the degree to which the child feels parents and peers disapprove of his or her gender-related traits. Because such pressure reduces the likelihood that children will explore options related to their interests and talents, children who feel strong gender-typed pressure are often distressed.

In a longitudinal study of third through seventh graders, *gender-typical* and *gender-contented* children gained in self-esteem over the following year. In contrast, children who were *gender-atypical* and *gender-discontented* declined in self-worth. Furthermore, gender-atypical children who reported *intense pressure to conform to gender roles* experienced serious difficulties—withdrawal, sadness, disappointment, and anxiety (Yunger, Carver, & Perry, 2004).

Clearly, how children feel about themselves in relation to their gender group becomes vitally important in middle childhood, and those who experience rejection because of their gender-atypical traits suffer profoundly. Researchers and therapists are debating how best to help children who feel gender-atypical. Some favor providing these children with therapy that reinforces them for engaging in traditional gender-role activities so they will feel more compatible with same-sex peers (Zucker, 2006). Others oppose this approach on grounds that it promotes a pathological view of gender atypicality, is likely to heighten felt pressure to conform (which predicts maladjustment), and—for children who fail to change—may result in parental rejection. These experts advocate intervening with parents and peers to help them become more accepting of children's gender-atypical interests and behaviors (Bigler, 2007; Conway, 2007; Crawford,

2003). *TAKE A MOMENT...* In view of what you have learned about the development of children's gender typing, which approach do you think would be more successful, and why?

ASK YOURSELF

REVIEW Why are girls more androgynous than boys in middle childhood?

CONNECT Describe similarities in development of self-concept, attitudes toward ethnic minorities, and gender-stereotyped beliefs in middle childhood.

APPLY What changes in parent–child relationships are probably necessary to help rejected children?

REFLECT As a school-age child, did you have classmates you would classify as popular-aggressive? What were they like, and why do you think peers admired them?

Family Influences

As children move into school, peer, and community contexts, the parent–child relationship changes. At the same time, children's well-being continues to depend on the quality of family interaction. In the following sections, we will see that contemporary diversity in family life—divorce, remarriage, maternal employment, and dual-earner families—can have positive as well as negative effects on children. In later chapters, we take up other family structures, including gay and lesbian families, never-married single-parent families, and the increasing numbers of grandparents rearing grandchildren.

Parent–Child Relationships

In middle childhood, the amount of time children spend with parents declines dramatically. Children's growing independence means that parents must deal with new issues. "I've struggled with how many chores to assign, how much allowance to give, whether their friends are good influences, and what to do about problems at school," Rena remarked. "And then there's the challenge of keeping track of them when they're out—or even when they're home and I'm not there to see what's going on."

Despite these new concerns, child rearing becomes easier for those parents who established an authoritative style during the early years. Reasoning is more effective with school-age children because of their greater capacity for logical thinking and their increased respect for parents' expert knowledge (Collins, Madsen, & Susman-Stillman, 2002). And children of parents who engage in joint decision making where possible are more likely to listen to parents' perspectives in situations where compliance is vital (Russell, Mize, & Bissaker, 2004).

As children demonstrate that they can manage daily activities and responsibilities, effective parents gradually shift control from adult to child. They do not let go entirely but, rather, engage in **coregulation,** a form of supervision in which parents exercise general oversight while letting children take charge of moment-by-moment decision making. Coregulation grows out of a warm, cooperative relationship between parent and child based on give-and-take. Parents must guide and monitor from a distance and effectively communicate expectations when they are with their children. And children must inform parents of their whereabouts, activities, and problems so parents can intervene when necessary (Maccoby, 1984). Coregulation supports and protects children while preparing them for adolescence, when they will make many important decisions themselves.

As at younger ages, mothers tend to spend more time than fathers with school-age children. Mothers also are more knowledgeable about children's everyday activities. Still, many fathers are highly involved (Galinsky, Aumann, & Bond, 2009). Each parent, however, tends to devote more time to children of their own sex (Lamb & Lewis, 2004; Tucker, McHale, & Crouter, 2003). And parents are more vigilant about monitoring the activities of same-sex children while their children are away from home.

Although school-age children often press for greater independence, they know how much they need their parents' support. In one study, fifth and sixth graders described parents as the most influential people in their lives (Furman & Buhrmester, 1992). They often turned to mothers and fathers for affection, advice, enhancement of self-worth, and assistance with everyday problems.

Siblings

In addition to parents and friends, siblings continue to be important sources of support. Yet sibling rivalry tends to increase in middle childhood. As children participate in a wider range of activities, parents often compare siblings' traits and accomplishments (Dunn, 2004; Tamrouti-Makkink et al., 2004). The child who gets less parental affection, more disapproval, or fewer material resources is likely to be resentful and show poorer adjustment.

Although sibling rivalry tends to increase in middle childhood, siblings also provide each other with emotional support and help with difficult tasks.

BRUCE LAURANCE/GETTY IMAGES/BLEND IMAGES

For same-sex siblings who are close in age, parental comparisons are more frequent, resulting in more quarreling and antagonism. This effect is particularly strong when parents are under stress as a result of financial worries, marital conflict, single parenthood, or child negativity (Jenkins, Rasbash, & O'Connor, 2003). Parents whose energies are drained become less careful about being fair.

To reduce this rivalry, siblings often strive to be different from one another. For example, two brothers I know deliberately selected different athletic pursuits and musical instruments. If the older one did especially well at an activity, the younger one did not want to try it. Parents can limit these effects by making an effort not to compare children, but some feedback about their competencies is inevitable. As siblings strive to win recognition for their own uniqueness, they shape important aspects of each other's development.

Although conflict rises, school-age siblings continue to rely on each other for companionship, assistance, and emotional support (Seibert & Kerns, 2009). When researchers asked siblings about shared daily activities, children mentioned that older siblings often helped younger siblings with academic and peer challenges. And both offered each other help with family issues (Tucker, McHale, & Crouter, 2001). But for siblings to reap these benefits, parental encouragement of warm, considerate sibling ties is vital. The more positive their relationship, the more siblings resolve disagreements constructively, provide emotional support and concrete forms of assistance, and contribute to resilience in the face of major stressors, such as parental divorce (Conger, Stocker, & McGuire, 2009; Soli, McHale, & Feinberg, 2009).

When siblings get along well, the older sibling's academic and social competence tends to "rub off on" the younger sibling, fostering more favorable achievement and peer relations (Brody & Murry, 2001; Lamarche et al., 2006). But destructive sibling conflict in middle childhood is associated with negative outcomes, including conflict-ridden peer relationships, anxiety, depressed mood, and later substance use and delinquency, even after other family relationship factors are controlled (Criss & Shaw, 2005; Kim et al., 2007; Stocker, Burwell, & Briggs, 2002).

Only Children

Although sibling relationships bring many benefits, they are not essential for healthy development. Contrary to popular belief, only children are not spoiled, and in some respects, they are advantaged. U.S. children growing up in one-child and multi-child families do not differ in self-rated personality traits (Mottus, Indus, & Allik, 2008). And compared to children with siblings, only children are higher in self-esteem and achievement motivation, do better in school, and attain higher levels of education. One reason may be that only children have somewhat closer relationships with parents, who may exert more pressure for mastery and accomplishment (Falbo, 1992). However, only children tend to be less well-accepted in the peer group, perhaps because they have not had opportunities to learn effective conflict-resolution strategies through sibling interactions (Kitzmann, Cohen, & Lockwood, 2002).

Limiting family size has been a national policy in China for more than three decades. In urban areas, the majority of couples have no more than one child.

Favorable development also characterizes only children in China, where a one-child family policy has been strictly enforced in urban areas for more than three decades to control population growth (Yang, 2008). Compared with agemates who have siblings, Chinese only children are advanced in cognitive development and academic achievement. They also feel more emotionally secure, perhaps because government disapproval promotes tension in families with more than one child (Falbo & Poston, 1993; Jiao, Ji, & Jing, 1996; Yang et al., 1995). Chinese mothers usually ensure that their children have regular contact with first cousins (who are considered siblings). Perhaps as a result, Chinese only children do not differ from agemates with siblings in social skills and peer acceptance (Hart, Newell, & Olsen, 2003). The next generation of Chinese only children, however, will have no first cousins.

China's birth rate, at 1.5 overall and 0.7 in its largest cities, is now lower than that of many developed nations. As a result, its elderly population is rapidly increasing while its working-age population has leveled off—an imbalance that threatens the country's economic progress. And because sons are more highly valued than daughters, the policy has resulted in an epidemic of abortions of female fetuses and abandonment of girl babies, yielding a vastly skewed population sex ratio (130 male births for every 100 female births) that jeopardizes social stability (Zhu & Hesketh, 2009). Consequently, China is considering relaxing the one-child policy, but it is now so culturally ingrained that couples typically say they would not have a second child, even if offered the opportunity (LaFraniere, 2011).

Divorce

Children's interactions with parents and siblings are affected by other aspects of family life. Joey and Lizzie's relationship, Rena told me, had been particularly negative only a few years before.

Joey pushed, hit, and taunted Lizzie and called her names. Although she tried to retaliate, she was no match for Joey's larger size. The arguments usually ended with Lizzie running in tears to her mother. Joey and Lizzie's fighting coincided with their parents' growing marital unhappiness. When Joey was 8 and Lizzie 5, their father, Drake, moved out.

Between 1960 and 1985, divorce rates in Western nations rose dramatically before stabilizing in most countries. The United States has experienced a decline in divorces over the past decade, largely due to a rise in age at first marriage (Amato & Dorius, 2010). Nevertheless, the United States continues to have the highest divorce rate in the world (see Figure 10.3). Of the 45 percent of American marriages that end in divorce, half involve children. At any given time, one-fourth of U.S. children live in single-parent households. Although most reside with their mothers, the percentage in father-headed households has increased steadily, to about 12 percent (Federal Interagency Forum on Child and Family Statistics, 2011).

Children of divorce spend an average of five years in a single-parent home—almost a third of childhood. For many, divorce leads to new family relationships. About two-thirds of divorced parents marry again. Half their children eventually experience a third major change—the end of a parent's second marriage (Hetherington & Kelly, 2002).

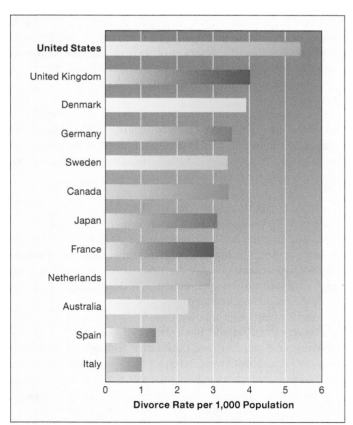

FIGURE 10.3 Divorce rates in 12 industrialized nations. The U.S. divorce rate is the highest in the industrialized world, far exceeding divorce rates in other countries. (Adapted from U.S. Census Bureau, 2012b.)

These figures reveal that divorce is not a single event in the lives of parents and children. Instead, it is a transition that leads to a variety of new living arrangements, accompanied by changes in housing, income, and family roles and responsibilities. Since the 1960s, many studies have reported that marital breakup is stressful for children. But the research also reveals great individual differences (Fine, Ganong, & Demo, 2010). How well children fare depends on many factors: the custodial parent's psychological health, the child's characteristics, and social supports within the family and surrounding community.

Immediate Consequences. "Things were worst during the period Drake and I decided to separate," Rena reflected. "We fought over division of our belongings and custody of the children, and the kids suffered. Sobbing, Lizzie told me she was 'sorry she made Daddy go away.' Joey kicked and threw things at home and didn't do his work at school. In the midst of everything, I could hardly deal with their problems. We had to sell the house, and I needed a better-paying job."

Family conflict often rises around the time of divorce as parents try to settle disputes over children and possessions. Once one parent moves out, additional events threaten supportive interactions between parents and children. Many mother-headed households experience a sharp drop in income. In the United States, 27 percent of divorced mothers with young children live in poverty, and more are low-income, getting less than the full amount of child support from the absent father or none at all (Grall, 2011). They usually must move to lower-cost housing, reducing supportive ties to neighbors and friends.

The transition from marriage to divorce typically leads to high maternal stress, depression, and anxiety and to a disorganized family situation. Declines in well-being are greatest for mothers of young children (Williams & Dunne-Bryant, 2006). "Meals and bedtimes were at all hours, the house didn't get cleaned, and I stopped taking Joey and Lizzie on weekend outings," said Rena. As children react with distress and anger to their less secure home lives, discipline may become harsh and inconsistent. Contact with noncustodial fathers often decreases over time (Hetherington & Kelly, 2002). Fathers who see their children only occasionally are inclined to be permissive and indulgent, making the mother's task of managing the child even more difficult.

The more parents argue and fail to provide children with warmth, involvement, and consistent guidance, the poorer children's adjustment. About 20 to 25 percent of children in divorced families display severe problems, compared with about 10 percent in nondivorced families (Lansford, 2009; Noller et al., 2008). At the same time, reactions vary with children's age, temperament, and sex.

Children's Age. Five-year-old Lizzie's fear that she had caused her father to leave is not unusual. Preschool and young school-age children often blame themselves for a marital breakup and fear that both parents may abandon them. And although older children have the cognitive maturity to understand that they are not responsible for their parents' divorce, many react strongly, declining in school performance, becoming unruly, and escaping into undesirable peer activities, especially when family conflict is high and parental supervision is low (D'Onofrio et al., 2006; Lansford et al., 2006). Some older children—especially the oldest child in the family—display more mature behavior, willingly taking on extra family and household tasks as well as emotional support of a depressed, anxious mother. But if these demands are too great, these children may eventually become resentful, withdraw from the family, and engage in angry, acting-out behavior (Hetherington, 1999).

Children's Temperament and Sex. Exposure to stressful life events and inadequate parenting magnifies the problems of temperamentally difficult children (Lengua et al., 2000). In contrast, easy children are less often targets of parental anger and also cope more effectively with adversity.

These findings help explain sex differences in response to divorce. Girls sometimes respond as Lizzie did, with internalizing reactions such as crying, self-criticism, and withdrawal. More often, children of both sexes show demanding, attention-getting behavior. But in mother-custody families, boys are at slightly greater risk for serious adjustment problems (Amato, 2010). Recall from Chapter 8 that boys are more active and noncompliant—behaviors that increase with exposure to parental conflict and inconsistent discipline. Coercive maternal behavior and defiance by sons are common in divorcing households.

Perhaps because their behavior is so unruly, boys receive less emotional support from mothers, teachers, and peers. And as Joey's behavior toward Lizzie illustrates, the coercive cycles of interaction between boys and their divorced mothers soon spread to sibling relationships, compounding adjustment difficulties (Hetherington & Kelly, 2002; Sheehan et al., 2004). After divorce, children who are challenging to rear generally get worse.

Long-Term Consequences.
Rena eventually found better-paying work and gained control over the daily operation of the household. And after several meetings with a counselor, Rena and Drake realized the harmful impact of their quarreling on Joey and Lizzie. Drake visited regularly and handled Joey's unruliness with firmness and consistency. Soon Joey's school performance improved, his behavior problems subsided, and both children seemed calmer and happier.

Most children show improved adjustment by two years after divorce. Yet overall, children and adolescents of divorced parents continue to score slightly lower than children of continuously married parents in academic achievement, self-esteem, social competence, and emotional and behavior problems (Lansford, 2009). And divorce is linked to problems with adolescent sexuality and development of intimate ties. Young people who experienced parental divorce—especially more than once—display higher rates of early sexual activity and adolescent parenthood (Wolfinger, 2000). Some experience other lasting difficulties—reduced educational attainment, troubled romantic relationships and marriages, divorce in adulthood, and unsatisfying parent–child relationships (Amato, 2006, 2010).

The overriding factor in positive adjustment following divorce is effective parenting—shielding the child from family conflict and using authoritative child rearing (Leon, 2003; Wolchik et al., 2000). Where the custodial parent is the mother, contact with fathers is important. In the United States, paternal contact has risen over the past three decades, with about one-third of children today experiencing at least weekly visits (Amato & Dorius, 2010).

The more paternal contact and the warmer the father–child relationship, the less children react with defiance and aggression (Dunn et al., 2004). For girls, a good father–child relationship protects against early sexual activity and unhappy romantic involvements. For boys, it seems to affect overall psychological well-being. In fact, several studies indicate that outcomes for sons are better when the father is the custodial parent (Clarke-Stewart & Hayward, 1996; McLanahan, 1999). Fathers' greater economic security and image of authority seem to help them engage in effective parenting with sons. And boys in father-custody families may benefit from greater involvement of both parents because noncustodial mothers participate more in their children's lives than do noncustodial fathers.

Although divorce is painful for children, remaining in an intact but high-conflict family is much worse than making the transition to a low-conflict, single-parent household (Greene et al., 2003; Strohschein, 2005). However, more parents today are divorcing because they are moderately (rather than extremely) dissatisfied with their relationship. Research suggests that children in these low-discord homes are especially puzzled and upset. Perhaps these youngsters' inability to understand the marital breakup and grief over the loss of a seemingly happy home life explain why the adjustment problems of children of divorce have intensified over time (Amato, 2001; Lansford, 2009).

Regardless of the extent of their friction, divorcing parents who manage to engage in *coparenting* (see page 60 in Chapter 2), supporting each other in their child-rearing roles, greatly improve their children's chances of growing up competent, stable, and happy. Caring extended-family members, teachers, siblings, and friends also reduce the likelihood that divorce will result in long-term difficulties (Hetherington, 2003).

Divorce Mediation, Joint Custody, and Child Support.
Awareness that divorce is highly stressful for children and families has led to community-based services aimed at helping them through this difficult time. One such service is *divorce mediation,* a series of meetings between divorcing adults and a trained professional aimed at reducing family conflict, including legal battles over property division and child custody. Research reveals that mediation increases out-of-court settlements, cooperation and involvement of both parents in child rearing, and parents' and children's feelings of well-being (Emery, Sbarra, & Grover, 2005).

Joint custody, which grants parents equal say in important decisions about the child's upbringing, is becoming increasingly common. Children usually reside with one parent and see the other on a fixed schedule, similar to the typical sole-custody situation. In other cases, parents share physical custody, and children move between homes and sometimes schools and peer groups. These transitions can be especially hard on some

Applying What We Know

Helping Children Adjust to Their Parents' Divorce

Suggestion	Explanation
Shield children from conflict.	Witnessing intense parental conflict is very damaging to children. If one parent insists on expressing hostility, children fare better if the other parent does not respond in kind.
Provide children with as much continuity, familiarity, and predictability as possible.	Children adjust better during the period surrounding divorce when their lives have some stability—for example, the same school, bedroom, babysitter, playmates, and daily schedule.
Explain the divorce, and tell children what to expect.	Children are more likely to develop fears of abandonment if they are not prepared for their parents' separation. They should be told that their parents will not be living together anymore, which parent will be moving out, and when they will be able to see that parent. If possible, parents should explain the divorce together, providing a reason that each child can understand and assuring children that they are not to blame.
Emphasize the permanence of the divorce.	Fantasies of parents getting back together can prevent children from accepting the reality of their current life. Children should be told that the divorce is final and that they cannot change this fact.
Respond sympathetically to children's feelings.	Children need a supportive and understanding response to their feelings of sadness, fear, and anger. For children to adjust well, their painful emotions must be acknowledged, not denied or avoided.
Engage in authoritative parenting.	Parents who engage in authoritative parenting—providing affection and acceptance, reasonable demands for mature behavior, and consistent, rational discipline—greatly reduce their children's risk of maladjustment following divorce.
Promote a continuing relationship with both parents.	When parents disentangle their lingering hostility toward the former spouse from the child's need for a continuing relationship with the other parent, children adjust well. Grandparents and other extended-family members can help by not taking sides.

Source: Teyber, 2001.

children. Joint-custody parents report little conflict—fortunately so, since the success of the arrangement depends on coparenting. And their children—regardless of living arrangements—tend to be better-adjusted than children in sole-maternal-custody homes (Bauserman, 2002).

Finally, many single-parent families depend on child support from the noncustodial parent to relieve financial strain. All U.S. states have procedures for withholding wages from parents who fail to make these payments. Although child support is usually not enough to lift a single-parent family out of poverty, it can ease its burdens substantially. Noncustodial fathers who have generous visitation schedules and who often see their children are more likely to pay child support regularly (Amato & Sobolewski, 2004). Applying What We Know above summarizes ways to help children adjust to their parents' divorce.

Blended Families

"If you get married to Wendell, and Daddy gets married to Carol," Lizzie wondered aloud to Rena, "then I'll have two sisters and one more brother. And let's see, how many grandmothers and grandfathers? A lot!" exclaimed Lizzie.

About 60 percent of divorced parents remarry within a few years. Others *cohabit,* or share a sexual relationship and a residence with a partner outside of marriage. Parent, stepparent, and children form a new family structure called the **blended,** or **reconstituted, family.** For some children, this expanded

family network is positive, bringing greater adult attention. But children in blended families usually have more adjustment problems than children in stable, first-marriage families (Jeynes, 2007; Nicholson et al., 2008). Switching to stepparents' new rules and expectations can be stressful, and children often view steprelatives as intruders. How well they adapt is, again, related to the quality of family functioning (Hetherington & Kelly, 2002). This depends on which parent forms a new relationship, the child's age and sex, and the complexity of blended-family relationships. As we will see, older children and girls seem to have the hardest time.

Mother–Stepfather Families. Because mothers generally retain custody of children, the most common form of blended family is a mother–stepfather arrangement. Boys tend to adjust quickly, welcoming a stepfather who is warm, who refrains from exerting his authority too quickly, and who offers relief from coercive cycles of mother–son interaction. Mothers' friction with sons also declines as a result of greater economic security, another adult to share household tasks, and an end to loneliness (Visher, Visher, & Pasley, 2003). Stepfathers who marry rather than cohabit are more involved in parenting, perhaps because men who choose to marry a mother with children are more interested in and skilled at child rearing (Hofferth & Anderson, 2003). Girls, however, often have difficulty with their custodial mother's remarriage. Stepfathers disrupt the close ties many girls have established with their mothers, and girls often react with sulky, resistant behavior (Bray, 1999; Ganong, Coleman, & Jamison, 2011).

But age affects these findings. Older school-age children and adolescents of both sexes display more irresponsible, acting-out behavior than their peers not in stepfamilies (Hetherington & Stanley-Hagan, 2000; Robertson, 2008). If parents are warmer and more involved with their biological children than with their stepchildren, older children are more likely to notice and challenge unfair treatment. And adolescents often view the new stepparent as a threat to their freedom, especially if they experienced little parental monitoring in the single-parent family. But when teenagers have affectionate, cooperative relationships with their mothers, many eventually develop good relations with their stepfathers—a circumstance linked to better adjustment (King, 2009; Yuan & Hamilton, 2006).

Father–Stepmother Families. Remarriage of noncustodial fathers often leads to reduced contact with their biological children, especially when fathers remarry quickly, before they have established post-divorce parent–child routines (Dunn, 2002; Juby et al., 2007). When fathers have custody, children typically react negatively to remarriage. One reason is that children living with fathers often start out with more problems. Perhaps the biological mother could no longer handle the difficult child (usually a boy), so the father and his new partner are faced with a youngster who has behavior problems. In other instances, the father has custody because of a very close relationship with the child, and his remarriage disrupts this bond (Buchanan, Maccoby, & Dornbusch, 1996).

Girls, especially, have a hard time getting along with their stepmothers, either because the remarriage threatens the girl's bond with her father or because she becomes entangled in loyalty conflicts between the two mother figures. But the longer girls live in father–stepmother households, the more positive their interaction with stepmothers becomes (King, 2007). With time and patience, most girls benefit from the support of a second mother figure.

Support for Blended Families. Parenting education and couples counseling can help parents and children adapt to the complexities of blended families. Effective approaches encourage stepparents to move into their new roles gradually by first building a warm relationship with the child (Nicholson et al., 2008). Counselors can offer couples guidance in coparenting to limit loyalty conflicts and provide consistency in child rearing. This allows children to benefit from the increased diversity that stepparent relationships bring to their lives.

Unfortunately, the divorce rate for second marriages is even higher than for first marriages. Parents with antisocial tendencies and poor child-rearing skills are particularly likely to have several divorces and remarriages. The more marital transitions children experience, the greater their adjustment difficulties (Amato, 2010). These families usually require prolonged, intensive therapy.

To help these teenagers adapt to life in a complex blended family, both father and stepmother must avoid favoring their much younger children, born after remarriage.

Maternal Employment and Dual-Earner Families

Today, U.S. single and married mothers are in the labor market in nearly equal proportions, and more than three-fourths of those with school-age children are employed (U.S. Census Bureau, 2012b). In previous chapters, we saw that the impact of maternal employment on early development depends on the quality of child care and the continuing parent–child relationship. The same is true in middle childhood.

Maternal Employment and Child Development. When mothers enjoy their work and remain committed to parenting, children show favorable adjustment—higher self-esteem, more positive family and peer relations, less gender-stereotyped beliefs, and better grades in school. Girls, especially, profit from the image of female competence. Regardless of SES, daughters of employed mothers perceive women's roles as involving more freedom of choice and satisfaction and are more achievement- and career-oriented (Hoffman, 2000).

Parenting practices contribute to these benefits. Employed mothers who value their parenting role are more likely to use authoritative child rearing and coregulation. Also, children in dual-earner households devote more daily hours to doing homework under parental guidance and participate more in household chores. And maternal employment leads fathers—especially those who believe in the importance of the paternal role and who feel successful at parenting—to take on greater child-care responsibilities (Gottfried, Gottfried, & Bathurst, 2002; Jacobs & Kelley, 2006). Paternal involvement is associated in childhood and adolescence with higher intelligence and achievement, more mature social behavior, and a flexible view of gender roles; and in adulthood with generally better mental health (Pleck & Masciadrelli, 2004).

But when employment places heavy demands on a mother's or a father's schedule or is stressful for other reasons, children are at risk for ineffective parenting. Working many hours or experiencing a negative workplace atmosphere is associated with reduced parental sensitivity, fewer joint parent–child activities, and poorer cognitive development throughout childhood and adolescence (Brooks-Gunn, Han, & Waldfogel, 2002; Bumpus, Crouter, & McHale, 2006; Strazdins et al., 2006). Negative consequences are magnified when low-SES mothers spend long days at low-paying, physically exhausting jobs— conditions linked to maternal depression and harsh, inconsistent discipline (Raver, 2003). In contrast, part-time employment and flexible work schedules are associated with sensitive, involved parenting and good child adjustment (Buehler & O'Brien, 2011). By preventing work–family role conflict, these arrangements help parents meet children's needs.

Support for Employed Parents and Their Families.

In dual-earner families, the father's willingness to share responsibilities is a crucial factor. If he helps little or not at all, the mother carries a double load, at home and at work, leading to fatigue, distress, and little time and energy for children. Fortunately, compared to three decades ago, today's U.S. fathers are far more involved in child care (see pages 202–203 in Chapter 6). But their increased participation has resulted in a growing number of fathers who also report work–family life conflict (Galinsky, Aumann, & Bond, 2009).

Employed parents need assistance from work settings and communities in their child-rearing roles. Part-time employment, flexible schedules, job sharing, and paid leave when children are ill help parents juggle the demands of work and child rearing. Equal pay and employment opportunities for women are also important. Because these policies enhance financial status and morale, they improve the way mothers feel and behave when they arrive home at the end of the working day.

Child Care for School-Age Children.

High-quality child care is vital for parents' peace of mind and children's well-being, even in middle childhood. An estimated 5 million 5- to 14-year-olds in the United States are **self-care children,** who regularly look after themselves for some period of time after school (Afterschool Alliance, 2009). Self-care increases with age and also with SES, perhaps because of the greater safety of higher-income neighborhoods. But when lower-SES parents lack alternatives to self-care, their children spend more hours on their own (Casper & Smith, 2002).

The implications of self-care for development depend on children's maturity and the way they spend their time. Among younger school-age children, those who spend more hours alone have more emotional and social difficulties (Vandell & Posner, 1999). As children become old enough to look after themselves, those who have a history of authoritative child rearing, are monitored by parental telephone calls, and have regular after-school chores appear responsible and well-adjusted. In contrast, children left to their own devices are more likely to

High-quality after-school programs with enrichment activities yield academic and social benefits for low-SES children.

bend to peer pressures and engage in antisocial behavior (Coley, Morris, & Hernandez, 2004; Vandell et al., 2006).

Before age 8 or 9, most children need supervision because they are not yet competent to handle emergencies (Galambos & Maggs, 1991). Also, throughout middle childhood, attending after-school programs with well-trained staffs, generous adult–child ratios, and skill-building activities is linked to good school performance and emotional and social adjustment (Durlak & Weissberg, 2007; Granger, 2008). Low-SES children who participate in "after-care" programs offering academic assistance and enrichment activities (scouting, music and art lessons, clubs) show special benefits. They exceed their self-care counterparts in classroom work habits, academic achievement, and prosocial behavior and display fewer behavior problems (Lauer et al., 2006; Vandell et al., 2006).

Unfortunately, good after-care is in especially short supply in low-income neighborhoods (Afterschool Alliance, 2009; Dearing et al., 2009). A special need exists for well-planned programs in these areas—ones that provide safe environments, warm relationships with adults, and enjoyable, goal-oriented activities.

ASK YOURSELF

REVIEW Describe and explain changes in sibling relationships during middle childhood.

CONNECT How does each level in Bronfenbrenner's ecological systems theory—microsystem, mesosystem, exosystem, and macrosystem—contribute to the effects of maternal employment on children's development?

APPLY Steve and Marissa are in the midst of an acrimonious divorce. Their 9-year-old son Dennis has become hostile and defiant. How can Steve and Marissa help Dennis adjust?

REFLECT What after-school child-care arrangements did you experience in elementary school? How do you think they influenced your development?

Some Common Problems of Development

We have considered a variety of stressful experiences that place children at risk for future problems. Next, we address two more areas of concern: school-age children's fears and anxieties and the consequences of child sexual abuse. Finally, we sum up factors that help children cope effectively with stress.

Fears and Anxieties

Although fears of the dark, thunder and lightning, and supernatural beings persist into middle childhood, older children's anxieties are also directed toward new concerns. Common fears of the school years include poor academic performance, peer rejection, the possibility of personal harm (being robbed or shot), threats to parents' health, and media events (Gullone, 2000; Weems & Costa, 2005).

Children's fears are shaped in part by their culture. Children in Western nations mention exposure to negative information in the media as the most common source of their fears, followed by direct exposure to frightening events (Muris et al., 2001). In China, where self-restraint and compliance with social standards are highly valued, more children mention failure and adult criticism as salient fears than in Australia or the United States (Ollendick et al., 1996). Chinese children, however, are not more fearful overall. The number and intensity of fears they report resemble those of Western children.

Most children handle fears constructively, using the more sophisticated emotion regulation strategies that develop in middle childhood. Consequently, fears decline with age, especially for girls, who express more fears than boys throughout childhood and adolescence (Gullone, 2000). But about 5 percent of school-age children develop an intense, unmanageable fear called a **phobia.** Children with inhibited temperaments are at high risk, displaying phobias five to six times as often as other children (Ollendick, King, & Muris, 2002).

For example, in *school phobia,* children feel severe apprehension about attending school, often accompanied by physical complaints (dizziness, nausea, stomachaches, and vomiting). About one-third of children with school phobia are 5- to 7-year-olds for whom the real fear is maternal separation. Family therapy helps these children, whose difficulty can often be traced to parental overprotection (Elliott, 1999).

Most cases of school phobia appear around age 11 to 13, in children who usually find a particular aspect of school frightening—an overcritical teacher, a school bully, or too much parental pressure to achieve. A change in school environment or parenting practices may be needed. Firm insistence that the child return to school, along with training in how to cope with difficult situations, is also helpful (Silverman & Pina, 2008).

Severe childhood anxieties may arise from harsh living conditions. In inner-city ghettos and in war-torn areas of the world, large numbers of children live in the midst of constant danger, chaos, and deprivation. As the Cultural Influences box on the following page reveals, these youngsters are at risk for long-term emotional distress and behavior problems. Finally, as we saw in our discussion of child abuse in Chapter 8, too often violence and other destructive acts become part of adult–child relationships. During middle childhood, child sexual abuse increases.

Child Sexual Abuse

Until recently, child sexual abuse was considered rare, and adults often dismissed children's claims of abuse. In the 1970s, efforts by professionals and media attention led to recognition of child sexual abuse as a serious and widespread problem. About 65,000 cases in the United States were confirmed in the most recently reported year (U.S. Department of Health and Human Services, 2011b).

Characteristics of Abusers and Victims. Sexual abuse is committed against children of both sexes, but more often against girls. Most cases are reported in middle childhood, but for some victims, abuse begins early in life and continues for many years (Hoch-Espada, Ryan, & Deblinger, 2006; Goodyear-Brown, Fath, & Myers, 2012).

Typically, the abuser is male, either a parent or someone the parent knows well—a father, stepfather, or live-in boyfriend, somewhat less often an uncle or older brother. But in about 25 percent of cases, mothers are the offenders, more often with sons (Boroughs, 2004). If the abuser is a nonrelative, the person is usually someone the child has come to know and trust. However, the Internet and mobile phones have become avenues through which other adults commit sexual abuse—for example, by exposing children and adolescents to pornography and online sexual advances as a way of "grooming" them for sexual acts offline (Wolak et al., 2008).

Abusers make the child comply in a variety of distasteful ways, including deception, bribery, verbal intimidation, and physical force. You may wonder how any adult—especially a parent or close relative—could violate a child sexually. Many offenders deny their own responsibility, blaming the abuse on the willing participation of a seductive youngster. Yet children are not capable of making a deliberate, informed decision to enter into a sexual relationship! Even older children and adolescents are not free to say yes or no. Rather, the responsibility lies with abusers, who tend to have characteristics that predispose them toward sexual exploitation of children. They have great difficulty controlling their impulses and may suffer from psychological disorders, including alcohol and drug abuse. Often they pick out children who are unlikely to defend themselves or to be believed—those who are physically weak, emotionally deprived, socially isolated, or affected by disabilities (Bolen, 2001).

Reported cases of child sexual abuse are linked to poverty, marital instability, and resulting weakening of family ties. Children who live in homes with a constantly changing cast of characters—repeated marriages, separations, and new partners—are especially vulnerable (Goodyear-Brown, Fath, & Myers, 2012). But children in economically advantaged, stable families are also victims, although their abuse is more likely to escape detection.

Cultural Influences

Impact of Ethnic and Political Violence on Children

Around the world, many children live with armed conflict, terrorism, and other acts of violence stemming from ethnic and political tensions. Some children may participate in fighting, either because they are forced or because they want to please adults. Others are kidnapped, assaulted, and tortured. Those who are bystanders often come under direct fire and may be killed or physically maimed. And many watch in horror as family members, friends, and neighbors flee, are wounded, or die. In the past decade, wars have left 6 million children physically disabled, 20 million homeless, and more than 1 million separated from their parents (UNICEF, 2011).

When war and social crises are temporary, most children can be comforted and do not show long-term emotional difficulties. But chronic danger requires children to make substantial adjustments that can seriously impair their psychological functioning. Many children of war lose their sense of safety, become desensitized to violence, are haunted by terrifying intrusive memories, display immature moral reasoning, and build a pessimistic view of the future. Anxiety and depression increase, as do aggression and antisocial behavior (Eisenberg & Silver, 2011; Klingman, 2006). These outcomes appear to be culturally universal, observed among children in every war zone studied—from Bosnia, Angola, Rwanda, and the Sudan to the West Bank, Gaza, Afghanistan, and Iraq (Barenbaum, Ruchkin, & Schwab-Stone, 2004).

Parental affection and reassurance are the best protection against lasting problems.

When parents offer security, discuss traumatic experiences sympathetically, and serve as role models of calm emotional strength, most children can withstand even extreme war-related violence (Gewirtz, Forgatch, & Wieling, 2008). Children who are separated from parents must rely on help from their communities. Orphans in Eritrea who were placed in residential settings where they could form a close emotional tie with an adult showed less emotional stress five years later than orphans placed in impersonal settings (Wolff & Fesseha, 1999). Education and recreation programs are powerful safeguards, too, providing children with consistency in their lives along with teacher and peer supports.

With the September 11, 2001, terrorist attacks on the World Trade Center, some U.S. children experienced extreme wartime violence firsthand. Most children, however, learned about the attacks indirectly—from the media or from caregivers or peers. Although both direct and indirect exposure triggered child and adolescent distress, extended exposure—having a family member affected or repeatedly witnessing the attacks on TV—resulted in more severe symptoms (Agronick et al., 2007; Otto et al., 2007; Rosen & Cohen, 2010). During the following months, distress reactions declined, though more slowly for children with conflict-ridden parent–

KHALIL MAZRAAWI/AFP/GETTY IMAGES

At a refugee camp in Jordan, Syrian children wearing face-masks to protect against blowing sand play games with a caring adult. Most have witnessed violent atrocities and lost family members in Syria's civil war. Sensitive adult support can help them regain a sense of safety.

child relationships or preexisting adjustment problems.

Unlike many war-traumatized children in the developing world, students in New York's Public School 31, who watched from their classroom windows as the towers collapsed, received immediate intervention—a "trauma curriculum" in which they expressed their emotions through writing, drawing, and discussion and participated in experiences aimed at restoring trust and tolerance (Lagnado, 2001). Older children learned about the feelings of their Muslim classmates, the dire condition of children in Afghanistan, and ways to help victims as a means of overcoming a sense of helplessness.

When wartime drains families and communities of resources, international organizations must step in and help children. Efforts to preserve children's physical, psychological, and educational well-being may be the best way to stop transmission of violence to the next generation.

Consequences. The adjustment problems of child sexual abuse victims—including anxiety, depression, low self-esteem, mistrust of adults, and anger and hostility—are often severe and can persist for years after the abusive episodes. Younger children frequently react with sleep difficulties, loss of appetite, and generalized fearfulness. Adolescents may run away and show suicidal reactions, eating disorders, substance abuse, and delinquency. At all ages, persistent abuse accompanied by force, violence, and a close relationship to the perpetrator (incest) has a

more severe impact (Hornor, 2010; Wolfe, 2006). And repeated sexual abuse, like physical abuse, is associated with central nervous system damage (Gaskill & Perry, 2012).

Sexually abused children frequently display precocious sexual knowledge and behavior. In adolescence, abused young people often become promiscuous, and as adults, they show increased arrest rates for sex crimes (mostly against children) and prostitution (Salter et al., 2003; Whipple, 2006). Furthermore, women who were sexually abused are likely to choose partners

Children in Hyderabad, India, participate in a "Stay Safe" campaign against child abuse and sexual exploitation—part of a global effort to prevent all forms of abuse.

who abuse them and their children. As mothers, they often engage in irresponsible and coercive parenting, including child abuse and neglect (Pianta, Egeland, & Erickson, 1989). In all these ways, the harmful impact of sexual abuse is transmitted to the next generation.

Prevention and Treatment. Because sexual abuse typically appears in the midst of other serious family problems, long-term therapy with both children and parents is often needed (Saunders, 2012). The best way to reduce the suffering of victims is to prevent sexual abuse from continuing. Today, courts are prosecuting abusers more vigorously and taking children's testimony more seriously (see the Social Issues: Health box on the following page).

Educational programs that teach children to recognize inappropriate sexual advances and identify sources of help reduce the risk of abuse (Finkelhor, 2009). Yet because of controversies over educating children about sexual abuse, few schools offer these interventions. New Zealand is the only country with a national, school-based prevention program targeting sexual abuse. In Keeping Ourselves Safe, children and adolescents learn that abusers are rarely strangers. Parent involvement ensures that home and school collaborate in teaching children self-protection skills. Evaluations reveal that virtually all New Zealand parents and children support the program and that it has helped many children avoid or report abuse (Sanders, 2006).

Fostering Resilience in Middle Childhood

Throughout middle childhood—and other periods of development—children encounter challenging and sometimes threatening situations that require them to cope with psychological stress. In this and the previous chapter, we have considered such topics as chronic illness, learning disabilities, achievement expectations, divorce, harsh living conditions and wartime trauma, and sexual abuse. Each taxes children's coping resources, creating serious risks for development.

Nevertheless, only a modest relationship exists between stressful life experiences and psychological disturbance in childhood (Masten & Reed, 2002). In our discussion in Chapter 3 of the long-term consequences of birth complications, we noted that some children manage to overcome the combined effects of birth trauma, poverty, and troubled family life. The same is true for school difficulties, family transitions, the experience of war, and child maltreatment. Recall from Chapter 1 that four broad factors protect against maladjustment: (1) the child's personal characteristics, including an easy temperament and a mastery-oriented approach to new situations; (2) a warm parental relationship; (3) an adult outside the immediate family who offers a support system; and (4) community resources, such as good schools, social services, and youth organizations and recreation centers (Commission on Children at Risk, 2008; Wright & Masten, 2005).

Often just one or a few of these ingredients account for why one child is "stress-resilient" and another is not. Usually, however, personal and environmental factors are interconnected: Each resource favoring resilience strengthens others. For example, safe, stable neighborhoods with family-friendly community services reduce parents' daily hassles and stress, thereby promoting good parenting (Chen, Howard, & Brooks-Gunn, 2011). In contrast, unfavorable home and neighborhood experiences increase the chances that children will act in ways that expose them to further hardship. And when negative conditions pile up, such as marital discord, poverty, crowded living conditions, neighborhood violence, and abuse and neglect, the rate of maladjustment multiplies (Wright & Masten, 2005).

Rather than a preexisting attribute, *resilience* is a capacity that develops, enabling children to use internal and external resources to cope with adversity (Dessel, 2010; Riley & Masten, 2004). Throughout our discussion, we have seen how families, schools, communities, and society as a whole can enhance or undermine school-age children's developing sense of competence. As the next two chapters will reveal, young people whose childhood experiences helped them learn to control impulses, overcome obstacles, strive for self-direction, and respond considerately and sympathetically to others meet the challenges of the next period—adolescence—quite well.

ASK YOURSELF

REVIEW When children must testify in court cases, what factors increase the chances of accurate reporting?

CONNECT Explain how factors that promote resilience contribute to favorable adjustment following divorce.

APPLY Claire told her 6-year-old daughter never to talk to or take candy from strangers. Why will Claire's warning not protect her daughter from sexual abuse?

REFLECT Describe a challenging time during your childhood. What aspects of the experience increased stress? What resources helped you cope with adversity?

Social Issues: Health

Children's Eyewitness Testimony

Increasingly, children are being called on to testify in court cases involving child abuse and neglect, child custody, and similar matters. The experience can be traumatic, requiring children to report on highly stressful events and sometimes to speak against a parent or other relative to whom they feel loyal. In some family disputes, they may fear punishment for telling the truth. In addition, child witnesses are faced with an unfamiliar situation—at the very least an interview in the judge's chambers and at most an open courtroom with judge, jury, spectators, and the possibility of unsympathetic cross-examination. Not surprisingly, these conditions can compromise the accuracy of children's recall.

Age Differences

As a result of societal reactions to rising rates of child abuse and the difficulty of prosecuting perpetrators, age requirements for child testimony have been relaxed in the United States (Sandler, 2006). Children as young as age 3 frequently serve as witnesses.

Compared with preschoolers, school-age children are better at giving accurate, detailed narrative accounts of past experiences and correctly inferring others' motives and intentions. Older children are also more resistant to misleading questions that attorneys may ask when probing for more information or, in cross-examination, trying to influence the child's response (Roebers & Schneider, 2001). Inhibition (ability to ignore irrelevant information), which improves from early to middle childhood, predicts children's resistance to suggestion (Melinder, Endestad, & Magnussen, 2006).

Nevertheless, when properly questioned, even 3-year-olds can recall recent events accurately (Peterson & Rideout, 1998). And in the face of biased interviewing, adolescents and adults often form elaborate, false memories of events (Ceci et al., 2007).

Suggestibility

Court testimony often involves repeated interviews, which by itself impairs children's response consistency and accuracy (Krähenbühl, Blades, & Eiser, 2009). When adults lead witnesses by suggesting incorrect "facts," interrupt their denials, reinforce them for giving desired answers, or use a confrontational questioning style, they increase the likelihood of incorrect reporting (Bruck & Ceci, 2004; Owen-Kostelnik, Reppucci, & Meyer, 2006).

By the time children appear in court, weeks, months, or even years have passed since the target events. When a long delay is combined with biased interviewing and with stereotyping of the accused ("He's in jail because he's been bad"), children can easily be misled into giving false information (Gilstrap & Ceci, 2005; Quas et al., 2007). The more distinctive and personally relevant an event is, the more likely children are to recall it accurately over time. For example, a year later, even when exposed to misleading information, children correctly reported details of an injury that required emergency room treatment (Peterson, Parsons, & Dean, 2004).

In many sexual abuse cases, anatomically correct dolls are used to prompt children's recall. Although this method helps older children provide more detail about experienced events, it increases the suggestibility of preschoolers, who report physical and sexual contact that never happened (Goodman & Melinder, 2007).

Interventions

Adults must prepare child witnesses so they understand the courtroom process and know what to expect. In some places, "court schools" take children through the setting and give them an opportunity to role-play court activities. Practice interviews—in which children learn to provide the most accurate, detailed information possible and

School-age eyewitnesses are better able than preschoolers to give accurate, detailed descriptions and correctly infer others' motives and intentions. This police officer can promote accurate recall by using a warm, supportive tone and avoiding leading questions.

to admit not knowing rather than agreeing or guessing—are helpful (Saywitz, Goodman, & Lyon, 2002).

At the same time, legal professionals must use interviewing procedures that increase children's accurate reporting. Unbiased, open-ended questions that prompt children to disclose details—"Tell me what happened" or "You said there was a man; tell me about the man"—reduce suggestibility (Steele, 2012). Also, a warm, supportive interview tone fosters accurate recall, perhaps by easing children's anxiety so they feel freer to disagree with an interviewer's false suggestions (Ceci, Bruck, & Battin, 2000).

If children are likely to experience emotional trauma or later punishment (as in a family dispute), courtroom procedures can be adapted to protect them. For example, children can testify over closed-circuit TV so they do not have to face an abuser. When it is not wise for a child to participate directly, impartial expert witnesses can provide testimony that reports on the child's psychological condition and includes important elements of the child's story.

SUMMARY

Erikson's Theory: Industry versus Inferiority (p. 330)

What personality changes take place during Erikson's stage of industry versus inferiority?

- According to Erikson, children who successfully resolve the psychological conflict of **industry versus inferiority** develop a sense of competence at useful skills and tasks, learn the value of division of labor, and develop a sense of moral commitment and responsibility.

Self-Understanding (p. 330)

Describe school-age children's self-concept and self-esteem, and discuss factors that affect their achievement-related attributions.

- During middle childhood, children's self-concepts include personality traits, competencies, and **social comparisons.** The content of self-concept varies from culture to culture.

- Self-esteem differentiates further, becoming hierarchically organized and more realistic. Cultural forces, gender-stereotyped expectations, and child-rearing practices contribute to variations in self-esteem. Authoritative parenting is linked to favorable self-esteem.

- Children who hold **mastery-oriented attributions** believe ability can be improved by trying hard and attribute failure to controllable factors, such as insufficient effort. In contrast, children who receive negative feedback about their ability are likely to develop **learned helplessness,** attributing success to external factors, such as luck, and failure to low ability.

Emotional Development (p. 335)

Cite changes in self-conscious emotions, emotional understanding, and management of emotion in middle childhood.

- Self-conscious emotions of pride and guilt become clearly governed by personal responsibility. Intense shame is particularly destructive, yielding both internalizing and externalizing problems.

- School-age children develop an appreciation of mixed emotions and can reconcile contradictory cues in interpreting another's feelings. Empathy increases and includes sensitivity to both people's immediate distress and their general life condition.

- By age 10, most children shift adaptively between **problem-centered** and **emotion-centered coping** to regulate emotion. Children who acquire a sense of emotional self-efficacy are upbeat, empathic, and prosocial.

Moral Development (p. 336)

Describe changes in moral understanding during middle childhood, including children's understanding of diversity and inequality.

- By middle childhood, children have internalized rules for good conduct. They clarify and link moral imperatives and social conventions and develop a better understanding of personal choice and individual rights.

- Children of all races pick up prevailing societal attitudes about race and ethnicity. With age, they come to understand that people who look different need not think, feel, or act differently. Consequently, voicing of prejudice typically declines though automatic prejudice may persist. Children most likely to hold biases are those who believe that personality traits are fixed, who have inflated self-esteem, and who live in a social world that highlights group differences. Long-term intergroup contact is most effective at reducing prejudice.

Peer Relations (p. 339)

How do peer sociability and friendship change in middle childhood?

- Peer interaction becomes more prosocial, and physical aggression declines. By the end of middle childhood, children organize themselves into **peer groups.**

- Friendships develop into mutual relationships based on trust. Children tend to select friends similar to themselves in many ways.

Describe major categories of peer acceptance and ways to help rejected children.

- On measures of **peer acceptance, popular children** are well-liked by many agemates; **rejected children** are actively disliked; **controversial children** are both liked and disliked; and **neglected children** arouse little response, either positive or negative.

- **Popular-prosocial children** combine academic and social competence, while **popular-antisocial children** are aggressive but admired. **Rejected-aggressive children** are especially high in conflict and hostility; in contrast, **rejected-withdrawn children** are passive, socially awkward, and frequent targets of **peer victimization.**

- Coaching in social skills, academic tutoring, and training in perspective taking and social problem solving have been used to help rejected children gain in social competence and peer acceptance. Intervening to improve the quality of parent–child interaction is often necessary.

Gender Typing (p. 343)

What changes in gender-stereotyped beliefs and gender identity occur during middle childhood?

- School-age children extend their awareness of gender stereotypes to personality traits and academic subjects. But they also develop a more open-minded view of what males and females can do.

- Boys strengthen their identification with masculine traits, whereas girls more often experiment with "other-gender" activities. Gender identity includes self-evaluations of gender typicality, contentedness, and felt pressure to conform to gender roles—each of which affects adjustment.

Family Influences (p. 345)

How do parent–child communication and sibling relationships change in middle childhood?

- Despite declines in time spent with parents, **coregulation** allows parents to exercise general oversight over children, who increasingly make their own decisions.

- Sibling rivalry tends to increase with participation in a wider range of activities and more frequent parental comparisons. Only children do not differ from children with siblings in self-rated personality traits and are higher in self-esteem, school performance, and educational attainment.

What factors influence children's adjustment to divorce and blended family arrangements?

- Marital breakup is often quite stressful for children. Individual differences are affected by parental psychological health, child characteristics (age, temperament, and sex), and social supports. Children with difficult temperaments are at greater risk for adjustment problems. Divorce is linked to early sexual activity, adolescent parenthood, and long-term relationship difficulties.

- The overriding factor in positive adjustment following divorce is effective parenting. Positive father–child relationships are protective, as are supports from extended-family members, teachers, siblings, and friends. Divorce mediation can foster parental conflict resolution in the period surrounding divorce. The success of joint custody depends on effective coparenting.

- When divorced parents enter new relationships and form **blended,** or **reconstituted, families,** girls, older children, and children in father–stepmother families tend to have more adjustment problems. Stepparents who move into their roles gradually help children adjust.

How do maternal employment and life in dual-earner families affect school-age children?

- When employed mothers enjoy their work and remain committed to parenting, their children benefit from higher self-esteem, more positive family and peer relations, less gender-stereotyped beliefs, and better school grades. In dual-earner families, the father's willingness to share responsibilities is a crucial factor. Workplace supports help parents in their child-rearing roles.

- Authoritative child rearing, parental monitoring, and regular after-school chores lead **self-care children** to be responsible and well-adjusted. Good "after-care" programs also aid school performance and emotional and social adjustment, with special benefits for low-SES children.

Some Common Problems of Development (p. 352)

Cite common fears and anxieties in middle childhood.

- School-age children's fears are directed toward new concerns, including physical harm, media events, academic failure, parents' health, and peer rejection. Children with inhibited temperaments are at higher risk of developing **phobias.** Harsh living conditions can also cause severe anxiety.

Discuss factors related to child sexual abuse, its consequences for children's development, and its prevention and treatment.

- Child sexual abuse is typically committed by male family members, more often against girls than boys. Abusers have characteristics that predispose them toward sexual exploitation of children. Reported cases are strongly associated with poverty and marital instability. Abused children often have severe adjustment problems.

- Treatment for abused children typically requires long-term therapy with both children and parents. Educational programs that teach children to recognize inappropriate sexual advances and identify sources of help reduce the risk of sexual abuse.

Cite factors that foster resilience in middle childhood.

- Only a modest relationship exists between stressful life experiences and psychological disturbance in childhood. Children's personal characteristics, a warm family life, authoritative parenting, and school, community, and societal resources predict resilience.

Important Terms and Concepts

blended, or reconstituted, families (p. 349)
controversial children (p. 341)
coregulation (p. 345)
emotion-centered coping (p. 336)
industry versus inferiority (p. 330)
learned helplessness (p. 333)
mastery-oriented attributions (p. 333)

neglected children (p. 341)
peer acceptance (p. 341)
peer group (p. 339)
peer victimization (p. 342)
phobia (p. 352)
popular-antisocial children (p. 341)
popular children (p. 341)

popular-prosocial children (p. 341)
problem-centered coping (p. 336)
rejected-aggressive children (p. 341)
rejected children (p. 341)
rejected-withdrawn children (p. 341)
self-care children (p. 351)
social comparisons (p. 330)

milestones

Development in Middle Childhood

■ Self-concept begins to include personality traits, competencies, and social comparisons. (330)

■ Self-esteem differentiates, becomes hierarchically organized, and declines to a more realistic level. (331)

■ Self-conscious emotions of pride and guilt are governed by personal responsibility. (335)

■ Recognizes that individuals can experience more than one emotion at a time and that people's expressions may not reflect their true feelings. (335)

6–8 years

PHYSICAL

■ Slow gains in height and weight continue until adolescent growth spurt. (290)

■ Permanent teeth gradually replace primary teeth. (290)

■ Legibility of writing increases, preparing children to master cursive writing. (295)

■ Drawings become more organized and detailed and include some depth cues. (295)

■ Games with rules and rough-and-tumble play become common. (296, 297)

COGNITIVE

■ Thought becomes more logical, as shown by the ability to pass Piagetian conservation, class inclusion, and seriation problems. (299–300)

■ Attention becomes more selective, adaptable, and planful. (303)

■ Uses memory strategies of rehearsal and then organization. (304)

■ Views the mind as an active, constructive agent, capable of transforming information. (306)

■ Awareness of memory strategies and the impact of psychological factors, such as mental inferences, on performance improves. (306)

■ Appreciates second-order false beliefs. (306)

■ Uses informal knowledge of number concepts and counting to master increasingly complex mathematical skills. (308)

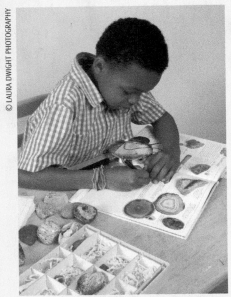

LANGUAGE

■ Vocabulary increases rapidly throughout middle childhood, eventually exceeding comprehension of 40,000 words. (316)

■ Word definitions are concrete, referring to functions and appearance. (316)

■ Narratives increase in organization, detail, and expressiveness. (317)

■ Transitions from emergent literacy to conventional reading. (308)

■ Language awareness improves. (316)

■ Conversational strategies become more refined. (316–317)

■ Reconciles contradictory facial and situational cues in understanding another's feelings. (335)

■ Empathy increases. (335)

■ Becomes more independent and trustworthy. (336)

■ Constructs a flexible appreciation of moral rules, taking prosocial and antisocial intentions into account. (336)

■ Physical aggression declines; verbal and relational aggression continue. (339)

■ Resolves conflicts more effectively. (339)

9–11 years

PHYSICAL

■ Adolescent growth spurt begins two years earlier in girls than in boys. (290)

Note: Numbers in parentheses indicate the page or pages on which each milestone is discussed.

- Executes gross-motor skills of running, jumping, throwing, catching, kicking, batting, and dribbling more quickly and with better coordination. (294)
- Steady gains in attention and reaction time contribute to improved motor performance. (295)
- Representation of depth in drawings expands. (295)
- Dominance hierarchies become more stable, especially among boys. (297)

COGNITIVE

- Continues to master Piagetian tasks in a step-by-step fashion. (301)
- Spatial reasoning improves; readily draws and reads maps of large-scale spaces, and grasps the notion of scale. (300)

- Selective attention and planning improve further. (303–304)
- Uses memory strategies of rehearsal and organization more effectively. (303)
- Applies several memory strategies simultaneously; begins to use elaboration. (304)
- Long-term knowledge base grows larger and becomes better organized. (305–306)
- Theory of mind becomes more elaborate and refined. (306)
- Cognitive self-regulation improves. (307)

LANGUAGE

- Thinks about and uses words more precisely; word definitions emphasize synonyms and categorical relations. (316)

- Grasps double meanings of words, as reflected in comprehension of metaphors and humor. (316)
- Continues to master complex grammatical constructions. (316)
- Continues to refine conversational strategies. (317)
- Narratives lengthen, become more coherent, and include more evaluative comments. (317)

EMOTIONAL/SOCIAL

- Self-esteem tends to rise (331)
- Distinguishes ability, effort, and external factors (such as luck) in attributions for success and failure. (333)
- Empathic responding extends to general life conditions. (335–336)

- Shifts adaptively between problem-centered and emotion-centered strategies in regulating emotion. (336)

- Becomes more knowledgeable about socially approved ways to display negative emotion. (336)
- Clarifies and links moral rules and social conventions. (337)
- Convictions about matters of personal choice strengthen, and understanding of individual rights expands. (337)
- Overt expressions of outgroup prejudice decline. (338)
- Friendships become more selective and are based on mutual trust. (340)
- Peer groups emerge. (339)

- Becomes aware of more gender stereotypes, including personality traits and achievement, but has a flexible appreciation of what males and females can do. (343–344)
- Gender identity expands to include self-evaluations of typicality, contentedness, and felt pressure to conform. (344)
- Sibling rivalry tends to increase. (345–346)

© TIM PANNELL/CORBIS

The dramatic physical and cognitive changes of adolescence make it both an exhilarating and apprehensive period of development. Although their bodies are full-grown and sexually mature, these exuberant teenagers have many skills to acquire and hurdles to surmount before they are ready for full assumption of adult roles.

Physical and Cognitive Development in Adolescence

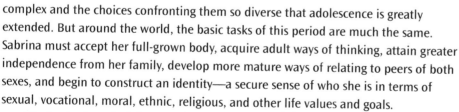

On Sabrina's eleventh birthday, her friend Joyce gave her a surprise party, but Sabrina seemed somber during the celebration. Although Sabrina and Joyce had been close friends since third grade, their relationship was faltering. Sabrina was a head taller and some 20 pounds heavier than most girls in her sixth-grade class. Her breasts were well-developed, her hips and thighs had broadened, and she had begun to menstruate. In contrast, Joyce still had the short, lean, flat-chested body of a school-age child.

Ducking into the bathroom while the other girls put candles on the cake, Sabrina frowned at her image in the mirror. "I'm so big and heavy," she whispered. At church youth group on Sunday evenings, Sabrina broke away from Joyce and joined the eighth-grade girls. Around them, she didn't feel so large and awkward.

Once a month, parents gathered at Sabrina's and Joyce's school to discuss child-rearing concerns. Sabrina's parents, Franca and Antonio, attended whenever they could. "How you know they are becoming teenagers is this," volunteered Antonio. "The bedroom door is closed, and they want to be alone. Also, they contradict and disagree. I tell Sabrina, 'You have to go to Aunt Gina's on Saturday for dinner with the family.' The next thing I know, she's arguing with me."

© DANIEL GRILL/TETRA IMAGES/CORBIS

Sabrina has entered **adolescence**, the transition between childhood and adulthood. In industrialized societies, the skills young people must master are so complex and the choices confronting them so diverse that adolescence is greatly extended. But around the world, the basic tasks of this period are much the same. Sabrina must accept her full-grown body, acquire adult ways of thinking, attain greater independence from her family, develop more mature ways of relating to peers of both sexes, and begin to construct an identity—a secure sense of who she is in terms of sexual, vocational, moral, ethnic, religious, and other life values and goals.

The beginning of adolescence is marked by **puberty**, a flood of biological events leading to an adult-sized body and sexual maturity. As Sabrina's reactions suggest, entry into adolescence can be an especially trying time for some young people. In this chapter, we trace the events of puberty and take up a variety of health concerns—physical exercise, nutrition, sexual activity, substance abuse, and other challenges that many teenagers encounter on the path to maturity.

chapter outline

PHYSICAL DEVELOPMENT

Conceptions of Adolescence

The Biological Perspective • The Social Perspective • A Balanced Point of View

Puberty: The Physical Transition to Adulthood

Hormonal Changes • Body Growth • Motor Development and Physical Activity • Sexual Maturation • Individual Differences in Pubertal Growth • Brain Development • Changing States of Arousal

The Psychological Impact of Pubertal Events

Reactions to Pubertal Changes • Pubertal Change, Emotion, and Social Behavior • Pubertal Timing

Health Issues

Nutritional Needs • Eating Disorders • Sexuality • Sexually Transmitted Diseases • Adolescent Pregnancy and Parenthood • Substance Use and Abuse

■ **SOCIAL ISSUES: HEALTH** Lesbian, Gay, and Bisexual Youths: Coming Out to Oneself and Others

COGNITIVE DEVELOPMENT

Piaget's Theory: The Formal Operational Stage

Hypothetico-Deductive Reasoning • Propositional Thought • Follow-Up Research on Formal Operational Thought

An Information-Processing View of Adolescent Cognitive Development

Scientific Reasoning: Coordinating Theory with Evidence • How Scientific Reasoning Develops

Consequences of Adolescent Cognitive Changes

Self-Consciousness and Self-Focusing • Idealism and Criticism • Decision Making

Sex Differences in Mental Abilities
Verbal Abilities • Mathematical Abilities

■ **BIOLOGY AND ENVIRONMENT** Sex Differences in Spatial Abilities

Learning in School

School Transitions • Academic Achievement • Dropping Out

■ **SOCIAL ISSUES: EDUCATION** Media Multitasking Disrupts Attention and Learning

Adolescence also brings with it vastly expanded powers of reasoning. Teenagers can grasp complex scientific and mathematical principles, grapple with social and political issues, and delve deeply into the meaning of a poem or story. The second part of this chapter traces these extraordinary changes from both Piaget's and the information-processing perspective. Next, we examine sex differences in mental abilities. Finally, we turn to the main setting in which adolescent thought takes shape: the school. ●

PHYSICAL DEVELOPMENT

Conceptions of Adolescence

Why is Sabrina self-conscious, argumentative, and in retreat from family activities? Historically, theorists explained the impact of puberty on psychological development by resorting to extremes—either a biological or a social explanation. Today, researchers realize that biological and social forces jointly determine adolescent psychological change.

The Biological Perspective

TAKE A MOMENT... Ask several parents of young children what they expect their sons and daughters to be like as teenagers. You will probably get answers like these: "Rebellious and irresponsible," "Full of rages and tempers." This widespread storm-and-stress view dates back to major early-twentieth-century theorists. The most influential, G. Stanley Hall, based his ideas on Darwin's theory of evolution. Hall (1904) described adolescence as a period so turbulent that it resembled the era in which humans evolved from savages into civilized beings. Similarly, in Freud's psychosexual theory, sexual impulses reawaken in the *genital stage,* triggering psychological conflict and volatile behavior. As adolescents find intimate partners, inner forces gradually achieve a new, mature harmony, and the stage concludes with marriage, birth, and child rearing. In this way, young people fulfill their biological destiny: sexual reproduction and survival of the species.

The Social Perspective

Contemporary research suggests that the storm-and-stress notion of adolescence is exaggerated. Certain problems, such as eating disorders, depression, suicide, and lawbreaking, do occur more often than earlier (Farrington, 2009; Graber, 2004). But the overall rate of serious psychological disturbance rises only slightly from childhood to adolescence, reaching 15 to 20

percent (Merikangas et al., 2010). Though much greater than the adulthood rate (about 6 percent), emotional turbulence is not a routine feature of the teenage years.

The first researcher to point out the wide variability in adolescent adjustment was anthropologist Margaret Mead (1928). She returned from the Pacific islands of Samoa with a startling conclusion: Because of the culture's relaxed social relationships and openness toward sexuality, adolescence "is perhaps the pleasantest time the Samoan girl (or boy) will ever know" (p. 308). Mead offered an alternative view in which the social environment is entirely responsible for the range of teenage experiences, from erratic and agitated to calm and stress-free. Later researchers found that Samoan adolescence was not as untroubled as Mead had assumed (Freeman, 1983). Still, she showed that to understand adolescent development, researchers must pay greater attention to social and cultural influences.

A Balanced Point of View

Today we know that biological, psychological, and social forces combine to influence adolescent development (Susman & Dorn, 2009). Biological changes are universal—found in all primates and all cultures. These internal stresses and the social expectations accompanying them—that the young person give up childish ways, develop new interpersonal relationships, and take on greater responsibility—are likely to prompt moments of uncertainty, self-doubt, and disappointment in all teenagers. Adolescents' prior and current experiences affect their success in surmounting these challenges.

At the same time, the length of adolescence and its demands and pressures vary substantially among cultures. Most tribal and village societies have only a brief intervening phase between childhood and full assumption of adult roles (Weisfield, 1997). In industrialized nations, young people face prolonged dependence on parents and postponement of sexual gratification while they prepare for a productive work life. As a result, adolescence is greatly extended—so much so that researchers commonly divide it into three phases:

1. *Early adolescence* (11–12 to 14 years): This is a period of rapid pubertal change.
2. *Middle adolescence* (14 to 16 years): Pubertal changes are now nearly complete.
3. *Late adolescence* (16 to 18 years): The young person achieves full adult appearance and anticipates assumption of adult roles.

The more the social environment supports young people in achieving adult responsibilities, the better they adjust. For all the biological tensions and uncertainties about the future that teenagers feel, most negotiate this period successfully. With this in mind, let's look closely at puberty, the dawning of adolescent development.

Puberty: The Physical Transition to Adulthood

The changes of puberty are dramatic: Within a few years, the body of the school-age child is transformed into that of a full-grown adult. Genetically influenced hormonal processes regulate pubertal growth. Girls, who have been advanced in physical maturity since the prenatal period, reach puberty, on average, two years earlier than boys.

Hormonal Changes

The complex hormonal changes that underlie puberty occur gradually and are under way by age 8 or 9. Secretions of *growth hormone (GH)* and *thyroxine* (see Chapter 7, page 219) increase, leading to tremendous gains in body size and to attainment of skeletal maturity.

Sexual maturation is controlled by the sex hormones. Although we think of *estrogens* as female hormones and *androgens* as male hormones, both types are present in each sex but in different amounts. The boy's testes release large quantities of the androgen *testosterone,* which leads to muscle growth, body and facial hair, and other male sex characteristics. Androgens (especially testosterone for boys) exert a GH-enhancing effect, contributing greatly to gains in body size. Because the testes secrete small amounts of estrogen as well, 50 percent of boys experience temporary breast enlargement. In both sexes, estrogens also increase GH secretion, adding to the growth spurt and, in combination with androgens, stimulating gains in bone density, which continue into early adulthood (Cooper, Sayer, & Dennison, 2006; Styne, 2003).

Estrogens released by girls' ovaries cause the breasts, uterus, and vagina to mature, the body to take on feminine proportions, and fat to accumulate. Estrogens also contribute to regulation of the menstrual cycle. *Adrenal androgens,* released from the adrenal glands on top of each kidney, influence girls' height spurt and stimulate growth of underarm and pubic hair. They have little impact on boys, whose physical characteristics are influenced mainly by androgen and estrogen secretions from the testes.

As you can see, pubertal changes are of two broad types: (1) overall body growth and (2) maturation of sexual characteristics. We have seen that the hormones responsible for sexual maturity also affect body growth, making puberty the time of greatest sexual differentiation since prenatal life.

Body Growth

The first outward sign of puberty is the rapid gain in height and weight known as the **growth spurt**. On average, it is under way for North American girls shortly after age 10, for boys around age 12½. Because estrogens trigger and then restrain GH secretion more readily than androgens, the typical girl is taller and

Sex differences in pubertal growth are obvious among these 11-year-olds. Compared with the boys, the girls are taller and more mature-looking.

heavier during early adolescence (Archibald, Graber, & Brooks-Gunn, 2006; Bogin, 2001). At age 14, however, she is surpassed by the typical boy, whose adolescent growth spurt has now started, whereas hers is almost finished. Growth in body size is complete for most girls by age 16 and for boys by age 17½, when the epiphyses at the ends of the long bones close completely (see Chapter 7, page 217). Altogether, adolescents add 10 to 11 inches in height and 50 to 75 pounds—nearly 50 percent of adult body weight. Figure 11.1 on page 364 illustrates pubertal changes in general body growth.

Body Proportions. During puberty, the cephalocaudal growth trend of infancy and childhood reverses. The hands, legs, and feet accelerate first, followed by the torso, which accounts for most of the adolescent height gain. This pattern helps explain why early adolescents often appear awkward and out of proportion—long-legged, with giant feet and hands.

Large sex differences in body proportions also appear, caused by the action of sex hormones on the skeleton. Boys' shoulders broaden relative to the hips, whereas girls' hips broaden relative to the shoulders and waist. Of course, boys also end up larger than girls, and their legs are longer in relation to the rest of the body—mainly because boys have two extra years of preadolescent growth, when the legs are growing the fastest.

Muscle–Fat Makeup and Other Internal Changes. Sabrina worried about her weight because compared with her later-developing girlfriends, she had accumulated much more fat. Around age 8, girls start to add fat on their arms, legs, and trunk, a trend that accelerates between ages 11 and 16. In contrast, arm and leg fat decreases in adolescent boys. Although both sexes gain in muscle, this increase is much greater in boys, who develop larger skeletal muscles, hearts, and lung capacity (Rogol, Roemmich, & Clark, 2002). Also, the number of red blood cells—and therefore the ability to carry oxygen from the lungs to the muscles—increases in boys but not in girls.

Kate at 13

Kate at 17

Kate at 11

Steven at 13

Steven at 16

Steven at 18

FIGURE 11.1 **Body growth during adolescence.** Because the pubertal growth spurt takes place earlier for girls than for boys, Kate reached her adult body size earlier than Steven. Rapid pubertal growth is accompanied by large sex differences in body proportions.

Altogether, boys gain far more muscle strength than girls, a difference that contributes to teenage boys' superior athletic performance (Ramos et al., 1998).

Motor Development and Physical Activity

Puberty brings steady improvements in gross motor performance, but the pattern of change differs for boys and girls. Girls' gains are slow and gradual, leveling off by age 14. In contrast, boys show a dramatic spurt in strength, speed, and endurance that continues through the teenage years. By midadolescence, few girls perform as well as the average boy in running speed, broad jump, or throwing distance, and practically no boys score as low as the average girl (Haywood & Getchell, 2005; Malina & Bouchard, 1991).

Because girls and boys are no longer well-matched physically, gender-segregated physical education usually begins in middle school. Athletic options for both sexes expand as new sports—including track and field, wrestling, tackle football, weight lifting, floor hockey, archery, tennis, and golf—are added to the curriculum.

Among boys, athletic competence is strongly related to peer admiration and self-esteem. Some adolescents become so obsessed with physical prowess that they turn to performance-enhancing drugs. In recent large-scale studies, about 8 percent of U.S. high school seniors, mostly boys, reported using creatine, an over-the-counter substance that enhances short-term muscle power but carries a risk of serious side effects, including muscle tissue disease, brain seizures, and heart irregularities (Castillo & Comstock, 2007). About 2 percent of seniors, again mostly boys, have taken anabolic steroids or a related substance, androstenedione—powerful prescription medications that boost muscle mass and strength (Johnston et al., 2012). Teenagers usually obtain steroids illegally, ignoring side effects, which range from acne, excess body hair, and high blood pressure to mood swings, aggressive behavior, and damage to the liver, circulatory system, and reproductive organs (Casavant et al., 2007). Coaches and health professionals should inform teenagers of the dangers of these performance-enhancing substances.

In 1972, the U.S. federal government required schools receiving public funds to provide equal opportunities for males and females in all educational programs, including athletics. Since then, high school girls' sports participation has increased, but it still falls far short of boys'. According to a recent survey of all 50 U.S. state high school athletic associations, 41 percent of sports participants are girls, 59 percent boys (National

Federation of State High School Associations, 2012). In Chapter 9, we saw that girls get less encouragement and recognition for athletic achievement, a pattern that starts early and persists into the teenage years (see page 296).

Furthermore, when researchers followed a large, representative sample of U.S. youths from ages 9 to 15, physical activity declined by about 40 minutes per day each year until, at age 15, less than one-third met the U.S. government recommendation of at least 60 minutes of moderate to strenuous physical activity per day (see Figure 11.2) (Nader et al., 2008). In high school, only 57 percent of U.S. boys and 47 percent of girls are enrolled in any physical education, with 31 percent of all students experiencing a daily physical education class (U.S. Department of Health and Human Services, 2012f).

Besides improving motor performance, sports and exercise influence cognitive and social development. Interschool and intramural athletics provide important lessons in teamwork, problem solving, assertiveness, and competition. And regular, sustained physical activity—which required physical education can ensure—is associated with lasting physical and mental health benefits and enjoyment of sports and exercise (Brand et al., 2010). In one study, participating in team or individual sports at age 14 at least once a week for girls and twice a week for boys predicted high physical activity rates at age 31. Endurance sports, such as running and cycling—activities that do not require expensive equipment or special facilities—were especially likely to continue into adulthood (Tammelin et al., 2003). And adolescent exertion during exercise, defined as

High school girls' participation in sports has increased but still falls far short of boys'. Yet athletic participation yields many benefits—not just gains in motor skills but important lessons in teamwork, problem solving, assertiveness, and competition.

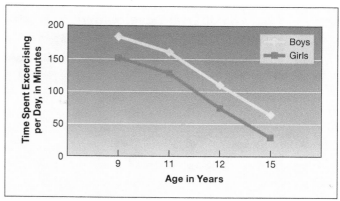

FIGURE 11.2 **Decline in physical activity from ages 9 to 15 among U.S. boys and girls.** In a large representative sample of youths followed over six years, time spent exercising dropped sharply until, at age 15, most youths did not meet government recommendations of at least 60 minutes of moderate to vigorous physical activity per day. At all ages, boys spent more time exercising than girls. (Adapted from Nader et al., 2008.)

sweating and breathing heavily, is one of the best predictors of adult physical exercise, perhaps because it fosters high *physical self-efficacy*—belief in one's ability to sustain an exercise program (Motl et al., 2002; Telama et al., 2005).

Sexual Maturation

Accompanying rapid body growth are changes in physical features related to sexual functioning. Some, called **primary sexual characteristics**, involve the reproductive organs (ovaries, uterus, and vagina in females; penis, scrotum, and testes in males). Others, called **secondary sexual characteristics**, are visible on the outside of the body and serve as additional signs of sexual maturity (for example, breast development in females and the appearance of underarm and pubic hair in both sexes). As Table 11.1 on page 366 shows, these characteristics develop in a fairly standard sequence, although the ages at which each begins and is completed vary greatly. Typically, pubertal development takes about four years, but some adolescents complete it in two years, whereas others take five to six years.

Sexual Maturation in Girls. Female puberty usually begins with the budding of the breasts and the growth spurt. **Menarche**, or first menstruation, typically occurs around age 12½ for North American girls, 13 for Western Europeans. But the age range is wide, from 10½ to 15½ years. Following menarche, breast and pubic hair growth are completed, and underarm hair appears.

Notice in Table 11.1 that nature delays sexual maturity until the girl's body is large enough for childbearing; menarche takes place after the peak of the height spurt. As an extra measure of security, for 12 to 18 months following menarche, the menstrual cycle often occurs without the release of an ovum from the ovaries (Archibald, Graber, & Brooks-Gunn, 2006; Bogin, 2001). But this temporary period of sterility does not

TABLE 11.1 **Pubertal Development in North American Girls and Boys**

GIRLS	AVERAGE AGE ATTAINED	AGE RANGE	BOYS	AVERAGE AGE ATTAINED	AGE RANGE
Breasts begin to "bud"	10	8–13	Testes begin to enlarge	11.5	9.5–13.5
Height spurt begins	10	8–13	Pubic hair appears	12	10–15
Pubic hair appears	10.5	8–14	Penis begins to enlarge	12	10.5–14.5
Peak strength spurt	11.6	9.5–14	Height spurt begins	12.5	10.5–16
Peak height spurt	11.7	10–13.5	Spermarche (first ejaculation) occurs	13.5	12–16
Menarche (first menstruation) occurs	12.5	10.5–14	Peak height spurt	14	12.5–15.5
Peak weight spurt	12.7	10–14	Peak weight spurt	14	12.5–15.5
Adult stature reached	13	10–16	Facial hair begins to grow	14	12.5–15.5
Pubic hair growth completed	14.5	14–15	Voice begins to deepen	14	12.5–15.5
Breast growth completed	15	10–17	Penis and testes growth completed	14.5	12.5–16
			Peak strength spurt	15.3	13–17
			Adult stature reached	15.5	13.5–17.5
			Pubic hair growth completed	15.5	14–17

Sources: Chumlea et al., 2003; Herman-Giddens, 2006; Rogol, Roemmich, & Clark, 2002; Rubin et al., 2009; Wu, Mendola, & Buck, 2002.
Photos: (left) © Laura Dwight Photography; (right) Rob Melnychuk/Taxi/Getty Images

occur in all girls, and it does not provide reliable protection against pregnancy.

Sexual Maturation in Boys. The first sign of puberty in boys is the enlargement of the testes (glands that manufacture sperm), accompanied by changes in the texture and color of the scrotum. Pubic hair emerges soon after, about the same time the penis begins to enlarge (Rogol, Roemmich, & Clark, 2002).

As Table 11.1 reveals, the growth spurt occurs much later in the sequence of pubertal events for boys than for girls. When it reaches its peak around age 14, enlargement of the testes and penis is nearly complete, and underarm hair appears. So do facial and body hair, which increase gradually for several years. Another landmark of male physical maturity is the deepening of the voice as the larynx enlarges and the vocal cords lengthen. (Girls' voices also deepen slightly.) Voice change usually takes place at the peak of the male growth spurt and is often not complete until puberty is over (Archibald, Graber, & Brooks-Gunn, 2006).

While the penis is growing, the prostate gland and seminal vesicles (which together produce semen, the fluid containing sperm) enlarge. Then, around age 13½, **spermarche**, or first ejaculation, occurs (Rogol, Roemmich, & Clark, 2002). For a while, the semen contains few living sperm. So, like girls, boys have an initial period of reduced fertility.

Individual Differences in Pubertal Growth

Heredity contributes substantially to the timing of pubertal changes. Identical twins are more similar than fraternal twins in attainment of most pubertal milestones (Eaves et al., 2004; Mustanski et al., 2004). Nutrition and exercise also make a difference. In females, a sharp rise in body weight and fat may trigger sexual maturation. Fat cells release a protein called *leptin,* which is believed to signal the brain that the girl's energy stores are sufficient for puberty—a likely reason that breast and pubic hair growth and menarche occur earlier for heavier and, especially, obese girls. In contrast, girls who begin rigorous athletic training at an early age or who eat very little (both of which reduce the percentage of body fat) usually experience later puberty (Kaplowitz, 2007; Lee et al., 2007; Rubin et al., 2009). Few studies, however, report a link between body fat and puberty in boys.

Variations in pubertal growth also exist among regions of the world and among SES and ethnic groups. Physical health plays a major role. In poverty-stricken regions where malnutrition and infectious disease are common, menarche is greatly delayed, occurring as late as age 14 to 16 in many parts of Africa. Within developing countries, girls from higher-income families reach menarche 6 to 18 months earlier than those living in economically disadvantaged homes (Parent et al., 2003).

But in industrialized nations where food is abundant, the joint roles of heredity and environment in pubertal growth are apparent. For example, breast and pubic hair growth begin, on average, around age 9 in African-American girls—a year earlier than in Caucasian-American girls. And African-American girls reach menarche about six months earlier, around age 12. Although widespread overweight and obesity in the black population contribute, a genetically influenced faster rate of physical maturation is also involved. Black girls usually reach menarche before white girls of the same age and body weight (Chumlea et al., 2003; Herman-Giddens, 2006; Hillard, 2008).

Early family experiences may also affect pubertal timing. One theory suggests that humans have evolved to be sensitive to the emotional quality of their childhood environments. When children's safety and security are at risk, it is adaptive for them to reproduce early. Research indicates that girls and (less consistently) boys with a history of family conflict, harsh parenting, or parental separation tend to reach puberty early. In contrast, those with warm, stable family ties reach puberty relatively late (Belsky et al., 2007; Bogaert, 2005; Ellis, 2004; Ellis & Essex, 2007; Mustanski et al., 2004; Tremblay & Frigon, 2005). Critics offer an alternative explanation—that mothers who reached puberty early are more likely to bear children earlier, which increases the likelihood of marital conflict and separation (Mendle et al., 2006). But two longitudinal studies confirm the former chain of influence among girls: from adverse family environments in childhood to earlier pubertal timing to increased sexual risk taking (Belsky et al., 2010; James et al., 2012).

In the research we have considered, threats to emotional health accelerate puberty, whereas threats to physical health delay it. A **secular trend**, or generational change, in pubertal timing lends added support to the role of physical well-being in pubertal development. In industrialized nations, age of menarche declined steadily—by about 3 to 4 months per decade—from 1900 to 1970, a period in which nutrition, health care, sanitation, and control of infectious disease improved greatly. Boys, too, have reached puberty earlier in recent decades (Herman-Giddens et al., 2012). And as developing nations make socioeconomic progress, they also show secular gains (Ji & Chen, 2008).

In the United States and a few European countries, soaring rates of overweight and obesity are responsible for a modest, continuing trend toward earlier menarche (Kaplowitz, 2006; Parent et al., 2003). A worrisome consequence is that girls who reach sexual maturity at age 10 or 11 will feel pressure to act much older than they are. As we will see shortly, early-maturing girls are at risk for unfavorable peer involvements, including sexual activity.

Brain Development

The physical transformations of adolescence include major changes in the brain. Brain-imaging research reveals continued pruning of unused synapses in the cerebral cortex, especially in the prefrontal cortex. In addition, linkages between the two cerebral hemispheres through the corpus callosum, and between

the prefrontal cortex and other areas in the cerebral cortex and the inner brain (including the amygdala), expand, myelinate, and attain rapid communication. As a result, the prefrontal cortex becomes a more effective "executive"—overseeing and managing the integrated functioning of various areas, yielding more complex, flexible, and adaptive thinking and behavior (Blakemore & Choudhury, 2006; Lenroot & Giedd, 2006). Consequently, adolescents gain in diverse cognitive skills, including processing speed and executive function.

But these advances occur gradually over the teenage years. fMRI evidence reveals that adolescents recruit the prefrontal cortex's network of connections with other brain areas less effectively than adults do. Because the *prefrontal cognitive-control network* still requires fine-tuning, teenagers' performance on executive function tasks requiring inhibition, planning, and future orientation (rejecting a smaller immediate reward in favor of a larger delayed reward) is not yet fully mature (McClure et al., 2004; Smith, Xiao, & Bechara, 2012; Steinberg et al., 2009).

Adding to these self-regulation difficulties are changes in the brain's *emotional/social network*. In humans and other mammals, neurons become more responsive to excitatory neurotransmitters during puberty. As a result, adolescents react more strongly to stressful events and experience pleasurable stimuli more intensely. But because the cognitive control network is not yet functioning optimally, most teenagers find it hard to manage these powerful feelings (Ernst & Spear, 2009; Steinberg et al., 2008). This imbalance contributes to teenagers' drive for novel experiences, including drug taking, reckless driving, unprotected sex, and delinquent activity (Pharo et al., 2011). In a longitudinal study of a nationally representative sample of 7,600 U.S. youths, researchers tracked changes in self-reported impulsivity and sensation seeking between ages 12 and 24 (Harden & Tucker-Drob, 2011). As Figure 11.3 on page 368 shows, impulsivity declined steadily with age—evidence for gradual improvement of the cognitive-control network. But

In adolescence, changes in the brain's emotional/social network outpace development of the cognitive-control network. As a result, teenagers do not yet have the capacity to control their powerful drive for new—and sometimes risky—experiences.

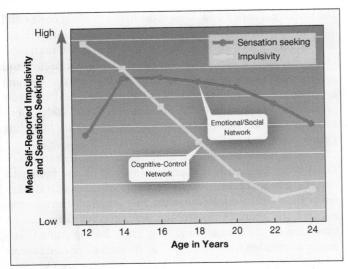

FIGURE 11.3 Development of impulsivity and sensation seeking from 12 to 24 years. In this longitudinal study of a large, nationally representative U.S. sample, impulsivity declined steadily, while sensation seeking increased in early adolescence and then diminished more gradually. Findings confirm the challenge posed by the emotional/social network to the cognitive control network. (From K. P. Harden and E. M. Tucker-Drob, 2011, "Individual Differences in the Development of Sensation Seeking and Impulsivity During Adolescence: Further Evidence for a Dual Systems Model," *Developmental Psychology, 47,* p. 742. Copyright © 2011 by the American Psychological Association. Adapted with permission of the American Psychological Association.)

sensation seeking increased from 12 to 16, followed by a more gradual decline through age 24, reflecting the challenge posed by the emotional/social network.

In sum, changes in the adolescent brain's emotional/social network outpace development of the cognitive-control network. Only over time are young people able to effectively manage their emotions and reward-seeking behavior. Of course, wide individual differences exist in the extent to which teenagers manifest this rise in risk-taking in the form of careless, dangerous acts—some not at all, and others extremely so (Pharo et al., 2011). But transformations in the adolescent brain enhance our understanding of both the cognitive advances and the worrisome behaviors of this period, along with teenagers' need for adult patience, oversight, and guidance.

Changing States of Arousal

At puberty, revisions occur in the way the brain regulates the timing of sleep, perhaps because of increased neural sensitivity to evening light. As a result, adolescents go to bed much later than they did as children. Yet they need almost as much sleep as they did in middle childhood—about nine hours. When the school day begins early, their sleep needs are not satisfied.

This sleep "phase delay" strengthens with pubertal growth. But today's teenagers—who often have evening social activities, part-time jobs, and bedrooms equipped with TVs, computers, and phones—get much less sleep than teenagers of previous

generations (Carskadon et al., 2002; Jenni, Achermann, & Carskadon, 2005). Sleep-deprived adolescents display declines in executive function, performing especially poorly on cognitive tasks during morning hours. And they are more likely to achieve less well in school, suffer from anxiety and depressed mood, and engage in high-risk behaviors (Dahl & Lewin, 2002; Hansen et al., 2005; Talbot et al., 2010). Sleep rebound on weekends sustains the pattern by leading to difficulty falling asleep on subsequent evenings. Later school start times ease but do not eliminate sleep loss. Educating teenagers about the importance of sleep is vital.

The Psychological Impact of Pubertal Events

TAKE A MOMENT... Think back to your late elementary and middle school days. As you reached puberty, how did your feelings about yourself and your relationships with others change? Research reveals that pubertal events affect adolescents' self-image, mood, and interaction with parents and peers. Some outcomes are a response to dramatic physical change, whenever it occurs. Others have to do with pubertal timing.

Reactions to Pubertal Changes

Two generations ago, menarche was often traumatic. Today, girls commonly react with "surprise," undoubtedly due to the sudden onset of the event. Otherwise, they typically report a mixture of positive and negative emotions (DeRose & Brooks-Gunn, 2006). Yet wide individual differences exist that depend on prior knowledge and support from family members, which in turn are influenced by cultural attitudes toward puberty and sexuality.

For girls who have no advance information, menarche can be shocking and disturbing. Unlike 50 to 60 years ago, today few girls are uninformed, a shift that is probably due to parents' greater willingness to discuss sexual matters and to the spread of health education classes (Omar, McElderry, & Zakharia, 2003). Almost all girls get some information from their mothers. And some evidence suggests that compared with Caucasian-American families, African-American families may better prepare girls for menarche, treat it as an important milestone, and express less conflict over girls reaching sexual maturity—factors that lead African-American girls to react more favorably (Martin, 1996).

Like girls' reactions to menarche, boys' responses to spermarche reflect mixed feelings. Virtually all boys know about ejaculation ahead of time, but many say that no one spoke to them before or during puberty about physical changes (Omar, McElderry, & Zakharia, 2003). Usually they get their information from reading material or websites. Even boys who had advance information often say that their first ejaculation occurred earlier than they expected and that they were unprepared for it. As with girls, boys who feel better prepared tend to react more positively (Stein & Reiser, 1994). But whereas almost all girls eventually tell a friend that they are menstruating, far fewer boys tell anyone about spermarche (DeRose & Brooks-Gunn, 2006; Downs & Fuller, 1991). Overall, boys get much less social support than girls for the physical changes of puberty. They might benefit, especially, from opportunities to ask questions and discuss feelings with a sympathetic parent or health professional.

Many tribal and village societies celebrate the onset of puberty with an *initiation ceremony,* a ritualized announcement to the community that marks an important change in privilege and responsibility. Consequently, young people know that reaching puberty is valued in their culture. In contrast, Western societies grant little formal recognition to movement from childhood to adolescence or from adolescence to adulthood. Ceremonies such as the Jewish bar or bat mitzvah and the *quinceañera* in Hispanic communities (celebrating a 15-year-old girl's sexual maturity and marriage availability), resemble initiation ceremonies, but only within the ethnic or religious subculture. They do not mark a significant change in social status in the larger society.

Instead, Western adolescents are granted partial adult status at many different ages—for example, an age for starting employment, for driving, for leaving high school, for voting, and for drinking. And in some contexts (at home and at school), they may still be regarded as children. The absence of a widely accepted marker of physical and social maturity makes the process of becoming an adult more confusing.

This 13-year-old's bat mitzvah ceremony recognizes her as an adult with moral and religious responsibilities in the Jewish community. In the larger society, however, she will experience no change in status.

Pubertal Change, Emotion, and Social Behavior

A common belief is that puberty has something to do with adolescent moodiness and the desire for greater physical and psychological separation from parents. Let's see what research says about these relationships.

Adolescent Moodiness. Higher pubertal hormone levels are linked to greater moodiness, but only modestly so (Buchanan, Eccles, & Becker, 1992; Graber, Brooks-Gunn, & Warren, 2006). What other factors might contribute? In several studies, the moods of children, adolescents, and adults were monitored by having them carry electronic pagers. Over a one-week period, they were beeped at random intervals and asked to write down what they were doing, whom they were with, and how they felt.

As expected, adolescents reported less favorable moods than school-age children and adults (Larson et al., 2002; Larson & Lampman-Petraitis, 1989). But negative moods were linked to a greater number of negative life events, such as difficulty getting along with parents, disciplinary actions at school, and breaking up with a boyfriend or girlfriend. Negative events increased steadily from childhood to adolescence, and teenagers also seemed to react to them with greater emotion than children (Larson & Ham, 1993). (Recall that stress reactivity is heightened by changes in the brain's emotional/social network during puberty.)

Compared with the moods of older adolescents and adults, those of younger adolescents (ages 12 to 16) were less stable, often shifting between cheerful and sad. These mood swings were strongly related to situational changes. High points of adolescents' days were times spent with peers and in self-chosen leisure activities. Low points tended to occur in adult-structured settings—class, job, and religious services. Furthermore, emotional highs coincided with Friday and Saturday evenings, especially in high school. Going out with friends and romantic partners increases so dramatically during adolescence that it becomes a "cultural script" for what is *supposed* to happen (Larson & Richards, 1998). Consequently, teenagers who spend weekend evenings at home often feel profoundly lonely.

Fortunately, frequent reports of negative mood level off in late adolescence (Natsuaki, Biehl, & Ge, 2009). And overall, teenagers with supportive family and peer relationships more often report positive and less often negative moods than their agemates with few social supports (Weinstein et al., 2006). In contrast, poorly adjusted young people—with low self-esteem, conduct difficulties, or delinquency—tend to react with stronger negative emotion to unpleasant daily experiences, perhaps compounding their adjustment problems (Schneiders et al., 2006).

Parent–Child Relationships. Sabrina's father noticed that as his children entered adolescence, they kept their bedroom doors closed, resisted spending time with the family, and became more argumentative. Sabrina and her mother squabbled over Sabrina's messy room ("It's *my* room, Mom. You don't have to live in it!"). And Sabrina protested the family's regular weekend visit to Aunt Gina's ("Why do I have to go *every* week?"). Research in cultures as diverse as the United States and Turkey shows that puberty is related to a rise in intensity of parent–child conflict, which persists into middle adolescence (Gure, Ucanok, & Sayil, 2006; Laursen, Coy, & Collins, 1998; McGue et al., 2005).

Why should a youngster's more adultlike appearance trigger these disputes? The association may have adaptive value. Among nonhuman primates, the young typically leave the family group around the time of puberty. The same is true in many nonindustrialized cultures (Caine, 1986; Schlegel & Barry, 1991). Departure of young people discourages sexual relations between close blood relatives. But adolescents in industrialized nations, who are still economically dependent on parents, cannot leave the family. Consequently, a substitute seems to have emerged: psychological distancing.

As children become physically mature, they demand to be treated in adultlike ways. And as we will see, adolescents' new powers of reasoning may also contribute to a rise in family tensions. Parent–adolescent disagreements focus largely on everyday matters such as driving, dating partners, and curfews (Adams & Laursen, 2001). But beneath these disputes lie serious concerns: parental efforts to protect teenagers from substance use, auto accidents, and early sex. The larger the gap between parents' and adolescents' views of teenagers' readiness for new responsibilities, the more they quarrel (Deković, Noom, & Meeus, 1997).

Parent–daughter conflict tends to be more intense than conflict with sons, perhaps because parents place more restrictions on girls (Allison & Schultz, 2004). But most disputes are mild and diminish by late adolescence. Parents and teenagers display both conflict and affection, and they usually agree on important values, such as honesty and the importance of education. And as the teenage years conclude, parent–adolescent interactions are less hierarchical, setting the stage for mutually supportive relationships in adulthood (Laursen & Collins, 2009).

LOOK AND LISTEN

Interview several parents and/or their 12- to 14-year-olds about recent changes in parent–child relationships. Has conflict increased? Over what topics? ●

Pubertal Timing

"All our children were early maturers," said Franca during the parents' discussion group. "The three boys were tall by age 12 or 13, but it was easier for them. They felt big and important. Sabrina was skinny as a little girl, but now she says she is too fat and needs to diet. She thinks about boys and doesn't concentrate on her schoolwork."

Findings of several studies match the experiences of Sabrina and her brothers. Both adults and peers viewed early-maturing boys as relaxed, independent, self-confident, and physically attractive. Popular with agemates, they tended to hold leadership positions in school and to be athletic stars. In contrast,

African-American early-maturing girls are more likely to report a positive body image than their Caucasian counterparts. Perhaps because their families and friends tend to welcome menarche, they may escape the adjustment difficulties commonly associated with early pubertal timing.

late-maturing boys expressed more anxiety and depressed mood than their on-time counterparts (Brooks-Gunn, 1988; Huddleston & Ge, 2003). But early-maturing boys, though viewed as well-adjusted, reported more psychological stress, depressed mood, and problem behaviors (sexual activity, smoking, drinking, aggression, delinquency) than both their on-time and later-maturing agemates (Ge, Conger, & Elder, 2001; Natsuaki, Biehl, & Ge, 2009; Susman & Dorn, 2009).

In contrast, early-maturing girls were unpopular, withdrawn, lacking in self-confidence, anxious (especially about others' negative evaluations), and prone to depression, and they held few leadership positions (Blumenthal et al., 2011; Ge, Conger, & Elder, 1996; Graber, Brooks-Gunn, & Warren, 2006; Jones & Mussen, 1958). And like early-maturing boys, they were more involved in deviant behavior (smoking, drinking, sexual activity) (Caspi et al., 1993; Dick et al., 2000; Ge et al., 2006). In contrast, their later-maturing counterparts were regarded as physically attractive, lively, sociable, and leaders at school. In one study of several hundred eighth graders, however, negative effects were not evident among early-maturing African-American girls, whose families—and perhaps friends as well—tend to be more unconditionally welcoming of menarche (see page 365) (Michael & Eccles, 2003).

Two factors largely account for these trends: (1) how closely the adolescent's body matches cultural ideals of physical attractiveness, and (2) how well young people fit in physically with their peers.

The Role of Physical Attractiveness. *TAKE A MOMENT...* Flip through your favorite popular magazine. You will see evidence of our society's view of an attractive female as thin and long-legged and of a good-looking male as tall, broad-shouldered, and muscular. The female image is a girlish shape that favors the late developer. The male image fits the early-maturing boy.

Consistent with these preferences, early-maturing Caucasian girls tend to report a less positive **body image**—conception of and attitude toward their physical appearance—than their on-time and late-maturing agemates. Compared with African-American and Hispanic girls, Caucasian girls are more likely to have internalized the cultural ideal of female attractiveness. Most want to be thinner (Rosen, 2003; Stice, Presnell, & Bearman, 2001; Williams & Currie, 2000). Although boys are less consistent, early, rapid maturers are more likely to be satisfied with their physical characteristics (Alsaker, 1995; Sinkkonen, Anttila, & Siimes, 1998).

Body image is a strong predictor of young people's self-esteem (Harter, 2006). But the negative effects of pubertal timing on body image and—as we will see next—emotional adjustment are greatly amplified when accompanied by other stressors (Stice, 2003).

The Importance of Fitting in with Peers. Physical status in relation to peers also explains differences in adjustment between early and late maturers. From this perspective, early-maturing girls and late-maturing boys have difficulty because they fall at the extremes of physical development and feel out of place when with their agemates. Not surprisingly, adolescents feel most comfortable with peers who match their own level of biological maturity (Stattin & Magnusson, 1990).

Because few agemates of the same pubertal status are available, early-maturing adolescents of both sexes seek out older companions, who often encourage them into activities they are not ready to handle emotionally. And hormonal influences on the brain's emotional/social network are stronger for early maturers, further magnifying their receptiveness to sexual activity, drug and alcohol use, and delinquent acts (Ge et al., 2002; Steinberg, 2008). Perhaps as a result, early maturers of both sexes more often report feeling stressed and show declines in academic performance (Mendle, Turkheimer, & Emery, 2007; Natsuaki, Biehl, & Ge, 2009).

At the same time, the young person's context greatly increases the likelihood that early pubertal timing will lead to negative outcomes. Early maturers in economically disadvantaged neighborhoods are especially vulnerable to establishing ties with deviant peers, which heightens their defiant, hostile behavior. And because families in such neighborhoods tend to be exposed to chronic, severe stressors and to have few social supports, these early maturers are also more likely to experience harsh, inconsistent parenting, which, in turn, predicts both deviant peer associations and antisocial behavior (Ge et al., 2002, 2011).

Long-Term Consequences. Do the effects of pubertal timing last? Follow-ups reveal that early-maturing girls, especially, are prone to lasting difficulties. In one study, depression subsided by age 13 in early-maturing boys but tended to persist in early-maturing girls (Ge et al., 2003). In another study, which followed young people from ages 14 to 24, early-maturing boys again showed good adjustment. But early-maturing girls

reported poorer-quality relationships with family and friends, smaller social networks, and lower life satisfaction into early adulthood than their on-time counterparts (Graber et al., 2004).

Recall that childhood family conflict and harsh parenting are linked to earlier pubertal timing, more so for girls than for boys (see page 367). Perhaps many early-maturing girls enter adolescence with emotional and social difficulties. As the stresses of puberty interfere with school performance and lead to unfavorable peer pressures, poor adjustment extends and deepens (Graber, 2003). Clearly, interventions that target at-risk early-maturing youths are needed. These include educating parents and teachers and providing adolescents with counseling and social supports so they will be better prepared to handle the emotional and social challenges of this transition.

ASK YOURSELF

REVIEW Summarize the impact of pubertal timing on adolescent development.

CONNECT How might adolescent moodiness contribute to psychological distancing between parents and adolescents? (*Hint:* Think about bidirectional influences in parent–child relationships.)

APPLY As a school-age child, Chloe enjoyed leisure activities with her parents. Now, at age 14, she spends hours in her room and resists going on weekend family excursions. Explain Chloe's behavior.

REFLECT Recall your own reactions to the physical changes of puberty. Are they consistent with research findings? Explain.

 Health Issues

The arrival of puberty brings new health issues related to the young person's efforts to meet physical and psychological needs. As adolescents attain greater autonomy, their personal decision making becomes important, in health as well as other areas. Yet none of the health concerns we are about to discuss can be traced to a single cause. Rather, biological, psychological, family, peer, and cultural factors jointly contribute.

Nutritional Needs

When their sons reached puberty, Franca and Antonio reported a "vacuum cleaner effect" in the kitchen as the boys routinely emptied the refrigerator. Rapid body growth leads to a dramatic increase in nutritional requirements, at a time when the diets of many young people are the poorest. Of all age groups, adolescents are the most likely to skip breakfast (a practice linked to obesity), eat on the run, and consume empty calories (Ritchie et al., 2007; Striegel-Moore & Franko, 2006). Fast-food restaurants, where teenagers often gather, have begun to offer some healthy menu options. But adolescents need guidance in choosing these alternatives. Eating fast food and school purchases from snack bars and vending machines is strongly associated with consumption of soft drinks and foods high in fat and sugar, indicating that teenagers often make unhealthy food choices (Bowman et al., 2004; Kubik et al., 2003).

The most common nutritional problem of adolescence is iron deficiency. Iron requirements increase to a maximum during the growth spurt and remain high among girls because of iron loss during menstruation. A tired, irritable teenager may be suffering from anemia rather than unhappiness and should have a medical checkup. Most adolescents do not get enough calcium and are also deficient in riboflavin (vitamin B2) and magnesium, both of which support metabolism (Cavadini, Siega-Riz, & Popkin, 2000).

Frequency of family meals is strongly associated with greater intake of fruits, vegetables, grains, and calcium-rich foods and reduced soft drink and fast-food consumption (Burgess-Champoux et al., 2009; Fiese & Schwartz, 2008). But compared to families with younger children, those with adolescents eat fewer meals together. In addition to their other benefits (see page 63 in Chapter 2 and page 291 in Chapter 9), family meals can greatly improve teenagers' diets.

Adolescents—especially girls concerned about their weight—tend to be attracted to fad diets. Unfortunately, most are too limited in nutrients and calories to be healthy for fast-growing, active teenagers (Donatelle, 2012). Parents should encourage young people to consult a doctor or dietitian before trying any special diet.

Eating Disorders

Concerned about her daughter's desire to lose weight, Franca explained to Sabrina that she was really quite average in build for an adolescent girl and reminded her that her Italian ancestors had considered a plump female body more beautiful than a thin one. Girls who reach puberty early, who are very dissatisfied with their body image, and who grow up in homes where concern with weight and thinness is high are at risk for eating problems. Severe dieting is the strongest predictor of the onset of an eating disorder in adolescence (Lock & Kirz, 2008). The two most serious are anorexia nervosa and bulimia nervosa.

Anorexia Nervosa. **Anorexia nervosa** is a tragic eating disorder in which young people starve themselves because of a compulsive fear of getting fat. It affects about 1 percent of North American and Western European teenage girls. During the past half-century, cases have increased sharply, fueled by cultural admiration of female thinness. Anorexia nervosa is equally common in all SES groups, but Asian-American, Caucasian-American, and Hispanic girls are at greater risk than African-American girls, who tend to be more satisfied with their size and shape (Granillo, Jones-Rodriguez, & Carvajal, 2005; Ozer & Irwin, 2009; Steinhausen, 2006). Boys account for 10 to 15 percent of anorexia cases; about half of these are gay or bisexual

Aiva, a 16-year-old anorexia nervosa patient, is shown at left on the day she entered treatment—weighing just 77 pounds—and, at right, after a 10-week treatment program. Less than 50 percent of young people with anorexia recover fully.

young people who are uncomfortable with a strong, muscular appearance (Raevuori et al., 2009; Robb & Dadson, 2002).

Individuals with anorexia have an extremely distorted body image. Even after they have become severely underweight, they see themselves as too heavy. Most go on self-imposed diets so strict that they struggle to avoid eating in response to hunger. To enhance weight loss, they exercise strenuously.

In their attempt to reach "perfect" slimness, individuals with anorexia lose between 25 and 50 percent of their body weight. Because a normal menstrual cycle requires about 15 percent body fat, either menarche does not occur or menstrual periods stop. Malnutrition causes pale skin, brittle discolored nails, fine dark hairs all over the body, and extreme sensitivity to cold. If it continues, the heart muscle can shrink, the kidneys can fail, and irreversible brain damage and loss of bone mass can occur. About 6 percent of individuals with anorexia die of the disorder, as a result of either physical complications or suicide (Katzman, 2005).

Forces within the person, the family, and the larger culture give rise to anorexia nervosa. Identical twins share the disorder more often than fraternal twins, indicating a genetic influence. Abnormalities in neurotransmitters in the brain, linked to anxiety and impulse control, may make some individuals more susceptible (Kaye, 2008; Lock & Kirz, 2008). Many young people with anorexia have unrealistically high standards for their own behavior and performance, are emotionally inhibited, and avoid intimate ties outside the family. Consequently, they are often excellent students who are responsible and well-behaved. But as we have also seen, the societal image of "thin is beautiful" contributes to the poor body image of many girls—especially early-maturing girls, who are at greatest risk for anorexia nervosa (Hogan & Strasburger, 2008).

In addition, parent–adolescent interactions reveal problems related to adolescent autonomy. Often the mothers of these girls have high expectations for physical appearance, achievement, and social acceptance and are overprotective and controlling. Fathers tend to be emotionally distant. These parental attributes may contribute to affected girls' persistent anxiety and fierce pursuit of perfection in achievement, respectable behavior, and thinness (Kaye, 2008). Nevertheless, it remains unclear whether maladaptive parent–child relationships precede the disorder, emerge in response to it, or both.

Because individuals with anorexia typically deny or minimize the seriousness of their disorder, treating it is difficult (Couturier & Lock, 2006). Hospitalization is often necessary to prevent life-threatening malnutrition. The most successful treatment is family therapy plus medication to reduce anxiety and neurotransmitter imbalances (Robin & Le Grange, 2010; Treasure & Schmidt, 2005). Still, less than 50 percent of young people with anorexia recover fully. For many, eating problems continue in less extreme form. About 10 percent show signs of a less severe, but nevertheless debilitating, disorder: bulimia nervosa.

Bulimia Nervosa. In **bulimia nervosa**, young people (again, mainly girls, but gay and bisexual boys are also vulnerable) engage in strict dieting and excessive exercise accompanied by binge eating, often followed by deliberate vomiting and purging with laxatives (Herzog, Eddy, & Beresin, 2006; Wichstrøm, 2006). Bulimia typically appears in late adolescence and is more common than anorexia nervosa, affecting about 2 to 4 percent of teenage girls, only 5 percent of whom previously suffered from anorexia.

Twin studies show that bulimia, like anorexia, is influenced by heredity (Klump, Kaye, & Strober, 2001). Overweight and early menarche increase the risk. Some adolescents with bulimia, like those with anorexia, are perfectionists. But most are impulsive, sensation-seeking young people who lack self-control in many areas, engaging in petty shoplifting, alcohol abuse, and other risky behaviors (Kaye, 2008). And although girls with bulimia, like those with anorexia, are pathologically anxious about gaining weight, they may have experienced their parents as disengaged and emotionally unavailable rather than controlling (Fairburn & Harrison, 2003).

In contrast to young people with anorexia, those with bulimia usually feel depressed and guilty about their abnormal eating habits and desperately want help. As a result, bulimia is usually easier to treat than anorexia, through support groups, nutrition education, training in changing eating habits, and anti-anxiety, antidepressant, and appetite-control medication (Hay & Bacaltchuk, 2004).

Sexuality

Sabrina's 16-year-old brother Louis and his girlfriend Cassie hadn't planned to have intercourse—it "just happened." But before and after, a lot of things passed through their minds. After they had dated for three months, Cassie began to wonder, "Will Louis think I'm normal if I don't have sex with him? If he wants to and I say no, will I lose him?" Both young people knew

Cultural attitudes will profoundly affect the way these young teenagers, who are just beginning to explore their sexual attraction to each other, learn to manage sexuality in social relationships.

their parents wouldn't approve. In fact, when Franca and Antonio noticed how attached Louis was to Cassie, they talked to him about the importance of waiting and the dangers of pregnancy. But that Friday evening, Louis and Cassie's feelings for each other seemed overwhelming. "If I don't make a move," Louis thought, "will she think I'm a wimp?"

With the arrival of puberty, hormonal changes—in particular, the production of androgens in young people of both sexes—lead to an increase in sex drive (Halpern, Udry, & Suchindran, 1997). In response, adolescents become very concerned about managing sexuality in social relationships. New cognitive capacities involving perspective taking and self-reflection affect their efforts to do so. Yet like the eating behaviors we have just discussed, adolescent sexuality is heavily influenced by the young person's social context.

The Impact of Culture. *TAKE A MOMENT...* When did you first learn the "facts of life"—and how? Was sex discussed openly in your family, or was it treated with secrecy? Exposure to sex, education about it, and efforts to limit the sexual curiosity of children and adolescents vary widely around the world.

Despite the prevailing image of sexually free adolescents, sexual attitudes in North America are relatively restrictive. Typically, parents provide little or no information about sex, discourage sex play, and rarely talk about sex in children's presence. When young people become interested in sex, only about half report getting information from parents about intercourse, pregnancy prevention, and sexually transmitted disease. Many parents avoid meaningful discussions about sex out of fear of embarrassment or concern that the adolescent will not take them seriously (Wilson et al., 2010). Yet warm, open give-and-take is associated with teenagers' adoption of parents' views and with reduced sexual risk taking (Jaccard, Dodge, & Dittus, 2003; Usher-Seriki, Bynum, & Callands, 2008).

Adolescents who do not get information about sex from their parents are likely to learn from friends, books, magazines, movies, TV, and the Internet (Jaccard, Dodge, & Dittus, 2002; Sutton et al., 2002). On prime-time TV shows, which adolescents watch more than other TV offerings, 80 percent of programs contain sexual content. Most depict partners as spontaneous and passionate, taking no steps to avoid pregnancy or sexually transmitted disease, and experiencing no negative consequences (Roberts, Henriksen, & Foehr, 2004). In several studies, teenagers' media exposure to sexual content predicted current sexual activity, intentions to be sexually active in the future, and subsequent sexual activity, pregnancies, and sexual harassment behaviors (offensive name-calling or touching, pressuring a peer for a date) even after many other relevant factors were controlled (Brown & L'Engle, 2009; Chandra et al., 2008; Roberts, Henriksen, & Foehr, 2009).

Not surprisingly, adolescents who are prone to early sexual activity choose to consume more sexualized media (Steinberg & Monahan, 2011). The Internet is an especially hazardous "sex educator." In a survey of a large sample of U.S. 10- to 17-year-old Web users, 42 percent said they had viewed online pornographic websites (images of naked people or people having sex) while surfing the Internet in the past 12 months. Of these, 66 percent indicated they had encountered the images accidentally and did not want to view them (Wolak, Mitchell, & Finkelhor, 2007). Youths who felt depressed, had been bullied by peers, or were involved in delinquent activities had more encounters with Internet pornography, which may have intensified their adjustment problems.

Consider the contradictory messages young people receive. On one hand, adults express disapproval of sex at a young age and outside of marriage. On the other hand, the social environment extols sexual excitement, experimentation, and promiscuity. American teenagers are left bewildered, poorly informed about sexual facts, and with little sound advice on how to conduct their sex lives responsibly.

Adolescent Sexual Attitudes and Behavior.
Although differences between subcultural groups exist, sexual attitudes of U.S. adolescents and adults have become more liberal over the past 40 years. Compared with a generation ago, more people believe that sexual intercourse before marriage is all right, as long as two people are emotionally committed to each other (ABC News, 2004; Hoff, Greene, & Davis, 2003). During the past two decades, adolescents have swung back slightly toward more conservative sexual beliefs, largely in response to the risk of sexually transmitted disease, especially AIDS, and to teenage sexual abstinence programs sponsored by schools and religious organizations (Akers et al., 2011; Ali & Scelfo, 2002).

Trends in adolescents' sexual behavior are consistent with their attitudes. Rates of extramarital sex among U.S. young

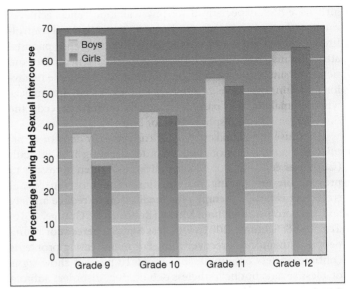

FIGURE 11.4 **U.S. adolescents who report ever having had sexual intercourse.** Many young adolescents are sexually active—more than in other Western nations. Boys tend to have their first intercourse earlier than girls. By the end of high school, rates of boys and girls having had sexual intercourse are similar. (From U.S. Department of Health and Human Services, 2012f.)

people rose for several decades, declined during the 1990s, and then stabilized (U.S. Department of Health and Human Services, 2012f). Nevertheless, as Figure 11.4 illustrates, a substantial percentage of U.S. young people are sexually active by ninth grade (age 14 to 15).

Overall, teenage sexual activity rates are similar in the United States and other Western countries: Nearly half of adolescents have had intercourse. But quality of sexual experiences differs. U.S. youths become sexually active earlier than their Canadian and European counterparts (Boyce et al., 2006; U.S. Department of Health and Human Services, 2012f). And about 18 percent of U.S. adolescent boys and 13 percent of girls—more than in other Western nations—have had sexual relations with four or more partners in the past year. Most teenagers, however, have had only one or two sexual partners by the end of high school.

Characteristics of Sexually Active Adolescents.
Early and frequent teenage sexual activity is linked to personal, family, peer, and educational characteristics. These include childhood impulsivity, weak sense of personal control over life events, early pubertal timing, parental divorce, single-parent and stepfamily homes, large family size, little or no religious involvement, weak parental monitoring, disrupted parent–child communication, sexually active friends and older siblings, poor school performance, lower educational aspirations, and tendency to engage in norm-violating acts, including alcohol and drug use and delinquency (Coley, Votruba-Drzal, & Schindler, 2009; Crockett, Raffaelli, & Shen, 2006; Siebenbruner, Zimmer-Gembeck, & Egeland, 2007; Zimmer-Gembeck & Helfand, 2008).

Because many of these factors are associated with growing up in a low-income family, it is not surprising that early sexual activity is more common among young people from economically disadvantaged homes. Living in a neighborhood high in physical deterioration, crime, and violence also increases the likelihood that teenagers will be sexually active (Ge et al., 2002). In such neighborhoods, social ties are weak, adults exert little oversight and control over adolescents' activities, and negative peer influences are widespread. In fact, the high rate of sexual activity among African-American teenagers—60 percent report having had sexual intercourse, compared with 47 percent of all U.S. young people—is largely accounted for by widespread poverty in the black population (Darroch, Frost, & Singh, 2001; U.S. Department of Health & Human Services, 2012b).

Contraceptive Use. Although adolescent contraceptive use has increased in recent years, about 20 percent of sexually active teenagers in the United States are at risk for unintended pregnancy because they do not use contraception consistently (see Figure 11.5) (Fortenberry, 2010). Why do so many fail to take precautions? Typically, teenagers respond, "I was waiting until I had a steady boyfriend," or "I wasn't planning to have sex." As we will see when we take up adolescent cognitive development, although adolescents can consider multiple possibilities when faced with a problem, they often fail to apply this advanced reasoning to everyday situations.

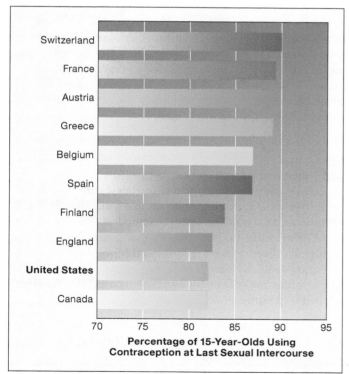

FIGURE 11.5 Contraceptive use by sexually active 15-year-olds in 10 industrialized nations. Sexually active U.S. teenagers are less likely to use contraception (condom, contraceptive pill, or both) consistently than teenagers in other industrialized nations. (Adapted from Godeau et al., 2008; U.S. Department of Health and Human Services, 2012f.)

One reason is that advances in perspective taking lead teenagers, for a time, to be extremely concerned about others' opinions of them. Recall how Cassie and Louis each worried about what the other would think if they decided not to have sex. Also, in the midst of everyday social pressures, adolescents often overlook the potential consequences of risky behaviors. And many teenagers—especially those from troubled, low-income families—do not have realistic expectations about the impact of early parenthood on their current and future lives (Stevens-Simon, Sheeder, & Harter, 2005).

As these findings suggest, the social environment also contributes to teenagers' reluctance to use contraception. Those without the rewards of meaningful education and work are especially likely to engage in irresponsible sex, sometimes within relationships characterized by exploitation. About 12 percent of U.S. girls and 5 percent of boys say they were pressured to have intercourse when they were unwilling (U.S. Department of Health and Human Services, 2012f).

In contrast, teenagers who report good relationships with parents and who talk openly with them about sex and contraception are more likely to use birth control (Henrich et al., 2006; Kirby, 2002a). But few adolescents believe their parents would be understanding and supportive. School sex education classes, as well, often leave teenagers with incomplete or incorrect knowledge. Some do not know where to get birth control counseling and devices. And those engaged in high-risk sexual behaviors are especially likely to worry that a doctor or family planning clinic might not keep their visits confidential (Lehrer et al., 2007). Most of these young people forgo essential health care but continue to have sex without contraception.

Sexual Orientation. So far, we have focused only on heterosexual behavior. About 4 percent of U.S. 15- to 44-year-olds identify as lesbian, gay, or bisexual (Mosher, Chandra, & Jones, 2005). An unknown number experience same-sex attraction but have not come out to friends or family (see the Social Issues: Health box on page 376). Adolescence is an equally crucial time for the sexual development of these young people, and societal attitudes, again, loom large in how well they fare.

Heredity makes an important contribution to homosexuality: Identical twins of both sexes are much more likely than fraternal twins to share a homosexual orientation; so are biological (as opposed to adoptive) relatives (Kendler et al., 2000; Kirk et al., 2000). Furthermore, male homosexuality tends to be more common on the maternal than on the paternal side of families, suggesting that it may be X-linked (see Chapter 2). Indeed, one gene-mapping study found that among 40 pairs of homosexual brothers, 33 (82 percent) had an identical segment of DNA on the X chromosome (Hamer et al., 1993). One or several genes in that region might predispose males to become homosexual.

How might heredity lead to homosexuality? According to some researchers, certain genes affect the level or impact of prenatal sex hormones, which modify brain structures in ways that induce homosexual feelings and behavior (Bailey et al., 1995; LeVay, 1993). Keep in mind, however, that environmental

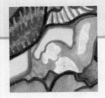

Social Issues: Health

Lesbian, Gay, and Bisexual Youths: Coming Out to Oneself and Others

Cultures vary as much in their acceptance of homosexuality as in their approval of extramarital sex. In the United States, homosexuals are stigmatized, as shown by the degrading language often used to describe them. This makes forming a sexual identity a much greater challenge for lesbian, gay, and bisexual youths than for their heterosexual counterparts.

Wide variations in sexual identity formation exist, depending on personal, family, and community factors. Yet interviews with gay and lesbian adolescents and adults reveal that many (though not all) move through a three-phase sequence in coming out to themselves and others.

Feeling Different

Many gay men and lesbians recall feeling different from other children when they were young. Typically, this first sense of their biologically determined sexual orientation appears between ages 6 and 12, in play interests more like those of the other gender (Rahman & Wilson, 2003). Boys may find that they are less interested in sports,

more drawn to quieter activities, and more emotionally sensitive than other boys; girls that they are more athletic and active than other girls.

By age 10, many of these children start to engage in *sexual questioning*—wondering why the typical heterosexual orientation does not apply to them. Often, they experience their sense of being different as deeply distressing. Compared with children who are confident of their homosexuality, sexual-questioning children report greater anxiety about peer relationships and greater dissatisfaction with their biological gender over time (Carver, Egan, & Perry, 2004).

Confusion

With the arrival of puberty, feeling different clearly encompasses feeling sexually different. In research on ethnically diverse lesbian, gay, and bisexual youths, awareness of a same-sex physical attraction occurred, on average, between ages 11 and 12 for boys and 14 and 15 for girls, perhaps because adolescent social pressures toward hetero-

sexuality are particularly intense for girls (D'Augelli, 2006; Diamond, 1998).

Realizing that homosexuality has personal relevance generally sparks additional confusion. A few adolescents resolve their discomfort by crystallizing a gay, lesbian, or bisexual identity quickly, with a flash of insight into their sense of being different. But most experience an inner struggle and a deep sense of isolation—outcomes intensified by lack of role models and social support (D'Augelli, 2002; Safren & Pantalone; 2006).

Some throw themselves into activities they associate with heterosexuality. Boys may go out for athletic teams; girls may drop softball and basketball in favor of dance. And many homosexual youths (more females than males) try heterosexual dating, sometimes to hide their sexual orientation and at other times to develop intimacy skills that they later apply to same-sex relationships (D'Augelli, 2006; Dubé, Savin-Williams, & Diamond, 2001). Those who are extremely troubled and guilt-ridden may escape into alcohol, drugs, and suicidal thinking. Suicide attempts are unusually high among lesbian, gay, and bisexual young people (Morrow, 2006; Teasdale & Bradley-Engen, 2010).

---

factors can also alter prenatal hormones. Girls exposed prenatally to very high levels of androgens or estrogens—either because of a genetic defect or from drugs given to the mother to prevent miscarriage—are more likely to become lesbian or bisexual (Meyer-Bahlburg et al., 1995). Furthermore, gay men tend to be later in birth order and to have a higher-than-average number of older brothers (Blanchard & Bogaert, 2004). One possibility is that mothers with several male children sometimes produce antibodies to androgens, reducing the prenatal impact of male sex hormones on the brains of later-born boys.

Stereotypes and misconceptions about homosexuality persist. For example, most homosexual adolescents are not "gender-deviant" in dress or behavior. And attraction to members of the same sex is not limited to lesbian, gay, and bisexual teenagers. About 50 to 60 percent of adolescents who report having engaged in homosexual acts identify as heterosexual (Savin-Williams & Diamond, 2004). And in a study of lesbian, bisexual,

and "unlabeled" young women over a 10-year period, most reported stable proportions of same-sex versus other-sex attractions over time, providing evidence that bisexuality is not, as often assumed, a transient state (Diamond, 2008).

The evidence to date suggests that genetic and prenatal biological influences are largely responsible for homosexuality. In our evolutionary past, homosexuality may have served the adaptive function of reducing aggressive competition for other-sex mates (Rahman & Wilson, 2003).

Sexually Transmitted Diseases

Sexually active adolescents, both homosexual and heterosexual, are at risk for sexually transmitted diseases (STDs). Adolescents have the highest rates of STDs of all age groups. Despite a recent decline in STDs in the United States, one out of five to six sexually active teenagers contracts one of these illnesses each year—a rate three or more times as high as that of Canada and Western

Self-Acceptance

By the end of adolescence, the majority of gay, lesbian, and bisexual teenagers accept their sexual identity. But they face another crossroad: whether to tell others. The powerful stigma against their sexual orientation leads some to decide that disclosure is impossible: While self-defining as gay, they otherwise "pass" as heterosexual (Savin-Williams, 2001). When homosexual youths do come out, they often face intense hostility, including verbal abuse and physical attacks, because of their sexual orientation. These experiences trigger intense emotional distress, depression, suicidal thoughts, school truancy, and drug use in victims (Almeida et al., 2009; Birkett, Espelage, & Koenig, 2009).

Nevertheless, many young people eventually acknowledge their sexual orientation publicly, usually by telling trusted friends first. Once teenagers establish a same-sex sexual or romantic relationship, many come out to parents. Although few parents respond with severe rejection, lesbian, gay, and bisexual young people report lower levels of family support than their heterosexual agemates (Needham & Austin, 2010; Savin-Williams & Ream, 2003). Yet parental understanding is the strongest predictor of favorable adjustment—including reduced

internalized homophobia, or societal prejudice turned against the self (D'Augelli, Grossman, & Starks, 2008).

When people react positively, coming out strengthens the young person's view of homosexuality as a valid, meaningful, and fulfilling identity. Contact with other gays and lesbians is important for reaching this phase, and changes in society permit many adolescents in urban areas to attain it earlier than their counterparts did a decade or two ago. Gay and lesbian communities exist in large cities, along with specialized interest groups, social clubs, religious groups, newspapers, and periodicals. But teenagers in small towns and rural areas may have difficulty meeting other homosexuals and finding a supportive environment. These adolescents have a special need for caring adults and peers who can help them find self- and social acceptance.

Lesbian, gay, bisexual, and transgender high school students and their allies participate in an annual Youth Pride Festival and March. When peers react with acceptance, coming out strengthens the young person's view of homosexuality as a valid and fulfilling identity.

Lesbian, gay, and bisexual teenagers who succeed in coming out to themselves and others integrate their sexual orientation into a broader sense of identity, a process we will address in Chapter 12. As a result, energy is freed for other aspects of psychological growth. In sum, coming out can foster many facets of adolescent development, including self-esteem, psychological well-being, and relationships with family and friends.

Europe (Centers for Disease Control and Prevention, 2011d). Teenagers at greatest risk are the same ones most likely to engage in irresponsible sexual behavior: poverty-stricken young people who feel a sense of hopelessness (Niccolai et al., 2004). Left untreated, STDs can lead to sterility and life-threatening complications.

By far the most serious STD is AIDS. In contrast to other Western nations, where the incidence of AIDS among people under age 30 is low, about 15 percent of U.S. AIDS cases occur in young people between ages 20 and 29. Because AIDS symptoms typically do not emerge until 8 to 10 years after infection with the HIV virus, nearly all these cases originated in adolescence. Drug-abusing teenagers who share needles and male adolescents who have sex with HIV-positive same-sex partners account for most cases, but heterosexual spread of the disease remains high, especially among teenagers with more than one partner in the previous 18 months. It is at least twice as easy for a male to infect a female with any STD, including HIV,

as for a female to infect a male. Currently, females account for about 25 percent of new U.S. cases among adolescents and young adults (Centers for Disease Control and Prevention, 2011b).

As a result of school courses and media campaigns, most adolescents are aware of basic facts about AIDS. But they have limited understanding of other STDs, tend to underestimate their own susceptibility, and are poorly informed about how to protect themselves (Copen, Chandra, & Martinez, 2012; Ethier et al., 2003; Centers for Disease Control and Prevention, 2007).

Furthermore, high school students report engaging in oral sex as early and about as often as intercourse. But few report consistently using STD protection during oral sex, which is a significant mode of transmission of several STDs (Copen, Chandra, & Martinez, 2012). Concerted efforts are needed to educate young people about the full range of STDs and risky sexual behaviors.

Adolescent Pregnancy and Parenthood

Cassie didn't get pregnant after having sex with Louis, but some of her classmates were less fortunate. About 727,000 U.S. teenage girls (12,000 of them younger than age 15)—an estimated 20 percent of those who had sexual intercourse—became pregnant in the most recently reported year. Despite a decline of almost one-half since 1990, the U.S. adolescent pregnancy rate remains higher than that of most other industrialized countries (Ventura, Curtin, & Abma, 2012). Three factors heighten the incidence of adolescent pregnancy: (1) Effective sex education reaches too few teenagers; (2) convenient, low-cost contraceptive services for adolescents are scarce; and (3) many families live in poverty, which encourages young people to take risks without considering the future implications of their behavior.

Because about one-fourth of U.S. adolescent pregnancies end in abortion, the number of American teenage births is considerably lower than it was 50 years ago (Ventura, Curtin, & Abma, 2012). Still, it is up to nine times higher than in most other developed nations (see Figure 11.6). But teenage parenthood is a much greater problem today because adolescents are far less likely to marry before childbirth. In 1960, only 15 percent of teenage births were to unmarried females, compared with 87 percent today (Child Trends, 2011). Increased social acceptance of single motherhood, along with the belief of many teenage girls that a baby might fill a void in their lives, means that very few girls give up their infants for adoption.

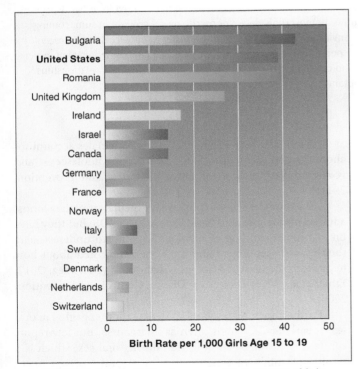

FIGURE 11.6 **Birth rates among 15- to 19-year-olds in 15 industrialized nations.** The U.S. adolescent birth rate greatly exceeds that of most other industrialized nations. (From Centers for Disease Control and Prevention, 2011c.)

Correlates and Consequences of Adolescent Parenthood. Becoming a parent is especially challenging for adolescents, who have not yet established a clear sense of direction for their own lives. Life conditions and personal attributes jointly contribute to adolescent childbearing and also interfere with teenagers' capacity to parent effectively.

Teenage parents are far more likely to be poor than agemates who postpone parenthood. Their backgrounds often include low parental warmth and involvement, domestic violence and child abuse, repeated parental divorce and remarriage, adult models of unmarried parenthood, and residence in neighborhoods where other adolescents also display these risks. Girls at risk for early pregnancy do poorly in school, engage in alcohol and drug use, have a childhood history of aggressive and antisocial behavior, associate with deviant peers, and experience high rates of depression (Elfenbein & Felice, 2003; Hillis et al., 2004; Luster & Haddow, 2005). A high percentage of out-of-wedlock births are to low-income ethnic minority teenagers. Many turn to early parenthood as a way to move into adulthood when educational and career avenues are unavailable.

The lives of expectant teenagers, already troubled in many ways, tend to worsen in several respects after the baby is born:

- *Educational attainment.* Parenthood before age 18 reduces the likelihood of finishing high school. Only about 70 percent of U.S. adolescent mothers graduate, compared with 95 percent of girls who wait to become parents (National Women's Law Center, 2007).

- *Marital patterns.* Teenage motherhood reduces the chances of marriage and, for those who do marry, increases the likelihood of divorce compared with peers who delay childbearing (Moore & Brooks-Gunn, 2002). Consequently, teenage mothers spend more of their parenting years as single parents. About 35 percent become pregnant again within two years. Of these, about half go on to deliver a second child (Child Trends, 2011).

- *Economic circumstances.* Because of low educational attainment, marital instability, and poverty, many teenage mothers are on welfare or work in unsatisfying, low-paid jobs. Similarly, many adolescent fathers are unemployed or earn too little to provide their children with basic necessities (Bunting & McAuley, 2004). An estimated 50 percent have committed illegal offenses resulting in imprisonment (Elfenbein & Felice, 2003). And for both mothers and fathers, reduced educational and occupational attainment often persists well into adulthood (Taylor, 2009).

Because many pregnant teenage girls have inadequate diets, smoke, use alcohol and other drugs, and do not receive early prenatal care, their babies often experience pregnancy and birth complications—especially preterm and low birth weight (Khashan, Baker, & Kenny, 2010). And compared with adult mothers, adolescent mothers know less about child development, have unrealistically high expectations of infants, perceive their babies as more difficult, interact less effectively with them, and more often engage in child abuse (Moore & Florsheim, 2001;

Pomerleau, Scuccimarri, & Malcuit, 2003; Sieger & Renk, 2007). Their children tend to score low on intelligence tests, achieve poorly in school, and engage in disruptive social behavior.

Furthermore, adolescent parenthood frequently is repeated in the next generation (Brooks-Gunn, Schley, & Hardy, 2002). In longitudinal studies that followed mothers—some who gave birth as teenagers, others who postponed parenting—and their children for several decades, mothers' age at first childbirth strongly predicted the age at which their daughters and sons became parents. The researchers found that adolescent parenthood was linked to a set of related unfavorable family conditions and personal characteristics that negatively influenced development over an extended time and, therefore, often transferred to the next generation. Among influential factors was father absence (Barber, 2001a; Campa & Eckenrode, 2006; Meade, Kershaw, & Ickovics, 2008). Consistent with findings reported earlier for sexual activity and pregnancy, far greater intergenerational continuity, especially for daughters, occurred when teenage mothers remained unmarried.

Even when children born to teenage mothers do not become early childbearers, their development is often compromised, in terms of likelihood of high school graduation, financial independence in adulthood, and long-term physical and mental health (Moore, Morrison, & Greene, 1997; Pogarsky, Thornberry, & Lizotte, 2006). Still, outcomes vary widely. If a teenage parent finishes high school, secures gainful employment, avoids additional births, and finds a stable partner, long-term disruptions in her own and her child's development will be less severe.

Prevention Strategies. Preventing teenage pregnancy means addressing the many factors underlying early sexual activity and lack of contraceptive use. Too often, sex education courses are given late (after sexual activity has begun), last only a few sessions, and are limited to a catalog of facts about anatomy and reproduction. Sex education that goes beyond this minimum does not encourage early sex, as some opponents claim (Kirby, 2002c). It does improve awareness of sexual facts—knowledge that is necessary for responsible sexual behavior.

Knowledge, however, is not enough: Sex education must also help teenagers build a bridge between what they know and what they do. Effective sex education programs include several key elements:

- They teach techniques for handling sexual situations—including refusal skills for avoiding risky sexual behaviors and communication skills for improving contraceptive use—through role-playing and other activities.

- They deliver clear, accurate messages that are appropriate in view of participating adolescents' culture and sexual experiences.

- They last long enough to have an impact.

- They provide specific information about contraceptives and ready access to them.

Many studies show that sex education with these components can delay the initiation of sexual activity, reduce the frequency of sex and the number of sexual partners, increase contraceptive use, change attitudes (for example, strengthen future orientation), and reduce pregnancy rates (Kirby, 2002b; Kirby & Laris, 2009; Thomas & Dimitrov, 2007).

LOOK AND LISTEN

Contact a nearby public school district for information about its sex education curriculum. Considering research findings, do you think it is likely to be effective in delaying initiation of sexual activity and reducing adolescent pregnancy rates? ●

Proposals to increase access to contraceptives are the most controversial aspect of U.S. adolescent pregnancy prevention efforts. Many adults argue that placing birth control pills or condoms in the hands of teenagers is equivalent to approving of early sex. Yet sex education programs encouraging abstinence without encouraging contraceptive use have little or no impact on delaying teenage sexual activity or preventing pregnancy (Rosenbaum, 2009; Underhill, Montgomery, & Operario, 2007). In Canada and Western Europe, where community- and school-based clinics offer adolescents contraceptives and where universal health insurance helps pay for them, teenage sexual activity is no higher than in the United States—but pregnancy, childbirth, and abortion rates are much lower (Schalet, 2007).

Efforts to prevent adolescent pregnancy and parenthood must go beyond improving sex education and access to contraception to build academic and social competence (Allen, Seitz, & Apfel, 2007). In one study, researchers randomly assigned at-risk high school students either to a year-long community service class, called Teen Outreach, or to regular classroom experiences in health or social studies. In Teen Outreach, adolescents spent at least 20 hours per week in volunteer work tailored to their interests. They returned to school for discussions that focused on enhancing their community service skills and their ability to cope with everyday challenges. At the end of the school year, rates of pregnancy, school failure, and school suspension were substantially lower among participants in Teen Outreach, which fostered social skills, connection to the community, and self-respect (Allen et al., 1997).

Finally, teenagers who look forward to a promising future are far less likely to engage in early and irresponsible sex. By expanding educational, vocational, and employment opportunities, society can give young people good reasons to postpone childbearing.

Intervening with Adolescent Parents. The most difficult and costly way to deal with adolescent parenthood is to wait until it happens. Young parents need health care, encouragement to stay in school, job training, instruction in parenting and life-management skills, and high-quality, affordable child care. Schools that provide these services reduce the incidence of low-birth-weight babies, increase educational success, and prevent additional childbearing (Key et al., 2008; Seitz & Apfel, 2005).

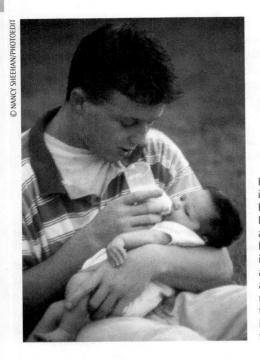

Early parenthood imposes lasting hardships on adolescent parents and their newborn babies. But the involvement of a caring father and a stable partnership between the parents can improve outcomes for young families.

Adolescent mothers also benefit from relationships with family members and other adults who are sensitive to their developmental needs. In one study, African-American teenage mothers who had a long-term "mentor" relationship—an aunt, neighbor, or teacher who provided emotional support and guidance—were far more likely than those without a mentor to stay in school and graduate (Klaw, Rhodes, & Fitzgerald, 2003). Home visiting programs are also effective. Return to page 94 in Chapter 3 to review the Nurse–Family Partnership, which helps launch teenage mothers and their babies on a favorable life course.

Programs focusing on fathers attempt to increase their financial and emotional commitment to the baby. Although nearly half of young fathers visit their children during the first few years, contact usually diminishes. By the time the child starts school, fewer than one-fourth have regular paternal contact. As with teenage mothers, support from family members helps fathers stay involved (Bunting & McAuley, 2004). Teenage mothers who receive financial and child-care assistance and emotional support from their child's father are less distressed and more likely to sustain a relationship with him (Cutrona et al., 1998; Gee & Rhodes, 2003). And infants with lasting ties to their teenage fathers show better long-term adjustment (Florsheim & Smith, 2005; Furstenberg & Harris, 1993).

Substance Use and Abuse

At age 14, Louis waited until he was alone at home, took some cigarettes from his uncle's pack, and smoked. At an unchaperoned party, he and Cassie drank several cans of beer and lit up marijuana joints. Louis got little physical charge out of these experiences. A good student, who was well-liked by peers and got along well with his parents, he did not need drugs as an escape valve. But he knew of other teenagers who started with alcohol and cigarettes, moved on to harder substances, and eventually were hooked.

Teenage alcohol and drug use is pervasive in industrialized nations. According to the most recent nationally representative survey of U.S. high school students, by tenth grade, 33 percent of U.S. young people have tried cigarette smoking, 58 percent drinking, and 37 percent at least one illegal drug (usually marijuana). At the end of high school, 11 percent smoke cigarettes regularly, and 27 percent have engaged in heavy drinking during the past month. About 25 percent have tried at least one highly addictive and toxic substance, such as amphetamines, cocaine, phencyclidine (PCP), Ecstasy (MDMA), inhalants, heroin, sedatives (including barbiturates), or OxyContin (a narcotic painkiller) (Johnston et al., 2011).

These figures represent a substantial decline since the mid-1990s, probably resulting from greater parent, school, and media focus on the hazards of drug use. But use of marijuana, inhalants, sedatives, and OxyContin has risen slightly in recent years (Johnston et al., 2011). Other drugs, such as LSD, PCP, and Ecstasy, have made a comeback as adolescents' knowledge of their risks faded.

In part, drug taking reflects the sensation seeking of the teenage years. But adolescents also live in drug-dependent cultural contexts. They see adults relying on caffeine to stay alert, alcohol and cigarettes to cope with daily hassles, and other remedies to relieve stress, depression, and physical discomfort. And compared to a decade or two ago, today doctors more often prescribe—and parents frequently seek—medication to treat children's problems (Olfman & Robbins, 2012). In adolescence, these young people may readily "self-medicate" when stressed.

Most teenagers who dabble in alcohol, tobacco, and marijuana are not headed for a life of addiction. These *minimal experimenters* are usually psychologically healthy, sociable, curious young people (Shedler & Block, 1990). As Figure 11.7 shows, tobacco and alcohol use is somewhat greater among European than U.S. adolescents, perhaps because European adults more often smoke and drink. But illegal drug use is far more prevalent among U.S. teenagers. A greater percentage of American young people live in poverty, which is linked to family and peer contexts that promote illegal drug use. At the same time, use of diverse drugs is lower among African Americans than among Hispanic and Caucasian Americans; Native-American youths rank highest in drug taking (Johnston et al., 2011). Researchers have yet to explain these variations.

Adolescent experimentation with any drug should not be taken lightly. Because most drugs impair perception and thought processes, a single heavy dose can lead to permanent injury or death. And a worrisome minority of teenagers move from substance *use* to *abuse*—taking drugs regularly, requiring increasing amounts to achieve the same effect, moving on to harder substances, and using enough to interfere with their ability to meet daily responsibilities.

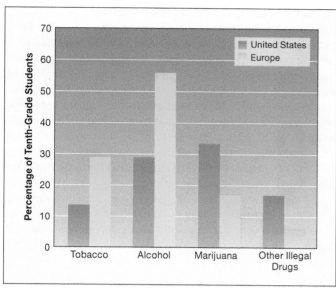

FIGURE 11.7 Tenth-grade students in the United States and Europe who have used various substances. Rates for tobacco and alcohol are based on any use in the past 30 days. Rates for marijuana and other illegal drugs are based on any lifetime use. Tobacco use and alcohol use are greater for European adolescents, whereas illegal drug use is greater for U.S. adolescents. (Adapted from ESPAD, 2012; Johnson et al., 2011.)

Correlates and Consequences of Adolescent Substance Abuse.

Unlike experimenters, drug abusers are seriously troubled young people. Their impulsive, disruptive, hostile style is often evident in early childhood, and they are inclined to express their unhappiness through antisocial acts. Compared with other young people, their drug taking starts earlier and may have genetic roots (Dick, Prescott, & McGue, 2008; Tarter, Vanyukov, & Kirisci, 2008). But environmental factors also contribute. These include low SES, family mental health problems, parental and older sibling drug abuse, lack of parental warmth and involvement, physical and sexual abuse, and poor school performance. Especially among teenagers with family difficulties, encouragement from friends who use and provide drugs increases substance abuse (Ohannessian & Hesselbrock, 2008; U.S. Department of Health and Human Services, 2010c).

Introducing drugs while the adolescent brain is still a work-in-progress can have profound, lasting consequences, impairing neurons and their connective networks. At the same time, teenagers who use substances to deal with daily stresses fail to learn responsible decision-making skills and alternative coping techniques. They show serious adjustment problems, including chronic anxiety, depression, and antisocial behavior, that are both cause and consequence of heavy drug taking (Kassel et al., 2005; U.S. Department of Health and Human Services, 2010c). And they often enter into marriage, childbearing, and the work world prematurely and fail at them—painful outcomes that further promote addictive behavior.

Prevention and Treatment. School and community programs that reduce drug experimentation typically combine several components:

- They promote effective parenting, including monitoring of teenagers' activities.
- They teach skills for resisting peer pressure.
- They reduce the social acceptability of drug taking by emphasizing health and safety risks (Cuijpers, 2002; Stephens et al., 2009).

But given that adolescent drug taking is widespread, interventions that prevent teenagers from harming themselves and others when they do experiment are essential. Many communities offer weekend on-call transportation services that any young person can contact for a safe ride home, with no questions asked.

Because drug abuse has different roots than occasional use, different prevention strategies are required. One approach is to work with parents early, reducing family adversity and improving parenting skills, before children are old enough for drug involvement (Velleman, Templeton, & Copello, 2005). Programs that teach at-risk teenagers effective strategies for handling life stressors and that build competence through community service reduce alcohol and drug abuse, just as they reduce teenage pregnancy.

When an adolescent becomes a drug abuser, family and individual therapy are generally needed to treat maladaptive parent–child relationships, impulsivity, low self-esteem, anxiety, and depression. Academic and vocational training to improve life success also helps. But even comprehensive programs have alarmingly high relapse rates—from 35 to 85 percent (Brown & Ramo, 2005; Sussman, Skara, & Ames, 2008). One recommendation is to start treatment gradually, through support-group sessions that focus on reducing drug taking (Myers et al., 2001). Modest improvements may increase young people's motivation to make longer-lasting changes through intensive treatment.

Teenagers enjoy a community party sponsored by Drug Free Youth in Town (DFYIT), a substance abuse prevention program. DFYIT trains high school students as peer educators, who teach middle school students life skills and strategies for resisting peer pressure.

ASK YOURSELF

REVIEW Compare risk factors for anorexia nervosa and bulimia nervosa. How do treatments and outcomes differ for the two disorders?

CONNECT What unfavorable life experiences do teenagers who engage in early and frequent sexual activity have in common with those who abuse drugs?

APPLY After 17-year-old Veronica gave birth to Ben, her parents told her they didn't have room for the baby. Veronica dropped out of school and moved in with her boyfriend, who soon left. Why are Veronica and Ben likely to experience long-term hardships?

REFLECT Describe your experiences with peer pressure to experiment with alcohol and drugs. What factors influenced your response?

COGNITIVE DEVELOPMENT

One mid-December evening, a knock at the front door announced the arrival of Franca and Antonio's oldest son, Jules, home for vacation after the fall semester of his sophomore year at college. The family gathered around the kitchen table. "How did it all go, Jules?" asked Antonio as he served slices of apple pie.

"Well, physics and philosophy were awesome," Jules responded with enthusiasm. "The last few weeks, our physics prof introduced us to Einstein's theory of relativity. Boggles my mind, it's so incredibly counterintuitive."

"Counter-what?" asked 11-year-old Sabrina.

"Counterintuitive. Unlike what you'd normally expect," explained Jules. "Imagine you're on a train, going unbelievably fast, like 160,000 miles a second. The faster you go, approaching the speed of light, the slower time passes and the denser and heavier things get relative to on the ground. The theory revolutionized the way we think about time, space, matter—the entire universe."

Sabrina wrinkled her forehead, baffled by Jules's other-worldly reasoning. "Time slows down when I'm bored, like right now, not on a train when I'm going somewhere exciting. No speeding train ever made me heavier, but this apple pie will if I eat any more of it," Sabrina announced, leaving the table.

Sixteen-year-old Louis reacted differently. "Totally cool, Jules. So what'd you do in philosophy?"

"It was a course in philosophy of technology. We studied the ethics of futuristic methods in human reproduction. For example, we argued the pros and cons of a world in which all embryos develop in artificial wombs."

"What do you mean?" asked Louis. "You order your kid at the lab?"

"That's right. I wrote my term paper on it. I had to evaluate it in terms of principles of justice and freedom. I can see some advantages but also lots of dangers. . . ."

As this conversation illustrates, adolescence brings with it vastly expanded powers of reasoning. At age 11, Sabrina finds it difficult to move beyond her firsthand experiences to a world of possibilities. Over the next few years, her thinking will acquire the complex qualities that characterize the cognition of her older brothers. Jules and Louis consider multiple variables simultaneously and think about situations that are not easily detected in the real world or that do not exist at all. As a result, they can grasp advanced scientific and mathematical principles and grapple with social and political issues. Compared with school-age children's thinking, adolescent thought is more enlightened, imaginative, and rational.

Systematic research on adolescent cognitive development began with testing of Piaget's ideas (Kuhn, 2009). Recently, information-processing research has greatly enhanced our understanding.

Piaget's Theory: The Formal Operational Stage

According to Piaget, around age 11 young people enter the **formal operational stage**, in which they develop the capacity for abstract, systematic, scientific thinking. Whereas concrete operational children can "operate on reality," formal operational adolescents can "operate on operations." They no longer require concrete things or events as objects of thought. Instead, they can come up with new, more general logical rules through internal reflection (Inhelder & Piaget, 1955/1958). Let's look at two major features of the formal operational stage.

Hypothetico-Deductive Reasoning

Piaget believed that at adolescence, young people first become capable of **hypothetico-deductive reasoning**. When faced with a problem, they start with a *hypothesis,* or prediction about variables that might affect an outcome, from which they *deduce* logical, testable inferences. Then they systematically isolate and combine variables to see which of these inferences are confirmed in the real world. Notice how this form of problem solving begins with possibility and proceeds to reality. In contrast, concrete operational children start with reality—with the most obvious predictions about a situation. If these are not confirmed, they usually cannot think of alternatives and fail to solve the problem.

Adolescents' performance on Piaget's famous *pendulum problem* illustrates this approach. Suppose we present several school-age children and adolescents with strings of different lengths, objects of different weights to attach to the strings, and a bar from which to hang the strings (see Figure 11.8). Then we ask each of them to figure out what influences the speed with which a pendulum swings through its arc.

Formal operational adolescents hypothesize that four variables might be influential: (1) the length of the string, (2) the weight of the object hung on it, (3) how high the object is raised before it is released, and (4) how forcefully the object is pushed.

FIGURE 11.8 Piaget's pendulum problem. Adolescents who engage in hypothetico-deductive reasoning think of variables that might possibly affect the speed with which a pendulum swings through its arc. Then they isolate and test each variable, as well as testing the variables in combination. Eventually they deduce that the weight of the object, the height from which it is released, and how forcefully it is pushed have no effect on the speed with which the pendulum swings through its arc. Only string length makes a difference.

By varying one factor at a time while holding the other three constant, they test each variable separately and, if necessary, also in combination. Eventually they discover that only string length makes a difference.

In contrast, concrete operational children cannot separate the effects of each variable. They may test for the effect of string length without holding weight constant—comparing, for example, a short, light pendulum with a long, heavy one. Also, they typically fail to notice variables that are not immediately suggested by the concrete materials of the task—for example, how high the object is raised or how forcefully it is released.

Propositional Thought

A second important characteristic of Piaget's formal operational stage is **propositional thought**—adolescents' ability to evaluate the logic of propositions (verbal statements) without referring to real-world circumstances. In contrast, children can evaluate the logic of statements only by considering them against concrete evidence in the real world.

In a study of propositional reasoning, a researcher showed children and adolescents a pile of poker chips and asked whether statements about the chips were true, false, or uncertain (Osherson & Markman, 1975). In one condition, the researcher hid a chip in her hand and presented the following propositions:

> "*Either* the chip in my hand is green or it is not green."
> "The chip in my hand is green *and* it is not green."

In another condition, the experimenter made the same statements while holding either a red or a green chip in full view.

School-age children focused on the concrete properties of the poker chips. When the chip was hidden, they replied that they were uncertain about both statements. When it was visible, they judged both statements to be true if the chip was green and false if it was red. In contrast, adolescents analyzed the logic of the statements. They understood that the "either-or" statement is always true and the "and" statement is always false, regardless of the poker chip's color.

Although Piaget did not view language as playing a central role in children's cognitive development (see Chapter 7), he acknowledged its importance in adolescence. Formal operations require language-based and other symbolic systems that do not stand for real things, such as those in higher mathematics. Secondary school students use such systems in algebra and geometry. Formal operational thought also involves verbal reasoning about abstract concepts. Jules was thinking in this way when he pondered relationships among time, space, and matter in physics and wondered about justice and freedom in philosophy.

Follow-Up Research on Formal Operational Thought

Research on formal operational thought poses questions similar to those we discussed with respect to Piaget's earlier stages: Does formal operational thinking appear earlier than Piaget expected? Do all individuals reach formal operations during their teenage years?

Are Children Capable of Hypothetico-Deductive and Propositional Thinking?
School-age children show the glimmerings of hypothetico-deductive reasoning, although they are less competent at it than adolescents. In simplified situations involving no more than two possible causal variables, 6-year-olds understand that hypotheses must be confirmed by appropriate evidence (Ruffman et al., 1993). But school-age children cannot sort out evidence that bears on three or more variables at once. And as we will see when we take up information-processing research, children have difficulty explaining why a pattern of observations supports a hypothesis, even when they recognize the connection between the two.

With respect to propositional thought, when a simple set of premises defies real-world knowledge ("All cats bark. Rex is a cat. Does Rex bark?"), 4- to 6-year-olds can reason logically in make-believe play. To justify their answer, they are likely to say, "We can pretend cats bark!" (Dias & Harris, 1988, 1990). But in an entirely verbal mode, children have great difficulty reasoning from premises that contradict reality or their own beliefs.

Consider this set of statements: "If dogs are bigger than elephants and elephants are bigger than mice, then dogs are bigger than mice." Children younger than 10 judge this reasoning to be false because some of the relations specified do not occur in real life (Moshman & Franks, 1986; Pillow, 2002). They have more difficulty than adolescents inhibiting activation of well-learned knowledge ("Elephants are larger than dogs") that impedes effective reasoning (Klaczynski, Schuneman, & Daniel,

As these students discuss problems in a social studies class, they reason logically from premises that do not refer to real-world circumstances. They are far better at propositional thought than they were as children.

2004; Simoneau & Markovits, 2003). Partly for this reason, they fail to grasp the *logical necessity* of propositional reasoning—that the accuracy of conclusions drawn from premises rests on the rules of logic, not on real-world confirmation.

As with hypothetico-deductive reasoning, in early adolescence, young people become better at analyzing the *logic* of propositions irrespective of their *content*. And as they get older, they handle problems requiring increasingly complex mental operations. In justifying their reasoning, they more often explain the logical rules on which it is based (Müller, Overton, & Reese, 2001; Venet & Markovits, 2001). But these capacities do not appear suddenly at puberty. Rather, gains occur gradually from childhood on—findings that call into question the emergence of a new stage of cognitive development at adolescence (Kuhn, 2009; Moshman, 2005).

Do All Individuals Reach the Formal Operational Stage? TAKE A MOMENT... Try giving one or two of the formal operational tasks just described to your friends. How well do they do? Even well-educated adults often have difficulty (Kuhn, 2009; Markovits & Vachon, 1990).

Why are so many adults not fully formal operational? One reason is that people are most likely to think abstractly and systematically on tasks in which they have had extensive guidance and practice in using such reasoning. This conclusion is supported by evidence that taking college courses leads to improvements in formal reasoning related to course content. Math and science prompt gains in propositional thought, social science in methodological and statistical reasoning (Lehman & Nisbett, 1990). Like concrete reasoning in children, formal operations do not emerge in all contexts at once but are specific to situation and task (Keating, 2004).

Individuals in tribal and village societies rarely do well on tasks typically used to assess formal operational reasoning (Cole, 1990). Piaget acknowledged that without the opportunity to solve hypothetical problems, people in some societies might not display formal operations. Still, researchers ask, Does formal operational thought largely result from children's and adolescents' independent efforts to make sense of their world, as Piaget claimed? Or is it a culturally transmitted way of thinking that is specific to literate societies and taught in school? In an Israeli study, after controlling for participants' age, researchers found that years of schooling fully accounted for early adolescent gains in propositional thought (Artman, Cahan, & Avni-Babad, 2006). School tasks, the investigators speculated, provide crucial experiences in setting aside the "if . . . then" logic of everyday conversations that is often used to convey intentions, promises, and threats ("If you don't do your chores, then you won't get your allowance") but that conflicts with the logic of academic reasoning. In school, then, adolescents encounter rich opportunities to realize their neurological potential to think more effectively.

An Information-Processing View of Adolescent Cognitive Development

Information-processing theorists refer to a variety of specific mechanisms, including diverse aspects of executive function, as underlying cognitive gains in adolescence. Each was discussed in previous chapters (Kuhn, 2009; Kuhn & Franklin, 2006; Luna et al., 2004). Now let's draw them together:

- *Attention* becomes more selective (focused on relevant information) and better-adapted to the changing demands of tasks.
- *Inhibition*—both of irrelevant stimuli and of well-learned responses in situations where they are inappropriate—improves, supporting gains in attention and reasoning.
- *Strategies* become more effective, improving storage, representation, and retrieval of information.
- *Knowledge* increases, easing strategy use.
- *Metacognition* (awareness of thought) expands, leading to new insights into effective strategies for acquiring information and solving problems.
- *Cognitive self-regulation* improves, yielding better moment-by-moment monitoring, evaluation, and redirection of thinking.
- *Speed of thinking* and *processing capacity* increase. As a result, more information can be held at once in working memory and combined into increasingly complex, efficient representations, "opening possibilities for growth" in the capacities just listed and also improving as a result of gains in those capacities (Demetriou et al., 2002, p. 97).

As we look at influential findings from an information-processing perspective, we will see some of these mechanisms of change in action. And we will discover that researchers regard one of them—*metacognition*—as central to adolescent cognitive development.

Scientific Reasoning: Coordinating Theory with Evidence

During a free moment in physical education class, Sabrina wondered why more of her tennis serves and returns passed the net and dropped into her opponent's court when she used a particular brand of balls. "Is it something about their color or size?" she asked herself. "Hmm . . . or maybe it's their surface texture—that might affect their bounce."

The heart of scientific reasoning is coordinating theories with evidence. Deanna Kuhn (2002) has conducted extensive research into the development of scientific reasoning, using problems that, like Piaget's tasks, involve several variables that might affect an outcome. In one series of studies, third, sixth, and ninth graders and adults were first given evidence—sometimes consistent and sometimes conflicting with theories—and then questioned about the accuracy of each theory.

For example, participants were given a problem much like Sabrina's: to theorize about which of several features of sports balls—size (large or small), color (light or dark), texture (rough or smooth), or presence or absence of ridges on the surface—influences the quality of a player's serve. Next, they were told about the theory of Mr. (or Ms.) S, who believes that the ball's size is important, and the theory of Mr. (or Ms.) C, who thinks color matters. Finally, the interviewer presented evidence by placing balls with certain characteristics in two baskets, labeled "good serve" and "bad serve" (see Figure 11.9).

The youngest participants often discounted obviously causal variables, ignored evidence conflicting with their own initial judgments, and distorted evidence in ways consistent with their preferred theory. These findings, and others like them, suggest that on complex, multivariable tasks, children—instead of viewing evidence as separate from and bearing on a theory—often blend the two into a single representation of "the way things are." Children are especially likely to overlook evidence that does not match their prior beliefs when a causal variable is implausible (like color affecting the performance of a sports ball) and when task demands (number of variables to be evaluated) are high (Yang & Tsai, 2010; Zimmerman, 2007). The ability to distinguish theory from evidence and use logical rules to examine their relationship improves steadily from childhood into adolescence, continuing into adulthood (Kuhn & Dean, 2004; Kuhn & Pearsall, 2000).

How Scientific Reasoning Develops

What factors support skill at coordinating theory with evidence? Greater working-memory capacity, permitting a theory and the effects of several variables to be compared at once, is vital. Adolescents also benefit from exposure to increasingly complex problems and to teaching that highlights critical features of scientific reasoning—for example, why a scientist's expectations in a particular situation are inconsistent with everyday beliefs and experiences (Chinn & Malhotra, 2002). This explains why scientific reasoning is strongly influenced by years of schooling, whether individuals grapple with traditional scientific tasks (like the sports-ball problem) or engage in informal reasoning—for example, justifying a theory about what causes children to fail in school (Amsel & Brock, 1996).

Researchers believe that sophisticated *metacognitive understanding* is vital for scientific reasoning (Kuhn, 2009; Kuhn & Pease, 2006). When adolescents regularly pit theory against evidence over many weeks, they experiment with various strategies, reflect on and revise them, and become aware of the nature of logic. Then they apply their appreciation of logic to an increasingly wide variety of situations. The ability to *think about* theories, *deliberately isolate* variables, *consider all influential* variables, and *actively seek* disconfirming evidence is rarely present before adolescence (Kuhn, 2000; Kuhn et al., 2008; Moshman, 1998).

But adolescents and adults vary widely in scientific reasoning skills. Many continue to show a self-serving bias, applying logic more effectively to ideas they doubt than to ideas they favor (Klaczynski & Narasimham, 1998). Reasoning scientifically requires the metacognitive capacity to evaluate one's objectivity—to be fair-minded rather than self-serving (Moshman, 2005). As we will see in Chapter 12, this flexible, open-minded approach is not just a cognitive attainment but a personality trait—one that assists teenagers greatly in forming an identity and developing morally.

Adolescents develop scientific reasoning skills in a similar step-by-step fashion on different types of tasks. In a series of studies, 10- to 20-year-olds were given sets of problems graded in difficulty. One set consisted of quantitative-relational tasks like the pendulum problem in Figure 11.8. Another contained

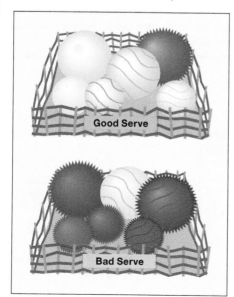

FIGURE 11.9 Which features of these sports balls—size, color, surface texture, or presence or absence of ridges—influence the quality of a player's serve? This set of evidence suggests that color might be important, since light-colored balls are largely in the good-serve basket and dark-colored balls in the bad-serve basket. But the same is true for texture! The good-serve basket has mostly smooth balls; the bad-serve basket, rough balls. Since all light-colored balls are smooth and all dark-colored balls are rough, we cannot tell whether color or texture makes a difference. But we can conclude that size and presence or absence of ridges are not important, since these features are equally represented in the good-serve and bad-serve baskets. (Adapted from Kuhn, Amsel, & O'Loughlin, 1988.)

Applying What We Know

Handling Consequences of Teenagers' New Cognitive Capacities

Thought expressed as . . .	Suggestion
Sensitivity to public criticism	Refrain from finding fault with the adolescent in front of others. If the matter is important, wait until you can speak to the teenager alone.
Exaggerated sense of personal uniqueness	Acknowledge the adolescent's unique characteristics. At opportune times, encourage a more balanced perspective by pointing out that you had similar feelings as a teenager.
Idealism and criticism	Respond patiently to the adolescent's grand expectations and critical remarks. Point out positive features of targets, helping the teenager see that all societies and people are blends of virtues and imperfections.
Difficulty making everyday decisions	Refrain from deciding for the adolescent. Model effective decision making and offer diplomatic suggestions about the pros and cons of alternatives, the likelihood of various outcomes, and learning from poor choices.

propositional tasks like the poker chip problem on page 384. Still another consisted of causal-experimental tasks like the sports-ball problem in Figure 11.9 (Demetriou et al., 1993, 1996, 2002). In each type of task, adolescents mastered component skills in sequential order by expanding their metacognitive awareness. For example, on causal-experimental tasks, they first became aware of the many variables—separately and in combination—that could influence an outcome. This enabled them to formulate and test hypotheses. Over time, adolescents combined separate skills into a smoothly functioning system, constructing a general model that they could apply to many instances of a given type of problem.

LOOK AND LISTEN

Describe one or more memorable experiences from your high school classes that helped you advance in scientific reasoning—pit theory against evidence and become receptive to disconfirming evidence even for theories you favored. ●

Piaget underscored the role of metacognition in formal operational thought when he spoke of "operating on operations" (see page 382). But information-processing findings confirm that scientific reasoning does not result from an abrupt, stagewise change. Instead, it develops gradually out of many specific experiences that require children and adolescents to match theories against evidence and reflect on and evaluate their thinking.

Consequences of Adolescent Cognitive Changes

The development of increasingly complex, effective thinking leads to dramatic revisions in the way adolescents see themselves, others, and the world in general. But just as adolescents are occasionally awkward in using their transformed bodies,

so they initially falter in their abstract thinking. Teenagers' self-concern, idealism, criticism, and faulty decision making, though perplexing to adults, are usually beneficial in the long run. Applying What We Know above suggests ways to handle the everyday consequences of teenagers' newfound cognitive capacities.

Self-Consciousness and Self-Focusing

Adolescents' ability to reflect on their own thoughts, combined with physical and psychological changes, leads them to think more about themselves. Piaget believed that a new form of egocentrism arises, in which adolescents again have difficulty distinguishing their own and others' perspectives (Inhelder & Piaget, 1955/1958). Piaget's followers suggest that two distorted images of the relation between self and other appear.

The first is called the **imaginary audience**, adolescents' belief that they are the focus of everyone else's attention and concern (Elkind & Bowen, 1979). As a result, they become extremely self-conscious. The imaginary audience helps explain why adolescents spend long hours inspecting every detail of their appearance and why they are so sensitive to public criticism. To teenagers, who believe that everyone is monitoring their performance, a critical remark from a parent or teacher can be mortifying.

A second cognitive distortion is the **personal fable**. Certain that others are observing and thinking about them, teenagers develop an inflated opinion of their own importance—a feeling that they are special and unique. Many adolescents view themselves as reaching great heights of omnipotence and also sinking to unusual depths of despair—experiences that others cannot possibly understand (Elkind, 1994). One teenager wrote in her diary, "My parents' lives are so ordinary, so stuck in a rut. Mine will be different. I'll realize my hopes and ambitions." Another, upset when a boyfriend failed to return her affections, rebuffed her mother's comforting words: "Mom, you don't know what it's like to be in love!"

ANTONIO MO/PHOTODISC/GETTY IMAGES

This teenager's swagger reflects self-confidence and delight that all eyes are on him. When the personal fable engenders a view of one-self as highly capable and influential, it may help young people cope with the challenges of adolescence.

Although imaginary-audience and personal-fable ideation is common in adolescence, these distorted visions of the self do not result from egocentrism, as Piaget suggested. Rather, they are partly an outgrowth of advances in perspective taking, which cause young teenagers to be more concerned with what others think (Vartanian & Powlishta, 1996).

In fact, certain aspects of the imaginary audience may serve positive, protective functions. When asked why they worry about the opinions of others, adolescents responded that others' evaluations have important *real* consequences—for self-esteem, peer acceptance, and social support (Bell & Bromnick, 2003). The idea that others care about their appearance and behavior also has emotional value, helping teenagers hold onto important relationships as they struggle to establish an independent sense of self (Vartanian, 1997).

With respect to the personal fable, in a study of sixth through tenth graders, sense of omnipotence predicted self-esteem and overall positive adjustment. Viewing the self as highly capable and influential helps young people cope with challenges of adolescence. In contrast, sense of personal unique-ness was modestly associated with depression and suicidal thinking (Aalsma, Lapsley, & Flannery, 2006). Focusing on the distinctiveness of one's own experiences may interfere with forming close, rewarding relationships, which provide social support in stressful times. And when combined with a sensa-tion-seeking personality, the personal fable seems to contribute to adolescent risk taking by reducing teenagers' sense of vulner-ability (Alberts, Elkind, & Ginsberg, 2007). Young people with high personal-fable and sensation-seeking scores tend to take more sexual risks, more often use drugs, and commit more delinquent acts than their agemates (Greene et al., 2000).

Idealism and Criticism

Adolescents' capacity to think about possibilities opens up the world of the ideal. Teenagers can imagine alternative family, religious, political, and moral systems, and they want to explore them. They often construct grand visions of a world with no injustice, discrimination, or tasteless behavior. The disparity between teenagers' idealism and adults' greater realism creates tension between parent and child. Envisioning a perfect family against which their parents and siblings fall short, adolescents become fault-finding critics.

Overall, however, teenage idealism and criticism are advan-tageous. Once adolescents come to see other people as having both strengths and weaknesses, they have a much greater capac-ity to work constructively for social change and to form positive, lasting relationships (Elkind, 1994).

Decision Making

Recall that changes in the brain's emotional/social network out-pace development of the prefrontal cortex's cognitive-control network. Consequently, teenagers often perform less well than adults in decision making, where they must inhibit emotion and impulses in favor of thinking rationally.

Good decision making involves: (1) identifying the pros and cons of each alternative, (2) assessing the likelihood of vari-ous outcomes, (3) evaluating their choice in terms of whether their goals were met and, if not, (4) learning from the mistake and making a better future decision. When researchers modified a card game to trigger strong emotion by introducing immedi-ate feedback about gains and losses after each choice, teenagers behaved more irrationally, taking far greater risks than adults in their twenties (Figner et al., 2009). They were more influenced by the possibility of immediate reward (see page 367).

Nevertheless, teenagers are less effective than adults at decision making even under "cool," unemotional conditions (Huizenga, Crone, & Jansen, 2007). They less often carefully

© JEFF GREENBERG/PHOTOEDIT

These high school students attending a college fair will face many choices over the next few years. But in making decisions, teenagers are less likely than adults, to carefully weigh the pros and cons of each alternative.

evaluate alternatives, instead falling back on well-learned intuitive judgments (Jacobs & Klaczynski, 2002). Consider a hypothetical problem requiring a choice, on the basis of two arguments, between taking a traditional lecture class and taking a computer-based class. One argument contains large-sample information: course evaluations from 150 students, 85 percent of whom liked the computer class. The other argument contains small-sample personal reports: complaints of two honor-roll students who both hated the computer class and enjoyed the traditional class. Most adolescents, even those who knew that selecting the large-sample argument was "more intelligent," based their choice on the small-sample argument, which resembled the informal opinions they depend on in everyday life (Klaczynski, 2001).

Earlier we noted that processing skills governed by the prefrontal cortex's cognitive-control system, such as decision making, develop gradually. But like other aspects of brain development, the cognitive-control system is affected by experience (Kuhn, 2009). As "first-timers" in many situations, adolescents do not have sufficient knowledge to consider pros and cons and predict likely outcomes. And after engaging in risky behavior without negative consequences, teenagers rate its benefits higher and its risks lower than peers who have not tried it—judgments that increase the chances of continued risk-taking (Halpern-Felsher et al., 2004).

Over time, young people learn from their successes and failures, gather information from others about factors that affect decision making, and reflect on the decision-making process (Byrnes, 2003; Reyna & Farley, 2006). But because taking risks without experiencing harm can heighten adolescents' sense of invulnerability, they need supervision and protection from high-risk experiences until their decision making improves.

ASK YOURSELF

REVIEW Describe research findings that challenge Piaget's notion of a new stage of cognitive development at adolescence.

CONNECT How does evidence on adolescent decision making help us understand teenagers' risk taking in sexual activity and drug use?

APPLY Clarissa, age 14, is convinced that no one appreciates how hurt she feels at not being invited to the homecoming dance. Meanwhile, 15-year-old Justine, alone in her room, pantomimes being sworn in as student body president with her awestruck parents looking on. Which aspect of the personal fable is each girl displaying? Which girl is more likely to be well-adjusted, which poorly adjusted? Explain.

REFLECT Cite examples of your own idealistic thinking or poor decision making as a teenager. How has your thinking changed?

Sex Differences in Mental Abilities

Sex differences in mental abilities have sparked almost as much controversy as the ethnic and SES differences in IQ considered in Chapter 9. Although boys and girls do not differ in general intelligence, they do vary in specific mental abilities.

Verbal Abilities

Throughout the school years, girls attain higher scores in reading achievement and account for a lower percentage of children referred for remedial reading instruction. Girls continue to score slightly higher on tests of verbal ability in middle childhood and adolescence in every country in which assessments have been conducted (Bussière, Knighton, & Pennock, 2007; Mullis et al., 2007; Wai et al., 2010). And when verbal tests are heavily weighted with writing, girls' advantage is large (Halpern et al., 2007).

A special concern is that girls' advantage in reading and writing achievement increases in adolescence, with boys doing especially poorly in writing—trends evident in the United States and other industrialized nations (OECD, 2010a; U.S. Department of Education, 2007b, 2010). These differences in literacy skills are believed to be major contributors to a widening gender gap in college enrollments. Whereas 40 years ago, males accounted for 60 percent of U.S. undergraduate students, today they are in the minority, at 43 percent (U.S. Department of Education, 2012b).

Recall from Chapter 5 that girls have a biological advantage in earlier development of the left hemisphere of the cerebral cortex, where language is usually localized. And fMRI research indicates that in tackling language tasks (such as deciding whether two spoken or written words rhyme), 9- to 15-year-old girls show concentrated activity in language-specific brain areas. Boys, in contrast, display more widespread activation—in addition to language areas, considerable activity in auditory and visual areas, depending on how words are presented (Burman, Bitan, & Booth, 2007). This suggests that girls are more efficient language processors than boys, who rely heavily on sensory brain regions and process spoken and written words differently.

But girls also receive more verbal stimulation from the preschool years through adolescence (Peterson & Roberts, 2003). Furthermore, children view language arts as a "feminine" subject. And as a result of the high-stakes testing movement, students today spend more time at their desks being taught in a regimented way—an approach particularly at odds with boys' higher activity level, assertiveness, and incidence of learning problems. Clearly, reversing boys' weakening literacy skills is a high priority, requiring a concerted effort by families, schools, and communities.

Mathematical Abilities

Studies of sex differences in mathematical abilities in the early school grades are inconsistent. Some find no disparities, others slight disparities depending on the skill assessed (Lachance & Mazzocco, 2006). Girls tend to be advantaged in counting, arithmetic computation, and mastery of basic concepts, perhaps because of their better verbal skills and more methodical approach to problem solving. But by late childhood to early adolescence, when math concepts become more abstract and spatial, boys start to outperform girls, with the difference especially evident on tests of complex reasoning and geometry (Bielinski & Davison, 1998; Gibbs, 2010; Lindberg et al., 2010). In science achievement, too, boys' advantage increases as problems become more difficult (Penner, 2003).

The male advantage is evident in most countries where males and females have equal access to secondary education. But the gap is typically small, varies considerably across nations, and has diminished over the past 30 years (Aud et al., 2011; Lindberg et al., 2010; U.S. Department of Education, 2009). Among the most capable, however, the gender gap is greater. In widely publicized research on more than 100,000 bright seventh and eighth graders invited to take the Scholastic Assessment Test (SAT), boys outscored girls on the mathematics subtest year after year. Yet even this disparity has been shrinking. A quarter-century ago, 13 times as many boys as girls scored over 700 (out of a possible 800) on the math portion of the SAT; today, the ratio is about 4 to 1 for seventh graders and 2 to 1 for high school students (Benbow & Stanley, 1983; Wai et al., 2010).

Some researchers believe that heredity contributes substantially to the gender gap in math, especially to the tendency for more boys to be extremely talented. Accumulating evidence indicates that boys' advantage originates in two skill areas: (1) their more rapid numerical memory, which permits them to devote more energy to complex mental operations; and (2) their superior spatial reasoning, which enhances their mathematical problem solving (Geary et al., 2000; Halpern et al., 2007). Longitudinal evidence on nationally representative samples of U.S. high school students tracked for a decade or more reveals that high spatial ability consistently predicts subsequent advanced educational attainment in math-intensive fields and entry into science, technology, engineering and math (STEM) careers (Wai, Lubinski, & Benbow, 2009). See the Biology and Environment box on page 390 for further consideration of this issue.

Social pressures are also influential. Long before sex differences in math achievement appear, many children view math as a "masculine" subject. Also, many parents think boys are better at it—an attitude that encourages girls to blame their errors on lack of ability and to consider math less useful for their future lives. These beliefs, in turn, reduce girls' confidence and interest in math and their willingness to consider STEM careers in college (Ceci & Williams, 2010; Kenney-Benson et al., 2006; Parker et al., 2012). Furthermore, *stereotype threat*—fear of being judged on the basis of a negative stereotype (see pages 314–315 in Chapter 9)—causes girls to do worse than their abilities allow on difficult math problems (Ben-Zeev et al., 2005; Muzzatti & Agnoli, 2007). As a result of these influences, even girls who are highly talented are less likely to develop effective math reasoning skills.

A positive sign is that today, American boys and girls reach advanced levels of high school math and science study in equal proportions—a crucial factor in reducing sex differences in knowledge and skill (Gallagher & Kaufman, 2005). But boys spend more time than girls with computers, and they tend to use them differently. Whereas girls typically focus on information gathering and social networking, boys more often play video games, create web pages, write computer programs, analyze data, and use graphics programs (Lenhart et al., 2010; Looker & Thiessen, 2003; Rideout, Foehr, & Roberts, 2010). As a result, boys acquire more specialized computer knowledge.

Clearly, extra steps must be taken to promote girls' interest in and confidence at math and science. As Figure 11.10 shows, in cultures that value gender equality, sex differences in math achievement are much smaller and, in one nation, reversed! Icelandic high school girls exceed boys in math scores (Guiso et al., 2008). Similarly, in countries where few individuals view science as "masculine," secondary school girls equal or exceed boys in science achievement (Nosek et al., 2009).

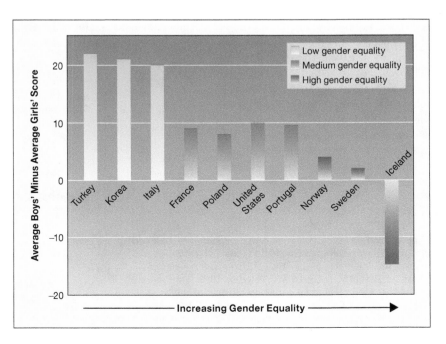

FIGURE 11.10 **Math achievement gender gaps in 10 industrialized nations, arranged in order of increasing gender equality.** Math achievement scores are based on 15-year-olds' performance on an identical test in each country. Country gender equality is a composite measure that includes cultural attitudes toward women, women's participation in the labor force and in politics and government, and women's educational attainment and economic opportunities. As country gender equality increases, boys' advantage in math achievement declines; in Iceland, girls' math scores exceed boys'. (Adapted from Guiso et al., 2008.)

Biology and Environment

Sex Differences in Spatial Abilities

Spatial skills are a key focus of researchers' efforts to explain sex differences in complex mathematical reasoning. The gender gap favoring males is large for *mental rotation tasks,* in which individuals must rotate a three-dimensional figure rapidly and accurately inside their heads (see Figure 11.11). Males also do considerably better on *spatial perception tasks,* in which people must determine spatial relationships by considering the orientation of the surrounding environment. Sex differences on *spatial visualization tasks,* involving analysis of complex visual forms, are weak or nonexistent. Because many strategies can be used to solve these tasks, both sexes may come up with effective procedures (Collaer & Hill, 2006; Voyer, Voyer, & Bryden, 1995).

Sex differences in spatial abilities emerge as early as the first few months of life, in male infants' superior ability to recognize a familiar object from a new perspective—a capacity requiring mental rotation (Moore & Johnson, 2008; Quinn & Liben, 2008). The male spatial advantage is present throughout childhood, adolescence, and adulthood in many cultures (Levine et al., 1999; Silverman, Choi, & Peters, 2007). One explanation is that heredity, perhaps by exposing the brain to androgen hormones, enhances right hemispheric functioning, giving males a spatial advantage. (Recall that for most people, spatial skills are housed in the right hemisphere of the cerebral cortex.) In support of this idea, girls and women whose prenatal androgen levels were abnormally high show superior performance on spatial rotation tasks (Berenbaum, 2001; Halpern & Collaer, 2005). And women with a male twin brother,

who are exposed to slightly higher levels of prenatal androgens, outperform women with a female twin sister in spatial rotation (Heil et al., 2011; Vuoksimaa et al., 2010).

Why might a biologically based sex difference in spatial abilities exist? Evolutionary theorists point out that mental rotation skill predicts rapid, accurate map drawing and interpretation, areas in which boys and men do better than girls and women. Over the course of human evolution, the cognitive abilities of males became adapted for hunting, which required generating mental representations of large-scale spaces to find one's way (Jones, Braithwaite, & Healy, 2003). But this explanation is controversial: Critics point out that female gatherers also needed to travel long distances to find fruits and vegetables that ripened in different seasons (Newcombe, 2007).

Experience also contributes to males' superior spatial performance. Children who engage in manipulative activities, such as block play, model building, and carpentry, do better on spatial tasks (Baenninger & Newcombe, 1995). Furthermore, playing action video games enhances many cognitive processes important for spatial skills, including visual discrimination, speed of thinking, attention shifting, tracking of multiple

This 17-year-old science fair winner plans a career in physics. With supportive experiences, girls can excel in math and science.

objects, mental rotation, and wayfinding—gains that persist and generalize to diverse situations (Spence & Feng, 2010). Boys spend far more time than girls at these pursuits.

Furthermore, spatial skills respond readily to training, with improvements often larger than the sex differences themselves. But because boys and girls show similar training effects, sex differences persist (Liu et al., 2008; Newcombe & Huttenlocher, 2006). In one study of first-graders, however, training in mental rotation strategies over several months—a more intensive approach than previously tried—led girls to reach the same performance level as boys (Tzuriel & Egozi, 2010). These findings suggest that the right kind of early intervention can override biologically based sex differences in spatial skills.

FIGURE 11.11 **Types of spatial tasks.** Large sex differences favoring males appear in mental rotation, and males do considerably better than females in spatial perception. In contrast, sex differences in spatial visualization are weak or nonexistent. (From M. C. Linn & A. C. Petersen, 1985, "Emergence and Characterization of Sex Differences in Spatial Ability: A Meta-Analysis," *Child Development, 56,* pp. 1482, 1483, 1485. © The Society for Research in Child Development. Reprinted with permission of John Wiley & Sons Ltd.)

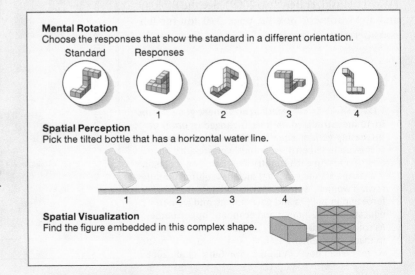

Mental Rotation
Choose the responses that show the standard in a different orientation.

Standard   Responses

1   2   3   4

Spatial Perception
Pick the tilted bottle that has a horizontal water line.

1   2   3   4

Spatial Visualization
Find the figure embedded in this complex shape.

Furthermore, a math curriculum beginning in kindergarten that teaches children how to apply effective spatial strategies—drawing diagrams, mentally manipulating visual images, searching for numerical patterns, and graphing—is vital (Nuttall, Casey, & Pezaris, 2005). Because girls are biased toward verbal processing, they may not attain their math and science potential unless they are taught how to think spatially.

 ## Learning in School

In complex societies, adolescence coincides with entry into secondary school. Most young people move into either a middle or a junior high school and then into a high school. With each change, academic achievement increasingly determines higher education options and job opportunities. In the following sections, we take up various aspects of secondary school life.

School Transitions

When Sabrina started middle school, she left a small, intimate, self-contained sixth-grade classroom for a much larger school. "I don't know most of the kids in my classes, and my teachers don't know me," Sabrina complained to her mother at the end of the first week. "Besides, there's too much homework. I get assignments in all my classes at once. I can't do all this!" she shouted, bursting into tears.

Impact of School Transitions. As Sabrina's reactions suggest, school transitions can create adjustment problems. With each school change—from elementary to middle or junior high and then to high school—adolescents' grades decline. The drop is partly due to tighter academic standards. At the same time, the transition to secondary school often means less personal attention, more whole-class instruction, and less chance to participate in classroom decision making (Seidman, Aber, & French, 2004).

It is not surprising, then, that students rate their middle- and high school learning experiences less favorably than their elementary-school experiences (Wigfield & Eccles, 1994). They also report that their teachers care less about them, are less friendly, grade less fairly, and stress competition more. Consequently, many young people feel less academically competent, and their liking for school and motivation decline (Barber & Olsen, 2004; Gutman & Midgley, 2000; Otis, Grouzet, & Pelletier, 2005).

Inevitably, students must readjust their feelings of self-confidence and self-worth as they encounter revised academic expectations and a more complex social world. In several studies that followed students across the middle- and high-school transitions, grade point average declined and feelings of anonymity increased after each school change. Girls fared less well than boys. On entering middle school, girls' self-esteem dropped sharply, perhaps because the transition tended to coincide with

On the first day of school, a teacher's caring attention helps this sixth grader deal with the stress of moving from a small, self-contained elementary school classroom to a large middle school.

other life changes: the onset of puberty and dating (Simmons & Blyth, 1987). And after starting high school, girls felt lonelier and more anxious than boys, and—although they were doing better academically—their grades declined more rapidly (Benner & Graham, 2009; Russell, Elder, & Conger, 1997).

Adolescents facing added strains at either transition—family disruption, poverty, low parental involvement, or learned helplessness on academic tasks—are at greatest risk for self-esteem and academic difficulties (de Bruyn, 2005; Rudolph et al., 2001; Seidman et al., 2003). Furthermore, high-school transition is especially challenging for African-American and Hispanic students who move to a new school with substantially fewer peers of the same ethnicity (Benner & Graham, 2009). Under these conditions, minority adolescents report decreased feelings of belonging and school liking, and they show steeper declines in grades.

Distressed youths whose school performance either remains low or drops sharply after school transition often show a persisting pattern of poor self-esteem, motivation, and achievement. In another study, researchers compared "multiple-problem" youths (those with both academic and mental health problems), youths with difficulties in just one area (either academic or mental health), and well-adjusted youths (those doing well in both areas) across the transition to high school. Although all groups declined in grade point average, well-adjusted students continued to get high marks and multiple-problem youths low marks, with the others falling in between. And as Figure 11.12 on page 392 shows, the multiple-problem youths showed a far greater rise in truancy and out-of-school problem behaviors (Roeser, Eccles, & Freedman-Doan, 1999). For some, school transition initiates a downward spiral in academic performance and school involvement that leads to dropping out.

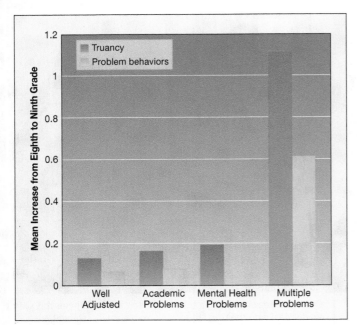

FIGURE 11.12 Increase in truancy and out-of-school problem behaviors across the transition to high school in four groups of students. Well-adjusted students, students with only academic problems, and students with only mental health problems showed little change. (Good students with mental health problems actually declined in problem behaviors, so no orange bar is shown for them.) In contrast, multiple-problem students—with both academic and mental health difficulties—increased sharply in truancy and problem behaviors after changing schools from eighth to ninth grade. (Adapted from Roeser, Eccles, & Freedman-Doan, 1999.)

Helping Adolescents Adjust to School Transitions. As these findings reveal, school transitions often lead to environmental changes that fit poorly with adolescents' developmental needs (Eccles & Roeser, 2009). They disrupt close relationships with teachers at a time when adolescents need adult support. They emphasize competition during a period of heightened self-focusing. They reduce decision making and choice as the desire for autonomy is increasing. And they interfere with peer networks as young people become more concerned with peer acceptance.

LOOK AND LISTEN

Ask several secondary school students to describe their experiences after school transition. What supports for easing the stress of transition did their teachers and school provide?

Support from parents, teachers, and peers can ease these strains. Parental involvement, monitoring, gradual autonomy granting, and emphasis on mastery rather than merely good grades are associated with better adjustment (Grolnick et al., 2000; Gutman, 2006). Adolescents with close friends are more likely to sustain these friendships across the transition, which increases social integration and academic motivation in the new school (Aikens, Bierman, & Parker, 2005). Forming smaller

units within larger schools promotes closer relationships with both teachers and peers and—as we will see later—greater extracurricular involvement (Seidman, Aber, & French, 2004). And a "critical mass" of same-ethnicity peers—according to one suggestion, at least 15 percent of the student body—helps teenagers feel socially accepted and reduces fear of out-group hostility (National Research Council, 2007).

Other, less extensive changes are also effective. In the first year after a school transition, homerooms can be provided in which teachers offer academic and personal counseling. Assigning students to classes with several familiar peers or a constant group of new peers strengthens emotional security and social support. In schools that took these steps, students were less likely to decline in academic performance or display other adjustment problems (Felner et al., 2002).

Academic Achievement

Adolescent achievement is the result of a long history of cumulative effects. Early on, positive educational environments, both family and school, lead to personal traits that support achievement—intelligence, confidence in one's own abilities, the desire to succeed, and high educational aspirations. Nevertheless, improving an unfavorable environment can foster resilience among poorly performing young people. See Applying What We Know on the following page for a summary of environmental factors that enhance achievement during the teenage years.

Child-Rearing Styles. Authoritative parenting is linked to higher grades in school among adolescents varying widely in SES, just as it predicts mastery-oriented behavior in childhood. In contrast, authoritarian and permissive styles are associated with lower grades (Collins & Steinberg, 2006; Vazsonyi, Hibbert, & Snider, 2003). Uninvolved parenting (low in both warmth and maturity demands) predicts the poorest grades and worsening school performance over time (Glasgow et al., 1997; Kaisa, Stattin, & Nurmi, 2000).

The link between authoritative parenting and adolescents' academic competence has been confirmed in countries with diverse value systems, including Argentina, Australia, China, Hong Kong, the Netherlands, Pakistan, and Scotland (de Bruyn, Deković, & Meijnen, 2003; Heaven & Ciarrochi, 2008; Steinberg, 2001). In Chapter 8, we noted that authoritative parents adjust their expectations to children's capacity to take responsibility for their own behavior. Adolescents whose parents engage in joint decision making, gradually permitting more autonomy with age, achieve especially well (Spera, 2005; Wang, Pomerantz, & Chen, 2007). Warmth, open discussion, firmness, and monitoring of the adolescents' whereabouts and activities make young people feel cared about and valued, encourage reflective thinking and self-regulation, and increase awareness of the importance of doing well in school. These factors, in turn, are related to mastery-oriented attributions, effort, achievement, and high educational aspirations (Aunola, Stattin, & Nurmi, 2000; Gregory & Weinstein, 2004; Trusty, 1999).

Applying **What We Know**

Supporting High Achievement in Adolescence

Factor	Description
Child-rearing practices	Authoritative parenting
	Joint parent–adolescent decision making
	Parent involvement in the adolescent's education
Peer influences	Peer valuing of and support for high achievement
School characteristics	Teachers who are warm and supportive, develop personal relationships with parents, and show them how to support their teenager's learning
	Learning activities that encourage high-level thinking
	Active student participation in learning activities and classroom decision making
Employment schedule	Job commitment limited to less than 15 hours per week
	High-quality vocational education for non-college-bound adolescents

Parent–School Partnerships. High-achieving students typically have parents who keep tabs on their child's progress, communicate with teachers, and make sure their child is enrolled in challenging, well-taught classes. These efforts are just as important during adolescence as they were earlier (Hill & Taylor, 2004). In a large, nationally representative sample of U.S. adolescents, parents' school involvement in eighth grade strongly predicted students' grade point average in tenth grade, beyond the influence of SES and previous academic achievement (Keith et al., 1998). Parents who are in frequent contact with the school send a message to their child about the value of education, model constructive solutions to academic problems, and promote wise educational decisions.

The daily stresses of living in low-income, high-risk neighborhoods reduce parents' energy for school involvement (Bowen, Bowen, & Ware, 2002). Yet stronger home–school links could relieve some of this stress. Schools can build parent–school partnerships by strengthening personal relationships between teachers and parents, tapping parents' talents to improve the quality of school programs, and including parents in school governance so they remain invested in school goals.

Peer Influences. Peers play an important role in adolescent achievement, in a way that relates to both family and school. Teenagers whose parents value achievement generally choose friends who share those values (Kiuru et al., 2009; Woolley, Kol, & Bowen, 2009). For example, when Sabrina began to make new friends in middle school, she often studied with her girlfriends. Each girl wanted to do well and reinforced this desire in the others.

Peer support for high achievement also depends on the overall climate of the peer culture, which, for ethnic minority youths, is powerfully affected by the surrounding social order. In one study, integration into the school peer network predicted higher grades among Caucasians and Hispanics but not among Asians and African Americans (Faircloth & Hamm, 2005). Asian cultural values stress respect for family and teacher expectations over close peer ties (Chao & Tseng, 2002; Chen, 2005). African-American minority adolescents may observe that their ethnic group is worse off than the white majority in educational attainment, jobs, income, and housing. And discriminatory treatment by teachers and peers, often resulting from stereotypes that they are "not intelligent," triggers anger, anxiety, self-doubt, declines in achievement, association with peers who are not interested in school, and increases in problem behaviors (Wong, Eccles, & Sameroff, 2003).

Schools that build close networks of support between teachers and peers can prevent these negative outcomes. One high school with a largely low-income ethnic minority student body (65 percent African American) reorganized into "career academies"—learning communities within the school, each

By attending parent–teacher conferences and keeping tabs on her daughter's academic progress, this mother sends her child a message about the importance of education and builds a bridge between the worlds of home and school.

© MICHAEL DWYER/ALAMY

Social Issues: Education

Media Multitasking Disrupts Attention and Learning

"Mom, I'm going to study for my biology test now," called 16-year-old Cassie while shutting her bedroom door. Sitting down at her desk, she accessed a popular social-networking website on her laptop, donned headphones and began listening to a favorite song on her MP3 player, and placed her cell phone next to her elbow so she could hear it chime if any text messages arrived. Only then did she open her textbook and begin to read.

In a survey of a nationally representative sample of U.S. 8- to 18-year-olds, more than two-thirds reported engaging in two or more media activities at once, some or most of the time (Rideout, Foehr, & Roberts, 2010). Their most frequent type of media multitasking is listening to music while doing homework, but many also report watching TV or using the Internet while studying (Jeong & Fishbein, 2007). The presence of a television or computer in the young person's bedroom is a strong predictor of this behavior (Foehr, 2006). And it extends into classrooms, where students can be seen text-messaging under their desks or surfing the Internet on cell phones.

Research confirms that media multitasking greatly reduces learning. In one experiment, participants were given two tasks: learning to predict the weather in

two different cities using colored shapes as cues and keeping a mental tally of how many high-pitched beeps they heard through headphones. Half the sample performed the tasks simultaneously, the other half separately. Both groups learned to predict the weather in the two-city situation, but the multitaskers were unable to apply their learning to new weather problems (Foerde, Knowlton, & Poldrack, 2006).

fMRI evidence revealed that the participants working only on the weather task activated the hippocampus, which plays a vital role in *explicit memory*—conscious, strategic recall, which enables new information to be used flexibly and adaptively in contexts outside the original learning situation (see page 218 in Chapter 7). In contrast, the multitaskers activated subcortical areas involved in *implicit memory*—a shallower, automatic form of learning that takes place unconsciously.

As early as 1980, studies linked heavy media use with executive-function difficulties (Nunez-Smith et al., 2008). Frequent media multitaskers, who are accustomed

Media multitasking while doing homework fragments attention, yielding superficial learning. Frequent multitaskers are likely to have trouble filtering out irrelevant stimuli even when they are not multitasking.

to continuously shifting their attention between tasks, have a harder time filtering out irrelevant stimuli when they are not multitasking (Ophir, Nass, & Wagner, 2009).

Beyond superficial preparation for her biology test, Cassie is likely to have trouble concentrating and strategically processing new information after turning off her computer and MP3 player. Experienced teachers often complain that compared to students of a generation ago, today's teenagers are more easily distracted and learn less thoroughly. One teacher reflected, "It's the way they've grown up—working short times on many different things at one time" (Clay, 2009, p. 40).

---

offering a different career-related curriculum (for example, one focusing on health, medicine, and life sciences, another on computer technology). The smaller-school climate and common theme helped create caring teacher–student relationships and a peer culture that focused on valuing school engagement, collaborating on projects, and academic success (Conchas, 2006). High school graduation and college enrollment rates rose from a small minority to over 90 percent.

Finally, teenagers' use of text messaging and e-mail to remain continuously in touch with peers—even during class and while working on homework—is an aspect of contemporary peer-group life that poses risks to achievement. Turn to the Social Issues: Education box above to find out about the impact of "media multitasking" on attention and learning.

School Characteristics. Adolescents need school environments that are responsive to their expanding powers of reasoning and their emotional and social needs. Without appropriate learning experiences, their cognitive potential is unlikely to be realized.

Classroom Learning Experiences. As noted earlier, in large, departmentalized secondary schools, many adolescents report that their classes lack warmth and supportiveness, which dampens their motivation. Of course, an important benefit of separate classes in each subject is that adolescents can be taught by experts, who are more likely to encourage high-level thinking, teach effective learning strategies, and emphasize content relevant to students' experiences—factors that contribute to interest, effort, and achievement (Eccles, 2004). But many classrooms do not consistently provide stimulating, challenging teaching.

Wide variability in quality of instruction has contributed to increasing numbers of seniors who graduate from high school deficient in basic academic skills. Although the achievement gap separating African-American, Hispanic, and Native-American students from white students has declined since the 1970s, mastery of reading, writing, mathematics, and science by low-SES ethnic minority students remains disappointing (U.S. Department of Education, 2007a, 2009, 2010). Too often these young people attend underfunded schools with rundown buildings, outdated equipment, and textbook shortages. In some, crime and discipline problems receive more attention than teaching and learning. By middle school, many low-SES minority students have been placed in low academic tracks, compounding their learning difficulties.

Tracking. Ability grouping, as we saw in Chapter 9, is detrimental during the elementary school years. At least into middle school, mixed-ability classes are desirable. They support the motivation and achievement of students who vary widely in academic progress (Gillies, 2003; Gillies & Ashman, 1996).

By high school, some grouping is unavoidable because certain aspects of education must dovetail with the young person's future educational and vocational plans. In the United States, high school students are counseled into college preparatory, vocational, or general education tracks. Unfortunately, low-SES minority students are assigned in large numbers to noncollege tracks, perpetuating educational inequalities of earlier years.

Longitudinal research following thousands of U.S. students from eighth to twelfth grade reveals that assignment to a college preparatory track accelerates academic progress, whereas assignment to a vocational or general education track decelerates it (Hallinan & Kubitschek, 1999). Even in secondary schools with no formal tracking program, low-SES minority students tend to be assigned to lower course levels in most or all academic subjects, resulting in *de facto* (unofficial) *tracking* (Lucas & Behrends, 2002).

Breaking out of a low academic track is difficult. Track or course enrollment is generally based on past performance, which is limited by placement history. Interviews with African-American students revealed that many thought their previous performance did not reflect their ability. Yet teachers and counselors, overburdened with other responsibilities, had little time to reconsider individual cases (Ogbu, 2003). And compared to students in higher tracks, those in low tracks exert substantially less effort—a difference due in part to less stimulating classroom experiences (Worthy, Hungerford-Kresser, & Hampton, 2009).

High school students are separated into academic and vocational tracks in virtually all industrialized nations. In China, Japan, and most Western European countries, students' placement in high school is determined by a national exam, which

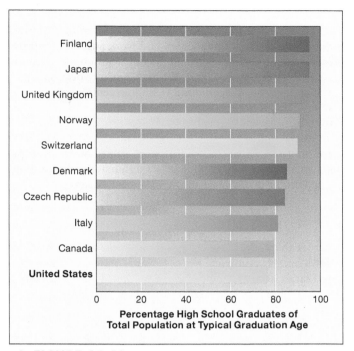

FIGURE 11.13 High school graduation rates in 10 industrialized nations. The United States ranks below many other developed countries. (From OECD, 2011a.)

usually establishes the young person's future possibilities. In the United States, students who are not assigned to a college preparatory track or who do poorly in high school can still attend college. Ultimately, however, many young people do not benefit from the more open U.S. system. By adolescence, SES differences in quality of education and academic achievement are greater in the United States than in most other industrialized countries (Marks, Cresswell, & Ainley, 2006). And the United States has a higher percentage of young people who see themselves as educational failures and drop out of high school (see Figure 11.13).

Part-Time Work. In high school, about one-fourth of U.S. adolescents are employed—a greater percentage than in other developed countries. But most are middle-SES adolescents in pursuit of spending money rather than vocational exploration and training. Low-income teenagers who need to contribute to family income or to support themselves find it harder to get jobs (U.S. Department of Education, 2012b).

Adolescents typically hold jobs that involve low-level, repetitive tasks and provide little contact with adult supervisors. A heavy commitment to such jobs is harmful. The more hours students work, the poorer their school attendance, the lower their grades, the less likely they are to participate in extra-curricular activities, and the more likely they are to drop out (Marsh & Kleitman, 2005). Students who spend many hours at such jobs also tend to feel more distant from their parents and report more drug and alcohol use and delinquent acts (Samuolis et al., 2011; Staff & Uggen, 2003).

In contrast, participation in work–study programs or other jobs that provide academic and vocational learning opportunities is related to positive school and work attitudes, improved achievement, and reduced delinquency (Hamilton & Hamilton, 2000; Staff & Uggen, 2003). Yet high-quality vocational preparation for non-college-bound U.S. adolescents is scarce. Unlike some European nations, the United States has no widespread training system to prepare youths for skilled business and industrial occupations and manual trades. Although U.S. federal and state governments support some job-training programs, most are too brief to make a difference and serve only a small minority of young people who need assistance.

Dropping Out

Across the aisle from Louis in math class sat Norman, who daydreamed, crumpled his notes into his pocket after class, and rarely did his homework. On test days, he twirled a rabbit's foot for good luck but left most questions blank. Louis and Norman had been classmates since fourth grade, but they had little to do with each other. To Louis, who was quick at schoolwork, Norman seemed to live in another world. Once or twice a week, Norman cut class; one spring day, he stopped coming altogether.

Norman is one of about 8 percent of U.S. 16- to 24-year-olds who dropped out of high school and remain without a diploma or a GED (U.S. Department of Education, 2012b). The dropout rate is higher among boys than girls and is particularly high among low-SES ethnic minority youths, especially Native-American and Hispanic teenagers (15 and 18 percent, respectively). The decision to leave school has dire consequences. Youths without upper secondary education have much lower literacy scores than high school graduates; they lack the skills employers value in today's knowledge-based economy. Consequently, dropouts have much lower employment rates than high school graduates. Even when employed, dropouts are far more likely to remain in menial, low-paying jobs and to be out of work from time to time.

Factors Related to Dropping Out. Although many dropouts achieve poorly and show high rates of norm-violating acts, a substantial number, like Norman, have few behavior problems, experience academic difficulties, and quietly disengage from school (Janosz et al., 2000; Newcomb et al., 2002). The pathway to dropping out starts early. Risk factors in first grade predict dropout nearly as well as risk factors in secondary school (Entwisle, Alexander, & Olson, 2005).

Norman had a long history of marginal-to-failing school grades and low academic self-esteem. Faced with a challenging task, he gave up, relying on luck—his rabbit's foot—to get by. As Norman got older, he attended class less regularly, paid little attention when he was there, and rarely did his homework. He didn't join school clubs or participate in sports. As a result, few teachers or students knew him well. By the day he left, Norman felt alienated from all aspects of school life.

As with other dropouts, Norman's family background contributed to his problems. Compared with other students, even those with the same grade profile, dropouts are more likely to have parents who are uninvolved in their teenager's education and engage in little monitoring of their youngster's daily activities (Englund, Egeland, & Collins, 2008; Pagani et al., 2008). Many are single parents, never finished high school themselves, and are unemployed.

Students who drop out often have school experiences that undermine their chances for success: grade retention, which marks them as academic failures; large, impersonal secondary schools; and classes with unsupportive teachers and few opportunities for active participation (Brown & Rodriguez, 2009). In such schools, rule breaking is common and often results in suspension, which—by excluding students from classes—contributes further to academic failure (Christie, Jolivette, & Nelson, 2007). Students in general education and vocational tracks, where teaching tends to be the least stimulating, are three times as likely to drop out as those in a college preparatory track (U.S. Department o f Education, 2012).

Prevention Strategies. Among the diverse strategies available for helping teenagers at risk of dropping out, several common themes are related to success:

- *Remedial instruction and counseling that offer personalized attention.* Most potential dropouts need academic assistance combined with social support—intensive remedial instruction in small classes that foster warm, caring teacher–student relationships (Christenson & Thurlow, 2004). In one successful approach, at-risk students are matched with retired adults, who serve as tutors, mentors, and role models in addressing academic and vocational needs (Prevatt, 2003).

- *High-quality vocational training.* For many marginal students, the real-life nature of vocational education is more comfortable and effective than purely academic work (Harvey, 2001). To work well, vocational education must carefully integrate academic and job-related instruction so students see the relevance of classroom experiences to their future goals.

- *Efforts to address the many factors in students' lives related to leaving school early.* Programs that strengthen parent involvement, offer flexible work–study arrangements, and provide on-site child care for teenage parents can make staying in school easier for at-risk adolescents.

- *Participation in extracurricular activities.* Another way of helping marginal students is to draw them into the community life of the school. The most powerful influence on extracurricular involvement is small school size (Crosnoe, Johnson, & Elder, 2004; Feldman & Matjasko, 2007). As high school student body declines—dropping from 2,000 students to 500 to 700 students—at-risk youths are more likely to be needed to help staff activities. As a result, they feel more attached to their school. In large schools, creation of smaller "schools within schools" has the same effect.

St. Paul, Minnesota, police chief Thomas Smith warmly greets one of his student mentees following a high school fundraising event for a charitable organization. Support from a caring adult and extracurricular involvement are effective ways to prevent school dropout.

Moderate (but not excessive) participation in arts, community service, or vocational development activities promotes improved academic performance, reduced antisocial behavior, more favorable self-esteem and initiative, and increased peer acceptance (Fredricks, 2012; Fredricks & Eccles, 2006). Adolescents with academic, emotional, and social problems are especially likely to benefit (Marsh & Kleitman, 2002).

As we conclude our discussion of academic achievement, let's place the school dropout problem in historical perspective. Over the second half of the twentieth century, the percentage of U.S. young people completing high school by age 24 increased steadily, from less than 50 percent to just over 90 percent. Although many dropouts get caught in a vicious cycle in which their lack of self-confidence and skills prevents them from seeking further education and training, about one-third return to finish their secondary education within a few years (U.S. Department of Education, 2012b). And some extend their schooling further as they come to realize how essential education is for a rewarding job and a satisfying adult life.

ASK YOURSELF

REVIEW List ways that parents can promote their adolescent's academic achievement. Explain why each is effective.

CONNECT How are educational practices that prevent school dropout similar to those that improve learning for adolescents in general?

APPLY Tanisha is finishing sixth grade. She can either continue in her current school through eighth grade or switch to a much larger seventh- to ninth-grade middle school. Which choice would you suggest, and why?

REFLECT Describe your own experiences in making the transition to middle or junior high school and then to high school. What did you find stressful? What helped you adjust?

SUMMARY

PHYSICAL DEVELOPMENT

Conceptions of Adolescence
(p. 362)

How have conceptions of adolescence changed over the past century?

- **Adolescence** is the transition between childhood and adulthood. Early theorists viewed adolescence as either a biologically determined period of storm and stress or entirely influenced by the social environment. Contemporary researchers view adolescence as a joint product of biological, psychological, and social forces.

- In industrialized societies, adolescence is greatly extended.

Puberty: The Physical Transition to Adulthood
(p. 363)

Describe body growth, motor performance, and sexual maturation during puberty.

- Hormonal changes under way in middle childhood initiate **puberty**, on average, two years earlier for girls than for boys. The first outward sign is the **growth spurt**. As the body enlarges, girls' hips and boys' shoulders broaden. Girls add more fat, boys more muscle.

- Puberty brings slow, gradual improvements in gross-motor performance for girls, dramatic gains for boys. Nevertheless, participation in regular physical activity declines sharply with age.

- At puberty, changes in **primary** and **secondary sexual characteristics** accompany rapid body growth. **Menarche** occurs late in the girl's sequence of pubertal events, after the growth spurt peaks. In boys, the peak in growth occurs later, preceded by enlargement of the sex organs and **spermarche**.

What factors influence the timing of puberty?

- Heredity, nutrition, exercise, and overall physical health influence the timing of puberty. The emotional quality of family experiences may play a role.

- A **secular trend** toward earlier puberty has occurred in industrialized nations as physical well-being increased. In some countries, rising obesity rates have extended this trend.

What changes in the brain take place during adolescence?

● Pruning of unused synapses in the cerebral cortex continues, and linkages between areas of the brain expand and myelinate. As the prefrontal cortex becomes a more effective "executive," adolescents gradually gain in processing speed and executive function. But performance on tasks requiring inhibition, planning, and future orientation is not yet fully mature.

● During puberty, neurons become more responsive to excitatory neurotransmitters, heightening emotional reactivity and reward-seeking. Changes in the brain's emotional/social network outpace development of the cognitive-control network, resulting in self-regulation difficulties.

● Revisions also occur in brain regulation of sleep timing, leading to a sleep "phase delay." Sleep deprivation contributes to poorer achievement, depressed mood, and high-risk behaviors.

The Psychological Impact of Pubertal Events (p. 368)

Explain adolescents' reactions to the physical changes of puberty.

● Girls typically react to menarche with mixed emotions, although those who receive advance information and support from family members respond more positively. Boys, who receive little social support for pubertal changes, react to spermarche with mixed feelings.

● Besides higher hormone levels, negative life events and adult-structured situations are associated with adolescents' negative moods. Psychological distancing between parent and child at puberty may be a modern substitute for physical departure from the family.

Describe the impact of pubertal timing on adolescent adjustment, noting sex differences.

● Early-maturing boys and late-maturing girls have a more positive **body image** and usually adjust well. In contrast, early-maturing girls and late-maturing boys tend to experience emotional and social difficulties, which—for girls—persist into early adulthood.

Health Issues (p. 371)

Describe nutritional needs during adolescence, and cite factors related to eating disorders.

● Nutritional requirements increase with rapid body growth, and vitamin and mineral deficiencies may result from poor eating habits. Frequency of family meals is associated with healthy eating.

● Early puberty, certain personality traits, maladaptive family interactions, and societal emphasis on thinness heighten risk of eating disorders such as **anorexia nervosa** and **bulimia nervosa**. Heredity also plays a role.

Discuss social and cultural influences on adolescent sexual attitudes and behavior.

● Although sexual attitudes of U.S. adolescents and adults have become more liberal over the past 40 years, North American attitudes toward adolescent sex remain relatively restrictive. Parents and the mass media deliver contradictory messages.

● Early, frequent sexual activity is linked to factors associated with economic disadvantage. Adolescent cognitive processes and weak social supports for responsible sexual behavior underlie the failure of many sexually active teenagers to practice contraception consistently.

Cite factors involved in the development of homosexuality.

● Biological factors, including heredity and prenatal hormone levels, play an important role in homosexuality. Lesbian, gay, and bisexual teenagers face special challenges in establishing a positive sexual identity.

Discuss factors related to sexually transmitted disease and teenage pregnancy and parenthood, noting prevention and intervention strategies.

● Early sexual activity, combined with inconsistent contraceptive use, results in high rates of sexually transmitted diseases (STDs) among U.S. adolescents.

● Life conditions linked to poverty and personal attributes jointly contribute to adolescent childbearing. Teenage parenthood is associated with school dropout, reduced chances of marriage, greater likelihood of divorce, and long-term economic disadvantage.

● Effective sex education, access to contraceptives, and programs that build academic and social competence help prevent early pregnancy. Adolescent mothers need school programs that provide job training, instruction in life-management skills, and child care. When teenage fathers stay involved, children develop more favorably.

What personal and social factors are related to adolescent substance use and abuse?

● Teenage alcohol and drug use is pervasive in industrialized nations. Drug taking reflects adolescent sensation seeking and drug-dependent cultural contexts. The minority who move to substance abuse tend to start using drugs early and to have serious personal, family, school, and peer problems.

● Effective prevention programs work with parents early to reduce family adversity, strengthen parenting skills, and build teenagers' competence.

COGNITIVE DEVELOPMENT

Piaget's Theory: The Formal Operational Stage (p. 382)

What are the major characteristics of formal operational thought?

● In Piaget's **formal operational stage**, adolescents become capable of **hypothetico-deductive reasoning**. To solve problems, they start with a hypothesis; deduce logical, testable inferences; and systematically isolate and combine variables to see which inferences are confirmed.

● Adolescents also develop **propositional thought**—the ability to evaluate the logic of verbal statements without referring to real-world circumstances.

Discuss follow-up research on formal operational thought and its implications for the accuracy of Piaget's formal operational stage.

● Adolescents, like adults, are most likely to think abstractly and systematically in situations in which they have had extensive guidance and practice in using such reasoning. Individuals in tribal and village societies rarely do well on tasks typically used to assess formal operational reasoning. Learning activities in school provide adolescents with rich opportunities to acquire formal operations.

An Information-Processing View of Adolescent Cognitive Development (p. 384)

How do information-processing researchers account for cognitive changes in adolescence?

● Information-processing researchers believe that a variety of specific mechanisms underlie cognitive gains in adolescence: improved attention, inhibition, strategies, knowledge, metacognition, cognitive self-regulation, speed of thinking, and processing capacity.

● The ability to coordinate theory with evidence improves as adolescents solve increasingly complex problems and acquire more sophisticated metacognitive understanding.

Consequences of Adolescent Cognitive Changes (p. 386)

Describe typical reactions of adolescents that result from their advancing cognition.

● As adolescents reflect on their own thoughts, two distorted images of the relation between self and other appear—the **imaginary audience** and the **personal fable**. Both result from heightened social sensitivity and gains in perspective taking.

● Teenagers' capacity to think about possibilities prompts idealistic visions at odds with reality, and they often become fault-finding critics.

● Adolescents are less effective at decision making than adults. They take greater risks in emotionally charged situations, less often weigh alternatives, and more often fall back on intuitive judgments.

Sex Differences in Mental Abilities (p. 388)

What factors contribute to sex differences in mental abilities at adolescence?

● Girls' advantage in reading and writing achievement increases, probably due to earlier development of the left hemisphere of the cerebral cortex, more efficient language processing, and greater verbal stimulation. Gender stereotyping of language arts as "feminine" and regimented teaching may weaken boys' literacy skills.

● By early adolescence, when concepts become more abstract and spatial, boys surpass girls in mathematical performance. Overall, the gender difference is small, but it is greater among the most capable. Boys' superior spatial reasoning enhances their mathematical problem solving. Gender stereotyping of math as "masculine" contributes to boys' greater self-confidence and interest in pursuing STEM careers.

Learning in School (p. 391)

Discuss the impact of school transitions on adolescent adjustment.

● School transitions bring larger, more impersonal school environments, in which grades and feelings of competence decline. Girls experience more adjustment difficulties. Teenagers coping with added stressors are at greatest risk for self-esteem and academic problems.

Discuss family, peer, school, and employment influences on academic achievement during adolescence.

● Authoritative parenting and parents' school involvement promote high achievement. Teenagers whose parents value achievement generally choose friends who share those values. Schools can help by promoting a peer culture that values school engagement.

● Warm, supportive classroom environments that encourage student interaction, and high-level thinking enable adolescents to reach their academic potential.

● By high school, separate educational tracks that dovetail with students' future plans are necessary. However, U.S. high school tracking usually extends the educational inequalities of earlier years.

● The more hours students work at a part-time job, the poorer their school attendance, academic performance, and extracurricular participation. But work–study programs that provide academic and vocational learning opportunities predict positive school and work attitudes and better academic achievement.

What factors increase the risk of high school dropout?

● Factors contributing to the high U.S. dropout rate include lack of parental support for achievement, a history of poor school performance, large impersonal secondary schools, and unsupportive teachers.

Important Terms and Concepts

adolescence (p. 361)
anorexia nervosa (p. 372)
body image (p. 371)
bulimia nervosa (p. 373)
formal operational stage (p. 382)
growth spurt (p. 363)

hypothetico-deductive reasoning (p. 382)
imaginary audience (p. 386)
menarche (p. 365)
personal fable (p. 386)
primary sexual characteristics (p. 365)
propositional thought (p. 383)

puberty (p. 361)
secondary sexual characteristics (p. 365)
secular trend (p. 367)
spermarche (p. 366)

As adolescents spend less time with family members, peer groups become more tightly knit into cliques. Mixed-sex cliques prepare teenagers for dating by providing models of how to interact and opportunities to do so without having to be intimate.

Emotional and Social Development in Adolescence

chapter outline

Erikson's Theory: Identity versus Role Confusion

Self-Understanding

Changes in Self-Concept • Changes in Self-Esteem • Paths to Identity • Identity Status and Psychological Well-Being • Factors Affecting Identity Development

■ **CULTURAL INFLUENCES** Identity Development Among Ethnic Minority Adolescents

Moral Development

Kohlberg's Theory of Moral Development • Are There Sex Differences in Moral Reasoning? • Coordinating Moral, Social-Conventional, and Personal Concerns • Influences on Moral Reasoning • Moral Reasoning and Behavior • Religious Involvement and Moral Development • Further Challenges to Kohlberg's Theory

■ **SOCIAL ISSUES: EDUCATION** Development of Civic Engagement

Gender Typing

The Family

Parent–Child Relationships • Family Circumstances • Siblings

Peer Relations

Friendships • Cliques and Crowds • Dating

Problems of Development

Depression • Suicide • Delinquency

■ **BIOLOGY AND ENVIRONMENT** Two Routes to Adolescent Delinquency

Louis sat on the grassy hillside overlooking the high school, waiting for his best friend, Darryl, to arrive from his fourth-period class. The two boys often had lunch together. Watching as hundreds of students poured onto the school grounds, Louis reflected on what he had learned in government class that day. "Suppose I *had* been born in the People's Republic of China. I'd be sitting here, speaking a different language, being called by a different name, and thinking about the world in different ways. Wow," Louis pondered. "I am who I am through some quirk of fate."

Louis awoke from his thoughts with a start to see Darryl standing in front of him. "Hey, dreamer! I've been shouting and waving from the bottom of the hill for five minutes. How come you're so spaced out lately, Louis?"

"Oh, just wondering about stuff—what I want, what I believe in. My older brother Jules—I envy him. He seems to know more about where he's going. I'm up in the air about it. You ever feel that way?"

"Yeah, a lot," Darryl admitted, looking at Louis seriously. "I wonder, what am I really like? Who will I become?"

© MARY KATE DENNY/ALAMY

Louis and Darryl's introspective remarks are signs of a major reorganization of the self at adolescence: the development of identity. Both young people are attempting to formulate who they are—their personal values and the directions they will pursue in life.

We begin this chapter with Erikson's account of identity development and the research it has stimulated on teenagers' thoughts and feelings about themselves. The quest for identity extends to many aspects of development. We will see how a sense of cultural belonging, moral understanding, and masculine and feminine self-images are refined during adolescence. And as parent–child relationships are revised and young people become increasingly independent of the family, friendships and peer networks become crucial contexts for bridging the gap between childhood and adulthood. Our chapter concludes with a discussion of several serious adjustment problems of adolescence: depression, suicide, and delinquency. ●

Erikson's Theory: Identity versus Role Confusion

Erikson (1950, 1968) was the first to recognize **identity** as the major personality achievement of adolescence and as a crucial step toward becoming a productive, content adult. Constructing an identity involves defining who you are, what you value, and the directions you choose to pursue in life. One expert described it as an explicit theory of oneself as a rational agent—one who acts on the basis of reason, takes responsibility for those actions, and can explain them (Moshman, 2005). This search for what is true and real about the self drives many choices—vocation, interpersonal relationships, community involvement, ethnic-group membership, and expression of one's sexual orientation, as well as moral, political, and religious ideals.

Although the seeds of identity formation are planted early, not until late adolescence and early adulthood do young people become absorbed in this task. According to Erikson, in complex societies, teenagers experience an *identity crisis*—a temporary period of distress as they experiment with alternatives before settling on values and goals. They go through a process of inner soul-searching, sifting through characteristics that defined the self in childhood and combining them with emerging traits, capacities, and commitments. Then they mold these into a solid inner core that provides a mature identity—a sense of self-continuity as they move through various roles in daily life. Once formed, identity continues to be refined in adulthood as people reevaluate earlier commitments and choices.

Erikson called the psychological conflict of adolescence **identity versus role confusion.** If young people's earlier conflicts were resolved negatively or if society limits their choices to ones that do not match their abilities and desires, they may appear shallow, directionless, and unprepared for the challenges of adulthood.

Current theorists agree with Erikson that questioning of values, plans, and priorities is necessary for a mature identity, but they no longer describe this process as a "crisis" (Côté, 2009; Kroger, 2007). For most young people, identity development is not traumatic and disturbing but, rather, a process of *exploration* followed by *commitment.* As young people try out life possibilities, they gather important information about themselves and their environment and move toward making enduring decisions. In doing so, they forge an organized self-structure (Arnett, 2000, 2006; Moshman, 2005). In the following sections, we will see that adolescents go about the task of defining the self in ways that closely match Erikson's description.

Self-Understanding

During adolescence, the young person's vision of the self becomes more complex, well-organized, and consistent. Compared with younger children, adolescents engage in evaluations of an increasing variety of aspects of the self. Over time, they construct a balanced, integrated representation of their strengths and limitations (Harter, 2003, 2006). Changes in self-concept and self-esteem set the stage for developing a unified personal identity.

Changes in Self-Concept

Recall that by the end of middle childhood, children can describe themselves in terms of personality traits. In early adolescence, they unify separate traits ("smart" and "curious") into more abstract descriptors ("intelligent"). But these generalizations are not interconnected and are often contradictory. For example, 12- to 14-year-olds might mention opposing traits—"intelligent" and "dork," "extrovert" and "introvert." These disparities result from the expansion of adolescents' social world, which creates pressure to display different selves in different relationships. As adolescents' awareness of these inconsistencies grows, they frequently agonize over "which is the real me" (Harter, 1998, 2003, 2006).

From middle to late adolescence, cognitive changes enable teenagers to combine their traits into an organized system. Their use of qualifiers ("I have a *fairly* quick temper," "I'm not *thoroughly* honest") reveals an increasing awareness that psychological qualities can vary from one situation to the next. Older adolescents also add integrating principles that make sense of formerly troublesome contradictions. "I'm very adaptable," said one young person. "When I'm around my friends, who think what I say is important, I'm talkative; but around my family I'm quiet because they're never interested enough to really listen to me" (Damon, 1990, p. 88).

Compared with school-age children, teenagers place more emphasis on social virtues, such as being friendly, considerate, kind, and cooperative—traits that reflect adolescents' increasing concern with being viewed positively by others. Among older adolescents, personal and moral values also appear as key themes. As young people revise their views of themselves to include enduring beliefs and plans, they move toward the unity of self that is central to identity development.

Changes in Self-Esteem

Self-esteem, the evaluative side of self-concept, continues to differentiate in adolescence. Teenagers add several new dimensions of self-evaluation—close friendship, romantic appeal, and job competence—to those of middle childhood (see Chapter 10, pages 330–331) (Harter, 1999, 2003, 2006).

Level of self-esteem also changes. Though some adolescents experience temporary or persisting declines after school transitions (see Chapter 11, page 391), self-esteem rises for most young people, who report feeling especially good about their peer relationships and athletic capabilities (Impett et al., 2008; Twenge & Campbell, 2001). Teenagers often assert that they have become more mature, capable, personable, and attractive than in the past. In longitudinal research on a nationally representative sample of U.S. youths, an increasing sense of mastery—feeling competent and in control of one's life—strongly predicted this age-related rise in self-esteem (Erol & Orth, 2011).

During adolescence, self-esteem rises for most young people, who feel especially good about their peer relationships and athletic capabilities.

As in middle childhood, individuals with mostly favorable self-esteem profiles tend to be well-adjusted, sociable, and conscientious, whereas low self-esteem in all areas is linked to adjustment difficulties. But certain self-esteem factors are more strongly related to adjustment. Teenagers who feel highly dissatisfied with parental relationships often are aggressive and antisocial. Those with poor academic self-esteem tend to be anxious and unfocused, and those with negative peer relationships are likely to be anxious and depressed (Marsh, Parada, & Ayotte, 2004; Rudolph, Caldwell, & Conley, 2005).

In adolescence, authoritative parenting continues to predict high self-esteem, as does encouragement from teachers (Lindsey et al., 2008; McKinney, Donnelly, & Renk, 2008; Wilkinson, 2004). In contrast, teenagers whose parents are critical and insulting have unstable and generally low self-esteem (Kernis, 2002). Feedback that is negative, inconsistent, or not contingent on performance triggers, at best, uncertainty about the self's capacities and, at worst, a sense of being incompetent and unloved. Teenagers who experience such parenting tend to rely only on peers, not on adults, to affirm their self-esteem—a risk factor for adjustment difficulties (DuBois et al., 1999, 2002).

Paths to Identity

Adolescents' well-organized self-descriptions and differentiated sense of self-esteem provide the cognitive foundation for forming an identity. Using a clinical interviewing procedure devised by James Marcia (1980) or briefer questionnaire measures, researchers commonly evaluate progress in identity development on two key criteria derived from Erikson's theory: *exploration* and *commitment*. Their various combinations yield four *identity statuses*, summarized in Table 12.1: **identity achievement**, commitment to values, beliefs, and goals following a period of exploration; **identity moratorium**, exploration without having reached commitment; **identity foreclosure**, commitment in the absence of exploration; and **identity diffusion**, an apathetic state characterized by lack of both exploration and commitment.

Identity development follows many paths. Some young people remain in one status, whereas others experience many

TABLE 12.1

The Four Identity Statuses

IDENTITY STATUS	DESCRIPTION	EXAMPLE
Identity achievement	Having already explored alternatives, identity-achieved individuals are committed to a clearly formulated set of self-chosen values and goals. They feel a sense of psychological well-being, of sameness through time, and of knowing where they are going.	When asked how willing she would be to give up going into her chosen occupation if something better came along, Lauren responded, "Well, I might, but I doubt it. I've thought long and hard about law as a career. I'm pretty certain it's for me."
Identity moratorium	*Moratorium* means "delay or holding pattern." These individuals have not yet made definite commitments. They are in the process of exploring—gathering information and trying out activities, with the desire to find values and goals to guide their lives.	When asked whether he had ever had doubts about his religious beliefs, Ramón said, "Yes, I guess I'm going through that right now. I just don't see how there can be a God and yet so much evil in the world."
Identity foreclosure	Identity-foreclosed individuals have committed themselves to values and goals without exploring alternatives. They accept a ready-made identity chosen for them by authority figures—usually parents but sometimes teachers, religious leaders, or romantic partners.	When asked if she had ever reconsidered her political beliefs, Emily answered, "No, not really, our family is pretty much in agreement on these things."
Identity diffusion	Identity-diffused individuals lack clear direction. They are not committed to values and goals, nor are they actively trying to reach them. They may never have explored alternatives or may have found the task too threatening and overwhelming.	When asked about his attitude toward nontraditional gender roles, Justin responded, "Oh, I don't know. It doesn't make much difference to me. I can take it or leave it."

status transitions. And the pattern often varies across *identity domains,* such as sexual orientation, vocation, and religious and political values. Most young people change from "lower" statuses (foreclosure or diffusion) to higher ones (moratorium or achievement) between their mid-teens and mid-twenties, but as many remain stable, and some move in the reverse direction (Kroger, 2007; Kroger, Martinussen, & Marcia, 2010; Meeus et al., 2012).

Because attending college provides opportunities to explore values, career options, and lifestyles, college students make more identity progress than they did in high school (Klimstra et al., 2010; Montgomery & Côté, 2003). After college, they often sample a broad range of life experiences before choosing a life course. Those who go to work immediately after high school graduation often settle on a self-definition earlier. But if non-college-bound youths encounter obstacles to realizing their occupational goals because of lack of training or vocational choices, they are at risk for identity foreclosure or diffusion (Cohen et al., 2003; Eccles et al., 2003).

At one time, researchers thought that adolescent girls postponed establishing an identity, focusing instead on Erikson's next stage, intimacy development. Some girls do show more sophisticated reasoning than boys in identity domains related to intimacy, such as sexuality and family versus career priorities. Otherwise, adolescents of both sexes typically make progress on identity concerns before experiencing genuine intimacy in relationships (Berman et al., 2006; Kroger, 2007).

Identity Status and Psychological Well-Being

A wealth of research verifies that both identity achievement and moratorium are psychologically healthy routes to a mature self-definition. Long-term foreclosure and diffusion, in contrast, are maladaptive.

Adolescents in moratorium resemble identity-achieved individuals in using an active, *information-gathering cognitive style* to make personal decisions and solve problems: They seek out relevant information, evaluate it carefully, and critically reflect on and revise their views (Berzonsky, 2003, 2011). Young people who are identity-achieved or exploring have higher self-esteem, feel more in control of their lives, are more likely to view school and work as feasible avenues for realizing their aspirations, and are more advanced in moral reasoning (Berzonsky et al., 2011; Kroger, 2007; Serafini & Adams, 2002).

Adolescents stuck in either foreclosure or diffusion are passive in the face of identity concerns and have adjustment difficulties. Foreclosed individuals display a *dogmatic, inflexible cognitive style,* internalizing the values and beliefs of parents and others without deliberate evaluation and resisting information that threatens their position (Berzonsky & Kuk, 2000; Berzonsky et al., 2011). Most fear rejection by people on whom they depend for affection and self-esteem. A few foreclosed teenagers who are alienated from their families and society may join cults or other extremist groups, uncritically adopting a way of life different from their past.

Long-term diffused individuals are the least mature in identity development. They typically use a *diffuse-avoidant cognitive style* in which they avoid dealing with personal decisions and problems and, instead, allow current situational pressures to dictate their reactions (Berzonsky & Kuk, 2000; Krettenauer, 2005). Taking an "I don't care" attitude, they entrust themselves to luck or fate, tend to go along with the crowd, and are focused on short-term personal pleasures. As a result, they experience time management and academic difficulties and, of all young people, are most likely to commit antisocial acts and to use and abuse drugs (Berzonsky et al., 2011; Schwartz et al., 2005). Often at the heart of their apathy is a sense of hopelessness about the future.

Factors Affecting Identity Development

Adolescent identity formation begins a lifelong, dynamic process in which a change in either the individual or the context opens up the possibility of reformulating identity (Kunnen & Bosma, 2003). A wide variety of factors influence identity development.

Identity status, as we have just seen, is both cause and consequence of personality characteristics. Adolescents who assume that absolute truth is always attainable tend to be foreclosed, while those who doubt that they will ever feel certain about anything are more often identity-diffused. Young people who appreciate that they can use rational criteria to choose among alternatives are likely to be in a state of moratorium or identity achievement (Berzonsky & Kuk, 2000; Berzonsky et al., 2011).

Teenagers' identity development is enhanced when their families serve as a "secure base" from which they can confidently move out into the wider world. Adolescents who feel attached to their parents but also free to voice their own opinions tend to be in a state of moratorium or identity achievement (Berzonsky, 2004; Luyckx, Goossens, & Soenens, 2006; Schwartz

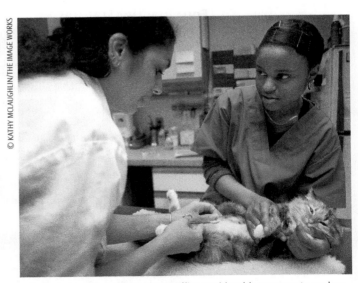

An internship in a veterinary office enables this teenager to explore a real-world career related to her love of animals, thereby fostering identity development.

Applying **What We Know**

Supporting Healthy Identity Development

Strategy	Explanation
Engage in warm, open communication.	Provides both emotional support and freedom to explore values and goals.
Initiate discussions that promote high-level thinking at home and at school.	Encourages rational and deliberate selection among beliefs and values.
Provide opportunities to participate in extracurricular activities and vocational training programs.	Permits young people to explore the real world of adult work.
Provide opportunities to talk with adults and peers who have worked through identity questions.	Offers models of identity achievement and advice on how to resolve identity concerns.
Provide opportunities to explore ethnic heritage and learn about other cultures in an atmosphere of respect.	Fosters identity achievement in all areas and ethnic tolerance, which supports the identity explorations of others.

et al., 2005). Foreclosed teenagers usually have close bonds with parents but lack opportunities for healthy separation. And diffused young people report the lowest levels of parental support and of warm, open communication (Reis & Youniss, 2004; Zimmerman & Becker-Stoll, 2002).

Interaction with diverse peers through school and community activities encourages adolescents to explore values and role possibilities (Barber et al., 2005). And close friends, like parents, can act as a secure base, providing emotional support, assistance, and models of identity development. In one study, 15-year-olds with warm, trusting peer ties were more involved in exploring relationship issues—for example, thinking about what they valued in close friends and in a life partner (Meeus, Oosterwegel, & Vollebergh, 2002). In another study, young people's attachment to friends predicted progress in choosing a career (Felsman & Blustein, 1999).

Identity development also depends on schools and communities that offer rich and varied opportunities for exploration. Supportive experiences include classrooms that promote high-level thinking, teachers and counselors who encourage low-SES students to go to college, extracurricular activities that offer teenagers responsible roles consistent with their interests and talents, and vocational training that immerses adolescents in the real world of adult work (Coatsworth et al., 2005; Hardy et al., 2011; McIntosh, Metz, & Youniss, 2005).

Culture strongly influences an aspect of mature identity not captured by the identity-status approach: constructing a sense of self-continuity despite major personal changes. In one study, researchers asked Native Canadian and cultural-majority 12- to 20-year-olds to describe themselves in the past and in the present and then to justify why they regarded themselves as the same continuous person (Lalonde & Chandler, 2005). Most cultural-majority adolescents used an individualistic approach: They described an *enduring personal essence,* a core self that remained the same despite change. In contrast, Native Canadian youths took an interdependent approach that emphasized a *constantly transforming self,* resulting from new roles and relationships.

They typically constructed a *coherent narrative* in which they linked together various time slices of their life with a thread that explained how they had changed in meaningful ways.

Finally, societal forces also are responsible for the special challenges faced by gay, lesbian, and bisexual youths (see Chapter 11) and by ethnic minority adolescents in forming a secure identity (see the Cultural Influences box on page 406). Applying What We Know above summarizes ways that adults can support adolescents in their quest for identity.

ASK YOURSELF

REVIEW List personal and contextual factors that promote identity development.

CONNECT Explain the close link between adolescent identity development and cognitive processes.

APPLY Return to the conversation between Louis and Darryl in the opening of this chapter. Which identity status best characterizes each of the two boys, and why?

REFLECT Does your identity status vary across the domains of sexuality, close relationships, vocation, religious beliefs, and political values? Describe factors that may have influenced your identity development in an important domain.

Moral Development

Eleven-year-old Sabrina sat at the kitchen table reading the Sunday newspaper, her eyes wide with interest. "Look at this!" she said to 16-year-old Louis, who was munching cereal. Sabrina held up a page of large photos showing a 70-year-old woman standing in her home. The floor and furniture were piled with stacks of newspapers, cardboard boxes, tin cans,

Cultural Influences

Identity Development Among Ethnic Minority Adolescents

Most adolescents are aware of their cultural ancestry but relatively unconcerned about it. However, for teenagers who are members of minority groups, **ethnic identity**—a sense of ethnic group membership and attitudes and feelings associated with that membership— is central to the quest for identity. As they develop cognitively and become more sensitive to feedback from the social environment, minority youths become painfully aware that they are targets of prejudice and discrimination. This discovery complicates their efforts to develop a sense of cultural belonging and a set of personally meaningful goals.

In many immigrant families from collectivist cultures, adolescents' commitment to obeying their parents and fulfilling family obligations lessens the longer the family has been in the immigrant-receiving country— a circumstance that induces **acculturative stress**, psychological distress resulting from conflict between the minority and the host culture (Phinney, Ong, & Madden, 2000). When immigrant parents tightly restrict their teenagers through fear that assimilation into the larger society will undermine their cultural traditions, their youngsters often rebel, rejecting aspects of their ethnic background.

At the same time, discrimination can interfere with the formation of a positive ethnic identity. In one study, Mexican-American youths who had experienced more discrimination were less likely to explore their ethnicity and to report feeling good about it (Romero & Roberts, 2003). Those with low ethnic pride showed a sharp drop in self-esteem in the face of discrimination.

With age, many minority young people strengthen their ethnic identity. But because the process of forging an ethnic identity can be painful and confusing, others show no change, and still others regress (Huang & Stormshak, 2011). Young people with parents of different ethnicities face extra challenges.

In a large survey of high school students, part-black biracial teenagers reported as much discrimination as their monoracial black counterparts, yet they felt less positively about their ethnicity. And compared with monoracial minorities, many biracial young people—including black–white, black–Asian, white–Asian, black–Hispanic, and white–Hispanic— regarded ethnicity as less central to their identities (Herman, 2004). Perhaps these adolescents encountered fewer opportunities in their homes and communities to forge a strong sense of belonging to either culture.

Adolescents whose family members encourage them to disprove ethnic stereotypes of low achievement or antisocial behavior typically surmount the threat that discrimination poses to a favorable ethnic identity. These young people manage experiences of unfair treatment effectively, by seeking social support and engaging in direct problem solving (Phinney & Chavira, 1995; Scott, 2003). Also, adolescents whose families taught them the history, traditions, values, and language of their ethnic group and who frequently interact with same-ethnicity peers are more likely to forge a favorable ethnic identity (Hughes et al., 2006; McHale et al., 2006).

How can society help minority adolescents resolve identity conflicts constructively? Here are some relevant approaches:

- Promote effective parenting, in which children and adolescents benefit from family ethnic pride yet are encouraged to explore the meaning of ethnicity in their own lives.

- Ensure that schools respect minority youths' native languages, unique learning styles, and right to high-quality education.

- Foster contact with peers of the same ethnicity, along with respect between ethnic groups (García Coll & Magnuson, 1997).

Stilt walkers celebrate their heritage at a Caribbean youth festival. Minority youths whose culture is respected in their community are more likely to incorporate ethnic values and customs into their identity.

A strong, secure ethnic identity is associated with higher self-esteem, optimism, a sense of mastery over the environment, and more positive attitudes toward one's ethnicity (St. Louis & Liem, 2005; Umana-Taylor & Updegraff, 2007; Worrell & Gardner-Kitt, 2006). For these reasons, adolescents with a positive connection to their ethnic group are better-adjusted. They cope more effectively with stress, show higher achievement in school, and have fewer emotional and behavior problems than agemates who identify only weakly with their ethnicity (Ghavami et al., 2011; Greene, Way, & Pahl, 2006; Seaton, Scottham, & Sellers, 2006; Umana-Taylor & Alfaro, 2006).

Forming a **bicultural identity**—by exploring and adopting values from both the adolescent's subculture and the dominant culture—offers added benefits. Biculturally identified adolescents tend to be achieved in other areas of identity as well and to have especially favorable relations with members of other ethnic groups (Phinney, 2007; Phinney et al., 2001). In sum, achievement of ethnic identity enhances many aspects of emotional and social development.

glass containers, food, and clothing. The accompanying article described crumbling plaster on the walls, frozen pipes, and nonfunctioning sinks, toilet, and furnace. The headline read: "Loretta Perry: My Life Is None of Their Business."

"Look what they're trying to do to this poor lady," exclaimed Sabrina. "They wanna throw her out of her house and tear it down! Those city inspectors must not care about anyone. Here it says, 'Mrs. Perry has devoted much of her life to doing favors for people.' Why doesn't someone help *her?*"

"Sabrina, you're missing the point," Louis responded. "Mrs. Perry is violating 30 building code standards. The law says you're supposed to keep your house clean and in good repair."

"But Louis, she's old, and she needs help. She says her life will be over if they destroy her home."

"The building inspectors aren't being mean, Sabrina. She's refusing to obey the law. And she's not just a threat to herself—she's a danger to her neighbors, too. Suppose her house caught on fire. You can't live around other people and say your life is nobody's business."

"You don't just knock someone's home down," Sabrina replied angrily. "Why aren't her friends and neighbors over there fixing up that house? You're just like those building inspectors, Louis. You've got no feelings!"

As Louis and Sabrina's disagreement over Loretta Perry's plight illustrates, cognitive development and expanding social experiences permit adolescents to better understand larger social structures—societal institutions and law-making systems—that govern moral responsibilities. As their grasp of social arrangements expands, adolescents construct new ideas about what should be done when the needs and desires of people conflict. As a result, they move toward increasingly just, fair, and balanced solutions to moral problems.

Kohlberg's Theory of Moral Development

Early work by Piaget on the moral judgment of the child inspired Lawrence Kohlberg's more comprehensive cognitive-developmental theory of moral understanding. Kohlberg used a clinical interviewing procedure in which he presented a sample of 10- to 16-year-old boys with hypothetical *moral dilemmas*—stories involving a conflict between two moral values—and asked them what the main actor should do and why. Then he followed the participants longitudinally, reinterviewing them at 3- to 4-year intervals over the next 20 years. The best known of Kohlberg's dilemmas, the "Heinz dilemma," pits the value of obeying the law (not stealing) against the value of human life (saving a dying person):

> In Europe a woman was near death from cancer. There was one drug the doctors thought might save her. A druggist in the same town had discovered it, but he was charging ten times what the drug cost him to make. The sick woman's husband, Heinz, went to everyone he knew to borrow the money, but he could only get together half of what it cost. The druggist refused to sell the drug for less or let Heinz pay later. So Heinz became desperate and broke into the man's store to steal the drug for his wife. Should

Heinz have done that? Why or why not? (paraphrased from Colby et al., 1983, p. 77)

Kohlberg emphasized that it is *the way an individual reasons about the dilemma,* not *the content of the response* (whether or not to steal), that determines moral maturity. Individuals who believe Heinz should take the drug and those who think he should not can be found at each of Kohlberg's first four stages. Only at the two highest stages do moral reasoning and content come together in a coherent ethical system (Kohlberg, Levine, & Hewer, 1983). Given a choice between obeying the law and preserving individual rights, the most advanced moral thinkers support individual rights (in the Heinz dilemma, stealing the drug to save a life). *TAKE A MOMENT...* Does this remind you of adolescents' efforts to formulate a sound, well-organized set of personal values in constructing an identity? According to some theorists, the development of identity and moral understanding are part of the same process (Bergman, 2004; Blasi, 1994).

Kohlberg's Stages of Moral Understanding. Kohlberg organized moral development into three levels, each with two stages, yielding six stages in all. He believed that moral understanding is promoted by the same factors Piaget thought were important for cognitive development: (1) actively grappling with moral issues and noticing weaknesses in one's current reasoning, and (2) gains in perspective taking, which permit individuals to resolve moral conflicts in more effective ways. *TAKE A MOMENT...* As we examine Kohlberg's developmental sequence and illustrate it with responses to the Heinz dilemma, look for changes in perspective taking that each stage assumes.

The Preconventional Level. At the **preconventional level,** morality is externally controlled. Children accept the rules of authority figures and judge actions by their consequences. Behaviors that result in punishment are viewed as bad, those that lead to rewards as good.

● *Stage 1: The punishment and obedience orientation.* Children at this stage find it difficult to consider two points of view in a moral dilemma. As a result, they overlook people's intentions. Instead, they focus on fear of authority and avoidance of punishment as reasons for behaving morally.

> *Prostealing:* "If you let your wife die, you will . . . be blamed for not spending the money to help her and there'll be an investigation of you and the druggist for your wife's death." (Kohlberg, 1969, p. 381)

> *Antistealing:* "You shouldn't steal the drug because you'll be caught and sent to jail if you do. If you do get away, [you'd be scared that] the police would catch up with you any minute." (Kohlberg, 1969, p. 381)

● *Stage 2: The instrumental purpose orientation.* Children become aware that people can have different perspectives in a moral dilemma, but at first this understanding is concrete. They view right action as flowing from self-interest and understand reciprocity as equal exchange of favors: "You do this for me and I'll do that for you."

If the child on the right expects a favor in return for helping her friend, she is at Kohlberg's preconventional level. If she is motivated by ideal reciprocity, as in the Golden Rule, she has advanced to the conventional level.

Prostealing: "[I]f Heinz decides to risk jail to save his wife, it's his life he's risking; he can do what he wants with it. And the same goes for the druggist; it's up to him to decide what he wants to do." (Rest, 1979, p. 26)

Antistealing: "[Heinz] is running more risk than it's worth [to save a wife who is near death]." (Rest, 1979, p. 27)

The Conventional Level. At the **conventional level,** individuals continue to regard conformity to social rules as important, but not for reasons of self-interest. Rather, they believe that actively maintaining the current social system ensures positive relationships and societal order.

- **Stage 3: The "good boy–good girl" orientation, or the morality of interpersonal cooperation.** The desire to obey rules because they promote social harmony first appears in the context of close personal ties. Stage 3 individuals want to maintain the affection and approval of friends and relatives by being a "good person"—trustworthy, loyal, respectful, helpful, and nice. The capacity to view a two-person relationship from the vantage point of an impartial, outside observer supports this new approach to morality. At this stage, individuals understand *ideal reciprocity:* They express the same concern for the welfare of another as they do for themselves—a standard of fairness summed up by the Golden Rule: "Do unto others as you would have them do unto you."

  Prostealing: "No one will think you're bad if you steal the drug, but your family will think you're an inhuman husband if you don't. If you let your wife die, you'll never be able to look anyone in the face again." (Kohlberg, 1969, p. 381)

  Antistealing: "It isn't just the druggist who will think you're a criminal, everyone else will too. . . . [Y]ou'll feel bad thinking how you've brought dishonor on your family and yourself." (Kohlberg, 1969, p. 381)

- **Stage 4: The social-order-maintaining orientation.** At this stage, the individual takes into account a larger perspective—that of societal laws. Moral choices no longer depend on close ties to others. Instead, rules must be enforced in the same evenhanded fashion for everyone, and each member of society has a personal duty to uphold them. The Stage 4 individual believes that laws should never be disobeyed because they are vital for ensuring societal order and cooperation between people.

  Prostealing: "Heinz has a duty to protect his wife's life; it's a vow he took in marriage. But it's wrong to steal, so he would have to take the drug with the idea of paying the druggist for it and accepting the penalty for breaking the law later." (Rest, 1979, p. 30)

  Antistealing: "Even if his wife is dying, it's still [Heinz's] duty as a citizen to obey the law. . . . If everyone starts breaking the law in a jam, there'd be no civilization, just crime and violence." (Rest, 1979, p. 30)

The Postconventional or Principled Level. Individuals at the **postconventional level** move beyond unquestioning support for their own society's rules and laws. They define morality in terms of abstract principles and values that apply to all situations and societies.

- **Stage 5: The social contract orientation.** At Stage 5, individuals regard laws and rules as flexible instruments for furthering human purposes. They can imagine alternatives to their own social order, and they emphasize fair procedures for interpreting and changing the law. When laws are consistent with individual rights and the interests of the majority, each person follows them because of a *social contract orientation*—free and willing participation in the system because it brings about more good for people than if it did not exist.

  Prostealing: "Although there is a law against stealing, the law wasn't meant to violate a person's right to life. . . . If Heinz is prosecuted for stealing, the law needs to be reinterpreted to take into account situations in which it goes against people's natural right to keep on living."

  Antistealing: At this stage, there are no antistealing responses.

- **Stage 6: The universal ethical principle orientation.** At this highest stage, right action is defined by self-chosen ethical principles of conscience that are valid for all people, regardless of law and social agreement. Stage 6 individuals typically mention such abstract principles as respect for the worth and dignity of each person.

  Prostealing: "It doesn't make sense to put respect for property above respect for life itself. [People] could live together without private property at all. Respect for human life and personality is absolute and accordingly [people] have a mutual duty to save one another from dying." (Rest, 1979, p. 37)

  Antistealing: At this stage, there are no antistealing responses.

Research on Kohlberg's Stage Sequence. Kohlberg's original research and other longitudinal studies provide the most convincing evidence for his stage sequence. With few exceptions, individuals move through the first four stages in the predicted order (Boom, Wouters, & Keller, 2007; Dawson, 2002; Walker & Taylor, 1991b). Moral development is slow and gradual: Reasoning at Stages 1 and 2 decreases in early adolescence, while Stage 3 increases through midadolescence and then declines. Stage 4 reasoning rises over the teenage years until, among college-educated young adults, it is the typical response.

Few people move beyond Stage 4. In fact, postconventional morality is so rare that no clear evidence exists that Kohlberg's Stage 6 actually follows Stage 5. This poses a key challenge to Kohlberg's theory: If people must reach Stages 5 and 6 to be considered truly morally mature, few individuals anywhere would measure up! According to one reexamination of Kohlberg's stages, moral maturity can be found in a revised understanding of Stages 3 and 4 (Gibbs, 1991, 2010b). These stages are not "conventional"—based on social conformity—as Kohlberg assumed. Rather, they require profound moral constructions—an understanding of ideal reciprocity as the basis for relationships (Stage 3) and for widely accepted moral standards, set forth in rules and laws (Stage 4). In this view, "postconventional" morality is a highly reflective endeavor limited to a handful of people who have attained advanced education, usually in philosophy.

TAKE A MOMENT... Think of an actual moral dilemma you faced recently. How did you solve it? Did your reasoning fall at the same stage as your thinking about Heinz? Real-life conflicts often elicit moral reasoning below a person's actual capacity because they involve practical considerations and mix cognition with intense emotion (Carpendale, 2000). Although adolescents and adults mention reasoning as their most frequent strategy for resolving these dilemmas, they also refer to other strategies—talking through issues with others, relying on intuition, and calling on religious and spiritual ideas. And they report feeling drained, confused, and torn by temptation—an emotional side of moral judgment not tapped by hypothetical situations, which evoke the upper limits of moral thought because they allow reflection without the interference of personal risk (Walker, 2004).

The influence of situational factors on moral judgments indicates that like Piaget's cognitive stages, Kohlberg's moral stages are loosely organized and overlapping. Rather than developing in a neat, stepwise fashion, people draw on a range of moral responses that vary with context. With age, this range shifts upward as less mature moral reasoning is gradually replaced by more advanced moral thought.

Are There Sex Differences in Moral Reasoning?

As we have seen, real-life moral dilemmas often highlight the role of emotion in moral judgment. In the discussion at the beginning of this section, notice how Sabrina's moral argument focuses on caring and commitment to others. Carol Gilligan (1982) is the best-known of those who have argued that Kohlberg's theory does not adequately represent the morality of girls and women. Gilligan believes that feminine morality emphasizes an "ethic of care" that Kohlberg's system devalues. Sabrina's reasoning falls at Stage 3 because it is based on mutual trust and affection, whereas Louis's is at Stage 4 because he emphasizes following the law. According to Gilligan, a concern for others is a *different* but no less valid basis for moral judgment than a focus on impersonal rights.

Many studies have tested Gilligan's claim that Kohlberg's approach underestimates the moral maturity of females, and most do not support it (Turiel, 2006; Walker, 2006). On hypothetical dilemmas as well as everyday moral problems, adolescent and adult females display reasoning at the same stage as their male agemates and often at a higher stage. And themes of justice and caring appear in the responses of both sexes (Jadack et al., 1995; Walker, 1995). These findings suggest that although Kohlberg emphasized justice rather than caring as the highest moral ideal, his theory taps both sets of values.

Nevertheless, some evidence indicates that although the morality of males and females taps both orientations, females tend to emphasize care, whereas males either stress justice or focus equally on justice and care (Jaffee & Hyde, 2000; Wark & Krebs, 1996; Weisz & Black, 2002). This difference in emphasis, which appears more often in real-life dilemmas than in hypothetical ones, may reflect women's greater involvement in daily activities involving care and concern for others.

Indeed, cultural context profoundly affects use of a care orientation. In one study, U.S. and Canadian 17- to 26-year-old females exceeded their male counterparts in complex reasoning about care issues. But Norwegian males were just as advanced as Norwegian females in care-based understanding (Skoe, 1998). Perhaps Norwegian culture, which explicitly endorses gender equality, induces boys and men to think deeply about interpersonal obligations.

Coordinating Moral, Social-Conventional, and Personal Concerns

Adolescents' moral advances are also evident in their reasoning about situations that raise competing moral, social-conventional, and personal issues. In diverse Western and non-Western cultures, concern with matters of personal choice strengthens during the teenage years—a reflection of adolescents' quest for identity and increasing independence (Neff & Helwig, 2002; Nucci, 2002). As young people firmly insist that parents not encroach on the personal arena (dress, hairstyle, diary records, friendships), disputes over these issues increase. Teenagers whose parents frequently intrude into their personal affairs report greater psychological stress (Hasebe, Nucci, & Nucci, 2004). In contrast, adolescents typically say that parents have a right to tell them what to do in moral and social-conventional situations. And when these issues spark disagreements, teenagers seldom challenge parental authority (Smetana & Daddis, 2002).

As they enlarge the range of issues they regard as personal, adolescents think more intently about conflicts between personal choice and community obligations—for example, whether,

These teenagers participate in a demonstration in favor of gun control. Adolescent moral development involves thinking intently about conflicts between personal choice and community obligation—for example, whether, and under what conditions, individuals' right to bear arms should be restricted.

and under what conditions, it is permissible to restrict speech, religion, marriage, childbearing, group membership, and other individual rights (Wainryb, 1997). When asked if it is OK to exclude a child from a peer group on the basis of race or gender, fourth graders usually say exclusion is always unfair. But by tenth grade, young people, though increasingly mindful of fairness, indicate that under certain conditions—in intimate relationships (friendship) and private contexts (at home or in a small club), and on the basis of gender more often than race—exclusion is OK (Killen et al., 2002, 2007; Rutland, Killen, & Abrams, 2010). In explaining, they mention the right to personal choice as well as concerns about effective group functioning. Justifying her opinion that members of an all-boys music club need not let a girl in, one tenth grader commented, "[The girl and the boys] probably wouldn't relate on very many things" (Killen et al., 2002, p. 62; 2007).

As adolescents integrate personal rights with ideal reciprocity, they demand that the protections they want for themselves extend to others. For example, with age, they are more likely to defend the government's right to limit the individual freedom to engage in risky health behaviors such as smoking and drinking, in the interest of the larger public good (Flanagan, Stout, & Gallay, 2008). Similarly, they eventually realize that violating strongly held conventions in favor of asserting personal choices—showing up at a wedding in a T-shirt, talking out of turn at a student council meeting—can harm others, either by inducing distress or by undermining fair treatment (Nucci, 2001). As their grasp of fairness deepens, young people realize that many social conventions have moral implications: They are vital for maintaining a just and peaceful society. Notice how this understanding is central to Kohlberg's Stage 4, which is typically attained as adolescence draws to a close.

Influences on Moral Reasoning

Many factors influence moral understanding, including child-rearing practices, schooling, peer interaction, and culture. Growing evidence suggests that, as Kohlberg believed, these experiences work by presenting young people with cognitive challenges, which stimulate them to think about moral problems in more complex ways.

Child-Rearing Practices. As in childhood, parenting practices associated with moral maturity in adolescence combine warmth, exchange of ideas, and appropriate demands for maturity. Adolescents who gain most in moral understanding have parents who engage in moral discussions, encourage prosocial behavior, and create a supportive atmosphere by listening sensitively, asking clarifying questions, and presenting higher-level reasoning (Carlo et al., 2011; Pratt, Skoe, & Arnold, 2004; Wyatt & Carlo, 2002). In one study, 11-year-olds were asked what they thought an adult would say to justify a moral rule, such as not lying, stealing, or breaking a promise. Those with warm, demanding, communicative parents were far more likely than their agemates to point to the importance of ideal reciprocity: "You wouldn't like it if I did it to you" (Leman, 2005). In contrast, when parents lecture, use threats, or make sarcastic remarks, adolescents show little or no change in moral reasoning over time (Walker & Taylor, 1991a).

Schooling. Years of schooling is a powerful predictor of movement to Kohlberg's Stage 4 or higher (Dawson et al., 2003; Gibbs et al., 2007). Higher education introduces young people to social issues that extend beyond personal relationships to entire political or cultural groups. Consistent with this idea, college students who report more perspective-taking opportunities (for example, classes that emphasize open discussion of opinions, friendships with others of different cultural backgrounds) and who indicate that they have become more aware of social diversity tend to be advanced in moral reasoning (Comunian & Gielen, 2006; Mason & Gibbs, 1993a, 1993b).

Peer Interaction. Interaction among peers who present differing viewpoints promotes moral understanding. When young people negotiate and compromise, they realize that social life can be based on cooperation between equals rather than authority relations (Killen & Nucci, 1995). Adolescents who report more close friendships and who more often participate in conversations with their friends are advanced in moral reasoning (Schonert-Reichl, 1999). The mutuality and intimacy of friendship, which foster decisions based on consensual agreement, may be particularly important for moral development. Furthermore, recall from Chapter 10 that intergroup contact—cross-race friendships and interactions in schools and communities—reduces racial and ethnic prejudice. It also affects young people morally, strengthening their conviction that race-based and other forms of peer exclusion are wrong (Crystal, Killen, & Ruck, 2008).

Peer discussions and role playing of moral problems have provided the basis for interventions aimed at improving high school and college students' moral understanding. For these discussions to be effective, young people must be highly engaged—confronting, critiquing, and attempting to clarify one another's viewpoints, as Sabrina and Louis did when they argued over Mrs. Perry's plight (Berkowitz & Gibbs, 1983; Comunian & Gielen, 2006). And because moral development occurs gradually, many peer interaction sessions over weeks or months typically are needed to produce moral change.

Culture. Individuals in industrialized nations move through Kohlberg's stages more quickly and advance to a higher level than individuals in village societies, who rarely move beyond Stage 3. One explanation of these cultural differences is that in village societies, moral cooperation is based on direct relations between people and does not allow for the development of advanced moral understanding (Stages 4 to 6), which depends on appreciating the role of larger social structures, such as laws and government institutions (Gibbs et al., 2007).

A second possible reason for cultural variation is that responses to moral dilemmas in collectivist cultures (including village societies) are often more other-directed than in Western Europe and North America (Miller, 2006). In both village and industrialized cultures that highly value interdependency, statements portraying the individual as vitally connected to the social group are common. In one study, Japanese adolescents, who almost always integrated care- and justice-based reasoning, placed greater weight on care, which they regarded as a communal responsibility (Shimizu, 2001). Similarly, in research conducted in India, even highly educated people

© ATLANTIDE PHOTOTRAVEL/CORBIS

Members of this small village community in Mozambique experience moral cooperation as based on direct relations between people. Consequently, their moral reasoning is unlikely to advance beyond Kohlberg's Stage 3.

(expected to have attained Kohlberg's Stages 4 and 5) viewed solutions to moral dilemmas as the responsibility of the entire society, not of a single person (Miller & Bersoff, 1995).

These findings raise the question of whether Kohlberg's highest level represents a culturally specific way of thinking—one limited to Western societies that emphasize individualism and an appeal to an inner, private conscience. At the same time, a review of over 100 studies confirmed an age-related trend consistent with Kohlberg's Stages 1 to 4 across diverse societies (Gibbs et al., 2007). A common justice morality is clearly evident in the dilemma responses of people from vastly different cultures.

Moral Reasoning and Behavior

A central assumption of the cognitive-developmental perspective is that moral understanding should affect moral action. According to Kohlberg, mature moral thinkers realize that behaving in line with their beliefs is vital for creating and maintaining a just social world (Gibbs, 2010b). Consistent with this idea, higher-stage adolescents more often act prosocially by helping, sharing, and defending victims of injustice and by volunteering in their communities (Carlo et al., 1996, 2011; Comunian & Gielen, 2000, 2006). Also, they less often engage in cheating, aggression, and other antisocial behaviors (Gregg, Gibbs, & Fuller, 1994; Raaijmakers, Engels, & van Hoof, 2005; Stams et al., 2006).

Yet the connection between mature moral reasoning and action is only modest. As we have seen, moral behavior is influenced by many factors besides cognition, including the emotions of empathy, sympathy, and guilt; individual differences in temperament; and a long history of cultural experiences and intuitive beliefs that affect moral decision making (Haidt & Kesebir, 2010). **Moral identity**—the degree to which morality is central to self-concept—also affects moral behavior (Hardy & Carlo, 2011). In a study of low-SES African-American and Hispanic teenagers, those who emphasized moral traits and goals in their self-descriptions displayed exceptional levels of community service (Hart & Fegley, 1995). But they did not differ from their agemates in moral reasoning.

Researchers have begun to identify factors that strengthen moral identity in hopes of capitalizing on them to promote moral commitment. Certain parenting practices—inductive discipline (see page 264 in Chapter 8) and clearly conveyed moral expectations—augment adolescents' moral identity (Patrick & Gibbs, 2011). And *just educational environments*—in which teachers guide students in democratic decision making and rule setting, resolving disputes civilly, and taking responsibility for others' welfare—are influential (Atkins, Hart, & Donnelly, 2004). In one study, tenth graders who reported fair teacher treatment were more likely than those who had experienced unjust treatment (an unfair detention or a lower grade than they deserved) to regard excluding a peer on the basis of race as a moral transgression (Crystal, Killen, & Ruck, 2010).

Schools can also foster students' opportunities to experience and explore moral emotions, thoughts, and actions through civic engagement. As the Social Issues: Education box on the following page reveals, civic engagement can help young people see the connection between their personal interests and the public interest—an insight that may foster all aspects of morality.

LOOK AND LISTEN

Would you characterize your high school as a *just educational environment?* Cite specific features and experiences that may have contributed to students' moral development and civic engagement. ●

Religious Involvement and Moral Development

Recall that in resolving real-life moral dilemmas, many people voice notions of religion and spirituality. Religion is especially important in U.S. family life. In recent national polls, nearly two-thirds of Americans reported actively practicing religion, compared with one-half of those in Canada, one-third of those in Great Britain and Italy, and even fewer elsewhere in Europe (CIA, 2012; Gallup News Service, 2006; Jones, 2003). People who regularly attend religious services include many parents with children. But as adolescents search for a personally meaningful identity, formal religious involvement declines—for U.S. youths, from 55 percent at ages 13 to 15 to 40 percent at ages 17 to 18 (Kerestes & Youniss, 2003; Pew Research Center, 2010b).

Nevertheless, teenagers who remain part of a religious community are advantaged in moral values and behavior. Compared with nonaffiliated youths, they are more involved in community service activities aimed at helping the less fortunate (Kerestes, Youniss, & Metz, 2004). And religious involvement promotes responsible academic and social behavior and discourages

Playing in a brass quartet at church gives these adolescents a sense of connection to their faith. Religious involvement promotes teenagers' moral development, encouraging responsible academic work and community service.

misconduct (Dowling et al., 2004). It is associated with lower levels of drug and alcohol use, early sexual activity, and delinquency (Regnerus, Smith, & Fritsch, 2003).

A variety of factors probably contribute to these favorable outcomes. In a study of inner-city high school students, religiously involved young people were more likely to report trusting relationships with parents, adults, and friends who hold similar worldviews. The more activities they shared with this network, the higher they scored in empathy and prosocial behavior (King & Furrow, 2004). Furthermore, religious education and youth activities directly teach concern for others and provide opportunities for moral discussions and civic engagement. And adolescents who feel connected to a higher being may develop certain inner strengths, including prosocial values and a strong moral identity, that help them translate their thinking into action (Hardy & Carlo, 2005; Sherrod & Spiewak, 2008).

Because most teenagers, regardless of formal affiliation, identify with a religious denomination and say they believe in a higher being, religious institutions may be uniquely suited to foster moral and prosocial commitments. For youths in inner-city neighborhoods with few alternative sources of social support, outreach by religious institutions can lead to life-altering involvement (Jang & Johnson, 2001). An exception is seen in religious cults, where rigid indoctrination into the group's beliefs, suppression of individuality, and estrangement from society all work against moral maturity (Scarlett & Warren, 2010).

Further Challenges to Kohlberg's Theory

Although much evidence is consistent with the cognitive-developmental approach to morality, Kohlberg's theory has faced major challenges. The most radical opposition comes from researchers who—referring to wide variability in moral reasoning across situations—claim that Kohlberg's stage sequence inadequately accounts for morality in everyday life (Krebs and Denton, 2005). These investigators favor abandoning Kohlberg's stages for a *pragmatic approach to morality*. They assert that each person makes moral judgments at varying levels of maturity, depending on the individual's current context and motivations: Conflict over a business deal is likely to evoke Stage 2 (instrumental purpose) reasoning, a friendship or romantic dispute Stage 3 (ideal reciprocity) reasoning, and a breach of contract Stage 4 (social-order-maintaining) reasoning (Krebs et al., 1991).

According to the pragmatic view, everyday moral judgments—rather than being efforts to arrive at just solutions—are practical tools that people use to achieve their goals. To benefit personally, they often must advocate cooperation with others. But people often act first and then invoke moral judgments to rationalize their actions, regardless of whether their behavior is self-centered or prosocial (Haidt, 2001; Haidt & Kesebir, 2010). And sometimes people use moral judgments for immoral purposes—for example, to excuse their transgressions.

Is the pragmatic approach correct that people strive to resolve moral conflicts fairly only when they themselves have nothing to lose? Supporters of the cognitive-developmental

Social Issues: Education

Development of Civic Engagement

On Thanksgiving Day, Jules, Martin, Louis, and Sabrina joined their parents to serve a holiday dinner to poverty-stricken people. Throughout the year, Sabrina volunteered on Saturday mornings at a nursing home. During a congressional election campaign, all four adolescents raised questions about issues at special youth meetings with candidates. At school, Louis and his girlfriend, Cassie, formed an organization devoted to promoting ethnic and racial tolerance.

These young people show a strong sense of *civic engagement*—a complex combination of cognition, emotion, and behavior. Civic engagement involves knowledge of political issues, commitment to making a difference in the community, and skills for achieving civic goals, such as how to resolve differing views fairly (Zaff et al., 2010).

When young people engage in community service that exposes them to people in need or to public issues, they are especially likely to express a commitment to future service. And youth volunteers—who tend to be advanced in moral reasoning—gain further in moral maturity as a result of participating (Gibbs et al., 2007; Hart, Atkins, & Donnelly, 2006). Family, school, and community experiences contribute to adolescents' civic engagement.

Family Influences

Teenagers whose parents encourage their children to form opinions about controversial issues are more knowledgeable about civic issues and better able to see them from more than one perspective (Santoloupo & Pratt, 1994). Also, adolescents whose parents engage in community service and stress compassion for the less fortunate tend to hold socially responsible values. When asked what causes unemployment or poverty, they more often mention situational and societal factors (lack of education, government policies, or the state of the economy) than individual factors (low intelligence or personal problems). Youths who endorse situational and societal causes, in turn, have more altruistic life goals (Flanagan & Tucker, 1999). And

they engage in more civic activities into early adulthood (Zaff, Malanchuk, & Eccles, 2008).

School and Community Influences

A democratic climate at school, in which teachers promote respectful discussion of controversial issues, fosters knowledge and critical analysis of political issues and commitment to social causes (Torney-Purta, Barber, & Wilkenfeld, 2007). Furthermore, high school students who view their community as one in which adults care about youths and work to make the community better report higher levels of civic participation (Kahne & Sporte, 2008). Participation in extracurricular activities at school whose primary objectives are to induce social change outside the organization itself is also associated with civic commitment that persists into adulthood (Obradović & Masten, 2007; Zaff et al., 2003).

Two aspects of these involvements seem to account for their lasting impact. First, they introduce adolescents to the vision and skills required for mature civic engagement. Within student government, political and vocational clubs, music and drama groups, and student newspaper and yearbook staffs, young people see how their actions affect the wider school and community. They realize that collectively they can achieve results greater than any one person can achieve alone. And they learn to work together, balancing strong convictions with compromise (Atkins, Hart, & Donnelly, 2004; Kirshner, 2009). Second, while producing a weekly newspaper, participating in a school play, or implementing a service project, young people explore political and moral ideals. Often they redefine their identities to include a responsibility to combat others' misfortunes (Wheeler, 2002).

The power of family, school, and community to promote civic engagement may lie in discussions, educational practices, and activities that jointly foster moral thought,

For this young teenager, planting a tree during an Earth Day celebration in Los Angeles promotes a sense of civic engagement—an effect that may persist into adulthood.

emotion, and behavior. In a comparison of nationally representative samples of 14-year-olds in 28 nations, U.S. young people excelled at community service, with 50 percent reporting membership in organizations devoted to volunteering (Torney-Purta, 2002).

Currently, two-thirds of U.S. public schools provide students with community service opportunities. Nearly half of these have *service-learning programs*, which integrate service activities into the academic curriculum, and about one-third of students enroll. High school students who are required to serve their communities express as strong a desire to remain engaged as do students who volunteer. And when they reach early adulthood, they are equally likely to vote and participate in community organizations (Hart et al., 2007; Metz & Youniss, 2005).

Still, most U.S. schools offering service learning do not have policies encouraging or mandating such programs. Furthermore, low-SES, inner-city youths—although they express high interest in contributing to society—attend schools and live in neighborhoods with fewer civic-training opportunities. As a result, they score substantially lower than higher-SES youths in civic knowledge and participation (Balsano, 2005; Zaff et al., 2010). A broad societal commitment to fostering civic character must pay special attention to supportive experiences for these young people, so their eagerness to make a difference can be realized.

perspective point out that people frequently rise above self-interest to defend others' rights. For example, moral leaders in business—rather than resorting to Stage 2 reasoning—endorse trust, integrity, good faith, and just laws and codes of conduct (Damon, 2004; Gibbs, 2006). Also, adolescents and adults are well aware of the greater adequacy of higher-stage moral reasoning, which some people act on despite highly corrupt environments. And individuals who engage in sudden altruistic action may have previously considered relevant moral issues so thoroughly that their moral judgment activates automatically, triggering an immediate response (Gibbs et al., 2009a; Pizarro & Bloom, 2003). In these instances, people who appear to be engaging in after-the-fact moral justification are actually behaving with great forethought.

In sum, the cognitive-developmental approach to morality has done much to clarify our profound moral potential. And despite opposition, Kohlberg's central assumption—that with age, humans everywhere construct a deeper understanding of fairness and justice that guides moral action—remains powerfully influential.

Gender Typing

As Sabrina entered adolescence, she began to worry about walking, talking, eating, dressing, laughing, and competing in ways consistent with a feminine gender role. According to one hypothesis, the arrival of adolescence is typically accompanied by **gender intensification**—increased gender stereotyping of attitudes and behavior, and movement toward a more traditional gender identity. Research on gender intensification, however, is mixed, with some studies finding evidence for it and others reporting few instances (Basow & Rubin, 1999; Galambos, Almeida, & Petersen, 1990; Huston & Alvarez, 1990; Priess, Lindberg, & Hyde, 2009). When gender intensification is evident, it seems to be stronger for adolescent girls. Although girls continue to be less gender-typed than boys, some may feel less free to experiment with "other-gender" activities and behaviors than they did in middle childhood.

In young people who do exhibit gender intensification, biological, social, and cognitive factors likely are involved. As puberty magnifies sex differences in appearance, teenagers may spend more time thinking about themselves in gender-linked ways. Pubertal changes might also prompt gender-typed pressures from others. Parents with traditional gender-role beliefs may encourage "gender-appropriate" activities and behavior more than they did earlier (Crouter et al., 2007; Shanahan et al., 2007). And when adolescents start to date, they may become more gender-typed as a way of increasing their attractiveness (Maccoby, 1998). Finally, cognitive changes—in particular, greater concern with what others think—might make young teenagers more responsive to gender-role expectations.

Gender intensification declines by late adolescence, but not all affected young people move beyond it to the same degree. Teenagers who are encouraged to explore non-gender-typed options and to question the value of gender stereotypes for

For some young people, early adolescence is a time of gender intensification. Pubertal changes in appearance, traditional gender-role expectations of parents, and increased concern with what others think can prompt a move toward a more traditional gender identity.

themselves and society are more likely to build an androgynous gender identity (see Chapter 8, page 276). Overall, androgynous adolescents, especially girls, tend to be psychologically healthier—more self-confident, more willing to speak their own mind, better-liked by peers, and identity-achieved (Bronstein, 2006; Dusek, 1987; Harter, 2006).

ASK YOURSELF

REVIEW How does an understanding of ideal reciprocity contribute to moral development? Why are Kohlberg's Stages 3 and 4 morally mature?

CONNECT How might the exploration of values and goals associated with healthy identity development contribute to a decline in adolescent gender intensification?

APPLY Tam grew up in a small village culture, Lydia in a large industrial city. At age 15, Tam reasons at Kohlberg's Stage 3, Lydia at Stage 4. What factors might account for the difference?

REFLECT Do you favor a cognitive-developmental or a pragmatic approach to morality, or both? Explain, drawing on research evidence and personal experiences.

The Family

Franca and Antonio remember their son Louis's freshman year of high school as a difficult time. Because of a demanding project at work, Franca was away from home many evenings and weekends. In her absence, Antonio took over, but when business declined and he had to cut costs at his hardware store, he, too, had less time for the family. That year, Louis and two friends used their computer know-how to gain entry to their classmates' systems to pirate video game software. Louis's grades fell, and he often left the house without saying where he was going. Franca and Antonio began to feel uncomfortable about the long hours Louis spent at his computer and their lack of contact with him. One day, when Franca and Antonio noticed the video-game icons covering Louis's computer desktop, they knew they had cause for concern.

During adolescence, striving for **autonomy**—a sense of one-self as a separate, self-governing individual—becomes a salient task. Autonomy has two vital aspects: (1) an *emotional component*—relying more on oneself and less on parents for support and guidance, and (2) a *behavioral component*—making decisions independently by carefully weighing one's own judgment and the suggestions of others to arrive at a well-reasoned course of action (Collins & Laursen, 2004; Steinberg & Silk, 2002). As we will see, parent–child relationships remain vital for helping adolescents become autonomous, responsible individuals.

Parent–Child Relationships

A variety of changes within the adolescent support autonomy. In Chapter 11, we saw that puberty triggers psychological distancing from parents. In addition, as young people look more mature, parents give them more freedom to think and decide for themselves, more opportunities to regulate their own activities, and more responsibility (McElhaney et al., 2009). Cognitive development also paves the way toward autonomy: Gradually, adolescents solve problems and make decisions more effectively. And an improved ability to reason about social relationships leads teenagers to *deidealize* their parents, viewing them as "just people." Consequently, they no longer bend as easily to parental authority as they did when younger.

Yet as Franca and Antonio's episode with Louis reveals, teenagers still need guidance and protection from dangerous situations. (Recall from Chapter 11 our discussion of adolescent brain development, in which changes in the emotional/social network outpace gains in the cognitive-control network.) Warm, supportive parenting that grants young people freedom to explore while making appropriate demands for maturity fosters autonomy—in diverse ethnic and SES groups, nations, and family structures (including single-parent, two-parent, and stepparent). Autonomy, in turn, predicts high self-reliance, effortful control, academic achievement, positive work orientation, favorable self-esteem, and ease of separation in the transition to college (Bean, Barber, & Crane, 2007; Eisenberg et al., 2005b; Supple et al., 2009; Vazsonyi, Hibbert, & Snider, 2003; Wang, Pomerantz, & Chen, 2007).

Conversely, parents who are coercive or psychologically controlling interfere with the development of autonomy. These tactics are linked to low self-esteem, depression, drug and alcohol use, and antisocial behavior—outcomes that often persist into early adulthood (Barber, Stolz, & Olsen, 2005; Bronte-Tinkew, Moore, & Carrano, 2006; Wissink, Deković, & Meijer, 2006).

In Chapter 2, we described the family as a *system* that must adapt to changes in its members. The rapid physical and

Parent–child relationships are vital for helping adolescents attain autonomy. Though teenagers benefit from freedom to explore ideas and make their own decisions, they need guidance and protection from dangerous situations.

psychological changes of adolescence trigger conflicting expectations in parent–child relationships. Earlier we noted that interest in making choices about personal matters strengthens in adolescence. Yet parents and teenagers—especially young teenagers—differ sharply on the appropriate age for granting certain privileges, such as control over clothing, school courses, going out with friends, and dating (Smetana, 2002). Consistent parental monitoring of the young person's daily activities, through a cooperative relationship in which the adolescent willingly discloses information, is linked to a variety of positive outcomes—prevention of delinquency, reduction in sexual activity, improved school performance, and positive psychological well-being (Crouter & Head, 2002; Jacobson & Crockett, 2000).

LOOK AND LISTEN

Ask an early adolescent and his or her parent for their views on when the young person is mature enough to begin dating, own a cell phone, create a Facebook page, and be given other privileges. Do adolescent and parent perspectives differ? ●

Parents' own development can also lead to friction with teenagers. While their children face a boundless future and a wide array of choices, middle-aged parents must accept the fact that their own possibilities are narrowing (Holmbeck, 1996). Often parents can't understand why the adolescent wants to skip family activities to be with peers. And teenagers fail to appreciate that parents want the family to spend as much time together as possible because an important period in their adult life—child rearing—will soon end.

Immigrant parents from cultures that place a high value on family closeness and obedience to authority have greater difficulty adapting to their teenagers' push for autonomy, often reacting more strongly to adolescent disagreement. And as adolescents acquire the host culture's language and are increasingly exposed to its individualistic values, immigrant parents may become even more critical, causing teenagers to rely less on the family network for social support, disclosing less about peer relationships, potentially risky activities, and personal feelings (Yau, Tasopoulos-Chan, & Smetana, 2009). The resulting *acculturative stress* is associated with a decline in self-esteem and a rise in anxiety, depressive symptoms, and deviant behavior, including alcohol use and delinquency (Park, 2009; Suarez-Morales & Lopez, 2009; Warner et al., 2006).

Throughout adolescence, the quality of the parent–child relationship is the single most consistent predictor of mental health. In well-functioning families, teenagers remain attached to parents and seek their advice, but they do so in a context of greater freedom (Collins & Steinberg, 2006). The mild conflict that typically arises facilitates adolescent identity and autonomy by helping family members express and tolerate disagreement. Conflicts also inform parents of teenagers' changing needs and expectations, signaling a need for adjustments in the parent–child relationship.

By middle to late adolescence, most parents and children achieve this mature, mutual relationship, and harmonious interaction is on the rise. The reduced time that Western teenagers spend with parents—for U.S. youths, a drop from 33 percent of waking hours in fifth grade to 14 percent in twelfth grade—has little to do with conflict (Larson et al., 1996). Rather, it results from the large amount of unstructured time available to teenagers in North America and Western Europe—on average, nearly half their waking hours (Larson, 2001). Young people tend to fill these hours with activities that take them away from home—part-time jobs, leisure and volunteer pursuits, and time with friends.

But this drop in family time is not universal. In one study, urban low- and middle-SES African-American youths showed no decline in hours spent with family—a pattern typical in cultures with collectivist values (Larson et al., 2001). Furthermore, teenagers living in risky neighborhoods tend to have more trusting relationships with parents and adjust more favorably when parents maintain tighter control and pressure them not to engage in worrisome behaviors (McElhaney & Allen, 2001). In harsh surroundings, young people seem to interpret more measured granting of autonomy as a sign of parental caring.

Family Circumstances

As Franca and Antonio's experience with Louis reminds us, adult life stress can interfere with warm, involved parenting and, in turn, with children's adjustment at any period of development. But parents who are financially secure, not overloaded with job pressures, and content with their marriages usually find it easier to grant teenagers appropriate autonomy and experience less conflict with them (Cowan & Cowan, 2002; Crouter & Bumpass, 2001). When Franca and Antonio's work stress eased and they recognized Louis's need for more involvement and guidance, his problems subsided.

Among the minority of families with seriously troubled parent–adolescent relationships, most difficulties began in childhood (Collins & Laursen, 2004). Table 12.2 summarizes family

TABLE 12.2 **Family Circumstances with Implications for Adolescent Adjustment**

FAMILY CIRCUMSTANCE	TO REVIEW, TURN TO . . .
TYPE OF FAMILY	
Adoptive	Chapter 2, pages 57–59
Divorced single-parent	Chapter 10, pages 346–349
Blended	Chapter 10, pages 349–350
Employed mother and dual-earner	Chapter 10, pages 350–351
FAMILY CONDITIONS	
Economic hardship	Chapter 2, pages 61–62
Child maltreatment	Chapter 8, pages 281–283 Chapter 10, pages 352–354
Adolescent parenthood	Chapter 11, pages 378–380

conditions considered in earlier chapters that pose challenges for adolescents. Teenagers who develop well despite family stress continue to benefit from factors that fostered resilience in earlier years: an appealing, easy-going disposition; a parent who combines warmth with high expectations; and (especially if parental supports are lacking) bonds with prosocial adults outside the family who care deeply about the adolescent's well-being (Masten, 2001; Masten & Shaffer, 2006).

Siblings

Like parent–child relationships, sibling interactions adapt to development at adolescence. As younger siblings become more self-sufficient, they accept less direction from their older brothers and sisters, and sibling influence declines. Also, as teenagers become more involved in friendships and romantic relationships, they invest less time and energy in siblings, who are part of the family from which they are trying to establish autonomy. As a result, sibling relationships often become less intense, in both positive and negative feelings (Hetherington, Henderson, & Reiss, 1999; Kim et al., 2006).

Nevertheless, attachment between siblings remains strong for most young people. Overall, siblings who established a positive bond in early childhood continue to display greater affection and caring, which contribute to more favorable adolescent adjustment (Kim et al., 2007; Samek & Rueter, 2011). Culture also influences quality of sibling relationships. In one study, Mexican-American adolescents who expressed a strong Mexican cultural orientation resolved sibling conflicts more cooperatively than did those more oriented toward U.S. individualistic values (Killoren, Thayer, & Updegraff, 2008).

Finally, mild sibling differences in perceived parental affection no longer trigger jealousy but, instead, predict greater sibling warmth (Feinberg et al., 2003). Perhaps adolescents interpret a unique relationship with parents, as long as it is generally accepting, as a gratifying sign of their own individuality.

Peer Relations

As adolescents spend less time with family members, peers become increasingly important. In industrialized nations, young people spend most of each weekday with agemates in school. Teenagers also spend much out-of-class time together, more in some cultures than others. For example, U.S. young people have about 50 hours of free time per week, Europeans about 45 hours, and East Asians about 33 hours (Larson, 2001). A shorter school year and less demanding academic standards, which lead American youths to devote much less time to schoolwork, account for this difference.

In the following sections, we will see that adolescent peer relations can be both positive and negative. At their best, peers serve as critical bridges between the family and adult social roles.

Friendships

Number of best friends declines from about four to six in early adolescence to one or two in adulthood (Hartup & Stevens, 1999). At the same time, the nature of the relationship changes.

Characteristics of Adolescent Friendships.
When asked about the meaning of friendship, teenagers stress three characteristics. The most important is *intimacy,* or psychological closeness, which is supported by *mutual understanding* of each other's values, beliefs, and feelings. In addition, more than younger children, teenagers want their friends to be *loyal*—to stick up for them and not leave them for somebody else (Collins & Madsen, 2006).

As frankness and faithfulness increase, *self-disclosure* (sharing of private thoughts and feelings) between friends rises over the adolescent years (see Figure 12.1). As a result, teenage friends get to know each other better as personalities. In addition to the many characteristics that school-age friends share (see page 340 in Chapter 10), adolescent friends tend to be alike in identity status, educational aspirations, political beliefs, and willingness to try drugs and engage in lawbreaking acts. Over time, they become increasingly similar in these ways (Berndt & Murphy, 2002; Selfhout, Branje, & Meeus, 2008). Occasionally, however, teenagers choose friends with differing attitudes and values, which permits them to explore new perspectives within the security of a compatible relationship.

During adolescence, cooperation and mutual affirmation between friends increase—changes that reflect greater skill at preserving the relationship and sensitivity to a friend's needs and desires (De Goede, Branje, & Meeus, 2009). Adolescents also are less possessive of their friends than they were in childhood (Parker et al., 2005). Desiring a certain degree of autonomy for themselves, they recognize that friends need this, too.

Sex Differences in Friendships. *TAKE A MOMENT...*
Ask several adolescent girls and boys to describe their close friendships. You are likely to find a consistent sex difference: Emotional closeness is more common between girls than between boys (Markovits, Benenson, & Dolensky, 2001). Girls frequently get together to "just talk," and their interactions contain more self-disclosure and supportive statements. In contrast, boys more often gather for an activity—usually sports and competitive games. Boys' discussions usually focus on achievements in sports and school and involve more competition and conflict (Brendgen et al., 2001; Rubin, Bukowski, & Parker, 2006).

Because of gender-role expectations, girls' friendships typically focus on communal concerns, boys' on achievement and status. Boys do form close friendship ties, but the quality of their friendships is more variable. Gender identity plays a role: Androgynous boys are just as likely as girls to form intimate same-sex ties, whereas highly "masculine" boys are less likely to do so (Jones & Dembo, 1989).

FIGURE 12.1 Age changes in reported self-disclosure to parents and peers, based on findings of several studies. Self-disclosure to friends increases steadily during adolescence, reflecting intimacy as a major basis of friendship. Self-disclosure to romantic partners also rises, but it does not surpass intimacy with friends until the college years. Self-disclosure to parents declines in early adolescence, a time of mild parent–child conflict. As family relationships readjust to the young person's increasing autonomy, self-disclosure to parents rises. (From D. Buhrmester, 1996, "Need Fulfillment, Interpersonal Competence, and the Developmental Contexts of Early Adolescent Friendship," in W. M. Bukowski, A. F. Newcomb, & W. W. Hartup [Eds.], *The Company They Keep: Friendship in Childhood and Adolescence,* New York: Cambridge University Press, p. 168. Reprinted with permission of Cambridge University Press.)

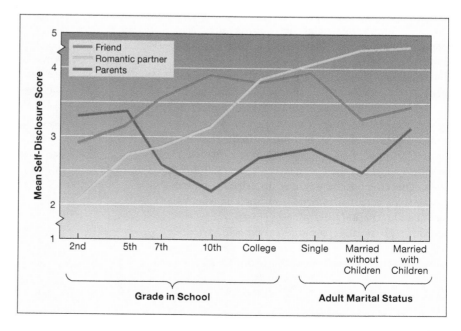

Compared to boys, adolescent girls place a higher value on emotional closeness, engaging in more self-disclosure and supportive statements with friends.

Friendship closeness has costs as well as benefits. When friends focus on deeper thoughts and feelings, they tend to *coruminate,* or repeatedly mull over problems and negative emotions. Corumination, while contributing to high friendship quality, also triggers anxiety and depression—symptoms more common among girls than among boys (Hankin, Stone, & Wright, 2010; Rose, Carlson, & Waller, 2007). And when conflict arises between intimate friends, more potential exists for one party to harm the other through relational aggression—for example, by divulging sensitive personal information to outsiders. Partly for this reason, girls' closest same-sex friendships tend to be of shorter duration than boys' (Benenson & Christakos, 2003).

Friendships on the Internet. Teenagers frequently use cell phones and the Internet to communicate with friends. About 75 percent of U.S. 12- to 17-year-olds own a cell phone, a rate that has nearly doubled during the past decade. Cell-phone texting has become the preferred means of electronic interaction between teenage friends, with cell calling second, followed by social networking sites and instant messaging (see Figure 12.2). Girls use cell phones to text and call their friends considerably more often than boys (Lenhart et al., 2010). These forms of online interaction seem to support friendship closeness. In several studies, as amount of online messaging between preexisting friends increased, so did young people's perceptions of intimacy in the relationship and feelings of well-being (Reich, Subrahmanyam, & Espinoza, 2012; Valkenburg & Peter, 2007a, 2007b, 2009). The effect is largely due to friends' online disclosure of personal information, such as worries, secrets, and romantic feelings.

Although mostly communicating with friends they know, teenagers are also drawn to meeting new people over the Internet. Social networking sites such as Facebook and MySpace (used by nearly three-fourths of U.S. teenagers) along with blogs, message boards, and chat rooms open up vast alternatives

beyond their families, schools, and communities (Lenhart et al., 2010). Through these online ties, young people explore central adolescent issues—sexuality, challenges in parent and peer relationships, and identity issues, including attitudes and values—in contexts that grant anonymity and, therefore, may feel less threatening than similar everyday conversations (Subrahmanyam, Smahel, & Greenfield, 2006; Valkenburg & Peter, 2011). Online interactions with strangers also offer some teenagers vital social support. Young people suffering from depression, eating disorders, and other problems can access message boards where participants provide mutual assistance, including a sense of group belonging and acceptance (Whitlock, Powers, & Eckenrode, 2006).

But online communication also poses dangers. In unmonitored chat rooms, teenagers are likely to encounter degrading racial and ethnic slurs and sexually obscene and harassing remarks (Subrahmanyam & Greenfield, 2008). Furthermore, in a survey of a nationally representative sample of U.S. 10- to 17-year-olds, 14 percent reported having formed online close friendships or romances. Although some of these youths were well-adjusted, many reported high levels of conflict with parents, peer victimization, depression, and delinquency (Wolak, Mitchell, & Finkelhor, 2003). They also more often had been asked by online friends for face-to-face meetings and had attended those meetings—without telling their parents.

Finally, time devoted to social media is rising among older children and adolescents. For example, nearly 45 percent send more than 50 texts per day, and more than 70 percent use social networking sites for an average of 37 minutes per day. Some evidence suggests that very high social media use is linked to unsatisfying face-to-face social experiences, boredom, unhappiness, and Internet addiction (obsessive Internet use) (Pea et al., 2012; Rideout, Foehr, & Roberts, 2010; Smahel, Brown, & Blinka, 2012). Furthermore, high Internet consumers often engage in "face-to-face multitasking," such as texting at the dinner table or web surfing while chatting with friends (Abelson,

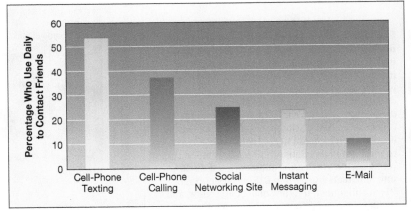

FIGURE 12.2 Percentage of U.S. 12- to 17-year-olds who use various communication channels daily to contact friends. A nationally representative sample of 800 U.S. 12- to 17-year-olds responded to a survey about their communication strategies with friends. Cell-phone texting emerged as the preferred channel, with over half of teenagers reporting that they used it daily. (Adapted from Lenhart et al., 2010.)

Ledeen, & Lewis, 2008). These behaviors detract from high-quality face-to-face communication.

In sum, the Internet's value for enabling convenient and satisfying interaction among teenage friends must be weighed against its potential for facilitating harmful social consequences. Parents are wise to point out the risks of Internet communication, including excessive use, harassment, and exploitation, and to insist that teenagers follow Internet safety rules (see *www.safeteens.com*).

Friendship and Adjustment. As long as adolescent friendships are high in trust, intimate sharing, and support and not characterized by relational aggression or attraction to antisocial behavior, they contribute to many aspects of psychological health and competence into early adulthood (Bukowski, 2001; Waldrip, 2008), for several reasons:

- *Close friendships provide opportunities to explore the self and develop a deep understanding of another.* Through open, honest communication, friends become sensitive to each other's strengths and weaknesses, needs and desires—a process that supports the development of self-concept, perspective taking, and identity.

- *Close friendships provide a foundation for future intimate relationships.* Recall from Figure 12.1 that self-disclosure to friends precedes disclosure to romantic partners. Conversations with teenage friends about sexuality and romance, along with the intimacy of friendship itself, may help adolescents establish and work out problems in romantic partnerships (Connolly & Goldberg, 1999).

- *Close friendships help young people deal with the stresses of adolescence.* By enhancing sensitivity to and concern for another, supportive friendships promote empathy, sympathy, and prosocial behavior. As a result, friendships contribute to involvement in constructive youth activities, avoidance of antisocial acts, and psychological well-being (Lansford et al., 2003; Wentzel, Barry, & Caldwell, 2004).

- *Close friendships can improve attitudes toward and involvement in school.* Close friendships promote good school adjustment, academically and socially (Wentzel, Barry, & Caldwell, 2004). When teenagers enjoy interacting with friends at school, they may begin to view all aspects of school life more positively.

LOOK AND LISTEN

Interview several adolescents about qualities they value most in their best friends. Ask how friendships have helped them cope with stress and resulted in other personal benefits. •

Cliques and Crowds

In early adolescence, *peer groups* (see Chapter 10) become increasingly common and tightly knit. They are organized into **cliques,** groups of about five to seven members who are friends and, therefore, usually resemble one another in family background, attitudes, and values (Brown & Dietz, 2009). At first,

These high school drama club members form a crowd, establishing relationships on the basis of shared abilities and interests. Crowd membership grants them an identity within the larger social structure of the school.

cliques are limited to same-sex members. Among girls but not boys, being in a clique predicts academic and social competence. Clique membership is more important to girls, who use it as a context for expressing emotional closeness (Henrich et al., 2000). By midadolescence, mixed-sex cliques are common.

Among Western adolescents attending high schools with complex social structures, often several cliques with similar values form a larger, more loosely organized group called a **crowd.** Unlike the more intimate clique, membership in a crowd is based on reputation and stereotype, granting the adolescent an identity within the larger social structure of the school. Prominent crowds in a typical high school might include "brains" (nonathletes who enjoy academics), "jocks" (who are very involved in sports), "populars" (class leaders who are highly social and involved in activities), "partyers" (who value socializing but care little about schoolwork), "nonconformists" (who like unconventional clothing and music), "druggies" (who frequently use substances, engage in sexual risk-taking, and otherwise get into trouble), and "normals" (average to good students who get along with most other peers) (Kinney, 1999; Stone & Brown, 1999).

What influences the sorting of teenagers into cliques and crowds? Crowd affiliations are linked to strengths in adolescents' self-concepts, which reflect their abilities and interests (Prinstein & La Greca, 2002). Ethnicity also plays a role. Minority teenagers who associate with an ethnically defined crowd, as opposed to a crowd reflecting their abilities and interests, may be motivated by discrimination in their school or neighborhood. Alternatively, they may be expressing a strong ethnic identity (Brown et al., 2008). Family factors are important, too. In a study of 8,000 ninth to twelfth graders, adolescents who described their parents as authoritative were members of "brain," "jock," and "popular" groups that accepted both adult and peer reward systems. In contrast, boys with permissive parents aligned themselves with the "partyers" and "druggies," suggesting lack of identification with adult reward systems (Durbin et al., 1993).

These findings indicate that many peer-group values are extensions of ones acquired at home. Once adolescents join a clique or crowd, it can modify their beliefs and behavior. But the positive impact of having academically and socially skilled peers is greatest for teenagers whose own parents are authoritative. And the negative impact of having antisocial, drug-using friends is strongest for teenagers whose parents use less effective child-rearing styles (Mounts & Steinberg, 1995). In sum, family experiences affect the extent to which adolescents become like their peers over time.

As interest in dating increases, boys' and girls' cliques come together. Mixed-sex cliques provide boys and girls with models of how to interact and a chance to do so without having to be intimate (Connolly et al., 2004). By late adolescence, when boys and girls feel comfortable enough about approaching each other directly, the mixed-sex clique disappears (Connolly & Goldberg, 1999).

Crowds also decline in importance. As adolescents settle on personal values and goals, they no longer feel a need to broadcast, through dress, language, and activities, who they are. From tenth to twelfth grade, about half of young people switch crowds, mostly in favorable directions (Strouse, 1999). "Brains" and "normal" crowds grow and deviant crowds lose members as teenagers focus more on their future.

Dating

The hormonal changes of puberty increase sexual interest, but cultural expectations determine when and how dating begins. Asian youths start dating later and have fewer dating partners than young people in Western societies, which tolerate and even encourage romantic involvements from middle school on (see Figure 12.3). At age 12 to 14, these relationships are usually

For this young couple out shopping together, dating extends the benefits of adolescent friendships, promoting sensitivity, empathy, self-esteem, and identity development.

casual, lasting only five months on average. By age 16, they have become steady relationships, continuing, on average, for nearly two years (Carver, Joyner, & Udry, 2003). Early adolescents tend to mention recreation and achieving peer status as reasons for dating. By late adolescence, as young people are ready for greater psychological intimacy, they seek dating partners who offer personal compatibility, companionship, affection, and social support (Collins & van Dulmen, 2006b; Meier & Allen, 2009).

The achievement of intimacy between dating partners typically lags behind that between friends. And positive relationships with parents and friends contribute to the development of warm romantic ties, whereas conflict-ridden parent–adolescent and peer relationships forecast hostile dating interactions (Connolly, Furman, & Konarski, 2000; Furman & Collins, 2009). Recall from Chapter 6 that according to ethological theory, early attachment bonds lead to an *internal working model*, or set of expectations about attachment figures, that guides later close relationships. Consistent with this idea, secure attachment to parents in infancy and childhood—together with recollections of that security in adolescence—predicts quality of teenagers' friendship and romantic ties (Collins & van Dulmen, 2006a; Collins, Welsh, & Furman, 2009). And in a study of high school seniors, secure models of parental attachment and supportive interactions with parents predicted secure models of friendship, which, in turn, were related to the security of romantic relationships (Furman et al., 2002).

Perhaps because early adolescent dating relationships are shallow and stereotyped, early dating is related to drug use, delinquency, and poor academic achievement (Eaton et al., 2007; Miller et al., 2009). These factors, along with a history of uninvolved parenting and aggression in family and peer relationships, increase the likelihood of dating violence. About 10 to 20 percent of adolescents are physically or sexually abused

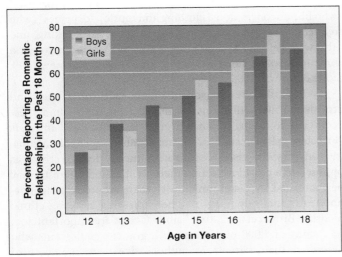

FIGURE 12.3 Increase in romantic relationships in adolescence. More than 16,000 U.S. youths responded to an interview in which they indicated whether they had been involved in a romantic relationship during the past 18 months. At age 12, about one-fourth of young people reported them, a figure that rose to about three-fourths at age 18. (Adapted from Carver, Joyner, & Udry, 2003.)

by dating partners, with boys and girls equally likely to report being victims, and violence by one partner often returned by the other (Cyr, McDuff, & Wright, 2006; Williams et al., 2008). Mental health consequences are severe, including increased anxiety, depression, suicide attempts, and risky sexual behavior (Wekerle & Avgoustis, 2003). Young teenagers are better off sticking with group activities, such as parties and dances, before becoming involved with a steady boyfriend or girlfriend.

Gay and lesbian youths face special challenges in initiating and maintaining visible romances. Their first dating relationships seem to be short-lived and to involve little emotional commitment, but for reasons different from those of heterosexuals: They fear peer harassment and rejection (Diamond & Lucas, 2004). Recall from Chapter 11 that because of intense prejudice, homosexual adolescents often retreat into heterosexual dating. In addition, many have difficulty finding a same-sex partner because their gay and lesbian peers have not yet come out. Often their first contacts with other sexual-minority youths occur in support groups, where they are free to date publicly and can discuss concerns about coming out (Diamond, 2003).

As long as it does not begin too soon, dating provides lessons in cooperation, etiquette, and dealing with people in a wide range of situations. Among older teenagers, close romantic ties promote sensitivity, empathy, self-esteem, social support, and identity development. In addition, teenagers' increasing capacity for interdependence and compromise within dating enhances the quality of other peer relationships (Collins, Welsh, & Furman, 2009).

Still, about half of first romances do not survive high school graduation, and those that do usually become less satisfying (Shaver, Furman, & Buhrmester, 1985). Because young people are still forming their identities, high school couples often find that they have little in common after graduation. Nevertheless, warm, caring romantic ties in adolescence can have long-term implications. They are positively related to gratifying, committed relationships in early adulthood (Meier & Allen, 2009).

ASK YOURSELF

REVIEW Describe the distinct positive functions of friendships, cliques, and crowds in adolescence. What factors lead some friendships and peer-group ties to be harmful?

CONNECT How might gender intensification contribute to the shallow quality of early adolescent dating relationships?

APPLY Thirteen-year-old Mattie's parents are warm, firm in their expectations, and consistent in monitoring her activities. At school, Mattie met some girls who want her to tell her parents she's going to a friend's house and then, instead, join them at the beach for a party. Is Mattie likely to comply? Explain.

REFLECT How did family experiences influence your crowd membership in high school? How did your crowd membership influence your behavior?

 # Problems of Development

Most young people move through adolescence with little disturbance. But as we have seen, some encounter major disruptions in development, such as early parenthood, substance abuse, and school failure. In each instance, biological and psychological changes, families, schools, peers, communities, and culture combine to yield particular outcomes. Serious difficulties rarely occur in isolation but are usually interrelated—as is apparent in three additional problems of the teenage years: depression, suicide, and delinquency.

Depression

Depression—feeling sad, frustrated, and hopeless about life, accompanied by loss of pleasure in most activities and disturbances in sleep, appetite, concentration, and energy—is the most common psychological problem of adolescence. Among U.S. teenagers, 20 to 50 percent experience mild to moderate feelings of depression, bouncing back after a short time. More worrisome are the 15 to 20 percent who have had one or more major depressive episodes, a rate comparable to that of adults. From 2 to 8 percent are chronically depressed—gloomy and self-critical for many months and sometimes years (Graber & Sontag, 2009; Rushton, Forcier, & Schectman, 2002).

Serious depression affects only 1 to 2 percent of children, many of whom (especially girls) remain depressed in adolescence. In addition, depression increases sharply from ages 12 to 16 in industrialized nations, with many more girls than boys displaying adolescent onset. Teenage girls are twice as likely as boys to report persistent depressed mood—a difference sustained throughout the lifespan (Dekker et al., 2007; Hankin & Abela, 2005; Nolen-Hoeksema, 2006). If allowed to continue, depression seriously impairs social, academic, and vocational functioning. Unfortunately, the stereotypical view of adolescence as a period of storm and stress leads many adults to minimize the seriousness of adolescent depression, misinterpreting it as just a passing phase.

Factors Related to Depression. The precise combination of biological and environmental factors leading to depression varies from one individual to the next. Kinship studies reveal that heredity plays an important role (Glowinski et al., 2003). Genes can induce depression by affecting the balance of neurotransmitters in the brain, the development of brain regions involved in inhibiting negative emotion, or the body's hormonal response to stress.

But experience can also activate depression, promoting any of these biological changes. Parents of depressed children and adolescents display a high incidence of depression and other psychological disorders. Although a genetic risk may be passed from parent to child, in earlier chapters we saw that depressed or otherwise stressed parents often engage in maladaptive parenting. As a result, their child's emotional self-regulation,

EERE VAN DE VELDE/BRAND X PICTURES/GETTY IMAGES

In industrialized nations, stressful life events and gender-typed coping styles—passivity, dependency, and rumination—make adolescent girls more prone to depression than boys.

attachment, and self-esteem may be impaired, with serious consequences for many cognitive and social skills (Abela et al., 2005; Yap, Allen, & Ladouceur, 2008). Depressed youths usually display a learned-helpless attributional style (see Chapter 10) (Graber, 2004). In a vulnerable young person, numerous events can spark depression—for example, failing at something important, parental divorce, or the end of a close friendship or romantic partnership.

Sex Differences. Why are girls more prone to depression than boys? Biological changes associated with puberty cannot be responsible because the gender difference is limited to industrialized nations. In developing countries, rates of depression are similar for males and females and occasionally higher in males (Culbertson, 1997). Even in nations where females exceed males in depression, the size of the difference varies.

Instead, stressful life events and gender-typed coping styles seem to be responsible. Early-maturing girls are especially prone to depression (see Chapter 11). Adolescent gender intensification may strengthen girls' passivity, dependency, and tendency to ruminate on their anxieties and problems—maladaptive approaches to tasks expected of teenagers in complex cultures. Consistent with this explanation, adolescents who identify strongly with "feminine" traits ruminate more and are more depressed, regardless of their sex (Lopez, Driscoll, & Kistner, 2009; Papadakis et al., 2006). And having friends with depressive symptoms is linked to a rise in teenagers' own depressive symptoms, perhaps because corumination is high in such relationships (Conway et al., 2011).

Girls who repeatedly feel troubled and insecure develop an overly reactive physiological stress response and cope more poorly with future challenges (Hyde, Mezulis, & Abramson, 2008; Nolen-Hoeksema, 2006). In this way, stressful experiences and stress reactivity feed on one another, sustaining depression. Profound depression can lead to suicidal thoughts, which all too often are translated into action.

Suicide

The suicide rate increases from childhood to old age, but it jumps sharply at adolescence. Currently, suicide is the third-leading cause of death among American youths, after motor vehicle collisions and homicides. Perhaps because U.S. teenagers experience more stress and fewer supports than in the past, the adolescent suicide rate tripled between the mid-1960s and mid-1990s, followed by a slight decline (Spirito & Esposito-Smythers, 2006; U.S. Census Bureau, 2012b). At the same time, rates of adolescent suicide vary widely among industrialized nations—low in Greece, Italy, the Netherlands, and Spain; intermediate in Australia, Canada, Japan, and the United States; and high in Finland, New Zealand, and Singapore (Bridge, Goldstein, & Brent, 2006). These international differences remain unexplained.

Factors Related to Adolescent Suicide. Despite girls' higher rates of depression, the number of boys who kill themselves exceeds the number of girls by a ratio of 3 or 4 to 1. Girls make more unsuccessful suicide attempts and use methods from which they are more likely to be revived, such as a sleeping pill overdose. In contrast, boys tend to choose techniques that lead to instant death, such as firearms or hanging (Langhinrichsen-Rohling, Friend, & Powell, 2009). Gender-role expectations may contribute; less tolerance exists for feelings of helplessness and failed efforts in males than in females.

Possibly due to higher levels of support from extended families, African Americans and Hispanics have lower suicide rates than Caucasian Americans. Recently, however, suicide has risen among African-American adolescent males; the current rate approaches that of Caucasian-American males. And Native-American youths commit suicide at rates two to six times national averages (Balis & Postolache, 2008; U.S. Census Bureau, 2012b). High rates of profound family poverty, school failure, alcohol and drug use, and depression probably underlie these trends.

Gay, lesbian, and bisexual youths are also at high risk, attempting suicide three times as often as other adolescents. Those who have tried to kill themselves report more family conflict over their gender-atypical behavior, inner turmoil about their sexuality, and peer victimization due to their sexual orientation (D'Augelli et al., 2005).

Suicide tends to occur in two types of young people. The first group includes adolescents who are highly intelligent but solitary, withdrawn, and unable to meet their own standards or those of important people in their lives. Members of the second, larger group show antisocial tendencies and express their unhappiness through bullying, fighting, stealing, increased risk taking, and drug abuse (Evans, Hawton, & Rodham, 2004). Besides being hostile and destructive, they turn their anger and disappointment inward.

Suicidal adolescents often have a family history of emotional and antisocial disorders. In addition, they are likely to have experienced multiple stressful life events, including economic disadvantage, parental divorce, frequent parent–child conflict, and abuse and neglect. Stressors typically increase during the period preceding a suicide attempt or completion (Beautrais, 2003; Kaminski et al., 2010). Triggering events include parental blaming of the teenager for family problems, the breakup of an important peer relationship, or the humiliation of having been caught engaging in antisocial acts.

Public policies resulting in cultural disintegration have amplified suicide rates among Native-American youths. From the late 1800s to the 1970s, Native-American families were forced to enroll their children in government-run residential boarding schools designed to erase tribal affiliations. In these repressive institutions, children were not allowed to "be Indian" in any way—culturally, linguistically, artistically, or spiritually (Goldston et al., 2008). The experience left many young people academically unprepared and emotionally scarred, contributing to family and community disorganization in current and succeeding generations (Barnes, Josefowitz, & Cole, 2006; Howell & Yuille, 2004). Consequently, alcohol abuse, youth crime, and suicide rates escalated.

Why does suicide increase in adolescence? One factor seems to be teenagers' improved ability to plan ahead. Although some act impulsively, many young people take purposeful steps toward killing themselves. Other cognitive changes also contribute. Belief in the personal fable (see Chapter 11) leads many depressed young people to conclude that no one could possibly understand their intense pain. As a result, despair, hopelessness, and isolation deepen.

Prevention and Treatment. To prevent suicides, parents and teachers must be trained to pick up on the signals that a troubled teenager sends (see Table 12.3). Schools and community settings, such as recreational and religious organizations, can help by strengthening adolescents' connection with their cultural heritage and providing counseling and support (Goldston et al., 2008; Miller, 2011). Once a teenager takes steps toward suicide, staying with the young person, listening, and expressing compassion and concern until professional help can be obtained are essential.

Treatments for depressed and suicidal adolescents range from antidepressant medication to individual, family, and group therapy. Until the adolescent improves, removing weapons, knives, razors, scissors, and drugs from the home is vital. On a broader scale, gun-control legislation that limits adolescents' access to the most frequent and deadly suicide method in the United States would greatly reduce both the number of suicides and the high teenage homicide rate (Commission on Adolescent Suicide Prevention, 2005).

After a suicide, family and peer survivors need support to help them cope with grief, anger, and guilt over not having been able to help the victim. Teenage suicides often occur in clusters, with one death increasing the likelihood of others among depressed peers who knew the young person or heard about the

TABLE 12.3 **Warning Signs of Suicide**

Efforts to put personal affairs in order—smoothing over troubled relationships, giving away treasured possessions
Verbal cues—saying goodbye to family members and friends, making direct or indirect references to suicide ("I won't have to worry about these problems much longer"; "I wish I were dead")
Feelings of sadness, despondency, "not caring" anymore
Extreme fatigue, lack of energy, boredom
No desire to socialize; withdrawal from friends
Easily frustrated
Emotional outbursts—spells of crying or laughing, bursts of energy
Inability to concentrate, distractible
Decline in grades, absence from school, discipline problems
Neglect of personal appearance
Sleep change—loss of sleep or excessive sleepiness
Appetite change—eating more or less than usual
Physical complaints—stomachaches, backaches, headaches

suicide through the media (Bearman & Moody, 2004; Feigelman & Gorman, 2008). In view of this trend, an especially watchful eye must be kept on vulnerable adolescents after a suicide happens. Restraint by journalists in publicizing teenage suicides also aids prevention.

Delinquency

Juvenile delinquents are children or adolescents who engage in illegal acts. Although youth crime has declined in the United States since the mid-1990s, 12- to 17-year-olds account for about 14 percent of police arrests, although they constitute only 8 percent of the population (U.S. Department of Justice, 2010). When asked directly and confidentially about lawbreaking, almost all teenagers admit to having committed some sort of offense—usually a minor crime, such as petty stealing or disorderly conduct (Flannery et al., 2003).

Both police arrests and self-reports show that delinquency rises over early and middle adolescence and then declines (Farrington, 2009; U.S. Department of Justice, 2010). Recall that antisocial behavior increases among teenagers as a result of heightened reward seeking and desire for peer approval. Over time, peers become less influential; decision making, emotional self-regulation, and moral reasoning improve; and young people enter social contexts (such as higher education, work, marriage, and career) that are less conducive to lawbreaking.

For most adolescents, a brush with the law does not forecast long-term antisocial behavior. But repeated arrests are cause for concern. Teenagers are responsible for 15 percent of violent offenses in the United States (U.S. Department of Justice, 2010).

Biology and Environment

Two Routes to Adolescent Delinquency

Persistent adolescent delinquency follows two paths of development, one involving a small number of youths with an onset of conduct problems in childhood, the second a larger number with an onset in adolescence. The early-onset type is far more likely to lead to a life-course pattern of aggression and criminality (Moffitt, 2007). The late-onset type usually does not persist beyond the transition to early adulthood.

Both childhood-onset and adolescent-onset youths engage in serious offenses; associate with deviant peers; participate in substance abuse, unsafe sex, and dangerous driving; and spend time in correctional facilities. Why does antisocial activity more often continue and escalate into violence in the first group? Longitudinal studies yield similar answers to this question. Most research has focused on boys, but several investigations report that girls who were physically aggressive in childhood are also at risk for later problems—occasionally violent delinquency but more often other norm-violating behaviors and psychological disorders

(Broidy et al., 2003; Chamberlain, 2003). Early relational aggression is linked to adolescent conduct problems as well.

Early-Onset Type

Early-onset youngsters seem to inherit traits that predispose them to aggressiveness (Pettit, 2004). For example, violence-prone boys are emotionally negative, restless, willful, and physically aggressive as early as age 2. They also show subtle deficits in cognitive functioning that seem to contribute to disruptions in the development of language, memory, and cognitive and emotional self-regulation (Moffitt, 2007; Shaw et al., 2003). Some have attention-deficit hyperactivity disorder (ADHD), which compounds their learning and self-control problems (see Chapter 9, pages 304–305).

Yet these biological risks are not sufficient to sustain antisocial behavior: Most early-onset boys decline in aggression over time. Among those who follow the life-course path, inept parenting transforms their undercontrolled style into defiance and persistent

aggression (Brame, Nagin, & Tremblay, 2001; Broidy et al., 2003). As they fail academically and are rejected by peers, they befriend other deviant youths, who facilitate one another's violent behavior while relieving loneliness (see Figure 12.4) (Hughes, 2010; Lacourse et al., 2003). Limited cognitive and social skills result in high rates of school dropout and unemployment, contributing further to antisocial involvements. Often these boys experience their first arrest before age 14—a good indicator that they will be chronic offenders by age 18 (Patterson & Yoerger, 2002).

Preschoolers high in relational aggression also tend to be hyperactive and frequently in conflict with peers and adults (Willoughby, Kupersmidt, & Bryant, 2001). As these behaviors trigger peer rejection, relationally aggressive girls befriend other girls high in relational hostility, and their relational aggression rises (Werner & Crick, 2004). Adolescents high in relational aggression are often angry, vengeful, and defiant of adult rules. Among teenagers who combine physical and relational hostility, these oppositional reactions intensify, increasing the likelihood of serious antisocial activity (Harachi et al., 2006; Prinstein, Boergers, & Vernberg, 2001).

Delinquency—usually petty stealing and disorderly conduct—rises over early and middle adolescence and then declines. But a small percentage of young people engage in repeated, serious offenses and are at risk for a life of crime.

A small percentage become recurrent offenders, who commit most of these crimes, and some enter a life of crime. As the Biology and Environment box above reveals, childhood-onset conduct problems are far more likely to persist than conduct problems that first appear in adolescence.

Factors Related to Delinquency. In adolescence, the gender gap in physical aggression widens. Although girls account for about one in five adolescent arrests for violence, their offenses are largely limited to simple assault (such as pushing and spitting). Serious violent crime is mostly the domain of boys (Dahlberg & Simon, 2006). SES and ethnicity are strong predictors of arrests but only mildly related to teenagers' self-reports of antisocial acts. The difference is due to the tendency to arrest, charge, and punish low-SES ethnic minority youths more often than their higher-SES white and Asian counterparts (Farrington, 2009; U.S. Department of Justice, 2010).

Difficult temperament, low intelligence, poor school performance, peer rejection in childhood, and association with antisocial peers are linked to chronic delinquency (Laird et al.,

Late-Onset Type

Other youths first display antisocial behavior around the time of puberty, gradually increasing their involvement. Their conduct problems arise from the peer context of early adolescence, not from biological deficits and a history of unfavorable development. For some, quality of parenting may decline for a time, perhaps due to family stresses or the challenges of disciplining an unruly teenager (Moffitt, 2007). When age brings gratifying adult privileges, these youths draw on pro-social skills mastered before adolescence and abandon their antisocial ways.

A few late-onset youths do continue to engage in antisocial acts. The seriousness of their adolescent offenses seems to trap them in situations that close off opportunities for responsible behavior. Being employed or in school and forming positive, close relationships predict an end to criminal offending by age 20 to 25 (Clingempeel & Henggeler, 2003; Stouthamer-Loeber et al., 2004). In contrast, the longer antisocial young people spend in prison, the more likely they are to sustain a life of crime.

These findings suggest a need for a fresh look at policies aimed at stopping youth crime. Keeping youth offenders locked up for many years disrupts their vocational lives and access to social support during a crucial period of development, condemning them to a bleak future.

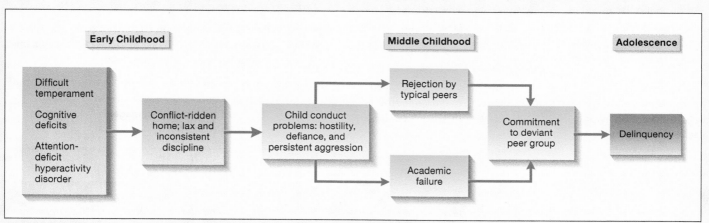

FIGURE 12.4 Path to chronic delinquency for adolescents with childhood-onset antisocial behavior. Difficult temperament and cognitive deficits characterize many of these youths in early childhood; some have attention-deficit hyperactivity disorder. Inept parenting transforms biologically based self-control difficulties into hostility and defiance.

2005). How do these factors fit together? One of the most consistent findings about delinquent youths is that their families are low in warmth, high in conflict, and characterized by harsh, inconsistent discipline and low monitoring (Barnes et al., 2006; Capaldi et al., 2002a). Because marital transitions often contribute to family discord and disrupted parenting, boys who experience parental separation and divorce are especially prone to delinquency (Farrington, 2004). And youth crime peaks on weekdays between 2:00 and 8:00 P.M., when many teenagers are unsupervised (U.S. Department of Justice, 2010).

Our discussion on page 259 in Chapter 8 explained how ineffective parenting can promote and sustain children's aggression, with boys—who are more active and impulsive—more often targets of parental anger, physical punishment, and inconsistency. When these child temperamental traits combine with emotionally negative, inept parenting, aggression rises sharply during childhood, leads to violent offenses in adolescence, and persists into adulthood (again, see the Biology and Environment box).

Teenagers commit more crimes in poverty-stricken neighborhoods with limited recreational and employment opportuni-

ties and high adult criminality (Leventhal, Duprere, & Brooks-Gunn, 2009). In such neighborhoods, adolescents have easy access to deviant peers, drugs, and firearms and are likely to be recruited into antisocial gangs, whose members commit the vast majority of violent delinquent acts. Furthermore, schools in these locales typically fail to meet students' developmental needs (Chung, Mulvey, & Steinberg, 2011; Flannery et al., 2003). Large classes, weak instruction, rigid rules, and reduced academic expectations and opportunities are associated with higher rates of lawbreaking, even after other influences are controlled.

Prevention and Treatment. Because delinquency has roots in childhood and results from events in several contexts, prevention must start early and take place at multiple levels (Frey et al., 2009). Positive family relationships, authoritative parenting, high-quality teaching in schools, and communities with healthy economic and social conditions go a long way toward reducing adolescent antisocial acts.

Lacking resources for effective prevention, many U.S. schools have implemented *zero tolerance policies,* which severely punish all disruptive and threatening behavior, major and minor, usually with suspension or expulsion. Yet often these policies are implemented inconsistently: Low-SES minority students are two to three times as likely to be punished, especially for minor misbehaviors (Goode & Goode, 2007; Reppucci, Meyer, & Kostelnik, 2011). No evidence exists that zero tolerance achieves its objective of reducing youth aggression and other forms of misconduct (Stinchcomb, Bazemore, & Riestenberg, 2006). To the contrary, some studies find that by excluding students from school, zero tolerance heightens high school dropout and antisocial behavior.

Treating serious offenders requires an intensive, often lengthy approach, also directed at the multiple determinants of delinquency. The most effective methods include training parents in communication, monitoring, and discipline strategies and providing youths with experiences that improve cognitive and social skills, moral reasoning, anger management, and other aspects of emotional self-regulation (DiBiase et al., 2011; Heilbrun, Lee, & Cottle, 2005).

Yet even these multidimensional treatments can fall short if young people remain embedded in hostile home lives, antisocial peer groups, and fragmented neighborhoods. In a program called *multisystemic therapy*, counselors combined family intervention with integrating violent youths into positive school, work, and leisure activities and disengaging them from deviant peers. Compared with conventional services or individual therapy, the intervention led to greater improvement in parent–adolescent relationships and school performance, a dramatic drop in number of arrests, and—when participants did commit crimes—a reduction in their severity. Multisystemic therapy also helped limit family instability once youth offenders reached adulthood, as measured by involvement in civil suits over divorce, paternity, or child support (Borduin, 2007; Henggeler et al., 2009; Sawyer & Borduin, 2011). Efforts to create nonaggressive environments—at the family, community, and cultural levels—are needed to help delinquent youths and to foster healthy development of all young people.

ASK YOURSELF

REVIEW Why are adolescent girls at greater risk for depression and adolescent boys at greater risk for suicide?

CONNECT Reread the sections on adolescent pregnancy and substance abuse in Chapter 11. What factors do these problems have in common with suicide and delinquency?

APPLY Zeke had been well-behaved in elementary school, but at age 13 he started spending time with the "wrong crowd." At 16, he was arrested for property damage. Is Zeke likely to become a long-term offender? Why or why not?

SUMMARY

Erikson's Theory: Identity versus Role Confusion (p. 402)

According to Erikson, what is the major personality achievement of adolescence?

- Erikson viewed **identity** as the major personality achievement of adolescence. Young people who successfully resolve the psychological conflict of **identity versus role confusion** construct a unified self-definition based on self-chosen values and goals.

Self-Understanding (p. 402)

Describe changes in self-concept and self-esteem during adolescence.

- Cognitive changes enable adolescents to develop more organized, consistent self-descriptions, with social, personal, and moral values as key themes.

- Self-esteem further differentiates and, for most adolescents, rises. Authoritative parenting and encouragement from teachers support positive self-esteem.

Describe the four identity statuses, along with factors that promote identity development.

- Researchers evaluate progress in identity development on two key criteria: exploration and commitment. **Identity achievement** (exploration followed by commitment to values, beliefs, and goals) and **identity moratorium** (exploration without having reached commitment) are psychologically healthy identity statuses. Long-term **identity foreclosure** (commitment without exploration) and **identity diffusion** (lack of both exploration and commitment) are related to adjustment difficulties.

- An information-gathering cognitive style, healthy parental attachment, interaction with diverse peers, close friendships, and schools and communities offering rich and varied opportunities promote healthy identity development. Supportive parents, peers, and schools can foster a strong, secure **ethnic identity** among minority adolescents, who often must overcome **acculturative stress.** A **bicultural identity** offers additional emotional and social benefits.

Moral Development (p. 405)

Describe Kohlberg's theory of moral development, and evaluate its accuracy.

- Kohlberg organized moral development into three levels, each with two stages. At the **preconventional level,** morality is externally controlled and actions are judged by their consequences; at the **conventional level,** conformity to laws and rules is regarded as necessary for positive human relationships and societal order; and at the **postconventional level,** morality is defined by abstract, universal principles.

- A reexamination of Kohlberg's stages suggests that moral maturity can be found at Stages 3 and 4; few people attain the postconventional level. Because situational factors influence moral judgments, Kohlberg's stages are best viewed as loosely organized and overlapping.

- Contrary to Gilligan's claim, Kohlberg's theory does not underestimate the moral maturity of females but instead taps both justice and caring orientations.

- Compared with children, teenagers display more subtle reasoning about conflicts between personal choice and community obligation and are increasingly aware of the moral implications of following social conventions.

Describe influences on moral reasoning and its relationship to moral behavior.

- Factors contributing to moral maturity include warm, rational child-rearing practices, education level, and peer discussions of moral issues. In village societies, where moral cooperation is based on direct relations between people, moral reasoning rarely moves beyond Kohlberg's Stage 3. In collectivist cultures, moral dilemma responses are more other-directed than in Western societies.

- The connection between mature moral reasoning and action is only modest. Moral behavior is also influenced by empathy and guilt, temperament, history of morally relevant experiences, and **moral identity.** Although formal religious involvement declines in adolescence, most religiously affiliated teenagers are advantaged in moral values and behavior.

- Researchers favoring a pragmatic approach to morality assert that moral maturity varies depending on context and motivations.

Gender Typing (p. 414)

How does gender typing change in adolescence?

- Some research suggests that adolescence is a time of **gender intensification,** in which gender stereotyping of attitudes and behavior increases, though evidence is mixed.

The Family (p. 414)

Discuss changes in parent–child and sibling relationships during adolescence.

- In their quest for **autonomy,** adolescents rely more on themselves and less on parents for decision making. Teenagers deidealize their parents, often questioning parental authority. Warm, supportive parenting, appropriate demands for maturity, and consistent monitoring predict favorable outcomes.

- Sibling influence declines as adolescents separate from the family and turn toward peers. Still, attachment to siblings remains strong for most young people.

Peer Relations (p. 417)

Describe adolescent friendships, peer groups, and dating relationships and their consequences for development.

- Adolescent friendships are based on intimacy, mutual understanding, and loyalty and contain more self-disclosure. Girls place greater emphasis on emotional closeness, boys on shared activities and accomplishments.

- Online communication supports closeness with existing friends. Though online communication with strangers provides some teenagers with vital social support, it also poses risks. High social media use is linked to unsatisfying face-to-face social experiences.

- Adolescent friendships—when not characterized by relational aggression or attraction to antisocial behavior—promote self-concept, perspective taking, identity, and the capacity for intimate relationships. They also help young people deal with stress and can foster improved attitudes toward and involvement in school.

- Adolescent peer groups are organized into **cliques,** particularly important to girls, and **crowds,** which grant teenagers an identity within the larger social structure of the school. With interest in dating, mixed-sex cliques increase in importance. Both cliques and crowds diminish as teenagers settle on personal values and goals.

- Intimacy in dating relationships lags behind that between friends. Positive relationships with parents and friends contribute to secure romantic ties.

© SCOTT HORTOP/ALAMY

Problems of Development (p. 421)

Describe factors related to adolescent depression and suicide.

- Depression is the most common psychological problem of adolescence, with girls at greater risk in industrialized nations. Combinations of biological and environmental factors are implicated, including heredity, maladaptive parenting, a learned-helpless attributional style, and negative life events.

- The suicide rate increases sharply at adolescence. Although teenage girls make more unsuccessful suicide attempts, boys account for more deaths. Teenagers at risk for suicide may be withdrawn but more often are antisocial. Family turmoil is common in the backgrounds of suicidal adolescents.

Discuss factors related to delinquency.

- Delinquency rises over early and middle adolescence and then declines. But only a few teenagers are serious repeat offenders—usually boys with a childhood history of conduct problems.

- A family environment low in warmth, high in conflict, and characterized by inconsistent discipline and low monitoring is consistently related to delinquency, as are poverty-stricken neighborhoods with high crime rates and ineffective schools.

Important Terms and Concepts

acculturative stress (p. 406)
autonomy (p. 415)
bicultural identity (p. 406)
clique (p. 419)
conventional level (p. 408)
crowd (p. 419)

ethnic identity (p. 406)
gender intensification (p. 414)
identity (p. 402)
identity achievement (p. 403)
identity diffusion (p. 403)
identity foreclosure (p. 403)

identity moratorium (p. 403)
identity versus role confusion (p. 402)
moral identity (p. 411)
postconventional level (p. 408)
preconventional level (p. 407)

milestones

Development in Adolescence

■ Becomes more self-conscious and self-focused. (386–387)

■ Becomes more idealistic and critical. (387)

■ Metacognition and self-regulation continue to improve. (367–368, 385)

EMOTIONAL/SOCIAL

■ Self-concept includes abstract descriptors unifying separate personality traits, but these are not interconnected and often contradictory. (402)

■ In striving for autonomy, spends less time with parents and siblings, more time with peers. (416–417)

■ Friendships decline in number and are based on intimacy, mutual understanding, and loyalty. (417)

■ Peer groups become organized around same-sex cliques. (419)

■ In high schools with complex social structures, cliques with similar values form crowds. (419)

Early Adolescence: 11–14

PHYSICAL

■ If a girl, reaches peak of growth spurt. (363)

■ If a girl, adds more body fat than muscle. (363–364)

■ If a girl, starts to menstruate. (366)

■ If a boy, begins growth spurt. (363)

■ If a boy, starts to ejaculate seminal fluid. (366)

■ Is likely to be aware of sexual orientation. (376)

■ If a girl, motor performance increases gradually, leveling off by age 14. (364)

■ Reacts more strongly to stressful events; shows heightened sensation-seeking and risk-taking behavior. (367–368)

COGNITIVE

■ Gains in hypothetico-deductive reasoning and propositional thought. (383–384)

■ Gains in scientific reasoning—coordinating theory with evidence—on complex, multivariable tasks. (385)

Middle Adolescence: 14–16

PHYSICAL

■ If a girl, completes growth spurt. (363)

■ If a boy, reaches peak of growth spurt. (363)

■ If a boy, voice deepens. (366)

■ If a boy, adds muscle while body fat declines. (363)

■ If a boy, motor performance improves dramatically. (364)

■ May have had sexual intercourse. (375)

COGNITIVE

■ Continues to improve in hypothetico-deductive reasoning and propositional thought. (383–384)

■ Continues to improve in scientific reasoning, following a similar sequential order on different types of tasks. (385–386)

Note: Numbers in parentheses indicate the page or pages on which each milestone is discussed.

- Becomes less self-conscious and self-focused. (386–387)
- Improves in decision making. (387–388)

EMOTIONAL/SOCIAL

- Combines features of the self into an organized self-concept. (402)
- Self-esteem differentiates further and tends to rise. (402–403)
- In most cases, begins to move from "lower" to "higher" identity statuses. (404)
- Increasingly emphasizes ideal reciprocity and societal laws as the basis for resolving moral dilemmas. (408–409)
- Engages in more subtle reasoning about conflicts between moral, social-conventional, and personal-choice issues. (409–410)

- Mixed-sex cliques become common. (420)
- Has probably started dating. (420)

Late Adolescence: 16–18

PHYSICAL

- If a boy, completes growth spurt. (363)
- If a boy, gains in motor performance continue. (364)

COGNITIVE

- Continues to improve in metacognition, scientific reasoning, and decision making. (385–386, 387–388)

EMOTIONAL/SOCIAL

- Self-concept emphasizes personal and moral values. (402)
- Continues to construct an identity, typically moving to higher identity statuses. (404–405)
- Continues to advance in maturity of moral reasoning. (408–409)
- Cliques and crowds decline in importance. (420)
- Seeks psychological intimacy in romantic ties, which last longer. (420–421)

© CEZARO DE LUCA/EPA/CORBIS

Early adulthood brings momentous changes—among them, choosing a vocation, starting full-time work, and attaining economic independence. This Argentinean forensic anthropologist, who recently completed her higher education, has joined a team identifying people who went missing several decades ago, during a dark period of her country's history.

Physical and Cognitive Development in Early Adulthood

The back seat and trunk piled high with belongings, 23-year-old Sharese hugged her mother and brother goodbye, jumped in the car, and headed toward the interstate with a sense of newfound freedom mixed with apprehension. Three months earlier, the family had watched proudly as Sharese received her bachelor's degree in chemistry from a small university 40 miles from her home. Her college years had been a time of gradual release from economic and psychological dependency on her family. She returned home periodically on weekends and lived there during the summer months. Her mother supplemented Sharese's loans with a monthly allowance. But this day marked a turning point. She was moving to her own apartment in a city 800 miles away, with plans to work on a master's degree. With a teaching assistantship and a student loan, Sharese felt more "on her own" than at any previous time in her life.

During her college years, Sharese made lifestyle changes and settled on a vocational direction. Overweight throughout high school, she lost 20 pounds in her sophomore year, revised her diet, and began an exercise regimen by joining the university's Ultimate Frisbee team, eventually becoming its captain. A summer spent as a counselor at a camp for chronically ill children helped convince Sharese to apply her background in science to a career in public health.

Still, two weeks before she was to leave, Sharese confided in her mother that she had doubts about her decision. "Sharese," her mother advised, "we never know if our life choices are going to suit us just right, and most times they aren't perfect. It's what we make of them—how we view and mold them—that turns them into successes." So Sharese embarked on her journey and found herself face-to-face with a multitude of exciting challenges and opportunities.

In this chapter, we take up the physical and cognitive sides of early adulthood, which extends from about age 18 to 40. As noted in Chapter 1, the adult years are difficult to divide into discrete periods because the timing of important milestones varies greatly among individuals—much more so than in childhood and adolescence. But for most people, early adulthood involves a common set of tasks: leaving home, completing education, beginning full-time work, attaining economic independence, establishing a long-term sexually and emotionally intimate relationship, and starting a family. These are energetic decades filled with momentous decisions that, more than any other time of life, offer the potential for living to the fullest. ●

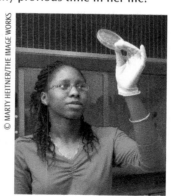

© MARTY HEITNER/THE IMAGE WORKS

chapter outline

PHYSICAL DEVELOPMENT

Biological Aging Is Under Way in Early Adulthood

Aging at the Level of DNA and Body Cells ● Aging at the Level of Tissues and Organs

■ **BIOLOGY AND ENVIRONMENT** Telomere Length: A Marker of the Impact of Life Circumstances on Biological Aging

Physical Changes

Cardiovascular and Respiratory Systems ● Motor Performance ● Immune System ● Reproductive Capacity

Health and Fitness

Nutrition ● Exercise ● Substance Abuse ● Sexuality ● Psychological Stress

■ **SOCIAL ISSUES: HEALTH** The Obesity Epidemic: How Americans Became the Heaviest People in the World

COGNITIVE DEVELOPMENT

Changes in the Structure of Thought

Perry's Theory: Epistemic Cognition ● Labouvie-Vief's Theory: Pragmatic Thought and Cognitive-Affective Complexity

Expertise and Creativity

The College Experience

Psychological Impact of Attending College ● Dropping Out

Vocational Choice

Selecting a Vocation ● Factors Influencing Vocational Choice ● Vocational Preparation of Non-College-Bound Young Adults

■ **SOCIAL ISSUES: EDUCATION** Masculinity at Work: Men Who Choose Nontraditional Careers

PHYSICAL DEVELOPMENT

We have seen that throughout childhood and adolescence, the body grows larger and stronger, coordination improves, and sensory systems gather information more effectively. Once body structures reach maximum capacity and efficiency, **biological aging,** or **senescence,** begins—genetically influenced declines in the functioning of organs and systems that are universal in all members of our species. Like physical growth, however, biological aging varies widely across parts of the body, and individual differences are great—variation that the *lifespan perspective* helps us understand. A host of contextual factors— including each person's genetic makeup, lifestyle, living environment, and historical period—influence biological aging, each of which can accelerate or slow age-related declines (Arking, 2006). As a result, the physical changes of the adult years are, indeed, *multidimensional* and *multidirectional* (see page 9 in Chapter 1).

In the following sections, we examine the process of biological aging. Then we turn to physical and motor changes already under way in early adulthood. As you will see, biological aging can be modified substantially through behavioral and environmental interventions. During the twentieth century, improved nutrition, medical treatment, sanitation, and safety added 25 to 30 years to *average life expectancy* in industrialized nations, a trend that is continuing (see Chapter 1, page 8). We will take up life expectancy in greater depth in Chapter 17.

Biological Aging Is Under Way in Early Adulthood

At an intercollegiate tournament, Sharese dashed across the playing field for hours, leaping high to catch Frisbees sailing her way. In her early twenties, she is at her peak in strength, endurance, sensory acuteness, and immune system responsiveness. Yet over the next two decades, she will age and, as she moves into middle and late adulthood, will show more noticeable declines.

Biological aging is the combined result of many causes, some operating at the level of DNA, others at the level of cells, and still others at the level of tissues, organs, and the whole organism. Hundreds of theories exist, indicating that our understanding is incomplete (Arking, 2006). For example, one popular idea—the *"wear-and-tear" theory*—is that the body wears out from use. But no relationship exists between physical activity and early death. To the contrary, regular, moderate-to-vigorous exercise predicts healthier, longer life for people differing widely in SES and ethnicity (Ruiz et al., 2011; Stessman et al., 2005). We now know that this "wear-and-tear" theory is an oversimplification.

This whitewater kayaker, in his early twenties, is at his peak in strength, endurance, and sensory acuteness.

Aging at the Level of DNA and Body Cells

Current explanations of biological aging at the level of DNA and body cells are of two types: (1) those that emphasize the *programmed effects of specific genes* and (2) those that emphasize the *cumulative effects of random events* that damage genetic and cellular material. Support for both views exists, and a combination may eventually prove to be correct.

Genetically programmed aging receives some support from kinship studies indicating that longevity is a family trait. People whose parents had long lives tend to live longer themselves. And greater similarity exists in the lifespans of identical than fraternal twins. But the heritability of longevity is modest, ranging from .15 to .35 for age at death and from .27 to .57 for various measures of current biological age, such as strength of hand grip, respiratory capacity, blood pressure, and bone density (Cevenini et al., 2008; Dutta et al., 2011; Gögele et al., 2011). Rather than inheriting longevity directly, people probably inherit risk and protective factors, which influence their chances of dying earlier or later.

One "genetic programming" theory proposes the existence of "aging genes" that control certain biological changes, such as menopause, gray hair, and deterioration of body cells. The strongest evidence for this view comes from research showing that human cells allowed to divide in the laboratory have a lifespan of 50 divisions, plus or minus 10 (Hayflick, 1998). With each duplication, a special type of DNA called **telomeres**— located at the ends of chromosomes, serving as a "cap" to protect the ends from destruction—shortens. Eventually, so little remains that the cells no longer duplicate at all. Telomere shortening acts as a brake against somatic mutations (such as those involved in cancer), which become more likely as cells duplicate (Shay & Wright, 2011). But an increase in the number of senescent cells (ones with short telomeres) also contributes to age-related disease, loss of function, and earlier mortality (Epel et al., 2009; Shin et al., 2006). As the Biology and Environment box on the following page reveals, researchers have begun to

Biology and Environment

Telomere Length: A Marker of the Impact of Life Circumstances on Biological Aging

In the not-too-distant future, your annual physical exam may include an assessment of the length of your *telomeres*—DNA at the ends of chromosomes, which safeguard the stability of your cells. Telomeres shorten with each cell duplication; when they drop below a critical length, the cell can no longer divide and becomes senescent (see Figure 13.1). Although telomeres shorten with age, the rate at which they do so varies greatly. An enzyme called *telomerase* prevents shortening and can even reverse the trend, causing telomeres to lengthen and, thus, protecting the aging cell.

Over the past decade, research examining the influence of life circumstances on telomere length has exploded. A well-established finding is that chronic illnesses, such as cardiovascular disease and cancer, hasten telomere shortening in white blood cells, which play a vital role in the immune response (see page 437). Telomere shortening, in turn, predicts more rapid disease progression and earlier death (Fuster & Andres, 2006).

Accelerated telomere shortening has been linked to a variety of unhealthy behaviors, including cigarette smoking and the physical inactivity and overeating that lead to obesity and to insulin resistance, which often precedes type 2 diabetes (Epel et al., 2006; Gardner et al., 2005). Unfavorable health conditions may alter telomere length as early as the prenatal period, with possible long-term negative consequences for biological aging. In research on rats, poor maternal nutrition during pregnancy resulted in low birth weight and development of shorter telomeres in kidney and heart tissue

(Jennings et al., 1999; Tarry-Adkins et al., 2008). In a related human investigation, preschoolers who had been low-birth-weight as infants had shorter telomeres in their white blood cells than did their normal-birth-weight agemates (Raqib et al., 2007).

Persistent psychological stress—in childhood, abuse or bullying; in adulthood, parenting a child with a chronic illness or caring for an elder with dementia—is linked to reduced telomerase activity and telomere shortness in white blood cells (Damjanovic et al., 2007; McEwen, 2007; Shalev, 2012; Simon et al., 2006). Can stress actually modify telomeres? In a laboratory experiment, researchers exposed human white blood cells to the stress hormone cortisol. The cells responded by decreasing production of telomerase (Choi, Fauce, & Effros, 2008).

Fortunately, when adults make positive lifestyle changes, telomeres seem to respond accordingly. In a study of obese women, those who responded to a lifestyle intervention with reduced psychological stress and healthier eating behaviors also displayed gains in telomerase activity (Daubenmier et al., 2012). In another investigation of men varying widely in age, greater maximum vital capacity of the lungs (a measure of physical

fitness) was associated with reduced age-related accumulation of senescent white blood cells (Spielmann et al., 2011).

Currently, researchers are working on identifying sensitive periods of telomere change—times when telomeres are most susceptible to modification. Early intervention—for example, enhanced prenatal care and interventions to reduce obesity in childhood—may be particularly powerful. But telomeres are changeable well into late adulthood (Epel et al., 2009). As our understanding of predictors and consequences of telomere length expands, it may become an important index of health and aging throughout life.

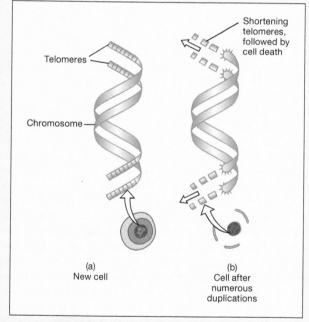

FIGURE 13.1 Telomeres at the ends of chromosomes. (a) Telomeres in a newly created cell. (b) With each cell duplication, telomeres shorten; when too short, they expose DNA to damage, and the cell dies.

---

identify health behaviors and psychological states that accelerate telomere shortening—powerful biological evidence that certain life circumstances compromise longevity.

According to an alternative, "random events" theory, DNA in body cells is gradually damaged through spontaneous or externally caused mutations. As these accumulate, cell repair and replacement become less efficient, and abnormal cancerous

cells are often produced. Animal studies confirm an increase in DNA breaks and deletions and damage to other cellular material with age. Similar evidence is accruing for humans (Freitas & Magalhães, 2011).

One hypothesized cause of age-related DNA and cellular abnormalities is the release of **free radicals**—naturally occurring, highly reactive chemicals that form in the presence of oxygen.

RONNIE KAUFMAN/LARRY HIRSHOWITZ/BLEND IMAGES/GETTY IMAGES

Kinship studies indicate that longevity is a family trait. In addition to favorable heredity, these grandsons will likely benefit from the model of a fit, active grandfather who buffers stress by enjoying life.

(Radiation and certain pollutants and drugs can trigger similar effects.) When oxygen molecules break down within the cell, the reaction strips away an electron, creating a free radical. As it seeks a replacement from its surroundings, it destroys nearby cellular material, including DNA, proteins, and fats essential for cell functioning. Free radicals are thought to be involved in more than 60 disorders of aging, including cardiovascular disease, neurological disorders, cancer, cataracts, and arthritis (Cutler & Mattson, 2006; Stohs, 2011). Although our bodies produce substances that neutralize free radicals, some harm occurs, and it accumulates over time.

Some researchers believe that genes for longevity work by defending against free radicals. In support of this view, animal species with longer life expectancies tend to display slower rates of free-radical damage to DNA (Sanz, Pamplona, & Barja, 2006). But contrary evidence also exists. Experimental manipulation of the mouse genome, by either augmenting or deleting antioxidant genes, has no impact on longevity. And scientists have identified a cave-dwelling salamander with exceptional longevity—on average, 68 years, making it the longest-living amphibian—with no unusual genetic defenses against free-radical damage (Speakman & Selman, 2011).

Research suggests that foods low in saturated fat and rich in vitamins can forestall free-radical damage (Bullo, Lamuela-Raventos, & Salas-Salvado, 2011). Nevertheless, the role of free radicals in aging is controversial.

Aging at the Level of Tissues and Organs

What consequences might age-related DNA and cellular deterioration have for the overall structure and functioning of organs and tissues? There are many possibilities. Among those with clear support is the **cross-linkage theory of aging**. Over time, protein fibers that make up the body's connective tissue form bonds, or links, with one another. When these normally separate fibers cross-link, tissue becomes less elastic, leading to many negative outcomes, including loss of flexibility in the skin and other organs, clouding of the lens of the eye, clogging of arteries, and damage to the kidneys. Like other aspects of aging, cross-linking can be reduced by external factors, including regular exercise and a healthy diet (Kragstrup, Kjaer, & Mackey, 2011; Wickens, 2001).

Gradual failure of the endocrine system, which produces and regulates hormones, is yet another route to aging. An obvious example is decreased estrogen production in women, which culminates in menopause. Because hormones affect many body functions, disruptions in the endocrine system can have widespread effects on health and survival. For example, a gradual drop in growth hormone (GH) is associated with loss of muscle and bone mass, addition of body fat, thinning of the skin, and decline in cardiovascular functioning. In adults with abnormally low levels of GH, hormone therapy can slow these symptoms, but it has serious side effects, including increased risk of fluid retention in tissues, muscle pain, and cancer (Harman & Blackman, 2004; Ceda et al., 2010). So far, diet and physical activity are safer ways to limit these aspects of biological aging.

Finally, declines in immune system functioning contribute to many conditions of aging, including increased susceptibility to infectious disease and cancer and changes in blood vessel walls associated with cardiovascular disease. Decreased vigor of the immune response seems to be genetically programmed, but other aging processes we have considered (such as weakening of the endocrine system) can intensify it (Alonso-Férnandez & De la Fuente, 2011; Hawkley & Cacioppo, 2004). Indeed, combinations of theories—the ones just reviewed as well as others—are needed to explain the complexities of biological aging. With this in mind, let's turn to physical signs and other characteristics of aging.

Physical Changes

During the twenties and thirties, changes in physical appearance and declines in body functioning are so gradual that most are hardly noticeable. Later, they will accelerate. The physical changes of aging are summarized in Table 13.1. We will examine several in detail here and take up others in later chapters. Before we begin, let's note that these trends are derived largely from cross-sectional studies. Because younger cohorts have experienced better health care and nutrition, cross-sectional evidence can exaggerate impairments associated with aging. Fortunately, longitudinal evidence is expanding, helping to correct this picture.

Cardiovascular and Respiratory Systems

During her first month in graduate school, Sharese pored over research articles on cardiovascular functioning. In her African-American extended family, her father, an uncle, and three aunts had died of heart attacks in their forties and fifties. These tragedies prompted Sharese to enter the field of public health in hopes

TABLE 13.1

Physical Changes of Aging

ORGAN OR SYSTEM	TIMING OF CHANGE	DESCRIPTION
Sensory		
Vision	From age 30	As the lens stiffens and thickens, ability to focus on close objects declines. Yellowing of the lens, weakening of muscles controlling the pupil, and clouding of the vitreous (gelatin-like substance that fills the eye) reduce light reaching the retina, impairing color discrimination and night vision. Visual acuity, or fineness of discrimination, decreases, with a sharp drop between ages 70 and 80.
Hearing	From age 30	Sensitivity to sound declines, especially at high frequencies but gradually extending to all frequencies. Change is more than twice as rapid for men as for women.
Taste	From age 60	Sensitivity to the four basic tastes—sweet, salty, sour, and bitter—is reduced. This may be due to factors other than aging, since number and distribution of taste buds do not change.
Smell	From age 60	Loss of smell receptors reduces ability to detect and identify odors.
Touch	Gradual	Loss of touch receptors reduces sensitivity on the hands, particularly the fingertips.
Cardiovascular	Gradual	As the heart muscle becomes more rigid, maximum heart rate decreases, reducing the heart's ability to meet the body's oxygen requirements when stressed by exercise. As artery walls stiffen and accumulate plaque, blood flow to body cells is reduced.
Respiratory	Gradual	Under physical exertion, respiratory capacity decreases and breathing rate increases. Stiffening of connective tissue in the lungs and chest muscles makes it more difficult for the lungs to expand to full volume.
Immune	Gradual	Shrinking of the thymus limits maturation of T cells and disease-fighting capacity of B cells, impairing the immune response.
Muscular	Gradual	As nerves stimulating them die, fast-twitch muscle fibers (responsible for speed and explosive strength) decline in number and size to a greater extent than slow-twitch fibers (which support endurance). Tendons and ligaments (which transmit muscle action) stiffen, reducing speed and flexibility of movement.
Skeletal	Begins in the late thirties, accelerates in the fifties, slows in the seventies	Cartilage in the joints thins and cracks, leading bone ends beneath it to erode. New cells continue to be deposited on the outer layer of the bones, and mineral content of bone declines. The resulting broader but more porous bones weaken the skeleton and make it more vulnerable to fracture. Change is more rapid in women than in men.
Reproductive	In women, accelerates after age 35; in men, begins after age 40	Fertility problems (including difficulty conceiving and carrying a pregnancy to term) and risk of having a baby with a chromosomal disorder increase.
Nervous	From age 50	Brain weight declines as neurons lose water content and die, mostly in the cerebral cortex, and as ventricles (spaces) within the brain enlarge. Development of new synapses and limited generation of new neurons can, in part, compensate for these declines.
Skin	Gradual	Epidermis (outer layer) is held less tightly to the dermis (middle layer); fibers in the dermis and hypodermis (inner layer) thin; fat cells in the hypodermis decline. As a result, the skin becomes looser, less elastic, and wrinkled. Change is more rapid in women than in men.
Hair	From age 35	Grays and thins.
Height	From age 50	Loss of bone strength leads to collapse of disks in the spinal column, leading to a height loss of as much as 2 inches by the seventies and eighties.
Weight	Increases to age 50; declines from age 60	Weight change reflects a rise in fat and a decline in muscle and bone mineral. Since muscle and bone are heavier than fat, the resulting pattern is weight gain followed by loss. Body fat accumulates on the torso and decreases on the extremities.

Sources: Arking, 2006; Lemaitre et al., 2012; Whitbourne, 1996.

of finding ways to relieve health problems among black Americans. *Hypertension,* or high blood pressure, occurs 12 percent more often in the U.S. black than in the U.S. white population; the rate of death from heart disease among African Americans is 30 percent higher (American Heart Association, 2012).

Sharese was surprised to learn that fewer age-related changes occur in the heart than we might expect, given that heart disease is a leading cause of death throughout adulthood, responsible for as many as 10 percent of U.S. male and 5 percent of U.S. female deaths between ages 20 and 34—figures that more than double in the following decade and, thereafter, continue to rise steadily with age (American Heart Association, 2012). In healthy individuals, the heart's ability to meet the body's oxygen requirements under typical conditions (as measured by heart rate in relation to volume of blood pumped) does not change during adulthood. Only during stressful exercise does heart performance decline with age—a change due to a decrease in maximum heart rate and greater rigidity of the heart muscle (Arking, 2006). Consequently, the heart has difficulty delivering enough oxygen to the body during high activity and bouncing back from strain.

One of the most serious diseases of the cardiovascular system is *atherosclerosis,* in which heavy deposits of plaque containing cholesterol and fats collect on the walls of the main arteries. If present, it usually begins early in life, progresses during middle adulthood, and culminates in serious illness. Atherosclerosis is multiply determined, making it hard to separate the contributions of biological aging from individual genetic and environmental influences. The complexity of causes is illustrated by research indicating that before puberty, a high-fat diet produces only fatty streaks on the artery walls (Oliveira, Patin, & Escrivao, 2010). In sexually mature adults, however, it leads to serious plaque deposits, suggesting that sex hormones may heighten the insults of a high-fat diet.

Heart disease has decreased considerably since the mid-twentieth century, with a larger drop in the last 25 years due to a decline in cigarette smoking, to improved diet and exercise among at-risk individuals, and to better medical detection and treatment of high blood pressure and cholesterol (American Heart Association, 2012). And as a longitudinal follow-up of an ethnically diverse sample of U.S. black and white 18- to 30-year-olds revealed, those at low risk—defined by not smoking, normal body weight, healthy diet, and regular physical activity—were far less likely to be diagnosed with symptoms of heart disease over the succeeding two decades (Liu et al., 2012). Later, when we consider health and fitness, we will see why heart attacks were so common in Sharese's family—and why they occur at especially high rates in the African-American population.

Like the heart, the lungs show few age-related changes in functioning at rest, but during physical exertion, respiratory volume decreases and breathing rate increases with age. Maximum vital capacity (amount of air that can be forced in and out of the lungs) declines by 10 percent per decade after age 25 (Mahanran et al., 1999; Wilkie et al., 2012). Connective tissue in the lungs, chest muscles, and ribs stiffens with age, making it more difficult for the lungs to expand to full volume (Smith & Cotter, 2008). Fortunately, under normal conditions, we use less than half our vital capacity. Nevertheless, aging of the lungs contributes to older adults' difficulty in meeting the body's oxygen needs while exercising.

Motor Performance

Declines in heart and lung functioning under conditions of exertion, combined with gradual muscle loss, lead to changes in motor performance. In most people, the impact of biological

aging on motor skills is difficult to separate from decreases in motivation and practice. Therefore, researchers study competitive athletes, who try to attain their very best performance in real life (Tanaka & Seals, 2003). As long as athletes continue intensive training, their attainments at each age approach the limits of what is biologically possible.

Many athletic skills peak between ages 20 and 35, then gradually decline. In several investigations, the mean ages for best performance of Olympic and professional athletes in a variety of sports were charted over time. Absolute performance in most events improved over the past century. Athletes continually set new world records, suggesting improved training methods. But ages of best performance remained relatively constant. Athletic tasks that require speed of limb movement, explosive strength, and gross-motor coordination—sprinting, jumping, and tennis—typically peak in the early twenties. Those that depend on endurance, arm–hand steadiness, and aiming—long-distance running, baseball, and golf—usually peak in the late twenties and early thirties (Bradbury, 2009; Schulz & Curnow, 1988). Because these skills require either stamina or precise motor control, they take longer to perfect.

Research on outstanding athletes tells us that the upper biological limit of motor capacity is reached in the first part of early adulthood. How quickly do athletic skills weaken in later years? Longitudinal research on master runners reveals that as long as practice continues, speed drops only slightly from the mid-thirties into the sixties, when performance falls off at an accelerating pace (see Figure 13.2) (Tanaka & Seals, 2003; Trappe, 2007). In the case of long-distance swimming—a non-weight-bearing exercise with a low incidence of injury—the decline in speed is even more gradual: The accelerating performance drop-off is delayed until the seventies (Tanaka & Seals, 1997).

In her early thirties, professional tennis champion Serena Williams recently became the oldest player to be ranked World No. 1 in the history of the Women's Tennis Association. Sustained training leads to adaptations in body structures that minimize motor decline into the sixties.

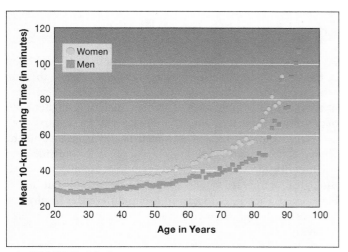

FIGURE 13.2 Ten-kilometer running times with advancing age, based on longitudinal performances of hundreds of master athletes. Runners maintain their speed into the mid-thirties, followed by modest increases in running times into the sixties, with a progressively steeper increase thereafter. (From H. Tanaka & D. R. Seals, 2003, "Dynamic Exercise Performance in Masters Athletes: Insight into the Effects of Primary Human Aging on Physiological Functional Capacity," *Journal of Applied Physiology, 5,* p. 2153. © The American Physiological Society (APS). All rights reserved. Adapted with permission.)

Indeed, sustained training leads to adaptations in body structures that minimize motor declines. For example, vital capacity is one-third greater in both younger and older people who participate actively in sports than in healthy inactive age-mates (Pimentel et al., 2003; Zaccagni, Onisto, & Gualdi-Russo, 2009). Training also slows muscle loss, increases speed and force of muscle contraction, and leads fast-twitch muscle fibers to be converted into slow-twitch fibers, which support excellent long-distance running performance and other endurance skills (Faulkner et al., 2007). In a study of hundreds of thousands of amateur marathon competitors, 25 percent of the 65- to 69-year-old runners were faster than 50 percent of the 20- to 54-year-old runners (Leyk et al., 2010). Yet many of the older runners had begun systematic marathon training only in the past five years.

In sum, although athletic skills are at their best in early adulthood, biological aging accounts for only a small part of age-related declines until advanced old age. Lower levels of performance by healthy people into their sixties and seventies largely reflect reduced capacities resulting from adaptation to a less physically demanding lifestyle.

Immune System

The immune response is the combined work of specialized cells that neutralize or destroy antigens (foreign substances) in the body. Two types of white blood cells play vital roles. *T cells,* which originate in the bone marrow and mature in the thymus (a small gland located in the upper part of the chest), attack antigens directly. *B cells,* manufactured in the bone marrow, secrete antibodies into the bloodstream that multiply, capture antigens, and permit the blood system to destroy them. Because

receptors on their surfaces recognize only a single antigen, T and B cells come in great variety. They join with additional cells to produce immunity.

The capacity of the immune system to offer protection against disease increases through adolescence and declines after age 20. The trend is partly due to changes in the thymus, which is largest during the teenage years, then shrinks until it is barely detectable by age 50. As a result, production of thymic hormones is reduced, and the thymus is less able to promote full maturity and differentiation of T cells (Fülöp et al., 2011). Because B cells release far more antibodies when T cells are present, the immune response is compromised further.

Withering of the thymus is not the only reason that the body gradually becomes less effective in warding off illness. The immune system interacts with the nervous and endocrine systems. For example, psychological stress can weaken the immune response. During final exams, for example, Sharese was less resistant to colds. And in the month after her father died, she had great difficulty recovering from the flu. Conflict-ridden relationships, caring for an ill aging parent, sleep deprivation, and chronic depression can also reduce immunity (Fagundes et al., 2011; Robles & Carroll, 2011). And physical stress—from pollution, allergens, poor nutrition, and rundown housing—undermines immune functioning throughout adulthood (Friedman & Lawrence, 2002). When physical and psychological stressors combine, the risk of illness is magnified.

The link between stress and illness makes sense when we consider that stress hormones mobilize the body for action, whereas the immune response is fostered by reduced activity. But this also means that increased difficulty coping with physical and psychological stress can contribute to age-related declines in immune system functioning.

Reproductive Capacity

Sharese was born when her mother was in her early twenties. At the same age a generation later, Sharese was still single and entering graduate school. Many people believe that pregnancy during the twenties is ideal, not only because of lower risk of miscarriage and chromosomal disorders (see Chapter 2) but also because younger parents have more energy to keep up with active children. Nevertheless, as Figure 13.3 on page 438 reveals, first births to women in their thirties have increased greatly over the past three decades. Many people are delaying childbearing until their education is complete, their careers are well-established, and they know they can support a child.

Nevertheless, reproductive capacity does decline with age. Between ages 15 and 29, 11 percent of U.S. married childless women report fertility problems, a figure that rises to 14 percent among 30- to 34-year-olds and to over 40 percent among 35- to 44-year-olds, when the success of reproductive technologies drops sharply (see page 54 in Chapter 2) (U.S. Department of Health and Human Services, 2012b). Because the uterus shows no consistent changes from the late thirties through the forties, the decline in female fertility is largely due to reduced number and quality of ova. In many mammals, including humans, a

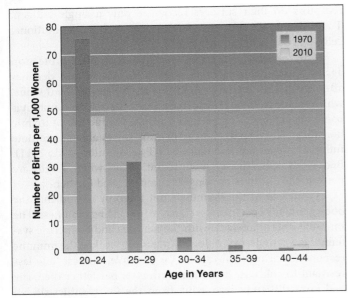

FIGURE 13.3 **First births to American women of different ages in 1970 and 2010.** The birthrate decreased during this period for women 20 to 24 years of age, whereas it increased for women 25 years of age and older. For women in their thirties, the birthrate increased six-fold, and for those in their early forties, it doubled. Similar trends have occurred in other industrialized nations. (From U.S. Census Bureau, 2012b.)

certain level of reserve ova in the ovaries is necessary for conception (Balasch, 2010; Djahanbakhch, Ezzati, & Zosmer, 2007). Some women have normal menstrual cycles but do not conceive because their reserve of ova is too low.

In males, semen volume, sperm motility, and percentage of normal sperm decrease gradually after age 35, contributing to reduced fertility rates in older men (Lambert, Masson, & Fisch, 2006). Although there is no best time in adulthood to begin parenthood, individuals who postpone childbearing until their late thirties or their forties risk having fewer children than they desired or none at all.

ASK YOURSELF

REVIEW How does research on life conditions that accelerate telomere shortening illustrate the concept of epigenesis, discussed in Chapter 2 (see pages 73–75)?

CONNECT How do heredity and environment jointly contribute to age-related changes in cardiovascular, respiratory, and immune system functioning?

APPLY Penny is a long-distance runner for her college track team. What factors will affect Penny's running performance 30 years from now?

REFLECT Before reading this chapter, had you thought of early adulthood as a period of aging? Why is it important for young adults to be aware of influences on biological aging?

Health and Fitness

Figure 13.4 displays leading causes of death in early adulthood in the United States. Death rates for all causes exceed those of other industrialized nations (OECD, 2012b). The difference is likely due to a combination of factors, including higher rates of poverty and extreme obesity, more lenient gun-control policies, and historical lack of universal health insurance in the United States. In later chapters, we will see that homicide rates decline with age, while disease and physical disability rates rise. Biological aging clearly contributes to this trend. But, as we have noted, wide individual and group differences in physical changes are linked to environmental risks and health-related behaviors.

SES variations in health over the lifespan reflect these influences. With the transition from childhood to adulthood, health inequalities associated with SES increase; income, education, and occupational status show strong, continuous relationships with almost every disease and health indicator (Braveman et al., 2010; Smith & Infurna, 2011). Furthermore, SES largely accounts for the sizable health advantage of white over ethnic minority adults in the United States (Phuong, Frank, & Finch, 2012). Consequently, improving socioeconomic conditions is essential for closing ethnic gaps in health.

Health-related circumstances and habits—stressful life events, crowding, pollution, diet, exercise, overweight and obesity, substance abuse, jobs with numerous health risks, availability of supportive social relationships, and (in the United States) access to affordable health care—underlie SES health disparities (Ertel, Glymour, & Berkman, 2009; Smith & Infurna, 2011). Furthermore, poor health in childhood, which is linked to low SES, affects health in adulthood. The overall influence of

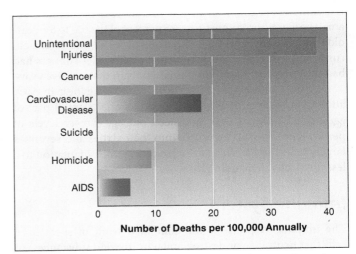

FIGURE 13.4 **Leading causes of death between 25 and 44 years of age in the United States.** Nearly half of unintentional injuries are motor vehicle accidents. As later chapters will reveal, unintentional injuries remain a leading cause of death at older ages, rising sharply in late adulthood. Rates of cancer and cardiovascular disease rise steadily during middle and late adulthood. (Adapted from U.S. Department of Health and Human Services, 2011b.)

SES variations in health in the United States—larger than in other industrialized nations— are in part due to lack of access to affordable health care. This Los Angeles free clinic helps address the problem by offering preventive services, including eye exams, to over 1,200 patients per day.

childhood factors lessens if SES improves. But in most instances, child and adult SES remain fairly consistent, exerting a cumulative impact that amplifies SES differences in health with age (Herd, Robert, & House, 2011).

Why are SES variations in health and mortality larger in the United States than in other industrialized nations? Besides lack of universal health insurance, low-income and poverty-stricken U.S. families are financially less well-off than families classified in these ways in other countries (Wilkinson & Pickett, 2006). In addition, SES groups are more likely to be segregated by neighborhood in the United States, resulting in greater inequalities in environmental factors that affect health, such as housing, pollution, education, and community services.

These findings reveal, once again, that the living conditions that nations and communities provide combine with those that people create for themselves to affect physical aging. Because the incidence of health problems is much lower during the twenties and thirties than later on, early adulthood is an excellent time to prevent later problems. In the following sections, we take up a variety of major health concerns—nutrition, exercise, substance abuse, sexuality, and psychological stress.

Nutrition

Bombarded with advertising claims and an extraordinary variety of food choices, adults find it increasingly difficult to make wise dietary decisions. An abundance of food, combined with a heavily scheduled life, means that most Americans eat because

they feel like it or because it is time to do so rather than to maintain the body's functions (Donatelle, 2012). As a result, many eat the wrong types and amounts of food. Overweight and obesity and a high-fat diet are widespread nutritional problems with long-term consequences for adult health.

Overweight and Obesity. In Chapter 9, we noted that obesity (a greater than 20 percent increase over average body weight, based on age, sex, and physical build) has increased dramatically in many Western nations, and it is on the rise in the developing world as well. Among adults, a body mass index (BMI) of 25 to 29 constitutes overweight, a BMI of 30 or greater (amounting to 30 or more excess pounds) constitutes obesity. Today, 36 percent of U.S. adults are obese. The rate rises to 38 percent among Hispanics, 39 percent among Native Americans, and 50 percent among African Americans (Flegal et al., 2012). The overall prevalence of obesity is similar among men and women.

Overweight—a less extreme but nevertheless unhealthy condition—affects an additional 33 percent of Americans. Combine the rates of overweight and obesity and the total, 69 percent, makes Americans the heaviest people in the world. *TAKE A MOMENT...* Notice in these figures that the U.S. obesity rate now exceeds its rate of overweight, a blatant indicator of the growing severity of the problem.

Recall from Chapter 9 that overweight children are very likely to become overweight adults. But a substantial number of people show large weight gains in adulthood, most often between ages 25 and 40. And young adults who were already overweight or obese typically get heavier, leading obesity rates to rise steadily between ages 20 and 65 (Flegel et al., 2012).

Causes and Consequences. As noted in Chapter 9, heredity makes some people more vulnerable to obesity than others. But environmental pressures underlie the rising rates of obesity in industrialized nations: With the decline in need for physical labor in the home and workplace, our lives have become more sedentary. Meanwhile, the average number of calories and amount of sugar and fat consumed by Americans rose over most of the twentieth and early twenty-first century, with a sharp increase after 1970 (see the Social Issues: Health box on pages 440–441).

Adding some weight between ages 25 and 50 is a normal part of aging because **basal metabolic rate (BMR),** the amount of energy the body uses at complete rest, gradually declines as the number of active muscle cells (which create the greatest energy demand) drops off. But excess weight is strongly associated with serious health problems (see page 291 in Chapter 9)—including type 2 diabetes, heart disease, and many forms of cancer—and with early death.

Furthermore, overweight adults suffer enormous social discrimination. Compared with their normal-weight agemates, they are less likely to find mates, be rented apartments, receive financial aid for college, or be offered jobs. And they report frequent mistreatment by family members, peers, co-workers, and health professionals (Ickes, 2011; Puhl, Heuer, & Brownell,

Social Issues: Health

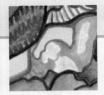

The Obesity Epidemic: How Americans Became the Heaviest People in the World

In the late 1980s, obesity in the United States started to soar. As the maps in Figure 13.5 show, it quickly engulfed the nation and has continued to expand. The epidemic also spread to other Western nations and, more recently, to developing countries. For example, as noted in Chapter 9, obesity was rare in China 30 years ago, but today it affects 7 percent of Chinese children and adolescents and 11 percent of adults; an additional 15 percent of the Chinese population is overweight (Xi et al., 2012). Yet China is a low-prevalence country! Worldwide, overweight afflicts more than 1.4 billion adults, 500 million of whom are obese. American Samoa leads the globe in overweight and obesity, with a staggering 94 percent of people affected (World Health Organization, 2013a). Among industrialized nations, no country matches the United States in prevalence of this life-threatening condition.

A Changing Food Environment and Lifestyle

Several societal factors have encouraged widespread rapid weight gain:

- *Availability of cheap commercial fat and sugar.* The 1970s saw two massive changes in the U.S. food economy: (1) the discovery and mass production of high-fructose corn syrup, a sweetener six times as sweet as ordinary sugar and therefore far less expensive; and (2) the importing from Malaysia of large quantities of palm oil, which is lower in cost than other vegetable oils and also tastier because of its high saturated fat content. Use of corn syrup and palm oil in soft drinks and calorie-dense convenience foods lowered production costs for these items, launching a new era of "cheap, abundant, and tasty calories" (Critser, 2003).

- *Portion supersizing.* Fast-food chains discovered a successful strategy for attracting customers: increasing portion sizes substantially and prices just a little for foods that had become inexpensive to produce. Customers thronged to buy "value meals," jumbo burgers and burritos, and 20-ounce Cokes (Critser, 2003). Research reveals that when presented with larger portions, individuals 2 years and older increase their intake, on average, by 25 to 30 percent (Fisher, Rolls, & Birch, 2003; Steenhuis & Vermeer, 2009).

- *Increasingly busy lives.* Between the 1970s and 1990s, women entered the labor force in record numbers, and the average amount of time Americans worked increased dramatically. Today, 86 percent of employed U.S. men and 66 percent of employed women work over 40 hours per week—substantially more than in most other countries (Schor, 2002; United Nations, 2012). As time for meal preparation shrank, eating out increased (Midlin, Jenkins, & Law, 2009). In addition, Americans became frequent snackers, tempted by a growing assortment of high-calorie snack foods on supermarket shelves. And the number of calories Americans consumed away from home doubled, with dietary fat increasing from 19 to 38 percent (Nielsen & Popkin, 2003).

- *Declining rates of physical activity.* During the 1980s, physical activity, which had risen since the 1960s, started to fall as Americans spent more time in sedentary transportation and jobs—driving to and from work and sitting throughout the work day, often behind a computer. At home, a rise in TV viewing to an average of more than four hours per day has been linked to weight gain in adults and children alike (Foster, Gore, & West, 2006).

Combating the Obesity Epidemic

Obesity is responsible for $150 billion in health expenditures and an estimated 2010). Since the mid-1990s, discrimination experienced by overweight Americans has increased, with serious physical and mental health consequences. Weight stigma triggers anxiety, depression, and low self-esteem, which increase the chances that that unhealthy eating behaviors will persist and even worsen (Puhl & Heuer, 2010). The widespread but incorrect belief, perpetuated by the media, that obesity is a personal choice promotes negative stereotyping of obese persons.

Treatment. Because obesity climbs in early and middle adulthood, treatment for adults should begin as soon as possible—preferably in the early twenties. Even moderate weight loss reduces health problems substantially (Poobalan et al., 2010). But successful intervention is difficult. Most individuals who start a weight-loss program return to their original weight, and often to a higher weight, within two years (Vogels, Diepvens, & Westerterp-Plantenga, 2005). The high rate of failure is partly due to limited evidence on just how obesity disrupts the complex neural, hormonal, and metabolic factors that maintain a normal body-weight set point. Until more information is available, researchers are examining the features of treatments and participants associated with greater success. The following elements promote lasting behavior change:

- *A lifestyle change to a nutritious diet lower in calories, sugar, and fat, plus regular exercise.* To lose weight, Sharese sharply reduced calories, sugar, and fat in her diet and exercised regularly. The precise balance of dietary protein, carbohydrates, and fats that best helps adults lose weight is a matter of heated debate. Although scores of diet books offer different recommendations, no clear-cut evidence exists for

300,000 premature deaths per year in the United States alone (Finkelstein et al., 2009; Flegal et al., 2007). Because multiple social and economic influences have altered the environment to promote this epidemic, broad societal efforts are needed to combat it. Effective policies include

- Government funding to support massive public education efforts about healthy eating and physical activity

- A high priority placed on building parks and recreation centers and replacing unhealthy fast-food outlets with access to healthy, affordable foods in low-income neighborhoods, where overweight and obesity are highest
- Laws that mandate prominent posting of the calorie, sugar, and fat content of foods sold in restaurants, movie theaters, and convenience stores

- Incentives to schools and workplaces for promoting healthy eating and daily exercise and for offering weight-management programs
- Increased obesity-related medical coverage in government-sponsored health insurance programs for low-income families

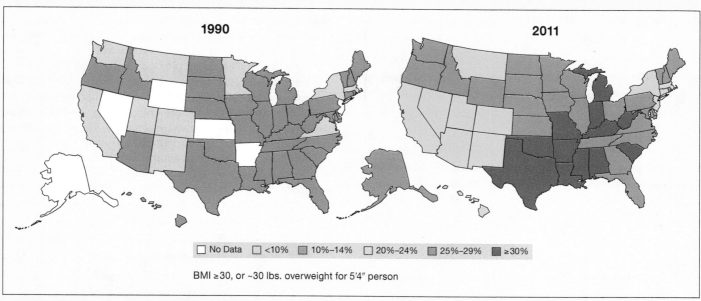

FIGURE 13.5 Obesity trends among U.S. adults, 1990 and 2011. The maps show that obesity has increased sharply. In 2011, twelve states (Alabama, Arkansas, Indiana, Kentucky, Louisiana, Michigan, Mississippi, Missouri, Oklahoma, South Carolina, Texas, and West Virginia) had rates equal to or greater than 30 percent. (From Centers for Disease Control and Prevention, 2012a.)

the long-term superiority of one approach over others (Tsai & Wadden, 2005).

Research does confirm that a permanent lifestyle alteration that restricts calorie intake and fat (to no more than 20 to 30 percent of calories) and that increases physical activity is essential for reducing the impact of a genetic tendency toward overweight. But most people mistakenly believe that only temporary lifestyle changes are needed (MacLean et al., 2011).

- *Training participants to keep an accurate record of food intake and body weight.* About 30 to 35 percent of obese people sincerely believe they eat less than they do. And although they have continued to gain weight, American adults generally report weight losses—suggesting that they are in denial about the seriousness of their weight condition

(Wetmore & Mokdad, 2012). Furthermore, from 25 to 45 percent report problems with binge eating—a behavior associated with weight-loss failure (Blaine & Rodman, 2007). As Sharese recognized how often she ate when not actually hungry and regularly recorded her weight, she was better able to limit food intake.

- *Social support.* Group or individual counseling and encouragement from friends and relatives help sustain weight-loss efforts by fostering self-esteem and self-efficacy (Poobalan et al., 2010). Once Sharese decided to act, with the support of her family and a weight-loss counselor, she felt better about herself even before the first pounds were shed.

- *Teaching problem-solving skills.* Most overweight adults do not realize that because their body has adapted to overweight, difficult periods requiring high self-control and

© RADIUS IMAGES/ALAMY

A permanent lifestyle change that includes an increase in physical activity is essential for treating obesity.

patience are inevitable in successful weight loss (MacLean et al., 2011). Acquiring cognitive and behavioral strategies for coping with tempting situations and periods of slowed progress is associated with long-term change (Cooper & Fairburn, 2002). Weight-loss maintainers are more likely than individuals who relapse to be conscious of their behavior, to use social support, and to confront problems directly.

- *Extended intervention.* Longer treatments (from 25 to 40 weeks) that include the components listed here grant people time to develop new habits.

Although many Americans on weight-reduction diets are overweight, about one-third of dieters are within normal range (Mokdad et al., 2001). Recall from Chapter 11 that the high value placed on thinness creates unrealistic expectations about desirable body weight and contributes to anorexia and bulimia, dangerous eating disorders that remain common in early adulthood (see pages 372–373). Throughout adulthood, both underweight and obesity are associated with increased mortality (Ringbäck, Eliasson, & Rosén, 2008). A sensible body weight—neither too low nor too high—predicts physical and psychological health and longer life.

Dietary Fat. During college, Sharese altered the diet of her childhood and adolescent years, sharply limiting red meat, eggs, butter, and fried foods. U.S. national dietary recommendations include reducing fat to 30 percent of total caloric intake, with no more than 7 percent made up of saturated fat, which generally comes from meat and dairy products and is solid at room temperature (U.S. Department of Agriculture, 2011a). Many researchers believe that dietary fat plays a role in the age-related

rise in breast cancer and (when it includes large amounts of red meat) is linked to colon cancer (Ferguson, 2010; Turner, 2011). But the main reasons for limiting dietary fat are the strong connection of total fat with obesity and of saturated fat with cardiovascular disease (Hooper et al., 2012). Nevertheless, despite a slight drop in fat consumption, most American adults eat too much.

Moderate fat consumption is essential for normal body functioning. But when we consume too much fat, especially saturated fat, some is converted to cholesterol, which accumulates as plaque on the arterial walls in atherosclerosis. Earlier in this chapter, we noted that atherosclerosis is determined by multiple biological and environmental factors. But excess fat consumption (along with other societal conditions) is an important contributor to the high rate of heart disease in the U.S. black population. As Figure 13.6 shows, when researchers compared Africans in West Africa, the Caribbean, and the United States (the historic path of the slave trade), dietary fat increased, and so did high blood pressure and heart disease (Luke et al., 2001).

The best rule of thumb is to eat less fat of all kinds, replacing saturated fat with unsaturated fat (which is derived from vegetables or fish and is liquid at room temperature) and with complex carbohydrates (whole grains, fruits, and vegetables), which are beneficial to cardiovascular health and protective against colon cancer (Kaczmarczyk, Miller, & Freund, 2012). Furthermore, regular exercise can reduce the harmful influence of saturated fat because it creates chemical byproducts that help eliminate cholesterol from the body.

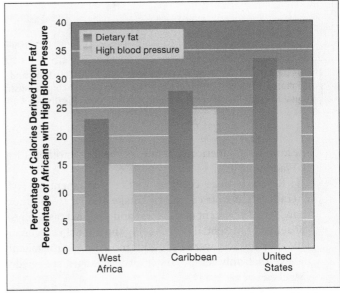

FIGURE 13.6 Dietary fat and prevalence of high blood pressure among Africans in West Africa, the Caribbean, and the United States. The three regions represent the historic path of the slave trade and, therefore, have genetically similar populations. As dietary fat increases, high blood pressure and heart disease rise. Both are particularly high among African Americans. (Adapted from Luke et al., 2001.)

Exercise

Three times a week, over the noon hour, Sharese delighted in running, making her way to a wooded trail that cut through a picturesque area of the city. Regular exercise kept her fit and slim, and she noticed that she caught fewer respiratory illnesses than in previous years, when she had been sedentary and overweight. As Sharese explained to a friend, "Exercise gives me a positive outlook and calms me down. Afterward, I feel a burst of energy that gets me through the day."

Although most Americans are aware of the health benefits of exercise, only 47 percent engage in the nationally recommended 150 minutes per week of at least moderately intense leisure-time physical activity. And just 24 percent engage in the recommended two sessions per week of resistance exercises, which place a moderately stressful load on each of the major muscle groups. Over half of Americans are inactive, with no regular brief sessions of even light activity (U.S. Department of Health and Human Services, 2011c). More women than men are inactive. And inactivity is greater among low-SES adults, who live in less safe neighborhoods, have more health problems, experience less social support for exercising regularly, and feel less personal control over their health.

Regular exercise of at least moderate intensity predicts a healthier, longer life. Participants in this kickboxing class reap both physical and mental health benefits.

LOOK AND LISTEN

Contact your local parks and recreation department to find out what community supports and services exist to increase adult physical activity. Are any special efforts made to reach low-SES adults? ●

Besides reducing body fat and building muscle, exercise fosters resistance to disease. Frequent bouts of moderate-intensity exercise enhance the immune response, lowering the risk of colds or flu and promoting faster recovery from these illnesses (Donatelle, 2012). Furthermore, animal and human evidence indicates that physical activity is linked to reduced incidence of several types of cancer, with the strongest findings for breast and colon cancer (Anzuini, Battistella, & Izzotti, 2011). Physically active people are also less likely to develop diabetes and cardiovascular disease (Bassuk & Manson, 2005). If they do, these illnesses typically occur later and are less severe than among their inactive agemates.

How does exercise help prevent these serious illnesses? First, it reduces the incidence of obesity—a risk factor for heart disease, diabetes, and cancer. In addition, people who exercise probably adopt other healthful behaviors, thereby lowering the risk of diseases associated with high-fat diets, alcohol consumption, and smoking. In animal studies, exercise directly inhibits growth of cancerous tumors—beyond the impact of diet, body fat, and the immune response (de Lima et al., 2008). Exercise also promotes cardiovascular functioning by strengthening the heart muscle, decreasing blood pressure, and producing a form of "good cholesterol" (high-density lipoproteins, or HDLs) that helps remove "bad cholesterol" (low-density lipoproteins, or LDLs) from the artery walls (Donatelle, 2012).

Yet another way that exercise guards against illness is through its mental health benefits. Physical activity reduces anxiety and depression and improves mood, alertness, and energy. Furthermore, EEG and fMRI evidence indicates that exercise enhances neural activity in the cerebral cortex, and it improves overall cognitive functioning (Carek, Laibstain, & Carek, 2011; Etnier & Labban, 2012; Hillman, Erickson, & Kramer, 2008). The impact of exercise on a "positive outlook," as Sharese expressed it, is most obvious just after a workout and can last for several hours (Acevedo, 2012). The stress-reducing properties of exercise undoubtedly strengthen immunity to disease. And as physical activity enhances cognitive functioning and psychological well-being, it promotes on-the-job productivity, self-esteem, ability to cope with stress, and life satisfaction.

When we consider the evidence as a whole, it is not surprising that physical activity is associated with substantially lower death rates from all causes. The contribution of exercise to longevity cannot be accounted for by preexisting illness in inactive people. In a Danish longitudinal study of a nationally representative sample of 7,000 healthy 20- to 79-year-olds followed over several decades, mortality was lower among those who increased their leisure-time physical activity from low to either moderate or high than among those who remained consistently inactive (Schnohr, Scharling, & Jensen, 2003).

How much exercise is recommended for a healthier, happier, and longer life? Moderately intense physical activity—for example, 30 minutes of brisk walking—on most days leads to health benefits for previously inactive people. Adults who exercise at greater intensity—enough to build up a sweat—derive even greater protection (American College of Sports Medicine, 2011). Regular, vigorous exercisers show large reductions in risk of cardiovascular disease, diabetes, colon cancer, and obesity.

Substance Abuse

Alcohol and drug use peaks among U.S. 19- to 25-year-olds and then declines steadily with age. Eager to try a wide range of experiences before settling down to the responsibilities of adulthood, young people of this age are more likely than younger or older individuals to smoke cigarettes, chew tobacco, use marijuana, and take stimulants to enhance cognitive or physical performance (U.S. Department of Health and Human Services, 2011e). Binge drinking, driving under the influence, and experimentation with prescription drugs (such as OxyContin, a highly addictive painkiller) and "party drugs" (such as LSD and MDMA, or Ecstasy) also increase, at times with tragic consequences. Risks include brain damage, lasting impairments in mental functioning, and unintentional injury and death (Montoya et al., 2002; National Institute on Drug Abuse, 2012).

Furthermore, when alcohol and drug taking become chronic, they intensify the psychological problems that underlie addiction. As many as 12 percent of 19- to 25-year-old men and 6 percent of women are substance abusers (U.S. Department of Health and Human Services, 2011e). Return to Chapter 11, pages 380–381, to review factors that lead to alcohol and drug abuse in adolescence. The same personal and situational conditions are predictive in the adult years. Cigarette smoking and alcohol consumption are the most commonly abused substances.

Cigarette Smoking. Dissemination of information on the harmful effects of cigarette smoking has helped reduce its prevalence among U.S. adults from 40 percent in 1965 to 19 percent in 2010 (Centers for Disease Control and Prevention, 2012e). Still, smoking has declined very slowly, and most of the drop is among college graduates, with very little change for those who did not finish high school. Furthermore, although more men than women smoke, the gender gap is much smaller today than in the past, reflecting a sharp increase in smoking among young women who did not finish high school. Smoking among college students has also risen—for students of both sexes and of diverse ethnicities. More than 90 percent of men and 85 percent of women who smoke started before age 21 (U.S. Department of Health and Human Services, 2011e). And the earlier people start smoking, the greater their daily cigarette consumption and likelihood of continuing, an important reason that preventive efforts with adolescents and young adults are vital.

The ingredients of cigarette smoke—nicotine, tar, carbon monoxide, and other chemicals—leave their damaging mark throughout the body. As smokers inhale, oxygen delivery to tissues is reduced, and heart rate and blood pressure rise. Over time, exposure to toxins and insufficient oxygen result in damage to the retina of the eye; constriction of blood vessels leading to painful vascular disease; skin abnormalities, including premature aging, poor wound healing, and hair loss; decline in bone mass; decrease in reserve ova, uterine abnormalities, and earlier menopause in women; and reduced sperm count and higher rate of sexual impotence in men (Dechanet et al., 2011; Freiman et al., 2004; Thornton et al., 2005). Other deadly outcomes include increased risk of heart attack, stroke, acute leukemia, melanoma, and cancer of the mouth, throat, larynx, esophagus, lungs, stomach, pancreas, kidneys, and bladder.

Cigarette smoking is the single most important preventable cause of death in industrialized nations. One out of every three young people who become regular smokers will die from a smoking-related disease, and the vast majority will suffer from at least one serious illness (Adhikari et al., 2009). The chances of premature death rise with the number of cigarettes consumed. At the same time, the benefits of quitting include return of most disease risks to nonsmoker levels within one to ten years. In a study of 1.2 million British women, those who had been regular smokers but stopped before they reached age 45 avoided 90 percent of the elevated risk of premature death from cigarettes (Pirie et al., 2012). And those who quit before age 35 avoided 97 percent of the added risk.

Nearly 70 percent of U.S. smokers say they want to quit completely, but less than half who saw their doctors in the past year received advice to do so (Centers for Disease Control and Prevention, 2012e). Although millions have stopped without help, those who use cessation aids (for example, nicotine gum, nasal spray, or patches, designed to reduce dependency gradually) or enter treatment programs often fail: As many as 90 percent start smoking again within six months (Aveyard & Raw, 2012). Unfortunately, too few treatments last long enough, effectively combine counseling with medications that reduce nicotine withdrawal symptoms, and teach skills for avoiding relapse.

Alcohol. National surveys reveal that about 10 percent of men and 3 percent of women in the United States are heavy drinkers (U.S. Department of Health and Human Services, 2011e). About one-third of them are *alcoholics*—people who cannot limit their alcohol use. In men, alcoholism usually begins in the teens and early twenties and worsens over the following decade. In women, its onset is typically later, in the twenties and thirties, and its course is more variable. Many alcoholics are also addicted to other substances, including nicotine and illegal mood-altering drugs.

Twin and adoption studies support a genetic contribution to alcoholism. Genes moderating alcohol metabolism and those influencing impulsivity and sensation seeking (temperamental traits linked to alcohol addiction) are involved (Buscemi & Turchi, 2011). But whether a person comes to deal with life's problems through drinking is greatly affected by environment: Half of alcoholics have no family history of problem drinking. Alcoholism crosses SES and ethnic lines but is higher in some groups than others (Schuckit, 2009). In cultures where alcohol is a traditional part of religious or ceremonial activities, people are less likely to abuse it. Where access to alcohol is carefully controlled and viewed as a sign of adulthood, dependency is more likely—factors that may, in part, explain why college students drink more heavily than young people not enrolled in college (Slutske et al., 2004). Poverty, hopelessness, and a history of physical or sexual abuse in childhood are among factors that sharply increase the risk of excessive drinking (Donatelle, 2012; Lown et al., 2011; U.S. Department of Health and Human Services, 2011e).

PHOTO RESEARCHERS/GETTY IMAGES

In cultures where alcohol is a traditional part of religious or ceremonial activities, people are less likely to abuse it. For Jewish families, holiday celebrations, such as this Passover Seder, include blessing and drinking wine.

Alcohol acts as a depressant, impairing the brain's ability to control thought and action. In a heavy drinker, it relieves anxiety at first but then induces it as the effects wear off, so the alcoholic drinks again. Chronic alcohol use does widespread physical damage. Its best-known complication is liver disease, but it is also linked to cardiovascular disease, inflammation of the pancreas, irritation of the intestinal tract, bone marrow problems, disorders of the blood and joints, and some forms of cancer. Over time, alcohol causes brain damage, leading to confusion, apathy, inability to learn, and impaired memory (O'Connor, 2012). The costs to society are enormous. About 30 percent of fatal motor vehicle crashes in the United States involve drivers who have been drinking (U.S. Department of Transportation, 2012). Nearly half of convicted felons are alcoholics, and about half of police activities in large cities involve alcohol-related offenses (McKim & Hancock, 2013). Alcohol frequently plays a part in sexual coercion, including date rape, and in domestic violence.

The most successful treatments combine personal and family counseling, group support, and aversion therapy (use of medication that produces a physically unpleasant reaction to alcohol, such as nausea and vomiting). Alcoholics Anonymous, a community support approach, helps many people exert greater control over their lives through the encouragement of others with similar problems. Nevertheless, breaking an addiction that has dominated a person's life is difficult; about 50 percent of alcoholics relapse within a few months (Kirshenbaum, Olsen, & Bickel, 2009).

Sexuality

At the end of high school, about 65 percent of U.S. young people have had sexual intercourse; by age 25, nearly all have done so, and the gender and SES differences that were apparent in adolescence (see page 374 in Chapter 11) have diminished (U.S. Department of Health and Human Services, 2012d). Compared

with earlier generations, contemporary adults display a wider range of sexual choices and lifestyles, including cohabitation, marriage, extramarital experiences, and orientation toward a heterosexual or homosexual partner. In this chapter, we explore the attitudes, behaviors, and health concerns that arise as sexual activity becomes a regular event in young people's lives. In Chapter 14, we focus on the emotional side of close relationships.

Heterosexual Attitudes and Behavior. One Friday evening, Sharese accompanied her roommate Heather to a young singles bar, where two young men soon joined them. Faithful to her boyfriend, Ernie, whom she had met in college and who worked in another city, Sharese remained aloof for the next hour. In contrast, Heather was talkative and gave one of the men, Rich, her phone number. The next weekend, Heather went out with Rich. On the second date, they had intercourse, but the romance lasted only a few weeks. Aware of Heather's more adventurous sex life, Sharese wondered whether her own was normal. Only after several months of dating exclusively had she and Ernie slept together.

Since the 1950s, public display of sexuality in movies, newspapers, magazines, and books has steadily increased, fostering the impression that Americans are more sexually active than ever before. What are contemporary adults' sexual attitudes and behaviors really like? Answers were difficult to find until the National Health and Social Life Survey, the first in-depth study of U.S. adults' sex lives based on a nationally representative sample, was carried out in the early 1990s. Nearly four out of five randomly chosen 18- to 59-year-olds agreed to participate— 3,400 in all. Findings were remarkably similar to those of surveys conducted at about the same time in France, Great Britain, and Finland, and to a more recent U.S. survey (Langer, 2004; Laumann et al., 1994; Michael et al., 1994).

Recall from Chapter 11 that the sex lives of most teenagers do not dovetail with exciting media images. The same is true of adults in Western nations. Although their sexual practices are diverse, they are far less sexually active than we have come to believe. Monogamous, emotionally committed couples like Sharese and Ernie are more typical (and more satisfied) than couples like Heather and Rich.

Sexual partners, whether dating, cohabiting, or married, tend to be similar in age (within five years), education, ethnicity, and (to a lesser extent) religion. In addition, people who establish lasting relationships often meet in conventional ways— through friends or family members, or at school or social events where people similar to themselves congregate. The powerful influence of social networks on sexual choice is adaptive. Sustaining an intimate relationship is easier when adults share interests and values and people they know approve of the match.

Over the past decade, the Internet has become an increasingly popular way to initiate relationships: More than one-third of single adults go to dating websites or other online venues in search of romantic partners. In a survey of a nationally representative sample of 4,000 Americans, most of whom were married or in a romantic relationship, 22 percent said they had met on the Internet, making it the second most common way

© MAMADUKE ST. JOHN/ALAMY

The Internet is an increasingly popular way to initiate romantic relationships. Here, young people attend a "speed dating" event, organized online, where they have brief conversations with potential partners.

to meet a partner, just behind meeting through friends (Finkel et al., 2012). In fact, knowing someone who has successfully engaged in Internet dating strongly predicts single adults' willingness to look for a partner on dating websites (Sautter, Tippett, & Morgan, 2010; Sprecher, 2011). As reports of dating success spread through social networks, use of Internet dating services is likely to increase further.

Nevertheless, the services of online dating sites sometimes undermine, rather than enhance, the chances of forming a successful romantic relationship. Relying on Internet dating profiles and computer-mediated communication omits aspects of direct social interaction that are vital for assessing one's compatibility with a potential partner. Especially when computer-mediated communication persists for a long time (six weeks or more), people form idealized impressions that often lead to disappointment at face-to-face meetings (Finkel et al., 2012; Ramirez & Zhang, 2007). Furthermore, having a large pool of potential partners from which to choose can promote a persistent "shopping mentality," which reduces online daters' willingness to make a commitment (Heino, Ellison, & Gibbs, 2010). Finally, the techniques that matching sites claim to use to pair partners—sophisticated analyses of information daters provide—have not demonstrated any greater success than conventional off-line means of introducing people.

Consistent with popular belief, Americans today have more sexual partners over their lifetimes than they did a generation ago. For example, one-third of adults over age 50 have had five or more partners, whereas half of 30- to 50-year-olds have accumulated that many in much less time. And although women are more opposed to casual sex then men, after excluding a small number of men (less than 3 percent) with a great many sexual partners, contemporary men and women differ little in average number of lifetime sexual partners (Langer,

2004). Why is this so? From an evolutionary perspective, contemporary effective contraception has permitted sexual activity with little risk of pregnancy, enabling women to have as many partners as men without risking the welfare of their offspring.

But when adults of any age are asked how many partners they have had in the past year, the usual reply (for about 70 percent) is one. What explains the trend toward more relationships in the context of sexual commitment? In the past, dating several partners was followed by marriage. Today, dating more often gives way to cohabitation, which leads either to marriage or to breakup. In addition, people are marrying later, and the divorce rate remains high. Together, these factors create more opportunities for new partners. Still, survey evidence indicates that most U.S. 18- to 29-year-olds want to settle down eventually with a mutually exclusive lifetime sexual partner (Arnett, 2012). In line with this goal, most people spend the majority of their lives with one partner.

How often do Americans have sex? Not nearly as frequently as the media would suggest. One-third of 18- to 59-year-olds have intercourse as often as twice a week, another third have it a few times a month, and the remaining third have it a few times a year or not at all. Three factors affect frequency of sexual activity: age, whether people are cohabiting or married, and how long the couple has been together. Single people have more partners, but this does not translate into more sex! Sexual activity increases through the twenties and (for men) the thirties as people either cohabit or marry. Then it declines, even though hormone levels have not changed much (Herbenick et al., 2010; Langer, 2004). The demands of daily life—working, commuting, taking care of home and children—are probably responsible. Despite the common assumption that sexual practices vary greatly across social groups, the patterns just described are unaffected by education, SES, or ethnicity.

Most adults say they are happy with their sex lives. For those in committed relationships, more than 80 percent report feeling "extremely physically and emotionally satisfied," a figure that rises to 88 percent for married couples. In contrast, as number of sex partners increases, satisfaction declines sharply. These findings challenge two stereotypes—that marriage is sexually dull and that people who engage in casual dating have the "hottest" sex (Paik, 2010). In actuality, individuals prone to unsatisfying relationships are more likely to prefer "hookups" or "friends with benefits."

A minority of U.S. adults—women more often than men—report persistent sexual problems. For women, the two most frequent difficulties are lack of interest in sex (39 percent) and inability to achieve orgasm (20 percent) (Shifren et al., 2008). Most often mentioned by men are climaxing too early (29 percent) and anxiety about performance (16 percent). Sexual difficulties are linked to low SES and psychological stress and are more common among people who are not married, have had more than five partners, and have experienced sexual abuse during childhood or (for women) sexual coercion in adulthood (Laumann, Paik, & Rosen, 1999). As these findings suggest, a history of unfavorable relationships and sexual experiences increases the risk of sexual dysfunction.

But overall, a completely untroubled physical experience is not essential for sexual happiness. Surveys of adults repeatedly show that satisfying sex involves more than technique; it is attained in the context of love, affection, and fidelity (Bancroft, 2002; Santtila et al., 2008). In sum, happiness with partnered sex is linked to an emotionally fulfilling relationship, good mental health, and overall contentment with life.

Homosexual Attitudes and Behavior. The majority of Americans support civil liberties and equal employment opportunities for gay men, lesbians, and bisexuals. And attitudes toward sex and romantic relationships between adults of the same sex have gradually become more accepting: Nearly half of U.S. adults say same-sex sexual relations are "not wrong at all" or only "sometimes wrong" and support same-sex marriage, and three-fourths favor same-sex civil unions (Pew Research Center, 2013; Smith, 2011b).

Homosexuals' political activism and greater openness about their sexual orientation have contributed to gains in acceptance. Exposure and interpersonal contact reduce negative attitudes. But perhaps because they are especially concerned with gender-role conformity, heterosexual men judge homosexuals (and especially gay men) more harshly than do heterosexual women (Herek, 2009). Also, the United States lags behind Western Europe in positive attitudes. Nations with greatest acceptance tend to have a greater proportion of highly educated, economically well-off citizens who are low in religiosity (Smith, 2011a).

An estimated 3.5 percent of U.S. men and women—more than 8 million adults—identify as lesbian, gay, or bisexual, with women substantially more likely than men to report a bisexual orientation. Estimates from national surveys conducted in Australia, Canada, and Western Europe tend to be lower, at 1.5 to 2 percent (Gates, 2011). But many people who are gay, lesbian, or bisexual do not report themselves as such in survey research. This unwillingness to answer questions, engendered by a climate of persecution, has limited researchers' access to

Gay and lesbian romantic partners, like heterosexual partners, tend to be similar in education and background. With greater openness and political activism, attitudes toward same-sex relationships have become more accepting.

information about the sex lives of gay men and lesbians. The little evidence available indicates that homosexual sex follows many of the same rules as heterosexual sex: People tend to seek out partners similar in education and background to themselves; partners in committed relationships have sex more often and are more satisfied; and the overall frequency of sex is modest (Laumann et al., 1994; Michael et al., 1994).

Homosexuals tend to live in or near large cities, where many others share their sexual orientation, or in college towns, where attitudes are more accepting. Living in small communities where prejudice is intense and no social network exists through which to find compatible homosexual partners is isolating, lonely, and predictive of mental health problems (Meyer, 2003).

People who identify themselves as gay or lesbian also tend to be well-educated (Mercer et al., 2007). In the National Health and Social Life Survey, twice as many college-educated as high-school-educated men and eight times as many college-educated as high-school-educated women reported a same-sex orientation. Although the reasons for these findings are not clear, they probably reflect greater social and sexual liberalism among the more highly educated and therefore greater willingness to disclose homosexuality.

Sexually Transmitted Diseases. In the United States, one in every four individuals is likely to contract a sexually transmitted disease (STD) at some point in life (U.S. Department of Health and Human Services, 2011b). Although the incidence is highest in adolescence, STDs continue to be prevalent in early adulthood. During the teens and twenties, people accumulate most of their sexual partners, and they often do not take appropriate precautions to prevent the spread of STDs (see page 377 in Chapter 11). The overall rate of STDs is higher among women than men because it is at least twice as easy for a man to infect a woman with any STD, including AIDS, than for a woman to infect a man.

Although AIDS, the most deadly STD, remains concentrated among gay men and intravenous drug abusers, many homosexuals have responded to its spread by changing their sexual practices—limiting number of sexual partners, choosing partners more carefully, and using latex condoms consistently and correctly. Heterosexuals at high risk due to a history of many partners have done the same. Still, the annual number of U.S. new HIV infections—about 48,000—has remained stable since the late 1990s, and AIDS remains the sixth-leading cause of death among U.S. young adults (refer to Figure 13.4 on page 438). The incidence of HIV-positive adults is higher in the United States than in any other industrialized nation (OECD, 2012b). The disease is spreading most rapidly through men having sex with men and through heterosexual contact in poverty-stricken minority groups, among whom high rates of intravenous drug abuse coexist with poor health, inadequate education, high life stress, and hopelessness (Centers for Disease Control and Prevention, 2012c). People overwhelmed by these problems are least likely to take preventive measures.

Yet AIDS can be contained and reduced—through sex education extending from childhood into adulthood and through access to health services, condoms, and clean needles and syringes for high-risk individuals. In view of the rise in AIDS among women, who currently account for one-fourth of cases in North America and Western Europe and more than half in developing countries, a special need exists for female-controlled preventive measures. Drug-based vaginal gels that kill or inactivate the virus have shown promising results and are undergoing further testing.

Sexual Coercion. After a long day of classes, Sharese flipped on the TV and caught a talk show on sex without consent. Karen, a 25-year-old woman, described her husband Mike pushing, slapping, verbally insulting, and forcing her to have sex. "It was a control thing," Karen explained tearfully. "He complained that I wouldn't always do what he wanted. I was confused and blamed myself. I didn't leave because I was sure he'd come after me and get more violent."

One day, as Karen was speaking long distance to her mother on the phone, Mike grabbed the receiver and shouted, "She's not the woman I married! I'll kill her if she doesn't shape up!" Alarmed, Karen's parents arrived by plane the next day to rescue her and helped her start divorce proceedings and get treatment.

An estimated 18 percent of U.S. women, sometime in their lives, have endured *rape*, legally defined as intercourse by force, by threat of harm, or when the victim is incapable of giving consent (because of mental illness, mental retardation, or alcohol consumption). About 45 percent of women have experienced other forms of sexual aggression. The majority of victims (eight out of ten) are under age 30 (Black et al., 2011; Schewe, 2007). Women are vulnerable to partners, acquaintances, and strangers, but in most instances their abusers are men they know well. Sexual coercion crosses SES and ethnic lines; people of all walks of life are offenders and victims.

In 2012, in New Delhi, India, the brutal gang rape of a 23-year-old student, who died a month later from her injuries, prompted candle-light vigils and other protests throughout the country. Participants demanded increased government and police action to prevent sexual violence against women.

Personal characteristics of the man with whom a woman is involved are far better predictors of her chances of becoming a victim than her own characteristics. Men who engage in sexual assault tend to be manipulative of others, lack empathy and remorse, pursue casual sexual relationships rather than emotional intimacy, approve of violence against women, and accept rape myths (such as "Women really want to be raped"). Perpetrators also tend to interpret women's social behaviors inaccurately, viewing friendliness as seductiveness, assertiveness as hostility, and resistance as desire (Abbey & Jacques-Tiura, 2011; Abbey & McAuslan, 2004). Furthermore, sexual abuse in childhood, promiscuity in adolescence, and alcohol abuse in adulthood are associated with sexual coercion. Approximately half of all sexual assaults take place while people are intoxicated (Black et al., 2011).

LOOK AND LISTEN

Obtain from your campus student services or police department the number of sexual assaults reported by students during the most recent year. What percentage involved alcohol? What prevention and intervention services does your college offer? ●

Cultural forces also contribute. When men are taught from an early age to be dominant, competitive, and aggressive and women to be submissive and cooperative, the themes of rape are reinforced. Societal acceptance of violence also sets the stage for rape, which typically occurs in relationships in which other forms of aggression are commonplace. Exposure to sexually aggressive pornography and other media images, which portray women desiring and enjoying the assault, also promote sexual coercion by dulling sensitivity to its harmful consequences.

About 7 percent of men have been victims of coercive sexual behavior. Although rape victims report mostly male perpetrators, women are largely responsible for other forms of sexual coercion against men (Black et al, 2011). Victimized men often say that women who committed these acts used threats of physical force or actual force, encouraged them to get drunk, or threatened to end the relationship unless they complied (Anderson & Savage, 2005). Unfortunately, authorities rarely recognize female-initiated forced sex as illegal, and few men report these crimes.

Consequences. Women's and men's psychological reactions to rape resemble those of survivors of extreme trauma. Immediate responses—shock, confusion, withdrawal, and psychological numbing—eventually give way to chronic fatigue, tension, disturbed sleep, depression, substance abuse, social anxiety, and suicidal thoughts (Black et al., 2011; Schewe, 2007). Victims of ongoing sexual coercion may fall into a pattern of extreme passivity and fear of taking any action.

One-third to one-half of female rape victims are physically injured. From 4 to 30 percent contract sexually transmitted diseases, and pregnancy results in about 5 percent of cases. Furthermore, victims of rape (and other sexual crimes) report more symptoms of illness across almost all body systems. And they are more likely to engage in negative health behaviors, including smoking and alcohol use (McFarlane et al., 2005; Schewe, 2007).

Applying What We Know

Preventing Sexual Coercion

Suggestion	Description
Reduce gender stereotyping and gender inequalities.	The roots of men's sexual coercion of women lie in the historically subordinate status of women. Unequal educational and employment opportunities keep women economically dependent on men and therefore poorly equipped to avoid partner violence. At the same time, increased public awareness that women sometimes commit sexually aggressive acts is needed.
Mandate treatment for men and women who physically or sexually assault their partners.	Ingredients of effective intervention include combating rape myths and inducing personal responsibility for violent behavior; teaching social awareness, social skills, and anger management; and developing a support system to prevent future attacks.
Expand interventions for children and adolescents who have witnessed violence between their parents.	Although most child witnesses to parental violence do not become involved in abusive relationships as adults, they are at increased risk.
Teach both men and women to take precautions that lower the risk of sexual assault.	Risk of sexual assault can be reduced by communicating sexual limits clearly to a date; developing supportive ties to neighbors; increasing the safety of the immediate environment (for example, installing deadbolt locks, checking the back seat of the car before entering); avoiding deserted areas; not walking alone after dark; and leaving parties where alcohol use is high.
Broaden definitions of rape to be gender-neutral.	In some U.S. states, where the definition of rape is limited to vaginal or anal penetration, a woman legally cannot rape a man. A broader definition is needed to encompass women as both victims and perpetrators of sexual aggression.

Sources: Anderson & Savage, 2005; Schewe, 2007.

Prevention and Treatment. Many female rape victims are less fortunate than Karen because anxiety about provoking another attack keeps them from confiding even in trusted family members and friends. A variety of community services, including safe houses, crisis hotlines, support groups, and legal assistance, exist to help women take refuge from abusive partners, but most are underfunded and cannot reach out to everyone in need. Practically no services are available for victimized men, who are often too embarrassed to come forward.

The trauma induced by rape is severe enough that therapy is important—both individual treatment to reduce anxiety and depression and group sessions where contact with other survivors helps counter isolation and self-blame (Street, Bell, & Ready, 2011). Other critical features that foster recovery include

- *Routine screening for victimization* during health-care visits to ensure referral to community services and protection from future harm
- *Validation of the experience,* by acknowledging that many others have been physically and sexually assaulted by intimate partners; that such assaults lead to a wide range of persisting symptoms, are illegal and inappropriate, and should not be tolerated; and that the trauma can be overcome
- *Safety planning,* even when the abuser is no longer present, to prevent recontact and reassault. This includes information about how to obtain police protection, legal intervention, a safe shelter, and other aid should a rape survivor be at risk again.

Finally, many steps can be taken at the level of the individual, the community, and society to prevent sexual coercion. Some are listed in Applying What We Know above.

Psychological Stress

A final health concern, threaded throughout previous sections, has such a broad impact that it merits a comment of its own. Psychological stress, measured in terms of adverse social conditions, traumatic experiences, negative life events, or daily hassles, is related to a wide variety of unfavorable health outcomes—both unhealthy behaviors and clear physical consequences. And recall from earlier chapters that intense, persistent stress, from the prenatal period on, disrupts the brain's inherent ability to manage stress, with long-term consequences. For individuals with childhood histories of stress, continuing stressful experiences combine with an impaired capacity to cope with stress, heightening the risk of adult health impairments.

As SES decreases, exposure to diverse stressors rises—an association that likely plays an important role in the strong connection between low SES and poor health (see pages 438–439) (Chandola & Marmot, 2011). Chronic stress is linked to overweight and obesity, diabetes, hypertension, and atherosclerosis. And in susceptible individuals, acute stress can trigger cardiac events, including heart-beat rhythm abnormalities and heart attacks (Bekkouche et al., 2011; Brooks, McCabe, & Schneiderman, 2011). These relationships contribute to the high incidence of heart disease in low-income groups, especially African Americans. Compared with higher-SES individuals, low-SES adults show a stronger cardiovascular response to stress, perhaps because they more often perceive stressors as unsolvable (Almeida et al., 2005; Carroll et al., 2007). Earlier we mentioned that stress interferes with immune system functioning, a link that may underlie its relationship to several forms of cancer. And by reducing digestive activity as blood flows to the brain, heart, and extremities, stress can cause gastrointestinal difficulties, including constipation, diarrhea, colitis, and ulcers (Donatelle, 2012).

The many challenging tasks of early adulthood make it a particularly stressful time of life. Young adults more often report depressive feelings than middle-aged people, many of whom have attained vocational success and financial security and are enjoying more free time as parenting responsibilities decline (Nolen-Hoeksema & Aldao, 2011). Also, as we will see in Chapters 15 and 16, middle-aged and older adults are better than young adults at coping with stress (Blanchard-Fields, Mienaltowski, & Baldi, 2007). Because of their longer life experience and greater sense of personal control over their lives, they are more likely to engage in problem-centered coping when stressful conditions can be changed and emotion-centered coping when nothing can be done.

In previous chapters, we repeatedly noted the stress-buffering effect of social support, which continues throughout life. Helping stressed young adults establish and maintain satisfying, caring social ties is as important a health intervention as any we have mentioned.

ASK YOURSELF

REVIEW List as many factors as you can that may have contributed to heart attacks and early death among Sharese's African-American relatives.

REVIEW Why are people in committed relationships likely to be more sexually active and satisfied than those who are dating several partners?

CONNECT Describe history-graded influences that have contributed to the obesity epidemic. (To review this aspect of the lifespan perspective, refer to page 11 in Chapter 1.)

APPLY Tom had been going to a health club three days a week after work, but job pressures convinced him that he no longer had time for regular exercise. Explain to Tom why he should keep up his exercise regimen, and suggest ways to fit it into his busy life.

COGNITIVE DEVELOPMENT

The cognitive changes of early adulthood are supported by further development of the cerebral cortex, especially the prefrontal cortex and its connections with other brain regions. Pruning of synapses along with growth and myelination of stimulated neural fibers continue, though at a slower pace than

in adolescence (Nelson, Thomas, & De Haan, 2006; Zelazo & Lee, 2010). These changes result in continued fine-tuning of the *prefrontal cognitive-control network* (see page 367 in Chapter 11). Consequently, planning, reasoning, and decision making improve, supported by major life events of this period—including attaining higher education, establishing a career, and grappling with the demands of marriage and child rearing. Furthermore, fMRI evidence reveals that as young adults become increasingly proficient in a chosen field of endeavor, regions of the cerebral cortex specialized for those activities undergo further *experience-dependent brain growth* (see page 128 in Chapter 4). Besides more efficient functioning, structural changes occur as greater knowledge and refinement of skills result in more cortical tissue devoted to the task and, at times, reorganization of brain areas governing the activity (Hill & Schneider, 2006; Lenroot & Giedd, 2006).

How does cognition change in early adulthood? Lifespan theorists have examined this question from three familiar vantage points. First, they have proposed transformations in the structure of thought—new, qualitatively distinct ways of thinking that extend the cognitive-developmental changes of adolescence. Second, adulthood is a time of acquiring advanced knowledge in a particular area, an accomplishment that has important implications for information processing and creativity. Finally, researchers have been interested in the extent to which the diverse mental abilities assessed by intelligence tests remain stable or change during the adult years—a topic addressed in Chapter 15.

 ## Changes in the Structure of Thought

Sharese described her first year in graduate school as a "cognitive turning point." As part of her internship in a public health clinic, she observed firsthand the many factors that affect human health-related behaviors. For a time, the realization that everyday dilemmas did not have clear-cut solutions made her intensely uncomfortable. "Working in this messy reality is so different from the problem solving I did in my undergraduate classes," she told her mother over the phone one day.

Piaget (1967) recognized that important advances in thinking follow the attainment of formal operations. He observed that adolescents prefer an idealistic, internally consistent perspective on the world to one that is vague, contradictory, and adapted to particular circumstances (see Chapter 11, pages 367–368). Sharese's reflections fit the observations of researchers who have studied **postformal thought**—cognitive development beyond Piaget's formal operational stage. To clarify how thinking is restructured in adulthood, let's look at some influential theories, along with supportive research. Together, they show how personal effort and social experiences combine to spark increasingly rational, flexible, and practical ways of thinking that accept uncertainties and vary across situations.

Perry's Theory: Epistemic Cognition

The work of William Perry (1981, 1970/1998) provided the starting point for an expanding research literature on the development of *epistemic cognition. Epistemic* means "of or about knowledge," and **epistemic cognition** refers to our reflections on how we arrived at facts, beliefs, and ideas. When mature, rational thinkers reach conclusions that differ from those of others, they consider the justifiability of their conclusions. When they cannot justify their approach, they revise it, seeking a more balanced, adequate route to acquiring knowledge.

Development of Epistemic Cognition. Perry wondered why young adults respond in dramatically different ways to the diversity of ideas they encounter in college. To find out, he interviewed Harvard University undergraduates at the end of each of their four years, asking "what stood out" during the previous year. Responses indicated that students' reflections on knowing changed as they experienced the complexities of university life and moved closer to adult roles—findings confirmed in many subsequent studies (King & Kitchener, 1994, 2002; Magolda, Abes, & Torres, 2009; Moore, 2002).

Younger students regarded knowledge as made up of separate units (beliefs and propositions), whose truth could be determined by comparing them to objective standards—standards that exist apart from the thinking person and his or her situation. As a result, they engaged in **dualistic thinking,** dividing information, values, and authority into right and wrong, good and bad, we and they. As one college freshman put it, "When I went to my first lecture, what the man said was just like God's word. I believe everything he said because he is a professor . . . and this is a respected position" (Perry, 1981, p. 81). And when asked, "If two people disagree on the interpretation of a poem, how would you decide which one is right?" a sophomore replied, "You'd have to ask the poet. It's his poem" (Clinchy, 2002, p. 67). Dualistic thinkers, who believe knowledge is certain and teachers have that knowledge, approach learning by accepting what they are given.

Older students, in contrast, had moved toward **relativistic thinking,** viewing all knowledge as embedded in a framework of thought. Aware of a diversity of opinions on many topics, they gave up the possibility of absolute truth in favor of multiple truths, each relative to its context. As a result, their thinking became more flexible and tolerant. As one college senior put it, "Just seeing how [famous philosophers] fell short of an all-encompassing answer, [you realize] that ideas are really individualized. And you begin to have respect for how great their thought could be, without its being absolute" (Perry, 1970/1998, p. 90). Relativistic thinking leads to the realization that one's own beliefs are often subjective, since several frameworks may satisfy the criterion of internal logical consistency (Moore, 2002; Sinnott, 2003). And from constructing, interpreting, and evaluating evidence from diverse frames of reference, relativistic thinkers become acutely aware that each person, in arriving at a position, creates her own "truth."

Eventually, the most mature individuals progress to **commitment within relativistic thinking.** Instead of choosing between opposing views, they try to formulate a more personally satisfying perspective that synthesizes contradictions. When considering which of two theories studied in a college course is better, or which of several movies most deserves an Oscar, the individual moves beyond the stance that everything is a matter of opinion and generates rational criteria against which options can be evaluated (Moshman, 2003, 2005). At the same time, mature thinkers willingly revise their internal belief system when presented with relevant evidence.

By the end of the college years, some students reach this extension of relativism. Adults who attain it generally display a more sophisticated approach to learning, in which they actively seek differing perspectives to deepen their knowledge and understanding and to clarify the basis for their own perspective. *TAKE A MOMENT...* Notice how commitment within relativistic thinking involves the information-gathering cognitive style (see page 404 in Chapter 12) and pursuit of personally meaningful beliefs, values, and goals essential to healthy identity development. Mature epistemic cognition also contributes greatly to effective decision making and problem solving.

Importance of Peer Interaction and Reflection. Advances in epistemic cognition depend on further gains in metacognition, which are likely to occur in situations that challenge young peoples' perspectives and induce them to consider the rationality of their thought processes (Magolda, Abes, & Torres, 2009). In a study of the college learning experiences of seniors scoring low and high in epistemic cognition, high-scoring students frequently reported activities that encouraged them to struggle with realistic but ambiguous problems in a supportive environment, in which faculty were committed to helping them understand how knowledge is constructed and why it must be subject to revision. For example, an engineering

When college students challenge one another's reasoning while tackling realistic, ambiguous problems, they are likely to gain in epistemic cognition.

major, describing an airplane-design project that required advanced epistemic cognition, noted his discovery that "you can design 30 different airplanes and each one's going to have its benefits and there's going to be problems with each one" (Marra & Palmer, 2004, p. 116). Low-scoring students rarely mentioned such experiences.

In tackling challenging, ill-structured problems, interaction among individuals who are roughly equal in knowledge and authority is beneficial because it prevents acceptance of another's reasoning simply because of greater power or expertise. When college students were asked to devise the most effective solution to a difficult logical problem, only 3 out of 32 students (9 percent) in a "work alone" condition succeeded. But in an "interactive" condition, 15 out of 20 small groups (75 percent) arrived at the correct solution following extensive discussion (Moshman & Geil, 1998). Whereas few students working alone reflected on their solution strategies, most groups engaged in a process of "collective rationality" in which members challenged one another to justify their reasoning and collaborated in working out the most defensible strategy.

Of course, reflection on one's own thinking can also occur individually. But peer interaction fosters the necessary type of individual reflection: arguing with oneself over competing ideas and strategies and coordinating opposing perspectives into a new, more effective structure. *TAKE A MOMENT…* Return to page 320 in Chapter 9 to review how peer collaboration fosters cognitive development in childhood. It remains a highly effective basis for education in early adulthood.

LOOK AND LISTEN

Describe learning experiences in one of your college courses that advanced your epistemic cognition. How did your thinking change? ●

Perry's theory and the research it stimulated are based on samples of highly educated young adults. These investigators acknowledge that progress in epistemic cognition is probably limited to people confronting the multiplicity of viewpoints typically encountered during a college education and that the most advanced attainment—commitment within relativism—often requires advanced graduate study (Greene, Torney-Purta, & Azevedo, 2010; King & Kitchener, 2002). But the underlying theme—thought less constrained by the need to find one answer to a question and more responsive to its context—is also evident in another theory of adult cognition.

Labouvie-Vief's Theory: Pragmatic Thought and Cognitive-Affective Complexity

Gisella Labouvie-Vief's (1980, 1985) portrait of adult cognition echoes features of Perry's theory. Adolescents, she points out, operate within a world of possibility. Adulthood involves movement from hypothetical to **pragmatic thought,** a structural advance in which logic becomes a tool for solving real-world problems.

According to Labouvie-Vief, the need to specialize motivates this change. As adults select one path out of many alternatives, they become more aware of the constraints of everyday life. And in the course of balancing various roles, they accept contradictions as part of existence and develop ways of thinking that thrive on imperfection and compromise. Sharese's friend Christy, a married graduate student and parent of her first child at age 26, illustrates:

> I've always been a feminist, and I wanted to remain true to my beliefs in family and career. But this is Gary's first year of teaching high school, and he's saddled with four preparations and coaching the school's basketball team. At least for now, I've had to settle for "give-and-take feminism"—going to school part-time and shouldering most of the child-care responsibilities while he gets used to his new job. Otherwise, we'd never make it financially.

Labouvie-Vief (2003, 2006) also points out that young adults' enhanced reflective capacities alter the dynamics of their emotional lives: They become more adept at integrating cognition with emotion and, in doing so, again make sense of discrepancies. Examining the self-descriptions of 10- to 80-year-olds diverse in SES, Labouvie-Vief found that from adolescence through middle adulthood, people gained in **cognitive-affective complexity**—awareness of conflicting positive and negative feelings and coordination of them into a complex, organized structure that recognizes the uniqueness of individual experiences (see Figure 13.7) (Labouvie-Vief, 2008; Labouvie-Vief et al., 1995, 2007). For example, one 34-year-old combined roles, traits, and diverse emotions into this coherent self-description: "With the recent birth of our first child, I find myself more fulfilled than ever, yet struggling in some ways. My elation is

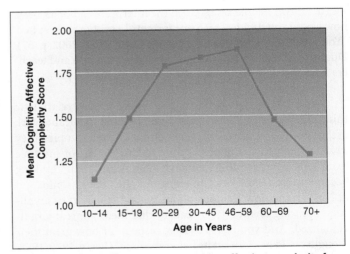

FIGURE 13.7 Changes in cognitive-affective complexity from adolescence to late adulthood. Performance, based on responses of several hundred 10- to 80-year-olds' descriptions of their roles, traits, and emotions, increased steadily from adolescence through early adulthood, peaked in middle age, and fell off in late adulthood when (as we will see in later chapters) basic information-processing skills decline. (From G. Labouvie-Vief, 2003, "Dynamic Integration: Affect, Cognition, and the Self in Adulthood," *Current Directions in Psychological Science, 12,* p. 203, copyright © 2003, Sage Publications. Reprinted by permission of SAGE Publications.)

tempered by my gnawing concern over meeting all my responsibilities in a satisfying way while remaining an individualized person with needs and desires."

Cognitive-affective complexity promotes greater awareness of one's own and others' perspectives and motivations. As Labouvie-Vief (2003) notes, it is a vital aspect of adult *emotional intelligence* (see page 313 in Chapter 9) and is valuable in solving many pragmatic problems. Individuals high in cognitive-affective complexity view events and people in a tolerant, open-minded fashion. And because cognitive-affective complexity involves accepting and making sense of both positive and negative feelings, it helps people regulate intense emotion and, therefore, think rationally about real-world dilemmas, even those that are laden with negative information (Labouvie-Vief, Grühn, & Studer, 2010).

Awareness of multiple truths, integration of logic with reality, and cognitive-affective complexity sum up qualitative transformations in thinking under way in early adulthood (Sinnott, 1998, 2003, 2008). As we will see next, adults' increasingly specialized and context-bound thought, although it closes off certain options, opens new doors to higher levels of competence.

Expertise and Creativity

In Chapter 9, we noted that children's expanding knowledge improves their ability to remember new information related to what they already know. For young adults, **expertise**—acquisition of extensive knowledge in a field or endeavor—is supported by the specialization that begins with selecting a college major or an occupation, since it takes many years to master any complex domain. Once attained, expertise has a profound impact on information processing.

Compared with novices, experts remember and reason more quickly and effectively. The expert knows more domain-specific concepts and represents them in richer ways—at a deeper and more abstract level and as having more features that can be linked to other concepts. As a result, unlike novices, whose understanding is superficial, experts approach problems with underlying principles in mind. For example, a highly trained physicist notices when several problems deal with conservation of energy and can therefore be solved similarly. In contrast, a beginning physics student focuses only on surface features—whether the problem contains a disk, a pulley, or a coiled spring (Chi, 2006; Chi, Glaser, & Farr, 1988). Experts can use what they know to arrive at many solutions automatically—through quick and easy remembering. And when a problem is challenging, they tend to plan ahead, systematically analyzing and categorizing elements and selecting the best from many possibilities, while the novice proceeds more by trial and error.

Expertise is necessary for creativity as well as problem solving (Weissberg, 2006). The creative products of adulthood differ from those of childhood in that they are not just original but also directed at a social or aesthetic need. Mature creativity requires a unique cognitive capacity—the ability to formulate new, culturally meaningful problems and to ask significant

A sculptor works on a statue to honor those who died in the Asian tsunami of 2004. The creative products of adulthood often are not just original but also directed at a social or aesthetic need.

questions that have not been posed before. According to Patricia Arlin (1989), movement from *problem solving* to *problem finding* is a core feature of postformal thought evident in highly accomplished artists and scientists.

Case studies support the 10-year rule in development of master-level creativity—a decade between initial exposure to a field and sufficient expertise to produce a creative work (Simonton, 2000; Winner, 2003). Furthermore, a century of research reveals that creative productivity typically rises in early adulthood, peaks in the late thirties or early forties, and gradually declines, though creative individuals near the end of their careers are usually more productive than those just starting their careers (see Figure 13.8) (Simonton, 2012). But

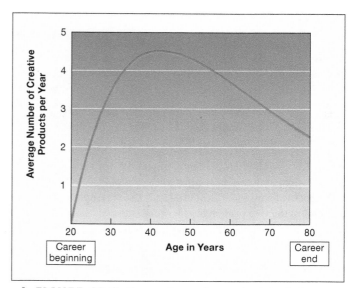

FIGURE 13.8 Changes in creative productivity during adulthood. Productivity typically rises over early adulthood and then declines, though creative older adults continue to produce more than adults just starting their careers. (Adapted from Simonton, 2012.)

exceptions exist. Those who get an early start in creativity tend to peak and drop off sooner, whereas "late bloomers" reach their full stride at older ages. This suggests that creativity is more a function of "career age" than of chronological age.

The course of creativity also varies across disciplines and individuals (Simonton, 2006, 2012). For example, poets, visual artists, and musicians typically show an early rise in creativity, perhaps because they do not need extensive formal education before they begin to produce. Academic scholars and scientists, who must earn higher academic degrees and spend years doing research to make worthwhile contributions, tend to display their achievements later and over a longer time. And whereas some creators are highly productive, others make only a single life-time contribution.

Though creativity is rooted in expertise, not all experts are creative. Creativity also requires other qualities. A vital ingredient is an innovative thinking style. In one study, college students who preferred to think intuitively (rely on "first impression") were told to solve a real-world problem using rational approach (be as "analytical" as possible) (Dane et al., 2011). Compared to controls who used their natural style, students required to use a style that differed sharply from their typical approach—who thought "outside the box"—generated many more creative ideas. Creative individuals are also tolerant of ambiguity, open to new experiences, persistent and driven to succeed, and willing to try again after failure (Lubart, 2003; Zhang & Sternberg, 2011). Finally, creativity demands time and energy. For women especially, it may be postponed or disrupted by child rearing, divorce, or an unsupportive partner (Vaillant & Vaillant, 1990).

In sum, creativity is multiply determined. When personal and situational factors jointly promote it, creativity can continue for many decades, well into old age.

ASK YOURSELF

REVIEW How does expertise affect information processing? Why is expertise necessary for, but not the same as, creativity?

CONNECT Our discussion in Chapter 9 noted that emotional intelligence is associated with life satisfaction and success in the workplace. How might cognitive–affective complexity contribute to these outcomes?

APPLY For her human development course, Marcia wrote a paper discussing the differing implications of Piaget's and Vygotsky's theories for education. Next, she reasoned that combining the two perspectives is more effective than relying on either position by itself. Explain how Marcia's reasoning illustrates advanced epistemic cognition.

REFLECT Describe a classroom experience or assignment in one of your college courses that promoted relativistic thinking.

 # The College Experience

Looking back at the trajectory of their lives, many people view the college years as formative—more influential than any other period of adulthood. This is not surprising. College serves as a "developmental testing ground," a time for devoting full attention to exploring alternative values, roles, and behaviors. To facilitate this exploration, college exposes students to a form of "culture shock"—encounters with new ideas and beliefs, new freedoms and opportunities, and new academic and social demands. More than 70 percent of U.S. high school graduates enroll in an institution of higher education (U.S. Department of Education, 2012b). Besides offering a route to a high-status career and its personal and monetary rewards, colleges and universities have a transforming impact on young people.

Psychological Impact of Attending College

Thousands of studies reveal broad psychological changes from the freshman to the senior year of college (Montgomery & Côté, 2003; Pascarella & Terenzini, 1991, 2005). As research inspired by Perry's theory indicates, students become better at reasoning about problems that have no clear solution, identifying the strengths and weaknesses of opposing sides of complex issues, and reflecting on the quality of their thinking. Their attitudes and values also broaden. They show increased interest in literature, the performing arts, and philosophical and historical issues and greater tolerance for racial and ethnic diversity. Also, as noted in Chapter 12, college leaves its mark on moral reasoning by fostering concern with individual rights and human welfare, sometimes expressed in political activism. Finally, exposure to multiple worldviews encourages young people to look more closely at themselves. During the college years, students develop greater self-understanding, enhanced self-esteem, and a firmer sense of identity.

How do these interrelated changes come about? The type of four-year institution attended—public versus private, highly selective versus relatively open in enrollment—makes little difference in psychological outcomes or even in ultimate career success and earnings (Montgomery & Côté, 2003). And cognitive growth seems to be similar at two-year community colleges and at four-year institutions (Pascarella, 2001).

Rather, the impact of college is jointly influenced by the person's involvement in academic and nonacademic activities and the richness of the campus environment. The more students interact with diverse peers in academic and extracurricular settings, the more they benefit cognitively—in grasping the complex causes of events, thinking critically, and generating effective problem solutions (Bowman, 2011a). Also, interacting with racially and ethnically mixed peers—both in courses exploring diversity issues and in out-of-class settings—predicts gains in civic engagement. And students who connect their community

Community college students join in a Peace Week activity, keeping pace with the beat of a drum circle. The more students interact with diverse peers in academic and extracurricular settings, the more they benefit cognitively from attending college.

service experiences with their classroom learning show large cognitive gains (Bowman, 2011b). These findings underscore the importance of programs that integrate commuting students into out-of-class campus life.

Dropping Out

Completing a college education has enduring effects on people's cognitive development, worldview, and postcollege opportunities. In the 1970s, the United States ranked first in the world in percentage of young adults with college degrees; today it is sixteenth, with just 41 percent of 25- to 34-year-olds having graduated. It lags far behind such countries as Canada, Japan, and South Korea, the global leader—where the rate is 63 percent (OECD, 2012a). Major contributing factors are the high U.S. child poverty rate; poor-quality elementary and secondary schools in low-income neighborhoods; and the high rate of high school dropout among teenagers. College leaving is also influential: 44 percent of U.S. students at two-year institutions and 32 percent of students at four-year institutions drop out, most within the first year and many within the first six weeks (ACT, 2010). Dropout rates are higher in colleges with less selective admission requirements; in some, first-year dropout approaches 50 percent. And ethnic minority students from low-SES families are, once again, at increased risk of dropping out (Feldman, 2005).

Both personal and institutional factors contribute to college leaving. Most entering freshmen have high hopes for college life but find the transition difficult. Those who have trouble adapting—because of lack of motivation, poor study skills, financial pressures, or emotional dependence on parents—quickly develop negative attitudes toward the college environment.

Often these exit-prone students do not meet with their advisers or professors. At the same time, colleges that do little to help high-risk students, through developmental courses and other support services, have a higher percentage of dropouts (Moxley, Najor-Durack, & Dumbrigue, 2001).

Beginning to prepare young people in early adolescence with the necessary visions and skills can do much to improve college success. In a study that followed up nearly 700 young people from sixth grade until two years after high school graduation, a set of factors—grade point average, academic self-concept, persistence in the face of challenge, parental SES and valuing of a college education, and the individual's plans to attend college—predicted college enrollment at age 20 (Eccles, Vida, & Barber, 2004). Although parental SES is difficult to modify, improving parents' attitudes and behaviors and students' academic motivation and educational aspirations is within reach, through a wide array of strategies considered in Chapters 11 and 12.

Once young people enroll in college, reaching out to them, especially during the early weeks and throughout the first year, is crucial. Programs that forge bonds between teachers and students and that generously fund student services—providing academic support, counseling to address academic and personal challenges, part-time work opportunities, and meaningful extracurricular roles—increase retention. Membership in campus-based social and religious organizations is especially helpful in strengthening minority students' sense of belonging (Chen, 2012; Fashola & Slavin, 1998). Young people who feel that their college community is concerned about them as individuals are far more likely to graduate.

 ## Vocational Choice

Young adults, college-bound or not, face a major life decision: the choice of a suitable work role. Being a productive worker calls for many of the same qualities as being an active citizen and a nurturant family member—good judgment, responsibility, dedication, and cooperation. What influences young people's decisions about careers? What is the transition from school to work like, and what factors make it easy or difficult?

Selecting a Vocation

In societies with an abundance of career possibilities, occupational choice is a gradual process that begins long before adolescence. Major theorists view the young person as moving through several periods of vocational development (Gottfredson, 2005; Super, 1990, 1994):

1. The **fantasy period:** In early and middle childhood, children gain insight into career options by fantasizing about them (Howard & Walsh, 2010). Their preferences, guided largely by familiarity, glamour, and excitement, bear little relation to the decisions they will eventually make.

2. The **tentative period:** Between ages 11 and 16, adolescents think about careers in more complex ways, at first in terms of their *interests,* and soon—as they become more aware of personal and educational requirements for different vocations—in terms of their *abilities* and *values.* "I like science and the process of discovery," Sharese thought as she neared high school graduation. "But I'm also good with people, and I'd like to do something to help others. So maybe teaching or medicine would suit my needs."

3. The **realistic period:** By the late teens and early twenties, with the economic and practical realities of adulthood just around the corner, young people start to narrow their options. A first step is often further *exploration*—gathering more information about possibilities that blend with their personal characteristics. In the final phase, *crystallization,* they focus on a general vocational category and experiment for a time before settling on a single occupation (Stringer, Kerpelman, & Skorikov, 2011). As a college sophomore, Sharese pursued her interest in science, but she had not yet selected a major. Once she decided on chemistry, she considered whether to pursue teaching, medicine, or public health.

Factors Influencing Vocational Choice

Most, but not all, young people follow this pattern of vocational development. A few know from an early age just what they want to be and follow a direct path to a career goal. Some decide and later change their minds, and still others remain undecided for an extended period. College students are granted added time to explore various options. In contrast, the life conditions of many low-SES youths restrict their range of choices.

Making an occupational choice is not simply a rational process in which young people weigh abilities, interests, and values against career options. Like other developmental milestones, it is the result of a dynamic interaction between person and environment (Gottfredson & Duffy, 2008). A great many influences feed into the decision, including personality, family, teachers, and gender stereotypes, among others.

Personality. People are attracted to occupations that complement their personalities. John Holland (1985, 1997) identified six personality types that affect vocational choice:

- The *investigative person,* who enjoys working with ideas, is likely to select a scientific occupation (for example, anthropologist, physicist, or engineer).

- The *social person,* who likes interacting with people, gravitates toward human services (counseling, social work, or teaching).

- The *realistic person,* who prefers real-world problems and working with objects, tends to choose a mechanical occupation (construction, plumbing, or surveying).

- The *artistic person,* who is emotional and high in need for individual expression, looks toward an artistic field (writing, music, or the visual arts).

- The *conventional person,* who likes well-structured tasks and values material possessions and social status, has traits well-suited to certain business fields (accounting, banking, or quality control).

- The *enterprising person,* who is adventurous, persuasive, and a strong leader, is drawn to sales and supervisory positions or to politics.

TAKE A MOMENT... Does one of these personality types describe you? Or do you have aspects of more than one type? Research confirms a relationship between personality and vocational choice in diverse cultures, but it is only moderate. Many people are blends of several personality types and can do well at more than one kind of occupation (Holland, 1997; Spokane & Cruza-Guet, 2005).

Furthermore, career decisions are made in the context of family influences, financial resources, educational and job opportunities, and current life circumstances. For example, Sharese's friend Christy scored high on Holland's investigative dimension. But after she married, had her first child, and faced increasing financial pressures, she postponed her dream of becoming a college professor and chose a human services career that required fewer years of education and offered reasonable likelihood of employment after graduation. During the late-2000s recession, which substantially increased unemployment among new college graduates, increasing numbers of U.S. college students chose to major in business, physical or biological sciences, health professions, or computer science, where the chances of securing a job—particularly a better-paying one—were greatest (U.S. Department of Education, 2012b). Thus, personality takes us only partway in understanding vocational choice.

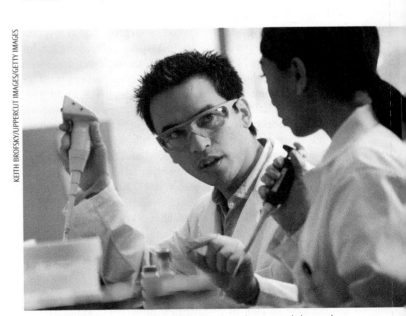

These young technicians in a genetics lab, who entered the workforce during the late-2000s recession, prepare DNA samples for analysis. They chose a career in the biological sciences, where employment opportunities were greater than in many other fields.

Family Influences. Young people's vocational aspirations correlate strongly with their parents' jobs. Individuals who grew up in higher-SES homes are more likely to select high-status, white-collar occupations, such as doctor, lawyer, scientist, or engineer. In contrast, those with lower-SES backgrounds tend to choose less prestigious, blue-collar careers—for example, plumber, construction worker, food service employee, or office worker. Parent–child vocational similarity is partly a function of similarity in personality, intellectual abilities, and—especially—educational attainment (Ellis & Bonin, 2003; Schoon & Parsons, 2002). Number of years of schooling completed powerfully predicts occupational status.

Other factors also promote family resemblance in occupational choice. Higher-SES parents are more likely to give their children important information about the worlds of education and work and to have connections with people who can help the young person obtain a high-status position (Kalil, Levine, & Ziol-Guest, 2005). In a study of African-American mothers' influence on their daughters' academic and career goals, college-educated mothers engaged in a wider range of strategies to promote their daughters' progress, including gathering information on colleges and areas of study and identifying knowledgeable professionals who could help (Kerpelman, Shoffner, & Ross-Griffin, 2002).

Parenting practices also shape work-related preferences. Recall from Chapter 2 that higher-SES parents tend to promote curiosity and self-direction, which are required in many high-status careers. Still, all parents can foster higher aspirations. Parental guidance, pressure to do well in school, and encouragement toward high-status occupations predict confidence in career choice and career attainment beyond SES (Bryant, Zvonkovic, & Reynolds, 2006; Stringer & Kerpelman, 2010).

Teachers. Young adults preparing for or engaged in careers requiring extensive education often report that teachers influenced their choice (Bright et al., 2005; Reddin, 1997). High school students who say that most of their teachers are caring and accessible, interested in their future, and expect them to work hard feel more confident about choosing a personally suitable career and succeeding at it (Metheny, McWhirter, & O'Neil, 2008). College-bound high school students tend to have closer relationships with teachers than do other students—relationships that are especially likely to foster high career aspirations in young women (Wigfield et al., 2002).

These findings provide yet another reason to promote positive teacher–student relations, especially for high school students from low-SES families. Teachers who offer encouragement and act as role models can serve as an important source of resilience for these young people.

Gender Stereotypes. Over the past four decades, young women have expressed increasing interest in occupations largely held by men (Gottfredson, 2005). Changes in gender-role attitudes, along with a dramatic rise in numbers of employed mothers who serve as career-oriented models for their daugh-

TABLE 13.2	Percentage of Women in Various Professions in the United States, 1983 and 2010	
PROFESSION	**1983**	**2010**
Architect or engineer	5.8	12.9
Lawyer	15.8	31.5
Doctor	15.8	32.3
Business executive	32.4	38.2[a]
Author, artist, entertainer	42.7	46.2
Social worker	64.3	80.8
Elementary or middle school teacher	93.5	81.8
Secondary school teacher	62.2	57.0
College or university professor	36.3	45.9
Librarian	84.4	82.8
Registered nurse	95.8	91.1
Psychologist	57.1	66.7

Source: U.S. Census Bureau, 2012.

[a]This percentage includes executives and managers at all levels. As of 2010, women made up only 4 percent of chief executive officers at Fortune 500 companies, although that figure represents more than 2½ times as many as in 2003.

ters, are common explanations for women's attraction to nontraditional careers.

But women's progress in entering and excelling at male-dominated professions has been slow. As Table 13.2 shows, although the percentage of women engineers, lawyers, doctors, and business executives has increased in the United States over the past quarter-century, it still falls far short of equal representation. Women remain concentrated in less-well-paid, traditionally feminine professions such as writing, social work, education, and nursing (U.S. Census Bureau, 2012). In virtually all fields, their achievements lag behind those of men, who write more books, make more discoveries, hold more positions of leadership, and produce more works of art.

Ability cannot account for these dramatic sex differences. Recall from Chapter 11 that girls are advantaged in reading and writing achievement, and the gender gap favoring boys in math is small and has been shrinking. Rather, gender-stereotyped messages play a key role. Although girls earn higher grades than boys, they reach secondary school less confident of their abilities, more likely to underestimate their achievement, and less likely to express interest in STEM careers (see page 389).

In college, the career aspirations of many women decline further as they question their capacity and opportunities to succeed in male-dominated fields and worry about combining a highly demanding career with family responsibilities (Chhin, Bleeker, & Jacobs, 2008; Wigfield et al., 2006). In a recent study, science professors at a broad sample of U.S. universities were

Social Issues: Education

Masculinity at Work: Men Who Choose Nontraditional Careers

Ross majored in engineering through his sophomore year of college, when he startled his family and friends by switching to nursing. "I've never looked back," Ross said. "I love the work." He noted some benefits of being a male in a female work world, including rapid advancement and the high regard of women colleagues. "But as soon as they learn what I do," Ross remarked with disappointment, "guys on the outside question my abilities and masculinity."

What factors influence the slowly increasing number of men who, like Ross, enter careers dominated by women? Compared to their traditional-career counterparts, these men are more liberal in their social attitudes, less gender-typed, less focused on the social status of their work, and more interested in working with people (Dodson & Borders, 2006; Jome, Surething, & Taylor, 2005). Perhaps their gender-stereotype flexibility allows them to choose occupations they find satisfying, even if those jobs are not typically regarded as appropriate for men.

In one investigation, 40 men who were primary school teachers, nurses, airline stewards, or librarians, when asked how they arrived at their choice, described diverse pathways (Simpson, 2005). Some actively sought the career, others happened on it while exploring possibilities, and still others first spent time in another occupation (usually male-dominated), found it

unsatisfying, and then settled into their current career.

The men also confirmed Ross's observations: Because of their male minority status, co-workers often assumed they were more knowledgeable than they actually were. They also had opportunities to move quickly into supervisory positions, although many did not seek advancement (Simpson, 2004). As one teacher commented, "I just want to be a good classroom teacher. What's wrong with that?" Furthermore, while in training and on the job, virtually all the men reported feeling socially accepted—relaxed and comfortable working with women.

But when asked to reflect on how others reacted to their choice, many men expressed anxiety about being stigmatized—by other men, not by women, whom they reported as generally accepting. To reduce these feelings, the men frequently described their job in ways that minimized its feminine image. Several librarians emphasized technical requirements by referring to their title as "information scientist" or "researcher." The nurses sometimes distanced themselves from a feminine work identity by specializing in "adrenaline-charged" areas such as accident or emergency. Despite these tensions, as with Ross, their high level of

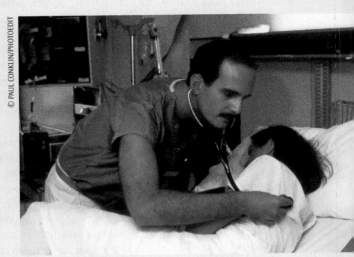

© PAUL CONKLIN/PHOTOEDIT

This nurse exemplifies the increasing number of men entering careers dominated by women. Compared with his traditional-career counterparts, he is likely to be less gender-typed and more interested in working with people.

private comfort seemed to prevail over uneasiness about the feminine public image of their work.

Still, men face certain barriers that resemble those of women preparing for nontraditional careers. For example, male students in college nursing programs often mention lack of male mentors and a "cooler" educational climate, which they attribute to implicit gender discrimination and unsupportive behaviors of women nurse educators (Bell-Scriber, 2008; Meadus & Twomey, 2011). These findings indicate that to facilitate entry into nontraditional careers, men, too, would benefit from supportive relationships with same-gender role models and an end to faculty gender-biased beliefs and behaviors.

---

sent an undergraduate student's application for a lab manager position. For half, the application bore a male name; for the other half, a female name (Moss-Racusin et al., 2012). Professors of both genders viewed the female student as less competent, less deserving of mentoring, and meriting a lower salary, though her accomplishments were identical to those of the male! In line with these findings, many mathematically talented college women settle on nonscience majors. And partly because of their strong interest in working with people, women who remain in the sciences more often choose medicine or another health

profession, and less often choose engineering or a math or physical science career, than their male counterparts (Robertson et al., 2010).

These findings reveal a pressing need for programs that sensitize educators to the special problems women face in developing and maintaining high vocational aspirations and selecting nontraditional careers. Young women's aspirations rise in response to career counseling that encourages them to set goals that match their abilities and faculty who take steps to enhance their experiences in math and science courses. Supportive relationships with women scientists and engineers add to female students' interest in and expectancies for success in STEM fields (Holdren & Lander, 2012). And such mentoring may help them see how altruistic values—which are particularly important to females—can be fulfilled within STEM occupations.

Compared to women, men have changed little in their interest in nontraditional occupations. See the Social Issues: Education box on the previous page for research on the motivations and experiences of men who do choose female-dominated careers.

Vocational Preparation of Non-College-Bound Young Adults

Sharese's younger brother Leon graduated from high school in a vocational track. Like approximately one-third of U.S. young people with a high school diploma, he had no current plans to go to college. While in school, Leon held a part-time job selling candy at the local shopping mall. He hoped to work in data processing after graduation, but six months later he was still a part-time sales clerk at the candy store. Although Leon had filled out many job applications, he got no interviews or offers.

Leon's inability to find a job other than the one he held as a student is typical for U.S. non-college-bound high school graduates. Although they are more likely to find employment than youths who drop out, they have fewer work opportunities than high school graduates of several decades ago. With rising unemployment during the late-2000s recession, these conditions worsened as entry-level positions went to the large pool of available college graduates. About 30 percent of recent U.S. high school graduates who do not continue their education are unemployed (Shierholz, Sabadish, & Wething, 2012). When they do find work, most hold low-paid, unskilled jobs. In addition, they have few alternatives for vocational counseling and job placement as they transition from school to work.

American employers regard recent high school graduates as unprepared for skilled business and industrial occupations and manual trades. And there is some truth to this impression. As noted in Chapter 11, unlike European nations, the United States has no widespread training system for non-college-bound youths. As a result, most graduate without work-related skills and experience a "floundering period" that lasts for several years.

In Germany, young people who do not go to a Gymnasium (college-preparatory high school) have access to one of the most successful work–study apprenticeship systems in the world for entering business and industry. About two-thirds of German youths participate. After completing full-time schooling at age 15 or 16, they spend the remaining two years of compulsory education in the Berufsschule, combining part-time vocational courses with an apprenticeship that is jointly planned by educators and employers. Students train in work settings for more than 350 blue- and white-collar occupations (Deissinger, 2007). Apprentices who complete the program and pass a qualifying examination are certified as skilled workers and earn union-set

wages. Businesses provide financial support because they know that the program guarantees a competent, dedicated work force (Kerckhoff, 2002). Many apprentices are hired into well-paid jobs by the firms that train them.

The success of the German system—and of similar systems in Austria, Denmark, Switzerland, and several East European countries—suggests that a national apprenticeship program would improve the transition from high school to work for U.S. young people. The many benefits of bringing together the worlds of schooling and work include helping non-college-bound young people establish productive lives right after graduation, motivating at-risk youths to stay in school, and contributing to the nation's economic growth. Nevertheless, implementing an apprenticeship system poses major challenges: overcoming the reluctance of employers to assume part of the responsibility for vocational training, ensuring cooperation between schools and businesses, and preventing low-SES youths from being concentrated in the lowest-skilled apprenticeship placements, an obstacle that Germany itself has not yet fully overcome (Lang, 2010). Currently, small-scale school-to-work projects in the United States are attempting to solve these problems and build bridges between learning and working.

Although vocational development is a lifelong process, adolescence and early adulthood are crucial periods for defining occupational goals and launching a career. Young people who are well-prepared for an economically and personally satisfying work life are much more likely to become productive citizens, devoted family members, and contented adults. The support of families, schools, businesses, communities, and society as a whole can contribute greatly to a positive outcome. In Chapter 14, we will take up the challenges of establishing a career and integrating it with other life tasks.

ASK YOURSELF

REVIEW What student and college-environment characteristics contribute to favorable psychological changes during the college years?

CONNECT What have you learned in previous chapters about development of gender stereotypes that helps explain women's slow progress in entering and excelling at male-dominated professions? (*Hint:* See Chapter 10, pages 343–344, and Chapter 11, page 389.)

APPLY Diane, a college freshman, knows that she wants to "work with people" but doesn't yet have a specific career in mind. Diane's father is a chemistry professor, her mother a social worker. What steps can Diane's parents take to broaden her awareness of the world of work and help her focus on an occupational goal?

REFLECT Describe personal and environmental influences on your progress in choosing a vocation.

SUMMARY

PHYSICAL DEVELOPMENT

Biological Aging Is Under Way in Early Adulthood
(p. 432)

Describe current theories of biological aging, both at the level of DNA and body cells and at the level of tissues and organs.

- Once body structures reach maximum capacity and efficiency in the teens and twenties, **biological aging,** or **senescence,** begins.

- The programmed effects of specific genes may control certain age-related biological changes. For example, **telomere** shortening results in senescent cells, which contribute to disease and loss of function.

- DNA may also be damaged as random mutations accumulate, leading to less efficient cell repair and replacement and to abnormal cancerous cells. Release of highly reactive **free radicals** is a possible cause of age-related DNA and cellular damage.

- The **cross-linkage theory of aging** suggests that over time, protein fibers form links and become less elastic, producing negative changes in many organs. Declines in the endocrine and immune systems may also contribute to aging.

Physical Changes (p. 434)

Describe the physical changes of aging, paying special attention to the cardiovascular and respiratory systems, motor performance, the immune system, and reproductive capacity.

- Gradual physical changes take place in early adulthood and later accelerate. Declines in heart and lung performance are evident during exercise. Heart disease is a leading cause of death in adults, although it has decreased since the mid-twentieth century due to lifestyle changes and medical advances.

- Athletic skills requiring speed, strength, and gross-motor coordination peak in the early twenties; those requiring endurance, arm–hand steadiness, and aiming peak in the late twenties and early thirties. Less active lifestyles rather than biological aging are largely responsible for age-related declines in motor performance.

- The immune response declines after age 20 because of shrinkage of the thymus gland and increased difficulty coping with physical and psychological stress.

- Women's reproductive capacity declines with age due to reduced quality and quantity of ova. In men, semen volume and sperm quality decrease gradually after age 35.

Health and Fitness (p. 438)

Describe the impact of SES, nutrition, and exercise on health, and discuss obesity in adulthood.

- Health inequalities associated with SES increase in adulthood. Health-related circumstances and habits underlie these disparities.

- Today, Americans are the heaviest people in the world. Sedentary lifestyles and diets high in sugar and fat contribute to obesity, which is associated with serious health problems, social discrimination, and early death.

- Some weight gain in adulthood reflects a decrease in **basal metabolic rate (BMR),** but many young adults add excess weight. Effective treatment includes a nutritious diet low in calories, sugar, and fat, plus regular exercise, recording of food intake and body weight, social support, and teaching problem-solving skills.

- Regular exercise reduces body fat, builds muscle, fosters resistance to disease, and enhances psychological well-being. Health benefits increase with greater intensity of exercise.

What are the two most commonly abused substances, and what health risks do they pose?

- Cigarette smoking and alcohol consumption are the most commonly abused substances. Smokers, most of whom began before age 21, are at increased risk for many health problems, including decline in bone mass, heart attack, stroke, and numerous cancers.

- About one-third of heavy drinkers suffer from alcoholism, to which both heredity and environment contribute. Alcohol is implicated in liver and cardiovascular disease, certain cancers and other physical disorders, highway fatalities, crime, and sexual coercion.

Describe sexual attitudes and behavior of young adults, and discuss sexually transmitted diseases and sexual coercion.

- Most adults are less sexually active than media images suggest, but they display a wider range of sexual choices and lifestyles and have had more sexual partners than earlier generations. The Internet has become a popular way to initiate relationships.

- Adults in committed relationships report high satisfaction with their sex lives. Only a minority report persistent sexual problems—difficulties linked to low SES and psychological stress.

- Attitudes toward same-sex couples have become more accepting. Homosexual relationships, like heterosexual relationships, are characterized by similarity between partners in education and background, greater satisfaction in committed relationships, and modest frequency of sexual activity.

- Sexually transmitted diseases (STDs) continue to be prevalent in early adulthood; women are more vulnerable to infection than men. AIDS, the most deadly STD, is spreading most rapidly through men having sex with men and through heterosexual contact in poverty-stricken minority groups.

- Most rape victims are under age 30 and have been harmed by men they know well. Men who commit sexual assault typically support traditional gender roles, approve of violence against women, accept rape myths, and misinterpret women's social behaviors. Cultural acceptance of strong gender typing and of violence contributes to sexual coercion, which leads to psychological trauma. Female-initiated coercive sexual behavior also occurs but is less often reported and recognized by authorities.

How does psychological stress affect health?

- Chronic psychological stress induces physical responses that contribute to heart disease, several types of cancer, and gastrointestinal problems. Because the challenges of early adulthood make it a highly stressful time of life, interventions that help stressed young people form supportive social ties are especially important.

COGNITIVE DEVELOPMENT

Changes in the Structure of Thought (p. 450)

Explain how thinking changes in early adulthood.

- Development of the cerebral cortex in early adulthood results in continued fine-tuning of the prefrontal cognitive-control network, contributing to improvements in planning, reasoning, and decision making.

- Cognitive development beyond Piaget's formal operations is known as **postformal thought.** In early adulthood, personal effort and social experiences combine to spark increasingly rational, flexible, and practical ways of thinking.

- In Perry's theory of **epistemic cognition,** college students move from **dualistic thinking,** dividing information into right and wrong, to **relativistic thinking,** awareness of multiple truths. The most mature individuals progress to **commitment within relativistic thinking,** which synthesizes contradictions.

- Advances in epistemic cognition depend on gains in metacognition. Peer collaboration on challenging, ill-structured problems is especially beneficial.

© IAN SHAW/ALAMY

- In Labouvie-Vief's theory, the need to specialize motivates adults to move from hypothetical to **pragmatic thought,** which uses logic as a tool for solving real-world problems and accepts contradiction, imperfection, and compromise. Adults' enhanced reflective capacities permit gains in **cognitive-affective complexity**—coordination of positive and negative feelings into a complex, organized structure.

Expertise and Creativity (p. 453)

What roles do expertise and creativity play in adult thought?

- Specialization in college and in an occupation leads to **expertise,** which is necessary for both problem solving and creativity. Although creativity tends to rise in early adulthood and to peak in the late thirties or early forties, its development varies across disciplines and individuals. Diverse personal and situational factors jointly promote creativity.

The College Experience (p. 454)

Describe the impact of a college education on young people's lives, and discuss the problem of dropping out.

- College students' explorations, both academic and nonacademic, yield gains in knowledge and reasoning ability, broadening of attitudes and values, enhanced self-understanding and self-esteem, and a firmer sense of identity.

- Personal and institutional factors contribute to college dropout, which is more common in less selective colleges and among ethnic minority students from low-SES families. High-risk students benefit from interventions that show concern for them as individuals.

Vocational Choice (p. 455)

Trace the development of vocational choice, and cite factors that influence it.

- Vocational choice moves through a **fantasy period,** in which children explore career options by fantasizing about them; a **tentative period,** in which teenagers evaluate careers in terms of their interests, abilities, and values; and a **realistic period,** in which young people settle on a vocational category and then a specific occupation.

- Vocational choice is influenced by personality; parents' provision of educational opportunities, vocational information, and encouragement; and close relationships with teachers. Women's progress in male-dominated professions has been slow, and their achievements lag behind those of men in virtually all fields. Gender-stereotyped messages play a key role.

KEITH BROFSKY/UPPERCUT IMAGES/GETTY IMAGES

What problems do U.S. non-college-bound young people face in preparing for a vocation?

- Most U.S. non-college-bound high school graduates are limited to low-paid, unskilled jobs, and too many are unemployed. Work–study apprenticeships, like those widely available in European countries, would improve the transition from school to work for these young people.

Important Terms and Concepts

basal metabolic rate (BMR) (p. 439)
biological aging, or senescence (p. 432)
cognitive-affective complexity (p. 452)
commitment within relativistic thinking (p. 451)
cross-linkage theory of aging (p. 434)
dualistic thinking (p. 451)

epistemic cognition (p. 451)
expertise (p. 453)
fantasy period (p. 455)
free radicals (p. 433)
postformal thought (p. 450)
pragmatic thought (p. 452)

realistic period (p. 456)
relativistic thinking (p. 451)
telomeres (p. 432)
tentative period (p. 456)

THE WASHINGTON POST/GETTY IMAGES

This college student, a volunteer for a nonprofit organization called FoodCorps, helps children in economically disadvantaged communities plant a school garden, teaching them about healthy foods and how they grow. For many young people in industrialized nations, the transition to early adulthood is a time of prolonged exploration of attitudes, values, and life possibilities.

Emotional and Social Development in Early Adulthood

chapter outline

A Gradual Transition: Emerging Adulthood

Unprecedented Exploration • Cultural Change, Cultural Variation, and Emerging Adulthood • Risk and Resilience in Emerging Adulthood

■ **CULTURAL INFLUENCES** Is Emerging Adulthood Really a Distinct Period of Development?

Erikson's Theory: Intimacy versus Isolation

Other Theories of Adult Psychosocial Development

Levinson's Seasons of Life • Vaillant's Adaptation to Life • The Social Clock

Close Relationships

Romantic Love • Friendships • Loneliness

■ **SOCIAL ISSUES: HEALTH** Childhood Attachment Patterns and Adult Romantic Relationships

The Family Life Cycle

Leaving Home • Joining of Families in Marriage • Parenthood

■ **SOCIAL ISSUES: HEALTH** Partner Abuse

The Diversity of Adult Lifestyles

Singlehood • Cohabitation • Childlessness • Divorce and Remarriage • Varied Styles of Parenthood

Career Development

Establishing a Career • Women and Ethnic Minorities • Combining Work and Family

After completing her master's degree at age 26, Sharese returned to her hometown, where she and Ernie would soon be married. During their year-long engagement, Sharese had vacillated about whether to follow through. At times, she looked with envy at Heather, still unattached and free to choose from an array of options before her. After graduating from college, Heather accepted a Peace Corps assignment in a remote region of Ghana, forged a romance with another Peace Corps volunteer that she ended at the conclusion of her tour of duty, and then traveled for eight months before returning to the United States to contemplate next steps.

Sharese also pondered the life circumstances of Christy and her husband, Gary—married and first-time parents by their mid-twenties. Despite his good teaching performance, Gary's relationship with the high school principal deteriorated, and he quit his job at the end of his first year. A tight job market impeded Gary's efforts to find another teaching position, and financial pressures and parenthood put Christy's education and career plans on hold. Sharese wondered whether it was really possible to combine family and career.

© RADIUS IMAGES/ALAMY

As her wedding approached, Sharese's ambivalence intensified, and she admitted to Ernie that she didn't feel ready to marry. Ernie's admiration for Sharese had strengthened over their courtship, and he reassured her of his love. His career as an accountant had been under way for two years, and at age 28, he looked forward to marriage and starting a family. Uncertain and conflicted, Sharese felt swept toward the altar as relatives and friends began to arrive. On the appointed day, she walked down the aisle.

In this chapter, we take up the emotional and social sides of early adulthood. Notice that Sharese, Ernie, and Heather moved toward adult roles slowly, at times vacillating along the way. Not until their mid- to late twenties did they make lasting career and romantic choices and attain full economic independence—broadly accepted markers of adulthood that young people of previous generations reached considerably earlier. Each received financial and other forms of support from parents and other family members, which enabled them to postpone taking on adult roles. We consider whether prolonged exploration of life options has become so widespread that it merits a new developmental period—*emerging adulthood*—to describe and understand it.

Recall from Chapter 12 that identity development continues to be a central focus from the late teens into the mid-twenties (see page 404). As they achieve a secure identity and independence from parents, young adults seek close, affectionate ties. Yet the decade of the twenties is accompanied by a rise in feelings of personal control over events in their lives—in fact, a stronger sense of control than they will ever experience again (Grob, Krings, & Bangerter, 2001). Perhaps for this reason, like Sharese, they often fear losing their freedom. Once this struggle is resolved, early adulthood leads to new family units and parenthood, accomplished in the context of diverse lifestyles. At the same time, young adults must master the tasks of their chosen career.

Our discussion will reveal that identity, love, and work are intertwined. In negotiating these arenas, young adults do more choosing, planning, and changing course than any other age group. When their decisions are in tune with themselves and their social and cultural worlds, they acquire many new competencies, and life is full and rewarding. ●

A Gradual Transition: Emerging Adulthood

TAKE A MOMENT... Think about your own development. Do you consider yourself to have reached adulthood? When a large sample of American 18- to 25-year-olds was asked this question, the majority gave an ambiguous answer: "yes and no." Only after reaching their late twenties and early thirties did most feel that they were truly adult—findings evident in a wide range of industrialized nations, including Argentina, Austria, the Czech Republic, Finland, Germany, Italy, Romania, Spain, and Israel (Arnett, 2001, 2003, 2007a; Buhl & Lanz, 2007; Macek, Bejĉek, & Vaníĉková, 2007; Nelson, 2009; Sirsch et al., 2009). The life pursuits and subjective judgments of many contemporary young people indicate that the transition to adult roles has become so delayed and prolonged that it has spawned a new transitional period extending from the late teens to the mid- to late-twenties, called **emerging adulthood.**

Unprecedented Exploration

Psychologist Jeffrey Arnett is the leader of a movement that regards emerging adulthood as a distinct period of life. As Arnett explains, emerging adults have left adolescence but are still a considerable distance from taking on adult responsibilities. Their parents agree: In a survey of parents of a large sample of ethnically and religiously diverse U.S. undergraduate and graduate students, most viewed their children as not yet fully adult (Nelson et al., 2007). Furthermore, 18- to 25-year-olds who do not consider themselves adults are less adultlike in life goals and behavior—less certain about their identity and

the qualities they desire in a romantic partner and more likely to engage in risk taking, including substance use and unprotected sex (Nelson & Barry, 2005). During these years, young people who have the economic resources to do so explore alternatives in education, work, and personal values and behavior more intensely than they did as teenagers.

Not yet immersed in adult roles, many emerging adults can engage in activities of the widest possible scope. Because so little is normative, or socially expected, routes to adult responsibilities are highly diverse in timing and order across individuals (Côté, 2006). For example, more college students than in past generations pursue their education in a drawn-out, nonlinear way—changing majors as they explore career options, taking courses while working part-time, or interrupting school to work, travel, or participate in national or international service programs. About one-third of U.S. college graduates enter graduate school, taking still more years to settle into their desired career track (U.S. Department of Education, 2012b).

As a result of these experiences, young people's interests, attitudes, and values broaden (see page 454 in Chapter 13). Exposure to multiple viewpoints also encourages young people to look more closely at themselves. Consequently, they develop a more complex self-concept that includes awareness of their own changing traits and values over time, and self-esteem rises (Labouvie-Vief, 2006; Orth, Robins, & Widaman, 2012). Together, these changes contribute to advances in identity.

Identity Development. During the college years, young people refine their approach to constructing an identity. Besides exploring in *breadth* (weighing multiple possibilities), they also explore in *depth*—evaluating existing commitments (Luyckx et al., 2006). For example, if you have not yet selected your major, you may be taking classes in a broad array of disciplines. Once you choose a major, you are likely to embark on an in-depth evaluation of your choice—reflecting on your interest, motivation, and performance and on your career prospects as you take additional classes in that field. Depending on the outcome of your evaluation, either your commitment to your major strengthens, or you return to a broad exploration of options.

In a longitudinal study extending over the first two years of college, most students cycled between making commitments and evaluating commitments in various identity domains. Fluctuations in students' certainty about their commitments sparked movement between these two states (Luyckx, Goossens, & Soenens, 2006). *TAKE A MOMENT...* Consider your own identity progress. Does it fit this *dual-cycle model,* in which identity formation is a lengthy process of feedback loops? Notice how the model helps explain the movement between identity statuses displayed by many young people, described in Chapter 12. College students who move toward exploration in depth and certainty of commitment are higher in self-esteem, psychological well-being, and academic, emotional, and social adjustment. Those who spend much time exploring in breadth without making commitments, or who are identity diffused (engaging in no exploration), tend to be poorly adjusted—anxious, depressed, and higher in alcohol and drug use, casual and unprotected sex, and other health-compromising behaviors (Kunnen et al., 2008; Schwartz et al., 2011).

Many aspects of the life course that were once socially structured—marriage, parenthood, religious beliefs, and career paths—are increasingly left to individuals to decide on their own. As a result, emerging adults are required to "individualize" their identities—a process that requires a sense of self-efficacy, purpose, determination to overcome obstacles, and responsibility for outcomes. Among young people of diverse ethnicities and SES levels, this set of qualities, termed *personal agency,* is positively related to an information-gathering cognitive style and identity exploration followed by commitment (Schwartz, Côté, & Arnett, 2005; Stringer & Kerpelman, 2010).

Religion and Worldview. Most emerging adults say that constructing a worldview, or a set of beliefs and values to live by, is essential for attaining adult status—even more important than finishing their education and settling into a career and marriage (Arnett, 2006, 2007b). During the late teens and twenties, attendance at religious services drops to its lowest level throughout the lifespan as young people continue to question the beliefs they acquired in their families (Kunnen et al., 2008; Schwartz et al., 2011). About one-fourth of U.S. 18- to 29-year-olds are unaffiliated with a particular faith—considerably more than in their parents' generation at the same age (see Figure 14.1).

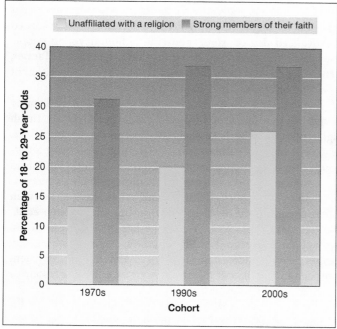

FIGURE 14.1 **U.S. 18- to 29-year-olds' religiosity across generations. The percentage of unaffiliated young people rose substantially from the 1970s to 2000s.** At the same time, among those in the 2000s cohort who are religiously affiliated, about one-third say they are strong members of their faith—similar to the 1990s cohort. (Adapted from Pew Forum on Religion and Public Life, 2010.)

Yet about 50 percent of U.S. young people remain stable in their religious commitment (or lack thereof) from adolescence into emerging adulthood (Smith & Snell, 2009). And in certain ways, U.S. emerging adults are quite traditional in their religious beliefs and practices. Religion is more important in their lives than it is for young people in other developed countries. More than half of U.S. 18- to 29-year-olds say they believe in God with certainty, and more than one-third of those who are religiously affiliated say they are "strong" members of their faith—equivalent to same-age individuals who said so a decade earlier (Pew Forum on Religion and Public Life, 2010). Women are more religious than men, a difference evident in other Western nations and throughout the lifespan. Also among the more religious are immigrants and certain ethnic minorities, including African Americans and Hispanics (Barry et al., 2010). Of the small number of young people who increase in religiosity during the late teens and early twenties, many are women, African American, and Hispanic.

Whether or not they are involved in organized religion, many young people begin to construct their own individualized faith and, if attending college, discuss religious beliefs and experiences more often with friends than with parents or other adults (Montgomery-Goodnough & Gallagher, 2007; Stoppa & Lefkowitz, 2010). Often they weave together beliefs and practices from diverse sources, including Eastern and Western religious traditions, science, and popular culture, including music and other media images.

As with adolescents, U.S. emerging adults who are religious or spiritual tend to be better adjusted. They are higher in self-esteem, less likely to engage in substance use and antisocial acts, and more likely to become involved in community service (Barry & Nelson, 2008; Knox, Langehough, & Walters, 1998; White et al., 2006). But outcomes vary: Among sexual minority young people, religiosity does not protect against drug taking (Rostosky, Danner, & Riggle, 2007). A possible explanation is that their religious communities often do not support (and sometimes condemn) their sexual orientation.

Perhaps because emerging adults are so focused on exploring and "finding themselves," a widespread view among older adults is that that they forge self-centered worldviews, as the descriptor "generation me" suggests (Arnett, 2010). This issue has generated heated controversy. Analyses of large, nationally representative samples of U.S. young people, collected repeatedly over several decades, suggest that compared to past generations, the Millennial generation reports greater narcissism (egotistical self-admiration) and materialism—valuing of money and leisure and reduced empathy for the less fortunate (Gentile, Twenge, & Campbell, 2010; O'Brien, Hsing, & Konrath, 2010; Twenge, Campbell, & Freeman, 2012).

But other researchers claim that generational changes in egotism and other traits are too small to be meaningful (Trzesniewski & Donnellan, 2009, 2010). And gradual, age-related gains in self-esteem extending from adolescence through emerging adulthood and into mid-life are similar across generations, with average self-esteem of today's young people no

© SYRACUSE NEWSPAPERS/PETER CHEN/THE IMAGE WORKS

Volunteers with Habitat for Humanity's Brush with Kindness program help low-income home owners with major repairs. Despite a widespread view of today's young adults as self-centered, many emerging adults are committed to improving their communities, nation, and world.

higher than that of past cohorts (Orth, Robins, & Widaman, 2012; Orth, Trzesniewski, & Robins, 2010). Over these years, adults derive a greater sense of competence from making identity commitments, entering and succeeding at their careers, and becoming involved in their communities.

Additional evidence supports the view that many emerging adults are committed to improving their communities, nation, and world. In a survey of several hundred thousand first-year students enrolled in nearly 300 U.S. colleges and universities, a record number—nearly 30 percent—said that there is "a very good chance" they will participate in community service—nearly double the number two decades earlier (Pryor et al., 2009). An additional 41 percent expressed "some chance" of participating, and only 6 percent said they would not volunteer.

Among college students who expect to volunteer, the overwhelming majority actually do so within their first year (DeAngelo, Hurtado, & Pryor, 2010). And compared with their nonvolunteer counterparts, volunteers have a stronger pluralistic orientation—disposition for living in a diverse society that includes respect for others with differing beliefs and willingness to discuss and negotiate controversial issues (Pryor et al., 2009).

LOOK AND LISTEN

Ask 10 to 15 of your college classmates to answer the following question: What would you do if you had a million dollars? How often do respondents mention prosocial as opposed to self-centered acts? ●

Finally, compared to previous generations, contemporary 18- to 29-year-olds have been labeled "apathetic no shows" when it comes to voting. But in the 2012 U.S. presidential election, they made up more of the total electorate (19 percent) than did citizens over age 65 (16 percent), who traditionally have been the highest participants. In this respect, emerging adults' civic involvement appears to have strengthened.

Cultural Change, Cultural Variation, and Emerging Adulthood

Rapid cultural change explains the recent appearance of emerging adulthood. First, entry-level positions in many fields require more education than in the past, prompting young adults to seek higher education in record numbers and thus delaying financial independence and career commitment. Second, wealthy nations with longer-lived populations have no pressing need for young people's labor, freeing those who are financially able for rich, extended exploration.

Indeed, emerging adulthood is limited to cultures that postpone entry into adult roles until the twenties. In developing nations such as Brazil, China, India, and Mexico, only a privileged few—usually those from wealthier families who are admitted to universities—experience it, often for a shorter time than their Western counterparts (Arnett, 2011; Nelson & Chen, 2007). Furthermore, the overwhelming majority of young people in traditional non-Western countries—those who have few economic resources or who remain in the rural regions where they grew up—have no emerging adulthood. With limited education, they typically enter marriage, parenthood, and lifelong work early (UNICEF, 2010c).

In industrialized countries, many young people experience these transitional years. Typically, their families are sufficiently well-off to provide them with financial support, without which few could advance their education, explore career possibilities, or travel the country and world to—as one emerging adult put it—"experience as much as possible." And although most emerging adults are pursuing higher education or have earned an advanced degree, some non-college-bound young people also benefit from this extended transition to adult roles (Tanner, Arnett, & Leis, 2009). But they may do so by trying out different types of work rather than college majors or travel.

Nevertheless, for the large numbers of U.S. low-SES young people who are burdened by early parenthood, do not finish high school, are otherwise academically unprepared for college, or do not have access to vocational training, emerging adulthood is limited or nonexistent (see Chapters 11 and 13). Instead of excitement and personal expansion, these individuals encounter a "floundering period" during which they alternate between unemployment and dead-end, low-paying jobs (Cohen et al., 2003; Eccles et al., 2003). When the late-2000s recession hit, work opportunities for low-SES high school graduates declined further, leaving increasing numbers in search of employment (see page 459 in Chapter 13) and without the economic resources for intensive exploration.

Because of its strong association with SES and higher education, some researchers reject the notion of emerging adulthood as a distinct period of development (see the Cultural Influences box on the following page). Others disagree, predicting that emerging adulthood will become increasingly common as *globalization*—the exchange of ideas, information, trade, and immigration among nations—accelerates. As globalization proceeds, gains in higher education and the formation of a common "global identity" among young people may lead to the spread of

Cultural Influences

Is Emerging Adulthood Really a Distinct Period of Development?

Although broad consensus exists that cultural change has prolonged the transition to adult roles for many young people, disagreement exists over whether these years of "emergence" merit the creation of a new developmental period (Hendry & Kloep, 2007, 2011). Critics of the concept of emerging adulthood offer the following arguments.

First, burgeoning higher education enrollment, delayed career entry, and later marriage and parenthood are cultural trends that began as early as the 1970s in industrialized nations, only gradually becoming more conspicuous. At no time has adulthood in complex societies been attained at a distinct moment (Côté & Bynner, 2008). Rather, young people in the past reached adult status earlier in some domains and later in others, just as they do today. They also may reverse direction—for example, move back to the parental home to get their bearings after finishing college or being laid off from a job. In accord with the lifespan perspective, development is multidimensional and multidirectional, for 18- to 29-year-olds as it is for adults of all ages. Transitions occur during all periods of adult life, with societal conditions heavily influencing their timing, length, and complexity.

Second, the term *emerging adulthood* fails to describe the experiences of the majority of the world's youths (Galambos & Martinez, 2007). In most developing countries, young people—particularly women— are limited in education and marry and have children early. According to one estimate, over 1 billion individuals—nearly 70 percent of young people—follow this

traditional route to adulthood (World Health Organization, 2011). We have also seen that many low-SES youths in industrialized nations lack the academic preparation and financial resources to experience an emerging adulthood.

Third, research on emerging adulthood largely emphasizes its personal and societal benefits. But the extended exploration that defines this period can be risky for those who have not developed the personal agency to make good choices and acquire adult skills. These young people may remain uncommitted for too long—an outcome that impedes the focused learning required for a successful work life. A favorable emerging adulthood, then, depends on whether it is used to acquire competencies essential for contemporary living.

Finally, the financial upheaval of the late 2000s has left large numbers of bachelor's degree holders under age 25 with restricted options. In 2011, over 9 percent were unemployed and 20 percent underemployed—in low-paid jobs not requiring a college degree and, thus, without experiences necessary for advancing their skills (Shierholz, Sabadish, & Wething, 2012). Rather than a period of unparalleled opportunities, these graduates' delayed leap into adult roles is filled with anxiety and frustration. One young person, who might have been high in personal agency in a stable economy, remarked, "It has been tough finding a job that keeps me wanting to stick with something" (Kotkin, 2012).

Proponents of emerging adulthood as a distinct developmental period respond that, though not universal, it applies to most young people in industrialized societies and is spreading in developing nations that play

With few economic resources, this young woman in Burma already has adult responsibilities, caring for her baby while working as a food vendor. Like the majority of young people in developing countries, she has no emerging adulthood.

major roles in our global economy (Tanner & Arnett, 2011). But skeptics counter that emerging adulthood is unlikely to become a prominent period of life in developing countries with high concentrations of poverty or, in industrialized countries, among low-income youths or those not involved in higher education (Côté & Bynner, 2008; Kloep & Hendry, 2011). And for college graduates, societal conditions can readily restrict the prospects and rewards of this period.

Critics also emphasize that in developed nations, age-graded influences have declined in favor of nonnormative influences throughout contemporary adulthood (see page 12 in Chapter 1 to review) (Hendry & Kloep, 2010). In their view, rather than being unique, emerging adults are part of a general trend toward blurring of age-related expectations, yielding multiple transitions and increased diversity in development across the adult years.

emerging adulthood (Arnett, 2007a; Nelson & Chen, 2007). But, as the Cultural Influences box points out, the recession's weak labor market has also left large numbers of college graduates with limited options. In sum, societal conditions enabling an emerging adulthood abundant in opportunity have recently contracted.

Risk and Resilience in Emerging Adulthood

In grappling with momentous choices and acquiring the skills to succeed in demanding life roles, emerging adults often encounter disappointments in love and work that require them to

Applying What We Know

Resources That Foster Resilience in Emerging Adulthood

Type of Resource	Description
Cognitive attributes	Effective planning and decision making
	Information-gathering cognitive style and mature epistemic cognition
	Good school performance
	Knowledge of vocational options and necessary skills
Emotional and social attributes	Positive self-esteem
	Good emotional self-regulation and flexible coping strategies
	Good conflict-resolution skills
	Confidence in one's ability to reach one's goals
	Sense of personal responsibility for outcomes
	Persistence and effective use of time
	Healthy identity development—movement toward exploration in depth and commitment certainty
	Strong moral character
	Sense of meaning and purpose in life, engendered by religion, spirituality, or other sources
	Desire to contribute meaningfully to one's community
Social supports	Positive relationships with parents, peers, teachers, and mentors
	Financial assistance from parents or others
	Sense of connection to social institutions, such as school, church, workplace, and community center

Sources: Benson et al., 2006; Eccles and Gootman, 2002.

adjust, and sometimes radically change, their life path (Arnett, 2006). Their vigorous explorations also extend earlier risks, including unprotected sexual activity, substance use, and hazardous driving behavior (see Chapter 13). And later in this chapter, we will see that feelings of loneliness are higher at this time than at any other time of life. As emerging adults move through school and employment settings, they must constantly separate from friends and forge new relationships.

Longitudinal research shows that the personal attributes and social supports listed in Applying What We Know above foster successful passage through these years, as indicated by completing a college education, forging a warm, stable intimate relationship, finding and keeping a well-paying job, and volunteering in one's community (Benson et al., 2006; Eccles & Gootman, 2002). Notice how the resources in the table overlap with ones discussed in previous chapters that promote development through *resilience,* the capacity to overcome challenge and adversity. Young people with more of these resources—and with resources in all three categories—probably make an especially smooth transition to adulthood. But many emerging adults with only a few resources also fare well.

As in childhood, certain resources strengthen others. Relationships with parents have an especially wide-ranging influence. A secure, affectionate parent–emerging adult bond that extends the balance of connection and separation established in adolescence—an empathic approach in which parents recognize

the weighty challenges the young person faces and encourage personally valued choices—predicts many aspects of adaptive functioning: favorable self-esteem, identity progress, successful transition to college life, higher academic achievement, more rewarding friendships and romantic ties, and positive psychological well-being. As one reviewer of research summed up, "What seems advantageous for emerging adults' achievement of independence is feeling connected, secure, understood, and loved in their families, and having the willingness to call on parental resources" (Aquilino, 2006, p. 201).

In contrast, excessive parental rule-setting and regulation of the young person's daily life (including taking over when the young person encounters challenges) and psychological control (invalidating the young person's thoughts and feelings and, when dissatisfied, withdrawing love) are linked to poor adjustment, including low self-esteem, inability to make commitments in identity formation, and increased anxiety, depression, and alcohol use (Luyckz et al., 2007; Nelson et al., 2011; Patock-Peckam & Morgan-Lopez, 2009). In another form of parenting—called *helicopter parenting* in popular culture—warm, well-intentioned parents "hover" over the emerging adult out of excessive concern for his or her well-being. They might, for example, take the child to college but refuse to leave, attend classes with the child for the first week, and contact professors to discuss the child's grades. Perhaps because helicopter parenting is motivated by strong parental affection and involvement,

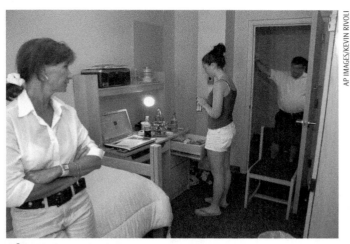

Although well-intentioned, these hovering "helicopter" parents make it harder for their daughter to acquire the skills she needs to manage the challenges of college life on her own.

it is not associated with the negative outcomes just noted. But it is related to reduced school engagement (going to class, completing assignments) (Padilla-Walker & Nelson, 2012). And it likely interferes with emerging adults' ability to acquire the skills they need to act on their own.

Finally, exposure to multiple negative life events—family conflict, abusive intimate relationships, repeated romantic breakups, academic or employment difficulties, and financial strain—undermines development, even in emerging adults whose childhood and adolescence prepared them well for this transition (Masten et al., 2004). In sum, supportive family, school, and community environments are crucial, just as they were at earlier ages. The overwhelming majority of young people with access to these resources are optimistic about their future and likely to transition successfully to adult roles (Arnett, 2006). Now let's turn to theories of psychosocial development in early adulthood.

ASK YOURSELF

REVIEW What cultural changes have led to the emergence of the period known as emerging adulthood?

CONNECT How are resources that foster resilience in emerging adulthood similar to those that promote resilience in childhood and adolescence? (See pages 10–11 in Chapter 1, page 354 in Chapter 10, and page 416 in Chapter 12.)

APPLY List supports that your college environment offers emerging adults in its health and counseling services, academic advising, residential living, and extracurricular activities. How does each help young people transition to adult roles?

REFLECT Should emerging adulthood be considered a distinct developmental period? Why or why not?

Erikson's Theory: Intimacy versus Isolation

Erikson's vision has influenced all contemporary theories of adult personality development. His psychological conflict of early adulthood is **intimacy versus isolation,** reflected in the young person's thoughts and feelings about making a permanent commitment to an intimate partner.

As Sharese discovered, establishing a mutually gratifying close relationship is challenging. Most young adults are still grappling with identity issues. Yet intimacy requires that they give up some of their independent self and redefine their identity to include both partners' values and interests. Those in their late teens and early twenties frequently say they don't feel ready for a lasting tie (Carroll et al., 2009). During their first year of marriage, Sharese separated from Ernie twice as she tried to reconcile her desire for self-determination with her desire for intimacy. Maturity involves balancing these forces. Without intimacy, young adults face the negative outcome of Erikson's early adulthood stage: loneliness and self-absorption. Ernie's patience and stability helped Sharese realize that committed love requires generosity and compromise but not total surrender of the self.

Research confirms that—as Erikson emphasized—a secure identity fosters attainment of intimacy. Commitment to personally meaningful values and goals prepares young adults for interpersonal commitments, which increase as early adulthood progresses. Among large samples of college students, identity achievement was positively correlated with fidelity (loyalty in relationships) and love, for both men and women. In contrast, identity moratorium—a state of searching prior to commitment—was negatively associated with fidelity and love (Markstrom et al., 1997; Markstrom & Kalmanir, 2001). Other studies show that advanced identity development strongly predicts involvement in a deep, committed love partnership or readiness to establish such a partnership (Beyers & Seiffge-Krenke, 2010; Montgomery, 2005). Still, the coordination of identity and intimacy is more complex for women, who are more likely than men to consider the impact of their personal goals on important relationships (Archer, 2002).

In friendships and work ties, too, young people who have achieved intimacy are cooperative, tolerant, and accepting of differences in background and values. In contrast, people with a sense of isolation hesitate to form close ties because they fear loss of their own identity, tend to compete rather than cooperate, are not accepting of differences, and are easily threatened when others get too close (Marcia, 2002).

Erikson believed that successful resolution of intimacy versus isolation prepares the individual for the middle adulthood stage, which focuses on *generativity*—caring for the next generation and helping to improve society. But as noted previously, few adults follow a fixed series of tasks tied neatly to age. Some aspects of generativity—childbearing and child rearing, as well as contributions to society through work and community service—are under way in the twenties and thirties. Still, in line with Erikson's ideas, high friendship or romantic intimacy in early adulthood does predict a stronger generative orientation (Mackinnon et al., 2011).

In sum, identity, intimacy, and generativity are concerns of early adulthood, with shifts in emphasis that differ among individuals. Recognizing that Erikson's theory provides only a broad sketch of adult personality development, other theorists have expanded his stage approach, adding detail.

Other Theories of Adult Psychosocial Development

In the 1970s, growing interest in adult development led to several widely read books on the topic. Daniel Levinson's *The Seasons of a Man's Life* (1978) and *The Seasons of a Woman's Life* (1996), and George Vaillant's *Adaptation to Life* (1977) and *Aging Well* (2002), present psychosocial theories in the tradition of Erikson.

Levinson's Seasons of Life

On the basis of in-depth biographical interviews with 35- to 45-year-old men—and, later, similar interviews with women in the same age range—Levinson (1978, 1996) depicted adult development as a sequence of qualitatively distinct eras (or "seasons") coinciding with Erikson's stages and separated by *transitions*. The *life structure,* a key concept in Levinson's theory, is the underlying design of a person's life, consisting of relationships with significant others—individuals, groups, and institutions. Of its many components, usually only a few, relating to family, close friendships, and occupation, are central. But wide individual differences exist in the weights of central and peripheral components.

Levinson found that during the transition to early adulthood, most young people constructed a *dream*—an image of themselves in the adult world that guides their decision making. For men, the dream usually emphasized achievement in a career, whereas most career-oriented women had "split dreams" involving both marriage and career. Young adults also formed a relationship with a *mentor* who facilitated realization of their dream—often a senior colleague at work but occasionally a more experienced friend, neighbor, or relative. According to Levinson, men oriented toward high-status careers spent their twenties acquiring professional skills, values, and credentials. In contrast, for many women, career development extended into middle age.

Around age 30, a second transition occurred: Young people who had been preoccupied with career and were single usually focused on finding a life partner, while women who had emphasized marriage and family often developed more individualistic goals. For example, Christy, who had dreamed of becoming a

A digital archives specialist shows an apprentice librarian how to proofread a scanned text. For young people starting out in a career, an experienced colleague can be an especially effective mentor, serving as a role model and guide in overcoming challenges.

professor, finally earned her doctoral degree in her mid-thirties and secured a college teaching position. Married women tended to expect their spouse to recognize and accommodate their career interests and aspirations. For young people without a satisfying intimate tie or a vocational direction, this can be a time of crisis.

To create an early adulthood culminating life structure, men usually "settled down" by focusing on certain relationships and aspirations, in an effort to establish a niche in society consistent with their values, whether those be wealth, prestige, artistic or scientific achievement, or forms of family or community participation. In his late thirties, Ernie became a partner in his firm, coached his son's soccer team, and was elected treasurer of his church. He paid less attention to golf, travel, and playing the guitar than previously.

Many women, however, remained unsettled in their thirties, often because they added an occupational or relationship commitment. When her two children were born, Sharese felt torn between her research position in the state health department and her family. She took three months off after the arrival of each baby. When she returned to work, she did not pursue attractive administrative openings that required travel and time away from home. And shortly after Christy began teaching, she and Gary divorced. Becoming a single parent while starting her professional life introduced new strains. Not until middle age did many women reach career maturity and take on more authority in the community.

Vaillant's Adaptation to Life

Vaillant (1977) followed the development of nearly 250 men born in the 1920s, selected for study while they were students at a competitive liberal arts college. Participants were interviewed extensively while in college and answered lengthy questionnaires during each succeeding decade. Then Vaillant (2002) interviewed them at ages 47, 60, and 70 about work, family, and physical and mental health.

Looking at how the men altered themselves and their social world to adapt to life, Vaillant—like Levinson—confirmed Erikson's stages but filled gaps between them. After focusing on intimacy concerns in their twenties, the men turned to career consolidation in their thirties. During their forties, they became more generative. In their fifties and sixties, they extended that generativity; they became "keepers of meaning," or guardians of their culture, expressing a deep need to preserve and pass on cultural traditions by teaching others what they had learned from life experience (Vaillant & Koury, 1994). Finally, in their seventies, the men became more spiritual and reflective, contemplating the meaning of life and accepting its finiteness. In a later lifelong study of a sample of well-educated women, Vaillant (2002) identified a similar series of changes.

Nevertheless, the developmental patterns Vaillant and Levinson described are based largely on interviews with people born in the first few decades of the twentieth century. As our discussion of emerging adulthood illustrates, development is far more variable today—so much so that some researchers doubt that adult psychosocial changes can be organized into distinct stages (Newton & Stewart, 2010). Rather, people may assemble the themes and dilemmas identified by these theorists into individualized arrangements, in a *dynamic system* of interacting biological, psychological, and social forces. Studies of new generations—both men and women of diverse backgrounds—are needed to shed light on the extent of commonality and variation among young people in psychosocial development.

Because the social clock has become increasingly flexible, this 30-year-old attorney, committed to her challenging, demanding career, may not feel pressure to conform to a strict timetable for major life events such as marriage and parenthood.

The Social Clock

As we have seen, changes in society from one generation to the next can affect the life course. Bernice Neugarten (1968a, 1979) identified an important cultural and generational influence on adult development: the **social clock**—age-graded expectations for major life events, such as beginning a first job, getting married, birth of the first child, buying a home, and retiring. All societies have such timetables. Research of two to three decades ago revealed that conformity to or departure from the social clock can be a major source of adult personality change, affecting self-esteem, independence, responsibility, and other attributes because adults (like children and adolescents) make social comparisons, measuring their progress against that of agemates (Helson, 1992; Vandewater & Stewart, 1997).

But as noted earlier, age-graded expectations for appropriate behavior have become increasingly flexible. Among economically better-off young people, finishing one's education, marrying, and having children occur much later in the lifespan than they did a generation or two ago. Furthermore, departures from social-clock life events have become increasingly

common. As we will see later, a growing number of women, mostly of lower income, are not marrying and, instead, rearing children as single mothers, turning not to a spouse but rather to their own parents and extended families for assistance (Furstenberg, 2010).

LOOK AND LISTEN

Describe your social clock, listing major life events along with the age you expect to attain each. Then ask a parent and/or grandparent to recall his or her own early adulthood social clock. Analyze generational differences. ●

These conditions can create intergenerational tensions when parents expect their young-adult children to attain adult milestones on an outdated schedule, at odds with their children's current opportunities and desires. Young adults may also feel distressed because their own timing of major milestones is not widely shared by their contemporaries or supported by current public policies, thereby weakening the availability of both informal and formal social supports. (Settersten, 2007). And while rendering greater flexibility and freedom to young people's lives, an ill-defined social clock likely causes them to feel inadequately grounded—unsure of what others expect and of what to expect of themselves.

In sum, following a social clock of some kind seems to foster confidence and social stability because it guarantees that young people will develop skills, engage in productive work, and gain in understanding of self and others (Hendry & Kloep, 2007). In contrast, "crafting a life of one's own," whether self-chosen or the result of circumstances, is risky—more prone to breakdown (Settersten, 2007, p. 244). With this in mind, let's take a closer look at how men and women traverse major tasks of young adulthood.

ASK
YOURSELF

REVIEW According to Levinson, how do the life structures of men and women differ?

CONNECT Return to pages 403–404 in Chapter 12 and review the contributions of exploration and commitment to a mature identity. Using the two criteria, explain why identity achievement is positively related to attainment of intimacy (fidelity and love), whereas identity moratorium is negatively predictive.

APPLY In view of contemporary changes in the social clock, explain Sharese's conflicted feelings about marrying Ernie.

REFLECT Describe your early adulthood dream. Then ask a friend or classmate of the other gender to describe his or her dream, and compare the two. Are they consistent with Levinson's findings?

 # Close Relationships

To establish an intimate tie to another person, people must find a partner and build an emotional bond that they sustain over time. Although young adults are especially concerned with romantic love, the need for intimacy can also be satisfied through other relationships involving mutual commitment—with friends, siblings, and co-workers.

Romantic Love

At a party during her junior year of college, Sharese fell into conversation with Ernie, a senior and one of the top students in her government class. Sharese had already noticed Ernie in class, and as they talked, she discovered that he was as warm and interesting as he had seemed from a distance. Ernie found Sharese to be lively, intelligent, and attractive. By the end of the evening, the two realized that they had similar opinions on important social issues and liked the same leisure activities. They began dating steadily. Six years later, they married.

Finding a life partner is a major milestone of early adult development, with profound consequences for self-concept and psychological well-being (Meeus et al., 2007). As Sharese and Ernie's relationship reveals, it is also a complex process that unfolds over time and is affected by a variety of events.

Selecting a Mate. Recall from Chapter 13 that intimate partners generally meet in places where they are likely to find people of their own age, level of education, ethnicity, and religion, or they connect through dating websites. People usually select partners who resemble themselves in other ways—attitudes, personality, educational plans, intelligence, physical attractiveness, and even height (Keith & Schafer, 1991; Simpson & Harris, 1994). Romantic partners sometimes have complementary

personality traits—one self-assured and dominant, the other hesitant and submissive. Because this difference permits each to sustain their preferred style of behavior, it contributes to compatibility (Sadler, Ethier, & Woody, 2011). But partners differing in other ways generally are not complementary! For example, a warm, agreeable person and an emotionally cool person usually react with discomfort to each other. Overall, little support exists for the idea that "opposites attract." Rather, adults typically indicate that their romantic ideal is someone with a personality similar to their own (Markey & Markey, 2007). And partners who are similar in personality and other attributes tend to be more satisfied with their relationship and more likely to stay together (Blackwell & Lichter, 2004; Furnham, 2009).

Nevertheless, in choosing a long-term partner, men and women differ in the importance they place on certain characteristics. In research carried out in diverse industrialized and developing countries, women assign greater weight to intelligence, ambition, financial status, and moral character, whereas men place more emphasis on physical attractiveness and domestic skills. In addition, women prefer a same-age or slightly older partner, men a younger partner (Buunk, 2002; Cramer, Schaefer, & Reid, 2003; Stewart, Stinnett, & Rosenfeld, 2000).

According to an evolutionary perspective, because their capacity to reproduce is limited, women seek a mate with traits, such as earning power and emotional commitment, that help ensure children's survival and well-being. In contrast, men look for a mate with traits that signal youth, health, sexual pleasure, and ability to give birth to and care for offspring. As further evidence for this difference, men often want a relationship to move quickly toward physical intimacy, whereas women typically prefer to take the time to achieve psychological intimacy first (Buss, 2012).

In an alternative, social learning view, gender roles profoundly influence criteria for mate selection. Beginning in childhood, men learn to be assertive and independent—behaviors needed for success in the work world. Women acquire nurturant behaviors, which facilitate caregiving. Then each sex learns to value traits in the other that fit with this traditional division of labor (Eagly & Wood, 2012). In support of this theory, in cultures and in younger generations experiencing greater gender equity, men and women are more alike in their mate preferences. For example, compared with men in China and Japan, American men place more emphasis on their mate's financial prospects, less on her domestic skills. Also, when either male or female young adults are asked to imagine themselves as a future homemaker, their preferences for a good provider and an older partner strengthen (Eagly, Eastwick, & Johannesen-Schmidt, 2009).

But neither men nor women put good looks, earning power, and mate's age relative to their own at the top of their wish list. Rather, they place a higher value on attributes that contribute to relationship satisfaction: mutual attraction, caring, dependability, emotional maturity, and a pleasing disposition (Buss et al., 2001; Toro-Morn & Sprecher, 2003). Nevertheless, men continue to emphasize physical attractiveness more than women do, and women earning capacity more than men do. Furthermore, these gender differences—along with gender similarity in desire for a caring partner—also characterize gay men and lesbians (Impett & Peplau, 2006; Regan, Medina, & Joshi, 2001). In sum, both biological and social forces contribute to mate selection.

As the Social Issues: Health box on page 474 reveals, young people's choice of an intimate partner and the quality of their relationship also are affected by memories of their early parent–child bond. Finally, for romance to lead to a lasting partnership, it must happen at the right time. Two people may be right for each other, but if one or both do not feel ready to marry, the relationship is likely to dissolve.

The Components of Love.

How do we know that we are in love? Robert Sternberg's (1988, 2000, 2006) **triangular theory of love** identifies three components—intimacy, passion, and commitment—that shift in emphasis as romantic relationships develop. *Intimacy,* the emotional component, involves warm, tender communication, expressions of concern about the other's well-being, and a desire for the partner to reciprocate. *Passion,* the desire for sexual activity and romance, is the physical- and psychological-arousal component. *Commitment* is the cognitive component, leading partners to decide that they are in love and to maintain that love.

At the beginning of a relationship, **passionate love**—intense sexual attraction—is strong. Gradually, passion declines in favor of intimacy and commitment, which form the basis for **companionate love**—warm, trusting affection and caregiving (Acker & Davis, 1992; Fehr, 1994). Each aspect of love, however, helps sustain the relationship. Early passionate love is a strong predictor of whether partners keep dating. But without the quiet intimacy, predictability, and shared attitudes and values of companionate love, most romances eventually break up (Hendrick & Hendrick, 2002).

An ongoing relationship requires effort from both partners. Research on newlyweds' feelings and behavior over the first year of marriage reveals that partners gradually felt less "in love" and less pleased with married life (Huston, McHale, & Crouter, 1986; Murray et al., 2011). A variety of factors contributed, including a sharp drop in time spent talking to each other and doing things that brought each other pleasure (for example, saying "I love you" or making the other person laugh). Joint leisure pursuits gave way to more household tasks and chores and, therefore, fewer enjoyable times together. Also, when discussing areas of conflict, partners declined in accurate reading of each other's thoughts and feelings (Kilpatrick, Bissonnette, & Rusbult, 2002). Perhaps after an increasing number of such interactions, they tried less hard to grasp the other's point of view and resorted to well-established habits, such as giving in or withdrawing.

But couples whose relationships endure generally report that they love each other more than they did earlier (Sprecher, 1999). In the transformation of romantic involvements from passionate to companionate, *commitment* may be the aspect of love that determines whether a relationship survives. Communicating that commitment in ways that strengthen *intimacy*—through warmth, attentiveness, empathy, caring, acceptance,

The warmth and intimacy of this couple's communication form the basis for mutual affection, caring, acceptance, and respect, which are vital for a satisfying, enduring bond.

and respect—strongly predicts relationship maintenance and satisfaction (Neff & Karney, 2008; Lavner & Bradbury, 2012). For example, Sharese's doubts about getting married subsided largely because of Ernie's expressions of commitment. In the most dramatic of these, he painted a large sign, reading "I LOVE SHARESE" and placed it in their front yard on her birthday. Sharese returned Ernie's sentiments, and the intimacy of their bond deepened.

Partners who consistently express their commitment report higher-quality and longer-lasting relationships (Fitzpatrick & Sollie, 1999; Madey & Rodgers, 2009). An important feature of their communication is constructive conflict resolution—directly expressing wishes and needs, listening patiently, asking for clarification, compromising, accepting responsibility, forgiving their partner, and avoiding the escalation of negative interaction sparked by criticism, contempt, defensiveness, and stonewalling (Johnson et al., 2005; Schneewind & Gerhard, 2002). In a longitudinal study, newlyweds' negativity during problem solving predicted marital dissatisfaction and divorce over the following decade (Sullivan et al., 2010). Those who displayed little warmth and caring often resorted to anger and contempt when dealing with problems.

These findings reveal that deficits in intimacy foreshadow poor conflict-resolution skills and eventual weakening of the marital tie. Although the capacity for constructive conflict resolution is a vital ingredient of enduring marriages, a tender, caring bond seems to energize that capacity, motivating couples to resolve conflicts in ways that preserve a gratifying sense of intimacy.

Compared with women, men are less skilled at communicating in ways that foster intimacy, offering less comfort and helpful support in their close relationships. Men also tend to be less effective at negotiating conflict, frequently avoiding discussion (Burleson & Kunkel, 2006; Wood, 2009).

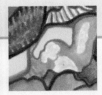

Social Issues: Health

Childhood Attachment Patterns and Adult Romantic Relationships

In Bowlby's ethological theory of attachment, the early attachment bond leads to construction of an *internal working model,* or set of expectations about attachment figures, that serves as a guide for close relationships throughout life. Adults' evaluations of their early attachment experiences are related to their parenting behaviors—specifically, to the quality of attachments they build with their children (see page 201 in Chapter 6). Additional evidence indicates that recollections of childhood attachment patterns predict romantic relationships in adulthood.

In studies carried out in Australia, Israel, and the United States, researchers asked people about their early parental bonds (attachment history), their attitudes toward intimate relationships (internal working model), and their actual experiences with romantic partners. In a few studies, investigators also observed couples' behaviors. Consistent with Bowlby's theory, adults' memories and interpretations of childhood attachment patterns were good indicators of internal working models and relationship experiences. (To review patterns of attachment, see pages 197–198.)

Secure Attachment

Adults who described their attachment history as secure (warm, loving, and supportive parents) had internal working models that reflected this security. They viewed themselves as likable and easy to get to know, were comfortable with intimacy, and rarely worried about abandonment. They characterized their most important love relationship in terms of trust, happiness, and friendship (Cassidy, 2001). Their behaviors toward their partner were empathic and supportive and their conflict resolution strategies constructive. They were also at ease in turning to their partner for comfort and assistance and reported mutually initiated, enjoyable sexual activity (Collins et al., 2006; Creasey & Jarvis, 2009; Roisman et al., 2002).

Avoidant Attachment

Adults who reported an avoidant attachment history (demanding, disrespectful, and critical parents) displayed internal working models that stressed independence, mistrust of love partners, and anxiety about people

getting too close. They were convinced that others disliked them and that romantic love is hard to find and rarely lasts. Jealousy, emotional distance, lack of support in response to their partner's distress, and little enjoyment of physical contact pervaded their most important love relationship (Collins et al., 2006). Avoidant adults often deny attachment needs through excessive work and brief sexual encounters and affairs (Feeney, 1998). They endorse many unrealistic beliefs about relationships—for example, that partners cannot change, that males' and females' needs differ, and that "mind reading" is expected (Stackert & Bursik, 2003).

Resistant Attachment

Adults recalling a resistant attachment history (parents who responded unpredictably and unfairly) presented internal working models in which they sought to merge completely with another person and fall in love quickly (Cassidy, 2001). At the same time, they worried that their intense feelings would overwhelm others, who really did not love them and would not want to stay with them. Their most important love relationship was riddled with jealousy, emotional highs and lows, and desperation about whether the partner would return their affection (Feeney, 1999). Resistant adults, though offering support, do so in ways that fit poorly with their partner's needs (Collins et al., 2006). They are also quick to express fear and anger, and they disclose information about themselves at inappropriate times (Brennan & Shaver, 1995).

Are adults' descriptions of their childhood attachment experiences accurate, or are they distorted or even completely invented? In several longitudinal studies, quality of parent–child interactions, observed or assessed through family interviews 5 to 23 years earlier, were good predictors of internal working models and romantic-relationship quality in early adulthood (Donnellan, Larsen-Rife, & Conger, 2005; Ogawa et al., 1997; Roisman et al., 2001). These findings suggest that adult recollections bear some resemblance to actual parent–child experiences. However, attributes of the current partner also influence internal working models and intimate ties. When generally insecure individuals

Did the internal working model constructed by this baby, held tenderly by his father, influence the relationship he later forged with his wife? Research indicates that early attachment pattern is one of several factors associated with the quality of later intimate ties.

manage to form a secure representation of their partner, they report stronger feelings of affection and concern and reduced relationship conflict and anxiety (Sibley & Overall, 2010; Sprecher & Fehr, 2011).

In sum, negative parent–child experiences can be carried forward into adult close relationships. At the same time, internal working models are continuously "updated." When adults with a history of unhappy love lives have a chance to form a satisfying intimate tie, they may revise their internal working model. As the new partner approaches the relationship with a secure state of mind and sensitive, supportive behavior, the insecure partner may reappraise her expectations and respond in kind (Creasey & Jarvis, 2009). This reciprocity creates a feedback loop through which a revised, more favorable internal working model, along with mutually gratifying interaction, persists over time.

Applying What We Know

Keeping Love Alive in a Romantic Partnership

Suggestion	Description
Make time for your relationship.	To foster relationship satisfaction and a sense of being "in love," plan regular times to be together.
Tell your partner of your love.	Express affection and caring, including the powerful words "I love you," at appropriate times. These messages increase perceptions of commitment, strengthen intimacy, and encourage your partner to respond in kind.
Be available to your partner in times of need.	Provide emotional support, giving of yourself when your partner is distressed.
Communicate constructively and positively about relationship problems.	When you or your partner is dissatisfied, suggest ways of overcoming difficulties, and ask your partner to collaborate in choosing and implementing a course of action. Avoid the four enemies of a gratifying, close relationship: criticism, contempt, defensiveness, and stonewalling.
Show an interest in important aspects of your partner's life.	Ask about your partner's work, friends, family, and hobbies and express appreciation for his or her special abilities and achievements. In doing so, you grant your partner a sense of being valued.
Confide in your partner.	Share innermost feelings, keeping intimacy alive.
Forgive minor offenses and try to understand major offenses.	Whenever possible, overcome feelings of anger through forgiveness. In this way, you acknowledge unjust behavior but avoid becoming preoccupied with it.

Sources: Donatelle, 2012; McCarthy & McCarthy, 2004.

Finally, for gay and lesbian couples, widespread social stigma complicates the process of forging a satisfying, committed bond. Those who worry most about being stigmatized, try to conceal their romance, or harbor negative attitudes toward their own sexual orientation report lower-quality and less enduring love relationships (Mohr & Daly, 2008; Mohr & Fassinger, 2006). Applying What We Know above lists ways to help keep the embers of love aglow in a romantic partnership.

Culture and the Experience of Love. Passion and intimacy, which form the basis for romantic love, became the dominant basis for marriage in twentieth-century Western nations as the value of individualism strengthened. From this vantage point, mature love is based on autonomy, appreciation of the partner's unique qualities, and intense emotion (Hatfield, Rapson, & Martel, 2007). Trying to satisfy dependency needs through an intimate bond is regarded as immature.

This Western view contrasts sharply with the perspectives of Eastern cultures. In Japan, for example, lifelong dependency is accepted and viewed positively. The Japanese word *amae,* or love, means "to depend on another's benevolence." The traditional Chinese collectivist view defines the self through role relationships—son or daughter, brother or sister, husband or wife. Feelings of affection are distributed across a broad social network, reducing the intensity of any one relationship.·

In choosing a mate, Chinese and Japanese young people are expected to consider obligations to others, especially parents. As one writer summarized, "An American asks, 'How does my heart feel?' A Chinese asks, 'What will other people say?'" (Hsu, 1981, p. 50). College students of Asian heritage are less likely than those of American or European descent to endorse a view of love based solely on physical attraction and deep emotion

(Hatfield, Rapson, & Martel, 2007; Hatfield & Sprecher, 1995). Instead, compared to Westerners, they place greater weight on companionship and practical matters—similarity of background, career promise, and likelihood of being a good parent. Similarly, compared with American couples, dating couples in China report less passion but equally strong feelings of intimacy and commitment (Gao, 2001).

Although arranged marriages are still common in parts of Southeast Asia, young couples increasingly expect love to be a prerequisite for marriage, and their parents are likely to acquiesce.

Still, even in countries where arranged marriages are still fairly common (including China, India, and Japan), parents and prospective brides and grooms consult one another before moving forward (Goodwin & Pillay, 2006). If parents try to force their children into an unappealing marriage with little chance of love, sympathetic extended family members may come to children's defense. And in developing countries, women who attain higher education are more likely to insist on actively participating in an arranged marriage. They have acquired more of an autonomous identity, along with knowledge and skills from which to bargain for a greater say (Bhopal, 2011). In sum, today young people in many countries consider love to be a prerequisite for marriage, though Westerners assign greater importance to love—especially, its passionate component.

Friendships

Like romantic partners and childhood friends, adult friends are usually similar in age, sex, and SES—factors that contribute to common interests, experiences, and needs and therefore to the pleasure derived from the relationship. As in earlier years, friends in adulthood enhance self-esteem and psychological well-being through affirmation, acceptance, autonomy support (permitting disagreement and choice), and support in times of stress (Collins & Madsen, 2006; Deci et al., 2006). Friends also make life more interesting by expanding social opportunities and access to knowledge and points of view.

Trust, intimacy, and loyalty, along with shared interests and values and enjoyment of each other's company, continue to be important in adult friendships, as they were in adolescence (Blieszner & Roberto, 2012). Sharing thoughts and feelings is sometimes greater in friendship than in marriage, although commitment is less strong as friends come and go over the life course. Even so, some adult friendships continue for many years, at times throughout life. Seeing each other with frequency contributes to friendship continuity and—because female friends get together more than male friends do—to longer-lasting friendship ties among women (Sherman, de Vries, & Lansford, 2000).

But because of the dramatic rise in social media use, today's friendships are no longer as constrained by physical proximity. Nearly three-fourths of 18- to 29-year-olds who access the Internet use social networking sites; Facebook reports more than 500 million active users worldwide. Consequently, networks of "friends" have expanded. These include new types of friends—for example, people who meet through an interest-group chat room or blog and may never meet in person but who offer emotional support (Lefkowitz, Vukman, & Loken, 2012). As yet, little is known about the role of these online ties in adults' lives.

Do social networking sites lead young adults to form a large number of acquaintances at the expense of intimate friendships? Research reveals that people with 500 or more Facebook friends actually interact individually—by "liking" posts, leaving comments on walls, or engaging in Facebook chats—with far fewer. Among these large-network Facebook users, men engaged in one-on-one communication with an average of just 10 friends, women with just 16 (Henig & Henig, 2012). Facebook led passive tracking of casual relationships to rise while core friendships remained limited.

LOOK AND LISTEN

Ask your Facebook friends to indicate the size of their Facebook network along with the number of friends they interacted with individually during the past month. Do large-network users have only a limited number of core friendships? ●

Same-Sex Friendships. Throughout life, women have more intimate same-sex friendships than men. Extending a pattern evident in childhood and adolescence, female friends often say they prefer to "just talk," whereas male friends say they like to "do something" such as play sports (see Chapter 12, page 417). Barriers to intimacy between male friends include competitiveness, which may make men unwilling to disclose weaknesses, and concern that if they tell about themselves, their friends will not reciprocate (Reid & Fine, 1992). Because of greater intimacy and give-and-take, women generally evaluate their same-sex friendships more positively than men do. But they also have higher expectations of friends (Blieszner & Roberto, 2012). Thus, they are more disapproving if friends do not meet their expectations.

Of course, individual differences in friendship quality exist. The longer-lasting men's friendships are, the closer they become and the more they include disclosure of personal information (Sherman, de Vries, & Lansford, 2000). Furthermore, involvement in family roles affects reliance on friends. For single adults, friends are the preferred companions and confidants. The more intimate young adults' same-sex friendships are in terms of warmth, exchange of social support, and self-disclosure, the more satisfying and longer-lasting the relationship and the

Male friends usually like to "do something" together, whereas female friends prefer to "just talk." But the longer-lasting men's friendships are, the more intimate they become, increasingly including disclosure of personal information.

greater its contribution to psychological well-being (Sanderson, Rahm, & Beigbeder, 2005; Sherman, Lansford, & Volling, 2006). Gay and lesbian romantic relationships often develop out of close same-sex friendships, with lesbians, especially, forging compatible friendships before becoming involved romantically (Diamond, 2006).

As they develop romantic ties and marry, young adults—especially men—direct more of their disclosures toward their partners (Carbery & Buhrmester, 1998). Still, friendships continue to be vital contexts for personal sharing throughout adulthood. A best friendship can augment well-being when a marriage is not fully satisfying (but not when the marriage is low in quality) (Birditt & Antonucci, 2007). Turn back to Figure 12.2 on page 418 to view developmental trends in self-disclosure to romantic partners and friends.

Other-Sex Friendships.

From the college years through career exploration and settling into work roles, other-sex friendships increase. After marriage, they decline for men but continue to rise for women, who more often form them in the workplace. Highly educated, employed women have the largest number of other-sex friends. Through these relationships, young adults often gain in companionship and self-esteem and learn about masculine and feminine styles of intimacy (Bleske & Buss, 2000). Because men confide especially easily in their female friends, such friendships offer them a unique opportunity to broaden their expressive capacity. And women sometimes say male friends offer objective points of view on problems and situations—perspectives not available from female friends (Monsour, 2002).

Many people try to keep other-sex friendships platonic to safeguard their integrity (Messman, Canary, & Hause, 2000). But sometimes the relationship changes into a romantic bond. When a solid other-sex friendship does evolve into a romance, it may be more stable and enduring than a romantic relationship formed without a foundation in friendship. And emerging adults, especially, are flexible about people they include in their friendship networks (Barry & Madsen, 2010). After a breakup, they may even keep a former romantic partner on as a friend.

Siblings as Friends.

Whereas intimacy is essential to friendship, commitment—willingness to maintain a relationship and care about the other—is the defining characteristic of family ties. As young people marry and invest less time in developing a romantic partnership, siblings—especially sisters whose earlier bond was positive—become more frequent companions than in adolescence (Birditt & Antonucci, 2007). Often, friend and sibling roles merge. For example, Sharese described Heather's practical assistance—helping with moving and running errands during an illness—in kinship terms: "She's like a sister to me. I can always turn to her." And adult sibling ties resemble friendships, in which the main concerns are staying in contact, offering social support, and enjoying being together.

A childhood history of intense parental favoritism and sibling rivalry can disrupt sibling bonds in adulthood (Panish & Stricker, 2002). But when family experiences have been positive, relationships between adult siblings can be especially close and are important sources of psychological well-being (Sherman, Lansford, & Volling, 2006). A shared background promotes similarity in values and perspectives and the possibility of deep mutual understanding.

In families with five to ten siblings, common in industrialized nations in the past and still widespread in some cultures, close sibling bonds may replace friendships (Fuller-Iglesias, 2010). One 35-year-old with five siblings, who all—with their partners and children—resided in the same small city, remarked, "With a family like this, who needs friends?"

Loneliness

Young adults are at risk for **loneliness**—unhappiness resulting from a gap between the social relationships we currently have and those we desire—when they either do not have an intimate partner or lack gratifying friendships. Though both situations give rise to similar emotions, they are not interchangeable. For example, even though she had several enjoyable friendships, Heather sometimes felt lonely because she was not dating someone she cared about. And although Sharese and Ernie were happily married, they felt lonely after moving to a new town where they did not know anyone.

Loneliness peaks in the late teens and early twenties and then declines steadily into the seventies. Figure 14.2 shows this trend, based on a large Canadian sample ranging in age from 13 to 80 (Rokach, 2001). The rise in loneliness during early adulthood is understandable. As young people move through school and employment settings, they must constantly develop new relationships. Also, young adults may expect more from their intimate ties than older adults, who have learned to live with imperfections (Rokach, 2003). With age, people become better at accepting loneliness and using it for positive ends—to sharpen awareness of their personal fears and needs.

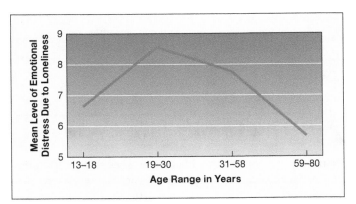

FIGURE 14.2 Changes in emotional distress due to loneliness from adolescence to late adulthood. More than 700 Canadian 13- to 80-year-olds responded to a questionnaire assessing the extent to which they experienced emotional distress due to loneliness. Loneliness rose sharply from the early teens to the late teens and early twenties and then declined. (Adapted from Rokach, 2001.)

Loneliness is intense after loss of an intimate tie: Separated, divorced, or widowed adults are lonelier than their married, co-habiting, or single counterparts. And immigrants from collectivist cultures report higher levels of loneliness than people born in the United States and Canada (DiTommaso, Brannen, & Burgess, 2005). Leaving a large, close-knit family system for an individualistic society seems to prompt intense feelings of isolation.

Personal characteristics also contribute to loneliness. Young adults who are socially anxious or who have insecure working models of attachment to parents are more often intensely lonely (Jackson et al., 2002). When extreme loneliness persists, it is associated with self-defeating attitudes and behaviors. To prevent anticipated rejection, people who are chronically lonely tend to be socially unresponsive, insensitive, and even hostile to others (Cacioppo & Patrick, 2008). These defensive responses, whether cause or consequence of loneliness, promote further isolation.

As long as loneliness is not overwhelming, it can motivate young people to reach out to others. It can also encourage them to find ways to be comfortably alone and to use this time to understand themselves better (Rokach & Neto, 2006). Healthy personality development involves striking this balance between gratifying relationships with others and contentment within ourselves.

ASK YOURSELF

REVIEW Describe gender differences in traits usually desired in a long-term partner. What findings indicate that *both* biological and social forces contribute to those differences?

CONNECT How might recollections and evaluations of childhood attachment history, discussed on page 474, affect intimate partners' readiness to develop companionate love?

APPLY After dating for two years, Mindy and Graham reported greater love and relationship satisfaction than during their first few months of dating. What features of communication probably deepened their bond, and why is it likely to endure?

REFLECT Do you have a nonromantic, close other-sex friendship? If so, how has it enhanced your emotional and social development?

 ## The Family Life Cycle

For most young people, the life course takes shape within the **family life cycle**—a series of phases characterizing the development of most families around the world. In early adulthood, people typically live on their own, marry, and bear and rear children. In middle age, as their children leave home, their parenting responsibilities diminish. Late adulthood brings retirement, growing old, and (more often for women) death of one's spouse (McGoldrick & Shibusawa, 2012). Stress tends to be greatest during transitions between phases, as family members redefine and reorganize their relationships.

But as our earlier discussion made clear, we must be careful not to view the family life cycle as a fixed progression. Wide variations exist in the sequence and timing of its phases—high rates of out-of-wedlock births, delayed marriage and childbearing, divorce, and remarriage, among others. And some people, voluntarily or involuntarily, do not experience all family life-cycle phases. Still, the family life-cycle model is useful. It offers an organized way of thinking about how the family system changes over time and the impact of each phase on the family unit and the individuals within it.

Leaving Home

During her first semester of college, Sharese noticed a change in how she related to her mother. She found it more enjoyable to discuss daily experiences and life goals, sought advice and listened with greater openness, and expressed affection more freely.

Departure from the parental home is a major step toward assuming adult responsibilities. The average age of leaving has risen since the 1960s; today, it resembles the departure age at the beginning of the twentieth century. But reasons for coresidence have changed: Early twentieth-century young adults resided with parents so they could contribute to the family economy. Twenty-first-century young adults living at home are typically financially dependent on their parents. This trend toward later home-leaving is evident in most industrialized nations, though substantial variation in timing exists. Because government support is available, young adults in the Scandinavian countries move out relatively early (Furstenberg, 2010). In contrast, cultural traditions in Mediterranean countries promote lengthy coresidence, extending for men into the mid-thirties.

Departures for education tend to occur at earlier ages, those for full-time work and marriage later. Because the majority of U.S. young adults enroll in higher education, many leave home around age 18. Those from divorced, single-parent homes tend to be early leavers, perhaps because of family stress (Cooney & Mortimer, 1999). Compared with the previous generation, fewer North American and Western European young people leave home to marry; more do so just to be "independent"—to express their adult status.

Slightly over half of U.S. 18- to 25-year-olds return to their parents' home for brief periods after first leaving (U.S. Census Bureau, 2012b). Usually, role transitions, such as the end of college or military service, bring young people back. But tight job markets, high housing costs, or failures in work or love can also prompt a temporary return home. Also, young people who left because of family conflict often return—largely because they were not ready for independent living.

Residential independence rises steadily with age; by the early thirties, 90 percent of U.S. young adults live on their own (U.S. Census Bureau, 2012b). Contrary to popular belief, returning home usually is not a sign of weakness (Ward & Spitze, 2007). Rather, as people encounter unexpected twists and turns

A father helps his son, a recent college graduate, move belongings back into the parental home. Parents usually respond to their children's return with generous financial and emotional support, doing everything possible to help them move into adult roles.

on the road to independence, the parental home offers a safety net and base of operations for launching adult life.

The extent to which young people live on their own before marriage varies with SES and ethnicity. Those who are economically well-off are more likely to establish their own residence. Among African-American, Hispanic, and Native-American groups, poverty and a cultural tradition of extended-family living lead to lower rates of leaving home, even among young people in college or working (De Marco & Berzin, 2008; Fussell & Furstenberg, 2005). Unmarried Asian young adults also tend to live with their parents. But the longer Asian families have lived in the United States, where they are exposed to individualistic values, the more likely young people are to move out before marriage (Lou, Lalonde, & Giguère, 2012).

Parents of young adults living at home are usually highly committed to helping their children move into adult roles. Many provide wide-ranging assistance—not just financial support, but material resources, advice, companionship, and emotional support as well. A survey of large sample of U.S. parents diverse in SES and ethnicity and their adult children revealed that parents gave more to those with greater needs (because of problems or younger age) and to those they perceived as more successful in education and career progress. Furthermore, most parents and young-adult children judged the amount of parental support to be appropriate, though a sizable minority viewed intense support (provided several times a week) as excessive (Fingerman et al., 2009, 2012a). Nevertheless, children receiving intense support adjusted especially well, expressing firmer goals and greater life satisfaction—perhaps because the intense support matched their needs.

Still, in homes where parents and young adults live together, conflict over personal and moral values related to the young person's future tends to rise (Rodríguez & López, 2011).

But when young adults feel securely attached to parents and well-prepared for independence, departure from the home is linked to more satisfying parent–child interaction and successful transition to adult roles, even among ethnic minorities that strongly emphasize family loyalty and obligations (Smetana, Metzger, & Campione-Barr, 2004; Whiteman, McHale, & Crouter, 2010). And regardless of living arrangements, young people doing well often have close, enjoyable relationships with their parents, who offer help because they see it as key to their child's future success (Fingerman et al., 2012b).

Finally, leaving home very early can contribute to long-term disadvantage because it is associated with lack of parental financial and emotional support, job seeking rather than education, and earlier childbearing (Furstenberg, 2010). Not surprisingly, non-college-bound youths who move out in their late teens tend to have less successful educational, marriage, and work lives. U.S. poverty-stricken young people are more likely than their nonpoor counterparts to leave home by age 18 (Berzin & De Marco, 2010). But if still at home beyond that age, they are less likely to move out well into their thirties—a trend that may reflect the steep challenges they face in attaining self-sufficiency and exiting poverty.

Joining of Families in Marriage

The average age of first marriage in the United States has risen from about 20 for women and 23 for men in 1960 to 26½ for women and 29 for men today. Consequently, just 20 percent of contemporary U.S. 18- to 29-year-olds are married, compared to 60 percent a half-century ago (U.S. Census Bureau, 2012b). Postponement of marriage is even more marked in Western Europe—to the early thirties for men and the late twenties for women.

The number of first and second marriages has declined over the last few decades as more people stay single, cohabit, or do not remarry after divorce. In 1960, 85 percent of Americans had been married at least once; today, the figure is 70 percent. At present, 51 percent of U.S. adults, only a slight majority, live together as married couples (U.S. Census Bureau, 2012b). In one recent survey, 4 out of 10 American adults agreed that "marriage is becoming obsolete." Nevertheless, marriage remains a central life goal for young people (Pew Forum on Religion and Public Life, 2010; Smith & Snell, 2009). Irrespective of SES and ethnicity, most U.S. 18- to 23-year-olds say they want to marry and have children.

Same-sex marriages are recognized nationwide in Argentina, Belgium, Brazil, Canada, Denmark, France, Iceland, the Netherlands, New Zealand, Norway, Portugal, South Africa, Spain, and Sweden. In the United States, twelve states—Connecticut, Delaware, Iowa, Maine, Maryland, Massachusetts, Minnesota, New Hampshire, New York, Rhode Island, Vermont, and Washington—as well as the District of Columbia have legalized same-sex marriage. Several other states either grant people in same-sex unions the same legal status as married couples or extend nearly all spousal rights to same-sex partnerships.

Because legalization is so recent, research on same-sex couples in the context of marriage is scant. But evidence on cohabiting same-sex couples suggests that the same factors that contribute to happiness in other-sex marriages do so in same-sex unions (Diamond, 2006).

Marriage is more than the joining of two individuals. It also requires that two systems—the spouses' families—adapt and overlap to create a new subsystem. Consequently, marriage presents complex challenges. This is especially so today because husband–wife roles are only gradually moving toward true partnership—educationally, occupationally, and in emotional connectedness. Among same-sex couples, acceptance of the relationship by parents, inclusion of the partner in family events, and living in a supportive community where they can be open about their bond benefit relationship satisfaction and durability (Diamond, 2006).

Marital Roles. Their honeymoon over, Sharese and Ernie turned to a multitude of issues they had previously decided individually or their families of origin had prescribed—from everyday matters (when and how to eat, sleep, talk, work, relax, have sex, and spend money) to family traditions and rituals (which to retain, which to work out for themselves). And as they related to their social world as a couple, they modified relationships with parents, siblings, extended family, friends, and co-workers.

Contemporary alterations in the context of marriage, including changing gender roles and living farther from family members, mean that couples must work harder than in the past to define their relationships. Although partners are usually similar in religious and ethnic background, "mixed" marriages are increasingly common today. Among new marriages in the United States, 15 percent are between partners of a different race or ethnicity, more than double the rate in 1980 (Taylor et al., 2012). Because of increased opportunities for interracial contact in colleges, workplaces, and neighborhoods and more positive attitudes toward intermarriage, highly educated young adults are more likely than their less educated counterparts to marry partners of another race or ethnicity (Qian & Lichter, 2011). Nevertheless, couples whose backgrounds differ face extra challenges in transitioning to married life.

Because many couples live together beforehand, marriage has become less of a turning point in the family life cycle. Still, defining marital roles can be difficult. Age of marriage is the most consistent predictor of marital stability. Young people who marry in their teens to mid-twenties are more likely to divorce than those who marry later (Lehrer & Chen, 2011). Most of those who marry early have not developed a secure identity or sufficient independence to form a mature marital bond. Both early marriage followed by childbirth and childbirth before marriage are more common among low-SES adults (U.S. Census Bureau, 2012b). This acceleration of family formation complicates adjustment to life as a couple.

Despite progress in the area of women's rights, **traditional marriages,** involving a clear division of roles—husband as head of household responsible for family economic well-being, wife as caregiver and homemaker—still exist in Western nations. In

Arms laden with her toddler, a briefcase, and a bag of groceries, an employed mother heads home to prepare dinner. In industrialized nations, women in dual-earner marriages continue to shoulder most housework responsibilities.

recent decades, however, these marriages have changed, with many women who focused on motherhood while their children were young returning to the work force later.

In **egalitarian marriages,** partners relate as equals, sharing power and authority. Both try to balance the time and energy they devote to their occupations, their children, and their relationship. Most well-educated, career-oriented women expect this form of marriage. And college-student couples who eventually intend to marry often plan in advance how they will coordinate work and family roles, especially if the woman intends to enter a male-dominated career (Peake & Harris, 2002).

In Western nations, men in dual-earner marriages participate much more in child care than in the past. U.S. fathers in such marriages put in 85 percent as much time as mothers do (see pages 202–203 in Chapter 6). But housework—cleaning, cooking, laundry, and picking up clutter, which (unlike children) do not require immediate attention—reveals a different story. Recent surveys indicate that women in the United States and most Western European nations spend nearly twice as much time as men on housework, and women in Australia spend four times as much (Sayer, 2010). In Sweden, which places a high value on gender equality, men do more than in other nations. In contrast, men typically do little housework or child care in Japan, where corporate jobs demand long work hours and traditional marriages are common (Geist, 2010; Shwalb et al., 2004).

Women's housework hours do decline as their employment hours increase. But a close look at gender differences in most industrialized countries reveals that men fail to compensate (Cooke, 2010; Lippe, 2010). As Figure 14.3 shows for Australia, the United Kingdom, and the United States, men spend the same amount of time at housework, irrespective of their partners' employment schedules. Therefore, employed women's reduced housework hours are made possible by either purchase of time-saving services (cleaning help, prepackaged meals) or greater tolerance for unkempt homes, or both. Perhaps women continue to do the lion's share of housework because their paid

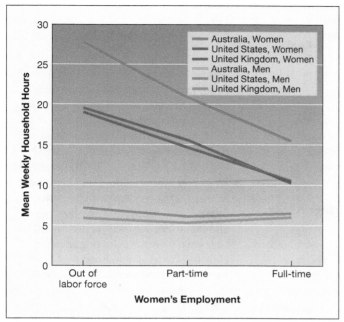

FIGURE 14.3 Women's and men's housework hours by women's employment for couples in Australia, the United Kingdom, and the United States. In each nation, as women's employment hours increase, they devote less time to housework. Men's contribution to housework is substantially less than women's. And women's level of employment has no influence on men's housework hours. (From L. P. Cooke, 2010, "The Politics of Housework," in J. Treas & S. Drobnic, [Eds.], *Dividing the Domestic: Men, Women, and Household Work in Cross-National Perspective*, p. 70. Copyright © 2010 by the Board of Trustees of the Leland Stanford Jr. University. Adapted with the permission of Stanford University Press, www.sup.org.)

work is viewed as secondary to their husband's, regardless of how much they earn (Lachance-Grzela & Bouchard, 2010). In sum, true equality in marriage is still rare, and couples who strive for it usually attain a form of marriage in between traditional and egalitarian.

Marital Satisfaction. Despite its rocky beginnings, Sharese and Ernie's marriage grew to be especially happy. In contrast, Christy and Gary became increasingly discontented. What distinguishes satisfying marriages from less successful partnerships? Differences between these two couples mirror the findings of a large body of research on personal and contextual factors, summarized in Table 14.1.

Christy and Gary had children early and struggled financially. Gary's negative, critical personality led him to get along poorly with Christy's parents and to feel threatened when he and Christy disagreed. Christy tried to offer Gary encouragement and support, but her own needs for nurturance and individuality were not being met. Gary was uncomfortable with Christy's career aspirations. As she came closer to attaining them, the couple grew further apart. In contrast, Sharese and Ernie married later, after their educations were complete. They postponed having children until their careers were under way and they had built a sense of togetherness that allowed each to thrive as an individual. Patience, caring, common values and interests, humor, affection, sharing of personal experiences through conversation, cooperating in household responsibilities, and good conflict-resolution skills contributed to their compatibility.

Men tend to report feeling slightly happier with their marriages than women do (Howard, Galambos, & Krahn, 2010; Kurdek, 2005). In the past, quality of the marital relationship had a greater impact on women's psychological well-being, but today it predicts mental health similarly for both genders. Women, however, feel particularly dissatisfied with marriage when the demands of husband, children, housework, and career are overwhelming (Forry, Leslie, & Letiecq, 2007; Saginak & Saginak, 2005). Research in both Western and non-Western industrialized nations reveals that equal power in the relationship and sharing of family responsibilities usually enhance both partners' satisfaction, largely by strengthening marital harmony (Amato & Booth, 1995; Xu & Lai, 2004).

TABLE 14.1
Factors Related to Marital Satisfaction

FACTOR	HAPPY MARRIAGE	UNHAPPY MARRIAGE
Family backgrounds	Partners similar in SES, education, religion, and age	Partners very different in SES, education, religion, and age
Age at marriage	After mid-20s	Before mid-20s
Timing of first pregnancy	After first year of marriage	Before or within first year of marriage
Relationship to extended family	Warm and positive	Negative; wish to maintain distance
Marital patterns in extended family	Stable	Unstable; frequent separations and divorces
Financial and employment status	Secure	Insecure
Family responsibilities	Shared; perception of fairness	Largely the woman's responsibility; perception of unfairness
Personality characteristics and behavior	Emotionally positive; common interests; good conflict-resolution skills	Emotionally negative and impulsive; lack of common interests; poor conflict-resolution skills

Note: The more factors present, the greater the likelihood of marital happiness or unhappiness.
Sources: Diamond, Fagundes, & Butterworth, 2010; Gere et al., 2011; Johnson et al., 2005.

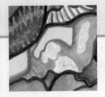

Social Issues: Health

Partner Abuse

Violence in families is a widespread health and human rights issue, occurring in all cultures and SES groups. Often one form of domestic violence is linked to others. Recall the story of Karen in Chapter 13. Her husband, Mike, not only assaulted her sexually and physically but also abused her psychologically—isolating, humiliating, and demeaning her. Violent adults also break their partner's favorite possessions, punch holes in walls, or throw objects. If children are present, they may become victims.

Partner abuse in which husbands are perpetrators and wives are physically injured is most likely to be reported to authorities. But many acts of family violence are not reported. When researchers ask American couples about fights that led to acts of hostility, men and women report similar rates of assault (Dutton, 2007). Women victims are more often physically injured, but sex differences in severity of abuse are small (Dutton, 2012; Ehrensaft, Moffitt, & Caspi, 2004). Partner abuse occurs at about the same rate in same-sex relationships as in heterosexual relationships (Schwartz & Waldo, 2004).

Although self-defense is a frequently reported cause of domestic assault by women, American men and women are equally likely to "strike first" (Currie, 1999; Dutton, 2007). "Getting my partner's attention," "gaining control," and "expressing anger" are reasons that partners typically give for abusing each other.

Factors Related to Partner Abuse

In abusive relationships, dominance–submission sometimes proceeds from husband to wife, sometimes from wife to husband. In about one-third to one-half of cases, both partners are violent (Dutton, Nicholls, & Spidel, 2005). Marvin's and Pat's relationship helps us understand how partner abuse escalates. Shortly after their wedding, Pat began complaining about the demands of Marvin's work and insisted that he come home early to spend time with her. When he resisted, she hurled epithets, threw objects, and slapped him. One evening, Marvin became so angry at Pat's hostilities that he smashed a dish against the wall, threw his wedding ring at her, and left the house. The next morning, Pat apologized and promised not to attack again. But her outbursts became more frequent and desperate.

These violence–remorse cycles, in which aggression escalates, characterize many abusive relationships. Why do they occur?

Personality and developmental history, family circumstances, and cultural factors combine to make partner abuse more likely (Diamond, Fagundes, & Butterworth, 2010).

Many abusers are overly dependent on their spouses as well as jealous, possessive, and controlling. For example, the thought of Karen ever leaving induced such high anxiety in Mike that he monitored all her activities. Depression, anxiety, and low self-esteem also characterize abusers. And because they have great difficulty managing anger, trivial events—such as an unwashed shirt or a late meal—can trigger abusive episodes. When asked to explain their offenses, they attribute greater blame to their partner than to themselves (Henning, Jones, & Holdford, 2005).

A high proportion of spouse abusers grew up in homes where parents engaged in hostile interactions, used coercive discipline, and were abusive toward their children (Ehrensaft, 2009). Perhaps this explains why conduct problems in childhood and violent delinquency in adolescence also predict partner abuse (Dutton, 2007). Adults with childhood exposure to domestic violence are not doomed to repeat it. But their parents provided them with negative expectations and behaviors that they often transfer to their close relationships. Stressful life events, such as job loss or financial difficulties, increase the likelihood of partner abuse (Emery &

Of course, from time to time, individuals are bound to say or do something upsetting to their partner. When this happens, the partner's attributions, or explanations for the behavior, make a difference. For example, a wife who interprets her husband's critical remark about her weight as unintentional ("He just isn't aware I'm sensitive about that") is far more likely to express both current and long-term marital satisfaction than a wife who views such comments as malicious ("He's trying to hurt my feelings") (Barelds & Dijkstra, 2011; Fincham & Bradbury, 2004). In fact, partners who hold overly positive (but still realistic) biases concerning each other's attributes are happier with their relationships (Claxton et al., 2011). As they turn to each other for feedback about themselves, these "positive illusions" enhance self-esteem and psychological well-being. And over time, positive illusions favorably influence behavior, as partners modify their actions to bring them closer to their partner's generous perceptions. In contrast, people who feel devalued by their partner tend to react with anxiety and insecurity—more so when they are low in self-esteem, which heightens fear of rejection. To protect themselves, they often mete out criticism and contempt in kind, setting in motion hostile, defensive exchanges that create the very rejection they fear (Murray, 2008). Alternatively, individuals may disengage emotionally, suppressing negative feelings so as not to poison the relationship (Driver et al., 2012). In the process, shared positive emotion also declines, and intimacy erodes.

At their worst, marital relationships can become contexts for intense opposition, dominance–submission, and emotional and physical violence. As the Social Issues: Health box above explains, although women are more often targets of severe partner abuse, both men and women play both roles: perpetrator and victim.

High school and college courses in family life education can promote better mate selection and teach communication

Laumann-Billings, 1998). Because of widespread poverty, African Americans and Native Americans report high rates of partner violence (Hoff, 2001). Alcohol abuse is another related factor.

At a societal level, cultural norms that endorse male dominance and female submissiveness promote partner abuse (Kaya & Cook, 2010). As Figure 14.4 shows, in countries with widespread poverty that also sanction gender inequality, partner violence against women is especially high, affecting nearly half or more of the female population.

Victims are chronically anxious and depressed and experience frequent panic attacks (Warshaw, Brashler, & Gil, 2009). Why don't they simply leave these destructive relationships? A variety of situational factors discourage them from leaving. A victimized wife may depend on her husband's earning power or fear even worse harm to herself or her children. Extreme assaults, including homicide, tend to occur after partner separation (Campbell & Glass, 2009). And victims of both sexes, but especially men, are deterred by the embarrassment of going to the police. Also, victims may falsely believe that their partner will change.

Intervention and Treatment

Community services available to battered women include crisis telephone lines that provide anonymous counseling and social support and shelters that offer safety and treatment (see page 449). Because many women return to their abusive partners several times before making their final move, community agencies usually offer therapy to male batterers. Most rely on several months to a year of group sessions that confront rigid gender stereotyping; teach communication, problem solving, and anger control; and use social support to motivate behavior change (Whitaker, Baker, & Arias, 2007).

Although existing treatments are better than none, most are not effective at dealing with relationship difficulties or alcohol abuse. Consequently, many treated perpetrators repeat their violent behavior with the same or a new partner (Hamberger et al., 2009). At present, few interventions acknowledge that men also are victims. Yet ignoring their needs perpetuates domestic violence. When victims do not want to separate from a violent partner, a whole-family treatment approach that focuses on changing partner interaction and reducing high life stress is crucial.

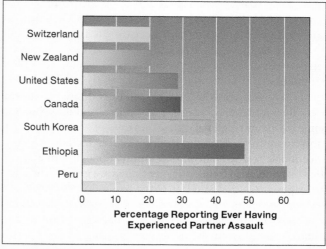

FIGURE 14.4 Assaults by intimate partners against women in seven nations. In each country, samples of women were asked to indicate whether they had ever experienced partner physical abuse. The incidence, always underreported, is high in all nations. It is especially high in countries that endorse traditional gender roles and suffer from widespread poverty. (From Kaya & Cook, 2010; World Health Organization, 2000, 2005.)

skills that contribute to gratifying romantic partnerships and marriages. And counseling aimed at helping couples listen to each other with understanding and empathy, focus on positive traits and memories, and use effective conflict-resolution strategies can cultivate the self-esteem, affection, and respect needed for the relationship to be resilient and enduring (Gottman, 2011).

Parenthood

In the past, the issue of whether to have children was, for many adults, a biological given or a compelling social expectation. Today, in Western industrialized nations, it is a matter of true individual choice. Effective birth control techniques enable adults to avoid having children in most instances. And changing cultural values allow people to remain childless with far less fear of social criticism and rejection than a generation or two ago.

In 1950, 78 percent of American married couples were parents. Today, 70 percent bear children, and they tend to be older when they have their first child. Consistent with this pattern of delayed childbearing and with the decision of most women to divide their energies between family and work, family size in industrialized nations has declined. In 1950, the average number of children per woman was 3.1. Currently, it is 2.1 in the United States and Canada; 1.9 in the United Kingdom, 1.7 in Sweden; 1.6 in Canada, 1.4 in Germany; and 1.3 in Italy and Japan (U.S. Census Bureau, 2012a, 2012b). Nevertheless, the vast majority of married people continue to embrace parenthood as one of life's most meaningful experiences. Why do they do so, and how do the challenges of child rearing affect the adult life course?

The Decision to Have Children. The choice of parenthood is affected by a complex array of factors, including financial circumstances, personal and religious values, and health conditions. Women with traditional gender identities usually decide to have children. Whether a woman is employed has less impact on childbearing than her occupation. Women in high-status, demanding careers less often choose parenthood and, when they do, more often delay it than women with less consuming jobs. Parenthood typically reduces work hours and slows career progress among career-oriented women but has no impact on men (Abele & Spurk, 2011). Professional women seem to consider these consequences in decision making about parenthood.

When Americans are asked about their desire to have children, they mention a variety of advantages and disadvantages. Some ethnic and regional differences exist, but in all groups, the most important reasons for having children include the warm, affectionate relationship and the stimulation and fun that children provide. Also frequently mentioned are growth and learning experiences that children bring to the lives of adults, the desire to have someone carry on after one's own death, and feelings of accomplishment and creativity that come from helping children grow (Cowan & Cowan, 2000; O'Laughlin & Anderson, 2001).

Most young adults also realize that having children means years of extra burdens and responsibilities. Among disadvantages of parenthood, they cite loss of freedom most often, followed by concerns about role overload (not enough time for both family and work responsibilities) and about the financial strains of child rearing. According to a conservative estimate, today's new parents in the United States will spend about $280,000 to rear a child from birth to age 18, and many will incur substantial additional expense for higher education and financial dependency during emerging adulthood (U.S. Department of Agriculture, 2012).

Greater freedom to choose whether and when to have children makes family planning more challenging today than in the past. With each partner expecting an equal say, childbearing often becomes a matter of delicate negotiation (Cowan & Cowan, 2000). Yet carefully weighing the pros and cons of parenthood means that many more couples are making informed and personally meaningful choices—a trend that should increase the chances that they will have children when ready and will find parenting an enriching experience.

Transition to Parenthood. The early weeks after a baby enters the family are full of profound changes: constant caregiving, added financial responsibilities, and less time for the couple's relationship. In response, gender roles of husband and wife usually become more traditional—even for couples like Sharese and Ernie who are strongly committed to gender equality (Katz-Wise, Priess, & Hyde, 2010; Lawrence et al., 2010).

First and Second Births. For most new parents, the arrival of a baby—though often associated with mild declines in relationship satisfaction and communication quality—does not cause significant marital strain. Marriages that are gratifying and supportive tend to remain so (Doss et al., 2009; Feeney et al., 2001; Miller, 2000). And the small decrease in satisfaction from

Compared to a first birth, a second birth typically requires that fathers become more actively involved in parenting, sharing in the high demands of tending to both a baby and a young child.

pregnancy to post-birth may not be unique to early parenthood (Mitnick, Heyman, & Slep, 2009). Couples who do not become parents also experience a slight decrease in relationship satisfaction across a similar time frame.

Nevertheless, troubled marriages usually become even more distressed after childbirth (Houts et al., 2008; Kluwer & Johnson, 2007). And when expectant mothers anticipate lack of partner support in parenting, their prediction generally becomes reality, yielding an especially difficult post-birth adjustment (Driver et al., 2012; McHale & Rotman, 2007).

Violated expectations about division of labor in the home powerfully affect new parents' well-being. In dual-earner marriages, the larger the difference in men's and women's caregiving responsibilities, the greater the decline in marital satisfaction after childbirth, especially for women—with negative consequences for parent–infant interaction. In contrast, sharing caregiving predicts greater parental happiness and sensitivity to the baby (McHale et al., 2004; Moller, Hwang, & Wickberg, 2008). An exception exists, however, for employed lower-SES women who endorse traditional gender roles. When their husbands take on considerable child-care responsibilities, these mothers tend to report more distress, perhaps because of disappointment at being unable to fulfill their desire to do most of the caregiving (Goldberg & Perry-Jenkins, 2003).

Postponing childbearing until the late twenties or thirties, as more couples do today, eases the transition to parenthood. Waiting permits couples to pursue occupational goals, gain life experience, and strengthen their relationship. Under these circumstances, men are more enthusiastic about becoming fathers and therefore more willing to participate. And women whose careers are well under way and whose marriages are happy are more likely to encourage their husbands to share housework and child care, which fosters fathers' involvement (Lee & Doherty, 2007; Schoppe-Sullivan et al., 2008).

A second birth typically requires that fathers take an even more active role in parenting—by caring for the firstborn while the mother is recuperating and by sharing in the high demands of tending to both a baby and a young child. Consequently, well-functioning families with a newborn second child typically pull back from the traditional division of responsibilities that occurred after the first birth. Fathers' willingness to place greater emphasis on the parenting role is strongly linked to mothers' adjustment after the arrival of a second baby (Stewart, 1990). And the support and encouragement of family, friends, and spouse are crucial for fathers' well-being.

Interventions. Couples' groups led by counselors are effective in easing the transition to parenthood (Gottman, Gottman, & Shapiro, 2010). Therapists report that many couples know little about caring for infants, perhaps because they grew up in small families where they had few sibling caregiving responsibilities. They are also unaware of the potential impact of a new baby on their relationship.

In one program, first-time expectant couples gathered once a week for six months to discuss their dreams for the family and changes in relationships sparked by the baby's arrival. Eighteen months after the program ended, participating fathers described themselves as more involved with their child than did fathers in a no-intervention condition. Perhaps because of fathers' caregiving assistance, participating mothers maintained their prebirth satisfaction with family and work roles. Three years after the birth, the marriages of participating couples were intact and just as happy as they had been before parenthood. In contrast, 15 percent of couples receiving no intervention had divorced (Cowan & Cowan, 1997; Schulz, Cowan, & Cowan, 2006). For high-risk parents struggling with poverty or the birth of a child with disabilities, interventions must be more intensive, focusing on enhancing social support and parenting skills (Petch & Halford, 2008).

Generous, paid employment leave—widely available in industrialized nations but not in the United States—is crucial for parents of newborns (see Chapter 3, pages 104–105). But financial pressures mean that many new mothers who are eligible for unpaid work leave take far less than they are guaranteed by U.S. federal law, while new fathers take little or none. When favorable workplace policies exist and parents take advantage of them, couples are more likely to support each other and experience family life as gratifying (Feldman, Sussman, & Zigler, 2004; Han & Waldfogel, 2003). As a result, the stress caused by the birth of a baby stays at manageable levels.

Families with Young Children.
A year after the birth of their first child, Sharese and Ernie received a phone call from Heather, who asked how they liked parenthood: "Is it a joy, a dilemma, a stressful experience—how would you describe it?"

Chuckling, Sharese and Ernie responded in unison, "All of the above!"

In today's complex world, men and women are less certain about how to rear children than in previous generations. Clarifying child-rearing values and implementing them in warm, involved, and appropriately demanding ways are crucial for the welfare of the next generation and society. Yet cultures do not always place a high priority on parenting, as indicated by lack of many societal supports for children and families (see Chapter 2, pages 66–67). Furthermore, changing family forms mean that the lives of today's parents differ substantially from those of past generations.

In previous chapters, we discussed a wide variety of influences on child-rearing styles, including personal characteristics of children and parents, SES, and ethnicity. The couple's relationship is also vital. Parents who engage in effective coparenting, collaborating and showing solidarity and respect for each other in parenting roles, are more likely to gain in warm marital interaction, feel competent as parents, use effective child-rearing practices, and have children who are developing well (McHale et al., 2002a; Schoppe-Sullivan et al., 2004). When parents forge this supportive coparenting alliance within the first few months after childbirth, it is more likely to persist (Fivaz-Depeursinge & Corboz-Warnery, 1999).

For employed parents, a major struggle is finding good child care and, when their child is ill or otherwise in need of emergency care, taking time off from work or making other urgent arrangements. The younger the child, the greater parents' sense of risk and difficulty—especially low-income parents, who must work longer hours to pay bills; who often, in the United States, have no workplace benefits (health insurance or paid sick leave); who typically cannot afford the cost of child care; and who experience more immediate concerns about their children's safety (Halpern, 2005b; Nomaguchi & Brown, 2011). When competent, convenient child care is not available, the woman usually faces added pressures. She must either curtail or give up her work, with profound financial consequences in low-income families, or endure unhappy children, missed workdays, and constant searches for new arrangements.

Despite its challenges, rearing young children is a powerful source of adult development. Parents report that it expands their emotional capacities, enriches their lives, and enhances psychological well-being (Nomaguchi & Milkie, 2003; Schindler, 2010). For example, Ernie remarked that through sharing in child rearing, he felt "rounded out" as a person. Other involved parents say that parenthood helped them tune in to others' feelings and needs, required that they become more tolerant, self-confident, and responsible, and broadened their extended family, friendship, and community ties. In a survey of a large, nationally representative sample of U.S. fathers, paternal history of engagement with children predicted greater community service and assistance of extended family members in middle adulthood (Eggebeen, Dew, & Knoester, 2010).

Families with Adolescents.
Adolescence brings sharp changes in parental roles. In Chapters 11 and 12, we noted that parents must establish a revised relationship with their adolescent children—blending guidance with freedom and gradually loosening control. As adolescents gain in autonomy and explore values and goals in their search for identity, parents often complain that their teenager is too focused on peers and no longer

cares about being with the family. Heightened parent–child bickering over everyday issues takes a toll, especially on mothers, who do most of the negotiating with teenagers.

Overall, children seem to navigate the challenges of adolescence more easily than parents, many of whom report a dip in marital and life satisfaction. More people seek family therapy during this period of the family life cycle than during any other (Steinberg & Silk, 2002).

Parent Education. In the past, family life changed little from one generation to the next, and adults learned what they needed to know about parenting through modeling and direct experience. Today's world confronts adults with a host of factors that impinge on their ability to succeed as parents.

Contemporary parents eagerly seek information on child rearing. In addition to popular parenting books, magazines, and websites, new mothers access knowledge about parenting through social media, including chat rooms and blogs. They also reach out to networks of other women for knowledge and assistance. Fathers, by contrast, rarely have social networks through which they can learn about child care and child rearing. Consequently, they frequently turn to mothers to figure out how to relate to their child, especially if they have a close, confiding marriage (Lamb & Lewis, 2004; McHale, Kuersten-Hogan, & Rao, 2004). Recall from Chapter 6 that marital harmony fosters both parents' positive engagement with babies, but it is especially important for fathers.

Parent education courses exist to help parents clarify child-rearing values, improve family communication, understand how children develop, and apply more effective parenting strategies. A variety of programs yield positive outcomes, including enhanced knowledge of effective parenting practices, improved parent–child interaction, and heightened awareness by parents of their role as educators of their children (Bert, Ferris, & Borkowski, 2008; Smith, Perou, & Lesesne, 2002). Another benefit is social support—opportunities to discuss concerns

Men are less likely than women to learn about child rearing through informal social networks. Fathers especially may benefit from parent education programs that help them clarify child-rearing values, learn about child development, and parent effectively.

with experts and other dedicated parents, who share the view that no job is more important to the future of society than child rearing.

ASK YOURSELF

REVIEW What strategies can couples use to ease the transition to parenthood?

CONNECT What aspects of adolescent development make rearing teenagers stressful for parents, leading to a dip in marital and life satisfaction? (See Chapter 11, pages 369–370, and Chapter 12, pages 415–416.)

APPLY After her wedding, Sharese was convinced she had made a mistake. Cite factors that sustained her marriage and led it to become especially happy.

REFLECT Do you live with your parents or on your own? Describe factors that contributed to your current living arrangements. How would you characterize the quality of your relationship with your parents? Do your responses match the findings of research?

The Diversity of Adult Lifestyles

The current array of adult lifestyles dates back to the 1960s, when young people began to question the conventional wisdom of previous generations and to ask, "How can I find happiness? What kinds of commitments should I make to live a full and rewarding life?" As the public became more accepting of diverse lifestyles, choices such as staying single, cohabiting, remaining childless, and divorcing seemed more available.

Today, nontraditional family options have penetrated the American mainstream. Many adults experience not just one but several. As we will see, some adults make a deliberate decision to adopt a lifestyle, whereas others drift into it. The lifestyle may be imposed by society, as is the case for cohabiting same-sex couples in the United States, who cannot marry legally in most states. Or people may choose a certain lifestyle because they feel pushed away from another, such as a marriage gone sour. In sum, the adoption of a lifestyle can be within or beyond the person's control.

Singlehood

On finishing her education, Heather joined the Peace Corps and spent four years in Ghana. Though open to a long-term relationship, she had only fleeting romances. After she returned to the United States, she went from one temporary job to another until, at age 30, she finally found steady employment in a large international travel company as a tour director. A few years later, she

Compared with single men, single women more easily come to terms with their lifestyle, in part because of the greater social support available to women through intimate same-sex friendships.

advanced into a management position. At age 35, over lunch with Sharese, she reflected on her life: "I was open to marriage, but after I got my career going, it would have interfered. Now I'm so used to independence that I question whether I could adjust to living with another person. I like being able to pick up and go where I want, when I want, without having to ask anyone or think about caring for anyone. But there's a tradeoff: I sleep alone, eat most of my meals alone, and spend a lot of my leisure time alone."

Singlehood—not living with an intimate partner—has increased in recent years, especially among young adults. For example, the rate of never-married Americans in their twenties has nearly tripled since 1960, to 75 percent of young people. As they move into their thirties, more people marry: By 30 to 34 years of age, about 32 percent remain single. Today, more people marry later or not at all, and divorce has added to the numbers of single adults—slightly more than half when adults of all ages are considered. In view of these trends, it is likely that most Americans will spend a substantial part of their adult lives single, and a growing minority—about 8 to 10 percent—will stay that way (Pew Research Center, 2010a; U.S. Census Bureau, 2012b).

Because they marry later, more young-adult men than women are single. But women are far more likely than men to remain single for many years or their entire life. With age, fewer men are available with characteristics that most women seek in a mate—the same age or older, equally or better educated, and professionally successful. In contrast, men can choose partners from a large pool of younger unmarried women. Because of the tendency for women to "marry up" and men to "marry down," men with a high school diploma or less and highly educated women in prestigious careers are overrepresented among singles after age 30.

Ethnic differences also exist. For example, the percentage of never-married African Americans is nearly twice as great as that of Caucasian Americans in early adulthood (U.S. Census Bureau, 2012b). As we will see later, high unemployment among black men interferes with marriage. Many African Americans eventually marry in their late thirties and forties, a period in which black and white marriage rates come closer together.

Singlehood can have a variety of meanings. At one extreme are people who choose it deliberately; at the other those who see themselves as single because of circumstances beyond their control. Most, like Heather, are in the middle—adults who wanted to marry but made choices that took them in a different direction. In interview studies of never-married women, some said they focused on occupational goals instead of marriage. Others reported that they found singlehood preferable to their disappointing intimate relationships. And still others commented that they just did not meet "the right person" (Baumbusch, 2004; Lewis, 2000).

The most commonly mentioned advantages of singlehood are freedom and mobility. But singles also recognize drawbacks—loneliness, the dating grind, limited sexual and social life, reduced sense of security, and feelings of exclusion from the world of married couples. Single men have more physical and mental health problems than single women, who more easily come to terms with their lifestyle, in part because of the greater social support available to women through intimate same-sex friendships (Pinquart, 2003). But overall, people over age 35 who have always been single are content with their lives (DePaulo & Morris, 2005; Lucas et al., 2003). Though not quite as happy as married people, they report feeling considerably happier than people recently widowed or divorced.

Nevertheless, many single people go through a stressful period in their late twenties or early thirties, when most of their friends have married. Widespread veneration of marriage, along with negative stereotyping of singles as socially immature and self-centered, contributes (Morris et al., 2008). The mid-thirties is another trying time, as the biological deadline for pregnancy approaches. Interviews with 28- to 34-year-old single women revealed that they were acutely aware of pressures from family members, the shrinking pool of eligible men, the risks of later childbearing, and a sense of being different (Sharp & Ganong, 2011). A few decide to become parents through artificial insemination or a love affair. And an increasing number are adopting, often from overseas countries.

Cohabitation

Cohabitation refers to the lifestyle of unmarried couples who have a sexually intimate relationship and who share a residence. Until the 1960s, cohabitation in Western nations was largely limited to low-SES adults. Since then, it has increased in all groups, with an especially dramatic rise among well-educated, economically advantaged young people. Today's young adults are much more likely than those of a generation ago to form their first conjugal union through cohabitation. Among American young people, cohabitation is now the preferred mode of entry into a committed intimate partnership, chosen by over 60 percent of couples (U.S. Census Bureau, 2012b). Cohabitation rates are even higher among adults with failed marriages; about one-third of these households include children.

© RICK GOMEZ/BLEND IMAGES/CORBIS

For some couples, cohabitation serves as *preparation for marriage*—a time to test the relationship and get used to living together. For others, however, it is an *alternative to marriage*, offering the rewards of sexual intimacy and companionship along with the possibility of easy departure if satisfaction declines. It is not surprising, then, that cohabiters vary greatly in the extent to which they share money and possessions and take responsibility for each other's children.

Although Americans are more open to cohabitation than in the past, their attitudes are not as positive as those of Western Europeans. In the Netherlands, Norway, and Sweden, cohabitation is thoroughly integrated into society, with cohabiters having many of the same legal rights and responsibilities as married couples. Between 70 and 90 percent of young people cohabit in their first intimate partnership, and cohabiters are nearly as committed to each other as married people (Fussell & Gauthier, 2005; Perelli-Harris & Gassen, 2012). Whereas about 50 percent of American cohabiting unions break up within two years, only 6 to 16 percent dissolve in Western Europe (Jose, O'Leary, & Moyer, 2010; Kiernan, 2002). When they decide to marry, Dutch, Norwegian, and Swedish cohabiters more often do so to legalize their relationships, especially for the sake of children. American cohabiters typically marry to confirm their love and commitment—sentiments that Western Europeans attach to cohabitation.

Furthermore, U.S. couples who cohabit before they are engaged to be married are more prone to divorce than couples who wait to live together until after they have made a commitment to each other. But this association is less strong or absent in Western European nations (Jose, O'Leary, & Moyer, 2010; Kline et al., 2004; Rhoades, Stanley, & Markman, 2006). U.S. young people who cohabit prior to engagement tend to have less conventional values. They have had more sexual partners and are more politically liberal, less religious, and more androgynous. In addition, a larger number have parents who divorced (Kurdek, 2006).

These personal characteristics may contribute to the negative outcomes associated with cohabitation. But the cohabitation experience itself also plays a role. Cohabiters are less likely than married people to pool finances or jointly own a house. In addition, both preengagement cohabiters and formerly cohabiting married couples have poorer-quality relationships (Cohan & Kleinbaum, 2002; Kline et al., 2004). Perhaps the open-ended nature of the cohabiting relationship reduces motivation to develop effective conflict-resolution skills. When cohabiters carry negative communication into marriage, it undermines marital satisfaction. Finally, a history of parental divorce may increase cohabiters' willingness to dissolve a union when it becomes less satisfying.

Certain couples, however, are exceptions to the trends just described. People who cohabit after separation or divorce often test a new relationship carefully to prevent another failure, especially when children are involved. As a result, they cohabit longer and are less likely to move toward marriage. Similarly, cohabitation is often an alternative to marriage among low-SES couples (Pew Research Center, 2010a). Many regard their earn-

Among U.S. couples, making a long-term commitment by becoming engaged before cohabiting predicts an enduring marriage. U.S. young people who cohabit prior to engagement are at increased risk for divorce.

ing power as too uncertain for marriage and continue living together, sometimes giving birth to children and marrying when their financial status improves.

Finally, cohabiting gay and lesbian couples report strong relationship commitment (Kurdek, 2006). When their relationships become difficult, they end more often than those of heterosexual cohabiters and married couples because of fewer barriers to separating. For example, in 37 U.S. states, same-sex cohabiters cannot plan to legalize their relationship because of laws or constitutional provisions that limit marriage to a man and a woman. Furthermore, same-sex cohabiters are less likely to have children in common and more likely to have extended family members who are unsupportive (Lau, 2012; Rothblum, Balsam, & Solomon, 2011). In a study in which same-sex couples in Vermont were followed over three years, cohabiters were more likely than couples in civil unions to have ended their relationships (Balsam et al., 2008). Civil unions were as stable as heterosexual marriages.

For people not ready for marriage, cohabitation combines the rewards of a close relationship with the opportunity to avoid the legal obligations of marriage. But cohabiting couples can encounter difficulties precisely because they do not have these obligations. Bitter fights over property, money, rental contracts, and responsibility for children are the rule rather than the exception when unmarried couples split up.

Childlessness

At work, Sharese got to know Beatrice and Daniel. Married for seven years and in their mid-thirties, they did not have children and were not planning any. To Sharese, their relationship seemed especially caring and affectionate. "At first, we were open to becoming parents," Beatrice explained, "but eventually we decided to focus on our marriage."

Childlessness in the United States has increased steadily, from 9 percent of women between ages 20 and 44 in 1975 to about 20 percent today, with similar trends occurring in other Western nations (Livingston & Cohn, 2010). Some people are *involuntarily childless* because they did not find a partner with whom to share parenthood or their efforts at fertility treatments did not succeed. Beatrice and Daniel are in another category—men and women who are *voluntarily childless*. But voluntary childlessness is not always a permanent condition. A few people decide early that they do not want to be parents and stick to their plans. But most, like Beatrice and Daniel, make their decision after they are married and have developed a lifestyle they do not want to give up. Later, some change their minds.

Besides marital satisfaction and freedom from child-care responsibilities, common reasons for not having children include the woman's career and economic security (Amba & Martinez, 2006; Kemkes-Grottenhaler, 2003). Consistent with these motives, the voluntarily childless are usually college-educated, have prestigious occupations, and are highly committed to their work.

Negative stereotypes of nonparenthood—as a sign of self-indulgence and irresponsibility—have weakened in Western nations as people have become more accepting of diverse lifestyles (Dykstra & Hagestad, 2007). Acceptance is greatest among highly educated women, who—while not necessarily embracing childlessness—may be more attuned to the demands of parenthood, which are still borne mostly by women (Koropeckyj-Cox & Pendell, 2007).

In line with this trend, voluntarily childless adults are just as content with their lives as parents who have warm relationships with their children. But adults who cannot overcome infertility are likely to be dissatisfied—some profoundly disappointed, others more ambivalent, depending on compensations in other areas of their lives (Letherby, 2002; Nichols & Pace-Nichols, 2000). Childlessness seems to interfere with adjustment and life satisfaction only when it is beyond a person's control.

Divorce and Remarriage

Divorce rates have stabilized since the mid-1980s, partly because of rising age of marriage, which is linked to greater financial stability and marital satisfaction. In addition, the increase in cohabitation has curtailed divorce: Many relationships that once would have been marriages now break up before marriage. Still, 45 percent of U.S. marriages dissolve (U.S. Census Bureau, 2012b). Because most divorces occur within seven years of marriage, many involve young children. Divorces are also common during the transition to midlife, when people have adolescent children—a period (as noted earlier) of reduced marital satisfaction.

Nearly two-thirds of divorced adults remarry. But marital failure is even greater during the first few years of second marriages—10 percent above that for first marriages. Afterward, the divorce rates for first and second marriages are similar (U.S. Census Bureau, 2012b).

Factors Related to Divorce. Why do so many marriages fail? As Christy and Gary's divorce illustrates, the most obvious reason is a disrupted husband–wife relationship.

Christy and Gary did not argue more than Sharese and Ernie. But their problem-solving style was ineffective, and it weakened their attachment to each other. When Christy raised concerns, Gary reacted with contempt, resentment, defensiveness, and retreat. This demand–withdraw pattern is found in many partners who split up, with women more often insisting on change and men more often retreating (Birditt et al., 2010; Haltzman, Holstein, & Moss, 2007). Another typical style involves little conflict, but partners increasingly lead separate lives because they have different expectations of family life and few shared interests, activities, or friends (Gottman & Levenson, 2000).

What problems underlie these maladaptive communication patterns? In a nine-year longitudinal study, researchers asked a U.S. national sample of 2,000 married people about marital problems and followed up three, six, and nine years later to find out who had separated or divorced (Amato & Rogers, 1997). Wives reported more problems than husbands, with the gender difference largely involving the wife's emotions, such as anger and hurt feelings. Husbands seemed to have difficulty sensing their wife's distress, which contributed to her view of the marriage as unhappy. Regardless of which spouse reported the problem or was judged responsible for it, the strongest predictors of divorce during the following decade were infidelity, spending money foolishly, drinking or using drugs, expressing jealousy, engaging in irritating habits, and moodiness.

Background factors that increase the chances of divorce are younger age at marriage, not attending religious services, being previously divorced, and having parents who had divorced—all of which are linked to marital difficulties. For example, couples who married at younger ages are more likely to report infidelity and jealousy. Low religious involvement subtracts an influential context for instilling positive marital attitudes and behaviors. And research following families over two decades reveals that parental divorce elevates risk of divorce in at least two succeeding generations, in part because it promotes child adjustment problems and reduces commitment to the norm of lifelong marriage (Amato & Cheadle, 2005; Wolfinger, 2005). As a result, when

FREDERICK BASS/GETTY IMAGES

An ineffective problem-solving style can lead to divorce. Partners who split up often follow a pattern in which one partner raises concerns, and the other reacts with resentment, anger, and retreat.

adult children marry, they are more likely to engage in inconsiderate behaviors and to have conflict-ridden relationships and less likely to try to work through these difficulties or (if they do try) to have the skills to do so. Marriage to a caring spouse from a stable family background reduces these negative outcomes.

Poorly educated, economically disadvantaged couples who suffer multiple life stresses are especially likely to split up (Clarke-Stewart & Brentano, 2006). But Christy's case represents another trend—rising marital breakup among well-educated, career-oriented, economically independent women. When a woman's workplace status and income exceed her husband's, the risk of divorce increases—an association explained by differing gender-role beliefs between the spouses (Popenoe, 2006). A husband's lack of support for his wife's career can greatly heighten her unhappiness and, therefore, the chances that she will end the marriage. Overall, women are twice as likely as men to initiate divorce proceedings.

In addition to the relationship factors just described, American individualism—which includes the belief that each person has the right to pursue self-expression and personal happiness—contributes to the unusually high U.S. divorce rate (see page 346 in Chapter 10) (Cherlin, 2009). Whether cohabiting or married, Americans partner, split up, and repartner more often than anywhere else in the industrialized world. When people are dissatisfied with their intimate relationship, the cultural value of individualism encourages moving on.

Consequences of Divorce. Divorce involves the loss of a way of life and therefore a part of the self sustained by that way of life. As a result, it provides opportunities for both positive and negative change. Immediately after separation, both men and women experience disrupted social networks, a decline in social support, and increased anxiety, depression, and impulsivity (Amato, 2000). For most, these reactions subside within two years. Nonworking women who organized their identities around their husbands have an especially hard time. And some noncustodial fathers feel disoriented and rootless as a result of decreased contact with their children (Coleman, Ganong, & Leon, 2006). Others distract themselves with a frenzy of social activity.

Finding a new partner contributes most to the life satisfaction of divorced adults (Forste & Heaton, 2004; Wang & Amato, 2000). But it is more crucial for men, who adjust less well than women to living on their own. Despite loneliness and a drop in income (see Chapter 10), women tend to bounce back more easily from divorce. Christy, for example, developed new friendships and a gratifying sense of self-reliance. However, a few women—especially those who are anxious and fearful, who remain strongly attached to their ex-spouses, or who lack education and job skills—experience a drop in self-esteem and persistent depression (Amato, 2000; Coleman, Ganong, & Leon, 2006). Job training, continued education, career advancement, and social support from family and friends play vital roles in the economic and psychological well-being of many divorced women.

Remarriage. On average, people remarry within four years of divorce, men somewhat faster than women. As noted earlier, remarriages are especially vulnerable to breakup, for several reasons. First, practical matters—financial security, help in rearing children, relief from loneliness, and social acceptance—figure more heavily into a second marriage than a first. These concerns do not provide a sound footing for a lasting partnership. Second, some people transfer the negative patterns of interaction learned in their first marriage to the second. Third, people with a failed marriage behind them are even more likely to view divorce as an acceptable solution when marital difficulties resurface. Finally, remarried couples experience more stress from stepfamily situations (Coleman, Ganong, & Leon, 2006). As we will see, stepparent–stepchild ties are powerful predictors of marital happiness.

Blended families generally take three to five years to develop the connectedness and comfort of intact biological families. Family life education, couples counseling, and group therapy can help divorced and remarried adults adapt to the complexities of their new circumstances (Whiteside, 2006).

Varied Styles of Parenthood

Diverse family forms result in varied styles of parenthood. Each type of family—blended, never-married, gay or lesbian, among others—presents unique challenges to parenting competence and adult psychological well-being.

Stepparents. Whether stepchildren live in the household or visit only occasionally, stepparents are in a difficult position. Stepparents enter the family as outsiders and, too often, move into their new parental role too quickly. Lacking a warm attachment bond to build on, their discipline is usually ineffective. Stepparents frequently criticize the biological parent for being too lenient, while the biological parent may view the stepparent as too harsh (Ganong & Coleman, 2004). Compared with first-marriage parents, remarried parents typically report higher levels of tension and disagreement, most centering on child-rearing issues. When both adults have children from prior marriages, rather than only one, more opportunities for conflict exist and relationship quality is poorer.

Stepmothers are especially likely to experience conflict. Those who have not previously been married and had children may have an idealized image of family life, which is quickly shattered. Expected to be in charge of family relationships, stepmothers quickly find that stepparent–stepchild ties do not develop instantly. After divorce, biological mothers are frequently jealous, uncooperative, and possessive of their children. Even when their husbands do not have custody, stepmothers feel stressed. As stepchildren go in and out of the home, stepmothers find life easier without resistant children and then may feel guilty about their "unmaternal" feelings (Church, 2004; MacDonald & DeMaris, 1996). No matter how hard a stepmother tries to build a close parent–child bond, her efforts are probably doomed to failure in the short run.

Stepfathers with children of their own tend to establish positive bonds with stepchildren relatively quickly, perhaps because they are experienced in building warm parent–child ties and feel less pressure than stepmothers to plunge into parenting (Ganong et al., 1999). But stepfathers without biological children (like their stepmother counterparts) can have unrealistic expectations. Or their wives may push them into the father role, sparking negativity from children. After making several overtures that are ignored or rebuffed, these stepfathers frequently withdraw from parenting (Hetherington & Clingempeel, 1992).

In interviews in which young-adult stepchildren provided retrospective accounts of their stepparent relationships, the quality of these ties varied widely, from warm and loving, to ambivalent, to coexisting, to critical and rejecting. A caring husband–wife bond, sensitive relationship-building behaviors by the stepparent, cooperation from the biological parent, and supportive extended family members all affected the development of stepparent–stepchild ties. Over time, many couples built a coparenting partnership that improved interactions with stepchildren (Ganong, Coleman, & Jamison, 2011). But because stepparent–stepchild bonds are hard to establish, the divorce rate is higher for remarried couples with stepchildren than for those without them.

Never-Married Single Parents. Over the past several decades, births to unmarried mothers in industrialized nations have increased dramatically. Today, about 40 percent of U.S. births are to single mothers, more than double the percentage in 1980. Whereas teenage parenthood has declined (see page 378 in Chapter 11), unwed parenthood among mothers in their twenties and older has risen. About 11 percent of U.S. children live with a single mother who has never married (U.S. Census Bureau, 2012b). In recent years, more single women over age 30 in high-status occupations have become parents. But they are still few in number, and little is known about how they and their children fare.

In the United States, African-American young women make up the largest group of never-married parents. About 64 percent of births to black mothers in their twenties are to women without a partner, compared with 28 percent of births to white women (U.S. Census Bureau, 2012b). African-American women postpone marriage more and childbirth less than women in other U.S. ethnic groups. Job loss, persisting unemployment, and consequent inability of many black men to support a family have contributed to the number of African-American never-married, single-mother families.

Never-married African-American mothers tap the extended family, especially their own mothers and sometimes male relatives, for help in rearing their children (Gasden, 1999; Jayakody & Kalil, 2002). For about one-third, marriage—not necessarily to the child's biological father—occurs within nine years after birth of the first child (Wu, Bumpass, & Musick, 2001). These couples function much like other first-marriage parents. Their children are often unaware that the father is a stepfather, and

parents do not report the child-rearing difficulties typical of blended families (Ganong & Coleman, 1994).

Still, for low-SES women, never-married parenthood generally increases financial hardship; about half live in poverty (Mather, 2010). Nearly 50 percent of white mothers and 60 percent of black mothers have a second child while unmarried. And they are far less likely than divorced mothers to receive paternal child support payments, although child support enforcement both reduces financial stress and increases father involvement (Huang, 2006).

Children of never-married mothers who lack father involvement achieve less well in school and display more antisocial behavior than children in low-SES, first-marriage families—problems that make life more difficult for mothers (Waldfogel, Craigie, & Brooks-Gunn, 2010). But marriage to the child's biological father benefits children only when the father is a reliable source of economic and emotional support. For example, adolescents who feel close to their nonresident father fare better in school performance and emotional and social adjustment than do those in two-parent homes where a close father tie is lacking (Booth, Scott, & King, 2009).

Unfortunately, most unwed fathers—who usually have no more than a modest education and are doing poorly financially—gradually spend less and less time with their children (Lerman, 2010). Strengthening parenting skills, social support, education, and employment opportunities for low-SES parents would greatly enhance the well-being of unmarried mothers and their children.

Gay and Lesbian Parents. According to recent estimates, about 20 to 35 percent of lesbian couples and 5 to 15 percent of gay couples are parents, most through previous heterosexual

Gay and lesbian parents are as committed to and effective at child rearing as heterosexual parents. Overall, families headed by same-sex partners can be distinguished from other families only by issues related to living in a nonsupportive society.

marriages, some through adoption, and a growing number through reproductive technologies (Gates et al., 2007; Goldberg, 2010; Patterson & Riskind, 2010). In the past, because of laws assuming that homosexuals could not be adequate parents, those who divorced a heterosexual partner lost custody of their children. Today, some U.S. states hold that sexual orientation by itself is irrelevant to custody. A few U.S. states, however, ban gay and lesbian couples from adopting children. Among other countries, gay and lesbian adoptions are legal in Argentina, Belgium, Brazil, Canada, Iceland, Mexico, the Netherlands, Norway, South Africa, Spain, Sweden, the United Kingdom, and Uruguay.

Most research on homosexual parents and children is limited to volunteer samples. Findings indicate that gay and lesbian parents are as committed to and effective at child rearing as heterosexual parents and sometimes more so (Bos, van Balen, & van den Boom, 2007; Tasker, 2005). Also, whether born to or adopted by their parents or conceived through donor insemination, children in gay and lesbian families did not differ from the children of heterosexuals in mental health, peer relations, or gender-role behavior (Allen & Burrell, 1996; Bos & Sandfort, 2010; Farr, Forssell, & Patterson, 2010; Goldberg, 2010). Two additional studies, which surmounted the potential bias associated with a volunteer sample by including all lesbian-mother families who had conceived children at a fertility clinic, also reported that children were developing favorably (Brewaeys et al., 1997; Chan, Raboy, & Patterson, 1998). Likewise, among participants drawn from a representative sample of British mothers and their 7-year-olds, children reared in lesbian-mother families did not differ from children reared in heterosexual families in adjustment and gender-role preferences (Golombok et al., 2003).

Furthermore, children of gay and lesbian parents are similar to other children in sexual orientation; the large majority are heterosexual (Tasker, 2005). But some evidence suggests that more adolescents from homosexual families experiment for a time with partners of both sexes, perhaps as a result of being reared in families and communities especially tolerant of nonconformity and difference (Bos, van Dalen, & Van den Boom, 2004; Stacey & Biblarz, 2001).

When extended-family members withhold acceptance, homosexual mothers and fathers often build "families of choice" through friends, who assume the roles of relatives. Usually, however, parents of gays and lesbians cannot endure a permanent rift (Fisher, Easterly, & Lazear, 2008). With time, interactions between homosexual parents and their families of origin become more positive and supportive.

A major concern of gay and lesbian parents is that their children will be stigmatized by their parents' sexual orientation. Most studies indicate that incidents of teasing or bullying are rare because parents and children carefully manage the information they reveal to others (Tasker, 2005). Overall, families headed by homosexuals can be distinguished from other families only by issues related to living in a nonsupportive society.

ASK YOURSELF

REVIEW Why is never-married single parenthood especially high among African Americans? What conditions affect parent and child well-being in these families?

CONNECT Return to Chapter 10, pages 346–350, and review the impact of divorce and remarriage on children and adolescents. How do those findings resemble outcomes for adults? What might account for the similarities?

APPLY After dating for three months, Wanda and Scott decided to live together. Their parents worried that cohabitation would reduce the couple's chances for a successful marriage. Is this fear justified? Why or why not?

REFLECT Do your own experiences or those of your friends match research findings on cohabitation, singlehood, never-married parents, or gay and lesbian parents? Select one instance and discuss.

 ## Career Development

Besides family life, vocational life is a vital domain of social development in early adulthood. After choosing an occupation, young people must learn how to perform its tasks well, get along with co-workers, respond to authority, and protect their own interests. When work experiences go well, adults develop new competencies, feel a sense of personal accomplishment, make new friends, and become financially independent and secure. And as we have seen, especially for women but also for men who support their partner's career development, aspirations and accomplishments in the workplace and the family are interwoven.

Establishing a Career

Our discussion earlier in this chapter highlighted diverse paths and timetables for career development. *TAKE A MOMENT...* Consider, once again, the wide variations among Sharese, Ernie, Christy, and Gary. Notice that Sharese and Christy, like many women, had *discontinuous* career paths—ones that were interrupted or deferred by child rearing and other family needs (Huang & Sverke, 2007; Moen & Roehling, 2005). Furthermore, not all people embark on the vocation of their dreams. As noted in our consideration of emerging adulthood, the late-2000s recession greatly increased the number of young people in jobs that do not match their educational preparation.

Over half of adults in their twenties with bachelor's or graduate degrees do manage to enter their chosen field. Even so, initial experiences can be discouraging. At the health department, Sharese discovered that paperwork consumed much of her day. Because each project had a deadline, the pressure of productivity weighed heavily on her. Adjusting to unanticipated disappointments in salary, supervisors, and co-workers is difficult.

As new employees become aware of the gap between their expectations and reality, resignations are common. Furthermore, in careers with opportunities for promotion, high aspirations must often be revised downward because the structure of most work settings resembles a pyramid, with fewer management and supervisory jobs. For these reasons—in addition to layoffs due to financial exigencies—workers in their twenties change jobs often; five or six changes are not unusual.

Recall from our discussion of Levinson's theory that career progress often depends on the quality of a mentoring relationship. Access to an effective mentor—a person with advanced experience and knowledge who is invested in the junior person's career success and who fosters a bond of trust—is jointly affected by the availability of willing people and the individual's capacity to select an appropriate individual (Ramaswami & Dreher, 2007). The best mentors are seldom top executives, who tend to be preoccupied and therefore less helpful and sympathetic. Usually, young adults fare better with mentors who are just above them in experience and advancement or who are members of their professional associations (Allen & Finkelstein, 2003). Furthermore, mentoring early in a worker's career increases the likelihood of mentoring later on (Bozionelos et al., 2011). The professional and personal benefits of mentoring induce employees to provide it to others and to seek it again for themselves.

Women and Ethnic Minorities

Women and ethnic minorities have penetrated nearly all professions, but their talents often are not developed to the fullest. Women, especially those who are members of economically disadvantaged minorities, remain concentrated in occupations that offer little opportunity for advancement, and they are underrepresented in executive and managerial roles (see Chapter 13, page 457). And although the overall difference between men's and women's earnings is smaller today than 30 years ago, it remains considerable in all industrialized countries (Rampell, 2010). U.S. government surveys following 9,000 U.S. college-educated workers for a decade revealed that a year after receiving their bachelor's degrees, women working full time earned just 80 percent as much as men. The difference was largely (but not entirely) due to gender differences in college majors: Women more often chose education and service fields, men higher-paying scientific and technical fields. Ten years after graduation, the gender pay gap had widened: Women's pay was only 69 percent of men's, and in no profession did women's earnings equal men's (Dey & Hill, 2007). Gender disparities in career development accounted for about 90 percent of the gap, with the remaining 10 percent attributed to on-the-job discrimination.

Especially for women in traditionally feminine occupations, career planning is often short-term and subject to change. Unlike the continuous career lives of most well-educated men, many women enter and exit the labor market several times, or reduce their work hours from full-time to part-time as they give birth to and rear children (Furchtgott-Roth, 2009; Lips, 2013). Time away from a career greatly hinders advancement—a major reason that women in prestigious, male-dominated careers tend to delay or avoid childbearing (Blair-Loy & DeHart, 2003). Yet an increasing number of accomplished professional women are leaving their jobs to devote themselves full-time to child rearing—a trend that has generated mistaken, gender-stereotyped interpretations of their "choice." Interviews with such women reveal that the decision to leave their careers is almost always agonizing (Rubin & Wooten, 2007; Stone & Lovejoy, 2004). The most common reason given was a high-pressured, inflexible work environment that offered no leeway for work–family life balance.

In addition, low self-efficacy with respect to male-dominated fields limits women's career progress. Women who pursue nontraditional careers usually have "masculine" traits—high achievement orientation, self-reliance, and belief that their efforts will result in success. But even those with high self-efficacy are less certain than their male counterparts that they can overcome barriers to career success. In a study of women scientists on university faculties, those reporting a sexist work climate (sexual harassment or discrimination in salary, promotion, or resources) were less satisfied with their jobs and less productive (Settles et al., 2006).

Gender-stereotyped images of women as followers rather than leaders slow advancement into top-level management positions. And because men dominate high-status fields, they must be willing to mentor women into leadership positions and take time from their work responsibilities to do so. Mentoring by a senior-male executive predicts progress into management roles and pay gains more strongly for women in male-dominated industries than for men (Ramaswami et al., 2010). When a powerful male leader *sponsors* the advancement of a talented woman, designating her as having the qualities to succeed, senior-level decision makers are far more likely to take notice.

Despite laws guaranteeing equality of opportunity, racial and ethnic bias in career opportunities remains strong (Smith, Brief, & Colella, 2010). In one study, researchers recruited two three-member teams consisting of a white, a black, and a Hispanic male job applicant, each 22 to 26 years old and matched

Women in male-dominated fields, such as this scientist, usually have "masculine" traits, such as high achievement orientation and self-reliance. Nevertheless, many encounter workplace barriers to career success.

Despite his strong résumé, this African-American job seeker is less likely than white applicants—even those with fewer qualifications—to receive a callback or job offer.

on verbal and interpersonal skills and physical attractiveness. The applicants were assigned identical fictitious résumés (with the exception that the résumé of the white member of the second team disclosed a criminal record) and sent out to apply for 170 entry-level jobs in New York City (Pager, Western, & Bonikowski, 2009). Findings revealed that the white applicant received callbacks or job offers from employers slightly more often than the Hispanic applicant, with the black applicant trailing far behind. When the experiment was repeated with the second team, the white felon remained slightly preferred over both minority applicants, despite their clean records.

In another similar investigation, which varied applicant qualifications within résumés, white men and women with high-quality résumés received substantially more employer callbacks than those with low-quality résumés. In contrast, having a high-quality résumé made little difference for blacks. As the researchers noted, "Discrimination appears to bite twice, making it harder for African Americans to find a job and to improve their employability" (Bertrand & Mullainathan, 2004, p. 3). Consistent with this conclusion, African Americans spend more time searching for work, experience less stable employment, and acquire less work experience than Caucasian Americans with equivalent job qualifications (Pager & Shepherd, 2008).

Ethnic minority women often must surmount combined gender and racial discrimination to realize their career potential. Those who succeed frequently display an unusually high sense of self-efficacy, attacking problems head-on despite repeated obstacles to achievement. In interviews with African-American women who had become leaders in diverse fields, all reported intense persistence, fueled by supportive relationships with other women, including teachers and peers. Many described their mothers as inspiring role models who had set high standards for them (Richie et al., 1997). Others felt empowered by a deep sense of connection to their African-American communities.

Despite obstacles to success, women who have developed rewarding careers generally report higher levels of psychological well-being and life satisfaction (Erdogan et al., 2012). This finding suggests that some of the discontent frequently expressed by married women may not be due to marriage per se but, rather, to lack of a gratifying work life. Consistent with this idea, most women prefer to blend work and family (Barnett & Hyde, 2001). And those in financially stressed families must do so.

Combining Work and Family

The majority of women with children are in the work force (see page 350 in Chapter 10), most in dual-earner marriages or cohabiting relationships. More women than men report moderate to high levels of stress in trying to meet both work and family responsibilities (Higgins, Duxbury, & Lyons, 2010; Zhao, Settles, & Sheng, 2011).

TAKE A MOMENT... Think about a dual-earner family you know well. What are the main sources of strain? When Sharese returned to her job after her children were born, she felt a sense of *role overload,* or conflict between the demands of work and family responsibilities. In addition to a challenging career, she also (like most employed women) shouldered more household and child-care tasks. And both Sharese and Ernie felt torn between the desire to excel at their jobs and the desire to spend more time with each other, their children, and their friends and relatives. Role overload is linked to increased psychological stress, physical health problems, poorer marital relations, less effective parenting, child behavior problems, and poorer job performance (Perry-Jenkins, Repetti, & Crouter, 2000; Saginak & Saginak, 2005; ten Brummelhuis et al., 2012).

Role overload is magnified for women in low-status work roles with rigid schedules and little autonomy (Marshall, 1997).

Time-flexible policies enabling employees to work from home help parents adjust work roles to meet family needs. As a result, employees work harder, take less time off, and feel more committed to their jobs.

Applying What We Know

Strategies That Help Dual-Earner Couples Combine Work and Family Roles

Strategy	Description
Devise a plan for sharing household tasks.	As soon as possible in the relationship, discuss relative commitment to work and family and division of household responsibilities. Decide who does a particular chore on the basis of who has the needed skill and time, not on the basis of gender. Schedule regular times to rediscuss your plan.
Begin sharing child care right after the baby's arrival.	For fathers, strive to spend equal time with the baby early. For mothers, refrain from imposing your standards on your partner. Instead, share the role of "child-rearing expert" by discussing parenting values and concerns often. Attend a parent education course together.
Talk over conflicts about decision making and responsibilities.	Face conflict through communication. Clarify your feelings and needs and express them to your partner. Listen and try to understand your partner's point of view. Then be willing to negotiate and compromise.
Establish a balance between work and family.	Critically evaluate the time you devote to work in view of your family values and priorities. If it is too much, cut back.
Make sure your relationship receives regular loving care.	See Applying What We Know on page 475.
Press for workplace and public policies that assist dual-earner-family roles.	Difficulties faced by dual-earner couples are partly due to lack of workplace and societal supports. Encourage your employer to provide benefits that help combine work and family, such as flexible work hours, parental leave with pay, and on-site high-quality, affordable child care. Communicate with lawmakers and other citizens about improving public policies for children and families.

Couples in prestigious careers have more control over both work and family domains. For example, Sharese and Ernie devised ways to spend more time with their children. They picked them up at child care early one day a week, compensating by doing certain occupational tasks on evenings and weekends. But in a Canadian study of more than 3,000 individuals in dual-earner families who were employed full-time, most coped with role overload by scaling back at home (leaving things undone) or restructuring family roles (taking over responsibilities for each other, as needed), with women doing more of this than men (Higgins, Duxbury, & Lyons, 2010). Overall, couples expected family life to accommodate to work demands. They seldom adjusted work roles to meet family needs. Although some had little flexibility at work, others simply prioritized work over family life.

Workplace supports can greatly reduce role overload, yielding substantial payoffs for employers. Among a large, nationally representative sample of U.S. working adults, the greater the number of time-flexible policies available in their work settings (for example, time off to care for a sick child, choice in start and stop times, and opportunities to work from home), the better their work performance (Halpern, 2005a). Employees with several time-flexible options missed fewer days of work, less often arrived at work late or left early, felt more committed to their employer, and worked harder. They also reported fewer stress-related health symptoms.

LOOK AND LISTEN

Talk with one or more dual-earner couples about workplace supports for good parenting. Which policies are available? Which additional ones would they find especially helpful? ●

Effectively balancing work and family brings many benefits—a better standard of living, improved work productivity, enhanced psychological well-being, greater self-fulfillment, and happier marriages. Ernie took great pride in Sharese's dedication to both family life and career. And the skills, maturity, and self-esteem each derived from coping successfully with challenges at home strengthened their capacity to surmount difficulties at work (Graves, Ohlott, & Ruderman, 2007). Applying What We Know above lists strategies that help dual-earner couples attain mastery and pleasure in both spheres of life.

ASK YOURSELF

REVIEW Why do professionally accomplished women, especially those who are members of economically disadvantaged minorities, typically display high self-efficacy?

CONNECT Generate a list of capacities and skills derived from high commitment to family roles (both partner and parent) that could enhance work performance and satisfaction.

APPLY Write an essay aimed at convincing a company executive that family-friendly policies are "win-win" situations for both workers and employers.

REFLECT Ask someone who has succeeded in a career of interest to you to describe mentoring relationships that aided his or her progress.

SUMMARY

A Gradual Transition: Emerging Adulthood (p. 464)

What is emerging adulthood, and how has cultural change contributed to it?

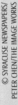

- In **emerging adulthood,** young adults from about age 18 to 25 have not yet taken on adult responsibilities and do not view themselves as fully adult. Instead, those with economic resources engage in extended exploration of alternatives in education, work, and personal values. Identity development extends into the college years, with young people exploring possibilities in breadth and depth.

© SYRACUSE NEWSPAPERS/
PETER CHEN/THE IMAGE WORKS

- During the late teens and early twenties, religious attendance drops to its lowest level, though women and ethnic minority young people express greater religiosity. Regardless of whether they participate in organized religion, many emerging adults begin to construct an individualized faith. They are also committed to improving their world, often engaging in community service.

- Increased education required for entry-level positions in many fields, gains in economic prosperity, and reduced need for young people's labor in industrialized nations have prompted the appearance of emerging adulthood. But because of its strong association with SES and higher education, some researchers do not view emerging adulthood as a distinct period of development.

- In exploring possibilities, emerging adults must adjust to disappointments in love and work, and their explorations may extend risky behaviors of adolescence. A wide array of personal attributes and social supports foster resilience. Relationships with parents are especially influential: A secure, affectionate bond that balances connection and separation predicts many aspects of adaptive functioning.

Erikson's Theory: Intimacy versus Isolation (p. 469)

According to Erikson, what personality changes take place during early adulthood?

- In Erikson's theory, young adults must resolve the conflict of **intimacy versus isolation** as they form a close relationship with a partner. The negative outcome is loneliness and self-absorption.

- Young people also focus on aspects of generativity, including parenting and contributions to society through work and community service.

Other Theories of Adult Psychosocial Development (p. 470)

Describe and evaluate Levinson's and Vaillant's psychosocial theories of adult personality development.

- Expanding Erikson's stage approach, Levinson described a series of eras in which people revise their life structure. Young adults usually construct a dream, typically involving career for men and both marriage and career for women, and form a relationship with a mentor. In their thirties, men tend to settle down, whereas many women remain unsettled into middle adulthood.

- Also in the tradition of Erikson, Vaillant portrayed the twenties as devoted to intimacy, the thirties to career consolidation, the forties to generativity, and the fifties and sixties to passing on cultural values.

- Young adults' development is far more variable today than Levinson's and Vaillant's theories depict.

What is the social clock, and how does it affect personality in adulthood?

- Following a **social clock**—age-graded expectations for major life events—grants confidence to young adults. Deviating from it can bring psychological distress.

- As age-graded expectations for appropriate behavior have become increasingly flexible, departures from social-clock life events are common and can create intergenerational tensions.

Close Relationships (p. 472)

Describe factors affecting mate selection and the role of romantic love in the young adult's quest for intimacy.

- Romantic partners tend to resemble each other in age, education level, ethnicity, religion, and various personal and physical attributes.

- According to an evolutionary perspective, women seek a mate with traits that help ensure children's survival, while men look for characteristics signaling sexual pleasure and ability to bear offspring. From a social learning perspective, gender roles profoundly influence criteria for mate selection. Research suggests that both biological and social forces are involved.

- According to Sternberg's **triangular theory of love,** the balance among intimacy, passion, and commitment changes as romantic relationships move from **passionate love** toward **companionate love.** The Western emphasis on romantic love in mate selection does not characterize all cultures.

Describe adult friendships and sibling relationships, and the role of loneliness in adult development.

- Adult friendships, like earlier friendships, are based on trust, intimacy, and loyalty. Women's same-sex friendships tend to be more intimate than men's. After marriage, other-sex friendships decline with age for men but increase for women, who tend to form them in the workplace. When family experiences have been positive, adult sibling relationships often resemble friendships

ROB LANG/GETTY IMAGES

- Young adults are vulnerable to **loneliness,** which peaks in the late teens and early twenties. Loneliness that is not overwhelming can encourage young people to reach out to others and better understand themselves.

The Family Life Cycle (p. 478)

Trace phases of the family life cycle that are prominent in early adulthood, and cite factors that influence these phases today.

- Wide variations exist in the sequence and timing of the **family life cycle.** A trend toward later home-leaving has occurred in most industrialized nations. Departures generally occur earlier for education than for full-time work or marriage; role transitions may prompt a move back. Parents of young adults living at home are usually highly committed to helping their children move into adult roles.

- The average age of first marriage in the United States and Western Europe has risen. Many countries and a growing number of U.S. states recognize same-sex marriages.

- Both **traditional marriages** and **egalitarian marriages** are affected by women's participation in the work force. Women in Western nations spend nearly twice as much time as men on housework, although men participate much more in child care than in the past. Women feel particularly dissatisfied when the combined demands of work and family roles are overwhelming. Partners who hold overly positive (but still realistic) biases concerning each other's attributes express greater relationship satisfaction.

- Although most couples in industrialized nations become parents, they do so later and have fewer children than in the past. The arrival of a child brings increased responsibilities, often prompting a shift to more traditional roles. After the birth of a second child, this may reverse. Gratifying marriages tend to remain so after childbirth, but troubled marriages usually become more distressed. Shared caregiving predicts greater parental happiness and positive parent–infant interaction.

- Couples with young children face challenges of clarifying and implementing child-rearing values. Those who engage in effective coparenting are more likely to gain in warm marital interaction, use effective child-rearing practices, and have children who are developing well.

- Parents of adolescents must establish revised relationships with their increasingly autonomous teenagers, blending guidance with freedom and gradually loosening control. Marital satisfaction often declines in this phase.

The Diversity of Adult Lifestyles (p. 486)

Discuss the diversity of adult lifestyles, focusing on singlehood, cohabitation, and childlessness.

- Postponement of marriage and a high divorce rate have contributed to a rise in singlehood. Despite an array of drawbacks, singles typically appreciate their freedom and mobility.

- **Cohabitation** among U.S. couples has increased, becoming the preferred mode of entry into a committed intimate partnership for young people. Compared with their Western European counterparts, Americans who cohabit before marriage tend to be less conventional in values and less committed to their partner, and their subsequent marriages are more likely to fail. But gay and lesbian couples who cohabit because they cannot legally marry report commitment equal to that of married couples.

© TAMPA BAY TIMES/EVE EDELHEIT/ THE IMAGE WORKS

- Voluntarily childless adults tend to be college-educated, career-oriented, and content with their lives. But involuntary childlessness interferes with adjustment and life satisfaction.

Cite factors that contribute to today's high rates of divorce and remarriage.

- Almost half of U.S. marriages dissolve. Although nearly two-thirds of divorced people remarry, many divorce again. Maladaptive communication patterns, younger ages at marriage, a family history of divorce, poverty, the changing status of women, and American individualism all contribute to divorce.

- Remarriages are especially vulnerable to breakup. Reasons include the prominence of practical concerns in the decision to remarry, the persistence of negative styles of communication, the acceptance of divorce as a solution to marital difficulties, and problems adjusting to a stepfamily.

Discuss the challenges associated with varied styles of parenthood, including stepparents, never-married parents, and gay and lesbian parents.

- Establishing stepparent–stepchild ties is difficult, especially for stepmothers and for stepfathers without children of their own. A caring husband–wife bond that includes a coparenting partnership, cooperation from the biological parent, and extended-family support promote positive stepparent–stepchild ties.

- Never-married single parenthood is especially high among African-American women in their twenties. Unemployment among black men contributes to this trend. Even with help from extended family members, these mothers find it difficult to overcome poverty.

- Gay and lesbian parents are as effective at child rearing as heterosexual parents, and their children are as well-adjusted as those reared by heterosexual parents.

Career Development (p. 492)

Discuss patterns of career development, and cite difficulties faced by women, ethnic minorities, and couples seeking to combine work and family.

- Men's career paths are usually continuous, whereas women's are often interrupted by family needs. Once young adults settle into an occupation, their progress is affected by opportunities for promotion, the broader economic environment, and access to an effective mentor.

- Women and ethnic minorities have penetrated most professions, but their career advancement has been hampered by time away from the labor market, low self-efficacy, lack of mentoring, and gender stereotypes. Racial and ethnic bias remains strong. Ethnic minority women who succeed display an unusually high sense of self-efficacy.

- Couples in dual-earner marriages often experience role overload. Effectively balancing work and family enhances standard of living, psychological well-being, marital happiness, and work performance.

Important Terms and Concepts

cohabitation (p. 487)
companionate love (p. 473)
egalitarian marriage (p. 480)
emerging adulthood (p. 464)

family life cycle (p. 478)
intimacy versus isolation (p. 469)
loneliness (p. 477)
passionate love (p. 473)

social clock (p. 471)
traditional marriage (p. 480)
triangular theory of love (p. 473)

milestones

Development in Early Adulthood

18–30 years

PHYSICAL

- Athletic skills that require speed of limb movement, explosive strength, and gross motor coordination peak early in this decade, then decline. (436)
- Athletic skills that depend on endurance, arm–hand steadiness, and aiming peak at the end of this decade, then decline. (436)
- Declines in touch sensitivity, cardiovascular and respiratory capacity, immune system functioning, and skin elasticity begin and continue throughout adulthood. (435)

- As basal metabolic rate declines, gradual weight gain begins in the middle of this decade and continues through middle adulthood. (439)
- Sexual activity increases. (446)

COGNITIVE

- If college educated, dualistic thinking declines in favor of relativistic thinking. (451)
- Moves from hypothetical to pragmatic thought. (452)
- Narrows vocational options and settles on a specific career. (456)

- Gains in cognitive–affective complexity. (452)
- Develops expertise in a field of endeavor, which enhances problem solving. (453)
- May increase in creativity. (453–454)

EMOTIONAL/SOCIAL

- In the first half of this decade, if life circumstances permit, may engage in the extended exploration that characterizes emerging adulthood. (464–465)
- Forms a more complex self-concept that includes awareness of own changing traits and values. (464)
- Is likely to achieve a personally meaningful identity. (464–465)
- Leaves the parental home permanently. (478–479)
- Strives to make a permanent commitment to an intimate partner. (469–470, 472–473)

- Usually constructs a dream—an image of the self in the adult world that guides decision making. (470)

Note: Numbers in parentheses indicate the page or pages on which each milestone is discussed.

- Typically forms a relationship with a mentor. (470)
- If in a high-status career, acquires professional skills, values, and credentials. (470)
- Develops mutually gratifying adult friendships and work ties. (476–477)
- May cohabit, marry, and bear children. (479–480, 483–484)
- Sibling relationships become more companionate. (477)

HUMMER/DIGITAL VISION/GETTY IMAGES

- Loneliness peaks early in this decade, then declines steadily throughout adulthood. (477)

30–40 years

PHYSICAL

- Declines in vision, hearing, and the skeletal system begin and continue throughout adulthood. (435)
- In women, reproductive capacity declines, and fertility problems increase sharply after the middle of this decade. (437–438)

GEORGE DOYLE/GETTY IMAGES

- In men, semen volume, sperm motility, and percentage of normal sperm decrease gradually in the second half of this decade. (438)
- Hair begins to gray and thin in the middle of this decade. (435)
- Sexual activity declines, probably as a result of the demands of daily life. (446)

COGNITIVE

- May develop commitment within relativistic thinking. (451)
- Creative accomplishment often peaks in the second half of this decade, although this varies across disciplines. (453)

ANDREW BROOKES, NATIONAL PHYSICAL LABORATORY/SCIENCE SOURCE

EMOTIONAL/SOCIAL

- May cohabit, marry, and bear children. (479–480, 483–484)

© ST. PETERSBURG TIMES/DIRK SHADD/THE IMAGE WORKS

- Increasingly establishes a stable niche in society through family, occupation, and community activities. (470)

© BIG CHEESE PHOTO LLC/ALAMY

© RIA NOVOSTI/ALAMY

A principal dancer at the Grand Opera of Paris teaches a master class for young professional dancers, transferring knowledge, skill, and passion for his art to a new generation. In middle adulthood, expertise reaches its height.

Physical and Cognitive Development in Middle Adulthood

chapter outline

PHYSICAL DEVELOPMENT

Physical Changes

Vision • Hearing • Skin • Muscle–Fat Makeup • Skeleton • Reproductive System

■ **BIOLOGY AND ENVIRONMENT** Anti-Aging Effects of Dietary Calorie Restriction

■ **CULTURAL INFLUENCES** Menopause as a Biocultural Event

Health and Fitness

Sexuality • Illness and Disability • Hostility and Anger

Adapting to the Physical Challenges of Midlife

Stress Management • Exercise • An Optimistic Outlook • Gender and Aging: A Double Standard

COGNITIVE DEVELOPMENT

Changes in Mental Abilities

Cohort Effects • Crystallized and Fluid Intelligence • Individual and Group Differences

Information Processing

Speed of Processing • Attention • Memory • Practical Problem Solving and Expertise • Creativity • Information Processing in Context

■ **SOCIAL ISSUES: EDUCATION** The Art of Acting Improves Memory in Older Adults

Vocational Life and Cognitive Development

Adult Learners: Becoming a Student in Midlife

Characteristics of Returning Students • Supporting Returning Students

On a snowy December evening, Devin and Trisha sat down to read the holiday cards piled high on the kitchen counter. Devin's 55th birthday had just passed; Trisha would turn 48 in a few weeks. During the past year, they had celebrated their 24th wedding anniversary. These milestones, along with the annual updates they received from friends, brought the changes of midlife into bold relief.

Instead of new births, children starting school, or a first promotion at work, holiday cards and letters sounded new themes. Jewel's recap of the past year reflected growing awareness of a finite lifespan, one in which time had become more precious. She wrote:

> My mood has been lighter ever since my birthday. There was some burden I laid down by turning 49. My mother passed away when she was 48, so it all feels like a gift now. Blessed be!

COMSTOCK IMAGES/GETTY IMAGES

George and Anya reported on their son's graduation from law school and their daughter Michelle's first year of university:

> Anya is filling the gap created by the children's departure by returning to college for a nursing degree. After enrolling this fall, she was surprised to find herself in the same psychology class as Michelle. At first, Anya worried about handling the academic work, but after a semester of success, she's feeling more confident.

Tim's message reflected continuing robust health, acceptance of physical changes, and a new burden: caring for aging parents—a firm reminder of the limits of the lifespan:

> I used to be a good basketball player in college, but recently I noticed that my 20-year-old nephew, Brent, can dribble and shoot circles around me. It must be my age! But I ran our city marathon in September and came in seventh in the over-50 division. Brent ran, too, but he opted out a few miles short of the finish line to get some pizza while I pressed on. That must be my age, too!

The saddest news is that my dad had a bad stroke. His mind is clear, but his body is partially paralyzed. It's really upsetting because he was getting to enjoy the computer I gave him, and it was so upbeat to talk with him about it in the months before the stroke.

Middle adulthood, which begins around age 40 and ends at about 65, is marked by narrowing life options and a shrinking future as children leave home and career paths become more determined. In other ways, middle age is hard to define because wide variations in attitudes and behaviors exist. Some individuals seem physically and mentally young at age 65—active and optimistic, with a sense of serenity and stability. Others feel old at age 40—as if their lives had peaked and were on a downhill course.

Another reason middle adulthood eludes definition is that it is a contemporary phenomenon. Before the twentieth century, only a brief interval separated the tasks of early adulthood from those of old age. Women were often widows by their mid-fifties, before their youngest child left home. And harsh living conditions led people to accept a ravaged body as a natural part of life. As life expectancy—and, with it, health and vigor—increased over the past century, adults became more aware of their own aging and mortality.

In this chapter, we trace physical and cognitive development in midlife. In both domains, we will encounter not just progressive declines but also sustained performance and compensating gains. As in earlier chapters, we will see that change occurs in manifold ways. Besides heredity and biological aging, our personal approach to passing years combines with family, community, and cultural contexts to affect the way we age. ●

PHYSICAL DEVELOPMENT

Physical development in middle adulthood is a continuation of the gradual changes under way in early adulthood. Even the most vigorous adults notice an older body when looking in the mirror or at family photos. Hair grays and thins, new lines appear on the face, and a fuller, less youthful body shape is evident. During midlife, most individuals begin to experience life-threatening health episodes—if not in themselves, then in their partners and friends. And a change in time orientation, from "years since birth" to "years left to live," adds to consciousness of aging (Neugarten, 1968b).

These factors lead to a revised physical self-image, with somewhat less emphasis on hoped-for gains and more on feared declines (Bybee & Wells, 2003; Frazier, Barreto, & Newman, 2012). Prominent concerns of 40- to 65-year-olds include get-

ting a fatal disease, being too ill to maintain independence, and losing mental capacities. Unfortunately, many middle-aged adults fail to embrace realistic alternatives—becoming more physically fit and developing into healthy, energetic older adults. Although certain aspects of aging cannot be controlled, people can do much to promote physical vigor and good health in midlife.

 ## Physical Changes

As she dressed for work one morning, Trisha remarked jokingly to Devin, "I think I'll leave the dust on the mirror so I can't see the wrinkles and gray hairs." Catching sight of her image, she continued in a more serious tone. "And look at this fat—it just doesn't want to go! I need to fit some regular exercise into my life." In response, Devin glanced soberly at his own enlarged midriff.

At breakfast, Devin took his glasses on and off and squinted while reading the paper. "Trish—what's the eye doctor's phone number? I've got to get these bifocals adjusted again." As they conversed between the kitchen and the adjoining den, Devin sometimes asked Trisha to repeat herself. And he kept turning up the radio and TV volume. "Does it need to be that loud?" Trisha would ask. Apparently Devin couldn't hear as clearly as before.

In the following sections, we look closely at the major physical changes of midlife. As we do so, you may find it helpful to refer back to Table 13.1 on page 435, which provides a summary.

Vision

By the forties, difficulty reading small print is common, due to thickening of the lens combined with weakening of the muscle that enables the eye to *accommodate* (adjust its focus) to nearby objects. As new fibers appear on the surface of the lens, they compress older fibers toward the center, creating a thicker, denser, less pliable structure that eventually cannot be transformed at all. By age 50, the accommodative ability of the lens is one-sixth of what it was at age 20. Around age 60, the lens loses its capacity to adjust to objects at varying distances entirely, a condition called **presbyopia** (literally, "old eyes"). As the lens enlarges, the eye rapidly becomes more farsighted between ages 40 and 60 (Charman, 2008). Corrective lenses—or, for nearsighted people, bifocals—ease reading problems.

A second set of changes limits ability to see in dim light, which declines at twice the rate of daylight vision (Jackson & Owsley, 2000). Throughout adulthood, the size of the pupil shrinks and the lens yellows. In addition, starting at age 40, the *vitreous* (transparent gelatin-like substance that fills the eye) develops opaque areas, reducing the amount of light reaching the retina. Changes in the lens and vitreous also cause light to scatter within the eye, increasing sensitivity to glare. Devin had always enjoyed driving at night, but now he sometimes had trouble making out signs and moving objects (Owsley, 2011). And his vision was more disrupted by bright light sources, such as headlights of oncoming cars. Yellowing of the lens and increasing density of the vitreous also limit color discrimination, especially at the green–blue–violet end of the spectrum (Paramei, 2012). Occasionally, Devin had to ask whether his sport coat, tie, and socks matched.

Besides structural changes in the eye, neural changes in the visual system occur. Gradual loss of rods and cones (light- and color-receptor cells) in the retina and of neurons in the optic nerve (the pathway between the retina and the cerebral cortex) contributes to visual declines. By midlife, half the *rods* (which enable vision in dim light) are lost (Owsley, 2011). And because rods secrete substances necessary for survival of *cones* (which enable daylight and color vision), gradual loss of cones follows.

Middle-aged adults are at increased risk of **glaucoma**, a disease in which poor fluid drainage leads to a buildup of pressure within the eye, damaging the optic nerve. Glaucoma affects nearly 2 percent of people over age 40, more often women than men. It typically progresses without noticeable symptoms and is a leading cause of blindness. Heredity contributes to glaucoma, which runs in families: Siblings of people with the disease have a tenfold increased risk, and it occurs three to four times as often in African Americans and Hispanics as in Caucasians (Guedes, Tsai, & Loewen, 2011; Kwon et al., 2009). Starting in midlife, eye exams should include a glaucoma test. Drugs that promote release of fluid and surgery to open blocked drainage channels prevent vision loss.

Hearing

An estimated 14 percent of Americans between ages 45 and 64 suffer from hearing loss, often resulting from adult-onset hearing impairments (Center for Hearing and Communication, 2012). Although some conditions run in families and may be hereditary, most are age-related, a condition called **presbycusis** ("old hearing").

As we age, inner-ear structures that transform mechanical sound waves into neural impulses deteriorate through natural cell death or reduced blood supply caused by atherosclerosis. Processing of neural messages in the auditory cortex also declines. Age-related cognitive changes—in processing speed, attention, and memory—that we will take up shortly are also associated with hearing loss (Lin et al., 2011). The first sign, around age 50, is a noticeable decline in sensitivity to high-frequency sounds, which gradually extends to all frequencies. Late in life, human speech becomes more difficult to make out, especially rapid speech and speech against a background of voices (Humes et al., 2012). Still, throughout middle adulthood, most people hear reasonably well across a wide frequency range. And African tribal peoples display little age-related hearing loss (Jarvis & van Heerden, 1967; Rosen, Bergman, & Plester, 1962). These findings suggest factors other than biological aging are involved.

Men's hearing tends to decline earlier and more rapidly than women's, a difference associated with cigarette smoking,

A worker uses a grinder to smooth a metal surface in a steel manufacturing facility. Men's hearing declines more rapidly than women's, a difference associated with several factors, including intense noise in some male-dominated occupations.

intense noise and chemical pollutants in some male-dominated occupations, and (at older ages) high blood pressure and cerebrovascular disease, or strokes that damage brain tissue (Heltzner et al., 2005; Van Eyken, Van Camp, & Van Laer, 2007). Government regulations requiring industries to implement such safeguards as noise monitoring, provision of earplugs, pollution control, and regular hearing tests have greatly reduced hearing damage, but some employers do not comply fully (Daniell et al., 2006; Ohlmiller, 2008).

Most middle-aged and elderly people with hearing difficulties benefit from sound amplification with hearing aids. When perception of the human voice is affected, speaking to the person patiently, clearly, and with good eye contact, in an environment with reduced background noise, aids understanding.

Skin

Our skin consists of three layers: (1) the *epidermis*, or outer protective layer, where new skin cells are constantly produced; (2) the *dermis*, or middle supportive layer, consisting of connective tissue that stretches and bounces back, giving the skin flexibility; and (3) the *hypodermis*, an inner fatty layer that adds to the soft lines and shape of the skin. As we age, the epidermis becomes less firmly attached to the dermis, fibers in the dermis thin, cells in both the epidermis and dermis decline in water content, and fat in the hypodermis diminishes, leading the skin to wrinkle, loosen, and feel dry.

In the thirties, lines develop on the forehead as a result of smiling, furrowing the brow, and other facial expressions. In the forties, these become more pronounced, and "crow's-feet" appear around the eyes. Gradually, the skin loses elasticity and begins to sag, especially on the face, arms, and legs (Khavkin & Ellis, 2011). After age 50, "age spots," collections of pigment under the skin, increase. Blood vessels in the skin become more visible as the fatty layer thins.

Because sun exposure hastens wrinkling and spotting, individuals who have spent much time outdoors without proper skin protection look older than their contemporaries. And partly because the dermis of women is not as thick as that of men, women's skin ages more quickly (Makrantonaki & Xouboulis, 2007).

Muscle–Fat Makeup

As Trisha and Devin make clear, weight gain—"middle-age spread"—is a concern for both men and women. A common pattern of change is an increase in body fat and a loss of lean body mass (muscle and bone). The rise in fat largely affects the torso and occurs as fatty deposits within the body cavity; as noted earlier, fat beneath the skin on the limbs declines. On average, size of the abdomen increases 7 to 14 percent. Although a large portion is due to weight gain, age-related changes in muscle–fat makeup also contribute (Stevens, Katz, & Huxley, 2010). In addition, sex differences in fat distribution appear. Men accumulate more on the back and upper abdomen, women around the waist and upper arms (Sowers et al., 2007). Muscle mass declines very gradually in the forties and fifties, largely due to atrophy of fast-twitch fibers, responsible for speed and explosive strength.

Yet, as indicated in Chapter 13, large weight gain and loss of muscle power are not inevitable. With age, people must gradually reduce caloric intake to adjust for the age-related decline in basal metabolic rate (see page 440). In a longitudinal study of nearly 30,000 U.S. 50- to 79-year-old women diverse in SES and ethnicity, a low-fat diet involving increased consumption of vegetables, fruits, and grains was associated with greater initial weight loss and success at maintaining that loss over a seven-year period (Howard et al., 2006). In nonhuman animals, dietary restraint dramatically increases longevity while sustaining health and vitality. Currently, researchers are identifying the biological mechanisms involved and studying their relevance to humans (see the Biology and Environment box on the following page).

Furthermore, weight-bearing exercise that includes resistance training (placing a moderately stressful load on the muscles) can offset both excess weight and muscle loss. Within the same individual, strength varies between often-used and little-used muscles (Macaluso & De Vito, 2004; Rivlin, 2007). Consider Devin's 57-year-old friend Tim, who for years has ridden his bike to and from work and jogged on weekends, averaging an hour of vigorous activity per day. Like many endurance athletes, he maintained the same weight and muscular physique throughout early and middle adulthood.

Skeleton

As new cells accumulate on their outer layers, the bones broaden, but their mineral content declines, so they become more porous. This leads to a gradual loss in bone density that begins around age 40 and accelerates in the fifties, especially among women (Clarke & Khosla, 2010). Women's reserve of bone minerals is lower than men's to begin with. And following menopause, the favorable impact of estrogen on bone mineral absorption is lost. Reduction in bone density during adulthood is substantial—about 8 to 12 percent in men and 20 to 30 percent in women (Seeman, 2008).

Loss of bone strength causes the disks in the spinal column to collapse. Consequently, height may drop by as much as 1 inch by age 60, a change that will hasten thereafter. In addition, the weakened bones cannot support as much load: They fracture more easily and heal more slowly. A healthy lifestyle—including weight-bearing exercise, adequate calcium and vitamin D intake, and avoidance of smoking and heavy alcohol consumption—can slow bone loss in postmenopausal women by as much as 30 to 50 percent (Cooper et al., 2009).

When bone loss is very great, it leads to a debilitating disorder called *osteoporosis*. We will take up this condition shortly when we consider illness and disability.

Reproductive System

The midlife transition in which fertility declines is called the **climacteric**. In women, it brings an end to reproductive capacity; in men, by contrast, fertility diminishes but is retained.

Reproductive Changes in Women. The changes involved in women's climacteric occur gradually over a 10-year period, during which the production of estrogen drops. As a result, the number of days in a woman's monthly cycle shortens from about 28 in her twenties and thirties to perhaps 23 by her late forties, and her cycles become more irregular. In some, ova are not released; when they are, more are defective (see Chapter 2, page 53). The climacteric concludes with **menopause**, the end of menstruation and reproductive capacity. This occurs, on average, in the early fifties among North American, European, and East Asian women, although the age range extends from the late thirties to the late fifties (Avis, Crawford, & Johannes, 2002; Rossi, 2005). Women who smoke or who have not borne children tend to reach menopause earlier.

Following menopause, estrogen declines further, causing the reproductive organs to shrink in size, the genitals to be less easily stimulated, and the vagina to lubricate more slowly during arousal. As a result, complaints about sexual functioning increase, with about 35 to 40 percent of women reporting difficulties, especially among those with health problems or whose partners have sexual performance difficulties (Lindau et al., 2007; Walsh & Berman, 2004). The drop in estrogen also contributes to decreased elasticity of the skin and loss of bone mass. Also lost is estrogen's ability to help protect against accumulation of plaque on the walls of the arteries, by boosting "good cholesterol" (high-density lipoprotein).

The period leading up to and following menopause is often accompanied by emotional and physical symptoms, including mood fluctuations and *hot flashes*—sensations of warmth accompanied by a rise in body temperature and redness in the face, neck, and chest, followed by sweating. Hot flashes—which may occur during the day and also, as *night*

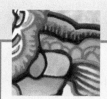

Biology and Environment

Anti-Aging Effects of Dietary Calorie Restriction

For nearly 70 years, scientists have known that dietary calorie restriction in nonprimate animals slows aging while maintaining good health and body functions. Rats and mice fed 30 to 40 percent fewer calories than they would freely eat beginning in early life show various physiological health benefits, lower incidence of chronic diseases, and a 60 percent increase in length of life (Fontana, 2009). Mild to moderate calorie restriction begun after rodents reach physical maturity also slows aging and extends longevity, though to a lesser extent. Other studies reveal similar dietary-restriction effects in mice, fleas, spiders, worms, fish, and yeast.

Nonhuman Primate Research

Would primates, especially humans, also benefit from a restricted diet? Researchers have been tracking health indicators in rhesus monkeys after placing some on regimens of 30 percent reduced calories at young, middle, and older ages. More than two decades of longitudinal findings revealed that, compared with freely eating controls, dietary-restricted monkeys were smaller but not overly thin. They accumulated body fat differently—less on the torso, a type of fat distribution that reduces middle-aged humans' risk of heart disease.

Calorie-restricted monkeys also had a lower body temperature and basal metabolic rate—changes that suggest they shifted physiological processes away from growth to life-maintaining functions. Consequently, like calorie-restricted rodents, they seemed better able to withstand severe physical stress, such as surgery and infectious disease (Weindruch et al., 2001).

Among physiological processes mediating these benefits, two seem most powerful. First, calorie restriction inhibited production of free radicals, thereby limiting cellular deterioration, which contributes to many diseases of aging (see page 433 in Chapter 13) (Carter et al., 2007; Yu, 2006). Second, calorie

restriction reduced blood glucose and improved insulin sensitivity, offering protection against diabetes and cardiovascular disease. Lower blood pressure and cholesterol and a high ratio of "good" to "bad" cholesterol in calorie-restricted primates strengthened these effects (Fontana, 2008).

Nevertheless, long-term tracking of the monkeys' age of death revealed no difference in length of survival between the calorie-restricted and control groups, regardless of the age at which restriction began. Limiting food intake delayed the onset of age-related diseases, including cancer, cardiovascular disease, and arthritis, but it did not extend the monkeys' longevity (Mattison et al., 2012). In sum, the calorie-restricted monkeys benefited from more years of healthy life, not from an extended lifespan.

Human Research

Prior to World War II, residents of the island of Okinawa consumed an average of 20 percent fewer calories (while maintaining a healthy diet) than mainland Japanese citizens. Their restricted diet was associated with a 60 to 70 percent reduction in incidence of deaths due to cancer and cardiovascular disease. Recent generations of Okinawans no longer show these health and longevity advantages (Gavrilova & Gavrilov, 2012). The reason, some researchers speculate, is the introduction of Westernized food, including fast food, to Okinawa.

Similarly, normal-weight and overweight people who have engaged in self-imposed calorie restriction for 1 to 12 years display health benefits—reduced blood glucose, cholesterol, and blood pressure and a stronger immune-system response than individuals eating a typical Western diet (Fontana et al., 2004, 2010; Redman et al., 2008). Furthermore, in the first experiment involving random assignment of human participants to calorie-restricted and nonrestricted conditions, the restricted group again displayed

An Okinawan grandfather and grandson enjoy an afternoon of kite flying. Before World War II, residents of Okinawa consumed a restricted diet that was associated with health benefits and longer life. Recent generations no longer show these advantages, possibly due to the introduction of Westernized food to Okinawa.

improved cardiovascular and other health indicators, suggesting reduced risk of age-related disease (Redman & Ravussin, 2011).

Because nonhuman primates (unlike nonprimate animals) show no gains in length of life, researchers believe that calorie restriction is also unlikely to prolong human longevity. But the health benefits that accrue from limiting calorie intake are now well-established. They seem to result from a physiological response to food scarcity that evolved to increase the body's capacity to survive adversity.

Nevertheless, very few people would be willing to maintain a substantially reduced diet for most of their lifespan. As a result, scientists have begun to explore *calorie-restriction mimetics*—agents such as natural food substances, herbs, and vigorous exercise regimens—that might yield the same health effects as calorie restriction, without dieting (Rizvi & Jha, 2011). These investigations are still in their early stages.

sweats, during sleep—affect more than 50 percent of women in Western industrialized nations (Nelson, 2008). Typically, they are not severe: Only about 1 in 12 women experiences them every day.

Although menopausal women tend to report increased irritability and less satisfying sleep, research using EEG and other neurobiological measures finds no links between menopause and changes in quantity or quality of sleep (Lamberg, 2007; Young et al., 2002). Also, most studies reveal no association between menopause and depression in the general population (Soares, 2007; Vesco et al., 2007; Woods et al., 2008). Rather, women who have a previous history of depression, are physically inactive, or are experiencing highly stressful life events are more likely to experience depressive episodes during the climacteric. In view of these findings, sleep difficulties or depression should not be dismissed as temporary byproducts of menopause: These problems merit serious evaluation and treatment.

As Figure 15.1 illustrates, compared with North American, European, African, and Middle Eastern women, Asian women report fewer menopausal complaints, including hot flashes (Obermeyer, 2000). Asian diets, which are low in fat and high in soy-based foods (a rich source of plant estrogen) may be involved.

Hormone Therapy. To reduce the physical discomforts of menopause, doctors may prescribe **hormone therapy,** or low daily doses of estrogen. Hormone therapy comes in two types: (1) estrogen alone, or *estrogen replacement therapy (ERT),* for women who have had hysterectomies (surgical removal of the uterus); and (2) estrogen plus progesterone, or *hormone replacement therapy (HRT),* for other women. Combining estrogen

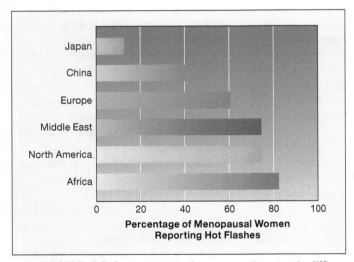

FIGURE 15.1 Percentage of menopausal women in different regions of the world reporting hot flashes. Findings are derived from interviews with large samples in each region. Women in Asian nations, especially Japanese women, are less likely to suffer from hot flashes, perhaps because they eat soy-based foods, a rich source of plant estrogen. See the Cultural Influences box on page 508 for additional evidence on the low rates of menopausal symptoms among Japanese women. (Adapted from Obermeyer, 2000; Shea, 2006.)

with progesterone lessens the risk of cancer of the endometrium (lining of the uterus), which has long been known as a serious side effect of hormone therapy.

Hormone therapy is highly successful at counteracting hot flashes and vaginal dryness. It also offers some protection against bone deterioration. Nevertheless, more than twenty experiments, in which nearly 43,000 peri- or postmenopausal women had been randomly assigned to take hormone therapy (ERT or HRT) or a sugar pill for at least one year and were followed for an average of seven years, revealed an array of negative consequences. Hormone therapy was associated with an increase in heart attack, stroke, blood clots, breast cancer, gallbladder disease, and deaths from lung cancer. ERT, when compared with HRT, intensified the risk of blood clots, stroke, and gallbladder disease. And women age 65 and older taking HRT showed an elevated risk of Alzheimer's disease and other dementias (Marjoribanks et al., 2012).

On the basis of available evidence, women and their doctors should make decisions about hormone therapy carefully. Women with family histories of cardiovascular disease or breast cancer are advised against it. Fortunately, the number of alternative treatments is increasing. A relatively safe migraine-headache medication, gabapentin, substantially reduces hot flashes, perhaps by acting on the brain's temperature regulation center. At high doses, which still appear safe, gabapentin is nearly as effective as hormone therapy. Several antidepressant drugs and black cohosh, an herbal medication, are helpful as well (Guttuso, 2012; Thacker, 2011). Alternative medications are also available to protect the bones, although their long-term safety is not yet clear.

Women's Psychological Reactions to Menopause. How do women react to menopause—a clear-cut signal that their childbearing years are over? The answer lies in how they interpret the event in relation to their past and future lives.

For Jewel, who had wanted marriage and family but never attained these goals, menopause was traumatic. Her sense of physical competence was still bound up with the ability to have children. Physical symptoms can also make menopause a difficult time (Elavsky & McAuley, 2007). And in a society that values a youthful appearance, some women respond to the climacteric with disappointment about a loss of sex appeal (Howell & Beth, 2002).

Many women, however, find menopause to be little or no trouble, regard it as a new beginning, and report improved quality of life (George, 2002; Mishra & Kuh, 2006). When more than 2,000 U.S. women were asked what their feelings were about no longer menstruating, nearly 50 percent of those currently experiencing changes in their menstrual cycles, and 60 percent of those whose periods had ceased, said they felt relieved (Rossi, 2005). Most do not want more children and are thankful to be freed from worry about birth control. And highly educated women usually have more positive attitudes toward menopause than those with less education (Pitkin, 2010).

Compared with previous generations, the baby-boom generation seems more accepting of menopause (Avis & Crawford,

African-American women, who generally view menopause as normal, inevitable, even welcome, experience less irritability and moodiness during this transition than Caucasian-American women.

2006). Their strong desire to cast aside old, gender-stereotyped views (such as menopause as a sign of decay and disease), their more active approach to seeking health information, and their greater willingness to openly discuss sexual topics may contribute to their generally positive adaptation.

Other research suggests that African-American and Mexican-American women hold especially favorable views. In several studies, African-American women experienced less irritability and moodiness than Caucasian Americans (Melby, Lock, & Kaufert, 2005). They rarely spoke of menopause in terms of physical aging but, instead, regarded it as normal, inevitable, and even welcome (Sampselle et al., 2002, p. 359). Several African Americans expressed exasperation at society's readiness to label as "crazy" middle-aged women's authentic reactions to work- or family-based stressors that often coincide with menopause. Among Mexican-American women who have not yet adopted the language (and perhaps certain beliefs) of the larger society, attitudes toward menopause are especially positive (Bell, 1995). And in an investigation of more than 13,000 40- to 55-year-old U.S. women diverse in ethnicity, other factors—SES, physical health, lifestyle factors (smoking, diet, exercise, weight gain), and especially psychological stress—overshadowed menopausal status and three common symptoms (hot flashes, night sweats, and vaginal dryness) in impact on self-rated quality of life (Avis et al., 2004).

The wide variation in physical symptoms and attitudes indicates that menopause is not just a hormonal event; it is also affected by cultural beliefs and practices. The Cultural Influences box on page 508 provides a cross-cultural look at women's experience of menopause.

Reproductive Changes in Men. Although men also experience a climacteric, no male counterpart to menopause exists. Both quantity and motility of sperm decrease from the twenties on, and quantity of semen diminishes after age 40, negatively affecting fertility in middle age (Sloter et al., 2006). Still, sperm production continues throughout life, and men in their nineties have fathered children. Testosterone production also declines with age, but the change is minimal in healthy men who continue to engage in sexual activity, which stimulates cells that release testosterone.

Nevertheless, because of reduced blood flow to and changes in connective tissue in the penis, more stimulation is required for an erection, and it may be harder to maintain. The inability to attain an erection when desired can occur at any age, but it becomes more common in midlife, affecting about 34 percent of U.S. men by age 60 (Shaeer & Shaeer, 2012).

An episode or two of impotence is not serious, but frequent bouts can lead some men to fear that their sex life is over and undermine their self-image. Viagra and other drugs that increase blood flow to the penis offer temporary relief from erectile dysfunction. Publicity surrounding these drugs has prompted open discussion of erectile dysfunction and encouraged more men to seek treatment (Berner et al., 2008). But those taking the medications are often not adequately screened for the host of factors besides declining testosterone that contribute to impotence, including disorders of the nervous, circulatory, and endocrine systems; anxiety and depression; pelvic injury; and loss of interest in one's sexual partner (Montorsi, 2005). Although drugs for impotence are generally safe, a few users have experienced serious vision loss (O'Malley, 2006). In men with high blood pressure or atherosclerosis, the medications heighten the risk of constricting blood vessels in the optic nerve, permanently damaging it.

ASK YOURSELF

REVIEW Describe cultural influences on the experience of menopause.

CONNECT Compare ethnic variations in attitudes toward menopause with ethnic variations in reactions to menarche and early pubertal timing (pages 368 and 370 in Chapter 11). Did you find similarities? Explain.

APPLY Between ages 40 and 50, Nancy gained 20 pounds. She also began to have trouble opening tightly closed jars, and her calf muscles ached after climbing a flight of stairs. "Exchanging muscle for fat must be an inevitable part of aging," Nancy thought. Is she correct? Why or why not?

REFLECT In view of the benefits and risks of hormone therapy, what factors would you consider, or advise others to consider, before taking such medication?

Cultural Influences

Menopause as a Biocultural Event

Biology and culture join forces to influence women's response to menopause, making it a *biocultural event*. In Western industrialized nations, menopause is "medicalized"—assumed to be a syndrome requiring treatment. Many women experience physical and emotional symptoms (Chrisler, 2008; Houck, 2006). The more symptoms they report, the more negative their attitude toward menopause tends to be.

Yet change the circumstances in which menopause is evaluated, and attitudes change as well. In one study, nearly 600 men and women between ages 19 and 85 described their view of menopause in one of three contexts—as a medical problem, as a life transition, or as a symbol of aging (Gannon & Ekstrom, 1993). The medical context evoked many more negative statements than the other contexts.

Research in non-Western cultures reveals that middle-aged women's social status also affects the experience of menopause. In societies where older women are respected and the mother-in-law and grandmother roles bring new privileges and responsibilities, complaints about menopausal symptoms are rare (Fuh et al., 2005). Perhaps in part for this reason, women in Asian nations report fewer discomforts (Shea, 2006). And their symptoms usually differ from those of Western women.

Though they rarely complain of hot flashes, the most frequent symptoms of Asian women are back, shoulder, and joint pain, a possible biological variation from other ethnic groups (Haines et al., 2005; Huang, 2010). In midlife, women in Asian cultures attain peak respect and responsi-

bility. Typically their days are filled with monitoring the household economy, attending to grandchildren, caring for dependent parents-in-law, and employment. Asian women seem to interpret menopausal distress in light of these socially valued commitments. In Japan, neither women nor their doctors consider menopause to be a significant marker of female middle age. Rather, midlife is viewed as an extended period of "socially recognized, productive maturity" (Menon, 2001, p. 58).

A comparison of rural Mayan women of the Yucatán with rural Greek women on the island of Evia reveals additional biocultural influences on the menopausal experience (Beyene, 1992; Beyene & Martin, 2001; Mahady et al., 2008). In both societies, old age is a time of increased status, and menopause brings release from child rearing and more time for leisure activities. Otherwise, Mayan and Greek women differ greatly.

Mayan women marry as teenagers. By 35 to 40, they have given birth to many children but rarely menstruated because of repeated pregnancies and breastfeeding. They also experience menopause up to 10 years earlier than their counterparts in developed nations, perhaps because of additional physical stressors, such as poor nutrition and heavy physical work. Eager for childbearing to end, they welcome menopause, describing it with such phrases as "being happy" and "free like a young girl again." None report hot flashes or any other symptoms.

For these rural Mayan women of the Yucatán, menopause brings freedom. After decades of childbearing, Mayan women welcome menopause, describing it as "being happy" and "free like a young girl again."

Like North Americans, rural Greek women use birth control to limit family size, and most report hot flashes and sweating at menopause. But they regard these as temporary discomforts that will stop on their own, not as medical symptoms requiring treatment. When asked what they do about hot flashes, the Greek women reply, "Pay no attention," "Go outside for fresh air," and "Throw off the covers at night."

Does frequency of childbearing affect menopausal symptoms, as this contrast between Mayan and Greek women suggests? More research is needed to be sure. At the same time, the difference between North American and Greek women in attitudes toward and management of hot flashes is striking (Melby, Lock, & Kaufert, 2005). This—along with other cross-cultural findings—highlights the combined impact of biology and culture on menopausal experiences.

Health and Fitness

In midlife, nearly 85 percent of Americans rate their health as either "excellent" or "good"—still a large majority, but lower than the 95 percent figure in early adulthood (U.S. Department of Health and Human Services; 2012c). Whereas younger

people usually attribute health complaints to temporary infections, middle-aged adults more often point to chronic diseases. As we will see, among those who rate their health unfavorably, men are more likely to suffer from fatal illnesses, women from nonfatal, limiting health problems.

In addition to typical negative indicators—major diseases and disabling conditions—our discussion takes up sexuality as a positive indicator of health. Before we begin, it is important to note that our understanding of health in middle and late adulthood is limited by insufficient research on women and ethnic minorities. Most studies of illness risk factors, prevention, and treatment have been carried out on men. Fortunately, this situation is changing. For example, the Women's Health Initiative (WHI)—a commitment by the U.S. federal government, extending from 1993 to 2005, to study the impact of various lifestyle and medical prevention strategies on the health of nearly 162,000 postmenopausal women of all ethnic groups and SES levels—has led to important findings, including health risks associated with hormone therapy, discussed earlier. Two five-year extensions, involving annual health updates from 115,000 WHI participants in 2005–2010, and 94,000 participants in 2010–2015, continue to yield vital information.

Sexuality

Frequency of sexual activity among married couples tends to decline in middle adulthood, but for most, the drop is slight. In the National Social Life, Health, and Aging Project, a nationally representative sample of 3,000 U.S. middle-aged and older adults was surveyed about their sex lives. Even in the latter years of midlife (ages 57 to 64), the overwhelming majority of married and cohabiting adults were sexually active (90 percent of men and 80 percent of women) (Waite et al., 2009). About two-thirds reported having sex several times a month, one-third once or twice a week.

Longitudinal research reveals that stability of sexual activity is far more typical than dramatic change. Couples who have sex often in early adulthood continue to do so in midlife (Dennerstein & Lehert, 2004; Walsh & Berman, 2004). And the best predictor of sexual frequency is marital happiness, an association that is probably bidirectional (DeLamater, 2012). Sex is more likely to occur in the context of a good marriage, and couples who have sex often probably view their relationship more positively.

Nevertheless, *intensity* of sexual response diminishes in midlife due to physical changes of the climacteric. Both men and women take longer to feel aroused and to reach orgasm (Bartlik & Goldstein, 2001; Walsh & Berman, 2004). If partners perceive each other as less attractive, this may contribute to a drop in sexual desire. Yet in the context of a positive outlook, sexual activity can become more satisfying. Devin and Trisha, for example, viewed each other's aging bodies with acceptance and affection—as a sign of their enduring and deepening relationship. And with greater freedom from the demands of work and family, their sex life became more spontaneous. The majority of married people over age 50 say that their sex life is an important component of their relationship (Waite et al., 2009). And most find ways to overcome difficulties with sexual functioning. One happily married 52-year-old woman commented, "We know what we are doing, we've had plenty of practice (laughs), and I would never have believed that it gets better as you get older, but it does" (Gott & Hinchliff, 2003, p. 1625; Kingsberg, 2002).

When surveys include both married and unmarried people, a striking gender difference in age-related sexual activity appears. The proportion of U.S. men with no sexual partners in the previous year increases only slightly, from 8 percent in the thirties to 12 percent in the late fifties. In contrast, the rise for women is dramatic, from 9 percent to 40 percent—a gender gap that becomes even greater in late adulthood (Laumann & Mahay, 2002; Lindau et al., 2007; Waite et al., 2009). A higher male mortality rate and the value women place on affection and continuity in sexual relations make partners less available to them. Taken as a whole, the evidence reveals that sexual activity in midlife, as in earlier periods, is the combined result of biological, psychological, and social forces.

Illness and Disability

As Figure 15.2 shows, cancer and cardiovascular disease are the leading causes of U.S. deaths in middle age. Unintentional injuries, though still a major health threat, occur at a lower rate than in early adulthood, largely because motor vehicle collisions decline. Despite a rise in vision problems, older adults' many years of driving experience and greater cautiousness may reduce these deaths. In contrast, falls resulting in bone fractures and death nearly double from early to middle adulthood (U.S. Census Bureau, 2012).

As in earlier decades, economic disadvantage is a strong predictor of poor health and premature death, with SES differences widening in midlife (Smith & Infurna, 2011). And largely because of more severe poverty and lack of universal health insurance, the United States continues to exceed most other industrialized nations in death rates from major causes (OECD, 2012). Furthermore, men are more vulnerable than women to most health problems. Among middle-aged men, cancer deaths exceed cardiovascular disease deaths by a small margin; among

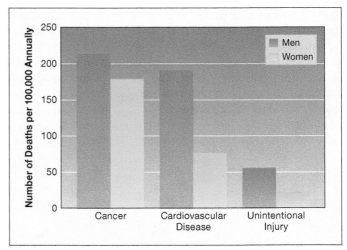

FIGURE 15.2 Leading causes of death among people age 45 to 64 in the United States. Men are more vulnerable than women to each leading cause of death. Cancer is the leading killer of both sexes, by a far smaller margin over cardiovascular disease for men than for women. (Adapted from U.S. Census Bureau, 2012.)

FIGURE 15.3 Incidence of 10 leading cancer types among men and women in the United States, 2012. (From R. Siegel, D. Naishadham, & A. Jemal, 2012, "Cancer Statistics, 2012," *CA: A Cancer Journal for Clinicians, 62,* p. 13. Copyright © 2012 American Cancer Society, Inc. Reproduced with permission of Wiley Inc.)

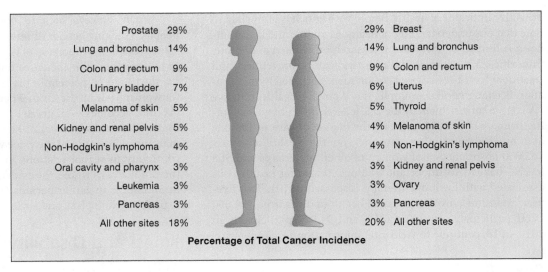

Prostate	29%		29%	Breast
Lung and bronchus	14%		14%	Lung and bronchus
Colon and rectum	9%		9%	Colon and rectum
Urinary bladder	7%		6%	Uterus
Melanoma of skin	5%		5%	Thyroid
Kidney and renal pelvis	5%		4%	Melanoma of skin
Non-Hodgkin's lymphoma	4%		4%	Non-Hodgkin's lymphoma
Oral cavity and pharynx	3%		3%	Kidney and renal pelvis
Leukemia	3%		3%	Ovary
Pancreas	3%		3%	Pancreas
All other sites	18%		20%	All other sites

Percentage of Total Cancer Incidence

women, cancer is by far the leading cause of death (refer again to Figure 15.2). Finally, as we take a closer look at illness and disability in the following sections, we will encounter yet another familiar theme: the close connection between psychological and physical well-being. Personality traits that magnify stress—especially hostility and anger—are serious threats to health in midlife.

Cancer. From early to middle adulthood, the death rate due to cancer multiplies tenfold, accounting for about one-third of all midlife deaths in the United States. Although the incidence of many types of cancer is currently leveling off or declining, cancer mortality was on the rise for many decades, largely because of a dramatic increase in lung cancer due to cigarette smoking. Lung cancer is the most common cause of cancer deaths in both genders, worldwide. In the past two decades, its incidence dropped in men; 50 percent fewer smoke today than in the 1950s. In contrast, lung cancer has just begun to decrease in women after a long period of increase, due to large numbers of women taking up smoking in the decades after World War II (American Cancer Society, 2012).

Cancer occurs when a cell's genetic program is disrupted, leading to uncontrolled growth and spread of abnormal cells that crowd out normal tissues and organs. Why does this happen? Mutations of three main kinds contribute to cancer. Some result in *oncogenes* (cancer genes) that directly undergo abnormal cell duplication. Others interfere with the activity of *tumor suppressor genes* so they fail to keep oncogenes from multiplying. And a third type of mutation disrupts the activity of *stability genes,* which normally keep genetic alterations to a minimum by repairing subtle DNA mistakes that occur either during normal cell duplication or as a result of environmental agents (Ewald & Ewald, 2012). When stability genes do not function, mutations in many other genes occur at a higher rate.

Each of these cancer-linked mutations can be either *germline* (due to an inherited predisposition) or *somatic* (occurring in a single cell, which then multiplies) (see page 52 in Chapter 2 to review). Recall from Chapter 13 that according to one theory, error in DNA duplication increases with age, either occurring spontaneously or resulting from the release of free radicals or breakdown of the immune system. Environmental toxins may initiate or intensify this process.

Figure 15.3 shows the incidence of the most common types of cancer. For cancers that affect both sexes, men are generally more vulnerable than women. The difference may be due to genetic makeup, exposure to cancer-causing agents as a result of lifestyle or occupation, and men's greater tendency to delay going to the doctor. Although the relationship of SES to cancer varies with site (for example, lung and stomach cancers are linked to lower SES, breast and prostate cancers to higher SES), cancer death rates increase sharply as SES decreases and are especially high among low-income ethnic minorities (Clegg et al., 2009). Poorer medical care and reduced ability to fight the disease, due to inadequate diet and high life stress, underlie this trend.

Overall, a complex interaction of heredity, biological aging, and environment contributes to cancer. For example, many patients with familial breast cancer who respond poorly to treatment have defective forms of particular tumor-suppressor genes (either BRCA1 or BRCA2). Women with these mutations are especially likely to develop early-onset breast cancer, before age 30 (Ripperger et al., 2009). But their risk remains elevated throughout middle and late adulthood, when breast cancer rises among women in general. Genetic screening is available, permitting prevention efforts to begin early. Nevertheless, breast cancer susceptibility genes account for only 5 to 10 percent of all cases; most women with breast cancer do not have a family history (American Cancer Society, 2012). Other genes and lifestyle factors—including alcohol consumption, overweight, physical inactivity, never having had children, use of oral contraceptives, and hormone therapy to treat menopausal symptoms—heighten their risk.

People often fear cancer because they believe it is incurable. Yet nearly 60 percent of affected individuals are cured—free of the disease for five years or longer. Survival rates, however, vary

Applying What We Know

Reducing Cancer Incidence and Deaths

Intervention	Description
Know the seven warning signs of cancer.	The signs are change in bowel or bladder habits, sore that does not heal, unusual bleeding or discharge, thickening or lump in a breast or elsewhere in your body, indigestion or swallowing difficulty, obvious change in a wart or mole, nagging cough or hoarseness. If you have any of these signs, consult your doctor immediately.
Schedule regular medical checkups and cancer-screening tests.	Women should have a mammogram and Pap test every one to two years. Beginning at age 50, men should have an annual prostate screening test. Both men and women should be screened periodically for colon cancer, as recommended by their doctor.
Avoid tobacco.	Cigarette smoking causes 90 percent of lung cancer deaths and 30 percent of all cancer deaths. Smokeless (chewing) tobacco increases risk of cancers of the mouth, larynx, throat, and esophagus.
Limit alcohol consumption.	Consuming more than one drink per day for women or two drinks per day for men increases risk of cancers of the breast, kidney, liver, head, and neck.
Avoid excessive sun exposure.	Sun exposure causes many cases of skin cancer. When in the sun for an extended time, wear sunglasses, use sunscreen that protects against both UVA and UVB rays, and cover exposed skin.
Avoid unnecessary X-ray exposure.	Excessive exposure to X-rays increases risk of many cancers. Most medical X-rays are adjusted to deliver the lowest possible dose but should not be used unnecessarily.
Avoid exposure to industrial chemicals and other pollutants.	Exposure to nickel, chromate, asbestos, vinyl chloride, radon, and other pollutants increases risk of various cancers.
Weigh the benefits versus risks of hormone therapy.	Because estrogen replacement increases risk of uterine and breast cancers, carefully consider hormone therapy with your doctor.
Maintain a healthy diet.	Eating vegetables, fruits, and whole grains, while avoiding excess dietary fat and salt-cured, smoked, and nitrite-cured foods, reduces risk of colon and rectal cancers.
Avoid excessive weight gain.	Overweight and obesity increase risk of cancers of the breast, colon, esophagus, uterus, and kidney.
Adopt a physically active lifestyle.	Physical activity offers protection against cancers at all body sites except the skin, with the strongest evidence for cancers of the breast, rectum, and colon.

Source: American Cancer Society, 2012.

widely with type of cancer (Siegel, Naishadham, & Jemal, 2012). For example, they are relatively high for breast and prostate cancers, intermediate for cervical and colon cancers, and low for lung and pancreatic cancers.

Breast cancer is the leading malignancy for women, prostate cancer for men. Lung cancer ranks second for both sexes; it causes more deaths (largely preventable through avoiding tobacco) than any other cancer type. It is followed closely in incidence by colon and rectal cancer. Scheduling annual medical checkups that screen for these and other forms of cancer and taking the additional steps listed in Applying What We Know above can reduce cancer illness and death rates considerably. An increasing number of cancer-promoting mutations are being identified, and promising new therapies targeting these genes are being tested.

Surviving cancer is a triumph, but it also brings emotional challenges. During cancer treatment, relationships focus on the illness. Afterward, they must refocus on health and full participation in daily life. Unfortunately, stigmas associated with

cancer exist (Daher, 2012). Friends, family, and co-workers may need reminders that cancer is not contagious and that with patience and support from supervisors and co-workers, cancer survivors regain their on-the-job productivity.

Cardiovascular Disease. Despite a decline over the last few decades (see Chapter 13), each year about 25 percent of middle-aged Americans who die succumb to cardiovascular disease (U.S. Department of Health and Human Services, 2012c). We associate cardiovascular disease with heart attacks, but Devin, like many middle-aged and older adults, learned of the condition during an annual checkup. His doctor detected high blood pressure, high blood cholesterol, and *atherosclerosis*—a buildup of plaque in his coronary arteries, which encircle the heart and provide its muscles with oxygen and nutrients. These indicators of cardiovascular disease are known as "silent killers" because they often have no symptoms.

When symptoms *are* evident, they take different forms. The most extreme is a *heart attack*—blockage of normal blood

Applying What We Know

Reducing the Risk of Heart Attack

Intervention	Risk Reduction
Quit smoking.	Five years after quitting, greatly reduces risk compared to current smokers. Chemicals in tobacco smoke damage the heart and blood vessels and greatly increase the risk of atherosclerosis.
Reduce blood cholesterol level.	Reductions in cholesterol average 10 percent with transition to a healthy diet.
Treat high blood pressure.	Places added force against the artery walls, which can damage the arteries over time. Combination of healthy diet and drug therapy can lower blood pressure substantially.
Maintain ideal weight.	Greatly reduced risk for people who maintain ideal body weight compared to those who are obese.
Exercise regularly.	Greatly reduced risk for people who maintain an active rather than a sedentary lifestyle. In addition to contributing to healthy weight, lowers cholesterol and blood pressure and helps prevent type 2 diabetes, which is strongly linked to heart disease.
Drink an occasional glass of wine or beer.[a]	Modestly reduced risk for people who consume small-to-moderate amounts of alcohol. Believed to promote high-density lipoproteins (a form of "good cholesterol" that lowers "bad cholesterol") and to prevent clot formation.
If medically recommended, take low-dose aspirin.	Modestly reduced risk for people with a previous heart attack or stroke, by lowering the likelihood of blood clots (should be doctor advised; long-term use can have serious side effects).
Reduce hostility and other forms of psychological stress.	People under stress are more likely to engage in high-risk behaviors, such as overeating and smoking, and to display high-risk symptoms, such as high blood pressure.

[a]Recall from Chapter 13 that heavy alcohol use increases the risk of cardiovascular disease as well as many other diseases.
Source: Go et al., 2013.

supply to an area of the heart, usually brought on by a blood clot in one or more plaque-filled coronary arteries. Intense pain results as muscle in the affected region dies. A heart attack is a medical emergency; over 50 percent of victims die before reaching the hospital, another 15 percent during treatment, and an additional 15 percent over the next few years (Go et al., 2013). Among other, less extreme symptoms of cardiovascular disease are *arrhythmia,* or irregular heartbeat. When it persists, it can prevent the heart from pumping enough blood and result in faintness. It can also allow clots to form within the heart's chambers, which may break loose and travel to the brain. In some individuals, indigestion-like pain or crushing chest pain, called *angina pectoris,* reveals an oxygen-deprived heart.

Today, cardiovascular disease can be treated in many ways—including coronary bypass surgery, medication, and pacemakers to regulate heart rhythm. To relieve arterial blockage, Devin had *angioplasty,* a procedure in which a surgeon threaded a needle-thin catheter into his arteries and inflated a balloon at its tip, which flattened fatty deposits to allow blood to flow more freely. Unless Devin took other measures to reduce his risk, his doctor warned, the arteries would clog again within a year. As Applying What We Know above indicates, adults can do much to prevent heart disease or slow its progress.

Some risks, such as heredity, advanced age, and being male, cannot be changed. But cardiovascular disease is so disabling and deadly that people must be alert for it where they least expect it—for example, in women. Because men account for

over 70 percent of cases in middle adulthood, doctors often view a heart condition as a "male problem" and frequently overlook women's symptoms, which tend to be milder, more often taking the form of angina than a heart attack (Go et al., 2013). In follow-ups of victims of heart attacks, women—especially African-American women, who are at increased risk—were less likely to be offered drugs to treat blood clots and costly, invasive therapies, such as angioplasty and bypass surgery (Lawton, 2011; Mosca, Conner, & Wenger, 2012; Poon et al., 2012). As a result, treatment outcomes—including rehospitalization and death—tend to be worse for women, particularly black women.

Osteoporosis. When age-related bone loss is severe, a condition called **osteoporosis** develops. The disorder, affecting about 10 million U.S. adults, 80 percent of whom are women, greatly magnifies the risk of bone fractures. An estimated 55 percent of people over age 50 are at risk for osteoporosis because they have bone density levels low enough to be of concern, and 12 percent have been diagnosed with it (American Academy of Orthopaedic Surgeons, 2009). After age 70, osteoporosis affects the majority of people of both sexes. Although we associate it with a slumped-over posture, a shuffling gait, and a "dowager's hump" in the upper back, this extreme is rare. Because the bones gradually become more porous over many years, osteoporosis may not be evident until fractures—typically in the spine, hips, and wrist—occur or are discovered through X-rays.

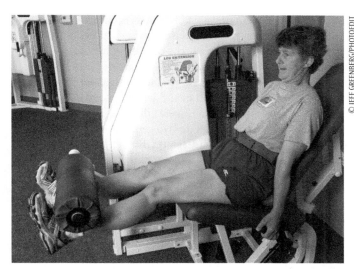

© JEFF GREENBERG/PHOTOEDIT

Physical inactivity increases the chances of osteoporosis. More than half of people over age 50, mostly women, are at risk. Weight-bearing exercise and strength training are recommended for both prevention and treatment.

A major factor related to osteoporosis is the decline in estrogen associated with menopause. In middle and late adulthood, women lose about 50 percent of their bone mass, about half of it in the first 10 years following menopause—a decline that, by the late sixties, is two to five times greater than in men (Bonnick, 2008). The earlier a woman reaches menopause, the greater her chances of developing osteoporosis related to estrogen loss. In men, the age-related decrease in testosterone—though much more gradual than estrogen loss in women—contributes to bone loss because the body converts some to estrogen.

Heredity plays an important role. A family history of osteoporosis increases risk, with identical twins more likely than fraternal twins to share the disorder (Ralston & Uitterlinden, 2010). People with thin, small-framed bodies are more likely to be affected because they typically attain a lower peak bone mass in adolescence. In contrast, higher bone density makes African Americans less susceptible than Asian Americans, Caucasians, Hispanics, and Native Americans (Cauley, 2011). An unhealthy lifestyle also contributes: A diet deficient in calcium and vitamin D (essential for calcium absorption), excess intake of sodium and caffeine, and physical inactivity reduce bone mass. Cigarette smoking and alcohol consumption are also harmful because they interfere with replacement of bone cells (Body et al., 2011; Langsetmo et al., 2012).

When major bone fractures (such as the hip) occur, 10 to 20 percent of patients die within a year (Marks, 2010). Osteoporosis usually develops earlier in women than in men, so it has become known as a "women's disease." Men are far less likely to be screened and treated for it, even after a hip fracture. Compared with women, men with hip fractures tend to be older and to lack a history of interventions aimed at preserving bone density. Probably for these reasons, the one-year mortality rate after hip fracture is nearly twice as great for men as for women—a gap that widens with age (Haentjens et al., 2010).

To treat osteoporosis, doctors recommend a diet enriched with calcium and vitamin D, weight-bearing exercise (walking rather than swimming), resistance training, and bone-strengthening medications (American Academy of Orthopaedic Surgeons, 2009). A better way to reduce lifelong risk is through early prevention: maximizing peak bone density by increasing calcium and vitamin D intake and engaging in regular exercise in childhood, adolescence, and early adulthood.

Hostility and Anger

Whenever Trisha's sister Dottie called, she seemed like a powder keg ready to explode. Dottie was critical of her boss at work and dissatisfied with the way Trisha, a lawyer, had handled the family's affairs after their father died. Inevitably, Dottie's anger surfaced, exploding in hurtful remarks: "Any lawyer knows that, Trisha. How could you be so stupid! I should have called a *real* lawyer." "You and Devin are so stuck in your privileged lives that you can't think of anyone else. You don't know what work *is.*"

After listening as long as she could bear, Trisha would warn, "Dottie, if you continue, I'm going to hang up. . . . Dottie, I'm ending this right now!"

At age 53, Dottie had high blood pressure, difficulty sleeping, and back pain. In the past five years, she had been hospitalized five times—twice for treatment of digestive problems, twice for an irregular heartbeat, and once for a benign tumor on her thyroid gland. Trisha often wondered whether Dottie's personal style was partly responsible for her health problems.

That hostility and anger might have negative effects on health is a centuries-old idea. Several decades ago, researchers first tested this notion by identifying 35- to 59-year-old men who displayed the **Type A behavior pattern**—extreme competitiveness, ambition, impatience, hostility, angry outbursts, and a sense of time pressure. They found that within the next eight years, Type As were more than twice as likely as Type Bs (people with a more relaxed disposition) to develop heart disease (Rosenman et al., 1975).

Later studies, however, often failed to confirm these results. Type A is actually a mix of behaviors, only one or two of which affect health. Current evidence pinpoints hostility as a "toxic" ingredient of Type A, since isolating it from global Type A consistently predicts heart disease and other health problems in both men and women (Aldwin et al., 2001; Eaker et al., 2004; Matthews et al., 2004; Smith et al., 2004). The risks of high blood pressure, atherosclerosis, and stroke are several times greater in adults scoring high on hostility measures than in those scoring low (Räikkönen et al., 2004; Williams et al., 2002; Yan et al., 2003).

Expressed hostility in particular—frequent angry outbursts; rude, disagreeable behavior; critical and condescending nonverbal cues during social interaction, including glares; and expressions of contempt and disgust—predicts greater cardiovascular arousal, coronary artery plaque buildup, and heart disease (Haukkala et al., 2010; Julkunen & Ahlström, 2006; Smith & Cundiff, 2011; Smith et al., 2012). As people get angry, heart rate, blood pressure, and stress hormones escalate until the body's response is extreme.

Of course, people who are repeatedly enraged are more likely to be depressed and dissatisfied with their lives, to lack social supports, and to engage in unhealthy behaviors. But hostility predicts health problems even after such factors as smoking, alcohol consumption, overweight, general unhappiness, and negative life events are controlled (Smith & Mackenzie, 2006).

Another unhealthy feature of the Type A pattern, which also predicts heart disease, is a socially dominant style, evident in rapid, loud, insistent speech and a tendency to cut off and talk over others (Smith, 2006; Smith, Gallo, & Ruiz, 2003). And because men score higher in hostility and dominance than women (Dottie is an exception), emotional style may contribute to the sex differences in heart disease described earlier.

Can Dottie preserve her health by bottling up her hostility instead of expressing it? Repeatedly suppressing overt anger or ruminating about past anger-provoking events is also associated with high blood pressure and heart disease (Eaker et al., 2007; Hogan & Linden, 2004). A better alternative, as we will see, is to develop effective ways of handling stress and conflict.

Adapting to the Physical Challenges of Midlife

Middle adulthood is often a productive time of life, when people attain their greatest accomplishments and satisfactions. Nevertheless, it takes considerable stamina to cope with the full array of changes this period can bring. Devin responded to his expanding waistline and cardiovascular symptoms by leaving his desk twice a week to attend a low-impact aerobics class and by reducing job-related stress through daily 10-minute meditation sessions. Aware of her sister Dottie's difficulties, Trisha resolved to handle her own hostile feelings more adaptively. And her generally optimistic outlook enabled her to cope successfully with the physical changes of midlife, the pressures of her legal career, and Devin's cardiovascular disease.

Stress Management

TAKE A MOMENT... Turn back to Chapter 13, pages 449–450, and review the negative consequences of psychological stress on the cardiovascular, immune, and gastrointestinal systems. As adults encounter problems at home and at work, daily hassles can add up to a serious stress load. Stress management is important at any age, but in middle adulthood it can limit the age-related rise in illness and, when disease strikes, reduce its severity.

Applying What We Know on the following page summarizes effective ways to reduce stress. Even when stressors cannot be eliminated, people can change how they handle some and view others. At work, Trisha focused on problems she could control—not on her boss's irritability but on ways to delegate routine tasks to her staff so she could focus on challenges that required her knowledge and skills. When Dottie phoned, Trisha

learned to distinguish normal emotional reactions from unreasonable self-blame. Instead of interpreting Dottie's anger as a sign of her own incompetence, she reminded herself of Dottie's difficult temperament and hard life. And greater life experience helped her accept change as inevitable, so that she was better-equipped to deal with the jolt of sudden events, such as Devin's hospitalization for treatment of heart disease.

Notice how Trisha called on two general strategies for coping with stress, discussed in Chapter 10: (1) *problem-centered coping,* in which she appraised the situation as changeable, identified the difficulty, and decided what to do about it; and (2) *emotion-centered coping,* which is internal, private, and aimed at controlling distress when little can be done about a situation. Longitudinal research shows that adults who effectively reduce stress move flexibly between problem-centered and emotion-centered techniques, depending on the situation (Zakowski et al., 2001). Their approach is deliberate, thoughtful, and respectful of both themselves and others.

Notice, also, that problem-focused and emotion-focused coping, though they have different immediate goals, facilitate each other. Effective problem-focused coping reduces emotional distress, while effective emotion-focused coping helps people face problems more calmly and, thus, generate better solutions. Ineffective coping, in contrast, is largely emotion-centered and self-blaming, impulsive, or escapist.

Constructive approaches to anger reduction are a vital health intervention (refer again to Applying What We Know). Teaching people to be assertive rather than hostile and to

Stress management in middle adulthood helps limit the age-related rise in illness. This midlifer reduces stress by periodically leaving her high-pressure office environment to work in a tranquil, picturesque setting.

Applying What We Know

Managing Stress

Strategy	Description
Reevaluate the situation.	Learn to differentiate normal reactions from those based on irrational beliefs.
Focus on events you can control.	Don't worry about things you cannot change or that may never happen; focus on strategies for handling events under your control.
View life as fluid.	Expect change and accept it as inevitable; then many unanticipated changes will have less emotional impact.
Consider alternatives.	Don't rush into action; think before you act.
Set reasonable goals for yourself.	Aim high, but be realistic about your capacities, motivation, and the situation.
Exercise regularly.	A physically fit person can better handle stress, both physically and emotionally.
Master relaxation techniques.	Relaxation helps refocus energies and reduce the physical discomfort of stress. Classes and self-help books teach these techniques.
Use constructive approaches to anger reduction.	Delay responding ("Let me check into that and get back to you"); use mentally distracting behaviors (counting to 10 backwards) and self-instruction (a covert "Stop!") to control anger arousal; then engage in calm, self-controlled problem solving ("I should call him rather than confront him personally").
Seek social support.	Friends, family members, co-workers, and organized support groups can offer information, assistance, and suggestions for coping with stressful situations.

negotiate rather than explode interrupts the intense physiological response that intervenes between psychological stress and illness. Sometimes it is best to delay responding by simply leaving a provocative situation, as Trisha did when she told Dottie that she would hang up after one more insult.

As noted in Chapter 13, people tend to cope with stress more effectively as they move from early to middle adulthood. They may become more realistic about their ability to change situations and more skilled at anticipating stressful events and at preparing to manage them (Aldwin, Yancura, & Boeninger, 2010). Furthermore, when middle-aged adults surmount a highly stressful experience, they often report lasting personal benefits as they look back with amazement at what they were able to accomplish under extremely trying conditions. A serious illness and brush with death commonly brings changes in values and perspectives, such as clearer life priorities, a greater sense of personal strength, and closer ties to others. Interpreting trauma as growth-promoting is related to more effective coping with current stressors and with increased physical and mental health years later (Aldwin & Yancura, 2011; Carver, 2011). In this way, managing intense stress can serve as a context for positive development.

But for people who do have difficulty handling midlife's challenges, communities provide fewer social supports than for young adults or senior citizens. For example, Jewel had little knowledge of what to expect during the climacteric. "It would have helped to have a support group so I could have learned about menopause and dealt with it more easily," she told Trisha. Community programs addressing typical midlife concerns, such as those of adult learners returning to college and caregivers of elderly parents, can reduce stress during this period.

LOOK AND LISTEN

Interview a middle-aged adult who has overcome a highly stressful experience, such as a serious illness, about how he or she coped. Inquire about any resulting changes in outlook on life. Do the adult's responses fit with research findings? ●

Exercise

Regular exercise, as noted in Chapter 13, has a range of physical and psychological benefits—among them, equipping adults to handle stress more effectively and reducing the risk of many diseases. Heading for his first aerobics class, Devin wondered, Can starting to exercise at age 50 counteract years of physical inactivity? His question is important: Nearly 70 percent of U.S. middle-aged adults are sedentary, and half of those who begin an exercise program discontinue it within the first six months. Even among those who stay active, fewer than 20 percent exercise at levels that lead to health benefits (U.S. Department of Health and Human Services, 2011c).

A person beginning to exercise in midlife must overcome initial barriers and ongoing obstacles—lack of time and energy, inconvenience, work conflicts, and health factors (such as overweight). *Self-efficacy*—belief in one's ability to succeed—is just as vital in adopting, maintaining, and exerting oneself in an exercise regimen as it is in career progress (see Chapter 14). An

In cities across the United States, barriers to physical activity are being overcome through the creation of attractive, safe parks and trails. But low-SES adults need greater access to convenient, pleasant exercise environments.

important outcome of starting an exercise program is that sedentary adults gain in self-efficacy, which further promotes physical activity (McAuley & Elavsky, 2008; Wilbur et al., 2005). Enhanced physical fitness, in turn, prompts middle-aged adults to feel better about their physical selves. Over time, their physical self-esteem—sense of body conditioning and attractiveness—rises (Elavsky & McAuley, 2007; Gothe et al., 2011).

The exercise format that works best depends on the beginning exerciser's characteristics. Normal-weight adults are more likely to stick with group classes than are overweight adults, who may feel embarrassed and struggle to keep up with the pace. Overweight people do better with an individualized, home-based routine planned by a consultant (King, 2001). However, adults with highly stressful lives are more likely to persist in group classes, which offer a regular schedule and the face-to-face support of others (King et al., 1997). Yet when stressed people do manage to sustain a home-based program, it substantially reduces stress—more so than the group format (King, Taylor, & Haskell, 1993). Perhaps succeeding on their own helps stressed adults gain better control over their lives. A small digital monitor that tracks physical activity and gives feedback motivates inactive middle-aged adults to increase their activity levels (King et al., 2008). And most say they enjoy using the device.

Accessible, attractive, and safe exercise environments—parks, walking and biking trails, and community recreation centers—and frequent opportunities to observe others using them also promote physical activity. Besides health problems and daily stressors, low-SES adults often mention inconvenient access to facilities, expense, unsafe neighborhoods, and unclean streets as barriers to exercise—important reasons that activity level declines sharply with SES (Taylor et al., 2007; Wilbur et al., 2003). Interventions aimed at increasing physical activity among low-SES adults must address these issues in addition to lifestyle and motivational factors.

An Optimistic Outlook

What type of individual is likely to cope adaptively with stress brought on by the inevitable changes of life? Researchers interested in this question have identified a set of three personal qualities—control, commitment, and challenge—that, together, they call **hardiness** (Maddi, 2005, 2007, 2011).

Trisha fit the pattern of a hardy individual. First, she regarded most experiences as *controllable*. "You can't stop all bad things from happening," she advised Jewel after hearing about her menopausal symptoms, "but you can try to do something about them." Second, Trisha displayed a *committed*, involved approach to daily activities, finding interest and meaning in almost all of them. Finally, she viewed change as a *challenge*—a normal, welcome, even exciting part of life.

Hardiness influences the extent to which people appraise stressful situations as manageable, interesting, and enjoyable. These optimistic appraisals, in turn, predict health-promoting behaviors, tendency to seek social support, reduced physiological arousal to stress, and fewer physical and emotional symptoms (Maddi, 2006; Maruta et al., 2002; Räikkönen et al., 1999; Smith, Young, & Lee, 2004). Furthermore, high-hardy individuals are likely to use active, problem-centered coping strategies in situations they can control. In contrast, low-hardy people more often use emotion-centered and avoidant coping strategies—for example, saying, "I wish I could change how I feel," denying that the stressful event occurred, or eating and drinking to forget about it (Maddi, 2007; Soderstrom et al., 2000).

In this and previous chapters, we have seen that many factors act as stress-resistant resources—among them heredity, diet, exercise, social support, and coping strategies. Research on hardiness adds yet another ingredient: a generally optimistic outlook and zest for life.

Gender and Aging: A Double Standard

Negative stereotypes of aging, which lead many middle-aged adults to fear physical changes, are more likely to be applied to women than to men, yielding a double standard (Antonucci, Blieszner, & Denmark, 2010). Though many women in midlife say they have "hit their stride"—feel assertive, confident, versatile, and capable of resolving life's problems—people often rate them as less attractive and as having more negative personality characteristics than middle-aged men (Canetto, Kaminski, & Felicio, 1995; Denmark & Klara, 2007; Kite et al., 2005).

These effects appear more often when people rate photos as opposed to verbal descriptions of men and women. The ideal of a sexually attractive woman—smooth skin, good muscle tone, lustrous hair—may be at the heart of the double standard of aging. Some evidence suggests that the end of a woman's ability to bear children contributes to negative judgments of physical appearance, especially by men (Marcus-Newhall, Thompson, & Thomas, 2001). Yet societal forces exaggerate this view. For example, middle-aged people in media ads are usually male executives, fathers, and grandfathers—handsome images of competence and security. And many more cosmetic products designed to hide signs of aging are offered for women than for men.

At one time in our evolutionary history, this double standard may have been adaptive. Today, as many couples limit childbearing and devote more time to career and leisure pursuits, it has become irrelevant. Some recent surveys suggest that the double standard is declining—that more people are viewing middle age as a potentially upbeat, satisfying time for both genders, sometimes even more so for women than for men (Menon, 2001; Narayan, 2008). Models of older women with lives full of intimacy, accomplishment, hope, and imagination are promoting acceptance of physical aging and a new vision of growing older—one that emphasizes gracefulness, fulfillment, and inner strength.

ASK YOURSELF

REVIEW Cite evidence that biological aging, individual heredity, and environmental factors contribute to osteoporosis.

CONNECT According to the lifespan perspective, development is multidimensional—affected by biological, psychological, and social forces. Provide examples of how this assumption characterizes health at midlife.

APPLY During a routine physical exam, Dr. Furrow gave 55-year-old Bill a battery of tests for cardiovascular disease but did not assess his bone density. In contrast, when 60-year-old Cara complained of chest pains, Dr. Furrow opted to "wait and see" before initiating further testing. What might account for Dr. Furrow's different approaches to Cara and Bill?

REFLECT Which midlife health problem is of greatest personal concern to you? What steps can you take now to help prevent it?

COGNITIVE DEVELOPMENT

In middle adulthood, the cognitive demands of everyday life extend to new and sometimes more challenging situations. Consider a typical day in the lives of Devin and Trisha. Recently appointed dean of faculty at a small college, Devin was at his desk by 7:00 A.M. In between strategic-planning meetings, he reviewed files of applicants for new positions, worked on the coming year's budget, and spoke at an alumni luncheon. Meanwhile, Trisha prepared for a civil trial, participated in jury selection, and then joined the other top lawyers at her firm for

a conference about management issues. That evening, Trisha and Devin advised their 20-year-old son, Mark, who had dropped by to discuss his uncertainty over whether to change his college major. By 7:30 P.M., Trisha was off to an evening meeting of the local school board. And Devin left for a biweekly gathering of an amateur quartet in which he played the cello.

Middle adulthood is a time of expanding responsibilities—on the job, in the community, and at home. To juggle diverse roles effectively, Devin and Trisha called on a wide array of intellectual abilities, including accumulated knowledge, verbal fluency, memory, rapid analysis of information, reasoning, problem solving, and expertise in their areas of specialization. What changes in thinking take place in middle adulthood? How does vocational life—a major arena in which cognition is expressed—influence intellectual skills? And what can be done to support the rising tide of adults who are returning to higher education in hopes of enhancing their knowledge and quality of life?

Changes in Mental Abilities

At age 50, when he occasionally couldn't recall a name or had to pause in the middle of a lecture or speech to think about what to say next, Devin wondered, Are these signs of an aging mind? Twenty years earlier, he had taken little notice of the same events. His questioning stems from widely held stereotypes of older adults as forgetful and confused. Most cognitive aging research has focused on deficits while neglecting cognitive stability and gains.

As we examine changes in thinking in middle adulthood, we will revisit the theme of diversity in development. Different aspects of cognitive functioning show different patterns of change. Although declines occur in some areas, most people display cognitive competence, especially in familiar contexts, and some attain outstanding accomplishment. As we will see, certain apparent decrements in cognitive aging result from weaknesses in the research itself! Overall, the evidence supports an optimistic view of adult cognitive potential.

The research we are about to consider illustrates core assumptions of the lifespan perspective: development as *multidimensional,* or the combined result of biological, psychological, and social forces; development as *multidirectional,* or the joint expression of growth and decline, with the precise mix varying across abilities and individuals; and development as *plastic,* or open to change, depending on how a person's biological and environmental history combines with current life conditions. You may find it helpful to return to pages 9–10 in Chapter 1 to review these ideas.

Cohort Effects

Research using intelligence tests sheds light on the widely held belief that intelligence inevitably declines in middle and late adulthood as the brain deteriorates. Many early cross-sectional

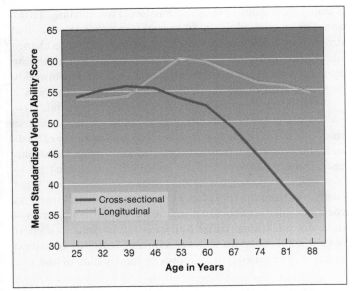

FIGURE 15.4 Cross-sectional and longitudinal trends in verbal ability, illustrating cohort effects. The steep cross-sectional decline is largely due to better health and education in younger generations. When adults are followed longitudinally, their verbal scores rise during early and middle adulthood and gradually decline during later years. However, this longitudinal trend does not hold for all abilities. (From K. W. Schaie, 1988, "Variability in Cognitive Functioning in the Elderly," in M. A. Bender, R. C. Leonard, & A. D. Woodhead [Eds.], *Phenotypic Variation in Populations*, p. 201. Adapted with kind permission from Springer Science+Business Media B. V. and K. W. Schaie.)

studies showed this pattern—a peak in performance at age 35 followed by a steep drop into old age. But widespread testing of college students and soldiers in the 1920s provided a convenient opportunity to conduct longitudinal research, retesting participants in middle adulthood. These findings revealed an age-related increase! To explain this contradiction, K. Warner Schaie (1998, 2005) used a sequential design, combining longitudinal and cross-sectional approaches (see page 38 in Chapter 1) in the Seattle Longitudinal Study.

In 1956, people ranging in age from 22 to 70 were tested cross-sectionally. Then, at regular intervals, longitudinal follow-ups were conducted and new samples added, yielding a total of 5,000 participants, five cross-sectional comparisons, and longitudinal data spanning more than 60 years. Findings on five mental abilities showed the typical cross-sectional drop after the mid-thirties. But longitudinal trends for those abilities revealed modest gains in midlife, sustained into the fifties and the early sixties, after which performance decreased gradually.

Figure 15.4 illustrates Schaie's cross-sectional and longitudinal outcomes for just one intellectual factor: verbal ability. How can we explain the seeming contradiction in findings? *Cohort effects* are largely responsible for this difference. In cross-sectional research, each new generation experienced better health and education than the one before it (Schaie, 2011). Also, the tests given may tap abilities less often used by older individuals, whose lives no longer require that they learn information for its own sake but, instead, skillfully solve real-world problems.

Crystallized and Fluid Intelligence

A close look at diverse mental abilities shows that only certain ones follow the longitudinal pattern identified in Figure 15.4. To appreciate this variation, let's consider two broad mental abilities, each of which includes an array of specific intellectual factors.

The first of these broad abilities, **crystallized intelligence**, refers to skills that depend on accumulated knowledge and experience, good judgment, and mastery of social conventions—abilities acquired because they are valued by the individual's culture. Devin made use of crystallized intelligence when he expressed himself articulately at the alumni luncheon and suggested effective ways to save money in budget planning. On intelligence tests, vocabulary, general information, verbal comprehension, and logical reasoning items measure crystallized intelligence.

In contrast, **fluid intelligence** depends more heavily on basic information-processing skills—ability to detect relationships among visual stimuli, speed of analyzing information, and capacity of working memory. Though fluid intelligence often combines with crystallized intelligence to support effective reasoning and problem solving, it is believed to be influenced less by culture than by conditions in the brain and by learning unique to the individual (Horn & Noll, 1997). Intelligence test items reflecting fluid abilities include spatial visualization, digit span, letter–number sequencing, and symbol search. (Refer to page 302 in Chapter 9 for examples.)

Many cross-sectional studies show that crystallized intelligence increases steadily through middle adulthood, whereas fluid intelligence begins to decline in the twenties. These trends have been found repeatedly in investigations in which younger and older participants had similar education and general health status, largely correcting for cohort effects (Horn, Donaldson,

Don Clarke, who flew attack helicopters in the U.S. army, fulfilled a long-held dream when he became an emergency medical service helicopter pilot. Flying search-and-rescue missions requires Clarke, now in his early sixties, to make use of complex mental abilities that are at their peak in midlife.

& Engstrom, 1981; Kaufman & Horn, 1996; Park et al., 2002). In one such investigation, including nearly 2,500 mentally and physically healthy 16- to 85-year-olds, verbal (crystallized) IQ peaked between ages 45 and 54 and did not decline until the eighties! Nonverbal (fluid) IQ, in contrast, dropped steadily over the entire age range (Kaufman, 2001).

The midlife rise in crystallized abilities makes sense because adults are constantly adding to their knowledge and skills at work, at home, and in leisure activities. In addition, many crystallized skills are practiced almost daily. But does longitudinal evidence confirm the progressive falloff in fluid intelligence? And if so, how can we explain it?

Schaie's Seattle Longitudinal Study. Figure 15.5 shows Schaie's longitudinal findings in detail. The five factors that gained in early and middle adulthood—verbal ability, inductive reasoning, verbal memory, spatial orientation, and numeric ability—include both crystallized and fluid skills. Their paths of change confirm that midlife is a time when some of the most complex mental abilities are at their peak (Willis & Schaie, 1999). According to these findings, middle-aged adults are intellectually "in their prime," not—as stereotypes would have it— "over the hill."

Figure 15.5 also shows a sixth ability, *perceptual speed*— a fluid skill in which participants must, for example, identify

within a time limit which of five shapes is identical to a model or whether pairs of multidigit numbers are the same or different. Perceptual speed decreased from the twenties to the late eighties—a pattern that fits with a wealth of research indicating that cognitive processing slows as people get older (Schaie, 1998, 2005). Also notice in Figure 15.5 how, late in life, fluid factors (spatial orientation, numeric ability, and perceptual speed) show greater decrements than crystallized factors (verbal ability, inductive reasoning, and verbal memory). These trends have been confirmed in short-term longitudinal follow-ups of individuals varying widely in age (McArdle et al., 2002).

Explaining Changes in Mental Abilities. Some theorists believe that a general slowing of central nervous system functioning underlies nearly all age-related declines in cognitive performance (Salthouse, 1996, 2006). Many studies offer at least partial support for this idea. For example, Kaufman (2001) reported that scores on speeded tasks mirror the regular, age-related decline in fluid-task performance. Researchers have also identified other important changes in information processing, some of which may be triggered by declines in speed.

Before we turn to this evidence, let's clarify why research reveals gains followed by stability in crystallized abilities, despite a much earlier decline in fluid intelligence, or basic information-processing skills. First, the decrease in basic processing, while substantial after age 45, may not be great enough to affect many well-practiced performances until quite late in life. Second, as we will see, adults can often compensate for cognitive limitations by drawing on their cognitive strengths. Finally, as people discover that they are no longer as good as they once were at certain tasks, they accommodate, shifting to activities that depend less on cognitive efficiency and more on accumulated knowledge. Thus, the basketball player becomes a coach, the once quick-witted salesperson a manager.

Individual and Group Differences

The age trends just described mask large individual differences. Some adults, because of illness or unfavorable environments, decline intellectually much earlier than others. And others sustain high functioning, even in fluid abilities, at advanced ages.

Adults who use their intellectual skills seem to maintain them longer. In the Seattle Longitudinal Study, declines were delayed for people with above-average education; complex, self-directed occupations; and stimulating leisure pursuits that included reading, traveling, attending cultural events, and participating in clubs and professional organizations. People with flexible personalities, lasting marriages (especially to a cognitively high-functioning partner), and absence of cardiovascular and other chronic diseases were also likely to maintain mental abilities well into late adulthood (Schaie, 1996, 2000, 2011; Yu et al., 2009). And being economically well-off was linked to favorable cognitive development, undoubtedly because SES is associated with many of the factors just mentioned.

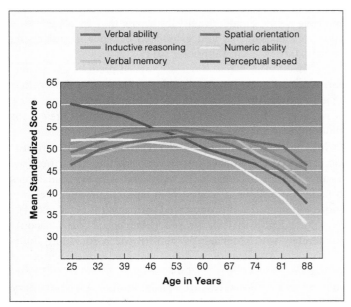

FIGURE 15.5 Longitudinal trends in six mental abilities, from the Seattle Longitudinal Study. In five abilities, modest gains occurred into the fifties and early sixties, followed by gradual declines. The sixth ability—perceptual speed—decreased steadily from the twenties to the late eighties. And late in life, fluid factors (spatial orientation, numeric ability, and perceptual speed) showed greater decrements than crystallized factors (verbal ability, inductive reasoning, and verbal memory). (From K. W. Schaie, 1994, "The Course of Adult Intellectual Development," *American Psychologist, 49,* p. 308. Copyright © 1994 by the American Psychological Association. Reprinted with permission of American Psychological Association.)

Several sex differences also emerged, consistent with those found in childhood and adolescence. In early and middle adulthood, women outperformed men on verbal tasks and perceptual speed, while men excelled at spatial skills (Maitland et al., 2000). Overall, however, changes in mental abilities over the adult years were remarkably similar for the two sexes, defying the stereotype that older women are less competent than older men.

Furthermore, when the baby-boom generation, now middle-aged, was compared with the previous generation at the same age, cohort effects were evident. On verbal memory, inductive reasoning, and spatial orientation, baby boomers performed substantially better, reflecting generational advances in education, technology, environmental stimulation, and health care (Schaie, 2011; Willis & Schaie, 1999). These gains are expected to continue: Today's children, adolescents, and adults of all ages attain substantially higher mental test scores than same-age individuals born just a decade or two earlier—differences that are largest for fluid-ability tasks (Flynn, 2007, 2011; Zelinski & Kennison, 2007).

Finally, adults who maintained higher levels of perceptual speed tended to be advantaged in other cognitive capacities. As we turn to information processing in midlife, we will pay special attention to the impact of processing speed on other aspects of cognitive functioning.

Information Processing

Many studies confirm that as processing speed slows, certain basic aspects of executive function, including attention and working memory, decline. Yet midlife is also a time of great expansion in cognitive competence as adults apply their vast knowledge and life experience to problem solving in the everyday world.

Speed of Processing

Devin watched with fascination as his 20-year-old son, Mark, played a computer game, responding to multiple on-screen cues in rapid-fire fashion. When Devin tried it, though he practiced over several days, his performance remained well behind Mark's. Similarly, on a family holiday in Australia, Mark adjusted quickly to driving on the left side of the road, but after a week, Trisha and Devin still felt confused at intersections, where rapid responses were needed.

These real-life experiences fit with laboratory findings. On both simple reaction-time tasks (pushing a button in response to a light) and complex ones (pushing a left-hand button to a blue light, a right-hand button to a yellow light), response time increases steadily from the early twenties into the nineties. The more complex the situation, the more disadvantaged older adults are. Although the decline in speed is gradual and quite small—less than 1 second in most studies—it is nevertheless of practical significance (Der & Deary, 2006; Dykiert et al., 2012).

What causes this age-related slowing of cognitive processing? Researchers agree that changes in the brain are responsible but disagree on the precise explanation (Hartley, 2006; Salthouse & Caja, 2000). According to the **neural network view**, as neurons in the brain die, breaks in neural networks occur. The brain adapts by forming bypasses—new synaptic connections that go around the breaks but are less efficient (Cerella, 1990). In support of this hypothesis, aging is accompanied by withering of the myelin coating on neural fibers within the cerebral cortex, especially in the frontal lobes and the corpus callosum. Reduced myelination appears as small, high-intensity bright spots within fMRIs (Raz et al., 2007). The bright spots, a sign of deteriorating neuronal connections, are believed to be caused by reduced cerebral blood flow (often associated with high blood pressure and atherosclerosis). Extent of myelin breakdown, however, does not consistently predict decrements in reaction time or other cognitive functions (Rodrigue & Kennedy, 2011).

Another approach to age-related cognitive slowing, the **information-loss view**, suggests that older adults experience greater loss of information as it moves through the cognitive system. As a result, the whole system must slow down to inspect and interpret the information. Imagine making a photocopy, then using it to make another copy. Each subsequent copy is less clear. Similarly, with each step of thinking, information degrades. The older the adult, the more exaggerated this effect (Myerson et al., 1990). Complex tasks, which have more processing steps, are more affected by information loss. Possibly, multiple neural changes that vary across individuals underlie such information loss and associated declines in processing speed (Hartley, 2006; Salthouse, 2011).

What is clear is that processing speed predicts adults' performance on many tests of complex abilities. The slower their reaction time, the lower people's scores on tests of memory, reasoning, and problem solving, with relationships greater for fluid- than crystallized-ability items (Finkel et al., 2007; Salthouse, 2006). Indeed, as adults get older, correlations between processing speed and other cognitive performances strengthen (see Figure 15.6). This suggests that processing speed contributes broadly to declines in cognitive functioning, which become more widespread and pronounced with aging (Li et al., 2004).

Yet as Figure 15.6 shows, processing speed correlates only moderately with older adults' performances, including fluid-ability tasks. And it is not the only major predictor of age-related cognitive changes. Other factors—declines in vision and hearing and in attentional resources, inhibition, working-memory capacity, and use of memory strategies—also predict diverse age-related cognitive performances (Hartley, 2006; Luo & Craik, 2008). Nevertheless, processing speed, as we will see in the following sections, does contribute to the decrements in attention and memory just mentioned (Levitt, Fugelsang, & Crossley, 2006). But disagreement persists over whether age-related cognitive changes have just one common cause, best represented by processing speed, or multiple independent causes.

Furthermore, processing speed is a weak predictor of the skill with which older adults perform complex, familiar tasks in

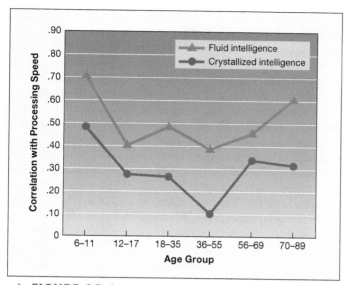

FIGURE 15.6 Age-related changes in correlations of processing speed with measures of fluid and crystallized intelligence. Correlations are higher at younger and at older ages. During childhood, gains in processing speed support development of other abilities and are related to mental test performance (see Chapter 9, page 302). As people age, declines in processing speed limit many abilities, but more so for fluid than crystallized skills. Note, however, that even at the oldest ages, correlations between processing speed and other abilities are moderate. (From S.-C. Li et al., 2004, "Transformations in the Couplings Among Intellectual Abilities and Constituent Cognitive Processes Across the Life Span," *Psychological Science, 15,* p. 160. Copyright © 2004, Sage Publications. Reprinted by Permission of SAGE Publications.)

everyday life, which they continue to do with considerable proficiency. Devin, for example, played a Mozart quartet on his cello with great speed and dexterity, keeping up with three other players 10 years his junior. How did he manage? Compared with the others, he more often looked ahead in the score (Krampe & Charness, 2007). Using this compensatory approach, he could prepare a response in advance, thereby minimizing the importance of speed. In one study, researchers asked 19- to 72-year-olds to perform a variety of typing tasks and also tested their reaction time. Although reaction time slowed with age, typing speed did not change (Salthouse, 1984). Like Devin, older typists look further ahead in the material to be typed, anticipating their next keystrokes. Knowledge and experience can also compensate for impairments in processing speed. Devin's many years of playing the cello undoubtedly supported his ability to play swiftly and fluidly.

Because older adults find ways to compensate for cognitive slowing on familiar tasks, their reaction time is considerably better on verbal items (indicating as quickly as possible whether a string of letters forms a word) than on nonverbal items (responding to a light or other signal) (Hultsch, MacDonald, & Dixon, 2002; Verhaeghen & Cerella, 2008). Finally, as we will see in Chapter 17, older adults' processing speed can be improved through training, though age differences remain.

Attention

Studies of attention focus on how much information adults can take into their mental systems at once; the extent to which they can attend selectively, ignoring irrelevant information; and the ease with which they can adapt their attention, switching from one task to another as the situation demands. When Dottie telephoned, Trisha sometimes tried to prepare dinner or check her e-mail inbox while talking on the phone. But with age, she found it harder to engage in the two activities simultaneously.

Consistent with Trisha's experience, laboratory research reveals that sustaining two tasks at once, when at least one of the tasks is complex, becomes more challenging with age. Older adults have difficulty even when they have recently engaged in extensive practice of one of the activities and it is therefore expected to be automatic (Maquestiaux et al., 2010). An age-related decrement also occurs in the ability to focus on relevant information and to switch back and forth between mental operations, such as judging one of a pair of numbers as "odd or even" on some trials, "more or less" on others (Kramer & Kray, 2006; Verhaeghen & Cerella, 2008).

These declines in attention might be due to the slowdown in information processing described earlier, which limits the amount of information a person can focus on at once (Allen, Ruthruff, & Lien, 2007; Verhaeghen, 2012). Reduced processing speed may also contribute to a related finding: a decrement with age in the ability to combine many pieces of visual information into a meaningful pattern. When the mind inspects stimuli slowly, they are more likely to remain disconnected (Pilz, Bennett, & Sekuler, 2010; Plude & Doussard-Roosevelt, 1989). This problem, in turn, can intensify attentional difficulties.

As adults get older, *inhibition*—resistance to interference from irrelevant information—is also harder (Gazzaley et al., 2005; Hasher, Lustig, & Zacks, 2007). On *continuous performance tasks,* in which participants are shown a series of stimuli on a computer screen and asked to press the space bar only after a particular sequence occurs (for example, the letter *K* immediately followed by the letter *A*), performance declines steadily from the thirties into old age, with older adults making more errors of commission (pressing the space bar in response to incorrect letter sequences). And when extraneous noise is introduced, errors of omission (not pressing the space bar after a *K–A* sequence) also rise with age (Mani, Bedwell, & Miller, 2005). In everyday life, inhibitory difficulties cause older adults to appear distractible—inappropriately diverted from the task at hand by a thought or a feature of the environment.

Again, adults can compensate for these changes. People highly experienced in attending to critical information and performing several tasks at once, such as air traffic controllers and pilots, know exactly what to look for. As a result, they show smaller age-related attentional declines (Tsang & Shaner, 1998). Similarly, older adults focus on relevant information and handle two tasks proficiently when they have extensively practiced those activities over their lifetimes (Kramer & Madden, 2008).

Conductors and teachers must focus on relevant information within a complex field of stimulation and divide their attention among competing tasks—well-practiced skills that may help slow age-related declines in attention.

Finally, practice can improve the ability to divide attention between two tasks, selectively focus on relevant information, and switch back and forth between mental operations. When older adults receive training in these skills, their performance improves as much as that of younger adults, although training does not close the gap between age groups (Bherer et al., 2006; Erickson et al., 2007; Kramer, Hahn, & Gopher, 1998).

Memory

Memory is crucial for all aspects of information processing—an important reason that we place great value on a good memory in middle and late adulthood. From the twenties into the sixties, the amount of information people can retain in working memory diminishes. Whether given lists of words or digits (verbal tasks) or serial location stimuli (spatial tasks involving retaining each location on a screen of a series of stimuli), middle-aged and older adults recall less than young adults, although verbal memory suffers much less than spatial memory (Hale et al., 2011; Old & Naveh-Benjamin, 2008a). Verbal memory may be better preserved because the older adults tested have previously formed and often used verbal representations of the to-be-learned information (Kalpouzos & Nyberg, 2012). The necessary spatial representations, in contrast, are far less familiar.

These changes are affected by a decline in use of memory strategies. Older individuals rehearse less than younger individuals—a difference believed to be due to a slower rate of thinking (Salthouse, 1996). Older people cannot repeat new information to themselves as quickly as younger people. A reduction in basic working-memory capacity is another influence, leading to difficulties in retaining to-be-remembered items and processing them at the same time (Basak & Verhaeghen, 2011).

Memory strategies of organization and elaboration, which require people to link incoming information with already stored information, are also applied less often and less effectively with age (Dunlosky & Hertzog, 2001; Troyer et al., 2006). An additional reason older adults are less likely to use these techniques is that they find it harder to retrieve information from long-term memory that would help them recall. For example, given a list of words containing *parrot* and *blue jay*, they don't immediately access the category "bird," even though they know it well (Hultsch et al., 1998). Why does this happen? Greater difficulty keeping one's attention on relevant information seems to be involved (Hasher, Lustig, & Zacks, 2007). As irrelevant stimuli take up space in working memory, less is available for the memory task at hand.

But keep in mind that the memory tasks given by researchers require strategies that many adults seldom use and may not be motivated to use, since most are not in school (see Chapter 9, page 306). When a word list has a strong category-based structure, older adults organize as well as younger adults do (Naveh-Benjamin, 2000; Naveh-Benjamin et al., 2005). And when given training in strategic memorizing, middle-aged and older people use strategies willingly, and they show improved performance over long periods, though age differences remain (Derwinger, Neely, & Bäckman, 2005).

Furthermore, tasks can be designed to help older people compensate for age-related declines in working memory—for example, by slowing the pace at which information is presented or cuing the link between new and previously stored information ("To learn these words, try thinking of the category 'bird'") (Hay & Jacoby, 1999). In one study, adults ranging in age from 19 to 68 were shown a video and immediately tested on its content (a pressured, classroomlike condition). Then they were given a packet of information on the same topic as the video to study at their leisure and told to return three days later to be tested (a self-paced condition) (Beier & Ackerman, 2005). Performance declined with age only in the pressured condition, not in the self-paced condition. And although topic-relevant knowledge predicted better recall in both conditions, it did so more strongly in the self-paced condition, which granted participants ample time to retrieve and apply what they already knew.

LOOK AND LISTEN

Ask several adults in their fifties or early sixties to list their top three everyday memory challenges and to explain what they do to enhance recall. How knowledgeable are these midlifers about effective memory strategies? ●

As these findings illustrate, assessing older adults in highly structured, constrained conditions substantially underestimates what they can remember when given opportunities to pace and direct their own learning. (Refer to the Social Issues: Education box on the following page for a "dramatic" illustration.) When we consider the variety of memory skills we call on in daily life, the decrements just described are limited in scope. General *factual knowledge* (such as historical events), *procedural*

Social Issues: Education

The Art of Acting Improves Memory in Older Adults

Actors face a daunting task: They must memorize massive quantities of dialogue and then reproduce it accurately and spontaneously, as if they genuinely mean what they say. No wonder the most common question asked of actors is, "How did you learn all those lines?"

Interviews with professional actors reveal that most don't memorize lines in the way students typically learn a historic speech or a poem in school—by rote, or rehearsing the lines many times. Instead, they focus on the meaning of the words, an approach that produces much better recall. First, they analyze the script for the character's intentions, breaking it down into what they call "beats"—small, goal-directed chunks of dialogue. Then they represent the role as a sequence of goals, one leading to the next. When actors recall this chain of goals, lines become easier to remember (Noice & Noice, 2006). For example, one actor divided a half-page of dialogue into three beats: "to put [the other character] at ease," "to start a conversation with him," "to flatter/draw him out."

To create a beat sequence, actors engage in extensive elaboration of dialogue segments. For example, to the line, "Perhaps he's in love with me but doesn't know it," an actor might create a visual image of an uncertain lover, relate the material to a past love affair of her own, and match her own mood to feeling tone of the statement. Deep elaborative processing of the dialogue segment, along with analysis of its beat goal, yields substantial verbatim recall without rote memorization.

Actors' script learning is so successful that on stage, they are free to "live in the moment," focusing on communicating authentic meaning through action, emotion, and utterance while speaking verbatim lines. This intermodal integration of spoken word with facial expression, tone of voice, and body language contributes further to script retention.

Can aging adults benefit from exercises that teach the essence of acting—thorough mastery of a script, enabling complete immersion in performance? To find out, researchers gave middle-aged and older adults nine 90-minute cognitively demanding group sessions of theater training over a month's time. Each session required them to analyze the goals of brief scenes so they could become fully engrossed in acting out their meaning (Noice, Noice, & Staines, 2004). Compared with no-intervention controls, theater-training participants showed greater gains on tests of working-memory capacity, word recall, and problem solving—improvements still evident four months after the intervention ended.

The theater training required highly effortful intermodal processing, which may explain its cognitive benefits. fMRI research

© JESSE FOLKS

These community-theater actors master their lines through deep, elaborate processing of goal-oriented segments of dialogue. Teaching these script-learning techniques to aging adults yields lasting gains in memory performance.

indicates that deeply processing verbal meanings strongly activates certain areas in the frontal lobes of the cerebral cortex in middle-aged adults, restoring them to patterns close to those of young adults (Park, 2002). These findings lend neurobiological support to the power of acting, with its challenging intermodal processing of meaning, to enhance human memory.

---

knowledge (such as how to drive a car or solve a math problem), and knowledge related to one's occupation either remain unchanged or increase into midlife.

Furthermore, middle-aged people who have trouble recalling something often draw on decades of accumulated *metacognitive knowledge* about how to maximize memory—reviewing major points before an important presentation, organizing notes and files so information can be found quickly, and parking the car in the same area of the parking lot each day. Research confirms that aging has little impact on metacognitive knowledge and the ability to apply such knowledge to improve learning (Hertzog & Dunlosky 2011; Schwartz & Frazier, 2005).

In sum, age-related changes in memory vary widely across tasks and individuals as people use their cognitive capacities to meet the requirements of their everyday worlds. *TAKE A MOMENT...* Does this remind you of Sternberg's *theory of successful intelligence*, described in Chapter 9—in particular, his notion of *practical intelligence* (see page 311)? Intelligent people adapt their information-processing skills to fit with their personal desires and the demands of their environments. Therefore, to understand memory development (and other aspects of cognition) in adulthood, we must view it in context. As we turn to problem solving, expertise, and creativity, we will encounter this theme again.

Practical Problem Solving and Expertise

One evening, as Devin and Trisha sat in the balcony of the Chicago Opera House awaiting curtain time, the announcement came that 67-year-old Ardis Krainik, the opera company's general director and "life force," had died. After a shocked hush, members of the audience began turning to one another, asking about the woman who had made the opera company into one of the world's greatest.

Starting as a chorus singer and clerk typist, Ardis rose rapidly through the ranks, becoming assistant to the director and developing a reputation for tireless work and unmatched organizational skill. When the opera company fell deeply in debt, Ardis—now the newly appointed general director—erased the deficit within a year and restored the company's sagging reputation. She charmed donors into making large contributions, attracted world-class singers, and filled the house to near capacity.

Ardis's story is a dramatic one, but all middle-aged adults encounter opportunities to display continued cognitive growth in the realm of **practical problem solving**, which requires people to size up real-world situations and analyze how best to achieve goals that have a high degree of uncertainty. Gains in *expertise*—an extensive, highly organized, and integrated knowledge base that can be used to support a high level of performance—help us understand why practical problem solving takes this leap forward.

The development of expertise is under way in early adulthood and reaches its height in midlife, leading to highly efficient and effective approaches to solving problems that are organized around abstract principles and intuitive judgments. Saturated with experience, the expert intuitively feels when an approach to a problem will work and when it will not. This rapid, implicit application of knowledge is the result of years of learning, experience, and effortful practice (Birney & Sternberg, 2006; Krampe & Charness, 2007). It cannot be assessed by laboratory tasks or mental tests that do not call on this knowledge.

Expertise is not just the province of the highly educated and of those who rise to the top of administrative ladders. In a study of food service workers, researchers identified the diverse ingredients of expert performance in terms of physical skills (strength and dexterity); technical knowledge (of menu items, ordering, and food presentation); organizational skills (setting priorities, anticipating customer needs); and social skills (confident presentation and a pleasant, polished manner). Next, 20- to 60-year-olds with fewer than two to more than ten years of experience were evaluated on these qualities. Although physical strength and dexterity declined with age, job knowledge and organizational and social skills increased (Perlmutter, Kaplan, & Nyquist, 1990). Compared to younger adults with similar years of experience, middle-aged employees performed more competently, serving customers in especially adept, attentive ways.

Age-related advantages are also evident in solutions to everyday problems (Denney, 1990; Denney & Pearce, 1989). *TAKE A MOMENT...* Consider the following dilemma:

> What would you do if you had a landlord who refused to make some expensive repairs you want done because he or she thinks they are too costly?
>
> **a.** Try to make the repairs yourself.
> **b.** Try to understand your landlord's view and decide whether they are necessary repairs.
> **c.** Try to get someone to settle the dispute between you and your landlord.
> **d.** Accept the situation and don't dwell on it. (Cornelius & Caspi, 1987, p. 146)

In this example, the preferred choice is (b), a problem-centered approach that involves seeking information and using it to guide action. From middle age on, adults place greater emphasis on thinking through a practical problem with multiple potential solutions—trying to understand it better, interpreting it from different perspectives, and solving it through logical analysis. On such tasks, middle-aged and older adults select strategies that (as rated by independent judges) are at least as good as and sometimes better than those of young adults (Kim & Hasher, 2005; Mienaltowski, 2011). Perhaps for this reason, they are more rational decision makers—less likely than young adults to select attractive-looking options that, on further reflection, are not the best.

Creativity

As noted in Chapter 13, creative accomplishment tends to peak in the late thirties or early forties and then decline, but with considerable variation across individuals and disciplines. Some people produce highly creative works in later decades: In her early sixties, Martha Graham choreographed *Clytemnestra,* recognized as one of the great full-length modern-dance dramas. Igor Stravinsky composed his last major musical work at age 84. Charles Darwin finished *On the Origin of Species* at age 50 and continued to write groundbreaking books and papers in his sixties and seventies. Harold Gregor, who painted the dazzling image on the cover of this book, continues to invent new styles and to be a highly productive artist at age 83. And as with problem solving, the *quality* of creativity may change with advancing age—in at least three ways.

First, youthful creativity in literature and the arts is often spontaneous and intensely emotional, while creative works produced after age 40 often appear more deliberately thoughtful (Lubart & Sternberg, 1998). Perhaps for this reason, poets produce their most frequently cited works at younger ages than do authors of fiction and nonfiction (Cohen-Shalev, 1986). Poetry depends more on language play and "hot" expression of feelings, whereas story- and book-length works require extensive planning and molding.

Second, with age, many creators shift from generating unusual products to combining extensive knowledge and expe-

In midlife, creativity often shifts to more altruistic goals. Author Masha Hamilton's travels to northeastern Kenya to research her novel, *The Camel Bookmobile,* led her to help organize the Camel Book Drive. It has funded the purchase of camels, books, and equipment for nomadic schools in the area.

rience into unique ways of thinking (Abra, 1989; Sasser-Coen, 1993). Creative works by older adults more often sum up or integrate ideas. Mature academics typically devote less energy to new discoveries in favor of writing memoirs, histories of their field, and other reflective works. And in older creators' novels, scholarly writings, and commentaries about their paintings and musical compositions, learning from life experience and living with old age are common themes (Beckerman, 1990; Lindauer, Orwoll, & Kelley, 1997; Sternberg & Lubart, 2001).

Finally, creativity in middle adulthood frequently reflects a transition from a largely egocentric concern with self-expression to more altruistic goals (Tahir & Gruber, 2003). As the middle-aged person overcomes the youthful illusion that life is eternal, the desire to give to humanity and enrich the lives of others increases.

Taken together, these changes may contribute to an overall decline in creative output in later decades. In reality, however, creativity takes new forms.

Information Processing in Context

Cognitive gains in middle adulthood are especially likely in areas involving experience-based buildup and transformation of knowledge and skills. As the evidence just reviewed confirms, processing speed varies with the situation. When given challenging real-world problems related to their expertise, middle-aged adults are likely to win out in both efficiency and excellence of thinking. Furthermore, on tasks and test items relevant to their real-life endeavors, intelligent, cognitively active midlifers respond as competently and nearly as quickly as their younger counterparts do!

By middle age, people's past and current experiences vary enormously—more so than in previous decades—and thinking is characterized by an increase in specialization as people branch out in various directions. Yet to reach their cognitive potential, adults must have opportunities for continued growth. Let's see how vocational and educational environments can support cognition in midlife.

ASK YOURSELF

REVIEW How do slowing of cognitive processing, reduced working-memory capacity, and difficulties with inhibition affect memory in midlife? What can older adults do to compensate for these declines?

CONNECT In which aspects of cognition did Devin decline, and in which did he gain? How do changes in Devin's thinking reflect assumptions of the lifespan perspective?

APPLY Asked about hiring middle-aged sales personnel, a department store manager replied, "They're my best employees!" Why does this manager find older employees desirable, despite age-related declines in processing speed, attention, and working memory?

 ## Vocational Life and Cognitive Development

Vocational settings are vital contexts for maintaining previously acquired skills and learning new ones. Yet work environments vary in the degree to which they are cognitively stimulating and promote autonomy. And inaccurate, negative stereotypes of age-related problem-solving and decision-making skills can result in older employees being assigned less challenging work.

Recall from Chapter 13 that cognitive and personality characteristics affect occupational choice. Once a person is immersed in a job, it influences cognition. In a study of a large sample of U.S. men in diverse occupations, researchers asked about the complexity and self-direction of their jobs. During the interview, they also assessed cognitive flexibility, based on logical reasoning, awareness of both sides of an issue, and independence of judgment. Two decades later, the job and cognitive variables were remeasured, permitting a look at their effects on each other (Schooler, Mulatu, & Oates, 2004). Findings revealed that complex work augmented later cognitive flexibility more than cognitive flexibility influenced preference for complex work.

Similar findings emerged in large-scale studies carried out in Japan and Poland—cultures quite different from the United States (Kohn, 2006; Kohn et al., 1990; Kohn & Slomczynski, 1990). In each nation, having a stimulating, nonroutine job helped explain the relationship between SES and flexible, abstract thinking. Furthermore, people in their fifties and early sixties benefit cognitively from challenging work just as much as those in their twenties and thirties (Avolio & Sosik, 1999; Miller, Slomczynski, & Kohn, 1985).

Mentally stimulating work requires middle-aged and older adults to grapple with novel situations. Research suggests that continuously confronting complex, novel tasks contributes importantly to cognitive development, predicting gains in cognitive flexibility and reducing the age-related decline in fluid abilities (Bowen, Noack, & Staudinger, 2011). Once again, we are reminded of the plasticity of development. Cognitive flexibility is responsive to work experiences well into middle adulthood and perhaps beyond. Designing jobs to promote intellectual stimulation and challenge may be a powerful means of fostering higher cognitive functioning later in the lifespan.

Adult Learners: Becoming a Student in Midlife

Adults are returning to undergraduate and graduate study in record numbers. During the past three decades, students age 25 and older in U.S. colleges and universities increased from 27 to 39 percent of total enrollment, with an especially sharp rise in those over age 35 (U.S. Department of Education, 2012). Life transitions often trigger a return to formal education, as with Devin and Trisha's friend Anya, who entered a nursing program after her last child left home. Early marriage (which often disrupts women's educational pathways), divorce, widowhood, a job layoff, a family move, a youngest child reaching school age, older children entering college, and rapid changes in the job market are other events that commonly precede reentry (Hostetler, Sweet, & Moen, 2007; Moen & Roehling, 2005). Among a sample of African-American women, additional motivations included serving as a role model for children and enriching their ethnic community as a whole (Coker, 2003).

This 50-year-old, a full-time undergraduate at Mount Holyoke College, is one of many nontraditional students in U.S. colleges and universities. Appropriate academic advising and encouragement from family members, friends, and faculty help middle-aged learners succeed.

Characteristics of Returning Students

About 60 percent of adult learners are women (U.S. Department of Education, 2012). As Anya's fear of not being able to handle class work suggests (see page 501), reentry women report feeling especially self-conscious, inadequate, and hesitant to talk in class (Compton, Cox, & Laanan, 2006). Their anxiety stems partly from not having practiced academic learning for many years and partly from negative aging and gender stereotypes—erroneous beliefs that traditional-age students are smarter or that men are more logical and therefore more academically capable. And for minority students, ethnic stereotypes about ability to learn and prejudicial treatment are also factors (Coker, 2003).

Role demands outside of school—from children, spouses, other family members, friends, and employers—pull many returning women in conflicting directions. Those reporting high psychological stress typically are single parents with limited financial resources, or married women with high career aspirations, young children, and nonsupportive partners (Deutsch & Schmertz, 2011; Padula & Miller, 1999). When couples fail to rework divisions of household and child-care responsibilities to accommodate the woman's return to school, marital satisfaction declines (Sweet & Moen, 2007). As a classmate remarked to Anya, "I tried keeping the book open and reading, cooking, and talking to the kids. It didn't work. So I had to say to Bill, 'Can't you put in a load of laundry once in a while, get home earlier on just some nights?' He forgets—I went through his going to graduate school!"

Because of multiple demands on their time, mature-age women tend to take fewer credits, experience more interruptions in their academic programs, and progress at a slower pace than mature-age men. Role overload is the most common reason for not completing their degrees (Jacobs & King, 2002). But many express high motivation to work through those difficulties, referring to the excitement of learning, to the fulfillment academic success brings, and to their hope that a college education will improve both their work and family lives (Kinser & Deitchman, 2007).

LOOK AND LISTEN

Interview a nontraditional student on your campus about the personal challenges and rewards of working toward a degree at a later age. ●

Supporting Returning Students

As these findings suggest, social supports for returning students can make the difference between continuing in school and dropping out. Adult students need family members and friends who encourage their efforts and enable them to find time for uninterrupted study. Anya's classmate explained, "My doubts subsided when one day, Bill volunteered, 'You take your books and do what you need to do. I can cook dinner and do the laundry.'" Institutional services for returning students are also essential. Personal relationships with faculty, peer networks enabling adults to build a social community with other non-

Applying What We Know

Facilitating Adult Reentry to College

Sources of Support	Description
Partner and children	Value and encourage educational efforts.
	Help with household tasks to permit time for uninterrupted study.
Extended family and friends	Value and encourage educational efforts.
Educational institution	Provide orientation programs and literature that inform adult students about services and social supports.
	Provide counseling and intervention addressing academic weaknesses, self-doubts about success, and matching courses to career goals.
	Facilitate peer networks through regular meetings, phone, and online contacts.
	Promote personal relationships with faculty.
	Encourage active engagement and discussion in classes and integration of course content with real-life experiences.
	Offer evening, Saturday, and off-campus classes and online courses.
	Provide financial aid for part-time students.
	Initiate campaigns to recruit returning students, including those from low-income families and ethnic minority groups.
	Help students with young children find child-care arrangements and provide on-campus child care.
Workplace	Value and encourage educational efforts.
	Offer flexible work schedules to make possible coordination of work, class, and family responsibilities.

traditional students who understand their daily struggles, conveniently scheduled evening and Saturday classes, online courses, and financial aid for part-time students increase the chances of academic success.

Although nontraditional students rarely require assistance in settling on career goals, they report a strong desire for help in choosing the most appropriate courses and for small, discussion-based classes that meet their learning and relationship needs. Academic advising and professional internship opportunities are vital. Students from low-SES backgrounds often need special assistance, such as academic tutoring, sessions in confidence building and assertiveness, and—in the case of ethnic minorities—help adjusting to styles of learning that are at odds with their cultural background.

Applying What We Know above suggests ways to facilitate adult reentry to college. When support systems are in place, most returning students reap great personal benefits and do well academically. Succeeding at coordinating education, family, and work demands leads to gains in self-efficacy and admiration from family members, friends, and co-workers (Chao & Good, 2004). Nontraditional students especially value forming new relationships, sharing opinions and experiences, and relating subject matter to their own lives. Their greater ability to integrate knowledge results in an enhanced appreciation of classroom experiences and assignments. And their presence in college classes provides valuable intergenerational contact. As younger students observe the capacities and talents of older classmates, unfavorable stereotypes of aging decline.

After finishing her degree, Anya secured a position as a parish nurse with creative opportunities to counsel members of

a large congregation about health concerns. Education granted her new life options, financial rewards, and higher self-esteem as she reevaluated her own competencies. Sometimes (though not in Anya's case) these revised values and increased self-reliance can spark other changes, such as a divorce or a new intimate partnership (Esterberg, Moen, & Dempster-McClain, 1994). In middle adulthood as in earlier years, education transforms development, often profoundly reshaping the life course.

ASK YOURSELF

REVIEW In view of the impact of vocational and educational experiences on midlife cognitive development, evaluate the saying "You can't teach an old dog new tricks."

CONNECT Most high-level government and corporate positions are held by middle-aged and older adults rather than by young adults. What cognitive capacities enable mature adults to perform these jobs well?

APPLY Marcella completed one year of college in her twenties. Now, at age 42, she has returned to earn a degree. Plan a set of experiences for Marcella's first semester that will increase her chances of success.

REFLECT What range of services does your institution offer to support returning students? What additional supports would you recommend?

SUMMARY

PHYSICAL DEVELOPMENT

Physical Changes (p. 502)

Describe the physical changes of middle adulthood, paying special attention to vision, hearing, the skin, muscle–fat makeup, and the skeleton.

- The gradual physical changes begun in early adulthood continue in midlife, contributing to a revised physical self-image, with less emphasis on hoped-for gains and more on feared declines.

- Vision is affected by **presbyopia** (loss of the accommodative ability of the lens), reduced vision in dim light, increased sensitivity to glare, and diminished color discrimination. After age 40, risk of **glaucoma**, a buildup of pressure in the eye that damages the optic nerve, increases.

- Age-related hearing loss, or **presbycusis**, begins with a decline in detection of high frequencies and then spreads to other tones. Eventually, human speech becomes harder to decipher.

- The skin wrinkles, loosens, and dries. Age spots develop, especially in women and in people exposed to the sun.

- Muscle mass declines and fat deposits increase, with notable sex differences in fat distribution. A low-fat diet and regular exercise, including resistance training, can offset both excess weight and muscle loss.

- Bone density declines, especially in women after menopause. Height loss and bone fractures can result.

Describe reproductive changes in both sexes during middle adulthood.

- The **climacteric** in women, which occurs gradually as estrogen production drops, concludes with **menopause**, often accompanied by emotional and physical symptoms. These reactions, however, vary widely with ethnicity, SES, physical health, psychological stress, and other factors.

- **Hormone therapy** can reduce the discomforts of menopause, but its use increases the risk of cardiovascular disease, certain cancers, and cognitive declines.

- Although sperm production continues throughout life, quantity of semen diminishes and erections become harder to attain and maintain. Drugs are available to combat impotence.

Health and Fitness (p. 508)

Discuss sexuality in middle adulthood and its association with psychological well-being.

- Frequency of sexual activity among married couples declines only slightly in middle adulthood. Intensity of sexual response diminishes due to physical changes of the climacteric. Most married people over age 50 find ways to overcome difficulties with sexual functioning.

Discuss cancer, cardiovascular disease, and osteoporosis, noting risk factors and interventions.

- The death rate from cancer multiplies tenfold from early to middle adulthood. A complex interaction of heredity, biological aging, and environment contributes to cancer. Today, nearly 60 percent of affected individuals are cured. Regular screenings and various preventive steps can reduce the incidence of cancer and cancer deaths.

- Despite a decline in recent decades, cardiovascular disease remains a major cause of death in middle adulthood, especially among men. Symptoms include high blood pressure, high blood cholesterol, atherosclerosis, heart attack, arrhythmia, and angina pectoris. Quitting smoking, reducing blood cholesterol, exercising, and reducing stress can decrease risk and aid in treatment.

- **Osteoporosis** affects 12 percent of people over age 50; most are postmenopausal women. Adequate calcium and vitamin D, weight-bearing exercise, resistance training, and bone-strengthening medications can help prevent and treat osteoporosis.

Discuss the association of hostility and anger with heart disease and other health problems.

- Expressed hostility, a component of the **Type A behavior pattern**, predicts heart disease and other health problems, largely due to physiological arousal associated with anger. Anger suppression is also related to health problems; a better alternative is to develop effective ways of handling stress and conflict.

Adapting to the Physical Challenges of Midlife (p. 514)

Discuss the benefits of stress management, exercise, and an optimistic outlook in dealing effectively with the physical challenges of midlife.

- Effective stress management includes both problem-centered and emotion-centered coping, depending on the situation; constructive approaches to anger reduction; and social support. In middle adulthood, people tend to cope with stress more effectively, often reporting lasting personal benefits.

- Regular exercise offers physical and psychological advantages, making it worthwhile for sedentary middle-aged people to begin exercising. Developing a sense of self-efficacy, choosing an appropriate exercise format, and having access to accessible, attractive, and safe exercise environments promote physical activity.

- **Hardiness** is made up of three personal qualities: control, commitment, and challenge. By inducing a generally optimistic outlook, hardiness helps people cope with stress adaptively.

Explain the double standard of aging.

● Although negative stereotypes of aging discourage both men and women, middle-aged women are more likely to be viewed unfavorably, especially by men. New surveys suggest that this double standard is declining.

COGNITIVE DEVELOPMENT

Changes in Mental Abilities
(p. 517)

Describe cohort effects on intelligence revealed by Schaie's Seattle Longitudinal Study.

● Early cross-sectional research showed a peak in intelligence test performance at age 35 followed by a steep decline, whereas longitudinal evidence revealed modest gains in midlife. Using a sequential design, Schaie found that the cross-sectional, steep drop-off largely resulted from cohort effects, as each new generation experienced better health and education.

Describe changes in crystallized and fluid intelligence in middle adulthood, and discuss individual and group differences in intellectual development.

● **Crystallized intelligence**, which depends on accumulated knowledge and experience, gains steadily through middle adulthood. In contrast, **fluid intelligence**, which depends more on basic information-processing skills, begins to decline in the twenties.

● In the Seattle Longitudinal Study, perceptual speed shows steady, continuous decline. But other fluid skills, in addition to crystallized abilities, increase through middle adulthood, confirming that midlife is a time of peak performance on a variety of complex abilities.

● Large individual differences among middle-aged adults remind us that intellectual development is multidimensional, multidirectional, and plastic. Illness and unfavorable environments are linked to intellectual declines; stimulating occupations and leisure pursuits, flexible personalities, lasting marriages, good health, and economic advantage predict favorable cognitive development.

● Women outperform men on verbal tasks and perceptual speed, whereas men excel at spatial skills. Gains in certain intellectual skills by the baby-boomers relative to the previous generation reflect advances in education, technology, environmental stimulation, and health care.

Information Processing
(p. 520)

How does information processing change in midlife?

● Speed of cognitive processing slows with age. According to the **neural network view**, as neuronal connections deteriorate, the brain adapts by forming new, less efficient synaptic connections. The **information-loss view** states that older adults experience greater loss of information as it moves through the cognitive system, resulting in slower processing to interpret the information.

● As processing speed slows, people perform less well on memory, reasoning, and problem-solving tasks, especially fluid-ability items. But other factors also predict age-related cognitive performances.

● Middle-aged people show declines in ability to divide their attention, focus on relevant stimuli, and switch from one task to another as the situation demands. Inhibition becomes harder, at times prompting distractibility.

© ELLIOTT FRANKS/ARENAPAL/TOPHAM/THE IMAGE WORKS

● Adults in midlife retain less information in working memory, largely due to a decline in use of memory strategies. But training, improved design of tasks, and metacognitive knowledge enable older adults to compensate for age-related decrements.

Discuss the development of practical problem solving, expertise, and creativity in middle adulthood.

● Middle-aged adults display continued growth in **practical problem solving**, largely due to gains in expertise. Creativity becomes more deliberately thoughtful and often shifts from generating unusual products to integrating ideas, and from concern with self-expression to more altruistic goals.

Vocational Life and Cognitive Development
(p. 525)

Describe the relationship between vocational life and cognitive development.

● Well into middle adulthood, stimulating, complex work augments flexible, abstract thinking. It also reduces the age-related decline in fluid abilities.

Adult Learners: Becoming a Student in Midlife (p. 526)

Discuss the challenges that adults face in returning to college, ways to support returning students, and benefits of earning a degree in midlife.

● Adults are returning to college and graduate school in record numbers. The majority are women, often motivated by life transitions. Returning students must cope with a lack of recent practice at academic work, stereotypes of aging and ethnicity, and demands of multiple roles.

● Social support from family and friends and institutional services suited to their needs can help returning students succeed. Further education results in enhanced competencies, new relationships, intergenerational contact, and reshaped life paths.

Important Terms and Concepts

climacteric (p. 504)
crystallized intelligence (p. 518)
fluid intelligence (p. 518)
glaucoma (p. 503)
hardiness (p. 516)

hormone therapy (p. 506)
information-loss view (p. 520)
menopause (p. 504)
neural network view (p. 520)
osteoporosis (p. 512)

practical problem solving (p. 524)
presbycusis (p. 503)
presbyopia (p. 502)
Type A behavior pattern (p. 513)

Midlife is a time of increased generativity—giving to and guiding younger generations. Charles Callis, director of New Zealand's Olympic Museum, shows visiting schoolchildren how to throw a discus. His enthusiastic demonstration conveys the deep sense of satisfaction he derives from generative activities.

Emotional and Social Development in Middle Adulthood

chapter outline

Erikson's Theory: Generativity versus Stagnation

■ **SOCIAL ISSUES: HEALTH** Generative Adults Tell Their Life Stories

Other Theories of Psychosocial Development in Midlife

Levinson's Seasons of Life • Vaillant's Adaptation to Life • Is There a Midlife Crisis? • Stage or Life Events Approach

Stability and Change in Self-Concept and Personality

Possible Selves • Self-Acceptance, Autonomy, and Environmental Mastery • Coping with Daily Stressors • Gender Identity • Individual Differences in Personality Traits

■ **BIOLOGY AND ENVIRONMENT** What Factors Promote Psychological Well-Being in Midlife?

Relationships at Midlife

Marriage and Divorce • Changing Parent–Child Relationships • Grandparenthood • Middle-Aged Children and Their Aging Parents • Siblings • Friendships

■ **SOCIAL ISSUES: HEALTH** Grandparents Rearing Grandchildren: The Skipped-Generation Family

Vocational Life

Job Satisfaction • Career Development • Career Change at Midlife • Unemployment • Planning for Retirement

One weekend when Devin, Trisha, and their 24-year-old son, Mark, were vacationing together, the two middle-aged parents knocked on Mark's hotel room door. "Your dad and I are going off to see a crafts exhibit," Trisha explained. "Feel free to stay behind," she offered, recalling Mark's antipathy toward attending such events as an adolescent. "We'll be back around noon for lunch."

"That exhibit sounds great!" Mark replied. "I'll meet you in the lobby."

"Sometimes I forget he's an adult!" exclaimed Trisha as she and Devin returned to their room to grab their coats. "It's been great to have Mark with us—like spending time with a good friend."

In their forties and fifties, Trisha and Devin built on earlier strengths and intensified their commitment to leaving a legacy for those who would come after them. When Mark faced a difficult job market after graduating from college, he returned home to live with Trisha and Devin and remained there for several years. With their support, he took graduate courses while working part-time, found steady employment in his late twenties, fell in love, and married in his mid-thirties. With each milestone, Trisha and Devin felt a sense of pride at having escorted a member of the next generation into responsible adult roles. Family activities, which had declined during Mark's adolescent and college years, increased as Trisha and Devin related to their son as an enjoyable adult companion. Challenging careers and more time for community involvement, leisure pursuits, and each other contributed to a richly diverse and gratifying time of life.

The midlife years were not as smooth for two of Trisha and Devin's friends. Fearing that she might grow old alone, Jewel frantically pursued her quest for an intimate partner. She attended singles events, registered with dating services, and traveled in hopes of meeting a like-minded companion. "I can't stand the thought of turning 50," she lamented in a letter to Trisha. Jewel also had compensating satisfactions—friendships that had grown more meaningful, a warm relationship with a nephew and niece, and a successful consulting business.

Tim, Devin's best friend from graduate school, had been divorced for over five years. Recently, he had met Elena and had come to love her deeply. But Elena was in the midst of major life changes. In addition to her own divorce, she was dealing with a troubled daughter, a career change, and a move away from the city that served as a

PHOTOALTO/ODILON DIMIER/GETTY IMAGES

constant reminder of her unhappy past. Whereas Tim had reached the peak of his career and was ready to enjoy life, Elena wanted to recapture much of what she had missed in earlier decades, including opportunities to realize her talents. "I don't know where I fit into Elena's plans," Tim wondered aloud on the phone with Trisha.

With the arrival of middle adulthood, half or more of the lifespan is over. Increasing awareness of limited time ahead prompts adults to reevaluate the meaning of their lives, refine and strengthen their identities, and reach out to future generations. Most middle-aged people make modest adjustments in their outlook, goals, and daily lives. But a few experience profound inner turbulence and initiate major changes, often in an effort to make up for lost time. Together with advancing years, family and work transitions contribute greatly to emotional and social development.

More midlifers are addressing these tasks than ever before, now that the baby boomers have reached their forties, fifties, and sixties (see page 12 in Chapter 1 to review how baby boomers have reshaped the life course). Indeed, 45- to 54-year-olds are currently the largest age sector of the U.S. population, and they are healthier, better educated, and— despite the late-2000s recession—more financially secure than any previous midlife cohort (U.S. Census Bureau, 2012b; Whitbourne & Willis, 2006). As our discussion will reveal, they have brought increased self-confidence, social consciousness, and vitality—along with great developmental diversity— to this period of the lifespan.

A monumental survey called *Midlife Development in the United States (MIDUS),* conducted in the mid-1990s, has contributed enormously to our understanding of midlife emotional and social development. Conceived by a team of researchers spanning diverse fields, including psychology, sociology, anthropology, and medicine, the aim of MIDUS was to generate new knowledge on the challenges faced by middle-aged adults. Its nationally representative sample included over 7,000 U.S. 25- to 75-year-olds, enabling those in the middle years to be compared with younger and older individuals. Through telephone interviews and self-administered questionnaires, participants responded to over 1,100 items addressing wide-ranging psychological, health, and background factors, yielding unprecedented breadth of information in a single study (Brim, Ryff, & Kessler, 2005). The research endeavor also included "satellite" studies, in which subsamples of respondents were questioned in greater depth on key topics. And it has been extended longitudinally, with 75 percent of the sample recontacted at first follow-up, in the mid-2000s (Radler & Ryff, 2010).

MIDUS has greatly expanded our knowledge of the *multidimensional* and *multidirectional* nature of midlife change, and it promises to be a rich source of information about middle adulthood and beyond for many years to come. Hence, our discussion repeatedly draws on MIDUS, at times delving into its findings, at other times citing them alongside those of other investigations. Let's turn now to Erikson's theory and related research, to which MIDUS has contributed. ●

Erikson's Theory: Generativity versus Stagnation

Erikson's psychological conflict of midlife is called **generativity versus stagnation.** Generativity involves reaching out to others in ways that give to and guide the next generation. Recall from Chapter 14 that generativity is under way in early adulthood through work, community service, and childbearing and child rearing. Generativity expands greatly in midlife, when adults focus more intently on extending commitments beyond oneself (identity) and one's life partner (intimacy) to a larger group— family, community, or society. The generative adult combines the need for self-expression with the need for communion,

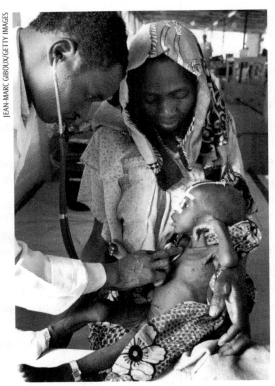

Through his work with severely malnourished children in Niger, this nurse, affiliated with the Nobel Prize–winning organization Doctors Without Borders, integrates personal goals with a broader concern for society.

integrating personal goals with the welfare of the larger social world (McAdams & Logan, 2004). The resulting strength is the capacity to care for others in a broader way than previously.

Erikson (1950) selected the term *generativity* to encompass everything generated that can outlive the self and ensure society's continuity and improvement: children, ideas, products, works of art. Although parenting is a major means of realizing generativity, it is not the only means: Adults can be generative in other family relationships (as Jewel was with her nephew and niece), as mentors in the workplace, in volunteer endeavors, and through many forms of productivity and creativity.

Notice, from what we have said so far, that generativity brings together personal desires and cultural demands. On the personal side, middle-aged adults feel a need to be needed—to attain symbolic immortality by making a contribution that will survive their death (Kotre, 1999; McAdams, Hart, & Maruna, 1998). This desire may stem from a deep-seated evolutionary urge to protect and advance the next generation. On the cultural side, society imposes a social clock for generativity in midlife, requiring adults to take responsibility for the next generation through their roles as parents, teachers, mentors, leaders, and coordinators (McAdams & Logan, 2004). And according to Erikson, a culture's "belief in the species"—the conviction that life is good and worthwhile, even in the face of human destructiveness and deprivation—is a major motivator of generative action. Without this optimistic worldview, people would have no hope of improving humanity.

The negative outcome of this stage is stagnation: Once people attain certain life goals, such as marriage, children, and career success, they may become self-centered and self-indulgent. Adults with a sense of stagnation express their self-absorption in many ways—through lack of interest in young people (including their own children), through a focus on what they can get from others rather than what they can give, and through taking little interest in being productive at work, developing their talents, or bettering the world in other ways.

Some researchers study generativity by asking people to rate themselves on generative characteristics, such as feelings of duty to help others in need or obligation to be an involved citizen. Others ask open-ended questions about life goals, major high points, and most satisfying activities, rating people's responses for generative references. And still others look for generative themes in people's narrative descriptions of themselves (Keyes & Ryff, 1998a, 1998b; McAdams, 2006, 2011; Newton & Stewart, 2010; Rossi, 2001, 2004). Whichever method is used, generativity tends to increase in midlife. For example, in longitudinal and cross-sectional studies of college-educated women, and in an investigation of middle-aged adults diverse in SES, self-rated generativity rose throughout middle adulthood (see Figure 16.1). At the same time, participants expressed greater concern about aging, increased security with their identities, and a stronger sense of competence (Miner-Rubino, Winter, & Stewart, 2004; Stewart, Ostrove, & Helson, 2001; Zucker, Ostrove, & Stewart, 2002). As the Social Issues: Health box on page 534 illustrates, generativity is also a major unifying theme in middle-aged adults' life stories.

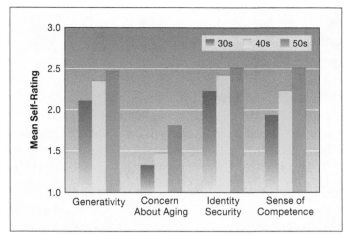

FIGURE 16.1 Age-related changes in self-rated generativity, concern about aging, identity security, and sense of competence. In a longitudinal study of over 300 college-educated women, self-rated generativity increased from the thirties to the fifties, as did concern about aging. The rise in generativity was accompanied by other indicators of psychological health—greater security with one's identity and sense of competence. (Adapted from Stewart, Ostrove, & Helson, 2001.)

Just as Erikson's theory suggests, highly generative people appear especially well-adjusted—low in anxiety and depression; high in autonomy, self-acceptance, and life satisfaction; and more likely to have successful marriages and close friends (Ackerman, Zuroff, & Moskowitz, 2000; An & Cooney, 2006; Grossbaum & Bates, 2002; Westermeyer, 2004). They are also more open to differing viewpoints, possess leadership qualities, desire more from work than financial rewards, and care greatly about the welfare of their children, their partner, their aging parents, and the wider society (Peterson, 2002; Peterson, Smirles, & Wentworth, 1997). Furthermore, generativity is associated with more effective child rearing—higher valuing of trust, open communication, transmission of generative values to children, and an authoritative style (Peterson, 2006; Peterson & Duncan, 2007; Pratt et al., 2008). Generative midlifers are also more involved in political activities, including voting, campaigning, and contacting public officials (Cole & Stewart, 1996).

Although these findings characterize adults of all backgrounds, individual differences in contexts for generativity exist. Having children seems to foster generative development in both men and women. In several studies, including the MIDUS survey, fathers scored higher in generativity than childless men (Marks, Bumpass, & Jun, 2004; McAdams & de St. Aubin, 1992; Snarey et al., 1987). Similarly, in an investigation of well-educated women from ages 43 to 63, those with family commitments (with or without a career) expressed greater generative concerns than childless women who were solely focused on their careers (Newton & Stewart, 2010). Parenting seems to spur especially tender, caring attitudes toward succeeding generations.

For low-SES men with troubled pasts as sons, students, workers, and intimate partners, fatherhood can provide a context for highly generative, positive life change (Roy & Lucas, 2006). At times, these fathers express this generativity as a

Social Issues: Health

Generative Adults Tell Their Life Stories

In research aimed at understanding how highly generative adults make sense of their lives, Dan McAdams and his colleagues interviewed two groups of midlifers: those who often behave generatively and those who seldom do. Participants were asked to relate their life stories, including a high point, a low point, a turning point, and important scenes from childhood, adolescence, and adulthood (McAdams, 2006, 2011; McAdams et al., 2001). Analyses of story lines and themes revealed that adults high and low in generativity reconstruct their past and anticipate their future in strikingly different ways.

Narratives of highly generative people usually contained an orderly sequence of events that the researchers called a commitment story, in which adults give to others as a means of giving back to family, community, and society (McAdams, 2006). The generative storyteller typically describes an early special advantage (such as a good family or a talent), along with early awareness of the suffering of others. This clash between blessing and suffering motivates the person to view the self as "called," or committed, to being good to others. In commitment stories, the theme of redemption is prominent. Highly generative adults frequently describe scenes in which extremely negative life events, involving frustration, failure, loss, or death, are redeemed, or made better, by good outcomes—personal renewal, improvement, and enlightenment.

Consider a story related by Diana, a 49-year-old fourth-grade teacher. Born in a small town to a minister and his wife, Diana was a favorite among the parishioners, who showered her with attention and love. When she was 8, however, her life hit its lowest point: As she looked on in horror, her younger brother ran into the street and was hit by a car; he died later that day. Afterward, Diana, sensing her father's anguish, tried—unsuccessfully—to be the

"son" he had lost. But the scene ends on an upbeat note, with Diana marrying a man who forged a warm bond with her father and who became accepted "as his own son." One of Diana's life goals was to improve her teaching, because "I'd like to give something back . . . to grow and help others grow" (McAdams et al., 1997, p. 689). Her interview overflowed with expressions of generative commitment.

Whereas highly generative adults tell stories in which bad scenes turn good, less generative adults relate stories with themes of contamination, in which good scenes turn bad. For example, a good first year of college turns sour when a professor grades unfairly. A young woman loses weight and looks good but can't overcome her low self-esteem.

Why is generativity connected to life-story redemption events? First, some adults may view their generative activities as a way to redeem negative aspects of their lives. In a study of the life stories of ex-convicts who turned away from crime, many spoke of a strong desire to do good works as penance for their transgressions (Maruna, 2001; Maruna, LeBel, & Lanier, 2004). Second, generativity seems to entail the conviction that the imperfections of today can be transformed into a better tomorrow. Through guiding and giving to the next generation, mature adults increase the chances that the mistakes of the past will not happen again. Finally, interpreting one's own life in terms of redemption offers hope that hard work will lead to

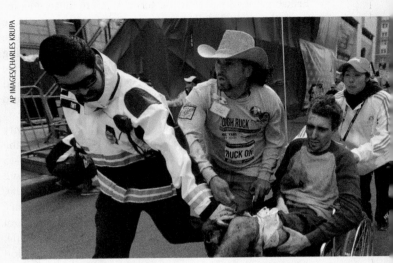

Carlos Arredondo, who lost his older son in the Iraq War and his younger son to suicide, now travels the country, telling the story of how he overcame despair and committed himself to campaigning for peace in his sons' memory. After the Boston Marathon bombings in April 2013, Arredondo, a spectator, leapt into action and rescued this gravely injured bystander.

future benefits—an expectation that may sustain generative efforts of all kinds, from rearing children to advancing communities and societies.

Life stories offer insight into how people imbue their lives with meaning and purpose. Adults high and low in generativity do not differ in the number of positive and negative events included in their narratives. Rather, they interpret those events differently. Commitment stories, filled with redemption, involve a way of thinking about the self that fosters a caring, compassionate approach to others (McAdams & Logan, 2004). Such stories help people realize that although their own personal story will someday end, other stories will follow, due in part to their own generative efforts.

The more redemptive events adults include in their life stories, the higher their self-esteem, life satisfaction, and certainty that the challenges of life are meaningful, manageable, and rewarding (Lilgendahl & McAdams, 2011; McAdams, 2001). Researchers still have much to learn about factors that lead people to view good as emerging from adversity.

refusal to pass on their own history of suffering. As one former gang member, who earned an associate's degree and struggled to keep his teenage sons off the streets, explained, "I came through the depths of hell to try to be a father. I let my sons know, 'You're never without a daddy, don't you let anybody tell you that.' I tell them that if me and your mother separate, I make sure that wherever I go, I build something for you to come to" (p. 153).

Finally, compared with Caucasians, African Americans more often engage in certain types of generativity. They are more involved in religious groups and activities, offer more social support to members of their community, and are more likely to view themselves as role models and sources of wisdom for their children (Hart et al., 2001). A life history of strong support from church and extended family may strengthen these generative values and actions. Among Caucasian Americans, religiosity and spirituality are also linked to greater generative activity (Dillon & Wink, 2004; Son & Wilson, 2011; Wink & Dillon, 2008). Highly generative middle-aged adults often indicate that as children and adolescents, they internalized moral values rooted in a religious tradition and sustained their commitment to those values, which provided lifelong encouragement for generative action (McAdams, 2006). Especially in individualistic societies, belonging to a religious community or believing in a higher being may help preserve generative commitments.

Other Theories of Psychosocial Development in Midlife

Erikson's broad sketch of psychosocial change in midlife has been extended by Levinson and Vaillant. Let's revisit their theories, which were introduced in Chapter 14.

Levinson's Seasons of Life

Return to page 470 to review Levinson's eras (seasons of life). His interviews with adults revealed that middle adulthood begins with a transition, during which people evaluate their success in meeting early adulthood goals. Realizing that from now on, more time will lie behind than ahead, they regard the remaining years as increasingly precious. Consequently, some make drastic revisions in their life structure: divorcing, remarrying, changing careers, or displaying enhanced creativity. Others make smaller changes in the context of marital and occupational stability.

Whether these years bring a gust of wind or a storm, most people turn inward for a time, focusing on personally meaningful living (Neugarten, 1968b). According to Levinson, to reassess and rebuild their life structure, middle-aged adults must confront four developmental tasks. Each requires the individual to reconcile two opposing tendencies within the self, attaining greater internal harmony.

- *Young–old:* The middle-age person must seek new ways of being both young and old. This means giving up certain youthful qualities, transforming others, and finding positive meaning in being older. Perhaps because of the double standard of aging (see pages 516–517 in Chapter 15), most middle-aged women express concern about appearing less attractive as they grow older (Rossi, 2005). But middle-aged men—particularly non-college-educated men, who often hold blue-collar jobs requiring physical strength and stamina—are also highly sensitive to physical aging. In one study, they were more concerned about physical changes than both college- and non-college-educated women, who exceeded college-educated men (Miner-Rubino, Winter, & Stewart, 2004).

  Compared with previous midlife cohorts, U.S. baby boomers are especially interested in controlling physical changes—a desire that has helped energize a huge industry of anti-aging cosmetic products and medical procedures (Jones, Whitbourne, & Skultety, 2006; Lachman, 2004). And sustaining a youthful *subjective age* (feeling younger than one's actual age) is more strongly related to self-esteem and psychological well-being among American than Western-European middle-aged and older adults (Westerhof & Barrett, 2005; Westerhof, Whitbourne, & Freeman, 2012). In the more individualistic U.S. context, a youthful self-image seems more important for viewing oneself as self-reliant and capable of planning for an active, fulfilling late adulthood.

- *Destruction–creation:* With greater awareness of mortality, the middle-aged person focuses on ways he or she has acted destructively. Past hurtful acts toward parents, intimate partners, children, friends, and co-workers are countered by a strong desire to participate in activities that advance human welfare and leave a legacy for future generations. The image of a legacy can be satisfied in many ways—through charitable gifts, creative products, volunteer service, or mentoring young people.

- *Masculinity–femininity:* The middle-aged person must create a better balance between masculine and feminine parts of the self. For men, this means greater acceptance of "feminine" traits of nurturance and caring, which enhance close relationships and compassionate exercise of authority in the workplace. For women, it generally means being more open to "masculine" characteristics of autonomy and assertiveness. Recall from Chapter 8 that people who combine masculine and feminine traits have an androgynous gender identity. Later we will see that androgyny is associated with favorable personality traits and adjustment.

- *Engagement–separateness:* The middle-aged person must forge a better balance between engagement with the external world and separateness. For many men, and for women who have had successful careers, this may mean reducing concern with ambition and achievement and attending more fully to oneself. But women who have been devoted to child rearing or an unfulfilling job often feel compelled to move in the other direction (Levinson, 1996). At age 48, Elena left her position as a reporter for a small-town newspaper, pursued an advanced degree in creative writing, accepted a college teaching position, and began writing a novel. Tim, in contrast, recognized his overwhelming desire for a gratifying romantic partnership. By scaling back his own career, he realized he could grant Elena the time and space she needed to build a rewarding work life—and that doing so might deepen their attachment to each other.

People who flexibly modify their identities in response to age-related changes yet maintain a sense of self-continuity are more aware of their own thoughts and feelings and are higher in self-esteem and life satisfaction (Jones, Whitbourne, & Skultety, 2006; Sneed et al., 2012). But adjusting one's life structure to incorporate the effects of aging requires supportive social contexts. When poverty, unemployment, and lack of a respected place in society dominate the life course, energies are directed toward survival rather than realistically approaching age-related changes. And even adults whose jobs are secure and who live in pleasant neighborhoods may find that employment conditions restrict possibilities for growth by placing too much emphasis on productivity and profit and too little on the meaning of work. In her early forties, Trisha left a large law firm, where she felt constant pressure to bring in high-fee clients and received little acknowledgment of her efforts, for a small practice.

Opportunities for advancement ease the transition to middle adulthood. Yet these are far less available to women than to men. Individuals of both sexes in blue-collar jobs also have few possibilities for promotion. Consequently, they make whatever vocational adjustments they can—becoming active union members, shop stewards, or mentors of younger workers (Christensen & Larsen, 2008; Levinson, 1978). Many men find compensating rewards in moving to the senior generation of their families.

Vaillant's Adaptation to Life

Whereas Levinson interviewed 35- to 45-year-olds, Vaillant (1977, 2002)—in his longitudinal research on well-educated men and women—followed participants past the half-century mark. Recall from Chapter 14 how adults in their late fifties and sixties extend their generativity, becoming "keepers of meaning," or guardians of their culture (see page 471). Vaillant reported that the most-successful and best-adjusted entered a calmer, quieter time of life. "Passing the torch"—concern that the positive aspects of their culture survive—became a major preoccupation.

In societies around the world, older people are guardians of traditions, laws, and cultural values. This stabilizing force holds in check too-rapid change sparked by the questioning and challenging of adolescents and young adults. As people approach the end of middle age, they focus on longer-term, less-personal goals, such as the state of human relations in their society. And they become more philosophical, accepting the fact that not all problems can be solved in their lifetime.

Is There a Midlife Crisis?

Levinson (1978, 1996) reported that most men and women in his samples experienced substantial inner turmoil during the transition to middle adulthood. Yet Vaillant (1977, 2002) saw few examples of crisis but, rather, slow and steady change. These contrasting findings raise the question of how much personal upheaval actually accompanies entry to midlife. Are self-doubt and stress especially great during the forties, and do they prompt major restructuring of the personality, as the term **midlife crisis** implies?

Consider the reactions of Trisha, Devin, Jewel, Tim, and Elena to middle adulthood. Trisha and Devin moved easily into this period, whereas Jewel, Tim, and Elena engaged in greater questioning of their situations and sought alternative life paths. Clearly, wide individual differences exist in response to midlife. *TAKE A MOMENT...* Now ask several individuals in their twenties and thirties whether they expect to encounter a midlife crisis between ages 40 and 50. You are likely to find that Americans often anticipate it, perhaps because of culturally induced apprehension of aging (Wethington, Kessler, & Pixley, 2004). Yet little evidence supports this view of middle age as a turbulent time.

When MIDUS participants were asked to describe "turning points" (major changes in the way they felt about an important aspect of their lives) that had occurred during the past five years, most of the ones reported concerned work. Women's work-related turning points peaked in early adulthood, when many adjusted their work lives to accommodate marriage and childrearing (see Chapter 14). The peak for men, in contrast, came at midlife, a time of increased career responsibility

Like many midlifers, elementary school teacher Jaime Malwitz modified his career in ways that resemble a turning point, not a crisis. He designed a scientist-in-residence program for elementary schools. Here he serves as a resident physicist, discussing a density experiment with a fifth grader.

and advancement. Other common turning points in early and middle adulthood were positive: They involved fulfilling a dream and learning something good about oneself (Wethington, Kessler, & Pixley, 2004). Overall, turning points rarely resembled midlife crises. Even negative work-related turning points generally led to personal growth—for example, a layoff that sparked a positive career change or a shift in energy from career to personal life.

Asked directly if they had ever experienced something they would consider a midlife crisis, only one-fourth of the MIDUS respondents said yes. And they defined such events much more loosely than researchers do. Some reported a crisis well before age 40, others well after age 50. And most attributed it not to age but rather to challenging life events (Wethington, 2000). Consistent with this view, Elena had considered both a divorce and a new career long before she initiated these changes. In her thirties, she separated from her husband; later she reconciled with him and told him that she desired to return to school, which he firmly opposed. She put her own life on hold because of her daughter's academic and emotional difficulties and her husband's resistance.

Another way of exploring midlife questioning is to ask adults about life regrets—attractive opportunities for career or other life-changing activities they did not pursue or lifestyle changes they did not make. In two investigations of women in their early forties, those who acknowledged regret without making life changes, compared to those who modified their lives, reported less favorable psychological well-being and poorer physical health over time (Landman et al., 1995; Stewart & Vandewater, 1999). The two groups did not differ in social or financial resources available to effect change. Rather, they differed in personality: Those who made changes were higher in confidence and assertiveness.

By late midlife, with less time ahead to make life changes, people's interpretation of regrets plays a major role in their well-being. Mature, contented adults acknowledge a past characterized by some losses, have thought deeply about them, and feel stronger because of them. At the same time, they are able to disengage from them, investing in current, personally rewarding goals (King & Hicks, 2007). Among a sample of several hundred 60- to 65-year-olds diverse in SES, about half expressed at least one regret. Compared to those who had not resolved their disappointments, those who had come to terms with them (accepted and identified some eventual benefits) or had "put the best face on things" (identified benefits but still had some lingering regret) reported better physical health and greater life satisfaction (Torges, Stewart, & Miner-Rubino, 2005).

In sum, life evaluation is common during middle age. Most people make changes that are best described as turning points rather than drastic alterations of their lives. Those who cannot modify their life paths often look for the "silver lining" in life's difficulties (King & Hicks, 2007; Wethington, Kessler, & Pixley, 2004). The few midlifers who are in crisis typically have had early adulthoods in which gender roles, family pressures, or low income and poverty severely limited their ability to fulfill personal needs and goals, at home or in the wider world.

Stage or Life Events Approach

That crisis and major restructuring in midlife are rare raises, once again, a question we considered in Chapter 14: Can adult psychosocial changes can be organized into stages, as Erikson's, Levinson's, and Vaillant's theories indicate? A growing number of researchers believe the midadult transition is not stagelike (Freund & Ritter, 2009; McCrae & Costa, 2003; Srivastava et al., 2003). Some regard it as simply an adaptation to normative life events, such as children growing up, reaching the crest of a career, and impending retirement.

Yet recall from earlier chapters that life events are no longer as age-graded as they were in the past. Their timing is so variable that they cannot be the sole cause of midlife change. Furthermore, in several studies, people were asked to trace their thoughts, feelings, attitudes, and hopes during early and middle adulthood. Psychosocial change, in terms of personal disruption followed by reassessment, coincided with both family life cycle events and chronological age. For this reason, most experts regard adaptation during midlife as the combined result of growing older and social experiences (Lachman, 2004; Sneed, Whitbourne, & Culang, 2006). *TAKE A MOMENT...* Return to our discussion of generativity and the midlife transition on page 533, and notice how both factors are involved.

Finally, in describing their lives, the large majority of middle-aged people report troubling moments that prompt new understandings and goals. As we look closely at emotional and social development in middle adulthood, we will see that this period, like others, is characterized by both continuity and change. Debate persists over whether midlife psychosocial changes are stagelike. With this in mind, let's turn to the diverse inner concerns and outer experiences that contribute to psychological well-being and decision making in midlife.

ASK YOURSELF

REVIEW What personal and cultural forces motivate generativity? Why does it increase and contribute vitally to favorable adjustment in midlife?

CONNECT How might the approach of many middle-aged adults to handling life regrets prevent the occurrence of midlife crises?

APPLY After years of experiencing little personal growth at work, 42-year-old Mel looked for a new job and received an attractive offer in another city. Although he felt torn between leaving close friends and pursuing a long-awaited career opportunity, after several weeks of soul searching, he took the new job. Was Mel's dilemma a midlife crisis? Why or why not?

REFLECT Think of a middle-aged adult whom you admire. Describe the various ways that individual expresses generativity.

Stability and Change in Self-Concept and Personality

Midlife changes in self-concept and personality reflect growing awareness of a finite lifespan, longer life experience, and generative concerns. Yet certain aspects of personality remain stable, revealing the persistence of individual differences established during earlier periods.

Possible Selves

On a business trip, Jewel found a spare afternoon to visit Trisha. Sitting in a coffee shop, the two women reminisced about the past and thought aloud about the future. "It's been tough living on my own and building the business," Jewel said. "What I hope for is to become better at my work, to be more community-oriented, and to stay healthy and available to my friends. Of course, I would rather not grow old alone, but if I don't find that special person, I suppose I can take comfort in the fact that I'll never have to face divorce or widowhood."

Jewel is discussing **possible selves**, future-oriented representations of what one hopes to become and what one is afraid of becoming. Possible selves are the temporal dimension of self-concept—what the individual is striving for and attempting to avoid. To lifespan researchers, these hopes and fears are just as vital in explaining behavior as people's views of their current characteristics. Indeed, possible selves may be an especially strong motivator of action in midlife, as adults attach increased meaning to time (Frazier & Hooker, 2006). As we age, we may rely less on social comparisons in judging our self-worth and more on temporal comparisons—how well we are doing in relation to what we had planned.

Throughout adulthood, the personality traits people assign to their current selves show considerable stability. A 30-year-old who says he is cooperative, competent, outgoing, or successful is likely to report a similar picture at a later age. But reports of possible selves change greatly. Adults in their early twenties mention many possible selves, and their visions are lofty and idealistic—being "perfectly happy," "rich and famous," "healthy throughout life," and not being "down and out" or "a person who does nothing important." With age, possible selves become fewer in number and more modest and concrete. Most middle-aged people no longer desire to be the best or the most successful. Instead, they are largely concerned with performance of roles and responsibilities already begun—"being competent at work," "being a good husband and father," "putting my children through the colleges of their choice," "staying healthy," and not being "a burden to my family" or "without enough money to meet my daily needs" (Bybee & Wells, 2003; Cross & Markus, 1991; Ryff, 1991).

What explains these shifts in possible selves? Because the future no longer holds limitless opportunities, adults preserve mental health by adjusting their hopes and fears. To stay motivated, they must maintain a sense of unachieved possibility, yet they must still manage to feel good about themselves and their lives despite disappointments (Lachman & Bertrand, 2002). For example, Jewel no longer desired to be an executive in a large company, as she had in her twenties. Instead, she wanted to grow in her current occupation. And although she feared loneliness in old age, she reminded herself that marriage can lead to equally negative outcomes, such as divorce and widowhood—possibilities that made not having attained an important interpersonal goal easier to bear.

Unlike current self-concept, which is constantly responsive to others' feedback, possible selves (though influenced by others) can be defined and redefined by the individual, as needed. Consequently, they permit affirmation of the self, even when things are not going well (Bolkan & Hooker, 2012). Researchers believe that possible selves may be the key to continued well-being in adulthood, as people revise these future images to achieve a better match between desired and achieved goals. Many studies reveal that the self-esteem of middle-aged and older individuals equals or surpasses that of younger people, perhaps because of the protective role of possible selves (Robins & Trzesniewski, 2005).

Self-Acceptance, Autonomy, and Environmental Mastery

An evolving mix of competencies and experiences leads to changes in certain aspects of personality during middle adulthood. In Chapter 15, we noted that midlife brings gains in expertise and practical problem solving. Middle-aged adults also offer more complex, integrated descriptions of themselves than do younger and older individuals (Labouvie-Vief, 2003). Furthermore, midlife is typically a period in which the number of social roles peaks—spouse, parent, worker, and engaged community member. And status at work and in the community typically rises, as adults take advantage of opportunities for leadership and other complex responsibilities (Helson, Soto, & Cate, 2006).

These changes in cognition and breadth of roles undoubtedly contribute to other gains in personal functioning. In research on adults ranging in age from the late teens into the seventies, and in cultures as distinct as the United States and Japan, three qualities increased from early to middle adulthood:

- *Self-acceptance:* More than young adults, middle-aged people acknowledged and accepted both their good and bad qualities and felt positively about themselves and life.

- *Autonomy:* Middle-aged adults saw themselves as less concerned about others' expectations and evaluations and more concerned with following self-chosen standards.

- *Environmental mastery:* Middle-aged people saw themselves as capable of managing a complex array of tasks easily and effectively (Karasawa et al., 2011; Ryff & Keyes, 1995).

As these findings indicate, midlife is generally a time of increased comfort with the self, independence, assertiveness, commitment to personal values, and life satisfaction (Helson, Jones, & Kwan, 2002; Keyes, Shmotkin, & Ryff, 2002; Stone et al., 2010). Perhaps because of this rise in overall psychological well-being, middle age is sometimes referred to as "the prime of life."

At the same time, factors contributing to psychological well-being differ substantially among cohorts, as self-reports gathered from 25- to 65-year-old MIDUS survey respondents reveal (Carr, 2004). Among women who were born during the baby-boom years or later, and who thus benefited from the women's movement, balancing career with family predicted greater self-acceptance and environmental mastery. But also consider that women born before or during World War II who sacrificed career to focus on child rearing—expected of young mothers in the 1950s and 1960s—were similarly advantaged in self-acceptance. Likewise, men who were in step with prevailing social expectations scored higher in well-being. Baby-boom and younger men who modified their work schedules to make room for family responsibilities—who fit their cohort's image of the "good father"—were more self-accepting. But older men who made this accommodation scored much lower in self-acceptance than those who focused on work and thus conformed to the "good provider" ideal of their times. (See the Biology and Environment box on pages 540–541 for additional influences on midlife psychological well-being.)

Notions of happiness, however, vary among cultures. In comparisons of Japanese and Korean adults with same-age U.S. MIDUS participants, the Japanese and Koreans reported lower levels of psychological well-being, largely because they were less willing than the Americans to endorse individualistic traits, such as self-acceptance and autonomy, as characteristic of themselves (Karasawa et al., 2011; Keyes & Ryff, 1998b). Consistent with their collectivist orientation, Japanese and Koreans' highest well-being scores were on positive relations with others. The Korean participants clarified that they viewed personal fulfillment as achieved through family, especially the success of children. Americans also regarded family relations as relevant to well-being but placed greater emphasis on their own traits and accomplishments than on their children's.

Coping with Daily Stressors

In Chapter 15, we discussed the importance of stress management in preventing illness. It is also vital for psychological well-being. In a MIDUS satellite study in which more than 1,000 participants were interviewed on eight consecutive evenings, researchers found an early- to mid-adulthood plateau in frequency of daily stressors, followed by a decline as work and family responsibilities ease and leisure time increases (see Figure 16.2) (Almeida & Horn, 2004). Women reported more frequent role overload (conflict among roles of employee, spouse, parent, and caregiver of an aging parent) and family-network and child-related stressors, men more work-related stressors, but both

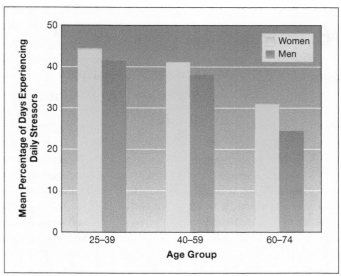

FIGURE 16.2 Age-related changes in daily stressors among men and women. In a MIDUS satellite study, researchers interviewed more than 1,000 adults on eight consecutive evenings. Findings revealed an early- to mid-adulthood plateau, followed by a decline as work and family responsibilities ease and leisure time increases. (From D. M. Almeida & M. C. Horn, 2004, "Is Daily Life More Stressful During Middle Adulthood?" in O. G. Brim, C. D. Ruff, and R. C. Kessler [Eds.], *How Healthy Are We? A National Study of Well-Being at Midlife.* Chicago: The University of Chicago Press, p. 438. Adapted by permission of The University of Chicago Press.)

genders experienced all varieties. Compared with older people, young and midlife adults also perceived their stressors as more disruptive and unpleasant, perhaps because they often experienced several at once, and many involved financial risks and children.

But recall, also, from Chapter 15 that midlife brings an increase in effective coping strategies. Middle-aged individuals are more likely to identify the positive side of difficult situations, postpone action to permit evaluation of alternatives, anticipate and plan ways to handle future discomforts, and use humor to express ideas and feelings without offending others (Diehl, Coyle, & Labouvie-Vief, 1996). Notice how these efforts flexibly draw on both problem-centered and emotion-centered strategies.

Why might effective coping increase in middle adulthood? Other personality changes seem to support it. Complex, integrated, coherent self-descriptions—which increase in midlife, indicating an improved ability to blend strengths and weaknesses into an organized picture—predict a stronger sense of personal control over outcomes and good coping strategies (Hay & Diehl, 2010; Labouvie-Vief & Diehl, 2000). Midlife gains in emotional stability and confidence in handling life's problems may also contribute (Roberts et al., 2007; Roberts & Mroczek, 2008). These attributes predict work and relationship effectiveness—outcomes that reflect the sophisticated, flexible coping of middle age.

Biology and Environment

What Factors Promote Psychological Well-Being in Midlife?

For Trisha and Devin, midlife brought contentment and high life satisfaction. But the road to happiness was rockier for Jewel, Tim, and Elena. What factors contribute to individual differences in psychological well-being at midlife? Consistent with the lifespan perspective, biological, psychological, and social forces are involved, and their effects are interwoven.

Good Health and Exercise

Good health affects energy and zest for life at any age. But during middle and late adulthood, taking steps to improve health and prevent disability becomes a better predictor of psychological well-being. Many studies confirm that engaging in regular exercise—walking, dancing, jogging, or swimming—is more strongly associated with self-rated health and a positive outlook in older than in younger adults (Bherer, 2012). Middle-aged people who maintain an exercise regimen are likely to perceive themselves as particularly active for their age and, therefore, to feel a special sense of accomplishment (Netz et al., 2005). In addition, physical activity enhances self-

efficacy and effective stress management (see page 515 in Chapter 15).

Sense of Control and Personal Life Investment

Middle-aged adults who report a high sense of control over events in various aspects of their lives—health, family, and work—also report more favorable psychological well-being. Sense of control contributes further to self-efficacy. It also predicts use of more effective coping strategies, including seeking of social support, and thereby helps sustain a positive outlook in the face of health, family, and work difficulties (Lachman, Neupert, & Agrigoroaei, 2011).

Personal life investment—firm commitment to goals and involvement in pursuit of those goals—also adds to mental health and life satisfaction (Staudinger & Bowen, 2010). According to Mihaly Csikszentmihalyi, a vital wellspring of

These yoga students express a sense of purpose and accomplishment. Maintaining an exercise regimen contributes greatly to midlife psychological well-being.

happiness is *flow*—the psychological state of being so engrossed in a demanding, meaningful activity that one loses all sense of time and self-awareness. People describe flow as the height of enjoyment, even as an ecstatic state. The more people experience flow, the more they judge their lives to be gratifying (Nakamura & Csikszentmihalyi, 2009). Although flow is common in people engaged in creative endeavors, many others report it—students who love studying, employees who like their jobs, adults involved in challenging leisure pursuits, and

Gender Identity

In her forties and early fifties, Trisha appeared more assertive at work. She spoke out more freely at meetings and took a leadership role when a team of lawyers worked on an especially complex case. She was also more dominant in family relationships, expressing her opinions to her husband and son more readily than she had 10 or 15 years earlier. In contrast, Devin's sense of empathy and caring became more apparent, and he was less assertive and more accommodating to Trisha's wishes than before.

Many studies report an increase in "masculine" traits in women and "feminine" traits in men across middle age (Huyck, 1990; James et al., 1995). Women become more confident, self-sufficient, and forceful, men more emotionally sensitive, caring, considerate, and dependent. These trends appear in cross-sectional and longitudinal research, in people varying in SES,

and in diverse cultures—not just Western industrialized nations but also village societies such as the Maya of Guatemala, the Navajo of the United States, and the Druze of the Middle East (Fry, 1985; Gutmann, 1977; Turner, 1982). Consistent with Levinson's theory, gender identity in midlife becomes more androgynous—a mixture of "masculine" and "feminine" characteristics.

Although the existence of these changes is well-accepted, explanations for them are controversial. A well-known evolutionary view, **parental imperative theory,** holds that identification with traditional gender roles is maintained during the active parenting years to help ensure the survival of children. Men become more goal-oriented, while women emphasize nurturance (Gutmann & Huyck, 1994). After children reach adulthood, parents are free to express the "other-gender" side of their personalities.

parents and grandparents engaged in pleasurable learning activities with children. Flow depends on perseverance and skill at complex endeavors that offer potential for growth. These qualities are well-developed in middle adulthood.

Positive Social Relationships

Developing gratifying social ties is closely linked to midlife psychological well-being. In a survey of college alumni, those who preferred occupational prestige and high income to close friends were twice as likely as other respondents to describe themselves as "fairly" or "very" unhappy (Perkins, 1991, as cited by Myers, 2000).

Supportive relationships, especially with friends and relatives, improve mental health by promoting positive emotions and protecting against stress (Fiori, Antonucci, & Cortina, 2006; Powdthavee, 2008). Enjoyable social ties can even strengthen the impact of an exercise regimen on well-being. Among an ethnically diverse sample of women using a private gym or an African Caribbean community center, exercising with likeminded companions contributed to their happiness and life satisfaction (Wray, 2007). The social side of going to the gym appeared especially important to minority women, who were less concerned with physical-appearance benefits than their Caucasian agemates.

A Good Marriage

Although friendships are important, a good marriage boosts psychological well-being even more. The role of marriage in mental health increases with age, becoming a powerful predictor by late midlife (Marks, Bumpass, & Jun, 2004; Marks & Greenfield, 2009).

Longitudinal studies tracking people as they move in and out of intimate relationships suggest that marriage actually brings about well-being. For example, when interviews with over 13,000 U.S. adults were repeated five years later, people who remained married reported greater happiness than those who remained single. Those who separated or divorced became less happy, reporting considerable depression (Marks & Lambert, 1998). Couples who married for the first time experienced a sharp increase in happiness, those who entered their second marriage a modest increase.

Although not everyone is better off married, the link between marriage and well-being is similar in many nations, suggesting that marriage changes people's behavior in ways that make them better off (Diener et al., 2000; Lansford et al., 2005). Married partners monitor each other's health and offer care in times of illness. They also earn and save more money than single people,

and higher income is modestly linked to psychological well-being (Myers, 2000; Waite, 1999). Furthermore, sexual satisfaction predicts mental health, and married couples have more satisfying sex lives than singles (see Chapter 13).

Mastery of Multiple Roles

Finally, success in handling multiple roles—spouse, parent, worker, community volunteer—is linked to psychological well-being. In the MIDUS survey, as role involvement increased, both men and women reported greater environmental mastery, more rewarding social relationships, heightened sense of purpose in life, and more positive emotion. Furthermore, adults who occupied multiple roles and who also reported high control (suggesting effective role management) scored especially high in well-being—an outcome that was stronger for less-educated adults (Ahrens & Ryff, 2006). Control over roles may be vital for individuals with lower educational attainment, whose role combinations may be particularly stressful and who have fewer economic resources.

Finally, among nonfamily roles, community volunteering in the latter part of midlife contributes uniquely to psychological well-being (Choi & Kim, 2011; Ryff et al., 2012). It may do so by strengthening self-efficacy, generativity, and altruism.

But this biological account has been criticized. As we discussed in earlier chapters, parents need both warmth and assertiveness (in the form of firmness and consistency) to rear children effectively. And although children's departure from the home is related to men's openness to the "feminine" side of their personalities, the link to a rise in "masculine" traits among women is less apparent (Huyck, 1996, 1998). In longitudinal research, college-educated women in the labor force became more independent by their early forties, regardless of whether they had children; those who were homemakers did not. Women attaining high status at work gained most in dominance, assertiveness, and outspokenness by their early fifties (Helson & Picano, 1990; Wink & Helson, 1993). Furthermore, cohort effects can contribute to this trend: In one study, middle-aged women of the baby-boom generation—who experienced new career opportunities as a result of the women's

movement—more often described themselves as having masculine and androgynous traits than did older women (Strough et al., 2007).

Additional demands of midlife may prompt a more androgynous orientation. For example, among men, a need to enrich a marital relationship after children have departed, along with reduced chances for career advancement, may be involved in the awakening of emotionally sensitive traits. Compared with men, women are far more likely to face economic and social disadvantages. A greater number remain divorced, are widowed, and encounter discrimination in the workplace. Self-reliance and assertiveness are vital for coping with these circumstances.

In sum, androgyny in midlife results from a complex combination of social roles and life conditions. In Chapter 8, we noted that androgyny predicts high self-esteem. In adulthood,

In middle age, gender identity becomes more androgynous for both sexes. Men tend to show an increase in "feminine" traits, becoming more emotionally sensitive, caring, considerate, and dependent.

it is also associated with cognitive flexibility, creativity, advanced moral reasoning, and psychosocial maturity (Prager & Bailey, 1985; Runco, Cramond, & Pagnani, 2010; Waterman & Whitbourne, 1982). People who integrate the masculine and feminine sides of their personalities tend to be psychologically healthier, perhaps because they are able to adapt more easily to the challenges of aging.

Individual Differences in Personality Traits

Although Trisha and Jewel both became more self-assured and assertive in midlife, in other respects they differed. Trisha had always been more organized and hard-working, Jewel more gregarious and fun-loving. Once, the two women traveled together. At the end of each day, Trisha was disappointed if she had not kept to a schedule and visited every tourist attraction. Jewel liked to "play it by ear"—wandering through streets and stopping to talk with shopkeepers and residents.

In previous sections, we considered personality changes common to many middle-aged adults, but stable individual differences also exist. Through factor analysis of self-report ratings, the hundreds of personality traits on which people differ have been reduced to five basic factors, often referred to as the **"big five" personality traits:** neuroticism, extroversion, openness to experience, agreeableness, and conscientiousness. Table 16.1 provides a description of each. Notice that Trisha is high in conscientiousness, whereas Jewel is high in extroversion.

Longitudinal and cross-sectional studies of U.S. men and women reveal that agreeableness and conscientiousness increase from the teenage years through middle age, whereas neuroticism declines, and extroversion and openness to experience do not change or decrease slightly—changes that reflect "settling down" and greater maturity. Similar trends have been identified in more than fifty countries varying widely in cultural traditions, including Canada, Germany, Italy, Japan, Russia, and South Korea (McCrae & Costa, 2006; Roberts, Walton, & Viechtbauer, 2006; Schmitt et al., 2007; Soto et al., 2011; Srivastava et al., 2003). The consistency of these cross-cultural findings has led some researchers to conclude that adult personality change is genetically influenced. They note that individual differences in the "big five" traits are large and highly stable: A person who scores high or low at one age is likely to do the same at another, over intervals ranging from 3 to 30 years (McCrae & Costa, 2006).

How can there be high stability in personality traits, yet significant changes in aspects of personality discussed earlier? Studies of the "big five" traits include very large samples and typically do not examine the impact of a host of contextual factors—including life events, the social clock, and cultural values—that shape aspirations, goals, and expectations for appropriate behavior (Caspi & Roberts, 2001). Look closely at the traits in Table 16.1, and you will see that they differ from the attributes considered in previous sections: They do not take into account motivations, preferred tasks, and coping styles, nor do they consider how certain aspects of personality, such as masculinity and femininity, are integrated. Theorists concerned

TABLE 16.1 The "Big Five" Personality Traits

TRAIT	DESCRIPTION
Neuroticism	Individuals who are high on this trait are worrying, temperamental, self-pitying, self-conscious, emotional, and vulnerable. Individuals who are low are calm, even-tempered, self-content, comfortable, unemotional, and hardy.
Extroversion	Individuals who are high on this trait are affectionate, talkative, active, fun-loving, and passionate. Individuals who are low are reserved, quiet, passive, sober, and emotionally unreactive.
Openness to experience	Individuals who are high on this trait are imaginative, creative, original, curious, and liberal. Individuals who are low are down-to-earth, uncreative, conventional, uncurious, and conservative.
Agreeableness	Individuals who are high on this trait are soft-hearted, trusting, generous, acquiescent, lenient, and good-natured. Individuals who are low are ruthless, suspicious, stingy, antagonistic, critical, and irritable.
Conscientiousness	Individuals who are high on this trait are conscientious, hard-working, well-organized, punctual, ambitious, and persevering. Individuals who are low are negligent, lazy, disorganized, late, aimless, and nonpersistent.

Source: McCrae, 2011; McCrae & Costa, 2006.

with change due to experience focus on how personal needs and life events induce new strategies and goals; their interest is in "the human being as a complex adaptive system" (Block, 1995, 2011, p. 19). In contrast, those who emphasize stability due to heredity measure personality traits on which individuals can easily be compared and that are present at any time of life.

To resolve this apparent contradiction, we can think of adults as changing in overall organization and integration of personality but doing so on a foundation of basic, enduring dispositions that support a coherent sense of self as people adapt to changing life circumstances. When more than 2,000 individuals in their forties were asked to reflect on their personalities during the previous six years, 52 percent said they had "stayed the same," 39 percent said they had "changed a little," and 9 percent said they had "changed a lot" (Herbst et al., 2000). Again, these findings contradict a view of middle adulthood as a period of great turmoil and change. But they also underscore that personality remains an "open system," responsive to the pressures of life experiences. Indeed, certain midlife personality changes may strengthen trait consistency! Improved self-understanding, self-acceptance, and skill at handling challenging situations may result in less need to modify basic personality dispositions over time.

ASK YOURSELF

REVIEW Summarize personality changes at midlife. How can these changes be reconciled with increasing stability of the "big five" personality traits?

CONNECT List cognitive gains that typically occur during middle adulthood. (See Chapter 15, pages 518–519 and 524–525.) How might they support midlife personality changes?

APPLY Jeff, age 46, suggested to his wife, Julia, that they set aside time once a year to discuss their relationship—both positive aspects and ways to improve. Julia was surprised because Jeff had never before expressed interest in working on their marriage. What midlife developments probably fostered this new concern?

REFLECT List your hoped-for and feared possible selves. Then ask family members in early and middle adulthood to do the same. Are their reports consistent with age-related research findings? Explain.

 ## Relationships at Midlife

The emotional and social changes of midlife take place within a complex web of family relationships and friendships and an intensified personal focus on generative concerns. Although some middle-aged people live alone, the vast majority—87 percent in the United States—live in families, most with a spouse

(U.S. Census Bureau, 2012b). Partly because they have ties to older and younger generations in their families and partly because their friendships are well-established, people tend to have a larger number of close relationships during midlife than at any other period (Antonucci, Akiyama, & Takahashi, 2004).

The middle adulthood phase of the family life cycle is often referred to as "launching children and moving on." In the past, it was called the "empty nest," but this phrase implies a negative transition, especially for women who have devoted themselves entirely to their children and for whom the end of active parenting can trigger feelings of emptiness and regret. But for most people, middle adulthood is a liberating time, offering a sense of completion and opportunities to strengthen social ties and rekindle interests.

As our discussion in Chapter 14 revealed, increasing numbers of young adults are living at home because of tight job markets and financial challenges, yielding launch–return–relaunch patterns for many middle-aged parents. Still, a declining birthrate and longer life expectancy mean that many contemporary parents do launch children a decade or more before retirement and then turn to other rewarding activities. As adult children depart and marry, middle-aged parents must adapt to new roles of parent-in-law and grandparent. At the same time, they must establish a different type of relationship with their aging parents, who may become ill or infirm and die.

Middle adulthood is marked by the greatest number of exits and entries of family members. Let's see how ties within and beyond the family change during this time of life.

Marriage and Divorce

Although not all couples are financially comfortable, middle-aged households are well-off economically compared with other age groups. Americans between 45 and 54 have the highest average annual income. And the baby boomers—more of whom have earned college and postgraduate degrees and live in dual-earner families—are financially better off than previous midlife generations (Eggebeen & Sturgeon, 2006; U.S. Census Bureau, 2012b). Partly because of increased education and financial security, the contemporary social view of marriage in midlife is one of expansion and new horizons.

These forces strengthen the need to review and adjust the marital relationship. For Devin and Trisha, this shift was gradual. By middle age, their marriage had permitted satisfaction of family and individual needs, endured many changes, and culminated in deeper feelings of love. Elena's marriage, in contrast, became more conflict-ridden as her teenage daughter's problems introduced added strains and as departure of children made marital difficulties more obvious. Tim's failed marriage revealed yet another pattern. With passing years, the number of problems declined, but so did the love expressed (Rokach, Cohen, & Dreman, 2004). As less happened in the relationship, good or bad, the couple had little to keep them together.

As the Biology and Environment box on pages 540–541 revealed, marital satisfaction is a strong predictor of midlife psychological well-being. Middle-aged men who have focused

For many middle-aged couples, having forged a relationship that permits satisfaction of both family and individual needs results in deep feelings of love.

only on career often realize the limited nature of their pursuits. At the same time, women may insist on a more gratifying relationship. And children fully engaged in adult roles remind middle-aged parents that they are in the latter part of their lives, prompting many to decide that the time for improving their marriages is now (Berman & Napier, 2000).

As in early adulthood, divorce is one way of resolving an unsatisfactory marriage in midlife. The divorce rate of U.S. 50- to 65-year-olds has doubled over the past two decades (Brown & Lin, 2012). Divorce at any age takes a heavy psychological toll, but midlifers seem to adapt more easily than younger people. A survey of more than 13,000 Americans revealed that following divorce, middle-aged men and women reported less decline in psychological well-being than their younger counterparts (Marks & Lambert, 1998). Midlife gains in practical problem solving and effective coping strategies may reduce the stressful impact of divorce.

Because the divorce rate is more than twice as great among remarried couples as among those in first marriages, about half of midlife divorces involve people who have had one or more previous unsuccessful marriages. Highly educated middle-aged adults are more likely to divorce, probably because their more comfortable economic circumstances make it easier to leave an unhappy marriage (Skaff, 2006). Nevertheless, for many women, marital breakup—especially when it is repeated—severely reduces standard of living (see page 347 in Chapter 10). For this reason, in midlife and earlier, it is a strong contributor to the **feminization of poverty**—a trend in which women who support themselves or their families have become the majority

of the adult population living in poverty, regardless of age and ethnic group. Because of weak public policies safeguarding families (see Chapter 2), the gender gap in poverty is higher in the United States than in other Western industrialized nations (U.S. Census Bureau, 2012b).

What do recently divorced middle-aged people say about why their marriages ended? Women frequently mention communication problems, inequality in the relationship, adultery, gradual distancing, substance abuse, physical and verbal abuse, or their own desire for autonomy. Men also bring up poor communication and sometimes admit that their "workaholic" lifestyle or emotional inattentiveness played a major role in their marital failure. Women are more likely than men to initiate divorce, and those who do fare somewhat better in psychological well-being. Men who initiate a split often already have another romantic involvement to turn to (Rokach, Cohen, & Dreman, 2004; Sakraida, 2005; Schneller & Arditti, 2004).

Longitudinal evidence reveals that middle-aged women who weather divorce successfully tend to become more tolerant, comfortable with uncertainty, nonconforming, and self-reliant in personality—factors believed to be fostered by divorce-forced independence. And both men and women reevaluate what they consider important in a healthy relationship, placing greater weight on equal friendship and less on passionate love than they had the first time. As in earlier periods, divorce represents both a time of trauma and a time of growth (Baum, Rahav, & Sharon, 2005; Schneller & Arditti, 2004). Little is known about long-term adjustment following divorce among middle-aged men, perhaps because most enter new relationships and remarry within a short time.

Changing Parent–Child Relationships

Parents' positive relationships with their grown children are the result of a gradual process of "letting go," starting in childhood, gaining momentum in adolescence, and culminating in children's independent living. As noted earlier, most parents "launch" adult children sometime in midlife. But because more people are delaying having children to their thirties and even forties (see page 438 in Chapter 13), the age at which midlifers experience their children's departure varies widely. Most parents adjust well; only a minority have difficulty (Mitchell & Lovegreen, 2009). Investment in nonparental relationships and roles, children's characteristics, parents' marital and economic circumstances, and cultural forces affect the extent to which this transition is expansive and rewarding or sad and distressing.

After their son Mark secured a career-entry job and moved out of the family home permanently, Devin and Trisha felt a twinge of nostalgia combined with a sense of pride in their grown son's maturity and success. Beyond this, they returned to rewarding careers and community participation and delighted in having more time for each other. Parents who have developed gratifying alternative activities typically welcome their children's adult status (Mitchell & Lovegreen, 2009). A strong work orientation, especially, predicts gains in life satisfaction after children depart from the home (Silverberg, 1996).

Wide cultural variations exist in the social clock for children's departure. Recall from Chapter 13 that many young people from low-SES homes and with cultural traditions of extended-family living do not leave home early. In the Southern European countries of Greece, Italy, and Spain, parents often actively delay their children's leaving. In Italy, for example, parents believe that moving out without a "justified" reason signifies that something is wrong in the family. Hence, many more Italian young adults reside with their parents until marriage than in other Western nations. At the same time, Italian adults grant their grown children extensive freedom within the parental home (Rusconi, 2004). Parent–adult-child relationships are usually positive, making living with parents attractive.

With the end of parent–child coresidence comes a substantial decline in parental authority. Devin and Trisha no longer knew of Mark's daily comings and goings or expected him to inform them. Nevertheless, Mark telephoned at regular intervals to report on events in his life and seek advice about major decisions. Although the parental role changes, its continuation is important to middle-aged adults. Departure of children is a relatively minor event as long as parent–child contact and affection are sustained (Mitchell & Lovegreen, 2009). When it results in little or no communication, parents' psychological well-being declines.

Whether or not they reside with parents, adolescent and young-adult children who are "off-time" in development—who deviate from parental expectations about how the path to adult responsibilities should unfold—can prompt parental strain (Pillemer & Suitor, 2002; Settersten, 2003). Consider Elena, whose daughter was doing poorly in her college courses and in danger of not graduating. The need for extensive parental guidance, at a time when she expected her daughter to be more responsible and independent, caused anxiety and unhappiness for Elena, who was ready to reduce time devoted to active parenting.

In one study, researchers asked a large sample of 40- to 60-year-old parents to report on their grown children's problems and successes along with their own psychological well-being. Consistent with the familiar saying, "parents are only as happy as their least happy child," having even one problematic child dampened parents' well-being, but having a successful child did not have a compensating positive effect. The more grown children with problems, the poorer parents' well-being. In contrast, it took multiple successful grown children to sway parents' well-being in a favorable direction (Fingerman et al., 2012a). As with marriages, negative, conflict-ridden experiences with grown children are particularly salient, profoundly affecting midlife parents' psychological states.

Throughout middle adulthood, parents continue to give more assistance to children than they receive, especially while children are unmarried or when they face difficulties, such as marital breakup or unemployment (Ploeg et al., 2004; Zarit & Eggebeen, 2002). Support in Western countries typically flows "downstream": Although ethnic variations exist, most middle-aged parents provide more financial, practical, emotional, and social support to their offspring than to their aging parents,

unless a parent has an urgent need (declining health or other crises) (Fingerman & Birditt, 2011; Fingerman et al., 2011a). In explaining their generous support of adult children, parents usually mention the importance of the relationship. And providing adult children with assistance enhances midlife psychological well-being (Marks & Greenfield, 2009). Clearly, middle-aged adults remain invested in their adult children's development and continue to reap deep personal rewards from the parental role.

When children marry, parents must adjust to an enlarged family network that includes in-laws. Difficulties occur when parents do not approve of their child's partner or when the young couple adopts a way of life inconsistent with parents' values. Parents who take steps to forge a positive tie with a future daughter- or son-in-law generally experience a closer relationship after the couple marries (Fingerman et al., 2012b). And when warm, supportive relationships endure, intimacy between parents and children increases over the adult years, with great benefits for parents' life satisfaction (Ryff, Singer, & Seltzer, 2002). Members of the middle generation, especially mothers, usually take on the role of **kinkeeper,** gathering the family for celebrations and making sure everyone stays in touch.

Parents of adult children expect a mature relationship, marked by tranquility and contentment. Yet many factors—on both the child's and the parent's side—affect whether that goal is achieved. Applying What We Know on page 546 suggests ways middle-aged parents can increase the chances that bonds with adult children will be loving and rewarding and serve as contexts for personal growth.

Grandparenthood

Two years after Mark married, Devin and Trisha were thrilled to learn that a granddaughter was on the way. Although the stereotypical image of grandparents as elderly persists, today the average age of becoming a grandparent is 50 years for American women, 52 for American men (Legacy Project, 2012). A longer life expectancy means that many adults will spend one-third or more of their lifespan in the grandparent role.

Meanings of Grandparenthood. Middle-aged adults typically rate grandparenthood as highly important, following closely behind the roles of parent and spouse but ahead of worker, son or daughter, and sibling (Reitzes & Mutran, 2002). Why did Trisha and Devin, like many others their age, greet the announcement of a grandchild with such enthusiasm? Most people experience grandparenthood as a significant milestone, mentioning one or more of the following gratifications:

- *Valued elder*—being perceived as a wise, helpful person
- *Immortality through descendants*—leaving behind not just one but two generations after death
- *Reinvolvement with personal past*—being able to pass family history and values to a new generation
- *Indulgence*—having fun with children without major child-rearing responsibilities (AARP, 2002; Hebblethwaite & Norris, 2011)

Applying What We Know

Ways Middle-Aged Parents Can Promote Positive Ties with Their Adult Children

Suggestion	Description
Emphasize positive communication.	Let adult children and their intimate partners know of your respect, support, and interest. This not only communicates affection but also permits conflict to be handled in a constructive context.
Avoid unnecessary comments that are a holdover from childhood.	Adult children, like younger children, appreciate an age-appropriate relationship. Comments that have to do with safety, eating, and self-care ("Be careful on the freeway," "Don't eat those foods," "Make sure you wear a sweater—it's cold out today") annoy adult children and can stifle communication.
Accept the possibility that some cultural values and practices and aspects of lifestyle will be modified in the next generation.	In constructing a personal identity, most adult children have gone through a process of evaluating the meaning of cultural values and practices for their own lives. Traditions and lifestyles cannot be imposed on adult children.
When an adult child encounters difficulties, resist the urge to "fix" things.	Accept the fact that no meaningful change can take place without the willing cooperation of the adult child. Stepping in and taking over communicates a lack of confidence and respect. Find out whether the adult child wants your help, advice, and decision-making skills.
Be clear about your own needs and preferences.	When it is difficult to arrange for a visit, babysit, or provide other assistance, say so and negotiate a reasonable compromise rather than letting resentment build.

Grandparent–Grandchild Relationships. Grand-parents' styles of relating to grandchildren vary as widely as the meanings they derive from their new role. The grandparent's and grandchild's age and sex make a difference. When their grand-daughter was young, Trisha and Devin enjoyed an affectionate, playful relationship with her. As she got older, she looked to them for information and advice in addition to warmth and caring. By the time their granddaughter reached adolescence,

Many grandparents derive great joy from an affectionate, playful relationship with young grandchildren. As this grandchild gets older, he may look to his grandfather for advice, as a role model, and for family history in addition to warmth and caring.

Trisha and Devin had become role models, family historians, and conveyers of social, vocational, and religious values.

Living nearby is the strongest predictor of frequent, face-to-face interaction with young grandchildren. Despite high family mobility in Western industrialized nations, most grand-parents live close enough to at least one grandchild to enable regular visits. But because time and resources are limited, number of "grandchild sets" (households with grandchildren) reduces grandparent visits (Uhlenberg & Hammill, 1998). A strong desire to affect the development of grandchildren can motivate grandparents' involvement. As grandchildren get older, distance becomes less influential and relationship quality more so: The extent to which adolescent or young-adult grand-children believe their grandparent values contact is a good predictor of a close bond (Brussoni & Boon, 1998).

As Figure 16.3 shows, maternal grandmothers report more frequent visits with grandchildren than do paternal grand-mothers, who are slightly advantaged over both maternal and paternal grandfathers (Uhlenberg & Hammill, 1998). Typically, relationships are closer between grandparents and grand-children of the same sex and, especially, between maternal grandmothers and granddaughters—a pattern found in many countries (Brown & Rodin, 2004). Grandmothers also report higher satisfaction with the grandparent role than grandfathers, perhaps because grandmothers are more likely to participate in recreational, religious, and family activities with grandchildren (Reitzes & Mutran, 2004; Silverstein & Marenco, 2001). The grandparent role may be a vital means through which women satisfy their kinkeeping function.

SES and ethnicity also influence grandparent–grandchild ties. In higher-income families, where the grandparent role is not central to family maintenance and survival, it is fairly

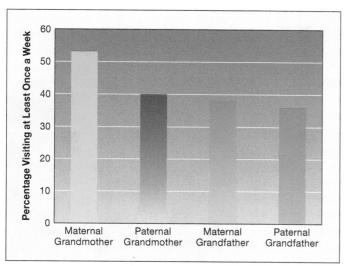

FIGURE 16.3 Influence of grandparent sex and lineage on frequent visiting of grandchildren. When a nationally representative sample of 4,600 U.S. grandparents were asked how often they visited a particular set of grandchildren, maternal grandmothers were especially likely to report visiting frequently (at least once a week). Paternal grandmothers slightly exceeded both maternal and paternal grandfathers. (From P. Uhlenberg & B. G. Hammill, 1998, "Frequency of Grandparent Contact with Grandchild Sets: Six Factors That Make a Difference," *Gerontologist, 38,* p. 281. Copyright © 1998 The Gerontological Society of America. Reprinted by permission of Oxford University Press and Peter Uhlenberg.)

unstructured and takes many forms. In low-income families, by contrast, grandparents often perform essential activities. For example, many single parents live with their families of origin and depend on grandparents' financial and caregiving assistance to reduce the impact of poverty. Compared with grandchildren in intact families, grandchildren in single-parent and stepparent families report engaging in more diverse, higher-quality activities with their grandparents (Kennedy & Kennedy, 1993). As children experience the stress of family transition, bonds with grandparents take on increasing importance.

In some cultures, grandparents are absorbed into an extended-family household and become actively involved in child rearing. When a Chinese, Korean, or Mexican-American maternal grandmother is a homemaker, she is the preferred caregiver while parents of young children are at work (Kamo, 1998; Williams & Torrez, 1998). Similarly, involvement in child care is high among Native-American grandparents. In the absence of a biological grandparent, an unrelated aging adult may be integrated into the family to serve as a mentor and disciplinarian for children (Werner, 1991). (See Chapter 2, page 66, for a description of the grandmother's role in the African-American extended family.)

Increasingly, grandparents have stepped in as primary caregivers in the face of serious family problems. As the Social Issues: Health box on page 548 reveals, a rising number of American children live apart from their parents in grandparent-headed households. Despite their willingness to help and their competence at child rearing, grandparents who take full responsibility for young children experience considerable emotional

and financial strain. They need more assistance from community and government agencies than is currently available.

Because parents usually serve as gatekeepers of grandparents' contact with grandchildren, relationships between grandparents and their daughter-in-law or son-in-law strongly affect the closeness of grandparent–grandchild ties. A positive bond with a daughter-in-law seems particularly important in the relationship between grandparents and their son's children (Fingerman, 2004). And after a marital breakup, grandparents who are related to the custodial parent (typically the mother) have more frequent contact with grandchildren.

When family relationships are positive, grandparenthood provides an important means of fulfilling personal and societal needs in midlife and beyond. Typically, grandparents are a frequent source of pleasure, support, and knowledge for children, adolescents, and young adults. They also provide the young with firsthand experience in how older people think and function. In return, grandchildren become deeply attached to grandparents and keep them abreast of social change. Clearly, grandparenthood is a vital context for sharing between generations.

Middle-Aged Children and Their Aging Parents

The percentage of middle-aged Americans with living parents has risen dramatically—from 10 percent in 1900 to over 50 percent in the first decade of the twenty-first century (U.S. Census Bureau, 2012b). A longer life expectancy means that adult children and their parents are increasingly likely to grow old together. What are middle-aged children's relationships with their aging parents like? And how does life change for adult children when an aging parent's health declines?

Frequency and Quality of Contact. A widespread myth is that adults of past generations were more devoted to their aging parents than are today's adults. Although adult children spend less time in physical proximity to their parents, the reason is not neglect or isolation. Because of a desire to be independent, made possible by gains in health and financial security, fewer aging adults live with younger generations now than in the past. Nevertheless, approximately two-thirds of older adults in the United States live close to at least one of their children, and frequency of contact is high through both visits and telephone calls (U.S. Census Bureau, 2012b). Proximity increases with age: Aging adults who move usually do so in the direction of kin, and younger people tend to move in the direction of their aging parents.

Middle age is a time when adults reassess relationships with their parents, just as they rethink other close ties. Many adult children become more appreciative of their parents' strengths and generosity and mention positive changes in the quality of the relationship, even after parents show physical declines. A warm, enjoyable relationship contributes to both parent and adult-child well-being (Fingerman et al., 2007, 2008; Pudrovska, 2009). Trisha, for example, felt closer to her parents and often asked them to tell her more about their earlier lives.

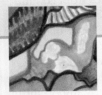

Social Issues: Health

Grandparents Rearing Grandchildren: The Skipped-Generation Family

Nearly 2.4 million U.S. children—4 to 5 percent of the child population—live with grandparents but apart from parents, in **skipped-generation families** (U.S. Census Bureau, 2012b). The number of grandparents rearing grandchildren has increased over the past two decades. The arrangement occurs in all ethnic groups, though more often in African-American, Hispanic, and Native-American families than in Caucasian families. Although grandparent caregivers are more likely to be women than men, many grandfathers participate (Fuller-Thomson & Minkler, 2005, 2007; Minkler & Fuller-Thomson, 2005). Grandparents generally step in when parents' troubled lives—as a result of substance abuse, child abuse and neglect, family violence, or physical or mental illness—threaten children's well-being (Langosch, 2012). Often these families take in two or more children.

As a result, grandparents usually assume the parenting role under highly stressful life circumstances. Unfavorable child-rearing experiences have left their mark on the children, who show high rates of learning difficulties, depression, and antisocial behavior. Absent parents' adjustment difficulties strain family relationships. Parents may interfere by violating the grandparents' behavioral limits, taking grandchildren away without permission, or making promises to children that they do not keep. These youngsters also introduce financial burdens into households that often are already low-income (Mills, Gomez-Smith, & De Leon, 2005; Williamson, Softas-Nall, & Miller, 2003). All these factors heighten grandparents' emotional distress.

Grandparents struggle with daily dilemmas—wanting to be grandparents, not parents; wanting the parent to be present in the child's life but fearing for the child's well-being if the parent returns and does not provide good care (Templeton, 2011). And grandparent caregivers, at a time when they anticipated having more time for spouses, friends, and leisure, instead have less. Many report feeling emotionally drained, depressed, and worried about what will happen to the children if their own health fails (Hayslip & Kaminski, 2005; Langosch, 2012). Some families are extremely burdened. Native-American caregiving grandparents are especially likely to be unemployed, to have a disability, to be caring for several grandchildren, and to be living in extreme poverty (Fuller-Thomson & Minkler, 2005).

Despite great hardship, these grandparents seem to realize their widespread image as "silent saviors," often forging close emotional bonds with their grandchildren and using effective child-rearing practices (Fuller-Thomson & Minkler, 2000; Gibson, 2005). Compared with children in divorced, single-parent families, blended families, or foster families, children reared by grandparents fare better in adjustment (Rubin et al., 2008; Solomon & Marx, 1995).

Skipped-generation families have a tremendous need for social and financial support and intervention services for troubled children. Custodial grandparents describe support groups—both for themselves and for their grandchildren—as especially

A custodial grandmother helps her 8-year-old granddaughter with homework. Although grandparents usually assume the parenting role under highly stressful circumstances, most find compensating rewards in rearing grandchildren.

helpful, yet only a minority make use of such interventions (Smith, Rodriguez, & Palmieri, 2010). This suggests that grandparents need special help in finding out about and accessing support services.

Although their everyday lives are often stressful, caregiving grandparents—even those rearing children with serious problems—report as much fulfillment in the grandparent role as typical grandparents do (Hayslip et al., 2002). The warmer the grandparent–grandchild bond, the greater grandparents' long-term life satisfaction (Goodman, 2012). Many grandparents mention joy from sharing children's lives and feelings of pride at children's progress, which help compensate for difficult circumstances. And some grandparents view the rearing of grandchildren as a "second chance"—an opportunity to make up for earlier, unfavorable parenting experiences and "do it right" (Dolbin-MacNab, 2006).

Research indicates that middle-aged daughters forge closer, more supportive relationships with aging parents, especially mothers, than do middle-aged sons (Fingerman, 2003). But this gender difference may be declining. Sons report closer ties and greater assistance to aging parents in recent than in previous studies (Fingerman et al., 2007, 2008). Changing gender roles are likely responsible. Because the majority of contemporary middle-aged women are employed, they face many competing demands on their time and energy. Consequently, men are becoming more involved in family responsibilities, including with aging parents (Fingerman & Birditt, 2011). Despite this shift, women's investment continues to exceed men's.

In midlife, many adults develop warmer, more supportive relationships with their aging parents. At a birthday party for her mother, this daughter expresses love and appreciation for her mother's strengths and generosity.

In collectivist cultures, older adults most often live with their married children. For example, traditionally, Chinese, Japanese, and Korean seniors moved in with a son and his wife and children; today, many live with a daughter and her family, too. This tradition of coresidence, however, is declining in some parts of Asia and in the United States, as more Asian and Asian-American aging adults choose to live on their own (Davey & Takagi, 2013; Zhan & Montgomery, 2003; Zhang, 2004). In African-American and Hispanic families as well, coresidence is common. Regardless of whether coresidence and daily contact are typical, relationship quality usually reflects patterns established earlier: Positive parent–child ties generally remain so, as do conflict-ridden interactions.

Help exchanged between adult children and their aging parents is responsive to past and current family circumstances. The more positive the history of the parent–child tie, the more help given and received. Also, aging parents give more help to unmarried adult children and to those with disabilities. Similarly, adult children give more to elderly parents who are widowed or in poor health—usually emotional support and practical help, less often financial assistance. At the same time, middle-aged parents do what they can to maximize the overall quantity of help offered, as needed: While continuing to provide generous assistance to their children because of the priority placed on the parent–child tie (see page 545), middle-aged adults augment the aid they give to elderly parents as parental health problems increase (Kunemund, Motel-Klingebiel, & Kohli, 2005; Stephens et al., 2009).

Even when parent–child relationships have been emotionally distant, adult children offer more support as parents age, out of a sense of altruism and family duty (Silverstein et al., 2002).

And although the baby-boom generation is often described as self-absorbed, baby-boom midlifers actually express a stronger commitment to caring for their aging parents than the preceding middle-aged generation (Gans & Silverstein, 2006).

In sum, as long as multiple roles are manageable and the experiences within each are high in quality, midlife intergenerational assistance as family members (aging parents) have increased needs is best characterized as *resource expansion* rather than as merely conflicting demands that inevitably drain energy and detract from psychological well-being (Grundy & Henretta, 2006; Stephens et al., 2009). Recall from the Biology and Environment box on pages 540–541 that midlifers derive great personal benefits from successfully managing multiple roles. Their enhanced self-esteem, mastery, and sense of meaning and purpose expand their motivation and energy to handle added family-role demands, from which they reap additional personal rewards.

Caring for Aging Parents. About 25 percent of U.S. adult children provide unpaid care to an aging adult (MetLife, 2011). The burden of caring for aging parents can be great. In Chapter 2, we noted that as birthrates have declined, the family structure has become increasingly "top-heavy," with more generations alive but fewer younger members. Consequently, more than one older family member is likely to need assistance, with fewer younger adults available to provide it.

The term **sandwich generation** is widely used to refer to the idea that middle-aged adults must care for multiple generations above and below them at the same time (Riley & Bowen, 2005). Although only a minority of contemporary middle-aged adults who care for aging parents have children younger than age 18 at home, many are providing assistance to young-adult children and to grandchildren—obligations that, when combined with work and community responsibilities, can lead middle-aged caregivers to feel "sandwiched," or squeezed, between the pressures of older and younger generations. As more baby boomers move into late adulthood and as their adult children continue to delay childbearing, the number of midlifers who are working, rearing young children, and caring for aging parents will increase.

Middle-aged adults living far from aging parents who are in poor health often substitute financial help for direct care, if they have the means. But when parents live nearby and have no spouse to meet their needs, adult children usually engage in direct care. Regardless of family income level, African-American, Asian-American, and Hispanic adults give aging parents more direct care and financial help than Caucasian-American adults do (Shuey & Hardy, 2003). Compared with their white counterparts, African Americans and Hispanics express a stronger sense of obligation, and find it more personally rewarding, to support their aging parents (Fingerman et al., 2011b; Swartz, 2009). And African Americans often draw on close, family-like relationships with friends and neighbors for caregiving assistance.

In all ethnic groups, responsibility for providing care to aging parents falls more on daughters than on sons. Why are

Caring for an aging parent with a chronic illness or disability is highly stressful. But social support reduces physical and emotional strain, enabling adult children to find satisfactions and rewards in tending to parents' needs.

women usually the principal caregivers? Families turn to the person who seems most available—living nearby and with fewer commitments that might interfere with the ability to assist. These unstated rules, in addition to parents' preference for same-sex caregivers (aging mothers live longer), lead more women to fill the role (see Figure 16.4). Daughters also feel more obligated than sons to care for aging parents (Gans & Silverstein, 2006; Stein, 2009). And although couples strive to be fair to both sides of the family, they tend to provide more direct care for the wife's parents. This bias, however, is weaker in ethnic minority families and is nonexistent in Asian nations where cultural norms specify that daughters-in-law provide care to their husband's parents (Shuey & Hardy, 2003; Zhan & Montgomery, 2003).

As Figure 16.4 shows, nearly one-fourth of American working women are caregivers; others quit their jobs to provide care. And the time they devote to caring for a disabled aging parent is substantial, averaging 10 to 20 hours per week (Metlife, 2011; Takamura & Williams, 2004). Nevertheless, men—although doing less than women—do contribute. In one investigation, employed men spent an average of 7½ hours per week caring for parents or parents-in-law (Neal & Hammer, 2007). Tim, for example, looked in on his father, a recent stroke victim, every evening, reading to him, running errands, making household repairs, and taking care of finances. His sister, however, provided more hands-on care—cooking, feeding, bathing, managing medication, and doing laundry. The care sons and daughters provide tends to be divided along gender-role lines. About 10 percent of the time—generally when no other family member

can do so—sons become primary caregivers, heavily involved in basic-care tasks (Harris, 1998; Pinquart & Sörensen, 2006).

As adults move from early to later middle age, the sex difference in parental caregiving declines. Perhaps as men reduce their vocational commitments and feel less need to conform to a "masculine" gender role, they grow more able and willing to provide basic care (Marks, 1996; MetLife, 2011). At the same time, parental caregiving may contribute to men's greater openness to the "feminine" side of their personalities. A man who cared for his mother, severely impaired by Alzheimer's disease, commented on how the experience altered his outlook: "It was so difficult to do these tasks; things a man, a son, is not supposed to do. I have definitely modified my views on conventional expectations" (Hirsch, 1996, p. 112).

Although most adult children help willingly, caring for a chronically ill or disabled parent is highly stressful. Over time, the parent usually gets worse, and the caregiving task escalates. As Tim explained to Devin and Trisha, "One of the hardest aspects is the emotional strain of seeing my father's physical and mental decline up close."

Caregivers who share a household with ill parents—about 23 percent of U.S. adult children—experience the most stress. When a parent and child who have lived separately for years must move in together, conflicts generally arise over routines and lifestyles. But the greatest source of stress is problem behavior, especially for caregivers of parents who have deteriorated mentally (Alzheimer's Association, 2012b). Tim's sister reported that their father would wake during the night, ask repetitive questions, follow her around the house, and become agitated and combative.

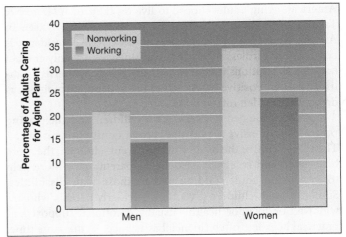

FIGURE 16.4 Baby boomers, by work status and gender, who provide basic personal care to an aging parent in poor health. A survey of a nationally representative sample of 1,100 U.S. men and women over age 50 with at least one parent living revealed that more nonworking than working adults engaged in basic personal care (assistance with such activities as dressing, feeding, and bathing). Regardless of work status, many more women than men were caregivers. (Adapted from *The MetLife Study of Caregiving Costs to Working Caregivers: Double Jeopardy for Baby Boomers Caring for Their Parents*, June 2011, Figure 3. Reprinted by permission of The MetLife Mature Market Institute, New York, NY.)

Applying What We Know

Relieving the Stress of Caring for an Aging Parent

Strategy	Description
Use effective coping strategies.	Use problem-centered coping to manage the parent's behavior and caregiving tasks. Delegate responsibilities to other family members, seek assistance from friends and neighbors, and recognize the parent's limits while calling on capacities the parent does have. Use emotion-centered coping to reinterpret the situation in a positive way, such as emphasizing the opportunity it offers for personal growth and for giving to parents in the last years of their lives. Avoid denial of anger, depression, and anxiety in response to the caregiving burden, which heightens stress.
Seek social support.	Confide in family members and friends about the stress of caregiving, seeking their encouragement and help. So far as possible, avoid quitting work to care for an ill parent; doing so is associated with social isolation and loss of financial resources.
Make use of community resources.	Contact community organizations to seek information and assistance, in the form of caregiver support groups, in-home respite help, home-delivered meals, transportation, and adult day care.
Press for workplace and public policies that relieve the emotional and financial burdens of caring for an aging parent.	Encourage your employer to provide care benefits, such as flexible work hours and employment leave for caregiving. Communicate with lawmakers and other citizens about the need for additional government funding to help pay for caregiving. Emphasize the need for improved health insurance plans that reduce the financial strain of caring for an aging parent on middle- and low-income families.

Parental caregiving often has emotional, physical, and financial consequences. It leads to role overload, high job absenteeism, exhaustion, inability to concentrate, feelings of hostility, anxiety about aging, and high rates of depression, with women more profoundly affected than men (Neal & Hammer, 2007; Pinquart & Sörensen, 2006). Caregivers who must reduce their employment hours or leave the labor force to provide care (mostly women) face not just lost wages but also diminished retirement benefits. Despite having more time to care for an ill parent, women who quit work fare especially poorly in adjustment, probably because of social isolation and financial strain (Bookman & Kimbrel, 2011). Positive experiences at work can actually reduce the stress of parental care as caregivers bring a favorable self-evaluation and a positive mood home with them.

In cultures and subcultures where adult children feel an especially strong sense of obligation to care for aging parents, the emotional toll is also high (Knight & Sayegh, 2010). In research on Korean, Korean-American, and Caucasian-American caregivers of parents with mental disabilities, the Koreans and Korean Americans reported higher levels of family obligation and care burden—and also higher levels of anxiety and depression—than the Caucasian Americans (Lee & Farran, 2004; Youn et al., 1999). And among African-American caregivers, women who strongly endorsed cultural reasons for providing care ("It's what my people have always done") fared less well in mental health two years later than women who moderately endorsed cultural reasons (Dilworth-Anderson, Goodwin, & Williams, 2004).

Social support is highly effective in reducing caregiver stress. Tim's encouragement, assistance, and willingness to listen helped his sister cope with in-home care of their father so that she could find satisfactions in it. When caregiving becomes a team effort with multiple family members trading off, caregivers cope more effectively. Under these conditions, despite being demanding and stressful, it can enhance psychological well-being (Roberto & Jarrott, 2008). Adult children feel gratified at having helped and gain in self-understanding, problem solving, and sense of competence.

LOOK AND LISTEN

Ask a middle-aged adult caring for an aging parent in declining health to describe both the stressful and rewarding aspects of caregiving. What strategies does he or she use to reduce stress? To what extent does the caregiver share caregiving burdens with family members and enlist the support of community organizations? ●

In Denmark, Sweden, and Japan, a government-sponsored home helper system eases the burden of parental care by making specially trained nonfamily caregivers available, based on seniors' needs (Saito, Auestad, & Waerness, 2010). In the United States, in-home care by a nonfamily caregiver is too costly for most families; only 10 to 20 percent arrange it (Family Caregiver Alliance, 2009). And unless they must, few people want to place their parents in formal care, such as nursing homes, which also are expensive. Applying What We Know above summarizes ways to relieve the stress of caring for an aging parent—at the individual, family, community, and societal levels. We will address additional care options, along with interventions for caregivers, in Chapter 17.

Siblings

As Tim's relationship with his sister reveals, siblings are ideally suited to provide social support. Nevertheless, a survey of a large sample of ethnically diverse Americans revealed that sibling contact and support decline from early to middle adulthood, rebounding only after age 70 for siblings living near each other (White, 2001). Decreased midlife contact is probably due to the demands of middle-aged adults' diverse roles. However, most adult siblings report getting together or talking on the phone at least monthly (Antonucci, Akiyama, & Merline, 2002).

Despite reduced contact, many siblings feel closer in midlife, often in response to major life events (Stewart et al., 2001). Launching and marriage of children seem to prompt siblings to think more about each other. As Tim commented, "It helped our relationship when my sister's children were out of the house and married. I'm sure she cared about me. I think she just didn't have time!" When a parent becomes seriously ill, brothers and sisters who previously had little to do with one another may find themselves in touch about parental care. And when parents die, adult children realize they have become the oldest generation and must look to each other to sustain family ties.

Not all sibling bonds improve, of course. Recall Trisha's negative encounters with her sister, Dottie (see page 513 in Chapter 15). Dottie's difficult temperament had made her hard to get along with since childhood, and her temper flared when their father died and problems arose over family finances. Large inequities in division of labor in parental caregiving can also unleash intense sibling conflict (Silverstein & Giarrusso, 2010). As siblings grow older, good relationships often get better and poor relationships get worse.

As in early adulthood, sister–sister relationships are closer than sister–brother and brother–brother ties, a difference apparent in many industrialized nations (Cicirelli, 1995; Fowler, 2009). But a comparison of middle-aged men of the baby-boom generation with those of the preceding cohort revealed warmer, more expressive ties between baby-boom brothers (Bedford &

Avioli, 2006). A contributing factor may be baby boomers' more flexible gender-role attitudes.

In industrialized nations, sibling relationships are voluntary. In village societies, they are generally involuntary and basic to family functioning. For example, among Asian Pacific Islanders, family social life is organized around strong brother–sister attachments. A brother–sister pair is often treated as a unit in exchange marriages with another family. After marriage, brothers are expected to protect sisters, and sisters serve as spiritual mentors to brothers. Families not only include biological siblings but bestow on other relatives, such as cousins, the status of brother or sister, creating an unusually large network of lifelong sibling support (Cicirelli, 1995). Cultural norms reduce sibling conflict, thereby ensuring family cooperation. In industrialized nations, promoting positive sibling ties in childhood is vital for warm sibling bonds in later years.

Friendships

As family responsibilities declined in middle age, Devin found he had more time to spend with friends. On Friday afternoons, he met several male friends at a coffee house, and they chatted for a couple of hours. But most of Devin's friendships were couple-based—relationships he shared with Trisha. Compared with Devin, Trisha more often got together with friends on her own.

Middle-aged friendships reflect the same trends discussed in Chapter 14. At all ages, men's friendships are less intimate than women's. Men tend to talk about sports, politics, and business, whereas women focus on feelings and life problems. Women report a greater number of close friends and say they both receive and provide their friends with more emotional support (Antonucci, Akiyama, & Takahashi, 2004).

Over the past decade, the average number of friendships rose among U.S. midlifers, perhaps because of ease of keeping in touch through social media (Wang & Wellman, 2010). Though falling short of young adults' use, connecting regularly with friends through Facebook or other social networking sites has risen rapidly among middle-aged adults (see Figure 16.5) (Brenner, 2013; Hampton et al., 2011). As in early adulthood, women are more active users. And users have more offline close relationships, sometimes using Facebook to revive "dormant" friendships.

Still, for both sexes, number of friends declines from middle to late adulthood, probably because people become less willing to invest in nonfamily ties unless they are very rewarding. As selectivity of friendship increases, older adults try harder to get along with friends (Antonucci & Akiyama, 1995). Having chosen a friend, middle-aged people attach great value to the relationship and take extra steps to protect it.

These brothers, both in their fifties, express their mutual affection at a family reunion. Even when they have only limited contact, siblings often feel closer in midlife.

© JEFF GREENBERG/THE IMAGE WORKS

LOOK AND LISTEN

Ask a middle-aged couple you know well to describe the number and quality of their friendships today compared with their friendships in early adulthood. Does their report match research findings? Explain. ●

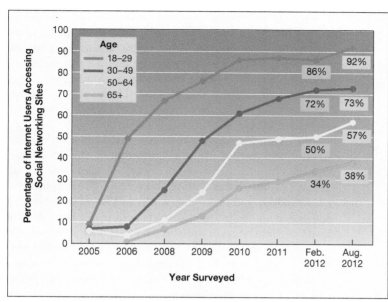

FIGURE 16.5 Gains in use of social networking sites by age group from 2005 to 2012. Repeated surveys of large representative samples of U.S. adults who use the Internet revealed that social networking site use increased substantially for all age groups. Though not as avid users as young adults, most middle-aged adults use social networking sites, primarily Facebook. (From J. Brenner, 2013, "Pew Internet: Social Networking." Pew Research Center's Internet & American Life Project, Washington, D.C. February 14, 2013, *www.pewinternet.org*. Adapted by permission.)

By midlife, family relationships and friendships support different aspects of psychological well-being. Family ties protect against serious threats and losses, offering security within a long-term timeframe. In contrast, friendships serve as current sources of pleasure and satisfaction, with women benefiting somewhat more than men (Levitt & Cici-Gokaltun, 2011). As middle-aged couples renew their sense of companionship, they may combine the best of family and friendship.

ASK YOURSELF

REVIEW How do age, sex, proximity, and culture affect grandparent–grandchild ties?

CONNECT Cite evidence that early family relationships affect middle-aged adults' bonds with adult children, aging parents, and siblings.

APPLY Raylene and her brother Walter live in the same city as their aging mother, Elsie. When Elsie could no longer live independently, Raylene took primary responsibility for her care. What factors probably contributed to Raylene's involvement in caregiving and Walter's lesser role?

REFLECT Ask one of your parents for his or her view of how the parent–child relationship changed as you transitioned to new adult roles, such as college student, career-entry worker, married partner, or parent. Do you agree?

 Vocational Life

As we have seen, the midlife transition typically involves vocational adjustments. For Devin, it resulted in a move up the career ladder to a demanding administrative post as college dean. Trisha reoriented her career from a large to a small law firm, where she felt her efforts were appreciated. Recall from Chapter 15 that after her oldest child left home, Anya earned a college degree and entered the work force for the first time. Jewel strengthened her commitment to an already successful business, while Elena changed careers. Finally, Tim reduced his career obligations as he prepared for retirement.

Work continues to be a salient aspect of identity and self-esteem in middle adulthood. More so than in earlier or later years, people attempt to increase the personal meaning and self-direction of their vocational lives. At the same time, certain aspects of job performance improve. Middle-aged employees have lower rates of absenteeism, turnover, and accidents. They are also more effective workplace citizens—more often helping colleagues and trying to improve group performance and less often complaining about trivial issues. And because of their greater knowledge and experience, their work productivity typically equals or exceeds that of younger workers (Ng & Feldman, 2008). Consequently, an older employee ought to be as valuable as a younger employee, and possibly more so.

The large tide of baby boomers currently moving through midlife and (as we will see in Chapter 18) the desire of most to work longer than the previous generation means that the number of older workers will rise dramatically over the next few decades (Leonesio et al., 2012). Yet a favorable transition from adult worker to older worker is hindered by negative stereotypes of aging—incorrect assumptions of limited learning capacity, slower decision making, and resistance to change and supervision (Posthuma & Campion, 2009). Furthermore, gender discrimination continues to restrict the career attainments of many women. Let's take a close look at middle-aged work life.

Job Satisfaction

Job satisfaction has both psychological and economic significance. If people are dissatisfied at work, the consequences include absenteeism, turnover, grievances, and strikes, all of which are costly to employers.

Research shows that job satisfaction increases in midlife in diverse nations and at all occupational levels, from executives to hourly workers (see Figure 16.6 on page 554). The relationship is weaker for women than for men, probably because women's reduced chances for advancement result in a sense of unfairness. It is also weaker for blue-collar than for white-collar workers, perhaps because blue-collar workers have less control over their own work schedules and activities (Avolio & Sosik, 1999). When different aspects of jobs are considered, intrinsic

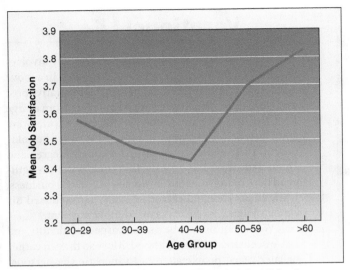

FIGURE 16.6 Age-related changes in job satisfaction.
In this study of more than 2,000 university employees at all levels, from secretary to university president, job satisfaction dropped slightly in early adulthood as people encountered some discouraging experiences (see Chapter 14). In middle age, job satisfaction showed a steady rise. (From W. A. Hochwarter et al., 2001, "A Note on the Nonlinearity of the Age–Job-Satisfaction Relationship," *Journal of Applied Social Psychology, 31,* p. 1232. Copyright © 2001, John Wiley and Sons. Reproduced with permission of Wiley Inc.)

satisfaction—happiness with the work itself—shows a strong age-related gain. Extrinsic satisfaction—contentment with supervision, pay, and promotions—changes very little (Barnes-Farrell & Matthews, 2007).

What explains the rise in job satisfaction during middle adulthood? An improved capacity to cope effectively with difficult situations and a broader time perspective probably contribute. "When I first started teaching, I complained about a lot of things," remarked Devin. "From my current vantage point, I can tell a big problem from a trivial one." Moving out of unrewarding work roles, as Trisha did, can also boost morale. Key characteristics that predict job well-being include involvement in decision making, reasonable workloads, and good physical working conditions. Older people may have greater access to jobs that are attractive in these ways. Furthermore, having fewer alternative positions into which they can move, older workers generally reduce their career aspirations (Barnes-Farrell & Matthews, 2007). As the perceived gap between actual and possible achievements narrows, job involvement—importance of one's work to self-esteem—increases (Warr, 2001).

Although emotional engagement with work is usually seen as psychologically healthy, it can also result in **burnout**—a condition in which long-term job stress leads to mental exhaustion, a sense of loss of personal control, and feelings of reduced accomplishment. Burnout occurs more often in the helping professions, including health care, human services, and teaching, which place high emotional demands on employees. Although people in interpersonally demanding jobs are as psychologi-

cally healthy as other people, sometimes a worker's dedication exceeds his or her coping skills, especially in an unsupportive work environment (Schmidt, Neubach, & Heuer, 2007). Burnout is associated with excessive work assignments for available time and lack of encouragement and feedback from supervisors. It tends to occur more often in the United States than in Western Europe, perhaps because of Americans' greater achievement orientation (Maslach, Schaufeli, & Leiter, 2001).

Burnout is a serious occupational hazard, linked to impaired attention and memory, severe depression, on-the-job injuries, physical illnesses, poor job performance, absenteeism, and turnover (Sandström et al., 2005; Wang, 2005). To prevent burnout, employers can make sure workloads are reasonable, provide opportunities for workers to take time out from stressful situations, limit hours of stressful work, and offer social support. Interventions that enlist employees' participation in designing higher-quality work environments show promise for increasing work engagement and effectiveness and reducing burnout (Leiter, Gascón, & Martínez-Jarreta, 2010). And provisions for working at home may respond to the needs of some people for a calmer, quieter work atmosphere.

Career Development

After several years as a parish nurse, Anya felt a need for additional training to do her job better. Trisha appreciated her firm's generous support of workshop and course attendance, which helped her keep abreast of new legal developments. And as college dean, Devin took a summer seminar each year on management effectiveness. As these experiences reveal, career development is vital throughout work life.

Job Training. Anya's 35-year-old supervisor, Roy, was surprised when she asked for time off to upgrade her skills. "You're in your fifties," he replied. "What're you going to do with so much new information at this point in your life?"

Roy's insensitive, narrow-minded response, though usually unspoken, is all too common among managers—even some who are older themselves! Research suggests that training and on-the-job career counseling are less available to older workers. And when career development activities are offered, older employees may be less likely to volunteer for them (Barnes-Farrell & Matthews, 2007; Hedge, Borman, & Lammlein, 2006). What influences willingness to engage in job training and updating?

Personal characteristics are important: With age, growth needs give way somewhat to security needs. Consequently, learning and challenge may have less intrinsic value to many older workers. Perhaps for this reason, older employees depend more on co-worker and supervisor encouragement for vocational development. Yet as we have seen, they are less likely to have supportive supervisors. Furthermore, negative stereotypes of aging reduce older workers' self-efficacy, or confidence that they can get better at their jobs (Maurer, 2001; Maurer,

Wrenn, & Weiss, 2003). Self-efficacy is a powerful predictor of employees' efforts to renew and expand career-relevant skills.

Workplace characteristics matter, too. An employee given work that requires new learning must pursue that learning to complete the assignment. Unfortunately, older workers sometimes receive more routine tasks than younger workers. Therefore, some of their reduced motivation to engage in career-relevant learning may be due to the type of assignments they receive. In companies with a more favorable *age climate* (view of older workers), mature employees participate frequently in further education and report greater self-efficacy and commitment to the organization (Bowen, Noack, & Staudinger, 2011).

Gender and Ethnicity: The Glass Ceiling.

In her thirties, Jewel became a company president by starting her own business. Having concluded that, as a woman, she had little chance of rising to a top executive position in a large corporation, she didn't even try. Although women and ethnic minorities have gradually gained in access to managerial careers, they remain a long distance from gender and ethnic equality (Huffman, 2012). From career entry on, inequalities in promotion between men and women and between whites and blacks become more pronounced over time—findings still evident after education, work skills, and work productivity have been controlled (Barreto, Ryan, & Schmitt, 2009; Maume, 2004). Women who are promoted usually get stuck in mid-level positions. When the most prestigious high-level management jobs are considered, white men are overwhelmingly advantaged: They account for 70 percent of chief executive officers at large corporations and 93 percent at Fortune 500 companies (U.S. Census Bureau, 2012b).

Facebook executive Sheryl Sandberg is among a handful of women who have attained top positions in major corporations. In her best-selling book, *Lean In*, she urges women to be more assertive in demonstrating qualities linked to leadership at work.

Women and ethnic minorities face a **glass ceiling,** or invisible barrier to advancement up the corporate ladder. Why is this so? Management is an art and skill that must be taught. Yet women and ethnic minorities have less access to mentors, role models, and informal networks that serve as training routes (Baumgartner & Schneider, 2010). And stereotyped doubts about women's career commitment and ability to become strong managers (especially women with children) also contribute, leading supervisors to underrate their competence and not to recommend them for formal management training programs (Hoobler, Lemmon, & Wayne, 2011). Furthermore, challenging, high-risk, high-visibility assignments that require leadership and open the door to advancement, such as startup ventures, international experience, and troubleshooting, are less often granted to both women and minorities.

Finally, women who demonstrate qualities linked to leadership and advancement—assertiveness, confidence, forcefulness, and ambition—encounter prejudice because they deviate from traditional gender roles, even though they more often combine these traits with a democratic, collaborative style of leading than do men (Cheung & Halpern, 2010; Eagly & Carli, 2007). To overcome this bias, women in line for top positions must demonstrate greater competence than their male counterparts. In an investigation of several hundred senior managers at a multinational financial services corporation, promoted female managers had earned higher performance ratings than promoted male managers (Lyness & Heilman, 2006). In contrast, no gender difference existed in performance of managers not selected for promotion.

Like Jewel, many women have dealt with the glass ceiling by going around it, leaving the corporate environment and going into business for themselves. Today, more than half of all startup businesses in the United States are owned and operated by women. The large majority are successful entrepreneurs and leaders, meeting or exceeding their expansion and earnings goals (Ahuja, 2005; U.S. Census Bureau, 2012b). But when women and ethnic minorities leave the corporate world to further their careers, companies not only lose valuable talent but also fail to address the leadership needs of an increasingly diverse work force.

Career Change at Midlife

Although most people remain in the same vocation through middle age, career change does occur, as with Elena's shift from journalism to teaching and creative writing. Recall that circumstances at home and at work motivated Elena's decision to pursue a new vocation. Like other career changers, she wanted a more satisfying life—a goal she attained by ending an unhappy marriage and initiating a long-awaited vocational move at the same time.

As noted earlier, midlife career changes are seldom radical; they typically involve leaving one line of work for a related one. Elena sought a more stimulating, involving job. But other people

After many years as a professor of ancient Greek philosophy, Abe Schoener found himself at a dead end in his career. In his mid-forties, he decided to transform his passion for winemaking into a new vocation as a vintner—a radical shift that prompted the breakup of his marriage but ultimately led to a more satisfying life.

move in the reverse direction—to careers that are more relaxing, free of painful decisions, and less demanding (Juntunen, Wegner, & Matthews, 2002). The decision to change is often difficult. The individual must weigh years invested in one set of skills, current income, and job security against present frustrations and hoped-for gains.

An extreme career shift, by contrast, usually signals a personal crisis (Young & Rodgers, 1997). In a study of professionals who abandoned their well-paid, prestigious positions for routine, poorly paid, semiskilled work, nonwork problems contributed to radical change. An eminent 55-year-old TV producer became a school bus driver, a New York banker a waiter in a ski resort (Sarason, 1977). Each was responding to feelings of personal meaninglessness—escaping from family conflict, difficult relationships with colleagues, and work that had become unsatisfying to a less burdensome life.

Among blue-collar workers—those in such occupations as construction, manufacturing, mining, maintenance, or food-service work—midlife career shifts are seldom freely chosen. In one investigation, researchers followed a large sample of blue-collar men in their fifties over a seven-year period; all were employed by Alcoa, the world's largest producer of aluminum. One-third had highly physically taxing jobs. Of the small minority who transitioned to less physically demanding work, an injury usually preceded the change (Modrek & Cullen, 2012). Transitioners appeared to change jobs to stay in the workforce, rather than being forced to retire early, at less than full pension benefits, because of their disability.

Yet opportunities to shift to less physically demanding work are limited, particularly in the late-2000s recession aftermath. A strong predictor of middle-aged workers' eligibility for such jobs for is education—at least a high school diploma (Blau & Goldstein, 2007). Less educated workers with a physical disability face greatly reduced chances of remaining in the labor force.

Unemployment

As companies downsize, eliminating jobs, the majority of people affected are middle-aged and older. Although unemployment is difficult at any time, middle-aged adults show a sharper decline in physical and mental health than their younger counterparts. Those who perceive a company's layoff process as unfair and inconsiderate—for example, giving them little time to prepare—often experience the event as highly traumatic (Breslin & Mustard, 2003; McKee-Ryan et al., 2009). Older workers affected by layoffs remain jobless longer, suffering substantial income loss. In addition, people over age 40 who must reestablish occupational security find themselves "off-time" in terms of the social clock. Consequently, job loss can disrupt major tasks of midlife, including generativity and reappraisal of life goals and accomplishments. Finally, having been more involved in and committed to an occupation, the older unemployed worker has also lost something of greater value.

People who lose their jobs in midlife, whether executives or blue-collar workers, seldom duplicate the status and pay of their previous positions. As they search, they encounter age discrimination and find that they are overqualified for many openings. Those also facing financial difficulties are at risk for deepening depression and physical health declines over time (Gallo et al., 2006; McKee-Ryan, 2011). Counseling that focuses on financial planning, reducing feelings of humiliation due to the stigma of unemployment, and encouraging personal flexibility can help people implement effective problem-centered coping strategies in their search for alternative work roles.

Planning for Retirement

One evening, Devin and Trisha met Anya and her husband, George, for dinner. Halfway through the meal, Devin inquired, "George, tell us what you and Anya are going to do about retirement. Are you planning to close down your business or work part-time? Do you think you'll stay here or move out of town?"

Three or four generations ago, the two couples would not have had this conversation. In 1900, about 70 percent of American men age 65 and over were in the labor force. By 1970, however, the figure had dropped to 27 percent, and in the early twenty-first century it declined to 16 percent (U.S. Census Bureau, 2012b). Because of government-sponsored retirement benefits (begun in the United States in 1935), retirement is no longer a privilege reserved for the wealthy. The federal government pays Social Security to the majority of the aged, and others are covered by employer-based private pension plans.

As the trend just noted suggests, the average age of retirement has declined over the past several decades. Currently, it is age 63 in the United States and hovers between 60 and 63 in other Western nations (U.S. Census Bureau, 2012b). The recent recession led to an increase in the number of Americans at

Applying What We Know

Ingredients of Effective Retirement Planning

Issue	Description
Finances	Ideally, financial planning for retirement should start with the first paycheck; at a minimum, it should begin 10 to 15 years before retirement.
Fitness	Starting a fitness program in middle age is important because good health is crucial for well-being in retirement.
Role adjustment	Retirement is harder for people who strongly identify with their work role. Preparing for a radical role adjustment reduces stress.
Where to live	The pros and cons of moving should be considered carefully because where one lives affects access to health care, friends, family, recreation, entertainment, and part-time employment.
Leisure and volunteer activities	A retiree typically gains an additional 50 hours per week of free time. Careful planning of what to do with that time has a major impact on psychological well-being.
Health insurance	Finding out about government-sponsored health insurance options helps protect quality of life after retirement.
Legal affairs	The preretirement period is an excellent time to finalize a will and begin estate planning.

risk for being unable to sustain their preretirement standard of living after leaving the workforce. Consequently, a survey of a large, nationally representative sample of baby boomers revealed that the majority expect to delay retirement (Jones, 2012). But current estimates indicate that most will need to work just a few extra years to be financially ready to retire (Munnell et al., 2012). For the healthy, active, long-lived baby-boom generation, up to one-fourth of their lives may lie ahead after they leave their jobs.

Retirement is a lengthy, complex process that begins as soon as the middle-aged person first thinks about it (Kim & Moen, 2002b). Planning is important because retirement leads to a loss of two important work-related rewards—income and status—and to a change in many other aspects of life. Like other life transitions, retirement can be stressful.

Nearly half of middle-aged people engage in no concrete retirement planning, yet research consistently shows that clarifying goals for the future and acquiring financial-planning knowledge result in better retirement savings, adjustment, and satisfaction (Hershey et al., 2007; Jacobs-Lawson, Hershey, & Neukam, 2004).

LOOK AND LISTEN

Contact the human resources division of a company or institution in your community, and inquire about the retirement planning services it offers. How comprehensive are those services, and what percentage of its recent retirees made use of them? •

Applying What We Know above lists the variety of issues addressed in a typical retirement preparation program. Financial planning is especially vital in the United States where (unlike Western European nations) the federal government does not offer a pension system that guarantees an adequate standard of living (see page 68 in Chapter 2). Hence, U.S. retirees' income typically drops by 50 percent. But although more people engage in financial planning than in other forms of preparation, even those who attend financial education programs often fail to look closely at their financial well-being and to make wise decisions (Keller & Lusardi, 2012). Many could benefit from an expert's financial analysis and counsel.

Retirement leads to ways of spending time that are largely guided by one's interests rather than one's obligations. Individuals who have not thought carefully about how to fill this time may find their sense of purpose in life seriously threatened. Research reveals that planning for an active life has an even greater impact on happiness after retirement than financial planning. Participation in activities promotes many factors essential for psychological well-being, including a structured time schedule, social contact, and self-esteem (Schlossberg, 2004). Carefully considering whether or not to relocate at retirement is related to an active life, since it affects access to health care, friends, family, recreation, entertainment, and part-time work.

Devin retired at age 62, George at age 66. Though several years younger, Trisha and Anya—like many married women—coordinated their retirements with those of their husbands. In contrast, Jewel—in good health but without an intimate partner to share her life—kept her consulting business going until age 75. Tim took early retirement and moved to be near Elena, where he devoted himself to public service—tutoring second graders in a public school, transporting inner-city children to museums, and coaching after-school and weekend youth sports. For Tim, retirement offered a new opportunity to give generously to his community.

Unfortunately, less well-educated people with lower life-time earnings are least likely to attend retirement preparation programs—yet they stand to benefit the most. And compared with men, women do less planning for retirement, instead relying on their husband's preparations. This gender gap seems to be narrowing, however, as women increasingly contribute to family income (Adams & Rau, 2011). Employers must take extra steps to encourage lower-paid workers and women to participate in planning activities. In addition, enhancing retirement adjustment among the economically disadvantaged depends on access to better vocational training, jobs, and health care at early ages. Clearly, a lifetime of opportunities and experiences affects the transition to retirement. In Chapter 18, we will consider the decision to retire and retirement adjustment in greater detail.

ASK YOURSELF

REVIEW What factors contribute to the rise in job satisfaction with age?

CONNECT Supervisors sometimes assign the more routine tasks to older workers, believing that they can no longer handle complex assignments. Cite evidence from this and the previous chapter indicating that this assumption is incorrect.

APPLY An executive wonders how his large corporation can foster advancement of women and ethnic minorities to upper management positions. What strategies would you recommend?

SUMMARY

Erikson's Theory: Generativity versus Stagnation (p. 532)

According to Erikson, how does personality change in middle age?

- Generativity expands as middle-aged adults face Erikson's psychological conflict of **generativity versus stagnation.** Personal desires and cultural demands jointly shape adults' generative activities.

- Highly generative people, who contribute to society through parenthood, other family relationships, the workplace, and volunteer endeavors, appear especially well-adjusted. Stagnation occurs when people become self-centered and self-indulgent in midlife.

Other Theories of Psychosocial Development in Midlife (p. 535)

Describe Levinson's and Vaillant's views of psychosocial development in middle adulthood, and discuss similarities and differences between men and women.

- According to Levinson, middle-aged adults confront four developmental tasks, each requiring them to reconcile two opposing tendencies within the self: young–old, destruction–creation, masculinity–femininity, and engagement–separateness.

- Middle-aged men show greater acceptance of "feminine" traits of nurturance and caring, while women are more open to "masculine" characteristics of autonomy and assertiveness. Men and successful career-oriented women may reduce their concern with ambition and

achievement, but women who have devoted themselves to child rearing or an unfulfilling job often seek rewarding work or community engagement.

- Vaillant found that adults in their late forties and fifties become guardians of their culture, seeking to "pass the torch" to later generations.

Does the term midlife crisis reflect most people's experience of middle adulthood, and is middle adulthood accurately characterized as a stage?

- Most people respond to midlife with changes that are better described as "turning points" than as a crisis. Only a minority experience a **midlife crisis** characterized by intense self-doubt and stress that lead to drastic life alterations.

- Some midlife changes are adaptations to life events that are less age-graded than in the past. Most middle-aged adults also report troubling moments that prompt new understandings and goals, but debate persists over whether these psychosocial changes are stagelike.

Stability and Change in Self-Concept and Personality (p. 538)

Describe changes in self-concept, personality, and gender identity in middle adulthood.

- Middle-aged individuals maintain self-esteem and stay motivated by revising their **possible selves,** which become fewer in number as well as more modest and concrete as people adjust their hopes and fears to their life circumstances.

- Midlife typically brings enhanced psychological well-being, through greater self-acceptance, autonomy, and environmental mastery. Factors contributing to well-being, however, vary widely among cohorts and cultures.

- Daily stressors plateau in early to mid-adulthood, and then decline as work and family responsibilities ease. Midlife gains in emotional stability and confidence in handling life's problems lead to increased effectiveness in coping with stressors.

- Both men and women become more androgynous in middle adulthood. Biological explanations, such as **parental imperative theory,** are controversial. A combination of social roles and life conditions is more likely responsible.

Discuss stability and change in the "big five" personality traits in adulthood.

- Among the **"big five" personality traits,** agreeableness and conscientiousness increase into middle age, while neuroticism declines, and extroversion and openness to experience do not change or decrease slightly. Individual differences are large and highly stable: Although adults change in overall organization and integration of personality, they do so on a foundation of basic, enduring dispositions.

Relationships at Midlife
(p. 543)

Describe the middle adulthood phase of the family life cycle.

- "Launching children and moving on" is the midlife phase of the family life cycle. Adults must adapt to many entries and exits of family members as their children launch—return—relaunch, marry, and produce grandchildren, and as their own parents age and die.

- When divorce occurs, middle-aged adults seem to adapt more easily than younger people. For women, midlife marital breakup often severely reduces standard of living, contributing to the **feminization of poverty.**

- Most middle-aged parents adjust well to launching adult children, especially if positive parent–child relationships are sustained, but adult children who are "off-time" in development can prompt parental strain. As children marry, middle-aged parents, especially mothers, often become **kinkeepers.**

- Grandparents' contact and closeness with grandchildren depend on proximity, number of grandchild sets, sex of grandparent and grandchild, and in-law relationships. In low-income families and in some ethnic groups, grandparents provide essential financial and child-care assistance. When serious family problems exist, grandparents may become primary caregivers in **skipped-generation families.**

- Middle-aged adults reassess their relationships with aging parents, often becoming more appreciative. Mother–daughter relationships tend to be closer than other parent–child ties. The more positive the history of the parent–child tie and the greater the need for assistance, the more help exchanged.

- Middle-aged adults, often caught between caring for aging parents, assisting young-adult children and grandchildren, and meeting work and community responsibilities, are called the **sandwich generation.** The burden of caring for ill or frail parents falls most heavily on adult daughters, though the sex difference declines in later middle age.

- Parental caregiving has emotional and health consequences, especially in cultures and subcultures where adult children feel a particularly strong obligation to provide care. Social support is highly effective in reducing caregiver stress and helping adult children derive benefits from caregiving.

Describe midlife sibling relationships and friendships.

- Sibling contact and support decline from early to middle adulthood, probably because of the demands of diverse roles. But many middle-aged siblings feel closer, often in response to major life events. Sister–sister ties are typically closest in industrialized nations. In nonindustrialized societies, strong brother–sister attachments may be basic to family functioning.

- In midlife, friendships become fewer, more selective, and more deeply valued. Men continue to be less expressive with their friends than women, who have more close friendships. Viewing a spouse as a best friend can contribute greatly to marital happiness.

Vocational Life (p. 553)

Discuss job satisfaction and career development in middle adulthood, with special attention to sex differences and experiences of ethnic minorities.

- Vocational readjustments are common as middle-aged people seek to increase the personal meaning and self-direction of their work lives. Certain aspects of job performance improve. Job satisfaction increases at all occupational levels, more so for men than for women.

- **Burnout** is a serious occupational hazard, especially for those in helping professions. It can be prevented by ensuring reasonable workloads, limiting hours of stressful work, providing workers with social support, and enlisting employees' participation in designing higher-quality work environments.

- Both personal and workplace characteristics influence the extent to which older workers engage in career development. In companies with a more favorable age climate, mature employees report greater self-efficacy and commitment to the organization.

- Women and ethnic minorities face a **glass ceiling** because of limited access to management training and prejudice against women who demonstrate strong leadership qualities. Many women further their careers by leaving the corporate world, often to start their own businesses.

Discuss career change and unemployment in middle adulthood.

- Midlife career change typically involves leaving one line of work for a related one. Radical career change often signals a personal crisis. Among blue-collar workers, midlife career shifts are seldom freely chosen.

- Unemployment is especially difficult for middle-aged adults, who constitute the majority of workers affected by corporate downsizing and layoffs. Counseling can help them find alternative, gratifying work roles, but these rarely match their previous status and pay.

Discuss the importance of planning for retirement.

- Retirement brings major life changes, including loss of income and status and an increase in free time. Besides financial planning, planning for an active life is vital, with a strong impact on happiness after retirement. Low-paid workers and women need extra encouragement to participate in retirement planning.

Important Terms and Concepts

"big five" personality traits (p. 542)
burnout (p. 554)
feminization of poverty (p. 544)
generativity versus stagnation (p. 532)

glass ceiling (p. 555)
kinkeeper (p. 545)
midlife crisis (p. 536)
parental imperative theory (p. 540)

possible selves (p. 538)
sandwich generation (p. 549)
skipped-generation family (p. 548)

milestones

Development in Middle Adulthood

40–50 years

PHYSICAL

- Accommodative ability of the lens of the eye, ability to see in dim light, and color discrimination decline; sensitivity to glare increases. (502–503)
- Hearing loss at high frequencies occurs. (503)
- Hair grays and thins. (502)
- Lines on the face become more pronounced; skin loses elasticity and begins to sag. (503)
- Weight gain continues, accompanied by a rise in fatty deposits in the torso, while fat beneath the skin declines. (504)
- Loss of lean body mass (muscle and bone) occurs. (504)
- In women, production of estrogen drops, leading to shortening and irregularity of the menstrual cycle. (504)

- In men, quantity of semen and sperm declines. (507)
- Intensity of sexual response declines, but frequency of sexual activity drops only slightly. (509)
- Rates of cancer and cardiovascular disease increase. (509–513)

COGNITIVE

- Consciousness of aging increases. (502, 535)
- Crystallized intelligence increases; fluid intelligence declines. (518–519)
- Speed of processing declines, but adults can compensate through experience and practice. (520–521)

- Ability to attend selectively and to adapt attention—switching from one task to another—declines, but adults can compensate through experience and practice. (521)
- Amount of information retained in working memory declines, in part because of reduced use of memory strategies. (522)
- Retrieving information from long-term memory becomes more difficult. (522)

- General factual knowledge, procedural knowledge, knowledge related to one's occupation, and metacognitive knowledge remain unchanged or may increase. (522–523)

- Practical problem solving and expertise increase. (524)
- Creativity may become more deliberately thoughtful, emphasize integrating ideas, and shift from self-expression to more altruistic goals. (524–525)

- If occupation offers challenge and autonomy, may show gains in cognitive flexibility. (525–526)

Note: Numbers in parentheses indicate the page or pages on which each milestone is discussed.

EMOTIONAL/SOCIAL

- Generativity increases. (532–533)
- Focus shifts toward personally meaningful living. (535)

- Possible selves become fewer in number and more modest and concrete. (538)
- Self-acceptance, autonomy, and environmental mastery increase. (538–539)
- Strategies for coping with stressors become more effective. (539)
- Gender identity becomes more androgynous; "masculine" traits increase in women, "feminine" traits in men. (535, 540–542)
- Agreeableness and conscientiousness increase, while neuroticism declines. (542)
- May launch children. (544–545)
- May become a kinkeeper, especially if a mother. (545)
- May become a parent-in-law and a grandparent. (545–547)
- Becomes more appreciative of parents' strengths and generosity; quality of relationships with parents increase. (547)
- May care for a parent with a disability or chronic illness. (549–551)
- Siblings may feel closer. (552)

- Number of friends generally declines. (552)
- Intrinsic job satisfaction—happiness with one's work—typically increases. (553–554)

50–65 years

PHYSICAL

- Lens of the eye loses its capacity to adjust to objects at varying distances entirely. (502)
- Hearing loss gradually extends to all frequencies but remains greatest for high frequencies. (503)
- Skin continues to wrinkle and sag, "age spots" increase, and blood vessels in the skin become more visible. (503)
- In women, menopause occurs; as estrogen declines further, genitals are less easily stimulated, and the vagina lubricates more slowly during arousal. (504)
- In men, inability to attain an erection when desired becomes more common. (507)
- Loss of bone mass continues; rates of osteoporosis rise. (504, 512–513)
- Collapse of disks in the spinal column causes height to drop by as much as 1 inch. (504)
- Rates of cancer and cardiovascular disease continue to increase. (509–513)

COGNITIVE

- Cognitive changes previously listed continue.

EMOTIONAL/SOCIAL

- Emotional and social changes previously listed continue.

- Parent-to-child help-giving declines, and child-to-parent support and practical assistance increase. (548–549)

- May retire. (556–557)

561

AP IMAGES/KHIN MAUNG WIN

Cultures around the world connect age with wisdom. Older adults' life experience enhances their ability to solve human problems and fill leadership positions. These are endeavors of South African anti-apartheid activist Archbishop Desmond Tutu and Myanmar opposition leader Aung San Suu Kyi. Each is a Nobel Peace laureate.

Physical and Cognitive Development in Late Adulthood

chapter outline

PHYSICAL DEVELOPMENT

Life Expectancy

Variations in Life Expectancy • Life Expectancy in Late Adulthood • Maximum Lifespan

■ **BIOLOGY AND ENVIRONMENT** What Can We Learn About Aging from Centenarians?

Physical Changes

Nervous System • Sensory Systems • Cardiovascular and Respiratory Systems • Immune System • Sleep • Physical Appearance and Mobility • Adapting to Physical Changes of Late Adulthood

■ **CULTURAL INFLUENCES** Cultural Variations in Sense of Usefulness in Late Life

Health, Fitness, and Disability

Nutrition and Exercise • Sexuality • Physical Disabilities • Mental Disabilities • Health Care

■ **SOCIAL ISSUES: HEALTH** Interventions for Caregivers of Older Adults with Dementia

COGNITIVE DEVELOPMENT

Memory

Deliberate versus Automatic Memory • Associative Memory • Remote Memory • Prospective Memory

Language Processing

Problem Solving

Wisdom

Factors Related to Cognitive Maintenance and Change

Cognitive Interventions

Lifelong Learning

Types of Programs • Benefits of Continuing Education

At age 67, Walt gave up his photography business and looked forward to more spare time with 64-year-old Ruth, who retired from her position as a social worker at the same time. For Walt and Ruth, this culminating period of life was filled with volunteer work, golfing three times a week, and joint vacations with Walt's older brother Dick and his wife, Goldie. Walt also took up activities he had always loved but had little time to pursue—writing poems and short stories, attending theater performances, enrolling in a class on world politics, and cultivating a garden that became the envy of the neighborhood. Ruth read voraciously, served on the board of directors of an adoption agency, and had more time to visit her sister Ida in a nearby city.

Over the next 20 years, Walt and Ruth amazed nearly everyone who met them with their energy and vitality. Their warmth, concern for others, and generosity with their time led not just their own children and grandchildren, but also nieces, nephews, children of friends, and former co-workers, to seek them out. On weekends, their home was alive with visitors.

© JEFF GREENBERG/ THE IMAGE WORKS

Then, in their early eighties, the couple's lives changed profoundly. Walt had surgery to treat a cancerous prostate gland and within 3 months was hospitalized again after a heart attack. He lingered for 6 weeks with Ruth at his side and then died. Ruth's grieving was interrupted by the need to care for Ida. Alert and spry at age 78, Ida deteriorated mentally in her seventy-ninth year, despite otherwise excellent physical health. Meanwhile, Ruth's arthritis worsened, and her vision and hearing weakened.

As Ruth turned 85, certain activities had become difficult—but not impossible. "It just takes a little adjustment!" Ruth exclaimed in her usual upbeat manner. Reading was harder, so she downloaded audiobooks to her MP3 player. Her gait was slower and her eyesight less reliable, making her hesitant to go out alone. At dinner in a noisy restaurant with her daughter and family, Ruth felt overwhelmed and participated little in the fast-moving conversation. But in one-to-one interactions in a calm environment, she showed the same intelligence, wit, and astute insights that she had displayed all her life.

Late adulthood stretches from age 65 to the end of the lifespan. Unfortunately, popular images fail to capture the quality of these final decades. Instead, many myths prevail—that older people have entered a period of deterioration and dependency, that they are no longer able to learn, and that their families isolate them in nursing homes. Young people who have little contact with older adults are often surprised that those like Walt and Ruth even exist—active and involved in the world around them.

As we trace physical and cognitive development in late adulthood, we will see that the balance of gains and declines shifts as death approaches. But in industrialized nations, the typical 65-year-old can anticipate nearly two healthy, rewarding decades before this shift affects everyday life. And as Ruth illustrates, even after older adults become frail, many find ways to surmount physical and cognitive challenges.

Late adulthood is best viewed as an extension of earlier periods, not a break with them. As long as social and cultural contexts give older adults support, respect, and purpose in life, these years are a time of continued potential. ●

PHYSICAL DEVELOPMENT

TAKE A MOMENT... Do you know an older person who "seems young" or "seems old" for his or her age? In using these descriptors, we acknowledge that chronological age is an imperfect indicator of **functional age**, or actual competence and performance. Because people age biologically at different rates, some 80-year-olds appear younger than many 65-year-olds. Also, recall from Chapter 13 that within each person, change differs across parts of the body. For example, Ruth became infirm physically but remained active mentally, whereas Ida, though physically fit for her age, found it hard to carry on a conversation, keep appointments, or complete familiar tasks.

So much variation exists between and within individuals that researchers have not yet identified any single biological measure that predicts the overall rate at which a person will age.

Two friends enjoy a stroll in Tokyo, Japan. How old are they? How old do they look and feel? Because people age biologically at different rates, the woman on the right appears younger, though both are in their early eighties.

But we do have estimates of how much longer older adults can expect to live, and our knowledge of factors affecting longevity in late adulthood has increased rapidly.

Life Expectancy

"I wonder how many years I have left," Ruth asked herself each time a major life event, such as retirement or widowhood, occurred. Dramatic gains in **average life expectancy**—the number of years that an individual born in a particular year can expect to live, starting at any given age—provide powerful support for the multiplicity of factors considered in previous chapters that slow biological aging, including improved nutrition, medical treatment, sanitation, and safety. Recall from Chapter 1 that in 1900, life expectancy was just under 50 years; in the United States today, it is 78.5—nearly 76 for men and 81 for women. A major factor in this extraordinary gain is a steady decline in infant mortality (see Chapter 3), but death rates among adults have decreased as well. For example, heart disease, the leading cause of overall adult death in the United States, has dropped by more than 60 percent in the past 50 years, due to declines in risk factors (such as high blood pressure and cigarette smoking) and, mostly, advances in medical treatment (U.S. Department of Health and Human Services, 2011c).

Variations in Life Expectancy

Consistent group differences in life expectancy underscore the joint contributions of heredity and environment to biological aging. In almost all cultures, women can look forward to 2 to 7 more years of life than men—a life expectancy advantage that characterizes females of most species (Kirkwood, 2010). The protective value of the female's extra X chromosome (see Chapter 2) is believed to be responsible. Yet since the early 1970s, the gender gap in life expectancy has narrowed in industrialized nations (Leung, Zhang, & Zhang, 2004). Because men are at higher risk for disease and early death, they reap somewhat larger generational gains from positive lifestyle changes and new medical discoveries.

Life expectancy varies substantially with SES, ethnicity, and nationality. As education and income increase, so does length of life (Whitfield, Thorpe, & Szanton, 2011). In the United States, a white child born in 2010 is likely to live 3 to 6 years longer than an African-American child (U.S. Department of Health and Human Services, 2011c). Accounting for this difference are higher rates of infant mortality, unintentional injuries, life-threatening disease, stress, and violent death linked to low SES.

Length of life—and, even more important, *quality of life* in old age—can be predicted by a country's health care, housing, and social services, along with lifestyle factors. When researchers estimate **average healthy life expectancy**, the number of years a person born in a particular year can expect to live in full health, without disease or injury, Japan ranks first,

In a Japanese seaside city, a spry aging couple practice their local tradition of net fishing. Japan's low rates of obesity and heart disease and favorable health-care policies contribute to its worldwide leading status in healthy life expectancy.

with the United States below the overwhelming majority of industrialized nations (see Figure 17.1). Japan's leading status in this overall measure of population health has been attributed to its low rates of obesity and heart disease, linked to its low-fat diet, along with its favorable health-care policies. Because the United States falls short in these respects, Americans spend somewhat more time disabled and die earlier than older adults in most other developed countries.

In developing nations with widespread poverty, malnutrition, disease, and armed conflict, average life expectancy hovers around 55 years. And healthy life expectancy is reduced by three to four decades compared with the industrialized world—for example, for males, 69 years in Japan, 67 years in Sweden, 65 years in the United States, but only 48 in Afghanistan, 47 in Sierra Leone, and 28 in Haiti, where overall health recently declined because of the 2010 catastrophic earthquake (Salomon et al., 2012).

Life Expectancy in Late Adulthood

Although poverty-stricken groups lag behind the economically advantaged, the proportion of older adults has risen dramatically in the industrialized world. From 1900 to 2010, people age 65 and older increased from 4 percent to 13 percent of the U.S. population. Because of aging baby boomers, older adults are projected to rise to nearly 20 percent by 2030. Among older Americans, the fastest-growing segment is the 85-and-older group, which has increased by 30 percent during the past decade and currently makes up nearly 3.5 percent of the U.S. population. By 2050, they are expected to swell to over three times their current number (U.S. Census Bureau, 2012b).

Americans reaching age 65 in the early twenty-first century can look forward, on average, to 19 more years of life. As at earlier ages, life expectancy is greater for older women than for men. Today, the 65- to 69-year age group includes 117 women

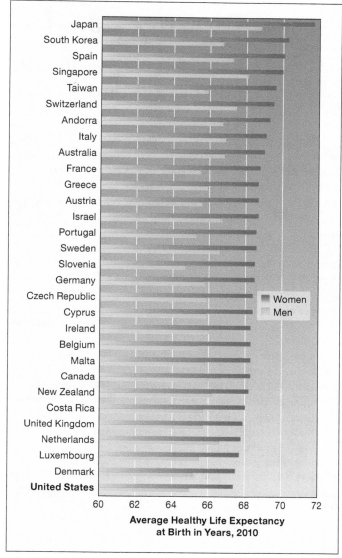

FIGURE 17.1 Average healthy life expectancy at birth in 30 nations, ranked on basis of measures for women. Japan ranks first, the United States a disappointing thirtieth. In each nation, women's healthy life expectancy is about 2 to 3 years longer than men's. (From Salomon et al., 2012.)

for every 100 men; for people age 85 and older, this number climbs to 210 (U.S. Census Bureau, 2012b). Similar discrepancies exist throughout the world, with the exception of a few developing countries where death rates of women during childbirth are high or women experience severe discrimination and deprivation.

Although women outnumber men by a greater margin as older adults advance in age, differences in average life expectancy between the sexes are declining. An American newborn girl can expect to live about 5 years longer than a newborn boy. At age 65, the difference narrows to just under 3 years; at age 85, to just over 1 year. Over age 100, the gender gap in life expectancy disappears (U.S. Census Bureau, 2012b). Similarly,

Biology and Environment

What Can We Learn About Aging from Centenarians?

Jeanne Louise Calment, listed in *Guinness World Records* as the longest-lived person whose age could be documented, was born in Arles, France, in 1875 and died there in 1997, 122 years later. Heredity undoubtedly contributed to her longevity: Her father lived to age 94, her mother to 86. Her family was middle-SES, and in her twenties, she married a prosperous merchant (Robine & Allard, 1999). As a young woman, she was healthy and energetic; she bicycled, swam, roller-skated, played tennis, and ran up the steps of the cathedral to attend daily Mass.

Jeanne attributed her longevity to a diet rich in olive oil and an occasional glass of port wine. Others credit her easy-going disposition and resistance to stress. "If you can't do anything about it," she once said, "don't worry about it." Jeanne took up fencing at age 85 and rode a bicycle until age 100. Shortly thereafter, she moved into assisted living (see page 589), where she blossomed, becoming a celebrity because of both her age and her charming personality. Alert and quick-witted until her final

year, she recommended laughter as the best recipe for long life. Asked once about the effects of aging, she quipped, "I've only one wrinkle, and I am sitting on it."

Because of stereotypes of aging, we tend to picture the most older people as extremely frail. Yet the past 30 years have seen a 65 percent increase in centenarians in the industrialized world. Currently, American centenarians, though still rare (a fraction of one percent of the population), number about 53,000 (Meyer, 2012). But the proportion of centenarians in the United States is smaller than in most other developed nations.

Among centenarians, women outnumber men by five to one. About 60 to 70 percent have physical and mental impairments that interfere with independent functioning. But the rest lead active, autonomous lives (Perls & Terry, 2003). These robust centenarians are of special interest because they represent the ultimate potential of the human species. What are they like? Results of several longitudinal studies reveal that they are diverse in years of education (none to postgraduate),

Jeanne Louise Calment, shown here at age 121, took up fencing at age 85, rode a bicycle until age 100, and maintained a quick wit until her final year. The longest-lived person on record, she died at age 122.

economic well-being (very poor to very rich), and ethnicity. At the same time, their physical condition and life stories reveal common threads.

---

differences in rates of chronic illness and in life expectancy between higher-SES whites and low-SES ethnic minorities decline with age. Around age 87, a *life expectancy crossover* occurs—surviving members of low-SES ethnic minority groups live longer than members of the white majority (Herd, Robert, & House, 2011; Masters, 2012; Sautter et al., 2012). Researchers speculate that among males and members of low-SES groups, only the biologically sturdiest survive into very old age.

Throughout this book, we have seen that genetic and environmental factors jointly affect aging. With respect to heredity, identical twins typically die within 3 years of each other, whereas fraternal twins of the same sex differ by more than 6 years. Also, longevity runs in families. When both parents survive to age 70 or older, the chances that their children will live to 90 or 100 are double that of the general population (Cevenini et al., 2008; Hayflick, 1994; Mitchell et al., 2001). At the same time, evidence from twin studies suggests that once people pass 75 to 80 years, the contribution of heredity to length of life decreases in favor of environmental factors—a healthy diet;

normal body weight; regular exercise; little or no tobacco, alcohol, and drug use; an optimistic outlook; low psychological stress; and social support (Yates et al., 2008; Zaretsky, 2003). As the Biology and Environment box above reveals, the study of centenarians—people who cross the 100-year mark—offers special insights into how biological, psychological, and social influences work together to promote a long, satisfying life.

Maximum Lifespan

Finally, perhaps you are wondering: For humans, what is the **maximum lifespan**, or species-specific biological limit to length of life (in years), corresponding to the age at which the oldest known individual died? As the Biology and Environment box indicates, the oldest verified age is 122 years.

Does this figure actually reflect the upper bound of human longevity, or can it be extended? Some scientists believe that 122 years is close to the maximum, and 85 to 90 years is as much as most humans can expect. They point out that gains in average

Health

Centenarians usually have grandparents, parents, and siblings who reached very old age, indicating a genetically based survival advantage. Likewise, their children, who are typically in their seventies and eighties, appear physically young for their age (Coles, 2004; Perls et al., 2002). Some centenarians share with siblings a segment of identical DNA on the fourth chromosome, suggesting that a certain gene, or several genes, may increase the likelihood of exceptionally long life (Perls & Terry, 2003).

Most robust centenarians greatly delay or escape age-related chronic illnesses. Genetic testing reveals a low incidence of genes associated with immune-deficiency disorders, cancer, and Alzheimer's disease. Consistent with these findings, robust centenarians usually have efficiently functioning immune systems, and after-death examinations reveal few brain abnormalities (Silver & Perls, 2000). Others function effectively despite underlying chronic disease—typically atherosclerosis, other cardiovascular problems, and brain pathology (Berzlanovich et al., 2005; Evert et al., 2003). Compared with the general population, about four times as many centenarian women gave birth to healthy children after age 40 (Perls et al., 2000). Late childbearing may indicate that the body, including the reproductive system, is aging slowly.

As a group, robust centenarians are of average or slender build and practice moderation in eating. Many have most or all of their own teeth—another sign of unusual physical health. The large majority report having never smoked, engaging in no more than moderate wine consumption, and sustaining a lifelong pattern of physical activity past age 100 (Hagberg & Samuelson, 2008; Kropf & Pugh, 1995).

Personality

In personality, these very senior citizens appear highly optimistic (Jopp & Rott, 2006). In a study in which robust centenarians retook personality tests after 18 months, they reported more fatigue and depression, perhaps in response to increased frailty at the very end of their lives. But they also scored higher in toughmindedness, independence, emotional security, and openness to experience—traits that may be vital for surviving beyond 100 (Martin, Long, & Poon, 2002). An important contributor to their favorable mental health and longevity is social support, especially close family bonds and a long and happy marriage (Margrett et al., 2011; Velkoff, 2000). An unusually large percentage of centenarian men—about one-fourth—are still married.

Activities

Robust centenarians have a history of community involvement—working for just causes that are central to their growth and happiness. Their past and current activities often include stimulating work, leisure pursuits, and learning, which may help sustain their good cognition and life satisfaction (Antonini et al., 2008). Writing letters, poems, plays, and memoirs; making speeches; teaching music lessons and Sunday school; nursing the sick; chopping wood; selling merchandise, bonds, and insurance; painting; practicing medicine; and preaching sermons are among robust centenarians' varied involvements. In several cases, illiterate centenarians learned to read and write.

In sum, robust centenarians illustrate typical development at its best. These independent, mentally alert, happy 100-year-olds reveal how a healthy lifestyle, personal resourcefulness, and close ties to family and community can build on biological strengths, thereby pushing the limits of an active, fulfilling life.

---

life expectancy are largely the result of reducing health risks in the first 20 or 30 years—especially, the harmful behavioral and environmental conditions linked to poverty, limited education, and weak access to health care (Olshansky, 2011). For people age 65 and older, life expectancy has increased very little—only about 5 months—over the past decade. And although the number of centenarians is rising (see the Biology and Environment box), the odds of becoming a centenarian have been extremely low throughout human history and remain so today—in the U.S. population, just 1.7 for every 10,000 people, with most centenarians dying by age 103 (Carnes, Olshansky, & Hayflick, 2013). Nevertheless, other researchers remain convinced that we can add to human maximum lifespan.

This controversy raises another issue: *Should* maximum lifespan be increased as far as possible? *TAKE A MOMENT...* How would you answer this question? Many people respond that the important goal is not just quantity of life, but quality—that is, doing everything possible to extend healthy life expectancy. Most experts agree that only after reducing the high rates of preventable illness and disability among low-SES individuals and wiping out age-related diseases should we invest in lengthening the maximum lifespan.

Physical Changes

The programmed effects of specific genes and the random cellular events believed to underlie biological aging (see Chapter 13) make physical declines more apparent in late adulthood. The majority of people age 65 and older are capable of living active, independent lives, but with age, growing numbers need assistance. After age 75, about 9 percent of Americans have difficulty carrying out **activities of daily living (ADLs)**—basic self-care tasks required to live on one's own, such as bathing, dressing, getting in and out of bed or a chair, or eating. And about 17 percent cannot carry out **instrumental activities of daily living (IADLs)**—tasks necessary to conduct the business of daily life and also requiring some cognitive competence, such as telephoning, shopping, food preparation, housekeeping, and paying bills. The proportion of older adults with these limitations rises sharply with age (U.S. Department of Health and Human Services, 2011c). Nevertheless, most body structures can last into our eighties and beyond, if we take good care of them. For an overview of the physical changes we are about to discuss, return to Table 13.1 on page 435.

Nervous System

On a routine office visit, 80-year-old Ruth's doctor asked her how she was getting along. "I think I might be losing my mind," Ruth replied anxiously. "Yesterday, I forgot the name of the family who just moved in next door. And the day before, I had trouble finding the right words to explain to a delivery service how to get to my house."

"Ruth, everyone forgets those sorts of things from time to time," Dr. Wiley reassured her. "When we were young and had a memory lapse, we reprimanded ourselves for being scatterbrained and thought no more about it. Now, when we do the same thing, we attribute it to having 'a senior moment,' and we worry."

Ruth also wondered why extremes of hot and cold weather felt more uncomfortable than in earlier years. And she needed more time to coordinate a series of movements and had become less sure of her balance.

Aging of the central nervous system affects a wide range of complex activities. Although brain weight declines throughout adulthood, brain-imaging research and after-death autopsies reveal that the loss becomes greater starting in the sixties and may amount to as much as 5 to 10 percent by age 80, due to withering of the myelin coating on neural fibers, loss of synaptic connections, death of neurons, and enlargement of ventricles (spaces) within the brain (Rodrigue & Kennedy, 2011; Zelazo & Lee, 2010).

Neuron loss occurs throughout the cerebral cortex but at different rates among different regions and often inconsistently within parts of those regions. In longitudinal studies, the frontal lobes, especially the prefrontal cortex (responsible for inhibition, integration of information, strategic thinking, and other aspects of executive function), and the corpus callosum (which connects the two cortical hemispheres) tended to show greater shrinkage than the parietal and temporal lobes, with the occipital lobes changing little (see page 124 in Chapter 4 for a visual image of these regions) (Fabiani, 2012; Smith et al., 2007). The cerebellum (which controls balance and coordination and supports cognitive processes) also loses neurons—in all, about 25 percent. And EEG measures reveal gradual slowing and reduced intensity of brain waves—signs of diminished efficiency of the central nervous system (Kramer, Fabiani, & Colcombe, 2006).

But brain-imaging research reveals wide individual differences in the extent of these losses, which are moderately associated with cognitive functioning (Raz et al., 2010). And the brain can overcome some decline. In several studies, growth of neural fibers in the brains of older adults unaffected by illness took place at the same rate as in middle-aged people. Aging neurons established new synapses after other neurons had degenerated

(Flood & Coleman, 1988). Furthermore, the aging cerebral cortex can, to a limited degree, generate new neurons (Gould, 2007; Snyder & Cameron, 2012). And fMRI evidence reveals that compared with younger adults, older people who do well on memory and other cognitive tasks show more widely distributed activity across areas of the cerebral cortex, particularly in the prefrontal cortex and in regions mirroring typically active sites but located in the opposite hemisphere (Fabiani, 2012; Reuter-Lorenz & Cappell, 2008). This suggests that one way older adults compensate for neuron loss is to call on additional brain regions to support cognitive processing.

The autonomic nervous system, involved in many life-support functions, also performs less well, putting the older adults at risk during heat waves and cold spells. For example, Ruth's reduced tolerance for hot weather was due to decreased sweating. And her body found it harder to raise its core temperature during cold exposure. However, among physically fit older people who are free of disease, these declines are mild (Blatteis, 2012). The autonomic nervous system also releases higher levels of stress hormones into the bloodstream than it did earlier, perhaps to arouse body tissues that have become less responsive to these hormones over the years (Whitbourne, 2002). As we will see, this change may contribute to decreased immunity and to sleep problems.

Sensory Systems

Changes in sensory functioning become increasingly noticeable in late life. Older adults see and hear less well, and their taste, smell, and touch sensitivity may also decline. As Figure 17.2

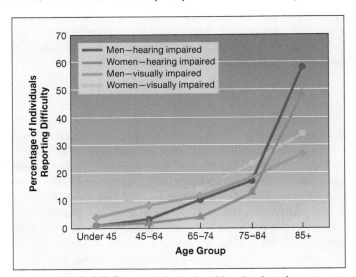

FIGURE 17.2 Rates of visual and hearing impairments among U.S. men and women by age. Among a large, nationally representative sample, those reporting that they had trouble seeing, even when wearing glasses or contact lenses, were judged visually impaired; those reporting "a lot of trouble" hearing were judged hearing impaired. Women report more visual impairments; men report more hearing impairments, a gap that widens considerably in late adulthood. In late life, hearing impairments become more common than visual impairments. (Adapted from U.S. Department of Health and Human Services, 2012d.)

shows, in late life, hearing impairments are more common than visual impairments. Extending trends in middle adulthood, more women than men report being visually impaired, more men than women hearing impaired.

Vision. In Chapter 15 (see pages 502–503), we noted that structural changes in the eye make it harder to focus on nearby objects, see in dim light, and perceive color. In late adulthood, vision diminishes further. The cornea (clear covering of the eye) becomes more translucent and scatters light, which blurs images and increases sensitivity to glare. The lens continues to yellow, leading to further impairment in color discrimination. The number of individuals with **cataracts**—cloudy areas in the lens, resulting in foggy vision and (without surgery) eventual blindness—increases tenfold from middle to late adulthood, affecting 25 percent of people in their seventies and 50 percent of those in their eighties (Owsley, 2011; U.S. Census Bureau, 2012b). Besides biological aging, heredity, sun exposure, cigarette smoking, alcohol consumption, and certain diseases (such as hypertension and diabetes) increase the risk of cataracts (Sacca et al., 2009). Fortunately, removal of the lens and replacement with an artificial lens implant is highly successful in restoring vision.

Impaired eyesight in late adulthood largely results from a reduction in light reaching the retina (caused by yellowing of the lens, shrinking of the pupil, and clouding of the vitreous) and from cell loss in the retina and optic nerve (refer again to Chapter 15). Dark adaptation—moving from a brightly lit to a dim environment, such as a movie theater—becomes harder. A decline in binocular vision (the brain's ability to combine images received from both eyes) makes depth perception less reliable. And visual acuity (fineness of discrimination) worsens, dropping sharply after age 70 (Owsley, 2011).

When light-sensitive cells in the macula, or central region of the retina, break down, older adults may develop **macular degeneration**, in which central vision blurs and gradually is lost. Macular degeneration is the leading cause of blindness among older adults. About 10 percent of 65- to 74-year-olds, and 30 percent of 75- to 85-year-olds, have symptoms. If diagnosed early, macular degeneration can sometimes be treated with laser therapy. As with cataracts, heredity (including several identified genes) increases risk, especially when combined with cigarette smoking or obesity (Chu et al., 2008; Rhone & Basu, 2008; Wysong, Lee, & Sloan, 2009). Atherosclerosis also contributes by constricting blood flow to the retina. Protective factors—believed to exert their effects by shielding cells in the macula from free-radical damage—include regular, brisk physical activity and a diet rich in green, leafy vegetables, which are excellent sources of vitamins A, C, E, and carotenoids (yellow and red plant pigments) (Feret et al., 2007).

Visual difficulties have a profound impact on older people's self-confidence and everyday behavior. As she approached age 80, Ruth gave up driving, and she worried about Walt, who found it hard to shift focus between the road and the dashboard or to make out pedestrians at dusk and at night. On foot, problems with depth perception and dark adaptation increase older adults' chances of stumbling.

When vision loss is extensive, it can affect leisure pursuits and be very isolating. Because of her poor vision, Ruth could no longer enjoy museums, movies, playing bridge, or working crossword puzzles, and she depended on others for help with housekeeping and shopping. But even among people age 85 and older, only 30 percent experience visual impairment severe enough to interfere with daily living (U.S. Department of Health and Human Services, 2011c). For many, however, reduced vision goes undetected. Treatment is vital for sustaining quality of life.

Hearing. "Mom, I'd like you to meet Joe's cousin Leona," said Ruth's daughter Sybil at a Thanksgiving gathering. But in the clamor of boisterous children, television sounds, and nearby conversations, 85-year-old Ruth didn't catch Leona's name or her relationship to Sybil's husband, Joe.

"Tell me your name again?" Ruth asked, adding, "Let's go into the other room, where it's quieter, so we can speak a bit."

Reduced blood supply and natural cell death in the inner ear and auditory cortex, discussed in Chapter 15, along with stiffening of membranes (such as the eardrum), cause hearing to decline in late adulthood. Decrements are greatest at high frequencies, although detection of soft sounds diminishes throughout the frequency range (see page 503). In addition, responsiveness to startling noises lessens, and discriminating complex tone patterns becomes harder (Hietanen et al., 2004; Kidd & Bao, 2012).

Although hearing loss has less impact on self-care than vision loss, it affects safety and enjoyment of life. In the din of city traffic, 80-year-old Ruth didn't always correctly interpret warnings, whether spoken ("Watch it, don't step out yet") or nonspoken (the beep of a horn). And when she turned up the radio or television volume, she sometimes missed the ring of the telephone or a knock at the door.

As hearing declines, older people report lower self-efficacy, more loneliness and depressive symptoms, and a smaller social

This adult son's patient guidance helps his father feel included at a boisterous family reunion. Declines in hearing make it difficult for older adults to socialize in noisy settings.

network than their normally hearing peers (Kramer et al., 2002). Of all hearing difficulties, the age-related decline in speech perception has the greatest impact on life satisfaction. After age 70, ability to detect the content and emotionally expressive features of conversation declines, especially in noisy settings (Gosselin & Gagne, 2011).

Although Ruth used problem-centered coping to increase her chances of hearing conversation, she wasn't always successful. At the family's Thanksgiving reunion, fewer relatives took time to talk with Ruth, and she felt some pangs of loneliness. And sometimes people were inconsiderate. On a dinner outing, when Ruth asked Joe to repeat himself, he turned to Sybil and said loudly, "Be honest, Syb, Ruth's going deaf, isn't she?" In one study, older adults' adoption of such negative stereotypes of aging predicted greater hearing loss over a three-year period (Levy, Slade, & Gill, 2006).

Most older adults do not suffer from hearing loss great enough to disrupt their daily lives until after age 85. For those who do, compensating with a hearing aid is helpful. Furthermore, recall from Chapter 4 (pages 145–146) that beginning at birth, our perception is *intermodal* (combines information from more than one sensory system). By attending to facial expressions, gestures, and lip movements, older adults can use vision to help interpret the spoken word. Finally, when family members and others speak in quiet environments, older people are far more likely to convey an image of alertness and competence than of reduced sensitivity to the surrounding world.

Taste and Smell. Walt's brother Dick was a heavy smoker. In his sixties, he poured salt and pepper over his food and asked for "extra hot" in Mexican and Indian restaurants.

Dick's reduced sensitivity to the four basic tastes—sweet, salty, sour, and bitter—is evident in many adults after age 60. Older adults also have greater difficulty recognizing familiar foods by taste alone (Fukunaga, Uematsu, & Sugimoto, 2005; Methven et al., 2012). But no change in the number or distribution of taste buds occurs late in life, so this drop in taste sensitivity may be due to factors other than aging. Cigarette smoking, dentures, medications, and environmental pollutants can affect taste perception (Drewnowski & Shultz, 2001). When taste is harder to detect, food is less enjoyable, increasing the likelihood of dietary deficiencies. Flavor additives can help make food more attractive.

Besides enhancing food enjoyment, smell has a self-protective function. An aging person who has difficulty detecting rancid food, gas fumes, or smoke may be in a life-threatening situation. A decrease in the number of smell receptors after age 60 contributes to declines in odor sensitivity (Seiberling & Conley, 2004). Researchers believe that odor perception not only wanes but becomes distorted, a change that may promote complaints that "food no longer smells and tastes right." But older adults experiencing greater difficulty with verbal recall, including retrieval of odor labels, have greater difficulty with odor recognition tasks (Larsson, Öberg, & Bäckman, 2005). So cognitive changes may make the decline in odor perception appear greater than it actually is.

Touch. Object recognition through touch occurs many times each day, as adults identify common objects after manually exploring them—keys or credit card in a pocket, corkscrew at the back of a drawer—within 2 to 3 seconds. Touch sensitivity is especially crucial for certain adults, such as the severely visually impaired reading Braille and people making fine judgments about texture—for example, in art and handicraft activities. In later life, capacity to discriminate detailed surface properties and identify unfamiliar objects by touch declines. Waning of touch perception on the hands, especially the fingertips—believed to be due to loss of touch receptors in certain regions of the skin and slowing of blood circulation to the extremities—contributes (Stevens & Cruz, 1996). In addition, decrements in fluid abilities, especially spatial orientation, are influential (see page 519 in Chapter 15) (Kalisch et al., 2012). Fluid skills are strongly correlated with older adults' tactile performance.

Compared to their sighted counterparts, blind Braille readers retain high touch sensitivity well into old age (Legge et al., 2008). Years of experience in picking up detailed tactile information seem to protect their tactile discrimination skills.

Cardiovascular and Respiratory Systems

Aging of the cardiovascular and respiratory systems proceeds gradually and usually unnoticed in early and middle adulthood. In late adulthood, changes become more apparent. In their sixties, Ruth and Walt noticed that they felt more physically stressed after running to catch a bus or to cross a street before the light changed.

As the years pass, the heart muscle becomes more rigid, and some of its cells die while others enlarge, leading the walls of the left ventricle (the largest heart chamber, from which blood is pumped to the body) to thicken. In addition, artery walls stiffen

These mountain hikers need frequent rests to catch their breath and regain their energy. With aging of the cardiovascular and respiratory systems, sufficient oxygen may not be delivered to body tissues during physical exertion.

and accumulate some plaque (cholesterol and fats) due to normal aging (much more in those with atherosclerosis). Finally, the heart muscle becomes less responsive to signals from pacemaker cells within the heart, which initiate each contraction (Larsen, 2009; Smith & Cotter, 2008).

As a combined result of these changes, the heart pumps with less force, maximum heart rate decreases, and blood flow throughout the circulatory system slows. This means that sufficient oxygen may not be delivered to body tissues during high physical activity. (Recall from Chapter 13 that a healthy heart supports typical levels of exertion well into old age.)

Changes in the respiratory system compound the effects of reduced oxygenation. Because lung tissue gradually loses its elasticity, vital capacity (amount of air that can be forced in and out of the lungs) is reduced by half between ages 25 and 80. As a result, the lungs fill and empty less efficiently, causing the blood to absorb less oxygen and give off less carbon dioxide. This explains why older people increase their breathing rate more and feel more out of breath while exercising.

Cardiovascular and respiratory deficiencies are more extreme in lifelong smokers and in people who have failed to reduce dietary fat or have had many years of exposure to environmental pollutants. As we have seen in previous chapters, exercise is a powerful means of slowing cardiovascular aging (Galetta et al., 2012). Exercise also facilitates respiratory functioning, as we will see later when we discuss health and fitness.

Immune System

As the immune system ages, T cells, which attack antigens (foreign substances) directly, become less effective (see Chapter 13, page 437). In addition, the immune system is more likely to malfunction by turning against normal body tissues in an **autoimmune response**. A less competent immune system can increase the risk of a variety of illnesses, including infectious diseases (such as the flu), cardiovascular disease, certain forms of cancer, and various autoimmune disorders, such as rheumatoid arthritis and diabetes (Larbi, Fülöp, & Pawelec, 2008). But an age-related decline in immune functioning is not the cause of most late-life illnesses. It merely permits disease to progress, whereas a stronger immune reaction would stamp out the disease agent.

Although older adults vary greatly in immunity, most experience some loss, ranging from partial to profound (Ponnappan & Ponnappan, 2011). The strength of the aging person's immune system seems to be a sign of overall physical vigor. Certain immune indicators, such as high T cell activity, predict better physical functioning and survival over the next two years in very old people (Moro-Garcia et al., 2012; Wikby et al., 1998).

Recall from Chapter 13 that stress hormones undermine immunity. With age, the autonomic nervous system releases higher levels of these into the bloodstream (refer back to page 437). As the immune response declines with age, stress-induced susceptibility to infection rises dramatically (Archer et al., 2011). A healthy diet and exercise help protect the immune response in old age, whereas obesity aggravates the age-related decline.

Sleep

When Walt went to bed at night, he usually lay awake for a half-hour to an hour before falling asleep, remaining in a drowsy state longer than when he was younger. During the night, he spent less time in the deepest phase of NREM sleep (see Chapter 3, page 108) and awoke several times—again sometimes lying awake for a half-hour or more before drifting back to sleep.

Older adults require about as much total sleep as younger adults: around 7 hours per night. Yet as people age, they have more difficulty falling asleep, staying asleep, and sleeping deeply. Insomnia affects nearly half of older adults at least a few nights per month. The timing of sleep tends to change as well, toward earlier bedtime and earlier morning wakening (Edwards et al., 2010). Changes in brain structures controlling sleep and higher levels of stress hormones in the bloodstream, which have an alerting effect on the central nervous system, are believed to be responsible.

Until age 70 or 80, men experience more sleep disturbances than women, for several reasons. First, enlargement of the prostate gland, which occurs in almost all aging men, constricts the urethra (the tube draining the bladder) and leads to a need to urinate more often, including during the night. Second, men—especially those who are overweight and use alcohol heavily—are more prone to **sleep apnea**, a condition in which breathing ceases for 10 seconds or longer, resulting in many brief awakenings. An estimated 45 to 60 percent of older adults are affected (Edwards et al., 2010).

Poor sleep can feed on itself. Walt's nighttime wakefulness led to daytime fatigue and short naps, which made it harder to fall asleep the following evening. And because Walt expected to have trouble sleeping, he worried about it, which also interfered with sleep. Insomnia in older adults is of special concern because it increases the risk of falls and cognitive impairments (Crowley, 2011). Those who are poor sleepers more often report slower reaction times and attention and memory difficulties.

Fortunately, there are ways to foster restful sleep, such as establishing a consistent bedtime and waking time, exercising regularly, and using the bedroom only for sleep (not for eating, reading, or watching TV) (McCurry et al., 2007). Older adults receive more prescription sedatives for sleep complaints than do people under age 60. Used briefly, these drugs can help relieve temporary insomnia. But long-term medication can make matters worse by increasing the frequency and severity of sleep apnea and by inducing rebound insomnia after the drug is discontinued (Feinsilver, 2003). Finally, discomfort due to an enlarged prostate, including frequent urination at night, can be corrected with laser surgical procedures that relieve symptoms without complications (Zhang et al., 2012).

Physical Appearance and Mobility

In earlier chapters, we saw that changes leading to an aged appearance are under way as early as the twenties and thirties. Because these occur gradually, older adults may not notice that they look older until changes have become obvious. Each year

Aging brings changes in appearance, evident in these portraits of Jimmy Carter, former U.S. president, at ages 52, 63, and 88. The skin creases and sags, "age spots" increase, the nose and ears broaden, and hair on the head thins.

during their summer travels, Walt and Ruth observed that Dick and Goldie's skin appeared more wrinkled. Their hair turned from gray to white as all pigment was lost; their bodies grew rounder and their arms and legs thinner. When they returned home, Walt and Ruth also were more aware that they themselves had aged.

Creasing and sagging of the skin, described in Chapter 15, extends into old age. In addition, oil glands that lubricate the skin become less active, leading to dryness and roughness. "Age spots" increase; in some individuals, the arms, backs of the hands, and face may be dotted with these pigmented marks. Blood vessels can be seen beneath the more transparent skin, which has largely lost its layer of fatty support (Whitbourne, 2002). This loss further limits the older adult's ability to adapt to hot and cold temperatures.

The face is especially likely to show these effects because it is frequently exposed to the sun, which accelerates aging. Other factors that contribute to facial wrinkling and age spots include long-term alcohol use, cigarette smoking, and psychological stress. Additional facial changes occur: The nose and ears broaden as new cells are deposited on the outer layer of the skeleton. And especially in older adults with a history of poor dental care, teeth may be yellowed, cracked, and chipped, and gums may have receded. As hair follicles under the skin's surface die, hair on the head thins in both sexes, and the scalp may be visible (Whitbourne, 2002). In men with hereditary pattern baldness, follicles do not die but, instead, begin to produce fine, downy hair.

Body build changes as well. Height continues to decline, especially in women, as loss of bone mineral content leads to further collapse of the spinal column. Weight generally drops after age 60 because of additional loss of lean body mass (bone density and muscle), which is heavier than the fat deposits accumulating on the torso.

Several factors affect mobility. The first is muscle strength, which generally declines at a faster rate in late adulthood than in middle age. On average, by 60 to 70 years of age, 10 to 20 percent of muscle power has been lost, a figure that climbs to 30 to 50 percent after age 70 to 80 (Reid & Fielding, 2012). Second, bone strength deteriorates because of reduced bone mass, and tiny cracks in response to stress weaken the bones further. Third, strength and flexibility of the joints and the ligaments and tendons (which connect muscle to bone) diminish. In her eighties, Ruth's reduced ability to support her body, flex her limbs, and rotate her hips made walking at a steady, moderate pace, climbing stairs, and rising from a chair difficult.

In Chapter 13, we noted that endurance athletes who continue training throughout adulthood retain their muscular physiques and much of their strength into their sixties and seventies. These especially active people, like other aging individuals, lose fast-twitch muscle fibers, but they compensate by strengthening remaining slow-twitch fibers so they work more efficiently. A history of regular physical activity translates into greater mobility in late life (Koster et al., 2007; Patel et al., 2006). At the same time, a carefully planned exercise program can enhance older adults' joint flexibility and range of movement.

Adapting to Physical Changes of Late Adulthood

Great diversity exists in older adults' adaptation to the physical changes of aging. People who are more anxious about growing older monitor their physical state more closely and are more concerned about their appearance (Montepare, 2006). Dick and Goldie took advantage of an enormous industry designed to stave off outward signs of old age, including cosmetics, wigs, and plastic surgery, plus various "anti-aging" dietary supplements, herbal products, and hormonal medications offered by "longevity" clinics—none with any demonstrated benefits and some of them harmful (Olshansky, Hayflick, & Perls, 2004). In contrast, Ruth and Walt were relatively unconcerned about their thinning white hair and wrinkled skin. Their identities were less bound up with their appearance than with their ability to remain actively engaged in their surroundings.

Most older people sustain a favorable *subjective age*—say they feel younger than they look and than they actually are (Kleinspehn-Ammerlahn, Kotter-Grühn, & Smith, 2008; Uotinen et al., 2006; Westerhof, 2008). In several investigations, 75-year-olds reported feeling about 15 years younger! A youthful self-evaluation is linked to satisfaction with growing older—better mental health and psychological well-being (Keyes & Westerhof, 2012).

Clearly, older adults vary in the aspects of physical aging that matter most to them. *Wanting* to be younger (as opposed to *feeling* younger) than one's actual age is associated with less positive mental health (Keyes & Westerhof, 2012). Compared with Dick and Goldie, Ruth and Walt approached aging with a more positive outlook and greater peace of mind, resolving to intervene in those aspects of physical aging that could be changed and to accept those that could not.

Research shows that the most obvious outward signs of aging—graying hair, facial wrinkles, and baldness—bear no relationship to sensory, cognitive, and motor functioning or to longevity (Schnohr et al., 1998). In contrast, neurological, sensory, cardiovascular, respiratory, immune-system, and skeletal and muscular health are strongly associated with cognitive performance and both quality and length of later life (Bergman, Blomberg, & Almkvist, 2007; Lin et al., 2011; Reyes-Ortiz et al., 2005; Schäfer, Huxhold, & Lindenberger, 2006). Furthermore, people can do more to prevent declines in the functioning of these internal body systems than they can do to prevent gray hair and baldness!

Effective Coping Strategies.
Think back to our discussion of problem-centered and emotion-centered coping in Chapter 15. It applies here as well. As Walt and Ruth prevented and compensated for age-related changes through diet, exercise, environmental adjustments, and an active, stimulating lifestyle, they felt a sense of personal control over their fates. This prompted additional active coping and improved physical functioning.

Older people who report a high sense of personal control usually deal with physical changes through problem-centered coping strategies. A 75-year-old who lost sight in one eye consulted an occupational therapist for advice and, to compensate for reduced depth perception and visual field, trained himself to use more side-to-side head movements. In contrast, older adults who consider age-related declines inevitable and uncontrollable tend to be passive when faced with them and to report more physical and psychological adjustment difficulties (Kempen et al., 2006; Lachman, Neupert, & Agrigoroaei, 2011).

Sense of control varies across cultures: U.S. individualistic values emphasize the power of one's own action and choices.

Consequently, Americans score higher in personal control than adults in Asian nations and in Mexico (Angel, Angel, & Hill, 2009; Yamaguchi et al., 2005). Furthermore, we have seen that the United States is less generous than other industrialized nations in government-supported health care and social security benefits (see pages 67–68 in Chapter 2). In one study, sense of personal control was a much stronger predictor of older adults' health status in the United States than it was in England, where government policies do more to support good health throughout the lifespan (Clarke & Smith, 2011).

When physical disabilities become severe, sense of control has diminishing returns, no longer having as much impact on health status. Older adults with substantial physical impairments cope more effectively when they acknowledge reduced control and accept the need for caregiver or equipment assistance (Clarke & Smith, 2011; Ross & Sastry, 1999). But doing so may be more difficult for many older Americans, who are accustomed to a "culture of personal control," than for older people elsewhere in the world.

Assistive Technology.
A rapidly expanding **assistive technology**, or array of devices that permit people with disabilities to improve their functioning, is available to help older people cope with physical declines. Computers are the greatest source of these innovative products. People with sensory impairments can use special software to enlarge text or have it read aloud. Phones that can be dialed and answered by voice commands help those with difficulty pushing buttons or getting across a room to answer the phone. And for older people who take multiple medications, a tiny computer chip called a "smart cap" can be placed on medicine bottles. It beeps on a programmed schedule as a reminder to take the drug and tracks how many and at what time pills have been taken.

A physical therapist helps a stroke patient master use of a tool for reaching and gripping small objects. Assistive devices help older adults with disabilities maintain their independence.

Architects have also designed homes that can adapt to changing physical needs—equipping them with movable walls that expand and contract, plumbing that enables a full bathroom to be added on the main floor, and "smart-home" technologies that promote safety and mobility, such as sensors in floors that activate room lights when an older person gets up at night and alarm systems that detect falls. Another remarkable device is a bathroom scale that helps monitor health status. It sends a signal to a control box, which reads the person's weight aloud. After comparing weight with previous readings, the box asks relevant questions—"Are you more tired than usual?" "Are you having trouble sleeping?"—that can be answered by pressing a "yes" or "no" button. The box also works with equipment that measures blood pressure, activity level, and other health indicators. Data collected are sent electronically to whomever the older adult gives access.

Use of assistive devices slows physical declines and reduces the need for personal caregiving (Hoenig, Taylor, & Sloan, 2003; Wilson et al., 2009). Do older adults with disabilities regard some technologies as invasions of privacy? The overwhelming majority weigh privacy concerns against potential benefits—saying for example, "If this [monitoring system] would keep me independent longer, I wouldn't mind" (Melenhorst et al., 2004; Rogers & Fisk, 2005). As these findings suggest, sustaining an effective *person–environment fit*, or match between older people's current capabilities and the demands of their living environments, enhances psychological well-being (Lawton, 1998). Modifying physical and social environments to boost older adults' ability to perform familiar tasks and master new ones contributes to their sense of competence and the quality of their lives.

At present, U.S. government-sponsored health-care coverage is largely limited to essential medical equipment; smart-home technologies are beyond the means of most older people. Sweden's health-care system, in contrast, covers many assistive devices that promote function and safety, and its building code requires that new homes include a full bathroom on the main floor (Hooyman & Kiyak, 2011). In this way, Sweden strives to maximize person–environment fit for its older adults, helping them remain as independent as possible.

Overcoming Stereotypes of Aging.

Negative stereotypes of late adulthood, which view older adults as weak, boring, and debilitated and "deterioration as inevitable," are widespread in Western nations (Staudinger & Bowen, 2010). Overcoming this pessimistic picture is vital for helping people adapt favorably to late-life physical changes. In a survey of older adults diverse in SES, many reported experiencing prejudice and discrimination (Palmore, 2001). For example, 30 to 40 percent had been ignored, talked down to, or assumed to be unable to hear or understand well because of their age.

Like gender stereotypes, aging stereotypes often operate automatically, without awareness; people "see" older adults in stereotypical ways, even when they appear otherwise (Kite et al., 2005). As seniors encounter these negative messages, they experience *stereotype threat*, which results in diminished

performance on tasks related to the stereotype (see pages 314–315 in Chapter 9). In several studies, researchers exposed older adults to words associated with either negative aging stereotypes ("decrepit," "confused") or positive aging stereotypes ("sage," "enlightened"). Those in negative-stereotype conditions displayed a more intense physiological response to stress, greater help-seeking and feelings of loneliness, and worse physical performance, recall memory, self-efficacy, and appraisals of their own health (Coudin & Alexopoulos, 2010; Hess & Hinson, 2006; Hess, Hinson, & Statham, 2004; Levy & Leifheit-Limson, 2009; Mazerolle et al., 2012). *TAKE A MOMENT...* How might stereotype threat explain the hearing loss linked to negative stereotypes of aging, mentioned on page 570?

As the findings just reviewed indicate, negative stereotypes have a stressful, disorganizing impact on older adults' functioning. Positive stereotypes, in contrast, reduce stress and foster physical and mental competence (Bolkan & Hooker, 2012). In a longitudinal investigation, people with positive self-perceptions of aging—who, for example, agreed with such statements as "As I get older, things are better than I thought they'd be"—lived, on average, 7½ years longer than those with negative self-perceptions. This survival advantage remained after gender, SES, loneliness, and physical health status were controlled (Levy et al., 2002). Adults with less education are especially susceptible to the detrimental effects of aging stereotypes, perhaps because they tend to accept those messages uncritically (Andreoletti & Lachman, 2004).

Older adults rarely appear in television programs and, when they do, typically play minor roles. But a positive sign is that negative portrayals of seniors on TV and in other media are rare. TV commercials featuring older people usually depict them in stereotypically positive roles, most commonly as an "adventurous golden ager" (fun-loving, sociable, and active), "perfect grandparent" (family-oriented, kind, and generous), or "productive golden ager" (intelligent, capable, and successful) (Lee, Carpenter, & Meyers, 2006). Still, the products promoted in such ads are mostly medications and medical services and "anti-aging" cosmetics and treatments—images that reinforce negative views of older adults as preoccupied with physical declines and dissatisfied with their appearance.

In cultures where older adults are treated with deference and respect, an aging appearance can be a source of pride. In one study, Chinese adults diverse in age were less likely than Canadian adults to stereotype older people, either positively or negatively (Ryan et al., 2004). In the native language of the Inuit people of Canada, the closest word to "elder" is *isumataq*, or "one who knows things"—a high status that begins when a couple becomes head of the extended family unit. When Inuit older adults were asked for their thoughts on aging well, they mentioned attitudes—a positive approach to life, interest in transmitting cultural knowledge to young people, and community involvement—nearly twice as often as physical health (Collings, 2001).

Japan honors its older citizens with an annual celebration, Respect for the Aged Day. Also, a ritual called *kanreki* recognizes

An Inuit senior of northern Canada teaches a young adult how to make sealskin kamiks, or boots. In Inuit culture, aging is associated with expert knowledge and high status. Hence, changes in physical appearance can be a source of pride.

the older person's new freedoms and competencies and senior place in the family and society. Japanese extended families in the United States often plan the kanreki as a surprise sixtieth birthday party, incorporating elements of both the traditional ritual (such as dress) and the Western birthday (a special cake). Cultural valuing of aging prompts a welcoming approach to late adulthood, including some of its physical transitions.

Despite inevitable declines, physical aging can be viewed with either optimism or pessimism. As Walt commented, "You can think of your glass as half full or half empty." As the Cultural Influences box on page 576 makes clear, cultural valuing of older adults greatly increases the likelihood that they will adopt the "half full" alternative.

ASK YOURSELF

REVIEW Cite examples of how older adults can compensate for age-related physical declines.

CONNECT Review research on stereotype threat on page 315 in Chapter 9. How do stereotypes of aging similarly affect older adults' behavior?

APPLY "The best way to adjust to this is to learn to like it," thought 65-year-old Herman, inspecting his thinning hair in the mirror. "I remember reading that bald older men are regarded as leaders." What type of coping is Herman using, and why is it effective?

REFLECT While watching TV during the coming week, keep a log of portrayals of older adults in commercials. How many images were positive? How many negative? Compare your observations with research findings.

Health, Fitness, and Disability

At Walt and Ruth's fiftieth wedding anniversary, 77-year-old Walt thanked a roomful of well-wishers for joining in the celebration. Then, with emotion, he announced, "I'm so grateful Ruth and I are still healthy enough to give to our family, friends, and community."

As Walt's remarks affirm, health is central to psychological well-being in late life. When researchers ask older adults about possible selves (see Chapter 16, page 538), number of hoped-for physical selves declines with age and number of feared physical selves increases. Nevertheless, because older people compare themselves to same-age peers, the majority rate their health favorably (U.S. Department of Health and Human Services, 2011c). In an investigation of more than 500 70- to 100-year-olds living in Berlin, Germany, subjective ratings of one's own health rose in late life, even though objective assessments by health professionals declined (Baltes & Smith, 2003). As for protecting their health, older adults' sense of self-efficacy is as high as that of young adults and higher than that of middle-aged people (Frazier, 2002).

Self-efficacy and optimism about one's health promote continued health-enhancing behaviors (Kubzansky et al., 2002; Morrison, 2008). Disability need not inevitably lead to further disability and dependency. In several longitudinal studies, 10 to 50 percent of older adults with disabilities showed substantial improvement two to six years later (Johnston et al., 2004; Ostir et al., 1999). Furthermore, good health permits older adults to remain socially active, thereby fostering psychological well-being (Fiori, Smith, & Antonucci, 2007).

As mentioned earlier, SES and ethnic variations in health diminish in late adulthood. Nevertheless, SES continues to predict physical functioning (House, Lantz, & Herd, 2005; Yao & Robert, 2008). African-American and Hispanic older people (one-fifth of whom live in poverty) remain at greater risk for various health problems, including cardiovascular disease, diabetes, and certain cancers. Native-American older adults are even worse off. The majority are poor, and chronic health conditions—including diabetes, kidney disease, liver disease, tuberculosis, and hearing and vision impairments—are so widespread that in the United States, the federal government grants Native Americans special health benefits. These begin as early as age 45, reflecting a much harder and shorter lifespan.

Unfortunately, low-SES older adults are more likely than their higher-SES counterparts to delay seeking medical treatment (Lee, Hasnain-Wynia, & Lau, 2011). Part of the reason is cost: On average, U.S. Medicare beneficiaries devote an estimated one-tenth of their income to out-of-pocket health-care expenses—a proportion that escalates among those with the fewest resources (Johnson & Mommaerts, 2010). Furthermore, low-SES older people often do not comply with doctors' directions because they feel less in control of their health and less optimistic that treatment will work. Their low sense of self-efficacy further impairs their physical condition.

Cultural Influences

Cultural Variations in Sense of Usefulness in Late Life

A wealth of evidence confirms that older adults fare best when they retain social status and opportunities for community participation, even after they become frail (Fry et al., 1997; Rossi, 2004). Yet cultures vary widely in the extent to which they include their oldest members in meaningful social roles.

Consider the Herero, a pastoral people of Botswana, Africa. Older people who are strong and active spend their days just as younger people do, tending the cattle and performing other chores. When older adults decline physically, they retain positions of seniority and are treated with respect. A status hierarchy makes the oldest man and his wife village leaders. They are responsible for preserving the sacred flame of the ancestors, who remain significant family members after death. Children are sent to live in the homes of frail community members to provide care—an assignment that is a source of great pride and prestige.

Old age is also a gratifying time of life in Momence, Illinois, a small, working-class farming and manufacturing town. The population is highly stable, so seniors hold positions of authority because of their length of residence and intimate knowledge of the community. Town, church, and club leaders tend to be older, and past leaders are included in decision making. And because frail older adults are embedded in family, neighborhood, and church networks that have persisted for many years, other community members often inquire about them, visit them, and monitor their condition.

The Herero and the residents of Momence seldom refer to older adults in terms of their age. Rather, they mention knowledge and social position (Keith et al., 1994). But in most of the Western world, old age is a salient attribute that readily triggers negative stereotypes, including the label "useless." For example, after a young anthropologist who was studying life at a senior center introduced several of his contemporaries to an 80-year-old man, one remarked, "He has outlived his usefulness. He would be happier dead" (Tsuji, 2005, p. 3). In line with this view, compared with younger and middle-aged adults, older adults typically score lower on measures of sense of purpose in life (Ryff & Singer, 2002).

Yet contributing to making life better for others, as we will see in Chapter 18, is an important component of older adults' life goals. It also affects their health and survival. Studies in diverse nations—Finland, France, Japan, and the United States—reveal that older people who often felt useless were more likely to display increasing disability and to die in the ensuing 4 to 10 years than those who felt needed, after initial health status, SES, and other relevant factors were controlled (Gruenewald et al.,

Among the Herero people of Botswana, Africa, children are assigned the prestigious responsibility of providing care to older adults who have declined physically. This Herero child helps a senior member of her village drink milk.

2007, 2009; Okamoto & Tanaka, 2004; Pitkala et al., 2004).

Fortunately, only a minority of Western older adults report feeling useless most or all of the time—7 percent in a U.S sample. But another 34 percent said that they sometimes feel that way (Gruenewald et al., 2009). Providing older people with opportunities to assume important roles readily combats this harmful self-perception. In one instance, seniors with arthritis were trained to become lay leaders, who delivered courses on coping with disease symptoms. Six months later, they reported a changed outlook: They highly valued their newly acquired status, felt more self-confident, better managed their own symptoms, and were more willing "to get on with life" (Hainsworth & Barlow, 2001). As one lay leader remarked, "It's almost as if I've stopped aging and started to get younger!"

The sex differences noted in Chapter 15 extend into late adulthood: Men are more prone to fatal diseases, women to non-life-threatening disabling conditions. By very old age (80 to 85 and beyond), women are more impaired than men because only the sturdiest men have survived (Crimmins, Kim, & Solé-Auró, 2011; Morrison, 2008). In addition, with fewer physical limitations, older men are better able to remain independent and to engage in exercise, hobbies, and involvement in the social world, all of which promote better health.

Widespread health-related optimism among older people suggests that substantial inroads into preventing disability can be made even in the last few decades of life. Ideally, as life expectancy extends, we want the average period of diminished vigor before death—especially, the number of months or years of ill-health and suffering—to decrease. This public health goal is called the **compression of morbidity**. Several large-scale studies indicate that over the past several decades, compression of morbidity has occurred in industrialized nations (Fries,

Bruce, & Chakravarty, 2011). Medical advances in treatment of disease and improved socioeconomic conditions are largely responsible.

In addition, the impact of good health habits on postponement of disability is large. In a longitudinal investigation, researchers followed university alumni from their late sixties over the next two decades. In those who were low risk (no risk factors of smoking, obesity, or lack of exercise), disability was delayed by nearly 5 years compared with those who were moderate risk (had one of these risk factors). Compared to high-risk participants (with two or three risk factors), postponement of disability in the low-risk group exceeded 8 years (see Figure 17.3) (Chakravarty et al., 2012). Those who were obese, sedentary, and addicted to tobacco surged to extremely high levels of disability in the two years before death. And although good health habits lengthened life by about 3½ years, their impact on functional ability was greater.

Consequently, researchers believe that the most promising route to further compression of morbidity in developed countries is to reduce negative lifestyle factors. Progress in this respect, however, has been disappointing. Certain unhealthy conditions—such as a high-fat diet, overweight and obesity, and a sedentary lifestyle—that contribute to earlier onset of disability have been increasing. Without modifying these factors, future gains in compression of morbidity will be hard to achieve. Rather, we may see a trend in the reverse direction: people surviving longer with debilitating illnesses because of new and improved medical treatments (Crimmins & Beltrán-Sánchez, 2010). As we look closely at health, fitness, and disability in late adulthood, we will add to our discussion of health promotion in earlier chapters, taking up additional routes to this vital objective.

Comprehensive strategies are needed in the developing world, where 70 percent of older people will reside by 2025. In these nations, poverty is rampant, chronic diseases occur earlier, even routine health interventions are unavailable or too costly for all but a few, and most public health programs do not focus on late adulthood (Rinaldo & Ferraro, 2012). As a result, disability rates among older adults are especially high, and as yet, no progress has been made in compression of morbidity.

Nutrition and Exercise

The physical changes of late life lead to an increased need for certain nutrients—calcium and vitamin D to protect the bones; zinc and vitamins B_6, C, and E to protect the immune system; and vitamins A, C, and E to prevent free radicals (see Chapter 13, pages 433–434). Yet declines in physical activity, in the senses of taste and smell, and in ease of chewing (because of deteriorating teeth) can reduce the quantity and quality of food eaten. Furthermore, the aging digestive system has greater difficulty absorbing certain nutrients, such as protein, calcium, and vitamin D. And older adults who live alone may have problems shopping or cooking and may feel less like eating by themselves. Together, these physical and environmental conditions increase the risk of dietary deficiencies, which are common among U.S. older adults.

Except for calcium and vitamin D, a daily vitamin–mineral supplement is recommended only for older adults suffering from malnutrition. Vitamin–mineral supplements do not reduce the incidence of cardiovascular disease or cancer (Neuhouser et al., 2009). Furthermore, supplemental nutrients and herbs identified as "cognitive enhancers"—including B and E vitamins, folic acid, and ginkgo biloba—do not improve cognitive functioning and neither prevent nor slow the progression of Alzheimer's disease (Aisen et al., 2008; DeKosky et al., 2008; McDaniel, Maier, & Einstein, 2002). Rather, a diet high in nutrients is most effective in fostering physical and cognitive health in late adulthood. And regularly eating fish high in polyunsaturated fatty acids (which promote vascular health) offers some protection against mental disabilities (Cannella, Savina, & Donini, 2009; Skully & Saleh, 2011).

In addition to a healthy diet, exercise continues to be a powerful health intervention. Sedentary healthy older adults up to age 80 who begin endurance training (walking, cycling, aerobic dance) show gains in vital capacity that compare favorably with those of much younger individuals. And

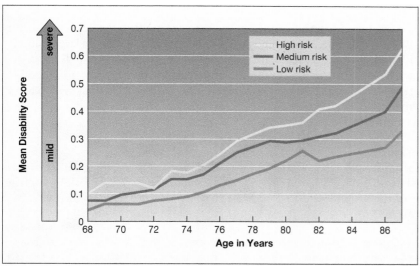

FIGURE 17.3 Development of disability in older adults with low, moderate, and high risk factors. More than 2,300 university alumni were followed from age 68 over the next two decades. The low-risk group had no risk factors (smoking, obesity, or lack of exercise). The moderate-risk group had one risk factor, and the high-risk group had two or three risk factors. Emergence of disability (at the 0.1 level) in the low-risk group was delayed by nearly 5 years compared to the moderate-risk group, and by more than 8 years compared to the high-risk group. Compression of morbidity occurred among the low-risk participants relative to their higher-risk counterparts, even though all participants were socioeconomically advantaged. (Adapted from E. F. Chakravarty et al., 2012, "Lifestyle Risk Factors Predict Disability and Death in Healthy Aging Adults," *American Journal of Medicine, 125,* p. 193. Copyright © 2012, Elsevier. Reprinted with permission from Elsevier, Inc.)

This spectacularly fit participant in the Senior Olympics has likely been exercising for most of her life. But even exercise programs begun in late adulthood can promote muscle size and strength and preservation of brain structures and behavioral capacities.

weight-bearing exercise begun in late adulthood—even as late as age 90—promotes muscle size and strength, blood flow to muscles, and ability of muscles to extract oxygen from blood (deJong & Franklin, 2004; Goldberg, Dengel, & Hagberg, 1996; Pyka et al., 1994). This translates into improved walking speed, balance, posture, and ability to carry out everyday activities, such as opening a stubborn jar lid, carrying an armload of groceries, or lifting a 30-pound grandchild.

Exercise also increases blood circulation to the brain, which helps preserve brain structures and behavioral capacities. Brain scans show that physically fit older people experience less tissue loss—in both neurons and glial cells—in diverse areas of the cerebral cortex (Erickson et al., 2010; Miller et al., 2012). And compared with physically inactive agemates, previously sedentary older adults who initiated a program of regular, moderate to vigorous exercise displayed increased activity in areas of the prefrontal cortex governing control of attention, as well as improved attention during mental testing, yielding better performance (Colcombe et al., 2004). They also showed gains in volume of the cerebral cortex—clear biological evidence for the role of physical activity in preserving central nervous system health (Colcombe et al., 2006).

Although good nutrition and physical activity are most beneficial when they are lifelong, it is never too late to change. Beginning in his sixties and until his death at age 94, Walt's Uncle Louie played tennis for an hour on most days and went ballroom dancing three nights a week. Exercise led Louie to

sustain a high sense of physical self-esteem. As a dancer, he dressed nattily and moved gracefully. He often commented on how dance and other sports could transform an older person's appearance from dowdy to elegant, expressing the beauty of the inner self.

Older people who come to value the intrinsic benefits of physical activity—feeling stronger, healthier, and more energetic—are likely to engage in it. Yet about 65 percent of U.S. 65- to 74-year-olds and 75 percent of those over age 75 do not exercise regularly (U.S. Department of Health and Human Services, 2011c). Often, those with chronic disease symptoms think "taking it easy" is the best treatment and believe that exercise actually will do harm. In planning exercise programs for older adults, it is important to instill a sense of control—by stressing the health-enhancing rewards of physical activity and by changing negative beliefs that interfere with sustained effort (Lachman, Neupert, & Agrigoroaei, 2011). Active seniors can serve as positive role models and sources of encouragement.

Sexuality

When Walt turned 60, he asked his 90-year-old Uncle Louie at what age sexual desire and activity cease. Walt's question stemmed from a widely held myth that sex drive disappears in late adulthood. Louie corrected this impression. "My sexual interest has never gone away," he explained to Walt. "I can't do it as often, and it's a quieter experience than it was in my youth. But Rachella and I have led a happy intimate life, and it's still that way."

As in other cross-sectional studies, the National Social Life, Health, and Aging Project, which surveyed a large, nationally representative sample of U.S. 57- to 85-year-olds, reported a decline in frequency of sexual activity in late adulthood—especially among women, who are less likely than men to be in

Most healthy older couples report continued, regular sexual enjoyment. In addition to intercourse, feeling sensual, enjoying close companionship, and being loved and wanted are all part of sexuality at the most advanced ages.

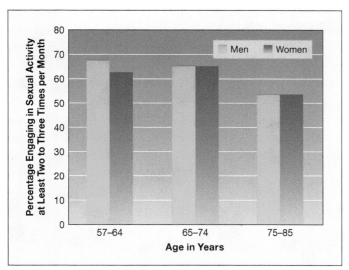

FIGURE 17.4 **Age-related changes in sexual activity among adults with an intimate partner.** In the National Social Life, Health, and Aging Project, which surveyed more than 3,000 U.S. 57- to 85-year-olds, most men and women with an intimate partner reported engaging in sexual activity (usually intercourse) at least two to three times per month. Sexual activity declined during late adulthood. Still, more than half of partnered 75- to 85-year-olds reported regular sexual activity. (Adapted from Waite et al., 2009.)

a marital or other intimate relationship. At the same time, the majority of respondents attributed at least some importance to sex, and those who had been sexually active in the previous year mostly rated sex as "very" or "extremely" important. Consistent with these attitudes, most healthy couples reported continued, regular sexual enjoyment. More than half of the oldest respondents with an intimate partner indicated that they engaged in some type of sexual activity (usually intercourse) at least two to three times per month (see Figure 17.4) (Waite et al., 2009). Note that these trends are probably influenced by cohort effects: A new generation of older adults, accustomed to viewing sexuality positively, will probably be more sexually active.

The same generalization we discussed for midlife applies to late life: Good sex in the past predicts good sex in the future. Furthermore, using intercourse as the only measure of sexual activity promotes a narrow view of pleasurable sex. Even at the most advanced ages, there is more to sexuality than the sex act itself—feeling sensual, enjoying close companionship, and being loved and wanted. Both older men and older women report that the male partner is usually the one who ceases to interact sexually (DeLamater, 2012; DeLamater & Moorman, 2007). In a culture that emphasizes an erection as necessary for being sexual, a man may withdraw from all erotic activity when he finds that erections are harder to achieve and more time must elapse between them.

Disabilities that disrupt blood flow to the penis—most often, disorders of the autonomic nervous system, cardiovascular disease, and diabetes—are largely responsible for dampening sexuality in older men. But as noted in Chapter 15, availability of drug treatments, such as Viagra, has increased men's willingness to discuss erectile dysfunction with their doctors. Cigarette smoking, excessive alcohol intake, and a variety of prescription medications also lead to diminished sexual performance. Among women, poor health and absence of a partner are major factors that reduce sexual activity (DeLamater, 2012; Huang et al., 2009). Because the sex ratio increasingly favors females, aging heterosexual women have fewer and fewer opportunities for sexual encounters. Older adults who lack partners for an extended time tend to drift into a state of sexual disinterest.

Physical Disabilities

TAKE A MOMENT... Compare the death rates shown in Figure 17.5 with those in Figure 15.2 on page 509. You will see that illness and disability climb as the end of the lifespan approaches. Cardiovascular disease and cancer remain the leading causes of death, increasing dramatically from mid- to late life. As before, death rates from heart disease and cancer are higher for men than for women, although the sex difference declines with advancing age (U.S. Census Bureau, 2012b).

Respiratory diseases, which rise sharply with age, are the third most common cause of death among the aged. Among such diseases is *emphysema*, caused by extreme loss of elasticity in lung tissue, which results in serious breathing difficulty. Although a few cases of emphysema are inherited, most result from long-term cigarette smoking. *Stroke* and *Alzheimer's disease* follow; both are unique in being more prevalent among women, largely because women live longer. Stroke occurs when

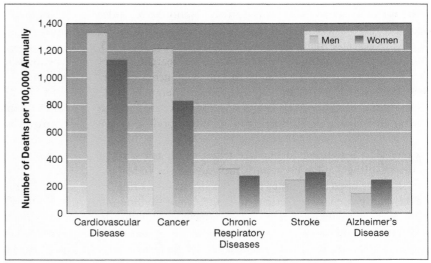

FIGURE 17.5 **Leading causes of death among people age 65 and older in the United States.** In late adulthood, heart disease is the leading cause of death, followed by cancer. Stroke (unique in being more prevalent among women), chronic respiratory diseases, pneumonia and flu, Alzheimer's disease, and unintentional injuries also claim the lives of many older adults. (Adapted from U.S. Census Bureau, 2012b.)

a blood clot blocks a blood vessel or a blood vessel hemorrhages in the brain, causing damage to brain tissue. It is a major cause of late-life disability and, after age 75, death. Alzheimer's disease, the leading cause of dementia, also rises sharply with age; we will consider it in-depth shortly.

Other diseases are less frequent killers, but they limit older adults' ability to live fully and independently. We have already noted the increase after age 65 in macular degeneration, which severely impairs vision and leads to blindness (see page 569). Osteoporosis, discussed in Chapter 15, continues to rise in late adulthood; recall that it affects the majority of men and women after age 70. Yet another bone disorder—*arthritis*—adds to the physical limitations of many older people. And *type 2 diabetes* and *unintentional injuries* also multiply in late adulthood. In the following sections, we take up these last three conditions.

Finally, an important point must be kept in mind as we discuss physical and mental disabilities of late adulthood: That these conditions are strongly *related to age* does not mean that they are *entirely caused by aging*. To clarify this distinction, experts distinguish between **primary aging** (another term for *biological aging*), or genetically influenced declines that affect all members of our species and take place even in the context of overall good health, and **secondary aging**, declines due to hereditary defects and negative environmental influences, such as poor diet, lack of exercise, disease, substance abuse, environmental pollution, and psychological stress.

Throughout this book, we have seen that it is difficult to distinguish primary from secondary aging. Undoubtedly you have, at one time or another, encountered a *frail older adult*—a person of extreme infirmity who displays wasted muscle mass and strength, weight loss, severe mobility problems, and perhaps cognitive impairment. **Frailty** involves weakened functioning of diverse organs and body systems, yielding symptoms that profoundly interfere with everyday competence—unintentional weight loss, self-reported exhaustion, muscle weakness, slow walking speed, and low physical activity. Frailty leaves older people highly vulnerable in the face of infection, extremely hot or cold weather, or injury (Masoro, 2011; Walston et al., 2006). Although primary aging contributes to frailty, researchers agree that secondary aging plays a larger role, through genetic disorders, unhealthy lifestyle, and chronic disease (Bergman et al., 2007; Fried et al., 2009). The serious conditions we are about to discuss are major sources of frailty in late adulthood.

Arthritis. Beginning in her late fifties, Ruth felt a slight morning stiffness in her neck, back, hips, and knees. In her sixties, she developed bony lumps on the end joints of her fingers. As the years passed, she experienced periodic joint swelling and some loss of flexibility—changes that affected her ability to move quickly and easily.

Arthritis, a condition of inflamed, painful, stiff, and sometimes swollen joints and muscles, becomes more common in late adulthood. It occurs in several forms. Ruth has **osteoarthritis**, the most common type, which involves deteriorating cartilage on the ends of bones of frequently used joints. Otherwise known

This frail 80-year-old, working with a physical therapist, suffers from wasted muscle mass and strength, weight loss, and severe mobility problems. In addition to biological aging, secondary aging—through genetic disorders, unhealthy lifestyle, and chronic disease—plays a major role in his frailty.

as "wear-and-tear arthritis" or "degenerative joint disease," it is one of the few age-related disabilities in which years of use make a difference. Although a genetic proneness exists, the disease usually does not appear until the forties or fifties. In frequently used joints, cartilage on the ends of the bones, which reduces friction during movement, gradually deteriorates. Or obesity places abnormal pressure on the joints and damages cartilage. Almost all older adults show some osteoarthritis on X-rays, although wide individual differences in severity exist (Zhang & Jordan, 2010). It is the most common cause of mobility problems and of surgical hip and knee replacements in older adults.

Unlike osteoarthritis, which is limited to certain joints, **rheumatoid arthritis** involves the whole body. An autoimmune response leads to inflammation of connective tissue, particularly the membranes that line the joints, resulting in overall stiffness, inflammation, and aching. Tissue in the cartilage tends to grow, damaging surrounding ligaments, muscles, and bones. The result is deformed joints and often serious loss of mobility. Sometimes other organs, such as the heart and lungs, are affected (Goronzy, Shao, & Weyand, 2010). Worldwide, about ½ to 1 percent of older adults have rheumatoid arthritis.

Overall, disability due to arthritis affects 45 percent of U.S. men over age 65 and rises modestly with age. Among women, the incidence is higher and increases sharply with age: About 50 percent of 65- to 84-year-olds and 70 percent of those over age 85 are affected (U.S. Census Bureau, 2012b). Although rheumatoid arthritis can strike at any age, it rises after age 60. Twin studies support a strong hereditary contribution. Presence of certain genes heightens disease risk, possibly by triggering a late-life defect in the immune system (Turesson & Matteson, 2006). However, identical twins differ widely in disease severity, indicating that environment makes a difference. So far, cigarette smoking is the only confirmed lifestyle influence, greatly increasing risk in people without a family history of the disease (Klareskog et al., 2006). Early treatment with powerful anti-inflammatory medications helps slow progression of rheumatoid arthritis.

Managing arthritis requires a balance of rest when the disease flares, pain relief, and physical activity. Regular aerobic exercise and strength training lessen pain and improve physical functioning (Semanik, Chang, & Dunlop, 2012). In obese people, weight loss is essential. Although osteoarthritis responds to these interventions more easily than rheumatoid arthritis, the course of each varies greatly. With proper analgesic medication, joint protection, lifestyle changes, and surgery to replace badly damaged hip or knee joints, many people with either form of the illness lead long, productive lives.

Diabetes.
After a meal, the body breaks down the food, releasing glucose (the primary energy source for cell activity) into the bloodstream. Insulin, produced by the pancreas, keeps the blood concentration of glucose within set limits by stimulating muscle and fat cells to absorb it. When this balance system fails, either because not enough insulin is produced or because body cells become insensitive to it, *type 2 diabetes* (otherwise known as *diabetes mellitus*) results. Over time, abnormally high blood glucose damages the blood vessels, increasing the risk of heart attack, stroke, circulatory problems in the legs (which impair balance and gait), and injury to the eyes, kidneys, and nerves.

Excessive blood glucose also reduces blood flow to the hippocampus, a brain structure that plays an important role in memory (see page 218 in Chapter 7) (Wu et al., 2008). In several longitudinal studies, diabetes was associated with more rapid cognitive declines in older people and an elevated risk of dementia, especially Alzheimer's disease—an association we will soon revisit when we take up Alzheimer's (Cole, Astell, & Sutherland, 2007; Williams, McNeilly, & Sutherland, 2012). Impaired glucose tolerance accelerates degeneration of neurons and synapses (Petrofsky, Berk, & Al-Nakhli, 2012). Cognitive deficits may even be under way in the prediabetic state, prior to a diabetic diagnosis.

From middle to late adulthood, the incidence of type 2 diabetes nearly doubles; it affects 20 percent of Americans age 65 and older (U.S. Census Bureau, 2012b). Diabetes runs in families, suggesting that heredity is involved. But inactivity and abdominal fat deposits greatly increase the risk. Higher rates of type 2 diabetes—exceeding 30 percent—are found among African-American, Mexican-American, and Native-American seniors for both genetic and environmental reasons, including high-fat diets and obesity associated with poverty.

Treating type 2 diabetes requires lifestyle changes, including a carefully controlled diet, regular exercise, and weight loss (Meneilly, 2006). By promoting glucose absorption and reducing abdominal fat, physical activity lessens disease symptoms.

Unintentional Injuries.
At age 65 and older, the death rate from unintentional injuries is at an all-time high—more than twice as great as in adolescence and early adulthood. Motor vehicle collisions and falls are largely responsible.

Motor Vehicle Accidents.
Motor vehicle collisions account for only one-fourth of U.S. injury mortality in late life, compared with one-half in middle adulthood. But a look at individual drivers tells a different story. Older adults have higher rates of traffic violations, accidents, and fatalities per mile driven than any other age group, with the exception of drivers under age 25. The high rate of injury persists, even though many older people, especially women, limit their driving after noticing that their ability to drive safely is slipping. Deaths due to injuries—motor vehicle and otherwise—continue to be much higher for men than for women (U.S. Census Bureau, 2012b).

Recall that visual declines led Walt to have difficulty seeing the dashboard and identifying pedestrians at night. The greater older adults' visual processing difficulties, the higher their rate of moving violations and crashes (Friedman et al., 2013). Compared with young drivers, older people are less likely to drive quickly and recklessly but more likely to fail to heed signs, yield the right of way, and turn appropriately. They often try to compensate for their difficulties by being more cautious. Slowed reaction time and indecisiveness pose hazards, too. In Chapter 15, we noted that with age, adults find it harder to attend selectively, engage in two activities at once, and switch back and forth between tasks—skills essential for safe driving (Makishita & Matsunaga, 2008). Hence, they are at high risk for collisions at busy intersections and in other complex traffic situations.

Nevertheless, older people usually try to drive as long as possible. Giving up driving results in loss of freedom, control over one's life, and self-esteem. Specially trained driver rehabilitation consultants—affiliated with hospitals, drivers licensing agencies, or U.S. Area Agencies on Aging (see page 67 in Chapter 2)—can help assess older adults' capacity to continue

Visual processing difficulties, slowed reaction time, and declines in selective attention contribute to the high rates of traffic violations, accidents, and fatalities per mile driven among older people. Still, seniors usually try to drive as long as possible.

driving, provide driver retraining, or counsel them to retire from driving and to arrange other transportation options.

Older adults also make up more than 30 percent of all U.S. pedestrian deaths (U.S. Census Bureau, 2012b). Confusing intersections, especially signals that do not allow older people enough time to cross the street, are often involved.

Falls. One day, Ruth fell down the basement steps and lay there with a broken ankle until Walt arrived home an hour later. Ruth's tumble represents the leading type of accident in late life. About 30 percent of adults over age 65 and 50 percent over age 80 have experienced a fall within the last year. Declines in vision, hearing, mobility, muscle strength, and cognitive functioning; depressed mood; use of medications that affect mental processing; and development of certain chronic illnesses, such as arthritis—all of which make it harder to avoid hazards and keep one's balance—increase the risk of falling (Rubenstein, Stevens, & Scott, 2008). The more of these factors that are present, the greater the risk of falling.

Because of weakened bones and difficulty breaking a fall, serious injury results about 10 percent of the time. Among the most common is hip fracture. It increases fifteenfold from age 65 to 85 and is associated with a 20 percent increase in mortality (Centers for Disease Control and Prevention, 2010). Of those who survive, half never regain the ability to walk without assistance.

Falling can also impair health indirectly, by promoting fear of falling. Almost half of older adults who have fallen admit that they purposefully avoid activities because they are afraid of falling again. In this way, a fall can limit mobility and social contact, undermining both physical and psychological well-being (Painter et al., 2012). Although an active lifestyle may expose older people to more situations that can cause a fall, the health benefits of activity far outweigh the risk of serious injury due to falling.

Preventing Unintentional Injuries. Many steps can be taken to reduce unintentional injury in late adulthood. Designing motor vehicles and street signs to accommodate seniors' visual needs is a goal for the future. Meanwhile, training that enhances visual and cognitive skills essential for safe driving and that helps older adults avoid high-risk situations (such as busy intersections and rush hour) can save lives.

Similarly, efforts to prevent falls must address risks within the person and the environment—through corrective eyewear, strength and balance training, and improved safety in homes and communities. Consult the National Resource Center for Safe Aging, *www.safeaging.org*, for a wealth of information on senior safety.

Mental Disabilities

Normal age-related cell death in the brain, described earlier, does not lead to loss of ability to engage in everyday activities. But when cell death and structural and chemical abnormalities are profound, serious deterioration of mental and motor functions occurs.

Dementia refers to a set of disorders occurring almost entirely in old age in which many aspects of thought and behavior are so impaired that everyday activities are disrupted. Dementia strikes 13 percent of adults over age 65. Approximately 2 to 3 percent of people age 65 to 69 are affected; the rate doubles every 5 to 6 years until it reaches about 22 percent among those age 85 to 89 and over half after age 90—trends that apply to the United States and other Western nations (Prince et al., 2013). Beyond age 80, a larger proportion of women than men have dementia, perhaps reflecting the biological sturdiness of the oldest men. Although dementia rates are similar across most ethnic groups, older African Americans have about twice the incidence, and Hispanics about one and one-half times the incidence, as whites (Alzheimer's Association, 2012b). Associated risk factors, not race, are responsible, as we will see shortly.

About a dozen types of dementia have been identified. Some are reversible with proper treatment, but most are irreversible and incurable. A few forms, such as Parkinson's disease,[1] involve deterioration in subcortical brain regions (primitive structures below the cortex) that often extends to the cerebral cortex and, in many instances, results in brain abnormalities resembling Alzheimer's disease. Research suggests that Parkinson's and Alzheimer's are related (Cai et al., 2012). But in the large majority of dementia cases, subcortical brain regions are intact, and progressive damage occurs only to the cerebral cortex. The two most common forms of *cortical dementia* are Alzheimer's disease and cerebrovascular dementia.

Alzheimer's Disease. When Ruth took 79-year-old Ida to the ballet, an occasion the two sisters anticipated eagerly each year, she noticed a change in Ida's behavior. Ida, who had forgotten the engagement, reacted angrily when Ruth arrived unannounced at her door. Driving to the theater, which was in a familiar part of town, Ida got lost—all the while insisting that she knew the way perfectly. As the lights dimmed and the music began, Ida talked loudly and dug noisily in her purse.

"Shhhhhh," responded a dozen voices from surrounding seats.

"It's just the music!" Ida snapped at full volume. "You can talk all you want until the dancing starts." Ruth was astonished and embarrassed at the behavior of her once socially sensitive sister.

Six months later, Ida was diagnosed with **Alzheimer's disease**, the most common form of dementia, in which structural and chemical brain deterioration is associated with gradual loss of many aspects of thought and behavior. Alzheimer's accounts for 60 percent of all dementia cases and, at older ages, for an even higher percentage. Approximately 8 to 10 percent

---

[1]In Parkinson's disease, neurons in the part of the brain that controls muscle movements deteriorate. Symptoms include tremors, shuffling gait, loss of facial expression, rigidity of limbs, difficulty maintaining balance, and stooped posture.

of people over age 65—about 5.2 million Americans—have the disorder. Of those over age 85, close to 45 percent are affected. In 2030, when all baby boomers will have reached late adulthood, the number of Americans with Alzheimer's is expected to rise to 7.7 million—an increase of more than 50 percent. About 5 to 15 percent of all deaths among older adults involve Alzheimer's, making it a significant cause of late-life mortality (Alzheimer's Association, 2012b).

Symptoms and Course of the Disease.

The earliest symptoms are often severe memory problems—forgetting names, dates, appointments, familiar routes of travel, or the need to turn off the kitchen stove. At first, recent memory is most impaired, but as serious disorientation sets in, recall of distant events and such basic facts as time, date, and place evaporates. Faulty judgment puts the person in danger. For example, Ida insisted on driving after she was no longer competent to do so. Personality changes occur—loss of spontaneity and sparkle, anxiety in response to uncertainties created by mental problems, aggressive outbursts, reduced initiative, and social withdrawal. Depression often appears in the early phase of Alzheimer's and other forms of dementia and seems to be part of the disease process (Serra et al., 2010; Yaari & Corey-Bloom, 2007). However, depression may worsen as the older adult reacts to disturbing mental changes.

As the disease progresses, skilled and purposeful movements disintegrate. When Ruth took Ida into her home, she had to help her dress, bathe, eat, brush her teeth, and (eventually) walk and use the bathroom. Ida's sleep was disrupted by delusions and imaginary fears. She often awoke in the night and banged on the wall, insisting that it was dinnertime, or cried out that someone was choking her. Over time, Ida lost the ability to comprehend and produce speech. And when her brain ceased to process information, she could no longer recognize objects and familiar people. In the final months, Ida became increasingly vulnerable to infections, lapsed into a coma, and died.

The course of Alzheimer's varies greatly, from a year to as long as 20 years, with those diagnosed in their sixties and early seventies typically surviving longer than those diagnosed at later ages (Brodaty, Seeher, & Gibson, 2012; Rait et al., 2010). The average life expectancy for a 70-year-old man with the disease is about 4½ years, for a 70-year-old woman about 8 years.

Brain Deterioration.

A diagnosis of Alzheimer's disease is made through exclusion, after ruling out other causes of dementia by a physical examination and psychological testing—an approach that is more than 90 percent accurate. To confirm Alzheimer's, doctors inspect the brain after death for a set of abnormalities that either cause or result from the disease (Hyman et al., 2012). In about 90 percent of cases, however, brain-imaging techniques (MRI and PET), which yield three-dimensional pictures of brain volume and activity, predict whether individuals will receive an after-death confirmation of Alzheimer's (Vitali et al., 2008). Researchers are also tracking changes in the chemical makeup of the blood and cerebrospinal

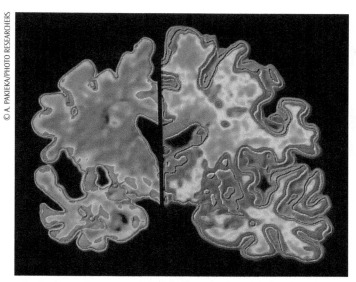

© A. PASIEKA/PHOTO RESEARCHERS

Computer images compare a brain scan of an Alzheimer's patient (left) with one of a healthy older adult (right). The Alzheimer's brain is shrunken, due to massive degeneration and death of neurons. Activity and blood flow (coded yellow and green in the right scan) are also greatly reduced in the Alzheimer's brain.

fluid in an effort to predict Alzheimer's long before cognitive symptoms appear (Sperling et al., 2011). These procedures offer hope of very early diagnosis, opening the door to more successful interventions.

Two major structural changes in the cerebral cortex, especially in memory and reasoning areas, are associated with Alzheimer's. Inside neurons, **neurofibrillary tangles** appear—bundles of twisted threads that are the product of collapsed neural structures and that contain abnormal forms of a protein called *tau*. Outside neurons, **amyloid plaques**, dense deposits of a deteriorated protein called *amyloid*, surrounded by clumps of dead nerve and glial cells, develop. Although some neurofibrillary tangles and amyloid plaques are present in the brains of normal middle-aged and older people and increase with age, they are far more abundant in Alzheimer's victims. A major thrust of current research is understanding exactly how abnormal amyloid and tau damage neurons, so treatments can be developed to slow or block these processes.

Researchers once thought that amyloid plaques contributed to the neuronal damage of Alzheimer's. But recent findings suggest that they reflect the brain's effort to get harmful amyloid away from neurons. Instead, a major culprit seems to be abnormal breakdown of amyloid remaining *within* neurons (National Institute on Aging, 2012). In both Alzheimer's disease and Parkinson's disease, disruptions occur in a key neuronal process responsible for chopping up and disposing of abnormal proteins (Cai et al., 2012). These damaged proteins (including amyloid) build to toxic levels. Studies suggest that abnormal amyloid causes the generation of signals within neurons and their transfer across synapses to malfunction (Kopeikina et al., 2011; Palop et al., 2007). Eventually, damaged

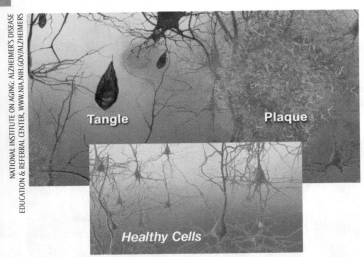

An image of tissue in the Alzheimer's brain reveals amyloid plaques between neurons, and dead and dying neurons containing neuro-fibrillary tangles. Compare these cell changes with healthy brain cells.

amyloid induces heightened, abnormal electrical activity throughout the brain, contributing to broad neural network malfunctioning.

Abnormal tau in neurofibrillary tangles adds to neuronal breakdown. Tangles disrupt the transport of nutrients and signals from the neuron to its connective fibers, thereby joining with amyloid to block synaptic communication. Furthermore, abnormal tau triggers disintegration of nearby normal tau (de Calignon et al., 2012; Liu et al., 2012). Gradually, tau pathology moves across synapses, spreading from neuron to neuron and, over time, from one brain region to the next—thereby amplifying damage.

As synapses deteriorate, levels of neurotransmitters decline, neurons die in massive numbers, and brain volume shrinks. Destruction of neurons that release the neurotransmitter acetylcholine, involved in transporting messages between distant brain regions, further disrupts neuronal networks. A drop in serotonin, a neurotransmitter that regulates arousal and mood, may contribute to sleep disturbances, aggressive outbursts, and depression (Rothman & Mattson, 2012). These problems may intensify cognitive and motor symptoms.

Risk Factors. Alzheimer's disease comes in two types: *familial*, which runs in families, and *sporadic*, which has no obvious family history. Familial Alzheimer's generally has an early onset—between ages 30 and 60—and progresses more rapidly than the later-appearing sporadic type, which typically appears after age 65. Researchers have identified genes on chromosomes 1, 14, and 21, involved in generation of harmful amyloid, that are related to familial Alzheimer's. In each case, the abnormal gene is dominant; if it is present in only one of the pair of genes inherited from parents, the person will develop early-onset Alzheimer's (Ertekin-Tanner, 2007; National Institute on Aging, 2012). Recall that chromosome 21 is involved in

Down syndrome. Individuals with this chromosomal disorder who live past age 40 almost always have the brain abnormalities and symptoms of Alzheimer's.

Heredity plays a different role in sporadic Alzheimer's, through somatic mutation. About half of people with this form of the disease have an abnormal gene on chromosome 19, which results in excess levels of *ApoE4*, a blood protein that carries cholesterol throughout the body. Researchers believe that a high blood concentration of ApoE4 affects the expression of a gene involved in regulating insulin. Deficient insulin and resulting glucose buildup in the bloodstream (conditions that, when extreme, lead to diabetes) are linked to brain damage, especially in areas regulating memory, and to high buildup of harmful amyloid in brain tissue (Liu et al., 2013; National Institute on Aging, 2012). In line with these findings, individuals with diabetes have a greatly increased risk of developing Alzheimer's.

At present, the abnormal ApoE4 gene is the most commonly known risk factor for sporadic Alzheimer's. But genetic testing has revealed many other genes that seem to make an equal or greater contribution. For example, in older adults with Alzheimer's, genes involved in clearing amyloid from neurons often are altered, enabling excessive amyloid buildup (Weeraratna et al., 2007). And some genes impair nutrient and signal transfer from neurons to connective fibers, without affecting amyloid (Conejero-Goldberg et al., 2011).

Nevertheless, many sporadic Alzheimer's victims show no known genetic marker, and some individuals with the ApoE4 gene do not develop the disease. Evidence is increasing for the role of a variety of other factors in susceptibility to Alzheimer's, including excess dietary fat, physical inactivity, overweight and obesity, smoking, chronic psychological stress, cardiovascular disease, stroke, and (as just noted) diabetes (Kivipelto et al., 2008; Pendlebury & Rothwell, 2009; Whitmer et al., 2008; Yaffe et al., 2011). Moderate to severe head injuries, possibly by accelerating deterioration of amyloid and tau, also increase Alzheimer's risk, especially among people with the ApoE4 gene (Jellinger, 2004). Individuals subjected to repeated instances, such as boxers, football players, and combat veterans, are especially likely to be affected.

Still, some older adults with an abundance of amyloid plaques in their brains never develop Alzheimer's (Rowe et al., 2007). The disease probably results from different combinations of genetic and environmental factors, each leading to a somewhat different course of the disease. The high incidence of Alzheimer's and other forms of dementia among African Americans illustrates the complexity of potential causes.

Compared with African Americans, Yoruba village dwellers of Nigeria show a much lower Alzheimer's incidence and no association between the ApoE4 gene and the disease (Gureje et al., 2006). Some investigators speculate that intermarriage with Caucasians heightened genetic risk among African Americans and that environmental factors translated that risk into reality (Hendrie, 2001). Whereas the Yoruba of Nigeria eat a low-fat diet, the African-American diet is high in fat. Eating fatty foods may increase the chances that the ApoE4 gene will lead to Alzheimer's. And even for Yoruba and African Americans without the ApoE4 gene, a high-fat diet is risky (Hall et al., 2006). The more fat consumed and the higher the blood level of "bad" cholesterol (low-density lipoproteins), the greater the incidence of Alzheimer's.

Protective Factors. Researchers are testing both drug and nondrug approaches to preventing or slowing the progress of Alzheimer's. Among promising drug therapies is immune globulin, a blood product delivered intravenously that contains naturally occurring antibodies against harmful amyloid (National Institute on Aging, 2012). Preliminary research suggests that it improves cognitive functioning and reduces amyloid buildup in the brain. Insulin therapy, delivered via a nasal spray to the brain, helps regulate neuronal use of glucose (Craft et al., 2012). New findings indicate that it has memory benefits and slows cognitive decline—at least in the short term—among older adults with mild cognitive impairment, which commonly precedes Alzheimer's.

A "Mediterranean diet" emphasizing fish, unsaturated fat (olive oil), and moderate consumption of red wine is linked to a 13 percent reduced incidence of Alzheimer's disease, to slower disease progression in diagnosed individuals, and also to a reduction in cerebrovascular dementia (which we will turn to next) (Scarmeas et al., 2007; Sofi et al., 2008). These foods contain fatty acids, antioxidants, and other substances that help promote the health of the cardiovascular and central nervous systems.

Education and an active lifestyle are beneficial as well. The rate of Alzheimer's is reduced by more than half in older adults with higher education, though this protective effect is not as great for those with the ApoE4 gene (Seeman et al., 2005; Stern, 2009). Some researchers speculate that the complex cognitive activities of better-educated people lead to more synaptic connections, which act as a *cognitive reserve,* giving the aging brain greater tolerance for injury before it crosses the threshold into mental disability. In support of this view, compared to their less educated counterparts, the highly educated display a faster rate of decline following an Alzheimer's diagnosis, suggesting that they show symptoms only after very advanced brain deterioration (Hall et al., 2007). Late-life engagement in cognitively stimulating social and leisure activities also reduces the risk of Alzheimer's and of dementia in general, perhaps by stimulating synaptic growth (Bennett et al., 2006; Hall et al., 2009).

Finally, persistence, intensity, and variety of physical activity are associated with decreased risk of Alzheimer's and cerebrovascular dementia, with larger benefits for older people with the ApoE4 gene. In longitudinal research, exercising regularly in midlife predicted reduced late-life dementia, after many other dementia-linked lifestyle factors were controlled (Ahlskog et al., 2011; Smith et al., 2013). Beginning regular exercise in late life is also protective. In one investigation, older adults with mild cognitive impairment and therefore judged to be at risk for Alzheimer's were randomly assigned to either a 24-week home-based physical activity program or to a usual home-care control group (Lautenschlager et al., 2008). At a six-month follow-up, those experiencing the intervention continued to engage in regular exercise and showed slight cognitive improvement, whereas controls had declined in cognitive functioning.

Helping Alzheimer's Victims and Their Caregivers. As Ida's Alzheimer's worsened, the doctor prescribed a mild sedative and an antidepressant to help control her behavior. Drugs that increase levels of the neurotransmitters acetylcholine and serotonin show promise in limiting challenging dementia symptoms—especially agitation and disruptiveness, which are particularly stressful for caregivers (National Institute on Aging, 2012). Providing stimulation through engaging activities, exercise, and sensory experiences (touch, music, and videos) also helps reduce inappropriate behaviors (Camp, Cohen-Mansfield, & Capezuti, 2002).

But with no cure available, family interventions ensure the best adjustment possible for the Alzheimer's victim, spouse, and other relatives. Dementia caregivers devote substantially more time to caregiving and experience more stress than do people caring for older adults with physical disabilities (Alzheimer's Association, 2012b). They need assistance and encouragement from extended-family members, friends, and community agencies. The Social Issues: Health box on pages 586–587 describes a variety of helpful interventions for family caregivers. In addition to these strategies, avoiding dramatic changes in living conditions, such as moving to a new location, rearranging furniture, or modifying daily routines, helps people with Alzheimer's disease feel as secure as possible in a cognitive world that is gradually disintegrating.

LOOK AND LISTEN

Investigate formal respite services, providing temporary relief to caregivers of older adults with dementia, in your community. Visit a respite program, and talk to several family caregivers about its impact on the patient's and their own adjustment. ●

Cerebrovascular Dementia. In **cerebrovascular dementia**, a series of strokes leaves areas of dead brain cells, producing step-by-step degeneration of mental ability, with each step occurring abruptly after a stroke. Approximately 10 to 20 percent of all cases of dementia in Western nations are cerebrovascular, and about 10 percent are due to a combination of Alzheimer's and repeated strokes (Gorelick et al., 2011).

Cerebrovascular dementia results from a combination of genetic and environmental forces. The effects of heredity are indirect, through high blood pressure, cardiovascular disease, and diabetes, each of which increases the risk of stroke. And environmental influences—including cigarette smoking, heavy alcohol use, high salt intake, very low dietary protein, obesity, inactivity, and psychological stress—also heighten stroke risk (Sahathevan, Brodtmann, & Donnan, 2011).

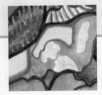

Social Issues: Health

Interventions for Caregivers of Older Adults with Dementia

Margaret, wife and caregiver of a 71-year-old Alzheimer's patient, sent a desperate plea to an advice columnist at her local newspaper: "My husband can't feed or bathe himself, or speak to anyone or ask for assistance. I must constantly anticipate his needs and try to meet them. Please help me. I'm at the end of my rope."

The effects of Alzheimer's disease are devastating not just to victims but also to family members who provide care with little or no outside assistance. Caregiving under these conditions has been called the "36-hour day" because of its constant demands. Although the majority of home caregivers are middle-aged, an estimated nearly 25 percent are older adults caring for a spouse or an aging parent. One-third of them are in poor health themselves, yet the number of hours dedicated to caregiving increases with caregiver age and is especially high among ethnic minority older adults, whose cultures emphasize care as a family obligation (Alzheimer's Association, 2012a).

Family members who exceed their caregiving capacities suffer greatly in physical and mental health and are at risk for early mortality (Sörensen & Pinquart, 2005). Severity of cognitive impairments and behavior problems in care recipients are strong predictors of weakening caregiver health. And the close relationship between the caregiver and the suffering individual—involving shared memories, experiences, and emotions—seems to heighten caregiver risk for physical and psychological problems (Monin & Schulz, 2009).

Most communities offer interventions designed to support family caregivers, but they need to be expanded and made more cost-effective. Those that work best address multiple needs: knowledge, coping strategies, caregiving skills, and respite.

Knowledge

Virtually all interventions try to enhance knowledge about the disease, caregiving challenges, and available community assistance. Knowledge is usually delivered through classes, but websites with wide-ranging information on caregiving, and online message boards and chat rooms through which caregivers can share information, also exist. Gains in knowledge, however, must be combined with other approaches to improve caregivers' well-being.

This daughter cares for her father, who has Alzheimer's disease. Although the task has compensating rewards, it is physically demanding and emotionally draining. A great need exists for interventions that support caregivers.

Coping Strategies

Many interventions teach caregivers everyday problem-solving strategies for managing the dependent person's behavior, along with techniques for dealing with their own negative thoughts and feelings, such as resentment about having to provide constant care. Modes of delivery include support groups, individual therapy, and "coping with frustration" classes. All yield improvements in caregivers' adjustment and in patients' disturbing behaviors, both immediately and in follow-ups more than a year

---

Because of their greater susceptibility to cardiovascular disease, more men than women have cerebrovascular dementia (Ruitenberg et al., 2001). The disease also varies among countries. For example, deaths due to stroke are high in Japan. Although a low-fat diet reduces Japanese adults' risk of cardiovascular disease, high intake of alcohol and salt and a diet very low in animal protein increase the risk of stroke. As Japanese consumption of alcohol and salt declined and intake of meat rose in recent decades, rates of cerebrovascular dementia and stroke-caused deaths dropped (Jellinger, 2008; Sekita et al., 2010). However, they remain higher than in other developed nations.

Although Japan presents a unique, contradictory picture (there, cardiovascular disease is low, and stroke is high), in most cases cerebrovascular dementia is caused by atherosclerosis. Prevention is the only effective way to stop the disease. The incidence of cerebrovascular dementia has dropped in the last two decades, largely as a result of the decline in heart disease and more effective stroke prevention methods (U.S. Department of Health and Human Services, 2011c). Signs that a stroke might be coming are weakness, tingling, or numbness in an arm, a leg, or the face; sudden vision loss or double vision; speech difficulty; and severe dizziness and imbalance. Doctors may prescribe drugs to reduce the tendency of the blood to clot.

later (Selwood et al., 2007). Individual approaches are most effective because assistance can be tailored to the specific caregiver–patient situation.

Caregiving Skills

Caregivers benefit from lessons in how to communicate with older adults who can no longer express thoughts and emotions clearly and handle everyday tasks—for example, sustaining good eye contact to convey interest and caring; speaking slowly, with short, simple words; using gestures to reinforce meaning; waiting patiently for a response; refraining from interrupting, correcting, criticizing, or talking about the older adult as if he or she isn't there; and introducing pleasant activities, such as music and slow-paced children's TV programs, that relieve agitation (Alzheimer's Association, 2012a). Interventions that teach communication skills through active practice reduce patients' troublesome behavior and, as a result, lessen caregivers' distress and boost their sense of self-efficacy (Done & Thomas, 2001; Irvine, Ary, & Bourgeois, 2003).

Respite

Caregivers usually say that *respite*—time away from providing care—is the assistance they most desire. But they may be reluctant to accept friends' and relatives' informal offers to help because of guilt, or to use formal services (such as adult day care or temporary placement in a care facility) because of cost or worries about the older

adult's adjustment. Yet respite at least twice a week for several hours improves physical and mental health for most caregivers by enabling them to maintain friendships, engage in enjoyable activities, and sustain a balanced life (Jeon, Brodaty, & Chesterson, 2005; Lund et al., 2010).

For respite to be most effective, caregivers must start using services before they become overwhelmed. Once a rewarding, enjoyable life has been lost, it is difficult to restore. Furthermore, frequent, regular respite is far more helpful than infrequent, irregular use. And planning how best to use respite time is crucial. Caregivers who end up spending respite hours doing housework, shopping, or working usually remain dissatisfied (Lund et al., 2009). Those who engage in activities they had wanted and planned to do gain in psychological well-being.

In addition to time away from the caregiving situation, caregivers benefit from short periods of relief from the unrelenting demands of in-home care. One group of researchers devised a unique tool called Video Respite—a series of videotapes suited to the interests of Alzheimer's patients that provide caregivers with a half-hour to an hour break. On each tape, an actor conducts a slow-paced, simple conversation about familiar experiences, people, and objects, pausing occasionally for the impaired person to respond (Lund et al., 1995). Evaluations show that the videos capture the attention of people with Alzheimer's and reduce problem behaviors, such as wandering, agitation, and aggression.

Intervention Programs

Multifaceted intervention programs that begin early in the caregiving process, that continue for many weeks or months, and that are tailored to caregivers' individual needs greatly reduce stress while helping them find satisfactions in caring for a declining loved one. And such interventions usually delay institutional placement of dementia patients as well.

The Resources for Enhancing Alzheimer's Caregiver Health (REACH) initiative was an evaluation of nine "active" intervention programs, each including some or all of the ingredients just described, versus five "passive" interventions providing only information and referral to community agencies. Among more than 1,200 participating caregivers, those receiving six months of active intervention declined more in self-reported burden. And one program providing family therapy in the home—through a telephone system facilitating frequent communication among therapist, caregiver, family members, and other support systems—substantially reduced caregiver depressive symptoms (Gitlin et al., 2003; Schultz et al., 2003). Caregivers with greater care responsibility—women versus men, lower-SES versus higher-SES, spouses versus nonspouses—benefited most from active intervention. In an additional evaluation with more than 600 participants, REACH active intervention programs enhanced quality of life among caregivers of diverse ethnicities—African American, Caucasian, and Hispanic (Belle et al., 2006).

Once strokes occur, paralysis and loss of speech, vision, coordination, memory, and other mental abilities are common.

Misdiagnosed and Reversible Dementia. Careful diagnosis of dementia is crucial because other disorders can be mistaken for it. And some forms of dementia can be treated and a few reversed.

Depression is the disorder most often misdiagnosed as dementia. The depressed (but not demented) older adult is likely to exaggerate his or her mental difficulties, whereas the demented person minimizes them and is not fully aware of cognitive declines. About 1 to 2 percent of people over age 65

are severely depressed, and another 2 percent are moderately depressed—rates lower than those for young and middle-aged adults (Nordhus, 2008). As we will see in Chapter 18, however, depression rises with age. It is often related to physical illness and pain and can lead to cognitive deterioration. As at younger ages, the support of family members and friends, antidepressant medication, and individual, family, and group therapy can help relieve depression. However, U.S. older adults often do not receive the mental health services they need—partly because Medicare offers reduced coverage for treating mental health problems and partly because doctors rarely refer seniors for mental health services (Robinson, 2010). These circumstances

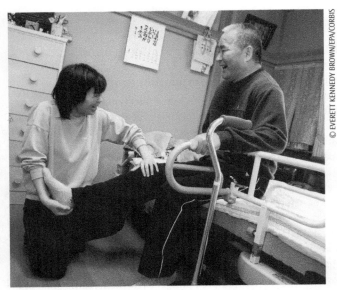

Depression—often related to physical illness and pain—may be misdiagnosed as dementia. With his therapist's support, this senior has a good chance of avoiding depression during his slow recovery from a leg injury.

increase the chances that depression will deepen and be confused with dementia.

The older we get, the more likely we are to be taking drugs that may have side effects resembling dementia. For example, some medications for coughs, diarrhea, and nausea inhibit the neurotransmitter acetylcholine, leading to Alzheimer's-like symptoms. In addition, some diseases can cause temporary memory loss and mental symptoms, especially among older people, who often become confused and withdrawn when ill (Fong, Tulevaev, & Inouye, 2009). Treatment of the underlying illness relieves the problem. Finally, environmental changes and social isolation can trigger mental declines (Hawton et al., 2011). When supportive ties are restored, cognitive functioning usually bounces back.

Health Care

Health-care professionals and lawmakers in industrialized nations worry about the economic consequences of rapid increase in the older population. Rising government-supported health-care costs and demand for certain health-care services, particularly long-term care, are of greatest concern.

Cost of Health Care for Older Adults.
Adults age 65 and older make up just 13 percent of the American population but account for over 40 percent of government health-care spending (U.S. Department of Health and Human Services, 2012d). According to current estimates, the cost of government-sponsored health insurance, or Medicare, for older people will nearly double by 2020 as more baby boomers enter late adulthood and average life expectancy extends further (Centers for Medicare and Medicaid Services, 2012).

Medicare expenses rise steeply with age. People age 75 and older receive, on average, 70 percent more benefits than younger senior citizens. Most of this increase reflects the need for long-term care—in hospitals and nursing homes—resulting from an age-related rise in disabling chronic diseases and acute illnesses. Because Medicare funds only about half of older adults' medical needs, American seniors spend several times as much on health care as their counterparts do in other industrialized nations (OECD, 2012b). And Medicare provides far less support for long-term care than U.S. older people with severe disabilities need.

Long-Term Care.
When Ida moved into Ruth's home, Ruth promised never to place Ida in an institution. But as Ida's condition worsened and Ruth faced health problems of her own, she couldn't keep her word. Ida needed round-the-clock monitoring. Reluctantly, Ruth placed her in a nursing home.

Advancing age is strongly associated with use of long-term care services, especially nursing homes. Nearly half of U.S. nursing home residents are age 85 and older (Centers for Disease Control and Prevention, 2012). Among disorders of aging, dementia—especially Alzheimer's disease—most often leads to nursing home placement, followed by arthritis, hip fracture, and stroke (Agüero-Torres et al., 2001). Greater use of nursing homes is also prompted by loss of informal caregiving support through widowhood—which mostly affects women—and aging of adult children and other relatives.

Overall, only 5 percent of Americans age 65 and older are institutionalized, about half the rate in other industrialized nations, such as the Netherlands and Sweden, which provide more generous public financing of institutional care (OECD, 2012). Unless nursing home placement follows hospitalization for an acute illness, older adults must pay for it until their resources are exhausted. At that point, Medicaid (health insur-

In a nursing home in the Netherlands, a patient enjoys moving landscapes displayed on a screen in an area resembling a train compartment. Institutional care is more common in other industrialized nations than in the United States, where Medicare usually does not cover it.

A resident greets a server in the dining room of an assisted living facility. This homelike environment enhances older adults' autonomy, social life, community involvement, and life satisfaction.

ance for the poor) takes over. Consequently, the largest users of nursing homes in the United States are people with either very low or high incomes. Middle-income seniors and their families are more likely to try to protect their savings from being drained by high nursing home costs.

Nursing home use also varies across ethnic groups. For example, Caucasian Americans are nearly twice as likely as African Americans to be institutionalized. African-American older adults are more likely to have large, close-knit extended families with a strong sense of caregiving responsibility and who care for them at home. Similarly, Asian, Hispanic, and Native-American seniors use nursing homes less often than Caucasian Americans (Andel, Hyer, & Slack, 2007; Yaffe et al., 2002). Overall, families provide at least 60 to 80 percent of all long-term care in Australia, Canada, New Zealand, the United States, and Western Europe. As we have seen, families of diverse ethnic and SES backgrounds willingly step in to care for older people in times of need.

To reduce institutionalized care of older adults and its associated high cost, experts advocate alternatives, such as publicly funded in-home help for family caregivers (see Chapter 16, page 551). Another option that has increased dramatically over the past two decades is **assisted living**—a homelike housing arrangement for seniors who require more care than can be provided at home but less than is usually provided in nursing homes. Assisted living is a cost-effective alternative to nursing homes that prevents unnecessary institutionalization (Stone & Reinhard, 2007). It also can enhance residents' autonomy, social life, community involvement, and life satisfaction—benefits that we will take up in Chapter 18.

In Denmark, the combination of a government-sponsored home-helper system and expansion of assisted-living housing resulted in a 30 percent reduction in the need for nursing home beds over a 15-year period. At the same time, the Danish government saved money: Public expenditures for long-term care

declined by 8 percent (Hastrup, 2007; Stuart & Weinrich, 2001). Strengthening caregiving and health-care services in U.S. assisted-living facilities would result in similarly favorable outcomes, while also enhancing older adults' happiness (Williams & Warren, 2008). The overwhelming majority of residents want to stay in assisted living rather than move to a nursing home.

When nursing home placement is necessary, steps can be taken to improve its quality. For example, the Netherlands has established separate facilities designed to meet the different needs of patients with mental and physical disabilities. And every older person, no matter how disabled, benefits from opportunities to maintain existing strengths and acquire new skills that can compensate for declines. Institutionalized individuals—like older people everywhere—desire a sense of personal control, gratifying social relationships, and meaningful and enjoyable daily activities (Alkema, Wilber, & Enguidanos, 2007). As Chapter 18 will reveal, designing nursing homes to meet these needs promotes both physical and psychological well-being.

ASK YOURSELF

REVIEW Cite evidence that both genetic and environmental factors contribute to Alzheimer's disease and cerebrovascular dementia.

CONNECT Explain how each level of ecological systems theory (Chapter 1, pages 24–25) contributes to caregiver well-being and quality of home care for older adults with dementia.

APPLY Marissa complained to a counselor that at age 68, her husband, Wendell, no longer initiated sex or cuddled her. Why might Wendell have ceased to interact sexually? What interventions—both medical and educational—could be helpful to Marissa and Wendell?

REFLECT What care and living arrangements have been made for seniors needing assistance in your family? How did culture, personal values, financial means, health, and other factors influence those decisions?

COGNITIVE DEVELOPMENT

Ruth's complaints to her doctor about difficulties with memory and verbal expression reflect common concerns about cognitive functioning in late adulthood. Decline in speed of processing, under way throughout the adult years, is believed to affect many aspects of cognition in old age. In Chapter 15, we noted that reduced efficiency of thinking contributes to (but may not fully explain) decrements in certain basic aspects of executive function, including attention and memory. Declines in working-memory capacity, inhibition of irrelevant information, use of

© JOURNAL-COURIER/STEVE WARMOWKSI/THE IMAGE WORKS

Older adults can sustain high levels of functioning through selective optimization with compensation. This retired theater teacher has done so by creating a studio at home where he focuses on composing music.

memory strategies, and retrieval from long-term memory continue in the final decades of life, affecting many aspects of cognitive aging.

TAKE A MOMENT... Return to Figure 15.5 on page 519, and note that the more a mental ability depends on fluid intelligence (biologically based information-processing skills), the earlier it starts to decline. In contrast, mental abilities that rely on crystallized intelligence (culturally based knowledge) are sustained longer. But maintenance of crystallized intelligence depends on continued opportunities to enhance cognitive skills. When these are available, crystallized abilities—vocabulary, general information, and expertise in specific endeavors—can offset losses in fluid intelligence.

Look again at Figure 15.5. In advanced old age, decrements in fluid intelligence limit what people can accomplish even with cultural supports, including a rich background of experience, knowledge of how to remember and solve problems, and a stimulating daily life (Berg & Sternberg, 2003; Kaufman, 2001). Consequently, crystallized intelligence shows a modest decline.

Generally, loss outweighs improvement and maintenance as people approach the end of life, but plasticity is still possible: Some individuals display high maintenance and minimal loss at very old ages (Baltes & Smith, 2003; Schaie, 2011). Research reveals greater individual variation in cognitive functioning in late adulthood than at any other time of life (Hultsch, MacDonald, & Dixon, 2002; Riediger & Lindenberger, 2006). Besides fuller expression of genetic and lifestyle influences, increased freedom to pursue self-chosen courses of action— some that enhance and others that undermine cognitive skills— may be responsible.

How can older adults make the most of their cognitive resources? According to one view, those who sustain high levels

of functioning engage in **selective optimization with compensation:** Narrowing their goals, they select personally valued activities to optimize (or maximize) returns from their diminishing energy. They also find new ways to *compensate* for losses (Baltes & Freund. 2003; Baltes, Lindenberger, & Staudinger, 2006).

One day, Ruth and Walt watched a public television rebroadcast of an interview with 80-year-old concert pianist Arthur Rubinstein. Asked how he managed to sustain such extraordinary piano playing at his advanced age, Rubinstein replied that he was *selective;* he played fewer pieces. This enabled him to *optimize* his energy; he could practice each piece more. Finally, he developed new, *compensatory* techniques for a decline in playing speed. For example, before a fast passage, he played extra slowly, so the fast section appeared to his audience to move more quickly.

Research confirms that in late adulthood, personal goals— while still including gains—increasingly focus on maintaining abilities and preventing losses (Freund & Ebner, 2005). In one study, researchers asked people to rate their most important physical and cognitive goals for emphasis on growth ("With this goal, I want to improve something or achieve something new") and maintenance/prevention of losses ("With this goal, I want to maintain something or prevent a loss") (Ebner, Freund, & Baltes, 2006). As Figure 17.6 shows, compared with young adults, older adults accentuated maintenance and loss prevention.

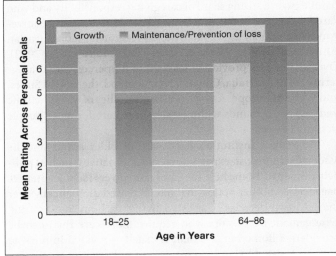

FIGURE 17.6 Personal goal orientation toward growth and maintenance/prevention of loss in young and older adults. Participants were asked to list two physical and two cognitive goals and then to rate each for emphasis on growth and on maintenance or prevention of loss, using an 8-point scale. Older adults—while continuing to pursue growth—placed much greater emphasis on maintenance and loss prevention than did young adults. (From N. C. Ebner, A. M. Freund, & P. B. Baltes, 2006, "Developmental Changes in Personal Goal Orientation from Young to Late Adulthood: From Striving for Gains to Maintenance and Prevention of Losses," *Psychology and Aging, 21,* p. 671. Adapted by permission of American Psychological Association.)

As we review major changes in memory, language processing, and problem solving, we will consider ways that older adults optimize and compensate in the face of declines. We will also see that certain abilities that depend on extensive life experience, not processing efficiency, are sustained or increase in old age. Last, we take up programs that recognize older people as lifelong learners empowered by new knowledge, just as they were at earlier periods of development.

LOOK AND LISTEN

Interview an older adult about memory and other cognitive challenges, asking for examples. For each instance, invite the older person to describe his or her efforts to optimize cognitive resources and compensate for losses. ●

Memory

As older adults take in information more slowly, retain less in working memory, and find it harder to inhibit irrelevant information, apply strategies, and retrieve relevant knowledge from long-term memory, the chances of memory failure increase (Luo & Craik, 2008; Naveh-Benjamin, 2012; Verhaeghen, 2012). A reduced capacity to hold material in working memory while operating on it means that memory problems are especially evident on complex tasks.

Deliberate versus Automatic Memory

"Ruth, you know that movie we saw—the one with the little 5-year-old boy who did such a wonderful acting job. I'd like to suggest it to Dick and Goldie. But what was it called?" asked Walt.

"I can't think of it, Walt. We've seen a few movies lately. Which theater was it at? Who'd we go with? Tell me more about the little boy—maybe it'll come to me."

Although we all occasionally have memory failures like this, difficulties with diverse aspects of *episodic memory,* or recall of everyday experiences, rise substantially in old age. When Ruth and Walt watched the movie, their slower cognitive processing meant that they retained fewer details. And because their working memories could hold less at once, they attended poorly to *context*—where they saw the movie and who went with them (Wegesin et al., 2000; Zacks & Hasher, 2006). When we try to remember, context serves as an important retrieval cue.

Because older adults take in less about a stimulus and its context, their recall is reduced in relation to that of younger people. For example, they sometimes cannot distinguish an imagined event from one they actually experienced (Rybash & Hrubi-Bopp, 2000). They find it harder to remember the source of information, particularly when potential sources are similar—which member of their bridge club made a certain statement, in what magazine they read about a particular news event, and to whom and on which occasion they previously told a certain joke or story (Simons et al., 2004). Temporal memory—recall of the order in which events occurred or how recently they happened—suffers as well (Dumas & Hartman, 2003; Hartman & Warren, 2005).

Older adults' limited working memories increase the likelihood of another type of episodic memory difficulty: They may, for example, travel from the den to the kitchen intending to get something but then not recall what they intended to get. When the context in which they formed the memory intention (the den) differs from the retrieval context (the kitchen), they often experience memory lapses (Verhaeghen, 2012). When they return to the first context (the den), it serves as a strong cue for their memory intention because that is where they first encoded it, and they say, "Oh, now I remember why I went to the kitchen!"

A few days later, when Ruth saw a TV ad for the movie whose title she had forgotten, she recognized its name immediately. Recognition—a fairly automatic type of memory that demands little mental effort—suffers less than recall in late adulthood because a multitude of environmental supports for remembering are present. Age-related memory declines are greatest on tasks that require effortful, strategic processing (Hoyer & Verhaeghen, 2006).

Consider another automatic form of memory: **implicit memory,** or memory without conscious awareness. In a typical implicit memory task, you would be shown a list of words, then asked to fill in a word fragment (such as t– –k). You would probably complete the sequence with a word you had just seen *(task)* rather than another word (*took* or *teak*). Without trying to do so, you would engage in recall.

Age differences in implicit memory are much smaller than in explicit, or deliberate, memory. Memory that depends on familiarity rather than on conscious use of strategies is largely spared in old age (Fleischman et al., 2004; Hudson, 2008). This helps explain why recall of vocabulary and general information—which are mostly well-learned and highly familiar—decline far less, and do so at later ages, than recall of everyday experiences (Small et al., 2012). The episodic memory problems seniors report—for names of people, places where they put important objects, directions for getting from one place to another, and (as we will see) appointments and medication schedules—all place high demands on their more limited working memories.

Associative Memory

The memory deficits just described are part of a general, age-related decline in binding information into complex memories (Naveh-Benjamin, 2012). Researchers call this an **associative memory deficit,** or difficulty creating and retrieving links between pieces of information—for example, two items or an item and its context, such as Ruth's attempt to remember the name of the movie with the child actor or where she had seen the movie.

To find out whether older adults have greater difficulty with associative memory than younger adults, researchers showed them pairs of unrelated words or pictures of objects (such as *table–overcoat* or *sandwich–radio*) and asked that they study the pairs for an upcoming memory test. During the test, one group

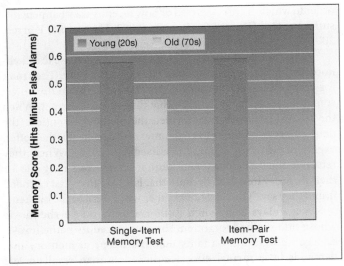

FIGURE 17.7 Young and older adults' performance on single-item and item-pair memory tests, supporting an associative memory deficit in late adulthood. After studying pairs of unrelated words or pictures, some participants were asked to identify single items they had seen. Others were asked to identify item pairs they had seen. Older adults performed almost as well as young adults on the single-item memory test. But they did far worse on the item-pair memory test. These findings support an associative memory deficit in late adulthood. (Adapted from Naveh-Benjamin, 2000.)

of participants was given a page of *single items,* some that had appeared in the study phase and some that had not, and asked to circle the ones they had studied. The other group was given a page of *item pairs,* some intact from the study phase *(table–overcoat)* and some that had been rearranged *(overcoat–radio),* and asked to circle pairs they had studied. As Figure 17.7 shows, older adults did almost as well as younger adults on the single-item memory test (Naveh-Benjamin, 2000; Naveh-Benjamin et al., 2003). But they performed far worse on the item-pair test—findings that support an associative memory deficit.

The memory tasks in the study just described relied on recognition. Older adults perform well when they are required only to recognize single pieces of information. But when researchers complicate recognition tasks by making them depend on associations between unrelated items, older people have difficulty with widely varying associations, including face–name, face–face, word–voice, and person–action pairings (Naveh-Benjamin, 2012).

Reducing task demands by providing older adults with helpful memory cues improves their associative memory (Naveh-Benjamin et al., 2003; Simons et al., 2004). For example, to associate names with faces, older people profit from mention of relevant facts about those individuals. And when older adults are directed to use the memory strategy of *elaboration* (relating word pairs by generating a sentence linking them) during both study and retrieval, the young–old difference in memory is greatly reduced (Naveh-Benjamin, Brav, & Levy, 2007). Clearly, associative deficits are greatly affected by lack of strategy use that helps bind information into integrated wholes.

Remote Memory

Although older people often say that their **remote memory,** or very long-term recall, is clearer than their memory for recent events, research does not support this conclusion. In several studies, adults ranging in age from their twenties to their seventies were asked to recall names of grade school teachers and high school classmates and Spanish vocabulary from high school—information very well learned early in life. Memory declined rapidly for the first 3 to 6 years, then changed little for the next 20 years (Bahrick, 1984; Bahrick, Bahrick, & Wittlinger, 1975). After that, additional modest forgetting occurred.

How about *autobiographical memory,* or memory for personally meaningful events, such as what you did on your first date or how you celebrated your college graduation? To test for this type of memory, researchers typically give a series of words (such as *book, machine, sorry, surprised*) and ask adults to report a personal memory cued by each. Or they present participants with a time line on a piece of paper, representing birth to present age, and ask them to place important life events on the line and note the age at which each occurred. People between ages 50 and 90 recall both remote and recent events more frequently than intermediate events, with recent events mentioned most often in the word-cue studies (see Figure 17.8). Among remote events recalled using either word-cue or time-line procedures, most happened between ages 10 and 30—a period of heightened autobiographical memory called the **reminiscence bump**

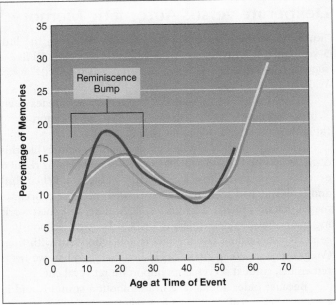

FIGURE 17.8 Distribution of older adults' autobiographical memories by reported age at time of the event. In the four studies of 50- to 90-year-olds represented here, later events were remembered better than early events. Among early events, most of those recalled occurred between ages 10 and 30. (From D. C. Rubin, T. A. Rahhal, & L. W. Poon, 1998, "Things Learned in Early Adulthood Are Remembered Best," *Memory and Cognition, 26,* p. 4. Copyright © 1998 by the Psychonomic Society, Inc. Adapted by permission of the Psychonomic Society.)

(Janssen, Rubin, & St. Jacques, 2011; Rubin, 2002; Schroots, van Dijkum, & Assink, 2004).

The reminiscence bump is evident in the autobiographical recall of older adults from diverse cultures—Bangladesh, China, Japan, Turkey, and the United States (Conway et al., 2005; Demiray, Gülgöz, & Bluck, 2009). Why are adolescent and early adulthood experiences retrieved more readily than those of middle adulthood? Youthful events occur during a period of rapid life change filled with novel experiences that stand out from the humdrum of daily life. Adolescence and early adulthood are also times of identity development, when many personally significant experiences occur (Glück & Bluck, 2007). Furthermore, the reminiscence bump characterizes emotionally positive, but not negative, memories. Culturally shared, important life events—school proms, graduations, marriage, birth of children—are usually positive and cluster earlier in life (Dickson, Pillemer, & Bruehl, 2011). In contrast, negative events—a serious illness, a car accident—are generally unanticipated and are not overrepresented during any life period.

Nevertheless, older people recall recent personal experiences more readily than remote ones, probably because of interference produced by years of additional experience (Verhaeghen, 2012). As we accumulate more memories, some inevitably resemble others. As a result, certain early memories become less clear than they once were. However, even when asked to recall an important event of the previous year, older adults—because of their episodic memory difficulties—provide considerably fewer details than do young adults (Levine et al., 2002).

Prospective Memory

Older people often complain that they have become more absent-minded about everyday events. Because Ruth and Walt knew they were prone to forget appointments, they asked about them repeatedly. "Sybil, what time is our dinner engagement?" Walt queried several times during the preceding two days. His questioning was not a sign of dementia. He simply wanted to be sure to remember an important date.

So far, we have considered various aspects of *retrospective memory* (remembrance of things past). **Prospective memory** refers to remembering to engage in planned actions in the future. The amount of mental effort required determines whether older adults have trouble with prospective memory. Remembering the dinner date was challenging for Walt because he typically ate dinner with his daughter on Thursday evenings at 6 P.M., but this time, dinner was set for Tuesday at 7:15 P.M.

In the laboratory, older adults do better on *event-based* than on *time-based* prospective memory tasks. In an event-based task, an event (such as a certain word appearing on a computer screen) serves as a cue for remembering to do something (pressing a key) while the participant engages in an ongoing activity (reading paragraphs). As long as the event-based task is not complex, older adults do as well as younger adults. But when researchers introduce extra attentional and working-memory demands (for example, press the key when any one of four cues appears), older adults' performance worsens (Kliegel, Jäger, & Phillips, 2008; McDaniel, Einstein, & Rendell, 2007). In time-based tasks, the adult must engage in an action after a certain time interval has elapsed, without any obvious external cue (for example, pressing a key every 10 minutes). Time-based prospective memory requires considerable initiative to keep the planned action in mind and monitor the passage of time while also performing an ongoing activity (Einstein, McDaniel, & Scullin, 2012). Consequently, declines in late adulthood are considerable.

But difficulties with prospective memory seen in the laboratory do not appear in real life, where adults are highly motivated to remember and good at setting up event-based reminders for themselves, such as a buzzer ringing in the kitchen to signal it's time to take medication or a note tacked up prominently displaying the time of a same-day meeting (Henry et al., 2004). In trying to remember a future activity, younger adults rely more on strategies like rehearsal, older adults on external memory aids (Dixon, de Frias, & Bäckman, 2001). In this way, the seniors compensate for their reduced-capacity working memories and the challenge of dividing attention between what they are doing now and what they must do in the future.

Nevertheless, once a prospective memory task is finished, older adults find it harder than younger adults to deactivate, or inhibit, their intention to engage in the future action, especially when cues are still present after the task has been performed. Hence, they sometimes repeat the task again (Scullin et al., 2011). Whereas forgetting whether one has washed one's hair and doing so a second time is harmless, repeating a dose of medication can be dangerous. Older adults benefit from a system of reminders that regularly scheduled tasks have been completed, and they often arrange such systems themselves.

 ## Language Processing

Language and memory skills are closely related. In language comprehension (understanding the meaning of spoken or written prose), we recollect what we have heard or read without conscious awareness. Like implicit memory, language comprehension changes little in late life, as long as conversational partners do not speak too quickly and older adults are given enough time to process written text accurately, enabling them to compensate for reduced working-memory capacity (Stine-Morrow & Miller, 2009). Older readers make a variety of adjustments to ensure comprehension, such as attending more closely to features of text prose, pausing more often to integrate information, and making good use of story organization to help them recall both main ideas and details. Those who have invested more time in reading and literacy activities over their lifetimes display faster and more accurate reading comprehension (Payne et al., 2012). They benefit from years of greater practice of this highly skilled activity.

In Alberta, Canada, a First Nations senior speaks out against environmental destruction caused by the oil industry. To compensate for language-production problems, older adults speak more slowly, use simplified grammatical structures, and represent information in terms of gist rather than details.

Two aspects of language production show age-related losses. The first is retrieving words from long-term memory (Connor et al., 2004). When conversing with others, Ruth and Walt sometimes had trouble finding the right words to convey their thoughts—even well-known words they had used many times in the past. Consequently, their speech contained more pronouns and other unclear references than it did at younger ages. They also spoke more slowly and paused more often, partly because they needed time to search their memories for certain words (Burke & Shafto, 2004). And compared to younger people, they more often reported a *tip-of-the-tongue state*—certainty that they knew a word accompanied by an inability to produce it.

Second, planning what to say and how to say it is harder in late adulthood. As a result, Walt and Ruth displayed slightly more hesitations, false starts, word repetitions, and sentence fragments as they aged (Bortfeld et al., 2001). Their statements were also less grammatically complex and less well-organized than before (Kemper, 2012).

What explains these changes? Whereas the meanings older people want to convey have many "mental connections" with other meanings, the sound of a word has only one mental connection to the word's underlying concept. Consequently, as associative memory declines with age, memory difficulties in everyday conversation are especially apparent in word retrieval (Burke & Shafto, 2004). Also, diminished working-memory capacity is involved. Because less information can be held at once, older adults have difficulty coordinating the multiple tasks required to produce complex, coherent speech.

As with memory, older adults develop compensatory techniques for their language production problems. For example, they speak more slowly so they can devote more effort to retrieving words and organizing their thoughts. Sacrificing efficiency for greater clarity, they use more sentences, but shorter ones, to convey their message (Griffin & Spieler, 2006; Kemper, Thompson, & Marquis, 2001). As older people monitor their word-retrieval failures and try hard to overcome them, they show a greater frequency of tip-of-the-tongue states—but they resolve tip-of-the-tongues at a higher rate than do younger people (Schwartz & Frazier, 2005).

Furthermore, older adults often compensate by representing information they want to communicate in terms of gist rather than details (Jepson & Labouvie-Vief, 1992). For example, when Walt told his granddaughter Marci fairytales, he left out many concrete facts while substituting personal inferences and a moral lesson—elements that appear less often in the storytelling of younger adults. Here is Walt's rendition of "Sleeping Beauty": "An evil fairy condemns Sleeping Beauty to death. But a kind fairy changes the curse from death to sleep. Then a handsome prince awakens the girl with a kiss. So you see, Marci, both good and bad exist in the world. The bad things instill in us the need to care for others."

Older adults often make the most of their limited working memories by extracting the essence of a message. Then, drawing on their extensive life experience, they enrich it with symbolic interpretations.

 ## Problem Solving

Problem solving is yet another cognitive skill that illustrates how aging brings not only deterioration but also adaptive changes. Problem solving in the laboratory, where tasks have goals set by the researcher, declines in late adulthood (Finucane et al., 2005). Older adults' memory limitations make it hard to keep all relevant facts in mind when dealing with a complex hypothetical problem.

Yet the everyday problems the seniors encounter differ from hypothetical problems devised by researchers—and also from the problems they experienced at earlier ages. After retirement, older adults do not have to deal with workplace problems. Their children are typically grown and living on their own, and their marriages have endured long enough to have fewer difficulties. With age, major concerns involve dealing with extended-family relationships (for example, expectations of adult children that they babysit grandchildren) and managing IADLs, such as preparing nutritious meals, handling finances, and attending to health concerns.

How do the older people solve problems of daily living? Their strategies extend the adaptive problem solving of midlife. As long as they perceive problems as under their control and as important, they are active and effective in solving them (Berg & Strough, 2011). Older adults generate a smaller number of strategies compared to young and middle-aged adults, but this may be due to their greater life experience. Among the strategies they do suggest, they may include only those they believe will be helpful (Strough et al., 2008). Furthermore, older adults are particularly good at adapting strategies to fit problem conditions—home, relatives, friends, and finances. And perhaps because they are especially concerned with maintaining positive relationships, they usually do what they can to avoid interpersonal conflicts (Blanchard-Fields, Chen, & Norris, 2007). As we will see in Chapter 18, this strategy also fits with their desire to conserve energy and limit stress.

The health arena illustrates the adaptiveness of everyday problem solving in late adulthood. Older adults make faster decisions about whether they are ill, seek medical care sooner, and select treatments more quickly. In contrast, young and middle-aged adults are more likely to adopt a "wait and see" approach in favor of gathering more facts, even when a health problem is serious (Meyer, Russo, & Talbot, 1995). This swift response of older people is interesting in view of their slower cognitive processing. Research reveals that they have accumulated more health-related knowledge, which enables them to move ahead with greater certainty (Meyer, Talbot, & Ranalli, 2007). Acting decisively when faced with health risks is sensible in old age.

Finally, older adults report that they often consult others—generally spouses and adult children, but also friends, neighbors, and members of their religious congregation—for advice about everyday problems (Strough et al., 2003). And compared with younger married couples, older married couples more often collaborate in problem solving, and researchers judge their jointly generated strategies as highly effective—even on demanding tasks that require complex memory and reasoning (Meegan & Berg, 2002; Peter-Wight & Martin, 2011). In jointly solving problems, older people seem to compensate for moments of cognitive difficulty, yielding enhanced performance.

 # Wisdom

We have seen that a wealth of life experience enhances the storytelling and problem solving of older adults. It also underlies another capacity believed to reach its height in old age: **wisdom**. When researchers ask people to describe wisdom, most mention breadth and depth of practical knowledge, ability to reflect on and apply that knowledge in ways that make life more bearable and worthwhile; emotional maturity, including the ability to listen patiently and empathetically and give sound advice; and the altruistic form of creativity discussed in Chapter 15 that involves contributing to humanity and enriching others' lives. One group of researchers summed up the multiple cognitive and personality traits that make up wisdom as "expertise in the conduct and meaning of life" (Baltes & Smith, 2008; Baltes & Staudinger, 2000, p. 124; Staudinger, Dörner, & Mickler, 2005).

During her college years, Ruth and Walt's granddaughter Marci telephoned with a pressing personal dilemma. Ruth's

advice reflected the features of wisdom just mentioned. After her boyfriend Ken moved to another city to attend medical school, Marci, unsure whether her love for Ken would endure, had begun dating another student. "I can't stand being pulled in two directions," she exclaimed. "I'm thinking of calling Ken and telling him about Steve. Do you think I should?"

"This is not a good time, Marci," Ruth advised. "You'll break Ken's heart before you've had a chance to size up your feelings for Steve. And you said Ken's taking some important exams in two weeks. If you tell him now and he's distraught, it could affect the rest of his life."

Wisdom—whether applied to personal problems or to community, national, and international concerns—requires the "pinnacle of insight into the human condition" (Baltes & Staudinger, 2000; Birren, 2009). Not surprisingly, cultures around the world assume that age and wisdom go together. In village and tribal societies, the most important social positions, such as chieftain and shaman (religious leader), are reserved for the old. Similarly, in industrialized nations, older adults are chief executive officers of large corporations, high-level religious leaders, members of legislatures, and supreme court justices. What explains this widespread trend? According to an evolutionary view, the genetic program of our species grants health, fitness, and strength to the young. Culture tames this youthful advantage in physical power with the insights of the old (Csikszentmihalyi & Nakamura, 2005; Csikszentmihalyi & Rathunde, 1990). As wise older adults identify useful knowledge and reflections to transmit to younger people, they ensure balance and interdependence between generations.

In the most extensive research to date on development of wisdom, adults ranging in age from 20 to 89 responded to uncertain real-life situations—for example, what to consider and do if a good friend is about to commit suicide or if, after reflecting on your life, you discover that you have not achieved your goals (Staudinger, 2008; Staudinger, Dörner, & Mickler, 2005). Responses were rated for five ingredients of wisdom:

- Knowledge about fundamental concerns of life, including human nature, social relations, and emotions
- Effective strategies for applying that knowledge to making life decisions, handling conflict, and giving advice
- A view of people that considers the multiple demands of their life contexts
- A concern with ultimate human values, such as the common good, as well as respect for individual differences in values
- Awareness and management of the uncertainties of life—that many problems have no perfect solution

Results revealed that age is no guarantee of wisdom. A small number of adults of diverse ages ranked among the wise. But type of life experience made a difference. People in human-service careers who had extensive training and practice in grappling with human problems tended to attain high wisdom scores. Other high-scorers held leadership positions (Staudinger,

TONY KARUMBA/AFP/GETTY IMAGES

Renowned British primatologist Dr. Jane Goodall—speaking with admirers after a presentation at the National Museum in Nairobi, Kenya—exemplifies wisdom. At age 79, she continues to be a tireless leader in efforts to protect chimpanzees and their African habitats and to promote humane treatment of animals everywhere.

Smith, & Baltes, 1992; Staudinger, 1996). And when age and relevant life experiences were considered together, more older than younger people scored in the top 20 percent.

In addition to age and life experience, having faced and overcome adversity appears to be an important contributor to late-life wisdom (Brugman, 2006; Linley, 2003). In an investigation of people who were young adults during the Great Depression of the 1930s, those who experienced economic hardship and surmounted it scored especially high in wisdom nearly 40 years later, as indicated by reflections on life events that included insights into their own motives and behavior and compassionate concern for the welfare of others (Ardelt, 1998).

Compared to their agemates, older adults with the cognitive, reflective, and emotional (compassionate) qualities that make up wisdom are better educated and physically healthier, forge more positive relations with others, and score higher on the personality dimension of openness to experience (Kramer, 2003). Wisdom also predicts sense of personal growth, generativity, favorable adjustment to aging, marital happiness, and life satisfaction (Ardelt, 2011; Le, 2011). Wise older people seem to flourish, even when faced with physical and cognitive challenges. This suggests that finding ways to promote wisdom would be a powerful means of both contributing to human welfare and fostering a gratifying old age.

Factors Related to Cognitive Maintenance and Change

Heritability research suggests a modest genetic contribution to individual differences in cognitive change in late adulthood (Deary et al., 2012). At the same time, as in middle adulthood, a mentally active life is vital for preserving cognitive resources.

Above-average education, frequent contact with family members and friends, stimulating leisure pursuits, community participation, and a flexible personality predict higher mental test scores and reduced cognitive decline into advanced old age (Bielak et al., 2012; Schaie, 2011). Today's seniors in industrialized nations are better educated than any previous generation. Since 1950, the rate of high school completion among U.S. adults age 65 and older has quadrupled, reaching 80 percent. Those with at least a bachelor's degree have increased sixfold, to 23 percent (U.S. Department of Health and Human Services, 2012d). As more baby boomers enter late adulthood, these trends are expected to continue, forecasting improved preservation of cognitive functions.

As noted earlier, health status powerfully predicts older adults' cognitive functioning. In longitudinal research, cigarette smokers declined cognitively at a faster rate than their non-smoking counterparts, as did overweight and obese people, even after initial health status, SES, and mental test performance were controlled (Dahl et al., 2010; Starr et al., 2007). And a wide variety of chronic conditions, including vision and hearing impairments, cardiovascular disease, diabetes, osteoporosis, and arthritis, are strongly associated with cognitive declines (Baltes, Lindenberger, & Staudinger, 2006). But we must be cautious in interpreting this link between physical and cognitive deterioration. The relationship may be exaggerated by the fact that brighter adults are more likely to engage in health-protective behaviors, which postpone the onset of serious disease.

Retirement also affects cognitive change, both positively and negatively. When people leave routine jobs for stimulating leisure activities, outcomes are favorable. In contrast, retiring from a highly complex job without developing challenging substitutes accelerates intellectual declines (Schaie, 1996). In fact, complex, challenging work in late adulthood may have an even stronger, facilitating impact on intellectual functioning than in middle adulthood (see pages 525–526 in Chapter 15) (Hertzog et al., 2009; Schooler, Mulatu, & Oates, 1999).

As seniors grow older, their cognitive scores show larger fluctuations from one occasion to the next. This rising instability of performance—especially in speed of response—accelerates in the seventies and is associated with cognitive declines, along with neurobiological signs of shrinkage in the prefrontal cortex and deficient brain functioning (Bielak et al., 2010; MacDonald, Li, & Bäckman, 2009; Lövdén et al., 2012). It seems to signal end-of-life brain degeneration.

In the year before Walt died, those close to him noticed that he had become less active and more withdrawn, even in the company of friends. **Terminal decline** refers to acceleration in deterioration of cognitive functioning prior to death. Some longitudinal studies indicate that it is limited to a few aspects of intelligence, others that it occurs generally, across many abilities. Findings also differ greatly in its estimated length—from 1 to 3 to as long as 14 years, with an average of 4 to 5 years (Lövdén et al., 2005; MacDonald, Hultsch, & Dixon, 2011; Rabbitt, Lunn, & Wong, 2008; Wilson et al., 2003). In one investigation, a sharp drop in life satisfaction predicted mortality. The downturn appeared, on average, four years in advance of death, was especially steep in people age 85 and older, and showed only a weak relationship to mental deterioration or chronic illnesses (Gerstorf et al., 2008).

Perhaps different kinds of terminal decline exist—one type arising from disease processes, another reflecting general biological breakdown due to normal aging. What we do know is that an extended falloff in cognitive performance or in emotional investment in life is a sign of loss of vitality and impending death.

 ## Cognitive Interventions

For most of late adulthood, cognitive declines are gradual. Although aging of the brain contributes to them, recall from our earlier discussion that the brain can compensate by growing new neural fibers. Furthermore, some cognitive decrements may be due to disuse of particular skills rather than biological aging. If plasticity of development is possible, then interventions that train older people in cognitive strategies should at least partially reverse the age-related declines we have discussed.

Older adults' relatively well-preserved *metacognition* is a powerful asset in training efforts. Most, for example, are aware of memory declines, report troublesome anxiety when faced with demanding memory situations, and know they must take extra steps to ensure recall of important information (Castel, McGillivray, & Friedman, 2011). Their impressive metacognitive understanding is also evident in the wide-ranging techniques they devise to compensate for everyday cognitive challenges.

The Adult Development and Enrichment Project (ADEPT) is the most extensive cognitive intervention program conducted to date (Schaie, 2005). By using participants in the Seattle Longitudinal Study (see Chapter 15, page 519), researchers were able to do what no other investigation has done: assess the effects of cognitive training on long-term development.

Intervention began with adults over age 64, some of whom had maintained their scores on tests of two mental abilities (inductive reasoning and spatial orientation) over the previous 14 years and others who had shown declines. After just five one-hour training sessions in one of two types of mental test items, two-thirds of participants improved their performance on the trained skill. Gains for decliners were dramatic: Forty percent returned to the level at which they had been functioning 14 years earlier! A follow-up after 7 years revealed that although scores dropped somewhat, participants remained advantaged in their trained skill over agemates trained in the other ability. Finally, "booster" training at this time led to further gains, although these were smaller than the earlier gains.

In another large-scale intervention study called ACTIVE (Advanced Cognitive Training for Independent and Vital Elderly), more than 2,800 65- to 84-year-olds were randomly assigned to a ten-session training program focusing on one of three abilities—speed of processing, memory, or reasoning—or to a no-intervention control group. Again, trained older adults showed an immediate advantage in the trained skill over con-

trols that was still evident—though smaller in magnitude—at one- and two-year follow-ups (Ball et al., 2002). Transfer to everyday functioning, unfortunately, was disappointing: For example, participants who improved on a laboratory processing-speed task were no faster at looking up numbers in a phone book. Nevertheless, five years after intervention, cognitive training was associated with reduced declines in general health and ability to perform IADLs—outcomes that were strongest for the speed-of-processing group (Wolinsky et al., 2006). The investigators speculated that speed-of-processing training induces a broad pattern of brain activation, affecting many regions.

Clearly, many cognitive skills can be enhanced in old age. A vital goal is to transfer intervention from the laboratory to the community, weaving it into the daily experiences of older people (Stine-Morrow & Basak, 2011). Broadening training programs by focusing not just on strategy use and practice but also on beliefs that promote sustained effort may be helpful. Seniors who are higher in self-efficacy benefit more from cognitive training, and targeting self-efficacy in training programs by emphasizing cognitive potential at any age boosts both self-efficacy and cognitive gains (West, Bagwell, & Dark-Freudeman, 2008). Furthermore, working in groups may offer unique opportunities for strengthening self-efficacy ("If they can do it, so can I") along with social support for persisting (Hastings & West, 2009). As we will see in the next section, a promising approach is to provide older adults with well-designed, highly interesting educational experiences in which cognitive training in socially rich contexts is an integral part.

 ## Lifelong Learning

Think about the competencies that older adults need to live in our complex, changing world. They are the same as those of younger people—communicating effectively through spoken and written systems; locating information, sorting through it, and selecting what is needed; using math strategies, such as estimation; planning and organizing activities, including making good use of time and resources; mastering new technologies; and understanding past and current events and the relevance of each to their own lives. Seniors also need to develop new, problem-centered coping strategies—ways to sustain health and operate their households efficiently and safely—and updated vocational skills, for those who continue to work.

Participation of older adults in continuing education has increased substantially over the past few decades. Successful programs include a wide variety of offerings responsive to the diversity of senior citizens and teaching methods suited to their developmental needs.

Types of Programs

One summer, Walt and Ruth attended a Road Scholar (formerly called Elderhostel) program at a nearby university. After moving into a dormitory room, they joined 30 other seniors for two weeks of morning classes on Shakespeare, afternoon visits to

Applying What We Know

Increasing the Effectiveness of Educational Experiences for Older Adults

Technique	Description
Provide a positive learning environment.	Many older adults have internalized negative stereotypes of their own abilities and come to the learning environment with low self-efficacy. A supportive group atmosphere helps convince older adults that they can learn.
Allow ample time to learn new information.	Rate of learning varies widely among older adults, and some master new material at a fairly slow rate. Presenting information over multiple sessions or allowing for self-paced instruction aids mastery.
Present information in a well-organized fashion.	Older adults do not organize information as effectively as younger adults. Material that is outlined, presented, and then summarized enhances memory and understanding. Digressions make a presentation harder to comprehend.
Relate information to older adults' experiences.	Relating new material to what older adults have already learned, by drawing on their extensive knowledge and experiences and giving many vivid examples, enhances recall.
Adapt the learning environment to fit changes in sensory systems.	Adequate lighting, availability of large-print reading materials, appropriate sound amplification, reduction in background noise, and clear, well-organized visual aids to supplement verbal teaching ease information processing.

points of interest, and evening performances of plays at a nearby Shakespeare festival.

In its most recently reported year, Road Scholar campus-based programs, and their recent extension to travel experiences around the world, attracted nearly 100,000 American and Canadian older adults. Some programs make use of community resources through classes on local ecology or folk life. Others focus on innovative topics and experiences—writing one's own life story, discussing contemporary films with screenwriters, whitewater rafting, Chinese painting and calligraphy, or acquiring French language skills. Travel programs are enriched by in-depth lectures and expert-led field trips.

Similar educational programs have sprung up in the United States and elsewhere. The Bernard Osher Foundation collaborates with more than 120 U.S. universities to establish Osher Lifelong Learning Institutes on campuses. Each offers older adults a wide array of stimulating learning experiences, from auditing regular courses, to forming learning communities that address common interests, to helping to solve community problems. Originating in France, the University of the Third Age[2] provides Western European, British, and Australian seniors with university- and community-sponsored courses, workshops on special topics, and excursions, with older adults often doing the teaching.

LOOK AND LISTEN

Find out if your college or university hosts Road Scholar or Osher Foundation programs. Attend a session of an on-campus program. What did you observe about older adults' capacity for complex learning? ●

Participants in the programs just mentioned tend to be active, well-educated, and financially well-off. Much less is available for older people with little education and limited income. Community senior centers with inexpensive offerings related to everyday living attract more low-SES people than programs such as Road Scholar. Regardless of course content and which seniors attend, using the techniques summarized in Applying What We Know above increases the effectiveness of educational experiences.

PHOTO BY CARL STUDNA/ROAD SCHOLAR

Active, adventurous seniors explore the sights, sounds, streets, and monuments of Dublin's authors, poets, and playwrights as part of a Road Scholar travel program to Ireland.

[2]The term *Third Age,* as we will see in Chapter 18, refers to the period after the "Second Age" of midlife, when older people are freed from responsibilities of earning a living and rearing children to focus on personal fulfillment.

Benefits of Continuing Education

Older participants in continuing education report a rich array of benefits—understanding new ideas in many disciplines, learning new skills that enrich their lives, making new friends, and developing a broader perspective on the world (Preece & Findsen, 2007). Furthermore, seniors come to see themselves differently. Many abandon their own ingrained stereotypes of aging when they realize that adults in late life—including themselves—can still engage in complex learning.

Older adults' willingness to acquire new knowledge and skills is apparent in the recent, rapid rise in their use of computers and the Internet. Seniors are now the fastest growing age group to embrace online technology as they discover its many practical benefits, including assistance with shopping, banking, health-care management, and communication. Currently, just over half of adults age 65 and older access the Internet, with 86 percent using e-mail and 38 percent social networking sites such as Facebook (Brenner, 2013; Zickuhr & Madden, 2012). Still, older people have joined the computer and Internet community to a lesser extent than younger people (see page 553 in Chapter 16). Those over age 75 are especially reluctant, with many perceiving the technology as too complicated—an attitude that continuing education can overcome (Wagner, Hassanein, & Head, 2010). With patient training, support, and modified equipment and software to suit their physical and cognitive needs, older adults readily enter the online world, often becoming just as devoted as younger users.

The educational needs of seniors are likely to be given greater attention in coming decades, as their numbers grow and they assert their right to lifelong learning. Once this happens, false stereotypes—"the elderly are too old to learn" or "education is for the young"—are likely to weaken and, perhaps, disappear.

ASK YOURSELF

REVIEW Describe cognitive functions that are maintained or improve in late adulthood. What aspects of aging contribute to them?

CONNECT What processes in brain development contribute to the success of older adults' efforts to compensate for cognitive declines? (See page 568.)

APPLY Estelle complained that she had recently forgotten two of her regular biweekly hair appointments and sometimes had trouble finding the right words to convey her thoughts. What cognitive changes account for Estelle's difficulties? What can she do to compensate?

REFLECT Interview an older adult in your family, asking about ways the individual engages in selective optimization with compensation to make the most of declining cognitive resources. Describe several examples.

SUMMARY

PHYSICAL DEVELOPMENT

Life Expectancy (p. 564)

Distinguish between chronological age and functional age, and discuss changes in life expectancy over the past century.

- People age biologically at different rates, making chronological age is an imperfect indicator of **functional age.** Dramatic twentieth-century gains in **average life expectancy** confirm that biological aging can be modified by environmental factors, including improved nutrition, medical treatment, sanitation, and safety.

- Length of life and, especially, **average healthy life expectancy** can be predicted by a country's health care, housing, and social services, along with lifestyle factors. In developing nations, both are shortened by poverty, malnutrition, disease, and armed conflict.

- With advancing age, the gender gap in average life expectancy declines, as do differences between higher-SES whites and low-SES ethnic minorities.

- Longevity runs in families, but environmental factors become increasingly important with age. Scientists disagree on whether **maximum lifespan** can be extended beyond 122 years—the oldest verified age.

Physical Changes (p. 567)

Describe physical declines of late adulthood, including changes in the nervous and sensory systems.

- With age, growing numbers of older adults experience physical declines, evident in difficulties carrying out **activities of daily living (ADLs),** or basic self-care tasks, and **instrumental activities of daily living (IADLs),** which are necessary to conduct the business of daily life.

- Neuron loss occurs throughout the cerebral cortex, with greater shrinkage in the frontal lobes and the corpus callosum. The cerebellum also loses neurons. The brain compensates by forming new synapses and, to some extent, generating new neurons. The autonomic nervous system functions less well in old age and releases more stress hormones.

- Older adults—more women than men—tend to suffer from impaired vision and may experience **cataracts** and **macular degeneration.** Hearing impairments are more common than visual impairments, especially in men, with decline in speech perception having the greatest impact on life satisfaction.

© JEFF GREENBERG/THE IMAGE WORKS

- Taste and odor sensitivity wane, making food less appealing. Touch sensitivity also deteriorates, particularly on the fingertips.

Describe cardiovascular, respiratory, and immune system changes and sleep difficulties in late adulthood.

- Reduced capacity of the cardiovascular and respiratory systems becomes more apparent in late adulthood, especially in lifelong smokers and in people who have not reduced dietary fat or who have had extensive exposure to environmental pollutants. Exercise can slow cardiovascular aging and facilitate respiratory functioning.

- The immune system functions less effectively in late life, permitting diseases to progress and making **autoimmune responses** and stress-induced infection more likely.

- Older adults find it harder to fall asleep, stay asleep, and sleep deeply. Until age 70 or 80, men have more trouble sleeping than women because of prostate enlargement (initiating frequent urination) and **sleep apnea.**

Describe changes in physical appearance and mobility in late adulthood, along with effective adaptations to these changes.

- Outward signs of aging—white hair, wrinkled and sagging skin, age spots, and decreased height and weight—become more noticeable. Mobility diminishes as muscle and bone strength and joint flexibility decline.

- "Anti-aging" dietary supplements, herbal products, and hormonal medications have shown no demonstrated benefits and may cause harm. Instead, problem-centered coping strategies yield improved physical functioning.

- A rapidly expanding **assistive technology** helps older people cope with physical declines, sustaining an effective person–environment fit that enhances psychological well-being.

- Negative stereotypes of aging have a stressful, disorganizing impact on older adults' functioning, whereas positive stereotypes reduce stress and foster physical and mental competence.

Health, Fitness, and Disability (p. 575)

Discuss health and fitness in late life, paying special attention to nutrition, exercise, and sexuality.

- Most older adults rate their health favorably and have a high sense of self-efficacy about protecting it. Low-SES ethnic minority older people remain at greater risk for certain health problems and are less likely to believe they can control their health.

- In late life, men continue to be more prone to fatal diseases and women to disabling conditions. In industrialized nations, **compression of morbidity** has occurred, largely as a result of medical advances and improved socioeconomic conditions; further gains will depend on reducing negative lifestyle factors. In the developing world, comprehensive strategies are needed.

- Risk of dietary deficiencies increases in late life, but except for calcium and vitamin D, a daily vitamin–mineral supplement is recommended only for those suffering from malnutrition. Exercise, even when begun in late adulthood, is a powerful health intervention.

- Though sexual activity declines, especially among women, most older couples report continued, regular sexual enjoyment.

JONATHAN KIRN/GETTY IMAGES

Discuss physical disabilities common in late adulthood.

- Illness and disability increase toward the end of life. Cardiovascular disease and cancer are the leading causes of death, followed by respiratory diseases. **Primary aging** contributes to **frailty** in the elderly, but **secondary aging** (declines due to hereditary defects and negative environmental influences) plays a larger role.

- **Osteoarthritis** and **rheumatoid arthritis** are widespread among older adults, especially women. Type 2 diabetes also increases.

- The death rate from unintentional injuries reaches an all-time high from age 65 on, largely due to motor vehicle collisions and falls. Visual declines and slowed reaction time often contribute.

Discuss mental disabilities common in late adulthood.

- **Alzheimer's disease**, the most common form of **dementia**, often starts with severe memory problems. It brings personality changes, depression, disintegration of purposeful movements, loss of ability to comprehend and produce speech, and death. Underlying these changes are abundant **neurofibrillary tangles** and **amyloid plaques** and lowered neurotransmitter levels in the brain.

- Familial Alzheimer's, related to genes involved in generation of harmful amyloid, generally has an early onset and progresses rapidly. About half of sporadic Alzheimer's victims have an abnormal gene that results in insulin deficiency linked to brain damage.

- Diverse environmental factors, including a high-fat diet, physical inactivity, overweight and obesity, smoking, chronic psychological stress, cardiovascular disease, stroke, diabetes, and head injuries increase the risk of Alzheimer's. A "Mediterranean diet," education, and an active lifestyle are associated with lower incidence.

- Heredity contributes to **cerebrovascular dementia** indirectly, through high blood pressure, cardiovascular disease, and diabetes. Many environmental influences also heighten stroke risk. Because of their greater susceptibility to cardiovascular disease, more men than women are affected.

- Treatable problems, such as depression, side effects of medication, and reactions to social isolation, can be mistaken for dementia.

Discuss health-care issues that affect senior citizens.

- Only a small percentage of U.S. seniors are institutionalized, about half the rate in other industrialized nations with more generous public financing of institutional care. Though ethnic differences exist, family members provide most long-term care in Western nations. Publicly funded in-home help and **assisted living** can reduce the high costs of institutional placement and increase older adults' life satisfaction.

COGNITIVE DEVELOPMENT

Describe overall changes in cognitive functioning in late adulthood.

- Individual differences in cognitive functioning are greater in late adulthood than at any other time of life. Older adults can make the most of their cognitive resources through **selective optimization with compensation**. Personal goals increasingly emphasize maintaining abilities and preventing loss.

Memory (p. 591)

How does memory change in late life?

- Memory failure is more likely in older adults, especially on tasks that are complex and require deliberate processing. Recall of context, source, and temporal order of episodic events declines. Automatic forms of memory, such as recognition and **implicit memory**, suffer less. In general, an **associative memory deficit**, or difficulty creating and retrieving links between pieces of information, characterizes older adults' memory deficits.

- Contrary to what older people often report, **remote memory** is not clearer than recent memory. Autobiographical memory is best for recent experiences, followed by personally meaningful events that occurred between ages 10 and 30, a period of heightened recall called the **reminiscence bump**. In the laboratory, older adults do better on event-based than on time-based **prospective memory** tasks. In everyday life, they compensate for declines in prospective memory by using external memory aids.

Language Processing (p. 593)

Describe changes in language processing in late adulthood.

- Language comprehension changes little in late life. Age-related losses occur in two aspects of language production: retrieving words from long-term memory and planning what to say and how to say it. Older people compensate by speaking more slowly, using shorter sentences, and communicating gist rather than details.

©ASHLEY COOPER/CORBIS

Problem Solving (p. 594)

How does problem solving change in late life?

- Hypothetical problem solving declines in late adulthood. In everyday problem solving, older adults are effective as long as they perceive problems as important and under their control. Older people make faster decisions about health than younger people and more often consult others about everyday problems.

Wisdom (p. 595)

What capacities make up wisdom, and how is it affected by age and life experience?

- **Wisdom** involves extensive practical knowledge, ability to reflect on and apply that knowledge in ways that make life more bearable and worthwhile, emotional maturity, and altruistic creativity. When age and life experience in grappling with human problems are combined, more older than younger people rank among the wise.

Factors Related to Cognitive Maintenance and Change (p. 596)

Cite factors related to cognitive maintenance and change in late adulthood.

- Mentally active people are likely to maintain their cognitive abilities into advanced old age. A wide array of chronic health conditions are associated with cognitive decline. Retirement can bring about either positive or negative changes. Stimulating leisure activities and complex, challenging work facilitate intellectual functioning.

- With age, older adults' cognitive scores become increasingly unstable. As death approaches, **terminal decline**—a marked acceleration in deterioration of cognitive functioning—often occurs.

Cognitive Interventions (p. 597)

Can cognitive interventions help older adults sustain their mental abilities?

- Large-scale interventions like ADEPT and ACTIVE demonstrate that training in cognitive skills can offer large benefits for older people who have experienced cognitive declines. Targeting self-efficacy enhances cognitive gains.

Lifelong Learning (p. 597)

Discuss types of continuing education and benefits of such programs in late life.

- Increasing numbers of older people continue their education through university courses, community offerings, and programs such as Road Scholar and Osher Lifelong Learning Institutes. Participants acquire new knowledge and skills, new friends, a broader perspective on the world, and an image of themselves as more competent. Unfortunately, fewer continuing-education opportunities are available to low-SES seniors.

Important Terms and Concepts

activities of daily living (ADLs) (p. 567)
Alzheimer's disease (p. 582)
amyloid plaques (p. 583)
assisted living (p. 589)
assistive technology (p. 573)
associative memory deficit (p. 591)
autoimmune response (p. 571)
average healthy life expectancy (p. 564)
average life expectancy (p. 564)
cataracts (p. 569)
cerebrovascular dementia (p. 585)

compression of morbidity (p. 576)
dementia (p. 582)
frailty (p. 580)
functional age (p. 564)
implicit memory (p. 591)
instrumental activities of daily living (IADLs) (p. 567)
macular degeneration (p. 569)
maximum lifespan (p. 566)
neurofibrillary tangles (p. 583)
osteoarthritis (p. 580)

primary aging (p. 580)
prospective memory (p. 593)
reminiscence bump (p. 592)
remote memory (p. 592)
rheumatoid arthritis (p. 580)
secondary aging (p. 580)
selective optimization with compensation (p. 590)
sleep apnea (p. 571)
terminal decline (p. 596)
wisdom (p. 595)

© DESIGN PICS/CORBIS

As family responsibilities and vocational pressures lessen, friendships—like the relaxed companionship of these Guatemalan seniors—take on increasing importance. Having friends is an especially strong predictor of mental health in late adulthood.

Emotional and Social Development in Late Adulthood

chapter outline

Erikson's Theory: Ego Integrity versus Despair

Other Theories of Psychosocial Development in Late Adulthood

Peck's Tasks of Ego Integrity and Joan Erikson's Gerotranscendence • Labouvie-Vief's Emotional Expertise • Reminiscence

■ **CULTURAL INFLUENCES** The New Old Age

Stability and Change in Self-Concept and Personality

Secure and Multifaceted Self-Concept • Agreeableness, Acceptance of Change, and Openness to Experience • Spirituality and Religiosity

■ **BIOLOGY AND ENVIRONMENT** Religious Involvement and Quality of Life in the Final Year

Contextual Influences on Psychological Well-Being

Control versus Dependency • Physical Health • Negative Life Changes • Social Support

■ **SOCIAL ISSUES: HEALTH** Elder Suicide

A Changing Social World

Social Theories of Aging • Social Contexts of Aging: Communities, Neighborhoods, and Housing

Relationships in Late Adulthood

Marriage • Gay and Lesbian Partnerships • Divorce, Remarriage, and Cohabitation • Widowhood • Never-Married, Childless Older Adults • Siblings • Friendships • Relationships with Adult Children • Relationships with Adult Grandchildren and Great-Grandchildren • Elder Maltreatment

Retirement

The Decision to Retire • Adjustment to Retirement • Leisure and Volunteer Activities

Optimal Aging

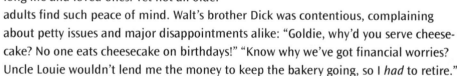

With Ruth at his side, Walt spoke to the guests at their sixtieth-anniversary party. "Even when things were hard," he reflected, "the time of life I liked best always seemed to be the current one. When I was a kid, I adored playing baseball. In my twenties, I loved learning the photography business. And of course," Walt continued, glancing affectionately at Ruth, "our wedding was the most memorable day of all."

He went on: "We never had much money for luxuries, but we found ways to have fun anyway—singing in the church choir and acting in community theater. And then Sybil was born. It meant so much to me to be a father—and now a grand-father and a great-grandfather. Looking back at my parents and grandparents and forward at Sybil, Marci, and Marci's son Jamel, I feel a sense of unity with past and future generations." With a smile, Walt added, "We keep up with Marci and Jamel on Facebook!"

PAUL BURNS/LIFESIZE/GETTY IMAGES

Walt and Ruth greeted old age with calm acceptance, grateful for the gift of long life and loved ones. Yet not all older adults find such peace of mind. Walt's brother Dick was contentious, complaining about petty issues and major disappointments alike: "Goldie, why'd you serve cheese-cake? No one eats cheesecake on birthdays!" "Know why we've got financial worries? Uncle Louie wouldn't lend me the money to keep the bakery going, so I *had* to retire."

A mix of gains and losses characterizes these twilight years, extending the multi-directionality of development begun early in life. On one hand, old age is a time of pleasure and tranquility, when children are grown, life's work is nearly done, and responsibilities are lightened. On the other hand, it brings concerns about declining physical functions, unwelcome loneliness, and the growing specter of imminent death.

In this chapter, we consider how older adults reconcile these opposing forces. Although some are weary and discontented, most traverse this period with poise and calm composure. They attach deeper significance to life and reap great benefits from family and friendship bonds, leisure activities, and community involvement. We will see how personal attributes and life history combine with home, neighbor-hood, community, and societal conditions to mold emotional and social development in late life. ●

Erikson's Theory: Ego Integrity versus Despair

The final psychological conflict of Erikson's (1950) theory, **ego integrity versus despair**, involves coming to terms with one's life. Adults who arrive at a sense of integrity feel whole, complete, and satisfied with their achievements. They have adapted to the mix of triumphs and disappointments that are an inevitable part of love relationships, child rearing, work, friendships, and community participation. They realize that the paths they followed, abandoned, and never selected were necessary for fashioning a meaningful life course.

The capacity to view one's life in the larger context of all humanity—as the chance combination of one person and one segment in history—contributes to the serenity and contentment that accompany integrity. "These last few decades have been the happiest," Walt murmured, clasping Ruth's hand—only weeks before the heart attack that would end his life. At peace with himself, his wife, and his children, Walt had accepted his life course as something that had to be the way it was.

In a study that followed a sample of women diverse in SES throughout adulthood, midlife generativity predicted ego integrity in late adulthood. Ego integrity, in turn, was associated with more favorable psychological well-being—a more upbeat mood, greater self-acceptance, higher marital satisfaction, closer rela-

Erik Erikson and his wife Joan exemplified the ideal of Erikson's final stage. They aged gracefully, felt satisfied with their achievements, and were often seen together, contented and deeply in love.

tionships with adult children, greater community involvement, and increased ease in accepting help from others when it is needed (James & Zarrett, 2007). As Erikson's theory indicates, psychosocial maturity in late life brings increased contentment, affectionate, enjoyable bonds with others, and continued service to society.

Scanning the newspaper, Walt pondered, "I keep reading these percentages: One out of five people will get heart disease, one out of three will get cancer. But the truth is, one out of one will die. We are all mortal and must accept this fate." The year before, Walt had given his granddaughter, Marci, his collection of prized photos, which had absorbed him for over half a century. With the realization that the integrity of one's own life is part of an extended chain of human existence, Erikson suggested, death loses its sting (Vaillant, 2002). In support of this view, older adults who report having attained intrinsic (personally gratifying) life goals typically express acceptance of their own death (Van Hiel & Vansteenkiste, 2009). Those who emphasize attainment of extrinsic goals (such as money or prestige) more often fear life's end.

The negative outcome of this stage, despair, occurs when aging adults feel they have made many wrong decisions, yet time is too short to find an alternate route to integrity. Without another chance, the despairing person finds it hard to accept that death is near and is overwhelmed with bitterness, defeat, and hopelessness. According to Erikson, these attitudes are often expressed as anger and contempt for others, which disguise contempt for oneself. Dick's argumentative, fault-finding behavior, tendency to blame others for his personal failures, and regretful view of his own life reflect this deep sense of despair.

Other Theories of Psychosocial Development in Late Adulthood

As with Erikson's stages of early and middle adulthood, other theorists have clarified and refined his vision of late adulthood, specifying the tasks and thought processes that contribute to a sense of ego integrity. All agree that optimal development involves greater integration and deepening of the personality.

Peck's Tasks of Ego Integrity and Joan Erikson's Gerotranscendence

According to Robert Peck (1968), attaining ego integrity involves three distinct tasks:

- *Ego differentiation:* For those who invested heavily in their careers, finding other ways to affirm self-worth—through family, friendship, and community life
- *Body transcendence:* Surmounting physical limitations by emphasizing the compensating rewards of cognitive, emotional, and social powers

- *Ego transcendence:* As contemporaries die, facing the reality of death constructively through efforts to make life more secure, meaningful, and gratifying for younger generations

In Peck's theory, ego integrity requires older adults to move beyond their life's work, their bodies, and their separate identities by investing in a future that extends beyond their own lifespan. Research suggests that as seniors grow older, both *body transcendence* (focusing on psychological strengths) and *ego transcendence* (orienting toward a larger, more distant future) increase. In a study of women, those in their eighties and nineties stated with greater certainty than those in their sixties that they "accept the changes brought about by aging," "have moved beyond fear of death," "have a clearer sense of the meaning of life," and "have found new, positive spiritual gifts to explore" (Brown & Lowis, 2003).

Erikson's widow Joan Erikson suggested that these attainments actually represent development beyond ego integrity (which requires satisfaction with one's past life) to an additional psychosocial stage that she calls **gerotranscendence**—a cosmic and transcendent perspective directed forward and outward, beyond the self. Drawing on her own experience of aging, her observations of her husband's final years, and the work of others on the positive potential of the years shortly before death, Joan Erikson speculated that success in attaining gerotranscendence is apparent in heightened inner calm and contentment and additional time spent in quiet reflection (Erikson, 1998; Tornstam, 2000, 2011).

Although interviews with people in their ninth and tenth decades reveal that many (but not all) experience this peaceful, contemplative state, more research is needed to confirm the existence of a distinct, transcendent late-life stage. Besides focusing more intently on life's meaning, many of the very old continue to report investments in the real world—visiting friends, keeping up with current events, striving to be a good neighbor, and engaging in leisure and volunteer pursuits.

Labouvie-Vief's Emotional Expertise

In Chapter 13, we discussed Gisella Labouvie-Vief's research on development of adults' reasoning about emotion (see page 453). Recall that cognitive-affective complexity (awareness and coordination of positive and negative feelings into an organized self-description) increases from adolescence through middle adulthood and then declines as basic information-processing skills diminish in late adulthood.

But older people display a compensating emotional strength: They gain in **affect optimization,** the ability to maximize positive emotion and dampen negative emotion (Labouvie-Vief, 2005; Labouvie-Vief et al., 2007; Labouvie-Vief, Grühn, & Studer, 2010). Compared with younger people, older adults selectively attend to and better recall emotionally positive over negative information (Mather & Carstensen, 2005). This bias toward the emotionally positive contributes to their remarkable

Despite serious medical problems, this aging adult asserts, "Being an invalid does not invalidate your life." Her adopted rescue dog gives her great pleasure. The ability to maximize positive emotion and dampen negative emotion contributes to older people's' remarkable resilience.

resilience. Despite physical declines, increased health problems, a restricted future, and death of loved ones, most older people sustain a sense of optimism, emotional stability, and good psychological well-being—an upbeat attitude linked to longer survival (Boyle et al., 2009; Carstensen et al., 2011). Furthermore, about 30 to 40 percent not only are high in affect optimization but also retain considerable capacity for cognitive-affective complexity—a combination related to especially effective emotional self-regulation.

Research also reveals that when asked to relate personal experiences in which they were happy, angry, fearful, or sad and to indicate how they knew they felt that emotion, aging individuals gave more vivid accounts than did younger people—evidence of being more in touch with their feelings. Consider this example:

> You have sunshine in your heart. During the wedding the candles were glowing. And that's just how I felt. I was glowing too. It was kind of dull outside. But that isn't how I felt. Everybody in the church felt like they were glowing. It was that kind of feeling. (Labouvie-Vief, DeVoe, & Bulka, 1989, p. 429)

Older adults' emotional perceptiveness helps them separate interpretations from objective aspects of situations. Consequently, their coping strategies often include making sure they fully understand their own feelings before deciding on a course of action. And they readily use emotion-centered coping strategies (controlling distress internally) in negatively charged situations (Blanchard-Fields, 2007). In sum, a significant late-life psychosocial attainment is becoming expert at reflecting on one's own feelings and regulating negative affect.

Reminiscence

We often think of older adults as engaged in **reminiscence**—telling stories about people and events from their past and reporting associated thoughts and feelings. Indeed, the widespread image of a reminiscing older person ranks among negative stereotypes of aging. In this common view, older people live in the past to escape the realities of a shortened future and the nearness of death. Yet research consistently reveals no age differences exist in total quantity of reminiscing! Rather, younger and older adults often use reminiscence for different purposes (Westerhof, Bohlmeijer, & Webster, 2010). And certain types of reminiscence are positive and adaptive.

In his comments on major events in his life at the beginning of this chapter, Walt was engaging in a special form of reminiscence called *life review*—calling up past experiences with the goal of achieving greater self-understanding. According to Robert Butler (1968), most older adults engage in life review as part of attaining ego integrity—a notion that has led many therapists to encourage life-review reminiscence. Older adults who participate in counselor-led life review report increased self-esteem, greater sense of purpose in life, and reduced depression (O'Rourke, Cappeliez, & Claxton, 2011; Westerhof, Bohlmeijer, & Webster, 2010). Life-review interventions can also help bereaved adults find a place for lost loved ones in their emotional lives, reinvest energy in other relationships, and move on with life (Worden, 2009).

Although life review occurs more often among older than younger adults, many older people who are high in self-acceptance and life satisfaction spend little time evaluating their past (Wink, 2007; Wink & Schiff, 2002). Indeed, in several studies in which older people were asked what they considered to be the best time of life, 10 to 30 percent identified one of the decades of late adulthood. Early and middle adulthood received especially high marks, whereas childhood and adolescence ranked as less satisfying (Field, 1997; Mehlson, Platz, & Fromholt, 2003). These findings challenge the widespread belief that older adults inevitably focus on the past and wish to be young again. To the contrary, today's seniors in industrialized nations are largely present- and future-oriented: They seek avenues for personal growth and fulfillment (see the Cultural Influences box on the following page).

Clearly, life review is not essential for adapting well to late adulthood. Indeed, reminiscence that is *self-focused,* engaged in to reduce boredom and revive bitter events, is linked to adjustment problems. Compared with younger people, older adults less often engage in this ruminative form of reminiscence, and those who do are often anxious and depressed from dwelling on painful past experiences (Bohlmeijer et al., 2007; O'Rourke, Cappeliez, & Claxton, 2011). Life review therapy aimed at helping these older adults focus on positive memories improves their psychological well-being.

In contrast, extroverted seniors favor *other-focused* reminiscence directed at social goals, such as solidifying family and friendship ties and reliving relationships with lost loved ones. And at times, older adults—especially those who score high in openness to experience—engage in *knowledge-based* reminiscence, drawing on their past for effective problem-solving strategies and for teaching younger people. These socially engaged, mentally stimulating forms of reminiscence help make life rich and rewarding (Cappeliez, Rivard, & Guindon, 2007). Perhaps because of their strong storytelling traditions, African-American and Chinese immigrant older adults are more likely than their Caucasian counterparts to use reminiscence to teach others about the past (Merriam, 1993; Webster, 2002).

For young and old alike, reminiscence often occurs during times of life transition. Older adults who have recently retired, been widowed, or moved to a new residence may turn temporarily to the past to sustain a sense of personal continuity (Cappeliez & Robitaille, 2010). As long as they do not get stuck in mulling over unresolved difficulties, reminiscence probably helps them recapture a sense of meaning.

Stability and Change in Self-Concept and Personality

Longitudinal research reveals continuing stability of the "big five" personality traits from mid- to late life (see Chapter 16, page 542). Yet the ingredients of ego integrity—wholeness, contentment, and image of the self as part of a larger world order—are reflected in several significant late-life changes in both self-concept and personality.

Secure and Multifaceted Self-Concept

Older adults have accumulated a lifetime of self-knowledge, leading to more secure and complex conceptions of themselves than at earlier ages (Diehl et al., 2011; Labouvie-Vief & Diehl, 1999). Ruth, for example, knew with certainty that she was good at growing a flower garden, budgeting money, counseling others, giving dinner parties, and figuring out who could be trusted and who couldn't. Furthermore, when young and older adults were asked for several life-defining memories, 65- to 85-year-olds were more likely to mention events with a consistent theme—such as the importance of relationships or personal independence—and to explain how the events were interrelated (McLean, 2008). Their autobiographical selves emphasized coherence and consistency, despite physical, cognitive, and occupational changes. As Ruth remarked humorously, "I know who I am. I've had plenty of time to figure it out!"

The firmness, stability, and multifaceted nature of Ruth's self-concept enabled her to compensate for lack of skill in domains she had never tried, had not mastered, or could no longer perform as well as before. Consequently, it allowed for self-acceptance—a key feature of integrity. In a study of old (70 to 84 years) and very old (85 to 103 years) German seniors asked to respond to the question "Who am I?," participants mentioned a broad spectrum of life domains, including hobbies, interests, social participation, family, health, and personality traits.

Cultural Influences

The New Old Age

After retiring, pediatrician Jack McConnell tried a relaxing lifestyle near a lake and golf course, but it worked poorly for the energetic 64-year-old. As his desire for a more fulfilling retirement grew, he noticed that outside his comfortable, gated neighborhood were many people serving community needs as gardeners, laborers, fast-food workers, and the like, yet who lived in or near poverty. The contrast galvanized Jack to found Volunteers in Medicine, a free clinic for working-poor adults and their families who lack health insurance (Croker, 2007). Five years later, at age 69, Jack was overseeing a highly cost-effective operation involving 200 retired doctors, nurses, and lay volunteers, who treat 6,000 patients a year.

Jack exemplifies a revised approach to late adulthood, one infused with new cultural meanings: Increasingly, older adults are using their freedom from work and parenting responsibilities to pursue personally enriching interests and goals. In doing so, they are giving back to their communities in significant ways, serving as role models for younger generations, and strengthening their sense of ego integrity with images of themselves as living ethical, worthy lives.

Added years of longevity and health plus financial stability have granted this active, opportunistic time of life to so many contemporary seniors that some experts believe a new phase of late adulthood has evolved called the **Third Age**—a term originating over a decade ago in France that spread through Western Europe and recently has stretched to North America. According to this view, the First Age is childhood, the Second Age is the adult period of earning a living

and rearing children, and the Third Age— extending from ages 65 to 79, and sometimes longer—is a time of personal fulfillment (James & Wink, 2007). The Fourth Age brings physical decline and need for care.

The baby boomers—healthier and financially better off than any preceding aging generation—are approaching late life with the conviction that their old age will not begin until 80 (Gergen & Gergen, 2003). This self-perception has helped define the Third Age as a time of self-realization and high life satisfaction. But even people a decade ahead of the oldest baby boomers are experiencing the Third Age as a phase of new goal setting and purpose rather than as an extended vacation (Winter et al., 2007). As we will see later in this chapter, retirement is no longer a one-way, age-graded event. In one survey of 300 older Americans, very few self-identified as retired (Trafford, 2004). Instead, they were building hybrid lives—leaving career jobs to work at different jobs that utilized their skills and devoting themselves to community service that they experienced as more meaningful than the paid work they left behind (Moen & Altobelli, 2007).

Although policy makers often express concern about the huge, impending baby-boomer burden on Social Security and Medicare, this large pool of vigorous, publicly minded future seniors has the potential to make enormous economic and social contributions. Today's Third Agers donate billions to the global economy in volunteer work, continue to participate in the work force in large numbers, and give generously to their families through monetary support and other forms of help—far more than they receive (see page 626).

For child-protection advocate Freda Briggs, late adulthood is a time of personal enrichment and new goal-setting. Since retiring from her faculty position at the University of South Australia, 82-year-old Briggs continues to write and speak on behalf of abused children while also embracing new adventures, such as parasailing and hot-air ballooning.

But as midlife roles shrink and terminate, too few alternatives are available for the many aging adults eager to make a difference (Bass, 2011). Societies need to provide abundant volunteer, national service, and other public interest opportunities, thereby harnessing their rich elder resources to solve pressing problems. The U.S. Serve America Act, signed into law in 2009, offers expanded service incentives and options to American adults of all ages and, thus, is a major step in that direction.

Finally, although the majority of U.S. adults in their sixties and seventies have more energy and choice than ever before, others—more often ethnic minorities, women, and those who live alone—suffer from financial hardship and distress and, thus, have little chance for new beginnings (Holstein, 2011). When social security, health care, and housing policies ensure a comfortable Third Age to all retiring adults, benefits accrue to the entire nation.

Adults in both age groups expressed more positive than negative self-evaluations, although a slight increase in negative comments occurred in the older group (Freund & Smith, 1999). Positive, multifaceted self-definitions predicted psychological well-being.

As the future shortens, most older adults, into their eighties and nineties, continue to mention—and actively pursue— hoped-for selves in the areas of physical health, cognitive functioning, personal characteristics, relationships, social responsibility, and leisure (Frazier, 2002; Markus & Herzog, 1992).

With respect to feared selves, physical health is even more prominent than it was in midlife.

At the same time, possible selves reorganize well into old age. When the German 70- to 103-year-olds just mentioned were followed longitudinally for four years, the majority deleted some possible selves and replaced them with new ones (Smith & Freund, 2002). Although future expectations become more modest with age, older adults often characterize hoped-for selves in terms of "improving," "achieving," or "attaining." Consistent with this view, they usually take concrete steps to attain their goals. Engaging in hope-related activities, in turn, is associated with gains in life satisfaction and with longer life (Hoppmann et al., 2007). Clearly, late adulthood is not a time of withdrawal from future planning!

Agreeableness, Acceptance of Change, and Openness to Experience

During late adulthood, shifts occur in personality characteristics that, once again, defy aging stereotypes. Old age is not a time in which the personality inevitably becomes rigid and morale declines. Rather, a flexible, optimistic approach to life, which fosters resilience in the face of adversity, is common.

Both open-ended interviews and personality tests reveal that older adults gain in *agreeableness,* becoming increasingly generous, acquiescent, and good-natured well into late life (Allemand, Zimprich, & Martin, 2008; Field & Millsap, 1991; Weiss et al., 2005). Agreeableness seems to characterize people who have come to terms with life despite its imperfections.

At the same time, older adults show modest age-related dips in *extroversion,* perhaps reflecting a narrowing of social contacts as people become more selective about relationships—a trend we will take up in a later section. Older people also tend to decline in *openness to experience,* likely due to their awareness of cognitive declines (Allemand, Zimprich, & Martin, 2008; Donnellan & Lucas, 2008). But engaging in cognitively challenging activities can promote openness to experience! In one study, 60- to 94-year-olds participated in a 16-week cognitive training program in reasoning, which included experience in solving challenging but enjoyable puzzles. During the program, the trained group showed steady gains in both reasoning and openness to experience not displayed by untrained controls. Sustained intellectual engagement seemed to induce seniors to view themselves as more open (Jackson et al., 2012). Openness, in turn, predicts pursuit of intellectual stimulation, thereby contributing to enhanced cognitive functioning.

Another late-life development is greater *acceptance of change*—an attribute older adults frequently mention as important to psychological well-being (Rossen, Knafl, & Flood, 2008). When asked about dissatisfactions in their lives, many seniors respond that they are not unhappy about anything! Acceptance of change is also evident in most older people' effective coping with the loss of loved ones, including death of a spouse, which they describe as the most stressful event they ever experienced (Lund, Caserta, & Dimond, 1993). The capacity to accept life's twists and turns, many of which are beyond one's control, is vital for adaptive functioning in late adulthood.

Most older adults are resilient, bouncing back in the face of adversity—especially if they did so earlier in their lives. And their heightened capacity for positive emotion contributes greatly to their resilience. Older adults' general cheerfulness strengthens their physiological resistance to stress, enabling them to conserve physical and mental resources needed for effective coping (Ong, Mroczek, & Riffin, 2011). The minority who are high in neuroticism—emotionally negative, short-tempered, and dissatisfied—tend to cope poorly with stressful events, experience mounting negative affect, and are at risk for health problems and earlier death (Mroczek & Spiro, 2007; Mroczek, Spiro, & Turiano, 2009).

Spirituality and Religiosity

How do older adults manage to accept declines and losses yet still feel whole and complete and anticipate death with calm composure? One possibility, consistent with Peck's and Erikson's emphasis on a transcendent perspective among seniors, is the development of a more mature sense of spirituality. Spirituality is not the same as religion: An inspirational sense of life's meaning can be found in art, nature, and social relationships. But for many people, religion provides beliefs, symbols, and rituals that guide this quest for meaning.

Older adults attach great value to religious beliefs and behaviors. In recent national surveys, over 70 percent of Americans age 65 and older said that religion is very important in their lives—the highest of any age group (Gallup News Service, 2006, 2012). Although health and transportation difficulties reduce organized religious participation in advanced old age, U.S. seniors generally become more religious or spiritual as they age.

The late-life increase in religiosity, however, is modest, and it is far from universal. Longitudinal research reveals that the majority of people show stability in religiosity throughout adulthood (Ai, Wink, & Ardelt, 2010; Dillon & Wink, 2007). Furthermore, in a British investigation following adults for two decades, one-fourth of seniors said they had become less religious, with some citing disappointment at the support they had received from their religious institution during stressful times (such as bereavement) as the reason (Coleman, Ivani-Chalian, & Robinson, 2004).

Despite these differences, spirituality and faith may advance to a higher level in late adulthood—away from prescribed beliefs toward a more reflective approach that emphasizes links to others and is at ease with mystery and uncertainty. According to James Fowler's theory of faith development, mature adults develop new faith capacities, including awareness of their own belief system as just one of many possible worldviews, contemplation of the deeper significance of religious symbols and rituals, openness to other religious perspectives as sources of inspiration, and (especially in late life) an enlarged vision of a common good that serves the needs of all humanity (Fowler & Dell, 2006). For example, as a complement to his Catholicism,

Biology and Environment

Religious Involvement and Quality of Life in the Final Year

Jane—deeply religious all her life—attended a Friday evening service at the synagogue on her eighty-ninth birthday, celebrating at a reception with close friends and congregants. "I love being here, but I'm tired at night so I don't come often," Jane said. Still, she found private ways to stay involved. An amateur poet, she composed a poetic ending to a religious school play at the request of student actors. At home, she read from her prayer book, describing certain excerpts as "incredibly thought-provoking." Despite escalating frailty, Jane sustained a gratifying connection with her faith and her people until she died in the middle of her ninetieth year.

Religiosity is linked to an array of psychological and physical benefits for older adults. Does it predict enhanced quality of life even in the final year—a time of increasing disability for most older people?

In a longitudinal investigation of 2,800 people age 65 and older, representing the senior population of New Haven, Connecticut, researchers conducted periodic interviews addressing religious participation and quality of life over the course of a decade,

while also noting any deaths (Idler, McLaughlin, & Kasl, 2009). The study offered a unique opportunity to look closely at a subsample of nearly 500, who had died within one year of being interviewed.

For religious seniors with greater disability, public involvement (attending services) declined. In the final year of life, private religiosity more powerfully predicted of quality of life. Compared with others, the deeply religious more often saw friends and scored higher in psychological well-being: They were more upbeat in mood, displayed fewer depressive symptoms, and experienced life as more exciting and enjoyable. They also felt better physically—had less difficulty sleeping, better appetite, and better self-rated health. And among the most disabled, this link between religiosity and self-rated heath was stronger!

Being deeply religious seems to fortify the mind–body connection near life's end, with the frailest displaying the greatest resilience. These findings help us understand another outcome of the New Haven study (as well as other research): Participants were more likely to die just after than just before

For this aging adult, the daily ritual of Tibetan Buddhist prayer is a powerful source of inner strength. For many people in late adulthood, religiosity is linked to physical and psychological benefits.

a major religious holiday—for Jews, Passover and Yom Kippur; for Christians, Christmas and Easter (Anson & Anson, 2001; Idler & Kasl, 1992). Religious beliefs and practices appeared to intercede in a biological pathway, extending and giving meaning to life even in its final days.

Walt became intensely interested in Buddhism, especially its focus on attaining perfect peace and happiness by mastering thoughts and feelings, never harming others, and resisting attachment to worldly objects.

Involvement in both organized and informal religious activities is especially high among low-SES ethnic minority older people, including African-American, Hispanic, and Native-American groups. In African-American communities, churches not only provide contexts for deriving meaning from life but also are centers for education, health, social welfare, and political activities aimed at improving life conditions. African-American seniors look to religion as a powerful resource for social support beyond the family and for the inner strength to withstand daily stresses and physical impairments (Armstrong & Crowther, 2002). Compared with their Caucasian agemates, more African-American older adults report collaborating with God to overcome life problems (Lee & Sharpe, 2007).

As at earlier ages, in late adulthood women are more likely than men to say that religion is very important to them, to participate in religious activities, and to engage in a personal quest for connectedness with a higher power (Gallup News Service, 2012; Wink & Dillon, 2002). Women's higher rates of poverty, widowhood, and participation in caregiving, including caring for chronically ill family members, expose them to higher levels of stress and anxiety. As with ethnic minorities, they turn to religion for social support and for a larger vision of community that places life's challenges in perspective.

Religious involvement is associated with diverse benefits, including better physical and psychological well-being, more time devoted to exercising and leisure activities, greater sense of closeness to family and friends, and greater generativity (care for others) (Boswell, Kahana, & Dilworth-Anderson, 2006; Gillum et al., 2008; Krause, 2012; Wink, 2006, 2007). In longitudinal research, both organized and informal religious participation predicted longer survival, after family background, health, social, and psychological factors known to affect mortality were controlled (Helm et al., 2000; Strawbridge et al., 2001). And as the Biology and Environment box above confirms, the benefits of religious involvement for quality of life are evident even in the final year of life.

But aspects of religion that make a difference in aging adults' lives are not always clear. In two investigations of Caucasian older adults, religious *activity*—not religious belief or membership in a congregation—was associated with favorable adjustment following loss of a spouse (Lund, Caserta, & Dimond, 1993). Increased social engagement brought about by religious participation, rather than the specifically religious nature of the activity, was the influential factor. Other evidence, however, indicates that belief in God's powers contributes substantially to self-esteem, optimism, and life satisfaction, especially among low-SES, ethnic minority seniors (Krause, 2005; Schieman, Bierman, & Ellison, 2010). Their personal relationship with God seems to help them cope with life's hardships.

Contextual Influences on Psychological Well-Being

As we have seen in this and the previous chapter, most adults adapt well to old age, yet some feel dependent, incompetent, and worthless. Personal and situational factors often combine to affect psychological well-being. Identifying these contextual influences is vital for designing interventions that foster positive adjustment.

Control versus Dependency

As Ruth's eyesight, hearing, and mobility declined in her eighties, Sybil visited daily to help with self-care and household tasks. During the hours mother and daughter were together, Sybil interacted most often with Ruth when she asked for help with activities of daily living. When Ruth handled tasks on her own, Sybil usually withdrew.

Observations of people interacting with older adults in both private homes and institutions reveal two highly predictable, complementary behavior patterns. In the first, called the **dependency–support script**, dependent behaviors are attended to immediately. In the second, the **independence–ignore script**, independent behaviors are mostly ignored. Notice how these sequences reinforce dependent behavior at the expense of independent behavior, regardless of the older person's competencies (Baltes, 1995, 1996). Even a self-reliant individual like Ruth did not always resist Sybil's unnecessary help because it brought about social contact.

Among older people who experience no difficulty with daily activities, opportunities to interact with others are related to high satisfaction with everyday life. In contrast, among older adults who have trouble performing daily activities, social contact is linked to a less positive everyday existence (Lang & Baltes, 1997). This suggests that social interaction while assisting seniors with physical care, household chores, and errands is often not meaningful and rewarding but, rather, demeaning and unpleasant. Consider these typical reactions of care recipients

to a spouse's help with daily activities: "felt dependent," "felt indebted," "felt like a weak, incapable person" (Newsom, 1999).

Longitudinal research shows that negative reactions to caregiving can result in persisting depression (Newsom & Schulz, 1998). But whether assistance from others undermines well-being depends on many factors, including the quality of help, the caregiver–older adult relationship, and the social and cultural context in which helping occurs. Why do family members and other caregivers often respond in ways that promote excessive dependency in old age? Stereotypes of older people as passive and incompetent appear to be responsible. After reading passages that activated these stereotypes (by portraying aging adults as inept), older people responded with more frequent help-seeking behavior (Coudin & Alexopoulos, 2010).

In Western societies, which highly value independence, many older adults fear relinquishing control and becoming dependent on others. This is especially so for those with a high need for self-determination (Curtiss, Hayslip, & Dolan, 2007; Frazier, 2002). As physical and cognitive limitations increase, granting older adults the freedom to choose those areas in which they desire help preserves their autonomy (Lachman, Neupert, & Agrigoroaei, 2011). Dependency can be adaptive if it permits older people to remain in control by choosing those areas in which they desire help. In this way, they can conserve their strength by investing it in self-chosen, highly valued activities, using a set of strategies considered in Chapter 17: *selective optimization with compensation.*

TAKE A MOMENT... Cite examples of the varied ways older adults optimize their functioning while compensating for

By letting her son help with grocery shopping, will this Mexican 80-year-old become too dependent? Not necessarily. When older adults assume personal control over areas of dependency, they can conserve their strength and invest it in highly valued activities.

declines. Notice how they adaptively modify their personal goals: They invest in goals that enable them to remain active and self-determining, adjust those goals to suit their changing capacities, and disengage from goals that overextend their capacities, turning toward other, attainable goals (Heckhausen, Wrosch, & Schultz, 2010). Using these strategies, older people strive to remain active agents in the direction of their own lives. When family and caregiving environments support their efforts, most older adults sustain a sense of self-efficacy, purpose, and investment in overcoming obstacles.

Assistance aimed at enabling older adults use their capacities fully in pursuit of their goals sustains an effective **person–environment fit**—a good match between their abilities and the demands of their living environments, which promotes adaptive behavior and psychological well-being. When people cannot maximize use of their capacities (have become excessively dependent), they react with boredom and passivity. When they encounter environmental demands that are too great (receive too little assistance), they experience overwhelming stress.

Physical Health

As noted in Chapter 16, physical health is a powerful predictor of psychological well-being. Physical declines and chronic disease can lead to a sense of loss of personal control—a powerful contributor to mental health problems. Physical illness resulting in disability is among the strongest risk factors for late-life depression (Morrison, 2008; Whitbourne & Meeks, 2011). Although fewer older than young and middle-aged adults are depressed (see Chapter 17), profound feelings of hopelessness rise with age as physical disability and consequent social isolation increase. But more than actual physical limitations, *perceived negative physical health* predicts depressive symptoms (Jang et al., 2007; Weinberger & Whitbourne, 2010). This helps explain the stronger physical impairment–depression relationship among higher-SES aging adults (Schieman & Plickert, 2007). Because of their lifetime of better physical health, they probably experience physical limitations as more unexpected and challenging.

The relationship between physical and mental health problems can become a vicious cycle, each intensifying the other. In survey research conducted in 15 countries, adults of all ages reported that mental health problems actually interfered more than physical disabilities with activities of daily living, including home management and social life (Ormel et al., 2008). At times, despondency and "giving up" trigger rapid physical decline in a sick aging adult. This downward spiral can be hastened by a move to a nursing home, requiring the older person to adjust to diminished control over daily life and greater distance from family and friends. In the months after admission, many residents judge their quality of life to have worsened substantially, become severely anxious and depressed, and deteriorate rapidly. The stress of illness together with institutionalization is associated with escalating physical and mental health problems and with mortality (Scocco, Rapattoni, & Fantoni, 2006).

Depression in old age is often lethal. People age 65 and older have the highest suicide rate of all age groups (see the Social Issues: Health box on pages 612–613). What factors enable people like Ruth to surmount the physical impairment–depression relationship, remaining content? Personal characteristics discussed in this and earlier chapters—optimism, sense of self-efficacy, and effective coping—are vitally important (Morrison, 2008). But for frail aging adults to display these attributes, families and caregivers must avoid the dependency-support script and, instead, grant them autonomy.

Unfortunately, older adults generally do not get the mental health care they need—even in nursing homes, where depression and other mental health problems are widespread (Grabowski et al., 2010; Karel, Gatz, & Smyer, 2012). More than half of U.S. nursing home residents receive no regular mental health intervention.

Negative Life Changes

Ruth lost Walt to a heart attack, cared for her sister Ida as her Alzheimer's symptoms worsened, and faced health problems of her own—all within a span of a few years. Older people are at risk for a variety of negative life changes—death of loved ones, illness and physical disabilities, declining income, and greater dependency. Negative life changes are difficult for everyone but may actually evoke less stress and depression in older than in younger adults (Charles, 2011). Many older people have learned to cope with hard times, to appraise negative changes as common and expected in late life, and to accept loss as part of human existence.

Still, when negative changes pile up, they test the coping skills of older adults. In very old age, such changes are greater for women than for men. Women over age 75 are far less likely to be married, more often have lower incomes, and suffer from more illnesses—especially ones that restrict mobility. Furthermore, older women (as at younger ages) more often say that others depend on them for caregiving and emotional support (see page 626 in Chapter 17). Thus, their social relations, even in very old age, are more often a source of stress (Antonucci, Ajrouch, & Birditt, 2008). And because of their own declining health, older women may not be able to meet others' needs for care—circumstances associated with chronic, high distress (Charles, 2010). Not surprisingly, women of advanced age tend to report lower psychological well-being than do men (Pinquart & Sörensen, 2001).

Social Support

In late adulthood, social support continues to reduce stress, thereby promoting physical health and psychological well-being. Availability of social support increases the odds of living longer (Fry & Debats, 2006; Temkin-Greener et al., 2004). And it helps explain the relationship of religious participation to survival, discussed earlier. Usually, older adults receive informal assistance with tasks of daily living from family members—first from their spouse or, if none exists, from children and then

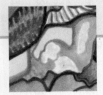

Social Issues: Health

Elder Suicide

When 65-year-old Abe's wife died, he withdrew from life. Living far from his two daughters, he spent his nonworking days alone, watching television and reading mystery novels. As grandchildren were born, Abe visited his daughters' homes from time to time, carrying his despondent behavior with him. "Look at my new pajamas, Grandpa!" Abe's 6-year-old grandson Tony exclaimed on one occasion. Abe didn't respond.

After arthritis made walking difficult, Abe retired. With more empty days, his depression deepened. Gradually, he developed painful digestive difficulties, but he refused to see a doctor. "Don't need to," he said abruptly when one of his daughters begged him to get medical attention. Answering her invitation to Tony's tenth birthday party, Abe wrote, "Maybe—if I'm still around next month. By the way, when I go, I want my body cremated." Two weeks later, Abe died from an intestinal blockage. His body was found in the living room chair where he habitually spent his days. Although it may seem surprising, Abe's self-destructive acts are a form of suicide.

Factors Related to Elder Suicide

Recall from Chapter 12 that suicide increases over the lifespan. Although age differences in adulthood rates are shrinking, suicide continues to climb in late adulthood. Older adults are at increased risk in most countries throughout the world (World Health Organization, 2013b).

The higher suicide rate among males persists in late life. Five times as many U.S. aging men as women take their own lives. Suicide among white men age 70 and older rises steeply with age, whereas it actually declines after age 75 in women (U.S. Census Bureau, 2012b). Compared with the white majority, most ethnic minority older adults have low suicide rates.

What explains these trends? Despite the lifelong pattern of higher rates of depression and more suicide attempts among females, older women's closer ties to family and friends, greater willingness to seek social support, and religiosity prevent many from taking their own lives. High levels of social support through extended families and church affiliations also may prevent suicide among ethnic minorities (Conwell, Van Orden, & Caine, 2011). And within certain groups, such as Alaskan Natives, deep

respect for and reliance on older adults to teach cultural traditions strengthen self-esteem and social integration (Kettl, 1998). This reduces elder suicide, making it nonexistent after age 80.

As in earlier years, the methods favored by older males (firearms, hanging) offer less chance of revival than those by older females (poisoning or drug overdose). Nevertheless, failed suicides are much rarer in old age than in adolescence. The ratio of attempts to completions for the young is as high as 300 to 1; for aging adults, it is 4 to 1 or lower (Conwell, Van Orden, & Caine, 2011). When seniors decide to die, they seem especially determined to succeed.

Underreporting of suicides probably occurs at all ages, but it is more common in old age. Medical examiners are less likely to pursue suicide as a cause of death when a person is old. And many older adults, like Abe, engage in indirect self-destructive acts rarely classified as suicide—deciding not to go to a doctor when ill or refusing to eat or take prescribed medications. Among institutionalized seniors, these efforts to hasten death are widespread (Reiss & Tishler, 2008b). Consequently, elder suicide is an even larger problem than official statistics indicate.

Two types of events prompt suicide in late life. Losses—retirement from a highly valued occupation, widowhood, or social

from siblings. If these individuals are not available, other relatives and friends may step in.

Nevertheless, many older people place such high value on independence that they do not want extensive help from others close to them unless they can reciprocate. When assistance is excessive or cannot be returned, it often results in reduced self-efficacy and psychological stress (Liang, Krause, & Bennett, 2001; Warner et al., 2011). Perhaps for this reason, adult children express a deeper sense of obligation toward their aging parents than their parents expect from them (see Chapter 16, page 549). Formal support—a paid home helper or agency-provided services—as a complement to informal assistance not only helps relieve caregiving burden but also spares aging adults from feeling overly dependent in their close relationships.

Ethnic minority older adults, however, do not readily accept formal assistance. But they are more willing to do so when home helpers are connected to a familiar neighborhood organization, especially the church. Although African-American seniors say they rely more on their families than on the church for assistance, those with support and meaningful roles in both contexts fare best in mental health (Coke, 1992; Taylor, Lincoln, & Chatters, 2005). Support from religious congregants has psychological benefits for older adults of all backgrounds, perhaps because recipients feel that it is motivated by genuine care and concern, not just obligation (Krause, 2001). Also, the warm atmosphere of religious organizations fosters a sense of social acceptance and belonging.

Overall, for social support to foster well-being, older adults must take personal control of it. This means consciously giving

isolation—place seniors who have difficulty coping with change at risk for persistent depression. Risks of another type arise when chronic and terminal illnesses severely reduce physical functioning or cause intense pain (Conwell et al., 2010). As comfort and quality of life diminish, feelings of hopelessness and helplessness deepen. Very old people, especially men, are particularly likely to take their own lives under these conditions. The chances are even greater when a sick older person is socially isolated—living alone or in a nursing home with high staff turnover, minimal caregiver support, and little opportunity for personal control over daily life (Reiss & Tishler, 2008a).

Prevention and Treatment

Warning signs of suicide in late adulthood, like those at earlier ages, include efforts to put personal affairs in order, statements about dying, despondency, and sleep and appetite changes. But family members, friends, and caregivers must also watch for indirect self-destructive acts that are unique to old age, such as refusing food or medical treatment. Too often, people in close touch with the elderly incorrectly assume that these symptoms are a "natural" consequence of aging. Older suicide victims are 2.5 times more likely to have visited their doctors within a month of

taking their lives (Vannoy et al., 2011). Yet their suicidal risk was not recognized.

When suicidal aging adults are depressed, the most effective treatment combines antidepressant medication with therapy, including help in coping with role transitions, such as retirement, widowhood, and dependency brought about by illness. Distorted ways of thinking ("I'm old—nothing can be done about my problems") must be countered and revised. Meeting with the family to find ways to reduce loneliness and desperation is also helpful.

Although youth suicide has risen (see Chapter 12, page 422), elder suicide has diminished during the past 50 years, as a result of increased economic security among older adults, improved medical care and social services, and more favorable cultural attitudes toward retirement. Communities are beginning to recognize the importance of additional preventive steps, such as programs that help older adults cope with life transitions, telephone hot lines with trained volunteers who provide emotional support, and agencies that arrange for regular home visitors or "buddy system" phone calls (Lapierr et al., 2011). But so far, most of these efforts benefit women more than men because women are more likely to tell health professionals about high-risk symptoms, such as despondency, and to use social resources.

Suicide reaches its highest rate among people age 75 and older. Warning signs include despondency, sleep and appetite changes, statements about dying, and efforts to put personal affairs in order.

Finally, elder suicide raises a controversial ethical issue: Do people with incurable illnesses have the right to take their own lives? We will take up this topic in Chapter 19.

---

up primary control in some areas to remain in control of other, highly valued pursuits (Heckhausen, Wrosch, & Schultz, 2010). For example, although she could handle financial matters, shopping, and food preparation on her own, Ruth allowed her daughter Sybil to assist with these activities, leaving Ruth with more stamina for pleasurable reading and gardening.

When we intervene with older adults, we must ask ourselves, What kind of assistance are we providing? Help that is not wanted or needed or that exaggerates weaknesses results in poor person–environment fit, undermines mental health, and—if existing skills fall into disuse—accelerates physical disability. In contrast, help that increases autonomy—that frees up energy for endeavors that are personally satisfying and that lead to growth—enhances quality of life. These findings clarify why *perceived social support* (older adults' sense of being able to

count on family or friends in times of need) is associated with a positive outlook in older adults with disabilities, whereas sheer *amount* of help family and friends provide has little impact (Uchino, 2009).

Finally, besides tangible assistance, older adults benefit from social support that offers affection, affirmation of their self-worth, and sense of belonging. Extroverted seniors are more likely to take advantage of opportunities to engage with others, thereby reducing loneliness and depression and fostering self-esteem and life satisfaction (Mroczek & Spiro, 2005). But as we will see in the next section, supportive social ties in old age have little to do with quantity of contact. Instead, high-quality relationships, involving expressions of kindness, encouragement, respect, and emotional closeness, have the greatest impact on mental health in late life.

A Changing Social World

Walt and Ruth's outgoing personalities led many family members and friends to seek them out, and they often reciprocated. In contrast, Dick's stubborn nature meant that he and Goldie, for many years, had had a far more restricted network of social ties.

As noted earlier, extroverts (like Walt and Ruth) continue to interact with a wider range of people than do introverts and people (like Dick) with poor social skills. Nevertheless, both cross-sectional and longitudinal research reveals that size of social networks and, therefore, amount of social interaction decline for virtually everyone (Antonucci, Akiyama, & Takahashi, 2004; Charles & Carstensen, 2009). This finding presents a curious paradox: If social interaction and social support are essential for mental health, how is it possible for older adults to interact less yet be generally satisfied with life and less depressed than younger adults?

Social Theories of Aging

Social theories of aging offer explanations for changes in aging adults' social activity. Two older perspectives—disengagement theory and activity theory—interpret declines in social interaction in opposite ways. More recent approaches—continuity theory and socioemotional selectivity theory—account for a wider range of findings.

Disengagement Theory. According to **disengagement theory,** mutual withdrawal between older adults and society takes place in anticipation of death (Cumming & Henry, 1961). Older people decrease their activity levels and interact less fre-

quently, becoming more preoccupied with their inner lives. At the same time, society frees the old from employment and family responsibilities. The result is viewed as beneficial for both sides. Older adults are granted a life of tranquility. And once they disengage, their deaths are less disruptive to society.

Clearly, however, most aging adults don't disengage! As we saw in Chapter 17 when we discussed wisdom, older people in many cultures move into new positions of prestige and power because of their long life experience. Even after retirement, many adults sustain aspects of their work; others develop new, rewarding roles in their communities. Disengagement, then, may represent not older peoples' personal preference but, rather, a failure of the social world to provide opportunities for engagement. The more social opportunities older adults report, the more strongly they believe they can create worthwhile social experiences for themselves (Lang, Featherman, & Nesselroade, 1997). Indeed, an obvious application of disengagement theory—encouraging older people to withdraw from vital roles—can have profound negative consequences for their sense of self-worth and, at a societal level, waste valuable social resources!

As we will see shortly, older adults' retreat from interaction is more complex than disengagement theory implies. Instead of disengaging from all social ties, they let go of unsatisfying contacts and maintain satisfying ones. And sometimes, they put up with less than satisfying relationships to remain engaged! For example, though Ruth often complained about Dick's insensitive behavior, she reluctantly agreed to travel with Dick and Goldie because she wanted to share the experience with Walt.

Activity Theory. Attempting to overcome the flaws of disengagement theory, **activity theory** states that social barriers to engagement, not the desires of aging adults, cause declining rates of interaction. When older people lose certain roles (for example, through retirement or widowhood), they try to find others in an effort to stay about as active and busy as they were in middle age (Maddox, 1963). In this view, older adults' life satisfaction depends on conditions that permit them to remain engaged in roles and relationships.

Although people do seek alternative sources of meaning in response to social losses, activity theory fails to acknowledge any psychological change in old age. Many studies show that merely offering seniors opportunities for social contact does not lead to greater social activity. In nursing homes, for example, where social partners are abundant, social interaction is very low, even among the healthiest residents—a circumstance we will examine when we discuss housing arrangements for aging adults. Especially troubling for activity theory is the repeated finding that when health status is controlled, older people who have larger social networks and engage in more activities are not necessarily happier (Charles & Carstensen, 2009; Ritchey, Ritchey, & Dietz, 2001). Recall that quality, not quantity, of relationships predicts psychological well-being in old age.

Continuity Theory. Unlike activity theory, **continuity theory** does not view older adults' efforts to remain active as simple replacement of lost social roles with new ones. Rather,

These sisters—ages 93 and 89—greet each other with enthusiasm. The one on the right traveled from Poland to New York City for this reunion. To preserve emotional equilibrium and reduce stress, older adults increasingly emphasize familiar, emotionally rewarding relationships.

according to this view, most aging adults strive to maintain a personal system—an identity and a set of personality dispositions, interests, roles, and skills—that promotes life satisfaction by ensuring consistency between their past and anticipated future. This striving for continuity does not mean that older people's lives are static. To the contrary, aging produces inevitable change, but most older adults try to minimize stress and disruptiveness by integrating those changes into a coherent, consistent life path. As much as possible, they choose to use familiar skills and engage in familiar activities with familiar people—preferences that provide a secure sense of routine and direction in life.

Research confirms a high degree of continuity in older adults' everyday pursuits and relationships. For most, friends and family members with whom they interact remain much the same, as do work, volunteer, leisure, and social activities. Even after a change (such as retirement), people usually make choices that extend the previous direction of their lives, engaging in new activities but often within familiar domains. For example, a retired manager of a children's bookstore collaborated with friends to build a children's library and donate it to an overseas orphanage. A musician who, because of arthritis, could no longer play the violin arranged regular get-togethers with musically inclined friends to listen to and talk about music. Robert Atchley (1989), originator of continuity theory, noted, "Everyday life for most older people is like long-running improvisational

theater in which . . . changes are mostly in the form of new episodes [rather] than entirely new plays" (p. 185).

Aging adults' reliance on continuity has many benefits. Participating in familiar activities with familiar people provides repeated practice that helps preserve physical and cognitive functioning, fosters self-esteem and mastery, and affirms identity (Finchum & Weber, 2000; Vacha-Haase, Hill, & Bermingham, 2012). Investing in long-standing, close relationships provides comfort, pleasure, and a network of social support. Finally, striving for continuity is essential for attaining Erikson's sense of ego integrity, which depends on preserving a sense of personal history (Atchley, 1999).

As we explore social contexts and relationships of aging, we will encounter many examples of how older adults use continuity to experience aging positively, as a "gentle slope." We will also address ways that communities can help them do so. As our discussion will reveal, people experiencing the greatest disruption to desired continuity in activities and lifestyle preferences have the most difficulty adapting to growing older.

Socioemotional Selectivity Theory. A final perspective addresses how people's social networks sustain continuity while also narrowing as they age. According to **socioemotional selectivity theory,** social interaction extends lifelong selection processes. In middle adulthood, marital relationships deepen, siblings feel closer, and number of friendships declines. In old age, contacts with family and long-term friends are sustained until the eighties, when they diminish gradually in favor of a few very close relationships. In contrast, as Figure 18.1 shows, contacts with acquaintances and willingness to form new social ties

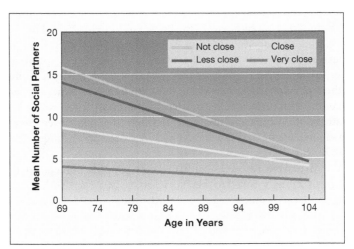

FIGURE 18.1 Age-related change in number of social partners varying in closeness. In interviews with over 500 older adults ranging in age from 69 to 104, the number of "not close" and "less close" partners fell off steeply with age, whereas the number of "close" and "very close" partners declined minimally. (From F. R. Lang, U. M. Staudinger, & L. L. Carstensen, 1998, "Perspectives on Socioemotional Selectivity in Late Life: How Personality and Social Context Do (and Do Not) Make a Difference," *Journal of Gerontology, 53B,* p. 24. Copyright © 1998 The Gerontological Society of America. Adapted by permission of Oxford University Press and F. R. Lang.)

fall off steeply from middle through late adulthood (Carstensen, 2006; Carstensen, Fung, & Charles, 2003; Fung, Carstensen, & Lang, 2001).

What explains these changes? Socioemotional selectivity theory states that physical and psychological aspects of aging lead to changes in the functions of social interaction. *TAKE A MOMENT...* Consider the reasons you interact with members of your social network. At times, you approach them to get information. At other times, you seek affirmation of your worth as a person. You also choose social partners to regulate emotion, approaching those who evoke positive feelings and avoiding those who make you feel sad, angry, or uncomfortable. For older adults, who have gathered a lifetime of information, the information-gathering function becomes less significant. Also, they realize it is risky to approach people they do not know for self-affirmation: Stereotypes of aging increase the odds of receiving a condescending, hostile, or indifferent response.

Instead, as physical fragility makes it more important to avoid stress, older adults emphasize the emotion-regulating function of interaction. In one study, younger and older adults were asked to categorize their social partners. Younger people more often sorted them on the basis of information seeking and future contact, whereas older people emphasized anticipated feelings (Frederickson & Carstensen, 1990). They appeared highly motivated to approach pleasant relationships and avoid unpleasant ones. Interacting mostly with relatives and friends increases the chances that emotional equilibrium will be preserved.

Within these close bonds, older adults actively apply their emotional expertise to promote harmony. They are less likely than younger people to respond to tensions with destructive tactics (yelling, arguing) and more likely to use constructive strategies, such as expressing affection or disengaging to calmly let the situation blow over (Birditt & Fingerman, 2005; Luong, Charles, & Fingerman, 2011). They also reinterpret conflict in less stressful ways—often by identifying something positive in the situation (Labouvie-Vief, 2003). Consequently, despite their smaller social networks, they are happier than younger people with their number of friends and report fewer problematic relationships and less distress when they encounter interpersonal tensions (Blanchard-Fields & Coats, 2008; Fingerman & Birditt, 2003).

Extensive research confirms that people's perception of time is strongly linked to their social goals. *TAKE A MOMENT...* If you faced a shortened future, with whom would you choose to spend time? When remaining time is limited, adults *of all ages* place more emphasis on the emotional quality of their social experiences. They shift from focusing on long-term goals to emphasizing emotionally fulfilling relationships in the here and now (Charles & Carstensen, 2010). Similarly, seniors—aware that time is "running out"—don't waste it on unlikely future payoffs but, instead, turn to close friends and family members. Furthermore, we generally take special steps to facilitate positive interaction with people dear to us whose time is limited—for example, treating older friends and relatives more kindly than younger ones, easily excusing or forgiving their social transgressions (Luong, Charles, & Fingerman, 2011). In this way,

social partners contribute to older adults' gratifying relationship experiences.

Aging adults' emphasis on *relationship quality* helps explain a cultural exception to the restriction of social relationships just described. In collectivist societies, where people value an interdependent self and, thus, attach great importance to remaining embedded in their social group, older people may be motivated to sustain high-quality ties with all partners! In line with this prediction, in a Hong Kong study, aging adults scoring high in interdependence both expanded their number of emotionally close social partners and sustained the same number of peripheral social partners into advanced old age (Yeung, Fung, & Lang, 2008). In contrast, Hong Kong older people scoring low in interdependence resembled their Western counterparts: They gradually limited their social ties to a few close relationships.

In sum, socioemotional selectivity theory views older adults' preference for high-quality, emotionally fulfilling relationships as resulting from changing life conditions. But the meaning of relationship quality and, therefore, the number and variety of people to whom older people turn for pleasurable interaction and self-affirmation vary with culture.

Social Contexts of Aging: Communities, Neighborhoods, and Housing

The physical and social contexts in which aging adults live affect their social experiences and, consequently, their development and adjustment. Communities, neighborhoods, and housing arrangements vary in the extent to which they enable aging residents to satisfy their social needs.

Communities and Neighborhoods. About half of U.S. ethnic minority older adults live in cities, compared with just one-third of Caucasians. The majority of seniors reside in suburbs, where they moved earlier in their lives and usually remain after retirement. Suburban older adults have higher incomes and report better health than their inner-city counterparts do. But inner-city older people are better off in terms of public transportation. As declines in physical functioning compromise out-of-home mobility, convenient bus, tram, and rail lines become increasingly important to life satisfaction and psychological well-being (Mollenkopf, Hieber, & Wahl, 2011; Oswald et al., 2010). Furthermore, city-dwelling seniors fare better in terms of health, income, and proximity of social services and cultural activities than do the one-fifth of U.S. older people who live in small towns and rural areas (U.S. Department of Health and Human Services, 2012e). In addition, small-town and rural seniors are less likely to live near their children, who often leave these communities in early adulthood.

Yet small-town and rural aging adults compensate for distance from children and social services by establishing closer relationships with nearby extended family and by interacting more with neighbors and friends (Hooyman & Kiyak, 2011; Shaw, 2005). Smaller communities have features that foster gratifying relationships—stability of residents, shared values and lifestyles, willingness to exchange social support, and frequent social visits as country people "drop in" on one another. And many suburban and rural communities have responded to aging residents' needs by developing transportation programs (such as special buses and vans) to take them to health and social services, senior centers, and shopping centers.

Both urban and rural older adults report greater life satisfaction when many senior citizens reside in their neighborhood and are available as like-minded companions. Presence of family is less crucial when neighbors and nearby friends provide social support (Gabriel & Bowling, 2004). This does not mean that neighbors replace family relationships. But older adults are content as long as their children and other relatives who live far away arrange occasional visits (Hooyman & Kiyak, 2011).

Compared with older adults in urban areas, those in quiet neighborhoods in small and midsized communities are more satisfied with life. In addition to a friendlier atmosphere, smaller communities have lower crime rates (AARP, 2006; Krause, 2004). As we will see next, fear of crime has profound, negative consequences for seniors' sense of security and comfort.

Victimization and Fear of Crime. Walt and Ruth's single-family home stood in an urban neighborhood, five blocks from the business district where Walt's photography shop had been prior to his retirement. As the neighborhood aged, some homes fell into disrepair, and the population became more transient. Although they had never been victimized, crime was on Walt and Ruth's minds and affected their behavior: They avoided neighborhood streets after sundown.

Media attention has led to a widely held belief that crime against seniors is common. In reality, older adults are less often targets of crime, especially violent crime, than other age groups. In urban areas, however, purse snatching and pickpocketing are more often committed against seniors (especially women) than younger people (U.S. Department of Justice, 2010). A single incident can strike intense anxiety into the hearts of seniors because of its potential for physical injury and its financial consequences for those with low incomes.

Among frail aging adults living alone and in inner-city areas, fear of crime, which is sometimes greater than worries about income, health, and housing, restricts activities and undermines morale (Beaulieu, Leclerc, & Dube, 2003). In one study, older adults who had experienced a violent crime were more likely than those with physical and cognitive impairments to enter a nursing home (Lachs et al., 2006). Neighborhood Watch and other programs that encourage residents to look out for one another increase communication among neighbors, strengthen sense of neighborhood cohesion, and reduce fear (Oh & Kim, 2009).

Housing Arrangements. Seniors' housing preferences reflect a strong desire for **aging in place**—remaining in a familiar

© ARIEL SKELLEY/CORBIS

Like many older adults, these dog lovers reap great satisfaction from residing in a neighborhood with like-minded senior residents. Presence of family is less crucial when neighbors and nearby friends provide social support.

setting where they have control over their everyday life. Overwhelmingly, older people in Western nations want to stay in the neighborhoods where they spent their adult lives; in fact, 90 percent remain in or near their old home. In the United States, fewer than 4 percent relocate to other communities (U.S. Department of Health and Human Services, 2012e). These moves are usually motivated by a desire to live closer to children or, among the more economically advantaged and healthy, a desire for a more temperate climate and a place to pursue leisure interests.

Most aging adults' relocations occur within the same town or city and are prompted by declining health, widowhood, or disability (Sergeant, Ekerdt, & Chapin, 2008). As we look at housing arrangements for older adults, we will see that the more a setting deviates from home life, the harder it is for older people to adjust.

Ordinary Homes. For the majority of older adults, who are not physically impaired, staying in their own homes affords the greatest possible personal control—freedom to arrange space and schedule daily events as one chooses. More seniors in Western countries live on their own today than ever before—a trend due to improved health and economic well-being (U.S. Department of Health and Human Services, 2012e). But when health and mobility problems appear, independent living poses risks to an effective person–environment fit. Most homes are designed for younger people. They are seldom modified to suit the physical capacities of their older residents. And living alone with a physical disability is linked to social isolation and loneliness (Adams, Sanders, & Auth, 2004).

When Ruth reached her mid-eighties, Sybil begged her to move into her home. Like many adult children of Southern, Central, and Eastern European descent (Greek, Italian, Polish, and others), Sybil felt an especially strong obligation to care for her frail mother. Older adults of these cultural backgrounds, as well as African Americans, Asians, Hispanics, and Native

Americans, more often live in extended families (see page 549 in Chapter 16).

Yet increasing numbers of ethnic minority older adults want to live on their own, although poverty often prevents them from doing so. For example, two decades ago, most Asian-American older adults were living with their children, whereas today 65 percent live independently—a trend also evident in certain Asian nations, such as Japan (Federal Interagency Forum on Aging Related Statistics, 2012; Takagi, Silverstein, & Crimmins, 2007). With sufficient income to keep her home, Ruth refused to move in with Sybil. Continuity theory helps us understand why many older adults react this way, even after health problems accumulate. As the site of memorable life events, the home strengthens continuity with the past, sustaining a sense of identity in the face of physical declines and social losses. And it permits older adults to adapt to their surroundings in familiar, comfortable ways (Atchley, 1999). Older people also value their independence, privacy, and network of nearby friends and neighbors.

During the past half century, the number of unmarried, divorced, and widowed seniors living alone has risen dramatically. Approximately 30 percent of U.S. older adults live by themselves, a figure that rises to nearly 50 percent for those age 85 and older (U.S. Census Bureau, 2012b). This trend, though evident in all segments of the aging population, is less pronounced among men, who are far more likely than women to be living with a spouse into advanced old age.

Over 40 percent of American seniors who live alone are poverty-stricken—rates many times greater than among older couples. More than 70 percent are widowed women. Because of lower earnings in earlier years, some entered old age this way.

Residents of a retirement community join visiting Girl Scouts to bake dog treats for animal shelters. By sustaining an effective person–environment fit as capacities change, residential communities enable older adults to enjoy a more active lifestyle.

Others became poor for the first time, often because they outlived a spouse who suffered a lengthy, costly illness. With age, their financial status worsens as their assets shrink and their own health-care costs rise (Biegel & Liebbrant, 2006; U.S. Census Bureau, 2012b). Under these conditions, isolation, loneliness, and depression can pile up. Poverty among lone aging women is deeper in the United States than in other Western nations because of less generous government-sponsored income and health benefits. Consequently, the feminization of poverty deepens in old age.

Residential Communities. About 7 percent of U.S. adults age 65 and older live in residential communities, a proportion that rises with age as functional limitations increase. Among people age 85 and older, 22 percent live in these communities, which come in great variety (U.S. Department of Health and Human Services, 2012e). Housing developments for the aged, either single-dwelling or apartment complexes, differ from ordinary homes only in that they have been modified to suit older adults' capacities (featuring, for example, single-level living space and grab bars in bathrooms). Some are federally subsidized units for low-income residents, but most are privately developed retirement villages with adjoining recreational facilities.

For older adults who need more help with everyday tasks, *assisted-living* arrangements are available (see Chapter 17, page 589). **Congregate housing**—an increasingly popular long-term care option—provides a variety of support services, including meals in a common dining room, along with watchful oversight of residents with physical and mental disabilities. **Life-care communities** offer a range of housing alternatives, from independent or congregate housing to full nursing home care. For a large initial payment and additional monthly fees, life care guarantees that seniors' changing needs will be met within the same facility as they age.

Unlike Ruth and Walt, who remained in their own home, Dick and Goldie decided in their late sixties to move to nearby congregate housing. For Dick, the move was a positive turn of events that permitted him to relate to peers on the basis of their current life together, setting aside past failures in the outside world. Dick found gratifying leisure pursuits—leading an exercise class, organizing a charity drive with Goldie, and using his skills as a baker to make cakes for birthday and anniversary celebrations.

By sustaining an effective person–environment fit as older adults' capacities change, residential communities have positive effects on physical and mental health. A specially designed physical space and care on an as-needed basis help seniors overcome mobility limitations, enabling greater social participation and a more active lifestyle (Fonda, Clipp, & Maddox, 2002; Jenkins, Pienta, & Horgas, 2002). And in societies where old age leads to reduced status, age-segregated living is gratifying to most seniors who choose it. It may open up useful roles and leadership opportunities. The more older adults perceive the environment as socially supportive, the more they collaborate with one another in coping with stressors of aging and in providing assistance to other residents (Lawrence & Schigelone, 2002). Congregate housing appears to be well-suited to promoting mutually supportive relationships among residents.

Nevertheless, no U.S. federal regulations govern assisted-living facilities, which vary widely in quality. Low-income ethnic minority seniors are less likely to use assisted living. When older people with limited financial resources do transition to assisted living, they usually lack control over when and where they move and enter lower-quality settings—conditions associated with high stress (Ball et al., 2009). And in some states, assisted-living facilities are prohibited from providing any nursing care and monitoring, requiring seniors to leave when their health declines (Hernandez & Newcomer, 2007). Yet physical designs and support services that enable aging in place are vital for aging adults' well-being. These include homelike surroundings, division of large environments into smaller units to facilitate meaningful activities, social roles and relationships, and the latest assistive technologies to permit adaptation to changing health needs (Cutler, 2007; Oswald & Wahl, 2013).

Shared values and goals among residents with similar backgrounds also enhance life satisfaction. Older adults who feel socially integrated into the setting are more likely to consider it their home. But those who lack like-minded companions are unlikely to characterize it as home and are at high risk for loneliness and depression (Adams, Sanders, & Auth, 2004; Cutchin, 2013).

LOOK AND LISTEN

Visit an assisted-living community, and explore its housing options, physical design, and social and leisure opportunities. Ask several residents about their satisfaction with daily life. How well does the living environment support aging in place and effective person–environment fit? ●

Nursing Homes. The 5 percent of Americans age 65 and older who live in nursing homes experience the most extreme restriction of autonomy and social integration. Although potential companions are abundant, interaction is low. To regulate emotion in social interaction (so important to aging adults), personal control over social experiences is vital. Yet nursing home residents have little opportunity to choose their social partners, and timing of contact is generally determined by staff rather than by residents' preferences. Social withdrawal is an adaptive response to these often overcrowded, hospital-like settings, which typically provide few ways for residents to use their competencies. Although interaction with people in the outside world predicts nursing home residents' life satisfaction, interaction within the institution does not (Baltes, Wahl, & Reichert, 1992). Not surprisingly, nursing home residents with physical but not mental impairments are far more depressed, anxious, and lonely than their community-dwelling counterparts (Guildner et al., 2001).

Designing more homelike nursing homes could help increase residents' sense of security and control. U.S. nursing homes, usually operated for profit, are often packed with resi-

THE GREEN HOUSE® model blurs distinctions among nursing home, assisted living, and "independent" living. In this homelike setting, residents determine their own daily schedules and help with household tasks. Green House living environments now exist in more than 20 U.S. states.

dents and institutional in their operation. In contrast, European facilities are liberally supported by public funds and resemble high-quality assisted living.

In a radically changed U.S. nursing-home concept called THE GREEN HOUSE® model, a large, outdated nursing home in Mississippi was replaced by ten small, self-contained houses (Rabig et al., 2006). Each is limited to ten or fewer residents, who live in private bedroom–bathroom suites that surround a family-style communal space. Besides providing personal care, a stable staff of nursing assistants fosters aging adults' control and independence. Residents determine their own daily schedules and are invited to join in both recreational and household activities, including planning and preparing meals, cleaning, gardening, and caring for pets. A professional support team—including licensed nurses, therapists, social workers, physicians, and pharmacists—visits regularly to serve residents' health needs. In a comparison of Green House residents with traditional nursing home residents, Green House older adults reported substantially better quality of life, and they also showed less decline over time in ability to carry out activities of daily living (Kane et al., 2007).

The Green House model—and other models like it—is blurring distinctions among nursing home, assisted living, and "independent" living. By making the home a central, organizing principle, the Green House approach includes all the aging-in-place and effective person–environment fit features that ensure late-life well-being: physical and emotional comfort, enjoyable daily pursuits enabling residents to maximize use of their capacities, and meaningful social relationships.

ASK YOURSELF

REVIEW Cite features of neighborhoods and residential communities that enhance aging adults' life satisfaction.

CONNECT According to socioemotional selectivity theory, when time is limited, adults focus on the emotional quality of their social relationships. How do older people apply their emotional expertise (discussed on page 616) to attain this goal?

APPLY Sam lives alone in the same home he has occupied for over 30 years. His adult children cannot understand why he won't move across town to a modern apartment. Using continuity theory, explain why Sam prefers to stay where he is.

REFLECT Imagine yourself as a resident in an assisted-living facility. List all the features you would want your living context to have, explaining how each helps ensure effective person–environment fit and favorable psychological well-being.

Relationships in Late Adulthood

The **social convoy** is an influential model of changes in our social networks as we move through life. *TAKE A MOMENT...* Picture yourself in the midst of a cluster of ships traveling together, granting one another safety and support. Ships in the inner circle represent people closest to you, such as a spouse, best friend, parent, or child. Those less close, but still important, travel on the outside. With age, ships exchange places in the convoy, and some drift off while others join the procession (Antonucci, Birditt, & Ajrouch, 2011; Antonucci, Birditt, & Akiyama, 2009). As long as the convoy continues to exist, you adapt positively.

In the following sections, we examine the ways older adults with diverse lifestyles sustain social networks of family members and friends. As ties are lost, older adults draw others closer and occasionally add replacements, though not at the rate they did at younger ages. Although size of the convoy decreases as agemates die, aging adults are rarely left without people in their inner circle who contribute to their well-being—a testament to their resilience in maintaining effective social networks (Fiori, Smith, & Antonucci, 2007). But for some, tragically, the social convoy breaks down. We will also explore the circumstances in which older people experience abuse and neglect at the hands of those close to them.

Marriage

Even with the high U.S. divorce rate, one in every four or five first marriages is expected to last at least 50 years. Walt's comment to Ruth that "the last few decades have been the happiest" characterizes the attitudes and behaviors of many aging couples who have spent their adult lives together. Marital satisfaction rises from middle to late adulthood, when it is at its peak (Ko

et al., 2007; Levenson, Carstensen, & Gottman, 1993). Several changes in life circumstance and couples' communication underlie this trend.

First, late-life marriages involve fewer stressful responsibilities that can negatively affect relationships, such as rearing children and balancing demands of career and family (Diamond, Fagundes, & Butterworth, 2010). Second, perceptions of fairness in the relationship increase as men participate more in household tasks after retirement. For older adults who experienced little social pressure for gender equality in their youth, division of labor in the home still reflects traditional roles. Men take on more home maintenance projects, whereas women's duties—cooking, cleaning, laundry, and shopping—continue as before. Among adults retiring today, "feminine" tasks are more equally shared than they were during work life (Kulik, 2001). In either case, men's increased involvement at home often results in a greater sense of equity in marriage than before. Third, with extra time together, the majority of couples engage in more joint leisure activities, which—especially for women—enhances sense of marital closeness (Trudel et al., 2008).

Fourth, greater emotional understanding and emphasis on regulating emotion in relationships lead to more positive interactions between spouses. Compared to younger couples, aging couples rate their relationship as higher in quality, disagree less often, and resolve their differences in more constructive ways. Even in unhappy marriages, older adults are less likely to let their disagreements escalate into expressions of anger and resentment (Hatch & Bulcroft, 2004). For example, when Dick complained about Goldie's cooking, Goldie tried to appease him: "All right, Dick, next birthday I won't make cheesecake." And when Goldie brought up Dick's bickering and criticism, Dick usually said, "I know, dear," and retreated to another room. As in other relationships, seniors protect themselves from stress by molding marital ties to make them as pleasant as possible.

As Dick and Goldie's exchanges illustrate, aging married couples do admit to times their partner gets on their nerves or

After retirement, couples have more time to devote to joint leisure activities, which contributes to the rise in marital satisfaction from middle to late adulthood.

makes too many demands—more so than they say their adult children or best friends do (Birditt, Jackey, & Antonucci, 2009). But these expressions are mild, and they likely result from frequent contact, yielding greater opportunity for minor annoyances.

Finally, compared to their single agemates, married seniors generally have larger social networks of both family members and friends, with whom they interact more frequently. As long as older adults report mostly high-quality ties, this relationship profile provides for social engagement and support from a variety of sources and is linked to higher psychological well-being (Birditt & Antonucci, 2007; Fiori, Smith, & Antonucci, 2007). Perhaps because of these benefits, simply having an intimate relationship is health-protective and is associated with increased longevity (Manzoli et al., 2007).

When marital dissatisfaction exists, however, even having close, high-quality friendships cannot reduce its profoundly negative impact on adjustment. A poor marriage often takes a greater toll on women than on men (Birditt & Antonucci, 2007; Whisman et al., 2006). Recall from Chapter 14 that women more often try to work on a troubling relationship, yet in late life, expending energy in this way is especially taxing, both physically and mentally. Men, in contrast, are more likely to protect themselves by withdrawing and avoiding discussion.

Gay and Lesbian Partnerships

Older gays and lesbians in long-term partnerships have sustained their relationships through a historical period of hostility and discrimination. Nevertheless, most report happy, highly fulfilling relationships, pointing to their partner as their most important source of social support. Compared with gay and lesbian seniors who live alone, couples rate their physical and mental health more favorably (Grossman, 2006).

A lifetime of effective coping with an oppressive social environment may have strengthened homosexuals' skill at dealing with late-life physical and social changes, thereby contributing to a satisfying partnership (Gabbay & Wahler, 2002). And changing social conditions, including the greater ease with which younger generations embrace their sexual minority identities and "come out," may have encouraged more older adults to do the same, with benefits for their well-being (Cohler & Hostetler, 2007). Also, greater gender-role flexibility enables gay and lesbian couples to adapt easily to sharing household tasks following retirement.

Because of imagined or real strain in family relationships when they told others about their homosexuality, gays and lesbians less often assume that family members will provide support in old age. Consequently, many have forged strong friendships to replace or supplement family ties (Richard & Brown, 2006). Homosexual couples with gratifying friendship networks report high life satisfaction and less fear of aging (Slusher, Mayer, & Dunkle, 1996).

Nevertheless, because of continuing prejudice and lack of societal recognition of their partnerships, aging gays and lesbians face unique challenges. Health-care systems are often unresponsive to their unique needs. And where gay and lesbian unions are not legally recognized (in most U.S. states), if one partner becomes frail or ill, the other may not be welcome in hospitals or nursing homes or be allowed to participate in health-care decisions—an issue we will return to in Chapter 19. These circumstances can make late-life declines and losses especially painful.

Divorce, Remarriage, and Cohabitation

When Walt's uncle Louie was 65, he divorced his wife Sandra after 32 years of marriage. Although she knew the marriage was far from perfect, Sandra had lived with Louie long enough that the divorce came as a shock. A year later, Louie married Rachella, a divorcée who shared his enthusiasm for sports and dance.

Couples who divorce in late adulthood constitute less than 5 percent of all U.S. divorces in any given year (Elliott & Simmons, 2011). But the divorce rate among people age 65 and older has increased over the past three decades as new generations of seniors—especially the baby boomers—have become accepting of marital breakup as a means of attaining self-fulfillment and as the divorce risk has risen for second and subsequent marriages.

Although one-fifth of older adults' dissolving marriages are of less than 10 years duration, about half are lengthy—30 years or more (Brown & Lin, 2012). Compared with younger adults, longtime married older people have given their adult lives to the relationship. Following divorce, they find it harder to separate their identity from that of their former spouse and, therefore, may experience a greater sense of personal failure. Relationships with family and friends shift at a time when close bonds are crucial for psychological well-being.

As in middle adulthood, aging women are more likely than men to initiate divorce. This is despite the fact that the financial consequences for women generally are severe—greater than for widowhood because many accumulated assets are lost in property settlements (McDonald & Robb, 2004; Wu & Schimmele, 2007). Still, older people of both genders seldom express regret over leaving an unhappy marriage (Bair, 2007). Usually, they experience a sense of relief.

Remarriage rates are low in late adulthood and decline with age, though remarriage is more likely after divorce than after widowhood. Aging baby boomers—accustomed to using the Internet for many purposes—are increasingly turning to contemporary ways of searching for new partners, including online dating services and personal ads, though they use dating sites far less often than younger people do. But older peoples' personal ads indicate that they are more selective with respect to the age, race, religion, and income of a potential dating partner (McIntosh et al., 2011). And as Figure 18.2 on page 622 shows, they more often refer to their own health issues and loneliness and less often to romance, sex, desire for a soulmate, and adventure than middle-aged people do (Alterovitz & Mendelsohn, 2013). In their search for the right person, seniors seem to take a candid, no-nonsense approach!

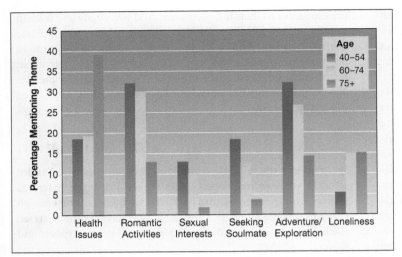

FIGURE 18.2 Themes in online personal ads of middle-aged and older adults seeking dating partners. An analysis of themes in 450 ads revealed that older adults more often mention health issues and loneliness, whereas middle-aged adults place greater emphasis on romance, sex, finding a soulmate, and adventure. Seniors appear to be practical and direct in their search for a partner. (From S. S. R. Alterovitz and G. A. Mendelsohn, 2013, "Relationship Goals of Middle-Aged, Young–Old, and Old–Old Internet Daters: An Analysis of Online Personal Ads." *Journal of Aging Studies, 27*, p. 163. Copyright © 2013, Elsevier. Reprinted by permission of Elsevier, Inc.)

Men more often succeed in finding a marriage partner than women, as their opportunities to do so are far greater. Nevertheless, increasing age makes remarriage less likely for both men and women, who frequently say they don't want to marry again (Calasanti & Kiecolt, 2007; Mahay & Lewin, 2007). Common reasons include poorer health, a shortened future (making it hard to justify radical life change), concerns about adult children's acceptance of the new partner, desire to protect their estate, and (especially for women) past negative experiences with marriage (Wu & Schimmele, 2007). Divorced men who remain single, however, no longer benefit from their former wives' kin-keeping role, are more likely to experience reduced contact and support from adult children, and more often move away from friends and neighbors (Daatland, 2007). For these reasons, they are at greater risk for adjustment difficulties.

Compared with younger people who remarry, seniors who do so enter more stable relationships, as their divorce rate is much lower. In Louie and Rachella's case, the second marriage lasted for 28 years! Perhaps late-life remarriages are more successful because they involve more maturity, patience, and a better balance of romantic with practical concerns. Remarried older couples are generally very satisfied with their new relationships, although men tend to be more content than women (Clarke, 2005; Connidis, 2010). With fewer potential mates, perhaps women who remarry in late life settle for less desirable partners.

Rather than remarrying, seniors who enter a new relationship are increasingly choosing cohabitation, a trend expected to continue as more baby boomers—the first generation to cohabit at high rates in early adulthood—reach late life. Like remarriage, cohabitation results in more stable relationships and higher relationship quality than it did at younger ages. And cohabiting seniors are as satisfied with their partnered lives as are their married counterparts (Brown & Kawamura, 2010). This suggests that cohabitation is distinctive in late adulthood, serving as a long-term alternative to marriage.

Widowhood

Walt died shortly after Ruth turned 80. Like over 70 percent of widowed seniors, Ruth described the loss of her spouse as the most stressful event of her life. As two researchers noted, being widowed means that the survivor has "lost the role and identity of being a spouse (being married and doing things as a couple), which is potentially one of the most pervasive, intense, intimate, and personal roles that they have ever had in their life" (Lund & Caserta, 2004a, p. 29). Ruth felt lonely, anxious, and depressed for several months after the funeral.

Widows make up about one-third of older adults in industrialized nations. Because women live longer than men and are less likely to remarry, more than 40 percent of U.S. women age 65 and older are widowed, compared with just 13 percent of men (U.S. Census Bureau, 2012b). Ethnic minorities with high rates of poverty and chronic disease are more likely to be widowed.

Earlier we mentioned that most widows and widowers live alone rather than in extended families, a trend that is stronger for whites than for ethnic minorities. Though less well-off financially than married seniors, most want to retain control over their time and living space and to avoid disagreements with

Because most men rely on their wives for social connectedness, they are less prepared than women to overcome the loneliness of widowhood. This widower, however, makes an effort to connect socially with neighbors by hosting a backyard barbecue.

their adult children. Widowed aging adults who relocate usually move closer to family but not into the same residence.

The greatest problem for recently widowed older people is profound loneliness (Connidis, 2010). But adaptation varies widely, depending on age, social support, and personality. Aging adults have fewer lasting problems than younger individuals who are widowed, probably because death in later life is viewed as less unfair (Bennett & Soulsby, 2012). And most widowed seniors—especially those with outgoing personalities and high self-esteem—are resilient in the face of loneliness (Moore & Stratton, 2002; van Baarsen, 2002). To sustain continuity with their past, they try to preserve social relationships that were important before the spouse's death and report that relatives and friends respond in kind, contacting them at least as often as before (Utz et al., 2002). Also, the stronger older adults' sense of self-efficacy in handling tasks of daily living, the more favorably they adjust (Fry, 2001).

Nevertheless, widowed individuals must reorganize their lives, reconstructing an identity that is separate from the deceased spouse. Wives whose roles depended on their husbands' typically find this harder than those who developed rewarding roles of their own. But overall, men show more physical and mental health problems and greater risk of mortality than women, for several reasons (Bennett, Smith, & Hughes, 2005; Shor et al., 2012). First, because most men relied on their wives for social connectedness, household tasks, promotion of healthy behaviors, and coping with stressors, they are less prepared than women for the challenges of widowhood. Second, because of gender-role expectations, men feel less free to express their emotions or to ask for help with meals, household tasks, and social relationships (Bennett, 2007; Lund & Caserta, 2004b). Finally, men tend to be less involved in religious activities—a vital source of social support and inner strength.

In two studies of older widowers, those in their seventies reported the most depression and showed the slowest rate of improvement over the following two years. The death of their wives occurred around the time they were adjusting to retirement, resulting in two major changes at once, with widowhood highly unexpected because most wives outlive their husbands (Lund & Caserta, 2001, 2004a). African-American widowers, however, show no elevated risk of mortality over their married agemates, and they report less depression than Caucasian widowers (Elwert & Christakis, 2006). Perhaps greater support from extended family and church is responsible.

Sex differences in the experience of widowhood contribute to men's higher remarriage rate. Women's kinkeeper role (see Chapter 16, page 545) and ability to form close friendships may lead them to feel less need to remarry. In addition, because many women share the widowed state, they probably offer one another helpful advice and sympathy. In contrast, men often lack skills for maintaining family relationships, forming emotionally satisfying ties outside marriage, and handling the chores of their deceased wives.

Still, most widowed seniors fare well within a few years, resembling their married counterparts in psychological well-being. Older widows and widowers who participated in several months of weekly classes providing information and support in acquiring daily living skills felt better prepared to manage the challenges of widowed life (Caserta, Lund, & Obray, 2004). Those who emerge from this traumatic event with a sense of purpose in life and with confidence in their ability to meet everyday challenges often experience stress-related personal growth (Caserta et al., 2009). Many report a new-found sense of inner strength, greater appreciation of close relationships, and reevaluation of life priorities. Applying What We Know on page 624 suggests a variety of ways to foster adaptation to widowhood in late adulthood.

Never-Married, Childless Older Adults

Shortly after Ruth and Walt's marriage in their twenties, Ruth's father died. Her sister Ida continued to live with and care for their mother, who was in ill health until she died 16 years later. When, at age 25, Ida received a marriage proposal, she responded, "I can't marry anybody while my mother is still living. I'm expected to look after her." Ida's decision was not unusual for a daughter of her day. She never married or had children.

About 5 percent of older Americans have remained unmarried and childless throughout their lives. Almost all are conscious of being different from the norm, but most have developed alternative meaningful relationships. Ida, for example, formed a strong bond with a neighbor's son. In his childhood, she provided emotional support and financial assistance, which helped him overcome a stressful home life. He included Ida in family events and visited her regularly until she died. Other nonmarried seniors speak of the centrality of extended family and of younger people in their social networks—often nieces and nephews—and of influencing them in enduring ways

For this never-married older adult, a warm relationship with his great-nephew provides a sense of family connection and an opportunity to influence a member of a younger generation.

Applying What We Know

Fostering Adaptation to Widowhood in Late Adulthood

Suggestion	Description
Self	
Mastery of new skills of daily living	Especially for men, learning how to perform household tasks such as shopping and cooking, to sustain existing family and friendship ties, and to build new relationships is vital for positive adaptation.
Family and Friends	
Social support and interaction	Social support and interaction must extend beyond the grieving period to ongoing assistance and caring relationships. Family members and friends can help most by making support available while encouraging the widowed older adult to use effective coping strategies.
Community	
Senior centers	Senior centers offer communal meals and other social activities, enabling widowed and other older adults to connect with people in similar circumstances and to gain access to other community resources, such as listings of part-time employment and available housing.
Support groups	Support groups can be found in senior centers, religious institutions, and other agencies. Besides new relationships, they offer an accepting atmosphere for coming to terms with loss, effective role models, and assistance with developing skills for daily living.
Religious activities	Involvement in a church, synagogue, or mosque can help relieve the loneliness associated with loss of a spouse and offer social support, new relationships, and meaningful roles.
Volunteer activities	One of the best ways for widowed older adults to find meaningful roles is through volunteer activities. Some are sponsored by formal service organizations, such as the Red Cross or the Retired and Senior Volunteer Program. Other volunteer programs exist in hospitals, senior centers, schools, and charitable organizations.

(Wenger, 2009; Wenger & Burholdt, 2001). In addition, same-sex friendships are key in never-married older women's lives (McDill, Hall, & Turell, 2006). These tend to be unusually close and often involve joint travel, periods of coresidence, and associations with each other's extended families.

Never-married, childless men are more likely than women to feel lonely and depressed. And without pressure from a partner to maintain a healthy lifestyle, they engage in more unhealthy behaviors. Hence, their physical and mental health is poor compared with their married counterparts (Kendig et al., 2007). Never-married older women report a level of well-being equivalent to that of married older adults and greater than that of divorcées and recently widowed seniors. Only when they cannot maintain social contacts because of declining health do they report feeling lonely (Dykstra, 2009).

Because friendships are not the same as blood ties when it comes to caregiving, being unmarried and childless in very old age reduces the likelihood of informal personal care (Chang, Wilber, & Silverstein, 2010; Wenger, 2009). And with close ties weighted toward friends, nonmarried childless seniors lose more network members with increasing age (Dykstra, 2006). Still, most say that some informal support is available.

Siblings

Nearly 80 percent of Americans age 65 and older have at least one living sibling. Most live within 100 miles of each other, communicate regularly, and visit at least several times a year. Both men and women describe closer bonds with sisters than with brothers. Perhaps because of women's greater emotional expressiveness and nurturance, the closer the tie to a sister, the higher older people's psychological well-being (Van Volkom, 2006).

Aging siblings in industrialized nations are more likely to socialize than to provide one another with direct assistance because most older adults turn first to their spouse and children. Nevertheless, siblings seem to be an important "insurance policy" in late adulthood. After age 70, aid from siblings living near one another rises (White, 2001). Widowed and never-married seniors have more contacts with siblings, perhaps because they have fewer competing family relationships, and they also are more likely to receive sibling support when their health declines (Connidis, 2010). For example, when Ida's Alzheimer's symptoms worsened, Ruth came to her aid. Although Ida had many friends, Ruth was her only living relative.

Friendships

As family responsibilities and vocational pressures lessen, friendships take on increasing importance. Having friends is an especially strong predictor of mental health among seniors (Rawlins, 2004). Older adults report more favorable experiences with friends than with family members, in part because of the pleasurable leisure activities shared with friends (Larson, Mannell, & Zuzanek, 1986). Unique qualities of friendship interaction—openness, spontaneity, mutual caring, and common interests—are also influential.

Functions of Late-Life Friendships. The diverse functions of friendship in late adulthood clarify its profound significance:

- *Intimacy and companionship are basic to meaningful late-life friendships.* As Ida and her best friend, Rosie, took walks, went shopping, or visited each other, they disclosed their deepest sources of happiness and worry, engaged in pleasurable conversation, laughed, and had fun. Older adults' descriptions of their close friendships reveal that mutual interests, feelings of belongingness, and opportunities to confide in each other sustain these bonds over time (Field, 1999).

- *Late-life friends help shield each other from negative judgments stemming from stereotypes of aging.* "Where's your cane, Rosie?" Ida asked when the two women were about to leave for a restaurant. "Come on, don't be self-conscious. When y'get one of those 'you're finished' looks from someone, just remember: In the Greek village where my mother grew up, there was no separation between generations, so the young ones got used to wrinkled skin and weak knees. And we older women were recognized as the wise ones (Deveson, 1994). Why, we were midwives, matchmakers, experts in herbal medicine; we knew about everything!"

- *Friendships link aging adults to the larger community.* For seniors who cannot go out as often, interactions with friends can keep them abreast of events in the wider world. "Rosie," Ida reported, "did you know the Thompson girl was named high school valedictorian . . . and the city council is voting on the living-wage act tonight?" Friends can also open up new experiences, such as travel or participation in community activities.

- *Friendships help protect seniors from the psychological consequences of loss.* Older people in declining health who remain in contact with friends through phone calls and visits show improved psychological well-being (Fiori, Smith, & Antonucci, 2007). Similarly, when close relatives die, friends offer compensating social supports.

Characteristics of Late-Life Friendships. Although older adults prefer familiar, established relationships over new ones, friendship formation continues throughout life. Ties to old and dear friends who live far away are maintained, with growing numbers of seniors staying in touch with the aid of e-mail and social networking sites, such as Facebook (see page 599 in Chapter 17). Nevertheless, with age, seniors report that the friends they interact with most often and feel closest to live in the same community.

As in earlier years, older people tend to choose friends whose age, sex, ethnicity, and values resemble their own. Compared with younger people, fewer report other-sex friendships. But some have them—usually long-standing ones dating back several decades. Seniors continue to benefit uniquely from these ties, obtaining an insider's view of the thoughts, feelings, and behavior of members of the other sex (Monsour, 2002). As age-mates die, the very old report more intergenerational friends—both same- and other-sex (Johnson & Troll, 1994). In her eighties, Ruth spent time with Margaret, a 55-year-old widow she met while serving on the board of directors of an adoption agency. Two or three times a month, Margaret came to Ruth's home for tea and lively conversation.

Sex differences in friendship, discussed in previous chapters, extend into late adulthood. Women are more likely to have intimate friends; men depend on their wives and, to a lesser extent, their sisters for warm, open communication (Waite & Das, 2013). Also, older women have more **secondary friends**—people who are not intimates but with whom they spend time occasionally, such as a group that meets for lunch, bridge, or museum tours. Through these associates, older adults meet new people, remain socially involved, and gain in psychological well-being (Blieszner & Roberto, 2012).

In late-life friendships, affection and emotional support are both given and received to maintain balance in the relationship. Although friends call on each other for help with tasks of daily living, they generally do so only in emergencies or for occasional, limited assistance. Seniors with physical limitations whose social networks consist mainly of friends and who therefore must rely frequently on them for help tend to report low psychological well-being (Fiori, Smith, & Antonucci, 2007). Feelings of excessive dependency and of being unable to reciprocate are probably responsible.

Relationships with Adult Children

About 80 percent of older adults in Western nations are parents of living children, most of whom are middle-aged. In Chapter 16, we noted that exchanges of help vary with the closeness of the parent–child bond and the needs of the parent and adult child. Recall, also, that over time, parent-to-child help declines, whereas child-to-parent assistance increases. Older adults and

AGE FOTOSTOCK/ROBERT HARDING

On a village street in Cyprus, these older adults often meet to play backgammon. Even after physical mobility declines, many seniors find ways to sustain ties with friends, who offer companionship, links to the larger community, and social support.

their adult children are often in touch, even when they live far from each other. But as with other ties, quality rather than quantity of interaction affects older adults' life satisfaction. In diverse ethnic groups and cultures, warm bonds with adult children reduce the negative impact of physical impairments and other losses (such as death of a spouse) on psychological well-being (Ajrouch, 2007; Milkie, Bierman, & Schieman, 2008). Alternatively, conflict or unhappiness with adult children contributes to poor physical and mental health.

Although aging parents and adult children in Western nations provide each other with various forms of help, level of assistance is typically modest. Older adults in their sixties and seventies—especially those who own their own home and who are married or widowed as opposed to divorced—are more likely to be providers than recipients of help, suggesting SES variations in the balance of support (Grundy, 2005). This balance shifts as older adults age, but well into late adulthood, seniors in Western nations give more than they receive, especially in financial support but also in practical assistance—a circumstance that contradicts stereotypes of older adults as "burdens" on younger generations (HSBC & Oxford Institute of Ageing, 2007).

Interviews with parents age 75 and older in five Western nations revealed that in all countries, aid received from adult children most often took the form of emotional support. Fewer than one-third said their children assisted with household chores and errands. Aging parents who provided more help of various kinds than they received scored highest in life satisfaction, those receiving more help than they gave scored lowest, while those in a balanced exchange fell in between (Lowenstein, Katz, & Gur-Yaish, 2007). To avoid dependency, older people usually do not seek children's practical assistance in the absence of a pressing need, and they express annoyance when children are overprotective or help unnecessarily (Spitze & Gallant, 2004). Moderate support, with many opportunities to reciprocate, is beneficial, fostering self-esteem and sense of family connection. Again, extensive support that cannot be returned is linked to poor well-being.

Sex differences in older parent–adult child interaction are evident. Both mothers and fathers feel ambivalent toward adult offspring with problematic lives—who are financially needy, emotionally troubled, or experiencing marital problems. But mothers are more likely to have adult children who feel similarly ambivalent toward them, perhaps because mothers more often express their mixed feelings (Fingerman et al., 2006).

Feelings of ambivalence undermine the psychological well-being of both adult children and their aging parents (Fingerman et al., 2008). But aging parents' ambivalence toward children is typically low. Consistent with socioemotional selectivity theory, older parents are more likely to describe their family ties as solely close rather than ambivalent (Fingerman, Hay, & Birditt, 2004; Willson et al., 2006). Mother–daughter ties are particularly warm, although competing demands in middle-aged daughters' busy lives may leave less time to devote to the relationship than each would like (see page 550 in Chapter 16).

As social networks shrink in size, relationships with adult children become more important sources of family involvement. People 85 years and older with children have substantially more contacts with relatives than do those without children (Hooyman & Kiyak, 2011). Why is this so? Consider Ruth, whose daughter Sybil linked her to grandchildren, great-grandchildren, and relatives by marriage. When childless adults reach their eighties, siblings, other same-age relatives, and close friends may have become frail or died and hence may no longer be available as companions.

Relationships with Adult Grandchildren and Great-Grandchildren

Seniors with adult grandchildren and great-grandchildren benefit from a wider potential network of support. Ruth and Walt saw their granddaughter, Marci, and their great-grandson, Jamel, at family gatherings. In between, they occasionally Skyped with Marci and Jamel, which enabled face-to-face communication despite physical distance. And Ruth and Walt used Facebook regularly to keep up with Marci and Jamel's activities. Staying in touch with grandchildren and other family members is the primary reason seniors say they use social networking sites (Zickuhr & Madden, 2012).

In developed nations, slightly more than half of adults over age 65 have a grandchild who is at least 18 years old (AARP, 2002). In the few studies available on grandparent–adult grandchild relationships, the overwhelming majority of grandchildren felt obligated to assist grandparents in need, more so if they had forged an affectionate bond (Even-Zohar, 2011; Fruhauf,

© AURORA PHOTOS/ROBERT HARDING

Grandparents regard ties with adult grandchildren as a vital link between themselves and the future. And great-grandparents comment that this new role reaffirms the continuity of their families. This Japanese 102-year-old describes meeting her great-great-grandchild as "like jumping into heaven."

Jarrott, & Allen, 2006). Grandparents expect affection (but not practical help) from grandchildren, and in most cases they receive it. They regard the adult grandchild tie as very gratifying—a vital link between themselves and the future.

Still, grandparent–adult grandchild relationships vary greatly. Degree of grandparent involvement during childhood strongly predicts the quality of the current relationship. Often, the tie with one grandchild is "special," characterized by more frequent contact, mutual expressions of affection, and enjoyable times together—factors that enhance older adults' psychological well-being (Fingerman, 1998). Relationships with grandmothers tend to be closer, with maternal grandmother–granddaughter bonds the closest, as was so when grandchildren were younger (Sheehan & Petrovic, 2008). However, as grandparents and grandchildren move through life, contact declines. Many grandchildren establish distant homes and become immersed in work, family, and friendship roles that compete for time with extended-family members.

LOOK AND LISTEN

Interview one or two seniors with adult grandchildren about the quality and personal meaning of those relationships. ●

But despite less contact, grandparents' affection for their adult grandchildren strengthens with age, usually exceeding grandchildren's expressed closeness toward their grandparents (which is still strong) (Giarrusso et al., 2001; Harwood, 2001). This difference in emotional investment reflects each generation's distinct needs and goals—adult grandchildren in establishing independent lives, grandparents in preserving family relationships and continuity of values across generations. Grandchildren become increasingly important sources of emotional meaning for seniors in the last decade or two of life.

About 40 percent of older adults have great-grandchildren (Hooyman & Kiyak, 2011). Although most describe their new role as limited and a sign of advancing age, they welcome it with enthusiasm, commenting that it reaffirms the continuity of their families. Parents mediate contact with great-grandchildren, as they did with young grandchildren (see Chapter 16).

Elder Maltreatment

Although the majority of older adults enjoy positive relationships with family members, friends, and professional caregivers, some suffer maltreatment at the hands of these individuals. Through recent media attention, elder maltreatment has become a serious public concern.

Reports from many industrialized nations reveal widely varying rates of maltreatment, from 3 to 28 percent in general population studies. Overall, 7 to 10 percent of U.S. older adults say they were targets during the past month, amounting to 3 to 4 million victims (Acierno et al., 2010). Elder maltreatment crosses ethnic lines, although it is lower in Asian, Hispanic, and Native-American groups with strong traditions of respect for and obligation to the aged and highly disapproving attitudes

toward harming them (Sherman, Rosenblatt, & Antonucci, 2008). Yet all figures substantially underestimate the actual incidence, because most abusive acts take place in private, and victims are often unable or unwilling to complain.

Elder maltreatment usually takes the following forms:

- *Physical abuse.* Intentional infliction of pain, discomfort, or injury, through hitting, cutting, burning, physical force, restraint, sexual assault, and other acts
- *Physical neglect.* Intentional or unintentional failure to fulfill caregiving obligations, resulting in lack of food, medication, or health services or in the older person being left alone or isolated
- *Emotional abuse.* Verbal assaults (such as name calling), humiliation (being treated as a child), and intimidation (threats of isolation or placement in a nursing home)
- *Sexual abuse.* Unwanted sexual contact of any kind
- *Financial abuse.* Illegal or improper exploitation of the aging person's property or financial resources, through theft or use without consent

Financial abuse, emotional abuse, and neglect are the most frequently reported types. Often several forms occur in combination (Anetzberger, 2005; National Academies Committee on National Statistics, 2010). The perpetrator is usually a person the older adult trusts and depends on for care and assistance.

Most abusers are family members—spouses (usually men), followed by children of both sexes and then by other relatives. Some are friends, neighbors, and in-home caregivers (National Center on Elder Abuse, 2013). Abuse in nursing homes is a major concern: From 6 to 40 percent of caregivers admit to having committed at least one act in the previous year (Schiamberg et al., 2011).

Over the past several decades, another form of neglect—referred to in the media as "granny dumping"—has risen: abandonment of older adults with severe disabilities by family caregivers, usually at hospital emergency rooms (Fulmer, 2008). Overwhelmed, their caregivers seem to have concluded that they have no other option but to take this drastic step. (See pages 549–551 in Chapter 16 and pages 586–587 in Chapter 17 for related research.)

Risk Factors. Characteristics of the victim, the abuser, their relationship, and its social context are related to the incidence and severity of elder maltreatment. The more of the following risk factors that are present, the greater the likelihood that abuse and neglect will occur.

Dependency of the Victim. Very old, frail, and mentally and physically impaired older adults are more vulnerable to maltreatment, with as many as 25 percent affected (Reay & Browne, 2008; Selwood & Cooper, 2009). This does not mean that declines in functioning cause abuse. Rather, when other conditions are ripe for maltreatment, older people with severe

This older adult, who suffers from depression and physical disabilities, lives in a dilapidated rooming house. When conditions are ripe for elder maltreatment, those with severe impairments are least able to protect themselves.

disabilities are least able to protect themselves. Those with physical or cognitive impairments may also have personality traits that make them vulnerable—a tendency to lash out when angry or frustrated, a passive or avoidant approach to handling problems, and a low sense of self-efficacy (Salari, 2011). The worse the caregiver–recipient relationship, the greater the risk of elder abuse of all kinds, particularly when that relationship has a long negative history.

Dependency of the Perpetrator. Many abusers are dependent, emotionally or financially, on their victims. This dependency, experienced as powerlessness, can lead to aggressive, exploitative behavior. Often the perpetrator–victim relationship is one of mutual dependency (Fryling, Summers, & Hoffman, 2006). The abuser needs the older person for money or housing, and the older person needs the abuser for assistance with everyday tasks or to relieve loneliness.

Psychological Disturbance and Stress of the Perpetrator. Abusers are more likely than other caregivers to have psychological problems and to be dependent on alcohol or other drugs (Nerenberg, 2010). Often they are socially isolated, have difficulties at work, or are unemployed, with resulting financial worries. These factors increase the likelihood that they will lash out when caregiving is highly demanding or the behavior of an older adult with dementia is irritating or hard to manage.

History of Family Violence. Elder abuse is often part of a long history of family violence. Adults who were abused as children are at increased risk of harming older adults (Reay & Browne, 2008). In Chapter 8, we showed how aggressive cycles between family members can easily become self-sustaining,

leading to the development of individuals who cope with anger through hostility toward others. In many instances, elder abuse is an extension of years of partner abuse (Walsh et al., 2007).

Institutional Conditions. Elder maltreatment is more likely to occur in nursing homes that are rundown and overcrowded and that have staff shortages, minimal staff supervision, high staff turnover, and few visitors (Schiamberg et al., 2011). Highly stressful work conditions combined with minimal oversight of caregiving quality set the stage for abuse and neglect.

Preventing Elder Maltreatment. Preventing elder maltreatment by family members is especially challenging. Victims may fear retribution; wish to protect abusers who are spouses, sons, or daughters; or feel embarrassed that they cannot control the situation. And they may be intimidated into silence or not know where to turn for help (Summers & Hoffman, 2006). Once abuse is discovered, intervention involves immediate protection and provision of unmet needs for the older adult and of mental health services and social support for the spouse or caregiver.

Prevention programs offer caregivers counseling, education, and respite services, such as elder day care and in-home help. Trained volunteer "buddies" who make visits to the home can combat social isolation of aging adults and assist them with problem solving to avoid further harm. Support groups help seniors identify abusive acts, practice appropriate responses, and form new relationships. And agencies that provide informal financial services to older people who are unable to manage on their own, such as writing and cashing checks and holding valuables in a safe, reduce financial abuse.

When elder abuse is extreme, legal action offers the best protection, yet it is rare. Many victims are reluctant to initiate court procedures or, because of mental impairments, cannot do so. In these instances, social service professionals must help caregivers rethink their role, even if it means that the aging person might be institutionalized. In nursing homes, improving staff selection, training, and working conditions can greatly reduce abuse and neglect.

LOOK AND LISTEN

Contact the your state's department of senior services. Find out about its policies and programs aimed at preventing elder abuse. ●

Combating elder maltreatment also requires efforts at the level of the larger society, including public education to encourage reporting of suspected cases and improved understanding of the needs of older people. As part of this effort, seniors benefit from information on where to go for help (National Center on Elder Abuse, 2013). Finally, countering negative stereotypes of aging reduces maltreatment because recognizing older adults' dignity, individuality, and autonomy is incompatible with acts of physical and psychological harm.

Retirement

In Chapter 16, we noted that the period of retirement has lengthened because of increased life expectancy and a steady decline in average age of retirement—trends that have occurred in all Western industrialized nations. These changes have also led to a blurring of the distinction between work and retirement. Because mandatory retirement no longer exists for most workers in Western countries, older adults have more choices about when to retire and how they spend their time.

The late-2000s recession has had only a modest impact on raising the retirement age of the baby boomers (see page 557). Still, according to surveys of adults in many countries, the majority of baby boomers say they want to work longer, with one-third indicating that devoting some time to work is important for a happy retirement (HSBC & Oxford Institute of Ageing, 2007, 2011). Currently, nearly 40 percent of U.S. adults age 65 to 69, and nearly 20 percent of those in their seventies, are still working in some capacity.

As these figures suggest, the contemporary retirement process is highly variable: It may include a planning period, the decision itself, diverse acts of retiring, and continuous adjustment and readjustment of activities for the rest of the life course. The majority of U.S. older adults with career jobs retire gradually by cutting down their hours and responsibilities. Many take *bridge jobs* (new part-time jobs or full-time jobs of shorter duration) that serve as transitions between full-time career and retirement (Wang, 2011). Others leave their jobs but later return to paid work and even start new careers, desiring to introduce interest and challenge into their lives, to supplement limited financial resources, or both. Today, retirement is not a single event but rather a dynamic process with multiple transitions serving different purposes.

In the following sections, we examine factors that affect the decision to retire, happiness during the retirement years, and leisure and volunteer pursuits. We will see that the process of retirement and retired life reflect an increasingly diverse retired population.

The Decision to Retire

When Walt and Ruth retired, both had worked long enough to be eligible for comfortable income-replacement benefits—Walt's through the government-sponsored Social Security program, Ruth's through a private pension plan. In addition, they had planned for retirement (see Chapter 16, pages 556–558), with a projected date for leaving the work force. They wanted to retire early enough to pursue leisure activities while both were in good health. In contrast, Walt's brother Dick was forced to retire as the operating costs of his bakery rose while his clientele declined. He looked for temporary employment in sales while his wife, Goldie, kept her part-time job as a bookkeeper to help cover living expenses.

Affordability of retirement is usually the first consideration in the decision to retire. Yet despite economic concerns, many preretirees decide to let go of a steady work life in favor of alternative, personally meaningful work, leisure, or volunteer activities. "I had been working since I was 10 years old," said one retired auto worker. "I wanted a rest." Exceptions to this favorable outlook are people like Dick—forced into retirement or earning very low wages—who often take bridge jobs reluctantly to make ends meet (Cahill, Giandrea, & Quinn, 2006).

Figure 18.3 on page 630 summarizes personal and workplace factors in addition to income that influence the decision to retire. People in good health, for whom vocational life is central to self-esteem, and whose work environments are pleasant and interesting are likely to keep on working. For these reasons, individuals in high-earning professional occupations usually retire later than those in blue-collar or clerical positions. And when they do retire, they more often shift to stimulating bridge jobs, with some retiring and returning to the work force multiple times (Feldman & Beehr, 2011; Wang et al., 2009). Self-employed older adults also work longer, probably because they can flexibly adapt their job's physical and cognitive demands and working hours to fit their changing capacities and needs (Feldman & Vogel, 2009). In contrast, people in declining health, who are engaged in routine, boring work, who have pleasurable leisure or family pursuits, or who otherwise perceive a decline in the fit of their work with their skills and interests often opt for retirement.

Societal factors also affect retirement decisions. When many younger, less costly workers are available to replace older workers, industries are likely to offer added incentives for people to retire, such as increments to pension plans and earlier benefits—a trend that has, until recently, contributed to many early retirements in Western nations. But when concern

Retire

- Adequate retirement benefits
- Compelling leisure interests or family pursuits
- Low work commitment
- Declining health
- Spouse retiring
- Routine, boring job

Continue Working

- Limited or no retirement benefits
- Few leisure interests or family pursuits
- High work commitment
- Good health
- Spouse working
- Flexible job demands and work schedule
- Pleasant, stimulating work environment

A recent retiree enjoys an adult-education class in bookbinding.

This doctor, in her 60s, continues to enjoy her fulfilling career.

| **FIGURE 18.3** Personal and workplace factors that influence the decision to retire.

increases about the burden on younger generations of an expanding population of retirees, eligibility for retirement benefits may be postponed to a later age.

Retirement decisions vary with gender. On average, women retire earlier than men, largely because family events—a spouse's retirement or the need to care for an ill partner or parent—play larger roles in their decisions (Moen et al., 2006). Women in or near poverty, however, are an exception (DeVaney, 2008). Lacking financial resources to retire, many continue working into old age.

In most Western nations, generous social security benefits make retirement feasible for the economically disadvantaged and sustain the standard of living of most workers after they retire. The United States is an exception: Many U.S. retirees, especially those who held low-income jobs without benefits, experience falling living standards. Denmark, France, Germany, Finland, and Sweden have gradual retirement programs in which older employees reduce their work hours, receive a partial pension to make up income loss, and continue to accrue pension benefits. Besides strengthening financial security, this approach introduces a transitional phase that fosters retirement planning and well-being (Peiró, Tordera, & Potocnik, 2012). And some countries' retirement policies are sensitive to women's more interrupted work lives. In Canada, France, and Germany, for example, time devoted to child rearing is given some credit when figuring retirement benefits (Service Canada, 2009).

In sum, individual preferences shape retirement decisions. At the same time, older adults' opportunities and limitations greatly affect their choices.

Adjustment to Retirement

Because retirement involves giving up roles that are a vital part of identity and self-esteem, it is often assumed to be a stressful process that contributes to declines in physical and mental health. Consider Dick, who reacted to the closing of his bakery with anxiety and depression. His adjustment difficulties resembled those of younger people experiencing job loss (see Chapter 16, page 556). But recall that Dick had a cranky, disagreeable personality. In this respect, his psychological well-being after retirement was similar to what it had been before!

We must be careful not to assume a cause-and-effect relationship each time retirement is paired with an unfavorable reaction. For example, a wealth of evidence confirms that physical health problems lead older adults to retire, rather than the reverse (Shultz & Wang, 2007). And for most people, mental health and perceived quality of life are fairly stable from the pre- to postretirement years, with little change prompted by retirement itself. The widely held belief that retirement inevitably leads to adjustment problems is contradicted by countless research findings indicating that most people adapt well. Contemporary seniors view retirement as a time of opportunity and personal growth and describe themselves as active and socially involved—major determinants of retirement satisfaction (Kloep & Hendry, 2007; Wang & Schultz, 2010). Still, about 10 to 30 percent mention some adjustment difficulties.

Workplace factors—especially financial worries and having to give up one's job—predict stress following retirement. Pressures at work also make a difference. Moving out of a high-stress job is associated with gains in psychological well-being following retirement, whereas leaving a pleasant, low-stress job or a highly satisfying job before one is ready is linked to greater difficulties during the retirement transition, typically followed by recovery (Wang, 2007). And especially for women, who take on greater caregiving responsibilities, retirement may not relieve the stress of family burdens (Coursolle et al., 2010). Rather, it may reduce work-based avenues of personal satisfaction, thereby triggering depressive symptoms and poorer psychological well-being.

Among psychological factors, a sense of personal control over life events, including deciding to retire for internally motivated reasons (to do other things), is strongly linked to retirement satisfaction (Kubicek et al., 2011; Quine et al., 2007). At the same time, those who find it hard to give up the predictable schedule and social contacts of the work setting or who have few nonwork social ties experience discomfort. Overall, however, well-educated people with complex jobs adjust more favorably (Kim & Moen, 2002a). Perhaps the satisfactions derived from challenging, meaningful work readily transfer to nonwork pursuits.

As with other major life events, social support reduces stress associated with retirement. Although social-network size typically shrinks as relationships with co-workers decline, quality of relationships remains fairly stable for most people. And many seniors add to their social networks through leisure and volunteer pursuits (Kloep & Hendry, 2007). In Dick's case, entering congregate housing eased a difficult postretirement period, leading to new friends and rewarding leisure activities, some of which he shared with Goldie.

Finally, earlier in this chapter we noted that marital happiness tends to rise after retirement. When a couple's relationship is positive, it can buffer the uncertainty of retirement (van Solinge & Henkens, 2008). And retirement can enhance marital satisfaction by granting husband and wife more time for companionship. Consequently, a good marriage not only promotes adjustment to retirement but also benefits from the greater freedom of the retirement years.

In line with continuity theory, people try to sustain lifestyle patterns, self-esteem, and values following retirement and, in favorable economic and social contexts, usually succeed (Atchley, 2003). Return to Chapter 16, page 557, for ways adults can plan ahead to increase the chances of a positive transition to retirement.

Leisure and Volunteer Activities

With retirement, most older adults have more time for leisure and volunteer activities than ever before. After a "honeymoon period" of trying out new options, many discover that interests and skills do not develop suddenly. Instead, meaningful leisure and community service pursuits are usually formed earlier and sustained or expanded during retirement (HSBC & Oxford Institute of Ageing, 2007; Pinquart & Schindler, 2009). For example, Walt's fondness for writing, theater, and gardening dated back to his youth. And Ruth's strong focus on her social work career led her to become an avid community volunteer.

Involvement in leisure activities and, especially, volunteer service is related to better physical and mental health and reduced mortality (Cutler, Hendricks, & O'Neill, 2011). But simply participating does not explain this relationship. Instead, older adults select these pursuits because they permit self-expression, new achievements, the rewards of helping others, pleasurable social interaction, and a structured daily life. And those high in sense of self-efficacy are more engaged (Diehl & Berg, 2007). These factors account for gains in well-being.

As mobility limitations increase, the frequency and variety of leisure pursuits tend to decline, especially travel, outdoor recreation, and exercise, with activities increasingly becoming more sedentary and home-based (Strain et al., 2002). Older adults in residential communities participate more than those in ordinary homes because activities are conveniently available. But regard-

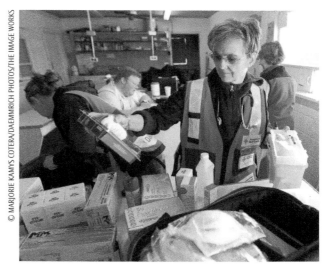

Time devoted to volunteering is higher in late adulthood than at any other time of life. As a Red Cross volunteer, this senior traveled to West, Texas, to provide services to those affected by the fertilizer plant explosion in April 2013.

less of living arrangements, seniors do not simply spend time in programs designed just for them. Rather, they choose activities on the basis of whether the activities are personally gratifying.

Older people contribute enormously to society through volunteer work, a trend that is strengthening. About one-third of 60- and 70-year-olds in industrialized nations report volunteering. Of those who do, over half give 200 or more hours per year (HSBC & Oxford Institute of Ageing, 2007; Kloep & Hendry, 2007). Younger, better-educated, and financially secure seniors with social interests are more likely to volunteer, women more often than men. Although most extend an earlier pattern of civic engagement, nonvolunteers are especially receptive to volunteer activities in the first few years after retiring as they look for ways to compensate for work-role losses (Mutchler, Burr, & Caro, 2003). The retirement transition is a prime time to recruit seniors into these personally rewarding, socially useful pursuits.

LOOK AND LISTEN

Interview an older adult participating in a significant community service role about the personal meaning of the experience at this time of life. ●

Volunteering grants seniors a continuing sense of making valuable contributions to society, and most sustain high commitment through their seventies. In a survey of a large, nationally representative U.S. sample, time spent volunteering did not decline until the eighties (see Figure 18.4 on page 632) (Hendricks & Cutler, 2004). Even then, it remained higher than at any other time of life! In accord with socioemotional selectivity theory, older adults eventually narrowed their volunteering to fewer roles, concentrating on one or two that meant the most to them (Windsor, Anstey, & Rodgers, 2008). They seemed to recognize that excessive volunteering reduces its emotional rewards and, thus, its benefits to life satisfaction.

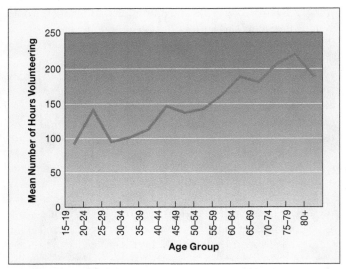

FIGURE 18.4 Age-related change in number of hours spent volunteering during the past year. A nationally representative sample of nearly 29,000 U.S. adolescents and adults reported on the amount of time they devoted to each of their volunteer activities. Time devoted to volunteering increased sharply in the early twenties, dipped in the late twenties and thirties as young people focused on establishing families and careers, and then rose steadily, peaking in the seventies. Even in the eighties, when volunteering declined slightly, it remained higher than at any other time of life. (From J. Hendricks and S. J. Cutler, 2004, "Volunteerism and Socioemotional Selectivity in Later Life," *Journal of Gerontology, 59B*, p. S255. Copyright © 2004 The Gerontological Society of America. Adapted by permission of Oxford University Press and Jon Hendricks.)

Finally, when Walt and Ruth got together with Dick and Goldie, the two couples often discussed politics. Older adults report greater awareness of and interest in public affairs and typically vote at a higher rate than any other age group. (The 2012 U.S. national election, in which 18- to 29-year-olds exceeded seniors in voter turnout, is an exception). Even in late old age, older people's political knowledge shows no sign of decline. After retiring, they have more time to keep abreast of current events. They also have a major stake in political debates over policies central to their welfare. But seniors' political concerns are far broader than those that serve their own age group, and their voting behavior is not driven merely by self-interest (Campbell & Binstock, 2011). Rather, their political involvement may stem from a deep desire for a safer, more secure world for future generations.

 # Optimal Aging

Walt, Ruth, Dick, Goldie, and Ida, and the research findings they illustrate, reveal great diversity in development during the final decades of life. Walt and Ruth fit contemporary experts' view of **optimal aging,** in which gains are maximized and losses minimized. Both were actively engaged with their families and communities, coped well with negative life changes, enjoyed a happy intimate partnership and other close relationships, and led daily lives filled with gratifying activities. Ida, too, experienced

optimal aging until the onset of Alzheimer's symptoms overwhelmed her ability to manage life's challenges. As a single adult, she built a rich social network that sustained her into old age, despite the hardship of having spent many years caring for her ailing mother. In contrast, Dick and Goldie reacted with despondency to physical aging and other losses (such as Dick's forced retirement). And Dick's angry outbursts restricted their social contacts, although the couple's move to congregate housing eventually led to an improved social life.

People age optimally when their growth, vitality, and striving limit and, at times, overcome physical, cognitive, and social declines. Researchers want to know more about factors that contribute to optimal aging so they can help more seniors experience it. Yet theorists disagree on the precise ingredients of a satisfying old age. Some focus on easily measurable outcomes, such as excellent cardiovascular functioning, absence of disability, superior cognitive performance, and creative achievements. But this view has been heavily criticized (Aldwin, Spiro, & Park, 2006). Not everyone can become an outstanding athlete, an innovative scientist, or a talented artist. And many older adults do not want to keep on accomplishing and producing—the main markers of success in Western nations. Each of us is limited by our genetic potential as it combines with a lifetime of environments we encounter and select for ourselves. Furthermore, outcomes valued in one culture may not be valued in others.

Recent views of a contented, fulfilling late adulthood have turned away from specific achievements toward processes people use to reach personally valued goals (Freund & Baltes, 1998; Lund, 1998; Kahana et al., 2005). Instead of identifying one set of standards as "successful," this perspective focuses on how people minimize losses while maximizing gains. In recent research on three samples of adults followed over the lifespan, George Vaillant looked at how various life-course factors contributed to late-life physical and psychological well-being. His findings revealed that factors people could control to some degree (such as health habits, coping strategies, marital stability, and years of education) far outweighed uncontrollable factors (parental SES, family warmth in childhood, early physical health, and longevity of family members) in predicting a happy, active old age (Vaillant & Mukamal, 2001).

Consider the following description of one participant, who in childhood had experienced low SES, parental discord, a depressed mother, and seven siblings crowded into a tenement apartment. Despite these early perils, he became happily married and, through the GI bill, earned an accounting degree. At 70, he was aging well:

Anthony Pirelli may have been *ill* considering his heart attack and open-heart surgery, but he did not feel *sick*. He was physically active as ever, and he continued to play tennis. Asked what he missed about his work, he exulted, "I'm so busy doing other things that I don't have time to miss work. . . . Life is not boring for me." He did not smoke or abuse alcohol; he loved his wife; he used mature [coping strategies]; he obtained 14 years of education; he watched his waistline; and he exercised regularly. (Adapted from Vaillant, 2002, pp. 12, 305.)

Vaillant concluded, "The past often predicts but never determines our old age" (p. 12). Optimal aging is an expression of remarkable resilience during this final phase of the lifespan.

In this and the previous chapter, we have considered the many ways that older adults realize their goals. *TAKE A MOMENT...* Look back and review the most important ones:

● Optimism and sense of self-efficacy in improving health and physical functioning (page 575)

● Selective optimization with compensation to make the most of limited physical energies and cognitive resources (pages 590 and 610)

● Strengthening of self-concept, which promotes self-acceptance and pursuit of hoped-for possible selves (pages 606–608)

● Enhanced emotional understanding and emotional self-regulation, which support meaningful, rewarding social ties (page 605)

● Acceptance of change, which fosters life satisfaction (page 608)

● A mature sense of spirituality and faith, permitting anticipation of death with calmness and composure (pages 608–609)

● Personal control over domains of dependency and independence (pages 610–611, 612)

● High-quality relationships, which offer social support and pleasurable companionship (page 616)

Optimal aging is facilitated by societal contexts that promote effective person–environment fit, enabling seniors to manage life changes effectively. Older adults need well-funded social security plans, good health care, safe housing, and diverse social services. (See, for example, the description of the U.S. Area Agencies on Aging in Chapter 2, page 67.) Yet because of inadequate funding and difficulties reaching rural communities, many older adults' needs remain unmet. Isolated aging adults with little education may not know how to gain access to available assistance. Furthermore, the U.S. Medicare system of sharing health-care costs with seniors strains the financial resources of many. And housing that adjusts to changes in older people's capacities, permitting them to age in place without disruptive and disorienting moves, is available only to the economically well-off.

Besides improving policies that meet older adults' basic needs, new future-oriented approaches must prepare for increased aging of the population. More emphasis on lifelong learning for workers of all ages would help people maintain and expand their skills as they grow older. Also, reforms that prepare for expected growth in the number of frail aging adults are vital, including affordable help for family caregivers, adapted housing, and sensitive nursing home care.

All these changes involve recognizing, supporting, and enhancing the contributions that seniors make to society—both the older adults of today and those of tomorrow. A nation that takes care of its aging citizens and grants them a multitude of opportunities for personal growth maximizes the chances that each of us, when our time comes to be old, will age optimally.

ASK YOURSELF

REVIEW What psychological and workplace factors predict favorable adjustment to retirement?

CONNECT Leisure and volunteer interests and skills usually form early and persist over the lifespan. Referring back to earlier parts of this book, cite examples of childhood, adolescent, and early adulthood experiences that are likely to foster meaningful pursuits after retirement.

APPLY Nate, happily married to Gladys, adjusted well to retirement, and his marriage became even happier. How can a good marriage ease the transition to retirement? How can retirement enhance marital satisfaction?

REFLECT Think of someone you know who is aging optimally. What personal qualities led you to select that person?

SUMMARY

Erikson's Theory: Ego Integrity versus Despair (p. 604)

According to Erikson, how does personality change in late adulthood?

● The final psychological conflict of Erikson's theory, **ego integrity versus despair,** involves coming to terms with one's life. Adults who arrive at a sense of integrity feel whole and satisfied with their achievements. Despair occurs when older people feel time is too short to find an alternate route to integrity.

Other Theories of Psychosocial Development in Late Adulthood (p. 604)

Describe Peck's, Joan Erikson's, and Labouvie-Vief's views of psychosocial development in late adulthood, and discuss reminiscence in older adults' lives.

● According to Robert Peck, attaining ego integrity involves three distinct tasks: ego differentiation, body transcendence, and ego transcendence.

● Joan Erikson believes these attainments represent an additional psychosocial stage, **gerotranscendence,** evident in inner calm and quiet reflection.

● Gisella Labouvie-Vief points out that older adults improve in **affect optimization,** the ability to maximize positive emotion and dampen negative emotion. This bias toward the emotionally positive contributes an upbeat attitude that is linked to longer survival.

- **Reminiscence** about people and events from one's past can be positive and adaptive for older people. But many well-adjusted older adults spend little time seeking greater self-understanding through life review. Rather, as the term **Third Age** conveys, they are largely present- and future-oriented, seeking opportunities for personal fulfillment.

Stability and Change in Self-Concept and Personality
(p. 606)

Cite stable and changing aspects of self-concept and personality, and discuss spirituality and religiosity in late adulthood.

- The "big five" personality traits remain stable from mid- to late life. Older adults' accumulation of a lifetime of self-knowledge leads to more secure and complex self-concepts. Those who continue to actively pursue hoped-for possible selves gain in life satisfaction. In late adulthood, resilience is fostered by gains in agreeableness and acceptance of change. Engaging in cognitively challenging activities promotes openness to experience.

- While U.S. seniors generally become more religious or spiritual as they age, this increase is modest and not universal. For the majority of people, religiosity is stable throughout adulthood. Faith and spirituality may move toward a more reflective approach that accepts uncertainty and emphasizes links to others. Religious involvement is especially high among low-SES ethnic minority older people and women and is linked to better physical and psychological well-being and longer survival.

Contextual Influences on Psychological Well-Being
(p. 610)

Discuss the influence of control versus dependency, physical health, negative life changes, and social support on older adults' psychological well-being.

- In patterns of behavior called the **dependency–support script** and the **independence–ignore script,** older adults' dependency behaviors are attended to immediately while their independent behaviors are ignored. But dependency can be adaptive if older adults remain in control by selecting areas in which they desire help while conserving their strength for highly valued activities. Assistance that enables older adults to use their capacities fully in pursuit of their goals sustains an effective **person–environment fit,** which fosters psychological well-being.

- Physical health is a powerful predictor of late-life psychological well-being. The relationship between physical and mental health problems can become a vicious cycle, each intensifying the other. Older adults have the highest suicide rate of all age groups.

- Although aging adults are at risk for a variety of negative life changes, these events evoke less stress and depression in older than in younger people. But when negative changes pile up, they test older adults' coping resources.

- By easing stress, social support promotes physical health and psychological well-being. But assistance that is excessive or cannot be returned often results in reduced self-efficacy and psychological stress. Consequently, perceived social support, rather than sheer amount of help, is associated with a positive outlook.

A Changing Social World
(p. 614)

Describe social theories of aging, including disengagement theory, activity theory, continuity theory, and socioemotional selectivity theory.

- **Disengagement theory** holds that mutual withdrawal between older adults and society occurs in anticipation of death. Most aging adults, however, do not disengage but let go of unsatisfying contacts and maintain satisfying ones.

- **Activity theory** states that social barriers to engagement, not the desires of older adults, cause declining rates of interaction. Yet opportunities for social contact do not guarantee greater social activity.

- **Continuity theory** proposes that most aging adults strive to maintain consistency between their past and anticipated future. By using familiar skills and engaging in familiar activities with familiar people, older people integrate late-life changes into a coherent, consistent life path.

- **Socioemotional selectivity theory** states that social networks become more selective with age. Older adults emphasize the emotion-regulating function of interaction, preferring high-quality, emotionally fulfilling relationships.

How do communities, neighborhoods, and housing arrangements affect older adults' social lives and adjustment?

- Suburban older adults have higher incomes and report better health than their inner-city counterparts, but the latter are better off in terms of public transportation. Small-town and rural aging adults, who are less likely to live near their children, compensate by interacting more with nearby relatives, neighbors, and friends. Living in neighborhoods with many like-minded seniors and in smaller communities promotes life satisfaction.

- Most older people prefer **aging in place,** remaining in a familiar setting where they have control over everyday life. But for those with health and mobility problems, independent living poses risks, and many older adults who live alone are poverty-stricken.

- Residential communities for older adults who need help with everyday tasks include assisted-living arrangements such as **congregate housing** and **life-care communities,** which guarantee that residents' changing needs will be met as they age.

- The small number of U.S. older adults who live in nursing homes experience extreme restriction of autonomy. Typically, social interaction among residents is low. Homelike nursing homes that achieve an effective person–environment fit foster late-life well-being.

Relationships in Late Adulthood (p. 620)

Describe changes in social relationships in late adulthood, including marriage, gay and lesbian partnerships, divorce, remarriage, and widowhood, and discuss never-married, childless older adults.

- The **social convoy** is an influential model of changes in individuals' social networks as they move through life. As ties are lost, aging adults seek ways to maintain gratifying relationships.

- Marital satisfaction peaks in late adulthood as stressful responsibilities decline and gains in perceptions of relationship fairness, joint leisure activities, and positive communication increase. Most gay and lesbian older adults also report happy, highly fulfilling relationships.

- Divorce in late life brings greater stress than for younger people. Although older adults' remarriage rates are low, those who do remarry enter into more stable relationships. Seniors are increasingly choosing cohabitation as a long-term alternative to marriage.

- Adaptation to widowhood varies widely, with age, social support, and personality making a difference. Aging adults fare better than younger individuals, and women better than men. Efforts to maintain social ties, an outgoing personality, high self-esteem, and a sense of self-efficacy in handling tasks of daily living promote resilience.

- Most older adults who remain unmarried and childless throughout their lives develop alternative meaningful relationships. Never-married childless women are better-adjusted than men, but—despite smaller social networks—both find social support.

How do sibling relationships and friendships change in late life?

- In late adulthood, most siblings live nearby, communicate regularly, and visit several times a year. Especially for widowed and never-married older people, siblings provide an important "insurance policy."

- Friendships in late adulthood serve diverse functions: intimacy and companionship, a shield against negative judgments, a link to the larger community, and protection from the psychological consequences of loss. Older adults prefer established relationships over new ones, and fewer older than younger people have other-sex friendships. Women, more than men, tend to have both intimate friends and **secondary friends,** with whom they spend time occasionally.

Describe older adults' relationships with adult children, adult grandchildren, and great-grandchildren.

- Older adults are often in touch with their adult children, who more often provide emotional support than direct assistance. Aging parents who provide more help than they receive score highest in life satisfaction.

- Seniors with adult grandchildren and great-grandchildren benefit from a wider potential network of support. Grandparents typically expect affection, but not practical help, from grandchildren. Although grandparent–grandchild contact declines over time, grandparents' emotional investment remains high and often strengthens.

Discuss elder maltreatment, including risk factors and strategies for prevention.

- Some older adults suffer maltreatment at the hands of family members, friends, or professional caregivers. Risk factors include a dependent perpetrator–victim relationship, perpetrator psychological disturbance and stress, a history of family violence, and inadequate institutional conditions. Abandonment of aging adults with severe disabilities by family caregivers has increased in recent decades.

- Elder-abuse prevention programs provide counseling, education, and respite services for caregivers. Trained volunteers and support groups can help older persons avoid future harm. Societal efforts that encourage reporting of suspected cases and increase understanding of older people's needs are also vital.

Retirement (p. 629)

Discuss the decision to retire, adjustment to retirement, and involvement in leisure and volunteer activities.

- The decision to retire depends on affordability, health status, nature of the work environment, opportunities to pursue meaningful activities, societal factors such as retirement benefits, and gender.

- On average, women retire earlier than men because family events play a larger role in their decisions. For most older adults, mental health and perceived quality of life are fairly stable before and after retirement. Factors affecting adjustment include health status, financial stability, satisfactions previously derived from work, caregiving responsibilities, a sense of personal control over life events (including the retirement decision), social support, and marital happiness.

- Meaningful leisure and volunteer pursuits are typically formed earlier and sustained or expanded during retirement. Involvement is related to better physical and mental health and to reduced mortality.

Optimal Aging (p. 632)

Discuss the meaning of optimal aging.

- Older adults who experience **optimal aging** have developed many ways to minimize losses and maximize gains. Societal contexts that permit older adults to manage life changes effectively foster optimal aging. These include well-funded social security plans, good health care, safe housing, diverse social services, and opportunities for lifelong learning.

Important Terms and Concepts

activity theory (p. 614)
affect optimization (p. 605)
aging in place (p. 617)
congregate housing (p. 618)
continuity theory (p. 614)
dependency–support script (p. 610)

disengagement theory (p. 614)
ego integrity versus despair (p. 604)
gerotranscendence (p. 605)
independence–ignore script (p. 610)
life-care communities (p. 618)
optimal aging (p. 632)

person–environment fit (p. 611)
reminiscence (p. 606)
secondary friends (p. 625)
social convoy (p. 620)
socioemotional selectivity theory (p. 615)
Third Age (p. 607)

milestones

Development in Late Adulthood

65–80 years

PHYSICAL

- Performance of autonomic nervous system declines, impairing tolerance for extremes of heat and cold. (568)
- Declines in vision continue, with increased sensitivity to glare and impaired color discrimination, dark adaptation, depth perception, and visual acuity. (569)
- Declines in hearing continue throughout the frequency range. (569)
- Sensitivity to taste and odor may decline. (570)
- Touch sensitivity declines on the hands, especially the fingertips. (570)
- Declines in cardiovascular and respiratory functioning lead to greater physical stress during exercise. (570–571)

- Aging of the immune system increases risk for a variety of illnesses, including infectious diseases, cardiovascular disease, certain forms of cancer, and several autoimmune disorders. (571)

- Timing of sleep shifts to earlier bedtime and earlier morning wakening; sleep difficulties increase. (571)
- Graying and thinning of the hair continue; the skin wrinkles and sags further and becomes more transparent as it loses its fatty layer of support; "age spots" increase. (572)
- Height and weight decline because of loss of lean body mass. (572)

- Continued loss of bone mass leads to rising rates of osteoporosis. (572, 580)
- Frequency of sexual activity and intensity of sexual response decline, although most healthy married couples report regular sexual enjoyment. (578–579)

COGNITIVE

- Processing speed continues to decline, but crystallized intelligence is largely sustained. (590)

- Ability to attend selectively and to adapt attention, switching from one task to another, continues to decline. (591)
- Amount of information that can be held in working memory, use of memory strategies, and retrieval from long-term memory diminish further; problems are greatest on tasks requiring deliberate processing and associative memory. (591–592)
- Modest forgetting of remote memories occurs. (593)
- Use of external aids for prospective memory increases. (593)
- Retrieving words from long-term memory and planning what to say and how to say it become more difficult. (594)

- More often represents to-be-communicated information in terms of gist rather than details. (594)
- Hypothetical problem solving declines, but everyday problem solving remains adaptive. (594–595)
- May hold an important position of leadership in society, such as chief executive officer, religious leader, or court justice. (595)
- May develop wisdom. (595–596)
- Can improve a wide range of cognitive skills through training. (597)

636

Note: Numbers in parentheses indicate the page or pages on which each milestone is discussed.

EMOTIONAL/SOCIAL

- Comes to terms with life, developing ego integrity. (604–605)
- Cognitive-affective complexity declines as basic information-processing skill diminish. (605)
- Affect optimization—the ability to maximize positive emotion and dampen negative emotion—increases. (605)
- May engage in reminiscence and life review, but continues to seek avenues for personal growth and fulfillment. (606)

- Self-concept strengthens, becoming more secure and complex. (606)
- Agreeableness and acceptance of change increase, while extroversion and openness to experience tend to decline modestly. (608)
- Spirituality and faith may advance to a higher level, away from prescribed beliefs toward a more reflective approach. (608–609)

- Size of social network and amount of social interaction decline. (614)
- Selection of social partners is based on anticipated feelings, including pursuit of pleasant relationships and avoidance of unpleasant ones. (615–616)
- Marital satisfaction increases, peaking in late adulthood. (620)
- May be widowed. (622)
- Visits and support from siblings living nearby may increase. (624)
- With additional time to devote to them, friendships take on increasing importance. (624–625)
- May become a great-grandparent. (627)

- May retire. (629–630)
- Likely to increase involvement in leisure and volunteer activities (631–632)
- More likely to be knowledgeable about politics and to vote. (632)

80 years and older

PHYSICAL

- Physical changes previously listed continue.
- Mobility diminishes as muscle and bone strength and joint flexibility decline. (572)

COGNITIVE

- Cognitive changes previously listed continue.
- Fluid abilities decline further; crystallized abilities drop as well, though only modestly. (590)

EMOTIONAL/SOCIAL

- Emotional and social changes previously listed continue.
- May develop gerotranscendence, a cosmic perspective directed beyond the self. (605)

- Relationships with adult children become more important. (626)
- Frequency and variety of leisure and volunteer activities decline slightly. (631–632)

BRUNO MORANDI/ROBERT HARDING

Mourners on the island of Bali, Indonesia, perform a traditional Hindu ceremony marking the passage of the dead into the spirit realm. All cultures have rituals for celebrating the end of life and helping the bereaved cope with profound loss.

Death, Dying, and Bereavement

chapter outline

How We Die

Physical Changes • Defining Death • Death with Dignity

Understanding of and Attitudes Toward Death

Childhood • Adolescence • Adulthood • Death Anxiety

Thinking and Emotions of Dying People

Do Stages of Dying Exist? • Contextual Influences on Adaptations to Dying

A Place to Die

Home • Hospital • Nursing Home • The Hospice Approach

■ **BIOLOGY AND ENVIRONMENT** Music as Palliative Care for Dying Patients

The Right to Die

Passive Euthanasia • Voluntary Active Euthanasia • Assisted Suicide

■ **SOCIAL ISSUES: HEALTH** Voluntary Active Euthanasia: Lessons from Australia and the Netherlands

Bereavement: Coping with the Death of a Loved One

Grief Process • Personal and Situational Variations • Bereavement Interventions

■ **CULTURAL INFLUENCES** Cultural Variations in Mourning Behavior

Death Education

As every life is unique, so each death is unique. The final forces of the human spirit separate themselves from the body in manifold ways.

My mother Sofie's death was the culmination of a five-year battle against cancer. In her last months, the disease invaded organs throughout her body, attacking the lungs in its final fury. She withered slowly, with the mixed blessing of time to prepare against certain knowledge that death was just around the corner. My father, Philip, lived another 18 years. At age 80, he was outwardly healthy, active, and about to depart on a long-awaited vacation when a heart attack snuffed out his life suddenly, without time for last words or deathbed reconciliations.

As I set to work on this chapter, my 65-year-old neighbor Nicholas gambled for a higher quality of life. To be eligible for a kidney transplant, he elected bypass surgery to strengthen his heart. Doctors warned that his body might not withstand the operation. But Nicholas knew that without taking a chance, he would live only a few years, in debilitated condition. Shortly after the surgery, infection set in, traveling throughout his system and so weakening him that only extreme measures—a respirator to sustain breathing and powerful drugs to elevate his fading blood pressure—could keep him alive.

"Come on, Dad, you can do it," encouraged Nicholas's daughter Sasha, standing by his bedside and stroking his hand. But Nicholas could not. After two months in intensive care, he experienced brain seizures and slipped into a coma. Three doctors met with his wife, Giselle, to tell her there was no hope. She asked them to disconnect the respirator, and within half an hour Nicholas drifted away.

Death is essential for the survival of our species. We die so that our own children and the children of others may live. When it comes to this fate, nature treats humankind, with all its unique capabilities, just as it treats every other living creature. As hard as it is to accept the reality that we too will die, our greatest solace lies in knowing that death is part of ongoing life.

In this chapter, we address the culmination of lifespan development. Over the past century, technology has provided so many means to keep death at bay that many people regard it as a forbidden topic. But pressing social and economic dilemmas that are an outgrowth of the dramatic increase in life expectancy are forcing us to attend to life's end—its quality, its timing, and ways to help people adjust to their own and others' final leave taking. The interdisciplinary field of **thanatology,** devoted to the study of death and dying, has expanded tremendously over the past 25 years.

Our discussion addresses the physical changes of dying; understanding of and attitudes toward death in childhood, adolescence, and adulthood; the thoughts and feelings of people as they stand face to face with death; where people die; hopelessly ill patients' right to die; and coping with the death of a loved one. The experiences of Sofie, Philip, Nicholas, their families, and others illustrate how each person's life history joins with social and cultural contexts to shape death and dying, lending great diversity to this universal experience. ●

How We Die

In industrialized countries, opportunities to witness the physical aspects of death are less available today than in previous generations. Most people in the developed world die in hospitals, where doctors and nurses, not loved ones, typically attend their last moments. Nevertheless, many want to know how we die, either to anticipate their own end or grasp what is happening to a dying loved one. As we look briefly at the physical dying, we must keep in mind that the dying person is more than a physical being requiring care of and attention to bodily functions. The dying are also mind and spirit—for whom the end of life is still life. They benefit profoundly in their last days and hours from social support responsive to their needs for emotional and spiritual closure.

Physical Changes

My father's fatal heart attack came suddenly during the night. When I heard the news, I longed for reassurance that his death had been swift and without suffering.

When asked how they would like to die, most people say they want "death with dignity"—either a quick, agony-free end during sleep or a clear-minded final few moments in which they can say farewell and review their lives. In reality, death is the culmination of a straightforward biological process. For about 20 percent of people, it is gentle—especially when narcotic drugs ease pain and mask the destructive events taking place (Nuland, 1993). But most of the time it is not.

Recall that unintentional injuries are the leading cause of death in childhood and adolescence, cardiovascular disease and cancer in adulthood. Of the one-quarter of deaths in industrialized nations that are sudden, 80 to 90 percent are due to heart attacks (American Heart Association, 2012; Winslow, Mehta, & Fuster, 2005). My yearning for a painless death for my father was probably not fulfilled. Undoubtedly he felt the sharp, crushing sensation of a heart deprived of oxygen. As his heart twitched uncontrollably (called *fibrillation*) or stopped entirely, blood circulation slowed and ceased, and he was thrust

into unconsciousness. A brain starved of oxygen for more than two to four minutes is irreversibly damaged—an outcome indicated by the pupils of the eyes becoming unresponsive to light and widening into large, black circles. Other oxygen-deprived organs stop functioning as well.

Death is long and drawn out for three-fourths of people—many more than in times past, as a result of life-saving medical technology. They succumb in different ways. Of those with heart disease, most have congestive heart failure, the cause of Nicholas's death (Gruenewald & White, 2006). His scarred heart could no longer contract with the force needed to deliver enough oxygen to his tissues. As it tried harder, its muscle weakened further. Without sufficient blood pressure, fluid backed up in Nicholas's lungs. This hampered his breathing and created ideal conditions for inhaled bacteria to multiply, enter the bloodstream, and run rampant in his system, leading many organs to fail.

Cancer also chooses diverse paths to inflict its damage. When it metastasizes, bits of tumor travel through the bloodstream and implant and grow in vital organs, disrupting their functioning. Medication made my mother's final days as comfortable as possible, granting a relatively easy death. But the preceding weeks involved physical suffering, including impaired breathing and digestion and turning and twisting to find a comfortable position in bed.

In the days or hours before death, activity declines; the person moves and communicates less and shows little interest in food, water, and surroundings. At the same time, body temperature, blood pressure, and circulation to the limbs fall, so the hands and feet feel cool and skin color changes to a duller, grayish hue (Hospice Foundation of America, 2005). When the transition from life to death is imminent, the person often moves through three phases:

1. The **agonal phase.** The Greek word *agon* means "struggle." Here agonal refers to gasps and muscle spasms during the first moments in which the regular heartbeat disintegrates (Manole & Hickey, 2006).
2. **Clinical death.** A short interval follows in which heartbeat, circulation, breathing, and brain functioning stop, but resuscitation is still possible.
3. **Mortality.** The individual passes into permanent death. Within a few hours, the newly lifeless being appears shrunken, not at all like the person he or she was when alive.

Defining Death

TAKE A MOMENT... Consider what we have said so far, and note the dilemma of identifying just when death occurs. Death is not an event that happens at a single point in time but, rather, a process in which organs stop functioning in a sequence that varies from person to person. Because the dividing line between life and death is fuzzy, societies need a definition of death to help doctors decide when life-saving measures should be terminated, to signal survivors that they must begin to grieve their loss and

A monk prays with mourners during a Shinto funeral in Japan. Shinto beliefs, emphasizing ancestor worship and time for the spirit to leave the corpse, may partly explain the Japanese discomfort with the brain death standard and organ donation.

reorganize their lives, and to establish when donated organs can be removed.

Several decades ago, loss of heartbeat and respiration signified death. But these criteria are no longer adequate because resuscitation techniques frequently permit vital signs to be restored. Today, **brain death,** irreversible cessation of all activity in the brain and the brain stem (which controls reflexes), is used in most industrialized nations.

But not all countries accept this standard. In Japan, for example, doctors rely on traditional criteria—absence of heartbeat and respiration. This approach has hindered the development of a national organ transplant program because few organs can be salvaged from bodies without artificially maintaining vital signs. Buddhist, Confucian, and Shinto beliefs about death, which stress ancestor worship and time for the spirit to leave the corpse, may be partly responsible for the Japanese discomfort with brain death and organ donation. Today, Japanese law allows organ donation using the standard of brain death, even if the wishes of the deceased are not clear, as long as the family does not object (Ida, 2010). Otherwise, people are considered to be alive until the heart stops beating.

Often the brain death standard does not solve the problem of when to halt treatment. Consider Nicholas, who, though not brain dead, had entered a **persistent vegetative state,** in which the cerebral cortex no longer registered electrical activity but the brain stem remained active. Doctors were certain they could not restore consciousness or body movement. Because thousands of people in the United States and other nations are in a persistent vegetative state, with health-care costs totaling many millions of dollars annually, some experts believe that absence of activity in the cerebral cortex should be sufficient to declare a person dead. But others point to a few cases in which patients who had been vegetative for months regained cortical responsiveness and consciousness, though usually with very limited functioning (Laureys & Boly, 2007). In still other instances of illness, a fully conscious but suffering person refuses life-saving

measures—an issue we will consider later when we take up the right to die.

Death with Dignity

We have seen that nature rarely delivers the idealized, easy end most people want, nor can medical science guarantee it. Therefore, the greatest dignity in death is in the integrity of the life that precedes it—an integrity we can foster by the way we communicate with and care for the dying person.

First, we can assure the majority of dying people, who succumb gradually, that we will support them through their physical and psychological distress. We can treat them with respect by taking interest in those aspects of their lives that they most value and by addressing their greatest concerns (Keegan & Drick, 2011). And we can do everything possible to ensure the utmost compassionate care through their last months, weeks, and even final hours—restful physical surroundings, soothing emotional and social support, closeness of loved ones, and pastoral care that helps relieve worries about the worth of one's life, important relationships, and mortality.

Second, we can be candid about death's certainty. Unless people are aware that they are dying and understand (as far as possible) the likely circumstances of their death, they cannot plan for end-of-life care and decision making and share the sentiments that bring closure to relationships they hold most dear. Because Sofie knew how and when her death would probably take place, she chose a time when she and Philip could express what their lives had meant to each other. Among those precious bedside exchanges was Sofie's last wish that Philip remarry after her death so he would not live out his final years alone. Openness about impending death granted Sofie a final generative act, helped her let go of the person closest to her, and offered comfort as she faced death.

Dying patient Dick Warner's wife, Nancy, wears a nurse's hat she crafted from paper to symbolize her dual roles as medical and emotional caregiver. The evening of this photo, Nancy heard Dick's breaths shortening. She kissed him and whispered, "It's time to let go." Dick died as he wished, with his loving wife at his bedside.

Finally, doctors and nurses can help dying people learn enough about their condition to make reasoned choices about whether to fight on or say no to further treatment. An understanding of how the normal body works simplifies comprehension of how disease affects it—education that can begin as early as the childhood years.

In sum, when the conditions of illness do not permit an easy death, we can still ensure the most dignified exit possible by offering the dying person care, affection, companionship, and esteem; the truth about diagnosis; and the maximum personal control over this final phase of life (American Hospice Foundation, 2013). These are essential ingredients of a "good death," and we will revisit them throughout this chapter.

Understanding of and Attitudes Toward Death

A century ago, when most deaths occurred at home, people of all ages, including children, helped with care of the dying family member and were present at the moment of death. They saw their loved one buried on family property or in the local cemetery, where the grave could be visited regularly. Because infant and childhood mortality rates were high, all people were likely to know someone their own age, or even younger, who had died. And it was common for children to experience the death of a parent.

Compared with earlier generations, today more young people reach adulthood without having experienced the death of someone they know well (Morgan, Laungani, & Palmer, 2009). When a death does occur, professionals in hospitals and funeral homes take care of most tasks that involve confronting it directly.

This distance from death undoubtedly contributes to a sense of uneasiness about it. Despite frequent images of death in television shows, movies, and news reports of accidents, murders, wars, and natural disasters, we live in a death-denying culture. Adults are often reluctant to talk about death with children and adolescents. And substitute expressions, such as "passing away," "going out," or "departing," permit us to avoid acknowledging it candidly. In the following sections, we examine the development of conceptions of and attitudes toward death, along with ways to foster increased understanding and acceptance.

Childhood

Five-year-old Miriam arrived at our university laboratory preschool the day after her dog Pepper died. Instead of joining the other children, she stayed close to her teacher, Leslie, who noticed Miriam's discomfort. "What's wrong?" Leslie asked.

"Daddy said Pepper was so sick the vet had to put him to sleep." For a moment, Miriam looked hopeful. "When I get home, Pepper might wake up."

Leslie answered directly, "No, Pepper won't get up again. He's not asleep. He's dead, and that means he can't sleep, eat, run, or play anymore."

Miriam wandered off but later returned to Leslie and, sobbing, confessed, "I chased Pepper too hard."

Leslie put her arm around Miriam. "Pepper didn't die because you chased him," she explained. "He was very old and sick."

Over the next few days, Miriam asked many questions: "When I go to sleep, will I die?" "Can a tummy ache make you die?" "Does Pepper feel better now?" "Will Mommy and Daddy die?"

Development of the Death Concept. An understanding of death is based on five ideas:

1. *Permanence*. Once a living thing dies, it cannot be brought back to life.
2. *Inevitability*. All living things eventually die.
3. *Cessation*. All living functions, including thought, feeling, movement, and bodily processes, cease at death.
4. *Applicability*. Death applies only to living things.
5. *Causation*. Death is caused by a breakdown of bodily functioning.

To understand death, children must acquire some basic notions of biology—that animals and plants contain body parts (brain, heart, stomach; leaf, stem, roots) essential for maintaining life. They must also break down their global category of *not alive* into *dead, inanimate, unreal,* and *nonexistent.* Until children grasp these ideas, they interpret death in terms of familiar experiences—as a change in behavior (Slaughter, Jaakkola, & Carey, 1999; Slaughter & Lyons, 2003). Consequently, they may believe that they caused a relative's or pet's death; that having a stomachache can cause someone to die; that dead people eat, go to the bathroom, see, and think; and that death is like sleep.

Permanence is the first understood component of the death concept. Preschoolers accept this fact quickly, perhaps because they have seen it in other situations—for example, in the dead butterflies and beetles they pick up and inspect while playing outside. Appreciation of *inevitability* soon follows. At first, children think that certain people do not die—themselves, people like themselves (other children), and people with whom they have close emotional ties. *Cessation, applicability,* and *causation* are more challenging ideas (Kenyon, 2001). Preschoolers and kindergartners say that the dead lose the capacity for most bodily processes. But the majority of 10- to 12-year-olds continue to say that the dead are able to perceive, think, and feel (Bering & Bjorklund, 2004).

Many adults, too, believe in the persistence of mental activity and consciousness after death. And they probably encourage these ideas in children when, in conversations with them about a dead relative or pet, they invite the child to think of the deceased's positive qualities and to sustain an emotional connection (Harris, 2011). It is not surprising, then, that most older children conclude that even if biological functions largely cease after death, thoughts and feelings continue in some form.

Because of exposure to the realities of death, these children in El Salvador—carrying the coffin of an infant during a funeral—likely exceed many agemates in their grasp of what death means.

Individual and Cultural Variations. Although children typically attain an adultlike understanding of death in middle childhood, wide individual differences exist (Speece & Brent, 1996). Terminally ill children under age 6 often have a well-developed concept of death (Linebarger, Sahler, & Egan, 2009; Nielson, 2012). If parents and health professionals have not been forthright, they discover that they are deathly ill in other ways—through nonverbal communication, eavesdropping, talking with other child patients, and perceiving physiological changes in their bodies. Children growing up on Israeli kibbutzim (agricultural settlements) who have witnessed terrorist attacks, family members' departure on army tours, and parental anxiety about safety express an adultlike grasp of death by age 5 (Mahon, Goldberg, & Washington, 1999).

Ethnic variations suggest that religious teachings affect children's understanding. In a comparison of four ethnic groups in Israel, Druze and Moslem children's death concepts differed from those of Christian and Jewish children (Florian & Kravetz, 1985). The Druze emphasis on reincarnation and the greater religiosity of both Druze and Moslem groups may have led more of their children to deny that death is permanent and that the body stops functioning. Similarly, children of U.S. Southern Baptist families, who believe in an afterlife, were less likely to endorse permanence than were children of Unitarian families, who do not dwell on an afterlife (Candy-Gibbs, Sharp, & Petrun, 1985).

Enhancing Children's Understanding. Parents often worry that discussing death candidly with children will fuel their fears. But children with a good grasp of the facts of death express less anxiety about it (Slaughter & Griffiths, 2007). Direct explanations, like Leslie's, that fit the child's capacity to

understand, work best. When adults use clichés or make misleading statements about the permanence of death, children may take these literally and react with confusion. For example, when a parent told her 5-year-old daughter, "Grandpa went on a long trip," the child wondered, "Why didn't he take me?" "When is he coming back?" Sometimes children ask difficult questions, such as "Will I die?" "Will you die?" Parents can be truthful as well as comforting by taking advantage of the child's sense of time. "Not for many, many years," they can say. "First I'm going to enjoy you as a grownup and be a grandparent."

Another way to foster an accurate appreciation of death is to teach young children about human biology. Three- to 5-year-olds given lessons in the role of the heart, brain, lungs, stomach, and other organs in sustaining life have more advanced death concepts than children not given such lessons (Slaughter & Lyons, 2003).

Adult–child discussions should also be culturally sensitive. Rather than presenting scientific evidence as negating religious beliefs, parents and teachers can help children blend the two sources of knowledge. Older children often combine their appreciation of the death concept with religious and philosophical views, which offer solace in times of bereavement (Talwar, 2011). As we will see later, open, honest discussions not only contribute to a realistic understanding of death but also facilitate grieving after a child has experienced a loss.

Adolescence

Recall that teenagers have difficulty integrating logical insights with the realities of everyday life. In this sense, their understanding of death is not yet fully mature, as both their reasoning and behavior reveal.

The Gap Between Logic and Reality. Teenagers can explain the permanence and cessation aspects of death, but they are attracted to alternatives. For example, adolescents often describe death as an enduring abstract state—"darkness," "eternal light," "transition," or "nothingness" (Brent et al., 1996). They also formulate personal theories about life after death. Besides images of heaven and hell influenced by their religious background, they speculate about reincarnation, transmigration of souls, and spiritual survival on earth or at another level (Noppe & Noppe, 1997; Yang & Chen, 2002).

Although mortality in adolescence is low compared with that in infancy and adulthood, teenage deaths are typically sudden and human-induced; unintentional injuries, homicide, and suicide are leading causes. Adolescents are clearly aware that death happens to everyone and can occur at any time. But as their high-risk activities suggest, they do not take death personally.

What explains teenagers' difficulty integrating logic with reality in the domain of death? First, adolescence is a period of rapid growth and onset of reproductive capacity—attainments that are the opposite of death! Second, recall the adolescent personal fable: Wrapped up in their own uniqueness, teenagers

Applying **What We Know**

Discussing Concerns About Death with Children and Adolescents

Suggestion	Description
Take the lead.	Be alert to the child's or adolescent's nonverbal behaviors, bringing up the subject sympathetically, especially after a death-related situation has occurred.
Listen perceptively.	Give full attention to the child or adolescent and the feelings underlying his or her words. When adults pretend to listen while thinking about other things, young people quickly pick up this sign of indifference and withdraw their confidence.
Acknowledge feelings.	Accept the child's or adolescent's emotions as real and important; avoid being judgmental. For example, paraphrase sentiments you detect, such as "I see you're very puzzled about that. Let's talk more about it."
Provide factual information in a candid, culturally sensitive fashion.	For children who do not yet have a realistic understanding of death, provide simple, direct, and accurate explanations. Avoid misleading statements, such as "went for a rest" or "sleeping." Do not contradict the young person's religious beliefs. Rather, assist him or her in blending biological with religious knowledge.
Engage in joint problem solving.	When questions do not have easy answers, such as "Where does your soul go when you die?," convey your belief in the young person's worth by indicating that you do not want to impose a point of view but rather to help him or her come to personally satisfying conclusions. To questions you cannot answer, say, "I don't know." Such honesty shows a willingness to generate and evaluate solutions jointly.

may conclude they are beyond reach of death. Finally, as teenagers construct a personal identity and experience their first freely chosen love relationships, they may be strongly attracted to romantic notions of death, which challenge logic (Noppe & Noppe, 1996). Not until early adulthood are young people

This teenager knows that death happens to everyone and can occur at any time, but his risk taking suggests otherwise. Wrapped up in their own uniqueness, adolescents may conclude they are beyond reach of death.

capable of the relativistic thinking needed to reconcile these conflicting ideas (see Chapter 13, page 451).

Enhancing Adolescents' Understanding. By encouraging adolescents to discuss concerns about death, adults can help them build a bridge between death as a logical concept and their personal experiences. In Chapter 12, we noted that teenagers with authoritative parents are more likely to turn to adults for guidance on important issues. But the majority of parents feel uncomfortable about addressing the topic of death and inadequately prepared to do so (Talwar, 2011).

Taking up adolescents' thoughts and feelings about death can be part of everyday conversation, sparked by a news report or the death of an acquaintance. Parents can capitalize on these moments to express their own views, listen closely, accept teenagers' feelings, and correct misconceptions. Such mutual sharing deepens bonds of love and provides the basis for further exploration when the need arises. Applying What We Know above suggests ways to discuss concerns about death with children and adolescents.

Adulthood

In early adulthood, many people brush aside thoughts of death (Corr & Corr, 2013). This avoidance may be prompted by death anxiety, which we will consider in the next section. Alternatively, it may be due to relative lack of interest in death-related issues, given that young adults typically do not know very many people who have died and (like adolescents) think of their own death as a long way off.

In Chapters 15 and 16, we described midlife as a time of stock taking in which people begin to view the lifespan in terms of time left to live and focus on tasks to be completed. Middle-aged people no longer have a vague conception of their own death. They know that in the not-too-distant future, it will be their turn to grow old and die.

In late adulthood, adults think and talk more about death because it is much closer. Increasing evidence of mortality comes from physical changes, higher rates of illness and disability, and loss of relatives and friends (see Chapter 17). Compared with middle-aged people, older adults spend more time pondering the process and circumstances of dying than the state of death (Kastenbaum, 2012). Nearness to death seems to lead to a practical concern with how and when it might happen.

Finally, although we have traced overall age-related changes, large individual differences exist. Some adults focus on life and death issues early on; others are less reflective, moving into old age without giving these matters much attention.

Death Anxiety

TAKE A MOMENT... As you read the following statements, do you find yourself agreeing, disagreeing, or reacting neutrally?

"Never feeling anything again after I die upsets me."

"I hate the idea that I will be helpless after I die."

"The total isolation of death is frightening to me."

"The feeling that I will be missing out on so much after I die disturbs me." (Thorson & Powell, 1994, pp. 38–39)

Items like these appear on questionnaires used to measure **death anxiety**—fear and apprehension of death. Even people who clearly accept the reality of death may fear it.

What predicts whether thoughts of our own demise trigger intense distress, relative calm, or something in between? To answer this question, researchers measure both general death anxiety and specific factors—fear of no longer existing, loss of control, a painful death, decay of the body, separation from loved ones, and the unknown (Neimeyer, 1994). Findings reveal large individual and cultural variations in aspects of death that arouse fear. For example, in a study of devout Islamic Saudi Arabians, certain factors that appear repeatedly in the responses of Westerners, such as fear of the body decaying and of the unknown, were entirely absent (Long, 1985).

Among Westerners, spirituality—a sense of life's meaning—seems to be more important than religious commitment in limiting death anxiety (Ardelt, 2003; Routledge & Juhl, 2010). People with a well-developed personal philosophy of death are also less fearful. And in two studies, Christian older adults whose religious beliefs and behavior were contradictory—who believed in a rewarding afterlife but rarely prayed or attended services, or who regularly prayed and attended services but doubted the existence of an afterlife—reported higher death anxiety (Wink, 2006; Wink & Scott, 2005). Together, these findings indicate that both firmness of beliefs and consistency between beliefs and practices, rather than religiousness itself, reduce fear of death. Death anxiety is especially low among adults with deep faith in some form of higher force or being—faith that may or may not be influenced by religion (Cicirelli, 2002; Neimeyer et al., 2011).

TAKE A MOMENT... From what you have learned about adult psychosocial development, how do you think death anxiety might change with age? If you predicted it would decline, reaching its lowest level in late adulthood, you are correct (see Figure 19.1) (Russac et al., 2007; Tomer, Eliason, & Smith, 2000). This age-related drop has been found in many cultures and ethnic groups. Recall from Chapter 18 that older adults are especially effective at regulating negative emotion. As a result, most cope with anxieties, including fear of death, effectively. Furthermore, attainment of ego integrity reduces death anxiety. Older people have had more time to develop symbolic immortality—the belief that one will continue to live on through one's children or through one's work or personal influence (see Chapter 16, page 533).

As long as it is not overly intense, death anxiety can motivate people to strive to live up to internalized cultural values—for example, to be kind to others and to work hard to reach one's goals. These efforts increase adults' sense of self-esteem, self-efficacy, and purpose in life—powerful antidotes against the terrifying thought that, in the overall scheme of things, they "are no more important or enduring than any individual potato, pineapple, or porcupine" (Fry, 2003; Pyszczynski et al., 2004, p. 436). In a study of Israeli adults, symbolic immortality predicted reduced fear of death, especially among those with secure attachments (Florian & Mikulincer, 1998). Gratifying, close interpersonal ties seem to help people feel worthwhile and forge a sense of symbolic immortality. And people who view death as an opportunity to pass a legacy to future generations are less likely to fear it (Cicirelli, 2001; Mikulincer, Florian, & Hirschberger, 2003).

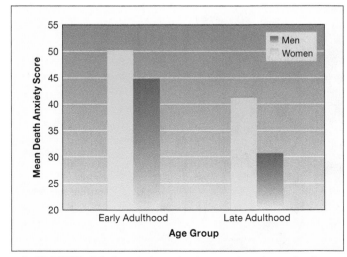

FIGURE 19.1 Relationship of age and gender to death anxiety. In this study comparing young and older adults, death anxiety declined with age. Women expressed greater fear of death than men. Many other studies show similar findings. (Adapted from Tomer, Eliason, & Smith, 2000.)

Regardless of age, in both Eastern and Western cultures, women appear more anxious about death than men do (refer again to Figure 19.1) (Madnawat & Kachhawa, 2007; Tomer, Eliason, & Smith, 2000). Women may be more likely to admit and men more likely to avoid troubled feelings about mortality—an explanation consistent with females' greater emotional expressiveness throughout the lifespan. Furthermore, in one study, women showed a temporary rise in death anxiety in their early fifties not seen in men (Russac et al., 2007). Perhaps menopause, in marking the end of reproductive capacity, provides women with a stark reminder of their mortality.

Experiencing some anxiety about death is normal and adaptive. But like other fears, very intense death anxiety can undermine effective adjustment. Although physical health in adulthood is not related to death anxiety, mental health clearly is. In cultures as different as China and the United States, people who are depressed or generally anxious are likely to have more severe death concerns (Neimeyer & Van Brunt, 1995; Wu, Tang, & Kwok, 2002). In contrast, people who are good at inhibition (keeping their minds from straying to irrelevant thoughts) and at emotional self-regulation report less death anxiety (Gailliot, Schmeichel, & Baumeister, 2006). They are better able to manage their concerns about death.

Death anxiety is largely limited to adolescence and adulthood. Children rarely display it unless they live in high-crime neighborhoods or war-torn areas where they are in constant danger (see the Cultural Influences box on the impact of ethnic and political violence on children on page 533 in Chapter 10). Terminally ill children are also at risk for high death anxiety. Compared with other same-age patients, children with cancer express more destructive thoughts and negative feelings about death (Malone, 1982). For those whose parents make the mistake of not telling them they are going to die, loneliness and death anxiety can be extreme (O'Halloran & Altmaier, 1996).

Death anxiety declines in old age, and this 81-year-old from the Netherlands seems to have very little! She had this coffin made to serve as a bookshelf because, she said, "It's a waste to use a coffin just for burial." The pillow on the top will support her head after she dies.

ASK YOURSELF

REVIEW Explain why older adults think and talk more about death than do younger people but feel less anxious about it.

CONNECT How do advances in cognition contribute to adolescents' concepts of death? (Refer to Chapter 11, pages 382–383 and 386–387.)

APPLY When 4-year-old Chloe's aunt died, Chloe asked, "Where's Aunt Susie?" Her mother explained, "Aunt Susie is taking a long, peaceful sleep." For the next two weeks, Chloe refused to go to bed, and, when finally coaxed into her room, lay awake for hours. What is the likely reason for Chloe's behavior? What might be a better way of answering her question?

REFLECT Ask members of earlier generations in your family about their childhood experiences with death. Compare these to your own experiences. What differences did you find, and how would you explain them?

Thinking and Emotions of Dying People

In the year before her death, Sofie did everything possible to surmount her illness. In between treatments to control the cancer, she tested her strength. She continued to teach high school, traveled to visit her children, cultivated a garden, and took weekend excursions with Philip. Hope pervaded Sofie's approach to her deadly condition, and she spoke often about the disease—so much so that her friends wondered how she could confront it so directly.

As Sofie deteriorated physically, she moved in and out of various mental and emotional states. She was frustrated, and at times angry and depressed, about her inability to keep on fighting. I recall her lamenting anxiously on a day when she was in pain, "I'm sick, so very sick! I'm trying so hard, but I can't keep on." Once she asked when my husband and I, who were newly married, would have children. "If only I could live long enough to hold them in my arms!" she cried. In the last week, she appeared tired but free of struggle. Occasionally, she spoke of her love for us and commented on the beauty of the hills outside her window. But mostly, she looked and listened, rather than actively participating in conversation. One afternoon, she fell permanently unconscious.

Do Stages of Dying Exist?

As dying people move closer to death, are their reactions predictable? Do they go through a series of changes that are the same for everyone, or are their thoughts and feelings unique?

Kübler-Ross's Theory. Although her theory has been heavily criticized, Elisabeth Kübler-Ross (1969) is credited with awakening society's sensitivity to the psychological needs of dying patients. From interviews with over 200 terminally ill people, she devised a theory of five typical responses—initially proposed as stages—to the prospect of death and the ordeal of dying:

- *Denial.* On learning of the terminal illness, the person denies its seriousness—refusing to accept the diagnosis, avoiding discussions with doctors and family members—to escape from the prospect of death. While the patient still feels reasonably well, denial is self-protective, allowing the individual to deal with the illness at his or her own pace. Most people move in and out of denial, making great plans one day and, the next, acknowledging that death is near (Rousseau, 2000). Although denial can reduce emotional distress, enabling patients to absorb the news while addressing unfinished life tasks, Kübler-Ross recommends that family members and health professionals not prolong denial by distorting the truth about the person's condition. In doing so, they prevent the dying person from adjusting to impending death and hinder necessary arrangements—for social support, for bringing closure to relationships, and for making decisions about medical interventions.

- *Anger.* Recognition that time is short promotes anger at having to die without having had a chance to do all one wants to do. Family members and health professionals may be targets of the patient's rage, resentment, and envy. Even so, they must tolerate rather than lash out at the patient's behavior, recognizing that the underlying cause is the unfairness of death.

- *Bargaining.* Realizing the inevitability of death, the terminally ill person attempts to bargain for extra time—a deal he or she may try to strike with family members, friends, doctors, nurses, or God. The best response to these efforts to sustain hope is to listen sympathetically, as one doctor did to the pleas of a young AIDS-stricken father, whose wish was to live long enough to dance with his daughter—then 8 years old—at her wedding (Selwyn, 1996). Sometimes, bargains are altruistic acts. Tony, a 15-year-old leukemia patient, expressed to his mother:

  > I don't want to die yet. Gerry [youngest brother] is only 3 and not old enough to understand. If I could live just one more year, I could explain it to him myself and he will understand. Three is just too young. (Komp, 1996, pp. 69–70)

  Although many dying patients' bargains are unrealistic and impossible to fulfill, Tony lived for exactly one year—a gift to those who survived him.

- *Depression.* When denial, anger, and bargaining fail to postpone the illness, the person becomes depressed about the loss of his or her life—a response that intensifies suffering. Unfortunately, many experiences associated with dying, including physical and mental deterioration, pain,

lack of control, certain medications, and being hooked to machines, contribute to despondency. Compassionate medical and psychological treatment, aimed at clarifying and alleviating the patients concerns, can limit hopelessness and despair.

- *Acceptance.* Most people who reach acceptance, a state of peace and quiet about upcoming death, do so only in the last weeks or days. The weakened patient yields to death, disengaging from all but a few family members, friends, and caregivers. Some dying people, in an attempt to pull away from all they have loved, withdraw into themselves for long periods of time. "I'm getting my mental and emotional house in order," one patient explained (Samarel, 1995, p. 101).

Evaluation of Kübler-Ross's Theory. Kübler-Ross cautioned that her five stages should not be viewed as a fixed sequence and that not all people display each response. But her use of the term *stages* has made it easy for her theory to be interpreted simplistically, as the series of steps a "normal" dying person follows. Some health professionals, unaware of diversity in dying experiences, have insensitively tried to push patients through Kübler-Ross's sequence. And caregivers, through callousness or ignorance, can too easily dismiss a dying patient's legitimate complaints about treatment as "just what you would expect in Stage 2" (Corr & Corr, 2013; Kastenbaum, 2012).

Research confirms that, in line with Kübler-Ross's observations, dying people are more likely to display denial after learning of their condition and acceptance shortly before death (Kalish, 1985). But rather than stages, the five reactions Kübler-Ross observed are best viewed as coping strategies that anyone may call on in the face of threat. Furthermore, dying people react in many additional ways—for example, through efforts to conquer the disease, as Sofie displayed; through an overwhelming need to control what happens to their bodies during the dying process; through acts of generosity and caring, as seen in Tony's concern for his 3-year-old brother, Gerry; and through shifting their focus to living in a fulfilling way—"seizing the day" because so little time is left (Silverman, 2004; Wright, 2003).

As these examples suggest, the most serious drawback to Kübler-Ross's theory is that it looks at dying patients' thoughts and feelings outside the contexts that give them meaning. As we will see next, people's adaptations to impending death can be understood only in relation to the multidimensional influences that have contributed to their life course and that also shape this final phase.

Contextual Influences on Adaptations to Dying

From the moment of her diagnosis, Sofie spent little time denying the deadliness of her disease. Instead, she met it head on, just as she had dealt with other challenges of life. Her impassioned plea to hold her grandchildren in her arms was

On September 18, 2007, Carnegie Mellon University computer science professor Randy Pausch, diagnosed with pancreatic cancer, gave his final lecture to a packed house. His message, which focused on achieving one's childhood dreams and enabling the dreams of others, can be viewed at *www.cmu.edu/homepage/multimedia/randy-pausch-lecture.shtml*. He died nine months later, at age 47, having approached his death in a way that suited his pattern of living and deepest values.

less a bargain with fate than an expression of profound defeat that on the threshold of late adulthood, she would not live to enjoy its rewards. At the end, her quiet, withdrawn demeanor was probably resignation, not acceptance. All her life, she had been a person with a fighting spirit, unwilling to give in to challenge.

According to recent theorists, a single strategy, such as acceptance, is not best for every dying patient. Rather, an **appropriate death** is one that makes sense in terms of the individual's pattern of living and values and, at the same time, preserves or restores significant relationships and is as free of suffering as possible (Worden, 2000). When asked about a "good death," most patients are clear about what, ideally, they would like to happen. They mention the following goals:

- Maintaining a sense of identity, or inner continuity with one's past
- Clarifying the meaning of one's life and death
- Maintaining and enhancing relationships
- Achieving a sense of control over the time that remains
- Confronting and preparing for death (Goldsteen et al., 2006; Kleespies, 2004; Proulx & Jacelon, 2004)

Research reveals that biological, psychological, and social and cultural forces affect people's coping with dying and, therefore, the extent to which they attain these goals. Let's look at some important influences on how people fare.

Nature of the Disease. The course of the illness and its symptoms affect the dying person's reactions. For example, the extended nature of Sofie's illness and her doctor's initial optimism about achieving a remission undoubtedly contributed to her attempts to try to conquer the disease. During the final

month, when cancer had spread to Sofie's lungs and she could not catch her breath, she was agitated and fearful until oxygen and medication relieved her uncertainty about being able to breathe. In contrast, Nicholas's weakened heart and failing kidneys so depleted his strength that he responded only with passivity.

Because of the toll of the disease, about one-third of cancer patients experience severe depression—reactions distinct from the sadness, grief, and worry that typically accompany the dying process. Profound depression amplifies pain, impairs the immune response, interferes with the patient's capacity for pleasure, meaning, and connection, and is associated with poorer survival (Satin, Linden, & Phillips, 2009; Williams & Dale, 2006). It therefore requires immediate treatment. Among the most successful approaches are meaning-focused life review (see page 606 in Chapter 18), medical control of pain, and advance care planning with the patient that ensures that his or her end-of-life wishes are known and respected (Rosenstein, 2011).

Personality and Coping Style. Understanding the way individuals view stressful life events and have coped with them in the past helps us appreciate the way they manage the dying process. In a study in which terminally ill patients discussed their images of dying, responses varied greatly. For example,

- Beth regarded *dying as imprisonment:* "I felt like the clock started ticking . . . like the future has suddenly been taken. . . . In a way, I feel like I'm already dead."
- To Faith, dying was *a mandate to live ever more fully:* "I have a saying: . . . 'You're not ready to live until you're ready to die.' . . . It never meant much to me until I . . . looked death in the eye, and now I'm living. . . . This life is a lot better than the one before."
- Dawn viewed dying as *part of life's journey:* "I learned all about my disease. . . . I would read, read, read. . . . I wanted to know as much as I can about it, and I don't think hiding . . . behind the door . . . could help me at all. And, I realized for the first time in my life—*really, really, really realized* that I could handle anything."
- Patty approached dying as *an experience to be transformed* so as to make it more bearable: "I am an avid, rabid fan of *Star Trek*, a trekkie like there never has been. . . . I watch it to the point that I've memorized it. . . . [In my mind, I play the various characters so] I'm not [always] thinking about cancer or dying. . . . I think that's how I get through it." (Wright, 2003, pp. 442–444, 447)

Each patient's view of dying helps explain her responses to worsening illness. Poorly adjusted individuals—those with conflict-ridden relationships and many disappointments in life—are usually more distressed (Kastenbaum, 2012).

Family Members' and Health Professionals' Behavior. Earlier we noted that a candid approach, in which everyone close to and caring for the dying person acknowledges

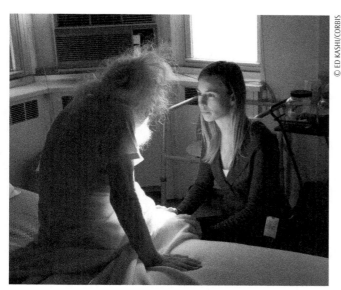

A doctor listens patiently to the concerns of a terminally ill 94-year-old. Through sensitive, open communication, health professionals help dying people prepare for death by bringing relationships to closure, reflecting on life, and dealing with fears and regrets.

the terminal illness, is best. Yet this also introduces the burden of participating in the work of dying with the patient—bringing relationships to closure, reflecting on life, and dealing with fears and regrets.

People who find it hard to engage in these tasks may pretend that the disease is not as bad as it is. In patients inclined toward denial, a "game" can be set in motion in which participants are aware that the patient is dying but act as though it were not so. Though this game softens psychological pain for the moment, it makes dying much more difficult. Besides impeding communication, it frequently leads to futile medical interventions, in which the patient has little understanding of what is happening and is subjected to great physical and emotional suffering. One attending physician provided this account of a cancer patient's death:

> The problem was that she had a young husband and parents who were pretty much in complete denial. We were trying to be aggressive up to the end. To the point that we actually hung a new form of chemotherapy about four hours before she died, even though everybody knew except her immediate family that she was going to die within the next four to eight hours. (Jackson et al., 2005, p. 653)

At other times, the patient suspects what he or she has not been told. In one instance, a terminally ill child flew into a rage because his doctor and a nurse spoke to him in ways that denied the fact that he would not grow up. Trying to get the child to cooperate with a medical procedure, the doctor said,

> "I thought you would understand, Sandy. You told me once you wanted to be a doctor."
>
> He screamed back, "I'm not going to be anything!" and threw an empty syringe at her.

The nurse standing nearby asked, "What are you going to be?"

"A ghost," said Sandy, and turned away from them. (Bluebond-Langner, 1977, p. 59)

The behavior of health professionals impeded Sandy's efforts to form a realistic time perspective and intensified his anger at the injustice of his premature death.

When doctors do want to inform patients of their prognosis, they may encounter resistance, especially within certain ethnic groups. Withholding information is common in Southern and Eastern Europe, Central and South America, much of Asia, and the Middle East. Japanese terminally ill cancer patients are seldom told the truth about their condition, partly because dying disrupts important interdependent relationships (Yamamoto, 2004). Many Mexican Americans and Korean Americans believe that informing patients is wrong and will hasten death (Blackhall et al., 1995, 2001). In these instances, providing information is complex. When a family insists that a patient not be told, the doctor can first offer information to the patient and then, if the patient refuses, ask who should receive information and make health-care decisions (Zane & Yeh, 2002). The patient's preference can be honored and reassessed at regular intervals.

Care of the terminally ill is demanding and stressful. Nurses who respond effectively to the psychological needs of dying patients and their families benefit from inservice training aimed at strengthening interpersonal skills, day-to-day mutual support among staff, and development of a personal philosophy of living and dying (Efstathiou & Clifford, 2011; Hebert, Moore, & Rooney, 2011; Morris, 2011. Extensive experience working with dying patients in a sensitive, supportive environment is associated with low death anxiety, perhaps because such caregivers observe their patients' distress decline and, thus, gradually learn that their own previous fears are less founded (Bluck et al., 2008; Peters et al., 2013).

Social support from family members also affects adaptation to dying. Dying patients who feel they have much unfinished business to attend to are more anxious about impending death. But family contact reduces their sense of urgency to prolong life (Mutran et al., 1997; Zimmerman, 2012). Perhaps it permits patients to work through at least some incomplete tasks.

Effective communication with the dying person is honest, fostering a trusting relationship, yet also oriented toward maintaining hope. Many dying patients move through a hope trajectory—at first, hope for a cure; later, hope for prolonging life; and finally, hope for a peaceful death with as few burdens as possible (Fanslow, 1981). Once patients near death stop expressing hope, those close to them must accept this. Family members who find letting go very difficult may benefit from expert guidance. Applying What We Know on page 650 offers suggestions for communicating with the dying.

Spirituality, Religion, and Culture. Earlier we noted that a sense of spirituality reduces fear of death. Research indicates that this is as true for the dying as for people in general.

Applying What We Know

Communicating with Dying People

Suggestion	Description
Be truthful about the diagnosis and course of the disease.	Be honest about what the future is likely to hold, thereby permitting the dying person to bring closure to his or her life by expressing sentiments and wishes and participating in decisions about treatment.
Listen perceptively and acknowledge feelings.	Be truly present, focusing full attention on what the dying person has to say and accepting the patient's feelings. Patients who sense another's presence and concern are more likely to relax physically and emotionally and express themselves.
Maintain realistic hope.	Assist the dying person in maintaining hope by encouraging him or her to focus on a realistic goal that might yet be achieved—for example, resolution of a troubled relationship or special moments with a loved one. Knowing the dying person's hope, family members and health professionals can often help fulfill it.
Assist in the final transition.	Assure the dying person that he or she is not alone, offering a sympathetic touch, a caring thought, or just a calm presence. Some patients who struggle may benefit from being given permission to die—the message that giving up and letting go is all right.

Source: Lugton, 2002.

Terminally ill patients who score higher in spiritual well-being (belief in life's meaning) experience less end-of-life despair (desire for a hastened death and suicidal thoughts) (McClain, Rosenfeld, & Breitbard, 2003; McClain-Jacobson et al., 2004). As one experienced nurse commented,

> At the end, those [patients] with a faith—it doesn't really matter in what, but a faith in something—find it easier. Not always, but as a rule. I've seen people with faith panic and I've seen those without faith accept it [death]. But, as a rule, it's much easier for those with faith. (Samarel, 1991, pp. 64–65)

Vastly different cultural beliefs, guided by religious ideas, also shape people's dying experiences:

- Buddhism, widely practiced in China, India, and Southeast Asia, fosters acceptance of death. By reading sutras (teachings of Buddha) to the dying person to calm the mind and emphasizing that dying leads to rebirth in a heaven of peace and relaxation, Buddhists believe that it is possible to reach Nirvana, a state beyond the world of suffering (Kubotera, 2004; Yeung, 1996).

- In many Native-American groups, death is met with stoic self-control, an approach taught at an early age through stories that emphasize a circular, rather than linear, relationship between life and death and the importance of making way for others (Cox, 2002).

- For African Americans, a dying loved one signals a crisis that unites family members in caregiving (Crawley et al., 2000; Jenkins et al., 2005). The terminally ill person remains an active and vital force within the family until he or she can no longer carry out this role—an attitude of respect that undoubtedly eases the dying process.

- Among the Maori of New Zealand, relatives and friends gather around the dying person to give spiritual strength and comfort. Older adults, clergy, and other experts in tribal customs conduct a *karakia* ceremony, in which they recite prayers asking for peace, mercy, and guidance from the creator. After the ceremony, the patient is encouraged to discuss important matters with those closest to her—giving away of personal belongings, directions for interment, and completion of other unfinished tasks (Ngata, 2004).

In sum, dying prompts a multitude of thoughts, emotions, and coping strategies. Which ones are emphasized depends on a wide array of contextual influences. A vital assumption of the lifespan perspective—that development is multidimensional and multidirectional—is just as relevant to this final phase as to each earlier period.

 ## A Place to Die

Whereas in the past most deaths occurred at home, in the United States today about 40 percent take place in hospitals and another 20 percent in long-term care facilities, mostly nursing homes (Centers for Disease Control and Prevention, 2013). In the large, impersonal hospital environment, meeting the human needs of dying patients and their families is secondary, not because professionals lack concern, but because the work to be done focuses on saving lives. A dying patient represents a failure.

In the 1960s, a death awareness movement arose as a reaction to hospitals' death-avoiding practices—attachment of complicated machinery to patients with no chance of survival and avoidance of communication with dying patients. This movement soon led to medical care better suited to the needs of dying people and also to hospice programs, which have spread to many countries in the industrialized world. Let's visit each of these settings for dying.

Home

Had Sofie and Nicholas been asked where they wanted to die, undoubtedly each would have responded, "At home"—the preference of 80 to 90 percent of Americans (NHPCO, 2005; O'Connor, 2003). The reason is clear: The home offers an atmosphere of intimacy and loving care in which the terminally ill person is unlikely to feel abandoned or humiliated by physical decline or dependence on others.

However, only about one-fourth of Americans experience home death (Centers for Disease Control and Prevention, 2013). And it is important not to romanticize dying at home. Because of dramatic improvements in medicine, dying people tend to be sicker or much older than in the past. Consequently, their bodies may be extremely frail, making ordinary activities—eating, sleeping, taking a pill, toileting, and bathing—major ordeals for informal caregivers (Singer et al., 2005). Health problems of aging spouses, work and other responsibilities of family members, and the physical, psychological, and financial strain of providing home care can make it difficult to honor a terminally ill person's wish to die at home.

For many people, the chance to be with the dying person until the very end is a rewarding tradeoff for the high demands of caregiving. But to make dying at home feasible, adequate support for the caregiver is essential (Karlsson & Berggren, 2011; Newbury, 2011). A specially trained home health aide is usually necessary—a service (as we will see shortly) that hospice programs have made more accessible. Still, when family relationships are conflict-ridden, a dying patient introduces additional family strains and is subjected to increased distress, negating the benefits of home death. Furthermore, even with professional help, most homes are poorly equipped to handle the medical and comfort-care needs of the dying. Hospital-based equipment and technical support often must be transported to the home.

For all these reasons, older adults—although they view home as their ideal place to die—express concerns about quality of care, about burdening family and friends, and about the need for adult children to engage in unduly intimate caregiving tasks (Gott et al., 2004). And 10 months after a home death, family members continue to report more psychological stress than do family members whose loved one died elsewhere (Addington-Hall, 2000).

Hospital

Hospital dying takes many forms. Each is affected by the physical state of the dying person, the hospital unit in which it takes place, and the goal and quality of care.

Sudden deaths, due to injury or critical illness, typically occur in emergency rooms. Doctors and nurses must evaluate the problem and take action quickly. Little time is available for contact with family members. When staff break the news of death in a sympathetic manner and provide explanations, family members are grateful. Otherwise, feelings of anger, frustra-

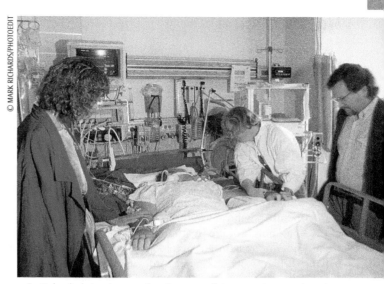

Dying in intensive care is a depersonalizing experience unique to technologically sophisticated societies. In such settings, medical responses supersede privacy and communication with patient and family.

tion, and confusion can add to their grief (Walsh & McGoldrick, 2004). Crisis intervention services are needed to help survivors cope with sudden death.

Nicholas died on an intensive care ward focused on preventing death in patients whose condition can worsen quickly. Privacy and communication with the family were secondary to monitoring his condition. To prevent disruption of nurses' activities, Giselle and Sasha could be at Nicholas's side only at scheduled times. Dying in intensive care—an experience unique to technologically sophisticated societies—is especially depersonalizing for patients like Nicholas, who linger between life and death while hooked to machines often for months.

Cancer patients, who account for most cases of prolonged dying, typically die in general or specialized cancer care hospital units. When hospitalized for a long time, they reach out for help with physical and emotional needs, too often with mixed success. In these hospital settings, as in intensive care, a conflict of values is apparent (Costello, 2006). The tasks associated with dying must be performed efficiently so that all patients can be served and health professionals are not drained emotionally by repeated attachments and separations.

Although hospital comprehensive treatment programs aimed at easing physical, emotional, and spiritual suffering at the end of life have increased steadily over the past decade, one-third of hospitals still do not have them (Center to Advance Palliative Care, 2012). And because just 16 percent of U.S. and Canadian medical schools offer even a single pain-focused course (usually an elective), few doctors and nurses are specially trained in managing pain in chronically ill and dying people (Mezei & Murinson, 2011). At present, many people die in painful, frightening, and depersonalizing hospital conditions, without their wishes being met.

Nursing Home

Though deaths in U.S. nursing homes—mostly elderly patients—are common, care emphasizes rehabilitation rather than high-quality terminal care. Too often, residents' end-of-life preferences are not gathered and recorded in medical records. The few studies that have addressed what it is like to die in nursing homes concur that many patients suffer from inattention to their emotional and spiritual needs and from high levels of untreated pain (Massachusetts Expert Panel on End of Life Care, 2010).

In one investigation, researchers conducted in-depth interviews with a nationally representative sample of nearly 600 family members whose loved one had spent at least 48 hours of the final month of life in a nursing home. Respondents frequently mentioned unsatisfactory physical care of the dying patient, difficulty obtaining basic information from staff members on the patient's condition, staff members' lack of compassion and attentiveness to the patient's medical deterioration, and physicians who were "missing in action"—rarely seen in the nursing home (Wetle et al., 2005; Shield et al., 2010). Relatives often felt the need to advocate for their dying relative, though their efforts met with limited success—circumstances that greatly increased both patient and family distress.

The hospice approach—which we consider next—aims to reduce profound caregiving failures in hospitals and nursing homes. When combined with hospice, nursing home care of the dying improves greatly in pain management, emotional and spiritual support, and family satisfaction. But referrals of dying nursing-home residents to hospice, though increasing, are often not made—or made too late to be useful (Zheng et al., 2012).

The Hospice Approach

In medieval times, a *hospice* was a place where travelers could find rest and shelter. In the nineteenth and twentieth centuries, the word referred to homes for dying patients. Today, **hospice** is not a place but a comprehensive program of support services for terminally ill people and their families. It aims to provide a caring community sensitive to the dying person's needs so patients and family members can prepare for death in ways that are satisfying to them. Quality of life is central to the hospice approach, which includes these main features:

- The patient and family as a unit of care
- Emphasis on meeting the patient's physical, emotional, social, and spiritual needs, including controlling pain, retaining dignity and self-worth, and feeling cared for and loved
- Care provided by an interdisciplinary team: a doctor, a nurse or home health aide, a chaplain, a counselor or social worker, and a trained volunteer
- The patient kept at home or in an inpatient setting with a homelike atmosphere where coordination of care is possible
- Focus on protecting the quality of remaining life with **palliative,** or **comfort, care** that relieves pain and other

A son and his dying mother share recollections as he shows her a photograph of her long-ago graduation. By creating opportunities for unpressured closeness and connection, hospice care enhances dying patients' quality of life rather than extending life.

symptoms (nausea, breathing difficulties, insomnia, and depression) rather than prolonging life

- In addition to regularly scheduled home care visits, on-call services available 24 hours a day, 7 days a week
- Follow-up bereavement services offered to families in the year after a death

Because hospice care is a philosophy, not a facility, it can be applied in diverse ways. In Great Britain, care in a special hospice inpatient unit, sometimes associated with a hospital, is typical. In the United States, home care has been emphasized: About 42 percent of hospice patients die in their own home, 26 percent in a hospice inpatient unit, 18 percent in a nursing home, 7 percent in another type of residential setting, and 7 percent in a typical hospital room (NHPCO, 2012).

But hospice programs everywhere have expanded to include a continuum of care, from home to inpatient options, including hospitals and nursing homes. Central to the hospice approach is that the dying person and his or her family be offered choices that guarantee an appropriate death. Some programs offer hospice day care, which enables caregivers to continue working or be relieved of the stresses of long-term care (Kernohan et al., 2006). Contact with others facing terminal illness is a supportive byproduct of many hospice arrangements. And to find out about a comforting musical intervention for patients near death, consult the Biology and Environment box on the following page.

LOOK AND LISTEN

Contact a nearby hospice program, and find out about its varied ways it delivers its comprehensive services to meet the needs of dying patients and their families. ●

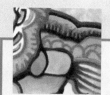

Biology and Environment

Music as Palliative Care for Dying Patients

When Peter visits 82-year-old Stuart to play the harp, Stuart reports being transported to an idyllic place with water, children, and trees—far from the lung tumors that will soon take his life. "When Peter plays for me, . . . I am no longer frightened," Stuart says.

Peter is a specialist in *music thanatology,* an emerging specialty in music therapy that focuses on providing palliative care to the dying through music. He uses his harp, and sometimes his voice, to induce calm and give solace to the dying, their families, and their caregivers. Peter applies music systematically—matching it to each patient's breathing patterns and other responses, delivering different sounds to uplift or comfort, depending on his assessment of the patient's moment-by-moment needs.

Chaplains and counselors informally report that after music vigils, patients' conversations indicate that they more easily

come to terms with their own death (Fyfe, 2006). And in a study of 65 dying patients in which pre- and post-intervention physiological measures were compared, music vigils averaging an hour in length resulted in decreased agitation and wakefulness and slower, deeper, less effortful breathing (Freeman et al., 2006). These physiological benefits extended to patients who, on the basis of their behavior, were clearly in pain.

Why is music effective in easing the distress of those who are dying? In patients close to death, hearing typically functions longer than other senses. Thus, responsiveness to music may persist until the individual's final moments. Besides

Music thanatology focuses on providing palliative care for the dying through music. This practitioner uses her harp, and sometimes her voice, to induce calm and provide solace.

reducing anxiety, music can, in some instances, enhance the effects of medication administered to control pain (Starr, 1999). For these reasons, music vigils may be an especially effective end-of-life therapy.

Currently, the United States has over 5,300 hospice programs serving approximately 1.6 million terminally ill patients annually. About 38 percent of hospice patients have cancer. The top noncancer diagnoses are extreme frailty in the elderly (14 percent), dementia (13 percent), heart disease (11 percent), and lung disease (9 percent) (NHPCO, 2012). Because hospice care is a cost-effective alternative to expensive life-saving treatments, U.S. government health-care benefits (Medicare and Medicaid) cover it, as do most private insurance plans. In addition, community and foundation contributions allow many hospices to provide free services to uninsured patients who cannot pay (Hospice Foundation of America, 2013). Consequently hospice is affordable for most dying patients and their families. Hospices also serve dying children—a tragedy so devastating that social support and bereavement intervention are vital.

Besides reducing patient physical suffering, hospice contributes to improved family functioning. The majority of patients and families report high satisfaction with quality of care and pain management, enhanced sense of social support, and (in the case of home hospice) increased ability to sustain patient care at home (Candy et al., 2011). In one study, family members

experiencing hospice scored higher than nonhospice family members in psychological well-being one to two years after their loved one's death (Ragow-O'Brien, Hayslip, & Guarnaccia, 2000).

As a long-range goal, hospice organizations are striving for broader acceptance of their patient- and family-centered approach. Culturally sensitive approaches are needed to reach more ethnic minority patients, who are far less likely than white patients to participate in hospice (NHPCO, 2012). Canada has a Web-based hospice outreach service, the Canadian Virtual Hospice (*www.virtualhospice.ca*), to support patients, families, and care providers—whether or not they are part of a hospice program—with information, resources, and connections to others with similar concerns.

In developing countries, where millions die of cancer and other devastating illnesses each year, community-based teams working under a nurse's supervision sometimes deliver palliative care. But they face many obstacles, including lack of funding, pain-relieving drugs, and professional and public education about hospice. As a result, they are small "islands of excellence," accessible to only a few families (Ddungu, 2011).

The Right to Die

In 1976, the parents of Karen Ann Quinlan, a young woman who had fallen into an irreversible coma after taking drugs at a party, sued to have her respirator turned off. The New Jersey Supreme Court, invoking Karen's right to privacy and her parents' power as guardians, complied with this request. Although Karen was expected to die quickly, she breathed independently, continued to be fed intravenously, and lived another 10 years in a persistent vegetative state.

In 1990, 26-year-old Terri Schiavo's heart stopped briefly, temporarily cutting off oxygen to her brain. Like Karen, Terri lay in a persistent vegetative state. Her husband and guardian, Michael, claimed that she had earlier told him she would not want to be kept alive artificially, but Terri's parents disagreed. In 1998, the Florida Circuit Court granted Michael's petition to have Terri's feeding tube removed. In 2001, after her parents had exhausted their appeals, the tube was taken out. But on the basis of contradictory medical testimony, Terri's parents convinced a circuit court judge to order the feeding tube reinserted, and the legal wrangling continued. In 2002, Michael won a second judgment to remove the tube.

By that time, publicity over the case and its central question—who should make end-of-life decisions when the patient's wishes are unclear—had made Terri a political issue. In 2003, the Florida legislature passed a law allowing the governor to stay the circuit court's order to keep Terri alive, but on appeal, the law was declared unconstitutional. In 2005, the U.S. Congress entered the fray, passing a bill that transferred Terri's fate to the U.S. District Court. When the judge refused to intervene, the feeding tube was removed for a third time. In 2005—15 years after losing consciousness—Terri Schiavo died. The autopsy confirmed the original persistent vegetative state diagnosis: Her brain was half normal size.

Before the 1950s, the right to die was of little concern because medical science could do little to extend the lives of terminally ill patients. Today, medical advances mean that the same procedures that preserve life can prolong inevitable death, diminishing both quality of life and personal dignity.

The Quinlan and Schiavo cases—and others like them—have brought right-to-die issues to the forefront of public attention. Today, all U.S. states have laws that honor patients' wishes concerning withdrawal of treatment in cases of terminal illness and, sometimes, in cases of a persistent vegetative state. But no uniform right-to-die policy exists, and heated controversy persists over how to handle the diverse circumstances in which patients and family members make requests.

Euthanasia is the practice of ending the life of a person suffering from an incurable condition. Its various forms are summarized in Table 19.1. As we will see, public acceptance of euthanasia is high, except when it involves ending the life of an anguished, terminally ill patient without his or her expressed permission.

Passive Euthanasia

In **passive euthanasia**, life-sustaining treatment is withheld or withdrawn, permitting a patient to die naturally. *TAKE A MOMENT...* Do you think Terri Schiavo should have been allowed to die sooner? Was it right for Nicholas's doctors to turn off his respirator at Giselle's request? When an Alzheimer's victim has lost all awareness and bodily functions, should life support be withheld?

TABLE 19.1 **Forms of Euthanasia**

FORM	DESCRIPTION
Passive euthanasia	At the patient's request, the doctor withholds or withdraws treatment, thereby permitting the patient to die naturally. For example, the doctor does not perform surgery or administer medication that could prolong life, or the doctor turns off the respirator of a patient who cannot breathe independently.
Voluntary active euthanasia	The doctor ends a suffering patient's life at the patient's request. For example, the doctor administers a lethal dose of drugs.
Assisted suicide	The doctor helps a suffering patient take his or her own life. For example, the doctor enables the patient to swallow or inject a lethal dose of drugs.
Involuntary active euthanasia	The doctor ends a suffering patient's life without the patient's permission. For example, without obtaining the patient's consent, the doctor administers a lethal dose of drugs.

FIGURE 19.2 Example of a living will. This document is legal in the State of Illinois. Each person completing a living will should use a form specific to the U.S. state or Canadian province in which he or she resides because laws vary widely. (Courtesy of Office of the Attorney General, State of Illinois.)

LIVING WILL

THIS DECLARATION is made this _____ day of _____, 20 ____ .

I, _____, being of sound mind, willfully and voluntarily make known my desires that my moment of death shall not be artificially postponed. If at any time I should have an incurable and irreversible injury, disease, or illness judged to be a terminal condition by my attending physician who has personally examined me and has determined that my death is imminent except for death delaying procedures, I direct that such procedures which would only prolong the dying process be withheld or withdrawn, and that I be permitted to die naturally with only the administration of medication, sustenance, or the performance of any medical procedure deemed necessary by my attending physician to provide me with comfort care.

In the absence of my ability to give directions regarding the use of such death delaying procedures, it is my intention that this declaration shall be honored by my family and physician as the final expression of my legal right to refuse medical or surgical treatment and accept the consequences from such refusal.

Signed: _____

City, County and State of Residence: _____

_____

_____

The declarant is personally known to me and I believe him or her to be of sound mind. I saw the declarant sign the declaration in my presence (or the declarant acknowledged in my presence that he or she had signed the declaration) and I signed the declaration as a witness in the presence of the declarant. At the date of this instrument, I am not entitled to any portion of the estate of the declarant according to the laws of intestate succession or, to the best of my knowledge and belief, under any will of declarant or other instrument taking effect at declarant's death, or directly financially responsible for declarant's medical care.

Witness: _____

Witness: _____

In recent polls, more 70 percent of U.S. adults and 95 percent of physicians supported the right of patients or family members to end treatment when there is no hope of recovery (Curlin et al., 2008; Pew Research Center, 2006). In 1986, the American Medical Association endorsed withdrawing all forms of treatment from the terminally ill when death is imminent and from those in a permanent vegetative state. Consequently, passive euthanasia is widely practiced as part of ordinary medical procedure, in which doctors exercise professional judgment.

Still, a minority of citizens oppose passive euthanasia. Religious denomination has surprisingly little effect on people's opinions. For example, most Catholics hold favorable views, despite slow official church acceptance because of fears that passive euthanasia might be a first step toward government-approved mercy killing. However, ethnicity makes a difference: Nearly twice as many African Americans as Caucasian Americans desire all medical means possible, regardless of the patient's condition, and African Americans more often receive life-sustaining intervention, such as feeding tubes (Haley, 2013; Johnson et al., 2008). Their reluctance to forgo treatment reflects strong cultural and religious beliefs in overcoming adversity and in the power of God to promote healing (Johnson, Elbert-Avila, & Tulsky, 2005).

Because of controversial court cases like Terri Schiavo's, some doctors and health-care institutions are unwilling to end treatment without legal protection. In the absence of national consensus on passive euthanasia, people can best ensure that their wishes will be followed by preparing an **advance medical directive**—a written statement of desired medical treatment should they become incurably ill. U.S. states recognize two types of advance directives: a *living will* and a *durable power of attorney for health care* (U.S. Living Will Registry, 2005). Sometimes these are combined into one document.

In a **living will,** people specify the treatments they do or do not want in case of a terminal illness, coma, or other near-death situation (see Figure 19.2). For example, a person might state that without reasonable expectation of recovery, he or she should not be kept alive through medical intervention of any kind. In addition, a living will sometimes specifies that pain-relieving medication be given, even though it might shorten life. In Sofie's case, her doctor administered a powerful narcotic to relieve labored breathing and quiet her fear of suffocation. The narcotic suppressed respiration, causing death to occur hours or days earlier than if the medication had not been prescribed, but without distress. Such palliative care is accepted as appropriate and ethical medical practice.

Although living wills help ensure personal control, they do not guarantee it. Recognition of living wills is usually limited to patients who are terminally ill or are otherwise expected to die shortly. Only a few U.S. states cover people in a persistent vegetative state or aging adults who linger with many chronic problems, including Alzheimer's disease, because these conditions are not classified as terminal. Even when terminally ill patients have living wills, doctors sometimes do not follow them for a variety of reasons (van Asselt, 2006). These include fear of lawsuits, their own moral beliefs, failure to inquire about patients' directives, and inaccessibility of those directives—for example, located in the family safe or family members unaware of them.

Because living wills cannot anticipate all future medical conditions and can easily be ignored, a second form of advance directive has become common. The **durable power of attorney for health care** authorizes appointment of another person (usually, though not always, a family member) to make health-care decisions on one's behalf. It generally requires only a short signed and witnessed statement like this:

I hereby appoint [name] as my attorney-in-fact (my "agent") to act for me and in my name (in any way I could act in person) to make any and all decisions for me concerning my personal care,

This couple discusses a durable power of attorney with a hospital chaplain. This advance directive authorizes a trusted spokesperson to make health-care decisions and helps ensure that one's desires will be granted.

medical treatment, hospitalization, and health care and to require, withhold, or withdraw any type of medical treatment or procedure, even though my death may ensue. (Courtesy of Office of the Attorney General, State of Illinois)

The durable power of attorney for health care is more flexible than the living will because it permits a trusted spokesperson to confer with the doctor as medical circumstances arise. Because authority to speak for the patient is not limited to terminal illnesses, more latitude exists for dealing with unexpected situations. And in gay and lesbian and other close relationships not sanctioned by law, the durable power of attorney can ensure the partner's role in decision making and in advocating for the patient's health-care needs.

Whether or not a person supports passive euthanasia, it is important to have a living will, durable power of attorney, or both, because most deaths occur in hospitals. Yet only about 30 percent of Americans have executed such documents, perhaps because of widespread uneasiness about bringing up the topic of death, especially with relatives (Harris Interactive, 2011; Pew Research Center, 2006). The percentage with advance directives does increase with age; almost two-thirds of adults over age 65 have them. To encourage people to make decisions about potential treatment while they are able, U.S. federal law now requires that all medical facilities receiving federal funds provide information at admission about state laws and institutional policies on patients' rights and advance directives.

As happened with Karen Quinlan and Terri Schiavo, health-care professionals—unclear about a patient's intent and fearing liability—will probably decide to continue treatment regardless of cost and a person's prior oral statements. Perhaps for this reason, some U.S. states permit appointment of a health-care proxy, or substitute decision maker, if a patient failed to provide an advance medical directive while competent. Proxies are an important means of covering children and adolescents, who cannot legally execute advance medical directives.

Voluntary Active Euthanasia

In recent years, the right-to-die debate has shifted from withdrawal of treatment for the hopelessly ill to more active alternatives. In **voluntary active euthanasia,** doctors or others act directly, at a patient's request, to end suffering before a natural end to life. The practice, a form of mercy killing, is a criminal offense in most countries, including almost all U.S. states. But support for voluntary active euthanasia has grown. As Figure 19.3 shows, about 70 to 90 percent of people in Western nations approve of it (World Federation of Right to Die Societies, 2006). In these countries, religiosity has little impact on acceptance. But in Eastern European nations where most of the population is religious, such as Croatia, Poland, Romania, and Turkey, approval rates tend to be lower (Cohen et al., 2006). In the United States and other Western nations, when doctors engage in voluntary active euthanasia, judges are usually lenient, granting suspended sentences or probation—a trend reflecting rising public interest in self-determination in death as in life.

Nevertheless, attempts to legalize voluntary active euthanasia have prompted heated controversy. Supporters believe it represents the most compassionate option for terminally ill people in severe pain. Opponents stress the moral difference between "letting die" and "killing" and point out that at times, even very sick patients recover. They also argue that involving doctors in taking the lives of suffering patients may impair people's trust in health professionals. Finally, a fear exists that legalizing this practice—even when strictly monitored to make sure it does not arise out of depression, loneliness, coercion, or a desire

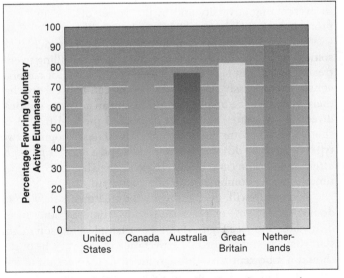

FIGURE 19.3 Public opinion favoring voluntary active euthanasia in five nations. A struggle exists between public opinion, which has increasingly favored voluntary active euthanasia over the past 30 years, and legal statutes, which prohibit it. The majority of people in Western nations believe that a hopelessly ill, suffering patient who asks for a lethal injection should be granted that request. Public support for voluntary active euthanasia is highest in the Netherlands—the only nation in the world where the practice is legal under certain conditions. (From Harris Interactive, 2011; Pew Research Center, 2006.)

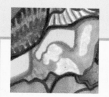

Social Issues: Health

Voluntary Active Euthanasia: Lessons from Australia and the Netherlands

In 1996, Australia's Northern Territory passed legislation allowing a terminally ill patient of sound mind and suffering from pain or other distress to ask a doctor to end his or her life. Two other doctors had to agree that the patient could not be cured, and a psychiatrist had to confirm the absence of treatable depression.

In the months that followed, four deaths occurred under the Northern Territory euthanasia statute, and it was heavily criticized. The Aborigines, valuing harmony and balance with nature, regarded it as culturally inappropriate. Their leaders claimed the law would discourage Aboriginal aging adults, many of whom had experienced a lifetime of persecution at the hands of European settlers, from seeking medical care (Fleming, 2000). Others considered the law to be a national issue because patients traveled from other states to make use of it. In 1997, the Northern Territory legislation was overturned by the Australian Parliament, which claimed that assemblies do not have the right to legislate intentional killing.

The episode placed Australia at the center of the debate over euthanasia—an issue that continues to spark high passions across the country. Opponents worry about error and abuse of the practice (Fickling, 2004). Supporters emphasize compassion and the right of individuals to control the course of their own lives. June Burns, an Australian woman with bladder cancer who participated in TV ads documenting the course of her illness, responded, "If I were a dog, they would have put me down by now. I feel life is very precious and . . . I wish I could go on, but I can't and I'd like to die with dignity." Eventually, she took her own life with a

lethal dose of a barbiturate, which she had kept for the purpose for nearly a decade (Voluntary Euthanasia Society of New South Wales, 2008).

For the past several decades, doctors in the Netherlands have engaged in voluntary active euthanasia without criminal prosecution. In 2002, the practice became legal under the following conditions: when physical or mental suffering is severe, with no prospect of relief; when no doubt exists about the patient's desire to die; when the patient's decision is voluntary, well-informed, and stable over time; when all other options for care have been exhausted or refused; and when another doctor has been consulted.

Over 50 percent of Dutch doctors say they perform euthanasia, most often with cancer patients. Despite safeguards, both voluntary and involuntary (without patient permission) active euthanasia have occurred. A small minority of doctors admit granting the euthanasia requests of physically healthy patients—usually older people who felt "weary of life" (Rurup et al., 2005; van Tol, Rietjens, & van der Heide, 2010). And some say they actively caused a death when a patient did not ask for it, defending their action by referring to the impossibility of treating pain, a low quality of life, or drawn-out dying in a patient near death.

Voluntary active euthanasia in the Netherlands has risen steadily over the past decade. Doctors report about 2,000 cases annually to medical examiners—nearly 2 percent of all deaths. But anonymous surveys reveal additional cases—as many as 20 percent of all such deaths—that probably

Australian Aboriginal peoples regard voluntary active euthanasia as contrary to the values of their culture. The natural images that permeate their artwork reflect the priority they place on harmony and balance with nature.

were voluntary active euthanasia but were not reported. In most of these, attending doctors said that they had not perceived their act (sedation to relieve pain) as ending a life. But for some, they expressed doubts about whether they had properly followed legal standards of practice, such as ascertaining patient consent or consulting a second doctor (Onwuteaka-Philipsen et al., 2005; van der Heide et al., 2007).

The Northern Territory and Dutch examples reveal that legalizing voluntary active euthanasia can spark both the fear and the reality of death without consent. And the Dutch experience highlights the challenges of monitoring euthanasia practices. Nevertheless, terminally ill individuals in severe pain continue to plead for such laws. Probably all would agree that when doctors feel compelled to relieve suffering and honor self-determination by assisting a patient in dying, they should be subject to the most stringent professional and legal oversight possible.

to diminish the burden of illness on others—could lead to a broadening of euthanasia. Initially limited to the terminally ill, it might be applied involuntarily to the frail, demented, or disabled—outcomes that most people find unacceptable and immoral.

Will legalizing voluntary active euthanasia lead us down a "slippery slope" to the killing of vulnerable people who did not ask to die? The Social Issues: Health box above presents lessons from the Australian state of the Northern Territory, where a law allowing voluntary active euthanasia was passed in 1996, and from the Netherlands, where doctors had practiced it for years before its 2002 legalization.

Assisted Suicide

After checking Diane's blood count, Dr. Timothy Quill gently broke the news: leukemia. If she were to have any hope of survival, a strenuous course of treatment with only a 25 percent success rate would have to begin immediately. Convinced that she would suffer unspeakably from side effects and lack of control over her body, Diane chose not to undergo chemotherapy and a bone marrow transplant.

Dr. Quill made sure that Diane understood her options. As he adjusted to her decision, Diane raised another issue: She wanted no part of a lingering death. She calmly insisted that when the time came, she desired to take her own life in the least painful way possible—a choice she had discussed with her husband and son, who respected it. Realizing that Diane could get the most out of the time she had left only if her fears of prolonged pain were allayed, Dr. Quill granted her request for sleeping pills, making sure she knew the amounts needed for both sleep and suicide.

Diane's next few months were busy and fulfilling. Her son took leave from college to be with her, and her husband worked at home as much as possible. Gradually, bone pain, fatigue, and fever set in. Saying goodbye to her family and friends, Diane asked to be alone for an hour, took a lethal dose of medication, and died at home (Quill, 1991).

Assisting a suicide is illegal in Canada and in most, but not all, U.S. states. In Western Europe, doctor-assisted suicide is legal in Belgium, the Netherlands, Luxembourg, and Switzerland and is tacitly accepted in many other countries. In the United States, Oregon's 1997 Death with Dignity Act explicitly allows physicians to prescribe drugs so terminally ill patients can end their lives. To get a prescription, patients must have two doctors

agree that they have less than six months to live and must request the drugs at least twice, with an interval of at least 15 days. In January 2006, the U.S. Supreme Court rejected a challenge to the Oregon law, but the Court has also upheld the right of other states to ban assisted suicide. In 2008, the state of Washington passed legislation—similar to Oregon's—permitting assisted suicide. In 2013, the Montana and Vermont legislatures also legalized the practice.

Nearly 60 percent of Americans approve of assisted suicide for terminally ill patients in great pain (Harris Interactive, 2011). In a review of studies carried out in the United States, Canada, and Western Europe, level of support among terminally ill patients was about the same as for the general public, with about one-third of patients saying they would consider it for themselves in particular circumstances (Hendry et al., 2012). People who support the practice tend to be higher in SES and less religious.

The number of Oregon residents dying by assisted suicide has increased since passage of the law, from 16 in 1998 to 77 in 2012. Most (68 percent) were age 65 or older, and the overwhelming majority (97 percent) were enrolled in hospice and died at home. Their most common diagnosis (75 percent) was cancer. Still, assisted suicide accounts for only one-fifth of 1 percent of Oregon deaths (Oregon Public Health Division, 2013). Doctors report that the most common reasons for assisted-suicide requests are loss of autonomy, decreasing ability to participate in activities that make life enjoyable, and loss of control of bodily functions (Oregon Department of Human Services, 2009). Ten times as many terminally ill people initiate the qualification process for assisted suicide as engage in it. But thousands of Oregonians say they find comfort in knowing the option is available should they suffer while dying (Hedberg et al., 2009).

Public interest in assisted suicide was sparked in the 1990s by Dr. Jack Kevorkian, a vigorous proponent of euthanasia who devised "suicide machines" that permitted more than 100 terminally ill patients, after brief counseling, to self-administer lethal drugs and carbon monoxide. Less publicity surrounded Dr. Quill's decision to assist Diane—a patient he knew well after serving for years as her personal doctor. After he told her story in a prestigious medical journal, reactions were mixed, as they are toward assisted suicide in general. Some view doctors who help suffering people who want to die as compassionate and respectful of patients' personal choices. Others oppose assisted suicide on religious and moral grounds or believe that the role of doctors should be limited to saving, not taking, lives.

Like euthanasia, assisted suicide poses grave dilemmas. Analyzing the practice, the American Academy of Hospice and Palliative Medicine (2007) advises great caution on the part of doctors practicing in regions where assisted suicide is legal, including making sure before engaging in it that the following conditions are met:

● The patient has access to the best possible palliative care and will continue to receive such care throughout the dying process.

In a prestigious medical journal, Dr. Timothy Quill explained how and why he aided a terminally ill patient in taking her own life. Doctor-assisted suicide is legal in the states of Oregon, Washington, Montana, and Vermont and in several Western European countries.

© BOB MAHONEY/THE IMAGE WORKS

- The patient has full decision-making capacity and requests assisted suicide voluntarily; health-care financial pressures and coercive influences from family members play no role.

- All reasonable alternatives to assisted suicide have been considered and implemented, if acceptable to the patient.

- The practice is consistent with the doctor's fundamental values, and he or she is willing to participate. (If not, the doctor should recommend transfer of care.)

Juries have seldom returned guilty verdicts in cases involving doctor-assisted suicide. Yet in April 1999, Kevorkian—after giving a terminally ill man a lethal injection, videotaping the death, and permitting the event to be broadcast on the CBS television program *60 Minutes*—was convicted of second-degree murder and served 8 years of a 10- to 25-year sentence. The murder indictment prevented Kevorkian from introducing evidence indicating that the man wanted to kill himself—evidence that would have been permissible had the charge been assisted suicide or voluntary active euthanasia.

Public opinion consistently favors voluntary active euthanasia over assisted suicide. Yet in assisted suicide, the final act is solely the patient's, reducing the possibility of coercion. For this reason, some experts believe that legalizing assisted suicide is preferable to legalizing voluntary active euthanasia. However, in an atmosphere of high family caregiving burdens and intense pressure to contain health-care costs (see Chapter 17), legalizing either practice poses risks. The American Medical Association opposes both voluntary active euthanasia and assisted suicide. In a survey of 1,140 U.S. doctors, only 18 percent objected to sedating a dying patient to unconsciousness if pain can be controlled in no other way, whereas nearly 70 percent opposed assisted suicide—attitudes resembling those of physicians in other Western nations (Curlin et al., 2008; Seale, 2009). Helping incurable, suffering patients who yearn for death poses profound moral and legal problems.

ASK YOURSELF

REVIEW What benefits and risks does legalizing voluntary active euthanasia pose?

APPLY Thinking ahead to the day she dies, Noreen imagines a peaceful scene in which she says goodbye to loved ones. What social and medical practices are likely to increase Noreen's chances of dying in the manner she desires?

APPLY Ramón is certain that, if he ever became terminally ill, he would want doctors to halt life-saving treatment. To best ensure that his wish will be granted, what should Ramón do?

REFLECT Do you approve of passive euthanasia, voluntary active euthanasia, or assisted suicide? If you were terminally ill, would you consider any of these practices? Explain.

Bereavement: Coping with the Death of a Loved One

Loss is an inevitable part of existence throughout the lifespan. Even when change is for the better, we must let go of some aspects of experience so we can embrace others. In this way, our development prepares us for profound loss.

Bereavement is the experience of losing a loved one by death. The root of this word means "to be robbed," suggesting unjust and injurious theft of something valuable. Consistent with this image, we respond to loss with **grief**—intense physical and psychological distress. When we say someone is grief-stricken, we imply that his or her total way of being is affected.

Because grief can be overwhelming, cultures have devised ways of helping their members move beyond it to deal with the life changes demanded by death of a loved one. **Mourning** is the culturally specified expression of the bereaved person's thoughts and feelings. Customs—such as gathering with family and friends, dressing in black, attending the funeral, and observing a prescribed mourning period with special rituals—vary greatly among societies and ethnic groups. But all have in common the goal of helping people work through their grief and learn to live in a world that does not include the deceased.

Clearly, grief and mourning are closely linked—in everyday language, we often use the two words interchangeably. Let's look closely at how people respond to the death of a loved one.

Grief Process

Theorists formerly believed that bereaved individuals—both children and adults—moved through three phases of grieving, each characterized by a different set of responses (Bowlby, 1980; Rando, 1995). In reality, however, people vary greatly in behavior and timing and often move back and forth between these reactions. A more accurate account compares grief to a roller-coaster ride, with many ups and downs and, over time, gradual resolution (Lund, 1996). Rather than phases, the grieving process can be conceived as a set of *tasks*—actions the person must take to recover and return to a fulfilling life: (1) to accept the reality of the loss; (2) to work through the pain of grief; (3) to adjust to a world without the loved one; and (4) to develop an inner bond with the deceased and move on with life (Worden, 2009). According to this view, people can take active steps to overcome grief—a powerful remedy for the overwhelming feelings of vulnerability that the bereaved often experience.

Avoidance. On hearing the news, the survivor experiences shock followed by disbelief, which may last from hours to weeks. A numbed feeling serves as "emotional anesthesia" while the person begins the first task of grieving: becoming painfully aware of the loss.

Confrontation. As the mourner confronts the reality of the death, grief is most intense. The person often experiences a cascade of emotional reactions, including anxiety, sadness, protest, anger, helplessness, frustration, abandonment, and yearning for the loved one. Common responses include obsessively reviewing the circumstances of death, asking how it might have been prevented, and searching for meaning in it (Neimeyer, 2001). In addition, the grief-stricken person may be absent-minded, unable to concentrate, and preoccupied with thoughts of the deceased, and may experience loss of sleep and appetite. Self-destructive behaviors, such as taking drugs or driving too fast, may occur. Most of these responses are symptoms of depression—an invariable component of grieving.

Although confrontation is difficult, it enables the mourner to grapple with the second task: working through the pain of grief. Each surge of anguish that results from an unmet wish to be reunited with the deceased brings the mourner closer to acceptance that the loved one is gone. After hundreds, perhaps thousands, of these painful moments, the grieving person comprehends that a cherished relationship must be transformed from a physical presence to an inner representation. As a result, the mourner makes progress on the third task: adjusting to a world in which the deceased is missing.

Restoration. Adjusting to the loss is more than an internal, emotional task. The bereaved must also deal with stressors that are secondary outcomes of the death—overcoming loneliness by reaching out to others; mastering skills (such as finances or cooking) that the deceased had performed; reorganizing daily life without the loved one; and revising one's identity from "spouse" to "widow" or from "parent" to "parent of a deceased child."

According to a recent perspective, called the **dual-process model of coping with loss,** effective coping requires people to oscillate between dealing with the emotional consequences of loss and attending to life changes, which—when handled successfully—have restorative, or healing, effects (Hansson & Stroebe, 2007; Stroebe & Schut, 1999, 2010). Moving back and forth offers temporary distraction and relief from painful grieving. Much research indicates that confronting grief without relief has severe negative consequences for physical and mental health (Corr & Corr, 2007). Consistent with the dual-process model, in a study that assessed widowed older adults at 6, 18, and 48 months after the death of their spouses, both loss-oriented and restoration-oriented activities occurred throughout bereavement. As predicted, restoration-oriented activities—such as visiting friends, attending religious services, and volunteering—reduced the stress of grieving (Richardson, 2007). Using the dual-process approach, one 14-session intervention for older adults grieving the loss of a spouse addresses both emotional and life-change issues, alternating between them (Lund et al., 2004, 2010).

As grief subsides, emotional energies increasingly shift toward the fourth task—forging a symbolic bond with the deceased and moving on with life by meeting everyday respon-

sibilities, investing in new activities and goals, strengthening old ties, and building new relationships. On certain days, such as family celebrations or the anniversary of death, grief reactions may resurface and require attention, but they do not interfere with a healthy, positive approach to life.

In fact, throughout the grieving process, individuals report experiencing positive as well as negative emotions, with expressions of happiness and humor aiding in coping with grief (Ong, Bergeman, & Bisconti, 2004). In an investigation of several hundred people age 50 and older whose spouse or partner had died within the previous six months, 90 percent agreed that "feeling happy" and "having humor" in daily life is important, and more than 75 percent said they had experienced humor, laughter, or happiness during the past week. The greater participants' valuing and experience of positive emotion, the better their bereavement adjustment, as indicated by reduced levels of grief and depression (Lund et al., 2008–2009). Expressions of happiness can be viewed as a restoration-oriented activity, offering distraction from grieving and strengthening bonds with others.

How long does grieving last? There is no single answer. Sometimes confrontation continues for a few months, at other times for several years. An occasional upsurge of grief may persist for a lifetime and is a common response to losing a much-loved spouse, partner, child, or friend.

Personal and Situational Variations

Like dying, grieving is affected by many factors, including personality, coping style, and religious and cultural background. Sex differences are also evident. Compared with women, men typically express distress and depression less directly and seek social support less readily—factors that may contribute to the much higher mortality rate among bereaved men than women (Doka & Martin, 2010; Lund & Caserta, 2004b; McGoldrick, 2004).

Furthermore, the quality of the mourner's relationship with the deceased is important. An end to a loving, fulfilling bond leads to more anguished grieving, but it is less likely to leave a long-term residue of anger, guilt, and regret than the dissolution of a conflict-ridden, ambivalent tie (Abakoumkin, Stroebe, & Stroebe, 2010; Mikulincer & Shaver, 2008). And end-of-life care makes a difference: Widowed older adults whose spouses experienced a painful death reported more anxiety, intrusive thoughts, and yearning for the loved one six months later (Carr, 2003).

Circumstances surrounding the death—whether it is sudden and unanticipated or follows a prolonged illness—also shape mourners' responses. The nature of the lost relationship and the timing of the death within the life course make a difference as well.

Sudden, Unanticipated Deaths versus Prolonged, Expected Deaths. In instances of sudden, unexpected deaths—usually the result of murder, suicide, war, accident, or natural disaster—avoidance may be especially pronounced and confrontation highly traumatic because shock and disbelief are extreme. In a survey of a representative sample of 18- to 45-year-old adults in a large U.S. city, the trauma most often reported as prompting an intense, debilitating stress reaction was the sudden, unanticipated death of a loved one (Breslau et al., 1998). In contrast, during prolonged dying, the bereaved person has had time to engage in **anticipatory grieving**—acknowledging that the loss is inevitable and preparing emotionally for it. Survivors may feel less overwhelmed immediately following the death (Johansson & Grimby, 2013). But they may display more persistent anxiety due to long-term stressors, such as highly demanding caregiving and having watched a loved one suffer from a debilitating illness (Carr et al., 2001).

Adjusting to a sudden death is easier when the survivor understands the reasons for it. This barrier to confronting loss is tragically apparent in cases of sudden infant death syndrome (SIDS), in which doctors cannot tell parents exactly why their apparently healthy baby died (see Chapter 3, page 110). That death seems "senseless" also complicates grieving after suicides, terrorist attacks, school and drive-by shootings, and natural disasters. In Western societies, people tend to believe that momentous events should be comprehensible and nonrandom (Lukas & Seiden, 2007). A death that is sudden and unexpected can threaten basic assumptions about a just, benevolent, and controllable world.

Suicide, particularly that of a young person, is especially hard to bear. Compared with survivors of other sudden deaths, people grieving a suicidal loss are more likely to conclude that they contributed to or could have prevented it—self-blame that can trigger profound guilt and shame. These reactions are likely to be especially intense and persisting when a mourner's culture or religion condemns suicide as immoral (Dunne & Dunne-Maxim, 2004). Individuals who have survived a suicide typically score higher than those who have experienced other types of losses in feelings of guilt and shame, sense of rejection by the deceased, and desire to conceal the cause of death (Sveen & Walby, 2008). Typically, recovery from grief after a suicide is prolonged.

Parents Grieving the Loss of a Child. The death of a child, whether unexpected or foreseen, is the most difficult loss an adult can face (Dent & Stewart, 2004). Children are extensions of parents' feelings about themselves—the focus of hopes and dreams, including parents' sense of immortality. Also, because children depend on, admire, and appreciate their parents in a deeply gratifying way, they are an unmatched source of love. Finally, the death of a child is unnatural: Children are not supposed to die before their parents.

Parents who have lost a child often report considerable distress many years later, along with frequent thoughts of the deceased. The guilt triggered by outliving their child frequently becomes a tremendous burden, even when parents "know" better (Murphy, 2008). For example, a mother whose daughter died of cancer said despairingly, "I gave her her genes, and her genes killed her. I had a hand in this."

A father weeps while holding the body of his son, killed during the Syrian armed conflict in 2012. The death of a child, whether unexpected or foreseen, is the most difficult loss an adult can face.

Although a child's death sometimes leads to marital breakup, this is likely to happen only when the relationship was already unsatisfactory (Wheeler, 2001). If parents can reorganize the family system and reestablish a sense of life's meaning through valuing the lost child's impact on their lives and investing in other children and activities, then the result can be firmer family commitments and personal growth. The process, which often takes years, is associated with improved physical and mental health and gains in marital satisfaction (Murphy, 2008; Price et al., 2011). Five years after her son's death, one parent reflected on her progress:

> I was afraid to let go [of my pain, which was] a way of loving him. . . . Finally I had to admit that his life meant more than pain, it also meant joy and happiness and fun—and living. . . . When we release pain we make room for happiness in our lives. My memories of S. became lighter and more spontaneous. Instead of hurtful, my memories brought comfort, even a chuckle. . . . realized S. was still teaching me things. (Klass, 2004, p. 87)

Children and Adolescents Grieving the Loss of a Parent or Sibling. The loss of an attachment figure has long-term consequences for children. When a parent dies, children's basic sense of security and being cared for is threatened. And the death of a sibling not only deprives children of a close emotional tie but also informs them, often for the first time, of their own vulnerability.

Children grieving a family loss describe frequent crying, trouble concentrating in school, sleep difficulties, headaches, and other physical symptoms several months to years after a death. And clinical studies reveal that persistent depression, anxiety, angry outbursts, social withdrawal, loneliness, and worries about dying themselves are common (Luecken, 2008;

Marshall & Davies, 2011). At the same time, many children say they have actively maintained mental contact with their dead parent or sibling, dreaming about and speaking to them regularly. In a follow-up seven to nine years after sibling loss, thinking about the deceased brother or sister at least once a day was common (Martinson, Davies, & McClowry, 1987; Silverman & Nickman, 1996). These images, reported by bereaved adults as well, seem to facilitate coping with loss.

Cognitive development contributes to the ability to grieve. For example, children with an immature understanding of death may believe the dead parent left voluntarily, perhaps in anger, and that the other parent may also disappear. For these reasons, young children need careful, repeated explanations assuring them that the parent did not want to die and was not angry at them (Christ, Siegel, & Christ, 2002). Keeping the truth from children isolates them and often leads to profound regrets. One 8-year-old who learned only a half-hour in advance that his sick brother was dying reflected, "If only I'd known, I could have said goodbye."

Regardless of children's level of understanding, honesty, affection, and reassurance help them tolerate painful feelings of loss. Grief-stricken school-age children are usually more willing than adolescents to confide in parents. To appear normal, teenagers tend to keep their grieving from both adults and peers. Consequently, they are more likely than children to become depressed or to escape from grief through acting-out behavior (Granot, 2005). Overall, effective parenting—warmth combined with rational discipline—fosters adaptive coping and positive long-term adjustment in both children and adolescents (Luecken, 2008).

Adults Grieving the Loss of an Intimate Partner. Recall from Chapter 18 that after the death of a spouse, adaptation to widowhood varies greatly, with age, social support, and personality making a difference. After a period of intense grieving, most widowed older adults in Western nations fare well, while younger individuals display more negative outcomes (see page 623 to review). Older widows and widowers have many more contemporaries in similar circumstances. And most have already attained important life goals or adjusted to the fact that some goals will not be attained.

In contrast, loss of a spouse or partner in early or middle adulthood is a nonnormative event that profoundly disrupts life plans. Interviews with a large, U.S. nationally representative sample of adults who had been widowed from less than 1 to 64 years previously (typically in middle adulthood) revealed that thoughts about and conversations with the lost spouse occurred often in the first few years, then declined gradually (Carnelley et al., 2006). But they did not reach their lowest level for several decades, when the typical respondent still thought about the deceased partner once every week or two and conversed with him or her about once a month.

In addition to dealing with feelings of loss, young and middle-aged widows and widowers often must assume a greater role in comforting others, especially children. They also face the stresses of single parenthood and rapid shrinking of the social network established during their life as a couple. The death of an intimate partner in a gay or lesbian relationship presents unique challenges. When relatives limit or bar the partner from participating in funeral services, the survivor experiences *disenfranchised grief*—a sense of loss without the opportunity to mourn publicly and benefit from others' support—which can profoundly disrupt the grieving process (Doka, 2008). Fortunately, gay and lesbian communities provide helpful alternative support in the form of memorial services and other rituals.

Bereavement Overload. When a person experiences several deaths at once or in close succession, bereavement overload can occur. Multiple losses deplete the coping resources of even well-adjusted people, leaving them emotionally overwhelmed and unable to resolve their grief (Lattanzi-Licht & Doka, 2003).

Because old age often brings the death of spouse, siblings, and friends in close succession, aging adults are at risk for bereavement overload (Kastenbaum, 2008). But recall from Chapter 18 that compared with young people, older adults are often better equipped to handle these losses. They know that decline and death are expected in late adulthood, and they have had a lifetime of experience through which to develop effective coping strategies.

Public tragedies—terrorist attacks, natural disasters, random murders in schools, or widely publicized kidnappings—can spark bereavement overload (Rynearson & Salloum, 2011). Many survivors who lost loved ones, co-workers, or friends in the September 11, 2001, terrorist attacks (including an estimated 3,000 children who lost a parent) experienced repeated images of horror and destruction, which impeded coming to terms with loss. Children and adolescents suffered profoundly—from intense shock, prolonged grief, frequent mental replays of

Villagers in Sichuan Province, China, grieve for relatives who died in a massive earthquake in 2013 that left nearly 200 dead. Public tragedies can spark bereavement overload, leaving mourners at risk for prolonged, overwhelming grief.

Applying What We Know

Suggestions for Resolving Grief After a Loved One Dies

Suggestion	Description
Give yourself permission to feel the loss.	Permit yourself to confront all thoughts and emotions associated with the death. Make a conscious decision to overcome your grief, recognizing that this will take time.
Accept social support.	In the early part of grieving, let others reach out to you by making meals, running errands, and keeping you company. Be assertive; ask for what you need so people who would like to help will know what to do.
Be realistic about the course of grieving.	Expect to have some negative and intense reactions, such as feeling anguished, sad, and angry, that last from weeks to months and may occasionally resurface years after the death. There is no one way to grieve, so find the best way for you.
Remember the deceased.	Review your relationship to and experiences with the deceased, permitting yourself to see that you can no longer be with him or her as before. Form a new bond based on memories, keeping it alive through photographs, commemorative donations, prayers, and other symbols and actions.
When ready, invest in new activities and relationships, and master new tasks of daily living.	Identify which roles you must give up and which ones you must assume as a consequence of the death, and take deliberate steps to modify daily life accordingly. Set small goals at first, such as a night at the movies, a dinner date with a friend, a cooking or household repair class, or a week's vacation.

the vicious attack and gruesome outcomes, and fear of the settings in which those events occurred (Nader, 2002; Webb, 2002). The greater the bereaved individual's exposure to the catastrophic death scene, the more severe these reactions.

Funerals and other bereavement rituals, illustrated in the Cultural Influences box on page 664, assist mourners of all ages in resolving grief with the help of family and friends. Bereaved individuals who remain preoccupied with loss and who have difficulty resuming interest in everyday activities benefit from special interventions designed to help them adjust.

Bereavement Interventions

Sympathy and understanding are sufficient to enable most people to undertake the tasks necessary to recover from grief (see Applying What We Know above). Yet effective support is often difficult to provide, and relatives and friends can benefit from training in how to respond. Sometimes they give advice aimed at hastening recovery or ask questions aimed at managing their own anxiety ("Were you expecting him to die?" "Was she in a lot of pain?")—approaches that most bereaved people dislike (Kastenbaum, 2012). Listening patiently and assuring the bereaved of "being there" for them—"I'm here if you need to talk," "Let me know what I can do"—are among the best ways to help.

Bereavement interventions typically encourage people to draw on their existing social network, while providing additional social support through group or individual counseling. Controversy exists over whether grief counseling benefits most bereaved people, or whether it helps only those experiencing

profound difficulties (CFAH, 2003; Jordan & Neimeyer, 2003). One analysis of research expressed optimism about broadly favorable effects (Larson & Hoyt, 2007). Furthermore, evidence is mounting that bereaved adults who struggle with and surmount challenges and losses often experience stress-related personal growth, including greater awareness of their own strengths, enhanced appreciation of close relationships, and new spiritual insights (Calhoun et al., 2010).

Support groups that bring together mourners who have experienced the same type of loss seem highly effective in promoting recovery. In a program for recently widowed older adults based on the dual-process model of coping with loss, in which group members helped one another resolve grief and master tasks of daily living, participants readily bonded with one another and gained in sense of self-efficacy at managing their own lives (Caserta, Lund, & Rice, 1999). A widow expressed the many lasting benefits:

> We shared our anger at being left behind, . . . our fright of that aloneness. We shared our favorite pictures, so each of us could know the others' families and the fun we used to have. We shared our feelings of guilt if we had fun . . . and found out that it was okay to keep on living! . . . We cheered when one of us accomplished a new task. We also tried to lend a helping hand and heart when we would have one of our bad days! . . . This group will always be there for me and I will always be there for them. I love you all! (Lund, 2005)

Follow-up research suggests that group sessions are best suited for fostering loss-oriented coping (confronting and resolving grief), whereas an individually tailored approach works best for restoration-oriented coping (reorganizing daily life) (Lund

Cultural Influences

Cultural Variations in Mourning Behavior

The ceremonies that commemorated Sofie's and Nicholas's deaths—the first Jewish, the second Quaker—were strikingly different. Yet they served common goals: announcing that a death had occurred, ensuring social support, commemorating the deceased, and conveying a philosophy of life after death.

At the funeral home, Sofie's body was washed and shrouded, a Jewish ritual signifying return to a state of purity. Then it was placed in a plain wooden (not metal) coffin, so as not to impede the natural process of decomposition. To underscore the finality of death, Jewish tradition does not permit viewing of the body; it remains in a closed coffin. Traditionally, the coffin is not left alone until burial; in honor of the deceased, the community maintains a day-and-night vigil.

To return the body quickly to the life-giving earth from which it sprang, Sofie's funeral was scheduled as soon as relatives could gather—just three days after death. Sofie's husband and children symbolized their anguish by cutting a black ribbon and pinning it to their clothing. The rabbi recited psalms of comfort, followed by a eulogy. The service continued at the graveside. Once the coffin had been lowered into the ground, relatives and friends took turns shoveling earth onto it, each participating in the irrevocable act of burial. The service concluded with the *Kaddish* prayer, which affirms life while accepting death.

At home, the family lit a memorial candle, which burned throughout *shiva,* the seven-day mourning period. A meal of consolation prepared by others followed, creating a warm feeling of community. Jewish custom prescribes that after 30 days, life should gradually return to normal. When a parent dies, the mourning period is extended to 12 months.

In the Quaker tradition of simplicity, Nicholas was cremated promptly. During the next week, relatives and close friends gathered with Giselle and Sasha at their home. Together, they planned a memorial service to celebrate Nicholas's life.

When people arrived on the appointed day, a clerk of the Friends (Quaker) Meeting welcomed them and explained to newcomers the Quaker custom of worshipping silently, with those who feel moved to speak rising at any time to share thoughts and feelings. Many mourners offered personal statements about Nicholas or read poems and selections from Scripture. After concluding comments from Giselle and Sasha, everyone joined hands to close the service. A reception for the family followed.

Variations in mourning behavior are vast, both within and across societies. At African-American funerals, for example, grief is expressed freely: Eulogies and music are usually designed to trigger release of deep emotion (McGoldrick et al., 2004). In contrast, the Balinese of Indonesia believe they must remain calm in the face of death so that the gods can hear their prayers. While acknowledging their underlying grief, Balinese mourners work hard to maintain their composure (Rosenblatt, 2008).

Religions also render accounts of the aftermath of death that console both dying and bereaved individuals. Beliefs of tribal and village cultures typically include an elaborate world of ancestor spirits and customs designed to ease the journey of the deceased to this afterlife (Rosenblatt, 2008). Jewish tradition emphasizes personal survival through giving life and care to others. Unlike other Christian groups, Quakers give little attention to hope of heaven or fear of hell, focusing mainly on "salvation by

Mourners light candles at a memorial service for six Sikhs who died in a shooting rampage in Wisconsin in 2012. Sikh funeral customs include singing hymns, saying prayers, and offering remembrances of the deceased, followed by cremation and scattering of the ashes.

© JIM WEST/THE IMAGE WORKS

character"—working for peace, justice, and a loving community.

In recent years, a new ritual has arisen: "virtual cemeteries" on the Internet, which allow postings whenever bereaved individuals feel ready to convey their thoughts and feelings, creation of tributes at little or no cost, and continuous, easy access to the memorial. Most creators of Web tributes choose to tell personal stories, highlighting a laugh, a favorite joke, or a touching moment. Some survivors use Web memorials to grieve openly, others to converse with the lost loved one. Cemetery guestbooks offer a place for visitors to connect with other mourners. Web cemeteries also provide a means for people excluded from traditional death rituals to engage in public mourning (Roberts, 2006; Stroebe, van der Houwen, & Schut, 2008). The following "gravesite" message captures the unique qualities of this highly flexible medium for mourning:

I wish I could maintain contact with you, to keep alive the vivid memories of your impact on my life. . . . Because I cannot visit your grave today, I use this means to tell you how much you are loved.

et al., 2010). Bereaved adults differ widely in the new roles, relationships, and life skills they need most, and in the formats and schedules best suited to acquiring them.

LOOK AND LISTEN

Arrange to sit in on a bereavement support group session sponsored by a local hospice program or hospital, noting both emotional and daily living challenges expressed by group members. Ask participants to explain how the group has helped them. ●

Interventions for children and adolescents following violent deaths must protect them from unnecessary reexposure and assist parents and teachers with their own distress so they can effectively offer comfort (Dowd, 2013). In the aftermath of horrific tragedies—such as the December 14, 2012, mass shooting at Sandy Hook Elementary School in Newtown, Connecticut, or the April 15, 2013, Boston Marathon bombings—nurturing and caring relationships with adults are the most powerful way to help children recover from trauma.

A sudden, violent, and unexplainable death; the loss of a child; a death that the mourner feels he or she could have prevented; or an ambivalent or dependent relationship with the deceased makes it harder for bereaved people to overcome their loss. In these instances, grief therapy, or individual counseling with a specially trained professional, can be helpful. Assisting bereaved adults in finding some value in the grieving experience—for example, gaining insight into the meaning of relationships, discovering their own capacity to cope with adversity, or crystallizing a sense of purpose in their lives—is particularly effective (Neimeyer et al., 2010).

Nevertheless, most bereaved individuals do not participate in bereavement interventions. In several studies, only 30 to 50 percent of family caregivers of dying patients made use of bereavement services—such as phone support, support groups, and referrals for counseling—even though these were readily available through hospice, hospitals, or other community organizations (Bergman, Haley, & Small, 2010, 2011; Cherlin et al., 2007). Many who refused bereavement services were severely distressed yet did not realize that intervention could be helpful.

 ## Death Education

Preparatory steps can help people of all ages cope with death more effectively. The death awareness movement that sparked increased sensitivity to the needs of dying patients has also led to the rise of college and university courses in death, dying, and bereavement. Instruction has been integrated into the training of doctors, nurses, psychologists, and social workers, although most professional offerings are limited to only a few lectures (Wass, 2004). Death education is also found in adult education programs in many communities and even in a few elementary and secondary schools.

Death education at all levels has the following goals:

- Increasing students' understanding of the physical and psychological changes that accompany dying
- Helping students learn how to cope with the death of a loved one
- Preparing students to be informed consumers of medical and funeral services
- Promoting understanding of social and ethical issues involving death

Educational format varies widely. Some programs simply convey information. Others are experiential and include activities such as role playing, discussions with the terminally ill, visits to mortuaries and cemeteries, and personal awareness exercises. Research reveals that although using a lecture style leads to gains in knowledge, it often leaves students more uncomfortable about death than when they entered. In contrast, experiential programs that help people confront their own mortality are less likely to heighten death anxiety and may sometimes reduce it (Hurtig & Stewin, 2006; Maglio & Robinson, 1994).

Whether acquired in the classroom or in our daily lives, our thoughts and feelings about death are forged through interactions with others. Becoming more aware of how we die and of our own mortality, we encounter our greatest loss, but we also gain. Dying people have at times confided in those close to them that awareness of the limits of their lifespan permitted them to dispense with superficial distractions and wasted energies and focus on what is truly important in their lives. As one terminally ill patient summed up, "[It's] kind of like life, just speeded up"—an accelerated process in which, over a period of weeks to months, one grapples with issues that normally would have taken years or decades to resolve (Selwyn, 1996, p. 36). Applying this lesson to ourselves, we learn that by being in touch with death and dying, we can live ever more fully.

ASK YOURSELF

REVIEW What circumstances are likely to induce bereavement overload? Cite examples.

CONNECT Compare grieving individuals' reactions with terminally ill patients' thoughts and feelings as they move closer to death, described on page 647. Can a dying person's reactions be viewed as a form of grieving? Explain.

APPLY List features of self-help groups that contribute to their effectiveness in helping people cope with loss.

REFLECT Visit a Web cemetery, such as Virtual Memorials (virtualmemorials.com). Select examples of Web tributes, guestbook entries, and testimonials that illustrate the unique ways in which virtual cemeteries help people cope with death.

SUMMARY

How We Die (p. 640)

Describe the physical changes of dying, along with their implications for defining death and the meaning of death with dignity.

- Death is long and drawn-out for three-fourths of people, many more than in times past, as a result of life-saving medical technology. Of those who die suddenly, 80 to 90 percent are victims of heart attacks.

- In general, dying takes place in three phases: the **agonal phase,** in which regular heartbeat disintegrates; **clinical death,** a short interval in which resuscitation is still possible; and **mortality,** or permanent death.

- In most industrialized nations, **brain death** is accepted as the definition of death. But for incurable patients who remain in a **persistent vegetative state,** the brain death standard does not solve the problem of when to halt treatment.

- We can best ensure death with dignity by supporting dying patients through their physical and psychological distress, being candid about death's certainty, and helping them learn enough about their condition to make reasoned choices about treatment.

Understanding of and Attitudes Toward Death (p. 642)

Discuss age-related changes in conceptions of and attitudes toward death, and cite factors that influence death anxiety.

- Compared with earlier generations, more young people reach adulthood having had little contact with death, contributing to a sense of unease about it.

- To understand death, children must have some basic notions of biology and must be able to distinguish between *dead, inanimate, unreal,* and *nonexistent.* Most children attain an adultlike concept of death in middle childhood, gradually mastering concepts of permanence, inevitability, cessation, applicability, and causation. Experiences with death and religious teachings affect children's understanding, as do open, honest discussions.

- Adolescents are aware that death happens to everyone and can occur at any time, but their high-risk activities suggest that they do not take death personally. Candid discussions can help teenagers build a bridge between death as a logical concept and their personal experiences.

- In early adulthood, many people avoid thinking about death, but in midlife, they become more conscious that their own lives are finite. In late adulthood, as death nears, people are more apt to ponder the process of dying than the state of death.

- Wide individual and cultural variations exist in **death anxiety.** People with a sense of spirituality or a well-developed personal philosophy of death are less fearful, as are those with deep faith in a higher force or being. Older adults' greater ability to regulate negative emotion and their sense of symbolic immortality reduce death anxiety. Across cultures, women exhibit more death anxiety than men.

Thinking and Emotions of Dying People (p. 646)

Describe and evaluate Kübler-Ross's theory of typical responses to dying, citing factors that influence dying patients' responses.

- Elisabeth Kübler-Ross proposed that dying people typically express five responses, initially proposed as stages: denial, anger, bargaining, depression, and acceptance. These reactions do not occur in fixed sequence, and dying people often display other coping strategies.

- An **appropriate death** is one that makes sense in terms of the individual's pattern of living and values, preserves or restores significant relationships, and is as free of suffering as possible. The extent to which people attain these goals depends on many contextual variables—nature of the disease, personality and coping style, family members' and health professionals' behavior, and spirituality, religion, and cultural background.

A Place to Die (p. 650)

Evaluate the extent to which homes, hospitals, nursing homes, and the hospice approach meet the needs of dying people and their families.

- Although most people say they want to die at home, only about one-fourth of Americans do. Even with professional help and hospital-supplied equipment, caring for a dying patient is highly demanding.

- Sudden deaths typically occur in hospital emergency rooms, where sympathetic explanations from staff can reduce family members' anger, frustration, and confusion. Intensive care is especially depersonalizing for patients, lingering between life and death while hooked to machines. Many U.S. hospitals still lack comprehensive treatment programs aimed at easing end-of-life suffering.

- Though deaths in U.S. nursing homes are common, high-quality terminal care is lacking. Too many patients die in pain without having their needs met.

- The **hospice** approach is a comprehensive program of support services designed to meet the dying person's physical, emotional, social, and spiritual needs by providing **palliative,** or **comfort, care,** rather than prolonging life. Hospice care also contributes to improved family functioning and better psychological well-being among family survivors.

The Right to Die (p. 654)

Discuss controversies surrounding euthanasia and assisted suicide.

- Modern medical procedures that preserve life can also prolong inevitable death, diminishing quality of life and personal dignity. **Euthanasia**—ending the life of a person suffering from an incurable condition—takes various forms.

- **Passive euthanasia,** withholding or withdrawing life-sustaining treatment from a hopelessly ill patient, is widely accepted and practiced. People can best ensure that their wishes will be followed by preparing a written **advance medical directive.** A **living will** contains instructions for treatment, whereas the **durable power of attorney for health care** names another person to make health care decisions on one's behalf.

© PENNY TWEEDIE/ALAMY

- Public support for **voluntary active euthanasia,** in which doctors or others act directly, at a patient's request, to end suffering before a natural end to life, is high. Nevertheless, the practice remains a criminal offense in most countries and has sparked heated controversy, fueled by fears that it will be applied involuntarily to vulnerable people.

- Less public support exists for assisted suicide. But because the final act is solely the patient's, some experts believe that legalizing assisted suicide is preferable to legalizing voluntary active euthanasia.

Bereavement: Coping with the Death of a Loved One (p. 659)

Describe the phases of grieving, factors that underlie individual variations, and bereavement interventions.

- **Bereavement** refers to the experience of losing a loved one by death, **grief** to the intense physical and psychological distress that accompanies loss. **Mourning** is the culturally prescribed expression of the bereaved person's thoughts and feelings.

- Although theorists previously believed that grieving occurred in orderly phases—avoidance, confrontation, and finally restoration—a more accurate image is a roller-coaster ride, with the mourner completing a set of tasks to overcome grief. According to the **dual-process model of coping with loss,** effective coping involves oscillating between dealing with the emotional consequences of loss and attending to life changes, which can have restorative effects. Bereaved individuals who experience positive as well as negative emotions cope more effectively.

- Like dying, grieving is affected by many personal and situational factors. Bereaved men express grief less directly than bereaved women. After a sudden, unanticipated death, avoidance may be especially pronounced and confrontation highly traumatic. In contrast, a prolonged, expected death grants the bereaved person time to engage in **anticipatory grieving.**

- When a parent loses a child or a child loses a parent or sibling, grieving is generally intense and prolonged. Because early loss of a life partner is a nonnormative event with a major impact on life plans, younger widowed individuals usually fare less well than widowed older people. Disenfranchised grief can profoundly disrupt the process of grieving.

- People who experience several deaths at once or in close succession may suffer from bereavement overload. Those at risk include aging adults, individuals who have lost loved ones to public tragedies, and people who have witnessed unexpected, violent deaths.

AP IMAGES/ZHANG HAO/COLOR CHINA PHOTO

- Sympathy and understanding are sufficient for most people to recover from grief. Support groups are highly effective in aiding recovery, whereas individually tailored approaches help mourners reorganize their daily lives. Interventions for children and adolescents following violent deaths must protect them from unnecessary reexposure and assist parents and teachers in offering comfort.

Death Education (p. 665)

Explain how death education can help people cope with death more effectively.

- Today, instruction in death, dying, and bereavement is integrated into training programs for doctors, nurses, psychologists, and social workers. It is also found in adult education programs and in a few elementary and secondary schools. Courses with an experiential component may reduce death anxiety.

Important Terms and Concepts

advance medical directive (p. 655)
agonal phase (p. 640)
anticipatory grieving (p. 661)
appropriate death (p. 648)
bereavement (p. 659)
brain death (p. 641)
clinical death (p. 640)

death anxiety (p. 645)
dual-process model of coping with loss (p. 660)
durable power of attorney for health care (p. 655)
euthanasia (p. 654)
grief (p. 659)
hospice (p. 652)
living will (p. 655)

mortality (p. 640)
mourning (p. 659)
palliative, or comfort, care (p. 652)
passive euthanasia (p. 654)
persistent vegetative state (p. 641)
thanatology (p. 640)
voluntary active euthanasia (p. 656)

Glossary

A

academic programs Preschool and kindergarten programs in which teachers structure children's learning, teaching academic skills through formal lessons that often involve repetition and drill. Distinguished from *child-centered programs*. (p. 244)

accommodation In Piaget's theory, that part of adaptation in which new schemes are created and old ones adjusted to produce a better fit with the environment. Distinguished from *assimilation*. (p. 152)

acculturative stress Psychological distress resulting from conflict between an individual's minority culture and the host culture. (p. 406)

activities of daily living (ADLs) Basic self-care tasks required to live on one's own, such as bathing, dressing, getting in and out of bed or a chair, and eating. (p. 567)

activity theory A social theory of aging that states that declining rates of interaction in late adulthood reflect social barriers to engagement, not the desires of aging adults. Older people try to preserve life satisfaction by finding roles that allow them to remain about as active and busy as they were in middle age. Distinguished from *disengagement theory, continuity theory,* and *socioemotional selectivity theory*. (p. 614)

adaptation In Piaget's theory, the process of building schemes through direct interaction with the environment. Consists of two complementary activities: *assimilation* and *accommodation*. (p. 152)

adolescence The transition between childhood and adulthood that begins with puberty. It involves accepting one's full-grown body, acquiring adult ways of thinking, attaining greater independence from one's family, developing more mature ways of relating to peers of both sexes, and beginning to construct an identity. (p. 361)

advance medical directive A written statement of desired medical treatment should a person become incurably ill. (p. 655)

affect optimization The ability to maximize positive emotion and dampen negative emotion. An emotional strength of late adulthood. (p. 605)

age-graded influences Influences on lifespan development that are strongly related to age and therefore fairly predictable in when they occur and how long they last. (p. 10)

age of viability The age at which the fetus can first survive if born early. Occurs sometime between 22 and 26 weeks. (p. 84)

aging in place In late adulthood, remaining in a familiar setting where one has control over one's everyday life. (p. 617)

agonal phase The phase of dying in which gasps and muscle spasms occur during the first moments in which the regular heart beat disintegrates. Distinguished from *clinical death* and *mortality*. (p. 640)

alcohol-related neurodevelopmental disorder (ARND) The least severe form of fetal alcohol spectrum disorder, involving brain injury but with typical physical growth and absence of facial abnormalities. Distinguished from *fetal alcohol syndrome (FAS)* and *partial fetal alcohol syndrome (p-FAS)*. (p. 89)

allele Each of two or more forms of a gene located at the same place on corresponding pairs of chromosomes. (p. 48)

Alzheimer's disease The most common form of dementia, in which structural and chemical brain deterioration is associated with gradual loss of many aspects of thought and behavior, including memory, skilled and purposeful movements, and comprehension and production of speech. (p. 582)

amnion The inner membrane that that encloses the prenatal organism in amniotic fluid, which helps keep temperature constant and provides a cushion against jolts caused by the mother's movements. (p. 81)

amyloid plaques A structural change in the cerebral cortex associated with Alzheimer's disease, in which dense deposits of a deteriorated protein called *amyloid* develop, surrounded by clumps of dead nerve and glial cells. (p. 583)

androgyny The gender identity held by individuals who score high on both traditionally masculine and traditionally feminine personality characteristics. (p. 276)

anorexia nervosa An eating disorder in which young people, mainly females, starve themselves because of a compulsive fear of getting fat and an extremely distorted body image. (p. 372)

anoxia Inadequate oxygen supply. (p. 100)

anticipatory grieving Before a prolonged, expected death, acknowledging the inevitability of the loss and preparing emotionally for it. (p. 661)

Apgar Scale A rating system used to assess a newborn baby's physical condition immediately after birth on the basis of five characteristics: heart rate, respiratory effort, reflex irritability, muscle tone, and color. (p. 98)

appropriate death A death that makes sense in terms of the individual's pattern of living and values, preserves or restores significant relationships, and is as free of suffering as possible. (p. 648)

assimilation In Piaget's theory, that part of adaptation in which the external world is interpreted in terms of current schemes. Distinguished from *accommodation*. (p. 152)

assisted living A homelike housing arrangement for older adults who require more care than can be provided at home but less than is usually provided in nursing homes. (p. 589)

assistive technology An array of devices that permits people with disabilities, including older adults, to improve their functioning. (p. 573)

associative memory deficit Age-related difficulty creating and retrieving links between pieces of information—for example, two items or an item and its context. (p. 591)

associative play A form of social interaction in which children engage in separate activities but interact by exchanging toys and commenting on one another's behavior. Distinguished from *nonsocial activity, parallel play,* and *cooperative play*. (p. 261)

attachment The strong affectionate tie that humans have with special people in their lives, which leads them to feel pleasure when interacting with those people and to be comforted by their nearness in times of stress. (p. 195)

Attachment Q-Sort A method for assessing the quality of attachment in children between 1 and 4 years of age through home observations of a variety of attachment-related behaviors. (p. 198)

attention-deficit hyperactivity disorder (ADHD) A childhood disorder involving inattention, impulsivity, and excessive motor activity, resulting in academic and social problems. (p. 304)

authoritarian child-rearing style A child-rearing style that is low in acceptance and involvement, high in coercive control, and low in autonomy granting. Distinguished from *authoritative, permissive,* and *uninvolved child-rearing styles*. (p. 279)

authoritative child-rearing style A child-rearing style that is high in acceptance and involvement, emphasizes adaptive control techniques, and includes gradual, appropriate autonomy granting. Distinguished from *authoritarian, permissive,* and *uninvolved child-rearing styles*. (p. 278)

autobiographical memory Long-lasting recollections of personally meaningful one-time events from both the recent and the distant past. (p. 164)

autoimmune response A malfunction of the immune system in which it turns against normal body tissues. (p. 571)

automatic processes Cognitive activities that are so well-learned that they require no space in working memory and, therefore, permit an individual to focus on other information while performing them. (p. 162)

autonomy At adolescence, a sense of oneself as a separate, self-governing individual. Involves relying more on oneself and less on parents for support and guidance and engaging in careful, well-reasoned decision making. (p. 415)

autonomy versus shame and doubt In Erikson's theory, the psychological conflict of toddlerhood, which is resolved favorably when parents provide young children with suitable guidance and reasonable choices. (p. 184)

autosomes The 22 matching chromosome pairs in each human cell. (p. 47)

average healthy life expectancy The number of years that an individual born in a particular year can expect to live in full health, without disease or injury. Distinguished from *maximum lifespan* and *average life expectancy*. (p. 564)

average life expectancy The number of years that an individual born in a particular year can expect to live, starting at any given age. Distinguished from *maximum lifespan* and *average healthy life expectancy*. (p. 564)

avoidant attachment The attachment pattern characterizing infants who seem unresponsive to the parent when she is present, are usually not distressed by parental separation, react to the stranger in much the same way as to the parent, and avoid or are slow to greet the parent when she returns. Distinguished from *secure, resistant,* and *disorganized/disoriented attachment.* (p. 197)

B

babbling Repetition of consonant–vowel combinations in long strings, beginning around 6 months of age. (p. 176)

basal metabolic rate (BMR) The amount of energy the body uses at complete rest. (p. 439)

basic emotions Emotions such as happiness, interest, surprise, fear, anger, sadness, and disgust that are universal in humans and other primates and have a long evolutionary history of promoting survival. (p. 185)

basic trust versus mistrust In Erikson's theory, the psychological conflict of infancy, which is resolved positively when the balance of care is sympathetic and loving. (p. 184)

behavioral genetics A field devoted to uncovering the contributions of nature and nurture to the diversity of human traits and abilities. (p. 69)

behaviorism An approach that regards directly observable events—stimuli and responses—as the appropriate focus of study and views the development of behavior as taking place through classical and operant conditioning. (p. 17)

behavior modification Procedures that combine conditioning and modeling to eliminate undesirable behaviors and increase desirable responses. (p. 18)

bereavement The experience of losing a loved one by death. (p. 659)

bicultural identity The identity constructed by individuals who explore and adopt values from both their family's subculture and the dominant culture. (p. 406)

"big five" personality traits Five basic factors into which hundreds of personality traits have been organized: neuroticism, extroversion, openness to experience, agreeableness, and conscientiousness. (p. 542)

biological aging, or senescence Genetically influenced, age-related declines in the functioning of organs and systems that are universal in all members of our species. Sometimes called *primary aging.* (p. 432)

blended, or reconstituted, family A family structure resulting from remarriage or cohabitation that includes parent, child, and steprelatives. (p. 349)

body image Conception of and attitude toward one's physical appearance. (p. 371)

brain death Irreversible cessation of all activity in the brain and the brain stem. The definition of death accepted in most industrialized nations. (p. 641)

brain plasticity The capacity of various parts of the cerebral cortex to take over functions of damaged regions. Declines as hemispheres of the cerebral cortex lateralize. (p. 124)

breech position A position of the baby in the uterus that would cause the buttocks or feet to be delivered first. (p. 100)

bulimia nervosa An eating disorder in which individuals, mainly females, engage in strict dieting and excessive exercise accompanied by binge eating, often followed by deliberate vomiting and purging with laxatives. (p. 373)

burnout A condition in which long-term job stress leads to mental exhaustion, a sense of loss of personal control, and feelings of reduced accomplishment. (p. 554)

C

canalization The tendency of heredity to restrict the development of some characteristics to just one or a few outcomes. (p. 72)

cardinality The mathematical principle specifying that the last number in a counting sequence indicates the quantity of items in the set. (p. 243)

carrier A heterozygous individual who can pass a recessive trait to his or her offspring. (p. 48)

cataracts Cloudy areas in the lens of the eye that increase from middle to old age, resulting in foggy vision and (without surgery) eventual blindness. (p. 569)

categorical self Classification of the self according to prominent ways in which people differ, such as age, sex, physical characteristics, and goodness and badness. Develops between 18 and 30 months. (p. 208)

central executive In information processing, the conscious, reflective part of our mental system that directs the flow of information, coordinating incoming information with information already in the system and selecting, applying, and monitoring strategies that facilitate memory storage, comprehension, reasoning, and problem solving. (p. 162)

centration In Piaget's theory, the tendency of preoperational children to focus on one aspect of a situation while neglecting other important features. (p. 229)

cephalocaudal trend An organized pattern of physical growth that proceeds from the upper to the lower part of the body ("head to tail"). Distinguished from *proximodistal trend.* (p. 121)

cerebellum A structure at the rear and base of the brain that aids in balance and control of body movements. (p. 218)

cerebral cortex The largest, most complex structure of the human brain, containing the greatest number of neurons and synapses and accounting for the highly developed intelligence of the human species. (p. 124)

cerebrovascular dementia A form of dementia that develops when a series of strokes leaves areas of dead brain cells, producing step-by-step degeneration of mental ability, with each step occurring abruptly after a stroke. (p. 585)

cesarean delivery A surgical delivery in which the doctor makes an incision in the mother's abdomen and lifts the baby out of the uterus. (p. 101)

child-centered programs Preschool and kindergarten programs in which teachers provide a variety of activities from which children select, and much learning takes place through play. Distinguished from *academic programs.* (p. 244)

child-rearing styles Combinations of parenting behaviors that occur over a wide range of situations, creating an enduring child-rearing climate. (p. 278)

chorion The outer membrane that forms a protective covering around the prenatal organism. It sends out tiny hairlike villi, from which the placenta begins to develop. (p. 82)

chromosomes Rodlike structures in the cell nucleus that store and transmit genetic information. (p. 46)

chronosystem In ecological systems theory, temporal changes in environments, either externally imposed or arising from within the person, that produce new conditions affecting development. Distinguished from *microsystem, mesosystem, exosystem,* and *macrosystem.* (p. 25)

circular reaction In Piaget's theory, a means of building schemes in which infants try to repeat a chance event caused by their own motor activity. (p. 153)

classical conditioning A form of learning that involves associating a neutral stimulus with a stimulus that leads to a reflexive response. Once the nervous system makes the connection between the two stimuli, the neutral stimulus alone produces the behavior. (p. 133)

climacteric The midlife transition in which fertility declines, bringing an end to reproductive capacity in women and diminished fertility in men. (p. 504)

clinical death The phase of dying in which heartbeat, circulation, breathing, and brain functioning stop, but resuscitation is still possible. Distinguished from *agonal phase* and *mortality.* (p. 640)

clinical interview An interview method in which the researcher uses a flexible, conversational style to probe for the participant's point of view. Distinguished from *structured interview.* (p. 30)

clinical, or case study, method A research method in which the aim is to obtain as complete a picture as possible of one individual's psychological functioning by bringing together interview data, observations, and sometimes test scores. (p. 30)

clique A group of about five to seven members who are good friends and, therefore, usually resemble one another in family background, attitudes, and values. (p. 419)

cognitive-affective complexity A form of thinking that increases from adolescence through middle adulthood, involving awareness of conflicting positive and negative feelings and coordination of them into a complex, organized structure that recognizes the uniqueness of individual experiences. (p. 452)

cognitive-developmental theory An approach introduced by Piaget that views children as actively constructing knowledge as they manipulate and explore their world and that regards cognitive development as taking place in stages. (p. 18)

cognitive maps Mental representations of familiar large-scale spaces, such as neighborhood or school. (p. 300)

cognitive self-regulation The process of continuously monitoring progress toward a goal, checking outcomes, and redirecting unsuccessful efforts. (p. 307)

cohabitation The lifestyle of unmarried couples who have a sexually intimate relationship and who share a residence. (p. 487)

cohort effects The effects of cultural–historical change on the accuracy of longitudinal and cross-sectional research findings. Results based on one cohort—individuals developing in the same time period, who are influenced by particular historical and cultural conditions—may not apply to other cohorts. (p. 37)

collectivist societies Societies in which people define themselves as part of a group and stress group goals over individual goals. Distinguished from *individualistic societies*. (p. 65)

commitment within relativistic thinking In Perry's theory, the mature individual's formulation of a perspective that synthesizes contradictions between opposing views, rather than choosing between them. (p. 451)

companionate love Love based on warm, trusting affection and caregiving. Distinguished from *passionate love*. (p. 473)

compliance Voluntary obedience to requests and commands. (p. 208)

compression of morbidity The public health goal of reducing the average period of diminished vigor before death as life expectancy extends. Medical advances, improved socioeconomic conditions, and good health habits all promote this goal. (p. 576)

concrete operational stage Piaget's third stage of cognitive development, extending from about 7 to 11 years of age, during which thought becomes logical, flexible, and organized in its application to concrete information, but the capacity for abstract thinking is not yet present. (p. 299)

conditioned response (CR) In classical conditioning, a new response produced by a conditioned stimulus (CS) that is similar to the unconditioned, or reflexive, response (UCR). (p. 134)

conditioned stimulus (CS) In classical conditioning, a neutral stimulus that, through pairing with an unconditioned stimulus (UCS), leads to a new, conditioned response. (CR). (p. 134)

congregate housing Housing for older adults that provides a variety of support services, including meals in a common dining room, along with watchful oversight of residents with physical and mental disabilities. (p. 618)

conservation The understanding that certain physical characteristics of objects remain the same, even when their outward appearance changes. (p. 229)

constructivist classroom A classroom grounded in Piaget's view of children as active agents who construct their own knowledge. Features include richly equipped learning centers, small groups and individuals solving self-chosen problems, a teacher who guides and supports in response to children's needs, and evaluation based on individual students' progress in relation to their own prior development. Distinguished from *traditional* and *social-constructivist classrooms*. (p. 319)

contexts Unique combinations of personal and environmental circumstances that can result in different paths of development. (p. 7)

continuity theory A social theory of aging that states that most aging adults, in their choice of everyday activities and social relationships, strive to maintain a personal system—an identity and a set of personality dispositions, interests, roles, and skills—that promotes life satisfaction by ensuring consistency between their past and anticipated future. Distinguished from *disengagement theory, activity theory,* and *socioemotional selectivity theory*. (p. 614)

continuous development The view that development is a process of gradually augmenting the same types of skills that were there to begin with. Distinguished from *discontinuous development*. (p. 6)

contrast sensitivity A general principle accounting for early pattern preferences, which states that if babies can detect a difference in contrast between two patterns, they will prefer the pattern with more contrast. (p. 144)

controversial children Children who receive many votes, both positive and negative, on self-report measures of peer acceptance, indicating that they are both liked and disliked. Distinguished from *popular, neglected,* and *rejected children*. (p. 341)

conventional level Kohlberg's second level of moral development, in which moral understanding is based on conforming to social rules to ensure positive human relationships and maintain societal order. (p. 408)

convergent thinking The type of cognition emphasized on intelligence tests, which involves arriving at a single correct answer to a problem. Distinguished from *divergent thinking*. (p. 322)

cooing Pleasant vowel-like noises made by infants beginning around 2 months of age. (p. 176)

cooperative learning Collaboration on a task by a small group of classmates who work toward common goals by resolving differences of opinion, sharing responsibilities, and providing one another with sufficient explanation to correct misunderstandings. (p. 320)

cooperative play A form of social interaction in which children orient toward a common goal, such as acting out a make-believe theme. Distinguished from *nonsocial activity, parallel play,* and *associative play*. (p. 261)

coparenting Parents' mutual support of each other's parenting behaviors. (p. 60)

coregulation A form of supervision in which parents exercise general oversight while letting children take charge of moment-by-moment decision making. (p. 345)

core knowledge perspective A perspective that states that infants are born with a set of innate knowledge systems, or core domains of thought, each of which permits a ready grasp of new, related information and therefore supports early, rapid development of certain aspects of cognition. (p. 159)

corpus callosum The large bundle of fibers connecting the two hemispheres of the cerebral cortex. (p. 218)

correlational design A research design in which the investigator gathers information on individuals without altering their experiences and then examines relationships between participants' characteristics and their behavior or development. Does not permit inferences about cause and effect. (p. 34)

correlation coefficient A number, ranging from +1.00 to –1.00, that describes the strength and direction of the relationship between two variables. (p. 34)

creativity The ability to produce work that is original yet appropriate— something others have not thought of that is useful in some way. (p. 322)

cross-linkage theory of aging A theory of biological aging asserting that the formation of bonds, or links, between normally separate protein fibers causes the body's connective tissue to become less elastic over time, leading to many negative physical outcomes. (p. 434)

cross-sectional design A research design in which groups of participants of different ages are studied at the same point in time. Distinguished from *longitudinal design*. (p. 37)

crowd A large, loosely organized social group consisting of several cliques with similar values. Membership is based on reputation and stereotype. (p. 419)

crystallized intelligence Intellectual skills that depend on accumulated knowledge and experience, good judgment, and mastery of social conventions—abilities acquired because they are valued by the individual's culture. Distinguished from *fluid intelligence*. (p. 518)

D

death anxiety Fear and apprehension of death. (p. 645)

deferred imitation The ability to remember and copy the behavior of models who are not present. (p. 154)

delay of gratification The ability to wait for an appropriate time and place to engage in a tempting act. (p. 209)

dementia A set of disorders occurring almost entirely in old age in which many aspects of thought and behavior are so impaired that everyday activities are disrupted. (p. 582)

deoxyribonucleic acid (DNA) Long, double-stranded molecules that make up chromosomes. (p. 46)

dependency–support script A typical pattern of interaction in which caregivers attend to older adults' dependent behaviors immediately, thereby reinforcing those behaviors. Distinguished from *independence-ignore script*. (p. 610)

dependent variable The variable the researcher expects to be influenced by the independent variable in an experiment. Distinguished from *independent variable*. (p. 35)

developmental cognitive neuroscience An area of investigation that brings together researchers from psychology, biology, neuroscience, and medicine to study the relationship between changes in the brain and the developing person's cognitive processing and behavior patterns. (p. 21)

developmentally appropriate practice A set of standards devised by the U.S. National Association for the Education of Young Children, specifying program characteristics that meet the developmental and individual needs of young children of varying ages, based on current research and consensus among experts. (p. 172)

developmental quotient (DQ) A score on an infant intelligence test, computed in the same manner as an IQ but labeled more conservatively because it does not tap the same dimensions of intelligence assessed in older children. (p. 170)

developmental science An interdisciplinary field devoted to understanding constancy and change throughout the lifespan. (p. 5)

differentiation theory The view that perceptual development involves the detection of increasingly fine-grained, invariant features in the environment. (p. 146)

difficult child A child whose temperament is characterized by irregular daily routines, slow acceptance of new experiences, and a tendency to react negatively and intensely. Distinguished from *easy child* and *slow-to-warm-up child*. (p. 190)

discontinuous development The view that development is a process in which new ways of understanding and responding to the world emerge at specific times. Distinguished from *continuous development*. (p. 6)

disengagement theory A social theory of aging that states that declines in social interaction in late adulthood are due to mutual withdrawal between older adults and society in anticipation of death. Distinguished from *activity theory, continuity theory,* and *socioemotional selectivity theory*. (p. 614)

disorganized/disoriented attachment The attachment pattern reflecting the greatest insecurity, characterizing infants who show confused, contradictory responses when reunited with the parent after a separation. Distinguished from *secure, avoidant,* and *resistant attachment*. (p. 198)

displaced reference The realization that words can be used to cue mental images of things that are not physically present. (p. 157)

divergent thinking The type of thinking associated with creativity, which involves generating multiple and unusual possibilities when faced with a task or problem. Distinguished from *convergent thinking*. (p. 322)

dominance hierarchy A stable ordering of group members that predicts who will win when conflict arises. (p. 297)

dominant cerebral hemisphere The hemisphere of the cerebral cortex responsible for skilled motor action and other important abilities. In right-handed individuals, the left hemisphere is dominant; in left-handed individuals, motor and language skills are often shared between the hemispheres. (p. 217)

dominant–recessive inheritance A pattern of inheritance in which, under heterozygous conditions, the influence of only one allele is apparent. (p. 48)

dualistic thinking In Perry's theory, the cognitive approach typical of younger college students, who divide information, values, and authority into right and wrong, good and bad, we and they. Distinguished from *relativistic thinking*. (p. 451)

dual-process model of coping with loss A perspective that assumes that people cope most effectively with loss when they oscillate between dealing with the emotional consequences of loss and attending to life changes, which—when handled successfully—have restorative, or healing, effects. (p. 660)

dual representation The ability to view a symbolic object as both an object in its own right and a symbol. (p. 227)

durable power of attorney for health care A written statement authorizing appointment of another person (usually, though not always, a family member) to make health care decisions on one's behalf. (p. 655)

dynamic assessment An approach to testing consistent with Vygotsky's zone of proximal development, in which purposeful teaching is introduced into the testing situation to find out what the child can attain with social support. (p. 315)

dynamic systems theory of motor development A theory that views new motor skills as reorganizations of previously mastered skills, which lead to more effective ways of exploring and controlling the environment. Each new skill is a joint product of central nervous system development, the body's movement capacities, the child's goals, and environmental supports for the skill. (p. 137)

E

easy child A child whose temperament is characterized by quick establishment of regular routines in infancy, general cheerfulness, and easy adaptation to new experiences. Distinguished from *difficult child* and *slow-to-warm-up child*. (p. 190)

ecological systems theory Bronfenbrenner's approach, which views the person as developing within a complex system of relationships affected by multiple levels of the surrounding environment, from immediate settings of family and school to broad cultural values and programs. (p. 24)

educational self-fulfilling prophecies Teachers' positive or negative views of individual children, who tend to adopt and start to live up to those views. (p. 320)

effortful control The self-regulatory dimension of temperament, involving the capacity to voluntarily suppress a dominant response in order to plan and execute a more adaptive response. (p. 191)

egalitarian marriage A form of marriage in which partners relate as equals, sharing power and authority. Both try to balance the time and energy they devote to their occupations, their children, and their relationship. Distinguished from *traditional marriage*. (p. 480)

egocentrism Failure to distinguish others' symbolic viewpoints from one's own. (p. 228)

ego integrity versus despair In Erikson's theory, the psychological conflict of late adulthood, which is resolved positively when older adults come to terms with their lives and feel whole, complete, and satisfied with their achievements, recognizing that the paths they followed, abandoned, or never selected were necessary for fashioning a meaningful life course. (p. 604)

elaboration A memory strategy that involves creating a relationship, or shared meaning, between two or more pieces of information that do not belong to the same category in order to improve recall. (p. 305)

embryo The prenatal organism from 2 to 8 weeks after conception—the period when the groundwork for all body structures and internal organs is laid down. (p. 82)

emergent literacy Children's active efforts to construct literacy knowledge through informal experiences. (p. 240)

emerging adulthood A new transitional period of development, extending from the late teens to the mid- to late twenties, during which young people have left adolescence but have not yet assumed adult responsibilities. Rather, they continue to explore alternatives in education, work, personal beliefs and values, and love. (p. 464)

emotional intelligence A set of emotional abilities that enable individuals to process and adapt to emotional information. Measured by tapping the emotional skills people use to manage their own emotions and interact competently with others. (p. 313)

emotional self-regulation Strategies for adjusting our emotional state to a comfortable level of intensity so we can accomplish our goals. (p. 189)

emotion-centered coping A strategy for managing emotion that is internal, private, and aimed at controlling distress when little can be done to change an outcome. Distinguished from *problem-centered coping*. (p. 336)

empathy The ability to understand another's emotional state and to *feel with* that person, or respond emotionally in a similar way. (p. 208)

epigenesis Development resulting from ongoing, bidirectional exchanges between heredity and all levels of the environment. (p. 73)

episodic memory Memory for everyday experiences. (p. 238)

epistemic cognition Reflections on how one arrived at facts, beliefs, and ideas. (p. 451)

ethnic identity A sense of ethnic group membership and attitudes and feelings associated with that membership, as an enduring aspect of the self. (p. 406)

ethnography A method in which the researcher attempts to understand a culture or a distinct social group through participant observation— living with its members and taking field notes for an extended time. (p. 32)

ethological theory of attachment Bowlby's theory, the most widely accepted view of attachment, which regards the infant's emotional tie to the caregiver as an evolved response that promotes survival. (p. 196)

ethology An approach concerned with the adaptive, or survival, value of behavior and its evolutionary history. (p. 22)

euthanasia The practice of ending the life of a person suffering from an incurable condition. (p. 654)

evolutionary developmental psychology An area of research that seeks to understand the adaptive value of specieswide cognitive, emotional, and social competencies as those competencies change with age. (p. 22)

executive function In information processing, the diverse cognitive operations and strategies that enable us to achieve our goals in cognitively challenging situations. Includes controlling attention, suppressing impulses, coordinating information in working memory, and flexibly directing and monitoring thought and behavior. (p. 162)

exosystem In ecological systems theory, social settings that do not contain the developing person but nevertheless affect experiences in immediate settings. Distinguished from *microsystem, mesosystem, macrosystem,* and *chronosystem.* (p. 25)

expansions Adult responses that elaborate on children's speech, increasing its complexity. (p. 251)

experience-dependent brain growth Growth and refinement of established brain structures as a result of specific learning experiences that vary widely across individuals and cultures. Distinguished from *experience-expectant brain growth.* (p. 128)

experience-expectant brain growth The young brain's rapidly developing organization, which depends on ordinary experiences—opportunities to explore the environment, interact with people, and hear language and other sounds. Distinguished from *experience-dependent brain growth.* (p. 127)

experimental design A research design in which the investigator randomly assigns participants to two or more treatment conditions and studies the effect that manipulating an independent variable has on a dependent variable. Permits inferences about cause and effect. (p. 35)

expertise Acquisition of extensive knowledge in a field or endeavor. (p. 453)

expressive style of language learning A style of early language learning in which toddlers use language mainly to talk about their own and others' feelings and needs, with an initial vocabulary emphasizing social formulas and pronouns. Distinguished from *referential style of language learning.* (p. 178)

extended-family household A household in which three or more generations live together. (p. 65)

F

family life cycle A series of phases characterizing the development of most families around the world. In early adulthood, people typically live on their own, marry, and bear and rear children. In middle age, parenting responsibilities diminish. Late adulthood brings retirement, growing old, and (more often for women) death of one's spouse. (p. 478)

fantasy period Period of vocational development in which children gain insight into career options by fantasizing about them. Distinguished from *tentative period* and *realistic period.* (p. 455)

fast-mapping Children's ability to connect new words with their underlying concepts after only a brief encounter. (p. 248)

feminization of poverty A trend in which women who support themselves or their families have become the majority of the adult population living in poverty, regardless of age and ethnic group. (p. 544)

fetal alcohol spectrum disorder (FASD) A range of physical, mental, and behavioral outcomes caused by prenatal alcohol exposure, including *fetal alcohol syndrome (FAS), partial fetal alcohol syndrome (p-FAS),* and *alcohol-related neurodevelopmental disorder (ARND).* (p. 88)

fetal alcohol syndrome (FAS) The most severe form of fetal alcohol spectrum disorder, distinguished by slow physical growth, facial abnormalities, and brain injury. Usually affects children whose mothers drank heavily throughout pregnancy. Distinguished from *partial fetal alcohol syndrome (p-FAS)* and *alcohol-related neurodevelopmental disorder (ARND).* (p. 88)

fetal monitors Electronic instruments that track the baby's heart rate during labor. (p. 100)

fetus The prenatal organism from the ninth week to the end of pregnancy— the period during which body structures are completed and dramatic growth in size occurs. (p. 83)

fluid intelligence Intellectual skills that largely depend on basic information-processing skills—ability to detect relationships among visual stimuli, speed of analyzing information, and capacity of working memory. Influenced less by culture than by conditions in the brain and by learning unique to the individual. Distinguished from *crystallized intelligence.* (p. 518)

formal operational stage Piaget's highest stage, beginning around 11 years of age, in which adolescents develop the capacity for abstract, systematic, scientific thinking. (p. 382)

frailty Weakened functioning of diverse organs and body systems, which profoundly interferes with everyday competence and leaves older adults highly vulnerable in the face of infection, extremely hot or cold weather, or injury. (p. 580)

fraternal, or dizygotic, twins Twins resulting from the release and fertilization of two ova. They are genetically no more alike than ordinary siblings. Distinguished from *identical,* or *monozygotic, twins.* (p. 47)

free radicals Naturally occurring, highly reactive chemicals that form in the presence of oxygen and destroy nearby cellular material, including DNA, proteins, and fats essential for cell functioning. Believed to be involved in many disorders of aging. (p. 433)

functional age Actual competence and performance of an older adult, as distinguished from chronological age. (p. 564)

G

gametes Sex cells, or sperm and ova, which contain half as many chromosomes as regular body cells. (p. 46)

gender constancy A full understanding of the biologically based permanence of one's gender, including the realization that sex remains the same even if clothing, hairstyle, and play activities change. (p. 276)

gender identity An image of oneself as relatively masculine or feminine in characteristics. (p. 276)

gender intensification Increased gender stereotyping of attitudes and behavior and movement toward a more traditional gender identity, typical of early adolescence. (p. 414)

gender schema theory An information-processing approach to gender typing that explains how environmental pressures and children's cognitions work together to shape gender-role development. (p. 277)

gender typing Any association of objects, roles, or traits with one sex or the other in ways that conform to cultural stereotypes. (p. 273)

gene A segment of a DNA molecule that contains instructions for production of various proteins that contribute to growth and functioning of the body. (p. 46)

gene–environment correlation The idea that heredity influences the environments to which individuals are exposed. (p. 72)

gene–environment interaction The view that people have unique, genetically influenced reactions to particular experiences and qualities of the environment. (p. 71)

generativity versus stagnation In Erikson's theory, the psychological conflict of midlife, which is resolved positively if the adult can integrate personal goals with the welfare of the larger social world. The resulting strength is the capacity to give to and guide the next generation. (p. 532)

genetic counseling A communication process designed to help couples assess their chances of giving birth to a baby with a hereditary disorder and choose the best course of action in view of risks and family goals. (p. 53)

genomic imprinting A pattern of inheritance in which alleles are imprinted, or chemically marked, in such a way that one pair member is activated, regardless of its makeup. (p. 51)

genotype An individual's genetic makeup. Distinguished from *phenotype*. (p. 45)

gerotranscendence According to Joan Erikson, a psychosocial stage characterizing the very old and representing development beyond ego integrity. Involves a cosmic, transcendent perspective directed forward and outward, beyond the self. Apparent in heightened inner calm and contentment and in additional time spent in quiet reflection. (p. 605)

gifted Displaying exceptional intellectual strengths, such as high IQ, high potential for creativity, and specialized talent. (p. 322)

glass ceiling Invisible barrier to advancement up the corporate ladder, faced by women and ethnic minorities. (p. 555)

glaucoma A disease in which poor fluid drainage leads to a buildup of pressure within the eye, damaging the optic nerve. A leading cause of blindness among older adults. (p. 503)

glial cells Cells that are responsible for myelination of neural fibers, improving the efficiency of message transfer. (p. 122)

goodness-of-fit model A model that describes how favorable adjustment depends on an effective match, or good fit, between a child's temperament and the child-rearing environment. (p. 194)

grief Intense physical and psychological distress following the death of a loved one. (p. 659)

growth hormone (GH) A pituitary hormone that affects the development of all body tissues except the central nervous system and the genitals. (p. 219)

growth spurt Rapid gain in height and weight that is the first outward sign of puberty. (p. 363)

guided participation Shared endeavors between more expert and less expert participants, without specifying the precise features of communication in order to allow for variations across situations and cultures. A broader concept than *scaffolding*. (p. 235)

H

habituation A gradual reduction in the strength of a response due to repetitive stimulation. (p. 134)

hardiness A set of three personal qualities—control, commitment, and challenge—that, together, help people cope adaptively with stress brought on by inevitable life changes. (p. 516)

heritability estimate A statistic that measures the extent to which individual differences in complex traits, such as intelligence or personality, in a specific population are due to genetic factors. (p. 70)

heterozygous Having two different alleles at the same place on a pair of chromosomes. Distinguished from *homozygous*. (p. 48)

hierarchical classification The organization of objects into classes and subclasses on the basis of similarities and differences. (p. 229)

hippocampus An inner-brain structure that plays a vital role in memory and in images of space that help us find our way. (p. 218)

history-graded influences Influences on lifespan development that are unique to a particular historical era and explain why people born around the same time (called a *cohort*) tend to be alike in ways that set them apart from people born at other times. (p. 11)

Home Observation for Measurement of the Environment (HOME) A checklist for gathering information about the quality of children's home lives through observation and parental interview. (p. 170)

homozygous Having two identical alleles at the same place on a pair of chromosomes. Distinguished from *heterozygous*. (p. 48)

hormone therapy Low daily doses of estrogen, either alone or in combination with progesterone, aimed at reducing the physical discomforts of menopause. (p. 506)

hospice A comprehensive program of support services for terminally ill people and their families, which regards the patient and family as a unit of care and emphasizes meeting the patient's physical, emotional, social, and spiritual needs while also providing follow-up bereavement services to the family. (p. 652)

hypothetico-deductive reasoning A formal operational problem-solving strategy in which adolescents begin with a *hypothesis*, or prediction, about variables that might affect an outcome. From the hypothesis, they *deduce* logical, testable inferences. Then they systematically isolate and combine variables to see which of those inferences are confirmed in the real world. (p. 382)

I

identical, or monozygotic, twins Twins that result when a zygote, during early cell duplication, separates into two clusters of cells with the same genetic makeup, which develop into two individuals. Distinguished from *fraternal, or dizygotic, twins*. (p. 48)

identity A well-organized conception of the self, consisting of values, beliefs, and goals, to which the individual is solidly committed. (p. 402)

identity achievement The identity status of individuals who, after a period of exploration, have committed themselves to a clearly formulated set of self-chosen values and goals. Distinguished from *identity moratorium, identity foreclosure,* and *identity diffusion*. (p. 403)

identity diffusion The identity status of individuals who do not engage in exploration and are not committed to values and goals. Distinguished from *identity achievement, identity moratorium,* and *identity foreclosure*. (p. 403)

identity foreclosure The identity status of individuals who do not engage in exploration but, instead, are committed to ready-made values and goals chosen for them by authority figures. Distinguished from *identity achievement, identity moratorium,* and *identity diffusion*. (p. 403)

identity moratorium The identity status of individuals who are exploring but not yet committed to self-chosen values and goals. Distinguished from *identity achievement, identity foreclosure,* and *identity diffusion*. (p. 403)

identity versus role confusion In Erikson's theory, the psychological conflict of adolescence, which is resolved positively when adolescents achieve an identity through a process of exploration and inner soul-searching. (p. 402)

imaginary audience Adolescents' belief that they are the focus of everyone else's attention and concern. (p. 386)

imitation Learning by copying the behavior of another person. Also known as *modeling* or *observational learning*. (p. 135)

implantation Attachment of the blastocyst to the uterine lining, which occurs 7 to 9 days after fertilization. (p. 81)

implicit memory Memory without conscious awareness. (p. 591)

inclusive classrooms Classrooms in which students with learning difficulties learn alongside typical students in a regular educational setting for all or part of the school day—a practice designed to prepare them for participation in society and to combat prejudices against individuals with disabilities. (p. 322)

incomplete dominance A pattern of inheritance in which both alleles are expressed in the phenotype, resulting in a combined trait, or one that is intermediate between the two. (p. 50)

independence–ignore script A typical pattern of interaction in which older adults' independent behaviors are mostly ignored and, as a result, occur less often. Distinguished from *dependency–support script*. (p. 610)

independent variable In an experiment, the variable the investigator expects to cause changes in another variable and that the researcher manipulates by randomly assigning participants to treatment conditions. Distinguished from *dependent variable*. (p. 35)

individualistic societies Societies in which people think of themselves as separate entities and are largely concerned with their own personal needs. Distinguished from *collectivist societies*. (p. 65)

induction A type of discipline in which an adult helps the child notice feelings by pointing out the effects of the child's misbehavior on others. (p. 264)

industry versus inferiority In Erikson's theory, the psychological conflict of middle childhood, which is resolved positively when experiences lead children to develop a sense of competence at useful skills and tasks. (p. 330)

infant-directed speech (IDS) A form of communication used by adults to speak to infants and toddlers, consisting of short sentences with high-pitched, exaggerated expression, clear pronunciation, distinct pauses between speech segments, and repetition of new words in a variety of contexts. (p. 178)

infantile amnesia The inability of most older children and adults to retrieve events that happened before age 3. (p. 164)

infant mortality The number of deaths in the first year of life per 1,000 live births. (p. 104)

information-loss view A view that attributes age-related slowing of cognitive processing to greater loss of information as it moves through the system. As a result, the whole system must slow down to inspect and interpret the information. Distinguished from *neural network view.* (p. 520)

information processing A perspective that views the human mind as a symbol-manipulating system through which information flows and that regards cognitive development as a continuous process. (p. 20)

inhibited, or shy, child A child whose temperament is such that he or she reacts negatively to and withdraws from novel stimuli. Distinguished from *uninhibited, or sociable, child.* (p. 191)

initiative versus guilt In Erikson's theory, the psychological conflict of early childhood, which is resolved positively through play experiences that foster a healthy sense of initiative and through development of a superego, or conscience, that is not overly strict and guilt-ridden. (p. 256)

instrumental activities of daily living (IADLs) Tasks necessary to conduct the business of daily life and also requiring some cognitive competence, such as telephoning, shopping, food preparation, housekeeping, and paying bills. (p. 567)

intelligence quotient (IQ) A score that permits an individual's performance on an intelligence test to be compared to the performances of other individuals of the same age. (p. 169)

intentional, or goal-directed, behavior A sequence of actions in which schemes are deliberately coordinated to solve a problem. (p. 154)

interactional synchrony A form of communication in which the caregiver responds to infant signals in a well-timed, rhythmic, appropriate fashion and both partners match emotional states, especially the positive ones. (p. 200)

intermodal perception The process of making sense of simultaneous input from more than one modality, or sensory system, perceiving them as an integrated whole. (p. 145)

internal working model A set of expectations about the availability of attachment figures and the likelihood that they will provide support in times of stress. It becomes a vital part of personality, serving as a guide for all future close relationships. (p. 197)

intimacy versus isolation In Erikson's theory, the psychological conflict of early adulthood, reflected in the young person's thoughts and feelings about making a permanent commitment to an intimate partner. (p. 469)

irreversibility The inability to mentally go through a series of steps in a problem and then reverse direction, returning to the starting point. Distinguished from *reversibility.* (p. 229)

J

joint attention A state in which the child attends to the same object or event as the caregiver, who often labels it. Supports language development. (p. 176)

K

kinkeeper Role assumed by members of the middle generation, especially mothers, who take responsibility for gathering the family for celebrations and making sure everyone stays in touch. (p. 545)

kinship studies Studies that compare the characteristics of family members to determine the importance of heredity in complex human characteristics. (p. 70)

kwashiorkor A disease caused by an unbalanced diet very low in protein that usually appears after weaning, between 1 and 3 years of age.

Symptoms include an enlarged belly, swollen feet, hair loss, skin rash, and irritable, listless behavior. (p. 132)

L

language acquisition device (LAD) In Chomsky's theory, an innate system containing a universal grammar, or set of rules common to all languages, that enables children, no matter which language they hear, to understand and speak in a rule-oriented fashion as soon as they pick up enough words. (p. 174)

lanugo White, downy hair that covers the entire body of the fetus, helping the vernix stick to the skin. (p. 83)

lateralization Specialization of functions in the two hemispheres of the cerebral cortex. (p. 124)

learned helplessness Attribution of success to external factors, such as luck, and failure to low ability, which is fixed and cannot be improved through effort. Distinguished from *mastery-oriented attributions.* (p. 333)

learning disabilities Great difficulty with one or more aspects of learning, usually reading, resulting in achievement considerably behind what would be expected on the basis of a child's IQ. (p. 322)

life-care communities Housing for older adults that offers a range of alternatives, from independent or congregate housing to full nursing home care, guaranteeing that residents' changing needs will be met within the same facility as they age. (p. 618)

lifespan perspective A dynamic systems approach to development that assumes development is lifelong, multidimensional and multidirectional, highly plastic, and affected by multiple interacting forces. (p. 8)

living will A written statement specifying the treatments a person does or does not want in case of a terminal illness, coma, or other near-death situation. (p. 655)

loneliness Unhappiness resulting from a gap between actual and desired social relationships. (p. 477)

longitudinal design A research design in which participants are studied repeatedly, and changes are noted as they get older. Distinguished from *cross-sectional design.* (p. 35)

long-term memory In information processing, the largest storage area in memory, containing our permanent knowledge base. (p. 162)

M

macrosystem In ecological systems theory, cultural values, laws, customs, and resources that influence experiences and interactions at inner levels of the environment. Distinguished from *microsystem, mesosystem, exosystem,* and *chronosystem.* (p. 25)

macular degeneration Blurring and eventual loss of central vision due to a breakdown of light-sensitive cells in the macula, or central region of the retina. (p. 569)

make-believe play A type of play in which children act out everyday and imaginary activities. (p. 154)

marasmus A wasted condition of the body caused by a diet low in all essential nutrients, which usually appears in the first year of life. (p. 132)

mastery-oriented attributions Attributions that credit success to ability, which can be improved through effort, and failure to insufficient effort. Distinguished from *learned helplessness.* (p. 333)

matters of personal choice Concerns that do not involve rights or others' welfare and, therefore, are up to the individual, such as choice of friends, hairstyle, and leisure activities. Distinguished from *moral imperatives* and *social conventions.* (p. 269)

maximum lifespan The species-specific biological limit to length of life (in years), corresponding to the age at which the oldest known individual died. Distinguished from *average life expectancy* and *average healthy life expectancy.* (p. 566)

meiosis The process of cell division through which gametes are formed and in which the number of chromosomes in each cell is halved. (p. 46)

memory strategies Deliberate mental activities that improve the likelihood of remembering. (p. 237)

menarche First menstruation. (p. 365)

menopause The end of menstruation and, therefore, of a woman's reproductive capacity. (p. 504)

mental representation An internal depiction of information that the mind can manipulate, including images and concepts. (p. 154)

mesosystem In ecological systems theory, connections between a person's microsystems, or immediate settings. Distinguished from *microsystem, exosystem, macrosystem,* and *chronosystem.* (p. 25)

metacognition Thinking about thought; a theory of mind, or coherent set of ideas about mental activities. (p. 239)

microsystem In ecological systems theory, the innermost level of the environment, consisting of activities and interaction patterns in the person's immediate surroundings. Distinguished from *mesosystem, exosystem, macrosystem,* and *chronosystem.* (p. 24)

midlife crisis Self-doubt and stress that prompt major restructuring of the personality during the transition to middle adulthood. Characterizes the experience of only a minority of adults. (p. 536)

mirror neurons Specialized cells in motor areas of the cerebral cortex in primates that underlie the ability to imitate by firing identically when a primate hears or sees an action and when it carries out the action on its own. (p. 136)

mitosis The process of cell duplication, in which each new cell receives an exact copy of the original chromosomes. (p. 46)

moral identity The degree to which morality is central to an individual's self-concept. (p. 411)

moral imperatives Rules and expectations that protect people's rights and welfare. Distinguished from *social conventions* and *matters of personal choice.* (p. 269)

mortality The phase of dying in which the individual passes into permanent death. Distinguished from *agonal phase* and *clinical death.* (p. 640)

mourning The culturally specified expression of the bereaved person's thoughts and feelings through funerals and other rituals. (p. 659)

mutation A sudden but permanent change in a segment of DNA. (p. 51)

myelination The coating of neural fibers with an insulating fatty sheath, called *myelin,* that improves the efficiency of message transfer. (p. 122)

N

naturalistic observation A research method in which the researcher goes into the field, or natural environment, and records the behavior of interest. Distinguished from *structured observation.* (p. 28)

natural, or **prepared, childbirth** A group of techniques designed to reduce pain and medical intervention and to make childbirth as rewarding an experience as possible. (p. 99)

nature–nurture controversy Disagreement among theorists about whether genetic or environmental factors are more important influences on development. (p. 7)

neglected children Children who are seldom mentioned, either positively or negatively, on self-report measures of peer acceptance. Distinguished from *popular, rejected,* and *controversial children.* (p. 341)

Neonatal Behavioral Assessment Scale (NBAS) A test used to evaluate a newborn infant's reflexes, muscle tone, state changes, responsiveness to physical and social stimuli, and other reactions. (p. 114)

neural network view A view that attributes age-related slowing of cognitive processing to breaks in neural networks as neurons die. The brain adapts by forming bypasses—new synaptic connections that go around the breaks but are less efficient. Distinguished from *information-loss view.* (p. 520)

neural tube During the period of the embryo, the primitive spinal cord that develops from the ectoderm, the top of which swells to form the brain. (p. 82)

neurofibrillary tangles A structural change in the cerebral cortex associated with Alzheimer's disease, in which bundles of twisted threads appear that are the product of collapsed neural structures. (p. 583)

neurons Nerve cells that store and transmit information. (p. 121)

neurotransmitters Chemicals released by neurons that cross the synapse to send messages to other neurons. (p. 121)

niche-picking A type of gene–environment correlation in which individuals actively choose environments that complement their heredity. (p. 72)

nonnormative influences Influences on lifespan development that are irregular, in that they happen to just one or a few individuals and do not follow a predictable timetable. (p. 12)

non-rapid-eye-movement (NREM) sleep A "regular" sleep state during which the body is almost motionless and heart rate, breathing, and brain-wave activity are slow and even. Distinguished from *rapid-eye-movement (REM) sleep.* (p. 108)

nonsocial activity Unoccupied, onlooker behavior and solitary play. Distinguished from *parallel, associative,* and *cooperative play.* (p. 261)

normal distribution The bell-shaped distribution that results when individual differences are measured in large samples. Most scores cluster around the mean, or average, with progressively fewer falling toward the extremes. (p. 169)

normative approach An approach in which measures of behavior are taken on large numbers of individuals, and age-related averages are computed to represent typical development. (p. 15)

O

obesity A greater-than-20-percent increase over healthy body weight, based on body mass index, a ratio of weight to height associated with body fat. (p. 291)

object permanence The understanding that objects continue to exist when out of sight. (p. 154)

operant conditioning A form of learning in which a spontaneous behavior is followed by a stimulus that changes the probability that the behavior will occur again. (p. 134)

optimal aging Aging in which gains are maximized and losses minimized. (p. 632)

ordinality The mathematical principle specifying order relationships (more than and less than) between quantities. (p. 242)

organization In Piaget's theory, the internal rearrangement and linking together of schemes to create a strongly interconnected cognitive system. In information processing, a memory strategy that involves grouping related items together to improve recall. (p. 152, p. 304)

osteoarthritis A form of arthritis that involves deteriorating cartilage on the ends of bones of frequently used joints, which leads to swelling, stiffness, and loss of flexibility. Also known as "wear-and-tear" arthritis or "degenerative joint disease." Distinguished from *rheumatoid arthritis.* (p. 580)

osteoporosis Severe age-related bone loss, which greatly magnifies the risk of bone fractures. (p. 512)

overextension An early vocabulary error in which young children apply a word too broadly, to a wider collection of objects and events than is appropriate. Distinguished from *underextension.* (p. 177)

overregularization Overextension of regular grammatical rules to words that are exceptions. (p. 249)

P

palliative, or **comfort, care** Care for terminally ill, suffering patients that relieves pain and other symptoms (such as nausea, breathing difficulties, insomnia, and depression), with the goal of protecting the patient's quality of remaining life rather than prolonging life. (p. 652)

parallel play A form of limited social participation in which a child plays near other children with similar materials but does not try to influence their behavior. Distinguished from *nonsocial, associative,* and *cooperative play.* (p. 261)

parental imperative theory A theory that claims that identification with traditional gender roles is maintained during the active parenting years to help ensure the survival of children but that after children reach adulthood, parents are free to express the "other-gender" side of their personalities. (p. 540)

partial fetal alcohol syndrome (p-FAS) A form of fetal alcohol spectrum disorder characterized by facial abnormalities and brain injury, but less severe than fetal alcohol syndrome. Usually affects children whose mothers drank alcohol in smaller quantities during pregnancy. Distinguished from *fetal alcohol syndrome (FAS)* and *alcohol-related neurodevelopmental disorder (ARND).* (p. 89)

passionate love Love based on intense sexual attraction. Distinguished from *companionate love.* (p. 473)

passive euthanasia The practice of withholding or withdrawing life-sustaining treatment, permitting a patient to die naturally. Distinguished from *voluntary active euthanasia.* (p. 654)

peer acceptance Likability, or the extent to which a child is viewed by a group of agemates as a worthy social partner. (p. 341)

peer group A collective of peers who generate unique values and standards for behavior and a social structure of leaders and followers. (p. 339)

peer victimization A destructive form of peer interaction in which certain children become frequent targets of verbal and physical attacks or other forms of abuse. (p. 342)

perceptual narrowing effect Perceptual sensitivity that becomes increasingly attuned with age to information most often encountered. (p. 141)

permissive child-rearing style A child-rearing style that is warm and accepting but uninvolved, low in control (either overindulgent or inattentive), and lenient rather than appropriate in autonomy granting. Distinguished from *authoritative, authoritarian,* and *uninvolved child-rearing styles.* (p. 279)

persistent vegetative state A state in which the cerebral cortex no longer registers electrical activity but the brain stem remains active. The person is unconscious and displays no voluntary movements. (p. 641)

personal fable Adolescents' inflated opinion of their own importance—a feeling that they are special and unique. (p. 386)

person–environment fit A good match between older adults' abilities and the demands of their living environments. Promotes adaptive behavior and psychological well-being. (p. 611)

phenotype An individual's directly observable physical and behavioral characteristics, which are determined by both genetic and environmental factors. Distinguished from *genotype.* (p. 45)

phobia An intense, unmanageable fear that leads to persistent avoidance of the feared situation. (p. 352)

phonics approach An approach to beginning reading instruction that emphasizes coaching children on phonics—the basic rules for translating written symbols into sounds—before exposing them to complex reading material. Distinguished from the *whole-language approach.* (p. 308)

phonological awareness The ability to reflect on and manipulate the sound structure of spoken language, as indicated by sensitivity to changes in sounds within words, to rhyming, and to incorrect pronunciation. A strong predictor of emergent literacy knowledge. (p. 242)

physical aggression A form of aggression that harms others through physical injury to themselves or their property. Distinguished from *verbal aggression* and *relational aggression.* (p. 269)

pituitary gland A gland located at the base of the brain that releases hormones that induce physical growth. (p. 219)

placenta The organ that permits exchange of nutrients and waste products between the bloodstreams of the mother and the embryo, while also preventing the mother's and embryo's blood from mixing directly. (p. 82)

plasticity Openness of development to change in response to influential experiences. (p. 7)

polygenic inheritance A pattern of inheritance in which many genes influence a characteristic. (p. 52)

popular-antisocial children A subgroup of popular children who are admired for their socially adept yet belligerent behavior. Includes "tough" boys who are athletically skilled, aggressive, and poor students, as well as relationally aggressive boys and girls. Distinguished from *popular-prosocial children.* (p. 341)

popular children Children who receive many positive votes on self-report measures of peer acceptance, indicating they are well-liked. Distinguished from *rejected, controversial,* and *neglected children.* (p. 341)

popular-prosocial children A subgroup of popular children who combine academic and social competence. Distinguished from *popular-antisocial children.* (p. 341)

possible selves Future-oriented representations of what one hopes to become and what one is afraid of becoming. The temporal dimension of self-concept. (p. 538)

postconventional level Kohlberg's highest level of moral development, in which individuals define morality in terms of abstract principles and values that apply to all situations and societies. (p. 408)

postformal thought Cognitive development beyond Piaget's formal operational stage. (p. 450)

practical problem solving Problem solving that requires people to size up real-world situations and analyze how best to achieve goals that have a high degree of uncertainty. (p. 524)

pragmatics The practical, social side of language, concerned with how to engage in effective and appropriate communication. (p. 250)

pragmatic thought In Labouvie-Vief's theory, a structural advance in thinking in adulthood, in which logic becomes a tool for solving real-world problems and contradictions are accepted as part of existence. (p. 452)

preconventional level Kohlberg's first level of moral development, in which children accept the rules of authority figures and judge actions by their consequences, viewing behaviors that result in punishment as bad and those that lead to rewards as good. (p. 407)

prefrontal cortex The region of the cerebral cortex, lying in front of areas controlling body movement, that is responsible for thought—in particular, for consciousness, inhibition of impulses, integration of information, and use of memory, reasoning, planning, and problem-solving strategies. (p. 124)

prenatal diagnostic methods Medical procedures that permit detection of developmental problems before birth. (p. 56)

preoperational stage Piaget's second stage of cognitive development, extending from about 2 to 7 years of age, in which children undergo an extraordinary increase in representational, or symbolic, activity, although thought is not yet logical. (p. 226)

presbycusis Age-related hearing impairment, beginning around age 50 with a noticeable decline in sensitivity to high-frequency sounds, which gradually extends to all frequencies. (p. 503)

presbyopia A condition of aging in which, around age 60, the lens of the eye loses its capacity to adjust to objects at varying distances. (p. 502)

preterm infants Infants born several weeks or more before their due date. (p. 102)

primary aging Genetically influenced age-related declines in the functioning of organs and systems that affect all members of our species and occur even in the context of overall good health. Also called *biological aging.* Distinguished from *secondary aging.* (p. 580)

primary sexual characteristics Physical features that involve the reproductive organs (ovaries, uterus, and vagina in females; penis, scrotum, and testes in males). Distinguished from *secondary sexual characteristics.* (p. 365)

private speech Self-directed speech that children use to plan and guide their own behavior. (p. 234)

proactive aggression A type of aggression in which children act to fulfill a need or desire—obtain an object, privilege, space, or social reward, such as adult or peer attention—and unemotionally attack a person to achieve their goal. Also called *instrumental aggression.* Distinguished from *reactive aggression.* (p. 269)

problem-centered coping A strategy for managing emotion that involves appraising the situation as changeable, identifying the difficulty, and deciding what to do about it. Distinguished from *emotion-centered coping.* (p. 336)

programmed cell death An aspect of brain growth whereby, as synapses form, many surrounding neurons die, making space for these connective structures. (p. 122)

Project Head Start A U.S. federal early intervention program that provides children from low-income families with a year or two of preschool, along with nutritional and health services, and that encourages parent involvement in children's learning and development. (p. 245)

propositional thought A type of formal operational reasoning involving the ability to evaluate the logic of propositions, or verbal statements, without referring to real-world circumstances. (p. 383)

prosocial, or **altruistic, behavior** Actions that benefit another person without any expected reward for the self. (p. 260)

prospective memory Recall that involves remembering to engage in planned actions in the future. (p. 593)

proximodistal trend An organized pattern of physical growth that proceeds from the center of the body outward. Distinguished from *cephalocaudal trend.* (p. 121)

psychoanalytic perspective An approach to personality development introduced by Freud that assumes people move through a series of stages in which they confront conflicts between biological drives and social expectations. How these conflicts are resolved determines the person's ability to learn, to get along with others, and to cope with anxiety. (p. 15)

psychological control Parental behaviors that intrude on and manipulate children's verbal expressions, individuality, and attachments to parents. (p. 279)

psychosexual theory Freud's theory, which emphasizes that how parents manage children's sexual and aggressive drives in the first few years is crucial for healthy personality development. (p. 15)

psychosocial theory Erikson's theory, which emphasizes that in each Freudian stage, individuals not only develop a unique personality but also acquire attitudes and skills that make them active, contributing members of their society. Recognizes the lifespan nature of development and the impact of culture. (p. 16)

puberty Biological changes at adolescence that lead to an adult-sized body and sexual maturity. (p. 361)

public policies Laws and government programs designed to improve current conditions. (p. 65)

punishment In operant conditioning, removal of a desirable stimulus or presentation of an unpleasant one to decrease the occurrence of a response. (p. 134)

R

random assignment An unbiased procedure for assigning participants to treatment conditions in an experiment, such as drawing numbers out of a hat or flipping a coin. Increases the chances that participants' characteristics will be equally distributed across treatment groups. (p. 35)

rapid-eye-movement (REM) sleep An "irregular" sleep state in which brain-wave activity is similar to that of the waking state. Distinguished from *non-rapid-eye-movement (NREM) sleep*. (p. 108)

reactive aggression An angry, defensive response to provocation or a blocked goal that is meant to hurt another person. Also called *hostile aggression*. Distinguished from *proactive aggression*. (p. 269)

realistic period Period of vocational development in which older adolescents and young adults narrow their vocational options, engaging in further exploration before focusing on a general vocational category and, slightly later, settling on a single occupation. Distinguished from *fantasy period* and *tentative period*. (p. 456)

recall A type of memory that involves remembering something that is not present. Distinguished from *recognition*. (p. 164)

recasts Adult responses that restructure children's grammatically inaccurate speech into correct form. (p. 251)

recognition A type of memory that involves noticing whether a stimulus is identical or similar to one previously experienced. Distinguished from *recall*. (p. 164)

recovery Following habituation, an increase in responsiveness to a new stimulus. (p. 134)

referential style of language learning A style of early language learning in which toddlers use language mainly to name things, producing many words that refer to objects. Distinguished from *expressive style of language learning*. (p. 178)

reflex An inborn, automatic response to a particular form of stimulation. (p. 106)

rehearsal A memory strategy that involves repeating information to oneself to improve recall. (p. 304)

reinforcer In operant conditioning, a stimulus that increases the occurrence of a response. (p. 134)

rejected-aggressive children A subgroup of rejected children who show high rates of conflict, physical and relational aggression, and hyperactive, inattentive, and impulsive behavior. Distinguished from *rejected-withdrawn children*. (p. 341)

rejected children Children who receive many negative votes on self-report measures of peer acceptance, indicating they are actively disliked. Distinguished from *popular, controversial,* and *neglected children*. (p. 341)

rejected-withdrawn children A subgroup of rejected children who are passive and socially awkward. Distinguished from *rejected-aggressive children*. (p. 341)

relational aggression A form of aggression that damages another's peer relationships through social exclusion, malicious gossip, or friendship manipulation. Distinguished from *physical aggression* and *verbal aggression*. (p. 269)

relativistic thinking In Perry's theory, the cognitive approach typical of older college students, who view all knowledge as embedded in a framework of thought and, therefore, give up the possibility of absolute truth in favor of multiple truths, each relative to its context. Distinguished from *dualistic thinking*. (p. 451)

reminiscence The process of telling stories about people and events from the past and reporting associated thoughts and feelings. (p. 606)

reminiscence bump Older adults' heightened autobiographical memory for events that occurred between ages 10 and 30. (p. 592)

remote memory Very long-term recall. (p. 592)

resilience The ability to adapt effectively in the face of threats to development. (p. 10)

resistant attachment The attachment pattern characterizing infants who remain close to the parent and fail to explore before separation, are usually distressed when the parent leaves, and combine clinginess with angry, resistive behavior when the parent returns. Distinguished from *secure, avoidant,* and *disorganized/disoriented attachment*. (p. 198)

reticular formation A structure in the brain stem that maintains alertness and consciousness. (p. 218)

reversibility The ability to think through a series of steps in a problem and then mentally reverse direction, returning to the starting point. Distinguished from *irreversibility*. (p. 299)

rheumatoid arthritis A form of arthritis in which an autoimmune response leads to inflammation of connective tissue, particularly the membranes that line the joints, resulting in overall stiffness, inflammation, and aching. Leads to deformed joints and often serious loss of mobility. Distinguished from *osteoarthritis*. (p. 580)

Rh factor incompatibility A condition that arises when the Rh protein is present in the fetus's blood but not in the mother's, causing the mother to build up antibodies. If these enter the fetus's system, they destroy red blood cells, reducing the oxygen supply to organs and tissues. Mental retardation, miscarriage, heart damage, and infant death can occur. (p. 93)

rough-and-tumble play A form of peer interaction involving friendly chasing and play-fighting that emerges in the preschool years and peaks in middle childhood. In our evolutionary past, it may have been important for developing fighting skill. (p. 297)

S

sandwich generation A term used to describe middle-aged adults who must care for multiple generations above and below them at the same time. (p. 549)

scaffolding Adjusting the support offered during a teaching session to fit the learner's current level of performance. Direct instruction is offered when a task is new; less help is provided as competence increases, thereby keeping the task within the zone of proximal development. (p. 234)

scale errors Toddlers' attempts to do things that their body size makes impossible, possibly indicating lack of an accurate understanding of their own body dimensions. (p. 207)

scheme In Piaget's theory, a specific psychological structure, or organized way of making sense of experience, that changes with age. (p. 152)

scripts General descriptions of what occurs and when it occurs in a particular situation, used to organize and interpret everyday experiences. (p. 238)

secondary aging Age-related declines due to hereditary defects and environmental influences, such as poor diet, lack of exercise, disease, substance abuse, environmental pollution, and psychological stress. Distinguished from *primary aging*. (p. 580)

secondary friends People who are not intimates but with whom an individual spends time occasionally, such as a group that meets for lunch, bridge, or museum tours. (p. 625)

secondary sexual characteristics Physical features visible on the outside of the body that serve as signs of sexual maturity but do not involve the reproductive organs (for example, breast development in females, appearance of underarm and pubic hair in both sexes). Distinguished from *primary sexual characteristics*. (p. 365)

secular trend A change from one generation to the next in an aspect of development, such as body size or pubertal timing. (p. 367)

secure attachment The attachment pattern characterizing infants who use the parent as a secure base from which to explore, may be distressed by parental separation, but actively seek contact and are easily comforted by the parent when she returns. Distinguished from *avoidant, resistant,* and *disorganized/disoriented attachment*. (p. 197)

secure base The familiar caregiver as a point from which the baby explores, venturing into the environment and then returning for emotional support. (p. 187)

selective optimization with compensation A set of strategies used by older adults who sustain high levels of functioning. Narrowing their goals, they *select* personally valued activities to *optimize* returns from their diminishing energy and also find new ways to *compensate* for losses. (p. 590)

self-care children Children who are without adult supervision for some period of time after school. (p. 351)

self-concept The set of attributes, abilities, attitudes, and values that an individual believes defines who he or she is. (p. 256)

self-conscious emotions Emotions involving injury to or enhancement of the sense of self, including guilt, shame, embarrassment, envy, and pride. (p. 188)

self-esteem An aspect of self-concept that involves judgments about one's own worth and the feelings associated with those judgments. (p. 257)

self-recognition Identification of the self as a physically unique being. (p. 207)

sensitive caregiving Caregiving that involves responding promptly, consistently, and appropriately to infants and holding them tenderly and carefully. (p. 199)

sensitive period A time that is optimal for certain capacities to emerge and in which the individual is especially responsive to environmental influences. (p. 22)

sensorimotor stage Piaget's first stage, spanning the first two years of life, during which infants and toddlers "think" with their eyes, ears, hands, and other sensorimotor equipment. (p. 152)

sensory register The part of the information-processing system in which sights and sounds are represented directly and stored briefly. (p. 161)

separation anxiety An infant's distressed reaction to the departure of the familiar caregiver. (p. 196)

seriation The ability to order items along a quantitative dimension, such as length or weight. (p. 300)

sequential designs Developmental designs in which investigators conduct several similar cross-sectional or longitudinal studies (called *sequences*) at varying times, sometimes combining longitudinal and cross-sectional strategies. (p. 38)

sex chromosomes The twenty-third pair of chromosomes, which determines the sex of the individual. In females, it is called *XX*; in males, *XY*. (p. 47)

short-term memory store The part of the mind in which attended-to-information is retained briefly so that we can actively "work" on it to achieve our goals. (p. 161)

skipped-generation family A family structure in which children live with grandparents but apart from parents. (p. 548)

sleep apnea A condition in which breathing ceases for 10 seconds or longer during sleep, resulting in many brief awakenings. (p. 571)

slow-to-warm-up child A child whose temperament is characterized by inactivity; mild, low-key reactions to environmental stimuli; negative mood; and slow adjustment to new experiences. Distinguished from *easy child* and *difficult child*. (p. 190)

small-for-date infants Infants whose birth weight is below their expected weight considering length of the pregnancy. Some are full-term; others are preterm infants who are especially underweight. (p. 102)

social clock Age-graded expectations for major life events, such as beginning a first job, getting married, birth of the first child, buying a home, and retiring. (p. 471)

social comparisons Judgments of one's own appearance, abilities, and behavior in relation to those of others. (p. 330)

social-constructivist classroom A classroom grounded in Vygotsky's sociocultural theory, in which children participate in a wide range of challenging activities with teachers and peers, with whom they jointly construct understandings. Distinguished from *traditional* and *constructivist classrooms*. (p. 319)

social conventions Customs determined solely by consensus within a society, such as table manners and politeness rituals. Distinguished from *moral imperatives* and *matters of personal choice*. (p. 269)

social convoy A model of age-related changes in social networks, which views the individual as moving through life within a cluster of relationships, with close ties in the inner circle and less close ties on the outside. With age, people change places in the convoy, new ties are added, and some are lost entirely. (p. 620)

social learning theory An approach that emphasizes the role of modeling, otherwise known as imitation or observational learning, in the development of behavior. (p. 18)

social referencing Actively seeking emotional information from a trusted person in an uncertain situation. (p. 188)

social smile The infant's broad grin, evoked by the parent's communication, that first appears between 6 and 10 weeks of age. (p. 185)

sociocultural theory Vygotsky's theory, in which children acquire the ways of thinking and behaving that make up their community's culture through social interaction—in particular, cooperative dialogues with more knowledgeable members of society. (p. 23)

sociodramatic play The make-believe with others that is under way by the end of the second year and increases rapidly in complexity during early childhood. (p. 227)

socioeconomic status (SES) A measure of an individual's or a family's social position and economic well-being that combines three related, but not completely overlapping, variables: years of education, the prestige of one's job and the skill it requires, and income. (p. 61)

socioemotional selectivity theory A social theory of aging that states that social interaction in late adulthood extends lifelong selection processes. Physical and psychological aspects of aging lead to an increased emphasis on the emotion-regulating function of social interaction, leading older adults to prefer familiar social partners with whom they have developed pleasurable relationships. Distinguished from *disengagement theory, activity theory,* and *continuity theory*. (p. 615)

spermarche First ejaculation of seminal fluid. (p. 366)

stage A qualitative change in thinking, feeling, and behaving that characterizes a specific period of development. (p. 6)

standardization The practice of giving a newly constructed test to a large, representative sample and using the results as the standard for interpreting individual scores. (p. 169)

states of arousal Different degrees of sleep and wakefulness. (p. 108)

statistical learning capacity The capacity to analyze the speech stream for regularly occurring sound sequences, through which infants acquire a stock of speech structures for which they will later learn meanings. (p. 142)

stereotype threat The fear of being judged on the basis of a negative stereotype, which can trigger anxiety that interferes with performance. (p. 314)

stranger anxiety The infant's expression of fear in response to unfamiliar adults, which appears in many babies in the second half of the first year. (p. 186)

Strange Situation A laboratory procedure used to assess the quality of attachment between 1 and 2 years of age by observing the baby's response to eight short episodes involving brief separations from and reunions with the caregiver in an unfamiliar playroom. (p. 197)

structured interview An interview method in which each participant is asked the same questions in the same way. Distinguished from *clinical interview*. (p. 30)

structured observation A research method in which the investigator sets up a laboratory situation that evokes the behavior of interest so that every participant has an equal opportunity to display the response. Distinguished from *naturalistic observation*. (p. 29)

subculture A group of people with beliefs and customs that differ from those of the larger culture. (p. 65)

sudden infant death syndrome (SIDS) The unexpected death, usually during the night, of an infant under 1 year of age that remains unexplained after thorough investigation. (p. 110)

sympathy Feelings of concern or sorrow for another's plight. (p. 260)

synapses The gaps between neurons, across which chemical messages are sent. (p. 121)

synaptic pruning Loss of synapses by seldom-stimulated neurons, a process that returns them to an uncommitted state so they can support future development. (p. 122)

T

talent Outstanding performance in a specific field. (p. 323)

telegraphic speech Toddlers' two-word utterances that, like a telegram, focus on high-content words while omitting smaller, less important words. (p. 177)

telomeres A special type of DNA located at the ends of chromosomes—serving as a "cap" to protect the ends from destruction—that shortens with each cell duplication. Eventually, so little remains that the cells no longer duplicate at all. (p. 432)

temperament Early-appearing, stable individual differences in reactivity (quickness and intensity of emotional arousal, attention, and motor activity) and self-regulation (strategies that modify that reactivity). (p. 190)

tentative period Period of vocational development in which adolescents begin to evaluate vocational options in terms of their interests, abilities, and values. Distinguished from *fantasy period* and *realistic period*. (p. 456)

teratogen Any environmental agent that causes damage during the prenatal period. (p. 85)

terminal decline Acceleration in deterioration of cognitive functioning prior to death. (p. 596)

thanatology An interdisciplinary field devoted to the study of death and dying. (p. 640)

theory An orderly, integrated set of statements that describes, explains, and predicts behavior. (p. 5)

theory of multiple intelligences Gardner's theory, which identifies eight independent intelligences, defined in terms of distinct sets of processing operations that permit individuals to engage in a wide range of culturally valued activities: linguistic, logico-mathematical, musical, spatial, bodily-kinesthetic, naturalist, interpersonal, and intrapersonal. (p. 311)

Third Age A new phase of late adulthood extending from ages 65 to 79 or longer, resulting from added years of longevity plus good health and financial stability, in which older adults pursue personally enriching interests and goals. (p. 607)

thyroid-stimulating hormone (TSH) A pituitary hormone that stimulates the thyroid gland to release thyroxine, which is necessary for brain development and for growth hormone to have its full impact on body size. (p. 219)

time out A form of mild punishment that involves removing children from the immediate setting until they are ready to act appropriately. (p. 266)

traditional classroom A classroom in which the teacher is the sole authority for knowledge, rules, and decision making and students are relatively passive learners whose progress is evaluated in relation to how well they keep pace with a uniform set of standards for their grade. Distinguished from *constructivist* and *social-constructivist classrooms*. (p. 319)

traditional marriage A form of marriage involving clear division of husband's and wife's roles, in which the man is the head of household and economic provider, and the woman devotes herself to caring for her husband and children and creating a nurturant, comfortable home. Distinguished from *egalitarian marriage*. (p. 480)

transitive inference The ability to seriate, or order items along a quantitative dimension, mentally. (p. 300)

triarchic theory of successful intelligence Sternberg's theory, in which intelligent behavior involves balancing three broad, interacting intelligences—analytical intelligence, creative intelligence, and practical intelligence—to achieve success in life according to one's personal goals and the requirements of one's cultural community. (p. 310)

triangular theory of love Sternberg's view of love as including three components—intimacy, passion, and commitment—that shift in emphasis as romantic relationships develop. (p. 473)

trimesters Three equal time periods, each lasting three months, into which prenatal development is sometimes divided. (p. 83)

Type A behavior pattern A behavior pattern characterized by extreme competitiveness, ambition, impatience, hostility, angry outbursts, and a sense of time pressure. (p. 513)

U

umbilical cord The long cord connecting the prenatal organism to the placenta that delivers nutrients and removes waste products. (p. 82)

unconditioned response (UCR) In classical conditioning, a reflexive response that is produced by an unconditioned stimulus (UCS). Distinguished from *conditioned response*. (p. 133)

unconditioned stimulus (UCS) In classical conditioning, a stimulus that leads to a reflexive response. Distinguished from *conditioned stimulus*. (p. 133)

underextension An early vocabulary error in which young children apply a word too narrowly, to a smaller number of objects and events than is appropriate. Distinguished from *overextension*. (p. 177)

uninhibited, or sociable, child A child whose temperament is such that he or she displays positive emotion to and approaches novel stimuli. Distinguished from *inhibited*, or *shy, child*. (p. 191)

uninvolved child-rearing style A child-rearing style that combines low acceptance and involvement with little control and general indifference to issues of autonomy. Distinguished from *authoritative, authoritarian*, and *permissive child-rearing styles*. (p. 280)

V

verbal aggression A type of aggression that harms others through threats of physical aggression, name-calling, or hostile teasing. Distinguished from *physical aggression* and *relational aggression*. (p. 269)

vernix A white, cheeselike substance that covers the fetus, preventing the skin from chapping due to constant exposure to amniotic fluid. (p. 83)

video deficit effect In toddlers, poorer performance on tasks after watching a video than after seeing a live demonstration. (p. 159)

violation-of-expectation method A method in which researchers show babies an expected event (one that follows physical laws) and an unexpected event (a variation of the first event that violates physical laws). Heightened attention to the unexpected event suggests that the infant is "surprised" by a deviation from physical reality and, therefore, is aware of that aspect of the physical world. (p. 155)

visual acuity Fineness of visual discrimination. (p. 113)

voluntary active euthanasia The practice of acting directly, at a patient's request, to end suffering before a natural end to life. Distinguished from *passive euthanasia*. (p. 656)

W

whole-language approach An approach to beginning reading instruction that exposes children to text in its complete form, using reading materials that are whole and meaningful, to promote appreciation of the communicative function of written language. Distinguished from *phonics approach*. (p. 308)

wisdom A capacity made up of multiple cognitive and personality traits, combining breadth and depth of practical knowledge; ability to reflect on and apply that knowledge in ways that make life more bearable and worthwhile; emotional maturity, including the ability to listen, evaluate, and give advice; and altruistic creativity, which involves contributing to humanity and enriching others' lives. (p. 595)

working memory The number of items that can be briefly held in mind while also engaging in some effort to monitor of manipulate those items—a "mental workspace" that we use to accomplish many activities in daily life. A contemporary view of the short-term memory store. (p. 161)

X

X-linked inheritance A pattern of inheritance in which a recessive gene is carried on the X chromosome, so that males are more likely than females to be affected. (p. 50)

Z

zone of proximal development In Vygotsky's theory, a range of tasks too difficult for a child to do alone but possible with the help of more-skilled partners. (p. 167)

zygote The newly fertilized cell formed by the union of sperm and ovum at conception. (p. 46)

References

A

Aalsma, M., Lapsley, D. K., & Flannery, D. J. (2006). Personal fables, narcissism, and adolescent adjustment. *Psychology in the Schools, 43,* 481–491.

Aarnoudse-Moens, C. S., Weisglas-Kuperus, N., & van Goudoever, J. B. (2009). Meta-analysis of neurobehavioral outcomes in very preterm and/or very low birth weight children. *Pediatrics, 124,* 717–728.

AARP (American Association of Retired Persons). (2002). *The Grandparent Study 2002 report.* Washington, DC: Author.

AARP (American Association of Retired Persons). (2006). *The state of 50+ America 2006.* Washington, DC: AARP Public Policy Institute.

Abakoumkin, G., Stroebe, W., & Stroebe, M. (2010). Does relationship quality moderate the impact of marital bereavement on depressive symptoms? *Journal of Social and Clinical Psychology, 29,* 510–526.

Abbey, A., & Jacques-Tiura, A. J. (2011). Sexual assault perpetrators' tactics: Associations with their personal characteristics and aspects of the incident. *Journal of Interpersonal Violence, 26,* 2866–2889.

Abbey, A., & McAuslan, P. (2004). A longitudinal examination of male college students' perpetration of sexual assault. *Journal of Consulting and Clinical Psychology, 72,* 747–756.

ABC News. (2004). *The American Sex Survey: A peek beneath the sheets.* Retrieved from abcnews.go.com/images/Politics/959a1AmericanSexSurvey.pdf

Abela, J. R. Z., Hankin, B. L., Haigh, E. A. P., Adams, P., Vinokuroff, T., & Trayhern, L. (2005). Interpersonal vulnerability to depression in high-risk children: The role of insecure attachment and reassurance seeking. *Journal of Clinical Child and Adolescent Psychology, 34,* 182–192.

Abele, A. E., & Spurk, D. (2011). The dual impact of gender and the influence of timing of parenthood on men's and women's career development: Longitudinal findings. *International Journal of Behavioral Development, 35,* 225–232.

Abelson, H., Ledeen, K., & Lewis, H. (2008). *Blown to bits: Your life, liberty and happiness after the digital explosion.* New York: Addison-Wesley.

Aber, J. L., Jones, S. M., & Raver, C. C. (2007). Poverty and child development: New perspectives on a defining issue. In J. L. Aber, S. J. Bishop-Josef, S. M. Jones, K. T. McLearn, & D. Phillips (Eds.), *Child development and social policy: Knowledge for action* (pp. 149–166). Washington, DC: American Psychological Association.

Aboud, F. E. (2008). A social-cognitive developmental theory of prejudice. In S. M. Quintana & C. McKown (Eds.), *Handbook of race, racism, and the developing child* (pp. 55–71). Hoboken, NJ: Wiley.

Aboud, F. E., & Doyle, A. (1996). Parental and peer influences on children's racial attitudes. *International Journal of Intercultural Relations, 20,* 371–383.

Abra, J. (1989). Changes in creativity with age: Data, explanations, and further predictions. *International Journal of Aging and Human Development, 28,* 105–126.

Abrams, K. Y., Rifkin, A., & Hesse, E. (2006). Examining the role of parental frightened/frightening subtypes in predicting disorganized attachment within a brief observational procedure. *Development and Psychopathology, 18,* 345–361.

Acevedo, E. O. (2012). Exercise psychology: Understanding the mental health benefits of physical activity and the public health challenges of inactivity. In E. O. Acevedo (Ed.), *Oxford handbook of exercise psychology* (pp. 3–8). New York: Oxford University Press.

Achenbach, T. M., Phares, V., Howell, C. T., Rauh, V. A., & Nurcombe, B. (1990). Seven-year outcome of the Vermont program for low-birthweight infants. *Child Development, 61,* 1672–1681.

Acierno R., Hernandez, M. A., Amstadter, A. B., Resnick, H. S., Steve, K., Muzzy, W., et al. (2010). Prevalence and correlates of emotional, physical, sexual, and financial abuse and potential neglect in the United States: The national elder mistreatment study. *American Journal of Public Health, 100,* 292–297.

Acker, M. M., & Davis, M. H. (1992). Intimacy, passion, and commitment in adult romantic relationships: A test of the triangular love theory. *Journal of Social and Personal Relationships, 9,* 21–50.

Acker, M. M., & O'Leary, S. G. (1996). Inconsistency of mothers' feedback and toddlers' misbehavior and negative affect. *Journal of Abnormal Child Psychology, 24,* 703–714.

Ackerman, S., Zuroff, D. C., & Moskowitz, D. S. (2000). Generativity in midlife and young adults: Links to agency, communion, and subjective well-being. *International Journal of Aging and Human Development, 50,* 17–41.

ACT. (2010). *2010 retention/completion summary tables.* Retrieved from www.act.org/research/policymakers/pdf/10retain_trends.pdf

Adachi-Mejia, A. M., Longacre, M. R., Gibson, J. J., Beach, M. L., Titus-Ernstoff, L. T., & Dalton, M. A. (2007). Children with a TV in their bedroom at higher risk for being overweight. *International Journal of Obesity, 31,* 644–651.

Adam, E. K., Snell, E. K., & Pendry, P. (2007). Sleep timing and quantity in ecological and family context: A nationally representative time-diary study. *Journal of Family Psychology, 21,* 4–19.

Adams, G. A., Rau, B. L. (2011). Putting off tomorrow to do what you want today: Planning for retirement. *American Psychologist, 66,* 180–192.

Adams, K. B., Sanders, S., & Auth, E. A. (2004). Loneliness and depression in independent living retirement communities: Risk and resilience factors. *Aging and Mental Health, 8,* 475–485.

Adams, R. G., & Laursen, B. (2001). The organization and dynamics of adolescent conflict with parents and friends. *Journal of Marriage and the Family, 63,* 97–110.

Adamson, D. (2005). Regulation of assisted reproductive technologies in the United States. *Family Law Quarterly, 39,* 727–744.

Addington-Hall, J. (2000). Do home deaths increase distress in bereavement? *Palliative Medicine, 14,* 161–162.

Adhikari, B., Kahende, J., Malarcher, A., Pechacek, T., & Tong, V. (2009). Smoking-attributable mortality, years of potential life lost, and productivity losses. *Oncology Times, 31,* 40–43.

Adolph, K. E. (2002). Learning to keep balance. In R. V. Kail (Ed.), *Advances in child development and behavior* (Vol. 30, pp. 1–40). Boston: Academic Press.

Adolph, K. E. (2008). Learning to move. *Current Directions in Psychological Science, 17,* 213–218.

Adolph, K. E., & Berger, S. E. (2006). Motor development. In D. Kuhn & R. Siegler (Eds.), *Handbook of child psychology: Vol. 2. Cognition, perception, and language* (6th ed., pp. 161–213). Hoboken, NJ: Wiley.

Adolph, K. E., & Eppler, M. A. (1998). Development of visually guided locomotion. *Ecological Psychology, 10,* 303–321.

Adolph, K. E., & Eppler, M. A. (1999). Obstacles to understanding: An ecological approach to infant problem solving. In E. Winograd, R. Fivush, & W. Hirst (Eds.), *Ecological approaches to cognition* (pp. 31–58). Mahwah, NJ: Erlbaum.

Adolph, K. E., & Joh, A. S. (2009). Multiple learning mechanisms in the development of action. In A. Woodward & A. Needham (Eds.), *Learning and the infant mind* (pp. 172–207). New York: Oxford University Press.

Adolph, K. E., Karasik, L. B., & Tamis-LeMonda, C. S. (2010). Motor skill. In M. H. Bornstein (Ed.), *Handbook of cultural developmental science* (pp. 61–88). New York: Psychology Press.

Adolph, K. E., Tamis-LeMonda, C. S., Ishak, S., Karasik, L. B., & Lobo, S. A. (2008). Locomotor experience and use of social information are posture specific. *Developmental Psychology, 44,* 1705–1714.

Adolph, K. E. A., Vereijken, B., & Shrout, P. E. (2003). What changes in infant walking and why. *Child Development, 74,* 475–497.

Afifi, T. O., Brownridge, D. A., Cox, B. J., & Sareen J. (2006). Physical punishment, childhood abuse and psychiatric disorders. *Child Abuse and Neglect, 30,* 1093–1103.

Afterschool Alliance. (2009). *America after 3 PM.* Retrieved from www.kidsdeservebetter.org/AA3PM.cfm

Aggarwal, R., Sentz, J., & Miller, M. A. (2007). Role of zinc administration in prevention of childhood diarrhea and respiratory illnesses: A meta-analysis. *Pediatrics, 119,* 1120–1130.

Agronick, G., Stueve, A., Vargo, S., & O'Donnell, L. (2007). New York City young adults' psychological reactions to 9/11: Findings from the Reach for Health longitudinal study. *American Journal of Community Psychology, 39,* 79–90.

Agüero-Torres, H., von Strauss, E., Viitanen, M., Winblad, B., & Fratiglioni, L. (2001). Institutionalization in the elderly: The role of chronic diseases and dementia. Cross-sectional and longitudinal data from a population-based study. *Journal of Clinical Epidemiology, 54,* 795–801.

Aguiar, A., & Baillargeon, R. (2002). Developments in young infants' reasoning about occluded objects. *Cognitive Psychology, 45,* 267–336.

Ahlskog, J. E., Geda, Y. E., Graff-Radford, N. R., & Petersen, R. C. (2011). Physical exercise as a preventive or disease-modifying treatment of dementia and brain aging. *Mayo Clinics Proceedings, 86,* 876–884.

Ahrens, C. J. C., & Ryff, C. D. (2006). Multiple roles and well-being: Sociodemographic and psychological moderators. *Sex Roles, 55,* 801–815.

Ahuja, J. (2005). *Women's entrepreneurship in the United States.* Kansas City, MO: Kauffman Center for Entrepreneurial Leadership, Clearinghouse on Entrepreneurship Education. Retrieved from www.celcee.edu

Ai, A. L., Wink, P., & Ardelt, M. (2010). Spirituality and aging: A journey for meaning through deep interconnection in humanity. In J. C. Cavanaugh & C. K. Cavanaugh (Eds.), *Aging in America: Vol. 3. Societal issues* (pp. 222–246). Santa Barbara, CA: Praeger.

Aikens, J. W., Bierman, K. L., & Parker, J. G. (2005). Navigating the transition to junior high school: The influence of pre-transition friendship and self-system characteristics. *Social Development, 14,* 42–60.

Aikens, J. W., Howes, C., & Hamilton, C. (2009). Attachment stability and the emergence of unresolved representations in adolescence. *Attachment & Human Development, 11,* 491–512.

Ainsworth, M. D. S., Blehar, M. C., Waters, E., & Wall, S. (1978). *Patterns of attachment.* Hillsdale, NJ: Erlbaum.

Aisen, P. S., Schneider, L. S., Sano, M., Diaz-Arrastia, R., van Dyck, C. H., & Weiner, M. F. (2008). High-dose B vitamin supplementation and cognitive decline in Alzheimer disease: A randomized controlled trial. *Journal of the American Medical Association, 15,* 1774–1783.

Ajrouch, K. (2007). Health disparities and Arab-American elders: Does intergenerational support buffer the inequality–health link? *Journal of Social Issues, 63,* 745–758.

Akers, A. Y., Gold, M. A., Bost, J. E., Adimore, A. A., Orr, D. P., & Fortenberry, J. D. (2011). Variation in sexual behaviors in a cohort of adolescent females: The role of personal, perceived peer, and perceived family attitudes. *Journal of Adolescent Health, 48,* 87–93.

Akhtar, N., & Tomasello, M. (2000). The social nature of words and word learning. In R. Golinkoff & K. Hirsh-Pasek (Eds.), *Becoming a word learner: A debate on lexical acquisition.* Oxford, UK: Oxford University Press.

Akimoto, S. A., & Sanbonmatsu, D. M. (1999). Differences in self-effacing behavior between European and Japanese Americans: Effect on competence evaluations. *Journal of Cross-Cultural Psychology, 30,* 159–177.

Akinbami, L. J., Moorman, J. E., Garbe, P. L., & Sondik, E. J. (2009). Status of childhood asthma in the United States, 1980–2007. *Pediatrics, 123,* S123–S145.

Aksan, N., & Kochanska, G. (2004). Heterogeneity of joy in infancy. *Infancy, 6,* 79–94.

Akshoomoff, N. A., Feroleto, C. C., Doyle, R. E., & Stiles, J. (2002). The impact of early unilateral brain injury on perceptual organization and visual memory. *Neuropsychologia, 40,* 539–561.

Albers, C. A., & Grieve, A. J. (2007). Test review: Bayley, N. (2006). Bayley Scales of Infant and Toddler Development–Third Edition. San Antonio, TX: Harcourt Assessment. *Journal of Psychoeducational Assessment, 25,* 180–190.

Alberts, A., Elkind, D., & Ginsberg, S. (2007). The personal fable and risk-taking in early adolescence. *Journal of Youth and Adolescence, 36,* 71–76.

Aldridge, M. A., Stillman, R. D., & Bower, T. G. R. (2001). Newborn categorization of vowel-like sounds. *Developmental Science, 4,* 220–232.

Aldwin, C. M., Spiro, A., III, Levenson, M. R., & Cupertino, A. P. (2001). Longitudinal findings from The Normative Aging Study: III. Personality, individual health trajectories, and mortality. *Psychology and Aging, 16,* 450–465.

Aldwin, C. M., Spiro, A., III, & Park, C. L. (2006). Health, behavior, and optimal aging: A life span developmental perspective. In J. E. Birren & K. W. Schaie (Eds.), *Handbook of the psychology of aging* (6th ed., pp. 85–104). Burlington, MA: Elsevier Academic Press.

Aldwin, C. M., & Yancura, L. (2011). Stress, coping, and adult development. In R. J. Contrada & A. Baum (Eds.), *Handbook of stress science: Biology, psychology, and health* (pp. 263–274). New York: Springer.

Aldwin, C. M., Yancura, L. A., & Boeninger, D. K. (2010). Coping across the life span. In M. E. Lamb, A. M. Freund, & R. M. Lerner (Eds.), *Handbook of life-span development. Vol. 2: Social and emotional development* (pp. 298–340). Hoboken, NJ: Wiley.

Alessandri, S. M., Sullivan, M. W., & Lewis, M. (1990). Violation of expectancy and frustration in early infancy. *Developmental Psychology, 26,* 738–744.

Alexander, J. M., Fabricius, W. V., Fleming, V. M., Zwahr, M., & Brown, S. A. (2003). The development of metacognitive causal explanations. *Learning and Individual Differences, 13,* 227–238.

Ali, L., & Scelfo, J. (2002, December 9). Choosing virginity. *Newsweek,* pp. 60–65.

Alink, L. R. A., Mesman, J., van Zeijl, J., Stolk, M. N., Juffer, F., & Koot, H. M. (2006). The early childhood aggression curve: Development of physical aggression in 10- to 50-month-old children. *Child Development, 77,* 954–966.

Alkema, G. E., Wilber, K. H., & Enguidanos, S. M. (2007). Community- and facility-based care. In J. A. Blackburn & C. N. Dulmus (Eds.), *Handbook*

of gerontology: Evidence-based approaches to theory, practice, and policy (pp. 455–497). Hoboken, NJ: Wiley.

Allemand, M., Zimprich, D., & Martin, M. (2008). Long-term correlated change in personality traits in old age. *Psychology and Aging, 23,* 545–557.

Allen, J. P., Philliber, S., Herrling, S., & Kuperminc, G. P. (1997). Preventing teen pregnancy and academic failure: Experimental evaluation of a developmentally based approach. *Child Development, 64,* 729–742.

Allen, J. P., Seitz, V., & Apfel, N. H. (2007). The sexually mature teen as a whole person. In J. L. Aber, S. J. Bishop-Josef, S. M. Jones, K. T. McLearn, & D. A. Phillips (Eds.), *New directions in prevention and intervention for teen pregnancy and parenthood* (pp. 185–199). Washington, DC: American Psychological Association.

Allen, M., & Burrell, N. (1996). Comparing the impact of homosexual and heterosexual parents on children: Meta-analysis of existing research. *Journal of Homosexuality, 32,* 19–35.

Allen, P. A., Ruthruff, E., & Lien, M.-C. (2007). Attention. In J. E. Birren (Ed.), *Encyclopedia of gerontology* (2nd ed., pp. 120–129). San Diego: Academic Press.

Allen, S. E. M., & Crago, M. B. (1996). Early passive acquisition in Inukitut. *Journal of Child Language, 23,* 129–156.

Allen, T. D., & Finkelstein, L. M. (2003). Beyond mentoring: Alternative sources and functions of developmental support. *Career Development Quarterly, 51,* 346–355.

Allison, B. N., & Schultz, J. B. (2004). Parent–adolescent conflict in early adolescence. *Adolescence, 39,* 101–119.

Alloway, T. P. (2009). Working memory, but not IQ, predicts subsequent learning in children with learning difficulties. *European Journal of Psychological Assessment, 25,* 92–98.

Almeida, D. M., & Horn, M. C. (2004). Is daily life more stressful during middle adulthood? In O. G. Brim, C. D. Ryff, & R. C. Kessler (Eds.), *How healthy are we? A national study of well-being at midlife* (pp. 425–451). Chicago: University of Chicago Press.

Almeida, D. M., Neupert, S. D., Banks, S. R., & Serido, J. (2005). Do daily stress processes account for socioeconomic health disparities? *Journal of Gerontology, 60B,* 34–39.

Almeida, J., Johnson, R. M., Corliss, H. L., Molnar, B. E., & Azrael, D. (2009). Emotional distress among LGBT youth: The influence of perceived discrimination based on sexual orientation. *Journal of Youth and Adolescence, 38,* 1001–1014.

Al-Namlah, A. S., Fernyhough, C., & Meins, E. (2006). Sociocultural influences on the development of verbal mediation: Private speech and phonological recoding in Saudi Arabian and British samples. *Developmental Psychology, 42,* 117–131.

Alonso-Fernández, P., & De la Fuente, M. (2011). Role of the immune system in aging and longevity. *Current Aging Science, 4,* 78–100.

Alsaker, F. D. (1995). Timing of puberty and reactions to pubertal changes. In M. Rutter (Ed.), *Psychosocial disturbances in young people* (pp. 37–82). New York: Cambridge University Press.

Alterovitz, S. S. R., & Mendelsohn, G. A. (2013). Relationship goals of middle-aged, young-old, and old-old Internet daters: An analysis of online personal ads. *Journal of Aging Studies, 27,* 159–165.

Althaus, J., & Wax, J. (2005). Analgesia and anesthesia in labor. *Obstetrics and Gynecology Clinics of North America, 32,* 231–244.

Alwan, S., & Friedman, J. M. (2009). Safety of selective serotonin reuptake inhibitors in pregnancy. *CNS Drugs, 23,* 493–509.

Alzheimer's Association. (2012a). *Communication: Best ways to interact with a person with dementia.* Chicago: Author.

Alzheimer's Association. (2012b). 2012 Alzheimer's disease facts and figures. *Alzeimer's and Dementia, 8* (Issue 2).

Amato, P. R. (2000). The consequences of divorce for adults and children. *Journal of Marriage and Family, 62,* 1269–1287.

Amato, P. R. (2001). Children of divorce in the 1990s: An update of the Amato and Keith (1991) meta-analysis. *Journal of Family Psychology, 15,* 355–370.

Amato, P. R. (2006). Marital discord, divorce, and children's well-being: Results from a 20-year longitudinal study of two generations. In A. Clarke-Stewart & J. Dunn (Eds.), *Families count: Effects on child and adolescent development* (pp. 179–202). New York: Cambridge University Press.

Amato, P. R. (2010). Research on divorce: Continuing trends and new developments. *Journal of Marriage and Family, 72,* 650–666.

Amato, P. R., & Booth, A. (1995). Change in gender role attitudes and perceived marital quality. *American Sociological Review, 60,* 58–66.

Amato, P. R., & Cheadle, J. (2005). The long reach of divorce: Divorce and child well-being across three generations. *Journal of Marriage and Family, 67,* 191–206.

Amato, P. R., & Dorius, C. (2010). Father, children, and divorce. In M. E. Lamb (Ed.), *The role of the father in child development* (5th ed., pp. 177–200). Hoboken, NJ: Wiley.

Amato, P. R., & Fowler, F. (2002). Parenting practices, child adjustment, and family diversity. *Journal of Marriage and the Family, 64,* 703–716.

Amato, P. R., & Rogers, S. J. (1997). A longitudinal study of marital problems and subsequent divorce. *Journal of Marriage and the Family, 59,* 612–624.

Amato, P. R., & Sobolewski, J. M. (2004). The effects of divorce on fathers and children: Nonresidential fathers and stepfathers. In M. E. Lamb (Ed.), *The role of the father in child development* (4th ed., pp. 341–367). Hoboken, NJ: Wiley.

Amba, J. C., & Martinez, G. M. (2006). Childlessness among older women in the United States: Trends and profiles. *Journal of Marriage and Family, 68,* 1045–1056.

American Academy of Hospice and Palliative Medicine. (2007). Position statement on physician-assisted death. *Journal of Pain and Palliative Care Pharmacotherapy, 21,* 55–57.

American Academy of Orthopaedic Surgeons. (2009). *Position statement: Osteoporosis/bone health in adults as a national health priority.* Retrieved from www.aaos.org/about/papers/position/1113.asp

American Academy of Pediatrics. (2001). Committee on Public Education: Children, adolescents, and television. *Pediatrics, 104,* 341–343.

American Academy of Pediatrics. (2005). Breastfeeding and the use of human milk. *Pediatrics, 115,* 496–506.

American Academy of Pediatrics. (2006). Folic acid for the prevention of neural tube defects. *Pediatrics, 104,* 325–327.

American Academy of Pediatrics. (2012). SIDS and other sleep-related infant deaths: Expansion of recommendations for a safe sleep environment *Pediatrics, 128,* e1341.

American Cancer Society. (2012). *Stay healthy.* Retrieved from www.cancer.org/healthy/index

American College of Sports Medicine. (2011). Quantity and quality of exercise for developing and maintaining cardiorespiratory, musculoskeletal, and neuromotor fitness in apparently healthy adults: Guidance for prescribing exercise. *Medicine and Science in Sports and Exercise, 43,* 1334–1359.

American Heart Association. (2012). Heart disease and stroke statistics—2012 update. *Circulation, 125,* e2–e220.

American Hospice Foundation. (2013). *Talking about hospice: Tips for physicians.* Washington, DC: Author.

American Psychiatric Association. (2000). *DSM-IV-TR: Diagnostic and statistical manual of mental disorders—Text revision* (4th ed.). Washington, DC: Author.

American Psychological Association. (2002). Ethical principles of psychologists and code of conduct. *American Psychologist, 57,* 1060–1073.

Amsel, E., & Brock, S. (1996). The development of evidence evaluation skills. *Cognitive Development, 11,* 523–550.

Amsterlaw, J., & Wellman, H. M. (2006). Theories of mind in transition: A micro-genetic study of the development of false belief understanding. *Journal of Cognition and Development, 7,* 139–172.

An, J. S., & Cooney, T. M. (2006). Psychological well-being in mid to late life: The role of generativity development and parent–child relationships across the lifespan. *International Journal of Behavioral Development, 30,* 410–421.

Anand, S. S., Yusuf, S., Jacobs, R., Davis, A. D., Yi, Q., & Gerstein, H. (2001). Risk factors, atherosclerosis, and cardiovascular disease among Aboriginal people in Canada: The study of health assessment and risk evaluation in Aboriginal peoples (SHARE-AP). *Lancet, 358,* 1147–1153.

Andel, R., Hyer, K., & Slack, A. (2007). Risk factors for nursing home placement in older adults with and without dementia. *Journal of Aging and Health, 19,* 213–228.

Anderman, E. M., Eccles, J. S., Yoon, K. S., Roeser, R., Wigfield, A., & Blumenfeld, P. (2001). Learning to value mathematics and reading: Relations to mastery and performance-oriented instructional practices. *Contemporary Educational Psychology, 26,* 76–95.

Anderson, C. A., Sakamoto, A., Gentile, D. A., Ihori, N., Shibuya, A., Yukawa, S., et al. (2008). Longitudinal effects of violent video games on aggression in Japan and the United States. *Pediatrics, 122,* e1067–e1072.

Anderson, D. M., Huston, A. C., Schmitt, K. L., Linebarger, D. L., & Wright, J. C. (2001). Early childhood television viewing and adolescent behavior. *Monographs of the Society for Research in Child Development, 66*(1, Serial No. 264).

Anderson, E. (2000). Exploring register knowledge: The value of "controlled improvisation." In L. Menn & N. B. Ratner (Eds.), *Methods for studying language production* (pp. 225–248). Mahwah, NJ: Erlbaum.

Anderson, J. L., Morgan, J. L., & White, K. S. (2003). A statistical basis for speech sound discrimination. *Language and Speech, 46,* 155–182.

Anderson, P. B., & Savage, J. S. (2005). Social, legal, and institutional context of heterosexual aggression by college women. *Trauma, Violence, and Abuse, 6,* 130–140.

Anderson, V. A., Catroppa, C., Dudgeon, P., Morse, S. A., Haritou, F., & Rosenfeld, J. V. (2006). Understanding predictors of functional recovery and outcome 30 months following early childhood head injury. *Neuropsychology, 20,* 42–57.

Andreoletti, C., & Lachman, M. E. (2004). Susceptibility and resilience to memory aging stereotypes: Education matters more than age. *Experimental Aging Research, 30,* 129–148.

Andrews, G., & Halford, G. S. (1998). Children's ability to make transitive inferences: The importance of premise integration and structural complexity. *Cognitive Development, 13,* 479–513.

Andrews, G., & Halford, G. S. (2002). A cognitive complexity metric applied to cognitive development. *Cognitive Psychology, 45,* 475–506.

Aneshensel, C. S., Wight, R. G., Miller-Martinez, D., Botticello, A. L., Karlamangla, A. S., & Seeman, T. E. (2007). Urban neighborhoods and depressive symptoms among older adults. *Journal of Gerontology, 62B,* S52–S59.

Anetzberger, G. J. (2005). The reality of elder abuse. *Clinical Gerontologist, 28,* 2–25.

Angel, R. J., Angel, J. L., & Hill, T. D. (2009). Subjective control and health among Mexican-origin elders in Mexico and the United States: Structural considerations in comparative research. *Journal of Gerontology, 64B,* 390–401.

Anisfeld, M., Turkewitz, G., Rose, S. A., Rosenberg, F. R., Shelber, F. J., Couturier-Fagan, D. A., Ger, J. S., & Sommer, I. (2001). No compelling evidence that newborns imitate oral gestures. *Infancy, 2,* 111–122.

Annett, M. (2002). *Handedness and brain asymmetry: The right shift theory.* Hove, UK: Psychology Press.

Anson, J., & Anson, O. (2001). Death rests awhile: Holy day and Sabbath effects of Jewish mortality in Israel. *Social Science and Medicine, 52,* 83–97.

Antonini, F. M., Magnolfi, S. U., Petruzzi, E., Pinzani, P., Malentacchi, F., Petruzzi, I., & Masotti, G. (2008). Physical performance and creative activities of centenarians. *Archives of Gerontology and Geriatrics, 46,* 253–261.

Antonucci, T. C., Ajrouch, K. J., & Birditt, K. (2008). Social relations in the Third Age: Assessing strengths and challenges using the convoy model. In J. B. James & P. Wink (Eds.), *Annual review of gerontology and geriatrics* (Vol. 26, pp. 193–209). New York: Springer.

Antonucci, T. C., & Akiyama, H. (1995). Convoys of social relations: Family and friendships within a life span context. In R. Blieszner & V. H. Bedford (Eds.), *Handbook of aging and the family* (pp. 355–371). Westport, CT: Greenwood Press.

Antonucci, T. C., Akiyama, H., & Merline, A. (2002). Dynamics of social relationships in midlife. In M. E. Lachman (Ed.), *Handbook of midlife development* (pp. 571–598). New York: Wiley.

Antonucci, T. C., Akiyama, H., & Takahashi, K. (2004). Attachment and close relationships across the lifespan. *Attachment and Human Development, 6,* 353–370.

Antonucci, T. C., Birditt, K. S., & Ajrouch, K. (2011). Convoys of social relations: Past, present, and future. In K. L. Fingerman, C. A. Berg, J. Smith, & T. C. Antonucci (Eds.), *Handbook of life-span development* (pp. 161–182). New York: Springer.

Antonucci, T. C., Birditt, K. S., & Akiyama, H. (2009). Convoys of social relations: An interdisciplinary approach. In V. Bengston, M. Silverstein, N. Putney, & D. Gans (Eds.), *Handbook of theories of aging* (pp. 247–260). New York: Springer.

Antonucci, T. C., Blieszner, R., & Denmark, F. L. (2010). Psychological perspectives on older women. In H. Landrine & N. F. Russo (Eds.), *Handbook of diversity in feminist psychology* (pp. 233–257). New York: Springer.

Anzuini, F., Battistella, A., & Izzotti, A. (2011). Physical activity and cancer prevention: A review of current evidence and biological mechanisms. *Journal of Preventive Medicine and Hygiene, 52,* 174–180.

Apfelbaum, E. P., Pauker, K., Ambady, N., Sommers, S. R., & Norton, M. I. (2008). Learning (not) to talk about race: When older children underperform in social categorization. *Developmental Psychology, 44,* 1513–1518.

Apgar, V. (1953). A proposal for a new method of evaluation in the newborn infant. *Current Research in Anesthesia and Analgesia, 32,* 260–267.

Aquilino, W. S. (2006). Family relationships and support systems in emerging adulthood. In J. J. Arnett & J. L. Tanner (Eds.), *Emerging adults in America: Coming of age in the 21st century* (pp. 193–218). Washington, DC: American Psychological Association.

Archer, J. (2002). Sex differences in aggression between heterosexual partners: A meta-analytic review. *Psychological Bulletin, 126,* 651–681.

Archer, T., Fredriksson, A., Schütz, E., & Kostrzewa, R. M. (2011). *Neurotoxicity Research, 20,* 69–83.

Archibald, A. B., Graber, J. A., & Brooks-Gunn, J. (2006). Pubertal processes and physiological growth in adolescence. In G. R. Adams & M. D. Berzonsky (Eds.), *Blackwell handbook of adolescence* (pp. 24–48). Malden, MA: Blackwell.

Arcus, D., & Chambers, P. (2008). Childhood risks associated with adoption. In T. P. Gullotta & G. M Blau (Eds.), *Family influences on childhood behavior and development* (pp. 117–142). New York: Routledge.

Ardelt, M. (1998). Social crisis and individual growth: The long-term effects of the Great Depression. *Journal of Aging Studies, 12,* 291–314.

Ardelt, M. (2003). Effects of religion and purpose in life on elders' subjective well-being and attitudes toward death. *Journal of Religious Gerontology, 14,* 55–77.

Ardelt, M. (2011). Wisdom, age, and well-being. In K. W. Schaie & S. L. Willis (Eds.), *Handbook of the psychology of aging* (7th ed., pp. 279–291). San Diego, CA: Academic Press.

Ardila-Rey, A., & Killen, M. (2001). Middle-class Colombian children's evaluations of personal, moral, and social-conventional interactions in the classroom. *International Journal of Behavioral Development, 25,* 246–255.

Arija, V., Esparó, G., Fernández-Ballart, J., Murphy, M. M., Biarnés, E., & Canals, J. (2006). Nutritional status and performance in test of verbal and non-verbal intelligence in 6 year old children. *Intelligence, 34,* 141–149.

Arking, R. (2006). *Biology of aging: Observations and principles* (3rd ed.). New York: Oxford University Press.

Arlin, P. K. (1989). Problem solving and problem finding in young artists and young scientists. In M. L. Commons, J. D. Sinnott, F. A. Richards, & C. Armon (Eds.), *Adult development: Vol 1. Comparisons and applications of developmental models* (pp. 197–216). New York: Praeger.

Armstrong, K. L., Quinn, R. A., & Dadds, M. R. (1994). The sleep patterns of normal children. *Medical Journal of Australia, 161,* 202–206.

Armstrong, T. D., & Crowther, M. R. (2002). Spirituality among older African Americans. *Journal of Adult Development, 9,* 3–12.

Arnett, J. J. (2000). Emerging adulthood: A theory of development from the late teens through the twenties. *American Psychologist, 55,* 469–480.

Arnett, J. J. (2001). Conceptions of the transition to adulthood: Perspectives from adolescence to midlife. *Journal of Adult Development, 8,* 133–143.

Arnett, J. J. (2003). Conceptions of the transition to adulthood among emerging adults in American ethnic groups. In J. J. Arnett & N. L. Galambos (Eds.), *New directions for child and adolescent development* (No. 100, pp. 63–75). San Francisco: Jossey-Bass.

Arnett, J. J. (2006). Emerging adulthood: Understanding the new way of coming of age. In J. J. Arnett & J. L. Tanner (Eds.), *Emerging adults in America: Coming of age in the 21st century* (pp. 3–19). Washington, DC: American Psychological Association.

Arnett, J. J. (2007a). Emerging adulthood, a 21st century theory: A rejoinder to Hendry and Kloep. *Child Development Perspectives, 1,* 80–82.

Arnett, J. J. (2007b). Emerging adulthood: What is it and what is it good for? *Child Development Perspectives, 1,* 68–73.

Arnett, J. J. (2010). Oh, grow up! Generational grumbling and the new life stage of emerging adulthood—commentary on Trzesniewski & Donnellan (2010). *Perspectives on Psychological Science, 5,* 89–92.

Arnett, J. J. (2011). Emerging adulthood(s): The cultural psychology of a new life stage. In L. A. Jensen (Ed.), *Bridging cultural and developmental psychology: New syntheses in theory, research, and policy* (pp. 255–275). New York: Oxford University Press.

Arnett, J. J. (2012). *New Clark Poll: 18- to 29-year-olds are traditional about roles in sex, marriage and raising children.* Retrieved from http://news.clarku.edu/news/2012/08/07/new-clark-poll-18-to-29-year-olds-are-traditional-about-roles-in-sex-marriage-and-raising-children

Arnon, S., Shapsa, A., Forman, L., Regev, R., Bauer, S., & Litmanovitz, I. (2006). Live music is beneficial to preterm infants in the neonatal intensive care unit. *Birth, 33,* 131–136.

Artman, L., & Cahan, S. (1993). Schooling and the development of transitive inference. *Developmental Psychology, 29,* 753–759.

Artman, L., Cahan, S., & Avni-Babad, D. (2006). Age, schooling, and conditional reasoning. *Cognitive Development, 21,* 131–145.

Asher, S. R., & Rose, A. J. (1997). Promoting children's social-emotional adjustment with peers. In P. Salovey & D. J. Sluyter (Eds.), *Emotional development and emotional intelligence* (pp. 193–195). New York: Basic Books.

Aslin, R. N., Jusczyk, P. W., & Pisoni, D. B. (1998). Speech and auditory processing during infancy: Constraints on and precursors to language. In D. Kuhn & R. S. Siegler (Eds.), *Handbook of child psychology: Vol. 2. Cognition, perception, and language* (5th ed., pp. 147–198). New York: Wiley.

Aslin, R. N., & Newport, E. L. (2009). What statistical learning can and can't tell us about language acquisition. In J. Colombo, P. McCardle, & L. Freund (Eds.), *Infant pathways to language: Methods, models, and research directions* (pp. 15–29). New York: Psychology Press.

Astington, J. W., & Pelletier, J. (2005). Theory of mind, language, and learning in the early years: Developmental origins of school readiness. In B. D. Homer & C. S. Tamis-LeMonda (Eds.), *The development of social cognition and communication* (pp. 205–230). Mahwah, NJ: Erlbaum.

Astington, J. W., Pelletier, J., & Homer, B. (2002). Theory of mind and epistemological development: The relation between children's second-order false belief understanding and their ability to reason about evidence. *New Ideas in Psychology, 20,* 131–144.

Atance, C. M., & Meltzoff, A. N. (2005). My future self: Young children's ability to anticipate and explain future states. *Cognitive Development, 20,* 341–361.

Atchley, R. C. (1989). A continuity theory of normal aging. *Gerontologist, 29,* 183–190.

Atchley, R. C. (1999). *Continuity and adaptation in aging: Creating positive experiences.* Baltimore, MD: Johns Hopkins University Press.

Atchley, R. C. (2003). Why people cope well with retirement. In J. L. Ronch & J. A. Goldfield (Eds.), *Mental wellness in aging: Strengths-based approaches* (pp. 123–138). Baltimore, MD: Health Professions Press.

Atkins, R., Hart, D., & Donnelly, T. M. (2004). Moral identity development and school attachment. In D. Lapsley & D. Narvaez (Eds.), *Moral development, self, and identity* (pp. 65–82). Mahwah, NJ: Erlbaum.

Au, T. K., Sidle, A. L., & Rollins, K. B. (1993). Developing an intuitive understanding of conservation and contamination: Invisible particles as a plausible mechanism. *Developmental Psychology, 29,* 286–299.

Aud, S., Hussar, W., Kena, G., Bianco, K., Frohlich, L., Kemp, J., & Tahan, K. (2011). *The condition of education 2011* (NCES 2011-033). U.S. Department of Education, National Center for Education Statistics. Washington, DC: U.S. Government Printing Office.

Aunola, K., Stattin, H., & Nurmi, J.-E. (2000). Parenting styles and adolescents' achievement strategies. *Journal of Adolescence, 23,* 205–222.

Averhart, C. J., & Bigler, R. S. (1997). Shades of meaning: Skin tone, racial attitudes, and constructive memory in African-American children. *Journal of Experimental Child Psychology, 67,* 368–388.

Aveyard, P., & Raw, M. (2012). Improving smoking cessation approaches at the individual level. *Tobacco Control, 21,* 252–257.

Avis, N. E., Assmann, S. F., Kravitz, H. M., Ganz, P. A., & Ory, M. (2004). Quality of life in diverse groups of midlife women: Assessing the influence of menopause, health status and psychosocial and demographic factors. *Quality of Life Research, 13,* 933–946.

Avis, N. E., & Crawford, S. (2006). Menopause: Recent research findings. In S. K. Whitbourne & S. L. Willis (Eds.), *The baby boomers grow up: Contemporary perspectives on midlife* (pp. 75–109). Mahwah, NJ: Erlbaum.

Avis, N. E., Crawford, S., & Johannes, C. B. (2002). Menopause. In G. M. Wingood & R. J. DiClemente (Eds.), *Handbook of women's sexual and reproductive health* (pp. 367–391). New York: Kluwer.

Avolio, B. J., & Sosik, J. J. (1999). A lifespan framework for assessing the impact of work on white-collar workers. In S. L. Willis & J. D. Reid (Eds.), *Life in the middle* (pp. 249–274). San Diego, CA: Academic Press.

Axelin, A., Salanterä, S., & Lehtonen, L. (2006). 'Facilitated tucking by parents' in pain management of preterm infants—a randomized crossover trial. *Early Human Development, 82,* 241–247.

Axia, G., & Baroni, R. (1985). Linguistic politeness at different age levels. *Child Development, 56,* 918–927.

Ayala, G. X., Rogers, M., Arredondo, E. M., Campbell, N. R., Baquero, B., Duerksen, S. C., & Elder, J. P. (2008). Away-from-home food intake and risk for obesity: Examining the influence of context. *Obesity, 16,* 1002–1008.

B

Bacallao, M. L., & Smokowski, P. R. (2007). The costs of getting ahead: Mexican family system changes after immigration. *Family Relations, 56,* 52–66.

Baenninger, M., & Newcombe, N. (1995). Environmental input to the development of sex-related differences in spatial and mathematical ability. *Learning and Individual Differences, 7,* 363–379.

Bagwell, C. L., & Coie, J. D. (2004). The best friendships of aggressive boys: Relationship quality, conflict management, and rule-breaking behavior. *Journal of Experimental Child Psychology, 88,* 5–24.

Bahrick, H. P. (1984). Semantic memory content in permastore: Fifty years of memory for Spanish learned in school. *Journal of Experimental Psychology: General, 113,* 1–29.

Bahrick, H. P., Bahrick, P. O., & Wittlinger, R. P. (1975). Fifty years of memory for names and faces: A cross-sectional approach. *Journal of Experimental Psychology: General, 104,* 54–75.

Bahrick, L. E. (2010). Intermodal perception and selective attention to intersensory redundancy: Implications for typical social development and autism. In G. Bremner & T. D. Wachs (Eds.), *Wiley-Blackwell handbook of infant development: Vol. 1. Basic research* (2nd ed., pp. 120–166). Malden, MA: Blackwell.

Bahrick, L. E., Gogate, L. J., & Ruiz, I. (2002). Attention and memory for faces and actions in infancy: The salience of actions over faces in dynamic events. *Child Development, 73,* 1629–1643.

Bahrick, L. E., Hernandez-Reif, M., & Flom, R. (2005). The development of infant learning about specific face–voice relations. *Developmental Psychology, 41,* 541–552.

Bahrick, L. E., Hernandez-Reif, M., & Pickens, J. N. (1997). The effect of retrieval cues on visual preferences and memory in infancy: Evidence for a four-phase attention function. *Journal of Experimental Child Psychology, 67,* 1–20.

Bahrick, L. E., Lickliter, R., & Flom, R. (2004). Intersensory redundancy guides the development of selective attention, perception, and cognition in infancy. *Current Directions in Psychological Science, 13,* 99–102.

Bahrick, L. E., Netto, D., & Hernandez-Reif, M. (1998). Intermodal perception of adult and child faces and voices by infants. *Child Development, 69,* 1263–1275.

Bai, D. L., & Bertenthal, B. I. (1992). Locomotor status and the development of spatial search skills. *Child Development, 63,* 215–226.

Bailar-Heath, M., & Valley-Gray, S. (2010). Accident prevention. In P. C. McCabe & S. R. Shaw (Eds.), *Pediatric disorders* (pp. 123–132). Thousand Oaks, CA; Corwin Press.

Bailey, J. M., Bobrow, D., Wolfe, M., & Mikach, S. (1995). Sexual orientation of adult sons of gay fathers. *Developmental Psychology, 31,* 124–129.

Baillargeon, R. (2004). Infants' reasoning about hidden objects: Evidence for event-general and event-specific expectations. *Developmental Science, 7,* 391–424.

Baillargeon, R., & DeVos, J. (1991). Object permanence in young infants: Further evidence. *Child Development, 62,* 1227–1246.

Baillargeon, R., Scott, R. M., & He, Z. (2010). False-belief understanding in infants. *Trends in Cognitive Sciences, 14,* 110–118.

Baillargeon, R. H., Zoccolillo, M., Keenan, K., Côté, S., Pérusse, D., Wu, H.-X., & Boivin, M. (2007). Gender differences in physical aggression: A prospective population-based survey of children before and after 2 years of age. *Developmental Psychology, 43,* 13–26.

Bair, D. (2007). *Calling it quits: Late-life divorce and starting over.* New York: Random House.

Baird, B. M., & Bergeman, C. S. (2011). Life-span developmental behavior genetics. In K. L. Fingerman, C. A. Berg, J. Smith, & T. C. Antonucci (Eds.), *Handbook of life-span development* (pp. 701–744). New York: Springer.

Baker, J. A. (2006). Contributions of teacher–child relationships to positive school adjustment during elementary school. *Journal of School Psychology, 44,* 211–229.

Balasch, J. (2010). Ageing and infertility: An overview. *Gynecological Endocrinology, 26,* 855–860.

Bale, J. F. (2009). Fetal infections and brain development. *Clinical Perinatology, 36,* 639–653.

Balis, T., & Postolache, T. T. (2008). Ethnic differences in adolescent suicide in the United States. *International Journal of Child Health and Human Development, 1,* 282–296.

Ball, H. (2006). Parent–infant bed-sharing behavior: Effects of feeding type and presence of father. *Human Nature, 17,* 301–318.

Ball, K., Berch, D. B., Helmers, K. F., Jobe, J. B., Leveck, M. D., & Marsiske, M. (2002). Effects of cognitive training interventions with older adults: A randomized controlled trial. *Journal of the American Medical Association, 288,* 2271–2281.

Ball, M. M., Perkins, M. M., Hollingsworth, C., Whittington, F. J., & King, S. V. (2009). Pathways to assisted living: The influence of race and class. *Journal of Applied Gerontology, 28,* 81–108.

Balsam, K. F., Beauchaine, T. P., Rothblum, E. D., & Solomon, S. E. (2008). Three-year follow-up of same-sex couples who had civil unions in Vermont, same-sex couples not in civil unions, and heterosexual married couples. *Developmental Psychology, 44,* 102–116.

Balsano, A. B. (2005). Youth civic engagement in the United States: Understanding and addressing the impact of social impediments on positive youth and community development. *Applied Developmental Science, 9,* 188–201.

Baltes, M. M. (1995, February). Dependency in old age: Gains and losses. *Psychological Science, 4*(1), 14–19.

Baltes, M. M. (1996). *The many faces of dependency in old age.* New York: Cambridge University Press.

Baltes, M. M., Wahl, H.-W., & Reichert, M. (1992). Successful aging in long-term care institutions. In K. W. Schaie & M. P. Lawton (Eds.), *Annual review of gerontology and geriatrics* (pp. 311–337). New York: Springer.

Baltes, P. B., & Freund, A. M. (2003). Human strengths as the orchestration of wisdom and selective optimization with compensation (SOC). In L. G. Aspinwall & U. M. Staudinger (Eds.), *A psychology of human strengths: Fundamental questions and future directions for a positive psychology* (pp. 23–25). Washington, DC: American Psychological Association.

Baltes, P. B., Lindenberger, U., & Staudinger, U. M. (2006). Life span theory in developmental psychology. In R. M. Lerner (Ed.), *Handbook of child psychology: Vol. 1. Theoretical models of human development* (6th ed., pp. 569–664). Hoboken, NJ: Wiley.

Baltes, P. B., & Smith, J. (2003). New frontiers in the future of aging: From successful aging of the young old to the dilemmas of the fourth age. *Gerontology, 49,* 123–135.

Baltes, P. B., & Smith, J. (2008). The fascination of wisdom. *Perspectives on Psychological Science, 3,* 56–64.

Baltes, P. B., & Staudinger, U. M. (2000). Wisdom: A metaheuristic (pragmatic) to orchestrate mind and virtue toward excellence. *American Psychologist, 55,* 122–136.

Bancroft, J. (2002). The medicalization of female sexual dysfunction: The need for caution. *Archives of Sexual Behavior, 31,* 451–455.

Bandstra, E. S., Morrow, C. E., Accornero, V. H., Mansoor, E., Xue, L., & Anthony, J. C. (2011). Estimated effects of in utero cocaine exposure on language development through early adolescence. *Neurotoxicology and Teratology, 33,* 25–35.

Bandstra, E. S., Morrow, C. E., Mansoor, E., & Accornero, V. H. (2010). Prenatal drug exposure: Infant and toddler outcomes. *Journal of Addictive Diseases, 29,* 245–258.

Bandura, A. (1977). *Social learning theory.* Englewood Cliffs, NJ: Prentice-Hall.

Bandura, A. (1992). Perceived self-efficacy in cognitive development and functioning. *Educational Psychologist, 28,* 117–148.

Bandura, A. (1999). Social cognitive theory of personality. In L. A. Pervin (Ed.), *Handbook of personality: Theory and research* (2nd ed., pp. 154–196). New York: Guilford.

Bandura, A. (2001). Social cognitive theory: An agentic perspective. *Annual Review of Psychology, 52,* 1–26.

Banish, M. T., & Heller, W. (1998). Evolving perspectives on lateralization of function. *Current Directions in Psychological Science, 7,* 1–2.

Banks, M. S. (1980). The development of visual accommodation during early infancy. *Child Development, 51,* 646–666.

Banks, M. S., & Ginsburg, A. P. (1985). Early visual preferences: A review and new theoretical treatment. In H. W. Reese (Ed.), *Advances in child development and behavior* (Vol. 19, pp. 207–246). New York: Academic Press.

Banse, R., Gawronski, B., Rebetez, C., Gutt, H., & Morton, J. B. (2010). The development of spontaneous gender stereotyping in childhood: Relations to stereotype knowledge and stereotype flexibility. *Developmental Science, 13,* 298–306.

Barber, B. K., & Olsen, J. A. (1997). Socialization in context: Connection, regulation, and autonomy in the family, school, and neighborhood, and with peers. *Journal of Adolescent Research, 12,* 287–315.

Barber, B. K., & Olsen, J. A. (2004). Assessing the transitions to middle and high school. *Journal of Adolescent Research, 19,* 3–30.

Barber, B. K., Stolz, H. E., & Olsen, J. A. (2005). Parental support, psychological control, and behavioral control: Assessing relevance across time, culture, and method. *Monographs of the Society for Research in Child Development, 70*(4, Serial No. 282).

Barber, B. L., Stone, M. R., Hunt, J. E., & Eccles, J. S. (2005). Benefits of activity participation: The roles of identity affirmation and peer group norm sharing. In J. L. Mahoney, R. W. Larson, & J. S. Eccles (Eds.), *Organized activities as contexts of development: Extracurricular activities, after-school and community programs* (pp. 185–210). Mahwah, NJ: Erlbaum.

Barber, J. S. (2001). Ideational influences on the transition to parenthood: Attitudes toward childbearing and competing alternatives. *Social Psychology Quarterly, 64,* 101–127.

Bard, K. A., Todd, B. K., Bernier, C., Love, J., & Leavens, D. A. (2006). Self-awareness in human and chimpanzee infants: What is measured and what is meant by the mark and mirror test? *Infancy, 9,* 191–219.

Barelds, D. P. H., & Dijkstra, P. (2011). Positive illusions about a partner's personality and relationship quality. *Journal of Research in Personality, 45,* 37–43.

Barenbaum, J., Ruchkin, V., & Schwab-Stone, M. (2004). The psychosocial aspects of children exposed to war: Practice and policy initiatives. *Journal of Child Psychology and Psychiatry, 45,* 41–62.

Bar-Haim, Y., Ziv, T., Lamy, D., & Hodes, R. M. (2006). Nature and nurture in own-race face processing. *Psychological Science, 17,* 159–163.

Barker, D. J. (2008). Human growth and cardiovascular disease. *Nestlé Nutrition Workshop Series, 61,* 21–38.

Barkley, R. A. (2002). Psychosocial treatments of attention-deficit/hyperactivity disorder in children. *Journal of Clinical Psychology, 63*(Suppl. 12), 36–43.

Barkley, R. A. (2003a). Attention-deficit/hyperactivity disorder. In E. J. Mash & R. A. Barkley (Eds.), *Child psychopathology* (2nd ed., pp. 75–143). New York: Guilford Press.

Barkley, R. A. (2003b). Issues in the diagnosis of attention-deficit hyperactivity disorder in children. *Brain and Development, 25,* 77–83.

Barkley, R. A. (2006). Attention-deficit/hyperactivity disorder. In R. A. Barkley, D. A. Wolfe, & E. J. Mash (Eds.), *Behavioral and emotional disorders in adolescents: Nature, assessment, and treatment* (pp. 91–152). New York: Guilford.

Barnes, G. M., Hoffman, J. H., Welte, J. W., Farrell, M. P., & Dintcheff, B. A. (2006). Effects of parental monitoring and peer deviance on substance use and delinquency. *Journal of Marriage and Family, 68,* 1084–1104.

Barnes, J., Katz, I., Korbin, J. E., & O'Brien, M. (2007). *Children and families in communities: Theory, research, policy and practice.* Hoboken, NJ: Wiley.

Barnes, R., Josefowitz, N., & Cole, E. (2006). Residential schools: Impact on Aboriginal students' academic and cognitive development. *Canadian Journal of School Psychology, 21,* 18–32.

Barnes-Farrell, J., & Matthews, R. A. (2007). Age and work attitudes. In K. S. Shultz & G. A. Adams (Eds.), *Aging and work in the 21st century* (pp. 139–162). Mahwah, NJ: Erlbaum.

Barnett, D., & Vondra, J. I. (1999). Atypical patterns of early attachment: Theory, research, and current directions. In J. I Vondra & D. Barnett (Eds.), *Atypical attachment in infancy and early childhood among children at developmental risk. Monographs of the Society for Research in Child Development, 64*(3, Serial No. 258), 1–24.

Barnett, R. C., & Hyde, J. S. (2001). Women, men, work, family: An expansionist theory. *American Psychologist, 56,* 781–796.

Barnett, W. S. (2011). Effectiveness of early educational intervention. *Science, 333,* 975–978.

Baron, I. S., & Rey-Casserly, C. (2010). Extremely preterm birth outcome: A review of four decades of cognitive research. *Neuropsychology Review, 20,* 430–452.

Baron-Cohen, S., Baldwin, D. A., & Crowson, M. (1997). Do children with autism use the speaker's direction of gaze strategy to crack the code of language? *Child Development, 68,* 48–57.

Baron-Cohen, S., & Belmonte, M. K. (2005). Autism: A window onto the development of the social and the analytic brain. *Annual Review of Neuroscience, 28,* 109–126.

Barr, H. M., Bookstein, F. L., O'Malley, K. D., Connor, P. D., Huggins, J. E., & Streissguth, A. P. (2006). Binge drinking during pregnancy as a predictor of psychiatric disorders on the structured clinical interview for DSM-IV in young adult offspring. *American Journal of Psychiatry, 163,* 1061–1065.

Barr, H. M., Streissguth, A. P., Darby, B. L., & Sampson, P. D. (1990). Prenatal exposure to alcohol, caffeine, tobacco, and aspirin: Effects on fine and gross motor performance in 4-year-old children. *Developmental Psychology, 26,* 339–348.

Barr, R., & Hayne, H. (2003). It's not what you know, it's who you know: Older siblings facilitate imitation during infancy. *International Journal of Early Years Education, 11,* 7–21.

Barr, R., Marrott, H., & Rovee-Collier, C. (2003). The role of sensory preconditioning in memory retrieval by preverbal infants. *Learning and Behavior, 31,* 111–123.

Barr, R., Muentener, P., & Garcia, A. (2007). Age-related changes in deferred imitation from television by 6- to 18-month-olds. *Developmental Science, 10,* 10–921.

Barr, R. G. (2001). "Colic" is something infants do, rather than a condition they "have": A developmental approach to crying phenomena patterns, pacification and (patho)genesis. In R. G. Barr, I. St. James-Roberts, & M. R. Keefe (Eds.), *New evidence on unexplained infant crying* (pp. 87–104). St. Louis: Johnson & Johnson Pediatric Institute.

Barr, R. G., Paterson, J. A., MacMartin, L. M., & Lehtonen, L. (2005). Prolonged and unsoothable crying bouts in infants with and without colic. *Journal of Developmental and Behavioral Pediatrics, 26,* 14–23.

Barratt, M. S., Roach, M. A., & Leavitt, L. A. (1996). The impact of low-risk prematurity on maternal behaviour and toddler outcomes. *International Journal of Behavioral Development, 19,* 581–602.

Barreto, M., Ryan, M. K., & Schmitt, M. T. (2009). *The glass ceiling in the 21st century: Understanding barriers to gender equality.* Washington, DC: American Psychological Association.

Barrett, K. C. (2005). The origins of social emotions and self-regulation in toddlerhood: New evidence. *Cognition and Emotion, 19,* 953–979.

Barrett, T. M., Traupman, E., & Needham, A. (2008). Infants' visual anticipation in grasp planning. *Infant Behavior and Development, 31,* 1–9.

Barros, R. M., Silver, E. J., & Stein, R. E. K. (2009). School recess and group classroom behavior. *Pediatrics, 123,* 431–436.

Barry, C. M., & Madsen, S. D. (2010). Friends and friendships in emerging adulthood. In T. Clydesdale (Ed.), *Who are emerging adults?* Washington, DC: Changing Spirituality of Emerging Adults Project. Retrieved from changingsea.org/barry.htm

Barry, C. M., & Nelson, L. J. (2008). The role of religious beliefs and practices in emerging adults' perceived competencies, perceived importance ratings, and global self-worth. *International Journal of Behavioral Development, 32,* 509–521.

Barry, C. M., Nelson, L., Davarya, S., & Urry, S. (2010). Religiosity and spirituality during the transition to adulthood. *International Journal of Behavioral Development, 34,* 311–324.

Bartlik, B., & Goldstein, M. Z. (2001). Men's sexual health after midlife. *Practical Geriatrics, 52,* 291–306.

Bartocci, M., Berggvist, L. L., Lagercrantz, H., & Anand, K. J. (2006). Pain activates cortical areas in the preterm newborn brain. *Pain, 122,* 109–117.

Bartrip, J., Morton, J., & de Schonen, S. (2001). Responses to mother's face in 3-week- to 5-month-old infants. *British Journal of Developmental Psychology, 19,* 219–232.

Bartsch, K., & Wellman, H. (1995). *Children talk about the mind.* New York: Oxford University Press.

Basak, C., & Verhaeghen, P. (2011). Aging and switching the focus of attention in working memory: Age differences in item availability but not in item accessibility. *Journal of Gerontology, 66B,* 519–526.

Basow, S. A., & Rubin, L. R. (1999). Gender influences on adolescent development. In N. G. Johnson & M. C. Roberts (Eds.), *Beyond appearance: A new look at adolescent girls* (pp. 25–52). Washington, DC: American Psychological Association.

Bass, S. (2011). From retirement to "productive aging" and back to work again. In D. C. Carr & K. Komp (Eds.), *Gerontology in the era of the Third Age: Implications and next steps* (pp. 169–188). New York: Springer.

Bassuk, S. S., & Manson, J. E. (2005). Epidemiological evidence for the role of physical activity in reducing risk of type 2 diabetes and cardiovascular disease. *Journal of Applied Physiology, 99,* 1193–1204.

Bates, E. (2004). Explaining and interpreting deficits in language development across clinical groups: Where do we go from here? *Brain and Language, 88,* 248–253.

Bates, E., Marchman, V., Thal, D., Fenson, L., Dale, P., Reznick, J. S., Reilly, J., & Hartung, J. (1994). Developmental and stylistic variation in the composition of early vocabulary. *Journal of Child Language, 21,* 85–123.

Bates, J. E., Wachs, T. D., & Emde, R. N. (1994). Toward practical uses for biological concepts. In J. E. Bates & T. D. Wachs (Eds.), *Temperament: Individual differences at the interface of biology and behavior* (pp. 275–306). Washington, DC: American Psychological Association.

Bauer, C. R., Langer, J. C., Shakaran, S., Bada, H. S., & Lester, B. (2005). Acute neonatal effects of cocaine exposure during pregnancy. *Archives of Pediatrics and Adolescent Medicine, 159,* 824–834.

Bauer, P. J. (2002). Early memory development. In U. Goswami (Ed.), *Blackwell handbook of child cognitive development* (pp. 127–150). Malden, MA: Blackwell.

Bauer, P. J. (2006). Event memory. In D. Kuhn & R. Siegler (Eds.), *Handbook of child psychology: Vol. 2. Cognition, perception, and language* (6th ed., pp. 373–425). Hoboken, NJ: Wiley.

Bauer, P. J. (2007). Recall in infancy: A neurodevelopmental account. *Current Directions in Psychological Science, 16,* 142–146.

Baum, N., Rahav, G., & Sharon, D. (2005). Changes in the self-concepts of divorced women. *Journal of Divorce and Remarriage, 43,* 47–67.

Baumbusch, J. L. (2004). Unclaimed treasures: Older women's reflections on lifelong singlehood. *Journal of Women and Aging, 16,* 105–121.

Baumeister, R. F. (1998). Inducing guilt. In J. Bybee (Ed.), *Guilt and children* (pp. 185–213). San Diego: Academic Press.

Baumeister, R. F., Campbell, J. D., Krueger, J. I., & Vohs, K. D. (2003). Does high self-esteem cause better performance, interpersonal success, happiness, or healthier lifestyles? *Psychological Science in the Public Interest, 4*(1), 1–44.

Baumgartner, M. S., & Schneider, D. E. (2010). Perceptions of women in management: A thematic analysis of razing the glass ceiling. *Journal of Career Development, 37,* 559–576.

Baumrind, D. (1971). Current patterns of parental authority. *Developmental Psychology Monograph, 4*(No. 1, Pt. 2).

Baumrind, D., Lazelere, R. E., & Owens, E. B. (2010). Effects of preschool parents' power assertive patterns and practices on adolescent development. *Parenting, 10,* 157–201.

Baumwell, L., Tamis-LeMonda, C. S., & Bornstein, M. H. (1997). Maternal verbal sensitivity and child language comprehension. *Infant Behavior and Development, 20,* 247–258.

Bauserman, R. (2002). Child adjustment in joint-custody versus sole-custody arrangements: A meta-analytic review. *Journal of Family Psychology, 16,* 91–102.

Baydar, N., Greek, A., & Brooks-Gunn, J. (1997). A longitudinal study of the effects of the birth of a sibling during the first 6 years of life. *Journal of Marriage and the Family, 59,* 939–956.

Bayer, A., & Tadd, W. (2000). Unjustified exclusion of elderly people from studies submitted to research ethics committee for approval: Descriptive study. *British Medical Journal, 321,* 992–993.

Bayley, N. (1969). *Bayley Scales of Infant Development.* New York: Psychological Corporation.

Bayley, N. (1993). *Bayley Scales of Infant Development* (2nd ed.). San Antonio, TX: Psychological Corporation.

Bayley, N. (2005). *Bayley Scales of Infant and Toddler Development, Third Edition* (Bayley-III). San Antonio, TX: Harcourt Assessment.

Bean, R. A., Barber, B. K., & Crane, D. R. (2007). Parental support, behavioral control, and psychological control among African American youth: The relationships to academic grades, delinquency, and depression. *Journal of Family Issues, 27,* 1335–1355.

Bearman, P. S., & Moody, J. (2004). Suicide and friendships among American adolescents. *American Journal of Public Health, 94,* 89–95.

Beaulieu, M., Leclerc, N., & Dube, M. (2003). Fear of crime among the elderly: An analysis of mental health issues. *Journal of Gerontological Social Work, 40,* 121–138.

Beautrais, A. L. (2003). Life course factors associated with suicidal behaviors in young people. *American Behavioral Scientist, 46,* 1137–1156.

Becker, G., Beyene, Y., Newsome, E., & Mayen, N. (2003). Creating continuity through mutual assistance: Intergenerational reciprocity in four ethnic groups. *Journal of Gerontology, 38B,* S151–S159.

Becker, K., El-Faddagh, M., Schmidt, M. H., Esser, G., & Laucht, M. (2008). Interaction of dopamine transporter genotype with prenatal smoke exposure on ADHD symptoms. *Journal of Pediatrics, 152,* 263–269.

Beckerman, M. B. (1990). Leos Janácek and "the late style" in music. *Gerontologist, 30,* 632–635.

Beckett, C., Maughan, B., Rutter, M., Castle, J., Colvert, E., & Groothues, C. (2006). Do the effects of early severe deprivation on cognition persist into early adolescence? Findings from the English and Romanian adoptees study. *Child Development, 77,* 696–711.

Bedford, O. A. (2004). The individual experience of guilt and shame in Chinese culture. *Culture and Psychology, 10,* 29–52.

Bedford, V. H., & Avioli, P. S. (2006). "Shooting the bull": Cohort comparisons of fraternal intimacy in midlife and old age. In V. H. Bedford & B. F. Turner (Eds.), *Men in relationships* (pp. 81–101). New York: Springer.

Behnke, M., Eyler, F. D., Warner, T. D., Garvan, C. W., Hou, W., & Wobie, K. (2006). Outcome from a prospective, longitudinal study of prenatal cocaine use: Preschool development at 3 years of age. *Journal of Pediatric Psychology, 31,* 41–49.

Behrens, K. Y., Hesse, E., & Main, M. (2007). Mothers' attachment status as determined by the Adult Attachment Interview predicts their 6-year-olds' reunion responses: A study conducted in Japan. *Developmental Psychology, 43*(6), 1553–1567.

Beier, M. E., & Ackerman, P. L. (2005). Age, ability, and the role of prior knowledge on the acquisition of new domain knowledge: Promising results in a real-world learning environment. *Psychology and Aging, 20,* 341–355.

Beilin, H. (1992). Piaget's enduring contribution to developmental psychology. *Developmental Psychology, 28,* 191–204.

Bekkouche, N. S., Holmes, S., Whittaker, K. S., & Krantz, D. S. (2011). Stress and the heart: Psychosocial stress and coronary heart disease. In R. J. Contrada & A. Baum (Eds.), *Handbook of stress science: Biology, psychology, and health* (pp. 385–398). New York: Springer.

Belcher, D., Lee, A., Solmon, M., & Harrison, L. (2003). The influence of gender-related beliefs and conceptions of ability on women learning the hockey wrist shot. *Research Quarterly for Exercise and Sport, 74,* 183–192.

Bell, J. H., & Bromnick, R. D. (2003). The social reality of the imaginary audience: A grounded theory approach. *Adolescence, 38,* 205–219.

Bell, M. A. (1998). Frontal lobe function during infancy: Implications for the development of cognition and attention. In J. E. Richards (Ed.), *Cognitive neuroscience of attention: A developmental perspective* (pp. 327–362). Mahwah, NJ: Erlbaum.

Bell, M. A., & Fox, N. A. (1996). Crawling experience is related to changes in cortical organization during infancy: Evidence from EEG coherence. *Developmental Psychobiology, 29,* 551–561.

Bell, M. L. (1995). Attitudes toward menopause among Mexican American women. *Health Care for Women International, 16,* 425–435.

Bellagamba, F., Camaioni, L., & Colonnesi, C. (2006). Change in children's understanding of others' intentional actions. *Developmental Science, 9,* 182–188.

Belle, S. H., Burgio, L., Burns, R., Coon, D., Czaja, S. J., Gallagher-Thompson, D., & Gitlin, L. N. (2006). Enhancing quality of life of dementia caregivers from different ethnic or racial groups: A randomized, controlled trial. *Annals of Internal Medicine, 145,* 727–738.

Bellinger, D. C. (2005). Teratogen update: Lead and pregnancy. *Birth Defects Research: Part A, Clinical and Molecular Teratology, 73,* 409–420.

Bell-Scriber, M. J. (2008). Warming the nursing education climate for traditional-age nurses who are male. *Nursing Education Perspectives, 29,* 143–150.

Belsky, J. (2001). Developmental risks (still) associated with early child care. *Journal of Child Psychology and Psychiatry, 42,* 845–859.

Belsky, J. (2005). Attachment theory and research in ecological perspective: Insights from the Pennsylvania Infant and Family Development Project and the NICHD Study of Early Child Care. In K. E. Grossmann, K. Grossmann, & E. Waters (Eds.), *Attachment from infancy to adulthood: The major longitudinal studies* (pp. 71–97). New York: Guilford.

Belsky, J. (2006). Early child care and early child development: Major findings of the NICHD Study of Early Child Care. *European Journal of Developmental Psychology, 3,* 95–110.

Belsky, J., Campbell, S. B., Cohn, J. F., & Moore, G. (1996). Instability of infant–parent attachment security. *Developmental Psychology, 32,* 921–924.

Belsky, J., & Fearon, R. M. P. (2002a). Early attachment security, subsequent maternal sensitivity, and later child development: Does continuity in development depend on caregiving? *Attachment and Human Development, 4,* 361–387.

Belsky, J., & Fearon, R. M. P. (2002b). Infant–mother attachment security, contextual risk, and early development: A moderational analysis. *Development and Pathology, 14,* 293–310.

Belsky, J., & Fearon, R. M. P. (2008). Precursors of attachment security. In J. Cassidy & P. R. Shaver (Eds.), *Handbook of attachment: Theory, research, and clinical applications* (2nd ed., pp. 295–316). New York: Guilford.

Belsky, J., Steinberg, L. D., Houts, R. M., Friedman, S. L., DeHart, G., Cauffman, E., Roisman, G. I., & Halpern-Felsher, B. (2007a). Family rearing antecedents of pubertal timing. *Child Development, 78,* 1302–1321.

Belsky, J., Steinberg, L., Houts, R. M., & Halpern-Felsher, B. L. (2010). The development of reproductive strategy in females: Early maternal harshness → earlier menarche → increased sexual risk taking. *Developmental Psychology, 46,* 120–128.

Belsky, J., Vandell, D. L., Burchinal, M., Clarke-Stewart, K. A., McCartney, K., & Owen, M. T. (2007b). Are there long-term effects of early child care? *Child Development, 78,* 681–701.

Benbow, C. P., & Stanley, J. C. (1983). Sex differences in mathematical reasoning: More facts. *Science, 222,* 1029–1031.

Bender, H. L., Allen, J. P., McElhaney, K. B., Antonishak, J., Moore, C. M., Kelly, H. L., & Davis, S. M. (2007). Use of harsh physical discipline and developmental outcomes in adolescence. *Development and Psychopathology, 19,* 227–242.

Benenson, J. F., & Christakos, A. (2003). The greater fragility of females' versus males' closest same-sex friendships. *Child Development, 74,* 1123–1129.

Bengtsson, H. (2005). Children's cognitive appraisal of others' distressful and positive experiences. *International Journal of Behavioral Development, 29,* 457–466.

Benner, A. D., & Graham, S. (2009). The transition to high school as a developmental process among multiethnic urban youth. *Child Development, 80,* 356–376.

Bennett, D. A., Schneider, J. A., Tang, Y., Arnold, S. E., & Wilson, R. S. (2006). The effect of social networks on the relation between Alzheimer's disease pathology and level of cognitive function in old people: A longitudinal cohort study. *Lancet Neurology, 5,* 406–412.

Bennett, K. M. (2007). "No sissy stuff": Toward a theory of masculinity and emotional expression in older widowed men. *Journal of Aging Studies, 21,* 347–356.

Bennett, K. M., Smith, P. T., & Hughes, G. M. (2005). Coping, depressive feelings and gender differences in late life widowhood. *Aging and Mental Health, 9,* 348–353.

Bennett, K. M., & Soulsby, L. K. (2012). Well-being in bereavement and widowhood. *Illness, Crisis & Loss, 20,* 321–337.

Bennett, M., Barrett, M., Karakozov, R., Kipiani, G., Lyons, E., Pavlenko, V., & Riazanova, T. (2004). Young children's evaluations of the ingroup and outgroups: A multi-national study. *Social Development, 13,* 124–141.

Benson, P. L., Scales, P. C., Hamilton, S. F., & Sesma, A., Jr. (2006). Positive youth development: Theory, research, and applications. In R. M. Lerner (Ed.), *Handbook of child psychology: Vol. 1. Theoretical models of human development* (6th ed., pp. 894–941). Hoboken, NJ: Wiley.

Ben-Zeev, T., Carrasquillo, C. M., Ching, A. M. L., Patton, G. E., Stewart, T. D., & Stoddard, T. (2005). "Math is hard!" (Barbie™, 1994): Responses of threat vs. challenge-mediated arousal to stereotypes alleging intellectual inferiority. In A. M. Gallagher & J. C. Kaufman (Eds.), *Gender differences in mathematics: An integrative psychological approach* (pp. 189–206). New York: Cambridge University Press.

Berenbaum, S. A. (2001). Cognitive function in congenital adrenal hyperplasia. *Endocrinology and Metabolism Clinics of North America, 30,* 173–192.

Berg, C. A., & Sternberg, R. J. (2003). Multiple perspectives on the development of adult intelligence. In J. Demick & C. Andreoletti (Eds.), *Handbook of adult development* (pp. 103–119). New York: Springer.

Berg, C. A., & Strough, J. (2011). Problem solving across the life span. In K. L. Fingerman, C. A. Berg, J. Smith, & T. C. Antonucci (Eds.), *Handbook of life-span development* (pp. 239–267). New York: Springer.

Bergen, D., & Mauer, D. (2000). Symbolic play, phonological awareness, and literacy skills at three age levels. In K. A. Roskos & J. F. Christie (Eds.), *Play and literacy in early childhood: Research from multiple perspectives* (pp. 45–62). Mahwah, NJ: Erlbaum.

Berger, L. M., Paxson, C., & Waldfogel, J. (2009). Income and child development. *Children and Youth Services Review, 31,* 978–989.

Berger, S. E. (2010). Locomotor expertise predicts infants' perseverative errors. *Developmental Psychology, 46,* 326–336.

Berger, S. E., Theuring, C., & Adolph, K. E. (2007). How and when infants learn to climb stairs. *Infant Behavior and Development, 30,* 36–49.

Bergman, E. J., Haley, W. E., & Small, B. J. (2010). The role of grief, anxiety, and depressive symptoms in the utilization of bereavement services. *Death Studies, 34,* 441–458.

Bergman, E. J., Haley, W. E., & Small, B. J. (2011). Who uses bereavement services? An examination of service use by bereaved dementia caregivers. *Aging and Mental Health, 15,* 531–540.

Bergman, H., Ferrucci, L., Guralnik, J., Hogan, D. B., Hummel, S., Karunananthan, S., & Wolfson. C. (2007). Frailty: An emerging research and clinical paradigm—issues and controversies. *Journal of Gerontology, 62A,* 731–737.

Bergman, I., Blomberg, M., & Almkvist, O. (2007). The importance of impaired physical health and age in normal cognitive aging. *Scandinavian Journal of Psychology, 48,* 115–125.

Bergman, R. (2004). Identity as motivation. In D. K. Lapsley & D. Narvaez (Eds.), *Moral development, self, and identity* (pp. 21–46). Mahwah, NJ: Erlbaum.

Bering, J. M., & Bjorklund, D. F. (2004). The natural emergence of reasoning about the afterlife as a developmental regularity. *Developmental Psychology, 40,* 217–233.

Berk, L. E. (2001). *Awakening children's minds: How parents and teachers can make a difference.* New York: Oxford University Press.

Berk, L. E. (2005). Why parenting matters. In S. Olfman (Ed.), *Childhood lost: How American culture is failing our kids* (pp. 19–53). New York: Guilford.

Berk, L. E. (2006). Looking at kindergarten children. In D. Gullo (Ed.), *K today: Teaching and learning in the kindergarten year* (pp. 11–25). Washington, DC: National Association for the Education of Young Children.

Berk, L. E., & Harris, S. (2003). Vygotsky, Lev. In L. Nadel (Ed.), *Encyclopedia of cognitive science.* London: Macmillan.

Berk, L. E., Mann, T., & Ogan, A. (2006). Make-believe play: Wellspring for development of self-regulation. In D. Singer, K. Hirsh-Pasek, & R. Golinkoff (Eds.), *Play = learning.* New York: Oxford University Press.

Berk, L. E., & Spuhl, S. (1995). Maternal interaction, private speech, and task performance in preschool children. *Early Childhood Research Quarterly, 10,* 145–169.

Berkowitz, M. W., & Gibbs, J. C. (1983). Measuring the developmental features of moral discussion. *Merrill-Palmer Quarterly, 29,* 399–410.

Berkowitz, R. L., Roberts, J., & Minkoff, H. (2006). Challenging the strategy of maternal age-based prenatal genetic counseling. *Journal of the American Medical Association, 295,* 1446–1448.

Berlin, L. J., Ipsa, J. M., Fine, M. A., Malone, P. S., Brooks-Gunn, J., Brady-Smith, C., et al. (2009). Correlates and consequences of spanking and verbal punishment for low-income white, African-American, and Mexican-American toddlers. *Child Development, 80,* 1403–1420.

Berman, E., & Napier, A. Y. (2000). The midlife family: Dealing with adolescents, young adults, and the marriage in transition. In W. C. Nichols, M. A. Pace-Nichols, D. S. Becvar, & A. Y. Napier (Eds.), *Handbook of family development and intervention* (pp. 208–234). New York: Wiley.

Berman, R. A. (2007). Developing linguistic knowledge and language use across adolescence. In K. Hirsh-Pasek & R. M. Golinkoff (Eds.), *Action meets word: How children learn verbs* (pp. 347–367). New York: Oxford University Press.

Berman, S. L., Weems, C. F., Rodriguez, E. T., & Zamora, I. J. (2006). The relation between identity status and romantic attachment style in middle and late adolescence. *Journal of Adolescence, 29,* 737–748.

Berndt, T. J. (2004). Children's friendships: Shifts over a half-century in perspectives on their development and effects. *Merrill-Palmer Quarterly, 50,* 206–223.

Berndt, T. J., & Murphy, L. M. (2002). Influences of friends and friendships: Myths, truths, and research recommendations. In R. V. Kail (Ed.), *Advances in child development and behavior* (Vol. 30, pp. 275–310). San Diego, CA: Academic Press.

Berner, M. M., Leiber, C., Kriston, L., Stodden, V., & Gunzler, C. (2008). Effects of written information material on help-seeking behavior in patients with erectile dysfunction: A longitudinal study. *Journal of Sexual Behavior, 5,* 436–447.

Bernier, J. C., & Siegel, D. H. (1994). Attention-deficit hyperactivity disorder: A family ecological systems perspective. *Families in Society, 75,* 142–150.

Bert, S. C., Farris, J. R., & Borkowski, J. G. (2008). Parent training: Implementation strategies for adventures in parenting. *Journal of Primary Prevention, 29,* 243–261.

Bertenthal, B. I. (1993). Infants' perception of biomechanical motions: Instrinsic image and knowledge-based constraints. In C. Granrud (Ed.), *Visual perception and cognition in infancy* (pp. 175–214). Hillsdale, NJ: Erlbaum.

Bertenthal, B. I., & Longo, M. R. (2007). Is there evidence of a mirror neuron system from birth? *Developmental Science, 10,* 513–523.

Bertenthal, B. I., Longo, M. R., & Kenny, S. (2007). Phenomenal permanence and the development of predictive tracking in infancy. *Child Development, 78,* 350–363.

Bertrand, M., & Mullainathan, S. (2004). *Are Emily and Brendan more employable than Lakisha and Jamal? A field experiment on labor market discrimination.* Unpublished manuscript, University of Chicago.

Berzin, S. C., & De Marco, A. C. (2010). Understanding the impact of poverty on critical events in emerging adulthood. *Youth and Society, 42,* 278–300.

Berzlanovich, A. M., Keil, W. W., Sim, T., Fasching, P., & Fazeny-Dorner, B. (2005). Do centenarians die healthy? An autopsy study. *Journal of Gerontology, 60A,* 862–865.

Berzonsky, M. D. (2003). Identity style and well-being: Does commitment matter? *Identity: An International Journal of Theory and Research, 3,* 131–142.

Berzonsky, M. D. (2004). Identity style, parental authority, and identity commitment. *Journal of Youth and Adolescence, 33,* 213–220.

Berzonsky, M. D. (2011). A social-cognitive perspective on identity construction. In S. J. Schwartz, K. Luyckx, & V. L. Vignoles (Eds.), *Handbook of identity theory and research* (pp. 55–76). New York: Springer.

Berzonsky, M. D., Cieciuch, J., Duriez, B., & Soenens, B. (2011). The how and what of identity formation: Associations between identity styles and value orientations. *Personality and Individual Differences, 50*, 295–299.

Berzonsky, M. D., & Kuk, L. S. (2000). Identity status, identity processing style, and the transition to university. *Journal of Adolescent Research, 15*, 81–98.

Best, D. (2009). From the American Academy of Pediatrics: Technical report—Secondhand and prenatal tobacco smoke exposure. *Pediatrics, 124*, e1017–e1044.

Best, D. L. (2001). Gender concepts: Convergence in cross-cultural research and methodologies. *Cross-cultural Research: The Journal of Comparative Social Science, 35*, 23–43.

Beyene, Y. (1992). Menopause: A biocultural event. In A. J. Dan & L. L. Lewis (Eds.), *Menstrual health in women's lives* (pp. 169–177). Urbana, IL: University of Illinois Press.

Beyene, Y., & Martin, M. C. (2001). Menopausal experiences and bone density of Mayan women in Yucatan, Mexico. *American Journal of Human Biology, 13*, 47–71.

Beyers, J. M., Bates, J. E., Pettit, G. S., & Dodge, K. A. (2003). Neighborhood structure, parenting processes, and the development of youths' externalizing behaviors: A multilevel analysis. *American Journal of Community Psychology, 31*, 35–53.

Beyers, W., & Seiffge-Krenke, I. (2010). Does identity precede intimacy? Testing Erikson's theory of romantic development in emerging adults of the 21st century. *Journal of Adolescent Research, 25*, 387–415.

Bhanot, R., & Jovanovic, J. (2005). Parents' academic gender stereotypes influence whether they intrude on their children's work. *Sex Roles, 52*, 597–607.

Bhat, A., Heathcock, J., & Galloway, J. C. (2005). Toy-oriented changes in hand and joint kinematics during the emergence of purposeful reaching. *Infant Behavior and Development, 28*, 445–465.

Bhatt, R. S., Rovee-Collier, C., & Weiner, S. (1994). Developmental changes in the interface between perception and memory retrieval. *Developmental Psychology, 30*, 151–162.

Bhatt, R. S., Wilk, A., Hill, D., & Rovee-Collier, C. (2004). Correlated attributes and categorization in the first half-year of life. *Developmental Psychobiology, 44*, 103–115.

Bherer, L. (2012). Physical activity and exercise in older adults. In E. O. Acevedo (Ed.), *Oxford handbook of exercise psychology* (pp. 359–384). New York: Oxford University Press.

Bherer, L., Kramer, A. F., Peterson, M. S., Colcombe, S., Erickson, K., & Becic, E. (2006). Training effects on dual-task performance: Are there age-related differences in plasticity of attentional control? *Psychology and Aging, 20*, 695–709.

Bhopal, K. (2011). "Education makes you have more say in the way your life goes": Indian women and arranged marriages in the United Kingdom. *British Journal of Sociology of Education, 32*, 431–447.

Bialystok, E., Craik, F. I. M., Green, D. W., & Gollan, T. H. (2009). Bilingual minds. *Psychological Science in the Public Interest, 3*, 89–129.

Bialystok, E., & Martin, M. M. (2003). Notation to symbol: Development in children's understanding of print. *Journal of Experimental Child Psychology, 86*, 223–243.

Bianchi, S. M., & Raley, S. B. (2005). Time allocation in families. In S. M. Bianchi, L. M. Casper, & R. B. King (Eds.), *Work, family, health, and well-being* (pp. 21–48). Mahwah, NJ: Erlbaum.

Bianco, A., Stone, J., Lynch, L., Lapinski, R., Berkowitz, G., & Berkowitz, R. L. (1996). Pregnancy outcome at age 40 and older. *Obstetrics and Gynecology, 87*, 917–922.

Biederman, J., Kwon, A., Aleardi, M., Chouinard, V. A., Marino, T., & Cole, H. (2005). Absence of gender effects on attention-deficit hyperactivity disorder: Findings in nonreferred subjects. *American Journal of Psychiatry, 162*, 1083–1089.

Biegel, D., & Liebbrant, S. (2006). Elders living in poverty. In B. Berkman & S. D'Ambruoso (Eds.), *Handbook of social work in health and aging* (pp. 161–180). New York: Oxford University Press.

Bielak, A. A. M., Anstey, K. J., Christensen, H., & Windsor, T. D. (2012). Activity engagement is related to level, but not change, in cognitive ability across adulthood. *Psychology and Aging, 27*, 219–228.

Bielak, A. A. M., Hultsch, D. F., Strauss, E., MacDonald, S. W. S., & Hunter, M. A. (2010). Intraindividual variability in reaction time predicts cognitive outcomes 5 years later. *Neuropsychology, 24*, 731–741.

Bielawska-Batorowicz, E., & Kossakowska-Petrycka, K. (2006). Depressive mood in men after the birth of their offspring in relation to a partner's depression, social support, fathers' personality and prenatal expectations. *Journal of Reproductive and Infant Psychology, 24*, 21–29.

Bielinski, J., & Davison, M. L. (1998). Gender differences by item difficulty interactions in multiple-choice mathematics items. *American Educational Research Journal, 35*, 455–476.

Bierman, K. L., & Powers, L. M. (2009). Social skills training to improve peer relations. In K. H. Rubin, W. M. Bukowski, & B. Laursen (Eds.), *Handbook of peer interactions, relationships, and groups* (pp. 603–621). New York: Guilford Press.

Bifulco, R., Cobb, C. D., & Bell, C. (2009). Can interdistrict choice boost student achievement? The case of Connecticut's interdistrict magnet school program. *Educational Evaluation and Policy Analysis, 31*, 323–345.

Bigelow, A. E., MacLean, K., Proctor, J., Myatt, T., Gillis, R., & Power, M. (2010). Maternal sensitivity throughout infancy: Continuity and relation to attachment security. *Infant Behavior and Development, 33*, 50–60.

Bigler, R. S. (2007, June). Personal communication.

Bigler, R. S., Brown, C. S., & Markell, M. (2001). When groups are not created equal: Effects of group status on the formation of intergroup attitudes in children. *Child Development, 72*, 1151–1162.

Bimmel, N., Juffer, F., van IJzendoorn, M. H., & Bakermans-Kranenburg, M. J. (2003). Problem behavior of internationally adopted adolescents: A review and meta-analysis. *Harvard Review of Psychiatry, 11*, 64–77.

Birch, E. E. (1993). Stereopsis in infants and its developmental relation to visual acuity. In K. Simons (Ed.), *Early visual development: Normal and abnormal* (pp. 224–236). New York: Oxford University Press.

Birch, L. L., & Fisher, J. A. (1995). Appetite and eating behavior in children. *Pediatric Clinics of North America, 42*, 931–953.

Birch, L. L., Fisher, J. O., & Davison, K. K. (2003). Learning to overeat: Maternal use of restrictive feeding practices promotes girls' eating in the absence of hunger. *American Journal of Clinical Nutrition, 78*, 215–220.

Birch, L. L., Zimmerman, S., & Hind, H. (1980). The influence of social–affective context on preschool children's food preferences. *Child Development, 51*, 856–861.

Birch, S. A. J., & Bloom, P. (2003). Children are cursed: An asymmetric bias in mental-state attribution. *Psychological Science, 14*, 283–285.

Bird, A., & Reese, E. (2006). Emotional reminiscing and the development of an autobiographical self. *Developmental Psychology, 42*, 613–626.

Birditt, K. S., & Antonucci, T. C. (2007). Relationship quality profiles and well-being among married adults. *Journal of Family Psychology, 21*, 595–604.

Birditt, K. S., Brown, E., Orbuch, T. L., & McIlvane, J. M. (2010). Marital conflict behaviors and implications for divorce over 16 years. *Journal of Marriage and Family, 72*, 1188–1204.

Birditt, K. S., & Fingerman, K. L. (2005). Do we get better at picking our battles? Age group differences in descriptions of behavioral reactions to interpersonal tensions. *Journal of Gerontology, 60B*, P121–P128.

Birditt, K. S., Jackey, L. M. H., & Antonucci, T. C. (2009). Longitudinal patterns of negative relationship quality across adulthood. *Journal of Gerontology, 64B*, 55–64.

Biringen, Z., Emde, R. N., Campos, J. J., & Appelbaum, M. I. (1995). Affective reorganization in the infant, the mother, and the dyad: The role of upright locomotion and its timing. *Child Development, 66*, 499–514.

Birkett, M., Espelage, D. L., & Koenig, B. (2009). LGB and questioning students in schools: The moderating effects of homophobic bullying and school climate on negative outcomes. *Journal of Youth and Adolescence, 38*, 989–1000.

Birney, D. P., & Sternberg, R. J. (2006). Intelligence and cognitive abilities as competencies in development. In E. Bialystok & F. I. M. Craik (Eds.), *Lifespan cognition: Mechanisms of change* (pp. 315–330). New York: Oxford University Press.

Birney, D. P., & Sternberg, R. J. (2011). The development of cognitive abilities. In M. H. Bornstein & M. E. Lamb (Eds.), *Developmental science: An advanced textbook* (6th ed., pp. 353–388). New York: Psychology Press.

Birren, J. E. (2009). Gifts and talents of elderly people: The persimmon's promise. In F. D. Horowitz, R. F. Subotnik, & D. J. Matthews (Eds.), *The development of giftedness and talent across the life span* (pp. 171–185). Washington, DC: American Psychological Association.

Bjorklund, D. F. (2012). *Children's thinking* (5th ed.). Belmont, CA: Wadsworth Cengage Learning.

Bjorklund, D. F., Causey, K., & Periss, V. (2009). The evolution and development of human social cognition. In P. Kappeler & J. Silk (Eds.), *Mind the gap: Racing the origins of human universals* (pp. 351–371). Berlin: Springer Verlag.

Bjorklund, D. F., Schneider, W., Cassel, W. S., & Ashley, E. (1994). Training and extension of a memory strategy: Evidence for utilization deficiencies in high- and low-IQ children. *Child Development, 65*, 951–965.

Black, M. C., Basile, K. C., Breiding, M. J., Smith, S. G., Walters, M. L., et al. (2011). *National intimate partner and sexual violence survey: 2010 summary report.* Atlanta, GA: U.S. Centers for Disease Control and Prevention.

Black, R. E., Williams, S. M., Jones, I. E., & Goulding, A. (2002). Children who avoid drinking cow milk have low dietary calcium intakes and poor bone health. *American Journal of Clinical Nutrition, 76*, 675–680.

Blackhall, L. J., Frank, G., Murphy, S., & Michel, V. (2001). Bioethics in a different tongue: The case of truth-telling. *Journal of Urban Health, 78*, 59–71.

Blackhall, L. J., Murphy, S. T., Frank, G., Michel, V., & Azen, S. (1995). Ethnicity and attitudes toward patient autonomy. *Journal of the American Medical Association, 274*, 820–825.

Blackwell, D. L., & Lichter, D. T. (2004). Homogamy among dating, cohabiting, and married couples. *Sociological Quarterly, 45*, 719–737.

Blackwell, L. S., Trzesniewski, K. H., & Dweck, C. S. (2007). Implicit theories of intelligence predict achievement across an adolescent transition: A longitudinal study and an intervention. *Child Development, 78*, 246–263.

Blaga, O. M., & Colombo, J. (2006). Visual processing and infant ocular latencies in the overlap paradigm. *Developmental Psychology, 42*, 1069–1076.

Blaine, B., & Rodman, J. (2007). Responses to weight loss treatment among obese individuals with and without BED: A matched-study meta-analysis. *Eating and Weight Disorders, 12,* 54–60.

Blair, C., & Raver, C. C. (2012). Child development in the context of adversity: Experiential canalization of brain and behavior. *American Psychologist, 67,* 309–318.

Blair, C., & Razza, R. P. (2007). Relating effortful control, executive function, and false belief understanding to emerging math and literacy ability in kindergarten. *Developmental Psychology, 78,* 647–663.

Blair-Loy, M., & DeHart, G. (2003). Family and career trajectories among African-American female attorneys. *Journal of Family Issues, 24,* 908–933.

Blakemore, J. E. O. (2003). Children's beliefs about violating gender norms: Boys shouldn't look like girls, and girls shouldn't act like boys. *Sex Roles, 48,* 411–419.

Blakemore, S.-J., & Choudhury, S. (2006). Development of the adolescent brain: Implications for executive function and social cognition. *Journal of Child Psychology and Psychiatry, 47,* 296–312.

Blanchard, R., & Bogaert, A. F. (2004). Proportion of homosexual men who owe their sexual orientation to fraternal birth order: An estimate based on two national probability samples. *American Journal of Human Biology, 16,* 151–157.

Blanchard-Fields, F. (2007). Everyday problem solving and emotion: An adult developmental perspective. *Current Directions in Psychological Science, 16,* 26–31.

Blanchard-Fields, F., Chen, Y., & Norris, L. (1997). Everyday problem solving across the adult life span: Influence of domain specificity and cognitive appraisal. *Psychology and Aging, 12,* 684–693.

Blanchard-Fields, F., & Coats, A. H. (2008). The experience of anger and sadness in everyday problems impacts age differences in emotion regulation. *Developmental Psychology, 44,* 1547–1556.

Blanchard-Fields, F., Mienaltowski, A., & Baldi, R. (2007). Age differences in everyday problem-solving effectiveness: Older adults select more effective strategies for interpersonal problems. *Journal of Gerontology, 62B,* P61–P64.

Blandon, A. Y., & Volling, B. L. (2008). Parental gentle guidance and children's compliance within the family: A replication study. *Journal of Family Psychology, 22,* 355–366.

Blasi, A. (1994). Moral identity: Its role in moral functioning. In B. Puka (Ed.), *Fundamental research in moral development: A compendium* (Vol. 2, pp. 123–167). New York: Garland.

Blasi, C. H., & Bjorklund, D. F. (2003). Evolutionary developmental psychology: A new tool for better understanding human ontogeny. *Human Development, 46,* 259–281.

Blass, E. M., Ganchrow, J. R., & Steiner, J. E. (1984). Classical conditioning in newborn humans 2–48 hours of age. *Infant Behavior and Development, 7,* 223–235.

Blatchford, P., Bassett, P., & Brown, P. (2005). Teachers' and pupils' behavior in large and small classes: A systematic observation study of pupils aged 10 and 11 years. *Journal of Educational Psychology, 97,* 454–467.

Blatchford, P., Bassett, P., Goldstein, H., & Martin, C. (2003). Are class size differences related to pupils' educational progress and classroom processes? Findings from the Institute of Education Class Size Study of Children Aged 5–7 years. *British Educational Research Journal, 29,* 709–730.

Blatchford, P., Russell, A., Bassett, P., Brown, P., & Martin, C. (2007). The effect of class size on the teaching of pupils aged 7–11 years. *School Effectiveness and School Improvement, 18,* 147–172.

Blatteis, C. M. (2012). Age-dependent changes in temperature regulation—a mini review. *Gerontology, 58,* 289–295.

Blau, D., & Goldstein, R. (2007). *What explains trends in labor force participation of older men in the United States?* Discussion Paper No. 2991. Bonn, Germany: Institute for the Study of Labor.

Bleeker, M. M., & Jacobs, J. E. (2004). Achievement in math and science: Do mothers' beliefs matter 12 years later? *Journal of Educational Psychology, 96,* 97–109.

Bleses, D., Vach, W., Slott, M., Wehberg, S., Thomsen, P., Madsen, T., et al. (2008). Early vocabulary development in Danish and other languages: A CDI-based comparison. *Journal of Child Language, 35,* 619–650.

Bleske, A. L., & Buss, D. M. (2000). Can men and women be just friends? *Personal Relationships, 7,* 131–151.

Blieszner, R., & Roberto, K. A. (2012). Partners and friends in adulthood. In S. K. Whitbourne & M. J. Sliwinski (Eds.), The Wiley-Blackwell handbook of adulthood and aging (pp. 381–398). Malden, MA: Wiley-Blackwell.

Block, J. (1995). A contrarian view of the five-factor approach to personality description. *Psychological Bulletin, 117,* 187–215.

Block, J. (2011). The five-factor framing of personality and beyond: Some ruminations. *Psychological Inquiry, 21,* 2–25.

Blood-Siegfried, J. (2009). The role of infection and inflammation in sudden infant death syndrome. *Immunopharmacology and Immunotoxicology, 31,* 516–523.

Bloom, L. (1998). Language acquisition in its developmental context. In D. Kuhn & R. S. Siegler (Eds.), *Handbook of child psychology: Vol. 2. Cognition, perception, and language* (5th ed., pp. 309–370). New York: Wiley.

Bloom, L. (2000). The intentionality model of language development: How to learn a word, any word. In R. Golinkoff, K. Hirsh-Pasek, N. Akhtar, L. Bloom, G. Hollich, L. Smith, M. Tomasello, & A. Woodward (Eds.), *Becoming a word learner: A debate on lexical acquisition.* New York: Oxford University Press.

Bluck, S., Dirk, J., Mackay, M. M., & Hux, A. (2008). Life experience with death: Relation to death attitudes and to the use of death-related memories. *Death Studies, 32,* 524–549.

Bluebond-Langner, M. (1977). Meanings of death to children. In H. Feifel (Ed.), *New meanings of death* (pp. 47–66). New York: McGraw-Hill.

Blumenfeld, P. C., Marx, R. W., & Harris, C. J. (2006). Learning environments. In K. A. Renninger & I. E. Sigel (Eds.), *Handbook of child psychology: Vol. 4. Child psychology in practice* (6th ed., pp. 297–342). Hoboken, NJ: Wiley.

Blumenthal, H., Leen-Feldner, E. W., Babson, K. A., Gahr, J. L., Trainor, C. D., & Frala, J. L. (2011). Elevated social anxiety among early maturing girls. *Developmental Psychology, 47,* 1133–1140.

Boardman, J. D. (2004). Stress and physical health: The role of neighborhoods as mediating and moderating mechanisms. *Social Science and Medicine, 58,* 2473–2483.

Bobb, A. J., Castellanos, F. X., Addington, A. M., & Rapoport, J. L. (2006). Molecular genetic studies of ADHD: 1991 to 2004. *American Journal of Medical Genetics Part B (Neuropsychiatric Genetics), 141B,* 551–565.

Bodrova, E., & Leong, D. J. (2007). *Tools of the mind: The Vygotskian approach to early childhood education* (2nd ed.). Upper Saddle River, NJ: Merrill/Prentice Hall.

Body, J. J., Bergmann, P., Boonen, S., Boutsen, Y., Bruyere, O., Devogelaer, J. P., et al. (2011). Non-pharmacological management of osteoporosis: A consensus of the Belgian Bone Club. *Osteoporosis International, 22,* 2769–2788.

Bogaert, A. F. (2005). Age at puberty and father absence in a national probability sample. *Journal of Adolescence, 28,* 541–546.

Bogin, B. (2001). *The growth of humanity.* New York: Wiley-Liss.

Bohannon, J. N., & Bonvillian, J. D. (2009). Theoretical approaches to language acquisition. In J. B. Gleason & B. Ratner (Ed.), *The development of language* (7th ed., pp. 227–284). Boston: Allyn and Bacon.

Bohannon, J. N., III, & Stanowicz, L. (1988). The issue of negative evidence: Adult responses to children's language errors. *Developmental Psychology, 24,* 684–689.

Bohlmeijer, E. T., Roemer, M., Cuijpers, P., & Smit, F. (2007). The effects of life-review on psychological well-being in older adults: A meta-analysis. *Aging and Mental Health, 11,* 291–300.

Boldizar, J. P. (1991). Assessing sex typing and androgyny in children: The children's sex role inventory. *Developmental Psychology, 27,* 505–515.

Bolen, R. M. (2001). *Child sexual abuse.* New York: Kluwer Academic.

Bolisetty, S., Bajuk, B., Me, A.-L., Vincent, T., Sutton, L., & Lui, K. (2006). Preterm outcome table (POT): A simple tool to aid counselling parents of very preterm infants. *Australian and New Zealand Journal of Obstetrics and Gynaecology, 46,* 189–192.

Bolkan, C., & Hooker, K. (2012). Self-regulation and social cognition in adulthood: The gyroscope of personality. In S. K. Whitbourne & M. J. Sliwinski (Eds.), *Wiley-Blackwell handbook of adulthood and aging* (pp. 357–380). Malden, MA: Wiley-Blackwell.

Bolzani, L. H., Messinger, D. S., Yale, M., & Dondi, M. (2002). Smiling in infancy. In M. H. Abel (Ed.), *An empirical reflection on the smile* (pp. 111–136). Lewiston, NY: Edwin Mellen Press.

Bonilla, S., Kehl, S., Kwong, K. Y., Morphew, T., Kachru, R., & Jones, C. A. (2005). School absenteeism in children with asthma in a Los Angeles inner-city school. *Journal of Pediatrics, 147,* 802–806.

Bonnick, S. L. (2008). Osteoporosis in men and women. *Management of Osteoporosis, 8,* 28–36.

Bono, M. A., & Stifter, C. A. (2003). Maternal attention-directing strategies and infant focused attention during problem solving. *Infancy, 4,* 235–250.

Bookman, A., & Kimbrel, D. (2011). Families and elder care in the twenty-first century. *Future of Children, 21,* 117–140.

Boom, J., Wouters, H., & Keller, M. (2007). A cross-cultural validation of stage development: A Rasch re-analysis of longitudinal socio-moral reasoning data. *Cognitive Development, 22,* 213–229.

Booth, A., Scott, M. E., & King, V. (2010). Father residence and adolescent problem behavior: Are youth always better off in two-parent families? *Journal of Family Issues, 31,* 585–605.

Borduin, C. M. (2007). Multisystemic treatment of violent youth and their families. In T. A. Cavell & K. T. Malcolm (Eds.), *Anger, aggression and interventions for interpersonal violence* (pp. 239–265). Mahwah, NJ: Erlbaum.

Bornstein, M. H. (1989). Sensitive periods in development: Structural characteristics and causal interpretations. *Psychological Bulletin, 105,* 179–197.

Bornstein, M. H. (2006). Parenting science and practice. In K. Renninger & I. E. Sigel (Eds.), *Handbook of child psychology: Vol. 4. Child psychology in practice* (6th ed., pp. 893–949). Hoboken, NJ: Wiley.

Bornstein, M. H., & Arterberry, M. E. (1999). Perceptual development. In M. H. Bornstein & M. E. Lamb (Eds.), *Developmental psychology: An advanced textbook* (pp. 231–274). Mahwah, NJ: Erlbaum.

Bornstein, M. H., & Arterberry, M. E. (2003). Recognition, discrimination, and categorization of smiling by 5-month-old infants. *Developmental Science, 6*, 585–599.

Bornstein, M. H., Arterberry, M. E., & Mash, C. (2010). Infant object categorization transcends object–context relations. *Infant Behavior and Development, 33*, 7–15.

Bornstein, M. H., & Sawyer, J. (2006). Family systems. In K. McCartney & D. Phillips (Eds.), *Blackwell handbook of early childhood development* (pp. 381–398). Malden, MA: Blackwell.

Boroughs, D. S. (2004). Female sexual abusers of children. *Children and Youth Services Review, 26*, 481–487.

Borst, C. G. (1995). *Catching babies: The professionalization of childbirth, 1870–1920.* Cambridge, MA: Harvard University Press.

Bortfeld, H., Leon, S., Bloom, J., Schober, M., & Brennan, S. (2001). Disfluency rates in conversation: Effects of age, relationship, topic, role, and gender. *Language and Speech, 44*, 123–147.

Bos, H. M. W., & Sandfort, T. G. M. (2010). Children's gender identity in lesbian and heterosexual two-parent families. *Sex Roles, 62*, 114–126.

Bos, H. M. W., van Balen, F., & van den Boom, D. C. (2004). Experience of parenthood, couple relationship, social support, and child-rearing goals in planned lesbian mother families. *Journal of Child Psychology and Psychiatry, 25*, 755–764.

Bos, H. M. W., van Balen, F., & van den Boom, D. C. (2007). Child adjustment and parenting in planned lesbian-parent families. *American Journal of Orthopsychiatry, 77*, 38–48.

Bosacki, S. L., & Moore, C. (2004). Preschoolers' understanding of simple and complex emotions: Links with gender and language. *Sex Roles, 50*, 659–675.

Bost, K. K., Shin, N., McBride, B. A., Brown, G. L., Vaughn, B. E., & Coppola, G. (2006). Maternal secure base scripts, children's attachment security, and mother–child narrative styles. *Attachment and Human Development, 8*, 241–260.

Boswell, G. H., Kahana, E., & Dilworth-Anderson, P. (2006). Spirituality and healthy lifestyle behaviors: Stress counter-balancing effects on the well-being of older adults. *Journal of Religion and Health, 45*, 587–602.

Botton, J., Heude, B., Maccario, J., Ducimetiére, P., & Charles, M. A. (2008). Postnatal weight and height growth velocities at different ages between birth and 5y and body composition in adolescent boys and girls. *American Journal of Clinical Nutrition, 87*, 1760–1768.

Bouchard, T. J. (2004). Genetic influence on human psychological traits: A survey. *Current Directions in Psychological Science, 13*, 148–151.

Bouchard, T. J., & Loehlin, J. C. (2001). Genes, evolution, and personality. *Behavior Genetics, 31*, 243–274.

Boucher, O., Bastien, C. H., Saint-Amour, D., Dewailly, E., Ayotte, P., Jacobson, J. L., Jacobson, et al. (2010). Prenatal exposure to methylmercury and PCBs affects distinct stages of information processing: An event-related potential study with Inuit children. *Neurotoxicology, 31*, 373–384.

Boucher, O., Muckle, G., & Bastien, C. H. (2009). Prenatal exposure to polychlorinated biphenyls: A neuropsychologic analysis. *Environmental Health Perspectives, 117*, 7–16.

Boukydis, C. F. Z., & Lester, B. M. (1998). Infant crying, risk status and social support in families of preterm and term infants. *Early Development and Parenting, 7*, 31–39.

Boulton, M. J. (1999). Concurrent and longitudinal relations between children's playground behavior and social preference, victimization, and bullying. *Child Development, 70*, 944–954.

Bowen, C. E., Noack, M. G., & Staudinger, U. M. (2011). Aging in the work context. In K. W. Schaie & S. L. Willis (Eds.), *Handbook of the psychology of aging* (7th ed., pp. 263–277). San Diego, CA: Academic Press.

Bowen, N. K., Bowen, G. L., & Ware, W. B. (2002). Neighborhood social disorganization, families, and the educational behavior of adolescents. *Journal of Adolescent Research, 17*, 468–490.

Bowkett, S., & Percival, S. (2011). *Coaching emotional intelligence in the classroom: A guide for 7–14.* New York: Routledge.

Bowlby, J. (1969). *Attachment and loss: Vol. 1. Attachment.* New York: Basic Books.

Bowlby, J. (1980). *Attachment and loss: Vol. 3. Loss: Sadness and depression.* New York: Basic Books.

Bowman, N. A. (2011a). College diversity experiences and cognitive development: A meta-analysis. *Review of Educational Research, 80*, 4–33.

Bowman, N. A. (2011b). Promoting participation in a diverse democracy: A meta-analysis of college diversity experiences and civic engagement. *Review of Educational Research, 81*, 29–68.

Bowman, S. A., Gortmaker, S. L., Ebbeling, C. B., Pereira, M. A., & Ludwig, D. S. (2004). Effects of fast-food consumption on energy intake and diet quality among children in a national household survey. *Pediatrics, 113*, 112–113.

Boyce, W., Doherty-Poirier, M., MacKinnon, D., Fortin, C., Saab, H., King, M., & Gallupe, O. (2006). Sexual health of Canadian youth: Findings from the Canadian Youth, Sexual Health and HIV/AIDS Study. *Canadian Journal of Human Sexuality, 15*, 59–68.

Boyd-Franklin, N. (2006). *Black families in therapy* (2nd ed.). New York: Guilford.

Boyle, P. A., Barnes, L. L., Buchman, A. S., & Bennett, D. A. (2009). Purpose in life is associated with mortality among community-dwelling older persons. *Psychosomatic Medicine, 71*, 574–579.

Boysson-Bardies, B. de, & Vihman, M. M. (1991). Adaptation to language: Evidence from babbling and first words in four languages. *Language, 67*, 297–319.

Bozionelos, N., Bozionelos, G., Kostopoulos, K., & Polychroniou, P. (2011). How providing mentoring relates to career success and organizational commitment: A study in the general managerial population. *Career Development International, 16*, 446–468.

Bracci, R., Perrone, S., & Buonocore, G. (2006). The timing of neonatal brain damage. *Biology of the Neonate, 90*, 145–155.

Bracken, B. A. (2000). Maximizing construct relevant assessment: The optimal preschool testing situation. In B. A. Bracken (Ed.), *The psychoeducational assessment of preschool children* (3rd ed., pp. 33–44). Upper Saddle River, NJ: Prentice-Hall.

Brackett, M. A., Mayer, J. D., & Warner, R. M. (2004). Emotional intelligence and the prediction of behavior. *Personality and Individual Differences, 36*, 1387–1402.

Bradbury, J. C. (2009). Peak athletic performance and ageing: Evidence from baseball. *Journal of Sports Sciences, 27*, 599–610.

Bradford, K., Barber, B. K., Olsen, J. A., Maughan, S. L., Erickson, L. D., Ward, D., & Stolz, H. E. (2003). A multi-national study of interparental conflict, parenting, and adolescent functioning: South Africa, Bangladesh, China, India, Bosnia, Germany, Palestine, Colombia, and the United States. *Marriage and Family Review, 35*, 107–137.

Bradley, R. H. (1994). The HOME Inventory: Review and reflections. In H. W. Reese (Ed.), *Advances in child development and behavior* (Vol. 25, pp. 241–288). San Diego, CA: Academic Press.

Bradley, R. H., & Caldwell, B. M. (1982). The consistency of the home environment and its relation to child development. *International Journal of Behavioral Development, 5*, 445–465.

Bradley, R. H., Corwyn, R. F., McAdoo, H. P., & Garcia-Coll, C. (2001). The home environments of children in the United States. Part I: Variations by age, ethnicity, and poverty status. *Child Development, 72*, 1844–1867.

Bradley, R. H., Whiteside, L., Mundfrom, D. J., Casey, P. H., Kelleher, K. J., & Pope, S. K. (1994). Early indications of resilience and their relation to experiences in the home environments of low birthweight, premature children living in poverty. *Child Development, 65*, 346–360.

Braine, L. G., Schauble, L., Kugelmass, S., & Winter, A. (1993). Representation of depth by children: Spatial strategies and lateral biases. *Developmental Psychology, 29*, 466–479.

Brainerd, C. J. (2003). Jean Piaget, learning, research, and American education. In B. J. Zimmerman (Ed.), *Educational psychology: A century of contributions* (pp. 251–287). Mahwah, NJ: Erlbaum.

Brame, B., Nagin, D. S., & Tremblay, R. E. (2001). Developmental trajectories of physical aggression from school entry to late adolescence. *Journal of Child Psychology and Psychiatry, 42*, 503–512.

Brand, S., Gerber, M., Beck, J., Hatzinger, M., Puhse, U., & Holsboer-Trachsler, E. (2010). High exercise levels are related to favorable sleep and psychological functioning in adolescence: A comparison of athletes and controls. *Journal of Adolescent Health, 46*, 133–141.

Branje, S. J. T., van Lieshout, C. F. M., van Aken, M. A. G., & Haselager, G. J. T. (2004). Perceived support in sibling relationships and adolescent adjustment. *Journal of Child Psychology and Psychiatry, 45*, 1385–1396.

Braswell, G. S. (2006). Sociocultural contexts for the early development of semiotic production. *Psychological Bulletin, 132*, 877–894.

Braswell, G. S., & Callanan, M. A. (2003). Learning to draw recognizable graphic representations during mother–child interactions. *Merrill-Palmer Quarterly, 49*, 471–494.

Braungart-Rieker, J. M., Hill-Soderlund, A. L., & Karrass, J. (2010). Fear and anger reactivity trajectories from 4 to 16 months: The roles of temperament, regulation, and maternal sensitivity. *Developmental Psychology, 46*, 791–804.

Braveman, P., Cubbin, C., Egerter, S., Williams, D. R., & Pamuk, E. (2010). Socioeconomic disparities in health in the United States: What the patterns tell us. *American Journal of Public Health, 100*, S186–S196.

Bray, J. H. (1999). From marriage to remarriage and beyond: Findings from the Developmental Issues in Stepfamilies Research Project. In E. M. Hetherington (Ed.), *Coping with divorce, single parenting, and remarriage: A risk and resiliency perspective* (pp. 295–319). Mahwah, NJ: Erlbaum.

Brazelton, T. B., Koslowski, B., & Tronick, E. (1976). Neonatal behavior among urban Zambians and Americans. *Journal of the American Academy of Child Psychiatry, 15*, 97–107.

Brazelton, T. B., & Nugent, J. K. (1995). *Neonatal Behavioral Assessment Scale.* London, Mac Keith Press.

Brazelton, T. B., Nugent, J. K., & Lester, B. M. (1987). Neonatal Behavioral Assessment Scale. In J. D. Osofsky (Ed.), *Handbook of infant development* (2nd ed., pp. 780–817). New York: Wiley.

Bremner, J. G. (2010). Cognitive development: Knowledge of the physical world. In J. G. Bremner & T. D. Wachs (Eds.), *Wiley-Blackwell handbook of infant development: Vol. 1. Basic research* (2nd ed., pp. 204–242). Oxford, UK: Wiley.

Brendgen, M., Markiewicz, D., Doyle, A. B., & Bukowski, W. M. (2001). The relations between friendship quality, ranked-friendship preference, and adolescents' behavior with their friends. *Merrill-Palmer Quarterly, 47*, 395–415.

Brennan, K. A., & Shaver, P. R. (1995). Dimensions of adult attachment, affect regulation, and romantic relationship functioning. *Personality and Social Psychology Bulletin, 21,* 267–283.

Brennan, W. M., Ames, E. W., & Moore, R. W. (1966). Age differences in infants' attention to patterns of different complexities. *Science, 151,* 354–356.

Brenner, E., & Salovey, P. (1997). Emotional regulation during childhood: Developmental, interpersonal, and individual considerations. In P. Salovey & D. Sluyter (Eds.), *Emotional literacy and emotional development* (pp. 168–192). New York: Basic Books.

Brenner, J. (2013). *Pew Internet: Social Networking.* Washington, DC: Pew Research Center.

Brenner, R. A., & Committee on Injury, Violence, and Poison Prevention. (2003). Prevention of drowning in infants, children, and adolescents. *Pediatrics, 112,* 440–445.

Brent, R. L., Christian, M. S., & Diener, R. M. (2011). Evaluation of the reproductive and developmental risks of caffeine. *Developmental and Reproductive Toxicology, 92,* 152–187.

Brent, S. B., Speece, M. W., Lin, C., Dong, Q., & Yang, C. (1996). The development of the concept of death among Chinese and U.S. children 3–17 years of age: From binary to "fuzzy" concepts? *Omega, 33,* 67–83.

Breslau, N., Kessler, R. C., Chilcoat, H. D., Schultz, L. R., Davis, G. C., & Andreski, P. (1998). Trauma and posttraumatic stress disorder in the community: The 1996 Detroit Area Survey of Trauma. *Archives of General Psychiatry, 55,* 626–632.

Breslin, F. C., & Mustard, C. (2003). Factors influencing the impact of unemployment on mental health among young and older adults in a longitudinal, population-based survey. *Scandinavian Journal of Work, Environment, and Health, 29,* 5–14.

Bretherton, I., & Munholland, K. A. (2008). Internal working models in attachment relationships. In J. Cassidy & P. R. Shaver (Eds.), *Handbook of attachment: Theory, research, and clinical applications* (2nd ed., pp. 102–127). New York: Guilford.

Brewaeys, A., Ponjaert, I., Van Hall, E. V., & Golombok, S. (1997). Donor insemination: Child development and family functioning in lesbian mother families. *Human Reproduction, 12,* 1349–1359.

Bridge, J. A., Goldstein, T. R., & Brent, D. A. (2006). Adolescent suicide and suicidal behavior. *Journal of Child Psychology and Psychiatry, 47,* 372–394.

Bridgett, D. J., Gartstein, M. A., Putnam, S. P., McKay, T., Iddins, R., Robertson, C., et al. (2009). Maternal and contextual influences and the effect of temperament development during infancy on parenting in toddlerhood. *Infant Behavior and Development, 32,* 103–116.

Bright, G. M., Mendoza, J. R., & Rosenfeld, R. G. (2009). Recombinant human insulin-like growth factor-1 treatment: Ready for primetime. *Endocrinology and Metabolism Clinics of North America, 38,* 625–638.

Bright, J. E. H., Pryor, R. G. L., Wilkenfeld, S., & Earl, J. (2005). The role of social context and serendipitous events in career decision making. *International Journal for Educational and Vocational Guidance, 5,* 19–36.

Brim, O. G., Ryff, C. D., & Kessler, R. C. (2005). The MIDUS National Survey: An overview. In O. G. Brim, C. D. Ryff, & R. C. Kessler (Eds.), *How healthy are we? A national study of well-being at midlife* (pp. 1–34). Chicago: University of Chicago Press.

Brisch, K. H., Bechinger, D., Betzler, S., Heineman, H., Kachele, H., Pohlandt, F., Schmucker, G., & Buchheim, A. (2005). Attachment quality in very low-birth-weight premature infants in relation to maternal attachment representations and neurological development. *Parenting: Science and Practice, 5,* 11–32.

Brodaty, H., Seeher, K., & Gibson, L. (2012). Dementia time to death: A systematic literature review on survival time and years of life lost in people with dementia. *International Psychogeriatrics, 24,* 1034–1045.

Brody, G. H., & Flor, D. L. (1998). Maternal resources, parenting practices, and child competence in rural, single-parent African American families. *Child Development, 69,* 803–816.

Brody, G. H., & Murry, V. M. (2001). Sibling socialization of competence in rural, single-parent African American families. *Journal of Marriage and Family, 63,* 996–1008.

Brody, G. H., Stoneman, Z., & McCoy, J. K. (1994). Forecasting sibling relationships in early adolescence from child temperaments and family processes in middle childhood. *Child Development, 65,* 771–784.

Brody, L. (1999). *Gender, emotion, and the family.* Cambridge, MA: Harvard University Press.

Brody, L. R. (1997). Gender and emotion: Beyond stereotypes. *Journal of Social Issues, 53,* 369–393.

Brody, N. (1997). Intelligence, schooling, and society. *American Psychologist, 52,* 1046–1050.

Brodzinsky, D. M. (2011). Children's understanding of adoption: Developmental and clinical implications. *Professional Psychology: Research and Practice, 42,* 200–207.

Broidy, L. M., Nagin, D. S., Tremblay, R. E., Bates, J. E., Brame, B., Dodge, K. A., Fergusson, D., Horwood, J. L., Loeber, R., Laird, R., Lynam, D. R., Moffitt, T. E., Pettit, G. S., & Vitaro, F. (2003). Developmental trajectories of childhood disruptive behaviors and adolescent delinquency: A six-site, cross-national study. *Developmental Psychology, 39,* 222–245.

Bronfenbrenner, U. (Ed.). (2005). *Making human beings human.* Thousand Oaks, CA: Sage.

Bronfenbrenner, U., & Morris, P. A. (2006). The bioecological model of human development. In R. M. Lerner (Ed.), *Handbook of child psychology: Vol. 1. Theoretical models of human development* (6th ed., pp. 297–342). Hoboken, NJ: Wiley.

Bronson, G. W. (1994). Infants' transitions toward adult-like scanning. *Child Development, 65,* 1243–1261.

Bronstein, P. (2006). The family environment: Where gender role socialization begins. In J. Worell & C. D. Goodheart (Eds.), *Handbook of girls' and women's psychological health: Gender and well-being across the lifespan* (pp. 262–271). New York: Oxford University Press.

Bronte-Tinkew, J., Moore, K. A., & Carrano, J. (2006). The father–child relationship, parenting styles, and adolescent risk behaviors in intact families. *Journal of Family Issues, 27,* 850–881.

Brooks, L., McCabe, P., & Schneiderman, N. (2011). Stress and cardiometabolic syndrome. In R. J. Contrada & A. Baum (Eds.), *Handbook of stress science: Biology, psychology, and health* (pp. 399–410). New York: Springer.

Brooks, P. J., Hanauere, J. B., Padowska, B., & Rosman, H. (2003). The role of selective attention in preschoolers' rule use in a novel dimensional card sort. *Cognitive Development, 18,* 195–215.

Brooks, R., & Meltzoff, A. N. (2005). The development of gaze following and its relation to language. *Developmental Science, 8,* 535–543.

Brooks, R., & Meltzoff, A. N. (2008). Infant gaze following and pointing predict accelerated vocabulary growth through two years of age: A longitudinal, growth curve modeling study. *Journal of Child Language, 35,* 207–220.

Brooks-Gunn, J. (1988). Antecedents and consequences of variations in girls' maturational timing. *Journal of Adolescent Health Care, 9,* 365–373.

Brooks-Gunn, J. (2003). Do you believe in magic? What we can expect from early childhood intervention programs. *Social Policy Report of the Society for Research in Child Development, 17,* 3–14.

Brooks-Gunn, J. (2004). Intervention and policy as change agents for young children. In P. L. Chase-Lansdale, K. Kiernan, & R. J. Friedman (Eds.), *Human development across lives and generations: The potential for change* (pp. 293–340). New York: Cambridge University Press.

Brooks-Gunn, J., Han, W.-J., & Waldfogel, J. (2002). Maternal employment and child cognitive outcomes in the first three years of life: The NICHD study of early child care. *Child Development, 73,* 1052–1072.

Brooks-Gunn, J., Han, W.-J., & Waldfogel, J. (2010). First-year maternal employment and child development in the first 7 years. *Monographs of the Society for research in Child Development, 75*(No. 2, Serial No. 296), 59–69.

Brooks-Gunn, J., Klebanov, P. K., Smith, J., Duncan, G. J., & Lee, K. (2003). The black–white test score gap in young children. Contributions of test and family characteristics. *Applied Developmental Science, 7,* 239–252.

Brooks-Gunn, J., Schley, S., & Hardy, J. (2002). Marriage and the baby carriage: Historical change and intergenerational continuity in early parenthood. In L. J. Crockett & R. K. Sibereisen (Eds.), *Negotiating adolescence in times of social change* (pp. 36–57). New York: Cambridge University Press.

Brown, A. M., & Miracle, J. A. (2003). Early binocular vision in human infants: Limitations on the generality of the Superposition Hypothesis. *Vision Research, 43,* 1563–1574.

Brown, A. S. (2006). Prenatal infection as a risk factor for schizophrenia. *Schizophrenia Bulletin, 32,* 200–202.

Brown, B. B., & Dietz, E. L. (2009). Informal peer groups in middle childhood and adolescence. In K. H. Rubin, W. M. Bukowski, & B. Laursen (Eds.), *Handbook of peer interactions, relationships, and groups* (pp. 361–376). New York: Guilford Press.

Brown, B. B., Herman, M., Hamm, J. V., & Heck, D. (2008). Ethnicity and image: Correlates of minority adolescents' affiliation with individual-based versus ethnically defined peer crowds. *Child Development, 79,* 529–546.

Brown, C., & Lowis, M. J. (2003). Psychosocial development in the elderly: An investigation into Erikson's ninth stage. *Journal of Aging Studies, 17,* 415–426.

Brown, C. S., & Bigler, R. S. (2004). Children's perceptions of gender discrimination. *Developmental Psychology, 40,* 714–726.

Brown, G. L., Schoppe-Sullivan, S. J., Mangelsdorf, S. C., & Neff, C. (2010). Observed and reported supportive coparenting as predictors of infant-mother and infant-father attachment security. *Early Child Development and Care, 180,* 121–137.

Brown, J. D., & L'Engle, K. L. (2009). X-rated: Attitudes and behaviors associated with U.S. early adolescents' exposure to sexually explicit media. *Communication Research, 36,* 129–151.

Brown, L. H., & Rodin, P. A. (2004). Grandparent-grandchild relationships and the life course perspective. In J. Demick & C. Andreoletti (Eds.), *Handbook of adult development* (pp. 459–474). New York: Springer.

Brown, R. W. (1973). *A first language: The early stages.* Cambridge, MA: Harvard University Press.

Brown, S. A., & Ramo, D. E. (2005). Clinical course of youth following treatment for alcohol and drug problems. In H. A. Liddle & C. L. Rowe (Eds.), *Adolescent substance abuse: Research and clinical advances* (pp. 79–103). Cambridge, UK: Cambridge University Press.

Brown, S. L., & Kawamura, S. (2010). Relationships quality among cohabitors and marrieds in older adulthood. *Social Science Research, 39,* 777–786.

Brown, S. L., & Lin, I.-F. (2012). *Divorce in middle and later life: New estimates from the 2009 American Community Survey.* Bowling Green, OH: Center for

Family and Demographic Research, Bowling Green University.

Brown, T. M., & Rodriguez, L. F. (2009). School and the co-construction of dropout. *International Journal of Qualitative Studies in Education, 22,* 221–242.

Browne, C. A., & Woolley, J. D. (2004). Preschoolers' magical explanations for violations of physical, social, and mental laws. *Journal of Cognition and Development, 5,* 239–260.

Browne, J. V., & Talmi, A. (2005). Family-based intervention to enhance infant–parent relationships in the neonatal intensive care unit. *Journal of Pediatric Psychology, 30,* 667–677.

Brownell, C. A., Zerwas, S., & Ramani, G. B. (2007). "So big": The development of body self-awareness in toddlers. *Child Development, 78,* 1426–1440.

Bruck, M., & Ceci, S. J. (2004). Forensic developmental psychology: Unveiling four common misconceptions. *Current Directions in Psychological Science, 13,* 229–232.

Brugman, G. M. (2006). Wisdom and aging. In J. E. Birren & K. W. Schaie (Eds.), *Handbook of the psychology of aging* (6th ed., pp. 445–476). Burlington, MA: Elsevier Academic Press.

Brühwiler, C., & Blatchford, P. (2011). Effects of class size and adaptive teaching competency on classroom processes and academic outcome. *Learning and Instruction, 21,* 95–108.

Bruschweiler-Stern, N. (2004). A multifocal neonatal intervention. In A. J. Sameroff, S. C. McDonough, & K. L. Rosenblum (Eds.), *Treating parent–infant relationship problems* (pp. 188–212). New York: Guilford.

Brussoni, M. J., and Boon, S. D. (1998). Grandparental impact in young adults' relationships with their closest grandparents: The role of relationship strength and emotional closeness. *International Journal of Aging and Human Development, 45,* 267–286.

Bruzzese, J.-M., & Fisher, C. B. (2003). Assessing and enhancing the research consent capacity of children and youth. *Applied Developmental Science, 7,* 13–26.

Bryan, A. E., & Dix, T. (2009). Mothers' emotions and behavioral support during interactions with toddlers: The role of child temperament. *Social Development, 18,* 647–670.

Bryant, B. K., Zvonkovic, A. M., & Reynolds, P. (2006). Parenting in relation to child and adolescent vocational development. *Journal of Vocational Behavior, 69,* 149–175.

Bryant, P., & Nunes, T. (2002). Children's understanding of mathematics. In U. Goswami (Ed.), *Blackwell handbook of childhood cognitive development* (pp. 412–439). Malden, MA: Blackwell.

Bryk, R. L., & Fisher, P. A. (2012). Training the brain: Practical applications of neural plasticity from the intersection of cognitive neuroscience, developmental psychology, and prevention science. *American Psychologist, 67,* 87–100.

Buchanan, A. (1996). *Cycles of child maltreatment.* Chichester, UK: Wiley.

Buchanan, C. M., Eccles, J. S., & Becker, J. B. (1992). Are adolescents the victims of raging hormones? Evidence for activational effects of hormones on moods and behavior at adolescence. *Psychological Bulletin, 111,* 62–107.

Buchanan, C. M., Maccoby, E. E., & Dornbusch, S. M. (1996). *Adolescents after divorce.* Cambridge, MA: Harvard University Press.

Buchanan-Barrow, E., & Barrett, M. (1998). Children's rule discrimination within the context of the school. *British Journal of Developmental Psychology, 16,* 539–551.

Buehler, C., & O'Brien, M. (2011). Mothers' part-time employment: Associations with mother and family well-being. *Journal of Family Psychology, 25,* 895–906.

Buescher, E. S. (2001). Anti-inflammatory characteristics of human milk: How, where, why.

Advances in Experimental Medicine and Biology, 501, 207–222.

Bugental, D. B., Ellerson, P. C., Lin, E. K., Rainey, B., & Kokotovic, A. (2002). A cognitive approach to child abuse prevention. *Journal of Family Psychology, 16,* 243–258.

Bugental, D. B., & Happaney, K. (2004). Predicting infant maltreatment in low-income families: The interactive effects of maternal attributions and child status at birth. *Developmental Psychology, 40,* 234–243.

Buhl, H. M., & Lanz, M. (2007). Emerging adulthood in Europe: Common traits and variability across five European countries. *Journal of Adolescent Research, 22,* 439–443.

Buhrmester, D. (1996). Need fulfillment, interpersonal competence, and the developmental contexts of early adolescent friendship. In W. M. Bukowski, A. F. Newcomb, & W. W. Hartup (Eds.), *The company they keep: Friendship during childhood and adolescence* (pp. 158–185). New York: Cambridge University Press.

Buhrmester, D., & Furman, W. (1990). Perceptions of sibling relationships during middle childhood and adolescence. *Child Development, 61,* 1387–1398.

Buhs, E. S., Ladd, G. W., & Herald-Brown, S. L. (2010). Victimization and exclusion: Links to peer rejection, classroom engagement, and achievement. In S. R. Jimerson, S. M. Swearer, & D. L. Espelage (Eds.), *Handbook of bullying in schools: An international perspective* (pp. 163–172). New York: Routledge.

Bukowski, W. M. (2001). Friendship and the worlds of childhood. In D. W. Nangle & C. A. Erdley (Eds.), *The role of friendship in psychological adjustment* (pp. 93–105). San Francisco: Jossey-Bass.

Bullo, M., Lamuela-Raventos, R., & Salas-Salvadó, J. (2011). Mediterranean diet and oxidation: Nuts and olive oil as important sources of fat and antioxidants. *Current Topics in Medicinal Chemistry, 11,* 1797–1810.

Bumpus, M. F., Crouter, A. C., & McHale, S. M. (2006). Linkages between negative work-to-family spillover and mothers' and fathers' knowledge of their young adolescents' daily lives. *Journal of Early Adolescence, 26,* 36–59.

Bunge, S. A., & Wright, S. B. (2007). Neurodevelopmental changes in working memory and cognitive control. *Current Opinion in Neurobiology, 17,* 243–250.

Bunting, L., & McAuley, C. (2004). Teenage pregnancy and parenthood: The role of fathers. *Child and Family Social Work, 9,* 295–303.

Burchinal, M., Vandergrift, N., & Pianta, R. (2010). Threshold analysis of association between child care quality and child outcomes for low-income children in prekindergarten programs. *Early Childhood Research Quarterly, 25,* 166–176.

Burden, M. J., Jacobson, S. W., & Jacobson, J. L. (2005). Relation of prenatal alcohol exposure to cognitive processing speed and efficiency in childhood. *Alcoholism: Clinical and Experimental Research, 29,* 1473–1483.

Burgess-Champoux, T. L., Larson, N., Neumark-Sztainer, D., Hannan, P. J., & Story, M. (2009). Are family meal patterns associated with overall diet quality during the transition from early to middle adolescence? *Journal of Nutrition Education and Behavior, 41,* 79–86.

Burke, D. M., & Shafto, M. A. (2004). Aging and language production. *Current Directions in Psychological Science, 13,* 21–24.

Burleson, B. R., & Kunkel, A. W. (2006). Revisiting the different cultures thesis: An assessment of sex differences and similarities in communication. In K. Dindia & D. J. Canary (Eds.), *Sex differences and similarities in communication* (2nd ed., pp. 137–159). Mahwah, NJ: Erlbaum.

Burman, D. D., Bitan, T., & Booth, J. R. (2007). Sex differences in neural processing of language among some children. *Neuropsychologia, 46,* 1349–1362.

Burts, D.C., Hart, C. H., Charlesworth, R., Fleege, P. O., Mosely, J., & Thomasson, R. H. (1992). Observed activities and stress behaviors of children in developmentally appropriate and inappropriate kindergarten classrooms. *Early Childhood Research Quarterly, 7,* 297–318.

Buscemi, L., & Turchi, C. (2011). An overview of the genetic susceptibility to alcoholism. *Medicine, Science, and the Law, 51,* S2–S6.

Bush, K. R., & Peterson, G. W. (2008). Family influences on child development. In T. P. Gullotta & G. M. Blau (Eds.), *Handbook of child behavioral issues: Evidence-based approaches to prevention and treatment* (pp. 43–67). New York: Routledge.

Bushman, B. J., & Huesmann, L. R. (2001). Effects of televised violence on aggression. In D. G. Singer & J. L. Singer (Eds.), *Handbook of children and the media* (pp. 223–254). Thousand Oaks, CA: Sage.

Bushnell, E. W., & Boudreau, J. P. (1993). Motor development and the mind: The potential role of motor abilities as a determinant of aspects of perceptual development. *Child Development, 64,* 1005–1021.

Buss, D. (2012). *Evolutionary psychology: The new science of the mind* (4th ed.). Upper Saddle River, NJ: Pearson.

Buss, D. M., Shackelford, T. K., Kirkpatrick, L. A., & Larsen, R. J. (2001). A half century of mate preferences: The cultural evolution of values. *Journal of Marriage and Family, 63,* 491–503.

Bussey, K. (1992). Lying and truthfulness: Children's definitions, standards, and evaluative reactions. *Child Development, 63,* 129–137.

Bussey, K. (1999). Children's categorization and evaluation of different types of lies and truths. *Child Development, 70,* 1338–1347.

Bussière, P., Knighton, T., & Pennock, D. (2007). *Measuring up: Canadian results of the OECD PISA Study: The performance of Canada's youth in science, reading, and mathematics: 2006.* First results for Canadians aged 15. Catalogue No. 81-590-XPE—No. 3. Ottawa: Human Resources and Social Development Canada, Council of Ministers of Education, Canada and Statistics Canada. Retrieved from www.statcan.ca/english/freepub/81-590-XIE/81-590-XIE2007001.htm

Buswell, S. D., & Spatz, D. L. (2007). Parent-infant co-sleeping and its relationship to breastfeeding. *Journal of Pediatric Health Care, 21,* 22–28.

Butler, M., & Meaney, J. (Eds.). (2005). *Genetics of developmental disabilities.* Boca Raton, FL: Taylor & Francis.

Butler, M. G. (2009). Genomic imprinting disorders in humans: A mini-review. *Journal of Assisted Reproduction and Genetics, 26,* 477–486.

Butler, R. (1998). Age trends in the use of social and temporal comparison for self-evaluation: Examination of a novel developmental hypothesis. *Child Development, 69,* 1054–1073.

Butler, R. N. (1968). The life review: An interpretation of reminiscence in the aged. In B. Neugarten (Ed.), *Middle age and aging* (pp. 486–496). Chicago: University of Chicago Press.

Buttelmann, D., Carpenter, M., & Tomasello, M. (2009). Eighteen-month-old infants show false belief understanding in an active helping paradigm. *Cognition, 112,* 337–342.

Buunk, B. P. (2002). Age and gender differences in mate selection criteria for various involvement levels. *Personal Relationships, 9,* 271–278.

Bybee, J. A., & Wells, Y. V. (2003). The development of possible selves during adulthood. In J. Demick & C. Andreoletti (Eds.), *Handbook of adult development* (pp. 257–270). New York: Springer.

Byrnes, J. P. (2003). Cognitive development during adolescence. In G. R. Adams & M. D. Berzonsky (Eds.), *Blackwell handbook of adolescence* (pp. 227–246). Malden, MA: Blackwell.

C

Cabrera, N. J., & Bradley, R. H. (2012). Latino fathers and their children. *Child Development Perspectives, 6,* 232–238.

Cabrera, N. J., & Garcia-Coll, C. (2004). Latino fathers: Uncharted territory in need of much exploration. In M. E. Lamb (Ed.), *The role of the father in child development* (4th ed., pp. 98–120). Hoboken, NJ: Wiley.

Cabrera, N. J., Shannon, J. D., & Tamis-LeMonda, C. (2007). Fathers' influence on their children's cognitive and emotional development: From toddlers to pre-K. *Applied Developmental Science, 11,* 208–213.

Cabrera, N. J., Tamis-LeMonda, C. S., Bradley, R. H., Hoferth, S., & Lamb, M. E. (2000). Fatherhood in the twenty-first century. *Child Development, 71,* 127–136.

Cacioppo, J. T., & Patrick, W. (2008). *Loneliness: Human nature and the need for social connection.* New York: Norton.

Cahill, A. G., & Macones, G. A. (2007). Vaginal birth after cesarean delivery: Evidence-based practice. *Clinical Obstetrics and Gynecology, 50,* 518–525.

Cahill, K. E., Giandrea, M. D., & Quinn, J. F. (2006). Retirement patterns from career employment. *Gerontologist, 46,* 514–523.

Cai, H., Cong, W., Ji, S., Rathman, S., Maudsley, S., & Martin, B. (2012). Metabolic dysfunction in Alzheimer's disease and related neurodegenerative disorders. *Current Alzheimer Research, 9,* 5–17.

Cain, K. M., & Dweck, C. S. (1995). The relation between motivational patterns and achievement cognitions through the elementary school years. *Merrill-Palmer Quarterly, 41,* 25–52.

Caine, N. (1986). Behavior during puberty and adolescence. In G. Mitchell & J. Erwin (Eds.), *Comparative primate biology: Vol. 2A. Behavior, conservation, and ecology* (pp. 327–361). New York: Liss.

Cairns, R. B., & Cairns, B. D. (2006). The making of developmental psychology. In R. M. Lerner (Ed.), *Handbook of child psychology: Vol. 1. Theoretical models of human development* (6th ed., pp. 89–165). Hoboken, NJ: Wiley.

Calasanti, T., & Kiecolt, K. J. (2007). Diversity among late-life couples. *Generations, 31,* 10–17.

Caldera, Y. M., & Lindsey, E. W. (2006). Coparenting, mother–infant interaction, and infant–parent attachment relationships in two-parent families. *Journal of Family Psychology, 20,* 275–283.

Caldwell, B. M., & Bradley, R. H. (1994). Environmental issues in developmental follow-up research. In S. L. Friedman & H. C. Haywood (Eds.), *Developmental follow-up* (pp. 235–256). San Diego: Academic Press.

Calhoun, L. G., Tedeschi, R. G., Cann, A., & Hanks, E. A. (2010). Positive outcomes following bereavement: Paths to posttraumatic growth. *Psychologica Belgica, 50,* 125–143.

Callaghan, T., Rochat, P., Lillard, A., Claux, M. L., Odden, H., Itakura, S., Tapanya, S., & Singh, S. (2005). Synchrony in the onset of mental-state reasoning: Evidence from five cultures. *Psychological Science, 16,* 378–384.

Callanan, M. A., & Oakes, L. M. (1992). Preschoolers' questions and parents' explanations: Causal thinking in everyday activity. *Cognitive Development, 7,* 213–233.

Callanan, M. A., & Sabbagh, M. A. (2004). Multiple labels for objects in conversations with young children: Parents' language and children's developing expectations about word meanings. *Developmental Psychology, 40,* 746–763.

Calvert, S. L., Rideout, V. J., Woolard, J. L., Barr, R. F., & Strouse, G. A. (2005). Age, ethnicity, and socioeconomic patterns in early computer use: A national survey. *American Behavioral Scientist, 48,* 590–607.

Cameron, C. A., & Lee, K. (1997). The development of children's telephone communication. *Journal of Applied Developmental Psychology, 18,* 55–70.

Cameron, P. A., & Gallup, G. G. (1988). Shadow recognition in human infants. *Infant Behavior and Development, 11,* 465–471.

Cameron-Faulkner, T., Lieven, E., & Tomasello, M. (2003). A construction based analysis of childdirected speech. *Cognitive Science, 27,* 843–873.

Camp, C. J., Cohen-Mansfield, J., & Capezuti, E. A. (2002). Use of nonpharmacologic interventions among nursing home residents with dementia. *Psychiatric Services, 53,* 1397–1401.

Campa, M. J., & Eckenrode, J. J. (2006). Pathways to intergenerational adolescent childbearing in a high-risk sample. *Journal of Marriage and Family, 68,* 558–572.

Campbell, A., Shirley, L., & Candy, J. (2004). A longitudinal study of gender-related cognition and behaviour. *Developmental Science, 7,* 1–9.

Campbell, A. L., & Binstock, R. H. (2011). Politics and aging in the United States. In R. H. Binstock & L. K. George (Eds.), *Handbook of aging and the social sciences* (pp. 265–280). San Diego, CA: Academic Press.

Campbell, D. A., Lake, M. F., Falk, M., & Backstrand, J. R. (2006). A randomized control trial of continuous support in labor by a lay doula. *Journal of Obstetrics and Gynecology and Neonatal Nursing, 35,* 456–464.

Campbell, D. A., Scott, K. D., Klaus, M. H., & Falk, M. (2007). Female relatives or friends trained as labor doulas: Outcomes at 6 to 8 weeks postpartum. *Birth, 34,* 220–227.

Campbell, F. A., Pungello, E. P., Miller-Johnson, S., Burchinal, M., & Ramey, C. T. (2001). The development of cognitive and academic abilities: Growth curves from an early childhood educational experiment. *Developmental Psychology, 37,* 231–242.

Campbell, F. A., & Ramey, C. T. (2010). Carolina Abecedarian Project. In A. Reynolds, A. J. Rolick, M. M. Englund, & J. A. Temple (Eds.), *Childhood programs and practices in the first decade of life: A human capital integration* (pp. 76–98). New York: Cambridge University Press.

Campbell, F. A., Ramey, C. T., Pungello, E. P., Sparling, J., & Miller-Johnson, S. (2002). Early childhood education: Young adult outcomes from the Abecedarian Project. *Applied Developmental Science, 6,* 42–57.

Campbell, J., & Glass, N. (2009). Safety planning, danger, and lethality assessment. In C. Mitchell & D. Anglin (Eds.), *Intimate partner violence: A health-based perspective* (pp. 319–334). New York: Oxford University Press.

Campbell, S. B., Brownell, C. A., Hungerford, A., Spieker, S. J., Mohan, R., & Blessing, J. S. (2004). The course of maternal depressive symptoms and maternal sensitivity as predictors of attachment security at 36 months. *Development and Psychopathology, 16,* 231–252.

Campos, J. J., Anderson, D. I., Barbu-Roth, M. A., Hubbard, E. M., Hertenstein, J. J., & Witherington, D. (2000). Travel broadens the mind. *Infancy, 1,* 149–219.

Campos, J. J., Frankel, C. B., & Camras, L. (2004). On the nature of emotion regulation. *Child Development, 75,* 377–394.

Campos, J. J., Witherington, D., Anderson, D. I., Frankel, C. I., Uchiyama, I., & Barbu-Roth, M. (2008). Rediscovering development in infancy. *Child Development, 79,* 1625–1632.

Campos, R. G. (1989). Soothing pain-elicited distress in infants with swaddling and pacifiers. *Child Development, 60,* 781–792.

Camras, L. A., Oster, H., Campos, J. J., & Bakeman, R. (2003). Emotional facial expressions in European-American, Japanese, and Chinese infants. *Annals of the New York Academy of Sciences, 1000,* 1–17.

Camras, L. A., Oster, H., Campos, J. J., Campos, R., Ujie, T., Miyake, K., Wang, L., & Meng, Z. (1998). Production of emotional and facial expressions in European American, Japanese, and Chinese infants. *Developmental Psychology, 34,* 616–628.

Camras, L. A., Oster, H., Campos, J. J., Miyake, K., & Bradshaw, D. (1992). Japanese and American infants' responses to arm restraint. *Developmental Psychology, 28,* 578–583.

Canada Campaign 2000. (2009). *2009 Report Card on Child and Family Poverty in Canada: 1989–2009.* Retrieved from www.campaign2000.ca/reportcards .html

Candy, B., Holman, A., Leurent, S., & Jones, D. L. (2011). Hospice care delivered at home, in nursing homes and in dedicated hospice facilities: A systematic review of quantitative and qualitative evidence. *International Journal of Nursing Studies, 48,* 113–133.

Candy-Gibbs, S., Sharp, K., & Petrun, C. (1985). The effects of age, object, and cultural/religious background on children's concepts of death. *Omega, 154,* 329–345.

Canetto, S. S., Kaminski, P. L., & Felicio, D. M. (1995). Typical and optimal aging in women and men: Is there a double standard? *International Journal of Aging and Human Development, 40,* 187–207.

Cannella, C., Savina, C., & Donini, L. M. (2009). Nutrition, longevity and behavior. *Archives of Gerontology and Geriatrics, 49*(Suppl. 1), 19–27.

Canobi, K. H. (2004). Individual differences in children's addition and subtraction knowledge. *Cognitive Development, 19,* 81–93.

Canobi, K. H., Reeve, R. A., & Pattison, P. E. (2003). The role of conceptual understanding in children's addition problem solving. *Developmental Psychology, 39,* 521–534.

Capaldi, D., DeGarmo, D., Patterson, G. R., & Forgatch, M. (2002). Contextual risk across the early life span and association with antisocial behavior. In J. B. Reid, G. R. Patterson, & J. Snyder (Eds.), *Antisocial behavior in children and adolescents* (pp. 123–145). Washington, DC: American Psychological Association.

Capirci, O., Contaldo, A., Caselli, M. C., & Volterra, V. (2005). From action to language through gesture. *Gesture, 5,* 155–177.

Cappeliez, P., Rivard, V., & Guindon, S. (2007). Functions of reminiscence in later life: Proposition of a model and applications. European *Review of Applied Psychology, 57,* 151–156.

Cappeliez, P., & Robitaille, A. (2010). Coping mediates the relationships between reminiscence and psychological well-being among older adults. *Aging and Mental Health, 14,* 807–818.

Carbery, J., & Buhrmester, D. (1998). Friendship and need fulfillment during three phases of young adulthood. *Journal of Social and Personal Relationships, 15,* 393–409.

Card, N. A., Stucky, B. D., Sawalani, G. M., & Little, T. D. (2008). Direct and indirect aggression during childhood and adolescence: A meta-analytic review of gender differences, intercorrelations, and relations to maladjustment. *Child Development, 79,* 1185–1229.

Carek, P. J., Laibstain, S. E., & Carek, S. M. (2011). Exercise for the treatment of depression and anxiety. *International Journal of Psychiatry in Medicine, 41,* 15–28.

Carey, S., & Markman, E. M. (1999). Cognitive development. In B. M. Bly & D. E. Rumelhart (Eds.), *Cognitive science* (pp. 201–254). San Diego: Academic Press.

Carlo, G., Koller, S. H., Eisenberg, N., Da Silva, M., & Frohlich, C. (1996). A cross-national study on the relations among prosocial moral reasoning, gender role orientations, and prosocial behaviors. *Developmental Psychology, 32,* 231–240.

Carlo, G., Mestre, M. V., Samper, P., Tur, A., & Armenta, B. E. (2011). The longitudinal relations among dimensions of parenting styles, sympathy, prosocial moral reasoning, and prosocial behaviors. *International Journal of Behavioral Development, 35,* 116–124.

Carlson, S. M., & Meltzoff, A. N. (2008). Bilingual experience and executive functioning in young children. *Developmental Science, 11,* 282–298.

Carlson, S. M., Moses, L. J., & Claxton, S. J. (2004). Individual differences in executive functioning and theory of mind: An investigation of inhibitory control and planning ability. *Journal of Experimental Child Psychology, 87,* 299–319.

Carlson, V. J., & Harwood, R. L. (2003). Attachment, culture, and the caregiving system: The cultural patterning of everyday experiences among Anglo and Puerto Rican mother–infant pairs. *Infant Mental Health Journal, 24,* 53–73.

Carnelley, K. B., Wortman, C. B., Bolger, N., & Burke, C. T. (2006). The time course of grief reactions to spousal loss: Evidence from a national probability sample. *Journal of Personality and Social Psychology, 91,* 476–492.

Carnes, B. A., Olshansky, S. J., & Hayflick, L. (2013). Can human biology allow most of us to become centenarians? *Journal of Gerontology, 68A,* 136–142.

Carpendale, J. I. M. (2000). Kohlberg and Piaget on stages and moral reasoning. *Developmental Review, 20,* 181–205.

Carpenter, M., Akhtar, N., & Tomasello, M. (1998). Fourteen- through eighteen-month-old infants differentially imitate intentional and accidental actions. *Infant Behavior and Development, 21,* 315–330.

Carpenter, M., Nagell, K., & Tomasello, M. (1998). Social cognition, joint attention, and communicative competence. *Monographs of the Society for Research in Child Development, 63*(4, Serial No. 255).

Carpenter, T. P., Fennema, E., Fuson, K., Hiebert, J., Human, P., & Murray, H. (1999). Learning basic number concepts and skills as problem solving. In E. Fennema & T. A. Romberg (Eds.), *Mathematics classrooms that promote understanding: Studies in mathematical thinking and learning series* (pp. 45–61). Mahwah, NJ: Erlbaum.

Carr, D. (2003). A "good death" for whom? Quality of spouse's death and psychological distress among older widowed persons. *Journal of Health and Social Behavior, 44,* 215–232.

Carr, D. (2004). Psychological well-being across three cohorts: A response to shifting work-family opportunities and expectations? In O. G. Brim, C. D. Ryff, & R. C. Kessler (Eds.), *How healthy are we? A national study of well-being at midlife* (pp. 452–484). Chicago: University of Chicago Press.

Carr, D., House, J. S., Wortman, C., Nesse, R., & Kessler, R. C. (2001). Psychological adjustment to sudden and anticipated spousal loss among older widowed persons. *Journal of Gerontology, 56B,* S237–S248.

Carr, J. (2002). Down syndrome. In P. Howlin & O. Udwin (Eds.), *Outcomes in neurodevelopmental and genetic disorders* (pp. 169–197). New York: Cambridge University Press.

Carroll, D., Phillips, A. C., Hunt, K., & Der, G. (2007). Symptoms of depression and cardiovascular reactions to acute psychological stress: Evidence from a population study. *Biological Psychology, 75,* 68–74.

Carroll, J. B. (2005). The three-stratum theory of cognitive abilities. In D. P. Flanagan & P. L. Harrison (Eds.), *Contemporary intellectual assessment:*

Theories, tests, and issues (2nd ed., pp. 69–76). New York: Guilford.

Carroll, J. S., Badger S., Willoughby, B. J., Nelson, L. J., Madsen, S. D., & Barry, C. M. (2009). Ready or not?: Criteria for marriage readiness among emerging adults. *Journal of Adolescent Research, 24,* 349–375.

Carskadon, M. A., Harvey, K., Duke, P., Anders, T. F., Litt, I. F., & Dement, W. C. (2002). Pubertal changes in daytime sleepiness. *Sleep, 25,* 525–605.

Carstensen, L. L. (2006). The influence of sense of time on human development. *Science, 312,* 1913–1915.

Carstensen, L. L., Fung, H. H., & Charles, S. T. (2003). Socioemotional selectivity theory and the regulation of emotion in the second half of life. *Motivation and Emotion, 27,* 103–123.

Carstensen, L. L., Turan, B., Scheibe, S., Ram, N., Ersner-Hershfield, H., Samanez-Larkin, G. R., et al. (2011). Emotional experience improves with age: Evidence based on over 10 years of experience sampling. *Psychology and Aging, 26,* 21–33.

Carter, C. S., Hofer, T., Seo, A. Y., & Leeuwenburgh, C. (2007). Molecular mechanisms of life- and healthspan extension: Role of calorie restriction and exercise intervention. *Applied Physiology, Nutrition, and Metabolism, 32,* 954–966.

Carver, C. S. (2011). Coping. In R. J. Contrada & A. Baum (Eds.), *Handbook of stress science: Biology, psychology, and health* (pp. 221–245). New York: Springer.

Carver, K., Joyner, K., & Udry, J. R. (2003). National estimates of adolescent romantic relationships. In P. Florsheim (Ed.), *Adolescent romantic relations and sexual behavior: Theory, research, and practical implications* (pp. 23–56). Mahwah, NJ: Erlbaum.

Carver, P. R., Egan, S. K., & Perry, D. G. (2004). Children who question their heterosexuality. *Developmental Psychology, 40,* 43–53.

CASA. (2006). *The importance of family dinners III.* New York: National Center on Addiction and Substance Abuse, Columbia University.

Casalis, S., & Cole, P. (2009). On the relationship between morphological and phonological awareness: Effects of training in kindergarten and in first-grade reading. *First Language, 29,* 113–142.

Casas, J. F., Weigel, S. M., Crick, N. R., Ostrov, J. M., Woods, K. E., Yeh, E. A. J., & Huddleston-Casas, C. A. (2006). Early parenting and children's relational and physical aggression in the preschool and home contexts. *Applied Developmental Psychology, 27,* 209–227.

Casasola, M., Cohen, L. B., & Chiarello, E. (2003). Six-month-old infants' categorization of containment spatial relations. *Child Development, 74,* 679–693.

Casavant, M. J., Blake, K., Griffith, J., Yates, A., & Copley, L. M. (2007). Consequences of use of anabolic androgenic steroids. *Pediatric Clinics of North America, 54,* 677–690.

Case, R. (1996). Introduction: Reconceptualizing the nature of children's conceptual structures and their development in middle childhood. In R. Case & Y. Okamoto (Eds.), The role of central conceptual structures in the development of children's thought. *Monographs of the Society for Research in Child Development, 246*(61, Serial No. 246), pp. 1–26.

Case, R. (1998). The development of central conceptual structures. In D. Kuhn & R. Siegler (Eds.), *Handbook of child psychology: Vol. 2. Cognition, perception, and language* (5th ed., pp. 745–800). New York: Wiley.

Case, R., & Okamoto, Y. (Eds.). (1996). The role of central conceptual structures in the development of children's thought. *Monographs of the Society for Research in Child Development, 61*(1–2, Serial No. 246).

Caserta, M., Lund, D., Utz, R., & de Vries, B. (2009). Stress-related growth among the recently bereaved. *Aging and Mental Health, 13,* 463–476.

Caserta, M. S., Lund, D. A., & Obray, S. J. (2004). Promoting self-care and daily living skills among older widows and widowers: Evidence from the Pathfinders Demonstration Project. *Omega, 49,* 217–236.

Caserta, M. S., Lund, D. A., & Rice, S. J. (1999). Pathfinders: A self-care and health education program for older widows and widowers. *Gerontologist, 39,* 615–620.

Casper, L. M., & Smith, K. E. (2002). Dispelling the myths: Self-care, class, and race. *Journal of Family Issues, 23,* 716–727.

Caspi, A., Elder, G. H., Jr., & Bem, D. J. (1987). Moving against the world: Life-course patterns of explosive children. *Developmental Psychology, 23,* 308–313.

Caspi, A., Elder, G. H., Jr., & Bem, D. J. (1988). Moving away from the world: Life-course patterns of shy children. *Developmental Psychology, 24,* 824–831.

Caspi, A., Harrington, H., Milne, B., Amell, J. W., Theodore, R. F., & Moffitt, T. E. (2003). Children's behavioral styles at age 3 are linked to their adult personality traits at age 26. *Journal of Personality, 71,* 495–513.

Caspi, A., Lynam, D., Moffitt, T. E., & Silva, P. A. (1993). Unraveling girls' delinquency: Biological, dispositional, and contextual contributions to adolescent misbehavior. *Developmental Psychology, 29,* 19–30.

Caspi, A., McClay, J., Moffitt, T. E., Mill, J., Martin, J., & Craig, I. W. (2002). Role of genotype in the cycle of violence in maltreated children. *Science, 297,* 851–854.

Caspi, A., Moffitt, T. E., Morgan, J., Rutter, M., Taylor, A., Kim-Cohen, J., & Polo-Tomas, M. (2004). Maternal expressed emotion predicts children's antisocial behavior problems: Using monozygotic-twin differences to identify environmental effects on behavioral development. *Developmental Psychology, 40,* 149–161.

Caspi, A., & Roberts, B. W. (2001). Personality development across the life course: The argument for change and continuity. *Psychological Inquiry, 12,* 49–66.

Caspi, A., & Shiner, R. L. (2006). Personality development. In N. Eisenberg (Ed.), *Handbook of child psychology: Vol. 3. Social, emotional, and personality development* (6th ed., pp. 300–365). Hoboken, NJ: Wiley.

Cassia, V. M., Turati, C., & Simion, F. (2004). Can a nonspecific bias toward top-heavy patterns explain newborns' face preference? *Psychological Science, 15,* 379–383.

Cassidy, J. (2001). Adult romantic attachments: A developmental perspective on individual differences. *Review of General Psychology, 4,* 111–131.

Cassidy, J., & Berlin, L. J. (1994). The insecure/ambivalent pattern of attachment: Theory and research. *Child Development, 65,* 971–991.

Castel, A. D., McGillivray, S., & Friedman, M. C. (2011). Metamemory and memory efficiency in older adults: Learning about the benefits of priority processing and value-directed remembering. In M. Naveh-Benjamin & N. Ohta (Eds.), *Memory and aging: Current issues and future directions* (pp. 245–270). New York: Psychology Press.

Castillo, E. M., & Comstock, R. D. (2007). Prevalence of use of performance-enhancing substances among United States adolescents. *Pediatric Clinics of North America, 54,* 663–675.

Catalano, R., Ahern, J., Bruckner, T., Anderson, E., & Saxton, K. (2009). Gender-specific selection in utero among contemporary human birth cohorts. *Paediatric and Perinatal Epidemiology, 23,* 273–278.

Catalano, R., Zilko, C. E., Saxton, K. B., & Bruckner, T. (2010). Selection in utero: A biological response to mass layoffs. *American Journal of Human Biology, 22,* 396–400.

Caton, D., Corry, M. P., Frigoletto, F. D., Hokins, D. P., Liberman, E., & Mayberry, L. (2002). The nature and management of labor pain: Executive summary. *American Journal of Obstetrics and Gynecology, 186,* S1–S15.

Cauley, J. A. (2011). Defining ethnic and racial differences in osteoporosis and fragility fractures. *Clinical Orthopedics and Related Research, 469,* 1891–1899.

Cavadini, C., Siega-Riz, A. M., & Popkin, B. M. (2000). U.S. adolescent food intake trends from 1965 to 1996. *Archives of Diseases in Childhood, 83,* 18–24.

Ceci, S. J. (1991). How much does schooling influence general intelligence and its cognitive components? A reassessment of the evidence. *Developmental Psychology, 27,* 703–722.

Ceci, S. J. (1999). Schooling and intelligence. In S. J. Ceci & W. M. Williams (Eds.), *The nature–nurture debate: The essential readings* (pp. 168–175). Oxford, UK: Blackwell.

Ceci, S. J., Bruck, M., & Battin, D. B. (2000). The suggestibility of children's testimony. In D. F. Bjorklund (Ed.), *False-memory creation in children and adults* (pp. 169–201). Mahwah, NJ: Erlbaum.

Ceci, S. J., Kulkofsky, S., Klemfuss, J. Z., Sweeney, C. D., & Bruck, M. (2007). Unwarranted assumptions about children's testimonial accuracy. *Annual Review of Clinical Psychology, 3,* 311–328.

Ceci, S. J., Rosenblum, T. B., & Kumpf, M. (1998). The shrinking gap between high- and low-scoring groups: Current trends and possible causes. In U. Neisser (Ed.), *The rising curve* (pp. 287–302). Washington, DC: American Psychological Association.

Ceci, S. J., & Williams, W. M. (1997). Schooling, intelligence, and income. *American Psychologist, 52,* 1051–1058.

Ceci, S. J., & Williams, W. M. (2010). *The mathematics of sex: How biology and society conspire to limit talented women and girls.* New York: Oxford University Press.

Cecil, J. E., Watt, P., Murrie, I. S. L., Wrieden, W., Wallis, D. J., Hetherington, M. M., Bolton-Smith, C., & Palmer, C. N. A. (2005). Childhood obesity and socioeconomic status: A novel role for height growth limitation. *International Journal of Obesity, 29,* 1199–1203.

Ceda, G. P., Dall'Aglio, E., Morganti, S., Denti, L., Maggio M., Lauretani, F., et al. (2010). Update on new therapeutic options for the somatopause. *Atenei Parmensis, 81*(Suppl. 1), 67–72.

Center for Hearing and Communication. (2012). *Facts about hearing loss.* Retrieved from www.chchearing.org/about-hearing-loss/facts-about-hearing-loss

Center to Advance Palliative Care. (2012). *Growth of palliative care in U.S. hospitals: 2012 snapshot.* Retrieved from www.capc.org/capc-growth-analysis-snapshot-2011.pdf

Centers for Disease Control and Prevention. (2007). *School Health Policies and Programs Study.* Atlanta, GA: Author.

Centers for Disease Control and Prevention. (2010). *Hip fractures in older adults.* Retrieved from www.cdc.gov/homeandrecreationalsafety/falls/adulthipfx.html

Centers for Disease Control and Prevention. (2011a). *Breastfeeding report card—United States 2011.* Retrieved from www.cdc.gov/breastfeeding/pdf/2011BreastfeedingReportCard.pdf

Centers for Disease Control and Prevention. (2011b). *HIV Surveillance Report: Diagnoses of HIV infection and AIDS in the United States and dependent areas, 2009.* Atlanta, GA: U.S. Department of Health and Human Services.

Centers for Disease Control and Prevention. (2011c, April). *CDC vital signs: Preventing teen pregnancy in the U.S.* Retrieved from www.cdc.gov/vitalsigns/pdf/2011-04-vitalsigns.pdf

Centers for Disease Control and Prevention. (2011d). *Sexually transmitted disease surveillance 2010.*

Atlanta, GA: U.S. Department of Health and Human Services.

Centers for Disease Control and Prevention. (2011e). *2009 assisted reproductive technology success rates: National summary and fertility clinic reports.* Atlanta, GA: Author.

Centers for Disease Control and Prevention. (2012a). *Adult obesity facts.* Retrieved from www.cdc.gov/obesity/data/adult.html

Centers for Disease Control and Prevention. (2012b). *CDC vital signs: Child injury.* Retrieved from www.cdc.gov/vitalsigns/ChildInjury

Centers for Disease Control and Prevention. (2012c). *HIV in the United States: An overview.* Retrieved from www.cdc.gov/hiv/topics/surveillance/resources/factsheets/pdf/HIV_overview_2012.pdf

Centers for Disease Control and Prevention. (2012d). Vital signs: Current cigarette smoking among adults aged ≥18 years—United States, 2005–2010. *Morbidity and Mortality Weekly Report, 60,* 1207–1212.

Centers for Disease Control and Prevention. (2013). *Multiple cause of death, 1999–2010.* Retrieved from wonder.cdc.gov/wonder/help/mcd.html

Centers for Medicare and Medicaid Services. (2012). *National health expenditure projections.* Retrieved from www.cms.gov/Research-Statistics-Data-and-Systems/Statistics-Trends-and-Reports/NationalHealthExpendData/NationalHealthAccountsProjected.html

Cerella, J. (1990). Aging and information processing rate. In J. E. Birren & K. W. Schaie (Eds.), *Handbook of the psychology of aging* (3rd ed.), (pp. 201–221). San Diego: Academic Press.

Cernoch, J. M., & Porter, R. H. (1985). Recognition of maternal axillary odors by infants. *Child Development 56,* 1593–1598.

Cevenini, E., Invidia, L., Lescai, F., Salvioli, S., Tieri, P., Castellani, G., & Franceschi, G. (2008). Human models of aging and longevity. *Expert Opinion on Biological Therapy, 8,* 1393–1405.

CFAH (Center for Advancement of Health). (2003). *Report on Phase 1 of the Grief Research Gaps, Needs and Actions Project.* Washington, DC: Author.

Chakravarty, E. F., Hubert, H. B., Krishnan, E., Bruce, B. B., Lingala, V. B., & Fries, J. F. (2012). Lifestyle risk factors predict disability and death in healthy aging adults. *American Journal of Medicine, 125,* 190–197.

Chalabaev, A., Sarrazin, P., & Fontayne, P. (2009). Stereotype endorsement and perceived ability as mediators of the girls' gender orientation–soccer performance relationship. *Psychology of Sport and Exercise, 10,* 297–299.

Chamberlain, P. (2003). Antisocial behavior and delinquency in girls. In P. Chamberlain (Ed.), *Treating chronic juvenile offenders* (pp. 109–127). Washington, DC: American Psychological Association.

Champion, T. B. (2003a). "A matter of vocabulary": Performances of low-income African-American Head Start children on the Peabody Picture Vocabulary Test. *Communication Disorders Quarterly, 24,* 121–127.

Champion, T. B. (2003b). *Understanding storytelling among African-American children: A journey from Africa to America.* Mahwah, NJ: Erlbaum.

Chan, A., Meints, K., Lieven, E., & Tomasello, M. (2010). Young children's comprehension of English SVO word order revisited: Testing the same children in act-out and intermodal preferential looking tasks. *Cognitive Development, 25,* 30–45.

Chan, L. K. S., & Moore, P. J. (2006). Development of attributional beliefs and strategic knowledge in years 5–9: A longitudinal analysis. *Educational Psychology, 26,* 161–185.

Chan, R. W., Raboy, B., & Patterson, C. J. (1998). Psychosocial adjustment among children conceived

via donor insemination by lesbian and heterosexual mothers. *Child Development, 69,* 443–457.

Chan, S. M. (2010). Aggressive behaviour in early elementary school children: Relations to authoritarian parenting, children's negative emotionality and coping strategies. *Early Child Development and Care, 180,* 1253–1269.

Chandola, T., & Marmot, M. G. (2011). Socioeconomic status and stress. In R. J. Contrada & A. Baum (Eds.), *Handbook of stress science: Biology, psychology, and health* (pp. 185–193). New York: Springer.

Chandra, A., Martino, S. C., Collins, R. L., Elliott, M. N., Berry, S. H., Kanouse, D. E., & Miu, A. (2008). Does watching sex on television predict teen pregnancy? Findings from a national longitudinal survey of youth. *Pediatrics, 122,* 1047–1054.

Chandra, R. K. (1991). Interactions between early nutrition and the immune system. In *Ciba Foundation Symposium No. 156* (pp. 77–92). Chichester, UK: Wiley.

Chang, E., Wilber, K. H., & Silverstein, M. (2010). The effects of childlessness on the care and psychological well-being of older adults with disabilities. *Aging and Mental Health, 14,* 712–719.

Chang, F., Dell, G. S., & Bock, K. (2006). Becoming syntactic. *Psychological Review, 113,* 234–272.

Chang, L., Schwartz, D., Dodge, D. A., & McBride-Chang, C. (2003). Harsh parenting in relation to child emotion regulation and aggression. *Journal of Family Psychology, 17,* 598–606.

Chao, R. K. (1994). Beyond parental control and authoritarian parenting style: Understanding Chinese parenting through the cultural notion of training. *Child Development, 65,* 1111–1119.

Chao, R. K., & Good, G. E. (2004). Nontraditional students' perspectives on college education: A qualitative study. *Journal of College Counseling, 7,* 5–12.

Chao, R. K., & Tseng, V. (2002). Parenting of Asians. In M. H. Bornstein (Ed.), *Handbook of parenting: Vol 4* (2nd ed., pp. 59–94). Mahwah, NJ: Erlbaum.

Chapman, R. S. (2006). Children's language learning: An interactionist perspective. In R. Paul (Ed.), *Language disorders from a developmental perspective* (pp. 1–53). Mahwah, NJ: Erlbaum.

Charles, S. T. (2010). Strength and vulnerability integration: A model of emotional well-being across adulthood. *Psychological Bulletin, 136,* 1068–1091.

Charles, S. T. (2011). Emotional experience and regulation in later life. In K. W. Schaie & S. L. Willis (Eds.), *Handbook of the psychology of aging* (7th ed., pp. 295–310). San Diego, CA: Academic Press.

Charles, S. T., & Carstensen, L. L. (2009). Socioemotional selectivity theory. In H. Reis & S. Sprecher (Eds.), *Encyclopedia of human relationships* (pp. 1578–1581). Thousand Oaks, CA: Sage.

Charles, S. T., & Carstensen, L. L. (2010). Social and emotional aging. *Annual Review of Psychology, 61,* 383–409.

Charman, T., Baron-Cohen, S., Swettenham, J., Baird, G., Cox, A., & Drew, A. (2001). Testing joint attention, imitation, and play as infancy precursors to language and theory of mind. *Cognitive Development, 15,* 481–49.

Charman, W. N. (2008). The eye in focus: Accommodation and presbyopia. *Optometry, 91,* 207–225.

Charpak, N., Ruiz-Peláez, J. G., & Figueroa, Z. (2005). Influence of feeding patterns and other factors on early somatic growth of healthy, preterm infants in home-based kangaroo mother care: A cohort study. *Journal of Pediatric Gastroenterology and Nutrition, 41,* 430–437.

Chase-Lansdale, P. L., Brooks-Gunn, J., & Zamsky, E. S. (1994). Young African-American multigenerational families in poverty: Quality of mothering and grandmothering. *Child Development, 65,* 373–393.

Chase-Lansdale, P. L., Gordon, R., Brooks-Gunn, J., & Klebanov, P. K. (1997). Neighborhood and family influences on the intellectual and behavioral competence of preschool and early school-age children. In J. Brooks-Gunn, G. Duncan, & J. L. Aber (Eds.), *Neighborhood poverty: Context and consequences for development* (pp. 79–118). New York: Russell Sage Foundation.

Chauhan, G. S., Shastri, J., & Mohite, P. (2005). Development of gender constancy in preschoolers. *Psychological Studies, 50,* 62–71.

Chavajay, P., & Rogoff, B. (1999). Cultural variation in management of attention by children and their caregivers. *Developmental Psychology, 35,* 1079–1090.

Chavajay, P., & Rogoff, B. (2002). Schooling and traditional collaborative social organization of problem solving by Mayan mothers and children. *Developmental Psychology, 38,* 55–66.

Chawarska, K., & Shic, F. (2009). Looking but not seeing: Atypical visual scanning and recognition of faces in 2- and 4-year-old children with autism spectrum disorder. *Journal of Autism and Developmental Disorders, 39,* 1663–1672.

Cheadle, J. E., & Amato, P. R. (2011). A quantitative assessment of Lareau's qualitative conclusions about class, race, and parenting. *Journal of Family Issues, 32,* 679–706.

Cheah, C. S. L., Leung, C. Y. Y., Tahseen, M., & Schultz, D. (2009). Authoritative parenting among immigrant Chinese mothers of preschoolers. *Journal of Family Psychology, 23,* 311–320.

Checkley, W., Epstein, L. D., Gilman, R. H., Cabrera, L., & Black, R. E. (2003). Effects of acute diarrhea on linear growth in Peruvian children. *American Journal of Epidemiology, 157,* 166–175.

Chen, E. S. L., & Rao, N. (2011). Gender socialization in Chinese kindergartens: Teachers' contributions. *Sex Roles, 64,* 103–116.

Chen, J. J. (2005). Relation of academic support from parents, teachers, and peers to Hong Kong adolescents' academic achievement: The mediating role of academic engagement. *Genetic, Social, and General Psychology Monographs, 131,* 77–127.

Chen, J. J., Howard, K. S., & Brooks-Gunn, J. (2011). How do neighborhoods matter across the life span? In K. L. Fingerman, C. A. Berg, J. Smith, & T. C. Antonucci (Eds.), *Handbook of life-span development* (pp. 805–836). New York: Springer.

Chen, L. -C., Metcalfe, J. S., Jeka, J. J., & Clark, J. E. (2007). Two steps forward and one back: Learning to walk affects infants' sitting posture. *Infant Behavior and Development, 30,* 16–25.

Chen, R. (2012). Institutional characteristics and college student dropout risks: A multilevel event history analysis. *Research in Higher Education, 53,* 487–505.

Chen, X., Cen, G., Li, D., & He, Y. (2005). Social functioning and adjustment in Chinese children: The imprint of historical time. *Child Development, 76,* 182–195.

Chen, X., DeSouza, A. T., Chen, H., & Wang, L. (2006). Reticent behavior and experiences in peer interactions in Chinese and Canadian children. *Developmental Psychology, 42,* 656–665.

Chen, X., & French, D. C. (2008). Children's social competence in cultural context. *Annual Review of Psychology, 59,* 591–616.

Chen, X., Hastings, P. D., Rubin, K. H., Chen, H., Cen, G., & Stewart, S. L. (1998). Childrearing attitudes and behavioral inhibition in Chinese and Canadian toddlers: A cross-cultural study. *Developmental Psychology, 34,* 677–686.

Chen, X., Rubin, K. H., & Li, Z. (1995). Social functioning and adjustment in Chinese children: A longitudinal study. *Developmental Psychology, 31,* 531–539.

Chen, X., Wang, L., & Cao, R. (2011). Shyness-sensitivity and unsociability in rural Chinese children: Relations with social, school, and psychological adjustment. *Child Development, 82,* 1531–1543.

Chen, X., Wang, L., & DeSouza, A. (2006). Temperament, socioemotional functioning, and peer relationships in Chinese and North American children. In X. Chen, D. C. French, & B. H. Schneider (Eds.), *Peer relationships in cultural context* (pp. 123–147). New York: Cambridge University Press.

Chen, X., Wu, H., Chen, H., Wang, L., & Cen, G. (2001). Parenting practices and aggressive behavior in Chinese children. *Parenting: Science and Practice, 1,* 159–184.

Chen, Y.-C., Yu, M.-L., Rogan, W., Gladen, B., & Hsu, C.-C. (1994). A 6-year follow-up of behavior and activity disorders in the Taiwan Yu-cheng children. *American Journal of Public Health, 84,* 415–421.

Chen, Y.-J., & Hsu, C.-C. (1994). Effects of prenatal exposure to PCBs on the neurological function of children: A neuropsychological and neurophysiological study. *Developmental Medicine and Child Neurology, 36,* 312–320.

Chen, Z., Sanchez, R. P., & Campbell, T. (1997). From beyond to within their grasp: The rudiments of analogical problem solving in 10- to 13-month-olds. *Developmental Psychology, 33,* 790–801.

Cherlin, A. J. (2009). *The marriage-go-round.* New York: Knopf.

Cherlin, E. J., Barry, C. L., Prigerson, H. G., Schulman-Green, D., Johnson-Hurzeler, R., Kasl, S. V., & Bradley, E. H. (2007). Bereavement services for family caregivers: How often used, why, and why not. *Journal of Palliative Medicine, 10,* 148–158.

Chess, S., & Thomas, A. (1984). *Origins and evolution of behavior disorders.* New York: Brunner/Mazel.

Cheung, F. M., & Halpern, D. F. (2010). Women at the top: Powerful leaders define success as work + family in a culture of gender. *American Psychologist, 65,* 182–193.

Chhin, C. S., Bleeker, M. M., & Jacobs, J. E. (2008). Gender-typed occupational choices: The long-term impact of parents' beliefs and expectations. In H. M. G. Watt & J. S. Eccles (Eds.), *Gender and occupational outcomes: Longitudinal assessments of individual, social, and cultural influences* (pp. 215–234). Washington, DC: American Psychological Association.

Chi, M. T. H. (2006). Laboratory methods for assessing experts' and novices' knowledge. In K. A. Ericsson, N. Charness, P. J. Feltovich, & R. R. Hoffman (Eds.), *The Cambridge handbook of expertise and expert performance* (pp. 167–184). New York: Cambridge University Press.

Chi, M. T. H., Glaser, R., & Farr, M. J. (Eds.). (1988). *The nature of expertise.* Hillsdale, NJ: Erlbaum.

Child Trends. (2007). *Late or no prenatal care.* Retrieved from www.childtrendsdatabank.org/indicators/25PrenatalCare.cfm

Child Trends. (2011). *Teen births.* Retrieved from www.childtrendsdatabank.org/?q=node/52

Child Trends. (2012). *Late or no prenatal care.* Retrieved from www.childtrendsdatabank.org/sites/default/files/25_Prenatal_Care.pdf

Children's Defense Fund. (2009). *State of America's children: 2008.* Washington, DC: Author.

Chin, T., & Phillips, M. (2004). Social reproduction and child-rearing practices: Social class, children's agency, and the summer activity gap. *Sociology of Education, 77*(3), 185–210.

Chinn, C. A., & Malhotra, B. A. (2002). Children's responses to anomalous scientific data: How is conceptual change impeded? *Journal of Educational Psychology, 94,* 327–343.

Choi, J., Fauce, S. R., & Effros, R. B. (2008). Reduced telomerase activity in human T lymphocytes exposed to cortisol. *Brain, Behavior, and Immunity, 22,* 600–605.

Choi, N., & Kim, J. (2011). The effect of time volunteering and charitable donations in later life on psychological well-being. *Ageing and Society, 31,* 590–611.

Choi, S., & Gopnik, A. (1995). Early acquisition of verbs in Korean: A cross-linguistic study. *Journal of Child Language, 22,* 497–529.

Choi, S., McDonough, L., Bowerman, M., & Mandler, J. M. (1999). Early sensitivity to language-specific spatial categories in English and Korean. *Cognitive Development, 14,* 241–268.

Chomsky, C. (1969). *The acquisition of syntax in children from five to ten.* Cambridge, MA: MIT Press.

Chomsky, N. (1957). *Syntactic structures.* The Hague: Mouton.

Chomtho, S., Wells, J. C., Williams, J. E., Davies, P. S., Lucas, A., & Fewtrell, M. S. (2008). Infant growth and later body composition: Evidence from the 4-component model. *American Journal of Clinical Nutrition, 87,* 1776–1784.

Chouinard, M. M. (2007). Children's questions: A mechanism for cognitive development. *Monographs of the Society for Research in Child Development, 72*(1, Serial No. 286).

Chouinard, M. M., & Clark, E. V. (2003). Adult reformulations of child errors as negative evidence. *Journal of Child Language, 30,* 637–669.

Chrisler, J. C. (2008). The menstrual cycle in a biopsychosocial context. In F. L. Denmark & M. Paludi (Eds.), *Psychology of women: A handbook of issues and theories* (2nd ed., pp. 400–439). Westport, CT: Praeger.

Christ, G. H., Siegel, K., & Christ, A. E. (2002). "It never really hit me . . . until it actually happened." *Journal of the American Medical Association, 288,* 1269–1278.

Christakis, D. A., Zimmerman, F. J., DiGiuseppe, D. L., & McCarty, C. A. (2004). Early television exposure and subsequent attentional problems in children. *Pediatrics, 113,* 708–713.

Christensen, A.-D., & Larsen, J. E. (2008). Gender, class, and family: Men and gender equality in a Danish context. *Social Politics: International Studies in Gender, State and Society, 15,* 53–78.

Christenson, S. L., & Thurlow, M. L. (2004). School dropouts: Prevention considerations, interventions, and challenges. *Current Directions in Psychological Science, 13,* 36–39.

Christiansen, M. H., & Chater, N. (2008). Language as shaped by the brain. *Behavioral and Brain Sciences, 31,* 489–558.

Christie, C. A., Jolivette, K., & Nelson, M. (2007). School characteristics related to high school dropout rates. *Remedial and Special Education, 28,* 325–339.

Chu, J., Zhou, C. C., Lu, N., Zhang, X., & Dong, F. T. (2008). Genetic variants in three genes and smoking show strong associations with susceptibility to exudative age-related macular degeneration in a Chinese population. *Chinese Medical Journal, 121,* 2525–2533.

Chudley, A. E., Conry, J., Cook, J. L., Loock, C., Rosales, T., & LeBlanc, N. (2005). Fetal alcohol spectrum disorder: Canadian guidelines for diagnosis. *Canadian Medical Association Journal, 172,* S1–S21.

Chumlea, W. C., Schubert, C. M., Roche, A. F., Kulin, H. E., Lee, P. A., Himes, J. H., & Sun, S. S. (2003). Age at menarche and racial comparisons in U.S. girls. *Pediatrics, 111,* 110–113.

Chung, H. L., Mulvey, E. P., & Steinberg, L. (2011). Understanding the school outcomes of juvenile offenders: An exploration of neighborhood influences and motivational resources. *Journal of Youth and Adolescence, 40,* 1025–1038.

Church, E. (2004). *Understanding stepmothers: Women share their struggles, successes, and insights.* Toronto: HarperCollins.

CIA (Central Intelligence Agency). (2012). *World fact book.* Retrieved from www.cia.gov/library/publications/download/download-2012/index.html

Cicchetti, D. (2007). Intervention and policy implications of research on neurobiological functioning in maltreated children. In J. L. Aber, S. J. Bishop-Josef, S. M. Jones, K. T. McLearn, & D. A. Phillips (Eds.), *Child development and social policy* (pp. 167–184). Washington, DC: American Psychological Association.

Cicirelli, V. G. (1995). *Sibling relationships across the life span.* New York: Plenum.

Cicirelli, V. G. (2001). Personal meanings of death in older adults and young adults in relation to their fears of death. *Death Studies, 25,* 663–683.

Cicirelli, V. G. (2002). *Older adults' views on death.* New York: Springer.

Cillessen, A. H. N., & Bellmore, A. D. (2004). Social skills and interpersonal perception in early and middle childhood. In P. K. Smith & C. H. Hart (Eds.), *Blackwell handbook of childhood social development* (pp. 355–374). Malden, MA: Blackwell.

Cipriano, E. A., & Stifter, C. A. (2010). Predicting preschool effortful control from toddler temperament and parenting behavior. *Journal of Applied Developmental Psychology, 31,* 221–230.

Clapp, J. F., III, Kim, H., Burciu, B., Schmidt, S., Petry, K., & Lopez, B. (2002). Continuing regular exercise during pregnancy: Effect of exercise volume on fetoplacental growth. *American Journal of Obstetrics and Gynecology, 186,* 142–147.

Clark, C. A., Woodward, L. J., Horwood, L. J., & Moor, S. (2008). Development of emotional and behavioral regulation in children born extremely preterm and very preterm: Biological and social influences. *Child Development, 79,* 1444–1462.

Clarke, B. L., & Khosla, S. (2010). Physiology of bone loss. *Radiologic Clinics of North America, 48,* 483–495.

Clarke, L. H. (2005). Remarriage in later life: Older women's negotiations of power, resources and domestic labor. *Journal of Women and Aging, 17,* 21–41.

Clarke, P., & Smith, J. (2011). Aging in a cultural context: Cross-national differences in disability and the moderating role of personal control among older adults in the United States and England. *Journal of Gerontology, 66B,* 457–467.

Clarkson, T. W., Magos, L., & Myers, G. J. (2003). The toxicology of mercury—current exposures and clinical manifestations. *New England Journal of Medicine, 349,* 1731–1737.

Clarke-Stewart, K. A., & Brentano, C. (2006). *Divorce: Causes and consequences.* New Haven: Yale University Press.

Clarke-Stewart, K. A., & Hayward, C. (1996). Advantages of father custody and contact for the psychological well-being of school-age children. *Journal of Applied Developmental Psychology, 17,* 239–270.

Claxton, A., O'Rourke, N., Smith, J. Z., & DeLongis, A. (2011). Personality traits and marital satisfaction within enduring relationships: An intra-couple discrepancy approach. *Journal of Social and Personal Relationships, 29,* 375–396.

Claxton, L. J., Keen, R., & McCarty, M. E. (2003). Evidence of motor planning in infant reaching behavior. *Psychological Science, 14,* 354–356.

Clay, R. A. (2009). Mini-multitaskers. *Monitor on Psychology, 40*(2), 38–40.

Clearfield, M. W., & Nelson, N. M. (2006). Sex differences in mothers' speech and play behavior with 6-, 9-, and 14-month-old infants. *Sex Roles, 54,* 127–137.

Clearfield, M. W., Obsborn, C. N., & Mullen, M. (2008). Learning by looking: Infants' social looking behavior across the transition from crawling to walking. *Journal of Experimental Child Psychology, 100,* 297–307.

Clegg, L. X., Reichman, M. E., Miller, B. A., Hankey, B. F., Singh, G. K., Lin, Y. D., et al. (2009). Impact of socioeconomic status on cancer incidence and stage at diagnosis: Selected findings from the surveillance, epidemiology, and end results: National Longitudinal Mortality Study. *Cancer Causes and Control, 20,* 417–435.

Clements, D. H., & Sarama, J. (2003). Young children and technology: What does the research say? *Young Children, 58*(6), 34–40.

Clements, D. H., & Sarama, J. (2008). Experimental evaluation of the effects of a research-based preschool mathematics curriculum. *American Educational Research Journal, 45,* 443–494.

Cleveland, E. S., & Reese, E. (2005). Maternal structure and autonomy support in conversations about the past: Contributions to children's autobiographical memory. *Developmental Psychology, 41,* 376–388.

Clifton, R. K., Rochat, P., Robin, D. J., & Berthier, N. E. (1994). Multimodal perception in the control of infant reaching. *Journal of Experimental Psychology: Human Perception and Performance, 20,* 876–886.

Clinchy, B. M. (2002). Revisiting women's ways of knowing. In B. K. Hofer & P. R. Pintrich (Eds.), *Personal epistemology: The psychological beliefs about knowledge and knowing* (pp. 63–87). Mahwah, NJ: Erlbaum.

Clingempeel, W. G., & Henggeler, S. W. (2003). Aggressive juvenile offenders transitioning into emerging adulthood: Factors discriminating persistors and desistors. *American Journal of Orthopsychiatry, 73,* 310–323.

Coatsworth, J. D., Sharp, E. H., Palen, L., Darling, N., Cumsille, P., & Marta, M. (2005). Exploring adolescent self-defining leisure activities and identity experiences across three countries. *International Journal of Behavioral Development, 29,* 361–370.

Cohan, C. L., & Kleinbaum, S. (2002). Toward a greater understanding of the cohabitation effect: Premarital cohabitation and marital communication. *Journal of Marriage and Family, 64,* 180–192.

Cohen, J., Marcoux, I., Bilsen, J., Deboosere, P., van der Wal, G., & Deliens, L. (2006). European public acceptance of euthanasia: Socio-demographic and cultural factors associated with the acceptance of euthanasia in 33 European countries. *Social Science and Medicine, 63,* 743–756.

Cohen, L. B. (2003). Commentary on Part I: Unresolved issues in infant categorization. In D. H. Rakison & L. M. Oakes (Eds.), *Early category and concept development: Making sense of the blooming, buzzing confusion* (pp. 193–209). New York: Oxford University Press.

Cohen, L. B. (2010). A bottom-up approach to infant perception and cognition: A summary of evidence and discussion of issues. In S. P. Johnson (Ed.), *Neoconstructivism: The new science of cognitive development* (pp. 335–346). New York: Oxford University Press.

Cohen, L. B., & Brunt, J. (2009). Early word learning and categorization: Methodological issues and recent empirical evidence. In J. Colombo, P. McCardle, & L. Freund (Eds.), *Infant pathways to language: Methods, models, and research disorders* (pp. 245–266). New York: Psychology Press.

Cohen, L. B., & Cashon, C. H. (2006). Infant cognition. In D. Kuhn & R. Siegler (Eds.), *Handbook of child psychology: Vol. 2. Cognition, perception, and language* (6th ed., pp. 214–251). Hoboken, NJ: Wiley.

Cohen, L. B., & Marks, K. S. (2002). How infants process addition and subtraction events. *Developmental Science, 5,* 186–201.

Cohen, P., Kasen, S., Chen, H., Hartmark, C., & Gordon, K. (2003). Variations in patterns of developmental transitions in the emerging adulthood period. *Developmental Psychology, 39,* 657–669.

Cohen-Bendahan, C. C. C., van de Beek, C., & Berenbaum, S. A. (2005). Prenatal sex hormones effects on child and adult sex-typed behavior: Methods and findings. *Neuroscience and Biobehavioral Reviews, 29,* 353–384.

Cohen-Shalev, A. (1986). Artistic creativity across the adult life span: An alternative approach. *Interchange, 17*(4), 1–16.

Cohler, B. J., & Hostetler, A. J. (2007). Gay lives in the Third Age: Possibilities and paradoxes. In J. B. James & P. Wink (Eds.), *Annual review of gerontology and geriatrics* (Vol. 26, pp. 193–209). New York: Springer.

Coie, J. D., Dodge, K. A., & Coppotelli, H. (1982). Dimensions and types of social status: A cross-age perspective. *Developmental Psychology, 18,* 557–570.

Coke, M. M. (1992). Correlates of life satisfaction among elderly African Americans. *Journal of Gerontology, 47,* P316–P320.

Coker, A. D. (2003). African American female adult learners: Motivations, challenges, and coping strategies. *Journal of Black Studies, 33,* 654–674.

Colby, A., Kohlberg, L., Gibbs, J., & Lieberman, M. (1983). A longitudinal study of moral judgment. *Monographs of the Society for Research in Child Development, 48*(1–2, Serial No. 200).

Colcombe, S. J., Erickson, K. I., Scalf, P. E., Kim, J. S., Prakash, R., & McAuley, E. (2006). Aerobic exercise training increases brain volume in aging humans. *Journal of Gerontology, 61A,* 1166–1170.

Colcombe, S. J., Kramer, A. F., Erickson, K. I., Scalf, P., McAuley, E., & Cohen, N. J. (2004). Cardiovascular fitness, cortical plasticity, and aging. *Proceedings of the National Academy of Sciences, 101,* 3316–3321.

Coldwell, J., Pike, A., & Dunn, J. (2008). Maternal differential treatment and child adjustment: A multi-informant approach. *Social Development, 17,* 596–612.

Cole, A., Astell, A., Green, C., & Sutherland, C. (2007). Molecular connections between dementia and diabetes. *Neuroscience and Biobehavioral Reviews, 31,* 1046–1063.

Cole, D. A., Martin, J. M., Peeke, L. A., Seroczynski, A. D., & Fier, J. (1999). Children's over- and underestimation of academic competence: A longitudinal study of gender differences, depression, and anxiety. *Child Development, 70,* 459–473.

Cole, E. R., & Stewart, A. J. (1996). Meanings of political participation among black and white women: Political identity and social responsibility. *Journal of Personality and Social Psychology, 71,* 130–140.

Cole, M. (1990). Cognitive development and formal schooling: The evidence from cross-cultural research. In L. C. Moll (Ed.), *Vygotsky and education* (pp. 89–110). New York: Cambridge University Press.

Cole, M. (2006). Culture and cognitive development in phylogenetic, historical, and ontogenetic perspective. In R. M. Lerner (Ed.), *Handbook of child psychology: Vol. 1. Theoretical models of human development* (6th ed., pp. 636–685). Hoboken, NJ: Wiley.

Cole, P. M., Armstrong, L. M., & Pemberton, C. K. (2010). The role of language in the development of emotion regulation. In S. D. Calkins & M. A. Bell (Eds.), *Child development at the intersection of emotion and cognition* (pp. 59–77). Washington, DC: American Psychological Association.

Coleman, M., Ganong, L., & Leon, K. (2006). Divorce and postdivorce relationships. In A. L. Vangelisti & D. Perlman (Eds.), *The Cambridge handbook of personal relationships* (pp. 157–173). New York: Cambridge University Press.

Coleman, P. G., Ivani-Chalian, C., & Robinson, M. (2004). Religious attitudes among British older people: Stability and change in a 20-year longitudinal study. *Ageing and Society, 24,* 167–188.

Coles, C. D., Goldstein, F. C., Lynch, M. E., Chen, X., Kable, J. A., Johnson, K. C., et al. (2011). Memory and brain volume in adults prenatally exposed to alcohol. *Brain and Cognition, 75,* 67–77.

Coles, L. (2004). Demography of human supercentenarians. *Journal of Gerontology, 59A*, 579–586.

Coley, R. L., Morris, J. E., & Hernandez, D. (2004). Out-of-school care and problem behavior trajectories among low-income adolescents: Individual, family, and neighborhood characteristics as added risks. *Child Development, 75*, 948–965.

Coley, R. L., Votruba-Drzal, E., & Schindler, H. S. (2009). Fathers' and mothers' parenting predicting and responding to adolescent sexual risk behaviors. *Child Development, 80*, 808–827.

Collaer, M. L., & Hill, E. M. (2006). Large sex difference in adolescents on a timed line judgment task: Attentional contributors and task relationship to mathematics. *Perception, 35*, 561–572.

Collings, P. (2001). "If you got everything, it's good enough": Perspectives on successful aging in a Canadian Inuit community. *Journal of Cross-Cultural Gerontology, 16*, 127–155.

Collins, N. L., Guichard, A. C., Ford, M. B., & Feeney, B. C. (2006). Responding to need in intimate relationships: Normative processes and individual differences. In M. Mikulincer & G. S. Goodman (Eds.), *Dynamics of romantic love* (pp. 149–189). New York: Guilford.

Collins, W. A., & Laursen, B. (2004). Parent–adolescent relationships and influences. In R. M. Lerner & L. Steinberg (Eds.), *Handbook of adolescent psychology* (2nd ed., pp. 331–361). New York: Wiley.

Collins, W. A., & Madsen, S. D. (2006). Personal relationships in adolescence and early adulthood. In A. L. Vangelisti & D. Perlman (Eds.), *The Cambridge handbook of personal relationships* (pp. 191–209). New York: Cambridge University Press.

Collins, W. A., Madsen, S. D., & Susman-Stillman, A. (2002). Parenting during middle childhood. In M. H. Bornstein (Ed.), *Handbook of parenting: Vol. 1* (2nd ed., pp. 73–101). Mahwah, NJ: Erlbaum.

Collins, W. A., & van Dulmen, M. (2006a). "The course of true love(s) . . .": Origins and pathways in the development of romantic relationships. In A. Booth & A. Crouter (Eds.), *Romance and sex in adolescence and emerging adulthood: Risks and opportunities* (pp. 63–86). Mahwah, NJ: Erlbaum.

Collins, W. A., & van Dulmen, M. (2006b). Friendships and romantic relationships in emerging adulthood: Continuities and discontinuities. In J. J. Arnett & J. Tanner (Eds.), *Emerging adults in America: Coming of age in the 21st century* (pp. 219–234). Washington, DC: American Psychological Association.

Collins, W. A., Welsh, D. P., & Furman, W. (2009). Adolescent romantic relationships. *Annual Review of Psychology, 60*, 631–652.

Collins, W. K., & Steinberg, L. (2006). Adolescent development in interpersonal context. In N. Eisenberg (Ed.), *Handbook of child psychology: Vol. 3. Social, emotional, and personality development* (6th ed., pp. 1003–1067). Hoboken, NJ: Wiley.

Colman, L. L., & Colman, A. D. (1991). *Pregnancy: The psychological experience.* New York: Noonday Press.

Colman, R. A., Hardy, S. A., Albert, M., Raffaelli, M., & Crockett, L. (2006). Early predictors of self-regulation in middle childhood. *Infant and Child Development, 15*, 421–437.

Colom, R., Escorial, S., Shih, P. C., & Privado, J. (2007). Fluid intelligence, memory span, and temperament difficulties predict academic performance of young adolescents. *Personality and Individual Differences, 42*, 1503–1514.

Colombo, J. (2002). Infant attention grows up: The emergence of a developmental cognitive neuroscience perspective. *Current Directions in Psychological Science, 11*, 196–199.

Colombo, J., Shaddy, D. J., Richman, W. A., Maikranz, J. M., & Blaga, O. M. (2004). The developmental

course of habituation in infancy and preschool outcome. *Infancy, 5*, 1–38.

Colson, E. R., Rybin, D. R., Smith, L. A., Colton, T., Lister, G., & Corwin, M. J. (2009). Trends and factors associated with infant sleeping position: The National Infant Sleep Position Study, 1993–2007. *Archives of Pediatric and Adolescent Medicine, 163*, 1122–1128.

Coltrane, S. (1996). *Family man.* New York: Oxford University Press.

Commission on Adolescent Suicide Prevention. (2005). Targeted youth suicide prevention programs. In D. L. Evans, E. B. Foa, R. E. Gur, H. Hending, & C. P. O'Brien (Eds.), *Treating and preventing adolescent mental health disorders: What we know and what we don't know* (pp. 463–469). New York: Oxford University Press.

Commission on Children at Risk. (2008). Hardwired to connect: The new scientific case for authoritative communities. In K. K. Kline (Ed.), *Authoritative communities: The scientific case for nurturing the whole child* (pp. 3–68). New York: Springer.

Compton, J. I., Cox, E., & Laanan, F. S. (2006). Adult learners in transition. In F. S. Lanaan (Eds.), *New directions for student services* (Vol. 114, pp. 73–800). San Francisco: Jossey-Bass.

Comstock, G., & Scharrer, E. (2006). Media and popular culture. In K. A. Renninger & I. E. Sigel (Eds.), *Handbook of child psychology: Vol. 4. Child psychology in practice* (6th ed., pp. 817–863). Hoboken, NJ: Wiley.

Comunian, A. L., & Gielen, U. P. (2000). Sociomoral reflection and prosocial and antisocial behavior: Two Italian studies. *Psychological Reports, 87*, 161–175.

Comunian, A. L., & Gielen, U. P. (2006). Promotion of moral judgment maturity through stimulation of social role-taking and social reflection: An Italian intervention study. *Journal of Moral Education, 35*, 51–69.

Conboy, B. T., & Thal, D. J. (2006). Ties between the lexicon and grammar: Cross-sectional and longitudinal studies of bilingual toddlers. *Child Development, 77*, 712–735.

Conchas, G. Q. (2006). *The color of success: Race and high-achieving urban youth.* New York: Teachers College Press.

Conde-Agudelo, A., Belizan, J. M., and Diaz-Rossello, J. (2011). Kangaroo mother care to reduce morbidity and mortality in low birthweight infants. *Cochrane Database of Systematic Reviews, 3*, CD002771.

Conejero-Goldberg C., Hyde T. M., Chen S., Dreses-Werringloer, U., Herman, M. M., Kleinman, J. E., Davies P., & Goldberg, T. E. (2011). Molecular signatures in post-mortem brain tissue of younger individuals at high risk for Alzheimer's disease as based on APOE genotype. *Molecular Psychiatry, 16*, 836–847.

Conger, K. J., Stocker, C., & McGuire, S. (2009). Sibling socialization: The effects of stressful life events and experiences. In L. Kramer & K. J. Conger (Eds.), *Siblings as agents of socialization: New directions for child and adolescent development* (No. 126, pp. 44–60). San Francisco: Jossey-Bass.

Conger, R. D., & Donnellan, M. B. (2007). An interactionist perspective on the socioeconomic context of human development. *Annual Review of Psychology, 58*, 175–199.

Connell, M. W., Sheridan, K., & Gardner, H. (2003). On abilities and domains. In R. J. Sternberg & E. Grigorenko (Eds.), *Perspectives on the psychology of abilities, competencies, and expertise* (pp. 126–155). New York: Cambridge University Press.

Conner, D. B., & Cross, D. R. (2003). Longitudinal analysis of the presence, efficacy, and stability of maternal scaffolding during informal problemsolving interactions. *British Journal of Developmental Psychology, 21*, 315–334.

Connidis, I. A. (2010). *Family ties and aging* (2nd ed.). Thousand Oaks, CA: Pine Forge Press.

Connolly, J., Craig, W., Goldberg, A., & Pepler, D. (2004). Mixed-gender groups, dating, and romantic relationships in early adolescence. *Journal of Research on Adolescence, 14*, 185–207.

Connolly, J., Furman, W., & Konarski, R. (2000). The role of peers in the emergence of romantic relationships in adolescence. *Child Development, 71*, 1395–1408.

Connolly, J., & Goldberg, A. (1999). Romantic relationships in adolescence: The role of friends and peers in their emergence and development. In W. Furman, B. B. Brown, & C. Feiring (Eds.), *The development of romantic relationships in adolescence* (pp. 266–290). New York: Cambridge University Press.

Connolly, J. A., & Doyle, A. B. (1984). Relations of social fantasy play to social competence in preschoolers. *Developmental Psychology, 20*, 797–806.

Connor, L. T., Spiro, A., Obler, L. K., & Albert, M. L. (2004). Change in object naming ability during adulthood. *Journal of Gerontology, 59B*, P203–P209.

Conway, C. C., Rancourt, D., Adelman, C. B., Burk, W. J., & Prinstein, M. J. (2011). Depression socialization within friendship groups at the transition to adolescence: The roles of gender and group centrality as moderators of peer influence. *Journal of Abnormal Psychology, 120*, 857–867.

Conway, L. (2007, April 5). Drop the Barbie: Ken Zucker's reparatist treatment of gender-variant children. *Trans News Updates.* Retrieved from ai.eecs.umich.edu/people/conway/TS/News/Drop%20the%20Barbie.htm

Conway, M. A., Wang, Q., Hanyu, K., & Haque, S. (2005). A cross-cultural investigation of autobiographical memory. On the universality and cultural variation of the reminiscence bump. *Journal of Cross-Cultural Psychology, 36*, 739–749.

Conwell, Y., Duberstein, P. R., Hirsch, J., & Conner, K. R. (2010). Health status and suicide in the second half of life. *Geriatric Psychiatry, 25*, 371–379.

Conwell, Y., Van Orden, K., & Caine, E. D. (2011). Suicide in older adults. *Psychiatric Clinics of North America, 34*, 451–468.

Cook, C. R., Williams, K. R., Guerra, N. G., & Kim, T. E. (2010). Variability in the prevalence of bullying and victimization: A cross-national and methodological analysis. In S. R. Jimerson, S. M. Swearer, & D. L. Espelage (Eds.), *Handbook of bullying in schools: An international perspective* (pp. 347–362). New York: Routledge.

Cooke, L. P. (2010). The politics of housework. In J. Treas & S. Drobnic (Eds.), *Dividing the Domestic: Men, women, and household work in cross-national perspective* (pp. 59–78). Stanford, CA: Stanford University Press.

Cooney, T. M., & Mortimer, J. T. (1999). Family structure differences in the timing of leaving home: Exploring mediating factors. *Journal of Research on Adolescence, 9*, 367–393.

Cooper, C., Harvey, N., Cole, Z., Hanson, M., & Dennison, E. (2009). Developmental origins of osteoporosis: The role of maternal nutrition. In B. Koletzko, T. Decsi, D. Molnár, & A. de la Hunty (Eds.), *Early nutrition programming and health outcomes in later life: Obesity and beyond* (pp. 31–39). New York: Springer Science + Business Media.

Cooper, C., Sayer, A. A., & Dennison, E. M. (2006). The developmental environment: Clinical perspectives on effects on the musculoskeletal system. In P. Gluckman & M. Hanson (Eds.), *Developmental origins of health and disease* (pp. 392–405). Cambridge, UK: Cambridge University Press.

Cooper, R., & Huh, C. R. (2008). Improving academic possibilities of students of color during the middle school to high school transition: Conceptual and strategic considerations in a U.S. context. In J. K.

Asamen, M. L. Ellis, & G. L. Berry (Eds.), *Sage handbook of child development, multiculturalism, and media* (pp. 143–162). Thousand Oaks, CA: Sage.

Cooper, Z., & Fairburn, C. G. (2002). Cognitive-behavioral treatment of obesity. In T. A. Wadden & A. J. Stunkard (Eds.), *Handbook of obesity treatment* (3rd ed., pp. 465–479). New York: Guilford.

Copen, C. E., Chandra A., & Martinez G. (2012). *Prevalence and timing of oral sex with opposite-sex partners among females and males aged 15–24 years: United States, 2007–2010*. National Health Statistics Reports, No. 56. Hyattsville, MD: U.S. Department of Health and Human Services.

Coplan, R. J., & Arbeau, K. A. (2008). The stresses of a "brave new world": Shyness and school adjustment in kindergarten. *Journal of Research in Childhood Education, 22*, 377–389.

Coplan, R. J., Arbeau, K. A., & Armer, M. (2008). "Don't fret, be supportive!" Maternal characteristics linking child shyness to psychosocial and school adjustment in kindergarten. *Journal of Abnormal Child Psychology, 36*, 359–371.

Coplan, R. J., & Armer, M. (2007). A "multitude" of solitude: A closer look at social withdrawal and nonsocial play in early childhood. *Child Development Perspectives, 1*, 26–32.

Coplan, R. J., Gavinsky-Molina, M. H., Lagace-Seguin, D., & Wichmann, C. (2001). When girls versus boys play alone: Gender differences in the associates of nonsocial play in kindergarten. *Developmental Psychology, 37*, 464–474.

Coplan, R. J., Prakash, K., O'Neil, K., & Armer, M. (2004). Do you "want" to play? Distinguishing between conflicted shyness and social disinterest in early childhood. *Developmental Psychology, 40*, 244–258.

Copple, C., & Bredekamp, S. (2009). *Developmentally appropriate practice in early childhood programs* (3rd ed.). Washington, DC: National Association for the Education of Young Children.

Corenblum, B. (2003). What children remember about ingroup and outgroup peers: Effects of stereotypes on children's processing of information about group members. *Journal of Experimental Child Psychology, 86*, 32–66.

Cornelius, S. W., & Caspi, A. (1987). Everyday problem solving in adulthood and old age. *Psychology and Aging, 2*, 144–153.

Cornish, A. M., McMahon, C. A., Ungerer, J. A., Barnett, B., Kowalenko, N., & Tennant, C. (2005). Postnatal depression and infant cognitive and motor development in the second postnatal year: The impact of depression chronicity and infant gender. *Infant Behavior and Development, 28*, 407–417.

Cornwell, A. C., & Feigenbaum, P. (2006). Sleep biological rhythms in normal infants and those at high risk for SIDS. *Chronobiology International, 23*, 935–961.

Corr, C. A., & Corr, D. M. (2007). Historical and contemporary perspectives on loss, grief, and mourning. In C. A. Corr & D. M. Corr (Eds.), *Handbook of thanatology* (pp. 131–142). New York: Routledge.

Corr, C. A., & Corr, D. M. (2013). *Death and dying, life and living* (2nd ed.). Belmont, CA: Cengage.

Correa-Chávez, M., Rogoff, B., & Mejía-Arauz, R. (2005). Cultural patterns in attending to two events at once. *Child Development, 76*, 664–678.

Costello, J. (2006). Dying well: Nurses' experiences of "good and bad" deaths in hospital. *Journal of Advanced Nursing, 54*, 594–601.

Côté, J. E. (2006). Emerging adulthood as an institutionalized moratorium: Risks and benefits to identity formation. In J. J. Arnett (Ed.), *Emerging adults in America: Coming of age in the 21st century* (pp. 85–116). Washington, DC: American Psychological Association.

Côté, J. E. (2009). Identity formation and self-development in adolescence. In R. M. Lerner &

L. Steinberg (Eds.), *Handbook of adolescent psychology: Vol. 1. Individual bases of adolescent development* (3rd ed., pp. 266–304). Hoboken, NJ: Wiley.

Côté, J. E., & Bynner, J. M. (2008). Changes in the transition to adulthood in the UK and Canada: The role of structure and agency in emerging adulthood. *Journal of Youth Studies, 11*, 251–268.

Côté, S. M., Vaillancourt, T., Barker, E. D., Nagin, D., & Tremblay, R. E. (2007). The joint development of physical and indirect aggression: Predictors of continuity and change during childhood. *Development and Psychopathology, 19*, 37–55.

Coudin, G., & Alexopoulos, T. (2010). "Help me! I'm old!": How negative aging stereotypes create dependency among older adults. *Aging and Mental Health, 14*, 516–523.

Coulton, C. J., Crampton, D. S., Irwin, M., Spilsbury, J. C., & Korbin, J. E. (2007). How neighborhoods influence child maltreatment: A review of the literature and alternative pathways. *Child Abuse and Neglect, 31*, 1117–1142.

Courage, M. L., & Howe, M. L. (1998). The ebb and flow of infant attentional preferences: Evidence for long-term recognition memory in 3-month-olds. *Journal of Experimental Child Psychology, 18*, 98–106.

Courage, M. L., & Howe, M. L. (2002). From infant to child: The dynamics of cognitive change in the second year of life. *Psychological Bulletin, 128*, 250–277.

Courage, M. L., & Howe, M. L. (2010). To watch or not to watch: Infants and toddlers in a brave new electronic world. *Developmental Review, 30*, 101–115.

Courchesne, E., Carper, R., & Akshoomoff, N. (2003). Evidence of brain overgrowth in the first year of life in autism. *Journal of the American Medical Association, 290*, 337–344.

Coursolle, K. M., Sweeney, M. M., Raymo, J. M., & Ho, J-H. (2010). The association between retirement and emotional well-being: Does prior work–family conflict matter? *Journal of Gerontology, 65B*, 609–620.

Couturier, J. L., & Lock, J. (2006). Denial and minimization in adolescents with anorexia nervosa. *International Journal of Eating Disorders, 39*, 212–216.

Covington, C. Y., Nordstrom-Klee, B., Ager, J., Sokol, R., & Delaney-Black, V. (2002). Birth to age 7 growth of children prenatally exposed to drugs: A prospective cohort study. *Neurotoxicology and Teratology, 24*, 489–496.

Cowan, C. P., & Cowan, P. A. (1997). Working with couples during stressful transitions. In S. Dreman (Ed.), *The family on the threshold of the 21st century* (pp. 17–47). Mahwah, NJ: Erlbaum.

Cowan, C. P., & Cowan, P. A. (2000). *When partners become parents: The big life change for couples*. Mahwah, NJ: Erlbaum.

Cowan, N., & Alloway, T. (2009). Development of working memory in childhood. In M. L. Courage & N. Cowan (Eds.), *Development of memory in infancy and childhood* (pp. 303–342). Hove, UK: Psychology Press.

Cowan, P. A., & Cowan, C. P. (2002). Interventions as tests of family systems theories: Marital and family relationships in children's development and psychopathology. *Development and Psychopathology, 14*, 731–759.

Cowan, P. A., & Cowan, C. P. (2004). From family relationships to peer rejection to antisocial behavior in middle childhood. In J. B. Kupersmidt & K. A. Dodge (Eds.), *Children's peer relations: From development to intervention* (pp. 159–177). Washington, DC: American Psychological Association.

Cox, G. (2002). The Native American patient. In R. B. Gilbert (Ed.), *Health care and spirituality: Listening, assessing, caring* (pp. 107–127). Amityville, NY: Baywood.

Cox, M., & Littlejohn, K. (1995). Children's use of converging obliques in their perspective drawings. *Educational Psychology, 15*, 127–139.

Cox, M. J., Owen, M. T., Henderson, V. K., & Margand, N. A. (1992). Prediction of infant–father and infant–mother attachment. *Developmental Psychology, 28*, 474–483.

Cox, S. M., Hopkins, J., & Hans, S. L. (2000). Attachment in preterm infants and their mothers: Neonatal risk status and maternal representations. *Infant Mental Health Journal, 21*, 464–480.

Coyl, D. D., Newland, L. A., & Freeman, H. (2010). Predicting preschoolers' attachment security from parenting behaviours, parents' attachment relationships and their use of social support. *Early Child Development and Care, 180*, 499–512.

Coyne, S. M., Robinson, S. L., & Nelson, D. A. (2010). Does reality backbite? Verbal and relational aggression in reality television programs. *Journal of Broadcasting and Electronic Media, 54*, 282–298.

Craft, S., Baker, L. D., Montine, T. J., Minoshima, S., Watson, G. S., Arbuckle, M., et al. (2012). Intranasal insulin therapy for Alzheimer disease and amnestic mild cognitive impairment: A pilot clinical trial. *Archives of Neurology, 69*, 29–38.

Crago, M. B., Annahatak, B., & Ningiuruvik, L. (1993). Changing patterns of language socialization in Inuit homes. *Anthropology and Education Quarterly, 24*, 205–223.

Craig, C. M., & Lee, D. N. (1999). Neonatal control of sucking pressure: Evidence for an intrinsic tau guide. *Experimental Brain Research, 124*, 371–382.

Craig, W. M., Pepler, D., & Atlas, R. (2000). Observations of bullying in the playground and in the classroom. *School Psychology International, 21*, 22–36.

Crain, W. (2005). *Theories of development* (5th ed.). Upper Saddle River, NJ: Prentice-Hall.

Crair, M. C., Gillespie, D. C., & Stryker, M. P. (1998). The role of visual experience in the development of columns in cat visual cortex. *Science, 279*, 566–570.

Cramer, R. E., Schaefer, J. T., & Reid, S. (2003). Identifying the ideal mate: More evidence for male–female convergence. In N. J. Pallone (Ed.), *Love, romance, sexual interaction: Research perspectives from current psychology* (pp. 61–73). New Brunswick, NJ: Transaction Publishers.

Cratty, B. J. (1986). *Perceptual and motor development in infants and children* (3rd ed.), Englewood Cliffs, NJ: Prentice-Hall.

Crawford, N. (2003, September). Understanding children's atypical gender behavior. *APA Monitor*, p. 40.

Crawley, L., Payne, R., Bolden, J., Payne, T., Washington, P., & Williams, S. (2000). Palliative and end-of-life care in the African American community. *Journal of the American Medical Association, 284*, 2518–2521.

Creasey, G., & Jarvis, P. (2009). Attachment and marriage. In M. C. Smith & N. DeFrates-Densch (Eds.), *Handbook of research on adult learning and development* (pp. 269–304). New York: Routledge/Taylor & Francis Group.

Creasey, G. L., Jarvis, P. A., & Berk, L. E. (1998). Play and social competence. In O. N. Saracho & B. Spodek (Eds.), *Multiple perspectives on play in early childhood education* (pp. 116–143). Albany: State University of New York Press.

Crick, N. R., Casas, J. F., & Nelson, D. A. (2002). Toward a more comprehensive understanding of peer maltreatment: Studies of relational victimization. *Current Directions in Psychological Science, 11*, 98–101.

Crick, N. R., & Nelson, D. A. (2002). Relational and physical victimization within friendships: Nobody told me there'd be friends like these. *Journal of Abnormal Child Psychology, 30*, 599–607.

Crick, N. R., Ostrov, J. M., Appleyard, K., Jansen, E., & Casas, J. F. (2004). Relational aggression in early childhood: You can't come to my birthday party unless. . . . In M. Putallaz & K. Bierman (Eds.), *Aggression, antisocial behavior, and violence among girls: A developmental perspective* (pp. 71–89). New York: Guilford.

Crick, N. R., Ostrov, J. M., Burr, J. E., Cullerton-Sen, C., Jansen-Yeh, E., & Ralston, P. (2006). A longitudinal study of relational and physical aggression in preschool. *Journal of Applied Developmental Psychology, 27,* 254–268.

Crick, N. R., Ostrov, J. M., & Werner, N. E. (2006). A longitudinal study of relational aggression, physical aggression, and social-psychological adjustment. *Journal of Abnormal Child Psychology, 34,* 131–142.

Crimmins, E. M., & Beltrán-Sánchez, H. (2010). Mortality and morbidity trends: Is there compression of morbidity? *Journal of Gerontology, 66B,* 75–86.

Crimmins, E. M., Kim, J. K., & Solé-Auró, A. (2011). Gender differences in health: Results from SHARE, ELSA and HRS. *European Journal of Public Health, 21,* 81–91.

Criss, M. M., & Shaw, D. S. (2005). Sibling relationships as contexts for delinquency training in low income families. *Journal of Family Psychology, 19,* 592–600.

Critser, G. (2003). *Fat land.* Boston: Houghton Mifflin.

Crockenberg, S., & Leerkes, E. (2003). Infant negative emotionality, caregiving, and family relationships. In A. C. Crouter & A. Booth (Eds.), *Children's influence on family dynamics* (pp. 57–78). Mahwah, NJ: Erlbaum.

Crockenberg, S., & Leerkes, E. (2004). Infant and maternal behaviors regulate infant reactivity to novelty at 6 months. *Developmental Psychology, 40,* 1123–1132.

Crockett, L. J., Raffaelli, M., & Shen, Y.-L. (2006). Linking self-regulation and risk proneness to risky sexual behavior: Pathways through peer pressure and early substance use. *Journal of Research on Adolescence, 16,* 503–525.

Croker, R. (2007). *The boomer century: 1946–2046: How America's most influential generation changed everything.* New York: Springboard Press.

Crosno, R., Kirkpatrick, M., & Elder, G. H., Jr. (2004). Intergenerational bonding in school: The behavioral and contextual correlates of student–teacher relationships. *Sociology of Education, 77,* 60–81.

Crosnoe, R., Johnson, M. K., & Elder, G. H., Jr. (2004). School size and the interpersonal side of education: An examination of race/ethnicity and organizational context. *Social Science Quarterly, 85,* 1259–1274.

Cross, S., & Markus, H. (1991). Possible selves across the life span. *Human Development, 34,* 230–255.

Crouch, J. L., Skowronski, J. J., Milner, J. S., & Harris, B. (2008). Parental responses to infant crying: The influence of child physical abuse risk and hostile priming. *Child Abuse and Neglect, 32,* 702–710.

Crouter, A. C., & Bumpus, M. F. (2001). Linking parents' work stress to children's and adolescents' psychological adjustment. *Current Directions in Psychological Science, 10,* 156–159.

Crouter, A. C., & Head, M. R. (2002). Parental monitoring and knowledge of children. In M. H. Bornstein (Ed.), *Handbook of parenting: Vol. 3. Being and becoming a parent* (2nd ed., pp. 461–483). Mahwah, NJ: Erlbaum.

Crouter, A. C., Whiteman, S. D., McHale, S. M., & Osgood, D. W. (2007). Development of gender attitude traditionality across middle childhood and adolescence. *Child Development, 78,* 911–926.

Crowley, K. (2011). Sleep and sleep disorders in older adults. *Neuropsychological Review, 21,* 41–53.

Crystal, D. S., Killen, M., & Ruck, M. D. (2008). It is who you know that counts: Intergroup contact and judgments about race-based exclusion. *British Journal of Developmental Psychology, 26,* 51–70.

Crystal, D. S., Killen, M., & Ruck, M. D. (2010). Fair treatment by authorities is related to children's and adolescents' evaluations of interracial exclusion. *Applied Developmental Science, 14,* 125–136.

Csikszentmihalyi, M., & Nakamura, J. (2005). The role of emotions in the development of wisdom. In R. J. Sternberg & J. Jordan (Eds.), *A handbook of wisdom: Psychological perspectives* (pp. 220–242). New York: Cambridge University Press.

Csikszentmihalyi, M., & Rathunde, K. (1990). The psychology of wisdom: An evolutionary interpretation. In R. J. Sternberg (Ed.), *Wisdom: Its nature, origins, and development* (pp. 25–51). New York: Cambridge University Press.

Cuijpers, P. (2002). Effective ingredients of school-based drug prevention programs: A systematic review. *Addictive Behaviors, 27,* 1009–1023.

Culbertson, F. M. (1997). Depression and gender: An international review. *American Psychologist, 52,* 25–51.

Cumming, E., & Henry, W. E. (1961). *Growing old: The process of disengagement.* New York: Basic Books.

Cummings, E. M., Goeke-Morey, M. C., & Papp, L. M. (2004). Everyday marital conflict and child aggression. *Journal of Abnormal Child Psychology, 32,* 91–202.

Cummings, E. M., & Merrilees, C. E. (2010). Identifying the dynamic processes underlying links between marital conflict and child adjustment. In M. S. Schulz, M. K. Pruett, P. K. Kerig, & R. D. Parke (Eds.), *Strengthening couple relationships for optimal child development* (pp. 27–40). Washington, DC: American Psychological Association.

Cunningham, A. E., & Stanovich, K. E. (1998, Spring/Summer). What reading does for the mind. *American Educator,* 8–15.

Curby, T. W., LoCasale-Crouch, J., Konold, T. R., Pianta, R. C., Howes, C., Burchinal, M., et al. (2009). The relations of observed pre-K classroom quality profiles to children's achievement and social competence. *Early Education and Development, 20,* 346–372.

Curlin, F. A., Nwodim, C., Vance, J. L., Chin, M. H., & Lantos, J. D. (2008). To die, to sleep: U.S. physicians' religious and other objections to physician-assisted suicide, terminal sedation, and withdrawal of life support. *American Journal of Hospice and Palliative Medicine, 25,* 112–120.

Currie, D. H. (1999). Violent men or violent women? Whose definition counts? In R. K. Bergen (Ed.), *Issues in intimate violence* (pp. 97–111). Thousand Oaks, CA: Sage.

Curtiss, K., Hayslip, B., Jr., & Dolan, D. C. (2007). Motivational style, length of residence, voluntariness, and gender as influences on adjustment to long term care: A pilot study. *Journal of Human Behavior in the Social Environment, 15,* 13–34.

Cutchin, M. P. (2013). The complex process of becoming at-home in assisted living. In G. D. Rowles & M. Bernard (Eds.), *Environmental gerontology: Making meaningful places in old age* (pp. 105–124). New York: Springer.

Cutler, L. J. (2007). Physical environments of assisted living: Research needs and challenges. *Gerontologist, 47*(Special Issue III), 68–82.

Cutler, R. G., & Mattson, M. P. (2006). Introduction: The adversities of aging. *Ageing Research Reviews, 5,* 221–238.

Cutler, S. J., Hendricks, J., & O'Neill, G. (2011). Civic engagement and aging. In R. H. Binstock & L. K. George (Eds.), *Handbook of aging and the social sciences* (7th ed., pp. 221–233). San Diego, CA: Academic Press.

Cutrona, C. E., Hessling, R. M., Bacon, P. L., & Russell, D. W. (1998). Predictors and correlates of continuing involvement with the baby's father among adolescent mothers. *Journal of Family Psychology, 12,* 369–387.

Cutter, W. J., Daly, E. M., Robertson, D. M. W., Chitnis, X. A., van Amelsvoort, T. A. M. J., & Simmons, A. (2006). Influence of X chromosome and hormones on human brain development: A magnetic resonance imaging and proton magnetic resonance spectroscopy study of Turner syndrome. *Biological Psychiatry, 59,* 273–283.

Cvencek, D., Meltzoff, A. N., & Greenwald, A. G. (2011). Math–gender stereotypes in elementary school children. *Child Development, 82,* 766–779.

Cyr, M., McDuff, P., & Wright, J. (2006). Prevalence and predictors of dating violence among adolescent female victims of child sexual abuse. *Journal of Interpersonal Violence, 21,* 1000–1017.

D

Daatland, S. O. (2007). Marital history and intergenerational solidarity: The impact of divorce and unmarried cohabitation. *Journal of Social Issues, 63,* 809–825.

Dabrowska, E. (2000). From formula to schema: The acquisition of English questions. *Cognitive Linguistics, 11,* 1–20.

Daher, M. (2012). Cultural beliefs and values in cancer patients. *Annals of Oncology, 23*(Suppl. 3), 66–69.

Dahl, A., Hassing, L. B., Fransson, E., Berg, S., Gatz, M., Reynolds, C. A., et al. (2010). Being overweight in midlife is associated with lower cognitive ability and steeper cognitive decline in late life. *Journal of Gerontology, 65A,* 57–62.

Dahl, R. E., & Lewin, D. S. (2002). Pathways to adolescent healthy sleep regulation and behavior. *Journal of Adolescent Health, 31,* 175–184.

Dahlberg, L. L., & Simon, T. R. (2006). Predicting and preventing youth violence: Developmental pathways and risk. In L. L. Dahlberg & T. R. Simon (Eds.), *Preventing violence: Research and evidence-based intervention strategies* (pp. 97–124). Washington, DC: American Psychological Association.

Dal Santo, J. A., Goodman, R. M., Glik, D., & Jackson, K. (2004). Childhood unintentional injuries: Factors predicting injury risk among preschoolers. *Journal of Pediatric Psychology, 29,* 273–283.

Damashek, A., & Peterson, L. (2002). Unintentional injury prevention efforts for young children: Levels, methods, types, and targets. *Developmental and Behavioral Pediatrics, 23,* 443–455.

Damjanovic, A. M., Yang, Y., Glaser, R., Kiecolt-Glaser, J. K., & Nguyen, H. (2007). Accelerated telomere erosion is associated with a declining immune function of caregivers of Alzheimer's disease patients. *Journal of Immunology, 179,* 4249–4254.

Damon, W. (1988a). *The moral child.* New York: Free Press.

Damon, W. (1988b). *Self-understanding in childhood and adolescence.* New York: Cambridge University Press.

Damon, W. (1990). Self-concept, adolescent. In R. M. Lerner, A. C. Petersen, & J. Brooks-Gunn (Eds.), *The encyclopedia of adolescence* (Vol. 2, pp. 87–91). New York: Garland.

Damon, W. (1995). *Greater expectations: Overcoming the culture of indulgence in America's homes and schools.* New York: Free Press.

Damon, W. (2004). *The moral advantage: How to succeed in business by doing the right thing.* San Francisco: Berrett-Koehler.

Damon, W., & Hart, D. (1988). *Self-understanding in childhood and adolescence.* New York: Cambridge University Press.

Dane, E., Baer, M., Pratt, M. G., & Oldham, G. R. (2011). Rational versus intuitive problem solving: How thinking "off the beaten path" can stimulate creativity. *Psychology of Aesthetics, Creativity, and the Arts, 5,* 3–12.

Daniell, W. E., Swan, S. S., McDaniel, M. M., Camp, J. E., Cohen, M. A., & Stebbins, J. G. (2006). Noise exposure and hearing loss prevention programs after twenty years of regulations in the United

States. *Occupational and Environmental Medicine, 63,* 343–351.

Daniels, E., & Leaper, C. (2006). A longitudinal investigation of sport participation, peer acceptance, and self-esteem among adolescent girls and boys. *Sex Roles, 55,* 875–880.

Daniels, P., Noe, G. F., & Mayberry, R. (2006). Barriers to prenatal care among black women of low socioeconomic status. *American Journal of Health Behavior, 30,* 188–198.

Dannemiller, J. L., & Stephens, B. R. (1988). A critical test of infant pattern preference models. *Child Development, 59,* 210–216.

Dapretto, M., & Bjork, E. L. (2000). The development of word retrieval abilities in the second year and its relation to early vocabulary growth. *Child Development, 71,* 635–648.

Darling-Hammond, L. (2010). *The flat world and education: How America's commitment to equity will determine our future.* New York: Teachers College Press.

Darroch, J. E., Frost, J. J., & Singh, S. (2001). *Teenage sexual and reproductive behavior in developed countries: Can more progress be made?* New York: Alan Guttmacher Institute.

Darwin, C. (1936). *On the origin of species by means of natural selection.* New York: Modern Library. (Original work published 1859)

Daubenmier, J., Lin, J., Blackburn, E., Hecht, F. M., Kristeller, J., Maninger, N., et al. (2012). Changes in stress, eating, and metabolic factors are related to changes in telomerase activity in a randomized mindfulness intervention pilot study. *Psychoneuroendocrinology, 37,* 917–928.

D'Augelli, A. R. (2002). Mental health problems among lesbian, gay, and bisexual youths ages 14 to 21. *Clinical Child Psychology and Psychiatry, 7,* 433–456.

D'Augelli, A. R. (2006). Developmental and contextual factors and mental health among lesbian, gay, and bisexual youths. In A. M. Omoto & H. S. Howard (Eds.), *Sexual orientation and mental health: Examining identity and development in lesbian, gay, and bisexual people* (pp. 37–53). Washington, DC: American Psychological Association.

D'Augelli, A. R., Grossman, A. H., Salter, N. P., Vasey, J. J., Starks, M. T., & Sinclair, K. O. (2005). Predicting the suicide attempts of lesbian, gay, and bisexual youth. *Suicide and Life-Threatening Behavior, 35,* 646–660.

D'Augelli, A. R., Grossman, A. H., & Starks, M. T. (2008). Families of gay, lesbian, and bisexual youth: What do parents and siblings know and how do they react? *Journal of GBLT Family Studies, 4,* 95–115.

Davey, A., & Takagi, E. (2013). Adulthood and aging in families. In G. W. Peterson & K. R. Bush (Eds.), *Handbook of marriage and family* (pp. 377–399). New York: Springer.

David, K. M., & Murphy, B. C. (2007). Interparental conflict and preschoolers' peer relations: The moderating roles of temperament and gender. *Social Development, 16,* 1–23.

Davidov, M., & Grusec, J. E. (2006). Untangling the links of parental responsiveness to distress and warmth to child outcomes. *Child Development, 77,* 44–58.

Davidson, R. J. (1994). Asymmetric brain function, affective style, and psychopathology: The role of early experience and plasticity. *Development and Psychopathology, 6,* 741–758.

Davies, J. (2008). Differential teacher positive and negative interactions with male and female pupils in the primary school setting. *Educational and Child Psychology, 25,* 17–26.

Davis, K. F., Parker, K. P., & Montgomery, G. L. (2004). Sleep in infants and young children. Part 1: Normal sleep. *Journal of Pediatric Health Care, 18,* 65–71.

Dawley, K., Loch, J., & Bindrich, I. (2007). The Nurse–Family Partnership. *American Journal of Nursing, 107,* 60–67.

Dawson, G., Ashman, S. B., Panagiotides, H., Hessl, D., Self, J., Yamada, E., & Embry, L. (2003). Preschool outcomes of children of depressed mothers: Role of maternal behavior, contextual risk, and children's brain activity. *Child Development, 74,* 1158–1175.

Dawson, T. L. (2002). New tools, new insights: Kohlberg's moral judgment stages revisited. *International Journal of Behavioral Development, 26,* 154–166.

Ddungu, H. (2011). Palliative care: What approaches are suitable in developing countries? *British Journal of Haematology, 154,* 728–735.

Deák, G. O. (2000). Hunting the fox of word learning: Why "constraints" fail to capture it. *Developmental Review, 20,* 29–80.

Deák, G. O., Ray, S. D., & Brenneman, K. (2003). Children's perseverative appearance–reality errors are related to emerging language skills. *Child Development, 74,* 944–964.

DeAngeleo, L., Hurtado, S., & Pryor, J. H. (2010). *Your first college year: National norms for the 2008 YFCY survey.* Los Angeles: Higher Education Research Institute, UCLA.

Dearing, E., Wimer, C., Simpkins, S. D., Lund, T., Bouffard, S. M., Caronongan, P., & Kreider, H. (2009). Do neighborhood and home contexts help explain why low-income children miss opportunities to participate in activities outside of school? *Developmental Psychology, 45,* 1545–1562.

Deary, I. J. (2001). *g* and cognitive elements of information progressing: An agnostic view. In R. J. Sternberg & E. L. Grigorenko (Eds.), *The general factor of intelligence: How general is it?* (pp. 447–479). Mahwah, NJ: Erlbaum.

Deary, I. J., Strand, S., Smith, P., & Fernandes, C. (2007). Intelligence and educational achievement. *Intelligence, 35,* 13–21.

Deary, I. J., Yang, J., Davies, G., Harris, S. E., Tenesa, A., Liewald, D., et al. (2012). Genetic contributions to stability and change in intelligence from childhood to old age. *Nature, 481,* 212–215.

Deater-Deckard, K., Lansford, J. E., Dodge, K. A., Pettit, G. S., & Bates, J. E. (2003). The development of attitudes about physical punishment: An 8-year longitudinal study. *Journal of Family Psychology, 17,* 351–360.

Deater-Deckard, K., Pike, A., Petrill, S. A., Cutting, A. L., Hughes, C., & O'Connor, T. G. (2001). Nonshared environmental processes in socialemotional development: An observational study of identical twin differences in the preschool period. *Developmental Science, 4,* F1–F6.

Debes, F., Budtz-Jorgensen, E., Weihe, P., White, R. F., & Grandjean, P. (2006). Impact of prenatal methylmercury exposure on neurobehavioral function at age 4 years. *Neurotoxicology and Teratology, 28,* 536–547.

DeBoer, T., Scott, L. S., & Nelson, C. A. (2007). Methods for acquiring and analyzing infant eventrelated potentials. In M. de Haan (Ed.), *Infant EEG and event-related potentials* (pp. 5–37). New York: Psychology Press.

de Bruyn, E. H. (2005). Role strain, engagement and academic achievement in early adolescence. *Educational Studies, 31,* 15–27.

de Bruyn, E. H., & Cillessen, A. H. N. (2006). Popularity in early adolescence: Prosocial and antisocial subtypes. *Journal of Adolescent Research, 21,* 607–627.

de Bruyn, E. H., Deković, M., & Meijnen, G. W. (2003). Parenting, goal orientations, classroom behavior, and school success in early adolescence. *Journal of Applied Developmental Psychology, 24,* 393–412.

de Calignon, A., Polydoro, M., Suárez-Calvet, M., William, C., Adamowicz, D. H., Kopeikina, K. J., et al. (2012). Propagation of tau pathology in a model of early Alzheimer's disease. *Neuron, 73,* 685–697.

DeCasper, A. J., & Spence, M. J. (1986). Prenatal maternal speech influences newborns' perception

of speech sounds. *Infant Behavior and Development, 9,* 133–150.

Dechanet, C., Anahory, T., Mathieu, T., Mathieu, D. J. C., Quantin, X., Ryftmann, L., et al. (2011). Effects of cigarette smoking on reproduction. *Human Reproduction Update, 17,* 76–95.

Deci, E. L., La Guardia, J. G., Moller, A. C., Scheiner, M. J., & Ryan, R. M. (2006). On the benefits of giving as well as receiving autonomy support: Mutuality in close friendships. *Personality and Social Psychology Bulletin, 32,* 313–327.

de Frias, C. M., & Dixon, R. A. (2005). Confirmatory factor structure and measurement invariance of the Memory Compensation Questionnaire. *Psychological Assessment, 17,* 168–178.

Degner, J., & Wentura, D. (2010). Automatic prejudice in childhood and early adolescence. *Journal of Personality and Social Psychology, 98,* 356–374.

De Goede, I. H. A., Branje, S. J. T., & Meeus, W. H. J. (2009). Developmental changes and gender differences in adolescents' perceptions of friendships. *Journal of Adolescence, 32,* 1105–1123.

de Haan, M., Bauer, P. J., Georgieff, M. K., & Nelson, C. A. (2000). Explicit memory in low-risk infants aged 19 months born between 27 and 42 weeks of gestation. *Developmental Medicine and Child Neurology, 42,* 304–312.

de Haan, M., & Johnson, M. H. (2003). Mechanisms and theories of brain development. In M. de Haan & M. H. Johnson (Eds.), *The cognitive neuroscience of development* (pp. 1–18). Hove, UK: Psychology Press.

Deissinger, T. (2007). "Making schools practical": Practice firms and their function in the full-time vocational school system in Germany. *Education + Training, 49,* 364–378.

deJong, A., & Franklin, B. A. (2004). Prescribing exercise for the elderly: Current research and recommendations. *Current Sports Medicine Reports, 3,* 337–343.

Dekker, M. C., Ferdinand, R. F., van Lang, D. J., Bongers, I. L., van der Ende, J., & Verhulst, F. C. (2007). Developmental trajectories of depressive symptoms from early childhood to late adolescence: Gender differences and adult outcome. *Journal of Child Psychology and Psychiatry, 48,* 657–666.

DeKosky, S. T., Williamson, J. D., Fitzpatrick, A. L., Kronmal, R. A., Ives, D. G., & Saxton, J. A. (2008). Ginkgo biloba for prevention of dementia: A randomized controlled trial. *Journal of the American Medical Association, 300,* 2253–2262.

Deković, M., & Buist, K. L. (2005). Multiple perspectives within the family: Family relationship patterns. *Journal of Family Issues, 26,* 467–490.

Deković, M., Noom, M. J., & Meeus, W. (1997). Expectations regarding development during adolescence: Parent and adolescent perceptions. *Journal of Youth and Adolescence, 26,* 253–271.

DeLamater, J. (2012). Sexual expression in later life: A review and synthesis. *Journal of Sex Research, 49,* 125–141.

DeLamater, J., & Moorman, S. M. (2007). Sexual behavior in later life. *Journal of Aging and Health, 19,* 921–945.

de Lima, C., Alves, L. E., Iagher, F., Machado, A. F., Bonatto, S. J., & Kuczera, D. (2008). Anaerobic exercise reduces tumor growth, cancer cachexia and increases macrophage and lymphocyte response in Walker 256 tumor-bearing rats. *European Journal of Applied Physiology, 104,* 957–964.

DeLoache, J. S. (1987). Rapid change in symbolic functioning of very young children. *Science, 238,* 1556–1557.

DeLoache, J. S. (2000). Dual representation and children's use of scale models. *Child Development, 71,* 329–338.

DeLoache, J. S. (2002). The symbol-mindedness of young children. In W. Hartup & R. A. Weinberg

(Eds.), *Minnesota Symposia on Child Psychology* (Vol. 32, pp. 73–101). Mahwah, NJ: Erlbaum.

DeLoache, J. S., & Ganea, P. A. (2009). Symbol-based learning in infancy. In A. Woodward & A. Needham (Eds.), *Learning and the infant mind* (pp. 263–285). New York: Oxford University Press.

DeLoache, J. S., Pierroutsakos, S. L., Uttal, D. H., Rosengren, K. S., & Gottlieb, A. (1988). Grasping the nature of pictures. *Psychological Science, 9,* 205–210.

DeLoache, J. S., Uttal, D. H., & Rosengren, K. S. (2004). Scale errors offer evidence for a perception–action dissociation early in life. *Science, 304,* 1027–1029.

Delobel-Ayoub, M., Arnaud, C., White-Koning, M., Casper, C., Pierrat, V., Garel, M., et al. (2009). Behavioral problems and cognitive performance at 5 years of age after very preterm birth: The EPIPAGE Study. *Pediatrics, 123,* 485–1492.

De Marco, A. C., & Berzin, S. C. (2008). The influence of family economic status on home-leaving patterns during emerging adulthood. *Families in Society, 89,* 208–218.

Demetriou, A., Christou, C., Spanoudis, G., & Platsidou, M. (2002). The development of mental processing: Efficiency, working memory, and thinking. *Monographs of the Society for Research in Child Development, 67*(1, Serial No. 268).

Demetriou, A., Efklides, A., Papadaki, M., Papantoniou, G., & Economou, A. (1993). Structure and development of causal thought: From early adolescence to youth. *Developmental Psychology, 29,* 480–497.

Demetriou, A., Pachaury, A., Metallidou, Y., & Kazi, S. (1996). Universals and specificities in the structure and development of quantitative-relational thought: A cross-cultural study in Greece and India. *International Journal of Behavioral Development, 19,* 255–290.

Demiray, B., Gülgöz, S., & Bluck, S. (2009). Examining the life story account of the reminiscence bump: Why we remember more from young adulthood. *Memory, 17,* 708–723.

DeNavas-Walt, C., Proctor, B. D., & Smith, J. C. (2011). Income, poverty, and health insurance coverage in the United States: 2010. *U.S. Census Bureau, Current Population Reports,* P60–P239. Washington, DC: U.S. Government Printing Office.

Denham, S. A. (2005). Emotional competence counts: Assessment as support for school readiness. In K. Hirsh-Pasek, A. Kochanoff, N. S. Newcombe, & J. de Villiers (Eds.), Using scientific knowledge to inform preschool assessment. *Social Policy Report of the Society for Research in Child Development, 19*(No.1), 12.

Denissen, J. J. A., Zarrett, N. R., & Eccles, J. S. (2007). I like to do it, I'm able, and I know I am: Longitudinal couplings between domain-specific achievement, self-concept, and interest. *Child Development, 78,* 430–447.

Denmark, F. L., & Klara, M. D. (2007). Empowerment: A prime time for women over 50. In V. Mulhbauer & J. C. Chrisler (Eds.), *Women over 50* (pp. 182–203). New York: Springer.

Dennerstein, L., & Lehert, P. (2004). Modeling midaged women's sexual functioning: A prospective, population-based study. *Journal of Sex and Marriage Therapy, 30,* 173–183.

Denney, N. W. (1990). Adult age differences in traditional and practical problem solving. *Advances in Psychology, 72,* 329–349.

Denney, N. W., & Pearce, K A. (1989). A developmental study of practical problem solving in adults. *Psychology and Aging, 4,* 438–442.

Dennis, T., Bendersky, M., Ramsay, D., & Lewis, M. (2006). Reactivity and regulation in children prenatally exposed to cocaine. *Developmental Psychology, 42,* 688–697.

Dennis, W. (1960). Causes of retardation among institutionalized children: Iran. *Journal of Genetic Psychology, 96,* 47–59.

Dent, A., & Stewart, A. (2004). *Sudden death in childhood: Support for the bereaved family.* London: Butterworth-Heinemann.

Deocampo, J. A. (2003, April). *Tools on TV: A new paradigm for testing dual representational understanding.* Poster presented at the biennial meeting of the Society for Research in Child Development, Tampa, FL.

DePaulo, B. M., & Morris, W. L. (2005). Singles in society and in science. *Psychological Inquiry, 16,* 142–149.

Deprest, J. A., Devlieger, R., Srisupundit, K., Beck, V., Sandaite, I., Rusconi, S., et al. (2010). Fetal surgery is a clinical reality. *Seminars in Fetal and Neonatal Medicine, 15,* 58–67.

Der, G., Batty, G. D., & Deary, I. J. (2006). Effect of breastfeeding on intelligence in children: Prospective study, sibling pairs analysis, and meta-analysis. *British Medical Journal, 333,* 945.

Der, G., & Deary, I. J. (2006). Age and sex differences in reaction time in adulthood: Results from the United Kingdom Health and Lifestyle Survey. *Psychology and Aging, 21,* 62–73.

deRegnier, R.-A. (2005). Neurophysiologic evaluation of early cognitive development in high-risk infants and toddlers. *Mental Retardation and Developmental Disabilities, 11,* 317–324.

deRegnier, R.-A., Long, J. D., Geogieff, M. K., & Nelson, C. A. (2007). Using event-related potentials and brain development in infants of diabetic mothers. *Developmental Neuropsychology, 31,* 379–396.

DeRoche, K., & Welsh, M. (2008). Twenty-five years of research on neurocognitive outcomes in early-treated phenylketonuria: Intelligence and executive function. *Developmental Neuropsychology, 33,* 474–504.

Derom, C., Thiery, E., Vlietinck, R., Loos, R., & Derom, R. (1996). Handedness in twins according to zygosity and chorion type: A preliminary report. *Behavior Genetics, 26,* 407–408.

DeRose, L. M., & Brooks-Gunn, J. (2006). Transition into adolescence: The role of pubertal processes. In L. Balter & C. S. Tamis-LeMonda (Eds.), *Child psychology: A handbook of contemporary issues* (2nd ed., pp. 385–414). New York: Psychology Press.

DeRosier, M. E. (2007). Peer-rejected and bullied children: A safe schools initiative for elementary school students. In J. E. Zins, M. J. Elias, & C. A. Maher (Eds.), *Bullying, victimization, and peer harassment* (pp. 257–276). New York: Haworth.

DeRosier, M. E., & Thomas, J. M. (2003). Strengthening sociometric prediction: Scientific advances in the assessment of children's peer relations. *Child Development, 75,* 1379–1392.

de Rosnay, M., Copper, P. J., Tsigaras, N., & Murray, L. (2006). Transmission of social anxiety from mother to infant: An experimental study using a social referencing paradigm. *Behavior Research and Therapy, 44,* 1165–1175.

de Rosnay, M., & Hughes, C. (2006). Conversation and theory of mind: Do children talk their way to socio-cognitive understanding? *British Journal of Developmental Psychology, 24,* 7–37.

Derwinger, A., Neely, A. S., & Bäckman, L. (2005). Design your own memory strategies! Self-generated strategy training versus mnemonic training in old age: An 8-month follow-up. *Neuropsychological Rehabilitation, 15,* 37–54.

De Souza, E., Alberman, E., & Morris, J. K. (2009). Down syndrome and paternal age, a new analysis of case-control data collected in the 1960s. *American Journal of Medical Genetics, 149A,* 1205–1208.

Desrochers, S. (2008). From Piaget to specific Genevan developmental models. *Child Development Perspectives, 2,* 7–12.

Dessel, A. (2010). Prejudice in schools: Promotion of an inclusive culture and climate. *Education and Urban Society, 42,* 407–429.

Deutsch, N. L., & Schmertz, B. (2011). "Starting from Ground Zero: Constraints and experiences of adult women returning to college. *Review of Higher Education, 34,* 477–504.

DeVaney, S. A. (2008). Financial issues of older adults. In J. J. Xiao (Ed.), *Handbook of consumer finance research* (pp. 209–221). New York: Springer Science + Business Media.

Deveson, A. (1994). *Coming of age: Twenty-one interviews about growing older.* Newham, Australia: Scribe.

Devi, N. P. G., Shenbagvalli, R., Ramesh, K., & Rathinam, S. N. (2009). Rapid progression of HIV infection in infancy. *Indian Pediatrics, 46,* 53–56.

de Villiers, J. G., & de Villiers, P. A. (1973). A crosssectional study of the acquisition of grammatical morphemes in child speech. *Journal of Psycholinguistic Research, 2,* 267–278.

DeVries, R. (2001). Constructivist education in preschool and elementary school: The sociomoral atmosphere as the first educational goal. In S. L. Golbeck (Ed.), *Psychological perspectives on early childhood education* (pp. 153–180). Mahwah, NJ: Erlbaum.

de Waal, F. B. M. (1993). Sex differences in chimpanzee (and human) behavior: A matter of social values? In M. Hechter, L. Nadel, & R. E. Michod (Eds.), *The origin of values* (pp. 285–303). New York: Aldine de Gruyter.

de Waal, F. B. M. (2001). *Tree of origin.* Cambridge, MA: Harvard University Press.

De Weerd, A. W., & van den Bossche, A. S. (2003). The development of sleep during the first months of life. *Sleep Medicine Reviews, 7,* 179–191.

de Weerth, C., & Buitelaar, J. K. (2005). Physiological stress reactivity in human pregnancy—a review. *Neuroscience and Biobehavioral Reviews, 29,* 295–312.

De Wolff, M. S., & van IJzendoorn, M. H. (1997). Sensitivity and attachment: A meta-analysis on parental antecedents of infant attachment. *Child Development, 68,* 571–591.

Dey, J. G., & Hill, C. A. (2007). *Behind the pay gap.* Washington, DC: American Association of University Women.

Diamond, A. (2000). Close interrelation of motor development and cognitive development and of the cerebellum and prefrontal cortex. *Child Development, 71,* 44–56.

Diamond, A. (2004). Normal development of prefrontal cortex from birth to young adulthood: Cognitive functions, anatomy, and biochemistry. In D. T. Stuff & R. T. Knight (Eds.), *Principles of frontal lobe function* (pp. 466–503). New York: Oxford University Press.

Diamond, A. (2009). The interplay of biology and the environment broadly defined. *Developmental Psychology, 45,* 1–8.

Diamond, A., Barnett, W. S., Thomas, J., & Munro, S. (2007). Preschool program improves cognitive control. *Science, 318,* 1387–1388.

Diamond, A., Cruttenden, L., & Neiderman, D. (1994). AB with multiple wells: 1. Why are multiple wells sometimes easier than two wells? 2. Memory or memory + inhibition. *Developmental Psychology, 30,* 192–205.

Diamond, L. M. (1998). Development of sexual orientation among adolescent and young adult women. *Developmental Psychology, 34,* 1085–1095.

Diamond, L. M. (2003). Love matters: Romantic relationships among sexual-minority adolescents. In P. Florsheim (Ed.), *Adolescent romantic relations and sexual behavior* (pp. 85–108). Mahwah, NJ: Erlbaum.

Diamond, L. M. (2006). The intimate same-sex relationships of sexual minorities. In A. L.

Vangelisti & D. Perlman (Eds.), *The Cambridge handbook of personal relationships* (pp. 293–312). New York: Cambridge University Press.

Diamond, L. M. (2008). Female bisexuality from adolescence to adulthood: Results from a 10-year longitudinal study. *Developmental Psychology, 44,* 5–14.

Diamond, L. M., Fagundes, C. P., & Butterworth, M. R. (2010). Intimate relationships across the lifespan. In M. E. Lamb, A. M. Freund, & R. M. Lerner, (Eds.), *The handbook of life-span development, Vol. 2: Social and emotional development* (pp. 379–433). Hoboken, NJ: Wiley.

Diamond, L. M., & Lucas, S. (2004). Sexual-minority and heterosexual youths' peer relationships: Experiences, expectations, and implications for well-being. *Journal of Research on Adolescence, 14,* 313–340.

Dias, M. G., & Harris, P. L. (1988). The effect of make-believe play on deductive reasoning. *British Journal of Developmental Psychology, 6,* 207–221.

DiBiase, A.-M., Gibbs, J. C., Potter, G. B., & Blount, M. R. (2011). Teaching adolescents to think and act responsibly: *The EQUIP approach.* Champaign, IL: Research Press.

Dick, D. M., Prescott, C., & McGue, M. (2008). The genetics of substance use and substance use disorders. In Y.-K. Kim (Ed.), *Handbook of behavior genetics* (pp. 433–453). New York: Springer.

Dick, D. M., Rose, R. J., Viken, R. J., & Kaprio, J. (2000). Pubertal timing and substance use: Associations between and within families across late adolescence. *Developmental Psychology, 36,* 180–189.

Dickinson, D. K., Golinkoff, R. M., & Hirsh-Pasek, K. (2010). Speaking out for language: Why language is central to reading development. *Educational Researcher, 39,* 305–310.

Dickinson, D. K., & McCabe, A. (2001). Bringing it all together: The multiple origins, skills, and environmental supports of early literacy. *Learning Disabilities Research and Practice, 16,* 186–202.

Dickinson, D. K., & Sprague, K. E. (2001). The nature and impact of early childhood care environments on the language and early literacy development of children from low-income families. In S. B. Neuman & D. K. Dickinson (Eds.), *Handbook of early literacy research.* New York: Guilford.

Dick-Read, G. (1959). *Childbirth without fear.* New York: Harper & Row.

Dickson, R. A., Pillemer, D. B., & Bruehl, E. C. (2011). The reminiscence bump for salient personal memories: Is a cultural life script required? *Memory and Cognition, 39,* 977–991.

Dickstein, M. (1992). After utopia: The 1960s today. In B. L. Tischler (Ed.), *Sights on the sixties* (pp. 13–24). New Brunswick, NJ: Rutgers University Press.

DiDonato, M. D., & Berenbaum, S. A. (2011). The benefits and drawbacks of gender typing: How different dimensions are related to psychological adjustment. *Archives of Sexual Behavior, 40,* 457–463.

Diehl, M., & Berg, K. M. (2007). Personality and involvement in leisure activities during the Third Age: Findings from the Ohio Longitudinal Study. In J. B. James & P. Wink (Eds.), *Annual review of gerontology and geriatrics* (Vol. 26, pp. 211–226). New York: Springer.

Diehl, M., Coyle, N., & Labouvie-Vief, G. (1996). Age and sex differences in strategies of coping and defense across the life span. *Psychology and Aging, 11,* 127–139.

Diehl, M., Youngblade, L. M., Hay, E. L., & Chui, H. (2011). The development of self-representations across the life span. In K. L. Fingerman, C. A. Berg, J. Smith, & H. Chui (Eds.), *Handbook of lifespan development* (pp. 611–646). New York: Springer.

Diener, E., Gohm, C. L., Suh, E., & Oishi, S. (2000). Similarity of the relations between marital status and subjective well-being across cultures. *Journal of Cross-Cultural Psychology, 31,* 419–436.

Dildy, G. A., Jackson, G. M., Fowers, G. K., Oshiro, B. T., Varner, M. W., & Clark, S. L. (1996). Very advanced maternal age. Pregnancy after age 45. *American Journal of Obstetrics and Gynecology, 175,* 668–674.

Dillon, M., & Wink, P. (2004). American religion, generativity, and the therapeutic culture. In E. de St. Aubin & D. P. McAdams (Eds.), *The generative society: Caring for future generations* (pp. 15–31). Washington, DC: American Psychological Association.

Dillon, M., & Wink, P. (2007). *In the course of a lifetime: Tracing religious belief, practice, and change.* Berkeley: University of California Press.

Dilworth-Anderson, P., Goodwin, P. Y., & Williams, S. W. (2004). Can culture help explain the physical health effects of caregiving over time among African American caregivers? *Journal of Gerontology, 59B,* S138–S145.

Ding, Z. Y. (2008). National epidemiological survey on childhood obesity, 2006. *Chinese Journal of Pediatrics, 46,* 179–184.

DiPietro, J. A., Bornstein, M. H., Costigan, K. A., Pressman, E. K., Hahn, C.-S., & Painter, K. (2002). What does fetal movement predict about behavior during the first two years of life? *Developmental Psychobiology, 40,* 358–371.

DiPietro, J. A., Caulfield, L. E., Irizarry, R. A., Chen, P., Merialdi, M., & Zavaleta, N. (2006). Prenatal development of intrafetal and maternal–fetal synchrony. *Behavioral Neuroscience, 120,* 687–701.

DiPietro, J. A., Hodgson, D. M., Costigan, K. A., & Hilton, S. C. (1996). Fetal neurobehavioral development. *Child Development, 67,* 2553–2567.

Dirix, C. E. H., Nijhuis, J. G., Jongsma, H. W., & Hornstra, G. (2009). Aspects of fetal learning and memory. *Child Development, 80,* 1251–1258.

Dirks, J. (1982). The effect of a commercial game on children's Block Design scores on the WISC-R test. *Intelligence, 6,* 109–123.

Dishion, T. J., Shaw, D., Connell, A., Gardner, F., Weaver, C., & Wilson, M. (2008). The Family Check-Up with high-risk indigent families: Preventing problem behavior by increasing parents' positive behavior support in early childhood. *Child Development, 79,* 1395–1414.

DiTommaso, E., Brannen, C., & Burgess, M. (2005). The universality of relationship characteristics: A cross-cultural comparison of different types of attachment and loneliness in Canadian and visiting Chinese students. *Social Behavior and Personality, 33,* 57–68.

Dix, T., Stewart, A. D., Gershoff, E. T., & Day, W. H. (2007). Autonomy and children's reactions to being controlled: Evidence that both compliance and defiance may be positive markers in early development. *Child Development, 78,* 1204–1221.

Dixon, R. A., de Frias, C. M., & Bäckman, L. (2001). Characteristics of self-reported memory compensation in older adults. *Journal of Clinical and Experimental Neuropsychology, 23,* 650–661.

Djahanbakhch, O., Ezzati, M., & Zosmer, A. (2007). Reproductive ageing in women. *Journal of Pathology, 211,* 219–231.

Dodd, V. L. (2005). Implications of kangaroo care for growth and development in preterm infants. *JOGNN, 34,* 218–232.

Dodge, K. A., Coie, J. D., & Lynam, D. (2006). Aggression and antisocial behavior in youth. In N. Eisenberg (Ed.), *Handbook of child psychology: Vol. 3. Social, emotional, and personality development* (6th ed., pp. 719–788). New York: Wiley.

Dodge, K. A., McLoyd, V. C., & Lansford, J. E. (2006). The cultural context of physically disciplining children. In V. C. McLoyd, N. E. Hill, & K. A. Dodge (Eds.), *African-American family life: Ecological and cultural diversity* (pp. 245–263). New York: Guilford.

Dodson, T. A., & Borders, L. D. (2006). Men in traditional and nontraditional careers: Gender role attitudes, gender role conflict, and job satisfaction. *Career Development Quarterly, 54,* 283–296.

Dohnt, H., & Tiggemann, M. (2006). The contribution of peer and media influences to the development of body satisfaction and self-esteem in young girls: A prospective study. *Developmental Psychology, 42,* 929–936.

Doka, K. J. (2008). Disenfranchised grief in historical and cultural perspective. In M. S. Stroebe, R. O. Hansson, H. Schut, & W. Stroebe (Eds.), *Handbook of bereavement research and practice* (pp. 223–240). Washington, DC: American Psychological Association.

Doka, K. J., & Martin, T. L. (2010). *Grieving beyond gender: Understanding the ways men and women mourn* (rev. ed.). New York: Routledge.

Dolbin-MacNab, M. L. (2006). Just like raising your own? Grandmothers' perceptions of parenting a second time around. *Family Relations, 55,* 564–575.

Dombrowski, S. C., Noonan, K., & Martin, R. P. (2007). Low birth weight and cognitive outcomes: Evidence for a gradient relationship in an urban, poor, African American birth cohort. *School Psychology Quarterly, 22,* 26–43.

Donatelle, R. J. (2012). *Health: The basics* (10th ed.). San Francisco: Benjamin Cummings.

Dondi, M., Simion, F., & Caltran, G. (1999). Can newborns discriminate between their own cry and the cry of another newborn infant? *Developmental Psychology, 35,* 418–426.

Done, D. J., & Thomas, J. A. (2001). Training in communication skills for informal carers of people suffering from dementia: A cluster randomized clinic trial comparing a therapist led workshop and booklet. *International Journal of Geriatric Psychiatry, 16,* 816–821.

Donnellan, M. B., Larsen-Rife, D., & Conger, R. D. (2005). Personality, family history, and competence in early adult romantic relationships. *Journal of Personality and Social Psychology, 88,* 562–576.

Donnellan, M. B., & Lucas, R. E. (2008). Age differences in the big five across the life span: Evidence from two national samples. *Psychology and Aging, 23,* 558–566.

Donnellan, M. B., Trzesniewski, K. H., Robins, R. W., Moffitt, T. E., & Caspi, A. (2005). Low self-esteem is related to aggression, antisocial behavior, and delinquency. *Psychological Science, 16,* 328–335.

D'Onofrio, B. M., Turkheimer, E., Emery, R. E., Slutske, W. S., Heath, A. C., Madden, P. A., & Martin, N. G. (2006). A genetically informed study of the processes underlying the association between parental marital instability and offspring adjustment. *Developmental Psychology, 42,* 486–499.

Dorris, M. (1989). *The broken cord.* New York: Harper & Row.

Doss, B. D., Rhoades, G. K., Stanley, S. M., & Markman, H. J. (2009). The effect of the transition to parenthood on relationship quality: An 8-year prospective study. *Journal of Personality and Social Psychology, 96,* 601–619.

Double, E. B., Mabuchi, K., Cullings, H. M., Preston, D. L., Kodama, K., Shimizu, Y., et al. (2011). Long-term radiation-related health effects in a unique human population: Lessons learned from the atomic bomb survivors of Hiroshima and Nagasaki. *Disaster Medicine and Public Health Preparedness, 5*(Suppl. 1), S122–S133.

Dowd, M. D. (2013). Prevention and treatment of traumatic stress in children: Few answers, many questions. *Pediatrics, 31,* 591–592.

Dowling, E. M., Gestsdottir, S., Anderson, P. M., von Eye, A., Almerigi, J., & Lerner, R. M. (2004). Structural relations among spirituality, religiosity, and thriving in adolescence. *Applied Developmental Psychology, 8,* 7–16.

Downing, J. E. (2010). *Academic instruction for students with moderate and severe intellectual disabilities.* Thousand Oaks, CA: Corwin.

Downs, A. C., & Fuller, M. J. (1991). Recollections of spermarche: An exploratory investigation. *Current Psychology: Research and Reviews, 10,* 93–102.

Dozier, M., Stovall, K. C., Albus, K. E., & Bates, B. (2001). Attachment for infants in foster care: The role of caregiver state of mind. *Child Development, 72,* 1467–1477.

Drabman, R. S., Cordua, G. D., Hammer, D., Jarvie, G. J., & Horton, W. (1979). Developmental trends in eating rates of normal and overweight preschool children. *Child Development, 50,* 211–216.

Drayton, S., Turley-Ames, K. J., & Guajardo, N. R. (2011). Counterfactual thinking and false belief: The role of executive function. *Journal of Experimental Child Psychology, 108,* 532–548.

Drewnowski, A., & Shultz, J. M. (2001). Impact of aging on eating behaviors, food choices, nutrition, and health status. *Journal of Nutrition, Health, and Aging, 5,* 75–79.

Driscoll, M. C. (2007). Sickle cell disease. *Pediatrics in Review, 28,* 259–268.

Driver, J., Tabares, A., Shapiro, A. F., & Gottman, J. M. (2012). Couple interaction in happy and unhappy marriages: Gottman Laboratory studies. In F. Walsh (Ed.), *Normal family processes: Growing diversity and complexity* (pp. 57–77). New York: Guilford.

Drotar, D., Witherspoon, D. O., Zebracki, K., & Peterson, C. C. (2006). *Psychological interventions in childhood chronic illness.* Washington, DC: American Psychological Association.

Dubé, E. M., Savin-Williams, R. C., & Diamond, L. M. (2001). Intimacy development, gender, and ethnicity among sexual-minority youths. In A. R. D'Augelli & C. J. Patterson (Eds.), *Lesbian, gay, and bisexual identities and youth* (pp. 129–152). New York: Oxford University Press.

DuBois, D. L., Burk-Braxton, C., Swenson, L. P., Tevendale, H. D., Lockerd, E. M., & Moran, B. L. (2002). Getting by with a little help from self and others: Self-esteem and social support as resources during early adolescence. *Developmental Psychology, 38,* 822–939.

DuBois, D. L., Felner, R. D., Brand, S., & George, G. R. (1999). Profiles of self-esteem in early adolescence: Identification and investigation of adaptive correlates. *American Journal of Community Psychology, 27,* 899–932.

Dubois, M-F., Bravo, C., Graham, J., Wildeman, S., Cohen, C., Painter, K., et al. (2011). Comfort with proxy consent to research involving decisionally impaired older adults: Do type of proxy and risk–benefit profile matter? *International Psychogeriatrics, 23,* 1479–1488.

Duckworth, A. L., & Seligman, M. E. P. (2005). Self-discipline outdoes IQ in predicting academic performance of adolescents. *Psychological Science, 12,* 939–944.

Dudani, A., Macpherson, A., & Tamim, H. (2010). Childhood behavior problems and unintentional injury: A longitudinal, population-based study. *Journal of Developmental and Behavioral Pediatrics, 31,* 276–285.

Duggan, A., McFarlane, E., Fuddy, L., Burrell, L., Higman, S. M., Windham, A., & Sia, C. (2004). Randomized trial of a statewide home visiting program: Impact in preventing child abuse and neglect. *Child Abuse and Neglect, 28,* 597–622.

Dumas, J. A., & Hartman, M. (2003). Age differences in temporal and item memory. *Psychology and Aging, 18,* 573–586.

Duncan, G. J., Dowsett, C. J., Claessens, A., Magnuson, K., Huston, A. C., Klebanov, P., et al. (2007). School readiness and later achievement. *Developmental Psychology, 43,* 1428–1446.

Duncan, G. J., & Magnuson, K. A. (2003). Off with Hollingshead: Socioeconomic resources, parenting, and child development. In M. H. Bornstein & R. H. Bradley (Eds.), *Socioeconomic status, parenting, and child development* (pp. 83–106). Mahwah, NJ: Erlbaum.

Duncan, S. R., Paterson, D. S., Hoffman, J. M., Mokler, D. J., Borenstein, M. S., Belliveau, R. A., et al. (2010). Brainstem serotonergic deficiency in sudden infant death syndrome. *Journal of the American Medical Association, 303,* 430–437.

Dundek, L. H. (2006). Establishment of a Somali doula program at a large metropolitan hospital. *Journal of Perinatal and Neonatal Nursing, 20,* 128–137.

Dunham, Y., Baron, A. S., & Banaji, M. R. (2006). From American city to Japanese village: A cross-cultural investigation of implicit race attitudes. *Child Development, 77,* 1129–1520.

Dunham, Y., Baron, A. S., & Carey, S. (2011). Consequences of "minimal" group affiliations in children. *Child Development, 82,* 793–811.

Dunlosky, J., & Hertzog, C. (2001). Measuring strategy production during associative learning: The relative utility of concurrent versus retrospective reports. *Memory and Cognition, 29,* 247–253.

Dunn, J. (1989). Siblings and the development of social understanding in early childhood. In P. G. Zukow (Ed.), *Sibling interaction across cultures* (pp. 106–116). New York: Springer-Verlag.

Dunn, J. (1994). Temperament, siblings, and the development of relationships. In W. B. Carey & S. C. McDevitt (Eds.), *Prevention and early intervention* (pp. 50–58). New York: Brunner/Mazel.

Dunn, J. (2002). The adjustment of children in stepfamilies: Lessons from community studies. *Child and Adolescent Mental Health, 7,* 154–161.

Dunn, J. (2004). Sibling relationships. In P. K. Smith & C. H. Hart (Eds.), *Handbook of childhood social development* (pp. 223–237). Malden, MA: Blackwell.

Dunn, J. (2005). Moral development in early childhood and social interaction in the family. In M. Killen & J. G. Smetana (Eds.), *Handbook of moral development* (pp. 331–350). Mahwah, NJ: Erlbaum.

Dunn, J., Brown, J. R., & Maguire, M. (1995). The development of children's moral sensibility: Individual differences and emotion understanding. *Developmental Psychology, 31,* 649–659.

Dunn, J., Cheng, H., O'Connor, T. G., & Bridges, L. (2004). Children's perspectives on their relationships with their nonresident fathers: Influences, outcomes and implications. *Journal of Child Psychology and Psychiatry, 45,* 553–566.

Dunn, J. R., Schaefer-McDaniel, N. J., & Ramsay, J. T. (2010). Neighborhood chaos and children's development: Questions and contradictions. In G. W. Evans & T. D. Wachs (Eds.), *Chaos and its influence on children's development: An ecological perspective* (pp. 173–189). Washington, DC: American Psychological Association.

Dunne, E. J., & Dunne-Maxim, K. (2004). Working with families in the aftermath of suicide. In F. Walsh & M. McGoldrick (Eds.), *Living beyond loss: Death in the family* (2nd ed., pp. 272–284). New York: Norton.

Durbin, D. L., Darling, N., Steinberg, L., & Brown, B. B. (1993). Parenting style and peer group membership among European-American adolescents. *Journal of Research on Adolescence, 3,* 87–100.

Durlak, J. A., & Weissberg, R. P. (2007). *The impact of after-school programs that promote personal and social skills.* Chicago: Collaborative for Academic, Social, and Emotional Learning.

Durston, S., & Casey, B. J. (2006). What have we learned about cognitive development from neuroimaging? *Neuropsychologia, 44,* 2149–2157.

Durston, S., & Conrad, K. (2007). Integrating genetic, psychopharmacological and neuroimaging studies: A converging methods approach to understanding the neurobiology of ADHD. *Developmental Review, 27,* 374–395.

Dusek, J. B. (1987). Sex roles and adjustment. In D. B. Carter (Ed.), *Current conceptions of sex roles and sex typing* (pp. 211–222). New York: Praeger.

Duszak, R. S. (2009). Congenital rubella syndrome—major review. *Optometry, 80,* 36–43.

Dutta, A., Henley, W., Lang, I., Llewellyn, D., Guralnik, J., Wallace, R. B., et al. (2011). Predictors of extraordinary survival in the Iowa Established Populations for Epidemiological Study of the Elderly: Cohort follow-up to "extinction." *Journal of the American Geriatrics Society, 59,* 963–971.

Dutton, D. G. (2007). *The abusive personality: Violence and control in intimate relationships* (2nd ed.). New York: Guilford.

Dutton, D. G. (2012). The case against the role of gender in intimate partner violence. *Aggression and Violent Behavior, 17,* 99–104.

Dutton, D. G., Nicholls, T. L., & Spidel, A. (2005). Female perpetrators of intimate abuse. In F. P. Buttell & M. M. Carney (Eds.), *Women who perpetrate relationship violence: Moving beyond political correctness* (pp. 1–31). New York: Haworth Press.

Dweck, C. S. (2002). Messages that motivate: How praise molds students' beliefs, motivation, and performance (in surprising ways). In J. Aronson (Ed.), *Improving academic achievement: Impact of psychological factors on education* (pp. 37–60). San Diego, CA: Academic Press.

Dweck, C. S. (2009). Prejudice: How it develops and how it can be undone. *Human Development, 52,* 371–376.

Dykiert, D., Der, G., Starr, J. M., & Deary, I. J. (2012). Sex differences in reaction time mean and intraindividual variability across the life span. *Developmental Psychology, 48,* 1262–1276.

Dykstra, P. A. (2006). Off the beaten track: Childlessness and social integration in late life. *Research on Aging, 28,* 749–767.

Dykstra, P. A. (2009). Older adult loneliness: Myths and realities. *European Journal of Ageing, 6,* 91–100.

Dykstra, P. A., & Hagestad, G. O. (2007). Roads less taken: Developing a nuanced view of older adults without children. *Journal of Family Issues, 28,* 1275–1310.

Dynarski, M., James-Burdumy, S., Moore, M., Rosenberg, L., Deke, J., & Mansfield, W. (2004). *When schools stay open late: The national evaluation of the 21st Century Community Learning Centers Program: New findings.* Washington, DC: U.S. Department of Education.

Dzurova, D., & Pikhart, H. (2005). Down syndrome, paternal age and education: Comparison of California and the Czech Republic. *BMC Public Health, 5,* 69.

E

Eagly, A. H., & Carli, L. L. (2007). *Through the labyrinth: The truth about how women become leaders.* Boston, MA: Harvard Business School Press.

Eagly, A. H., Eastwick, P. W., & Johannesen-Schmidt, M. (2009). Possible selves in marital roles: The impact of the anticipated division of labor on mate preferences of women and men. *Personality and Social Psychology Bulletin, 35,* 403–414.

Eagly, A. H., & Wood, W. (2012). Social role theory. In P. A. M. Van Lange, A. W. Kruglanski, & E. T. Higgins (Eds.), *Handbook of theories of social psychology* (Vol. 2, pp. 458–476). Thousand Oaks, CA: Sage.

Eaker, E. D., Sullivan, L. M., Kelly-Hayes, M., D'Agostino, R. B., & Benjamin, E. J. (2004). Anger and hostility predict the development of atrial fibrillation in men in the Framingham Offspring Study. *Circulation, 109,* 1267–1271.

Eaker, E. D., Sullivan, L. M., Kelly-Hayes, M., D'Agostino, R. B., & Benjamin, E. J. (2007). Marital status, marital strain, and risk of coronary heart disease or total mortality: The Framingham Offspring Study. *Psychosomatic Medicine, 69,* 509–513.

Early Head Start National Resource Center. (2011). *Early Head Start program fact sheet.* Retrieved from www.ehsnrc.org/AboutUs/ehs.htm

Eaton, D. K., Davis, K. S., Barrios, L., Brener, N. D., & Noonan, R. K. (2007). Associations of dating violence victimization with lifetime participation, cooccurrence, and early initiation of risk behaviors among U.S. high school students. *Journal of Interpersonal Violence, 22,* 585–602.

Eaves, L., Silberg, J., Foley, D., Bulik, C., Maes, H., & Erkanli, A. (2004). Genetic and environmental influences on the relative timing of pubertal change. *Twin Research, 7,* 471–481.

Ebeling, K. S., & Gelman, S. A. (1994). Children's use of context in interpreting "big" and "little." *Child Development, 65,* 1178–1192.

Ebner, N. C., Freund, A. M., & Baltes, P. B. (2006). Developmental changes in personal goal orientation from young to late adulthood: From striving for gains to maintenance and prevention of losses. *Psychology and Aging, 21,* 664–678.

Eccles, J. S., & Gootman, J. (Eds.). (2002). *Community programs to promote youth development.* Washington, DC: National Academy Press.

Eccles, J. S., Jacobs, J. E., & Harold, R. D. (1990). Gender-role stereotypes, expectancy effects, and parents' role in the socialization of gender differences in self-perceptions and skill acquisition. *Journal of Social Issues, 46,* 183–201.

Eccles, J. S., & Roeser, R. W. (2009). Schools, academic motivation, and stage–environment fit. In R. M. Lerner & L. Steinberg (Eds.), *Handbook of adolescent psychology* (Vol. 1, pp. 404–434). Hoboken, NJ: Wiley.

Eccles, J. S., Templeton, J., Barber, B., & Stone, M. (2003). Adolescence and emerging adulthood: The critical passageways to adulthood. In M. H. Bornstein, L. Davidson, C. L. M., Keyes, K. A. Moore, & the Center for Child Well-Being (Eds.), *Well-being: Positive development across the life course* (pp. 383–406). Mahwah, NJ: Erlbaum.

Eccles, J. S., Vida, M. N., & Barber, B. (2004). The relation of early adolescents' college plans and both academic ability and task-value beliefs to subsequent college enrollment. *Journal of Early Adolescence, 24,* 63–77.

Economic Policy Institute. (2010). *A broader, bolder approach to education.* Retrieved from www .boldapproach.org

Eder, R. A., & Mangelsdorf, S. C. (1997). The emotional basis of early personality development: Implications for the emergent self-concept. In R. Hogan, J. Johnson, & S. Briggs (Eds.), *Handbook of personality psychology* (pp. 209–240). San Diego, CA: Academic Press.

Edwards, B. A., O'Driscoll, D. M., Ali A., Jordan, A. S., Trinder, J., & Malhotra, A. (2010). Aging and sleep: Physiology and pathophysiology. *Seminars in Respiratory Critical Care Medicine, 31,* 618–633.

Edwards, O. W., & Oakland, T. D. (2006). Factorial invariance of Woodcock-Johnson III scores for African Americans and Caucasian Americans. *Journal of Psychoeducational Assessment, 24,* 358–366.

Efstathiou, N., & Clifford, C. (2011). The critical care nurse's role in end-of-life care: Issues and challenges. *Nursing in Critical Care, 16,* 116–123.

Egan, S. K., & Perry, D. G. (2001). Gender identity: A multidimensional analysis with implications for psychosocial adjustment. *Developmental Psychology, 37,* 451–463.

Eggebeen, D. J., Dew, J., & Knoester, C. (2010). Fatherhood and men's lives at middle age. *Journal of Family Issues, 31,* 113–130.

Eggebeen, D. J., & Sturgeon, S. (2006). Demography of the baby boomers. In S. K. Whitbourne & S. L. Willis (Eds.), *The baby boomers grow up: Contemporary perspectives on midlife* (pp. 3–21). Mahwah, NJ: Erlbaum.

Ehrensaft, M. K. (2009). Family and relationship predictors of psychological and physical aggression. In D. K. O'Leary & E. M. Woodin (Eds.), *Psychological and physical aggression in couples: Causes and interventions* (pp. 99–118). Washington, DC: American Psychological Association.

Ehrensaft, M. K., Moffitt, T. E., & Caspi, A. (2004). Clinically abusive relationships in an unselected birth cohort: Men's and women's participation and developmental antecedents. *Journal of Abnormal Psychology, 113,* 258–270.

Ehri, L. C., & Roberts, T. (2006). The roots of learning to read and write: Acquisition of letters and phonemic awareness. In D. K. Dikinson & S. B. Neuman (Eds.), *Handbook of early literacy research* (Vol. 2, pp. 113–131). New York: Guildford.

Eichstedt, J. A., Serbin, L. A., Poulin-Dubois, D., & Sen, M. G. (2002). Of bears and men: Infants' knowledge of conventional and metaphorical gender stereotypes. *Infant Behavior and Development, 25,* 296–310.

Einspieler, C., Marschik, P. B., & Prechtl, H. F. R. (2008). Human motor behavior: Prenatal origin and early postnatal development. *Zeitschrift für Psychologie, 216,* 147–153.

Einstein, G. O., McDaniel, M. A., & Scullin, M. K. (2012). Prospective memory and aging: Understanding the variability. In M. Naveh-Benjamin & N. Ohta (Eds.), *Memory and aging: Current issues and future directions* (pp. 153–179). New York: Psychology Press.

Eisenberg, N. (2003). Prosocial behavior, empathy, and sympathy. In M. H. Bornstein & L. Davidson (Eds.), *Well-being: Positive development across the life course* (pp. 253–265). Mahwah, NJ: Erlbaum.

Eisenberg, N. (2010). Empathy-related responding: Links with self-regulation, moral judgment, and moral behavior. In M. Mikulincer & P. R. Shaver (Eds.), *Prosocial motives, emotions, and behavior: The better angels of our nature* (pp. 129–148). Washington, DC: American Psychological Association.

Eisenberg, N., Eggum, N. D., & Edwards, A. (2010). Empathy-related responding and moral development. In W. F. Arsenio & E. A. Lemerise (Eds.), *Emotions, aggression, and morality in children* (pp. 115–135). Washington, DC: American Psychological Association.

Eisenberg, N., Fabes, R. A., Shepard, S. A., Murphy, B. C., Jones, S., & Guthrie, I. K. (1998). Contemporaneous and longitudinal prediction of children's sympathy from dispositional regulation and emotionality. *Developmental Psychology, 34,* 910–924.

Eisenberg, N., Fabes, R. A., & Spinrad, T. L. (2006). Prosocial development. In N. Eisenberg (Ed.), *Handbook of child psychology: Vol. 3. Social, emotional, and personality development* (6th ed., pp. 646–718). Hoboken, NJ: Wiley.

Eisenberg, N., Sadovsky, A., Spinrad, T. L., Fabes, R. A., Losoya, S., & Valiente, C. (2005a). The relations of problem behavior status to children's negative emotionality, effortful control, and impulsivity: Concurrent relations and prediction of change. *Developmental Psychology, 41,* 193–211.

Eisenberg, N., & Silver, R. C. (2011). Growing up in the shadow of terrorism. *American Psychologist, 66,* 468–481.

Eisenberg, N., Smith, C. L., Sadovsky, A., & Spinrad, T. L. (2004). Effortful control: Relations with emotion regulation, adjustment, and socialization in childhood. In R. Baumeister & K. D. Vohs (Eds.), *Handbook of self-regulation: Research,*

theory, and applications (pp. 259–282). New York: Guilford.

Eisenberg, N., & Spinrad, T. L. (2004). Emotion-related regulation: Sharpening the definition. *Child Development, 75,* 334–339.

Eisenberg, N., Zhou, Q., Spinrad, T. L., Valiente, C., Fabes, R. A., & Liew, J. (2005b). Relations among positive parenting, children's effortful control, and externalizing problems: A three-wave longitudinal study. *Child Development, 76,* 1055–1071.

Ekman, P. (2003). *Emotions revealed.* New York: Times Books.

Ekman, P., & Friesen, W. (1972). Constants across culture in the face of emotion. *Journal of Personality and Social Psychology, 17,* 124–129.

Elavsky, S., & McAuley, E. (2007). Physical activity and mental health outcomes during menopause: A randomized controlled trial. *Annals of Behavioral Medicine, 33,* 132–142.

Elder, G. H., Jr., & Conger, R. (2000). *Children of the land: Adversity and success in rural America.* Chicago: University of Chicago Press.

Elder, G. H., Jr., Nguyen, T. V., & Caspi, A. (1985). Linking family hardship to children's lives. *Child Development, 56,* 361–375.

Elder, G. H., Jr., & Shanahan, M. J. (2006). The life course and human development. In R. M. Lerner (Ed.), *Handbook of child psychology: Vol. 1. Theoretical models of human development* (6th ed., pp. 665–715). Hoboken, NJ: Wiley.

Elfenbein, D. S., & Felice, M. E. (2003). Adolescent pregnancy. *Pediatric Clinics of North America, 50,* 781–800.

Eliakim, A., Friedland, O., Kowen, G., Wolach, B., & Nemet, D. (2004). Parental obesity and higher pre-intervention BMI reduce the likelihood of a multidisciplinary childhood obesity program to succeed: A clinical observation. *Journal of Pediatric Endocrinology and Metabolism, 17,* 1055–1061.

Elias, C. L., & Berk, L. E. (2002). Self-regulation in young children: Is there a role for sociodramatic play? *Early Childhood Research Quarterly, 17,* 1–17.

Elicker, J., Englund, M., & Sroufe, L. A. (1992). Predicting peer competence and peer relationships in childhood from early parent–child relationships. In R. D. Parke & G. W. Ladd (Eds.), *Family–peer relationships: Modes of linkage* (pp. 77–106). Hillsdale, NJ: Erlbaum.

Elkind, D. (1994). *A sympathetic understanding of the child: Birth to sixteen* (3rd ed.). Boston: Allyn and Bacon.

Elkind, D., & Bowen, R. (1979). Imaginary audience behavior in children and adolescents. *Developmental Psychology, 15,* 33–44.

Elliott, D. B., & Simmons, T. (2011, August). *Marital events of Americans: 2009. American Community Survey Reports, ACS-13.* Washington, DC: U.S. Census Bureau. Retrieved from www.census.gov/prod/2011pubs/acs-13.pdf

Elliott, J. G. (1999). School refusal: Issues of conceptualization, assessment, and treatment. *Journal of Child Psychology and Psychiatry and Allied Disciplines, 40,* 1001–1012.

Ellis, A. E., & Oakes, L. M. (2006). Infants flexibly use different dimensions to categorize objects. *Developmental Psychology, 42,* 1000–1011.

Ellis, B. J. (2004). Timing of pubertal maturation in girls: An integrated life history approach. *Psychological Bulletin, 130,* 920–958.

Ellis, B. J., & Essex, M. J. (2007). Family environments, adrenarche, and sexual maturation: A longitudinal test of a life history model. *Child Development, 78,* 1799–1817.

Ellis, L., & Bonin, S. L. (2003). Genetics and occupation-related preferences: Evidence from adoptive and non-adoptive families. *Personality and Individual Differences, 35,* 929–937.

Ellis, W. E., & Zarbatany, L. (2007). Explaining friendship formation and friendship stability:

The role of children's and friends' aggression and victimization. *Merrill-Palmer Quarterly, 53,* 79–104.

Elman, J. L. (2001). Connectionism and language acquisition. In M. Tomasello & E. Bates (Eds.), *Language development* (pp. 295–306). Oxford, UK: Blackwell.

Else-Quest, N. M., Hyde, J. S., Goldsmith, H. H., & Van Hulle, C. A. (2006). Gender differences in temperament: A meta-analysis. *Psychological Bulletin, 132,* 33–72.

El-Sheikh, M., Cummings, E. M., & Reiter, S. (1996). Preschoolers' responses to ongoing interadult conflict: The role of prior exposure to resolved versus unresolved arguments. *Journal of Abnormal Child Psychology, 24,* 665–679.

Eltzschig, H. K., Lieberman, E. S., & Camann, W. R. (2003). Regional anesthesia and analgesia for labor and delivery. *New England Journal of Medicine, 384,* 319–332.

Eluvathingal, T. J., Chugani, H. T., Behen, M. E., Juhasz, C., Muzik, O., Maqbook, M., et al. (2006). Abnormal brain connectivity in children after early severe socioemotional deprivation: A diffusion tensor imaging study. *Pediatrics, 117,* 2093–2100.

Elwert, F., & Christakis, N. A. (2006). Widowhood and race. *American Sociological Review, 71,* 16–41.

Emery, R. E., & Laumann-Billings, L. (1998). An overview of the nature, causes, and consequences of abusive family relationships: Toward differentiating maltreatment and violence. *American Psychologist, 53,* 121–135.

Emery, R. E., Sbarra, D., & Grover, T. (2005). Divorce mediation: Research and reflections. *Family Court Review, 43,* 22–37.

Emory, E. K., Schlackman, L. J., & Fiano, K. (1996). Drug–hormone interactions on neurobehavioral responses in human neonates. *Infant Behavior and Development, 19,* 213–220.

Englund, M. E., Egeland, B., & Collins, W. A. (2008). Exceptions to high school dropout predictions in a low-income sample: Do adults make a difference? *Journal of Social Issues, 64,* 77–93.

Ennemoser, M., & Schneider, W. (2007). Relations of television viewing and reading: Findings from a 4-year longitudinal study. *Journal of Educational Psychology, 99,* 349–368.

Entringer, S., Kumsta, R., Hellhammer, D. H., Wadhwa, P. D., & Wüst, S. (2009). Prenatal exposure to maternal psychosocial stress and HPA axis regulation in young adults. *Hormones and Behavior, 55,* 292–298.

Entwisle, D. R., Alexander, K. L., & Olson, L. S. (2005). First grade and educational attainment by age 22: A new story. *American Journal of Sociology, 110,* 1458–1502.

Epel, E. S., Linn, J., Wilhelm, F., Mendes, W., Adler, N., & Dolbier, C. (2006). Cell aging in relation to stress arousal and cardiovascular disease risk factors. *Psychoneuroendocrinology, 31,* 277–287.

Epel, E. S., Merkin, S. S., Cawthon, R., Blackburn, E. H., Adler, N. E., Pletcher, M. J., & Seeman, T. S. (2009). The rate of leukocyte telomere shortening predicts mortality from cardiovascular disease in elderly men: A novel demonstration. *Aging, 1,* 81–88.

Epstein, L. H., Roemmich, J. N., & Raynor, H. A. (2001). Behavioral therapy in the treatment of pediatric obesity. *Pediatric Clinics of North America, 48,* 981–983.

Erath, S. A., Bierman, K. L., & the Conduct Problems Prevention Research Group. (2006). Aggressive marital conflict, maternal harsh punishment, and child aggressive-disruptive behavior: Evidence for direct and mediate relations. *Journal of Family Psychology, 20,* 217–226.

Erdogan, B., Bauer, T. N., Truxillo, D. M., & Mansfield, L. R. (2012). Whistle while you work: A review of the life satisfaction literature. *Journal of Management, 38,* 1038–1083.

Erickson, K. I., Colcombe, S. J., Wadhwa, R., Bherer, L., Peterson, M. S., & Scalf, P. E. (2007). Training-induced plasticity in older adults: Effects of training on hemispheric asymmetry. *Neurobiology of Aging, 28,* 272–283.

Erickson, K. I., Raji, C. A., Lopez, O. L., Becker, J. T., Rosano, C., Newman, A. B., et al. (2010). Physical activity predicts gray matter volume in late adulthood: The Cardiovascular Health Study. *Neurology, 75,* 1415–1422.

Erikson, E. H. (1950). *Childhood and society.* New York: Norton.

Erikson, E. H. (1968). *Identity, youth, and crisis.* New York: Norton.

Erikson, E. H. (1998). *The life cycle completed. Extended version with new chapters on the ninth stage by Joan M. Erikson.* New York: Norton.

Ernst, M., Moolchan, E. T., & Robinson, M. L. (2001). Behavioral and neural consequences of prenatal exposure to nicotine. *Journal of the American Academy of Child and Adolescent Psychiatry, 40,* 630–641.

Ernst, M., & Spear, L. (2009). Reward systems. In M. de Haan & M. Gunnar (Eds.), *Handbook of developmental social neuroscience* (pp. 324–341). New York: Guilford.

Erol, R. Y., & Orth, U. (2011). Self-esteem development from age 14 to 30 years: A longitudinal study. *Journal of Personality and Social Psychology, 101,* 607–619.

Ertekin-Tanner, N. (2007). Genetics of Alzheimer's disease: A centennial review. *Neurologic Clinics, 25,* 611–667.

Ertel, K. A., Glymour, M. M., & Berkman, L. F. (2009). Social networks and health: A life course perspective integrating observational and experimental evidence. *Journal of Social and Personal Relationships, 26,* 73–92.

ESPAD (European School Project on Alcohol and Other Drugs). (2012). *Keyresult generator, 2011.* Retrieved from www.espad.org/en/Keyresult-Generator/

Espy, K. A., Fang, H., Johnson, C., Stopp, C., & Wiebe, S. A. (2011). Prenatal tobacco exposure: Developmental outcomes in the neonatal period. *Developmental Psychology, 47,* 153–156.

Espy, K. A., Molfese, V. J., & DiLalla, L. F. (2001). Effects of environmental measures on intelligence in young children: Growth curve modeling of longitudinal data. *Merrill-Palmer Quarterly, 47,* 42–73.

Esterberg, K. G., Moen, P., & Dempster-McClain, D. (1994). Transition to divorce: A life-course approach to women's marital duration and dissolution. *Sociological Quarterly, 35,* 289–307.

Estourgie-van Burk, G. F., Bartels, M., van Beijsterveldt, T. C., Delemarre-van de Waal, H. A., & Boomsma, D. I. (2006). Body size in five-year-old twins: Heritability and comparison to singleton standards. *Twin Research and Human Genetics, 9,* 646–655.

Ethier, K. A., Kershaw, T., Niccolai, L., Lewis, J. B., & Ickovics, J. R. (2003). Adolescent women underestimate their susceptibility to sexually transmitted infections. *Sexually Transmitted Infections, 79,* 408–411.

Etnier, J. L., & Labban, J. D. (2012). Physical activity and cognitive function: Theoretical bases, mechanisms, and moderators. In E. O. Acebedo (Ed.), *Oxford Handbook of exercise psychology* (pp. 76–96). New York: Oxford University Press.

Evanoo, G. (2007). Infant crying: A clinical conundrum. *Journal of Pediatric Health Care, 21,* 333–338.

Evans, A. M. (2008). Growing pains: Contemporary knowledge and recommended practice. *Journal of Foot and Ankle Research, 1,* 4.

Evans, E., Hawton, K., & Rodham, K. (2004). Factors associated with suicidal phenomena in adolescents: A systematic review of population-based studies. *Clinical Psychology Review, 24,* 957–979.

Evans, G. W., & Schamberg, M A. (2009). Childhood poverty, chronic stress, and adult working memory. *Proceedings of the National Academy of Sciences, 106,* 6545–6549.

Evans, N., & Levinson, S. C. (2009). The myth of language universals: Language diversity and its importance for cognitive science. *Behavioral and Brain Sciences, 32,* 429–492.

Even-Zohar, A. (2011). Intergenerational solidarity between adult grandchildren and their grandparents with different levels of functional ability. *Journal of Intergenerational Relationships, 9,* 128–145.

Evert, J., Lawler, E., Bogan, H., & Perls, T. (2003). Morbidity profiles of centenarians: Survivors, delayers, and escapers. *Journal of Gerontology, 58A,* 232–237.

Ewald, P. W., & Ewald, H. A. S. (2012). Infection, mutation, and cancer evolution. *Journal of Molecular Medicine, 90,* 535–541.

F

Fabes, R. A., Eisenberg, N., Hanish, L. D., & Spinrad, T. L. (2001). Preschoolers' spontaneous emotion vocabulary: Relations to likeability. *Early Education and Development, 12,* 11–27.

Fabes, R. A., Eisenberg, N., McCormick, S. E., & Wilson, M. S. (1988). Preschoolers' attributions of the situational determinants of others' naturally occurring emotions. *Developmental Psychology, 24,* 376–385.

Fabes, R. A., Martin, C. L., & Hanish, L. D. (2003). Young children's play qualities in same-, other-, and mixed-sex peer groups. *Child Development, 74,* 921–932.

Fabiani, M. (2012). It was the best of times, it was the worst of times: A psychophysiologist's view of cognitive aging. *Psychophysiology, 49,* 283–304.

Fagan, J. F., III. (1973). Infants' delayed recognition memory and forgetting. *Journal of Experimental Child Psychology, 16,* 424–450.

Fagan, J. F., Holland, C. R., & Wheeler, K. (2007). The prediction, from infancy, of adult IQ and achievement. *Intelligence, 35,* 225–231.

Fagard, J., & Pezé, A. (1997). Age changes in interlimb coupling and the development of bimanual coordination. *Journal of Motor Behavior, 29,* 199–208.

Fagard, J., Spelke, E., & von Hofsten, C. (2009). Reaching and grasping a moving object in 6-, 8-, and 10-month-old infants: Laterality and performance. *Infant Behavior and Development, 32,* 137–146.

Fagot, B. I. (1985). Changes in thinking about early sex role development. *Developmental Review, 5,* 83–98.

Fagot, B. I., & Hagan, R. I. (1991). Observations of parent reactions to sex-stereotyped behaviors: Age and sex effects. *Child Development, 62,* 617–628.

Fagot, B. I., & Leinbach, M. D. (1989). The young child's gender schema: Environmental input, internal organization. *Child Development, 60,* 663–672.

Fagundes, C. P., Bennett, J. M., Derry, H. M., & Kiecolt-Glaser, J. K. (2011). Relationships and inflammation across the lifespan: Social developmental pathways to disease. *Social and Personality Psychology Compass, 5,* 891–903.

Fahrmeier, E. D. (1978). The development of concrete operations among the Hausa. *Journal of Cross-Cultural Psychology, 9,* 23–44.

Fairburn, C. G., & Harrison, P. J. (2003). Eating disorders. *Lancet, 361,* 407–416.

Faircloth, B. S., & Hamm, J. V. (2005). Sense of belonging among high school students representing four ethnic groups. *Journal of Youth and Adolescence, 34,* 293–309.

Falagas, M. E., & Zarkadoulia, E. (2008). Factors associated with suboptimal compliance to vaccinations in children in developed countries: A systematic review. *Current Medical Research and Opinion, 24,* 1719–1741.

Falbo, T. (1992). Social norms and the one-child family: Clinical and policy implications. In F. Boer & J. Dunn (Eds.), *Children's sibling relationships* (pp. 71–82). Hillsdale, NJ: Erlbaum.

Falbo, T., & Poston, D. L., Jr. (1993). The academic, personality, and physical outcomes of only children in China. *Child Development, 64,* 18–35.

Falbo, T., Poston, D. L., Jr., Triscari, R. S., & Zhang, X. (1997). Self-enhancing illusions among Chinese schoolchildren. *Journal of Cross-Cultural Psychology, 28,* 172–191.

Falk, D. (2005). Brain lateralization in primates and its evolution in hominids. *American Journal of Physical Anthropology, 30,* 107–125.

Family Caregiver Alliance. (2009). *Fact sheet: Selected caregiver statistics.* Retrieved from www.caregiver .org/caregiver/jsp/content_node.jsp?nodeid=439

Fanslow, C. A. (1981). Death: A natural facet of the life continuum. In D. Krieger (Ed.), *Foundations for holistic health nursing practices: The renaissance nurse* (pp. 249–272). Philadelphia: Lippincott.

Fantz, R. L. (1961, May). The origin of form perception. *Scientific American, 204*(5), 66–72.

Farah, M. J., Shera, D. M., Savage, J. H., Betancourt, L., Giannetta, J. M., Brodsky, N. L., et al. (2006). Childhood poverty: Specific associations with neurocognitive development. *Brain Research, 110,* 166–174.

Faraone, S. V. (2008). Statistical and molecular genetic approaches to developmental psychopathology: The pathway forward. In J. J. Hudziak (Ed.), *Developmental psychology and wellness: Genetic and environmental influences* (pp. 245–265). Washington, DC: American Psychiatric Publishing.

Faraone, S. V., & Mick, E. (2010). Molecular genetics of attention deficit hyperactivity disorder. *Psychiatric Clinics of North America, 33,* 159–180.

Farmer, T. W., Irvin, M. J., Leung, M.-C., Hall, C. M., Hutchins, B. C., & McDonough, E. (2010). Social preference, social prominence, and group membership in late elementary school: Homophilic concentration and peer affiliation configurations. *Social Psychology of Education, 13,* 271–293.

Farr, R. J., Forssell, S. L., & Patterson, C. J. (2010). Parenting and child development in adoptive families: Does parental sexual orientation matter? *Applied Developmental Science, 14,* 164–178.

Farrant, K., & Reese, E. (2000). Maternal style and children's participation in reminiscing: Stepping stones in children's autobiological memory development. *Journal of Cognition and Development, 1,* 193–225.

Farrington, D. P. (2004). Conduct disorder, aggression, and delinquency. In R. M. Lerner & L. Steinberg (Eds.), *Handbook of adolescent psychology* (2nd ed., pp. 627–664). New York: Wiley.

Farrington, D. P. (2009). Conduct disorder, aggression and delinquency. In R. M. Lerner & L. Steinberg (Eds.), *Handbook of adolescent psychology: Vol. 1. Individual bases of adolescent development* (3rd ed., pp. 683–722). Hoboken, NJ: Wiley.

Farroni, T., Csibra, G., Simion, F., & Johnson, M. H. (2002). Eye contact detection in humans from birth. *Proceedings of the National Academy of Sciences, 99,* 9602–9605.

Farroni, T., Massaccesi, S., Menon, E., & Johnson, M. H. (2007). Direct gaze modulates face recognition in young infants. *Cognition, 102,* 396–404.

Farver, J. M., & Branstetter, W. H. (1994). Preschoolers' prosocial responses to their peers' distress. *Developmental Psychology, 30,* 334–341.

Farver, J. M., Kim, Y. K., & Lee, Y. (1995). Cultural differences in Korean-and Anglo-American preschoolers' social interaction and play behaviors. *Child Development, 66,* 1088–1099.

Farver, J. M., & Wimbarti, S. (1995). Indonesian toddlers' social play with their mothers and older siblings. *Child Development, 66,* 1493–1503.

Fashola, O. S., & Slavin, R. E. (1998). Effective dropout prevention and college attendance programs for students placed at risk. *Journal of Education for Students Placed at Risk, 3,* 159–183.

Fasolo, M., Majorano, M., & D'Odorico, L. (2008). Babbling and first words in children with slow expressive development. *Clinical Linguistics and Phonetics, 22,* 83–94.

Fattibene, P., Mazzei, F., Nuccetelli, C., & Risica, S. (1999). Prenatal exposure to ionizing radiation: Sources, effects, and regulatory aspects. *Acta Paediatrica, 88,* 693–702.

Faulkner, J. A., Larkin, L. M., Claflin, D. R., & Brooks, S. V. (2007). Age-related changes in the structure and function of skeletal muscles. *Clinical and Experimental Pharmacology and Physiology, 34,* 1091–1096.

Fearon, R. P., Bakermans-Kranenburg, M. J., Lapsley, A., & Roisman, G. I. (2010). The significance of insecure attachment and disorganization in the development of children's externalizing behavior: A meta-analytic study. *Child Development, 81,* 435–456.

Federal Interagency Forum on Aging Related Statistics. (2012). *Older Americans: Key indicators of well-being.* Washington, DC: U.S. Government Printing Office.

Federal Interagency Forum on Child and Family Statistics. (2011). *America's children: Key national indicators of well-being, 2011.* Retrieved from www .childstats.gov

Federico, M. J., & Liu, A. H. (2003). Overcoming childhood asthma disparities of the inner-city poor. *Pediatric Clinics of North America, 50,* 655–675.

Feeney, J. A. (1998). Adult attachment and relationship-centered anxiety: Responses to physical and emotional distancing. In J. A. Simpson & W. S. Rholes (Eds.), *Attachment theory and close relationships* (pp. 189–218). New York: Guilford.

Feeney, J. A. (1999). Adult romantic attachment and couple relationships. In J. Cassidy & P. R. Shaver (Eds.), *Handbook of attachment* (pp. 355–377). New York: Guilford.

Feeney, J. A., Hohaus, L., Noller, P., & Alexander, R. P. (2001). *Becoming parents: Exploring the bonds between mothers, fathers, and their infants.* New York: Cambridge University Press.

Fehr, B. (1994). Prototype based assessment of laypeoples' views of love. *Personal Relationships, 1,* 309–331.

Feigelman, W., & Gorman, B. S. (2008). Assessing the effects of peer suicide on youth suicide. *Suicide and Life-Threatening Behavior, 38,* 181–194.

Feinberg, M. E., McHale, S. M., Crouter, A. C., & Cumsille, P. (2003). Sibling differentiation: Sibling and parent relationship trajectories in adolescence. *Child Development, 74,* 1261–1274.

Feinsilver, S. H. (2003). Sleep in the elderly: What is normal? *Clinical Geriatric Medicine, 19,* 177–188.

Feldkämper, M., & Schaeffel, F. (2003). Interactions of genes and environment in myopia. *Developmental Ophthalmology, 37,* 34–49.

Feldman, A. F., & Matjasko, J. L. (2007). Profiles and portfolios of adolescent school-based extracurricular activity participation. *Journal of Adolescence, 30,* 313–332.

Feldman, D. C., & Beehr, T. A. (2011). A three-phase model of retirement decision making. *American Psychologist, 66,* 193–203.

Feldman, D. C., & Vogel, R. M. (2009). The aging process and person–environment fit. In S. G. Baugh & S. E. Sullivan (Eds.), *Research in careers* (pp. 1–25). Charlotte, NC: Information Age Press.

Feldman, D. H. (2004). Child prodigies: A distinctive form of giftedness. In R. J. Sternberg (Ed.), *Definitions and conceptions of giftedness* (pp. 133–144). Thousand Oaks, CA: Corwin Press.

Feldman, P. J., & Steptoe, A. (2004). How neighborhoods and physical functioning are related:

The roles of neighborhood socioeconomic status, perceived neighborhood strain, and individual health risk factors. *Annals of Behavioral Medicine, 27,* 91–99.

Feldman, R. (2003). Infant–mother and infant–father synchrony: The coregulation of positive arousal. *Infant Mental Health Journal, 24,* 1–23.

Feldman, R. (2006). From biological rhythms to social rhythms: Physiological precursors of mother–infant synchrony. *Developmental Psychology, 42,* 175–188.

Feldman, R. (2007). Maternal versus child risk and the development of parent–child and family relationships in five high-risk populations. *Development and Psychopathology, 19,* 293–312.

Feldman, R., Eidelman, A. I., & Rotenberg, N. (2004). Parenting stress, infant emotion regulation, maternal sensitivity, and the cognitive development of triplets: A model for parent and child influences in a unique ecology. *Child Development, 75,* 1774–1791.

Feldman, R., Gordon, I., Schneiderman, I., Weisman, O., & Zagoory-Sharon, O. (2010). Natural variations in maternal and paternal care are associated with systematic changes in oxytocin following parent–infant contact. *Psychoneuroendocrinology, 35,* 1133–1141.

Feldman, R., Granat, A., Pariente, C., Kanety, H., Kuint, J., & Gilboa-Schechtman, E. (2009). Maternal depression and anxiety across the postpartum year and infant social engagement, fear regulation, and stress reactivity. *Journal of the American Academy of Child and Adolescent Psychiatry, 48,* 919–927.

Feldman, R., Greenbaum, C. W., & Yirmiya, N. (1999). Mother–infant affect synchrony as an antecedent of the emergence of self-control. *Developmental Psychology, 35,* 223–231.

Feldman, R., & Klein, P. S. (2003). Toddlers' self-regulated compliance to mothers, caregivers, and fathers: Implications for theories of socialization. *Developmental Psychology, 39,* 680–692.

Feldman, R., Sussman, A. L., & Zigler, E. (2004). Parental leave and work adaptation at the transition to parenthood: Individual, marital, and social correlates. *Applied Developmental Psychology, 25,* 459–479.

Feldman, R. S. (2005). *Improving the first year of college: Research and practice.* Mahwah, NJ: Erlbaum.

Felner, R. D., Favazza, A., Shim, M., Brand, S., Gu, K., & Noonan, N. (2002). Whole school improvement and restructuring as prevention and promotion: Lessons from STEP and the Project on High Performance Learning Communities. *Journal of School Psychology, 39,* 177–202.

Felsman, D. E., & Blustein, D. L. (1999). The role of peer relatedness in late adolescent career development. *Journal of Vocational Behavior, 54,* 279–295.

Feng, Q. (2005). Postnatal consequences of prenatal cocaine exposure and myocardial apoptosis: Does cocaine in utero imperil the adult heart? *British Journal of Pharmacology, 144,* 887–888.

Fenson, L., Dale, P. S., Reznick, J. S., Bates, E., Thal, D. J., & Pethick, S. J. (1994). Variability in early communicative development. *Monographs of the Society for Research in Child Development, 59*(5, Serial No. 242).

Feret, A., Steinweg, S., Griffin, H. C., & Glover, S. (2007). Macular degeneration: Types, causes, and possible interventions. *Geriatric Nursing, 28,* 387–392.

Ferguson, L. R. (2010). Meat and cancer. *Meat Science, 84,* 308–313.

Ferguson, T. J., Stegge, H., & Damhuis, I. (1991). Children's understanding of guilt and shame. *Child Development, 62,* 827–839.

Fergusson, D. M., & Woodward, L. J. (1999). Breastfeeding and later psychosocial adjustment. *Paediatric and Perinatal Epidemiology, 13,* 144–157.

Fernald, A., & Morikawa, H. (1993). Common themes and cultural variations in Japanese and American mothers' speech to infants. *Child Development, 64,* 637–656.

Fernald, A., Perfors, A., & Marchman, V. A. (2006). Picking up speed in understanding: Speech processing efficiency and vocabulary growth across the 2nd year. *Developmental Psychology, 42,* 98–116.

Fernald, A., Taeschner, T., Dunn, J., Papousek, M., Boyssen-Bardies, B., & Fukui, I. (1989). A cross-language study of prosodic modifications in mothers' and fathers' speech to preverbal infants. *Journal of Child Language, 16,* 477–502.

Fernald, L. C., & Grantham-McGregor, S. M. (1998). Stress response in school-age children who have been growth-retarded since early childhood. *American Journal of Clinical Nutrition, 68,* 691–698.

Ferrari, P. F., & Coudé, G. (2011). Mirror neurons and imitation from a developmental and evolutionary perspective. In A. Vilain, C. Abry, J.-L. Schwartz, & J. Vauclair (Eds.), *Primate communication and human language* (pp. 121–138). Amsterdam, Netherlands: John Benjamins.

Ferrari, P. F., Visalberghi E., Paukner A., Fogassi L., Ruggiero A., Suomi, S. (2006). Neonatal imitation in rhesus macaques. *PLoS Biology,* e302.

Ferry, A. L., Hespos, S. J., & Waxman, S. R. (2010). Categorization in 3- and 4-month-old infants: An advantage of words over tones. *Child Development, 81,* 472–479.

Ficca, G., Fagioli, I., Giganti, F., & Salzarulo, P. (1999). Spontaneous awakenings from sleep in the first year of life. *Early Human Development, 55,* 219–228.

Fickling, D. (2004). A happy ending? *Lancet, 364,* 831–832.

Field, D. (1997). "Looking back, what period of your life brought you the most satisfaction?" *International Journal of Aging and Human Development, 45,* 169–194.

Field, D. (1999). Stability of older women's friendships: A commentary on Roberto. *International Journal of Aging and Human Development, 48,* 81–83.

Field, D., & Millsap, R. E. (1991). Personality in advanced old age: Continuity or change? *Journal of Gerontology, 46,* 299–308.

Field, T. (1998). Massage therapy effects. *American Psychologist, 53,* 1270–1281.

Field, T. (2001). Massage therapy facilitates weight gain in preterm infants. *Current Directions in Psychological Science, 10,* 51–54.

Field, T. (2011). Prenatal depression effects on early development: A review. *Infant Behavior and Development, 34,* 1–14.

Field, T., Hernandez-Reif, M., Feijo, L., & Freedman, J. (2006). Prenatal, perinatal and neonatal stimulation: A survey of neonatal nurseries. *Infant Behavior and Development, 29,* 24–31.

Field, T., Hernandez-Reif, M., & Freedman, J. (2004). Stimulation programs for preterm infants. *Social Policy Report of the Society for Research in Child Development, 18*(1).

Fiese, B. H., Foley, K. P., & Spagnola, M. (2006). Routine and ritual elements in family mealtimes: Contexts for child well-being and family identity. *New Directions for Child and Adolescent Development, 111,* 67–90.

Fiese, B. H., & Schwartz, M. (2008). Reclaiming the family table: Mealtimes and child health and well-being. *Social Policy Report of the Society for Research in Child Development, 22*(4), 3–18.

Fiese, B. H., & Winter, M. A. (2010). The dynamics of family chaos and its relation to children's socioemotional well-being. In G. W. Evans & T. D. Wachs (Eds.), *Chaos and its influence on children's development: An ecological perspective* (pp. 49–66). Washington, DC: American Psychological Association.

Fifer, W. P., Byrd, D. L., Kaku, M., Eigsti, I. M., Isler, J. R., Grose-Fifer, J., et al. (2010). Newborn infants learn during sleep. *Proceedings of the National Academy of Sciences, 107,* 10320–10323.

Figner, B., Mackinlay, R. J., Wilkening, F., & Weber, E. U. (2009). Affective and deliberative processes in risky choice: Age differences in risk taking in the Columbia Card Task. *Journal of Experimental Psychology: Learning, Memory, and Cognition, 35,* 709–770.

Fincham, F. D., & Bradbury, T. N. (2004). Marital satisfaction, depression, and attributions: A longitudinal analysis. In R. M. Kowalski & M. R. Leary (Eds.), *The interface of social and clinical psychology: Key readings* (pp. 129–146). New York: Psychology Press.

Finchum, T., & Weber, J. A. (2000). Applying continuity theory to elder adult friendships. *Journal of Aging and Identity, 5,* 159–168.

Findlay, L. C., & Coplan, R. J. (2008). Come out and play: Shyness in childhood and the benefits of organized sports participation. *Canadian Journal of Behavioural Science, 40,* 153–161.

Fine, M. A., Ganong, L. H., & Demo, D. H. (2010). Divorce: A risk and resilience perspective. In S. J. Price, C. A. Price, & P. C. McKenry (Eds.), *Families and change: Coping with stressful events and transitions* (pp. 211–234). Thousand Oaks, CA: Sage.

Finger, B., Hans, S. L., Bernstein, V. J., & Cox, S. M. (2009). Parent relationship quality and infant-mother attachment. *Attachment and Human Development, 11,* 285–306.

Fingerman, K. L. (1998). The good, the bad, and the worrisome: Emotional complexities in grandparents' experiences with individual grandchildren. *Family Relations, 47,* 403–414.

Fingerman, K. L. (2003). *Mothers and their adult daughters: Mixed emotions, enduring bonds.* Amherst, NY: Prometheus Books.

Fingerman, K. L. (2004). The role of offspring and in-laws in grandparents' ties to their grandchildren. *Journal of Family Issues, 25,* 1026–1049.

Fingerman, K. L., & Birditt, K. S. (2003). Do we get better at picking our battles? Age group differences in descriptions of behavioral reactions to interpersonal tensions. *Journal of Gerontology, 60B,* P121–P128.

Fingerman, K. L., & Birditt, K. S. (2011). Relationships between adults and their aging parents. In K. W. Schaie & S. L. Willis (Eds.), *Handbook of the psychology of aging* (pp. 219–232). San Diego, CA: Academic Press.

Fingerman, K. L., Chen, P.-C., Hay, E., Cichy, K. E., & Lefkowitz, E. S. (2006). Ambivalent reactions in the parent and offspring relationship. *Journal of Gerontology, 61B,* P152–P160.

Fingerman, K. L., Cheng, Y.-P., Birditt, K., & Zarit, S. (2012a). Only as happy as the least happy child: Multiple grown children's problems and successes and middle-aged parents' well-being. *Journal of Gerontology, 67B,* 184–193.

Fingerman, K. L., Cheng, Y-P., Tighe, L., Birditt, K. S., & Zarit, S. (2012a). Relationships between young adults and their parents. In A. Booth, S. L. Brown, N. S. Landale, W. D. Manning, & S. M. McHale (Eds.), *Early adulthood in a family context* (pp. 59–85). New York: Springer.

Fingerman, K. L., Cheng, Y-P., Wesselmann, D., Zarit, S., Furstenberg, F., & Birditt, K. S. (2012b). Helicopter parents and landing pad kids: Intense parental support of grown children. *Journal of Marriage and Family, 74,* 880–896.

Fingerman, K. L., Gilligan, M., VanderDrift, L., & Pitzer, L. (2012b). In-law relationships before and after marriage: Husbands, wives, and their mothers-in-law. *Research in Human Development, 9,* 106–125.

Fingerman, K. L., Hay, E. L., & Birditt, K. S. (2004). The best of ties, the worst of ties: Close, problematic, and ambivalent social relationships. *Journal of Marriage and Family, 66,* 792–808.

Fingerman, K. L., Hay, E. L., Dush, C. M. K., Cichy, K. E., & Hosterman, S. J. (2007). Parents' and

offspring's perceptions of change and continuity when parents experience the transition to old age. *Advances in Life Course Research, 12,* 275–305.

Fingerman, K. L., Miller, L., Birditt, K., & Zarit, S. (2009). Giving to the good and the needy: Parental support of grown children. *Journal of Marriage and Family, 71,* 1220–1233.

Fingerman, K. L., Pitzer, L. M., Chan, W., Birditt, K., Franks, M. M., & Zarit, S. (2011a). Who gets what and why? Help middle-aged adults provide to parents and grown children. *Journal of Gerontology, 66B,* 87–98.

Fingerman, K. L., Pitzer, L., Lefkowitz, E. S., Birditt, K. S., & Mroczek, D. (2008). Ambivalent relationship qualities between adults and their parents: Implications for both parties' well-being. *Journal of Gerontology, 63B,* P362–P371.

Fingerman, K. L., VanderDrift, L. E., Dotterer, A. M., Birditt, K. S., & Zarit, S. H. (2011b). Support to aging parents and grown children in black and white families. *Gerontologist, 51,* 441–452.

Finkel, D., Reynolds, C. A., McArdle, J. J., & Pedersen, N. L. (2007). Age changes in processing speed as a leading indicator of cognitive aging. *Psychology and Aging, 22,* 558–568.

Finkel, E. J., Eastwick, P. W., Karney, B. R., Reis, H. T., & Sprecher, S. (2012). Online dating: A critical analysis from the perspective of psychological science. *Psychological Science in the Public Interest, 13,* 3–66.

Finkelhor, D. (2009). The prevention of childhood sexual abuse. *Future of Children, 19,* 169–194.

Finkelstein, E. A., Trogdon, J. G., Cohen, J. W., & Dietz, W. (2009). Annual medical spending attributable to obesity: Payer- and service-specific estimates. *Health Affairs, 28,* w822–w831.

Finn, J. D., Gerber, S. B., & Boyd-Zaharias, J. (2005). Small classes in the early grades, academic achievement, and graduating from high school. *Journal of Educational Psychology, 97,* 214–233.

Finucane, M. L., Mertz, C. K., Slovic, P., & Schmidt, E. S. (2005). Task complexity and older adults' decision-making competence. *Psychology and Aging, 20,* 71–84.

Fiori, K. L., Antonucci, T., & Cortina, K. S. (2006). Social network typologies and mental health among older adults. *Journal of Gerontology, 61B,* 25–32.

Fiori, K. L., Smith, J., & Antonucci, T. C. (2007). Social network types among older adults: A multidimensional approach. *Journal of Gerontology, 62B,* P322–P330.

Fischer, K. W., & Bidell, T. (1991). Constraining nativist inferences about cognitive capacities. In S. Carey & R. Gelman (Eds.), *The epigenesis of mind: Essays on biology and cognition* (pp. 199–235). Hillsdale, NJ: Erlbaum.

Fischer, K. W., & Bidell, T. R. (2006). Dynamic development of action and thought. In R. M. Lerner (Ed.), *Handbook of child psychology: Vol. 1. Theoretical models of human development* (6th ed., pp. 313–399). Hoboken, NJ: Wiley.

Fischman, M. G., Moore, J. B., & Steele, K. H. (1992). Children's one-hand catching as a function of age, gender, and ball location. *Research Quarterly for Exercise and Sport, 63,* 349–355.

Fish, M. (2004). Attachment in infancy and preschool in low socioeconomic status rural Appalachian children: Stability and change and relations to preschool and kindergarten competence. *Development and Psychopathology, 16,* 293–312.

Fisher, C. B. (1993, Winter). Integrating science and ethics in research with high-risk children and youth. *Social Policy Report of the Society for Research in Child Development, 7*(4), 1–27.

Fisher, C. B. (2005). Deception research involving children: Ethical practices and paradoxes. *Ethics and Behavior, 15,* 271–287.

Fisher, J. O., Rolls, B. J., & Birch, L. L. (2003). Children's bite size and intake of an entrée are greater with large portions than with age-appropriate or self-selected portions. *American Journal of Clinical Nutrition, 77,* 1164–1170.

Fisher, S. E., Francks, C., McCracken, J. T., McGough, J. J., Marlow, A. J., & MacPhie, I. L. (2002). A genomewide scan for loci involved in attention-deficit/hyperactivity disorder. *American Journal of Human Genetics, 70,* 1183–1196.

Fisher, S. K., Easterly, S., & Lazear, K. J. (2008). Lesbian, gay, bisexual and transgender families and their children. In T. P. Gullotta & G. M. Blau (Eds.), *Family influences on child behavior and development: Evidence-based prevention and treatment approaches* (pp. 187–208). New York: Routledge.

Fitzpatrick, J., & Sollie, D. L. (1999). Influence of individual and interpersonal factors on satisfaction and stability in romantic relationships. *Personal Relationships, 6,* 337–350.

Fivaz-Depeursinge, E., & Corboz-Warnery, A. (1999). *The primary triangle: A developmental systems view of mothers, fathers, and infants.* New York: Basic Books.

Fivush, R. (2001). Owning experience: Developing subjective perspective in autobiographical narratives. In C. Moore & K. Lemmon (Eds.), *The self in time: Developmental perspectives* (pp. 35–52). Mahwah, NJ: Erlbaum.

Fivush, R. (2009). Sociocultural perspectives on autobiographical memory. In M. L. Courage & N. Cowan (Eds.), *The development of memory in infancy and childhood* (pp. 283–301). Hove, UK: Psychology Press.

Fivush, R., & Haden, C. A. (2005). Parent–child reminiscing and the construction of a subjective self. In B. D. Homer & C. S. Tamis-LeMonda (Eds.), *The development of social cognition and communication* (pp. 315–336). Mahwah, NJ: Erlbaum.

Fivush, R., & Reese, E. (2002). Reminiscing and relating: The development of parent–child talk about the past. In J. D. Webster & B. K. Haight (Eds.), *Critical advances in reminiscence work: From theory to application* (pp. 109–122). New York: Springer.

Fivush, R., & Wang, Q. (2005). Emotion talk in mother-child conversations of the shared past: The effects of culture, gender, and event valence. *Journal of Cognition and Development, 6,* 489–506.

Flanagan, C. A., Stout, M., & Gallay, L. S. (2008). It's my body and none of your business: Developmental changes in adolescents' perceptions of rights concerning health. *Journal of Social Issues, 64,* 815–834.

Flanagan, C. A., & Tucker, C. J. (1999). Adolescents' explanations for political issues: Concordance with their views of self and society. *Developmental Psychology, 35,* 1198–1209.

Flannery, D. J., Hussey, D. L., Biebelhausen, L., & Wester, K. L. (2003). Crime, delinquency, and youth gangs. In G. R. Adams & M. D. Berzonsky (Eds.), *Blackwell handbook of adolescence* (pp. 502–522). Malden, MA: Blackwell.

Flannery, K. A., & Liederman, J. (1995). Is there really a syndrome involving the co-occurrence of neurodevelopmental disorder, talent, non-right handedness and immune disorder among children? *Cortex, 31,* 503–515.

Flavell, J. H., Flavell, E. R., & Green, F. L. (2001). Development of children's understanding of connections between thinking and feeling. *Psychological Science, 12,* 430–432.

Flavell, J. H., Green, F. L., & Flavell, E. R. (1987). Development of knowledge about the appearance-reality distinction. *Monographs of the Society for Research in Child Development, 51*(1, Serial No. 212).

Flavell, J. H., Green, F. L., & Flavell, E. R. (1993). Children's understanding of the stream of consciousness. *Child Development, 64,* 387–398.

Flavell, J. H., Green, F. L., & Flavell, E. R. (1995). Young children's knowledge about thinking. *Monographs of the Society for Research in Child Development, 60*(1, Serial No. 243).

Flavell, J. H., Green, F. L., & Flavell, E. R. (2000). Development of children's awareness of their own thoughts. *Journal of Cognition and Development, 1,* 97–112.

Flegal, K. M., Carroll, M. D., Kit, B. K., & Ogden, C. L. (2012). Prevalence of obesity and trends in the distribution of body mass index among U.S. adults, 1999–2010. *Journal of the American Medical Association, 307,* 491–497.

Flegal, K. M., Graubard, B. I., Williamson, D. F., & Gail, M. H. (2007). Cause-specific excess deaths associated with underweight, overweight, and obesity. *Journal of the American Medical Association, 299,* 1260–1261.

Fleischman, D. A., Wilson, R. S., Gabrieli, J. D. E., Bienias, J. L., & Bennett, D. A. (2004). A longitudinal study of implicit and explicit memory in old persons. *Psychology and Aging, 19,* 617–625.

Fleming, J. I. (2000). Death, dying, and euthanasia: Australia versus the Northern Territory. *Issues in Law and Medicine, 15,* 291–305.

Fletcher, A. C., Nickerson, P., & Wright, K. L. (2003). Structured leisure activities in middle childhood: Links to well-being. *Journal of Community Psychology, 31,* 641–659.

Floccia, C., Christophe, A., & Bertoncini, J. (1997). High-amplitude sucking and newborns: The quest for underlying mechanisms. *Journal of Experimental Child Psychology, 64,* 175–198.

Flom, R., & Bahrick, L. E. (2010). The effects of intersensory redundancy on attention and memory: Infants' long-term memory for orientation in audiovisual events. *Developmental Psychology, 46,* 428–436.

Flom, R., & Pick, A. D. (2003). Verbal encouragement and joint attention in 18-month-old infants. *Infant Behavior and Development, 26,* 121–134.

Flood, D. G., & Coleman, P. D. (1988). Cell type heterogeneity of changes in dendritic extent in the hippocampal region of the human brain in normal aging and in Alzheimer's disease. In T. L. Petit & G. O. Ivy (Ed.), *Neural plasticity: A lifespan approach* (pp. 265–281). New York: Alan R. Liss.

Florian, V., & Kravetz, S. (1985). Children's concepts of death: A cross-cultural comparison among Muslims, Druze, Christians, and Jews in Israel. *Journal of Cross-Cultural Psychology, 16,* 174–179.

Florian, V., & Mikulincer, M. (1998). Symbolic immortality and the management of the terror of death: The moderating role of attachment style. *Journal of Personality and Social Psychology, 74,* 725–734.

Florsheim, P., & Smith, A. (2005). Expectant adolescent couples' relations and subsequent parenting behavior. *Infant Mental Health Journal, 26,* 533–548.

Flynn, E. (2006). A microgenetic investigation of stability and continuity in theory of mind development. *British Journal of Developmental Psychology, 24,* 631–654.

Flynn, J. R. (2007). *What is intelligence? Beyond the Flynn effect.* New York: Cambridge University Press.

Flynn, J. R. (2011). Secular changes in intelligence. In R. J. Sternberg & S. B. Kaufman (Eds.), *Cambridge handbook of intelligence* (pp. 647–665). New York: Cambridge University Press.

Foehr, U. G. (2006). *Media multitasking among American youth: Prevalence, predictors, and pairings.* Menlo Park. CA: Kaiser Family Foundation.

Foerde, K., Knowlton, B. J., & Poldrack, R. A. (2006). Modulation of competing memory systems by distraction. *Proceedings of the National Academy of Sciences, 103,* 11778–11783.

Fogel, A. (1993). *Developing through relationships: Origins of communication, self and culture.* New York: Harvester Wheatsheaf.

Fomon, S. J., & Nelson, S. E. (2002). Body composition of the male and female reference infants. *Annual Review of Nutrition, 22,* 1–17.

Fonda, S. J., Clipp, E. C., & Maddox, G. L. (2002). Patterns in functioning among residents of an affordable assisted living housing facility. *Gerontologist, 42,* 178–187.

Fong, T. G., Tulebaev, S. R., & Inouye, S. K. (2009). Delirium in elderly adults: Diagnosis, prevention and treatment. *Nature Reviews Neurology, 5,* 210–220.

Fontana, L. (2008). Calorie restriction and cardiometabolic health. *European Journal of Cardiovascular Prevention and Rehabilitation, 15,* 3–9.

Fontana, L. (2009). The scientific basis of caloric restriction leading to longer life. *Current Opinion in Gastroenterology, 25,* 144–150.

Fontana, L., Klein, S., & Holloszy, J. O. (2010). Effects of long-term calorie restriction and endurance exercise on glucose tolerance, insulin action, and adipokine production. *Age, 32,* 97–108.

Fontana, L., Meyer, T. E., Klein, S., & Holloszy, J. O. (2004). Long-term calorie restriction is highly effective in reducing the risk for atherosclerosis in humans. *Proceedings of the National Academy of Sciences, 101,* 6659–6663.

Forman, D. R., Aksan, N., & Kochanska, G. (2004). Toddlers' responsive imitation predicts preschool-age conscience. *Psychological Science, 15,* 699–704.

Forman, D. R., O'Hara, M. W., Stuart, S., Gorman, L. L., Larsen, K. E., & Coy, K. C. (2007). Effective treatment for postpartum depression is not sufficient to improve the developing mother–child relationship. *Development and Psychopathology, 19,* 585–602.

Forry, N. D., Leslie, L. A., & Letiecq, B. L. (2007). Marital quality in interracial relationships: The role of sex role ideology and perceived fairness. *Journal of Family Issues, 28,* 1538–1552.

Forste, R., & Heaton, T. B. (2004). The divorce generation: Well-being, family attitudes, and socioeconomic consequences of marital disruption. *Journal of Divorce and Remarriage, 42,* 95–114.

Fortenberry, J. D. (2010). Fate, desire, and the centrality of the relationship to adolescent condom use. *Journal of Adolescent Health, 47,* 219–220.

Foster, J. A., Gore, S. A., & West, D. S. (2006). Altering TV viewing habits: An unexplored strategy for adult obesity intervention? *American Journal of Health Behavior, 30,* 3–14.

Foster, M. A., Lambert, R., Abbott-Shim, M., McCarty, F., & Franze, S. (2005). A model of home learning environment and social risk factors in relation to children's emergent literacy and social outcomes. *Early Childhood Research Quarterly, 20,* 13–36.

Fowler, C. (2009). Motives for sibling communication across the lifespan. *Communication Quarterly, 57,* 51–66.

Fowler, J. W., & Dell, M. L. (2006). Stages of faith from infancy through adolescence: Reflections on three decades of faith development theory. In E. C. Roehlkepartain, P. E. King, L. Wagener, & P. L. Benson (Eds.), *Handbook of spiritual development in childhood and adolescence* (pp. 34–45). Thousand Oaks, CA: Sage.

Fox, C. L., & Boulton, M. J. (2006). Friendship as a moderator of the relationship between social skills problems and peer victimization. *Aggressive Behavior, 32,* 110–121.

Fox, N. A. (1991). If it's not left, it's right: Electroencephalograph asymmetry and the development of emotion. *American Psychologist, 46,* 863–872.

Fox, N. A., & Calkins, S. D. (2003). The development of self-control of emotion: Intrinsic and extrinsic influences. *Motivation and Emotion, 27,* 7–26.

Fox, N. A., & Davidson, R. J. (1986). Taste-elicited changes in facial signs of emotion and the asymmetry of brain electrical activity in newborn infants. *Neuropsychologia, 24,* 417–422.

Fox, N. A., Henderson, H. A., Pérez-Edgar, K., & White, L. K. (2008). The biology of temperament: An integrative approach. In C. A. Nelson & M. Luciana (Eds.), *Handbook of developmental cognitive neuroscience* (2nd ed., pp. 839–853). Cambridge, MA: MIT Press.

Franchak, J. M., & Adolph, K. E. (2012). What infants know and what they do: Perceiving possibilities for walking through openings. *Developmental Psychology, 48,* 1254–1261.

Frank, D. A., Rose-Jacobs, R., Beeghly, M., Wilbur, M., Bellinger, D., & Cabral, H. (2005). Level of prenatal cocaine exposure and 48-month IQ: Importance of preschool enrichment. *Neurotoxicology and Teratology, 27,* 15–28.

Frankenburg, E., & Orfield, G. (2007). *Lessons in integration: Realizing the promise of racial diversity in American schools.* Charlottesville: University of Virginia Press.

Franklin, V. P. (2012). "The teachers' unions strike back?" No need to wait for "Superman": Magnet schools have brought success to urban public school students for over 30 years. In D. T. Slaughter-Defoe, H. C. Stevenson, E. G. Arrington, & D. J. Johnson (Eds.), *Black educational choice: Assessing the private and public alternatives to traditional K–12 public schools* (pp. 217–220). Santa Barbara, CA: Praeger.

Frazier, L., Barreto, M., & Newman, F. (2012). Self-regulation and eudaimonic well-being across adulthood. *Experimental Aging Research, 38,* 394–410.

Frazier, L. D. (2002). Perceptions of control over health: Implications for sense of self in healthy and ill older adults. In S. P. Shohov (Ed.), *Advances in psychology research* (Vol. 10, pp. 145–163). Huntington, NY: Nova Science Publishers.

Frazier, L. D., & Hooker, K. (2006). Possible selves in adult development: Linking theory and research. In C. Dunkel & J. Kerpelman (Eds.), *Possible selves: Theory, research and applications* (pp. 41–59). Hauppauge, NY: Nova Science.

Frederickson, B. L., & Carstensen, L. L. (1990). Relationship classification using grade of membership analysis: A typology of sibling relationships in later life. *Journal of Gerontology, 45,* S43–S51.

Fredricks, J. A. (2012). Extracurricular participation and academic outcomes: Testing the over-scheduling hypothesis. *Journal of Youth and Adolescence, 41,* 295–306.

Fredricks, J. A., & Eccles, J. S. (2002). Children's competence and value beliefs from childhood through adolescence: Growth trajectories in two male-sex-typed domains. *Developmental Psychology, 38,* 519–533.

Fredricks, J. A., & Eccles, J. S. (2006). Is extracurricular participation associated with beneficial outcomes? Concurrent and longitudinal relations. *Developmental Psychology, 42,* 698–713.

Freedman, M. (1999). *Prime time: How baby boomers will revolutionize retirement and transform America.* New York: Public Affairs.

Freeman, D. (1983). *Margaret Mead and Samoa: The making and unmaking of an anthropological myth.* Cambridge, MA: Harvard University Press.

Freeman, H., & Newland, L. A. (2010). New directions in father attachment. *Early Child Development and Care, 180,* 1–8.

Freeman, L., Caserta, M., Lund, D., Rossa, S., Dowdy, A., & Partenheimer, A. (2006). Music thanatology: Prescriptive harp music as palliative care for the dying patient. *American Journal of Hospice and Palliative Care, 23,* 100–104.

Freiman, A., Bird, G., Metelitsa, A. I., Barankin, B., & Lauzon, G. J. (2004). Cutaneous effects of smoking. *Journal of Cutaneous Medicine and Surgery, 8,* 415–423.

Freitag, C. M., Rohde, L. A., Lempp, T., & Romanos, M. (2010). Phenotypic and measurement influences on heritability estimates in childhood ADHD. *European Child and Adolescent Psychiatry, 19,* 311–323.

Freitas, A. A., & Magalhães, J. P. de. (2011). A review and appraisal of the DNA damage theory of ageing. *Mutation Research, 728,* 1–2, 12–22.

Freud, S. (1973). *An outline of psychoanalysis.* London: Hogarth. (Original work published 1938)

Freud, S. (1974). *The ego and the id.* London: Hogarth. (Original work published 1923)

Freund, A. M., & Baltes, P. B. (1998). Selection, optimization, and compensation as strategies of life management: Correlations with subjective indicators of successful aging. *Psychology and Aging, 13,* 531–543.

Freund, A. M., & Ebner, N. C. (2005). The aging self: Shifting from promoting gains to balancing losses. In W. Greve, K. Rothermund, & D. Wentura (Eds.), *The adaptive self: Personal continuity and intentional self-development* (pp. 185–202). New York: Hogrefe.

Freund, A. M., & Ritter, J. O. (2009). Midlife crisis: A debate. *Gerontology, 55,* 582–591.

Freund, A. M., & Smith, J. (1999). Content and function of the self-definition in old and very old age. *Journal of Gerontology, 54B,* P55–P67.

Frey, A., Ruchkin, V., Martin, A., & Schwab-Stone, M. (2009). Adolescents in transition: School and family characteristics in the development of violent behaviors entering high school. *Child Psychiatry and Human Development, 40,* 1–13.

Fried, L. P., Xue, Q.-L., Cappola, A. R., Ferrucci, L., Chaves, P., Varadhan, R., et al. (2009). Nonlinear multisystem physiological dysregulation associated with frailty in older women: Implications for etiology and treatment. *Journal of Gerontology, 64A,* 1049–1052.

Friedman, C., McGwin, G., Jr., Ball, K. K., & Owsley, C. (2013). Association between higher-order visual processing abilities and a history of motor vehicle collision involvement by drivers age 70 and over. *Investigative Ophthalmology and Visual Science, 54,* 778–782.

Friedman, E. M., & Lawrence, D. A. (2002). Environmental stress mediates changes in neuroimmunological interactions. *Toxicological Sciences, 67,* 4–10.

Friedman, J. M. (1996). *The effects of drugs on the fetus and nursing infant: A handbook for health care professionals.* Baltimore: Johns Hopkins University Press.

Friedman, S. L., & Scholnick, E. K. (1997). An evolving "blueprint" for planning: Psychological requirements, task characteristics, and social–cultural influences. In S. L. Friedman & E. K. Scholnick (Eds.), *The developmental psychology of planning: Why, how, and when do we plan?* (pp. 3–22). Mahwah, NJ: Erlbaum.

Fries, J. F., Bruce, B., & Chakravarty, E. (2011). Compression of morbidity 1980–2011: A focused review of paradigms and progress. *Journal of Aging Research,* Article ID 261702. Retrieved from www.hindawi.com/journals/jar/2011/261702

Frith, L. (2001). Gamete donation and anonymity: The ethical and legal debate. *Human Reproduction, 16,* 818–824.

Frith, U. (2003). *Autism: Explaining the enigma* (2nd ed.). Malden, MA: Blackwell.

Fruhauf, C. A., Jarrott, S. E., & Allen, K. R. (2006). Grandchildren's perception of caring for grandparents. *Journal of Family Issues, 27,* 887–911.

Fry, C. L. (1985). Culture, behavior, and aging in the comparative perspective. In J. E. Birren & K. W. Schaie (Eds.), *Handbook of the psychology of aging* (2nd ed., pp. 216–244). New York: Van Nostrand Reinhold.

Fry, C. L., Dickerson-Putman, J., Draper, P., Ikels, C., Keith, J., Glascock, A. P., & Harpending, H. C. (1997). Culture and the meaning of a good old age. In J. Sokolovsky (Ed.), *The cultural context of aging: Worldwide perspectives* (2nd ed., pp. 99–124). New York: Bergin & Garvey.

Fry, P. S. (2001). Predictors of health-related quality of life perspectives, self-esteem, and life satisfactions of older adults following spousal loss: An 18-month follow-up study of widows and widowers. *Gerontologist, 41,* 787–798.

Fry, P. S. (2003). Perceived self-efficacy domains as predictors of fear of the unknown and fear of dying among older adults. *Psychology and Aging, 18,* 474–486.

Fry, P. S., & Debats, D. L. (2006). Sources of life strengths as predictors of late-life mortality and survivorship. *International Journal of Aging and Human Development, 62,* 303–334.

Fryer, S. L., Crocker, N. A., & Mattson, S. N. (2008). Exposure to teratogenic agents as a risk factor for psychopathology. In T. P. Beauchaine & S. P. Hinshaw (Eds.), *Child and adolescent psychopathology* (pp. 180–207). Hoboken, NJ: Wiley.

Fryling, T., Summers, R., & Hoffman, A. (2006). Elder abuse: Definition and scope of the problem. In R. W. Summers & A. M. Hoffman (Eds.), *Elder abuse: A public health perspective* (pp. 5–18). Washington, DC: American Public Health Association.

Fu, G., Xu, F., Cameron, C. A., Heyman, G., & Lee, K. (2007). Cross-cultural differences in children's choices, categorizations, and evaluations of truths and lies. *Developmental Psychology, 43,* 278–293.

Fuchs, D., Fuchs, L. S., Mathes, P. G., & Martinez, E. A. (2002a). Preliminary evidence on the standing of students with learning disabilities in PALS and no-PALS classrooms. *Learning Disabilities Research and Practice, 17,* 205–215.

Fuchs, L. S., Fuchs, D., Yazkian, L., & Powell, S. R. (2002b). Enhancing first-grade children's mathematical development with peer-assisted learning strategies. *School Psychology Review, 31,* 569–583.

Fuh, M.-H., Wang, S.-J., Wang, P.-H., & Fuh, J.-L. (2005). Attitudes toward menopause among middle-aged women: A community survey in an island of Taiwan. *Maturitas, 52,* 348–355.

Fukunaga, A., Uematsu, H., & Sugimoto, K. (2005). Influences of aging on taste perception and oral somatic sensation. *Journal of Gerontology, 60A,* 109–113.

Fuligni, A. J. (1998). The adjustment of children from immigrant families. *Current Directions in Psychological Science, 7,* 99–103.

Fuligni, A. J. (2004). The adaptation and acculturation of children from immigrant families. In U. P. Gielen & J. Roopnarine (Eds.), *Childhood and adolescence: Cross-cultural perspectives* (pp. 297–318). Westport, CT: Praeger.

Fuligni, A. J., Yip, T., & Tseng, V. (2002). The impact of family obligation on the daily activities and psychological well-being of Chinese-American adolescents. *Child Development, 73,* 302–314.

Fuligni, A. S., Han, W.-J., & Brooks-Gunn, J. (2004). The Infant-Toddler HOME in the 2nd and 3rd years of life. *Parenting: Science and Practice, 4,* 139–159.

Fuller, C., Keller, L., Olson, J., Plymale, A., & Gottesman, M. (2005). Helping preschoolers become healthy eaters. *Journal of Pediatric Health Care, 19,* 178–182.

Fuller-Iglesias, H. (2010, November). Coping across borders: Transnational families in Mexico. In M. Mulso, *Families Coping across Borders.* Paper symposium presented at the National Council on Family Relations Annual Conference, Minneapolis, MN.

Fuller-Thomson, E., & Minkler, M. (2000). The mental and physical health of grandmothers who are raising their grandchildren. *Journal of Mental Health and Aging, 6,* 311–323.

Fuller-Thomson, E., & Minkler, M. (2005). Native American grandparents raising grandchildren: Findings from the Census 2000 Supplementary Survey and implications for social work practice. *Social Work, 50,* 131–139.

Fuller-Thomson, E., & Minkler, M. (2007). Mexican American grandparents raising grandchildren: Findings from the Census 2000 American Community Survey. *Families in Society, 88,* 567–574.

Fullerton, J. T., Navarro, A. M., & Young, S. H. (2007). Outcomes of planned home birth: An integrative review. *Journal of Midwifery and Women's Health, 52,* 323–333.

Fulmer, T. (2008). Screening for mistreatment of older adults. *American Journal of Nursing, 108,* 52–56.

Fülöp, T., Larbi, A., Kotb, R., de Angelis, F., & Pawelec, G. (2011). Aging, immunity, and cancer. *Discovery Medicine, 11,* 537–550.

Fung, H. H., Carstensen, L. L., & Lang, F. R. (2001). Age-related patterns in social networks among European Americans and African Americans: Implications for socioemotional selectivity across the life span. *International Journal of Aging and Human Development, 52,* 185–206.

Furchtgott-Roth, D. (2009). *Testimony on the gender pay gap* (testimony before the Joint Economic Committee, U.S. House of Representatives). Washington, DC: Hudson Institute.

Furman, W., & Buhrmester, D. (1992). Age and sex differences in perceptions of networks of personal relationships. *Child Development, 63,* 103–115.

Furman, W., & Collins, W. A. (2009). Adolescent romantic relationships and experiences. In K. Rubin, W. M. Bukowski, & B. Laursen (Eds.), *Handbook of peer interactions, relationships, and groups* (pp. 341–360). New York: Guilford Press.

Furman, W., Simon, V. A., Shaffer, L., & Bouchey, H. A. (2002). Adolescents' working models and styles for relationships with parents, friends, and romantic partners. *Child Development, 73,* 241–255.

Furnham, A. (2009). Sex differences in mate selection preferences. *Personality and Individual Differences, 47,* 262–267.

Furstenberg, F. F. (2010). On a new schedule: Transitions to adulthood and family change. *Future of Children, 20,* 67–87.

Furstenberg, F. F., Jr., & Harris, K. M. (1993). When and why fathers matter: Impact of father involvement on children of adolescent mothers. In R. I. Lerman & T. J. Ooms (Eds.), *Young unwed fathers* (pp. 117–138). Philadelphia: Temple University Press.

Fuson, K. C. (2009). Avoiding misinterpretations of Piaget and Vygotsky: Mathematical teaching without learning, learning without teaching, or helpful learning-path teaching? *Cognitive Development, 24,* 343–361.

Fuson, K. C., & Burghard, B. H. (2003). Multidigit addition and subtraction methods invented in small groups and teacher support of problem solving and reflection. In J. J. Baroody & A. Dowker (Eds.), *The development of arithmetic concepts and skills* (pp. 267–304). Mahwah, NJ: Erlbaum.

Fussell, E., & Furstenberg, F. F., Jr. (2005). The transition to adulthood during the twentieth century. In R. A. Settersten, Jr., F. F. Furstenberg, Jr., & R. G. Rumbaut (Eds.), *On the frontier of adulthood* (pp. 29–75). Chicago: University of Chicago Press.

Fussell, E., & Gauthier, A. H. (2005). American women's transition to adulthood in comparative perspective. In R. A. Settersten, Jr., F. F. Furstenberg, Jr., & R. G. Rumbaut (Eds.), *On the frontier of adulthood: Theory, research, and public policy* (pp. 76–109). Chicago: University of Chicago Press.

Fuster, J. J., & Andres, V. (2006). Telomere biology and cardiovascular disease. *Circulation Research, 99,* 1167–1180.

Fyfe, M. (2006, April). Music and love help defy the doctors. Retrieved from www.theage.com.au/news/national/music-and-love-help-dying-defy-thedoctors/2006/03/31/1143441339517.html

G

Gabbay, S. G., & Wahler, J. J. (2002). Lesbian aging: Review of a growing literature. *Journal of Gay and Lesbian Social Services, 14,* 1–21.

Gabriel, Z., & Bowling, A. (2004). Quality of life from the perspectives of older people. *Ageing and Society, 24,* 675–691.

Gailliot, M. T., Schmeichel, B. J., & Baumeister, R. F. (2006). Self-regulatory processes defend against the threat of death: Effects of self-control depletion and trait self-control on thoughts and fears of dying. *Journal of Personality and Social Psychology, 91,* 49–62.

Galambos, N. L., Almeida, D. M., & Petersen, A. C. (1990). Masculinity, femininity, and sex role attitudes in early adolescence: Exploring gender intensification. *Child Development, 61,* 1905–1914.

Galambos, N. L., & Maggs, J. L. (1991). Children in self-care: Figures, facts, and fiction. In J. V. Lerner & N. L. Galambos (Eds.), *Employed mothers and their children* (pp. 131–157). New York: Garland.

Galambos, N. L., & Martinez, M. L. (2007). Poised for emerging adulthood in Latin America: A pleasure for the privileged. *Child Development Perspectives, 1,* 109–114.

Galetta, F., Carpi, A., Abraham, N., Guidotti, E., Russo, M. A., Camici, M., et al. (2012). Age related cardiovascular dysfunction and effects of physical activity. *Frontiers in Bioscience, 4,* 2617–2637.

Galinsky, E., Aumann, K., & Bond, J. T. (2009). *Times are changing: Gender and generation at work and at home.* New York: Families and Work Institute.

Gallagher, A. M., & Kaufman, J. C. (2005). Gender differences in mathematics: What we know and what we need to know. In A. M. Gallagher & J. C. Kaufman (Eds.), *Gender differences in mathematics: An integrative psychological approach* (pp. 316–331). New York: Cambridge University Press.

Galler, J. R., Ramsey, C. F., Morley, D. S., Archer, E., & Salt, P. (1990). The long-term effects of early kwashiorkor compared with marasmus. IV. Performance on the National High School Entrance Examination. *Pediatric Research, 28,* 235–239.

Gallo, W. T., Bradley, E. H., Dubin, J. A., Jones, R. N., Falba, T. A., Teng, H.-M., & Kasl, S. V. (2006). The persistence of depressive symptoms in older workers who experience involuntary job loss: Results from the Health and Retirement Survey. *Journal of Gerontology, 61B,* S221–S228.

Galloway, J., & Thelen, E. (2004). Feet first: Object exploration in young infants. *Infant Behavior and Development, 27,* 107–112.

Gallup News Service. (2006). *Religion most important to blacks, women, and older Americans.* Retrieved from www.gallup.com/poll/25585/Religion-Most-Important-Blacks-Women-Older-Americans.aspx?version=print

Gallup News Service. (2012). *Seven in 10 Americans are very or moderately religious.* Retrieved from www.gallup.com/poll/159050/seven-americans-moderately-religious.aspx

Ganea, P. A., Allen, M. L., Butler, L., Carey, S., & DeLoache, J. S. (2009). Toddlers' referential understanding of pictures. *Journal of Experimental Child Psychology, 104,* 283–295.

Ganea, P. A., Pickard, M. B., & DeLoache, J. S. (2008). Transfer between picture books and the real world by very young children. *Journal of Cognition and Development, 9,* 46–66.

Ganea, P. A., Shutts, K., Spelke, E., & DeLoache, J. S. (2007). Thinking of things unseen: Infants' use of language to update object representations. *Psychological Science, 8,* 734–739.

Ganger, J., & Brent, M. R. (2004). Reexamining the vocabulary spurt. *Developmental Psychology, 40,* 621–632.

Ganji, V., Hampl, J. S., & Betts, N. M. (2003). Race-, gender-, and age-specific differences in dietary micronutrient intakes of U.S. children. *International Journal of Food Sciences and Nutrition, 54,* 485–490.

Gannon, L., & Ekstrom, B. (1993). Attitudes toward menopause: The influence of sociocultural paradigms. *Psychology of Women Quarterly, 17,* 275–288.

Ganong, L., Coleman, M., Fine, M., & Martin, P. (1999). Step-parents' affinity-seeking and affinitymaintaining strategies with stepchildren. *Journal of Family Issues, 20,* 299–327.

Ganong, L. H., & Coleman, M. (1994). *Remarried family relationships.* Thousand Oaks, CA: Sage.

Ganong, L. H., & Coleman, M. (2004). *Stepfamily relationships: Development, dynamics, and interventions.* New York: Kluwer/Plenum.

Ganong, L. H., Coleman, M., & Jamison, Y. (2011). Patterns of stepchild–stepparent relationship development. *Journal of Marriage and Family, 73,* 396–413.

Gans, D., & Silverstein, M. (2006). Norms of filial responsibility for aging parents across time and generations. *Journal of Marriage and Family, 68,* 961–976.

Gao, G. (2001). Intimacy, passion, and commitment in Chinese and U.S. American romantic relationships. *International Journal of Intercultural Relations, 25,* 329–342.

Garces, E., Thomas, D., & Currie, J. (2002). Longer-term effects of Head Start. *American Economic Review, 92,* 999–1012.

Garcia, M. M., Shaw, D. S., Winslow, E. B., & Yaggi, K. E. (2000). Destructive sibling conflict and the development of conduct problems in young boys. *Developmental Psychology, 36,* 44–53.

Garcia-Bournissen, F., Tsur, L., Goldstein, L. H., Staroselsky, A., Avner, M., & Asrar, F. (2008). Fetal exposure to isotretinoin—an international problem. *Reproductive Toxicology, 25,* 124–128.

García Coll, C., & Magnuson, K. (1997). The psychological experience of immigration: A developmental perspective. In A. Booth, A. C. Crouter, & N. Landale (Eds.), *Immigration and the family* (pp. 91–131). Mahwah, NJ: Erlbaum.

García Coll, C., & Marks, A. K. (2009). *Immigrant stories: Ethnicity and academics in middle childhood.* New York: Oxford University Press.

Gardner, H. (1983). *Frames of mind: The theory of multiple intelligences.* New York: Basic Books.

Gardner, H. (1993). *Multiple intelligences: The theory in practice.* New York: Basic Books.

Gardner, H. E. (1998). Are there additional intelligences? The case of the naturalist, spiritual, and existential intelligences. In J. Kane (Ed.), *Educational information and transformation.* Upper Saddle River, NJ: Prentice-Hall.

Gardner, H. E. (2000). *Intelligence reframed: Multiple intelligences for the twenty-first century.* New York: Basic Books.

Gardner, J. P., Li, S., Srinivasan, S. R., Chen, W., Kimura, M., & Lu, X. (2005). Rise in insulin resistance is associated with escalated telomere attrition. *Circulation, 111,* 2171–2177.

Garner, P. W. (1996). The relations of emotional role taking, affective/moral attributions, and emotional display rule knowledge to low-income school-age children's social competence. *Journal of Applied Developmental Psychology, 17,* 19–36.

Garner, P. W. (2003). Child and family correlates of toddlers' emotional and behavioral responses to a mishap. *Infant Mental Health Journal, 24,* 580–596.

Garner, P. W., & Estep, K. (2001). Emotional competence, emotion socialization, and young children's peer-related social competence. *Early Education and Development, 12,* 29–48.

Gartstein, M. A., & Rothbart, M. K. (2003). Studying infant temperament via the revised infant behavior questionnaire. *Infant Behavior and Development, 26*, 64–86.

Gartstein, M. A., Slobodskaya, H. R., Zylicz, P. O., Gosztyla, D., & Nakagawa, A. (2010). A cross-cultural evaluation of temperament: Japan, USA, Poland and Russia. *International Journal of Psychology and Psychological Therapy, 10*, 55–75.

Gasden, V. (1999). Black families in intergenerational and cultural perspective. In M. E. Lamb (Ed.), *Parenting and child development in "nontraditional" families* (pp. 221–246). Mahwah, NJ: Erlbaum.

Gaskill, R. L., & Perry, B. D. (2012). Child sexual abuse, traumatic experiences, and their impact on the developing brain. In P. Goodyear-Brown (Ed.), *Handbook of child sexual abuse: Identification, assessment, and treatment* (pp. 29–47). Hoboken, NJ: Wiley.

Gaskins, S. (1999). Children's daily lives in a Mayan village: A case study of culturally constructed roles and activities. In R. Göncü (Ed.), *Children's engagement in the world: Sociocultural perspectives* (pp. 25–61). Cambridge, UK: Cambridge University Press.

Gaskins, S. (2000). Children's daily activities in a Mayan village: A culturally grounded description. *Cross-Cultural Research, 34*, 375–389.

Gaskins, S., Haight, W., & Lancy, D. F. (2007). The cultural construction of play. In A. Göncü & S. Gaskins (Eds.), *Play and development: Evolutionary, sociocultural, and functional perspectives* (pp. 179–202). Mahwah, NJ: Erlbaum.

Gates, G. J. (2011). *How many people are lesbian, gay, bisexual, and transgender?* Berkeley, CA: The Williams Institute, University of California School of Law.

Gates, G. J., Badgett, M. V. L., Macomber, J. E., & Chambers, K. (2007). *Adoption and foster care by gay and lesbian parents in the United States.* Los Angeles, CA: Williams Institute of the UCLA School of Law.

Gathercole, S. E., Adams, A.-M., & Hitch, G. (1994). Do young children rehearse? An individual-differences analysis. *Memory and Cognition, 22*, 201–207.

Gathercole, S. E., & Alloway, T. P. (2008). Working memory and classroom learning. In S. K. Thurman & C. A. Fiorello (Eds.), *Applied cognitive research in K–3 classrooms* (pp. 17–40). New York: Routledge/Taylor & Francis Group.

Gathercole, S. E., Alloway, T. P., Willis, C., & Adams, A.-M. (2006). Working memory in children with reading disabilities. *Journal of Experimental Child Psychology, 93*, 265–281.

Gathercole, S. E., Lamont, E., & Alloway, T. P. (2006). Working memory in the classroom. In S. Pickering (Ed.), *Working memory and education* (pp. 219–240). San Diego: Elsevier.

Gathercole, S. E., Tiffany, C., Briscoe, J., Thorn, A., & ALSPAC Team. (2005). Developmental consequences of poor phonological short-term memory function in childhood: A longitudinal study. *Journal of Child Psychology and Psychiatry, 46*, 598–611.

Gathercole, V., Sebastián, E., & Soto, P. (1999). The early acquisition of Spanish verb morphology: Across-the-board or piecemeal knowledge? *International Journal of Bilingualism, 3*, 133–182.

Gauvain, M. (2004). Bringing culture into relief: Cultural contributions to the development of children's planning skills. In R. V. Kail (Ed.), *Advances in child development and behavior* (pp. 39–71). San Diego, CA: Elsevier.

Gauvain, M., de la Ossa, J. L., & Hurtado-Ortiz, M. T. (2001). Parental guidance as children learn to use cultural tools: The case of pictorial plans. *Cognitive Development, 16*, 551–575.

Gauvain, M., & Huard, R. D. (1999). Family interaction, parenting style, and the development of planning: A longitudinal analysis using archival data. *Journal of Family Psychology, 13*, 75–92.

Gauvain, M., & Rogoff, B. (1989). Ways of speaking about space: The development of children's skill in communicating spatial knowledge. *Cognitive Development, 4*, 295–307.

Gavrilova, N. S., & Gavrilov, L. A. (2012). Comments on dietary restriction, Okinawa diet and longevity. *Gerontology, 58*, 221–223.

Gazzaley, A., Cooney, J. W., Rissman, J., & D'Esposito, M. (2005). Top-down suppression deficit underlies working memory impairment in normal aging. *Nature Neuroscience, 8*, 1298–1300.

Ge, X., Brody, G. H., Conger, R. D., Simons, R. L., & Murry, V. (2002). Contextual amplification of the effects of pubertal transition on African American children's deviant peer affiliation and externalized behavioral problems. *Developmental Psychology, 38*, 42–54.

Ge, X., Conger, R. D., & Elder, G. H., Jr. (1996). Coming of age too early: Pubertal influences on girls' vulnerability to psychological distress. *Child Development, 67*, 3386–3400.

Ge, X., Conger, R. D., & Elder, G. H., Jr. (2001). The relation between puberty and psychological distress in adolescent boys. *Journal of Research on Adolescence, 11*, 49–70.

Ge, X., Jin, R., Natsuaki, M. N., Frederick, X., Brody, G. H., Cutrona, C. E., & Simons, R. L. (2006). Pubertal maturation and early substance use risks among African American children. *Psychology of Addictive Behaviors, 20*, 404–414.

Ge, X., Kim, I. J., Brody, G. H., Conger, R. D., & Simons, R. L. (2003). It's about timing and change: Pubertal transition effects on symptoms of major depression among African American youths. *Developmental Psychology, 39*, 430–439.

Ge, X., Natsuaki, M. N., Jin, R., & Biehl, M. C. (2011). A contextual amplification hypothesis: Pubertal timing and girls' emotional and behavior problems. In M. Kerr, H. Stattin, R. C. M. E. Engels, G. Overbeek, & A.-K. Andershed (Eds.), *Understanding girls' problem behavior* (pp. 11–28). Chichester, UK: Wiley-Blackwell.

Geangu, E., Benga, O., Stahl, D., & Striano, T. (2010). Contagious crying beyond the first days of life. *Infant Behavior and Development, 33*, 279–288.

Geary, D. C. (2006a). Development of mathematical understanding. In D. Kuhn & R. Siegler (Eds.), *Handbook of child psychology: Vol. 2. Cognition, perception, and language* (pp. 777–810). Hoboken, NJ: Wiley.

Geary, D. C. (2006b). Evolutionary developmental psychology: Current status and future directions. *Developmental Review, 26*, 113–119.

Geary, D. C., Saults, J. S., Liu, F., & Hoard, M. K. (2000). Sex differences in spatial cognition, computational fluency, and arithmetic reasoning. *Journal of Experimental Child Psychology, 77*, 337–353.

Gee, C. B., & Rhodes, J. E. (2003). Adolescent mothers' relationship with their children's biological fathers: Social support, social strain, and relationship continuity. *Journal of Family Psychology, 17*, 370–383.

Geerts, C. C., Bots, M. L., van der Ent, C. K., Grobbee, D. E., & Uiterwaal, C. S. (2012). Parental smoking and vascular damage in their 5-year-old children. *Pediatrics, 129*, 45–54.

Geist, C. (2010). Men's and women's reports about housework. In J. Treas & S. Drobnic (Eds.), *Dividing the Domestic: Men, women, and household work in cross-national perspective* (pp. 217–240). Stanford, CA: Stanford University Press.

Gelman, R. (1972). Logical capacity of very young children: Number invariance rules. *Child Development, 43*, 75–90.

Gelman, R., & Shatz, M. (1978). Appropriate speech adjustments: The operation of conversational constraints on talk to two-year-olds. In M. Lewis & L. A. Rosenblum (Eds.), *Interaction, conversation, and the development of language* (pp. 27–61). New York: Wiley.

Gelman, S. A. (2003). *The essential child.* New York: Oxford University Press.

Gelman, S. A., & Kalish, C. W. (2006). Conceptual development. In D. Kuhn & R. Siegler (Eds.), *Handbook of child psychology: Vol. 2. Cognition, perception, and language* (6th ed., pp. 687–733). Hoboken, NJ: Wiley.

Gelman, S. A., & Koenig, M. A. (2003). Theory-based categorization in early childhood. In D. H. Rakison & L. M. Oakes (Eds.), *Early category and concept development* (pp. 330–359). New York: Oxford University Press.

Gelman, S. A., Taylor, M. G., & Nguyen, S. P. (2004). Mother–child conversations about gender. *Monographs of the Society for Research in Child Development, 69*(1, Serial No. 275), pp. 1–127.

Gendler, M. N., Witherington, D. C., & Edwards, A. (2008). The development of affect specificity in infants' use of emotion cues. *Infancy, 13*, 456–468.

Genesee, F., & Nicoladis, E. (2007). Bilingual first language acquisition. In E. Hoff & M. Shatz (Eds.), *Blackwell handbook of language development* (pp. 324–342). Malden, MA: Blackwell.

Gentile, B., Twenge, J. M., & Campbell, W. K. (2010). Birth cohort differences in self-esteem, 1988–2008: A cross-temporal meta-analysis. *Review of General Psychology, 14*, 261–268.

George, S. A. (2002). The menopause experience: A woman's perspective. *Journal of Obstetric, Gynecologic, and Neonatal Nursing, 31*, 71–85.

Gerardi-Caulton, G. (2000). Sensitivity to spatial conflict and the development of self-regulation in children 24–36 months of age. *Developmental Science, 3*, 397–404.

Gere, J., Schimmack, U., Pinkus, R. T., & Lockwood, P. (2011). The effects of romantic partners' goal congruence on affective well-being. *Journal of Research in Personality, 45*, 549–559.

Gergely, G., & Watson, J. (1999). Early socioemotional development: Contingency perception and the social-biofeedback model. In P. Rochat (Ed.), *Early social cognition: Understanding others in the first months of life* (pp. 101–136). Mahwah, NJ: Erlbaum.

Gergen, M., & Gergen, K. J. (2003). Positive aging. In J. F. Gubrim & J. A. Holstein (Eds.), *Ways of aging* (pp. 203–224). Malden: Blackwell Publishers Ltd.

Gershoff, E. T. (2002a). Corporal punishment by parents and associated child behaviors and experiences: A meta-analytic and theoretical review. *Psychological Bulletin, 128*, 539–579.

Gershoff, E. T. (2002b). Corporal punishment, physical abuse, and the burden of proof: Reply to Baumrind, Larzelere, and Cowan (2002), Holden (2002), and Parke (2002). *Psychological Bulletin, 128*, 602–611.

Gershoff, E. T., Grogan-Kaylor, A., Lansford, J. E., Chang, L., Zelli, A., Deater-Deckard, K., et al. (2010). Parent discipline practices in an international sample: Associations with child behaviors and moderation by perceived normativeness. *Child Development, 81*, 487–502.

Gershoff, E. T., Lansford, J. E., Sexton, H. R., Davis-Kean, P., & Sameroff, A. J. (2012). Longitudinal links between spanking and children's externalizing behaviors in a national sample of white, black, Hispanic, and Asian American families. *Child Development, 83*, 838–843.

Gershoff-Stowe, L., & Hahn, E. R. (2007). Fast mapping skills in the developing lexicon. *Journal of Speech, Language, and Hearing Research, 50*, 682–697.

Gerstorf, D., Ram, N., Estabrook, R., Schupp, J., Wagner, G. G., & Lindenberger, U. (2008). Life satisfaction shows terminal decline in old age: Longitudinal evidence from the German socioeconomic panel study. *Developmental Psychology, 44*, 1148–1159.

Gervai, J. (2009). Environmental and genetic influences on early attachment. *Child and Adolescent Psychiatry and Mental Health, 3*, 25. Retrieved from www.capmh.com/content/3/1/25

Gesell, A. (1933). Maturation and patterning of behavior. In C. Murchison (Ed.), *A handbook of child psychology*. Worcester, MA: Clark University Press.

Gest, S. D., Domitrovich, C. E., & Welsh, J. A. (2005). Peer academic reputation in elementary school: Associations with changes in self-concept and academic skills. *Journal of Educational Psychology, 97*, 337–346.

Geuze, R. H., Schaafsma, S. M., Lust, J. M., Bouma, A., Schiefenhovel, W., Groothuis, T. G. G., et al. (2012). Plasticity of lateralization: Schooling predicts hand preference but not hand skill asymmetry in a non-industrial society. *Neuropsychologia, 50*, 612–620.

Gewirtz, A., Forgatch, M. S., & Wieling, E. (2008). Parenting practices as potential mechanisms for child adjustment following mass trauma. *Journal of Marital and Family Therapy, 34*, 177–192.

Ghavami, N., Fingerhut, A., Peplau, L. A., Grant, S. K., & Wittig, M. A. (2011). Testing a model of minority identity achievement, identity affirmation, and psychological well-being among ethnic minority and sexual minority individuals. *Cultural Diversity and Ethnic Minority Psychology, 17*, 79–88.

Ghim, H. R. (1990). Evidence for perceptual organization in infants: Perception of subjective contours by young infants. *Infant Behavior and Development, 13*, 221–248.

Giarrusso, R., Feng, D., Silverstein, M., & Bengtson, V. L. (2001). Grandparent–adult grandchild affection and consensus. *Journal of Family Issues, 22*, 456–477.

Gibbons, R., Dugaiczyk, L. J., Girke, T., Duistermars, B., Zielinski, R., & Dugaiczyk, A. (2004). Distinguishing humans from great apes with AluYb8 repeats. *Journal of Molecular Biology, 339*, 721–729.

Gibbs, B. G. (2010). Reversing fortunes or content change? Gender gaps in math-related skill throughout childhood. *Social Science Research, 39*, 540–569.

Gibbs, J. C. (1991). Toward an integration of Kohlberg's and Hoffman's theories of morality. In W. M. Kurtines & J. L. Gewirtz (Eds.), *Handbook of moral behavior and development* (Vol. 1, pp. 183–222). Hillsdale, NJ: Erlbaum.

Gibbs, J. C. (2006). Should Kohlberg's cognitive developmental approach to morality be replaced with a more pragmatic approach? Comment on Krebs and Denton (2005). *Psychological Review, 113*, 666–671.

Gibbs, J. C. (2010a). Beyond the conventionally moral. *Journal of Applied Developmental Psychology, 31*, 106–108.

Gibbs, J. C. (2010b). *Moral development and reality: Beyond the theories of Kohlberg and Hoffman* (2nd ed.). Boston: Pearson Allyn & Bacon.

Gibbs, J. C., Basinger, K. S., Grime, R. L., & Snarey, J. R. (2007). Moral judgment development across cultures: Revisiting Kohlberg's universality claims. *Developmental Review, 24*, 443–500.

Gibbs, J. C., Moshman, D., Berkowitz, M. W., Basinger, K. S., & Grime, R. L. (2009a). Taking development seriously: Critique of the 2008 *JME* special issue on moral functioning. *Journal of Moral Education, 38*, 271–282.

Gibson, E. J. (1970). The development of perception as an adaptive process. *American Scientist, 58*, 98–107.

Gibson, E. J. (2000). Perceptual learning in development: Some basic concepts. *Ecological Psychology, 12*, 295–302.

Gibson, E. J. (2003). The world is so full of a number of things: On specification and perceptual learning. *Ecological Psychology, 15*, 283–287.

Gibson, E. J., & Walk, R. D. (1960). The "visual cliff." *Scientific American, 202*, 64–71.

Gibson, J. J. (1979). *The ecological approach to visual perception*. Boston: Houghton Mifflin.

Gibson, P. A. (2005). Intergenerational parenting from the perspective of American grandmothers. *Family Relations, 54*, 280–297.

Giles, J. W., & Heyman, G. D. (2005). Young children's beliefs about the relationship between gender and aggressive behavior. *Child Development, 76*, 107–121.

Gill, M., Daly, G., Heron, S., Hawi, Z., & Fitzgerald, M. (1997). Confirmation of association between attention deficit hyperactivity disorder and a dopamine transporter polymorphism. *Molecular Psychiatry, 2*, 311–313.

Gillet, J.-P., Macadangdang, B., Rathke, R. L., Gottesman, M. M., & Kimchi-Sarfaty, C. (2009). The development of gene therapy: From monogenic recessive disorders to complex diseases such as cancer. *Methods in Molecular Biology, 542*, 5–54.

Gillies, R. M. (2000). The maintenance of cooperative and helping behaviours in cooperative groups. *British Journal of Educational Psychology, 70*, 97–111.

Gillies, R. M. (2003). The behaviors, interactions, and perceptions of junior high school students during small-group learning. *Journal of Educational Psychology, 95*, 137–147.

Gillies, R. M., & Ashman, A. F. (1996). Teaching collaborative skills to primary school children in classroom-based workgroups. *Learning and Instruction, 6*, 187–200.

Gilligan, C. F. (1982). *In a different voice*. Cambridge, MA: Harvard University Press.

Gilliom, M., Shaw, D. S., Beck, J. E., Schonberg, M. A., & Lukon, J. L. (2002). Anger regulation in disadvantaged preschool boys: Strategies, antecedents, and the development of self-control. *Developmental Psychology, 38*, 222–235.

Gillum, R. F., Dana, E. K., Thomas, O. O., & Harold, G. K. (2008). Frequency of attendance at religious services and mortality in a U.S. national cohort. *Annals of Epidemiology, 18*, 124–129.

Gilstrap, L. L., & Ceci, S. J. (2005). Reconceptualizing children's suggestibility: Bidirectional and temporal properties. *Child Development, 76*, 40–53.

Ginsburg, H. P., Lee, J. S., & Boyd, J. S. (2008). Mathematics education for young children: What it is and how to promote it. *Social Policy Report of the Society for Research in Child Development, 12*(1).

Ginsburg, K. R. (2007). The importance of play in promoting healthy child development and maintaining strong parent–child bonds. *Pediatrics, 119*, 182–191.

Ginsburg-Block, M. D., Rohrbeck, C. A., & Fantuzzo, J. W. (2006). A meta-analytic review of social, self-concept, and behavioral outcomes of peer-assisted learning. *Journal of Educational Psychology, 98*, 732–749.

Gitlin, L. N., Belle, S. H., Burgio, L. D., Szaja, S. J., Mahoney, D., & Gallagher-Thompson, D. (2003). Effect of multicomponent interventions on caregiver burden and depression: The REACH multisite initiative at 6-month follow-up. *Psychology and Aging, 18*, 361–374.

Giuliani, A., Schöll, W. M., Basver, A., & Tasmussino, K. F. (2002). Mode of delivery and outcome of 699 term singleton breech deliveries at a single center. *American Journal of Obstetrics and Gynaecology, 187*, 1649–1698.

Gladstone, I. M., & Katz, V. L. (2004). The morbidity of the 34- to 35-week gestation: Should we reexamine the paradigm? *American Journal of Perinatology, 21*, 9–13.

Glasgow, K. L., Dornbusch, S. M., Troyer, L., Steinberg, L., & Ritter, P. L. (1997). Parenting styles, adolescents' attributions, and educational outcomes in nine heterogeneous high schools. *Child Development, 68*, 507–523.

Gleason, J. B. (2009). The development of language. In J. B. Gleason (Ed.), *The development of language* (7th ed., pp. 1–33). Boston: Allyn and Bacon.

Gleitman, L. R., Cassidy, K., Nappa, R., Papfragou, A., & Trueswell, J. C. (2005). Hard words. *Language Learning and Development, 1*, 23–64.

Glover, V., Bergman, K., & O'Connor, T. G. (2008). The effects of maternal stress, anxiety, and depression during pregnancy on the neurodevelopment of the child. In S. D. Stone & A. E. Menken (Eds.), *Perinatal and postpartum mood disorders: Perspectives and treatment guide for the health care practitioner* (pp. 3– 5). New York: Springer.

Glowinski, A. L., Madden, P. A. F., Bucholz, K. K., Lynskey, M. T., & Heath, A. C. (2003). Genetic epidemiology of self-reported lifetime DSM-IV major depressive disorder in a population-based twin sample of female adolescents. *Journal of Child Psychology and Psychiatry and Allied Disciplines, 44*, 988–996.

Glück, J., & Bluck, S. (2007). Looking back across the lifespan: A life story account of the reminiscence bump. *Memory and Cognition, 35*, 1928–1939.

Gluckman, P. D., Sizonenko, S. V., & Bassett, N. S. (1999). The transition from fetus to neonate—an endocrine perspective. *Acta Paediatrica Supplement, 88*(428), 7–11.

Gnepp, J. (1983). Children's social sensitivity: Inferring emotions from conflicting cues. *Developmental Psychology, 19*, 805–814.

Go, A. S., Mozaffarian, V. L., Roger, E. J., Benjmin, J. D., Berry, J. D., Borden, W. B, et al. (2013). Heart disease and stroke statistics—2013 update. A report from the American Heart Association. *Circulation, 127*, e1–e241.

Godeau, E., Nic Gabhainn, S., Vignes, C., Ross, J., Boyce, W., & Todd, J. (2008). Contraceptive use by 15-year-old students at their last sexual intercourse. *Archives of Pediatric and Adolescent Medicine, 162*, 66–73.

Goering, J. (Ed.). (2003). *Choosing a better life? How public housing tenants selected a HUD experiment to improve their lives and those of their children: The Moving to Opportunity Demonstration Program.* Washington, DC: Urban Institute Press.

Gogate, L. J., & Bahrick, L. E. (1998). Intersensory redundancy facilitates learning of arbitrary relations between vowel sounds and objects in seven-month-old infants. *Journal of Experimental Child Psychology, 69*, 133–149.

Gogate, L. J., & Bahrick, L. E. (2001). Intersensory redundancy and 7-month-old infants' memory for arbitrary syllable–object relations. *Infancy, 2*, 219–231.

Gögele, M., Pattaro, C., Fuchsberger, C., Minelli, C., Pramstaller, P. P., & Wjst, M. (2011). Heritability analysis of life span in a semi-isolated population followed across four centuries reveals the presence of pleiotropy between life span and reproduction. *Journal of Gerontology, 66A*, 26–37.

Goh, Y. I., & Koren, G. (2008). Folic acid in pregnancy and fetal outcomes. *Journal of Obstetrics and Gynaecology, 28*, 3–13.

Goldberg, A. E. (2010). *Lesbian and gay parents and their children: Research on the family life cycle*. Washington, DC: American Psychological Association.

Goldberg, A. E., & Perry-Jenkins, M. (2003). Division of labor and working-class women's well-being across the transition to parenthood. *Journal of Family Psychology, 18*, 225–236.

Goldberg, A. P., Dengel, D. R., & Hagberg, J. M. (1996). Exercise physiology and aging. In E. L. Schneider & J. W. Rowe (Eds.), *Handbook of the biology of aging* (pp. 331–354). San Diego: Academic Press.

Goldenberg, C., Gallimore, R., Reese, L., & Garnier, H. (2001). Cause or effect? Immigrant Latino parents' aspirations and expectations, and their children's school performance. *American Educational Research Journal, 38*, 547–582.

Goldfield, B. A. (1987). The contributions of child and caregiver to referential and expressive language. *Applied Psycholinguistics, 8,* 267–280.

Goldschmidt, L., Richardson, G. A., Cornelius, M. D., & Day, N. L. (2004). Prenatal marijuana and alcohol exposure and academic achievement at age 10. *Neurotoxicology and Teratology, 26,* 521–532.

Goldsmith, H. H., Pollak, S. D., & Davidson, R. J. (2008). Developmental neuroscience perspectives on emotion regulation. *Child Development Perspectives, 2,* 132–140.

Goldsmith, L. T. (2000). Tracking trajectories of talent: Child prodigies growing up. In R. C. Friedman & B. M. Shore (Eds.), *Talents unfolding: Cognition and development* (pp. 89–122). Washington, DC: American Psychological Association.

Goldsteen, M., Houtepen, R., Proot, I. M., Abu-Saad, H. H., Spreeuwenberg, C., & Widdershoven, G. (2006). What is a good death? Terminally ill patients dealing with normative expectations around death and dying. *Patient Education and Counseling, 64,* 378–386.

Goldstein, M. H., & Schwade, J. A. (2008). Social feedback to infants' babbling facilitates rapid phonological learning. *Psychological Science, 19,* 515–523.

Goldstein, S. (2011). Attention-deficit/hyperactivity disorder. In S. Goldstein & C. R. Reynolds (Eds.), *Handbook of neurodevelopmental and genetic disorders in children* (2nd ed., pp. 131–150). New York: Guilford.

Goldston, D. B., Molock, S. D., Whitbeck, L. B., Murakami, J. L., Zayas, L. H., & Hall, G. C. N. (2008). Cultural considerations in adolescent suicide prevention and psychosocial treatment. *American Psychologist, 63,* 14–31.

Goleman, D. (1995). *Emotional intelligence.* New York: Bantam.

Goleman, D. (1998). *Working with emotional intelligence.* New York: Bantam.

Golinkoff, R. M., & Hirsh-Pasek, K. (2006). Baby wordsmith: From associationist to social sophisticate. *Current Directions in Psychological Science, 15,* 30–33.

Golinkoff, R. M., & Hirsh-Pasek, K. (2008). How toddlers begin to learn verbs. *Trends in Cognitive Sciences, 12,* 397–403.

Golomb, C. (2004). *The child's creation of a pictorial world* (2nd ed.). Mahwah, NJ: Erlbaum.

Golombok, S., Lycett, E., MacCallum, F., Jadva, V., Murray, C., Rust, J., Abdalla, H., Jenkins, J., & Margar, R. (2004). Parenting of infants conceived by gamete donation. *Journal of Family Psychology, 18,* 443–452.

Golombok, S., Perry, B., Burston, A., Murray, C., Mooney-Somers, J., Stevens, M., & Golding, J. (2003). Children with lesbian parents: A community study. *Developmental Psychology, 39,* 20–33.

Gomez-Perez, E., & Ostrosky-Solis, F. (2006). Attention and memory evaluation across the life span: Heterogeneous effects of age and education. *Journal of Clinical and Experimental Neuropsychology, 28,* 477–494.

Göncü, A. (1993). Development of intersubjectivity in the dyadic play of preschoolers. *Early Childhood Research Quarterly, 8,* 99–116.

Göncü, A., Patt, M. B., & Kouba E. (2004). Understanding young children's pretend play in context. In P. K. Smith & C. H. Hart (Eds.), *Blackwell handbook of childhood social development* (pp. 418–437). Malden, MA: Blackwell.

Gonzales, N. A., Cauce, A. M., Friedman, R. J., & Mason, C. A. (1996). Family, peer, and neighborhood influences on academic achievement among African-American adolescents: One-year prospective effects. *American Journal of Community Psychology, 24,* 365–387.

Gonzalez, A.-L., & Wolters, C. A. (2006). The relation between perceived parenting practices and achievement motivation in mathematics. *Journal of Research in Childhood Education, 21,* 203–217.

Good, T. L., & Brophy, J. (2003). *Looking in classrooms* (9th ed.). Boston: Allyn and Bacon.

Goode, V., & Goode, J. D. (2007). De facto zero tolerance: An exploratory study of race and safe school violations. In J. L. Kincheloe & K. Hayes (Eds.), *Teaching city kids: Understanding and appreciating them* (pp. 85–96). New York: Peter Lang.

Goodman, A. Schorge, J., & Greene, M. F. (2011). The long-term effects of in utero exposures—the DES story. *New England Journal of Medicine, 364,* 2083–2084.

Goodman, C. C. (2012). Caregiving grandmothers and their grandchildren: Well-being nine years later. *Children and Youth Services Review, 34,* 648–654.

Goodman, G. S., & Melinder, A. (2007). Child witness research and forensic interviews of young children: A review. *Legal and Criminological Psychology, 12,* 1–19.

Goodman, J., Dale, P., & Li, P. (2008). Does frequency count? Parental input and the acquisition of vocabulary. *Journal of Child Language, 35,* 515–531.

Goodnow, J. J. (2010). Culture. In M. H. Bornstein (Ed.), *Handbook of cultural developmental science* (pp. 3–20). New York: Psychology Press.

Goodvin, R., Meyer, S., Thompson, R. A., & Hayes, R. (2008). Self-understanding in early childhood: Associations with child attachment security and maternal negative affect. *Attachment and Human Development, 10,* 433–450.

Goodwin, M. H. (1998). Games of stance: Conflict and footing in hopscotch. In S. Hoyle & C. T. Adger (Eds.), *Language practices of older children* (pp. 23–46). New York: Oxford University Press.

Goodwin, R., & Pillay, U. (2006). Relationships, culture, and social change. In A. L. Vangelisti & D. Perlman (Eds.), *The Cambridge handbook of personal relationships* (pp. 760–779). New York: Cambridge University Press.

Goodyear-Brown, P., Fath, A., & Myers, L. (2012). Child sexual abuse: The scope of the problem. In P. Goodyear-Brown (Ed.), *Handbook of child sexual abuse: Identification, assessment, and treatment* (pp. 3–28). Hoboken, NJ: Wiley.

Gooren, E. M. J. C., Pol, A. C., Stegge, H., Terwogt, M. M., & Koot, H. M. (2011). The development of conduct problems and depressive symptoms in early elementary school children: The role of peer rejection. *Journal of Clinical Child and Adolescent Psychology, 40,* 245–253.

Gopnik, A., & Choi, S. (1990). Do linguistic differences lead to cognitive differences? A cross-linguistic study of semantic and cognitive development. *First Language, 11,* 199–215.

Gopnik, A., & Nazzi, T. (2003). Words, kinds, and causal powers: A theory theory perspective on early naming and categorization. In D. H. Rakison & L. M. Oakes (Eds.), *Early category and concept development* (p. 303–329). New York: Oxford University Press.

Gopnik, A., & Tenenbaum, J. B. (2007). Bayesian networks, Bayesian learning and cognitive development. *Developmental Science, 10,* 281–287.

Gordon, R. A., Chase-Lansdale, P. L., & Brooks-Gunn, J. (2004). Extended households and the life course of young mothers: Understanding the associations using a sample of mothers with premature, low-birth-weight babies. *Child Development, 75,* 1013–1038.

Gorelick, P. B., Scuteri A., Black S. E., DeCarli, C., Greenberg, S. M., Costantino, I., et al. (2011). Vascular contributions to cognitive impairment and dementia: A statement for healthcare professionals from the American Heart Association/American Stroke Association. *Stroke, 42,* 2672–2713.

Gormally, S., Barr, R. G., Wertheim, L., Alkawaf, R., Calinoiu, N., & Young, S. N. (2001). Contact and nutrient caregiving effects on newborn infant pain responses. *Developmental Medicine and Child Neurology, 43,* 28–38.

Goronzy, J. J., Shao, L., & Weyand, C. M. (2010). Immune aging and rheumatoid arthritis. *Rheumatoid Disease Clinics of North America, 36,* 297–310.

Gosselin, P. A., & Gagne, J.-P. (2011). Older adults expend more listening effort than young adults recognizing audiovisual speech in noise. *International Journal of Audiology, 50,* 786–792.

Goswami, U. (1996). Analogical reasoning and cognitive development. In H. Reese (Ed.), *Advances in child development and behavior* (Vol. 26, pp. 91–138). New York: Academic Press.

Gothe, N., Mullen, S. P., Wójcicki, T. R., Mailey, E. L., White, S. M., Olson, E. A. (2011). Trajectories of change in self-esteem in older adults: Exercise intervention effects. *Journal of Behavioral Medicine, 34,* 298–306.

Gott, M., & Hinchliff, S. (2003). How important is sex in later life? The views of older people. *Social Science and Medicine, 56,* 1617–1628.

Gott, M., Seymour, J., Bellamy, G., Clark, D., & Ahmedzai, S. (2004). Older people's views about home as a place of care at the end of life. *Palliative Medicine, 18,* 460–467.

Gottfredson, G. D., & Duffy, R. D. (2008). Using a theory of vocational personalities and work environments to explore subjective well-being. *Journal of Career Assessment, 16,* 44–59.

Gottfredson, L. S. (2005). Applying Gottfredson's theory of circumscription and compromise in career guidance and counseling. In S. D. Brown & R. W. Lent (Eds.), *Career development and counseling* (pp. 71–100). Hoboken, NJ: Wiley.

Gottfried, A. E., Gottfried, A. W., & Bathurst, K. (2002). Maternal and dual-earner employment status and parenting. In M. H. Bornstein (Ed.), *Handbook of parenting. Vol. 2: Biology and ecology of parenting* (2nd ed., pp. 207–229). Mahwah, NJ: Erlbaum.

Gottlieb, G. (1998). Normally occurring environmental and behavioral influences on gene activity: From central dogma to probabilistic epigenesis. *Psychological Review, 105,* 792–802.

Gottlieb, G. (2003). On making behavioral genetics truly developmental. *Human Development, 46,* 337–355.

Gottlieb, G. (2007). Probabilistic epigenesis. *Developmental Science, 10,* 1–11.

Gottlieb, G., Wahlsten, D., & Lickliter, R. (2006). The significance of biology for human development: A developmental psychobiological systems view. In R. M. Lerner (Ed.), *Handbook of child psychology: Vol. 1. Theoretical models of human development* (6th ed., pp. 210–257). Hoboken, NJ: Wiley.

Gottman, J. M., Gottman, J. S., & Shapiro, A. (2010). A new couples approach to interventions for the transition to parenthood. In M. S. Schulz, M. K. Pruett, P. K. Kerig, & R. D. Parke (Eds.), *Strengthening couple relationships for optimal child development* (pp. 165–179). Washington, DC: American Psychological Association.

Gottman, J. M. (2011). *The science of trust: Emotional attunement for couples.* New York: Norton.

Gottman, J. M., & Levenson, R. W. (2000). The timing of divorce: Predicting when a couple will divorce over a 14-year period. *Journal of Marriage and Family, 62,* 737–745.

Gould, E. (2007). How widespread is adult neurogenesis in mammals? *Nature Reviews: Neuroscience, 8,* 481–488.

Gould, F., Clarke, J., Heim, C., Harvey, P. D., Majer, M., & Nemeroff, C. B. (2010). The effects of child abuse and neglect on cognitive functioning in adulthood. *Journal of Psychiatric Research, 46,* 500–506.

Gould, J. L., & Keeton, W. T. (1996). *Biological science* (6th ed.). New York: Norton.

Graber, J. A. (2003). Puberty in context. In C. Hayward (Ed.), *Gender differences at puberty* (pp. 307–325). New York: Cambridge University Press.

Graber, J. A. (2004). Internalizing problems during adolescence. In R. M. Lerner & L. Steinberg (Eds.), *Handbook of adolescent psychology* (2nd ed., pp. 587–626). Hoboken, NJ: Wiley.

Graber, J. A., Brooks-Gunn, J., & Warren, M. P. (2006). Pubertal effects on adjustment in girls: Moving from demonstrating effects to identifying pathways. *Journal of Youth and Adolescence, 35,* 413–423.

Graber, J. A., Nichols, T., Lynne, S. D., Brooks-Gunn, J., & Botwin, G. J. (2006). A longitudinal examination of family, friend, and media influences on competent versus problem behaviors among urban minority youth. *Applied Developmental Science, 10,* 75–85.

Graber, J. A., Seeley, J. R., Brooks-Gunn, J., & Lewinsohn, P. M. (2004). Is pubertal timing associated with psychopathology in young adulthood? *Journal of the American Academy of Child and Adolescent Psychiatry, 43,* 718–726.

Graber, J. A., & Sontag, L. M. (2009). Internalizing problems during adolescence. In R. M. Lerner & L. Steinberg (Eds.), *Handbook of adolescent psychology: Vol. 1. Individual bases of adolescent development* (3rd ed., pp. 642–682). Hoboken, NJ: Wiley.

Grabowski, D. C., Aschbrenner, K. A., Rome, V. F., & Bartels, S. (2010). Quality of mental health care for nursing home residents: A literature review. *Medical Care Research and Review, 67,* 627–656.

Graham-Bermann, S. A., & Howell, K. H. (2011). Child maltreatment in the context of intimate partner violence. In J. E. B. Myers (Ed.), *Child maltreatment* (3rd ed., pp. 167–180). Thousand Oaks, CA: Sage.

Gralinski, J. H., & Kopp, C. B. (1993). Everyday rules for behavior: Mothers' requests to young children. *Developmental Psychology, 29,* 573–584.

Grall, T. S. (2011, December). *Custodial mothers and fathers and their child support: 2007. Current Population Reports,* P60–240. Washington, DC: U.S. Department of Commerce.

Granger, R. C. (2008). After-school programs and academics: Implications for policy, practice, and research. *Social Policy Report of the Society for Research in Child Development, 22*(2), 3–11.

Granier-Deferre, C., Bassereau, S., Ribeiro, A., Jacquet, A.-Y., & Lecanuet, J.-P. (2003). *Cardiac "orienting" response in fetuses and babies following in utero melody-learning.* Paper presented at the 11th European Conference on Developmental Psychology, Milan, Italy.

Granillo, T., Jones-Rodriguez, G., & Carvajal, S. C. (2005). Prevalence of eating disorders in Latina adolescents: Associations with substance use and other correlates. *Journal of Adolescent Health, 36,* 214–220.

Granot, T. (2005). *Without you: Children and young people growing up with loss and its effects.* London: Jessica Kingsley.

Grant, K., O'Koon, J., Davis, T., Roache, N., Poindexter, L., & Armstrong, M. (2000). Protective factors affecting low-income urban African American youth exposed to stress. *Journal of Early Adolescence, 20,* 388–418.

Grantham-McGregor, S., Powell, C., Walker, S., Chang, S., & Fletcher, P. (1994). The long-term follow-up of severely malnourished children who participated in an intervention program. *Child Development, 65,* 428–439.

Grantham-McGregor, S., Schofield, W., & Powell, C. (1987). Development of severely malnourished children who received psychosocial stimulation: Six-year follow-up. *Pediatrics, 79,* 247–254.

Grantham-McGregor, S., Walker, S. P., & Chang, S. (2000). Nutritional deficiencies and later behavioral development. *Proceedings of the Nutrition Society, 59,* 47–54.

Graves, L. M., Ohlott, P. J., & Ruderman, M. N. (2007). Commitment to family roles: Effects on managers'

attitudes and performance. *Journal of Applied Psychology, 92,* 44–56.

Gray, K. A., Day, N. L., Leech, S., & Richardson, G. A. (2005). Prenatal marijuana exposure: Effect on child depressive symptoms at ten years of age. *Neurotoxicology and Teratology, 27,* 439–448.

Gray, M. R., & Steinberg, L. (1999). Unpacking authoritative parenting: Reassessing a multidimensional construct. *Journal of Marriage and the Family, 61,* 574–587.

Gray-Little, B., & Carels, R. (1997). The effects of racial and socioeconomic consonance on self-esteem and achievement in elementary, junior high, and high school students. *Journal of Research on Adolescence, 7,* 109–131.

Gray-Little, B., & Hafdahl, A. R. (2000). Factors influencing racial comparisons of self-esteem: A quantitative review. *Psychological Bulletin, 126,* 26–54.

Green, G. E., Irwin, J. R., & Gustafson, G. E. (2000). Acoustic cry analysis, neonatal status and long-term developmental outcomes. In R. G. Barr, B. Hopkins, & J. A. Green (Eds.), *Crying as a sign, a symptom, and a signal* (pp. 137–156). Cambridge, UK: Cambridge University Press.

Greenberger, E., O'Neil, R., & Nagel, S. K. (1994). Linking workplace and homeplace: Relations between the nature of adults' work and their parenting behavior. *Developmental Psychology, 30,* 990–1002.

Greendorfer, S. L., Lewko, J. H., & Rosengren, K. S. (1996). Family and gender-based socialization of children and adolescents. In F. L. Smoll & R. E. Smith (Eds.), *Children and youth in sport: A biopsychological perspective* (pp. 89–111). Dubuque, IA: Brown & Benchmark.

Greene, J. A., Torney-Purta, J., & Azevedo, R. (2010). Empirical evidence regarding relations among a model of epistemic and ontological cognition, academic performance, and educational level. *Journal of Educational Psychology, 102,* 234–255.

Greene, K., Krcmar, M., Walters, L. H., Rubin, D. L., Hale, J., & Hale, L. (2000). Targeting adolescent risk-taking behaviors: The contributions of egocentrism and sensation-seeking. *Journal of Adolescence, 23,* 439–461.

Greene, M. L., Way, N., & Pahl, K. (2006). Trajectories of perceived adult and peer discrimination among black, Latino, and Asian American adolescents: Patterns and psychological correlates. *Developmental Psychology, 42,* 218–238.

Greene, S. M., Anderson, E., Hetherington, E. M., Forgatch, M. S., & DeGarmo, D. S. (2003). Risk and resilience after divorce. In R. Walsh (Ed.), *Normal family processes* (pp. 96–120). New York: Guilford.

Greenfield, P. (1992, June). *Notes and references for developmental psychology.* Conference on Making Basic Texts in Psychology More Culture-Inclusive and Culture-Sensitive, Western Washington University, Bellingham, WA.

Greenfield, P. M. (2004). *Weaving generations together: Evolving creativity in the Maya of Chiapas.* Santa Fe, NM: School of American Research.

Greenfield, P. M., Maynard, A. E., & Childs, C. P. (2000). History, culture, learning, and development. *Cross-Cultural Research, 34,* 351–374.

Greenhill, L. L., Halperin, J. M., & Abikoff, H. (1999). Stimulant medications. *Journal of the American Academy of Child and Adolescent Psychiatry, 38,* 503–512.

Greenough, W. T., & Black, J. E. (1992). Induction of brain structure by experience: Substrates for cognitive development. In M. R. Gunnar & C. A. Nelson (Eds.), *Minnesota Symposia on Child Psychology* (pp. 155–200). Hillsdale, NJ: Erlbaum.

Gregg, V., Gibbs, J. C., & Fuller, D. (1994). Patterns of developmental delay in moral judgment by male and female delinquents. *Merrill-Palmer Quarterly, 40,* 538–553.

Gregory, A., & Weinstein, R. S. (2004). Connection and regulation at home and in school: Predicting growth in achievement for adolescents. *Journal of Adolescent Research, 19,* 405–427.

Greve, W., & Bjorklund, D. F. (2009). The Nestor effect: Extending evolutionary developmental psychology to a lifespan perspective. *Developmental Review, 29,* 163–179.

Griffin, Z. M., & Spieler, D. H. (2006). Observing the what and when of language production for different age groups by monitoring speakers' eye movements. *Brain and Language, 99,* 272–288.

Grigorenko, E. L. (2000). Heritability and intelligence. In R. J. Sternberg (Ed.), *Handbook of intelligence* (pp. 53–91). Cambridge, UK: Cambridge University Press.

Grob, A., Krings, F., & Bangerter, A. (2001). Life markers in biographical narratives of people from three cohorts: A life span perspective in its historical context. *Human Development, 44,* 171–190.

Grolnick, W. S., Kurowski, C. O., Dunlap, K. G., & Hevey, C. (2000). Parental resources and the transition to junior high. *Journal of Research on Adolescence, 10,* 466–488.

Gropman, A. L., & Adams, D. R. (2007). Atypical patterns of inheritance. *Seminars in Pediatric Neurology, 14,* 34–45.

Grossbaum, M. F., & Bates, G. W. (2002). Correlates of psychological well-being at midlife: The role of generativity, agency and communion, and narrative themes. *International Journal of Behavioral Development, 26,* 120–127.

Grossman, A. H. (2006). Physical and mental health of older lesbian, gay, and bisexual adults. In D. Kimmel, T. Rose, & S. David (Eds.), *Lesbian, gay, bisexual, and transgender aging* (pp. 53–69). New York: Columbia University Press.

Grossmann, K., Grossmann, K. E., Fremmer-Bombik, E., Kindler, H., Scheueuu-Englisch, H., & Zimmerman, P. (2002). The uniqueness of the child–father attachment relationship: Fathers' sensitive and challenging play as a pivotable variable in a 16-year longitudinal study. *Social Development, 11,* 307–331.

Grossmann, K., Grossmann, K. E., Kindler, H., & Zimmermann, P. (2008). A wider view of attachment and exploration: The influence of mothers and fathers on the development of psychological security from infancy to young adulthood. In J. Cassidy & P. R. Shaver (Eds.), *Handbook of attachment: Theory, research, and clinical applications* (2nd ed., pp. 880–905). New York: Guilford.

Grossmann, K., Grossmann, K. E., Spangler, G., Suess, G., & Unzner, L. (1985). Maternal sensitivity and newborns' orientation responses as related to quality of attachment in Northern Germany. In I. Bretherton & E. Waters (Eds.), Growing points of attachment theory and research. *Monographs of the Society for Research in Child Development, 50*(1–2, Serial No. 209).

Gruendel J., & Aber, J. L. (2007). Bridging the gap between research and child policy change: The role of strategic communications in policy advocacy. In J. L. Aber, S. J. Bishop-Josef, S. M. Jones, K. T. McLearn, & D. Phillips (Eds.), *Child development and social policy: Knowledge for action* (pp. 43–58). Washington, DC: American Psychological Association.

Gruenewald, D. A., & White, E. J. (2006). The illness experience of older adults near the end of life: A systematic review. *Anesthesiology Clinics of North America, 24,* 163–180.

Gruenewald, T. L., Karlamangla, A. S., Greendale, G. A., Singer, B. H., & Seeman, T. E. (2007). Feelings of mortality in older adults: The MacArthur Study of Successful Aging. *Journal of Gerontology, 62B,* P28–P37.

Gruenewald, T. L., Karlamangla, A. S., Greendale, G. A., Singer, B. H., & Seeman, T. E. (2009). Increased mortality risk in older adults with persistently low or declining feelings of usefulness to others. *Journal of Aging and Health, 21,* 398–425.

Grundy, E. (2005). Reciprocity in relationships: Socio-economic and health influences on intergenerational exchanges between Third Age parents and their adult children in Great Britain. *British Journal of Sociology, 56,* 233–255.

Grundy, E., & Henretta, J. C. (2006). Between elderly parents and adult children: A new look at the "sandwich generation." *Aging and Society, 26,* 707–722.

Grusec, J. E. (1988). *Social development: History, theory, and research.* New York: Springer.

Grusec, J. E. (2006). The development of moral behavior and conscience from a socialization perspective. In M. Killen & J. Smetana (Eds.), *Handbook of moral development* (pp. 243–265). Philadelphia: Erlbaum.

Grusec, J. E., & Goodnow, J. J. (1994). Impact of parental discipline methods on the child's internalization of values: A reconceptualization of current points of view. *Developmental Psychology, 30,* 4–19.

Guedes, G. Tsai, J. C., & Loewen, N. A. (2011). Glaucoma and aging. *Current Aging Science, 4,* 110–117.

Guerra, N. G., Graham, S., & Tolan, P. H. (2011). Raising healthy children: Translating child development research into practice. *Child Development, 82,* 7–16.

Guglielmi, R. S. (2008). Native language proficiency, English literacy, academic achievement, and occupational attainment in limited-English-proficient students: A latent growth modeling perspective. *Journal of Educational Psychology, 100,* 322–342.

Guignard, J.-H., & Lubart, T. (2006). Is it reasonable to be creative? In J. C. Kaufman & J. Baer (Eds.), *Creativity and reason in cognitive development* (pp. 269–281). New York: Cambridge University Press.

Guildner, S. H., Loeb, S., Morris, D., Penrod, J., Bramlett, M., Johnston, L., & Schlotzhauer, P. (2001). A comparison of life satisfaction and mood in nursing home residents and community-dwelling elders. *Archives of Psychiatric Nursing, 15,* 232–240.

Guilford, J. P. (1985). The structure-of-intellect model. In B. B. Wolman (Ed.), *Handbook of intelligence* (pp. 225–266). New York: Wiley.

Guiso, L., Mont, F., Sapienza, P., & Zingales, L. (2008). Culture, gender, and math. *Science, 320,* 1164–1165.

Gullone, E. (2000). The development of normal fear: A century of research. *Clinical Psychology Review, 20,* 429–451.

Gulotta, T. P. (2008). How theory influences treatment and prevention practice within the family. In T. P. Gulotta (Ed.), *Family influences on child behavior and development: Evidence-based prevention and treatment approaches* (pp. 1–20). New York: Routledge.

Gunnar, M. R., & Cheatham, C. L. (2003). Brain and behavior interfaces: Stress and the developing brain. *Infant Mental Health Journal, 24,* 195–211.

Gunnar, M. R., Morison, S. J., Chisholm, K., & Schuder, M. (2001). Salivary cortisol levels in children adopted from Romanian orphanages. *Development and Psychopathology, 13,* 611–628.

Gunnarsdottir, I., Schack-Nielsen, L., Michaelson, K. F., Sørensen, T. I., & Thorsdottir, I. (2010). Infant weight gain, duration of exclusive breast-feeding, and childhood BMI—two similar follow-up cohorts. *Public Health Nutrition, 13,* 201–207.

Gunnoe, M. L., & Mariner, C. L. (1997). Toward a developmental-contextual model of the effects of parental spanking on children's aggression. *Archives of Pediatrics and Adolescent Medicine, 151,* 768–775.

Gunstad, J., Spitznagel, M. B., Luyster, F., Cohen, R. A., & Paul, R. H. (2007). Handedness and cognition across the healthy lifespan. *International Journal of Neuroscience, 117,* 477–485.

Gure, A., Ucanok, Z., & Sayil, M. (2006). The associations among perceived pubertal timing, parental relations and self-perception in Turkish adolescents. *Journal of Youth and Adolescence, 35,* 541–550.

Gureje, O., Ogunniyi, A., Baiyewu, O., Price, B., Unverzagt, F. W., & Evans, R. M. (2006). APOE epsilon-4 is not associated with Alzheimer's disease in elderly Nigerians. *Annals of Neurology, 59,* 182–185.

Gustafson, G. E., Green, J. A., & Cleland, J. W. (1994). Robustness of individual identity in the cries of human infants. *Developmental Psychobiology, 27,* 1–9.

Gustafson, G. E., Wood, R. M., & Green, J. A. (2000). Can we hear the causes of infants' crying? In R. G. Barr & B. Hopkins (Eds.), *Crying as a sign, a symptom, and a signal: Clinical, emotional, and developmental aspects of infant and toddler crying* (pp. 8–22). New York: Cambridge University Press.

Guterman, N. B., Lee, S. J., Taylor, C. A., & Rathouz, P. J. (2009). Parental perceptions of neighborhood processes, stress, personal control, and risk for physical child abuse and neglect. *Child Abuse and Neglect, 33,* 897–906.

Gutman, L. M. (2006). How student and parent goal orientations and classroom goal structures influence the math achievement of African Americans during the high school transition. *Contemporary Educational Psychology, 31,* 44–63.

Gutman, L. M., & Midgley, C. (2000). The role of protective factors in supporting the academic achievement of poor African-American students during the middle school transition. *Journal of Youth and Adolescence, 29,* 223–248.

Gutman, L. M., Sameroff, A. J., & Cole, R. (2003). Academic growth curve trajectories from 1st grade to 12th grade: Effects of multiple social risk factors and preschool child factors. *Developmental Psychology, 39,* 777–790.

Gutmann, D. (1977). The cross-cultural perspective: Notes toward a comparative psychology of aging. In J. E. Birren & K. W. Schaie (Eds.), *Handbook of the psychology of aging* (pp. 302–326). New York: Van Nostrand Reinhold.

Gutmann, D. L., & Huyck, M. H. (1994). Development and pathology in post-parental men: A community study. In E. Thompson, Jr. (Ed.), *Older men's lives* (pp. 65–84). Thousand Oaks, CA: Sage.

Gutteling, B. M., de Weerth, C., Zandbelt, N., Mulder, E. J. H., Visser, G. H. A., & Buitelaar, J. K. (2006). Does maternal prenatal stress adversely affect the child's learning and memory at age six? *Journal of Abnormal Child Psychology, 34,* 789–798.

Guttuso, T., Jr. (2012). Effective and clinically meaningful non-hormonal hot flash therapies. *Maturitas, 72,* 6–12.

Gwiazda, J., & Birch, E. E. (2001). Perceptual development: Vision. In E. B. Goldstein (Ed.), *Blackwell handbook of perception* (pp. 636–668). Oxford, UK: Blackwell.

H

Haentjens, P., Magaziner, J., Colón-Emeric, C. S., Vanderschueren, D., Milisen, K., Velkeniers, B., et al. (2010). Meta-analysis: Excess mortality after hip fracture among older women and men. *Annals of Internal Medicine, 16,* 380–390.

Hagberg, B., & Samuelsson, G. (2008). Survival after 100 years of age: A multivariate model of exceptional survival in Swedish centenarians. *Journal of Gerontology, 63A,* 1219–1226.

Hagerman, R. J., Berry-Kravis, E., Kaufmann, W. E., Ono, M. Y., Tartaglia, N., & Lachiewicz, A. (2009). Advances in the treatment of fragile X syndrome. *Pediatrics, 123,* 378–390.

Hahn, S., & Chitty, L. S. (2008). Noninvasive prenatal diagnosis: Current practice and future perspectives. *Current Opinion in Obstetrics and Gynecology, 20,* 146–151.

Haidt, J. (2001). The emotional dog and its rational tail: A social intuitionist approach to moral judgment. *Psychological Review, 108,* 814–834.

Haidt, J., & Kesebir, S. (2010). Morality. In S. T. Fiske & D. Gilbert (Eds.), *Handbook of social psychology* (5th ed., pp. 797–832). Hoboken, NJ: Wiley.

Haight, W. L., & Miller, P. J. (1993). *Pretending at home: Early development in a sociocultural context.* Albany, NY: State University of New York Press.

Haines, C. J., Xing, S. M., Park, K. H., Holinka, C. F., & Ausmanas, M. K. (2005). Prevalence of menopausal symptoms in different ethnic groups of Asian women and responsiveness to therapy with three doses of conjugated estrogens/medroxyprogesterone acetate: The pan-Asian menopause (PAM) study. *Maturitas, 52,* 264–276.

Hainline, L. (1998). The development of basic visual abilities. In A. Slater (Ed.), *Perceptual development: Visual, auditory, and speech perception in infancy* (pp. 37–44). Hove, UK: Psychology Press.

Hainsworth, J., & Barlow, J. (2001). Volunteers' experiences of becoming arthritis self-management lay leaders: "It's almost as if I've stopped aging and started to get younger!" *Arthritis and Rheumatism, 45,* 378–383.

Hakman, M., & Sullivan, M. (2009). The effect of task and maternal verbosity on compliance in toddlers. *Infant and Child Development, 18,* 195–205.

Hakuta, K., Bialystok, E., & Wiley, E. (2003). Critical evidence: A test of the critical-period hypothesis for second-language acquisitions. *Psychological Science, 14,* 31–38.

Halberstadt, A., Denham, S. A., & Dunsmore, J. (2001). Affective social competence. *Social Development, 10,* 79–119.

Hale, C. M., & Tager-Flusberg, H. (2003). The influence of language on theory of mind: A training study. *Developmental Science, 6,* 346–359.

Hale, S., Rose, N. S., Myerson, J., Strube, M. J., Sommers, M., Tye-Murray, N., et al. (2011). The structure of working memory abilities across the adult life span. *Psychology and Aging, 26,* 92–110.

Hales, C. N., & Ozanne, S. E. (2003). The dangerous road of catch-up growth. *Journal of Physiology, 547,* 5–10.

Haley, W. E. (2013). Family caregiving at end-of-life: Current status and future directions. In R. C. Talley & R. J. V. Montgomery (Eds.), *Caregiving across the lifespan: Research, practice, and policy* (pp. 157–175). New York: Springer.

Halfon, N., & McLearn, K. T. (2002). Families with children under 3: What we know and implications for results and policy. In N. Halfon & K. T. McLearn (Eds.), *Child rearing in America: Challenges facing parents with young children* (pp. 367–412). New York: Cambridge University Press.

Halford, G. S. (2005). Development of thinking. In K. J. Holyoak & R. G. Morrison (Eds.), *The Cambridge handbook of thinking and reasoning* (pp. 529–558). New York: Cambridge University Press.

Halford, G. S., & Andrews, G. (2006). Reasoning and problem solving. In D. Kuhn & R. Siegler (Eds.), *Handbook of child psychology: Vol. 2. Cognition, perception, and language* (6th ed., pp. 557–608). Hoboken, NJ: Wiley.

Halgunseth, L. C., Ispa, J. M., & Rudy, D. (2006). Parental control in Latino families: An integrated review of the literature. *Child Development, 77,* 1282–1297.

Hall, C. B., Derby, C., LeValley, A., Katz, M. J., Verghese, J., & Lipton, R. B. (2007). Education delays accelerated decline on a memory test in persons who develop dementia. *Neurology, 69,* 1657–1664.

Hall, C. B., Lipton, R. B., Sliwinski, M., Katz, M. J., Derby, C. A., & Verghese, J. (2009). Cognitive activities delay onset of memory decline in persons who develop dementia. *Neurology, 73,* 356–361.

Hall, D. G., & Graham, S. A. (1999). Lexical form class information guides word-to-object mapping in preschoolers. *Child Development, 70,* 78–91.

Hall, G. S. (1904). *Adolescence.* New York: Appleton.

Hall, J. G. (2003). Twinning. *Lancet, 362,* 735–743.

Hall, K., Murrell, J., Ogunniyi, A., Deeg, M., Baiyewu, O., & Gao, S. (2006). Cholesterol, APOE genotype, and Alzheimer disease: An epidemiologic study of Nigerian Yoruba. *Neurology, 66,* 223–227.

Halle, T. G. (2003). Emotional development and well-being. In M. H. Bornstein, L. Davidson, C. L. M. Keyes, K. A. Moore, & the Center for Child Well-Being (Eds.), *Well-being: Positive development across the life course* (pp. 125–138). Mahwah, NJ: Erlbaum.

Haller, J. (2005). Vitamins and brain function. In H. R. Lieberman, R. B. Kanarek, & C. Prasad (2005). *Nutritional neuroscience* (pp. 207–233). Philadelphia: Taylor & Francis.

Hallinan, M. T., & Kubitschek, W. N. (1999). Curriculum differentiation and high school achievement. *Social Psychology of Education, 3,* 41–62.

Halpern, C. T., Udry, J. R., & Suchindran, C. (1997). Testosterone predicts initiation of coitus in adolescent females. *Psychosomatic Medicine, 59,* 161–171.

Halpern, D. F. (2005a). How time-flexible work policies can reduce stress, improve health, and save money. *Stress and Health, 21,* 157–168.

Halpern, D. F. (2005b). Psychology at the intersection of work and family: Recommendations for employers, working families, and policymakers. *American Psychologist, 60,* 397–409.

Halpern, D. F., Benbow, C. P., Geary, D. C., Gur, R. C., Hyde, J. S., & Gernsbacher, M. A. (2007). The science of sex differences in science and mathematics. *Psychological Science in the Public Interest, 8,* 1–51.

Halpern, D. F., & Collaer, M. L. (2005). Sex differences in visuospatial abilities: More than meets the eye. In P. Shah & A. Miyake (Eds.), *Handbook of visuospatial thinking* (pp. 170–212). New York: Cambridge University Press.

Halpern-Felsher, B. L., Biehl, M., Kropp, R. Y., & Rubinstein, M. L. (2004). Perceived risks and benefits of smoking: Differences among adolescents with different smoking experiences and intentions. *Preventive Medicine, 39,* 559–567.

Haltzman, S., Holstein, N., & Moss, S. B. (2007). Men, marriage, and divorce. In J. E. Grant & M. N. Potenza (Eds.), *Textbook of men's mental health* (pp. 283–305). Washington, DC: American Psychiatric Publishing.

Hamberger, L. K., Lohr, J. M., Parker, L. M., & Witte, T. (2009). Treatment approaches for men who batter their partners. In C. Mitchell & D. Anglin (Eds.), *Intimate partner violence: A health-based perspective* (pp. 459–471). New York: Oxford University Press.

Hamer, D. H., Hu, S., Magnuson, V. L., Hu, N., & Pattatucci, A. M. L. (1993). A linkage between DNA markers on the X chromosome and male sexual orientation. *Science, 261,* 321–327.

Hamilton, S. F., & Hamilton, M. A. (2000). Research, intervention, and social change: Improving adolescents' career opportunities. In L. J. Crockett & R. K. Silbereisen (Eds.), *Negotiating adolescence in times of social change* (pp. 267–283). New York: Cambridge University Press.

Hammes, B., & Laitman, C. J. (2003). Diethylstilbestrol (DES) update: Recommendations for the identification and management of DES-exposed individuals. *Journal of Midwifery and Women's Health, 48,* 19–29.

Hampton, K. N., Goulet, L. S., Rainie, L., & Purcell, K. (2011). *Social networking sites and our lives.* Washington, DC: Pew Research Center Internet & American Life Project. Retrieved from www.pewinternet.org/Reports/2011/Technology-and-social-networks.aspx

Han, W.-J., & Waldfogel, J. (2003). Parental leave: The impact of recent legislation on parents' leave taking. *Demography, 40,* 191–200.

Hane, A. A., Cheah, C., Rubin, K. H., & Fox, N. A. (2008). The role of maternal behavior in the relation between shyness and social reticence in early childhood and social withdrawal in middle childhood. *Social Development, 17,* 795–811.

Hanioka, T., Ojima, M., Tanaka, K., & Yamamoto, M. (2011). Does secondhand smoke affect the development of dental caries in children? A systematic review. *International Journal of Environmental Research and Public Health, 8,* 1503–1509.

Hankin, B. L., & Abela, J. R. Z. (2005). Depression from childhood through adolescence and adulthood: A developmental vulnerability and stress perspective. In B. L. Hankin & J. R. Z. Abela (Eds.), *Development of psychopathology: A vulnerability-stress perspective* (pp. 245–288). Thousand Oaks, CA: Sage.

Hankin, B. L., Stone, L., & Wright, P. A. (2010). Co-rumination, interpersonal stress generation, and internalizing symptoms: Accumulating effects and transactional influences in a multiwave study of adolescents. *Development and Psychopathology, 22,* 217–235.

Hannon, E. E., & Johnson, S. P. (2004). Infants use meter to categorize rhythms and melodies: Implications for musical structure learning. *Cognitive Psychology, 50,* 354–377.

Hannon, E. E., & Trehub, S. E. (2005a). Metrical categories in infancy and adulthood. *Psychological Science, 16,* 48–55.

Hannon, E. E., & Trehub, S. E. (2005b). Tuning in to musical rhythms: Infants learn more readily than adults. *Proceedings of the National Academy of Sciences, 102,* 12639–12643.

Hannon, T. S., Rao, G., & Arslanian, S. A. (2005). Childhood obesity and type 2 diabetes mellitus. *Pediatrics, 116,* 473–480.

Hans, S. L., & Jeremy, R. J. (2001). Postneonatal mental and motor development of infants exposed in utero to opiate drugs. *Infant Mental Health Journal, 22,* 300–315.

Hansell, N. K., Wright, M. J., Geffen, G. M., Geffen, L. B., Smith, G. A., & Martin, N. G. (2001). Genetic influence on ERP slow wave measures of working memory. *Behavioral Genetics, 31,* 603–614.

Hansen, M., Janssen, I., Schiff, A., Zee, P. C., & Dubocovich, M. L. (2005). The impact of school daily schedule on adolescent sleep. *Pediatrics, 115,* 1555–1561.

Hansen, M. B., & Markman, E. M. (2009). Children's use of mutual exclusivity to learn labels for parts of objects. *Developmental Psychology, 45,* 592–596.

Hansson, R. O., & Stroebe, M. S. (2007). The dual process model of coping with bereavement and development of an integrative risk factor framework. In R. O. Hansson & M. S. Stroebe (Eds.), *Bereavement in late life: Coping, adaptation, and developmental influences* (pp. 41–60). Washington, DC: American Psychological Association.

Hao, L., & Woo, H. S. (2012). Distinct trajectories in the transition to adulthood: Are children of immigrants advantaged? *Child Development, 83,* 1623–1639.

Happé, F., & Frith, U. (2006). The weak coherence account: Detail-focused cognitive style in autism spectrum disorders. *Journal of Autism and Developmental Disorders, 1,* 1–21.

Harachi, T. W., Fleming, C. B., White, H. R., Ensminger, M. E., Abbott, R. D., Catalano, R. F., & Haggerty, K. P. (2006). Aggressive behavior among girls and boys during middle childhood: Predictors and sequelae of trajectory group membership. *Aggressive Behavior, 32,* 279–293.

Harden, K. Paige, & Tucker-Drob, E. M. (2011). Individual differences in the development of sensation seeking and impulsivity during adolescence: Further evidence for a dual systems model. *Developmental Psychology, 47,* 739–746.

Hardy, S. A., & Carlo, G. (2005). Religiosity and prosocial behaviours in adolescence: The mediating role of prosocial values. *Journal of Moral Education, 34,* 231–249.

Hardy, S. A., & Carlo, G. (2011). Moral identity: What is it, how does it develop, and is it linked to moral action? *Child Development Perspectives, 5,* 212–218.

Hardy, S. A., Pratt, M. W., Pancer, S. M., Olsen, J. A., & Lawford, H. L. (2011). Community and religious involvement as contexts of identity change across late adolescence and emerging adulthood. *International Journal of Behavioral Development, 35,* 125–135.

Harley, B., & Jean, G. (1999). Vocabulary skills of French immersion students in their second language. *Zeitschrift für Interkulturellen Fremdsprachenunterricht, 4*(2). Retrieved from www.ualberta.ca

Harley, K., & Reese, E. (1999). Origins of autobiographical memory. *Developmental Psychology, 35,* 1338–1348.

Harlow, H. F., & Zimmerman, R. (1959). Affectional responses in the infant monkey. *Science, 130,* 421–432.

Harman, S. M., & Blackman, M. R. (2004). Use of growth hormone for prevention or treatment of effects of aging. *Journal of Gerontology, 59,* 652–658.

Harris, G. (1997). Development of taste perception and appetite regulation. In G. Bremner, A. Slater, & G. Butterworth (Eds.), *Infant development: Recent advances* (pp. 9–30). East Sussex, UK: Erlbaum.

Harris, J. R. (1998). *The nurture assumption: Why children turn out the way they do.* New York: Free Press.

Harris, P. L. (2011). Death in Spain, Madagascar, and beyond. In V. Talwar, P. L. Harris, & M. Schleifer (Eds.), *Children's understanding of death* (pp. 19–40). New York: Cambridge University Press.

Harris, R. C., Robinson, J. B., Chang, F., & Burns, B. M. (2007). Characterizing preschool children's attention regulation in parent–child interactions: The roles of effortful control and motivation. *Journal of Applied Developmental Psychology, 28,* 25–39.

Harris, Y. R., & Graham, J. A. (2007). *The African American child: Development and challenges.* New York: Springer.

Harris Interactive. (2011). *Large majorities support doctor-assisted suicide for terminally ill patients in great pain.* Retrieved from www.harrisinteractive.com/NewsRoom/HarrisPolls/tabid/447/mid/1508/articleId/677/ctl/ReadCustom%20Default/Default.aspx

Hart, B., & Risley, T. R. (1995). *Meaningful differences in the everyday experience of young American children.* Baltimore: Paul H. Brookes.

Hart, C. H., Burts, D. C., Durland, M. A., Charlesworth, R., DeWolf, M., & Fleege, P. O. (1998). Stress behaviors and activity type participation of preschoolers in more and less developmentally appropriate classrooms: SES and sex differences. *Journal of Research in Childhood Education, 13,* 176–196.

Hart, C. H., Newell, L. D., & Olsen, S. F. (2003). Parenting skills and social–communicative competence in childhood. In J. O. Greene & B. R. Burleson (Eds.), *Handbook of communication and social interaction skills* (pp. 753–797). Mahwah, NJ: Erlbaum.

Hart, C. H., Yang, C., Charlesworth, R., & Burts, D. C. (2003, April). *Kindergarten teaching practices: Associations with later child academic and social/ emotional adjustment to school.* Paper presented at the biennial meeting of the Society for Research in Child Development, Tampa, FL.

Hart, C. H., Yang, C., Nelson, L. J., Robinson, C. C., Olsen, J. A., Nelson, D. A., Porter, C. L., Jin, S., Olsen, S. F., & Wu, P. (2000). Peer acceptance in early childhood and subtypes of socially withdrawn behavior in China, Russia, and the United States. *International Journal of Behavioral Development, 24,* 73–81.

Hart, D., Atkins, R., & Donnelly, T. M. (2006). Community service and moral development. In M. Killen & J. G. Smetana (Eds.), *Handbook of moral development* (pp. 633–656). Philadelphia: Erlbaum.

Hart, D., Atkins, R., & Matsuba, M. K. (2008). The association of neighborhood poverty with personality change in childhood. *Journal of Personality and Social Psychology, 44,* 1048–1061.

Hart, D., Donnelly, T. M., Youniss, J., & Atkins, R. (2007). High school community service as a predictor of adult voting and volunteering. *American Educational Research Journal, 44,* 197–219.

Hart, D., & Fegley, S. (1995). Prosocial behavior and caring in adolescence: Relations to self-understanding and social judgment. *Child Development, 66,* 1346–1359.

Hart, H., & Rubia, K. (2012). Neuroimaging of child abuse: A review. *Frontiers in Human Neuroscience, 6,* 52.

Hart, H. M., McAdams, D. P., Hirsch, B. J., & Bauer, J. J. (2001). Generativity and social involvement among African Americans and white adults. *Journal of Research in Personality, 35,* 208–230.

Harter, S. (1998). The development of self-representations. In N. Eisenberg (Ed.), *Handbook of child psychology: Vol. 3. Social, emotional, and personality development* (5th ed., pp. 553–618). New York: Wiley.

Harter, S. (1999). *The construction of self: A developmental perspective.* New York: Guilford.

Harter, S. (2003). The development of self-representations during childhood and adolescence. In M. R. Leary & J. P. Tangney (Eds.), *Handbook of self and identity* (pp. 610–642). New York: Guilford.

Harter, S. (2006). The self. In N. Eisenberg (Ed.), *Handbook of child psychology: Vol. 3. Social, emotional, and personality development* (6th ed., pp. 505–570). Hoboken, NJ: Wiley.

Harter, S., & Whitesell, N. (1989). Developmental changes in children's understanding of simple, multiple, and blended emotion concepts. In C. Saarni & P. Harris (Eds.), *Children's understanding of emotion* (pp. 81–116). Cambridge, UK: Cambridge University Press.

Hartley, A. (2006). Changing role of the speed of processing construct. In J. E. Birren & K. W. Schaie (Eds.), *Handbook of the psychology of aging* (6th ed., pp. 183–207). Burlington, MA: Academic Press.

Hartman, M., & Warren, L. H. (2005). Explaining age differences in temporal working memory. *Psychology and Aging, 20,* 645–656.

Hartshorn, K., Rovee-Collier, C., Gerhardstein, P., Bhatt, R. S., Wondoloski, T. L., Klein, P., Gilch, J., Wurtzel, N., & Campos-de-Carvalho, M. (1998). The ontogeny of long-term memory over the first year-and-a-half of life. *Developmental Psychobiology, 32,* 69–89.

Hartup, W. W. (2006). Relationships in early and middle childhood. In A. L. Vangelisti & D. Perlman (Eds.), *Cambridge handbook of personal relationships* (pp. 177–190). New York: Cambridge University Press.

Hartup, W. W., & Abecassis, M. (2004). Friends and enemies. In P. K. Smith & C. H. Hart (Eds.), *Blackwell handbook of childhood social development* (pp. 285–306). Malden, MA: Blackwell.

Hartup, W. W., & Stevens, N. (1999). Friendships and adaptation across the life span. *Current Directions in Psychological Science, 8,* 76–79.

Harvey, M. W. (2001). Vocational-technical education: A logical approach to dropout prevention for secondary special education. *Preventing School Failure, 45,* 108–113.

Harwood, J. (2001). Comparing grandchildren's and grandparents' stake in their relationship. *International Journal of Aging and Human Development, 53,* 195–210.

Harwood, M. D., & Farrar, M. J. (2006). Conflicting emotions: The connection between affective perspective taking and theory of mind. *British Journal of Developmental Psychology, 24,* 401–418.

Harwood, R., Leyendecker, B., Carlson, V., Asencio, M., & Miller, A. (2002). Parenting among Latino families in the U.S. In M. H. Bornstein (Ed.), *Handbook of parenting: Vol. 4. Social conditions and applied parenting* (4th ed., pp. 21–46). Mahwah, NJ: Erlbaum.

Hasebe, Y., Nucci, L., & Nucci, M. S. (2004). Parental control of the personal domain and adolescent symptoms of psychopathology: A cross-national study in the United States and Japan. *Child Development, 75,* 815–828.

Hasher, L., Lustig, C., & Zacks, R. T. (2007). Inhibitory mechanisms and the control of attention. In A. R. A. Conway, C. Jarrold, M. Kane, A. Miyake, & J. N. Towse (Eds.), *Variation in working memory* (pp. 227–249). New York: Oxford University Press.

Hastings, E. C., & West, R. L. (2009). The relative success of a self-help and a group-based memory training program for older adults. *Psychology and Aging, 24,* 586–594.

Hastrup, B. (2007). Healthy aging in Denmark? In M. Robinson, W. Novelli, C. Pearson, & L. Norris (Eds.), *Global health and global aging* (pp. 71–84). San Francisco: Jossey-Bass.

Hatch, L. R., & Bulcroft, K. (2004). Does long-term marriage bring less frequent disagreements? *Journal of Family Issues, 25,* 465–495.

Hatfield, E., Rapson, R. L., & Martel, L. D. (2007). Passionate love and sexual desire. In S. Kitayama & D. Cohen (Eds.), *Handbook of cultural psychology* (pp. 760–779). New York: Guilford.

Hatfield, E., & Sprecher, S. (1995). Men's and women's mate preferences in the United States, Russia, and Japan. *Journal of Cross-Cultural Psychology, 26,* 728–750.

Hau, K.-T., & Ho, I. T. (2010). Chinese students' motivation and achievement. In M. H. Bond (Ed.), *Oxford handbook of Chinese psychology* (pp. 187–204). New York: Oxford University Press.

Hauf, P., Aschersleben, G., & Prinz, W. (2007). Baby do–baby see! How action production influences action perception in infants. *Cognitive Development, 22,* 16–32.

Haukkala, A., Konttinen, H., Laatikainen, T., Kawachi, I., & Uutela, A. (2010). Hostility, anger control, and anger expression as predictors of cardiovascular disease. *Psychosomatic Medicine, 72,* 556–562.

Hausfather, A., Toharia, A., LaRoche, C., & Engelsmann, F. (1997). Effects of age of entry, daycare quality, and family characteristics on preschool behavior. *Journal of Child Psychology and Psychiatry, 38,* 441–448.

Hawkins, J. N. (1994). Issues of motivation in Asian education. In H. F. O'Neil, Jr., & M. Drillings (Eds.), *Motivation: Theory and research* (pp. 101–115). Hillsdale, NJ: Erlbaum.

Hawkley, L. C., & Cacioppo, J. T. (2004). Stress and the aging immune system. *Brain, Behavior and Immunity, 18,* 114–119.

Haworth, C. M. A., Wright, M. J., Luciano, M., Martin, N. G., de Geus, E. J. C., van Beijsterveldt, C. E. M., et al. (2010). The heritability of general cognitive ability increases linearly from childhood to young adulthood. *Molecular Psychiatry, 15,* 1112–1120.

Haws, R. A., Yakoob, M. Y., Soomro, T., Menezes, E. V., Darmstadt, G. L., & Bhutta, Z. A. (2009). Reducing stillbirths: Screening and monitoring during pregnancy and labour. *BMC Pregnancy and Childbirth, 9*(Suppl. S1).

Hawton, A., Green, C., Dickens, A. P., Richards, S. H., Taylor, R. S., & Edwards, R. (2011). The impact of social isolation on the health status and health-related quality of life of older people. *Quality of Life Research, 20,* 57–67.

Hay, D. F., Pawlby, S., Waters, C. S., Perra, O., & Sharp, D. (2010). Mothers' antenatal depression and their children's antisocial outcomes. *Child Development, 81,* 149–165.

Hay, E. L., & Diehl, M. (2010). Reactivity to daily stressors in adulthood: The importance of stressor type in characterizing risk factors. *Psychology and Aging, 25,* 118–131.

Hay, J. F., & Jacoby, L. L. (1999). Separating habit and recollection in young and older adults: Effects of elaborative processing and distinctiveness. *Psychology and Aging, 14,* 122–134.

Hay, P., & Bacaltchuk, J. (2004). Bulimia nervosa. *Clinical Evidence, 12,* 1326–1347.

Haycock, P. C. (2009). Fetal alcohol spectrum disorders: The epigenetic perspective. *Biology of Reproduction, 81,* 607–617.

Hayflick, L. (1994). *How and why we age.* New York: Ballantine.

Hayflick, L. (1998). How and why we age. *Experimental Gerontology, 33,* 639–653.

Hayne, H., Herbert, J., & Simcock, G. (2003). Imitation from television by 24- and 30-month-olds. *Developmental Science, 6,* 254–261.

Hayne, H., Rovee-Collier, C., & Perris, E. E. (1987). Categorization and memory retrieval by three-month-olds. *Child Development, 58,* 750–767.

Hayslip, B., Jr., Emick, M. A., Henderson, C. E., & Elias, K. (2002). Temporal variations in the experience of custodial grandparenting: A short-term longitudinal study. *Journal of Applied Gerontology, 21,* 139–156.

Hayslip, B., Jr., & Kaminski, P. L. (2005). Grandparents raising their grandchildren. *Marriage and Family Review, 37,* 147–169.

Haywood, H. C., & Lidz, C. S. (2007). *Dynamic assessment in practice.* New York: Cambridge University Press.

Haywood, K. M., & Getchell, N. (2005). *Life span motor development* (4th ed.). Champaign, IL: Human Kinetics.

Haywood, K. M., & Getchell, N. (2009). *Life span motor development* (5th ed.). Champaign, IL: Human Kinetics.

Hazen, N. L., McFarland, L., Jacobvitz, D., & Boyd-Soisson, E. (2010). Fathers' frightening behaviours and sensitivity with infants: Relations with fathers' attachment representations, father–infant attachment, and children's later outcomes. *Early Child Development and Care, 180,* 51–69.

Head Start Bureau. (2010). *Head Start Program fact sheet.* Retrieved from eclkc.ohs.acf.hhs.gov/hslc/mr/factsheets/fHeadStartProgr.htm

Healthy Families America. (2011). *Healthy Families America FAQ.* Retrieved from www.healthyfamiliesamerica.org/about_us/faq.shtml

Heath, S. B. (1990). The children of Trackton's children: Spoken and written in social change. In J. Stigler, G. Herdt, & R. A. Shweder (Eds.), *Cultural psychology: Essays on comparative human development* (pp. 496–519). New York: Cambridge University Press.

Heaven, P. C. L., & Ciarrochi, J. (2008). Parental styles, conscientiousness, and academic performance in high school: A three-wave longitudinal study. *Personality and Social Psychology Bulletin, 34,* 451–461.

Hebblethwaite, S., & Norris, J. (2011). Expressions of generativity through family leisure: Experiences of grandparents and adult grandchildren. *Family Relations, 60,* 121–133.

Hebert, K., Moore, H., & Rooney, J. (2011). The nurse advocate in end-of-life care. *Ochsner Journal, 11,* 325–329.

Heckhausen, J., Wrosch, C., & Schultz, R. (2010). A motivational theory of life-span development. *Psychological Review, 117,* 32–60.

Heckman, J. J., Seong, H. M., Pinto, R., Savelyev, P., & Yavitz, A. (2010). A new cost–benefit and rate of return for the Perry Preschool Program: A summary. In A. J. Reynolds, A. J. Rolnick, M. M. Englund, & J. Temple (Eds.), *Childhood programs and practices in the first decade of life: A human capital integration* (pp. 199–213). New York: Cambridge University Press.

Hedberg, K., Hopkins, D., Leman, R., & Kohn, M. (2009). The 10-year experience of Oregon's Death with Dignity Act: 1998–2007. *Journal of Clinical Ethics, 20,* 124–132.

Hedge, J. W., Borman, W. C., & Lammlein, S. E. (2006). *The aging workforce: Realities, myths, and* implications for organizations. Washington, DC: American Psychological Association.

Hediger, M. L., Overpeck, M. D., Ruan, W. J., & Troendle, J. F. (2002). Birthweight and gestational age effects on motor and social development. *Paediatric and Perinatal Epidemiology, 16,* 33–46.

Heil, M., Kavsek, Rolke, B., Best, C., & Jansen, P. (2011). Mental rotation in female fraternal twins: Evidence for intrauterine hormone transfer? *Biological Psychology, 86,* 90–93.

Heilbrun, K., Lee, R., & Cottle, C. C. (2005). Risk factors and intervention outcomes: Meta-analyses of juvenile offending. In K. Heilbrun, N. E. S. Goldstein, & R. E. Redding (Eds.), *Juvenile delinquency: Prevention, assessment, and intervention* (pp. 111–133). New York: Oxford University Press.

Heiman, N., Stallings, M. C., Hofer, S. M., & Hewitt, J. K. (2003). Investigating age differences in the genetic and environmental structure of the tridimensional personality questionnaire in later adulthood. *Behavior Genetics, 33,* 171–180.

Heino, R., Ellison, N., & Gibbs, J. (2010). Relationshopping: Investigating the market metaphor in online dating. *Journal of Social and Personal Relationships, 27,* 427–447.

Helburn, S. W. (Ed.). (1995). *Cost, quality and child outcomes in child care centers.* Denver: University of Colorado.

Hellemans, K. G., Sliwowska, J. H., Verma, P., & Weinberg, J. (2010). Prenatal alcohol exposure: Fetal programming and later life vulnerability to stress, expression and anxiety disorders. *Neuroscience and Biobehavioral Reviews, 34,* 791–807.

Helm, H. M., Hays, J. C., Flint, E. P., Koenig, H. G., & Blazer, D. G. (2000). Does private religious activity prolong survival? A six-year follow-up study of 3,851 older adults. *Journal of Gerontology, 55A,* M400–M405.

Helson, R. (1992). Women's difficult times and the rewriting of the life story. *Psychology of Women Quarterly, 16,* 331–347.

Helson, R., Jones, C. J., & Kwan, V. S. Y. (2002). Personality change over 40 years of adulthood: Hierarchical linear modeling analyses of two longitudinal samples. *Journal of Personality and Social Psychology, 83,* 752–766.

Helson, R., & Picano, J. (1990). Is the traditional role bad for women? *Journal of Personality and Social Psychology, 59,* 311–320.

Helson, R., Soto, C. J., & Cate, R. A. (2006). From young adulthood through the middle ages. In D. K. Mroczek & T. D. Little (Eds.), *Handbook of personality development* (pp. 337–352). Mahwah, NJ: Erlbaum.

Heltzner, E. P., Cauley, J. A., Pratt, S. R., Wisniewski, S. R., Zmuda, J. M., & Talbott, E. O. (2005). Race and sex differences in age-related hearing loss: The health, aging and body composition study. *Journal of the American Geriatrics Society, 53,* 2119–2127.

Helwig, C. C. (2006). Rights, civil liberties, and democracy across cultures. In M. Killen & J. G. Smetana (Eds.), *Handbook of moral development* (pp. 185–210). Philadelphia: Erlbaum.

Helwig, C. C., & Jasiobedzka, U. (2001). The relation between law and morality: Children's reasoning about socially beneficial and unjust laws. *Child Development, 72,* 1382–1393.

Helwig, C. C., & Kim, S. (1999). Children's evaluations of decision-making procedures in peer, family, and school contexts. *Child Development, 70,* 502–512.

Helwig, C. C., & Prencipe, A. (1999). Children's judgments of flags and flag-burning. *Child Development, 70,* 132–143.

Helwig, C. C., & Turiel, E. (2004). Children's social and moral reasoning. In P. K. Smith & C. H. Hart (Eds.), *Blackwell handbook of childhood social development* (pp. 476–490). Malden, MA: Blackwell.

Helwig, C. C., Zelazo, P. D., & Wilson, M. (2001). Children's judgments of psychological harm in normal and canonical situations. *Child Development, 72,* 66–81.

Henggeler, S. W., Schoenwald, S. K., Bourduin, C. M., Rowland, M. D., & Cunningham, P. B. (2009). *Multisystemic therapy for antisocial behavior in children and adolescents* (2nd ed.). New York: Guilford.

Hendrick, S. S., & Hendrick, C. (2002). Love. In C. R. Snyder & S. J. Lopez (Eds.), *Handbook of positive psychology* (pp. 472–484). New York: Oxford University Press.

Hendricks, J., & Cutler, S. J. (2004). Volunteerism and socioemotional selectivity in later life. *Journal of Gerontology, 59B,* S251–S257.

Hendrie, H. H. (2001). Exploration of environmental and genetic risk factors for Alzheimer's disease: The value of cross-cultural studies. *Current Directions in Psychological Science, 10,* 98–101.

Hendry, L. B., & Kloep, M. (2007). Conceptualizing emerging adulthood: Inspecting the emperor's new clothes? *Child Development Perspectives, 1,* 74–79.

Hendry, L. B., & Kloep, M. (2010). How universal is emerging adulthood? An empirical example. *Journal of Youth Studies, 13,* 169–179.

Hendry, M., Paserfield, D., Lewis, R., Carter, B., Hodgson, D., & Wilinson, C. (2012). Why do we want the right to die? A systematic review of the international literature on the views of patients, carers and the public on assisted dying. *Palliative Medicine, 27,* 13–26.

Henig, R. M., & Henig, S. (2012). *Twenty something: Why do young adults seem stuck?* New York: Hudson Street Press.

Henning, K., Jones, A. R., & Holdford, R. (2005). Attributions of blame among male and female domestic violence offenders. *Journal of Family Violence, 20,* 131–139.

Henrich, C. C., Brookmeyer, K. A., Shrier, L. A., & Shahar, G. (2006). Supportive relationships and sexual risk behavior in adolescence: An ecological-transactional approach. *Journal of Pediatric Psychology, 31,* 286–297.

Henrich, C. C., Kuperminc, G. P., Sack, A., Blatt, S. J., & Leadbeater, B. J. (2000). Characteristics and homogeneity of early adolescent friendship groups: A comparison of male and female clique and nonclique members. *Applied Developmental Science, 4,* 15–26.

Henricsson, L., & Rydell, A.-M. (2004). Elementary school children with behavior problems: Teacher-child relations and self-perception. A prospective study. *Merrill-Palmer Quarterly, 50,* 111–138.

Henry, J. D., MacLeod, M. S., Phillips, L. H., & Crawford, J. R. (2004). A meta-analytic review of prospective memory and aging. *Psychology and Aging, 19,* 27–39.

Heraghty, J. L., Hilliard, T. N., Henderson, A. J., & Fleming, P. J. (2008). The physiology of sleep in infants. *Archives of Disease in Childhood, 93,* 982–985.

Herbenick, D., Reece, M., Schick, V., Sanders, S. A., Dodge, B., & Fortenberry, J. D. (2010). Sexual behavior in the United States: Results from a national probability sample of men and women ages 14–94. *Journal of Sexual Medicine, 7*(Suppl. 5), 255–265.

Herbst, J. H., McCrae, R. R., Costa, P. T., Jr., Feaganes, J. R., & Siegler, I. C. (2000). Self-perceptions of stability and change in personality at midlife: The UNC Alumni Heart Study. *Assessment, 7,* 379–388.

Herd, P., Robert, S. A., & House, J. S. (2011). Health disparities among older adults: Life course influences and policy solutions. *Handbook of aging and the social sciences* (7th ed., pp. 121–134). San Diego: Academic Press.

Herek, G. M. (2009). Sexual prejudice. In T. Nelson (Ed.), *Handbook of prejudice, stereotyping,*

and discrimination (pp. 439–465). New York: Psychology Press.

Herman, M. (2004). Forced to choose: Some determinants of racial identification in multiracial adolescents. *Child Development, 75,* 730–748.

Herman-Giddens, M. E. (2006). Recent data on pubertal milestones in United States children: The secular trend toward earlier development. *International Journal of Andrology, 29,* 241–246.

Herman-Giddens, M. E., Steffes, J., Harris, D., Slora, E., Hussey, M., Dowshen, S. A., et al. (2012). Secondary sexual characteristics in boys: Data from the Pediatric Research in Office Settings Network. *Pediatrics, 130,* e1058–e1068.

Hernandez, D. J., Denton, N. A., & Macartney, S. E. (2008). Children in immigrant families: Looking to America's future. *Social Policy Report of the Society for Research in Child Development, 12*(11).

Hernandez, M., & Newcomer, R. (2007). Assisted living and special populations: What do we know about differences in use and potential access barriers? *Gerontologist, 47*(Special Issue III), 110–117.

Herrnstein, R. J., & Murray, C. (1994). *The bell curve.* New York: Free Press.

Hershey, D. A., Jacobs-Lawson, J. M., McArdle, J. J., & Hamagami, F. (2007). Psychological foundations of financial planning for retirement. *Journal of Adult Development, 14,* 26–36.

Hertzog, C., & Dunlosky, J. (2011). Metacognition in later adulthood: Spared monitoring can benefit older adults' self-regulation. *Current Directions in Psychological Science, 20,* 167–173.

Hertzog, C., Kramer, A. F., Wilson, R. S., & Lindenberger, U. (2009). Enrichment effects on adult cognitive development. *Psychological Science in the Public Interest, 9*(1), 1–65.

Herzog, D. B., Eddy, K. T., & Beresin, E. V. (2006). Anorexia and bulimia nervosa. In M. K. Dulcan & J. M. Wiener (Eds.), *Essentials of child and adolescent psychiatry* (pp. 527–560). Washington, DC: American Psychiatric Publishing.

Hespos, S. J., & Baillargeon, R. (2008). Young infants' actions reveal their developing knowledge of support variables: Converging evidence for violation-of-expectation findings. *Cognition, 107,* 304–316.

Hespos, S. J., Ferry, A. L., Cannistraci, C. J., Gore, J., & Park, S. (2010). Using optical imaging to investigate functional cortical activity in human infants. In A. W. Roe (Ed.), *Imaging the brain with optical methods* (pp. 159–176). New York: Springer Science + Business Media.

Hess, T. M., & Hinson, J. T. (2006). Age-related variation in the influences of aging stereotypes on memory in adulthood. *Psychology and Aging, 21,* 621–625.

Hess, T. M., Hinson, J. T., & Statham, J. A. (2004). Explicit and implicit stereotype activation effects on memory: Do age and awareness moderate the impact of priming? *Psychology and Aging, 19,* 495–505.

Hesse, E., & Main, M. (2000). Disorganized infant, child, and adult attachment: Collapse in behavioral and attentional strategies. *Journal of the American Psychoanalytic Association, 48,* 1097–1127.

Hetherington, E. M. (1999). Should we stay together for the sake of the children? In E. M. Hetherington (Ed.), *Coping with divorce, single-parenting, and remarriage: A risk and resiliency perspective* (pp. 93–116). Hillsdale, NJ: Erlbaum.

Hetherington, E. M. (2003). Social support and the adjustment of children in divorced and remarried families. *Childhood, 10,* 237–254

Hetherington, E. M., & Clingempeel, W. G. (1992). Coping with marital transitions: A family systems perspective. *Monographs of the Society for Research in Child Development, 57*(2–3, Serial No. 227).

Hetherington, E. M., Henderson, S. H., & Reiss, D. (1999). Adolescent siblings in stepfamilies: Family functioning and adolescent adjustment.

Monographs of the Society for Research in Child Development, 64(4, Serial No. 259).

Hetherington, E. M., & Kelly, J. (2002). *For better or for worse: Divorce reconsidered.* New York: Norton.

Hetherington, E. M., & Stanley-Hagan, M. (2000). Diversity among stepfamilies. In D. H. Demo, K. R. Allen, & M. A. Fine (Eds.), *Handbook of family diversity* (pp. 173–196). New York: Oxford University Press.

Hewlett, B. S. (1992). Husband–wife reciprocity and the father–infant relationship among Aka pygmies. In B. S. Hewlett (Ed.), *Father–child relations: Cultural and biosocial contexts* (pp. 153–176). New York: Aldine de Gruyter.

Hewlett, B. S. (2004). Fathers in forager, farmer, and pastoral cultures. In M. E. Lamb (Ed.), *The role of the father in child development* (4th ed., pp. 182–195). Hoboken, NJ: Wiley.

Hewlett, S. (2003). *Creating a life.* New York: Miramax.

Heyes, C. (2005). Imitation by association. In S. Hurley & N. Chater (Eds.), *From neuroscience to social science: Vol. 1. Mechanisms of imitation and imitation in animals* (pp. 157–177). Cambridge, MA: MIT Press.

Heyman, G. D., & Dweck, C. S. (1998). Children's thinking about traits: Implications for judgments of the self and others. *Child Development, 69,* 391–403.

Heyman, G. D., & Legare, C. H. (2004). Children's beliefs about gender differences in the academic and social domains. *Sex Roles, 50,* 227–239.

Hickling, A. K., & Wellman, H. M. (2001). The emergence of children's causal explanations and theories: Evidence from everyday conversation. *Developmental Psychology, 37,* 668–683.

Hietanen, A., Era, P., Sorri, M., & Heikkinen, E. (2004). Changes in hearing in 80-year-old people: A 10-year follow-up study. *International Journal of Audiology, 43,* 126–135.

Higginbottom, G. M. A. (2006). 'Pressure of life': Ethnicity as a mediating factor in mid-life and older peoples' experience of high blood pressure. *Sociology of Health and Illness, 28,* 583–610.

Higgins, C. A., Duxbury, L. E., & Lyons, S. T. (2010). Coping with overload and stress: Men and women in dual-earner families. *Journal of Marriage and Family 72,* 847–859.

High, P. C., LaGasse, L., Becker, S., Ahlgren, I., & Gardner, A. (2000). Literacy promotion in primary care pediatrics: Can we make a difference? *Pediatrics, 105,* 927–934.

Hildreth, K., & Rovee-Collier, C. (2002). Forgetting functions of reactivated memories over the first year of life. *Developmental Psychobiology, 41,* 277–288.

Hildreth, K., Sweeney, B., & Rovee-Collier, C. (2003). Differential memory-preserving effects of reminders at 6 months. *Journal of Experimental Child Psychology, 84,* 41–62.

Hilgers, K. K., Akridge, M., Scheetz, J. P., & Kinance, D. E. (2006). Childhood obesity and dental development. *Pediatric Dentistry, 28,* 18–22.

Hill, E. J., Mead, N. T., Dean, L. R., Hafen, D. M., Gadd, R., & Palmer, A. A. (2006). Researching the 60-hour dual-earner workweek. *American Behavioral Scientist, 49,* 1184–1203.

Hill, J. L., Brooks-Gunn, J., & Waldfogel, J. (2003). Sustained effects of high participation in an early intervention for low-birth-weight premature infants. *Developmental Psychology, 39,* 730–744.

Hill, N. E., & Taylor, L. C. (2004). Parental school involvement and children's academic achievement: Pragmatics and issues. *Current Directions in Psychological Science, 13,* 161–164.

Hill, N. M., & Schneider, W. (2006). Brain changes in the development of expertise: Neuroanatomical and neurophysiological evidence about skill-based adaptations. In K. A. Ericsson, N. Charness, P. J. Feltovich, & R. R. Hoffman (Eds.), *The Cambridge handbook of expertise and expert performance* (pp. 653–682). New York: Cambridge University Press.

Hillard, P. J. A. (2008). Menstruation in adolescents: What's normal, what's not. *Annals of the New York Academy of Sciences, 1135,* 29–35.

Hillis, S. D., Anda, R. F., Dube, S. R., Felitti, V. J., Marchbanks, P. A., & Marks, J. S. (2004). The association between adverse childhood experiences and adolescent pregnancy, long-term psychosocial consequences, and fetal death. *Pediatrics, 113,* 320–327.

Hillman, C. H., Erickson, K. I., & Kramer, A. F. (2008). Be smart, exercise your heart: Exercise effects on brain and cognition. *Nature Reviews Neuroscience, 9,* 58–65.

Hilt, L. M. (2004). Attribution retaining for therapeutic change: Theory, practice, and future directions. *Imagination, Cognition, and Personality, 23,* 289–307.

Hinojosa, T., Sheu, C.-F., & Michael, G. F. (2003). Infant hand-use preference for grasping objects contributes to the development of a hand-use preference for manipulating objects. *Developmental Psychobiology, 43,* 328–334.

Hirasawa, R., & Feil, R. (2010). Genomic imprinting and human disease. *Essays in Biochemistry, 48,* 187–200.

Hirsch, C. (1996). Understanding the influence of gender role identity on the assumption of family caregiving roles by men. *International Journal of Aging and Human Development, 42,* 103–121.

Hirsh-Pasek, K., & Burchinal, M. (2006). Mother and caregiver sensitivity over time: Predicting language and academic outcomes with variable- and person-centered approaches. *Merrill-Palmer Quarterly, 52,* 449–485.

Hirsh-Pasek, K., & Golinkoff, R. M. (2003). *Einstein never used flash cards.* New York: Rodale.

Hirsh-Pasek, K., Golinkoff, R. M., Berk, L. E., & Singer, D. G. (2009). *A mandate for playful learning in preschool: Presenting the evidence.* New York: Oxford University Press.

Hoch-Espada, A., Ryan, E., & Deblinger, E. (2006). Child sexual abuse. In J. E. Fisher & W. T. O'Donohue (Eds.), *Practitioner's guide to evidence-based psychotherapy* (pp. 177–188). New York: Springer.

Hochwarter, W. A., Ferris, G. R., Perrewe, P. L., Witt, L. A., & Kiewitz, C. (2001). A note on the nonlinearity of the age–job satisfaction relationship. *Journal of Applied Social Psychology, 31,* 1223–1237.

Hock, H. S., Park, C. L., & Bjorklund, D. F. (1998). Temporal organization in children's strategy formation. *Journal of Experimental Child Psychology, 70,* 187–206.

Hodges, J., & Tizard, B. (1989). Social and family relationships of ex-institutional adolescents. *Journal of Child Psychology and Psychiatry, 30,* 77–97.

Hodges, R. M., & French, L. A. (1988). The effect of class and collection labels on cardinality, class inclusion, and number conservation tasks. *Child Development, 59,* 1387–1396.

Hodnett, E. D., Gates, S., Hofmeyr, G. J., & Sakala, C. (2003). Continuous support for women during childbirth. *Cochrane Database of Systematic Reviews, 3,* CD003766.

Hoekstra, C., Zhao, Z. Z., Lambalk, C. B., Willemsen, G., Martin, N. G., Boomsma, D. I., & Montgomery, G. W. (2008). Dizygotic twinning. *Human Reproduction Update, 14,* 37–47.

Hoenig, H., Taylor, D. H., Jr., & Sloan, F. A. (2003). Does assistive technology substitute for personal assistance among the disabled elderly? *American Journal of Public Health, 93,* 330–337.

Hoerr, T. (2004). How MI informs teaching at New City School. *Teachers College Record, 106,* 40–48.

Hoff, B. (2001). *Full report of the prevalence, incidence, and consequences of violence against women.* Washington, DC: U.S. Department of Justice.

Hoff, E. (2003). The specificity of environmental influence: Socioeconomic status affects early vocabulary development via maternal speech. *Child Development, 74,* 1368–1378.

Hoff, E. (2006). How social contexts support and shape language development. *Developmental Review, 26,* 55–88.

Hoff, E. (2013). Interpreting the early language trajectories of children from low-SES and language minority homes: Implications for closing achievement gaps. *Developmental Psychology, 49,* 4–14.

Hoff, E., Laursen, B., & Tardif, T. (2002). Socioeconomic status and parenting. In M. H. Bornstein (Ed.), *Handbook of parenting* (pp. 231–252). Mahwah, NJ: Erlbaum.

Hoff, T., Greene, L., & Davis, J. (2003). *National survey of adolescents and young adults: Sexual health knowledge, attitudes and experiences.* Menlo Park, CA: Henry J. Kaiser Family Foundation.

Hofferth, S. L. (2010). Home media and children's achievement and behavior. *Child Development, 81,* 1598–1619.

Hofferth, S. L., & Anderson, K. G. (2003). Are all dads equal? Biology versus marriage as a basis for paternal investment. *Journal of Marriage and Family, 65,* 213–232.

Hoffman, L. W. (2000). Maternal employment: Effects of social context. In R. D. Taylor & M. C. Wang (Eds.), *Resilience across contexts: Family, work, culture, and community* (pp. 147–176). Mahwah, NJ: Erlbaum.

Hoffman, M. L. (2000). *Empathy and moral development.* New York: Cambridge University Press.

Hoffner, C., & Badzinski, D. M. (1989). Children's integration of facial and situational cues to emotion. *Child Development, 60,* 411–422.

Hogan, B. E., & Linden, W. (2004). Anger response styles and blood pressure: At least don't ruminate about it! *Annals of Behavioral Medicine, 27,* 38–49.

Hogan, M. J., & Strasburger, V. C. (2008). Body image, eating disorders, and the media. *Adolescent Medicine, 19,* 521–546.

Holden, G. W., Coleman, S. M., & Schmidt, K. L. (1995). Why 3-year-old children get spanked: Determinants as reported by college-educated mothers. *Merrill-Palmer Quarterly, 41,* 431–452.

Holditch-Davis, D., Belyea, M., & Edwards, L. J. (2005). Prediction of 3-year developmental outcomes from sleep development over the preterm period. *Infant Behavior and Development, 79,* 49–58.

Holdren, J. P., & Lander, E. (2012). *Engage to excel: Producing one million additional college graduates with degrees in science, technology, engineering, and mathematics.* Washington, DC: President's Council of Advisors on Science and Technology.

Holland, A. L. (2004). Plasticity and development. *Brain and Language, 88,* 254–255.

Holland, J. L. (1985). *Making vocational choices: A theory of vocational personalities and work environments.* Englewood Cliffs, NJ: Prentice-Hall.

Holland, J. L. (1997). *Making vocational choices: A theory of vocational personalities and work environments* (3rd ed.). Odessa, FL: Psychological Assessment Resources.

Hollich, G. J., Hirsh-Pasek, K., & Golinkoff, R. M. (2000). Breaking the language barrier: An emergentist coalition model for the origins of word learning. *Monographs of the Society for Research in Child Development, 65*(3, Serial No. 262).

Holmbeck, G. N. (1996). A model of family relational transformations during the transition to adolescence: Parent–adolescent conflict and adaptation. In J. A. Graber, J. Brooks-Gunn, & A. C. Petersen (Eds.), *Transitions through adolescence* (pp. 167–199). Mahwah, NJ: Erlbaum.

Holobow, N., Genesee, F., & Lambert, W. (1991). The effectiveness of a foreign language immersion program for children from different ethnic and social class backgrounds: Report 2. *Applied Psycholinguistics, 12,* 179–198.

Holstein, M. (2011). Cultural ideals, ethics, and agelessness: A critical perspective on the Third Age. In D. C. Carr & K. Komp (Eds.), *Gerontology in the era of the Third Age: Implications and next steps* (pp. 225–243). New York: Springer.

Honein, M. A., Paulozzi, L. J., & Erickson, J. D. (2001). Continued occurrence of Accutane exposed pregnancies. *Teratology, 64,* 142–147.

Hong, Z.-R., Veach, P. M., & Lawrenz, F. (2003). An investigation of the gender stereotyped thinking of Taiwanese secondary school boys and girls. *Sex Roles, 48,* 495–504.

Hoobler, J. M., Lemmon, G., & Wayne, S. J. (2011). Women's underrepresentation in upper management: New insights on a persistent problem. *Organizational Dynamics, 40,* 151–156.

Hood, M., Conlon, E., & Andrews, G. (2008). Preschool home literacy practices and children's literacy development: A longitudinal analysis. *Journal of Educational Psychology, 100,* 252–271.

Hooper, L., Summerbell, C. D., Thompson, R., Sills, F., Roberts, F. G., Moore, H. J., et al. (2012). Reduced or modified dietary fat for preventing cardiovascular disease. *Cochrane Database of Systematic Reviews* [Online], 5: CD002137.

Hooyman, N. R., & Kiyak, H. A. (2011). *Social gerontology: A multidisciplinary perspective* (9th ed.). Boston, MA: Pearson.

Hopkins, B., & Westra, T. (1988). Maternal handling and motor development: An intracultural study. *Genetic, Social and General Psychology Monographs, 14,* 377–420.

Hoppmann, C. A., Gerstorf, D., Smith, J., & Klumb, P. L. (2007). Linking possible selves and behavior: Do domain-specific hopes and fears translate into daily activities in very old age? *Journal of Gerontology, 62B,* P104–P111.

Horn, J. L., Donaldson, G., & Engstrom, R. (1981). Apprehension, memory, and fluid intelligence decline through the "vital years" of adulthood. *Research on Aging, 3,* 33–84.

Horn, J. L., & Noll, J. (1997). Human cognitive capabilities: Gf–Gc theory. In D. P. Flanagan, J. L., Genshaft, & P. L. Harrison (Eds.), *Beyond traditional intellectual assessment* (pp. 53–91). New York: Guilford.

Horner, T. M. (1980). Two methods of studying stranger reactivity in infants: A review. *Journal of Child Psychology and Psychiatry, 21,* 203–219.

Hornor, G. (2010). Child sexual abuse: Consequences and implications. *Journal of Pediatric Health Care, 24,* 358–364.

Horst, J. S., Oakes, L. M., & Madole, K. M. (2005). What does it look like and what can it do? Category structure influences how infants categorize. *Child Development, 76,* 614–631.

Hospice Foundation of America. (2005). *The dying process: A guide for caregivers.* Washington, DC: Author.

Hospice Foundation of America. (2013). *Hospice services and expenses.* Retrieved from www.hospicefoundation.org/servicesandexpenses

Hostetler, A. J., & Sweet, S., & Moen, P. (2007). Gendered career paths: A life course perspective on returning to school. *Sex Roles, 56,* 85–103.

Houck, J. A. (2006). *Hot and bothered: Women, medicine, and menopause in modern America.* Cambridge, MA: Harvard University Press.

Houlihan, J., Kropp. T., Wiles, R., Gray, S., & Campbell, C. (2005). *Body burden: The pollution in newborns.* Washington, DC: Environmental Working Group.

House, J. S., Lantz, P. M., & Herd, P. (2005). Continuity and change in the social stratification of aging and health over the life course: Evidence from a nationally representative longitudinal study from 1986 to 2001/2002 (Americans' Changing Lives Study). *Journal of Gerontology, 60B*(Special Issue II), 15–26.

Houts, R. M., Barnett-Walker, K. C., Paley, B., & Cox, M. J. (2008). Patterns of couple interaction during the transition to parenthood. *Personal Relationships, 15,* 103–122.

Hoven, C. W., Duarte, C. S., Lucas, C. P., Wu, P., Mandell, D. J., & Goodwin, R. D. (2005). Psychopathology among New York City school children 6 months after September 11. *Archives of General Psychiatry, 62,* 545–552.

Howard, A. L., Galambos, N. L., & Krahn, H. J. (2010). Paths to success in young adulthood from mental health and life transitions in emerging adulthood. *International Journal of Behavioral Development, 34,* 538–546.

Howard, B. V., Manson, J. E., Stefanick, M. L., Beresford, S. A., Frank, G., & Jones, B. (2006). Low-fat dietary pattern and weight change over 7 years: The Women's Health Initiative Dietary Modification Trial. *Journal of the American Medical Association, 295,* 39–49.

Howard, K., & Walsh, M. E. (2010). Conceptions of career choice and attainment: Developmental levels in how children think about careers. *Journal of Vocational Behavior, 76,* 143–152.

Howe, M. L., Courage, M. L., & Rooksby, M. (2009). The genesis and development of autobiographical memory. In M. L. Courage & N. Cowan (Eds.), *The development of memory in infancy and childhood* (pp. 177–196). Hove, UK: Psychology Press.

Howe, N., Aquan-Assee, J., & Bukowski, W. M. (2001). Predicting sibling relations over time: Synchrony between maternal management styles and sibling relationship quality. *Merrill-Palmer Quarterly, 47,* 121–141.

Howell, K. K., Coles, C. D., & Kable, J. A. (2008). The medical and developmental consequences of prenatal drug exposure. In J. Brick (Ed.), *Handbook of the medical consequences of alcohol and drug abuse* (2nd ed., pp. 219–249). New York: Haworth Press.

Howell, K. K., Lynch, M. E., Platzman, K. A., Smith, G. H., & Coles, C. D. (2006). Prenatal alcohol exposure and ability, academic achievement, and school functioning in adolescence: A longitudinal follow-up. *Journal of Pediatric Psychology, 31,* 116–126.

Howell, L. C., & Beth, A. (2002). Midlife myths and realities: Women reflect on their experiences. *Journal of Women and Aging, 14,* 189–204.

Howell, T. M., & Yuille, J. C. (2004). Healing and treatment of Aboriginal offenders: A Canadian example. *American Journal of Forensic Psychology, 22,* 53–76.

Hoyer, W. J., & Verhaeghen, P. (2006). Memory aging. In J. E. Birren & K. W. Schaie (Eds.), *Handbook of the psychology of aging* (6th ed., pp. 209–232). Burlington, MA: Elsevier Academic Press.

Hoza, B., Gerdes, A. C., Hinshaw, S. P., Bukowski, W. M., Gold, J. A., Kraemer, H. C., Pelham, W. E., Jr., Wigal, T., & Arnold, L. E. (2005). What aspects of peer relationships are impaired in children with attention-deficit/hyperactivity disorder? *Journal of Consulting and Clinical Psychology, 73,* 411–423.

HSBC & Oxford Institute of Ageing. (2007). *The future of retirement.* London: HSBC Insurance.

HSBC & Oxford Institute of Ageing. (2011). *The future of retirement: The power of planning.* London: HSBC Insurance.

Hsu, F. L. K. (1981). *Americans and Chinese: Passage to difference* (3rd ed.). Honolulu: University of Hawaii Press.

Huang, A. Subak, L., Thom, D., Van Den Eeden, S., Ragins, A., Kuppermann, M., et al. (2009). Sexual function and aging in racially and ethnically diverse women. *Journal of the American Geriatrics Society, 57,* 1362–1368.

Huang, C.-C. (2006). Child support enforcement and father involvement for children in never-married mother families. *Fathering, 4,* 97–111.

Huang, C. Y., & Stormshak, E. A. (2011). A longitudinal examination of early adolescence ethnic identity trajectories. *Cultural Diversity and Ethnic Minority Psychology, 17,* 261–270.

Huang, K-E. (2010). Menopause perspective and treatment of Asian women. *Seminars in Reproductive Medicine, 28,* 396–403.

Huang, Q., & Sverke, M. (2007). Women's occupational career patterns over 27 years: Relations to family of origin, life careers, and wellness. *Journal of Vocational Behavior, 70,* 369–397.

Hubbs-Tait, L., Nation, J. R., Krebs, N. F., & Bellinger, D. C. (2005). Neurotoxicants, micronurrients, and social environments: Individual and combined effects on children's development. *Psychological Science in the Public Interest, 6,* 57–121.

Huddleston, J., & Ge, X. (2003). Boys at puberty: Psychosocial implications. In C. Hayward (Ed.), *Gender differences at puberty* (pp. 113–134). New York: Cambridge University Press.

Hudson, J. A., Fivush, R., & Kuebli, J. (1992). Scripts and episodes: The development of event memory. *Applied Cognitive Psychology, 6,* 483–505.

Hudson, J. A., & Mayhew, E. M. Y. (2009). The development of memory for recurring events. In M. L. Courage & N. Cowan (Eds.), *The development of memory in infancy and childhood* (pp. 69–91). Hove, UK: Psychology Press.

Hudson, J. M. (2008). Automatic memory processes in normal ageing and Alzheimer's disease. *Cortex, 44,* 345–349.

Hudziak, J. J., & Rettew, D. C. (2009). Genetics of ADHD. In T. E. Brown (Ed.), *ADHD comorbidties: Handbook for ADHD complications in children and adults* (pp. 23–36). Arlington, VA: American Psychiatric Publishing.

Huebner, C. E., & Payne, K. (2010). Home support for emergent literacy: Follow-up of a community-based implementation of dialogic reading. *Journal of Applied Developmental Psychology, 31,* 195–201.

Huesmann, L. R. (1986). Psychological processes promoting the relation between exposure to media violence and aggressive behavior by the viewer. *Journal of Social Issues, 42,* 125–139.

Huesmann, L. R., Moise-Titus, J., Podolski, C. & Eron, L. D. (2003). Longitudinal relations between children's exposure to TV violence and their aggressive and violent behavior in young adulthood: 1977–1992. *Developmental Psychology, 39,* 201–221.

Huffman, M. L. (2012). Introduction: Gender, race, and management. *Annals of the American Academy of Political and Social Science, 639,* 6–12.

Hughes, C. (2010). Conduct disorder and antisocial behavior in the under-5s. In C. L. Cooper, J. Field, U. Goswami, R. Jenkins, & B. J. Sahakian (Eds.), *Mental capital and well-being* (pp. 821–827). Malden, MA: Wiley-Blackwell.

Hughes, C., & Dunn, J. (1998). Understanding mind and emotion: Longitudinal associations with mental-state talk between young friends. *Developmental Psychology, 34,* 1026–1037.

Hughes, C., & Ensor, R. (2007). Executive function and theory of mind: Predictive relations from ages 2 to 4. *Developmental Psychology, 43,* 1447–1459.

Hughes, C., & Ensor, R. (2010). Do early social cognition and executive function predict individual differences in preschoolers' prosocial and antisocial behavior? In B. W. Sokol, U. Müller, J. I. M. Carpendale, A. R. Young, & G. Iarocci (Eds.), *Social interaction and the development of social understanding and executive functions* (pp. 418–441). New York: Oxford University Press.

Hughes, C., Ensor, R., & Marks, A. (2010). Individual differences in false belief understanding are stable from 3 to 6 years of age and predict children's mental state talk with school friends. *Journal of Experimental Child Psychology, 108,* 96–112.

Hughes, D., Rodriguez, J., Smith, E. P., Johnson, D. J., Stevenson, H. C., & Spicer, P. (2006). Parents' ethnic-racial socialization practices: A review of research and directions for future study. *Developmental Psychology, 42,* 747–770.

Hughes, J. N., Cavell, T. A., & Grossman, P. B. (1997). A positive view of self: Risk or protection for aggressive children? *Development and Psychopathology, 9*, 75–94.

Hughes, J. N., & Kwok, O. (2006). Classroom engagement mediates the effect of teacher–student support on elementary students' peer acceptance. *Journal of School Psychology, 43*, 465–480.

Hughes, J. N., & Kwok, O. (2007). Influence of student–teacher and parent–teacher relationships on lower achieving readers' engagement and achievement in the primary grades. *Journal of Educational Psychology, 99*, 39–51.

Hughes, J. N., Zhang, D., & Hill, C. R. (2006). Peer assessments of normative and individual teacher–student support predict social acceptance and engagement among low-achieving children. *Journal of School Psychology, 43*, 447–463.

Huizenga, H., Crone, E. A., & Jansen, B. (2007). Decision making in healthy children, adolescents and adults explained by the use of increasingly complex proportional reasoning rules. *Developmental Science, 10*, 814–825.

Huizink, A. C., Bartels, M., Rose, R. J., Pulkkinen, L., Eriksson, C. J., & Kaprio, J. (2008). Chernobyl exposure as a stressor during pregnancy and hormone levels in adolescent offspring. *Journal of Epidemiology and Community Health, 62*, e5.

Huizink, A. C., & Mulder, E. J. (2006). Maternal smoking, drinking or cannabis use during pregnancy and neurobehavioral and cognitive functioning in human offspring. *Neuroscience and Biobehavioral Reviews, 30*, 24–41.

Hultsch, D. F., Hertzog, C., Dixon, R. A., & Small, B. J. (1998). *Memory change in the aged.* New York: Cambridge University Press.

Hultsch, D. F., MacDonald, S. W. S., & Dixon, R. A. (2002). Variability in reaction time performance of younger and older adults. *Journal of Gerontology, 57B*, P101–P115.

Human Genome Program. (2008). *How many genes are in the human genome?* Retrieved from www.ornl .gov/sci/techresources/Human_Genome/faq/ genenumber.shtml

Human Rights Campaign. (2008). *Surrogacy laws: State by state.* Retrieved from http://66.151.111.225/ issues/parenting/surrogacy/surrogacy_laws.asp

Humes, L. E., Dubno, J. R., Gordon-Salant, S., Lister, J. J., Cacace, A. T., Cruickshanks, K. J., et al. (2012). Central presbycusis: A review and evaluation of the evidence. *Journal of the American Academy of Audiology, 23*, 635–666.

Humphrey, T. (1978). Function of the nervous system during prenatal life. In U. Stave (Ed.), *Perinatal physiology* (pp. 651–683). New York: Plenum.

Hunnius, S., & Geuze, R. H. (2004a). Developmental changes in visual scanning of dynamic faces and abstract stimuli in infants: A longitudinal study. *Infancy, 6*, 231–255.

Hunnius, S., & Geuze, R. H. (2004b). Gaze shifting in infancy: A longitudinal study using dynamic faces and abstract stimuli. *Infant Behavior and Development, 27*, 397–416.

Hunt, C. E., & Hauck, F. R. (2006). Sudden infant death syndrome. *Canadian Medical Association Journal, 174*, 1861–1869.

Huotilainen, M., Kujala, A., Hotakainen, M., Parkkonen, L., Taulu, S., & Simola, J. (2005). Short-term memory functions of the human fetus recorded with magneto-encephalography. *NeuroReport, 16*, 81–84.

Hursti, U. K. (1999). Factors influencing children's food choice. *Annals of Medicine, 31*, 26–32.

Hurt, H., Betancourt, L. M., Malmud, E. K., Shera, D. M., Giannetta, J. M., Brodsky, N. L., et al. (2009). Children with and without gestational cocaine exposure: A neurocognitive systems analysis. *Neurotoxicology and Teratology, 31*, 334–341.

Hurtig, W. A., & Stewin, L. (2006). The effect of death education and eperience on nursing students' attitude toward death. *Journal of Advanced Nursing, 15*, 29–34.

Huston, A. C., & Alvarez, M. M. (1990). The socialization context of gender role development in early adolescence. In R. Montemayor, G. R. Adams, & T. P. Gullotta (Eds.), *From childhood to adolescence: A transitional period?* (pp. 156–179). Newbury Park, CA: Sage.

Huston, A. C., Wright, J. C., Marquis, J., & Green, S. B. (1999). How young children spend their time: Television and other activities. *Developmental Psychology, 35*, 912–925.

Huston, T. L., McHale, S. M., & Crouter, A. (1986). When the honeymoon's over: Changes in the marriage relationship over the first year. In R. Gilmour & S. Duck (Eds.), *The emerging field of personal relationships* (pp. 109–132). Hillsdale, NJ: Erlbaum.

Huttenlocher, P. R. (2002). *Neural plasticity: The effects of environment on the development of the cerebral cortex.* Cambridge, MA: Harvard University Press.

Huyck, M. H. (1990). Gender differences in aging. In J. E. Birren & K. W. Schaie (Eds.), *Handbook of the psychology of aging* (3rd ed., pp. 124–134). New York: Academic Press.

Huyck, M. H. (1996). Continuities and discontinuities in gender identity in midlife. In V. L. Bengtson (Ed.), *Adulthood and aging* (pp. 98–121). New York: Springer-Verlag.

Huyck, M. H. (1998). Gender roles and gender identity in midlife. In S. L. Willis & J. D. Reid (Eds.), *Life in the middle* (pp. 209–232). San Diego: Academic Press.

Hyde, J. S., Essex, M. J., Clark, R., & Klein, M. H. (2001). Maternity leave, women's employment, and marital incompatibility. *Journal of Family Psychology, 15*, 476–491.

Hyde, J. S., Mezulis, A. H., & Abramson, L. Y. (2008). The ABCs of depression: Integrating affective, biological, and cognitive models to explain the emergence of the gender difference in depression. *Psychological Review, 115*, 291–313.

Hyman, B. T., Phelps, C. H., Beach, T. G., Bigio, E. H., Cairns, N. J., Carrillo, M. C., et al. (2012). National Institute on Aging–Alzheimer's Association guidelines for the neuropathologic assessment of Alzheimer's disease. *Alzheimer's and Dementia, 8*, 1–13.

Hymel, S., Vaillancourt, T., McDougall, P., & Renshaw, P. D. (2004). Peer acceptance and rejection in childhood. In P. K. Smith & C. H. Hart (Eds.), *Blackwell handbook of childhood social development* (pp. 265–284). Malden, MA: Blackwell.

I

Iacoboni, M. (2009). Imitation, empathy, and mirror neurons. *Annual Review of Psychology, 60*, 653–670.

Ickes, M. J. (2011). Stigmatization of overweight and obese individuals: Implications for mental health promotion. *International Journal of Mental Health Promotion, 13*, 37–45.

Ida, M. (2010). [The concept of death in the revised Organ Transplant Law in Japan.] *Nihon Rinsho [Japanese Journal of Clinical Medicine], 68*, 2223–2228.

Idler, E. L., & Kasl, S. V. (1992). Religion, disability, depression, and the timing of death. *American Journal of Sociology, 97*, 1052–1079.

Idler, E. L., McLaughlin, J., & Kasl, S. (2009). Religion and the quality of life in the last year of life. *Journal of Gerontology, 64B*, 528–537.

Iglowstein, I., Jenni, O. G., Molinari, L., & Largo, R. H. (2003). Sleep duration from infancy to adolescence: Reference values and generational trends. *Pediatrics, 111*, 302–307.

Imai, M., & Haryu, E. (2004). The nature of word-learning biases and their roles for lexical development: From a cross-linguistic perspective.

In D. G. Hall & S. R. Waxman (Eds.), *Weaving a lexicon* (pp. 411–444). Cambridge, MA: MIT Press.

Impett, E. A., & Peplau, L. A. (2006). "His" and "her" relationships? A review of the empirical evidence. In A. L. Vangelisti & D. Perlman (Eds.), *The Cambridge handbook of personal relationships* (pp. 273–292). New York: Cambridge University Press.

Impett, E. A., Sorsoli, L., Schooler, D., Henson, J. M., & Tolman, D. L. (2008). Girls' relationship authenticity and self-esteem across adolescence. *Developmental Psychology, 44*, 722–733.

Inhelder, B., & Piaget, J. (1958). *The growth of logical thinking from childhood to adolescence: An essay on the construction of formal operational structures.* New York: Basic Books. (Original work published 1955)

Irvine, A. B., Ary, D. V., & Bourgeois, M. S. (2003). An interactive multimedia program to train professional caregivers. *Journal of Applied Gerontology, 22*, 269–288.

Isabella, R. (1993). Origins of attachment: Maternal interactive behavior across the first year. *Child Development, 64*, 605–621.

Isabella, R., & Belsky, J. (1991). Interactional synchrony and the origins of infant–mother attachment: A replication study. *Child Development, 62*, 373–384.

Isasi, R. M., Nguyen, T. M., & Knoppers, B. M. (2006). *National regulatory frameworks regarding human genetic modification technologies (somatic and germline modification).* Montréal, Québec: Centre de Recherché en Droit Public (CRDP), Université de Montréal.

Ishihara, K., Warita, K., Tanida, T., Sugawara, T., Kitagawa, H., & Hoshi, N. (2007). Does paternal exposure to 2, 3, 7, 8-tetrachlorodibenzo-p-dioxin (TCDD) affect the sex ratio of offspring? *Journal of Veterinary Medical Science, 69*, 347–352.

Israel, M., Johnson, C., & Brooks, P. J. (2000). From states to events: The acquisition of English passive participles. *Cognitive Linguistics, 11*, 103–129.

Itti, E., Gaw, G. I. T., Pawlikowska-Haddal, A., Boone, K. B., Mlikotic, A., & Itti, L. (2006). The structural brain correlates of cognitive deficits in adults with Klinefelter's syndrome. *Journal of Clinical Endocrinology and Metabolism, 91*, 1423–1427.

Ivorra, J. L., Sanjuan, J., Jover, M., Carot, J. M., de Frutos, R., & Molto, M. D. (2010). Gene-environment interaction of child temperament. *Journal of Developmental and Behavioral Pediatrics, 31*, 545–554.

Izard, C. E., & Ackerman, B. P. (2000). Motivational, organizational, and regulatory functions of discrete emotions. In M. Lewis & J. M. Haviland-Jones (Eds.), *Handbook of emotions* (2nd ed., pp. 253–264). New York: Guilford.

J

Jaakkola, J. J., & Gissler, M. (2004). Maternal smoking in pregnancy, fetal development, and childhood asthma. *American Journal of Public Health, 94*, 136–140.

Jaccard, J., Dodge, T., & Dittus, P. (2002). Parent-adolescent communication about sex and birth control: A conceptual framework. In S. S. Feldman & D. A. Rosenthal (Eds.), *Talking sexuality: Parent–adolescent communication* (pp. 9–41). San Francisco: Jossey-Bass.

Jaccard, J., Dodge, T., & Dittus, P. (2003). Maternal discussions about pregnancy and adolescents' attitudes toward pregnancy. *Journal of Adolescent Health, 33*, 84–87.

Jackson, G. R., & Owsley, C. (2000). Scotopic sensitivity during adulthood. *Vision Research, 40*, 2467–2473.

Jackson, J. J., Hill, P. L., Payne, B. R., Roberts, B. W., & Steine-Morrow, E. A. L. (2012). Can an old dog learn (and want to experience) new tricks? Cognitive training increases openness to experience in older adults. *Psychology and Aging, 27*, 286–292.

Jackson, T., Fritch, A., Nagaska, T., & Gunderson, J. (2002). Towards explaining the association between shyness and loneliness: A path analysis with American college students. *Social Behavior and Personality, 30,* 263–270.

Jackson, V. A., Sullivan, A. M., Gadmer, N. M., Seltzer, D., Mitchell, A. M., & Lakoma, M. D. (2005). "It was haunting . . . ": Physicians' descriptions of emotionally powerful patient deaths. *Academic Medicine, 80,* 648–656.

Jacobs, J. A., & King, R. B. (2002). Age and college completion: A life-history analysis of women aged 15–44. *Sociology of Education, 75,* 211–230.

Jacobs, J. E., & Klaczynski, P. A. (2002). The development of judgment and decision making during childhood and adolescence. *Current Directions in Psychological Science, 11,* 145–149.

Jacobs, J. E., Lanza, S., Osgood, D. W., Eccles, J. S., & Wigfield, A. (2002). Changes in children's self-competence and values: Gender and domain differences across grades one through twelve. *Child Development, 73,* 509–527.

Jacobs, J. N., & Kelley, M. L. (2006). Predictors of paternal involvement in childcare in dual-earner families with young children. *Fathering, 4,* 23–47.

Jacobs-Lawson, J. M., Hershey, D. A., & Neukam, K. A. (2004). Gender differences in factors that influence time spent planning for retirement. *Journal of Women and Aging, 16,* 55–69.

Jacobson, J. L., & Jacobson, S. W. (2003). Prenatal exposure to polychlorinated biphenyls and attention at school age. *Journal of Pediatrics, 143,* 780–788.

Jacobson, K. C., & Crockett, L. J. (2000). Parental monitoring and adolescent adjustment: An ecological perspective. *Journal of Research on Adolescence, 10,* 65–97.

Jacobson, S. W., Jacobson, J. L., Sokol, R. J., Chiodo, L. M., & Corobana, R. (2004). Maternal age, alcohol abuse history, and quality of parenting as moderators of the effects of prenatal alcohol exposure on 7.5-year intellectual function. *Alcoholism: Clinical and Experimental Research, 28,* 1732–1745.

Jacquet, P. (2004). Sensitivity of germ cells and embryos to ionizing radiation. *Journal of Biological Regulators and Homeostatic Agents, 18,* 106–114.

Jadack, R. A., Hyde, J. S., Moore, C. F., & Keller, M. L. (1995). Moral reasoning about sexually transmitted diseases. *Child Development, 66,* 167–177.

Jaffee, S. R., & Hyde, J. S. (2000). Gender differences in moral orientation: A meta-analysis. *Psychological Bulletin, 126,* 703–706.

James, J., Ellis, B. J., Schlomer, G. L., & Garber, J. (2012). Sex-specific pathways to early puberty, sexual debut, and sexual risk taking: Tests of an integrated evolutionary–developmental model. *Developmental Psychology, 48,* 687–702.

James, J. B., Lewkowicz, C., Libhaber, J., & Lachman, M. (1995). Rethinking the gender identity crossover hypothesis: A test of a new model. *Sex Roles, 32,* 185–207.

James, J. B., & Wink, P. (2007). The Third Age: A rationale for research. In J. B. James & P. Wink (Eds.), *Annual review of gerontology and geriatrics* (Vol. 26, pp. xix–xxxii). New York: Springer.

James, J. B., & Zarrett, N. (2007). Ego integrity in the lives of older women. *Journal of Adult Development, 13,* 61–75.

Jang, S. J., & Johnson, B. R. (2001). Neighborhood disorder, individual religiosity, and adolescent use of illicit drugs: A test of multilevel hypotheses. *Criminology, 39,* 109–143.

Jang, Y., Bergman, E., Schonfeld, L., & Molinari, V. (2007). The mediating role of health perceptions in the relation between physical and mental health: A study of older residents in assisted living facilities. *Journal of Aging and Health, 19,* 439–452.

Janosz, M., Le Blanc, M., Boulerice, B., & Tremblay, R. E. (2000). Predicting different types of school dropouts: A typological approach with two longitudinal samples. *Journal of Educational Psychology, 92,* 171–190.

Jansen, A., Theunissen, N., Slechten, K., Nederkoorn, C., Boon, B., Mulkens, S., & Roefs, A. (2003). Overweight children overeat after exposure to food cues. *Eating Behaviors, 4,* 197–209.

Jansen, J., de Weerth, C., & Riksen-Walraven, J. M. (2008). Breastfeeding and the mother–infant relationship. *Developmental Review, 28,* 503–521.

Janssen, S. M., Rubin, D. C., & St. Jacques, P. L. (2011). The temporal distribution of autobiographical memory: Changes in reliving and vividness over the life span do not explain the reminiscence bump. *Memory and Cognition, 39,* 1–11.

Janssens, J. M. A. M., & Deković, M. (1997). Child rearing, prosocial moral reasoning, and prosocial behaviour. *International Journal of Behavioral Development, 20,* 509–527.

Jarvis, J. F., & van Heerden, H. G. (1967). The acuity of hearing in the Kalahari Bushman: A pilot study. *Journal of Laryngology and Otology, 81,* 63–68.

Jaudes, P. K., & Mackey-Bilaver, L. (2008). Do chronic conditions increase young children's risk of being maltreated? *Child Abuse and Neglect, 32,* 671–681.

Jayakody, R., & Kalil, A. (2002). Social fathering in low-income, African-American families with preschool children. *Journal of Marriage and Family, 64,* 504–516.

Jedrychowski, W., Perera, F. P., Jankowski, J., Mrozek-Budzyn, D., Mroz, E., Flak, E., et al. (2009). Very low prenatal exposure to lead and mental development of children in infancy and early childhood. *Neuroepidemiology, 32,* 270–278.

Jeffrey, J. (2004, November). Parents often blind to their kids' weight. *British Medical Journal Online.* Retrieved from content.health.msn.com/content/article/97/104292.htm

Jellinger, K. A. (2004). Head injury and dementia. *Current Opinion in Neurology, 17,* 719–723.

Jellinger, K. A. (2008). Morphologic diagnosis of "vascular dementia"—a critical update. *Journal of the Neurological Sciences, 270,* 1–12.

Jenkins, C., Lapelle, N., Zapka, J. G., & Kurent, J. E. (2005). End-of-life care and African Americans: Voices from the community. *Journal of Palliative Medicine, 8,* 585–592.

Jenkins, J. M., Rasbash, J., & O'Connor, T. G. (2003). The role of the shared family context in differential parenting. *Developmental Psychology, 39,* 99–113.

Jenkins, J. M., Turrell, S. L., Kogushi, Y., Lollis, S., & Ross, H. S. (2003). A longitudinal investigation of the dynamics of mental state talk in families. *Child Development, 74,* 905–920.

Jenkins, K. R., Pienta, A. M., & Horgas, A. L. (2002). Activity and health-related quality of life in continuing care retirement communities. *Research on Aging, 24,* 124–149.

Jenni, O. G., Achermann, P., & Carskadon, M. A. (2005). Homeostatic sleep regulation in adolescents. *Sleep, 28,* 1446–1454.

Jennings, B. J., Ozanne, S. E., Dorling, M. W., & Hales, C. N. (1999). Early growth determines longevity in male rats and may be related to telomere shortening in the kidney. *FEBS Letters, 448,* 4–8.

Jensen, A. R. (1969). How much can we boost IQ and scholastic achievement? *Harvard Educational Review, 39,* 1–123.

Jensen, A. R. (1998). *The g factor: The science of mental ability.* New York: Praeger.

Jensen, A. R. (2001). Spearman's hypothesis. In J. M. Collis & S. Messick (Eds.), *Intelligence and personality: Bridging the gap in theory and measurement* (pp. 3–24). Mahwah, NJ: Erlbaum.

Jensen, A. R. (2002). Galton's legacy to research on intelligence. *Journal of Biosocial Science, 34,* 145–172.

Jeon, Y.-H., Brodaty, H., & Chesterson, J. (2005). Respite care for caregivers and people with severe mental illness: Literature review. *Journal of Advanced Nursing, 49,* 297–306.

Jeong, S.-H., & Fishbein, M. (2007). Predictors of multitasking with media: Media factors and audience factors. *Media Psychology, 10,* 364–384.

Jepson, K. L., & Labouvie-Vief, G. (1992). Symbolic processing of youth and elders. In R. L. West and J. D. Sinnott (Eds.), *Everyday memory and aging* (pp. 124–137). New York: Springer.

Jerome, E. M., Hamre, B. K., & Pianta, R. C. (2009). Teacher–child relationships from kindergarten to sixth grade: Early childhood predictors of teacher-perceived conflict and closeness. *Social Development, 18,* 915–945.

Jeynes, W. (2012). A meta-analysis of the efficacy of different types of parental involvement programs for urban students. *Urban Education, 47,* 706–742.

Jeynes, W. H. (2007). The impact of parental remarriage on children: A meta-analysis. *Marriage and Family Review, 40,* 75–102.

Ji, C. Y., & Chen, T. J. (2008). Secular changes in stature and body mass index for Chinese youth in sixteen major cities, 1950s–2005. *American Journal of Human Biology, 20,* 530–537.

Jiao, S., Ji, G., & Jing, Q. (1996). Cognitive development of Chinese urban only children and children with siblings. *Child Development, 67,* 387–395.

Jipson, J. L., & Gelman, S. A. (2007). Robots and rodents: Children's inferences about living and nonliving kinds. *Child Development, 78,* 1675–1688.

Joh, A. S., & Adolph, K. E. (2006). Learning from falling. *Child Development, 77,* 89–102.

Johansson, A. K., & Grimby, A. (2013). Anticipatory grief among close relatives of patients in hospice and palliative wards. *American Journal of Hospice and Palliative Medicine, 29,* 134–138.

Johnson, C. L., & Troll, L. E. (1994). Constraints and facilitators to friendships in late life. *Gerontologist, 34,* 79–87.

Johnson, E. K., & Seidl, A. (2008). Clause segmentation by 6-month-old infants: A crosslinguistic perspective. *Infancy, 13,* 440–455.

Johnson, J., Im-Bolter, N., & Pascual-Leone, J. (2003). Development of mental attention in gifted and mainstream children: The role of mental capacity, inhibition, and speed of processing. *Child Development, 74,* 1594–1614.

Johnson, J. G., Cohen, P., Smailes, E. M., Kasen, S., & Brook, J. S. (2002). Television viewing and aggressive behavior during adolescence and adulthood. *Science, 295,* 2468–2471.

Johnson, K. S., Elbert-Avila, K. I., & Tulsky, J. A. (2005). The influence of spiritual beliefs and practices on the treatment preferences of African Americans: A review of the literature. *Journal of the American Geriatrics Society, 53,* 711–719.

Johnson, K. S., Juchibhatla, M., Tanis, D., & Tulsky, J. A. (2008). Racial differences in hospice revocation to pursue aggressive care. *Archives of Internal Medicine, 168,* 218–224.

Johnson, M. D., Cohan, C. L., Davilla, J., Lawrence, E., Rogge, R. D., Karney, B. R., Sullivan, K. T., & Bradbury, T. N. (2005). Problem-solving skills and affective expressions as predictors of change in marital satisfaction. *Journal of Consulting and Clinical Psychology, 73,* 15–27.

Johnson, M. H. (1999). Ontogenetic constraints on neural and behavioral plasticity: Evidence from imprinting and face processing. *Canadian Journal of Experimental Psychology, 55,* 77–90.

Johnson, M. H. (2001). The development and neural basis of face recognition: Comment and speculation. *Infant and Child Development, 10,* 31–33.

Johnson, M. H. (2011). Developmental neuroscience, psychophysiology, and genetics. In M H. Bornstein & M. E. Lamb (Eds.), *Developmental science: An advanced textbook* (6th ed., pp. 187–222). Mahwah, NJ: Erlbaum.

Johnson, M. H., & Mareschal, D. (2001). Cognitive and perceptual development during infancy. *Current Opinion in Neurobiology, 11,* 213–218.

Johnson, R. W., & Mommaerts, C. (2010). *Will health care costs bankrupt aging boomers?* Washington, DC: Urban Institute.

Johnson, S. C., Dweck, C. S., & Chen, F. S. (2007). Evidence for infants' internal working models of attachment. *Psychological Science, 18,* 501–502.

Johnson, S. C., Dweck, C., Chen, F. S., Stern, H. L., Ok, S.-J., & Barth, M. (2010). At the intersection of social and cognitive development: Internal working models of attachment in infancy. *Cognitive Science, 34,* 807–825.

Johnson, S. P., Slemmer, J. A., & Amso, D. (2004). Where infants look determines how they see: Eye movements and object perception performance in 3-month-olds. *Infancy, 6,* 185–201.

Johnston, L. D., O'Malley, P. M., Bachman, J. G., & Schulenberg, J. E. (2011). *Monitoring the future: National results on adolescent drug use. Overview of key findings, 2010.* Bethesda, MD: National Institute on Drug Abuse.

Johnston, L. D., O'Malley, P. M., Bachman, J. G., & Schulenberg, J. E. (2012). *Monitoring the Future: National results on adolescent drug use: Overview of key findings, 2011.* Ann Arbor: Institute for Social Research, University of Michigan.

Johnston, M., Pollard, B., Morrison, V., & MacWalter, R. (2004). Functional limitations and survival following stroke: Psychological and clinical predictors of 3 year outcome. *International Journal of Behavioral Medicine, 11,* 187–196.

Johnston, M. V., Nishimura, A., Harum, K., Pekar, J., & Blue, M. E. (2001). Sculpting the developing brain. *Advances in Pediatrics, 48,* 1–38.

Jokhi, R. P., & Whitby, E. H. (2011). Magnetic resonance imaging of the fetus. *Developmental Medicine and Child Neurology, 53,* 18–28.

Jome, L. M., Surething, N. A., & Taylor, K. K. (2005). Relationally oriented masculinity, gender nontraditional interests, and occupational traditionality of employed men. *Journal of Career Development, 32,* 183–197.

Jones, C. M., Braithwaite, V. A., & Healy, S. D. (2003). The evolution of sex differences in spatial ability. *Behavioral Neuroscience, 117,* 403–411.

Jones, E. F., & Thompson, N. R. (2001). Action perception and outcome valence: Effects on children's inferences of intentionality and moral and liking judgments. *Journal of Genetic Psychology, 162,* 154–166.

Jones, F. (2003). *Religious commitment in Canada, 1997 and 2000. Religious Commitment Monograph No. 3.* Ottawa: Christian Commitment Research Institute.

Jones, G. P., & Dembo, M. H. (1989). Age and sex role differences in intimate friendships during childhood and adolescence. *Merrill-Palmer Quarterly, 35,* 445–462.

Jones, H. E. (2006). Drug addiction during pregnancy: Advances in maternal treatment and understanding child outcomes. *Current Directions in Psychological Science, 15,* 126–130.

Jones, J., Lopez, A., & Wilson, M. (2003). Congenital toxoplasmosis. *American Family Physician, 67,* 2131–2137.

Jones, J. M. (2012). *Expected retirement age in U.S.: Up to 67.* Princeton, NJ: Gallup. Retrieved from www.gallup.com/poll/154178/expected-retirement-age.aspx

Jones, K. M., Whitbourne, S. K., & Skultety, K. M. (2006). Identity processes and the transition to midlife among the baby boomers. In S. K. Whitbourne & S. L. Willis (Eds.), *The baby boomers grow up: Contemporary perspectives on midlife* (pp. 149–164). Mahwah, NJ: Erlbaum.

Jones, M. C., & Mussen, P. H. (1958). Self-conceptions, motivations, and interpersonal attitudes of early

and late-maturing girls. *Child Development, 29,* 491–501.

Jones, N. A., Field, T., & Davalos, M. (2000). Right frontal EEG asymmetry and lack of empathy in preschool children of depressed mothers. *Child Psychiatry and Human Development, 30,* 189–204.

Jones, S. (2009). The development of imitation in infancy. *Philosophical Transactions of the Royal Society B, 364,* 2325–2335.

Jongbloet, P. H., Zielhuis, G. A., Groenewoud, H. M., & Pasker-De Jong, P. C. (2001). The secular trends in male: female ratio at birth in postwar industrialized countries. *Environmental Health Perspectives, 109,* 749–752.

Jopp, D., & Rott, C. (2006). Adaptation in very old age: Exploring the role of resources, beliefs, and attitudes for centenarians' happiness. *Psychology and Aging, 21,* 266–280.

Jordan, B. (1993). *Birth in four cultures.* Prospect Heights, IL: Waveland.

Jordon, J., & Neimeyer, R. (2003). Does grief counseling work? *Death Studies, 27,* 765–786.

Jose, A., O'Leary, D., & Moyer, A. (2010). Does premarital cohabitation predict subsequent marital stability and martial quality? A meta-analysis. *Journal of Marriage and Family, 72,* 105–116.

Joseph, R. M., & Tager-Flusberg, H. (2004). The relationship of theory of mind and executive functions to symptom type and severity in children with autism. *Development and Psychopathology, 16,* 137–155.

Juby, H., Billette, J.-M., Laplante, B., & Le Bourdais, C. (2007). Nonresident fathers and children: Parents' new unions and frequency of contact. *Journal of Family Issues, 28,* 1220–1245.

Julkunen, J., & Ahlström, R. (2006). Hostility, anger, and sense of coherence as predictors of health-related quality of life. Results of an ASCOT substudy. *Journal of Psychosomatic Research, 61,* 33–39.

Juntunen, C. L., Wegner, K. E., & Matthews, L. G. (2002). Promoting positive career change in midlife. In C. L. Juntunen & D. R. Atkinson (Eds.), *Counseling across the lifespan* (pp. 329–347). Thousand Oaks, CA: Sage.

Jürgensen, M., Hiort, O., Holterhus, P.-M., & Thyen, U. (2007). Gender role behavior in children with XY karyotype and disorders of sex development. *Hormones and Behavior, 51,* 443–453.

Jusczyk, P. W. (2001). In the beginning, was the word. . . . In F. Lacerda & C. von Hofsten (Eds.), *Emerging cognitive abilities in early infancy* (pp. 173–192). Mahwah, NJ: Erlbaum.

Jusczyk, P. W. (2002). Some critical developments in acquiring native language sound organization. *Annals of Otology, Rhinology and Laryngology, 189,* 11–15.

Jusczyk, P. W., & Hohne, E. A. (1997). Infants' memory for spoken words. *Science, 277,* 1984–1986.

Jusczyk, P. W., & Luce, P. A. (2002). Speech perception. In H. Pashler & S. Yantis (Eds.), *Stevens' handbook of experimental psychology: Vol. 1. Sensation and perception* (3rd ed., pp. 493–536). New York: Wiley.

Jutras-Aswad, D., DiNieri, J. A., Harkany, T., & Hurd, Y. L. (2009). Neurobiological consequences of maternal cannabis on human fetal development and its neuropsychiatric outcome. *European Archives of Psychiatry and Clinical Neuroscience, 259,* 395–412.

K

Kaczmarczyk, M. M., Miller, M. J., & Freund, G. G. (2012). The health benefits of dietary fiber: Beyond the usual suspects of type 2 diabetes mellitus, cardiovascular disease and colon cancer. *Metabolism: Clinical and Experimental, 61,* 1058–1066.

Kagan, J. (2003). Behavioral inhibition as a temperamental category. In R. J. Davidson, K. R. Scherer, & H. H. Goldsmith (Eds.), *Handbook of*

affective science (pp. 320–331). New York: Oxford University Press.

Kagan, J. (2008a). Behavioral inhibition as a risk factor for psychopathology. In T. P. Beauchaine & S. P. Hinshaw (Eds.), *Child and adolescent psychopathology* (pp. 157–179). Hoboken, NJ: Wiley.

Kagan, J. (2008b). In defense of qualitative changes in development. *Child Development, 79,* 1606–1624.

Kagan, J. (2010). Emotions and temperament. In M. H. Bornstein (Ed.), *Handbook of cultural developmental science* (pp. 175–194). New York: Psychology Press.

Kagan, J., Arcus, D., Snidman, N., Feng, W. Y. Hendler, J., & Greene, S. (1994). Reactivity in infants: A cross-national comparison. *Developmental Psychology, 30,* 342–345.

Kagan, J., & Fox, N. A. (2006). Biology, culture, and temperamental biases. In N. Eisenberg (Ed.), *Handbook of child psychology: Vol. 3. Social, emotional, and personality development* (6th ed., pp. 167–225). Hoboken, NJ: Wiley.

Kagan, J., & Saudino, K. J. (2001). Behavioral inhibition and related temperaments. In R. N. Emde & J. K. Hewitt (Eds.), *Infancy to early childhood: Genetic and environmental influences on developmental change* (pp. 111–119). New York: Oxford University Press.

Kagan, J., Snidman, N., Kahn, V., & Towsley, S. (2007). The preservation of two infant temperaments into adolescence. *Monographs of the Society for Research in Child Development, 72*(2, Serial No. 287).

Kagan, J., Snidman, N., Zentner, M., & Peterson, E. (1999). Infant temperament and anxious symptoms in school-age children. *Development and Psychopathology, 11,* 209–224.

Kahana, E., King, C., Kahana, B., Menne, H., Webster, N. J., & Dan, A. (2005). Successful aging in the face of chronic disease. In M. L. Wykle, P. J. Whitehouse, & D. L. Morris (Eds.), *Successful aging through the life span* (pp. 101–126). New York: Springer.

Kahn, R. S., Khoury, J., Nichols, W. C., & Lanphear, B. M. (2003). Role of dopamine transporter genotype and maternal prenatal smoking in childhood hyperactive–impulsive, inattentive, and oppositional behaviors. *Journal of Pediatrics, 143,* 104–110.

Kahne, J. E., & Sporte, S. E. (2008). Developing citizens: The impact of civic learning opportunities on students' commitments to civic participation. *American Educational Research Journal, 45,* 738–766.

Kail, R. (1993). The role of a global mechanism in developmental change in speed of processing. In M. L. Howe & R. Pasnak (Eds.), *Emerging themes in cognitive development: Vol. 1. Foundations.* New York: Springer-Verlag.

Kail, R. (1997). Processing time, imagery, and spatial memory. *Journal of Experimental Child Psychology, 64,* 67–78.

Kail, R. V. (2003). Information processing and memory. In M. H. Bornstein, L. Davidson, C. L. M. Keyes, K. A. Moore, and the Center for Child Well-Being (Eds.), *Well-being: Positive development across the life course* (pp. 269–280). Mahwah, NJ: Erlbaum.

Kaisa, A., Stattin, H., & Nurmi, J. (2000). Parenting styles and adolescents' achievement strategies. *Journal of Adolescence, 23,* 205–222.

Kakihara, F., Tilton-Weaver, L., Kerr, M., & Stattin, H. (2010). The relationship of parental control to youth adjustment: Do youths' feelings about their parents play a role? *Journal of Youth and Adolescence, 39,* 1442–1456.

Kalil, A., Levine, J. A., & Ziol-Guest, K. M. (2005). Following in their parents' footsteps: How characteristics of parental work predict adolescents' interest in parents' working jobs. In B. Schneider & L. J. Waite (Eds.), *Being together, working apart: Dual-career families and the work-life balance* (pp. 422–442). New York: Cambridge University Press.

Kalisch, T., Kattenstroth, J.-C., Kowalewski, R., Tegenthoff, M., & Dinse, H. R. (2012). *PLoS ONE, 7*(1), e30420.

Kalish, R. A. (1985). The social context of death and dying. In R. H. Binstock & E. Shanas (Eds.), *Handbook of aging and the social sciences* (2nd ed., pp. 149–170). New York: Van Nostrand Reinhold.

Kaller, C. P., Rahm, B., Spreer, J., Mader, I., & Unterrainer, J. M. (2008). Thinking around the corner: The development of planning abilities. *Brain and Cognition, 67,* 360–370.

Kalpouzos, G., & Nyberg, L. (2012). *Multimodal neuroimaging in normal aging: Structure–function interactions* (pp. 273–304). New York: Psychology Press.

Kalra, L., & Ratan, R. (2007). Recent advances in stroke rehabilitation. *Stroke, 38,* 235–237.

Kaminski, J. W., Puddy, R. W., Hall, D. M., Cashman, S. Y., Crosby, A. E., & Ortega, L. G. (2010). The relative influence of different domains of social connectedness on self-directed violence in adolescence. *Journal of Youth and Adolescence, 39,* 460–473.

Kamo, Y. (1998). Asian grandparents. In M. E. Szinovacz (Ed.), *Handbook on grandparenthood* (pp. 97–112). Westport, CT: Greenwood Press.

Kane, P., & Garber, J. (2004). The relations among depression in fathers, children's psychopathology, and father–child conflict: A meta-analysis. *Clinical Psychology Review, 24,* 339–360.

Kane, R. A., Lum, T. Y., Cutler, L. J., Degenholtz, H. B., & Yu, T.-C. (2007). Resident outcomes in small-house nursing homes: A longitudinal evaluation of the initial Green House program. *Journal of the American Geriatrics Society, 55,* 836–839.

Kang, N. H., & Hong, M. (2008). Achieving excellence in teacher workforce and equity in learning opportunities in South Korea. *Educational Researcher, 37,* 200–207.

Kaplow, J. B., & Widom, C. S. (2007). Age of onset of child maltreatment predicts long-term mental health outcomes. *Journal of Abnormal Psychology, 116,* 176–187.

Kaplowitz, P. (2006). Pubertal development in girls: Secular trends. *Current Opinion in Obstetrics and Gynecology, 18,* 487–491.

Kaplowitz, P. B. (2007). Link between body fat and the timing of puberty. *Pediatrics, 121,* S208–S217.

Karafantis, D. M., & Levy, S. R. (2004). The role of children's lay theories about the malleability of human attributes in beliefs about and volunteering for disadvantaged groups. *Child Development, 75,* 236–250.

Karasawa, M., Curhan, K. B., Markus, H. R., Kitayama, S. S., Love, G. D., Radler, B. T., et al. (2011). Cultural perspectives on aging and well-being: A comparison of Japan and the U.S. *International Journal of Aging and Human Development, 73,* 73–98.

Karasik, L. B., Tamis-LeMonda, C. S., & Adolph, K. E. (2011). Transition from crawling to walking affects infants' social actions with objects. *Child Development, 82,* 1199–1209.

Karasik, L. B., Tamis-LeMonda, C. S., Adolph, K. E., & Dimitroupoulou, K. A. (2008). How mothers encourage and discourage infants' motor actions. *Infancy, 13,* 366–392.

Karel, M. J., Gatz, M., & Smyer, M. A. (2012). Aging and mental health in the decade ahead: What psychologists need to know. *American Psychologist, 67,* 184–198.

Karevold, E., Ystrom, E., Coplan, R. J., Sanson, A. V., & Mathiesen, K. S. (2012). A prospective longitudinal study of shyness from infancy to adolescence: Stability, age-related changes, and prediction of socio-emotional functioning. *Journal of Abnormal Child Psychology, 40,* 1167–1177.

Karger, H. J., & Stoesz, D. (2010). *American social welfare policy* (6th ed.). Upper Saddle River, NJ: Pearson Education.

Karlsson, C., & Berggren, I. (2011). Dignified end-of-life care in the patients' own homes. *Nursing Ethics, 18,* 374–385.

Kassel, J. D., Weinstein, S., Skitch, S. A., Veilleux, J., & Mermelstein, R. (2005). The development of substance abuse in adolescence: Correlates, causes, and consequences. In J. D. Kassel, S. Weinstein, S. A. Skitch, J. Veilleux, & R. Mermelstein (Eds.), *Development of psychopathology: A vulnerability-stress perspective* (pp. 355–384). Thousand Oaks, CA: Sage.

Kastenbaum, R. (2008). Grieving in contemporary society. In M. S. Stroebe, R. O. Hansson, H. Schut, & W. Stroebe (Eds.), *Handbook of bereavement research and practice* (pp. 67–85). Washington, DC: American Psychological Association.

Kastenbaum, R. J. (2012). *Death, society, and human experience* (11th ed.). Upper Saddle River, NJ: Pearson.

Kato, I., Franco, P., Groswasser, J., Scaillet, S., Kelmanson, I., Togari, H., & Kahn, A. (2003). Incomplete arousal processes in infants who were victims of sudden death. *American Journal of Respiratory and Critical Care, 168,* 1298–1303.

Katz, L. F., & Windecker-Nelson, B. (2004). Parental meta-emotion philosophy in families with conduct-problem children: Links with peer relations. *Journal of Abnormal Child Psychology, 32,* 385–398.

Katzman, D. K. (2005). Medical complications in adolescents with anorexia nervosa: A review of the literature. *International Journal of Eating Disorders, 37,* S52–S59.

Katz-Wise, S. L., Priess, H. A., & Hyde, J. S. (2010). Gender-role attitudes and behavior across the transition to parenthood. *Developmental Psychology, 46,* 18–28.

Kaufman, A. S. (2001). WAIS-III IQs, Horn's theory, and generational changes from young adulthood to old age. *Intelligence, 29,* 131–167.

Kaufman, A. S., & Horn, J. L. (1996). Age changes on tests of fluid and crystallized intelligence for females and males on the Kaufman Adolescent and Adult Intelligence Test (KAIT) at ages 17 to 94 years. *Archives of Clinical Neuropsychology, 11,* 97–121.

Kaufman, J., Csibra, G., & Johnson, M. H. (2005). Oscillatory activity in the infant brain reflects object maintenance. *Proceedings of the National Academy of Sciences, 102,* 15271–15274.

Kaufman, J. C., & Sternberg, R. J. (2007, July/August). Resource review: Creativity. *Change, 39,* 55–58.

Kavanaugh, R. D. (2006). Pretend play. In B. Spodek & O. N. Saracho (Eds.), *Handbook of research on the education of young children* (2nd ed., pp. 269–278). Mahwah, NJ: Erlbaum.

Kavšek, M., & Bornstein, M. H. (2010). Visual habituation and dishabituation in preterm infants: A review and meta-analysis. *Research in Developmental Disabilities, 31,* 951–975.

Kavšek, M., Yonas, A., & Granrud, C. E. (2012). Infants' sensitivity to pictorial depth cues: A review and meta-analysis. *Infant Behavior and Development, 35,* 109–128.

Kaya, Y., & Cook, K. J. (2010). A cross-national analysis of physical intimate partner violence against women. *International Journal of Comparative Sociology, 51,* 423–444.

Kaye, W. (2008). Neurobiology of anorexia and bulimia nervosa. *Physiology and Behavior, 94,* 121–135.

Kazdin, A. E., & Whitley, M. E. (2003). Treatment of parental stress to enhance therapeutic change among children referred for aggressive and antisocial behavior. *Journal of Consulting and Clinical Psychology, 71,* 504–515.

Keating, D. P. (2004). Cognitive and brain development. In R. M. Lerner & L. Steinberg (Eds.), *Handbook of adolescent psychology* (2nd ed., pp. 45–84). Hoboken, NJ: Wiley.

Keegan, L., & Drick, C. A. (2011). *End of life: Nursing solutions for death with dignity.* New York: Springer.

Keil, F. C. (1986). Conceptual domains and the acquisition of metaphor. *Cognitive Development, 1,* 73–96.

Keil, F. C., & Lockhart, K. L. (1999). Explanatory understanding in conceptual development. In E. K. Scholnick, K. Nelson, S. A. Gelman, & P. H. Miller (Eds.), *Conceptual development: Piaget's legacy* (pp. 103–130). Mahwah, NJ: Erlbaum.

Keith, J., Fry, C. L., Glascock, A. P., Ikels, C., Dickerson-Putman, J., Harpending, H. C., & Draper, P. (1994). *The aging experience: Diversity and commonality across cultures.* Thousand Oaks, CA: Sage.

Keith, P. M., & Schafer, R. B. (1991). *Relationships and well-being over the life stages.* New York: Praeger.

Keith, T. Z., Keith, P. B., Quirk, K. J., Sperduto, J., Santillo, S., & Killings, S. (1998). Longitudinal effects of parent involvement on high school grades: Similarities and differences across gender and ethnic groups. *Journal of School Psychology, 36,* 335–363.

Keller, H., Borke, Y. J., Kärtner, J., Jensen, H., & Papaligoura, Z. (2004). Developmental consequences of early parenting experiences: Self-recognition and self-regulation in three cultural communities. *Child Development, 75,* 1745–1760.

Keller, H., Kärtner, J., Borke, J., Yovsi, R., & Kleis, A. (2005). Parenting styles and the development of the categorical self: A longitudinal study on mirror self-recognition in Cameroonian Nso and German families. *International Journal of Behavioral Development, 29,* 496–504.

Keller, P. A., & Lusardi, A. (2012). Employee retirement savings: What we know and are discovering for helping people prepare for life after work. In G. D. Mick, S. Pettigrew, C. Pechmann, & J. L. Ozanne (Eds.), *Transformative consumer research for personal and collective well-being* (pp. 445–464). New York: Routledge.

Kelley, S. A., Brownell, C. A., & Campbell, S. B. (2000). Mastery motivation and self-evaluative affect in toddlers: Longitudinal relations with maternal behavior. *Child Development, 71,* 1061–1071.

Kellman, P. J., & Arterberry, M. E. (2006). Infant visual perception. In D. Kuhn & R. Siegler (Eds.), *Handbook of child psychology: Vol. 2. Cognition, perception, and language* (6th ed., pp. 109–160). Hoboken, NJ: Wiley.

Kelly, D. J., Liu, S., Ge, L., Quinn, P. C., Slater, A. M., Lee, K., Liu, Q., & Pascalis, O. (2007). Cross-race preferences for same-race faces extend beyond the African versus Caucasian contrast in 3-month-old infants. *Infancy, 11,* 87–95.

Kelly, D. J., Quinn, P. C., Slater, A. M., Lee, K., Ge, L., & Pascalis, O. (2009). Development of the other-race effect during infancy: Evidence toward universality? *Journal of Experimental Child Psychology, 104,* 105–114.

Kelly, N., & Norwich, B. (2004). Pupils' perceptions of self and of labels: Moderate learning difficulties in mainstream and special schools. *British Journal of Educational Psychology, 74,* 411–435.

Kemkes-Grottenhaler, A. (2003). Postponing or rejecting parenthood? Results of a survey among female academic professionals. *Journal of Biosocial Science, 35,* 213–226.

Kempe, C. H., Silverman, B. F., Steele, P. W., Droegemueller, P. W., & Silver, H. K. (1962). The battered-child syndrome. *Journal of the American Medical Association, 181,* 17–24.

Kempen, G., Ranchor, A. V., van Sonderen, E., van Jaarsveld, C. H. M., & Sanderman, R. (2006). Risk and protective factors of different functional trajectories in older persons: Are these the same? *Journal of Gerontology, 61B,* P95–P101.

Kemper, S. (2012). The interaction of linguistic constraints, working memory, and aging on language production and comprehension. In M. Naveh-Benjamin & N. Ohta (Eds.), *Memory and aging: Current issues and future directions* (pp. 31–47). New York: Psychology Press.

Kemper, S., Thompson, M., & Marquis, J. (2001). Longitudinal change in language production: Effects of aging and dementia on grammatical complexity and prepositional content. *Psychology and Aging, 16,* 600–614.

Kendig, H., Dykstra, P. A., van Gaalen, R. I., & Melkas, T. (2007). Health of aging parents and childless individuals. *Journal of Family Issues, 28,* 1457–1486.

Kendler, K. S., Thornton, L. M., Gilman, S. E., & Kessler, R. C. (2000). Sexual orientation in a U.S. national sample of twin and non-twin sibling pairs. *American Journal of Psychiatry, 157,* 1843–1846.

Kendrick, D., Barlow, J., Hampshire, A., Stewart-Brown, S., & Polnay, L. (2008). Parenting interventions and the prevention of unintentional injuries in childhood: Systematic review and meta-analysis. *Child: Care, Health and Development, 34,* 682–695.

Kennedy, A. M., & Gust, D. A. (2008). Measles outbreak associated with a church congregation: A study of immunization attitudes of congregation members. *Public Health Reports, 123,* 126–134.

Kennedy, G. E., & Kennedy, C. E. (1993). Grandparents: A special resource for children in stepfamilies. *Journal of Divorce and Remarriage, 19,* 45–68.

Kennell, J., Klaus, M., McGrath, S., Robertson, S., & Hinkley, C. (1991). Continuous emotional support during labor in a U.S. hospital. *Journal of the American Medical Association, 265,* 2197–2201.

Kenney, G. M., Lynch, V., Cook, A., & Phong, S. (2010). Who and where are the children yet to enroll in Medicaid and the Children's Health Insurance Program? *Health Affairs, 29,* 1920–1929.

Kenney-Benson, G. A., Pomerantz, E. M. Ryan, A. M., & Patrick, H. (2006). Sex differences in math performance: The role of children's approach to schoolwork. *Developmental Psychology, 42,* 11–26.

Kenyon, B. L. (2001). Current research in children's conceptions of death: A critical review. *Omega, 43,* 63–91.

Kerckhoff, A. C. (2002). The transition from school to work. In J. T. Mortimer & R. Larson (Eds.), *The changing adolescent experience* (pp. 52–87). New York: Cambridge University Press.

Keren, M., Feldman, R., Namdari-Weinbaum, I., Spitzer, S., & Tyano, S. (2005). Relations between parents' interactive style in dyadic and triadic play and toddlers' symbolic capacity. *American Journal of Orthopsychiatry, 75,* 599–607.

Kerestes, M., & Youniss, J. E. (2003). Rediscovering the importance of religion in adolescent development. In R. M. Lerner, F. Jacobs, & D. Wertlieb (Eds.), *Handbook of applied developmental science* (Vol. 1, pp. 165–184). Thousand Oaks, CA: Sage.

Kerestes, M., Youniss, J., & Metz, E. (2004). Longitudinal patterns of religious perspective and civic integration. *Applied Developmental Science, 8,* 39–46.

Kernis, M. H. (2002). Self-esteem as a multifaceted construct. In T. M. Brinthaupt & R. P. Lipka (Eds.), *Understanding early adolescent self and identity* (pp. 57–88). Albany: State University of New York Press.

Kernohan, W. G., Hasson, F., Hutchison, P., & Cochrane, B. (2006). Patient satisfaction with hospice day care. *Supportive Care in Cancer, 14,* 462–468.

Kerpelman, J. L., Shoffner, M. F., & Ross-Griffin, S. (2002). African American mothers' and daughters' beliefs about possible selves and their strategies for reaching the adolescent's future academic and career goals. *Journal of Youth and Adolescence, 31,* 289–302.

Kerr, D. C. R., Lopez, N. L., Olson, S. L., & Sameroff, A. J. (2004). Parental discipline and externalizing behavior problems in early childhood: The roles of moral regulation and child gender. *Journal of Abnormal Child Psychology, 32,* 369–383.

Kesler, S. R. (2007). Turner syndrome. *Child and Adolescent Psychiatric Clinics of North America, 16,* 709–722.

Kettl, P. (1998). Alaska Native suicide: Lessons for elder suicide. *International Psychogeriatrics, 10,* 205–211.

Key, J. D., Gebregziabher, M. G., Marsh, L. D., & O'Rourke, K. M. (2008). Effectiveness of an intensive, school-based intervention for teen mothers. *Journal of Adolescent Health, 42,* 394–400.

Keyes, C. L. M., & Ryff, C. D. (1998a). Generativity and adult lives: Social structural contours and quality of life consequences. In D. P. McAdams & E. de St. Aubin (Eds.), *Generativity and adult development: How and why we care for the next generation* (pp. 227–263). Washington, DC: American Psychological Association.

Keyes, C. L. M., & Ryff, C. D. (1998b). Psychological well-being in midlife. In S. L. Willis & J. D. Reid (Eds.), *Life in the middle* (pp. 161–180). San Diego: Academic Press.

Keyes, C. L. M., Shmotkin, D., & Ryff, C. D. (2002). Optimizing well-being: The empirical encounter of two traditions. *Journal of Personality and Social Psychology, 82,* 1007–1022.

Keyes, C. L. M., & Westerhof, G. J. (2012). Chronological and subjective age differences in flourishing mental health and major depressive episode. *Aging and Mental Health, 16,* 67–74.

Khashan, A. S., Baker, P. N., & Kenny, L. C. (2010). Preterm birth and reduced birthweight in first and second teenage pregnancies: A register-based cohort study. *BMC Pregnancy and Childbirth, 10,* 36.

Khavkin, J., & Ellis, D. A. (2011). Aging skin: Histology, physiology, and pathology. *Facial Plastic Surgery Clinics of North America, 19,* 229–234.

Kidd, A. R., III, & Bao, J. (2012). Recent advances in the study of age-related hearing loss: A mini-review. *Gerontology, 58,* 490–496.

Kieffer, M. J. (2008). Catching up or falling behind? Initial English proficiency, concentrated poverty and the reading growth of language minority learners in the United States. *Journal of Educational Psychology, 100,* 851–868.

Kiernan, K. (2002). Cohabitation in Western Europe: Trends, issues, and implications. In A. Booth & A. C. Crouter (Eds.), *Just living together* (pp. 3–32). Mahwah, NJ: Erlbaum.

Killen, M., Crystal, D., & Watanabe, H. (2002). The individual and the group: Japanese and American children's evaluations of peer exclusion, tolerance of difference, and prescriptions for conformity. *Child Development, 73,* 1788–1802.

Killen, M., Henning, A., Kelly, M. C., Crystal, D., & Ruck, M. (2007). Evaluations of interracial peer encounters by majority and minority U.S. children and adolescents. *International Journal of Behavioral Development, 31,* 491–500.

Killen, M., Kelly, M. C., Richardson, C., Crystal, D., & Ruck, M. (2010). European American children's and adolescents' evaluations of interracial exclusion. *Group Processes and Intergroup Relations, 13,* 283–300.

Killen, M., Lee-Kim, J., McGlothlin, H., & Stangor, C. (2002). How children and adolescents evaluate gender and racial exclusion. *Monographs of the Society for Research in Child Development, 67*(4, Serial No. 271).

Killen, M., Margie, N. G., & Sinno, S. (2006). Morality in the context of intergroup relationships. In M. Killen & J. G. Smetana (Eds.), *Handbook of moral development* (pp. 155–183). Mahwah, NJ: Erlbaum.

Killen, M., & Nucci, L. P. (1995). Morality, autonomy, and social conflict. In M. Killen & D. Hart (Eds.), *Morality in everyday life: Developmental perspectives* (pp. 52–86). Cambridge, UK: Cambridge University Press.

Killoren, S. E., Thayer, S. M., & Updegraff, K. A. (2008). Conflict resolution between Mexican origin adolescent siblings. *Journal of Marriage and Family, 70,* 1200–1212.

Kilpatrick, S. D., Bissonnette, V. L., & Rusbult, C. E. (2002). Empathic accuracy and accommodative behavior among newly married couples. *Personal Relationships, 9,* 369–393.

Kilpatrick, S. W., & Sanders, D. M. (1978). Body image stereotypes: A developmental comparison. *Journal of Genetic Psychology, 132,* 87–95.

Kim, G., Walden, T. A., & Knieps, L. J. (2010). Impact and characteristics of positive and fearful emotional messages during infant social referencing. *Infant Behavior and Development, 33,* 189–195.

Kim, J., & Cicchetti, D. (2006). Longitudinal trajectories of self-system processes and depressive symptoms among maltreated and nonmaltreated children. *Child Development, 77,* 624–639.

Kim, J. E., & Moen, P. (2002a). Is retirement good or bad for subjective well-being? *Current Directions in Psychological Science, 10,* 83–86.

Kim, J. E., & Moen, P. (2002b). Moving into retirement: Preparation and transitions in late midlife. In M. E. Lachman (Ed.), *Handbook of midlife development* (pp. 487–527). New York: Wiley.

Kim, J. M. (1998). Korean children's concepts of adult and peer authority and moral reasoning. *Developmental Psychology, 34,* 947–955.

Kim, J. M., & Turiel, E. (1996). Korean children's concepts of adult and peer authority. *Social Development, 5,* 310–329.

Kim, J.-Y., McHale, S. M., Crouter, A. C., & Osgood, D. W. (2007). Longitudinal linkages between sibling relationships and adjustment from middle childhood through adolescence. *Developmental Psychology, 43,* 960–973.

Kim, J.-Y., McHale, S. M., Osgood, D. W., & Crouter, A. C. (2006). Longitudinal course and family correlates of sibling relationships from childhood through adolescence. *Child Development, 77,* 1746–1761.

Kim, M., McGregor, K. K., & Thompson, C. K. (2000). Early lexical development in English-and Korean-speaking children: Language-general and language-specific patterns. *Journal of Child Language, 27,* 225–254.

Kim, S., & Hasher, L. (2005). The attraction effect in decision making: Superior performance by older adults. *Quarterly Journal of Experimental Psychology, 58A,* 120–133.

Kimbro, R. T. (2006). On-the-job moms: Work and breastfeeding initiation and duration for a sample of low-income women. *Maternal and Child Health Journal, 10,* 19–26.

King, A. C. (2001). Interventions to promote physical activity by older adults. *Journal of Gerontology, 56A,* 36A–46A.

King, A. C., Ahn, D. K., Oliveira, B. M., Atienza, A. A., Castro, C. M., & Gardner, C. D. (2008). Promoting physical activity through hand-held computer technology. *American Journal of Preventive Medicine, 34,* 138–142.

King, A. C., & Bjorklund, D. F. (2010). Evolutionary developmental psychology. *Psicothema, 22,* 22–27.

King, A. C., Kiernan, M., Oman, R. F., Kraemer, H., Hull, M., & Ahn, D. (1997). Can we identify who will adhere to long-term physical activity? Signal detection methodology as a potential aid to clinical decision making. *Health Psychology, 16,* 380–389.

King, A. C., Taylor, C. B., & Haskell, W. L. (1993). Effects of differing intensities and formats of 12 months of exercise training on psychological outcomes in older adults. *Health Psychology, 12,* 292–300.

King, L. A., & Hicks, J. A. (2007). Whatever happened to "What might have been"? *American Psychologist, 62,* 625–636.

King, P. E., & Furrow, J. L. (2004). Religion as a resource for positive youth development: Religion, social capital, and moral outcomes. *Developmental Psychology, 40*, 703–713.

King, P. M., & Kitchener, K. S. (1994). *Developing reflective judgment: Understanding and promoting intellectual growth and critical thinking in adolescents and adults.* San Francisco: Jossey-Bass.

King, P. M., & Kitchener, K. S. (2002). The reflective judgment model: Twenty years of research on epistemic cognition. In B. K. Hofer & P. R. Pintrich (Eds.), *Personal epistemology: The psychological beliefs about knowledge and knowing* (pp. 37–61). Mahwah, NJ: Erlbaum.

King, V. (2007). When children have two mothers: Relationships with nonresident mothers, stepmothers, and fathers. *Journal of Marriage and Family, 69*, 1178–1193.

King, V. (2009). Stepfamily formation: Implications for adolescent ties to mothers, nonresident fathers, and stepfathers. *Journal of Marriage and Family, 71*, 954–968.

Kingsberg, S. A. (2002). The impact of aging on sexual function in women and their partners. *Archives of Sexual Behavior, 31*, 431–437.

Kinney, D. (1999). From "headbangers" to "hippies": Delineating adolescents' active attempts to form an alternative peer culture. In J. A. McLellan & M. J. V. Pugh (Eds.), *The role of peer groups in adolescent social identity: Exploring the importance of stability and change* (pp. 21–35). San Francisco: Jossey-Bass.

Kinney, H. C. (2009). Brainstem mechanisms underlying the sudden infant death syndrome: Evidence from human pathologic studies. *Developmental Psychobiology, 51*, 223–233.

Kinnunen, M.-L., Pietilainen, K., & Rissanen, A. (2006). Body size and overweight from birth to adulthood. In L. Pulkkinen & J. Kaprio (Eds.), *Socioemotional development and health from adolescence to adulthood* (pp. 95–107). New York: Cambridge University Press.

Kinsella, M. T., & Monk, C. (2009). Impact of maternal stress, depression and anxiety on fetal neurobehavioral development. *Clinical Obstetrics and Gynecology, 52*, 425–440.

Kinser, K., & Deitchman, J. (2007). Tenacious persisters: Returning adult students in higher education. *Journal of College Student Retention, 9*, 75–94.

Kirby, D. (2002a). Antecedents of adolescent initiation of sex, contraceptive use, and pregnancy. *American Journal of Health Behavior, 26*, 473–485.

Kirby, D. (2002b). Effective approaches to reducing adolescent unprotected sex, pregnancy, and childbearing. *Journal of Sex Research, 39*, 51–57.

Kirby, D. (2002c). The impact of schools and school programs upon adolescent sexual behavior. *Journal of Sex Research, 39*, 27–33.

Kirby, D., & Laris, B. A. (2009). Effective curriculum-based sex and STD/HIV education programs for adolescents. *Child Development Perspectives, 3*, 21–29.

Kirchner, G. (2000). *Children's games from around the world.* Boston: Allyn and Bacon.

Kiriakidis, S. P., & Kavoura, A. (2010). Cyberbullying: A review of the literature on harassment through the Internet and other electronic means. *Family and Community Health, 33*, 82–93.

Kirk, K. M., Bailey, J. M., Dunne, M. P., & Martin, N. G. (2000). Measurement models for sexual orientation in a community twin sample. *Behavior Genetics, 30*, 345–356.

Kirkham, N. Z., Cruess, L., & Diamond, A. (2003). Helping children apply their knowledge to their behavior on a dimension-switching task. *Developmental Science, 6*, 449–476.

Kirkham, N. Z., Slemmer, J. A., & Johnson, S. P. (2002). Visual statistical learning in infancy: Evidence for a domain general learning mechanism. *Cognition, 83*, B35–B42.

Kirkwood, T. (2010, November). Why women live longer. *Scientific American, 303*, 34–35.

Kirshenbaum, A. P., Olsen, D. M., & Bickel, W. K. (2009). A quantitative review of the ubiquitous relapse curve. *Journal of Substance Abuse Treatment, 36*, 8–17.

Kirshner, B. (2009). "Power in numbers": Youth organizing as a context for exploring civic identity. *Journal of Research on Adolescence, 19*, 414–440.

Kisilevsky, B. S., Hains, S. M. J., Brown, C. A., Lee, C. T., Cowperthwaite, B., & Stutzman, S. S. (2009). Fetal sensitivity to properties of maternal speech and language. *Infant Behavior and Development, 32*, 59–71.

Kisilevsky, B. S., Hains, S. M. J., Lee, K., Xie, X., Huang, H., Ye, H. H., Zhang, K., & Wang, Z. (2003). Effects of experience on fetal voice recognition. *Psychological Science, 14*, 220–224.

Kisilevsky, B. S., & Low, J. A. (1998). Human fetal behvior: 100 years of study. *Developmental Review, 18*, 1–29.

Kite, M. E., Stockdale, G. D., Whitley, B. E., Jr., & Johnson, B. T. (2005). Attitudes toward younger and older adults: An updated meta-analytic review. *Journal of Social Issues, 61*, 241–266.

Kitzman, H. J., Olds, D. L., Cole, R. E., Hanks, C. A., Anson, E. A., Arcoleo, K. J., et al. (2010). Enduring effects of prenatal and infancy home visiting by nurses on children: Follow-up of a randomized trial among children at age 12 years. *Archives of Pediatric and Adolescent Medicine, 164*, 412–418.

Kitzmann, K. M., Cohen, R., & Lockwood, R. L. (2002). Are only children missing out? Comparison of the peer-related social competence of only children and siblings. *Journal of Social and Personal Relationships, 19*, 299–316.

Kiuru, N., Aunola, K., Vuori, J., & Nurmi, J.-E. (2009). The role of peer groups in adolescents' educational expectation and adjustment. *Journal of Youth and Adolescence, 36*, 995–1009.

Kivipelto, M., Rovio, S., Ngandu, T., Karenhold, I., Eskelinen, M., & Winblad, B. (2008). Apolipoprotein E epsilon4 magnifies lifestyle risks for dementia: A population-based study. *Journal of Cellular and Molecular Medicine, 12*, 2762–2771.

Kjønniksen, L., Anderssen, N., & Wold, B. (2009). Organized youth sport as a predictor of physical activity in adulthood. *Scandinavian Journal of Medicine and Science in Sports, 19*, 646–654.

Kjønniksen, L., Torsheim, T., & Wold, B. (2008). Tracking of leisure-time physical activity during adolescence and young adulthood: A 10-year longitudinal study. *International Journal of Behavioral Nutrition and Physical Activity, 5*, 69.

Klaczynski, P. A. (2001). Framing effects on adolescent task representations, analytic and heuristic processing, and decision making: Implications for the normative/descriptive gap. *Applied Developmental Psychology, 22*, 289–309.

Klaczynski, P. A., & Narasimham, G. (1998). Development of scientific reasoning biases: Cognitive versus ego-protective explanations. *Developmental Psychology, 34*, 175–187.

Klaczynski, P. A., Schuneman, M. J., & Daniel, D. B. (2004). Theories of conditional reasoning: A developmental examination of competing hypotheses. *Developmental Psychology, 40*, 559–571.

Klahr, D., & MacWhinney, B. (1998). Information processing. In D. Kuhn & R. S. Siegler (Eds.), *Handbook of child psychology: Vol. 2. Cognition, perception, and language* (5th ed., pp. 631–678). New York: Wiley.

Klahr, D., & Nigam, M. (2004). The equivalence of learning paths in early science instruction: Effects of direct instruction and discovery learning. *Psychological Science, 15*, 661–667.

Klareskog, L., Padyukov, L., Rönnelid, J., & Alfredsson, L. (2006). Genes, environment and immunity in the development of rheumatoid arthritis. *Current Opinion in Immunology, 18*, 650–655.

Klass, D. (2004). The inner representation of the dead child in the psychic and social narratives of bereaved parents. In R. A. Neimeyer (Ed.), *Meaning reconstruction and the experience of loss* (pp. 77–94). Washington, DC: American Psychological Association.

Klaw, E. L., Rhodes, J. E., & Fitzgerald, L. F. (2003). Natural mentors in the lives of African-American adolescent mothers: Tracking relationships over time. *Journal of Youth and Adolescence, 32*, 223–232.

Klebanov, P. K., Brooks-Gunn, J., McCarton, C., & McCormick, M. C. (1998). The contribution of neighborhood and family income to developmental test scores over the first three years of life. *Child Development, 69*, 1420–1436.

Kleespies, P. M. (2004). Concluding thoughts on suffering, dying and choice. In P. M. Kleespies (Ed.), *Life and death decisions: Psychological and ethical considerations in end-of-life care* (pp. 163–167). Washington, DC: American Psychological Association.

Klein, P. J., & Meltzoff, A. N. (1999). Long-term memory, forgetting, and deferred imitation in 12-month-old infants. *Developmental Science, 2*, 102–113.

Kleinspehn-Ammerlahn, A., Kotter-Grühn, D., & Smith, J. (2008). Self-perceptions of aging: Do subjective age and satisfaction with aging change during old age? *The Journals of Gerontology Series B: Psychological Sciences and Social Sciences, 63*, 377–385.

Klesges, L. M., Johnson, K. C., Ward, K. D., & Barnard, M. (2001). Smoking cessation in pregnant women. *Obstetrics and Gynecology Clinics of North America, 28*, 269–282.

Kliegel, M., Jäger, T., & Phillips, L. H. (2008). Adult age differences in event-based prospective memory: A meta-analysis on the role of focal versus nonfocal cues. *Psychology and Aging, 23*, 203–208.

Kliegman, R. M., Behrman, R. E., Jenson, H. B., & Stanton, B. F. (Eds.). (2008). *Nelson textbook of pediatrics e-dition.* Philadelphia: Saunders.

Kliewer, W., Fearnow, M. D., & Miller, P. A. (1996). Coping socialization in middle childhood: Tests of maternal and paternal influences. *Child Development, 67*, 2339–2357.

Klimes-Dougan, B., & Kistner, J. (1990). Physically abused preschoolers' responses to peers' distress. *Developmental Psychology, 26*, 599–602.

Klimstra, T. A., Hale, W. W., III, Raaijmakers, Q. A. W., Branje, S. J. T., & Meeus, W. H. J. (2010). Identity formation in adolescence: Change or stability? *Journal of Youth and Adolescence, 39*, 150–162.

Kline, G. H., Stanley, S. M., Markman, H. J., Olmos-Gallo, P. A., St. Peters, M., Whitton, S. W., & Prado, L. M. (2004). Timing is everything: Preengagement cohabitation and increased risk for poor marital outcomes. *Journal of Family Psychology, 18*, 311–318.

Klingman, A. (2006). Children and war trauma. In K. A. Renninger & I. E. Sigel (Eds.), *Handbook of child psychology: Vol. 4. Child psychology in practice* (6th ed., pp. 619–652). Hoboken, NJ: Wiley.

Kloep, M., & Hendry, L. B. (2007). Retirement: A new beginning? *The Psychologist, 20*, 742–745.

Kloep, M., & Hendry, L. B. (2011). A systemic approach to the transitions to adulthood. In J. J. Arnett, M. Kloep, L. B. Hendry, & J. L. Tanner (Eds.), *Debating emerging adulthood: Stage or process?* (pp. 53–75). New York: Oxford University Press.

Klomsten, A. T., Skaalvik, E. M., & Espnes, G. A. (2004). Physical self-concept and sports: Do gender differences exist? *Sex Roles, 50*, 119–127.

Klump, K. L., Kaye, W. H., & Strober, M. (2001). The evolving foundations of eating disorders. *Psychiatric Clinics of North America, 24*, 215–225.

Kluwer, E. S., & Johnson, M. D. (2007). Conflict frequency and relationship quality across the transition to parenthood. *Journal of Marriage and Family, 69,* 1089–1106.

Knafo, A., Zahn-Waxler, C., Davidov, M., Hulle, C. V., Robinson, J. L., & Rhee, S. H. (2009). Empathy in early childhood: Genetic, environmental, and affective contributions. In O. Vilarroya, S. Altran, A. Navarro, K. Ochsner, & A. Tobena (Eds.), *Values, empathy, and fairness across social barriers* (pp. 103–114). New York: New York Academy of Sciences.

Knickmeyer, R. C., Gouttard, S., Kang, C., Evans, D., Wilber, K., Smith, J. K., et al. (2008). A structural MRI study of human brain development from birth to 2 years. *Journal of Neuroscience, 28,* 12176–12182.

Knight, B. J., & Sayegh, P. (2010). Cultural values and caregiving: The updated sociocultural stress and coping model. *Journal of Gerontology, 65B,* 5–13.

Knobloch, H., & Pasamanick, B. (Eds.). (1974). *Gesell and Amatruda's Developmental Diagnosis.* Hagerstown, MD: Harper & Row.

Knopf, M., Kraus, U., & Kressley-Mba, R. A. (2006). Relational information processing of novel unrelated actions by infants. *Infant Behavior and Development, 29,* 44–53.

Knox, D., Langehough, S. O., & Walters, C. (1998). Religiosity and spirituality among college students. *College Student Journal, 32,* 430–432.

Ko, K. J., Berg, C. A., Butner, J., Uchino, B. N., & Smith, T. W. (2007). Profiles of successful aging in middle-age and older adult married couples. *Psychology and Aging, 22,* 705–718.

Kobayashi, T., Hiraki, K., & Hasegawa, T. (2005). Auditory-visual intermodal matching of small numerosities in 6-month-old infants. *Developmental Science, 8,* 409–419.

Kobayashi, T., Kazuo, H., Ryoko, M., & Hasegawa, T. (2004). Baby arithmetic: One object plus one tone. *Cognition, 91,* B23–B34.

Kobayashi, Y. (1994). Conceptual acquisition and change through social interaction. *Human Development, 37,* 233–241.

Kochanska, G. (1991). Socialization and temperament in the development of guilt and conscience. *Child Development, 62,* 1379–1392.

Kochanska, G., & Aksan, N. (2006). Children's conscience and self-regulation. *Journal of Personality, 74,* 1587–1617.

Kochanska, G., Aksan, N., & Carlson, J. J. (2005). Temperament, relationships, and young children's receptive cooperation with their parents. *Developmental Psychology, 41*(4), 648–660.

Kochanska, G., Aksan, N., & Joy, M. E. (2007). Children's fearfulness as a moderator of parenting in early socialization: Two longitudinal studies. *Developmental Psychology, 43,* 222–237.

Kochanska, G., Aksan, N., & Nichols, K. E. (2003). Maternal power assertion in discipline and moral discourse contexts: Commonalities, differences, and implications for children's moral conduct and cognition. *Developmental Psychology, 39,* 949–963.

Kochanska, G., Aksan, N., Prisco, T. R., & Adams, E. E. (2008). Mother–child and father–child mutually responsive orientation in the first 2 years and children's outcomes at preschool age: Mechanisms of influence. *Child Development, 79,* 30–44.

Kochanska, G., Casey, R. J., & Fukumoto, A. (1995). Toddlers' sensitivity to standard violations. *Child Development, 66,* 643–656.

Kochanska, G., Forman, D. R., Aksan, N., & Dunbar, S. B. (2005). Pathways to conscience: Early mother–child mutually responsive orientation and children's moral emotion, conduct, and cognition. *Journal of Child Psychology and Psychiatry, 46,* 19–34.

Kochanska, G., Gross, J. N., Lin, M.-H., & Nichols, K. E. (2002). Guilt in young children: Development, determinants, and relations with broader system standards. *Child Development, 73,* 461–482.

Kochanska, G., & Knaack, A. (2003). Effortful control as a personality characteristic of young children: Antecedents, correlates, and consequences. *Journal of Personality, 71,* 1087–1112.

Kochanska, G., Murray, K. T., & Harlan, E. T. (2000). Effortful control in early childhood: Continuity and change, antecedents, and implications for social development. *Developmental Psychology, 36,* 220–232.

Kochanska, G., Philibert, R. A., & Barry, R. A. (2009). Interplay of genes and early other–child relationship in the development of self-regulation from toddler to preschool age. *Journal of Child Psychology and Psychiatry, 50,* 1331–1338.

Kochenderfer-Ladd, B. (2003). Identification of aggressive and asocial victims and the stability of their peer victimization. *Merrill-Palmer Quarterly, 49,* 401–425.

Koestner, R., Franz, C., & Weinberger, J. (1990). The family origins of empathic concern: A 26-year longitudinal study. *Journal of Personality and Social Psychology, 58,* 709–717.

Kohen, D. E., Leventhal, T., Dahinten, V. S., & McIntosh, C. N. (2008). Neighborhood disadvantage: Pathways of effects for young children. *Child Development, 79,* 156–169.

Kohlberg, L. (1969). Stage and sequence: The cognitive-developmental approach to socialization. In D. A. Goslin (Ed.), *Handbook of socialization theory and research* (pp. 347– 480). Chicago: Rand McNally.

Kohlberg, L., Levine, C., & Hewer, A. (1983). *Moral stages: A current formulation and a response to critics.* Basel, Switzerland: Karger.

Kohn, M. L. (2006). *Change and stability: A crossnational analysis of social structure and personality.* Greenbrae, CA: Paradigm Press.

Kohn, M. L., Naoi, A., Schoenbach, C., Schooler, C., & Slomczynski, K. M. (1990). Position in the class structure and psychological functioning in the United States, Japan, and Poland. *American Journal of Sociology, 95,* 964–1008.

Kohn, M. L., & Slomczynski, K. M. (1990). *Social structure and self-direction: A comparative analysis of the United States and Poland.* Cambridge, MA: Blackwell.

Komp, D. M. (1996). The changing face of death in children. In H. M. Spiro, M. G. M. Curnen, & L. P. Wandel (Eds.), *Facing death: Where culture, religion, and medicine meet* (pp. 66–76). New Haven: Yale University Press.

Konner, M. (2010). *The evolution of childhood: Relationships, emotion, mind.* Cambridge, MA: Harvard University Press.

Konold, T. R., & Pianta, R. C. (2005). Empirically derived, person-oriented patterns of school readiness in typically developing children: Description and prediction to first-grade achievement. *Applied Developmental Science, 9,* 174–187.

Kopp, C. B., & Neufeld, S. J. (2003). Emotional development during infancy. In R. Davidson, K. R. Scherer, & H. H. Goldsmith (Eds.), *Handbook of affective sciences* (pp. 347–374). Oxford, UK: Oxford University Press.

Kooijman, V., Hagoort, P., & Cutler, A. (2009). Prosodic structure in early word segmentation: ERP evidence from Dutch ten-month-olds. *Infancy, 14,* 591–612.

Kopeikina, K. J., Carlson, G. A., Pitstick, R., Ludvigson, A. E., Peters, A., et al. (2011). Tau accumulation causes mitochondrial distribution deficits in neurons in a mouse model of tauopathy and in human Alzheimer's disease brain. *American Journal of Pathology 179,* 2071–2082.

Korkman, M., Kettunen, S., & Autti-Raemoe, I. (2003). Neurocognitive impairment in early adolescence following prenatal alcohol exposure of varying duration. *Child Neurology, 9,* 117–128.

Kornhaber, M. L. (2004). Using multiple intelligences to overcome cultural barriers to identification for gifted education. In D. Boothe & J. C. Stanley (Eds.), *In the eyes of the beholder: Critical issues for diversity in gifted education* (pp. 215–225). Waco, TX: Prufrock Press.

Koropeckyj-Cox, T., & Pendell, G. (2007). The gender gap in attitudes about childlessness in the United States. *Journal of Marriage and Family, 69,* 899–915.

Koster, A., Penninx, B. W., Newman, A. B., Visser, M., van Gool, C. H., & Harris, T. B. (2007). Lifestyle factors and incident mobility limitation in obese and non-obese older adults. *Obesity, 15,* 3122–3132.

Kotkin, J. (2012, July 16). Are Millennials the screwed generation? *Newsweek.* Retrieved from www .thedailybeast.com/newsweek/2012/07/15/are-millennials-the-screwed-generation.html

Kotre, J. (1999). *Make it count: How to generate a legacy that gives meaning to your life.* New York: Free Press.

Kowalski, R. M., Limber, S. P., & Agatston, P. W. (2008). *Cyber bullying: Bullying in the digital age.* Malden, MA: Blackwell.

Kozer, E., Costei, A. M., Boskovic, R., Nulman, I., Nikfar, S., & Koren, G. (2003). Effects of aspirin consumption during pregnancy on pregnancy outcomes: Meta-analysis. *Birth Defects Research, Part B, Developmental and Reproductive Toxicology, 68,* 70–84.

Kozol, J. (2005). *The shame of the nation: The restoration of apartheid schooling in America.* New York: Three Rivers Press.

Kozulin, A. (Ed.). (2003). *Vygotsky's educational theory in cultural context.* Cambridge, U.K.: Cambridge University Press.

Krafft, K., & Berk, L. E. (1998). Private speech in two preschools: Significance of open-ended activities and make-believe play for verbal self-regulation. *Early Childhood Research Quarterly, 13,* 637–658.

Kragstrup, T. W., Kjaer, M., & Mackey, A. L. (2011). Structural, biochemical, cellular, and functional changes in skeletal muscle extracellular matrix with aging. *Scandinavian Journal of Medicine and Science in Sports, 21,* 749–757.

Krähenbühl, S., Blades, M., & Eiser, C. (2009). The effect of repeated questioning on children's accuracy and consistency in eyewitness testimony. *Legal and Criminological Psychology, 14,* 263–278.

Kral, T. V. E., & Faith, M. S. (2009). Influences on child eating and weight development from a behavioral genetics perspective. *Journal of Pediatric Psychology, 34,* 596–605.

Kramer, A. F., Fabiani, M., & Colcombe, S. J. (2006). Contributions of cognitive neuroscience to the understanding of behavior and aging. In J. E. Birren & K. W. Schaie (Eds.), *Handbook of the psychology of aging* (6th ed., pp. 57–83). Burlington, MA: Elsevier Academic Press.

Kramer, A. F., Hahn, S., & Gopher, D. (1998). Task coordination and aging: Explorations of executive control processes in the task switching paradigm. *Acta Psychologica, 101,* 339–378.

Kramer, A. F., & Kray, J. (2006). Aging and attention. In E. Bialystok & F. I. M. Fergus (Eds.), *Lifespan cognition: Mechanisms of change* (pp. 57–69). New York: Oxford University Press.

Kramer, A. F., & Madden, D. J. (2008). Attention. In F. I. M. Craik & T. A. Salthouse (Eds.), *Handbook of aging and cognition* (pp. 189–249). New York: Psychology Press.

Kramer, D. A. (2003). The ontogeny of wisdom in its variations. In J. Demick & C. Andreoletti (Eds.), *Handbook of adult development* (pp. 131–151). New York: Springer.

Kramer, S. E., Kapteyn, T. S., Kuik, D. J., & Deeg, D. J. (2002). The association of hearing impairment and chronic diseases with psychosocial health status in older age. *Journal of Aging and Health, 14,* 122–137.

Krampe, R. T., & Charness, N. (2007). Aging and expertise. In K. A. Ericsson, N. Charness, P. J. Feltovich, & R. R. Hoffman (Eds.), *Cambridge handbook of expertise and expert performance* (pp. 723–742). New York: Cambridge University Press.

Krause, N. (2001). Social support. In R. H. Binstock & L. K. George (Eds.), *Handbook of aging and the social sciences* (5th ed., pp. 272–294). San Diego, CA: Academic Press.

Krause, N. (2004). Neighborhoods, health, and well-being in later life. In H.-W. Wahl, R. J. Scheidt, & P. G. Windley (Eds.), *Aging in context: Socio-physical environments* (pp. 223–249). New York: Springer.

Krause, N. (2005). God-mediated control and psychological well-being in late life. *Research on Aging, 27,* 136–164.

Krause, N. (2012). Religious involvement, humility, and change in self-rated health over time. *Journal of Psychology and Theology, 40,* 199–210.

Krcmar, M., Grela, B., & Linn, K. (2007). Can toddlers learn vocabulary from television? An experimental approach. *Media Psychology, 10,* 41–63.

Krebs, D., & Denton, K. (2005). Toward a more pragmatic approach to morality: A critical evaluation of Kohlberg's model. *Psychological Review, 112,* 629–649.

Krebs, D. L., Vermeulen, S. C., Carpendale, J. I., & Denton, K. (1991). Structural and situational influences on moral judgment: The interaction between stage and dilemma. In W. Kurtines & J. Gewirtz (Eds.), *Handbook of moral behavior and development: Theory, research, and application* (pp. 139–169). Hillsdale, NJ: Erlbaum.

Kreppner, J. M., Kumsta, R., Rutter, M., Beckett, C., Castle, J., Stevens, S., et al. (2010). Developmental course of deprivation specific psychological patterns: Early manifestations, persistence to age 15, and clinical features. *Monographs of the Society for Research in Child Development, 75*(1, Serial No. 295), 79–101.

Kreppner, J. M., Rutter, M., Beckett, C., Castle, J., Colvert, E., Groothues, C., Hawkins, A., & O'Connor, T. G. (2007). Normality and impairment following profound early institutional deprivation: A longitudinal follow-up into early adolescence. *Developmental Psychology, 43,* 931–946.

Krettenauer, T. (2005). The role of epistemic cognition in adolescent identity formation: Further evidence. *Journal of Youth and Adolescence, 34,* 185–198.

Krevans, J., & Gibbs, J. C. (1996). Parents' use of inductive discipline: Relations to children's empathy and prosocial behavior. *Child Development, 67,* 3263–3277.

Krishnamoorthy, J. S., Hart, C., & Jelalian, E. (2006). The epidemic of childhood obesity: Review of research and implications for public policy. *Social Policy Report of the Society for Research in Child Development, 9*(2).

Kroger, J. (2007). *Identity development: Adolescence through adulthood* (2nd ed.). Thousand Oaks, CA: Sage.

Kroger, J., Martinussen, M., & Marcia, J. E. (2010). Identity status change during adolescence and young adulthood: A meta-analysis. *Journal of Adolescence, 33,* 683–698.

Kropf, N. P., & Pugh, K. L. (1995). Beyond life expectancy: Social work with centenarians. *Journal of Gerontological Social Work, 23,* 121–137.

Krumhansl, C. L., & Jusczyk, P. W. (1990). Infants' perception of phrase structure in music. *Psychological Science, 1,* 70–73.

Kubicek, B., Korunka, C., Raymo, J. M., & Hoonakker, P. (2011). Psychological well-being in retirement: The effects of personal and gendered contextual resources. *Journal of Occupational Health Psychology, 16,* 230–246.

Kubik, M. Y., Lytle, L. A., Hannan, P. J., Perry, C. L., & Story, M. (2003). The association of the school food environment with dietary behaviors of young adolescents. *American Journal of Public Health, 93,* 1168–1173.

Kübler-Ross, E. (1969). *On death and dying.* New York: Macmillan.

Kubotera, T. (2004). Japanese religion in changing society: The spirits of the dead. In J. D. Morgan & P. Laungani (Eds.), *Death and bereavement around the world: Vol. 4. Asia, Australia, and New Zealand* (pp. 95–99). Amityville, NY: Baywood Publishing Company.

Kubzansky, L. D., Wright, R. J., Cohen, S., Weiss, S., Rosner, B., & Sparrow, D. (2002). Breathing easy: A prospective study of optimism and pulmonary function in the Normative Aging Study. *Annals of Behavioral Medicine, 24,* 345–353.

Kuchner, J. (1989, April). *Chinese-American and European-American mothers and infants: Cultural influences in the first three months of life.* Paper presented at the biennial meeting of the Society for Research in Child Development, Kansas City, MO.

Kuczynski, L. (1984). Socialization goals and mother-child interaction: Strategies for long-term and short-term compliance. *Developmental Psychology, 20,* 1061–1073.

Kuczynski, L., & Lollis, S. (2002). Four foundations for a dynamic model of parenting. In J. R. M. Gerris (Ed.), *Dynamics of parenting.* Hillsdale, NJ: Erlbaum.

Kudo, N., Nonaka, Y., Noriko, M., Katsumi, M., & Okanoya, K. (2011). On-line statistical segmentation of a non-speech auditory stream in neonates as demonstrated by event-related brain potentials. *Developmental Science, 14,* 1100–1106.

Kuebli, J., Butler, S., & Fivush, R. (1995). Mother–child talk about past emotions: Relations of maternal language and child gender over time. *Cognition and Emotion, 9,* 265–283.

Kugelmass, J., & Ainscow, M. (2004). Leadership for inclusion: A comparison of international practices. *Journal of Research in Special Educational Needs, 4,* 133–141.

Kuhl, P. K., Tsao, F.-M., & Liu, H.-M. (2003). Foreignlanguage experience in infancy: Effects of short-term exposure and social interaction on phonetic learning. *Proceedings of the National Academy of Sciences, 100,* 9096–9101.

Kuhn, D. (2000). Theory of mind, metacognition, and reasoning: A life-span perspective. In P. Mitchell & K. J. Riggs (Eds.), *Children's reasoning and the mind* (pp. 301–326). Hove, UK: Psychology Press.

Kuhn, D. (2002). What is scientific thinking, and how does it develop? In U. Goswami (Ed.), *Blackwell handbook of childhood cognitive development* (pp. 371–393). Malden, MA: Blackwell.

Kuhn, D. (2008). Formal operations from a twenty-first century perspective. *Human Development, 51,* 48–55.

Kuhn, D. (2009). Adolescent thinking. In R. M. Lerner & L. Steinberg (Eds.), *Handbook of adolescent psychology, Vol. 1: Individual bases of adolescent development* (3rd ed., pp. 152–186). Hoboken, NJ: Wiley.

Kuhn, D., Amsel, E., & O'Loughlin, M. (1988). *The development of scientific thinking skills.* Orlando, FL: Academic Press.

Kuhn, D., & Dean, D. (2004). Connecting scientific reasoning and causal inference. *Journal of Cognition and Development, 5,* 261–288.

Kuhn, D., & Franklin, S. (2006). The second decade: What develops (and how)? In D. Kuhn & R. S. Siegler (Eds.), *Handbook of child psychology: Vol. 2. Cognition, perception, and language* (6th ed.). Hoboken, NJ: Wiley.

Kuhn, D., Iordanou, K., Pease, M., & Wirkala, C. (2008). Beyond control of variables: What needs to develop to achieve skilled scientific thinking? *Cognitive Development, 23,* 435–451.

Kuhn, D., & Pearsall, S. (2000). Developmental origins of scientific thinking. *Journal of Cognition and Development, 1,* 113–129.

Kuhn, D., & Pease, M. (2006). Do children and adults learn differently? *Journal of Cognition and Development, 7,* 279–293.

Kuklinski, M. R., & Weinstein, R. S. (2001). Classroom and developmental differences in a path model of teacher expectancy effects. *Child Development, 72,* 1554–1578.

Kulik, K. (2001). Marital relationships in late adulthood: Synchronous versus asynchronous couples. *International Journal of Aging and Human Development, 52,* 323–339.

Kumar, S., & O'Brien, A. (2004). Recent developments in fetal medicine. *British Medical Journal, 328,* 1002–1006.

Kunemund, H., Motel-Klingebiel, A., & Kohli, M. (2005). Do intergenerational transfers from elderly parents increase social inequality among their middle-aged children? Evidence from the German Aging Survey. *Journal of Gerontology, 60B,* S30-S36.

Kunnen, E. S., & Bosma, H. A. (2003). Fischer's skill theory applied to identity development: A response to Kroger. *Identity, 3,* 247–270.

Kunnen, E. S., Sappa, V., van Gert, P. L. C., & Bonica, L. (2008). The shapes of commitment development in emerging adulthood. *Journal of Adult Development, 15,* 113–131.

Kuppens, S., Grietens, H., Onghena, P., & Michiels, D. (2009). Associations between parental control and children's overt and relational aggression. *British Journal of Developmental Psychology, 27,* 607–623.

Kurdek, L. A. (2005). Gender and marital satisfaction early in marriage: A growth curve approach. *Journal of Marriage and Family, 67,* 68–84.

Kurdek, L. A. (2006). Differences between partners from heterosexual, gay, and lesbian cohabiting couples. *Journal of Marriage and Family, 68,* 509–528.

Kurdek, L. A., & Fine, M. A. (1994). Family acceptance and family control as predictors of adjustment in young adolescents: Linear, curvilinear, or interactive effects? *Child Development, 65,* 1137–1146.

Kurganskaya, M. E. (2011). Manual asymmetry in children is related to parameters of early development and familial sinistrality. *Human Physiology, 37,* 654–657.

Kurtz-Costes, B., Rowley, S. J., Harris-Britt, A., & Woods, T. A. (2008). Gender stereotypes about mathematics and science and self-perceptions of ability in late childhood and early adolescence. *Merrill-Palmer Quarterly, 54,* 386–409.

Kwon, Y. H., Fingert, J. H., Kuehn, M. H., & Alward, W. L. (2009). Primary open-angle glaucoma. *New England Journal of Medicine, 360,* 1113–1124.

Kyratzis, A., & Guo, J. (2001). Preschool girls' and boys' verbal conflict strategies in the United States and China. *Research on Language and Social Interaction, 34,* 45–74.

L

Labouvie-Vief, G. (1980). Beyond formal operations: Uses and limits of pure logic in life-span development. *Human Development, 23,* 141–160.

Labouvie-Vief, G. (1985). Logic and self-regulation from youth to maturity: A model. In M. Commons, F. Richards, & C. Armon (Eds.), *Beyond formal operations: Late adolescent and adult cognitive development* (pp. 158–180). New York: Praeger.

Labouvie-Vief, G. (2003). Dynamic integration: Affect, cognition, and the self in adulthood. *Current Directions in Psychological Science, 12,* 201–206.

Labouvie-Vief, G. (2005). Self-with-other representations and the organization of the self. *Journal of Research in Personality, 39,* 185–205.

Labouvie-Vief, G. (2006). Emerging structures of adult thought. In J. J. Arnett & J. L. Tanner (Eds.), *Emerging adults in America: Coming of age in the 21st century* (pp. 59–84). Washington, DC: American Psychological Association.

Labouvie-Vief, G. (2008). When differentiation and negative affect lead to integration and growth. *American Psychologist, 63,* 564–565.

Labouvie-Vief, G., Chiodo, L. M., Goguen, L. A., Diehl, M., & Orwoll, L. (1995). Representations of self across the life span. *Psychology and Aging, 10,* 404–415.

Labouvie-Vief, G., DeVoe, M., & Bulka, D. (1989). Speaking about feelings: Conceptions of emotion across the life span. *Psychology and Aging, 4,* 425–437.

Labouvie-Vief, G., & Diehl, M. (1999). Self and personality development. In J. C. Kavanaugh & S. K. Whitbourne (Eds.), *Gerontology: An interdisciplinary perspective* (pp. 238–268). New York: Oxford University Press.

Labouvie-Vief, G., & Diehl, M. (2000). Cognitive complexity and cognitive-affective integration: Related or separate domains of adult development? *Psychology and Aging, 15,* 490–504.

Labouvie-Vief, G., Diehl, M., Jain, E., & Zhang, F. (2007). Six-year change in affect optimization and affect complexity across the adult life span: A further examination. *Psychology and Aging, 22,* 738–751.

Labouvie-Vief, G., Grühn, S., & Studer, J. (2010). Dynamic integration of emotion and cognition: Equilibrium regulation in development and aging. In W. Overton & R. M. Lerner (Eds.), *Handbook of life-span development: Vol. 2. Social and emotional development* (pp. 79–115). Hoboken, NJ: Wiley.

Lachance, J. A., & Mazzocco, M. M. M. (2006). A longitudinal analysis of sex differences in math and spatial skills in primary school age children. *Learning and Individual Differences, 16,* 195–216.

Lachance-Grzela, M., & Bouchard, G. (2010). Why do women do the lion's share of housework? A decade of research. *Sex Roles, 63,* 767–780.

Lachman, M. E. (2004). Development in midlife. *Annual Review of Psychology, 55,* 305–331.

Lachman, M. E., & Bertrand, R. M. (2002). Personality and self in midlife. In M. E. Lachman (Ed.), *Handbook of midlife development* (pp. 279–309). New York: Wiley.

Lachman, M. E., Neupert, S. D., & Agrigoroaei, S. (2011). The relevance of control beliefs for health and aging. In. K. W. Schaie & S. L. Willis (Eds.), *Handbook of the psychology of aging* (7th ed., pp. 175–190). San Diego, CA: Elsevier.

Lachs, M., Bachman, R., Williams, C. S., Kossack, A., Bove, C., & O'Leary, J. (2006). Violent crime victimization increases the risk of nursing home placement in older adults. *Gerontologist, 46,* 583–589.

Lacourse, E., Nagin, D., Tremblay, R. E., Vitaro, F., & Claes, M. (2003). Developmental trajectories of boys' delinquent group membership and facilitation of violent behaviors during adolescence. *Development and Psychopathology, 15,* 183–197.

Ladd, G. W. (2005). *Children's peer relationships and social competence: A century of progress.* New Haven, CT: Yale University Press.

Ladd, G. W., Birch, S. H., & Buhs, E. S. (1999). Children's social and scholastic lives in kindergarten: Related spheres of influence? *Child Development, 70,* 1373–1400.

Ladd, G. W., Buhs, E. S., & Seid, M. (2000). Children's initial sentiments about kindergarten: Is school liking an antecedent of early classroom participation and achievement? *Merrill-Palmer Quarterly, 46,* 255–279.

Ladd, G. W., & Burgess, K. B. (1999). Charting the relationship trajectories of aggressive, withdrawn, and aggressive/withdrawn children during early grade school. *Child Development, 70,* 910–929.

Ladd, G. W., Herald, S. L., & Kochel, K. P. (2006). School readiness: Are there social prerequisites? *Early Education and Development, 17,* 115–150.

Ladd, G. W., Kochenderfer-Ladd, B., Eggum, N. D., Kochel, K. P., & McConnell, E. M. (2011).

Characterizing and comparing the friendships of anxious-solitary and unsociable preadolescents. *Child Development, 82,* 1434–1453.

Ladd, G. W., LeSieur, K., & Profilet, S. M. (1993). Direct parental influences on young children's peer relations. In S. Duck (Ed.), *Learning about relationships* (Vol. 2, pp. 152–183). London: Sage.

Ladd, G. W., & Pettit, G. S. (2002). Parenting and the development of children's peer relationships. In M. Bornstein (Ed.), *Handbook of parenting* (2nd ed.). Mahwah, NJ: Erlbaum.

Ladd, G. W., & Price, J. M. (1987). Predicting children's social and school adjustment following the transition from preschool to kindergarten. *Child Development, 58,* 1168–1189.

LaFraniere, S. (2011, April 6). As China ages, birthrate policy may prove difficult to reverse. *New York Times.* Retrieved from www.nytimes.com/2011/04/07/world/asia/07population.html?pagewanted=all

Lagattuta, K. H., Wellman, H. M., & Flavell, J. H. (1997). Preschoolers' understanding of the link between thinking and feeling: Cognitive cuing and emotional change. *Child Development, 68,* 1081–1104.

Lagnado, L. (2001, November 2). Kids confront Trade Center trauma. *Wall Street Journal,* pp. B1, B6.

Laible, D. (2004). Mother–child discourse in two contexts: Links with child temperament, attachment security, and socioemotional competence. *Developmental Psychology, 40,* 979–992.

Laible, D. (2007). Attachment with parents and peers in late adolescence: Links with emotional competence and social behavior. *Personality and Individual Differences, 43,* 1185–1197.

Laible, D., & Song, J. (2006). Constructing emotional and relational understanding: The role of affect and mother–child discourse. *Merrill-Palmer Quarterly, 52,* 44–69.

Laible, D., & Thompson, R. A. (2002). Mother–child conflict in the toddler years: Lessons in emotion, morality, and relationships. *Child Development, 73,* 1187–1203.

Laird, R. D., Jordan, K. Y., Dodge, K. A., Pettit, G. S., & Bates, J. E. (2001). Peer rejection in childhood, involvement with antisocial peers in early adolescence, and the development of externalizing behavior problems. *Development and Psychopathology, 13,* 337–354.

Laird, R. D., Pettit, G. S., Dodge, K. A., & Bates, J. E. (2005). Peer relationship antecedents of delinquent behavior in late adolescence: Is there evidence of demographic group differences in developmental processes? *Development and Psychopathology, 17,* 127–144.

Lalonde, C. E., & Chandler, M. J. (2002). Children's understanding of interpretation. *New Ideas in Psychology, 20,* 163–198.

Lalonde, C. E., & Chandler, M. J. (2005). Culture, selves, and time: Theories of personal persistence in native and non-native youth. In C. Lightfoot, C. Lalonde, & M. Chandler (Eds.), *Changing conceptions of psychological life* (pp. 207–229). Mahwah, NJ: Erlbaum.

Lamarche, V., Brendgen, M., Boivin, M., Vitaro, F., Perusse, D., & Dionne, G. (2006). Do friendships and sibling relationships provide protection against peer victimization in a similar way? *Social Development, 15,* 373–393.

Lamaze, F. (1958). *Painless childbirth.* London: Burke.

Lamb, M. E., & Ahnert, L. (2006). Nonparental child care: Context, concepts, correlates, and consequences. In K. A. Renninger & I. E. Sigel (Eds.), *Handbook of child psychology: Vol. 4. Child psychology in practice* (6th ed., pp. 700–778). Hoboken, NJ: Wiley.

Lamb, M. E., & Lewis, C. (2004). The development and significance of father–child relationships in two-parent families. In M. E. Lamb (Ed.), *The role of the*

father in child development (4th ed., pp. 272–306). Hoboken, NJ: Wiley.

Lamb, M. E., & Oppenheim, D. (1989). Fatherhood and father–child relationships: Five years of research. In S. H. Cath, A. Gurwitt, & L. Gunsberg (Eds.), *Fathers and their families* (pp. 11–26). Hillsdale, NJ: Erlbaum.

Lamb, M. E., Thompson, R. A., Gardner, W., Charnov, E. L., & Connell, J. P. (1985). Infant–mother attachment: The origins and developmental significance of individual differences in the Strange Situation: Its study and biological interpretation. *Behavioral and Brain Sciences, 7,* 127–147.

Lamberg, L. (2007). Menopause not always to blame for sleep problems in midlife women. *Journal of the American Medical Association, 297,* 1865–1866.

Lambert, S. M., Masson, P., & Fisch, H. (2006). The male biological clock. *World Journal of Urology, 24,* 611–617.

Lampl, M. (1993). Evidence of saltatory growth in infancy. *American Journal of Human Biology, 5,* 641–652.

Lampl, M., Veldhuis, J. D., & Johnson, M. L. (1992). Saltation and stasis: A model of human growth. *Science, 258,* 801–803.

Landman, J., Vandewater, E. A., Stewart, A. J., & Malley, J. E. (1995). Missed opportunities: Psychological ramifications of counterfactual thought in midlife women. *Journal of Adult Development, 2,* 87–97.

Lang, F. R., & Baltes, M. M. (1997). Being with people and being alone in later life: Costs and benefits for everyday functioning. *International Journal of Behavioral Development, 21,* 729–749.

Lang, F. R., Featherman, D. L., & Nesselroade, J. R. (1997). Social self-efficacy and short-term variability in social relationships: The MacArthur Successful Aging Studies. *Psychology and Aging, 12,* 657–666.

Lang, F. R., Rohr, M. K., & Williger, B. (2010). Modeling success in life-span psychology: The principles of selection, optimization, and compensation. In L. Fingerman, C. A. Berg, J. Smith, & T. C. Antonucci (Eds.), *Handbook of life-span development* (pp. 57–85). New York: Springer.

Lang, F. R., Staudinger, U. M., & Carstensen, L. L. (1998). Perspectives on socioemotional selectivity in late life: How personality and social context do (and do not) make a difference. *Journal of Gerontology, 53B,* P21–P30.

Lang, I. A., Llewellyn, D. J., Langa, K. M., Wallace, R. B., Huppert, F. A., & Melzer, D. (2008). Neighborhood deprivation, individual socioeconomic status, and cognitive function in older people: Analyses from the English Longitudinal Study of Ageing. *Journal of the American Geriatric Society, 56,* 191–198.

Lang, M. (2010). Can mentoring assist in the school-to-work transition? *Education + Training, 52,* 359–367.

Langer, G. (2004). *ABC New Prime Time Live Poll: The American Sex Survey.* Retrieved from abcnews.go.com/Primetime/News/story?id=174461&page=1

Langer, J., Gillette, P., & Arriaga, R. I. (2003). Toddlers' cognition of adding and subtracting objects in action and in perception. *Cognitive Development, 18,* 233–246.

Langhinrichsen-Rohling, J., Friend, J., & Powell, A. (2009). Adolescent suicide, gender, and culture: A rate and risk factor analysis. *Aggression and Violent Behavior, 14,* 402–414.

Langosch, D. (2012). Grandparents parenting again: Challenges, strengths, and implications for practice. *Psychoanalytic Inquiry, 32,* 163–170.

Langsetmo, L., Hitchcock, C. L., Kingwell, E. J., Davison, K. S., Berger, C., Forsmo, S., et al., (2012). Physical activity, body mass index and bone mineral density-associations in a prospective population-based cohort of women and men: The Canadian Multicentre Osteoporosis Study. *Bone, 50,* 401–408.

Lansford, J. E. (2009). Parental divorce and children's adjustment. *Perspectives on Psychological Science, 4,* 140–152.

Lansford, J. E., Antonucci, T. C., Akiyama, H., & Takahashi, K. (2005). A quantitative and qualitative approach to social relationships and well-being in the United States and Japan. *Journal of Comparative Family Studies, 36,* 1–22.

Lansford, J. E., Criss, M. M., Dodge, K. A., Shaw, D. S., Pettit, G. S., & Bates, J. E. (2009). Trajectories of physical discipline: Early childhood antecedents and developmental outcomes. *Child Development, 80,* 1385–1402.

Lansford, J. E., Criss, M. M., Pettit, G. S., Dodge, K. A., & Bates, J. E. (2003). Friendship quality, peer group affiliation, and peer antisocial behavior as moderators of the link between negative parenting and adolescent externalizing behavior. *Journal of Research on Adolescence, 13,* 161–184.

Lansford, J. E., Deater-Deckard, K., Dodge, K. A., Bates, J. E., & Pettit, G. S. (2004). Ethnic differences in the link between physical discipline and later adolescent externalizing behaviors. *Journal of Child Psychology and Psychiatry, 45,* 801–812.

Lansford, J. E., Malone, P. S., Castellino, D. R., Dodge, K. A., Pettit, G., & Bates, J. E. (2006). Trajectories of internalizing, externalizing, and grades for children who have and have not experienced their parents' divorce or separation. *Journal of Family Psychology, 20,* 292–301.

Lapierr, S., Erlangsen, A., Waern, M., De Leo, D., Oyama, H., Scocco, P., et al. (2011). A systematic review of elderly suicide prevention programs. *Crisis, 32,* 88–98.

Larbi, A., Fülöp, T., & Pawelec, G. (2008). Immune receptor signaling, aging and autoimmunity. In A. B. Sigalov (Ed.), *Multichain immune recognition receptor signaling: From spatiotemporal organization to human disease* (pp. 312–324). New York: Springer.

Largo, R. H., Caflisch, J. A., Hug, F., Muggli, K., Molnar, A. A., & Molinari, L. (2001). Neuromotor development from 5 to 18 years. Part 1: Timed performance. *Developmental Medicine and Child Neurology, 43,* 436–443.

Larkin, S. (2010). *Metacognition in young children.* London: Routledge.

Larsen, J. A., & Nippold, M. A. (2007). Morphological analysis in school-age children: Dynamic assessment of a word learning strategy. *Language, Speech, and Hearing Services in Schools, 38,* 201–212.

Larsen, J. T., To, Y. M., & Fireman, G. (2007). Childen's understanding and experience of mixed emotions. *Psychological Science, 18,* 186–191.

Larsen, P. (2009, January). A review of cardiovascular changes in the older adult. *Gerontology Update, December 2008/January 2009, 3,* 9.

Larson, D. G., & Hoyt, W. T. (2007). What has become of grief counseling? An evaluation of the empirical foundations of the new pessimism. *Professional Psychology: Research and Practice, 38,* 347–355.

Larson, R. W. (2001). How U.S. children and adolescents spend time: What it does (and doesn't) tell us about their development. *Current Directions in Psychological Science, 10,* 160–164.

Larson, R. W., & Ham, M. (1993). Stress and "storm and stress" in early adolescence: The relationship of negative events with dysphoric affect. *Developmental Psychology, 29,* 130–140.

Larson, R. W., & Lampman-Petraitis, C. (1989). Daily emotional states as reported by children and adolescents. *Child Development, 60,* 1250–1260.

Larson, R. W., Mannell, R., & Zuzanek, J. (1986). Daily well-being of older adults with friends and family. *Psychology and Aging, 1,* 117–126.

Larson, R. W., Moneta, G., Richards, M. H., & Wilson, S. (2002). Continuity, stability, and change in daily emotional experience across adolescence. *Child Development, 73,* 1151–1165.

Larson, R. W., & Richards, M. (1998). Waiting for the weekend: Friday and Saturday night as the emotional climax of the week. In A. C. Crouter & R. Larson (Eds.), *Temporal rhythms in adolescence: Clocks, calendars, and the coordination of daily life* (pp. 37–51). San Francisco: Jossey-Bass.

Larson, R. W., Richards, M. H., Moneta, G., Holmbeck, G., & Duckett, E. (1996). Changes in adolescents' daily interactions with their families from ages 10 to 18: Disengagement and transformation. *Developmental Psychology, 32,* 744–754.

Larson, R. W., Richards, M. H., Sims, B., & Dworkin, J. (2001). How urban African-American young adolescents spend their time: Time budgets for locations, activities, and companionship. *American Journal of Community Psychology, 29,* 565–597.

Larsson, M., Öberg, C., & Bäckman, L. (2005). Odor identification in old age: Demographic, sensory and cognitive correlates. *Aging, Neuropsychology, and Cognition, 12,* 231–244.

Larzelere, R. E., Schneider, W. N., Larson, D. B., & Pike, P. L. (1996). The effects of discipline responses in delaying toddler misbehavior recurrences. *Child and Family Behavior Therapy, 18,* 35–57.

Lashley, F. R. (2007). Essentials of clinical genetics in nursing practice. New York: Springer.

Lattanzi-Licht, M., & Doka, K. J. (Eds.). (2003). *Living with grief: Coping with public tragedy.* New York: Brunner-Routledge.

Latz, S., Wolf, A. W., & Lozoff, B. (1999). Sleep practices and problems in young children in Japan and the United States. *Archives of Pediatric and Adolescent Medicine, 153,* 339–346.

Lau, C. Q. (2012). The stability of same-sex cohabitation, different-sex cohabitation, and marriage. *Journal of Marriage and Family, 74,* 973–988.

Laucht, M., Esser, G., & Schmidt, M. H. (1997). Developmental outcome of infants born with biological and psychosocial risks. *Journal of Child Psychology and Psychiatry, 38,* 843–853.

Lauer, P. A., Akiba, M., Wilkerson, S. B., Apthorp, H. S., Snow, D., & Martin-Glenn, M. (2006). Out-of-school time programs: A meta-analysis of effects for at-risk students. *Review of Educational Research, 76,* 275–313.

Laumann, E. O., Gagnon, J. H., Michael, R. T., & Michaels, S. (1994). *The social organization of sexuality.* Chicago: University of Chicago Press.

Laumann, E. O., & Mahay, J. (2002). The social organization of woman's sexuality. In G. M. Wingood & R. J. DiClemente (Eds.), *Handbook of women's sexual and reproductive health* (pp. 43–70). New York: Springer.

Laumann, E. O., Paik, A., & Rosen, R. C. (1999). Sexual dysfunction in the United States: Prevalence and predictors. *Journal of the American Medical Association, 281,* 537–544.

Laureys, S., & Boly, M. (2007). What is it like to be vegetative or minimally conscious? *Current Opinion in Neurology, 20,* 609–613.

Laursen, B., Bukowski, W. M., Aunola, K., & Nurmi, J.-E. (2007). Friendship moderates prospective associations between social isolation and adjustment problems in young children. *Child Development, 78,* 1395–1404.

Laursen, B., & Collins, W. A. (2009). Parent–child relationships during adolescence. In R. M. Lerner (Ed.), *Handbook of adolescent psychology: Vol. 2. Contextual influences on adolescent development* (3rd ed., pp. 3–42). Hoboken, NJ: Wiley.

Laursen, B., Coy, K., & Collins, W. A. (1998). Reconsidering changes in parent–child conflict across adolescence: A meta-analysis. *Child Development, 69,* 817–832.

Lautenschlager, N. T., Cox, K. L., Flicker, L., Foster, J. K., van Bockxmeer, F. M., Xiao, J., Greenop, K. R., & Almeida, O. P. (2008). Effect of physical activity on cognitive function in older adults at risk for Alzheimer disease: A randomized trial. *Journal of the American Medical Association, 300,* 1027–1037.

Lavelli, M., & Fogel, A. (2005). Developmental changes in the relationship between the infant's attention and emotion during early face-to-face communication: The 2-month transition. *Developmental Psychology, 41,* 265–280.

Lavner, J. A., & Bradbury, T. N. (2012). Why do even satisfied newlyweds eventually go on to divorce? *Journal of Family Psychology, 26,* 1–10.

Law, K. L., Stroud, L. R., Niaura, R., LaGasse, L. L., Giu, J., & Lester, B. M. (2003). Smoking during pregnancy and newborn neurobehavior. *Pediatrics, 111,* 1318–1323.

Lawn, J. E., Mwansa-Kambafwile J., Horta, B. L., Barros, F. C., & Cousens, S. (2010). Kangaroo mother care to prevent neonatal deaths due to preterm birth complications. *International Journal of Epidemiology, 39* (Supplement 1), i144–i154.

Lawrence, A. R., & Schigelone, A. R. S. (2002). Reciprocity beyond dyadic relationships: Aging-related communal coping. *Research on Aging, 24,* 684–704.

Lawrence, E., Rothman, A., Cobb, R. J., & Bradbury, T. N. (2010). Marital satisfaction across the transition to parenthood. In M. S. Schulz, M. K. Pruett, P. K. Kerig, & R. D. Parke (Eds.), *Strengthening couple relationships for optimal child development* (pp. 97–114). Washington, DC: American Psychological Association.

Lawrence, K., Kuntsi, J., Coleman, M., Campbell, R., & Skuse, D. (2003). Face and emotion recognition deficits in Turner syndrome: A possible role for X-linked genes in amygdala development. *Neuropsychology, 17,* 39–49.

Lawson, K. R., & Ruff, H. A. (2004). Early attention and negative emotionality predict later cognitive and behavioral function. *International Journal of Behavioral Development, 28,* 157–165.

Lawton, J. S. (2011). Sex and gender differences in coronary artery disease. *Seminars in Thoracic Surgery, 23,* 126–130.

Lawton, M. P. (1998). Environment and aging: Theory revisited. In R. J. Scheidt & P. G. Windley (Eds.), *Environment and aging theory: A focus on housing* (pp. 1–31). Westport, CT: Greenwood.

Lazar, I., & Darlington, R. (1982). Lasting effects of early education: A report from the Consortium for Longitudinal Studies. *Monographs of the Society for Research in Child Development, 47*(2–3, Serial No. 195).

Lazarus, R. S., & Lazarus, B. N. (1994). *Passion and reason.* New York: Oxford University Press.

Lazinski, M. J., Shea, A. K., & Steiner, M. (2008). Effects of maternal prenatal stress on offspring development: A commentary. *Archives of Women's Mental Health, 11,* 363–375.

Le, T. N. (2011). Life satisfaction, openness value, self-transcendence, and wisdom. *Journal of Happiness Studies, 12,* 171–182.

Leaper, C. (1994). Exploring the correlates and consequences of gender segregation: Social relationships in childhood, adolescence, and adulthood. In C. Leaper (Ed.), *New directions for child development* (No. 65, pp. 67–86). San Francisco: Jossey-Bass.

Leaper, C. (2000). Gender, affiliation, assertion, and the interactive context of parent–child play. *Developmental Psychology, 36,* 381–393.

Leaper, C., Anderson, K. J., & Sanders, P. (1998). Moderators of gender effects on parents' talk to their children: A meta-analysis. *Developmental Psychology, 34,* 3–27.

Leaper, C., & Friedman, C. K. (2007). The socialization of gender. In J. E. Grusec & P. D. Hastings (Eds.), *Handbook of socialization: Theory and research* (pp. 561–587). New York: Guilford.

Leaper, C., Tenenbaum, H. R., & Shaffer, T. G. (1999). Communication patterns of African-American girls and boys from low-income, urban backgrounds. *Child Development, 70,* 1489–1503.

LeBlanc, L. A., Goldsmith, T., & Patel, D. R. (2003). Behavioral aspects of chronic illness in children and adolescents. *Pediatric Clinics of North America, 50,* 859–878.

Lecanuet, J.-P., Granier-Deferre, C., Jacquet, A.-Y., Capponi, I., & Ledru, L. (1993). Prenatal discrimination of a male and female voice uttering the same sentence. *Early Development and Parenting, 2,* 217–228.

Lecuyer, E., & Houck, G. M. (2006). Maternal limit-setting in toddlerhood: Socialization strategies for the development of self-regulation. *Infant Mental Health Journal, 27,* 344–370.

Lee, C.-Y. S., & Doherty, W. J. (2007). Marital satisfaction and father involvement during the transition to parenthood. *Fathering, 5,* 75–96.

Lee, E. E., & Farran, C. J. (2004). Depression among Korean, Korean American, and Caucasian American family caregivers. *Journal of Transcultural Nursing, 15,* 18–25.

Lee, E. O., & Sharpe, T. (2007). Understanding religious/spiritual coping and support resources among African American older adults: A mixed method approach. *Journal of Religion, Spirituality and Aging, 19,* 55–75.

Lee, J. C., Hasnain-Wynia, R., & Lau, D. T. (2011). Delay in seeing a doctor due to cost: Disparity between older adults with and without disabilities in the United States. *Health Services Research, 47,* 698–720.

Lee, J. M., Appulgiese, D., Kaciroti, N., Corwyn, R. F., Bradley, R. H., & Lumeng, J. C. (2007). Weight status in young girls and the onset of puberty. *Pediatrics, 119,* e624–e630.

Lee, K., Cameron, C., Xu, F., Fu, G., & Board, J. (1997). Chinese and Canadian children's evaluations of lying and truth telling: Similarities and differences in the context of pro- and antisocial behaviors. *Child Development, 68,* 924–934.

Lee, K., Xu, F., Fu, G., Cameron, C. A., & Chen, S. (2001). Taiwan and Mainland Chinese and Canadian children's categorization and evaluation of lieand truth-telling: A modesty effect. *British Journal of Developmental Psychology, 19,* 525–542.

Lee, M. M., Carpenter, B., & Meyers, L. S. (2006). Representations of older adults in television advertisements. *Journal of Aging Studies, 21,* 23–30.

Lee, S. J., Ralston, H. J., Partridge, J. C., & Rosen, M. A. (2005). Fetal pain: A systematic multidisciplinary review of the evidence. *Journal of the American Medical Association, 294,* 947–954.

Lee, V. E., & Burkam, D. T. (2002). *Inequality at the starting gate.* Washington, DC: Economic Policy Institute.

Leerkes, E. M. (2010). Predictors of maternal sensitivity to infant distress. *Parenting: Science and Practice, 10,* 219–239.

Leet, T., & Flick, L. (2003). Effect of exercise on birth weight. *Clinical Obstetrics and Gynecology, 46,* 423–431.

Lefkowitz, E. S., Vukman, S. N., & Loken, E. (2012). Young adults in a wireless world. In A. Booth, S. L. Brown, N. S. Landale, W. D. Manning, & S. M. McHale (Eds.), *Early adulthood in a family context* (pp. 45–57). New York: Springer.

Legacy Project. (2012). *Fast facts on grandparenting and intergenerational mentoring.* Retrieved from www.legacyproject.org/specialreports/fastfacts .html

Legge, G. E., Madison, C., Vaughn, B. N., Cheong, A. M. Y., and Miller, J. C. (2008). Retention of high tactile acuity throughout the life span in blindness. *Perception and Psychophysics, 70,* 1471–1488.

Le Grand, R., Mondloch, C. J., Maurer, D., & Brent, H. P. (2003). Expert face processing requires input to the right hemisphere during infancy. *Nature Neuroscience, 6,* 1108–1112.

Lehman, D. R., & Nisbett, R. E. (1990). A longitudinal study of the effects of undergraduate training on reasoning. *Developmental Psychology, 26,* 952–960.

Lehman, M., & Hasselhorn, M. (2007). Variable memory strategy use in children's adaptive intratask learning behavior: Developmental changes and working memory influences in free recall. *Child Development, 78,* 1068–1082.

Lehman, M., & Hasselhorn, M. (2010). The dynamics of free recall and their relation to rehearsal between 8 and 10 years of age. *Child Development, 81,* 1006–1020.

Lehr, V. T., Zeskind, P. S., Ofenstein, J. P., Cepeda, E., Warrier, I., & Aranda, J. V. (2007). Neonatal facial coding system scores and spectral characteristics of infant crying during newborn circumcision. *Clinical Journal of Pain, 23,* 417–424.

Lehrer, E. L., & Chen, Y. (2011). *Women's age at first marriage and marital instability: Evidence from the 2006–2008 National Survey of Family Growth.* Discussion Paper No. 5954. Chicago: University of Illinois at Chicago.

Lehrer, J. A., Pantell, R., Tebb, K., & Shafer, M. A. (2007). Forgone health care among U.S. adolescents: Associations between risk characteristics and confidentiality. *Journal of Adolescent Health, 40,* 218–226.

Leiter, M. P., Gascón, S., & Martínez-Jarreta, B. (2010). Making sense of work life: A structural model of burnout. *Journal of Applied Social Psychology, 40,* 57–75.

Lemaitre, H., Goldman, A. L., Sambataro, F., Verchinski, B. A., Meyer-Lindenberg, A., & Mattay, V. S. (2012). Normal age-related brain morphometric changes: Nonuniformity across cortical thickness, surface area and gray matter volume? *Neurobiology of Aging, 33,* 617.

Leman, P. J. (2005). Authority and moral reasons: Parenting style and children's perceptions of adult rule justifications. *International Journal of Behavioral Development, 29,* 265–270.

Lemche, E., Lennertz, I., Orthmann, C., Ari, A., Grote, K., Hafker, J., & Klann-Delius, G. (2003). Emotion-regulatory process in evoked play narratives: Their relation with mental representations and family interactions. *Praxis der Kinderpsychologie und Kinderpsychiatrie, 52,* 156–171.

Lempert, H. (1990). Acquisition of passives: The role of patient animacy, salience, and lexical accessibility. *Journal of Child Language, 17,* 677–696.

Lengua, L. J., Wolchik, S., Sandler, I. N., & West, S. G. (2000). The additive and interactive effects of parenting and temperament in predicting problems of children of divorce. *Journal of Clinical Psychology, 29,* 232–244.

Lenhart, A., Ling, R., Campbell, S., & Purcell, K. (2010). *Teens and mobile phones.* Washington, DC: Pew Internet & American Life Project.

Lenroot, R. K., & Giedd, J. N. (2006). Brain development in children and adolescents: Insights from anatomical magnetic resonance imaging. *Neuroscience and Biobehavioral Reviews, 30,* 718–729.

Leon, K. (2003). Risk and protective factors in young children's adjustment to parental divorce: A review of the research. *Family Relations, 52,* 258–270.

Leonesio, M. V., Bridges, B., Gesumaria, R., & Del Bene, L. (2012). The increasing labor force participation of older workers and its effect on the income of the aged. *Social Security Bulletin, 72*(1). Retrieved from www.ssa.gov/policy/docs/ssb/v72n1/v72n1p59.html

Lepage, J.-F., & Théoret, H. (2007). The mirror neuron system: Grasping others' actions from birth? *Developmental Science, 10,* 513–523.

Lerman, R. I. (2010). Capabilities and contributions of unwed fathers. *Future of Children, 20,* 63–85.

Lerner, R. M. (2006). Developmental science, developmental systems, and contemporary theories of human development. In R. M. Lerner (Ed.), *Handbook of child psychology: Vol. 1. Theoretical models of human development* (6th ed., pp. 1–17). Hoboken, NJ: Wiley.

Lerner, R. M., Leonard, K., Fay, K., & Issac, S. S. (2011). Continuity and discontinuity in development across the life span: A developmental systems perspective. In K. L. Fingerman, C. A. Berg, J. Smith, & T. C. Antonucci (Eds.), *Handbook of life-span development* (pp. 141–160). New York: Springer.

Lerner, R. M., & Overton, W. F. (2008). Exemplifying the integrations of the relational developmental system. *Journal of Adolescent Research, 23,* 245–255.

Leslie, A. M. (2004). Who's for learning? *Developmental Science, 7,* 417–419.

Lester, B. M. (1985). Introduction: There's more to crying than meets the ear. In B. M. Lester & C. F. Z. Boukydis (Eds.), *Infant crying* (pp. 1–27). New York: Plenum.

Lester, B. M., & Lagasse, L. L. (2010). Children of addicted women. *Journal of Addictive Diseases, 29,* 259–276.

Lester, B. M., & Tronick, E. Z. (2004). *NICU Network Neurobehavioral Scale (NNNS).* Baltimore, MD: Brookes.

Letherby, G. (2002). Childless and bereft? Stereotypes and realities in relation to "voluntary" and "involuntary" childlessness and womanhood. *Sociological Inquiry, 72,* 7–20.

Leuner, B., Glasper, E. R., & Gould, E. (2010). Parenting and plasticity. *Trends in Neurosciencess, 33,* 465–473.

Leung, M. C. M., Zhang, J., & Zhang, J. (2004). An economic analysis of life expectancy by gender with application to the United States. *Journal of Health Economics, 23,* 737–759.

LeVay, S. (1993). *The sexual brain.* Cambridge, MA: MIT Press.

Levendosky, A. A., Bogat, G. A., Huth-Bocks, A. C., Rosenblum, K., & von Eye, A. (2011). The effects of domestic violence on the stability of attachment from infancy to preschool. *Journal of Clinical Child and Adolescent Psychology, 40,* 398–410.

Levenson, R. W., Carstensen, L. L., & Gottman, J. M. (1993). Long-term marriage: Age, gender, and satisfaction. *Psychology and Aging, 8,* 301–313.

Leventhal, T., & Brooks-Gunn, J. (2003). Children and youth in neighborhood contexts. *Current Directions in Psychological Science, 12,* 27–31.

Leventhal, T., Dupere, V., & Brooks-Gunn, J. (2009). Neighborhood influences on adolescent development. In R. M. Lerner & L. Steinberg (Eds.), *Handbook of adolescent psychology: Vol. 2* (3rd ed., pp. 411–443). Hoboken, NJ: Wiley.

Levi, J., Vinter, S., Richardson, L., St. Laurent, R., & Segal, L. M. (2009). *F as in fat: How obesity policies are failing in America.* Washington, DC: Trust for America's Health.

Levine, B., Svoboda, E., Hay, J. F., Winocur, G., & Moscovitch, M. (2002). Aging and autobiographical memory: Dissociating episodic from semantic retrieval. *Psychology and Aging, 17,* 677–689.

Levine, L. J. (1995). Young children's understanding of the causes of anger and sadness. *Child Development, 66,* 697–709.

LeVine, R. A., Dixon, S., LeVine, S., Richman, A., Leiderman, P. H., Keefer, C. H., & Brazelton, T. B. (1994). *Child care and culture: Lessons from Africa.* New York: Cambridge University Press.

Levine, S. C., Huttenlocher, J., Taylor, A., & Langrock, A. (1999). Early sex differences in spatial skill. *Developmental Psychology, 35,* 940–949.

Levinson, D. J. (1978). *The seasons of a man's life.* New York: Knopf.

Levinson, D. J. (1996). *The seasons of a woman's life.* New York: Knopf.

Levitt, M. J., & Cici-Gokaltun, A. (2011). Close relationships across the lifespan. In K. Fingerman, C. A. Berg, J. Smith, & T. C. Antonucci (Eds.),

Handbook of life-span development (pp. 457–486). New York: Springer.

Levitt, T., Fugelsang, J., & Crossley, M. (2006). Processing speed, attentional capacity, and age-related memory change. *Experimental Aging Research, 32,* 263–295.

Levy, B. R., & Leifheit-Limson, E. (2009). The stereotype-matching effect: Greater influence on functioning when age stereotypes correspond to outcomes. *Psychology and Aging, 24,* 230–233.

Levy, B. R., Slade, M. D., & Gill, T. M. (2006). Hearing decline predicted by elders' stereotypes. *Journal of Gerontology, 61B,* P82–P87.

Levy, B. R., Slade, M. D., Kunkel, S. R., & Kasl, S. V. (2002). Longevity increased by positive self-perceptions of aging. *Journal of Personality and Social Psychology, 83,* 261–270.

Levy, G. D., Taylor, M. G., & Gelman, S. A. (1995). Traditional and evaluative aspects of flexibility in gender roles, social conventions, moral rules, and physical laws. *Child Development, 66,* 515–531.

Levy, S. R., & Dweck, C. S. (1999). The impact of children's static vs. dynamic conceptions of people on stereotype formation. *Child Development, 70,* 1163–1180.

Levy-Shiff, R., & Israelashvili, R. (1988). Antecedents of fathering: Some further exploration. *Developmental Psychology, 24,* 434–440.

Lewis, K. G. (2000). *With or without a man: Single women taking control of their lives.* New York: Bull Publishing.

Lewis, M. (1992). *Shame: The exposed self.* New York: Free Press.

Lewis, M. (1995). Embarrassment: The emotion of self-exposure and evaluation. In J. P. Tangney & K. W. Fischer (Eds.), *Self-conscious emotions* (pp. 198–218). New York: Guilford.

Lewis, M. (1998). Emotional competence and development. In D. Pushkar, W. M. Bukowski, A. E. Schwartzman, E. M. Stack, & D. R. White (Eds.), *Improving competence across the lifespan* (pp. 27–36). New York: Plenum.

Lewis, M., & Brooks-Gunn, J. (1979). *Social cognition and the acquisition of self.* New York: Plenum.

Lewis, M., & Ramsay, D. (2004). Development of self-recognition, personal pronoun use, and pretend play during the 2nd year. *Child Development, 75,* 1821–1831.

Lewis, M., Ramsay, D. S., & Kawakami, K. (1993). Differences between Japanese infants and Caucasian American infants in behavioral and cortisol response to inoculation. *Child Development, 64,* 1722–1731.

Lewis, M., Sullivan, M. W., Stanger, C., & Weiss, M. (1989). Self development and self-conscious emotions. *Child Development, 60,* 146–156.

Lewis, M. D. (2000). The promise of dynamic systems approaches for an integrated account of human development. *Child Development, 71,* 36–43.

Lewis, M. D. (2008). Emotional habits in brain and behavior: A window on personality development. In A. Fogel, B. J. King, & S. G. Shanker (Eds.), *Human Development in the twenty-first century* (pp. 72–80). New York: Cambridge University Press.

Lewis, T. L., & Maurer, D. (2005). Multiple sensitive periods in human visual development: Evidence from visually deprived children. *Developmental Psychobiology, 46,* 163–183.

Leyk, D., Rüther, T., Wunderlich, M., Sievert, A., Ebfeld, D., Witzki, A., et al. (2010). Physical performance in middle age and old age. *Deutsches Ärzteblatt International, 107,* 809–816.

Li, D.-K., Willinger, M., Petitti, D. B., Odouli, R., Liu, L., & Hoffman, H. J. (2006). Use of a dummy (pacifier) during sleep and risk of sudden infant death syndrome (SIDS): Population based case-control study. *British Medical Journal, 332,* 18–21.

Li, S.-C., Lindenberger, U., Hommel, B., Aschersleben, G., Prinz, W., & Baltes, P. B. (2004). Transformation in the couplings among intellectual abilities and constituent cognitive processes across the life span. *Psychological Science, 15,* 155–163.

Liang, J., Krause, N. M., & Bennett, J. M. (2001). Social exchange and well-being: Is giving better than receiving? *Psychology and Aging, 16,* 511–523.

Liben, L. S. (2006). Education for spatial thinking. In K. A. Renninger & I. E. Sigel (Eds.), *Handbook of child psychology: Vol. 4. Child psychology in practice* (6th ed., pp. 197–247). Hoboken, NJ: Wiley.

Liben, L. S. (2009). The road to understanding maps. *Current Directions in Psychological Science, 18,* 310–315.

Liben, L. S., & Bigler, R. S. (2002). The developmental course of gender differentiation: Conceptualizing, measuring, and evaluating constructs and pathways. *Monographs of the Society for Research in Child Development, 6*(4, Serial No. 271).

Liben, L. S., Bigler, R. S., & Krogh, H. R. (2001). Pink and blue collar jobs: Children's judgments of job status and job aspirations in relation to sex of worker. *Journal of Experimental Child Psychology, 79,* 346–363.

Liben, L. S., & Downs, R. M. (1993). Understanding person–space–map relations: Cartographic and developmental perspectives. *Developmental Psychology, 29,* 739–752.

Lidstone, J. S. M., Meins, E., & Fernyhough, C. (2010). The roles of private speech and inner speech in planning during middle childhood: Evidence from a dual task paradigm. *Journal of Experimental Child Psychology, 107,* 438–451.

Lidz, J. (2007). The abstract nature of syntactic representations. In E. Hoff & M. Shatz (Eds.), *Blackwell handbook of language development* (pp. 277–303). Malden, MA: Blackwell.

Lidz, J., Gleitman, H., & Gleitman, L. (2004). Kidz in the 'hood: Syntactic bootstrapping and the mental lexicon. In D. G. Hall & S. R. Waxman (Eds.), *Weaving a lexicon* (pp. 603–636). Cambridge, MA: MIT Press.

Lieven, E., Pine, J., & Baldwin, G. (1997). Lexically based learning and early grammatical development. *Journal of Child Language, 24,* 187–220.

Li-Grining, C. P. (2007). Effortful control among low-income preschoolers in three cities: Stability, change, and individual differences. *Developmental Psychology, 43,* 208–221.

Lilgendahl, J. P., & McAdams, D. P. (2011). Constructing stories of self-growth: How individual differences in patterns of autobiographical reasoning relate to well-being in midlife. *Journal of Personality, 79,* 391–428.

Lillard, A. (2003). Pretend play and cognitive development. In U. Goswami (Ed.), *Blackwell handbook of childhood cognitive development* (pp. 189–205). Malden, MA: Blackwell.

Lillard, A. (2007). *Montessori: The science behind the genius.* New York: Oxford University Press.

Lillard, A., & Else-Quest, N. (2006). Evaluating Montessori education. *Science, 313,* 1893–1894.

Lillard, A. S., & Witherington, D. (2004). Mothers' behavior modifications during pretense snacks and their possible signal value for toddlers. *Developmental Psychology, 40,* 95–113.

Lin, F. R., Ferrucci, L., Metter, E. J., An, Y., Zonderman, A. B., & Resnick, S. M. (2011). Hearing loss and cognition in the Baltimore Longitudinal Study of Aging. *Neuropsychology, 25,* 763–770.

Linares, T. J., Singer, L. T., Kirchner, H., Lester, H., Short, E. J., & Min, M. O. (2006). Mental health outcomes of cocaine-exposed children at 6 years of age. *Journal of Pediatric Psychology, 31,* 85–97.

Lindblad, F., & Hjern, A. (2010). ADHD after fetal exposure to maternal smoking. *Nicotine and Tobacco Research, 12,* 408–415.

Lindau, S. T., Schumm, L. P., Laumann, E. O., Levinson, W., O'Muircheartaigh, C. A., & Waite, L. J. (2007). A study of sexuality and health among older adults in the United States. *New England Journal of Medicine, 357,* 762–774.

Lindauer, M. S., Orwoll, L., & Kelley, M. C. (1997). Aging artists on the creativity of their old age. *Creativity Research Journal, 10,* 133–152.

Lindberg, S. M., Hyde, J. S., Linn, M. C., & Petersen, J. L. (2010). New trends in gender and mathematics performance: A meta-analysis. *Psychological Bulletin, 136,* 1123–1135.

Lindsay-Hartz, J., de Rivera, J., & Mascolo, M. F. (1995). Differentiating guilt and shame and their effects on motivation. In J. P. Tangney & K. W. Fischer (Eds.), *Self-conscious emotions* (pp. 274–300). New York: Guilford.

Lindsey, E. W., & Colwell, M. J. (2003). Preschoolers' emotional competence: Links to pretend and physical play. *Child Study Journal, 33,* 39–52.

Lindsey, E. W., Colwell, M. J., Frabutt, J. M., Chambers, J. C., & MacKinnon-Lewis, C. (2008). Mother–child dyadic synchrony in European-American families during early adolescence: Relations with self-esteem and prosocial behavior. *Merrill-Palmer Quarterly, 54,* 289–315.

Lindsey, E. W., & Mize, J. (2000). Parent–child physical and pretense play: Links to children's social competence. *Merrill-Palmer Quarterly, 46,* 565–591.

Linebarger, D. L., Kosanic, A. Z., Greenwood, C. R., & Doku, N. S. (2004). Effects of viewing the television program *Between the Lions* on the emergent literacy skills of young children. *Journal of Educational Psychology, 96,* 297–308.

Linebarger, D. L., & Piotrowski, J. T. (2010). Structure and strategies in children's educational television: The roles of program type and learning strategies in children's learning. *Child Development, 81,* 1582–1597.

Linebarger, J. S., Sahler, O. J., & Egan, K. A. Coping with death. *Pediatrics in Review, 30,* 350–355.

Linley, P. A. (2003). Positive adaptation to trauma: Wisdom as both process and outcome. *Journal of Traumatic Stress, 16,* 601–610.

Linn, M. C., & Petersen, A. C. (1985). Emergence and characterization of sex differences in spatial ability: A meta-analysis. *Child Development, 56,* 1479–1498.

Linn, R. L., & Welner, K. G. (2007). *Race-conscious policies for assigning students to schools: Social science research and the Supreme Court cases.* Washington, DC: National Academy Press.

Linver, M. R., Martin, A., & Brooks-Gunn, J. (2004). Measuring infants' home environment: The ITHOME for infants between birth and 12 months in four national data sets. *Parenting: Science and Practice, 4,* 115–137.

Lippe, T. van der (2010). Women's employment and housework. In J. Treas & S. Drobnic (Eds.), *Dividing the Domestic: Men, women, and household work in cross-national perspective* (pp. 41–58). Stanford, CA: Stanford University Press.

Lips, H. M. (2013). The gender pay gap: Challenging the rationalizations. Perceived equity, discrimination, and the limits of human capital models. *Sex Roles, 68,* 169–185.

Lipsitt, L. P. (2003). Crib death: A biobehavioral phenomenon? *Psychological Science, 12,* 164–170.

Lipton, J., & Spelke, E. (2004). Discrimination of large and small numerosities by human infants. *Infancy, 5,* 271–290.

Liszkowski, U., Carpenter, M., & Tomasello, M. (2007). Pointing out new news, old news, and absent referents at 12 months of age. *Developmental Science, 10,* F1–F7.

Little, T. D., Jones, S. M., Henrich, C. C., & Hawley, P. H. (2003). Disentangling the "whys" from the "whats" of aggressive behavior. *International Journal of Behavioral Development, 27,* 122–133.

Liu, C.-C., Kanekiyo, T., Xu, H., & Bu, G. (2013). Apolipoprotein E and Alzheimer disease: Risk, mechanisms and therapy. *Nature Reviews Neurology, 9,* 106–118.

Liu, J., Raine, A., Venables, P. H., Dalais, C., & Mednick, S. A. (2003). Malnutrition at age 3 years and lower cognitive ability at age 11 years. *Archives of Paediatric and Adolescent Medicine, 157,* 593–600.

Liu, J., Raine, A., Venables, P. H., & Mednick, S. A. (2004). Malnutrition at age 3 years and externalizing behavior problems at age 8, 11, and 17 years. *American Journal of Psychiatry, 161,* 2006–2013.

Liu, K., Daviglus, M. L., Loria, C. M., Colangelo, L. A., Spring, B., Moller, A. C., et al. (2012). Healthy lifestyle through young adulthood and the presence of low cardiovascular disease risk profile in middle age: The Coronary Artery Risk Development in (Young) Adults (CARDIA) study. *Circulation, 125,* 996–1004.

Liu, L., Drouet, V., Wu, J. W., Witter, M. P., Small, S. A., Clelland C., et al. (2012). Trans-synaptic spread of tau pathology in vivo. *PLoS One, 7,* e31302.

Liu, L. L., Uttal, D. H., Marulis, L. M., & Newcombe, N. S. (2008). Training spatial skills: What works for whom, why and for how long? Poster presented at the annual meeting of the Association for Psychological Science, Chicago.

Livingston, G., & Cohn, D. (2010). *Childlessness up among all women; down among women with advanced degrees.* Washington, DC: Pew Research Center. Retrieved from pewresearch.org/pubs/1642/more-women-without-children

Lleras, C., & Rangel, C. (2009). Ability grouping practices in elementary school and African American/Hispanic achievement. *American Journal of Education, 115,* 279–304.

Lloyd, L. (1999). Multi-age classes and high ability students. *Review of Educational Research, 69,* 187–212.

Lloyd, M. E., Doydum, A. O., & Newcombe, N. S. (2009). Memory binding in early childhood: Evidence for a retrieval deficit. *Child Development, 80,* 1321–1328.

Lochman, J. E., & Dodge K. A. (1998). Distorted perceptions in dyadic interactions of aggressive and nonaggressive boys: Effects of prior expectations, context, and boys' age. *Development and Psychopathology, 10,* 495–512.

Lock, J., & Kirz, N. (2008). Eating disorders: Anorexia nervosa. In W. E. Graighead, D. J. Miklowitz, & L. W. Craighead (Eds.), *Psychopathology: History, diagnosis, and empirical foundations* (pp. 467–494). Hoboken, NJ: Wiley.

Loeb, S., Fuller, B., Kagan, S. L., & Carrol, B. (2004). Child care in poor communities: Early learning effects of type, quality, and stability. *Child Development, 75,* 47–65.

Loehlin, J. C., Horn, J. M., & Willerman, L. (1997). Heredity, environment, and IQ in the Texas Adoption Project. In R. J. Sternberg & E. L. Grigorenko (Eds.), *Intelligence, heredity, and environment* (pp. 105–125). New York: Cambridge University Press.

Loehlin, J. C., Jonsson, E. G., Gustavsson, J. P., Stallings, M. C., Gillespie, N. A., Wright, M. J., & Martin, N. G. (2005). Psychological masculinity–femininity via the gender diagnosticity approach: Heritability and consistency across ages and populations. *Journal of Personality, 73,* 1295–1319.

Loehlin, J. C., & Martin, N. G. (2001). Age changes in personality traits and their heritabilities during the adult years: Evidence from Australian twin registry samples. *Personality and Individual Differences, 30,* 1147–1160.

Loganovskaja, T. K., & Loganovsky, K. N. (1999). EEG, cognitive and psychopathological abnormalities in children irradiated in utero. *International Journal of Psychophysiology, 34,* 211–224.

Loganovsky, K. N., Loganovskaja, T. K., Nechayev, S. Y., Antipchuk, Y. Y., & Bomko, M. A. (2008). Disrupted devlopment of the dominant hemisphere following prenatal irradiation. *Journal of Neuropsychiatry and Clinical Neurosciences, 20,* 274–291.

Lohman, D. F. (2000). Measures of intelligence: Cognitive theories. In A. E. Kazdin (Ed.), *Encyclopedia of psychology: Vol. 5* (pp. 147–150). Washington, DC: American Psychological Association.

Lohrmann, S., & Bambara, L. M. (2006). Elementary education teachers' beliefs about essential supports needed to successfully include students with developmental disabilities who engage in challenging behaviors. *Research and Practice for Persons with Severe Disabilities, 31,* 157–173.

Loman, M. M., & Gunnar, M. R. (2010). Early experience and the development of stress reactivity and regulation in children. *Neuroscience and Biobehavioral Reviews, 34,* 867–876.

Long, D. D. (1985). A cross-cultural examination of fears of death among Saudi Arabians. *Omega, 16,* 43–50.

Loock, C., Conry, J., Cook, J. L., Chudley, A. E., & Rosales, T. (2005). Identifying fetal alcohol spectrum disorder in primary care. *Canadian Medical Association Journal, 172,* 628–630.

Looker, D., & Thiessen, V. (2003). *The digital divide in Canadian schools: Factors affecting student access to and use of information technology.* Ottawa: Canadian Education Statistics Council.

Loomans, E. M. Van der Stelt, O., van Eijsden, M., Gemke, R. J., Vrijkotte, T., & den Bergh, B. R. (2011). Antenatal maternal anxiety is associated with problem behaviour at age five. *Early Human Development, 87,* 565–570.

Lopez, C. M., Driscoll, K. A., & Kistner, J. A. (2009). Sex differences and response styles: Subtypes of rumination and associations with depressive symptoms. *Journal of Clinical Child and Adolescent Psychology, 38,* 27–35.

Lorenz, K. (1952). *King Solomon's ring.* New York: Crowell.

Lou, H., Lalonde, R. N., & Giguère, B. (2012). Making the decision to move out: Bicultural young adults and the negotiation of cultural demands and family relationships. *Journal of Cross-Cultural Psychology, 43,* 663–670.

Louie, V. (2001). Parents' aspirations and investment: The role of social class in the educational experiences of 1.5- and second generation Chinese Americans. *Harvard Educational Review, 71,* 438–474.

Louis, J., Cannard, C., Bastuji, H., & Challemel, M. J. (1997). Sleep ontogenesis revisited: A longitudinal 24-hour home polygraphic study on 15 normal infants during the first two years of life. *Sleep, 20,* 323–333.

Lourenco, O. (2003). Making sense of Turiel's dispute with Kohlberg: The case of the child's moral competence. *New Ideas in Psychology, 21,* 43–68.

Lövdén, M., Bergman, L., Adolfsson, R., Lindenberger, U., & Nilsson, L.-G. (2005). Studying individual aging in an interindividual context: Typical paths of age-related, dementia-related, and mortality-related cognitive development in old age. *Psychology and Aging, 20,* 303–316.

Lövdén, M., Schmiedek, F., Kennedy, K. M., Rodrigue, K. M., Lindenberger, U., & Raz, N. (2012). Does variability in cognitive performance correlated with frontal brain volume? *NeuroImage, 64,* 209–215.

Love, J. M., Chazan-Cohen, R., & Raikes, H. (2007). Forty years of research knowledge and use: From Head Start to Early Head Start and beyond. In. J. L. Aber, S. J. Bishop-Josef, S. M. Jones, K. T. McLearn, & D. Phillips (Eds.), *Child development and social policy: Knowledge for action* (pp. 79–95). Washington, DC: American Psychological Association.

Love, J. M., Harrison, L., Sagi-Schwartz, A., van IJzendoorn, M. H., Ross, C., & Ungerer, J. A. (2003). Child care quality matters: How conclusions may vary with context. *Child Development, 74,* 1021–1033.

Love, J. M., Kisker, E. E., Ross, C., Raikes, H., Constantine, J., Boller, K., & Brooks-Gunn, J. (2005). The effectiveness of Early Head Start for 3-year-old children and their parents: Lessons for policy and programs. *Developmental Psychology, 41,* 885–901.

Love, J. M., Tarullo, L. B., Raikes, H., & Chazan-Cohen, R. (2006). Head Start: What do we know about its effectiveness? What do we need to know? In K. McCartney & D. Phillips (Eds.), *Blackwell handbook of early childhood development* (pp. 550–575). Malden, MA: Blackwell.

Low, S. M., & Stocker, C. (2012). Family functioning and children's adjustment: Associations among parents' depressed mood, marital hostility, parent–child hostility, and children's adjustment. *Journal of Family Psychology, 19,* 394–403.

Lowenstein, A., Katz, R., & Gur-Yaish, N. (2007). Reciprocity in parent–child exchange and life satisfaction among the elderly: A cross-national perspective. *Journal of Social Issues, 63,* 865–883.

Lown, A. E., Nayak, M. B., Korcha, R. A., & Greenfield, T. K. (2011). Child physical and sexual abuse: A comprehensive look at alcohol consumption patterns, consequences, and dependence from the National Alcohol Survey. *Alcoholism: Clinical and Experimental Research, 35,* 317–325.

Lubart, T. I. (2003). In search of creative intelligence. In R. J. Sternberg, J. Lautrey, & T. I. Lubart (Eds.), *Models of intelligence: International perspectives* (pp. 279–292). Washington, DC: American Psychological Association.

Lubart, T. I., Georgsdottir, A., & Besançon, M. (2009). The nature of creative giftedness and talent. In T. Balchin, B. Hymer, & D. J. Matthews (Eds.), *The Routledge international companion to gifted education* (pp. 42–49). New York: Routledge.

Lubart, T. I., & Sternberg, R. J. (1998). Life span creativity: An investment theory approach. In C. E. Adams-Price (Ed.), *Creativity and successful aging.* New York: Springer.

Luby, J., Belden, A., Sullivan, J., Hayen, R., McCadney, A., & Spitznagel, E. (2009). Shame and guilt in preschool depression: Evidence for elevations in self-conscious emotions in depression as early as age 3. *Journal of Child Psychology and Psychiatry, 50,* 1156–1166.

Lucas, R. E., Clark, A. E., Georgellis, Y., & Diener, E. (2003). Reexamining adaptation and the set point model of happiness: Reactions to changes in marital status. *Journal of Personality and Social Psychology, 84,* 803–805.

Lucas, S. R., & Behrends, M. (2002). Sociodemographic diversity, correlated achievement, and de facto tracking. *Sociology of Education, 75,* 328–348.

Lucas-Thompson, R., & Clarke-Stewart, K. A. (2007). Forecasting friendship: How marital quality, maternal mood, and attachment security are linked to children's peer relationships. *Journal of Applied Developmental Psychology, 28,* 499–514.

Luciana, M. (2003). The neural and functional development of the human prefrontal cortex. In M. de Haan & M. H. Johnson (Eds.), *The cognitive neuroscience of development* (pp. 157–180). New York: Psychology Press.

Luciana, M. (2007). Special issue: Developmental cognitive neuroscience. *Developmental Review, 27,* 277–282.

Ludemann, P. M. (1991). Generalized discrimination of positive facial expressions by seven-and ten-month-old infants. *Child Development, 62,* 55–67.

Luecken, L. J. (2008). Long-term consequences of parental death in childhood: Psychological and physiological manifestations. In M. S. Stroebe, R. O. Hansson, H. Schut, & W. Stroebe (Eds.), *Handbook of bereavement research and practice* (pp. 397–416).

Washington, DC: American Psychological Association.

Lugton, J. (2002). *Communicating with dying people.* Oxon, UK: Radcliffe Medical Press.

Lukas, C., & Seiden, H. M. (2007). *Silent grief: Living in the wake of suicide* (rev. ed.). London, U.K.: Jessica Kingsley.

Luke, A., Cooper, R. S., Prewitt, T. E., Adeyemo, A. A., & Forrester, T. E. (2001). Nutritional consequences of the African diaspora. *Annual Review of Nutrition, 21,* 47–71.

Lukowski, A. F., Koss, M., Burden, M. J., Jonides, J., Nelson, C. A., Kaciroti, N., et al. (2010). Iron deficiency in infancy and neurocognitive functioning at 19 years: Evidence of long-term deficits in executive function and recognition memory. *Nutritional Neuroscience, 13,* 54–70.

Luna, B., Garver, K. E., Urban, T. A., Lazar, N. A., & Sweeney, J. A. (2004). Maturation of cognitive processes from late childhood to adulthood. *Child Development, 75,* 1357–1372.

Luna, B., Thulborn, K. R., Monoz, D. P., Merriam, E. P., Garver, K. E., Minshew, N. J., Keshavan, M. S., Genovese, C. R., Eddy, W. F., & Sweeney, J. A. (2001). Maturation of widely distributed brain function subserves cognitive development. *Neuroimage, 13,* 786–793.

Lund, D., Caserta, M., Utz, R., & de Vries, B. (2010). Experiences and early coping of bereaved spouses/partners in an intervention based on the dual process model (DPM). *Omega, 61,* 291–313.

Lund, D. A. (1996). Bereavement and loss. In J. E. Birren (Ed.), *Encyclopedia of gerontology* (pp. 173–183). San Diego: Academic Press.

Lund, D. A. (1998). Statements and perspectives from leaders in the field of aging in Utah. In *Utah sourcebook on aging.* Salt Lake City: Empire Publishing.

Lund, D. A. (2005). *My journey* [Sue's letter]. Unpublished document. Salt Lake City, UT: University of Utah.

Lund, D. A., & Caserta, M. S. (2001). When the unexpected happens: Husbands coping with the deaths of their wives. In D. Lund (Ed.), *Men coping with grief* (pp. 147–166). Amityville, NY: Baywood.

Lund, D. A., & Caserta, M. S. (2004a). Facing life alone: Loss of a significant other in later life. In D. Doda (Ed.), *Living with grief: Loss in later life* (pp. 207–223). Washington, DC: Hospice Foundation of America.

Lund, D. A., & Caserta, M. S. (2004b). Older men coping with widowhood. *Geriatrics and Aging, 7*(6), 29–33.

Lund, D. A., Caserta, M. S., de Vries, B., & Wright, S. (2004). Restoration after bereavement. *Generations Review, 14,* 9–15.

Lund, D. A., Caserta, M. S., & Dimond, M. F. (1993). The course of spousal bereavement in later life. In M. S. Stroebe, W. Stroebe, & R. O. Hansson (Eds.), *Handbook of bereavement* (pp. 240–245). New York: Cambridge University Press.

Lund, D. A., Hill, R. D., Caserta, M. S., & Wright, S. D. (1995). Video Respite™: An innovative resource for family, professional cargivers, and persons with dementia. *Gerontologist, 35,* 683–687.

Lund, D. A., Utz, R., Caserta, M., & de Vries, B. (2008–2009). Humor, laughter, and happiness in the daily lives of recently bereaved spouses. *Omega, 58,* 87–105.

Lund, D. A., Utz, R., Caserta, M. S., & Wright, S. D. (2009). Examining what caregivers do during respite time to make respite more effective. *Journal of Applied Gerontology, 28,* 109–131.

Lund, D. A., Wright, S. D., Caserta, M. S., Utz, R. L., Lindfelt, C., Bright, O., et al. (2010). *Respite services: Enhancing the quality of daily life for caregivers and care receivers.* San Bernardino, CA: California State University at San Bernardino.

Lund, N., Pedersen, L. H., & Henriksen, T. B. (2009). Selective serotonin reuptake inhibitor exposure in utero and pregnancy outcomes. *Archives of Pediatrics and Adolescent Medicine, 163,* 949–954.

Lundy, B. L. (2002). Paternal socio-psychological factors and infant attachment: The mediating role of synchrony in father–infant interactions. *Infant Behavior and Development, 25,* 221–236.

Lundy, B. L. (2003). Father– and mother–infant faceto-face interactions: Differences in mind-related comments and infant attachment? *Infant Behavior and Development, 26,* 200–212.

Luo, L., & Craik, F. I. M. (2008). Aging and memory: A cognitive approach. *Canadian Journal of Psychiatry, 53,* 346–353.

Luo, L. Z., Li, H., & Lee, K. (2011). Are children's faces really more appealing than those of adults? Testing the baby schema hypothesis beyond infancy. *Journal of Experimental Child Psychology, 110,* 115–124.

Luo, Y., & Baillargeon, R. (2005). When the ordinary seems unexpected: Evidence for incremental physical knowledge in young infants. *Cognition, 95,* 297–328.

Luong, G., Charles, S. T., & Fingerman, K. L. (2011). Better with age: Social relationships across adulthood. *Journal of Social and Personal Relationships, 28,* 9–23.

Luster, T., & Haddow, J. L. (2005). Adolescent mothers and their children: An ecological perspective. In T. Luster & J. L. Haddow (Eds.), *Parenting: An ecological perspective* (2nd ed., pp. 73–101). Mahwah, NJ: Erlbaum.

Luthar, S. S., & Becker, B. E. (2002). Privileged but pressured: A study of affluent youth. *Child Development, 73,* 1593–1610.

Luthar, S. S., & Goldstein, A. S. (2008). Substance use and related behaviors among suburban late adolescents: The importance of perceived parent containment. *Development and Psychopathology, 20,* 591–614.

Luthar, S. S., & Latendresse, S. J. (2005a). Children of the affluent: Challenges to well-being. *Current Directions in Psychological Science, 14,* 49–53.

Luthar, S. S., & Latendresse, S. J. (2005b). Comparable "risks" at the socioeconomic status extremes: Preadolescents' perceptions of parenting. *Development and Psychopathology, 17,* 207–230.

Luthar, S. S., & Sexton, C. (2004). The high price of affluence. In R. V. Kail (Ed.), *Advances in child development* (Vol. 32, pp. 126–162). San Diego, CA: Academic Press.

Luxembourg Income Study. (2011). *LIS key figures.* Retrieved from www.lisdatacenter.org/data-access/key-figures/download-key-figures

Luyckx, K., Goossens, L., & Soenens, B. (2006). A developmental contextual perspective on identity construction in emerging adulthood: Change dynamics in commitment formation and commitment evaluation. *Developmental Psychology, 42,* 366–380.

Luyckx, K., Goossens, L., Soenens, B., & Beyers, W. (2006). Unpacking commitment and exploration: Preliminary validation of an integrative model of late adolescent identity formation. *Journal of Adolescence, 29,* 361–378.

Luyckz, K., Soenens, B., Vansteenkiste, M., Goossens, L., & Berzonsky, M. D. (2007). Parental psychological control and dimensions of identity formation in emerging adulthood. *Journal of Family Psychology, 21,* 546–550.

Lynch, S. K., Turkheimer, E., D'Onofrio, B. M., Mendle, J., Emery, R. E., Slutske, W. S., & Martin, N. G. (2006). A genetically informed study of the association between harsh punishment and offspring behavioral problems. *Journal of Family Psychology, 20,* 190–198.

Lyness, K. S., & Heilman, M. E. (2006). When fit is fundamental: Performance evaluations and promotions of upper-level female and male managers. *Journal of Applied Psychology, 90,* 777–785.

Lyon, T. D., & Flavell, J. H. (1994). Young children's understanding of "remember" and "forget." *Child Development, 65,* 1357–1371.

Lyons-Ruth, K., Bronfman, E., & Parsons, E. (1999). Maternal frightened, frightening, or atypical behavior and disorganized infant attachment patterns. *Monographs of the Society for Research in Child Development, 64*(3, Serial No. 258), 67–96.

Lyons-Ruth, K., Easterbrooks, M. A., & Cibelli, C. (1997). Infant attachment strategies, infant mental lag, and maternal depressive symptoms: Predictors of internalizing and externalizing problems at age 7. *Developmental Psychology, 33,* 681–692.

Lytton, H., & Gallagher, L. (2002). Parenting twins and the genetics of parenting. In M. H. Bornstein (Ed.), *Handbook of parenting* (Vol. 1, pp. 227–253). Mahwah, NJ: Erlbaum.

M

Ma, F., Xu, F., Heyman, G. D., & Lee, K. (2011). Chinese children's evaluations of white lies: Weighing the consequences for recipients. *Journal of Experimental Child Psychology, 108,* 308–321.

Ma, L., & Lillard, A. S. (2006). Where is the real cheese? Young children's ability to discriminate between real and pretend acts. *Child Development, 77,* 1762–1777.

Maas, F. K. (2008). Children's understanding of promising, lying, and false belief. *Journal of General Psychology, 13,* 301–321.

Maas, F. K., & Abbeduto, L. J. (2001). Children's judgments about intentionally and unintentionally broken promises. *Journal of Child Language, 28,* 517–529.

Macaluso, A., & De Vito, G. (2004). Muscle strength, power and adaptations to resistance training in older people. *European Journal of Applied Physiology, 91,* 450–472.

Maccoby, E. E. (1984). Socialization and developmental change. *Child Development, 55,* 317–328.

Maccoby, E. E. (1998). *The two sexes: Growing up apart, coming together.* Cambridge, MA: Belknap.

Maccoby, E. E. (2002). Gender and group process: A developmental perspective. *Current Directions in Psychological Science, 11,* 54–58.

MacDonald, S. W. S., Hultsch, D. F., & Dixon, R. A. (2011). Aging and the shape of cognitive change before death: Terminal decline or terminal drop? *Journal of Gerontology, 66,* 292–301.

MacDonald, S. W. S., Li, S-C., & Bäckman, L. (2009). Neural underpinnings of within-person variability in cognitive functioning. *Psychology and Aging, 24,* 792–808.

MacDonald, W. L., & DeMaris, A. (1996). The effects of stepparent's gender and new biological children. *Journal of Family Issues, 17,* 5–25.

Macek, P., Bejček, J., & Vaníčková, J. (2007). Contemporary Czech emerging adults: Generation growing up in the period of social changes. *Journal of Adolescent Research, 22,* 444–475.

Machin, G. A. (2005). Multiple birth. In H. W. Taeusch, R. A. Ballard, & C. A. Gleason (Eds.), *Avery's diseases of the newborn* (8th ed., pp. 57–62). Philadelphia: Saunders.

Mackey, K., Arnold, M. L., & Pratt, M. W. (2001). Adolescents' stories of decision making in more and less authoritative families: Representing the voices of parents in narrative. *Journal of Adolescent Research, 16,* 243–268.

Mackie, S., Show, P., Lenroot, R., Pierson, R., Greenstein, D. K., & Nugent, T. F., III. (2007). Cerebellar development and clinical outcome in attention deficit hyperactivity disorder. *American Journal of Psychiatry, 164,* 647–655.

Mackinnon, S. P., Nosko, A., Pratt, M. W., & Norris, J. E. (2011). Intimacy in young adults' narratives of romance and friendship predicts Eriksonian generativity: A mixed mother analysis. *Journal of Personality, 79,* 587–617.

MacLean, P. S., Bergouignan, A., Cornier, M-A., & Jackman, M. R. (2011). Biology's response to dieting: The impetus for weight gain. *American Journal of Physiology—Regular, Integrated, and Comparative Physiology, 301,* R581–R600.

Macpherson, A., & Spinks, A. (2007). Bicycle helmet legislation for the uptake of helmet use and prevention of head injuries. *Cochrane Database of Systematic Reviews,* Issue 3. Chichester, UK: Wiley.

MacWhinney, B. (2005). Language development. In M. H. Bornstein & M. E. Lamb (Eds.), *Developmental science: An advanced textbook* (5th ed., pp. 359–387). Mahwah, NJ: Erlbaum.

Maddi, S. R. (2005). On hardiness and other pathways to resilience. *American Psychologist, 60,* 261–262.

Maddi, S. R. (2006). Hardiness: The courage to be resilient. In J. C. Thomas, D. L. Segal, & M. Hersen (Eds.), *Comprehensive handbook of personality and psychopathology: Vol. 1. Personality and everyday functioning* (pp. 306–321). Hoboken, NJ: Wiley.

Maddi, S. R. (2007). The story of hardiness: Twenty years of theorizing, research, and practice. In A. Monat, R. S. Lazarus, & G. Reevy (Eds.), *Praeger handbook on stress and coping* (Vol. 2, pp. 327–340). Wastport, CT: Praeger.

Maddi, S. R. (2011). Personality hardiness as a pathway to resilience under educational stresses. In G. M. Reevy & E. Frydenberg (Eds.), *Personality, stress, and coping: Implications for education* (pp. 293–313). Charlotte, NC: Information Age Publishing.

Maddox, G. L. (1963). Activity and morale: A longitudinal study of selected elderly subjects. *Social Forces, 42,* 195–204.

Madey, S. F., & Rodgers, L. (2009). The effect of attachment and Sternberg's triangular theory of love on relationship satisfaction. *Individual Differences Research, 7,* 76–84.

Madigan, S., Bakermans-Kranenburg, M. J., van IJzendoorn, M. H., Moran, G., Pederson, D. R., & Benoit, D. (2006). Unresolved states of mind, anomalous parental behavior, and disorganized attachment: A review and meta-analysis of a transmission gap. *Attachment and Human Development, 8,* 89–111.

Madigan, S., Moran, G., & Pederson, D. R. (2006). Unresolved states of mind, disorganized attachment relationships, and disrupted interactions of adolescent mothers and their infants. *Developmental Psychology, 42,* 293–304.

Madnawat, A. V. S., & Kachhawa, P. S. (2007). Age, gender, and living circumstances: Discriminating older adults on death anxiety. *Death Studies, 31,* 763–769.

Madon, S., Jussim, L., & Eccles, J. (1997). In search of the powerful self-fulfilling prophecy. *Journal of Personality and Social Psychology, 72,* 791–809.

Madsen, S. A., & Juhl, T. (2007). Paternal depression in the postnatal period assessed with traditional and male depression scales. *Journal of Men's Health and Gender, 4,* 26–31.

Maglio, C. J., & Robinson, S. E. (1994). The effects of death education on death anxiety: A meta-analysis. *Omega, 29,* 319–335.

Magnuson, K., & Shager H. (2010). Early education: Progress and promise for children from low-income families. *Children and Youth Services Review, 32,* 1186–1198.

Magolda, M. B., Abes, E., & Torres, V. (2009). Epistemological, intrapersonal, and interpersonal development in the college years and young adulthood. In M. C. Smith & N. DeFrates-Densch (Eds.), *Handbook of research on adult learning and development* (pp. 183–219). New York: Routledge.

Mahady, G. B., Locklear, T. D., Doyle, B. J., Huang, Y., Perez, A. L., & Caceres, A. (2008). Menopause, a universal female experience: Lessons from Mexico and Central America. *Current Women's Health Reviews, 4,* 3–8.

Mahanran, L. G., Bauman, P. A., Kalman, D., Skolnik, H., & Pele, S. M. (1999). Master athletes: Factors affecting performance. *Sports Medicine, 28,* 273–285.

Mahay, J., & Lewin, A. C. (2007). Age and the desire to marry. *Journal of Family Issues, 28,* 706–723.

Mahon, M. M., Goldberg, E. Z., & Washington, S. K. (1999). Concept of death in a sample of Israeli kibbutz children. *Death Studies, 23,* 43–59.

Main, M., & Goldwyn, R. (1998). *Adult attachment classification system.* London: University College.

Main, M., & Solomon, J. (1990). Procedures for identifying infants as disorganized/disoriented during the Ainsworth Strange Situation. In M. Greenberg, D. Cicchetti, & M. Cummings (Eds.), *Attachment in the preschool years: Theory, research, and intervention* (pp. 121–160). Chicago: University of Chicago Press.

Maitland, S. B., Intrieri, R. C., Schaie, K. W., & Willis, S. L. (2000). Gender differences and changes in cognitive abilities across the adult life span. *Aging, Neuropsychology, and Cognition, 7,* 32–53.

Majdandžić, M., & van den Boom, D. C. (2007). Multimethod longitudinal assessment of temperament in early childhood. *Journal of Personality, 75,* 12.

Majnemer, A., & Barr, R. G. (2005). Influence of supine sleep positioning on early motor milestone acquisition. *Developmental Medicine and Child Neurology, 47,* 370–376.

Makishita, H., & Matsunaga, K. (2008). Differences of drivers' reaction times according to age and mental workload. *Accident Analysis Prevention, 40,* 567–575.

Makrantonaki, E., & Xouboulis, C. C. (2007). Molecular mechanisms of skin aging: State of the art. *Annals of the New York Academy of Sciences, 1119,* 40–50.

Malatesta, C. Z., Grigoryev, P., Lamb, C., Albin, M., & Culver, C. (1986). Emotion socialization and expressive development in preterm and full-term infants. *Child Development, 57,* 316–330.

Malina, R. M., & Bouchard, C. (1991). *Growth, maturation, and physical activity.* Champaign, IL: Human Kinetics.

Malone, M. M. (1982). Consciousness of dying and projective fantasy of young children with malignant disease. *Developmental and Behavioral Pediatrics, 3,* 55–60.

Mandara, J., Varner, F., Greene, N., & Richman, S. (2009). Intergenerational family predictors of the black–white achievement gap. *Journal of Educational Psychology, 101,* 867–878.

Mandler, J. M. (2004). Thought before language. *Trends in Cognitive Sciences, 8,* 508–513.

Mandler, J. M., & McDonough, L. (1998). On developing a knowledge base in infancy. *Developmental Psychology, 34,* 1274–1288.

Mangelsdorf, S. C., Schoppe, S. J., & Buur, H. (2000). The meaning of parental reports: A contextual approach to the study of temperament and behavior problems. In V. J. Molfese & D. L. Molfese (Eds.), *Temperament and personality across the life span* (pp. 121–140). Mahwah, NJ: Erlbaum.

Mani, T. M., Bedwell, J. S., & Miller, L. S. (2005). Age-related decrements in performance on a brief continuous performance task. *Archives of Clinical Neuropsychology, 20,* 575–586.

Manole, M. D., & Hickey, R. W. (2006). Preterminal gasping and effects on the cardiac function. *Critical Care Medicine, 34*(Suppl.), S438–S441.

Manzoli, L., Villari, P., Pirone, G. M., & Boccia, A. (2007). Marital status and mortality in the elderly: A systematic review and meta-analysis. *Social Science and Medicine, 64,* 77–94.

Mao, A., Burnham, M. M., Goodlin-Jones, B. L., Gaylor, E. E., & Anders, T. F. (2004). A comparison of the sleep–wake patterns of cosleeping and solitarysleeping infants. *Child Psychiatry and Human Development, 35,* 95–105.

Maquestiaux, F., Lagué-Beauvais, M., Ruthruff, E., Hartley, A., & Bherer, L. (2010). Learning to bypass the central bottleneck: Declining automaticity with advancing age. *Psychology and Aging, 25,* 177–192.

Maratsos, M. (2000). More overregularizations after all: New data and discussion on Marcus, Pinker, Ullman, Hollander, Rosen, & Xu. *Journal of Child Language, 27,* 183–212.

Marchman, V. A., & Thal, D. J. (2005). Words and grammar. In M. Tomasello & D. I. Slobin (Eds.), *Beyond nature–nurture: Essays in honor of Elizabeth Bates* (pp. 141–164). Mahwah, NJ: Erlbaum.

Marcia, J. E. (1980). Identity in adolescence. In J. Adelson (Ed.), *Handbook of adolescent psychology* (pp. 159–187). New York: Wiley.

Marcia, J. E. (2002). Identity and psychosocial development in adulthood. *Identity, 2,* 7–28.

Marcon, R. A. (1999a). Differential impact of preschool models on development and early learning of inner-city children: A three-cohort study. *Developmental Psychology, 35,* 358–375.

Marcon, R. A. (1999b). Positive relationships between parent–school involvement and public school inner-city preschoolers' development and academic performance. *School Psychology Review, 28,* 395–412.

Marcus, G. F. (1995). Children's overregularization of English plurals: A quantitative analysis. *Journal of Child Language, 22,* 447–459.

Marcus-Newhall, A., Thompson, S., & Thomas, C. (2001). Examining a gender stereotype: Menopausal women. *Journal of Applied Social Psychology, 31,* 698–719.

Mardh, P. A. (2002). Influence of infection with *Chlamydia trachomatis* on pregnancy outcome, infant health and life-long sequelae in infected offspring. *Best Practice and Research in Clinical Obstetrics and Gynaecology, 16,* 847–964.

Margrett, J. A., Daugherty, K., Martin, P., MacDonald, M., Davey, A., Woodard, J. L., et al. (2011). Affect and loneliness among centenarians and the oldest old: The role of individual and social resources. *Aging and Mental Health, 15,* 385–396.

Marian, V., Neisser, U., & Rochat, P. (1996). *Can 2-month-old infants distinguish live from videotaped interactions with their mothers?* (Emory Cognition Project, Report #33). Atlanta, GA: Emory University.

Mariano, K. A., & Harton, H. C. (2005). Similarities in aggression, inattention/hyperactivity, depression, and anxiety in middle childhood friendships. *Journal of Social and Clinical Psychology, 24,* 471–496.

Marjoribanks, J., Farquhar, C., Roberts, H., & Lethaby, A. (2012). Long term hormone therapy for perimenopausal and postmenopausal women. *Cochrane Database of Systematic Reviews,* Issue 7, Art. No.: CD004143.

Markey, P. M., & Markey, C. N. (2007). Romantic ideas, romantic obtainment, and relationship experiences: The complementarity of interpersonal traits among romantic partners. *Journal of Social and Personal Relationships, 24,* 517–533.

Markman, E. M. (1992). Constraints on word learning: Speculations about their nature, origins, and domain specificity. In M. R. Gunnar & M. P. Maratsos (Eds.), *Minnesota Symposia on Child Psychology* (Vol. 25, pp. 59–101). Hillsdale, NJ: Erlbaum.

Markova, G., & Legerstee, M. (2006). Contingency, imitation, and affect sharing: Foundations of infants' social awareness. *Developmental Psychology, 42,* 132–141.

Markovits, H., Benenson, J., & Dolensky, E. (2001). Evidence that children and adolescents have internal models of peer interactions that are gender differentiated. *Child Development, 72,* 879–886.

Markovits, H., & Vachon, R. (1990). Conditional reasoning, representation, and level of abstraction. *Developmental Psychology, 26,* 942–951.

Marks, G. N., Cresswell, J., & Ainley, J. (2006). Explaining socioeconomic inequalities in student achievement: The role of home and school factors. *Educational Research and Evaluation, 12,* 105–128.

Marks, N. F. (1996). Caregiving across the lifespan: National prevalence and predictors. *Family Relations, 45,* 27–36.

Marks, N. F., Bumpass, L. L., & Jun, H. (2004). Family roles and well-being during the middle life course. In O. G. Brim, C. D. Ryff, & R.C. Kessler (Eds.), *How healthy are we? A national study of well-being at midlife* (pp. 514–549). Chicago: University of Chicago Press.

Marks, N. F., & Greenfield, E. A. (2009). The influence of family relationships on adult psychological well-being and generativity. In M. C. Smith & N. DeFrates-Densch (Eds.), *Handbook of research on adult learning and development* (pp. 306–349). New York: Routledge.

Marks, N. F., & Lambert, J. D. (1998). Marital status continuity and change among young and midlife adults. *Journal of Family Issues, 19,* 652–686.

Marks, R. (2010). Hip fracture epidemiological trends, outcomes, and risk factors, 1970–2009. *International Journal of General Medicine, 3,* 1–17.

Markstrom, C. A., & Kalmanir, H. M. (2001). Linkages between the psychosocial stages of identity and intimacy and the ego strengths of fidelity and love. *Identity, 1,* 179–196.

Markstrom, C. A., Sabino, V., Turner, B., & Berman, R. (1997). The Psychosocial Inventory of Ego Strengths: Development and validation of a new Eriksonian measure. *Journal of Youth and Adolescence, 26,* 705–732.

Markus, H. R., & Herzog, A. R. (1992). The role of self-concept in aging. In K. W. Schaie & M. P. Lawton (Eds.), *Annual review of gerontology and geriatrics* (pp. 110–143). New York: Springer.

Marlier, L., & Schaal, B. (2005). Human newborns prefer human milk: Conspecific milk odor is attractive without postnatal exposure. *Child Development, 76,* 155–168.

Marra, R., & Palmer, B. (2004). Encouraging intellectual growth: Senior college student profiles. *Journal of Adult Development, 11,* 111–122.

Marsee, M. A., & Frick, P. J. (2010). Callous-unemotional traits and aggression in youth. In W. F. Arsenio & E. A. Lemerise (Eds.), *Emotions, aggression, and morality in children: Bridging development and psychopathology* (pp. 137–156). Washington, DC: American Psychological Association.

Marsh, H. W. (1990). The structure of academic self-concept: The Marsh/Shavelson model. *Journal of Educational Psychology, 82,* 623–636.

Marsh, H. W., & Ayotte, V. (2003). Do multiple dimensions of self-concept become more differentiated with age? The differential distinctiveness hypothesis. *Journal of Educational Psychology, 95,* 687–706.

Marsh, H. W., Craven, R., & Debus, R. (1998). Structure, stability, and development of young children's self-concepts: A multicohort–multioccasion study. *Child Development, 69,* 1030–1053.

Marsh, H. W., Ellis, L. A., & Craven, R. G. (2002). How do preschool children feel about themselves? Unraveling measurement and multidimensional self-concept structure. *Developmental Psychology, 38,* 376–393.

Marsh, H. W., Gerlach, E., Trautwein, U., Lüdtke, O., & Brettschneider, W.-D. (2007). Longitudinal study of predadolescent sport self-concept and performance: Reciprocal effects and causal ordering. *Child Development, 78,* 1640–1656.

Marsh, H. W., & Kleitman, S. (2002). Extracurricular school activities: The good, the bad, and the nonlinear. *Harvard Educational Review, 72,* 464–514.

Marsh, H. W., & Kleitman, S. (2005). Consequences of employment during high school: Character building, subversion of academic goals, or a threshold? *American Educational Research Journal, 42,* 331–369.

Marsh, H. W., Parada, R. H., & Ayotte, V. (2004). A multidimensional perspective of relations between self-concept (Self Description Questionnaire II) and adolescent mental health (Youth Self Report). *Psychological Assessment, 16,* 27–41.

Marsh, H. W., Trautwein, U., Lüdtke, O., Koller, O., & Baumert, J. (2005). Academic self-concept, interest, grades, and standardized test scores: Reciprocal effects models of causal ordering. *Child Development, 76,* 397–416.

Marshall, B. J., & Davies, B. (2011). Bereavement in children and adults following the death of a sibling. In R. Neimeyer, D. Harris, H. Winokuer, G. Thornton (Eds.), *Grief and bereavement in contemporary society: Bridging research and practice* (pp. 107–116). New York: Routledge.

Marshall, N. L. (1997). Combining work and family. In S. J. Gallant, G. P. Keita, & R. Royak-Schaler (Eds.), *Health care for women* (pp. 163–174). Washington, DC: American Psychological Association.

Marshall-Baker, A., Lickliter, R. & Cooper, R. P. (1998). Prolonged exposure to a visual pattern may promote behavioral organization in preterm infants. *Journal of Perinatal and Neonatal Nursing, 12,* 50–62.

Martin, C. L., & Fabes, R. A. (2001). The stability and consequences of young children's same-sex peer interactions. *Developmental Psychology, 37,* 431–446.

Martin, C. L., Fabes, R. A., Evans, S. M., & Wyman, H. (1999). Social cognition on the playground: Children's beliefs about playing with girls versus boys and their relations to sex segregated play. *Journal of Social and Personal Relationships, 16,* 751–771.

Martin, C. L., & Halverson, C. F. (1987). The role of cognition in sex role acquisition. In D. B. Carter (Ed.), *Current conceptions of sex roles and sex typing: Theory and research* (pp. 123–137). New York: Praeger.

Martin, C. L., & Ruble, D. (2004). Children's search for gender cues: Cognitive perspectives on gender development. *Current Directions in Psychological Science, 13,* 67–70.

Martin, C. L., Ruble, D. N., & Szkrybalo, J. (2002). Cognitive theories of early gender development. *Psychological Bulletin, 128,* 903–933.

Martin, G. L., & Pear, J. (2011). *Behavior modification: What it is and how to do it* (9th ed.). Upper Saddle River, NJ: Pearson.

Martin, K. A. (1996). *Puberty, sexuality and the self: Girls and boys at adolescence.* New York: Routledge.

Martin, P., Long, M. V., & Poon, L. W. (2002). Age changes and differences in personality traits and states of the old and very old. *Journal of Gerontology, 57B,* P144–P152.

Martin, R. (2008). Meiotic errors in human oogenesis and spermatogenesis. *Reproductive Biomedicine Online, 16,* 523–531.

Martinez-Frias, M. L., Bermejo, E., Rodríguez-Pinilla, E., & Frías, J. L. (2004). Risk for congenital anomalies associated with different sporadic and daily doses of alcohol consumption during pregnancy: A case-control study. *Birth Defects Research, Part A, Clinical and Molecular Teratology, 70,* 194–200.

Martinot, D., & Désert, M. (2007). Awareness of a gender stereotype, personal beliefs, and self-perceptions regarding math ability: When boys do not surpass girls. *Social Psychology of Education, 10,* 455–471.

Martinson, I. M., Davies, E., & McClowry, S. G. (1987). The long-term effect of sibling death on self-concept. *Journal of Pediatric Nursing, 2,* 227–235.

Martlew, M., & Connolly, K. J. (1996). Human figure drawings by schooled and unschooled children in Papua New Guinea. *Child Development, 67,* 2743–2762.

Maruna, S. (2001). *Making good: How ex-convicts reform and rebuild their lives.* Washington, DC: American Psychological Association.

Maruna, S., LeBel, T. P., & Lanier, C. S. (2004). Generativity behind bars: Some "redemptive truths" about prison society. In E. de St. Aubin, D. P. McAdams, & T.-C. Kim (Eds.), *The generative society* (pp. 131–151). Washington, DC: American Psychological Association.

Maruta, T., Colligan, R. C., Malinchoc, M., & Offord, K. P. (2002). Optimism–pessimism assessed in the 1960s and self-reported health status 30 years later. *Mayo Clinic Proceedings, 77,* 748–753.

Marzolf, D. P., & DeLoache, J. S. (1994). Transfer in young children's understanding of spatial representations. *Child Development, 65,* 1–15.

Masataka, N. (1996). Perception of motherese in a signed language by 6-month-old deaf infants. *Developmental Psychology, 32,* 874–879.

Mascolo, M. F., & Fischer, K. W. (2007). The codevelopment of self and sociomoral emotions during the toddler years. In C. A. Brownell & C. B. Kopp (Eds.), *Socioemotional development in the toddler years: Transitions and transformations* (pp. 66–99). New York: Guilford.

Mashburn, A. J. (2008). Quality of social and physical environments in preschools and children's development of academic, language, and literacy skills. *Applied Developmental Science, 12,* 113–127.

Mashburn, A. J., Pianta, R. C., Mamre, B. K., Downer, J. T., Barbarin, O. A., Bryant, D., et al. (2008). Measures of classroom quality in prekindergarten and children's development of academic, language, and social skills. *Child Development, 79,* 732–749.

Maslach, C., Schaufeli, W. B., & Leiter, M. P. (2001). Job burnout. *Annual Review of Psychology, 52,* 397–422.

Mason, M. G., & Gibbs, J. C. (1993a). Role-taking opportunities and the transition to advanced moral judgment. *Moral Education Forum, 18,* 1–12.

Mason, M. G., & Gibbs, J. C. (1993b). Social perspective taking and moral judgment among college students. *Journal of Adolescent Research, 8,* 109–123.

Masoro, E. J. (2011). Terminal weight loss, frailty, and mortality. In E. J. Masoro & S. N. Austad (Eds.), *Handbook of the biology of aging* (7th ed., pp. 321–331). San Diego, CA: Academic Press.

Massachusetts Expert Panel on End-of-Life Care. (2010, October). *Patient-centered care and human mortality: The urgency of health system reforms to ensure respect for patients' wishes and accountability for excellence in care.* Retrieved from www.mass.gov/hqcc/docs/expert-panel/final-expert-panel-report.pdf

Masten, A. S. (2001). Ordinary magic: Resilience processes in development. *American Psychologist, 56,* 227–238.

Masten, A. S., Burt, K. B., Roisman, G. I., Obradovic, J., Long, J. D., & Tellegen, A. (2004). Resources and resilience in the transition to adulthood: Continuity and change. *Development and Psychopathology, 16,* 1071–1094.

Masten, A. S., & Gewirtz, A. H. (2006). Vulnerability and resilience in early child development. In K. McCartney & D. Phillips (Eds.), *Blackwell handbook of early childhood development* (pp. 22–43). Malden, MA: Blackwell.

Masten, A. S., & Powell, J. L. (2003). A resilience framework for research, policy, and practice. In S. S. Luthar (Ed.), *Resilience and vulnerability* (pp. 1–25). New York: Cambridge University Press.

Masten, A. S., & Reed, M. J. (2002). Resilience in development. In C. R. Snyder & S. J. Lopez (Eds.),

Handbook of positive psychology (pp. 74–88). New York: Oxford University Press.

Masten, A. S., & Shaffer, A. (2006). How families matter in child development: Reflections from research on risk and resilience. In A. S. Masten & A. Shaffer (Eds.), *Families count: Effects on child and adolescent development* (pp. 5–25). New York: Cambridge University Press.

Masters, R. K. (2012). Uncrossing the U.S. black-white mortality crossover: The role of cohort forces in life course mortality risk. *Demography, 49,* 773–796.

Mastropieri, D., & Turkewitz, G. (1999). Prenatal experience and neonatal responsiveness to vocal expression of emotion. *Developmental Psychobiology, 35,* 204–214.

Masur, E. F., McIntyre, C. W., & Flavell, J. H. (1973). Developmental changes in apportionment of study time among items in a multi-trial free recall task. *Journal of Experimental Child Psychology, 15,* 237–246.

Masur, E. F., & Rodemaker, J. E. (1999). Mothers' and infants' spontaneous vocal, verbal, and action imitation during the second year. *Merrill-Palmer Quarterly, 45,* 392–412.

Mather, M. (2010, May). *U.S. children in single-mother families* (PRB Data Brief). Washington, DC: Population Reference Bureau.

Mather, M., & Carstensen, L. L. (2005). Aging and motivated cognition: The positivity effect in attention and memory. *Trends in Cognitive Sciences, 9,* 496–502.

Mathews, T. J., & MacDorman, M. F. (2008). Infant mortality statistics from the 2005 period linked birth/infant death data set. *National Vital Statistics Reports, 57*(2), 1–32.

Matthews, K. A., Gump, B. B., Harris, K. F., Haney, T. L., & Barefoot, J. C. (2004). Hostile behaviors predict cardiovascular mortality among men enrolled in the Multiple Risk Factor Intervention Trial. *Circulation, 109,* 66–70.

Mattison, J. A., Roth, G. S., Beasley, T. M., Tilmont, E. M., Handy, A. M., Herbert, R. L., et al. (2012). Impact of caloric restriction on health and survival in rhesus monkeys from the NIA study. *Nature, 489,* 318–321.

Mattson, S. N., Calarco, K. E., & Lang, A. R. (2006). Focused and shifting attention in children with heavy prenatal alcohol exposure. *Neuropsychology, 20,* 361–369.

Maume, D. J., Jr. (2004). Is the glass ceiling a unique form of inequality? *Work and Occupations, 31,* 250–274.

Maupin, R., Lyman, R., Fatsis, J., Prystowiski, E., Nguyen, A., & Wright, C. (2004). Characteristics of women who deliver with no prenatal care. *Journal of Maternal-Fetal and Neonatal Medicine, 16,* 45–50.

Maurer, D., Mondloch, C. J., & Lewis, T. L. (2007). Sleeper effects. *Developmental Science, 10,* 40–47.

Maurer, T. J. (2001). Career-relevant learning and development, worker age, and beliefs about self-efficacy for development. *Journal of Management, 27,* 123–140.

Maurer, T. J., Wrenn, K. A., & Weiss, E. M. (2003). Toward understanding and managing stereotypical beliefs about older workers' ability and desire for learning and development. In J. J. Martocchio & G. R. Ferris (Eds.), *Research in personnel and human resources management* (Vol. 22, pp. 253–285). Stamford, CT: JAI Press.

Mavroveli, S., Petrides, K. V., Sangareau, Y., & Furnham, A. (2009). Exploring the relationships between trait emotional intelligence and objective socio-emotional outcomes in childhood. *British Journal of Educational Psychology, 79,* 259–272.

Mayberry, R. I. (2010). Early language acquisition and adult language ability: What sign language reveals about the critical period for language. In M. Marshark & P. E. Spencer (Eds.), *Oxford handbook of deaf studies, language, and education* (Vol. 2, pp. 281–291). New York: Oxford University Press.

Mayer, J. D., Salovey, P., & Caruso, D. R. (2003). *Mayer–Salovey–Caruso Emotional Intelligence Test (MSCEIT): User's manual.* Toronto, Ontario: Multi-Health Systems.

Mayer, J. D., Salovey, P., & Caruso, D. R. (2008). Emotional intelligence: New ability or eclectic traits? *American Psychologist, 63,* 503–517.

Mayeux, L., & Cillessen, A. H. N. (2003). Development of social problem solving in early childhood: Stability, change, and associations with social competence. *Journal of Genetic Psychology, 164,* 153–173.

Maynard, A. E. (2002). Cultural teaching: The development of teaching skills in Maya sibling interactions. *Child Development, 73,* 969–982.

Maynard, A. E., & Greenfield, P. M. (2003). Implicit cognitive development in cultural tools and children: Lessons from Maya Mexico. *Cognitive Development, 18,* 489–510.

Maynard, A. E., Subrahmanyam, K., & Greenfield, P. M. (2005). Technology and the development of intelligence: From the loom to the computer. In R. J. Sternberg & D. D. Preiss (Eds.), *Intelligence and technology: The impact of tools in the nature and development of human abilities* (pp. 29–53). Mahwah, NJ: Erlbaum.

Mazerolle, M., Régner, I., Morisset, P., Rigalleau, F., & Huguet, P. (2012). Stereotype threat strengthens automatic recall and undermines controlled processes in older adults. *Psychological Science, 23,* 723–727.

McAdams, D. P. (2001). Generativity in midlife. In M. E. Lachman (Ed.), *Handbook of midlife development* (pp. 395–443). New York: Wiley.

McAdams, D. P. (2006). The redemptive self: Generativity and the stories Americans live by. *Research in Human Development, 3,* 81–100.

McAdams, D. P. (2011). Life narratives. In K. L. Fingerman, C. A. Berg, J. Smith, & T. C. Antonucci (Eds.), *Handbook of life-span development* (pp. 589–610). New York: Springer.

McAdams, D. P., & Cox, K. S. (2010). Self and identity across the life span. In M. Lamb & A. Freund (Eds.), *Handbook of life-span development: Vol. 2. Social and emotional development* (pp. 158–207). Hoboken, NJ: Wiley.

McAdams, D. P., & de St. Aubin, E. (1992). A theory of generativity and its assessment through self-report, behavioral acts, and narrative themes in autobiography. *Journal of Personality and Social Psychology, 62,* 1003–1015.

McAdams, D. P., Diamond, A., de St. Aubin, E., & Mansfield, E. (1997). Stories of commitment: The psychosocial construction of generative lives. *Journal of Personality and Social Psychology, 72,* 678–694.

McAdams, D. P., Hart, H. M., & Maruna, S. (1998). The anatomy of generativity. In D. P. McAdams & E. de St. Aubin (Eds.), *Generativity and adult development* (pp. 7–43). Washington, DC: American Psychological Association.

McAdams, D. P., & Logan, R. L. (2004). What is generativity? In E. de St. Aubin & D. P. McAdams (Eds.), *The generative society: Caring for future generations* (pp. 15–31). Washington, DC: American Psychological Association.

McAdams, D. P., Reynolds, J., Lewis, M., Patten, A. H., & Bowman, P. J. (2001). When bad things turn good and good things turn bad: Sequences of redemption and contamination in life narrative and their relation to psychosocial adaptation in midlife adults and children. *Personality and Social Psychology Bulletin, 27,* 474–485.

McAdoo, H. P., & Younge, S. N. (2009). Black families. In H. A. Neville, B. M. Tynes, & S. O. Utsey (Eds.), *Handbook of African American psychology* (pp. 103–115). Thousand Oaks, CA: Sage.

McAlister, A., & Peterson, C. C. (2006). Mental playmates: Siblings, executive functioning and theory of mind. *British Journal of Developmental Psychology, 24,* 733–751.

McAlister, A., & Peterson, C. C. (2007). A longitudinal study of child siblings and theory of mind development. *Cognitive Development, 22,* 258–270.

McArdle, J. J., Ferrer-Caja, E., Hamagami, F., & Woodcock, R. W. (2002). Comparative longitudinal structural analyses of the growth and decline of multiple intellectual abilities over the life span. *Developmental Psychology, 38,* 115–142.

McAuley, E., & Elavsky, S. (2008). Self-efficacy, physical activity, and cognitive function. In W. W. Spirduso, L. W. Poon, & W. Chodzko-Zajko (Eds.). *Exercise and its mediating effects on cognition* (pp. 69–84). Champaign, IL: Human Kinetics.

McBee, M. T. (2006). A descriptive analysis of referral sources for gifted identification screening by race and socioeconomic status. *Journal of Secondary Gifted Education, 17,* 103–111.

McBride-Chang, C., & Kail, R. V. (2002). Cross-cultural similarities in the predictors of reading acquisition. *Child Development, 73,* 1392–1407.

McCabe, A. (1997). Developmental and cross-cultural aspects of children's narration. In M. Bamberg (Ed.), *Narrative development: Six approaches* (pp. 137–174). Mahwah, NJ: Erlbaum.

McCall, R. B., & Carriger, M. S. (1993). A meta-analysis of infant habituation and recognition memory performance as predictors of later IQ. *Child Development, 64,* 57–79.

McCarthy, B., & McCarthy, E. J. (2004). *Getting it right the first time: Creating a healthy marriage.* New York: Brunner-Routledge.

McCartney, K., Dearing, E., Taylor, B., & Bub, K. (2007). Quality child care supports the achievement of low-income children: Direct and indirect pathways through caregiving and the home environment. *Journal of Applied Developmental Psychology, 28,* 411–426.

McCartney, K., Harris, M. J., & Bernieri, F. (1990). Growing up and growing apart: A developmental meta-analysis of twin studies. *Psychological Bulletin, 107,* 226–237.

McCartney, K., Owen, M., Booth, C., Clarke-Stewart, A., & Vandell, D. (2004). Testing a maternal attachment model of behavior problems in early childhood. *Journal of Child Psychology and Psychiatry, 45,* 765–778.

McCarton, C. (1998). Behavioral outcomes in low birth weight infants. *Pediatrics, 102,* 1293–1297.

McCarty, M. E., & Ashmead, D. H. (1999). Visual control of reaching and grasping in infants. *Developmental Psychology, 35,* 620–631.

McCarty, M. E., & Keen, R. (2005). Facilitating problem-solving performance among 9- and 12-month-old infants. *Journal of Cognition and Development, 6,* 209–228.

McClain, C. S., Rosenfeld, B., & Breitbart, W. (2003). Effect of spiritual well-being on end-of-life despair in terminally ill cancer patients. *Lancet, 361,* 1603–1607.

McClain-Jacobson, C., Rosenfeld, B., Kosinski, A., Pessin, H., Cimino, J. E., & Breitbart, W. (2004). Belief in an afterlife, spiritual well-being and end-of-life despair in patients with advanced cancer. *General Hospital Psychiatry, 26,* 484–486.

McClure, S., Laibson, D., Loewenstein, G., & Cohen, J. (2004). Separate neural systems value immediate and delayed monetary rewards. *Science, 306,* 503–507.

McColgan, K. L., & McCormack, T. (2008). Searching and planning: Young children's reasoning about past and future event sequences. *Child Development, 79,* 1477–1479.

McCrae, R., & Costa, P. T., Jr. (2003). *Personality in adulthood: A five-factor theory perspective* (2nd ed.). New York: Guilford.

McCrae, R., & Costa, P. T., Jr. (2006). Cross-cultural perspectives on adult personality trait development. In D. K. Mroczek & T. D. Little (Eds.), *Handbook of personality development* (pp. 129–146). Mahwah, NJ: Erlbaum.

McCrae, R. R. (2011). Personality theories for the 21st century. *Teaching of Psychology, 38,* 209–214.

McCune, L. (1993). The development of play as the development of consciousness. In M. H. Bornstein & A. O'Reilly (Eds.), *New directions for child development* (No. 59, pp. 67–79). San Francisco: Jossey-Bass.

McCurry, S. M., Logsdon, R. G., Teri, L., & Vitello, M. V. (2007). Evidence-based psychological treatments for insomnia in older adults. *Psychology and Aging, 22,* 18–27.

McDaniel, M. A., Einstein, G. O., & Rendell, P. G. (2007). The puzzle of inconsistent age-related declines in prospective memory: A multiprocess explanation. In M. Kliegel, M. A. McDaniel, & G. O. Einstein (Eds.), *Prospective memory: Cognitive, neuroscience, developmental, and applied perspectives* (pp. 141–160). Mahwah, NJ: Erlbaum.

McDaniel, M. A., Maier, S. F., & Einstein, G. O. (2002). "Brain-specific" nutrients: A memory cure? *Psychological Science in the Public Interest, 3,* 12–38.

McDill, T., Hall, S. K., & Turell, S. C. (2006). Aging and creating families: Never-married heterosexual women over forty. *Journal of Women and Aging, 18,* 37–50.

McDonagh, M. S., Osterweil, P., & Guise, J. M. (2005). The benefits and risks of inducing labour in patients with prior cesarean delivery: A systematic review. *BJOG, 112,* 1007–1015.

McDonald, L., & Robb, A. L. (2004). The economic legacy of divorce and separation for women in old age. *Canadian Journal on Aging, 23*(Suppl. 1), S83–S97.

McDonough, L. (1999). Early declarative memory for location. *British Journal of Developmental Psychology, 17,* 381–402.

McDowell, D. J., & Parke, R. D. (2000). Differential knowledge of display rules for positive and negative emotions: Influences from parents, influences on peers. *Social Development, 9,* 415–432.

McElhaney, K. B., & Allen, J. P. (2001). Autonomy and adolescent social functioning: The moderating effect of risk. *Child Development, 72,* 220–235.

McElhaney, K. B., Allen, J. P., Stephenson, J. C., & Hare, A. L. (2009). Attachment and autonomy during adolescence. In R. M. Lerner & L. Steiberg (Eds.), *Handbook of adolescent psychology: Vol. 1. Individual bases of adolescent development* (3rd ed., pp. 358–403). Hoboken, NJ: Wiley.

McElwain, N. L., & Booth-LaForce, C. (2006). Maternal sensitivity to infant distress and nondistress as predictors of infant–mother attachment security. *Journal of Family Psychology, 20,* 247–255.

McEwen, B. S. (2007). Physiology and neurobiology of stress an adaptation: Central role of the brain. *Physiological Reviews, 87,* 873–904.

McFarlane, J., Malecha, A., Watson, K., Gist, J., Batten, E., Hall, I., & Smith, S. (2005). Intimate partner assault against women: Frequency, health consequences, and treatment outcomes. *Obstetrics and Gynecology, 105,* 99–108.

McGee, L. M., & Richgels, D. J. (2004). *Literacy's beginnings* (4th ed.). Boston: Allyn and Bacon.

McGee, L. M., & Richgels, D. J. (2012). *Literacy's beginnings: Supporting young readers and writers* (6th ed.). Boston: Allyn and Bacon.

McGoldrick, M. (2004). Echoes from the past: Helping families deal with their ghosts. In F. Walsh & M. McGoldrick (Eds.), *Living beyond loss* (pp. 99–118). New York: Norton.

McGoldrick, M., Schlesinger, J. M., Lee, E., Hines, P. M., Chan, J., & Almeida, R. (2004). Mourning in different cultures. In F. Walsh & M. McGoldrick (Eds.), *Living beyond loss* (pp. 1119–160). New York: Norton.

McGoldrick, M., & Shibusawa, T. (2012). The family life cycle. In F. Walsh (Ed.), *Normal family processes: Growing diversity and complexity* (pp. 375–398). New York: Guilford.

McGrath, S. K., & Kennell, J. H. (2008). A randomized controlled trial of continuous labor support for middle-class couples: Effect on cesarean delivery rates. *Birth: Issues in Perinatal Care, 35,* 9–97.

McGue, M., Elkins, I., Walden, B., & Iacono, W. G. (2005). Perceptions of the parent–adolescent relationship: A longitudinal investigation. *Developmental Psychology, 41,* 971–984.

McHale, J. P., Kazali, C., Rotman, T., Talbot, J., Carleton, M., & Lieberson, R. (2004). The transition to coparenthood: Parents' prebirth expectations and early coparental adjustment at 3 months postpartum. *Development and Psychopathology, 16,* 711–733.

McHale, J. P., Khazan, I., Erera, P., Rotman, T., DeCourcey, W., & McConnell, M. (2002a). Coparenting in diverse family systems. In M. H. Bornstein (Ed.), *Handbook of parenting: Vol. 3* (2nd ed., pp. 75–107). Mahwah, NJ: Erlbaum.

McHale, J. P., Kuersten-Hogan, R., & Rao, N. (2004). Growing points for coparenting theory and research. *Journal of Adult Development, 11,* 221–234.

McHale, J. P., Lauretti, A., Talbot, J., & Pouquette, C. (2002b). Retrospect and prospect in the psychological study of coparenting and family group process. In J. P. McHale & W. S. Grolnick (Eds.), *Retrospect and prospect in the psychological study of families* (pp. 127–165). Mahwah, NJ: Erlbaum.

McHale, J. P., & Rotman, T. (2007). Is seeing believing? Expectant parents' outlooks on coparenting and later coparenting solidarity. *Infant Behavior and Development, 30,* 63–81.

McHale, S. M., Crouter, A. C., Kim, J.-Y., Burton, L. M., Davis, K. D., Dotterer, A. M., & Swanson, D. P. (2006). Mothers' and fathers' racial socialization in African-American families: Implications for youth. *Child Development, 77,* 1387–1402.

McIntosh, H., Metz, E., & Youniss, J. (2005). Community service and identity formation in adolescents. In J. S. Mahoney, R. W. Larson, & J. S. Eccles (Eds.), *Organized activities as contexts of development: Extracurricular activities, after-school and community programs* (pp. 331–351). Mahwah, NJ: Erlbaum.

McIntosh, W. D., Locker, L., Briley, K., Ryan, R., & Scott, A. J. (2011). What do older adults seek in their potential romantic partners? Evidence from online personal ads. *International Journal of Aging and Human Development, 72,* 67–82.

McKee-Ryan, F. M. (2011). "I have a job, but . . . ": A review of underemployment. *Journal of Management, 37,* 962–996.

McKee-Ryan, F. M., Virick, M., Prussia, G. E., Harvey, J., & Lilly, J. D. (2009). Life after the layoff: Getting a job worth keeping. *Journal of Organizational Behavior, 30,* 561–580.

McKenna, J. J. (2001). Why we never ask "Is it safe for infants to sleep alone?" *Academy of Breast Feeding Medicine News and Views, 7*(4), 32, 38.

McKenna, J. J. (2002, September/October). Breast-feeding and bedsharing still useful (and important) after all these years. *Mothering, 114.* Retrieved from www.mothering.com/articles/new_baby/sleep/mckenna.html

McKenna, J. J., & McDade, T. (2005). Why babies should never sleep alone: A review of the co-sleeping controversy in relation to SIDS, bedsharing, and breastfeeding. *Paediatric Respiratory Reviews, 6,* 134–152.

McKenna, J. J., & Volpe, L. E. (2007). Sleeping with baby: An Internet-based sampling of parental experiences, choices, perceptions, and interpretations in a Western industrialized context. *Infant and Child Development, 16,* 359–385.

McKeown, M. G., & Beck, I. L. (2009). The role of metacognition in understanding and supporting reading comprehension. In D. J. Hacker, J. Dunlosky, & A. C. Graesser (Eds.), *Handbook of metacognition in education* (pp. 7–25). New York: Routledge.

McKim, W. A., & Hancock, S. (2013). *Drugs and behavior* (7th ed.). Upper Saddle River, NJ: Pearson.

McKinney, C., Donnelly, R., & Renk, K. (2008). Perceived parenting, positive and negative perceptions of parents, and late adolescent emotional adjustment. *Child and Adolescent Mental health, 13,* 66–73.

McKown, C., & Strambler, M. J. (2009). Developmental antecedents and social and academic consequences of stereotype-consciousness in middle childhood. *Child Development, 80,* 1643–1659.

McKown, C., & Weinstein, R. S. (2003). The development and consequences of stereotype consciousness in middle childhood. *Child Development, 74,* 498–515.

McKown, C., & Weinstein, R. S. (2008). Teacher expectations, classroom context, and the achievement gap. *Journal of School Psychology, 46,* 235–261.

McKusick, V. A. (2011). *Online Mendelian inheritance in man.* Retrieved from www.nslij-genetics.org/search_omim.html

McLanahan, S. (1999). Father absence and the welfare of children. In E. M. Hetherington (Ed.), *Coping with divorce, single parenting, and remarriage: A risk and resiliency perspective* (pp. 117–145). Mahwah, NJ: Erlbaum.

McLaughlin, K. A., Fox, N. A., Zeanah, C. H., & Nelson, C. A. (2011). Adverse rearing environments and neural development in children: The development of frontal electroencephalogram asymmetry. *Biological Psychiatry, 70,* 1008–1015.

McLean, K. C. (2008). Stories of the young and the old: Personal continuity and narrative identity. *Developmental Psychology, 44,* 254–264.

McLoyd, V. C., Aikens, N. L., & Burton, L. M. (2006). Child poverty, policy, and practice. In K. A. Renninger & I. E. Sigel (Eds.), *Handbook of child psychology: Vol. 4. Child psychology in practice* (6th ed., pp. 700–778). Hoboken, NJ: Wiley.

McLoyd, V. C., Kaplan, R., Hardaway, C. R., & Wood, D. (2007). Does endorsement of physical discipline matter? Assessing moderating influences on the maternal and child psychological correlates of physical discipline in African-American families. *Journal of Family Psychology, 21,* 165–175.

McLoyd, V. C., & Smith, J. (2002). Physical discipline and behavior problems in African-American, European-American, and Hispanic children: Emotional support as a moderator. *Journal of Marriage and Family, 64,* 40–53.

McMahon, C. A., Barnett, B., Kowalenko, N. M., & Tennant, C. C. (2006). Maternal attachment state of mind moderates the impact of postnatal depression on infant attachment. *Journal of Child Psychology and Psychiatry, 47,* 660–669.

MCR Vitamin Study Research Group. (1991). Prevention of neural tube defects: Results of the Medical Research Council Vitamin Study. *Lancet, 338,* 131–137.

Mead, G. H. (1934). *Mind, self, and society.* Chicago: University of Chicago Press.

Mead, M. (1928). *Coming of age in Samoa.* Ann Arbor, MI: Morrow.

Mead, M., & Newton, N. (1967). Cultural patterning of perinatal behavior. In S. Richardson & A. Guttmacher (Eds.), *Childbearing: Its social and psychological aspects* (pp. 142–244). Baltimore: Williams & Wilkins.

Meade, C. S., Kershaw, T. S., & Ickovics, J. R. (2008). The intergenerational cycle of teenage motherhood: An ecological approach. *Health Psychology, 27,* 419–429.

Meadus, R. J., & Twomey, J. C. (2011). Men student nurses: The nursing education experience. *Nursing Forum, 46,* 269–279.

Meegan, S. P., & Berg, C. A. (2002). Contexts, functions, forms, and processes of collaborative everyday problem solving in older adulthood. *International Journal of Behavioral Development, 26,* 6–15.

Meeus, W., Oosterwegel, A., & Vollebergh, W. (2002). Parental and peer attachment and identity development in adolescence. *Journal of Adolescence, 25,* 93–106.

Meeus, W., van de Schoot, R., Keijsers, L., & Branje, S. (2012). Identity statuses as developmental trajectories: A five-wave longitudinal study in early-to-middle and middle-to-late adolescents. *Journal of Youth and Adolescence, 41,* 1008–1021.

Meeus, W. H. J., Branje, S. J. T., van der Valk, I., & de Wied, M. (2007). Relationships with intimate partner, best friend, and parents in adolescence and early adulthood: A study of the saliency of the intimate partnership. *International Journal of Behavioral Development, 31,* 569–580.

Mehlmadrona, L., & Madrona, M. M. (1997). Physician- and midwife-attended home births—effects of breech, twin, and post-dates outcome data on mortality rates. *Journal of Nurse-Midwifery, 42,* 91–98.

Mehlson, M., Platz, M., & Fromholt, P. (2003). Life satisfaction across the life course: Evaluations of the most and least satisfying decades of life. *International Journal of Aging and Human Development, 57,* 217–236.

Meier, A., & Allen, G. (2009). Romantic relationships from adolescence to young adulthood: Evidence from the National Longitudinal Study of Adolescent Health. *Sociological Quarterly, 50,* 308–335.

Meins, E., Fernyhough, C., Russell, J., & Clark-Carter, D. (1998). Security of attachment as a predictor of symbolic and mentalizing abilities: A longitudinal study. *Social Development, 7,* 1–24.

Meins, E., Fernyhough, C., Wainwright, R., Clark-Carter, D., Gupta, M. D., Fradley, E., & Tucker, M. (2003). Pathways to understanding mind: Construct validity and predictive validity of maternal mind-mindedness. *Child Development, 74,* 1194–1211.

Melby, M. K., Lock, M., & Kaufert, P. (2005). Culture and symptom reporting at menopause. *Human Reproduction Update, 11,* 495–512.

Melby-Lervag, M., & Hulme, C. (2010). Serial and free recall in children can be improved by training: Evidence for the importance of phonological and semantic representations in immediate memory tasks. *Psychological Science, 21,* 1694–1700.

Melenhorst, A. S., Fisk, A. D., Mynatt, E. D., & Rogers, W. A. (2004). Potential intrusiveness of aware home technology: Perceptions of older adults. In *Proceedings of the Human Factors and Ergonomics Society 48th annual meeting* (pp. 266–270). Santa Monica, CA: Human Factors and Ergonomics Society.

Melinder, A., Endestad, T., & Magnusson, S. (2006). Relations between episodic memory, suggestibility, theory of mind, and cognitive inhibition in the preschool child. *Scandinavian Journal of Psychology, 47,* 485–495.

Meltzoff, A. N. (2007). "Like me": A foundation for social cognition. *Developmental Science, 10,* 126–134.

Meltzoff, A. N., & Kuhl, P. K. (1994). Faces and speech: Intermodal processing of biologically relevant signals in infants and adults. In D. J. Lewkowicz & R. Lickliter (Eds.), *The development of intersensory perception* (pp. 335–369). Hillsdale, NJ: Erlbaum.

Meltzoff, A. N., & Moore, M. K. (1977). Imitation of facial and manual gestures by human neonates. *Science, 198,* 75–78.

Meltzoff, A. N., & Moore, M. K. (1994). Imitation, memory, and the representation of persons. *Infant Behavior and Development, 17,* 83–99.

Meltzoff, A. N., & Moore, M. K. (1999). Persons and representations: Why infant imitation is important for theories of human development. In J. Nadel & G. Butterworth (Eds.), *Imitation in infancy* (pp. 9–35). Cambridge, UK: Cambridge University Press.

Meltzoff, A. N., & Williamson, R. A. (2010). The importance of imitation for theories of social-cognitive development. In J. G. Bremner & T. D. Wachs (Eds.), *Wiley-Blackwell handbook of infant development* (2nd ed., pp. 345–364). Oxford, UK: Wiley.

Melzi, G., & Ely, R. (2009). Language development in the school years. In J. B. Gleason & N. B. Ratner (Eds.), *The development of language* (7th ed., pp. 391–435). Boston: Allyn and Bacon.

Mendle, J., Turkheimer, E., D'Onofrio, B. M., Lynch, S., Emery, R. E., & Slutske, W. S. (2006). Family structure and age at menarche: A children-of-twins approach. *Developmental Psychology, 42,* 533–542.

Mendle, J., Turkheimer, E., & Emery, R. E. (2007). Detrimental psychological outcomes associated with early pubertal timing in adolescent girls. *Developmental Review, 27,* 151–171.

Meneilly, G. S. (2006). Diabetes in the elderly. *Medical Clinics of North America, 90,* 909–923.

Mennella, J. A., & Beauchamp, G. K. (1998). Early flavor experiences: Research update. *Nutrition Reviews, 56,* 205–211.

Menon, U. (2001). Middle adulthood in cultural perspective: The imagined and the experienced in three cultures. In M. E. Lachman (Ed.), *Handbook of midlife development* (pp. 40–74). New York: Wiley.

Ment, L. R., Vohr, B., Allan, W., Katz, K. H., Schneider, K. C., Westerveld, M., Cuncan, C., & Makuch, R. W. (2003). Change in cognitive function over time in very low-birth-weight infants. *Journal of the American Medical Association, 289,* 705–711.

Mercer, C. H., Bailey, J. V., Johnson, A. M., Erens, B., Wellings, K., Fenton, K., & Copas, A. J. (2007). Women who report having sex with women: British national probability data on prevalence, sexual behaviors, and health outcomes. *Research and Practice, 97,* 1126–1133.

Mergenhagen, P. (1996). Her own boss. *American Demographics, 18,* 36–41.

Merikangas, K. R., He, J-P. Burstein, M., Swanson, S. A. Avenevoli, S., Cui, L., Benjet, C., et al. (2010). Lifetime prevalence of mental disorders in U.S. adolescents: Results from the National Comorbidity Survey Replication—Adolescent Supplement (NCS-A). *Journal of the American Academy of Child and Adolescent Psychiatry, 49,* 980–989.

Merriam, S. B. (1993). The uses of reminiscence in older adulthood. *Educational Gerontology, 8,* 275–290.

Messinger, D. S., & Fogel, A. (2007). The interactive development of social smiling. In R. Kail (Ed.), *Advances in child development and behavior* (Vol. 35, pp. 327–366). Oxford, UK: Elsevier.

Messman, S. J., Canary, D. J., & Hause, K. S. (2000). Motives to remain platonic, equity, and the use of maintenance strategies in opposite-sex friendships. *Journal of Social and Personal Relationships, 17,* 67–94.

Methven, L., Allen, V. J., Withers, C. A., & Gosney, M. A. (2012). Aging and taste. *Proceedings of the Nutrition Society, 71,* 556–565.

MetLife. (2011). *MetLife study of caregiving costs to working caregivers: Double jeopardy for baby boomers caring for their parents.* Westport, CT: National Alliance for Caregiving and MetLife Mature Market Institute.

Metheny, J., McWhirter, E. H., & O'Neil, M. E. (2008). Measuring perceived teacher support and its influence on adolescent career development. *Journal of Career Assessment, 16,* 218–237.

Metz, E. C., & Youniss, J. (2005). Longitudinal gains in civic development through school-based required service. *Political Psychology, 26,* 413–437.

Meyer, B. J. F., Russo, C., & Talbot, A. (1995). Discourse comprehension and problem solving: Decisions about the treatment of breast cancer by women across the lifespan. *Psychology and Aging, 10,* 84–103.

Meyer, B. J. F., Talbot, A. P., & Ranalli, C. (2007). Why older adults make more immediate treatment decisions about cancer than younger adults. *Psychology and Aging, 22,* 505–524.

Meyer, I. H. (2003). Prejudice, social stress, and mental health in lesbian, gay, and bisexual populations: Conceptual issues and research evidence. *Psychological Bulletin, 129,* 674–697.

Meyer, J. (2012). *Centenarians: 2010.* Washington, DC: U.S. Government Printing Office.

Meyer, R. (2009). Infant feeding in the first year. 1: Feeding practices in the first six months of life. *Journal of Family Health Care, 19,* 13–16.

Meyer-Bahlburg, H. F. L., Ehrhardt, A. A., Rosen, L. R., Gruen, R. S., Veridiano, N. P., Vann, F. H., & Neuwalder, H. F. (1995). Prenatal estrogens and the development of homosexual orientation. *Developmental Psychology, 31,* 12–21.

Mezei, L., & Murinson, B. B. (2011). Pain education in North American medical schools. *Journal of Pain, 12,* 1199–1208.

Mezulis, A. H., Hyde, J. S., & Clark, R. (2004). Father involvement moderates the effect of maternal depression during a child's infancy on child behavior problems in kindergarten. *Journal of Family Psychology, 18,* 575–588.

Michael, A., & Eccles, J. S. (2003). When coming of age means coming undone: Links between puberty and psychosocial adjustment among European American and African American girls. In C. Hayward (Ed.), *Gender differences at puberty* (pp. 277–303). New York: Cambridge University Press.

Michael, R. T., Gagnon, J. H., Laumann, E. O., & Kolata, G. (1994). *Sex in America.* Boston: Little, Brown.

Michalik, N. M., Eisenberg, N., Spinrad, T. L., Ladd, B., Thompson, M., & Valiente, C. (2007). Longitudinal relations among parental emotional expressivity and sympathy and prosocial behavior in adolescence. *Social Development, 16,* 286–309.

Michels, K. B., Willett, W. C., Graubard, B. I., Vaidya, R. L., Cantwell, M. M., Sansbury, L. B., & Forman, M. R. (2007). A longitudinal study of infant feeding and obesity throughout the life course. *International Journal of Obesity, 31,* 1078–1085.

Michiels, D., Grietens, H., Onghena, P., & Kuppens, S. (2010). Perceptions of maternal and paternal attachment security in middle childhood: Links with positive parental affection and psychological adjustment. *Early Child Development and Care, 180,* 211–225.

Midlin, M., Jenkins, R., & Law, C. (2009). Maternal employment and indicators of child health: A systematic review in pre-school children in OECD countries. *Journal of Epidemiology and Community Health, 63,* 340–350.

Mienaltowski, A. (2011). Everyday problem solving across the adult life span. *Annals of the New York Academy of Sciences, 1235,* 75–85.

Mikami, A. Y., Lerner, M. D., & Lun, J. (2010). Social context influences on children's rejection by their peers. *Child Development Perspectives, 4,* 123–130.

Mikulincer, M., Florian, V., & Hirschberger, G. (2003). The existential function of close relationships: Introducing death into the science of love. *Personality and Social Psychology Review, 7,* 20–40.

Mikulincer, M., & Shaver, P. R. (2008). An attachment perspective on bereavement. In M. S. Stroebe, R. O. Hansson, H. Schut, & W. Stroebe (Eds.), *Handbook of bereavement research and practice* (pp. 87–112).

Washington, DC: American Psychological Association.

Milevsky, A., Schlechter, M., Netter, S., & Keehn, D. (2007). Maternal and paternal parenting styles in adolescents: Associations with self-esteem, depression, and life satisfaction. *Journal of Child and Family Studies, 16*, 39–47.

Milkie, M. A., Bierman, A., & Schieman, S. (2008). How adult children influence older parents' mental health: Integrating stress-process and life-course perspectives. *Social Psychology Quarterly, 71*, 86–105.

Miller, D. I., Taler, V., Davidson, P. S. R., & Messier, C. (2012). Measuring the impact of exercise on cognitive aging: Methodological issues. *Neurobiology of Aging, 33*, 622.e29–622.e43.

Miller, D. N. (2011). *Child and adolescent suicidal behavior: School-based prevention, assessment, and intervention.* New York: Guilford.

Miller, J., Slomczynski, K. M., & Kohn, M. L. (1985). Continuity of learning-generalization: The effect of job on men's intellective process in the United States and Poland. *American Journal of Sociology, 91*, 593–615.

Miller, J. G. (2006). Insights into moral development from cultural psychology. In M. Killen & J. Smetana (Eds.), *Handbook of moral development* (pp. 375–398). Philadelphia: Erlbaum.

Miller, J. G., & Bersoff, D. M. (1995). Development in the context of everyday family relationships: Culture, interpersonal morality, and adaptation. In M. Killen & D. Hart (Eds.), *Morality in everyday life: Developmental perspectives* (pp. 259–282). Cambridge, UK: Cambridge University Press.

Miller, L. T., & Vernon, P. A. (1992). The general factor in short-term memory, intelligence, and reaction time. *Intelligence, 16*, 5–29.

Miller, P. H. (2009). *Theories of developmental psychology* (5th ed.). New York: Worth.

Miller, P. J., Fung, H., & Koven, M. (2007). Narrative reverberations: How participation in narrative practices co-creates persons and cultures. In S. Kitayama & D. Cohen (Eds.), *Handbook of cultural psychology* (pp. 595–614). New York: Guilford.

Miller, P. J., Fung, H., Lin, S., Chen, E. C., & Boldt, B. R. (2012). How socialization happens on the ground: Narrative practices as alternate socializing pathways in Taiwanese and European-American families. *Monographs of the Society for Research in Child Development, 77*(1, Serial No. 302).

Miller, P. J., Fung, H., & Mintz, J. (1996). Self-construction through narrative practices: A Chinese and American comparison of early socialization. *Ethos, 24*, 1–44.

Miller, P. J., Hengst, J. A., & Wang, S. (2003). Ethnographic methods: Applications from developmental cultural psychology. In P. M. Carnic & J. E. Rhodes (Eds.), *Qualitative research in psychology* (pp. 219–242). Washington, DC: American Psychological Association.

Miller, P. J., Wang, S., Sandel, T., & Cho, G. E. (2002). Self-esteem as folk theory: A comparison of European American and Taiwanese mothers' beliefs. *Parenting: Science and Practice, 2*, 209–239.

Miller, P. J., Wiley, A. R., Fung, H., & Liang, C. H. (1997). Personal storytelling as a medium of socialization in Chinese and American families. *Child Development, 68*, 557–568.

Miller, R. B. (2000). Do children make a marriage unhappy? *Family Science Review, 13*, 60–73.

Miller, S., Lansford, J. E., Costanzo, P., Malone, P. S., Golonka, M., & Killeya-Jones, L. A. (2009). Early adolescent romantic partner status, peer standing, and problem behaviors. *Journal of Early Adolescence, 29*, 839–861.

Miller, S. A., Hardin, C. A., & Montgomery, D. E. (2003). Young children's understanding of the conditions for knowledge acquisition. *Journal of Cognition and Development, 4*, 325–356.

Milligan, K., Astington, J. W., & Dack, L. A. (2007). Language and theory of mind: Meta-analysis of the relation between language ability and falsebelief understanding. *Child Development, 78*, 622–646.

Mills, D., Plunkett, K., Prat, C., & Schafer, G. (2005). Watching the infant brain learn words: Effects of language and experience. *Cognitive Development, 20*, 19–31.

Mills, R., & Grusec, J. (1989). Cognitive, affective, and behavioral consequences of praising altruism. *Merrill-Palmer Quarterly, 35*, 299–326.

Mills, R. S. L. (2005). Taking stock of the developmental literature on shame. *Developmental Review, 25*, 26–63.

Mills, T. L., Gomez-Smith, Z., & De Leon, J. M. (2005). Skipped generation families: Sources of psychological distress among grandmothers of grandchildren who live in homes where neither parent is present. *Marriage and Family Review, 37*, 191–212.

Miner-Rubino, K., Winter, D. G., & Stewart, A. J. (2004). Gender, social class, and the subjective experience of aging: Self-perceived personality change from early adulthood to late midlife. *Personality and Social Psychology Bulletin, 30*, 1599–1610.

Minkler, M., & Fuller-Thomson, E. (2005). African American grandparents raising grandchildren: A national study using the Census 2000 American Community Survey. *Journal of Gerontology, 60B*, S82–S92.

Misailidi, P. (2006). Young children's display rule knowledge: Understanding the distinction between apparent and real emotions and the motives underlying the use of display rules. *Social Behavior and Personality, 34*, 1285–1296.

Mischel, W., & Liebert, R. M. (1966). Effects of discrepancies between observed and imposed reward criteria on their acquisition and transmission. *Journal of Personality and Social Psychology, 3*, 45–53.

Mishra, G., & Kuh, D. (2006). Perceived change in quality of life during the menopause. *Social Science and Medicine, 62*, 93–102.

Mistry, R. S., Biesanz, J. C., Chien, N., Howes, C., & Benner, A. D. (2008). Socioeconomic status, parental investments and the cognitive and behavioral outcomes of low-income children from immigrant and native households. *Early Childhood Research Quarterly, 23*, 193–212.

Mitchell, A., & Boss, B. J. (2002). Adverse effects of pain on the nervous systems of newborns and young children: A review of the literature. *Journal of Neuroscience Nursing, 34*, 228–235.

Mitchell, B. A., & Lovegreen, L. D. (2009). The empty nest syndrome in midlife families: A multimethod exploration of parental gender differences and cultural dynamics. *Journal of Family Issues, 30*, 1651–1670.

Mitchell, B. D., Hsueh, W. C., King, T. M., Pollin, T. I., Sorkin, J., Agarwala, R., Schäffer, A. A., & Shuldiner, A. R. (2001). Heritability of life span in the Old Order Amish. *American Journal of Medical Genetics, 102*, 346–352.

Mitchell, P., Teucher, U., Kikuno, H., & Bennett, M. (2010). Cultural variations in developing a sense of knowing your own mind: A comparison between British and Japanese children. *International Journal of Behavioral Development, 34*, 248–258.

Mitnick, D. M., Heyman, R. E., & Slep, A. M. S. (2009). Changes in relationship satisfaction across the transition to parenthood: A meta-analysis. *Journal of Family Psychology, 23*, 848–852.

Miura, I. T., & Okamoto, Y. (2003). Language supports for mathematics understanding and performance. In A. J. Baroody & A. Dowker (Eds.), *The development of arithmetic concepts and skills* (pp. 229–242). Mahwah, NJ: Erlbaum.

Mize, J., & Pettit, G. S. (2010). The mother–child playgroup as socialisation context: A short-

term longitudinal study of mother–child–peer relationship dynamics. *Early Child Development and Care, 180*, 1271–1284.

Modrek, S., & Cullen, M. R. (2012). *Job demand and early retirement.* Chestnut Hill, MA: Center for Retirement Research at Boston College. Retrieved from ssrn.com/abstract=2127722

Moen, P., & Altobelli, J. (2007). Strategic selection as a retirement project: Will Americans develop hybrid arrangements? In J. B. James & P. Wink (Eds.), *Annual review of gerontology and geriatrics* (Vol. 26, pp. 61–82). New York: Springer.

Moen, P., & Roehling, P. V. (2005). *The career mystique.* Bolder, CO: Rowman & Littlefield.

Moen, P., Huang, Q., Plassmann, V., & Dentinger, E. (2006). Deciding the future: Do dual-earner couples plan together for retirement? *American Behavioral Scientist, 49*, 1422–1443.

Moens, E., Braet, C., & Soetens, B. (2007). Observation of family functioning at mealtime: A comparison between families of children with and without overweight. *Journal of Pediatric Psychology, 32*, 52–63.

Moffitt, T. E. (2007). Life-course-persistent vs. adolescence-limited antisocial behavior. In D. Cicchetti & D. J. Cohen (Eds.), *Developmental psychopathology* (2nd ed., pp. 570–598). Hoboken, NJ; Wiley.

Mohr, J. J., & Daly, C. A. (2008). Sexual minority stress and changes in relationship quality in same-sex couples. *Journal of Social and Personal Relationships, 25*, 989–1007.

Mohr, J. J., & Fassinger, R. E. (2006). Sexual orientation identity and romantic relationship quality in same-sex couples. *Personality and Social Psychology Bulletin, 32*, 1085–1099.

Mok, M. M. C., Kennedy, K. J., & Moore, P. J. (2011). Academic attribution of secondary students: Gender, year level and achievement level. *Educational Psychology, 31*, 87–104.

Mokdad, A. H., Bowman, B. A., Ford, E. S., Vinicor, F., Marks, J. S., & Koplan, J. P. (2001). The continuing epidemics of obesity and diabetes in the United States. *Journal of the American Medical Association, 286*, 1195–1200.

Moll, H., & Meltzoff, A. N. (2011). How does it look? Level 2 perspective-taking at 36 months of age. *Child Development, 82*, 661–673.

Moll, H., & Tomasello, M. (2006). Level I perspective-taking at 24 months of age. *British Journal of Developmental Psychology, 24*, 603–613.

Moll, I. (1994). Reclaiming the natural line in Vygotsky's theory of cognitive development. *Human Development, 37*, 333–342.

Mollenkopf, H., Hieber, A., & Wahl, H-W. (2011). Continuity and change in older adults' perceptions of out-of-home mobility over ten years: A qualitative–quantitative approach. *Ageing and Society, 31*, 782–802.

Moller, K., Hwang, C. P., & Wickberg, B. (2008). Couple relationship and transition to parenthood: Does workload at home matter? *Journal of Reproductive and Infant Psychology, 26*, 57–68.

Mondloch, C. J., Lewis, T., Budreau, D. R., Maurer, D., Dannemiller, J. L., Stephens, B. R., & Kleiner-Gathercoal, K. A. (1999). Face perception during early infancy. *Psychological Science, 10*, 419–422.

Monin, J. K., & Schulz, R. (2009). Interpersonal effects of suffering in older adult caregiving relationships. *Psychology and Aging, 24*, 681–695.

Monk, C., Sloan, R., Myers, M. M., Ellman, L., Werner, E., Jeon, J., et al. (2010). Neural circuitry of emotional face processing in autism spectrum disorders. *Journal of Psychiatry and Neuroscience, 35*, 105–114.

Monsour, M. (2002). *Women and men as friends.* Mahwah, NJ: Erlbaum.

Montague, D. P. F., & Walker-Andrews, A. S. (2001). Peekaboo: A new look at infants' perception of emotion expressions. *Developmental Psychology, 37*, 826–838.

Montemayor, R., & Eisen, M. (1977). The development of self-conceptions from childhood to adolescence. *Developmental Psychology, 37,* 826–838.

Montepare, J. M. (2006). Body consciousness across the adult years: Variations with actual and subjective age. *Journal of Adult Development, 13,* 102–107.

Montgomery, M. J. (2005). Psychosocial intimacy and identity: From early adolescence to emerging adulthood. *Journal of Adolescent Research, 20,* 346–374.

Montgomery, M. J., & Côté, J. E. (2003). College as a transition to adulthood. In G. R. Adams & M. D. Berzonsky (Eds.), *Blackwell handbook of adolescence* (pp. 149–172). Malden, MA: Blackwell.

Montgomery-Goodnough, A., & Gallagher, S. J. (2007). Review of research on spiritual and religious formation in higher education. In S. M. Nielsen & M. S. Plakhotnik (Eds.), *Proceedings of the sixth annual College of Education Research Conference: Urban and international education section* (pp. 60–65). Miami, FL: International University.

Montorsi, F. (2005). Assessment, diagnosis, and investigation of erectile dysfunction. *Clinical Cornerstone, 7,* 29–35.

Montoya, A. G., Sorrentino, R., Lukas, S. E., & Price, B. H. (2002). Long-term neuropsychiatric consequences of "ecstasy" (MDMA): A review. *Harvard Review of Psychiatry, 10,* 212–220.

Moon, C., Cooper, R. P., & Fifer, W. P. (1993). Two-day-old infants prefer their native language. *Infant Behavior and Development, 16,* 495–500.

Moon, R. Y., Horne, R. S. C., & Hauck, F. R. (2007). Sudden infant death syndrome. *Lancet, 370,* 1578–1587.

Moore, A., & Stratton, D. C. (2002). *Resilient widowers.* New York: Springer.

Moore, D. R., & Florsheim, P. (2001). Interpersonal processes and psychopathology among expectant and nonexpectant adolescent couples. *Journal of Consulting and Clinical Psychology, 69,* 101–113.

Moore, D. S., & Johnson, S. P. (2008). Mental rotation in human infants: A sex difference. *Psychological Science, 19,* 1063–1066.

Moore, E. G. J. (1986). Family socialization and the IQ test performance of traditionally and transracially adopted black children. *Developmental Psychology, 22,* 317–326.

Moore, K. A., Morrison, D. R., & Greene, A. D. (1997). Effects on the children born to adolescent mothers. In R. A. Maynard (Ed.), *Kids having kids* (pp. 145–180). Washington, DC: The Urban Institute.

Moore, K. L., & Persaud, T. V. N. (2008). *Before we are born* (7th ed.). Philadelphia: Saunders.

Moore, K. L., Persaud, T. V. N., & Torchia, M. G. (2013). *Before we are born: Essentials of embryology and birth defects* (8th ed.). Philadelphia, PA: Saunders.

Moore, M. K., & Meltzoff, A. N. (1999). New findings on object permanence: A developmental difference between two types of occlusion. *British Journal of Developmental Psychology, 17,* 563–584.

Moore, M. K., & Meltzoff, A. N. (2004). Object permanence after a 24-hr delay and leaving the locale of disappearance: The role of memory, space, and identity. *Developmental Psychology, 40,* 606–620.

Moore, M. K., & Meltzoff, A. N. (2008). Factors affecting infants' manual search for occluded objects and the genesis of object permanence. *Infant Behavior and Development, 31,* 168–180.

Moore, M. R., & Brooks-Gunn, J. (2002). Adolescent parenthood. In M. H. Bornstein (Ed.), *Handbook of parenting: Vol. 3* (2nd ed., pp. 173–214). Mahwah, NJ: Erlbaum.

Moore, W. S. (2002). Understanding learning in a postmodern world: Reconsidering the Perry scheme of ethical and intellectual development. In B. K. Hofer & P. R. Pintrich (Eds.), *Personal epistemology* (pp. 17–36). Mahwah, NJ: Erlbaum.

Moran, G., Forbes, L., Evans, E., Tarabulsy, G. M., & Madigan, S. (2008). Both maternal sensitivity and atypical maternal behavior independently predict attachment security and disorganization in adolescent mother–infant relationships. *Infant Behavior and Development, 31,* 321–325.

Moran, S., & Gardner, H. (2006). Extraordinary achievements: A developmental and systems analysis. In D. Kuhn & R. Siegler (Eds.), *Handbook of child psychology: Vol. 2. Cognition, perception, and language* (6th ed., pp. 905–949). Hoboken, NJ: Wiley.

Morawska, A., & Sanders, M. (2011). Parental use of time out revisited: A useful or harmful parenting strategy? *Journal of Child and Family Studies, 20,* 1–8.

Morelli, G., Rogoff, B., Oppenheim, D., & Goldsmith, D. (1992). Cultural variation in infants' sleeping arrangements: Questions of independence. *Developmental Psychology, 28,* 604–613.

Morelli, G. A., Rogoff, B., & Angelillo, C. (2003). Cultural variation in young children's access to work or involvement in specialized child-focused activities. *International Journal of Behavioral Development, 27,* 264–274.

Moreno, A. J., Klute, M. M., & Robinson, J. L. (2008). Relational and individual resources as predictors of empathy in early childhood. *Social Development, 17,* 613–637.

Morgan, B., Maybery, M., & Durkin, K. (2003). Weak central coherence, poor joint attention, and low verbal ability: Independent deficits in early autism. *Developmental Psychology, 39,* 646–656.

Morgan, J. D., Laungani, P., & Palmer, S. (2009). General introduction to series. In J. D. Morgan, P. Laungani, & S. Palmer (Eds.), *Death and bereavement around the world: Vol. 5. Reflective essays* (pp. 1–4). Amityville, NY: Baywood.

Morgan, P. L., Farkas, G., Hillemeier, M. M., & Maczuga, S. (2009). Risk factors for learning-related behavior problems at 24 months of age: Population-based estimates. *Journal of Abnormal Child Psychology, 37,* 401–413.

Moro-García, M. A., Alonso-Arias, R., López-Vázquez, A., Suárez-García, F. M., Solano-Jaurrieta, J. J., Baltar, J., et al. (2012). Relationship between functional ability in older people, immune system status, and intensity of response to CMV. *Age, 34,* 479–495.

Morrill, M. I., Hines, D. A., Mahmood, S., & Córdova, J. V. (2010). Pathways between marriage and parenting for wives and husbands: The role of coparenting. *Family Process, 49,* 59–73.

Morris, A. S., Silk, J. S., Morris, M. D. S., & Steinberg, L. (2011). The influence of mother–child emotion regulation strategies on children's expression of anger and sadness. *Developmental Psychology, 47,* 213–225.

Morris, G., & Baker-Ward, L. (2007). Fragile but real: Children's capacity to use newly acquired words to convey preverbal memories. *Child Development, 78,* 448–458.

Morris, J. (2011). Communication skills training in end-of-life care. *Nursing Times, 107,* 16–17.

Morris, W. L., DePaulo, B. M., Hertel, J., & Taylor, L. C. (2008). Singlism—another problem that has no name: Prejudice, stereotypes and discrimination against singles. In M. A. Morrison & T. G. Morrison (Eds.), *The psychology of modern prejudice* (pp. 165–194). Hauppauge, NY: Nova Science Publishers.

Morrison, V. (2008). Ageing and physical health. In B. Woods & L. Clare (Eds.), *Handbook of the clinical psychology of ageing* (2nd ed., pp. 57–74). Chichester, UK: Wiley.

Morrongiello, B. A., Fenwick, K. D., & Chance, G. (1998). Crossmodal learning in newborn infants: Inferences about properties of auditory-visual events. *Infant Behavior and Development, 21,* 543–554.

Morrongiello, B. A., Midgett, C., & Shields, R. (2001). Don't run with scissors: Young children's knowledge of home safety rules. *Journal of Pediatric Psychology, 26,* 105–115.

Morrongiello, B. A., Ondejko, L., & Littlejohn, A. (2004). Understanding toddlers' in-home injuries: I. Context, correlates, and determinants. *Journal of Pediatric Psychology, 29,* 415–431.

Morrow, D. F. (2006). Gay, lesbian, and transgender adolescents. In D. F. Morrow & L. Messinger (Eds.), *Sexual orientation and gender expression in social work practice* (pp. 177–195). New York: Columbia University Press.

Morse, S. B., Zheng, H., Tang, Y., & Roth, J. (2009). Early school-age outcomes of late preterm infants. *Pediatrics, 123,* e622–e629.

Mosby, L., Rawls, A. W., Meehan, A. J., Mays, E., & Pettinari, C. J. (1999). Troubles in interracial talk about discipline: An examination of African American child rearing narratives. *Journal of Comparative Family Studies, 30,* 489–521.

Mosca, L., Barrett-Connor, E., & Wenger, N. K. (2012). Sex/gender differences in cardiovascular disease prevention: What a difference a decade makes. *Circulation, 124,* 2145–2154.

Mosely-Howard, G. S., & Evans, C. B. (2000). Relationships and contemporary experiences of the African-American family: An ethnographic case study. *Journal of Black Studies, 30,* 428–451.

Moses, L. J., Baldwin, D. A., Rosicky, J. G., & Tidball, G. (2001). Evidence for referential understanding in the emotions domain at twelve and eighteen months. *Child Development, 72,* 718–735.

Mosher, W. D., Chandra, A., & Jones, J. (2005). *Sexual behavior and selected health measures: Men and women 15–44 years of age, United States 2002,* Vol. 362. Atlanta: U.S. Centers for Disease Control and Prevention.

Moshman, D. (1998). Identity as a theory of oneself. *Genetic Epistemologist, 26*(3), 1–9.

Moshman, D. (2003). Developmental change in adulthood. In J. Demick & C. Andreoletti (Eds.), *Handbook of adult development* (pp. 43–61). New York: Plenum.

Moshman, D. (2005). *Adolescent psychological development: Rationality, morality, and identity* (2nd ed.). Mahwah, NJ: Erlbaum.

Moshman, D. (2011). *Adolescent rationality and development: Cognition, morality, and identity* (3rd ed.). New York: Psychology Press.

Moshman, D., & Franks, B. A. (1986). Development of the concept of inferential validity. *Child Development, 57,* 153–165.

Moshman, D., & Geil, M. (1998). Collaborative reasoning: Evidence for collective rationality. *Thinking and Reasoning, 4,* 231–248.

Moss, E., Cyr, C., Bureau, J.-F., Tarabulsy, G. M., & Dubois-Comtois, K. (2005). Stability of attachment during the preschool period. *Developmental Psychology, 41,* 773–783.

Moss, E., Smolla, N., Guerra, I., Mazzarello, T., Chayer, D., & Berthiaume, C. (2006). Attachment and self-reported internalizing and externalizing behavior problems in a school period. *Canadian Journal of Behavioural Science, 38,* 142–157.

Mossey, P. A., Little, J,, Munger, R. G., Dixon, M. J., & Shaw, W. C. (2009). Cleft lip and palate. *Lancet, 374,* 1773–1785.

Moss-Racusin, C. A., Dovidio, J. F., Brescoll, V. L., Graham, M. J., & Handelsman, J. (2012). Science faculty's subtle gender biases favor male students. *Proceedings of the National Academy of Sciences, 109,* 16474–16479.

Mosteller, F. (1995, Fall). The Tennessee Study of Class Size in the Early School Grades. *Future of Children, 5*(2), 113–127.

Motl, R. W., Dishman, R. K., Saunders, R. P., Dowda, M., Felton, G., Ward, D. S., & Pate, R. R. (2002).

Examining social–cognitive determinants of intention and physical activity among black and white adolescent girls using structural equation modeling. *Health Psychology, 21,* 459–467.

Mottus, R., Indus, K., & Allik, J. (2008). Accuracy of only children stereotype. *Journal of Research in Personality, 42,* 1047–1052.

Mounts, N. S., & Steinberg, L. (1995). An ecological analysis of peer influence on adolescent grade point average and drug use. *Developmental Psychology, 31,* 915–922.

Mounts, N. S., Valentiner, D. P., Anderson, K. L., & Boswell, M. K. (2006). Shyness, sociability, and parental support for the college transition: Relation to adolescents' adjustment. *Journal of Youth and Adolescence, 35,* 71–80.

Moxley, D. P., Najor-Durack, A., & Dumbrigue, C. (2001). *Keeping students in higher education.* London: Kogan Page.

Mroczek, D. K., & Spiro, A., III. (2005). Change in life satisfaction during adulthood: Findings from the Veterans Affairs Normative Aging Study. *Journal of Personality and Social Psychology, 88,* 189–202.

Mroczek, D. K., & Spiro, A., III. (2007). Personality change influences mortality in older men. *Psychological Science, 18,* 371–376.

Mroczek, D. K., Spiro, A., & Turiano, N. A. (2009). Do health behaviors explain the effect of neuroticism on mortality? *Journal of Research in Personality, 43,* 653–659.

Mrug, S., Hoza, B., & Gerdes, A. C. (2001). Children with attention-deficit/hyperactivity disorder: Peer relationships and peer-oriented interventions. In D. W. Nangle & C. A. Erdley (Eds.), *The role of friendship in psychological adjustment* (pp. 51–77). San Francisco: Jossey-Bass.

Mueller, C. M., & Dweck, C. S. (1998). Intelligence praise can undermine motivation and performance. *Journal of Personality and Social Psychology, 75,* 33–52.

Muenchow, S., & Marsland, K. W. (2007). Beyond baby steps: Promoting the growth and development of U.S. child-care policy. In J. L. Aber, S. J. Bishop-Josef, S. M. Jones, K. T. McLearn, & D. Phillips (Eds.), *Child development and social policy: Knowledge for action* (pp. 97–112). Washington, DC: American Psychological Association.

Müller, O., & Krawinkel, M. (2005). Malnutrition and health in developing countries. *Canadian Medical Association Journal, 173,* 279–286.

Müller, U., Liebermann-Finestone, D. P., Carpendale, J. I. M., Hammond, S. I., & Bibok, M. B. (2012). Knowing minds, controlling actions: The developmental relations between theory of mind and executive function from 2 to 4 years of age. *Journal of Experimental Child Psychology, 111,* 331–348.

Müller, U., Overton, W. F., & Reese, K. (2001). Development of conditional reasoning: A longitudinal study. *Journal of Cognition and Development, 2,* 27–49.

Mullett-Hume, E., Anshel, D., Guevara, V., & Cloitre, M. (2008). Cumulative trauma and posttraumatic stress disorder among children exposed to the 9/11 World Trade Center attack. *American Journal of Orthopsychiatry, 78,* 103–108.

Mullis, I. V. S., Martin, M. O., Kennedy, A. M., & Foy, P. (2007). *PIRLS 2006 international report: IEA's Progress in International Reading Literacy Study.* Boston: TIMSS & PIRLS International Study Center.

Mulvaney, M. K., McCartney, K., Bub, K. L., & Marshall, N. L. (2006). Determinants of dyadic scaffolding and cognitive outcomes in first graders. *Parenting: Science and Practice, 6,* 297–310.

Mumme, D. L., Bushnell, E. W., DiCorcia, J. A., & Lariviere, L. A. (2007). Infants' use of gaze cues to interpret others' actions and emotional reactions. In R. Flom, K. Lee, & D. Muir (Eds.), *Gaze-following:*

Its development and significance (pp. 143–170). Mahwah, NJ: Erlbaum.

Munakata, Y. (2001). Task-dependency in infant behavior: Toward an understanding of the processes underlying cognitive development. In F. Lacerda, C. von Hofsten, & M. Heimann (Eds.), *Emerging cognitive abilities in early infancy* (pp. 29–52). Mahwah, NJ: Erlbaum.

Munakata, Y. (2006). Information processing approaches to development. In D. Kuhn & R. S. Siegler (Eds.), *Handbook of child psychology: Vol. 3. Cognition, perception, and language* (6th ed., pp. 426–463). Hoboken, NJ: Wiley.

Mundy, P., & Stella, J. (2000). Joint attention, social orienting, and nonverbal communication in autism. In A. M. Wetherby & B. M. Prizant (Eds.), *Autism spectrum disorders* (Vol. 9, pp. 55–77). Baltimore, MD: Paul H. Brookes.

Munnell, A. H., Webb, A., Delorme, L., & Golub-Sass, F. (2012). *National retirement risk index: How much longer do we need to work?* Chestnut Hill, MA: Center for Retirement Research at Boston College. Retrieved from crr.bc.edu/briefs/national-retirement-risk-index-how-much-longer-do-we-need-to-work

Munroe, R. L., & Romney, A. K. (2006). Gender and age differences in same-sex aggregation and social behavior. *Journal of Cross-Cultural Psychology, 37,* 3–19.

Muret-Wagstaff, S., & Moore, S. G. (1989). The Hmong in America: Infant behavior and rearing practices. In J. K. Nugent, B. M. Lester, & T. B. Brazelton (Eds.), *Biology, culture, and development* (Vol. 1, pp. 319–339). Norwood, NJ: Ablex.

Muris, P., Merckelbach, H., Ollendick, T. H., King, N. J., & Bogie, N. (2001). Children's nighttime fears: Parent–child ratings of frequency, content, origins, coping behaviors, and severity. *Behaviour Research and Therapy, 39,* 13–28.

Murphy, S. A. (2008). The loss of a child: Sudden death and extended illness perspectives. In M. S. Stroebe, R. O. Hansson, H. Schut, & W. Stroebe (Eds.), *Handbook of bereavement research and practice* (pp. 375–396). Washington, DC: American Psychological Association.

Murphy, T. H., & Corbett, D. (2009). Plasticity during recovery: From synapse to behaviour. *Nature Reviews Neuroscience, 10,* 861–872.

Murray, A. D. (1985). Aversiveness is in the mind of the beholder. In B. M. Lester & C. F. Z. Boukydis (Eds.), *Infant crying* (pp. 217–239). New York: Plenum.

Murray, S. L. (2008). Risk regulation in relationships: Self-esteem and the if-then contingencies of interdependent life. In J. V. Wood, A. Tesser, & J. G. Holmes (Eds.), *The self and social relationships* (pp. 3–25). New York: Psychology Press.

Murray, S. L., Griffin, D. W., Derrik, J. L., Harris, B., Aloni, M., & Leder, S. (2011). Tempting fate or inviting happiness? Unrealistic idealization prevents the decline of marital satisfaction. *Psychological Science, 22,* 619–626.

Mussen, P., & Eisenberg-Berg, N. (1977). *Roots of caring, sharing, and helping.* San Francisco: Freeman.

Mustanski, B. S., Viken, R. J., Kaprio, J., Pulkkinen, L., & Rose, R. J. (2004). Genetic and environmental influences on pubertal development: Longitudinal data from Finnish twins at ages 11 and 14. *Developmental Psychology, 40,* 1188–1198.

Mutchler, J. E., Burr, J. A., & Caro, F. G. (2003). From paid worker to volunteer: Leaving the paid workforce and volunteering in later life. *Social Forces, 81,* 1267–1293.

Mutran, E. J., Danis, M., Bratton, K. A., Sudha, S., & Hanson, L. (1997). Attitudes of the critically ill toward prolonging life: The role of social support. *Gerontologist, 37,* 192–199.

Muzzatti, B., & Agnoli, F. (2007). Gender and mathematics: Attitudes and stereotype threat

susceptibility in Italian children. *Developmental Psychology, 43,* 747–759.

Myers, D. G. (2000). The funds, friends, and faith of happy people. *American Psychologist, 55,* 56–67.

Myers, M. G., Brown, S. A., Tate, S., Abrantes, A., & Tomlinson, K. (2001). *Adolescents, alcohol, and substance abuse* (pp. 275–296). New York: Guilford.

Myerson, J., Hale, S., Wagstaff, D., Poon, L. W., & Smith, G. A. (1990). The information-loss model: A mathematical theory of age-related cognitive slowing. *Psychological Review, 97,* 475–487.

Myowa-Yamakoshi, M., Tomonaga, M., Tanaka, M., & Matsuzawa, T. (2004). Imitation in neonatal chimpanzees *(Pan troglodytes). Developmental Science, 7,* 437–442.

N

Nadel, J., Prepin, K., & Okanda, M. (2005). Experiencing contingency and agency: First step toward self-understanding in making a mind? *Interaction Studies, 6,* 447–462.

Nader, K. (2002). Treating children after violence in schools and communities. In N. B. Webb (Ed.), *Helping bereaved children: A handbook for practitioners* (pp. 214–244). New York: Guilford.

Nader, P. R., Bradley, R. H., Houts, R. M., McRitchie, S. L., & O'Brien, M. (2008). Moderate-to-vigorous physical activity from ages 9 to 15 years. *Journal of the American Medical Association, 16,* 295–305.

Nagy, E., Compagne, H., Orvos, H., Pal, A., Molnar, P., & Janszky, I. (2005). Index finger movement imitation by human neonates: Motivation, learning, and left-hand preference. *Pediatric Research, 58,* 749–753.

Nagy, W. E., & Scott, J. A. (2000). Vocabulary processes. In M. L. Kamil & P. B. Mosenthal (Eds.), *Handbook of reading research* (Vol. 3, pp. 269–284). Mahwah, NJ: Erlbaum.

Naigles, L. G., & Gelman, S. A. (1995). Overextensions in comprehension and production revisited: Preferential-looking in a study of dog, cat, and cow. *Journal of Child Language, 22,* 19–46.

Naigles, L. R., & Swenson, L. D. (2007). Syntactic supports for word learning. In E. Hoff & M. Shatz (Eds.), *Blackwell handbook of language development* (pp. 212–231). Malden, MA: Blackwell.

Naito, M., & Seki, Y. (2009). The relationship between second-order false belief and display rules reasoning: Integration of cognitive and affective social understanding. *Developmental Science, 12,* 150–164.

Nakamura, J., & Csikszentmihalyi, M. (2009). Flow theory and research. In C. R. Snyder & S. J. Lopez (Eds.), *Oxford handbook of positive psychology* (2nd ed., pp. 195–206). New York: Oxford University Press.

Nánez, J., Sr., & Yonas, A. (1994). Effects of luminance and texture motion on infant defensive reactions to optical collision. *Infant Behavior and Development, 17,* 165–174.

Narayan, C. (2008). Is there a double standard of aging? Older men and women and ageism. *Educational Gerontology, 34,* 782–787.

Narr, K. L., Woods, R. P., Lin J., Kim, J., Phillips, O. R., Del'Homme, M., et al. (2009). Widespread cortical thinning is a robust anatomical marker for attention-deficit/hyperactivity disorder. *Journal of the American Academy of Child and Adolescent Psychiatry, 48,* 1014–1022.

Nastasi, B. K., & Clements, D. H. (1994). Effectance motivation, perceived scholastic competence, and higher-order thinking in two cooperative computer environments. *Journal of Educational Computing Research, 10,* 249–275.

Natale, K., Viljaranta, J., Lerkkanen, M.-K., Poikkeus, A.-M., & Nurmi, J.-E. (2009). Cross-lagged associations between kindergarten teachers' causal attributions and children's task motivation and performance in reading. *Educational Psychology, 29,* 603–619.

Natale, R., & Dodman, N. (2003). Birth can be a hazardous journey: Electronic fetal monitoring does not help. *JOGC, 25,* 1007–1009.

National Academies Committee on National Statistics. (2010, January). *Meeting on research issues in elder mistreatment and abuse and financial fraud: Meeting report.* Washington, DC: National Institute on Aging.

National Association for Sport and Physical Education. (2010). *2010 Shape of the nation report: Status of physical education in the USA.* Reston, VA: Author.

National Center for Biotechnology Information, National Institutes of Health. (2007). *Genes and disease: Sickle cell anemia.* Retrieved from www .ncbi.nlm.nih.gov/bookshelf/br.fcgi?book=gnd&par t=anemiasicklecell

National Center for Injury Prevention and Control. (2012). *WISQAR fatal injury reports, national and regional, 1999–2010.* Retrieved from webappa.cdc .gov/sasweb/ncipc/mortrate10_us.html

National Center on Elder Abuse, U.S. Administration on Aging. (2013). *Frequently asked questions.* Retrieved from www.ncea.aoa.gov/faq/index.aspx

National Coalition for the Homeless. (2009). How many people experience homelessness? *National Coalition for the Homeless.* Retrieved from www .nationalhomeless.org/factsheets/How_Many.html

National Council of Youth Sports. (2008). *Report on trends and participation in organized youth sports.* Stuart, FL: Author.

National Federation of State High School Associations. (2012). *2010–2011 High School Athletics Participation Survey.* Retrieved from www.nfhs.org

National Institute on Aging. (2012). *2011–2012 Alzheimer's disease progress report: Intensifying the research effort.* Retrieved from www.nia.nih .gov/alzheimers/publication/2011-2012- alzheimers-disease-progress-report

National Institute on Drug Abuse. (2012). *Drug facts: MDMA (Ecstasy).* Retrieved from www.drugabuse .gov/publications/drugfacts/mdma-ecstasy

National Institutes of Health. (2011). *Dental caries (tooth decay) in children (age 2 to 11).* Retrieved from www.nidcr.nih.gov/ DataStatistics/FindDataByTopic/DentalCaries/ DentalCariesChildren2to11

National Institutes of Health. (2012). *Genes and disease.* Retrieved from www.ncbi.nlm.nih.gov/books/ NBK22183

National Research Council. (2007). *Race conscious policies for assigning students to schools: Social science research and the Supreme Court cases.* Washington, DC: National Academy Press.

National Women's Law Center. (2007). *When girls don't graduate we all fail.* Washington, DC: Author.

Natsuaki, M. N., Biehl, M. C., & Ge, X. (2009). Trajectories of depressed mood from early adolescence to young adulthood: The effects of pubertal timing and adolescent dating. *Journal of Research on Adolescence, 19,* 47–74.

Naveh-Benjamin, M. (2000). Adult age differences in memory performance: Tests of an associative deficit hypothesis. *Journal of Experimental Psychology: Learning, Memory, and Cognition, 26,* 1170–1187.

Naveh-Benjamin, M. (2012). Age-related differences in explicit associative memory: Contributions of effortful-strategic and automatic processes. In M. Naveh-Benjamin & N. Ohta (Eds.), *Memory and aging: Current issues and future directions* (pp. 71–95). New York: Psychology Press.

Naveh-Benjamin, M., Brav, T. K., & Levy, D. (2007). The associative memory deficit of older adults: The role of strategy utilization. *Psychology and Aging, 22,* 202–208.

Naveh-Benjamin, M., Craik, F. I. M., Guez, J., & Kreuger, S. (2005). Divided attention in younger and older adults: Effects of strategy and relatedness on memory performance and secondary task costs.

Journal of Experimental Psychology: Learning, Memory, and Cognition, 31, 520–537.

Naveh-Benjamin, M., Hussain, Z., Guez, J., & Bar-On, M. (2003). Adult age differences in episodic memory: Further support for an associative-deficit hypothesis. *Journal of Experimental Psychology: Learning, Memory, and Cognition, 29,* 826–837.

Neal, M. B., & Hammer, L. B. (2007). *Working couples caring for children and aging parents.* Mahwah, NJ: Erlbaum.

Needham, B. L., & Austin, E. L. (2010). Sexual orientation, parental support, and health during the transition to young adulthood. *Journal of Youth and Adolescence, 39,* 1189–1198.

Neff, K. D., & Helwig, C. C. (2002). A constructivist approach to understanding the development of reasoning about rights and authority within cultural contexts. *Cognitive Development, 17,* 1429–1450.

Neff, L. A., & Karney, B. R. (2008). Compassionate love in early marriage. In B. Fehr, S. Sprecher, & L. G. Underwood, (Eds.), *The science of compassionate love: Theory, research, and applications* (pp. 201–221). Malden, MA: Wiley-Blackwell.

Neimeyer, R., Currier, J. M., Coleman, R., Tomer, A., & Samuel, E. (2011). Confronting suffering and death at the end of life: The impact of religiosity, psychosocial factors, and life regret among hospice patients. *Death Studies, 35,* 777–800.

Neimeyer, R. A. (Ed.). (1994). *Death anxiety handbook.* Washington, DC: Taylor & Francis.

Neimeyer, R. A. (2001). The language of loss: Grief therapy as a process of meaning reconstruction. In R. A. Neimeyer (Ed.), *Meaning reconstruction and the experience of loss* (pp. 261–292). Washington, DC: American Psychological Association.

Neimeyer, R. A., Burke, L. A., Mackay, M. M., & Stringer, J G. van D. (2010). Grief therapy and the reconstruction of meaning: From principles to practice. *Journal of Contemporary Psychotherapy, 40,* 73–83.

Neimeyer, R. A., & Van Brunt, D. (1995). Death anxiety. In H. Waas & R. A. Neimeyer (Eds.), *Dying: Facing the facts* (3rd ed., pp. 49–88). Washington, DC: Taylor & Francis.

Neitzel, C., & Stright, A. D. (2003). Mothers' scaffolding of children's problem solving: Establishing a foundation of academic self-regulatory competence. *Journal of Family Psychology, 17,* 147–159.

Nelson, C. A. (1995). The ontogeny of human memory: A cognitive neuroscience perspective. *Developmental Psychology, 31,* 723–738.

Nelson, C. A. (2001). The development and neural bases of face recognition. *Infant and Child Development, 10,* 3–18.

Nelson, C. A. (2002). Neural development and lifelong plasticity. In R. M. Lerner, F. Jacobs, & D. Wertlieb (Eds.), *Handbook of applied developmental science* (Vol. 1, pp. 31–60). Thousand Oaks, CA: Sage.

Nelson, C. A. (2007a). A developmental cognitive neuroscience approach to the study of atypical development: A model system involving infants of diabetic mothers. In D. Coch, G. Dawson, & K. W. Fischer (Eds.), *Human behavior, learning, and the developing brain: Atypical development* (pp. 1–27). New York: Guilford.

Nelson, C. A. (2007b). A neurobiological perspective on early human deprivation. *Child Development Perspectives, 1,* 13–18.

Nelson, C. A. (2011). Neural development and lifelong plasticity. In D. P. Keating (Ed.), *Nature and nurture in early child development* (pp. 45–69). New York: Cambridge University Press.

Nelson, C. A., & Bosquet, M. (2000). Neurobiology of fetal and infant development: Implications for infant mental health. In C. H. Zeanah, Jr. (Ed.), *Handbook of infant mental health* (2nd ed., pp. 37–59). New York: Guilford.

Nelson, C. A., Thomas, K. M., & de Haan, M. (2006). Neural bases of cognitive development. In D. Kuhn & R. Siegler (Eds.), *Handbook of child psychology: Vol. 2. Cognition, perception, and language* (6th ed., pp. 3–57). Hoboken, NJ: Wiley.

Nelson, C. A., Zeanah, C. H., Fox, N. A., Marshall, P. J., Smyke, A. T., & Guthrie, D. (2007). Cognitive recovery in socially deprived young children: The Bucharest Early Intervention Project. *Science, 318,* 1937–1940.

Nelson, D. A., & Coyne, S. M. (2009). Children's intent attributions and feelings of distress: Associations with maternal and paternal parenting practices. *Journal of Abnormal Child Psychology, 37,* 223–237.

Nelson, D. A., Hart, C. H., Yang, C., Olsen, J. A., & Jin, S. (2006a). Aversive parenting in China: Associations with child physical and relational aggression. *Child Development, 77,* 554–572.

Nelson, D. A., Nelson, L. J., Hart, C. H., Yang, C., & Jin, S. (2006b). Parenting and peer-group behavior in cultural context. In X. Chen, D. French, & B. Schneider (Eds.), *Peer relations in cultural context* (pp. 213–246). New York: Cambridge University Press.

Nelson, D. A., Robinson, C. C., & Hart, C. H. (2005). Relational and physical aggression of preschool-age children: Peer status linkages across informants. *Early Education and Development, 16,* 115–139.

Nelson, H. D. (2008). Menopause. *Lancet, 371,* 760–770.

Nelson, K. (2003). Narrative and the emergence of a consciousness of self. In G. D. Fireman & T. E. McVay, Jr. (Eds.). *Narrative and consciousness: Literature, psychology, and the brain* (pp. 17–36). London: Oxford University Press.

Nelson, L. J. (2009). An examination of emerging adulthood in Romanian college students. *International Journal of Behavioral Development, 33,* 402–411.

Nelson, L. J., & Barry, C. M. (2005). Distinguishing features of emerging adulthood: The role of self-classification as an adult. *Journal of Adolescent Research, 20,* 242–262.

Nelson, L. J., & Chen, X. (2007). Emerging adulthood in China: The role of social and cultural factors. *Child Development Perspectives, 1,* 86–91.

Nelson, L. J., Padilla-Walker, L. M., Carroll, J. S., Madsen, S. D., Barry, C. M., & Badger, S. (2007). "If you want me to treat you like an adult, start acting like one!" Comparing the criteria that emerging adults and their parents have for adulthood. *Journal of Family Psychology, 21,* 665–674.

Nelson, L. J., Padilla-Walker, L. M., Christensen, K. J., Evans, C. A., & Carroll, J. S. (2011). Parenting in emerging adulthood: An examination of parenting clusters and correlates. *Journal of Youth and Adolescence, 40,* 730–743.

Nemet, D., Barkan, S., Epstein, Y., Friedland, O., Kowen, G., & Eliakim, A. (2005). Short- and long-term beneficial effects of a combined dietary–behavioral–physical activity intervention for the treatment of childhood obesity. *Pediatrics, 115,* e443–e449.

Nepomnyaschy, L., & Waldfogel, J. (2007). Paternity leave and fathers' involvement with their young children. *Community, Work and Family, 10,* 427–453.

Nerenberg, L. (2010). Elder abuse prevention: A review of the field. In J. C. Cavanaugh & C. K. Cavanaugh (Eds.), *Aging in America. Vol. 3: Societal issues* (pp. 53–80). Santa Barbara, CA: Praeger.

Neri, Q., Takeuchi, T., & Palermo, G. D. (2008). An update of assisted reproductive technologies in the United States. *Annals of the New York Academy of Sciences, 1127,* 41–48.

Nesdale, D., Durkin, K., Maas, A., & Griffiths, J. (2004). Group status, outgroup ethnicity, and children's ethnic attitudes. *Applied Developmental Psychology, 25,* 237–251.

Nesdale, D., Durkin, K., Maas, A., & Griffiths, J. (2005). Threat, group identification, and children's ethnic prejudice. *Social Development, 14,* 189–205.

Nettelbeck, T., & Burns, N. R. (2010). Processing speed, working memory and reasoning ability from childhood to old age. *Personality and Individual Differences, 48,* 379–384.

Netz, Y., Wu, M.-J., Becker, B. J., & Tenenbaum, G. (2005). Physical activity and psychological well-being in advanced age: A meta-analysis of intervention studies. *Psychology and Aging, 20,* 272–284.

Neugarten, B. L. (1968a). Adult personality: Toward a psychology of the life cycle. In B. Neugarten (Ed.), *Middle age and aging* (pp. 137–147). Chicago: University of Chicago Press.

Neugarten, B. L. (1968b). The awareness of middle aging. In B. L. Neugarten (Ed.), *Middle age and aging* (pp. 93–98). Chicago: University of Chicago Press.

Neugarten, B. L. (1979). Time, age, and the life cycle. *American Journal of Psychiatry, 136,* 887–894.

Neuhouser, M. L., Wassertheil-Smoller, S., Thomson, C., Aragaki, A., Anderson, G. L., & Manson, J. E. (2009). Multivitamin use and risk of cancer and cardiovascular disease in the Women's Health Initiative cohorts. *Archives of Internal Medicine, 169,* 294–304.

Neuman, S. B. (2003). From rhetoric to reality: The case for high-quality compensatory prekindergarten programs. *Phi Delta Kappan, 85*(4), pp. 286–291.

Neville, H. J., & Bavelier, D. (2002). Human brain plasticity: Evidence from sensory deprivation and altered language experience. In M. A. Hofman, G. J. Boer, A. J. G. D. Holtmaat, E. J. W. van Someren, J. Berhaagen, & D. F. Swaab (Eds.), *Plasticity in the adult brain: From genes to neurotherapy* (pp. 177–188). Amsterdam: Elsevier Science.

Newbury, J. (2011). The drama of end of life care at home. *Nursing Times, 107*(11), 20–23.

Newcomb, A. F., Bukowski, W. M., & Pattee, L. (1993). Children's peer relations: A meta-analytic review of popular, rejected, neglected, controversial, and average sociometric status. *Psychological Bulletin, 113,* 99–128.

Newcomb, M. D., Abbott, R. D., Catalano, R. F., Hawkins, J. D., Battin-Pearson, S., & Hill, K. (2002). Mediational and deviance theories of late high school failure: Process roles of structural strains, academic competence, and general versus specific problem behavior. *Journal of Counseling Psychology, 49,* 172–186.

Newcombe, N. S. (2007). Taking science seriously: Straight thinking about spatial sex differences. In S. J. Ceci & W. Williams (Eds.), *Why aren't more women in science?* (pp. 69–77). Washington, DC: American Psychological Association.

Newcombe, N. S., & Huttenlocher, J. (2006). Development of spatial cognition. In D. Kuhn & R. Siegler (Eds.), *Handbook of child psychology: Vol. 2. Cognition, perception, and language* (6th ed., pp. 734–776). Hoboken, NJ: Wiley.

Newcombe, N. S., Sluzenski, J., & Huttenlocher, J. (2005). Preexisting knowledge versus on-line learning: What do young infants really know about spatial location? *Psychological Science, 16,* 222–227.

Newland, L. A., Coyl, D. D., & Freeman, H. (2008). Predicting preschoolers' attachment security from fathers' involvement, internal working models, and use of social support. *Early Child Development and Care, 178,* 785–801.

Newnham, C. A., Milgrom, J., & Skouteris, H. (2009). Effectiveness of a modified mother–infant transaction program on outcomes for preterm infants from 3 to 24 months of age. *Infant Behavior and Development, 32,* 17–26.

Newport, E. L. (1991). Contrasting conceptions of the critical period for language. In S. Cary & R. Gelman (Eds.), *The epigenesis of mind: Essays on biology and cognition* (pp. 111–130). Hillsdale, NJ: Erlbaum.

Newsom, J. T. (1999). Another side to caregiving: Negative reactions to being helped. *Current Directions in Psychological Science, 8,* 183–187.

Newsom, J. T., & Schulz, R. (1998). Caregiving from the recipient's perspective: Negative reactions to being helped. *Health Psychology, 17,* 172–181.

Newton, N. J., & Stewart, A. J. (2010). The middle ages: Change in women's personalities and social roles. *Psychology of Women Quarterly, 34,* 75–84.

Newton, N. J., & Stewart, A. J. (2012). Personality development in adulthood. In S. K. Whitbourne & M. J. Sliwinski (Eds.), *Wiley-Blackwell handbook of adulthood and aging* (pp. 211–235). Malden, MA: Wiley-Blackwell.

Ng, F. F., Pomerantz, E. M., & Lam, S. (2007). European American and Chinese parents' responses to children's success and failure: Implications for children's responses. *Developmental Psychology, 43,* 1239–1255.

Ng, T. W. H., & Feldman, D. C. (2008). The relationship of age to ten dimensions of job performance. *Journal of Applied Psychology, 93,* 392–423.

Ngata, P. (2004). Death, dying, and grief: A Maori perspective. In J. D. Morgan & P. Laungani (Eds.), *Death and bereavement around the world: Vol. 4. Asia, Australia, and New Zealand* (pp. 95–99). Amityville, NY: Baywood.

Nguyen, U.-S. D. T., Rothman, K. J., Demissie, S., Jackson, D. J., Lang, J. M., & Ecker, J. L. (2010). Epidural analgesia and risks of cesarean and operative vaginal deliveries in nulliparous and multiparous women. *Maternal and Child Health Journal, 14,* 705–712.

NHPCO (National Hospice and Palliative Care Organization). (2005). 83% of Americans want to die at home. Retrieved from www.nhpco.org/templates/1/homepage.cfm

NHPCO (National Hospice and Palliative Care Organization). (2012). *Hospice care in America.* Retrieved from www.nhpco.org/sites/default/files/public/Statistics_Research/2012_Facts_Figures.pdf

Ni, Y. (1998). Cognitive structure, content knowledge, and classificatory reasoning. *Journal of Genetic Psychology, 159,* 280–296.

Niccolai, L. M., Ethier, K. A., Kershaw, T. S., Lewis, J. B., Meade, C. S., & Ickovics, J. R. (2004). New sex partner acquisition and sexually transmitted disease risk among adolescent females. *Journal of Adolescent Health, 34,* 216–223.

NICHD (National Institute of Child Health and Human Development) Early Child Care Research Network. (1997). The effects of infant child care on infant–mother attachment security: Results of the NICHD Study of Early Child Care. *Child Development, 68,* 860–879.

NICHD (National Institute of Child Health and Human Development) Early Child Care Research Network. (1998). Relations between family predictors and child outcomes: Are they weaker for children in child care? *Developmental Psychology, 34,* 1119–1128.

NICHD (National Institute of Child Health and Human Development) Early Child Care Research Network. (1999). Child care and mother–child interaction in the first 3 years of life. *Developmental Psychology, 35,* 1399–1413.

NICHD (National Institute of Child Health and Human Development) Early Child Care Research Network. (2000a). Characteristics and quality of child care for toddlers and preschoolers. *Applied Developmental Science, 4,* 116–135.

NICHD (National Institute of Child Health and Human Development) Early Child Care Research Network. (2000b). The relation of child care to cognitive and language development. *Child Development, 71,* 960–980.

NICHD (National Institute of Child Health and Human Development) Early Child Care Research Network.

(2001). Before Head Start: Income and ethnicity, family characteristics, child care experiences, and child development. *Early Education and Development, 12,* 545–575.

NICHD (National Institute of Child Health and Human Development) Early Child Care Research Network. (2002a). Child-care structure → process → outcome: Direct and indirect effects of childcare quality on young children's development. *Psychological Science, 13,* 199–206.

NICHD (National Institute of Child Health and Human Development) Early Child Care Research Network. (2002b). The interaction of child care and family risk in relation to child development at 24 and 36 months. *Applied Developmental Science, 6,* 144–156.

NICHD (National Institute of Child Health and Human Development) Early Child Care Research Network. (2003a). Does amount of time spent in child care predict socioemotional adjustment during the transition to kindergarten? *Child Development, 74,* 976–1005.

NICHD (National Institute of Child Health and Human Development) Early Child Care Research Network. (2003b). Does quality of child care affect child outcomes at age 4½? *Developmental Psychology, 39,* 451–469.

NICHD (National Institute of Child Health and Human Development) Early Child Care Research Network. (2004). Trajectories of physical aggression from toddlerhood to middle childhood. *Monographs of the Society for Research in Child Development, 69*(4, Serial No. 278).

NICHD (National Institute of Child Health and Human Development) Early Child Care Research Network. (2006). Child-care effect sizes for the NICHD Study of Early Child Care and Youth Development. *American Psychologist, 61,* 99–116.

Nichols, W. C., & Pace-Nichols, M. A. (2000). Childless married couples. In W. C. Nichols, M. A. Pace-Nichols, D. S. Becvar, & A. Y. Napier (Eds.), *Handbook of family development and intervention* (pp. 171–188). New York: Wiley.

Nicholson, J. M., Sanders, M. R., Halford, W. K., Phillips, M., & Whitton, S. W. (2008). The prevention and treatment of children's adjustment problems in stepfamilies. In J. Pryor (Ed.), *International handbook of stepfamilies: Policy and practice in legal, research, and clinical environments* (pp. 485–521). Hoboken, NJ: Wiley.

Nickman, S. L., Rosenfeld, A. A., Fine, P., MacIntyre, J. C., Pilowsky, D. J., & Howe, R. A. (2005). Children in adoptive families: Overview and update. *Journal of the American Academy of Child and Adolescent Psychiatry, 44,* 987–995.

Niehaus, M. D., Moore, S. R., Patrick, P. D., Derr, L. L., Lorntz, B., Lima, A. A., & Gurerrant, R. L. (2002). Early childhood diarrhea is associated with diminished cognitive function 4 to 7 years later in children in a northeast Brazilian shanty-town. *American Journal of Tropical Medicine and Hygiene, 66,* 590–593.

Nielsen, L. S., Danielsen, K. V., & Sørensen, T. I. (2011). Short sleep duration as a possible cause of obesity: Critical analysis of the epidemiological evidence. *Obesity Reviews, 12,* 78–92.

Nielsen, N. M., Hansen, A. V., Simonsen, J., & Hviid, A. (2011). Prenatal stress and risk of infectious diseases in offspring. *American Journal of Epidemiology, 173,* 990–997.

Nielsen, S. J., & Popkin, B. M. (2003). Patterns and trends in food portion sizes. *Journal of the American Medical Association, 289,* 450–453.

Nielson, D. (2012). Discussing death with pediatric patients: Implications for nurses. *Journal of Pediatric Nursing, 27,* e59–e64.

Nievar, M. A., & Becker, B. J. (2008). Sensitivity as a privileged predictor of attachment: A second perspective on De Wolff & van IJzendoorn's meta-analysis. *Social Development, 17*, 102–114.

Nippold, M. A., Taylor, C. L., & Baker, J. M. (1996). Idiom understanding in Australian youth: A cross-cultural comparison. *Journal of Speech and Hearing Research, 39*, 442–447.

Nisbett, R. E. (2009). *Intelligence and how to get it.* New York: Norton.

Nishitani, S., Miyamura, T., Tagawa, M., Sumi, M., Takase, R., Doi, H., et al. (2009). The calming effect of a maternal breast milk odor on the human newborn infant. *Neuroscience Research, 63*, 66–71.

Noble, K. G., Fifer, W. P., Rauh, V. A., Nomura, Y., & Andrews, H. F. (2012). Academic achievement varies with gestational age among children born at term. *Pediatrics, 130*, e257–e264.

Noble, K. G., McCandliss, B. D., & Farah, M. J. (2007). Socioeconomic gradients predict individual differences in neurocognitive abilities. *Developmental Science, 10*, 464–480.

Noguera, P. (2010, June 14). A new vision for school reform. *The Nation,* pp. 11–14.

Noice, H., & Noice, T. (2006). What studies of actors and acting can tell us about memory and cognitive functioning. *Current Directions in Psychological Science, 15*, 14–18.

Noice, H., Noice, T., & Staines, G. (2004). A short-term intervention to enhance cognitive and affective functioning in older adults. *Journal of Aging and Health, 16*, 562–585.

Nolen-Hoeksema, S. (2006). The etiology of gender differences in depression. In C. M. Mazure & G. Puryear (Eds.), *Understanding depression in women: Applying empirical research to practice and policy* (pp. 9–43). Washington, DC: American Psychological Association.

Nolen-Hoeksema, S., & Aldao, A. (2011). Gender and age differences in emotion regulation and their relationship to depressive symptoms. *Personality and Individual Differences, 51*, 704–708.

Noller, P., Feeney, J. A., Sheehan, G., Darlington, Y., & Rogers, C. (2008). Conflict in divorcing and continuously married families: A study of marital, parent–child and sibling relationships. *Journal of Divorce and Remarriage, 49*, 1–24.

Nomaguchi, K. M., & Brown, S. L. (2011). Parental strains and rewards among mothers: The role of education. *Journal of Marriage and Family, 73*, 621–636.

Nomaguchi, K. M., & Milkie, M. A. (2003). Costs and rewards of children: The effects of becoming a parent on adults' lives. *Journal of Marriage and Family, 65*, 356–374.

Noppe, I. C., & Noppe, L. D. (1997). Evolving meanings of death during early, middle, and later adolescence. *Death Studies, 21*, 253–275.

Noppe, L. D., & Noppe, I. C. (1996). Ambiguity in adolescent understandings of death. In C. A. Corr & D. E. Balk (Eds.), *Handbook of adolescent death and bereavement* (pp. 25–41). New York: Springer.

Nordhus, I. H. (2008). Manifestations of depression and anxiety in older adults. In B. Woods & L. Clare (Eds.), *Handbook of the clinical psychology of ageing* (pp. 97–110). Hoboken, NJ: Wiley-Interscience.

Nosarti, C., Walshe, M., Rushe, T. M., Rifkin, L., Wyatt, J., Murray, R. M., et al. (2011). Neonatal ultrasound results following very preterm birth predict adolescent behavioral and cognitive outcome. *Developmental Neuropsychology, 36*, 118–135.

Nosek, B. A., Smyth, F. L., Siriram, N., Lindner, N. M., Devos, T., Ayala, A., et al. (2009). National differences in gender–science stereotypes predict national sex differences in science and math achievement. *Proceedings of the National Academy of Sciences, 106*, 10593–10597.

Noterdaeme, M., Mildenberger, K., Minow, F., & Amorosa, H. (2002). Evaluation of neuromotor deficits in children with autism and children with a specific speech and language disorder. *European Child and Adolescent Psychiatry, 11*, 219–225.

Nucci, L. (2008). *Nice is not enough: Facilitating moral development.* Upper Saddle River, NJ: Prentice Hall.

Nucci, L. P. (1996). Morality and the personal sphere of action. In E. Reed, E. Turiel, & T. Brown (Eds.), *Values and knowledge* (pp. 41–60). Hillsdale, NJ: Erlbaum.

Nucci, L. P. (2001). *Education in the moral domain.* New York: Cambridge University Press.

Nucci, L. P. (2002). The development of moral reasoning. In U. Goswami (Ed.), *Blackwell handbook of childhood cognitive development* (pp. 303–325). Malden, MA: Blackwell.

Nucci, L. P. (2005). Culture, context, and the psychological sources of human rights concepts. In W. Edelstein & G. Nunner-Winkler (Eds.), *Morality in context* (pp. 365–394). Amsterdam, Netherlands: Elsevier.

Nuland, S. B. (1993). *How we die.* New York: Random House.

Numan, M., & Insel, T. (2003). *Neurobiology of parental behavior.* New York: Springer-Verlag.

Nunez-Smith, M., Wolf, E., Huang, H. M., Chen, P. G., Lee, L., Emanuel, E. J., et al. (2008). *The impact of media on child and adolescent health.* Retrieved from www.commonsensemedia.org/sites/default/files/media_child_health_exec_summary_0.pdf

Nuttall, R. L., Casey, M. B., & Pezaris, E. (2005). Spatial ability as a mediator of gender differences on mathematics tests: A biological–environmental framework. In A. M. Gallagher & J. C. Kaufman (Eds.), *Gender differences in mathematics: An integrated psychological approach* (pp. 121–142). New York: Cambridge University Press.

Nye, B., Hedges, L. V., & Konstantopoulos, S. (2001). Are effects of small classes cumulative? Evidence from a Tennessee experiment. *Journal of Educational Research, 94*, 336–345.

O

Oakes, L. M., Coppage, D. J., & Dingel, A. (1997). By land or by sea: The role of perceptual similarity in infants' categorization of animals. *Developmental Psychology, 33*, 396–407.

Oakes, L. M., Horst, J. S., Kovack-Lesh, K. A., & Perone, S. (2009). How infants learn categories. In A. Woodward & A. Needham (Eds.), *Learning and the infant mind* (pp. 144–171). New York: Oxford University Press.

Oberecker, R., & Friederici, A. D. (2006). Syntactic event-related potential components in 24-month-olds' sentence comprehension. *NeuroReport, 17*, 1017–1021.

Oberecker, R., Friedrich, M., & Friederici, A. D. (2005). Neural correlates of syntactic processing in two-year-olds. *Journal of Cognitive Neuroscience, 17*, 1667–1678.

Obermeyer, C. M. (2000). Menopause across cultures: A review of the evidence. *Menopause, 7*, 184–192.

Obradović, J., Long, J. D., Cutuli, J. J., Chan, C. K., Hinz, E., Heistad, D., & Masten, A. S. (2009). Academic achievement of homeless and highly mobile children in an urban school district: Longitudinal evidence on risk, growth, and resilience. *Development and Psychopathology, 21*, 493–518.

Obradović, J., & Masten, A. S. (2007). Developmental antecedents of young adult civic engagement. *Applied Developmental Science, 11*, 2–19.

O'Brien, M. A., Hsing, C., & Konrath, S. (2010, May). *Empathy is declining in American college students.* Poster presented at the annual meeting of the Association for Psychological Science, Boston.

O'Connor, A. R., Stephenson, T., Johnson, A., Tobin, M. J., Ratib, S., Ng, Y., & Fielder, A. R. (2002). Long-term ophthalmic outcome of low birth weight children with and without retinopathy of prematurity. *Pediatrics, 109*, 12–18.

O'Connor, E., & McCartney, K. (2007). Examining teacher–child relationships and achievement as part of an ecological model of development. *American Educational Research Journal, 44*, 340–369.

O'Connor, P. (2003). Dying in the hospital. In I. Corless, B. B. Germino, & M. A. Pitman (Eds.), *Dying, death, and bereavement: A challenge for the living* (2nd ed., pp. 87–103). New York: Springer.

O'Connor, P. G. (2012). Alcohol abuse and dependence. In L. Goldman & D. A. Ausiello (Eds.), *Cecil Medicine* (23rd ed.), Philadelphia, PA: Elsevier.

O'Connor, T. G., Rutter, M., Beckett, C., Keaveney, L., Dreppner, J. M., & the English and Romanian Adoptees Study Team. (2000). The effects of global severe privation on cognitive competence: Extension and longitudinal follow-up. *Child Development, 71*, 376–390.

O'Dea, J. A. (2003). Why do kids eat healthful food? Perceived benefits of and barriers to healthful eating and physical activity among children and adolescents. *Journal of the American Dietetic Association, 103*, 497–501.

OECD (Organisation for Economic Cooperation and Development). (2006). *Starting strong II: Early childhood education and care.* Paris: OECD Publishing. Retrieved from www.sourceoecd.org/education/9264035451

OECD (Organisation for Economic Cooperation and Development). (2010a). *Education at a glance 2010: OECD indicators.* Paris: Author. Retrieved from www.oecd.org/document/52/0,3746,en_2649_39263238_45897844_1_1_1_1,00.html

OECD (Organisation for Economic Cooperation and Development). (2010b). *OECD Health data: 2010.* Retrieved from www.oecd.org/document/44/0,3746,en_2649_37407_2085228_1_1_1_37407,00.html

OECD (Organisation for Economic Cooperation and Development). (2011a). *Education at a glance 2011: OECD indicators.* Paris: Author.

OECD (Organisation for Economic Cooperation and Development). (2011b). *OECD health data 2011.* Retrieved from stats.oecd.org/index.aspx?DataSetCode=HEALTH_STAT

OECD (Organisation for Economic Cooperation and Development). (2012a). *Education at a glance 2012: OECD indicators.* Paris: Author.

OECD (Organisation for Economic Cooperation and Development). (2012b). *Health data: 2012.* Retrieved from www.oecd.org/health/healthpoliciesanddata/oecdhealthdata2012.htm

Ogan, A., & Berk, L. E. (2009, April). *Effects of two approaches to make-believe play training on self-regulation in Head Start children.* Paper presented at the biennial meeting of the Society for Research in Child Development, Denver, CO.

Ogawa, J. R., Sroufe, L. A., Weinfield, N. S., Carlson, E. A., & Egeland, B. (1997). Development and the fragmented self: Longitudinal study of dissociative symptomatology in a nonclinical sample. *Development and Psychopathology, 9*, 855–879.

Ogbu, J. U. (2003). *Black American students in an affluent suburb: A study of academic disengagement.* Mahwah, NJ: Erlbaum.

Ogden, C. L., Carroll, M. D., Curtin, L. R., Lamb, M. M., & Flegal, K. M. (2010). Prevalence of high body mass index in U.S. children and adolescents, 2007–2008. *Journal of the American Medical Association, 303*, 242–249.

Oh, J.-H., & Kim, S. (2009). Aging, neighborhood attachment, and fear of crime: Testing reciprocal effects. *Journal of Community Psychology, 37*, 21–40.

O'Halloran, C. M., & Altmaier, E. M. (1996). Awareness of death among children: Does a life-threatening illness alter the process of discovery? *Journal of Counseling and Development, 74*, 259–262.

Ohannessian, C. M., & Hesselbrock, V. M. (2008). Paternal alcoholism and youth substance abuse: The indirect effects of negative affect, conduct problems, and risk taking. *Journal of Adolescent Health, 42,* 198–200.

Ohgi, S., Arisawa, K., Takahashi, T., Kusumoto, T., Goto, Y., Akiyama, T., & Saito, H. (2003a). Neonatal behavioral assessment scale as a predictor of later developmental disabilities of low-birth-weight and/or premature infants. *Brain and Development, 25,* 313–321.

Ohgi, S., Takahashi, T., Nugent, J. K., Arisawa, K., & Akiyama, T. (2003b). Neonatal behavioral characteristics and later behavioral problems. *Clinical Pediatrics, 42,* 679–686.

Ohlemiller, K. K. (2008). Recent findings and emerging questions in cochlear noise injury. *Hearing Research, 245,* 5–17.

Okagaki, L., & Sternberg, R. J. (1993). Parental beliefs and children's school performance. *Child Development, 64,* 36–56.

Okami, P., Weisner, T., & Olmstead, R. (2002). Outcome correlates of parent–child bedsharing: An eighteen-year longitudinal study. *Developmental and Behavioral Pediatrics, 23,* 244–253.

Okamoto, K., & Tanaka, Y. (2004). Subjective usefulness and 6-year mortality risks among elderly persons in Japan. *Journal of Gerontology, 59B,* P246–P249.

O'Keefe, M. J., O'Callaghan, M., Williams, G. M., Najman, J. M., & Bor, W. (2003). Learning, cognitive, and attentional problems in adolescents born small for gestational age. *Pediatrics, 112,* 301–307.

O'Laughlin, E. M., & Anderson, V. N. (2001). Perceptions of parenthood among young adults: Implications for career and family planning. *American Journal of Family Therapy, 29,* 95–108.

Old, S. R., & Naveh-Benjamin, M. (2008a). Age-related changes in memory: Experimental approaches. In S. M. Hofer & D. F. Alwin (Eds.), *Handbook of cognitive aging: Interdisciplinary perspectives* (pp. 151–167). Thousand Oaks, CA: Sage.

Olds, D. L., Kitzman, H., Cole, R., Robinson, J., Sidora, K., Luckey, D. W., et al. (2004). Effects of nurse home-visiting on maternal life course and child development: Age 6 follow-up results of a randomized trial. *Pediatrics, 114,* 1550–1559.

Olds, D. L., Kitzman, H., Hanks, C., Cole, R., Anson, E., Sidora-Arcoleo, K., et al. (2007). Effects of nurse home visiting on maternal and child functioning: Age-9 follow-up of a randomized trial. *Pediatrics, 120,* e832–e845.

Olds, D. L., Robinson, J., O'Brien, R., Luckey, D. W., Pettitt, L. M., Henderson, C. R., Jr., et al. (2002). Home visiting by paraprofessionals and by nurses: A randomized, controlled trial. *Pediatrics, 110,* 486–496.

Olfman, S., & Robbins, B. D. (Eds.). (2012). *Drugging our children.* New York: Praeger.

Olineck, K. M., & Poulin-Dubois, D. (2007). Imitation of intentional actions and internal state language in infancy predict preschool theory of mind skills. *European Journal of Developmental Psychology, 4,* 14–30.

Olineck, K. M., & Poulin-Dubois, D. (2009). Infants' understanding of intention from 10 to 14 months: Interrelations among violation of expectancy and imitation tasks. *Infant Behavior and Development, 32,* 404–415.

Oliveira, F. L., Patin, R. V., & Escrivao, M. A. (2010). Atherosclerosis prevention and treatment in children and adolescents. *Expert Review of Cardiovascular Therapy, 8,* 513–528.

Ollendick, T. H., King, N. J., & Muris, P. (2002). Fears and phobias in children: Phenomenology, epidemiology, and aetiology. *Child and Adolescent Mental Health, 7,* 98–106.

Ollendick, T. H., Yang, B., King, N. J., Dong, Q., & Akande, A. (1996). Fears in American, Australian, Chinese, and Nigerian children and adolescents: A cross-cultural study. *Journal of Child Psychology and Psychiatry, 37,* 213–220.

Oller, D. K. (2000). *The emergence of the speech capacity.* Mahwah, NJ: Erlbaum.

Olshansky, S. J. (2011). Trends in longevity and prospects for the future. In R. H. Binstock & L. K. George (Eds.), *Handbook of aging and the social sciences* (7th ed., pp. 47–56). San Diego, CA: Academic Press.

Olshansky, S. J., Hayflick, L., & Perls, T. T. (2004). Antiaging medicine: The hype and the reality—Part II. *Journal of Gerontology, 59A,* 649–651.

Olson, D., Sikka, R. S., Hayman, J., Novak, M., & Stavig, C. (2009). Exercise in pregnancy. *Current Sports Medicine Reports, 8,* 147–153.

O'Malley, P. (2006). Viagra and vision loss: What is known and unknown. *Clinical Nurse Specialist, 20,* 227–228.

Omar, H., McElderry, D., & Zakharia, R. (2003). Educating adolescents about puberty: What are we missing? *International Journal of Adolescent Medicine and Health, 15,* 79–83.

Ondrusek, N., Abramovitch, R., Pencharz, P., & Koren, G. (1998). Empirical examination of the ability of children to consent to clinical research. *Journal of Medical Ethics, 24,* 158–165.

O'Neill, M., Bard, K. A., Kinnell, M., & Fluck, M. (2005). Maternal gestures with 20-month-old infants in two contexts. *Developmental Science, 8,* 352–359.

O'Neill, R., Welsh, M., Parke, R. D., Wang, S., & Strand, C. (1997). A longitudinal assessment of the academic correlates of early peer acceptance and rejection. *Journal of Clinical Child Psychology, 26,* 290–303.

Ong, A. D., Bergeman, C. S., & Bisconti, T. L. (2004). The role of daily positive emotions during conjugal bereavement. *Journal of Gerontology, 59B,* 168–176.

Ong, A. D., Mroczek, D. K., & Riffin, C. (2011). The health significance of positive emotions in adulthood and later life. *Social and Personality Psychology Compass, 5/8,* 538–551.

Ong, W., Allison, J., & Haladyna, T. M. (2000). Student achievement of third graders in comparable single-age and multiage classrooms. *Journal of Research in Childhood Education, 14,* 205–215.

Ontai, L. L., & Thompson, R. A. (2008). Attachment, parent–child discourse and theory-of-mind development. *Social Development, 17,* 47–60.

Onwuteaka-Philipsen, B. D., van der Heide, A., Muller, M. T., Rurup, M., Rietjens, J. A. C., & Georges, J.-J. (2005). Dutch experience of monitoring euthanasia. *British Medical Journal, 331,* 691–693.

Ophir, E., Nass, C., & Wagner, A. D. (2009). Cognitive control in media multitaskers. *Proceedings of the National Academy of Sciences, 106,* 15583–15587.

Oosterwegel, A., & Oppenheimer, L. (1993). *The self-system: Developmental changes between and within self-concepts.* Hillsdale, NJ: Erlbaum.

Opinion Research Corporation. (2009). *American teens say they want quality time with parents.* Retrieved from www.napsnet.com/pdf_archive/47/68753.pdf

O'Rahilly, R., & Müller, F. (2001). *Human embryology and teratology.* New York: Wiley-Liss.

Orbio de Castro, B., Veerman, J. W., Koops, W., Bosch, J. D., & Monshouwer, H. J. (2002). Hostile attribution of intent and aggressive behavior: A meta-analysis. *Child Development, 73,* 916–934.

Ordonana, J. R., Caspi, A., & Moffitt, T. E. (2008). Unintentional injuries in a twin study of preschool children: Environmental, not genetic risk factors. *Journal of Pediatric Psychology, 33,* 185–194.

Oregon Department of Human Services. (2009). *Death with Dignity Act annual report: 2008 summary.* Retrieved from oregon.gov/DHS/ph/pas/ar-index.shtml

Oregon Public Health Division. (2013). *Oregon's Death with Dignity Act—2012.* Retrieved from public.health.oregon.gov/ProviderPartnerResources/EvaluationResearch/DeathwithDignityAct/Documents/year15.pdf

O'Reilly, A. W. (1995). Using representations: Comprehension and production of actions with imagined objects. *Child Development, 66,* 999–1010.

Ormel, J., Petukhova, M., Chatterji, S., Aguilar-Gaxiola, S., Alonso, J., & Angermeyer, M. C. (2008). Disability and treatment of specific mental and physical disorders across the world. *British Journal of Psychiatry, 192,* 368–375.

Ornstein, P. A., Haden, C. A., & Elischberger, H. B. (2006). Children's memory development: Remembering the past and preparing for the future. In E. Bialystok & F. I. M. Craik (Eds.), *Lifespan cognition: Mechanisms of change* (pp. 143–161). New York: Oxford University Press.

O'Rourke, N., Cappeliez, P., & Claxton, A. (2011). Functions of reminiscence and the psychological well-being of young-old and older adults over time. *Aging and Mental Health, 15,* 272–281.

Orth, U., Robins, R. W., & Widaman, K. F. (2012). Life-span development of self-esteem and its effects on important life outcomes. *Personality Processes and Individual Differences, 102,* 1271–1288.

Orth, U., Trzesniewski, K. H., & Robins, R. W. (2010). Self-esteem development from young adulthood to old age: A cohort-sequential longitudinal study. *Journal of Personality and Social Psychology, 98,* 645–658.

Osherson, D. N., & Markman, E. M. (1975). Language and the ability to evaluate contradictions and tautologies. *Cognition, 2,* 213–226.

Ostir, G. V., Carlson, J. E., Black, S. A., Rudkin, L., Goodwin, J. S., & Markides, K. S. (1999). Disability in older adults 1: Prevalence, causes, and consequences. *Behavioral Medicine, 24,* 147–156.

Ostrov, J. M., Crick, N. R., & Stauffacher, K. (2006). Relational aggression in sibling and peer relationships during early childhood. *Applied Developmental Psychology, 27,* 241–253.

Ostrov, J. M., Gentile, D. A., & Crick, N. R. (2006). Media exposure, aggression, and prosocial behavior during early childhood: A longitudinal study. *Social Development, 15,* 612–627.

Oswald, F., Jopp, D., Rott, C., & Wahl, H.-W. (2010). Is aging in place a resource for or risk to life satisfaction? *Gerontologist, 51,* 238–250.

Oswald, F., & Wahl, H.-W. (2013). Creating and sustaining homelike places in residential living. In G. D. Rowles & M. Bernard (Eds.), *Environmental gerontology: Making meaningful places in old age* (pp. 53–78). New York: Springer.

Otis, N., Grouzet, F. M. E., & Pelletier, L. G. (2005). Latent motivational change in an academic setting: A three-year longitudinal study. *Journal of Educational Psychology, 97,* 170–183.

Otto, M. W., Henin, A., Hirshfeld-Becker, D. R., Pollack, M. H., Biederman, J., & Rosenbaum, J. (2007). Posttraumatic stress disorder symptoms following media exposure to tragic events: Impact of 9/11 on children at risk for anxiety disorders. *Journal of Anxiety Disorders, 21,* 888–902.

Oude, L. H., Baur, L., Jansen, H., Shrewsbury, V. A., O'Malley, C., Stolk, R. P., & Summerbell, C. D. (2009). Interventions for treating obesity in children. *Cochrane Database of Systematic Reviews, Issue 4.* Chichester, UK: Wiley.

Ouko, L. A., Shantikumar, K., Knezovich, J., Haycock, P., Schnugh, D. J., & Ramsay, M. (2009). Effect of alcohol consumption on CpG methylation in the differentially methylated regions of H19 and IG-DMR in male gametes: Implications for fetal alcohol spectrum disorders. *Alcoholism, Clinical and Experimental Research, 33,* 1615–1627.

Ovando, C. J., & Collier, V. P. (1998*). Bilingual and ESL classrooms: Teaching in multicultural contexts.* Boston: McGraw-Hill.

Overton, W. F. (2010). Life-span development: Concepts and issues. In W. F. Overton (Ed.), *Handbook of life-span development: Cognition, biology, and methods* (pp. 1–29). Hoboken, NJ: Wiley.

Owen, C. G., Whincup, P. H., Kaye, S. J., Martin, R. M., Smith, G. D., Cook, D. G., et al. (2008). Does initial breastfeeding lead to lower blood cholesterol in adult life? A quantitative review of the evidence. *American Journal of Clinical Nutrition, 88,* 305–314.

Owen-Kostelnik, J., Reppucci, N. D., & Meyer, J. R. (2006). Testimony and interrogation of minors: Assumptions about maturity and morality. *American Psychologist, 61,* 286–304.

Owsley, C. (2011). Aging and vision. *Vision Research, 51,* 1610–1622.

Oyserman, D., Bybee, D., Mowbray, C., & Hart-Johnson, T. (2005). When mothers have serious mental health problems: Parenting as a proximal mediator. *Journal of Adolescence, 28,* 443–463.

Özçaliskan, S. (2005). On learning to draw the distinction between physical and metaphorical motion: Is metaphor an early emerging cognitive and linguistic capacity? *Journal of Child Language, 32,* 291–318.

Özçaliskan, S., & Goldin-Meadow, S. (2005). Gesture is at the cutting edge of early language development. *Cognition, 96,* B101–B113.

Ozer, E. M., & Irwin, C. E., Jr. (2009). Adolescent and young adult health: From basic health status to clinical interventions. In R. M. Lerner & L. Steinberg (Eds.), *Handbook of adolescent psychology: Vol. 1. Individual bases of adolescent development* (pp. 618–641). Hoboken, NJ: Wiley.

P

Pacella, R., McLellan, M., Grice, K., Del Bono, E. A., Wiggs, J. L., & Gwiazda, J. E. (1999). Role of genetic factors in the etiology of juvenile-onset myopia based on a longitudinal study of refractive error. *Optometry and Vision Science, 76,* 381–386.

Padilla-Walker, L. M., & Nelson, L. J. (2012). Black Hawk down?: Establishing helicopter parenting as a distinct construct from other forms of parental control during emerging adulthood. *Journal of Adolescence, 35,* 1177–1190.

Padula, M. A., & Miller, D. L. (1999). Understanding graduate women's reentry experiences. *Psychology of Women Quarterly, 23,* 327–343.

Pagani, L. S., Japel, C., Vitaro, F., Tremblay, R. E., Larose, S., & McDuff, P. (2008). When predictions fail: The case of unexpected pathways toward high school dropout. *Journal of Social Issues, 64,* 175–193.

Pager, D., & Shepherd, H. (2008). The sociology of discrimination: Racial discrimination in employment, housing, credit, and consumer markets. *Annual Review of Sociology, 34,* 181–209.

Pager, D., Western, B., & Bonkowski, B. (2009), Discrimination in a low-wage labor market: A field experiment, *American Sociological Review, 74,* 777–799.

Paik, A. (2010). "Hookups," dating, and relationship quality: Does the type of sexual involvement matter? *Social Science Research, 39,* 739–753.

Painter, J. A., Allison, L., Dhingra, P., Daughtery, J., Cogdill, K., & Trujillo, L. G. (2012). Fear of falling and its relationship with anxiety, depression, and activity engagement among community-dwelling older adults. *American Journal of Occupational Therapy, 66,* 169–176.

Palincsar, A. S. (2003). Advancing a theoretical model of learning and instruction. In B. J. Zimmerman (Ed.), *Educational psychology: A century of contributions* (pp. 459–475). Mahwah, NJ: Erlbaum.

Palmore, E. (2001). The ageism survey: First findings. *Gerontologist, 41,* 572–575.

Palop, J. J., Chin, J., Roberson, E. D., Wang, J., Thwin, M. T., & Bien-Ly, N. (2007). Aberrant excitatory neuronal activity and compensatory remodeling of inhibitory hippocampal circuits in mouse models of Alzheimer's disease. *Neuron, 55,* 697–711.

Pan, B. A., & Snow, C. E. (1999). The development of conversation and discourse skills. In M. Barrett (Ed.), *The development of language* (pp. 229–249). Hove, UK: Psychology Press.

Pan, C. W. Ramamurthy, D., & Saw, S. M. (2012). Worldwide prevalence and risk factors for myopia. *Ophthalmic and Physiological Optics, 32,* 3–16.

Pan, H. W. (1994). Children's play in Taiwan. In J. L. Roopnarine, J. E. Johnson, & F. H. Hooper (Eds.), *Children's play in diverse cultures* (pp. 31–50). Albany, NY: SUNY Press.

Panish, J. B., & Stricker, G. (2002). Perceptions of childhood and adult sibling relationships. *NYS Psychologist, 14,* 33–36.

Papadakis, A. A., Prince, R. P., Jones, N. P., & Strauman, T. J. (2006). Self-regulation, rumination, and vulnerability to depression in adolescent girls. *Development and Psychopathology, 18,* 815–829.

Paquette, D. (2004). Theorizing the father–child relationship: Mechanisms and developmental outcomes. *Human Development, 47,* 193–219.

Paradis, J. (2007). Second language acquisition in childhood. In E. Hoff & M. Shatz (Eds.), *Blackwell handbook of language development* (pp. 387–405). Malden, MA: Blackwell.

Paradise, R., & Rogoff, B. (2009). Side by side: Learning by observing and pitching in. *Ethos, 27,* 102–138.

Paramei, G. V. (2012). Color discrimination across four life decades assessed by the Cambridge Color Test. *Journal of the Optical Society of America, 29,* A290–A297.

Parameswaran, G. (2003). Experimenter instructions as a mediator in the effects of culture on mapping one's neighborhood. *Journal of Environmental Psychology, 23,* 409–417.

Pardeck, J. T. (2005). An exploration of child maltreatment among homeless families: Implications for family policy. *Early Child Development and Care, 175,* 335–342.

Pardini, D. A., Fite, P. J., & Burke, J. D. (2008). Bidirectional associations between parenting practices and conduct problems in boys from childhood to adolescence: The moderating effect of age and African-American ethnicity. *Journal of Abnormal Child Psychology, 36,* 647–662.

Parent, A., Teilmann, G., Juul, A., Skakkebaek, N. E., Toppari, J., & Bourguignon, J. (2003). The timing of normal puberty and the age limits of sexual precocity: Variations around the world, secular trends, and changes after migration. *Endocrine Reviews, 24,* 668–693.

Paris, S. G., & Paris, A. H. (2006). Assessments of early reading. In K. A. Renninger & I. E. Sigel (Eds.), *Handbook of child psychology: Vol. 4. Child psychology in practice* (6th ed., pp. 48–74). Hoboken, NJ: Wiley.

Park, D. C. (2002). Judging meaning improves function in the aging brain. *Trends in Cognitive Sciences, 6,* 227–229.

Park, D. C., Lautenschlager, G., Hedden, T., Davidson, N. S., Smith, A. D., & Smith, P. K. (2002). Models of visuospatial and verbal memory across the adult life span. *Psychology and Aging, 17,* 299–320.

Park, W. (2009). Acculturative stress and mental health among Korean adolescents in the United States. *Journal of Human Behavior in the Social Environment, 19,* 626–634.

Parke, R. D. (2002). Fathers and families. In M. H. Bornstein (Ed.), *Handbook of parenting: Vol. 3* (2nd ed., pp. 27–73). Mahwah, NJ: Erlbaum.

Parke, R. D., & Buriel, R. (2006). Socialization in the family: Ethnic and ecological perspectives. In N. Eisenberg (Ed.), *Handbook of child psychology: Vol. 3. Social, emotional, and personality development* (6th ed., pp. 429–504). Hoboken, NJ: Wiley.

Parke, R. D., Simpkins, S. D., McDowell, D. J., Kim, M., Killian, C., Dennis, J., Flyr, M. L., Wild, M., & Rah, Y. (2004b). Relative contributions of families and peers to children's social development. In P. K. Smith & C. H. Hart (Eds.), *Blackwell handbook of childhood social development* (pp. 156–177). Malden, MA: Blackwell.

Parker, F. L., Boak, A. Y., Griffin, K. W., Ripple, C., & Peay, L. (1999). Parent–child relationship, home learning environment, and school readiness. *School Psychology Review, 28,* 413–425.

Parker, J. G., Low, C. M., Walker, A. R., & Gamm, B. K. (2005). Friendship jealousy in young adolescents: Individual differences and links to sex, self-esteem, aggression, and social adjustment. *Developmental Psychology, 41,* 235–250.

Parker, P. D., Schoon, I., Tsai, Y-M., Nagy, G., Trautwein, U., & Eccles, J. (2012). Achievement, agency, gender, and socioeconomic background as predictors of postschool choices: A multicontext study. *Developmental Psychology, 48,* 1629–1642.

Parten, M. (1932). Social participation among preschool children. *Journal of Abnormal and Social Psychology, 27,* 243–269.

Pascalis, O., de Haan, M., & Nelson, C. A. (1998). Long-term recognition memory for faces assessed by visual paired comparison in 3- and 6-month-old infants. *Journal of Experimental Psychology: Learning, Memory, and Cognition, 24,* 249–260.

Pascalis, O., de Haan, M., & Nelson, C. A. (2002). Is face processing species-specific during the first year of life? *Science, 296,* 1321–1323.

Pascarella, E. T. (2001). Cognitive growth in college: Surprising and reassuring findings from the National Study of Student Learning. *Change, 22*(6), 20–27.

Pascarella, E. T., & Terenzini, P. T. (1991). *How college affects students.* San Francisco: Jossey-Bass.

Pascarella, E. T., & Terenzini, P. T. (2005). *How college affects students: Vol. 2. A third decade of research.* San Francisco: Jossey-Bass.

Pasterski, V. L., Geffner, M. E., Brain, C., Hindmarsh, P., & Brook, C. (2005). Prenatal hormones and postnatal socialization by parents as determinants of male-typical toy play in girls with congenital adrenal hyperplasia. *Child Development, 76,* 264–278.

Patel, K. V., Coppin, A. K., Manini, T. M., Lauretani, F., Bandinelli, S., Ferrucci, L., & Guralnik, J. M. (2006). Midlife physical activity and mobility in older age: The InCHIANTI Study. *American Journal of Preventive Medicine, 31,* 217–224.

Patock-Peckam, J. A., & Morgan-Lopez, A. A. (2009). Mediational links among parenting styles, perceptions of parental confidence, self-esteem, and depression on alcohol-related problems in emerging adulthood. *Journal of Studies on Alcohol and Drugs, 70,* 215–226.

Patrick, R. B., & Gibbs, J. C. (2011). Inductive discipline, parental expression of disappointed expectations, and moral identity in adolescence. *Journal of Youth and Adolescence, 41,* 973–983.

Pattenden, S., Antova, T., Neuberger, M., Nikiforov, B., De Sario, M., Grize, L., & Heinrich, J. (2006). Parental smoking and children's respiratory health: Independent effects of prenatal and postnatal exposure. *Tobacco Control, 15,* 294–301.

Patterson, C. J., & Riskind, R. G. (2010). To be a parent: Issues in family formation among gay and lesbian adults. *Journal of GLBT Family Studies, 6,* 326–340.

Patterson, G. R., & Fisher, P. A. (2002). Recent developments in our understanding of parenting: Bidirectional effects, causal models, and the search for parsimony. In M. H. Bornstein (Ed.), *Handbook of parenting* (Vol. 5, pp. 59–88). Mahwah, NJ: Erlbaum.

Patterson, G. R., & Yoerger, K. (2002). A developmental model for early-and late-onset delinquency. In J. B.

Reid & G. R. Patterson (Eds.), *Antisocial behavior in children and adolescents* (pp. 147–172). Washington, DC: American Psychological Association.

Paukner, A., Ferrari, P. F., & Suomi, S. J. (2011). Delayed imitation of lipsmacking gestures by infant rhesus macaques (*Macaca mulatta*). *PLoS ONE 6*(12), e28848.

Paul, J. J., & Cillessen, A. H. N. (2003). Dynamics of peer victimization in early adolescence: Results from a four-year longitudinal study. *Journal of Applied School Psychology, 19,* 25–43.

Pauli, S. A., Berga, S. L., Shang, W., & Session, D. R. (2009). Current status of the approach to assisted reproduction. *Pediatric Clinics of North America, 56,* 467–488.

Paulussen-Hoogeboom, M. C., Stams, G. J. J. M., Hermanns, J. M. A., & Peetsma, T. T. D. (2007). Child negative emotionality and parenting from infancy to preschool: A meta-analytic review. *Developmental Psychology, 43,* 438–453.

Payne, B. R., Gao, X., Noh, S. R., Anderson, C. J., & Stine-Morrow, E. A. L. (2012). The effects of print exposure on sentence processing and memory in older adults: Evidence for efficiency and reserve. *Aging, Neuropsychology, and Cognition, 19,* 122–149.

Pea, R., Nass, C., Meheula, L., Rance, M., Kumar, A., Bamford, H., et al. (2012). Media use, face-to-face communication, media multitasking, and social well-being among 8- to 12-year-old girls. *Developmental Psychology, 48,* 327–336.

Peake, A., & Harris, K. L. (2002). Young adults' attitudes toward multiple role planning: The influence of gender, career traditionality, and marriage plans. *Journal of Vocational Behavior, 60,* 405–421.

Pearlman, D. N., Zierler, S., Meersman, S., Kim, H. K., Viner-Brown, S. I., & Caron, C. (2006). Race disparities in childhood asthma: Does where you live matter? *Journal of the National Medical Association, 98,* 239–247.

Peck, R. C. (1968). Psychological developments in the second half of life. In B. L. Neugarten (Ed.), *Middle age and aging* (pp. 88–92). Chicago: University of Chicago Press.

Pedersen, S., Vitaro, F., Barker, E. D., & Anne, I. H. (2007). The timing of middle-childhood peer rejection and friendship: Linking early behavior to early adolescent adjustment. *Child Development, 78,* 1037–1051.

Pederson, D. R., & Moran, G. (1996). Expressions of the attachment relationship outside of the Strange Situation. *Child Development, 67,* 915–927.

Peets, K., Hodges, E. V. E., Kikas, E., & Salmivalli, C. (2007). Hostile attributions and behavioral strategies in children: Does relationship type matter? *Developmental Psychology, 43,* 889–900.

Peirano, P., Algarin, C., & Uauy, R. (2003). Sleep–wake states and their regulatory mechanisms throughout early human development. *Journal of Pediatrics, 43,* S70–S79.

Peiró, J., Tordera, N., & Potocnik, K. (2012). Retirement practices in different countries. In M. Wang (Ed.), *Oxford handbook of retirement* (pp. 509–540). New York: Oxford University Press.

Pellegrini, A. D. (1992). Kindergarten children's social cognitive status as a predictor of first grade success. *Early Childhood Research Quarterly, 7,* 565–577.

Pellegrini, A. D. (2003). Perceptions and functions of play and real fighting in early adolescence. *Child Development, 74,* 1522–1533.

Pellegrini, A. D. (2004). Rough-and-tumble play from childhood through adolescence: Development and possible functions. In P. K. Smith & C. H. Hart (Eds.), *Blackwell handbook of childhood social development* (pp. 438–453). Malden, MA: Blackwell.

Pellegrini, A. D., & Holmes, R. M. (2006). The role of recess in primary school. In D. G. Singer, R. M. Golinkoff, & K. Hirsh-Pasek (Eds.), *Play = learning* (pp. 36–53). New York: Oxford University Press.

Pellegrini, A. D., Huberty, P. D., & Jones, I. (1995). The effects of recess timing on children's playground and classroom behaviors. *American Educational Research Journal, 32,* 845–864.

Pellegrini, A. D., Kato, K., Blatchford, P., & Baines, E. (2002). A short-term longitudinal study of children's playground games across the first year of school: Implications for social competence and adjustment to school. *American Educational Research Journal, 39,* 991–1015.

Pellegrini, A. D., & Smith, P. K. (1998). Physical activity play: The nature and function of a neglected aspect of play. *Child Development, 69,* 577–598.

Pellicano, E., Maybery, M., Durkin, K., & Maley, A. (2006). Multiple cognitive capabilities/deficits in children with an autism spectrum disorder: "Weak" central coherence and its relationship to theory of mind and executive control. *Development and Psychopathology, 18,* 77–98.

Pendlebury, S. T., Rothwell, P. M. (2009). Prevalence, incidence, and factors associated with pre-stroke and post-stroke dementia: A systematic review and meta-analysis. *Lancet Neurology, 8,* 1006–1018.

Penner, A. M. (2003). International gender item difficulty interactions in mathematics and science achievement tests. *Journal of Educational Psychology, 95,* 650–655.

Pennington, B. F., Snyder, K. A., & Roberts, R. J., Jr. (2007). Developmental cognitive neuroscience: Origins, issues, and prospects. *Developmental Review, 27,* 428–441.

Penny, H., & Haddock, G. (2007). Anti-fat prejudice among children: The 'mere proximity' effect in 5–10 year olds. *Journal of Experimental Social Psychology, 43,* 678–683.

Pepler, D. J., Craig, W. M., Connolly, J. A., Yuile, A., McMaster, L., & Jiang, D. (2006). A developmental perspective on bullying. *Aggressive Behavior, 32,* 376–384.

Peralta de Mendoza, O. A., & Salsa, A. M. (2003). Instruction in early comprehension and use of a symbol–referent relation. *Cognitive Development, 18,* 269–284.

Perelli-Harris, B., & Gassen, N. S. (2012). How similar are cohabitation and marriage? Legal approaches to cohabitation across Western Europe. *Population and Development Review, 38,* 435–467.

Perkins, H. W. (1991). Religious commitment, yuppie values, and well-being in post-collegiate life. *Review of Religious Research, 32,* 244–251.

Perlmutter, M. (1984). Continuities and discontinuities in early human memory: Paradigms, processes, and performances. In R. V. Kail, Jr., & N. R. Spear (Eds.), *Comparative perspectives on the development of memory* (pp. 253–287). Hillsdale, NJ: Erlbaum.

Perlmutter, M., Kaplan, M., & Nyquist, L. (1990). Development of adaptive competence in adulthood. *Human Development, 33,* 185–197.

Perls, T., Levenson, R., Regan, M., & Puca, A. (2002). What does it take to live to 100? *Mechanisms of Ageing and Development, 123,* 231–242.

Perls, T., & Terry, D. (2003). Understanding the determinants of exceptional longevity. *Annals of Internal Medicine, 139,* 445–449.

Perls, T., Terry, D. F., Silver, M., Shea, M., Bowen, J., & Joyce, E. (2000). Centenarians and the genetics of longevity. *Results and Problems in Cell Differentiation, 29,* 1–20.

Perone, S., Madole, K. L., Ross-Sheehy, S., Carey, M., & Oakes, L. M. (2008). The relation between infants' activity with objects and attention to object appearance. *Developmental Psychology, 44,* 1242–1248.

Perry, W. G., Jr. (1981). Cognitive and ethical growth. In A. Chickering (Ed.), *The modern American college* (pp. 76–116). San Francisco: Jossey-Bass.

Perry, W. G., Jr. (1998). *Forms of intellectual and ethical development in the college years: A scheme.*

San Francisco: Jossey-Bass. (Originally published 1970)

Perry-Jenkins, M., Repetti, R. L., & Crouter, A. C. (2000). Work and family in the 1990s. *Journal of Marriage and the Family, 62,* 981–998.

Peshkin, A. (1997). *Places of memory: Whiteman's schools and Native American communities.* Mahwah, NJ: Erlbaum.

Pesonen, A.-K., Räikkönen, K., Heinonen, K., & Komsi, N. (2008). A transactional model of temperamental development: Evidence of a relationship between child temperament and maternal stress over five years. *Social Development, 17,* 326–340.

Petch, J., & Halford, W. K. (2008). Psychoeducation to enhance couples' transition to parenthood. *Clinical Psychology Review, 28,* 1125–1137.

Peters, L., Cant, R., Payne, S., O'Connor, M., McDermott, F., Hood, K., et al. (2013). How death anxiety impacts nurses' caring for patients at the end of life: A review of literature. *Open Nursing Journal, 7,* 14–21.

Peters, R. D. (2005). A community-based approach to promoting resilience in young children, their families, and their neighborhoods. In R. D. Paters, B. Leadbeater, & R. J. McMahon (Eds.), *Resilience in children, families, and communities: Linking context to practice and policy* (pp. 157–176). New York: Kluwer Academic.

Peters, R. D., Bradshaw, A. J., Petrunka, K., Nelson, G., Herry, Y., Craig, W. M., et al. (2010). The Better Beginnings, Better Futures Project: Findings from grade 3 to grade 9. *Monographs of the Society for Research in Child Development, 75*(3, Serial No. 297).

Peters, R. D., Petrunka, K., & Arnold, R. (2003). The Better Beginnings, Better Futures Project: A universal, comprehensive, community-based prevention approach for primary school children and their families. *Journal of Clinical Child and Adolescent Psychology, 32,* 215–227.

Peterson, B. E. (2002). Longitudinal analysis of midlife generativity, intergenerational roles, and caregiving. *Psychology and Aging, 17,* 161–168.

Peterson, B. E. (2006). Generativity and successful parenting: An analysis of young adult outcomes. *Journal of Personality, 74,* 847–869.

Peterson, B. E., & Duncan, L. E. (2007). Midlife women's generativity and authoritarianism: Marriage, motherhood, and 10 years of aging. *Psychology and Aging, 22,* 411–419.

Peterson, B. E., Smirles, K. A., & Wentworth, P. A. (1997). Generativity and authoritarianism: Implications for personality, political involvement, and parenting. *Journal of Personality and Social Psychology, 72,* 1202–1216.

Peterson, C., Parsons, T., & Dean, M. (2004). Providing misleading and reinstatement information a year after it happened: Effects on long-term memory. *Memory, 12,* 1–13.

Peterson, C., & Rideout, R. (1998). Memory for medical emergencies experienced by 1- and 2-year-olds. *Developmental Psychology, 34,* 1059–1072.

Peterson, C., & Roberts, C. (2003). Like mother, like daughter: Similarities in narrative style. *Developmental Psychology, 39,* 551–562.

Peterson, C., Warren, K. L., & Short, M. M. (2011). Infantile amnesia across the years: A 2-year follow-up of children's earliest memories. *Child Development, 82,* 1092–1105.

Peter-Wight, M., & Martin, M. (2011). Older spouses' individual and dyadic problem solving. *European Psychologist, 16,* 288–294.

Petitto, L. A., Holowka, S., Sergio, L. E., Levy, B., & Ostry, D. J. (2004). Baby hands that move to the rhythm of language: Hearing babies acquiring sign languages babble silently on the hands. *Cognition, 93,* 43–73.

Petitto, L. A., Holowka, S., Sergio, L. E., & Ostry, D. (2001, September 6). Language rhythms in babies' hand movements. *Nature, 413,* 35–36.

Petitto, L. A., & Marentette, P. F. (1991). Babbling in the manual mode: Evidence for the ontogeny of language. *Science, 251,* 1493–1496.

Petrides, K. V., Sangareau, Y., Furnham, A., & Fredrickson, N. (2006). Trait emotional intelligence and children's peer relations at school. *Social Development, 15,* 537–547.

Petrill, S. A., & Deater-Deckard, K. (2004). The heritability of general cognitive ability: A within-family adoption design. *Intelligence, 32,* 403–409.

Petrofsky, J., Berk, L., & Al-Nakhli, H. (2012). The influence of autonomic dysfunction associated with aging and type 2 diabetes on daily life activities. *Experimental Diabetes Research,* Article ID 657103.

Pettigrew, T. F., & Tropp, L. R. (2006). A meta-analytic test of intergroup contact theory. *Journal of Personality and Social Psychology, 90,* 751–783.

Pettit, G. S. (2004). Violent children in developmental perspective. *Current Directions in Psychological Science, 13,* 194–197.

Pettit, G. S., Brown, E. G., Mize, J., & Lindsey, E. (1998). Mothers' and fathers' socializing behaviors in three contexts: Links with children's peer competence. *Merrill-Palmer Quarterly, 44,* 173–193.

Pettit, G. S., Keiley, M. K., Laird, R. D., Bates, J. E., & Dodge, K. A. (2007). Predicting the developmental course of mother-reported monitoring across childhood and adolescence from early proactive parenting, child temperament, and parents' worries. *Journal of Family Psychology, 21,* 206–217.

Pew Forum on Religion and Public Life. (2010). *Religion among the Millennials.* Washington, DC: Pew Research Center.

Pew Research Center. (2006). *Strong public support for right to die.* Retrieved from http://people-press.org/reports

Pew Research Center. (2010a). *The decline of marriage and rise of new families.* Washington, DC: Author.

Pew Research Center. (2010b). *Religion among the millennials.* Washington, DC: Pew Form on Religion and Public Life.

Pew Research Center. (2013). *Growing support for gay marriage: Changed minds and changing demographics.* Washington, DC: Author. Retrieved from www.people-press.org/files/legacy-pdf/3-20-13%20Gay%20Marriage%20Release%20UPDATE.pdf

Pfeffer, C. R., Altemus, M., Heo, M., & Jiang, H. (2007). Salivary cortisol and psychopathology in children bereaved by the September 11, 2001, terror attacks. *Biological Psychiatry, 61,* 957–965.

Pfeifer, J. H., Ruble, D. N., Bachman, M. A., Alvarez, J. M., Cameron, J. A., & Fuligni, A. J. (2007). Social identities and intergroup bias in immigrant and nonimmigrant children. *Developmental Psychology, 43,* 496–507.

Pharo, H., Sim, C., Graham, M., Gross, J., & Hayne, H. (2011). Risky business: Executive function, personality, and reckless behavior during adolescence and emerging adulthood. *Behavioral Neuroscience, 125,* 970–978.

Philips, S. U. (1983). *The invisible culture: Communication in classroom and community on the Warm Springs Indian Reservation.* Prospect Heights, IL: Waveland.

Phinney, J. S. (2007). Ethnic identity exploration in emerging adulthood. In J. J. Arnett & J. L. Tanner (Eds.), *Emerging adults in America: Coming of age in the 21st century* (pp. 117–134). Washington, DC: American Psychological Association.

Phinney, J. S., & Chavira, V. (1995). Parental ethnic socialization and adolescent outcomes in ethnic minority families. *Journal of Research on Adolescence, 5,* 31–53.

Phinney, J. S., Horenczyk, G., Liebkind, K., & Vedder, P. (2001). Ethnic identity, immigration, and well-being: An interactional perspective. *Journal of Social Issues, 57,* 493–510.

Phinney, J. S., & Ong, A. (2001). *Family obligations and life satisfaction among adolescents from immigrant and non-immigrant families: Direct and moderated effects.* Unpublished manuscript, California State University.

Phinney, J. S., Ong, A., & Madden, T. (2000). Cultural values and intergenerational value discrepancies in immigrant and non-immigrant families. *Child Development, 71,* 528–539.

Phuong, D. D., Frank, R., & Finch, B. R. (2012). Does SES explain more of the black/white health gap than we thought? Revisiting our approach toward understanding racial disparities in health. *Social Science and Medicine, 74,* 1385–1393.

Piaget, J. (1926). *The language and thought of the child.* New York: Harcourt, Brace & World. (Original work published 1923)

Piaget, J. (1930). *The child's conception of the world.* New York: Harcourt, Brace, & World. (Original work published 1926)

Piaget, J. (1951). *Play, dreams, and imitation in childhood.* New York: Norton. (Original work published 1945)

Piaget, J. (1952). *The origins of intelligence in children.* New York: International Universities Press. (Original work published 1936)

Piaget, J. (1967). *Six psychological studies.* New York: Vintage.

Piaget, J. (1971). *Biology and knowledge.* Chicago: University of Chicago Press.

Pianta, R., Egeland, B., & Erickson, M. F. (1989). The antecedents of maltreatment: Results of the Mother–Child Interaction Research Project. In D. Cicchetti & V. Carlson (Eds.), *Child maltreatment* (pp. 203–253). New York: Cambridge University Press.

Pianta, R. C., Hamre, B., & Stuhlman, M. (2003). Relationships between teachers and children. In W. M. Reynolds & G. E. Miller (Eds.), *Handbook of psychology: Educational psychology* (Vol. 7, pp. 199–234). New York: Wiley.

Pickens, J., Field, T., & Nawrocki, T. (2001). Frontal EEG asymmetry in response to emotional vignettes in preschool age children. *International Journal of Behavioral Development, 25,* 105–112.

Pickett, K. E., Luo, Y., & Lauderdale, D. S. (2005). Widening social inequalities in risk for sudden infant death syndrome. *American Journal of Public Health, 95,* 1976–1981.

Pierce, S. H., & Lange, G. (2000). Relationships among metamemory, motivation and memory performance in young school-age children. *British Journal of Developmental Psychology, 18,* 121–135.

Pierroutsakos, S. L., & Troseth, G. L. (2003). Video verité: Infants' manual investigation of objects on video. *Infant Behavior and Development, 26,* 183–199.

Pietz, J., Peter, J., Graf, R., Rauterberg, R. I., Rupp, A., & Sontheimer, D. (2004). Physical growth and neurodevelopmental outcome of nonhandicapped low-risk children born preterm. *Early Human Development, 79,* 131–143.

Piirto, J. (2007). *Talented children and adults* (3rd ed.). Waco, TX: Prufrock Press.

Pillemer, K., & Suitor, J. (2002). Explaining mothers' ambivalence toward their adult children. *Journal of Marriage and the Family, 64,* 602–613.

Pillow, B. (2002). Children's and adults' evaluation of the certainty of deductive inferences, inductive inferences, and guesses. *Child Development, 73,* 779–792.

Pilz, K. S., Bennett, P. J., & Sekuler, A. B. (2010). Effects of aging on biological motion discrimination. *Vision Research, 50,* 211–219.

Pimentel, A. E., Gentiel, C. L., Tanaka, H., Seals, D. R., & Gates, P. E. (2003). Greater rate of decline in maximal aerobic capacity with age in endurancetrained vs. sedentary men. *Journal of Applied Physiology, 94,* 2406–2413.

Ping, R. M., & Goldin-Meadow, S. (2008). Hands in the air: Using ungrounded iconic gestures to teach children conservation of quantity. *Developmental Psychology, 44,* 1277–1287.

Pinker, S. (1999). *Words and rules: The ingredients of language.* New York: Basic Books.

Pinquart, M. (2003). Loneliness in married, widowed, divorced, and never-married older adults. *Journal of Social and Personal Relationships, 20,* 31–53.

Pinquart, M., & Schindler, I. (2009). Change of leisure satisfaction in the transition to retirement: A latent-class analysis. *Leisure Sciences, 31,* 311–329.

Pinquart, M., & Sörensen, S. (2001). Gender differences in self-concept and psychological well-being in old age: A meta-analysis. *Journal of Gerontology, 56B,* P195–P213.

Pinquart, M., & Sörensen, S. (2006). Gender differences in caregiver stressor, social resources, and health: An updated meta-analysis. *Journal of Gerontology, 61B,* P33–P45.

Pirie, K., Peto, R., Reeves, G. K., Green, J., Beral, V., & the Million Women Study Collaborators. (2012). The 21st century hazards of smoking and benefits of stopping: A prospective study of one million women in the UK. *Lancet, 308,* 133–141.

Pitkala, K. H., Laakkonen, M. L., Strandberg, T. E., & Tilvis, R. S. (2004). Positive life orientation as a predictor of 10-year outcome in an aged population. *Journal of Clinical Epidemiology, 57,* 409–414.

Pitkin, J. (2010). Cultural issues and the menopause. *Menopause International, 16,* 156–161.

Pizarro, D. A., & Bloom, P. (2003). The intelligence of the moral intuitions: Comment on Haidt (2001). *Psychological Review, 110,* 193–196.

Plante, I., Théoret, M., & Favreau, O. E. (2009). Student gender stereotypes: Contrasting the perceived maleness and femaleness of mathematics and language. *Educational Psychology, 29,* 385–405.

Pleck, J. H., & Masciadrelli, B. P. (2004). Paternal involvement by U.S. residential fathers: Levels, sources, and consequences. In M. E. Lamb (Ed.), *The role of the father in child development* (4th ed., pp. 222–271). Hoboken, NJ: Wiley.

Ploeg, J., Campbell, L., Denton, M., Joshi, A., & Davies, S. (2004). Helping to build and rebuild secure lives and futures: Financial transfers from parents to adult children and grandchildren. *Canadian Journal on Aging, 23,* S131–S143.

Plomin, R. (1994). *Genetics and experience: The interplay between nature and nurture.* Thousand Oaks, CA: Sage.

Plomin, R. (2003). General cognitive ability. In R. Plomin & J. C. DeFries (Eds.), *Behavioral genetics in the postgenomic era* (pp. 183–201). Washington, DC: American Psychological Association.

Plomin, R. (2009). The nature of nurture. In K. McCartney & R. A. Weinberg (Eds.), *Experience and development: A festschrift in honor of Sandra Wood Scarr* (pp. 61–80). New York: Psychology Press.

Plomin, R., & Davis, O. S. P. (2009). The future of genetics in psychology and psychiatry: Microarrays, genome-wide association, and non-coding RNA. *Journal of Child Psychology and Psychiatry, 50,* 63–71.

Plomin, R., DeFries, J. C., McClearn, G. E., & McGuffin, P. (2001). *Behavioral genetics* (4th ed.). New York: Worth.

Plomin, R., & Spinath, F. M. (2004). Intelligence: Genetics, genes, and genomics. *Journal of Personality and Social Psychology, 86,* 112–129.

Plucker, J. A., & Makel, M. C. (2010). Assessment of creativity. In J. C. Kaufman & R. J. Sternberg (Eds.), *Cambridge handbook of creativity* (pp. 48–73). New York: Cambridge University Press.

Plude, D. J., & Doussard-Roosevelt, J. A. (1989). Aging, selective attention, and feature integration. *Psychology and Aging, 4,* 98–105.

Pluess, M., & Belsky, J. (2011). Prenatal programming of postnatal plasticity? *Development and Psychopathology, 23,* 29–38.

Poehlmann, J., & Fiese, B. H. (2001). The interaction of maternal and infant vulnerabilities on developing attachment relationships. *Development and Psychopathology, 13,* 1–11.

Poehlmann, J., Schwichtenberg, A. J. M., Shlafer, R. J., Hahn, E., Bianchi, J.-P., & Warner, R. (2011). Emerging self-regulation in toddlers born preterm or low birth weight: Differential susceptibility to parenting. *Developmental and Psychopathology, 23,* 177–193.

Pogarsky, G., Thornberry, T. P., & Lizotte, A. J. (2006). Developmental outcomes for children of young mothers. *Journal of Marriage and Family, 68,* 332–344.

Polderman, T. J. C., de Geus, J. C., Hoekstra, R. A., Bartels, M., van Leeuwen, M., Verhulst, F. C., et al. (2009). Attention problems, inhibitory control, and intelligence index overlapping genetic factors: A study in 9-, 12-, and 18-year-old twins. *Neuropsychology, 23,* 381–391.

Polka, L., & Werker, J. F. (1994). Developmental changes in perception of non-native vowel contrasts. *Journal of Experimental Psychology: Human Perception and Performance, 20,* 421–435.

Pollitt, E. (1996). A reconceptualization of the effects of undernutrition on children's biological, psychosocial, and behavioral development. *Social Policy Report of the Society for Research in Child Development, 10*(5).

Pomerantz, E. M., & Dong, W. (2006). Effects of mothers' perceptions of children's competence: The moderating role of mothers' theories of competence. *Developmental Psychology, 42,* 950–961.

Pomerantz, E. M., & Eaton, M. M. (2000). Developmental differences in children's conceptions of parental control: "They love me, but they make me feel incompetent." *Merrill-Palmer Quarterly, 46,* 140–167.

Pomerantz, E. M., Ng, F. F., & Wang, Q. (2008). Culture, parenting, and motivation: The case of East Asia and the United States. In M. L. Maehr, S. A., Karabenick, & T. C. Urdan (Eds.), *Advances in motivation and achievement: Social psychological perspectives* (Vol. 15, pp. 209–240). Bingley, UK: Emerald Group.

Pomerantz, E. M., & Ruble, D. N. (1998). The multidimensional nature of control: Implications for the development of sex differences in self-evaluation. In J. Heckhausen & C. S. Dweck (Eds.), *Motivation and self-regulation across the lifespan* (pp. 159–184). New York: Cambridge University Press.

Pomerantz, E. M., & Saxon, J. L. (2001). Conceptions of ability as stable and self-evaluative processes: A longitudinal examination. *Child Development, 72,* 152–173.

Pomerleau, A., Scuccimarri, C., & Malcuit, G. (2003). Mother–infant behavioral interactions in teenage and adult mothers during the first six months postpartum: Relations with infant development. *Infant Mental Health Journal, 24,* 495–509.

Pong, S., Johnston, J., & Chen, V. (2010). Authoritarian parenting and Asian adolescent school performance. *International Journal of Behavioral Development, 34,* 62–72.

Pong, S., & Landale, N. S. (2012). Academic achievement of legal immigrants' children: The roles of parents' pre- and postmigration characteristics in origin-group differences. *Child Development, 83,* 1543–1559.

Ponnappan, S., & Ponnappan, U. (2011). Aging and immune function: Molecular mechanisms to interventions. *Antioxidants & Redox Signaling, 14,* 1551–1585.

Pons, F., Lawson, J., Harris, P. L., & de Rosnay, M. (2003). Individual differences in children's emotion understanding: Effects of age and language. *Scandinavian Journal of Psychology, 44,* 347–353.

Poobalan, A. S., Aucott, L. S., Precious, E., Crombie, I. K., & Smith, W. C. S. (2010). Weight loss interventions in young people (18 to 25 year olds): A systematic review. *Obesity Reviews, 11,* 580–592.

Poon, S., Goodman, S. G., Bugiardini, R., Bierman, A. S., Eagle, K. A., Johnston, N., et al. (2012). Bridging the gender gap: Insights from a contemporary analysis of sex-related differences in the treatment and outcomes of patients with acute coronary syndromes. *American Heart Journal, 163,* 66–73.

Popenoe, D. (2006). *Debunking divorce myths.* Retrieved from health.discovery.com/centers/loverelationships/articles/divorce.html

Portes, A., & Rumbaut, R. G. (2005), Introduction: The second generation and the Children of Immigrants Longitudinal Study. *Ethnic and Racial Studies, 28,* 983–999.

Posner, M. I., & Rothbart, M. K. (2007). Temperament and learning. In M. I. Posner & M. K. Rothbart (Eds.), *Educating the human brain* (pp. 121–146). Washington, DC: American Psychological Association.

Posthuma, R. A., & Campion, M. A. (2009). Age stereotypes in the workplace: Common stereotypes, moderators, and future research directions. *Journal of Management, 35,* 158–188.

Poti, J. M., & Popkin, B. M. (2011). Trends in energy intake among U.S. children by eating location and food source, 1977–2006. *Journal of the American Dietetic Association, 111,* 1156–1164.

Poudevigne, M., & O'Connor, P. J. (2006). A review of physical activity patterns in pregnant women and their relationship to psychological health. *Sports Medicine, 36,* 19–38.

Poulin-Dubois, D., Serbin, L. A., Eichstedt, J. A., Sen, M. G., & Beissel, C. F. (2002). Men don't put on make-up: Toddlers' knowledge of the gender stereotyping of household activities. *Social Development, 11,* 166–181.

Povinelli, D. J. (2001). The self—Elevated in consciousness and extended in time. In C. Moore & K. Lemmon (Eds.), *The self in time: Developmental perspectives* (pp. 75–95). Mahwah, NJ: Erlbaum.

Powdthavee, N. (2008). Putting a price tag on friends, relatives, and neighbors: Using surveys of life satisfaction to value social relationships. *Journal of Socio-economics, 37,* 1459–1480.

Power, T. G. (2000). *Play and exploration in children and animals.* Mahwah, NJ: Erlbaum.

Powlishta, K. K., Serbin, L. A., & Moller, L. C. (1993). The stability of individual differences in gender typing: Implications for understanding gender segregation. *Sex Roles, 29,* 723–737.

Prager, K. J., & Bailey, J. M. (1985). Androgyny, ego development, and psychological crisis resolution. *Sex Roles, 13,* 525–535.

Pratt, M. W., Norris, J. E., Hebblethwaite, S., & Arnold, M. L. (2008). Intergenerational transmission of values: Family generativity and adolescents' narratives of parent and grandparent value teaching. *Journal of Personality, 76,* 171–198.

Pratt, M. W., Skoe, E. E., & Arnold, M. L. (2004). Care reasoning development and family socialization patterns in later adolescence: A longitudinal analysis. *International Journal of Behavioral Development, 28,* 139–147.

Prechtl, H. F. R., & Beintema, D. (1965). *The neurological examination of the full-term newborn infant.* London: Heinemann Medical Books.

Preece, J., & Findsen, B. (2007). Keeping people active: Continuing education programs that work. In M. Robinson, W. Novelli, C. Pearson, & L. Norris (Eds.), *Global health and global aging* (pp. 313–322). San Francisco: Jossey-Bass.

Preissler, M. A., & Carey, S. (2004). Do both pictures and words function as symbols for 18- and 24-month-old children? *Journal of Cognition and Development, 5,* 185–212.

Pressley, M., & Hilden, D. (2006). Cognitive strategies. In D. Kuhn & R. Siegler (Eds.), *Handbook of child psychology: Vol. 2. Cognition, perception, and language* (6th ed., pp. 511–556). Hoboken, NJ: Wiley.

Pressley, M., Wharton-McDonald, R., Raphael, L. M., Bogner, K., & Roehrig, A. (2002). Exemplary firstgrade teaching. In B. M. Taylor & P. D. Pearson (Eds.), *Teaching reading: Effective schools, accomplished teachers* (pp. 73–88). Mahwah, NJ: Erlbaum.

Prevatt, F. (2003). Dropping out of school: A review of intervention programs. *Journal of School Psychology, 41,* 377–399.

Previc, F. H. (1991). A general theory concerning the prenatal origins of cerebral lateralization. *Psychological Review, 98,* 299–334.

Price, J., Jordan, J., Prior, L., & Parkes, J. (2011). Living through the death of a child: A qualitative study of bereaved parents' experiences. *International Journal of Nursing Studies, 48,* 1384–1392.

Priess, H. A., Lindberg, S. M., & Hyde, J. S. (2009). Adolescent gender-role identity and mental health: Gender intensification revisited. *Child Development, 80,* 1531–1544.

Prince, M., Bryce, R., Albanese, E., Wimo, A., Ribeiro, W., & Ferri, C. P. (2013). The global prevalence of dementia: A systematic review and meta-analysis. *Alzheimer's and Dementia, 9,* 63–75.

Prinstein, M. J., Boergers, J., & Vernberg, E. M. (2001). Overt and relational aggression in adolescents: Social–psychological adjustment of aggressors and victims. *Journal of Clinical Child Psychology, 30,* 479–491.

Prinstein, M. J., & Cillessen, A. H. N. (2003). Forms and functions of adolescent peer aggression associated with high levels of peer status. *Merrill-Palmer Quarterly, 49,* 310–342.

Prinstein, M. J., & La Greca, A. M. (2002). Peer crowd affiliation and internalizing distress in childhood and adolescence: A longitudinal follow-back study. *Journal of Research on Adolescence, 12,* 325–351.

Prinstein, M. J., & La Greca, A. (2004). Childhood peer rejection and aggression as predictors of adolescent girls' externalizing and health risk behaviors: A 6-year longitudinal study. *Journal of Consulting and Clinical Psychology, 72,* 103–112.

Proctor, M. H., Moore, L. L., Gao, D., Cupples, L. A., Bradlee, M. L., Hood, M. Y., & Ellison, R. C. (2003). Television viewing and change in body fat from preschool to early adolescence: The Framingham Children's Study. *International Journal of Obesity, 27,* 827–833.

Programme for International Student Assessment. (2009). *PISA profiles by country/economy.* Retrieved from stats.oecd.org/PISA2009Profiles

Proulx, K., & Jacelon, C. (2004). Dying with dignity: The good patient versus the good death. *American Journal of Hospice and Palliative Care, 21,* 116–120.

Pruden, S. M., Hirsh-Pasek, K., Golinkoff, R. M., & Hennon, E. A. (2006). The birth of words: Ten-month-olds learn words through perceptual salience. *Child Development, 77,* 266–280.

Pryor, J. H., Hurtado, S., DeAngelo, L., Blake, L. P., & Tran, S. (2009). *The American freshman: National norms for fall 2009.* Los Angeles: Higher Education Research Institute, UCLA.

Prysak, M., Lorenz, R. P., & Kisly, A. (1995). Pregnancy outcome in nulliparous women 35 years and older. *Obstetrics and Gynecology, 85,* 65–70.

Pudrovska, T. (2009). Parenthood, stress, and mental health in late midlife and early old age. *International*

Journal of Aging and Human Development, 68, 127–147.

Puhl, R. M., & Heuer, C. A. (2010). Obesity stigma: Important considerations for public health. *American Journal of Public Health, 100,* 1019–1028.

Puhl, R. M., Heuer, C. A., & Brownell, D. K. (2010). Stigma and social consequences of obesity. In P. G. Kopelman, I. D. Caterson, & W. H. Dietz (Eds.), *Clinical obesity in adults and children* (3rd ed., pp. 25–40). Hoboken, NJ: Wiley.

Puhl, R. M., & Latner, J. D. (2007). Stigma, obesity, and the health of the nation's children. *Psychological Bulletin, 133,* 557–580.

Pujol, J., Soriano-Mas, C., Ortiz, H., Sebastián-Gallés, N., Losilla, J. M., & Deus, J. (2006). Myelination of language-related areas in the developing brain. *Neurology, 66,* 339–343.

Punamaki, R. L. (2006). Ante-and perinatal factors and child characteristics predicting parenting experience among formerly infertile couples during the child's first year: A controlled study. *Journal of Family Psychology, 20,* 670–679.

Putallaz, M., Grimes, C. L., Foster, K. J., Kupersmidt, J. B., Coie, J. D., & Dearing, K. (2007). Overt and relational aggression and victimization: Multiple perspectives within the school setting. *Journal of School Psychology, 45,* 523–547.

Putnam, S. P., Samson, A. V., & Rothbart, M. K. (2000). Child temperament and parenting. In V. J. Molfese & D. L. Molfese (Eds.), *Temperament and personality across the life span* (pp. 255–277). Mahwah, NJ: Erlbaum.

Pyka, G., Lindenberger, E., Charette, S., & Marcus, R. (1994). Muscle strength and fiber adaptations to a year-long resistance training program in elderly men and women. *Journal of Gerontology, 49,* M22–27.

Pyszczynski, T., Greenberg, J., Solomon, S., Arndt, J., & Schimel, J. (2004). Why do people need self-esteem? A theoretical and empirical view. *Psychological Bulletin, 130,* 435–468.

Q

Qian, Z., & Lichter, D. T. (2011). Changing patterns of interracial marriage in a multiracial society. *Journal of Marriage and Family, 73,* 1065–1084.

Quas, J. A., Malloy, L. C., Melinder, A., Goodman, G. S., & D'Mello, M. (2007). Developmental differences in the effects of repeated interviews and interviewer bias on young children's event memory and false reports. *Developmental Psychology, 43,* 823–837.

Quill, T. E. (1991). Death and dignity: A case of individualized decision making. *New England Journal of Medicine, 324,* 691–694.

Quine, S., Wells, Y., de Vaus, D., & Kendig, H. (2007). When choice in retirement decisions is missing: Qualitative and quantitative findings of impact on well-being. *Australasian Journal on Ageing, 26,* 173–179.

Quinn, P. C. (2008). In defense of core competencies, quantitative change, and continuity. *Child Development, 79,* 1633–1638.

Quinn, P. C., Kelly, D. J., Lee, K., Pascalis, O., & Slater, A. (2008). Preference for attractive faces extends beyond conspecifics. *Developmental Science, 11,* 76–83.

Quinn, P. C., & Liben, L. S. (2008). A sex difference in mental rotation in young infants. *Psychological Science, 19,* 1067–1070.

Quinn, P. C., Yahr, J., Kuhn, A., Slater, A. M., & Pascalis, O. (2002). Representation of the gender of human faces by infants: A preference for female. *Perception, 31,* 1109–1121.

R

Raaijmakers, Q. A. W., Engels, R. C. M. E., & van Hoof, A. (2005). Delinquency and moral reasoning in adolescence and young adulthood. *International Journal of Behavioral Development, 29,* 247–258.

Rabbitt, P., Lunn, M., & Wong, D. (2008). Death, dropout, and longitudinal measurements of cognitive change in old age. *Journal of Gerontology, 63B,* P271–P278.

Rabig, J., Thomas, W., Kane, R., Cutler, L. J., & McAlilly, S. (2006). Radical redesign of nursing homes: Applying the Green House concept in Tupelo, Mississippi. *Gerontologist, 46,* 533–539.

Radler, B. T., & Ryff, C. D. (2010). Who participates? Accounting for longitudinal retention in the MIDUS national study of health and well-being. *Journal of Aging and Health, 22,* 307–331.

Raevuori, A., Hoek, H. W., Susser, E., Kaprio, J., Rissanen, A., & Keski-Rahkonen, A. (2009). Epidemiology of anorexia nervosa in men: A nationwide study of Finnish twins. *PLoS ONE, 4,* e4402.

Ragow-O'Brien, D., Hayslip, B., Jr., & Guarnaccia, C. A. (2000). The impact of hospice on attitudes toward funerals and subsequent bereavement adjustment. *Omega, 41,* 291–305.

Rahi, J. S., Cumberland, P. M., & Peckham, C. S. (2011). Myopia over the life course: Prevalence and early life influences in the 1958 British birth cohort *Ophthalmology, 118,* 797–804.

Rahman, Q., & Wilson, G. D. (2003). Born gay? The psychobiology of human sexual orientation. *Personality and Individual Differences, 34,* 1337–1382.

Raikes, H. A., Robinson, J. L., Bradley, R. H., Raikes, H. H., & Ayoub, C. C. (2007). Developmental trends in self-regulation among low-income toddlers. *Social Development, 16,* 128–149.

Raikes, H. A., & Thompson, R. A. (2005). Links between risk and attachment security: Models of influence. *Journal of Applied Developmental Psychology, 26,* 440–455.

Raikes, H. A., & Thompson, R. A. (2006). Family emotional climate, attachment security, and young children's emotion knowledge in a high-risk sample. *British Journal of Developmental Psychology, 24,* 89–104.

Raikes, H. H., Chazan-Cohen, R., Love, J. M., & Brooks-Gunn, J. (2010). Early Head Start impacts at age 3 and a description of the age 5 follow-up study. In A. J. Reynolds, A. J. Rolnick, M. M. Englund, & J. Temple (Eds.), *Childhood programs and practices in the first decade of life: A human capital integration* (pp. 99–118). New York: Cambridge University Press.

Räikkönen, K., Matthews, K. A., Flory, J. D., Owens, J. F., & Gump, B. B. (1999). Effects of optimism, pessimism, and trait anxiety on ambulatory blood pressure and mood during everyday life. *Journal of Personality and Social Psychology, 76,* 104–113.

Räikkönen, K., Matthews, K. A., Sutton-Tyrrell, K., & Kuller, L. H. (2004). Trait anger and the metabolic syndrome predict progression of carotid atherosclerosis in healthy middle-aged women. *Psychosomatic Medicine, 66,* 903–908.

Rait, G., Walters, K., Bottomley, C., Petersen, I., Iliffe, S., & Nazareth, I. (2010). Survival of people with clinical diagnosis of dementia in primary care: Cohort study. *British Medical Journal, 341,* c3584.

Rakison, D. H. (2005). Developing knowledge of objects' motion properties in infancy. *Cognition, 96,* 183–214.

Rakison, D. H. (2006). Make the first move: How infants learn about self-propelled objects. *Developmental Psychology, 42,* 900–912.

Rakison, D. H. (2010). Perceptual categorization and concepts. In J. G. Bremner & T. D. Wachs (Eds.), *Wiley-Blackwell handbook of infant development* (2nd ed., pp. 243–270). Oxford, UK: Wiley.

Rakison, D. H., & Lupyan, G. (2008). Developing object concepts in infancy: An associative learning perspective. *Monographs of the Society for Research in Child Development, 73*(1, Serial No. 289).

Rakoczy, H., Tomasello, M., & Striano, T. (2004). Young children know that trying is not pretending: A test of the "behaving-as-if" construal of children's early concept of pretense. *Developmental Psychology, 40,* 388–399.

Rakoczy, H., Tomasello, M., & Striano, T. (2005). How children turn objects into symbols: A cultural learning account. In L. Namy (Ed.), *Symbol use and symbol representation* (pp. 67–97). New York: Erlbaum.

Ralston, S. H., & Uitterlinden, A. G. (2010). Genetics of osteoporosis. *Endocrine Reviews, 31,* 629–662.

Ramaswami, A., & Dreher, G. F. (2007). The benefits associated with workplace mentoring relationships. In T. D. Allen & L. T. Eby (Eds.), *Blackwell handbook of mentoring: A multiple perspectives approach* (pp. 211–231). Malden, MA: Blackwell.

Ramaswami, A., Dreher, G. F., Bretz, R., & Wiethoff, C. (2010). Gender, mentoring, and career success: The importance of organizational context. *Personnel Psychology, 63,* 385–405.

Ramchandani, P. G., Stein, A., O'Connor, T. G., Heron, J., Murray, L., & Evans, J. (2008). Depression in men in the postnatal period and later child psychopathology: A population cohort study. *Journal of the American Academy of Child and Adolescent Psychiatry, 47,* 390–398.

Ramey, C. T., Ramey, S. L., & Lanzi, R. G. (2006). Children's health and education. In K. A. Renninger & I. E. Sigel (Eds.), *Handbook of child psychology: Vol. 4. Child psychology in practice* (6th ed., pp. 864–892). Hoboken, NJ: Wiley.

Ramirez, A., & Zhang, S. (2007). When online meets offline: The effect of modality switching on relational communication. *Communication Monographs, 74,* 287–310.

Ramos, E., Frontera, W. R., Llorpart, A., & Feliciano, D. (1998). Muscle strength and hormonal levels in adolescents: Gender related differences. *International Journal of Sports Medicine, 19,* 526–531.

Ramos, M. C., Guerin, D. W., Gottfried, A. W., Bathurst, K., & Oliver, P. H. (2005). Family conflict and children's behavior problems: The moderating role of child temperament. *Structural Equation Modeling, 12,* 278–298.

Rampell, C. (2010, March 9). The gender wage gap, around the world. *New York Times online.* Retrieved from economix.blogs.nytimes.com/2010/03/09/the-gender-wage-gap-around-the-world

Ramsey-Rennels, J. L., & Langlois, J. H. (2006). Differential processing of female and male faces. *Current Directions in Psychological Science, 15,* 59–62.

Ramus, F. (2002). Language discrimination by newborns: Teasing apart phonotactic, rhythmic, and intonational cues. *Annual Review of Language Acquisition, 2,* 85–115.

Rando, T. A. (1995). Grief and mourning: Accommodating to loss. In H. Wass & R. A. Neimeyer (Eds.), *Dying: Facing the facts* (3rd ed., pp. 211–241). Washington, DC: Taylor & Francis.

Raqib, R., Alam, D. S., Sarker, P., Ahmad, S. M., Ara, G., & Yunus, M. (2007). Low birth weight is associated with altered immune function in rural Bangladeshi children: A birth cohort study. *American Journal of Clinical Nutrition, 85,* 845–852.

Rasmussen, C., Ho, E., & Bisanz, J. (2003). Use of the mathematical principle of inversion in young children. *Journal of Experimental Child Psychology, 85,* 89–102.

Rasmussen, E. R., Neuman, R. J., Heath, A. C., Levy, F., Hay, D. A., & Todd, R. D. (2004). Familial clustering of latent class and DSM-IV defined attention-deficit hyperactivity disorder (ADHD) subtypes. *Journal of Child Psychology and Psychiatry, 45,* 589–598.

Rathunde, K., & Csikszentmihalyi, M. (2005). The social context of middle school: Teachers, friends, and activities in Montessori and traditional school environments. *Elementary School Journal, 106,* 59–79.

Rauber, M. (2006, May 18). Parents aren't sitting still as recess disappears. *Parents in Action*. Retrieved from http://healthyschoolscampaign.org/news/media/food/2006-05_recess_disappears.php

Raver, C. C. (2003). Does work pay psychologically as well as economically? The role of employment in predicting depressive symptoms and parenting among low-income families. *Child Development, 74*, 1720–1736.

Ravid, D., & Tolchinsky, L. (2002). Developing linguistic literacy: A comprehensive model. *Journal of Child Language, 29*, 417–447.

Ravitch, D. (2010). *The death and life of the great American school system: How testing and choice are undermining education*. New York: Basic Books.

Rawlins, W. K. (2004). Friendships in later life. In J. F. Nussbaum & J. Coupland (Eds.), *Handbook of communication and aging research* (2nd ed., pp. 273–299). Mahwah, NJ: Erlbaum.

Rayner, K., Pollatsek, A., & Starr, M. S. (2003). Reading. In A. F. Healy & R. W. Proctor (Eds.), *Handbook of psychology: Experimental psychology* (Vol. 4, pp. 549–574). New York: Wiley.

Raz, N., Ghisletta, P., Rodrigue, K. M., Kennedy, K. M., & Lindenberger, U. (2010). Trajectories of brain aging in middle-aged and older adults: Regional and individual differences. *NeuroImage, 51*, 501–511.

Raz, N., Rodrigue, K. M., Kennedy, K. M., & Acker, J. D. (2007). Vascular health and longitudinal changes in brain and cognition in middle-aged and older adults. *Neuropsychology, 21*, 149–157.

Reay, A. C., & Browne, K. D. (2008). Elder abuse and neglect. In B. Woods & L. Clare (Eds.), *Handbook of the clinical psychology of ageing* (pp. 311–322). Chichester, UK: Wiley.

Reddin, J. (1997). High-achieving women: Career development patterns. In H. S. Farmer (Ed.), *Diversity and women's career development* (pp. 95–126). Thousand Oaks, CA: Sage.

Redman, L. M., Martin, C. K., Williamson, D. A., & Ravussin, E. (2008). Effect of caloric restriction in non-obese humans on physiological, psychological and behavioral outcomes. *Physiology and Behavior, 94*, 643–648.

Redman, L. M., & Ravussin, E. (2011). Caloric restriction in humans: Impact on physiological, psychological, and behavioral outcomes. *Antioxidants & Redox Signaling, 14*, 275–287.

Regan, P. C., Medina, R., & Joshi, A. (2001). Partner preferences among homosexual men and women: What is desirable in a sex partner is not necessarily desirable in a romantic partner. *Social Behavior and Personality, 29*, 625–634.

Regnerus, M., Smith, C., & Fritsch, M. (2003). *Religion in the lives of American adolescents: A review of the literature*. Chapel Hill, NC: National Study of Youth and Religion.

Reich, S. M., Subrahmanyam, K., & Espinoza, G. (2012). Friending, IMing, and hanging out face-to-face: Overlap in adolescents' online and offline social networks. *Developmental Psychology, 48*, 356–368.

Reid, H. M., & Fine, A. (1992). Self-disclosure in men's friendships: Variations associated with intimate relations. In P. M. Nardi (Ed.), *Men's friendships* (pp. 153–171). Newbury Park, CA: Sage.

Reid, K. F., & Fielding, R. A. (2012). Skeletal muscle power: A critical determinant of physical functioning in older adults. *Exercise and Sports Sciences Reviews, 40*, 4–12.

Reilly, J. S., Bates, E. A., & Marchman, V. A. (1998). Narrative discourse in children with early focal brain injury. *Brain and Language, 61*, 335–375.

Reilly, J. S., Losh, M., Bellugi, U., & Wulfeck, B. (2004). "Frog, where are you?" Narratives in children with specific language impairment, early focal brain injury, and Williams syndrome. *Brain and Language, 88*, 229–247.

Reis, O., & Youniss, J. (2004). Patterns in identity change and development in relationships with mothers and friends. *Journal of Adolescent Research, 19*, 31–44.

Reis, S. M. (2004). We can't change what we don't recognize: Understanding the special needs of gifted females. In S. Baum (Ed.), *Twice-exceptional and special populations of gifted students* (pp. 67–80). Thousand Oaks, CA: Corwin Press.

Reisman, J. E. (1987). Touch, motion, and proprioception. In P. Salapatek & L. Cohen (Eds.), *Handbook of infant perception: Vol. 1. From sensation to perception* (pp. 265–303). Orlando, FL: Academic Press.

Reiss, D. (2003). Child effects on family systems: Behavioral genetic strategies. In A. C. Crouter & A. Booth (Eds.), *Children's influence on family dynamics: The neglected side of family relationships* (pp. 3–36). Mahwah, NJ: Erlbaum.

Reiss, N. S., & Tishler, C. L. (2008a). Suicidality in nursing home residents: Part I. Prevalence, risk factors, methods, assessment, and management. *Professional Psychology: Research and Practice, 39*, 264–270.

Reiss, N. S., & Tishler, C. L. (2008b). Suicidality in nursing home residents: Part II. Prevalence, risk factors, methods, assessment, and management. *Professional Psychology: Research and Practice, 39*, 271–275.

Reitzes, D. C., & Mutran, E. J. (2002). Self-concept as the organization of roles: Importance, centrality, and balance. *Sociological Quarterly, 43*, 647–667.

Reitzes, D. C., & Mutran, E. J. (2004). Grandparenthood: Factors influencing frequency of grandparent–grandchildren contact and grandparent role satisfaction. *Journal of Gerontology, 59*, S9–S16.

Renninger, K. A. (1998). Developmental psychology and instruction: Issues from and for practice. In I. Sigel & K. A. Renninger (Eds.), *Handbook of child psychology: Vol. 4. Child psychology and practice* (pp. 211–274). New York: Wiley.

Repacholi, B. M., & Gopnik, A. (1997). Early reasoning about desires: Evidence from 14- and 18-month-olds. *Developmental Psychology, 33*, 12–21.

Repetti, R., & Wang, S. (2010). Parent employment and chaos in the family. In G. W. Evans & T. D. Wachs (Eds.), *Chaos and its influence on children's development: An ecological perspective* (pp. 191–208). Washington, DC: American Psychological Association.

Reppucci, N. D., Meyer, J. R., & Kostelnik, J. O. (2011). Tales of terror from juvenile justice and education. In M. S. Aber, K. I. Maton, & E. Seidman (Eds.), *Empowering settings and voices for social change* (pp. 155–172). New York: Oxford University Press.

Resnick, M., & Silverman, B. (2005). *Some reflections on designing construction kits for kids*. Proceedings of the Conference on Interaction Design and Children, Boulder, CO.

Resnick, M. B., Gueorguieva, R. V., Carter, R. L., Ariet, M., Sun, Y., Roth, J., Bucciarelli, R. L., Curran, J. S., & Mahan, C. S. (1999). The impact of low birth weight, perinatal conditions, and sociodemographic factors on educational outcome in kindergarten. *Pediatrics, 104*, e74.

Rest, J. R. (1979). *Development in judging moral issues*. Minneapolis: University of Minnesota Press.

Resta, R., Biesecker, B. B., Bennett, R. L., Blum, S., Hahn, S. E., Strecker, M. N., & Williams, J. L. (2006). A new definition of genetic counseling: National Society of Genetic Counselors' Task Force Report. *Journal of Genetic Counseling, 15*, 77–83.

Reuter-Lorenz, P. A., & Cappell, K. A. (2008). Neurocognitive aging and the compensation hypothesis. *Current Directions in Psychological Science, 17*, 177–182.

Reyes-Ortiz, C. A., Kuo, Y.-F., DiNuzzo, A. R., Ray, L. A., Raji, M. A., & Markides, K. S. (2005). Near vision impairment predicts cognitive decline: Data from the Hispanic established populations for epidemiologic studies of the elderly. *Journal of the American Geriatric Society, 53*, 681–686.

Reyna, V. F., & Farley, F. (2006). Risk and rationality in adolescent decision making: Implications for theory, practice, and public policy. *Psychological Science in the Public Interest, 7*, 1–44.

Reynolds, A. J., & Temple, J. A. (1998). Extended early childhood intervention and school achievement: Age 13 findings from the Chicago Longitudinal Study. *Child Development, 69*, 231–246.

Rhoades, B. L., Greenberg, M. T., & Domitrovich, C. E. (2009). The contribution of inhibitory control to preschoolers' social-emotional competence. *Journal of Applied Developmental Psychology, 30*, 310–320.

Rhoades, G. K., Stanley, S. M., & Markman, H. J. (2006). Pre-engagement cohabitation and gender asymmetry in marital commitment. *Journal of Family Psychology, 20*, 553–560.

Rhone, M., & Basu, A. (2008). Phytochemicals and age-related eye diseases. *Nutrition Reviews, 66*, 465–472.

Richard, C. A., & Brown, A. H. (2006). Configurations of informal social support among older lesbians. *Journal of Women and Aging, 18*, 49–65.

Richardson, H. L., Walker, A. M., & Horne, R. S. C. (2008). Sleep position alters arousal processes maximally at the high-risk age for sudden infant death syndrome. *Journal of Sleep Research, 17*, 450–457.

Richardson, H. L., Walker, A. M., & Horne, R. S. C. (2009). Maternal smoking impairs arousal patterns in sleeping infants. *Pediatric Sleep, 32*, 515–521.

Richardson, V. E. (2007). A dual process model of grief counseling: Findings from the changing lives of older couples (CLOC) study. *Journal of Gerontological Social Work, 48*, 311–329.

Richie, B. S., Fassinger, R. E., Linn, S. G., Johnson, J., Prosser, J., & Robinson, S. (1997). Persistence, connection, and passion: A qualitative study of the career development of highly achieving African American–black and white women. *Journal of Counseling Psychology, 44*, 133–148.

Richler, J., Luyster, R., Risi, S., Hsu, W.-L., Dawson, G., & Bernier, R. (2006). Is there a "regressive phenotype" of autism spectrum disorder associated with the measles-mumps-rubella vaccine? A CPEA study. *Journal of Autism and Developmental Disorders, 36*, 299–316.

Richmond, J., Colombo, M., & Hayne, H. (2007). Interpreting visual preferences in the visual paired-comparison task. *Journal of Experimental Psychology: Learning, Memory, and Cognition, 33*, 823–831.

Ridenour, T. A. (2000). Genetic epidemiology of antisocial behavior. In D. H. Fishbein (Ed.), *The science, treatment, and prevention of antisocial behaviors* (pp. 7.1–7.24). Kingston, NJ: Civic Research Institute.

Rideout, V., & Hamel, E. (2006). *The media family: Electronic media in the lives of infants, toddlers, preschoolers and their parents*. Menlo Park, CA: Henry J. Kaiser Family Foundation.

Rideout, V. J., Foehr, U. G., & Roberts, D. F. (2010). *Generation M^2: Media in the lives of 8- to 18-year-olds*. Menlo Park. CA: Henry J. Kaiser Family Foundation.

Riediger, M., Li, S.-C., & Lindenberger, U. (2006). Selection, optimization, and compensation as developmental mechanisms of adaptive resource allocation: Review and preview. In J. E. Birren & K. W. Schaire (Eds.), *Handbook of the psychology of aging* (6th ed.) (pp. 289–313). Burlington, MA: Academic Press.

Riley, J. R., & Masten, A. S. (2004). Resilience in context. In R. D. Peters, B. Leadbeater, & R. McMahon (Eds.), *Resilience in children, families, and communities: Linking context to practice and policy* (pp. 13–25). New York: Kluwer Academic.

Riley, L. D., & Bowen, C. P. (2005). The sandwich generation: Challenges and coping strategies of multigenerational families. *Counseling and Therapy for Couples and Families, 13,* 52–58.

Rinaldo, L. A., & Ferraro, K. F. (2012). Inequality, health. In G. Ritzer (Ed.), *Wiley-Blackwell encyclopedia of globalization.* Hoboken, NJ: Wiley-Blackwell.

Ringbäck, W. G., Eliasson, M., & Rosén, M. (2008). Underweight, overweight and obesity as risk factors for mortality and hospitalization. *Scandinavian Journal of Public Health, 36,* 169–176.

Ripperger, T., Gadzicki, D., Meindl, A. & Schlegelberger, B. (2009). Breast cancer susceptibility: Current knowledge and implications for genetic counseling. *European Journal of Human Genetics, 17,* 722–731.

Ripple, C. H., & Zigler, E. (2003). Research, policy, and the federal role in prevention initiatives for children. *American Psychologist, 58,* 482–490.

Ritchey, L. H., Ritchey, P. N., & Dietz, B. E. (2001). Clarifying the measurement of activity. *Activities, Adaptation, and Aging, 26,* 1–21.

Ritchie, L. D., Spector, P., Stevens, M. J., Schmidt, M. M., Schreiber, G. B., Striegel-Moore, R. H., et al. (2007). Dietary patterns in adolescence are related to adiposity in young adulthood in black and white females. *Journal of Nutrition, 137,* 399–406.

Riva, D., & Giorgi, C. (2000). The cerebellum contributes to higher functions during development: Evidence from a series of children surgically treated for posterior fossa tumours. *Brain, 123,* 1051–1061.

Rivkees, S. A. (2003). Developing circadian rhythmicity in infants. *Pediatrics, 112,* 373–381.

Rivlin, R. S. (2007). Keeping the young–elderly healthy: Is it too late to improve our health through nutrition? *American Journal of Clinical Nutrition, 86*(Suppl.), 1572S–1576S.

Rizvi, S. I., & Jha, R. (2011). Strategies for the discovery of anti-aging compounds. *Expert Opinion on Drug Discovery, 6,* 89–102.

Rizzolatti, G., & Craighero, L. (2004). The mirror-neuron system. *Annual Review of Neuroscience, 27,* 169–192.

Robb, A. S., & Dadson, M. J. (2002). Eating disorders in males. *Child and Adolescent Psychiatric Clinics of North America, 11,* 399–418.

Roberto, K. A., & Jarrott, S. E. (2008). Family caregivers of older adults: A life span perspective. *Family Relations, 57,* 100–111.

Roberts, B. W., & DelVecchio, W. E. (2000). The rank-order consistency of personality traits from childhood to old age: A quantitative review of longitudinal studies. *Psychological Bulletin, 126,* 3–25.

Roberts, B. W., Kuncel, N., Shiner, R., Caspi, A., & Goldberg, L. R. (2007). The power of personality: A comparative analysis of the predictive validity of personality traits, SES, and IQ. *Perspectives on Psychological Science, 2,* 313–345.

Roberts, B. W., & Mroczek, D. (2008). Personality and trait change in adulthood. *Current Directions in Psychological Science, 17,* 31–35.

Roberts, B. W., Walton, K. E., & Viechtbauer, W. (2006). Patterns of mean-level change in personality traits across the life course: A meta-analysis of longitudinal studies. *Psychological Bulletin, 132,* 3–25.

Roberts, D. F., Henriksen, L., & Foehr, U. G. (2004). Adolescents and media. In R. M. Lerner & L. Steinberg (Eds.), *Handbook of adolescent psychology* (2nd ed., pp. 627–664). Hoboken, NJ: Wiley.

Roberts, D. F., Henriksen, L., & Foehr, U. G. (2009). Adolescence, adolescents, and media. In R. M. Lerner & L. Steinberg (Eds.), *Handbook of adolescent psychology: Vol. 2. Contextual influences on adolescent development* (3rd ed., pp. 314–344). Hoboken, NJ: Wiley.

Roberts, J. E., Burchinal, M. R., & Durham, M. (1999). Parents' report of vocabulary and grammatical development of American preschoolers: Child and environment associations. *Child Development, 70,* 92–106.

Roberts, P. (2006). From my space to our space: The functions of Web memorials in bereavement. *The Forum, 32,* 1–4.

Robertson, J. (2008). Stepfathers in families. In J. Pryor (Ed.), *International handbook of stepfamilies: Policy and practice in legal, research, and clinical environments* (pp. 125–150). Hoboken, NJ: Wiley.

Robertson, K. F., Smeets, S., Lubinski, D., & Benbow, C. P. (2010). Beyond the threshold hypothesis: Even among the gifted and top math/science graduate students, cognitive abilities, vocational interests, and lifestyle preferences matter for career choice, performance, and persistence. *Current Directions in Psychological Science, 19,* 346–351.

Robin, A. L., & Le Grange, D. (2010). Family therapy for adolescents with anorexia nervosa. In J. R. Weisz & A. E. Kazdin (Eds.), *Evidence-based psychotherapies for children and adolescents* (2nd ed., pp. 359–374). New York: Guilford.

Robine, J.-M., & Allard, M. (1999). Jeanne Louise Calment: Validation of the duration of her life. In B. Jeune & J. W. Vaupel (Ed.), *Validation of exceptional longevity.* Odense, Denmark: Odense University Press.

Robins, R. W., Tracy, J. L., Trzesniewski, K., Potter, J., & Gosling, S. D. (2001). Personality correlates of self-esteem. *Journal of Research in Personality, 35,* 463–482.

Robins, R. W., & Trzesniewski, K. H. (2005). Self-esteem development across the lifespan. *Current Directions in Psychological Science, 14,* 158–162.

Robinson, C. C., Anderson, G. T., Porter, C. L., Hart, C. H., & Wouden-Miller, M. (2003). Sequential transition patterns of preschoolers' social interactions during child-initiated play: Is parallel-aware play a bi-directional bridge to other play states? *Early Childhood Research Quarterly, 18,* 3–21.

Robinson, K. M. (2010). Policy issues in mental health among the elderly. *Nursing Clinics of North America, 45,* 627–634.

Robinson, S., Goddard, L., Dritschel, B., Wisley, M., & Howlin, P. (2009). Executive functions in children with autism spectrum disorders. *Brain and Cognition, 71,* 362–368.

Robles, T. F., & Carroll, J. E. (2011). Restorative biological processes and health. *Social and Personality Psychology Compass, 5,* 518–537.

Roca, A. Carcia-Esteve, L., Imaz, M. L., Torres, A., Hernández, S., & Botet, F. (2011). Obstetrical and neonatal outcomes after prenatal exposure to selective serotonin reuptake inhibitors: The relevance of dose. *Journal of Affective Disorders, 135,* 208–215.

Rochat, P. (1989). Object manipulation and exploration in 2- to 5-month-old infants. *Developmental Psychology, 25,* 871–884.

Rochat, P. (1998). Self-perception and action in infancy. *Experimental Brain Research, 123,* 102–109.

Rochat, P. (2001). *The infant's world.* Cambridge, MA: Harvard University Press.

Rochat, P. (2003). Five levels of self-awareness as they unfold early in life. *Consciousness and Cognition, 12,* 717–731.

Rochat, P., & Goubet, N. (1995). Development of sitting and reaching in 5- to 6-month-old infants. *Infant Behavior and Development, 18,* 53–68.

Rochat, P., & Hespos, S. J. (1997). Differential rooting responses by neonates: Evidence for an early sense of self. *Early Development and Parenting, 6,* 105–112.

Rochat, P., Querido, J. G., & Striano, T. (1999). Emerging sensitivity to the timing and structure of proto-conversation. *Developmental Psychology, 35,* 950–957.

Rochat, P., & Striano, T. (2002). Who's in the mirror? Self–other discrimination in specular images by four- and nine-month-old infants. *Infant and Child Development, 11,* 289–303.

Rochat, P., Striano, T., & Blatt, L. (2002). Differential effects of happy, neutral, and sad still-faces on 2-, 4-, and 6-month-old infants. *Infant and Child Development, 11,* 289–303.

Rodkin, P. C., Farmer, T. W., Pearl, R., & Van Acker, R. (2000). Heterogeneity of popular boys: Antisocial and prosocial configurations. *Developmental Psychology, 36,* 14–24.

Rodkin, P. C., Farmer, T. W., Pearl, R., & Van Acker, R. (2006). They're cool: Social status and peer group supports for aggressive boys and girls. *Social Development, 15,* 175–204.

Rodrigue, K. M., & Kennedy, K. M. (2011). The cognitive consequences of structural changes to the aging brain. In K. W. Schaie & S. L. Willis (Eds.), *Handbook of the psychology of aging* (7th ed., pp. 73–91). San Diego, CA: Academic Press.

Rodriguez, A., & Waldenström, U. (2008). Fetal origins of child non-right-handedness and mental health. *Child Psychology and Psychiatry, 49,* 967–976.

Rodríguez, B., & López, M. J. R. (2011). El "nido repleto": La resolución de conflictos familiares cuando los hijos mayores se quedan en el hogar. [The 'full nest': The resolution of family conflicts when older children remain in the home.] *Cultura y Educación, 23,* 89–104.

Roebers, C. M., & Schneider, W. (2001). Individual differences in children's eyewitness recall: The influence of intelligence and shyness. *Applied Developmental Science, 5,* 9–20.

Roelfsema, N. M., Hop, W. C., Boito, S. M., & Wladimiroff, J. W. (2004). Three-dimensional sonographic measurement of normal fetal brain volume during the second half of pregnancy. *American Journal of Obstetrics and Gynecology, 190,* 275–280.

Roeser, R. W., Eccles, J. S., & Freedman-Doan, C. (1999). Academic functioning and mental health in adolescence: Patterns, progressions, and routes from childhood. *Journal of Adolescent Research, 14,* 135–174.

Rogers, W. A., & Fisk, A. D. (2005). Aware home technology: Potential benefits for older adults. *Public Policy and Aging Report, 15*(4), 28–30.

Rogoff, B. (1998). Cognition as a collaborative process. In D. Kuhn & R. S. Siegler (Eds.), *Handbook of child psychology: Vol. 2. Cognition, perception, and language* (5th ed., pp. 679–744). New York: Wiley.

Rogoff, B. (2003). *The cultural nature of human development.* New York: Oxford University Press.

Rogoff, B., & Chavajay, P. (1995). What's become of research on the cultural basis of cognitive development? *American Psychologist, 50,* 859–877.

Rogoff, B., Malkin, C., & Gibride, K. (1984). Interaction with babies as guidance in development. In B. Rogoff & J. V. Wertsch (Eds.), *Children's learning in the "zone of proximal development" (New directions for child development,* No. 23, pp. 31–44). San Francisco: Jossey-Bass.

Rogoff, B., Paradise, R., Arauz, R. M., Correa-Chávez, M., & Angelillo, C. (2003). Firsthand learning through intent participation. *Annual Review of Psychology, 54,* 175–203.

Rogoff, B., & Waddell, K. J. (1982). Memory for information organized in a scene by children from two cultures. *Child Development, 53,* 1224–1228.

Rogol, A. D., Roemmich, J. N., & Clark, P. A. (2002). Growth at puberty. *Journal of Adolescent Health, 31,* 192–200.

Rohner, R. P., & Veneziano, R. A. (2001). The importance of father love: History and contemporary evidence. *Review of General Psychology, 5,* 382–405.

Roid, G. (2003). *The Stanford-Binet Intelligence Scales, Fifth Edition, interpretive manual.* Itasca, IL: Riverside Publishing.

Roisman, G. I., & Fraley, R. C. (2008). Behavior-genetic study of parenting quality, infant-attachment security, and their covariation in a nationally representative sample. *Developmental Psychology, 44,* 831–839.

Roisman, G. I., Madsen, S. D., Hennighausen, K. H., Sroufe, L. A., & Collins, W. A. (2001). The coherence of dyadic behavior across parent–child and romantic relationships as mediated by the internalized representation of experience. *Attachment and Human Development, 3,* 156–172.

Roisman, G. I., Padron, E., Sroufe, L. A., & Egeland, B. (2002). Earned-secure attachment status in retrospect and prospect. *Child Development, 73,* 1204–1219.

Rokach, A. (2001). Perceived causes of loneliness in adulthood. *Journal of Social Behavior and Personality, 15,* 67–84.

Rokach, A. (2003). Strategies of coping with loneliness throughout the lifespan. In N. J. Pallone (Ed.), *Love, romance, sexual interaction: Research perspectives from current psychology* (pp. 225–344). New Brunswick, NJ: Transaction.

Rokach, A., & Neto, F. (2006). Age, culture, and coping with loneliness. *Psychology and Education, 43,* 1–21.

Rokach, R., Cohen, O., & Dreman, S. (2004). Who pulls the trigger? Who initiates divorce among over 45-year-olds. *Journal of Divorce and Remarriage, 42,* 61–83.

Romano, E., Babchishin, L., Pagani, L. S., & Kohen, D. (2010). School readiness and later achievement: Replication and exgtension using a nationwide Canadian survey. *Developmental Psychology, 46,* 995–1007.

Rome-Flanders, T., & Cronk, C. (1995). A longitudinal study of infant vocalizations during mother–infant games. *Journal of Child Language, 22,* 259–274.

Romero, A. J., & Roberts, R. E. (2003). The impact of multiple dimensions of ethnic identity on discrimination and adolescents' self-esteem. *Journal of Applied Social Psychology, 33,* 2288–2305.

Rönnqvist, L., & Domellöf, E. (2006). Quantitative assessment of right and left reaching movements in infants: A longitudinal study from 6 to 36 months. *Developmental Psychobiology, 48,* 444–459.

Roopnarine, J. L., & Evans, M. E. (2007). Family structural organization, mother–child and father–child relationships and psychological outcomes in English-speaking African Caribbean and Indo Caribbean families. In M. Sutherland (Ed.), *Psychological of development in the Caribbean.* Kingston, Jamaica: Ian Randle.

Roopnarine, J. L., Hossain, Z., Gill, P., & Brophy, H. (1994). Play in the East Indian context. In J. L. Roopnarine, J. E. Johnson, & F. H. Hooper (Eds.), *Children's play in diverse cultures* (pp. 9–30). Albany: State University of New York Press.

Roopnarine, J. L., Krishnakumar, A., Metindogan, A., & Evans, M. (2006). Links between parenting styles, parent–child academic interaction, parent–school interaction, and early academic skills and social behaviors in young children of English-speaking Caribbean immigrants. *Early Childhood Research Quarterly, 21,* 238–252.

Roopnarine, J. L., Talukder, E., Jain, D., Joshi, P., & Srivastav, P. (1990). Characteristics of holding, patterns of play, and social behaviors between parents and infants in New Delhi, India. *Developmental Psychology, 26,* 667–673.

Rosander, K., & von Hofsten, C. (2002). Development of gaze tracking of small and large objects. *Experimental Brain Research, 146,* 257–264.

Rosander, K., & von Hofsten, C. (2004). Infants' emerging ability to represent occluded object motion. *Cognition, 91,* 1–22.

Rose, A. J., Carlson, W., & Waller, E. M. (2007). Prospective associations of co-rumination with friendship and emotional adjustment: Considering the socioemotional trade-offs of corumination. *Developmental Psychology, 43,* 1019–1031.

Rose, A. J., Swenson, L. P., & Waller, E. M. (2004). Overt and relational aggression and perceived popularity: Developmental differences in concurrent and prospective relations. *Developmental Psychology, 40,* 378–387.

Rose, S. A., Feldman, J. F., & Jankowski, J. J. (2001). Attention and recognition memory in the 1st year of life: A longitudinal study of preterm and full-term infants. *Developmental Psychology, 37,* 135–151.

Rose, S. A., Jankowski, J. J., & Senior, G. J. (1997). Infants' recognition of contour-deleted figures. *Journal of Experimental Psychology: Human Perception and Performance, 23,* 1206–1216.

Rosen, A. B., & Rozin, P. (1993). Now you see it, now you don't: The preschool child's conception of invisible particles in the context of dissolving. *Developmental Psychology, 29,* 300–311.

Rosen, C. S., & Cohen, M. (2010). Subgroups of New York City children at high risk of PTSD after the September 11 attacks: A signal detection analysis. *Psychiatric Services, 61,* 64–69.

Rosen, D. (2003). Eating disorders in children and young adolescents: Etiology, classification, clinical features, and treatment. *Adolescent Medicine: State of the Art Reviews, 14,* 49–59.

Rosen, S., Bergman, M., & Plester, D. (1962). Presbycusis study of a relatively noise-free population in the Sudan. *Transactions of the American Otological Society, 50,* 135–152.

Rosenbaum, J. E. (2009). Patient teenagers? A comparison of the sexual behavior of virginity pledgers and matched nonpledgers. *Pediatrics, 123,* e110–e120.

Rosenblatt, P. C. (2008). Grief across cultures: A review and research agenda. In M. S. Stroebe, R. O. Hansson, H. Schut, & W. Stroebe (Eds.), *Handbook of bereavement research and practice* (pp. 207–222). Washington, DC: American Psychological Association.

Rosengren, K. S., & Hickling, A. K. (2000). The development of children's thinking about possible events and plausible mechanisms. In K. S. Rosengren, C. N. Johnson, & P. L. Harris (Eds.), *Imagining the impossible* (pp. 75–98). Cambridge, UK: Cambridge University Press.

Rosenman, R. H., Brand, R. J., Jenkins, C. D., Friedman, M., Strauss, R., & Wurm, M. (1975). Coronary heart disease in the Western Collaborative Group Study: Final follow-up experience of 8½ years. *Journal of the American Medical Association, 223,* 872–877.

Rosenstein, D. L. (2011). Depression and end-of-life care for patients with cancer. *Dialogues in Clinical Neuroscience, 13,* 101–108.

Roseth, C. J., Pellegrini, A. D., Bohn, C. M., van Ryzin, M., & Vance, N. (2007). Preschoolers' aggression, affiliation, and social dominance relationships: An observational, longitudinal study. *Journal of School Psychology, 45,* 479–497.

Rosetta, L., & Baldi, A. (2008). On the role of breastfeeding in health promotion and the prevention of allergic diseases. *Advances in Experimental Medicine and Biology, 606,* 467–483.

Ross, C. E., & Sastry, J. (1999). The sense of personal control: Social-structural causes and emotional consequences. In C. S. Aneshensel & J. C. Phelan (Eds.), *Handbook of the sociology of mental health* (pp. 369–394). New York: Springer.

Rossen, E. K., Knafl, K. A., & Flood, M. (2008). Older women's perceptions of successful aging. *Activities, Adaptation and Aging, 32,* 73–88.

Rossi, A. S. (2001). (Ed.). *Caring and doing for others: Social responsibility in the domains of family, work, and community.* Chicago: University of Chicago Press.

Rossi, A. S. (2004). Social responsibility to family and community. In O. G. Brim, C. D. Ryff, & R. C. Kessler (Eds.), *How healthy are we? A national study of well-being at midlife* (pp. 550–585). Chicago: University of Chicago Press.

Rossi, A. S. (2005). The menopausal transition and aging processes. In O. G. Brim, C. D. Ryff, & R. C. Kessler (Eds.), *How healthy are we? A national study of well-being at midlife* (pp. 153–201). Chicago: University of Chicago Press.

Rostosky, S. S., Danner, F., & Riggle, E. (2007). Is religiosity a protective factor against substance use in young adulthood? Only if you're straight! *Journal of Adolescent Health, 40,* 440–447.

Rothbart, M. K. (2003). Temperament and the pursuit of an integrated developmental psychology. *Merrill-Palmer Quarterly, 50,* 492–505.

Rothbart, M. K., Ahadi, S. A., & Evans, D. E. (2000). Temperament and personality: Origins and outcome. *Journal of Personality and Social Psychology, 78,* 122–135.

Rothbart, M. K., & Bates, J. E. (2006). Temperament. In N. Eisenberg (Ed.), *Handbook of child psychology: Vol. 3. Social, emotional, and personality development* (6th ed., pp. 99–166). Hoboken, NJ: Wiley.

Rothbart, M. K., & Mauro, J. A. (1990). Questionnaire approaches to the study of infant temperament. In J. W. Fagen & J. Colombo (Eds.), *Individual differences in infancy: Reliability, stability and prediction* (pp. 411–429). Hillsdale, NJ: Erlbaum.

Rothbart, M. K., Posner, M. I., & Kieras, J. (2006). Temperament, attention, and the development of self-regulation. In K. McCartney & D. Phillips (Eds.), *Blackwell handbook of early childhood development* (pp. 338–357). Malden, MA: Blackwell.

Rothbaum, F., Kakinuma, M., Nagaoka, R., & Azuma, H. (2007). Attachment and amae: Parent–child closeness in the United States and Japan. *Journal of Cross-Cultural Psychology, 38,* 465–486.

Rothbaum, F., Pott, M., Azuma, H., Miyake, K., & Weisz, J. (2000a). The development of close relationships in Japan and the United States: Paths of symbiotic harmony and generative tension. *Child Development, 71,* 1121–1142.

Rothblum, E. D., Balsam, K. F., & Solomon, S. E. (2011). The longest "legal" U.S. same-sex couples reflect on their relationships. *Journal of Social Issues, 67,* 302–315.

Rothman, S. M., & Mattson, M. P. (2012). Sleep disturbances in Alzheimer's and Parkinson's diseases. *Neuromolecular Medicine, 14,* 194–204.

Rouselle, L., Palmers, E., & Noël, M.-P. (2004). Magnitude comparison in preschoolers: What counts? Influence of perceptual variables. *Journal of Experimental Child Psychology, 87,* 57–84.

Rousseau, P. (2000). Death denial. *Journal of Clinical Oncology, 18,* 3998–3999.

Routledge, C., & Juhl, J. (2010). When death thoughts lead to death fears: Mortality salience increases death anxiety for individuals who lack meaning in life. *Cognition and Emotion, 24,* 848–854.

Rovee-Collier, C. K. (1999). The development of infant memory. *Current Directions in Psychological Science, 8,* 80–85.

Rovee-Collier, C. K., & Barr, R. (2001). Infant learning and memory. In G. Bremner & A. Fogel (Eds.), *Blackwell handbook of infant development* (pp. 139–168). Oxford, UK: Blackwell.

Rovee-Collier, C. K., & Bhatt, R. S. (1993). Evidence of long-term memory in infancy. *Annals of Child Development, 9,* 1–45.

Rovee-Collier, C. K., & Cuevas, K. (2009). Multiple memory systems are unnecessary to account for infant memory development: An ecological model. *Developmental Psychology, 45,* 160–174.

Rowe, C. C., Ng, S., Ackermann, U., Gong, S. J., Pike, K., & Savage, G. (2007). Hippocampal expression analyses reveal selective association of immediate-early, neuroenergetic, and myelinogenic pathways with cognitive impairment in aged rats. *Journal of Neuroscience, 27,* 3098–3110.

Rowe, M. L. (2008). Child-directed speech: Relation to socioeconomic status, knowledge of child development and child vocabulary skill. *Journal of Child Language, 35,* 185–205.

Rowe, M. L., & Goldin-Meadow, S. (2009). Early gesture selectively predicts later language learning. *Developmental Science, 12,* 182–187.

Rowland, C. F. (2007). Explaining errors in children's questions. *Cognition, 104,* 106–134.

Rowland, C. F., & Pine, J. M. (2000). Subject-auxiliary inversion errors and wh-question acquisition: "What children do know?" *Journal of Child Language, 27,* 157–181.

Rowley, S. J., Kurtz-Costes, B., Mistry, R., & Feagans, L. (2007). Social status as a predictor of race and gender stereotypes in late childhood and early adolescence. *Social Development, 16,* 150–168.

Roy, K. M., & Lucas, K. (2006). Generativity as second chance: Low-income fathers and transformation of the difficult past. *Research in Human Development, 3,* 139–159.

Rubenstein, L. Z., Stevens, J. A., & Scott, V. (2008). Interventions to prevent falls among older adults. In L. S. Doll, S. E. Bonzo, D. A. Sleet, J. A. Mercy, & E. N. Haas (Eds.), *Handbook of injury and violence prevention* (pp. 37–53). New York: Springer.

Rubin, C., Maisonet, M., Kieszak, S., Monteilh, C., Holmes A., Flanders, D., et al. (2009). Timing of maturation and predictors of menarche in girls enrolled in a contemporary British cohort. *Paediatric and Perinatal Epidemiology, 23,* 492–504.

Rubin, D., Downes, B., O'Reilly, A., Mekonnen, R., Luan, X., & Localio, R. (2008). Impact of kinship care on behavioral well-being for children in out of home care. *Archives of Pediatrics and Adolescent Medicine, 162,* 550–556.

Rubin, D. C. (2002). Autobiographical memory across the lifespan. In P. Graf & N. Ohta (Eds.), *Lifespan development of human memory* (pp. 159–184). Cambridge, MA: MIT Press.

Rubin, D. C., Rahhal, T. A., & Poon, L. W. (1998). Things learned in early adulthood are remembered best. *Memory and Cognition, 26,* 3–19.

Rubin, D. M., O'Reilly, A. L., Luan, X., Dai, D., Localio, A. R., et al. (2011). Variation in pregnancy outcomes following statewide implementation of a prenatal home visitation program. *Archives of Pediatrics and Adolescent Medicine, 165,* 198–204.

Rubin, K. H., Bowker, J., & Gazelle, H. (2010). Social withdrawal in childhood and adolescence: Peer relationships and social competence. In K. H. Rubin & R. J. Coplan (Eds.), *The development of shyness and social withdrawal* (pp. 131–156). New York: Guilford.

Rubin, K. H., Bukowski, W. M., & Parker, J. G. (2006). Peer interactions, relationships, and groups. In N. Eisenberg (Ed.), *Handbook of child psychology: Vol. 3. Social, emotional, and personality development* (6th ed., pp. 571–645). Hoboken, NJ: Wiley.

Rubin, K. H., & Burgess, K. B. (2002). Parents of aggressive and withdrawn children. In M. Bornstein (Ed.), *Handbook of parenting* (2nd ed., pp. 383–418). Hillsdale, NJ: Erlbaum.

Rubin, K. H., Burgess, K. B., & Coplan, R. (2002). Social withdrawal and shyness. In P. K. Smith & C. H. Hart (Eds.), *Blackwell handbook of child social development* (pp. 329–352). Oxford, UK: Blackwell.

Rubin, K. H., Coplan, J., Chen, X., Buskirk, A. A., & Wojslawowicz, J. C. (2005). Peer relationships in childhood. In M. H. Bornstein & M. E. Lamb (Eds.), *Developmental science: An advanced textbook* (pp. 469–512). Mahwah, NJ: Erlbaum.

Rubin, K. H., Fein, G. G., & Vandenberg, B. (1983). Play. In E. M. Hetherington (Ed.), *Handbook of child psychology: Vol. 4. Socialization, personality, and social development* (4th ed., pp. 693–744). New York: Wiley.

Rubin, K. H., Watson, K. S., & Jambor, T. W. (1978). Free-play behaviors in preschool and kindergarten children. *Child Development, 49,* 539–536.

Rubin, S. E., & Wooten, H. R. (2007). Highly educated stay-at-home mothers: A study of commitment and conflict. *Counseling and Therapy for Couples and Families, 15,* 336–345.

Ruble, D. N., Alvarez, J., Bachman, M., Cameron, J., Fuligni, A., García Coll, C., & Rhee, E. (2004). The development of a sense of "we": The emergence and implications of children's collective identity. In M. Bennett & F. Sani (Eds.), *The development of the social self* (pp. 29–76). Hove, UK: Psychology Press.

Ruble, D. N., Martin, C. L., & Berenbaum, S. A. (2006). Gender development. In N. Eisenberg (Ed.), *Handbook of child psychology: Vol. 3. Social, emotional, and personality development* (6th ed., pp. 226–299). Hoboken, NJ: Wiley.

Ruble, D. N., Taylor, L. J., Cyphers, L., Greulich, F. K., Lurye, L. E., & Shrout, P. E. (2007). The role of gender constancy in early gender development. *Child Development, 78,* 1121–1136.

Rudolph, K. D., Caldwell, M. S., & Conley, C. S. (2005). Need for approval and children's well-being. *Child Development, 76,* 309–323.

Rudolph, K. D., Lambert, S. F., Clark, A. G., & Kurlakowsky, K. D. (2001). Negotiating the transition to middle school: The role of self-regulatory processes. *Child Development, 72,* 929–946.

Ruff, H. A., & Capozzoli, M. C. (2003). Development of attention and distractibility in the first 4 years of life. *Developmental Psychology, 39,* 877–890.

Ruffman, T., & Langman, L. (2002). Infants' reaching in a multi-well A not B task. *Infant Behavior and Development, 25,* 237–246.

Ruffman, T., Perner, J., Olson, D. R., & Doherty, M. (1993). Reflecting on scientific thinking: Children's understanding of the hypothesis– evidence relation. *Child Development, 64,* 1617–1636.

Ruffman, T., Slade, L., Devitt, K., & Crowe, E. (2006). What mothers say and what they do: The relation between parenting, theory of mind, language, and conflict/cooperation. *British Journal of Developmental Psychology, 24,* 105–124.

Ruitenberg, A., Ott, A., van Swieten, J. C., Hofman, A., & Breteler, M. M. B. (2001). Incidence of dementia: Does gender make a difference? *Neurobiology of Aging, 22,* 575–580.

Ruiz, J. R., Morán, M., Arenas, J., & Lucia, A. (2011). Strenuous endurance exercise improves life expectancy: It's in our genes. *British Journal of Sports Medicine, 45,* 159–161.

Runco, M. A. (1992). Children's divergent thinking and creative ideation. *Developmental Review, 12,* 233–264.

Runco, M. A., Cramond, B., & Pagnani, A. R. (2010). Gender and creativity. In J. C. Chrisler & D. R. McCreary (Eds.), *Handbook of gender research in psychology* (Vol. 1, pp. 343–357). New York: Springer.

Rurup, M. L., Muller, M. T., Onwuteaka-Philipsen, B. D., van der Heide, A., van der Wal, G., & van der Maas, P. J. (2005). Requests for euthanasia or physician-assisted suicide from older persons who do not have a severe disease: An interview study. *Psychological Medicine, 35,* 665–671.

Rusconi, A. (2004). Different pathways out of the parental home: A comparison of West Germany and Italy. *Journal of Comparative Family Studies, 35,* 627–649.

Rushton, J. L., Forcier, M., & Schectman, R. M. (2002). Epidemiology of depressive symptoms in the National Longitudinal Study of Adolescent Health. *Journal of the American Academy of Child and Adolescent Psychiatry, 41,* 199–205.

Rushton, J. P., & Bons, T. A. (2005). Mate choice and friendship in twins. *Psychological Science, 16,* 555–559.

Rushton, J. P., & Jensen, A. R. (2005). Thirty years of research on race differences in cognitive ability. *Psychology, Public Policy, and Law, 11,* 235–294.

Rushton, J. P., & Jensen, A. R. (2006). The totality of available evidence shows the race IQ gap still remains. *Psychological Science, 17,* 921–924.

Rushton, J. P., & Jensen, A. R. (2010). The rise and fall of the Flynn effect as a reason to expect a narrowing of the black–white IQ gap. *Intelligence, 38,* 213–219.

Russac, R. J., Gatliff, C., Reece, M., & Spottswood, D. (2007). Death anxiety across the adult years: An examination of age and gender effects. *Death Studies, 31,* 549–561.

Russell, A., Mize, J., & Bissaker, K. (2004). Parent–child relationships. In P. K. Smith & C. H. Hart (Eds.), *Blackwell handbook of childhood social development* (pp. 204–222). Malden, MA: Blackwell.

Russell, J. A. (1990). The preschooler's understanding of the causes and consequences of emotion. *Child Development, 61,* 1872–1881.

Russell, J. A., Douglas, A. J., & Ingram, C. D. (2001). Brain preparations for maternity—adaptive changes in behavioral and neuroendocrine systems during pregnancy and lactation. *Progress in Brain Research, 133,* 1–38.

Russell, R. B., Petrini, J. R., Damus, K., Mattison, D. R., & Schwarz, R. H. (2003). The changing epidemiology of multiple births in the United States. *Obstetrics and Gynecology, 101,* 129–135.

Russell, S. T., Elder, G. H., & Conger, R. D. (1997). *School transitions and academic achievement.* Paper presented at the annual meeting of the American Sociological Association, Toronto, Canada.

Rutland, A., Killen, M., & Abrams, D. (2010). A new social-cognitive developmental perspective on prejudice: The interplay between morality and group identity. *Perspectives on Psychological Science, 5,* 279–291.

Rutter, M. (2007). Gene–environment interdependence. *Developmental Science, 10,* 12–18.

Rutter, M. (2011). Biological and experiential influences on psychological development. In D. P. Keating (Ed.), *Nature and nurture in early child development* (pp. 7–44). New York: Cambridge University Press.

Rutter, M., Colvert, E., Kreppner, J., Beckett, C., Castle, J., & Groothues, C. (2007). Early adolescent outcomes for institutionally deprived and nondeprived adoptees. I: Disinhibited attachment. *Journal of Child Psychology and Psychiatry, 48,* 17–30.

Rutter, M., & the English and Romanian Adoptees Study Team. (1998). Developmental catch-up, and deficit, following adoption after severe global early privation. *Journal of Child Psychology and Psychiatry, 39,* 465–476.

Rutter, M., O'Connor, T. G., & English and Romanian Adoptees (ERA) Study Team. (2004). Are there biological programming effects for psychological development? Findings from a study of Romanian adoptees. *Developmental Psychology, 40,* 81–94.

Rutter, M., Pickles, A., Murray, R., & Eaves, L. (2001). Testing hypotheses on specific environmental causal effects on behavior. *Psychological Bulletin, 127,* 291–324.

Rutter, M., Sonuga-Barke, E. J, Beckett, C., Castle, J., Kreppner, J., Kumsta, R., et al. (2010). Deprivation-specific psychological patterns: Effects of institutional deprivation. *Monographs of the Society for Research in Child Development, 75*(1, Serial No. 295), 48–78.

Ryan, E. B., Jin, Y., Anas, A. P., & Luh, J. J. (2004). Communication beliefs about youth and old age in Asia and Canada. *Journal of Cross-Cultural Gerontology, 19,* 343–360.

Ryan, R. M., Fauth, R. C., & Brooks-Gunn, J. (2006). Childhood poverty: Implications for school readiness and early childhood education In B. Spodek & O. N. Saracho (Eds.), *Handbook of research on the education of young children* (2nd ed., pp. 323–346). Mahwah, NJ: Erlbaum.

Rybash, J. M., & Hrubi-Bopp, K. L. (2000). Isolating the neural mechanisms of age-related changes in human working memory. *Nature Neuroscience, 3,* 509–515.

Ryding, M., Konradsson, K., Kalm, O., & Prellner, K. (2002). Auditory consequences of recurrent acute purulent otitis media. *Annals of Otology, Rhinology, and Laryngology, 111*(3, Pt. 1), 261–266.

Ryff, C. D. (1991). Possible selves in adulthood and old age: A tale of shifting horizons. *Psychology and Aging, 6,* 286–295.

Ryff, C. D., Friedman, E., Fuller-Rowell, T., Love, G., Miyamoto, Y., Morozink, J., et al. (2012). Varieties of resilience in MIDUS. *Social and Personality Psychology Compass, 6,* 792–806.

Ryff, C. D., & Keyes, C. L. M. (1995). The structure of psychological well-being revisited. *Journal of Personality and Social Psychology, 69,* 719–727.

Ryff, C. D., & Singer, B. H. (2002). From social structure to biology. In S. J. L. C. R. Snyder (Ed.), *Handbook of positive psychology* (pp. 541–555). Oxford: Oxford University Press.

Ryff, C. D., Singer, B. H., & Seltzer, M. M. (2002). Pathways through challenge: Implications for well-being and health. In L. Pulkkinen & A. Caspi (Eds.), *Paths to successful development* (pp. 302–328). Cambridge, UK: Cambridge University Press.

Rynearson, E. K., & Salloum, A. (2011). Restorative retelling: Revising the narrative of violent death. In R. A. Neimeyer, D. L. Harris, H. R. Winokuer, & G. F. Thornton (Eds.), *Grief and bereavement in contemporary society: Bridging research and practice* (pp. 177–188). New York: Routledge.

S

Saarni, C. (1999). *The development of emotional competence.* New York: Guilford.

Saarni, C. (2000). Emotional competence: A developmental perspective. In R. Bar-On & J. D. A. Parker (Eds.), *Handbook of emotional intelligence* (pp. 68–91). San Francisco: Jossey-Bass.

Saarni, C., Campos, J. J., Camras, L. A., & Witherington, D. (2006). Emotional development: Action, communication, and understanding. In N. Eisenberg (Ed.), *Handbook of child psychology: Vol. 3. Social, emotional, and personality development* (6th ed., pp. 226–299). Hoboken, NJ: Wiley.

Sabo, D. and Veliz, P. (2011). *Progress without equity: The provision of high school athletic opportunity in the United States, by gender 1993–94 through 2005–06.* East Meadow, NY: Women's Sports Foundation.

Sacca, S. C., Bolognesi, C., Battistella, A., Bagnis, A., & Izzotti, A. (2009). Gene–environment interactions in ocular diseases. *Mutation Research, 667,* 98–117.

Sacks, P. (2005). "No child left": What are schools for in a democratic society? In S. Olfman (Ed.), *Childhood lost: How American culture is failing our kids* (pp. 185–202). Westport, CT: Praeger.

Sadeh, A. (1997). Sleep and melatonin in infants: A preliminary study. *Sleep, 20,* 185–191.

Sadeh, A., Flint-Ofir, E., Tirosh, T., & Tikotzky, L. (2007). Infant sleep and parental sleep-related cognitions. *Journal of Family Psychology, 21,* 74–87.

Sadler, P., Ethier, N., & Woody, E. (2011). Interpersonal complementarity. In L. M. Horowitz & S. Strack (Eds.), *Handbook of interpersonal psychology* (pp. 123–156). Hoboken, NJ: Wiley.

Sadler, T. W. (2010). *Langman's medical embryology* (11th ed.). Baltimore, MD: Lippincott Williams & Wilkins.

Safe Kids USA. (2008). *Report to the nation: Trends in unintentional childhood injury mortality and parental views on child safety.* Retrieved from www.safekids.org/assets/docs/ourwork/research/research-report-safe-kids-week-2008.pdf

Safe Kids USA. (2011a). *A look inside American family vehicles: National study of 79,000 car seats, 2009–2010.* Retrieved from www.safekids.org/assets/docs/safety-basics/safety-tips-by-risk-area/sk-car-seat-report-2011.pdf

Safe Kids USA. (2011b). *Injury trends fact sheet.* Retrieved from www.safekids.org/our-work/research/fact-sheets/injury-trends-fact-sheet.html

Saffran, J. R. (2009). Acquiring grammatical patterns: Constraints on learning. In J. Colombo, P. McCardle, & L. Freund (Eds.), *Infant pathways to language: Methods, models, and research disorders* (pp. 31–47). New York: Psychology Press.

Saffran, J. R., Aslin, R. N., & Newport, E. L. (1996). Statistical learning by 8-month-old infants. *Science, 27,* 1926–1928.

Saffran, J. R., & Thiessen, E. D. (2003). Pattern induction by infant language learners. *Developmental Psychology, 39,* 484–494.

Saffran, J. R., Werker, J. F., & Werner, L. A. (2006). The infant's auditory world: Hearing, speech, and the beginnings of language. In D. Kuhn & R. Siegler (Eds.), *Handbook of child psychology: Vol. 2. Cognition, perception, and language* (6th ed., pp. 58–108). Hoboken, NJ: Wiley.

Safren, S. A., & Pantalone, D. W. (2006). Social anxiety and barriers to resilience among lesbian, gay, and bisexual adolescents. In A. M. Omoto & H. S. Kurtzman (Eds.), *Sexual orientation and mental health: Examining identity and development in lesbian, gay, and bisexual young people* (pp. 55–71). Washington, DC: American Psychological Association.

Saginak, K. A., & Saginak, M. A. (2005). Balancing work and family: Equity, gender, and marital satisfaction. *Counseling and Therapy for Couples and Families, 13,* 162–166.

Sahathevan, R., Brodtmann, A., & Donnan, G. (2011). Dementia, stroke, and vascular risk factors: A review. *International Journal of Stroke, 7,* 61–73.

Sahlberg, P. (2010). Educational change in Finland. In A. Hargreaves, M. Fullan, A. Lieberman, & D. Hopkins (Eds.), *Second international handbook of educational change.* New York: Springer.

Saito, Y., Auestad, R. A., & Waerness, K. (2010). *Meeting the challenges of elder care: Japan and Norway.* Kyoto, Japan: Kyoto University Press.

Sakraida, T. J. (2005). Divorce transition differences of midlife women. *Issues in Mental Health Nursing, 26,* 225–249.

Salari, S. (2011). Elder mistreatment. In R. A. Settersten, Jr., & J. L. Angel (Eds.), *Handbook of sociology of aging* (pp. 415–430). New York: Springer.

Sale, A., Berardi, N., & Maffei, L. (2009). Enrich the environment to empower the brain. *Trends in Neurosciences, 32,* 233–239.

Salerno, M., Micillo, M., Di Maio, S., Capalbo, D., Ferri, P., & Lettiero, T. (2001). Longitudinal growth, sexual maturation and final height in patients with congenital hypothyroidism detected by neonatal screening. *European Journal of Endocrinology, 145,* 377–383.

Salihu, H. M., Shumpert, M. N., Slay, M., Kirby, R. S., & Alexander, G. R. (2003). Childbearing beyond maternal age 50 and fetal outcomes in the United States. *Obstetrics and Gynecology, 102,* 1006–1014.

Salisbury, A. L., Ponder, K. L., Padbury, J. F., & Lester, B. M. (2009). Fetal effects of psychoactive drugs. *Clinics in Perinatology, 36,* 595–619.

Salley, B. J., & Dixon, W. E., Jr. (2007). Temperamental and joint attentional predictors of language development. *Merrill-Palmer Quarterly, 53,* 131–154.

Salmivalli, C., & Voeten, M. (2004). Connections between attitudes, group norms, and behaviour in bullying situations. *International Journal of Behavioral Development, 28,* 246–258.

Salomon, J. A., Wang, H., Freeman, M. K., Vos, T., Flaxman, A. D., Lopez, A. D., et al. (2012). Healthy life expectancy for 187 countries, 1990–2010: A systematic analysis for the Global Burden Disease Study 2010. *Lancet, 380,* 2144–2162.

Salovey, P., & Pizarro, D. A. (2003). The value of emotional intelligence. In R. J. Sternberg, J.

Lautrey, & T. I. Lubart (Eds.), *Models of intelligence: International perspectives* (pp. 263–278). Washington, DC: American Psychological Association.

Salter, D., McMillan, D., Richards, M., Talbot, T., Hodges, J., Bentovim, A., & Hastings, R. (2003). Development of sexually abusive behavior in sexually victimized males: A longitudinal study. *Lancet, 361,* 471–476.

Salthouse, T. A. (1984). Effects of age and skill in typing. *Journal of Experimental Psychology: General, 113,* 345–371.

Salthouse, T. A. (1996). Constraints on theories of cognitive aging. *Psychonomic Bulletin and Review, 3,* 287–299.

Salthouse, T. A. (2006). Aging of thought. In E. Bialystok & F. I. M. Craik (Eds.), *Lifespan cognition: Mechanisms of change* (pp. 274–284). New York: Oxford University Press.

Salthouse, T. A. (2011). Neuroanatomical substrates of age-related cognitive decline. *Psychological Bulletin, 137,* 753–784.

Salthouse, T. A., & Caja, S. J. (2000). Structural constraints on process explanations in cognitive aging. *Psychology and Aging, 15,* 44–55.

Salvioli, S., Capri, M., Santoro, A., Raule, N., Sevini, F., & Lukas, S. (2008). The impact of mitochondrial DNA on human lifespan: A view from studies on centenarians. *Biotechnology Journal, 3,* 740–749.

Samarel, N. (1991). *Caring for life and death.* Washington, DC: Hemisphere.

Samarel, N. (1995). The dying process. In H. Wass & R. A. Neimeyer (Eds.), *Dying: Facing the facts* (3rd ed., pp. 89–116). Washington, DC: Taylor & Francis.

Samek, D. R., & Rueter, M. A. (2011). Considerations of elder sibling closeness in predicting younger sibling substance use: Social learning versus social bonding explanations. *Journal of Family Psychology, 25,* 931–941.

Sameroff, A. (2006). Identifying risk and protective factors for healthy child development. In A. Clarke-Stewart & J. Dunn (Eds.), *Families count: Effects on child and adolescent development* (pp. 53–76). New York: Cambridge University Press.

Sampselle, C. M., Harris, V., Harlow, S. D., & Sowers, M. (2002). Midlife development and menopause in African-American and Caucasian women. *Health Care for Women International, 23,* 351–363.

Samuolis, J., Griffin, K. W., Williams, C., Cesario, B., & Botvin, G. J. (2011). Work intensity and substance use among adolescents employed part-time in entry-level jobs. *International Journal of Child and Adolescent Health, 4,* 67–73.

Sanchez, M. M., & Pollak, S. D. (2009). Socioemotional development following early abuse and neglect: Challenges and insight from translational research. In M. de Haan & M. R. Gunnar (Eds.), *Handbook of developmental social neuroscience* (pp. 497–520). New York: Guilford.

Sanders, O. (2006). *Evaluating the Keeping Ourselves Safe Programme.* Wellington, NZ: Youth Education Service, New Zealand Police. Retrieved from www.nzfvc.org.nz/accan/papers-presentations/abstract11v.shtml

Sanderson, C. A., Rahm, K. B., & Beigbeder, S. A. (2005). The link between the pursuit of intimacy goals and satisfaction in close same-sex friendships: An examination of the underlying processes. *Journal of Social and Personal Relationships, 22,* 75–98.

Sanderson, J. A., & Siegal, M. (1988). Conceptions of moral and social rules in rejected and nonrejected preschoolers. *Journal of Clinical Child Psychology, 17,* 66–72.

Sandler, J. C. (2006). Alternative methods of child testimony: A review of law and research. In C. R. Bartol & A. M. Bartol (Eds.), *Current perspectives in forensic psychology and criminal justice* (pp. 203–212). Thousand Oaks, CA: Sage.

Sandnabba, N. K., & Ahlberg, C. (1999). Parents' attitudes and expectations about children's crossgender behavior. *Sex Roles, 40*, 249–263.

Sandström, A., Rhodin, N., Lundberg, M., Olsson, T., & Nyberg, L. (2005). Impaired cognitive performance in patients with chronic burnout syndrome. *Biological Psychology, 69*, 271–279.

Sangrigoli, S., Pallier, C., Argenti, A. M., Ventureyra, V. A. G., & de Schonen, S. (2005). Reversibility of the other-race effect in face recognition during childhood. *Psychological Science, 16*, 440–444.

San Juan, V., & Astington, J. W. (2012). Bridging the gap between implicit and explicit understanding: How language development promotes the processing and representation of false belief. *British Journal of Developmental Psychology, 30*, 105–122.

Sann, C., & Streri, A. (2007). Perception of object shape and texture in human newborns: Evidence from cross-modal transfer tasks. *Developmental Science, 10*, 399–410.

Sann, C., & Streri, A. (2008). The limits of newborn's grasping to detect texture in a cross-modal transfer task. *Infant Behavior and Development, 31*, 523–531.

Sansavini, A., Bertoncini, J., & Giovanelli, G. (1997). Newborns discriminate the rhythm of multisyllabic stressed words. *Developmental Psychology, 33*, 3–11.

Santoloupo, S., & Pratt, M. (1994). Age, gender, and parenting style variations in mother–adolescent dialogues and adolescent reasoning about political issues. *Journal of Adolescent Research, 9*, 241–261.

Santtila, P., Wager, I., Witting, K., Harlaar, N., Jern, P., Johansson, A., Varjonen, M., & Sandnabba, K. (2008). Discrepancies between sexual desire and sexual activity: Gender differences and associations with relationship satisfaction. *Journal of Sex and Marital Therapy, 34*, 31–44.

Sanz, A., Pamplona, R., & Barja, G. (2006). Is the mitochondrial free radical theory of aging intact? *Antioxidants and Redox Signaling, 8*, 582–599.

Sarason, S. B. (1977). *Work, aging, and social change.* New York: Free Press.

Sarnecka, B. W., & Gelman, S. A. (2004). Six does not just mean a lot: Preschoolers see number words as specific. *Cognition, 92*, 329–352.

Sasser-Coen, J. A. (1993). Qualitative changes in creativity in the second half of life: A life-span developmental perspective. *Journal of Creative Behavior, 27*, 18–27.

Satin, J. R., Linden, W., Phillips, M. J. (2009). Depression as a predictor of disease progression and mortality in cancer patients. *Cancer, 115*, 5349–5361.

Sato, T., Matsumoto, T., Kawano, H., Watanabe, T., Uematsu, Y., & Semine, K. (2004). Brain masculinization requires androgen receptor function. *Proceedings of the National Academy of Sciences, 101*, 1673–1678.

Saucier, J. F., Sylvestre, R., Doucet, H., Lambert, J., Frappier, J. Y., Charbonneau, L., & Malus, M. (2002). Cultural identity and adaptation to adolescence in Montreal. In F. J. C. Azima & N. Grizenko (Eds.), *Immigrant and refugee children and their families: Clinical, research, and training issues* (pp. 133–154). Madison, WI: International Universities Press.

Saudino, K. J. (2003). Parent ratings of infant temperament: Lessons from twin studies. *Infant Behavior and Development, 26*, 100–107.

Saudino, K. J., & Plomin, R. (1997). Cognitive and temperamental mediators of genetic contributions to the home environment during infancy. *Merrill-Palmer Quarterly, 43*, 1–23.

Saunders, B. E. (2012). Determining best practice for treating sexually victimized children. In P. Goodyear-Brown (Ed.), *Handbook of child sexual abuse: Identification, assessment, and treatment* (pp. 173–198). Hoboken, NJ: Wiley.

Sautter, J. M., Thomas, P. A., Dupre, M., & George, L. K. (2012). Socioeconomic status and the black–white mortality crossover. *American Journal of Public Health, 102*, 1566–1571.

Sautter, J. M., Tippett, R. M., & Morgan, S. P. (2010). The social demography of internet dating in the United States. *Social Science Quarterly, 91*, 554–575.

Savin-Williams, R. C. (2001). A critique of research on sexual minority youths. *Journal of Adolescence, 24*, 5–13.

Savin-Williams, R. C., & Diamond, L. M. (2004). Sex. In R. M. Lerner & L. Steinberg (Eds.), *Handbook of adolescent development* (2nd ed., pp. 189–231). Hoboken, NJ: Wiley.

Savin-Williams, R. C., & Ream, G. L. (2003). Sex variations in the disclosure to parents of same-sex attractions. *Journal of Family Psychology, 17*, 429–438.

Sawyer, A. M., & Borduin, C. M. (2011). Effects of multisystemic therapy through midlife: A 21.9-year follow-up to a randomized clinical trial with serious and violent juvenile offenders. *Journal of Consulting and Clinical Psychology, 79*, 643–652.

Saxe, G. B. (1988, August–September). Candy selling and math learning. *Educational Researcher, 17*(6), 14–21.

Saxton, M., Backley, P., & Gallaway, C. (2005). Negative input for grammatical errors: Effects after a lag of 12 weeks. *Journal of Child Language, 32*, 643–672.

Sayer, L. C. (2010). Trends in housework. In J. Treas & S. Drobnic (Eds.), *Dividing the domestic: Men, women, and household work in cross-national perspective* (pp. 19–38). Stanford, CA: Stanford University Press.

Saygin, A. P., Leech, R., & Dick, F. (2010). Nonverbal auditory agnosia with lesion to Wernicke's area. *Neuropsychologia, 48*, 107–113.

Saygin, A. P., Wilson, S. M., Dronkers, N. F., & Bates, E. (2004). Action comprehension in aphasia: Linguistic and non-linguistic deficits and their lesion correlates. *Neuropsychologia, 42*, 1788–1804.

Saylor, M. M. (2004). Twelve- and 16-month-old infants recognize properties of mentioned absent things. *Developmental Science, 7*, 599–611.

Saylor, M. M., Baldwin, D. A., & Sabbagh, M. A. (2005). Word learning: A complex product. In G. Hall & S. Waxman (Eds.), *Weaving a lexicon.* Cambridge, MA: MIT Press.

Saylor, M. M., & Troseth, G. L. (2006). Preschoolers use information about speakers' desires to learn new words. *Cognitive Development, 21*, 214–231.

Saywitz, K. J., Goodman, G. S., & Lyon, T. D. (2002). Interviewing children in and out of court: Current research and practice implications. In J. E. B. Myers & L. Berliner (Eds.), *The APSAC handbook on child maltreatment* (2nd ed., pp. 349–377). Thousand Oaks, CA: Sage.

Scarlett, W. G., & Warren, A. E. A. (2010). Religious and spiritual development across the life span: A behavioral and social science perspective. In M. Lamb & A. Freund (Eds.), *Handbook of life-span development: Vol. 2. Social and emotional development* (pp. 631–682). Hoboken, NJ: Wiley.

Scarmeas, N., Luchsinger, J. A., Mayeux, R., & Stern, Y. (2007). Mediterranean diet and Alzheimer disease mortality. *Neurology, 69*, 1084–1093.

Scarr, S., & McCartney, K. (1983). How people make their own environments: A theory of genotype environment effects. *Child Development, 54*, 424–435.

Scarr, S., & Weinberg, R. A. (1983). The Minnesota Adoption Studies: Genetic differences and malleability. *Child Development, 54*, 260–267.

Schaal, B., Marlier, L., & Soussignan, R. (2000). Human fetuses learn odours from their pregnant mother's diet. *Chemical Senses, 25*, 729–737.

Schacht, P. M., Cummings, E. M., & Davies, P. T. (2009). Fathering in family context and child adjustment: A longitudinal analysis. *Journal of Family Psychology, 23*, 790–797.

Schäfer, S., Huxhold, O., & Lindenberger, U. (2006). Healthy mind in healthy body? A review of sensorimotor–cognitive interdependencies in old age. *European Review of Aging and Physical Activity, 3*, 45–54.

Schaie, K. W. (1994). The course of adult intellectual development. *American Psychologist, 49*, 304–313.

Schaie, K. W. (1996). *Intellectual development in adulthood: The Seattle Longitudinal Study.* New York: Cambridge University Press.

Schaie, K. W. (1998). The Seattle Longitudinal Studies of Adult Intelligence. In M. P. Lawton & T. A. Salthouse (Eds.), *Essential papers on the psychology of aging* (pp. 263–271). New York: New York University Press.

Schaie, K. W. (2000). The impact of longitudinal studies on understanding development from young adulthood to old age. *International Journal of Behavioral Development, 24*, 257–266.

Schaie, K. W. (2005). *Developmental influences on adult intelligence: The Seattle Longitudinal Study.* New York: Oxford University Press.

Schaie, K. W. (2011). Historical influences on aging and behavior. In K. W. Schaie & S. L. Willis (Eds.), *Handbook of the psychology of aging* (7th ed., pp. 41–55). San Diego, CA: Academic Press.

Schalet, A. (2007). Adolescent sexuality viewed through two different cultural lenses. In M. S. Tepper & A. F. Owens (Eds.), *Sexual health: Vol. 3. Moral and cultural foundations* (pp. 365–387). Westport, CT: Praeger.

Scheibe, S., Freund, A. M., & Baltes, P. B. (2007). Toward a developmental psychology of Sehnsucht (life longings): The optimal (utopian) life. *Developmental Psychology, 43*, 778–795.

Scher, A., Epstein, R., & Tirosh, E. (2004). Stability and changes in sleep regulation: A longitudinal study from 3 months to 3 years. *International Journal of Behavioral Development, 28*, 268–274.

Scher, A., Tirosh, E., Jaffe, M., Rubin, L., Sadeh, A., & Lavie, P. (1995). Sleep patterns of infants and young children in Israel. *International Journal of Behavioral Development, 18*, 701–711.

Schewe, P. A. (2007). Interventions to prevent sexual violence. In L. S. Doll, S. E. Bonzo, D. A. Sleet, & J. A. Mercy (Eds.), *Handbook of injury and violence prevention* (pp. 223–240). New York: Springer Science + Business Media.

Schiamberg, L. B., Barboza, G. G., Oehmke, J., Zhang, Z., Griffore, R. J., Weatherill, R. P., et al. (2011). Elder abuse in nursing homes: An ecological perspective. *Journal of Elder Abuse and Neglect, 23*, 190–211.

Schieman, S., Bierman, A., & Ellison, C. G. (2010). Religious involvement, beliefs about God, and the sense of mattering among older adults. *Journal for the Scientific Study of Religion, 49*, 517–535.

Schieman, S., & Plickert, G. (2007). Functional limitations and changes in levels of depression among older adults: A multiple-hierarchy stratification perspective. *Journal of Gerontology, 62B*, S36–S42.

Schindler, H. S. (2010). The importance of parenting and financial contributions in promoting fathers' psychological health. *Journal of Marriage and Family, 72*, 318–332.

Schlaggar, B. L., & McCandliss, B. D. (2007). Development of neural systems for reading. *Annual Review of Neuroscience, 30*, 475–503.

Schlagmüller, M., & Schneider, W. (2002). The development of organizational strategies in children: Evidence from a microgenetic longitudinal study. *Journal of Experimental Child Psychology, 81*, 298–319.

Schlegel, A., & Barry, H., III. (1991). *Adolescence: An anthropological inquiry.* New York: Free Press.

Schlossberg, N. (2004). *Retire smart, retire happy: Finding your true path in life.* Washington, DC: American Psychological Association.

Schmidt, K.-H., Neubach, B., & Heuer, H. (2007). Self-control demands, cognitive control deficits, and burnout. *Work and Stress, 21*, 142–154.

Schmidt, L. A., Fox, N. A., Rubin, K. H., Sternberg, E. M., Gold, P. W., & Smith, C. C. (1997). Behavioral and neuroendocrine responses in shy children. *Developmental Psychobiology, 35,* 119–135.

Schmidt, L. A., Fox, N. A., Schulkin, J., & Gold, P. W. (1999). Behavioral and psychophysiological correlates of self-presentation in temperamentally shy children. *Developmental Psychology, 30,* 127–140.

Schmidt, L. A., Santesso, D. L., Schulkin, J., & Segalowitz, S. J. (2007). Shyness is a necessary but not sufficient condition for high salivary cortisol in typically developing 10-year-old children. *Personality and Individual Differences, 43,* 1541–1551.

Schmidt, M. E., Crawley-Davis, A. M., & Anderson, D. R. (2007). Two-year-olds' object retrieval based on television: Testing a perceptual account. *Media Psychology, 9,* 389–409.

Schmitt, D. P., Allik, J., McCrae, R. R., & Benet-Martínez, V. (2007). The geographic distribution of the Big Five personality traits: Patterns and profiles of human self-description across 56 countries. *Journal of Cross-Cultural Psychology, 38,* 173–212.

Schmitz, S., Fulker, D. W., Plomin, R., Zahn-Waxler, C., Emde, R. N., & DeFries, J. C. (1999). Temperament and problem behaviour during early childhood. *International Journal of Behavioural Development, 23,* 333–355.

Schneewind, K. A., & Gerhard, A. (2002). Relationship personality, conflict resolution, and marital satisfaction in the first 5 years of marriage. *Family Relations, 51,* 63–71.

Schneider, B. H., Atkinson, L., & Tardif, C. (2001). Child–parent attachment and children's peer relations: A quantitative review. *Developmental Psychology, 37,* 87–100.

Schneider, W. (2002). Memory development in childhood. In U. Goswami (Ed.), *Blackwell handbook of childhood cognitive development* (pp. 236–256). Malden, MA: Blackwell.

Schneider, W., & Bjorklund, D. F. (1992). Expertise, aptitude, and strategic remembering. *Child Development, 63,* 461–473.

Schneider, W., & Bjorklund, D. F. (1998). Memory. In D. Kuhn & R. S. Siegler (Eds.), *Handbook of child psychology: Vol. 2. Cognition, perception, and language* (5th ed., pp. 467–521). New York: Wiley.

Schneider, W., & Pressley, M. (1997). *Memory development between two and twenty* (2nd ed.). Mahwah, NJ: Erlbaum.

Schneiders, J., Nicolson, N. A., Berkhof, J., Feron, F. J., van Os, J., & deVries, M. W. (2006). Mood reactivity to daily negative events in early adolescence: Relationship to risk for psychopathology. *Developmental Psychology, 42,* 543–554.

Schneller, D. P., & Arditti, J.A. (2004). After the breakup: Interpreting divorce and rethinking intimacy. *Journal of Divorce and Remarriage, 42,* 1–37.

Schnohr, P., Nyboe, J., Lange, P., & Jensen, G. (1998). Longevity and gray hair, baldness, facial wrinkles, and arcus senilis in 13,000 men and women: The Copenhagen City Heart Study. *Journal of Gerontology, 53,* M347–350.

Schnohr, P., Scharling, H., & Jensen, J. S. (2003). Changes in leisure-time physical activity and risk of death: An observational study of 7,000 men and women. *American Journal of Epidemiology, 158,* 639–644.

Scholl, B. J., & Leslie, A. M. (2000). Minds, modules, and meta-analysis. *Child Development, 72,* 696–701.

Scholl, T. O., Hediger, M. L., & Belsky, D. H. (1996). Prenatal care and maternal health during adolescent pregnancy: A review and meta-analysis. *Journal of Adolescent Health, 15,* 444–456.

Scholnick, E. K. (1995, Fall). Knowing and constructing plans. *SRCD Newsletter,* pp. 1–2, 17.

Schonberg, R. L., & Tifft, C. J. (2007). Birth defects and prenatal diagnosis. In M. L. Batshaw, L. Pellegrino, & N. J. Roizen (Eds.), *Children with*

disabilities (6th ed., pp. 83–96). Baltimore: Paul H. Brookes.

Schöner, G., & Thelen, E. (2006). Using dynamic field theory to rethink infant habituation. *Psychological Review, 113,* 273–299.

Schonert-Reichl, K. A. (1999). Relations of peer acceptance, friendship adjustment, and social behavior to moral reasoning during early adolescence. *Journal of Early Adolescence, 19,* 249–279.

Schooler, C., Mulatu, M. S., & Oates, G. (1999). The continuing effects of substantively complex work on the intellectual functioning of older workers. *Psychology and Aging, 14,* 483–506.

Schooler, C., Mulatu, M. S., & Oates, G. (2004). Occupational self-direction, intellectual functioning, and self-directed orientation in older workers: Findings and implications for individuals and societies. *American Journal of Sociology, 110,* 161–197.

Schoon, L., & Parsons, S. (2002). Teenage aspirations for future careers and occupational outcomes. *Journal of Vocational Behavior, 60,* 262–288.

Schoppe-Sullivan, S. J., Brown, G. L., Cannon, E. A., Mangelsdorf, S. C., & Sokolowski, M. S. (2008). Maternal gatekeeping, coparenting quality, and fathering behavior in families with infants. *Journal of Family Psychology, 22,* 389–398.

Schoppe-Sullivan, S. J., Mangelsdorf, S. C., Frosch, C. A., & McHale, J. (2004). Associations between coparenting and marital behavior from infancy to the preschool years. *Journal of Family Psychology, 18,* 194–207.

Schor, J. B. (2002). Time crunch among American parents. In S. A. Hewlett, N. Rankin, & C. West (Eds.), *Taking parenting public* (pp. 83–102). Boston: Rowman & Littlefield.

Schott, J. M., & Rossor, M. N. (2003). The grasp and other primitive reflexes. *Journal of Neurological and Neurosurgical Psychiatry, 74,* 558–560.

Schroeder, R. D., Bulanda, R. E., Giordano, P. C., & Cernkovich, S. A. (2010). Parenting and adult criminality: An examination of direct and indirect effects by race. *Journal of Adolescent Research, 25,* 64–98.

Schroots, J. J. F., van Dijkum, C., & Assink, M. H. J. (2004). Autobiographical memory from a life span perspective. *International Journal of Aging and Human Development, 58,* 69–85.

Schuckit, M. A. (2009). Alcohol-use disorders. *Lancet, 373,* 492–501.

Schuetze, P., & Eiden, R. D. (2006). The association between maternal cocaine use during pregnancy and physiological regulation in 4- to 8-week-old infants: An examination of possible mediators and moderators. *Journal of Pediatric Psychology, 31,* 15–26.

Schull, W. J. (2003). The children of atomic bomb survivors: A synopsis. *Journal of Radiological Protection, 23,* 369–394.

Schulte-Ruther, M., Markowitsch, H. J., Fink, G. R., & Piefke, M. (2007). Mirror neuron and theory of mind mechanisms involved in face-to-face interactions: A functional magnetic resonance imaging approach to empathy. *Journal of Cognitive Neuroscience, 19,* 1354–1372.

Schultz, R., Burgio, L., Burns, R., Eisdorfer, C., Gallagher-Thompson, D., Gitlin, L. N., & Mahoney, D. F. (2003). Resources for enhancing Alzheimer's caregiver health (REACH): Overview, site-specific outcomes, and future directions. *Gerontologist, 43,* 514–520.

Schulz, M. S., Cowan, C. P., & Cowan, P. A. (2006). Promoting healthy beginnings: A randomized controlled trial. *Journal of Consulting and Clinical Psychology, 74,* 20–31.

Schulz, R., & Curnow, C. (1988). Peak performance and age among superathletes: Track and field, swimming, baseball, tennis, and golf. *Journal of Gerontology, 43,* P113–P120.

Schumann, C. M., & Amaral, D. G. (2010). The human amygdala in autism. In P. J. Whalen & E. A. Phelps

(Eds.), *The human amygdala* (pp. 362–381). New York: Guilford.

Schumann, C. M., Barnes, C. C., Lord, C., & Courchesne, E. (2009). Amygdala enlargement in toddlers and autism related to severity of social and communication impairments. *Biological Psychiatry, 66,* 942–949.

Schwanenflugel, P. J., Henderson, R. L., & Fabricius, W. V. (1998). Developing organization of mental verbs and theory of mind in middle childhood: Evidence from extensions. *Developmental Psychology, 34,* 512–524.

Schwarte, A. R. (2008). Fragile X syndrome. *School Psychology Quarterly, 23,* 290–300.

Schwartz, B. L., & Frazier, L. D. (2005). Tip-of-the-tongue states and aging: Contrasting psycholinguistic and metacognitive perspectives. *Journal of General Psychology, 132,* 377–391.

Schwartz, C. E., Wright, C. I., Shin, L. M., Kagan, J., & Rauch, S. L. (2003). Inhibited and uninhibited infants "grown up": Adult amygdalar response to novelty. *Science, 300,* 1952–1953.

Schwartz, J. P., & Waldo, M. (2004). Group work with men who have committed partner abuse. In J. L. DeLucia-Waack, D. A. Gerrity, C. R. Kalodner, & M. T. Riva (Eds.), *Handbook of group counseling and psychotherapy* (pp. 576–592). Thousand Oaks, CA: Sage.

Schwartz, S. J., Beyers, W., Luyckz, K., Soenens, B. Zamboanga, B. L., Forthun, L. F., et al. (2011). Examining the light and dark sides of emerging adults' identity: A study of identity status differences in positive and negative psychosocial functioning. *Journal of Youth and Adolescence, 40,* 839–859.

Schwartz, S. J., Côté, J. E., & Arnett, J. J. (2005). Identity and agency in emerging adulthood: Two developmental routes in the individualization process. *Youth and Society, 37,* 201–229.

Schwartz, S. J., Pantin, H., Prado, G., Sullivan, S., & Szapocznik, J. (2005). Family functioning, identity, and problem behavior: Immigrant early adolescents. *Journal of Early Adolescence, 25,* 392–420.

Schwarz, N. (1999). Self-reports: How the questions shape the answers. *American Psychologist, 54,* 93–105.

Schwebel, D. C., & Bounds, M. L. (2003). The role of parents and temperament on children's estimation of physical ability: Links to unintentional injury prevention. *Journal of Pediatric Psychology, 28,* 505–516.

Schwebel, D. C., & Brezausek, C. M. (2007). Father transitions in the household and young children's injury risk. *Psychology of Men and Masculinity, 8,* 173–184.

Schwebel, D. C., & Gaines, J. (2007). Pediatric unintentional injury: Behavioral risk factors and implications for prevention. *Journal of Developmental and Behavioral Pediatrics, 28,* 245–254.

Schwebel, D. C., Roth, D. L., Elliott, M. N., Chien, A. T., Mrug, S., Shipp, E., et al. (2012). Marital conflict and fifth-graders' risk for injury. *Accident Analysis and Prevention, 47,* 30–35.

Schwebel, D. C., Roth, D. L., Elliott, M. N., Windle, M., Grunbaum, J. A., Low, B., et al. (2011). The association of activity level, parent mental distress, and parental involvement and monitoring with unintentional injury risk in fifth graders. *Accident Analysis and Prevention, 43,* 848–852.

Schweiger, W. K., & O'Brien, M. (2005). Special needs adoption: An ecological systems approach. *Family Relations, 54,* 512–522.

Schweinhart, L. J. (2010). The challenge of the High/Scope Perry Preschool study. In A. J. Reynolds, A. J. Rolnick, M. M. Englund, & J. Temple (Eds.), *Childhood programs and practices in the first decade of life: A human capital integration* (pp. 199–213). New York: Cambridge University Press.

Schweinhart, L. J., Montie, J., Xiang, Z., Barnett, W. S., Belfield, C. R., & Nores, M. (2005). *Lifetime effects:*

The High/Scope Perry Preschool Study through age 40. Ypsilanti, MI: High/Scope Press.

Schweizer, K., Moosbrugger, H., & Goldhammer, F. (2006). The structure of the relationship between attention and intelligence. *Intelligence, 33,* 589–611.

Schwenck, C., Bjorklund, D. F., & Schneider, W. (2007). Factors influencing the incidence of utilization deficiencies and other patterns of recall/strategy-use relations in a strategic memory task. *Child Development, 22,* 197–212.

Schwier, C., van Maanen, C., Carpenter, M., & Tomasello, M. (2006). Rational imitation in 12-month-old infants. *Infancy, 10,* 303–311.

Scocco, P., Rapattoni, M., & Fantoni, G. (2006). Nursing home institutionalization: A source of eustress or distress for the elderly? *International Journal of Geriatric Psychiatry, 21,* 281–287.

Scott, L. D. (2003). The relation of racial identity and racial socialization to coping with discrimination among African Americans. *Journal of Black Studies, 20,* 520–538.

Scott, L. S., & Monesson, A. (2009). The origin of biases in face perception. *Psychological Science, 20,* 676–680.

Scrutton, D. (2005). Influence of supine sleep positioning on early motor milestone acquisition. *Developmental Medicine and Child Neurology, 47,* 364.

Scullin, M. K., Bugg, J. M., McDaniel, M. A., & Einstein, G. O. (2011). Prospective memory and aging: Preserved spontaneous retrieval, but impaired deactivation, in older adults. *Memory and Cognition, 39,* 1232–1240.

Seale, C. (2009). Legalisation of euthanasia or physician-assisted suicide: Survey of doctors' attitudes. *Palliative Medicine, 23,* 205–212.

Seaton, E. K., Scottham, K. M., & Sellers, R. M. (2006). The status model of racial identity development in African American adolescents: Evidence of structure, trajectories, and well-being. *Child Development, 77,* 1416–1426.

Seeman, E. (2008). Structural basis of growth-related gain and age-related loss of bone strength. *Rheumatology, 47,* iv2–iv8.

Seeman, T. E., Huang, M.-H., Bretsky, P., Crimmins, E., Launer, L., & Guralnik, J. M. (2005). Education and APOE-e4 in longitudinal cognitive decline: MacArthur Studies of Successful Aging. *Journal of Gerontology, 60B,* P74–P83.

Seiberling, K. A., & Conley, D. B. (2004). Aging and olfactory and taste function. *Otolaryngologic Clinics of North America, 37,* 1209–1228.

Seibert, A. C., & Kerns, K. A. (2009). Attachment figures in middle childhood. *International Journal of Behavioral Development, 33,* 347–355.

Seidman, E., Aber, J. L., & French, S. E. (2004). Assessing the transitions to middle and high school. *Journal of Adolescent Research, 19,* 3–30.

Seidman, E., Lambert, L. E., Allen, L., & Aber, J. L. (2003). Urban adolescents' transition to junior high school and protective family transactions. *Journal of Early Adolescence, 23,* 166–193.

Seifer, R., & Schiller, M. (1995). The role of parenting sensitivity, infant temperament, and dyadic interaction in attachment theory and assessment. In E. Waters, B. E. Vaughn, G. Posada, & K. Kondo-Ikemura (Eds.), *Caregiving, cultural, and cognitive perspectives on secure-base behavior and working models: New growing points of attachment theory and research. Monographs of the Society for Research in Child Development, 60*(2–3, Serial No. 244).

Seitz, V., & Apfel, N. H. (2005). Creating effective school-based interventions for pregnant teenagers. In R. DeV. Peters, B. Leadbeater, & R. J. McMahon (Eds.), *Resilience in children, families, and communities: Linking context to practice and policy* (pp. 65–82). New York: Kluwer Academic.

Sekita, A., Ninomiya, T., Tanizaki, Y., Doi, Y., Hata, J., Yonemoto, K., et al. (2010). Trends in prevalence of Alzheimer's disease and vascular dementia in a Japanese community: the Hisayama Study. *Acta Psychiatrica Scandivavica, 122,* 319–325.

Selfhout, M. H. W., Branje, S. J. T., & Meeus, W. H. J. (2008). The development of delinquency and perceived friendship quality in adolescent best friendship dyads. *Journal of Abnormal Child Psychology, 36,* 471–485.

Selwood, A., & Cooper, C. (2009). Abuse of people with dementia. *Reviews in Clinical Gerontology, 19,* 35–43.

Selwood, A., Johnston, K., Katona, C., Lyketsos, C., & Livingston, G. (2007). Systematic review of the effect of psychological interventions on family caregivers of people with dementia. *Journal of Affective Disorders, 101,* 75–89.

Selwyn, P. A. (1996). Before their time: A clinician's reflections on death and AIDS. In H. M. Spiro, M. G. M. Curnen, & L. P. Wandel (Eds.), *Facing death: Where culture, religion, and medicine meet* (pp. 33–37). New Haven, CT: Yale University Press.

Semanik, P. A., Chang, R. W., & Dunlop, D. D. (2012). Aerobic activity in prevention and symptom control of osteoarthritis. *PM&R, 4,* S37–S44.

Senechal, M., & LeFevre, J. (2002). Parental involvement in the development of children's reading skill: A five-year longitudinal study. *Child Development, 73,* 445–460.

Senju, A., Csibra, G., & Johnson, M. H. (2008). Understanding the referential nature of looking: Infants' preference for object-directed gaze. *Cognition, 108,* 303–319.

Senju, A., Southgate, V., Snape, C., Leonard, M., & Csibra, G. (2011). Do 18-month-olds really attribute mental states to others? A critical test. *Psychological Science, 22,* 878–880.

Serafini, T. E., & Adams, G. R. (2002). Functions of identity: Scale construction and validation. *Identity: An International Journal of Theory and Research, 2,* 361–389.

Serbin, L. A., Powlishta, K. K., & Gulko, J. (1993). The development of sex typing in middle childhood. *Monographs of the Society for Research in Child Development, 58*(2, Serial No. 232).

Sergeant, J. F., Ekerdt, D. J., & Chapin, R. (2008). Measurement of late-life residential relocation: Why are rates for such a manifest event so varied? *Journal of Gerontology, 63B,* S92–S98.

Sermon, K., Van Steirteghem, A., & Liebaers, I. (2004). Preimplantation genetic diagnosis. *Lancet, 363,* 1633–1641.

Serpell, R., Sonnenschein, S., Baker L., & Ganapathy, H. (2002). Intimate culture of families in the early socialization of literacy. *Journal of Family Psychology, 16,* 391–405.

Serra, L., Perri, R., Cercignani, M., Spano, B., Fadda, L., Marra, C. et al. (2010). Are behavioral symptoms of Alzheimer's disease directly associated with neurodegeneration? *Journal of Alzheimer's Disease, 21,* 627–639.

Service Canada. (2009). *Guide to Canada Pension Plan disability benefits.* Retrieved from www.servicecanada.gc.ca/eng/isp/pub/cpp/disability/guide/sectionb.shtml

Sesame Workshop. (2009). *Sesame Workshop Annual Report 2009.* Retrieved from www.sesameworkshop.org/assets/290/src/Annual%20Report%202009.pdf

Settersten, R. A. (2003). Age structuring and the rhythm of the life course. In J. T. Mortimer & M. J. Shanahan (Eds.), *Handbook of the life course* (pp. 81–98). New York: Kluwer Academic.

Settersten, R. A. (2007). The new landscape of adult life: Road maps, signposts, and speed lines. *Research in Human Development, 4,* 239–252.

Settles, I. H., Cortina, L. M., Malley, J., & Stewart, A. J. (2006). The climate for women in academic science: The good, the bad, and the changeable. *Psychology of Women Quarterly, 30,* 47–58.

Sevigny, P. R., & Loutzenhiser, L. (2010). Predictors of parenting self-efficacy in mothers and fathers of toddlers. Child Care, *Health and Development, 36,* 179–189.

Seymour, S. C. (1999). *Women, family, and child care in India.* Cambridge, UK: Cambridge University Press.

Shaeer, O., & Shaeer, K. (2012). The Global Online Sexual Survey (GOSS): The United States of America in 2011. Chapter I: Erectile dysfunction among English-speakers. *Journal of Sexual Medicine, 9,* 3018–3027.

Shafer, V. L., & Garrido-Nag, K. (2007). The neurodevelopmental bases of language. In E. Hoff & M. Shatz (Eds.), *Blackwell handbook of language development* (pp. 21–45). Malden, MA: Blackwell.

Shah, T., Sullivan, K., & Carter, J. (2006). Sudden infant death syndrome and reported maternal smoking during pregnancy. *American Journal of Public Health, 96,* 1757–1759.

Shalev, I. (2012). Early life stress and telomere length: Investigating the connection and possible mechanisms. *BioEssays, 34,* 943–952.

Shanahan, L., McHale, S. M., Crouter, A. C., & Osgood, D. W. (2007). Warmth with mothers and fathers from middle childhood to late adolescence: Within- and between-families comparisions. *Developmental Psychology, 43,* 551–563.

Shapka, J. D., & Keating, D. P. (2005). Structure and change in self-concept during adolescence. *Canadian Journal of Behavioural Science, 37,* 83–96.

Sharp, E. A., & Ganong, L. (2011). "I'm a loser, I'm not married, let's just all look at me": Ever-single women's perceptions of their social environment. *Journal of Family Issues, 32,* 956–980.

Shatz, M. (2007). On the development of the field. In E. Hoff & M. Shatz (Eds.), *Blackwell handbook of language development* (pp. 1–20). Malden, MA: Blackwell.

Shaver, P., Furman, W., & Buhrmester, D. (1985). Transition to college: Network changes, social skills, and loneliness. In S. Duck & D. Perlman (Eds.), *Understanding personal relationships: An interdisciplinary approach* (pp. 193–219). London: Sage.

Shaw, B. A. (2005). Anticipated support from neighbors and physical functioning during later life. *Research on Aging, 27,* 503–525.

Shaw, D. S., Gilliom, M., Ingoldsby, E. M., & Nagin, D. S. (2003). Trajectories leading to school-age conduct problems. *Developmental Psychology, 39,* 189–200.

Shaw, P., Eckstrand, K., Sharp, W., Blumenthal, J., Lerch, J. P., & Greenstein, D. (2007, November 16). Attention-deficit/hyperactivity disorder is characterized by a delay in cortical maturation. *Proceedings of the National Academy of Sciences Online.* Retrieved from www.pnas.org/cgi/content/abstract/0707741104v1

Shay, J. W., & Wright, W. E. (2011). Role of telomeres and telomerase in cancer. *Seminars in Cancer Biology, 21,* 349–353.

Shea, J. L. (2006). Cross-cultural comparison of women's midlife symptom-reporting: A China study. *Culture, Medicine, and Psychiatry, 30,* 331–362.

Shedler, J., & Block, J. (1990). Adolescent drug use and psychological health: A longitudinal inquiry. *American Psychologist, 45,* 612–630.

Sheehan, G., Darlington, Y., Noller, P., & Feeney, J. (2004). Children's perceptions of their sibling relationships during parental separation and divorce. *Journal of Divorce and Remarriage, 41,* 69–94.

Sheehan, N. W., & Petrovic, K. (2008). Grandparents and their adult grandchildren: Recurring themes from the literature. *Marriage and Family Review, 44,* 99–124.

Sherman, A. M., de Vries, B., & Lansford, J. E. (2000). Friendship in childhood and adulthood: Lessons across the life span. *International Journal of Aging and Human Development, 51*, 31–51.

Sherman, A. M., Lansford, J. E., & Volling, B. L. (2006). Sibling relationships and best friendships in young adulthood: Warmth, conflict, and well-being. *Personal Relationships, 13*, 151–165.

Sherman, C. W., Rosenblatt, D. E., & Antonucci, T. C. (2008). Elder abuse and mistreatment: A life span and cultural context. *Indian Journal of Gerontology, 22.*

Sherman, S. L., Freeman, S. B., Allen, E. G., & Lamb, N. E. (2005). Risk factors for nondisjunction of trisomy 21. *Cytogenetic Genome Research, 111*, 273–280.

Sherrod, L. R., & Spiewak, G. S. (2008). Possible interrelationships between civic engagement, positive youth development, and spirituality/religiosity. In R. M. Lerner, R. W. Roeser, & E. Phelps (Eds.), *Positive youth development and spirituality: From theory to research* (pp. 322–338). West Conshohocken, PA: Templeton Foundation Press.

Sherry, B., McDivitt, J., Brich, L. L., Cook, F. H., Sanders, S., Prish, J. L., Francis, L. A., & Scanlon, K. S. (2004). Attitudes, practices, and concerns about child feeding and child weight status among socioeconomically diverse white, Hispanic, and African-American mothers. *Journal of the American Dietetic Association, 104*, 215–221.

Shield, R. R., Wetle, T., Teno, J., Miller, S. C., & Welch, L. C. (2010). Vigilant at the end of life: Family advocacy in the nursing home. *Journal of Palliative Medicine, 13*, 573–579.

Shields, G., King, W., Fulks, S., & Fallon, L. F. (2002). Determinants of perceived safety among the elderly: An exploratory study. *Journal of Gerontological Social Work, 38*, 73–83.

Shierholz, H., Sabadish, N., & Wething, H. (2012, May 3). *The class of 2012: Labor market for young graduates remains grim.* EPI Briefing Paper #340. Washington, DC: Economic Policy Institute.

Shifren, J. L., Monz, B. U., Russo, P. A., Segreti, A., & Johannes, C. B. (2008). Sexual problems and distress in United States women. *Obstetrics and Gynecology, 112*, 970–978.

Shimada, S., & Hiraki, K. (2006). Infant's brain responses to live and televised action. *NeuroImage, 32*, 930–939.

Shimizu, H. (2001). Japanese adolescent boys' senses of empathy (omoiyari) and Carol Gilligan's perspectives on the morality of care: A phenomenological approach. *Culture and Psychology, 7*, 453–475.

Shin, J. A., Hong, A., Solomon, M. J., & Lee, C. S. (2006). The role of telomeres and telomerase in the pathology of human cancer and aging. *Pathology, 38*, 103–113.

Shinn, M., Schteingart, J. S., Williams, N. C., Carlin-Mathis, J., Bialo-Karagis, N., Becker-Klein, R., & Weitzman, B. C. (2008). Long-term associations of homelessness with children's well-being. *American Behavioral Scientist, 51*, 789–809.

Shipman, K. L., Zeman, J., Nesin, A. E., & Fitzgerald, M. (2003). Children's strategies for displaying anger and sadness: What works with whom? *Merrill-Palmer Quarterly, 49*, 100–122.

Shonkoff, J. P., & Bales, S. N. (2011). Science does not speak for itself: Translating child development research for the public and its policymakers. *Child Development, 82*, 17–32.

Shonkoff, J. P., & Phillips, D. (Eds.). (2001). *Neurons to neighborhoods: The science of early childhood development.* Washington, DC: National Academy Press.

Shor, E., Roelfs, D. J., Curreli, M., Clemow, L., Burg, M. M., & Schwartz, J. E. (2012). Widowhood and mortality: A meta-analysis and meta-regression. *Demography, 49*, 575–606.

Shuey, K., & Hardy, M. A. (2003). Assistance to aging parents and parents-in-law: Does lineage affect family allocation decisions? *Journal of Marriage and Family, 65*, 418–431.

Shultz, K. S., & Wang, M. (2007). The influence of specific physical health conditions on retirement decisions. *International Journal of Aging and Human Development, 65*, 149–161.

Shure, M. B., & Aberson, B. (2005). Enhancing the process of resilience through effective thinking. In S. Goldstein & R. B. Brooks (Eds.), *Handbook of resilience in children* (pp. 373–394). New York: Kluwer Academic.

Shuwairi, S. M., Albert, M. K., & Johnson, S. P. (2007). Discrimination of possible and impossible objects in infancy. *Psychological Science, 18*, 303–307.

Shwalb, D. W., Nakawaza, J., Yamamoto, T., & Hyun, J.-H. (2004). Fathering in Japanese, Chinese, and Korean cultures: A review of the research literature. In M. E. Lamb (Ed.), *The role of the father in child development* (4th ed., pp. 146–181). Hoboken, NJ: Wiley.

Shweder, R. A., Goodnow, J. J., Hatano, G., LeVine, R. A., Markus, H. R., & Miller, P. J. (2006). The cultural psychology of development: One mind, many mentalities. In R. M. Lerner (Ed.), *Handbook of child psychology: Vol. 1. Theoretical models of human development* (6th ed., pp. 716–792). Hoboken, NJ: Wiley.

Sibley, C. G., & Overall, N. C. (2010). Modeling the hierarchical structure of personality–attachment associations: Domain diffusion versus domain differentiation. *Journal of Social and Personal Relationships, 27*, 47–70.

Sidebotham, P., Heron, J., & the ALSPAC Study Team. (2003). Child maltreatment in the "children of the nineties": The role of the child. *Child Abuse and Neglect, 27*, 337–352.

Siebenbruner, J., Zimmer-Gembeck, M. J., & Egeland, B. (2007). Sexual partners and contraceptive use: A 16-year prospective study predicting abstinence and risk behavior. *Journal of Research on Adolescence, 17*, 179–206.

Siebert, A. C., & Kerns, K. A. (2009). Attachment figures in middle childhood. *International Journal of Behavioral Development, 33*, 347–355.

Siegal, M., Iozzi, L., & Surian, L. (2009). Bilingualism and conversational understanding in young children. *Cognition, 110*, 115–122.

Siega-Riz, A. M., Deming, D. M., Reidy, K. C., Fox, M. K., Condon, E., & Briefel, R. R. (2010). Food consumption patterns of infants and toddlers: Where are we now? *Journal of the American Dietetic Association, 110*, S38–S51.

Siegel, R., Naishadham, D., & Jemal, A. (2012). Cancer statistics, 2012. *CA: A Cancer Journal for Clinicians, 62*, 10–29.

Sieger, K., & Renk, K. (2007). Pregnant and parenting adolescents: A study of ethnic identity, emotional and behavioral functioning, child characteristics, and social support. *Journal of Youth and Adolescence, 36*, 567–581.

Siegler, R. S. (1996). *Emerging minds: The process of change in children's thinking.* New York: Oxford University Press.

Siegler, R. S. (2007). Cognitive variability. *Developmental Science, 10*, 104–109.

Siegler, R. S. (2009). Improving preschoolers' number sense using information-processing theory. In O. A. Barbarin & B. H. Wasik (Eds.), *Handbook of child development and early education* (pp. 429–454). New York: Guilford.

Siegler, R. S., & Mu, Y. (2008). Chinese children excel on novel mathematics problems even before elementary school. *Psychological Science, 19*, 759–763.

Siegler, R. S., & Svetina, M. (2006). What leads children to adopt new strategies? A microgenetic/cross-sectional study of class inclusion. *Child Development, 77*, 997–1015.

Siervogel, R. M., Maynard, L. M., Wisemandle, W. A., Roche, A. F., Guo, S. S., Chumlea, W. C., & Towne, B. (2000). Annual changes in total body fat and fat-free mass in children from 8 to 18 years in relation to changes in body mass index: The Fels Longitudinal Study. *Annals of the New York Academy of Sciences, 904*, 420–423.

Silk, J. S., Morris, A. S., Kanaya, T., & Steinberg, L. (2003). Psychological control and autonomy granting: Opposite ends of a continuum or distinct constructs? *Journal of Research on Adolescence, 13*, 113–128.

Silvén, M. (2001). Attention in very young infants predicts learning of first words. *Infant Behavior and Development, 24*, 229–237.

Silver, M. H., & Perls, T. T. (2000). Is dementia the price of a long life? An optimistic report from centenarians. *Journal of Geriatric Psychiatry, 33*, 71–79.

Silverberg, S. B. (1996). Parents' well-being at their children's transition to adolescence. In C. D. Ryff & M. M. Seltzer (Eds.), *The parental experience in midlife* (pp. 215–254). Chicago: University of Chicago Press.

Silverman, I., Choi, J., & Peters, M. (2007). The hunter-gatherer theory of sex differences in spatial abilities. *Archives of Sexual behavior, 36*, 261–268.

Silverman, P. R. (2004). Dying and bereavement in historical perspective. In J. Berzoff & P. R. Silverman (Eds.), *Living with dying: A handbook for end-of-life healthcare practitioners* (pp. 128–149). New York: Columbia University Press.

Silverman, P. R., & Nickman, S. L. (1996). Children's construction of their dead parents. In D. Klass, P. R. Silverman, & S. L. Nickman (Eds.), *Continuing bonds: New understandings of grief* (pp. 73–86). Washington, DC: Taylor & Francis.

Silverman, W. K., & Pina, A. A. (2008). Psychosocial treatments for phobic and anxiety disorders in youth. In R. G. Steele, T. D. Elkin, & M. Roberts (Eds.), *Handbook of evidence-based therapies for children and adolescents: Bridging science and practice* (pp. 65–82). New York: Springer.

Silverstein, M., Conroy, S., Wang, H., Giarrusso, R., & Bengtson, V. L. (2002). Reciprocity in parent–child relations over the adult life course. *Journal of Gerontology, 57B*, S3–S13.

Silverstein, M., & Giarrusso, R. (2010). Aging and family life: A decade review. *Journal of Marriage and Family, 72*, 1039–1058.

Silverstein, M., & Marenco, A. (2001). How Americans enact the grandparent role across the family life course. *Journal of Family Issues, 22*, 493–522.

Simcock, G., & DeLoache, J. (2006). Get the picture? The effects of iconicity on toddlers' reenactment from picture books. *Developmental Psychology, 42*, 1352–1357.

Simcock, G., & Hayne, H. (2002). Breaking the barrier? Children fail to translate their preverbal memories into language. *Psychological Science, 13*, 225–231.

Simcock, G., & Hayne, H. (2003). Age-related changes in verbal and nonverbal memory during early childhood. *Developmental Psychology, 39*, 805–814.

Simmons, R. G., & Blyth, D. A. (1987). *Moving into adolescence.* New York: Aldine De Gruyter.

Simon, N. M., Smoller, J. W., McNamara, K. L., Maser, R. S., Zlata, A. K., & Pollack, M. H. (2006). Telomere shortening and mood disorders: Preliminary support for a chronic stress model of accelerated aging. *Biological Psychiatry, 60*, 432–435.

Simoneau, M., & Markovits, H. (2003). Reasoning with premises that are not empirically true: Evidence for the role of inhibition and retrieval. *Developmental Psychology, 39*, 964–975.

Simons, J. S., Dodson, C. S., Bell, D., & Schachter, D. L. (2004). Specific-and partial-source memory: Effects of aging. *Psychology and Aging, 19*, 689–694.

Simons, L. G., Chen, Y. F., Simons, R. L., Brody, G., & Cutrona, C. (2006). Parenting practices and child adjustment in different types of households: A study of African-American families. *Journal of Family Issues, 27,* 803–825.

Simons, R. L., Whitbeck, L. B., Conger, R. D., & Wu, C. -I. (1991). Intergenerational transmission of harsh parenting. *Developmental Psychology, 27,* 159–171.

Simonton, D. K. (2000). Creativity: Cognitive, personal, developmental, and social aspects. *American Psychologist, 55,* 151–158.

Simonton, D. K. (2006). Historiometric methods. In K. A. Ericsson, N. Charness, P. J. Feltovich, & R. R. Hoffman (Eds.), *The Cambridge handbook of expertise and expert performance* (pp. 319–335). New York: Cambridge University Press.

Simonton, D. K. (2012). Creative productivity and aging. In S. K. Whitbourne & M. J. Sliwinski (Eds.), *Wiley-Blackwell handbook of adulthood and aging* (pp. 477–496). Malden, MA: Blackwell Publishing.

Simpson, E. A., Varga, K., Frick, J. E., & Fragaszy, D. (2011). Infants experience perceptual narrowing for nonprimate faces. *Infancy, 16,* 318–328.

Simpson, J. A., & Harris, B. A. (1994). Interpersonal attraction. In A. L. Weber & J. H. Harvey (Eds.), *Perspectives on close relationships* (pp. 45–66). Boston: Allyn and Bacon.

Simpson, J. A., Rholes, W. S., Campbell, L., Tran, S., & Wilson, C. L. (2003). Adult attachment, the transition to parenthood, and depressive symptoms. *Journal of Personality and Social Psychology, 84,* 1172–1187.

Simpson, J. L., de la Cruz, F., Swerdloff, R. S., Samango-Sprouse, C., Skakkebaek, N. E., & Graham, J. M., Jr. (2003). Klinefelter syndrome: Expanding the phenotype and identifying new research directions. *Genetic Medicine, 5,* 460–468.

Simpson, R. (2004). Masculinity at work: The experiences of men in female dominated occupations. *Work, Employment and Society, 18,* 349–368.

Simpson, R. (2005). Men in non-traditional occupations: Career entry, career orientation and experience of role strain. *Gender, Work and Organization, 12,* 363–380.

Singer, D. G., & Singer, J. L. (2005). *Imagination and play in the electronic age.* Cambridge, MA: Harvard University Press.

Singer, Y., Bachner, Y. G., Shvartzman, P., & Carmel, S. (2005). Home death—the caregivers' experiences. *Journal of Pain and Symptom Management, 30,* 70–74.

Singleton, J. L., & Newport, E. L. (2004). When learners surpass their models: The acquisition of American Sign Language from inconsistent input. *Cognitive Psychology, 49,* 370–407.

Sinkkonen, J., Anttila, R., & Siimes, M. A. (1998). Pubertal maturation and changes in self-image in early adolescent Finnish boys. *Journal of Youth and Adolescence, 27,* 209–218.

Sinnott, J. D. (1998). *The development of logic in adulthood: Postformal thought and its applications.* New York: Plenum.

Sinnott, J. D. (2003). Postformal thought and adult development: Living in balance. In J. Demick & C. Andreoletti (Eds.), *Handbook of adult development* (pp. 221–238). New York: Kluwer Academic.

Sinnott, J. D. (2008). Cognitive and representational development in adults. In K. B. Cartwright (Ed.), *Literacy processes: Cognitive flexibility in learning and teaching* (pp. 42–61). New York: Guilford.

Sirois, S., & Jackson, I. R. (2012). Pupil dilation and object permanence in infants. *Infancy, 17,* 61–78.

Sirsch, U., Erher, E., Mayr, E., & Willinger, U. (2009). What does it take to be an adult in Austria? *Journal of Adolescent Research, 24,* 275–292.

Skaff, M. M. (2006). The view from the driver's seat: Sense of control in the baby boomers at midlife. In. S. K. Whitbourne & S. L. Willis (Eds.), *The baby boomers grow up: Contemporary perspectives on midlife* (pp. 185–204). Mahwah, NJ: Erlbaum.

Skinner, E. A., Zimmer-Gembeck, M. J., & Connell, J. P. (1998). Individual differences and the development

of perceived control. *Monographs of the Society for Research in Child Development, 63*(2–3, Serial No. 254).

Skoe, E. E. A. (1998). The ethic of care: Issues in moral development. In E. E. A. Skoe & A. L. von der Lippe (Eds.), *Personality development in adolescence* (pp. 143–171). London: Routledge.

Skully, R., & Saleh, A. S. (2011). Aging and the effects of vitamins and supplements. *Clinical Geriatric Medicine, 27,* 591–607.

Slack, K. S., & Yoo, J. (2005). Food Hardship and child behavior problems among low-income children. *Social Service Review, 79,* 511–536.

Slater, A., Brown, E., Mattock, A., & Bornstein, M. H. (1996). Continuity and change in habituation in the first 4 months from birth. *Journal of Reproductive and Infant Psychology, 14,* 187–194.

Slater, A., Quinn, P. C., Kelly, D. J., Lee, K., Longmore, C. A., McDonald, P. R., & Pascalis, O. (2011). The shaping of the face space in early infancy: Becoming a native face processor. *Child Development Perspectives, 4,* 205–211.

Slater, A., Riddell, P., Quinn, P. C., Pascalis, O., Lee, K., & Kelly, D. J. (2010). Visual perception. In J. G. Bremner & T. D. Wachs (Eds.), *Wiley-Blackwell handbook of infant development: Vol. 1. Basic research* (2nd ed., pp. 40–80). Chichester, UK: Wiley-Blackwell.

Slaughter, V., & Griffiths, M. (2007). Death understanding and fear of death in young children. *Clinical Child Psychology and Psychiatry, 12,* 525–535.

Slaughter, V., Jaakkola, R., & Carey, S. (1999). Constructing a coherent theory: Children's biological understanding of life and death. In M. Siegel & C. C. Petersen (Eds.), *Children's understanding of biology and health* (pp. 71–96). Cambridge, UK: Cambridge University Press.

Slaughter, V., & Lyons, M. (2003). Learning about life and death in early childhood. *Cognitive Psychology, 46,* 1–30.

Sleet, D. A., & Mercy, J. A. (2003). Promotion of safety, security, and well-being. In M. H. Bornstein, L. Davidson, C. M. M. Keyes, K. A. Moore, & the Center for Child Well-Being (Eds.), *Well-being: Positive development across the life course* (pp. 81–97). Mahwah, NJ: Erlbaum.

Slobin, D. I. (1985). Crosslinguistic evidence for the language-making capacity. In D. I. Slobin (Ed.), *The crosslinguistic study of language acquisition: Vol. 2. Theoretical issues.* Hillsdale, NJ: Erlbaum.

Slobin, D. I. (1997). *The crosslinguistic study of language acquisition: Vol. 5. Expanding the contexts.* Mahwah, NJ: Erlbaum.

Slonims, V., & McConachie, H. (2006). Analysis of mother-infant interaction in infants with Down syndrome and typically developing infants. *American Journal of Mental Retardation, 111,* 273–289.

Sloter, E., Schmid, T. E., Marchetti, F., Eskenazi, B., & Nath, J. (2006). Quantitative effects of male age on sperm motion. *Human Reproduction, 21,* 2868–2875.

Slusher, M. P., Mayer, C. J., & Dunkle, R. E. (1996). Gays and lesbians older and wiser (GLOW): A support group for older gay people. *Gerontologist, 36,* 118–123.

Slutske, W. S., Hunt-Carter, E. E., Nabors-Oberg, R. E., Sher, K. J., Bucholz, K. K., & Madden, P. A. F. (2004). Do college students drink more than their non-college-attending peers? Evidence from a population-based longitudinal female twin study. *Journal of Abnormal Psychology, 113,* 530–540.

Smahel, D., Brown, B. B., & Blinka, L. (2012). Associations between online friendship and Internet addiction among adolescents and emerging adults. *Developmental Psychology, 48,* 381–388.

Small, B. J., Rawson, K. S., Eisel, S., & McEvoy, C. L. (2012). Memory and aging. In S. K. Whitbourne &

M. J. Sliwinski (Eds.), *Wiley-Blackwell handbook of adulthood and aging* (pp. 174–189). Malden, MA: Wiley-Blackwell.

Small, M. (1998). *Our babies, ourselves.* New York: Anchor.

Smart, J., & Hiscock, H. (2007). Early infant crying and sleeping problems: A pilot study of impact on parental well-being and parent-endorsed strategies for management. *Journal of Paediatrics and Child Health, 43,* 284–290.

Smetana, J. G. (2002). Culture, autonomy, and personal jurisdiction in adolescent–parent relationships. In R. V. Kail & H. W. Reese (Eds.), *Advances in child development and behavior* (Vol. 29, pp. 51–87). San Diego, CA: Academic Press.

Smetana, J. G. (2006). Social-cognitive domain theory: Consistencies and variations in children's moral and social judgments. In M. Killen & J. G. Smetana (Eds.), *Handbook of moral development* (pp. 119–154). Mahwah, NJ: Erlbaum.

Smetana, J. G., & Daddis, C. (2002). Domain-specific antecedents of parental psychological control and monitoring: The role of parenting beliefs and practices. *Child Development, 73,* 563–580.

Smetana, J. G., Metzger, A., & Campione-Barr, N. (2004). African-American late adolescents' relationships with parents: Developmental transitions and longitudinal patterns. *Child Development, 75,* 932–947.

Smith, A. N., Brief, A. P., & Colella, A. (2010). Bias in organizations. In J. F. Dovidio, M. Hewstone, P. Glick, & V. M. Esses (Eds.), *Treatment of childhood disorders* (3rd ed., pp. 65–136). New York: Guilford.

Smith, B. H., Barkley, R. A., & Shapiro, C. J. (2006). Attention-deficit/hyperactivity disorder. In E. J. Mash & R. A. Barkley (Eds.), *Treatment of childhood disorders* (3rd ed., pp. 65–136). New York: Guilford.

Smith, C., Perou, R., & Lesesne, C. (2002). Parent education. In M. H. Bornstein (Ed.), *Handbook of parenting* (Vol. 4, pp. 389–410). Mahwah, NJ: Erlbaum.

Smith, C., & Snell, P. (2009). *Souls in transition: The religious & spiritual lives of emerging adults.* New York: Oxford University Press.

Smith, C. D., Chebrolu, H., Wekstein, D. R., Schmitt, F. A., & Markesbery, W. R. (2007). Age and gender effects on human brain anatomy: A voxel-based morphometric study in healthy elderly. *Neurobiology of Aging, 28,* 1075–1087.

Smith, C. L., Calkins, S. D., Keane, S. P., Anastopoulos, A. D., & Shelton, T. L. (2004). Predicting stability and change in toddler behavior problems: Contributions of maternal behavior and child gender. *Developmental Psychology, 40,* 29–42.

Smith, C. M., & Cotter, V. T. (2008). Age-related changes in health. In E. Capezuti, D. Zwicker, M. Mezey, T. T. Fulmer, & D. Gray-Miceli (Eds.), *Evidence-based geriatric nursing protocols for best practice* (3rd ed., pp. 431–458). New York: Springer.

Smith, D. G., Xiao, L., & Bechara, A. (2012). Decision making in children and adolescents: Impaired Iowa gambling task performance in early adolescence. *Developmental Psychology, 48,* 1180–1187.

Smith, G. C., Rodriguez, J. M., & Palmieri, P. A. (2010). Patterns and predictors of support group use by custodial grandmothers and grandchildren. *Families in Society, 91,* 385–393.

Smith, J., & Baltes, P. B. (1999). Life-span perspectives on development. In M. H. Bornstein & M. E. Lamb (Eds.), *Developmental psychology: An advanced textbook* (4th ed., pp. 275–311). Mahwah, NJ: Erlbaum.

Smith, J., & Freund, A. M. (2002). The dynamics of possible selves in old age. *Journal of Gerontology, 57P,* P492–P500.

Smith, J., & Infurna, F. J. (2011). Early precursors of later health. In K. L. Fingerman, C. A. Berg, J. Smith, & T. C. Antonucci (Eds.), *Handbook of life-span development* (pp. 213–238). New York: Springer.

Smith, J. C., Nielson, K. A., Woodard, J. L., Seidenberg, M., & Rao, S. M. (2013). Physical activity and brain function in older adults at increased risk for Alzheimer's disease. *Brain Science, 3,* 54–83.

Smith, L. B., Jones, S. S., Gershkoff-Stowe, L., & Samuelson, L. (2002). Object name learning provides on-the-job training for attention. *Psychological Science, 13,* 13–19.

Smith, N., Young, A., & Lee, C. (2004). Optimism, health-related hardiness and well-being among older Australian women. *Journal of Health Psychology, 9,* 741–752.

Smith, T. W. (2006). Personality as risk and resilience in physical health. *Current Directions in Psychological Science, 15,* 227–231.

Smith, T. W. (2011a). *Cross-national differences in attitudes toward homosexuality.* Chicago: National Opinion Research Center/University of Chicago.

Smith, T. W. (2011b). *Public attitudes toward homosexuality.* Chicago: National Opinion Research Center/University of Chicago.

Smith, T. W., & Cundiff, J. M. (2011). An interpersonal perspective on risk for coronary heart disease. In L. Horowitz & S. Strack (Eds.), *Handbook of interpersonal psychology: Theory, research, assessment, and therapeutic interventions* (pp. 471–489). Hoboken, NJ: Wiley.

Smith, T. W., Gallo, L. C., & Ruiz, J. M. (2003). Toward a social psychophysiology of cardiovascular reactivity: Interpersonal concepts and methods in the study of stress and coronary disease. In J. Suls & K. Wallston (Eds.), *Social psychological foundations of health and illness* (pp. 335–366). Oxford, U.K.: Blackwell.

Smith, T. W., Glazer, K., Ruiz, J. M., & Gallo, L. C. (2004). Hostility, anger, aggressiveness, and coronary heart disease: An interpersonal perspective on personality, emotion, and health. *Journal of Personality, 72,* 1217–1270.

Smith, T. W., & Mackenzie, J. (2006). Personality and risk of physical illness. *Annual Review of Clinical Psychology, 2,* 435–467.

Smith, T. W., Uchino, B. N., Berg, C. A., & Florsheim, P. (2012). Marital discord and coronary artery disease: A comparison of behaviorally defined discrete groups. *Journal of Consulting and Clinical Psychology, 80,* 87–92.

Smyke, A. T., Zeanah, C. H., Fox, N. A., & Nelson, C. A. (2009). A new model of foster care for young children: The Bucharest Early Intervention Project. *Child and Adolescent Psychiatric Clinics of North America, 18,* 721–734.

Smyke, A. T., Zeanah, C. H., Fox, N. A., Nelson, C. A., & Guthrie, D. (2010). Placement in foster care enhances quality of attachment among young institutionalized children. *Child Development, 81,* 212–223.

Snarey, J., Son, L., Kuehne, V. S., Hauser, S., & Vaillant, G. (1987). The role of parenting in men's psychosocial development: A longitudinal study of early adulthood infertility and midlife generativity. *Developmental Psychology, 23,* 593–603.

Sneed, J. R., Whitbourne, S. K., & Culang, M. E. (2006). Trust, identity, and ego integrity: Modeling Erikson's core stages over 34 years. *Journal of Adult Development, 13,* 148–157.

Sneed, J. R., Whitbourne, S. K., Schwartz, S. J., & Huang, S. (2012). The relationship between identity, intimacy, and midlife well-being: Findings from the Rochester Adult Longitudinal Study. *Psychology and Aging, 27,* 318–323.

Snidman, N., Kagan, J., Riordan, L., & Shannon, D. C. (1995). Cardiac function and behavioral reactivity. *Psychophysiology, 32,* 199–207.

Snow, C. E., & Beals, D. E. (2006). Mealtime talk that supports literacy development. In R. W. Larson, A. R. Wiley, & K. R. Branscomb (Eds.), *Family mealtime as a context of development and socialization* (pp. 51–66). San Francisco: Jossey-Bass.

Snow, C. E., & Kang, J. Y. (2006). Becoming bilingual, biliterate, and bicultural. In K. A. Renninger & I. E. Sigel (Eds.), *Handbook of child psychology: Vol. 4. Child psychology in practice* (6th ed., pp. 75–102). Hoboken, NJ: Wiley.

Snyder, J., Brooker, M., Patrick, M. R., Snyder, A., Schrepferman, L., & Stoolmiller, M. (2003). Observed peer victimization during early elementary school: Continuity, growth, and relation to risk for child antisocial and depressive behavior. *Child Development, 74,* 1881–1898.

Snyder, J. S., & Cameron, H. A. (2012). Could adult hippocampal neurogenesis be relevant for human behavior? *Behavioural Brain Research, 227,* 384–390.

Soares, C. N. (2007). Menopausal transition and depression: Who is at risk and how to treat it? *Expert Review of Neurotherapeutics, 7,* 1285–1293.

Sobel, D. M. (2006). How fantasy benefits young children's understanding of pretense. *Developmental Science, 9,* 63–75.

Society for Research in Child Development. (2007). *SRCD ethical standards for research with children.* Retrieved from www.srcd.org/index.php?option=com_content&task=view&id=68&Itemid=110

Soderstrom, M., Dolbier, C., Leiferman, J., & Steinhardt, M. (2000). The relationship of hardiness, coping strategies, and perceived stress to symptoms of illness. *Journal of Behavioral Medicine, 23,* 311–328.

Soderstrom, M., Seidl, A., Nelson, D. G. K., & Jusczyk, P. W. (2003). The prosodic bootstrapping of phrases: Evidence from prelinguistic infants. *Journal of Memory and Language, 49,* 249–267.

Sofi, F., Cesari, F., Abbate, R., Gensini, G. F., & Casini, A. (2008). Adherence to Mediterranean diet and health status: Meta-analysis. *British Medical Journal, 337,* a1344.

Soli, A. R., McHale, S. M., & Feinberg, M. E. (2009). Risk and protective effects of sibling relationships among African American adolescents. *Family Relations, 58,* 578–592.

Solomon, J. C., & Marx, J. (1995). "To grandmother's house we go": Health and school adjustment of children raised solely by grandparents. *Gerontologist, 35,* 386–394.

Son, J., & Wilson, J. (2011). Generativity and volunteering. *Sociological Forum, 26,* 644–667.

Sondergaard, C., Henriksen, T. B., Obel, C., & Wisborg, K. (2002). Smoking during pregnancy and infantile colic. *Journal of the American Academy of Child and Adolescent Psychiatry, 41,* 147.

Sophian, C. (1995). Representation and reasoning in early numerical development: Counting, conservation, and comparisons between sets. *Child Development, 66,* 559–577.

Sörensen, S., & Pinquart, M. (2005). Racial and ethnic differences in the relationship of caregiving stressors, resources, and sociodemographic variables to caregiver depression and perceived physical health. *Aging and Mental Health, 9,* 482–495.

Sosa, R., Kennell, J., Klaus, M., Robertson, S., & Urrutia, J. (1980). The effect of a supportive companion on perinatal problems, length of labor, and mother–infant interaction. *New England Journal of Medicine, 303,* 597–600.

Soska, K. C., Adolph, K. E., & Johnson, S. P. (2010). Systems in development: Motor skill acquisition facilitates three-dimensional object completion. *Developmental Psychology, 46,* 129–138.

Soto, C. J., John, O. P., Gosling, S. D., & Potter, J. (2011). Age differences in personality traits from 10 to 65: Big five domains and facets in a large cross-sectional sample. *Journal of Personality and Social Psychology, 100,* 330–348.

South African Department of Health. (2009). *2008 National Antenatal Sentinel HIV and Syphilis Prevalence Survey.* Retrieved from www.info.gov.za/view/DownloadFileAction?id=109007

Sowell, E. R., Thompson, P. M., Welcome, S. E., Henkenius, A. L., Toga, A. W., & Peterson, B. S. (2003). Cortical abnormalities in children and adolescents with attention-deficit hyperactivity disorder. *Lancet, 362,* 1699–1707.

Sowell, E. R., Trauner, D. A., Gamst, A., & Jernigan, T. (2002). Development of cortical and subcortical brain structures in childhood and adolescence: A structural MRI study. *Developmental Medicine and Child Neurology, 44,* 4–16.

Sowers, M. F., Zheng, H., Tomey, K., Karvonen-Gutierrez, M. J., Li, X., Matheos, Y., & Symons, J. (2007). Changes in body composition in women over six years at midlife: Ovarian and chronological aging. *Journal of Clinical Endocrinology and Metabolism, 92,* 895–901.

Speakman, J. R., & Selman, C. (2011). The free-radical damage theory: Accumulating evidence against a simple link of oxidative stress to ageing and lifespan. *Bioessays, 33,* 255–259.

Speece, D. L., Ritchey, K. D., Cooper, D. H., Roth, F. P., & Schatschneider, C. (2004). Growth in early reading skills from kindergarten to third grade. *Contemporary Educational Psychology, 29,* 312–332.

Speece, M. W., & Brent, S. B. (1996). The development of children's understanding of death. In C. A. Corr & D. M. Corr (Eds.), *Handbook of childhood death and bereavement* (pp. 29–50). New York: Springer.

Spelke, E. S. (2000). Core knowledge. *American Psychologist, 55,* 1233–1242.

Spelke, E. S. (2004). Core knowledge. In N. Kanwisher & J. Duncan (Eds.), *Attention and performance* (Vol. 20, pp. 29–56). Oxford, UK: Oxford University Press.

Spelke, E. S., & Kinzler, K. D. (2007). Core knowledge. *Developmental Science, 10,* 89–96.

Spelke, E. S., Phillips, A. T., & Woodward, A. L. (1995). Infants' knowledge of object motion and human action. In A. Premack (Ed.), *Causal understanding in cognition and culture* (pp. 4–78). Oxford, UK: Clarendon Press.

Spence, I., & Feng, J. (2010). Video games and spatial cognition. *Review of General Psychology, 14,* 92–104.

Spence, M. J., & DeCasper, A. J. (1987). Prenatal experience with low-frequency maternal voice sounds influences neonatal perception of maternal voice samples. *Infant Behavior and Development, 10,* 133–142.

Spencer, J. P., & Perone, S. (2008). Defending qualitative change: The view from dynamical systems theory. *Child Development, 79,* 1639–1647.

Spencer, J. P., Verejiken, B., Diedrich, F. J., & Thelen, E. (2000). Posture and the emergence of manual skills. *Developmental Science, 3,* 216–233.

Spera, C. (2005). A review of the relationship among parenting practices, parenting styles, and adolescent school achievement. *Educational Psychology Review, 17,* 125–146.

Spere, K. A., Schmidt, L. A., Theall-Honey, L. A., & Martin-Chang, S. (2004). Expressive and receptive language skills of temperamentally shy preschoolers. *Infant and Child Development, 13,* 123–133.

Sperling R. A., Aisen, P. S., Beckett, L. A., Bennett D. A., Craft, S., Fagan, A. M., et al. (2011). Toward defining the preclinical stages of Alzheimer's disease: Recommendations from the National Institute on Aging–Alzheimer's Association workgroups on diagnostic guidelines for Alzheimer's disease. *Alzheimer's and Dementia, 7,* 280–292.

Spielmann, G., McFarlin, B. K., O'Connor, D. P., Smith, P. J., Pircher, H., & Simpson, R. J. (2011). Aerobic fitness is associated with lower proportions of senescent blood T-cells in man. *Brain, Behavior, and Immunity, 25,* 1521–1529.

Spinrad, T. L., & Eisenberg, N. (2009). Empathy, prosocial behavior, and positive development in schools. In R. Gilman, E. S. Huebner, & M. J.

Furlong (Eds.), *Handbook of positive psychology in schools* (pp. 119–129). New York: Routledge

Spirito, A., & Esposito-Smythers, C. (2006). Attempted and completed suicide. *Annual Review of Clinical Psychology, 2*, 237–266.

Spitze, G., & Gallant, M. P. (2004). "The bitter with the sweet": Older adults' strategies for handling ambivalence in relations with their adult children. *Research on Aging, 26*, 387–412.

Spock, B., & Needlman, R. (2012). *Dr. Spock's baby and child care* (9th ed.). New York: Gallery Books.

Spokane, A. R., & Cruza-Guet, M. C. (2005). Holland's theory of vocational personalities in work environments. In S. D. Brown & R. W. Lent (Eds.), *Career development and counseling* (pp. 24–41). Hoboken, NJ: Wiley.

Sprecher, S. (1999). "I love you more today than yesterday": Romantic partners' perceptions of changes in love and related affect over time. *Journal of Personality and Social Psychology, 76*, 46–53.

Sprecher, S. (2011). The influence of social networks on romantic relationships: Through the lens of the social network. *Personal Relationships, 18*, 630–644.

Sprecher, S., & Fehr, B. (2011). Dispositional attachment and relationship-specific attachment as predictors of compassionate love for partner. *Journal of Social and Personal Relationships, 28*, 558–574.

Srivastava, S., John, O. P., Gosling, S. D., & Potter, J. (2003). Development of personality in early and middle adulthood: Set like plaster or persistent change? *Journal of Personality and Social Psychology, 84*, 1041–1053.

Sroufe, L. A. (2002). From infant attachment to promotion of adolescent autonomy: Prospective, longitudinal data on the role of parents in development. In J. G. Borkowski & S. L. Ramey (Eds.), *Parenting and the child's world* (pp. 187–202). Mahwah, NJ: Erlbaum.

Sroufe, L. A., Coffino, B., & Carlson, E. A. (2010). Conceptualizing the role of early experience: Lessons from the Minnesota Longitudinal Study. *Developmental Review, 30*, 36–51.

Sroufe, L. A., Egeland, B., Carlson, E., & Collins, W. (2005). *Minnesota Study of Risk and Adaptation from birth to maturity: The development of the person.* New York: Guilford.

Sroufe, L. A., & Waters, E. (1976). The ontogenesis of smiling and laughter: A perspective on the organization of development in infancy. *Psychological Review, 83*, 173–189.

Sroufe, L. A., & Wunsch, J. P. (1972). The development of laughter in the first year of life. *Child Development, 43*, 1324–1344.

Stacey, J., & Biblarz, T. (2001). (How) Does the sexual orientation of parents matter? *American Sociological Review, 66*, 159–183.

Stackert, R. A., & Bursik, K. (2003). Why am I unsatisfied? Adult attachment style, gendered irrational relationship beliefs, and young adult romantic relationship satisfaction. *Personality and Individual Differences, 34*, 1419–1434.

Staff, J., & Uggen, C. (2003). The fruits of good work: Early work experiences and adolescent deviance. *Journal of Research in Crime and Delinquency, 40*, 263–290.

Stahl, S. A., & Miller, P. D. (2006). Whole language and language experience approaches for beginning reading: A quantitative research synthesis. In K. A. Dougherty Stahl & M. C. McKenna (Eds.), *Reading research at work: Foundations of effective practice* (pp. 9–35). New York: Guilford.

Stams, G. J. M., Brugman, D., Deković, M., van Rosmalen, L., van der Laan, P., & Gibbs, J. C. (2006). The moral judgment of juvenile delinquents: A meta-analysis. *Journal of Abnormal Child Psychology, 34*, 697–713.

Stams, G. J. M., Juffer, F., & van IJzendoorn, M. H. (2002). Maternal sensitivity, infant attachment, and temperament in early childhood predict adjustment in middle childhood: The case of adopted children and their biologically unrelated parents. *Developmental Psychology, 38*, 806–821.

Stanovich, K. E. (2013). *How to think straight about psychology* (10th ed.). Upper Saddle River, NJ: Pearson.

Starr, J. M., Deary, I. J., Fox, H. C., & Whalley, L. J. (2007). Smoking and cognitive change from age 11 to 66: A confirmatory investigation. *Addictive Behaviors, 32*, 63–68.

Starr, R. J. (1999). Music therapy in hospice care. *American Journal of Hospice and Palliative Care, 16*, 739–742.

Stattin, H., & Magnusson, D. (1990). *Pubertal maturation in female development.* Hillsdale, NJ: Erlbaum.

Staudinger, U. M. (1996). Wisdom and the social-interactive foundation of the mind. In P. B. Baltes & U. M. Staudinger (Eds.), *Interactive minds: Life-span perspectives on the social foundation of cognition* (pp. 276–315). New York: Cambridge University Press.

Staudinger, U. M. (2008). A psychology of wisdom: History and recent developments. *Research in Human Development, 5*, 107–120.

Staudinger, U. M., & Bowen, C. E. (2010). Life-span perspectives on positive personality development in adulthood and old age. In M. E. Lamb, A. M. Freund, & R. M. Lerner (Eds.), *Handbook of life-span development: Vol. 2. Social and emotional development* (pp. 254–297). Hoboken, NJ: Wiley.

Staudinger, U. M., Dörner, J., & Mickler, C. (2005). Wisdom and personality. In R. J. Sternberg & J. Jordan (Eds.), *A handbook of wisdom: Psychological perspectives* (pp 191–219). New York: Cambridge University Press.

Staudinger, U. M., & Lindenberger, U. (2003). Understanding human development takes a metatheory and multiple disciplines. In U. M. Staudinger & U. Lindenberger (Eds.), *Understanding human development: Dialogues with life span psychology* (pp. 1–13). Norwell, MA: Kluwer.

Staudinger, U. M., Smith, J., & Baltes, P. B. (1992). Wisdom-related knowledge in a life-review task: Age differences and the role of professional specialization. *Psychology and Aging, 7*, 271–281.

Steele, C. M. (1997). A threat in the air: How stereotypes shape intellectual identity and performance. *American Psychologist, 52*, 613–629.

Steele, H., Steele, M., & Fonagy, P. (1996). Associations among attachment classifications of mothers, fathers, and their infants. *Child Development, 67*, 541–555.

Steele, L. C. (2012). The forensic interview: A challenging intervention. In P. Goodyear-Brown (Ed.), *Handbook of child sexual abuse: Identification, assessment, and treatment* (pp. 99–119). Hoboken, NJ: Wiley.

Steele, S., Joseph, R. M., & Tager-Flusberg, H. (2003). Developmental change in theory of mind abilities in children with autism. *Journal of Autism and Developmental Disorders, 33*, 461–467.

Steenhuis, I. H., & Vermeer, W. M. (2009). Portion size: Review and framework for interventions. *International Journal of Behavioral Nutrition and Physical Activity, 6*, 58.

Stehr-Green, P., Tull, P., Stellfeld, M., Mortenson, P. B., & Simpson, D. (2003). Autism and thimerosal-containing vaccines: Lack of consistent evidence for an association. *American Journal of Preventive Medicine, 25*, 101–106.

Stein, C. H. (2009). "I owe it to them": Understanding felt obligation toward parents in adulthood. In K. Shifren (Ed.), *How caregiving affects development* (pp. 119–145). Washington, DC: American Psychological Association.

Stein, J. H., & Reiser, L. W. (1994). A study of white middle-class adolescent boys' responses to

"semenarche" (the first ejaculation). *Journal of Youth and Adolescence, 23*, 373–384.

Stein, N., & Levine, L. J. (1999). The early emergence of emotional understanding and appraisal: Implications for theories of development. In T. Dalgleish & M. J. Power (Eds.), *Handbook of cognition and emotion* (pp. 383–408). Chichester, UK: Wiley.

Steinberg, L. (2008). A social neuroscience perspective on adolescent risk-taking. *Developmental Review, 28*, 78–106.

Steinberg, L., Albert, D., Cauffman, E., Banich, M., & Graham, S. (2008). Age differences in sensation seeking and impulsivity as indexed by behavior and self-report: Evidence for a dual systems model. *Developmental Psychology, 44*, 1764–1778.

Steinberg, L., Blatt-Eisengart, I., & Cauffman, E. (2006). Patterns of competence and adjustment among adolescents from authoritative, authoritarian, indulgent, and neglectful homes: A replication in a sample of serious juvenile offenders. *Journal of Research on Adolescence, 16*, 47–58.

Steinberg, L., Graham, S., O'Brien, L., Woolard, J., Cauffman, E., & Banich, M. (2009). Age differences in future orientation and delay discounting. *Child Development, 80*, 28–44.

Steinberg, L., & Monahan, K. C. (2011). Adolescents' exposure to sexy media does not hasten the initiation of sexual intercourse. *Developmental Psychology, 47*, 562–576.

Steinberg, L. D. (2001). We know some things: Parent-adolescent relationships in retrospect and prospect. *Journal of Research on Adolescence, 11*, 1–19.

Steinberg, L. D., Darling, N. E., & Fletcher, A. C. (1995). Authoritative parenting and adolescent development: An ecological journey. In P. Moen, G. H. Elder, Jr., & K. Luscher (Eds.), *Examining lives in context* (pp. 423–466). Washington, DC: American Psychological Association.

Steinberg, L. D., & Silk, J. S. (2002). Parenting adolescents. In M. H. Bornstein (Ed.), *Handbook of parenting* (Vol. 1, pp. 103–134). Mahwah, NJ: Erlbaum.

Steiner, J. E. (1979). Human facial expression in response to taste and smell stimulation. In H. W. Reese & L. P. Lipsitt (Eds.), *Advances in child development and behavior* (Vol. 13, pp. 257–295). New York: Academic Press.

Steiner, J. E., Glaser, D., Hawilo, M. E., & Berridge, D. C. (2001). Comparative expression of hedonic impact: Affective reactions to taste by human infants and other primates. *Neuroscience and Biobehavioral Review, 25*, 53–74.

Steinhausen, H.-C. (2006). Eating disorders: Anorexia nervosa and bulimia nervosa. In C. Gillberg, R. Harrington, & H. Steinhausen (Eds.), *A clinician's handbook of child and adolescent psychiatry* (pp. 272–303). New York: Cambridge University Press.

Stenberg, C. (2003). Effects of maternal inattentiveness on infant social referencing. *Infant and Child Development, 12*, 399–419.

Stenberg, C., & Campos, J. J. (1990). The development of anger expressions in infancy. In N. Stein, B. Leventhal, & T. Trabasso (Eds.), *Psychological and biological approaches to emotion* (pp. 247–282). Hillsdale, NJ: Erlbaum.

Stephens, B. E., & Vohr, B. R. (2009). Neurodevelopmental outcome of the premature infant. *Pediatric Clinics of North America, 56*, 631–646.

Stephens, M. A. P., Franks, M. M., Martire, L. M., Norton, T. R., & Atienza, A. A. (2009). Women at midlife: Stress and rewards of balancing parent care with employment and family roles. In K. Shifren (Ed.), *How caregiving affects development* (pp. 147–167). Washington, DC: American Psychological Association.

Stephens, P. C., Sloboda, Z., Stephens, R. C., Teasdale, B., Grey, S. F., Hawthorne, R. D., & Williams, J. (2009).

Universal school-based substance abuse prevention programs: Modeling targeted mediators and outcomes for adolescent cigarette, alcohol, and marijuana use. *Drug and Alcohol Dependence, 102,* 19–29.

Stern, D. (1985). *The interpersonal world of the infant.* New York: Basic Books.

Stern, Y. (2009). Cognitive reserve. *Neuropsychologia, 47,* 2015–2028.

Sternberg, R. J. (1988). Triangulating love. In R. J. Sternberg & M. L. Barnes (Eds.), *The psychology of love* (pp. 119–138). New Haven, CT: Yale University Press.

Sternberg, R. J. (2000). *Cupid's arrow: The course of love through time.* Cambridge, UK: Cambridge University Press.

Sternberg, R. J. (2001). Why schools should teach for wisdom: The balance theory of wisdom in educational settings. *Educational Psychologist, 36,* 227–245.

Sternberg, R. J. (2003). The development of creativity as a decision-making process. In R. K. Sawyer, V. John-Steiner, S. Moran, R. J. Sternberg, D. H. Feldman, J. Nakamura, & M. Csikszentmihalyi (Eds.), *Creativity and development* (pp. 91–138). New York: Oxford University Press.

Sternberg, R. J. (2005). The triarchic theory of successful intelligence. In D. P. Flanagan & P. L. Harrison (Eds.), *Contemporary intellectual assessment: Theories, tests, and issues* (pp. 103–119). New York: Guilford.

Sternberg, R. J. (2006). A duplex theory of love. In R. J. Sternberg & K. Weis (Eds.), *The new psychology of love* (pp. 184–199). New Haven, CT: Yale University Press.

Sternberg, R. J. (2008). The triarchic theory of successful intelligence. In N. Salkind (Ed.), *Encyclopedia of educational psychology* (Vol. 2, pp. 988–994). Thousand Oaks, CA: Sage.

Sternberg, R. J., Forsythe, G. B., Hedlund, J., Horvath, J. A., Wagner, R. K., Williams, W. M., Snook, S. A., & Grigorenko, E. L. (2000). *Practical intelligence in everyday life.* Cambridge, UK: Cambridge University Press.

Sternberg, R. J., & Grigorenko, E. L. (2002). *Dynamic testing.* New York: Cambridge University Press.

Sternberg, R. J., & Lubart, T. I. (2001). Wisdom and creativity. In J. E. Birren & K. W. Schaie (Eds.), *Handbook of the psychology of aging* (pp. 500–522). San Diego: Academic Press.

Stessman, J., Hammerman-Rozenberg, R., Maaravi, Y., Azoulai, D., & Cohen, A. (2005). Strategies to enhance longevity and independent function: The Jerusalem Longitudinal Study. *Mechanisms of Ageing and Development, 126,* 327–331.

Stevens, J., Katz, E. G., & Huxley, R. R. (2010). Associations between gender, age and waist circumference. *European Journal of Clinical Nutrition, 64,* 6–15.

Stevens, J. C., & Cruz, L. A. (1996). Spatial acuity of touch: Ubiquitous decline with aging revealed by repeated threshold testing. *Somatosensory and Motor Research, 13,* 1–10.

Stevenson, H. W., Lee, S., & Mu, X. (2000). Successful achievement in mathematics: China and the United States. In C. F. M. van Lieshout & P. G. Heymans (Eds.), *Developing talent across the life span* (pp. 167–183). Philadelphia: Psychology Press.

Stevenson, R., & Pollitt, C. (1987). The acquisition of temporal terms. *Journal of Child Language, 14,* 533–545.

Stevens-Simon, C., Sheeder, J., & Harter, S. (2005). Teen contraceptive decisions: Childbearing intentions are the tip of the iceberg. *Women and Health, 42,* 55–73.

Stewart, A. J., & Malley, J. E. (2004). Women of the greatest generation. In C. Daiute & C. Lightfoot (Eds.), *Narrative analysis: Studying the development of individuals in society* (pp. 223–244). Thousand Oaks, CA: Sage.

Stewart, A. J., & Ostrove, J. M. (1998). Women's personality in middle age: Gender, history and midcourse correction. *American Psychologist, 53,* 1185–1194.

Stewart, A. J., Ostrove, J. M., & Helson, R. (2001). Middle aging in women: Patterns of personality change from the 30s to the 50s. *Journal of Adult Development, 8,* 23–37.

Stewart, A. J., & Vandewater, E. A. (1999). "If I had to do over again . . .": Midlife review, midcourse corrections, and women's well-being in midlife. *Journal of Personality and Social Psychology, 76,* 270–283.

Stewart, A. L., Verboncoeur, C. J., McLellan, B. Y., Gillis, D. E., Rush, S., & Mills, K. M. (2001). Physical activity outcomes of CHAMPS II: A physical activity promotion program for older adults. *Journal of Gerontology, 56A,* M465–M470.

Stewart, P. W., Lonky, E., Reihman, J., Pagano, J., Gump, B. B., & Darvill, T. (2008). The relationship between prenatal PCB exposure and intelligence (IQ). *Environmental Health Perspectives, 116,* 1416–1422.

Stewart, R. B., Jr. (1990). *The second child: Family transition and adjustment.* Newbury Park, CA: Sage.

Stewart, S., Stinnett, H., & Rosenfeld, L. B. (2000). Sex differences in desired characteristics of short-term and long-term relationship partners. *Journal of Social and Personal Relationships, 17,* 843–853.

Stewart-Brown, S., & Edmunds, L. (2007). *Educating people to be emotionally intelligent* (pp. 241–257). Westport, CT: Praeger.

Stice, E. (2003). Puberty and body image. In C. Hayward (Ed.), *Gender differences at puberty* (pp. 61–76). New York: Cambridge University Press.

Stice, E., Presnell, K., & Bearman, S. K. (2001). Relation of early menarche to depression, eating disorders, substance abuse, and comorbid psychopathology among adolescent girls. *Developmental Psychology, 37,* 608–619.

Stiles, J. (2001a). Neural plasticity in cognitive development. *Developmental Neuropsychology, 18,* 237–272.

Stiles, J. (2001b). Spatial cognitive development. In C. A. Nelson & M. Luciana (Eds.), *Handbook of developmental cognitive neuroscience* (pp. 399–414). Cambridge, MA: MIT Press.

Stiles, J. (2008). *Fundamentals of brain development.* Cambridge, MA: Harvard University Press.

Stiles, J. (2012). The effects of injury to dynamic neural networks in the mature and developing brain. *Developmental Psychobiology, 54,* 343–349.

Stiles, J., Bates, E. A., Thal, D., Trauner, D. A., & Reilly, J. (2002). Linguistic and spatial cognitive development in children with pre- and perinatal focal brain injury: A ten-year overview from the San Diego longitudinal project. In M. H. Johnson & Y. Munakata (Eds.), *Brain development and cognition: A reader* (2nd ed., pp. 272–291). Malden, MA: Blackwell.

Stiles, J., Moses, P., Roe, K., Akshoomoff, N. A., Trauner, D., & Hesselink, J. (2003). Alternative brain organization after prenatal cerebral injury: Convergent fMRI and cognitive data. *Journal of the International Neuropsychological Society, 9,* 604–622.

Stiles, J., Reilly, J., Paul, B., & Moses, P. (2005). Cognitive development following early brain injury: Evidence for neural adaptation. *Trends in Cognitive Sciences, 9,* 136–143.

Stiles, J., Stern, C., Appelbaum, M., & Nass, R. (2008). Effects of early focal brain injury on memory for visuospatial patterns: Selective deficits of global–local processing. *Neuropsychology, 22,* 61–73.

Stilson, S. R., & Harding, C. G. (1997). Early social context as it relates to symbolic play: A longitudinal investigation. *Merrill-Palmer Quarterly, 43,* 682–693.

Stinchcomb, J. B., Bazemore, G., & Riestenberg, N. (2006). Beyond zero tolerance: Restoring justice in secondary schools. *Youth Violence and Juvenile Justice, 4,* 123–147.

Stine-Morrow, E. A. L., & Basak, C. (2011). Cognitive interventions. In K. W. Schaie & S. L. Willis (Eds.), *Handbook of the psychology of aging* (7th ed., pp. 153–171). New York: Elsevier.

Stine-Morrow, E. A. L., & Miller, L. M. S. (2009). Aging, self-regulation, and learning from text. *Psychology of Learning and Motivation, 51,* 255–285.

Stipek, D. J., Feiler, R., Daniels, D., & Milburn, S. (1995). Effects of different instructional approaches on young children's achievement and motivation. *Child Development, 66,* 209–223.

Stipek, D. J., Gralinski, J. H., & Kopp, C. B. (1990). Self-concept development in the toddler years. *Developmental Psychology, 26,* 972–977.

St James-Roberts, I. (2007). Helping parents to manage infant crying and sleeping: A review of the evidence and its implications for services. *Child Abuse Review, 16,* 47–69.

St James-Roberts, I., Alvarez, M., Csipke, E., Abramsky, T., Goodwin, J., & Sorgenfrei, E. (2006). Infant crying and sleeping in London, Copenhagen and when parents adopt a "proximal" form of care. *Pediatrics, 117,* e1146–e1155.

St James-Roberts, I., Goodwin, J., Peter, B., Adams, D., & Hunt, S. (2003). Individual differences in responsivity to a neurobehavioural examination predict crying patterns of 1-week-old infants at home. *Developmental Medicine and Child Neurology, 45,* 400–407.

St. Louis, G. R., & Liem, J. H. (2005). Ego identity, ethnic identity, and the psychosocial well-being of ethnic minority and majority college students. *Identity, 5,* 227–246.

Stoch, M. B., Smythe, P. M., Moodie, A. D., & Bradshaw, D. (1982). Psychosocial outcome and CT findings after growth undernourishment during infancy: A 20-year developmental study. *Developmental Medicine and Child Neurology, 24,* 419–436

Stocker, C. M., Burwell, R. A., & Briggs, M. L. (2002). Sibling conflict in middle childhood predicts children's adjustment in early adolescence. *Journal of Family Psychology, 16,* 50–57.

Stohs, S. J. (2011). The role of free radicals in toxicity and disease. *Journal of Basic and Clinical Physiology and Pharmacology, 6,* 205–228.

Stone, A. A., Schwartz, J. E., Broderick, J. E., & Deaton, A. (2010). A snapshot of the age distribution of psychological well-being in the United States. *Proceedings of the National Academy of Sciences, 107,* 9985–9990.

Stone, M. R., & Brown, B. B. (1999). Identity claims and projections: Descriptions of self and crowds in secondary school. In J. A. McLellan & M. J. V. Pugh (Eds.), *The role of peer groups in adolescent social identity: Exploring the importance of stability and change* (pp. 7–20). San Francisco: Jossey-Bass.

Stone, P., & Lovejoy, M. (2004). Fast-track women and the "choice" to stay home. *Annals of the American Academy of Political and Social Science, 596,* 62–83.

Stone, R. I., & Reinhard, S. C. (2007). The place of assisted living in long-term care and related service systems. *Gerontologist, 47,* 23–32.

Stoppa, T. M., & Lefkowitz, E. S. (2010). Longitudinal changes in religiosity among emerging adult college students. *Journal of Research on Adolescence, 20,* 23–38.

Storch, S. A., & Whitehurst, G. J. (2001). The role of family and home in the literacy development of children from low-income backgrounds. In P. R. Britto & J. Brooks-Gunn (Eds.), *New directions for child and adolescent development* (No. 92, pp. 53–71). San Francisco: Jossey-Bass.

Stormshak, E. A., Bierman, K. L., McMahon, R. J., Lengua, L. J., & the Conduct Problems Prevention Research Group. (2000). Parenting practices and child disruptive behavior problems in early elementary school. *Journal of Clinical Child Psychology, 29,* 17–29.

Story, R. (2007). Asthma and obesity in children. *Current Opinion in Pediatrics, 19,* 680–684.

Stouthamer-Loeber, M., Wei, E., Loeber, R., & Masten, A. S. (2004). Desistance from persistent serious delinquency in the transition to adulthood. *Development and Psychopathology, 16,* 897–918.

Strain, L. A., Grabusic, C. C., Searle, M. S., & Dunn, N. J. (2002). Continuing and ceasing leisure activities in later life: A longitudinal study. *Gerontologist, 42,* 217–223.

Strapp, C. M., & Federico, A. (2000). Imitations and repetitions: What do children say following recasts? *First Language, 20,* 273–290.

Straus, M. A., & Stewart, J. H. (1999). Corporal punishment by American parents: National data on prevalence, chronicity, severity, and duration, in relation to child and family characteristics. *Clinical Child and Family Psychology Review, 2,* 55–70.

Strawbridge, W. J., Shema, S. J., Cohen, R. D., & Kaplan, G. A. (2001). Religious attendance increases survival by improving and maintaining good health behaviors. *Annals of Behavioral Medicine, 23,* 68–74.

Strayer, J., & Roberts, W. (2004). Children's anger, emotional expressiveness, and empathy: Relations with parents' empathy, emotional expressiveness, and parenting practices. *Social Development, 13,* 229–254.

Strazdins, L., Clements, M. S., Korda, R. J., Broom, D. H., & D'Souza, R. M. (2006). Unsociable work? Nonstandard work schedules, family relationships, and children's well-being. *Journal of Marriage and the Family, 68,* 394–410.

Street, A. E., Bell, M., & Ready, C. B. (2011). Sexual assault. In D. Benedek & G. Wynn (Eds.), *Clinical manual for the management of PTSD* (pp. 325–348). Arlington, VA: American Psychiatric Press.

Streissguth, A. P., Bookstein, F. L., Barr, H. M., Sampson, P. D., O'Malley, K., & Young, J. K. (2004). Risk factors for adverse life outcomes in fetal alcohol syndrome and fetal alcohol effects. *Journal of Developmental and Behavioral Pediatrics, 25,* 228–238.

Streissguth, A. P., Treder, R., Barr, H. M., Shepard, T., Bleyer, W. A., Sampson, P. D., & Martin, D. (1987). Aspirin and acetaminophen use by pregnant women and subsequent child IQ and attention decrements. *Teratology, 35,* 211–219.

Striano, T., & Rochat, P. (2000). Emergence of selective social referencing in infancy. *Infancy, 1,* 253–264.

Striano, T., Tomasello, M., & Rochat, P. (2001). Social and object support for early symbolic play. *Developmental Science, 4,* 442–455.

Striegel-Moore, R. H., & Franko, D. L. (2006). Adolescent eating disorders. In R. H. Striegel-Moore & D. L. Franko (Eds.), *Child and adolescent psychopathology: Theoretical and clinical implications* (pp. 160–183). New York: Routledge.

Stright, A. D., Herr, M. Y., & Neitzel, C. (2009). Maternal scaffolding of children's problem solving and children's adjustment in kindergarten: Hmong families in the United States. *Journal of Educational Psychology, 101,* 207–218.

Stright, A. D., Neitzel, C., Sears, K. G., & Hoke-Sinex, L. (2002). Instruction begins in the home: Relations between parental instruction and children's self-regulation in the classroom. *Journal of Educational Psychology, 93,* 456–466.

Stringer, K., Kerpelman, J., & Skorikov, V. (2011). Career preparation: A longitudinal, process-oriented examination. *Journal of Vocational Behavior, 79,* 158–169.

Stringer, K. J., & Kerpelman, J. L. (2010). Career identity development in college students: Decision making, parental support, and work experience. *Identity, 10,* 181–200.

Stroebe, M., & Schut, H. (2010). The dual process model of coping with bereavement: A decade on. *Omega, 61,* 273–289.

Stroebe, M. S., & Schut, H. (1999). The dual process model of coping with bereavement: Rationale and description. *Death Studies, 23,* 197–224.

Stroebe, M. S., van der Houwen, K., & Schut, H. (2008). Bereavement support, intervention, and research on the Internet: A critical review. In M. S. Stroebe, R. O. Hansson, H. Schut, & W. Stroebe (Eds.), *Handbook of bereavement research and practice* (pp. 551–574). Washington, DC: American Psychological Association.

Strohschein, L. (2005). Parental divorce and child mental health trajectories. *Journal of Marriage and Family, 67,* 1286–1300.

Stromswold, K. (2000). The cognitive neuro-science of language acquisition. In M. S. Gazzaniga (Ed.), *The new cognitive neuro-sciences* (pp. 909–932). Cambridge, MA: MIT Press.

Strough, J., Hicks, P. J., Swenson, L. M., Cheng, S., & Barnes, K. A. (2003). Collaborative everyday problem solving: Interpersonal relationships and problem dimensions. *International Journal of Aging and Human Development, 56,* 43–66.

Strough, J., Leszczynski, J. P., Neely, T. L., Flinn, J. A., & Margrett, J. (2007). From adolescence to later adulthood: Femininity, masculinity, and androgyny in six age groups. *Sex Roles, 57,* 385–396.

Strough, J., McFall, J. P., Flinn, J. A., & Schuller, K. L. (2008). Collaborative everyday problem solving among same-gender friends in early and later adulthood. *Psychology and Aging, 23,* 517–530.

Strouse, D. L. (1999). Adolescent crowd orientations: A social and temporal analysis. In J. A. McLellan & M. J. V. Pugh (Eds.), *The role of peer groups in adolescent social identity: Exploring the importance of stability and change* (pp. 37–54). San Francisco: Jossey-Bass.

Stuart, M., & Weinrich, M. (2001). Home-and community-based long-term care: Lessons from Denmark. *Gerontologist, 41,* 474–480.

Sturaro, C., van Lier, P. A. C., Cuijpers, P., & Koot, H. M. (2011). The role of peer relationships in the development of early school-age externalizing problems. *Child Development, 82,* 758–765.

Sturge-Apple, M. L., Davies, P. T., Winter, M. A., Cummings, E. M., & Schermerhorn, A. (2008). Interparental conflict and children's school adjustment: The explanatory role of children's internal representations of interparental and parent–child relationships. *Developmental Psychology, 44,* 1678–1690.

Styne, D. M. (2003). The regulation of pubertal growth. *Hormone Research, 60*(Suppl. 1), 22–26.

Su, T. F., & Costigan, C. L. (2008). The development of children's ethnic identity in immigrant Chinese families in Canada: The role of parenting practices and children's perceptions of parental family obligation expectations. *Journal of Early Adolescence, 29,* 638–663.

Suarez-Morales, L., & Lopez, B. (2009). The impact of acculturative stress and daily hassles on preadolescent psychological adjustment: Examining anxiety symptoms. *Journal of Primary Prevention, 30,* 335–349.

Suárez-Orozco, C., Todorova, I., & Qin, D. B. (2006). The well-being of immigrant adolescents: A longitudinal perspective on risk and protective factors. In F. A. Villarruel & T. Luster (Eds.), *The crisis in youth mental health: Critical issues and effective programs: Vol. 2. Disorders in adolescence* (pp. 53–83). Westport, CT: Praeger.

Subbotsky, E. (2004). Magical thinking in judgments of causation: Can anomalous phenomena affect ontological causal beliefs in children and adults? *British Journal of Developmental Psychology, 22,* 123–152.

Subrahmanyam, K., Gelman, R., & Lafosse, A. (2002). Animate and other separably moveable things. In G. Humphreys (Ed.), *Category-specificity in brain and mind* (pp. 341–371). London: Psychology Press.

Subrahmanyam, K., & Greenfield, P. M. (2008). Online communication and adolescent relationships. *Future of Children, 18,* 119–146.

Subrahmanyam, K., Smahel, D., & Greenfield, P. (2006). Connecting developmental constructions to the Internet: Identity presentation and sexual exploration in online teen chat rooms. *Developmental Psychology, 42,* 395–406.

Substance Abuse and Mental Health Services Administration. (2011). *Results from the 2010 National Survey on Drug Use and Health: Vol. 1. Summary of national findings.* Rockville, MD: Author.

Suddendorf, T., Simcock, G., & Nielsen, M. (2007). Visual self-recognition in mirrors and live videos: Evidence for a developmental asynchrony. *Cognitive Development, 22,* 185–196.

Sullivan, K. T., Pasch, L. A., Johnson, M. D., & Bradbury, T. N. (2010). Social support, problem solving, and the longitudinal course of newlywed marriage. *Journal of Personality and Social Psychology, 98,* 631–644.

Sullivan, M. C., McGrath, M. M. Hawes, K., & Lester, B. M. (2008). Growth trajectories of preterm infants: Birth to 12 years. *Journal of Pediatric Health Care, 22,* 83–93.

Sullivan, M. W., & Lewis, M. (2003). Contextual determinants of anger and other negative expressions in young infants. *Developmental Psychology, 39,* 693–705.

Summers, R. W., & Hoffman, A. M. (Eds.). (2006). *Elder abuse: A public health perspective.* Washington, DC: American Public Health Association.

Super, C. M. (1981). Behavioral development in infancy. In R. H. Monroe, R. L. Monroe, & B. B. Whiting (Eds.), *Handbook of cross-cultural human development* (pp. 181–270). New York: Garland.

Super, C. M., & Harkness, S. (2002). Culture structures the environment for development. *Human Development 45,* 270–274.

Super, C. M., & Harkness, S. (2009). The developmental niche of the newborn in rural Kenya. In J. K. Nugent, B. J. Petrauskas, & T. B. Brazelton (Eds.), *The newborn as a person: Enabling healthy development worldwide* (pp. 85–97). Hoboken, NJ: Wiley.

Super, C. M., & Harkness, S. (2010). Culture and infancy. In J. G. Bremner & T. D. Wachs (Eds.), *Wiley-Blackwell handbook of infant development: Vol. 1. Basic research* (2nd ed., pp. 623–649). Chichester, UK: Wiley-Blackwell.

Super, C. M., Harkness, S., van Tijen, N., van der Vlugt, E., Fintelman, M., & Dijkstra, J. (1996). The three R's of Dutch childrearing and the socialization of infant arousal. In S. Harkness & C. M. Super (Eds.), *Parents' cultural belief systems* (pp. 447–466). New York: Guilford.

Super, D. E. (1990). A life span, life space approach to career development. In D. Brown & L. Brooks (Eds.), *Career choice and development* (2nd ed., pp. 197–261). San Francisco: Jossey-Bass.

Supple, A. J., Ghazarian, S. R., Peterson, G. W., & Bush, K. R. (2009). Assessing the cross-cultural validity of a parental autonomy granting measure: Comparing adolescents in the United States, China, Mexico, and India. *Journal of Cross-Cultural Psychology, 40,* 816–833.

Supple, A. J., & Small, S. A. (2006). The influence of parental support, knowledge, and authoritative parenting on Hmong and European American adolescent development. *Journal of Family Issues, 27,* 1214–1232.

Susman, E. J., & Dorn, L. D. (2009). Puberty: Its role in development. In R. M. Lerner & L. Steinberg (Eds.), *Handbook of adolescent psychology: Vol. 1. Individual bases of adolescent development* (3rd ed., pp. 116–151). Hoboken, NJ: Wiley.

Sussman, S., Skara, S., & Ames, S. L. (2008). Substance abuse among adolescents. *Substance Use and Misuse, 43,* 1802–1828.

Sutton, M. J., Brown, J. D., Wilson, K. M., & Klein, J. D. (2002). Shaking the tree of forbidden fruit: Where adolescents learn about sexuality and contraception. In J. D. Brown, J. R. Steele, & K. Walsh-Childers (Eds.), *Sexual teens, sexual media* (pp. 25–55). Mahwah, NJ: Erlbaum.

Sveen, C.-A., & Walby, F. A. (2008). Suicide survivors' mental health and grief reactions: A systematic review of controlled studies. *Suicide and Life-Threatening Behavior, 38,* 13–29.

Swartz, T. T. (2009). Intergenerational family relations in adulthood: Patterns, variations, and implictions in the contemporary United States. *Annual Review of Sociology, 25,* 191–212.

Sweet, M. A., & Appelbaum, M. L. (2004). Is home visiting an effective strategy? A meta-analytic review of home visiting programs for families with young children. *Child Development, 75,* 1435–1456.

Sweet, S., & Moen, P. (2007). Integrating educational careers in work and family. *Community, Work and Family, 10,* 231–250.

Swingley, D. (2005). Statistical clustering and the contents of the infant vocabulary. *Cognitive Psychology, 50,* 86–132.

Swinson, J., & Harrop, A. (2009). Teacher talk directed to boys and girls and its relationship to their behaviour. *Educational Studies, 35,* 515–524.

Symons, D. K. (2001). A dyad-oriented approach to distress and mother–child relationship outcomes in the first 24 months. *Parenting: Science and Practice, 1,* 101–122.

Szaflarski, J. P., Rajogopal, A., Altaye, M., Byars, A. W., Jacola, L., Schmithorst, V. J., et al. (2012). Left-handedness and language lateralization in children. *Brain Research, 1433,* 85–97.

Szkrybalo, J., & Ruble, D. N. (1999). "God made me a girl": Sex-category constancy judgments and explanations revisited. *Developmental Psychology, 35,* 392–402.

Szlemko, W. J., Wood, J. W., & Thurman, P. J. (2006). Native Americans and alcohol: Past, present, and future. *Journal of General Psychology, 133,* 435–451.

T

Tabibi, Z., & Pfeffer, K. (2007). Finding a safe place to cross the road: The effect of distractors and the role of attention in children's identification of safe and dangerous road-crossing sites. *Infant and Child Development, 16,* 193–206.

Tacon, A., & Caldera, Y. (2001). Attachment and parental correlates in late adolescent Mexican American women. *Hispanic Journal of Behavioral Sciences, 23,* 71–88.

Taga, G., Asakawa, K., Maki, A., Konishi, Y., & Koizumi, H. (2003). Brain imaging in awake infants by near-infrared optical topography. *Proceedings of the National Academy of Sciences, 100,* 10722–10727.

Tager-Flusberg, H., & Zukowski, A. (2009). Putting words together: Morphology and syntax in the preschool years. In J. B. Gleason & B. Ratner (Ed.), *The development of language* (7th ed., pp. 139–191). Boston: Allyn and Bacon.

Tahir, L., & Gruber, H. E. (2003). Developmental trajectories and creative work in late life. In J. Demick & C. Andreoletti (Eds.), *Handbook of adult development* (pp. 239–255). New York: Springer.

Takagi, E., Silverstein, M., & Crimmins, E. (2007). Intergenerational coresidence of older adults in Japan: Conditions for cultural plasticity. *Journal of Gerontology, 62B,* S330–S339.

Takahashi, K. (1990). Are the key assumptions of the "Strange Situation" procedure universal? A view from Japanese research. *Human Development, 33,* 23–30.

Takamura, J., & Williams, B. (2002). *Informal caregiving: Compassion in action.* Arlington, TX: Arc of the United States.

Talbot, L. S., McGlinchey, E. L., Kaplan, K. A., & Dahl, R. E. (2010). Sleep deprivation in adolescents and adults: Changes in affect. *Emotion, 10,* 831–841.

Talwar, V. (2011). Talking to children about death in educational settings. In V. Talwar, P. L. Harris, & M. Schleifer (Eds.), *Children's understanding of death: From biological to religious conceptions* (pp. 98–115). Cambridge, UK: Cambridge University Press.

Tamis-LeMonda, C. S., & Bornstein, M. H. (1989). Habituation and maternal encouragement of attention in infancy as predictors of toddler language, play, and representational competence. *Child Development, 60,* 738–751.

Tamis-LeMonda, C. S., Way, N., Hughes, D., Yoshikawa, H., Kalman, R. K., & Niwa, E. Y. (2008). Parents' goals for children: The dynamic coexistence of individualism and collectivism in cultures and individuals. *Social Development, 17,* 183–209.

Tammelin, T., Näyhä, S., Hills, A. P., & Järvelin, M. (2003). Adolescent participation in sports and adult physical activity. *American Journal of Preventive Medicine, 24,* 22–28.

Tamrouti-Makkink, I. D., Dubas, J. S., Gerris, J. R. M., & van Aken, A. G. (2004). The relation between the absolute level of parenting and differential parental treatment on adolescent siblings' adjustment. *Journal of Child Psychology and Psychiatry, 45,* 1397–1406.

Tanaka, H., & Seals, D. R. (1997). Age and gender interactions in physiological functional capacity: Insight from swimming performance. *Journal of Applied Physiology, 82,* 846–851.

Tanaka, H., & Seals, D. R. (2003). Dynamic exercise performance in master athletes: Insight into the effects of primary human aging on physiological functional capacity. *Journal of Applied Physiology, 95,* 2152–2162.

Tangney, J. P., Stuewig, J., & Mashek, D. J. (2007). Moral emotions and moral behavior. *Annual Review of Psychology, 58,* 345–372.

Tanimura, M., Takahashi, K., Kataoka, N., Tomita, K., Tanabe, I., Yasuda, M., et al. (2004). Proposal: Heavy television and video viewing poses a risk for infants and young children. *Nippon Shonika Gakkai Zasshi, 108,* 709–712 (in Japanese).

Tanner, J. M., Healy, M., & Cameron, N. (2001). *Assessment of skeletal maturity and prediction of adult height (TW3 method)* (3rd ed.). Philadelphia: Saunders.

Tanner, J. L., & Arnett, J. J. (2011). Presenting "emerging adulthood": What makes it developmentally distinctive? In J. J. Arnett, M. Kloep, L. B. Hendry, & J. L. Tanner (Eds.), *Debating emerging adulthood: Stage or process?* (pp. 13–30). New York: Oxford University Press.

Tanner, J. L., Arnett, J. J., & Leis, J. A. (2009). Emerging adulthood: Learning and development during the first stage of adulthood. In M. C. Smith & N. DeFrates-Densch (Eds.), *Handbook of research on adult learning and development* (pp. 34–67). New York: Routledge.

Tardif, T. (2006). But are they really verbs? Chinese words for action. In K. Hirsh-Pasek & R. M. Golinkoff (Eds.), *Action meets word: How children learn verbs* (pp. 477–498). New York: Oxford University Press.

Tardif, T., Fletcher, P., Liang, W., & Kaciroti, N. (2009). Early vocabulary development in Mandarin (Putonghua) and Cantonese. *Journal of Child Language, 36,* 1115–1144.

Tardif, T., Fletcher, P., Liang, W., Zhang, Z., Kaciroti, N., & Marchman, V. A. (2008). Baby's first 10 words. *Developmental Psychology, 44,* 929–938.

Tardif, T., Gelman, S. A., & Xu, F. (1999). Putting the "noun bias" in context: A comparison of English and Mandarin. *Child Development, 70,* 620–635.

Tardif, T., Wellman, H. M., & Cheung, K. M. (2004). False belief understanding in Cantonese-speaking children. *Journal of Child Language, 31,* 779–800.

Tarry-Adkins, J. L., Martin-Gronert, M. S., Chen, J. H., Cripps, R. L., & Ozanne, S. E. (2008). Maternal diet influences DNA damage, aortic telomere length, oxidative stress, and antioxidant defense capacity in rats. *FASEB Journal, 22,* 2037–2044.

Tarter, R. E., Vanyukov, M., & Kirisci, L. (2008). Etiology of substance use disorder: Developmental perspective. In Y. Kaminer & O. G. Bukstein (Eds.), *Adolescent substance abuse: Psychiatric comorbidity and high-risk behaviors* (pp. 5–27). New York: Routledge.

Tasker, F. (2005). Lesbian mothers, gay fathers, and their children: A review. *Developmental and Behavioral Pediatrics, 26,* 224–240.

Taumoepeau, M., & Ruffman, T. (2006). Mother and infant talk about mental states relates to desire language and emotion understanding. *Child Development, 77,* 465–481.

Taylor, C. A., Manganello, J. A., Lee, S. J., & Rice, J. C. (2010). Mother's spanking of 3-year-old children and subsequent risk of children's aggressive behavior. *Pediatrics, 125,* e1057–e1065.

Taylor, J. L. (2009). Midlife impacts of adolescent parenthood. *Journal of Family Issues, 30,* 484–510.

Taylor, M. C., & Hall, J. A. (1982). Psychological androgyny: Theories, methods, and conclusions. *Psychological Bulletin, 92,* 347–366.

Taylor, M. G., Rhodes, M., & Gelman, S. A. (2009). Boys will be boys; cows will be cows: Children's essentialist reasoning about gender categories and animal species. *Child Development, 80,* 461–481.

Taylor, P., Wang, W., Parker, K., Passel, J. S., Patten, E., & Motel, S. (2012). *The rise of intermarriage.* Washington, DC: Pew Research Center.

Taylor, R. D. (2010). Risk and resilience in low-income African American families: Moderating effects of kinship social support. *Cultural Diversity and Ethnic Minority Psychology, 16,* 344–351.

Taylor, R. J., Lincoln, K. D., & Chatters, L. M. (2005). Supportive relationships with church members among African Americans. *Family Relations, 54,* 501–511.

Taylor, R. L. (2000). Diversity within African-American families. In D. H. Demo & K. R. Allen (Eds.), *Handbook of family diversity* (pp. 232–251). New York: Oxford University Press.

Taylor, W. C., Sallis, J. F., Lees, E., Hepworth, J. T., Feliz, K., Volding, D. C., Cassels, A., & Tobin, J. N. (2007). Changing social and built environments to promote physical activity: Recommendations from low-income, urban women. *Journal of Physical Activity and Health, 4,* 54–65.

Teasdale, B., & Bradley-Engen, M. S. (2010). Adolescent same-sex attraction and mental health: The role of stress and support. *Journal of Homosexuality, 57,* 287–309.

Teinonen, T., Fellman, V., Näätänen, R., Alku, P., & Huotilainen, M. (2009). Statistical language learning in neonates revealed by event-related brain potentials. *BMC Neuroscience, 10,* 21.

Telama, R., Yang, X., Viikari, J., Valimaki, I., Wanne, O., & Raitakari, O. (2005). Physical activity from childhood to adulthood: A 21-year tracking study. *American Journal of Preventive Medicine, 28,* 267–273.

Temkin-Greener, H., Bajorska, A., Peterson, D. R., Kunitz, S. J., Gross, D., & Williams, T. F. (2004). Social support and risk-adjusted mortality in a frail older population. *Medical Care, 42,* 779–788.

Temple, J. L., Giacomelli, A. M., Roemmich, J. N., & Epstein, L. H. (2007). Overweight children habituate slower than nonoverweight children to food. *Physiology and Behavior, 9,* 250–254.

Templeton, L. (2011). Dilemmas facing grandparents with grandchildren affected by parental substance misuse. *Drugs: Education, Prevention, and Policy, 19,* 11–18.

ten Brummelhuis, L. L., ter Hoeven, C. L., De Jong, M. D. T., & Peper, B. (in press). Exploring the linkage between the home domain and absence from work: Health, motivation, or both? *Journal of Organizational Behavior, 33.* Accessed online at http://onlinelibrary.wiley.com/doi/10.1002/job.1789/abstract

Tenenbaum, H. R., Hill, D., Joseph, N., & Roche, E. (2010). "It's a boy because he's painting a picture": Age differences in children's conventional and unconventional gender schemas. *British Journal of Psychology, 101,* 137–154.

Tenenbaum, H. R., & Leaper, C. (2002). Are parents' gender schemas related to their children's gender-related cognitions? A meta-analysis. *Developmental Psychology, 38,* 615–630.

Tenenbaum, H. R., & Leaper, C. (2003). Parent–child conversations about science: The socialization of gender inequities? *Developmental Psychology, 39,* 34–47.

Tenenbaum, H. R., Snow, C. E., Roach, K. A., & Kurland, B. (2005). Talking and reading science: Longitudinal data on sex differences in mother–child conversations in low-income families. *Journal of Applied Developmental Psychology, 26,* 1–19.

ten Tusscher, G. W., & Koppe, J. G. (2004). Perinatal dioxin exposure and later effects—a review. *Chemosphere, 54,* 1329–1336.

Terwel, J., Gillies, R. M., van den Eeden, P., & Hoek, D. (2001). Cooperative learning processes of students: A longitudinal multilevel perspective. *British Journal of Educational Psychology, 71,* 619–645.

Teti, D. M., Saken, J. W., Kucera, E., & Corns, K. M. (1996). And baby makes four: Predictors of attachment security among preschool-age firstborns during the transition to siblinghood. *Child Development, 67,* 579–596.

Teyber, E. (2001). *Helping children cope with divorce* (rev. ed.). San Francisco: Jossey-Bass.

Thacker, H. L. (2011). Assessing risks and benefits of nonhormonal treatments for vasomotor symptoms in perimenopausal and postmenopausal women. *Journal of Women's Health, 20,* 1007–1016.

Thacker, S. B., & Stroup, D. F. (2003). Revisiting the use of the electronic fetal monitor. *Lancet, 361,* 445–446.

Tharpe, A. M., & Ashmead, D. H. (2001). A longitudinal investigation of infant auditory sensitivity. *American Journal of Audiology, 10,* 104–112.

Thatcher, R. W., Walker, R. A., & Giudice, S. (1987). Human cerebral hemispheres develop at different rates and ages. *Science, 236,* 1110–1113.

Thelen, E., & Adolph, K. E. (1992). Arnold Gesell: The paradox of nature and nurture. *Developmental Psychology, 28,* 368–380.

Thelen, E., Fisher, D. M., & Ridley-Johnson, R. (1984). The relationship between physical growth and a newborn reflex. *Infant Behavior and Development, 7,* 479–493.

Thelen, E., Schöner, G., Scheier, C., & Smith, L. B. (2001). The dynamics of embodiment: A field theory of infant perseverative reaching. *Behavioral and Brain Sciences, 24,* 1–34.

Thelen, E., & Smith, L. B. (1998). Dynamic systems theories. In R. M. Lerner (Ed.), *Handbook of child psychology: Vol. 1. Theoretical models of human development* (5th ed., pp. 563–634). New York: Wiley.

Thelen, E., & Smith, L. B. (2006). Dynamic systems theories. In R. M. Lerner (Ed.), *Handbook of child psychology: Vol. 1. Theoretical models of human development* (6th ed., pp. 258–312). Hoboken, NJ: Wiley.

Théoret, E., Halligan, M., Kobayashi, F., Fregni, H., Tager-Flusberg, H., & Pascual-Leone, A. (2005). Impaired motor facilitation during action observation in individuals with autism spectrum disorder, *Current Biology, 15,* R84–R85.

Thiessen, E. D., & Saffran, J. R. (2007). Learning to learn: Infants' acquisition of stress-based strategies for work segmentation. *Language Learning and Development, 3,* 73–100.

Thoermer, C., Sodian, B., Vuori, M., Perst, H,., & Kristen, S. (2012). Continuity from an implicit to an explicit understanding of false belief from infancy to preschool age. *British Journal of Developmental Psychology, 30,* 172–187.

Thomaes, S., Stegge, H., Bushman, B. J., & Olthof, T. (2008). Trumping shame by blasts of noise: Narcissism, self-esteem, shame, and aggression in young adolescents. *Child Development, 79,* 1792–1801.

Thomas, A., & Chess, S. (1977). *Temperament and development.* New York: Brunner/Mazel.

Thomas, A., Chess, S., & Birch, H. G. (1968). *Temperament and behavior disorders in children.* New York: New York University Press.

Thomas, C. L., & Dimitrov, D. M. (2007). Effects of a teen pregnancy prevention program on teens' attitudes toward sexuality: A latent trait modeling approach. *Developmental Psychology, 43,* 173–185.

Thomas, K. A., & Tessler, R. C. (2007). Bicultural socialization among adoptive families: Where there is a will, there is a way. *Journal of Family Issues, 28,* 1189–1219.

Thomas, R. M. (2005). *Comparing theories of child development* (6th ed.). Belmont, CA: Wadsworth.

Thombs, B. D., Roseman, M., & Arthurs, E. (2010). Prenatal and postpartum depression in fathers and mothers. *Journal of the American Medical Association, 304,* 961.

Thompson, A., Hollis, C., & Richards, D. (2003). Authoritarian parenting attitudes as a risk for conduct problems: Results of a British national cohort study. *European Child and Adolescent Psychiatry, 12,* 84–91.

Thompson, P. M., Giedd, J. N., Woods, R. P., MacDonald, D., Evans, A. C., & Toga, A. W. (2000). Growth patterns in the developing brain detected by using continuum mechanical tensor maps. *Nature, 404,* 190–192.

Thompson, R. A. (2000). The legacy of early attachments. *Child Development, 71,* 145–152.

Thompson, R. A. (2006). The development of the person: Social understanding, relationships, conscience, self. In N. Eisenberg (Ed.), *Handbook of child psychology: Vol. 3. Social, emotional, and personality development* (6th ed., pp. 24–98). Hoboken, NJ: Wiley.

Thompson, R. A. (2008). Early attachment and later development. In J. Cassidy & P. R. Shaver (Eds.), *Handbook of attachment: Theory, research, and clinical applications* (2nd ed., pp. 348–365). New York: Guilford.

Thompson, R. A., & Goodman, M. (2010). Development of emotion regulation: More than meets the eye. In A. M. Kring & D. M. Sloan (Eds.), *Emotion regulation and psychopathology: A transdiagnostic approach to etiology and treatment* (pp. 38–58). New York: Guilford.

Thompson, R. A., & Goodvin, R. (2007). Taming the tempest in the teapot. In C. A. Brownell & C. B. Kopp (Eds.), *Socioemotional development in the toddler years: Transitions and transformations* (pp. 320–341). New York: Guilford.

Thompson, R. A., & Meyer, S. (2007). Socialization of emotion regulation in the family. In J. J. Gross (Ed.), *Handbook of emotion regulation* (pp. 249–268). New York: Guilford.

Thompson, R. A., Meyer, S., & McGinley, M. (2006). Understanding values in relationships: The development of conscience. In M. Killen & J. G.

Smetana (Eds.), *Handbook of moral development* (pp. 267–298). Mahwah, NJ: Erlbaum.

Thompson, R. A., & Nelson C. A. (2001). Developmental science and the media. *American Psychologist, 56,* 5–15.

Thompson, R. A., & Raikes, H. A. (2007). The social and emotional foundations of school readiness. In D. F. Perry, R. K. Kaufmann, & J. Knitzer (Eds.), *Social and emotional health in early childhood: Building bridges between services and systems* (pp. 13–35). Baltimore, MD: Paul H. Brookes.

Thompson, R. A., Winer, A. C., & Goodvin, R. (2011). The individual child: Temperament, emotion, self, and personality. In M. H. Bornstein & M. E. Lamb (Eds.), *Developmental science: An advanced textbook* (6th ed.). New York: Psychology Press.

Thompson, W. W., Price, C., Goodson, B., Shay, D. K., Benson, P., Hinrichsen, V. L., et al. (2007). Early thimerosal exposure and neuropsychological outcomes at 7to 10 years. *New England Journal of Medicine, 357,* 1281–1292.

Thorne, B. (1993). *Gender play: Girls and boys in school.* New Brunswick, NJ: Rutgers University Press.

Thornton, J., Edwards, R., Mitchell, P., Harrison, R. A., Buchan, I., & Kelly, S. P. (2005). Smoking and age-related macular degeneration: A review of association. *Eye, 19,* 935–944.

Thornton, S. (1999). Creating conditions for cognitive change: The interaction between task structures and specific strategies. *Child Development, 70,* 588–603.

Thorson, J. A., & Powell, F. C. (1994). A revised death anxiety scale. In R. A. Neimeyer (Ed.), *Death anxiety handbook* (pp. 31–43). Washington, DC: Taylor & Francis.

Tienari, P., Wahlberg, K. E., & Wynne, L. C. (2006). Finnish adoption study of schizophrenia: Implications for family interventions. *Families, Systems, and Health, 24,* 442–451.

Tienari, P., Wynne, L. C., Lasky, K., Moring, J., Nieminen, P., & Sorri, A. (2003). Genetic boundaries of the schizophrenia spectrum: Evidence from the Finnish adoptive family study of schizophrenia. *American Journal of Psychiatry, 160,* 1587–1594.

Tiet, Q. Q., Huizinga, D., & Byrnes, H. F. (2010). Predictors of resilience among inner city youths. *Journal of Child and Family Studies, 19,* 360–378.

Tiggemann, M., & Anesbury, T. (2000). Negative stereotyping of obesity in children: The role of controllability beliefs. *Journal of Applied Social Psychology, 30,* 1977–1993.

Tincoff, R., & Jusczyk, P. W. (1999). Some beginnings of word comprehension in 6-month-olds. *Psychological Science, 10,* 172–175.

Tizard, B., & Rees, J. (1975). The effect of early institutional rearing on the behaviour problems and affectional relationships of four-year-old children. *Journal of Child Psychology and Psychiatry, 16,* 61–73.

Tofler, I. R., Knapp, P. K., & Drell, M. J. (1998). The achievement by proxy spectrum in youth sports: Historical perspective and clinical approach to pressured and high-achieving children and adolescents. *Child and Adolescent Psychiatric Clinics of North America, 7,* 803–820.

Tokunaga, R. S. (2010). Following you home from school: A critical review and synthesis of research on cyberbullying victimization. *Computers in Human behavior, 26,* 277–287.

Tomasello, M. (1992). *First verbs: A case study of early grammatical development.* New York: Cambridge University Press.

Tomasello, M. (1999). Having intentions, understanding intentions, and understanding communicative intentions. In P. D. Zelazo, J. W. Astington, & J. Wilde (Eds.), *Developing theories of intention: Social understanding and self-control* (pp. 63–75). Mahwah, NJ: Erlbaum.

Tomasello, M. (2003). *Constructing a language: A usage-based theory of language acquisition.* Cambridge, MA: Harvard University Press.

Tomasello, M. (2005). Beyond formalities: The case of language acquisition. *Linguistic Review, 22,* 183–197.

Tomasello, M. (2006). Acquiring linguistic constructions. In D. Kuhn & R. Siegler (Eds.), *Handbook of child psychology: Vol. 2: Cognition, perception, and language* (6th ed., pp. 255–298). Hoboken, NJ: Wiley.

Tomasello, M. (2011). Language development. In U. Goswami (Ed.), *Wiley-Blackwell handbook of childhood cognitive development* (2nd ed., pp. 239–257). Malden, MA: Wiley-Blackwell.

Tomasello, M., & Akhtar, N. (1995). Two-year-olds use pragmatic cues to differentiate reference to objects and actions. *Cognitive Development, 10,* 201–224.

Tomasello, M., & Brandt, S. (2009). Flexibility in the semantics and syntax of children's early verb use. *Monographs of the Society for Research in Child Development, 72*(2, Serial No. 293), 113–126.

Tomasello, M., Call, J., & Hare, B. (2003). Chimpanzees understand psychological states—the question is which ones and to what extent. *Trends in Cognitive Sciences, 7,* 153–156.

Tomasello, M., Carpenter, M., & Liszkowski, U. (2007). A new look at infant pointing. *Child Development, 78,* 705–722.

Tomer, A., Eliason, G., & Smith, J. (2000). Beliefs about the self, life, and death: Testing aspects of a comprehensive model of death anxiety and death attitudes. *Death attitudes and the older adult: Theories, concepts, and applications* (pp. 109–122). Philadelphia: Taylor & Francis.

Tong, S., Baghurst, P., Vimpani, G., & McMichael, A. (2007). Socioeconomic position, maternal IQ, home environment, and cognitive development. *Journal of Pediatrics, 151,* 284–288.

Tong, V. T., Jones, J. R., Dietz, P. M., D'Angelo, D., & Bombard, J. M. (2009, May 29). Trends in smoking before, during, and after pregnancy—Pregnancy Risk Assessment Monitoring System (PRAMS), United States, 31 Sites, 2000–2005. *Morbidity and Mortality Weekly Report, 58* (No. SS-4).

Torges, C. M., Stewart, A. J., & Miner-Rubino, K. (2005). Personality after the prime of life: Men and women coming to terms with regrets. *Journal of Research in Personality, 39,* 148–165.

Torney-Purta, J. (2002). The school's role in developing civic engagement: A study of adolescents in twenty-eight countries. *Applied Developmental Science, 6,* 203–212.

Torney-Purta, J., Barber, C. H., & Wilkenfeld, B. (2007). Latino adolescents' civic development in the United States: Research results from the IEA Civic Education Study. *Journal of Youth and Adolescence, 36,* 111–125.

Tornstam, L. (2000). Transcendence in later life. *Generations, 23*(10), 10–14.

Tornstam, L. (2011). Maturing into gerotranscendence. *Journal of TransPersonal Psychology, 43,* 166–180.

Toro-Morn, M., & Sprecher, S. (2003). A cross-cultural comparison of mate preferences among university students: The United States vs. the People's Republic of China (PRC). *Journal of Comparative Family Studies, 34,* 151–170.

Torrance, E. P. (1988). The nature of creativity as manifest in its testing. In R. J. Sternberg (Ed.), *The nature of creativity: Contemporary psychological perspectives* (pp. 43–75). New York: Cambridge University Press.

Tottenham, N., Hare, T. A., Millner, A., Gilhooly, T., Zevin, J. D., & Casey, B. J. (2011). Elevated amygdala response to faces following early deprivation. *Developmental Science, 14,* 190–204.

Touwslager, R. N., Gielen, M., Derom, C., Mulder, A. L., Gerver, W. J., Zimmermann, L. J., et al. (2011).

Determinants of infant growth in four age windows: A twin study. *Journal of Pediatrics, 158,* 566–572.

Tracy, J. L., Robins, R. W., & Lagattuta, K. H. (2005). Can children recognize pride? *Emotion, 5,* 251–257.

Trafford, A. (2004). *My time: Making the most of the rest of your life.* New York: Basic Books.

Trappe, S. (2007). Marathon runners: How do they age? *Sports Medicine, 37,* 302–305.

Trautner, H. M., Gervai, J., & Nemeth, R. (2003). Appearance–reality distinction and development of gender constancy understanding in children. *International Journal of Behavioral Development, 27,* 275–283.

Trautner, H. M., Ruble, D. N., Cyphers, L., Kirsten, B., Behrendt, R., & Hartmann, P. (2005). Rigidity and flexibility of gender stereotypes in childhood: Developmental or differential? *Infant and Child Development, 14,* 365–381.

Treasure, J., & Schmidt, U. (2005). Anorexia nervosa. *Clinical Evidence, 13,* 1148–1157.

Trehub, S. E. (2001). Musical predispositions in infancy. *Annals of the New York Academy of Sciences, 930,* 1–16.

Tremblay, L., & Frigon, J.-Y. (2005). Precocious puberty in adolescent girls: A biomarker of later psychosocial adjustment problems. *Child Psychiatry and Human Development, 36,* 73–94.

Tremblay, R. E. (2000). The development of aggressive behaviour during childhood: What have we learned in the past century? *International Journal of Behavioral Development, 24,* 129–141.

Tremblay, R. E., Japel, C., Perusse, D., Voivin, M., Zoccolillo, M., Montplaisir, J., & McDuff, P. (1999). The search for the age of "onset" of physical aggression: Rousseau and Bandura revisited. *Criminal Behavior and Mental Health, 9,* 8–23.

Trent, K., & Harlan, S. L. (1994). Teenage mothers in nuclear and extended households. *Journal of Family Issues, 15,* 309–337.

Trentacosta, C. J., & Shaw, D. S. (2009). Emotional self-regulation, peer rejection, and antisocial behavior: Developmental associations from early childhood to early adolescence. *Journal of Applied Developmental Psychology, 30,* 356–365.

Triandis, H. C. (1995). *Individualism and collectivism.* Boulder, CO: Westview Press.

Triandis, H. C. (2005). Issues in individualism and collectivism research. In R. M. Sorrentino, D. Cohen, J. M. Olson, & M. P. Zanna (Eds.), *Culture and social behavior: The Ontario Symposium* (Vol. 10, pp. 207–225). Mahwah, NJ: Erlbaum.

Triandis, H. C. (2007). Culture and psychology: A history of the study of their relationship. In S. Kitayama & D. Cohen (Eds.), *Handbook of cultural psychology* (pp. 59–76). New York: Guilford.

Trocomé, N., & Wolfe, D. (2002). *Child maltreatment in Canada: The Canadian Incidence Study of Reported Child Abuse and Neglect.* Retrieved from www.hc-sc.gc.ca/pphb-dgspsp/cm-vee

Tronick, E., Morelli, G., & Ivey, P. (1992). The Efe forager infant and toddler's pattern of social relationships: Multiple and simultaneous. *Developmental Psychology, 28,* 568–577.

Tronick, E. Z., Thomas, R. B., & Daltabuit, M. (1994). The Quechua manta pouch: A caretaking practice for buffering the Peruvian infant against the multiple stressors of high altitude. *Child Development, 65,* 1005–1013.

Troop-Gordon, W., & Asher, S. R. (2005). Modifications in children's goals when encountering obstacles to conflict resolution. *Child Development, 76,* 568–582.

Troseth, G. L. (2003). Getting a clear picture: Young children's understanding of a televised image. *Developmental Psychology, 6,* 247–253.

Troseth, G. L., & DeLoache, J. S. (1998). The medium can obscure the message: Young children's understanding of video. *Child Development, 69,* 950–965.

Troseth, G. L., Saylor, M. M., & Archer, A. H. (2006). Young children's use of video as a source of socially

relevant information. *Child Development, 77,* 786–799.

Troutman, D. R., & Fletcher, A. C. (2010). Context and companionship in children's short-term versus long-term friendships. *Journal of Social and Personal Relationships, 27,* 1060–1074.

Troyer, A. K., Häfliger, A., Cadieux, M. J., & Craik, F. I. M. (2006). Name and face learning in older adults: Effects of level of processing, self-generation, and intention to learn. *Journal of Gerontology, 61B,* P67–P74.

Trudel, G., Villeneuve, V., Anderson, A., & Pilon, G. (2008). Sexual and marital aspects of old age: An update. *Sexual and Relationship Therapy, 23,* 161–169.

True, M. M., Pisani, L., & Oumar, F. (2001). Infant–mother attachment among the Dogon of Mali. *Child Development, 72,* 1451–1466.

Trusty, J. (1999). Effects of eighth-grade parental involvement on late adolescents' educational expectations. *Journal of Research and Development in Education, 32,* 224–233.

Trzesniewski, K. H., & Donnellan, M. B. (2009). Reevaluating the evidence for increasingly positive self-views among high school students: More evidence for consistency across generations. *Psychological Science, 20,* 920–922.

Trzeniewski, K. H., & Donnellan, M. B. (2010). Rethinking "generation me": A study of cohort effects from 1976–2006. *Perspectives on Psychological Science, 5,* 58–75.

Trzesniewski, K. H., Donnellan, M. B., & Robins, R. W. (2003). Stability of self-esteem across the life span. *Journal of Personality and Social Psychology, 84,* 205–220.

Tsai, A. G., & Wadden, T. A. (2005). Systematic review: An evaluation of major commercial weight loss programs in the United States. *Annals of Internal Medicine, 142,* 56–66.

Tsang, P. S., & Shaner, T. L. (1998). Age, attention, expertise, and time-sharing performance. *Psychology and Aging, 13,* 323–347.

Tsuji, Y. (2005). Time is not up: Temporal complexity of older Americans' lives. *Journal of Cross-Cultural Gerontology, 20,* 3–26.

Tsujimoto, S. (2008). The prefrontal cortex: Functional neural development during early childhood. *Neuroscientist, 14,* 345–358.

Tucker, C. J., McHale, S. M., & Crouter, A. C. (2001). Conditions of sibling support in adolescence. *Journal of Family Psychology, 15,* 254–271.

Tucker, C. J., McHale, S. M., & Crouter, A. C. (2003). Dimensions of mothers' and fathers' differential treatment of siblings: Links with adolescents' sex-typed personal qualities. *Family Relations, 52,* 82–89.

Tudge, J. R. H. (1992). Processes and consequences of peer collaboration: A Vygotskian analysis. *Child Development, 63,* 1364–1397.

Tudge, J. R. H., Hogan, D. M., Snezhkova, I. A., Kulakova, N. N., & Etz, K. E. (2000). Parents' child-rearing values and beliefs in the United States and Russia: The impact of culture and social class. *Infant and Child Development, 9,* 105–121.

Turati, C. (2004). Why faces are not special to newborns: An account of the face preference. *Current Directions in Psychological Science, 13,* 5–8.

Turati, C., Cassia, V. M., Simion, F., & Leo, I. (2006). Newborns' face recognition: Role of inner and outer facial features. *Child Development, 77,* 297–311.

Turesson, C., & Matteson, E. L. (2006). Genetics of rheumatoid arthritis. *Mayo Clinic Proceedings, 81,* 94–101.

Turiel, E. (2006). The development of morality. In N. Eisenberg (Ed.), *Handbook of child psychology: Vol. 3. Social, emotional, and personality development* (6th ed., pp. 789–857). Hoboken, NJ: Wiley.

Turiel, E., & Killen, M. (2010). Taking emotions seriously: The role of emotions in moral development. In W. F. Arsenio & E. A. Lemerise (Eds.), *Emotions, aggression, and morality in children: Bridging development and psychopathology* (pp. 33–52). Washington, DC: American Psychological Association.

Turkheimer, E., Haley, A., Waldron, M., D'Onofrio, B., & Gottesman, I. I. (2003). Socioeconomic status modifies heritability of IQ in young children. *Psychological Science, 14*, 623–628.

Turnbull, K. P., Anthony, A. B., Justice, L., & Bowles, R. (2009). Preschoolers' exposure to language stimulation in classrooms serving at-risk children: The contribution of group size and activity context. *Early Education and Development, 20*, 53–79.

Turnbull, M., Hart, D., & Lapkin, S. (2003). Grade 6 French immersion students' performance on large-scale reading, writing, and mathematics tests: Building explanations. *Alberta Journal of Educational Research, 49*, 6–23.

Turner, B. F. (1982). Sex-related differences in aging. In B. B. Wolman (Ed.), *Handbook of developmental psychology* (pp. 912–936). Englewood Cliffs, NJ: Prentice-Hall.

Turner, L. B. (2011). A meta-analysis of fat intake, reproduction, and breast cancer risk: An evolutionary perspective. *American Journal of Human Biology, 23*, 601–608.

Turner, P. J., & Gervai, J. (1995). A multidimensional study of gender typing in preschool children and their parents: Personality, attitudes, preferences, behavior, and cultural differences. *British Journal of Developmental Psychology, 11*, 323–342.

Turner, R. N., Hewstone, M., & Voci, A. (2007). Reducing explicit and implicit outgroup prejudice via direct and extended contact: The mediating role of self-disclosure and intergroup anxiety. *Journal of Personality and Social Psychology, 93*, 369–388.

Tuyen, J. M., & Bisgard, K. (2003). Community setting: Pertussis outbreak. Atlanta, GA: U.S. Centers for Disease Control and Prevention. Retrieved from www.cdc.gov/nip/publications/pertussis/chapter10.pdf

Twenge, J. M. (1997). Changes in masculine and feminine traits over time: A meta-analysis. *Sex Roles, 36*, 305–325.

Twenge, J. M. (2001). Changes in women's assertiveness in response to status and roles: A crosstemporal meta-analysis, 1931–1993. *Journal of Personality and Social Psychology, 81*, 133–145.

Twenge, J. M., & Campbell, W. K. (2001). Age and birth cohort differences in self-esteem: A crosstemporal meta-analysis. *Personality and Social Psychology Review, 5*, 321–344.

Twenge, J. M., Campbell, W. K., & Freeman, E. C. (2012). Generational differences in young adults' life goals, concern for others, and civic orientation, 1966–2009. *Journal of Personality and Social Psychology, 102*, 1045–1062.

Twenge, J. M., & Crocker, J. (2002). Race and self-esteem: Meta-analyses comparing whites, blacks, Hispanics, Asians, and America Indians and comment on Gray-Little and Hafdahl (2000). *Psychological Bulletin, 128*, 371–408.

Tzuriel, D., & Egozi, G. (2010). Gender differences in spatial ability of young children: The effects of training and processing strategies. *Child Development, 81*, 1417–1430.

Tzuriel, D., & Kaufman, R. (1999). Mediated learning and cognitive modifiability: Dynamic assessment of young Ethiopian immigrant children to Israel. *Journal of Cross-Cultural Psychology, 30*, 359–380.

U

Uauy, R., Kain, J., Mericq, V., Rojas, J., & Corvalán, C. (2008). Nutrition, child growth, and chronic disease prevention. *Annals of Medicine, 40*, 11–20.

Uchino, B. N. (2009). Understanding the links between social support and physical health. *Perspectives on Psychological Science, 4*, 236–255.

Udechuku, A., Nguyen, T., Hill, R., & Szego, K. (2010). Antidepressants in pregnancy: A systematic review. *Australian and New Zealand Journal of Psychiatry, 44*, 978–996.

Uhlenberg, P., & Hammill, B. G. (1998). Frequency of grandparent contact with grandchild sets: Six factors that make a difference. *Gerontologist, 38*, 276–285.

Ukrainetz, T. A., Justice, L. M., Kaderavek, J. N., Eisenberg, S. L., Gillam, R., & Harm, H. M. (2005). The development of expressive elaboration in fictional narratives. *Journal of Speech, Language, and Hearing Research, 48*, 1363–1377.

Umana-Taylor, A. J., & Alfaro, E. C. (2006). Ethnic identity among U.S. Latino adolescents: Measurement and implications for well-being. In F. A. Villarruel & T. Luster (Eds.), *The crisis in youth mental health: Critical issues and effective programs: Vol. 2. Disorders in adolescence* (pp. 195–211). Westport, CT: Praeger.

Umana-Taylor, A. J., & Updegraff, K. A. (2007). Latino adolescents' mental health: Exploring the interrelations among discrimination, ethnic identity, cultural orientation, self-esteem, and depressive symptoms. *Journal of Adolescence, 30*, 549–567.

Underhill, K., Montgomery, P., & Operario, D. (2007). Sexual abstinence only programmes to prevent HIV infection in high-income countries: Systematic review. *British Medical Journal, 335*, 248.

Underwood, M. K. (2003). *Social aggression among girls*. New York: Guilford.

UNICEF (United Nations Children's Fund). (2007). *An overview of child well-being in rich countries, Innocenti Report Card 7*. Florence, Italy: UNICEF Innocenti Research Centre.

UNICEF (United Nations Children's Fund). (2009). *Infant and young child feeding 2000–2007*. Retrieved from www.childinfo.org/breastfeeding_countrydata.php

UNICEF (United Nations Children's Fund). (2010a). *Children and AIDS: Fifth stocktaking report*. New York: United Nations.

UNICEF (United Nations Children's Fund). (2010b). *The children left behind: A league table of inequality in the world's richest countries, Innocenti Report Card*. Florence, Italy: UNICEF Innocenti Research Centre.

UNICEF (United Nations Children's Fund). (2010c). *Young champions for education: A progress review*. Retrieved from www.ungei.org/resources/files/Young_Champions_Evaluation_7_Jan.pdf

UNICEF (United Nations Children's Fund). (2011). *Children in conflict and emergencies*. Retrieved from www.unicef.org/protection/armedconflict.html

United Nations. (2011). *World population prospects: The 2011 revision. Population database*. Retrieved from esa.un.org/wpp/unpp/panel_population.htm

United Nations. (2012). *UN data: A world of information*. Retrieved from data.un.org

Uotinen, V., Rantanen, T., Suutama, T., & Ruoppila, I. (2006). Change in subjective age among older people over an eight-year follow-up: "Getting older and feeling younger"? *Experimental Aging Research, 32*, 381–393.

U.S. Census Bureau. (2012a). International database. Retrieved from sasweb.ssd.census.gov/idb/ranks.html

U.S. Census Bureau. (2012b). *Statistical abstract of the United States* (131st ed.). Washington, DC: U.S. Government Printing Office.

U.S. Department of Agriculture. (2011a). *Food security in the United States: Key statistics and graphics*. Retrieved from www.ers.usda.gov/Briefing/FoodSecurity/stats_graphs.htm

U.S. Department of Agriculture. (2011b). *WIC: The Special Supplemental Nutrition Program for Women, Infants, and Children*. Nutrition Program Facts. Retrieved from www.fns.usda.gov/wic/wic-fact-sheet.pdf

U.S. Department of Agriculture. (2012). *Expenditures on children by families, 2011*. Retrieved from www.cnpp.usda.gov/Publications/CRC/crc2011.pdf

U.S. Department of Education. (2007a). *The Nation's Report Card: Mathematics 2007*. Retrieved from nces.ed.gov/pubsearch/pubsinfo.asp?pubid=2007494

U.S. Department of Education. (2007b). *The Nation's Report Card: Reading 2007*. Retrieved from nces.ed.gov/pubSearch/pubsinfo.asp?pubid=2007496

U.S. Department of Education. (2009). *The Nation's Report Card: Mathematics 2009*. Retrieved from nces.ed.gov/nationsreportcard/mathematics/

U.S. Department of Education. (2010). *The nation's report card: Reading 2009*. Retrieved from nces.ed.gov/pubsearch/pubsinfo.asp?pubid=2010458

U.S. Department of Education. (2012a). *The condition of education 2012*. Retrieved from nces.ed.gov/pubsearch/pubsinfo.asp?pubid=2012045

U.S. Department of Education. (2012b). *Digest of education statistics: 2011*. Washington, DC: U.S. Government Printing Office.

U.S. Department of Health and Human Services. (2010a). Births: Final data for 2008. *National Vital Statistics Reports, 59*(1).

U.S. Department of Health and Human Services. (2010b). *Breastfeeding*. Retrieved from www.womenshealth.gov/breastfeeding/index.cfm

U.S. Department of Health and Human Services. (2010c). *Drugs, brains, and behavior: The science of addiction*. Bethesda, MD: National Institute of Drug Abuse.

U.S. Department of Health and Human Services. (2010d). *Head Start Impact Study: Final report*. Washington, DC: U.S. Government Printing Office.

U.S. Department of Health and Human Services. (2010e). National, state, and local vaccination coverage among children aged 19–35 months—United States, 2009. *Morbidity and Mortality Weekly Report, 59*, 1171–1177.

U.S. Department of Health and Human Services. (2010f). *A profile of older Americans: 2009*. Retrieved from www.aoa.gov/AoAroot/Aging_Statistics/Profile/2009/docs/2009profile_508.pdf

U.S. Department of Health and Human Services. (2011a). *Births: Preliminary data for 2010*. Retrieved from www.cdc.gov/nchs/data/nvsr/nvsr60/nvsr60_02.pdf

U.S. Department of Health and Human Services. (2011b). *Child maltreatment 2010*. Retrieved from www.acf.hhs.gov/programs/cb/resource/child-maltreatment-2010

U.S. Department of Health and Human Services. (2011c). *Health, United States 2010: With special feature on death and dying*. Washington, DC: U.S. Government Printing Office.

U.S. Department of Health and Human Services. (2011d). *Premenstrual syndrome (PMS) fact sheet*. Retrieved from womenshealth.gov/publications/our-publications/fact-sheet/premenstrual-syndrome.cfm

U.S. Department of Health and Human Services. (2011e). *Results from the 2010 National Survey on Drug Use and Health: Summary of national findings*. Rockville, MD: Substance Abuse and Mental Health Services Administration.

U.S. Department of Health and Human Services. (2011f). *The Surgeon General's call to action to prevent and decrease overweight and obesity: Overweight children and adolescents*. Retrieved from www.surgeongeneral.gov/library/calls/obesity/fact_adolescents.html

U.S. Department of Health and Human Services. (2011g). *Your Medicare coverage.* Retrieved from www.medicare.gov/coverage/Home.asp

U.S. Department of Health and Human Services. (2012a). *Facts about Down syndrome.* Retrieved from www.education.com/reference/article/Ref_Facts_About_Down

U.S. Department of Health and Human Services. (2012b). *Key statistics from the National Survey of Family Growth: Impaired fecundity.* Retrieved from www.cdc.gov/nchs/nsfg/abc_list_i.htm#impaired

U.S. Department of Health and Human Services. (2012c). *Morbidity and mortality: 2012 chart book on cardiovascular, lung and blood diseases.* Bethesda, MD: Author.

U.S. Department of Health and Human Services. (2012d). *Older persons' health: Health care utilization.* Retrieved from www.cdc.gov/nchs/fastats/older_americans.htm

U.S. Department of Health and Human Services. (2012e). *A profile of older Americans 2012: Key indicators of well-being.* Washington, DC: U.S. Government Printing Office.

U.S. Department of Health and Human Services. (2012f). Youth Risk Behavior Surveillance—United States, 2011. *Morbidity and Mortality Weekly Report, 61*(No. 4). Retrieved from www.cdc.gov/mmwr/pdf/ss/ss6104.pdf

U.S. Department of Justice. (2010). *Crime in the United States, 2009.* Retrieved from www2.fbi.gov/ucr/cius2009

U.S. Department of Transportation. (2012). *Traffic safety facts: Research note. 2011 motor vehicle crashes: Overview.* Retrieved from www-nrd.nhtsa.dot.gov/Pubs/811701.pdf

U.S. Living Will Registry. (2005). *Advance directive forms.* Retrieved from www.uslivingwillregistry.com/forms.shtm

Usher-Seriki, K. K., Bynum, M. S., & Callands, T. A. (2008). Mother–daughter communication about sex and sexual intercourse among middle- to upper-class African American girls. *Journal of Family Issues, 29,* 901–917.

Usta, I. M., & Nassar, A. H. (2008). Advanced maternal age. Part I: Obstetric complications. *American Journal of Perinatology, 25,* 521–534.

Utz, R. L., Carr, D., Nesse, R., & Wortman, C. B. (2002). The effect of widowhood on older adults' social participation: An evaluation of activity, disengagement, and continuity theories. *Gerontologist, 42,* 522–533.

V

Vacha-Haase, T., Hill, R. D., & Bermingham, D. W. (2012). Aging theory and research. In N. A. Fouad, J. A. Carter, & L. M. Subich (Eds.), *APA handbook of counseling psychology: Vol. 1. Theories, research, and methods* (pp. 491–505). Washington, DC: American Psychological Association.

Vaillancourt, T., Brendgen, M., Boivin, M., & Tremblay, R. E. (2003). A longitudinal confirmatory factor analysis of indirect and physical aggression: Evidence of two factors over time? *Child Development, 74,* 1628–1638.

Vaillancourt, T., Brittain, H., Bennett, L., Arnocky, S., McDougall, P., Hymel, S., et al. (2010a). Places to avoid: Population-based study of student reports of unsafe and high bullying areas at school. *Canadian Journal of School Psychology, 25,* 40–54.

Vaillancourt, T., Clinton, J., McDougall, P., Schmidt, L. A., & Hymel, S. (2010b). The neurobiology of peer victimization and rejection. In S. Jimerson, S. M. Swearer, & D. L. Espelage (Eds.), *Handbook of bullying in schools: An international perspective* (pp. 293–304). New York: Routledge.

Vaillancourt, T., & Hymel, S. (2006). Aggression and social status: The moderating roles of sex and peer-valued characteristics. *Aggressive Behavior, 32,* 396–408.

Vaillancourt, T., McDougall, P., Hymel, S., & Sunderani, S. (2010c). Respect or fear? The relationship between power and bullying behavior. In Jimerson, S. M. Swearer, & D. L. Espelage (Eds.), *Handbook of bullying in schools: An international perspective* (pp. 211–222). New York: Routledge.

Vaillant, G. E. (1977). *Adaptation to life.* Boston: Little, Brown.

Vaillant, G. E. (2002). *Aging well.* Boston: Little, Brown.

Vaillant, G. E., & Koury, S. H. (1994). Late midlife development. In G. H. Pollock & S. I. Greenspan (Eds.), *The course of life* (pp. 1–22). Madison, CT: International Universities Press.

Vaillant, G. E., & Mukamal, K. (2001). Successful aging. *American Journal of Psychiatry, 158,* 839–847.

Vaillant, G. E., & Vaillant, C. O. (1990). Determinants and consequences of creativity in a cohort of gifted women. *Psychology of Women Quarterly, 14,* 607–616.

Vaish, A., & Striano, T. (2004). Is visual reference necessary? Contributions of facial versus vocal cues in 12-month-olds' social referencing behavior. *Developmental Science, 7,* 261–269.

Vakil, E., Blachstein, H., Sheinman, M., & Greenstein, Y. (2009). Developmental changes in attention tests norms: Implications for the structure of attention. *Child Neuropsychology, 15,* 21–39.

Valdés, G. (1998). The world outside and inside schools: Language and immigrant children. *Educational Researcher, 27*(6), 4–18.

Valentine, J. C., DuBois, D. L., & Cooper, H. (2004). The relation between self-beliefs and academic achievement: A meta-analytic review. *Educational Psychologist, 39,* 111–133.

Valian, V. (1999). Input and language acquisition. In W. C. Ritchie & T. K. Bhatia (Eds.), *Handbook of child language acquisition* (pp. 497–530). San Diego: Academic Press.

Valiente, C., Eisenberg, N., Fabes, R. A., Shepard, S. A., Cumberland, A., & Losoya, S. H. (2004). Prediction of children's empathy-related responding from their effortful control and parents' expressivity. *Developmental Psychology, 40,* 911–926.

Valiente, C., Lemery-Chalfant, K., Swanson, J., & Reiser, M. (2008). Prediction of children's academic competence from their effortful control, relationships, and classroom participation. *Journal of Educational Psychology, 100,* 67–77.

Valiente, C., Lemery-Chalfant, K., Swanson, J., & Reiser, M. (2010). Prediction of kindergartners' academic achievement from their effortful control and emotionality: Evidence for direct and moderated relations. *Journal of Educational Psychology, 102,* 550–560.

Valkenburg, P. M., & Peter, J. (2007a). Internet communication and its relation to well-being: Identifying some underlying mechanisms. *Media Psychology, 9,* 43–58.

Valkenburg, P. M., & Peter, J. (2007b). Preadolescents' and adolescents' online communication and their closeness to friends. *Developmental Psychology, 43,* 267–277.

Valkenburg, P. M., & Peter, J. (2009). Social consequences of the Internet for adolescents: A decade of research. *Current Directions in Psychological Science, 18,* 1–5.

Valkenburg, P. M., & Peter, J. (2011). Online communication among adolescents: An integrated model of its attraction, opportunities, and risks. *Journal of Adolescent Health, 48,* 121–127.

van Aken, C., Junger, M., Verhoeven, M., van Aken, M. A. G., & Deković, M. (2007). The interactive effects of temperament and maternal parenting on toddlers' externalizing behaviours. *Infant and Child Development, 16,* 553–572.

van Asselt, D. (2006). Advance directives: Prerequisites and usefulness. *Zeitschrift für Gerontologie und Geriatrie, 39,* 371–375.

van Baarsen, B. (2002). Theories on coping with loss: The impact of social support and self-esteem on adjustment to emotional and social loneliness following a partner's death in later life. *Journal of Gerontology, 57B,* S33–S42.

Van Cleave, J., Gortmaker, S. L., & Perrin, J. M. (2010). Dynamics of obesity and chronic health conditions among children and youth. *Journal of the American Medical Association, 303,* 623–630.

Vandell, D. L., Belsky, J., Burchinal, M., Steinberg, L., Vandergrift, N., & NICHD Early Child Care Research Network. (2010). Do effects of early child care extend to age 15 years? Results from the NICHD Study of Early Child Care and Youth Development. *Child Development, 81,* 737–756.

Vandell, D. L., & Posner, J. K. (1999). Conceptualization and measurement of children's after-school environments. In S. L. Friedman & T. D. Wachs (Eds.), *Measuring environment across the life span* (pp. 167–196). Washington, DC: American Psychological Association.

Vandell, D. L., Reisner, E. R., & Pierce, K. M. (2007). *Outcomes linked to high-quality after-school programs: Longitudinal findings from the Study of Promising After-School Programs.* Retrieved from www.gse.uci.edu/childcare/pdf/afterschool/PP%20Longitudinal%20Findings%20Final%20Report.pdf

Vandell, D. L., Reisner, E. R., Pierce, K. M., Brown, B. B., Lee, D., Bolt, D., & Pechman, E. M. (2006). *The study of promising after-school programs: Examination of longer term outcomes after two years of program experiences.* Madison, WI: University of Wisconsin. Retrieved from www.wcer.wisc.edu/childcare/statements.html

Vandell, D. L., & Shumow, L. (1999). After-school child care programs. *Future of Children, 9*(2), 64–80.

van den Akker, A. L. Deković, M., Prinzie, P., & Asscher, J. J. (2010). Toddlers' temperament profiles: Stability and relations to negative and positive parenting. *Journal of Abnormal Child Psychology, 38,* 485–495.

Van den Bergh, B. R. H., & De Rycke, L. (2003). Measuring the multidimensional self-concept and global self-worth of 6- to 8-year-olds. *Journal of Genetic Psychology, 164,* 201–225.

Van den Bergh, B. R. H., Van Calster, B., Smits, T., Van Huffel, S., & Lagae, L. (2008). Antenatal maternal anxiety is related to HPA-axis dysregulation and self-reported depressive symptoms in adolescence: A prospective study on the fetal origins of depressed mood. *Neuropsychopharmacology, 33,* 536–545.

van den Dries, L., Juffer, F., van IJzendoorn, M. H., & Bakermans-Kranenburg, M. J. (2009). Fostering security? A meta-analysis of attachment in adopted children. *Children and Youth Services Review, 31,* 410–421.

Vanderbilt-Adriance, E., & Shaw, D. S. (2008). Protective factors and the development of resilience in the context of neighborhood disadvantage. *Journal of Abnormal Child Psychology, 36,* 887–901.

van der Heide, A., Onwuteaka-Philipsen, B. D., Rurup, M. L., Buiting, H. M., van Delden, J. J. M., & Hanssen-de Wolf, J. E. (2007). End-of-life practices in the Netherlands under the Euthanasia Act. *New England Journal of Medicine, 356,* 1957–1965.

van der Wal, M. F., van Eijsden, M., & Bonsel, G. J. (2007). Stress and emotional problems during pregnancy and excessive infant crying. *Developmental and Behavioral Pediatrics, 28,* 431–437.

Van de Vijver, P. J. R., Hofer, J., & Chasiotis, A. (2010). Methodology. In M. H. Bornstein (Ed.), *Handbook of cultural developmental science* (pp. 21–37). New York: Psychology Press.

Vandewater, E. A., & Stewart, A. J. (1997). Women's career commitment patterns and personality development. In M. E. Lachman & J. B. James (Eds.), *Multiple paths of midlife development* (pp. 375–410). Chicago: University of Chicago Press.

Van Eyk, J., & Dunn, M. J. (Eds.). (2008). *Clinical proteomics.* Weinheim, Germany: Wiley-VCH.

Van Eyken, E., Van Camp, G., & Van Laer, L. (2007). The complexity of age-related hearing impairment: Contributing environmental and genetic factors. *Audiology and Neurotology, 12,* 345–358.

Van Hiel, A., & Vansteenkiste, M. (2009). Ambitions fulfilled? The effects of intrinsic and extrinsic goal attainment on older adults' ego integrity and death attitudes. *International Journal of Aging and Human Development, 68,* 27–51.

Van Hulle, C. A., Goldsmith, H. H., & Lemery, K. S. (2004). Genetic, environmental, and gender effects on individual differences in toddler expressive language. *Journal of Speech, Language, and Hearing Research, 47,* 904–912.

van IJzendoorn, M. H. (1995). Adult attachment representations, parental responsiveness, and infant attachment: A meta-analysis on the predictive validity of the Adult Attachment Interview. *Psychological Bulletin, 117,* 387–403.

van IJzendoorn, M. H., & Bakermans-Kranenburg, M. J. (2006). DRD4 7-repeat polymorphism moderates the association between maternal unresolved loss or trauma and infant disorganization. *Attachment and Human Development, 8,* 291–307.

van IJzendoorn, M. H., & Hubbard, F. O. A. (2000). Are infant crying and maternal responsiveness during the first year related to infant–mother attachment at 15 months? *Attachment and Human Development, 2,* 371–391.

van IJzendoorn, M. H., Juffer, F., & Poelhuis, C. W. K. (2005). Adoption and cognitive development: A meta-analytic comparison of adopted and nonadopted children's IQ and school performance. *Psychological Bulletin, 131,* 301–316.

van IJzendoorn, M. H., & Kroonenberg, P. M. (1988). Cross-cultural patterns of attachment: A meta-analysis of the Strange Situation. *Child Development, 59,* 147–156.

van IJzendoorn, M. H., & Sagi-Schwartz, A. (2008). Cross-cultural patterns of attachment: Universal and contextual dimensions. In J. Cassidy & P. R. Shaver (Eds.), *Handbook of attachment* (2nd ed., pp. 880–905). New York: Guilford.

van IJzendoorn, M. H., Schuengel, C., & Bakermans-Kranenburg, M. J. (1999). Disorganized attachment in early childhood: Meta-analysis of precursors, concomitants, and sequelae. *Development and Psychopathology, 11,* 225–249.

van IJzendoorn, M. H., Vereijken, C. M. J. L., Bakermans-Kranenburg, M. J., & Riksen-Walraven, J. M. (2004). Assessing attachment security with the Attachment Q Sort: Meta-analytic evidence for the validity of the Observer AQS. *Child Development, 75,* 1188–1213.

Vannoy, S. D., Tai-Seale, M., Duberstein, P., Eaton, L. J., & Cook, M. A. (2011). Now what should I do? Primary care physicians' responses to older adults expressing thoughts of suicide. *Journal of General Internal Medicine, 26,* 1005–1011.

van Solinge, H., & Henkens, K. (2008). Adjustment to and satisfaction with retirement: Two of a kind? *Psychology and Aging, 23,* 422–434.

van Tol, D., Rietjens, J., & van der Heide, A. (2010). Judgment of unbearable suffering and willingness to grant a euthanasia request by Dutch general practitioners. *Health Policy, 97,* 166–172.

Van Volkom, M. (2006). Sibling relationships in middle and older adulthood: A review of the literature. *Marriage and Family Review, 40,* 151–170.

Varendi, H., & Porter, R. H. (2001). Breast odour as the only maternal stimulus elicits crawling toward the odour source. *Acta Paediatrica, 90,* 372–375.

Varnhagen, C. (2007). Children and the Web. In J. Gackenbach (Ed.), *Psychology and the Internet* (2nd ed., pp, 37–54). Amsterdam: Elsevier.

Vartanian, L. R. (1997). Separation–individuation, social support, and adolescent egocentrism: An exploratory study. *Journal of Early Adolescence, 17,* 245–270.

Vartanian, L. R., & Powlishta, K. K. (1996). A longitudinal examination of the social-cognitive foundations of adolescent egocentrism. *Journal of Early Adolescence, 16,* 157–178.

Vaughn, B. E., Bost, K. K., & van IJzendoorn, M. H. (2008). Attachment and temperament. In J. Cassidy & P. R. Shaver (Eds.), *Handbook of attachment: Theory, research, and clinical applications* (2nd ed., pp. 192–216). New York: Guilford.

Vaughn, B. E., Colvin, T. N., Azria, M. R., Caya, L., & Krzysik, L. (2001). Dyadic analyses of friendship in a sample of preschool-age children attending Head Start: Correspondence between measures and implications for social competence. *Child Development, 72,* 862–878.

Vaughn, B. E., Kopp, C. B., & Krakow, J. B. (1984). The emergence and consolidation of self-control from eighteen to thirty months of age: Normative trends and individual differences. *Child Development, 55,* 990–1004.

Vazsonyi, A. T., Hibbert, J. R., & Snider, J. B. (2003). Exotic enterprise no more? Adolescent reports of family and parenting processes from youth in four countries. *Journal of Research on Adolescence, 13,* 129–160.

Veenstra, R., Lindenberg, S., Munniksma, A., & Dijkstra, J. K. (2010). The complex relation between bullying, victimization, acceptance, and rejection: Giving special attention to status, affection, and sex differences. *Child Development, 81,* 480–486.

Velderman, M. K., Bakermans-Kranenburg, M. J., Juffer, F., & van IJzendoorn, M. H. (2006). Effects of attachment-based interventions on maternal sensitivity and infant attachment: Differential susceptibility of highly reactive infants. *Journal of Family Psychology, 20,* 266–274.

Velkoff, V. (2000, January–March). Centenarians in the United States, 1990 and beyond. *Statistical Bulletin, U.S. Bureau of the Census.* Washington, DC: U.S. Government Printing Office.

Velleman, R. D. B., Templeton, L. J., & Copello, A. G. (2005). The role of the family in preventing and intervening with substance use and misuse: A comprehensive review of family interventions, with a focus on young people. *Drug and Alcohol Review, 24,* 93–109.

Venet, M., & Markovits, H. (2001). Understanding uncertainty with abstract conditional premises. *Merrill-Palmer Quarterly, 47,* 74–99.

Venezia, M., Messinger, D. S., Thorp, D., & Mundy, P. (2004). The development of anticipatory smiling. *Infancy, 6,* 397–406.

Veneziano, R. A. (2003). The importance of paternal warmth. *Cross-Cultural Research, 37,* 265–281.

Ventura, S. J., Curtin, S. C., & Abma, J. C. (2012). Estimated pregnancy rates and rates of pregnancy outcomes for the United States, 1990–2008. *National Vital Statistics Reports, 60*(7). Retrieved from www.cdc.gov/nchs/data/nvsr/nvsr60/nvsr60_07.pdf

Vereijken, B., & Adolph, K. E. (1999). Transitions in the development of locomotion. In G. J. P. Savelsbergh, H. L. J. van der Maas, & P. C. L. van Geert (Eds.), *Non-linear analyses of developmental processes* (pp. 137–149). Amsterdam: Elsevier.

Verhaeghen, P. (2012). Age-related differences in working-memory functioning and cognitive control. In M. Naveh-Benjamin & N. Ohta (Eds.), *Memory and aging: Current issues and future directions* (pp. 3–30). New York: Psychology Press.

Verhaeghen, P., & Cerella, J. (2008). Everything we know about aging and response times: A meta-analytic integration. In S. M. Hofer & D. F. Alwin (Eds.), *Handbook of cognitive aging: Interdisciplinary perspectives* (pp. 134–150). Thousand Oaks, CA: Sage.

Verhulst, F. C. (2008). International adoption and mental health: Long-term behavioral outcome. In M. E. Garralda & J.-P. Raynaud (Eds.), *Culture and conflict and adolescent mental health* (pp. 83–105). Lanham, MD: Jason Aronson.

Vernon-Feagans, L., Pancsofar, N., Willoughby, M., Odom, E., Quade, A., & Cox, M. (2008). Predictors of maternal language to infants during a picture book task in the home: Family SES, child characteristics and the parenting environment. *Journal of Applied Developmental Psychology, 29,* 213–226.

Veríssimo, M., & Salvaterra, F. (2006). Maternal secure-base scripts and children's attachment security in an adopted sample. *Attachment and Human Development, 8,* 261–273.

Vesco, K. K., Haney, E. M., Humphrey, L., Fu, R., & Nelson, H. D. (2007). Influence of menopause on mood: A systematic review of cohort studies. *Climacteric, 10,* 448–465.

Vidaeff, A. C., Carroll, M. A., & Ramin, S. M. (2005). Acute hypertensive emergencies in pregnancy. *Critical Care Medicine, 33,* S307–S312.

Vinden, P. G. (1996). Junín Quechua children's understanding of mind. *Child Development, 67,* 1707–1716.

Vinden, P. G. (2002). Understanding minds and evidence for belief: A study of Mofu children in Cameroon. *International Journal of Behavioral Development, 26,* 445–452.

Visher, E. B., Visher, J. S., & Pasley, K. (2003). Remarriage, families and stepparenting. In F. Walsh (Ed.), *Normal family processes* (pp. 153–175). New York: Guilford.

Vitali, P., Migliaccio, R., Agosta, F., Rosen, H. J., & Geschwind, M. D. (2008). Neuroimaging in dementia. *Seminars in Neurology, 28,* 467–483.

Vitrup, B., & Holden, G. W. (2010). Children's assessments of corporal punishment and other disciplinary practices: The role of age, race, SES, and exposure to spanking. *Journal of Applied Developmental Psychology, 31,* 211–220.

Vivanti, G., Nadig, A., Ozonoff, S., & Rogers, S. J. (2008). What do children with autism attend to during imitation tasks? *Journal of Experimental Psychology, 101,* 186–205.

Vogels, N., Diepvens, K., & Westerterp-Plantenga, M. S. (2005). Predictors of long-term weight maintenance. *Obesity Research, 13,* 2162–2168.

Volling, B. L. (2001). Early attachment relationships as predictors of preschool children's emotion regulation with a distressed sibling. *Early Education and Development, 12,* 185–207.

Volling, B. L., & Belsky, J. (1992). Contribution of mother–child and father–child relationships to the quality of sibling interaction: A longitudinal study. *Child Development, 63,* 1209–1222.

Volling, B. L., Mahoney, A., & Rauer, A. J. (2009). Sanctification of parenting, moral socialization, and young children's conscience development. *Psychology of Religion and Spirituality, 1,* 53–68.

Volling, B. L., McElwain, N. L., & Miller, A. L. (2002). Emotion regulation in context: The jealousy complex between young siblings and its relations with child and family characteristics. *Child Development, 73,* 581–600.

Volling, B. L., McElwain, N. L., Notaro, P. C., & Herrera, C. (2002). Parents' emotional availability and infant emotional competence: Predictors of parent–infant attachment and emerging self-regulation. *Journal of Family Psychology, 16,* 447–465.

Voluntary Euthanasia Society of New South Wales. (2008). *Australian timeline.* Retrieved from www.vesnsw.org.au/articles/facts-Aust_timeline.php

Vondra, J. I., Shaw, D. S., Searingen, L., Cohen, M., & Owens, E. B. (2001). Attachment stability and emotional and behavioral regulation from infancy to preschool age. *Development and Psychopathology, 13,* 13–33.

von Hofsten, C. (2004). An action perspective on motor development. *Trends in Cognitive Sciences, 8,* 266–272.

von Hofsten, C., & Rosander, K. (1998). The establishment of gaze control in early infancy. In S. Simion & S. G. Butterworth (Eds.), *The development of sensory, motor and cognitive capacities in early infancy* (pp. 49–66). Hove, UK: Psychology Press.

Votruba-Drzal, E. (2003). Income changes and cognitive stimulation in young children's home learning environments. *Journal of Marriage and Family, 65,* 341–355.

Vouloumanos, A., & Werker, J. F. (2004). Tuned to the signal: The privileged status of speech for young infants. *Developmental Science, 7,* 270–276.

Voyer, D., Voyer, S., & Bryden, M. P. (1995). Magnitude of sex differences in spatial abilities: A meta-analysis and consideration of critical variables. *Psychological Bulletin, 117,* 250–270

Vuoksimaa, E., Kaprio, J., Kremen, W. S., Hokkanen, L., Viken, R. J., Tuulio-Henriksson, A., et al. (2010). Having a male co-twin masculinizes mental rotation performance in females. *Psychological Science, 21,* 1069–1071.

Vuoksimaa, E., Koskenvuo, M., Rose, R. J., & Kaprio, J. (2009). Origins of handedness: A nationwide study of 30,1671 adults. *Neuropsychologia, 47,* 1294–301.

Vygotsky, L. S. (1978). *Mind in society: The development of higher mental processes.* Cambridge, MA: Harvard University Press. (Original works published 1930, 1933, and 1935)

Vygotsky, L. S. (1987). Thinking and speech. In R. W. Rieber & A. S. Carton (Eds.), & N. Minick (Trans.), *The collected works of L. S. Vygotsky: Vol. 1. Problems of general psychology* (pp. 37–285). New York: Plenum. (Original work published 1934)

W

Waber, D. P. (2010). *Rethinking learning disabilities.* New York: Guilford.

Wachs, T. D., & Bates, J. E. (2001). Temperament. In G. Bremner & A. Fogel (Eds.), *Blackwell handbook of infant development* (pp. 465–501). Oxford, UK: Blackwell.

Waddington, C. H. (1957). *The strategy of the genes.* London: Allen & Unwin.

Wadsworth, M. E., & Santiago, C. D. (2008). Risk and resiliency processes in ethnically diverse families in poverty. *Journal of Family Psychology, 22,* 399–410.

Wagenaar, K., van Wessenbruch, M. M., van Leeuwen, F. E., Cohen-Kettenis, P. T., Delemarre-van de Waal, H. A., Schats, R., et al. (2011). Self-reported behavioral and socioemotional functioning of 11- to 18-year-old adolescents conceived by in vitro fertilization. *Fertility and Sterility, 95,* 611–616.

Wagner, N., Hassanein, K., & Head, M. (2010). Computer use by older adults: A multidisciplinary review. *Computers in Human Behavior, 26,* 870–882.

Wai, J., Cacchio, M., Putallaz, M., & Makel, M. C. (2010). Sex differences in the right tail of cognitive abilities: A 30-year examination. *Intelligence, 38,* 412–423.

Wai, J., Lubinski, D., & Benbow, C. P. (2009). Spatial ability for STEM domains: Aligning over 50 years of cumulative psychological knowledge solidifies its importance. *Journal of Educational Psychology, 101,* 817–835.

Wainryb, C. (1997). The mismeasure of diversity: Reflections on the study of cross-cultural differences. In H. D. Saltzstein (Ed.), *New directions for child development* (No. 76, pp. 51–65). San Francisco: Jossey-Bass.

Waite, L., & Das, A. (2013). Families, social life, and well-being at older ages. *Demography, 47,* S87–S109.

Waite, L. J. (1999, July). *Debunking the marriage myth: It works for women, too.* Paper presented at the annual Smart Marriages Conference, Washington, DC.

Waite, L. J., Laumann, E. O., Das, A., & Schumm, L. P. (2009). Sexuality: Measures of partnerships, practices, attitudes, and problems in the National Social Life, Health, and Aging Study. *Journal of Gerontology, 64B,* i56–i66.

Wakeley, A., Rivera, S., & Langer, J. (2000). Can young infants add and subtract? *Child Development, 71,* 1477–1720.

Walberg, H. J. (1986). Synthesis of research on teaching. In M. C. Wittrock (Ed.), *Handbook of research on teaching* (3rd ed., pp. 214–229). New York: Macmillan.

Waldfogel, J. (2001). International policies toward parental leave and child care. *Future of Children 11,* 52–61.

Waldfogel, J., Craigie, T. A., & Brooks-Gunn, J. (2010). Fragile families and child well-being. *Future of Children, 20,* 87–112.

Waldman, I. D., Rowe, D. C., Abramowitz, A., Kozel, S. T., Mohr, J. H., & Sherman, S. L. (1998). Association and linkage of the dopamine transporter gene and attention-deficit hyperactivity disorder in children: Heterogeneity owing to diagnostic subtype and severity. *American Journal of Human Genetics, 63,* 1767–1776.

Waldrip, A. M. (2008). With a little help from your friends: The importance of high-quality friendships on early adolescent adjustment. *Social Development, 17,* 832–852.

Walenski, M., Tager-Flusberg, H., & Ullman, M. T. (2006). Language in autism. In S. O. Moldin & J. L. R. Rubenstein (Eds.), *Understanding autism: From basic neuroscience to treatment* (pp. 175–203). Boca Raton, FL: CRC Press.

Walker, L. J. (1995). Sexism in Kohlberg's moral psychology? In W. M. Kurtines & J. L. Gewirtz (Eds.), *Moral development: An introduction* (pp. 83–107). Boston: Allyn and Bacon.

Walker, L. J. (2004). Progress and prospects in the psychology of moral development. *Merrill-Palmer Quarterly, 50,* 546–557.

Walker, L. J. (2006). Gender and morality. In M. Killen & J. G. Smetana (Eds.), *Handbook of moral development* (pp. 93–118). Philadelphia: Erlbaum.

Walker, L. J., & Taylor, J. H. (1991a). Family interactions and the development of moral reasoning. *Child Development, 62,* 264–283.

Walker, L. J., & Taylor, J. H. (1991b). Stage transitions in moral reasoning: A longitudinal study of developmental processes. *Developmental Psychology, 27,* 330–337.

Walker-Andrews, A. (1997). Infants' perception of expressive behaviors: Differentiation of multimodal information. *Psychological Bulletin, 121,* 437–456.

Wall, M., & Côté, J. (2007). Developmental activities that lead to dropout and investment in sport. *Physical Education and Sport Pedagogy, 12,* 77–87.

Walsh, C. A., Ploeg, J., Lohfeld, L., Horne, J., MacMillan, H., & Lai, D. (2007). Violence across the lifespan: Interconnections among forms of abuse as described by marginalized Canadian elders and their caregivers. *British Journal of Social Work, 37,* 491–514.

Walsh, F., & McGoldrick, M. (2004). Loss and the family: A systemic perspective. In F. Walsh & M. McGoldrick (Eds.), *Living beyond loss: Death in the family* (2nd ed., pp. 3–26). New York: Norton.

Walsh, K. E., & Berman, J. R. (2004). Sexual dysfunction in the older woman: An overview of the current understanding and management. *Therapy in Practice, 21,* 655–675.

Walston, J., Hadley, E. C., Ferrucci, L., Guralnik, J. M., Newman, A. B., Studenski, S. A., Ershler, W. B., Harris, T., & Fried, L. P. (2006). Research agenda for frailty in older adults: Toward a better understanding of physiology and etiology: Summary from the American Geriatrics Society/

National Institute on Aging Research Conference on Frailty in Older Adults. *Journal of the American Geriatrics Society, 54,* 991–1001.

Wang, H., & Amato, P. R. (2000). Predictors of divorce adjustment: Stressors, resources, and definitions. *Journal of Marriage and Family, 62,* 655–668.

Wang, H., & Wellman, B. (2010). Social connectivity in America: Changes in adult friendship network size from 2002 to 2007. *American Behavioral Scientist, 53,* 1148–1169.

Wang, J. (2005). Work stress as a risk factor for major depressive episode(s). *Psychological Medicine, 35,* 865–871.

Wang, M. (2007). Profiling retirees in the retirement transition and adjustment process: Examining the longitudinal change patterns of retirees' psychological well-being. *Journal of Applied Psychology, 92,* 455–474.

Wang, M. (2011). Retirement: An adult development perspective. In S. K. Whitbourne & M. J. Sliwinski (Eds.), *Wiley-Blackwell handbook of adulthood and aging* (pp. 416–429). Malden, MA: Wiley-Blackwell.

Wang, M., Adams, G. A., Beehr, T. A., & Shultz, K. S. (2009). Career issues at the end of one's career: Bridge employment and retirement. In S. G. Baugh & S. E. Sullivan (Eds.), *Maintaining focus, energy, and options over the life span* (pp. 135–162). Charlotte, NC: Information Age Publishing.

Wang, M., & Shultz, K. (2010). Employee retirement: A review and recommendations for future investigation. *Journal of Management, 36,* 172–206.

Wang, Q. (2006a). Earliest recollections of self and others in European American and Taiwanese young adults. *Psychological Science, 17,* 708–714.

Wang, Q. (2006b). Relations of maternal style and child self-concept to autobiographical memories in Chinese, Chinese immigrant, and European American 3-year-olds. *Child Development, 77,* 1794–1809.

Wang, Q. (2008). Emotion knowledge and autobiographical memory across the preschool years: A cross-cultural longitudinal investigation. *Cognition, 108,* 117–135.

Wang, Q., Pomerantz, E. M., & Chen, H. (2007). The role of parents' control in early adolescents' psychological functioning: A longitudinal investigation in the United States and China. *Child Development, 78,* 1592–1610.

Wang, Q., Shao, Y., & Li, Y. J. (2010). "My way or mom's way?" The bilingual and bicultural self in Hong Kong Chinese children and adolescents. *Child Development, 81,* 555–567.

Wang, S., Baillargeon, R., & Paterson, S. (2005). Detecting continuity violations in infancy: A new account and new evidence from covering and tube events. *Cognition, 95,* 129–173.

Wang, Z., & Deater-Deckard, K. (2013). Resilience in gene–environment transactions. In S. Goldstein & R. Brooks (Eds.), *Handbook of resilience in children* (2nd ed., pp. 57–72). New York: Springer Science + Business Media.

Ward, R. A., & Spitze, G. D. (2007). Nest-leaving and coresidence by young adult children: The role of family relations. *Research on Aging, 29,* 257–277.

Wark, G. R., & Krebs, D. L. (1996). Gender and dilemma differences in real-life moral judgment. *Developmental Psychology, 32,* 220–230.

Warner, L. A., Valdez, A., Vega, W. A., de la Rosa, M., Turner, R. J., & Canino, G. (2006). Hispanic drug abuse in an evolving cultural context: An agenda for research. *Drug and Alcohol Dependence, 84*(Suppl. 1), S8–S16.

Warner, L. M., Ziegelmann, J. P., Schüz, B., Wurm, S., Tesch-Römer, C., & Schwarzer, R. (2011). Maintaining autonomy despite multimorbidity: Self-efficacy and the two faces of social support. *European Journal of Ageing, 8,* 3–12.

Warnock, F., & Sandrin, D. (2004). Comprehensive description of newborn distress behavior in response to acute pain (newborn male circumcision). *Pain, 107,* 242–255.

Warr, P. (2001). Age and work behavior: Physical attributes, cognitive abilities, knowledge, personality traits, and motives. *International Review of Industrial and Organizational Psychology, 16,* 1–36.

Warren, A. R., & Tate, C. S. (1992). Egocentrism in children's telephone conversations. In R. M. Diaz & L. E. Berk (Eds.), *Private speech: From social interaction to self-regulation* (pp. 245–264). Hillsdale, NJ: Erlbaum.

Warshaw, C., Brashler, P., & Gil, J. (2009). Mental health consequences of intimate partner violence. In C. Mitchell & D. Anglin (Eds.), *Intimate partner violence: A health-based perspective* (pp. 147–171). New York: Oxford University Press.

Wass, H. (2004). A perspective on the current state of death education. *Death Studies, 28,* 289–308.

Wasserman, E. A., & Rovee-Collier, C. (2001). Pick the flowers and mind your As and 2s! Categorization by pigeons and infants. In M. E. Carroll & J. B. Overmier (Eds.), *Animal research and human health: Advancing human welfare through behavioral science* (pp. 263–279). Washington, DC: American Psychological Association.

Watamura, S. E., Donzella, B., Alwin, J., & Gunnar, M. R. (2003). Morning-to-afternoon increases in cortisol concentrations for infants and toddlers at child care: Age differences and behavioral correlates. *Child Development, 74,* 1006–1020.

Watamura, S. E., Phillips, D., Morrissey, T. W., McCartney, K., & Bub, K. (2011). Double jeopardy: Poorer social-emotional outcomes for children in the NICHD SECCYD experiencing home and childcare environments that confer risk. *Child Development, 82,* 48–65.

Waterman, A. S., & Whitbourne, S. K. (1982). Androgyny and psychosocial development among college students and adults. *Journal of Personality, 50,* 121–133.

Waters, E., & Cummings, E. M. (2000). A secure base from which to explore close relationships. *Child Development, 71,* 164–172.

Waters, E., Merrick, S., Treboux, D., Crowell, J., & Albersheim, L. (2000). Attachment security in infancy and early adulthood: A twenty-year longitudinal study. *Child Development, 71,* 684–689.

Waters, E., Vaughn, B. E., Posada, G., & Kondo-Ikemura, K. (Eds.). (1995). Caregiving, cultural, and cognitive perspectives on secure-base behavior and working models: New growing points of attachment theory and research. *Monographs of the Society for Research in Child Development, 60*(2–3, Serial No. 244).

Watson, J. B., & Raynor, R. (1920). Conditioned emotional reactions. *Journal of Experimental Psychology, 3,* 1–14.

Watson, M. (1990). Aspects of self development as reflected in children's role playing. In D. Cicchetti & M. Beeghly (Eds.), *The self in transition: Infancy to childhood* (pp. 281–307). Chicago: University of Chicago Press.

Wax, J. R., Pinette, M. G., & Cartin, A. (2010). Home versus hospital birth—process and outcome. *Obstetric and Gynecological Survey, 65,* 132–140.

Waxman, S. R. (2003). Links between object categorization and naming: Origins and emergence in human infants. In D. H. Rakison & L. M. Oakes (Eds.), *Early category and concept development: Making sense of the blooming, buzzing confusion* (pp. 193–209). New York: Oxford University Press.

Waxman, S. R., & Senghas, A. (1992). Relations among word meanings in early lexical development. *Developmental Psychology, 28,* 862–873.

Webb, N. B. (2002). September 11, 2001. In N. B. Webb (Ed.), *Helping bereaved children: A handbook for practitioners* (pp. 365–384). New York: Guilford.

Webb, N. M., Franke, M. L., Ing, M., Chan, A., De, T., Freund, D., & Battey, D. (2008). The role of teacher instructional practices in student collaboration. *Contemporary Educational Psychology, 35,* 360–381.

Webb, S. J., Monk, C. S., & Nelson, C. A. (2001). Mechanisms of postnatal neurobiological development: Implications for human development. *Developmental Neuropsychology, 19,* 147–171.

Weber, C., Hahne, A., Friedrich, M., & Friederici, A. (2004). Discrimination of word stress in early infant perception: Electrophysiological evidence. *Cognitive Brain Research, 18,* 149–161.

Webster, J. D. (2002). Reminiscence function in adulthood: Age, ethnic, and family dynamics correlates. In J. D. Webster & B. K. Haight (Eds.), *Critical advances in reminiscence work* (pp. 140–142). New York: Springer.

Webster-Stratton, C., & Herman, K. C. (2010). Disseminating Incredible Years series early-intervention programs: Integrating and sustaining services between school and home. *Psychology in the Schools, 47,* 36–54.

Webster-Stratton, C., & Reid, M. J. (2010a). The Incredible Years Parents, Teachers, and Children Training Series: A multifaceted treatment approach for young children with conduct disorders. In J. R. Weisz & A. E. Kazdin (Eds.), *Evidence-based psychotherapies for children and adolescents* (2nd ed., pp. 194–210). New York: Guilford.

Webster-Stratton, C., & Reid, M. J. (2010b). The Incredible Years program for children from infancy to pre-adolescence: Prevention and treatment of behavior problems. In R. C. Murrihy, A. D. Kidman, & T. H. Ollendick (Eds.), *Clinical handbook of assessing and treating conduct problems in youth* (pp. 117–138). New York: Springer Science + Business Media.

Webster-Stratton, C., Rinaldi, J., & Reid, J. M. (2011). Long-term outcomes of Incredible Years parenting program: Predictors of adolescent adjustment. *Child and Adolescent Mental Health, 16,* 38–46.

Wechsler, D. (2002). *WPPSI-III: Wechsler Preschool and Primary Scale of Intelligence* (3rd ed.). San Antonio, TX: Psychological Corporation.

Wechsler, D. (2003). *WISC-IV: Wechsler Intelligence Scale for Children* (4th ed.). San Antonio, TX: Psychological Corporation.

Weems, C. F., & Costa, N. M. (2005). Developmental differences in the expression of childhood anxiety symptoms and fears. *Journal of the American Academy of Child and Adolescent Psychiatry, 44,* 656–663.

Weeraratna, A. T., Kalehua, A., Deleon, I., Bertak, D., Maher, G., & Wade, M. S. (2007). Alterations in immunological and neurological gene expression patterns in Alzheimer's disease tissues. *Experimental Cell Research, 313,* 450–461.

Wegesin, D. J., Jacobs, D. M., Zubin, N. R., & Ventura, P. R. (2000). Source memory and encoding strategy in normal aging. *Journal of Clinical and Experimental Neuropsychology, 22,* 455–464.

Wehren, A., De Lisi, R., & Arnold, M. (1981). The development of noun definition. *Journal of Child Language, 8,* 165–175.

Weikum, W. M., Vouloumanos, A., Navarra, J., Soto-Faraco, S., Sebastián-Gallés, N., & Werker, J. F. (2007). Visual language discrimination in infancy. *Science, 316,* 1159.

Weinberg, M. K., & Tronick, E. Z. (1994). Beyond the face: An empirical study of infant affective configurations of facial, vocal, gestural, and regulatory behaviors. *Child Development, 65,* 1503–1515.

Weinberger, M. I., & Whitbourne, S. K. (2010). Depressive symptoms, self-reported physical functioning, and identity in community-dwelling older adults. *Aging International, 35,* 276–285.

Weindruch, R., Keenan, K. P., Carney, J. M., Fernandes, G., Feuers, R. J., & Floyd, R. A. (2001). Caloric restriction mimetics: Metabolic interventions. *Journal of Gerontology, 56A,* 20–33.

Weiner, J., & Tardif, C. (2004). Social and emotional functioning of children with learning disabilities: Does special education placement make a difference? *Learning Disabilities Research and Practice, 19,* 20–32.

Weinfield, N. S., Sroufe, L. A., & Egeland, B. (2000). Attachment from infancy to early adulthood in a high-risk sample: Continuity, discontinuity, and their correlates. *Child Development, 71,* 695–702.

Weinfield, N. S., Whaley, G. J. L., & Egeland, B. (2004). Continuity, discontinuity, and coherence in attachment from infancy to late adolescence: Sequelae of organization and disorganization. *Attachment and Human Development, 6,* 73–97.

Weinstein, R. S. (2002). *Reaching higher: The power of expectations in schooling.* Cambridge, MA: Harvard University Press.

Weinstein, S. M., Mermelstein, R. J., Hedeker, D., Hankin, B. L., & Flay, B. R. (2006). The time-varying influences of peer and family support on adolescent daily positive and negative affect. *Journal of Clinical Child and Adolescent Psychology, 35,* 420–430.

Weinstock, M. (2008). The long-term behavioural consequences of prenatal stress. *Neuroscience and Biobehavioral Reviews, 32,* 1073–1086.

Weisfield, G. E. (1997). Puberty rites as clues to the nature of human adolescence. *Cross-Cultural Research, 31,* 27–54.

Weisgram, E. S., Bigler, R. S., & Liben, L. S. (2010). Gender, values, and occupational interests among children, adolescents, and adults. *Child Development, 81,* 778–796.

Weiss, A., Costa, P. T., Jr., Karuza, J., Duberstein, P. R., Friedman, B., & McCrae, R. M. (2005). Crosssectional age differences in personality among Medicare patients aged 65 to 100. *Psychology and Aging, 20,* 182–185.

Weiss, K. M. (2005). Cryptic causation of human disease: Reading between the germ lines. *Trends in Genetics, 21,* 82–88.

Weissberg, R. W. (2006). Modes of expertise in creative thinking: Evidence from case studies. In K. A. Ericsson, N. Charness, P. J. Feltovich, & R. R. Hoffman (Eds.), *The Cambridge handbook of expertise and expert performance* (pp. 761–787). New York: Cambridge University Press.

Weisz, A. N., & Black, B. M. (2002). Gender and moral reasoning: African American youths respond to dating dilemmas. *Journal of Human Behavior in the Social Environment, 6,* 17–34.

Weizman, Z. O., & Snow, C. E. (2001). Lexical output as related to children's vocabulary acquisition: Effects of sophisticated exposure and support for meaning. *Developmental Psychology, 37,* 265–279.

Wekerle, C., & Avgoustis, E. (2003). Child maltreatment, adolescent dating, and adolescent dating violence. In P. Florsheim (Ed.), *Adolescent romantic relations and sexual behavior: Theory, research, and practical implications* (pp. 213–242). Mahwah, NJ: Erlbaum.

Wekerle, C., Wall, A.-M., Leung, E., & Trocmé, N. (2007). Cumulative stress and substantiated maltreatment: The importance of caregiver vulnerability and adult partner violence. *Child Abuse and Neglect, 31,* 427–443.

Wekerle, C., & Wolfe, D. A. (2003). Child maltreatment. In E. J. Mash & R. A. Barkley (Eds.), *Child psychopathology* (2nd ed., pp. 632–684). New York: Guilford.

Wellman, H. M. (2002). Understanding the psychological world: Developing a theory of mind. In U. Goswami (Ed.), *Blackwell handbook of child cognitive development* (pp. 167–187). Malden, MA: Blackwell.

Wellman, H. M. (2011). Developing a theory of mind. In U. Goswami (Ed.), *Wiley-Blackwell handbook of childhood cognitive development* (2nd ed., pp. 258–284). Malden, MA: Wiley-Blackwell.

Wellman, H. M., & Hickling, A. K. (1994). The mind's "I": Children's conception of the mind as an active agent. *Child Development, 65,* 1564–1580.

Wellman, H. M., Lopez-Duran, S., LaBounty, J., & Hamilton, B. (2008). Infant attention to intentional action predicts preschool theory of mind. *Developmental Psychology, 44,* 618–623.

Welsh, M. C. (2002). Developmental and clinical variations in executive functions. In U. Kirk & D. Molfese (Eds.), *Developmental variations in language and learning* (pp. 139–185). Mahwah, NJ: Erlbaum.

Welsh, M. C., Friedman, S. L., & Spieker, S. J. (2008). Executive functions in developing children: Current conceptualizations and questions for the future. In K. McCartney & D. Phillips (Eds.), *Blackwell handbook of early childhood development* (pp. 167–187). Malden, MA: Blackwell Publishing.

Welsh, M. C., Pennington, D. F., & Groisser, D. B. (1991). A normative-developmental study of executive function: A window on prefrontal function in children. *Developmental Neuropsychology, 7,* 131–149.

Wenger, G. C. (2009). Childlessness at the end of life: Evidence from rural Wales. *Ageing and Society, 29,* 1243–1259.

Wenger, G. C., & Burholdt, V. (2001). Differences over time in older people's relationships with children, grandchildren, nieces and nephews in rural North Wales. *Ageing and Society, 21,* 567–590.

Wentworth, N., Benson, J. B., & Haith, M. M. (2000). The development of infants' reaches for stationary and moving targets. *Child Development, 71,* 576–601.

Wentzel, K. R., Barry, C. M., & Caldwell, K. A. (2004). Friendships in middle school: Influences on motivation and school adjustment. *Journal of Educational Psychology, 96,* 195–203.

Werner, E. E. (1989, April). Children of the garden island. *Scientific American, 260*(4), 106–111.

Werner, E. E. (1991). Grandparent–grandchild relationships amongst U.S. ethnic groups. In P. K. Smith (Ed.), *The psychology of grandparenthood: An international perspective* (pp. 68–82). London: Routledge.

Werner, E. E. (2001). *Journeys from childhood to midlife: Risk, resilience, and recovery.* Ithaca, NY: Cornell University Press.

Werner, E. E. (2013). What can we learn about resilience from large-scale longitudinal studies? In S. Goldstein & R. Brooks (Eds.), *Handbook of resilience in children* (2nd ed., pp. 87–102). New York: Springer Science + Business Media.

Werner, E. E., & Smith, R. S. (1982). *Vulnerable but invincible.* New York: McGraw-Hill.

Werner, E. E., & Smith, R. S. (1992). *Overcoming the odds: High-risk children from birth to adulthood.* Ithaca, NY: Cornell University Press.

Werner, N. E., & Crick, N. R. (2004). Maladaptive peer relationships and the development of relational and physical aggression during middle childhood. *Social Development, 13,* 495–514.

Wesson, D. E., Stephens, D., Lam, K., Parsons, D., Spence, L, & Parkin, P. C. (2008). Trends in pediatric and adult bicycling deaths before and after passage of a bicycle helmet law. *Pediatrics, 122,* 605–610.

West, R. L., Bagwell, D. K., & Dark-Freudeman, A. (2008). Memory and goal-setting: The response of older and younger adults to positive and objective feedback. *Psychology and Aging, 20,* 195–201.

Westerhof, G. J. (2008). Age identity. In D. Carr (Ed.), *Encyclopedia of the life course and human development* (pp. 10–14). Farmington Hills, MI: Macmillan.

Westerhof, G. J., & Barrett, A. E. (2005). Age identity and subjective well-being: A comparison of the United States and Germany. *Journal of Gerontology, 60S,* 129–136.

Westerhof, G. J., Bohlmeijer, E., & Webster, J. D. (2010). Reminiscence and mental health: A review of recent progress in theory, research and interventions. *Ageing and Society, 30,* 697–721.

Westerhof, G. J., Whitbourne, S. K., & Freeman, G. P. (2012). The aging self in a cultural context: The relation of conceptions of aging to identity processes and self-esteem in the United States and the Netherlands. *Journal of Gerontology, 67B,* 52–60.

Westermann, G., Mareschal, D., Johnson, M. H., Sirois, S., Spratling, M. W., & Thomas, M. S. C. (2007). Neuroconstructivism. *Developmental Science, 10,* 75–83.

Westermann, G., Sirois, S., Shultz, T. R., & Mareschal, D. (2006). Modeling developmental cognitive neuroscience. *Trends in Cognitive Sciences, 10,* 227–232.

Westermeyer, J. F. (2004). Predictors and characteristics of Erikson's life cycle model among men: A 32-year longitudinal study. *International Journal of Aging and Human Development, 58,* 29–48.

Wethington, E. (2000). Expecting stress: Americans and the "midlife crisis." *Motivation and Emotion, 24,* 85–103.

Wethington, E., Kessler, R. C., & Pixley, J. E. (2004). Turning points in adulthood. In O. G. Brim, C. D. Ryff, & R. C. Kessler (Eds.), *How healthy are we? A national study of well-being at midlife* (pp. 586–613). Chicago: University of Chicago Press.

Wetle, T., Shield, R., Teno, J., Miller, S. C., & Welch, L. (2005). Family perspectives on end-of-life care experiences in nursing homes. *Gerontologist, 45,* 642–650.

Wetmore, C. M., & Mokdad, A. H. (2012). In denial: Misperceptions of weight change among adults in the United States. *Preventive Medicine, 55,* 93–100.

Weyermann, M., Rothenbacher, D., & Brenner, H. (2006). Duration of breast-feeding and risk of overweight in childhood: A prospective birth cohort study from Germany. *International Journal of Obesity, 30,* 1281–1287.

Wheeler, I. (2001). Parental bereavement: The crisis of meaning. *Death Studies, 25,* 51–66.

Wheeler, W. (2002). Youth leadership for development: Civic activism as a component of youth development programming and a strategy for strengthening civil society. In R. M. Lerner, F. Jacobs, & D. Wertlieb (Eds.), *Handbook of applied developmental science* (Vol. 2, pp. 491–506). Thousand Oaks, CA: Sage.

Whincup, P. H., Kaye, S. G., Owen, C. G., Huxley, R., Cook, D. G., Anazawa, S., et al. (2008). Birth weight and risk of type 2 diabetes: A systematic review. *Journal of the American Medical Association, 24,* 2886–2897.

Whipple, E. E. (2006). Child abuse and neglect: Consequences of physical, sexual, and emotional abuse of children. In H. E. Fitzgerald, B. M. Lester, & B. Zuckerman (Eds.), *The crisis in youth mental health: Critical issues and effective programs: Vol. 1. Childhood disorders* (pp. 205–229). Westport, CT: Praeger.

Whipple, N., Bernier, A., & Mageau, G. A. (2011). Broadening the study of infant security of attachment: Maternal autonomy-support in the context of infant exploration. *Social Development, 20,* 17–32.

Whisman, M. A., Uebelacker, L. A., Tolejko, N., Chatav, Y., & McKelvie, M. (2006). Marital discord and well-being in older adults: Is the association confounded by personality? *Psychology and Aging, 21,* 626–631.

Whitaker, D. J., Baker, C. K., & Arias, I. (2007). Interventions to prevent intimate partner violence. In L. S. Doll, S. E., Bonzo, D. A. Sleet, & J. A. Mercy (Eds.), *Handbook of injury and violence prevention* (pp. 203–221). New York: Springer Science + Business Media.

Whitbourne, S. K. (1996). *The aging individual: Physical and psychological perspectives.* New York: Springer.

Whitbourne, S. K. (2002). *The aging individual: Physical and psychological perspectives.* New York: Springer.

Whitbourne, S. K., & Meeks, S. (2011). Psychopathology, bereavement, and aging. In K. W. Schaie & S. L. Willis (Eds.), *Handbook of the psychology of aging* (7th ed., pp. 311–323). San Diego, CA: Elsevier.

Whitbourne, S. K., & Willis, S. L. (2006). Preface. In S. K. Whitbourne & S. L. Willis (Eds.), *The baby boomers grow up* (pp. vii–ix). Mahwah, NJ: Erlbaum.

Whitbourne, S. K., Zuschlag, M. K., Elliot, L. B., & Waterman, A. S. (1992). Psychosocial development in adulthood: A 22-year sequential study. *Journal of Personality and Social Psychology, 63,* 260–271.

White, H. R., McMorris, B. J., Catalano, R. F., Fleming, C. B., Haggerty, K. P., & Abbott, R. D. (2006). Increases in alcohol and marijuana use during the transition out of high school into emerging adulthood: The effects of leaving home, going to college, and high school protective factors. *Journal of Studies on Alcohol, 67,* 810–822.

White, L. (2001). Sibling relationships over the life course: A panel analysis. *Journal of Marriage and Family, 63,* 555–568.

White, Y. A., Woods, D. C., Takai, Y., Ishihara, O., Seki, H., & Tilly, J. L. (2012). Oocyte formation by mitotically active germ cells purified from ovaries of reproductive-age women. *Nature Medicine, 18,* 413–421.

Whiteman, S. D., & Loken, E. (2006). Comparing analytic techniques to classify dyadic relationships: An example using siblings. *Journal of Marriage and Family, 68,* 1370–1382.

Whiteman, S. D., McHale, S. M., & Crouter, A. C. (2010). Family relationships from adolescence to early adulthood: Changes in the family system following firstborns' leaving home. *Journal of Research on Adolescence, 21,* 461–474.

Whitesell, N. R., Mitchell, C. M., Spicer, P., and the Voices of Indian Teens Project Team. (2009). A longitudinal study of self-esteem, cultural identity, and academic success among American Indian adolescents. *Cultural Diversity and Ethnic Minority Psychology, 15,* 38–50.

Whiteside, M. F. (2006). Remarried systems. In L. Combrinck-Graham (Ed.), *Children in family contexts: Perspectives on treatment* (pp. 163–189). New York: Guilford.

Whiteside-Mansell, L., Bradley, R. H., Owen, M. T., Randolph, S. M., & Cauce, A. M. (2003). Parenting and children's behavior at 36 months: Equivalence between African-American and European-American mother–child dyads. *Parenting: Science and Practice, 3,* 197–234.

Whitfield, K. E., Thorpe, R., & Szanton, S. (2011). Health disparities, social class, and aging. In K. Warner Schaie & S. L. Willis (Eds.), *Handbook of the psychology of aging* (7th ed., pp. 207–218). San Diego, CA: Academic Press.

Whiting, B., & Edwards, C. P. (1988). A cross-cultural analysis of sex differences in the behavior of children aged 3 through 11. In G. Handel (Ed.), *Childhood socialization* (pp. 281–297). New York: Aldine de Gruyter.

Whitlock, J. L., Powers, J. L., & Eckenrode, J. (2006). The virtual cutting edge: The Internet and adolescent self-injury. *Developmental Psychology, 42,* 407–417.

Whitmer, R. A., Gustafson, D. R., Barrett-Connor, E., Haan, M. N., Gunderson, E. P., & Yaffe, K. (2008). Central obesity and increased risk of dementia more than three decades later. *Neurology, 71,* 1057–1064.

Wichmann, C., Coplan, R. J., & Daniels, T. (2004). The social cognitions of socially withdrawn children. *Social Development, 13,* 377–392.

Wichstrøm, L. (2006). Sexual orientation as a risk factor for bulimic symptoms. *International Journal of Eating Disorders, 39,* 448–453.

Wickens, A. P. (2001). Aging and the free radical theory. *Respiration Physiology, 128,* 379–391.

Wigfield, A., Battle, A., Keller, L. B., & Eccles, J. S. (2002). Sex differences in motivation, self-concept, career aspiration, and career choice: Implications for cognitive development. In A. McGillicudy-De Lisi & R. De Lisi (Eds.), *Biology, society, and behavior: The development of sex differences in cognition* (pp. 93–124). Westport, CT: Ablex.

Wigfield, A., & Eccles, J. S. (1994). Children's competence beliefs, achievement values, and general self-esteem change across elementary and middle school. *Journal of Early Adolescence, 14,* 107–138.

Wigfield, A., Eccles, J. S., Schiefele, U., Roeser, R. W., & Davis-Kean, P. (2006). Development of achievement motivation. In N. Eisenberg (Ed.), *Handbook of child psychology: Vol. 3. Social, emotional, and personality development* (6th ed., pp. 933–1002). Hoboken, NJ: Wiley.

Wigfield, A., Eccles, J. S., Yoon, K. S., Harold, R. D., Arbreton, A. J., Freedman-Doan, C., & Blumenfeld, P. C. (1997). Changes in children's competence beliefs and subjective task values across the elementary school years: A three-year study. *Journal of Educational Psychology, 89,* 451–469.

Wikby, A., Maxson, P., Olsson, J., Johansson, B., & Ferguson, F. G. (1998). Changes in CD8 and CD4 lymphocyte subsets, T cell proliferation responses and non-survival in the very old: The Swedish longitudinal OCTO-immune study. *Mechanisms of Ageing and Development, 102,* 187–198.

Wilbur, J., Chandler, P. J., Dancy, B., & Lee, H. (2003). Correlates of physical activity in urban Midwestern African-American women. *American Journal of Preventive Medicine, 25,* 45–52.

Wilbur, J., Vassalo, A., Chandler, P., McDevitt, J., & Miller, A. M. (2005). Midlife women's adherence to home-based walking during maintenance. *Nursing Research, 54,* 33–40.

Wilcox, A. J., Weinberg, C. R., & Baird, D. D. (1995). Timing of sexual intercourse in relation to ovulation: Effects on the probability of conception, survival of the pregnancy, and sex of the baby. *New England Journal of Medicine, 333,* 1517–1519.

Wilkie, S. S., Guenette, J. A., Dominelli, P. B., & Sheel, A. W. (2012). Effects of an aging pulmonary system on expiratory flow limitation and dyspnoea during exercise in healthy women. *European Journal of Applied Physiology, 112,* 2195–2204.

Wilkinson, K., Ross, E., & Diamond, A. (2003). Fast mapping of multiple words: Insights into when "the information provided" does and does not equal "the information perceived." *Applied Developmental Psychology, 24,* 739–762.

Wilkinson, R. B. (2004). The role of parental and peer attachment in the psychological health and self-esteem of adolescents. *Journal of Youth and Adolescence, 33,* 479–493.

Wilkinson, R. G., & Pickett, K. E. (2006). Income inequality and population health: A review and explanation of the evidence. *Social Science and Medicine, 62,* 1768–1784.

Willatts, P. (1999). Development of means–end behavior in young infants: Pulling a support to retrieve a distant object. *Developmental Psychology, 35,* 651–667.

Williams, J. E., Nieto, F. J., Sanford, C. P., Couper, D. J., & Tyroler, H. A. (2002). The association between trait anger and incident stroke risk: The Atherosclerosis Risk in Communities (ARIC) Study. *Stroke, 33,* 13–20.

Williams, J. M., & Currie, C. (2000). Self-esteem and physical development in early adolescence: Pubertal timing and body image. *Journal of Early Adolescence, 20,* 129–149.

Williams, K., & Dunne-Bryant, A. (2006). Divorce and adult psychological well-being: Clarifying the role of gender and age. *Journal of Marriage and Family, 68,* 1178–1196.

Williams, K. N., & Warren, C. A. B. (2008). Assisted living and the aging trajectory. *Journal of Women and Aging, 20,* 309–327.

Williams, N., & Torrez, D. J. (1998). Grandparenthood among Hispanics. In M. E. Szinovacz (Ed.), *Handbook on grandparenthood* (pp. 87–96). Westport, CT: Greenwood Press.

Williams, P. E., Weis, L. G., & Rolfhus, E. (2003). *WISC-IV: Theoretical model and test blueprint.* San Antonio, TX: Psychological Corporation.

Williams, R., McNeilly, A., & Sutherland, C. (2012). Insulin resistance in the brain: An old-age or new-age problem? *Biochemical Pharmacology, 84,* 737–745.

Williams, S., & Dale, J. (2006). The effectiveness of treatment for depression/depressive symptoms in adults with cancer: A systematic review. *British Journal of Cancer, 94,* 372–390.

Williams, T. S., Connolly, J., Pepler, D., Craig, W., & Loporte, L. (2008). Risk models of dating aggression across different adolescent relationships: A developmental psychopathology approach. *Journal of Consulting and Clinical Psychology, 76,* 622–632.

Williamson, J., Softas-Nall, B., & Miller, J. (2003). Grandmothers raising grandchildren: An exploration of their experiences and emotions. *Counseling and Therapy for Couples with Families, 11,* 23–32.

Willinger, M., Ko, C.-W., Hoffman, H. J., Kessler, R. C., & Corwin, M. J. (2003). Trends in infant bed sharing in the United States. *Archives of Pediatrics and Adolescent Medicine, 157,* 43–49.

Willis, S. L., & Schaie, K. W. (1999). Intellectual functioning in midlife. In S. L. Willis & J. D. Reid (Eds.), *Life in the middle* (pp. 105–146). San Diego: Academic Press.

Willoughby, J., Kupersmidt, J. B., & Bryant, D. (2001). Overt and covert dimensions of antisocial behavior. *Journal of Abnormal Child Psychology, 29,* 177–187.

Willson, A. E., Shuey, K. M., Elder, G. H., Jr., & Wickrama, K. A. S. (2006). Ambivalence in mother–adult child relations: A dyadic analysis. *Social Psychology Quarterly, 69,* 235–252.

Wilson, D. J., Mitchell, J. M., Kemp, B. J., Adkins, R. H., & Mann, W. (2009). Effects of assistive technology on functional decline in people aging with a disability. *Assistive Technology, 21,* 208–217.

Wilson, E. K., Dalberth, B. T., Koo, H. P., & Gard, J. C. (2010). Parents' perspectives on talking to preteenage children about sex. *Perspectives on Sexual and Reproductive Health, 42,* 56–63.

Wilson, R. S., Beckett, L. A., Evans, D. A., & Bennett, D. A. (2003). Terminal decline in cognitive function. *Neurology, 60,* 1782–1787.

Windsor, T. D., Anstey, K. J., & Rodgers, B. (2008). Volunteering and psychological well-being among young-old adults: How much is too much? *Gerontologist, 48,* 59–70.

Wink, P. (2006). Who is afraid of death? Religiousness, spirituality, and death anxiety in late adulthood. *Journal of Religion, Spirituality and Aging, 18,* 93–110.

Wink, P. (2007). Everyday life in the Third Age. In J. B. James & P. Wink (Eds.), *Annual review of gerontology and geriatrics* (Vol. 26, pp. 243–261). New York: Springer.

Wink, P., & Dillon, M. (2002). Spiritual development across the adult life course: Findings from a longitudinal study. *Journal of Adult Development, 9,* 79–94.

Wink, P., & Dillon, M. (2008). Religiousness, spirituality, and psychosocial functioning in late adulthood: Findings from a longitudinal study. *Psychology of Religion and Spirituality 5,* 102–115.

Wink, P., & Helson, R. (1993). Personality change in women and their partners. *Journal of Personality and Social Psychology, 65,* 597–605.

Wink, P., & Schiff, B. (2002). To review or not to review? The role of personality and life events in life review and adaptation to older age. In J. D. Webster & B. K. Haight (Eds.), *Critical advances in reminiscence work* (pp. 44–75). New York: Springer.

Wink, P., & Scott, J. (2005). Does religiousness buffer against the fear of death and dying in late adulthood? Findings from a longitudinal study. *Journal of Gerontology, 60B,* P207–P214.

Winkler, I., Háden, G. P., Ladinig, O., Sziller, I., & Honing, H. (2009). Newborn infants detect the beat in music. *Proceedings of the National Academy of Sciences, 106,* 2468–2471.

Winner, E. (1986, August). Where pelicans kiss seals. *Psychology Today, 20*(8), 25–35.

Winner, E. (1988). *The point of words: Children's understanding of metaphor and irony.* Cambridge, MA: Harvard University Press.

Winner, E. (2000). The origins and ends of giftedness. *American Psychologist, 55,* 159–169.

Winner, E. (2003). Creativity and talent. In M. H. Bornstein, L. Davidson, C. L. M. Keyes, K. A. Moore, & the Center for Child Well-Being (Eds.), *Well-being: Positive development across the life course* (pp. 371–380). Mahwah, NJ: Erlbaum.

Winsler, A. (2009). Still talking to ourselves after all these years: A review of current research on private speech. In A. Winsler, C. Fernyhough, & I. Montero (Eds.), *Private speech executive functioning, and the development of self-regulation.* New York: Cambridge University Press.

Winsler, A., Fernyhough, C., & Montero, I. (Eds.). (2009). *Private speech, executive functioning, and the development of verbal self-regulation.* New York: Cambridge University Press.

Winsler, A., Naglieri, J., & Manfra, L. (2006). Children's search strategies and accompanying verbal and motor strategic behavior: Developmental trends and relations with task performance among children age 5 to 17. *Cognitive Development, 21,* 232–248.

Winslow, R. D., Mehta, D., & Fuster, V. (2005). Sudden cardiac death: Mechanisms, therapies and challenges. *Cardiovascular Medicine, 2,* 352–360.

Winter, D. G., Torges, C. M., Stewart, A. J., Henderson-King, D., & Henderson-King, E. (2007). Pathways toward the Third Age: Studying a cohort from the "golden age." In J. B. James & P. Wink (Eds.), *The crown of life: Dynamics of the early postretirement period* (pp. 103–130). New York: Springer.

Wiseman, F. K., Alford, K. A., Tybulewicz, V. L. J., & Fisher, E. M. C. (2009). Down syndrome—recent progress and future prospects. *Human Molecular Genetics, 8,* R75–R83.

Wissink, I. B., Deković, M., & Meijer, A. M. (2006). Parenting behavior, quality of the parent–adolescent relationship, and adolescent functioning in four ethnic groups. *Journal of Early Adolescence, 26,* 133–159.

Witherington, D. C. (2005). The development of prospective grasping control between 5 and 7 months: A longitudinal study. *Infancy, 7,* 143–161.

Wolak, J., Finkelhor, D., Mitchell, K. J., & Ybarra, M. L. (2008). Online "predators" and their victims: Myths, realities, and implications for prevention and treatment. *American Psychologist, 63,* 111–128.

Wolak, J., Mitchell, K. J., & Finkelhor, D. (2003). Escaping or connecting? Characteristics of youth who form close online relationships. *Journal of Adolescence, 26,* 105–119.

Wolak, J., Mitchell, K., & Finkelhor, D. (2007). Unwanted and wanted exposure to online pornography in a national sample of youth Internet users. *Pediatrics, 119,* 247–257.

Wolchik, S. A., Wilcox, K. L., Tein, J.-Y. & Sandler, I. N. (2000). Maternal acceptance and consistency of discipline as buffers of divorce stressors on children's psychological adjustment problems. *Journal of Abnormal Child Psychology, 28,* 87–102.

Wolfe, D. A. (2005). *Child abuse* (2nd ed.). Thousand Oaks, CA: Sage.

Wolfe, V. V. (2006). Child sexual abuse. In E. J. Mash & R. A. Barkley (Eds.), *Treatment of childhood disorders* (3rd ed., pp. 647–727). New York: Guilford.

Wolff, P. H. (1966). The causes, controls and organization of behavior in the neonate. *Psychological Issues, 5*(1, Serial No. 17).

Wolff, P. H., & Fesseha, G. (1999). The orphans of Eritrea: A five-year follow-up study. *Journal of Child Psychology and Psychiatry and Allied Disciplines, 40,* 1231–1237.

Wolfinger, N. H. (2000). Beyond the intergenerational transmission of divorce: Do people replicate the patterns of marital instability they grew up with? *Journal of Family Issues, 21,* 1061–1086.

Wolfinger, N. H. (2005). *Understanding the divorce cycle.* New York: Cambridge University Press.

Wolinsky, F. D., Unverzagt, F. W., Smith, D. M., Jones R., Stoddard, A., & Tennstedt, S. L. (2006). The ACTIVE cognitive training trail and health-related quality of life: Protection that lasts for 5 years. *Journal of Gerontology, 61A,* 1324–1329.

Wong, C. A., Eccles, J. S., & Sameroff, A. (2003). The influence of ethnic discrimination and ethnic identification on African American adolescents' school and socioemotional adjustment. *Journal of Personality, 71,* 1197–1232.

Wood, E., Desmarais, S., & Gugula, S. (2002). The impact of parenting experience on gender stereotyped toy play of children. *Sex Roles, 47,* 39–49.

Wood, J. J., Emmerson, N. A., & Cowan, P. A. (2004). Is early attachment security carried forward into relationships with preschool peers? *British Journal of Developmental Psychology, 22,* 245–253.

Wood, J. T. (2009). Communication, gender differences in. In H. T. Reis & S. K. Sprecher (Eds.), *Encyclopedia of human relationships* (Vol. 1, pp. 252–256). Thousand Oaks, CA: Sage.

Wood, R. M. (2009). Changes in cry acoustics and distress ratings while the infant is crying. *Infant and Child Development, 18,* 163–177.

Woods, N. F., Smith-DiJulio, K., Percival, D. B., Tao, E. Y., Mariella, A., & Mitchell, E. S. (2008). Depressed mood during the menopausal transition and early postmenopause: Observations from the Seattle Midlife Women's Health Study. *Menopause, 15,* 223–232.

Woodward, A. L., & Markman, E. M. (1998). Early word learning. In D. Kuhn & R. S. Siegler (Eds.), *Handbook of child psychology: Vol. 2. Cognition, perception, and language* (5th ed., pp. 371–420). New York: Wiley.

Woolley, J. D., & Cox, V. (2007). Development of beliefs about storybook reality. *Developmental Science, 10,* 681–693.

Woolley, M. E., Kol, K. L., & Bowen, G. L. (2009). The social context of school success for Latino middle school students: Direct and indirect influences of teachers, family, and friends. *Journal of Early Adolescence 29,* 43–70.

Worden, J. W. (2000). Toward an appropriate death. In T. A. Rando (Ed.), *Clinical dimensions of anticipatory mourning* (pp. 267–277). Champaign, IL: Research Press.

Worden, J. W. (2009). *Grief counseling and grief therapy* (4th ed.). New York: Springer.

World Cancer Research Fund/American Institute for Cancer Research. (2007). *Food, nutrition, physical activity, and the prevention of cancer: A global perspective.* Washington, DC: American Institute for Cancer Research.

World Federation of Right to Die Societies. (2006). *Public opinion.* Retrieved from www.worldrtd.net

World Health Organization. (2000). *Violence against women information pack.* Retrieved from www .who.int/frh-whd/VAW/infopack/English

World Health Organization. (2005). *WHO multi-country study on women's health and domestic violence against women.* Geneva: Author.

World Health Organization. (2008). *World report on child injury prevention.* Geneva, Switzerland: Author.

World Health Organization. (2010). *World health statistics 2010.* Geneva, Switzerland: Author.

World Health Organization. (2011). *The world's women 2010: Trends and statistics.* Retrieved from unstats.un.org/unsd/demographic/products/ Worldswomen/Executive%20summary.htm

World Health Organization. (2012a). *Countdown to 2015: Building a future for women and children.* Geneva, Switzerland: Author.

World Health Organization. (2012b). *The World Health Organization's infant feeding recommendation.* Retrieved from www.who.int/nutrition/topics/ infantfeeding_recommendation/en/index.html

World Health Organization. (2012c). *World health statistics 2012.* Geneva: Author.

World Health Organization. (2013a). *Obesity and overweight.* Retrieved from www.who.int/ mediacentre/factsheets/fs311/en

World Health Organization. (2013b). *Suicide prevention (SUPRE).* Retrieved from www.who.int/mental_ health/prevention/suicide/suicideprevent/en

Worrell, F. C., & Gardner-Kitt, D. L. (2006). The relationship between racial and ethnic identity in black adolescents: The cross-racial identity scale and the multigroup ethnic identity measure. *Identity, 6,* 293–315.

Worthy, J., Hungerford-Kresser, H., & Hampton, A. (2009). Tracking and ability grouping. In L. Christenbury, R. Bomer, & P. Smargorinsky (Eds.), *Handbook of adolescent literacy research* (pp. 220–235). New York: Guilford.

Wray, S. (2007). Health, exercise, and well-being: The experiences of midlife women from diverse ethnic backgrounds. *Social Theory and Health, 5,* 126–144.

Wright, B. C. (2006). On the emergence of the discriminative mode for transitive inference. *European Journal of Cognitive Psychology, 18,* 776–800.

Wright, J. C., Huston, A. C., Murphy, K. C., St. Peters, M., Pinon, M., Scantlin, R., & Kotler, J. (2001). The relations of early television viewing to school readiness and vocabulary of children from low-income families: The Early Window Project. *Child Development, 72,* 1347–1366.

Wright, K. (2003). Relationships with death: The terminally ill talk about dying. *Journal of Marital and Family Therapy, 29,* 439–454.

Wright, M. J., Gillespie, N. A., Luciano, M., Zhu, G., & Martin, N. G. (2008). Genetics of personality and cognition in adolescents. In J. J. Hudziak (Eds.), *Developmental psychology and wellness: Genetic and environmental influences* (pp. 85–107). Washington, DC: American Psychiatric Publishing.

Wright, M. O., & Masten, A. S. (2005). Resilience processes in development. In S. Goldstein & R. B. Brooks (Eds.), *Handbook of resilience in children* (pp. 17–37). New York: Springer.

Wrotniak, B. H., Epstein, L. H., Raluch, R. A., & Roemmich, J. N. (2004). Parent weight change as a predictor of child weight change in family-based behavioral obesity treatment. *Archives of Pediatric and Adolescent Medicine, 158,* 342–347.

Wu, A. M. S., Tang, C. S. K., & Kwok, T. C. Y. (2002). Death anxiety among Chinese elderly people in Hong Kong. *Journal of Aging and Health, 14,* 42–56.

Wu, L. L., Bumpass, L. L., & Musick, K. (2001). Historical and life course trajectories of nonmarital childbearing. In L. L. Wu & B. Wolfe (Eds.), *Out of wedlock: Causes and consequences of nonmarital fertility* (pp. 3–48). New York: Russell Sage Foundation.

Wu, P., Robinson, C. C., Yang, C., Hart, C. H., Olsen, S. F., Porter, C. L., Jin, S., Wo, J., & Wu, X. (2002). Similarities and differences in mothers' parenting of preschoolers in China and the United States. *International Journal of Behavioral Development, 26,* 481–491.

Wu, T., Mendola, P., & Buck, G. M. (2002). Ethnic differences in the presence of secondary sex characteristics and menarche among U.S. girls: The Third National Health and Nutrition Examination Survey, 1988–1994. *Pediatrics, 110,* 752–757.

Wu, W., Brickman, A. M., Luchsinger, J., Ferrazzano, P., Pichiule, P., Yoshita, M., & Brown, T. (2008). The brain in the age of old: The hippocampal formation is targeted differentially by diseases of late life. *Annals of Neurology, 64,* 698–706.

Wu, Z., & Schimmelle, C. M. (2007). Uncoupling in late life. *Generations, 31,* 41–46.

Wulczyn, F. (2009). Epidemiological perspectives on maltreatment prevention. *Future of Children, 19,* 39–66.

Wust, S., Entringer, S., Federenko, I. S., Schlotz, W., Helhammer, D. H. (2005). Birth weight is associated with salivary cortisol responses to psychosocial stress in adult life. *Psychoneuroendocrinology, 30,* 591–598.

Wyatt, J. M., & Carlo, G. (2002). What will my parents think? Relations among adolescents' expected parental reactions, prosocial moral reasoning, and prosocial and antisocial behaviors. *Journal of Adolescent Research, 16,* 646–666.

Wyman, E., Rakoczy, H., & Tomasello, M. (2009). Normativity and context in young children's pretend play. *Cognitive Development, 24,* 146–155.

Wynn, K. (1992). Addition and subtraction by human infants. *Nature, 358,* 749–750.

Wynn, K., Bloom, P., & Chiang, W.-C. (2002). Enumeration of collective entities by 5-month-old infants. *Cognition, 83,* B55–B62.

Wynne-Edwards, K. E. (2001). Hormonal changes in mammalian fathers. *Hormones and Behavior, 40,* 139–145.

Wysong, A., Lee, P. P., & Sloan, F. A. (2009). Longitudinal incidence of adverse outcomes of age-related macular degeneration. *Archives of Ophthalmology, 127,* 320–327.

X

Xi, B., Liang, Y., He, T., Reilly, K. H., Hu, Y., Wang, Q., et al. (2012). Secular trends in the prevalence of general and abdominal obesity among Chinese adults, 1993–2009. *Obesity Reviews, 13,* 287–296.

Xu, F., Spelke, E. S., & Goddard, S. (2005). Number sense in human infants. *Developmental Science, 8,* 88–101.

Xu, X., & Lai, S.-C. (2004). Gender ideologies, marital roles, and marital quality in Taiwan. *Journal of Family Issues, 25,* 318–355.

Xue, Y., & Meisels, S. J. (2004). Early literacy instruction and learning in kindergarten: Evidence from the early childhood longitudinal study—kindergarten classes of 1998–1999. *American Educational Research Journal, 41,* 191–229.

Y

Yaari, R., & Corey-Bloom, J. (2007). Alzheimer's disease. *Seminars in Neurology, 27,* 32–41.

Yaffe, K., Fox, P., Newcomer, R., Sands, L., Lindquist, K., Dane, K., & Covinsky, K. E. (2002). Patient and caregiver characteristics and nursing home placement in patients with dementia. *Journal of the American Medical Association, 287,* 2090–2097.

Yaffe, K., Lindquist K., Schwartz, A. V., Vitartas C., Vittinghoff, E., Satterfield, S., et al. (2011). Advanced glycation end product level, diabetes, and accelerated cognitive aging. *Neurology, 77,* 1351–1356.

Yale, M. E., Messinger, D. S., Cobo-Lewis, A. B., Oller, D. K., & Eilers, R. E. (1999). An event-based analysis of the coordination of early infant vocalizations and facial actions. *Developmental Psychology, 35,* 505–513.

Yamaguchi, S., Gelfand, M., Ohashi, M. M., & Zemba, Y. (2005). The cultural psychology of control: Illusions of personal versus collective control in the United States and Japan. *Journal of Cross-Cultural Psychology, 36,* 750–761.

Yamamoto, K. (2004). The care of the dying and the grieving in Japan. In J. D. Morgan & P. Laungani (Eds.), *Death and bereavement around the world: Vol. 4. Death and bereavement in Asia, Australia, and New Zealand* (pp. 101–107). Amityville, NY: Baywood Publishing Company.

Yan, L. L., Liu, K., Matthews, K. A., Daviglus, M. L., Ferguson, T. F., & Kiefe, C. I. (2003). Psychosocial factors and risk of hypertension: The Coronary Artery Risk Development in Young Adults (CARDIA) study. *Journal of the American Medical Association, 290,* 2138–2148.

Yang, B., Ollendick, T. H., Dong, Q., Xia, Y., & Lin, L. (1995). Only children and children with siblings in the People's Republic of China: Levels of fear, anxiety, and depression. *Child Development, 66,* 1301–1311.

Yang, C. (2008, April). *The influence of one-child policy on child rearing, family, and society in post-Mao China.* Invited address, Illinois State University.

Yang, C.-K., & Hahn, H.-M. (2002). Cosleeping in young Korean children. *Developmental and Behavioral Pediatrics, 23,* 151–157.

Yang, F.-Y., & Tsai, C.-C. (2010). Reasoning about science-related uncertain issues and epistemological perspectives among children. *Instructional Science, 38,* 325–354.

Yang, S. C., & Chen, S.-F. (2002). A phenomenographic approach to the meaning of death: A Chinese perspective. *Death Studies, 26,* 143–175.

Yao, L., & Robert, S. A. (2008). The contributions of race, individual socioeconomic status, and neighborhood socioeconomic context to the self-rated health trajectories and mortality of older adults. *Research on Aging, 30,* 251–273.

Yap, M. B. H., Allen, N. B., & Ladouceur, C. D. (2008). Maternal socialization of positive affect: The impact of invalidation on adolescent emotion regulation and depressive symptomatology. *Child Development, 79,* 1415–1431.

Yarrow, M. R., Scott, P. M., & Waxler, C. Z. (1973). Learning concern for others. *Developmental Psychology, 8,* 240–260.

Yates, L. B., Djoussé, L., Kurth, T., Buring, J. E., & Gaziano, J. M. (2008). Exceptional longevity in men: Modifiable factors associated with survival and function to age 90 years. *Archives of Internal Medicine, 168,* 284–290.

Yau, J. P., Tasopoulos-Chan, M., & Smetana, J. G. (2009). Disclosure to parents about everyday activities among American adolescents from Mexican, Chinese, and European backgrounds. *Child Development, 80,* 1481–1498.

Yeh, C. J., Kim, A. B., Pituc, S. T., & Atkins, M. (2008). Poverty, loss, and resilience: The story of Chinese immigrant youth. *Journal of Counseling Psychology, 55,* 34–48.

Yeh, S. S. (2010). Understanding and addressing the achievement gap through individualized instruction and formative assessment. *Assessment in Education: Principles, Policy and Practice, 17,* 169–182.

Yeung, D. Y., Fung, H. H., & Lang, F. R. (2008). Self-construal moderates age differences in social network characteristics. *Psychology and Aging, 23,* 222–226.

Yeung, W. (1996). Buddhism, death, and dying. In J. K. Parry & A. S. Ryan (Eds.), *A cross-cultural look at death, dying, and religion* (pp. 74–83). Chicago: Nelson-Hall.

Yip, R., Scanlon, K., & Trowbridge, F. (1993). Trends and patterns in height and weight status of low-income U.S. children. *Critical Reviews in Food Science and Nutrition, 33,* 409–421.

Yirmiya, N., Erel, O., Shaked, M., & Solomonica-Levi, D. (1998). Meta-analyses comparing theory of mind abilities of individuals with autism, individuals with mental retardation, and normally developing individuals. *Psychological Bulletin, 124,* 283–307.

Yoshida, H., & Smith, L. B. (2003). Known and novel noun extensions: Attention at two levels of abstraction. *Child Development, 74,* 564–577.

Yoshikawa, H., Weisner, T. S., Kalil, A., & Way, N. (2008). Mixing qualitative and quantitative research in developmental science: Uses and methodological choices. *Developmental Psychology, 44,* 344–354.

Youn, G., Knight, B. G., Jeon, H., & Benton, D. (1999). Differences in familism values and caregiving outcomes among Korean, Korean American, and White American dementia caregivers. *Psychology and Aging, 14,* 355–364.

Young, J. B., & Rodgers, R. F. (1997). A model of radical career change in the context of psychosocial development. *Journal of Career Assessment, 5,* 167–172.

Young, J. F., & Mroczek, D. K. (2003). Predicting intraindividual self-concept trajectories during adolescence. *Journal of Adolescence, 26,* 589–603.

Young, S. E., Friedman, N. P., Miyake, A., Willcutt, E. G., Corley, R. P., Haberstick, B. C., et al. (2009). Behavioral disinhibition: Liability for externalizing spectrum disorders and its genetic and environmental relation to response inhibition across adolescence. *Journal of Abnormal Psychology, 118,* 117–130.

Young, T., Rabago, D., Zgierska, A., Austin, D., & Finn, L. (2002). Objective and subjective sleep quality in premenopausal, perimenopausal, and postmenopausal women in the Wisconsin Sleep Cohort Study. *Epidemiology, 26,* 667–672.

Youngblade, L. M., & Dunn, J. (1995). Individual differences in young children's pretend play with mother and sibling: Links to relationships and understanding of other people's feelings and beliefs. *Child Development, 66,* 1472–1492.

Young-Hyman, D., Tanofsky-Kraff, M., Yanovski, S. Z., Keil, M., Cohen, M. L., & Peyrot, M. (2006). Psychological status and weight-related distress in overweight or at-risk-for-overweight children. *Obesity, 14,* 2249–2258.

Yu, B. P. (2006). Why calorie restriction would work for human longevity. *Biogerontology, 7,* 179–182.

Yu, F., Ryan, L. H., Schaie, K. W., Willis, S. L., & Kolanowski, A. (2009). Factors associated with cognition in adults: The Seattle Longitudinal Study. *Research in Nursing and Health, 32,* 540–550.

Yu, R. (2002). On the reform of elementary school education in China. *Educational Exploration, 129,* 56–57.

Yuan, A. S. V., & Hamilton, H. A. (2006). Stepfather involvement and adolescent well-being: Do mothers and nonresidential fathers matter? *Journal of Family Issues, 27,* 1191–1213.

Yumoto, C., Jacobson, S. W., & Jacobson, J. L. (2008). Fetal substance exposure and cumulative environmental risk in an African American cohort. *Child Development, 79,* 1761–1776.

Yunger, J. L., Carver, P. R., & Perry, D. G. (2004). Does gender identity influence children's psychological well-being? *Developmental Psychology, 40,* 572–582.

Z

Zaccagni, L., Onisto, N., & Gualdi-Russo, E. (2009). Biological characteristics and ageing in former elite volleyball players. *Journal of Science and Medicine in Sport, 12,* 667–672.

Zacks, R. T., & Hasher, L. (2006). Aging and long-term memory: Deficits are not inevitable. In E. Bialystok & F. I. M. Craik (Eds.), *Lifespan cognition: Mechanisms of change* (pp. 162–177). New York: Oxford University Press.

Zafeiriou, D. I. (2000). Plantar grasp reflex in high-risk infants during the first year of life. *Pediatric Neurology, 22,* 75–76.

Zaff, J. F., Hart, D., Flanagan, C. A., Youniss, J., & Levine, P. (2010). Developing civic engagement within a civic context. In M. Lamb & A. Freund (Eds.), *Handbook of life-span development: Vol. 2. Social and emotional development* (pp. 590–630). Hoboken, NJ: Wiley.

Zaff, J. F., Malanchuk, O., & Eccles, J. S. (2008). Predicting positive citizenship from adolescence to young adulthood: The effects of a civic context. *Applied Developmental Science, 12,* 38–53.

Zaff, J. F., Moore, K. A., Papillo, A. R., & Williams, S. (2003). Implications of extracurricular activity participation during adolescence on positive outcomes. *Journal of Adolescent Research, 18,* 599–630.

Zahn-Waxler, C., Kochanska, G., Krupnick, J., & McKnew, D. (1990). Patterns of guilt in children of depressed and well mothers. *Developmental Psychology, 26,* 51–59.

Zahn-Waxler, C., Radke-Yarrow, M., & King, R. M. (1979). Child-rearing and children's prosocial initiations toward victims of distress. *Child Development, 50,* 319–330.

Zakowski, S. G., Hall, M. H., Klein, L. C., & Baum, A. (2001). Appraised control, coping, and stress in a community sample: A test of the goodness-of-fit hypothesis. *Annals of Behavioral Medicine, 23,* 158–165.

Zane, N., & Yeh, M. (2002). The use of culturally based variables in assessment: Studies on loss of face. In K. Kurasaki, S. Okazaki, & S. Sue (Eds.), *Asian American mental health: Assessment theories and methods* (pp. 123–138). Dordrecht, Netherlands: Kluwer Academic.

Zaretsky, M. D. (2003). Communication between identical twins: Health behavior and social factors are associated with longevity that is greater among identical than fraternal U.S. World War II veteran twins. *Journal of Gerontology, 58,* 566–572.

Zarit, S. H., & Eggebeen, D. J. (2002). Parent–child relationships in adulthood and later years. In M. H. Bornstein (Ed.), *Handbook of parenting, Vol. 1* (2nd ed., pp. 135–161). Mahwah, NJ: Erlbaum.

Zaslow, M. J., Weinfield, N. S., Gallagher, M., Hair, E. C., Ogawa, J. R., Egeland, B., Tabors, P. O., & De Temple, J. M. (2006). Longitudinal prediction of child outcomes from differing measures of parenting in a low-income sample. *Developmental Psychology, 42,* 27–37.

Zeanah, C. H. (2000). Disturbances of attachment in young children adopted from institutions. *Journal of Developmental and Behavioral Pediatrics, 21,* 230–236.

Zeifman, D. M. (2003). Predicting adult responses to infant distress: Adult characteristics associated with perceptions, emotional reactions, and timing of intervention. *Infant Mental Health Journal, 24,* 597–612.

Zelazo, N. A., Zelazo, P. R., Cohen, K. M., & Zelazo, P. D. (1993). Specificity of practice effects on elementary neuromotor patterns. *Developmental Psychology, 29,* 686–691.

Zelazo, P. D., Carlson, S. M., & Kesek, A. (2008). The development of executive function in childhood. In C. A. Nelson & M. Luciana (Eds.), *Handbook of cognitive developmental neuroscience* (2nd ed., pp. 553–574). Cambridge, MA: MIT Press.

Zelazo, P. D., & Lee, W. S. C. (2010). Brain development: An overview. In W. Overton & R. M. Lerner (Eds.), *Handbook of life-span development: Vol. 1. Cognition* biology, and methods (pp. 89–114). Hoboken, NJ: Wiley.

Zelinski, E., & Kennison, R. F. (2007). Not your parents' test scores: Cohort reduces psychometric aging effects. *Psychology and Aging, 22*, 546–557.

Zeman, J., Shipman, K., & Suveg, C. (2002). Anger and sadness regulation: Predictions to internalizing and externalizing symptoms in children. *Journal of Clinical Child and Adolescent Psychology, 31*, 393–398.ioooou8ko

Zeskind, P. S., & Barr, R. G. (1997). Acoustic characteristics of naturally occurring cries of infants with "colic." *Child Development, 68*, 394–403.

Zhan, H. J., & Montgomery, R. J. V. (2003). Gender and elder care in China: The influence of filial piety and structural constraints. *Gender and Society, 17*, 209–229.

Zhang, L., & Sternberg, R. J. (2011). Revisiting the investment theory of creativity. *Creativity Research Journal, 23*, 229–238.

Zhang, Q. F. (2004). Economic transition and new patterns of parent–adult child coresidence in urban China. *Journal of Marriage and Family, 66*, 1231–1245.

Zhang, T.-Y., & Meaney, M. J. (2010). Epigenetics and the environmental regulation of the genome and its function. *Annual Review of Psychology, 61*, 439–466.

Zhang, X., Geng, J., Zheng, J., Peng, B., Che, J., & Liang, C. (2012). Photoselective vaporization versus transurethral resection of the prostate for benign prostatic hyperplasia: A meta-analysis. *Journal of Endourology, 26*, 1109–1117.

Zhang, Y., & Jordan, J. M. (2010). Epidemiology of osteoarthritis. *Clinics of Geriatric Medicine, 26*, 355–369.

Zhao, J., Settles, B. H., & Sheng, X. (2011). Family-to-work conflict: Gender, equity and workplace policies. *Journal of Comparative Family Studies, 42*, 723–738.

Zheng, N. T., Mukamel, D. B., Caprio, T. V., & Temkin-Greener, H. (2012). Hospice utilization in nursing homes: Association with facility end-of-life care practices. *Gerontologist, 52*. Retrieved from gerontologist.oxfordjournals.org.libproxy.lib.ilstu.edu/search?fulltext=Zheng&submit=yes&x=13&y=9

Zhou, M., & Bankston, C. L. (1998). *Growing up American: How Vietnamese children adapt to life in the United States*. New York: Russell Sage Foundation.

Zhou, Q., Lengua, L. J., & Wang, Y. (2009). The relations of temperament reactivity and effortful control to children's adjustment problems in China and the United States. *Developmental Psychology, 45*, 724–739.

Zhou, X., Huang, J., Wang, Z., Wang, B., Zhao, Z., Yang, L., & Zheng-zheng, Y. (2006). Parent–child interaction and children's number learning. *Early Child Development and Care, 176*, 763–775.

Zhu, W. X., & Hesketh, T. (2009). China's excess males, sex selective abortion, and one child policy: Analysis of data from 2005 national intercensus survey. *British Medical Journal, 338*, b1211.

Zickuhr, K., & Madden, M. (2012). *Pew Internet: Older adults and Internet use*. Washington, DC: Pew Research Center.

Zimmer-Gembeck, M., & Helfand, M. J. (2008). Ten years of longitudinal research on U.S. adolescent sexual behavior: Developmental correlates of sexual intercourse, and the importance of age, gender and ethnic background. *Developmental Review, 28*, 153–224.

Zimmerman, B. J., & Cleary, T. J. (2009). Motives to self-regulate learning: A social cognitive account. In K. R. Wenzel & A. Wigfield (Eds.), *Handbook of motivation at school* (pp. 247–264). New York: Routledge.

Zimmerman, B. J., & Moylan, A. R. (2009). Self-regulation: Where metacognition and motivation intersect. In D. J. Hacker, J. Dunlosky, & A. C. Graesser (Eds.), *Handbook of metacognition in education* (pp. 299–315). New York: Routledge.

Zimmerman, C. (2007). The development of scientific thinking skills in elementary and middle school. *Developmental Review, 27*, 172–223.

Zimmerman, C. (2012). Acceptance of dying: A discourse analysis of palliative care literature. *Social Science and Medicine, 78*, 217–224.

Zimmerman, F. J., & Christakis, D. A. (2005). Children's television viewing and cognitive outcomes. *Archives of Pediatrics and Adolescent Medicine, 159*, 619–625.

Zimmerman, F. J., Christakis, D. A., & Meltzoff, A. N. (2007). Television and DVD/video viewing in children younger than 2 years. *Archives of Pediatrics and Adolescent Medicine, 161*, 473–479.

Zimmerman, F. J., Gilkerson, J., Richards, J. A., Christakis, D. A., Xu, D., Gray, S., & Yapanel, U. (2009). Teaching by listening: The importance of adult–child conversations to language development. *Pediatrics, 124*, 342–348.

Zimmerman, L. K., & Stansbury, K. (2004). The influence of emotion regulation, level of shyness, and habituation on the neuroendocrine response of three-year-old children. *Psychoneuroendocrinology, 29*, 973–982.

Zimmerman, P., & Becker-Stoll, F. (2002). Stability of attachment representations during adolescence: The influence of ego-identity status. *Journal of Adolescence, 25*, 107–124.

Zins, J. E., Garcia, V. F., Tuchfarber, B. S., Clark, K. M., & Laurence, S. C. (1994). Preventing injury in children and adolescents. In R. J. Simeonsson (Ed.), *Risk, resilience, and prevention: Promoting the well-being of all children* (pp. 183–202). Baltimore: Paul H. Brookes.

Zolotor, A. J., & Puzia, M. E. (2010). Bans against corporal punishment: A systematic review of the laws, changes in attitudes and behaviours. *Child Abuse Review, 19*, 229–247.

Zosuls, K. M., Ruble, D. N., Bornstein, M. H., & Greulich, F. K. (2009). The acquisition of gender labels in infancy: Implications for gender-typed play. *Developmental Psychology, 45*, 688–701.

Zucker, A. N., Ostrove, J. M., & Stewart, A. J. (2002). College-educated women's personality development in adulthood: Perceptions and age differences. *Psychology and Aging, 17*, 236–244.

Zucker, K. J. (2006). "I'm half-boy, half-girl": Play psychotherapy and parent counseling for gender identity disorder. In R. L. Spitzer, M. B. First, J. B. W. Williams, & M. Gibbon (Eds.), *DSM-IV-TR Casebook: Vol. 2. Experts tell how they treated their own patients* (pp. 322–334). Washington, DC: American Psychiatric Publishing.

Zukow-Goldring, P. (2002). Sibling caregiving. In M. H. Bornstein (Ed.), *Handbook of parenting: Vol. 3* (2nd ed., pp. 253–286). Hillsdale, NJ: Erlbaum.

Zwart, M. (2007). The Dutch system of perinatal care. *Midwifery Today with International Midwife, 81*(Spring), 46.

Name Index

Italic n following page number indicates page with an illustration or table.

A

Aalsma, M., 387
Aarnoudse-Moens, C. S., 101
AARP, 545, 617, 626
Abakoumkin, G., 660
Abbeduto, L. J., 269
Abbey, A., 448
ABC News, 374
Abecassis, M., 340
Abela, J. R. Z., 421, 422
Abele, A. E., 484
Abelson, H., 418
Aber, J. L., 62, 65, 391, 392
Aberson, B., 272
Abes, E., 451
Abikoff, H., 305
Abma, J. C., 378
Aboud, F. E., 337, 338
Abra, J., 525
Abrams, D., 339, 410
Abrams, K. Y., 200
Abramson, L. Y., 422
Acevedo, E. O., 443
Achenbach, T. M., 103
Achermann, P., 368
Acierno, R., 627
Acker, M. M., 267, 473
Ackerman, B. P., 186
Ackerman, P. L., 522
Ackerman, S., 533
ACT, 455
Adachi-Mejia, A. M., 292
Adam, E. K., 26
Adams, A.-M., 237
Adams, D. R., 51
Adams, G. A., 558
Adams, G. R., 404
Adams, K. B., 617, 619
Adams, R. G., 370
Addington-Hall, J., 651
Adhikari, B., 444
Adolph, K. E., 15, 106, 137, 138, 139, 143,
    147, 207
Afifi, T. O., 266
Afterschool Alliance, 351
Agatston, P. W., 342
Aggarwal, R., 220
Agnoli, F., 389
Agrigoroaei, S., 540, 573, 578, 610
Agronick, G., 353
Agüero-Torres, H., 588
Aguiar, A., 155
Ahadi, S. A., 191
Ahlberg, C., 274
Ahlskog, J. E., 585
Ahlström, R., 513
Ahnert, L., 67, 171, 172, 246
Ahrens, C. J. C., 541
Ahuja, J., 555
Ai, A. L., 608
Aikens, J. W., 198, 392
Aikens, N. L., 173, 246
Ainley, J., 395
Ainscow, M., 322
Ainsworth, M. D. S., 197, 197n, 199
Aisen, P. S., 577
Ajrouch, K. J., 611, 620, 626
Akers, A. Y., 374
Akhtar, N., 157, 248, 249
Akimoto, S. A., 189
Akinbami, L. J., 293
Akiyama, H., 543, 552, 614, 620

Aksan, N., 185, 191, 209, 265, 266
Akshoomoff, N. A., 126, 241
Alberman, E., 53
Albers, C. A., 170
Albert, M. K., 143
Alberts, A., 387
Aldao, A., 450
Aldridge, M. A., 113
Aldwin, C. M., 513, 515, 632
Alessandri, S. M., 186
Alexander, J. M., 306
Alexander, K. L., 396
Alexopoulos, T., 574, 610
Alfaro, E. C., 406
Algarin, C., 109
Ali, L., 374
Alink, L. R. A., 269
Alkema, G. E., 589
Allard, M., 566
Allemand, M., 608
Allen, G., 420, 421
Allen, J. P., 379, 416
Allen, K. R., 627
Allen, M., 492
Allen, N. B., 422
Allen, P. A., 521
Allen, S. E. M., 316
Allen, T. D., 493
Allik, J., 346
Allison, B. N., 370
Allison, J., 322
Alloway, T. P., 162, 302, 303
Almeida, D. M., 414, 450, 539
Almeida, J., 377
Almkvist, O., 573
Al-Nakhli, H., 581
Al-Namlah, A. S., 234
Alonso-Férnandez, P., 433
Alsaker, F. D., 371
Alterovitz, S. S. R., 621, 622
Althaus, J., 100
Altmaier, E. M., 646
Altobelli, J., 607
Alvarez, M. A., 414
Alzheimer's Association, 550, 582, 583,
    585, 586, 587
Amaral, D. G., 241
Amato, P. R., 61, 279, 347, 348, 349, 350,
    481, 489, 490
Amba, J. C., 489
American Academy of Hospice and
    Palliative Medicine, 658
American Academy of Orthopaedic
    Surgeons, 512, 513
American Academy of Pediatrics, 92,
    129, 131n, 159
American Cancer Society, 510, 511n
American College of Sports Medicine,
    443
American Heart Association, 435, 436,
    640
American Hospice Foundation, 642
American Psychiatric Association, 304,
    322
American Psychological Association,
    39, 39n
Ames, E. W., 144
Ames, S. L., 381
Amsel, E., 385
Amso, D., 142
Amsterlaw, J., 239
An, J. S., 533

Anand, S. S., 291
Andel, R., 589
Anderman, E. M., 333
Anderson, C. A., 271
Anderson, D. M., 246
Anderson, D. R., 159
Anderson, J. L., 141
Anderson, K. G., 349
Anderson, K. J., 178, 343
Anderson, P. B., 448, 449n
Anderson, V. A., 126
Anderson, V. N., 484
Anderssen, N., 296
Andreoletti, C., 574
Andres, V., 433
Andrews, G., 20, 232, 233, 242, 300,
    301, 302
Anesbury, T., 292
Aneshensel, C. S., 63
Anetzberger, G. J., 627
Angel, J. L., 573
Angel, R. J., 573
Angelillo, C., 236
Anisfeld, M., 135
Annahatak, B., 314
Annett, M., 218
Anstey, K. J., 631
Antonini, F. M., 567
Antonucci, T. C., 477, 516, 541, 543, 552,
    575, 611, 614, 620, 621, 625, 627
Anttila, R., 371
Anzuini, F., 443
Apfel, N. H., 379
Apfelbaum, E. P., 338
Apgar, V., 98, 98n
Appelbaum, M. I., 173
Aquan-Assee, J., 205
Aquilino, W. S., 468
Arbeau, K. A., 192, 261
Archer, A. H., 159
Archer, J., 469
Archer, T., 571
Archibald, A. B., 363, 365, 366
Arcus, D., 58
Ardelt, M., 596, 608, 645
Ardila-Rey, A., 337
Arditti, J. A., 544
Arias, I., 483
Arija, V., 291
Arking, R., 432, 435n, 436
Arlin, P. K., 453
Armer, M., 192, 262
Armstrong, K. L., 128
Armstrong, L. M., 190, 259
Armstrong, T. D., 609
Arnett, J. J., 402, 446, 464, 465, 466, 467,
    468, 469
Arnold, M., 316
Arnold, M. L., 279, 410
Arnold, R., 63, 64
Arnon, S., 103
Arriaga, R. I., 161
Arslanian, S. A., 291
Arterberry, M. E., 113, 142, 145, 165, 225
Arthurs, E., 186
Artman, L., 301, 384
Ary, D. V., 587
Aschersleben, G., 140
Asher, S. R., 341, 343
Ashman, A. F., 395
Ashmead, D. H., 113, 140
Aslin, R. N., 142, 175, 179

Assink, M. H. J., 593
Astell, A., 581
Astington, J. W., 239, 306, 307
Atance, C. M., 257
Atchley, R. C., 615, 618, 631
Atkins, R., 62, 411, 413
Atkinson, L., 206
Atlas, R., 30
Au, T. K., 230
Aud, S., 389
Auestad, R. A., 551
Aumann, K., 26, 202, 203, 345, 351
Aunola, K., 279, 280, 392
Austin, E. L., 377
Auth, E. A., 617, 619
Autti-Raemoe, I., 89
Averhart, C. J., 338
Aveyard, P., 444
Avgoustis, E., 421
Avioli, P. S., 552
Avis, N. E., 504, 506, 507
Avni-Babad, D., 384
Avolio, B. J., 526, 553
Axelin, A., 112
Axia, G., 317
Ayala, G. X., 292
Ayotte, V., 331, 332, 403
Azevedo, R., 452

B

Bacallao, M. L., 33
Bacaltchuk, J., 373
Backley, P., 251
Bäckman, L., 522, 570, 593, 596
Badzinski, D. M., 258
Baenninger, M., 390
Bagwell, C. L., 340
Bagwell, D. K., 597
Bahrick, H. P., 592
Bahrick, L. E., 135, 146, 158, 163
Bahrick, P. O., 592
Bai, D. L., 143
Bailar-Heath, M., 294
Bailey, J. M., 375, 542
Baillargeon, R., 155, 159, 160, 239
Baillargeon, R. H., 270
Bair, D., 621
Baird, B. M., 70
Baird, D. D., 80
Baker, C. K., 483
Baker, J. A., 320
Baker, J. M., 316
Baker, P. N., 378
Bakermans-Kranenburg, M. J., 200
Baker-Ward, L., 164
Balasch, J., 438
Baldi, A., 131n
Baldi, R., 450
Baldwin, D. A., 241, 249
Baldwin, G., 249
Bale, J. F., 90
Bales, S. N., 69
Balis, T., 422
Ball, H., 129
Ball, K., 597
Ball, M. M., 619
Balsam, K. F., 488
Balsano, A. B., 413
Baltes, M. M., 610, 619
Baltes, P. B., 7, 8, 9, 71, 575, 590, 595,
    596, 632
Bambara, L. M., 322

Banaji, M. R., 338
Bancroft, J., 447
Bandstra, E. S., 87
Bandura, A., 18, 265
Bangerter, A., 464
Banish, M. T., 124
Banks, M. S., 113, 144
Bankston, C. L., 33
Banse, R., 273
Bao, J., 569
Barber, B., 455
Barber, B. K., 280, 391, 415
Barber, B. L., 279
Barber, C. H., 413
Barber, J. S., 379
Bard, K. A., 207
Barelds, D. P. H., 482
Barenbaum, J., 353
Bar-Haim, Y., 145
Barja, G., 433
Barker, D. J., 92
Barkley, R. A., 304, 305
Barlow, J., 576
Barnes, G. M., 425
Barnes, J., 63
Barnes, R., 423
Barnes-Farrell, J., 554
Barnett, D., 197
Barnett, R. C., 494
Barnett, W. S., 246
Baron, A. S., 338
Baron, I. S., 101
Baroni, R., 317
Baron-Cohen, S., 241
Barr, H. M., 87, 89
Barr, R., 134, 156, 159, 163, 168
Barr, R. G., 109, 111, 139
Barratt, M. S., 102
Barreto, M., 502, 555
Barrett, A. E., 535
Barrett, K. C., 188
Barrett, M., 337
Barrett, T. M., 140
Barros, R. M., 298
Barry, C. M., 419, 464, 465, 477
Barry, H., III, 370
Barry, R. A., 194, 280
Bartlik, B., 509
Bartocci, M., 112
Bartrip, J., 145
Bartsch, K., 239
Basak, C., 10, 522, 597
Basow, S. A., 414
Bass, S., 607
Bassett, N. S., 97
Bassett, P., 318
Bassuk, S. S., 443
Bastien, C. H., 90
Basu, A., 569
Bates, E. A., 126, 174, 178
Bates, G. W., 533
Bates, J. E., 70, 190, 191, 193
Bathurst, K., 25, 350
Battin, D. B., 355
Battistella, A., 443
Batty, G. D., 131
Bauer, C. R., 87
Bauer, P. J., 156, 164, 165, 238
Baum, N., 544
Baumbusch, J. L., 487
Baumeister, R. F., 265, 338, 646
Baumgartner, M. S., 555
Baumrind, D., 278, 280
Baumwell, L., 179
Bauserman, R., 349
Bavelier, D., 125

Baydar, N., 205
Bayer, A., 40
Bayley, N., 137n, 139, 169
Bazemore, G., 426
Beals, D. E., 317
Bean, R. A., 415
Bearman, P. S., 423
Bearman, S. K., 371
Beauchamp, G. K., 112
Beaulieu, M., 617
Beautrais, A. L., 423
Bechara, A., 367
Beck, I. L., 308
Becker, B. E., 62, 63
Becker, B. J., 200
Becker, G., 65
Becker, J. B., 369
Becker, K., 74
Beckerman, M. B., 525
Becker-Stoll, F., 405
Beckett, C., 125, 127
Bedford, O. A., 260
Bedford, V. H., 552
Bedwell, J. S., 521
Beehr, T. A., 629
Behnke, M., 87
Behrends, M., 395
Behrens, K. Y., 201
Beier, M. E., 522
Beigbeder, S. A., 477
Beilin, H., 228
Beintema, D., 107n
Bejĉek, J., 464
Bekkouche, N. S., 449
Belcher, D., 296
Belizan, J. M., 103
Bell, C., 321
Bell, J. H., 387
Bell, M., 449
Bell, M. A., 144, 156
Bell, M. L., 507
Bellagamba, F., 157
Belle, S. H., 587
Bellinger, D. C., 90
Bellmore, A. D., 341
Bell-Scriber, M. J., 458
Belmonte, M. K., 241
Belsky, D. H., 92
Belsky, J., 71, 171, 194, 198, 199, 200, 201,
    202, 205, 206, 246, 367
Beltrán-Sánchez, J., 577
Belyea, M., 109
Bem, D. J., 36
Benbow, C. P., 389
Bender, H. L., 266
Benenson, J. F., 340, 417, 418
Bengtsson, H., 260
Benner, A. D., 391
Bennett, D. A., 585
Bennett, J. M., 612
Bennett, K. M., 623
Bennett, M., 337
Bennett, P. J., 521
Benson, J. B., 140
Benson, P. L., 11, 468, 468n
Ben-Zeev, T., 389
Berardi, N., 125
Berenbaum, S. A., 193, 208, 274, 276,
    278, 390
Beresin, E. V., 373
Berg, C. A., 590, 594, 595
Berg, K. M., 631
Bergeman, C. S., 70, 660
Bergen, D., 227
Berger, L. M., 244
Berger, S. E., 106, 138, 156

Berggren, I., 651
Bergman, E. J., 665
Bergman, H., 580
Bergman, I., 573
Bergman, K., 93
Bergman, M., 503
Bergman, R., 407
Bering, J. M., 642
Berk, L., 581
Berk, L. E., 23, 168, 226, 227, 234, 235,
    268n, 323, 333
Berkman, L. F., 438
Berkowitz, M. W., 411
Berkowitz, R. L., 54
Berlin, L. J., 200, 266
Berman, E., 544
Berman, J. R., 504, 509
Berman, R. A., 316
Berman, S. L., 404
Bermingham, D. W., 615
Berndt, T. J., 340, 417
Berner, M. M., 507
Bernier, A., 200
Bernier, J. C., 305
Bernieri, F., 194
Bersoff, D. M., 411
Bert, S. C., 486
Bertenthal, B. I., 136, 143, 144, 155
Bertoncini, J., 113, 134
Bertrand, M., 494
Bertrand, R. M., 538
Berzin, S. C., 479
Berzlanovich, A. M., 567
Berzonsky, M. D., 404
Besançon, M., 323
Best, D., 88
Best, D. L., 343
Beth, A., 506
Betts, N. M., 220
Beyene, Y., 508
Beyers, J. M., 280
Beyers, W., 469
Bhat, A., 140
Bhatt, R. S., 163, 165, 166
Bherer, L., 522, 540
Bhopal, K., 476
Bialystok, E., 240, 317
Bianchi, S. M., 26
Bianco, A., 93
Biblarz, T., 492
Bickel, W. K., 445
Bidell, T. R., 20, 301, 302
Biederman, J., 304
Biegel, D., 618
Biehl, M. C., 369, 370, 371
Bielak, A. A. M., 596
Bielawska-Batorowicz, E., 187
Bielinski, J., 389
Bierman, A., 610, 626
Bierman, K. L., 272, 343, 392
Bifulco, R., 321
Bigelow, A. E., 200
Bigler, R. S., 273, 277, 278, 338, 344
Bimmel, N., 58
Bindrich, I., 94
Binet, A., 15
Binstock, R. H., 632
Birch, E. E., 142, 144
Birch, H. G., 190
Birch, L. L., 219, 220, 440
Birch, S. A. J., 240
Birch, S. H., 263
Bird, A., 238
Birditt, K. S., 477, 489, 545, 548, 611, 616,
    620, 621, 626
Birkett, M., 377

Birney, D. P., 20, 161, 524
Birren, J. E., 595
Bisanz, J., 243
Bisconti, T. L., 660
Bisgard, K., 221
Bissaker, K., 279, 345
Bissonnette, V. L., 473
Bitan, T., 388
Bjork, E. L., 177
Bjorklund, D. F., 22, 23, 161, 304, 305,
    306, 642
Black, B. M., 409
Black, J. E., 128
Black, M. C., 448
Black, R. E., 219
Blackhall, L. J., 649
Blackman, M. R., 433
Blackwell, D. L., 472
Blackwell, L. S., 333
Blades, M., 355
Blaga, O. M., 163
Blaine, B., 441
Blair, C., 75, 189, 237, 303
Blair-Loy, M., 493
Blakemore, J. E. O., 273, 344
Blakemore, S.-J., 367
Blanchard, R., 376
Blanchard-Fields, F., 450, 595, 605, 616
Blandon, A. Y., 209
Blasi, A., 407
Blasi, C. H., 23
Blass, E. M., 134
Blatchford, P., 318
Blatt, L., 188
Blatteis, C. M., 568
Blatt-Eisengart, I., 279, 280
Blau, D., 556
Bleeker, M. M., 334, 457
Bleses, D., 178
Bleske, A. L., 477
Blieszner, R., 476, 516, 625
Blinka, L., 418
Block, J., 380, 543
Blomberg, M., 573
Blood-Siegfried, J., 110
Bloom, L., 177, 248
Bloom, P., 160, 240, 414
Bluck, S., 593, 649
Blumenfeld, P. C., 21
Blumenthal, H., 370
Blustein, D. L., 405
Blyth, D. A., 391
Boardman, J. D., 64
Bobb, A. J., 305
Bock, K., 250
Bodrova, E., 24, 167, 237, 320
Body, J. J., 513
Boeninger, D. K., 515
Boergers, J., 424
Bogaert, A. F., 367, 376
Bogin, B., 121, 219, 363, 365
Bohannon, J. N., III, 175, 251
Bohlmeijer, E. T., 606
Boldizar, J. P., 276
Bolen, R. M., 352
Bolisetty, S., 101, 102
Bolkan, C., 538, 574
Boly, M., 641
Bolzani, L. H., 185
Bond, J. T., 26, 202, 203, 345, 351
Bonilla, S., 293
Bonin, S. L., 457
Bonnick, S. L., 513
Bono, M. A., 171
Bons, T. A., 72

Bonsel, G. J., 92
Bonvillian, J. D., 175
Bookman, A., 551
Boom, J., 409
Boon, S. D., 546
Booth, A., 481, 491
Booth, J. R., 388
Booth-LaForce, C., 199
Borders, L. D., 458
Borduin, C. M., 426
Borkowski, J. G., 486
Borman, W. C., 554
Bornstein, M. H., 22, 59, 134, 145, 165, 167, 179, 201, 225
Boroughs, D. S., 352
Borst, C. G., 99
Bortfeld, H., 594
Bos, H. M. W., 492
Bosacki, S. L., 273
Bosma, H. A., 404
Bosquet, M., 124
Boss, B. J., 112
Bost, K. K., 200, 238
Boswell, G. H., 609
Botton, J., 131
Bouchard, C., 223n, 364
Bouchard, G., 481
Bouchard, T. J., 72, 193
Boucher, O., 90
Boudreau, J. P., 143
Boukydis, C. F. Z., 111
Boulton, M. J., 342
Bounds, M. L., 294
Bourgeois, M. S., 587
Bowen, C. E., 526, 540, 555, 574
Bowen, C. P., 549
Bowen, G. L., 393
Bowen, N. K., 393
Bowen, R., 386
Bower, T. G. R., 113
Bowker, J., 341
Bowkett, S., 313
Bowlby, J., 7, 22, 196, 197, 201, 659
Bowling, A., 617
Bowman, N. A., 454, 455
Bowman, S. A., 372
Boyce, W., 374
Boyd, J. S., 242, 243
Boyd-Franklin, N., 66
Boyd-Zaharias, J., 318
Boyle, P. A., 605
Boysson-Bardies, B. de, 176
Bozionelos, N., 493
Bracci, R., 100
Bracken, B. A., 243
Brackett, M. A., 313
Bradbury, J. C., 436
Bradbury, T. N., 473, 482
Bradford, K., 270
Bradley, R. H., 104, 170, 171n, 173, 244, 244n, 281
Bradley-Engen, M. S., 376
Braet, C., 291
Braine, L. G., 295
Brainerd, C. J., 233
Braithwaite, V. A., 390
Brame, B., 424
Brand, S., 365
Brandt, S., 177
Branje, S. J. T., 37, 417
Brannen, C., 478
Branstetter, W. H., 28
Brashler, P., 483
Braswell, G. S., 224, 225
Braungart-Rieker, J. M., 186, 189
Brav, T. K., 592

Braveman, P., 438
Bray, J. H., 350
Brazelton, T. B., 114
Bredekamp, S., 172n, 247n, 319n
Breitbard, W., 650
Bremner, J. G., 155
Brendgen, M., 417
Brennan, K. A., 474
Brennan, W. M., 144
Brenneman, K., 228
Brenner, E., 336
Brenner, H., 131n
Brenner, J., 552, 553, 599
Brenner, R. A., 222
Brent, D. A., 422
Brent, M. R., 177
Brent, R. L., 87
Brent, S. B., 643
Brentano, C., 490
Breslau, N., 661
Breslin, F. C., 556
Bretherton, I., 197, 201
Brewaeys, A., 492
Brezausek, C. M., 222
Bridge, J. A., 422
Bridgett, D. J., 193, 194
Brief, A. P., 493
Briggs, M. L., 346
Bright, G. M., 219
Bright, J. E. H., 457
Brim, O., 532
Brisch, K. H., 200
Brock, S., 385
Brodaty, H., 583, 587
Brodtmann, A., 585
Brody, G. H., 205, 281, 346
Brody, L. R., 274, 309
Brodzinsky, D. M., 58
Broidy, L. M., 424
Bromnick, R. D., 387
Bronfenbrenner, U., 24, 59, 71
Bronfman, E., 200
Bronson, G. W., 144
Bronstein, P., 414
Bronte-Tinkew, J., 415
Brooks, L., 449
Brooks, P. J., 303, 316
Brooks, R., 176
Brooks-Gunn, J., 62, 63, 66, 104, 170, 171, 173, 203, 205, 207, 246, 312, 351, 354, 363, 365, 366, 368, 369, 370, 378, 379, 425, 491
Brophy, J., 343
Brown, A. H., 621
Brown, A. M., 142
Brown, A. S., 90, 304
Brown, B. B., 256, 418, 419
Brown, C., 605
Brown, C. S., 278, 338
Brown, G. L., 204
Brown, J. D., 374
Brown, J. R., 259
Brown, L. H., 546
Brown, P., 318
Brown, R. W., 249
Brown, S. A., 381
Brown, S. L., 485, 544, 621, 622
Brown, T. M., 396
Browne, C. A., 230
Browne, J. V., 114
Browne, K. D., 627, 628
Brownell, C. A., 207, 258, 260
Brownell, D. K., 439
Bruce, B., 577
Bruck, M., 355
Bruehl, E. C., 593

Brugman, G. M., 596
Brühwiler, C., 318
Brunt, J., 166
Bruschweiler-Stern, N., 114
Brussoni, M. J., 546
Bruzzese, J.-M., 40
Bryan, A. E., 193
Bryant, B. K., 457
Bryant, D., 424
Bryant, P., 243
Bryden, M. P., 390
Bryk, R. L., 122
Buchanan, A., 282
Buchanan, C. M., 350, 369
Buchanan-Barrow, E., 337
Buck, G. M., 366n
Buehler, C., 351
Buescher, E. S., 131n
Bugental, D. B., 282, 283
Buhl, H. M., 464
Buhrmester, D., 37, 345, 417, 421, 477
Buhs, E. S., 263, 340, 341
Buist, K. L., 59
Buitelaar, J. K., 93
Bukowski, W. M., 205, 261, 339, 341, 343, 417, 419
Bulcroft, K., 620
Bulka, D., 605
Bullo, M., 433
Bumpass, L. L., 491, 533, 541
Bumpass, M. F., 416
Bumpus, M. F., 351
Bunge, S. A., 217
Bunting, L., 378, 380
Buonocore, G., 100
Burchinal, M. R., 29, 244, 246
Burden, M. J., 89
Burgess, K. B., 192, 280, 343
Burgess, M., 478
Burgess-Champoux, T. L., 291, 372
Burghard, B. H., 309
Burholdt, V., 624
Buriel, R., 59
Burkam, D. T., 178, 242
Burke, D. M., 594
Burke, J. D., 267
Burleson, B. R., 473
Burman, D. D., 388
Burns, N. R., 302
Burr, J. A., 631
Burrell, N., 492
Bursik, K., 474
Burton, L. M., 173, 246
Burts, D. C., 245
Burwell, R. A., 346
Buscemi, L., 444
Bush, K. R., 61
Bushman, B. J., 271
Bushnell, E. W., 143
Buss, D. M., 472, 477
Bussey, K., 269, 336
Bussière, P., 388
Buswell, S. D., 129
Butler, M. G., 51
Butler, R., 330
Butler, R. N., 606
Butler, S., 274
Buttelmann, D., 239
Butterworth, M. R., 481n, 482, 620
Buunk, B. P., 472
Buur, H., 191
Bybee, J. A., 502, 538
Bynner, J. M., 467
Bynum, M. S., 374
Byrnes, H. F., 11
Byrnes, J. P., 388

C
Cabrera, N. J., 179, 202, 204, 281
Cacioppo, J. T., 433, 478
Cahan, S., 301, 384
Cahill, A. G., 101
Cahill, K. E., 629
Cai, H., 582, 583
Cain, K. M., 333
Caine, E. D., 612
Caine, N., 370
Cairns, B. D., 14, 18
Cairns, R. B., 14, 18
Caja, S. J., 520
Calarco, K. E., 89
Calasanti, T., 622
Caldera, Y. M., 25, 60, 204
Caldwell, B. M., 170, 244
Caldwell, K. A., 419
Caldwell, M. S., 403
Calhoun, L. G., 663
Calkins, S. D., 189
Call, J., 174
Callaghan, T., 239
Callanan, M. A., 224, 249
Callands, T. A., 374
Caltran, G., 109
Calvert, S. L., 247
Camaioni, L., 157
Camann, W. R., 101
Cameron, C. A., 250
Cameron, H. A., 568
Cameron, N., 121
Cameron, P. A., 207
Cameron-Faulkner, T., 179
Camp, C. J., 585
Campa, M. J., 379
Campbell, A., 276
Campbell, A. L., 632
Campbell, D. A., 99, 270
Campbell, F. A., 173, 173n
Campbell, J., 483
Campbell, S. B., 200, 258, 260
Campbell, T., 157
Campbell, W. K., 331, 333, 402, 465
Campion, M. A., 553
Campione-Barr, N., 479
Campos, J. J., 137, 143, 155, 158, 185, 186
Campos, R. G., 111n
Camras, L. A., 185, 186, 189
Canada Campaign 2000, 67n
Canary, D. J., 477
Candy, B., 653
Candy, J., 276
Candy-Gibbs, S., 643
Canetto, S. S., 516
Cannella, C., 577
Canobi, K. H., 308
Cao, R., 195
Capaldi, D., 425
Capezuti, E. A., 585
Capirci, O., 176
Capozzoli, M. C., 163, 227
Cappeliez, P., 606
Cappell, K. A., 568
Carbery, J., 477
Card, N. A., 270
Carek, P. J., 443
Carek, S. M., 443
Carels, R., 332
Carey, S., 153, 159, 228, 338, 642
Carli, L. L., 555
Carlo, G., 410, 411, 412
Carlson, J. J., 209
Carlson, S. M., 240, 303, 317
Carlson, V. J., 200

Carlson, W., 418
Carnelley, K. B., 662
Carnes, B. A., 567
Caro, F. G., 631
Carpendale, J. I. M., 409
Carpenter, B., 574
Carpenter, M., 157, 176, 177, 239
Carpenter, T. P., 309
Carper, R., 241
Carr, D., 539, 660, 661
Carr, J., 53
Carrano, J., 415
Carriger, M. S., 170
Carroll, D., 450
Carroll, J. B., 309
Carroll, J. E., 437
Carroll, J. S., 469
Carroll, M. A., 95
Carskadon, L. L., 368
Carskadon, M. A., 368
Carstensen, L. L., 605, 614, 615,
    616, 620
Carter, C. S., 505
Carter, J., 110
Cartin, A., 100
Caruso, D. R., 313
Carvajal, S. C., 372
Carver, C. S., 515
Carver, K., 420
Carver, P. R., 344, 376
CASA, 26
Casalis, S., 308
Casas, J. F., 270, 341
Casasola, M., 165
Casavant, M. J., 364
Case, R., 20, 162, 233, 295, 301, 302
Caserta, M. S., 608, 610, 622, 623, 660,
    663
Casey, B. J., 217
Casey, M. B., 391
Casey, R. J., 264
Cashon, C. H., 156, 158
Casper, L. M., 351
Caspi, A., 12, 36, 37, 70, 73, 191, 193,
    221, 370, 482, 524, 542
Cassia, V. M., 145
Cassidy, J., 200, 474
Castel, A. D., 597
Castillo, E. M., 364
Catalano, R., 51
Cate, R. A., 538
Caton, D., 101
Cauffman, E., 279, 280
Cauley, J. A., 513
Causey, K., 23
Cavadini, C., 372
Cavell, T. A., 333
Ceci, S. J., 220, 312, 314, 355, 389
Ceda, G. P., 433
Center for Communication and Social
    Policy, 271
Center for Hearing and Communication,
    503
Center to Advance Palliative Care, 651
Centers for Disease Control and
    Prevention, 54, 131, 221, 377, 378,
    441, 444, 447, 582, 588, 650, 651
Centers for Medicare and Medicaid
    Services, 588
Cerella, J., 520, 521
Cernoch, J. M., 112
Cevenini, E., 432, 566
CFAH (Center for Advancement of
    Health), 663
Chakravarty, E. F., 577
Chalabaev, A., 296

Chamberlain, P., 424
Chambers, P., 58
Champion, T. B., 314, 317
Chan, A., 249
Chan, L. K. S., 333
Chan, R. W., 492
Chan, S. M., 281
Chance, G., 146
Chandler, M. J., 306, 405
Chandola, T., 449
Chandra, A., 375, 377
Chandra, R. K., 92, 374
Chang, E., 624
Chang, F., 250
Chang, L., 259
Chang, R. W., 581
Chang, S., 291
Chao, R. K., 281, 393, 527
Chapin, R., 617
Chapman, R. S., 175
Charles, S. T., 611, 614, 616
Charman, T., 167
Charman, W. N., 502
Charness, N., 521, 524
Charpak, N., 103
Chase-Lansdale, P. L., 66, 171
Chasiotis, A., 32
Chater, N., 174
Chatters, L. M., 612
Chauhan, G. S., 277
Chavajay, P., 167, 306, 314
Chavira, V., 406
Chawarska, K., 241
Chazan-Cohen, R., 173
Cheadle, J. E., 61, 489
Cheah, C. S. L., 281
Cheatham, C. L., 127
Checkley, W., 220
Chen, E. S. L., 276
Chen, F. S., 197
Chen, H., 392, 415
Chen, J. J., 63, 354, 393
Chen, L.-C., 138
Chen, R., 455
Chen, S.-F., 643
Chen, T. J., 367
Chen, V., 281
Chen, X., 193, 194, 195, 262, 281, 466,
    467
Chen, Y., 480, 595
Chen, Y.-C., 90
Chen, Y.-J., 90
Chen, Z., 157
Cherlin, A. J., 490
Cherlin, E. J., 665
Chess, S., 190, 194
Chesterson, J., 587
Cheung, F. M., 555
Cheung, K. M., 240
Chhin, C. S., 457
Chi, M. T. H., 453
Chiang, W.-C., 160
Chiarello, E., 165
Chiang, W.-C., 160
Child Trends, 95, 378
Children's Defense Fund, 172
Childs, C. P., 24
Chin, T., 61
Chinn, C. A., 385
Chitty, L. S., 56n
Choi, J., 390, 433
Choi, N., 541
Choi, S., 166, 178
Chomsky, C., 316
Chomsky, N., 174
Chomtho, S., 131
Choudhury, S., 367

Chouinard, M. M., 232, 251
Chrisler, J. C., 508
Christ, A. E., 662
Christ, G. H., 662
Christakis, D. A., 159
Christakis, N. A., 623
Christakos, A., 418
Christensen, A.-D., 536
Christenson, S. L., 396
Christian, M. S., 87
Christiansen, M. H., 174
Christie, C. A., 396
Christophe, A., 134
Chu, J., 569
Chudley, A. E., 89
Chumlea, W. C., 366n, 367
Chung, H. L., 425
Church, E., 490
CIA (Central Intelligence Agency), 412
Ciarrochi, J., 392
Cibelli, C., 206
Cicchetti, D., 283, 331
Cici-Gokaltun, A., 553
Cicirelli, V. G., 552, 645
Cillessen, A. H. N., 339, 341, 342, 343
Cipriano, E. A., 194, 280
Clapp, J. F., III, 92
Clark, C. A., 101
Clark, E. V., 251
Clark, P. A., 363, 366, 366n
Clark, R., 187
Clarke, B. L., 504
Clarke, L. H., 622
Clarke, P., 573
Clarke-Stewart, K. A., 263, 348, 490
Clarkson, T. W., 90
Claxton, A., 482, 606
Claxton, L. J., 140
Claxton, S. J., 240
Clay, R. A., 394
Clearfield, M. W., 136, 274
Cleary, T. J., 307
Clegg, L. X., 510
Cleland, J. W., 109
Clements, D. H., 243, 247
Cleveland, E. S., 238
Clifford, C., 649
Clifton, R. K., 140
Clinchy, B. M., 451
Clingempeel, W. G., 425, 491
Clipp, E. C., 618
Coats, A. H., 616
Coatsworth, J. D., 405
Cobb, C. D., 321
Cohan, C. L., 488
Cohen, J., 656
Cohen, L. B., 155, 156, 158, 161, 165, 166
Cohen, M., 37, 353
Cohen, O., 543, 544
Cohen, P., 404, 466
Cohen, R., 346
Cohen-Bendahan, C. C. C., 274
Cohen-Mansfield, J., 585
Cohen-Shalev, A., 524
Cohler, B. J., 621
Cohn, D., 489
Coie, J. D., 269, 270, 340, 341
Coke, M. M., 612
Coker, A. D., 526
Colby, A., 407
Colcombe, S. J., 568, 578
Coldwell, J., 26
Cole, A., 581
Cole, D. A., 334
Cole, E., 423
Cole, E. R., 13, 533

Cole, M., 201, 384
Cole, P., 308
Cole, P. M., 190, 259
Cole, R., 173
Colella, A., 493
Coleman, M., 350, 490, 491
Coleman, P. D., 568
Coleman, P. G., 608
Coleman, S. M., 266
Coles, C. D., 87, 88, 89
Coles, L., 567
Coley, R. L., 351, 374
Collaer, M. L., 390
Collier, V. P., 318
Collings, P., 574
Collins, N. L., 474
Collins, W. A., 345, 370, 396, 415, 416,
    417, 420, 421, 476
Collins, W. K., 392, 416
Colman, A. D., 115
Colman, L. L., 115
Colman, R. A., 259
Colom, R., 302
Colombo, J., 163, 170
Colombo, M., 135
Colonnesi, C., 157
Colson, E. R., 110
Colwell, M. J., 227
Commission on Adolescent Suicide
    Prevention, 423
Commission on Children at Risk, 354
Committee on Injury, Violence, and
    Poison Protection, 222
Compton, J. I., 526
Comstock, G., 271
Comstock, R. D., 364
Comunian, A. L., 410, 411
Conboy, B. T., 317
Conchas, G. Q., 394
Conde-Agudelo, A., 103
Conejero-Goldberg, C., 584
Conger, K. J., 346
Conger, R. D., 61, 62, 64, 370, 391, 474
Conley, C. S., 403
Conley, D. B., 570
Conlon, E., 242
Connell, J. P., 334
Connell, M. W., 312
Conner, D. B., 234
Connidis, I. A., 622, 623, 624
Connolly, J., 419, 420
Connolly, J. A., 227
Connolly, K. J., 225
Connor, E., 512
Connor, L. T., 594
Conrad, K., 22
Conway, C. C., 422
Conway, L., 344
Conway, M. A., 593
Conwell, Y., 612, 613
Cook, C. R., 342
Cook, K. J., 483
Cooke, L. P., 480, 481
Cooney, T. M., 478, 533
Cooper, C., 363, 504, 627
Cooper, H., 331
Cooper, R., 315
Cooper, R. P., 103, 113
Cooper, Z., 442
Copello, A. G., 381
Copen, C. E., 377
Coplan, R. J., 192, 261, 262, 280, 296, 343
Coppage, D. J., 165
Copple, C., 172n, 247n, 319n
Coppotelli, H., 341
Corbett, D., 126

Corboz-Warnery, A., 485
Corenblum, B., 338
Corey-Bloom, J., 583
Cornelius, S. W., 524
Cornish, A. M., 186
Cornwell, A. C., 110
Corr, C. A., 644, 647, 660
Corr, D. M., 644, 647, 660
Correa-Chávez, M., 167
Cortina, K. S., 541
Costa, N. M., 352
Costa, P. T., Jr., 537, 542, 542n
Costello, J., 651
Costigan, C. L., 33
Côté, J. E., 297, 402, 404, 454, 464, 465, 467
Côté, S. M., 269, 270, 339
Cotter, V. T., 436, 571
Cottle, C. C., 426
Coudé, G., 136
Coudin, G., 574, 610
Coulton, C. J., 25, 282
Courage, M. L., 135, 161, 165, 247
Courchesne, E., 241
Coursolle, K. M., 630
Couturier, J. L., 373
Covington, C. Y., 87
Cowan, C. P., 341, 416, 484, 485
Cowan, N., 162
Cowan, P. A., 263, 341, 416, 484, 485
Cox, E., 526
Cox, G., 650
Cox, K. S., 65
Cox, M., 224
Cox, M. J., 204
Cox, S. M., 200
Cox, V., 230
Coy, K., 370
Coyl, D. D., 201, 202
Coyle, N., 539
Coyne, S. M., 204, 271
Craft, S., 585
Crago, M. B., 314, 316
Craig, C. M., 106
Craig, W. M., 30
Craighero, L., 136
Craigie, T. A., 491
Craik, F. I. M., 520, 591
Crain, W., 17
Crair, M. C., 125
Cramer, R. E., 472
Cramond, B., 542
Crane, D. R., 415
Cratty, B. J., 223n, 296
Craven, R. G., 257, 331
Crawford, N., 344
Crawford, S., 504, 506
Crawley, L., 650
Crawley-Davis, A. M., 159
Creasey, G. L., 227, 474
Cresswell, J., 395
Crick, N. R., 270, 271, 339, 340, 341, 424
Crimmins, E. M., 576, 577, 618
Criss, M. M., 346
Critser, G., 440
Crockenberg, S., 25, 189
Crocker, J., 331
Crocker, N. A., 88, 89
Crockett, L. J., 374, 415
Croker, R., 12, 607
Crone, E. A., 387
Cronk, C., 176
Crosno, R., 320
Crosnoe, R., 396
Cross, D. R., 234
Cross, S., 538

Crossley, M., 520
Crouch, J. L., 282
Crouter, A. C., 344, 345, 346, 351, 414, 415, 416, 473, 479, 494
Crowley, K., 571
Crowson, M., 241
Crowther, M. R., 609
Cruess, L., 237
Cruttenden, L., 156
Cruz, L. A., 570
Cruza-Guet, M. C., 456
Crystal, D. S., 339, 410, 411
Csibra, G., 155, 176
Csikszentmihalyi, M., 319, 540, 595
Cuevas, K., 156, 164
Cuijpers, P., 381
Culang, M. E., 38, 537
Culbertson, F. M., 422
Cullen, M. R., 556
Cumberland, P. M., 293
Cumming, E., 614
Cummings, E. M., 35, 60, 196
Cundiff, J. M., 513
Cunningham, A. E., 316
Curby, T. W., 263
Curlin, F. A., 655, 659
Curnow, C., 436
Currie, C., 371
Currie, D. H., 482
Currie, J., 246
Curtin, S. C., 378
Curtiss, K., 610
Cutchin, M. P., 619
Cutler, A., 142
Cutler, L. J., 619
Cutler, R. G., 433
Cutler, S. J., 631, 632
Cutrona, C. E., 380
Cutter, W. J., 53
Cvencek, D., 343
Cyr, M., 421

D
Daatland, S. O., 622
Dabrowska, E., 249
Dack, L. A., 239
Daddis, C., 409
Dadds, M. R., 128
Dadson, M. J., 372
Daher, M., 511
Dahl, A., 596
Dahl, R. E., 368
Dahlberg, L. L., 424
Dale, J., 648
Dale, P., 177
Dal Santo, J. A., 222
Daltabuit, M., 109
Daly, C. A., 475
Damashek, A., 222
Damhuis, I., 335
Damjanovic, A. M., 433
Damon, W., 262, 330, 333, 340, 402, 414
Dane, E., 454
Daniel, D. B., 383
Daniell, W. E., 503
Daniels, E., 296
Daniels, P., 95
Daniels, T., 343
Danielsen, K. V., 292
Dannemiller, J. L., 145
Danner, F., 465
Dapretto, M., 177
Dark-Freudeman, A., 597
Darling, N. E., 279
Darling-Hammond, L., 319, 321, 324
Darlington, R., 245

Darroch, J. E., 375
Darwin, C., 14
Das, A., 625
Daubenmier, J., 433
Davey, A., 549
David, K. M., 191
Davidov, M., 336
Davidson, R. J., 125, 193
Davies, B., 662
Davies, E., 662
Davies, J., 276
Davies, P. T., 60
Davis, J., 374
Davis, K. F., 108, 128
Davis, M. H., 473
Davis, O. S. P., 69
Davison, K. K., 220
Davison, M. L., 389
Dawley, K., 94
Dawson, G., 410
Dawson, T. L., 409
Ddungu, H., 653
Deák, G. O., 228, 249
Dean, D., 385
Dean, M., 355
DeAngeleo, L., 466
Dearing, E., 63, 351
Deary, I. J., 131, 309, 310, 520, 596
Deater-Deckard, K., 11, 70, 194, 266
Debats, D. L., 611
Debes, F., 90
Deblinger, E., 352
DeBoer, T., 123
de Bruyn, E. H., 343, 391, 392
Debus, R., 331
de Calignon, A., 584
DeCasper, A. J., 85, 113
Dechanet, C., 444
Deci, E. L., 476
de Frias, C. M., 9, 593
Degner, J., 338
De Goede, I. H. A., 417
de Haan, M., 122, 124, 126, 141, 163, 164, 217, 218, 450
DeHart, G., 493
Deissinger, T., 459
Deitchman, J., 526
deJong, A., 578
Dekker, M. C., 421
DeKosky, S. T., 577
Deković, M., 59, 269, 370, 392, 415
De la Fuente, M., 433
DeLamater, J., 509, 579
de la Ossa, J. L., 237
De Leon, J. M., 548
de Lima, C., 443
De Lisi, R., 316
Dell, G. S., 250
Dell, M. L., 608
DeLoache, J. S., 158, 159, 207, 227, 228
Delobel-Ayoub, M., 101
DelVecchio, W. E., 193
De Marco, A. C., 479
DeMaris, A., 490
Dembo, M. H., 417
Demetriou, A., 20, 302, 384, 386
Demiray, B., 593
Demo, D. H., 347
Dempster-McClain, D., 527
DeNavas-Walt, C., 61
Dengel, D. R., 578
Denham, S. A., 258, 313
Denissen, J. J. A., 331
Denmark, F. L., 516

Dennerstein, L., 509
Denney, N. W., 524
Dennis, T., 87
Dennis, W., 138
Dennison, E. M., 363
Dent, A., 661
Denton, K., 412
Denton, N. A., 32, 33
Deocampo, J. A., 159
DePaulo, B. M., 487
Deprest, J. A., 56
Der, G., 131, 520
deRegnier, R.-A., 95, 123
de Rivera, J., 260
DeRoche, K., 50
Derom, C., 218
DeRose, L. M., 368, 369
DeRosier, M. E., 343
de Rosnay, M., 188, 240
Derwinger, A., 522
De Rycke, L., 331
de Schonen, S., 145
Désert, M., 343
Desmarais, S., 274
DeSouza, A., 193, 195
De Souza, E., 53
Desrochers, S., 20
Dessel, A., 354
de St. Aubin, E., 533
Deutsch, N. L., 526
DeVaney, S. A., 630
Deveson, A., 625
Devi, N. P. G., 91
de Villiers, J. G., 249
de Villiers, P. A., 249
De Vito, G., 504
DeVoe, M., 605
DeVos, J., 155
de Vries, B., 476
DeVries, R., 319
Dew, J., 485
de Waal, F. B. M., 273
de Weerd, A. W., 109
de Weerth, C., 93, 131
De Wolff, M. S., 199
Dey, J. G., 493
Diamond, A., 73, 156, 218, 237, 248
Diamond, L. M., 376, 421, 477, 480, 481n, 482, 620
Dias, M. G., 383
Diaz-Rossello, J., 103
DiBiase, A.-M., 426
Dick, D. M., 370, 381
Dick, F., 175
Dickinson, D. K., 242
Dick-Read, G., 99
Dickson, R. A., 593
Dickstein, M., 13
DiDonato, M. D., 276
Diehl, M., 539, 606, 631
Diener, E., 541
Diener, R. M., 87
Diepvens, K., 440
Dietz, B. E., 614
Dietz, E. L., 419
Dijkstra, P., 482
DiLalla, L. F., 244
Dildy, G. A., 93
Dillon, M., 535, 608, 609
Dilworth-Anderson, P., 551, 609
Dimitrov, D. M., 379
Dimond, M. F., 608, 610
Ding, Z. Y., 291
Dingel, A., 165
DiPietro, J. A., 84
Dirix, C. E. H., 85

Dirks, J., 314
Dishion, T. J., 35
DiTommaso, E., 478
Dittus, P., 374
Dix, T., 193, 208
Dixon, R. A., 9, 521, 590, 593, 596
Dixon, W. E., Jr., 177
Djahanbakhch, O., 438
Dodd, V. L., 103
Dodge, K. A., 267, 269, 270, 341
Dodge, T., 374
Dodman, N., 100
D'Odorico, L., 178
Dodson, T. A., 458
Doherty, W. J., 484
Dohnt, H., 332
Doka, K. J., 660, 662
Dolan, D. C., 610
Dolbin-MacNab, M. L., 548
Dolensky, E., 340, 417
Dombrowski, S. C., 101
Domellöf, E., 217
Domitrovich, C. E., 237, 333
Donaldson, G., 518
Donatelle, R. J., 372, 443, 444, 450, 475n
Dondi, M., 109
Done, D. J., 587
Dong, W., 333
Donini, L. M., 577
Donnan, G., 585
Donnellan, M. B., 61, 62, 331, 333, 465, 474, 608
Donnelly, R., 403
Donnelly, T. M., 411, 413
D'Onofrio, B. M., 348
Dorius, C., 347, 348
Dorn, L. D., 362, 370
Dornbusch, S. M., 350
Dörner, J., 595
Dorris, M., 88
Doss, B. D., 484
Double, E. B., 89
Douglas, A. J., 115
Doussard-Roosevelt, J. A., 521
Dowd, M. D., 665
Dowling, E. M., 412
Downing, J. E., 322
Downs, A. C., 369
Downs, R. M., 300
Doydum, A. O., 238
Doyle, A. B., 227, 337
Dozier, M., 201
Drabman, R. S., 292
Drayton, S., 240
Dreher, G. F., 493
Drell, M. J., 296
Dreman, S., 543, 544
Drewnowski, A., 570
Drick, C. A., 641
Driscoll, K. A., 422
Driscoll, M. C., 50
Driver, J., 482, 484
Drotar, D., 294
Dubé, E. M., 376
Dube, M., 617
DuBois, D. L., 331, 403
Dubois, M.-F., 39, 40
Duckworth, A. L., 315
Dudani, A., 222
Duffy, R. D., 456
Duggan, A., 283
Dumas, J. A., 591
Dumbrigue, C., 455
Duncan, G. J., 61, 237, 243
Duncan, L. E., 533
Duncan, S. R., 110

Dundek, L. H., 99
Dunham, Y., 338
Dunkle, R. E., 621
Dunlop, D. D., 581
Dunlosky, J., 522, 523
Dunn, J. R., 26, 63, 204, 205, 208, 258, 259, 264, 345, 348, 350
Dunn, M. J., 57
Dunne, E. J., 661
Dunne-Bryant, A., 347
Dunne-Maxim, K., 661
Dunsmore, J., 258
Duprere, V., 425
Durbin, D. L., 419
Durham, M., 244
Durkin, K., 241
Durlak, J. A., 351
Durston, S., 22, 217
Dusek, J. B., 414
Duszak, R. S., 90
Dutta, A., 432
Dutton, D. G., 482
Duxbury, L. E., 494, 495
Dweck, C. S., 197, 333, 338, 339
Dykiert, D., 520
Dykstra, P. A., 489, 624
Dynarski, M., 63
Dzurova, D., 53

E
Eagly, A. H., 472, 555
Eaker, E. D., 513, 514
Early Head Start National Resource Center, 173
Easterbrooks, M. A., 206
Easterly, S., 492
Eastwick, P. W., 472
Eaton, D. K., 420
Eaton, M. M., 333
Eaves, L., 366
Ebeling, K. S., 230
Ebner, N. C., 590
Eccles, J. S., 296, 320, 331, 332, 343, 369, 370, 391, 392, 393, 395, 397, 404, 413, 455, 466, 468, 468n
Eckenrode, J. J., 379, 418
Eckenrode, J. J., 379, 418
Economic Policy Institute, 325
Eddy, K. T., 373
Eder, R. A., 256
Edmunds, L., 313
Edwards, A., 188, 265, 270
Edwards, B. A., 571
Edwards, C. P., 273
Edwards, L. J., 109
Edwards, O. W., 312, 314
Effros, R. B., 433
Efstathiou, N., 649
Egan, K. A., 643
Egan, S. K., 344, 376
Egeland, B., 198, 201, 354, 374, 396
Eggebeen, D. J., 485, 543, 545
Eggum, N. D., 265, 270
Egozi, G., 390
Ehrensaft, M. K., 482
Ehri, L. C., 225, 242
Eichstedt, J. A., 273
Eidelman, A. I., 48
Eiden, R. D., 87
Einspieler, C., 83
Einstein, G. O., 577, 593
Eisen, M., 330
Eisenberg, N., 189, 191, 193, 259, 260, 261, 265, 270, 353, 415
Eisenberg-Berg, N., 265
Eiser, C., 355
Ekerdt, D. J., 617

Ekman, P., 185
Ekstrom, B., 508
Elavsky, S., 506, 516
Elbert-Avila, K. I., 655
Elder, G. H., Jr., 5, 12, 36, 64, 320, 370, 391, 396
Elfenbein, D. S., 378
Eliakim, A., 293
Elias, C. L., 227
Eliason, G., 645, 646
Eliasson, M., 442
Elicker, J., 206
Elischberger, H. B., 237
Elkind, D., 386, 387
Elliott, D. B., 621
Elliott, J. G., 352
Ellis, A. E., 166
Ellis, B. J., 367
Ellis, D. A., 503
Ellis, L., 457
Ellis, L. A., 257
Ellis, W. E., 340
Ellison, C. G., 610
Ellison, N., 446
Elman, J. L., 174
Else-Quest, N. M., 189, 193, 209, 245, 273
El-Sheikh, M., 35
Eltzschig, H. K., 101
Eluvathingal, T. J., 127
Elwert, F., 623
Ely, R., 317
Emde, R. N., 190
Emery, R. E., 348, 371, 482
Emmerson, N. A., 263
Emory, E. K., 101
Endestad, T., 355
Engels, R. C. M. E., 411
Englund, M. E., 206, 396
Engstrom, R., 519
Enguidanos, S. M., 589
Ennemoser, M., 246, 247
Ensor, R., 239, 240, 259
Entringer, S., 93
Entwisle, D. R., 396
Epel, E. S., 432, 433
Eppler, M. A., 147
Epstein, L. H., 293
Epstein, R., 128
Erath, S. A., 266
Erdogan, B., 494
Erickson, J. D., 87
Erickson, K. I., 443, 522, 578
Erickson, M. F., 354
Erikson, E. H., 16, 184, 256, 330, 402, 533, 604, 605
Erol, R. Y., 402
Ernst, M., 74, 367
Ertekin-Tanner, N., 584
Ertel, K. A., 438
Escrivao, M. A., 436
ESPAD (European School Project on Alcohol and Other Drugs), 381
Espelage, D. L., 377
Espinoza, G., 418
Espnes, G. A., 331
Esposito-Smythers, C., 422
Espy, K. A., 88, 244
Esser, G., 106
Essex, M. J., 367
Estep, K., 259
Esterberg, K. G., 527
Estourgie-van Burk, G. F., 130
Ethier, N., 472
Etnier, J. L., 443
Evanoo, G., 111n

Evans, A. M., 290
Evans, C. B., 66
Evans, D. E., 191
Evans, E., 422
Evans, G. W., 303
Evans, M. E., 281
Evans, N., 174
Even-Zohar, A., 626
Evert, J., 567
Ewald, H. A. S., 510
Ewald, P. W., 510
Ezzati, M., 438

F
Fabes, R. A., 258, 259, 265, 274, 276
Fabiani, M., 568
Fabricius, W. V., 306
Fagan, J. F., III, 163, 170
Fagard, J., 140
Fagot, B. I., 270, 274, 277
Fagundes, C. P., 437, 481n, 482, 620
Fahrmeier, E. D., 301
Fairburn, C. G., 373, 442
Faircloth, B. S., 393
Faith, M. S., 291
Falagas, M. E., 221
Falbo, T., 331, 346
Falk, D., 124
Family Caregiver Alliance, 551
Fanslow, C. A., 649
Fantoni, G., 611
Fantuzzo, J. W., 320
Fantz, R. L., 144
Farah, M. J., 303
Faraone, S. V., 70, 305
Farley, F., 388
Farmer, T. W., 339
Farr, M. J., 453
Farr, R. J., 492
Farran, C. J., 551
Farrant, K., 238
Farrar, M. J., 239
Farrington, D. P., 362, 423, 424, 425
Farris, J. R., 486
Farroni, T., 145
Farver, J. M., 28, 262
Fashola, O. S., 455
Fasolo, M., 178
Fassinger, R. E., 475
Fath, A., 352
Fattibene, P., 90
Fauce, S. R., 433
Faulkner, J. A., 437
Fauth, R. C., 62
Favreau, O. E., 343
Fearnow, M. D., 336
Fearon, R. M. P., 199, 200, 201, 206
Featherman, D. L., 614
Federal Interagency Forum on Aging Related Statistics, 618
Federal Interagency Forum on Child and Family Statistics, 244, 347
Federico, A., 251
Federico, M. J., 293
Feeney, J. A., 474, 484
Fegley, S., 411
Fehr, B., 473, 474
Fehr, B., 473, 474
Feigelman, W., 423
Feigenbaum, P., 110
Feil, R., 51
Fein, G. G., 261, 262n
Feinberg, M. E., 346, 416
Feinsilver, S. H., 571
Feldkämper, M., 293
Feldman, A. F., 396
Feldman, D. C., 553, 629

Feldman, D. H., 31
Feldman, J. F., 163
Feldman, P. J., 64
Feldman, R., 34, 48, 102, 103, 105, 109, 115, 186, 189, 194, 202, 485
Feldman, R. S., 455
Felice, M. E., 378
Felicio, D. M., 516
Felner, R. D., 392
Felsman, D. E., 405
Feng, J., 390
Feng, Q., 87
Fenson, L., 177
Fenwick, K. D., 146
Feret, A., 569
Ferguson, L. R., 442
Ferguson, T. J., 335
Fergusson, D. M., 131
Fernald, A., 177, 178
Fernald, L. C., 132
Fernyhough, C., 23, 234
Ferrari, P. F., 135, 136
Ferraro, K. F., 577
Ferry, A. L., 166
Fesseha, G., 353
Fiano, K., 101
Ficca, G., 128
Fickling, D., 657
Field, D., 606, 608, 625
Field, T., 92, 103, 186, 260
Fielding, R. A., 572
Fiese, B. H., 26, 200, 291, 372
Fifer, W. P., 108, 113
Figner, B., 387
Figueroa, Z., 103
Finch, B. R., 438
Fincham, F. D., 482
Finchum, T., 615
Findlay, L. C., 296
Findsen, B., 599
Fine, A., 476
Fine, M. A., 280, 347
Finger, B., 201
Fingerman, K. L., 479, 545, 547, 548, 549, 616, 626, 627
Finkel, D., 520
Finkel, E. J., 446
Finkelhor, D., 354, 374, 418
Finkelstein, E. A., 441
Finkelstein, L. M., 493
Finn, J. D., 318
Finucane, M. L., 594
Fiori, K. L., 541, 575, 620, 621, 625
Fireman, G., 335
Fisch, H., 438
Fischer, K. W., 20, 186, 189, 260, 301, 302
Fischman, M. G., 225
Fish, M., 198
Fishbein, M., 394
Fisher, C. B., 40
Fisher, D. M., 107, 107n
Fisher, J. A., 219
Fisher, J. O., 220, 440
Fisher, P. A., 122, 178
Fisher, S. E., 74
Fisher, S. K., 492
Fisk, A. D., 574
Fite, P. J., 267
Fitzgerald, L. F., 380
Fitzpatrick, J., 473
Fivaz-Depeursinge, E., 485
Fivush, R., 238, 258, 274
Flanagan, C. A., 410, 413
Flannery, D. J., 387, 423, 425
Flannery, K. A., 218
Flavell, E. R., 228, 239, 240, 335

Flavell, J. H., 228, 239, 240, 258, 303, 335
Flegal, K. M., 439, 441
Fleischman, D. A., 591
Fleming, J. I., 657
Fletcher, A. C., 279, 296, 340
Flick, L., 92
Floccia, C., 134
Flom, R., 135, 146, 176
Flood, D. G., 568
Flood, M., 608
Flor, D. L., 281
Florian, V., 643, 645
Florsheim, P., 378, 380
Flynn, E., 239
Flynn, J. R., 312, 314, 520
Foehr, U. G., 246, 247, 271, 374, 389, 394, 418
Foerde, K., 394
Fogel, A., 185, 189
Foley, K. P., 26
Fomon, S. J., 121
Fonagy, P., 201
Fonda, S. J., 618
Fong, T. G., 588
Fontana, L., 505
Fontayne, P., 296
Forcier, M., 421
Forgatch, M. S., 353
Forman, D. R., 186, 187, 265
Forry, N. D., 481
Forssell, S. L., 492
Forste, R., 490
Fortenberry, J. D., 375
Foster, J. A., 440
Foster, M. A., 244
Fowler, C., 552
Fowler, F., 279
Fowler, J. W., 608
Fox, C. L., 342
Fox, N. A., 125, 144, 185, 189, 192
Fraley, R. C., 201
Franchak, J. M., 207
Frank, D. A., 87
Frank, R., 438
Frankel, C. B., 185
Frankenburg, E., 321
Franklin, B. A., 578
Franklin, S., 384
Franklin, V. P., 321
Franko, D. L., 371
Franks, B. A., 383
Franz, C., 260
Frazier, L. D., 502, 523, 538, 575, 594, 607
Frederickson, B. L., 616
Fredricks, J. A., 296, 332, 397
Freedman, J., 103
Freedman, M., 13
Freedman-Doan, C., 391, 392
Freeman, J., 362
Freeman, E. C., 465
Freeman, G. P., 535
Freeman, H., 201, 202
Freeman, L., 653
Freiman, A., 444
Freitag, C. M., 304
Freitas, A. A., 433
French, D. C., 262
French, L. A., 299
French, S. E., 391, 392
Freud, S., 15, 184
Freund, A. M., 9, 537, 590, 607, 608, 632
Freund, G. G., 442
Frey, A., 425
Frick, P. J., 270
Fried, L. P., 580
Friederici, A. D., 175

Friedman, C., 581
Friedman, C. K., 274
Friedman, E. M., 437
Friedman, M. C., 597
Friedman, S. L., 162, 236, 237
Friedrich, M., 175
Friend, J., 422
Fries, J. F., 576
Friesen, W., 185
Frigon, J.-Y., 367
Frith, L., 55
Frith, U., 241
Fritsch, M., 412
Fromholt, P., 606
Frost, J. J., 375
Fruhauf, C. A., 626
Fry, C. L., 540, 576
Fry, P. S., 611, 623, 645
Fryer, S. L., 88, 89
Fryling, T., 628
Fu, G., 337
Fuchs, D., 322
Fuchs, L. S., 322
Fugelsang, J., 520
Fuh, M.-H., 508
Fukumoto, A., 264
Fukunaga, A., 570
Fuligni, A. J., 32, 33
Fuligni, A. S., 170
Fuller, C., 219
Fuller, D., 411
Fuller, M. J., 369
Fuller-Iglesias, H., 477
Fuller-Thomson, E., 548
Fullerton, J. T., 100
Fulmer, T., 627
Fülöp, T., 437, 571
Fung, H. H., 257, 616
Furchtgott-Roth, D., 493
Furman, W., 37, 345, 420, 421
Furnham, A., 472
Furrow, J. L., 412
Furstenberg, F. F., Jr., 380, 471, 478, 479
Fuson, K. C., 308, 309
Fussell, E., 479, 488
Fuster, J. J., 433
Fuster, V., 640
Fyfe, M., 653

G
Gabbay, S. G., 621
Gabriel, Z., 617
Gagne, J.-P., 570
Gailliot, M. T., 646
Gaines, J., 221
Galambos, N. L., 351, 414, 467, 481
Galetta, F., 571
Galinsky, E., 26, 202, 203, 345, 351
Gallagher, A. M., 389
Gallagher, L., 48
Gallagher, S. J., 465
Gallant, M. P., 626
Gallaway, C., 251
Gallay, L. S., 410
Galler, J. R., 132
Gallo, L. C., 514
Gallo, W. T., 556
Galloway, J. C., 138, 140
Gallup, G. G., 207
Gallup News Service, 412, 608, 609
Ganchrow, J. R., 134
Ganea, P. A., 157, 158
Ganger, J., 177
Ganji, V., 220
Gannon, L., 508
Ganong, L. H., 347, 350, 487, 490, 491

Gans, D., 549, 550
Gao, G., 475
Garber, J., 187
Garces, E., 246
Garcia, A., 159
Garcia, M. M., 270
Garcia-Bournissen, F., 87
García Coll, C., 33, 204, 406
Gardner, H. E., 31, 311, 312, 312n, 323
Gardner, J. P., 433
Gardner-Kitt, D. L., 406
Garner, P. W., 29, 188, 259, 336
Garrido-Nag, K., 174
Gartstein, M. A., 189, 191
Gascón, S., 554
Gasden, V., 491
Gaskill, R. L., 353
Gaskins, S., 236, 262
Gassen, N. S., 488
Gates, G. J., 447, 492
Gathercole, S. E., 237, 302, 303
Gathercole, V., 249
Gatz, M., 611
Gauthier, A. H., 488
Gauvain, M., 237, 300, 303, 304
Gavrilov, L. A., 505
Gavrilova, N. S., 505
Gazelle, H., 341
Gazzaley, A., 521
Ge, X., 369, 370, 371, 375
Geangu, E., 109
Geary, D. C., 22, 243, 389
Gee, C. B., 380
Geerts, C. C., 88
Geil, M., 452
Geist, C., 480
Gelman, R., 230
Gelman, S. A., 177, 178, 230, 231, 243, 275, 275n, 344
Gendler, M. N., 188
Genesee, F., 317
Gentile, B., 465
Gentile, D. A., 271
George, S. A., 506
Georgsdottir, A., 323
Gerardi-Caulton, G., 193
Gerber, S. B., 318
Gerdes, A. C., 343
Gere, J., 481n
Gergely, G., 185
Gergen, K. J., 607
Gergen, M., 607
Gerhard, A., 473
Gershoff, E. T., 266, 267, 270
Gershoff-Stowe, L., 248
Gerstorf, D., 597
Gervai, J., 200, 274, 277
Gesell, A., 14
Gest, S. D., 333
Getchell, N., 223n, 225, 295, 296, 364
Geuze, R. H., 144, 218
Gewirtz, A. H., 10, 353
Ghavami, N., 406
Ghim, H. R., 144
Giandrea, M. D., 629
Giarrusso, R., 552, 627
Gibbons, R., 46
Gibbs, B. G., 389
Gibbs, J. C., 265, 268, 409, 410, 411, 413, 414, 446
Gibride, K., 167
Gibson, E. J., 142, 147
Gibson, J. J., 147
Gibson, L., 583
Gibson, P. A., 548
Giedd, J. N., 367, 450

Gielen, U. P., 410, 411
Giguère, B., 479
Gil, J., 483
Giles, J. W., 273
Gill, M., 74
Gill, T. M., 570
Gillespie, D. C., 125
Gillet, J.-P., 57
Gillette, P., 161
Gillies, R. M., 320, 395
Gilligan, C. F., 409
Gilliom, M., 259
Gillum, R. F., 609
Gilstrap, L. L., 355
Ginsberg, S., 387
Ginsburg, A. P., 144
Ginsburg, H. P., 242, 243
Ginsburg, K. R., 298
Ginsburg-Block, M. D., 320
Giorgi, C., 218
Giovanelli, G., 113
Gissler, M., 88
Gitlin, L. N., 587
Giudice, S., 217
Giuliani, A., 101
Gladstone, I. M., 102
Glaser, R., 453
Glasgow, K. L., 392
Glasper, E. R., 115
Glass, N., 483
Gleason, J. B., 174
Gleitman, H., 249
Gleitman, L. R., 248, 249
Glover, V., 93
Glowinski, A. L., 421
Glück, J., 593
Gluckman, P. D., 97
Glymour, M. M., 438
Gnepp, J., 258
Go, A. S., 512, 512n
Goddard, S., 160
Godeau, E., 375
Goeke-Morey, M. C., 60
Goering, J., 63
Gogate, L. J., 146, 163
Gögele, M., 432
Goh, Y. I., 92
Goldberg, A., 419, 420
Goldberg, A. E., 484, 492
Goldberg, A. P., 578
Goldberg, E. Z., 643
Goldenberg, C., 33
Goldfield, B. A., 178
Goldhammer, F., 310
Goldin-Meadow, S., 176, 232
Goldschmidt, L., 88
Goldsmith, H. H., 177, 193
Goldsmith, L. T., 31
Goldsmith, T., 294
Goldsteen, M., 648
Goldstein, A. S., 62
Goldstein, M. H., 176
Goldstein, M. Z., 509
Goldstein, R., 556
Goldstein, S., 305
Goldstein, T. R., 422
Goldston, D. B., 423
Goldwyn, R., 201
Goleman, D., 313
Golinkoff, R. M., 127, 177, 242, 249
Golomb, C., 224
Golombok, S., 54, 492
Gomez-Perez, E., 303
Gomez-Smith, Z., 548
Göncü, A., 227, 256
Gonzales, N. A., 63

Gonzalez, A.-L., 279
Good, G. E., 527
Good, T. L., 343
Goode, J. D., 426
Goode, V., 426
Goodman, A., 86
Goodman, C. C., 548
Goodman, G. S., 355
Goodman, J., 177
Goodman, M., 259, 336
Goodnow, J. J., 23, 266
Goodvin, R., 185, 189, 256, 259
Goodwin, M. H., 276
Goodwin, P. Y., 551
Goodwin, R., 476
Goodyear-Brown, P., 352
Gooren, E. M. J. C., 341
Goossens, L., 404, 464
Gootman, J., 468, 468n
Gopher, D., 522
Gopnik, A., 21, 166, 178, 188, 231
Gordon, R. A., 66
Gore, S. A., 440
Gorelick, P. B., 585
Gormally, S., 112
Gorman, B. S., 423
Goronzy, J. J., 580
Gortmaker, S. L., 293
Gosselin, P. A., 570
Goswami, U., 230
Gothe, N., 516
Gott, M., 509, 651
Gottfredson, G. D., 456
Gottfredson, L. S., 455, 457
Gottfried, A. E., 25, 350
Gottfried, A. W., 25, 350
Gottlieb, G., 7, 70, 71, 73
Gottman, J. M., 483, 485, 489, 620
Gottman, J. S, 485
Goubet, N., 140
Gould, E., 115, 568
Gould, F., 283
Gould, J. L., 47
Graber, J. A., 271, 362, 363, 365, 366, 369, 370, 371, 421, 422
Grabowski, D. C., 611
Graham, J. A., 334
Graham, S., 27, 391
Graham, S. A., 248
Graham-Bermann, S. A., 283
Gralinski, J. H., 208, 209
Grall, T. S., 347
Granger, R. C., 351
Granier-Deferre, C., 85
Granillo, T., 372
Granot, T., 662
Granrud, C. E., 143
Grant, K., 204
Grantham-McGregor, S. M., 92, 132, 291
Graves, L. M., 495
Gray, K. A., 88
Gray, M. R., 278
Gray-Little, B., 332
Greek, A., 205
Green, F. L., 228, 239, 240, 335
Green, G. E., 111
Green, J. A., 109
Greenbaum, C. W., 194
Greenberg, M. T., 237
Greenberger, E., 61
Greendorfer, S. L., 225
Greene, A. D., 379
Greene, J. A., 452
Greene, K., 387
Greene, L., 374
Greene, M. F., 86

Greene, M. L., 406
Greene, S. M., 348
Greenfield, E. A., 541, 545
Greenfield, P. M., 24, 139, 301, 314, 418
Greenhill, L. L., 305
Greenough, W. T., 128
Greenwald, A. G., 343
Gregg, V., 411
Gregory, A., 392
Grela, B., 159
Greve, W., 23
Grieve, A. J., 170
Griffin, Z. M., 594
Griffiths, M., 643
Grigorenko, E. L., 313, 315
Grimby, A., 661
Grob, A., 464
Groisser, D. B., 303
Grolnick, W. S., 392
Gropman, A. L., 51
Grossbaum, M. F., 533
Grossman, A. H., 377, 621
Grossman, P. B., 333
Grossmann, K., 199, 202, 204
Grouzet, F. M. E., 391
Grover, T., 348
Gruber, H. E., 525
Gruendel, J., 65
Gruenewald, D. A., 640
Gruenewald, T. L., 576
Grühn, S., 453, 605
Grundy, E., 549, 626
Grusec, J. E., 265, 266, 268n, 336
Gualdi-Russo, E., 437
Guarnaccia, C. A., 653
Guedes, G., 503
Guerra, N. G., 27
Guglielmi, R. S., 318
Gugula, S., 274
Guignard, J.-H., 323
Guildner, S. H., 619
Guilford, J. P., 322
Guindon, S., 606
Guise, J. M., 101
Guiso, L., 389
Gülgöz, S., 593
Gulko, J., 343, 344
Gullone, E., 352
Gulotta, T. P., 11
Gunnar, M. R., 127
Gunnarsdottir, I., 131
Gunnoe, M. L., 267
Gunstad, J., 218
Guo, J., 276
Gure, A., 370
Gureje, O., 584
Gur-Yaish, N., 626
Gust, D. A., 221
Gustafson, G. E., 109, 111
Guterman, N. B., 282
Gutman, L. M., 173, 391, 392
Gutmann, D. L., 540
Gutteling, B. M., 93
Guttuso, T., Jr., 506
Gwiazda, J., 144

H

Haddock, G., 292
Haddow, J. L., 378
Haden, C. A., 237, 258
Haentjens, P., 513
Hafdahl, A. R., 332
Hagan, R. I., 274
Hagberg, B., 567
Hagberg, J. M., 578
Hagerman, R. J., 51

Hagestad, G. O., 489
Hagoort, P., 142
Hahn, E. R., 248
Hahn, H.-M., 129
Hahn, S., 56n, 522
Haidt, J., 411, 412
Haight, W. L., 168., 236
Haines, C. J., 508
Hainline, L., 113
Hainsworth, J., 576
Haith, M. M., 140
Hakman, M., 209
Hakuta, K., 317
Haladyna, T. M., 322
Halberstadt, A., 258
Hale, C. M., 239
Hale, S., 522
Hales, C. N., 130
Haley, W. E., 655, 665
Halfon, N., 65
Halford, G. S., 20, 21, 232, 233, 300, 301, 302
Halford, W. K., 485
Halgunseth, L. C., 281
Hall, C. B., 585
Hall, D. G., 248
Hall, G. S., 14, 362
Hall, J. A., 276
Hall, J. G., 47n, 48
Hall, K., 585
Hall, S. K., 624
Halle, T. G., 185
Haller, J., 132
Hallinan, M. T., 395
Halperin, J. M., 305
Halpern, C. T., 373
Halpern, D. F., 388, 389, 390, 485, 495, 555
Halpern-Felsher, B. L., 388
Haltzman, S., 489
Halverson, C. F., 277
Ham, M., 369
Hamberger, L. K., 483
Hamel, E., 247, 271
Hamer, D. H., 375
Hamilton, C., 198
Hamilton, H. A., 350
Hamilton, M. A., 396
Hamilton, S. F., 396
Hamm, J. V., 393
Hammer, L. B., 550, 551
Hammes, B., 86
Hammill, B. G., 546, 547
Hampl, J. S., 220
Hampton, A., 321, 395
Hampton, K. N., 552
Hamre, B. K., 320
Han, W.-J., 170, 203, 351, 485
Hancock, S., 445
Hane, A. A., 192
Hanioka, T., 217
Hanish, L. D., 274
Hankin, B. L., 418, 421
Hannon, E. E., 140, 141
Hannon, T. S., 291
Hans, S. L., 87, 200
Hansell, N. K., 303
Hansen, M., 368
Hansen, M. B., 248
Hansson, R. O., 660
Hao, L., 32, 33
Happaney, K., 282
Happé, F., 241
Harachi, T. W., 424
Harden, K., 367, 368
Hardin, C. A., 240, 306

Harding, C. G., 171
Hardy, J., 379
Hardy, M. A., 549, 550
Hardy, S. A., 405, 411, 412
Hare, B., 174
Harkness, S., 114, 128
Harlan, E. T., 193, 208
Harlan, S. L., 66
Harley, B., 317
Harley, K., 165
Harlow, H. F., 196
Harman, S. M., 433
Harold, R. D., 343
Harris, B. A., 472
Harris, C. J., 21
Harris, G., 112
Harris, J. R., 550
Harris, K. L., 480
Harris, K. M., 380
Harris, M. J., 194
Harris, P. L., 383, 642
Harris, R. C., 191
Harris, S., 23, 234
Harris, Y. R., 334
Harris Interactive, 656, 658
Harrison, P. J., 373
Harrop, A., 276
Hart, B., 170, 250
Hart, C., 291
Hart, C. H., 245, 270, 278, 279, 280,
    341, 346
Hart, D., 62, 317, 330, 411, 413
Hart, H., 283
Hart, H. M., 533, 535
Harter, S., 256, 258, 276, 330, 331, 335,
    371, 375, 402, 414
Hartley, A., 520
Hartman, J., 591
Hartman, M., 591
Harton, H. C., 340
Hartshorn, K., 163
Hartup, W. W., 262, 263, 340, 417
Harvey, M. W., 396
Harwood, J., 627
Harwood, M. D., 239
Harwood, R. L., 65, 200
Haryu, E., 248
Hasebe, Y., 409
Hasegawa, T., 160
Hasher, L., 521, 522, 524, 591
Haskell, W. L., 516
Hasnain-Wynia, R., 575
Hassanein, K., 599
Hasselhorn, M., 304
Hastings, E. C., 597
Hastrup, B., 589
Hatch, L. R., 620
Hatfield, E., 475
Hau, K.-T., 324
Hauck, F. R., 110
Hauf, P., 140
Haukkala, A., 513
Hause, K. S., 477
Hausfather, A., 171
Hawkins, J. N., 331
Hawkley, L. C., 433
Haworth, C. M. A., 70
Haws, R. A., 100
Hawton, A., 588
Hawton, K., 422
Hay, D. F., 187
Hay, E. L., 539, 626
Hay, J. F., 522
Hay, P., 373
Haycock, P. C., 89
Hayflick, L., 432, 566, 567, 573

Hayne, H., 135, 159, 164, 165, 166, 168
Hayslip, B., Jr., 548, 610, 653
Hayward, C., 348
Haywood, H. C., 315
Haywood, K. M., 223n, 225, 295, 296,
    364
Hazen, N. L., 202
He, Z., 239
Head, M., 599
Head, M. R., 415
Head Start Bureau, 245
Healthy Families America, 283
Healy, M., 121
Healy, S. D., 390
Heathcock, J., 140
Heaton, T. B., 490
Heaven, P. C. L., 392
Hebblethwaite, S., 545
Hebert, K., 649
Heckhausen, J., 611, 613
Heckman, J. J., 246
Hedberg, K., 658
Hedge, J. W., 554
Hedges, L. V., 318
Hediger, M. L., 92, 102
Heil, M., 390
Heilbrun, K., 426
Heilman, M. E., 555
Heiman, N., 70
Heino, R., 446
Helburn, S. W., 172
Helfand, M. J., 374
Hellemans, K. G., 89
Heller, W., 124
Helm, H. M., 609
Helson, R., 471, 533, 538, 539, 541
Heltzner, E. P., 503
Helwig, C. C., 269, 337, 409
Henderson, R. L., 306
Henderson, S. H., 416
Hendrick, C., 473
Hendrick, S. S., 473
Hendricks, J., 631, 632
Hendrie, H. H., 584
Hendry, L. B., 467, 471, 630, 631
Hendry, M., 658
Henggeler, S. W., 425, 426
Hengst, J. A., 32
Henig, R. M., 476
Henig, S., 476
Henkens, K., 631
Henning, K., 482
Henretta, J. C., 549
Henrich, C. C., 375, 419
Henricsson, L., 320
Henriksen, L., 374
Henriksen, T. B., 87
Henry, J. D., 593
Henry, W. E., 614
Heraghty, J. L., 108
Herald, S. L., 263
Herald-Brown, S. L., 340, 341
Herbenick, D., 446
Herbert, J., 159
Herbst, J. H., 543
Herd, P., 439, 566, 575
Herek, G. M., 447
Herman, K. C., 272
Herman, M., 406
Herman-Giddens, M. E., 366n, 367
Hernandez, D., 351
Hernandez, D. J., 32, 33
Hernandez, M., 619
Hernandez-Reif, M., 103, 135, 146, 163
Herr, M. Y., 234
Herrnstein, R. J., 312

Hershey, D. A., 557
Hertzog, C., 522, 523, 596
Herzog, A. R., 607
Herzog, D. B., 373
Hesketh, T., 346
Hespos, S. J., 106, 124, 125, 159, 166, 206
Hess, T. M., 574
Hesse, E., 198, 200, 201
Hesselbrock, V. M., 381
Hetherington, E. M., 347, 348, 349, 350,
    416, 491
Heuer, C. A., 439, 440
Heuer, H., 554
Hewer, A., 407
Hewlett, B. S., 202, 204
Hewlett, S., 105
Hewstone, M., 338
Heyes, C., 136
Heyman, G. D., 273, 333, 343
Heyman, R. E., 484
Hibbert, J. R., 392, 415
Hickey, R. W., 640
Hickling, A. K., 230, 316
Hicks, J. A., 537
Hieber, A., 616
Hietanen, A., 569
Higginbottom, G. M. A., 33
Higgins, C. A., 494, 495
High, P. C., 242
Hilden, D., 162
Hildreth, K., 163
Hilgers, K. K., 217
Hill, C. A., 493
Hill, C. R., 320
Hill, E. J., 259
Hill, E. M., 390
Hill, J. L., 104
Hill, N. E., 64, 393
Hill, N. M., 450
Hill, R. D., 615
Hill, T. D., 573
Hillard, P. J. A., 367
Hillis, S. D., 378
Hillman, C. H., 443
Hill-Soderlund, A. L., 186, 189
Hilt, L. M., 334, 335n
Hinchliff, S., 509
Hind, H., 219
Hinojosa, T., 217
Hinson, J. T., 574
Hiraki, K., 136, 160
Hirasawa, R., 51
Hirsch, C., 550
Hirschberger, G., 645
Hirsh-Pasek, K., 29, 127, 177, 227,
    242, 249
Hiscock, H., 108
Hitch, G., 237
Ho, E., 243
Ho, I. T., 324
Hoch-Espada, A., 352
Hochwarter, W. A., 554
Hock, H. S., 305
Hodges, J., 199
Hodges, R. M., 299
Hodnett, E. D., 99
Hoekstra, C., 47n
Hoenig, H., 574
Hoerr, T., 323
Hofer, J., 32
Hoff, B., 483
Hoff, E., 34, 61, 178, 242
Hoff, T., 374
Hofferth, S. L., 271, 349
Hoffman, A. M., 628

Hoffman, L. W., 350
Hoffman, M. L., 208, 264, 335
Hoffner, C., 258
Hogan, B. E., 514
Hogan, M. J., 372
Hohne, E. A., 142
Holden, G. W., 266
Holdford, R., 482
Holditch-Davis, D., 109
Holdren, J. P., 459
Holland, A. L., 126
Holland, C. R., 170
Holland, J. L., 456
Hollich, G. J., 249
Hollis, C., 279
Holmbeck, G. N., 415
Holmes, R. M., 298
Holobow, N., 317
Holstein, M., 607
Holstein, N., 489
Homer, B., 306, 307
Honein, M. A., 87
Hong, M., 325
Hoobler, J. M, 555
Hood, M., 242
Hooker, K., 538, 574
Hooper, L., 442
Hooyman, N. R., 13, 64, 67, 574, 616,
    617, 626, 627
Hopkins, B., 139
Hopkins, J., 200
Hoppmann, C. A., 608
Horgas, A. L., 618
Horn, J. L., 518, 519
Horn, J. M., 72, 313
Horn, M. C., 539
Horne, R. S. C., 110
Horner, T. M., 186
Hornor, G., 353
Horst, J. S., 164
Hospice Foundation of America, 640,
    653
Hostetler, A. J., 526, 621
Houck, G. M., 190
Houck, J. A., 508
Houlihan, J., 90
House, J. S., 439, 566, 575
Houts, R. M., 484
Hoven, C. W., 37
Howard, A. L., 481
Howard, B. V., 504
Howard, K., 455
Howard, K. S., 63, 354
Howe, M. L., 135, 161, 165, 247
Howe, N., 205
Howell, K. H., 283
Howell, K. K., 87, 88, 89
Howell, L. C., 506
Howell, T. M., 423
Howes, C., 198
Hoyer, W. J., 591
Hoyt, W. T., 663
Hoza, B., 341, 343
Hrubi-Bopp, K. L., 591
HSBC (HSBC Insurance), 626, 629,
    631
Hsing, C., 465
Hsu, C.-C., 90
Hsu, F. L. K., 475
Huang, A., 579
Huang, C.-C., 491
Huang, C. Y., 406
Huang, K.-E., 508
Huang, Q., 492
Huard, R. D., 304
Hubbard, F. O. A., 111

Hubbs-Tait, L., 90
Huberty, P. D., 298
Huddleson, J., 370
Hudson, J. A., 238
Hudson, J. M., 591
Hudziak, J. J., 74
Huebner, C. E., 242
Huesmann, L. R., 271
Huffman, M. L., 555
Hughes, C., 239, 240, 258, 259, 424
Hughes, D., 406
Hughes, G. M., 623
Hughes, J. N., 320, 333
Huh, C. R., 315
Huizenga, H., 387
Huizinga, D., 11
Huizink, A. C., 88
Hulme, C., 237
Hultsch, D. F., 521, 522, 590, 596
Human Genome Program, 46
Human Rights Campaign, 55
Humes, L. E., 503
Humphrey, T., 112
Hungerford-Kresser, H., 321, 395
Hunnius, S., 144
Hunt, C. E., 110
Hursti, U. K., 219
Hurt, H., 87
Hurtado, S., 466
Hurtado-Ortiz, M. T., 237
Hurtig, W. A., 665
Huston, A. C., 247, 414
Huston, T. L., 473
Huttenlocher, J., 155, 390
Huttenlocher, P. R., 122, 126, 128,
    158, 217
Huxhold, O., 573
Huxley, R. R., 504
Huyck, M. H., 276, 540, 541
Hwang, C. P., 484
Hyde, J. S., 105, 187, 409, 414, 422,
    484, 494
Hyer, K., 589
Hyman, B. T., 583
Hymel, S., 341

I

Iacoboni, M., 136
Ickes, M. J., 439
Ickovics, J. R., 379
Ida, M., 641
Iglowstein, I., 128
Imai, M., 248
Im-Bolter, N., 237
Impett, E. A., 331, 402, 473
Indus, K., 346
Infurna, F. J., 438, 509
Ingram, C. D., 115
Inhelder, B., 382, 386
Inouye, S. K., 588
Insel, T., 115
Iozzi, L., 317
Irvine, A. B., 587
Irwin, C. E., Jr., 372
Irwin, J. R., 111
Isabella, R., 199, 200
Isasi, R. M., 55
Ishihara, K., 90
Ispa, J. M., 281
Israel, M., 316
Israelashvili, R., 204
Itti, E., 53
Ivani-Chalian, C., 608
Ivey, P., 187
Ivorra, J. L., 194

Izard, C. E., 186
Izzotti, A., 443

J

Jaakkola, J. J., 88
Jaakkola, R., 642
Jaccard, J., 374
Jacelon, C., 648
Jackey, L. M. H., 621
Jackson, G. R., 502
Jackson, I. R., 155
Jackson, J. J., 608
Jackson, T., 478
Jackson, V. A., 649
Jacobs, J. A., 526
Jacobs, J. E., 331, 332, 334, 343, 388, 457
Jacobs, J. N., 350
Jacobs-Lawson, J. M., 557
Jacobson, J. L., 86, 89, 90
Jacobson, K. C., 415
Jacobson, S. W., 86, 89, 90
Jacoby, L. L., 522
Jacques-Tiura, A. J., 448
Jacquet, P., 51
Jadack, R. A., 409
Jaffee, S. R., 409
Jäger, T., 593
Jambor, T. W., 261
James, J., 367
James, J. B., 540, 604, 607
Jamison, Y., 350, 491
Jang, S. J., 412
Jang, Y., 611
Jankowski, J. J., 144, 163
Janosz, M., 396
Jansen, A., 292
Jansen, B., 387
Jansen, J., 131
Janssen, S. M., 593
Janssens, J. M. A. M., 269
Jarrott, S. E., 551, 627
Jarvis, J. F., 503
Jarvis, P. A., 227, 474
Jasiobedzka, U., 337
Jaudes, P. K., 282
Jayakody, R., 491
Jean, G., 317
Jedrychowski, W., 90
Jeffrey, J., 293
Jelalian, E., 291
Jellinger, K. A., 584, 586
Jemal, A., 510, 511
Jenkins, C., 650
Jenkins, J. M., 240, 346
Jenkins, K. R., 618
Jenkins, R., 440
Jenni, O. G., 368
Jennings, B. J., 433
Jensen, A. R., 71, 312, 314
Jensen, J. S., 443
Jeon, Y.-H., 587
Jeong, S.-H., 394
Jepson, K. L., 594
Jeremy, R. J., 87
Jerome, E. M., 320
Jeynes, W. H., 25, 349
Jha, R., 505
Ji, C. Y., 367
Ji, G., 346
Jiao, S., 346
Jing, Q., 346
Jipson, J. L., 230
Joh, A. S., 143, 147
Johannes, C. B., 504
Johannesen-Schmidt, M., 472
Johansson, A. K., 661

Johnson, B. R., 412
Johnson, C., 316
Johnson, C. L., 625
Johnson, E. K., 142
Johnson, J., 237
Johnson, J. G., 271, 271n
Johnson, K. S., 655
Johnson, M. D., 473, 481n, 484
Johnson, M. H., 21, 122, 124, 145,
    155, 176
Johnson, M. K., 396
Johnson, M. L., 121
Johnson, R. W., 575
Johnson, S. C., 197
Johnson, S. P., 140, 142, 143, 390
Johnston, J., 281
Johnston, L. D., 364, 380, 381
Johnston, M., 575
Johnston, M. V., 122
Jokhi, R. P., 56n
Jolivette, K., 396
Jome, L. M., 458
Jones, A. R., 482
Jones, C. J., 539
Jones, C. M., 390
Jones, E. F., 269
Jones, F., 412
Jones, G. P., 417
Jones, H. E., 87
Jones, I., 298
Jones, J., 91n, 92, 375
Jones, J. M., 557
Jones, K. M., 535, 536
Jones, M. C., 370
Jones, N. A., 260
Jones, S., 136
Jones, S. M., 62
Jones-Rodriguez, G., 372
Jongbloet, P. H., 51
Jopp, D., 567
Jordan, B., 98
Jordan, J., 663
Jordan, J. M., 580
Jose, A., 488
Josefowitz, N., 423
Joseph, R. M., 241
Joshi, A., 473
Joy, M. E., 265
Joyner, K., 420
Juby, H., 350
Juffer, F., 58, 206, 313
Juhl, J., 645
Juhl, T., 186
Julkunen, J., 513
Jun, H., 533, 541
Juntunen, C. L., 556
Jürgensen, M., 274
Jusczyk, P. W., 113, 140, 142, 176, 179
Jussim, L., 320
Jutras-Aswad, D., 88

K

Kable, J. A., 87, 88
Kachhawa, P. S., 646
Kaczmarczyk, M. M., 442
Kagan, J., 7, 155, 158, 192, 193
Kahana, E., 609, 632
Kahn, R. S., 74
Kahne, J. E., 413
Kail, R. V., 162, 295, 302, 308
Kaisa, A., 392
Kakihara, F., 279
Kalil, A., 457, 491
Kalisch, T., 570
Kalish, C. W., 231
Kalish, R. A., 647

Kaller, C. P., 237
Kalmanir, H. M., 469
Kalpouzos, G., 522
Kalra, L., 126
Kaminski, J. W., 423
Kaminski, P. L., 516, 548
Kamo, Y., 547
Kane, P., 187
Kane, R. A., 619
Kang, J. Y., 317
Kang, N. H., 325
Kaplan, M., 524
Kaplow, J. B., 283
Kaplowitz, P. B., 366, 367
Karafantis, D. M., 339
Karasawa, M., 538, 539
Karasik, L. B., 136, 137, 139
Karel, M. J., 611
Karevold, E., 37
Karger, H. J., 67
Karlsson, C., 651
Karney, B. R., 473
Karrass, J., 186, 189
Kassel, J. D., 381
Kastenbaum, R. J., 645, 647, 648, 662,
    663
Kato, I., 110
Katz, E. G., 504
Katz, L. F., 259
Katz, R., 626
Katz, V. L., 102
Katz-Wise, S. L., 484
Katzman, D. K., 372
Kaufert, P., 507, 508
Kaufman, A. S., 519, 590
Kaufman, J., 155
Kaufman, J. C., 322, 389
Kaufman, R., 315
Kavanaugh, R. D., 227
Kavoura, A., 342
Kavšek, M., 134, 143, 170
Kawakami, K., 193
Kawamura, S., 622
Kaya, Y., 483
Kaye, W. H., 372, 373
Kazdin, A. E., 272
Keating, D. P., 331, 384
Keegan, L., 641
Keen, R., 140, 157
Keeton, W. T., 47
Keil, F. C., 230, 248
Keith, J., 576
Keith, P. M., 472
Keith, T. Z., 393
Keller, H., 207, 208
Keller, M., 409
Keller, P. A., 557
Kelley, M. C., 525
Kelley, M. L., 350
Kelley, S. A., 258, 260
Kellman, P. J., 113, 142
Kelly, D. J., 145
Kelly, J., 347, 348, 349
Kelly, N., 322
Kemkes-Grottenhaler, A., 489
Kempe, C. H., 282
Kempen, G., 573
Kemper, S., 594
Kendig, H., 624
Kendler, K. S., 375
Kendrick, D., 222
Kennedy, A. M., 221
Kennedy, C. E., 547
Kennedy, G. E., 547
Kennedy, K. J., 334
Kennedy, K. M., 520, 568

Kennell, J. H., 99
Kenney, G. M., 67
Kenney-Benson, G. A., 389
Kennison, R. F., 520
Kenny, L. C., 378
Kenny, S., 155
Kenyon, B. L., 642
Kerckhoff, A. C., 459
Keren, M., 168
Kerestes, M., 412
Kernis, M. H., 333, 403
Kernohan, W. G., 652
Kerns, K. A., 205, 346
Kerpelman, J. L., 456, 457, 465
Kerr, D. C. R., 264
Kershaw, T. S., 379
Kesebir, S., 411, 412
Kesek, A., 303
Kesler, S. R., 53
Kessler, R. C., 532, 536, 537
Kettl, P., 612
Kettunen, S., 89
Key, J. D., 379
Keyes, C. L. M., 533, 538, 539, 573
Khashan, A. S., 378
Khavkin, J., 503
Khosla, S., 504
Kidd, A. R., III, 569
Kiecolt, K. J., 622
Kieffer, M. J., 318
Kieras, J., 189
Kiernan, K., 488
Killen, M., 269, 337, 338, 339, 410, 411
Killoren, S. E., 416
Kilpatrick, S. D., 473
Kilpatrick, S. W., 292
Kim, G., 188
Kim, J., 541
Kim, J. E., 331, 557, 631
Kim, J. K., 576
Kim, J. M., 337
Kim, J.-Y., 37, 346, 416
Kim, M., 248
Kim, S., 337, 524, 617
Kim, Y. K., 262
Kimbrel, D., 551
Kimbro, R. T., 131
King, A. C., 22, 516
King, L. A., 537
King, N. J., 352
King, P. E., 412
King, P. M., 451, 452
King, R. B., 526
King, R. M., 264
King, V., 350, 491
Kingsberg, S. A., 509
Kinney, D., 419
Kinney, H. C., 110
Kinnunen, M.-L., 130
Kinsella, M. T., 93
Kinser, K., 526
Kinzler, K. D., 159
Kirby, D., 375, 379
Kirchner, G., 296
Kiriakidis, S. P., 342
Kirisci, L., 381
Kirk, K. M., 375
Kirkham, N. Z., 142, 237
Kirkpatrick, M., 320
Kirkwood, T., 564
Kirshenbaum, A. P., 445
Kirshner, B., 413
Kirz, N., 372
Kisilevsky, B. S., 85
Kisly, A., 93
Kistner, J. A., 261, 422

Kitchener, K. S., 451, 452
Kite, M. E., 516, 574
Kitzman, H. J., 94
Kitzmann, K. M., 346
Kiuru, N., 393
Kivipelto, M., 584
Kiyak, H. A., 13, 64, 67, 574, 616, 617, 626, 627
Kjaer, M., 433
Kjønniksen, L., 296, 299
Klaczynski, P. A., 383, 385, 388
Klahr, D., 20
Klara, M. D., 516
Klareskog, L., 581
Klass, D., 661
Klaw, E. L., 380
Klebanov, P. K., 171
Kleespies, P. M., 648
Klein, P. J., 156
Klein, P. S., 34
Kleinbaum, S., 488
Kleinspehn-Ammerlahn, A., 573
Kleitman, S., 395, 397
Klesges, L. M., 88
Kliegel, M., 593
Kliegman, R. M., 49n, 91n
Kliewer, W., 336
Klimes-Dougan, B., 261
Klimstra, T. A., 404
Kline, G. H., 488
Klingman, A., 353
Kloep, M., 467, 471, 630, 631
Klomsten, A. T., 331
Klump, K. L., 373
Klute, M. M., 208
Kluwer, E. S., 484
Knaack, A., 191, 193, 209, 265
Knafl, K. A., 608
Knafo, A., 265
Knapp, P. K., 296
Knickmeyer, R. C., 122
Knieps, L. J., 188
Knight, B. J., 551
Knighton, T., 388
Knobloch, H., 107n
Knoester, C., 485
Knopf, M., 156
Knoppers, B. M., 55
Knowlton, B. J., 394
Knox, D., 465
Ko, K. J., 620
Kobayashi, T., 160
Kobayashi, Y., 235
Kochanska, G., 185, 191, 193, 194, 208, 209, 264, 265, 266, 268, 280
Kochel, K. P., 263
Kochenderfer-Ladd, B., 342
Koenig, B., 377
Koenig, M. A., 231
Koestner, R., 260
Kohen, D. E., 62
Kohlberg, L., 407, 408
Kohli, M., 549
Kohn, M. L., 525, 526
Kol, K. L., 393
Komp, D. M., 647
Konarski, R., 420
Konner, M., 273
Konold, T. R., 263
Konrath, S., 465
Konstantopoulos, S., 318
Kooijman, V., 142
Kopeikina, K. J., 583
Kopp, C. B., 189, 208, 209
Koppe, J. G., 90
Koren, G., 92

Korkman, M., 89
Kornhaber, M. L., 323
Koropeckyj-Cox, T., 489
Koslowski, B., 114
Kossakowska-Petrycka, K., 187
Kostelnik, J. O., 426
Koster, A., 572
Kotkin, J., 467
Kotre, J., 533
Kotter-Grühn, D., 573
Kouba, E., 256
Koury, S. H., 471
Koven, M., 257
Kowalski, R. M., 342
Kozer, E., 87
Kozol, J., 321
Kozulin, A., 24
Krafft, K., 235
Kragstrup, T. W., 433
Krähenbühl, S., 355
Krahn, H. J., 481
Krakow, J. B., 209
Kral, T. V. E., 291
Kramer, A. F., 443, 521, 522, 568
Kramer, D. A., 596
Kramer, S. E., 570
Krampe, R. T., 521, 524
Kraus, U., 156
Krause, N. M., 609, 610, 612, 617
Kravetz, S., 643
Krawinkel, M., 132
Kray, J., 521
Krcmar, M., 159
Krebs, D. L., 409, 412
Kreppner, J. M., 127, 199
Kressley-Mba, R. A., 156
Krettenauer, T., 404
Krevans, J., 265
Krings, F., 464
Krishnamoorthy, J. S., 291
Kroger, J., 402, 404
Krogh, H. R., 344
Kroonenberg, P. M., 198
Kropf, N. P., 567
Krumhansl, C. L., 140
Kubicek, B., 630
Kubik, M. Y., 372
Kubitschek, W. N., 395
Kübler-Ross, E., 647
Kubotera, T., 650
Kubzansky, L. D., 575
Kuchner, J., 189
Kuczynski, L., 266, 279
Kudo, N., 142
Kuebli, J., 238, 274
Kuersten-Hogan, R., 486
Kugelmass, J., 322
Kuh, D., 506
Kuhl, P. K., 135, 141
Kuhn, D., 20, 306, 382, 384, 385, 388
Kuk, L. S., 404
Kuklinski, M. R., 320
Kulik, K., 620
Kumar, S., 56n
Kumpf, M., 312
Kunemund, H., 549
Kunkel, A. W., 473
Kunnen, E. S., 404, 465
Kupersmidt, J. B., 424
Kuppens, S., 270, 279
Kurdek, L. A., 280, 481, 488
Kurganskaya, M. E., 218
Kurtz-Costes, B., 332
Kwan, V. S. Y., 539
Kwok, O., 320
Kwok, T. C. Y., 646

Kwon, Y. H., 503
Kyratzis, A., 276

L
Laanan, F. S., 526
Labban, J. D., 443
Labouvie-Vief, G., 20, 452, 453, 464, 538, 539, 594, 605, 606, 616
Lachance, J. A., 389
Lachance-Grzela, M., 481
Lachman, M. E., 535, 537, 538, 540, 573, 574, 578, 610
Lachs, M., 617
Lacourse, E., 424
Ladd, G. W., 263, 340, 341, 343
Ladouceur, C. D., 422
Lafosse, A., 230
LaFraniere, S., 346
Lagasse, L. L., 87
Lagattuta, K. H., 258, 335
Lagnado, L., 353
La Greca, A. M., 341, 419
Lai, S.-C., 481
Laible, D., 258, 263
Laibstain, S. E., 443
Laird, R. D., 341, 424
Laitman, C. J., 86
Lalonde, C. E., 306, 405
Lalonde, R. N., 479
Lam, S., 334
Lamarche, V., 346
Lamaze, F., 99
Lamb, M. E., 67, 171, 172, 204, 206, 246, 345, 486
Lamberg, L., 506
Lambert, J. D., 541, 544
Lambert, S. M., 438
Lambert, W., 317
Lammlein, S. E., 554
Lamont, E., 302
Lampl, M., 121
Lampman-Petraitis, C., 369
Lamuela-Raventos, R., 433
Lancy, D. F., 236
Landale, N. S., 33
Lander, E., 459
Landman, J., 537
Lang, A. R., 89
Lang, F. R., 9, 610, 614, 615, 616
Lang, I. A., 63
Lang, M., 459
Lange, G., 307
Langehough, S. O., 465
Langer, G., 445, 446
Langer, J., 161
Langhinrichsen-Rohling, J., 422
Langlois, J. H., 145
Langman, L., 156
Langosch, D., 548
Langsetmo, L., 513
Lanier, C. S., 534
Lansford, J. E., 266, 267, 341, 347, 348, 419, 476, 477, 541
Lantz, P. M., 575
Lanz, M., 464
Lanzi, R. G., 173, 246
Lapierr, S., 613
Lapkin, S., 317
Lapsley, D. K., 387
Larbi, A., 571
Largo, R. H., 295
Laris, B. A., 379
Larkin, S., 307
Larsen, J. A., 316
Larsen, J. E., 536
Larsen, J. T., 335

Larsen, P., 571
Larsen-Rife, D., 474
Larson, D. G., 663
Larson, R. W., 369, 416, 417, 624
Larsson, M., 570
Larzelere, R. E., 267, 280
Lashley, F. R., 46, 47n, 48, 49n
Latendresse, S. J., 62, 63
Latner, J. D., 292
Lattanzi-Licht, M., 662
Latz, S., 129
Lau, C. Q., 488
Lau, D. T., 575
Laucht, M., 106
Lauderdale, D. S., 110
Lauer, P. A., 351
Laumann, E. O., 445, 446, 447, 509
Laumann-Billings, L., 483
Laungani, P., 642
Laureys, S., 641
Laursen, B., 61, 342, 370, 415, 416
Lautenschlager, N. T., 585
Lavelli, M., 185
Lavner, J. A., 473
Law, C., 440
Law, K. L., 88
Lawn, J. E., 103
Lawrence, A. R., 619
Lawrence, D. A., 437
Lawrence, E., 484
Lawrence, K., 53
Lawson, K. R., 189
Lawton, J. S., 512
Lawton, M. P., 574
Lazar, I., 245
Lazarus, B. N., 336
Lazarus, R. S., 336
Lazear, K. J., 492
Lazinski, M. J., 92, 93
Le, T. N., 596
Leaper, C., 178, 274, 276, 296, 343
Leavitt, L. A., 102
LeBel, T. P., 534
LeBlanc, L. A., 294
Lecanuet, J.-P., 85
Leclerc, N., 617
Lecuyer, E., 190
Ledeen, K., 419
Lee, C., 516
Lee, C.-Y. S., 484
Lee, D. N., 106
Lee, E. E., 551
Lee, E. O., 609
Lee, J. C., 575
Lee, J. M., 366
Lee, J. S., 242, 243
Lee, K., 98, 250, 336
Lee, M. M., 574
Lee, P. P., 569
Lee, R., 426
Lee, S., 324
Lee, S. J., 85
Lee, V. E., 178, 242
Lee, W. S. C., 450, 568
Lee, Y., 262
Leech, R., 175
Leerkes, E. M., 25, 109, 189
Leet, T., 92
LeFevre, J., 242
Lefkowitz, E. S., 465, 476
Legacy Project, 545
Legare, C. H., 343
Legerstee, M., 188
Legge, G. E., 570
Le Grand, R., 125
Le Grange, D., 373

Lehert, P., 509
Lehman, D. R., 384
Lehman, M., 304
Lehr, V. T., 112
Lehrer, E. L., 480
Lehrer, J. A., 375
Lehtonen, L., 112
Leifheit-Limson, E., 574
Leinbach, M. D., 270
Leis, J. A., 466
Leiter, M. P., 554
Lemaitre, H., 435n
Leman, P. J., 410
Lemche, E., 235
Lemery, K. S., 177
Lemmon, G., 555
Lempert, H., 250
L'Engle, K. L., 374
Lengua, L. J., 191, 348
Lenhart, A., 389, 418
Lenroot, R. K., 367, 450
Leon, K., 348, 490
Leonesio, M. V., 553
Lepage, J.-F., 136
Lerner, M. D., 343
Lerner, R. M., 5, 8, 70
Lesesne, C., 486
LeSieur, K., 263
Leslie, A. M., 159, 241
Leslie, L. A., 481
Lester, B. M., 87, 111, 111n, 114
Letherby, G., 489
Letiecq, B. L., 481
Leuner, B., 115
Leung, M. C. M., 564
LeVay, S., 375
Levendosky, A. A., 198
Levenson, R. W., 489, 620
Leventhal, T., 62, 63, 425
Levi, J., 293
Levine, B., 593
Levine, C., 407
Levine, J. A., 457
Levine, L. J., 258
LeVine, R. A., 200
Levine, S. C., 390
Levinson, D. J., 470, 536
Levinson, S. C., 174
Levitt, M. J., 553
Levitt, T., 520
Levy, B. R., 570, 574
Levy, D., 592
Levy, G. D., 344
Levy, S. R., 338, 339
Levy-Shiff, R., 204
Lewin, A. C., 622
Lewin, D. S., 368
Lewis, C., 204, 345, 486
Lewis, H., 419
Lewis, K. G., 487
Lewis, M., 186, 188, 189, 193, 207, 260
Lewis, M. D., 185
Lewis, T. L., 125
Lewko, J. H., 225
Leyk, D., 437
Li, D.-K., 110
Li, H., 98
Li, P., 177
Li, S.-C., 310, 520, 521, 590, 596
Li, Y. J., 331
Li, Z., 194
Liang, J., 612
Liben, L. S., 273, 277, 278, 300, 344, 390
Lichter, D. T., 472, 480
Lickliter, R., 70, 71, 103, 146

Lidstone, J. S. M., 234
Lidz, C. S., 315
Lidz, J., 175, 249, 250
Liebaers, I., 56n
Liebbrant, S., 618
Lieberman, E. S., 101
Lieberman, R. M., 265
Liederman, J., 218
Liem, J. H., 406
Lien, M.-C., 521
Lieven, E., 179, 249
Li-Grining, C. P., 193
Lilgendahl, J. P., 534
Lillard, A. S., 168, 227, 245
Limber, S. P., 342
Lin, F. R., 503, 573
Lin, I.-F., 544, 621
Linares, T. J., 87
Lincoln, K. D., 612
Lindau, S. T., 504, 509
Lindauer, M. S., 525
Lindberg, S. M., 389, 414
Lindblad, F., 88
Linden, W., 514, 648
Lindenberger, U., 7, 8, 71, 573, 590, 596
Lindsay-Hartz, J., 260
Lindsey, E. W., 25, 60, 227, 263, 332, 403
Linebarger, D. L., 246
Linebarger, J. S., 643
Linley, P. A., 596
Linn, K., 159
Linn, M. C., 390
Linn, R. L., 321
Linver, M. R., 170
Lippe, T. van der, 480
Lips, H. M., 493
Lipsitt, L. P., 110
Lipton, J., 160
Liszkowski, U., 176, 177
Little, T. D., 269
Littlejohn, A., 222
Littlejohn, K., 224
Liu, A. H., 293
Liu, C.-C., 584
Liu, H.-M., 141
Liu, J., 132, 220, 291
Liu, K., 584
Liu, L., 436
Liu, L. L., 390
Livingston, G., 489
Lizotte, A. J., 379
Lleras, C., 321
Lloyd, L., 322
Lloyd, M. E., 238
Loch, J., 94
Lochman, J. E., 270
Lock, J., 372, 373
Lock, M., 507, 508
Lockhart, K. L., 230
Lockwood, R. L., 346
Loeb, S., 246
Loehlin, J. C., 70, 72, 193, 194, 313
Loewen, N. A., 503
Logan, R. L., 533, 534
Loganovskaja, T. K., 90
Loganovsky, K. N., 90
Lohman, D. F., 310
Lohrmann, S., 322
Loken, E., 37, 476
Lollis, S., 279
Loman, M. M., 127
Long, D. D., 645
Long, M. V., 567
Longo, M. R., 136, 155
Loock, C., 89
Looker, D., 389

Loomans, E. M., 93
Lopez, A., 91n, 92
Lopez, B., 416
Lopez, C. M., 422
López, M. J. R., 479
Lorenz, K., 22, 196
Lorenz, R. P., 93
Lou, E., 479
Louie, V., 32
Louis, J., 108
Lourenco, O., 269
Loutzenhiser, L., 204
Lövdén, M., 596
Love, J. M., 173, 203, 246
Lovegreen, L. D., 544, 545
Lovejoy, M., 493
Low, J. A., 85
Low, S. M., 25
Lowenstein, A., 626
Lowis, M. J., 605
Lown, A. E., 444
Lozoff, B., 129
Lubart, T. I., 323, 454, 524, 525
Lubinski, D., 389
Luby, J., 260
Lucas, K., 533
Lucas, R. E., 487, 608
Lucas, S., 421
Lucas, S. R., 395
Lucas-Thompson, R., 263
Luce, P. A., 113
Luciana, M., 22, 303
Ludemann, P. M., 145
Luecken, L. J., 661, 662
Lugton, J., 650n
Lukas, C., 661
Luke, A., 442
Lukowski, A. F., 220
Lun, J., 343
Luna, B., 125, 302, 384
Lund, D. A., 587, 608, 610, 622, 623, 632, 659, 660, 663
Lund, N., 87
Lundy, B. L., 201, 204
Lunn, M., 596
Luo, L., 520, 591
Luo, L. Z., 98
Luo, Y., 110, 160
Luong, G., 616
Lupyan, G., 166
Lusardi, A., 557
Luster, T., 378
Lustig, C., 521, 522
Luthar, S. S., 62, 63
Luxembourg Income Study, 68
Luyckx, K., 404, 464, 468
Lynam, D., 269, 270, 341
Lynch, S. K., 266
Lyness, K. S., 555
Lyon, T. D., 240, 355
Lyons, M., 642, 643
Lyons, S. T., 494, 495
Lyons-Ruth, K., 200, 206
Lytton, H., 48

M
Ma, F., 336
Ma, L., 168
Maas, F. K., 269
Macaluso, A., 504
Macartney, S. E., 32, 33
Maccoby, E. E., 273, 274, 276, 345, 350, 414
MacDonald, S. W. S., 521, 590, 596
MacDonald, W. L., 490
MacDorman, M. F., 110

Macek, P., 464
Machin, G. A., 48, 54
Mackenzie, J., 514
Mackey, A. L., 433
Mackey, K., 279
Mackey-Bilaver, L., 282
Mackie, S., 305
Mackinnon, S. P., 470
MacLean, P. S., 441, 442
Macones, G. A., 101
Macpherson, A., 222, 294
MacWhinney, B., 20, 177
Madden, D. J., 521
Madden, M., 599, 626
Madden, T., 406
Maddi, S. R., 516
Maddox, G. L., 614, 618
Madey, S. F., 473
Madigan, S., 200
Madnawat, A. V. S., 646
Madole, K. M., 164
Madon, S., 320
Madrona, M. M., 100
Madsen, S. A., 186
Madsen, S. D., 345, 417, 476, 477
Maffei, L., 125
Magalhães, J. P. de, 433
Mageau, G. A., 200
Maggs, J. L., 351
Maglio, C. J., 665
Magnuson, K. A., 61, 246, 406
Magnussen, S., 355
Magnusson, D., 371
Magolda, M. B., 451
Magos, L., 90
Maguire, M., 259
Mahady, G. B., 508
Mahanran, L. G., 436
Mahay, J., 509, 622
Mahon, M. M., 643
Mahoney, A., 264
Maier, S. F., 577
Main, M., 197, 198, 201
Maitland, S. B., 520
Majdandžic, M., 191
Majnemer, A., 139
Makel, M. C., 323
Makishita, H., 581
Makrantonaki, E., 504
Malanchuk, O., 413
Malatesta, C. Z., 189
Malcuit, G., 379
Malhotra, B. A., 385
Malina, R. M., 223n, 364
Malkin, C., 167
Malley, J. E., 12
Malone, M. M., 646
Mandara, J., 61
Mandler, J. M., 165, 166
Manfra, L., 234
Mangelsdorf, S. C., 191, 256
Mani, T. M., 521
Mann, T., 168, 227, 235
Mannell, R., 624
Manole, M. D., 640
Manson, J. E., 443
Manzoli, L., 621
Mao, A., 129
Maquestiaux, F., 521
Maratsos, M., 249
Marchman, V. A., 126, 177, 250
Marcia, J. E., 403, 404, 469
Marcon, R. A., 245, 246
Marcus, G. F., 249
Marcus-Newhall, A., 517
Mardh, P. A., 91n

Marenco, A., 546
Marentette, P. F., 176
Mareschal, D., 21
Margie, N. G., 269
Margrett, J. A., 567
Marian, V., 159
Mariano, K. A., 340
Mariner, C. L., 267
Marjorano, M., 178
Marjoribanks, J., 506
Markell, M., 338
Markey, C. N., 472
Markey, P. M., 472
Markman, E. M., 153, 159, 248, 249, 383
Markman, H. J., 488
Markova, G., 188
Markovits, H., 340, 384, 417
Marks, A., 239
Marks, A. K., 33
Marks, G. N., 395
Marks, K. S., 155
Marks, N. F., 533, 541, 544, 545, 550
Marks, R., 513
Markstrom, C. A., 469
Markus, H. R., 538, 607
Marlier, L., 112, 113
Marmot, M. G., 449
Marquis, J., 594
Marra, R., 452
Marrott, H., 156
Marschik, P. B., 83
Marsee, M. A., 270
Marsh, H. W., 257, 296, 331, 332, 333, 395, 397, 403
Marshall, B. J., 662
Marshall, N. L., 494
Marshall-Baker, A., 103
Marsland, K. W., 67
Martel, L. D., 475
Martin, A., 170
Martin, C. L., 193, 208, 274, 276, 277, 278
Martin, G. L., 18
Martin, K. A., 368
Martin, M., 595, 608
Martin, M. C., 508
Martin, M. M., 240
Martin, N. G., 194
Martin, P., 567
Martin, R., 53
Martin, R. P., 101
Martin, T. L., 660
Martinez, G., 377
Martinez, G. M., 489
Martinez, M. L., 467
Martinez-Frias, M. L., 89
Martínez-Jarreta, B., 554
Martinot, D., 343
Martinson, I. M., 662
Martinussen, M., 404
Martlew, M., 225
Maruna, S., 533, 534
Maruta, T., 516
Marx, J., 548
Marx, R. W., 21
Marzolf, D. P., 228
Masataka, N., 178
Masciadrelli, B. P., 350
Mash, C., 165
Mashburn, A. J., 246, 263
Mashek, D. J., 260
Maslach, C., 554
Mason, M. G., 410
Masoro, E. J., 580
Massachusetts Expert Panel on End of Life Care, 652

Masson, P., 438
Masten, A. S., 10, 11, 354, 413, 416, 469
Masters, R. K., 566
Mastropieri, D., 113
Masur, E. F., 178, 303
Mather, M., 605
Mathews, T. J., 110
Matjasko, J. L., 396
Matsuba, M. K., 62
Matsunaga, K., 581
Matteson, E. L., 581
Matthews, K. A., 513
Matthews, L. G., 556
Matthews, R. A., 554
Mattison, S. N., 505
Mattson, M. P., 433, 584
Mattson, S. N., 88, 89
Mauer, D., 227
Maume, D. J., Jr., 555
Maupin, R., 95
Maurer, D., 125
Maurer, T. J., 554
Mauro, J. A., 191
Mavroveli, S., 313
Mayberry, R., 95
Mayberry, R. I., 174
Maybery, M., 241
Mayer, C. J., 621
Mayer, J. D., 313
Mayeux, L., 339
Mayhew, E. M. Y., 238
Maynard, A. E., 24, 168, 301, 314
Mazerolle, M., 574
Mazzocco, M. M. M., 389
McAdams, D. P., 65, 533, 534, 535
McAdoo, H. P., 66
McAlister, A., 240
McArdle, J. J., 519
McAuley, C., 378, 380
McAuley, E., 506, 516
McAuslan, P., 448
McBee, M. T., 323
McBride-Chang, C., 308
McCabe, A., 242, 317
McCabe, P., 449
McCall, R. B., 170
McCandliss, B. D., 22, 303
McCarthy, B., 475n
McCarthy, E. J., 475n
McCartney, K., 72, 171, 194, 203, 206, 320
McCarton, C., 104
McCarty, M. E., 140, 157
McClain, C. S., 650
McClain-Jacobson, C., 650
McClowry, S. G., 662
McClure, S., 367
McColgan, K. L., 237
McConachie, H., 53
McCormack, T., 237
McCoy, J. K., 205
McCrae, R., 537, 542, 542n
McCune, L., 227
McCurry, S. M., 571
McDade, T., 129
McDaniel, M. A., 577, 593
McDill, T., 624
McDonagh, M. S., 101
McDonald, L., 621
McDonough, L., 156, 166
McDowell, D. J., 336
McDuff, P., 421
McElderry, D., 368
McElhaney, K. B., 415, 416
McElwain, N. L., 199, 205
McEwen, B. S., 433

McFarlane, J., 448
McGee, L. M., 242
McGillivray, S., 597
McGinley, M., 260
McGoldrick, M., 478, 651, 660, 664
McGrath, S. K., 99
McGregor, K. K., 248
McGue, M., 370, 381
McGuire, S., 346
McHale, J. P., 60, 484, 485, 486
McHale, S. M., 345, 346, 351, 406, 473, 479
McIntosh, H., 405
McIntosh, W. D., 621
McIntyre, C. W., 303
McKee-Ryan, F. M., 556
McKenna, J. J., 129
McKeown, M. G., 308
McKim, W. A., 445
McKinney, C., 403
McKown, C., 315, 321
McKusick, V. A., 48n, 49n, 51
McLanahan, S., 348
McLaughlin, K. A., 127
McLean, K. C., 606
McLearn, K. T., 65
McLoyd, V. C., 173, 246, 267
McMahon, C. A., 186
McNeilly, A., 581
MCR Vitamin Study Research Group, 92
McWhirter, E. H., 457
Mead, G. H., 330
Mead, M., 98, 362
Meade, C. S., 379
Meadus, R. J., 458
Meaney, J., 51
Meaney, M. J., 74
Medina, R., 473
Meegan, S. P., 595
Meeks, S., 611
Meeus, W. H. J., 370, 404, 405, 417, 472
Mehlmadrona, L., 100
Mehlson, M., 606
Mehta, D., 640
Meier, A., 420, 421
Meijer, A. M., 415
Meijnen, G. W., 392
Meins, E., 234, 240
Meisels, S. J., 308
Mejía-Arauz, R., 167
Melby, M. K., 507, 508
Melby-Lervag, M., 237
Melenhorst, A. S., 574
Melinder, A., 355
Meltzoff, A. N., 135, 136, 156, 159, 176, 188, 230, 257, 317, 343
Melzi, G., 317
Mendelsohn, G. A., 621, 622
Mendle, J., 367, 371
Mendola, P., 366n
Mendoza, J. R., 219
Meneilly, G. S., 581
Mennella, J. A., 112
Menon, U., 508, 517
Ment, L. R., 102
Mercer, C. H., 447
Mercy, J. A., 221
Merikangas, K. R., 362
Merline, A., 552
Merriam, S. B., 606
Merrilees, C. E., 60
Messinger, D. S., 185
Messman, S. J., 477
Metheny, J., 457
Methven, L., 570
MetLife, 549, 550

Metz, E. C., 405, 412, 413
Metzger, A., 479
Meyer, B. J. F., 595
Meyer, I. H., 447
Meyer, J., 566
Meyer, J. R., 355, 426
Meyer, R., 130
Meyer, S., 259, 260
Meyer-Bahlburg, H. F. L., 376
Meyers, L. S., 574
Mezei, L., 651
Mezulis, A. H., 187, 422
Michael, A., 370
Michael, G. F., 217
Michael, R. T., 445, 447
Michalik, N. M., 260
Michels, K. B., 131n
Michiels, D., 204
Mick, E., 305
Mickler, C., 595
Midgett, C., 222
Midgley, C., 391
Midlin, M., 440
Mienaltowski, A., 450, 524
Mikami, A. Y., 343
Mikulincer, M., 645, 660
Milevsky, A., 279
Milgrom, J., 103
Milkie, M. A., 485, 626
Miller, A. L., 205
Miller, D. L., 526
Miller, D. N., 423
Miller, J., 526, 548
Miller, J. G., 411
Miller, L. M. S., 593
Miller, L. S., 521
Miller, L. T., 310
Miller, M. A., 220
Miller, M. J., 442
Miller, P. A., 336
Miller, P. D., 308
Miller, P. H., 161, 235, 306
Miller, P. J., 32, 168, 257, 578
Miller, R. B., 484
Miller, S., 420
Miller, S. A., 240, 306
Milligan, K., 239
Mills, R., 265
Mills, R. S. L., 260
Mills, T. L., 125, 548
Millsap, R. E., 608
Miner-Rubino, K., 533, 535, 537
Minkler, M., 548
Minkoff, H., 54
Mintz, J., 257
Miracle, J. A., 142
Misailidi, P., 335
Mischel, W., 265
Mishra, S., 506
Mistry, R. S., 61, 244
Mitchell, A., 112
Mitchell, B. A., 544, 545
Mitchell, B. D., 566
Mitchell, K. J., 374, 418
Mitchell, P., 331
Mitnick, D. M., 484
Miura, I. T., 309
Mize, J., 263, 279, 345
Modrek, S., 556
Moen, P., 492, 526, 527, 557, 607, 630, 631
Moens, E., 291
Moffitt, T. E., 221, 424, 425, 482
Mohite, P., 277
Mohr, J. J., 475
Mok, M. M. C., 334

Mokdad, A. H., 441, 442
Molfese, V. J., 244
Moll, H., 230
Moll, I., 235
Mollenkopf, H., 616
Moller, K., 484
Moller, L. C., 276
Mommaerts, C., 575
Monahan, K. C., 374
Mondloch, C. J., 125, 145
Monesson, A., 141
Monin, J. K., 586
Monk, C. S., 93, 122, 241
Monsour, M., 477, 625
Montague, D. P. F., 188
Montemayor, R., 330
Montepare, J. M., 572
Montero, I., 23
Montgomery, D. E., 240, 306
Montgomery, G. L., 108, 128
Montgomery, M. J., 404, 454, 469
Montgomery, P., 379
Montgomery, R. J. V., 549, 550
Montgomery-Goodnough, A., 465
Montorsi, F., 507
Montoya, A. G., 444
Moody, J., 423
Moolchan, E. T., 74
Moon, C., 113
Moon, R. Y., 110
Moore, A., 623
Moore, C., 273
Moore, D. R., 378
Moore, D. S., 390
Moore, E. G. J., 314
Moore, H., 649
Moore, J. B., 225
Moore, K. A., 379, 415
Moore, K. L., 47, 56n, 81, 81n, 82, 83, 84, 86, 122
Moore, M. K., 135, 136, 156
Moore, M. R., 378
Moore, P. J., 333, 334
Moore, R. W., 144
Moore, S. G., 114
Moore, W. S., 451
Moorman, S. M., 579
Moosbrugger, H., 310
Moran, C., 199, 200
Moran, S., 31, 323
Morawska, A., 267
Morelli, G. A., 129, 187, 236
Moreno, A. J., 208
Morgan, B., 241
Morgan, J. D., 642
Morgan, J. L., 141
Morgan, P. L., 62
Morgan, S. P., 446
Morgan-Lopez, A. A., 468
Morikawa, H., 178
Moro-García, M. A., 571
Morrill, M. I., 60
Morris, A. S., 259
Morris, G., 164
Morris, J., 649
Morris, J. E., 351
Morris, J. K., 53
Morris, P. A., 24, 59, 71
Morris, W. L., 487
Morrison, D. R., 379
Morrison, V., 575, 576, 611
Morrongiello, B. A., 146, 222
Morrow, D. F., 376
Morse, S. B., 102
Mortimer, J. T., 478
Morton, J., 145

Mosby, L., 267
Mosca, L., 512
Mosely-Howard, G. S., 66
Moses, L. J., 188, 240
Mosher, W. D., 375
Moshman, D., 20, 383, 384, 385, 402, 451, 452
Moskowitz, D. S., 533
Moss, E., 200, 201, 206
Moss, S. B., 489
Mossey, P. S., 88
Moss-Racusin, C. A., 458
Mosteller, F., 318
Motel-Klingebiel, A., 549
Motl, R. W., 365
Mottus, R., 346
Mounts, N. S., 37, 420
Moxley, D. P., 455
Moyer, A., 488
Moylan, A. R., 307
Mroczek, D. K., 332, 539, 608, 613
Mrug, S., 343
Mu, X., 324
Mu, Y., 309
Muckle, G., 90
Mueller, C. M., 333
Muenchow, S., 67
Muentener, P., 159
Mukamal, K., 632
Mulatu, M. S., 525, 596
Mulder, E. J., 88
Mullainathan, S., 494
Mullen, M., 136
Müller, F., 91n
Müller, O., 132
Müller, U., 240, 384
Mullett-Hume, E., 37
Mullis, I. V. S., 388
Mulvaney, M. K., 234
Mulvey, E. P., 425
Mumme, D. L., 188
Mummey, P., 241
Munakata, Y., 20, 21, 155, 174
Mundy, P., 241
Munholland, K. A., 197, 201
Munnell, A. H., 557
Munroe, R. L., 273
Muret-Wagstaff, S., 114
Murinson, B. B., 651
Muris, P., 352
Murphy, B. C., 191
Murphy, L. M., 417
Murphy, S. A., 661
Murphy, T. H., 126
Murray, A. D., 109
Murray, C., 312
Murray, K. T., 193, 208
Murray, S. L., 473, 482
Murry, V. M., 346
Musick, K., 491
Mussen, P. H., 265, 370
Mustanski, B. S., 366, 367
Mustard, C., 556
Mutchler, J. E., 631
Mutran, E. J., 545, 546, 649
Muzzatti, B., 389
Myers, D. G., 541
Myers, G. J., 90
Myers, L., 352
Myers, M. G., 381
Myerson, J., 520
Myowa-Yamakoshi, M., 135

N
Nadel, J., 207
Nader, K., 663
Nader, P. R., 365

Nagel, S. K., 61
Nagell, K., 176
Nagin, D. S., 424
Naglieri, J., 234
Nagy, E., 135
Nagy, W. E., 316
Naigles, L. G., 177
Naigles, L. R., 248
Naishadham, D., 510, 511
Naito, M., 306
Najor-Durack, A., 455
Nakamura, J., 540, 595
Nánez, J., Sr., 142
Napier, A. Y., 544
Narasimham, G., 385
Narayan, C., 517
Narr, K. L., 305
Nass, C., 394
Nassar, A. H., 93
Nastasi, B. K., 247
Natale, K., 333
Natale, R., 100
National Academies Committee on National Statistics, 627
National Association for Sport and Physical Education, 298
National Center for Biotechnology Information, 50
National Center for Injury Prevention and Control, 294
National Center on Elder Abuse, 627, 628
National Coalition for the Homeless, 62
National Council of Youth Sports, 296
National Federation of State High School Associations, 364
National Institute on Aging, 583, 584, 585
National Institute on Drug Abuse, 444
National Institutes of Health, 57, 217
National Research Council, 392
National Women's Law Center, 378
Natsuaki, M. N., 369, 370, 371
Navarro, A. M., 100
Naveh-Benjamin, M., 522, 591, 592
Nawrocki, T., 260
Nazzi, T., 231
Neal, M. B., 550, 551
Needham, B. L., 377
Needham, E., 140
Needlman, R., 129
Neely, A. S., 522
Neff, K. D., 337, 409
Neff, L. A., 473
Neiderman, D., 156
Neimeyer, R. A., 645, 646, 660, 663, 665
Neisser, U., 159
Neitzel, C., 234
Nelson, C. A., III, 24, 83, 122, 123, 124, 126, 127, 141, 145, 163, 164, 217, 218, 450, 464
Nelson, D. A., 204, 270, 271, 279, 281, 340, 341
Nelson, H. D., 506
Nelson, K., 257
Nelson, L. J., 464, 465, 466, 467, 468, 469
Nelson, M., 396
Nelson, N. M., 274
Nelson, S. E., 121
Nemet, D., 293
Nemeth, R., 277
Nepomnyaschy, L., 105
Nerenberg, L., 628
Neri, Q., 54
Nesdale, D., 337, 338
Nesselroade, J. R., 614

Neto, F., 478
Nettelbeck, T., 302
Netto, D., 146
Netz, Y., 540
Neubach, B., 554
Neufeld, S. J., 189
Neugarten, B. L., 471, 502, 535
Neuhouser, M. L., 577
Neukam, K. A., 557
Neuman, S. B., 178
Neupert, S. D., 540, 573, 578, 610
Neville, H. J., 125
Newbury, J., 651
Newcomb, A. F., 343, 417
Newcomb, M. D., 396
Newcombe, N. S., 155, 238, 390
Newcomer, R., 619
Newell, L. D., 280
Newell, L. L., 278, 279, 346
Newland, L. A., 201, 202
Newman, F., 502
Newnham, C. A., 103
Newport, E. L., 142, 174, 175
Newsom, J. T., 610
Newton, N., 98
Newton, N. J., 471, 533
Ng, F. F., 334
Ng, T. W. H., 553
Ngata, P., 650
Nguyen, S. P., 275, 275n
Nguyen, T. M., 55
Nguyen, T. V., 12
Nguyen, U.-S. D. T., 101
NHPCO (National Hospice and
  Palliative Care Organization), 651,
  652, 653
Ni, Y., 299
Niccolai, L. M., 377
NICHD (National Institute of Child
  Health and Human Development)
  Early Child Care Research Network,
  171, 172, 202, 203,
  246, 250
Nicholls, T. L., 482
Nichols, K. E., 266
Nichols, W. C., 489
Nicholson, J. M., 349, 350
Nickerson, P., 296
Nickman, S. L., 58, 662
Nicoladis, E., 317
Niehaus, M. D., 220
Nielsen, L. S., 292
Nielsen, M., 207
Nielsen, N. M., 93
Nielsen, S. J., 440
Nielson, D., 643
Nievar, M. A., 200
Nigam, M., 20
Ningiuruvik, L., 314
Nippold, M. A., 316
Nisbett, R. E., 312, 314, 384
Nishitani, S., 112
Noack, M. G., 526, 555
Noble, K. G., 102, 303
Noe, G. F., 95
Noël, M.-P., 232
Noguera, P., 324
Noice, H., 523
Noice, T., 523
Nolen-Hoeksema, S., 421, 422, 450
Noll, J., 518
Noller, P., 347
Nomaguchi, K. M., 485
Noom, M. J., 370
Noonan, K., 101
Noppe, I. C., 643, 644

Noppe, L. D., 643, 644
Nordhus, I. H., 587
Norris, J., 545
Norris, L., 595
Norwich, B., 322
Nosarti, C., 101
Nosek, B. A., 389
Noterdaeme, M., 218
Nucci, L. P., 269, 337, 409, 410
Nucci, M. S., 409
Nugent, J. K., 114
Nuland, S. B., 640
Numan, M., 115
Nunes, T., 243
Nunez-Smith, M., 394
Nurmi, J.-E., 279, 280, 392
Nuttall, R. L., 391
Nyberg, L., 522
Nye, B., 318
Nyquist, L., 524

O

Oakes, L. M., 164, 165, 166
Oakland, T. D., 312, 314
Oates, G., 525, 596
Oberecker, R., 175
Öberg, C., 570
Obermeyer, C. M., 506
Obradović, J., 11, 62, 413
Obray, S. J., 623
O'Brien, A., 56n
O'Brien, M., 58, 351
O'Brien, M. A., 465
O'Connor, A. R., 293
O'Connor, E., 320
O'Connor, P., 651
O'Connor, P. G., 445
O'Connor, P. J., 92
O'Connor, T. G., 93, 125, 346
O'Dea, J. A., 291
OECD (Organisation for Economic
  Cooperation and Development),
  67n, 101, 105, 388, 395, 438, 447,
  455, 509, 588
Ogan, A., 168, 227, 235
Ogawa, J. R., 474
Ogbu, J. U., 395
Ogden, C. L., 291
Oh, J.-H., 617
O'Halloran, C. M., 646
Ohannessian, C. M., 381
Ohgi, S., 114
Ohlemiller, K. K., 503
Ohlott, P. J., 495
Okagaki, L., 311
Okami, P., 129
Okamoto, K., 576
Okamoto, Y., 233, 295, 309
Okanda, M., 207
O'Keefe, M. J., 102
O'Laughlin, E. M., 484
Old, S. R., 522
Olds, D. L., 94
O'Leary, D., 488
O'Leary, S. G., 267
Olfman, S., 380
Olineck, K. M., 157
Oliveira, F. L., 436
Ollendick, T. H., 352
Oller, D. K., 176
Olmstead, R., 129
O'Loughlin, M., 385
Olsen, D. M., 445
Olsen, J. A., 280, 391, 415
Olsen, S. F., 278, 279, 280, 346
Olshansky, S. J., 567, 573

Olson, D., 92
Olson, L. S., 396
O'Malley, P., 507
Omar, H., 368
Ondejko, L., 222
Ondrusek, N., 40
O'Neil, M. E., 457
O'Neil, R., 61
O'Neill, G., 631
O'Neill, M., 178
O'Neill, R., 343
Ong, A., 406
Ong, A. D., 608, 660
Ong, W., 322
Onisto, N., 437
Ontai, L. L., 240
Onwuteaka-Philipsen, B. D., 657
Oosterwegel, A., 331, 405
Operario, D., 379
Ophir, E., 394
Opinion Research Corporation, 26
Oppenheim, D., 204
Oppenheimer, L., 331
O'Rahilly, R., 91n
Orbio de Castro, B., 270
Ordonana, J. R., 221
Oregon Department of Human Services,
  658
Oregon Public Health Division, 658
O'Reilly, A. W., 227
Orfield, G., 321
Ormel, J., 611
Ornstein, P. A., 237
O'Rourke, N., 606
Orth, U., 402, 464, 466
Orwoll, L., 525
Osborn, C. N., 136
Osherson, D. N., 383
Osterweil, P., 101
Ostir, G. V., 575
Ostrosky-Solis, F., 303
Ostrov, J. M., 270, 271
Ostrove, J. M., 13, 533
Oswald, F., 616, 619
Otis, N., 391
Otto, M. W., 353
Oude, L. H., 293
Ouko, L. A., 89
Oumar, F., 199
Ovando, C. J., 318
Overall, N. C., 474
Overton, W. F., 7, 70, 384
Owen, C. G., 131n
Owen-Kostelnik, J., 355
Owens, E. B., 280
Owsley, C., 502, 503, 569
Oxford Institute of Ageing, 626, 629, 631
Oyserman, D., 279
Ozanne, S. E., 130
Özçaliskan, S., 176, 248
Ozer, E. M., 372

P

Pacella, R., 293
Pace-Nichols, M. A., 489
Padilla-Walker, L. M., 469
Padula, M. A., 526
Pagani, L. S., 396
Pager, D., 494
Pagnani, A. R., 542
Pahl, K., 406
Paik, A., 446
Painter, J. A., 582
Palermo, G. D., 54
Palincsar, A. S., 320
Palmer, B., 452

Palmer, S., 642
Palmers, E., 232
Palmieri, P. A., 548
Palmore, E., 574
Palop, J. J., 583
Pamplona, R., 433
Pan, B. A., 250
Pan, C. S., 293
Pan, H. W., 261
Panish, J. B., 477
Pantalone, D. W., 376
Papadakis, A. A., 422
Papp, L. M., 60
Paquette, D., 202
Parada, R. H., 403
Paradis, J., 317
Paradise, R., 235, 314
Paramei, G. V., 503
Parameswaran, G., 300
Pardeck, J. T., 62
Pardini, D. A., 267
Parent, A., 366, 367
Paris, A. H., 242, 308
Paris, S. G., 242, 308
Park, C. L., 305, 632
Park, D. C., 519, 523
Park, W., 416
Parke, R. D., 59, 201, 204, 263, 336
Parker, F. L., 246
Parker, J. G., 199, 261, 339, 341, 392, 417
Parker, K. P., 108, 128
Parker, P. D., 389
Parsons, E., 200
Parsons, S., 457
Parsons, T., 355
Parten, M., 261
Pasamanick, B., 107n
Pascalis, O., 141, 163
Pascarella, E. T., 454
Pascual-Leone, J., 237
Pasley, K., 349
Pasterski, V. L., 274
Patel, D. R., 294
Patel, K. V., 572
Paterson, S., 155
Patin, R. V., 436
Patock-Peckam, J. A., 468
Patrick, R. B., 411
Patrick, W., 478
Patt, M. B., 256
Pattee, L., 343
Pattenden, S., 88
Patterson, C. J., 492
Patterson, G. R., 178, 424
Pattison, P. E., 308
Paukner, A., 136
Paul, J. J., 342
Pauli, S. A., 54
Paulozzi, L. J., 87
Paulussen-Hoogeboom, M. C., 194
Pawelec, G., 571
Paxson, C., 244
Payne, B. R., 593
Payne, K., 242
Pea, R., 418
Peake, A., 480
Pear, J., 18
Pearce, K. A., 524
Pearlman, D. N., 293
Pearsall, S., 385
Pease, M., 385
Peck, R. C., 604
Peckham, C. S., 293
Pedersen, L. H., 87
Pedersen, S., 341
Pederson, D. R., 199

Peets, K., 343
Peirano, P., 109
Peiró, J., 630
Pellegrini, A. D., 297, 298
Pelletier, J., 239, 306, 307
Pelletier, L. G., 391
Pellicano, E., 241
Pemberton, C. K., 190, 259
Pendell, G., 489
Pendlebury, S. T., 584
Pendry, P., 26
Penner, A. M., 389
Pennington, B. F., 21
Pennington, D. F., 303
Pennock, D., 388
Penny, H., 292
Peplau, L. A., 473
Pepler, D. J., 30, 342
Peralta de Mendoza, O. A., 228
Percival, S., 313
Perelli-Harris, B., 488
Perfors, A., 177
Periss, V., 23
Perkins, H. W., 541
Perlmutter, M., 237, 524
Perls, T. T., 566, 567, 573
Perone, S., 147, 166
Perou, R., 486
Perrin, J. M., 293
Perris, E. E., 166
Perrone, S., 100
Perry, B. D., 353
Perry, D. G., 344, 376
Perry, W. G., Jr., 20, 451
Perry-Jenkins, M., 484, 494
Persaud, T. V. N., 47, 56n, 81, 81n, 82, 83, 84, 86, 122
Peshkin, A., 33
Pesonen, A.-K., 194
Petch, J., 485
Peter, J., 418
Peters, L., 649
Peters, M., 390
Peters, R. D., 63, 64
Petersen, A. C., 390, 414
Peterson, B. E., 533
Peterson, C., 164, 355, 388
Peterson, C. C., 240
Peterson, G. W., 61
Peterson, L., 222
Peter-Wight, M., 595
Petitto, L. A., 176
Petrides, K. V., 313
Petrill, S. A., 70
Petrofsky, J., 581
Petrovic, K., 627
Petrun, C., 643
Petrunka, K., 63, 64
Pettigrew, T. F., 338
Pettit, G. S., 263, 280
Pew Forum on Religion and Public Life, 465, 479
Pew Research Center, 412, 447, 487, 488, 655, 656
Pezaris, E., 391
Pezé, A., 140
Pfeffer, C. R., 37
Pfeffer, K., 303
Pfeifer, J. H., 338
Pharo, H., 367, 368
Philibert, R. A., 194, 280
Philips, S. U., 167
Phillips, A. T., 165
Phillips, D., 128
Phillips, L. H., 593
Phillips, M., 61

Phillips, M. J., 648
Phinney, J. S., 406
Phuong, D. D., 438
Piaget, J., 18, 30, 152, 153, 154, 155, 161, 226, 228, 230, 233, 382, 386, 450
Pianta, R. C., 246, 263, 320, 354
Picano, J., 541
Pick, A. D., 176
Pickard, M. B., 158
Pickens, J. N., 135, 163, 260
Pickett, K. E., 110, 439
Pienta, A. M., 618
Pierce, K. M., 63
Pierce, S. H., 307
Pierroutsakos, S. L., 159
Pietilainen, K., 130
Pietz, J., 102
Piirto, J., 312
Pike, A., 26
Pikhart, H., 53
Pillay, U., 476
Pillemer, D. B., 593
Pillemer, K., 545
Pillow, B., 383
Pilz, K. S., 521
Pimentel, A. E., 437
Pina, A. A., 352
Pine, J. M., 249
Pinette, M. G., 100
Ping, R. M., 232
Pinker, S., 250
Pinquart, M., 487, 550, 551, 586, 611, 631
Piotrowski, J. T., 247
Pirie, K., 444
Pisani, L., 199
Pisoni, D. B., 179
Pitkala, K. H., 576
Pitkin, J., 506
Pixley, J. E., 536, 537
Pizarro, D. A., 313, 414
Plante, I., 343
Platz, M., 606
Pleck, J. H., 350
Plester, D., 503
Plickert, G., 611
Ploeg, J., 545
Plomin, R., 69, 70, 72, 73, 171, 313
Plucker, J. A., 323
Plude, D. J., 521
Pluess, M., 71, 194
Poehlmann, J., 102, 200
Poelhuis, C. W. K., 58, 313
Pogarsky, G., 379
Polderman, T. J. C., 303
Poldrack, R. A., 394
Polka, L., 141
Pollak, S. D., 193, 283
Pollatsek, A., 308
Pollitt, C., 248
Pollitt, E., 92
Pomerantz, E. M., 333, 334, 343, 392, 415
Pomerleau, A., 379
Pong, S., 33, 281
Ponnappan, S., 571
Ponnappan, U., 571
Pons, F., 335
Poobalan, A. S., 440, 441
Poon, L. W., 567, 592
Poon, S., 512
Popenoe, D., 490
Popkin, B. M., 292, 372, 440
Porter, R. H., 112
Portes, A., 32
Posner, J. K., 351
Posner, M. I., 163, 189, 191
Posthuma, R. A., 553

Postolache, T. T., 422
Poston, D. L., Jr., 346
Poti, J. M., 292
Potocnik, K., 630
Poudevigne, M., 92
Poulin-Dubois, D., 157, 273
Powdthavee, N., 541
Powell, A., 422
Powell, C., 92
Powell, F. C., 645
Powell, J. L., 10
Power, T. G., 297
Powers, J. L., 418
Powers, L. M., 272, 343
Powlishta, K. K., 276, 343, 344, 387
Prager, K. J., 542
Pratt, M. W., 279, 410, 413, 533
Prechtl, H. F. R., 83, 107n
Preece, J., 599
Preissler, M. A., 228
Prencipe, A., 337
Prepin, K., 207
Prescott, C., 381
Presnell, K., 371
Pressley, M., 162, 305, 308
Prevatt, F., 396
Previc, F. H., 218
Price, J., 661
Price, J. M., 263
Priess, H. A., 414, 484
Prince, M., 582
Prinstein, M. J., 341, 419, 424
Prinz, W., 140
Proctor, B. D., 61
Proctor, M. H., 292
Profilet, S. M., 263
Programme for International Student Assessment, 324
Proulx, K., 648
Pruden, S. M., 249
Pryor, J. H., 466
Prysak, M., 93
Pudrovska, T., 547
Pugh, K. L., 567
Puhl, R. M., 292, 439, 440
Pujol, J., 124
Punamaki, R. L., 54
Putallaz, M., 343
Putnam, S. P., 191
Puzia, M. E., 283
Pyka, G., 578
Pyszczynski, T., 645

Q
Qian, Z., 480
Qin, D. B., 32
Quas, J. A., 355
Querido, J. G., 176
Quill, T. E., 658
Quine, S., 630
Quinn, J. F., 629
Quinn, P. C., 145, 158, 165, 390
Quinn, R. A., 128

R
Raaijmakers, Q. A. W., 411
Rabbitt, P., 596
Rabig, J., 619
Raboy, B., 492
Radke-Yarrow, M., 264
Radler, B. T., 532
Raevuori, A., 372
Raffaelli, M., 374
Ragow-O'Brien, D., 653
Rahav, G., 544

Rahhal, T. A., 592
Rahi, J. S., 293
Rahm, K. B., 477
Rahman, Q., 376
Raikes, H. A., 194, 201, 258, 259, 263
Raikes, H. H., 173
Räikkönen, K., 513, 516
Rait, G., 583
Rakison, D. H., 158, 164, 166
Rakoczy, H., 227
Raley, S. B., 26
Ralston, S. H., 513
Ramamurthy, D., 293
Ramani, G. B., 207
Ramaswami, A., 493
Ramchandani, P. G., 187
Ramey, C. T., 173, 246
Ramey, S. L., 173, 246
Ramin, S. M., 95
Ramirez, A., 446
Ramo, D. E., 381
Ramos, E., 364
Ramos, M. C., 190
Rampell, C., 493
Ramsay, D. S., 193, 207
Ramsay, J. T., 63
Ramsey-Rennels, J. L., 145
Ramus, F., 113
Ranalli, C., 595
Rando, T. A., 659
Rangel, C., 321
Rao, G., 291
Rao, N., 276, 486
Rapattoni, M., 611
Rapson, R. L., 475
Raqib, R., 433
Rasbash, J., 346
Rasmussen, C., 243
Rasmussen, E. R., 304
Ratan, R., 126
Rathunde, K., 319, 595
Rau, B. L., 558
Rauber, M., 298
Rauer, A. J., 264
Raver, C. C., 62, 75, 189, 303, 351
Ravid, D., 316
Ravitch, D., 319, 324
Ravussin, E., 505
Raw, M., 444
Rawlins, W. K., 624
Ray, S. D., 228
Rayner, K., 308
Raynor, H. A., 293
Raynor, R., 17
Raz, N., 520, 568
Razza, R. P., 237
Ready, C. B., 449
Ream, G. L., 377
Reay, A. C., 627, 628
Reddin, J., 457
Redman, L. M., 505
Reed, M. J., 11, 354
Rees, J., 199
Reese, E., 165, 238
Reese, K., 384
Reeve, R. A., 308
Regan, P. C., 473
Regnerus, M., 412
Reich, S. M., 418
Reichert, M., 619
Reid, H. M., 476
Reid, J. M., 272
Reid, K. F., 572
Reid, M. J., 272
Reid, S., 472
Reilly, J. S., 126

Reinhard, S. C., 589
Reis, O., 405
Reis, S. M., 323
Reiser, L. W., 369
Reisman, J. E., 111*n*
Reisner, E. R., 63
Reiss, D., 72, 416
Reiss, N. S., 612, 613
Reiter, S., 35
Reitzes, D. C., 545, 546
Rendell, P. G., 593
Renk, K., 379, 403
Renninger, K. A., 320
Repacholi, B. M., 188
Repetti, R. L., 26, 494
Reppucci, N. D., 355, 426
Resnick, M., 247
Resnick, M. B., 106
Rest, J. R., 408
Resta, R., 53
Rettew, D. C., 74
Reuter-Lorenz, P. A., 568
Rey-Casserly, C., 101
Reyes-Ortiz, C. A., 573
Reyna, V. F., 388
Reynolds, A. J., 246
Reynolds, P., 457
Rhoades, B. L., 237
Rhoades, G. K., 488
Rhodes, J. E., 380
Rholdes, M., 344
Rhone, M., 569
Rice, S. J., 663
Richard, C. A., 621
Richards, D., 279
Richards, M., 369
Richardson, H. L., 110
Richardson, V. E., 660
Richgels, D. J., 242
Richie, B. S., 494
Richler, J., 221
Richmond, J., 135
Ridenour, T. A., 70
Rideout, R., 355
Rideout, V. J., 246, 247, 271, 389, 394, 418
Ridley-Johnson, R., 107, 107*n*
Riediger, M., 590
Riestenberg, N., 426
Rietjens, J., 657
Riffin, C., 608
Rifkin, A., 200
Riggle, E., 465
Riksen-Walraven, J. M., 131
Riley, J. R., 354
Riley, L. D., 549
Rinaldi, J., 272
Rinaldo, L. A., 577
Ringbäck, W. G., 442
Ripperger, T., 510
Ripple, C. H., 67
Riskind, R. G., 492
Risley, T. R., 170, 250
Rissanen, A., 130
Ritchey, L. H., 614
Ritchey, P. N., 614
Ritchie, L. D., 371
Ritter, J. O., 537
Riva, D., 218
Rivard, V., 606
Rivera, S., 161
Rivkees, S. A., 84
Rivlin, R. S., 504
Rizvi, S. I., 505
Rizzolatti, G., 136
Roach, M. A., 102
Robb, A. L., 621

Robb, A. S., 372
Robbins, B. D., 380
Robert, S. A., 439, 566, 575
Roberto, K. A., 476, 551, 625
Roberts, B. W., 36, 193, 539, 542
Roberts, C., 388
Roberts, D. F., 246, 247, 271, 374, 389, 394, 418
Roberts, J., 54
Roberts, J. E., 244
Roberts, P., 664
Roberts, R. E., 406
Roberts, R. J., Jr., 21
Roberts, T., 225, 242
Roberts, W., 260
Robertson, J., 350
Robertson, K. F., 458
Robin, A. L., 373
Robine, J.-M., 566
Robins, R. W., 331, 335, 464, 466, 538
Robinson, C. C., 261, 270
Robinson, J. L., 208
Robinson, K. M., 587
Robinson, M., 608
Robinson, M. L., 74
Robinson, S., 241
Robinson, S. E., 665
Robinson, S. L., 271
Robitaille, A., 606
Robles, T. F., 437
Roca, A., 87
Rochat, P., 106, 139, 140, 159, 176, 188, 206, 207, 227
Rodemaker, J. E., 178
Rodgers, B., 631
Rodgers, L., 473
Rodgers, R. F., 556
Rodham, K., 422
Rodin, P. A., 546
Rodkin, P. C., 341
Rodman, J., 441
Rodrigue, K. M., 520, 568
Rodriguez, A., 218
Rodríguez, B., 479
Rodriguez, J. M., 548
Rodriguez, L. F., 396
Roebers, C. M., 355
Roehling, P. V., 492, 526
Roelfsema , N. M., 83
Roemmich, J. N., 293, 363, 366, 366*n*
Roeser, R. W., 391, 392
Rogers, S. J., 489
Rogers, W. A., 574
Rogoff, B., 24, 167, 235, 236, 300, 301, 306, 314
Rogol, A. D., 363, 366, 366*n*
Rohner, R. P., 204
Rohr, M. K., 9
Rohrbeck, C. A., 320
Roid, G., 243, 309
Roisman, G. I., 201, 474
Rokach, A., 477, 478
Rokach, R., 543, 544
Rolfhus, E., 310
Rollins, K. B., 230
Rolls, B. J., 440
Romano, E., 243
Rome-Flanders, T., 176
Romero, A. J., 406
Romney, A. K., 273
Rönnqvist, L., 217
Rooksby, M., 165
Rooney, J., 649
Roopnarine, J. L., 201, 262, 281
Rosander, K., 113, 140, 142, 155
Rose, A. J., 341, 343, 418

Rose, S. A., 144, 163
Roseman, M., 186
Rosen, A. B., 230
Rosen, C. S., 37, 353
Rosen, D., 371
Rosén, M., 442
Rosen, R. C., 446
Rosen, S., 503
Rosenbaum, J. E., 379
Rosenblatt, D. E., 627
Rosenblatt, P. C., 664
Rosenblum, T. B., 312
Rosenfeld, B., 650
Rosenfeld, L. B., 472
Rosenfeld, R. G., 219
Rosengren, K. S., 207, 225, 230
Rosenman, R. H., 513
Rosenstein, D. L., 648
Roseth, C. J., 298
Rosetta, L., 131*n*
Ross, C. E., 573
Ross, E., 248
Rossen, E. K., 608
Ross-Griffin, S., 457
Rossi, A. S., 504, 506, 533, 535, 576
Rossor, M. N., 108
Rostosky, S. S., 465
Rotenberg, K., 48
Rothbart, M. K., 70, 163, 189, 190, 191, 193
Rothbaum, F., 193, 199
Rothblum, E. D., 488
Rothenbacher, D., 131*n*
Rothman, S. M., 584
Rothwell, P. M., 584
Rotman, T., 484
Rott, C., 567
Rouselle, L., 232
Rousseau, P., 647
Routledge, C., 645
Rovee-Collier, C. K., 134, 156, 163, 164, 165, 166
Rowe, C. C., 584
Rowe, M. L., 176, 179
Rowland, C. F., 249, 250
Rowley, S. J., 343
Roy, K. M., 533
Rozin, P., 230
Rubenstein, L. Z., 582
Rubia, K., 283
Rubin, C., 366, 366*n*
Rubin, D., 548
Rubin, D. C., 592, 593
Rubin, D. M., 94
Rubin, K. H., 192, 194, 261, 262*n*, 263, 280, 339, 341, 417
Rubin, L. R., 414
Rubin, S. E., 493
Ruble, D. N., 193, 208, 273, 277, 278, 338, 343
Ruchkin, V., 353
Ruck, M. D., 410, 411
Ruderman, M. N., 495
Rudolph, K. D., 391, 403
Rudy, D., 281
Rueter, M. A., 416
Ruff, H. A., 163, 189, 227
Ruffman, T., 156, 240, 383
Ruitenberg, A., 586
Ruiz, I., 163
Ruiz, J. M., 514
Ruiz, J. R., 432
Ruiz-Peláez, J. G., 103
Rumbaut, R. G., 32
Runco, M. A., 323, 542
Rurup, M. L., 657

Rusbult, C. E., 473
Rusconi, A., 545
Rushton, J. L., 421
Rushton, J. P., 71, 72, 312
Russac, R. J., 645, 646
Russell, A., 279, 345
Russell, J. A., 115, 258
Russell, R. B., 48
Russell, S. T., 391
Russo, C., 595
Ruthruff, E., 521
Rutland, A., 339, 410
Rutter, M., 7, 70, 71, 72, 73, 125, 199
Ryan, E., 352
Ryan, E. B., 574
Ryan, M. K., 555
Ryan, R. M., 62
Rybash, J. M., 591
Rydell, A.-M., 320
Ryding, M., 293
Ryff, C. D., 532, 533, 538, 539, 541, 545, 576
Rynearson, E. K., 662

S

Saarni, C., 185, 187, 188, 258, 335, 336
Sabadish, N., 459, 467
Sabbagh, M. A., 249
Sabo, D., 296
Sacca, S. C., 569
Sacks, P., 320
Sadeh, A., 108, 128
Sadler, P., 472
Sadler, T. W., 81, 83
Safe Kids USA, 221, 222
Saffran, J. R., 85, 113, 142, 174
Safren, S. A., 376
Saginak, K. A., 481, 494
Saginak, M. A., 481, 494
Sagi-Schwartz, A., 198, 199
Sahathevan, R., 585
Sahlberg, P., 324
Sahler, O. J., 643
St. Jacques, P. L., 593
St James-Roberts, I., 111, 112
St. Louis, G. R., 406
Saito, Y., 551
Sakraida, T. J., 544
Salanterä, S., 112
Salapatek, P., 144
Salari, S., 628
Salas-Salvadó, J., 433
Sale, A., 125
Saleh, A. S., 577
Salerno, M., 219
Salihu, H. M., 93
Salisbury, A. L., 87
Salley, B. J., 177
Salloum, A., 662
Salmivalli, C., 342
Salomon, J. A., 565
Salovey, P., 313, 336
Salsa, A. M., 228
Salter, D., 353
Salthouse, T. A., 519, 520, 521, 522
Salvaterra, F., 58
Salvioli, S., 52
Samarel, N., 647, 650
Samek, D. R., 8
Sameroff, A. J., 10, 173, 393
Sampselle, C. M., 507
Samson, A. V., 191
Samuelson, G., 567
Samuolis, J., 395
Sanbonmatsu, D. M., 189
Sanchez, M. M., 283

Sanchez, R. P., 157
Sanders, D. M., 292
Sanders, M., 267
Sanders, O., 354
Sanders, P., 178, 343
Sanders, S., 617, 619
Sanderson, C. A., 477
Sanderson, J. A., 269
Sandfort, T. G. M., 492
Sandler, J. C., 355
Sandnabba, N. K., 274
Sandrin, D., 112
Sandström, A., 554
Sangrigoli, S., 145
San Juan, V., 239
Sann, C., 112, 146
Sansavini, A., 113
Santiago, C. D., 10
Santoloupo, S., 413
Santtila, P., 447
Sanz, A., 433
Sarama, J., 243, 247
Sarason, S. B., 556
Sarnecka, B. W., 243
Sarrazin, P., 296
Sasser-Coen, J. A., 525
Sastry, J., 573
Satin, J. R., 648
Sato, T., 274
Saucier, J. F., 32
Saudino, K. J., 171, 192, 194
Saunders, B. E., 354
Sautter, J. M., 446, 566
Savage, J. S., 448, 449n
Savina, C., 577
Savin-Williams, R. C., 376, 377
Saw, S. M., 293
Sawyer, A. M., 426
Sawyer, J., 59
Saxe, G. B., 24
Saxon, J. L., 333
Saxton, M., 251
Sayegh, P., 551
Sayer, A. A., 363
Sayer, L. C., 480
Saygin, A. P., 175
Sayil, M., 370
Saylor, M. M., 157, 159, 249
Saywitz, K. J., 355
Sbarra, D., 348
Scanlon, K., 220
Scarlett, W. G., 412
Scarmeas, N., 585
Scarr, S., 72, 314
Scelfo, J., 374
Schaal, B., 112, 113
Schacht, P. M., 60
Schaefer, J. T., 472
Schaefer-McDaniel, N. J., 63
Schafer, R. B., 472
Schäfer, S., 573
Schaie, K. W., 518, 519, 520, 590, 596, 597
Schalet, A., 379
Schamberg, M. A., 303
Scharling, H., 443
Scharrer, E., 271
Schaufeli, W. B., 554
Schectman, R. M., 421
Scheibe, S., 9
Scher, A., 128
Schewe, P. A., 448, 449n
Schiamberg, L. B., 627, 628
Schieman, S., 610, 611, 626
Schiff, B., 606
Schigelone, A. R. S., 619

Schiller, M., 201
Schimmele, C. M., 621, 622
Schindler, H. S., 374, 485
Schindler, I., 631
Schlackman, L. J., 101
Schlaggar, B. L., 22
Schlagmüller, M., 307
Schlegel, A., 370
Schley, S., 379
Schlossberg, N., 557
Schmeichel, B. J., 646
Schmertz, B., 526
Schmidt, K.-H., 554
Schmidt, K. L., 266
Schmidt, L. A., 192
Schmidt, M. E., 159
Schmidt, M. H., 106
Schmidt, U., 373
Schmitt, D. P., 542
Schmitt, M. T., 555
Schmitz, S., 190
Schneewind, K. A., 473
Schneider, B. H., 206
Schneider, D. E., 555
Schneider, W., 246, 247, 304, 305, 306, 307, 355, 450
Schneiderman, N., 449
Schneiders, J., 369
Schneller, D. P., 544
Schnohr, P., 443, 573
Schofield, W., 92
Scholl, B. J., 241
Scholl, T. O., 92
Scholnick, E. K., 237, 303
Schonberg, R. L., 53, 56
Schöner, G., 155
Schonert-Reichl, K. A., 410
Schooler, C., 525, 596
Schoon, L., 457
Schoppe, S. J., 191
Schoppe-Sullivan, S. J., 484, 485
Schor, J. B., 440
Schorge, J., 86
Schott, J. M., 108
Schroeder, R. D., 280
Schroots, J. J. F., 593
Schuckit, M. A., 444
Schuengel, C., 200
Schuetze, P., 87
Schull, W. J., 89
Schulte-Ruther, M., 136
Schultz, J. B., 370
Schultz, K., 630
Schultz, R., 587, 611, 613
Schulz, M. S., 485
Schulz, R., 436, 586, 610
Schumann, C. M., 241
Schuneman, M. J., 383
Schut, H., 660, 664
Schwab-Stone, M., 353
Schwade, J. A., 176
Schwanenflugel, P. J., 306
Schwarte, A. R., 51
Schwartz, B. L., 523, 594
Schwartz, C. E., 192
Schwartz, J. P., 482
Schwartz, M., 26, 291, 372
Schwartz, S. J., 404, 465
Schwarz, N., 30
Schwebel, D. C., 221, 222, 294
Schweiger, W. K., 58
Schweinhart, L. J., 245
Schweizer, K., 310
Schwenck, C., 305
Schwier, C., 157
Scocco, P., 611

Scott, J., 645
Scott, J. A., 316
Scott, L. D., 406
Scott, L. S., 123, 141
Scott, M. E., 491
Scott, P. M., 265
Scott, R. M., 239
Scott, V., 582
Scottham, K. M., 406
Scrutton, D., 139
Scuccimarri, C., 379
Scullin, M. K., 593
Seale, C., 659
Seals, D. R., 436, 437
Seaton, E. K., 406
Sebastián, E., 249
Seeher, K., 583
Seeman, E., 504
Seeman, T. E., 585
Seiberling, K. A., 570
Seibert, A. C., 205, 346
Seid, M., 263
Seiden, H. M., 661
Seidl, A., 142
Seidman, E., 391, 392
Seifer, R., 201
Seiffge-Krenke, I., 469
Seitz, V., 379
Seki, Y., 306
Sekita, A., 586
Sekuler, A. B., 521
Selfhout, M. H. W., 417
Seligman, M. E. P., 315
Sellers, R. M., 406
Selman, C., 433
Selman, C., 433
Seltzer, M. M., 545
Selwood, A., 587, 627
Selwyn, P. A., 647, 665
Semanik, P. A., 581
Senechal, M., 242
Senghas, A., 248
Senior, G. J., 144
Senju, A., 176, 239
Sentz, J., 220
Serafini, T. E., 404
Serbin, L. A., 276, 343, 344
Sergeant, J. F., 617
Sermon, K., 56n
Serpell, R., 26
Serra, L., 583
Service Canada, 630
Sesame Workshop, 246
Settersten, R. A., 471, 545
Settles, B. H., 494
Settles, I. H., 493
Sevigny, P. R., 204
Sexton, C., 62
Seymour, S. C., 139
Shaeer, K., 507
Shaeer, O., 507
Shafer, V. L., 174
Shaffer, A., 11, 416
Shaffer, T. G., 276
Shafto, M. A., 594
Shager, H., 246
Shah, T., 110
Shalev, I., 433
Shanahan, L., 414
Shanahan, M. J., 5
Shaner, T. L., 521
Shannon, J. D., 179
Shao, L., 580
Shao, Y., 331
Shapiro, A., 485
Shapiro, C. J., 305
Shapka, J. D., 331

Sharon, D., 544
Sharp, E. A., 487
Sharp, K., 643
Sharpe, T., 609
Shastri, J., 277
Shatz, M., 175, 230
Shaver, P., 421
Shaver, P. R., 474, 660
Shaw, B. A., 616
Shaw, D. S., 11, 341, 346, 424
Shaw, P., 305
Shay, J. W., 432
Shea, A. K., 92, 93
Shea, J. L., 506, 508
Shedler, J., 380
Sheeder, J., 375
Sheehan, G., 348
Sheehan, N. W., 627
Shen, Y.-L., 374
Sheng, X., 494
Shepherd, H., 494
Sheridan, K., 312
Sherman, A. M., 476, 477
Sherman, C. W., 627
Sherman, S. L., 53
Sherrod, L. R., 412
Sherry, B., 292
Sheu, C.-F., 217
Shibusawa, T., 478
Shic, F., 241
Shield, R. R., 652
Shields, G., 65
Shields, R., 222
Shierholz, H., 459, 467
Shifren, J. L., 446
Shimada, S., 136
Shimizu, H., 411
Shin, J. S., 432
Shiner, R. L., 70, 193
Shinn, M., 62
Shipman, K. L., 336
Shirley, L., 276
Shmotkin, D., 539
Shoffner, M. F., 457
Shonkoff, J. P., 69, 128
Shor, E., 623
Short, M. M., 164
Shrout, P. E., 138
Shuey, K., 549, 550
Shultz, J. M., 570
Shultz, K. S., 630
Shumow, L., 340
Shure, M. B., 272
Shuwairi, S. M., 143
Shwalb, D. W., 281, 480
Shweder, R. A., 7, 32
Sibley, C. G., 474
Sidebotham, P., 282
Sidle, A. L., 230
Siebenbruner, J., 374
Siegal, M., 269, 317
Siega-Riz, A. M., 131, 372
Siegel, D. H., 305
Siegel, K., 662
Siegel, R., 510, 511
Sieger, K., 379
Siegler, R. S., 20, 21, 232, 305, 309
Siervogel, R. M., 290
Siimes, M. A., 371
Silk, J. S., 279, 415, 486
Silvén, M., 176
Silver, E. J., 298
Silver, M. H., 567
Silver, R. C., 353
Silverberg, S. B., 544
Silverman, B., 247

Silverman, I., 390
Silverman, P. R., 647, 662
Silverman, W. K., 352
Silverstein, M., 546, 549, 550, 552, 618, 624
Simcock, G., 159, 164, 165, 207, 228
Simion, F., 109, 145
Simmons, R. G., 391
Simmons, T., 621
Simon, N. M., 433
Simon, T. R., 424
Simoneau, M., 384
Simons, J. S., 591, 592
Simons, L. G., 66
Simons, R. L., 282
Simonton, D. K., 453, 454
Simpson, E. A., 141
Simpson, J. A., 472
Simpson, J. L., 53, 186
Simpson, R., 458
Singer, B. H., 545, 576
Singer, D. G., 247
Singer, J. L., 247
Singer, Y., 651
Singh, S., 375
Singleton, J. L., 174
Sinkkonen, J., 371
Sinno, S., 269
Sinnott, J. D., 451, 453
Sirois, S., 155
Sirsch, U., 464
Sizonenko, S. V., 97
Skaalvik, E. M., 331
Skaff, M. M., 544
Skara, S., 381
Skinner, B. F., 17
Skinner, E. A., 334
Skoe, E. E. A., 409, 410
Skorikov, V., 456
Skouteris, H., 103
Skully, R., 577
Skultety, K. M., 535, 536
Slack, A., 589
Slack, K. S., 220
Slade, M. D., 570
Slater, A., 113, 142, 145, 163
Slaughter, V., 642, 643
Slavin, R. E., 455
Sleet, D. A., 221
Slemmer, J. A., 142
Slep, A. M. S., 484
Sloan, F. A., 569, 574
Slobin, D. I., 250
Slomcynski, K. M., 525, 526
Slonims, V., 53
Sloter, E., 507
Slusher, M. P., 621
Slutske, W. S., 444
Sluzenski, J., 155
Smahel, D., 418
Small, B. J., 591, 665
Small, M., 114
Small, S. A., 32
Smart, J., 108
Smetana, J. G., 269, 409, 415, 416, 479
Smirles, K. A., 533
Smith, A., 380
Smith, A. N., 493
Smith, B. H., 305
Smith, C. (Camille), 486
Smith, C. (Christian), 412, 465, 479
Smith, C. D., 568
Smith, C. L., 34, 513
Smith, C. M., 436, 571
Smith, D. G., 367
Smith, G. C., 548

Smith, J. (Jacqui), 8, 438, 509, 575, 590, 595, 596, 607, 608, 620, 621, 625
Smith, J. (James), 573
Smith, J. (Jason), 645, 646
Smith, J. (Julia), 267
Smith, J. C., 61, 585
Smith, K. E., 351
Smith, L. B., 138, 166, 248
Smith, N., 516
Smith, P. K., 297
Smith, P. T., 623
Smith, R. S., 106
Smith, T. W., 447, 513, 514
Smokowski, P. R., 33
Smyer, M. A., 611
Smyke, A. T., 127, 199
Snarey, J., 533
Sneed, J. R., 38, 536, 537
Snell, E. K., 26
Snell, P., 465, 479
Snider, J. B., 392, 415
Snidman, N., 192
Snow, C. E., 250, 316, 317
Snyder, J., 342
Snyder, J. S., 568
Snyder, K. A., 21
Soares, C. N., 506
Sobel, D. M., 227
Sobolewski, J. M., 349
Society for Research in Child Development, 39, 39n
Soderstrom, M., 142, 516
Soenens, B., 404, 464
Soetens, B., 292
Sofi, F., 585
Softas-Nall, B., 548
Solé-Auró, A., 576
Soli, A. R., 346
Sollie, D. L., 473
Solomon, J., 197
Solomon, J. C., 548
Solomon, S. E., 488
Son, J., 535
Sondergaard, C., 88
Song, J., 258
Sontag, L. M., 421
Sophian, C., 232
Sörensen, S., 550, 551, 586, 611
Sørensen, T. I., 292
Sosa, R., 99
Sosik, J. J., 526, 553
Soska, K. C., 143
Soto, C. J., 538, 542
Soto, P., 249
Soulsby, L. K., 623
Soussignan, R., 112, 113
South African Department of Health, 90
Sowell, E. R., 124, 305
Sowers, M. F., 504
Spagnola, M., 26
Spatz, D. L., 129
Speakman, J. R., 433
Spear, L., 367
Speece, D. L., 242
Speece, M. W., 643
Spelke, E. S., 140, 159, 160, 165
Spence, I., 390
Spence, M. J., 85, 113
Spencer, J. P., 140, 166
Spera, C., 392
Spere, K. A., 177
Sperling, R. A., 583
Spidel, A., 482
Spieker, S. J., 162, 236
Spieler, D. H., 594
Spielmann, G., 433

Spiewak, G. S., 412
Spinath, F. M., 70
Spinks, A., 294
Spinrad, T. L., 189, 260, 265
Spirito, A., 422
Spiro, A., III, 608, 613, 632
Spitze, G. D., 478, 626
Spock, B., 15, 129
Spokane, A. R., 456
Sporte, S. E., 413
Sprague, K. E., 242
Sprecher, S., 446, 472, 473, 474, 475
Spuhl, S., 234
Spurk, D., 484
Srivastava, S., 537, 542
Sroufe, L. A., 7, 185, 198, 201, 206
Stacey, J., 492
Stackert, R. A., 474
Staff, J., 395, 396
Stahl, S. A., 308
Staines, G., 523
Stams, G. J. M., 58, 206, 411
Stanley, J. C., 389
Stanley, S. M., 488
Stanley-Hagan, M., 350
Stanovich, K. E., 31, 316
Stanowicz, L., 251
Stansbury, K., 192
Starks, M. T., 377
Starr, J. M., 596
Starr, M. S., 308
Starr, R. J., 653
Statham, J. A., 574
Stattin, H., 279, 280, 371, 392
Staudinger, U. M., 7, 8, 71, 526, 540, 555, 574, 590, 595, 596, 615
Stauffacher, K., 270
Steele, C. M., 315
Steele, H., 201
Steele, K. H., 225
Steele, L. C., 355
Steele, M., 201
Steele, S., 241
Steenhuis, I. H., 440
Stegge, H., 335
Stehr-Green, P., 221
Stein, C. H., 550
Stein, J. H., 369
Stein, N., 258
Stein, R. E. K., 298
Steinberg, L. D., 278, 279, 280, 367, 371, 374, 392, 415, 416, 420, 425, 486
Steiner, J. E., 112, 134
Steiner, M., 92, 93
Steinhausen, C., 372
Stella, J., 241
Stenberg, C., 186, 188
Stephens, B. E., 102
Stephens, B. R., 145
Stephens, M. A. P., 549
Stephens, P. C., 381
Steptoe, A., 64
Stern, D., 188
Stern, Y., 585
Sternberg, R. J., 20, 161, 243, 309, 310, 311, 314, 315, 322, 323, 454, 473, 524, 525, 590
Stessman, J., 432
Stevens, J., 504
Stevens, J. A., 582
Stevens, J. C., 570
Stevens, N., 417
Stevenson, H. W., 324
Stevenson, R., 248
Stevens-Simon, C., 375
Stewart, A., 661

Stewart, A. J., 12, 13, 471, 533, 535, 537
Stewart, A. L., 552
Stewart, J. H., 266, 266n
Stewart, P. W., 90
Stewart, R. B., Jr., 485
Stewart, S., 472
Stewart-Brown, S., 313
Stewin, L., 665
Stice, E., 371
Stifter, C. A., 171, 194, 280
Stiles, J., 122, 126
Stillman, R. D., 113
Stilson, S. R., 171
Stinchcomb, J. B., 426
Stine-Morrow, E. A. L., 10, 593, 597
Stinnett, H., 472
Stipek, D. J., 208, 245
Stoch, M. B., 132
Stocker, C. M., 25, 346
Stoesz, D., 67
Stohs, S. J., 433
Stolz, H. E., 415
Stone, A. A., 539
Stone, L., 418
Stone, M. R., 419
Stone, P., 493
Stone, R. I., 589
Stoneman, Z., 205
Stoppa, T. M., 465
Storch, S. A., 242
Stormshak, E. A., 60, 406
Story, R., 293
Stout, M., 410
Stouthamer-Loeber, M., 425
Strain, L. A., 631
Strambler, M. J., 315
Strapp, C. M., 251
Strasburger, V. C., 372
Stratton, D. C., 623
Straus, M. A., 266, 266n
Strawbridge, W. J., 609
Strayer, J., 260
Strazdins, L., 351
Street, A. E., 449
Streissguth, A. P., 87, 89
Streri, A., 112, 146
Striano, T., 176, 188, 207, 227
Stricker, G., 477
Striegel-Moore, R. H., 371
Stright, A. D., 234, 307
Stringer, K. J., 456, 457, 465
Strober, M., 373
Stroebe, M. S., 660, 664
Stroebe, W., 660
Strohschein, L., 348
Stromswold, K., 175
Strough, J., 541, 594, 595
Stroup, D. F., 100
Strouse, D. L., 420
Stryker, M. P., 125
Stuart, M., 589
Studer, J., 453, 605
Stuewig, J., 260
Stuhlman, M., 320
Sturaro, C., 341
Sturge-Apple, M. L., 187
Sturgeon, S., 543
Styne, D. M., 363
Su, T. F., 33
Suarez-Morales, L., 416
Suárez-Orozco, C., 32
Subbotsky, E., 230
Subrahmanyam, K., 230, 314, 418
Substance Abuse and Mental Health Services Administration, 87
Suchindran, C., 373

Suddendorf, T., 207
Sugimoto, K., 570
Suitor, J., 545
Sullivan, K., 110
Sullivan, K. T., 473
Sullivan, M., 209
Sullivan, M. C., 102
Sullivan, M. W., 186
Summers, R. W., 628
Suomi, S. J., 136
Super, C. M., 114, 128, 139
Supple, A. J., 32, 415
Surething, N. A., 458
Surian, L., 317
Susman, E. J., 362, 370
Susman-Stillman, A., 345
Sussman, A. L., 105, 485
Sussman, S., 381
Sutherland, C., 581
Sutton, M. J., 374
Suveg, C., 336
Sveen, C.-A., 661
Sverke, M., 492
Svetina, M., 20, 232
Swartz, T. T., 549
Sweeney, B., 163
Sweet, M. A., 173
Sweet, S., 526
Swenson, L. D., 248
Swenson, L. P., 341
Swingley, D., 142
Swinson, J., 276
Symons, D. K., 200
Szaflarski, J. P., 218
Szanton, S., 564
Szkrybalo, J., 277
Szlemko, W. J., 89

T

Tabibi, Z., 303
Tacon, A., 204
Tadd, W., 40
Taga, G., 123
Tager-Flusberg, H., 174, 239, 241, 250
Tahir, L., 525
Takagi, E., 549, 618
Takahashi, K., 129, 199, 543, 552, 614
Takamura, J., 550
Takeuchi, T., 54
Talbot, A. P., 595
Talbot, L. S., 368
Talmi, A., 114
Talwar, V., 643, 644
Tamim, H., 222
Tamis-LeMonda, C. S., 65, 137, 139, 167, 170, 179
Tammelin, T., 299, 365
Tamrouti-Makkink, I. D., 345
Tanaka, H., 436, 437
Tanaka, Y., 576
Tang, C. S. K., 646
Tangney, J. P., 260
Tanimura, M., 159
Tanner, J. L., 466, 467
Tanner, J. M., 121
Tardif, C., 206, 322
Tardif, T., 61, 177, 178, 240, 248
Tarry-Adkins, J. L., 433
Tarter, R. E., 381
Tasker, F., 492
Tasopoulos-Chan, M., 416
Tate, C. S., 250
Taumoepeau, M., 240
Taylor, C. A., 266
Taylor, C. B., 516
Taylor, C. L., 316

Taylor, D. H., Jr., 574
Taylor, J. H., 269, 409, 410
Taylor, J. L., 378
Taylor, K. K., 458
Taylor, L. C., 64, 393
Taylor, M. C., 276
Taylor, M. G., 275, 275n, 344
Taylor, P., 480
Taylor, R. D., 11, 66
Taylor, R. J., 612
Taylor, R. L., 66
Taylor, W. C., 516
Teasdale, B., 376
Teinonen, T., 142
Telama, R., 365
Temkin-Greener, H., 611
Temple, J. A., 246
Temple, J. L., 292
Templeton, L. J., 381, 548
ten Brummelhuis, L. L., 494
Tenenbaum, H. R., 274, 276, 343
Tenenbaum, J. B., 21
Tennenbaum, H. R., 278
ten Tusscher, G. W., 90
Terenzini, P. T., 454
Terry, D., 566, 567
Terwel, J., 320
Tessler, R. C., 58
Teyber, E., 349n
Thacker, H. L., 506
Thacker, S. B., 100
Thal, D. J., 250, 317
Tharpe, A. M., 113
Thatcher, R. W., 217
Thayer, S. M., 416
Thelen, E., 15, 107, 107n, 138, 155, 156, 166
Théoret, E., 241
Théoret, H., 136
Théoret, M., 343
Theuring, C., 138
Thiessen, E. D., 142
Thiessen, V., 389
Thoermer, C., 239
Thomaes, S., 333
Thomas, A., 190, 194
Thomas, C., 517
Thomas, C. L., 379
Thomas, D., 246
Thomas, J. A., 587
Thomas, J. M., 343
Thomas, K. A., 58
Thomas, K. M., 124, 126, 164, 217, 218, 450
Thomas, R. B., 109
Thomas, R. M., 17
Thombs, B. D., 186
Thompson, A., 279
Thompson, C. K., 248
Thompson, M., 594
Thompson, N. R., 269
Thompson, P. M., 217, 218
Thompson, R. A., 22, 122, 124, 185, 189, 197, 198, 201, 206, 240, 258, 259, 260, 263, 336
Thompson, S., 517
Thompson, W. W., 221
Thornberry, T. P., 379
Thorne, B., 276
Thornton, J., 444
Thornton, S., 21
Thorpe, R., 564
Thorson, J. A., 645
Thurlow, M. L., 396
Thurman, P. J., 89
Tienari, P., 70, 73

Tiet, Q. Q., 11
Tifft, C. J., 53, 56
Tiggemann, M., 292, 332
Tinbergen, N., 22
Tincoff, R., 176
Tirosh, E., 128
Tishler, C. L., 612, 613
Tizard, B., 199
To, Y. M., 335
Todorova, I., 32
Tofler, I. R., 296
Tokunaga, R. S., 342
Tolan, P. H., 27
Tolchinsky, L., 316
Tomasello, M., 157, 174, 175, 176, 177, 179, 188, 227, 230, 239, 248, 249, 250, 316
Tomer, A., 645, 646
Tong, S., 170
Tong, V. T., 88, 89
Torchia, M. G., 81, 81n, 82, 83, 84, 86, 122
Tordera, N., 630
Torges, C. M., 537
Torney-Purta, J., 413, 452
Tornstam, L., 605
Toro-Morn, M., 472
Torrance, E. P., 323
Torres, V., 451
Torrez, D. J., 547
Torsheim, T., 299
Tottenham, N., 199
Touwslager, R. N., 130
Tracy, J. L., 335
Trafford, A., 607
Trappe, S., 436
Traupman, E., 140
Trautner, H. M., 273, 277, 344
Treasure, J., 373
Trehub, S. E., 113, 140, 141
Tremblay, L., 367
Tremblay, R. E., 269, 424
Trent, K., 66
Trentacosta, C. J., 341
Triandis, H. C., 31, 65
Trocomé, N., 281
Troll, L. E., 625
Tronick, E. Z., 109, 114, 185, 187
Troop-Gordon, W., 341
Tropp, L. R., 338
Troseth, G. L., 159, 249
Troutman, D. R., 340
Trowbridge, F., 220
Troyer, A. K., 522
Trudel, G., 620
True, M. M., 199
Trusty, J., 392
Trzesniewski, K. H., 331, 333, 465, 466, 538
Tsai, A. G., 441
Tsai, C.-C., 385
Tsai, J. C., 503
Tsang, P. S., 521
Tsao, F.-M., 141
Tseng, V., 33, 393
Tsuji, Y., 576
Tsujimoto, S., 217
Tucker, C. J., 345, 346, 413
Tucker-Drob, E. M., 367, 368
Tudge, J. R. H., 61, 235
Tulevaev, S. R., 588
Tulsky, J. A., 655
Turati, C., 145
Turchi, C., 444
Turell, S. C., 624

Turesson, C., 581
Turiano, N. A., 608
Turiel, E., 268, 269, 337, 409
Turkewitz, G., 113
Turkheimer, E., 71, 371
Turnbull, K. P., 242
Turnbull, M., 317
Turner, B. F., 540
Turner, L. B., 442
Turner, P. J., 274
Turner, R. N., 338
Tuyen, J. M., 221
Twenge, J. M., 13, 331, 333, 402, 465
Twomey, J. C., 458
Tzuriel, D., 315, 390

U

Uauy, R., 109, 132
Ucanok, Z., 370
Uchino, B. N., 613
Udechuku, A., 87
Udry, J. R., 373, 420
Uematsu, H., 570
Uggen, C., 395, 396
Uhlenberg, P., 546, 547
Uitterlinden, A. G., 513
Ukrainetz, T. A., 317
Ullman, M. T., 241
Umana-Taylor, A. J., 406
Underhill, K., 379
Underwood, M. K., 270, 273
UNICEF (United Nations Children's Fund), 62, 65, 91, 130, 353, 466
United Nations, 51, 440
Uotinen, V., 573
Updegraff, K. A., 406, 416
U.S. Census Bureau, 8, 12, 55, 61, 64, 67n, 68, 104, 105, 171, 244, 246, 317, 347, 350, 422, 438, 457, 457n, 478, 479, 480, 483, 487, 489, 491, 509, 532, 543, 544, 547, 548, 555, 556, 565, 569, 579, 580, 581, 582, 612, 618, 622
U.S. Department of Agriculture, 92, 132, 442, 484
U.S. Department of Education, 67, 67n, 244, 298, 325, 388, 389, 395, 396, 397, 454, 456, 464, 526
U.S. Department of Health and Human Services, 48, 51, 52, 67, 68, 93, 99, 101, 131, 221, 246, 281, 282n, 283, 291, 352, 365, 374, 375, 381, 437, 438, 443, 444, 445, 447, 508, 511, 515, 564, 568, 569, 575, 578, 586, 588, 596, 616, 617, 618
U.S. Department of Justice, 423, 424, 425, 617
U.S. Department of Transportation, 445
U.S. Living Will Registry, 655
Usher-Seriki, K. K., 374
Usta, I. M., 93
Uttal, D. H., 207
Utz, R. L., 623

V

Vacha-Haase, T., 615
Vachon, R., 384
Vaillancourt, T., 270, 341, 342
Vaillant, C. O., 454
Vaillant, G. E., 454, 470, 471, 536, 604, 632
Vaish, A., 188
Vakil, E., 303
Valdés, G., 33
Valentine, J. C., 331

Valian, V., 251
Valiente, C., 191, 260, 261, 307
Valkenburg, P. M., 418
Valley-Gray, S., 294
van Aken, C., 194
van Asselt, D., 655
van Baarsen, B., 623
van Balen, F., 492
Van Brunt, D., 646
Van Camp, G., 503
Van Cleave, J., 293
van de Beek, C., 274
Vandell, D. L., 63, 246, 340, 351
van den Akker, A. L., 191
Vandenberg, B., 261, 262n
Van den Bergh, B. R. H., 93, 331
van den Boom, D. C., 191, 492
van den Bossche, A. S., 109
van den Dries, L., 58, 199
Vanderbilt-Adriance, E., 11
Vandergrift, N., 246
van der Heide, A., 657
van der Houwen, K., 664
van der Wal, M. F., 92
Van de Vijver, P. J. R., 32
Vandewater, E. A., 471, 537
van Dijkum, C., 593
van Dulmen, M., 420
van Eijsden, M., 92
Van Eyk, J., 57
Van Eyken, E., 503
van Goudoever, J. B., 101
van Heerden, H. G., 503
Van Hiel, A., 604
Van Hoof, A., 411
Van Hulle, C. A., 177
Vaníčková, J., 464
van IJzendoorn, M. H., 58, 111, 198, 199, 200, 201, 206, 313
Van Laer, L., 503
Vannoy, S. D., 613
Van Orden, K., 612
van Solinge, H., 631
Vansteenkiste, M., 604
Van Steirteghem, A., 56n
van Tol, D., 657
Van Volkom, M., 624
Vanyukov, M., 381
Varendi, H., 112
Varnhagen, C. K., 271
Vartanian, L. R., 387
Vaughn, B. E., 200, 209, 263
Vazsonyi, A. T., 392, 415
Veenstra, R., 342
Velderman, M. K., 201
Veldhuis, J. D., 121
Veliz, P., 296
Velkoff, V., 567
Velleman, R. D. B., 381
Venet, M., 384
Venezia, M., 185
Veneziano, R. A., 204
Ventura, S. J., 378
Vereijken, B., 138
Verhaeghen, P., 521, 522, 591, 593
Verhulst, F. C., 58
Veríssimo, M., 58
Vermeer, W. M., 440
Vernberg, E. M., 424
Vernon, P. A., 310
Vernon-Feagins, L., 61
Vesco, K. K., 506
Vida, M. N., 455
Vidaeff, A. C., 95
Viechtbauer, W., 542
Vihman, M. M., 176

Vinden, P. G., 239, 306
Visher, E. B., 349
Visher, J. S., 349
Vitali, P., 583
Vitrup, B., 266
Vivanti, G., 241
Voci, A., 338
Voeten, M., 342
Vogel, R. M., 629
Vogels, N., 440
Vohr, B. R., 102
Vol=berg, W., 405
Volling, B. L., 189, 205, 209, 264, 477
Volpe, L. E., 129
Voluntary Euthanasia Society of New South Wales, 657
Vondra, J. I., 197, 198
von Hofsten, C., 113, 140, 142, 155
Votruba-Drzal, E., 61, 374
Vouloumanos, A., 113
Voyer, D., 390
Voyer, S., 390
Vukman, S. N., 476
Vuoksimaa, E., 218, 390
Vygotsky, L. S., 23, 233, 234, 235

W
Waber, D. P., 322
Wachs, T. D., 190, 191, 193
Wadden, T. A., 441
Waddington, C. H., 72
Wadell, K. J., 306
Wadsworth, M. E., 10
Waerness, K., 551
Wagenaar, K., 54
Wagner, A. D., 394
Wagner, N., 599
Wahl, H.-W., 616, 619
Wahlberg, K. E., 73
Wahler, J. J., 621
Wahlsten, D., 70, 71
Wai, J., 388, 389
Wainryb, C., 410
Waite, L. J., 509, 541, 579, 625
Wakeley, A., 161
Walberg, H. J., 319
Walby, F. A., 661
Walden, T. A., 188
Waldenström, U., 218
Waldfogel, J., 104, 105, 203, 244, 351, 485, 491
Waldman, I. D., 74
Waldo, M., 482
Waldrip, A. M., 419
Walenski, M., 241
Walk, R. D., 142
Walker, A. M., 110
Walker, L. J., 269, 409, 410
Walker, R. A., 217
Walker, S. P., 291
Walker-Andrews, A. S., 146, 188
Wall, M., 296
Waller, E. M., 341, 418
Walsh, C. A., 628
Walsh, F., 651
Walsh, K. E., 504, 509
Walsh, M. E., 455
Walston, J., 580
Walters, C., 465
Walton, K. E., 542
Wang, H., 490
Wang, J., 552, 554
Wang, L., 193, 195
Wang, M., 629, 630
Wang, Q., 238, 331, 334, 392, 415
Wang, S., 26, 32, 155

Wang, Y., 191
Wang, Z., 11
Ward, R. A., 478
Ware, W. B., 393
Wark, G. R., 409
Warner, L. A., 416
Warner, L. M., 612
Warner, R. M., 313
Warnock, F., 112
Warr, P., 554
Warren, A. E. A., 412
Warren, A. R., 250
Warren, C. A. B., 589
Warren, K. L., 164
Warren, L. H., 591
Warren, M. P., 369, 370
Warshaw, C., 483
Washington, S. K., 643
Wass, H., 665
Wasserman, E. A., 165
Watamura, S. E., 202, 203
Watanabe, H., 339
Waterman, A. S., 542
Waters, E., 185, 196, 198, 201
Watson, J., 185
Watson, J. B., 17
Watson, K. S., 261
Watson, M., 256
Wax, J. R., 100
Waxler, C. Z., 265
Waxman, S. R., 166, 248
Way, N., 406
Wayne, S. J., 555
Webb, N. B., 663
Webb, N. M., 320
Webb, S. J., 122
Weber, C., 141
Weber, J. A., 615
Webster, J. D., 606
Webster-Stratton, C., 272
Wechsler, D., 243, 310
Weems, C. F., 352
Weeraratna, A. T., 584
Wegesin, D. J., 591
Wegner, K. E., 556
Wehren, A., 316
Weiglas-Kuperus, N., 101
Weikum, W. M., 317
Weinberg, C. R., 80
Weinberg, M. K., 185
Weinberg, R. A., 314
Weinberger, J., 260
Weinberger, M. I., 611
Weindruch, R., 505
Weiner, J., 322
Weiner, S., 166
Weinfield, N. S., 198, 201
Weinrich, M., 589
Weinstein, R. S., 315, 320, 321, 392
Weinstein, S. M., 369
Weinstock, M., 93
Weis, L. G., 310
Weisfield, G. E., 362
Weisgram, E. S., 344
Weisner, T., 129
Weiss, A., 608
Weiss, E. M., 555
Weiss, K. M., 52
Weissberg, R. P., 351
Weissberg, R. W., 453
Weisz, A. N., 409
Weizman, Z. O., 316
Wekerle, C., 282, 282n, 421
Wellman, B., 552
Wellman, H. M., 230, 239, 240, 258, 316

Wells, Y. V., 502, 538
Welner, K. G., 321
Welsh, D. P., 420, 421
Welsh, J. A., 333
Welsh, M. C., 50, 162, 236, 303
Wenger, G. C., 624
Wenger, N. K., 512
Wentura, D., 338
Wentworth, N., 140
Wentworth, P. A., 533
Wentzel, K. R., 419
Werker, J. F., 85, 113, 141, 142
Werner, E. E., 10, 106, 547
Werner, L. A., 85, 113, 142
Werner, N. E., 270, 339, 340, 424
Wesson, D. E., 294
West, D. S., 440
West, R. L., 597
Westerhof, G. J., 535, 573, 606
Westermann, G., 21
Westermeyer, J. F., 533
Western, B., 494
Westerterp-Plantenga, M. S., 440
Westra, T., 139
Wething, H., 459, 467
Wethington, E., 536, 537
Wetle, T., 652
Wetmore, C. M., 441
Weyand, C. M., 580
Weyermann, M., 131n
Whaley, G. J. L., 198
Wheeler, I., 661
Wheeler, K., 170
Wheeler, W., 413
Whincup, P. H., 92
Whipple, E. E., 282n, 353
Whipple, N., 200
Whisman, M. A., 621
Whitaker, D. J., 483
Whitbourne, S. K., 13, 38, 435n, 532, 535, 536, 537, 542, 568, 572, 611
Whitby, E. H., 56n
White, E. J., 640
White, H. R., 465
White, K. S., 141
White, L., 552, 624
White, Y. A., 47
Whitehurst, G. J., 242
Whiteman, S. D., 37, 479
Whitesell, N. R., 331, 335
Whiteside, M. F., 490
Whiteside-Mansell, L., 60
Whitfield, K. E., 564
Whiting, B., 273
Whitley, M. E., 272
Whitlock, J. L., 418
Whitmer, R. A., 584
Wichmann, C., 343
Wichstrøm, L., 373
Wickberg, B., 484
Wickens, A. P., 433
Widaman, K. F., 464, 466
Widom, C. S., 283
Wieling, E., 353
Wigfield, A., 331, 334, 335n, 391, 457
Wikby, A., 571
Wilber, K. H., 589, 624
Wilbur, J., 516
Wilcox, A. J., 80
Wiley, E., 317
Wilkenfeld, B., 413
Wilkie, S. S., 436
Wilkinson, K., 248
Wilkinson, R. B., 332, 403
Wilkinson, R. G., 439

Willatts, P., 157
Willerman, L., 72, 313
Williams, B., 550
Williams, J. E., 513
Williams, J. M., 371
Williams, K., 347
Williams, K. N., 589
Williams, N., 547
Williams, P. E., 310
Williams, R., 581
Williams, S., 648
Williams, S. W., 551
Williams, T. S., 421
Williams, W. M., 314, 389
Williamson, J., 548
Williamson, R. A., 156
Williger, B., 9
Willinger, M., 129
Willis, S. L., 13, 519, 520, 532
Willoughby, J., 424
Willson, A. E., 626
Wilson, D. J., 574
Wilson, E. K., 374
Wilson, G. D., 376
Wilson, J., 535
Wilson, M., 91n, 92, 269
Wilson, R. S., 596
Wimbarti, S., 262
Windecker-Nelson, B., 259
Windsor, T. D., 631
Winer, A. C., 185
Wink, P., 535, 541, 606, 607, 608, 609, 645
Winkler, I., 113
Winner, E., 224, 248, 323, 453
Winsler, A., 23, 234
Winslow, R. D., 640
Winter, D. G., 533, 535, 607
Winter, M. A., 26
Wiseman, F. K., 52
Wissink, I. B., 415
Witherington, D. C., 140, 168, 188
Wittlinger, R. P., 592
Wolak, J., 352, 374, 418
Wolchik, S. A., 348
Wold, B., 296, 299
Wolf, A. W., 129
Wolfe, D. A., 281, 282, 282n, 283
Wolfe, V. V., 353
Wolff, P. H., 108n, 353
Wolfinger, N. H., 348, 489
Wolinsky, F. D., 597
Wolters, C. A., 279
Wong, C. A., 393
Wong, D., 596
Woo, H. S., 32, 33
Wood, E., 274
Wood, J. J., 263

Wood, J. T., 473
Wood, J. W., 89
Wood, R. M., 109
Wood, W., 472
Woods, N. F., 506
Woodward, A. L., 165, 249
Woodward, L. J., 131
Woody, E., 472
Woolley, J. D., 230
Woolley, M. E., 393
Wooten, H. R., 493
Worden, J. W., 606, 648, 659
World Cancer Research Fund, 291
World Federation of Right to Die Societies, 656
World Health Organization, 130, 132, 220, 221, 222, 291, 440, 467, 483, 612
Worrell, F. C., 406
Worthy, J., 321, 395
Wouters, H., 409
Wray, S., 541
Wrenn, K. A., 555
Wright, B. C., 300
Wright, J., 421
Wright, J. C., 246, 247
Wright, K., 647, 648
Wright, K. L., 296
Wright, M. J., 54, 70
Wright, M. O., 354
Wright, P. A., 418
Wright, S. B., 217
Wright, W. E., 432
Wrosch, C., 611, 613
Wrotniak, B. H., 293
Wu, A. M. S., 646
Wu, L. L., 491
Wu, P., 32, 281
Wu, T., 366n
Wu, W., 581
Wu, Z., 621, 622
Wulczyn, F., 282
Wunsch, J. P., 185
Wust, S., 102
Wyatt, J. M., 410
Wyman, E., 227
Wynn, K., 160
Wynne, L. C., 73
Wynne-Edwards, K. E., 115
Wysong, A., 569

X

Xi, B., 440
Xiao, L., 367
Xouboulis, C. C., 504
Xu, F., 160, 178
Xu, X., 481
Xue, Y., 308

Y

Yaari, R., 583
Yaffe, K., 584, 589
Yale, M. E., 185
Yamaguchi, S., 573
Yamamoto, K., 649
Yan, L. L., 513
Yancura, L. A., 515
Yang, B., 346
Yang, C., 346
Yang, C.-K., 129
Yang, F.-Y., 385
Yang, S. C., 643
Yao, L., 575
Yap, M. B. H., 422
Yarrow, M. R., 265
Yates, L. B., 566
Yau, J. P., 416
Yeh, C. J., 33
Yeh, M., 649
Yeh, S. S., 334
Yeung, D. Y., 616
Yeung, W., 650
Yip, R., 220
Yip, T., 33
Yirmiya, N., 194, 241
Yoerger, K., 424
Yonas, A., 142, 143
Yoo, J., 220
Yoshida, H., 248
Yoshikawa, H., 30
Youn, G., 551
Young, A., 516
Young, J. B., 556
Young, J. F., 332
Young, S. E., 303
Young, S. H., 100
Young, T., 506
Youngblade, L. M., 258
Younge, S. N., 66
Young-Hyman, D., 292
Youniss, J. E., 405, 412, 413
Yu, B. P., 505
Yu, F., 519
Yu, H., 195
Yuan, A. S. V., 350
Yuille, J. C., 423
Yumoto, C., 86
Yunger, J. L., 344

Z

Zaccagni, L., 437
Zacks, R. T., 521, 522, 591
Zafeiriou, D. I., 108
Zaff, J. F., 413
Zahn-Waxler, C., 264
Zakharia, R., 368
Zakowski, S. G., 514

Zamsky, E. S., 66
Zane, N., 649
Zarbatany, L., 340
Zaretsky, M. D., 566
Zarit, S. H., 545
Zarkadoulia, E., 221
Zarrett, N. R., 331, 604
Zaslow, M. J., 244
Zeanah, C. H., 199
Zeifman, D. M., 109
Zelazo, N. A., 107
Zelazo, P. D., 269, 303, 450, 568
Zelinski, E., 520
Zeman, J., 336
Zerwas, S., 207
Zeskind, P. S., 111
Zhan, H. J., 549, 550
Zhang, D., 320
Zhang, J. (Jie), 564
Zhang, J. (Junsen), 564
Zhang, L., 454
Zhang, Q. F., 549
Zhang, S., 446
Zhang, T.-Y., 74
Zhang, X., 571
Zhang, Y., 580
Zhao, J., 494
Zheng, N. T., 652
Zhou, M., 33
Zhou, Q., 191
Zhou, X., 309
Zhu, W. X., 346
Zickuhr, K., 599, 626
Zigler, E., 67, 105, 485
Zimmer-Gembeck, M. J., 334, 374
Zimmerman, B. J., 307
Zimmerman, C. (Camilla), 649
Zimmerman, C. (Corinne), 385
Zimmerman, F. J., 159, 177
Zimmerman, P., 405
Zimmerman, R., 196
Zimmerman, S., 219
Zimmermann, L. K., 192
Zimprich, D., 608
Zins, J. E., 294
Ziol-Guest, K. M., 457
Zolotor, A. J., 283
Zosmer, A., 438
Zosuls, K. M., 208
Zucker, A. N., 533
Zucker, K. J., 344
Zukow-Goldring, P., 168
Zukowski, A., 174, 250
Zuroff, D. C., 533
Zuzanek, J., 624
Zvonkovic, A. M., 457
Zwart, M., 104

Subject Index

Figures and tables are indicated by f and t following page numbers.

A

A-not-B search error in sensorimotor stage, 154, 156
AARP, 69
Aboriginals, Australian, 657
Abortion
　in adolescent pregnancy, 378, 379
　spontaneous. *See* Miscarriage
Abstinence from sexual activity, 374, 379
Abstract thinking
　consequences of changes in, 386
　and expertise, 453, 524
　in formal operational stage, 19, 382–384
　and mathematical abilities, 389
　and moral development, 408
　and self-concept, 402
　and work experiences, 525
Abuse
　of child. *See* Child maltreatment
　in dating relationship, 420–421
　of elderly, 627–628
　of substances. *See* Substance abuse
Academic achievement
　in adolescence, 392–396
　child-rearing style affecting, 392
　class size affecting, 318
　cultural influences on, 393
　divorce of parents affecting, 348
　early intervention programs affecting, 245f, 245–246
　family beliefs on, 33
　gender stereotypes on, 276, 334, 343
　of immigrant youths, 32–33
　intelligence quotient as predictor of, 243, 309
　international comparison of, 324, 324t
　mathematical abilities affecting, 243
　parent–school partnership affecting, 393–394
　part-time work affecting, 395–396
　reading skills affecting, 242
　recess time affecting, 298
　of rejected children, 343
　school characteristics affecting, 394–395
　school transitions affecting, 391
　and self-esteem, 331
　and social skills, 263
　in teenage pregnancy, 378
Academic learning, 318–325, 391–397. *See also* Education
Academic programs in preschool and kindergarten, 244
Acceptance
　of change in late adulthood, 608
　in child rearing, 278, 279, 279t, 280
　in coping with dying, 604, 605, 647, 648
　in peer relations. *See* Peer acceptance
　of self. *See* Self-acceptance
Accidental injuries. *See* Injuries, unintentional
Accommodation in cognitive development, 152, 228

Accommodation of eyes, 502
Acculturative stress, 406, 416
Accutane (isotretinoin), 87
Acetylcholine
　in Alzheimer's disease, 584, 585
　drug therapy affecting, 588
Achievement
　ability and effort in, 333, 334
　academic. *See* Academic achievement
　attributions related to, 333–334
　gender stereotypes on, 276, 334, 343
　and identity, 403, 403t, 404
　and learned helplessness, 333
　and self-esteem, 333–334
Acquired immune deficiency syndrome. *See* AIDS
ACTIVE (Advanced Cognitive Training for Independent and Vital Elderly) study, 597
Active correlation, 72
Activities of daily living in late adulthood, 567–568
　cognitive interventions affecting, 597
　control versus dependency in, 610–611, 613
　problem solving in, 594–595
Activity level and temperament, 191, 191t, 193
Activity theory of aging, 614
Actors, memory strategies of, 523
Adaptation
　of baby to labor and delivery, 97
　coping strategies in. *See* Coping strategies
　Darwin on, 14
　to dying, contextual influences on, 647–650
　in early adulthood, 470–471
　ethology of, 22
　evolutionary developmental psychology on, 22–23
　to family changes, 60–61, 115
　and habituation, 85
　of immigrant youths, 32–33
　in late adulthood, 572–575, 595, 623, 624
　in middle adulthood, 514–517, 536, 537
　Piaget on, 18–19, 152
　and practical intelligence, 311
　and resilience, 10–11
　Vaillant on, 470–471, 536
　in widowhood, 623, 624
Adaptation to Life (Vaillant), 470
Addiction
　to alcohol, 444–445
　of infants, 87
　to nicotine, 444
Adjustment
　in adolescence, 362, 391–392, 419
　affluence affecting, 62–63, 63f
　child-care facilities affecting, 202–203
　child maltreatment affecting, 283
　child-rearing styles affecting, 279, 280

divorce of parents affecting, 347, 348, 349
　early intervention programs affecting, 246
　family mealtimes affecting, 63, 63f
　and friendships, 419
　of immigrant youths, 32–33
　and infant sleeping arrangements, 129
　to parenthood, 115
　peer acceptance affecting, 341, 343
　to retirement, 630–631
　and shyness, 195, 195f
Adolescence (11 to 18 years old), 8t, 361–427
　academic achievement in, 392–396
　in adoption, 58
　aggression in, 298
　arousal states in, 368
　autonomy in, 372–373, 415–416, 485–486
　bereavement interventions in, 665
　biological perspective of, 362
　in blended families, 350
　body composition in, 363–364
　body proportions in, 363
　body size in, 363, 364f
　brain development in, 367–368, 381, 387
　causes of death in, 643
　cognitive-affective complexity in, 452, 452f
　cognitive development in, 367, 382–397
　conflicts in, 369–370, 415, 418
　cultural influences on, 362, 369, 370, 373–374, 415–416
　dating in, 420–421
　death concept in, 643–644, 646
　death of parent or sibling during, 661–662
　decision making in, 387–388
　delinquency in, 423–426
　depression in, 421–423
　divorce of parents during, 348
　dropping out of school during, 396–397
　early phase of, 362
　eating disorders in, 372–373
　emotional and social development in, 401–427
　employment in, 459
　family in, 414–416, 485–486
　fetal alcohol exposure affecting, 89
　formal operational stage in, 382–384
　free time in, 417
　friendships in, 417–419
　gender typing in, 414
　health issues in, 371–381
　hormone changes in, 363, 369, 373
　hypothetico-deductive reasoning in, 382–383
　idealism and criticism in, 387
　identity development in, 402, 403–405
　identity versus role confusion in, 16t, 402
　of immigrant youths, 32, 33

impulsivity and sensation seeking in, 367–368, 368f
　information processing in, 384–386
　initiation ceremonies in, 369
　language development in, 383
　late phase of, 362
　learning in school during, 391–397
　mathematical abilities in, 388–391
　media multitasking in, 394
　memory of events in late adulthood, 593
　middle phase of, 362
　milestones of development, 428–429
　moodiness in, 369
　moral development in, 405–414
　motor development in, 364–365
　nutrition in, 366–367, 371–373
　obesity in, 291, 292
　parent relationship in, 369–370, 415. *See also* Parent–adolescent relationship
　peer relations in, 370, 371, 417–421
　physical attractiveness in, 370–371
　physical development in, 362–381
　play in, 298
　pregnancy in, 93, 378–380. *See also* Teenage pregnancy and parenthood
　propositional thought in, 383
　psychosexual and psychosocial development in, 16t, 362
　puberty in, 363–371. *See also* Puberty
　school transitions in, 391–392
　scientific reasoning in, 385–386
　self-consciousness and self-focusing in, 386–387
　self-understanding in, 402–405
　sex differences in, 363, 364, 365–366, 366f, 368–369, 388–391, 417–418
　sexual abuse in, 353
　sexuality in, 373–380
　sexually transmitted diseases in, 376–377
　sexual maturation in, 365–366
　shyness in, 192
　sibling relationship in, 416
　sleep schedule in, 368
　social perspective of, 362
　spatial abilities in, 390
　substance use and abuse in, 364, 370, 376, 380–381, 419, 420
　suicide in, 422–423
　time spent with family in, 416, 417
　verbal abilities in, 388
　vocational choice in, 456
Adoption, 57–59, 416t
　attachment security in, 199
　deprivation prior to, 125–127, 127f
　and environmental influences on gene expression, 73
　by gay and lesbian couples, 492
　heritability research in, 70
　intelligence and IQ research in, 70, 313–314
　schizophrenia research in, 70, 73
　in surrogate motherhood, 54–55
Adrenal androgens, 363

Adult Development and Enrichment
  Project (ADEPT), 597
Adulthood
  brain plasticity in, 126
  death concept in, 644–645, 646
  death of intimate partner in, 662
  diversity of lifestyles in, 486–492
  early, 8t, 430–497. See also Early
    adulthood
  late, 8t, 562–635. See also Late
    adulthood
  middle, 8t, 501–559. See also
    Middle adulthood
Advanced Cognitive Training for
  Independent and Vital Elderly
  (ACTIVE) study, 597
Advance medical directives, 655–656
Affect optimization in late adulthood,
  605
Affluence, 62–63
Afghanistan, life expectancy in, 565
Africa. See also specific countries
  breastfeeding and bottle-feeding
    in, 130
  late adulthood in, 576
  menopause in, 506, 506f
  neonatal behavioral assessment
    in, 114
African Americans
  academic achievement of, 393, 395
  adolescent, 367, 375, 380, 416
  as adolescent parents, 380
  as adult learners, 526
  aging parents of, 549, 551, 617
  Alzheimer's disease of, 584–585
  anorexia nervosa of, 372
  asthma of, 293
  body image of, 371
  body size of, 121
  cardiovascular diseases of, 434–
    435, 436, 442, 442f
  caregivers for older adults, 612
  child-rearing practices of, 267, 281
  communication style of, 314, 317
  cosleeping of parents and infants,
    129
  death beliefs of, 650, 664
  dementia of, 582, 584–585
  departure from parental home, 479
  diabetes mellitus of, 581
  discipline and punishment of
    children, 267, 281
  discrimination in career
    opportunities, 493–494, 494f
  drug use of, 380
  extended families of, 65, 66, 332,
    422, 434, 479, 491, 589
  food insecurity of, 132
  funerals of, 664
  gender stereotypes of, 276
  generativity of, 535
  glaucoma of, 503
  grandparents as caregivers of, 547,
    548
  health problems in late adulthood,
    575
  infant mortality rate of, 104
  intelligence quotient of, 312,
    313–314, 315
  long-term care of older adults, 589
  menarche of, 368
  menopause of, 507
  in mixed-race schools, 321

moral reasoning of, 411
narrative style of, 317
never-married, 487, 491
osteoporosis of, 513
overweight and obese, 291, 439
partner abuse of, 483
passive euthanasia beliefs of, 655
poverty of, 61
puberty of, 367
religiosity of, 465, 609
reminiscence in late adulthood,
  606
school transitions of, 391
self-esteem of, 332
sexual activity in adolescence, 375
sickle cell anemia of, 50
singlehood lifestyle of, 487
in single-parent families, 491
skeletal age of, 121
stereotype threat affecting, 315,
  315f
suicide rate of, 422
teacher–student interaction of,
  320–321
vocabulary development affecting
  intelligence testing of, 314
vocational choice of, 457
widowhood of, 623
Afterlife beliefs, 643, 645, 650, 664
After-school programs, 351
Age
  in adolescence (11 to 18 years old).
    See Adolescence
  in departure from parental home,
    478–479, 545
  during divorce of parents, 347–348,
    350
  in early adulthood (18 to 40 years
    old). See Early adulthood
  in early childhood (2 to 6 years
    old). See Early childhood
  in emerging adulthood (18 to 25
    to 29 years old). See Emerging
    adulthood
  in eyewitness testimony of
    children, 355
  of fetal viability, 84
  First Age, 607
  Fourth Age, 607
  functional, 564
  in infancy and toddlerhood (birth
    to 2 years old). See Infancy and
    toddlerhood
  in late adulthood (65 years old to
    death). See Late adulthood
  in lifespan perspective of
    development, 10–11
  in major periods of development,
    8t
  maternal, 93, 93f. See also Maternal
    age
  and maximum lifespan, 566–567
  in middle adulthood (40 to 65
    years old). See Middle adulthood
  in middle childhood (6 to 11 years
    old). See Middle childhood
  paternal, 438
  Second Age, 598n, 607
  skeletal, 121, 217
  and social clock, 471, 533
  subjective, 535, 573
  Third Age, 598, 598n, 607
Age-graded influences, 10–11, 12

Age spots on skin, 503, 572
Aggression
  in adolescence, 298
  androgens in, 270
  bullying in, 342
  and delinquency, 424, 425
  in early childhood, 269–272
  family influences on, 270
  friendships in, 340
  interventions in, 272
  partner abuse in, 482
  physical, 269, 270
  of popular children, 341
  proactive (instrumental), 269
  and punishment, 266, 267, 270
  reactive (hostile), 269
  of rejected children, 341, 342, 343
  relational, 269, 270, 424
  sex differences in, 269–270, 271
  and television viewing, 270–271,
    271f
  verbal, 269
  and victimization, 342
  and violence in media, 270–271,
    271f
Agility in motor development, 295
Aging
  activity theory of, 614
  of baby boomer generation, 13
  continuity theory of, 614–615,
    618, 631
  cross-linkage theory of, 434
  cumulative effects of random
    events in, 432, 433
  disengagement theory of, 614
  at DNA and cellular level, 432–434,
    433f
  double standard of, 516–517, 535
  in early adulthood, 432–438
  functional age in, 564
  in late adulthood, 567–575
  multidimensional and
    multidirectional influences in,
    432
  optimal, 632–633
  of parents, 547–551
  plasticity of development in, 9–10
  primary or biological, 432–438,
    580
  secondary, 580
  social contexts of, 616–619
  social theories of, 614–616
  socioemotional selectivity theory
    of, 615–616, 626, 631
  stereotypes of, 566, 570, 574–575,
    576, 606, 625
  subjective age in, 535, 573
  at tissue and organ level, 434
  wear-and-tear theory of, 432
Aging in place, 617
Aging Well (Vaillant), 470
Agonal phase in dying, 640
Agreeableness
  in late adulthood, 608
  in middle adulthood, 542, 542t
AIDS
  in adolescence, 377
  death rate in, 438f, 447
  in early adulthood, 438f, 447–448
  in middle childhood, 293
  in pregnancy, 90–91, 91t
Air pollution, and asthma, 293
Aka of Central Africa, 204

Alaskan Natives, cultural traditions
  of, 612
Alcoholics Anonymous, 445
Alcoholism, 444
Alcohol-related neurodevelopmental
  disorder (ARND), 89
Alcohol use and abuse
  in adolescence, 380, 381f
  in early adulthood, 444–445
  genetic factors in, 444
  health consequences of, 445
  impact on sexual performance, 579
  osteoporosis in, 513
  partner abuse in, 483
  paternal, at time of conception, 89
  in pregnancy, 88–90
Alertness of infants, 108t
Alleles, 48
  dominant and recessive, 48–50
  genomic imprinting of, 51
Altruistic behavior. See also Prosocial
  behavior
  in adolescence, 413, 414
  in early childhood, 260
Alzheimer's disease, 52, 577, 579,
  579f, 580, 582–585
  caregivers in, 585, 586–587
  familial, 584
  glucose blood levels in, 581, 584
  long-term care in, 588
  protective factors in, 585
  recognition of living will in, 655
  risk factors for, 584–585
  sporadic, 584
  symptoms and course of, 583
American Medical Association, 655,
  659
American Sign Language, 174
Amnesia, infantile, 164–165
Amniocentesis, 56, 56t
Amnion, 81
Amniotic fluid, 81
Amodal sensory properties, 146, 147
Amphetamine use in adolescence,
  380
Amygdala
  in adopted children, 199
  in autism, 241
  in shyness and sociability, 192
Amyloid plaque in Alzheimer's
  disease, 583, 584, 585
Anabolic steroid use in adolescence,
  364
Analgesic drugs
  in arthritis, 581
  in childbirth, 100–101
  living will on, 655
Analogical problem solving
  in preoperational stage, 230
  in sensorimotor stage, 157
Anal stage of psychosexual
  development, 16t
Analytical intelligence, 310, 311, 311f
Andorra, life expectancy in, 565f
Androgen
  adrenal, 363
  and aggression, 270
  and gender roles, 273, 274
  in new fathers, 115
  in puberty, 363
Androgyny, 276, 541–542
  and friendship intimacy of boys,
    417

Andrus, Ethel Percy, 69
Anemia
 Cooley's, 49t
 sickle cell, 49t, 50, 293
Anencephaly, 92
Anesthesia
 during childbirth, 100
 for newborns, 112
Anger
 coping strategies in, 514–515
 in coping with dying, 647, 649
 experimental research on, 35
 in infancy and toddlerhood, 185–186
 in middle adulthood, 513–514
Angina pectoris, 512
Angioplasty, 512
Animals, nonhuman
 anti-aging effects of dietary calorie restriction in, 505
 attachment of, 195–196
 brain plasticity in, 126
 free radicals in, 434
 imitation by, 135, 135f, 136
 imprinting in, 22
 language acquisition of, 174
 life expectancy variations in, 434, 564
 sensory deprivation studies of, 125
 sex differences in behavior of, 273–274
Animistic thinking in preoperational stage, 228, 230
Anorexia nervosa, 372–373, 442
Anoxia of infant during childbirth, 100, 101
Antibodies, 437
 in Alzheimer's disease, 585
 in prenatal development, 85, 93, 376
Anticipatory grieving, 661
Antidepressant drugs, 423, 506, 587
 in Alzheimer's disease, 585
 in bulimia, 373
 in parental depression, 187
 in pregnancy, 87
Antisocial behavior
 delinquency in, 423–426
 in depression of parent, 186–187
 environmental influences on gene expression for, 73
 of popular children, 341
 suicide in, 422–423
Anxiety
 death anxiety, 644, 645f, 645–646
 in middle childhood, 352
 in pregnancy, 92–93
 in separation, 196
 stranger anxiety, 186–187
Apathy
 in adolescence, 404
 in alcohol use, 445
Apgar Scale, 98, 98t
Apnea, sleep, 571
ApoE4 gene in Alzheimer's disease, 584, 585
Appearance and attractiveness
 in adolescence, 370–371
 and body image, 370–371, 372
 in late adulthood, 571–572, 573
 of newborn, assessment of, 97–98
Appearance–reality tasks in preoperational stage, 228

Appetite
 in adolescence, 371–373
 of dying person, 640
 in early childhood, 219
Applicability, and death concept, 642
Apprenticeship programs in vocational preparation, 459
Appropriate or good death, 648
Area Agencies on Aging, 67
Argentina
 adoption by gay and lesbian families in, 492
 child-rearing styles and academic achievement in, 392
 marriage of same-sex couples in, 479
Arithmetic abilities. See Mathematical abilities
Arousal states
 in adolescence, 368
 in infancy and toddlerhood, 108t, 108–112, 128
Arrhythmias, 512
 fibrillation in dying, 640
Arthritis
 calorie restricted diet affecting risk for, 505
 free radicals in, 434
 in late adulthood, 576, 580–581, 588
 in middle childhood, 293
Artistic expression
 creativity in. See Creativity
 drawing in. See Drawing
 in early childhood, 224f, 224–225
 in middle childhood, 295, 295f, 322–323
Artistic personality, vocational choice in, 456
Asia. See also specific countries
 academic achievement in, 324t, 324–325
 achievement-related attributions in, 334
 aging parents in, 549
 autobiographical memory in, 238
 dating in, 420
 departure from family home in, 479
 free time of adolescents in, 417
 immigrant youths from, 32
 language development in, 178
 math instruction in, 309
 menopause in, 506, 506f, 508
 myopia in, 293
 neonatal behavioral assessment in, 114
 romantic relationships in, 475
 self-concept in, 331
 self-conscious emotions in, 260
 self-esteem in, 331
 sense of control in, 573
 temperament of children in, 193
 terminally ill patients in, 649
Asian Americans
 academic achievement of, 393
 aging parents of, 549, 617, 618
 anorexia nervosa of, 372
 extended-family households of, 65
 intelligence quotient of, 312
 long-term care of older adults, 589
 osteoporosis in, 513
 respect for older adults, 627

Asian Pacific Islanders
 child-rearing practices of, 281
 sibling relationships of, 552
Aspirin in pregnancy, 87
Assimilation, Piaget's cognitive-developmental theory of, 152
Assisted discovery learning, 235
Assisted living facilities, 589, 618, 619
Assisted suicide, 654t, 658–659
Assistive technology and devices, 573–574
Associative memory in late adulthood, 591–592, 592f, 594
Associative play, 261
Asthma, 51, 293
Atherosclerosis, 436, 442, 511, 571
 cerebrovascular dementia in, 586
Athletic activities
 in adolescence, 364–365, 365f, 376, 419
 and clique membership, 419
 developmentally appropriate, 297
 in early adulthood, 436–437, 437f
 gender stereotypes in, 296, 365
 of lesbian, gay, and bisexual youths, 376
 in middle adulthood, 504
 in middle childhood, 295, 296–297
 parental involvement in, 296
 in pregnancy, 92
 and self-esteem, 296, 331, 365
 sex differences in, 296, 364–365
Attachment, 195–206
 avoidant, 197–198, 474
 Bowlby on, 22, 196–197, 201
 continuity of caregiving affecting, 199, 206
 cultural differences in, 198f, 198–199
 and dating, 420
 disorganized/disoriented, 198, 200, 206
 employment of parents affecting, 202–204, 203f
 ethological theory of, 196–197, 206
 fathers affecting, 201–204
 infant characteristics affecting, 200–201
 internal working models of, 197, 201, 420, 474
 and later development, 206, 420, 474
 and loneliness, 478
 maltreatment as child affecting, 200
 multiple, 201–205
 phases of development, 196–197
 psychoanalytic perspective on, 195, 206
 quality of caregiving affecting, 199–200
 resistant, 198, 474
 and romantic relationships of adults, 474
 secure, 197, 474
 security of, 197–198, 199–201. See also Security of attachment
 and self-concept, 256
 stability of, 198
 theory of, 5
 and theory of mind, 240
Attachment-in-the-making phase, 196

Attachment Q-Sort, 198
Attendance to school, 396–397
 and dropping out, 396–397, 455
 school transitions affecting, 391, 392f
Attention
 in autism, 241
 in continuous performance tasks, 521
 in early childhood, 236–237
 and emotional self-regulation, 189
 and habituation of infants, 163
 in infancy and toddlerhood, 144, 161, 163, 176
 information processing in, 161, 163, 236–237, 303–305, 384, 521–522
 and inhibition, 236–237, 237f, 521
 and intelligence quotient, 310
 joint attention of infant and caregiver, 176
 and memory, 304–305
 in middle adulthood, 521–522
 in middle childhood, 303–304
 in multitasking, 394, 521, 522
 and pattern perception of infants, 144
 in planning tasks, 237, 303–304
 selective, 303
 sustained, 163
 and temperament, 190, 191, 191t
Attention-deficit hyperactivity disorder (ADHD), 303, 304–305
 delinquency in, 424
 genetic factors in, 74, 304, 305
 maternal smoking during pregnancy as risk factor for, 74, 305
 origins of, 304–305
 symptoms of, 304
 treatment of, 305
Attractiveness. See Appearance and attractiveness
Attributions
 achievement-related, 333–334
 definition of, 333
 mastery-oriented, 333, 334, 335
 retraining of, 334
Australia
 academic achievement in, 324, 392
 adolescent suicide in, 422
 caregiving roles of parents in, 201
 cesarean delivery rate in, 101
 child care in, 171, 201, 203
 childhood attachment patterns and adult romantic relationships in, 474
 divorce rate in, 347f
 fears of children in, 352
 infant mortality rate in, 105f
 life expectancy in, 565f
 lifelong learning in, 598
 marital roles in, 480, 481f
 poverty rate in, 68f
 sleep patterns of infants in, 128
 unintentional childhood injuries in, 221f
 voluntary active euthanasia in, 656t, 657
Austria
 adolescent contraceptive use in, 375f
 corporal punishment in, 282–283

Austria (cont.)
    infant mortality rate in, 105f
    life expectancy in, 565f
    unintentional childhood injuries in, 221f
    vocational education in, 459
Authoritarian child-rearing style, 279, 279t
Authoritative child-rearing style, 278–279, 279t, 280–281
    academic achievement in, 392
    effectiveness of, 280
    self-esteem in, 332, 403
Authority understanding in moral development, 407
Autism
    false beliefs in, 240
    in fragile X syndrome, 51
    and mindblindness, 241
    and vaccinations, 221
Autobiographical memory, 164–165
    in early childhood, 238
    and infantile amnesia, 164–165
    in late adulthood, 592f, 592–593, 606
    reminiscence bump in, 592–593
Autoimmune disorders, 571
    rheumatoid arthritis in, 580
Automatic processes in information processing, 162
Autonomic nervous system, 568, 571
Autonomy issues
    in adolescence, 372–373, 415–416, 485–486
    in anorexia nervosa, 372–373
    in authoritarian child rearing, 279
    in authoritative child rearing, 278, 279
    behavioral component of, 415
    emotional component of, 189, 415
    in immigrant families, 415–416
    in infancy and toddlerhood, versus shame and doubt, 16t, 184
    in late adulthood, 610
    in middle adulthood, 538
    in permissive child rearing, 279
    in uninvolved child rearing, 280
Autosomes, 47
    diseases related to, 49t
Average life expectancy, 8, 432, 564–565, 565f
Avoidance in grief process, 659
Avoidant attachment, 197–198
    and romantic relationships of adults, 474

B
Babbling, 176, 178
Babinski reflex, 107t
Baby and Child Care (Spock), 15, 129
Baby boomer generation, 12–13
    aging of, 535
    caring for aging parents, 550f
    cognitive changes in late adulthood of, 596
    cohort effects in, 11, 12–13
    environmental mastery of, 539
    history-graded influences on, 11–12
    leading-edge of, 12–13
    life expectancy in, 565
    midlife of, 13
    retirement of, 557, 629

    self-acceptance of, 539
    sibling relationships in, 552
    Third Age of, 607
    trailing edge of, 13
    vocational life of, 553
Baby fat, 121, 216
Baby teeth, 217
Bacterial diseases in pregnancy, 91t, 92
Baka of West Africa, childhood play activities of, 256
Balance in motor development, 294
Balinese of Indonesia, mourning behavior of, 664
Ball skills in motor development, 223, 295
Bandura, Albert, 18
Baptist families, 643
Bargaining, in coping with dying, 647
Bar mitzvah, 369
Basal metabolic rate, 439, 504
    calorie restriction affecting, 505
Bases in DNA, 46, 47f
Bat mitzvah, 369
Bayley Scales of Infant and Toddler Development, 169
B cells, 437
Behavior
    antisocial. See Antisocial behavior
    conditioning of, 17, 133f, 133–134, 265
    and moral development, 411–412
    of newborn, assessment of, 114
    prosocial. See Prosocial behavior
    sexual. See Sexual attitudes and behavior
Behavioral control in child rearing
    in authoritarian style, 279
    in authoritative style, 278–279
    in permissive style, 279–280
    in uninvolved style, 280
Behavioral genetics, 69
Behaviorism, 17
    attachment in, 195
    compared to other human development theories, 28t
    contributions and limitations of, 18
Behavior modification, 18
Belgium
    adolescent contraceptive use in, 375f
    adoption by gay and lesbian families in, 492
    assisted suicide in, 658
    life expectancy in, 565f
    marriage of same sex couples in, 479
Beliefs
    and desires in theory of mind, 239
    false, 239f, 239–240, 241, 306, 307f
    gender stereotypes in, 273
    religious. See Religion
The Bell Curve (Herrnstein & Murray), 312
Bell-shaped distribution of intelligence test scores, 169–170, 170f
Bereavement, 659–665
    anticipatory, 661
    avoidance in, 659
    confrontation task in, 660
    cultural variations in, 663, 664
    in disenfranchised grief, 662

    dual-process model of coping in, 660
    duration of, 660
    interventions in, 663–665
    overload in multiple deaths, 662–663
    personal and situational factors in, 660–663
    restoration task in, 660
    in sudden unexpected death, 660–661, 665
Better Beginnings, Better Futures Project, 64
Bhatto Bhatto game in India, 262
Bias
    in clinical or case study research, 31
    cultural, in intelligence tests, 243, 314–315
    egocentric, 228
    in ethnographic research, 33
    in longitudinal research, 37
    mutual exclusivity, in vocabulary development, 248, 249
    racial and ethnic, 337–338
    self-serving, 385
    shape, in vocabulary development, 248
    stereotypes in. See Stereotypes
Bicultural identity, 406
Bicycle riding, childhood injuries in, 222, 294
Bidirectional influences
    in ecological systems theory, 25, 59
    in epigenetic framework, 73, 73f, 75
    in family, 59
    in prenatal development, 86
"Big five" personality traits, 542–543, 542t, 606
Bilingualism, 317–318
Binet, Alfred, 15, 169
Binge eating, 373, 441
Binocular depth cues, 142
Biocultural event, menopause as, 508
Bioecological model, 24
Biological aging, 432–438, 580. See also Aging
Biological influences
    on adolescence, 362
    on gender typing, 273–274
    genetic. See Genetic factors
Biracial identity, 406
Birth
    complications of. See Birth complications
    defects at time of. See Birth defects
    labor and delivery in, 96–101. See also Childbirth
    low weight at time of, 101–105. See also Low birth weight
    preterm. See Preterm infants
Birth centers, freestanding, 99
Birth complications, 101–106
    in fetal medicine interventions, 56
    Kauai study on, 106
    prenatal health care reducing, 95
    in preterm and low-birth-weight infants, 101–105
    resilience of children with, 106
    in teenage pregnancy, 93, 94
Birth control. See Contraception
Birth defects
    in chromosomal abnormalities, 52–53
    folic acid in prevention of, 92

    in malnutrition, 92
    neonatal mortality rates in, 104
    in teratogen exposure, 85–92
Birth order, and sexual orientation, 376
Birthrate by maternal age, 438f
Birth weight
    low, 101–105. See also Low birth weight
    of small-for-date infants, 102
    and survival rate, 101
Bisexuals. See Gay, lesbian, and bisexual people
Black Americans. See African Americans
Blastocyst, 80f, 81
Blended families, 349–350, 416t, 490–491
Blindness
    in cataracts, 569
    in diabetes mellitus, 291
    in glaucoma, 503
    in macular degeneration, 569, 580
    touch sensitivity in, 570
Blood pressure
    caloric restriction affecting, 505
    dietary fat affecting, 442, 442f
    in hypertension, 435, 436, 442, 442f, 511
    in shyness and sociability, 192
Blood tests
    in phenylketonuria, 50
    in pregnancy, 56, 56t
Blood types, inheritance of, 48t
Bodily-kinesthetic intelligence, 312t, 323
Body composition changes
    in early childhood, 216, 216f
    in infancy and toddlerhood, 121
    in late adulthood, 572
    in middle adulthood, 504
    in middle childhood, 290
    in puberty, 363–364
Body image
    in anorexia nervosa, 372
    in puberty, 370–371
Body mass index in obesity, 291, 439
Body proportion changes
    in adolescence, 363, 364f
    in infancy and toddlerhood, 120f, 121
    in middle childhood, 290
Body size
    in early childhood, 216, 216f
    genetic factors affecting, 130
    height in. See Height
    in infancy and toddlerhood, 120f, 120–121, 131–132
    in middle childhood, 290, 290f
    nutrition affecting, 130–132
    in puberty, 363, 364f
    scale errors in awareness of, 207
    weight in. See Weight
Body transcendence in late adulthood, 604, 605
Bonding. See Attachment
Bones, 435t
    in early childhood, 217
    epiphyses of, 217
    in late adulthood, 572, 577
    in middle adulthood, 504, 512–513
    osteoporosis of, 504, 512–513
    skeletal age, 121, 217

Bosnia, violence in, 353
Boston Marathon bombings, 665
Botswana
  Herero people of, 576
  !Kung society of, 129
Bottle-feeding, 130–131, 131*t*
Boundaries, subjective, in pattern
    perception, 144, 144*f*
Bowlby, John, 22
  on attachment, 22, 196–197, 201,
    474
Braille reading, touch sensitivity in,
    570
Brain
  in adolescence, 367–368, 381, 387
  alcohol use affecting, 445
  in Alzheimer's disease, 582–585
  in arousal states, 128
  in attention-deficit hyperactivity
    disorder, 304–305
  in autism, 241
  cerebellum of. *See* Cerebellum
  cerebral cortex of, 124–125. *See
    also* Cerebral cortex
  cerebral hemispheres of, 124–125,
    174, 217–218
  in cerebrovascular dementia,
    585–587
  childhood maltreatment affecting,
    283
  developmental cognitive
    neuroscience research on, 21–22
  in early adulthood, 450
  in early childhood, 126, 217*f*,
    217–219, 218*f*
  electroencephalography of, 122,
    123*f*, 192, 568
  experience-dependent growth of,
    128, 450
  experience-expectant growth of,
    127–128
  in fetal alcohol spectrum disorder,
    88–89
  in handedness, 217–218
  hormones affecting development
    of, 219
  imaging of, 123*f*, 123*t*, 123–124
  in infancy and toddlerhood,
    121–130
  information processing speed,
    520
  language areas in, 124, 125, 126,
    174, 175
  in late adulthood, 568, 578, 582–
    588, 596
  lateralization of, 124, 125, 217–218
  milestones of development, 122,
    122*f*
  neurobiological research on,
    122–124
  neurons in, 121–122, 136
  in Parkinson's disease, 582
  in persistent vegetative state, 641
  plasticity of, 21–22, 124–125, 126
  prenatal development of, 84, 85,
    88–89, 122
  programmed cell death in, 122
  sensitive periods in development
    of, 125–128
  size changes, 122
  in small-for-date infants, 102
  stimulation affecting development
    of, 122, 125–128

Brain death, 641
Brazil
  adoption by gay and lesbian
    families in, 492
  early adulthood in, 466
  infectious diseases and physical
    development in, 220
  mathematical abilities of child
    candy sellers in, 24
  unintentional childhood injuries
    in, 221*f*
Breast cancer, 442, 443, 510, 511
Breast development, 363, 365, 366
  age at time of, 366*f*
  variations in, 366, 367
Breastfeeding
  classical conditioning in, 133*f*,
    133–134
  compared to bottle-feeding, 130–
    131, 131*t*
  in cosleeping parents and infants,
    129
  operant conditioning in, 134
  and rooting reflex, 106, 107*t*
  and smell sense of newborn,
    112–113
  and sucking reflex, 106, 107*t*, 133*f*,
    133–134
  by Yurok Indians, 16–17
Breathing techniques in natural
    childbirth, 99
Breech position, 100
Bridge jobs prior to retirement, 629
The Broken Cord (Dorris), 88
Bronfenbrenner, Urie, 24
  ecological systems theory of, 24*f*,
    24–27, 59, 60
Bucharest Early Intervention Project,
    127
Buddhism, 609, 641, 650
Building Blocks math curriculum,
    243
Bulgaria, teenage pregnancy in, 378*f*
Bulimia nervosa, 373, 442
Bullying, 341, 342, 343
  cyberbullying in, 342
  sexual orientation of parents as
    factor in, 492
  systematic observation of, 30
Burial practices, 664
Burnout from job stress, 554

C

Caffeine, and prenatal development,
    87
Calcium
  in adolescence, 372
  in late adulthood, 577
  in osteoporosis, 513
Caloric intake
  anti-aging effects of restriction, 505
  in infancy, 130
  in middle adulthood, 504, 505
  in obesity, 440, 441
Calorie-restriction mimetics, 505
Cambodia, intelligence definition of
    immigrants from, 311
Cameroon
  self-recognition by toddlers in,
    207, 208*f*
  theory of mind in, 306–307
Canada
  academic achievement in, 324

adolescent contraceptive use in,
    375*f*, 379
  adolescent pregnancy in, 378*f*
  adolescent sexual activity in, 374,
    375*f*, 376, 378*f*, 379
  adolescent suicide in, 422
  adoption by gay and lesbian
    families in, 492
  aging stereotypes in, 574
  assisted suicide in, 658
  bilingualism in, 317, 318
  caregiving roles of parents in, 201
  cesarean delivery rate in, 101
  college education in, 455
  communication styles in, 314
  cosleeping of parents and infants,
    129
  divorce rate in, 347*f*
  dual-earner families in, 495
  family size in, 483
  fetal death rate in, 51
  gender stereotypes in, 343
  grammatical development in, 316
  high school graduation rate in,
    395*f*
  hospice programs in, 653
  identity development in, 405
  immunization rate in, 221
  infant mortality rate in, 105*f*
  life expectancy in, 8, 565*f*
  lifelong learning in, 598
  loneliness in, 477, 477*f*, 478
  marriage of same-sex couples in,
    479
  moral development in, 336, 409
  natives of. *See* Native Canadians
  out-group prejudice in, 338
  overweight and obesity rate in, 291
  parental leave in, 104
  partner abuse in, 483*f*
  personality traits in, 542
  poverty rate in, 68*f*
  religion in, 412
  respect for elders in, 574
  retirement programs in, 630
  sexually transmitted diseases in,
    376
  unintentional childhood injuries
    in, 221*f*
  voluntary active euthanasia
    opinions in, 656*t*
Canadian Virtual Hospice, 653
Canalization, 72
Cancer
  in alcohol use, 445
  assisted suicide in, 658
  calorie restricted diet affecting risk
    for, 505
  as cause of death, 438*f*, 509, 509*f*,
    510, 579, 579*f*, 640, 646, 648,
    649, 651
  in children, 293, 299, 646, 661
  and dietary fat, 442
  in diethylstilbestrol exposure, 86
  in dioxin exposure, 90
  in early adulthood, 438*f*, 439, 442,
    443
  exercise affecting risk for, 443
  free radicals in, 434
  genetic factors in, 51, 52, 57, 432,
    433, 510, 511, 567, 661
  in growth hormone therapy, 434
  hospice care in, 653

in immune system changes, 434,
    450, 571
  incidence of different types, 510,
    510*f*
  in late adulthood, 571, 575, 577,
    579, 579*f*
  in menopausal hormone therapy,
    506
  in middle adulthood, 509, 509*f*,
    510*f*, 510–511
  moral dilemma in, 407
  in obesity, 291, 439
  in radiation exposure, 51, 90
  sex differences in, 510*f*
  in smoking, 88, 444
  in stress, 450
  survival rate in, 510–511
  voluntary active euthanasia in, 657
Car accidents
  childhood injuries in, 221, 222
  in late adulthood, 581–582
Cardinality, 243
Cardiovascular system
  caloric restriction affecting, 505
  death from diseases of, 564, 579,
    579*f*, 640, 648
  dietary fat affecting, 436, 442, 442*f*
  in early adulthood, 434–436, 438*f*
  exercise affecting, 443
  in late adulthood, 570–571,
    579–580
  in middle adulthood, 509, 509*f*,
    511–512, 513–514
  of newborn, Apgar Scale on, 98*t*
  in physical changes of aging, 434–
    436, 435*t*, 570–571
  prenatal development of, 84, 85,
    100
  stress affecting, 449–450, 513–514
Career. *See also* Employment
  changes in midlife, 555–556
  discontinuous path in, 492
  in early adulthood, 470, 492–495
  educational preparation for, 393–
    394, 395, 396, 459, 554–555
  establishment of, 492–493
  glass ceiling in, 555
  mentoring relationship in, 493
  in middle adulthood, 553–558
  nontraditional, of men, 458
  and selection of vocation, 455–459
Caregivers
  abandonment of older adults with
    severe disabilities, 627
  of aging parents, 550–551, 617–
    618, 623, 626
  bereavement interventions for, 665
  of dementia victims, 585, 586–587
  dependency and control issues in
    late adulthood, 610–611
  of dying person, 651–653, 665
  elder maltreatment by, 627–628
  and social support in late
    adulthood, 611–613
Care orientation in moral
    development, 409
Caribbean families, child-rearing
    practices of, 281
Carolina Abecedarian Project, 173,
    173*f*
Carriers of inherited traits, 50, 50*f*, 51*f*
  genetic counseling of, 55
Case studies, 17, 29*t*, 30–31

Cataracts
free radicals in, 434
in infancy, 125
in late adulthood, 569
Catch-up growth, 130, 132
Categorical self, 208
Categorization abilities
Animate–inanimate distinction in, 166, 230
basic-level categories in, 231
in concrete operational stage, 299
general categories in, 231
and memory, 304
in preoperational stage, 229, 229f, 230–231
and self-awareness, 208
in sensorimotor stage, 164–166, 166f
subcategories in, 231
Catholicism, 608, 655
The Cat in the Hat (Seuss), 85
Caucasian Americans
academic achievement of, 393
aging parents of, 549, 551
anorexia nervosa of, 372
body image of, 371
communication style of, 317
discipline and punishment of children, 267
drug use of, 380
gender stereotypes of, 276
generativity of, 535
glaucoma of, 503
grandparents as caregivers of, 548
in-group favoritism of, 337
intelligence definition of, 311
intelligence quotient of, 312, 313–314, 315
long-term care of older adults, 589
menarche of, 368
menopause of, 507
never-married, 487
osteoporosis of, 513
passive euthanasia beliefs of, 655
play and peer sociability of, 262
religiosity of, 609, 610
scaffolding interactions of, 234
self-esteem of, 332
stereotype threat affecting, 315, 315f
suicide rate of, 422
Causation, and death concept, 642
Cell phone use, 418
and media multitasking, 394, 418
Cells, 46
aging at level of, 432–434
duplication in zygote period, 80f, 80–81
glial, 83, 122
in immune system, 437
meiosis of, 46–47
mitosis of, 46
nerve. *See* Neurons
programmed death of, 122
sex cells, 46–47
Cemeteries, 664
virtual, 664
Centenarians, 566–567
Central conceptual structures in concrete operational stage, 302
Central executive component of information processing system, 162, 162f

Central nervous system
brain in. *See* Brain
in late adulthood, 568
Centration in preoperational stage, 229
Cephalocaudal trend in growth, 121
Cerebellum
childhood maltreatment affecting, 283
in early childhood, 218, 218f
in late adulthood, 568
Cerebral cortex
in adolescence, 367
in Alzheimer's disease, 583–584
in autism, 241
in early childhood, 217, 237
electrical activity in, 122, 123t
in infancy and toddlerhood, 124–125
language areas in, 124, 125, 126, 174, 175
in late adulthood, 568
lateralization of, 124, 125, 217–218
mirror neurons in, 136
in persistent vegetative state, 641
plasticity of, 124–125
prenatal development of, 84, 85
regions of, 124, 124f
Cerebral hemispheres
dominant, 217
in early childhood, 217–218
in infancy and toddlerhood, 124–125
language functions in, 126, 174, 217
lateralization of, 124, 217–218
Cerebral palsy, 100
Cerebrovascular disorders, stroke in, 579f, 579–580
and brain plasticity, 126
and dementia, 585–587
signs and symptoms of, 586
Ceremonies. *See* Rituals and ceremonies
Certified nurse-midwives, 100
Cervix of uterus, 80, 80f
dilation and effacement in childbirth, 96, 97f
Cesarean delivery, 101
Cessation, and death concept, 642
Cessation of smoking, 444
Chaos in family, 26
Chemicals, prenatal exposure to, 90
Chernobyl nuclear power plant accident, 89
Chicago Child–Parent Centers, 246
Chickenpox in pregnancy, 91t
Child abuse. *See* Child maltreatment
Childbearing
decisions about, 483–484
maternal age in. *See* Maternal age
pregnancy in. *See* Pregnancy
transition to parenthood in, 484–485
Childbirth, 96–101
adaptation of baby to, 97
and appearance of newborn, 97–98
breech position in, 100
cesarean delivery in, 101
complications during. *See* Birth complications
cultural influences on, 98–99
fetal monitoring during, 101

in freestanding birth centers, 99
at home, 98, 99–100
medications during, 100–101
natural or prepared, 99
oxygen deprivation of infant in, 97, 100
parental leave from employment after, 104–105, 203, 485
of preterm and low-birth-weight infant, 101–105
stages of, 96, 97f
and transition to parenthood, 115, 484–485
Child care
and cognitive development, 171–173
employment affecting, 104–105, 202–204, 350–351, 485, 494–495
for preterm infants, 103–105
and self-care by children, 351
Child-care programs, 244, 246
and attachment, 202–203
compared to preschool programs, 244
developmentally appropriate practice standards in, 172, 247
quality of care in, 171–173, 202–203, 246, 247
weekly hours in, 202
for young children, 485
Child-centered programs in preschool and kindergarten, 244, 245
Childlessness, 488–489
late adulthood in, 623–624
Child maltreatment, 281–283, 282t, 416t
attachment insecurity in, 200
consequences of, 283
in corporal punishment, 266, 283
in emotional abuse, 281
eyewitness testimony of children on, 355
factors contributing to, 282t, 282–283
incidence of, 281, 283
in neglect, 280, 281, 282
origins of, 282–283
in physical abuse, 281
of preterm infants, 102, 112, 282
prevention of, 283
in sexual abuse, 281, 352–354
by teenage parents, 378
terminology related to, 281
Child-rearing costs, 484
Child-rearing practices
and academic achievement, 392
and adjustment to emerging adulthood, 468–469
and attachment security of child, 199–205
in attention-deficit hyperactivity disorder, 305
and clique membership, 419
cultural influences on, 16–17, 65, 194–195, 200, 204, 207, 280–281
and delinquency, 425
discipline in. *See* Discipline
early availability of consistent caregiver in, 199
education on, 485, 486
effective coparenting in, 60, 485

and emotional self-regulation of child, 259
experimental research on, 35
in extended families, 66
of fathers, 201–204
feeding and nutrition in, 291–292
gender typing in, 274, 275
goodness-of-fit model on, 194, 195
of grandparents, 546–547, 548
helicopter parenting in, 468–469
in maternal employment, 202–204
in middle childhood, 345
and moral development, 410, 411
and newborn behavior, 114
normative approach to, 15
positive parenting in, 268
quality of caregiving in, 199–200
and self-conscious emotions, 260
and self-control, 209
and self-esteem, 258, 332–333, 403
sensitivity in, 199–200, 201, 206
and sibling relationships, 205
socioeconomic status affecting, 61
sources of information on, 486
and stranger anxiety, 187
and temperament of child, 192, 194–195
and vocational choice, 457
warmth in, 204
Child-rearing styles, 278–280
authoritarian, 279, 279t
authoritative, 278–279, 279t, 280–281. *See also* Authoritative child-rearing style
distal and proximal, 207
permissive, 279t, 279–280
uninvolved, 279t, 280, 392
Children's Defense Fund, 68
Child support
in divorce, 349
in single-parent families, 491
Chimpanzees
imitation by, 135, 135f, 136
language acquisition of, 174
China
academic achievement in, 324, 324t, 392
academic and vocational tracks in, 395
achievement attributions in, 334, 334f
aging parents in, 549
aging stereotypes in, 574
autobiographical memory in, 238
child-rearing practices in, 194–195, 280–281, 392
death anxiety in, 646
early adulthood in, 466
emotional self-regulation in, 189, 193
fears of children in, 352
first words of infants in, 176–177
gender typing in, 276, 346
immigrant youths from, 32, 33
language development in, 176–177, 178
mate selection in, 472
mathematics instruction in, 309
menopause in, 506f
moral development in, 336
obesity in, 291, 440
one-child families in, 346
peer relations in, 262, 276

play activities in, 262
romantic relationships in, 475, 476
self-concept in, 331
self-conscious emotions in, 189
self-esteem in, 331
storytelling practices in, 257
temperament of children in, 193, 194–195
unintentional childhood injuries in, 221f
Chinese language, and false belief tasks, 239–240
Chlamydia in pregnancy, 91t
Cholesterol
  and atherosclerosis, 436, 442, 511
  caloric restriction affecting, 505
  exercise affecting, 443
Chomsky, Noam, language development theory of, 174
Chorion, 82
Chorionic villi, 82
  sampling of, 56, 56t, 82
Christian beliefs, 608
  death concept in, 643, 645, 664
  and passive euthanasia attitudes, 655
Chromosomes, 46
  abnormalities of, 52–53, 53f
  autosomes, 47
  biological aging of, 432, 433, 433f
  karyotype of, 46f
  in meiosis, 47
  and patterns of inheritance, 48–52
  sex, 47
  telomeres of, 432, 433, 433f
Chronosystem in ecological systems theory, 24f, 25, 60
Cigarette smoking. See Smoking
Circular reactions in sensorimotor development, 153, 153t, 154
Circumcision, 112
Civic engagement, development of, 413
Civil unions, 488
Classical conditioning, 17, 133f, 133–134
Classification
  categorization abilities in. See Categorization abilities
  in concrete operational stage, 299
Class inclusion problems, 229, 229f, 299
Classrooms. See Schools
Class size in school, 318
Cleft lip and palate, 88, 92
Climacteric, 504, 515. See also Menopause
Clinical death, 640
Clinical interviews, 20, 29t, 30
Clinical research method, 17, 29t, 30–31
Cliques and crowds in adolescence, 419–420
Cocaine, 87–88, 380
Coercion, sexual, 448–449
Cognitive-affective complexity, 452f, 452–453, 605
Cognitive development, 8, 9f
  and academic learning, 307–309, 318–325, 526–527
  accommodation in, 152, 228
  adaptation in, 18–19, 152
  in adolescence, 367, 382–397

assimilation in, 152
attention in, 303–304, 521–522
  in autism, 241
brain injury affecting, 126
central conceptual structures in, 302
child-care quality affecting, 171–173
cognitive-affective complexity in, 452f, 452–453
in college experience, 454–455
concrete operational stage in, 299–302. See also Concrete operational stage
as continuous or discontinuous process, 6, 302
core knowledge perspective of, 159–161
creativity in, 453–454, 524–525
crystallized and fluid intelligence in, 518–519, 590
cultural influences on, 167–168, 384
death concept in, 642–644, 662
decision making in, 387–388
definition of, 9f
disequilibrium in, 152
in dynamic systems perspective, 166
in early adulthood, 450–459
in early childhood, 19, 224, 226–251, 231t
early interventions in, 173, 173f, 245f, 245–246
emotional intelligence in, 453
environmental influences on, 170–173, 244–248
epistemic cognition in, 451–452
equilibrium in, 19, 152
ethological theory of, 22
executive function in, 303. See also Executive function
expertise in, 453–454, 524. See also Expertise
in fetal alcohol spectrum disorder, 89
formal operational stage in, 382–384. See also Formal operational stage
hypothetico-deductive reasoning in, 382–383, 384
idealism and criticism in, 387
imitation in, 156–157, 157f
individual differences in, 169–173, 243–248, 309–316, 519–520
in infancy and toddlerhood, 19, 151–181
information-processing approach to, 20–21, 161–167, 236–243, 302–309, 384–386, 520–525. See also Information processing
intelligence tests of, 169–170, 309–316
and language development, 174–179, 226, 239, 248–251, 316–318, 593–594
in late adulthood, 589–599
lateralization of brain functions in, 124
lifelong learning in, 597–599
in lifespan perspective, 13f
linguistic knowledge in, 160
in low birth weight, 101

maintenance and loss prevention in late adulthood, 590, 590f, 596–597
malnutrition affecting, 132
mathematical abilities in, 160f, 160–161, 388–391
memory in, 302–303, 304–306, 522–523, 591–593
mental representations in, 154, 156–158
in middle adulthood, 517–527
in middle childhood, 299–325
and moral development, 268–269
neo-Piagetian theory of, 233
neuroscience approach to, 21–22
numerical knowledge in, 160f, 160–161
object permanence in, 154, 155f, 155–156
organization in, 152–153
oxygen deprivation during childbirth affecting, 100
and perceptual development, 146–147
in phenylketonuria, 50
physical knowledge in, 159
Piaget on, 18–20, 19t, 152–161, 226–233, 382–384
play in, 168, 235, 261, 262t
postformal thought in, 450
pragmatic thought in, 452
prenatal drug exposure affecting, 86, 87, 88, 89
preoperational stage in, 226–233. See also Preoperational stage
problem solving in, 157, 524, 594–595
propositional thought in, 383
psychological knowledge in, 160
and questions asked by preschoolers, 232
reaching by infants in, 139–140
of returning students, 526–527
schemes in, 152, 154
scientific reasoning in, 385–386
self-concept in, 386–387
and self-regulation, 307
sensorimotor stage in, 152, 153–154. See also Sensorimotor stage
sex differences in, 388–391
social context of, 167, 234–235
social learning theory on, 18
sociocultural theory on, 23–24, 233–235, 319–320
spatial abilities in, 390
and suicidal behavior, 423
symbolic understanding in, 157–158, 227–228
theory of mind in, 238–240, 306–307
verbal abilities in, 388
and vocational choice, 455–459
and vocational life, 525–526
Vygotsky on, 233–235
wisdom in, 595–596
Cognitive-developmental theory, 18–20, 19t, 152–161
  compared to other human development theories, 28t
  concrete operational stage in, 299–302
  contributions and limitations of, 20

formal operational stage in, 382–384
  on gender identity, 276–277
  on gender typing, 273
  on moral behavior, 264, 268–269
  preoperational stage in, 226–233
  sensorimotor stage in, 153–158
Cognitive maps in concrete operational stage, 300
Cognitive neuroscience, developmental, 21–22
Cognitive reserve, 585
Cognitive self-regulation, 307, 384
Cognitive styles
  diffuse-avoidant, 404
  dogmatic and inflexible, 404
  information-gathering, 404
Cohabitation, 349, 487–488
  in late adulthood, 622
Cohort effects, 517–518, 518f
  in baby boomer generation, 11, 12–13
  in cross-sectional research, 37–38, 517–518, 518f
  history-graded influences in, 11–12
  in longitudinal research, 37, 518, 518f
  in sequential research, 38, 38f
Coinage of words in vocabulary development, 248
Colic, 111
Collaboration
  as communication style, 314
  in late adulthood, 595
Collectivist societies
  academic achievement in, 324
  aging parents in, 549
  autobiographical memory in, 238
  compared to individualistic societies, 65
  identity development in, 406
  infant sleeping arrangements in, 129
  loneliness in, 478
  moral development in, 411
  peer sociability in, 262
  psychological well-being in, 539
  romantic relationships in, 475
  self-conscious emotions in, 189, 260
  social relationships of older adults in, 616
  temperament of children in, 194–195
College experience, 454–455, 466
  of adults as returning students, 526–527
  friendships in, 477
  identity development in, 464
  leaving parental home for, 478
  sex differences in, 457–458
  vocational choice in, 456
Colombia, moral development in, 337
Colon cancer, 442, 443, 511
Color of skin of newborn, Apgar Scale on, 98t
Color vision
  in infancy and toddlerhood, 113, 142
  in middle adulthood, 503
Comfort care in hospice programs, 652

Commercials on television, roles of older adults in, 574
Commitment
  and generativity in middle adulthood, 534
  and hardiness as personal quality, 516
  in triangular theory of love, 473
  and well-being in middle adulthood, 540
Communication
  with cell phones, 394, 418, 418f
  collaborative style of, 314
  conversational. See Conversation
  cultural influences on, 314, 317
  with dying person, 643, 646, 648–649, 650, 662
  expressive, 178
  hierarchical style of, 314
  infant-directed speech in, 178–179
  interactional synchrony in, 200
  and language development. See Language development
  in late adulthood, 593–594
  in marital relationship, 473, 482, 489
  in online interactions, 418f, 418–419
  referential, 178
  sociocultural theory on, 23–24
  speech in. See Speech
  topic-associating style of, 317
  topic-focused style of, 317
Community influences, 63–65
  on child maltreatment, 282
  ecological systems theory on, 25, 63
  on immigrant youths, 33
  in late adulthood, 616–617
  on resilient children, 11
  in widowhood, 624
Community service. See Volunteer work
Companionate love, 473
Compensatory techniques of older adults, 9, 521, 590, 594
Compliance in toddlerhood, 208, 209
Componential analysis of intelligence tests, 310
Comprehension
  compared to production of language, 177
  of reading, 308
Compression of morbidity in late adulthood, 576–577
Computer use
  in assistive technology and devices, 573, 574
  Internet in. See Internet use
  in late adulthood, 599
  learning in, 247–248
  parental supervision of, 271, 272
Conception, 46, 80, 80f
  maternal age at time of. See Maternal age
  paternal alcohol use at time of, 89
Conceptual categorization in infancy and toddlerhood, 166
Concrete operational stage, 19, 19t, 299–302
  classification in, 299
  compared to formal operational stage, 382, 383

conservation in, 299
  continuum of acquisition in, 301
  cultural influences on, 300, 300f, 301
  evaluation of, 302
  information processing view of, 301–302
  limitations of thought in, 301
  research on, 301–302
  school influences on, 301
  seriation in, 300
  spatial reasoning in, 300, 300f
Conditioned response, 133f, 134
Conditioned stimulus, 133f, 134
Conditioning
  classical, 17, 133f, 133–134
  operant, 17, 134, 265
  social learning theory on, 265
Confidentiality in research, 39t
Conflict
  in adolescence, 369–370, 418
  in divorce of parents, 347, 348
  in late adulthood, 616, 620–621
  in marital relationship, 473, 482–483, 489–490, 620–621
Confrontation in grief process, 660
Confucian beliefs, 641
Congo, Republic of
  observational learning in, 236
  stranger anxiety of infants in, 187
Congregate housing, 618, 619
Connective tissue changes in aging, 434, 436
Conscience
  and moral development, 264. See also Moral development
  and superego, 15, 264
Conscientiousness, as personality trait, 542, 542t
Consent to research, 39t, 40
Conservation
  in concrete operational stage, 299, 301
  in preoperational stage, 229, 229f, 230, 232
Constancy, gender, 276–277
Constructivist classrooms, 319
Contexts for development, 7, 59–69
  in adaptations to dying, 647–650
  cultural influences in. See Cultural influences
  ecological systems theory on, 24–27. See also Ecological systems theory
  environmental, 59–69. See also Environmental influences
  ethology of, 22
  evolutionary development psychology on, 22–23
  in late adulthood, 616–619
  relative influence of nature and nurture in, 7, 28t, 69–75
  sociocultural theory on, 23–24. See also Sociocultural theory
Continuity theory of aging, 614–615, 618
  retirement in, 631
Continuous course of development, 28t
  compared to discontinuous development, 6, 6f, 302
  in lifespan perspective, 7
Continuous performance tasks, 521

Contraception
  in adolescence, 375, 375f, 379
  and decision to have children, 483
  in early adulthood, 446
Contractions of uterus in childbirth, 96, 97f
Contrast sensitivity, 144, 144f
Control
  in child rearing, 278–279, 280
  effortful. See Effortful control
  and hardiness as personal quality, 516
  in late adulthood, 573, 578, 610–613, 619, 633
  in middle adulthood, 540
  of self, 208–209, 264. See also Self-regulation
Controversial children, 341, 343
Conventional level of moral development, 408
Conventional personality type, vocational choice in, 456
Convergent thinking, 322
Conversation
  in early childhood, 250, 275
  generic references to gender in, 275, 275f
  in infancy and toddlerhood, 176
  in late adulthood, 570, 593, 594
  in middle childhood, 316–317
  in pragmatic language development, 316–317
Cooing, 176
Cooley's anemia, 49t
Cooperation
  in adolescent friendships, 417
  in learning, 320, 322
  morality of, 408
  in play, 261
Coparenting
  in divorce, 348, 349
  effective, 60, 485
Coping strategies
  in bereavement interventions, 663
  for caregivers of older adults with dementia, 586–587
  in caring for aging parents, 551
  in death of loved one, 659–665
  dual-process model of, 660
  of dying people, 647, 648
  emotion-centered, 336, 514, 516, 539, 573, 605
  in late adulthood, 570, 573, 605, 611, 613
  in middle adulthood, 514–515, 539
  in middle childhood, 336, 354
  problem-centered, 336, 514, 516, 539, 570, 573
Coregulation in middle childhood, 345
Core knowledge perspective, 159–161
  domains of thought in, 159
  linguistic knowledge in, 160
  numerical knowledge in, 160
  physical knowledge in, 159
  psychological knowledge in, 160
  theory of mind in, 240
Corporal punishment, 266, 266f
  cultural influences on, 267, 283
  prevalence of, 266, 266f
Corpus callosum
  in early childhood, 218, 218f
  in late adulthood, 568

Corpus luteum, 80
Correlational research, 34–35
  compared to other research designs, 36t
  correlation coefficient in, 34, 34f
  gene–environment correlation, 72, 72f
Correlation coefficient, 34, 34f
Cortex, cerebral. See Cerebral corte
Cortisol
  in bullying victims, 342
  in childbirth, 97
  child-care effects on, 203
  in child maltreatment victims, 283
  in early deprivation, 127
  in flight or fight response, 93
  in maternal depression, 186
  in poverty, 303
  in pregnancy, 93
  in shyness and sociability, 192
  and telomerase production, 433
Corumination, 418, 422
Cosleeping arrangements, 129
Cost
  of child rearing, 484
  of health care, 588
Costa Rica, life expectancy in, 565f
Counseling
  in alcoholism, 445
  in assisted suicide, 658
  in bereavement interventions, 663, 665
  on birth control, 375
  of blended families, 350, 490
  in chronic childhood illness, 294
  in dropout prevention programs, 396, 455
  in early pubertal timing, 371
  in elder maltreatment prevention, 628
  genetic, 53–55, 58
  on infant care, 104, 127
  on marital relationship, 272, 483
  in school transitions, 392
  in smoking cessation, 444
  in suicide prevention, 423
  in unemployment, 556
  vocational, 458, 459, 554
  in weight loss programs, 441
Counting skills in early childhood, 242–243
Course of development, 28t
  context affecting, 7
  as continuous or discontinuous process, 28t
  as dynamic system, 8
  Hall and Gesell on, 14–15
  in information processing approach, 21
  in lifespan perspective, 7–13
  as one course or many, 6–7, 28t
  relative influence of nature and nurture in, 7, 8, 28t, 69–75
  resilience in, 10–11
  stability and plasticity in, 7
Court proceedings, eyewitness testimony of children in, 355
Crawling, 136, 138, 139, 158
  and depth perception, 143–144
  and differentiation theory of perceptual development, 147, 147f

and emotional self-regulation by infants, 189
and temperament, 193
Creativity
  drawing in. *See* Drawing
  in early adulthood, 453*f,* 453–454
  of gifted children, 322–323
  and intelligence, 310, 311, 311*f*
  in middle adulthood, 524–525
Criminal behavior
  in adolescence, 423–426
  and alcohol use, 445
  assisted suicide as, 659
  fear of, in late adulthood, 617
  and homicide rates, 438, 438*f*
  voluntary active euthanasia as, 656
Crisis in midlife, 536–537
Critical periods of development, 22
Croatia
  corporal punishment in, 282–283
  infant mortality rate in, 105*f*
  voluntary active euthanasia attitudes in, 656
Cross-cultural research, 24, 31. *See also* Cultural influences; *specific cultures*
Cross-linkage theory of aging, 434
Cross-sectional research, 37–38
  cohort effects in, 37–38, 517–518, 518*f*
  compared to other research designs, 36*t,* 37
  limitations of, 37–38
  sequential designs, 38, 38*f*
Crowds and cliques in adolescence, 419–420
Crying of infants, 108*t,* 109–112
  abnormal patterns in, 111–112
  adult responsiveness to, 109, 111, 112
  in drug addiction, 87
  empathy of other infants in, 109
  and maternal smoking during pregnancy, 88
  soothing techniques in, 109–111, 112
Crystallized intelligence, 518–519, 521*f,* 590
Cuba, infant mortality rate in, 105*f*
Cults, religious, 412
Cultural bias in intelligence tests, 243, 310, 314–315
Cultural influences, 65–69
  on academic achievement, 393
  on achievement attributions, 334, 334*f*
  on adolescence, 362, 369, 370, 373–374, 415–416
  on aging stereotypes, 574–575
  on alcohol use, 444
  on attachment patterns, 198*f,* 198–199
  on bereavement, 663, 664
  on breastfeeding practices, 16–17
  on caring for aging parent, 551, 617–618
  on categorization skills, 166
  on childbirth practices, 98–99
  on child maltreatment, 282–283
  on child-rearing practices, 16–17, 65, 194–195, 200, 204, 207, 280–281

on cognitive development, 167–168, 384
on cohabitation, 488
on communication style, 314, 317
on concrete operational stage, 300, 300*f,* 301
on dating, 420
on death understanding and attitudes, 643, 645, 650, 656, 657, 658
on departure from parental home, 478, 479, 545
on drawings in early childhood, 225
ecological systems theory on, 25
on education and schools, 235, 236
on emerging adulthood, 464, 466–467
on emotional development, 185
on emotional self-regulation, 189
ethnographic research on, 32–33
on extended families, 66
on false beliefs, 239–240
on fathers as caregivers, 201–204
on fears of children, 352
on food preferences, 219
on formal operational stage, 384
on gender identity, 540
on gender stereotypes, 276
on grandparents as caregivers, 547
on hand preference, 218
on identity development, 405, 406
on immigrant youths, 32–33
on intelligence assessment, 311, 314–315
on language development, 177–178, 248, 314
on learned helplessness, 334
on learning, 141, 167, 236
in macrosystem, 25, 65
on make-believe play, 168, 236
on map making, 300, 300*f*
on mate selection, 472, 475
on memory and memory strategies, 238, 306
on menopause, 506, 506*f,* 507, 508
on moral development, 264, 336–337, 409, 411
on motor development, 138–139
multicultural research on, 31
on neonatal behavior, 114
on observational learning, 167
on one-child families, 346
on parenthood decisions, 483
on partner abuse, 483
on personality traits, 542
on play, 168, 236, 256, 261, 262
on psychological well-being, 539
on punishment, 267, 281
on religiosity, 465, 609
research methods on, 31–33
on respect for older adults, 574–575, 576
on romantic relationships, 475–476
on scaffolding, 234
on self-concept, 331–332
on self-conscious emotions, 188–189, 260
on self-esteem, 331–332, 333
on self-recognition, 207, 208*f*
on sense of control over health, 573
on sensitivity toward infants, 200
on sexual coercion, 448

on sexuality, 373–374, 376
on sibling relationships, 416, 477, 552
on sleep, 128, 129
sociocultural theory on, 23–24, 167
on soothing of crying infants, 111
on stereotypes of aging, 574–575, 576
on storytelling practices, 257
on stranger anxiety, 187
in subcultures, 65
on suicidal behavior, 422, 423
on temperament, 193, 194–195
on transition to adulthood, 464
in tribal and village societies, 236
on wisdom, 595
Custody of children
  in blended families, 348–349, 350
  in divorce, 347, 348–349
Cyberbullying, 342
Cyprus
  corporal punishment in, 282–283
  life expectancy in, 565*f*
Cystic fibrosis, 49*t,* 57, 293
Cytomegalovirus infection in pregnancy, 91, 91*t*
Cytoplasm, 46
Czech Republic
  high school graduation rate in, 395*f*
  infant mortality rate in, 105*f*
  life expectancy in, 565*f*
  poverty rate in, 68*f*

D
Daily living activities in late adulthood, 567–568
  cognitive interventions affecting, 597
  control versus dependency in, 610–611, 613
  problem solving in, 594–595
Dark adaptation in late adulthood, 569
Darwin, Charles, 14
Dating
  in adolescence, 420*f,* 420–421
  in early adulthood, 445–446
  in late adulthood, 621
  online services in, 445–446, 621, 622*f*
  personal ads for, 621, 622*f*
Day care programs. *See* Child-care programs
Death and dying, 639–667
  acceptance of, in late adulthood, 604, 605
  in adolescence, common causes of, 643
  adolescent concept of, 643–644, 646
  adult concept of, 644–645, 646
  advance medical directives on, 655–656
  and afterlife beliefs, 643, 645, 664
  agonal phase in, 640
  anxiety about, 644, 645*f,* 645–646
  appropriate or good death in, 648
  in assisted suicide, 658–659
  bereavement in, 659–665
  brain death in, 641
  cancer as cause of, 438*f,* 509, 509*f,* 510, 579, 579*f,* 640, 646, 648, 649, 651

cardiovascular disease as cause of, 564, 579, 579*f,* 640, 648
of child, parent grief in, 661
childhood concept of, 642–643
clinical death in, 640
communication with dying person in, 643, 646, 648–649, 650, 662
contextual influences on adaptations to, 647–650
coping of dying person in, 647, 648
coping with death of loved one, 659–665
cultural variations in beliefs on, 645, 650, 656, 664
definition of, 640–641
with dignity, 640, 641–642
and disengagement theory of aging, 614
in early adulthood, leading causes of, 438, 438*f*
education on, 643, 644, 662, 665
end-of-life care decisions in, 641, 642
in family, 648–649, 661–662
at home, 642, 650, 651
hospice approach to, 652–653
in hospital, 650, 651
in infancy, 104. *See also* Infant mortality
in infectious diseases, 220
of intimate partner, 662
in late adulthood, leading causes of, 579, 579*f*
and music as palliative care, 653
nature of disease in, 648
in nursing home, 650, 652
palliative care in, 652, 653
of parent, 661–662
in passive euthanasia, 654–656
physical changes in, 640
place of, 650–653
religious and spiritual beliefs on, 641, 643, 645, 649–650
and right to die, 654–659
of sibling, 661–662
of spouse, widowhood in, 621, 622–623, 660, 662
stages of, 646–647
sudden death in, 651, 660–661, 665
in sudden infant death syndrome, 109, 110, 129, 139, 661
in suicide, 422. *See also* Suicide
terminal decline prior to, 596–597
and thoughts and emotions of dying people, 646–650
understanding of and attitudes toward, 642–646
unintentional injuries as cause of, 221, 221*f,* 222, 294, 294*f,* 640
in voluntary active euthanasia, 656–658
Debriefing in research, 40
Decentration in concrete operational stage, 299
Deception in research, 40
Decision making
  in adolescence, 387–388
  in assisted suicide, 658–659
  on end-of-life care, 641, 642, 655–656
  on health care in gay and lesbian partnerships, 621, 656
  moral judgments in, 405–414

Decision making (*cont.*)
  on parenthood, 483–484, 488–489
  on retirement, 629–630, 630*f*
Deferred imitation in sensorimotor
    stage, 154, 156, 157*f*
Delay of gratification, 209
Deliberate memory, 591
Delinquency, 423–426
  and aggression, 424, 425
  child-rearing practices associated
    with, 425
  early-onset, 424, 425*f*
  in early pubertal maturation, 370,
    371
  late-onset, 424, 425
  prevention and treatment
    strategies, 425–426
Delivery of baby, 96, 97*f*. *See also*
    Childbirth
Dementia, 582–588
  in Alzheimer's disease, 582–585.
    See also Alzheimer's disease
  caregivers in, 585, 586–587
  cerebrovascular, 585–587
  hospice care in, 653
  incidence of, 582
  misdiagnosed and reversible,
    587–588
Denial, in coping with dying, 647, 649
Denmark
  caring for aging parents in, 551
  corporal punishment in, 282–283
  divorce rate in, 347*f*
  high school graduation rate in,
    395*f*
  immunization rate in, 221
  infant mortality rate in, 105*f*
  life expectancy in, 565*f*
  long-term care of older adults in,
    589
  marriage of same-sex couples in,
    479
  poverty rate in, 62, 68*f*
  retirement programs in, 630
  teenage pregnancy in, 378*f*
  vocational education in, 459
Dental development, 217, 290
Dentures, and taste sensitivity, 570
Deoxyribonucleic acid. *See* DNA
Dependency in late adulthood, 610–
    613, 626, 633
  dependency–support script in, 610
  independence–ignore script in, 610
  in nursing homes, 619
  risk for maltreatment in, 627–628
  suicide in, 613
Dependency–support script, 610
Dependent variables in experimental
    research, 35
Depression
  in adolescence, 421–423
  in Alzheimer's disease, 583
  in bulimia nervosa, 373
  in children with depressed parent,
    186
  drug therapy in, 187, 423, 587
  in dying, 647, 648
  of fathers, 186, 187
  in late adulthood, 587–588, 611,
    612–613, 623, 624
  in menopause, 506
  misdiagnosed as dementia,
    587–588

of mothers, 186–187, 200
of never-married childless older
    adults, 624
in obesity, 292, 440
suicide in, 422–423. *See also*
    Suicide
in widowhood, 623
Deprivation
  attachment security in, 199
  in sensitive periods of
    development, 125–127
  temperament in, 193
Depth perception in infancy, 142–
    144, 143*f*
  binocular cues in, 142
  and independent movement,
    143–144
  motion cues in, 142
  pictorial cues in, 142
  visual cliff studies of, 142, 143*f*
Dermis, 503
Design of research, 34–38
Desires, in theory of mind, 239
Despair in late adulthood, versus
    integrity, 16*t*, 604
Destruction–creation developmental
    tasks in seasons of life theory,
    535
Development, 5–7
  cognitive. *See* Cognitive
    development
  contextual influences on. *See*
    Contexts for development
  as continuous or discontinuous
    process, 6, 6*f*
  course of. *See* Course of
    development
  determinants of, 7
  emotional and social. *See*
    Emotional and social
    development
  historical views of, 14–20
  physical. *See* Physical development
  research on, 27–40
  as scientific, applied, and
    interdisciplinary field, 5
  theories of. *See* Theories of
    development
Developmental cognitive
    neuroscience, 21–22
Developmentally appropriate practice
    standards, 172
Developmental quotients (DQs), 170
Developmental science, 5–6
  applications of, 5
  definition of, 5
  historical studies in, 14–20
  interdisciplinary studies in, 5
  recent theories in, 20–27
Diabetes
  exercise reducing risk for, 443
  genetic factors in, 51
  in late adulthood, 580, 581
  in middle childhood, 293, 299
  in obesity, 291
  in pregnancy, 95
  type 2 (diabetes mellitus), 291, 581
Diabetes insipidus, 49*t*
Diarrhea, 220
Diet. *See* Nutrition
Diethylstilbestrol (DES), 86
Differentiation theory of perceptual
    development, 146–147, 147*f*

Difficult child, as temperament type,
    190
  attachment security in, 200
  child-rearing practices and, 194
Diffuse-avoidant cognitive style, 404
Diffusion of identity, 403, 403*t*, 404,
    405
Dignity, death with, 640, 641–642
Dilation and effacement of cervix in
    childbirth, 96, 97*f*
Dinner and mealtimes in family, 29,
    63, 63*f*
  in adolescence, 372
  in middle childhood, 291
Dioxins, prenatal exposure to, 90
Disabilities
  assistive technology and devices in,
    573–574
  in late adulthood, 573–574, 575,
    577, 577*f*, 579–588, 611
  learning, 322
  of preterm infants, 102, 102*f*
Discipline
  in authoritarian child rearing, 279
  in authoritative child rearing, 279
  in delinquency, 426
  inductive, 264–265
  and moral development, 266–268
  in permissive child rearing,
    279–280
  in positive parenting, 268
  punishment in. *See* Punishment
  and temperament, 194
  in uninvolved child rearing, 280
Discontinuous course of
    development, 28*t*
  compared to continuous
    development, 6, 6*f*, 302
  in lifespan perspective, 7
  qualitative changes in, 6
  stages in, 6
Discovery learning, 233
  assisted, 235
Discrimination
  in career opportunities, 493–494,
    494*f*, 555
  ethnic and racial, 338, 406, 493–
    494, 494*f*
  gender-related, 493–494
  in homosexuality, 447
  in obesity, 292, 439–440
Diseases, infectious. *See* Infectious
    diseases
Disenfranchised grief, 662
Disengagement theory of aging, 614
Disequilibrium in cognitive
    development, 152
Disorganized/disoriented attachment,
    198
  later development in, 206
  mother–infant relationship in, 200
  stability of, 198
Displaced reference, and symbolic
    understanding of infants, 157
Distal parenting style, 207
Distractibility, temperament in, 190
Divergent thinking, 322–323, 323*f*
Diversity and inequality, childhood
    understanding of, 337–339
Divorce, 346–349, 416*t*, 489–490
  age at time of marriage in, 480, 489
  age differences in response to
    parental divorce, 347–348

child support payments in, 349
cohabitation after, 488
departure from parental home in,
    478
in early adulthood, 489–490
gender roles in, 490
joint custody in, 348–349
in late adulthood, 621–622
long-term consequences of
    parental divorce, 348, 490
mediation services in, 348
in middle adulthood, 544
remarriage in, 347, 349–350, 489,
    490, 544
in second marriage, 350, 489, 490
sex differences in response to, 348,
    544
singlehood lifestyle after, 487
temperament affecting response to
    parental divorce, 348
Dizygotic twins, 47*f*, 47–48. *See also*
    Twins
DNA (deoxyribonucleic acid), 46, 47*f*
  aging at level of, 432–434, 433*f*
  free radicals affecting, 433–434
  mutations in, 51–52
Dogmatic inflexible cognitive style in
    identity development, 404
Dogon people of Mali, attachment
    patterns of, 199
Domains of development, 7
  cognitive, 8, 9*f*. *See also* Cognitive
    development
  emotional and social, 8, 9*f*. *See
    also* Emotional and social
    development
  in lifespan perspective, 13*f*
  multidirectional and
    multidimensional changes in, 9,
    432, 467, 517, 532
  physical, 8, 9*f*. *See also* Physical
    development
Domestic violence, 482–483, 483*f*
Dominance hierarchy in peer
    relations, 297–298
Dominant cerebral hemisphere,
    217–218
Dominant–recessive inheritance, 48*t*,
    48–50, 49*t*
  characteristics related to, 48, 48*t*
  diseases related to, 49*t*, 50
  incomplete dominance in, 50
Donor insemination, 54
Dorris, Michael, 88
Double standard of aging, 516–517,
    535
Doula support during childbirth, 99
Down syndrome, 52–53, 53*f*
  and Alzheimer's disease, 584
  maternal age in, 53, 53*f*
  mosaic pattern in, 52
  translocation pattern in, 52
Drawing
  cultural variations in, 225
  in early childhood, 224*f*, 224–225
  and early printing, 225
  of human figures, 224, 224*f*, 225
  in middle childhood, 295, 295*f*
Dreaming in REM sleep, 108
Dream of adult life in early
    adulthood, 470
Dressing skills in early childhood,
    224

Dropping out
 from college, 455
 from high school, 396–397
 prevention strategies, 396–397, 455
Drowsiness of infants, 108t
Drug abuse. *See* Substance abuse
Drug therapy
 in Alzheimer's disease, 585
 analgesic. *See* Analgesic drugs
 antidepressant. *See* Antidepressant
  drugs
 assistive technology in, 573
 in attention-deficit hyperactivity
  disorder, 305
 in bulimia, 373
 during childbirth, 100–101
 dementia-like symptoms from, 588
 in depression, 187, 423, 587
 in infertility, fraternal twinning
  related to, 47t, 48
 in menopause, 506
 taste changes from, 570
Druze culture, 540, 643
Dual-cycle model of identity
 development, 464
Dual-earner households, 350–351,
 416t, 494–495
 combining work and family in,
  494–495
 marital roles in, 480
 transition to parenthood in, 484
Dualistic thinking, 451
Dual-process model of coping with
 loss, 660
Dual representation in preoperational
 stage, 227–228
Duchenne muscular dystrophy, 49t,
 57
Duplication of cells, 80f, 80–81
Durable power of attorney for health
 care, 655–656
Dutch children
 ethnic bias of, 338
 sleep schedule for infants, 128
Dying, 639–665. *See also* Death and
 dying
Dynamic assessment of intelligence,
 315
Dynamic systems perspective, 8
 cognitive development in, 166
 emerging adulthood in, 471
 emotional development in, 185
 motor development in, 137–139

E
Ear, and hearing. *See* Hearing
Early adolescence, 362
Early adulthood (18 to 40 years old),
 8t, 430–497
 adaptation to life in, 470–471
 age range in, 8t
 biological aging in, 432–434
 cardiovascular and respiratory
  changes in, 434–436
 career development in, 492–495
 childlessness in, 488–489
 cognitive-affective complexity in,
  452f, 452–453
 cognitive development in, 450–459
 cohabitation in, 487–488
 college experience in, 454–455,
  464, 466
 cultural influences in, 464, 466–467

diversity of lifestyles in, 486–492
 divorce and remarriage in, 489–490
 emotional and social development
  in, 463–497
 endocrine system in, 434
 epistemic cognition in, 451–452
 exercise in, 443
 expertise and creativity in, 453–454
 family life cycle in, 478–486
 friendships in, 476–477
 health and fitness in, 438–450
 immune system in, 434, 437
 intimacy versus isolation in, 16t,
  469–470, 472–478
 loneliness in, 477f, 477–478
 marriage in, 479–483
 mate selection in, 472–473
 memory of events in, in late
  adulthood, 593
 milestones of development in,
  498–499
 motor performance in, 436–437
 nutrition in, 439–442
 parenthood in, 470, 483–486,
  490–492
 physical development in, 432–450
 pragmatic thought and cognitive-
  affective complexity in, 452–453
 pregnancy in, 437, 438f
 psychosocial development in, 16t,
  469–471
 reproductive capacity in, 437–438
 romantic relationships in, 445–446,
  472–476
 sexuality in, 445–449
 singlehood in, 486–487
 social clock in, 471
 stress in, 449–450, 469
 substance abuse in, 444–445
 vocational choice in, 455–459
Early childhood (2 to 6 years old),
 215–285
 aggression in, 269–272
 body composition in, 216, 216f
 body proportions in, 216, 216f
 brain in, 126, 217f, 217–219, 218f
 child-rearing practices of parents
  during, 278–283
 cognitive development in, 19, 224,
  226–251, 231t
 definition of, 8t
 emotional and social development
  in, 255–285
 emotional self-regulation in, 259
 empathy in, 260–261
 family issues in, 485
 fear in, 259
 friendships in, 262–263
 gender typing in, 273–278
 home environment in, 244
 information processing in, 236–243
 initiative versus guilt in, 16t, 256
 injuries in, 221–222
 language development in, 217, 226,
  233–234, 239, 240–242, 248–251
 milestones of development in,
  286–287
 moral development in, 264–272
 motor development in, 223t,
  223–226
 nutrition in, 217, 219–220
 parent relationship in. *See* Parent-
  child relationship

peer relations in, 261–264
 physical development in, 216–226
 play in, 225, 226–227, 235, 256,
  261, 262t, 263
 preoperational stage in, 226–233.
  See also Preoperational stage
 questions asked in, 232
 self-concept in, 256–258
 self-control in, 259
 sociocultural theory on, 233–235
 theory of mind in, 238–240
 vocational choice in, 455
Early Head Start program, 173,
 245–246
Early intervention programs, 173,
 173f, 245f, 245–246
 costs and benefits of, 246
 Project Head Start in, 173, 245–246
Easy child, as temperament type, 190
Eating habits. *See also* Nutrition
 in adolescence, 371–373
 in anorexia nervosa, 372–373
 in bulimia nervosa, 373
 in early childhood, 219–220
 in middle childhood, 291–292, 293
 in obesity, 291–292, 293, 440–442
 portion size in, 440
 record keeping on, 441
Ecological systems theory, 24f, 24–27,
 59
 bidirectional relationships in, 25, 59
 childhood injuries in, 221
 child maltreatment in, 282
 chronosystem in, 24f, 25, 60
 compared to other human
  development theories, 28t
 exosystem in, 24f, 25, 29, 63
 macrosystem in, 24f, 25, 59
 mesosystem in, 24f, 25, 29, 63
 microsystem in, 24f, 24–25, 29, 59
 third-party influences in, 60
Economic status. *See* Socioeconomic
 status
Ecstasy (MDMA), 380
Ectoderm, 82
Edelman, Marian Wright, 68
Education
 academic achievement in. *See*
  Academic achievement
 in adolescence, 391–397
 and adolescent pregnancy, 378
 of adult students, 526–527
 on aggression interventions, 272
 and Alzheimer's disease risk, 585
 back to basics movement in, 319
 bilingual, 317–318
 for caregivers of older adults with
  dementia, 586, 587
 of children with special needs,
  322–323
 and civic engagement, 413
 and cognitive changes of late
  adulthood, 596
 college experience in, 454–455. *See*
  also College experience
 cultural influences on, 235, 236
 on death, 643, 644, 662, 665
 in early adulthood, 454–455, 471
 in early childhood, 232, 233
 early interventions for at-risk
  children in, 173, 245–246
 in elder maltreatment prevention,
  628

equal access to, 321
 of gifted children, 322–323
 grouping practices in, 321–322
 high-quality, signs of, 319
 on immunizations, 221
 international comparisons of,
  323–325, 324f
 in late adulthood, 597–599
 in least restrictive environment,
  322
 in magnet schools, 321
 in Montessori approach, 245
 and moral development, 410,
  411–412
 on obesity, 441
 on parenthood, 485, 486
 philosophies on, 319–320
 in Piagetian classrooms, 233
 in preschool and kindergarten
  programs, 244–246
 on preterm infant caregiving skills,
  103–105
 in public education programs,
  221, 441
 and questions asked as catalyst for
  cognitive development, 232
 religious, 412
 in schools. *See* Schools
 self-fulfilling prophecies in,
  320–321
 in sexual abuse prevention and
  treatment, 354
 on sexuality. *See* Sex education
 sociocultural theory on, 235,
  319–320
 socioeconomic variations in, 61
 in substance abuse prevention, 381
 on sudden infant death syndrome,
  110
 television programs in, 246–247
 vocational, 393–394, 395, 396, 459,
  554–555
EEG (electroencephalography), 122,
 123t
Efe of Republic of Congo
 observational learning of, 236
 stranger anxiety of infants, 187
Effortful control
 and delay of gratification, 209
 and emotional self-regulation,
  189, 259
 and self-awareness, 208
 and temperament, 189, 191, 191t,
  193
Egalitarian marriages, 480
Ego, 15
Egocentrism
 in adolescence, 386, 387
 generational changes in, 465
 in preoperational stage, 228, 230
 in speech, 233
 and three-mountains problem,
  228, 228f
Ego differentiation in late adulthood,
 604
Ego integrity in late adulthood, 607
 and continuity theory of aging,
  615
 Erikson on, 16t, 604
 Peck on, 604–605
Ego transcendence in late adulthood,
 605
Ejaculation, first. *See* Spermarche.

Elaboration as memory strategy, 238, 305, 522, 592
for autobiographical memory of children, 238
Elderly. *See* Late adulthood
Elder maltreatment, 627–628
Electra conflict, 16*t*, 256
Electroencephalography. *See* EEG.
Embarrassment, in infancy and toddlerhood, 188, 189
Embryonic development, 82–83
teratogen exposure affecting, 85, 86*f*
Embryonic disk, 81, 82
Emerging adulthood, 464–469
cultural influences on, 466–467
as distinct period of development, 467
exploration in, 464–466, 467, 468
identity development in, 464–465, 469
parent relationship in, 468–469
religion and worldview in, 465–466
risk and resilience in, 467–469
Emotional abuse
of children, 281
of elderly, 627
Emotional and social development, 8, 9*f*, 16*t*, 16–17, 38
acceptance of change in, 608
adaptation to life in, 470–471, 536
in adolescence, 401–427
affect optimization in, 605
agreeableness in, 608
attachment in, 195–206. *See also* Attachment
in autism, 241
autonomy versus shame and doubt in, 16*t*, 184
basic emotions in, 185–188
categorical self in, 208
child-care quality affecting, 202–203
child-rearing practices affecting, 278–283
cognitive-affective complexity in, 452*f*, 452–453
common problems in, 352–354, 421–426
continuity theory of, 614–615
dating in, 420–421
and delinquency, 423–426
depression in, 421–423
depression of parent affecting, 186–187
disengagement theory of, 614
dynamic systems perspective of, 185
in early adulthood, 463–497
in early childhood, 255–285
early deprivation affecting, 127
ego integrity in, 604–605
emotional competence in, 258
emotional expertise in, 605
emotional intelligence in, 313
empathy and sympathy in, 260–261
ethology on, 22
evolutionary developmental psychology on, 22
family influences on, 345–351, 414–416
fear in, 259, 352

friendships in, 417–419. *See also* Friendships
gender typing in, 273–278, 343–345, 414
generativity versus stagnation in, 16*t*, 532–535
gerotranscendence in, 605
identity development in, 402, 403–405
identity versus role confusion in, 16*t*, 402
indirect influences on, 60
industry versus inferiority in, 16*t*, 330, 350
in infancy and toddlerhood, 183–211
initiative versus guilt in, 16*t*, 256
integrity versus despair in, 16*t*, 604
intimacy versus isolation in, 16*t*, 469–470, 472–478
in late adulthood, 603–635
in lifespan perspective, 13*f*
in middle adulthood, 531–559
in middle childhood, 329–357
and moral development, 264–272, 336–339, 405–414
nonsocial activities in, 261
openness to experience in, 608
in optimal aging, 632–633
parental warmth affecting, 205
parent–infant relationship affecting, 184
peer relations in, 261–264, 339–343, 417–421. *See also* Peer relations
personality in, 184
psychological well-being in, 610–613
and relationships in late adulthood, 620–628
reminiscence in, 606
in retirement, 629–632
in seasons of life, 470, 535–536
self-awareness in, 206–208, 256–258
self-concept in, 606–608
self-conscious emotions in, 188–189, 258, 259–260, 335
self-control in, 208–209
self-regulation of emotions in, 189–190, 259, 336, 605
self-understanding in, 330–334, 402–405
sequential research on, 38
sexual abuse affecting, 352–354
shyness and sociability in, 192
and social contexts of aging, 616–619
and social theories of aging, 614–616
socioemotional selectivity theory of, 615–616
spirituality and religiosity in, 412, 465, 608–610
and suicide, 422–423
temperament in, 190–195
trust versus mistrust in, 16*t*, 184
understanding and responding to emotions of others in, 188, 258, 260–261, 335–336
Emotional expertise in late adulthood, 605, 616
Emotional expression, facial, 185, 335

Emotional intelligence, 313, 453
Emotional self-regulation
coping strategies in, 336
in early childhood, 259
in infancy and toddlerhood, 189–190
in late adulthood, 605
in middle childhood, 336
Emotional well-being. *See* Psychological well-being
Emotion-centered coping
in late adulthood, 573, 605
in middle adulthood, 514, 516, 539
in middle childhood, 336
Emotions. *See also specific emotions*
in adolescence, 369
anger, 185–186
of dying people, 646–650
facial expressions of, 185, 335
fear, 186–188, 259
happiness, 185
in infancy and toddlerhood, 185–190
of others, understanding and responding to, 188, 258, 260–261, 335–336
sadness, 186
self-conscious, 188–189, 258, 259–260, 335
self-regulation of, 189–190, 259, 336, 605
Empathy
in early childhood, 258, 260–261, 265
and guilt, 265
in infancy and toddlerhood, 109, 208
in middle childhood, 335
and moral behavior, 265
and self-awareness, 208
Emphysema, 579
Employment
in adolescence, 395–396, 459
apprenticeship programs in, 459
bridge jobs prior to retirement in, 629
burnout from job stress in, 554
changes at midlife, 555–556
and child care, 104–105, 202–204, 350–351, 485, 494–495
combining family with, 494–495
discontinuous path in, 492
in dual-earner families, 494–495. *See also* Dual-earner households
in early adulthood, 466, 467, 470, 471, 492–495
educational preparation for, 393–394, 395, 396, 459, 554–555
establishment of career in, 492–493
ethnic and racial differences in, 555
in families with young children, 485
flexible time policies in, 495
gender stereotypes in, 344, 457*t*, 457–459, 493–494
glass ceiling in, 555
and marital roles, 350–351, 480–481, 481*f*, 494–495
and meal preparation time, 440
mentoring relationship in, 493
in middle adulthood, 525–526, 536, 553–558

of mothers, 202–204, 350–351, 416*t*, 494–495
nontraditional jobs of men in, 458
observation and participation of children in, 236
parental leave from, 104–105, 203, 485
and parenthood decisions, 484
part-time, affecting academic achievement, 395–396
retirement from, 556–558, 629–632. *See also* Retirement
satisfaction with job in, 553–554, 554*f*
selection of vocation in, 455–459
and self-care children, 351
sex differences in, 457–459, 492, 493–494, 536, 553, 555
and socioeconomic status, 61
and time spent per day with children, 203, 203*f*, 351
and unemployment, 556
Empty nest phase, 543
Endocrine system. *See* Hormones
Endoderm, 82
End-of-life care, 648–659
advance medical directives on, 655–656
communication with dying person in, 643, 646, 648–649, 650
decision making on, 641, 642, 655–656
dignity in, 641–642
informing patient of prognosis in, 649
and right to die, 654–659
Endorphins, 112
Engagement
and activity theory of aging, 614
and disengagement theory of aging, 614
and separateness, developmental task in seasons of life theory, 535–536
England
adolescent contraceptive use in, 375*f*
home births in, 99
lifelong learning in, 598
sense of control in, 573
Enterprising personality, vocational choice in, 456
Environmental influences, 59–69
on Alzheimer's disease, 584
on antisocial behavior, 73
on attention-deficit hyperactivity disorder, 74, 305
canalization concept on, 72
on cerebrovascular dementia, 585
on childhood injuries, 222
on cognitive development, 170–173, 244–248
cultural. *See* Cultural influences
on delinquency, 425
ecological systems theory on, 24*f*, 24–27
in epigenetic framework, 73*f*, 73–75
evolutionary developmental psychology on, 23
evolutionary theory of Darwin on, 14
on executive function, 303

family as, 59–63
  on gender typing, 274–276
  and gene correlation, 72, 72f, 193
  on gene expression, 73–75
  and gene interactions, 71, 71f
  on health in early adulthood, 438–439
  on hearing loss, 503
  in home, 244. See also Home environment
  on intelligence and IQ, 71, 71f, 170–171, 312–315
  on life expectancy, 565, 566
  on multiple births, 47t, 48
  neighborhood, town, and city as factors in, 64–65
  and person–environment fit, 574, 611, 618–619
  on prenatal development, 85–92
  on pubertal development, 366–367, 371
  and relative influence of nature and nurture, 7, 28t, 69–75
  and resilience, 10–11
  in sensitive periods, 22, 125–128
  on sexual activity of adolescents, 375
  on sexual orientation, 375–376
  socioeconomic, 61–63. See also Socioeconomic status
  on substance abuse, 381
  on sudden infant death syndrome, 110
  on temperament, 193–194
  teratogens in, 85–92
Environmental mastery in middle adulthood, 538, 539
Envy in infancy and toddlerhood, 188
Epidermis, 503
Epidural analgesia during childbirth, 100–101
Epigenesis, 73–75
Epigenetic framework, 73f, 73–75
Epinephrine in stress response, 93
Epiphyses, 217
Episodic memory
  in early childhood, 238
  in late adulthood, 591, 593
Epistemic cognition, 451–452
Equilibrium in cognitive development, 19, 152
Erectile dysfunction, 507, 579
Erikson, Erik, 16t, 16–17, 38
  on autonomy versus shame and doubt in infancy and toddlerhood, 16t, 184
  on generativity versus stagnation in middle adulthood, 16t, 532–535
  on identity versus role confusion in adolescence, 16t, 402
  on industry versus inferiority in middle childhood, 16t, 330
  on initiative versus guilt in early childhood, 16t, 256
  on integrity versus despair in late adulthood, 16t, 604
  on intimacy versus isolation in early adulthood, 16t, 469–470
  on trust versus mistrust in infancy and toddlerhood, 16t, 184
Eritrea, emotional stress of orphans in, 353
Estonia, poverty rate in, 68f

Estrogen, 115
  in menopause, 434, 504, 506
  in middle adulthood, 504, 513
  in osteoporosis, 513
  in puberty, 363
Ethical issues
  in reproductive technologies, 54, 55
  in research, 17, 39t, 39–40
  in right to die, 654–659
  and universal principles in moral development, 408
Ethiopia
  dynamic assessment of immigrant children from, 315
  malnutrition in, 132
  partner abuse in, 483f
Ethnic and racial differences
  in body size, 121
  in career opportunities, 493–494, 494f
  in caregiving for older adults, 549, 612
  in caring for aging parents, 549, 617–618
  in cliques and crowds, 419
  in community and neighborhood, 616
  in death concept of children, 643
  in dementia, 582
  in departure from parental home, 479
  in early adulthood health, 438–439
  in elder maltreatment, 627
  in employment, 493–494, 494f, 555
  in fraternal twinning, 47t
  in grandparents as primary caregivers, 548
  heritability research on, 71
  in identity, 406
  in late adulthood health, 575
  in life expectancy, 564, 566
  in long-term care of older adults, 589
  in marriage partners, 480
  and middle childhood understanding of diversity, 337–338
  in passive euthanasia beliefs, 655
  in religiosity, 465, 609
  in singlehood, 487
  in socioeconomic status, 61
  stereotypes on, 406
  in suicide, 612
  in temperament, 193
Ethnographic research, 29t, 32–33
  on immigrant youths, 33
Ethology, 22
  attachment theory in, 196–197, 206, 474
  compared to other human development theories, 28t
Europe. See also specific countries
  academic and vocational tracks in, 395
  assisted suicide in, 658
  caring for aging parents in, 617
  child care in, 171
  cohabitation in, 488
  contraceptive availability for adolescents in, 379
  departure from parental home in, 478, 545

drug use in, 381f
  free time of adolescents in, 417
  job stress in, 554
  lifelong learning in, 598
  marital roles in, 480
  menopause in, 506, 506f
  moral development in, 411
  nursing home care in, 619
  prenatal health care in, 104
  sexual activity of adolescents in, 374, 377, 379
  sexually transmitted diseases in, 377
  terminally ill patients in, 649
  vocational education in, 396, 459
Eustachian tube, 293
Euthanasia, 654, 654t
  and assisted suicide, 654t, 658–659
  involuntary active, 654t
  passive, 654t, 654–656
  voluntary active, 654t, 656–658, 659
Event-based prospective memory tasks, 593
Event-related potentials (ERPs), 123, 123t
  in emotional responses, 199
Evidence and theory, scientific reasoning on, 385
Evocative correlation of genetic and environmental factors, 72
Evolution, theories of
  attachment in, 22, 196
  of Darwin, 14
  in ethology, 22
  gender roles in, 273–274, 540
  generativity in, 533
  mate selection in, 472
  play activities in, 297–298
  spatial abilities in, 390
Evolutionary developmental psychology, 22–23, 28t
Executive function
  in attention-deficit hyperactivity disorder, 304
  in autism, 241
  in early childhood, 236
  in infancy and toddlerhood, 162
  in late adulthood, 568, 589–590
  and media multitasking, 394
  in middle adulthood, 520
  in middle childhood, 303
  and planning, 303–304
  and theory of mind, 240
Exercise
  in adolescence, 364–365, 365f
  and Alzheimer's disease risk, 585
  athletic activities in, 295, 296–297. See also Athletic activities
  daily amount recommended, 365, 443
  in early adulthood, 436–437, 437f, 443
  health benefits of, 443, 515, 578
  in late adulthood, 571, 572, 577–578
  and longevity, 567
  in middle adulthood, 504, 513, 515–516, 540, 541
  in obesity, 292, 440, 441, 443
  in osteoporosis, 513
  in physical education classes, 298–299

in pregnancy, 92
  in school recess, 298
  self-efficacy in, 515–516
Exosystem in ecological systems theory, 24f, 25, 63
  in family chaos, 29
Expansion strategy in grammar development, 251
Experience-dependent brain growth, 128, 450
Experience-expectant brain growth, 127–128
Experimental research, 35
  on classical conditioning, 17
  combined with developmental research, 38
  compared to other research designs, 36t
  ethical issues in, 17
  in natural settings, 35
  random assignment in, 35
Expertise
  creativity in, 454
  in early adulthood, 453
  emotional, in late adulthood, 605, 616
  in middle adulthood, 524
  practical problem solving in, 524
Explicit memory, 164, 394
Exploration in early adulthood, 464–466, 467, 468
  and vocational choice, 456
Exploration in infancy and toddlerhood
  attachment security affecting, 198
  circular reactions in, 153
  intentional behavior in, 154
  and motor development, 136–140
  and perceptual development, 142, 143–144, 147
  secure base for, 187–188
  and temperament, 193
  visual cliff studies of, 142, 143f
Expressive style of communication, 178
Extended families
  of African Americans, 65, 66, 332, 422, 434, 479, 491, 589
  Alzheimer's disease in, 585
  caregiving for older adults in, 589
  and departure from parental home, 479, 545
  in divorce, 348
  in exosystem, 25
  of families with young children, 485
  of gay and lesbian couples, 488, 492
  and generativity in middle adulthood, 535
  grandparents in, 65, 66, 547
  marital roles in, 480
  of never-married childless older adults, 623–624
  problem solving in, 594
  respect for older adults in, 574, 575
  of single mothers, 471, 491
  and social context of aging, 616, 618
  of stepfamilies, 491
  suicide prevention in, 422, 612
  in widowhood, 622, 623
Externalizing difficulties, 60

Extinction in classical conditioning, 134
Extracurricular activities
    and civic engagement, 413
    in dropout prevention, 396–397
Extroversion, 542, 542t
    in late adulthood, 606, 608, 613, 614
Eye blink reflex, 107t
Eye movements
    in non-rapid-eye-movement (NREM) sleep, 108, 108t, 109, 571
    in object permanence studies, 155
    in rapid-eye-movement (REM) sleep, 108t, 108–109, 128
    and visual acuity of infants, 113
Eyes
    accommodation of, 502
    in late adulthood, 569
    in middle adulthood, 502–503
    and vision. See Vision
Eyewitness testimony by children, 355

F
Fables, personal, 386–387
Face, aging of, 572
Facebook use
    in adolescence, 418
    in early adulthood, 476
    in late adulthood, 599, 625, 626
    in middle adulthood, 552, 553f
Face perception, 145, 145f
    early vision loss affecting, 125
    and sensitive period for culture-specific learning, 141
Facial expressions
    brain activity in response to, 199
    emotions associated with, 185, 335
    infant perception of, 188
    newborn imitation of, 135f, 135–136
    in odor response of infants, 112, 113f
    systematic observation of, 29
    in taste response of infants, 112
Facial hair development, 363, 366, 366f
Factor analysis of intelligence tests, 309
Factual knowledge in middle adulthood, 522–523
Faith, spiritual and religious
    death concept in, 645, 650
    in late adulthood, 608, 633
Fallopian tubes, 80, 80f
Falls
    in infancy and toddlerhood, 143, 147, 147f
    in late adulthood, 582
False beliefs
    in autism, 241
    in early childhood, 239f, 239–240
    in middle childhood, 306, 307f
    second-order, 306, 307f
    social interactions affecting, 240
Familiarity preference of infants, 134, 135f, 163
Family, 59–63
    adaptation to changes in, 60–61, 115
    adjustment to parenthood in, 115, 484–485

of adolescents, 414–416, 485–486
    adoptive, 416t. See also Adoption
    and aggression, 270
    aging parents in, 547–551, 623
    Alzheimer's disease in, 584, 585, 586–587
    attachment quality in, 201, 202
    attention-deficit hyperactivity disorder in, 305
    blended, 349–350, 416t, 490–491
    chaos in, 26
    child maltreatment in, 281–283
    child-rearing practices in. See Child-rearing practices
    chronic illness in, 294
    and civic engagement, 413
    combining work with, 494–495
    death and dying in, 648–649, 652, 661–662
    direct influences of, 59–60
    divorce in, 346–349. See also Divorce
    dual-earner, 494–495. See also Dual-earner households
    elder maltreatment in, 627–628
    extended, 65, 66. See also Extended families
    gay and lesbian, 491–492, 621
    and generativity in middle adulthood, 533, 534
    grandparents in, 545–547, 548, 626–627. See also Grandparents
    home environment of. See Home environment
    in hospice care, 652, 653
    of immigrant children, 33
    indirect influences of, 60
    kinkeeper role in, 545
    in late adulthood, 615–616, 617, 624, 625–627
    life cycle of, 478–486
    long-term care of older adults in, 589
    marital roles in, 480–481
    mealtimes in, 29, 63, 63f, 291, 372
    in middle adulthood, 543–552
    in middle childhood, 345–351
    with one child, 346
    parents in. See Parent(s)
    partner abuse in, 283
    and pubertal growth, 367, 371
    sexual abuse in, 352, 353
    siblings in, 204–205, 345–346. See also Siblings
    single-parent, 491. See also Single-parent families
    size of, 204, 483
    skipped-generation, 548
    socioeconomic status of, 61–63. See also Socioeconomic status
    stepparents in, 349–350, 490–491
    stressful circumstances in, 416, 416t
    and substance abuse, 381
    as system, 59, 415
    twins in, 47t, 48. See also Twins
    violence in, 482–483, 483f
    and vocational choice, 457
    in widowhood, 622–623, 624
    with young children, 485
Family Check-Up intervention, 35
Family tree (pedigree) in genetic counseling, 54–55

Fantasy period in vocational choice, 455
Fast-mapping process in vocabulary development, 248
Fast-twitch muscle fibers, 572
Fat, body
    baby fat, 121, 216
    in middle adulthood, 504
    in puberty, 366
    and television viewing, 292, 292f
Fat, dietary, 442, 442f
    in cardiovascular disease, 436, 442, 442f
    in middle adulthood, 504
    in obesity, 440, 441
Fathers
    adjustment to role as, 115, 484–485
    adolescent, 378, 380
    age of, 438
    alcohol use of, at time of conception, 89
    and attachment security of infant, 201–204
    in blended families, 349–350, 491
    cultural influences on role of, 201–204
    depression of, 186, 187
    dioxin in bloodstream of, 90
    divorce of, 347, 348
    in dual-earner marriages, 480
    education on child rearing, 486
    gender typing of children by, 274, 343
    generativity in middle adulthood, 533, 535
    leave time from employment, 105
    marital roles of, 480
    in maternal employment, 350–351
    play activities of, 201–202, 204
    self-acceptance of, 539
    as stepparents, 349–350, 491
    time spent with sons, 345
    unwed, 491
    warmth of, 204
Father–stepmother families, 350
Fatty acids, polyunsaturated, 577
Favoritism
    sibling preference in, 345–346
    toward in-groups, 276, 337–338
    toward out-groups, 338
Fear
    in early childhood, 259
    in infancy and toddlerhood, 134, 186–188, 190
    in late adulthood, of crime, 617
    in middle childhood, 352
    and temperament, 190, 191t
Feeding practices
    and attachment, 195–196
    bottle-feeding in, 130–131, 131t
    breastfeeding in. See Breastfeeding
    and obesity, 291–292
Feet-first reaching, 138, 138f
Feminine traits
    in adolescence, 422
    in caring for aging parents, 550
    in gender identity, 276, 540–542
    in middle adulthood, 535, 540–542
    in middle childhood, 344
Feminization of poverty, 544, 618
Fertility
    and childlessness in infertility, 489
    in early adulthood, 437–438

prenatal DES exposure affecting, 86
    in puberty, 365–366
    and reproductive technologies, 47t, 48, 54–55
Fertilization, 46, 80, 80f
    in vitro, 47t, 48, 54
    in reproductive technologies, 54, 56t
Fetal alcohol spectrum disorder (FASD), 88–89
Fetal alcohol syndrome (FAS), 88–89
    partial, 89
Fetal development, 83–85
    age of viability in, 84
    alcohol exposure affecting, 88–90
    diagnosis and treatment of problems in, 56t, 56–57
    habituation in, 85, 134
    nicotine exposure affecting, 88
    stress hormones affecting, 93
    teratogens affecting, 85, 86f
Fetal medicine, 56t, 56–57
Fetal monitoring, 100
Fetoscopy, 56t
Fibrillation, 640
Fibrosis, cystic, 49t, 57, 293
Field experiments, 35
Fiji, moral development in, 264
Filipinos
    as immigrants, 32
    intelligence definition of, 311
Financial abuse of elderly, 627, 628
Financial planning for retirement, 556–558, 629–630
Fine-motor development
    drawing in, 224f, 224–225, 295, 295f
    in early childhood, 223t, 224f, 224–225
    individual differences in, 225
    in infancy and toddlerhood, 137, 137t, 139–140
    in middle childhood, 295, 295f
    self-help skills in, 224
    sex differences in, 296
Finland
    academic achievement in, 324–325
    adolescent contraceptive use in, 375f
    adolescent suicide rate in, 422
    cesarean delivery rate in, 101
    corporal punishment in, 282–283
    high school graduation rate in, 395f
    infant mortality rate in, 105f
    late adulthood in, 576
    poverty rate in, 62, 68f
    retirement programs in, 630
    sexual attitudes and behavior in, 445
First Age, 607
Firstborn
    arrival of new sibling affecting, 204–205
    transition to parenthood in, 115, 484–485
First marriage, age at time of, 479
First pregnancy, 115, 438f, 484–485
First words, 176–177
Flexibility changes in motor development, 294
Flight or fight response, 93
Flowcharts on information processing, 20–21, 21f, 161, 162f

Flow state in middle adulthood, 540–541

Fluid intelligence, 518–519, 521*f*, 590

Fluoride treatments and fluoridated water, 217

Folic acid in prenatal nutrition, 92

Food. *See also* Eating habits; Nutrition
  insecurity concerning, 132
  mercury exposure from, 90
  supplement programs, 92
  taste and odor preferences of newborn, 112
  toxoplasmosis from, 92

Foot reaching of infants, 138, 138*f*

Foreclosure status in identity development, 403, 403*t*, 404, 405

Formal operational stage, 19, 19*t*, 382–384
  cultural influences on, 384
  hypothetico-deductive reasoning in, 382–383, 384
  pendulum problem in, 382–383, 383*f*
  and postformal thought, 450
  propositional thought in, 383, 384
  research on, 383–384

Formula feeding of infants, 130–131, 131*t*

Foster care, 127
  grandparents providing, 548

Fourth Age, 607

Fowler, James, on faith development, 608

Fractures
  in falls in late adulthood, 582
  in osteoporosis, 513

Fragile X syndrome, 51

Frailty in late adulthood, 580

France
  adolescent contraceptive use in, 375*f*
  adolescent pregnancy in, 378*f*
  corporal punishment in, 283
  divorce rate in, 347*f*
  gender stereotypes in, 343
  infant mortality rate in, 105*f*
  late adulthood in, 576
  life expectancy in, 565*f*
  lifelong learning in, 598
  math achievement scores in, 389*f*
  poverty rate in, 68*f*
  retirement programs in, 630
  sexual attitudes and behavior in, 445
  smell sense of newborn in, 112

Fraternal twins, 47*f*, 47–48. *See also* Twins

Free radicals, 433–434
  caloric restriction affecting, 505

Freestanding birth centers, 99

Freud, Sigmund, 15–16, 184
  on attachment, 195
  on moral development, 264–265
  on psychosexual stages of development, 15–16, 16*t*, 256

Friendships
  and adjustment, 419
  in adolescence, 405, 417–419
  of bullying victims, 342
  cell phone use in, 418, 418*f*
  cliques in, 419–420
  corumination in, 418, 422

in divorce, 490
  in early adulthood, 469, 476–477
  in early childhood, 262–263
  functions of, 625
  and identity development, 405
  intergenerational, 625
  intimacy in, 417, 417*f*, 419, 469
  in late adulthood, 615*f*, 615–616, 624–625
  in middle adulthood, 541, 543, 552–553
  in middle childhood, 340
  and moral development, 410
  of never-married childless older adults, 624
  online. *See* Online friendships
  with other sex, 477
  and peer acceptance, 341
  same-sex, 417–418, 476–477
  in school transitions, 392
  secondary, 625
  self-disclosure in, 417, 417*f*, 476, 477
  sex differences in, 340, 417–418, 476, 477, 552, 553, 625
  siblings in, 477
  in widowhood, 623, 624

Frontal lobes, 124, 124*f*

Full inclusion of students with learning difficulties, 322

Functional age, 564

Functional magnetic resonance imaging (fMRI), 123*t*, 123*f*, 123–124
  in multitasking, 394
  in neuron loss in late adulthood, 568
  of prefrontal cortex in early childhood, 217
  in visual stimulation of infants, 123*f*

Functional play, 262*t*

Funerals, 664

G

Gabapentin in menopause, 506

Games, 296–297. *See also* Play

Gametes, 46–47
  in reproductive technologies, 54

Gardner, Howard, theory of multiple intelligences, 311–312, 312*t*, 323

Gastrointestinal system
  cancer of, 444, 510
  stress affecting, 450, 514

Gay, lesbian, and bisexual people
  adolescence in, 375–377, 421
  bulimia in, 373
  cohabitation in, 488
  dating in, 421
  death of intimate partner in, 662
  early adulthood in, 447, 475
  friendships in, 477
  health care decisions for partners in, 621, 656
  identity development in, 405
  late adulthood in, 621
  marriage in, 479–480
  mate selection in, 473
  parenthood in, 491–492
  partner abuse in, 482
  romantic relationships in, 475
  sexually transmitted diseases in, 447
  suicide in, 376, 422

Gender constancy, 276–277

Gender contentedness, 344

Gender differences. *See* Sex differences

Gender identity, 276–278
  in adolescence, 414, 417
  androgynous, 276, 344, 414, 541–542
  constancy in, 276–277
  contentedness with, 344
  cultural influences on, 540
  emergence of, 276–277
  feminine traits in, 535, 540–542
  intensification of, 414, 422
  masculine traits in, 535, 540–542
  in middle adulthood, 535, 540–542
  in middle childhood, 344–345
  in parenthood, 540–541
  and parenthood decisions, 484
  personality traits in, 276
  typicality in, 344

Gender intensification, 414, 422

Gender roles
  in combining work and family, 350–351, 494–495
  conformity to, 344
  in employment opportunities, 555
  in friendships, 417
  in gay and lesbian partnerships, 621
  and gender identity, 344, 540
  hormones affecting, 273, 274
  in marital relationships, 350, 480–481, 481*f*, 490, 494, 620
  in maternal employment, 350–351, 494
  and mate selection, 472
  of parents, 278, 350, 494
  and partner abuse, 483
  in play activities, 273, 274, 276, 344
  for returning students, 526
  stereotypes on. *See* Gender stereotypes
  in transition to parenthood, 484–485
  in widowhood, 623

Gender-salience filter, 277, 277*f*

Gender schema theory, 273, 277*f*, 277–278

Gender stereotypes
  in achievement, 276, 334, 343
  in aggression, 270
  in athletic activities, 296, 365
  and double standard of aging, 516–517, 535
  in early childhood, 273, 278
  in employment, 344, 457*t*, 457–459, 493–494
  and gender schema theory, 277–278
  in language development, 275
  in mathematical abilities, 389
  in middle adulthood, 516–517, 535
  in middle childhood, 343–344
  reduction of, 278
  and self-esteem, 332
  and vocational choice, 457*t*, 457–459

Gender typing, 414
  biological influences on, 273–274
  in early childhood, 273–278

environmental influences on, 274–276
  evolution of, 273
  and gender identity, 276–278
  identity and behavior in, 344–345
  in middle childhood, 343–345
  peer relations in, 276
  stereotypes in, 343–344. *See also* Gender stereotypes

"Generation me," 465

Generativity, 469–470, 471
  ego integrity in, 604
  life stories in, 534
  in middle adulthood, versus stagnation, 16*t*, 532–535, 533*t*

Generic utterances, 275

Genes, 46–53
  dominant and recessive, 48*t*, 48–50, 49*t*
  expression of, 73–75
  heterozygous, 48
  homozygous, 48
  Human Genome Project on, 56
  mutations of, 51–52, 510
  programmed effects of, 432–433

Gene therapy, 57

Genetic engineering, 56

Genetic factors, 46–53
  in aggression, 424
  in aging, 432–434, 433*f*
  in alcoholism, 444
  in Alzheimer's disease, 584, 585
  in antisocial behavior, 73
  in attachment security, 200–201
  in attention-deficit hyperactivity disorder, 74, 74*f*, 304, 305
  in behavioral genetics, 69
  in cancer, 51, 52, 57, 432, 433, 510, 511, 567, 661
  in cerebrovascular dementia, 585
  in cognitive changes of late adulthood, 596
  counseling on, 53–55
  in depression, 186, 421
  dominant and recessive genes in, 48*t*, 48–50, 49*t*
  and environment correlation, 72, 72*f*, 171, 193
  and environment interactions, 71, 71*f*
  in epigenetic framework, 73*f*, 73–75
  in executive function, 303
  in glaucoma, 503
  in hand preference, 218
  heritability estimates on, 70–71
  in intelligence and IQ, 70, 71, 170–171, 312–315
  in life expectancy, 566, 567
  in multiple offspring, 47*f*, 47–48
  in obesity, 291
  in osteoporosis, 513
  in patterns of inheritance, 48–52
  in physical growth, 130, 219
  in pubertal changes, 366
  and relative influence of nature and nurture, 69–75
  and resilience, 10
  in rheumatoid arthritis, 580–581
  in sexual orientation, 375
  in temperament, 193–194
  and teratogen impact, 85
  in X-linked inheritance, 50–51, 51*f*

Genitals
  herpes simplex virus infection of, 91, 91*t*
  in menopause, 504
  prenatal DES exposure affecting, 86
  prenatal development of, 83
  in puberty, 366, 366*t*
Genital stage of psychosexual development, 16*t*, 362
Genomic imprinting, 51
Genotype, 45
German measles in pregnancy, 90, 91*t*
Germany
  attachment patterns in, 198*f*, 198–199
  caregiving roles of parents in, 201, 204
  corporal punishment in, 283
  divorce rate in, 347*f*
  ethnic bias in, 338
  family size in, 483
  infant mortality rate in, 105*f*
  life expectancy in, 565*f*
  overweight and obesity in, 291
  parental leave in, 105
  personality traits in, 542
  retirement programs in, 630
  self-recognition by toddlers in, 207
  teenage pregnancy in, 378*f*
  unintentional childhood injuries in, 221*f*
  vocational education in, 459
Germline mutations, 52, 510
Gerotranscendence, 605
Gesell, Arnold, 14–15
Gestures
  preverbal, 176
  in sign language, 174, 176, 178
Gifted children and prodigies, 31, 322–323
Gilligan, Carol, 409
Glass ceiling in employment opportunities, 555
Glaucoma, 503
Glial cells, 83, 122
Global identity, 466
Globalization, 466
Glucose blood levels
  in Alzheimer's disease, 581, 584
  in diabetes, Type 2, 581
Goal-directed behavior in sensorimotor stage, 154
Golden Rule, 408
Good boy–good girl orientation in moral development, 408
Goodness-of-fit model on child rearing, 194, 195
Government policy. *See* Public policy
Graduation rates for high schools, 395*f*
Grammatical development
  adult feedback in, 250–251
  complex structures in, 249–250
  in early childhood, 249–250
  first word combinations in, 177
  information processing theory of, 175, 250
  in middle childhood, 316
  nativist theory of, 174
  overregularization in, 249
  questions in, 249–250
  recast and expansion strategies in, 251
  universal, 174

Grandparents, 545–547, 548, 626–627
  in extended family, 65, 66, 547
  as indirect influence, 60
  of resilient children, 11
  in skipped-generation families, 548
Grasping of infants and newborn, 139*f*, 139–140
  pincer grasp in, 139*f*, 140
  as reflex, 107*t*
  ulnar grasp in, 139*f*, 140
Gratification, delayed, 209
Great Britain
  hospice care in, 652
  religion in, 412
  sexual attitudes and behavior in, 445
  voluntary active euthanasia opinions in, 656*t*
Great-grandchildren, 626–627
Greece
  adolescent contraceptive use in, 375*f*
  adolescent suicide in, 422
  departure from parental home in, 545
  infant mortality rate in, 105*f*
  life expectancy in, 565*f*
  menopause in, 508
  obesity in, 291
  poverty in, 68*f*
  toddler self-recognition in, 207, 208*f*
  unintentional childhood injuries in, 221*f*
Green House model of nursing-home care, 619
Grief and bereavement, 659–665. *See also* Bereavement
Gross-motor development
  in early childhood, 223, 223*t*
  individual differences in, 225
  in infancy and toddlerhood, 137, 137*t*
  in middle childhood, 294–295
  sex differences in, 296
Groups
  peer. *See* Peer groups
  in schools, 321–322, 395
Growing pains in middle childhood, 290
Growth, physical. *See* Physical development
Growth hormone (GH), 219
  in early adulthood, 434
  in puberty, 363
Growth norms, 121
Growth spurts
  in infancy and toddlerhood, 120–121
  in puberty, 363, 366
  in vocabulary, 177
Guatemala
  attention style in, 167
  childbirth practices in, 99
  communication style in, 314
  cosleeping of parents and infants in, 129
  memory strategies in, 306
  observational learning in, 167
Guidance Study, 36
Guided participation, 235

Guilt
  in bulimia nervosa, 373
  in early childhood, 16*t*, 256, 259, 260
  empathy-based, 265
  in infancy and toddlerhood, 188
  versus initiative, 16*t*, 256
  in middle childhood, 335
  in moral development, 264, 265
  of parents in death of child, 661
  in suicidal loss, 661
Gun control legislation in suicide prevention, 423
Gusii of Kenya
  Mother–infant relationship and attachment security in, 200
  motor development of infants, 139

H
Habituation, 134–135, 135*f*
  and attention, 163
  and categorization, 165
  definition of, 134
  and discrimination of human and monkey faces, 141, 141*f*
  and intelligence, 170
  in prenatal development, 85, 134
  and violation-of-expectation method, 155, 155*f*
Hair
  facial and body, in adolescence, 363, 365, 366, 366*f*, 367
  inheritance of characteristics, 48, 48*t*
  in physical changes of aging, 435*t*
Haiti, life expectancy in, 565
Hall, G. Stanley, 14–15
Hand preference, 217–218
Happiness
  in infancy and toddlerhood, 185
  in marital relationships, 481*t*, 481–483
  in middle adulthood, 539, 540–541
Hardiness, as personal quality, 516
Hausa of Nigeria, 301
Hawaii
  birth complications in, 105–106
  child maltreatment prevention programs in, 283
  parental leave time from employment in, 105
  same-sex marriage in, 479
Head Start programs, 173, 245–246
Health
  in adolescence, 371–381
  and cognitive changes of late adulthood, 596
  and compression of morbidity, 576–577
  in early adulthood, 438–450
  in early childhood, 219–222
  in infancy and toddlerhood, 130–132
  international comparisons of indicators on, 66–67, 67*t*
  in late adulthood, 567, 575–589, 611
  in middle adulthood, 508–514, 540
  in middle childhood, 290–294
  in prenatal period, 95–96
  in retirement decisions, 629
  stress affecting, 449–450
  and telomere length, 433

Health care
  advance medical directives on, 655–656
  in Alzheimer's disease, 585
  in arthritis, 581
  assistive technology and devices in, 573–574
  cost of, 588
  in diarrhea, 220
  drug therapy in. *See* Drug therapy
  durable power of attorney for, 655–656
  fetal medicine in, 56–57
  immunizations in, 90, 220–221
  in late adulthood, 574, 575, 588–589, 595
  in menopause, 506
  in osteoporosis, 513
  palliative, 652, 653, 655
  for parents and newborn, 104–105
  prenatal. *See* Prenatal health care
  reproductive technologies in. *See* Reproductive technologies
  and right to die, 654–659
  universal access to, 66–67
Health insurance
  hospice benefits in, 653
  lack of, 66–67, 438, 439
  obesity-related coverage in, 441
  for older adults, 588–589
  public policies on, 66–67
Health professionals
  in assisted suicide, 658–659
  behavior toward dying person, 649
  recognition of advance medical directives, 655, 656
  in voluntary active euthanasia, 656, 657
  in withholding or withdrawal of life-sustaining treatment, 655, 656
Healthy Families America, 283
Hearing
  and brain development, 125
  genetic factors affecting, 48*t*
  in infancy and toddlerhood, 113, 140–142
  in intermodal perception, 146
  and language development, 125, 176, 178
  in late adulthood, 568*f*, 569–570
  in middle adulthood, 503
  in middle childhood, 293
  in physical changes of aging, 435*t*, 503, 568*f*, 569–570
  in prenatal development, 85
  sign language in loss of, 174, 176
  and speech perception, 141–142
Heart, 434–436, 435*t*. *See also* Cardiovascular system
Heart attack, 511–512
  as cause of death, 640
  reducing risk of, 512
Heart rate
  age-related changes in, 436
  in arrhythmias, 512, 640
  fetal, 84, 85, 100
  of newborn, Apgar Scale on, 98*t*
  in shyness and sociability, 192
Height
  in early childhood, 216, 216*f*
  in infancy and toddlerhood, 120, 121

in late adulthood, 572
in middle adulthood, 504
in middle childhood, 290, 290f
in physical changes of aging, 435t,
504, 572
in puberty, 363, 366f
Heinz dilemma, 407–408
Helicopter parenting, 468–469
Helmet use, 294
Helpfulness. See Prosocial behavior
Helplessness, learned. See Learned
helplessness
Hemispheres, cerebral. See Cerebral
hemispheres
Hemophilia, 49t, 50
gene therapy in, 57
Heredity. See also Genetic factors
and heritability estimates, 70–71,
193, 312–313
and physical growth, 130
and relative influence of nature and
nurture, 69–75
stability of characteristics in, 7
Herero people of Botswana, 576
Heritability estimates, 70–71
of intelligence, 70, 71, 312–313
limitations of, 70–71
of temperament, 193
Heroin, 87, 88, 380
Herpes simplex virus, 91, 91t, 101
Heterogeneity of student groups,
322
Heterozygous genes, 48
Hidden objects, searching for, in
sensorimotor stage, 154, 155,
156
Hierarchical classification in
preoperational stage, 229, 229f
Hierarchical communication style,
314
Hierarchical structure of self-esteem,
331, 332f
High-density lipoproteins, 443, 504
High/Scope Perry Preschool Project,
245, 245f
High-stakes testing movement, 388
Hip fractures, 513, 582, 588
Hippocampus, 218, 218f, 394
Hispanics
academic achievement of, 393, 395
aging parents of, 549, 617
anorexia nervosa of, 372
bilingual, 318
body image of, 371
child-rearing practices of, 281
communication style of, 314
dementia of, 582
departure from parental home,
479
discrimination in career
opportunities, 493–494, 494f
dropout rates for, 396
drug use of, 380
extended-family households of, 65
father–child relationships of,
203–204
food insecurity of, 132
glaucoma of, 503
grandparents as caregivers of, 548
health problems in late adulthood,
575
intelligence quotient of, 312
long-term care of older adults, 589

Mexican American. See Mexican
Americans
moral reasoning of, 411
osteoporosis of, 513
overweight and obese, 291, 439
poverty of, 61
religiosity of, 465, 609
respect for older adults, 627
school transitions of, 391
stereotype threat affecting, 315,
315f
suicide rate of, 422
teacher–student interaction of,
320–321
Historical development of child
development theories, 14–20
History-graded influences, 11–12
HIV infection and AIDS. See AIDS
Hmong immigrants, scaffolding
interactions of, 234
Home births, 98, 99–100
Home environment
assisted living facilities as, 589
caring for aging parent in, 551
chaos in, 26
childbirth in, 98, 99–100
death and dying in, 642, 650, 651,
652
hospice care in, 652
and intelligence, 170–171
in late adulthood, 574, 589,
617–619
leaving parental home, 478–479,
543, 544–545
marital roles in, 480–481
and mental development, 244
person–environment fit in, 574,
611, 618–619
and reading readiness, 242, 242f
in residential communities for
older adults, 618–619, 631
siblings in. See Siblings
Homelessness, 62
*Home Observation for Measurement
of the Environment* (HOME),
170–171, 244
Home visitation program in Nurse–
Family Partnership, 94, 380
Homicide rates, 438, 438f
Homophobia, 377
Homosexuals. See Gay, lesbian, and
bisexual people
Homozygous genes, 48
Hong Kong
child-rearing styles and academic
achievement in, 392
social relationships of older adults
in, 616
Hope in dying people, 649
Hopi Indians, play activities in early
childhood, 256
Hormones
androgen. See Androgen
cortisol. See Cortisol
in early adulthood, 434
in early childhood, 219
estrogen. See Estrogen
growth hormone, 219, 363, 434
and immune response, 437
in late adulthood, 568, 571
in menopause, 434, 504, 506
in middle adulthood, 504, 506
in new parents, 115

prenatal exposure to, 376, 390
in puberty, 363, 369, 373
and sexual orientation, 376
testosterone, 363, 507
Hospice programs, 652–653
Hospitals
childbirth in, 99, 100, 101
death and dying in, 650, 651, 652
hospice care in, 652
Hostile aggression, 269
Hot flashes and night sweats in
menopause, 504, 506, 507, 508
Housework and household chores
in dual-earner families, 350, 480,
481f, 494–495
in late adulthood, 620
marital roles in, 480–481, 481f, 620
Human Genome Project, 56
Human immunodeficiency virus
(HIV) infections. See AIDS
Humor, and language development,
316
Hunger, infant crying in, 109
Huntington disease, 49t, 50, 57
Hyperactivity, in attention-deficit
hyperactivity disorder, 304
Hypertension, 435, 436, 511
and dietary fat, 442, 442f
Hypodermis, 503
Hypotheses, 27, 382
Hypothetico-deductive reasoning
in formal operational stage,
382–383, 384

I
Iceland
adoption by gay and lesbian
families in, 492
marriage of same-sex couples in,
479
math achievement scores in, 389f
Id, 15
Idealism in adolescence, 387
Ideal reciprocity, 408, 409, 410
Ideal self, 331
Identical twins, 48. See also Twins
Identity
achievement of, 403, 403t, 404
in adolescence, 402, 403–405
bicultural, 406
and cognitive style, 404
commitment to, 402, 403
crisis in, 402
cultural influences on, 405, 406
diffusion status, 403, 403t, 404, 405
domains of, 404
dual-cycle model of, 464
in emerging adulthood, 464–465,
469
ethnic, 406
exploration in, 402, 403, 464–465
foreclosure status, 403, 403t, 404,
405
gender-related, 276–278. See also
Gender identity
global, 466
in middle adulthood, 535–536,
540–542
moral, 264, 411
moratorium status, 403, 403t, 404
and personal agency, 465
and psychological well-being, 404
religious, 412

versus role confusion in
adolescence, 16t, 402
sequential design of research on, 38
sex differences in development
of, 404
sexual, 375–377, 405
Imaginary audience in adolescence,
386, 387
Imitation
deferred, 154, 156, 157f
emotional self-regulation in, 189
infant memory of, 156–157, 157f
inferred, 157
mirror neurons in, 136
by newborn, 135f, 135–136
social learning theory on, 18
Immigrants
academic achievement of, 32–33
acculturative stress of, 406, 416
adaptation of, 32–33
child-rearing styles of, 415–416
dynamic assessment of intelligence,
315
feeding practices and nutrition
of, 291
identity development of, 406
loneliness of, 478
prejudice against, 338
Immune system
in early adulthood, 434, 437
exercise affecting, 443
in late adulthood, 571
malnutrition affecting, 92, 220
in physical changes of aging, 435t,
437, 571
stress affecting, 93, 450, 571
Immunization, 90, 220–221
Implantation of blastocyst, 80f, 81
Implicit memory, 164, 394
in late adulthood, 591
Impotence, 444, 507
Imprinting, 22, 196
genomic, 51
Impulsivity
in adolescence, 367–368, 368f
in attention-deficit hyperactivity
disorder, 304, 305
and maternal prenatal smoking,
74, 74f
temperament in, 265
Incest, 353
Inclusive classrooms, 322
Incomplete dominance in genetic
inheritance, 50
Incredible Years program, 272
Independence–ignore script, 610
Independent living
in late adulthood, 566–567, 568,
622–623
in leaving parental home, 478–479,
543, 544–545
in widowhood, 622–623
Independent self in individualistic
societies, 65, 129
Independent variables in
experimental research, 35
India
caregiving roles of parents in, 201
early adulthood in, 466
maps drawn in, 300, 300f
moral development in, 411
play and peer sociability in, 262
romantic relationships in, 476

Individualistic societies
compared to collectivist societies, 65
divorce in, 490
infant sleeping arrangements in, 129
moral development in, 411
peer sociability in, 262
psychological well-being in, 539
romantic love in, 475
self-conscious emotions in, 188–189
Indonesia
make-believe play in, 168
mourning behavior in, 664
Inductive discipline, 264–265, 278, 411
Inductive reasoning, 519, 519f, 520, 597
Industry versus inferiority in middle childhood, 16t, 330
Inequality, understanding of, in middle childhood, 337–339
Inevitability, and death concept, 642
Infancy and toddlerhood (birth to 2 years old), 8t, 101–211
adjustment of parents in, 115, 484–485
amnesia about events in, 164–165
arousal states in, 108t, 108–112, 128
attachment in, 195–206. See also Attachment
attention in, 144, 163
autonomy versus shame and doubt in, 16t, 184
behavioral assessment in, 114
body composition in, 121
body proportions in, 120f, 121
body size in, 120f, 120–121, 131–132
brain development in, 121–128
breastfeeding and bottle-feeding in, 130–131, 131t
categorical self in, 208
categorization in, 164–166
child-care settings in, 171–173
cognitive development in, 19, 151–181
cosleeping arrangements in, 129
crying in, 87, 88, 108t, 109–112
definition of, 8t
deprivation and enrichment in, 125–128
early intervention programs in, 127, 173, 173f
emotional development in, 185–190
empathy in, 109, 208
fear in, 134
growth spurts in, 120–121
habituation and recovery in, 134–135, 141, 141f, 155, 163, 165, 170
heredity affecting growth in, 130
home environment in, 170–171
imitation in, 135f, 135–136, 156–157, 157f, 189
individual and group differences in, 121, 169–173, 177–178
intelligence tests in, 169–170
language development in, 125, 126, 141–142, 157–158, 160, 169, 174–179

learning capacities in, 133–136, 142
mathematics in, 160f, 160–161
memory in, 134–135, 161–162, 163–164
mental representations in, 153t, 154, 156–158
milestones of development in, 212–213
mortality in. See Infant mortality
motor development in, 136–140, 169
newborn infants. See Newborns
novelty preference in, 134, 135f, 141, 141f, 155, 163
nutrition in, 130–133
object permanence in, 154, 155f, 155–156
pain sensitivity in, 112
parent relationship in. See Parent–infant relationship
perceptual development in, 140–147
personality in, 184
physical development in, 119–149
physical knowledge in, 159
plasticity of brain in, 126
play in, 168
preterm infants, 101–105. See also Preterm infants
problem solving in, 157
reflexes in, 106–108, 107t, 153, 153t
self-awareness in, 206–208
self-control in, 208–209
as sensitive period of development, 125–128
sensorimotor stage in, 152, 153–154. See also Sensorimotor stage
sensory system in, 112–113, 140–147
sleep in, 108t, 108–109, 128, 129
sociocultural theory on, 167
statistical learning capacity in, 142
sudden infant death syndrome in, 109, 110, 129, 139, 661
symbolic understanding in, 157–158
television viewing in, 159
temperament in, 190–195
trust versus mistrust in, 16t, 184
visual impairment in, 125
Infant Health and Development Project, 103–104
Infantile amnesia, 164–165
Infant mortality, 104
in cosleeping of parents and infants, 129
in home delivery, 100
international differences in, 104, 105f
in Rh factor incompatibility, 93
of small-for-date infants, 102
in sudden infant death syndrome, 109, 110, 129, 139, 661
Infant–parent relationship. See Parent–infant relationship
Infectious diseases
AIDS. See AIDS
in early childhood, 220–221
immune response to, 437, 571
immunization against, 90, 220–221
in middle childhood, 293
and physical development, 220–221

in pregnancy, 90–92, 91t
sexually transmitted, 376–377, 447–448
Inferiority versus industry in middle childhood, 16t, 330
Inferred imitation, 157
Infertility
childlessness in, 489
in prenatal DES exposure, 86
reproductive technologies in, 47t, 48, 54–55
Infinitive phrases in language development, 316
Information-gathering cognitive style in identity development, 404
Information-loss view of information processing speed, 520
Information processing, 20–21
in academic learning, 302–303, 307–309
in adolescence, 384–386
and analytical intelligence, 311
attention in, 161, 163, 236–237, 303–305, 384, 521–522
in autism, 241
automatic, 162
capacity of working memory in, 161, 162, 302–303
categorization in, 162, 164–166, 166f
and cognitive self-regulation, 307
compared to other human development theories, 28t
compensatory strategies in, 521
and concrete operational thought, 301–302
in early childhood, 236–243
executive function in, 162, 162f, 236, 303
flowcharts on, 20–21, 21f, 161, 162f
general model of, 161–162, 162f
in infancy and toddlerhood, 161–167
and language development, 174–175, 250
and literacy development, 240–242
mathematical reasoning in, 242–243
memory in, 161, 162, 162f, 163–164, 237–238, 302–303, 304–306, 522–523
mental strategies in, 161
in middle adulthood, 519, 520–525
in middle childhood, 302–309
neural network view of, 520
scientific reasoning in, 385–386
sensory register in, 161, 162, 162f
speed of, 162, 519, 520–521, 521f
and theory of mind, 238–240, 306–307
Informed consent of research participants, 39t, 40
In-groups, 339
favoritism toward, 337–338
Inhalant drug use in adolescence, 380
Inheritance, 48–52. See also Genetic factors
of chromosomal abnormalities, 52–53
dominant–recessive, 48t, 48–50, 49t

genomic imprinting in, 51
of mutations, 51–52
polygenic, 52
X-linked, 50–51, 51f
Inhibition
and attention, 236–237, 237f, 310, 521
in early childhood, 236–237, 237f
and effortful control, 209
and eyewitness testimony by children, 355
and false-belief tasks, 240
in information processing, 384
temperament in, 191, 192
Initiation ceremonies in adolescence, 369
Initiative versus guilt in early childhood, 16t, 256
Injuries, unintentional
death rate in, 221, 221f, 294, 294f, 438f, 509, 509f, 640
in early childhood, 221–222
in late adulthood, 580, 581–582
in middle adulthood, 509, 509f
in middle childhood, 294, 294f
prevention of, 222, 294
Inner speech, 234
Insomnia in late adulthood, 571
Institutionalization
attachment security in, 199
early deprivation in, 125–127, 127f
for long-term care in late adulthood, 588–589
motor development in, 138–139
stress in, 127
temperament development in, 193
Institutional review boards, 40
Instrumental activities of daily living, 567–568, 597
Instrumental aggression, 269
Instrumental purpose orientation in moral development, 407–408
Insulin, 291, 433, 505, 581, 584, 585
Insurance, health. See Health insurance
Integration of schools, 321
Intellectual development. See Cognitive development
Intelligence
analytical, 310, 311, 311f
creative, 310, 311, 311f
crystallized, 518–519, 521f, 590
definitions of, 309–312
dynamic assessment of, 315
emotional, 313, 453
environmental influences on, 71, 71f, 170–171, 312–315
fluid, 518–519, 521f, 590
gene–environment interactions in, 71, 71f, 170–171, 312–315
general (g), 309
genetic factors in, 70, 71, 170–171, 312–315
heritability estimates on, 70, 71, 312–313
home environment affecting, 170–171
measurement of, 169–170, 309–312
multiple intelligences theory of Gardner, 311–312, 312t, 323
practical, 310, 311, 311f, 523
triarchic theory of, 310–311, 311f

Intelligence quotient (IQ), 169–170,
309–316
and academic achievement, 243, 309
bell-shaped distribution of, 169–
170, 170f
and early intervention programs,
246
environmental influences on,
170–173
ethnic and racial differences in,
312–315
genetic influences on, 170–171,
312–313
of gifted children, 322
heritability estimates of, 312–313
home environment affecting,
170–171
in learning disabilities, 322
normal distribution of, 169–170,
170f
predictive value of, 170, 243, 309
secular trends in, 314
and socioeconomic status, 173,
243, 312, 314
in twins, 314
Intelligence tests, 309–316
in attention-deficit hyperactivity
disorder, 304
componential analysis of, 310
cultural bias in, 243, 310, 314–315
dynamic assessment in, 315
factor analysis of, 309
group administered, 309
historical development of, 15
individually administered, 309
for infants, 169–170
intelligence quotient derived from.
See Intelligence quotient
normal distribution of scores,
169–170, 170f
predictive value of, 170, 243, 309
socioeconomic status affecting
performance on, 173, 243, 312,
314
standardization of, 169, 310
stereotype threat affecting
performance on, 314–315, 315f
verbal and nonverbal components
of, 243, 309–310, 310f
Interactional synchrony, and
attachment security, 200
Interactionist theories of language
development, 174–175
Intercourse
frequency of, 446, 509, 578, 579f
sexual dysfunction in, 446, 507
Interdependent self in collectivist
societies, 65, 129
Interdisciplinary study of
development, 5
Intergenerational patterns
in divorce, 489–490
in intelligence quotient, 313
in partner abuse, 482
social clock in, 471
in teenage parenthood, 379
Intermodal perception, 145–146, 147,
206, 570
Internalizing difficulties, 60
Internal working models of
attachment, 197, 201
and dating relationships, 420
and romantic relationships, 474

Internet use
in bereavement, 664
cyberbullying in, 342
dating services in, 445–446, 621,
622f
in late adulthood, 621, 625, 626
media multitasking in, 394, 418
of older adults, 599, 621
online friendships in, 418–419, 476
parent regulation of, 419
personal ads placed in, 621, 622f
romantic partners found in,
445–446, 621
sex education in, 374
social networking sites in. See
Social networking sites
Interpersonal intelligence, 312, 312t
Interventions
in adolescent delinquency, 425–426
in aggression, 272
in alcoholism, 445
in anorexia nervosa, 373
in attention-deficit hyperactivity
disorder, 305
attribution retraining in, 334
in bereavement, 663–665
in bulimia nervosa, 373
in cardiovascular disease risk
reduction, 512
for caregivers of adults with
dementia, 585, 586–587
in child maltreatment, 354
cognitive, in late adulthood, 597
counseling in. See Counseling
in depression, 187, 423, 587
in divorce, 348
in dropout prevention, 396–397,
455
early intervention programs in,
173, 173f, 245f, 245–246
in elder maltreatment prevention,
628
in injury prevention, 222, 294
in obesity, 292–293, 440–442
in partner abuse, 483
in peer victimization, 342
for preterm infants, 102–105
public education programs in,
221, 441
for rejected children, 343
in sexual abuse prevention, 354
in suicide prevention, 423, 423t,
613
in teenage pregnancy and
parenthood, 379–380
in transition to parenthood, 485
Interviews
clinical, 20, 29t, 30
structured, 29t, 30
suggestibility of children in, 355
Intimacy, 38
in adolescence, 404, 417, 417f,
419, 420
cohabitation in, 487–488
in dating, 420
in early adulthood, 16t, 469–470,
472–478
in friendships, 417, 417f, 419, 469,
476, 477, 625
versus isolation, 16t, 469–470,
472–478
in late adulthood, 578–579, 621, 625
loneliness after loss of, 478

in romantic love, 472–476
in triangular theory of love, 473
Intrapersonal intelligence, 312, 312t
Inuit
communication style of, 314
cosleeping of parents and infants,
129
grammatical development of, 316
respect for elders of, 574
Invariant features in differentiation
theory, 146, 147
Investigative personality, vocational
choice in, 456
Invisible displacement in
sensorimotor stage, 154
In vitro fertilization, 54
and fraternal twinning, 47t, 48
preimplantation genetic diagnosis
in, 56t
Involuntary active euthanasia, 654t
Involvement in child rearing, 278,
279, 279f
in uninvolved style, 279t, 280, 392
Iranian orphans, motor development
of, 138–139
Ireland
infant mortality rate in, 105f
life expectancy in, 565f
obesity in, 291
poverty rate in, 68f
teenage pregnancy in, 378f
Irish American storytelling practices,
257
Iron deficiency, 372
Irreversibility of thought in
preoperational stage, 229
Irritability
and effortful control, 209
temperament in, 190, 191, 191f,
193, 194
Islam, death concept in, 645
Isolation
in early adulthood, versus intimacy,
16t, 469–470, 472–478
of gay and lesbian youths, 376
of gifted children, 323
loneliness in, 477–478
Isotretinoin, 87
Israel
attachment patterns and romantic
relationships in, 474
caregiving roles of parents in, 201
corporal punishment in, 283
death concept in, 643, 645
infant mortality rate in, 105f
intelligence quotient in, 315
life expectancy in, 565f
obesity in, 291
sleep patterns of infants in, 128
stranger anxiety of infants in, 187
teenage pregnancy in, 378f
unintentional childhood injuries
in, 221f
Italy
adolescent suicide in, 422
caregiving roles of parents in, 201
corporal punishment in, 283
departure from parental home in,
545
divorce rate in, 347f
family size in, 483
high school graduation rate in, 395f
infant mortality rate in, 105f

life expectancy in, 565f
math achievement scores in, 389f
personality traits in, 542
poverty rate in, 68f
religion in, 412
teenage pregnancy in, 378f
unintentional childhood injuries
in, 221f

J
Jamaican West Indian infants, motor
development of, 139
Japan
academic achievement in, 324, 324t
academic and vocational tracks
in, 395
adolescent suicide in, 422
aging parents in, 549, 551
attachment patterns in, 198f, 199
caregiving roles of parents in, 201,
202
cerebrovascular dementia in, 586
college education in, 455
cosleeping of parents and infants
in, 129
death definition in, 641
divorce rate in, 347f
emotional self-regulation in, 189,
193
family size in, 483
high school graduation rate in, 395f
immigrant youths from, 32
infant mortality rate in, 105f
late adulthood in, 574–575, 576
life expectancy in, 564–565, 565f
mate selection in, 472
menopause in, 506f
moral development in, 411
personality traits in, 542
psychological well-being in, 539
respect for older adults in, 574–575
romantic relationships in, 475, 476
self-concept in, 331
self-conscious emotions in, 189
self-esteem in, 331
stroke in, 586
temperament of infants in, 193
terminally ill patients in, 649
unintentional childhood injuries
in, 221f
vocational life and cognitive
development in, 525
Jarara of South America, childbirth
practices of, 98
Jealousy
in avoidant attachment, 474
in friendships, 340
in marital relationships, 489
in resistant attachment, 474
in sibling relationships, 115, 205,
416
Jewish beliefs, 609
adolescent rites of passage in, 369
death concept in, 643, 664
Jimi Valley (Papua New Guinea),
drawings of children in, 225
Job. See Employment
Joint attention in language
development, 176
Joint custody of children, 348–349
Judaism, 609
adolescent rites of passage in, 369
death concept in, 643, 664

Justice, and moral reasoning, 269, 337, 409
Juvenile delinquency, 423–426. *See also* Delinquency

K
Kaddish prayer, 664
Kangaroo care for preterm infants, 103
Kanreki ritual, 574–575
Karakia ceremony, 650
Karyotype, 46*f*
Kauai study on birth complications, 106
Keeping Ourselves Safe, 354
Kenya
   mother–infant relationship and attachment security in, 200
   motor development in infancy, 114, 139
Kevorkian, Jack, 658, 659
Kibbutzim
   death concept of children in, 643
   stranger anxiety of infants in, 187
Kindergarten, 244–246
   types of programs in, 244–245
Kinesthetic intelligence, 312*t*, 323
Kinkeeper role, 545
Kinship studies
   of biological aging, 432
   of depression, 421
   heritability estimates in, 70, 313
   of intelligence, 70, 313
   twins in, 70. *See also* Twins
Kipsigis of Kenya, motor development in infancy, 114, 139
Klinefelter syndrome, 53
Knowledge
   core, 159–161, 240
   and creativity in early adulthood, 453–454
   cultural influences on, 314
   and expertise in early adulthood, 453
   factual, in middle adulthood, 522–523
   and information processing, 384
   and memory, 305–306
   metacognitive. *See* Metacognition
   procedural, in middle adulthood, 522–523
   and reminiscence in late adulthood, 606
   and wisdom in late adulthood, 595–596
Kohlberg, Lawrence, on moral development, 407–409, 410, 411, 412
Korea
   academic achievement in, 324, 324*t*
   aging parents in, 549, 551
   categorization skills in, 166
   college education in, 455
   immigrant youths from, 32
   infant mortality rate in, 105*f*
   life expectancy in, 565*f*
   math achievement scores in, 389*f*
   moral development in, 337
   partner abuse in, 483*f*
   personality traits in, 542
   psychological well-being in, 539
   unintentional childhood injuries in, 221*f*

Korean Americans
   caring for aging parents of, 551
   death and dying concept of, 649
   play and peer sociability of, 262
Kübler-Ross, Elisabeth, on stages of dying, 647
!Kung of Botswana, cosleeping of parents and infants, 129
Kwashiorkor, 132

L
Labor and delivery, 96–101. *See also* Childbirth
Laboratory experiments, 35
   on classical conditioning, 17
Labouvie-Vief, Gisella
   on emotional expertise in late adulthood, 605
   on pragmatic thought and cognitive-affective complexity, 452–453
Lamaze childbirth method, 99
Language acquisition device (LAD), 174
Language areas in cerebral cortex, 124, 125, 126, 174, 175
Language development
   in adolescence, 383, 388
   in autism, 241
   babbling in, 176
   in bilingualism, 317–318
   brain areas in, 124, 125, 126, 174, 175
   and categorization skills, 166, 208
   comprehension and production of words in, 177
   conversational skills in, 176, 250
   core knowledge perspective of, 160
   correlational study of, 34
   cultural influences on, 177–178, 248, 314
   in early childhood, 217, 226, 233–234, 239, 240–242, 248–251
   early intervention programs affecting, 246
   early printing in, 225
   emergent literacy in, 240–242, 242*f*
   and emotional self-regulation, 190–191
   emotion words in, 258
   and false beliefs, 239–240
   first speech sounds in, 175–176
   first words in, 176–177, 239
   and gender typing, 274, 275
   generic references to gender in, 275, 275*f*
   grammar in, 249–250. *See also* Grammatical development
   in hearing loss, 125, 176, 178
   home environment affecting, 170
   individual differences in, 177–178
   in infancy and toddlerhood, 125, 126, 141–142, 157–158, 160, 169, 174–179
   infant-directed speech in, 178–179
   information-processing theories of, 174–175, 250
   interactionist theories of, 174–175
   joint attention in, 176
   in late adulthood, 593–594
   and memory, 164, 165*f*, 237
   in middle childhood, 316–318
   milestones of, 175*t*

nativist theory of, 174, 250
phonological, 242, 308
pragmatic, 250, 316–317
private speech in, 233–234
reading in, 307–308. *See also* Reading
recall memory in, 237
sensitive period in, 174, 317
sex differences in, 388
in social interaction, 175, 248–249, 250–251
special language-making capacity in, 250
speech perception and analysis in, 141–142
and symbolic understanding, 157–158
theories of, 174–175
two-word utterances in, 177
vocabulary in, 248–249. *See also* Vocabulary
Language immersion programs in bilingualism, 317, 318
Lanugo, 83
Late adolescence, 362
Late adulthood (65 years old to death), 8*t*, 562–635
   acceptance of change in, 608, 633
   activities of daily living in, 567–568
   activity theory of, 614
   adaptation in, 572–575, 595
   adult children as caregivers in, 549–551
   aging in place in, 617
   agreeableness in, 608
   Alzheimer's disease in, 580, 582–585, 586–587
   appearance in, 571–572, 573
   arthritis in, 576, 580–581, 588
   assistive technology in, 573–574
   bereavement overload in, 662
   body composition changes in, 572
   cardiovascular system in, 570–571, 579–580
   causes of death in, 579*f*, 579–580
   cerebrovascular dementia in, 585–587
   cognitive development in, 589–599
   cognitive interventions in, 597
   cognitive maintenance and loss prevention in, 590, 590*f*, 596–597
   cohabitation in, 622
   community and neighborhood in, 64, 576, 616–617
   compression of morbidity in, 576–577
   contact with adult children in, 547–549
   continuity theory of, 614–615, 618, 631
   control versus dependency in, 610–611
   coping strategies in, 573, 611, 613
   cultural influences on, 574–575, 576
   death concept in, 604, 605, 645
   dementia in, 582–588
   dependency in, 610–613
   depression in, 587–588, 611, 612–613, 623, 624
   diabetes mellitus in, 581
   disabilities in, 573–574, 575, 577, 577*f*, 579–588, 611

disengagement theory of, 614
divorce in, 621
emotional and social development in, 603–635
emotional expertise in, 605, 616
ethical issues in research on, 39, 40
exercise in, 571, 572, 577–578
falls in, 582
family relationships in, 615–616, 617
frailty in, 580
friendships in, 615*f*, 615–616, 624–625
functional age in, 564
gay and lesbian partnerships in, 621
gerotranscendence in, 605
grandchildren and great-grandchildren in, 626–627
health and fitness in, 567, 575–589, 611
health care in, 574, 575, 588–589, 595
hearing changes in, 568*f*, 569–570
housing arrangements in, 617–619
immune system in, 571
integrity versus despair in, 16*t*, 604
language processing in, 593–594
leisure and volunteer activities in, 567, 569, 631–632
life expectancy in, 564–567
lifelong learning in, 597–599
long-term care in, 588–589
maltreatment in, 627–628
marriage in, 567, 620–622
maximum lifespan in, 566–567
memory in, 9, 568, 589–590, 591–593, 594, 606
mental disabilities in, 582–588
milestones of development in, 636–637
mobility in, 569, 572, 580, 582, 631
motor vehicle accidents in, 581–582
negative life changes in, 611
nervous system in, 568, 571, 578, 582–588, 596
of never-married childless adults, 623–624
number of social partners in, 615*f*, 615–616
nursing home care in, 588–589, 611, 619–620
nutrition in, 577–578
one-child policy in China affecting, 346
openness to experience in, 608
optimal aging in, 632–633
personality traits in, 566, 567, 608
person–environment fit in, 574, 611, 618–619
physical development in, 564–589
physical disabilities in, 579–582
plasticity of development in, 9–10
problem solving in, 594–595
psychological well-being in, 575, 576, 610–613
psychosocial theories of, 16*t*, 604–606
public policies on, 67–68, 68*f*, 69
quality of life in, 609–610, 611, 612–613
quality of relationships in, 616

relationship with adult children in, 547–551, 612, 617–618, 623, 625–626
remarriage in, 621–622
reminiscence in, 592–593, 606
respiratory system in, 570–571, 579
retirement in, 629–632
self-concept in, 574, 576, 606–610
sense of usefulness in, 576
sensory system changes in, 568–570
sexuality in, 578–579, 579f
siblings in, 624
in singlehood, 623–624
sleep in, 571
smell sense in, 570
social context of aging in, 616–619
social support in, 567, 611–613, 616–617, 623–625
social theories of aging in, 614–616
socioemotional selectivity theory of, 615–616, 626, 631
spirituality and religiosity in, 608–610, 611, 633
stereotypes of aging in, 566, 570, 574–575, 576, 606, 625
stroke in, 579–580
subjective age in, 573
suicide in, 611, 612–613
taste sense in, 570
terminal decline in, 596–597
as Third Age, 598, 598n, 607
unintentional injuries in, 581–582
victimization and fear of crime in, 617
vision changes in, 568f, 569, 581
widowhood in, 621, 622–623, 624
wisdom in, 595–596
Latency stage of psychosexual development, 16t
Lateralization of brain, 124, 125, 217
and handedness, 217–218
and language development, 125
Latin America
adaptation of immigrant youths from, 32
breastfeeding and bottle-feeding in, 130
Latvia, corporal punishment in, 283
Laughter in infancy and toddlerhood, 185
Layoff from job, 493, 526, 537, 556
Lead exposure, prenatal, 90
Learned helplessness
achievement-related attributions in, 333, 334
attribution retraining in, 334
and cognitive self-regulation, 307
cultural influences on, 334
and depression, 422
of rejected-withdrawn children, 343
Learning
in adolescence, 391–397
in classical conditioning, 17, 133f, 133–134
cognitive developmental theory on, 152–161
and cognitive self-regulation, 307
with computers, 247–248
cooperative, 320, 322
cultural influences on, 141, 167, 236
definition of, 133

by discovery, 233, 235
early interventions for, 173, 245–246
in guided participation, 235
in habituation, 134–135, 135f, 163
in imitation, 135f, 135–136, 156–157
individual differences in, 233
in infancy and toddlerhood, 133–136, 142
information processing in, 161–167, 302–303, 307–309
in job training during middle adulthood, 554–555
of language, 174–179
in late adulthood, 597–599
lifelong, 597–599
malnutrition affecting, 132
mathematics in, 308–309
media multitasking affecting, 394
and memory, 163–164, 302–303
observational, 18, 167, 236
in operant conditioning, 134, 163
in Piagetian classrooms, 233
readiness for, 233
reading in, 307–308
by returning students in middle adulthood, 526–527
in scaffolding, 167, 234, 235
in school, 318–325, 391–397
of second language, 317–318
in service-learning programs, 413
social, 18. See also Social learning
social-cognitive, 18
sociocultural theory on, 23–24, 167, 235, 320
statistical learning capacity in infants, 142
symbolic understanding in, 157–158
from television and videos, 159
vocabulary development in, 176–177, 248–249, 316
working memory in, 302–303
Learning disabilities, 322
Left-handedness, 124, 218
Legal issues
in child maltreatment, 283
in elder maltreatment, 628
eyewitness testimony by children in, 355
in health care decisions for gay and lesbian partnerships, 621
No Child Left Behind Act in, 319, 324
in right to die, 654–659
in school integration, 321
Leisure activities in late adulthood, 567, 569
in retirement, 631–632
Lens of eye, 113, 569
Leptin, 366
Lesbians. See Gay, lesbian, and bisexual people
Letters, early printing of, 225
Levinson, Daniel, seasons of life approach, 470, 535–536
Life-care communities, 618
Life cycle of family, 478–486
Life expectancy, 564–567
and adaptive value of longevity, 23
and aging parents of middle-aged children, 547

and anti-aging effects of caloric restriction, 505
average, 8, 432, 564–565, 565f
genetic factors in, 432
and maximum lifespan, 566–567
and retirement trends, 629
in sickle cell anemia, 50
variations in, 564–565, 565f
worldwide trends in, 8
Lifelong learning, 597–599
Life review in late adulthood, 606
Lifespan perspective, 7–13, 13f, 28t
age-graded influences in, 10–11
biological aging in, 432
history-graded influences in, 11–12
as lifelong process, 8
major periods of development in, 8, 8t
multidimensional and multidirectional influences in, 9, 432, 467, 517, 532
nonnormative influences in, 12–13
plasticity in, 9–10
and public policies, 65–69
Life structure, Levinson on, 470
Lifestyle
of adults, diversity of, 486–492
and Alzheimer's disease risk, 585
in cohabitation, 487–488
and compression of morbidity in late adulthood, 577
in diabetes mellitus, 581
in obesity, 440–442
in singlehood, 486–487
Life-sustaining treatment, withholding or withdrawal of, 654–656
Linguistic intelligence, 312, 312t, 323
Linguistic knowledge in core-knowledge perspective, 160
Lipoproteins
high-density, 443, 504
low-density, 443, 585
Literacy
emergent, 240–242, 307–308
reading skills in. See Reading
writing skills in. See Writing
Lithuania, infant mortality rate in, 105f
Liver disorders
from alcohol abuse, 445
from anabolic steroids, 364
Living will, 655, 655f, 656
Logical necessity in propositional thought, 384
Logical thought
in formal operational stage, 384
in preoperational stage, 230
Logico-mathematical intelligence, 312, 312t
Loneliness
in divorce, 490
in early adulthood, 477f, 477–478
in late adulthood, 623
Longevity. See Life expectancy
Longitudinal research, 35–37
on adaptation to life, 536
on adolescent delinquency, 424
on Alzheimer's disease, 585
on athletic performance in aging, 437f

on attachment, 201, 202, 206, 474
on authoritative child rearing, 280
on calorie restriction diets, 504, 505
on centenarians, 566
on cognitive maintenance and change in late adulthood, 596, 597
cohort effects in, 37, 518, 518f
compared to other research designs, 36t, 37
on corporal punishment, 266
on diabetes mellitus, 581
on divorce, 544
on early pubertal timing, 367
on exercise benefits, 443, 585
on gender identity and behavior, 344, 540
on gender typing, 344
on generativity, 533, 533f
on health and disability in late adulthood, 575, 577
on identity development, 464
on impulsivity and sensation-seeking behavior, 367, 368f
limitations of, 37
on marital relationships, 473, 489, 541
on maternal age at first childbirth, 379
on math achievement, 389
on mental abilities, 518, 518f, 519, 519f
on moral development, 407, 409
in New York Longitudinal Study, 190
on peer sociability, 261, 263
on personality traits, 36, 542, 606
on physical changes of aging, 434, 436, 568
on possible selves, 608
practice effects in, 37
on psychological well-being, 610
on resilience, 468
in Seattle Longitudinal Study, 519, 519f, 597
on self-esteem, 402
sequential design, 38, 38f
on sexual activity, 509
on smoking, 596
on social interactions in late adulthood, 614
on spirituality and religiosity, 608, 609
on stereotypes of aging, 574
on stress management, 514
on television viewing, 271, 292f
on temperament, 190, 192
on theory of mind, 239, 240
on tracking programs in school, 395
on verbal ability, 518, 518f, 519
Long-term care in late adulthood, 588–589
in nursing homes. See Nursing home care
Long-term memory
categorization of contents in, 162
in information-processing model, 161, 162, 162f, 164
in late adulthood, 591, 592–593, 594
retrieval of information from, 162

Lorenz, Konrad, 22, 196
Love, 472–476
   companionate, 473
   and mate selection, 472–473
   passionate, 473
   triangular theory of, 473
Low birth weight, 101–105
   drugs associated with, 87
   and exercise during pregnancy, 92
   infectious diseases associated with, 91t
   mortality rate in, 104
   of small-for-date infants, 102
   and smoking during pregnancy, 88
   sudden infant death syndrome in, 110
   telomere length in, 433
Low-density lipoproteins, 443, 585
Loyalty in friendships, 417, 476
Lungs
   age-related changes in, 435t, 436, 571
   cancer of, 510
Luxembourg
   assisted suicide in, 658
   infant mortality rate in, 105f
   life expectancy in, 565f

M

Macrosystem, 24f, 25, 59, 65
Macular degeneration, 569, 580
Magical thinking in preoperational stage, 230
Magnesium deficiency in adolescence, 372
Magnetic resonance imaging
   functional. *See* Functional magnetic resonance imaging
   ultrafast, in pregnancy, 56t
Magnet schools, 321
Make-believe play
   benefits of, 227, 235
   cognitive-developmental theory of, 226–227, 262t
   cultural influences on, 168, 236
   in early childhood, 226–227, 235, 240, 258, 262t
   emergent literacy in, 240
   emotional understanding in, 258
   and false beliefs, 240
   in preoperational stage, 226–227
   in sensorimotor stage, 154
   social origins of, 168
   sociocultural theory on, 235
Malaria
   in pregnancy, 91t
   sickle cell allele and resistance to, 50, 52
Mali, attachment patterns in, 199
Malnutrition
   in anorexia nervosa, 372–373
   in early childhood, 220
   in infancy and toddlerhood, 132
   and infectious diseases, 220
   in middle childhood, 291
   prenatal, 92
   temperament development in, 193
Malta, life expectancy in, 565f
Maltreatment
   of children. *See* Child maltreatment
   of elderly, 627–628
Management positions, glass ceiling in, 555

Maori of New Zealand, death beliefs of, 650
Mapping of human genome, 56
Map skills, 300, 300f
Marasmus, 132
Marfan syndrome, 49t, 57
Marijuana use
   in adolescence, 380, 381f
   in pregnancy, 88
Marital relationship
   abuse in, 482–483
   and adolescent pregnancy, 378
   in blended families, 349–350, 490–491
   childlessness in, 488–489
   cohabitation as alternative to, 488
   cohabitation prior to, 488
   communication in, 473, 482, 489
   conflicts in, 473, 482–483, 489–490
   cultural influences on, 475–476
   death of child affecting, 661
   death of spouse in, 621, 622–623, 624, 660, 662, 663
   and divorce, 346–349, 489–490. *See also* Divorce
   in dual-earner families, 350–351, 494–495
   in early adulthood, 467, 469, 470, 471, 473, 479–483
   egalitarian, 480
   first, age at time of, 479
   gender roles in, 350, 480–481, 490, 620
   in late adulthood, 567, 620–623
   and mate selection, 472–473, 475, 487
   in middle adulthood, 509, 537, 541, 543–544
   and never-married adults, 487
   and remarriage, 347, 349–350, 479, 489, 490. *See also* Remarriage
   in retirement, 631
   of returning students, 526
   romantic love in, 473
   of same-sex couples, 479–480
   satisfaction in, 446, 481t, 481–483, 484–485, 543–544, 620–621
   sexual satisfaction in, 446
   traditional, 480
   in transition to parenthood, 484–485
   and widowhood, 621, 622–623, 624, 660, 662, 663
Masculine traits
   and friendship intimacy of boys, 417
   in gender identity, 276, 540–542
   in middle adulthood, 535, 540–542
Masculinity–femininity, developmental task in seasons of life theory, 535
Mastery-oriented attributions, 333, 334, 335
Maternal age
   in Down syndrome, 53, 53f
   in first pregnancy, 438f
   in fraternal twinning, 47t, 48
   late childbearing associated with longevity, 567
   and prenatal development, 93, 93f
   in teenage pregnancy, 378–380
   and transition to parenthood, 484
Maternal factors. *See* Mothers

Mate selection, 472–473, 475, 487
Mathematical abilities
   cross-national research on, 324, 324t
   in early childhood, 242–243
   gender stereotypes on, 343, 457, 458
   in infancy and toddlerhood, 160f, 160–161
   in middle childhood, 308–309
   sex differences in, 388–391, 389f
   social interactions in learning, 24
   and spatial skills, 389, 390, 391
Matters of personal choice, 269, 337, 409–410
Maturation,
   Hall and Gesell on, 14
   sexual, 363, 365–366
Maximum lifespan, 566–567
Mayans
   attention style of, 167
   childbirth practices of, 98
   communication style of, 314
   cosleeping of parents and infants, 129
   gender identity of, 540
   memory strategies of, 306
   menopause of, 508
   observational learning of, 167, 236
   play of, 262
MDMA (Ecstasy), 380
Mead, Margaret, 362
Mealtimes in family, 29, 63, 63f
   in adolescence, 372
   in middle childhood, 291
Means–end action sequences in sensorimotor stage, 154
Measles, 220
Media
   and cell phone use, 394, 418
   computers, 247–248. *See also* Computer use
   educational, 246–248
   and Internet use. *See* Internet use
   and multitasking, 394, 418
   television. *See* Television
   violence on, 270–271, 271f
Mediation services in divorce, 348
Medicaid, for long-term care of older adults, 588–589
Medical care. *See* Health care
Medical insurance. *See* Health insurance
Medicare, 67, 588
Medications. *See* Drug therapy
Mediterranean countries
   diet in, 585
   leaving parental home in, 478
Meiosis, 46–47
Melatonin, 128
Memorial services and funerals, 664
Memory
   of actors, 523
   in Alzheimer's disease, 583
   associative, 591–592, 592f, 594
   and attention, 163, 304–305
   autobiographical. *See* Autobiographical memory
   automatic, 591
   and cognitive self-regulation, 307
   cultural influences on, 238, 306
   and deferred imitation, 156, 157f

in early childhood, 237–238
elaboration strategy for, 238, 305, 522, 592
episodic, 238, 591, 593
explicit, 164, 394
and eyewitness testimony by children, 355
for familiar events, 238
in habituation, 134–135, 163
implicit, 164, 394, 591
in infancy, 134–135, 163–164
and infantile amnesia, 164–165
and information-loss view of information-processing speed, 520
in information processing, 161, 162, 162f, 163–164, 237–238, 520, 522–523
and knowledge, 305–306
and language processing, 593–594
in late adulthood, 9, 568, 589–590, 591–593, 594, 606
long-term. *See* Long-term memory
in middle adulthood, 520, 522–523
in middle childhood, 301, 302–303, 304–306
and narratives in pragmatic language development, 317
nonverbal, 164, 165f
for one-time events, 238
in operant conditioning, 163, 163f
organization strategy for, 237, 304, 522
prospective, 593
recall. *See* Recall memory
recognition, 164, 237, 591, 592
reconstructed, 201
rehearsal strategy for, 237
remote, 135, 592–593
repetitive strategy for, 238, 304
retrieval of information from, 162
scripts in, 238
short-term, 161, 162, 162f
strategies for, 237–238, 522, 523
working. *See* Working memory
Menarche, 365, 366
   age at time of, 366f
   individual and group differences in, 366, 367
   reactions to, 368, 369
Menopause, 504–507, 508
   as biocultural event, 508
   cultural differences in, 506, 506f, 507, 508
   hormone changes in, 434, 504, 506
   psychological reactions to, 506–507
   reproductive technologies in, 55
   skeletal changes in, 504, 512–513
Menstrual cycle
   in early adulthood, 438
   eating disorders affecting, 372
   estrogen in, 363
   first, 365. *See also* Menarche
   in middle adulthood, 504, 506
Mental development. *See* Cognitive development
Mental representations
   and categorization skills, 164–166
   dual, 227–228
   in preoperational stage, 226, 227–228
   in problem solving, 157

in sensorimotor stage, 153t, 154, 156–158
and symbolic understanding, 157–158, 227–228
Mental retardation
classroom inclusion in, 322
in Down syndrome, 52
in fragile X syndrome, 51
handedness in, 218
infectious diseases during pregnancy associated with, 91t
in phenylketonuria, 50
in Prader-Willi syndrome, 51
Mental rotation tasks, sex differences in, 390, 390f
Mental strategies in information processing, 161
Mental testing movement, 15. See also Intelligence tests
Mentor relationships in early adulthood, 470, 493
Mercury
prenatal exposure to, 90
in vaccines, 221
Mercy killing, 655, 656
Mesoderm, 82
Mesosystem, 24f, 25, 63
in family chaos, 29
Metabolic rate, basal, 439, 504
calorie restriction affecting, 505
Metacognition
in adolescence, 384, 385
and cognitive self-regulation, 307
in early adulthood, 451
in late adulthood, 597
in middle adulthood, 523
in middle childhood, 306
and reading, 308
and scientific reasoning, 385
and theory of mind, 306
Metaphors in vocabulary development, 248
Methadone in pregnancy, 87
Mexican Americans
death and dying concept of, 649
diabetes mellitus of, 581
ethnic identity of, 406
grandparents as caregivers, 547
intelligence definition of, 311
menopause of, 507
sibling relationships of, 416
Mexico
adoption by gay and lesbian families in, 492
attention style in, 167
concrete operational stage in, 301
early adulthood in, 466
food preferences in, 219
immigrant youths from, 32, 33
make-believe play in, 168
motor development of infants in, 139
observational learning in, 167
sense of control in, 573
social interaction and learning in, 24
unintentional childhood injuries in, 221f
Zinacanteco Indians in, 24, 139, 168, 301
Microsystem, 24f, 24–25, 59
in family chaos, 29
Middle adolescence, 362

Middle adulthood (40 to 65 years old), 8t, 501–559
adaptation in, 514–517, 536, 537
age range in, 8t
attention in, 521–522
autonomy in, 538
body composition changes in, 504
career changes in, 555–556
career development in, 554–555
cognitive development in, 517–527
cohort effects in, 517–518
creativity in, 524–525
crystallized and fluid intelligence in, 518–519
death concept in, 644–645
death of spouse in, 662
divorce in, 544
emotional and social development in, 531–559
environmental mastery in, 538
exercise in, 504, 515–516, 540, 541
expertise in, 524
family in, 543–552
flow state in, 540–541
friendships in, 541, 543, 552–553
gender identity in, 540–542
gender stereotypes on aging in, 516–517
generativity versus stagnation in, 16t, 532–535
grandparenthood in, 545–547
health and fitness in, 508–514, 515–516, 540
hearing changes in, 503
hostility and anger in, 513–514
illness and disability in, 509–513
individual and group differences in, 519–520, 542–543
information processing in, 519, 520–525
job satisfaction in, 553–554, 554f
job training in, 554–555
learning as returning student in, 526–527
marital relationship in, 509, 541, 543–544
memory in, 520, 522–523
menopause in, 504–507, 508
mental abilities in, 517–520
midlife crisis in, 536–537
milestones of development in, 560–561
multiple roles in, 541
nutrition in, 504, 505
optimism in, 516
parent–child relationship in, with adult children, 544–545, 546
parent–child relationship in, with aging parents, 547–551, 625–626
personality traits in, 538, 542–543
personal life investment in, 540–541
physical development in, 502–517
possible selves in, 538
practical problem solving in, 524
psychological well-being in, 539, 540–541, 544, 545
reproductive system in, 504–508
retirement planning in, 556–558
as sandwich generation, 549
seasons of life in, 535–536
self-acceptance in, 538
self-concept in, 535–536, 538–542

sense of control in, 540
sexuality in, 509, 541
siblings in, 552
skeletal changes in, 504
skin changes in, 503–504
social relationships in, 541, 543–553
speed of information processing in, 519, 520–521, 521f
stage or life events approach to, 537
stress in, 513, 514–515, 516, 539, 539f, 544
turning points in, 536–537
unemployment in, 556
vision changes in, 502–503
vocational life in, 525–526, 536, 553–558
Middle childhood (6 to 11 years old), 8t, 289–357
attention in, 303–304
body composition in, 290
body growth in, 290
body proportions in, 290
cognitive development in, 299–325
cognitive self-regulation in, 307
concrete operational stage in, 299–302. See also Concrete operational stage
emotional and social development in, 329–357
executive function in, 303
eyewitness testimony during, 355
family influences in, 345–351
fears and anxieties in, 352
gender typing in, 343–345
grammar in, 316
health problems in, 290–294
hearing in, 293
height in, 290, 290f
individual differences in, 309–316
industry versus inferiority in, 16t, 330
information processing in, 302–309
intelligence in, 309–316
language development in, 316–318
learning in, 317–325
memory in, 301, 302–303, 304–306
milestones of development in, 358–359
moral development in, 336–339
motor development in, 294–299
nutrition in, 291–293
parent relationship in. See Parent–child relationship
peer relations in, 339–343
physical development in, 290–299
physical education in, 298–299
play in, 294–299
resilience in, 354
school attendance in, 318–325
self-care in, 351
self-conscious emotions in, 335
self-regulation in, emotional, 336
self-understanding in, 330–334
sex differences in, 290, 290f
sexual abuse during, 352–354
theory of mind in, 306–307
unintentional injuries in, 294
vision in, 293
vocabulary in, 316
vocational choice in, 455
weight in, 290, 290f, 291–293

Middle East
breastfeeding and bottle-feeding in, 130
menopause in, 506, 506f
Midlife crisis, 536–537
Midlife Development in the United States (MIDUS) survey, 532, 533, 536, 537, 539
Midwives, 100
Milestones of development
in adolescence, 428–429
in brain development, 122, 122f
in cognitive development of infants and toddlers, 158t
in early adulthood, 498–499
in early childhood, 286–287
in infancy and toddlerhood, 158t, 212–213
in language development, 175t
in late adulthood, 636–637
in middle adulthood, 560–561
in middle childhood, 358–359
prenatal, 81t
Mind, theory of. See Theory of mind
Mindblindness and autism, 241
Minerals, dietary, 92, 220, 577
Mirror neurons, 136
Mirror self-recognition of infants, 207
Miscarriage
in early adulthood, reduced risk for, 437
in fetal medicine and diagnostic procedures, 56
genetic factors in, 51, 53, 54
in infectious diseases, 91t
maternal age in, 93
prevention measures, 86, 376
in radiation exposure, 89
in Rh factor incompatibility, 93
in smoking, 88
in stress, 92
Mistrust, 16t, 184
Mitosis, 46
chromosomal abnormalities occurring in, 52
Mobility in late adulthood, 572
arthritis affecting, 580
falls affecting, 582
and leisure activities, 631
vision affecting, 569
Modeling
of empathy and sympathy, 260
gender typing in, 278
of moral behavior, 265
social learning theory on, 18
Monkeys
anti-aging effects of calorie restriction in, 505
attachment of, 195–196
discrimination of human and monkey faces, 141.141f
Monozygotic twins, 48. See also Twins
Montessori schools, 245
Moods
in adolescence, 369
in menopause, 506
Moral development
in adolescence, 405–414
and aggression, 269–272
and behavior, 411–412
care orientation in, 409
child-rearing practices affecting, 410, 411

Moral development *(cont.)*
and civic engagement, 413
cognitive-developmental theory of, 268–269
conventional level of, 408
cultural influences on, 336–337, 409, 411
diversity and inequality understanding in, 337–339
in early childhood, 269–272
ethical issues in research on, 39
good boy–good girl orientation in, 408
identity in, 411
individual rights in, 337
instrumental purpose orientation in, 407–408
Kohlberg on, 407–409, 410, 411, 412–414
in middle childhood, 336–339
peer interaction affecting, 410–411
postconventional or principled level of, 408, 409
pragmatic approach to, 412
preconventional level of, 407–408
psychoanalytic theory of, 264–265
punishment and obedience orientation in, 407
religion in, 412
schooling affecting, 410, 411–412
sex differences in, 409
social contract orientation in, 408
social conventions in, 336–337
social learning theory on, 265–268
social order-maintaining orientation in, 408
universal ethical principle orientation in, 408–409
Moral imperatives, 269
Morality
of cooperation, 408
postconventional, 409
pragmatic approach to, 412
Moratorium in identity development, 403, 403*t*, 404
Morbidity compression in late adulthood, 576–577
Moro reflex, 107*t*
Mortality. *See* Death and dying
Moslem children, death concept of, 643
Mothers
adolescent, 378
age of. *See* Maternal age
and attachment security of infant, 199–200
in blended families, 349–350, 490
depression of, 186–187, 200
divorce of, 347, 348
in dual-earner marriages, 480, 494–495
education on child rearing, 486
emotional sensitivity of, 34
employment of, 202–203, 203*f*, 204, 350–351, 416*t*, 494–495
gender typing of children by, 275, 343
marital roles of, 480
play activities of, 201–202
pregnancy of. *See* Pregnancy
in single-parent families, 347
as stepparents, 350, 490
time spent with daughters, 345

transition to parenthood, 484–485
and vocational choice of daughters, 457
Mother–stepfather families, 349–350
Motion, infant perception of, 142, 147
Motivation
attachment affecting, 206
awareness of, in emotional intelligence, 453
in career, 555
classroom experiences affecting, 394
grouping practices affecting, 321
for imitation, 18
maltreatment in childhood affecting, 283
moral, 265, 412
and motor performance, 436
of only children, 346
and personality traits, 542
and physical activity in middle adulthood, 516
preschool and kindergarten programs affecting, 244, 319
recess time affecting, 298
of returning students, 526
of school dropouts, 455
school transitions affecting, 391, 392
and self-esteem, 333, 346
stereotypes affecting, 315, 321
teacher–student interactions affecting, 320
tracking programs affecting, 395
unconscious, 15
Motor development
aging and, 435*t*, 436–437, 437*f*
cultural variations in, 138–139
dynamic systems perspective of, 137–139
in early adulthood, 436–437, 437*f*
in early childhood, 223*t*, 223–226
evolution of, 297–298
fine-motor skills in, 137, 139–140, 224–225, 295. *See also* Fine-motor skills
gross-motor skills in, 137, 223, 294–295. *See also* Gross-motor development
individual differences in, 225–226
in infancy and toddlerhood, 136–140, 169
in late adulthood, 572, 578
in middle childhood, 294–299
and physical education classes, 298–299
in puberty, 364–365
sequence of development, 137, 137*t*
sex differences in, 296
Motor vehicle accidents
childhood injuries in, 221, 222
in late adulthood, 581–582
Mourning behavior, 664. *See also* Bereavement
Multicultural research, 31. *See also* Cultural influences
Multidimensional aspect of lifespan development, 9
in early adulthood, 432, 467
in middle adulthood, 517, 532
Multidirectional aspect of lifespan development, 9, 12
in early adulthood, 432, 467
in middle adulthood, 517, 532

Multigrade classrooms, 322
Multiple attachments, 201–205
Multiple births, 47*f*, 47–48, 54
low birth weight in, 101
in reproductive technologies, 47*t*, 48, 54
twin. *See* Twins
Multiple intelligences theory of Gardner, 311–312, 312*t*, 323
Multiplication problems in mathematics, 308
Multisystemic therapy in delinquency, 426
Multitasking, media, 418
impact on learning, 394
in middle adulthood, 521, 522
Mumps in pregnancy, 91*t*
Muscles
in infancy and toddlerhood, 121
in late adulthood, 572, 578
in middle adulthood, 504
in middle childhood, 290
of newborn, Apgar Scale on, 98*t*
in physical changes of aging, 435*t*, 437, 504, 572
slow-twitch and fast-twitch fibers of, 572
Muscular dystrophy, Duchenne, 49*t*, 57
Music
in Alzheimer's disease, 585, 587
in multiple intelligences theory, 312*t*
as palliative care for dying person, 653
perception in infancy, 113, 140, 141
Mutations, 51–52
cancer in, 510
germline, 52, 510
somatic, 52, 510
Mutual exclusivity bias in vocabulary development, 248, 249
Myelination of nerves, 122, 122*f*, 218, 450
in aging, 520, 568
and information-processing speed in middle childhood, 302
malnutrition in infancy and toddlerhood affecting, 132
Myopia in middle childhood, 293

N

Narcissism of Millennial generation, 465
Narratives
cultural variations in, 317
in pragmatic language development, 317
Narrowing effect in perceptual development, 141, 145
National Association for the Education of Young Children, 172, 246
National Center for Children in Poverty, 68
National Health and Social Life Survey, 445, 447
National Institute of Child Health and Development, 202
National Social Life, Health, and Aging Project, 578
Native Americans
academic achievement of, 395
adolescent suicide of, 423

aging parents of, 617–618
attention style of, 167
communication style of, 314
death beliefs of, 650
departure from parental home, 479
diabetes mellitus of, 581
drug use of, 380
extended-family households of, 65
fetal alcohol syndrome of, 89
gender identity of, 540
grandparents as caregivers of, 547, 548
health problems in late adulthood, 575
infant mortality rate of, 104
long-term care of older adults, 589
neonatal behavioral assessment of, 114
osteoporosis of, 513
overweight and obese, 291, 439
partner abuse of, 483
poverty of, 61
religiosity of, 609
respect for older adults of, 627
school dropout rates of, 396
Native Canadians
communication style of, 314
cosleeping of parents and infants, 129
grammatical development of, 316
identity development of, 405
respect for elders of, 574
Nativist theory of language development, 174, 250
limitations of, 174
Natural childbirth, 99
Natural experiments, 35
Naturalistic observation research method, 28–29, 29*t*
Naturalist intelligence, 312*t*
Natural selection, 14
Nature, and relative influence of nurture, 7, 28*t*, 69–75
in behavioral genetics, 69
bidirectional influences in, 73–75
in canalization concept, 72
definition of, 7
and environmental influences on gene expression, 73–75
in epigenetic framework, 73
gene–environment correlation in, 72
gene–environment interactions in, 71, 71*f*
heritability estimates on, 70–71
in intelligence, 312–315
Near-infrared spectroscopy (NIRS), 123*f*, 123*t*, 124
Nearsightedness in middle childhood, 293
Neglect, 281
in child maltreatment, 281, 282
in elder maltreatment, 627
by peers, 341, 343
in uninvolved child rearing, 280
Neighborhood influences, 63–64, 616–617. *See also* Community influences
Neighborhood Watch programs, 617
Neonatal Behavioral Assessment Scale (NBAS), 114

Neonatal Intensive Care Unit Network Neurobehavioral Scale (NNNS), 114
Neonates. *See* Newborns
Neo-Piagetian theory, 233, 301–302
Nervous system
autonomic, 568, 571
brain in. *See* Brain
in late adulthood, 568, 571, 578, 582–588, 596
in middle adulthood, 519, 520
neurons in. *See* Neurons
in physical changes of aging, 435*t*, 519, 520
Netherlands
academic achievement in, 324, 392
adolescent pregnancy in, 378*f*
adolescent suicide rate in, 422
adoption in, 58, 492
assisted suicide in, 658
cohabitation in, 488
divorce rate in, 347*f*
gay and lesbian marriage and parenthood in, 479, 492
home births in, 99
immunization rate in, 221
infant mortality rate in, 105*f*
life expectancy in, 565*f*
long-term care for older adults in, 588, 589
marriage of same-sex couples in, 479
poverty rate in, 68*f*
voluntary active euthanasia in, 656*t*, 657, 658
Neural network view of information processing, 520
Neural tube, 82, 122
in fetal alcohol spectrum disorder, 89
folic acid affecting, 92
Neurobiological research, 122–124, 123*f*, 123*t*
on temperament, 191, 192
Neurofibrillary tangles in Alzheimer's disease, 583, 584
Neuroimaging techniques, 123*f*, 123*t*, 123–124
Neurons
and brain plasticity, 125
development of, 83, 121*f*, 121–122
in fetal alcohol spectrum disorder, 89
in late adulthood, 568
mirror, 136
stimulation of, 122
synapses of, 83, 121, 121*f*, 122
Neuroscience, developmental cognitive, 21–22
Neuroticism, 542, 542*t*
Neurotransmitters, 121
in Alzheimer's disease, 584
Neutral stimulus in classical conditioning, 133*f*, 134
Never-married adults
as childless older adults, 623–624
in single-parent families, 491
Newborns
adaptation to labor and delivery, 97
Apgar Scale on, 98, 98*t*
appearance of, 97–98
arousal states of, 108*t*, 108–112
behavioral assessment of, 114

breastfeeding of, 112–113. *See also* Breastfeeding
crying of, 109–112
empathy of, 109
face perception of, 145, 145*f*
family adjustment to, 115
and first-time parents, 115, 484–485
habituation and recovery of, 134
hand movements and prereaching of, 139*f*, 140
imitation by, 135*f*, 135–136
intermodal perception of, 146, 206
low birth weight of. *See* Low birth weight
mortality rate for, 104
pain sensitivity of, 112, 185
pattern perception of, 144
perceptual development of, 112–113, 140–147
preterm, 101–105. *See also* Preterm infants
reflexes of, 106–108, 107*t*, 153, 153*t*, 206
self-awareness of, 206–207
sensory capacities of, 112–113, 140–147
sleep patterns of, 108*t*, 108–109
small for date, 102
New York Longitudinal Study, 190
New Zealand
adolescent suicide in, 422
cesarean delivery in, 101
child care in, 171
death beliefs in, 650
infant mortality rate in, 105*f*
life expectancy in, 565*f*
make-believe play in, 168
obesity in, 291
partner abuse in, 483*f*
sexual abuse prevention programs in, 354
unintentional childhood injuries in, 221*f*
Niche-picking, 72
Nicotine, 444. *See also* Smoking
Nigeria
Alzheimer's disease in, 584–585
performance on conservation tasks in, 301
Night sweats, 504, 506, 507
Night vision in late adulthood, 569
No Child Left Behind Act, 319, 324
Nonnormative influences, 12–13
Non-rapid-eye-movement (NREM) sleep, 108, 108*t*, 109
in late adulthood, 571
Nonsocial activities, 261
Nonverbal memory, 164, 165*f*
Normal distribution of intelligence test scores, 169–170, 170*f*
Normative approach of Hall and Gesell, 14–15
Normative influences, 12
age-graded, 10–11
history-graded, 11–12
Norms
in intelligence test scores, 169–170, 170*f*
in physical growth, 121
Norway
adoption by gay and lesbian families in, 492

child poverty rate in, 62
cohabitation in, 488
corporal punishment in, 283
high school graduation rate in, 395*f*
immunization rate in, 221
infant mortality rate in, 105*f*
marriage of same-sex couples in, 479
math achievement scores in, 389*f*
moral reasoning in, 409
teenage pregnancy in, 378*f*
unintentional childhood injuries in, 221*f*
Nouns in vocabulary development, 248
Novelty
preference for, 134, 135*f*, 141, 141*f*, 155, 163
temperament affecting reaction to, 192
Nso people of Cameroon, self-recognition by toddlers, 207, 208*f*
Nuclear power plant accidents, radiation exposure in, 89–90
Nucleus of cells, 46
Numerical knowledge, 160–161, 242–243. *See also* Mathematical abilities
Nurse–Family Partnership, 94, 380
Nurse-midwives, certified, 100
Nursing home care, 588–589, 611, 619–620
and activity theory of aging, 614
death and dying in, 650, 652
maltreatment in, 627, 628
Nurture
definition of, 7
and relative influence of nature, 28*t*, 69–75. *See also* Nature, and relative influence of nurture
Nutrition
in adolescence, 366–367, 371–373
and Alzheimer's disease risk, 584–585
and anti-aging effects of calorie restriction, 505
and atherosclerosis, 436
in breastfeeding and bottle-feeding, 130–131, 131*t*
and cerebrovascular dementia risk, 585, 586
in early adulthood, 439–442
in early childhood, 217, 219–220
and free-radical damage, 434
in infancy and toddlerhood, 130–133
in late adulthood, 577–578
and longevity, 505, 567
and malnutrition, 132. *See also* Malnutrition
and menopause symptoms, 506, 506*f*
mercury exposure from seafood in, 90
in middle adulthood, 504, 505, 506, 506*f*, 513
in middle childhood, 291–293
and obesity, 291–293, 439, 440–442
in osteoporosis, 513
in phenylketonuria, 50
and physical growth, 130–133, 219–220

in pregnancy, 90, 92, 102
and telomere length, 433
and temperament development, 193
and tooth decay, 217
toxoplasmosis from food in, 92
and vision changes in aging, 569
vitamins in. *See* Vitamins
WIC program for, 92

O
Obedience, in preconventional level of moral development, 407
Obesity
in adolescence, 291, 292, 367
body mass index in, 291, 439
causes of, 291–292, 439
discrimination in, 292, 439–440
in early adulthood, 439–442
as epidemic, 440–441
health consequences of, 291, 439
in middle childhood, 291–293
osteoarthritis in, 580, 581
telomere length in, 433
treatment of, 292–293, 440–442
trends in, 441*f*
and weight in infancy, 131–132
Object permanence in sensorimotor stage, 154, 155*f*, 155–156
Observational learning, 18, 167, 236
Observational research, 28–30, 29*t*
naturalistic, 28–29, 29*t*
participant observations in, 32
structured, 29*t*, 29–30
on temperament, 191
Occupation. *See* Employment
Odor perception
in infancy and toddlerhood, 112–113, 113*f*
in late adulthood, 570
in physical changes of aging, 435*t*, 570
Oedipus conflict, 16*t*, 256
Older adults. *See* Late adulthood
Oncogenes, 510
One-child families, 346
Online friendships, 553*f*
in adolescence, 418–419
by age groups, 553*f*
in early adulthood, 445–446, 476
in middle adulthood, 552
Openness to experience as personality trait, 542, 542*t*
in late adulthood, 608
Operant conditioning, 17, 134
and categorization by infants, 164–165, 166*f*
and emotional expressions, 188
and memory of infants, 163, 163*f*
and moral development, 265
Operations, 228
and concrete operational stage, 299, 301
and formal operational stage, 382–384
and preoperational stage, 226–233
Optimal aging, 632–633
Optimism
in late adulthood, 575, 633
in middle adulthood, 516
Oral rehydration therapy (ORT), 220
Oral stage of psychosexual development, 16*t*

Ordinality, 242
Organ donation, death definition for, 641
Organization
    in cognitive development, 152–153
    as memory strategy, 237, 304, 522
Orphans
    attachment insecurity of, 199
    early deprivation of, 125–126, 127, 193, 199
    genetic and environmental influences on, 193
    motor development of, 138–139
    stress of, 127, 353
Osher Lifelong Learning Institutes, 598
Osteoarthritis, 580, 581
Osteoporosis, 504, 512–513
Other-focused reminiscence in late adulthood, 606
Other-sex friendships, 477
Out-groups, 339–340
    favoritism toward, 338
    prejudice against, 338
Ovaries, 80, 80f, 363
    age-related changes in, 437–438
Overextensions in language development, 177
Overregularization in grammatical development, 249
Overweight
    in adolescence, 367
    body mass index in, 439
    in early adulthood, 439–442
    in infancy, 131–132
    in middle childhood, 291–293
Ovulation, 80
Ovum, 46, 47, 80
    aging of, 47
    and conception, 80
    in multiple offspring, 47
    in reproductive technologies, 54, 55
Oxygen deprivation
    in cocaine use during pregnancy, 87
    in fetal alcohol syndrome, 89
    of infant during childbirth, 97, 100
    in sickle cell anemia, 50
Oxytocin, 115

P
Pacific Islanders
    adolescence of, 362
    childbirth practices of, 98
    child-rearing practices of, 281
    sibling relationships of, 552
Pain
    assisted suicide in, 658
    in childbirth, 99, 100–101
    of dying person, 640, 651, 652, 655
    fetal sensitivity to, 85
    newborn sensitivity to, 112, 185
Pakistan, child-rearing styles and academic achievement in, 392
Palate, cleft, 88, 92
Palliative care
    advance medical directives on, 655
    in hospice programs, 652
    music in, 653
Palmar grasp reflex, 107t
Papua New Guinea, drawings of children in, 225

Parallel play, 261
Parasitic diseases in pregnancy, 91t, 92
Parent(s), 483–486. See also Fathers; Mothers
    adjustment to role as, 115, 484–485
    and adolescent relationship. See Parent–adolescent relationship
    adolescents as, 378–380. See also Teenage pregnancy and parenthood
    adoption by. See Adoption
    aging, 547–551
    attachment experiences of, 201
    in blended families, 349–350, 490–491
    child-rearing practices of. See Child-rearing practices
    and child relationship. See Parent–child relationship
    children leaving home of, 478–479, 543, 544–545
    combining work and family, 494–495
    consent to research on children, 40
    and decision to have children, 483–484
    depression of, 186–187, 200, 421–422
    direct influence of, 59–60
    divorce of, 346–349
    in dual-earner families, 494–495. See also Dual-earner households
    early adults as, 470, 483–486, 490–492
    education on child rearing, 485, 486
    employment of, 104–105, 202–204, 350–351, 416t, 485, 494–495
    gay and lesbian, 491–492
    gender identity of, 540–541
    generativity of, 533
    as grandparents, 545–547
    grief in death of child, 661
    grief of children in death of, 661–662
    and infant relationship. See Parent–infant relationship
    leave time from employment, 104–105, 203, 485
    moral behavior of, 264, 265
    never-married, 491
    in observational research, 29–30
    overweight, 293
    of preterm infants, 103–105
    in single-parent families, 491. See also Single-parent families
    as stepparents, 349–350, 490–491
    warmth of, 204
Parent–adolescent relationship, 369–370, 415–416, 485–486
    and academic achievement, 392
    in anorexia nervosa, 372–373
    autonomy issues in, 372–373, 415
    cultural influences on, 415–416
    death discussions in, 644
    in delinquency, 425
    and dropout rates, 396
    of homosexual youths, 377
    and identity development, 404–405
    and moral development, 410, 411
    in school transitions, 392
    and self-esteem, 403

    and sexual activity of adolescents, 373–374
Parental imperative theory, 540
Parent–child relationship
    and achievement attributions, 333, 334, 334f
    in adolescence. See Parent–adolescent relationship
    in adoption, 58
    and aggression, 270
    attachment in. See Attachment
    in attention-deficit hyperactivity disorder, 305
    in blended families, 349–350, 490–491
    and childhood injuries, 221, 222
    child-rearing practices in, 278–283. See also Child-rearing practices
    communication style in, 314
    coregulation in, 345
    death explanations in, 643, 644
    depression of parent affecting, 186–187
    direct influences of, 59–60
    divorce affecting, 348
    in early adulthood of child, 468–469, 478–479
    and eating habits, 219–220
    and emotional development, 258, 259, 260, 278–283
    and emotional self-regulation of child, 259
    and empathy development, 260–261
    family chaos affecting, 29
    gender typing in, 274, 275
    and grandparent–grandchild relationship, 546–547, 547f
    in infancy. See Parent–infant relationship
    and language development, 177–178
    in late adulthood, with adult children, 547–551, 612, 617–618, 623, 625–626
    maltreatment in, 281–283
    in maternal employment, 350–351
    in middle adulthood, of child with aging parents, 547–551, 625–626
    in middle adulthood, of parents, 544–545, 546
    in middle childhood, 345
    and moral development, 264–272
    of older parent and adult child, 625–626
    in one-child families, 346
    and peer relations, 263, 342
    in planning tasks, 237
    play in, 201–202, 204, 263
    in positive parenting, 268
    in psychosexual theory of development, 15, 256
    punishment in, 267
    questions asked by children in, 232
    of resilient children, 11
    and romantic relationships as adults, 474
    in sandwich generation, 549
    scaffolding in, 234
    and self-concept, 256–257
    and self-conscious emotions, 260
    and self-esteem, 332–333
    socioeconomic status affecting, 61

    storytelling practices in, 257
    and theory of mind, 240
    warmth and attention in, 11
    in war-related violence, 353
Parent–infant relationship
    attachment in, 22, 195–206
    classical conditioning in, 133f, 133–134
    cultural variations in, 16–17
    depression of parent affecting, 186
    and emotional self-regulation by infant, 189–190
    facial expressions in, 188
    in first child, 115, 484
    infant-directed speech in, 178–179
    interactional synchrony in, 200
    and language development, 176
    make-believe play in, 168
    and motor development of infants, 136–137
    operant conditioning in, 134
    in preterm infants, 102–105
    quality of caregiving in, 199–200
    reflexes affecting, 107
    in sensitive caregiving, 199–200, 201
    and sleeping arrangements, 129
    social referencing in, 188
    transition to parenthood affecting, 484–485
    trust in, 184
Parenting practices. See Child-rearing practices
Parenting styles. See Child-rearing styles
Parents Anonymous, 283
Parent–school partnership, 393
Parietal lobe, 568
Parkinson's disease, 582, 583
Partial fetal alcohol syndrome, 89
Participant observation in ethnography, 32
Partner abuse, 482–483, 483f
    interventions and treatment in, 483
    violence–remorse cycle in, 482
Passion, in triangular theory of love, 473
Passive correlation of genetic and environmental factors, 72
Passive euthanasia, 654t, 654–656
Passive smoking, 88
Passive voice in language development, 174, 250, 316
Paternal factors. See Fathers
Pattern perception, 144, 144f
    contrast sensitivity in, 144, 144f
    and face perception, 145, 145f
    subjective boundaries in, 144, 144f
Pavlov, Ivan, 17
PCBs (polychlorinated biphenyls), 90
Peck, Robert, on ego integrity in late adulthood, 604–605
Pedigree in genetic counseling, 54–55
Peer acceptance, 341–343, 410
    categories of, 341
    determinants of, 341–343
    learning disability affecting, 322
    in nontraditional careers of men, 458
    pubertal timing affecting, 370–371
    in school transitions, 392
Peer collaboration in education, 235
Peer culture, 339

Peer groups, 419–420
  cliques and crowds in, 419–420
  exclusion from, 410
  in middle childhood, 339–340
Peer relations
  and academic achievement,
    393–394
  acceptance in, 341–343. See also
    Peer acceptance
  in adolescence, 370, 371, 393–394,
    405, 417–421
  aggression in, 270
  bullying in, 341, 342, 343
  cliques and crowds in, 419–420
  in college experience, 454
  cooperative learning in, 320
  dating in, 420–421
  in delinquency, 424
  dominance hierarchy in, 297–298
  in early adulthood, 451–452,
    476–477
  in early childhood, 261–264
  emotional intelligence in, 313
  and epistemic cognition, 451–452
  friendships in, 262–263, 340,
    417–419
  of gay, lesbian, and bisexual youths,
    377
  gender roles in, 276
  of gifted children, 323
  and identity development, 405
  in inclusive classrooms, 322
  in-group favoritism in, 276
  learning disability affecting, 322
  in middle childhood, 339–343
  and moral development, 410–411
  in nontraditional careers of men,
    458
  in obesity, 291, 292
  parental influences on, 263
  of resilient children, 11
  and school readiness, 263
  in school recess, 298
  in school transitions, 391, 392
  sex differences in, 274
  sociability in, 261–262
  and substance abuse, 381
  victimization in, 342
Peer sociability, 261–262
Peer victimization, 342
Pendulum problem, 382–383, 383f
Penis, 366, 366f, 507
Perception
  amodal, 146, 147
  deprivation affecting, 125
  differentiation theory of, 146–147,
    147f
  hearing in, 140–142. See also
    Hearing
  in infancy and toddlerhood,
    140–147
  intermodal, 145–146, 147, 206,
    570
  narrowing effect in, 141, 145
  smell sense in, 112–113. See also
    Smell sense
  taste sense in, 112–113. See also
    Taste sense
  touch sense in, 103, 112. See also
    Touch
  vision in, 142–145. See also Vision
Performance-enhancing drug use in
  adolescence, 364

Periods of development, 8, 8t
  adolescence. See Adolescence
  early adulthood. See Early
    adulthood
  early childhood. See Early
    childhood
  infancy and toddlerhood. See
    Infancy and toddlerhood
  late adulthood. See Late adulthood
  middle adulthood. See Middle
    adulthood
  middle childhood. See Middle
    childhood
  prenatal. See Prenatal development
Permanence
  and death concept, 642, 643
  of objects, in sensorimotor stage,
    154, 155f, 155–156
Permissive child-rearing style, 279t,
    279–280
Perry, William, on epistemic
  cognition, 451–452
Persistence, and temperament, 190,
    191, 191t
Persistent vegetative state, 641, 654
  recognition of living will in, 655
Personal agency, 465, 467
Personal choice, matters of, 269, 337,
    409–410
Personal fable, 386–387
Personality traits
  in Alzheimer's disease, 583
  in baby boomer generation, 12
  "big five" personality traits, 542–
    543, 542t, 606
  of dying people, and coping styles,
    648
  in ethnic and racial biases, 338
  and gender identity, 276
  and gender stereotypes, 343, 344
  gene–environment interactions
    in, 71
  heritability research on, 70
  and identity development, 404
  individual differences in, 542–543
  in infancy and toddlerhood, 184
  in late adulthood, 566, 567, 606,
    608
  longitudinal research on, 36, 542,
    606
  in middle adulthood, 538, 542–543
  in possible selves, 538
  prenatal development of, 84
  of resilient children, 10–11
  in self-concept, 402
  stability of, 542–543
  type A pattern, 513, 514
  type B pattern, 513
  in vocational choice, 456
Person–environment fit, 574, 611,
    618–619
Perspective taking
  in adolescence, 375, 387, 407
  in middle childhood, 296, 330–331,
    335
  and moral reasoning, 407
Peru
  infectious diseases and physical
    development in, 220
  partner abuse in, 483f
Phallic stage of psychosexual
  development, 16t
Phencyclidine (PCP), 380

Phenotype, 45, 50, 74
Phenylalanine, 49t, 50
Phenylketonuria (PKU), 49t, 50
  carriers of, 50, 50f
Philippines, unintentional childhood
  injuries in, 221f
Phobias in middle childhood, 352
Phonics approach to reading, 308
Phonological awareness, 242, 308
  in bilingualism, 317
Physical abuse
  of children, 281. See also Child
    maltreatment
  of elderly, 627
Physical activities. See Exercise
Physical aggression, 269, 270
Physical development, 8, 9f
  adaptation to changes in, 514–517,
    572–575
  in adolescence, 362–381
  and biological aging, 432–434
  body composition changes in. See
    Body composition changes
  body proportion changes in. See
    Body proportion changes
  body size changes in. See Body size
  cardiovascular and respiratory
    changes in, 434–436, 570–571
  cephalocaudal trend in, 121
  in early adulthood, 432–450
  in early childhood, 216–226
  exercise affecting, 443, 577–578
  genetic influences on, 219
  health and fitness in, 438–450,
    508–514, 575–589
  hearing changes in, 503, 569–570
  hormonal influences on, 219
  illness and disability in, 509–513
  immune system in, 437, 571
  in infancy and toddlerhood,
    119–149
  infectious diseases affecting,
    220–221
  in late adulthood, 564–589f
  in lifespan perspective, 13f
  in middle adulthood, 502–517
  in middle childhood, 290–299
  motor skills in, 436–437. See also
    Motor development
  of newborn, assessment of, 98, 98t
  nutrition affecting, 219–220, 439–
    442, 577–578
  prenatal. See Prenatal development
  proximodistal trend in, 121
  reproductive system in, 437–438,
    504–508
  sex differences in, 290, 290f
  sexuality in, 445–449, 509, 578–579
  skeletal changes in, 504
  skin changes in, 503–504, 572
  stress affecting, 449–450
  substance abuse affecting, 444–445
  vision changes in, 502–503, 569
Physical education classes, 298–299
Physical knowledge in infancy, 159
Piaget, Jean, 18
  clinical interviews of, 20, 30
  cognitive-developmental theory of,
    18–20, 28t, 152–161, 226–233,
    299–302, 382–384
  legacy of, 161
Pictorial depth cues, 142
Pincer grasp, 139f, 140

Pituitary hormones, 219
Placenta, 82
  delivery of, 96, 97f
Planning
  in early childhood, 237
  in middle childhood, 303–304
  for retirement, 556–558, 629–630
Plasticity
  of brain, 21–22, 124–125, 126
  of development, 7, 9–10, 517
Play
  in adolescence, 298
  associative, 261
  and attachment security, 202, 204
  benefits of, 227, 235
  categorization skills in, 166
  and cognitive development, 168,
    226–227, 235, 261, 262t
  constructive, 262t
  cooperative, 261
  cross-gender activities in, 276
  cultural influences on, 168, 236,
    256, 261, 262
  in early childhood, 225, 226–227,
    235, 240, 256, 258, 261, 262t,
    263
  emergent literacy in, 240
  emotional understanding in, 258
  and false beliefs, 240
  functional, 262t
  games with rules in, 296–297
  gender roles in, 273, 274, 276, 344
  gender segregation in, 276
  give-and-take interactions in, 176
  in infancy and toddlerhood, 176
  and language development, 176
  make-believe, 154, 226–227. See
    also Make-believe play
  in middle childhood, 294–299
  with mothers and fathers,
    differences in, 201–202
  and motor development, 225,
    294–299
  nonsocial activities in, 261
  parallel, 261
  parental influences on, 263
  of parent and child, 201–202, 204,
    263
  rough-and-tumble, 297–298
  in school recess, 298
  in sensorimotor stage, 154
  sex differences in, 201–202, 273–
    274, 276, 297–298, 344
  social origins of, 168
  sociocultural theory on, 235
  sociodramatic, 227, 235
  solitary, 261, 262
Playground safety, 222
Poland
  math achievement scores in, 389f
  poverty rate in, 68f
  vocational life and cognitive
    development in, 525
  voluntary active euthanasia beliefs
    in, 656
The Policy Book of AARP, 69
Political involvement
  in early adulthood, 466
  in late adulthood, 632
  in middle adulthood, 533
Pollution, prenatal exposure to, 90
Polychlorinated biphenyls (PCBs), 90
Polygenic inheritance, 52, 69

Popular children, 341
  antisocial, 341
  prosocial, 341
Pornography
  Internet access to, 374
  and sexual coercion, 448
Portion size in eating habits, 440
Portugal
  infant mortality rate in, 105*f*
  life expectancy in, 565*f*
  math achievement scores in, 389*f*
  same-sex marriage in, 479
Positive parenting, 268
Positron emission tomography (PET),
  123,123*t*, 124
Possible selves
  in late adulthood, 575, 608
  in middle adulthood, 538
Postconventional level of moral
  development, 408, 409
Postformal thought, 450, 453
Postpartum depression, 186
Poverty, 61–62
  attachment stability in, 198
  childhood injuries in, 222
  community influences in, 63–64
  early intervention and intellectual
    development in, 173, 245–246
  feminization of, 544, 618
  fetal alcohol syndrome in, 89
  and health problems in middle
    childhood, 291, 293
  homelessness in, 62
  immunizations in, 221
  infant mortality rate in, 104
  international differences in, 68, 68*f*
  in late adulthood, 68, 68*f*, 618
  life expectancy in, 565
  malnutrition in, 92, 220, 291
  physical development in, 220
  pubertal growth in, 366
  of single-parent families, 347, 544
  supplemental food program in, 92
  teenage pregnancy in, 94
  working-memory capacity in, 303
Power of attorney for health care,
  655–656
Practical intelligence, 310, 311, 311*f*,
  523
Practical problem solving in middle
  adulthood, 524
Practice effects in longitudinal
  research, 37
Prader-Willi syndrome, 51
Pragmatic approach to morality,
  412
Pragmatic language development,
  250, 316–317
Pragmatic thought, 452
Preattachment phase, 196
Preconventional level of moral
  development, 407–408
Preeclampsia, 95
Prefrontal cortex, 124, 124*f*
  in adolescence, 367, 387, 388
  in attention-deficit hyperactivity
    disorder, 305
  cognitive-control network in, 367,
    387, 388, 450
  in early adulthood, 450
  in early childhood, 217, 237
  in inhibitory tasks, 237
  in late adulthood, 568, 578

Pregnancy, 79–101
  in adolescence, 93, 375, 378–380.
    See also Teenage pregnancy and
    parenthood
  age at time of, 93, 93*f. See also*
    Maternal age
  alcohol use in, 88–90
  childbirth in, 96–101. *See also*
    Childbirth
  counseling on parenthood during,
    485
  diabetes in, 95
  diagnosis and treatment of fetal
    problems in, 56*t*, 56–57
  drug use in, 86–89, 110
  in early adulthood, 437, 438*f*
  embryo period in, 82–83, 85, 86*f*
  fetal period in, 83–85, 86*f*
  first, 115, 438*f*, 484–485
  infectious diseases in, 90–92, 91*t*
  leave time from employment in, 104
  miscarriage in. *See* Miscarriage
  nutrition in, 90, 92, 102
  prenatal development in, 80–96.
    See also Prenatal development
  prenatal health care in. *See* Prenatal
    health care
  radiation exposure in, 51, 89–90
  in reproductive technologies,
    54–55
  Rh factor incompatibility in, 93
  smoking in, 74, 74*f*, 110
  social support in, 93, 94
  stress in, 51, 92–93, 94
  in surrogate motherhood, 54–55
  teratogen exposure in, 85–92
  toxemia of, 95
  and transition to parenthood,
    484–485
  trimesters in, 81*t*, 83–85
  zygote period in, 80–82, 85, 86*f*
Preimplantation genetic diagnosis,
  56*t*
Prejudice, 338–339
Premature infants. *See* Preterm
  infants
Prenatal development, 8*t*, 80–96
  age of viability in, 84
  and conception, 80, 80*f*
  definition of, 8*t*
  diagnosis and treatment of
    problems in, 56*t*, 56–57
  drug exposure affecting, 86–89
  embryonic, 82–83, 85, 86*f*
  environmental influences on, 74,
    74*f*, 85–92
  fetal, 83–85, 86*f*
  habituation in, 85, 134
  hormone exposure affecting, 376,
    390
  infectious diseases affecting, 90–92,
    91*t*
  maternal age affecting, 93, 93*f*, 378
  milestones of, 81*t*
  nutrition affecting, 90, 92, 102
  Rh factor incompatibility affecting,
    93
  sensitive periods in, 85, 86*f*
  of small-for-date infants, 102
  stress affecting, 92–93, 94
  teratogens affecting, 85–92, 305
  trimesters in, 81*t*, 83–85
  zygote period in, 80–82, 85, 86*f*

Prenatal health care, 95
  barriers to, 95
  diagnostic tests in, 56*t*, 56–57
  exercise in, 92
  and infant mortality rates, 104
  nutrition in, 90, 92
  recommendations on, 57*t*, 96
  in teenage pregnancy, 94
Preoperational stage, 19, 19*t*, 226–233
  animistic thinking in, 228, 230
  categorization in, 229, 229*f*,
    230–231
  centration in, 229
  class inclusion problem in, 229,
    229*f*
  conservation in, 229, 229*f*, 230,
    232
  egocentrism in, 228, 230
  evaluation of, 231–233
  limitations of thought in, 228–229
  logical thought in, 230
  magical thinking in, 230
  make-believe play in, 226–227
  mental representations in, 226,
    227–228
  problem solving in, 228, 228*f*, 229,
    229*f*, 230, 232
  research on, 230–231
  symbol–real-world relations in,
    227–228
  three-mountains problem in, 228,
    228*f*
Prepared childbirth, 99
Prereaching movements of newborn,
  139*f*, 140
Presbycusis, 503
Presbyopia, 502
Preschool programs, 244–246
  compared to child care, 244
  early interventions for at-risk
    children in, 245–246
  types of, 244–245
Preschool years. *See* Early childhood
Preterm infants, 101–105
  in adolescent pregnancy, 378
  caregiving for, 102, 103–105
  disabilities of, 102, 102*f*
  and drug use during pregnancy, 87
  and infectious diseases during
    pregnancy, 91*t*
  interventions for, 102–105
  "kangaroo" care of, 103
  maltreatment and abuse of, 102,
    112, 282
  sudden infant death syndrome
    in, 110
  twins, 48
Preverbal gestures, 176
Pride
  in early childhood, 260
  in infancy and toddlerhood,
    188–189
  in middle childhood, 335
Primary aging, 432–438, 580. *See also*
  Aging
Primary circular reactions in
  sensorimotor stage, 153, 153*t*
Primary sexual characteristics, 365
Primary teeth, 217
Principled level of moral
  development, 408
Private speech, 233–234
Proactive aggression, 269

Problem-centered coping
  in late adulthood, 570, 573
  in middle adulthood, 514, 516, 539
  in middle childhood, 336
Problem solving
  analogical, 157, 230
  in class inclusion problem, 229,
    229*f*, 299
  cognitive self-regulation in, 307
  epistemic cognition in, 452
  in late adulthood, 594–595
  in mathematics, 308–309
  in middle adulthood, 524
  in moral dilemmas, 407–408
  in obesity, 441–442
  in pendulum problem, 382–383,
    383*f*
  practical, 524
  in preoperational stage, 228, 228*f*,
    229, 229*f*, 230, 232
  scientific reasoning in, 385*f*,
    385–386
  in sensorimotor stage, 157
  in three-mountains problem, 228,
    228*f*
Procedural knowledge in middle
  adulthood, 522–523
Processing capacity, 161, 162,
  302–303
Processing speed, 162, 519, 520–521,
  521*f*
Prodigies and gifted children, 31,
  322–323
Production of language, compared to
  comprehension, 177
Programmed cell death in brain
  development, 122
Project Head Start, 173, 245–246
Prolactin, 115
Prolonged death, compared to sudden
  unexpected death, 660–661
Propositional thought, 383, 384
  logical necessity of, 384
  in scientific reasoning, 386
Prosocial behavior
  in adolescence, 411, 412, 413, 414
  civic engagement in, 413
  in early childhood, 260
  empathy in, 260
  in middle childhood, 340, 341
  moral reasoning in, 411
  in peer relations, 340
  of popular children, 341
  and religious involvement, 412
Prospective memory, 593
Prostate gland
  cancer of, 511
  enlargement of, 571
Protein
  absorption in late adulthood, 577
  in Alzheimer's disease, 583, 584
  in breastfeeding, 131
  cross-linkage theory of aging on,
    434
  free radicals affecting, 434
  and gene activity, 46, 56, 57
  in kwashiorkor, 132
  leptin, 366
  in phenylketonuria, 49*t*, 50
  Rh factor, 93
  and stroke risk, 585, 586
  in weight loss diets, 440
Proteomics, 57

Proximal parenting style, 207
Proximodistal trend in growth, 121
Pruning, synaptic, 122, 217, 450
Psychoanalytic perspective, 15–17
  attachment in, 195, 206
  clinical or case study research in, 17, 30
  compared to other human development theories, 28t
  contributions and limitations of, 17
  on moral development, 264–265
  stages of development in, 16t
Psychological control in authoritarian child-rearing style, 279
Psychological knowledge in infancy, 160
Psychological well-being
  of caregivers in Alzheimer's disease, 587
  child-care experiences affecting, 202
  contextual influences on, 610–613
  in departure of children from parental home, 545
  in divorce, 544
  and ego integrity, 604
  and exercise, 443, 540
  and friendships, 418, 419, 541, 553
  of gay, lesbian, and bisexual youths, 377
  and gerotranscendence, 605
  and health, 540, 575, 611
  and identity status in adolescence, 404
  in late adulthood, 573, 574, 575, 610–613
  and marital relationship, 431, 543
  in mastery of multiple roles, 541, 549
  in middle adulthood, 535, 537, 539, 540–541, 544, 545, 547
  in nursing homes, 589
  and optimal aging, 632–633
  in person–environment fit, 574, 611
  in religious involvement, 609
  in retirement, 557, 630
  and sense of control, 540, 574, 610–611
  and sense of usefulness, 576
  and social support, 541, 551, 611–613
  and subjective age, 535, 573
Psychosexual stages of development, 15–16, 16t, 256
  compared to psychosocial stages, 16t, 256
Psychosocial development, 16t, 16–17, 38
  adaptation to life in, 470–471, 536
  autonomy versus shame and doubt in, 16t, 184
  compared to psychosexual development, 16t, 256
  emotional expertise in, 605
  generativity versus stagnation in, 16t, 532–535
  gerotranscendence in, 605
  identity versus role confusion in, 16t, 402
  industry versus inferiority in, 16t, 330
  initiative versus guilt in, 16t, 256
  integrity versus despair in, 16t, 604

intimacy versus isolation in, 16t, 469–470, 472–478
  reminiscence in, 606
  in seasons of life, 470, 535–536
  sequential research on, 38
  trust versus mistrust in, 16t, 184
Puberty, 361, 363–371
  arousal states in, 368
  body composition in, 363–364
  body proportions in, 363
  body size in, 363, 364f
  brain development in, 367–368
  depression in, 422
  early versus late timing of, 370–371, 422
  gender identity in, 414
  hormone changes in, 363, 369, 373
  individual and group differences in, 366–367
  moodiness in, 369
  motor development in, 364–365
  peer relations in, 370, 371
  psychological impact of, 368–371
  reactions to changes in, 368–369
  relationship with parents in, 369–370
  secular trends in, 367
  sex differences in, 363, 364, 365–366, 366f, 368–369
  sexual maturation in, 365–366
  timing of, 367, 370–371
Pubic hair development, 363, 365, 366
  age at time of, 366f
  variations in, 366, 367
Public education programs
  on immunizations, 221
  on obesity, 441
Public policy, 65–69
  on adolescent suicide, 423
  on advance medical directives, 655–656
  on assisted living facilities, 619
  on assistive technology, 574
  on bilingual education, 317–318
  on caring for aging parents, 551
  for children, youths, and families, 66–67, 67t
  and compression of morbidity in late adulthood, 576, 577
  on early intervention programs, 173, 245–246
  for elderly, 67–68, 68f, 69
  and feminization of poverty, 544
  future trends in, 68–69
  on health care in late adulthood, 588–589
  on hospice care, 653
  on immunizations, 221
  on long-term care in late adulthood, 588–589, 619
  on Nurse–Family Partnership, 94
  and obesity trends, 441
  on parental leave time from employment, 105
  on reproductive technologies, 55
  on right to die, 654–659
  and social clock in early adulthood, 471
  on surrogate motherhood, 55
  on universal health care, 66–67
Puerto Rico, mother–infant relationship and attachment security in, 200

Pukapukans of Pacific Islands, childbirth practices of, 98
Punishment
  and aggression, 266, 267, 270
  consistency in, 267
  corporal, 266, 266f, 267
  cultural influences on, 267, 281
  in delinquency, 425, 426
  explanations to child for, 267
  and moral development, 265–267, 407
  in operant conditioning, 17, 134
  in social learning theory, 18, 265–267
  time out technique in, 266–267
  undesirable effects of, 266
  withdrawal of privileges in, 267

Q
Q-Sort method in attachment assessment, 198
Quaker beliefs, 664
Quality of life, 611
  in hospice programs, 652
  in nursing homes, 619
  in religious involvement, 609–610
  in retirement, 630
  and right to die, 654
  and suicide, 612–613
Quasi-experimental research, 35
Quechua of Peru
  mental state words and false-belief tasks of, 239
  swaddling of infants, 109
Questionnaires in research, 29t, 30, 37
Questions
  and cognitive development in early childhood, 232
  in grammatical development, 249–250
Quinceañera, 369
Quinlan, Karen Ann, 654, 656

R
Racial differences. See Ethnic and racial differences
Radiation exposure
  genetic mutations in, 51
  in pregnancy, 51, 89–90
Random assignment in experimental research, 35
Random events theory of aging, 432
Rape, 448–449
Rapid-eye-movement (REM) sleep, 108t, 108–109, 128
Reaching in infancy and toddlerhood, 138, 138f, 139f, 139–140
  feet first, 138, 138f
  and grasping, 139f, 139–140
REACH (Resources for Enhancing Alzheimer's Caregiver Health) initiative, 587
Reactive aggression, 269
Reactivity, and temperament, 190, 192, 193
Readiness
  for learning, 233
  for reading, 242, 242f
  for school, 263
Reading
  comprehension of, 308
  in early childhood, 240–242, 242f
  and early printing, 225

and emergent literacy, 240–242, 242f
  information processing in, 307–308
  interactive, 242
  in late adulthood, 593
  in middle childhood, 307–308, 316
  phonics approach to, 308
  readiness for, 242, 242f
  sex differences in, 388, 457
  vocabulary growth in, 316
  whole-language approach to, 308
Realistic period in vocational choice, 456
Realistic personality, vocational choice in, 456
Real self, and ideal self, 331
Reasoning
  abstract. See Abstract thinking
  by analogy, 230
  hypothetico-deductive, 382–383, 384
  mathematical, 242–243. See also Mathematical abilities
  in middle childhood, 300
  moral, 405–414
  in preoperational stage, 230
  propositional thought in, 383, 384
  scientific, 385f, 385–386
  spatial. See Spatial reasoning and skills
Recall memory
  automatic, 591
  in early childhood, 237
  episodic, 591, 593
  in infancy and toddlerhood, 164
  in language development, 237
  in late adulthood, 591, 593
Recast strategy in grammar correction, 251
Recent memory of infants, in habituation, 134–135
Recessive and dominant inheritance, 48t, 48–50, 49t
Recess time at school, 298
Reciprocal relationships
  ecological systems theory on, 25
  ethological theory of attachment on, 196
  morality of cooperation in, 408
Reciprocity, ideal, 408, 409, 410
Recognition memory
  in early childhood, 237
  in infancy and toddlerhood, 164
  in late adulthood, 591, 592
Reconstituted families, 349–350
Recovery and habituation, 134
Rectal cancer, 511
Redemption themes in life stories, 534
Referential communication, 178
Reflexes
  Apgar Scale on, 98t
  classical conditioning of, 17
  of infants and newborn, 98t, 106–108, 107t, 153, 153t
Regrets
  in late adulthood, despair in, 604
  in middle adulthood, 537
Rehearsal as memory strategy, 237, 304
Reinforcement
  in operant conditioning, 17, 134
  in social learning theory, 18

Rejected children, 341
  aggressive, 341, 342, 343
  bullying of, 342
  interventions for, 343
  withdrawn, 341, 343
Relational aggression, 269, 424
  sex differences in, 270
Relativistic thinking, 451
  commitment within, 451
Relaxation techniques in natural
    childbirth, 99
Religion
  adolescent rites of passage in, 369
  death concept in, 641, 643, 645,
    649–650, 664
  in emerging adulthood, 465f,
    465–466
  freedom in choice of, 337, 410
  and generativity, 535
  in late adulthood, 608–610, 611,
    612
  of marriage partners, 480
  in middle adulthood, 535
  and moral development, 412
  and mourning behavior, 664
  and passive euthanasia beliefs, 655
  and quality of life, 609–610
  and voluntary active euthanasia
    beliefs, 656
Remarriage, 347, 349–350, 479, 489,
    490
  blended families in, 349–350,
    490–491
  in late adulthood, 621–622, 623
  in middle adulthood, 544
  in widowhood, 623
Reminiscence in late adulthood,
    592–593, 606
  knowledge-based, 606
  life review in, 606
  other-focused, 606
  self-focused, 606
Remote memory
  in infancy and toddlerhood, 135
  in late adulthood, 592–593
Repetition as memory strategy, 238,
    304
Representations, mental. See Mental
    representations
Reproductive capacity, age-related
    changes in, 437–438, 438f
Reproductive choices, 53–59
  adoption in, 57–59
  genetic counseling on, 53–55
  prenatal diagnosis and fetal
    medicine in, 56–57
Reproductive system
  in conception, 80, 80f
  in early adulthood, 437–438
  in middle adulthood, 504–508
  in physical changes of aging, 435t,
    437–438, 504–508
  in puberty, 365–366
Reproductive technologies, 54–55,
    437
  for gay and lesbian families, 492
  multiple births in, 47t, 48, 54
  preimplantation genetic diagnosis
    in, 56t
  sex sorter methods in, 54
  in singlehood, 487
Research, 27–40
  applications of, 5

behavioral conditioning in, 17
clinical or case study method, 17,
    29t, 30–31
confidentiality in, 39t
correlational, 34–35, 36t
cross-sectional, 36t, 37–38
on cultural influences, 31–33
of Darwin, 14
debriefing on, 40
designs of, 34–38
ethical issues in, 17, 39t, 39–40
ethnographic, 29t
experimental, 35, 36t, 38
hypothesis in, 27
longitudinal, 35–37, 36t. See also
    Longitudinal research
neurobiological, 122–124, 123f,
    123t
in normative approach, 14–15
observational, 28–30, 29t
rights of participants in, 39t, 39–40
risks and benefits of, 40
scientific verification of theories
    in, 5
self-report measures in, 29t, 30
sequential designs, 36t, 38, 38f
strengths and limitations of
    common methods, 29t
on temperament, 191
violation-of-expectation method
    in, 155, 158–161
Residential communities, older adults
    in, 618–619, 631
Resilience, 10–11
  in authoritative child-rearing style,
    280
  in birth complications, 106
  definition of, 10
  in emerging adulthood, 467–469
  in late adulthood, 605, 608, 623
  in middle childhood, 354
Resistant attachment, 198
  and romantic relationships of
    adults, 474
Resource room, 322
Resources for Enhancing Alzheimer's
    Caregiver Health (REACH)
    initiative, 587
Respiratory system
  death rate from disorders of, 579,
    579f
  in early adulthood, 436
  in late adulthood, 570–571, 579
  in newborn, Apgar Scale on, 98t
  in physical changes of aging, 435t,
    436, 570–571
  sudden infant death syndrome in
    disorders of, 110
Respite services
  for caregivers of older adults with
    dementia, 587
  in elder maltreatment prevention,
    628
Restoration task in grief process, 660
Reticular formation in early
    childhood, 218, 218f
Retina
  in infancy, 113
  in late adulthood, 569
Retirement, 629–632
  adjustment to, 630–631
  average age of, 556, 629
  bridge jobs to, 629

cognitive changes in, 596
community service and volunteer
    work in, 607
decision making on, 629–630, 630f
planning for, 556–558, 629–630
residential communities in, 618
Third Age in, 607
Retrieval of information from long-
    term memory, 162
Reversibility
  in concrete operational stage, 299
  in preoperational stage, 229
Rheumatoid arthritis, 580–581
Rh factor incompatibility, 93, 101
Riboflavin deficiency in adolescence,
    372
Right-handedness, 217–218
Rights
  adolescent understanding of,
    409–410
  childhood understanding of, 337
  in death and dying issues, 654–659
  of research participants, 39t, 39–40
Risks and benefits of research, 40
Risk-taking behavior in adolescence,
    367–368, 368f, 387, 388
Rituals and ceremonies
  in mourning, 664
  in puberty onset, 369
  respect for older adults in, 574–575
Road Scholar program, 597–598
Rods and cones, 503
Role confusion and identity in
    adolescence, 16t, 402
Romania
  early deprivation of orphan
    children in, 125–127, 127f
  teenage pregnancy in, 378f
  voluntary active euthanasia beliefs
    in, 656
Romantic relationships
  in adolescence, 420f, 420–421
  childhood attachment patterns
    affecting, 474
  cultural influences on, 475–476
  in early adulthood, 445–446,
    472–476
  in friendships, 477
  mate selection in, 472–473, 475
Rooting reflex, 106, 107t, 206
Rothbart model of temperament,
    190–191, 191t
Rough-and-tumble play, 297–298
Rubella, 221
  in pregnancy, 90, 91t
Running, age-related changes in,
    436–437, 437f
Rural areas, community influences
    in, 64
  in late adulthood, 616–617
Russia
  personality traits in, 542
  poverty rate in, 68f

S
Sadness in infancy, 186
Safety seats in cars, 221, 222
Same-sex friendships, 417–418,
    476–477
Same-sex marriage, 479–480
Samoans
  adolescence of, 362
  overweight and obesity, 440

Sandwich generation, 549
Satisfaction
  in job, 553–554, 554f
  in marital relationship, 446, 481t,
    481–483, 484–485, 543–544,
    620–621
SAT scores, sex differences in, 389
Saudi Arabia, death concept in, 645
Scaffolding, 303
  in sociocultural theory, 167, 234,
    235, 237
Scale errors, 207
Schemes in cognitive development,
    152, 154
Schiavo, Terri, 654, 655, 656
Schizophrenia
  adoption studies of, 70, 73
  heritability research on, 70
Scholastic Assessment Test (SAT)
    scores, sex differences in, 389
School phobia, 352
Schools
  academic achievement in, 392–396.
    See also Academic achievement
  achievement attributions in,
    333–334
  adult learners in, 526–527
  bilingual programs in, 317–318
  bullying in, 342
  career-related curriculum in,
    393–394
  child-centered programs in, 244,
    245
  children with special needs in,
    322–323
  and civic engagement, 413
  class size in, 318
  cliques and crowds in, 419–420
  cognitive self-regulation in, 307
  college, 454–455. See also College
    experience
  community service opportunities
    in, 413
  concrete operational thought in,
    301
  constructivist classrooms in, 319
  cooperative learning in, 320, 322
  corporal punishment in, 283
  delinquency prevention and
    treatment strategies in, 425–426
  dropping out from, 396–397, 455
  educational philosophies in,
    319–320
  ethnic and racial diversity in, 339,
    340, 406
  gender typing in, 274–276
  gifted children in, 322–323
  graduation rate from, 395f
  grouping practices in, 321–322
  heterogeneous groups in, 322
  high-quality, signs of, 319
  homogeneous groups in, 321
  identity development in, 405
  inclusive classrooms in, 322
  information processing in, 307–309
  integration of, 321
  international comparisons of,
    323–325, 324t
  just educational environment of,
    411–412
  learning in, 307–309, 318–325,
    391–397
  literacy activities in, 242

magnet, 321
mathematics instruction in, 308–309
meals served in, 293
memory strategies in, 306
Montessori, 245
moral development in, 410, 411–412
multigrade classes in, 322
parent partnership with, 393
peer relations in, 342, 343
physical education classes in, 298–299
Piagetian classrooms in, 233
preschool and kindergarten programs in, 244–246
readiness for, 263
reading instruction in, 307–308
recess time in, 298
resource rooms in, 322
service-learning programs in, 413
size of, 396
social-constructivist classrooms in, 319–320
suicide prevention strategies in, 423
teacher–student interactions in, 320–321. *See also* Teacher–student interactions
tracking in, 395
traditional classrooms in, 319
transitions in, 391–392, 392*f*
violent deaths in, 665
Vygotskian classrooms in, 235
zero tolerance policies in, 425–426
Science achievement, sex differences in, 389
Scientific reasoning, 385*f*, 385–386
Scotland, child-rearing styles and academic achievement in, 392
Scripts
  dependency–support, 610
  independence–ignore, 610
  memory of, 238
Scrotum, 80
The Seasons of a Man's Life (Levinson), 470
The Seasons of a Woman's Life (Levinson), 470
Seasons of life theory
  on early adulthood, 470
  on middle adulthood, 535–536
Seattle Longitudinal Study, 519, 519*f*, 597
Second Age of midlife, 598*n*, 607
Secondary aging, 580
Secondary circular reactions in sensorimotor stage, 153*t*, 154
Secondary friends, 625
Secondary sexual characteristics, 365
Second language learning, 317–318
Second-order false beliefs, 306, 307*f*
Secure base for infant exploration, 187–188
Security of attachment, 197–198, 199–201
  child-care facilities affecting, 202–203
  and dating, 420
  factors affecting, 199–201
  and later development, 206, 420, 474
  and loneliness, 478

measurement of, 197*f*, 197*t*, 197–198, 198*f*
parent experience of attachment affecting, 201
and peer relations, 263
and romantic relationships of adults, 474
and self-concept, 256
Self-acceptance
  of gay, lesbian, and bisexual youths, 377
  in late adulthood, 606, 633
  in middle adulthood, 538, 539
Self-awareness
  in early childhood, 256–258
  and empathy, 208
  in infancy and toddlerhood, 206–208
  scale errors in, 207
  and self-conscious emotions, 188–189
Self-care children, 351
Self-concept
  in adolescence, 402–403
  cultural influences on, 331–332
  in early childhood, 256–258
  gender identity in. *See* Gender identity
  ideal self in, 331
  in late adulthood, 574, 576, 606–608, 633
  in middle adulthood, 535–536, 538–542
  in middle childhood, 330–334
  morality in, 411
  perspective-taking skills affecting, 330–331
  possible selves in, 538, 575, 608
  in seasons of life theory, 470, 535–536
  self-esteem in. *See* Self-esteem
  and social comparisons, 330, 331
  storytelling practices affecting, 257
Self-conscious emotions
  in early childhood, 258, 259–260
  in infancy and toddlerhood, 188–189
  in middle childhood, 335
Self-consciousness in adolescence, 386–387
Self-control. *See also* Self-regulation
  in early childhood, and moral development, 264
  in infancy and toddlerhood, 208–209
Self-disclosure in friendships, 417, 417*f*, 476, 477
Self-efficacy
  academic, 307
  emotional, 336
  in late adulthood, 575, 597
  physical, 365, 515–516
  social learning theory on, 18
Self-esteem
  academic, 307, 331, 332, 333, 403
  achievement-related attributions in, 333–334
  in adolescence, 371, 387, 391, 402–403
  in athletic or physical competence, 296, 331, 332
  body image affecting, 371
  changes in level of, 331, 402–403

child-rearing practices affecting, 258, 332–333
cultural influences on, 331–332, 333
and dropout rates, 396
in early childhood, 257–258
in ethnic and racial biases, 338
and ethnic identity, 406
and gender identity, 276, 344
hierarchical structure of, 331, 332*f*
in middle adulthood, 553
in middle childhood, 331–334
in obesity, 440, 441
physical appearance affecting, 331
school transitions affecting, 391
Self-fulfilling prophecy, educational, 320–321
Self-help skills in early childhood, 224
Self-recognition, 207
Self-regulation
  in adolescence, 367–368, 368*f*
  cognitive, 307, 384
  in early childhood, and moral development, 264
  emotional, 189–190, 259, 336, 605
  in infancy and toddlerhood, 208–209
  in temperament, 189, 190, 191, 191*t*, 193
Self-report research methods, 29*t*, 30
Semen, 438, 507
Senescence, 432. *See also* Aging
Sensation-seeking behavior in adolescence, 367–368, 368*f*, 387
Sensitive caregiving, 199–200, 201, 206
Sensitive periods of development, 22
  of brain, 125–128
  in culture-specific learning, 141
  deprivation in, 125–127
  in language development, 174, 317
  teratogen exposure in, 85, 86*f*
Sensorimotor stage, 19, 19*t*, 152, 153–154
  circular reactions in, 153, 153*t*, 154
  evaluation of, 158–160
  imitation in, 156–157, 157*f*
  intentional behavior in, 154
  mental representation in, 153*t*, 154, 156–158
  object permanence in, 154, 155*f*, 155–156
  problem solving in, 157
  searching for hidden objects in, 154, 155, 156
  substages in, 153*t*
  symbolic understanding in, 157–158
Sensory register in information processing, 161, 162, 162*f*
Separation, marital. *See* Divorce
Separation anxiety, 196
September 11, 2001 terrorist attacks, 37, 353
Sequential research designs, 38, 38*f*
  compared to other research designs, 36*t*
Seriation in concrete operational stage, 300
Serotonin
  in Alzheimer's disease, 584, 585
  in sudden infant death syndrome, 110
  and temperament, 194

Serve America Act, 607
Service-learning programs, 413
Sesame Street, 246
Sex cells, 46–47
Sex chromosomes, 47
  abnormalities of, 53
  diseases linked to, 49*t*
Sex differences
  in achievement attributions, 334
  in aggression, 269–270, 271
  in aging stereotypes, 516–517, 535
  in AIDS, 448
  in alcohol use, 444
  in athletic activities, 296, 364–365
  in attention-deficit hyperactivity disorder, 304
  in autobiographical memory, 238
  in blended families, 349–350
  in body composition of muscle and fat, 363–364, 504
  in body proportion changes, 363
  in body size, 121
  in bullying, 342
  in cancer incidence, 510*f*, 511
  in cardiovascular disease, 512, 514
  in careers, 492, 493–494
  in caring for aging parents, 549–550, 550*f*
  in childhood injuries, 221
  in cliques, 420
  in death anxiety, 645*f*, 646
  in delinquency, 424
  in depression, 421, 422, 612
  in divorce, 490, 544, 621, 622
  in education on child rearing, 486
  in emotional expression, 189
  in exercise, 443
  in friendships, 340, 417–418, 476, 477, 552, 553, 625
  and gender typing, 273–278
  in generativity in middle adulthood, 533, 535
  in grandparent–grandchild relationship, 546, 547*f*, 548, 627
  in hearing loss, age-related, 503
  in identity development, 404
  in intimacy, 473
  in language development, 177
  in life expectancy, 564, 565, 566
  in marital roles, 480–481, 481*f*, 620
  in marital satisfaction, 481, 489, 490, 543–544, 621
  in mate selection, 472–473, 487
  in mathematical abilities, 388–391, 389*f*
  in mental abilities, 388–391, 520
  in moral development, 409
  in motor development, 225, 296
  in number of sexual partners, 446
  in older parent–adult child relationship, 626
  in osteoporosis, 512–513
  in physical growth, 121, 290
  in play activities, 201–202, 273–274, 276, 297–298, 344
  in puberty, 363, 364, 365–366, 366*f*, 368–369
  in relationship with aging parents, 548, 549–550
  in religiosity, 465, 609
  in remarriage, 622
  in reproductive system changes, 365–366, 437–438, 504–507

Sex differences (*cont.*)
in response to divorce of parents, 348, 544
in retirement decisions, 630
in retirement planning, 558
in school transitions, 391
in self-acceptance, 539
in self-control, 209
in self-esteem, 332
in sensory system changes in aging, 568*f*
in sexual abuse, 352
in sexual attitudes and behaviors, 446, 447, 448
in sexual coercion, 448
in sexual maturation, 365–366
in shyness, 36
in sibling relationships, 552
in singlehood, 487
in skeletal changes, age-related, 504
in sleep disturbances, 571
in smoking, 444
in spatial reasoning and skills, 389, 390
stereotyped beliefs on, 343–344. *See also* Gender stereotypes
in stress, 539, 539*f*
in suicidal behavior, 422, 612, 613
in temperament, 193
in verbal abilities, 388
in vocation, 457*t*, 457–459, 536, 553, 555
in widowhood, 622, 623
in X-linked inheritance, 51
Sex education
on contraception, 375
cultural influences on, 373–374
in prevention of teenage pregnancy, 379
and reactions to pubertal changes, 368–369
on sexually transmitted diseases, 377, 447–448
Sex hormones, 363
estrogen. *See* Estrogen
in puberty, 363
and sexual orientation, 376
testosterone, 363, 507
Sex roles. *See* Gender roles
Sex stereotypes. *See* Gender stereotypes
Sex typing. *See* Gender typing
Sexual abuse
in adolescent dating relationships, 420–421
consequences of, 353–354
in early adulthood, 448–449
in early childhood, 281, 355
eyewitness memory of children on, 355
in late adulthood, 627
in middle childhood, 352–354, 355
prevention and treatment of, 354
Sexual attitudes and behavior, 373–380
coercion in, 448–449
and contraceptive use, 375, 375*f*, 446
cultural influences on, 373–374, 376
divorce of parents affecting, 348
in early adulthood, 445–449

frequency of intercourse in, 446, 509, 578, 579*f*
in late adulthood, 578–579, 579*f*
in middle adulthood, 504, 509, 541
in passionate love, 473
psychosexual theory of Freud on, 15–16
sexual abuse affecting, 353–354
and sexually transmitted diseases, 376–377
and sexual orientation, 375–376
and teenage pregnancy, 378–380
trends in, 374, 374*f*
Sexual characteristics, primary and secondary, 365
Sexual coercion, 448–449
prevention and treatment of, 449
Sexual dysfunction
in early adulthood, 446
in middle adulthood, 507
Sexual identity of homosexual youths, 375–377
Sexually transmitted diseases
in adolescence, 376–377
AIDS. *See* AIDS
in early adulthood, 447–448
Sexual maturation, 365–366
hormone changes in, 363
Sexual orientation
in adolescence, 375–377
of children of homosexual parents, 492
in early adulthood, 447
of gay, lesbian, and bisexual. *See* Gay, lesbian, and bisexual people
and identity development, 376–377, 405
and suicidal behavior, 376
Shame
in early childhood, 259, 260
in infancy and toddlerhood, 16*t*, 184, 188, 189
in suicidal loss, 661
Shape bias in vocabulary development, 248
Shinto beliefs about death, 641
Shiva mourning period, 664
Short-term memory in information processing, 161, 162, 162*f*
Shyness, 192
and adjustment, 195, 195*f*
cultural influences on, 195, 195*f*
longitudinal study of, 36, 37
neurobiological correlates of, 192
temperament in, 191, 193, 195
Siblings
in adolescence, 416
arrival of new sibling, 204–205
attachment patterns of, 201, 204–205
in blended families, 349–350
cross-sectional studies of, 37
death of, 661–662
in early adulthood, 477
emotional understanding of, 258
and false beliefs, 240
as friends, 477
gene–environment correlation in studies of, 72, 72*f*
glaucoma in, 503
in late adulthood, 624
longitudinal studies of, 37
in middle adulthood, 552

in middle childhood, 345–346
number of, 204, 483
and one-child families, 346
play of, 168
rivalry between, 345–346
temperament and personality of, 194
twin. *See* Twins
Sickle cell anemia, 49*t*, 50, 293
Sickle cell trait, 50, 52
SIDS (sudden infant death syndrome), 109, 110, 129, 139, 661
Sierra Leone, life expectancy in, 565
Sign language
in hearing loss, 174, 176, 178
and sensitive periods in language development, 174
Simon, Theodore, 15
Singapore
adolescent suicide rate in, 422
infant mortality rate in, 105*f*
life expectancy in, 565*f*
Singlehood, 486–487, 623–624
and widowhood, 621, 622–623, 624, 660, 662, 663
Single-parent families
chaos in, 29
in divorce, 347, 349
extended family relationships of, 66
food insecurity in, 132
grandparents in, 547
leave time from employment, 105
in never-married parents, 491
poverty of, 61, 62, 544
in teenage pregnancy, 378
Size of family, 204, 483
Skeletal age, 121, 217
Skeletal system, 435*t*
in early childhood, 217
in late adulthood, 572, 577
in middle adulthood, 504, 512–513
osteoporosis of, 504, 512–513
Skin
age spots of, 503, 572
in late adulthood, 503, 572
in middle adulthood, 503–504
in physical changes of aging, 435*t*, 503–504, 572
Skinner, B. F., 17
Skipped-generation families, 548
Sleep
in adolescence, 368
apnea in, 571
cultural influences on, 128, 129
of fetus, 84
insufficient, weight gain in, 292
in late adulthood, 571
in menopause, 506
of newborn and infants, 108*t*, 108–109, 110, 128
non-rapid-eye-movement, 108, 108*t*, 109, 571
rapid-eye-movement, 108*t*, 108–109, 128
sudden infant death in, 110
Slovenia
infant mortality rate in, 105*f*
life expectancy in, 565*f*
poverty rate in, 68*f*
Slow-to-warm-up temperament, 190
Slow-twitch muscle fibers, 572
Small-for-date infants, 102

Smell sense
in aging, 435*t*, 570
in infancy and toddlerhood, 112–113, 113*f*
Smiling in infancy, 185, 188, 189
Smoking
in adolescence, 380, 381*f*
and attention-deficit hyperactivity disorder, 74, 74*f*
cessation of, 444
in early adulthood, 444
and erectile dysfunction, 579
health consequences of, 436, 444, 510, 571
heart disease in, 436
lung cancer in, 510
osteoporosis in, 513
in pregnancy, 74, 74*f*, 88, 110
and sudden infant death syndrome, 110
taste sense in, 570
telomere length in, 433
Sociability, 192
neurobiological correlates of, 192
parental influences on, 263
in peer relations, 261–262, 263
temperament in, 191, 193
Social clock, 471, 533
Social-cognitive learning theory, 18
Social comparisons
gender identity in, 344
in-group and out-group biases in, 337–338
in middle childhood, 330, 331, 337–338, 344
and self-esteem, 331
Social-constructivist classrooms, 319–320
Social contract orientation in moral development, 408
Social conventions and moral development, 269, 336–337
Social convoy model, 620
Social development. *See* Emotional and social development
Social learning theory, 18, 28*t*
gender identity in, 276
gender stereotypes in, 273
mate selection in, 472
moral development in, 264, 265–268
Social networking sites
in adolescence, 418, 418*f*
in early adulthood, 476
Facebook. *See* Facebook use
in late adulthood, 599, 625, 626
in middle adulthood, 552, 553*f*
online friendships in. *See* Online friendships
romantic partners found on, 445–446
Social order-maintaining orientation in moral development, 408
Social personality, vocational choice in, 456
Social preference measure of peer acceptance, 341
Social prominence measure of peer acceptance, 341, 342
Social referencing in infancy and toddlerhood, 188
Social security benefits, 67, 68, 607, 629, 630, 633

Social smile, 185
Social support
    and attachment security of
        children, 201
    in bereavement interventions, 663
    for caregivers of older adults with
        dementia, 587
    in caring for aging parents, 551
    during childbirth, 99
    in child maltreatment prevention,
        283
    in elder maltreatment prevention,
        628
    in emerging adulthood, 468
    in late adulthood, 567, 611–613,
        616–617, 623–625
    of never-married childless older
        adults, 623–624
    in obesity treatment, 441
    in partner abuse interventions, 483
    perceptions of, 613
    during pregnancy, 93, 94
    of resilient children, 11
    in retirement, 631
    for returning students, 526–527
    in singlehood, 623–624
    in widowhood, 623, 624
Social theories of aging, 614–616
Sociocultural theory, 23–24, 233–235
    compared to other human
        development theories, 28t
    on education, 235, 319–320
    evaluation of, 235
    on make-believe play, 235
    on private speech, 233–234
    on scaffolding, 167, 234, 235, 237
    on zone of proximal development,
        167, 234
Sociodramatic play in early
    childhood, 227, 235
Socioeconomic status, 61–63
    and academic achievement, 395
    and access to high quality
        education, 321
    in adolescent pregnancy, 378
    and adolescent sexual activity, 375
    in affluence, 62–63
    and attachment security, 198
    and cancer incidence, 510
    and child-care quality, 246
    and child-rearing practices, 281
    and cognitive development, 71–
        172, 173, 243, 244
    and computer use, 247
    and delinquency, 424, 425, 426
    and departure from parental home,
        479
    divorce affecting, 347, 349
    and dropout rates, 396, 455
    and early intervention programs
        for at-risk preschoolers, 173,
        245–246
    and emerging adulthood, 466
    factors considered in, 61
    and family functioning, 61
    and grandparent–grandchild
        relationship, 546–547
    and grouping practices in schools,
        321
    and health in early adulthood,
        438–439
    and health in late adulthood, 68,
        68f, 575

and health in middle adulthood,
    509
and IQ, 173, 243, 312, 314
and knowledge development, 314
and life expectancy, 565, 566
and lifelong learning programs,
    598
and mathematics skills, 243
and myopia, 293
and neighborhood influences,
    63–64
and nutrition problems, 220
in poverty, 61–62. See also Poverty
and pubertal growth variations,
    366–367, 371
and reading skills, 242, 242f
and religious activities, 609
and retirement decisions, 630
and self-esteem, 332, 334
and service-learning programs, 413
of single-parent families, 491
and storytelling practices, 257
and stress, 449–450
and teacher–student interactions,
    320
and television viewing time, 247
and vocabulary development, 178
and vocational choice, 457
Socioemotional selectivity theory of
    aging, 615–616, 626
    retirement in, 631
Somatic mutation, 52, 510
Soothing of child
    in crying, 109–111, 112
    and emotional self-regulation, 189
South Africa
    adoption by gay and lesbian
        families in, 492
    marriage of same-sex couples in,
        479
    unintentional childhood injuries
        in, 221f
South Korea
    college education in, 455
    infant mortality rate in, 105f
    life expectancy in, 565f
    partner abuse in, 483f
    personality traits in, 542
    unintentional childhood injuries
        in, 221f
Spain
    adolescent contraceptive use in,
        375f
    adolescent suicide rate in, 422
    adoption by gay and lesbian
        families in, 492
    departure from parental home in,
        545
    divorce rate in, 347f
    infant mortality rate in, 105f
    life expectancy in, 565f
    poverty rate in, 68f
    unintentional childhood injuries
        in, 221f
Spatial reasoning and skills, 390, 390f
    in concrete operational stage, 300,
        300f
    early brain injury affecting, 126
    lateralization of brain functions
        in, 126
    in multiple intelligences theory,
        312t, 323
    sex differences in, 389, 390

Special needs, teaching children with,
    322–323
Special Supplemental Food Program
    for Women, Infants, and
    Children, U.S. (WIC), 92
Spectroscopy, near-infrared (NIRS),
    123f, 123t, 124
Speech
    egocentric, 233
    first sounds of, 175–177
    infant attention to, 113
    infant-directed, 178–179
    infant perception of, 141–142
    inner, 234
    in late adulthood, 594
    private, 233–234
    telegraphic, 177
    two-word utterances in, 177
Speed of information processing, 162,
    519, 520–521, 521f, 589, 596
Sperm, 46, 47, 80
    age-related changes in, 438, 507
    and conception, 80
    in middle adulthood, 507
    in reproductive technologies, 54,
        55
Spermarche, 366, 366f
    reactions to, 368–369
Spina bifida, 92
Spirituality
    death concept in, 645, 649–650
    in emerging adulthood, 465f,
        465–466
    in late adulthood, 608–610, 633
Spock, Benjamin, 15, 129
Sports activities, 295, 296–297. See
    also Athletic activities
Spouses. See Marital relationship
Stability genes in cancer, 510
Stages of development
    cognitive, 18–20, 19t
    concrete operational. See Concrete
        operational stage
    in discontinuous perspective, 6
    formal operational. See Formal
        operational stage
    in middle adulthood, 537
    moral, 407–409
    preoperational. See Preoperational
        stage
    psychosexual, 15–16, 16t, 256
    psychosocial, 16, 16t
    sensorimotor. See Sensorimotor
        stage
    in sociocultural theory, 24
Stagnation versus generativity in
    middle adulthood, 16t, 532–535
Standardization of intelligence tests,
    169
Stanford-Binet Intelligence Scale, 15,
    309–310
States of arousal in infants, 108t,
    108–112, 128
Statistical learning capacity in infants,
    142
Stepfamilies, 349–350, 490–491
Stepping reflex, 106–107, 107t
Stereotypes
    of aging, 566, 570, 574–575, 576,
        606, 625
    ethnic and racial, 406
    gender-related. See Gender
        stereotypes

and stereotype threat, 314–315,
    315f, 321, 389, 574
Sternberg triarchic theory of
    successful intelligence, 310–311,
    311f, 523
Steroids, anabolic, adolescents using,
    364
Stimulant drug use
    in adolescence, 380
    in attention-deficit hyperactivity
        disorder, 305
Storytelling practices, cultural
    variations in, 257
Stranger anxiety, 186–187
Strange Situation procedure for
    measuring attachment security,
    197, 197t, 198, 198f, 199, 202
Stress
    acculturative, 406, 416
    in adolescence, 362, 416, 419
    in attending child-care center, 203
    in bereavement, 661
    of bullying victims, 342
    for caregivers of older adults with
        dementia, 585, 586–587
    in caring for aging parents,
        550–551
    in childbirth, 97
    of child maltreatment victims, 283
    coping strategies in, 514–515. See
        also Coping strategies
    cortisol levels in. See Cortisol
    depression in, 422
    in divorce of parents, 347, 348
    in early adulthood, 449–450, 469
    in early deprivation, 127
    in ethnic and political violence, 353
    exercise benefits in, 443, 516
    in family circumstances, 416, 416t
    of grandparents rearing
        grandchildren, 548
    health effects of, 437, 449–450, 571
    immune response in, 437, 571
    job burnout in, 554
    in late adulthood, 568, 571, 611
    male fetal death rate in, 51
    in middle adulthood, 513, 514–515,
        516, 539, 539f, 544
    in middle childhood, 352
    in pain of infants, 112
    in poverty, 62, 303
    in pregnancy, 92–93, 94
    resilience in, 10–11, 354
    in retirement, 630
    of returning students, 526
    sex differences in, 539, 539f
    of shy children, 192
    in singlehood, 487
    suicidal behavior in, 422–423
    telomere length in, 433
    in unemployment, 556
    working memory capacity in, 303
Stress hormones. See Cortisol
Stroke, 579f, 579–580
    brain plasticity in, 126
    dementia in, 585–587
    signs and symptoms of, 586
Structured interviews research
    method, 29t, 30
Structured observation research
    method, 29t, 29–30
Subcultures, 65
Subjective age, 535, 573

Substance abuse
  in adolescence, 364, 370, 376,
      380–381, 419, 420
  in affluence, 62
  AIDS in, 377
  of alcohol. *See* Alcohol use and
      abuse
  of anabolic steroids, 364
  and dating, 420
  in early adulthood, 444–445, 465
  in early pubertal maturation, 370
  of lesbian, gay, and bisexual youths,
      376
  in peer group, 419, 420
  during pregnancy, 86–89, 110
  prevention and treatment of, 381
  and smoking. *See* Smoking
Subtraction problems in mathematics,
    308, 309
Sucking reflex, 106, 107*t*, 133*f*,
    133–134
Sudden infant death syndrome
    (SIDS), 109, 110, 129, 139, 661
Suggestibility affecting eyewitness
    memory of children, 355
Suicide
  in adolescence, 422–423
  assisted, 654*t*, 658–659
  bereavement of survivors in, 661
  in clusters, 423
  in early adulthood, 438*f*
  of homosexual youths, 376, 422
  in incurable illness, 613
  in late adulthood, 611, 612–613
  of maltreatment victims, 283
  in obesity, 292
  prevention and treatment
      strategies, 423, 423*t*, 613
  warning signs in, 613
Sun exposure, skin aging in, 504
Superego, 15, 256, 264
Surrogate motherhood, 54–55
Swaddling of infants, 109
Sweden
  adoption by gay and lesbian
      families in, 492
  assistive technology in, 574
  caring for aging parents in, 551
  cohabitation in, 488
  corporal punishment in, 283
  divorce rate in, 347*f*
  family size in, 483
  health care in, 574
  home births in, 99
  immunization rate in, 221
  infant mortality rate in, 105*f*
  language development in, 178
  life expectancy in, 565, 565*f*
  long-term care for older adults
      in, 588
  marital roles in, 480
  math achievement scores in, 389*f*
  parental leave in, 104
  poverty rate in, 62, 68*f*
  retirement programs in, 630
  teenage pregnancy in, 378*f*
  unintentional childhood injuries
      in, 221*f*
Swimming, 72, 92, 436, 513, 540
Switzerland
  academic achievement in, 324
  adolescent contraceptive use in,
      375*f*

  adolescent pregnancy in, 378*f*
  assisted suicide in, 658
  high school graduation rate in, 395*f*
  infant mortality rate in, 105*f*
  life expectancy in, 565*f*
  partner abuse in, 483*f*
  poverty rate in, 68*f*
  vocational education in, 459
Symbolic understanding
  dual representation in, 227–228
  in preoperational stage, 227–228
  in sensorimotor stage, 157–158
Sympathy, 260–261
Synapses, 121, 121*f*, 122
  pruning process, 122, 217, 450
Syphilis in pregnancy, 91*t*
Systems approach
  in dynamic systems perspective,
      8. *See also* Dynamic systems
      perspective
  in ecological systems theory, 24–27
  family as system, 59, 415

T

Taiwan
  academic achievement in, 324, 324*t*
  infant mortality rate in, 105*f*
  life expectancy in, 565*f*
  play activities in, 261
Talent and creativity, 323
Taste sense
  in infancy and toddlerhood,
      112–113
  in physical changes of aging, 435*t*,
      570
Tau in neurofibrillary tangles, 584
Taxonomic categories as memory
      strategy, 304
Tay-Sachs disease, 49*t*, 53, 58–59
T cells, 437, 571
Teacher–student interactions,
      320–321
  achievement attributions in,
      333–334
  class size affecting, 318
  in college experience, 455, 457–458
  and dropout rates, 396
  gender typing in, 274–276, 278
  in just educational environment,
      411–412
  in school transitions, 392
  self-fulfilling prophecies in,
      320–321
  in social-constructivist classrooms,
      320
  suicide prevention strategies in,
      423
  and vocational choice, 457
Teenage pregnancy and parenthood,
      378–380, 416*t*
  and contraceptive use, 375
  incidence of, 378, 378*f*
  intergenerational continuity in, 379
  interventions in, 379–380
  Nurse–Family Partnership in, 94
  prenatal development in, 93, 94
  prevention strategies, 379
Teen Outreach, 379
Teeth
  decay problems, 217
  in middle childhood, 290
  permanent, 217
  primary or baby, 217

Telegraphic speech, 177
Television, 159
  daily viewing time, 132, 159, 247,
      271*f*, 292, 292*f*
  educational programs on, 159,
      246–247
  infant and toddler learning from,
      159
  and media multitasking, impact on
      learning, 394
  and obesity, 132, 292, 292*f*, 440
  roles of older adults on, 574
  sexual content of programs on,
      374
  and video deficit effect, 159
  violence on, 270–271, 271*f*
Telomerase, 433
Telomeres, 432, 433, 433*f*
  length of, 433
Temperament
  and attachment security, 200
  and child-rearing practices, 192,
      194–195
  cultural variations in, 193, 194–195
  definition of, 190
  and delinquency, 425
  and effortful control, 189, 191,
      191*t*, 193, 209
  and emotional self-regulation, 189
  and empathy, 260
  environmental influences on,
      193–194
  genetic influences on, 193–194
  in infancy and toddlerhood,
      190–195
  and language development,
      177–178
  measurement of, 191
  models of, 190–191, 191*t*
  and moral development, 265
  New York Longitudinal Study of,
      190
  of resilient children, 10–11
  and response to divorce of parents,
      348
  Rothbart model, 190–191, 191*t*
  stability of, 191–193
Temper tantrums, 189–190
Temporal lobes, 155, 175, 241, 568
Tentative period in vocational choice,
      456
Teratogens, 85–92, 305
Terminal decline in late adulthood,
      596–597
Terminal illness
  in children, 643, 646, 649
  coping with dying in, 646–650
  in family member, 648–649
  hospice care in, 652–653
  informing patient about, 649, 650
  personality and coping style in,
      648
  religious and spiritual beliefs in,
      650
  right to die in, 654–659
Terrorism
  bereavement overload in, 662–663
  impact on children, 353
Tertiary circular reactions in
      sensorimotor stage, 153*t*, 154
Testes, 80, 363, 366, 366*f*
Testimony, eyewitness, by children,
      355

Testing methods, 29*t*, 30
  on intelligence. *See* Intelligence tests
  practice effects in, 37
Testosterone
  in middle adulthood, 507
  in puberty, 363
Text messaging, 394, 418
Thalidomide, 86
Thanatology, 640
  music, 653
Theories of development, 5–27, 28*t*.
      See also specific theories
  on attachment, 5
  behaviorism, 17
  cognitive-developmental, 18–20
  comparison of, 27, 28*t*
  as continuous or discontinuous
      process, 6, 6*f*
  on course of development, 6–7
  definition of, 5
  developmental cognitive
      neuroscience, 21–22
  ecological systems, 24–27
  ethology, 22
  evolutionary developmental
      psychology, 22–23
  historical foundations of, 14–20
  information processing, 20–21
  psychoanalytic, 15–17
  recent perspectives, 20–27
  on relative influence of nature and
      nurture, 7
  scientific verification of, 5
  social learning, 18
  sociocultural, 23–24
Theory of mind
  in autism, 241
  in early childhood, 238–240
  in middle childhood, 306–307, 307*f*
Third Age, 598, 598*n*, 607
Third-party influences in ecological
      systems theory, 25, 60
Three-mountains problem, 228, 228*f*
Thymus, 437
Thyroid-stimulating hormone (TSH),
      219
Thyroxine, 219
  in puberty, 363
Time-based prospective memory
      tasks, 593
Time out as punishment technique,
      266–267
Tinbergen, Niko, 22
Tip-of-the-tongue state in late
      adulthood, 594
Tobacco use. *See* Smoking
Toddlerhood. *See* Infancy and
      toddlerhood
Toilet training, 184
Tonic neck reflex, 107*t*
Tools of the Mind curriculum, 237
Tooth conditions. *See* Teeth
Topic-associating narrative style, 317
Topic-focused narrative style, 317
Touch
  in blindness, 570
  in infancy, 103, 112
  in intermodal perception, 146
  in late adulthood, 570
  in physical changes of aging, 435*t*,
      570
  for preterm infant stimulation,
      103, 112

Toxemia of pregnancy, 95
Toxoplasmosis in pregnancy, 91*t*, 92
Tracking, academic, 395
Traditional classrooms, 319
Traditional marriages, 480
Training. *See* Education
Traits
  carriers of, 50, 50*f*, 51*f*
  dominant and recessive, 48*t*,
    48–50, 49*t*
  personality. *See* Personality traits
  polygenic inheritance of, 52, 69
  sickle cell, 50, 52
Transitive inferences in concrete
  operational stage, 300, 301
Triangular theory of love, 473
Triarchic theory of successful
  intelligence, 310–311, 311*f*
Tribal and village societies
  adolescent initiation ceremonies
    in, 369
  cognitive development in, 236
  concrete operational stage in, 301
  conservation in, 301
  formal operational stage in, 384
  gender identity in, 540
  hearing loss in, 503
  moral development in, 411
  mourning in, 664
  observation and participation in
    adult work by children in, 236
  sibling relationships in, 552
  wisdom in, 595
Trimesters in prenatal development,
  81*t*, 83–85
Triplets, 48, 101
Triple X syndrome, 53
Trisomy 21 (Down syndrome),
  52–53, 53*f*, 584
Trophoblast, 80*f*, 81, 82
Trust
  and attachment, 196
  in friendships, 340, 419, 476
  and mistrust in psychosocial
    development, 16*t*, 184
Tuberculosis in pregnancy, 91*t*
Tumor suppressor genes, 510
  in breast cancer, 510
Turkey
  math achievement scores in, 389*f*
  voluntary active euthanasia beliefs
    in, 656
Turner syndrome, 53
Twins, 47*f*, 47–48
  anorexia nervosa of, 372
  empathy of, 265
  environmental influences on gene
    expression in, 73
  gene–environment correlation in
    studies of, 72, 72*f*
  hand preference of, 218
  heritability estimate studies of,
    70–71
  intelligence quotient of, 313
  kinship studies of, 70
  life expectancy of, 566
  lifespan of, 432
  low birth weight of, 101
  maternal factors linked to, 47*t*
  myopia of, 293
  niche-picking of, 72
  obesity of, 291
  osteoporosis of, 513

physical growth of, 130
puberty of, 366
rheumatoid arthritis of, 580–581
schizophrenia of, 70
sexual orientation of, 375
spatial abilities of, 390
temperament and personality of,
  193, 194

U

Ulnar grasp, 139*f*, 140
Ultrasound in pregnancy, 56*t*
Umbilical cord, 82
Unconditioned response, 133, 133*f*
Unconditioned stimulus, 133, 133*f*,
  134
Underarm hair growth in puberty,
  363, 365, 366
Underextensions in language
  development, 177
Unemployment, 556
Uninhibited child, temperament of,
  191
Unintentional injuries. *See* Injuries,
  unintentional
Uninvolved child-rearing style, 279*t*,
  280
  academic achievement in, 392
United Kingdom
  adoption by gay and lesbian
    families in, 492
  divorce rate in, 347*f*
  family size in, 483
  high school graduation rate in, 395*f*
  immunization rate in, 221
  infant mortality rate in, 105*f*
  life expectancy in, 565*f*
  marital roles in, 480, 481*f*
  overweight and obesity rate in, 291
  poverty rate in, 68*f*
  teenage pregnancy in, 378*f*
  unintentional childhood injuries
    in, 221*f*
United States
  academic achievement in, 388, 389*f*
  academic tracks in, 395
  adjustment of immigrant youths
    in, 33
  adolescent contraceptive use in,
    375, 375*f*
  adolescent pregnancy and
    parenthood in, 378, 378*f*, 379
  adolescent sexual activity in, 374,
    375, 379
  adolescent substance abuse in, 381*f*
  adolescent suicide in, 422, 423
  age at first marriage in, 479
  alcohol use in, 444, 445
  assisted suicide in, 658
  attachment patterns in, 198*f*, 201,
    474
  baby boomer generation in, 11
  bilingual education in, 317–318
  birth complications in, 105–106
  breastfeeding in, 16
  cancer in, 510, 510*f*
  caregiving roles of mothers and
    fathers in, 201, 202–203
  centenarians in, 566
  cesarean delivery rate in, 101
  child-care facilities in, 171–173
  childhood injuries in, 221, 221*f*,
    222

childlessness in, 488–489
child maltreatment in, 283, 352
child-rearing costs in, 484
college dropout rate in, 455
concrete operational stage in, 300,
  300*f*, 301
corporal punishment in, 283
cultural values and practices in, 65
death anxiety in, 646
delinquency in, 423
dementia in, 582
divorce in, 347, 347*f*, 348
early adulthood health in, 438,
  438*f*, 439, 442, 442*f*
early intervention programs in,
  245, 246
education in, 317–318, 319,
  323–325
environmental pollution in, 90
family size in, 483
fears of children in, 352
fetal monitoring in, 100
first words of infants in, 176–177
gender identity in, 540
gender stereotypes in, 343
health care in, 66, 67, 95, 439, 573
high school graduation rate in,
  395*f*
hospice programs in, 652, 653
immunization rate in, 221
indicators of children's health and
  well-being in, 66, 67*t*
individualism in, 65, 469
infant child care in, 172, 202
infant mortality rate in, 104, 105*f*
job burnout in, 554
job training in, 396, 459
leading causes of death in, 438,
  438*f*, 509, 509*f*, 579, 579*f*
lesbian, gay, and bisexual people
  in, 376, 447, 479, 486
life expectancy in, 8, 564, 565,
  565*f*
lifelong learning in, 598
loneliness in, 478, 618
marital roles in, 480, 481*f*
marriage of same-sex couples in,
  479
maternal age in, 93
mathematics instruction in, 309
middle adulthood health in, 509,
  509*f*
middle-aged children and aging
  parents in, 547, 549, 551
midlife emotional and social
  development in, 532, 538, 543
never-married single parents in,
  491
nursing homes in, 589
nutrition in, 220, 291
overweight and obesity rate in, 291,
  367, 440, 441, 441*f*
parental leave from employment
  in, 105, 485
partner abuse in, 483*f*
place of death in, 650
poverty rate in, 61, 62, 68*f*, 544
prenatal health care in, 95, 100
preschool programs in, 244, 245,
  246
professions of women in, 457, 457*f*,
  555
puberty in, 370

public policies for children and
  elderly in, 65, 66, 67, 68
reproductive technologies in, 54, 55
retirement in, 556, 557, 630
scaffolding in, 234
self-care children in, 351
sexual abuse in, 352
sexually transmitted diseases in,
  376, 447
singlehood in, 486
sleep patterns of infants in, 128
Strange Situation reactions of
  infants in, 198*f*
sudden infant death syndrome
  in, 110
teacher–student interactions in,
  276
television programs in, 270, 271
temperament of children in, 193
twins in, 48
unintentional childhood injuries
  in, 221, 221*f*, 222
voluntary active euthanasia in,
  656, 656*f*
Universal ethical principle orientation
  in moral development, 408
Universal grammar, 174
University education. *See* College
  experience
University of the Third Age, 598
Urban areas, community influences
  in, 64
  in late adulthood, 616–617
Uruguay
  adoption by gay and lesbian
    families in, 492
  corporal punishment in, 283
Usefulness, sense of, in late
  adulthood, 576
Uterus, 80, 80*f*, 81
  age-related changes in, 437
  contractions in childbirth, 96, 97*f*
Utku Indians, moral development
  in, 264

V

Vaccinations, 90, 220–221
Vaillant, George, on adaptation to life,
  470–471, 536
Values, cultural. *See* Cultural
  influences
Variables in research, 35
  dependent, 35
  independent, 35
V-chip for television, 271
Vegetative state, persistent, 641, 654
  recognition of living will in, 655
Verbal abilities
  cohort effects in, 518, 518*f*
  sex differences in, 388
Verbal aggression, 269
Verbs, and grammatical development,
  249
Vernix, 83
Victims
  of child maltreatment, 352,
    353–354
  of elder abuse, 628
  of partner abuse, 483
  of peer bullying, 342
  of sexual coercion, 448–449
Video deficit effect, 159
Video games, violence in, 271

Video viewing
   infant and toddler learning from, 159
   interactive experiences in, 159
Vietnam
   immigrant youths from, 32, 33
   unintentional childhood injuries in, 221f
Vietnamese Americans, intelligence definition of, 311
Village societies. *See* Tribal and village societies
Violation-of-expectation research method, 155, 158–161
   on numerical knowledge, 160, 160f
   on object permanence, 155, 155f
   on physical knowledge, 159
Violence
   bereavement interventions in, 665
   bereavement overload in, 662
   in family, risk for elder maltreatment in, 628
   fear of, in late adulthood, 617
   in juvenile delinquency, 423, 424
   in partner abuse, 482–483, 483f
   in sexual coercion, 448–449
   on television, 270–271, 271f
   in video games, 271
   war-related, impact on children, 353
Viral diseases
   AIDS. *See* AIDS
   in pregnancy, 90–91, 91t
Vision
   color, 113, 142, 503
   and depth perception, 142–144, 143f
   and face perception, 125, 145, 145f
   genetic factors affecting, 48t
   in infancy and toddlerhood, 113, 142–145
   in intermodal perception, 146
   in late adulthood, 568f, 569, 581
   in middle adulthood, 502–503
   in middle childhood, 293
   and pattern perception, 144, 144f
   in physical changes of aging, 435t, 502–503, 568f, 569
Visual acuity
   in infancy, 113, 142
   in late adulthood, 569
Visual cliff, 142, 143f
Vital capacity of lungs, 436, 437
Vitamins
   in adolescence, 372
   in early adulthood, 434
   in early childhood, 220
   in late adulthood, 569, 577
   in middle adulthood, 504, 513
   in osteoporosis, 513
   in pregnancy, 87, 92
Vitreous changes
   in late adulthood, 569
   in middle adulthood, 502–503

Vocabulary
   and categorization skills, 166
   coalition of cues in development of, 249
   comprehension and production of, 177
   cultural influences on, 178, 248, 314
   decoding of, 308
   in early childhood, 248–249, 258
   and emotional self-regulation, 189
   emotion words in, 258
   fast-mapping process in development of, 248
   first words in, 176–177
   and grammatical development, 249–250
   growth of, 177, 248, 316
   learning strategies for, 248–249
   metaphors in, 248
   in middle childhood, 316
   two-word utterances in, 177
   types of words in, 248
   word coinage in, 248
Vocation. *See also* Employment
   apprenticeship programs on, 459
   burnout from job stress in, 554
   and career changes at midlife, 555–556
   choice of, 455–459, 525
   and cognitive development, 525–526
   educational preparation for, 393–394, 395, 396, 459, 554–555
   glass ceiling in, 555
   and job satisfaction, 553–554, 554f
   in middle adulthood, 525–526, 536, 553–558
   and nontraditional careers of men, 458
   and retirement planning, 556–558
   tracks for, 395
Voice
   effortful control of, 193
   and emotional expression, 185, 188
   fetal response to, 85
   hearing loss affecting perception of, 503
   infant response to, 113, 146, 147, 165, 188, 196
   in preterm infant stimulation, 103
   in puberty, 366, 366f
Voluntary active euthanasia, 654t, 656–658, 659
   public opinion on, 656, 656f
Volunteer work
   in adolescence, 413
   and civic engagement, 413
   in early adulthood, 466
   in late adulthood, 567, 607, 631, 632f
   in middle adulthood, 541
   in middle childhood, 339
   and resilience, 11
   in retirement, 631, 632f

Voting participation
   in early adulthood, 466
   in late adulthood, 632
   in middle adulthood, 533
Vygotsky, Lev, 23
   sociocultural theory of, 23–24, 28t, 167, 233–235, 237, 319–320

W
Walking
   in early childhood, 223
   in infancy, 133–137, 138, 139
   and stepping reflex, 106–107, 107t
War, and impact of violence on children, 353
Water, fluoridated, 217
Watson, John, 17
Wear-and-tear theory on biological aging, 432
Wechsler Intelligence Scale for Children, 309, 310
Weight
   in anorexia nervosa, 372
   at birth, low, 101–105. *See also* Low birth weight
   in early adulthood, 439–442
   in early childhood, 216
   genetic factors affecting, 130
   in infancy and toddlerhood, 120, 121, 131–132
   in late adulthood, 572
   in middle adulthood, 504, 516
   in middle childhood, 290, 290f, 291–293
   in obesity. *See* Obesity
   in physical changes of aging, 435t, 572
   in puberty, 363, 366f, 367
   sleep affecting, 292
Welfare benefits, 65, 66, 94
   in adolescent pregnancy and parenthood, 378
Well-being
   and health. *See* Health
   international comparisons of indicators on, 66–67, 67t
   psychological. *See* Psychological well-being
White Americans. *See* Caucasian Americans
White blood cells
   in immune system, 437
   telomere length in, 433
Whole-language approach to reading, 308
Whooping cough, 221
WIC (Special Supplemental Food Program for Women, Infants, and Children), 92
Widowhood, 621, 622–623, 624
   bereavement in, 660, 662, 663
Wisdom, 9
   in late adulthood, 595–596
Withdrawal of privileges as punishment technique, 267

Withholding or withdrawal of life-sustaining treatment, 654–656
Work. *See* Employment
Working memory, 301, 302–303
   capacity of, 161, 162, 302–303
   in information processing, 161, 162, 302–303
   and intelligence quotient, 310
   in late adulthood, 591, 594
   in middle adulthood, 522
   in middle childhood, 301, 302–303
   in neo-Piagetian theory, 301
World Health Organization, 130
World Trade Center terrorist attacks, 37, 353
Writing
   and early printing, 225
   and emergent literacy, 240–242, 242f
   in middle childhood, 295
   sex differences in, 388, 457

X
X chromosome, 47
   abnormalities of, 53
   diseases linked to, 49t, 50–51, 51f
   in fragile X syndrome, 51
XX chromosomes, 47
XXX syndrome, 53
XY chromosomes, 46, 46f, 48
XYY syndrome, 53

Y
Y chromosome, 47
   abnormalities of, 53
Yolk sac, 81
Yoruba of Nigeria, Alzheimer's disease in, 584–585
Young–old developmental tasks in seasons of life theory, 535
Yucatán Mayans
   childbirth practices of, 98
   menopause of, 508
   observational learning of, 236
Yurok Indians, breastfeeding and child-rearing practices of, 16–17

Z
Zambia, child-rearing practices and newborn behavior in, 114
Zero tolerance policies, 425–426
Zinacanteco Indians
   adult guidance and child learning among, 24
   concrete operational stage of, 301
   make-believe play of, 168
   motor development of infants, 139
Zinc, 220, 577
Zone of proximal development, 179
   sociocultural theory on, 167, 234, 320
Zygote, 46, 80f, 80–82
   in fraternal or dizygotic twins, 47
   in identical or monozygotic twins, 48
   teratogen exposure affecting, 85, 86f

Mt. Sac CHLD 10
Observation Guide

The Role of Play in Children's Development

৶ Observation Assignment ৻

Mt. San Antonio College
CHLD 10 Observation Guide: Observation Assignment

Assignment Introduction

This observation assignment is intended to sharpen the student's understanding of the role of play in a child's development and deepen the student's awareness of the many aspects and contributing factors to play. Additional consideration will be given to the deficits resulting from deprivation in play.

The assignment calls for the student to make an appointment at a licensed child care center after obtaining proof of being free from Tuberculosis, in accordance with California state law. Toward this end, the professor will issue a Letter of Introduction to the student, which will also serve as a verification of observation hours form. The making and keeping of appointments is solely the student's responsibility.

The observation is to be done on one particular child, so as to formulate an idea of the play preferences of this child and the contribution of play to his or her development. It requires observation of indoor and outdoor play periods on two different days. Each observation should be between 30 minutes and an hour, the range being attributable to the different arrangements that child care centers have for play periods. To clarify, this assignment requires two indoor play observations and two outdoor play observations of not less than 30 minutes each and spanning at least two separate dates. It will be important in meeting this criteria that the student make careful choices in scheduling when to visit the center. The target age for this assignment is 3-4 years.

Principles of confidentiality and courtesy should be observed while doing this observation. This assignment does not call for participation with the children, but rather observing their play without intrusion.

The forms that follow will provide a framework for observing the child's play preferences and making inferences based on this data.

Mt. San Antonio College
CHLD 10 Observation Guide: Observation Assignment

OBSERVATION FORM

Activity: Indoor—Outdoor   Identify the activity and give a description of the play dynamics.

Number of Participants:

Duration of Activity: Start:_____   End:_____

Functions of play addressed: List all that apply:

Mt. San Antonio College
CHLD 10 Observation Guide: Observation Assignment

ASSIGNMENT INFORMATION

Child—Male or female

Child's age (years and months)

Physical appearance of child:

Name of Center:

Teacher's name:

Hours per week child is at the center:

FUNCTIONS OF PLAY

Sensorimotor Development:

large and small muscle development

release of energy

exploration of the physical world

joy of bodily movement

joy of bodily movement with a vehicle

Creativity and Imagination

product oriented

process oriented

alone

with others

reflective of life situations

fantasy

Socialization

give and take within the play (e.g. sharing, deciding rules of the game, winning and losing)

give and take outside the play (e.g. deciding what game to play, what the rules will be)

sex roles

actions allowed and not allowed by adults (e.g. rough play, dangerous play, war play, or other restrictions on play, no running, no toys at school)

values perception reflective of the adult world (e.g. "I am good at baseball")

Self-Awareness

> physical limitations
>
> preferences
>
> self-regulation, control of temper
>
> skill comparison to others
>
> persistence in the face of failure
>
> empathy (aware of how my actions affect others)

Therapeutic Value

> release of tension and stress
>
> expression of emotions
>
> release of anger in a socially accepted way
>
> test fear
>
> mastery of roles

Moral Value

> adherence to rules
>
> fair teams
>
> including and excluding people
>
> running up the score
>
> criticizing and hurtful words

Mt. San Antonio College
CHLD 10 Observation Guide: Observation Assignment

ASSIGNMENT SUMMARY

Use the data collected in your observations to answer the following questions:

1) What aspects of play contribute to this child's physical development?

2) What aspects of play contribute to this child's cognitive development?

3) What aspects of play contribute to this child's social and emotional development?

4) Speculate on a microsystem influence on this child's play

5) Speculate on a macrosystem influence on this child's play

6) Articulate how a future illness, Injury, or disability might affect this child's ability to participate in the play you observed.

Mt. San Antonio College
CHLD 10 Observation Guide: Adolescent Interview

Interview: Adolescent Development (Ages 13-19)

Introduction: Who did you interview? What is his or her name, age, grade in school and relation to you? Why did you choose to interview this person? Where did the interview take place and how long did it take. What method did you use to record the answers?

Interview Transcript: (When this assignment is turned in, all of these questions and answers will be typed out. Use as much space as you need for each question)

1. Since you have become a teen ager, have you noted any changes in your body?

2. How much do you enjoy sports activities, and what types do you enjoy?

3. What kinds of activities do you enjoy? Do you have any special interests or hobbies?

4. What kind of food do you like, and how often do you find yourself feeling hungry?

5. There was recently a famine in the African country Somalia. How do you think the United States might help in this crisis? Give some details of your idea.

6. Do you have an idea what kind of career you might want to pursue?

7. What do you enjoy most about school? (he or she might ask if you mean social or academic. Get an answer for both)

8. Some teenagers engage in risky behavior. Have you ever? Do you know someone who has?

9. Do you think there is a difference in male and female sports abilities in the teen years.

10. In what ways do you define yourself on your own terms? For example, your style of dress, your free-time activities, your faith, your choice of friends, your career interests. (get an answer for each)

11. Where do you fit in socially?

12. During the American Revolutionary War, some of the Iroquois Confederacy assisted the Americans in fighting the British. After the war ended in American victory, these same people had their land settled by the Americans. They were pushed off their land. What do you think of this? Should anything be done about it today?

13. Do you practice a particular faith, and how do you feel about it?

14. How is your relationship with your parents? (get an answer for both mom and dad if there are two parents)

15. How do you get along with your brothers and sisters? Who is your favorite? What are some problems that arise with your siblings?

16. What responsibilities do you have at home?

17. Who is your best friend? Tell me a little about this person. How much time do you spend together, and what do you do in your time together?

18. Do you have a boyfriend or a girlfriend? What is the most difficult part of this relationship? What is the best part?

19. Do you have any role models, someone who you admire?

20. Do you think it's a good idea that teenagers can drive at age 16 or would you change this law?

Mt. San Antonio College
CHLD 10 Observation Guide: Adolescent Interview

Interview 2 Adolescent Interview Summary:

These questions and their answers will be typed when you hand them in. Remember to give evidence from the interview answers each time you answer a question. Consult your text if you need to remember some of the details of each theory being asked about.

1. What aspect of adolescent problem solving does this teenager exhibit?

2. Which of Erikson's identity statuses does this adolescent seem to be in?

3. What dynamics do you see between parent and child?

4. What is the social status of this teenager?

5. Give your speculation on the greatest challenge in the next few years for this teenager.

Mt. San Antonio College
CHLD 10 Observation Guide: Geriatric Interview

This assignment will be known as the Geriatric Interview. Its focus is on late adulthood, from 65 years on. In this assignment, the student will make his or her own questions, conforming to the areas of development under consideration. This will necessitate reviewing chapters 17 and 18 in the text. Of course if you feel more comfortable providing guidance in the form of specific questions you are free to do so. Because this assignment is more involved than the previous adult interview, you may wish to assign more point value to it than before.

Geriatric Interview

In this assignment, you will interview an adult 65 years of age or older. Use your text, chapters 17 and 18, to guide your completion of this assignment. You will write your own questions. The person you interview can be someone familiar to you or a stranger. If you want to make an appointment at an elder care facility, to interview one of the residents, you can do so.

Your finished assignment should be typed and fully address each area of development under consideration. Provide subject headings to distinguish one section from another. It is up to you to develop interview questions that accomplish this. In your finished work, include both your questions and the subject's answers. Some students are apprehensive about asking questions, but you will find that most older adults will enjoy the chance to talk with you.

Part 1. Physical Development

Ascertain the subject's vision, hearing, and sleep patterns. Discover any current health problems or orthopedic impairments, and what measures are being taken to address them. Assess how this impacts mobility, both on foot or in a vehicle. Ask about favorite physical activities enjoyed in the past.

Part 2. Cognitive Development

Discover if there are any mentally challenging games that the subject enjoys playing, such as cards, dominoes, board games, or Crossword puzzles. Discover if he or she enjoys reading, and if so what type of material? Reminiscence is a common activity of elders. Ask the subject to recall a memorable event (or events) from earlier in life. Ask the subject to recall what he or she was doing when he or she was your age. Of course you have to supply your age. Ask about popular and memorable music from his or her past. Does he or she have a favorite song?

Part 3. Social and Emotional Development

Explore Control vs Dependency: Inquire about the subject's current living situation. Provide details of the current situation and the subject's feelings about it.

Explore Integrity vs Despair: Ask questions that elicit evidence of satisfaction with a life well lived, or regrets over choices that were made.

Explore Spirituality and Religiosity: Ask questions that elicit evidence of a belief in what happens after this life.

Explore Ego Differentiation: As people age, former means of self-worth no longer hold up. Beauty and strength disappear. Earning power is diminished. Social accomplishments are curtailed. Ask questions that seek to discover how this older adult has re-calibrated self-worth in light of these changes.

Theories of late adulthood: Choose one of the following and show how your interview subject fits into it, citing evidence from the answers to the questions you have asked. Ask questions that explore one or another of these theories.

Disengagement Theory

Activity Theory

Continuity Theory

Socio-emotional Selectivity Theory

What follows is a list of questions you may draw from while considering your late adulthood interview. They are taken from The Legacy Project at www.legacyproject.org

---

Life Interview Questions – Geriatric Interview

Did you go to university or college? How did you decide what you wanted to study?

Did you serve in the military? What did you do and what kind of experience was it?

How did you decide what you wanted to do with your life? How do you feel about that choice?

What was your first job? What did you like or not like about it?

What job did you do most of your life? What did you like most about it? Least?

How did you meet your spouse? What did you like about him/her?

How and when did you get engaged?

When did you get married? How old were you? Where did you get married? What was your wedding like?

What was the first big purchase you made with your spouse?

What makes your spouse special or unique?

How many children do you have? When were they born? How did you decide what to name each?

What's your favorite story about each of your children?

What is something funny or embarrassing one of your children said at an early age that you'll never forget?

What's the most memorable family vacation you took?

What do you remember about holiday celebrations? Is there one holiday memory that stands out for you?

How did you feel about raising your children? What was the best part? The hardest part?

What makes you proud of your children?

How is my father/mother like me? Unlike me?

What do you remember about me when I was born? What about when I was younger than I am now?

What the best thing about being a parent? A grandparent?

Do you know the meaning of your family name? Are there stories about the origins of your family name?

Have you ever had any nicknames as a child or as an adult? Where did they come from?

How are you like your mother? Unlike her? How are you like your father? Unlike him?

What was most important to your parents?

Do you feel you're like any of your grandparents? In what ways?

How are your children like you? Unlike you?

What do you think are your three best qualities? Your three worst?

Which do you think you have the most of: talent, intelligence, education, or persistence? How has it helped
you in your life?

Do you have any special sayings or expressions?

What's your favorite book and why? What's your favorite movie and why?

Who are three people in history you admire most and why?

What have been the three biggest news events during your lifetime and why?

If you could travel into the future, would you rather see something that specifically relates to you, or
something that relates to the future of the country in general? Why?

If you could have three wishes, what would they be?

If you won $1 million tomorrow, what would you do with the money?

What's the highest honor or award you've ever received?

What's the most memorable phone call you've ever received?

What's the best compliment you ever received?

What kinds of things bring you the most pleasure now? When you were a younger adult? A child?

What things frighten you now? What frightened you when you were a younger adult? A child?

What's the one thing you've always wanted but still don't have?

Do you feel differently about yourself now from how you felt when you were younger? How?

What do you think has stayed the same about you throughout life? What do you think has changed?

Life Interview Questions – The Present, Aging, Life Lessons and Legacies

Do you have any hobbies or special interests? Do you enjoy any particular sports?

What's your typical day like now? How is it different from your daily routines in the past?

Is the present better or worse than when you were younger?

What do you do for fun?

Who do you trust and depend on?

What things are most important to you now? Why?

How have your dreams and goals changed through your life?

What do you see? (Hold a mirror up to the person)

What do you remember about your 20s? 30s? 40s? 50s? 60s? What events stand out in your mind? How
was each age different from the one before it?

There are some ages we don't look forward to. What birthday were you least enthusiastic about? Why?

If you could go back to any age, which age would it be and why?

How do you feel now about growing old? What's the hardest thing about growing older? The best thing?

What were your parents like when they got older?

Did you have any expectations at points in your life about what growing older would be like for you?

How should a person prepare for old age? Is there anything you wish you'd done differently?

Do you think about the future and make plans? What are your concerns for the future?

If you live another 20-30 years, what will you do? Do you want to live another 20-30 years?

What do you look forward to now?

What's your most cherished family tradition? Why is it important?

What have you liked best about your life so far? What's your happiest or proudest moment?

What do you feel have been the important successes in your life? The frustrations?

What's the most difficult thing that ever happened to you? How did you deal with it?

What do you think the turning points have been in your life? What were you like then?

Are there times of your life that you remember more vividly than others? Why?

What have been the most influential experiences in your life?

Describe a person or situation from your childhood that had a profound effect on the way you look at life.

If you were writing the story of your life, how would you divide it into chapters?

What, if anything, would you have done differently in your life?

What do you know now that you wish you'd known when you were young?

What have you thrown away in your life that you wish you hadn't? What have you held on to that's

important and why is it important? What "junk" have you held on to and why?

Over time, how have you changed the way you look at life/people?

What advice did your grandparents or parents give you that you remember best?

Do you have a philosophy of life? What's your best piece of advice for living? If a young person came to you

asking what's the most important thing for living a good life, what would you say?

How do you define a "good life" or a "successful life"?

Do you think a person needs to first overcome serious setbacks or challenges to be truly successful?

In what way is it important to know your limitations in your life or career?

If you had the power to solve one and only one problem in the world, what would it be and why?

What do you see as your place or purpose in life? How did you come to that conclusion?

What would you like your children and grandchildren to remember about you?

If you could write a message to each of your children and grandchildren and put it in a time capsule for

them to read 20 years from now, what would you write to each?

Birth to 36 months: Boys
Length-for-age and Weight-for-age percentiles

NAME _____

RECORD # _____

AGE (MONTHS)

Birth 3 6 9 12 15 18 21 24 27 30 33 36

LENGTH

LENGTH

95
90
75
50
25
10
5

95
90
75
50
25
10
5

WEIGHT

WEIGHT

AGE (MONTHS)

| | 12 | 15 | 18 | 21 | 24 | 27 | 30 | 33 | 36 | kg | lb |

Mother's Stature _____ Gestational
Father's Stature _____ Age: _____ Weeks   Comment

Date	Age	Weight	Length	Head Circ.	
	Birth				

Birth 3 6 9

Published May 30, 2000 (modified 4/20/01).
SOURCE: Developed by the National Center for Health Statistics in collaboration with
the National Center for Chronic Disease Prevention and Health Promotion (2000).
http://www.cdc.gov/growthcharts

SAFER · HEALTHIER · PEOPLE™

Birth to 36 months: Girls
Length-for-age and Weight-for-age percentiles

NAME _____

RECORD # _____

AGE (MONTHS)

Birth 3 6 9 12 15 18 21 24 27 30 33 36

LENGTH

WEIGHT

95
90
75
50
25
10
5

AGE (MONTHS)

12 15 18 21 24 27 30 33 36

Mother's Stature _____			Gestational		Comment
Father's Stature _____			Age: _____ Weeks		
Date	Age	Weight	Length	Head Circ.	
	Birth				

Birth 3 6 9

Published May 30, 2000 (modified 4/20/01).
SOURCE: Developed by the National Center for Health Statistics in collaboration with
the National Center for Chronic Disease Prevention and Health Promotion (2000).
http://www.cdc.gov/growthcharts

SAFER · HEALTHIER · PEOPLE™

2 to 20 years: Boys
Stature-for-age and Weight-for-age percentiles

NAME _____

RECORD # _____

Mother's Stature		Father's Stature		
Date	Age	Weight	Stature	BMI*

*To Calculate BMI: Weight (kg) ÷ Stature (cm) ÷ Stature (cm) x 10,000
or Weight (lb) ÷ Stature (in) ÷ Stature (in) x 703

AGE (YEARS)

12 13 14 15 16 17 18 19 20

STATURE

cm — in
190 — 74
185 — 72
180 — 70
175
170 — 68
165 — 66
160 — 64
155 — 62
150 — 60

in cm
3 4 5 6 7 8 9 10 11

STATURE

62 — 160
— 155
60 — 150
58 — 145
56 — 140
54 — 135
52 — 130
50 — 125
48 — 120
46 — 115
44 — 110
42 — 105
40 — 100
38 — 95
36 — 90
34 — 85
32 — 80
30

Percentile curves: 95, 90, 75, 50, 25, 10, 5

WEIGHT

105 — 230
100 — 220
95 — 210
90 — 200
85 — 190
80 — 180
75 — 170
70 — 160
65 — 150
60 — 140
55 — 130
50 — 120
45 — 110
40 — 100
35 — 90
lb — kg

WEIGHT

80 — 35
70 — 30
60 — 25
50 — 20
40 — 15
30 — 10
lb — kg

AGE (YEARS)

2 3 4 5 6 7 8 9 10 11 12 13 14 15 16 17 18 19 20

Published May 30, 2000 (modified 11/21/00).
SOURCE: Developed by the National Center for Health Statistics in collaboration with
the National Center for Chronic Disease Prevention and Health Promotion (2000).
http://www.cdc.gov/growthcharts

SAFER · HEALTHIER · PEOPLE™

2 to 20 years: Girls
Stature-for-age and Weight-for-age percentiles

NAME _____

RECORD # _____

Mother's Stature		Father's Stature		
Date	Age	Weight	Stature	BMI*

*To Calculate BMI: Weight (kg) ÷ Stature (cm) ÷ Stature (cm) x 10,000
or Weight (lb) ÷ Stature (in) ÷ Stature (in) x 703

AGE (YEARS)

STATURE

WEIGHT

Percentile lines: 95, 90, 75, 50, 25, 10, 5

Published May 30, 2000 (modified 11/21/00).
SOURCE: Developed by the National Center for Health Statistics in collaboration with
the National Center for Chronic Disease Prevention and Health Promotion (2000).
http://www.cdc.gov/growthcharts

SAFER · HEALTHIER · PEOPLE™